THE POCKET OXFORD RUSSIAN DICTIONARY

D0186090

THE POCKET OXFORD RUSSIAN DICTIONARY

RUSSIAN–ENGLISH

compiled by Jessie Coulson

ENGLISH–RUSSIAN

compiled by Nigel Rankin
and Della Thompson

CLARENDON PRESS · OXFORD
1981

Oxford University Press, Walton Street, Oxford OX2 6DP
London Glasgow New York Toronto
Delhi Bombay Calcutta Madras Karachi
Kuala Lumpur Singapore Hong Kong Tokyo
Nairobi Dar es Salaam Cape Town
Melbourne Wellington
and associate companies in
Beirut Berlin Ibadan Mexico City

Published in the United States
by Oxford University Press, New York

Pocket Oxford Russian–English Dictionary © Oxford University Press 1975
Pocket Oxford English–Russian Dictionary © Oxford University Press 1981

All rights reserved. No part of this publication may be reproduced, stored in a retrieval system, or transmitted, in any form or by any means, electronic, mechanical, photocopying, recording, or otherwise, without the prior permission of Oxford University Press

British Library Cataloguing in Publication Data
Coulson, Jessie
The pocket Oxford Russian dictionary.
1. Russian language—Dictionaries—English
2. English language—Dictionaries—Russian
I. Title II. Rankin, Nigel III. Thompson, Della IV. The pocket Oxford Russian–English dictionary
491.73'21 PG2640

ISBN 0–19–864122–2

Printed and bound in Great Britain by
William Clowes (Beccles) Limited, Beccles and London

THE
POCKET OXFORD
RUSSIAN – ENGLISH
DICTIONARY

THE POCKET OXFORD RUSSIAN – ENGLISH DICTIONARY

COMPILED BY
JESSIE COULSON

CLARENDON PRESS · OXFORD
1975

Oxford University Press, Ely House, London W. 1

GLASGOW NEW YORK TORONTO MELBOURNE WELLINGTON
CAPE TOWN IBADAN NAIROBI DAR ES SALAAM LUSAKA ADDIS ABABA
DELHI BOMBAY CALCUTTA MADRAS KARACHI LAHORE DACCA
KUALA LUMPUR SINGAPORE HONG KONG TOKYO

ISBN 0 19 864113 3

© *Oxford University Press 1975*

All rights reserved. No part of this publication may be reproduced, stored in a retrieval system, or transmitted, in any form or by any means, electronic, mechanical, photocopying, recording or otherwise, without the prior permission of Oxford University Press

Printed in Great Britain
by William Clowes & Sons Limited
London, Beccles and Colchester

PREFACE

THIS dictionary is based on the *Oxford Russian–English Dictionary* (Oxford, 1972), and like it is designed primarily for English-speaking users. It offers, as far as possible, translations rather than definitions or explanations. Its vocabulary is as large and as wide in range as its size allows, and has been supplemented and brought more nearly up to date by the fullest possible use of the new dictionaries, new editions of existing dictionaries, and other (chiefly Soviet) sources, that have become available in the past three or four years. Unlike most bilingual dictionaries, this is not intended exclusively for students of Russian, but caters also for those whose needs will be served if they can find and translate a limited number of words connected with their own special field, and whose interest in the language as such is minimal.

For such readers, and others whose study of Russian has not advanced very far, there is one respect in which the language presents peculiar difficulties. It has many words of which different parts, such as the oblique cases of pronouns, tenses and aspects of verbs, or alternative forms of prepositions, have different alphabetical positions from the nominative, imperfective infinitive, or simple preposition concerned. For example, the imperfective идти́ *go* has an alternative infinitive итти́, a past tense шёл, шла derived from a different root, and a perfective пойти́. Because of this characteristic of Russian we have been particularly careful to supply adequate cross-references to enable those who consult the dictionary to find and identify the word they are looking for from the form in which they have come across it.

Pronunciation. Russian spelling is almost entirely phonetic, and it seems unnecessary for a small dictionary to record the pronunciation of most words. Those abbreviations, however, which consist of groups of capital letters are likely, because the names of the letters of the alphabet are comparatively unfamiliar, to present some difficulties of pronunciation to English-speaking readers. As in English, abbreviations of this kind which do not readily form acceptable syllables must be pronounced by spelling them out, and we give some indication of this pronunciation in italic type within parentheses immediately after the head-word of the entry; as in **СССР** (*esesesér*) U.S.S.R., **АВМ** (*aveém*) analogue computer.

Stress. There are some classes of words—prepositions, conjunctions, particles—which are normally unstressed; stress is indicated for all others, except monosyllables, by the placing of a mark like an acute accent over the vowel of the stressed syllable or, if it is a capital letter, immediately after it, thus: **го́род, городско́й; ОО'Н**. The vowel ё, pronounced *yo* or *o*, is always stressed except in a few compound words, and so has no stress-mark. When two stress-marks are found in the same word or form (as in **о́бли́тый**), either of the two syllables may be stressed.

Treatment of individual words or entries. An article in this dictionary consists of a word, prefix, abbreviation or other lexical element, or occasionally of two or more synonymous words or forms, or corresponding masculine and feminine forms, with necessary grammatical information, translation(s), and sometimes illustrative examples of usage. In order to save space, related and alphabetically consecutive words may be grouped together in paragraphs, as may consecutive but unrelated entries each consisting only of a cross-reference, and compound words of which the first element is a prefix or other combining form. All head-words, including those grouped together in paragraphs, are printed in bold type to make them easily distinguishable.

Another device to save space is the use of the tilde (~ or ∼), which may be substituted in the body of an article for the whole of the head-word or, in a list of compound words, for the prefix or other combining form which is common to all of them. In some adjectives the adjectival ending -ый, -ой or -ий may be separated from the stem by a thin vertical stroke; the tilde will then represent the stem only, and the appropriate form of the ending will be appended to it, as in са́харн|ый sugar; sugary; ∼ая голова́, sugar-loaf; ∼ый заво́д, sugar-refinery.

The head-word of an article in this dictionary is usually the nominative case of nouns or pronouns, the nominative singular masculine of adjectives, the infinitive of verbs; the grammatical information that follows the head-word is not intended to enable the user to complete the paradigm but only to identify the specific form he has in mind, or assist him to translate it. The genitive ending of every noun is given, and followed by that of any case showing an irregularity of ending or a change of stress; in the singular any case cited is named, but in the plural the cases can be identified by their endings. The alternative genitive ending in -у is in round brackets immediately after the genitive (see examples below); the term locative (*loc.*) is used as a distinctive name for the prepositional form ending in -у́ after в or на. In those pronouns in which a list of case-endings is given, the accusative is never included and the order of the cases is genitive, dative, instrumental, prepositional. The gender of nouns can usually be deduced from the endings of the nominative and genitive, and it is indicated here only in exceptional instances, as of masculine nouns in -а and neuters in -мя; nouns ending in a soft consonant should be assumed to be feminine unless labelled *m.* Knowledge of their aspect is essential for the translation of verbs, and all verbs are labelled *imp.* or *perf.* or sometimes *perf.* and *imp.* The form and stress of the first person singular of the present or future tense are indicated immediately after the infinitive, and other forms of the present (or future) and past tenses are noted if they show a change of stress or an irregularity of ending or contain the vowel ё. When a perfective verb is formed by the addition of a prefix to a simple imperfective, the prefix is divided from the rest of the infinitive by a light vertical stroke. A single bracket, (, before the reflexive ending of an infinitive indicates, especially in cross-references, that the cross-reference, etc., applies to both the active and the reflexive infinitive. When the construction of a verb demands the use of a case other than the accusative or genitive the case required is indicated as in **маха́ть...** *imp.*, **махну́ть...** *perf.* + *instr.* wave; brandish.

Some adjectives have shifting stress in the short forms; in these the full nominative singular masculine form of the head-word is followed immediately by a semicolon and then by the short forms, as in **худо́й** below.

If a compound word cannot be found in the dictionary its meaning may often be deduced from those of its prefix and its second element. To assist this process full and careful translations and definitions are given of many prefixes, especially verbal prefixes, and other combining forms, all of which are distinguished by a head-word ending with a hyphen.

Examples illustrating many of the points mentioned in this preface follow:

адресова́ть, -су́ю *perf.* and *imp.* address, send; **~ся,** address oneself.

нали́ть, -лью́, -льёшь; на́ли́л, -а, -о *perf.* (*imp.* налива́ть) pour (out).

пла́мя, -мени *n.* flame; fire, blaze.

по́вод², -а (-у), *loc.* -у́; *pl.* -о́дья, -ьев, rein.
по|проси́ть(ся, -ошу́(сь, -о́сишь(ся *perf.*
прозва́ть, -зову́, -зовёшь; -а́л, -а́, -о *perf.* (*imp.* прозыва́ть) nickname, name.
проси́ть, -ошу́, -о́сишь *imp.* (*perf.* по~) ask; beg; invite; **~ся**, ask; apply.
про|слу́шать, -аю *perf.*, **прослу́шивать**, -аю *imp.* hear; listen to.
сестра́, -ы́; *pl.* сёстры, сестёр, сёстрам, sister.
сок, -а (-у), *loc.* -у́, juice; sap; в (по́лном) ~у́, in the prime of life.
худо́й; худ, -а́, -о, thin, lean.

ACKNOWLEDGEMENTS

THE compiler wishes to record her gratitude for the patience and kindness of the many scholars and friends in Oxford, Moscow, and elsewhere who have answered her questions and given her generous help and guidance, and in particular her debt to Professor J. G. Nicholson, Chairman of the Department of Russian at McGill University, Montreal, and Professor M. C. C. Wheeler, of the Queen's University of Belfast, author of the *Oxford Russian-English Dictionary*.

ABBREVIATIONS

abbr. abbreviation (of)
acc. accusative
adj. adjective(s)
adv., *advs.* adverb(s)
approx. approximately
collect. collective(ly)
comb. combination
comp. comparative
conj. conjunction
dat. dative
dim. diminutive(s)
etc. etcetera
f. feminine
fut. future
gen. genitive
imp. imperfective
impers. impersonal
indecl. indeclinable
inf. infinitive
instr. instrumental
int. interjection
loc. locative
m. masculine
n. neuter
neg. negative(s)
nom. nominative
part. particle
perf. perfective
pl. plural
predic. predicative adjective
pref. prefix
prep. prepositional, preposition(s)
pron. pronoun(s)
refl. reflexive
sb., *sbs.* substantive(s)
sing. singular
sl. slang
superl. superlative
usu. usually
vb., *vbs.* verb(s)
vbl. verbal
voc. vocative
= equals, the same as
\+ plus

A

a *n. indecl.* the letter a.
a *conj.* and, but; a (не) то́, or else, otherwise.
a *part.* eh?
a *int.* oh, ah.
абажу́р, -а, lampshade.
абба́т, -а, abbot; abbé. **аббати́са, -ы,** abbess. **абба́тство, -а,** abbey.
аббревиату́ра, -ы, abbreviation; acronym.
абза́ц, -а, indention; paragraph; сде́лать ~, indent.
абонеме́нт, -а, subscription, season ticket; сверх ~а, extra. **абоне́нт, -а,** subscriber. **абони́ровать, -рую** *perf.* and *imp.* subscribe for, subscribe to, take a (season-)ticket for; **~ся,** subscribe, take out a subscription, be a subscriber.
або́рт, -а, abortion; abort, failure, cancellation. **аборти́вный,** abortive; causing abortion. **аборти́ст, -а, -и́стка, -и,** abortionist.
абрико́с, -а, apricot.
а́брис, -а, outline, contour.
абсолю́т, -а, absolute. **абсолю́тно** *adv.* absolutely, utterly. **абсолю́тный,** absolute; utter; ~ слух, perfect pitch.
абсу́рд, -а, absurdity; the absurd. **абсу́рдный,** absurd.
аванга́рд, -а, advanced guard, van; vanguard; avantgarde. **авангарди́стский,** avantgarde. **аванпо́ст, -а,** outpost; forward position.
ава́нс, -а, advance, advance payment; *pl.* advances, overtures. **аванси́ровать, -рую** *perf.* and *imp.* advance. **ава́нсом,** *adv.* in advance, on account.
авансце́на, -ы, proscenium.
авантю́ра, -ы, adventure; venture; escapade; shady, risky, or speculative enterprise. **авантюри́ст, -а,** adventurer. **авантюри́стка, -и,** adventuress. **авантю́рный,** adventurous; adventure, of adventure.
авари́йка, -и, breakdown vehicle. **авари́йный,** accident, breakdown, crash; emergency; spare; ~ сигна́л, distress signal. **ава́рия, -и,** accident, crash, wreck; breakdown; damage; loss; потерпе́ть ава́рию, have an accident.
а́вгуст, -а, August.
а́виа *abbr.* авиапо́чтой, by airmail.
авиа- *abbr.* in *comb.* of авиацио́нный, air-, aero-; aircraft; aviation. **авиали́ния, -и,** air-route, airway. **~но́сец,** -сца, aircraft carrier. **~по́чта, -ы,** airmail. **~разве́дка, -и,** air reconnaissance. **~съёмка, -и,** aerial survey.
авиацио́нный, aviation; flying; aircraft. **авиа́ция, -и,** aviation, flying; aircraft; air-force.
АВМ (*авеэ́м*) *abbr.* анало́говая вычисли́тельная маши́на, analogue computer.
аво́сь *adv.* perhaps, maybe; на ~, at random, on the off-chance. **аво́ська,** -и, shopping-bag.
авра́л, -а, work involving all hands; emergency; rush job; *int.* all hands on deck! all hands to the pump! **авра́льный,** rush, emergency.
австрали́ец, -и́йца, **австрали́йка, -и,** Australian. **австрали́йский,** Australian.
австри́ец, -и́йца, **австри́йка, -и,** Austrian. **австри́йский,** Austrian.
авто́ *n. indecl.* car.
авто- in *comb.*, self-; auto-; automatic; motor-; bus. **автоба́за, -ы,** motor-transport depot. **~биогра́фия, -и,**

autobiography. **автóбус**, -а, bus. **~вокзáл**, -а, bus-station. **автóграф**, -а, autograph. **~запрáвочная** стáнция, petrol station. **~кáр**, -а, motor trolley. **~клáв**, -а, autoclave. **~крáт**, -а, autocrat. **~кратúческий**, autocratic. **~магистрáль**, -и, motor highway. **~машúна**, -ы, motor vehicle. **~нóмия**, -и, autonomy. **~нóмный**, autonomous; self-contained. **~павильóн**, -а, (long-distance) bus halt. **~пилóт**, -а, automatic pilot. **~рýчка**, -и, fountain-pen. **~стáнция**, -и, bus station. **~стóп**, -а, automatic brakes; hitch-hiking, hitch-hike. **~стрáда**, -ы, motorway.

автомáт, -а, slot-machine; automatic device, weapon, etc.; sub-machine gun; robot; automaton; (телефóн-)~, dial telephone, automatic telephone; public call-box. **автоматизáция**, -и, automation. **автоматизúровать**, -рую *perf.* and *imp.* automate; make automatic; **~ся**, become automatic. **автоматúческий**, **автоматúчный**, **автомáтный**, automatic.

áвтор, -а, author; composer, producer, inventor; ~ предложéния, ~ резолю́ции, mover of a resolution.

авторизáция, -и, authorization. **авторизóванный**, authorized. **авторизовáть**, -зýю *perf.* and *imp.* authorize.

авторитéт, -а, authority; prestige. **авторитéтный**, authoritative.

áвторск|ий, author's; ~ий гонорáр, royalty; ~ое прáво, copyright; ~ие правá заявлены, all rights reserved; **~ие** *sb. pl.* royalties. **áвторство**, -а, authorship.

агá *int.* ah; aha.

агéнт, -а, agent; attaché. **агéнтство**, -а, agency. **агентýра**, -ы, secret service; agents, network of agents.

агитáтор, -а, agitator, propagandist; canvasser. **агитациóнный**, propaganda. **агитáция**, -и, propaganda, agitation; campaign. **агитúровать**, -рую *imp.* (*perf.* с~) agitate, campaign; (try to) persuade, win over. **агúтка**, -и, piece of propaganda. **агитпрóп**, -а *abbr.* agitation and propaganda section. **агитпýнкт**, -а *abbr.* agitation centre; committee-rooms.

агонизúровать, -рую *perf.* and *imp.* be in the throes of death. **агóния**, -и, agony of death, death-pangs.

агрегáт, -а, aggregate; assembly, unit, outfit, set.

агронóм, -а, **-нóмша**, -и, agronomist. **агронóмия**, -и, agriculture.

ад, -а, *loc.* -ý, hell.

адвокáт, -а, lawyer, advocate. **адвокатýра**, -ы, legal profession; lawyers.

адéпт, -а, adherent, follower, disciple.

администратúвный, administrative. **администрáтор**, -а, administrator, manager. **администрáция** -и, administration; management. **администрúрование**, -я, bureaucracy, red tape. **администрúровать**, -рую *imp.* act as administrator or manager (of); send into exile.

адмирáл, -а, admiral. **адмиралтéйский**, Admiralty. **адмиралтéйство**, -а, Admiralty; naval dockyard. **адмирáльский**, admiral's; flag. **адмирáльша**, -и, admiral's wife.

áдов *adj.* infernal, diabolical.

áдрес, -а; *pl.* -á, -óв, address; не по ~у, to the wrong address. **адресáнт**, -а, sender. **адресáт**, -а, addressee. **áдресн|ый**, address; ~ая кнúга, directory; ~ый стол, address bureau. **адресовáть**, -сýю *perf.* and *imp.* address, send: **~ся**, address oneself.

áдский, infernal, hellish, fiendish, devilish.

адъю́нкт, -а, service student.

адъютáнт, -а, aide-de-camp; стáрший ~, adjutant.

ажýр, -а, openwork; up-to-date; в ~е, in order, (all) correct. **ажýрн|ый**, openwork; delicate, lacy; ~ая рабóта, openwork; tracery.

азáрт, -а, heat; excitement; fervour, ardour, passion. **азáртн|ый**, reckless, venturesome; heated; excitable; ~ая игрá, game of chance.

áзбука, -и, alphabet; ABC; ~ Мóрзе, Morse code. **áзбучный**, alphabetical; elementary.

азóт, -а, nitrogen; зáкись ~а, nitrous oxide.

а́ист, -а, stork.
ай *int.* oh; oo; ай да молоде́ц! well done! good lad!
айва́, -ы́, quince, quinces.
айда́, *int.* come on! let's go!
акаде́мик, -а, Academician; member or student of academy. **академи́ческий, академи́чный**, academic. **акаде́мия**, -и, academy.
аквала́нг, -а, aqualung.
акварели́ст, -а, water-colour painter. **акваре́ль**, -и, water-colour, water-colours.
акведу́к, -а, aqueduct.
аккомпанеме́нт, -а, accompaniment; под ~ +*gen.* to the accompaniment of. **аккомпаниа́тор**, -а, **-а́торша**, -и, accompanist. **аккомпани́ровать**, -рую *imp.* + *dat.* accompany.
акко́рд, -а chord; взять ~, strike a chord.
акко́рдн|ый, agreed, by agreement; ~ая рабо́та, piece-work.
аккредити́в, -а, letter of credit; credentials. **аккредитова́ть**, -ту́ю *perf.* and *imp.* accredit.
аккура́тный, accurate, neat, careful; punctual; exact, thorough.
аксельба́нт, -а, aiguillette.
аксессуа́р, -а, accessory; (stage) property.
аксио́ма, -ы, axiom; truism.
акт, -а, act; deed, document; обвини́тельный ~, indictment.
актёр, -а, actor. **актёрский**, actor's. **актёрство**, -а, acting; posing.
акти́в, -а, activists; assets; advantages. **активиза́ция**, -и, stirring up, making (more) active. **активизи́ровать**, -рую *perf.* and *imp.* make (more) active, stir up, arouse **акти́вный**, active; ~ бала́нс, favourable balance.
акти́ровать, -рую *perf.* and *imp.* (*perf.* also с~) register, record, presence or absence of; (*sl.*) write off. **актиро́вка**, -и (*sl.*) writing off, write-off; cancellation.
а́ктов|ый; ~ая бума́га. official document, stamped paper; ~ый зал, assembly hall.
актри́са, -ы, actress.
актуа́льный, actual; up-to-date, topical; urgent.
аку́ла, -ы, shark.
аку́стика, -и, acoustics. **акусти́ческий**, acoustic.
акушёр, -а, obstetrician. **акуше́рка**, -и, midwife. **акуше́рский**, obstetric, obstetrical. **акуше́рство**, -а, obstetrics; midwifery.
акце́нт, -а, accent, stress. **акценти́ровать**, -рую *perf.* and *imp.* accent; accentuate.
акци́з, -а, duty; Excise. **акци́зный**, excise.
акционе́р, -а, shareholder. **акционе́рн|ый**, joint-stock; ~ое о́бщество, joint-stock company. **а́кция**[1], -и, share; *pl.* stock. **а́кция**[2], -и, action.
але́ть, -е́ет *imp.* (*perf.* за~) redden, flush, blush; show red.
алле́я, -и, avenue; path, walk.
аллю́р, -а, pace, gait.
алма́з, -а, diamond. **алма́зный**, diamond; of diamonds.
алта́рь, -я́ *m.* altar; chancel, sanctuary.
а́лчный, greedy, grasping.
а́лый, scarlet.
альбино́с, -а, **альбино́ска**, -и, albino.
альбо́м, -а, album; sketch-book.
альмана́х, -а, literary miscellany; almanac.
альпи́йск|ий. Alpine; ~ие луга́, alps, mountain meadows. **альпини́зм**, -а, mountaineering. **альпини́ст**, -а, **альпини́стка**, -и, (mountain-)climber.
альт, -а́; *pl.* -ы́, alto, contralto; viola. **альтера́ция**, -и, change in pitch; зна́ки альтера́ции, accidentals. **альти́ст**, -а, **-и́стка**, -и, viola-player. **альто́вый**, alto, contralto; viola.
алюми́ниевый, aluminium. **алюми́ний**, -я, aluminium.
амазо́нка, -и, Amazon; horsewoman; riding-habit.
а́мба, *f. indecl.* (*sl.*) finish, curtains, kibosh.
амба́р, -а, barn; storehouse, warehouse. **амба́рный**, barn.
амби́ция, -и, pride; arrogance. **амбицио́зный**, vainglorious, conceited; self-loving, egoistic.
а́мбра, -ы, ambergris; scent, perfume,

fragrance. **амбре́** *n. indecl.* scent, perfume.
амбулато́рия, -и, out-patients' department; surgery. **амбулато́рный**; ~ больно́й, out-patient.
амбушю́р, -а, **амбушю́ра**, -ы, mouthpiece.
америка́нец, -нца, American. **америка́нка**, -и, American; racing sulky; snack bar, (*sl.*) vodka stand. **америка́нск|ий**, American; U.S.; ~ие го́ры, switchback; ~ий замо́к, Yale lock; ~ий оре́х Brazil nut.
ами́нь, -я *m.* amen; finis, finish, kibosh.
аммиа́к, -а, ammonia. **аммиа́чный**, ammonia, ammoniac, ammoniacal. **аммо́ний**, -я, ammonium.
амнисти́ровать, -рую *perf.* and *imp.* amnesty. **амни́стия**, -и, amnesty.
амора́льный, amoral; immoral.
амортиза́тор, -а, shock-absorber. **амортиза́ция**, -и, depreciation, wear and tear; shock-absorption. **амортизи́ровать**, -рую *perf.* and *imp.* amortize; damp, make shock-proof.
ампи́р, -а, Empire style. **ампи́рный**, Empire.
амплуа́ *n. indecl.* type; role; occupation, job.
АМС *f. indecl. abbr.* автомати́ческая межпланéтная ста́нция, automatic space station.
аму́р, -а, cupid; *pl.* amours, love-affairs. **аму́рный**, love.
амфитеа́тр, -а, amphitheatre; circle.
АН (*аэ́н* or *ан*) *abbr.* Акаде́мия Нау́к, Academy of Sciences.
ана́лиз, -а, analysis; ~ кро́ви, blood-test. **анализи́ровать**, -рую *perf.* and *imp.* analyse. **анали́тик**, -а, analyst. **аналити́ческий**, analytic, analytical.
анало́й, -я, lectern.
анана́с, -а, pineapple. **анана́сный**, **анана́совый**, pineapple.
анархи́ст, -а, **-и́стка**, -и, anarchist. **анархи́ческий**, anarchic, anarchical. **ана́рхия**, -и, anarchy.
анга́р, -а, hangar.
а́нгел, -а, angel; день ~а name-day. **а́нгельский**, angels'; angelic.
анги́на, -ы, quinsy, tonsillitis, ulcerated sore throat.
англизи́ровать, -рую *perf.* and *imp.* anglicize. **англи́йск|ий**, English; ~ая була́вка, safety-pin; ~ая соль, Epsom salts; ~ий рожо́к cor anglais. **англици́зм**, -а, anglicism, English loan-word. **англича́нин**, -а; *pl.* -ча́не, -чан, Englishman. **англича́нка**, -и, Englishwoman.
андре́евский, St. Andrew's.
анекдо́т, -а, anecdote, story; funny thing. **анекдоти́ческий**, anecdotal; unlikely; funny, comical. **анекдоти́чный**, improbable; odd; amusing, funny.
анестезио́лог, -а, anaesthetist. **анестезúровать**, -рую *perf.* and *imp.* anaesthetize. **анестези́рующ|ий**, anaesthetizing, anaesthetic; ~ее сре́дство, anaesthetic. **анестези́я**, -и, anaesthesia.
ани́с, -а, anise; kind of apple. **ани́сов|ый**; ~ое се́мя aniseed.
анке́та, -ы, questionnaire, form; (opinion) poll, inquiry, survey.
аннули́ровать, -рую *perf.* and *imp.* annul, nullify; cancel, repeal, revoke, abolish. **аннуля́ция**, -и, annulment, nullification; cancellation, revocation, repeal.
анони́м, -а, anonymous author, work, letter. **анони́мка**, -и, anonymous letter. **анони́мный**, anonymous.
ано́нс, -а, announcement, notice; advertisement. **анонси́ровать**, -рую *perf.* and *imp.* announce, make an announcement.
анса́мбль, -я, *m.* ensemble; company, troupe.
анте́нна, -ы, antenna; aerial.
антивещество́, -а́, anti-matter.
антидетона́тор -а, anti-knock (compound). **антидетонацио́нный**, anti-knock.
антиква́р, -а, **антиква́рий**, -я, antiquary, antiquarian; antique-dealer. **антиквариа́т**, -а, antique-dealer's, antique-shop. **антиква́рный**, antiquarian; antique.
анти́чность, -и, antiquity. **анти́чный** ancient, antique
антираке́та, -ы, anti-missile missile.
антите́ло, -а; *pl.* -а́, antibody.
антра́кт, -а, interval; entr'acte.
антрепренёр, -а, impresario.

антресо́ли, -ей *pl.* mezzanine; attic floor; attics; gallery.
антропофа́г, -а, cannibal. **антропофа́гия**, -и, cannibalism.
антура́ж, -а, surroundings, environment; entourage, associates.
анфа́с *adv.* full face.
анфила́да, -ы, suite.
анчо́ус, -а, anchovy.
аншла́г, -а, 'house full' notice; пройти́ с ~ом, play to full houses.
АО (*аó*) *abbr.* автоно́мная о́бласть, Autonomous Region.
апелли́ровать, -рую *perf.* and *imp.* appeal. **апелляцио́нный**; ~ суд, Court of Appeal. **апелля́ция**, -и, appeal.
апельси́н, -а, orange, orange-tree. **апельси́нный**, **апельси́новый**, orange; апельси́нное варе́нье, (orange) marmalade.
аплике́ *indecl. adj.* plated; appliqué.
аплоди́ровать, -рую *imp.* + *dat.* applaud. **аплодисме́нт**, -а, clap; *pl.* applause; под ~ы, to applause.
аполити́зм, -а, political apathy. **аполити́чный**, politically apathetic.
апо́стол, -а, apostle; Acts and Epistles. **апо́стольский**, apostolic.
аппара́т, -а, apparatus, apparat; machinery, organs; staff, establishment; camera. **аппарату́ра**, -ы, apparatus, gear. **аппара́тчик**, -а, operator; apparatchik, functionary.
аппликату́ра, -ы, fingering. **аппликá́ция**, -и, appliqué, appliqué-work. **аппликацио́нный**, appliqué.
апре́ль, -я *m.* April. **апре́льский**, April.
апроба́ция, -и, approval. **апроби́ровать**, -рую *perf.* and *imp.* approve.
апси́да, -ы, apse.
апте́ка, -и, (dispensing) chemist's; medicine chest; first-aid kit. **апте́карский**, chemist's; pharmaceutical. **апте́карь**, -я *m.* chemist, pharmacist. **апте́карша**, -и, pharmacist; chemist's wife. **апте́чка**, -и, medicine chest; first-aid kit. **апте́чный**, medicine, drug.
ара́б, -а, **ара́бка**, -и, Arab. **ара́бский**, Arab, Arabian, Arabic; arabic. **арави́йский**, Arabian.
ара́п, -а, Negro; trickster, swindler.
ара́пник, -а, (huntsman's) whip.
арба́, -ы́; *pl.* -ы, (bullock-)cart.
арби́тр, -а, arbitrator. **арбитра́ж**, -а, arbitration.
арбу́з, -а, water-melon.
аргуме́нт, -а, argument. **аргумента́ция**, -и, reasoning; arguments. **аргументи́ровать**, -рую *perf.* and *imp.* argue, (try to) prove.
аре́на, -ы, arena, ring.
аре́нда, -ы, lease; rent; в аре́нду, on lease. **аренда́тор**, -а, leaseholder, tenant. **арендова́ть**, -ду́ю *perf.* and *imp.* lease, take or hold on lease.
аре́ст, -а, arrest; seizure, sequestration. **аре́ста́нт**, -а, -а́нтка, -и prisoner. **ареста́нтская** *sb.* lock-up, cells. **арестова́ть**, -ту́ю *perf.*, **аресто́вывать**, -аю *imp.* arrest; seize, sequestrate.
арифме́тика, -и, arithmetic. **арифмети́ческий**, arithmetical. **арифмо́граф**, -а, **арифмо́метр**, -а, calculating machine.
а́рка, -и, arch. **арка́да**, -ы, arcade.
арка́н, -а, lasso. **арка́нить**, -ню *imp.* (*perf.* за~) lasso.
армату́ра, -ы, fittings, accessories, equipment; reinforcement; armature; trophy (of arms). **армату́рщик**, -а, fitter.
арме́ец, -е́йца, soldier; *pl.* Soviet Army Sports-Club team. **арме́йский**, army.
а́рмия, -и, army.
армя́к, -а́, peasant's heavy overcoat.
армяни́н, -а; *pl.* -я́не, -я́н, **армя́нка**, -и, Armenian. **армя́нский**, Armenian.
арома́т, -а, scent, odour, aroma. **аромати́ческий**, **аромати́чный**, **арома́тный**, aromatic, fragrant.
а́рочный, arched, vaulted.
арсена́л, -а, arsenal.
арта́читься, -чусь *imp.* jib, be restive; dig one's heels in; be pigheaded, be obstinate.
арте́ль, -и, artel. **арте́льный**, of an artel; common, collective. **арте́льщик**, -а, **арте́льщица**, -ы, member, leader, of an artel.
артериа́льный, arterial. **арте́рия**, -и, artery.
артиллери́йский, artillery, ordnance. **артилле́рия**, -и, artillery.
арти́ст, -а, -**и́стка**, -и, artiste, artist,

performer; expert. **артисти́ческая** *sb.* dressing-room, green-room, artists' room. **артисти́ческий,** artistic.

áрфа, -ы, harp. **арфи́ст,** -а, **-и́стка,** -и, harpist.

архи́в, -а, archives. **архива́риус,** -а, **архиви́ст,** -а, archivist. **архи́вный,** archive, archival.

архидья́кон, -а, archdeacon. **архиепи́скоп,** -а, archbishop. **архиере́й,** -я, bishop.

архите́ктор, -а, architect. **архитекту́ра,** -ы, architecture. **архитекту́рный,** architectural.

арши́н, -а; *gen. pl.* -ши́н(ов), arshin (71 cm.); arshin-rule; как бу́дто ~ проглоти́л, bolt upright, as stiff as a poker.

асе́ссор, -а; колле́жский ~, Collegiate Assessor (8th grade: see чин).

аске́т, -а, ascetic. **аскети́зм,** -а, asceticism. **аскети́ческий,** ascetic.

áспид[1], -а, asp; viper.

áспид[2], -а, slate. **áспидн|ый;** ~ая доска́, slate.

аспира́нт, -а, **-а́нтка,** -и, post-graduate student. **аспиранту́ра** -ы, post-graduate course; post-graduate students.

ассигна́ция, -и, banknote.

ассамбле́я, -и, assembly; ball.

ассисте́нт, -а, assistant; junior lecturer, research assistant. **ассисти́ровать,** -рую, *imp.*+*dat.* assist.

ассоциа́ция, -и, association. **ассоции́ровать,** -рую *perf.* and *imp.* associate.

АССР (*a-esesér*) *abbr.* автоно́мная сове́тская социалисти́ческая респу́блика, Autonomous Soviet Socialist Republic.

астрона́вт, -а, astronaut. **астрона́втика,** -и, space-travel. **астроно́м,** -а, astronomer. **астрономи́ческий,** astronomical. **астроно́мия,** -и, astronomy.

ась *int.* eh?

атама́н, -а, ataman; Cossack chieftain, commander; (gang-)leader, robber chieftain.

ателье́ *n. indecl.* studio; atelier.

áтлас[1], -а, atlas.

атла́с[2], -а, satin. **атла́систый, атла́сный,** satin; like satin, satiny.

атле́т, -а, athlete; acrobat; strong man. **атле́тика,** -и, athletics; лёгкая ~, track and field sports; тяжёлая ~, weight-lifting, boxing, wrestling. **атлети́ческий,** athletic.

атмосфе́ра, -ы, atmosphere. **атмосфери́ческий, атмосфе́рный,** atmospheric; атмосфе́рные оса́дки, rainfall.

áтом, -а, atom. **атоми́стика,** -и, atomics; atomic theory. **атомисти́ческий,** atomistic. **áтомник,** -а, atomic scientist. **áтомный,** atomic.

АТС (*ateés*) *abbr.* автомати́ческая телефо́нная ста́нция, automatic telephone exchange.

аттеста́т, -а, testimonial, recommendation, reference; certificate: pedigree. **аттеста́ция,** -и, attestation; testimonial; confidential report. **аттестова́ть,** -ту́ю *perf.* and *imp.* attest; recommend.

ау́ *int.* halloo, cooee.

аудито́рия, -и, auditorium, lecture-room; audience.

а́укать(ся, -аю(сь *imp.*, **а́укнуть(ся,** -ну(сь *perf.* halloo, cooee.

ау́л, -а, aul, Caucasian or Central Asian village.

áутборт, -а, outboard motor.

афи́нский, Athenian. **афи́нянин,** -а; *pl.* -яне, **афи́нянка,** -и, Athenian.

афи́ша, -и, placard, poster. **афиши́ровать,** -рую *perf.* and *imp.* parade, advertise; **~ся,** be exhibitionist, seek the limelight.

африка́нец, -нца, **африка́нка,** -и, African. **африка́нский,** African.

аффе́кт, -а, fit of passion, rage, nervous excitement; temporary insanity.

ах *int.* ah, oh. **áхи,** -ов *pl.* ahs, ohs. **áханье,** -я, sighing; exclamations. **áхать,** -аю *imp.* (*perf.* áхнуть) sigh; exclaim; gasp.

ахине́я, -и, nonsense, rubbish; нести́ ахине́ю, talk nonsense.

áхнуть, -ну *perf.* (*imp.* áхать) gasp, exclaim; bang; strike.

аэро- in *comb.* aero-, air-, aerial. **аэровокза́л,** -а, air terminal, airport

building. **~дро́м,** -а, aerodrome, airfield. **~зо́ль,** -я *m.* aerosol. **~на́вт,** -а, aeronaut. **~по́рт,** -а airport. **~по́чта,** -и, air-mail. **~сни́мок,** -мка, aerial photograph. **~ста́т,** -а, balloon. **~съёмка,** -и, aerial photography.
АЭС (*a-és*) *abbr.* а́томная электроста́нция, atomic power-station.

Б

б *letter*: see бэ.
б *part.*: see бы.
ба *int.* expressing surprise.
ба́ба, -ы, (married) peasant woman; woman; ка́менная ~, ancient stone image; сне́жная ~, snowman. **ба́б|ий;** ~ье ле́то, Indian summer; ~ьи ска́зки, old wives' tales. **ба́бка**[1], -и, grandmother; (повива́льная) ~, midwife.
ба́бка[2], -и, knucklebone; pastern; игра́ть в ба́бки, play at knucklebones.
ба́бочка, -и, butterfly; ночна́я ~, moth.
ба́бушка, -и, grandmother; granny.
бага́ж, -а́, luggage. **бага́жник,** -а, carrier; luggage-rack; boot. **бага́жный,** luggage; ~ ваго́н, luggage-van.
багрове́ть, -е́ю *imp.* (*perf.* по~) crimson, flush, go red. **багро́вый, багря́ный,** crimson, purple.
бадья́, -и́; *gen. pl.* -де́й, tub, bucket, pail.
ба́за, -ы, base; centre; stock, stores; basis.
база́р, -а, market, fair; bazaar; row, din. **база́рный,** market.
бази́ровать, -рую *imp.* base; **~ся,** be based, rest (on).
байда́рка, -и, canoe; kayak. **байда́рочный,** canoe.
ба́йка, flannelette flannel. **ба́йковый,** flannelette, flannel; ~ плато́к, woollen shawl.
бак[1], -а, tank, cistern; can, billy.
бак[2], -а, forecastle.
бакале́йный, grocer's, grocery. **бакале́йщик,** -а, grocer. **бакале́я,** -и, groceries.
ба́кан, -а, **ба́кен,** -а, buoy.
бакенба́рды, -ба́рд *pl.*, **ба́кены,** -ов *pl.* whiskers; side-whiskers. **ба́ки,** бак *pl.* sideburns, (short) side-whiskers.
баклажа́н, -а; *gen. pl.* -ов or -жа́н aubergine.
бактериа́льный, бактери́йный, bacterial. **бактерио́лог,** -а, bacteriologist.
бакте́рия, -и, bacterium.
бал, -а, *loc.* -у́; *pl.* -ы́, dance, ball.
балага́н, -а, booth; side-show; popular show; farce, buffoonery. **балага́нить,** -ню *imp.* play the fool. **балага́нщик,** -а, showman; clown, buffoon.
балала́ечник, -а, balalaika-player.
балала́йка, -и, balalaika.
баламу́т, -а, trouble-maker. **баламу́тить,** -у́чу *imp.* (*perf.* вз~) stir up, trouble; disturb; upset.
бала́нда, -ы, (*sl.*) watery soup, skilly, swill.
балансёр, -а, rope-walker.
баланси́р, -а, balance, balance-wheel. **баланси́ровать,** -рую *imp.* (*perf.* с~) balance; keep one's balance.
балахо́н, -а, loose overall; shapeless garment.
балбе́с, -а, booby.
балдахи́н, -а, canopy.
балери́на, -ы, ballerina. **бале́т,** -а, ballet.
ба́лка[1], -и. beam, girder.
ба́лка[2], -и, ravine, gully.
балл, -а, mark, number, point, degree; force; ве́тер в пять ~ов, wind force 5.
балла́ст, -а, ballast; lumber.
балло́н, -а, container, carboy, cylinder; balloon tyre.
баллоти́ровать, -рую *imp.* ballot, vote; put to the vote; **~ся,** stand, be a candidate (в or на + *acc.* for). **баллотиро́вка,** -и, vote, ballot, poll; polling, voting.

бало́ванный, spoilt. **балова́ть,** -лу́ю *imp.* (*perf.* из~) spoil; indulge, pamper; play about, play up; +*instr.* play with, play at, amuse oneself with; **~ся,** play about, get up to tricks; amuse oneself, play; +*instr.* indulge in. **ба́ловень,** -вня *m.* spoilt child; pet, favourite. **баловство́,** -а́, spoiling, over-indulgence; pampering; monkey tricks, mischief.

балти́йский, Baltic.

бальза́м, -а, balsam; balm. **бальзами́ровать,** -рую *imp.* (*perf.* на~) embalm.

ба́льный, ball, dance.

балюстра́да, -ы, balustrade; banister. **баля́сина,** -ы, baluster, banister. **баля́сы,** -я́с *pl.* banisters; точи́ть ~, jest, joke.

бамбу́к, -а, bamboo. **бамбу́ков|ый,** bamboo; ~ое положе́ние, awkward situation.

бан, -а, *loc.* -у́, (*sl.*) railway station.

ба́нда, -ы, band, gang.

банда́ж, -а́, truss; belt, bandage; tyre.

бандеро́ль, -и, wrapper; printed matter, book-post.

банди́т, -а, bandit, brigand; gangster.

банк, -а, bank.

ба́нка[1], -и, jar; tin.

ба́нка[2], -и, (sand-)bank, shoal.

банки́р, -а, banker. **банкро́т,** -а, bankrupt.

бант, -а, bow. **ба́нтик,** -а, bow; гу́бки ~ом, Cupid's bow. **бантов|о́й;** ~а́я скла́дка, box-pleat.

ба́ня, -и, bath, bath-house.

бар, -а, bar; snack-bar.

бараба́н, -а, drum. **бараба́нить,** -ню *imp.* drum, thump. **бараба́нн|ый,** drum; ~ая дробь, drum-roll; ~ая перепо́нка, ear-drum. **бараба́нщик,** -а, drummer.

бара́к, -а, barrack; *pl.* hutments.

бара́н, -а, ram; sheep. **бара́ний,** sheep's; sheepskin; mutton. **бара́нина,** -ы, mutton.

бара́нка, -и, baranka, ring-shaped roll; (steering-)wheel.

барахли́ть, -лю́ *imp.* pink, knock; talk rubbish.

барахло́, -а́, old clothes, jumble; odds and ends; trash, junk; rubbish. **барахо́лка,** -и, second-hand market, junk-stall.

бара́хтаться, -аюсь *imp.* flounder, wallow, thrash about.

бара́шек, -шка, young ram; lamb; lambskin; wing nut; catkin; *pl.* white horses; fleecy clouds. **бара́шковый,** lambskin.

баржа́, -и or -и́; *gen. pl.* барж(е́й), barge.

ба́рин, -а; *pl.* -ре or -ры, бар, barin; land-owner; gentleman; master; sir.

ба́рка, -и, barge.

баро́чный, baroque.

барс, -а, ounce, snow-leopard.

ба́рский, gentleman's; lordly; grand. **ба́рственный,** lordly, grand, arrogant.

барсу́к, -а́, badger. **барсу́чий,** badger; badger-skin.

барха́н, -а, sand-hill, dune.

ба́рхат, -а (-у), velvet. **бархати́стый,** velvety. **ба́рхатка,** -и, velvet ribbon. **ба́рхатный,** velvet; velvety.

барчо́нок, -нка; *pl.* -ча́та -ча́т, **барчу́к,** -а́, barin's son; young master, young gentleman.

барыга, -и, (*sl.*) fence.

ба́рыня, -и, barin's wife; lady; mistress; madam.

бары́ш, -а́, profit. **бары́шник,** -а, dealer; buyer for re-sale; jobber; (ticket) speculator. **бары́шничать,** -аю *imp.* deal, speculate, job (+*instr.* in).

ба́рышня, -и; *gen. pl.* -шень, barin's daughter; young lady, young mistress; miss.

барье́р, -а, barrier; obstacle; bar; fence, jump, hurdle. **барьери́ст,** -а, -и́стка, -и, hurdler. **барье́рный,** hurdle; ~ бег hurdle-race.

бас, -а; *pl.* -ы́, bass. **баси́стый,** bass.

баскетбо́л, -а, basket-ball. **баскетболи́ст,** -а, -и́стка, -и, basket-ball player. **баскетбо́льный,** basket-ball.

баснопи́сец, -сца, fabulist, writer of fables. **баснословный,** mythical, legendary; fabulous. **ба́сня,** -и; *gen. pl.* -сен, fable; legend; fabrication.

басо́вый, bass.

бассе́йн, -а, basin; pool, pond; reser-

voir; swimming-pool; каменноуго́льный ~, у́гольный ~, coal-field.
бастова́ть, -ту́ю *imp.* be on strike.
батаре́ец, -е́йца, gunner. **батаре́йка,** -и, **батаре́я,** -и, battery; radiator.
бати́ст, -а (-у), batiste, cambric, lawn.
бато́н, -а, long loaf; stick, bar. **бато́нчик,** -а, stick, bar; шокола́дный ~, bar of chocolate.
батра́к, -а́, **батра́чка,** -и, farm-hand, farm-worker, farm labourer. **батра́цкий,** farm, farm labourer's.
ба́тька, -и *m.*, **ба́тюшка,** -и *m.*, **ба́тя,** -и *m.* father; my dear chap. **ба́тюшки** *int.* expressing amazement or fright.
бах *int.* bang! **ба́хать(ся,** -аю(сь *imp.* of ба́хнуть(ся.
бахва́л, -а, boaster, braggart. **бахва́льство,** -а, bragging, boasting.
ба́хнуть, -ну *perf.* (*imp.* ба́хать) bang; thump; **~ся,** fall or bump heavily and noisily; let oneself fall, plump down; ~ся голово́й, bang one's head.
бахрома́, -ы́ fringe. **бахро́мчатый,** fringed.
бац *int.* bang! crack! **ба́цать,** -аю *imp.*, **ба́цнуть,** -ну *perf.* crack, bang, bash.
баци́лла, -ы, bacillus. **бациллоноси́тель,** -я *m.* carrier.
ба́шенка, -и, turret. **ба́шенный,** tower, turret.
башка́, -и́, head. **башкови́тый,** brainy.
башлы́к, -а́, hood.
башма́к, -а́, shoe; chock; под ~о́м у+*gen.* under the thumb of.
ба́шня, -и; *gen. pl.* -шен, tower, turret.
ба́ю-бай, ба́юшки-баю́ *int.* hushabye, lullaby. **баю́кать,** -аю *imp.* (*perf.* у~) lull, rock, sing to sleep.
БГДТ (*begedeté*) *abbr.* Большо́й госуда́рственный драмати́ческий теа́тр, Great State Dramatic Theatre.
бде́ние, -я, vigil, wakefulness. **бди́тельность,** -и, vigilance, watchfulness. **бди́тельный,** vigilant, watchful.
бег, -а, *loc.* -у́; *pl.* -а́, run, running; double; race; *pl.* trotting-races. **бе́гать,** -аю *indet.* (*det.* бежа́ть) *imp.* run; move quickly.
бегемо́т, -а, hippopotamus.
бегле́ц, -а́, **бегля́нка,** -и, fugitive. **бе́глость,** -и, speed, fluency, dexterity. **бе́глый,** fugitive; quick, rapid, fluent; fleeting, cursory, passing; ~ гла́сный, fugitive vowel, fill-vowel; *sb.* fugitive, runaway. **беговóй,** running; race; ~ круг, race-course, ring. **бего́м** *adv.* running, at a run, at the double. **беготня́,** -и́, running about; bustle. **бе́гство,** -а, flight, hasty retreat; escape. **бегу́н,** -а́, **бегу́нья,** -и; *gen. pl.* -ний, runner.
беда́, -ы́; *pl.* -ы, misfortune; calamity, disaster; trouble; ~ в том, что, the trouble is (that); ~ как, terribly, awfully; на беду́, unfortunately; не ~, it doesn't matter; что за ~! what does it matter? so what? **бедне́ть,** -е́ю *imp.* (*perf.* о~) grow poor. **бе́дность,** -и, poverty, the poor. **бе́дный;** -ден, -дна́, -дно, poor; poverty-stricken. **бедня́га,** -и *m.*, **бедня́жка,** -и *m.* and *f.* poor thing, poor creature. **бедня́к,** -а́, **бедня́чка,** -и, poor peasant; poor man, poor woman. **бедня́чество,** -а, poor peasants.
бе́дренный, femoral, thigh-. **бедро́,** -а́; *pl.* бёдра, -дер, thigh; hip; leg.
бе́дственный, disastrous, calamitous. **бе́дствие,** -я, disaster, calamity; сигна́л бе́дствия, distress signal. **бе́дствовать,** -твую *imp.* be in want, live in poverty.
бежа́ть, бегу́ *det.* (*indet.* бе́гать) *imp.* (*perf.* по~) run; flow; fly; boil over; *perf.* and *imp.* escape. **бе́женец,** -нца, **бе́женка,** -и, refugee.
без, безо *prep.*+*gen.* without; in the absence of; minus, less, short of; ~ вас, in your absence; ~ ма́лого, almost, all but; ~ пяти́ (мину́т), five (minutes) to; ~ ума́ (от+*gen.*) mad, crazy (about); ~ че́тверти, a quarter to.
без-, безъ-, бес- in *comb.* in-, un-; non-; -less. **безавари́йный,** accident-free; without breakdowns. **~ала́берный,** disorderly, unsystematic; slovenly, careless. **~алкого́льный,** non-alcoholic, soft. **~апелляцио́нный,** without appeal; peremptory, categorical. **~биле́тник,** -а, **-ница,** -ы, passenger without a ticket; stowaway. **~бо́жие,** -я,

atheism, **~бо́жный**, atheistic; irreligious, anti-religious; godless; shameless, scandalous, outrageous. **~боле́зненный**, painless. **~бра́чность, -и**, unmarried state, living in sin. **~бра́чный**. celibate. **~бре́жный**, boundless. **~ве́рие, -я**, unbelief. **~ве́стный**, unknown; obscure. **~ве́тренный**, calm, windless. **~ви́нный**, guiltless, innocent. **~вку́сие**, -я, **~вку́сица**, -ы lack of taste bad taste. **~вку́сный**, tasteless. **~вла́стие**, -я, anarchy. **~во́дный** arid, waterless; anhydrous. **~возвра́тный**, irrevocable; irretrievable; irrecoverable. **~возме́здный**, free, gratis; unpaid. **~во́лие** -я, weakness of will, lack of will-power. **~во́льный**, weak-willed, spineless. **~вре́дный**, harmless, innocuous. **~време́нный**, untimely, premature. **~вы́ходный**, hopeless, desperate; without going out; uninterrupted. **~гла́зый**, one-eyed, eyeless. **~гла́сный**, silent, dumb; powerless to protest **~голо́сный** voiceless, unvoiced. **~гра́мотный**, illiterate; ignorant. **~грани́чный**, boundless, limitless, infinite. **~гре́шный**, innocent, sinless, without sin. **~да́рный**, ungifted, untalented. **~де́йственный**, inactive; idle, passive. **~де́йствие, -я**, inaction, inactivity, inertia, idleness; negligence. **~де́йствовать**, -твую *imp.* be idle, be inactive; stand idle, not work.

безде́лица, -ы, **безде́лка**, -и, trifle, bagatelle. **безделу́шка**, -и, trinket, knick-knack, toy. **безде́льник**, -а, idler, loafer; ne'er-do-well. **безде́льничать**, -аю *imp.* idle, loaf. **безде́льный**, idle; trifling.

бе́здна, -ы, abyss, chasm; enormous numbers, a multitude, masses.

без-. **бездо́ждье**, -я, dry weather, drought. **~доказа́тельный**, unsupported, unsubstantiated, unproved. **~до́мный**, homeless. **~до́нный**, bottomless, fathomless. **~доро́жный**, without roads. **~доро́жье**, -я, lack of (good) roads; season when roads are impassable. **~ду́шный**, heartless, callous; soulless, lifeless. **~жа́лостный**, pitiless, ruthless. **~жи́зненный**, lifeless. **~забо́тный**, carefree, untroubled, careless. **~заве́тный**, selfless, whole-hearted. **~зако́ние**, -я, lawlessness; unlawful act. **~зако́нный**, illegal, unlawful; lawless. **~засте́нчивый**, shameless, unblushing, barefaced. **~защи́тный**, defenceless, unprotected. **~земе́льный**, landless. **~зло́бный**, good-natured, kindly. **~ли́чный**, characterless without personality, without individuality; impersonal. **~лу́нный**, moonless. **~лю́дный**, uninhabited; sparsely populated; lonely, solitary; empty, unfrequented.

безме́н, -а, steelyard; spring balance.

без-. **безме́рный**, boundless, limitless. **~мо́зглый**, brainless. **~мо́лвие**, -я, silence. **~мо́лвный**, silent, mute. **~мото́рный**, engineless; ~мото́рный самолёт, glider. **~мяте́жный**, serene, placid. **~надёжный**, hopeless. **~надзо́рный**, neglected. **~нака́занно** *adv.* with impunity, unpunished. **~нака́занный**, unpunished. **~но́гий**, legless; one-legged. **~нра́вственный**, immoral.

безо *prep.*: see без.

безобра́зие, -я, ugliness; outrage; disgrace, scandal. **безобра́зить**, -а́жу *imp.* (*perf.* о~) disfigure, mutilate; create a disturbance, make a nuisance of oneself. **безобра́зничать**, -аю *imp.* behave outrageously; make a nuisance of oneself.

без-. **безогово́рочный**, unconditional. **~опа́сность**, -и, safety, security. **~опа́сный**, safe; secure; ~опа́сная бри́тва, safety razor. **~ору́жный**, unarmed. **~оско́лочный**, unsplinterable; splinter-proof, shatter-proof. **~основа́тельный**, groundless. **~остано́вочный**, unceasing, continuous; without a break; sustained; non-stop. **~отве́тный**, meek, unanswering; unanswered; dumb. **~отве́тственный**, irresponsible. **~отка́зно** *adv.* without a hitch. **~отка́зный**, trouble-free, smooth(-running). **~отлага́тельный**, **~отло́жный**, urgent. **~отлу́чный**, uninterrupted; continual, continuous; ever-present. **~относи́тельно** *adv.* + к + *dat.* irrespective of. **~относи́тель-**

ный, absolute, unconditional. **~отра́дный**, cheerless, dreary. **~отчётный**, uncontrolled; unaccountable; instinctive. **~оши́бочный**, unerring, faultless; correct. **~рабо́тица**, -ы, unemployment. **~рабо́тный**, unemployed. **~разде́льный**, undivided; wholehearted; complete. **~разли́чие**, -я, indifference. **~разли́чно** *adv.* indifferently; it is all the same. **~разли́чный**, indifferent; neutral. **~разме́рный**, one-size, stretch. **~рассу́дный**, reckless, foolhardy, imprudent. **~ро́дный**, alone in the world; without relatives; of unknown antecedents. **~ро́потный**, uncomplaining, unmurmuring; meek, resigned. **~рука́вка**, -и, sleeveless jacket, jerkin. **~ру́кий**, armless; one-armed; awkward. **~уда́рный**, unstressed, unaccented. **~у́держный**, unrestrained, uncontrolled; uncontrollable. **~укори́зненный**, irreproachable, impecable.

безу́мец, -мца, madman. **безу́мие**, -я, madness, insanity; distraction. **безу́мный**, mad, insane; crazy, senseless; terrible. **~у́мство**, -а, madness.

без-. **безупре́чный**, irreproachable, faultless. **~уря́дица**, -ы, disorder, confusion. **~уса́дочный**, non-shrink. **~слу́овно** *adv.* unconditionally, absolutely; of course, undoubtedly, certainly. **~усло́вный**, unconditional, absolute; undoubted, indisputable. **~успе́шный**, unsuccessful. **~уста́нный**, tireless; ceaseless, unremitting. **~уте́шный**, inconsolable. **~уча́стие**, -я, **~уча́стность**, -и, indifference, apathy. **~уча́стный**, indifferent, apathetic, unconcerned. **~ыде́йный**, without ideas or ideals; unideological; unprincipled. **~ызве́стный**, unknown, obscure. **~ымённый**, **~ымя́нный**, nameless, anonymous; ~ымя́нный па́лец, third finger, ring-finger. **~ынтере́сный**, uninteresting. **~ыску́сственный**, **~ыску́сный**, artless, ingenuous, unsophisticated. **~ысхо́дный**, hopeless, inconsolable; irreparable; interminable.

бейсбо́л, -а, baseball. **бейсболи́ст**, -а, baseball player.

бека́р, -а, **бека́р** *indecl. adj.* natural.

бека́с, -а, snipe. **бекаси́нник**, -а, small shot.

беко́н, -а, bacon.

беле́ть, -е́ю *imp.* (*perf.* по~) grow white, turn white; show white; **~ся**, show white.

белизна́, -ы́, whiteness. **бели́ла**, -и́л *pl.* whitewash, whiting; ceruse. **бели́льный**, bleaching. **бели́ть**, -лю́, бе́ли́шь *imp.* (*perf.* вы~, на~, по~) whitewash; whiten; bleach; **~ся**, put ceruse on.

бе́личий, squirrel, squirrel's. **бе́лка**, -и, squirrel.

белко́вый, albuminous.

беллетри́ст, -а, writer of fiction. **беллетри́стика**, -и, fiction.

бело- in *comb.*, white-, leuco-. **белогварде́ец**, -е́йца, White Guard. **~кро́вие**, -я, leukaemia. **~ку́рый**, fair, blonde. **~ру́с**, -а, **~ру́ска**, -и, **~ру́сский**, Belorussian. **~ры́бица**, white salmon. **~сне́жный**, snow-white.

белови́к, -а́, fair copy. **белово́й**, clean fair.

бело́к, -лка́, white; albumen, protein.

белошве́йка, -и, seamstress. **белошве́йн|ый**, linen; ~ая рабо́та, plain sewing.

белу́га, -и, beluga, white sturgeon.

белу́ха, -и, white whale.

бе́л|ый; бел, -а́, бе́ло́, white; clean, blank; ~ая берёза, silver birch; ~ый день, broad daylight; ~ое кале́ние, white heat; ~ый медве́дь polar bear; ~ые но́чи, white nights, midnight sun; ~ые стихи́, blank verse.

бельё, -я́, linen; bedclothes, underclothes, underclothing; washing.

бельмо́, -а́; *pl.* -а, cataract; wall-eye.

бельэта́ж, -а, first floor; dress circle

бемо́ль, -я *m.*, **бемо́ль** *indecl. adj.* flat.

бенефи́с, -а, benefit (performance).

бензи́н, -а, petrol; benzine. **бензи́нов|ый**, petrol; ~ая коло́нка, petrol pump. **бензиноме́р**, -а, petrol-gauge. **бензинопрово́д**, -а, petrol pipe.

бензо- in *comb.*, petrol. **бензоба́к**, -а, petrol-tank. **~запра́вка**, -и, **~запра́вочная** *sb.*, filling-station, petrol-station. **~запра́вщик**, -а, petrol bowser,

~коло́нка, -и, petrol pump. **~ме́р,** -а, fuel gauge. **~очисти́тель,** -я *m.* petrol filter. **~прово́д,** -а, petrol pipe, fuel line. **~храни́лище** -а, petrol (storage) tank. **~цисте́рна,** -ы, petrol tanker.
бензо́л, -а, benzene; benzol.
берёг etc.: see бере́чь.
бе́рег, -а, *loc.* -у́; *pl.* -а́, bank, shore; coast; на ~у́ мо́ря, at the seaside.
берегов|о́й, coast; coastal; ~о́е судохо́дство, coastal shipping.
бережёшь, etc.: see бере́чь. **бережли́вый,** thrifty, economical; careful. **бе́режный,** careful; cautious; solicitous.
берёза, -ы, birch. **бере́зник,** -а, **березня́к,** -а́, birch grove, birch wood. **берёзовый,** birch.
бере́йтор, -а, horse-breaker; riding-master.
бере́менеть, -ею *imp.* (*perf.* за~) become pregnant; be pregnant. **бере́менный,** pregnant (+*instr.*, with). **бере́менность,** -и, pregnancy; gestation.
бере́чь, -регу́, -режёшь; -рёг, -ла́ *imp.* take care of, look after; keep; cherish; husband; be sparing of; **~ся,** be careful, take care; beware; береги́(те)сь! look out!
берли́нск|ий, Berlin; ~ая лазу́рь, Prussian blue.
берло́га, -и, den, lair.
беру́, etc.: see брать.
бес, -а, devil; the devil.
бес-: see без-.
бесе́да, -ы, talk, conversation; discussion. **бесе́дка,** -и, summer-house. **бесе́довать,** -дую *imp.* talk, converse. **бесе́дчик,** -а, discussion-leader.
беси́ть, бешу́, бе́сишь *imp.* (*perf.* вз~) enrage, madden, infuriate; **~ся,** go mad; rage, be furious.
бес-. бескла́ссовый, classless. **~коне́чный,** endless; infinite; interminable; ~коне́чная дробь, recurring decimal. **~коры́стие,** -я, disinterestedness. **~коры́стный,** disinterested. **~кра́йний,** boundless. **~кро́вный,** bloodless.
бесноватый, like one possessed; raving, frenzied. **бесноваться,** -ну́юсь *imp.* rage, storm, rave; be possessed. **бесо́вский,** devilish, devil's.
бес-. беспа́мятный, forgetful. **~па́мятство,** -а, unconsciousness; forgetfulness; delirium. **~пардо́нный,** shameless, brazen. **~парти́йный,** non-party. **~перспекти́вный,** without prospects; hopeless. **~пе́чность,** -и, carelessness, unconcern. **~пе́чный,** carefree; careless, unconcerned. **~пла́тно** *adv.* free. **~пла́тный,** free; rent-free; complimentary. **~пло́дие,** -я, sterility, barrenness. **~пло́дность,** -и, fruitlessness, futility. **~пло́дный,** sterile, barren; fruitless, futile. **~поворо́тный,** irrevocable, final. **~подо́бный,** incomparable, superb, magnificent. **~позвоно́чный,** invertebrate.
беспоко́ить, -о́ю *imp.* (*perf.* о~, по~) disturb, make anxious, make uneasy; trouble; **~ся,** worry, be anxious; trouble, put oneself out. **беспоко́йный,** restless; anxious; uneasy; troubled; disturbing; fidgety.
бес-. бесполе́зный, useless. **~по́лый,** sexless, asexual. **~по́мощный,** helpless, powerless; feeble. **~поро́дный,** mongrel, not thoroughbred. **~поро́чный,** blameless, irreproachable; immaculate. **~поря́док,** -дка, disorder; untidy state; *pl.* disorders, disturbances, rioting. **~поря́дочный,** disorderly; untidy. **~поса́дочный,** non-stop. **~по́чвенный,** groundless; unsound. **~по́шлинный,** duty-free; ~по́шлинная торго́вля, free trade. **~поща́дный,** merciless, relentless. **~пра́вный,** without rights, deprived of civil rights. **~преде́льный,** boundless, infinite. **~предме́тный,** aimless, purposeless; abstract. **~прекосло́вный,** unquestioning, absolute. **~препя́тственный,** unhindered; free, clear, unimpeded. **~преры́вный,** continuous, uninterrupted. **~преста́нный,** continual, incessant.
беспризо́рник, -а, **-ница,** -ы, waif, homeless child. **беспризо́рный,** neglected, stray; homeless; *sb.* waif, homeless child or young person.

бес-. **беспримéрный,** unexampled, unparalleled. **~пристрáстие, -я, ~пристрáстность,** -и, impartiality. **~пристрáстный,** impartial, unbiased. **~прию́тный,** homeless; not affording shelter. **~прóволочный,** wireless. **~просвéтный,** pitch-dark, pitch-black; hopeless, gloomy; unrelieved. **~пу́тный,** debauched, dissipated, dissolute. **~свя́зный,** incoherent. **~семя́нный,** seedless. **~сердéчие, -я, ~сердéчность,** -и, heartlessness, callousness. **~сердéчный,** heartless; callous, unfeeling, hard-hearted. **~си́лие, -я,** impotence; debility, feebleness. **~си́льный** weak, feeble; impotent, powerless. **~слáвие,** -я, infamy. **~слáвный,** ignominious; infamous; inglorious. **~слéдно** *adv.* without trace; utterly, completely. **~слéдный,** without leaving a trace, complete. **~словéсный** dumb, speechless; silent, unmurmuring, meek, humble; walking-on. **~смéнный,** permanent, continuous. **~смéртие,** -я, immortality. **~смéртный,** immortal, undying. **~смы́сленный,** senseless; foolish; meaningless, nonsensical. **~смы́слица,** -ы, nonsense. **~сóвестный,** unscrupulous; shameless. **~сознáтельный,** unconscious; involuntary. **~сóнница,** -ы, insomnia, sleeplessness. **~сóнный,** sleepless. **~спóрный,** indisputable, undeniable, unquestionable; incontrovertible. **~срóчный,** indefinite; indeterminate; unlimited. **~стрáстный,** impassive. **~стрáшный,** intrepid, fearless. **~талáнный,** untalented, without talent.

бестолкóвщина, -ы muddle, confusion, disorder. **бестолкóвый,** muddle-headed, slow, stupid; confused, incoherent. **бéстолочь,** -и, confusion, muddle; stupid creature; blockheads.

бес-. **бестрéпетный,** dauntless, undaunted, intrepid. **~фóрменный,** shapeless, formless. **~харáктерный,** weak, spineless. **~хи́тростный,** artless; ingenuous; unsophisticated. **~цвéтный,** colourless. **~цéльный,** aimless; pointless. **~цéнный,** priceless. **~цéнок;** за ~цéнок, very cheap, for a song. **~церемóнный,** unceremonious; free and easy, familiar, off-hand. **~человéчный,** inhuman. **~чéстить,** -éщу *imp.* (*perf.* о~чéстить) dishonour, disgrace. **~чéстный,** dishonourable, disgraceful. **~чи́сленный,** innumerable, countless.

бесчу́вственный, insensible, unconscious; insensitive, unfeeling. **бесчу́вствие,** -я, unconsciousness, insensibility; callousness, heartlessness; пьян до бесчу́вствия, dead drunk.

бес-. **бесшóвный,** seamless. **~шу́мный,** noiseless.

бетóн, -а, concrete. **бетони́ровать,** -рую *imp.* (*perf.* за-), concrete. **бетóнный,** concrete. **бетономешáлка,** -и, concrete-mixer. **бетóнщик,** -а, concrete-worker, concreter.

бечевá, бичевá, -ы́, tow-rope; rope, cord, twine. **бечёвка, бичёвка,** -и, twine, cord, string. **бечевни́к,** -á, tow-path, towing-path. **бечев|óй,** tow, towing; **~áя** *sb.* tow-path, towing-path.

бéшенство, -а, hydrophobia, rabies; fury, rage. **бéшеный,** rabid, mad; furious, violent.

бешу́ etc.: see беси́ть.

бибабó *n. indecl.* glove puppet.

библéйский, biblical. **библиóграф,** -а, bibliographer. **библиографи́ческий,** bibliographical. **библиотéка,** -и, library; ~-читáльня, reading-room. **библиотéкарь,** -я *m.*, **-тéкарша,** -и, librarian. **библиотéчный,** library. **би́блия.** -и, bible.

бивáк, -а, bivouac, camp.

би́вень, -вня *m.* tusk.

бигуди́ *pl. indecl.* curlers.

бидóн, -а, can; milk-churn.

биéние, -я beating; beat.

бижутéрия, -и, costume jewellery.

би́кса, -ы, (*sl.*) whore.

билéт, -а, ticket; card; pass, permit; креди́тный ~, bank-note. **билетёр,** -а, **-тёрша,** -и, ticket-collector; usherette. **билéтный,** ticket.

бинóкль -я *m.* binoculars; полевóй ~, field-glasses; театрáльный ~, opera-glasses. **бинокуля́рный,** binocular.

бинт, -á, bandage. **бинтовáть,** -ту́ю

imp. (*perf.* за~) bandage. **бинто́вка,** -и, bandaging.

би́ржа, -и, exchange.

би́рка, -и, tally; name-plate; label.

бирюза́, -ы́, turquoise.

бис *int.* encore; спеть на ~, repeat as encore. **биси́ровать,** -рую *perf.* and *imp.* repeat; give an encore.

би́сер, -а, glass beads, bugles. **би́серина,** -ы, **би́серинка,** -и, (small) glass bead.

бискви́т, -а, sponge cake; biscuit. **бискви́тный,** sponge; biscuit.

би́тва, -ы, battle.

битко́м *adv.*; ~ наби́т, crowded, packed.

бито́к -тка́, rissole, hamburger.

би́т|ый, beaten; broken, cracked; ~ые сли́вки, whipped cream; ~ый час, a full hour; hours, ages. **бить,** бью, бьёшь *imp.* (*perf.* за~, по~, про~, уда́рить) beat; hit; defeat; strike; whip; sound; thump, bang; kill, slaughter; smash, shatter; fight, struggle, wage war (по+*dat.* on, against); spurt, gush; shoot, fire; ~ в бараба́н, beat a drum; ~ в ладо́ши, clap one's hands; ~ (в) наба́т, sound, raise, the alarm; ~ в цель, hit the target; ~ за́дом, kick; ~ключо́м, gush out, well up; be in full swing; ~ на+*acc.* strive for, after; have a range of; ~ отбо́й, beat a retreat; ~ по+*dat.*, damage, injure, wound; ~ трево́гу, sound, raise, the alarm; ~ хвосто́м, lash its tail; **~ся,** fight; beat; writhe, struggle; break; +*instr.* knock, hit, strike; +над+*instr.* struggle with, rack one's brains over; ~ голово́й об сте́ну, be up against a blank wall; ~ об закла́д, bet, wager. **битьё,** -я́, beating, thrashing; thumping, banging; smashing.

бич, -а́, whip, lash; scourge. **бичева́,** **бичёвка**: see бечева́, бечёвка. **бичева́ть,** -чу́ю *imp.* flog; lash, castigate.

бишь *part.* expressing effort to remember name, etc.: как ~ его́? what was the name again? what's-his-name, thingamy; то ~, that is to say.

бла́го, -а, good; blessing; всех благ! all the best! **бла́го** *conj.* since.

бла́го- in *comb.* well-, good-. **Благове́щение,** -я, Annunciation. **~ве́щенский,** of the Annunciation. **~ви́дный,** comely; plausible, specious. **~воле́ние,** -я, goodwill; favour. **~воспи́танный,** well-bred.

благодаре́ние, -я, gratitude, thanks. **благодари́ть,** -рю́ *imp.* (*perf.* по~) thank; благодарю́ вас, thank you. **благода́рность,** -и, gratitude; thanks; bribe; не сто́ит благода́рности, don't mention it, not at all. **благода́рный,** grateful; rewarding, promising. **благода́рственный,** of gratitude, of thanks; thanksgiving. **благодаря́** *prep.*+*dat.* thanks to, owing to; because of.

благо-. **благоде́тель,** -я *m.*, **-ница,** -ы, benefactor. **~де́тельный,** beneficial; beneficent. **~ду́шный,** placid, equable; good-humoured. **~жела́тель,** -я *m.* well-wisher. **~жела́тельный,** well-disposed; benevolent. **~зву́чный,** melodious, harmonious. **~мы́слящий,** right-thinking, right-minded. **~надёжный,** reliable, trustworthy, sure; loyal. **~наме́ренный,** well-intentioned. **~нра́вие,** -я, good behaviour. **~нра́вный,** well-behaved; high-principled. **~полу́чие,** -я, well-being; happiness. **~полу́чно** *adv.* all right, well; happily; safely. **~полу́чный,** happy, successful; safe. **~присто́йный,** decent, seemly, decorous. **~прия́тный,** favourable. **~прия́тствовать** *imp.*+*dat.* favour; наибо́лее ~прия́тствуемая держа́ва, most-favoured nation. **~разу́мие,** -я, sense; prudence. **~разу́мный,** judicious; sensible, prudent. **~ро́дие,** -я; ва́ше ~ро́дие, your Honour. **~ро́дный,** noble. **~ро́дство,** -а, nobility. **~скло́нность,** -и favour, good graces. **~скло́нный,** favourable; gracious. **~слови́ть,** -влю́ *perf.*, благословля́ть, -я́ю *imp.* bless. **~состоя́ние,** -я, prosperity. **~твори́тель,** -я *m.*, **-ница,** -ы, philanthopist. **~твори́тельный,** charitable, charity. **~тво́рный,** salutary; beneficial; wholesome. **~устро́енный,** well-equipped, well-arranged, well-planned; with all amenities.

блаже́нный, blessed; blissful; simple-minded. **блаже́нство,** -а, bliss, blessedness.

бланк, -а, form; анке́тный ~, questionnaire. **бла́нков|ый**, form; ~ая на́дпись, endorsement.

блат, -а, (*sl.*) thieves' cant, criminals' slang; pull, protection; racket, fiddle. **блата́рь**, -я́ *m.*, **блатня́к**, -а́, **блатя́га**, -и *m.* professional criminal; racketeer. **блатн|о́й**, criminal; soft, cushy; ~а́я му́зыка, thieves' cant; ~**о́й** *sb.* criminal, thief.

бледне́ть, -е́ю *imp.* (*perf.* по~), grow pale; pale. **бледноли́цый**, pale; *sb.* paleface. **бле́дность**, -и, **бледнота́**, -ы, paleness, pallor. **бле́дный**; -ден, -дна́, -о, pale; colourless; ~ как полотно́, as white as a sheet.

блёклый, faded. **блёкнуть**, -ну; блёк(нул) *imp.* (*perf.* по~) fade, wither.

блеск, -а (-у), brightness, brilliance, lustre, shine; splendour, magnificence.

блесну́ть, -ну́, -нёшь *perf.* flash, gleam; shine. **блесте́ть**, -ещу́, -сти́шь or бле́щешь *imp.* shine; glitter; sparkle. **блёстка**, -и, sparkle, flash; spangle, sequin. **блестя́щий**, shining, bright; brilliant.

бле́яние, -я, bleat, bleating. **бле́ять**, -е́ет *imp.* bleat.

ближа́йший, nearest, closest; next; immediate; ~ ро́дственник, next of kin. **бли́же** *comp.* of бли́зкий, бли́зко. **бли́жний**, near, close; neighbouring; *sb.* neighbour. **близ** *prep.*+*gen.* near, close to, by. **бли́зиться**, -зится *imp.* approach, draw near. **бли́зкий**; -зок, -изка́, -о, near, close; imminent; intimate; ~**кие** *sb. pl.* one's nearest and dearest, near relatives. **бли́зко** *adv.* near, close (от+*gen.* to); nearly, closely. **близне́ц**, -а́, twin; *pl.* Gemini. **близору́кий**, short-sighted. **бли́зость**, -и, nearness, closeness, proximity; intimacy.

блик, -а, spot or patch of light; light, high-light.

блин, -а́, pancake.

блинда́ж, -а́, dug-out.

блиста́тельный, brilliant, splendid. **блиста́ть**, -а́ю *imp.* shine; glitter; sparkle.

блок[1], -а, block, pulley, sheave.

блок[2], -а, bloc; block; section, unit; slab. **блоки́ровать**, -рую *perf.* and *imp.* blockade; block; ~**ся**, form a bloc. **блокиро́вка**, -и, block system.

блокно́т, -а, writing-pad, note-pad, note-book.

блонди́н, -а, **блонди́нка**, -и, blond(e).

блоха́, -и́; *pl.* -и, -а́м flea. **блоши́ный**, flea. **бло́шки**, -шек *pl.* tiddlywinks.

блудни́ца, -ы, whore.

блужда́ть, -а́ю *imp.* roam, wander, rove. **блужда́ющ|ий**, wandering; ~ий огонёк, will-o'-the-wisp; ~ая по́чка, floating kidney.

блу́за, -ы, **блу́зка**, -и, blouse.

блю́дечко, -а, saucer; small dish; на блю́дечке, on a plate. **блю́до**, -а, dish; course. **блю́дце**, -а, saucer.

блюсти́, -юду́, -дёшь; блюл, -а́ *imp.* (*perf.* со~), guard, keep; watch over; observe. **блюсти́тель**, -я *m.* keeper, guardian.

БНТИ (*be-entei*) *abbr.* бюро́ нау́чно-техни́ческой информа́ции, Scientific and Technical Information Bureau.

боб, -а́, bean. **бобо́в|ый**, bean; ~**ые** *sb. pl.* leguminous plants. **бобо́к**, -бка́, bean.

бобр, -а́, beaver. **бо́брик**, -а, beaver cloth; во́лосы ~ом, crew cut. **бобро́вый**, beaver.

бобы́ль, -я́ *m.* poor landless peasant; solitary person.

бог, -а, *voc.* Бо́же, god; God; дай ~, God grant; ~ его́ зна́ет, who knows? не дай ~, God forbid; Бо́же (мой)! my God! good God!; ра́ди ~а, for God's sake; с ~ом! good luck!; сла́ва ~у, thank God. **богаде́льня**, -и, almshouse, workhouse.

богате́й, -я, rich man. **богате́ть**, -е́ю *imp.* (*perf.* раз~), grow rich. **бога́тство**, -а, riches, wealth; richness. **бога́тый**, rich, wealthy; *sb.* rich man. **бога́ч**, -а́, rich man.

боги́ня, -и, goddess. **богома́терь**, -и, Mother of God. **богомо́лец**, -льца, -мо́лка, -и, devout person; pilgrim. **богомо́лье**, -я, pilgrimage. **богомо́льный**, religious, devout. **богоро́дица**, -ы, the Virgin Mary. **богосло́в**, -а, theologian. **богосло́вие**, -я, theology.

боготвори́ть, -рю́ *imp.* worship, idolize; deify.

бода́ть(ся, -а́ю(сь *imp.*, **боднуть,** -ну́, -нёшь *perf.* (*perf.* also забода́ть) butt. **бодли́вый,** inclined to butt.

бодри́ть, -рю́ *imp.* stimulate, invigorate, brace up; **~ся,** try to keep up one's spirits. **бо́дрость,** -и, cheerfulness, good spirits, courage. **бо́дрствовать,** -твую *imp.* be awake; stay awake, keep awake; sit up. **бо́дрый;** бодр, -а́, -о, cheerful, brisk, bright; hale and hearty. **бодря́щий,** invigorating, bracing.

боеви́к, -а́, active revolutionary, militant; smash hit. **боев|о́й,** fighting, battle, war; urgent; militant, determined, unyielding; ~о́й клич, war-cry; ~о́е креще́ние, baptism of fire; ~о́й механи́зм, striking mechanism. **боеголо́вка,** -и, warhead. **боеприпа́сы,** -ов *pl.* ammunition. **бое́ц,** бойца́, soldier; fighter, warrior; butcher, slaughterer; *pl.* men.

Бо́же: see бог. **бо́жеский,** divine; fair, just. **божество́,** -а́, deity; divinity. **бо́ж|ий,** God's; ~ья коро́вка, ladybird; ка́ждый ~ий день, every blessed day. **божи́ться,** -жу́сь *imp.* (*perf.* по~), swear. **божо́к,** -жка́ idol.

бой, -я (-ю), *loc.* -ю́; *pl.* -и́, -ёв. battle, action, fight; bout; fighting; killing, slaughtering; striking; breakage(s), broken glass, crockery, etc.; бараба́нный ~, drumbeat; ~ быко́в bullfight; ~ кито́в, whaling; ~ тюле́ней, sealing; с бо́ю, by force; часы́ с бо́ем, striking clock.

бо́й|кий; бо́ек, бойка́, -о, bold, spry, smart, sharp; glib; lively, animated; busy.

бойни́ца, -ы, loophole, embrasure.

бо́йня, -и; *gen. pl.* бо́ен, slaughter-house, abattoir, shambles; massacre, slaughter, butchery.

бо́йче, *comp.* of бо́йкий.

бок, -а (-у), *loc.* -у́; *pl.* -а́, side; flank; ~ о́ ~, side by side; в ~, sideways; на́ ~, sideways, to the side; на ~у́, on one side; по́д ~ом, near by, close by; с ~у from the side, from the flank; с ~у на́ бок, from side to side.

бока́л, -а, glass; goblet.

боково́й, side, flank; lateral; sidelong. **бо́ком** *adv* sideways.

бокс, -а, boxing. **боксёр,** -а, boxer. **боксёрский,** boxing. **бокси́ровать,** -рую *imp.* box.

болва́н, -а, block; blockhead; dummy; idol. **болва́нка,** -и, block; pig; желе́зо в ~х, pig-iron.

болево́й, of pain painful.

бо́лее *adv.* more; ~ всего́, most of all; тем ~, что, especially as.

боле́знен|ный, sickly; unhealthy; abnormal morbid; painful. **боле́знь,** -и, illness, disease, ailment; abnormality; ~ ро́ста, growing pains.

боле́льщик, -а, **-щица,** -ы, fan, supporter. **боле́ть**[1], -е́ю *imp.* be ill, suffer; be worried; +за+*acc.* support, be a fan of. **боле́ть**[2], -ли́т *imp.* ache, hurt.

боло́нья, -и, (cape of) waterproof nylon.

боло́тистый, marshy, boggy, swampy. **боло́то,** -а, marsh, bog, swamp. **боло́тный,** marsh, bog.

болта́нка, -и, air-pocket. **болта́ть**[1], -а́ю *imp.* stir; shake; dangle; **~ся,** dangle, swing; hang loosely; hang about; fly bumpily, bump.

болта́ть[2], -а́ю *imp.* chatter, jabber, natter. **болтли́вый,** garrulous, talkative; indiscreet. **болтну́ть,** -ну́, -нёшь *perf.* blurt out. **болтовня́,** -и́, talk; chatter; gossip. **болту́н**[1], -а́, **болту́нья,** -и, talker, chatterer; chatterbox; gossip.

болту́н[2], -а́, addled egg.

болту́шка, -и, scrambled eggs; mixture; swill, mash; whisk.

боль, -и, pain; ache; ~ в боку́, stitch. **больни́ца,** -ы, hospital. **больни́чный,** hospital; ~ листо́к, medical certificate. **бо́льно**[1] *adv.* painfully, badly; *predic.* + *dat.* it hurts. **бо́льно**[2] *adv.* very, extremely, terribly. **больно́й;** -лен, -льна́, ill, sick; diseased; sore; *sb.* patient, invalid.

больша́к, -а́, high road. **бо́льше** *comp.* of большо́й, вели́кий, мно́го; bigger, larger; greater; more; ~ не, not any more, no more, no longer; ~ того́, and what is more; *adv.* for the most part. **бо́льш|ий,** greater, larger; ~ей ча́стью for the most part; са́мое ~ее, at most, at the utmost, at the outside. **большинство́,** -á, majority; most people. **больш|о́й,** big, large; great; grown-up; ~áя бу́ква, capital letter; ~áя доро́га, high road; ~о́й па́лец, thumb, big toe; ~о́й свет, high society, the world; **~и́е** *sb. pl.* grown-ups. **большу́щий,** huge, enormous.

боля́чка, -и, sore, scab; defect, weakness.

бо́мба, -ы, bomb. **бомбардирова́ть,** -ру́ю *imp.* bombard; bomb. **бомбардиро́вка,** -и, bombardment, bombing. **бомбардиро́вщик,** -а, bomber; bomber pilot. **бомбёжка,** -и, bombing. **бомби́ть,** -блю́ *imp.* bomb. **бомбово́з,** -а, bomber. **бо́мбовый,** bomb. **бомбоубе́жище,** -а, bomb shelter.

бо́на, -ы, bond, bill; money order; *pl.* paper money.

бор, -а, *loc.* -у́; *pl.* -ы́, pine-wood, coniferous forest.

бордо́ *n. indecl.* claret; red Bordeaux. **бордо́** *indecl. adj.*, **бордо́вый,** wine-red, claret-coloured.

бордю́р, -а, border.

боре́ц, -рца́, fighter; wrestler.

борза́я *sb.* borzoi. **бо́рзый,** swift.

бормота́ние, -я, muttering, mumbling; mutter, mumble. **бормота́ть,** -очу́, -о́чешь *imp.* (*perf.* про~), mutter, mumble.

бо́рный, boric, boracic.

бо́ров, -а, hog.

борови́к, -á, boletus.

борода́, -ы́, *acc.* бо́роду; *pl.* бо́роды, -ро́д, -а́м, beard; wattles. **борода́вка,** -и, wart. **борода́тый,** bearded. **борода́ч,** -á, bearded man. **боро́дка,** -и, small beard, tuft; (key-)bit.

борозда́, -ы; *pl.* бо́розды, -о́зд, -а́м, furrow; fissure. **борозди́ть,** -зжу́ *imp.* (*perf.* вз~) furrow; plough; leave wake or track on; score. **боро́здка,** -и, furrow, groove. **боро́здчатый,** furrowed; grooved, scored.

борона́, -ы́, *acc.* бо́рону; *pl.* бо́роны, -ро́н, -а́м, harrow. **борони́ть,** -ню́ *imp.* (*perf.* вз~) harrow.

боро́ться, -рю́сь, бо́решься *imp.* wrestle, grapple; struggle, fight.

борт, -а, *loc.* -у́; *pl.* -á, -о́в, side, ship's side; front; cushion; за́ ~, за ~ом, overboard; на ~, на ~у́, on board. **борт-** in *comb.* ship's; air, flight, flying. **бортов|о́й,** ship's; side; onboard; flight, flying; ~áя ка́чка, rolling. **бортпроводни́к,** -á, air steward. **бортпроводни́ца,** -ы, air hostess.

борщ, -á, borshch.

борьба́, -ы́, wrestling; struggle, fight; conflict.

босико́м *adv.* barefoot. **бос|о́й;** бос, -á, -о, **босоно́гий,** barefooted; на бо́су но́гу, on one's bare feet. **босоно́жка,** -и, barefooted woman or girl; barefoot dancer; *pl.* sandals, mules. **턴ося́к,** -á, **턴ося́чка,** -и, tramp; down-and-out.

бот[1], -а, **бо́тик**[1], -а, small boat.

бот[2], -а, **бо́тик**[2], -а, high overshoe.

боти́нок, -нка, boot.

боца́ть, буца́ть, -а́ю *imp.* (*perf.* за~) clatter, tramp.

бо́цман, -а, boatswain, boatswain's mate.

боча́г, -á, pool; deep puddle.

бочко́м *adv.* sideways.

бо́чка, -и, barrel, cask. **бочо́нок,** -нка, keg, small barrel.

боязли́вый, timid, timorous. **боя́знь,** -и, fear, dread.

боя́рин, -а; *pl.* -я́ре, -я́р, boyar. **боя́рск|ий,** boyar's, boyars'; ~ие де́ти, small landowners.

боя́рышник, -а, hawthorn.

боя́ться, бою́сь *imp.* +*gen.* be afraid of, fear; dislike, be intolerant of.

бр. *abbr.* бра́тья, brothers.

бра, *n. indecl.* sconce, bracket.

бра́га, -и, home-brewed beer.

брак[1], -а, marriage.

брак[2], -а, defective goods, defect, defective part; reject, waste. **браке́р,** -а, inspector. **бракова́ть,** -ку́ю *imp.* (*perf.* за~), reject. **бракоде́л,** -а, bad workman.

бракоразво́дный, divorce.

брандахлы́ст, -а, slops, swipes.

брани́ть, -ню́ *imp.* (*perf.* вы́~) scold; abuse, curse; **~ся** (*perf.* по~ся) swear, curse; quarrel. **бра́нн|ый**[1], abusive, profane; ~ое сло́во, swear-word.

бра́нный[2], martial, battle. **брань**[1], -и, war; battle.
брань[2], -и, swearing, bad language; abuse.
брасле́т, -а, bracelet; *pl.* (*sl.*) handcuffs.
брасс, -а, breast stroke. **брасси́ст**, -а, **-и́стка**, -и, breast-stroke swimmer.
брат, -а; *pl.* -тья, -тьев, brother; comrade; old man, my lad, mate; lay brother, monk, friar; *pl.* friends, boys; на ~а, per head; наш ~, we, the likes of us, our sort. **брата́ние**, -я, fraternization. **брата́ться**, -а́юсь *imp.* (*perf.* по~) fraternize. **братва́**, -ы́, comrades, friends. **бра́тия**, -и; *gen. pl.* -тий, **бра́тья**, -и, brotherhood, fraternity. **братоуби́йство**, -а, **братоуби́йца**, -ы, *m.* and *f.* fratricide. **бра́тский**, brotherly, fraternal. **бра́тство**, -а, brotherhood, fraternity.
брать, беру́, -рёшь; брал, -а́, -о *imp.* (*perf.* взять) take; get, obtain, book; hire; seize, grip; exact, demand, require; surmount, clear; work; be effective; take bribes; +*instr.* succeed through, succeed by means of; +*adv.* bear; ~ верх, get the upper hand; ~ в ско́бки, put in brackets; ~ на+*acc.* have a range of; ~ на букси́р, take in tow; ~ на пору́ки, go bail for; ~ но́ту, sing (play) a note; ~ под аре́ст, put under arrest; ~ своё, get one's (own) way; take its toll, tell; ~ сло́во, take the floor; **~ся**+за+*acc.* touch; take hold of, seize; take up; get down to; +за+*acc.* or *inf.* undertake, take on oneself; appear, come; ~ся за ум, come to one's senses; ~ся нарасхва́т, go (sell) like hot cakes.
бра́чный, marriage; mating.
бреве́нчатый, log. **бревно́**, -а́; *pl.* -ёвна, -вен, log, beam.
бред, -а, *loc.* -у́, delirium; raving(s); gibberish. **бре́дить**, -е́жу *imp.* be delirious, rave; +*instr.* rave about, be infatuated with. **бре́дни**, -ей *pl.* ravings; fantasies. **бредово́й**, **бредо́вый**, delirious; fantastic, nonsensical.
бреду́, etc.: see брести́. **бре́жу**, etc.: see бре́дить.
бре́згать, -аю *imp.* (*perf.* по~)+*inf.* or *instr.* be squeamish about, be fastidious about; be nauseated by, be sickened by; shrink from, scruple or hesitate to. **брезгли́вый**, squeamish, fastidious.
брезе́нт, -а, tarpaulin.
бре́зжить(ся, -ит(ся *imp.* dawn; gleam faintly, glimmer.
брёл, etc.: see брести́.
брело́к, -а, charm, trinket.
бремени́ть, -ню́ *imp.* (*perf.* о~) burden. **бре́мя**, -мени *n.* burden; load.
бренча́ть, -чу́ *imp.* strum; jingle.
брести́, -еду́, -едёшь; брёл, -а́ *imp.* stroll, amble; struggle along, drag oneself along.
брете́ль, -и, **брете́лька**, -и, shoulder-strap.
бре́ю etc.: see брить.
брига́да, -ы, brigade; squadron; crew, team, gang, squad. **бригади́р**, -а, brigadier; brigade-leader team-leader; foreman. **брига́дник**, -а, **-ница**, -ы, member of brigade, crew, team.
бри́джи, -ей *pl.* breeches.
бриза́нтный, high-explosive.
бриллиа́нт, -а, **брилья́нт**, -а, brilliant, diamond.
брита́нец, -нца, **брита́нка**, -и, Briton, British subject; Englishman, Englishwoman. **брита́нский**, British.
бри́тва, -ы, razor. **бри́твенный**, shaving. **бри́тый**, shaved; clean-shaven. **бри́ть**, бре́ю *imp.* (*perf.* по~) shave; **~ся**, shave (oneself). **бритьё**, -я́, shave; shaving.
бри́чка, -и, britzka, trap.
бро́вка, -и, brow; edge. **бровь**, -и; *pl.* -и, -е́й, eyebrow; brow.
брод, -а, ford.
броди́ть, -ожу́, -о́дишь *imp.* wander, roam, stray; amble, stroll; ferment. **бродя́га**, -и *m.* and *f.*, **бродя́жка**, -и *m.* and *f.* tramp, vagrant, down-and-out; wanderer. **бродя́жничать**, -аю *imp.* be on the road, be a tramp. **бродя́жничество**, -а, vagrancy. **бродя́чий**, vagrant; wandering, roving; strolling; stray; restless. **броже́ние**, -я, ferment, fermentation.
бром, -а, bromine; bromide. **бро́мистый**, bromic, bromidic; ~ ка́лий, potassium bromide. **бро́мный**, **бро́мовый**, bromine.

броне- in *comb.*, armoured, armour. **бронебо́йный,** armour-piercing. **~ви́к,** -а́, armoured car. **~во́й,** armoured, armour. **~но́сец,** -сца, battleship, ironclad; armadillo. **~но́сный, ~та́нковый,** armoured.

бро́нза, -ы, bronze; (collection of) bronzes. **бронзирова́ть,** -ру́ю, *perf.* and *imp.* bronze. **бронциро́вка,** -и, bronzing. **бро́нзовый,** bronze; bronzed.

брониро́ванный, armoured. **бронирова́ть**[1], -ру́ю *perf.* and *imp.* (*perf.* also за~) armour.

брони́ровать[2], -рую *perf.* and *imp.* (*perf.* also за~), reserve, book. **бро́ня**[2], -и, reservation; commandeering; warrant, permit; exemption.

броня́[1], -и́ armour.

броса́ть, -а́ю *imp.*, **бро́сить,** -о́шу *perf.* throw, cast, fling; drop, throw down; leave, abandon, desert; give up, leave off; бро́сь(те)! stop it! drop it!; **~ся,** throw oneself, fling oneself, rush; + *inf.* begin, start; + *instr.* throw away, squander; throw at one another, pelt one another with; ~ся в глаза́, be striking, arrest the attention; ~ся на коле́ни, fall on one's knees; ~ся на по́мощь+*dat.* rush to the assistance of. **бро́ский,** arresting, striking; loud, garish, glaring. **бро́сов|ый,** worthless, rubbishy; ~ая цена́, giveaway price; ~ый э́кспорт, dumping. **бросо́к,** -ска́, throw; burst; bound, spurt; thrust.

бро́шка, -и, **брошь,** -и, brooch.

брошю́ра, -ы, pamphlet, booklet, brochure. **брошюрова́ть,** -ру́ю *imp.* (*perf.* с~) stitch. **брошюро́вка,** -и, stitching. **брошюро́вщик,** -а, stitcher.

брус, -а; *pl.* -сья, -сьев, squared timber; beam, joist; bar; (паралле́льные) ~ья, parallel bars. **бруско́вый,** bar.

брусни́ка, -и, cowberry, red whortleberry; cowberries, red whortleberries.

брусо́к, -ска́, bar; ingot; slug.

бру́ствер, -а, breastwork, parapet.

бру́тто *indecl. adj.* gross.

бры́згать, -зжу or -гаю *imp.*, **бры́знуть,** -ну *perf.* splash, spatter; sprinkle; spurt, gush; ~ слюно́й sputter, splutter; **~ся,** splash; splash oneself, splash one another; spray oneself. **бры́зги,** брызг *pl.* spray, splashes; fragments; sparks.

брыка́ть, -а́ю *imp.*, **брыкну́ть,** -ну́, -нёшь *perf.* kick; **~ся,** kick, rebel.

брысь *int.* shoo.

БРЭ *m. indecl., abbr.* биологи́ческий ре́нтген-эквивале́нт, man roentgen equivalent.

брюзга́, -и́ *m.* and *f.* grumbler. **брюзгли́вый,** grumbling, peevish. **брюзжа́ть,** -жу́ *imp.* grumble.

брю́ква, -ы, swede.

брю́ки, брюк *pl.* trousers.

брюне́т, -а, dark man, dark-haired man. **брюне́тка,** -и, brunette.

брюха́стый, брюха́тый, big-bellied. **брю́хо** -а; *pl.* -и, belly; paunch, corporation; stomach.

брю́чный, trouser; ~ костю́м, trouser suit.

брюшко́, -а́; *pl.* -и́, -о́в, abdomen; paunch. **брюшно́й,** abdominal; ~ тиф, typhoid.

бря́канье, -я, clatter. **бря́кать,** -аю *imp.*, **бря́кнуть,** -ну *perf.* crash down, drop with a crash; blurt out; (+*instr.*) clatter, make a clatter; **~ся,** crash, fall heavily. **бряца́ние,** -я, rattling, rattle; clanking, clank; clang. **бряца́ть,** -а́ю *imp.* rattle; clank, clang.

бу́бен, -бна, tambourine. **бубене́ц,** -нца́, **бубе́нчик,** -а, small bell.

бу́бны, -бён, -бна́м *pl.* diamonds. **бубно́вый,** diamond; ~ вале́т, knave of diamonds.

бугóр, -гра́, mound, hillock, knoll; bump, lump. **бугоро́к,** -рка́, small mound or lump; protuberance; tubercle. **бугорча́тка,** -и, tuberculosis, consumption. **бугри́стый,** hilly, bumpy.

бу́дет, that's enough, that will do; +*inf.* it's time to stop; ~ вам писа́ть, don't do any more writing.

буди́льник, -а, alarm-clock. **буди́ть,** бужу́, бу́дишь *imp.* (*perf.* про~ раз~) wake, awaken; rouse, arouse.

бу́дка, -и, box, booth; hut; stall; соба́чья ~, dog-kennel.

бу́дни, -ней *pl.* weekdays; workdays,

working days; humdrum existence. **бу́дний, бу́дничный,** weekday; everyday; dull, humdrum.
бу́дто *conj.* as if, as though; ~ (бы), (как) ~, apparently, allegedly, ostensibly; *part.* really?
бу́ду, etc.: see быть. **бу́дучи,** being. **бу́дущ|ий,** future; next, coming; to be, to come; **~ее** *sb.* future. **бу́дущность,** -и, future. **бу́дь(те)**: see быть.
бу́ер, -а; *pl.* -а́, -о́в, ice-boat, ice-yacht.
бужу́: see буди́ть.
буза́, -ы́, home brew; (*sl.*) row, shindy; rubbish.
бузина́, -ы́, elder. **бузи́нник,** -а, thicket of elders. **бузи́нный, бузи́новый,** elder.
бузи́ть, -и́шь *imp.* (*sl.*) kick up a row.
бузотёр -а, (*sl.*) rowdy; trouble-maker.
буй, -я; *pl.* -и́, -ёв, buoy.
бу́йвол -а buffalo.
бу́йный; бу́ен, буйна́, -о, violent, turbulent; tempestuous; ungovernable; wild; luxuriant, lush. **бу́йство,** -а, tumult, uproar; unruly conduct, riotous behaviour. **бу́йствовать,** -твую *imp.* create an uproar, behave violently.
бук, -а, beech.
бука́шка, -и, small insect.
бу́ква, -ы; *gen. pl.* букв, letter; ~ в бу́кву, literally, word for word. **буква́льно** *adv.* literally. **буква́льный,** literal. **буква́рь,** -я́, ABC. **буквое́д,** -а, pedant. **буквое́дство,** -а, pedantry.
букети́ровать, -рую *imp.* thin out.
букини́ст, -а, second-hand bookseller.
буклиро́ванн|ый, bouclé; ~ая ткань, bouclé fabric. **бу́кля,** -и, curl, ringlet.
бу́ковый, beech, beech-wood.
букс, -а, box(-tree).
букси́р, -а, tug, tug-boat; tow-rope, hawser. **букси́ровать,** -рую *imp.* tow, be towing, have in tow.
буксова́ние, -я, wheel-spin. **буксова́ть,** -су́ет *imp.* spin, slip.
булава́, -ы́, mace. **була́вка,** -и, pin; англи́йская ~, safety-pin. **була́вочный,** pin.
бу́лка, -и, roll; сдо́бная ~, bun. **бу́лочная** *sb.* bakery; baker's shop. **бу́лочник,** -а, baker.
бултых *int.* splash, plump. **бултыха́ться,** -а́юсь *imp.*, **бултыхну́ться,** -ну́сь, -нёшься *perf.* fall with heavy splash, plunge, plump.
булы́жник, -а, cobble-stone, cobbles. **булы́жный,** cobbled.
бульва́р, -а, avenue; boulevard. **бульва́рный,** boulevard, avenue; trashy, rubbishy; vulgar.
бу́льканье, -я, gurgling, gurgle. **бу́лькать,** -аю *imp.* gurgle.
бум, -а, beam.
бума́га, -и, cotton; paper; document; *pl.* securities. **бумагодержа́тель,** -я *m.* security-holder, bond-holder; paper-clip. **бума́жка,** -и, piece of paper; paper; note. **бума́жник,** -а, wallet; paper-maker. **бума́жн|ый,** cotton; paper; ~ая волоки́та, red tape; ~ый змей, kite; ~ая фа́брика, paper-mill.
бумажо́нка, -и, scrap of paper.
бунт[1], -а, bale; package; bundle.
бунт[2], -а; *pl.* -ы́, rebellion, revolt, rising; riot; mutiny. **бунта́рский,** seditious, mutinous; rebellious; turbulent. **бунта́рь,** -я́ *m.* rebel; insurgent; mutineer; rioter; inciter to rebellion or mutiny.
бунтова́ть(ся, -ту́ю(сь *imp.* (*perf.* вз~), revolt, rebel; mutiny, riot; incite to rebellion or mutiny. **бунтовско́й,** rebellious, mutinous. **бунтовщи́к,** -а́, **-щи́ца,** -ы, rebel, insurgent; mutineer; rioter.
бур, -а, auger; bore; drill.
бура́, -ы́, borax.
бура́в, -а́; *pl.* -а́, auger; gimlet. **бура́вить,** -влю *imp.* (*perf.* про~) bore, drill. **бура́вчик,** -а, gimlet.
буран, -а, snowstorm.
бурда́, -ы́, (*sl.*) slops, swill, hog-wash.
буреве́стник, -а, stormy petrel. **бурево́й,** storm; stormy. **бурело́м,** -а, wind-fallen trees.
буре́ние, -я, boring, drilling.
буржуа́, *m. indecl.* bourgeois. **буржуа́зия,** -и, bourgeoisie. **буржуа́зный,** bourgeois. **буржу́й,** -я, bourgeois. **буржу́йка,** -и, bourgeois; small stove. **буржу́йский,** bourgeois.
бури́льный, boring, drilling. **бури́льщик,** -а, borer, driller, drill-operator.
бури́ть, -рю́ *imp.* bore, drill.
бу́ркать, -аю *imp.*, **бу́ркнуть,** -ну *perf.* growl, grumble, mutter.

бурли́вый, stormy; seething, turbulent. **бурли́ть,** -лю́ *imp.* boil, seethe.

бу́рный; -рен, -рна́, -о, stormy, rough; impetuous; rapid; energetic.

буров|о́й, boring, bore, drilling; ~а́я вы́шка, derrick; ~а́я (сква́жина), borehole; ~о́й стано́к, ~а́я устано́вка, drilling rig.

бурт, -а, clamp. **буртова́ние,** -я, storing in clamps.

бурча́ть, -чу́ *imp.* (*perf.* про~) grumble; mumble, mutter; rumble; bubble.

бу́р|ый; бур, -а́, -о, brown; liver chestnut, (dark) chestnut; ~ая лиси́ца, red fox.

бурья́н, -а, tall weeds.

бу́ря, -и, storm; tempest; gale.

бу́сать, -аю *imp.* (*sl.*) drink, swallow.

бу́сина, -ы, **бу́синка,** -и, bead. **бу́сы,** бус *pl.* beads.

бутафо́р, -а, property-man, props. **бутафо́рия,** -и, properties, props; window-dressing. **бутафо́рский,** property.

бутербро́д, -а, open sandwich.

буто́н, -а, bud. **бутонье́рка,** -и, button--hole, spray of flowers.

бу́тсы, бу́цы, -ов *pl.* football boots.

буты́лка, -и, bottle. **буты́лочный,** bottle; ~ цвет, bottle green. **буты́ль,** -и, large bottle; demijohn; carboy.

буфе́т, -а, sideboard; buffet, refreshment room; bar, counter. **буфе́тная** *sb.* pantry. **буфе́тчик,** -а, barman; steward. **буфе́тчица,** -ы, barmaid.

бу́фы, буф *pl.* gathered fullness, close gathering, puffs.

бух *int.* thump, thud. **бу́хать,** -аю *imp.* (*perf.* бу́хнуть) thump, bang; drop noisily, bang down; thunder, thud; blurt out; **~ся**, fall heavily; plump oneself down.

бухга́лтер, -а, book-keeper, accountant. **бухгалте́рия,** -и, book-keeping, accountancy; counting-house; accounts office, department. **бухга́лтерский,** book-keeping, account.

бу́хнуть[1] -ну; бух *imp.* swell.

бу́хнуть[2]**(ся,** -ну(сь *perf.* of бу́хать(ся.

бу́хта, -ы bay, bight. **бу́хточка,** -и, cove, creek, inlet.

буца́ть: see боца́ть. **бу́цы:** see бу́тсы.

бушева́ть, -шу́ю *imp.* rage, storm.

бушла́т, -а, pea-jacket; wadded jacket; (*sl.*) деревя́нный ~, coffin.

буя́н, -а, rowdy, brawler. **буя́нить,** -ню *imp.* make a row, create an uproar, brawl. **буя́нство,** -а, rowdyism, brawling.

бы, б *part.* I. +*pa. t.* or *inf.* indicates the conditional or subjunctive, expresses possibility, a wish, a polite suggestion or exhortation; II. (+ни), forms indefinite pronouns and conjunctions; see е́сли, как, когда́, кто, etc.

быва́ло: see быва́ть. **быва́лый,** experienced; worldly-wise; past, former; not new; habitual, familiar. **быва́ть,** -а́ю *imp.* be, be present; happen; take place; be inclined to be, tend to be; как не быва́ло +*gen.* have completely disappeared; как ни в чём не быва́ло, as if nothing had happened, as though everything was all right; **быва́ло** *part.* used to, would; мать быва́ло ча́сто пе́ла э́ту пе́сню, my mother would often sing this song. **бы́вший,** former, formerly, ex-.

бык, -а́, bull, ox; stag; pier.

были́на, -ы, bylina. **были́нный,** of byliny; epic, heroic.

бы́ло *part.* nearly, on the point of; (only) just; чуть ~ не, very nearly, all but. **был|о́й,** former, past, bygone; **~**о́е *sb.* the past. **быль,** -и, the past, what really happened; true story, true happening.

быстрина́, -ы́; *pl.* -ы, rapids. **быстроно́гий,** swift-footed, fleet-footed; fast. **быстрота́,** -ы́, quickness, swiftness, rapidity; speed. **быстроте́чный,** fleeting, transient. **быстрохо́дный,** fast, high-speed. **бы́стрый;** быстр, -а́, -о, rapid, fast, quick; prompt.

быт, -а, *loc.* -у́, way of life, life; everyday life; слу́жба ~а, consumer services. **бытие́,** -я́ being, existence; objective reality; кни́га Бытия́, Genesis. **бытова́ть,** -ту́ет *imp.* exist; occur; be current. **бытови́к,** -а (*sl.*) criminal, non-political prisoner. **бытов|о́й** of everyday life; everyday; domestic; social; ~а́я жи́вопись, genre painting

~óе **обслу́живание**. consumer services. **бытописа́ние, -я**, annals, chronicles. **бытописа́тель, -я** *m*. annalist, chronicler; writer on social themes.

быть, *pres. 3rd sing.* есть, *pl.* суть; *fut.* бу́ду; *past* был, -á, -о; *imper.* бу́дь(те) *imp.* be; exist; be situated; happen, take place; *impers.*+*dat.* be sure to happen, be inevitable; будь, что бу́дет, come what may; ~беде́, there's sure to be trouble; должно́ ~, probably, very likely; как ~? what is to be done?; не будь его́, but for him, if it weren't for him; так и ~, so be it; all right, very well, have it your own way. **бытьё, -я́,** way of life.

быча́чий, бы́чий, bull, ox. **бычо́к**[1], -чка́, young ox, steer.

бычо́к[2], -чка́, (*sl.*) cigarette end, fag-end.

бью etc.: see бить.

бэ *n. indecl.* the letter б.

БЭР, бэр, -а; *gen. pl.* бэр *abbr.* биологи́ческий эквивале́нт рентге́на, man roentgen equivalent.

бюллете́нь, -я *m.* bulletin; voting-paper, ballot-paper; medical certificate; быть на бюллете́не, be on the sick-list, be on sick-leave.

бюро́ *n. indecl.* bureau; office; writing-desk. **бюрокра́т,** -а, bureaucrat. **бюрократи́зм,** -а, bureaucracy. **бюрократи́ческий,** bureaucratic. **бюрокра́тия, -и,** bureaucracy; bureaucrats.

бюст, -а, bust; bosom. **бюстга́льтер,** -а, brassière, bra.

В

в *letter:* see вэ.

в, во *prep.* I.+*acc.* into, to; on; at; within; for, as; through; быть в, take after, be like; в два ра́за бо́льше, twice as big, twice the size; в на́ши дни, in our day; войти́ в дом, go into the house; в понеде́льник, on Monday; в тече́ние+*gen.* during, in the course of; в четы́ре часа́, at four o'clock; высото́й в три ме́тра, three metres high; игра́ть в ша́хматы, play chess; моро́з в де́сять гра́дусов, ten degrees of frost; пое́хать в Москву́, go to Moscow; положи́ть в я́щик стола́, put in(to) a drawer; преврати́ть во́ду в лёд, turn water into ice; разби́ть в куски́, smash to pieces; руба́шка в кле́тку check(ed) shirt; сесть в ваго́н, get into the carriage; сказа́ть в шу́тку, say as a joke; смотре́ть в окно́, look out of the window; это мо́жно сде́лать в неде́лю, it can be done in a week. II.+*prep.* in; on; at; of; at a distance of; в двадца́том ве́ке, in the twentieth century; в теа́тре, at the theatre; в трёх киломе́трах от го́рода, three kilometres from the town; в четвёртом часу́, between three (o'clock) and four; в э́том году́, this year; в январе́, in January; лицо́ в весну́шках, freckled face; пье́са в пяти́ а́ктах, a play in five acts, a five-act play; роди́ться в Москве́, be born in Moscow; са́хар в куска́х, lump sugar; служи́ть в куха́рках, be a cook.

в. *abbr.* век, century; восто́к, E.

в *abbr.* вольт, volt.

в-, во-, въ- *vbl. pref.* expressing direction of action or motion inwards or upwards; occurrence wholly within the agent.

ваго́н, -а, (railway-)carriage, coach; van; car; wagon-load; loads, an awful lot; ~-рестора́н, restaurant car, dining-car. **ваготе́тка, -и,** truck, trolley. **вагоновожа́тый** *sb.* tram-driver.

ва́жничанье, -я, airs. **ва́жничать, -аю** *imp.* give oneself airs; +*instr.* plume oneself, pride oneself, on. **ва́жность, -и,** importance, consequence; significance; pomposity, pretentiousness. **ва́жный;** -жен, -жна́, -о, important;

weighty, consequential; pompous, pretentious.
ва́за, -ы, vase, bowl.
ва́кса, -ы,(shoe-) polish, blacking; чи́стить ва́ксой, polish. **ва́ксить**, -кшу *imp.* (*perf.* на~) black, polish.
вал[1], -а, *loc.* -у́; *pl.* -ы́, bank, earthen wall; rampart; billow, roller, wave; barrage.
вал[2], -а, *loc.* -у́; *pl.* -ы́, shaft, spindle.
вал[3], -а, gross output.
вала́ндаться, -аюсь *imp.* loiter, hang about; mess about.
валёк, -лька́, battledore; swingle-tree; roll; roller; flail; loom.
ва́ленок, -нка; *gen. pl.* -нок, felt boot. **ва́леный**, felt.
вале́т, -а, knave, Jack.
ва́лик, -а, bolster; roller; cylinder; spindle, shaft; platen.
вали́ть[1], -ли́т *imp.* flock, throng; pour; вало́м ~, throng, flock; вали́(те)! go on! have a go!
вали́ть[2], -лю́, -лишь *imp.* (*perf.* по~, с~), throw down, bring down, knock down; overthrow; fell; lay low; heap, pile up; **~ся**, fall, collapse; drop; topple; у него́ всё из рук ва́лится, his fingers are all thumbs; he can't give his mind to anything.
ва́лка, -и, felling. **ва́лкий**; -лок, -лка́, -о, unsteady, shaky.
валово́й, gross; wholesale.
валто́рна, -ы, French horn. **валторни́ст**, -а, French-horn (player).
валу́н, -а́, boulder.
вальс, -а, waltz. **вальси́ровать**, -и́рую *imp.* waltz.
вальцева́ть, -цу́ю *imp.* roll. **вальцо́вка**, -и, rolling; rolling press. **вальцо́вый**, rolling. **вальцы́**, *pl.* -о́в, rolling press. **вальцо́вщик**, -а, roller.
валю́та, -ы, currency; foreign currency. **валю́тчик**, -а, **-чица**, -ы, speculator in foreign currency.
ва́ляный, felt. **валя́ть**, -я́ю *imp.* (*perf.* на~, с~) drag; roll; shape; full, felt; botch, bungle; make a mess (of), mess about; ~ дурака́, play the fool; валя́й(те)! go ahead! carry on!; **~ся**, lie, lie about, loll; roll, wallow; ~ся в нога́х у+*gen.* fall at the feet of.
вам, ва́ми: see вы.
вани́ль, -и, vanilla, vanilla-pod.
ва́нна, -ы, **ва́нночка**, -и, bath. **ва́нный**, bath; **~ая** *sb.* bathroom.
ва́нька, -и *m.* cabby.
ва́рвар, -а, barbarian. **варвари́зм**, -а, loan-word; barbarism. **ва́рварский**, barbarian; barbarous; barbaric. **ва́рварство**, -а, barbarity; vandalism.
ва́режка, -и, mitten.
варёный, boiled; limp. **варе́нье**, -я, jam, marmalade. **вари́ть**, -рю́, -ришь *imp.* (*perf.* с~) boil; cook; brew; make; digest; **~ся**, boil; cook. **ва́рка**, -и, boiling; cooking; making, brewing.
вас: see вы.
василёк, -лька́, cornflower. **василько́вый**, cornflower; cornflower blue.
ва́та, -ы, cotton wool; wadding.
вата́га, -и, band, gang.
ватерли́ния, -и, water-line. **ватерпа́с**, -а, level, spirit-level.
вати́н, -а, (sheet) wadding, quilting. **ва́тник**, -а, quilted jacket. **ва́тный**, quilted, wadded.
ватру́шка, -и, open tart; curd tart, cheese-cake.
ватт, -а; *gen. pl.* ватт, watt.
ва́фельный, waffle. **ва́фля**, -и, *gen. pl.* -фель, waffle.
вахла́к, -а, lout; sloven; (*sl.*) goner, wreck.
ва́хта, -ы, watch. **ва́хтенн|ый**, watch; ~ журна́л, log, log-book; ~ команди́р, officer of the watch, duty officer.
ваш, -его *m.*, **ва́ша**, -ей *f.*, **ва́ше**, -его *n.*, **ва́ши**, -их *pl.*, *pron.* your, yours.
вая́ние, -я, sculpture. **вая́тель**, -я *m.* sculptor. **вая́ть**, -я́ю *imp.* (*perf.* из~) sculpture; carve, model.
вбега́ть, -а́ю *imp.*, **вбежа́ть**, вбегу́ *perf.* run in, rush in.
вберу́ etc.: see вобра́ть.
вбива́ть, -а́ю *imp.* of вбить. **вби́вка**, -и, knocking in, driving in, hammering in.
вбира́ть, -а́ю, *imp.* of вобра́ть.
вбить, вобью́, -бьёшь *perf.* (*imp.* вбива́ть) drive in, hammer in, knock in.
вблизи́ *adv.* (+от+*gen.*), close (to), near (to), not far (from); closely.
вбок *adv.* sideways, to one side.

вбра́сывание, -я, throw-in. **вбра́сывать, -аю** *imp.* of вбро́сить.
вброд *adv.* by fording or wading; переходи́ть ~, ford, wade.
вбро́сить, -о́шу *perf.* (*imp.* вбра́сывать) throw in.
вв. *abbr.* века́, centuries.
вва́ливать, -аю *imp.*, **ввали́ть, -лю́, -лишь** *perf.* throw heavily, heave, fling, bundle, tumble; **~ся,** fall heavily; sink, become hollow or sunken; burst in. **ввали́вшийся,** sunken, hollow.
введе́ние, -я, leading in; introduction.
введу́, etc.: see ввести́.
ввезти́, -зу́, -зёшь; ввёз, -ла́ *perf.* (*imp.* ввози́ть) import; bring in, take in, carry in.
ввек *adv.* ever; for ever.
вве́рить, -рю *perf.* (*imp.* вверя́ть) entrust, confide; **~ся**+*dat.* trust in, put one's faith in; put oneself in the hands of.
ввернýть, -нý, -нёшь *perf.*, **ввёртывать, -аю** *imp.* screw in; insert; put in.
вверх *adv.* up, upward(s); ~ дном, ~ нога́ми, ~ тормашками, upside down, topsy-turvy; ~ (по ле́стнице), upstairs; ~ (по тече́нию) upstream. **вверху́** *adv.* above, overhead; upstairs; upstream; at the top.
вверя́ть(ся, -я́ю(сь *imp.* of вве́рить(ся.
ввести́, -еду́, -едёшь; ввёл, -а́ *perf.* (*imp.* вводи́ть) bring in, lead in; introduce; insert, interpolate, incorporate; administer.
ввечеру́ *adv.* in the evening.
ввиду́ *prep.*+*gen.* in view of.
ввинти́ть, -нчу́ *perf.*, **вви́нчивать, -аю** *imp.* screw in.
ввод, -а, bringing in, leading in; lead-in, lead; input, intake. **вводи́ть, -ожу́ -о́дишь** *imp.* of ввести́. **вво́дн|ый,** introductory; parenthetic; ~ое предложе́ние, ~ое сло́во, parenthesis; ~ый тон, leading note.
ввожу́: see вводи́ть, ввози́ть.
ввоз, -а, importation, importing; import, imports. **ввози́ть, -ожу́, -о́зишь** *imp.* of ввезти́. **вво́зный,** imported; import.
вво́лю *adv.* to one's heart's content; enough and to spare; ad lib.
вво́сьмеро *adv.* eight times. **ввосьмеро́м** *adv.* eight together; мы ~, eight of us.
ВВС (*veve-és*) *abbr.* вое́нно-возду́шные си́лы, air force.
ввысь *adv.* up, upward(s).
ввяза́ть, -яжу́, -я́жешь *perf.*, **ввя́зывать, -аю** *imp.* knit in; involve; **~ся,** meddle, get involved, get or be mixed up (in).
вгиб, -а, inward bend; concavity, dent, sag. **вгиба́ть(ся, -а́ю(сь** *imp.* of вогну́ть(ся.
вглубь *adv.* deep, deep into, into the depths.
вгляде́ться, -яжу́сь *perf.*, **вгля́дываться, -аюсь** *imp.* peer, look closely or intently (в+*acc.* at).
вгоня́ть, -я́ю *imp.* of вогна́ть. **вдава́ться, вдаю́сь, -ёшься** *imp* of вда́ться.
вдави́ть, -авлю́, -а́вишь *perf.*, **вда́вливать, -аю** *imp.* press in, crush in; **~ся,** give, give way; be crushed or pressed in; press in.
вдалеке́, вдали́ *adv.* in the distance, far away; ~ от, a long way from. **вдаль** *adv.* into the distance.
вда́ться, -а́мся, -а́шься, -а́стся, -ади́мся; -а́лся, -ла́сь *perf.* (*imp.* вдава́ться) jut out; penetrate, go in; ~ в то́нкости, split hairs.
ВДВ (*vedevé*) *abbr.* возду́шно-деса́нтные войска́, airborne troops.
вдвига́ть(ся, -а́ю(сь *imp.*, **вдви́нуть(ся, -ну(сь** *perf.* push in, move in, thrust in.
вдво́е *adv.* twice; double; ~ бо́льше, twice as big, as much, as many. **вдвоём** *adv.* (the) two together, both. **вдвойне́** *adv.* twice as much, double; doubly.
вдева́ть, -а́ю, *imp.* of вдеть.
вдёжка, -и, threading; thread, tape, cord, lace.
вде́лать, -аю *perf.*, **вде́лывать, -аю** *imp.* set in, fit in.
вдёржка, -и, bodkin; threading. **вдёргивать, -аю** *imp.*, **вдёрнуть, -ну** *perf.* в+*acc.* thread through, pull through.
вде́сятеро *adv.* ten times; ~ бо́льше, ten times as much, as many. **вдесятеро́м** *adv.* ten together; мы ~, ten of us.

вдеть, -е́ну *perf.* (*imp.* вдева́ть) put in, thread.

ВДНХ (*vede-enkhá*) *abbr.* Вы́ставка достиже́ний наро́дного хозя́йства, Exhibition of National Economic Achievements.

вдоба́вок *adv.* in addition; besides, as well, into the bargain.

вдова́, -ы́; *pl.* -ы, widow. **вдове́ц,** -вца́, widower. **вдо́вий,** widow's, widows'. **вдови́ца,** -ы, widow.

вдо́воль *adv.* enough; in abundance; plenty (of).

вдо́вствующая *sb.* dowager. **вдо́вый,** widowed.

вдого́нку *adv.* (за+*instr.*) after, in pursuit (of).

вдоль *adv.* lengthways, lengthwise; ~ и поперёк, in all directions, far and wide; minutely, in detail; *prep.*+*gen.* or по+*dat.* along.

вдох, -а, breath. **вдохнове́ние,** -я, inspiration. **вдохнове́нный,** inspired. **вдохнови́тель,** -я *m.*, **-тельница,** -ы inspirer, inspiration. **вдохнови́ть,** -влю́ *perf.*, **вдохновля́ть,** -я́ю *imp.* inspire. **вдохну́ть,** -ну́, -нёшь *perf.* (*imp.* вдыха́ть) breathe in, inhale; +в+*acc.* inspire with, breathe into.

вдре́безги *adv.* to pieces, to smithereens; ~ пьян dead drunk.

вдруг *adv.* suddenly; all at once; what if? suppose; все ~, all together.

вдува́ть, -а́ю *imp.* of вду́нуть, вдуть.

вду́маться, -аюсь *perf.*, **вду́мываться,** -аюсь *imp.* ponder, meditate; +в+*acc.* think over. **вду́мчивый,** thoughtful.

вду́нуть, -ну *perf.*, **вдуть,** -у́ю *perf.* (*imp.* вдува́ть) blow in pump in.

вдыха́ние, -я, inhalation, inspiration. **вдыха́тельный,** respiratory. **вдыха́ть,** -а́ю *imp.* of вдохну́ть.

ве́дать, -аю *imp.* know; +*instr.* manage, handle; be in charge of. **ве́дение**[1], -я, authority, jurisdiction; в ве́дении +*gen.* under the jurisdiction of; вне моего́ ве́дения, outside my province.

веде́ние[2]. -я, conducting, conduct, management; ~ книг, book-keeping.

ведёрный, bucket, pail; holding a bucketful, holding one vedro.

ве́домость, -и; *gen. pl.* -е́й, list, register; *pl.* gazette. **ве́домственный,** departmental. **ве́домство,** -а, department.

ведро́, -а́; *pl.* вёдра, -дер, bucket, pail; vedro (approx. 12 litres).

веду́ *etc.*: see вести́. **веду́щ|ий,** leading; ~ее колесо́, driving-wheel.

ведь *part.* and *conj.* you see, you know; but; why; isn't it? is it?

ве́дьма, -ы witch; old bitch, hag.

ве́ер, -а; *pl.* -а́, fan. **веерообра́зный,** fan-shaped; ~ свод, fan vault(ing).

ве́жливость, -и, politeness, courtesy, civility. **ве́жливый,** polite, courteous, civil.

везде́ *adv.* everywhere. **вездехо́д,** -а, cross-country vehicle. **вездехо́дный,** cross-country.

везе́ние, -я, luck. **везу́чий,** fortunate, lucky. **везти́,** -зу́, -зёшь; вёз, -ла́ *imp.* (*perf.* по~), cart, convey, carry; bring, take; *impers.*+*dat.* be lucky, be in luck, have luck; ему́ не везло́, he had no luck.

век, -а (-у), *loc.* -у́; *pl.* -а́, century; age; life, lifetime; испоко́н ~о́в, from time immemorial. **век** *adv.* for ages, for ever; always, constantly.

ве́ко, -а; *pl.* -и, век, eyelid.

векове́чный, eternal, everlasting. **вековóй,** ancient, age-old, secular.

ве́ксель, -я; *pl.* -я́, -е́й *m.* promissory note, bill (of exchange). **ве́ксельный;** ~ курс, rate of exchange.

вёл, etc.: see вести́.

веле́ть, -лю́ *perf.* and *imp.* order, tell; не ~, forbid, not allow.

велика́н, -а, giant. **велика́нша,** -и, giantess. **велика́нский,** gigantic. **вели́к|ий;** вели́к, -а or -а́, great; big, large; too big; ~ие держа́вы, Great Powers; ~ий князь, grand prince, grand duke; ~ий пост, Lent.

велико- in *comb.* great. **великодержа́вный,** great-power. **~ду́шие,** -я, magnanimity, generosity. **~ду́шный,** magnanimous; generous. **~ле́пие,** -я, splendour, magnificence. **~ле́пный,** splendid, magnificent; excellent. **~по́стный,** Lenten. **~ру́с,** -а, **-ру́ска,** -и, Great Russian. **~ру́сский,** Great Russian.

величáвый, stately, majestic. **величáйший**, greatest, extreme, supreme. **вели́чественный**, majestic, grand. **вели́чество**, -а, Majesty. **вели́чие**, -я, greatness, grandeur, sublimity. **величинá**, -ы́; *pl.* -ы, size; quantity, magnitude; value; great figure.

велосипéд, -а, cycle; bicycle, tricycle. **велосипеди́ст**, -а, cyclist.

вельвéт, -а, velveteen, cotton velvet; ~ в рýбчик, corduroy. **вельвéтовый**, velveteen.

вельмóжа, -и *m.* grandee, dignitary, magnate.

вéна, -ы, vein.

венгéрка, -и, Hungarian; dolman; Hungarian ballroom dance. **венгéрский**, Hungarian. **венгр**, -а, Hungarian.

Венéра -ы, Venus. **венéрин** *adj.* Venusian, of Venus; ~ волосóк, maidenhair fern.

вéнец[1], -нца, Viennese.

венéц[2], -нцá, crown; wreath, garland; corona; halo. **венéчный**, coronal; coronary.

вéнзель, -я; *pl.* -я́, -éй *m.* monogram.

вéник, -а, besom, (birch-)broom, birch-whisk.

вéнка, -и, Viennese.

венóзный, venous.

венóк, -нкá, wreath, garland.

вéнский, Viennese; ~ стул, ballroom chair.

вéнтиль, -я *m.* valve.

венчáльный, wedding. **венчáние**, -я, wedding; coronation. **венчáть**, -áю *imp.* (*perf.* об~, по~, у~) crown; marry; **~ся**, be married, marry. **вéнчик**, -а, halo, nimbus; corolla; edge, rim; crown; ring, bolt.

вéра, -ы, faith, belief; trust, confidence; на ~у, on trust.

вéрба, -ы, willow, osier, pussy-willow; willow branch. **вéрбн|ый**; ~ое воскресéнье, Palm Sunday.

верблю́д, -а, **-ю́дица**, -ы, camel. **верблю́ж|ий**, camel's; camelhair; ~ья шерсть, camel's hair.

вéрбный: see вéрба.

вербовáть, -бýю *imp.* (*perf.* за~) recruit, enlist. **вербóвка**, -и, recruitment.

вéрбовый, willow, osier; wicker.

верёвка, -и, rope; string; cord. **верёвочный**, rope.

вéред, -а, boil, abscess.

верени́ца, -ы, row, file, line, string.

вéреск, -а, heather.

веретенó, -á; *pl.* -тёна, spindle, shank, axle.

верещáть, -щý *imp.* squeal; chirp.

вéрить, -рю *imp.* believe, have faith; +*dat.* or в+*acc.* trust (in), believe in; ~ нá слово, take on trust.

вернéе *adv.* rather. **верноп́одданный**, loyal, faithful. **вéрно** *part.* probably, I suppose; that's right! **вéрность**, -и, faithfulness, loyalty; truth, correctness.

вернýть, -нý, -нёшь *perf.* (*imp.* возвращáть) give back, return; get back, recover, retrieve; **~ся**, return, revert.

вéрный; -рен, -рнá, -о, faithful, loyal; true; correct; sure; reliable; certain.

вéрование, -я, belief; creed. **вéровать**, -рую *imp.* believe. **вероисповéдание**, -я, religion; denomination. **верол́омный**, treacherous, perfidious. **вероотстýпник**, -а, apostate. **веротерпи́мость**, -и, (religious) toleration. **вероя́тно** *adv.* probably. **вероя́тность**, -и, probability. **вероя́тный**, probable, likely.

вéрсия, -и, version.

верстá, -ы́, *acc.* -ý or вёрсту; *pl.* вёрсты, verst (1·06 km.); verst-post; зá ~у, miles away.

верстáк, -á, bench.

верстовóй, verst; ~ столб, milestone.

вéртел, -а; *pl.* -á, spit, skewer. **вертéть**, -чý, -тишь *imp.* turn (round); twirl; spin; **~ся**, rotate, turn (round), revolve, spin; move about, hang about, go round; fidget; turn and twist, dodge. **вёрткий**; -ток, -тка, nimble, agile. **вертлю́г**, -á, swivel. **вертля́вый**, restless, fidgety; flighty, frivolous.

вертодрóм, -а, heliport. **вертолёт**, -а, helicopter.

вертýн, -á, fidget; tumbler-pigeon. **вертýшка**, -и, revolving door, revolving stand; flirt, coquette.

вéрующий *sb.* believer.

верфь, -и, dockyard, shipyard.

верх, -а (-у), *loc.* -ý; *pl.* -и́ or -á, top, summit; height; upper part, upper side; upper reaches; bonnet, hood; upper hand; outside; right side; *pl.* upper ten, bosses, leadership, management, top brass; high notes. **вéрхний,** upper; outer; top. **верхóвный,** supreme. **верховóй**[1], riding; *sb.* rider. **верховóй**[2], up-stream, up-river; upper. **верхóвье,** -я; *gen. pl.* -вьев, upper reaches, head. **верхолáз,** -а, steeple-jack. **вéрхом**[1] *adv.* on high ground; quite full, brim-full. **верхóм**[2] *adv.* on horseback; astride; éздить ~, ride. **верхýшка,** -и, top, summit; apex; bosses, top brass, management.

верчý, etc.: see вертéть.

верши́на, -ы, top, summit; peak; height; apex, vertex. **верши́ть,** -шý *imp.* top, top out; decide, settle; +*instr.* manage, control, direct; control, sway.

вершкóвый, a vershok long. **вершóк,** -шкá, vershok (4·4 cm.); inch; smattering.

вес, -а (-у), *loc.* -ý; *pl.* -á, weight; authority, influence; на ~, by weight; на ~ý, suspended, balanced.

веселéть, -éю *imp.* (*perf.* по~), cheer up, be cheerful. **весели́ть,** -лю́ *imp.* (*perf.* раз~) cheer up, gladden; amuse; **~ся,** enjoy oneself; amuse oneself. **вéсело** *adv.* gaily, merrily. **весёлость,** -и, gaiety; cheerfulness. **весёлый**; вéсел, -á, -о, gay, merry; cheerful, lively. **весéлье,** -я, gaiety, merriment.

весéнн|ий, spring; vernal; ~ее равнодéнствие, vernal equinox.

вéсить, вéшу *imp.* weigh. **вéский,** weighty.

веслó, -á; *pl.* вёсла, -сел, oar; scull; paddle.

веснá, -ы́; *pl.* вёсны, -сен, spring; spring-time. **веснóй,** -óю *adv.* in (the) spring. **веснýшка,** -и, freckle. **веснýшчатый,** freckled. **веснянка,** -и, may-fly.

весовóй, weight, of weight; sold by weight. **весóмый,** heavy, weighty; ponderable.

вести́, ведý, -дёшь; вёл, -á *imp.* (*perf.* по~) lead, take; conduct, carry on; be engaged in, wage; drive; conduct; direct, run; keep; +*instr.* pass, run (по+*dat.* over, across); ~ корáбль, navigate a ship; ~ (своё) начáло, originate, take rise; ~ огóнь, fire; ~ самолёт, pilot an aircraft; ~ свой род от, be descended from; ~ себя́, behave, conduct oneself; **~сь,** be observed, be the custom.

вéстник, -а, messenger, herald; bulletin. **вестовóй,** signal; *sb.* orderly. **весть,** -и; *gen. pl.* -éй, news; *pl.* tales, talk, gossip; бéз вести, without trace. **весть;** Бог ~, God knows; не ~, goodness knows, there's no knowing.

весы́, -óв *pl.* scales, balance; Libra.

весь, всегó *m.*, **вся,** всей *f.*, **всё,** всегó *n.*, **все,** всех *pl.*, *pron.* all, the whole of; all gone; бумáга вся, the paper is used up, there's no paper left; во~ гóлос, at the top of one's voice; во-всю́, like anything; вот и всё, that's all; при всём том, for all that; moreover; всегó хорóшего! goodbye; all the best!; **всё,** everything; без всегó, without anything, with nothing; **все,** everybody.

весьмá, *adv.* very, highly; very much.

ветви́стый, spreading, (many-) branched, branching. **ветви́ться,** -влю́сь *imp.* branch. **ветвь,** -и; *gen. pl.* -éй, branch; bough.

вéтер, -тра (-у), *loc.* -ý; *gen. pl.* ветрóв, wind; *pl.* wind; по вéтру, before the wind; down wind; подби́тый вéтром, empty-headed; light, flimsy; под вéтром, (to) leeward; прóтив вéтра, close to the wind, against the wind. **ветерóк,** -ркá, breeze.

вéтка, -и, branch; twig.

ветлá, -ы́; *pl.* вётлы, (white) willow.

вéточка, -и, twig, sprig, shoot.

ветóшка, -и, rag. **ветóшник,** -а, old-clothes dealer, rag-dealer. **вéтошь,** -и, old clothes, rags.

ветренéть, -éет *imp.* become windy, get windy. **вéтреный,** windy; frivolous, inconstant, unstable. **ветров|óй,** wind, of wind; ~óе окнó, ~óе стеклó, windscreen. **ветромéр,** -а, anemometer. **ветроуказáтель,** -я *m.* drogue, wind cone, wind sock. **ветрáк,** -á, wind motor; windmill. **ветряно́й, ве́тряный,** wind; ве́тряная о́спа, chicken-pox.

ве́тхий; ветх, -á, -o, old, ancient; dilapidated, ramshackle, tumbledown; decrepit; В~ заве́т, Old Testament. **ветхозаве́тный,** Old-Testament; antiquated, out-of-date. **ве́тхость,** -и, decrepitude, dilapidation, decay.

ветчина́, -ы́, ham.

ветша́ть, -а́ю *imp.* (*perf.* об~), decay; become dilapidated.

ве́ха, -и, landmark; marker post, stake; spar-buoy.

ве́чер, -а; *pl.* -а́, evening; party; soirée. **вече́рн|ий,** evening; ~яя заря́, sunset; dusk. **вече́рник,** -а, evening student, evening worker. **вече́рня,** -и; *gen. pl.* -рен, vespers. **ве́чером** *adv.* in the evening.

ве́чно *adv.* for ever, eternally; everlastingly. **вечнозелёный,** evergreen. **ве́чность,** -и, eternity; an age, ages. **ве́чн|ый,** eternal, everlasting; endless; perpetual; ~ая мерзлота́, permafrost; ~ое перо́, fountain-pen.

ве́шалка, -и, peg, rack, stand; hanger; cloak-room. **ве́шать,** -аю *imp.* (*perf.* взве́сить, пове́сить, све́шать) hang; weigh, weigh out; **~ся,** be hung, be hanged; hang oneself; weigh oneself.

ве́шний, spring, vernal.

ве́шу etc.: see ве́сить.

веща́ние, -я, radio; prophecy. **веща́ть,** -а́ю *imp.* broadcast; prophesy; pontificate.

вещево́й, clothing, kit; in kind; ~ мешо́к, knapsack; pack, hold-all, kit-bag; ~ склад, clothing store, stores. **веще́ственный,** substantial, material, real. **вещество́,** -а́, substance; matter. **вещмешо́к,** -шка́, rucksack. **вещь,** -и; *gen. pl.* -е́й, thing.

ве́ялка, -и, winnowing-fan; winnowing-machine. **ве́яние,** -я, winnowing; breathing, blowing; current, tendency, trend. **ве́ять,** ве́ю *imp.* (*perf.* про~) winnow, fan; blow, breathe; wave, flutter.

вз-, взо-, взъ-, вс- *vbl. pref.* expressing direction of motion or action upwards or on to; rapidity or suddenness of occurrence; completion or finality of action.

взад *adv.* backwards; ~ и вперёд, backwards and forwards, to and fro.

взаи́мность, -и, reciprocity; requital, return. **взаи́мный,** mutual, reciprocal.

взаимо- in *comb.* inter-. **взаимоде́йствие,** -я interaction; co-operation, coordination. **~де́йствовать,** -твую *imp.* interact; co-operate. **~отноше́ние,** -я, interrelation; *pl.* relations. **~по́мощь,** -и, mutual aid. **~свя́зь,** -и, intercommunication; interdependence, correlation.

взаймы́ *adv.* as a loan; взять ~, borrow; дать ~, lend.

взаме́н *prep.*+*gen.* instead of; in return for, in exchange for.

взаперти́ *adv.* under lock and key; in seclusion, in isolation.

взапра́вду *adv.* in truth, really and truly.

вз|баламу́тить, -у́чу *perf.*

взба́лмошный, unbalanced, eccentric.

взба́лтывание, -я, shaking (up). **взба́лтывать,** -аю *imp.* of взболта́ть.

взбега́ть, -а́ю *imp.*, **взбежа́ть,** -егу́ *perf.* run up.

взберу́сь, etc.: see взобра́ться. **вз|беси́ть(ся,** -ешу́(сь, -е́сишь(ся *perf.* **взбива́ть,** -а́ю *imp.* of взбить. **взбира́ться,** -а́юсь *imp.* of взобра́ться.

взби́тый, whipped, beaten. **взбить,** взобью́, -бьёшь *perf.* (*imp.* взбива́ть) beat (up), whip; shake up, fluff up.

взболта́ть, -а́ю *perf.* (*imp.* взба́лтывать) shake (up).

вз|борозди́ть, -зжу́ *perf.* **вз|борони́ть,** -ню́ *perf.* **взбра́сывать,** -аю *imp.* of взбро́сить.

взбреда́ть, -а́ю *imp.*, **взбрести́,** -еду́, -едёшь; -ёл, -ела́ *perf.*+на+*acc.* climb (up), mount, with difficulty; struggle up; ~ в го́лову, на ум, come into one's head.

взбро́сить, -о́шу *perf.* (*imp.* взбра́сывать) throw up, toss up.

вз|будора́жить, -жу *perf.* **вз|бунтова́ться,** -ту́юсь *perf.*

взбуха́ть, -а́ет *imp.*, **взбу́хнуть,** -нет; -ух *perf.* swell (out).

взва́ливать, -аю *imp.*, **взвали́ть,** -лю́,

-лишь *perf.* hoist, heave (up); load; +на+*acc.* saddle with.

взве́сить, -е́шу *perf.* (*imp.* ве́шать, взве́шивать) weigh.

взвести́, -еду́, -едёшь; -ёл, -а́ *perf.* (*imp.* взводи́ть) lead up, take up; lift up, raise; cock, arm; +на+*acc.* impute to, bring against.

взвесь, -и, suspension. **взве́шенный,** weighed; suspended, of suspension. **взве́шивать,** -аю *imp.* of взве́сить.

взвива́ть(ся, -а́ю(сь *imp.* of взви́ть(ся.

взвизг, -а, scream, squeal, screech; yelp. **взви́згивать,** -аю *imp.*, **взви́згнуть,** -ну *perf.* let out screams, a scream; scream, screech; yelp.

взвинти́ть, -нчу́ *perf.*, **взви́нчивать,** -аю *imp.* excite, work up; inflate; **~ся,** work oneself up; spiral up. **взви́нченный,** excited, worked up; nervy, on edge; highly strung; inflated.

взвить, взовью́ -ёшь; -ил, -а́, -о *perf.* (*imp.* взвива́ть) raise; **~ся,** rise, be hoisted; fly up, soar.

взвод[1], -а, platoon, troop.

взвод[2], -а, cocking; notch; на боево́м ~е, cocked; на пе́рвом ~е, at half-cock. **взводи́ть,** -ожу́, -о́дишь *imp.* of взвести́. **взводно́й,** cocking.

взво́дный, platoon; *sb.* platoon commander.

вз|двои́ть, -ою́ *perf.*

взволно́ванный, agitated, disturbed; ruffled; anxious, troubled, worried. **вз|волнова́ть(ся,** -ну́ю(сь *perf.*

взвыть, взво́ю *perf.* howl, set up a howl.

взгляд, -а, look; glance; gaze, stare; view; opinion; на ~, to judge from appearances; на пе́рвый ~, с пе́рвого ~а, at first sight. **взгля́дывать,** -аю *imp.*, **взгляну́ть,** -яну́, -я́нешь *perf.* look, glance.

взго́рок, -рка, **взго́рье,** -я, hill, hillock.

взгромозжда́ть, -а́ю *imp.*, **взгромозди́ть,** -зжу́ *perf.* pile up; **~ся,** clamber up.

вздёргивать, -аю *imp.*, **вздёрнуть,** -ну *perf.* hitch up; jerk up; turn up; hang.

вздор, -а, nonsense. **вздо́рный,** cantankerous, quarrelsome; foolish, stupid.

вздорожа́ние, -я, rise in price. **вз|дорожа́ть,** -а́ет *perf.*

вздох, -а, sigh; deep breath. **вздохну́ть,** -ну́, -нёшь *perf.* (*imp.* вздыха́ть) sigh; heave a sigh; take a deep breath; take a breather, pause for breath.

вздра́гивать, -аю *imp.* (*perf.* вздро́гнуть) shudder, quiver.

вздремну́ть, -ну́, нёшь *perf.* have a nap, doze.

вздро́гнуть, -ну *perf.* (*imp.* вздра́гивать) start, jump; wince, flinch.

вздува́ть(ся, -а́ю(сь *imp.* of вздуть[1](ся.

взду́мать, -аю *perf.* take it into one's head; не взду́май(те! mind you don't, don't you dare! **взду́маться,** -ается *impers.*+*dat.* come into one's head; как взду́мается, as the fancy takes one, as one likes.

взду́тие, -я, swelling; inflation. **взду́тый,** swollen. **взду́ть**[1], -у́ю *perf.* (*imp.* вздува́ть) blow up, swell, inflate; **~ся,** swell.

вздуть[2], -у́ю *perf.* thrash, lick, give a hiding.

вздыха́ние, -я, sighing; sigh. **вздыха́тель,** -я *m.* admirer, suitor. **вздыха́ть,** -а́ю *imp.* (*perf.* вздохну́ть) breathe; sigh.

взима́ть, -а́ю *imp.* levy, collect.

взла́мывать, -аю *imp.* of взлома́ть.

вз|леле́ять, -е́ю *perf.*

взлёт, -а, flight; taking wing; take-off. **взлета́ть,** -а́ю *imp.*, **взлете́ть,** -лечу́ *perf.* fly (up); take off. **взлётный,** flying; take-off; взлётно-поса́дочная полоса́, runway, landing-strip.

взлом, -а, breaking open, breaking in; break-in. **взлома́ть,** -а́ю *perf.* (*imp.* взла́мывать) break open, force; smash; break up, break through. **взло́мщик,** -а, burglar, house-breaker.

взлохма́ченный, dishevelled, tousled.

взмах, -а, stroke, sweep, wave, flap. **взма́хивать,** -аю *imp.*, **взмахну́ть,** -ну́, -нёшь *perf.*+*instr.* wave, flap.

взмо́рье, -я, (sea-)shore, coast; seaside, beach; coastal waters.

вз|мути́ть, -учу́, -у́ти́шь *perf.*

взнос, -а, payment; fee, dues; subscription; instalment.

взнуздáть, -áю *perf.*, **взнýздывать, -аю** *imp.* bridle.

взо-: see вз-.

взобрáться, взберýсь, -ёшься; -áлся, -лáсь, -áлóсь *perf.* (*imp.* взбирáться) на+*acc.* climb (up), clamber up.

взобью, etc.: see взбить. **взовью,** etc.: see взвить.

взойти, -йдý, -йдёшь; -ошёл, -шлá, *perf.* (*imp.* вос-, всходить), rise, go up, come up; на+*acc.* mount, ascend; enter.

взор, -а, look, glance.

взорвáть, -вý, -вёшь; -áл, -á, -о *perf.* (*imp.* взрывáть) blow up; blast; fire, explode, detonate; exasperate madden, make furiously angry; **~ся,** blow up, burst, explode.

взрóслый, grown-up, adult.

взрыв, -а, explosion; burst, outburst; plosion. **взрывáтель, -я** *m.* fuse. **взрывáть,** -áю *imp.*, **взрыть,** -рóю *perf.* (*perf.* also взорвáть) blow up; **~ся,** blow up, explode. **взрывн|óй,** explosive; explosion, blasting; plosive; ~áя волнá, shock wave, blast. **взрывчáтка,** -и, explosive. **взрывчатый,** explosive.

взъ-: see вз-.

взъерóшенный, tousled, dishevelled; ruffled. **взъерóшивать,** -аю *imp.*, **взъ|ерóшить,** -шу *perf.* tousle, ruffle, rumple; **~ся,** become dishevelled, bristle up, stand on end.

взывáть, -áю *imp.* of воззвáть.

взыскáние, -я, penalty, punishment; recovery, exaction; prosecution. **взыскáтельный,** exacting; demanding. **взыскáть,** -ыщý, -ыщешь *perf.*, **взыскивать,** -аю *imp.* exact, recover; call to account, make answer.

взятие, -я, taking, capture, seizure. **взятка,** -и, bribe; trick. **взяточничество,** -а, bribery, corruption. **взять(ся** возьмý(сь, -мёшь(ся; -ял(ся, -á(сь, -о(сь *perf.* of брать(ся; ни дать ни ~, exactly, neither more nor less than; откýда ни возьмись, out of the blue, from nowhere.

вибрировать, -рует *imp.* vibrate, oscillate.

вид[1], **-а (-у),** *loc.* **-ý, look**; appearance; air; shape, form; condition; view; prospect; sight; дéлать ~, pretend; имéть в ~ý, plan, intend; mean; bear in mind, not forget; из ~у, out of sight; на ~ý, in the public eye; потерять из ~у, lose sight of; под ~ом, under the pretext; при ~е, at the sight.

вид[2], -а, kind, sort; species.

виданный, seen; heard of. **видáть,** -áю *imp.* (*perf.* по~, у~) see; **~ся** meet; see one another. **видение**[1], -я, sight, vision. **видéние**[2], -я, vision, apparition. **видеть,** вижу *imp.* (*perf.* у~) see; ~ во сне dream (of); **~ся,** see one another, meet; appear. **видимо** *adv.* visibly; evidently; seemingly. **видимо-невидимо** *adv.* immense numbers of. **видимость,** -и, visibility, vision; appearance, semblance, show; appearances. **видимый,** visible, in sight; apparent, evident, seeming. **виднéться,** -éется, be visible. **видный;** -ден, -днá, -о, -ы or -ы́, visible; conspicuous; distinguished, prominent; stately, portly, dignified. **видовóй**[1], landscape; ~ фильм, travelogue, travel-film.

видовóй[2], specific; aspectual.

видоизменéние, -я modification; alteration; variety. **видоизменить,** -ню́ *perf.*, **видоизменять,** -яю *imp.* modify, alter; **~ся,** alter; be modified, be altered.

видоискáтель, -я *m.* view-finder.

вижу: see видеть.

виза, -ы, visa; official stamp.

визг, -а, squeal; scream; yelp. **визгливый,** shrill; screaming, squealing, squalling. **визжáть,** -жý *imp.* squeal, scream, yelp, squeak.

визировать, -рую *perf.* and *imp.* (*perf.* also за~) visa, visé.

визит, -а, visit; call. **визитáция,** -и, call; round; search. **визитка,** -и, morning coat.

викторина, -ы, quiz.

вилка, -и, fork; plug; bracket. **вилообрáзный,** forked. **вилочный,** fork-lift. **вилы,** вил *pl.* pitchfork.

вильнýть, -нý, -нёшь *perf.*, **вилять,** -яю *imp.* twist and turn; turn sharply; prevaricate, be evasive; +*instr.* wag.

винá, -ы́; *pl.* вины, fault, guilt; blame.

винегре́т, -а, Russian salad; medley, farrago.
вини́тельный, accusative. **вини́ть,** -ню *imp.* accuse, blame; reproach; **~ся** (*perf.* по~) confess.
ви́нкель, -я; *pl.* -я́ *m.* set-square.
виннока́менный, tartaric. **ви́нн|ый,** wine; winy; vinous; ~ый ка́мень, tartar; ~ая я́года, fig. **вино́,** -а́; *pl.* -а, wine; vodka.
винова́тый, guilty; to blame; винова́т(а)! (I'm) sorry. **вино́вник,** -а, author, initiator; culprit; ~ торжества́, founder of the feast. **вино́вный,** guilty.
виногра́д, -а (-у), vine; grapes. **виногра́дарь,** -я *m.* wine-grower. **виногра́дина,** -ы, grape. **виногра́дник,** -а, vineyard. **виногра́дный,** vine; grape; wine, vintage. **винoку́р,** -а, distiller. **винокуре́ние,** -я, distillation. **виноку́ренный,** distilling; ~ заво́д, distillery.
винт, -а́, screw; propeller; rotor; spiral; vint. **винти́ть,** -нчу́ *imp.* screw in; unscrew; turn. **винто́вка,** -и, rifle. **винтово́й,** screw; spiral; helical. **винто́вочный,** rifle-. **винто́м** *adv.* spirally.
вира́ж, -а, turn; bend, curve.
вис, -а, hang, hanging. **ви́селица,** -ы, gallows. **висе́ть,** вишу́ *imp.* hang; hover. **вислоу́хий,** lop-eared. **ви́снуть,** -ну; ви́с(нул) *imp.* hang; droop.
висо́к, -ска́, temple.
високо́сный; ~ год, leap-year.
висо́чный, temporal.
висю́лька, -и, pendant. **вися́чий,** hanging; ~ замо́к, padlock; ~ мост, suspension bridge.
вито́й, twisted, spiral. **вито́к,** -тка́, turn, coil, loop; orbit.
витра́ж, -а́, stained-glass window, panel, etc. **витри́на,** -ы, shop-window; showcase.
вить, вью, вьёшь; вил, -а́, -о *imp.* (*perf.* с~) twist, wind, weave; ~ гнездо́, build a nest; ~ верёвки из + *gen.* twist round one's little finger; **~ся,** wind, twine; curl, wave; hover, circle; twist, turn; whirl, eddy; writhe.
вихо́р, -хра́, tuft. **вихра́стый,** shaggy, wiry; shock-headed.
вихрево́й, vortical. **вихрь,** -я *m.* whirlwind; whirl, eddy, vortex; сне́жный ~, blizzard.
ви́це- *perf.* vice-. **вице-коро́ль,** -я́ *m.* viceroy. **~-президе́нт,** -а, vice-president.
вицмунди́р, -а, (dress) uniform.
ви́шенник, -а, **вишня́к,** -а́, cherry-orchard, cherry-grove; wild cherry. **вишнёвый,** cherry; cherry-coloured. **ви́шня,** -и; *gen. pl.* -шен, cherry, cherries; cherry-tree.
вишу́: see висе́ть.
вишь *part.* look, just look; well!
вка́лывать, -аю *imp.* (*perf.* вколо́ть) (*sl.*) work hard, slave; get stuck in.
вка́пывать, -аю *imp.* of вкопа́ть.
вкати́ть, -ачу́, -а́тишь *perf.*, **вка́тывать,** -аю *imp.* roll in, wheel in; roll up; put in, put on; administer; **~ся,** roll in; run in.
вклад, -а, deposit; investment; endowment; contribution. **вкла́дка,** -и, **вкла́дыш,** -а, supplementary sheet, inset. **вкладно́й,** deposit; supplementary, inserted; ~ лист, loose leaf, insert. **вкла́дчик,** -а, depositor; investor.
вкла́дывать, -аю *imp.* of вложи́ть.
вкла́дыш: see вкла́дка.
вкле́ивать, -аю *imp.*, **вкле́ить,** -е́ю *perf.* stick in, glue in, paste in; put in.
вкле́йка, -и, sticking in; inset.
вкли́нивать, -аю *imp.*, **вклини́ть,** -и́ню *perf.* wedge in; put in; **~ся,** edge one's way in; drive a wedge (into).
включа́тель, -я *m.* switch. **включа́ть,** -а́ю *imp.*, **включи́ть,** -чу́ *perf.* include; insert; switch on, turn on, start; plug in, connect; engage, let in; **~ся** в + *acc.* join in, enter into. **включа́я,** including. **включе́ние,** -я, inclusion insertion; switching on, turning on. **включи́тельно** *adv.* inclusive.
вкола́чивать, -аю *imp.*, **вколоти́ть,** -очу́, -о́тишь *perf.* hammer in, knock in.
вколо́ть, -олю́, -о́лешь *perf.* (*imp.* вка́лывать), stick (in), pin (in).
вконе́ц *adv.* completely, absolutely.
вко́панный, dug in; rooted to the ground. **вкопа́ть,** -а́ю *perf.* (*imp.* вка́пывать) dig in.

вкоренить, -ню́ *perf.*, **вкоренять**, -я́ю *imp.* inculcate; **~ся**, take root.
вкось *adv.* obliquely, slantwise; ~ и вкривь, вкривь и ~, at random, all over the place; indiscriminately.
ВКП(б) (*vekapebé*) *abbr.* Всесою́зная Коммунисти́ческая па́ртия (большевико́в), All-Union Communist Party (Bolsheviks).
вкра́дчивый, insinuating, ingratiating.
вкра́дываться, -аюсь *imp.*, **вкра́сться**, -аду́сь, -адёшься *perf.* steal in, creep in; worm oneself, insinuate oneself, (into).
вкра́тце *adv.* briefly, succinctly.
вкривь *adv.* aslant; wrongly, perversely; ~ и вкось: see вкось.
вкруг: see вокру́г.
вкруту́ю *adv.* hard(-boiled).
вку́пе *adv.* together.
вкус, -а, taste; manner, style; де́ло ~а, a matter of taste. **вкуси́ть**, -ушу́, -у́сишь *perf.*, **вкуша́ть**, -а́ю *imp.* taste; partake of; savour, experience. **вку́сный**; -сен, -сна́, -о, tasty, nice, good; appetizing.
вла́га, -и, moisture, damp, liquid.
влага́лище, -а, vagina; sheath.
влага́ть, -а́ю *imp.* of вложи́ть.
владе́лец, -льца, **-лица**, -ы, owner; proprietor. **владе́ние**, -я, ownership; possession; property; domain, estate. **владе́тель**, -я *m.*, **-ница**, -ы possessor; sovereign. **владе́тельный**, sovereign. **владе́ть**, -е́ю *imp.*+*instr.* own, possess; control; be in possession of; have (a) command of; have the use of.
влады́ка, -и *m.* master, sovereign; Orthodox prelate; my Lord. **влады́чество**, -а, dominion, rule, sway.
влажне́ть, -е́ет *imp.* (*perf.* по~) become humid, grow damp. **вла́жный**; -жен, -жна́, -о, damp moist, humid.
вла́мываться, -аюсь *imp.* of вломи́ться.
вла́ствовать, -твую *imp.*+(над+) *instr.* rule, hold sway over. **власти́тель**, -я *m.* sovereign, ruler. **вла́стный**, imperious, commanding; masterful; empowered competent. **власть**, -и; *gen. pl.* -е́й, power; authority; control; *pl.* authorities; ва́ша ~, as you like, please yourself, it's up to you.
вле́во *adv.* to the left.
влеза́ть, -а́ю *imp.*, **влезть**, -зу; влез *perf.* climb in, climb up; get in; fit in, go in, go on; ско́лько вле́зет, as much as will go in, any amount.
влёк, etc.: see влечь.
влепи́ть, -плю́, -пишь *perf.*, **влепля́ть**, -я́ю *imp.* stick in, fasten in; ~ пощёчину+*dat.* give a slap in the face.
влета́ть, -а́ю *imp.*. **влете́ть**, -ечу́ *perf.* fly in; rush in.
влече́ние, -я, attraction; bent, inclination. **влечь**, -еку́, -ечёшь; влёк, -ла́ *imp.* draw, drag; attract; ~ за собо́й, involve, entail; **~ся** к + *dat.* be drawn to, be attracted by.
влива́ть, -а́ю *imp.*, **влить**, волью́, -ёшь; влил, -а́, -о *perf.* pour in; infuse; instil; bring in; **~ся**, flow in.
влия́ние, -я, influence. **влия́тельный**, influential. **влия́ть**, -я́ю *imp.* (*perf.* по~) на+*acc.* influence, have an influence on, affect.
вложе́ние, -я, enclosure; investment. **вложи́ть**, -ожу́, -о́жишь *perf.* (*imp.* вкла́дывать, влага́ть) put in, insert; enclose; invest.
вломи́ться, -млю́сь, -мишься *perf.* (*imp.* вла́мываться) break in.
влюби́ть, -блю́, -бишь *perf.*, **влюбля́ть**, -я́ю *imp.* capture the heart of, make fall in love (в+*acc.* with); **~ся**, fall in love. **влюблённый**; -лён, -а́, in love; loving, tender; *sb.* lover. **влю́бчивый**, susceptible.
вма́зать, -а́жу *perf.*, **вма́зывать**, -аю *imp.* cement in, putty in, mortar in.
вм. *abbr.* вме́сто, instead of, in place of.
вмени́ть, -ню́ *perf.*, **вменя́ть**, -я́ю *imp.* impute; ~ в вину́, lay to the charge of; ~ в обя́занность, impose as a duty. **вменя́емый**, responsible, liable; of sound mind.
вме́сте *adv.* together; at the same time; ~ с тем, at the same time, also.
вмести́лище, -а, receptacle. **вмести́мость**, -и, capacity; tonnage. **вмести́тельный**, capacious; spacious, roomy. **вмести́ть**, -ещу́ *perf.* (*imp.* вмеща́ть)

contain, hold, accommodate; find room for; put, place; **~ся**, go in.
вмéсто *prep.*+*gen.* instead of, in place of.
вмешáтельство, -а interference; intervention. **вмешáть,** -áю *perf.*, **вмéшивать,** -аю *imp.* mix in; mix up, implicate; **~ся** interfere, meddle.
вмещáть(ся, -áю(сь *imp.* of вместúться.
вмиг *adv.* in an instant, in a flash.
вминáть, -áю *imp.*, **вмять,** вомнý, -нёшь *perf.* crush in, press in; dent. **вмя́тина,** -ы, dent.
ВМФ (*ve-eméf*) *abbr.* воéнно-морскóй флот, navy.
внаём, внаймы́ *adv.* to let; for hire; брать ~, hire rent; отдавáться ~, let, hire out, rent; сдавáться ~, be to let.
внакúдку *adv.* thrown over the shoulders.
вначáле *adv.* at first, in the beginning.
вне *prep.*+*gen.* outside; out of; without; ~ себя́, beside oneself; ~ сомнéния, without doubt, undoubtedly.
вне-, *pref.*, extra-; situated outside, lying outside the province or scope of; -less. **внебрáчный,** extra-marital; illegitimate, born outside wedlock. **~врéменный,** timeless. **~клáссный,** out-of-school, extracurricular. **~мáточный,** extra-uterine. **~очереднóй,** out of turn, out of order; extraordinary; extra. **~партúйный,** non-party. **~служéбный,** leisure-time, leisure. **~студúйный,** outside. **~шкóльный,** adult; extra-scholastic; out-of-school. **~штáтный,** not established; not permanent; part-time.
внедрéние, -я, introduction; inculcation, indoctrination; intrusion. **внедрúть,** -рю́ *perf.*, **внедря́ть,** я́ю *imp.* inculcate, instil; introduce; **~ся,** take root.
внезáпно *adv.* suddenly, all of a sudden, all at once. **внезáпный,** sudden, unexpected; surprise.
внéмлю, etc.: see внимáть.
внесéние, -я, bringing in, carrying in; paying in, deposit; entry, insertion; moving, submission. **внестú,** -сý, -сёшь; внёс, -лá *perf.* (*imp.* вносúть) bring in, carry in; introduce, put in; pay in, deposit; move, table; insert, enter; bring about, cause.
внéшне *adv.* outwardly. **внéшний,** outer, exterior; outward, external; outside; surface, superficial; foreign. **внéшность,** -и, exterior; surface; appearance.
вниз *adv.* down, downwards; downstream; ~ по+*dat.* down; ~ по течéнию, downstream. **внизý** *adv.* below; downstairs; *prep.*+*gen.* at the foot of, in the lower part of.
ВНИИ′ *abbr.* всесою́зный нayчно-исслéдовательский институ́т, All-Union Scientific-research Institute.
вникáть, -áю *imp.*, **вни́кнуть,** -ну; вник *perf.*+в+*acc.* go carefully into, investigate thoroughly, get to the heart or root of.
внимáние, -я, attention; notice, note; heed; consideration; attentions, kindness; ~! look out!; ~ на старт! get set! **внимáтельный,** attentive; thoughtful, considerate, kind. **внимáть,** -áю or внéмлю *imp.* (*perf.* внять) listen to, hear; heed.
вничью́ *adv.*; окóнчиться ~, end in a draw, be drawn; сыгрáть ~, draw.
вносúть, -ошý, -óсишь *imp.* of внестú.
внук, -а, grandson; *pl.* grandchildren, descendants.
вну́тренн|ий, inner, interior; internal; intrinsic; home, inland; -ие дохóды, inland revenue. **вну́тренность,** -и, interior; *pl.* entrails, intestines; internal organs; viscera. **внутрú** *adv.* and *prep.* +*gen.* inside, within. **внутрь** *adv.* and *prep*+*gen.* inside, in; inwards.
внучáта, -чáт *pl.* grandchildren. **внучáтный, внучáтый,** second, great-; ~ брат, second cousin; ~ племя́нник, great-nephew. **вну́чка,** -и, grand-daughter; grandchild.
внушáемость, -и, suggestibility. **внушáть,** -áю *imp.*, **внушúть,** -шý *perf.* instil; suggest; +*dat.* inspire with, fill with. **внушéние,** -я, suggestion; reproof reprimand. **внушúтельный,** inspiring, impressive; imposing, striking.
вня́тный, distinct; intelligible. **внять,** no *fut.*; -ял, -á, -о *perf.* of внимáть.
во: see в[2].

ВО *abbr.* вое́нный о́круг, military district.

во-: see в-.

вобра́ть, вберу́, -рёшь; -а́л, -а́, -о *perf.* (*imp.* вбира́ть) absorb, draw in, soak up, inhale.

вобью́, etc.: see вбить.

вове́к, вове́ки *adv.* for ever; ~ не, never.

во́время *adv.* in time; on time; не ~, at the wrong time.

во́все *adv.* quite; ~ не, not at all.

во-вторы́х *adv.* secondly, in the second place.

вогна́ть, вгоню́, -о́нишь; -гна́л, -а́, -о *perf.* (*imp.* вгоня́ть) drive in. **во́гнутый**, concave; dented. **вогну́ть**, -ну́, -нёшь *perf.* (*imp.* вгиба́ть) bend or curve inwards; **~ся**, bend inwards, curve inwards.

-вод in *comb.* -breeder, -grower, -raiser.

вода́, -ы́, *acc.* во́ду; *pl.* -ы, water; *pl.* the waters; watering-place, spa.

водворе́ние, -я, settlement; establishment. **водвори́ть**, -рю́ *perf.*, **водворя́ть**, -я́ю *imp.* settle, install, house; establish.

води́тель, -я *m.* driver; leader. **води́тельница**, -ы, (woman) driver. **води́тельство**, -а, leadership. **води́ть**, вожу́, во́дишь *imp.* lead; conduct; take; drive; + *instr.* (по + *dat.*) pass (over, across); ~ автомоби́ль, маши́ну, drive a car; ~ глаза́ми по + *dat.*, cast one's eyes over; **~ся**, be, be found; associate, play (with); be the custom, happen.

во́дка, -и, vodka. **воднолы́жник**, -а, -ница, -ы, water-skier. **во́дн|ый**, water; watery; aquatic; aqueous; ~ые лы́жи, water-skiing; water-skis.

водо- in *comb.* water, water-; hydraulic; hydro-. **водобоя́знь**, -и, hydrophobia. **~вмести́лище**, -а, reservoir. **~во́з**, -а, water-carrier. **~воро́т**, -а, whirlpool, eddy; vortex, maelstrom, whirl. **~ём**, -а, reservoir. **~измеще́ние**, -я, displacement. **~ка́чка**, -и, water-tower, pump-house, pumping station. **~ла́з**, -а, diver; Newfoundland. **~ла́зный**, diving. **~ле́й**, -я, Aquarius. **~непроница́емый**, watertight; waterproof. **~но́сный**, water-bearing. **~отво́д**, -а, drain, overflow. **~отво́дный**, drainage, overflow. **~отта́лкивающий**, water-repellent. **~па́д**, -а, waterfall; falls, cataract. **~по́й**, -я, watering-place; water-supply; watering. **~прово́д**, -а, water-pipe, water-main; water supply. **~прово́дный**, water-main, mains; tap-. **~прово́дчик**, -а, plumber. **~разде́л**, -а, watershed. **~распыли́тель**, -я *m.* sprinkler. **~ро́д**, -а, hydrogen. **во́доросль**, -и, water-plant, water-weed; seaweed; alga. **~снабже́ние**, -я, water-supply. **~сто́к**, -а, drain, gutter.

во́дочный, vodka.

водружа́ть, -а́ю *imp.*, **водрузи́ть**, -ужу́ *perf.* hoist; set up, fix up.

водяни́стый, watery. **водя́нка**, -и, dropsy. **водяно́й**, water; aquatic; ~ знак, watermark; *sb.* water-sprite. **водя́ночный**, dropsical.

воева́ть, вою́ю *imp.* wage war, make war, be at war; quarrel. **воево́да**, -ы *m.* voivode; commander of army; governor of province. **воево́дство**, -а, office of voivode; voivode's province.

воеди́но *adv.* together, into one.

воен- *abbr.* in *comb.* of вое́нный, military, war-. **военко́м**, -а, military commissar. **~ко́р**, -а, war-correspondent.

военииза́ция, -и, militarization. **военизи́рованный**, militarized, armed; paramilitary.

военно- in *comb.* military; war-. **вое́нно-возду́шный**, air-, air-force; ~-возду́шные си́лы, air force. **вое́нно-морско́й**, naval; ~-морско́й флот, navy. **~пле́нный** *sb.* prisoner of war. **вое́нно-полево́й**; ~-полево́й суд, (drumhead) court-martial. **~слу́жащий** *sb.* serviceman.

вое́нн|ый, military; war; army; ~ое положе́ние, martial law; ~ый суд, court-martial; *sb.* soldier, serviceman; *pl.* the military.

вожа́к, -а́, guide; leader. **вожа́тый** *sb.* guide; leader; tram-driver. **вожде́ние**, -я, leading; driving, steering, piloting. **вождь**, -я́ *m.* leader, chief.

вожжа́, -и́; *pl.* -и, -е́й, reins.

вожу́ etc.: see води́ть, вози́ть.

воз, -а (-у), *loc.* -у́; *pl.* -ы́ or -а́, cart, wagon; cart-load; loads, heaps.
воз-, возо-, вос- *vbl. pref.* indicates direction or movement upwards; renewed action; action in response; beginning of action; intensity, excitement, solemnity.
возбуди́мый, excitable, irritable. **возбуди́тель,** -я *m.* agent; stimulus; stimulant; exciter; instigator. **возбуди́ть,** -ужу́ *perf.*, **возбужда́ть,** -а́ю *imp.* excite, rouse, arouse; stimulate, whet; stir up, incite; provoke; institute, bring, raise. **возбужда́ющ|ий;** ~ее сре́дство, stimulant. **возбужде́ние,** -я, excitement, agitation. **возбуждённый,** excited, agitated.
возвести́, -еду́, -дёшь; -вёл, -ла́ *perf.* (*imp.* возводи́ть) elevate; raise; erect, put up; bring, advance, level; +к+*dat.* trace to, derive from.
возвести́ть, -ещу́ *perf.*, **возвеща́ть,** -а́ю *imp.* proclaim, announce.
возводи́ть, -ожу́, -о́дишь *imp.* of возвести́.
возвра́т, -а, return; repayment, reimbursement; restitution; ~ боле́зни, relapse; ~ со́лнца, solstice. **возврати́ть,** -ащу́ *perf.*, **возвраща́ть,** -а́ю *imp.* (*perf.* also верну́ть) return, give back, restore; pay back; recover, retrieve; send back, bring back; **~ся,** return; go back, come back; revert. **возвра́тный,** back, return; relapsing; recurrent; reflexive. **возвраще́ние,** -я, return; recurrence; restoration, restitution.
возвы́сить, -ы́шу *perf.*, **возвыша́ть,** -а́ю *imp.* raise; ennoble; **~ся,** rise, go up; tower. **возвыше́ние,** -я, rise; raising; eminence; raised place. **возвы́шенность,** -и, height; eminence; loftiness, sublimity. **возвы́шенный,** high, elevated; lofty, sublime.
возгла́вить, -влю *perf.*, **возглавля́ть,** -я́ю *imp.* head, be at the head of.
во́зглас, -а, cry, exclamation. **возгласи́ть,** -ашу́ *perf.*, **возглаша́ть,** -а́ю *imp.* proclaim. **возглаше́ние,** -я, proclamation; exclamation.
возгора́емость, -и, inflammability. **возгора́емый,** inflammable. **возгора́ние** -я, ignition; то́чка возгора́ния, flash-point. **возгора́ться,** -а́юсь *imp.*, **возгоре́ться,** -рюсь *perf.* flare up; be seized (with); be smitten.
воздава́ть, -даю́, -даёшь *imp.*, **возда́ть,** -а́м, -а́шь, -а́ст, -ади́м; -а́л, -а́, -о *perf.* render; ~ до́лжное+*dat.* do justice to.
воздвига́ть, -а́ю *imp.*, **воздви́гнуть,** -ну; -дви́г *perf.* raise, erect; **~ся,** rise, arise.
возде́йствие, -я, influence; физи́ческое ~, coercion. **возде́йствовать,** -твую *perf.* and *imp.* influence, affect; act on, work on.
возде́лать, -аю *perf.*, **возде́лывать,** -аю *imp.* cultivate till.
воздержа́вшийся *sb.* abstainer; abstention. **воздержа́ние,** -я, abstinence; abstention. **возде́ржанный, возде́ржный,** abstemious; temperate; abstinent. **воздержа́ться,** -жу́сь, -жишься *perf.*, **возде́рживаться,** -аюсь *imp.* refrain; abstain; withhold acceptance, decline.
во́здух, -а, air; в ~е, in the air; на ~, на ~е, out of doors. **воздуходу́вка,** -и, blower. **воздухонепроница́емый,** air-tight. **воздухоохлажда́емый,** air-cooled. **возду́шн|ый,** air, aerial; overhead; air-raid; airy, light; flimsy; ~ые за́мки, castles in the air; ~ый змей, kite; ~ая пе́тля, chain (stitch); ~ый пиро́г, soufflé; ~ый флот, air force; ~ый шар, balloon.
воззва́ние, -я, appeal. **воззва́ть,** -зову́, -вёшь *perf.* (*imp.* взыва́ть) appeal, call (о+*prep.* for).
воззре́ние, -я, view, opinion, outlook.
вози́ть, вожу́, во́зишь *imp.* cart, convey; carry; bring, take; drive; draw; beat, flog; **~ся,** romp, run about, play noisily; take trouble, spend time, busy oneself; potter about; tinker, fiddle about, mess about. **во́зка,** -и, carting, carriage.
возлага́ть, -а́ю *imp.* of возложи́ть.
во́зле *adv.* and *prep.*+*gen.* by, near; near by; past.
возложи́ть, -жу́, -жишь, *perf.* (*imp.* возлага́ть) lay; place.
возлю́бленный, beloved; *sb.* boy-friend, girl-friend; lover, mistress.

возме́здие, -я, retribution; requital; punishment.
возмести́ть, -ещу́ *perf.*, **возмеща́ть**, -а́ю *imp.* compensate for, make up for; refund, reimburse. **возмеще́ние**, -я, compensation, indemnity; damages; replacement; refund, reimbursement.
возмо́жно *adv.* possibly; +*comp.* as . . . as possible. **возмо́жность**, -и, possibility; opportunity; *pl.* means, resources; potentialities; по (ме́ре) возмо́жности, as far as possible; при пе́рвой возмо́жности, as soon as possible, at the first opportunity. **возмо́жный**, possible; greatest possible.
возмужа́лость, -и, maturity; manhood, womanhood. **возмужа́лый**, mature; grown up. **возмужа́ть**, -а́ю *perf.* grow up, reach maturity; gain strength, become strong.
возмути́тельный, disgraceful, scandalous; seditious, subversive. **возмути́ть**, -ущу́ *perf.*, **возмуща́ть**, -а́ю *imp.* disturb, trouble; stir up, incite; anger, rouse to indignation; **~ся**, be indignant, be roused to indignation, be exasperated; rebel, rise in revolt. **возмуще́ние**, -я, indignation; revolt, rebellion; perturbation; disturbance. **возмущённый**; -щён, -щена́, indignant, troubled, disturbed.
вознагради́ть, -ажу́ *perf.*, **вознагражда́ть**, -а́ю *imp.* reward; recompense; make up to (за+*acc.* for). **вознагражде́ние**, -я, reward, recompense; compensation; fee, remuneration.
возненави́деть, -и́жу *perf.* conceive a hatred for, come to hate.
вознесе́ние, -я, ascent; Ascension. **вознести́**, -несу́, -несёшь; -нёс, -ла́ *perf.* (*imp.* возноси́ть) raise, lift up; **~сь**, rise; ascend.
возника́ть, -а́ет *imp.*, **возни́кнуть**, -нет; -ни́к *perf.* arise, spring up. **возникнове́ние**, -я, rise, beginning, origin.
возни́ца, -ы *m.* coachman, driver. **возни́чий** *sb.* coachman, driver.
возноси́ть(ся, -ошу́(сь, -о́сишь(ся *imp.* of вознести́(сь. **вознoше́ние**, -я, raising, elevation.
возня́, -и́, row, noise; horse-play; bother, trouble.
возобнови́ть, -влю́ *perf.*, **возобновля́ть**, -я́ю *imp.* renew, resume; restore; **~ся**, begin again. **возобновле́ние**, -я, renewal, resumption; revival.
возража́ть, -а́ю *imp.*, **возрази́ть**, -ажу́ *perf.* object, have or raise an objection; take exception; retort; say. **возраже́ние**, -я, objection; retort; answer.
во́зраст, -а, age; на ~е, grown up. **возраста́ние**, -я, growth, increase; increment. **возраста́ть**, -а́ет *imp.*, **возрасти́**, -тёт; -ро́с, -ла́ *perf.* grow, increase.
возроди́ть, -ожу́ *perf.*, **возрожда́ть**, -а́ю *imp.* regenerate; revive; **~ся**, revive. **возрожде́ние**, -я, rebirth; revival; Renaissance.
возро́с etc.: see возрасти́. **возро́сший**, increased.
во́зчик, -а, carter, carrier; drayman.
возьму́ etc.: see взять.
во́ин, -а, warrior; soldier, serviceman. **во́инск|ий**, military; soldierly; army, troop; ~ая пови́нность, conscription. **вои́нственный**, warlike; bellicose. **вои́нствующий**, militant.
вои́стину *adv.* indeed; verily.
вой, -я, howl, howling; wail, wailing.
войду́ etc.: see войти́.
во́йлок, -а, felt; strip of felt. **во́йлочный**, felt.
война́, -ы́; *pl.* -ы, war.
во́йско, -а; *pl.* -а́, army; host; multitude; *pl.* troops, forces. **войсково́й**, military; of the (Cossack) host.
войти́, -йду́, -йдёшь; вошёл, -шла́ *perf.* (*imp.* входи́ть), go in, come in, enter; get in(to); ~ в аза́рт, grow heated; ~ в лета́, get on (in years); ~ в мо́ду, become fashionable; ~ во вкус, acquire a taste; ~ в си́лу, come into force.
вокза́л, -а, (railway) station.
вокру́г *adv.* and *prep.*+*gen.* round, around.
вол, -а́, ox, bullock.
вола́н, -а, flounce; shuttlecock.
волды́рь, -я́ *m.* blister; lump, bump.
волево́й, volitional; strong-willed.
во́лей-нево́лей *adv.* willy-nilly.
во́лжский, Volga, of the Volga.

волк, -а; -и, -о́в, wolf. **волкода́в**, -а, wolf-hound.

волна́, -ы́; *pl.* -ы, во́лна́м, wave. **волне́ние**, -я, roughness, choppiness; agitation, disturbance; emotion, excitement; (usu. *pl.*) unrest. **волни́стый**, wavy; undulating; corrugated; watered. **волнова́ть**, -ну́ю *imp.* (*perf.* вз~) disturb, agitate; excite; worry; **~ся**, be disturbed or agitated; fret, worry, be nervous, be excited; be in a state of ferment or unrest; be rough or choppy; ripple, wave. **волноло́м**, -а, breakwater. **волнообра́зный**, wave-like; undulatory; wavy, undulating. **волноре́з**, -а, breakwater. **волну́ющий**, disturbing, worrying; exciting, thrilling, stirring.

во́лок, -а; *pl.* -и or -а́, portage.

волоки́та, -ы, red tape.

волокни́стый, fibrous, stringy. **волокно́**, -а́; *pl.* -а, fibre, filament.

волоку́ etc.: see воло́чь.

во́лос, -а; *pl.* -ы or -а́, -о́с hair; *pl.* hair. **волоса́тый**, hairy; hirsute; pilose. **волоси́стый**, fibrous. **волосно́й**, capillary. **волосо́к**, -ска́, hair, fine hair; hair-spring; filament.

волостно́й, of a volost. **во́лость**, -и; *pl.* -и, -е́й, volost.

волосяно́й, hair.

волочи́ть, -очу́, -о́чишь *imp.* drag; draw; **~ся** drag, trail; +за+*instr.* run after. **воло́чь**, -оку́, -очёшь; -о́к, -ла́ *imp.* drag; **~ся**, drag, trail; drag oneself along; shuffle.

волча́та etc.: see волчо́нок. **во́лчий**, wolf, wolf's; wolfish. **волчи́ха**, -и, **волчи́ца**, -ы, she-wolf.

волчо́к, -чка́, top; gyroscope.

волчо́нок, -нка; *pl.* -ча́та, -ча́т, wolf-cub.

волше́бник, -а, magician; wizard. **волше́бница**, -ы, enchantress. **волше́бн|ый**, magic, magical; enchanted; bewitching, enchanting; ~ая па́лочка, magic wand; ~ое ца́рство, fairyland, enchanted kingdom. **волшебство́**, -а́, magic, enchantment.

во́льно *adv.* freely; ~! stand at ease! **вольнонаёмный**, civilian. **во́льность**, -и, freedom, liberty; license; familiarity. **во́льный**; -лен, -льна́ -о, -ы or -ы́, free; unrestricted; loose; free-style; familiar; private; at liberty; ~ ка́меньщик, Freemason.

вольт[1], -а, volt.

вольт[2], -а, *loc.* -у́, vault; volte. **вольтижёр**, -а, trick-rider. **вольтижи́ровать**, -рую *imp.* vault.

во́льтов *adj.* voltaic.

вольфра́м, -а, tungsten; wolfram.

волью́ etc.: see влить.

во́ля, -и, will; volition; wish(es); freedom, liberty; ~ ва́ша, as you please, as you like; дать во́лю+*dat.*, give rein, vent to; дать себе́ во́лю, let oneself go; на во́ле, at liberty; не по свое́й во́ле, against one's will; по до́брой во́ле, freely, of one's own free will.

вомну́ etc.: see вмять.

вон *adv.* out; off away.

вон *part.* there, over there.

вонза́ть, -а́ю *imp.*, **вонзи́ть** -нжу́ *perf.* plunge, thrust; **~ся** в + *acc.* pierce, penetrate.

вонь, -и, stink, stench. **воню́чий**, stinking, fetid. **воню́чка**, -и, stinker; skunk. **воня́ть**, -я́ю, stink, reek.

вообража́емый, imaginary; fictitious. **вообража́ть**, -а́ю *imp.*, **вообрази́ть**, -ажу́ *perf.* imagine; fancy; **~ся**, imagine oneself. **воображе́ние** -я, imagination; fancy. **вообрази́мый**, imaginable.

вообще́ *adv.* in general; generally (speaking); on the whole; always; altogether; at all; ~ говоря́, generally speaking; as a matter of fact.

воодушеви́ть, -влю́ *perf.*, **воодушевля́ть**, -я́ю *imp* inspire, rouse; inspirit, hearten. **воодушевле́ние**, -я, rousing; inspiration; inspiriting; animation; enthusiasm, fervour. **воодушевлённый**, animated; enthusiastic, fervent.

вооружа́ть, -а́ю *imp.*, **вооружи́ть**, -жу́ *perf.* arm equip; fit out; set turn; ~ про́тив себя́, antagonize; **~ся**, arm oneself take up arms; equip oneself, provide oneself. **вооруже́ние**, -я, arming; arms, armament; equipment.

вооружённый; -жён, -á, armed; equipped.
воо́чию *adv.* with one's own eyes, for oneself; clearly, plainly.
во-пе́рвых *adv.* first, first of all, in the first place.
вопи́ть, -плю́ *imp.* yell, howl, wail. **вопию́щий**, crying, glaring; flagrant, scandalous. **вопия́ть**, -ию́, -ие́шь *imp.* cry out, clamour.
воплоти́ть, -ощу́ *perf.*, **воплоща́ть**, -а́ю *imp.* embody, incarnate; ~ в себе́, be the embodiment of. **воплоще́ние**, -я, embodiment; incarnation. **воплощённый**; -щён, -щена́, incarnate; personified.
вопль, -я *m.* cry wail; wailing howling.
вопреки́ *prep.* + *dat.* despite, in spite of; against, contrary to.
вопро́с, -а question; problem; matter; ~ по существу́, substance of the matter; под ~ом in question, undecided; что за ~! of course! **вопроси́тельный**, interrogative; questioning; ~ знак, question-mark. **вопроша́ющий**, questioning, inquiring.
вопью́ etc.: see впить.
вор, -а; *pl.* -ы -о́в. thief; criminal.
ворва́ться, -ву́сь -вёшься; -а́лся, -ла́сь, -а́ло́сь *perf.* (*imp.* врыва́ться) burst in.
воркова́ть, -ку́ю *imp.* coo; bill and coo.
воркотня́, -и́, grumbling.
вороб́ей, -бья́ sparrow. **воробьи́ный** sparrow's; sparrow; passerine.
воро́ванный, stolen. **ворова́тый**, thievish; furtive. **ворова́ть**, -ру́ю *imp.* (*perf.* с~) steal; be a thief. **воро́вка**, -и woman thief. **воровски́** *adv.* furtively. **воровско́й**, thieves'; illegal. **воровство́** -а́, stealing; theft.
во́рон, -а, raven. **воро́на**, -ы, crow. **воронёный**, blued. **воро́ний**, crow's; corvine. **ворони́ть**, -ню́ *imp.* blue.
воро́нка, -и, funnel; crater.
вороно́й, black; *sb.* black horse.
воронье́, -я́, carrion crows.
во́рот[1], -а neckline; collar; neckband.
во́рот[2], -а winch; windlass.
воро́та, -ро́т *pl.* gate, gates; gateway; goal.
вороти́ть[1], -очу́, -о́тишь *imp.* + *instr.* be in charge of; ~ нос, turn up one's nose; меня́ воро́тит от э́того де́ла, this business makes me sick.
вороти́ть[2], -очу́, -о́тишь *perf.* bring back, get back; turn back, send back; **~ся**, return, come back, go back.
воротни́к, -а́, **воротничо́к**, -чка́, collar.
воро́тн|ый, gate; ~ая ве́на, portal vein.
во́рох, -а; *pl.* -а́, heap, pile; masses lots, heaps.
воро́чать, -аю *imp.* turn (over); move, shift; + *instr.* control, have control of; boss; ~ глаза́ми, roll one's eyes; ~ миллио́нами, deal in millions; **~ся**, move turn; toss and turn.
ворочу́(сь etc.: see вороти́ть(ся.
вороши́ть, -шу́ *imp.* stir stir up; turn (over); **~ся**, move about, stir.
ворс, -а, nap. pile. **ворси́нка**, -и hair, nap, lint; fibre. **ворси́стый**, fleecy.
ворча́ть, -чу́ *imp.* grumble growl. **ворчли́вый**, querulous, peevish; grumpy.
вос-: see воз-
восвоя́си *adv.* home; отпра́виться ~, go back home.
восемна́дцатый eighteenth. **восемна́дцать**, -и, eighteen. **во́семь**, -сьми́, *instr.* -сьмью́ or -семью́, eight. **во́семьдесят**, -сьми́десяти, eighty. **восемьсо́т**, -сьмисо́т, -ста́ми, eight hundred **во́семью** *adv.* eight times.
воск, -а (-у), wax, beeswax.
воскли́кнуть -ну *perf.*, **восклица́ть**, -а́ю *imp.* exclaim. **восклица́ние**, -я, exclamation. **восклица́тельный**, exclamatory; ~ знак, exclamation mark.
воско́вка, -и, waxed paper; stencil. **воскoв|о́й**, wax, waxen; waxy; waxed; ~а́я бума́га, greaseproof paper.
воскреса́ть, -а́ю *imp.*, **воскре́снуть**, -ну; -ес *perf.* rise again, rise from the dead; revive. **воскресе́ние**, -я, resurrection. **воскресе́нье**, -я Sunday. **воскреси́ть** -ешу́ *perf.*, **воскреша́ть**, -а́ю *imp.* raise from the dead, resurrect; revive. **воскре́сник**, -а voluntary Sunday work. **воскре́сный**, Sunday. **воскреше́ние**, -я, raising from the dead, resurrection; revival.
воспале́ние, -я, inflammation. **воспалённый**; -лён, -а́, inflamed; sore. **воспали́ть**, -лю́ *perf* **воспаля́ть**, -я́ю *imp.* inflame; **~ся** become inflamed.

воспита́ние, -я, upbringing, education; training; (good) breeding. **воспи́танник**, -а, **-ница**, -ы, pupil, schoolboy, schoolgirl; ward. **воспи́танность**, -и, (good) breeding. **воспи́танный**, well-brought-up. **воспита́тельный**, educational; ~ дом, foundling hospital. **воспита́ть**, -а́ю *perf*., **воспи́тывать**, -аю *imp*. bring up, rear; cultivate, foster; inculcate; educate; train.

воспламени́ть, -ню́ *perf*., **воспламеня́ть**, -я́ю *imp*. kindle, set on fire, ignite; fire, inflame; **~ся**, ignite catch fire; blaze up; take fire, flare up. **воспламеня́емый**, inflammable.

вос|по́льзоваться, -зуюсь *perf*.

воспомина́ние, -я, recollection, memory; *pl*. memoirs; reminiscences.

вос|препя́тствовать, -твую *perf*.

воспрети́ть, -ещу́ *perf*., **воспреща́ть**, -а́ю *imp*. forbid, prohibit. **воспреще́ние**, -я, prohibition. **воспрещённый**; -щён, -а, forbidden, prohibited.

восприе́мник, -а, godfather. **восприе́мница** -ы, godmother. **восприи́мчивый** receptive, impressionable; susceptible. **воспринима́емый**, perceptible, apprehensible. **воспринима́ть**, -а́ю *imp*., **восприня́ть**, -иму́, -и́мешь; -и́нял, -а́, -о *perf*. perceive, apprehend; grasp, take in; interpret take (как, for). **восприя́тие**, -я, perception.

воспроизведе́ние. -я, reproduction. **воспроизвести́**, -еду́, -едёшь; -вёл, -а́ *perf*., **воспроизводи́ть**, -ожу́, -о́дишь *imp*. reproduce; renew; recall. **воспроизводи́тельный**, reproductive. **воспроизво́дство**, reproduction.

вос|проти́виться, -влюсь *perf*.

воссоедине́ние, -я, reunion, reunification. **воссоедини́ть**, -ню́ *perf*., **воссоединя́ть**, -я́ю *imp*. reunite.

восстава́ть, -таю, -таёшь *imp*. of восста́ть. **восстана́вливать**, -аю *imp*. of восстанови́ть.

восста́ние, -я rising, insurrection.

восстанови́тельный, of restoration, of reconstruction. **восстанови́ть**, -влю́, -вишь *perf*. (*imp*. восстана́вливать) restore, renew, re-establish, reinstate; recall, recollect; reduce; ~ про́тив+*gen*. set against; ~ про́тив себя́, antagonize. **восстановле́ние**, -я, restoration, renewal, reinstatement; rehabilitation; reconstruction; reduction.

восста́ть, -а́ну *perf*. (*imp*. восстава́ть) rise (up), arise.

восто́к, -а, east. **востокове́дение**, -я, oriental studies.

восто́рг, -а, delight, rapture; в ~е от+*gen*. delighted with. **восторга́ть**, -а́ю *imp*. delight, enrapture; **~ся**+*instr*. be delighted with, go into raptures over. **восто́рженный**, enthusiastic. **восто́ржествовать**, -тву́ю *perf*. triumph.

восто́чник, -а, orientalist. **восто́чный**, east, eastern; oriental.

востре́бование, -я, claiming, demand; до востре́бования, to be called for, poste restante. **востре́бовать**, -бую *perf*. claim, call for.

восхвали́ть, -лю́, -лишь *perf*., **восхваля́ть**, -я́ю *imp*. praise, extol.

восхити́тельный, entrancing, ravishing; delightful; delicious. **восхити́ть**, -хищу́ *perf*., **восхища́ть**, -а́ю *imp*. carry away, delight, enrapture. **восхище́ние**, -я, delight, rapture; admiration. **восхищённый**; -щён. -а́, rapt, admiring.

восхо́д, -а, rising; east. **восходи́ть**, -ожу́, -о́дишь *imp*. of взойти́; ~ к+*dat*. go back to, date from. **восходи́тель**, -я *m*. mountaineer, climber. **восхожде́ние**, -я, ascent. **восходя́щий**, rising.

восше́ствие, -я, accession.

восьма́я *sb*. eighth; octave. **восьмёрка**, -и, eight; No. 8; figure of eight. **во́сьмеро**, -ры́х, eight; eight pairs.

восьми- in *comb*. eight-; octo-. **восьмигра́нник**, -а, octahedron. **~десяты́й**, eightieth. **~кла́ссник**, -а, **-ница**, -ы, eighth-year pupil. **~кра́тный**, eightfold, octuple. **~ле́тний**, eight-year; eight-year-old. **~со́тый**, eight-hundredth. **~уго́льник**, -а, octagon. **~уго́льный**, octagonal. **~часово́й**, eight-hour.

восьмо́й, eighth.

вот, *part*. here (is), there (is); this is; here's a . . ! there's a . . !; well!; ~ ещё! well, what next?; ~ и всё, and that's all; ~ как! no! really?; ~ та́к! that's it!; that's right!; ~ тебé! take that!; ~ тебé и . ., so much for . .; ~ что! no! not really? **вот-вóт** *adv.* a moment more, and . .; this moment, just; *part.* that's it, that's right!

воткнýть, -нý, -нёшь *perf.* (*imp.* втыкáть) stick in, drive in, thrust in.

вотрý etc.: see втерéть.

воцарéние, -я, accession. **воцари́ться**, -и́тся *perf.*, **воцаря́ться**, -я́ется *imp.* come to the throne; fall, set in, reign; establish oneself.

вошёл etc.: see войти́.

вошь, вши; *gen. pl.* вшей louse.

вошью́ etc.: see вшить.

вощáнка, -и, wax paper, wax(ed) cloth; cobbler's wax. **вощанóй**, wax. **вощи́ть**, -щý *imp.* (*perf.* на~) wax, wax-polish.

вóю, etc.: see выть.

вою́ю, etc.: see воевáть. **вою́ющий**, warring; belligerent.

впадáть, -áю *imp.*, **впасть** -адý *perf.* fall, flow; lapse, sink; fall in; + в + *acc.* verge on, approximate to. **впадéние**, -я, confluence, (river-)mouth. **впáдина**, -ы, cavity, hollow; socket. **впáлый**, hollow, sunken.

впервóй, впервы́е *adv.* for the first time, first.

вперёд, *adv.* forward(s), ahead; in future; in advance; идти́ ~, be fast. **впереди́** *adv.* in front, ahead; in (the) future; *prep.* + *gen.* in front of, ahead of, before.

вперемéшку *adv.* pell-mell, higgledy-piggledy.

вперить, -рю *perf.*, **вперя́ть**, -я́ю *imp.* fix, fasten; direct; **~ся**, be fixed; gaze fixedly, stare.

впечатлéние, -я, impression; effect. **впечатли́тельный**, impressionable sensitive.

впивáть(ся, -áю(сь *imp.* of впить(ся.

вписáть, -ишý, -и́шешь *perf.*, **вписывать**, -аю *imp.* enter insert; inscribe; **~ся**, be enrolled, join. **впи́ска**, -и, entry; insertion.

впитáть, -áю *perf.*, **впи́тывать**, -аю *imp.* absorb, take in; **~ся** soak.

впить, вопью, -ьёшь; -и́л, -á, -о *perf.* (*imp.* впивáть) imbibe, absorb; **~ся**, dig in, stick in; cling to; ~ся взóром, глазáми, fix one's gaze, one's eyes (on).

впи́хивать, -аю *imp.*, **впихнýть**, -нý, -нёшь *perf.* stuff in, cram in; shove in.

вплавь *adv.* (by) swimming; перепрáвиться ~, swim across.

вплести́, -етý, -етёшь; -ёл, -á *perf.*, **вплетáть**, -áю *imp.* plait in, intertwine; involve.

вплотнýю *adv.* close; closely; in earnest. **вплоть** *adv.*; ~ до + *gen.* (right) up to; ~ к + *dat.* right against, close to, right up to.

вполгóлоса *adv.* under one's breath, in an undertone.

вползáть, -áю *imp.*, **вползти́**, -зý, -зёшь; -з, -лá *perf.* creep in, creep up, crawl in.

вполнé *adv.* fully, entirely; quite.

вполови́ну *adv.* (by) half.

впопáд *adv.* to the point; opportunely.

впопыхáх *adv.* in a hurry, hastily; in one's haste.

впóру *adv.* at the right time, opportune(ly); just right, exactly; быть ~ (+ *dat.*) fit.

впослéдствии *adv.* subsequently afterwards.

впотьмáх *adv.* in the dark.

вправду *adv.* really.

впрáве *adv.*; быть ~, have a right.

впрáвить, -влю *perf.*, **вправля́ть**, -я́ю *imp.* set, reduce; tuck in. **впрáвка**, -и, setting, reduction.

впрáво *adv.* to the right (от + *gen.* of).

впредь *adv.* in (the) future; ~ до + *gen.* until.

впрóчем *conj.* however, but; though; or rather.

впры́гивать, -аю *imp.*, **впры́гнуть**, -ну *perf.* jump in, jump up (on).

впры́скивание, -я, injection. **впры́скивать**, -аю *imp.*, **впры́снуть**, -ну *perf.* inject.

впрягáть, -áю *imp.* **впрячь**, -ягý, -яжёшь; -яг, -лá *perf.* harness.

впуск, -а, admission, admittance. **впускáть**, -áю *imp.*, **впусти́ть**, -ущý -ýстишь *perf.* admit, let in. **впускнóй**, admittance; inlet.

впусту́ю *adv.* for nothing, to no purpose, in vain.
впу́тать, -аю *perf.*, **впу́тывать,** -аю *imp.* entangle, involve, implicate; **~ся,** get mixed up in.
впущу́, etc.: see впусти́ть.
впя́теро *adv.* five times. **впятеро́м** *adv.* five (together).
враг, -á, enemy; the Devil. **вражда́,** -ы́, enmity, hostility. **вражде́бный,** hostile; enemy. **враждова́ть,** -дую, be at war, be at enmity, be hostile, quarrel. **вра́жеский,** enemy. **вра́жий,** enemy, hostile.
вразби́вку *adv.* at random.
вразбро́д *adv.* separately not in concert, disunitedly.
вразре́з *adv.* contrary; идти́ ~ с + *instr.* go against.
вразуми́тельный, intelligible, clear; instructive; persuasive. **вразуми́ть,** -млю́ *perf.*, **вразумля́ть,** -я́ю *imp.* make understand make listen to reason, make see sense.
врасплóх *adv.* unexpectedly, unawares, by surprise.
враста́ть, -а́ет *imp.*, **врасти́,** -тёт; врос -ла́ *perf.* grow in; take root. **враста́ющий,** ingrowing.
врата́рь, -я́ *m.* gate-keeper; goalkeeper.
врать, вру, врёшь; -ал, -á, -о *imp.* (*perf.* на~, со~) lie, tell lies; talk nonsense.
врач, -á, doctor; medical officer; зубно́й ~, dentist. **враче́бный,** medical.
враща́тельный, rotary. **враща́ть,** -а́ю *imp.* turn rotate, revolve; ~ глаза́ми, roll one's eyes; **~ся,** turn, revolve, rotate; ~ся в худо́жественных круга́х, move in artistic circles. **враще́ние,** -я rotation, revolution, gyration.
вред, -á, harm, hurt, injury; damage. **вреди́тель,** -я *m.* pest; wrecker, saboteur; *pl.* vermin. **вреди́тельство,** -а, wrecking, (act of) sabotage. **вреди́ть,** -ежу́ *imp.* (*perf.* по~)+*dat.* injure, harm, hurt; damage. **вре́дный;** -ден, -дна́, -о, harmful, injurious; unhealthy.
врежу́: see вреди́ть. **вре́жу(сь,** etc.: see вре́зать(ся.
вре́зать, -ежу *perf.*, **вреза́ть,** -а́ю *imp.* cut in, engrave; set in, fit in, insert; (*sl.*) +*dat.* hit, smash; slang, curse; **~ся,** cut, force one's way, run (into); be engraved; fall in love; ~ся в зе́млю, plunge to the ground. **врезно́й,** inset; mortise; notch.
времена́ми *adv.* at times, now and then, from time to time. **временни́к,** -á, chronicle, annals. **вре́менно** *adv.* temporarily; ~ исполня́ющий обя́занности, acting; ~ пове́ренный в дела́х, acting chargé d'affaires. **временно́й,** temporal; time; of tense(s). **вре́менный,** temporary; provisional; acting. **времен́щик,** -á, favourite.
вре́мя, -мени; *pl.* -мена́, -мён, -а́м *n.* time, times; tense; ~ го́да, season; ~ от вре́мени, at times, from time to time, now and then; в своё ~, in one's time; once, at one time; in due course, in one's own time; до того́ вре́мени, till then, till that time; на ~, for a time; са́мое ~, just the time the (right) time; ско́лько вре́мени? what is the time?; тем вре́менем, meanwhile. **время́нка,** -и, portable or makeshift stove; temporary structure.
врид, -а *abbr.* вре́менно исполня́ющий до́лжность, temporary, acting (as).
вро́вень *adv.* level, on a level.
вро́де *prep.*+*gen.* like; не́что ~, a sort of, a kind of; *part.* such as, like; apparently, seemingly.
врождённый; -дён, -á, innate; congenital; inherent.
врозь, врозь *adv.* separately, apart.
вро́с, etc.: see врасти́. **вро́ю(сь,** etc.: see врыть(ся. **вру,** etc.: see врать.
врун, -á, **вру́нья,** -и, liar.
вруча́ть, -а́ю *imp.*, **вручи́ть,** -чу́ *perf.* hand, deliver; entrust; serve. **вручи́тель,** -я, *m.* bearer.
вручну́ю *adv.* by hand.
врыва́ть(ся, -а́ю(сь *imp.* of ворва́ться, врыть(ся.
врыть, вро́ю *perf.* (*imp.* врыва́ть) dig in, bury; **~ся,** dig oneself in.
вряд (ли) *adv.* it's not likely; hardly, scarcely; ~ ли сто́ит, it's hardly worth while.
вс-: see вз-.
всади́ть, -ажу́, -а́дишь *perf.*, **всажи́вать,** -аю *imp.* thrust in, plunge in; set in; put in, sink in. **вса́дник,** -а, rider,

horseman; knight. **всáдница,** -ы, rider, horsewoman.
всáсывание, -я, suction; absorption. **всáсывать(ся,** -аю(сь *imp.* of всосáть(ся.
всё, все *pron.*: see весь. **всё** *adv.* always, all the time; only, all; ~ (ещё), still; ~ из-за тебя́, all because of you; ~ лу́чше и лу́чше, better and better; *conj.* however, nevertheless; ~ же, all the same.
все- in *comb.* all-, omni-. **всевозмóжный,** of every kind; all possible. **~вóлновый,** all-wave. **~мéрно** *adv.* in every way, to the utmost. **всемéрный,** of every kind, every possible kind of. **~ми́рный,** world, world-wide, universal. **~могу́щий,** omnipotent, all-powerful. **~нарóдно** *adv.* publicly. **~нарóдный,** national; nation-wide. **~ору́жие;** во всеору́жии, completely ready; fully armed, equipped. **~побеждáющий,** all-conquering. **~российский,** All-Russian. **~си́льный,** omnipotent, all-powerful. **~славя́нский,** pan-Slav. **~сою́зный,** All-Union. **~сторóнний,** all-round; thorough, detailed; comprehensive.
всегдá, always, ever. **всегдáшний,** usual, habitual, customary.
всегó (*-vo*) *adv.* in all, all told; only.
вселéние, -я, installation, moving in.
вселéнная *sb.* universe. **вселéнский,** universal; oecumenical.
всели́ть, -лю́ *perf.*, **вселя́ть,** -я́ю *imp.* install, settle, lodge; move; inspire, instil!; **~ся,** move in, install oneself, settle in; be implanted.
всéмеро *adv.* seven times. **всемерóм** *adv.* seven (together).
всеóбуч, -а *abbr.* всеóбщее обучéние, compulsory education. **всеóбщий,** general, universal.
всерьёз *adv.* seriously, in earnest.
всё-таки *conj.* and *part.* all the same, for all that, still. **всецéло** *adv.* completely; exclusively.
вскáкивать, -аю *imp.* of вскочи́ть.
вс|карáбкаться, -аюсь *perf.*, **вскарáбкиваться,** -аюсь *imp.* scramble up, clamber up.
вскачь *adv.* at a gallop.
вски́дывать, -аю *imp.*, **вски́нуть,** -ну *perf.* throw up, toss; **~ся,** leap up; +на+*acc.* turn on, go for.
вскипáть, -áю *imp.*, **вс|кипéть,** -плю́ *perf.* boil up; flare up.
вс|кипяти́ть(ся, -ячу́(сь *perf.*
всклокóчивать, -аю *imp.*, **всклокóчить,** -чу *perf.* dishevel, tousle.
всколыхну́ть, -ну́, -нёшь *perf.* stir; stir up, rouse.
вскользь *adv.* slightly; in passing.
вскóре *adv.* soon, shortly after.
вскочи́ть, -очу́, óчишь *perf.* (*imp.* вскáкивать) jump up, spring up, leap up; come up.
вскри́кивать, -аю *imp.*, **вскри́кнуть,** -ну *perf.* cry out, shriek, scream. **вскричáть,** -чу́ *perf.* exclaim.
вскрывáть, -áю *imp.*, **вскрыть,** -рóю *perf.* open; reveal, disclose; turn up; lance; cut open, dissect; **~ся,** come to light, be revealed; become clear of ice, become open; burst. **вскры́тие,** -я, opening; revelation, disclosure; lancing; dissection, post-mortem.
вслед *adv.* and *prep.*+*dat.* after; ~ за+*instr.* after, following. **вслéдствие** *prep.*+*gen.* in consequence of, because of, on account of.
вслепу́ю *adv.* blindly; blindfold.
вслух *adv.* aloud.
вслу́шаться, -аюсь *perf.* **вслу́шиваться,** -аюсь *imp.* listen attentively, listen hard.
ВСМ (*ve-esém*) *abbr.* Всеми́рный Совéт Ми́ра, World Peace Council.
всмáтриваться, -аюсь *imp.*, **всмотрéться,** -рю́сь, -ришься *perf.* look closely, peer, look hard.
всмя́тку *adv.* soft(-boiled), lightly (boiled).
всóвывать, -аю *imp.* of всу́нуть.
всосáть, -су́, -сёшь *perf.* (*imp.* всáсывать) suck in; absorb; imbibe; **~ся,** be absorbed, soak in; sink in.
вспáрхивать, -аю *imp.* of вспорхну́ть.
вспáрывать, -аю *imp.* of вспорóть.
вс|пахáть, -ашу́, -áшешь *perf.*, **вспáхивать,** -аю *imp.* plough up. **вспáшка,** -и, ploughing.
вс|пéнить, -ню *perf.*
всплеск, -а, splash; blip. **всплёскивать,**

-аю *imp.*, **всплеснýть**, -нý, -нёшь *perf.* splash; ~ рукáми, fling up, throw up, one's hands.
всплывáть, -áю *imp.*, **всплыть**, -ывý, -ывёшь; -ыл, -á, о *perf.* rise to the surface, surface; arise, come up; come to light, be revealed.
вс|полошúть(ся, -шý(сь *perf.*
вспоминáть, -áю *imp.*, **вспóмнить**, -ню *perf.* remember, recall, recollect; **~ся** *impers.*+*dat.*: мне вспóмнилось, I remembered.
вспомогáтельный, auxiliary; subsidiary, branch.
вспорóть, -орю́, -óрешь *perf.* (*imp.* вспáрывать) rip open.
вспорхнýть, -нý, -нёшь *perf.* (*imp.* вспáрхивать) take wing, start up, fly up.
вс|потéть, -éю *perf.*
вспры́гивать, -аю *imp.*, **вспры́гнуть**, -ну *perf.* jump up, spring up.
вспры́скивать, -аю *imp.*, **вспры́снуть**, -ну *perf.* sprinkle.
вспухáть, -áет *imp.*, **вс|пýхнуть**, -нет; -ух *perf.* swell up.
вспылúть, -лю́ *perf.* flare up; fly into a rage (на+*acc.* with). **вспы́льчивый**, hot-tempered, irritable.
вспы́хивать, -аю *imp.*, **вспы́хнуть**, -ну *perf.* burst into flame blaze up; flare up; break out; blush. **вспы́шка**, -и, flash; flare, spurt; outburst, burst; outbreak.
вставáние, -я, rising, standing. **вставáть**, -таю́, -таёшь *imp.* of встать.
встáвить, -влю *perf.*, **вставля́ть**, -я́ю *imp.* put in, set in, insert. **встáвка**, -и, fixing, insertion; framing, mounting; inset; front: interpolation. **вставн|óй**, inserted; set in; ~ы́е зýбы, false teeth; ~ы́е рáмы, double window-frames.
встать, -áну *perf.* (*imp.* вставáть), get up, rise; stand up; stand; arise, come up; stop; go, fit (в+*acc.* into); ~ на колéни, kneel down; ~ с лéвой ногú, get out of bed on the wrong side.
встревóженный *adj.* anxious, worried, alarmed. **вс|тревóжить**, -жу *perf.*
встрёпанный, dishevelled.
встрепенýться, -нýсь, -нёшься *perf.* rouse oneself; shake its wings; start, start up; beat faster, begin to thump.
встрéтить, -éчу *perf.*, **встречáть**, -áю *imp.* meet, meet with, encounter; greet, welcome, receive; **~ся**, meet; be found, be met with. **встрéча**, -и, meeting; reception; encounter; match. **встрéчный**, coming to meet; contrary, head; counter; ~ вéтер, head wind; ~ иск, counter-claim; *sb.* person met with; кáждый ~ и поперéчный, anybody and everybody, every Tom, Dick, and Harry; пéрвый ~, the first person you meet, anybody.
встря́ска, -и, shaking; shock. **встря́хивать**, -аю *imp.*, **встряхнýть**, -нý, -нёшь *perf.* shake; shake up, rouse; **~ся**, shake oneself; rouse oneself, pull oneself together; have a good time.
вступáть, -áю *imp.*, **вступúть**, -плю́, -пишь *perf.*+в+*acc.* enter, enter into, join, join in; come into; +на+*acc.* go up, mount; ~ в брак, marry; ~ на престóл, ascend the throne; **~ся**, intervene; +за+*acc.* stand up for. **вступúтельный**, introductory; inaugural, opening; entrance. **вступлéние**, -я, entry, joining; accession; prelude, opening, introduction, preamble.
всýнуть, -ну *perf.* (*imp.* всóвывать) put in, stick in, push in; slip in.
всхлúпнуть, -ну *perf.*, **всхлúпывать**, -аю *imp.* sob. **всхлúпывание**, -я, sobbing; sobs.
всходúть, -ожý, -óдишь *imp.* of взойтú. **всхóды**, -ов *pl.* new growth, shoots.
всхрапнýть, -нý, -нёшь *perf.*, **всхрáпывать**, -аю *imp.* snore; snort; have a nap.
всю: see весь.
всю́ду *adv.* everywhere.
вся: see весь.
вся́к|ий, any; every, all kinds of; во ~ом слýчае, in any case, anyhow, at any rate; на ~ий слýчай, just in case, to be on the safe side; *pron.* anyone, everyone; anything. **вся́чески** *adv.* in every possible way, in all ways. **вся́ческий**, all kinds of.
вт *abbr.* ватт, watt.
втáйне *adv.* secretly, in secret.
втáлкивать, -аю *imp.* of втолкнýть.
втáптывать, -аю *imp.* of втоптáть.
втáскивать, -аю *imp.* of втащúть.

втачáть, -áю *perf.*, **втáчивать,** -аю *imp.* sew in, sew on; set in. **втáчка,** -и, sewing in, sewing on; patch. **втáчанный, втáчный** sewn in, sewn on; set in.

втащи́ть, -щý, -щишь *perf.* (*imp.* втáскивать) drag in, drag on, drag up; **~ся,** drag oneself.

втекáть, -áет *imp.* of втечь.

втерéть, вотрý, вотрёшь; втёр *perf.* (*imp.* втирáть) rub in; **~ся,** insinuate oneself, worm oneself.

втечь, -чёт; втёк, -лá *perf.* (*imp.* втекáть) flow in.

втирáние, -я rubbing in; embrocation, liniment. **втирáть(ся,** -áю(сь *imp.* of втерéть(ся.

вти́скивать, -аю *imp.*, **вти́снуть,** -ну *perf.* squeeze in; **~ся,** squeeze (oneself) in.

втихомóлку, втихýю *advs.* surreptitiously; on the quiet.

втолкнýть, -нý -нёшь *perf.* (*imp.* вткáлкивать) push in, shove in.

втоптáть -пчý, -пчешь *perf.* (*imp.* втáптывать) trample (in).

втóра, -ы, second voice, violin etc. **втóрить,** -рю *imp.* play or sing second; +*dat.* repeat, echo. **втори́чный,** second, secondary. **втóрник,** -а Tuesday. **втор|óй,** second; **~ое** *sb.* second course. **второочереднóй,** secondary. **второстепéнный,** secondary, minor.

в-трéтьих *adv.* thirdly, in the third place. **втрóе** *adv.* three times, treble. **втроём** *adv.* three (together). **втройнé** *adv.* three times as much, treble.

втуз -а *abbr.* вы́сшее техни́ческое учéбное заведéние, technical college.

втýлка, -и, bush; plug bung; liner, sleeve.

втыкáть, -áю *imp.* of воткнýть. **вты́чка** -и, thrusting in, driving in; plug, bung.

втя́гивать, -аю *imp.*, **втянýть,** -нý, -нишь *perf.* draw in, up; pull in, up; absorb take in; involve; **~ся,** sink, fall in; +в+*acc.* draw into enter; get used to; get keen on.

вуалéтка, -и, veil. **вуали́ровать,** -рую *imp.* (*perf.* за~), veil, draw a veil over; fog. **вуáль,** и, veil; fog.

вуз, -а *abbr.* вы́сшее учéбное заведéние, higher educational establishment; university, college, institute. **вýзовец,** -вца, **-овка,** -и, student.

вулкáн, -а, volcano. **вулкани́ческий,** volcanic.

вундерки́нд, -а, infant prodigy.

ВФП (*ve-efpé*) *abbr.* Всеми́рная федерáция профсою́зов, World Federation of Trade Unions.

вход, -а, entrance; entry. **входи́ть,** -ожý, -óдишь *imp.* of войти́. **вход|нóй,** entrance, input; ~óе отвéрстие, inlet, inlet port. **входя́щий,** incoming, entering; reentrant; male.

вхолостýю *adv.* idle, free; рабóтать ~, idle.

ВЦ (*vetsé*) *abbr.* вычисли́тельный центр, computer centre.

ВЦСПС (*vetse-espeés*) *abbr.* Всесою́зный Центрáльный Совéт Профессионáльных Сою́зов, All-Union Central Trade-Union Council.

вцепи́ться, -плю́сь, -пишься *perf.*, **вцепля́ться,** -я́юсь *imp.* clutch, cling to; seize, catch hold of.

ВЧ (*veché*) *abbr.* высокочастóтный, high-frequency, radio-frequency.

вчерá *adv.* yesterday. **вчерáшний,** yesterday's.

вчернé *adv.* in rough, roughly.

вчéтверо *adv.* four times, by four, in four. **вчетверóм** *adv.* four (together).

в-четвёртых *adv.* fourthly, in the fourth place.

вши, etc.: see вошь.

вшéстеро *adv.* six times, by six. **вшестерóм** *adv.* six (together).

вшивáть, -áю *imp.* of вшить. **вши́вка,** -и, sewing in; patch. **вшивнóй,** sewn in, set in.

вши́вый, lousy.

вширь *adv.* in breadth; widely.

вшить, вошью́, -ьёшь *perf.* (*imp.* вшивáть) sew in, set in.

въ-: see в-.

въедáться, -áется *imp.* of въéсться. **въéдливый, въéдчивый** *adjs.* corrosive; caustic; acid.

въезд, а, entry; entrance. **въезжáть,** -áю *imp.* of въéхать.

въéсться, -éстся, -едя́тся *perf.* (*imp.* въедáться) в+*acc.* eat into, corrode.

въе́хать, -е́ду *perf.* (*imp.* въезжа́ть), ride in, up; drive in, up; +в+*acc.* move into; run into.

въявь *adv.* in reality; before one's eyes, with one's own eyes.

вы, вас, вам, ва́ми, вас *pron.* you.

вы- *vbl. pref.* expressing direction of motion or action outwards; achievement or attainment by means of action; completion of action or process.

выбега́ть, -а́ю *imp.*, **вы́бежать,** -егу *perf.* run out.

вы́|белить, -лю *perf.* **вы́белка,** -и, bleaching; whitening.

вы́беру, etc.: see вы́брать. **выбива́ть(-ся,** -а́ю(сь *imp.* of вы́бить(ся. **выбира́ть(ся,** -а́ю(сь *imp.* of вы́брать(ся.

вы́бить, -бью *perf.* (*imp.* выбива́ть) knock out, kick out; dislodge; beat; beat down; beat out; stamp, strike; hammer out; **~ся,** get out; break loose; come out, show; ~ся из сил, exhaust oneself, be exhausted.

вы́боина, -ы, rut; pot-hole; dent; groove.

вы́бор, -а, choice, option; selection, assortment; *pl.* election, elections. **вы́борка,** -и, selection; excerpt. **вы́борн|ый,** elective; electoral; elected; ~ бюллете́нь, ballot-paper; **~ый, ~ая** *sb.* delegate. **вы́борочный,** selective.

вы́|бранить(ся, -ню(сь *perf.* **выбра́сывать(ся,** -аю(сь *imp.* of вы́бросить(ся.

вы́брать, -беру *perf.* (*imp.* выбира́ть) choose, select, pick out; elect; take out; haul in; **~ся,** get out; move, remove; manage to go out.

выбрива́ть, -а́ю *imp.*, **вы́брить,** -рею *perf.* shave; **~ся,** shave (oneself).

вы́брос, -а, blip, pip. **вы́бросить,** -ошу *perf.* (*imp.* выбра́сывать) throw out; reject, discard, throw away; put out; **~ся,** throw oneself out, leap out; ~ся с парашю́том, bale out.

выбыва́ть, -а́ю *imp.*, **вы́быть,** -буду *perf.* из+*gen.* leave, quit; be out of. **выбы́тие,** -я, departure, removal, absence.

выва́ливать, -аю *imp.*, **вы́валить,** -лю *perf.* throw out; pour out; **~ся,** fall out; pour out.

выва́ривать, -аю *imp.*, **вы́варить,** -рю *perf.* boil out; extract by boiling; boil thoroughly. **вы́варка,** -и, decoction, extraction; residue, concentrate.

вы́везти -зу; -ез *perf.* (*imp.* вывози́ть) take out, remove; bring out; export; save, rescue.

вы́верить, -рю *perf.* (*imp.* выверя́ть) verify; regulate.

вы́вернуть, -ну *perf.*, **вывёртывать,** -аю *imp.* turn inside out; unscrew; pull out; twist, wrench; dislocate; **~ся,** come unscrewed; slip out; get out, extricate oneself, wriggle out; be dislocated; emerge. **вы́верт,** -а, caper; mannerism; affectation.

выверя́ть, -я́ю *imp.* of вы́верить.

вы́весить, -ешу *perf.* (*imp.* выве́шивать) weigh; hang out; put up, post up. **вы́веска,** -и, sign, signboard; screen, pretext; mug.

вы́вести, -еду; -ел *perf.* (*imp.* выводи́ть) lead out, bring out; drive out; turn out, force out; remove; exterminate; deduce, conclude; hatch; grow, breed, raise; put up, erect; depict, portray; write, draw, trace out; **~сь,** go out of use; lapse; disappear; become extinct; come out; hatch out.

выве́тривание, -я, airing; weathering. **выве́тривать,** -аю *imp.*, **вы́ветрить,** -рю *perf.* air; drive out, remove, efface; weather, erode; **~ся,** weather; disappear, be driven out, be effaced.

выве́шивать, -аю *imp.* of вы́весить.

вы́вих, -а, dislocation; sprain; kink; oddity, quirk. **вы́вихнуть,** -ну *perf.* dislocate, put out; sprain.

вы́вод, -а, deduction, conclusion; withdrawal, removal. **выводи́ть(ся,** -ожу́(сь, -о́дишь(ся *imp.* of вы́вести(сь. **вы́водка,** -и, removal; exercising. **вы́водок,** -дка, brood; hatch litter.

вывожу́: see выводи́ть, вывози́ть.

вы́воз, -а, export; removal. **вывози́ть,** -ожу́, -о́зишь *imp.* of вы́везти. **вы́возка,** -и, carting out. **вывозно́й,** export.

вы́гарки, -ов *pl.* slag, dross.

вы́гиб, -а, curve, curvature. **выгиба́ть(ся,** -а́ю(сь *imp.* of **вы́гнуть(ся.**

вы́|гладить, -ажу *perf.*
вы́глядеть, -яжу *imp.* look look like.
выгля́дывать, -аю *imp.*, **вы́глянуть**, -ну *perf.* look out; peep out, emerge, become visible.
вы́гнать, -гоню *perf.* (*imp.* выгоня́ть) drive out; expel; distil; force.
вы́гнутый, curved, convex. **вы́гнуть**, -ну *perf.* (*imp.* выгиба́ть) bend, arch; **~ся**, arch up.
выгова́ривать, -аю *imp.* **вы́говорить**, -рю *perf.* pronounce, utter, speak; reserve; stipulate for; +*dat.* reprimand; **~ся**, speak out, have one's say out. **вы́говор**, -а, accent, pronunciation; reprimand, rebuke.
вы́года, -ы advantage, benefit; profit, gain; interest. **вы́годн|ый**, advantageous, beneficial; profitable; ~о, it pays.
вы́гон, -а pasture, common. **вы́гонка**, -и, distillation. **выгоня́ть**, -я́ю *imp.* of вы́гнать.
выгора́живать, -аю *imp.* of вы́городить.
выгора́ть, -а́ет *imp.*, **вы́гореть**, -рит *perf.* burn down; burn out; fade, bleach; turn out well, come off.
вы́городить, -ожу *perf.* (*imp.* выгора́живать) fence off; shield screen.
вы́|гравировать, -рую *perf.*
выгружа́ть, -а́ю *imp.*, **вы́грузить**, -ужу *perf.* unload; discharge; disembark; **~ся**, unload; disembark; detrain, debus. **вы́грузка**, -и unloading; disembarkation.
выдава́ть, -даю́, даёшь *imp.*, **вы́дать**, -ам, -ашь -аст, -адим *perf.* give out, issue, produce; give away, betray; deliver up, extradite; + за + *acc.* pass off as give out to be; ~ за́муж, give in marriage; **~ся**, protrude, project, jut out; stand out; present itself, happen to be. **вы́дача**, -и, issuing; issue; payment; extradition. **выдаю́щийся**, prominent; salient; eminent, outstanding.
выдвига́ть, -а́ю *imp.*, **вы́двинуть**, -ну *perf.* move out; pull out, open; put forward, advance; promote; nominate, propose; **~ся**, move forward, move out, come out; rise, get on. **выдвиже́нец**, -нца **-же́нка**, -и, worker promoted from rank and file. **выдвиже́ние**, -я, nomination; promotion, advancement.
выделе́ние -я, secretion; excretion; isolation; apportionment. **вы́делить**, -лю *perf.*, **выделя́ть**, -я́ю *imp.* pick out, single out; detach, detail; assign, earmark; allot; secrete; excrete; isolate; ~ курси́вом italicize; **~ся**, take one's share; ooze out exude; stand out, be noted (+*instr.* for).
вы́держанный consistent; self-possessed; firm; matured, seasoned. **вы́держать** -жу *perf.* **выде́рживать**, -аю *imp.* bear hold; stand, stand up to, endure; contain oneself; pass; keep; lay up; mature season; maintain, sustain. **вы́держка**[1], -и, endurance; self-possession; exposure.
вы́держка[2], -и, extract, excerpt, quotation.
вы́дох, -а, expiration. **вы́дохнуть**, -ну *perf.* (*imp.* выдыха́ть) breathe out; **~ся**, have lost fragrance or smell; be played out; be flat; be past one's best.
вы́дра, -ы, otter.
вы́|драть, -деру *perf.* **вы́|дрессировать**, -рую *perf.* **вы́|дубить**, -блю *perf.*
выдува́льщик, -а, glass-blower. **выдува́ть**, -а́ю *imp.* of вы́дуть. **вы́дувка**, -и glass-blowing. **выдувно́й**, blown.
вы́думанный, made-up, invented, fabricated. **вы́думать**, -аю *perf.*, **выду́мывать**, -аю *imp.* invent; make up, fabricate. **вы́думка**, -и, invention; idea, gadget, device; inventiveness; fabrication, fiction.
вы́|дуть, -ую *perf.* (*imp.* also выдува́ть) blow; blow out; blow up.
выдыха́ние, -я, expiration. **выдыха́ть(ся**, -а́ю(сь *imp.* of вы́дохнуть(ся.
вы́езд, -а, departure; exit; turn-out, equipage; going out. **выездн|о́й**, going-out; travelling, visiting; exit; away; ~о́й матч, away match; ~а́я се́ссия суда́, assizes. **выезжа́ть**, -а́ю *imp.* of вы́ехать.
вы́емка, -и taking out; seizure; collection; excavation; hollow, groove; fluting, flute; cutting, cut.

вы́ехать, -еду *perf.* (*imp.* выезжа́ть) go out depart; drive out, ride out; move, remove, leave; +на+*prep.* make use of, exploit take advantage of.

вы́жать, -жму *perf.* (*imp.* выжима́ть) squeeze out; wring out, press out; lift, press-lift.

вы́ждать, -ду *perf.* (*imp.* выжида́ть) wait for, wait out.

вы́жечь, -жгу *perf.* (*imp.* выжига́ть) burn low, burn out; burn, scorch; cauterize. **вы́жженн|ый**, ~ая земля́, scorched earth.

выжива́ние, -я, survival. **выжива́ть**, -а́ю *imp.* of вы́жить.

выжига́ние, -я, burning out, scorching; cauterization; ~ по де́реву poker--work. **выжига́ть**, -а́ю *imp.* of вы́жечь.

выжида́ние, -я, waiting, temporizing. **выжида́тельный**, waiting; expectant; temporizing. **выжида́ть**, -а́ю *imp.* of вы́ждать.

вы́жим, -а, press-up. **выжима́ние**, -я, squeezing; wringing (out); (weight-) -lifting. **выжима́ть**, -а́ю *imp.* of вы́жать. **вы́жимка**, -и, squeezing, pressing, wringing; abstract, brief summary.

вы́жить, -иву *perf.* (*imp.* выжива́ть) survive; live through; stay alive, hold out, stick it out; drive out, hound out; get rid of; ~ из ума́, become senile.

вы́звать, -зову *perf.* (*imp.* вызыва́ть) call, call out; send for; challenge; call forth, provoke; cause; stimulate, rouse; ~ по телефо́ну, ring up; **~ся**, volunteer, offer.

выздора́вливать, -аю *imp.*, **вы́здороветь**, -ею *perf.* recover get better. **выздоровле́ние**, -я, recovery; convalescence.

вы́зов, -а, call; summons; challenge.

вы́|золотить, -лочу *perf.* **вы́золоченный**, gilt.

вызу́бривать, -аю *imp.*, **вы́|зубрить**, -рю *perf.* learn by heart, cram.

вызыва́ть(ся, -а́ю(сь *imp.* of вы́звать(-ся. **вызыва́ющий**, defiant; challenging, provocative.

вы́играть, -аю *perf.*, **выи́грывать**, -аю *imp.* win; gain. **вы́игрыш**, -а, win; winning; winnings; gain; prize. **вы́игрышный**, winning; premium; lottery; advantageous; effective.

вы́йти, -йду; -шел, -шла *perf.* (*imp.* выходи́ть) go out; come out; get out; appear; turn out; come of; be used up; have expired; ~ в свет, appear; ~ в фина́л, reach the final; ~ за́муж (за+*acc.*) marry; ~ из грани́ц, ~ из преде́лов, exceed the bounds; ~ из себя́, lose one's temper, be beside oneself; ~ на вы́зовы, take a call; ~ на сце́ну, come on to the stage.

вы́казать, -ажу *perf.*, **выка́зывать**, -аю *imp.* show; display.

выка́лывать, -аю *imp.* of вы́колоть. **выка́пчивать**, -аю *imp.* of вы́коптить. **выка́пывать**, -аю *imp.* of вы́копать.

вы́карабкаться, -аюсь *perf.*, **выкара́бкиваться**, -аюсь *imp.* scramble out; get out.

вы́|катать, -аю *perf.*

вы́качать, -аю *perf.*, **выка́чивать**, -аю *imp.* pump out.

выки́дывать, -аю *imp.*, **вы́кинуть**, -ну *perf.* throw out, reject; put out; miscarry, abort; ~ флаг, hoist a flag. **вы́кидыш**, -а, miscarriage, abortion.

вы́кладка, -и, laying out; lay-out; facing; kit; computation, calculation. **выкла́дывать**, -аю *imp.* of вы́ложить.

выклика́ть, -а́ю *imp.*, **вы́кликнуть**, -ну *perf.* call out.

выключа́тель, -я *m.* switch. **выключа́ть**, -а́ю *imp.*, **вы́ключить**, -чу *perf.* turn off, switch off; remove, exclude; justify.

вы́|клянчить, -чу *perf.*

выкола́чивать, -аю *imp.*, **вы́колотить**, -лочу *perf.* knock out, beat out; beat; extort, wring out.

вы́колоть, -лю *perf.* (*imp.* выка́лывать) put out; gouge out; tattoo.

вы́|копать, -аю *perf.* (*imp.* also выка́пывать) dig; dig up, dig out; exhume; unearth; **~ся**, dig oneself out.

вы́коптить, -пчу *perf.* (*imp.* выка́пчивать) smoke.

вы́корчевать, -чую *perf.*, **выкорчёвывать**, -аю *imp.* uproot, root out; extirpate, eradicate.

выкра́ивать, -аю *imp.* of вы́кроить.

вы́|красить, -ашу *perf.*, **выкра́шивать**, -аю *imp.* paint; dye.
вы́крик, -а, cry, shout; yell. **выкри́кивать**, -аю *imp.*, **вы́крикнуть**, -ну *perf.* cry out; yell.
вы́кроить, -ою *perf.* (*imp.* выкра́ивать) cut out; (manage to) find. **вы́кройка**, -и, pattern.
вы́крутить, -учу *perf.*, **выкру́чивать**, -аю *imp.* unscrew; twist; **~ся**, extricate oneself, get oneself out.
вы́куп, -а, ransom; redemption.
вы́|купать[1]**(ся**, -аю(сь *perf.*
выкупа́ть[2], -а́ю *imp.*, **вы́купить**, -плю *perf.* ransom, redeem. **выкупно́й**, ransom; redemption.
выку́ривать, -аю *imp.*, **вы́курить**, -рю *perf.* smoke; smoke out; distil.
выла́вливать, -аю *imp.* of вы́ловить.
вы́лазка, -и, sally, sortie; raid; ramble, excursion outing.
вы́|лакать, -аю *perf.* **выла́мывать**, -аю *imp.* of вы́ломать. **выла́щивать**, -аю *imp.* of вы́лощить.
вылеза́ть, -а́ю *imp.*, **вы́лезти**, **вы́лезть**, -зу; -лез *perf.* crawl out; climb out; fall out, come out.
вы́|лепить, -плю *perf.*
вы́лет, -а, flight; take-off, departure; emission, escape; overhang. **вылета́ть**, -а́ю *imp.*, **вы́лететь**, -ечу *perf.* fly out, off, away; take off; rush out, dash out; escape.
выле́чивать, -аю *imp.*, **вы́лечить**, -чу *perf.* cure, heal; **~ся**, recover, be cured; ~ся от+*gen.* get over.
вылива́ть(ся, -а́ю(сь *perf.* of вы́лить(ся.
вы́|линять, -яет *perf.*
вы́лить, -лью *perf.* (*imp.* вылива́ть) pour out; empty (out); cast, found; mould; **~ся**, run out, flow (out); be expressed, express itself.
вы́ловить, -влю *perf.* (*imp.* выла́вливать) fish out, catch.
вы́ложить, -жу *perf.* (*imp.* выкла́дывать) lay out, spread out; cover, lay, face; tell, reveal.
вы́лом, -а, breaking down, in, out, open; breach, break, gap. **вы́ломать**, -аю, *perf.*, **вы́ломить**, -млю *perf.* (*imp.* выла́мывать) break down, break out, break open. **вы́ломка**, -и, breaking off.
вы́лощенный, glossy; polished, smooth. **вы́лощить**, -щу *perf.* (*imp.* выла́щивать) polish.
вы́|лудить, -ужу *perf.* **вы́лью**, etc.: see вы́лить.
вы́|мазать, -мажу *perf.*, **выма́зывать**, -аю *imp.* smear, daub, dirty; **~ся**, get dirty, make oneself dirty.
выма́ливать, -аю *imp.* of вы́молить.
выма́нивать, -аю *imp.*, **вы́манить**, -ню *perf.* entice, lure; +у+*gen.* swindle, cheat, out of; wheedle, coax, out of.
вы́|марать, -аю *perf.* **вы́мени**, etc.: see вы́мя.
вы́мереть, -мрет; -мер *perf.* (*imp.* вымира́ть) die out; become extinct; be, become, deserted. **вы́мерший**, extinct.
вымина́ть, -а́ю *imp.* of вы́мять. **вымира́ть**, -а́ю *imp.* of вы́мереть. **вы́мну**, etc.: see вы́мять.
вымога́тель, -я *m.*, **-ница**, -ы, blackmailer, extortioner. **вымога́тельство**, -а, blackmail, extortion. **вымога́ть**, -а́ю *imp.* extort, wring (out).
вымока́ть, -а́ю *imp.*, **вы́мокнуть**, -ну; -ок *perf.* be soaked, drenched, wet through; soak, steep; rot.
вымола́чивать, -аю *imp.* of вы́молотить.
вы́молвить, -влю *perf.* say, utter.
вы́молить, -лю *perf.* (*imp.* выма́ливать) beg; obtain by prayer(s).
вы́молот, -а, threshing; grain. **вы́молотить**, -очу *perf.* (*imp.* вымола́чивать) thresh. **вы́молотки**, -ток or -тков *pl.* chaff.
вы́|мостить, -ощу *perf.* **вы́мою** etc.: see вы́мыть.
вы́мпел, -а, pennant.
вы́мрет: see вы́мереть. **вымыва́ть(ся** *imp.* of вы́мыть(ся.
вы́мысел, -сла, invention, fabrication; fantasy, flight of fancy. **вы́мыслить**, -лю *perf.* (*imp.* вымышля́ть) think up, make up, invent; imagine.
вы́|мыть, -мою *perf.* (*imp.* also вымыва́ть) wash; wash out, off; wash away; **~ся**, wash, wash oneself.
вы́мышленный, fictitious, imaginary. **вымышля́ть**, -я́ю *imp.* of вы́мыслить.
вы́мя -мени *n.* udder.

вы́мять, -мну *perf.* (*imp.* вымина́ть) knead, work; trample down.
вы́нести, -су; -нес *perf.* (*imp.* выноси́ть) carry out, take out; take away; carry away; bear, stand, endure; pass; ~ вопро́с, submit a question; ~ на бе́рег, wash up; **~сь,** fly out, rush out.
вынима́ть(ся, -а́ю(сь *imp.* of вы́нуть(-ся.
вы́нос, -а, carrying out; removal; drift; trace. **выноси́ть,** -ошу́, -о́сишь *imp.* of вы́нести; не ~, be unable to bear, to stand; **~ся** *imp.* of вы́нестись. **вы́носка,** -и, taking out, carrying out; removal; marginal note, footnote. **выно́сливость,** -и, endurance, staying-power; hardiness.
вы́нудить, -ужу *perf.*, **вынужда́ть,** -а́ю *imp.* force, compel, oblige; extort. **вы́нужденный,** forced, compulsory.
вы́нуть, -ну *perf.* (*imp.* вынима́ть) take out; pull out; extract; draw out; **~ся,** come out, pull out.
вы́пад, -а, attack; lunge, thrust. **выпада́ть,** -а́ю *imp.* of вы́пасть. **выпаде́ние,** -я, falling out; fall-out; precipitation; prolapsus.
выпа́лывать, -аю *imp.* of вы́полоть.
выпа́ривать, -аю *imp.*, **вы́парить,** -рю, evaporate.
выпа́рывать, -аю *imp.* of вы́пороть[2].
вы́пасть, -аду; -ал *perf.* (*imp.* выпада́ть) fall out; fall; occur, turn out; lunge, thrust.
выпека́ть, -а́ю *imp.*, **вы́печь,** -еку; -ек *perf.* bake. **вы́печка,** -и, baking, batch.
выпива́ть, -а́ю *imp.* of вы́пить; enjoy a drink. **вы́пивка,** -и, drinking; drinks.
выпи́ливать, -аю *imp.*, **вы́пилить,** -лю *perf.* saw, cut out, make with fretsaw.
вы́писать, -ишу *perf.*, **выпи́сывать,** -аю *imp.* copy out, excerpt; trace out; write out; order; subscribe to; send for, write for; strike off the list; ~ из больни́цы, discharge from hospital; **~ся,** leave, be discharged. **вы́писка,** -и, copying out, making extracts; writing out; extract, excerpt, cutting; ordering, subscription; discharge. **вы́пись,** -и, extract, copy.
вы́|пить, -пью *perf.* (*imp.* also выпива́ть) drink; drink up, drink off.
вы́плавить, -влю *perf.*, **выплавля́ть,** -я́ю *imp.* smelt. **вы́плавка,** -и, smelting; smelted metal.
вы́плата, -ы, payment. **вы́платить,** -ачу *perf.*, **выпла́чивать,** -аю *imp.* pay, pay out; pay off.
выплёвывать, -аю *imp.* of вы́плюнуть.
вы́плести, -ету *perf.*, **выплета́ть,** -а́ю *imp.* undo, untie; unplait; weave.
выплыва́ть, -а́ю *imp.*, **вы́плыть,** -ыву *perf.* swim out, sail out; come to the surface, come up; emerge; appear, crop up.
вы́плюнуть, -ну *perf.* (*imp.* выплёвывать) spit out.
выполза́ть, -а́ю *imp.*, **вы́ползти,** -зу; -олз *perf.* crawl out, creep out.
выполне́ние, -я, execution, carrying out; fulfilment. **выполни́мый,** practicable, feasible. **вы́полнить,** -ню *perf.*, **выполня́ть,** -я́ю *imp.* execute, carry out; fulfil; discharge.
вы́|полоскать, -ощу *perf.*
вы́|полоть, -лю *perf.* (*imp.* also выпа́лывать) weed out; weed.
вы́|пороть[1], -рю *perf.*
вы́пороть[2], -рю *perf.* (*imp.* выпа́рывать) rip out, rip up.
вы́|потрошить, -шу *perf.*
вы́править, -влю *perf.*, **выправля́ть,** -я́ю *imp.* straighten (out); correct; improve; get, obtain; **~ся,** become straight; improve. **вы́правка,** -и, bearing; correction.
выпра́шивать, -аю *imp.* of вы́просить; solicit.
выпрова́живать, -аю *imp.*, **вы́проводить,** -ожу *perf.* send packing; show the door.
вы́просить, -ошу *perf.* (*imp.* выпра́шивать) (ask for and) get.
выпряга́ть, -а́ю *imp.* of вы́прячь.
выпрями́тель, -я *m.* rectifier. **вы́прямить,** -млю *perf.*, **выпрямля́ть,** -я́ю *imp.* straighten (out); rectify; **~ся,** become straight; straighten up, draw oneself up.
вы́прячь, -ягу; -яг *perf.* (*imp.* выпряга́ть) unharness.
выпу́гивать, -аю *imp.*, **вы́пугнуть,** -ну *perf.* scare off; start.

вы́пукло *adv.* in relief. **вы́пукло-**, convexo-. **вы́пуклость, -и,** protuberance; prominence, bulge; convexity; relief; clarity, distinctness. **вы́пуклый,** protuberant; prominent, bulging; convex; in relief; clear, distinct.

вы́пуск, -а, output; issue; discharge; part, number, instalment; final-year students, pupils; cut, omission; edging, piping. **выпуска́ть, -а́ю** *imp.*, **вы́пустить, -ущу** *perf.* let out, release; put out, issue; turn out, produce; cut, cut out, omit; let out, let down; show; see through the press. **выпускни́к, -а́,** final-year student, pupil. **выпускн|о́й,** output; discharge; exhaust; ~о́й экза́мен, finals, final examination; ~а́я цена́, market-price; **~о́й** *sb.* final-year student.

вы́путать, -аю *perf.*, **выпу́тывать, -аю** *imp.* disentangle; **~ся,** disentangle oneself, extricate oneself; ~ся из беды́, get out of a scrape.

вы́пушка, -и, edging, braid, piping.

вы́пытать, -аю *perf.*, **выпы́тывать, -аю** *imp.* elicit, worm out.

выпь, -и, bittern.

вы́пью, etc.: see вы́пить.

вы́пятить(ся, -ячу(сь *perf.*, **выпя́чивать(ся, -аю(сь** *imp.* stick out, protrude.

выраба́тывать, -аю *imp.*, **вы́работать, -аю** *perf.* work out; work up; draw up; elaborate; manufacture; produce, make; earn. **вы́работка, -и,** manufacture; production, making; working; working out, drawing up; output, yield; make.

выра́внивать(ся, -аю(сь *imp.* of вы́ровнять(ся.

выража́ть, -а́ю *imp.*, **вы́разить, -ажу** *perf.* express; convey; voice; **~ся,** express oneself; manifest itself; amount, come (в+*prep.* to). **выраже́ние, -я,** expression. **вы́раженный,** pronounced, marked. **вырази́тель, -я** *m.* spokesman, exponent; voice. **вырази́тельный,** expressive; significant.

выраста́ть, -а́ю *imp.*, **вы́расти, -ту; -рос** *perf.* grow, grow up; develop; increase; appear, rise up; ~ из+*gen.* grow out of. **вы́растить, -ащу** *perf.*, **выра́щивать, -аю** *imp.* bring up; rear, breed; grow, cultivate.

вы́рвать[1], **-ву** *perf.* (*imp.* вырыва́ть) pull out, tear out; extort, wring out; **~ся,** tear oneself away; break out, break loose, break free; get away; come loose, come out; break, burst, escape; shoot up, shoot (out).

вы́|рвать[2], **-ву** *perf.*

вы́рез, -а, cut; notch; décolletage. **вы́резать, -ежу** *perf.*, **выреза́ть, -а́ю** *imp.*, **выре́зывать, -аю** *imp.* cut out; excise; cut, carve; engrave; slaughter, butcher. **вы́резка, -и,** cutting-out, excision; carving; engraving; cutting; fillet. **вырезно́й,** cut; carved; low-necked, décolleté. **выре́зывание, -я,** cutting out; excision; carving; engraving.

вы́рисовать, -сую *perf.*, **вырисо́вывать, -аю** *imp.* draw carefully, draw in detail; **~ся,** appear; stand out.

вы́ровнять, -яю *perf.* (*imp.* выра́внивать) smooth level; straighten (out); draw up; **~ся,** become level, become even; form up; equalize; catch up, draw level; improve.

вы́родиться, -ится *perf.*, **вырожда́ться, -а́ется** *imp.* degenerate. **вы́родок, -дка,** degenerate; black sheep. **вырож-де́нец, -нца,** degenerate. **вырожде́ние, -я,** degeneration.

вы́ронить, -ню *perf.* drop.

вы́рос, etc.: see вы́расти. **вы́рост, -а,** growth, excrescence; offshoot. **вы́ростковый,** calf. **вы́росток, -тка,** yearling; calf.

вы́рою etc.: see вы́рыть.

вы́рубать, -а́ю *imp.*, **вы́рубить, -блю** *perf.* cut down, fell; hew out; cut (out); carve (out); **~ся,** cut one's way out. **вы́рубка, -и** cutting down, felling; hewing out; clearing.

вы́|ругать(ся, -аю(сь *perf.*

выру́ливать, -аю *imp.*, **вы́|рулить, -лю** *perf.* taxi.

выруча́ть, -а́ю *imp.*, **вы́ручить, -чу** *perf.* rescue; help out; gain; make. **вы́ручка, -и,** rescue, assistance; gain; proceeds, receipts; earnings.

вырыва́ние[1], **-я,** pulling out, extraction; uprooting.

вырыва́ние[2], -я, digging (up). **вырыва́ть**[2], -а́ю *imp.*, **вы́рыть**, -рою *perf.* dig up, dig out, unearth.

вырыва́ть[1](**ся** *imp.* of вы́рвать(ся.

вы́садить, -ажу *perf.*, **выса́живать**, -аю *imp.* set down; help down; put off; detrain, debus; put ashore, land; plant out, transplant; smash; break in; **~ся**, alight, get off; land; disembark; detrain, debus. **вы́садка**, -и, disembarkation; landing; transplanting, planting out.

выса́сывать, -аю *imp.* of вы́сосать.

высве́рливать, -аю *imp.*, **вы́сверлить**, -лю *perf.* drill, bore.

вы́свободить, -божу *perf.*, **высвобожда́ть**, -а́ю *imp.* free; disengage, disentangle; release; help to escape.

высека́ть, -а́ю *imp.* of вы́сечь[2]. **вы́секу** etc.: see вы́сечь.

выселе́нец, -нца, evacuee. **выселе́ние**, -я, eviction. **вы́селить**, -лю *perf.*, **выселя́ть**, -я́ю *imp.* evict; evacuate, move; **~ся**, move, remove. **вы́селок**, -лка, settlement.

вы́сечка, -и, carving; hewing. **вы́|сечь**[1], -еку; -сек *perf.* **вы́сечь**[2], -еку; -сек (*imp.* высека́ть) cut, cut out; carve; hew.

вы́сидеть, -ижу *perf.*, **выси́живать**, -аю *imp.* sit out; stay; hatch, hatch out.

вы́ситься, -сится *imp.* rise, tower.

вы́сказать, -кажу *perf.*, **выска́зывать**, -аю *imp.* express; state; **~ся**, speak out; speak one's mind, have one's say; speak. **выска́зывание**, -я, utterance; pronouncement, opinion.

выска́кивать, -аю *imp.* of вы́скочить.

выска́льзывать, -аю *imp.* of вы́скользнуть.

вы́скоблить, -лю *perf.* scrape out; erase; remove.

вы́скользнуть, -ну *perf.* (*imp.* выска́льзывать) slip out.

вы́скочить, -чу *perf.* (*imp.* выска́кивать) jump out; leap out, spring out, rush out; come up; drop out, fall out; ~ с + *instr.* come out with. **вы́скочка**, -и, upstart, parvenu.

вы́сланный *sb.* exile, deportee. **вы́слать** вы́шлю *perf.* (*imp.* высыла́ть) send, send out, dispatch; exile; deport.

вы́следить, -ежу *perf.*, **высле́живать**, -аю *imp.* trace, track; stalk; shadow.

вы́слуга, -и; ~ лет, long service. **выслу́живать**, -аю *imp.*, **вы́служить**, -жу *perf.* qualify for, earn; serve (out); **~ся**, gain promotion, be promoted; curry favour, get in (with).

вы́слушать, -аю *perf.*, **выслу́шивать**, -аю *imp.* hear out; sound; listen to. **выслу́шивание**, -я, auscultation.

вы́|смолить, -лю *perf.* **вы́|сморкать(ся**, -аю(сь *perf.* **сысо́вывать(ся**, -аю(сь *imp.* of вы́сунуть(ся.

высо́кий; -о́к, -а́, -о́ко́, high; tall; lofty; elevated, sublime.

высоко- in *comb.* high-, highly. **высокоблагоро́дие**, -я, (your) Honour, Worship. **~во́льтный**, high-tension. **~го́рный**, Alpine, mountain. **~ка́чественный**, high-quality. **~ме́рие**, -я, haughtiness, arrogance. **~ме́рный**, haughty, arrogant. **~па́рный**, high-flown, stilted; bombastic, turgid. **~про́бный**, sterling; standard; of high quality. **~со́ртный**, high-grade. **~часто́тный**, high-frequency.

вы́сосать, -осу *perf.* (*imp.* выса́сывать) suck out.

высота́, -ы́; *pl.* -ы, height, altitude; pitch; eminence; high level; high quality. **высо́тник**, -а, high-building worker; high-altitude flier. **высо́тн|ый**, high; high-altitude; tall, multi-storey, high-rise; ~ое зда́ние, tower block. **высотоме́р**, -а, altimeter, height-finder.

вы́|сохнуть, -ну; -ох *perf.* (*imp.* also высыха́ть) dry, dry out; dry up; wither, fade; waste away, fade away. **вы́сохший**, dried up; shrivelled; wizened.

вы́ставить, -влю *perf.*, **выставля́ть**, -я́ю *imp.* bring out, bring forward; display, exhibit; post; put forward; adduce; put down, set down; take out, remove; send out, turn out, throw out; + *instr.* represent as, make out to be; ~ свою́ кандидату́ру, stand for election; **~ся**, lean out, thrust oneself forward; show off. **вы́ставка**, -и, exhibition, show; display; showcase, (shop-)window. **выставно́й,** removable.

вы́|стегать, -аю *perf.* **вы́стелю,** etc.: see вы́стлать. **выстила́ть,** -а́ю *imp.* of вы́стлать. **вы́|стирать,** -а́ю *perf.*

вы́стлать, -телю *perf.* (*imp.* выстила́ть) cover; line; pave.

вы́страдать, -аю *perf.* suffer, go through; gain through suffering.

выстра́ивать(ся, -аю(сь *imp.* of вы́строить(ся. **выстра́чивать,** -аю *imp.* of вы́строчить.

вы́стрел, -а, shot; report. **вы́стрелить,** -лю *perf.* shoot, fire.

вы́|строгать, -аю *perf.*

вы́строить, -ою *perf.* (*imp.* выстра́ивать) build; draw up, order, arrange; form up; **~ся** form up.

вы́строчить, -чу *perf.* (*imp.* выстра́чивать) hemstitch; stitch.

вы́стукать, -аю *perf.* **высту́кивать,** -аю *imp.* tap, percuss; tap out. **высту́кивание,** -я, percussion; tapping.

вы́ступ, -а, protuberance, projection, ledge; bulge, salient; lug. **выступа́ть,** -а́ю *imp.* **вы́ступить,** -плю *perf.* come forward, go forward; come out; appear; perform; speak; +из+*gen.* go beyond exceed; ~ из берего́в, overflow its banks; ~ с докла́дом, give a talk; ~ с ре́чью, make a speech. **выступле́ние,** -я appearance, performance; speech; setting out.

вы́сунуть, -ну *perf.* (*imp.* высо́вывать) put out, thrust out; **~ся,** show oneself, thrust oneself forward; ~ся в окно́, lean out of the window.

вы́|сушить(ся, -шу(сь *perf.*

вы́сш|ий, highest; supreme; high; higher; ~ая то́чка, climax.

высыла́ть, -а́ю *imp.* of вы́слать. **вы́сылка,** -и, sending, dispatching; expulsion, exile.

вы́сыпать, -плю *perf.*, **высыпа́ть,** -а́ю *imp.* pour out; empty (out); spill; **~ся,** pour out, spill.

высыха́ть, -а́ю *imp.* of вы́сохнуть.

высь, -и, height; summit.

выта́лкивать, -аю *imp.* of вы́толкать, вы́толкнуть. **вы́|таращить,** -щу *perf.* **выта́скивать,** -аю *imp.* of вы́тащить.

вы́|тачать, -аю *perf.* **выта́чивать,** -аю *imp.* of вы́точить.

вы́тачка, -и, tuck; dart.

вы́|тащить, -щу *perf.* (*imp.* also выта́скивать) drag out; pull out, extract; steal, pinch.

вы́|твердить -ржу *perf.*

вытека́ть, -а́ю *imp.* (*perf.* вы́течь); ~ из+*gen.* flow from, out of; result from, follow from.

вы́|теребить, -блю *perf.*

вы́тереть, -тру; -тер *perf.* (*imp.* вытира́ть) wipe, wipe up; dry, rub dry; wear out.

вы́терпеть, -плю *perf.* bear, endure.

вы́тертый, threadbare.

вытесне́ние, -я, ousting; supplanting; displacement. **вы́теснить,** -ню *perf.*, **вытесня́ть,** -я́ю *imp.* crowd out; force out; oust; supplant; displace.

вы́течь, -чет; -ек *perf.* (*imp.* вытека́ть) flow out, run out.

вытира́ть, -а́ю *imp.* of вы́тереть.

вы́тиснить, -ню, *perf.*, **вытисня́ть,** -я́ю *imp.* stamp, imprint, impress.

вы́толкать, -аю *perf.*, **вы́толкнуть,** -ну *perf.* (*imp.* выта́лкивать) throw out, sling out; push out, force out.

вы́точенный, turned; сло́вно ~, chiselled; perfectly formed. **вы́|точить,** -чу *perf.* (*imp.*, also выта́чивать) turn; sharpen; gnaw through.

вы́|травить, -влю *perf.*, **вытра́вливать,** -аю, *imp.*, **вытравля́ть,** -я́ю *imp.* exterminate, destroy, poison; remove, get out; etch; trample down, damage.

вы́требовать, -бую *perf.* summon, send for; get on demand.

вытрезви́тель, -я *m.* sobering-up treatment, station. **вы́трезвить(ся,** -влю(сь *perf.*, **вытрезвля́ть(ся,** -я́ю(сь *imp.* sober up.

вы́тру etc.: see вы́тереть.

вытряса́ть, -а́ю *imp.*, **вы́|трясти,** -су; -яс *perf.* shake out.

вытря́хивать, -аю *imp.*, **вы́тряхнуть,** -ну *perf.* shake out.

выть, во́ю *imp.* howl; wail. **вытьё,** -я́, howling; wailing.

вытя́гивать, -аю *imp.*, **вы́тянуть,** -ну *perf.* stretch, stretch out; extend; draw out, extract; endure, stand, stick;

weigh; **~ся**, stretch, stretch out, stretch oneself; grow, shoot up; draw oneself up. **вы́тяжка**, -и, drawing out, extraction; extract; stretching extension. **вытяжно́й**, drawing; exhaust; ventilating; ~ шкаф, fume chamber.

вы́|утюжить, -жу *perf.*

выу́чивать, -аю *imp.*, **вы́|учить**, -чу *perf.* learn; teach; **~ся** + *dat.* or *inf.* learn. **вы́учка**, -и, teaching, training.

выха́живать, -аю *imp.* of вы́ходить.

вы́хватить, -ачу *perf.*, **выхва́тывать**, -аю *imp.* snatch out, up; snatch away; pull out, draw; take out; take up.

вы́хлоп, -а, exhaust.

выхлопа́тывать, -аю *imp.* of вы́хлопотать.

выхлопно́й, exhaust, discharge.

вы́хлопотать, -очу *perf.* (*imp.* выхлопа́тывать) obtain with much trouble.

вы́ход, -а, going out; leaving, departure; way out, exit; outlet, vent; appearance; entrance; output, yield; outcrop; все хо́ды и ~ы, all the ins and outs; ~ в отста́вку, retirement; ~ за́муж, marriage. **вы́ходец**, -дца, emigrant; immigrant. **выходи́ть**[1], -ожу́, -о́дишь *imp.* of вы́йти; +на+*acc.* look out on, give on, face.

вы́ходить[2], -ожу *perf.* (*imp.* выха́живать) tend, nurse; rear, bring up; grow.

вы́ходить[3], -ожу *perf.* (*imp.* выха́живать) pass through; go all over.

вы́ходка, -и, trick; escapade, prank. **выходн|о́й**, exit, outlet; going-out, outgoing; leaving, departure, discharge; publication, issue; output; ~а́я дверь, street door; ~о́й день, day off, free day, rest-day; ~о́й лист, title-page; ~а́я роль, walking-on part; ~ы́е све́дения, imprint; **~о́й** *sb.* person off duty; day off; **~а́я** *sb.* person off duty. **вы́хожу**, etc.: see вы́ходить. **выхожу́** etc.: see выходи́ть[1].

выхола́щивать, -аю *imp.*, **вы́холостить**, -ощу *perf.* castrate, geld; emasculate.

вы́хухоль, -я *m.*, musk-rat; musquash. **вы́хухолевый**, musquash.

вы́царапать, -аю *perf.*, **выцара́пывать**, -аю *imp.* scratch; scratch out; extract, get out.

вы́цвести, -ветет *perf.*, **выцвета́ть**, -а́ет *imp.* fade. **вы́цветший**, faded.

вы́цедить, -ежу *perf.*, **выце́живать**, -аю *imp.* filter, rack off; strain; decant; drink off, drain.

выче́канивать, -аю *imp.*, **вы́|чеканить**, -ню *perf.* mint; strike.

вычёркивать, -аю *imp.*, **вы́черкнуть**, -ну *perf.* cross out, strike out; expunge, erase.

вы́черпать, -аю *perf.*, **выче́рпывать**, -аю *imp.* bale out.

вы́честь, -чту; -чел, -чла *perf.* (*imp.* вычита́ть) subtract; deduct, keep back. **вы́чет**, -а, deduction; за ~ом, except; less, minus, allowing for.

вычисле́ние, -я, calculation. **вычисли́тель**, -я *m.* calculator; plotter; computer. **вычисли́тельн|ый**, calculating, computing; ~ая маши́на, computer. **вы́числить**, -лю *perf.*, **вычисля́ть**, -яю *imp.* calculate, compute.

вы́|чистить, -ищу *perf.* (*imp.* also вычища́ть) clean, clean up, clean out; purge.

вычита́емое *sb.* subtrahend. **вычита́ние**, -я, subtraction. **вычита́ть**, -а́ю *imp.* of вы́честь.

вычища́ть, -а́ю *imp.* of вы́чистить.

вы́чту, etc.: see вы́честь.

вы́швырнуть, -ну *perf.*, **вышвы́ривать**, -аю *imp.* throw out, hurl out; chuck out.

вы́ше, higher, taller; *prep.*+*gen.* above, beyond; over; *adv.* above.

вы́ше- in *comb.* above-, afore-. **вышеизло́женный**, foregoing. **~на́званный**, afore-named. **~озна́ченный**, aforesaid, above-mentioned. **~ска́занный**, **~ука́занный**, aforesaid. **~упомя́нутый**, afore-mentioned.

вы́шел, etc.: see вы́йти.

вышиба́ла, -ы *m.* chucker-out. **вышиба́ть**, -а́ю *imp.*, **вы́шибить**, -бу; -иб *perf.* knock out; chuck out.

вышива́льный, embroidery. **вышива́льщица**, -ы, embroideress, needlewoman. **вышива́ние**, -я, embroidery needlework. **вышива́ть**, -а́ю *imp.* of вы́шить. **вы́шивка** -и, embroidery.

вышина́, -ы́ height.
вы́шить, -шью *perf.* (*imp.* **вышива́ть**) embroider. **вы́шитый**, embroidered.
вы́шка, -и, turret; tower; (бурова́я) ~ derrick.
вы́|школить, -лю *perf.* **вы́шлю**, etc.: see вы́слать. **вы́шью**, etc.: see вы́шить.
вы́щипать, -плю *perf.* **вы́щипнуть**, -ну *perf.*, **выщи́пывать**, -аю *imp.* pluck out, pull out.
вы́явить, -влю *perf.*, **выявля́ть**, -я́ю *imp.* reveal; bring out; make known; display; show up, expose; **~ся**, appear, come to light, be revealed. **выявле́ние**, -я, revelation; showing up, exposure.
выясне́ние, -я, elucidation; explanation. **вы́яснить**, -ню *perf.* **выясня́ть**, -я́ю *imp.* elucidate; clear up, explain; **~ся**, become clear; turn out, prove.
вью etc.: see вить.
вью́га, -и, snow-storm, blizzard.
вьюк, -а, pack; load.
вьюно́к, -нка́, bindweed, convolvulus.
вью́чн|ый, pack; ~ое живо́тное, pack animal, beast of burden; ~ая ло́шадь, pack-horse; ~ое седло́, pack-saddle.
вью́шка, -и, damper.
вью́щийся, creeping, climbing; curly frizzy.
вэ *n. indecl.* the letter в.
вяжу́, etc.: see вяза́ть. **вя́жущий**, binding, cementing; astringent.
вяз, -а, elm.
вяза́льный, knitting, crochet. **вяза́ние**, -я, knitting, crocheting; binding, tying.
вя́занка[1], -и, knitted garment. **вяза́нка**[2], -и, bundle, truss. **вя́заный**, knitted, crocheted. **вяза́нье**, -я, knitting; crochet(-work). **вяза́ть**, вяжу́, вя́жешь *imp.* (*perf.* с~) tie, bind; clamp; knit, crochet; be astringent; **~ся**, accord, agree; fit in, be in keeping, tally. **вя́зка**, -и, tying, binding; knitting, crocheting; bunch, string.
вя́зкий; -зок, -зка́, -о, viscous, glutinous, sticky; boggy; ductile, malleable; tough; astringent. **вя́знуть**, -ну; вя́з(нул), -зла *imp.* (*perf.* за~, у~), stick, get stuck; sink.
вя́зовый, elm.
вя́зчик, -а, binder. **вязь**, -и, ligature; arabesque.
вял, etc.: see вя́нуть.
вя́ление, -я, dry-curing; drying. **вя́леный**, dried; sun-cured. **вя́лить**, -лю *imp.* (*perf.* про~) dry, dry-cure.
вя́лый, flabby, flaccid; limp; sluggish; inert; slack. **вя́нуть**, -ну; вял *imp.* (*pref.* за~, у~) fade, wither; droop, flag.

Г

г *letter:* see гэ.
г. *abbr.* год, year; гора́, mountain, mount; го́род, city, town; господи́н, Mr.
г *abbr.* грамм, gramme.
га *abbr.* гекта́р, hectare.
габари́т, -а, clearance; clearance diagram; size, dimension. **габари́тн|ый**, clearance; overall; ~ые воро́та, loading gauge; ~ая высота́, headroom.
га́вань, -и, harbour.
га́врик, -а, (*sl.*) petty crook; man, fellow, mate.
га́га, -и, eider(-duck).
гага́ра, -ы, loon, diver. **гага́рка**, -и, razorbill.
гага́т, -а, jet.
гага́чий, eider-; ~ пух, eiderdown.
гад, -а, reptile, amphibian; vile creature; *pl.* vermin.
гада́лка, -и, fortune-teller. **гада́ние**, -я, fortune-telling, divination; guess-work. **гада́тельный**, fortune-telling; problematical, conjectural, hypothetical. **гада́ть**, -а́ю *imp.* (*perf.* по~) tell fortunes; guess, conjecture, surmise.

га́дина, -ы, reptile; vile creature; *pl.* vermin. **га́дить**, га́жу *imp.* (*perf.* на∼) +в+*prep.*, на+*acc.*, *prep.* foul, dirty, defile. **га́дкий**; -док, -дка́, -о, nasty, vile, foul, loathsome; ∼ утёнок, ugly duckling. **гадли́вость**, -и, aversion, disgust. **гадли́вый**, of disgust, disgusted. **га́дость**, -и, filth, muck; dirty trick; *pl.* filthy expressions. **гадю́ка**, -и, adder, viper; repulsive person.

га́ер, -а, buffoon, clown. **га́ерничать**, -аю *imp.*, **га́ерствовать**, -твую *imp.* clown, play the fool.

га́ечный, nut; ∼ ключ, spanner, wrench.

га́же, *comp.* of га́дкий.

газ[1], -а, gauze.

газ[2], -а (-у), gas; wind; дать ∼, step on the gas; сба́вить ∼, reduce speed; на по́лном га́зе, at top speed. **газану́ть**, -ну́, -нёшь *perf.* (*imp.* газова́ть) accelerate; scram. **газа́ция**, -и, aeration. **газго́льдер**, -а, gasholder.

газе́та, -ы, newspaper, paper. **газе́тный**, newspaper, news. **газе́тчик**, -а, **-чица**, -ы, journalist; newspaper-seller.

газиро́ванный, aerated. **гази́ровать**, -рую *imp.* aerate. **газиро́вка**, -и, aeration; aerated water. **газова́ть**, -зу́ю *imp.* (*perf.* газану́ть) accelerate, step on it; scram. **га́зовый**[1], gas; ∼ счётчик, gas-meter.

га́зовый[2], gauze.

газокали́льный, incandescent. **газоли́н**, -а, gasolene. **газоме́р**, -а, gas-meter.

газо́н, -а, lawn, turf, grass. **газонокоси́лка**, -и, lawn-mower.

газообра́зный, gaseous. **газопрово́д**, -а, gas pipeline; gas-main. **газопрово́дный**, gas.

ГАИ′ *abbr.* Госуда́рсвтенная автомоби́льная инспе́кция, State Motor-vehicle Inspectorate.

гайду́к, -а́, heyduck.

га́йка, -и, nut; female screw.

гала́ктика, -и, galaxy.

галантере́йный, haberdasher's, haberdashery. **галантере́я**, -и, haberdashery fancy goods.

галанти́р, -а, galantine.

галдёж, -а́, din, racket, row. **галде́ть**, -ди́шь *imp.* make a din, make a row.

гале́ра, -ы, galley.

галере́я, -и, gallery. **галёрка**, -и, gallery, gods.

га́лечник, -а, shingle, pebbles.

галифе́ *indecl. pl.* riding-breeches; jodhpurs.

га́лка, -и, jackdaw, daw.

галл, -а, Gaul. **га́лльский**, Gaulish; Gallic.

гало́п, -а, gallop; galop. **галопи́ровать**, -рую *imp.* gallop.

га́лочий, jackdaw's, daw's. **га́лочка**, -и, tick.

гало́ша, -и, galosh.

галс, -а, tack.

га́лстук, -а, tie; neckerchief.

галу́шка, -и, dumpling.

га́лька, -и, pebble; pebbles, shingle.

гам, -а (-у), din, uproar.

га́мма, -ы, scale; gamut; range.

ганте́ль, -и, dumb-bell.

гардеро́б, -а, wardrobe; cloakroom. **гардеро́бная** *sb.* cloakroom. **гардеро́бщик**, -а, **-щица**, -ы, cloakroom attendant.

гарди́на, -ы, curtain.

гарев|о́й, **га́рев|ый**, cinder; ∼ая доро́жка, cinder track, cinder-path.

га́ркать, -аю *imp.*, **га́ркнуть**, -ну *perf.* shout, bark.

гармо́ника, -и, accordion, concertina; pleats; гармо́никой, (accordion-) pleated, in pleats. **гармони́ческий**, harmonic; harmonious; rhythmic. **гармони́чный**, harmonious. **гармо́ния**, -и, harmony; concord; accordion, concertina. **гармо́нь**, -и, **гармо́шка**, -и, accordion, concertina.

гарнизо́н, -а, garrison.

гарни́р, -а, garnish; trimmings; vegetables.

гарниту́р, -а, set; suite.

гарт, -а, type-metal.

гарь, -и, burning; cinders, ashes.

гаси́льник, -а, extinguisher, **гаси́тель**, -я *m.* extinguisher; damper; suppressor. **гаси́ть**, гашу́, га́сишь *imp.* (*perf.* за∼, по∼) put out, extinguish; slake; suppress, stifle; cancel; liquidate. **га́снуть**, -ну; га́с *imp.* (*perf.* за∼, по∼, у∼) be extinguished, go out; grow dim; sink.

гастролёр, -а, -ёрша, -и, guest-artist; touring actor, actress; casual worker. **гастроли́ровать, -рую** *imp.* tour, be on tour. **гастро́ль, -и,** tour; guest-appearance, performance; temporary engagement.

гастроно́м, -а, gastronome, gourmet; provision shop. **гастрономи́ческий,** gastronomic; provision. **гастроно́мия, -и,** gastronomy; provisions; delicatessen.

га́убица, -ы, howitzer.

гауптва́хта, -ы, guardhouse, guard-room.

гаше́ние, -я, extinguishing; slaking; cancellation, suppression. **гашёный,** slaked.

гаше́тка, -и, trigger; button.

гварде́ец, -е́йца, guardsman. **гварде́йский,** guards. **гва́рдия, -и,** Guards.

гво́здик, -а, tack; stiletto heel. **гвозди́ка, -и** pink(s), carnation(s); cloves. **гвоздь, -я́;** *pl.* -и, -е́й *m.* nail; tack; peg; crux; highlight, hit.

ГВФ (*geveéf*) *abbr.* Гражда́нский возду́шный флот СССР, U.S.S.R. Civil Air Fleet.

гг. *abbr.* го́ды, years.

где *adv.* where; somewhere; anywhere; how; ~ бы ни, wherever; ~ мне знать? how should I know? **где́-либо** *adv.* anywhere. **где́-нибудь** *adv.* somewhere; anywhere. **где́-то** *adv.* somewhere.

ГДР (*gede-ér*) *abbr.* Герма́нская Демократи́ческая Респу́блика, German Democratic Republic.

гекта́р, -а, hectare. **гекто-** in *comb.* hecto-.

ге́лий, -я, helium.

геморро́й, -я, haemorrhoids, piles. **гемофили́я, -и,** haemophilia.

ген, -а, gene.

ген- *abbr.* in *comb.* of генера́льный, general.

генера́л, -а, general; ~-губерна́тор, governor-general. **генералите́т, -а,** generals; high command. **генера́льн|ый,** general; radical, basic; ~ая репети́ция, dress rehearsal. **генера́льский,** general's. **генера́льша, -и,** general's wife.

генера́ция, -и, generation; oscillation.

гениа́льный, of genius, great; brilliant. **ге́ний, -я,** genius.

гео- in *comb.* geo-. **гео́граф, -а,** geographer. **~графи́ческий,** geographical. **~гра́фия, -и,** geography. **гео́лог, -а,** geologist. **~логи́ческий,** geological. **~ло́гия, -и,** geology. **гео́метр, -а,** geometrician. **~метри́ческий,** geometric, geometrical. **~ме́трия, -и,** geometry.

георги́н, -а, георги́на, -ы, dahlia.

гепа́рд, -а, cheetah.

гера́нь, -и, geranium.

герб, -а́, arms, coat of arms. **ге́рбов|ый,** heraldic; bearing coat of arms; stamped; ~ая печа́ть, official stamp; ~ый сбор, stamp-duty.

геркуле́с, -а, Hercules; rolled oats. **геркуле́совский,** Herculean.

герма́нец, -нца, Teuton, German. **герма́нский,** Germanic, Teutonic; German.

гермети́ческий, гермети́чный, hermetic, secret; hermetically sealed, air-tight, water-tight, pressurized.

герои́зм, -а, heroism. **геро́ика, -и,** heroics; heroic spirit; heroic style. **герои́ня, -и,** heroine. **герои́ческий,** heroic. **геро́й, -я,** hero. **геро́йский,** heroic. **геро́йство, -а,** heroism.

герц, -а; *gen. pl.* герц, hertz.

ге́тман, -а, hetman.

г-жа *abbr.* госпожа́, Mrs., Miss.

гиаци́нт, -а, hyacinth; jacinth.

ги́бель, -и, death; destruction, ruin; loss; wreck; downfall. **ги́бельный,** disastrous, fatal.

ги́бкий; -бок, -бка́, -бко, flexible, pliant; lithe; adaptable, versatile, resourceful; tractable. **ги́бкость, -и,** flexibility, pliancy; suppleness.

ги́бнуть, -ну; ги́б(нул) *imp.* (*perf.* по~) perish.

гига́нт, -а, giant. **гига́нтский,** gigantic.

гид, -а, гиде́сса, -ы, guide.

гидро- *perf.* hydro-. **гидро́лиз, -а,** hydrolysis. **~о́кись, -и,** hydroxide. **~ста́нция, -и,** hydro-electric power-station. **~те́хник, -а,** hydraulic engineer. **~те́хника, -и,** hydraulic engineering. **~фо́н, -а,** hydrophone.

гие́на, -ы, hyena.
гик, -а, whoop, whooping. **ги́кать**, -аю *imp.*, **ги́кнуть**, -ну *perf.* whoop.
гиль, -и, nonsense, rubbish.
ги́льдия, -и, guild.
ги́льза, -ы, case; cartridge-case; sleeve; liner; (cigarette-)wrapper.
гимн, -а, hymn.
гимнази́ст, -а, **-и́стка**, -и, grammar--school or high-school pupil. **гимна́зия**, -и, grammar school, high school.
гипно́з, -а, hypnosis. **гипнотизёр**, -а, hypnotist. **гипнотизи́ровать**, -рую *imp.* (*perf.* за~), hypnotize. **гипноти́зм**, -а, hypnotism. **гипноти́ческий**, hypnotic.
гипо́теза, -ы, hypothesis. **гипотети́ческий**, **гипотети́чный**, hypothetical.
гипс, -а, gypsum, plaster of Paris; plaster; plaster cast. **ги́псовый**, plaster.
гиреви́к, -а́, weight-lifter.
гирля́нда, -ы, garland.
ги́ря, -и, weight.
гита́ра, -ы, guitar.
гл. *abbr.* глава́, chapter.
гл *abbr.* гектоли́тр, hectolitre.
глав- *abbr.* in *comb.* of гла́вный, head, chief, main; гла́вное управле́ние, central administration, central board. **главбу́х**, -а, chief accountant. **главк**, -а, chief directorate; central committee, central administration. **~ре́ж**, -а, head producer, chief director.
глава́, -ы́; *pl.* -ы, head; chief; chapter; cupola. **глава́рь**, -я́ *m.* leader, ring-leader. **главе́нство**, -а, supremacy. **главе́нствовать**, -твую *imp.* be in command, lead, dominate. **главнокома́ндующий** *sb.* commander-in-chief. **гла́вн|ый**, chief, main, principal; head, senior; ~ая кни́га, ledger; ~ый нерв, nerve-centre; ~ым о́бразом, chiefly, mainly, for the most part; **~ое** *sb.* the chief thing, the main thing; the essentials; и са́мое ~ое, and above all.
глаго́л, -а, verb; word. **глаго́льный**, verbal.
глади́льный, ironing. **гла́дить**, -а́жу *imp.* (*perf.* вы́~, по~), stroke; iron, press. **гла́дкий**, smooth; sleek; plain; fluent, facile. **гла́дко** *adv.* smoothly; swimmingly; ~ вы́бритый, clean--shaven. **гладь**, -и, smooth surface; satin-stitch. **гла́же** *comp.* of гла́дкий, гла́дко. **гла́женье**, -я, ironing.
глаз, -а (-у), *loc.* -у́; *pl.* -а́, глаз, eye; eyesight; в ~а́, to one's face; за ~а́ + *gen.* in the absence of, behind the back of; на ~а́, на ~а́х, before one's eyes; с ~у на ~, without witnesses; смотре́ть во все ~а́, be all eyes. **глаза́стый**, big-eyed; quick-sighted.
глазиро́ванный, glazed; glossy; iced, glacé. **глазирова́ть**, -ру́ю *perf.* and *imp.* glaze; candy; ice. **глазиро́вка**, -и glazing; icing.
глазни́к, -а́, oculist. **глазни́ца**, -ы, eye--socket. **глазно́й**, eye; optic; ~ врач, oculist, eye-specialist.
глазу́нья, -и, fried eggs.
глазу́рь, -и, glaze; syrup; icing.
гла́нда, -ы, gland; tonsil.
глас, -а, voice. **гласи́ть**, -си́т *imp.* announce; say, run. **гла́сность**, -и, publicity. **гла́сный**, open, public; vowel vocalic; *sb.* vowel. **глаша́тай**, -я, crier; herald.
гле́тчер, -а, glacier.
гли́на, -ы, clay. **гли́нистый**, clay; clayey, argillaceous. **глинозём**, -а, alumina. **гли́нян|ый**, clay; earthenware, pottery; clayey; ~ая посу́да, earthenware.
гли́ссер, -а, speed-boat; hydroplane.
гл. обр. *abbr.* гла́вным о́бразом, chiefly, mainly.
гло́бус, -а, globe.
глода́ть, -ожу́, -о́жешь *imp.* gnaw.
глота́ть, -а́ю *imp.* swallow. **гло́тка**, -и, gullet; throat. **глото́к**, -тка́, gulp; mouthful.
гло́хнуть, -ну; глох *imp.* (*perf.* за~, о~) become deaf; die away, subside; decay; die; grow wild, become a wilderness, run to seed.
глу́бже *comp.* of глубо́кий, глубоко́.
глубина́, -ы́; *pl.* -ы. depth; depths, deep places; heart, interior; recesses; profundity; intensity. **глуби́нный**, deep; deep-laid; deep-sea; depth; remote, out-of-the-way. **глубо́к|ий**; -о́к, -а́, -о́ко́, deep; profound; intense; thorough, thorough-going; considerable,

serious; late, advanced, extreme; ~ий вира́ж, steep turn; ~ой о́сенью, in the late autumn; ~ая ста́рость, extreme old age; ~ая таре́лка, soup-plate. **глубоко́** *adv.* deep; deeply, profoundly. **глубоково́дный,** deep-water, deep-sea. **глубокомы́слие, -я,** profundity; perspicacity. **глубоме́р, -а,** depth gauge. **глубоча́йший** *superl.* of глубо́кий. **глубь, -и,** depth; (the) depths.

глуми́ться, -млю́сь *imp.* mock, jeer (над+*instr.* at). **глумле́ние, -я,** mockery; gibe, jeer. **глумли́вый,** mocking; gibing, jeering.

глупе́ть, -е́ю *imp.* (*perf.* по~) grow stupid. **глупе́ц,** -пца́, fool, blockhead. **глупи́ть,** -плю́ *imp.* (*perf.* с~) make a fool of oneself; do something foolish. **глупова́тый,** silly; rather stupid. **глу́пость, -и,** foolishness, stupidity; nonsense; глу́пости! (stuff and) nonsense! **глу́пый;** глуп, -á, -о, foolish, stupid, silly.

глуха́рь, -я́ *m.* capercailzie; deaf person; coach screw. **глухова́тый,** rather deaf, hard of hearing. **глухо́й;** глух, -á, -о, deaf; muffled, confused, indistinct; obscure, vague; voiceless; thick, dense; wild; remote, lonely, deserted; god-forsaken; sealed; blank, blind; buttoned up, done up; not open; late; ~а́я крапи́ва, dead-nettle; **~о́й, ~а́я** *sb.* deaf man, deaf woman. **глухонемо́й,** deaf and dumb; *sb.* deaf mute. **глухота́, -ы́** deafness. **глу́ше,** *comp.* of глухо́й. **глуши́лка, -и,** jamming, jammer. **глуши́тель, -я** *m.* silencer, damper; suppressor; jammer. **глуши́ть,** -шу́ *imp.* (*perf.* за~, о~) stun, stupefy; muffle; dull, deaden, damp; drown, jam; switch off; put out, extinguish; choke; stifle; suppress; soak up, swill. **глушь, -и,** backwoods; solitary place.

глы́ба, -ы, clod; lump, block.

гляде́ть, -яжу́ *imp.* (*perf.* по~, гля́нуть) look, gaze; heed, take notice; look for, seek; show, appear; +за+*instr.* look after, see to; +на+*acc.* look on (to), give on (to), face; take example from, imitate; +*instr.* or *adv.* look, look like; ~ в о́ба, be on one's guard; ~ ко́со на, take a poor view of; гляди́(те), mind (out); (того́ и) гляди́, it looks as if; I'm afraid; at any moment; гля́дя по+*dat.*, depending on; не гля́дя на+*acc.*, unmindful of, heedless of; **~ся,** look at oneself.

гля́нец, -нца, gloss, lustre; polish.

гля́нуть, -ну *perf.* (*imp.* гляде́ть) glance.

глянцеви́тый, glossy, lustrous.

гм, *int.* hm!

гнать, гоню́, го́нишь; гнал, -á, -о *imp.* drive; urge (on); whip up; drive hard; dash, tear; hunt, chase; persecute; turn out; distil; **~ся** за+*instr.* pursue; strive for, strive after; keep up with.

гнев, -а, anger, rage; wrath. **гне́ваться,** -аюсь *imp.* (*perf.* раз~) be angry. **гневи́ть,** -влю́ *imp.* (*perf.* про~) anger, enrage. **гневли́вый,** irascible. **гне́вный,** angry, irate.

гнедо́й, bay.

гнезди́ться, -зжу́сь *imp.* nest, build a nest; roost; have its seat; be lodged. **гнездо́, -á;** *pl.* гнёзда, nest; eyrie; den, lair; brood; cluster; socket; seat; housing. **гнездова́ние, -я,** nesting.

гнести́, -ету́, -етёшь *imp.* oppress, weigh down; press. **гнёт, -а,** press; weight; oppression. **гнету́щий,** oppressive.

гни́да, -ы nit.

гние́ние, -я, decay, putrefaction, rot. **гнило́й;** -ил, -á, -о, rotten; decayed; putrid; corrupt; damp, muggy. **гнить,** -ию́, -иёшь; -ил, -á, -о *imp.* (*perf.* с~), rot, decay; decompose. **гное́ние, -я,** suppuration. **гнои́ть,** -ою́ *imp.* (*perf.* с~) let rot, leave to rot; allow to decay; **~ся,** suppurate, discharge matter. **гной, -я** (-ю), *loc.* -ю́, pus, matter. **гнойни́к, -á,** abscess; ulcer. **гно́йный,** purulent.

гнуса́вить, -влю *imp.* talk, speak, through one's nose. **гнуса́вость, -и,** nasal twang. **гнуса́вый, гнусли́вый,** nasal.

гну́сный; -сен, -сна́, -о, vile, foul.

гну́т|ый, bent; ~ая ме́бель, bentwood furniture. **гнуть,** гну, гнёшь *imp.* (*perf.* со~) bend, bow; drive at, aim at; **~ся**, bend; be bowed; stoop; be flexible. **гнутьё**, -я́, bending.

гнуша́ться, -а́юсь *imp.* (*perf.* по~) disdain; +*gen.* or *instr.* shun; abhor, have an aversion to.

гобеле́н, -а, tapestry.

гобои́ст, -а, oboist. **гобо́й**, -я, oboe.

гове́нье, -я, fasting. **гове́ть**, -е́ю *imp.* fast.

говно́, -а́, shit.

го́вор, -а, sound of voices; murmur, babble; talk, rumour; pronunciation, accent; dialect. **говори́льня**, -и, talking-shop. **говори́ть**, -рю́ *imp.* (*perf.* сказа́ть) speak, talk; say; tell; mean, convey, signify; point, testify; говори́т Москва́! this is Moscow; ~ в по́льзу +*gen.* tell in favour of; support, back; не говоря́ уже́ о+*prep.*, not to mention; не́чего (и) ~, it goes without saying, needless to say; что и ~, it can't be denied; **~ся**; как говори́тся, as they say, as the saying goes. **говорли́вый**, garrulous, talkative. **говору́н**, -а́, **-ру́нья**, -и, talker, chatterer, chatterbox.

говя́дина, -ы, beef. **говя́жий**, beef.

го́гот, -а, cackle; shouts of laughter. **гогота́нье**, -я, cackling. **гогота́ть**, -очу́, -о́чешь *imp.* cackle; laugh aloud, shout with laughter.

год, -а (-у), *loc.* -у́; *pl.* -ы or -а́, *gen.* -о́в or лет, year; *pl.* years, age, time; бе́з ~у неде́ля, only a few days; в ~ы, in the days (of), during; в ~а́х, advanced in years; ~ о́т ~у, every year; из ~а в ~, year in, year out; не по ~а́м, beyond one's years, precocious(ly). **года́ми** *adv.* for years (on end). **годи́на**, -ы, time, period; year.

годи́ться, -жу́сь *imp.* be fit, suitable, suited; do, serve; +в+*nom.* or *acc.* be cut out for, be old enough to be; не годи́тся, it's no good, it won't do; +*inf.* it does not do to, one should not.

годи́чный, lasting a year, a year's; annual, yearly.

го́дный; -ден, -дна́, -о, -ы or -ы́, fit, suitable, valid.

годова́лый, a year old; yearling. **годови́к**, -а́, yearling. **годово́й**, annual, yearly. **годовщи́на**, -ы, anniversary.

гожу́сь etc.: see годи́ться.

гол, -а, goal.

гола́вль, -я́ *m.* chub.

голена́ст|ый, long-legged; **~ые** *sb. pl.* wading birds, Grallatores. **голени́ще**, -а, (boot-)top. **го́лень**, -и, shin.

голла́ндец, -дца, Dutchman. **голла́ндка**, -и, Dutchwoman; tiled stove; jumper. **голла́ндск|ий**, Dutch; ~ая печь, tiled stove; ~ое полотно́, holland.

голова́, -ы́, *acc.* го́лову; *pl.* го́ловы, -о́в, -а́м, head; brain, mind; wits; life; van; *m.* and *f.* person in charge, head; в пе́рвую го́лову, first of all; городско́й ~, mayor; ~ сы́ру, a cheese; на свою́ го́лову, to one's cost; с головы́, per head. **голова́стик**, -а, tadpole. **голо́вка**, -и, head; cap, nose, tip; head-scarf; *pl.* vamp. **головн|о́й**, head; brain, cerebral; leading, advance; ~а́я боль, headache; ~о́й го́лос, head-voice, falsetto; ~о́й мозг, brain, cerebrum; ~о́й убо́р, headgear, headdress. **головокруже́ние**, -я, giddiness, dizziness; vertigo. **головокружи́тельный**, dizzy, giddy. **головоло́мка**, -и, puzzle, riddle, conundrum. **головоло́мный**, puzzling. **головомо́йка**, -и, reprimand, dressing-down, telling-off. **головоно́гие** *sb. pl.* Cephalopoda. **головоре́з**, -а, cut-throat; bandit; blackguard, ruffian, rascal. **головотя́п**, -а, bungler, muddler.

го́лод, -а (-у), hunger; starvation; famine; dearth, acute shortage. **голода́ние**, -я, starvation; fasting. **голода́ть**, -а́ю *imp.* go hungry, hunger, starve; fast, go without food. **голо́дный**; го́лоден, -дна́, -о, -ы or -ы́, hungry; hunger, starvation; meagre, scanty, poor. **голодо́вка**, -и, starvation; hunger-strike.

голоно́гий, bare-legged; bare-foot.

го́лос, -а (-у); *pl.* -а́, -о́в, voice; part; word, opinion; say; vote; во весь ~, at the top of one's voice; пода́ть ~ за +*acc.*, vote for; пра́во ~а, vote, suffrage, franchise; с ~а, by ear. **голоси́стый**, loud-voiced; vociferous; loud. **голоси́ть**, -ошу́ *imp.* sing loudly; cry; wail, keen.

голосло́вный, unsubstantiated, unfounded; unsupported by evidence.
голосова́ние, -я, voting; poll; hitching lifts, hitch-hiking; всео́бщее ~, universal suffrage. **голосова́ть,** -су́ю *imp.* (*perf.* про~) vote; put to the vote, vote on; hitch lifts, hitch-hike. **голосово́й,** vocal.
голошта́нник, -а, ragamuffin.
голубе́ть, -е́ет *imp.* (*perf.* по~) turn blue, show blue. **голубизна́,** -ы́, blueness. **голу́бка,** -и, pigeon; (my) dear, darling. **голуб|о́й,** blue; light blue, pale blue; ~о́е то́пливо, natural gas; ~о́й экра́н, television screen. **голу́бчик,** -а, my dear, my dear fellow; darling. **го́лубь,** -я; *pl.* -и, -е́й *m.* pigeon, dove. **голубя́тник,** -а, pigeon-fancier; dovecote. **голубя́тня,** -и; *gen. pl.* -тен, dovecote, pigeon-loft.
го́лый; гол, -ла́, -ло, naked, bare; poor; unmixed, unadorned; pure, neat. **голытьба́,** -ы́, the poor. **голы́ш,** -а́, naked child, naked person; pauper; pebble, smooth round stone. **голышо́м** *adv.* stark naked. **голя́к,** -а́, beggar, tramp.
гомоге́нный, homogeneous.
го́мон, -а (-у), hubbub. **гомони́ть,** -ню́ *imp.* shout, talk noisily.
гондо́ла, -ы, gondola; car; nacelle.
гоне́ние, -я, persecution. **гони́тель,** -я *m.*, **~ница,** -ы, persecutor. **го́нка,** -и, race; dashing, rushing; haste, hurry. **го́нкий;** -нок, -нка́, -нко, fast, swift; fast-growing.
гонора́р, -а, fee.
го́ночный, racing.
гонча́р, -а́, potter.
го́нщик, -а, racer; drover. **гоню́,** etc.: see гнать. **гоня́ть,** -я́ю *imp.* drive; send on errands; **~ся,** race; +за+ *instr.* chase, pursue, hunt.
гор- *abbr.* in *comb.* of городско́й, го́рный.
гора́, -ы́, *acc.* го́ру; *pl.* го́ры, -а́м, mountain; hill; heap, pile, mass; в го́ру, uphill; по́д гору, downhill.
гора́здо *adv.* much, far, by far.
горб, -а́, *loc.* -у́, hump; protuberance, bulge. **горба́тый,** humpbacked, hunchbacked; ~ нос, hooked nose. **го́рбить,** -блю *imp.* (*perf.* с~) arch, hunch; **~ся,** stoop, become bent. **горбоно́сый,** hook-nosed. **горбу́н,** -а́ *m.*, **горбу́нья,** -и; *gen. pl.* -ний, humpback, hunchback. **горбу́шка,** -и; *gen. pl.* -шек, crust, heel of loaf.
горделйвый, haughty, proud. **горди́ться,** -ржу́сь *imp.* put on airs, be haughty; +*instr.* be proud of, pride oneself on. **го́рдость,** -и, pride. **го́рдый;** горд, -а́, -о, го́рды́, proud. **горды́ня,** -и, pride, arrogance.
го́ре, -я, grief, sorrow; distress; woe; misfortune, trouble. **горева́ть,** -рю́ю *imp.* grieve, mourn.
горе́лка, -и, burner. **горе́лый,** burnt.
горе́ние, -я, burning, combustion; enthusiasm.
го́рестный, sad, sorrowful; pitiful, mournful. **го́ресть,** -и, sorrow, grief; *pl.* afflictions, misfortunes, troubles.
горе́ть, -рю́ *imp.* (*perf.* с~) burn; be on fire, be alight; glitter, shine.
го́рец, -рца, mountain-dweller, highlander.
го́речь, -и, bitterness; bitter taste; bitter stuff.
горизо́нт, -а, horizon; skyline. **горизонта́ль,** -и, horizontal; contour line.
гори́стый, mountainous, hilly. **го́рка,** -и, hill; hillock; steep climb.
горла́н, -а, bawler. **горла́нить,** -ню *imp.* bawl, yell. **горла́стый,** noisy, loud-mouthed. **го́рло,** -а, throat; neck. **горлово́й,** throat; of the throat; guttural; raucous. **го́рлышко,** -а, neck.
горн[1], -а, furnace, forge.
горн[2], -а, bugle. **горни́ст,** -а, bugler.
го́рничная *sb.* maid, chambermaid; stewardess.
горново́й, furnace, forge; *sb.* furnaceman. **горнозаво́дский,** mining and metallurgical. **горнопромы́шленность,** -и, mining industry. **горнопромы́шленный,** mining. **горнорабо́чий** *sb.* miner.
горноста́евый, ermine. **горноста́й,** -я, ermine.
го́рный, mountain; mountainous; mineral; mining; ~ лён, asbestos; ~ хруста́ль, rock crystal.
го́род, -а; *pl.* -а́, town; city; base, home.
городи́ть, -ожу́, -о́дишь *imp.* fence,

enclose; ~ глýпости, talk nonsense; огорóд ~, make a fuss. **городовóй** *sb.* policeman. **городск|óй,** urban; city; municipal; **~áя** лáсточка, (house-) martin. **гóрод-спýтник,** -а, satellite town. **горожáнин,** -а; *pl.* -áне, -áн *m.*, **-жáнка,** -и, town-dweller; townsman, townswoman.

горóх, -а (-у), pea, peas. **горóховый,** pea. **горóшек,** -шка, spots, spotted pattern; души́стый ~, sweet peas; зелёный ~, green peas. **горóшина,** -ы, pea.

горсовéт, -а *abbr.* городскóй совéт, city soviet, town soviet.

гóрсточка, -и, **горсть,** -и; *gen. pl.* -éй, handful.

гортáнный, guttural; laryngeal. **гортáнь,** -и, larynx.

гóрче, *comp.* of гóрький. **горчи́ть,** -чи́т *imp.* taste bitter. **горчи́ца,** -ы, mustard. **горчи́чник,** -а, mustard plaster. **горчи́чница,** -ы, mustard-pot.

горшóк, -шкá, pot; chamber-pot.

гóрький; -рек, -рькá, -о, bitter; rancid; hapless, wretched.

горю́ч|ий, combustible, inflammable; **~ее** *sb.* fuel. **горю́чка,** -и, motor fuel.

горячелóмкий, hot-short. **горя́чий;** -ря́ч, -á, hot; passionate; ardent, fervent; hot-tempered; mettlesome; heated; impassioned; busy; high-temperature.

горячи́ть, -чý *imp.* (*perf.* раз~) excite, irritate; **~ся,** get excited, become impassioned. **горя́чка,** -и, fever; feverish activity; feverish haste; *m.* and *fem.* hothead; firebrand; порóть горя́чку, hurry, bustle; rush headlong. **горя́чность,** -и zeal, fervour, enthusiasm.

гос- *abbr.* in *comb.* of госудáрственный, state. **Госдепартáмент,** -а, State Department. **~издáт,** -а, State Publishing House. **~плáн,** -а, State Planning Commission. **~стрáх,** State Insurance.

гóспиталь, -я *m.* (military) hospital.

гóсподи (*ho-*) *int.* good heavens! good Lord! good gracious! **господи́н,** -а; *pl.* -одá, -óд, -áм, master; gentleman; Mr.; *pl.* gentlemen; ladies and gentlemen; Messrs. **господскóй,** seigniorial, manorial; ~ дом, manor-house; the big house. **господство,** -а, supremacy, dominion, mastery; predominance. **госпóдствовать,** -твую *imp.* hold sway, exercise dominion; predominate, prevail; ~ над+*instr.* command, dominate; tower above. **госпóдствующий,** ruling; predominant, prevailing; commanding. **госпóдь,** гóспода, *voc.* гóсподи *m.* God, the Lord. **госпожá,** -и́, mistress; lady; Mrs., Miss.

ГОСТ, гост, -а *abbr.* госудáрственный общесою́зный стандáрт, All-Union State Standard.

гостевóй, guest, guests'. **гостеприи́мный,** hospitable. **гостеприи́мство,** -а, hospitality. **гости́ная** *sb.* drawing-room, sitting-room; drawing-room suite. **гости́ница,** -ы, hotel; inn. **гости́ный;** ~ двор, arcade, bazaar. **гости́ть,** гощу *imp.* stay, be on a visit. **гость,** -я; *gen. pl.* -éй *m.*, **гóстья,** -и; *gen. pl.* -ий, guest, visitor.

госудáрственный, State, public. **госудáрство,** -а, State. **госудáрыня,** -и, **госудáрь,** -я *m.* sovereign; Your Majesty.

гот, -а, Goth. **готи́ческий,** Gothic; ~ шрифт, black-letter.

готóвить, -влю *imp.* (*perf.* с~) prepare, get ready; train; cook; lay in, store; have in store; **~ся,** get ready; prepare oneself, make preparations; be at hand, brewing, impending, imminent; loom ahead. **готóвность,** -и, readiness, preparedness, willingness. **готóв|ый,** ready, prepared; willing; on the point, on the verge; ready-made, finished; tight, plastered; на всём ~ом, and all found.

гофрирóванный, corrugated; crimped, waved; pleated; goffered. **гофрировáть,** -рýю *perf.* and *imp.* corrugate; wave, crimp; goffer. **гофрирóвка,** -и, corrugation; goffering; waving; waves.

гр. *abbr.* граждани́н, граждáнка, citizen.

граб, -а, hornbeam.

грабёж, -á, robbery; pillage, plunder. **грабитель,** -я *m.* robber. **граби́тельский,** extortionate, exorbitant. **граби́тельство,** -а, robbery. **грáбить,** -блю *imp.* (*perf.* о~) rob, pillage. **гра́бленый**, stolen.

гра́бли, -бель or -блей *pl.* rake.

грабо́вый, hornbeam.

гравёр, **-а**, **гравиро́вщик**, -а, engraver, etcher. **гравёрный**, engraver's, etcher's; engraving, etching.

гра́вий, -я, gravel. **гравийный**, gravel.

гравирова́льный, engraving, etching. **гравирова́ть**, -ру́ю *imp.* (*perf.* вы́~) engrave; etch. **гравиро́вка**, **-и**, engraving, print; etching. **гравю́ра**, -ы, engraving, print; etching; ~ на де́реве, woodcut; ~ на лино́леуме, linocut.

град[1], -а, city, town.

град[2], -а, hail; shower, torrent; volley; ~ом, thick and fast. **гра́дина**, -ы, hailstone.

гради́рня, -и, salt-pan; cooling tower. **гради́ровать**, -рую *perf.* and *imp.* evaporate.

градово́й, hail. **гра́дом**: see град.

градострои́тель, -я *m.* town-planner. **градострои́тельный**, **градострои́тельство**, -а, town(-)planning.

гра́дус, -а, degree; pitch; stage. **гра́дусник**, -а, thermometer. **гра́дусн|ый**, degree; grade; ~ая се́тка, grid.

граждани́н, -а; *pl.* гра́ждане, -дан, **гражда́нка**, **-и**, citizen. **гражда́нский**, civil; citizens'; civic; secular; civilian. **гражда́нство**, -а, citizenship, nationality.

грамза́пись, **-и**, gramophone recording.

гра́мота, -ы, ability to read and write, reading and writing; official document; deed. **гра́мотность**, -и, literacy. **гра́мотный**, literate; grammatically correct; competent.

грампласти́нка, -и, disc, (gramophone) record.

гран, -а; *gen. pl.* гран, grain.

грана́т, -а, pomegranate; garnet. **грана́та**, -ы, shell, grenade. **грана́тник**, -а, pomegranate. **грана́товый**, pomegranate; garnet; rich red.

гране́ние, -я, cutting. **гранёный**, cut, faceted; cut-glass. **грани́льный**, lapidary; diamond-cutting. **грани́льня**, -и; *gen. pl.* -лен, diamond-cutter's workshop. **грани́льщик**, -а, lapidary, diamond-cutter. **грани́ть**, -ню́ *imp.* cut, facet.

грани́ца, -ы, frontier, border; boundary, limit, bound; за грани́цей за грани́цу, abroad. **грани́чить**, -чит *imp.* border; verge.

гра́нка, -и, galley proof, galley, slip (proof).

грань, -и, border, verge; brink; side, facet; edge; period.

граф, -а, count; earl.

графа́, -ы́, column. **гра́фик**, -а, graph; chart; schedule; draughtsman, graphic artist. **гра́фика**, -и, drawing, graphic art; script.

графи́н, -а, carafe; decanter.

графи́ня, -и, countess.

графи́ть, -флю́ *imp.* (*perf.* раз-) rule.

графи́ческий, graphic.

графлёный, ruled.

гра́фство, -а, title of earl or count; county.

грацио́зный, graceful. **гра́ция**, -и, grace.

грач, -а́, rook.

гребёнка, -и, comb; rack; hackle. **гре́бень**, -бня *m.* comb; hackle; crest; ridge. **гребе́ц**, -бца́, rower, oarsman. **гребно́й**, rowing. **гребо́к**, -бка́, stroke; blade. **гребу́**, etc.: see грести́.

грёза, -ы, day-dream, dream. **гре́зить**, -е́жу *imp.* dream.

гре́йдер, -а, grader; unmetalled road.

грек, -а, Greek.

гре́лка, -и, heater; hot-water bottle, foot-warmer.

греме́ть, -млю́ *imp.* (*perf.* про~) thunder, roar; rumble; peal; rattle; resound, ring out. **грему́ч|ий**, roaring, rattling; fulminating; ~ий газ, fire-damp; ~ая змея́, rattlesnake; ~ая ртуть, fulminate of mercury; ~ий сту́день, nitro-gelatine. **гремýшка**, **-и**, rattle; sleigh-bell.

грести́, -ебу́, -ебёшь; грёб, -бла́ *imp.* row; scull, paddle; rake.

греть, -е́ю *imp.* warm, heat; give out heat; **~ся**, warm oneself, bask.

грех, -а́, sin. **грехо́вный**, sinful. **грехопаде́ние**, -я, the Fall; fall.

гре́цкий, Greek, Grecian; ~ оре́х, walnut. **греча́нка**, -и, Greek. **гре́ческий**, Greek, Grecian.

гречи́ха, -и, buckwheat. **гре́чневый**, buckwheat.

греши́ть, -шу́ *imp*. (*perf*. по~, со~) sin. **гре́шник**, -а, **-ница**, -ы, sinner. **гре́шный**; -шен, -шна́, -о, sinful; culpable.

гриб, -а́, mushroom, toadstool, fungus. **грибно́й**, mushroom.

гри́ва, -ы, mane; wooded ridge; spit, shelf, sandbank.

гри́венник, -а, ten-copeck piece.

грим, -а, make-up; grease-paint. **гримёр**, -а, **-ёрша**, -и, make-up man, woman. **гримирова́ть**, -ру́ю *imp*. (*perf*. за~, на~) make up; +*instr*. make up as; **~ся**, make up. **гримиро́вка**, -и, making up, make-up.

гриф[1], -а, gryphon; vulture.

гриф[2], -а, finger-board.

гриф[3], -а, seal, stamp.

гри́фель, -я *m*. slate-pencil. **гри́фельн|ый**, slate; ~ая доска́, slate.

гроб, -а, *loc*. -у́; *pl*. -ы́ or -а́, coffin; grave. **гробану́ть**, -ну́, -нёшь *perf*. damage, break; **~ся**, have an accident, be killed in an accident. **гробово́й**, coffin; deathly, sepulchral. **гробовщи́к**, -а́, coffin-maker; undertaker.

гроза́, -ы́; *pl*. -ы, (thunder-)storm; calamity, disaster; terror; threats.

гроздь, -и; *pl*. -ди or -дья, -де́й or -дьев, cluster, bunch.

грози́ть(ся, -ожу(сь *imp*. (*perf*. по~, при~) threaten; make a threatening gesture; ~ кулако́м+*dat*. shake one's fist at. **гро́зный**; -зен, -зна́, -о, menacing, threatening; dread, terrible; formidable; stern, severe. **грозово́й**, storm, thunder.

гром, -а; *pl*. -ы, -о́в, thunder.

грома́да, -ы, mass; bulk, pile; heaps. **грома́дина**, -ы, vast object. **грома́дный**, huge, vast, enormous, colossal.

громи́ть, -млю́ *imp*. destroy; smash, rout; thunder, fulminate, against. **гро́мкий**; -мок, -мка́, -о, loud; famous; notorious; fine-sounding, specious. **гро́мко** *adv*. loud(ly); aloud. **громкоговори́тель**, -я *m*. loud-speaker. **громово́й**, thunder, of thunder; thunderous, deafening; crushing, smashing.

громогла́сный, loud; loud-voiced; public, open.

громозди́ть, -зжу́ *imp*. (*perf*. на~), pile up, heap up; **~ся**, tower; clamber up. **громо́здкий**, cumbersome, unwieldy.

гро́мче, *comp*. of гро́мкий, гро́мко.

громыха́ть, -а́ю *imp*. rumble, clatter.

гроссме́йстер, -а, grand master.

гро́хать, -аю *imp*., **гро́хнуть**, -ну *perf*. crash, bang; drop with a crash, bang down; **~ся**, fall with a crash. **гро́хот**[1], -а, crash, din.

гро́хот[2], -а, screen, sieve, riddle.

грохота́ть, -очу́, -о́чешь *imp*. (*perf*. про~) crash; roll, rumble; thunder, roar; roar (with laughter).

грош, -а́, half-copeck piece; farthing, brass farthing, penny. **грошо́вый**, dirt-cheap; cheap, shoddy; insignificant, trifling.

грубе́ть, -е́ю *imp*. (*perf*. за~, о~, по~) grow coarse, coarsen; become rough. **груби́ть**, -блю́ *imp*. (*perf*. на~) be rude. **грубия́н**, -а, boor. **грубия́нить**, -ню *imp*. (*perf*. на~) be rude; behave boorishly. **гру́бо** *adv*. coarsely, roughly; crudely; rudely. **гру́бость**, -и, rudeness; coarseness; grossness; rude remark. **грубый**; груб, -а́, -о, coarse; rough; crude, rude; gross, flagrant.

гру́да, -ы, heap, pile.

груди́на, -ы, breastbone. **груди́нка**, -и, brisket; breast. **грудн|о́й**, breast, chest, pectoral; ~а́я жа́ба, angina pectoris; ~о́й ребёнок, infant in arms. **грудобрю́шн|ый**; ~ая прегра́да, diaphragm. **грудь**, -и́ or -и, *instr*. -ю, *loc*. -и́; *pl*. -и, -е́й, breast; bosom, bust; chest; (shirt-)front.

груз, -а, weight; load, cargo, freight; burden; bob. **грузи́ло**, -а, sinker.

грузи́н, -а; *gen*. *pl*. -и́н, **грузи́нка**, -и, Georgian. **грузи́нский**, Georgian.

грузи́ть, -ужу́, -у́зишь *imp*. (*perf*. за~, на~, по~) load, lade, freight; **~ся**, load, take on cargo. **гру́зка**, -и, lading. **гру́зный**; -зен, -зна́, -о, weighty, bulky; unwieldy; corpulent. **грузови́к**, -а́, lorry, truck. **грузово́й**, goods, cargo, freight, load. **грузопото́к**, -а, freight traffic, goods traffic.

грузотакси́ *n. indecl.* taxi-lorry. **гру́з-чик,** -а, stevedore, docker; loader.

грунт, -а, ground, soil, earth; subsoil; bottom; priming, primer. **грунтова́ть,** -ту́ю *imp.* (*perf.* за~) prime. **грунто́в-ка,** -и, priming, ground coat, ground. **грунтово́й,** soil, earth, ground; subsoil; bottom; priming; unpaved, unmetalled.

гру́ппа, -ы, group. **группирова́ть,** -ру́ю *imp.* (*perf.* с~), group, classify; **~ся,** group, form groups. **группиро́вка,** -и, grouping; classification; group. **груп-пово́й,** group; team.

грусти́ть, -ущу́ *imp.* grieve, mourn; +по+*dat.* pine for. **гру́стный;** -тен, -тна́, -о, sad; melancholy; grievous, distressing. **грусть,** -и, sadness, melancholy.

гру́ша, -и, pear; pear-shaped thing. **гру́шевый,** pear; ~ компо́т, stewed pears.

гры́жа, -и, hernia, rupture. **гры́жевый,** hernial; ~ банда́ж, truss.

грызня́, -и́, dog-fight, fight; squabble. **грызть,** -зу́, -зёшь; грыз *imp.* (*perf.* раз~) gnaw; nibble; nag; devour, consume; **~ся,** fight; squabble, bicker. **грызу́н,** -а́, rodent.

ГРЭС *abbr.* Госуда́рственная райо́нная электроста́нция, State District power-station.

гряда́, -ы́; *pl.* -ы, -а́м, ridge; bed; row, series; bank. **гря́дка,** -и, (flower-)bed.

гряду́щий, approaching; coming, future; to come; на сон ~, at bedtime; last thing at night.

грязево́й, mud. **грязни́ть,** -ню́ *imp.* (*perf.* за~, на~) dirty, soil; sully, besmirch; make a mess, be untidy; **~ся,** become dirty. **гря́зный;** -зен, -зна́, -о, muddy, mud-stained; dirty; untidy, slovenly; filthy; refuse, garbage, slop. **грязь,** -и, *loc.* -и́, mud; dirt, filth; *pl.* mud; mud-baths, mud-cure.

гря́нуть, -ну *perf.* burst out, crash out, ring out; strike up. **~ся,** crash (down).

грясти́, -яду́, -ядёшь *imp.* approach.

ГСП (*ge-espé*) *abbr.* городска́я слу-жёбная по́чта, urban postal service.

губа́, -ы́; *pl.* -ы, -а́м, lip; *pl.* pincers. **губа́стый,** thick-lipped.

губерна́тор, -а, governor. **губе́рния,** -и, province. **губе́рнский,** provincial; ~ секрета́рь, Provincial Secretary (12th grade: see чин).

губи́тельный, destructive, ruinous; baneful, pernicious. **губи́ть,** -блю́, -бишь *imp.* (*perf.* по~) destroy; be the undoing of; ruin, spoil; **~ся,** be destroyed; be wasted.

гу́бка, -и, sponge.

губн|о́й, lip; labial; ~а́я гармо́ника, harmonica, mouth organ.

гу́бчатый, porous, spongy; ~ каучу́к, foam rubber.

гуверна́нтка, -и, governess. **гувернёр,** -а, tutor.

гугу́; ни ~! not a sound! mum's the word!

гуде́ние, -я, hum; drone; buzzing; hooting, hoot. **гуде́ть,** гужу́ *imp.* (*perf.* про~) hum; drone; buzz; hoot. **гудо́к,** -дка́, hooter, siren, horn, whistle; hoot, hooting.

гудро́н, -а, tar. **гудрони́ровать,** -рую *perf.* and *imp.* (*perf.* also за~), tar. **гудро́нный,** tar, tarred.

гул, -а, rumble; hum; boom. **гу́лкий;** -лок, -лка́, -о, resonant; booming, rumbling.

гуля́нье, -я; *gen. pl.* -ний, walking, going for a walk, walk; fête; outdoor party. **гуля́ть,** -я́ю *imp.* (*perf.* по~) walk, stroll; go for a walk, take a walk; have time off, not be working; make merry, carouse, have a good time; +с+*instr.* go with.

ГУМ, -а *abbr.* Госуда́рственный универса́льный магази́н, State department store.

гумани́зм, -а, humanism. **гумани́ст,** -а, humanist. **гуманита́рный,** of the humanities; humane. **гума́нный,** humane.

гумно́, -а́; *pl.* -а, -мен or -мён, -ам, threshing-floor; barn.

гурт, -а́, herd, drove; flock. **гуртов-щи́к,** -а́, herdsman; drover. **гурто́м** *adv.* wholesale; in bulk; together; in a body, en masse.

гуса́к, -а́, gander.
гу́сеница, -ы, caterpillar; (caterpillar) track. **гу́сеничный**, track, tracked.
гусёнок, -нка; *pl.* -ся́та, -ся́т, gosling.
гуси́н|ый, goose; ~ая ко́жа, goose-flesh; ~ые ла́пки, crow's-feet.
густе́ть, -е́ет *imp.* (*perf.* за~, по~), thicken, get thicker. **густо́й**; густ, -а́, -о, thick, dense; deep, rich. **густота́**, -ы, thickness, density; deepness, richness.
гусы́ня, -и, goose. **гусь**, -я; *pl.* -и, -е́й *m.* goose. **гусько́м** *adv.* in single file. **гуся́тина**, -ы, goose.
гутали́н, -а, shoe-polish, boot-polish.
гу́ща, -и, dregs, lees, grounds, sediment; thicket; thick, centre, heart. **гу́ще**, *comp.* of густо́й. **гущина́**, -ы́, thickness; thicket.
гэ *n. indecl.* the letter г.
ГЭС *abbr.* гидроэлектроста́нция, hydro-electric power station.

Д

д *letter*: see дэ.
д. *abbr.* дере́вня, village; дом, house.
да *conj.* and; but; да (ещё), and what is more; да (и), and besides; да и то́лько, and that's all.
да *part.* yes; yes? really? indeed; well; +3rd pers. of vb., may, let; да здра́вствует . . ! long live . . !
дава́ть, даю́, -ёшь *imp.* of дать; **дава́й(те)**, let us, let's; come on; **~ся**, yield; let oneself be caught; come easy; не ~ся+*dat.* dodge, evade; ру́сский язы́к ему́ даётся легко́, Russian comes easy to him.
да́веча *adv.* lately, recently.
дави́ло, -а, press. **дави́ть**, -влю́, -вишь *imp.* (*perf.* за~, по~, раз~, у~) press; squeeze; weigh, lie heavy; crush; oppress; trample; strangle; **~ся**, choke; hang oneself. **да́вка**, -и, crushing, squeezing; throng, crush. **давле́ние**, -я, pressure.
да́вний, ancient; of long standing. **давно́** *adv.* long ago; for a long time; long since. **давнопроше́дший**, remote; long past; pluperfect. **да́вность**, -и, antiquity; remoteness; long standing; prescription. **давны́м-давно́** *adv.* long long ago, ages ago.
дади́м, etc.: see дать. **даю́**, etc.: see дава́ть.
да́же *adv.* even.
да́лее *adv.* further; и так ~, and so on, etc. **далёкий**; -ёк, -а́, -ёко́, distant, remote; far (away). **далёко́** *adv.* far; far off; by a long way; ~ за, long after; ~ не, far from. **даль**, -и, *loc.* -и́, distance.
да́льн|ий, distant, remote; long; без ~их слов, without more ado; ~ Восто́к, the Far East. **дальнозо́ркий**, long-sighted. **да́льность**, -и, distance; range. **да́льше** *adv.* farther; further; then, next; longer.
дам, etc.: see дать.
да́ма, -ы lady; partner; queen.
да́мба, -ы, dike, embankment; dam.
да́мка, -и, king. **да́мский**, ladies'.
да́нные *sb. pl.* data; facts, information; qualities, gifts; grounds. **да́нный**, given, present; in question, this. **дань**, -и, tribute; debt.
дар, -а; *pl.* -ы́, gift; donation; grant. **даре́ние**, -я, donation. **дари́тель**, -я *m.* donor. **дари́ть**, -рю́, -ришь *imp.* (*perf.* по~)+*dat.* give, make a present.
дармое́д, -а, **-е́дка**, -и, parasite, sponger, scrounger. **дармое́дничать**, -аю *imp.* sponge, scrounge.
ДАРМС *abbr.* дрейфу́ющая автомати́ческая радиометеорологи́ческая ста́нция, drifting radio weather-station.
дарова́ние, -я, gift, talent. **дарова́ть**, -ру́ю *perf.* and *imp.* grant, confer. **дарови́тый**, gifted, talented. **дарово́й**, free, gratuitous. **да́ром** *adv.* free, gratis; in vain, to no purpose.

да́та, -ы, date.
дта́ельный, dative.
дати́ровать, -рую *perf.* and *imp.* date.
да́тский, Danish. **датча́нин,** -а; *pl.* -а́не, -а́н, **датча́нка,** -и, Dane.
дать, дам, дашь, даст, дади́м; дал, -а́, да́ло́ *perf.* (*imp.* дава́ть) give; administer; grant; let; ~ взаймы́, lend; ~ газ, step on the gas; ~ доро́гу, make way; ~ кля́тву, take an oath; ~ нача́ло+*dat.* give rise to; ~ сло́во, give one's word; +*dat.* give the floor; ~ ход+*dat.* set in motion, get going; **~ся** *perf.* of дава́ться.
да́ча, -и, dacha; на да́че, in the country; на да́чу, (in)to the country. **да́чник,** -а, (holiday) visitor.
ДВ (*devé*) *abbr.* дли́нные во́лны, long waves; длинново́лновый, long-wave.
два *m.* and *n.*, **две** *f.*, двух, -ум, -умя́, -ух, two; ~-три, two or three, a couple; ка́ждые ~ дня, every other day. **двадцатиле́тний,** twenty-year; twenty-year-old. **двадца́т|ый,** twentieth; ~ые го́ды, the twenties. **два́дцать,** -и́, *instr.* -ью́, twenty. **два́дцатью** *adv.* twenty times. **два́жды** *adv.* twice; double. **двена́дцатый,** twelfth. **двена́дцать,** -и, twelve.
дверн|о́й, door; ~а́я коро́бка, door-frame. **две́рца,** -ы; *gen. pl.* -рец, door, hatch. **дверь,** -и, *loc.* -и́; *pl.* -и, -е́й, *instr.* -я́ми or -ьми́, door; *pl.* doors, door.
двёсти, двухсо́т, -умста́м, -умяста́ми, -ухста́х, two hundred.
дви́гатель, -я *m.* engine, motor; (prime) mover, motive force. **дви́гательный,** motive; motor. **дви́гать,** -аю or -и́жу *imp.*, **дви́нуть,** -ну *perf.* move; set in motion, get going; advance, further; **~ся,** move; advance; start, get started. **движе́ние,** -я, movement; motion; exercise; flow; traffic; promotion, advancement; impulse; железнодоро́жное ~, train service. **дви́жимость,** -и, movables, chattels; personal property. **дви́жимый,** movable; moved, prompted, activated. **дви́жущий,** motive; moving; driving.
двое, -и́х, two; two pairs.
двое- in *comb.*, two; double. **двоебо́рец,** -рца, competitor in double event. **~бо́рье,** -я, double event. **~ду́шие,** -я, duplicity, double-dealing. **~ду́шный,** two-faced. **~же́нец,** -нца, **~му́жница,** -ы, bigamist. **~жёнство,** -а, **~мужие,** -я, bigamy. **~то́чие,** -я, colon.
двои́ть, -ою́ *imp.* (*perf.* вз~) double; divide into two; **~ся,** divide in two; appear double. **двои́чный,** binary. **дво́йка,** -и, two; figure 2; No. 2; pair-oar. **двойни́к,** -а́, double; twin. **двойно́й,** double, twofold; binary. **дво́йня,** -и; *gen. pl.* -о́ен, twins. **дво́йственный,** double-dealing, two-faced; dual; bipartite.
двор, -а́, yard; courtyard; homestead; court; на ~е́, out of doors, outside; при ~е́, at court. **дворе́ц,** -рца́, palace. **дворе́цкий** *sb.* butler; major-domo. **дво́рник,** -а, dvornik, yardman; windscreen-wiper. **дво́рницк|ий,** dvornik's; **~ая** *sb.* dvornik's lodge. **дво́рня,** -и, servants, menials. **дворо́вый,** yard, courtyard; *sb.* house-serf. **дворцо́вый,** palace. **дворяни́н,** -а; *pl.* -я́не, -я́н, **дворя́нка,** -и, member of the nobility or gentry. **дворя́нство,** -а, nobility, gentry.
двою́родн|ый; ~ый брат, ~ая сестра́, (first) cousin; ~ый дя́дя, ~ая тётка, first cousin once removed. **двоя́кий,** double; ambiguous; in two ways, of two kinds. **двояко-,** double-, bi-, di-.
дву-, двух-, in *comb.* two-; bi-, di-; double; diplo-. **двубо́ртный,** double-breasted. **~гла́вый,** two-headed. **~гла́сный** *sb.* diphthong. **~гри́венный** *sb.* twenty-copeck piece. **~жи́льный,** strong; hardy; tough. **~зна́чный,** two-digit. **~ли́кий,** two-faced. **~ли́чие,** -я, double-dealing, duplicity. **~ли́чный,** two-faced; hypocritical. **~пла́нный,** two-dimensional. **~по́лый,** bisexual. **~ру́чный,** two-handed; two-handled. **~ру́шник,** -а, double-dealer. **~сло́жный,** disyllabic. **~сме́нный** in two shifts, two-shift. **~смы́сленный,** ambiguous, equivocal. **~(х)спа́льный,** double. **сторо́нний** double-sided; two-way; bilateral. **~хато́мный,** diatomic. **~хгоди́чный,** two-year. **~хкра́сочный,** two-colour;

two-tone. **~хле́тний,** two-year; two--year-old; biennial. **~хме́стный,** two--seater; two-berth. **~хмото́рный,** twin-engined, two-engined. **~хпала́тный,** bicameral. **~хсотле́тие,** -я, bicentenary. **~хсо́тый,** two-hundredth. **~хта́ктный,** two-beat; two--stroke. **~хъя́русный,** two-layer, two-storey, two-tier, double-deck; two-lever. **~хэта́жный,** two-storey; double-deck. **~чле́н,** -а, binomial. **~язы́чный,** bilingual.

деба́ты, -ов *pl.* debate.

де́бет, -а, debit. **дебетова́ть,** -ту́ю *perf.* and *imp.* debit.

деби́т, -а, discharge, flow, yield, output.

де́бри, -ей *pl.* jungle; thickets; the wilds; maze, labyrinth.

дебю́т, -а, début; opening.

де́ва, -ы, maid, maiden; girl; spinster; Virgo; ста́рая ~, old maid.

девальва́ция, -и, devaluation.

дева́ть(ся, -а́ю(сь *imp.* of деть(ся.

деви́з, -а, motto; device.

деви́ца, -ы, spinster; girl. **деви́ческий, де́вич|ий,** girlish, maidenly; ~ья фами́лия, maiden name. **де́вка,** -и, girl, wench, lass; tart, whore. **де́вочка,** -и, (little) girl. **де́вственник,** -а, **-ица,** -ы, virgin. **де́вственный,** virgin; virginal, innocent. **де́вушка,** -и, girl; maid.

девяно́сто, -а, ninety. **девяно́стый,** ninetieth. **де́вятеро,** -ы́х, nine; nine pairs. **девятисо́тый,** nine-hundredth. **девя́тка,** -и, nine; figure 9; No. 9; group of nine. **девятна́дцать,** -и, nineteen. **девя́тый,** ninth. **де́вять,** -и́, *instr.* -ью́, nine. **девятьсо́т** -тисо́т, -тиста́м, -тьюста́ми, -тиста́х, nine hundred. **де́вятью** *adv.* nine times.

дёготь, -гтя, tar, coal-tar, pitch. **дёгтебето́н,** -а, tarmac, tar concrete. **дегтя́рный,** tar, coal-tar, pitch; tarry.

дед, -а, grandfather; grandad, grandpa. **де́довский,** grandfather's; old-world; old-fashioned. **де́душка,** -и, grandfather; grandad.

дееприча́стие, -я, gerund, adverbial participle.

дежу́рить, -рю *imp.* be on duty, be in (constant) attendance. **дежу́рный,** duty; on duty. **дежу́рство,** -а, (being on) duty.

де́йственный, efficacious; effective.

де́йствие, -я, action; operation; activity; functioning; effect; act; под ~м under the influence. **действи́тельно** *adv.* really; indeed. **действи́тельность,** -и, reality; realities; conditions; validity; efficacy; в действи́тельности, in reality, in fact. **действи́тельный,** real, actual; true, authentic; valid, efficacious; effective; active; ~ та́йный сове́тник ~ ста́тский сове́тник, Actual Privy Councillor (2nd grade), Actual State Councillor (4th grade: see чин). **де́йствовать,** -твую *imp.* (*perf.* по~) affect, have an effect; act; work, function; operate; +*instr.* use; не ~, be out of order, not be working. **де́йствующ|ий,** active; in force; working; ~ее лицо́, character; active participant; ~ие ли́ца, dramatis personae, cast.

де́ка, -и, sounding-board.

декабри́ст, -а, Decembrist. **дека́брь,** -я́ *m.* December. **дека́брьский,** December.

дека́да, -ы, ten days; (ten-day) festival.

дека́н, -а, dean. **декана́т,** -а, office of dean.

деклама́тор, -а, reciter, declaimer. **деклама́ция,** -и, recitation, declamation. **деклами́ровать,** -рую *imp.* (*perf.* про~), recite, declaim.

декорати́вный, decorative, ornamental. **декора́тор,** -а, decorator; scene--painter. **декора́ция,** -и, scenery, décor; window-dressing.

де́ланный, artificial, forced, affected. **де́лать,** -аю *imp.* (*perf.* с~) make; do; give, produce; ~ вид, pretend, feign; ~ предложе́ние, propose; ~ честь + *dat.* honour; do credit to; **~ся,** become, get, grow; happen; be going on; break out, appear.

делёж, -а́, **делёжка,** -и, sharing, division; partition. **деле́ние,** -я, division; point, degree, unit.

деле́ц, -льца́, business man, dealer; smart operator.

дели́мое *sb.* dividend. **дели́мость,** -и, divisibility. **дели́тель,** -я *m.* divisor.

дели́ть, -лю́, -лишь *imp.* (*perf.* по~, раз~) divide; share; ~ шесть нá три, divide six by three; **~ся,** divide; be divisible; +*instr.* share; communicate, impart.

дéло, -а; *pl.* ~á, business; affair, affairs; cause; occupation; matter; point; fact; deed; thing; case, action; file, dossier; battle fighting; в сáмом дéле, really, indeed; ~ в том, the point is; в тóм-то и ~, that's just the point; ~ за вáми, it's up to you; как (вáши) делá? how are things going? how are you getting on?; на сáмом дéле, in actual fact, as a matter of fact; по дéлу, по делáм, on business; то и ~, continually, time and again. **делови́тый,** business-like, efficient. **деловóй,** business, work; business-like. **дéльный,** efficient, business-like; sensible, practical.

дельфи́н, -а, dolphin.

демокрáт, -а, democrat; plebeian. **демократизи́ровать,** -рую *perf.* and *imp.* democratize. **демократи́ческий,** democratic; plebeian. **демокрáтия,** -и, democracy; common people, lower classes.

демонстрáция, -и, demonstration; (public) showing; display, show.

дендрáрий, -я, arboretum.

дéнежн|ый, monetary; money; moneyed; ~ый перевóд, money order, postal order; ~ая рефóрма, currency reform; ~ый штраф, fine.

дéну, etc.: see деть.

день, дня *m.* day; afternoon; днём, in the afternoon; на днях, the other day; one of these days; чéрез ~, every other day.

дéньги, -нег, -ьгáм *pl.* money.

департáмент, -а, department.

депутáт, -а, deputy; delegate. **депутáция, -и,** deputation.

дёргать, -аю *imp.* (*perf.* дёрнуть) pull, tug; pull out; harass pester; +*instr.* move sharply, jerk shrug; **~ся,** twitch; jerk; move sharply.

дергáч, -á, corncrake, landrail.

деревенéть, -éю *imp.* (*perf.* за~, о~) grow stiff, grow numb. **деревéнский,** village; rural, country. **дерéвня, -и**; *pl.* -и, -вéнь, -вня́м, village; the country. **дéрево, -а**; *pl.* -éвья, -ьев, tree; wood. **деревýшка, -и,** hamlet. **деревя́нный,** wood; wooden; expressionless, dead; dull.

держáва, -ы, power; orb. **держáвный,** holding supreme power, sovereign; powerful. **держáть, -жý, -жишь** *imp.* hold; hold up, support; keep; ~ корректýру read proofs; ~ пари́, bet; ~ себя́, behave; ~ экзáмен, take an examination; **~ся,** hold; be held up, be supported; keep, stay, be; hold oneself; behave; last; hold together; hold out, stand firm, hold one's ground; +*gen.* keep to; adhere to, stick to; ~ся на ни́точке, hang by a thread.

дерзáние, -я, daring. **дерзáть, -áю** *imp.*, **дерзнýть, -нý, -нёшь** *perf.* dare. **дéрзкий,** impertinent, impudent, cheeky; insolent; daring, audacious. **дерзновéнный,** audacious, daring. **дéрзость,** -и, impertinence; cheek; rudeness; insolence; daring, audacity.

дёрн, -а (-у), turf. **дернóвый,** turf. **дерновáть, -нýю** *imp.* turf, edge with turf.

дёрнуть(ся, -ну(сь *perf.* of дёргать(ся.

дерý, etc.: see драть.

десáнт, -а, landing; landing force. **десáнтный,** landing.

десна́, -ы́; *pl.* дёсны, -сен, gum.

десятернóй, tenfold. **дéсятеро, -ы́х,** ten. **десятилéтие, -я,** decade; tenth anniversary. **десятилéтка, -и,** ten-year (secondary) school. **десятилéтний,** ten-year, decennial; ten-year-old. **десяти́чный,** decimal. **деся́тка, -и,** ten; No. 10; group of ten; ten-rouble note. **деся́ток, -тка,** ten; ten years, decade. **деся́тник, -а,** foreman. **деся́тский** *sb.* peasant policeman. **деся́тый,** tenth. **дéсять, -и́,** *instr.* -ью́, ten. **дéсятью** *adv.* ten times.

дет- *abbr.* in *comb.* of дéтский, children's. **детдóм, -а,** children's home. **~сáд, -а,** kindergarten, nursery school.

детáль, -и, detail; part, component. **детáльный,** detailed; minute.

детворá, -ы́, children. **детёныш, -а,** young animal; cub, whelp, etc.; *pl.*

young. **де́ти,** -те́й, -тям, -тьми́, -тях *pl.* children.

де́тская *sb.* nursery. **де́тский,** child's, children's; childish. **де́тство,** -а, childhood.

деть, де́ну *perf.* (*imp.* дева́ть) put; куда́ ты дел моё перо́? what have you done with my pen?; **~ся,** get to, disappear to; куда́ она́ де́лась? what has become of her?

дефи́с, -а, hyphen; писа́ть че́рез ~, hyphen, hyphenate.

дефици́т, -а, deficit; shortage, deficiency. **дефици́тный,** showing a loss; in short supply; scarce.

десима́льный, decimal.

дешеве́ть, -е́ет *imp.* (*perf.* по~), fall in price, get cheaper. **дешеви́зна,** -ы, cheapness; low price. **деше́вле,** *comp.* of дёшево, дешёвый. **дёшево** *adv.* cheap, cheaply; lightly. **дешёвый;** дёшев, -а́, -о, cheap; empty, worthless.

дешифри́ровать, -рую *perf.* and *imp.* decipher, decode. **дешифро́вка,** -и, decipherment, deciphering, decoding.

дея́ние, -я, act, deed. **де́ятель,** -я *m.*; госуда́рственный ~, statesman; ~ нау́ки, scientific worker, scientist; обще́ственный ~, public figure. **де́ятельность,** -и, activity; activities; work; operation. **де́ятельный,** active, energetic.

дже́мпер, -а, jumper, pullover, jersey.

джу́нгли, -ей *pl.* jungle.

диама́т, -а *abbr.* диалекти́ческий материали́зм, dialectical materialism.

диапазо́н, -а, diapason; range; compass; band.

диапозити́в, -а, slide, transparency.

дива́н, -а, sofa; divan.

диверса́нт, -а, saboteur. **диверсио́нный,** diversionary; sabotage, wrecking. **диве́рсия,** -и, diversion; sabotage.

ди́вный, amazing; marvellous, wonderful. **ди́во,** -а, wonder, marvel.

дие́з, -а, sharp.

ди́зель, -я *m.* diesel; diesel engine. **ди́зельный,** diesel.

дика́рь, -я́ *m.*, **дика́рка,** -и, savage; barbarian; shy person. **ди́кий,** wild; savage; shy, unsociable; queer absurd; fantastic, preposterous, ridiculous. **дикобра́з,** -а, porcupine. **дико́вина,** -ы, marvel, wonder. **дикорасту́щий,** wild. **ди́кость,** -и, wildness, savagery; shyness, unsociableness; absurdity, queerness.

дикта́нт, -а, dictation. **диктова́ть,** -ту́ю *imp.* (*perf.* про~) dictate. **дикто́вка,** -и, dictation. **ди́ктор,** -а, announcer.

дилижа́нс, -а, stage-coach.

ди́на, -ы, dyne.

диноза́вр, -а, dinosaur.

дипло́м, -а, diploma; degree; degree work, research; pedigree. **дипломи́рованный,** graduate; professionally qualified, certificated, diplomaed. **дипло́мный,** diploma, degree.

директи́ва, -ы, instructions; directions, directives.

дирижёр, -а, conductor. **дирижи́ровать,** -рую *imp.*+*instr.* conduct.

диск, -а, disc, disk; plate; dial; discus.

ди́скант, -а, treble.

дискре́тность, -и, discreteness, discontinuity. **дискре́тн|ый,** discrete; digital; ~ая маши́на, digital computer.

дискуссио́нный, discussion, debating; debatable, open to question. **диску́ссия,** -и, discussion, debate. **дискути́ровать,** -рую *perf.* and *imp.* discuss, debate.

диспансе́р, -а, clinic, (health) centre, dispensary.

диспе́тчер, -а, controller, dispatcher. **диспе́тчерская** *sb.* controller's office; control tower.

дистанцио́нн|ый, distance, distant, remote; remote-control; ~ый взрыва́тель, time fuse; ~ое управле́ние, remote control. **диста́нция,** -и, distance; range; division, region, sector.

дитя́, -я́ти; *pl.* де́ти, -е́й *n.* child; baby.

дифтери́т, -а, **дифтери́я,** -и, diphtheria.

дича́ть, -а́ю *imp.* (*perf.* о~) grow wild; become unsociable; run wild. **дичи́на,** -ы, game. **дичи́ться,** -чу́сь *imp.* be shy; +*gen.* shun, fight shy of. **дичь,** -и, *loc.* -и́, game; wildfowl; wilderness, wilds.

ДК (*deká*) *abbr.* Дворе́ц культу́ры, Дом культу́ры, Palace (House) of Culture.

длина́, -ы́, length; длино́й, in length, long. **дли́нный**; -нен, -нна́, -о, long; lengthy. **дли́тельность**, -и, duration. **дли́тельный**, long, protracted, long-drawn-out. **дли́ться**, -и́тся *imp.* (*perf.* про~), last, be protracted.

для *prep.*+*gen.* for; for the sake of; to; of; ~ ви́ду, for the sake of appearances; вре́дно ~ дете́й, bad for children; высо́к ~ свои́х лет, tall for his age; непроница́емый ~ воды́, waterproof, impervious to water; ~ того́, что́бы . ., in order to . .; э́то ~ вас, this is for you; э́то типи́чно ~ них, it is typical of them.

дм *abbr.* дециме́тр, decimetre.

днева́льный *sb.* orderly, man on duty. **дневни́к**, -а́, diary, journal. **дневн|о́й**, day; daylight; day's, daily; ~а́я сме́на, day shift; ~о́й спекта́кль, matinée. **днём** *adv.* in the day-time, by day; in the afternoon. **дни**, etc.: see день.

ДНК (*de-enká*) *abbr.* дезоксирибонуклеи́новая кислота́, DNA.

дно, дна; *pl.* до́нья, -ьев, bottom.

до *n. indecl.* C; doh.

до *prep.*+*gen.* to, up to; as far as; until, till; before; to the point of; under; about, approximately; with regard to, concerning; де́ти до пяти́ лет, children under five; до бо́ли, until it hurt(s); до войны́, before the war; до на́шей э́ры, B.C.; до сих пор, up to now, till now, hitherto; до тех пор, till then, before; до того́, как, before; до того́, что, to such an extent that, to the point where; мне не до, I don't feel like, I'm not in the mood for; от Ленингра́да до Москвы́, from Leningrad to Moscow; что до меня́, as far as I am concerned; ю́бка до коле́н, knee-length skirt.

до- *pref.* up (to); pre-; sub- in *comb.* I. with *vbs.* etc. expresses completion of action, indicates that action is carried to a certain point, expresses supplementary action; with *refl. vbs.* expresses eventual attainment of object, or continuation of action with injurious consequences; II. with *adjs.* indicates priority in time sequence.

доба́вить, -влю *perf.*, **добавля́ть**, -я́ю *imp.* (+*acc.* or *gen.*) add. **доба́вка**, -и, addition; second helping. **добавле́ние**, -я, addition; appendix, addendum, supplement; extra. **доба́вочный**, additional, supplementary; extra; extension, booster.

добега́ть, -а́ю *imp.*, **добежа́ть**, -егу́ *perf.*+до+*gen.* run to, run as far as; reach.

добела́ *adv.* to white heat, white-hot; clean, white.

добива́ть, -а́ю *imp.*, **доби́ть**, -бью́, -бьёшь *perf.* finish (off), kill off, deal the final blow to; **~ся**+*gen.* get, obtain, secure; achieve; ~ся своего́, get one's way, gain one's end.

добира́ться, -а́юсь *imp.* of добра́ться.

до́блестный, valiant, valorous, brave. **до́блесть**, -и, valour, prowess.

добра́ться, -беру́сь, -ёшься; -а́лся, -ла́сь, -а́ло́сь *perf.* (*imp.* добира́ться) +до+*gen.* get to, reach.

добро́, -а́, good; good deed; goods, property; э́то не к добру́, it is a bad sign, it augurs ill.

добро- in *comb.* good, well-. **доброво́лец**, -льца, volunteer. **~во́льно** *adv.* voluntarily, of one's own free will. **~во́льный**, voluntary. **~де́тель**, -и, virtue. **~де́тельный**, virtuous. **~ду́шие**, -я, good nature. **~ду́шный**, good-natured; genial. **~жела́тельный**, benevolent. **~ка́чественный**, of good quality; benign. **~со́вестный**, conscientious.

доброта́, -ы́, goodness, kindness. **до́бр|ый**; до́бр, -а́, -о, до́бры́, good; kind; бу́дте добры́+*imper.* please; would you be kind enough to; в ~ый час! good luck!; по ~ой во́ле, of one's own accord, of one's own free will.

добыва́ть, -а́ю *imp.*, **добы́ть**, -бу́ду; до́бы́л, -а́, -о *perf.* get, obtain, procure; extract, mine, quarry. **добы́ча**, -и, output; extraction, mining, quarrying; booty, spoils, loot; bag, catch; mineral products.

добью́, etc.: see доби́ть. **доведу́**, etc.: see довести́.

довезти́, -езу́, -езёшь; -вёз, -ла́ *perf.*

(*imp.* довози́ть) take (to), carry (to), drive (to).

дове́ренность, -и, warrant; power of attorney; trust. **дове́ренн|ый,** trusted; confidential; ~ое лицо́, confidential agent; **~ый** *sb.* agent, proxy. **дове́рие, -я,** trust, confidence. **дове́рить, -рю** *perf.* (*imp.* доверя́ть) entrust; trust, confide; **~ся**+*dat.* trust in; confide in. **дове́рчивый,** trustful, credulous.

доверша́ть, -а́ю *imp.*, **доверши́ть, -шу́** *perf.* complete. **доверше́ние, -я,** completion, accomplishment; в ~ всего́, to crown all.

доверя́ть(ся, -я́ю(сь *imp.* of дове́рить(-ся.

дове́сок, -ска, makeweight.

довести́, -еду́, -едёшь; -вёл, -а́ *perf.*, **доводи́ть, -ожу́, -о́дишь** *imp.* lead, take, accompany (to); bring, drive, reduce (to). **до́вод, -а,** argument, reason.

довое́нный, pre-war.

довози́ть, -ожу́, -о́зишь *imp.* of довезти́.

дово́льно *adv.* enough; quite, fairly; rather; pretty. **дово́льный,** contented, satisfied; content; pleased; considerable. **дово́льство, -а,** content, contentment; ease, prosperity. **дово́льствоваться, -ствуюсь** *imp.* (*perf.* у~) be content, be satisfied.

догада́ться, -а́юсь *perf.*, **дога́дываться, -аюсь** *imp.* guess; suspect. **дога́дка, -и,** surmise, conjecture; shrewdness; imagination. **дога́дливый,** quick-witted, shrewd.

догна́ть, -гоню́, -го́нишь; -гна́л, -а́, -о *perf.* (*imp.* догоня́ть), catch up (with); drive; push up.

догова́риваться, -аюсь *imp.*, **договори́ться, -рю́сь** *perf.* come to an agreement or understanding; arrange; negotiate, treat; догова́ривающиеся сто́роны, contracting parties. **до́говор, -а**; *pl.* -ы or -а́, -о́в, agreement; contract; treaty, pact. **догово́рный,** contractual; agreed; fixed by treaty.

догоня́ть, -я́ю *imp.* of догна́ть.

догорать, -а́ет *imp.*, **догоре́ть, -ри́т** *perf.* burn out, burn down.

дое́ду, etc.: see дое́хать. **доезжа́ть, -а́ю** *imp.* of дое́хать.

дое́ние, -я, milking.

дое́хать, -е́ду *perf.* (*imp.* доезжа́ть)+до+*gen.* reach, arrive at.

дожда́ться, -ду́сь, -дёшься; -а́лся, -ла́сь, -а́ло́сь *perf.* + *gen.* wait for, wait until.

дождеви́к, -а́, raincoat; puff-ball. **дождево́й,** rain; rainy; ~ червь, earthworm. **до́ждик, -а,** shower. **дождли́вый,** rainy. **дождь, -я́** *m.* rain; shower, hail; ~ идёт, it is raining.

дожива́ть, -а́ю *imp.*, **дожи́ть, -иву́, -ивёшь;** до́жил, -а́, -о *perf.* live out; spend; + до + *gen.* live until; reach; come to, be reduced to.

доза́тор, -а, metering device; hopper, feeder, dispenser.

дозволе́ние, -я, permission. **дозво́ленный,** permitted; legal. **дозво́лить, -лю** *perf.*, **дозволя́ть, -я́ю** *imp.* permit, allow.

дозвони́ться, -ню́сь *perf.* get through, reach by telephone; get bell answered.

дозо́р, -а, patrol; ночно́й ~, night watch. **дозо́рный,** patrol, scout.

дозрева́ть, -а́ет *imp.*, **дозре́ть, -е́ет** *perf.* ripen. **дозре́лый,** fully ripe.

доистори́ческий, prehistoric.

дои́ть, дою́, до́ишь *imp.* (*perf.* по~) milk; **~ся,** give milk. **до́йка, -и,** milking. **до́йный,** milch.

дойму́ etc.: see доня́ть.

дойти́, дойду́, -дёшь; дошёл, -шла́ *perf.* (*imp.* доходи́ть)+до+*gen.* reach; make an impression on, get through to, penetrate to, touch; come to, be a matter of.

доказа́тельный, demonstrative, conclusive. **доказа́тельство, -а,** proof, evidence; demonstration. **доказа́ть, -ажу́** *perf.*, **дока́зывать, -аю** *imp.* demonstrate, prove; argue, try to show. **доказу́емый,** demonstrable.

докати́ться, -ачу́сь, -а́тишься *perf.*, **дока́тываться, -аюсь** *imp.* roll; thunder, boom; +до+*gen.* sink into, come to.

докла́д, -а, report; lecture; paper; talk, address; announcement. **докла́дчик, -а,** speaker, lecturer; rapporteur.

докла́дывать(ся, -аю(сь *imp.* of доложи́ть(ся.

до́красна́ *adv.* to red heat, to redness; red-hot red.
до́ктор, -а; *pl.* -а́, doctor. **доктора́льный**, didactic. **доктора́нт**, -а, person working for doctorate. **до́кторский**, doctor's; doctoral. **до́кторша**, -и, woman doctor; doctor's wife.
докуме́нт, -а, document, paper; deed, instrument. **документа́льный**, documentary. **документа́ция**, -и, documentation; documents papers.
долби́ть, -блю́ *imp.* hollow; chisel, gouge; repeat, say over and over again; swot up; learn by rote.
долг, -а (-у), *loc.* -у́; *pl.* -и́, duty; debt; в ~, on credit; в ~у́, indebted; взять в ~, borrow; дать в ~, lend.
до́лгий; до́лог, -лга́, -о, long. **до́лго** *adv.* long, (for) a long time. **долгове́чный**, lasting; durable.
долголе́тие, -я, longevity. **долголе́тний**, of many years; long-standing.
долгота́, -ы́; *pl.* -ы, length; longitude.
долево́й, lengthwise. **до́лее** *adv.* longer.
должа́ть, -а́ю *imp.* (*perf.* за~) borrow.
до́лжен, -жна́ *predic.*+*dat.* in debt to; + *inf.* obliged, bound; likely; must, have to, ought to; он ~ мне три рубля́, he owes me three roubles; он ~ идти́, he must go; он ~ был отказа́ться, he had to refuse; он ~ ско́ро прийти́, he should be here soon; должно́ быть, probably. **должни́к**, -а́, **-ни́ца**, -ы, debtor. **должностн|о́й**, official; ~о́е лицо́, official, functionary, public servant. **до́лжность**, -и; *gen. pl.* -е́й, post, appointment, office; duties. **до́лжный**, due, fitting, proper.
доли́на, -ы, valley.
доложи́ть[1], -ожу́, -о́жишь *perf.* (*imp.* докла́дывать) add.
доложи́ть[2], -ожу́, -о́жишь *perf.* (*imp.* докла́дывать) + *acc.* or о + *prep.* report; give a report on; announce; **~ся**, announce one's arrival.
доло́й *adv.* away, off; + *acc.* down with!; с глаз ~, из се́рдца вон, out of sight, out of mind; с глаз мои́х ~! out of my sight!
долото́, -а́; *pl.* -а, chisel.
до́лька, -и, segment, section; clove.
до́льше *adv.* longer.
до́ля, -и; *gen. pl.* -е́й, part, portion; share; quota, allotment; lobe; lot, fate.
дом, -а (-у), *loc.* -у́; *pl.* -а́, building, house; home; household; lineage; family; на ~у́, at home. **до́ма** *adv.* at home; in. **дома́шн|ий**, house; home; domestic; home-made, homespun, home-brewed; tame; ~яя рабо́та, homework; housework; ~яя хозя́йка, housewife; **~ие** *sb. pl.* family, people.
до́менн|ый, blast-furnace, ironmaking; ~ая печь, blast-furnace.
домини́ровать, -рует *imp.* dominate, predominate; + над + *instr.* dominate, command.
домкра́т, -а, jack.
до́мна, -ы blast-furnace.
домовладе́лец, -льца, **-лица**, -ы, house-owner; landlord. **домово́дство**, -а, household management; domestic science. **домо́в|ый**, house; household; housing; ~ая кни́га, house-register, register of tenants; ~ая конто́ра, house-manager's office; ~ый трест, housing trust.
домога́тельство, -а, solicitation, importunity; demand, bid. **домога́ться**, -а́юсь *imp.*+*gen.* seek, solicit, covet, bid for.
домо́й *adv.* home, homewards. **домострое́ние**, -я, housebuilding. **домострои́тельный**, housebuilding. **домоуправле́ние**, -я, house management (committee). **домохозя́йка**, -и, housewife. **домрабо́тница**, -ы, domestic servant, (daily) maid. **дому́шник**, -а, (*sl.*) burglar, housebreaker.
дона́шиваться, -вается *imp.* of доноси́ться[2].
доне́льзя *adv.* in the extreme; to the utmost degree; он ~ упря́м, he's as stubborn as a mule, he couldn't be more pigheaded.
донесе́ние, -я, dispatch, report, message.
донести́, -су́, -сёшь; -нёс, -сла́ *perf.* (*imp.* доноси́ть) report, announce; + *dat.* inform; + на + *acc.* inform against, denounce; **~сь**, be heard; + до + *gen.* reach, reach the ears of; carry as far as.
до́низу *adv.* to the bottom; све́рху ~, from top to bottom.

донима́ть, -а́ю *imp.* of доня́ть.
до́нный, bottom, base; ~ лёд, ground ice.
до́нор, -а, blood-donor.
доно́с, -а, denunciation, information. **доноси́ть(ся**[1], -ношу́(сь, -но́сишь(ся *imp.* of донести́(сь.
доноси́ться[2], -но́сится *perf.* (*imp.* дона́шиваться) wear out, be worn out.
доно́счик, -а, informer.
донско́й, Don; ~ каза́к, Don Cossack.
до́нья, etc.: see дно.
до н.э. (*do-ené*) *abbr.* до на́шей э́ры, B.C.
доня́ть, дойму́, -мёшь; до́нял, -а́, -о *perf.* (*imp.* донима́ть), weary to death, pester.
допла́та, -ы, additional payment, extra charge, excess. **доплати́ть** -ачу́, -а́тишь *perf.*, **допла́чивать,** -аю *imp.* pay in addition; pay the rest.
доплыва́ть, -а́ю *imp.*, **доплы́ть,** -ыву́, -ывёшь; -ы́л, -а́, -о *perf.*+до+*gen.* swim to, sail to; reach.
допо́длинно *adv.* for certain. **допо́длинный,** authentic, genuine.
дополне́ние, -я, supplement, addition; appendix; addendum; object. **дополни́тельно** *adv.* in addition. **дополни́тельн|ый,** supplementary, additional, extra; complementary; ~ые вы́боры, by-election. **допо́лнить,** -ню *perf.*, **дополня́ть,** -я́ю *imp.* supplement, add to, amplify; complete; complement.
допото́пный, antediluvian.
допра́шивать, -аю *imp.*, **допроси́ть,** -ошу́, -о́сишь *perf.* interrogate, question, examine. **допро́с,** -а, interrogation, examination.
до́пуск, -а, right of entry, admittance; tolerance. **допуска́ть,** -а́ю *imp.*, **допусти́ть,** -ущу́, -у́стишь *perf.* admit; allow, permit; tolerate; grant, assume, suppose. **допусти́мый,** permissible, admissible, allowable, acceptable. **допуще́ние,** -я, assumption.
доро́га, -и, road; highway; way; journey; route; в доро́ге, on the journey, on the way, en route; по доро́ге, on the way; the same way; туда́ ему́ и ~! serves him right!
до́рого *adv.* dear, dearly. **дороговизна,** -ы, expensiveness; high cost, high prices. **дорого́й;** до́рог, -а́, -о, dear; expensive; costly.
доро́дный, portly, corpulent, stout; healthy, strong.
дорожа́ть, -а́ет *imp.* (*perf.* вз~, по~) rise in price, go up. **доро́же,** *comp.* of до́рого, дорого́й. **дорожи́ть,** -жу́ *imp.*+*instr.* value; prize; care about.
доро́жка, -и, path, walk; track; lane; runway; strip, runner, stair-carpet.
доро́жный, road; highway; travelling.
доса́да, -ы, annoyance; disappointment; nuisance, pity. **досади́ть,** -ажу́ *perf.*, **досажда́ть,** -а́ю *imp.* + *dat.* annoy. **доса́дливый,** annoyed, irritated, disappointed; of annoyance. **доса́дный,** annoying; disappointing. **доса́довать,** -дую, be annoyed (на+*acc.* with).
досе́ле *adv.* up to now.
доска́, -и́, *acc.* до́ску; *pl.* -и, -со́к, -ска́м, board; plank; slab; plaque, plate.
досло́вный, literal, verbatim; word-for-word.
досмо́тр, -а, inspection, examination. **досмо́трщик,** -а, inspector, examiner.
доспе́хи, -ов *pl.* armour.
досро́чный, ahead of time, ahead of schedule, early.
достава́ть(ся, -таю́(сь, -ёшь(ся *imp.* of доста́ть(ся.
доста́вить, -влю *perf.*, **доставля́ть,** -я́ю *imp.* deliver, convey; supply, furnish; cause, give. **доста́вка,** -и, delivery; conveyance. **доста́вщик,** -а, roundsman, delivery man.
доста́ну, etc.: see доста́ть.
доста́ток, -тка, sufficiency; prosperity; *pl.* income. **доста́точно** *adv.* enough, sufficiently. **доста́точный,** sufficient; adequate; prosperous, well-off.
доста́ть, -а́ну *perf.* (*imp.* достава́ть) fetch; get (out), take (out); obtain; + *gen.* or до + *gen.* touch; reach; (*impers.*) suffice, be sufficient; **~ся** + *dat.* pass to, be inherited by; fall to the lot of; ему́ доста́нется, he'll catch it.
достига́ть, -а́ю *imp.*, **дости́гнуть, дости́чь,** -и́гну; -сти́г *perf.*+*gen.* attain, achieve; + *gen.* or до + *gen.*

reach. **достиже́ние, -я,** achievement, attainment. **достижи́мый,** accessible; attainable.

досто- in *comb.*, worthy (of). **достове́рный,** reliable, trustworthy; authentic. **~па́мятный,** memorable. **~примеча́тельность,** -и, notable place or object; *pl.* sights; ~примеча́тельности Ленингра́да, What to see in Leningrad; осма́тривать ~примеча́тельности, go sightseeing. **~примеча́тельный,** noteworthy, remarkable, notable.

досто́инство, -а, dignity; merit, virtue; value; rank, title. **досто́йно** *adv.* suitably, fittingly, adequately, properly; with dignity. **досто́йный,** deserved; fitting, adequate; suitable, fit; worthy; +*gen.* worthy of, deserving.

достоя́ние, -я, property.

до́ступ, -а, access; entrance; admission, admittance. **досту́пный,** accessible; simple; easily understood; intelligible; approachable; moderate, reasonable; ~ для, open to; available to.

досу́г, -а, leisure, (spare) time. **досу́жий** leisure, spare; idle.

до́суха *adv.* dry.

досяга́емый, attainable accessible.

дота́ция, -и, grant, subsidy.

дотла́ *adv.* utterly, completely, out; to the ground.

дото́шный, meticulous.

дотра́гиваться, -аюсь *imp.*, **дотро́нуться,** -нусь *perf.* + до + *gen.* touch.

дотя́гивать, -аю *imp.*, **дотяну́ть,** -яну́, -я́нешь *perf.* draw out; stretch out; hold out; live, last; put off; + до + *gen.* draw, drag, haul as far as; reach, make; **~ся,** stretch, reach; drag on; + до + *gen.* reach, touch.

до́хлый, dead; sickly, puny. **до́хнуть,** -нет; дох (*perf.* из~, по~, с~) die; croak, kick the bucket.

дохну́ть, -ну́, -нёшь *perf.* draw a breath.

дохо́д, -а, income; receipts; revenue. **доходи́ть,** -ожу́, -о́дишь *imp.* of дойти́. **дохо́дность,** -и, profitability; income. **дохо́дный,** profitable, lucrative, paying; income-producing, revenue-producing. **дохо́дчивый,** intelligible, easy to understand.

доц. *abbr.*, **доце́нт,** -а, reader, senior lecturer.

до́чери, etc.: see дочь.

до́чиста *adv.* clean; completely.

до́чка, -и, daughter. **дочь,** -чери, *instr.* -черью; *pl.* -чери, -черéй, *instr.* -черьми́, daughter.

дошёл, etc.: see дойти́.

дошко́льник, -а, **-ница,** -ы, child under school age. **дошко́льный,** pre-school; nursery.

доща́тый, plank, board, wooden. **доще́чка,** -и, small plank, small board; door-plate, name-plate.

доя́рка, -и, milkmaid.

др. *abbr.* други́е, others.

драгоце́нность, -и, jewel; gem; precious stone; treasure; *pl.* jewellery; valuables. **драгоце́нный,** precious.

дразни́ть, -ню́, -нишь *imp.* tease.

дра́ка, -и, fight; доходи́ть до дра́ки, come to blows.

драко́н, -а, dragon; wyvern.

дра́ма, -ы, drama; tragedy, calamity. **драмати́зм,** -а, dramatic effect; dramatic character, dramatic quality; tension. **драмати́ческий,** dramatic; drama, theatre, of the theatre; theatrical; tense. **драмату́рг,** -а, playwright, dramatist. **драматурги́я,** -и, dramatic art; dramatic composition, play-writing; drama, plays.

драп, -а, heavy woollen cloth.

драпиро́вка, -и, draping; curtain; hangings. **драпиро́вщик,** -а, upholsterer. **драпри́** *indecl. pl.* curtain(s), hangings.

дра́повый, cloth.

драть, деру́, -рёшь; драл, -а́, -о *imp.* (*perf.* вы́~, за~, со~) tear, tear up; sting, irritate; run away, make off; tear off; kill; beat, flog, thrash; tear out; + с + *gen.* fleece; sting; ~ го́рло, bawl; ~ у́ши + *dat.* jar on; чёрт его́ (по)дери́! damn him!; **~ся,** fight; use one's fists; struggle.

дре́безги *pl.*; в ~, to smithereens. **дребезжа́ние,** -я, rattle, clink, jingle, tinkle. **дребезжа́ть,** -жи́т *imp.* rattle, jingle, tinkle, clink.

древеси́на, -ы, wood; wood-pulp; timber. **древе́сн|ый,** wood; ~ая ма́сса,

wood-pulp; ~ый питóмник, arboretum; ~ый ýголь, charcoal.
дрéвко, -а; *pl.* -и, -ов, pole, (flag-) staff; shaft.
древнееврéйский, Hebrew. **древнерýсский,** Old Russian. **дрéвний,** ancient; very old, aged. **дрéвность, -и,** antiquity.
дрези́на, -ы, trolley.
дрейф, -а, drift; leeway. **дрейфовáть,** -фýет *imp.* drift. **дрейфýющий,** drifting; ~ лёд, drift-ice.
дремá, -ы́, **дрёма,** -ы, drowsiness, sleepiness. **дремáть,** -млю́, -млешь *imp.* doze; slumber; drowse; не ~, be wakeful; be wide awake, on the alert. **дремóта,** -ы, drowsiness, somnolence.
дремýчий thick, dense.
дрессирóванный, trained; performing. **дрессировáть,** -рýю *imp.* (*perf.* вы́~) train, school. **дрессирóвка,** -и, training. **дрессирóвщик,** -а, trainer.
дроби́льный, crushing, grinding. **дроби́на,** -ы, pellet. **дроби́ть,** -блю́ *imp.* (*perf.* раз~) break up, smash; crush, grind; divide, split up; **~ся,** break to pieces, smash; crumble; divide, split up. **дроблёный,** splintered, crushed, ground, fragmented. **дрóбный,** separate; subdivided, split up; minute; staccato, abrupt; fractional; ~ дождь, fine rain. **дробови́к,** -á, shot-gun. **дробь,** -и, (small) shot, pellets; drumming; tapping; trilling; fraction.
дровá, дров *pl.* firewood. **дрóвни,** дрóвней *pl.* wood-sledge.
дрóги, дрог *pl.* dray; hearse.
дрóгнуть, -ну *perf.*, **дрожáть,** -жý *imp.* shake, move; tremble; shiver; quiver, quaver; flicker; waver, falter; +над+ *instr.* be concerned over, worry about; grudge.
дрожжевóй, yeast. **дрóжжи,** -éй *pl.* yeast.
дрóжки, -жек *pl.* droshky.
дрожь, -и, shivering, trembling; tremor, quaver.
дрозд, -á, thrush.
дрóссель, -я *m.* throttle, choke.
дрóтик, -а, javelin, dart.
друг[1], -а; *pl.* -узья́, -зéй, friend. **друг**[2]; ~ дрýга (дрýгу), each other, one another; ~ за ~ом, one after another; in single file. **другóй,** other, another; different; second; на ~ день, (the) next day. **дрýжба,** -ы, friendship. **дружелю́бный, дрýжеский, дрýжественный,** friendly. **дружи́ть,** -жý, -ýжишь *imp.* be friends. be on friendly terms; **~ся** (*perf.* по~ся) make friends. **дрýжно** *adv.* harmoniously, in concord; simultaneously, in concert; rapidly, smoothly. **дрýжный; -жен,** -жнá, -о, amicable; harmonious; simultaneous, concerted.
друммóндов свет, limelight.
дря́блый; дрябл, -á, -о, flabby; flaccid; sluggish.
дря́зги, -зг *pl.* squabbles; petty annoyances.
дряннóй, worthless, rotten; good-for--nothing. **дрянь,** -и, trash, rubbish.
дряхлéть, -éю *imp.* (*perf.* о~) become decrepit. **дря́хлый**; -хл, -лá, -о, decrepit, senile.
ДСО (*deseó*) *abbr.* доброво́льное спорти́вное óбщество, Voluntary Sports club.
дуб, -а; *pl.* -ы́, oak; blockhead. **дуби́льный,** tanning, tannic. **дуби́льня,** -и; *gen. pl.* -лен, tannery. **дуби́на,** -ы, club, cudgel; blockhead. **дуби́нка,** -и, truncheon, baton. **дуби́ть,** -блю́ *imp.* (*perf.* вы́~) tan.
дублёр, -а, understudy; actor dubbing a part. **дублéт,** -а, **дубликáт,** -а, duplicate. **дубли́ровать,** -рую *imp.* duplicate; understudy; dub.
дубовáтый, coarse; stupid, thick. **дубóвый,** oak; coarse; clumsy; thick.
дугá, -и́; *pl.* -и, shaft-bow; arc; arch.
дýдка, -и, pipe, fife.
дýжка, -и, small arch or bow; handle; (croquet-)hoop; wishbone.
дýло, -а, muzzle; barrel. **дýльце,** -а; *gen. pl.* -лец, mouthpiece.
дýма, -ы, thought; Duma; council. **дýмать,** -аю *imp.* (*perf.* по~) think; +*inf.* think of, intend.
дуновéние, -я, puff, breath. **дýнуть,** -ну *perf.* of дуть.
дупли́стый, hollow. **дуплó,** -á; *pl.* -а, -пел, hollow; hole; cavity.
дýра, -ы, **дурáк,** -á, fool. **дурáчить,** -чу

imp. (*perf.* о~) fool, dupe; **~ся**, play the fool.
дуре́ть, -е́ю *imp.* (*perf.* о~) grow stupid.
дурма́н, -а, datura; drug, narcotic; intoxicant. **дурма́нить**, -ню *imp.* (*perf.* о~) stupefy.
дурно́й; -рен, -рна́, -о, bad, evil; nasty; ill, faint; ugly; мне ду́рно, I'm going to faint. **дурнота́**, -ы́, faintness; nausea.
ду́тый, blown, blown up, hollow; inflated; pneumatic; exaggerated. **дуть**, ду́ю *imp.* (*perf.* вы́~, по~, ду́нуть) blow; ду́ет, there is a draught. **дутьё**, -я́, blowing; draught; blast; glass-blowing. **ду́ться**, ду́юсь *imp.* pout; sulk. be sulky.
дух, -а (-у), spirit; spirits; heart; mind; breath; air; ghost; smell; в ~е, in high spirits in a good mood; во весь ~, at full speed, flat out; не в моём ~е, not to my taste; ни слу́ху ни ~у, no news, not a word, not a whisper; одни́м ~ом, in one breath; at one go, at a stretch; па́дать ~ом, lose heart, grow despondent. **духи́**, -о́в *pl.* scent, perfume. **Ду́хов день**, Whit Monday. **духове́нство**, -а, clergy, priesthood. **духови́дец**, -дца, clairvoyant; medium. **духо́вка**, -и, oven. **духо́вный**, spiritual; inner, inward; ecclesiastical, church, religious. **духово́й**, wind; air; steam; steamed. **духота́**, -ы́, stuffiness, closeness; stuffy heat.
душ, -а, shower-bath.
душа́, -и́, *acc.* -у; *pl.* -и, soul; heart; feeling; spirit; moving spirit; inspiration; в глубине́ души́, in one's heart of hearts; в душе́, inwardly, secretly; at heart; за душо́й, to one's name; на ду́шу, per head; от всей души́, with all one's heart.
душева́я *sb.* shower-baths.
душевнобольно́й, mentally ill, insane; *sb.* mental patient; lunatic. **душе́вный**, mental; of the mind; sincere, cordial, heartfelt.
души́стый, fragrant; sweet-scented; ~ горо́шек, sweet pea(s). **души́ть**[1], -шу́, -шишь *imp.* (*perf.* на~) scent, perfume; **~ся**, use scent, put on scent.
души́ть[2], -шу́, -шишь *imp.* (*perf.* за~) strangle; stifle, smother, suffocate; suppress; choke.
ду́шный; -шен, -шна́, -о, stuffy, close; sultry; stifling, suffocating.
ды́бом *adv.* on end; у меня́ во́лосы вста́ли ~, my hair stood on end.
дыбы́: станови́ться на ~, rear; resist, jib, dig one's heels in.
дым, -а (-у), *loc.* -у́; *pl.* -ы́, smoke.
дыми́ть, -млю́ *imp.* (*perf.* на~) smoke; **~ся**, smoke, steam; billow. **ды́мка**, -и, haze, mist. **ды́мный**, smoky. **дымов|о́й**, smoke; ~а́я труба́, flue, chimney; smoke-stack, funnel. **дымо́к**, -мка́, puff of smoke. **дымохо́д**, -а, flue. **ды́мчатый**, smoky; smoked; smoke-coloured.
ды́ня, -и, melon.
дыра́, -ы́; *pl.* -ы **ды́рка**, -и; *gen. pl.* -рок, hole; gap. **дыря́вый**, full of holes; holed, perforated.
дыха́ние, -я, breathing, respiration; breath. **дыха́тельн|ый**, respiratory; breathing, breather; ~ое го́рло, windpipe. **дыша́ть**, -шу́, -шишь *imp.* breathe.
дья́вол, -а, devil. **дья́вольский**, devilish, diabolical; damnable.
дьяк, -а́, clerk, secretary. **дья́кон**, -а; *pl.* -а́, deacon. **дьячо́к**, -чка́, sacristan, sexton; reader.
дю́жина, -ы, dozen. **дю́жинный**, ordinary, commonplace.
дэ *n. indecl.* the letter д.
дя́денька, -и *m.*, **дя́дюшка**, -и *m.* uncle. **дя́дя**, -и; *gen. pl.* -ей *m.* uncle.
дя́тел, -тла, woodpecker.

Е

е *n. indecl.* the letter e.
ев- *pref.* eu-. **евге́ника,** -и, eugenics. **е́внух,** -а, eunuch. **евразийский,** Eurasian. **евста́хиев,** Eustachian.
ева́нгелие, -я gospel; the Gospels. **евангели́ческий,** evangelical. **ева́нгельский,** gospel.
евре́й, -я, Jew; Hebrew. **евре́йка,** -и Jewess. **евре́йский,** Jewish.
Еврови́дение, -я, Eurovision. **европе́ец,** -е́йца, European. **европе́йский,** European.
еги́петский, Egyptian. **египтя́нин,** -а; *pl.* -я́не, -я́н, **египтя́нка,** -и, Egyptian.
его́ (*-vo*): see он, оно́; *pron.* his; its, of it.
еда́, -ы́, food; meal; eating.
едва́ *adv.* and *conj.* hardly, barely; only just; scarcely; ~ . ., как, no sooner . . than; ~ ли, hardly, scarcely; ~ (ли) не, nearly, almost, all but.
еди́м, etc.: see есть[1].
едине́ние, -я, unity. **едини́ца,** -ы, one; figure one; unity; unit; individual. **едини́чность,** -и, singleness; single occurrence. **едини́чный,** single, unitary; solitary, isolated; individual.
едино- in *comb.* mono-, uni-; one; co-. **единобо́жие,** -я, monotheism. **~бо́рство,** -а, single combat. **~бра́чие,** -я, monogamy. **~бра́чный,** monogamous. **~вла́стие,** -я, autocracy, absolute rule. **~вла́стный,** autocratic; dictatorial; absolute. **~вре́менно** *adv.* only once; simultaneously. **~вре́менный,** extraordinary; unique; + *dat.* or с + *instr.* simultaneous with. **~гла́сие,** -я, **~ду́шие,** -я, unanimity. **~гла́сный,** **~ду́шный,** unanimous. **~кро́вный,** consanguineous; ~кро́вный брат, half-brother. **~мы́слие,** -я, like-mindedness; agreement in opinion. **~мы́шленник,** -а, like-minded person; accomplice; мы с ним ~мы́шленники, we are in agreement, we think the same way. **~нача́лие,** -я, unified management command. **~обра́зие,** -я uniformity. **~обра́зный,** uniform. **~ро́г,** -а, unicorn; narwhal. **~утро́бный,** uterine; ~утро́бный брат, half-brother.
еди́нственно *adv.* only, solely. **еди́нственный,** only, sole; singular; unique, unequalled. **еди́нство,** -а, unity. **еди́ный,** one; single, sole; united, unified; common.
е́дкий; е́док, едка́, -о, caustic, corrosive; acrid, pungent; sarcastic; ~ натр, caustic soda.
едо́к, -а́, mouth, head; eater.
е́ду, etc.: see е́хать. **е́дче,** *comp.* of е́дкий.
её: see она́; *pron.* her, hers; its.
ёж, ежа́, hedgehog.
еже- in *comb.* every; -ly. **ежего́дник,** -а, annual, year-book. **~го́дный,** annual, yearly. **~дне́вный,** daily; everyday; quotidian. **~ме́сячник,** -а, **~ме́сячный,** monthly. **~неде́льник,** -а, ~**неде́льный,** weekly. **~но́шный,** nightly.
ежеви́ка, -и, blackberries; blackberry bush, bramble. **ежеви́чный,** blackberry.
ёжиться, ёжусь *imp.* (*perf.* съ~) huddle up; shrivel; shrink away; hesitate.
езда́, -ы́, ride, riding; drive, driving; going; journey; traffic. **е́здить,** е́зжу *imp.* go; ride, drive; slip; ~ верхо́м, ride. **ездо́к,** -а́, rider; horseman.
ей: see она́.
ей-бо́гу *int.* really! I swear (to God).
ел, etc.: see есть[1].
е́ле *adv.* hardly, barely, scarcely; only just.
ёлка, -и, fir, fir-tree, spruce; Christmas tree, Christmas party; herring-bone pattern. **ело́вый,** fir, spruce; deal, white-wood. **ёлочка,** -и, herring-bone pattern, herring-boning. **ёлочный,** Christmas-tree; herring-bone; dendritic. **ель,** -и, fir, fir-tree; spruce; deal, white wood. **е́льник,** -а, fir (spruce) plantation; fir-wood, fir-twigs.
ем, etc.: see есть[1].
ёмкий, capacious. **ёмкость,** -и, capacity, cubic content; capacitance.
ему́: see он, оно́.

енóт, -а, **енóтовый**, raccoon.
епи́скоп, -а, bishop. **епи́скопский**, episcopal.
éресь, -и heresy. **ерети́к**, -á, heretic. **ерети́ческий**, heretical.
ёрзать, -аю *imp.* fidget.
ерóшить, -шу *imp.* (*perf.* взъ~) ruffle, rumple, tousle; dishevel; **~ся**, bristle, stand on end, stick up.
ерундá, -ы́, nonsense, rubbish; trifle, trifling matter.
éсли, if; ~ бы, if only; ~ бы не, but for, if it were not for; ~ не, unless; ~ тóлько, provided; if only; что, ~ бы, what about, how about.
ест: see есть[1].
естéственно *adv.* naturally. **естéственный**, natural. **естествó**, -á, nature; essence. **естествовéдение**, -я, естествознáние, -я, (natural) science; natural history; nature study.
есть[1], ем, ешь, ест, еди́м; ел *imp.* (*perf.* съ~) eat; corrode, eat away; sting, make smart; torment, nag (at).
есть[2]: see быть; is, are; there is, there are; и ~, yes, indeed; как ~, entirely, completely; *int.* yes, sir; very good, sir; aye, aye sir.
ефрéйтор, -а, lance-corporal.
éхать, éду *imp.* (*perf.* по~) go; ride, drive; travel, journey, voyage; ~ верхóм, ride.
ехи́дный, malicious, spiteful; venomous.
ешь: see есть[1].
ещё *adv.* still; yet; (some) more; any more; yet, further; again; +*comp.* still, yet even; всё ~, still; ~ бы! of course! oh yes! can you ask?; ~ не, нет ~, not yet; ~ раз, once more, again; encore!; покá ~, for the present, for the time being.
ЕЭС (*eés*) *abbr.* Европéйское экономи́ческое сообщество, E.E.C.
éю: see онá.

Ж

ж *letter*: see жэ.
ж *conj.*: see же.
жáба, -ы, toad; quinsy.
жáбра, -ы; *gen. pl.* -бр, gill, branchia.
жáворонок, -нка, lark.
жáдничать, -аю *imp.* be greedy; be mean. **жáдность**, -и, greed; greediness; avidity; avarice, meanness. **жáдный**; -ден, -днá, -о, greedy; avid; avaricious, mean.
жáжда, -ы, thirst; + *gen.* thirst for, craving for. **жáждать**, -ду *imp.* thirst, long, yearn.
жакéт -а, **жакéтка**, -и, jacket.
жалéть, -éю *imp.* (*perf.* по~) pity, feel sorry for; regret, be sorry; +*acc.* or *gen.* spare; grudge.
жáлить, -лю *imp.* (*perf.* у~) sting, bite.
жáлкий; -лок, -лкá, -о, pitiful, pitiable, pathetic, wretched. **жáлко** *predic.*: see жаль.
жáло, -а, sting.
жáлоба, -ы, complaint. **жáлобный**, plaintive; doleful mournful.
жáлованн|ый, granted, conferred; ~ая грáмота, charter, letters patent. **жáлованье**, -я, salary, pay, wage(s); reward; donation. **жáловать**, -лую *imp.* (*perf.* по~)+*acc.* or *dat.* of person, *instr.* or *acc.* of thing, grant, bestow on, confer on; +к+*dat.* come to see, visit; **~ся**, complain (на+*acc.* of, about).
жáлостливый, compassionate, sympathetic; pitiful. **жáлостный**, piteous; compassionate, sympathetic. **жáлость**, -и, pity, compassion. **жаль**, **жáлко**, *predic. impers.* (it is) a pity, a shame; + *dat.* it grieves; + *dat.* and *gen.* regret; feel sorry for; +*gen.* grudge; ей ~ бы́ло себя́, she felt sorry for herself; ~, что вас там нé было, it is a pity you were not there; как ~, what a pity; мне ~ егó, I'm sorry for him.

жанр, -а, genre; genre-painting. **жанри́ст,** -а, genre-painter.
жар, -а (-у), *loc.* -у́, heat; heat of the day; hot place; embers; fever; (high) temperature; ardour. **жара́,** -ы́, heat; hot weather.
жарго́н, -а, jargon; slang, cant.
жа́рен|ый, roast; grilled; fried; ~ый карто́фель, chips; **~ое** *sb.* roast (meat). **жа́рить,** -рю *imp.* (*perf.* за~, из~) roast; grill; fry; scorch, burn; **~ся,** roast, fry; ~ся на со́лнце, sunbathe. **жа́рк|ий;** -рок, -рка́, -о, hot; torrid; tropical; heated; ardent; passionate; **~ое** *sb.* roast (meat). **жаро́вня,** -и; *gen. pl.* -вен, brazier. **жар-пти́ца,** -ы, Firebird. **жа́рче,** *comp.* of жа́ркий.
жа́тва, -ы, harvest. **жа́твенн|ый,** harvest; reaping; ~ая маши́на, harvester, reaper. **жа́тка,** -и, harvester, reaper.
жать[1], жну, жнёшь *imp.* (*perf.* с~), reap, cut.
жать[2], жму, жмёшь *imp.* press, squeeze; pinch, be tight; oppress.
жва́чка, -и chewing, rumination; cud; chewing-gum. **жва́чн|ый,** ruminant; **~ое** *sb.* ruminant.
жгу, etc.: see жечь.
жгут, а́, plait; braid; tourniquet.
жгу́чий, burning, smarting; scalding, baking; hot; caustic, corrosive. **жёг,** etc.: see жечь.
ж.д. *abbr.* желе́зная доро́га, railway.
ждать, жду, ждёшь; -ал, -а́, -о *imp.*+ *gen.* wait for, await; expect.
же, ж *conj.* but; and; however; also; *part.* giving emphasis or expressing identity; мне же ка́жется, it seems to me, however; на пе́рвом же шагу́, at the very first step; оди́н и тот же, one and the same; он же ваш брат, he's your brother, after all; сего́дня же, this very day; так же, in the same way; тако́й же, тот же, the same, idem; там же, in the same place, ibid.; что же ты де́лаешь? what on earth are you doing?
жева́тельн|ый, chewing; ~ая рези́нка, chewing-gum. **жева́ть,** жую́, жуёшь *imp.* chew, masticate; ruminate.
жезл, -а́, rod; staff; baton; crozier.
жела́ние, -я wish, desire. **жела́нный,** wished-for, longed-for; desired; beloved. **жела́тельный,** desirable; advisable, preferable; optative. **жела́ть,** -а́ю *imp.* (*perf.* по~)+*gen.* wish for, desire; want; + что́бы or *inf.* wish, want. **жела́ющие** *sb. pl.* those who wish.
желе́ *n. indecl.* jelly.
железа́, -ы́; *pl.* же́лезы, -лёз, -за́м, gland; *pl.* tonsils. **желе́зистый**[1], glandular.
желе́зистый[2], iron; ferrous; ferriferous; chalybeate. **железнодоро́жник,** а, railwayman. **железнодоро́жн|ый,** railway; ~ая ве́тка, branch line; ~ое полотно́, permanent way; ~ый у́зел, junction. **желе́зн|ый,** iron; ferric; reliable, dependable; ~ая доро́га, railway; ~ый лом, scrap iron. **желе́зо,** -а, iron.
железо- in *comb.* iron, ferro-, ferri-, ferric. **железобето́н,** -а, reinforced concrete, ferro-concrete. **~бето́нный,** reinforced-concrete. **~плави́льный** заво́д, iron foundry. **~прока́тный,** steel-rolling; ~прока́тный заво́д, rolling mill. **~ру́дный,** iron-ore.
жёлоб, -а; *pl.* -а́, gutter; trough; chute; channel; groove. **желобо́к,** -бка́, groove, channel flute; slot; furrow.
желте́ть, -е́ю *imp.* (*perf.* по~) turn yellow; show yellow. **желтова́тый,** yellowish; sallow. **желто́к** -тка́, yolk. **желту́ха,** -и, jaundice. **желту́шный,** jaundiced. **жёлт|ый;** жёлт -а́, жёлто́, yellow; ~ая медь, brass.
желу́док, -дка, stomach. **желу́дочный,** stomach; gastric.
жёлудь, -я; *gen. pl.* -е́й *m.* acorn.
жёлчный, bilious; bile, gall; peevish, irritable. **жёлчь,** -и, bile, gall.
жема́ниться, -нюсь *imp.* mince, be affected, put on airs. **жема́нный,** mincing, affected.
же́мчуг, -а; *pl.* -а́, pearl, pearls. **жемчу́жина,** -ы, pearl. **жемчу́жный,** pearl; pearly.
жена́ -ы́; *pl.* жёны, wife. **жена́тик,** -а, married man; *pl.* married couple. **жена́тый,** married. **жени́ть,** -ню́, -нишь *perf.* and *imp.* (*perf.* also по~)

marry. **жени́тьба, -ы,** marriage, wedding. **жени́ться, -ню́сь, -нишься** *perf.* and *imp.* (+на+*prep.*) marry, get married (to). **жени́х, -а́,** fiancé; bridegroom. **же́нский,** woman's; feminine; female. **же́нственный,** womanly, feminine. **же́нщина, -ы,** woman.

жердь, -и; *gen. pl.* -е́й pole; stake.

жеребёнок, -нка; *pl.* -бя́та, -бя́т, foal. **жеребе́ц, -бца́,** stallion.

жеребьёвка, -и, casting of lots.

жерло́, -а́; *pl.* -а, muzzle; vent, pipe, crater.

жёрнов, -а; *pl.* -а́, -о́в, millstone.

же́ртва, -ы, sacrifice; victim; пасть же́ртвой+*gen.* fall victim to; принести́ в же́ртву, sacrifice. **же́ртвенный,** sacrificial. **же́ртвовать, -твую** *imp.* (*perf.* по~) present, donate, make a donation (of); +*instr.* sacrifice, give up.

жест, -а, gesture.

жёсткий; -ток, -тка́, -о hard, tough; rigid, strict.

жесто́кий; -то́к, -а́, -о, cruel; brutal; severe, sharp. **жестокосе́рдный, -се́рдый,** hard-hearted. **жесто́кость, -и,** cruelty, brutality.

жёстче *comp.* of жёсткий.

жесть, -и, tin(-plate). **жестя́нка, -и,** tin, can; piece of tin. **жестян|о́й,** tin; ~а́я посу́да, tinware.

жето́н, -а, medal; counter.

жечь, жгу, жжёшь; жёг жгла *imp.* (*perf.* с~) burn; **~ся,** burn, sting; burn oneself. **жжёный,** burnt; scorched; ~ ко́фе, roasted coffee.

живи́тельный, invigorating, revivifying; bracing. **жи́во** *adv.* vividly; with animation; keenly; strikingly; quickly promptly. **жив|о́й;** жив, -а́, -о, living, live, alive; lively; keen; brisk; animated; vivacious; poignant; bright, sparkling; ~а́я и́згородь, (quickset) hedge; ~о́й инвента́рь, livestock; на ~у́ю ни́тку, hastily, anyhow; шить на ~у́ю ни́тку, tack; оста́ться в ~ы́х, survive, escape with one's life. **живопи́сец, -сца,** painter. **живопи́сный,** pictorial; picturesque. **жи́вопись, -и,** painting; paintings, art. **жи́вость, -и,** liveliness, vivacity, animation.

живо́т, -а́, abdomen, belly; stomach. **живо́тик, -а,** tummy. **животново́дство, -а,** stock-breeding, animal husbandry. **живо́тное** *sb.* animal; beast; brute. **живо́тный,** animal.

живу́, etc.: see жить. **живу́чий,** tenacious of life; hardy; firm, stable. **живьём** *adv.* alive.

жи́дк|ий; -док, -дка́, -о, liquid; fluid; watery; weak, thin; sparse, scanty; feeble; ~ий криста́лл, liquid crystal; ~ое те́ло, liquid. **жи́дкостный,** liquid, fluid; liquid-fuel. **жи́дкость, -и,** liquid, fluid; liquor; wateriness, weakness, thinness. **жи́жа, -и, жи́жица, -ы,** sludge, slurry; slush; wash, swill; liquid, liquor. **жи́же,** *comp.* of жи́дкий.

жи́зненный, life, of life; vital; living; close to life; lifelike; vitally important; ~ые си́лы, vitality, sap; ~ый у́ровень, standard of living. **жизнеописа́ние, -я,** biography. **жизнера́достный,** full of the joy of living; cheerful, buoyant. **жизнеспосо́бный** capable of living; viable; vigorous, flourishing. **жизнь, -и,** life; existence.

жил- *abbr.* in *comb.* of жили́щный, жило́й; living; housing. **жилотде́л, -а,** housing department. **~пло́щадь, -и,** floor-space; housing, accommodation. **~строи́тельство, -а,** house-building. **~фо́нд, -а,** housing, accommodation.

жи́ла, -ы, vein; tendon, sinew; lode, seam; core, strand; catgut.

жиле́т, -а, жиле́тка, -и, waistcoat.

жиле́ц, -льца́, жили́ца, -ы, lodger; tenant; inhabitant; он не ~ (на бе́лом све́те), he is not long for this world.

жи́листый, sinewy; stringy; wiry.

жили́ца: see жиле́ц. **жили́ще, -а,** dwelling, abode; lodging; (living) quarters. **жили́щн|ый,** housing; living; ~ые усло́вия, living conditions.

жи́лка, -и, vein; fibre, rib; streak; bent.

жил|о́й, dwelling; residential; inhabited; habitable, fit to live in; ~о́й дом, dwelling house; block of flats; ~а́я пло́щадь, floor-space; housing, accommodation. **жильё, -я́,** habitation;

dwelling; lodging; (living) accommodation.

жим, -а, press.

жир, -а (-у), *loc.* -ý; *pl.* -ы́, fat; grease. **жирéть,** -éю *imp.* (*perf.* о∼, раз∼), grow fat, stout, plump. **жи́рный**; -рен, -рнá, -о, fatty; greasy; rich; plump; lush; bold, heavy. **жировáть,** -ру́ю *imp.* lubricate, oil, grease; fatten, grow fat. **жировóй,** fatty; adipose; fat.

житéйский, worldly; of life, of the world; everyday. **жи́тель,** -я *m.* inhabitant; dweller. **жи́тельство,** -а, residence; мéсто жи́тельства, residence, domicile; мéсто постоя́нного жи́тельства, permanent address. **жи́тница,** -ы, granary. **жи́тный,** cereal. **жи́то,** -а, corn, cereal. **жить,** живу́, -вёшь; жил, -á, -о *imp.* live; +*instr.* live for, live on, live in. **житьё,** -я́, life; existence; habitation, residence.

ЖКО (*zhekaó*) *abbr.* жили́щно-коммунáльный óтдел, department of housing and public utilities.

жму, etc.: see жать².

жму́риться, -рюсь *imp.* (*perf.* за∼) screw up one's eyes, frown. **жму́рки,** -рок *pl.* blind-man's-buff.

жмых, -á, **жмыхи́,** -óв *pl.* oil-cake.

жнéйка, -и, reaper. **жнец,** -á, **жни́ца,** -ы, reaper. **жну,** etc.: see жать¹.

жокéй, -я, jockey. **жокéйка,** -и, jockey cap.

жрéбий, -я, lot; fate, destiny; ∼ брóшен, the die is cast.

жрец, -á, priest. **жрéческий,** priestly. **жри́ца,** -ы, priestess.

жужжáние, -я, humming, buzzing; hum, buzz, drone. **жужжáть,** -жжу́, hum, buzz, drone; whiz(z).

жук, -á, beetle.

жу́лик, -а, petty thief; cheat, swindler; card-sharper. **жу́льничать,** -аю *imp.* (*perf.* с∼) cheat, swindle, defraud.

журáвль, -я́ *m.* crane.

жури́ть, -рю́ *imp.* reprove, take to task.

журнáл, -а, magazine, periodical; journal; diary; register; log; ∼ заседáний minute-book.

журчáние, -я, ripple, babble; murmur. **журчáть,** -чи́т *imp.* babble, ripple, murmur.

жу́ткий; -ток, -ткá, -о, awe-inspiring; uncanny; terrible, terrifying. **жу́тко** *adv.* terrifyingly; terribly, awfully.

жую́, etc.: see жевáть.

жэ *n. indecl.* the letter ж.

жюри́, *n. indecl.* jury, judges; umpire, referee; член ∼, judge.

З

з *letter*: see зэ.

з. *abbr.* зáпад, W.

за *prep.* I.+*acc.* (indicating motion or action) or *instr.* (indicating rest or state) behind; beyond; across, the other side of; at; to; вы́йти зáмуж за +*acc.* marry, get married to; зáмужем за+*instr.* married to; зá борт, за бóртом, overboard; зá городом, out of town; за рубежóм, abroad; сесть за роя́ль, sit down at the piano; сидéть за роя́лем. be at the piano; зá угол, за углóм, round the corner. II.+*acc.* after; over; during, in the space of; by; for; to; боя́ться за, fear for; за вáше здорóвье! your health!; вести́ зá руку, lead by the hand; далекó за пóлночь, long after midnight; за два дня до+ *gen.* two days before; емý ужé зá сорок, he is over forty already; есть за троих, eat enough for three; зá три киломéтра от дерéвни, three kilometres from the village; зá ночь, during the night, overnight; плати́ть за билéт, pay for a ticket; за послéднее врéмя, recently, lately, of late. III.+ *instr.* after; for; on account of, because of; at, during; год за гóдом, year after year; идти́ за молоко́м, go for milk; за неимéнием+*gen.* for want of; за обéдом, at dinner; óчередь за вáми, it is your turn; послáть за дóктором, send for a doctor; следи́ть за, look after; слéдовать за, follow.

за- *perf.* in *comb.* I. with *vbs.:* forms the perfective aspect; indicates beginning of action, direction of action beyond a given point, continuation of action to excess. II. with *sbs.* and *adjs.*, trans-, beyond, on the far side.

за|алéть, -éет *perf.* **за|аркáнить,** -ню *perf.*

забáва, -ы, amusement; game; pastime; fun. **забавля́ть,** -я́ю *imp.* amuse, entertain, divert; **~ся,** amuse oneself. **забáвный,** amusing, funny.

забаллоти́ровать, -рую *perf.* blackball, reject, fail to elect.

забастовáть, -тýю *perf.* strike; go on strike, come out on strike. **забастóвка,** -и, strike; stoppage. **забастóвщик,** -а, **-щица, -ы,** striker.

забвéние, -я, oblivion; unconsciousness; drowsiness. **забвéнный,** forgotten.

забéг, -а, heat, race; trial. **забегáть,** -áю *imp.*. **забежáть,** -егý *perf.* run up; run off; stray; +к+*dat.* drop in on, look in to see; ~ вперёд, run ahead; anticipate.

забелéть(ся, -éет(ся *perf.* (begin to) turn white.

за|берéменеть, -ею *perf.* become pregnant.

заберý, etc.: see забрать. **за|бетони́ровать,** -рую *perf.*

забивáние, -я, jamming. **забивáть(ся,** -áю(сь *imp.* of заби́ть(ся[1]. **заби́вка,** -и, driving in; blocking up, stopping up.

за|бинтовáть, -тýю *perf.*, **забинтóвывать** *imp.* bandage; **~ся,** bandage oneself.

забирáть(ся, -áю(сь *imp.* of забрáть(ся.

заби́тый, cowed, downtrodden. **заби́ть**[1], -бью, -бьёшь *perf.* (*imp.* забивáть), drive in, hammer in, ram in; score; seal, stop up, block up; obstruct; choke; jam; cram, stuff; beat up, knock senseless; render defenceless; beat; outdo, surpass; slaughter; ~ себé в гóлову, get it firmly fixed in one's head; **~ся,** hide, take refuge; become cluttered, become clogged; +в +*acc.* get into, penetrate. **за|би́ть(ся**[2] *perf.* begin to beat. **забия́ка,** -и *m.* and *f.* quarrelsome person; squabbler; trouble-maker; bully.

заблаговрéменно *adv.* in good time; well in advance. **заблаговрéменный,** done in good time.

заблагорассýдиться, -ится *perf. impers.* (+*dat.*) come into one's head; seem good (to); он придёт, когдá емý заблагорассýдится, he will come when he thinks fit, feels like it, feels so disposed.

заблестéть, -ещý, -ести́шь or -éщешь *perf.* begin to shine, glitter, glow.

заблуди́ться, -ужýсь, -ýдишься *perf.* lose one's way, get lost. **заблýдший,** lost, stray. **заблуждáться,** -áюсь *imp.* be mistaken. **заблуждéние,** -я, error; delusion.

за|бодáть, -áю *perf.*

забóй, -я, (pit-)face. **забóйщик,** -а, face-worker, cutter.

заболевáемость, -и, sickness rate; number of cases. **заболевáние,** -я, sickness, illness, disease; falling ill. **заболевáть**[1], -áю *imp.*, **заболéть**[1], -éю *perf.* fall ill, fall sick; be taken ill; +*instr.* go down with. **заболевáть**[2], -áет *imp.*, **заболéть**[2], -ли́т *perf.* (begin to) ache, (begin to) hurt; у меня́ заболéл зуб, I have tooth-ache.

забóр[1], -а, fence. **забóристый,** strong; pungent; risqué, racy. **забóрный,** fence; coarse, indecent; risqué.

забóр[2], -а, taking away; obtaining on credit.

забóртный, outboard.

забóта, -ы, concern; care, attention(s); cares, trouble(s). **забóтить,** -óчу *imp.* (*perf.* о~) trouble, worry, cause anxiety to; **~ся** *imp.* (*perf.* по~) worry, be troubled; take care (о+*prep.* of); take trouble; care. **забóтливый,** solicitous, thoughtful.

за|боцáть, -буцáть, -áю *perf.*

забракóванный, rejected; ~ товáр, rejects. **за|браковáть,** -кýю *perf.*

забра́сывать, -аю *imp.* of заброса́ть, забро́сить.
забра́ть, -беру́, -берёшь; -а́л, -а́, -о *perf.* (*imp.* забира́ть), take; take away; seize; appropriate; take in; turn off, turn aside; come over; catch; stop up, block up; **~ся,** climb; get to, get into; hide, go into hiding.
забреда́ть, -а́ю *imp.*, **забрести́,** -еду́, -едёшь; -ёл, -а́ *perf.* stray, wander; drop in.
за|брони́ровать[1] -рую *perf.* **за|брони́ровать**[2], -рую *perf.*
заброса́ть, -а́ю *perf.* (*imp.* забра́сывать), fill up; shower, bespatter, deluge. **забро́сить,** -о́шу *perf.* (*imp.* забра́сывать) throw; fling; cast; throw up, give up, abandon; neglect, let go; take, bring; leave behind; mislay. **забро́шенный,** neglected; deserted, desolate.
забры́згать, -аю *perf.*, **забры́згивать,** -аю *imp.* splash, spatter, bespatter.
забыва́ть, -а́ю *imp.*, **забы́ть,** -бу́ду *perf.* forget; **~ся,** doze off, drop off; lose consciousness; sink into a reverie; forget oneself. **забы́вчивый,** forgetful; absent-minded. **забытьё,** -я́, unconsciousness; drowsiness.
забью́, etc.: see заби́ть.
зав, -а *abbr.* заве́дующий, manager; chief, head.
зав- *abbr.* in *comb.* of заве́дующий, manager, director, superintendent; заводско́й, factory, works. **завга́р,** -а garage manager. **~ко́м,** -а, factory committee. **за́вуч,** -а, director of studies.
зава́ливать, -аю *imp.*, **завали́ть,** -лю́, -лишь *perf.* block up, obstruct; fill; pile; cram; overload; knock down, demolish; make a mess of; **~ся,** fall, tumble; collapse; overturn, tip up; come to grief.
зава́ривать, -аю *imp.*, **завари́ть,** -арю́, -а́ришь *perf.* make; brew; scald; weld. **зава́рка,** -и, brewing; scalding; welding.
заведе́ние, -я, establishment, institution; custom, habit. **заве́довать,** -дую *imp.* + *instr.* manage, superintend; be in charge of.
заве́домо *adv.* wittingly. **заве́домый,** notorious, undoubted; well-known.
заведу́ etc.: see завести́.
заве́дующий *sb.* (+ *instr.*) manager; head; director, superintendent; person in charge.
завезти́, -зу́, -зёшь; -ёз, -ла́ *perf.* (*imp.* завози́ть) convey, deliver; supply; leave.
за|вербова́ть, -бу́ю *perf.*
заве́ренн|ый, witnessed; certified; ~ая ко́пия, certified true copy. **завери́тель,** -я *m.* witness. **заве́рить,** -рю *perf.* (*imp.* заверя́ть) assure; certify; witness.
заверну́ть, -ну́, -нёшь *perf.* (*imp.* завёртывать, завора́чивать) wrap, wrap up; tuck up, roll up; screw tight, screw up; turn off; drop in, call in; turn; come on, come down; **~ся,** wrap oneself up, wrap up, muffle oneself.
заверте́ться, -рчу́сь, -ртишься *perf.* begin to turn, begin to spin; become flustered, lose one's head.
завёртка, -и, wrapping up; package. **завёртывать(ся,** -аю(сь *imp.* of заверну́ть(ся.
заверша́ть, -а́ю *imp.*, **заверши́ть,** -шу́ *perf.* complete, conclude, crown. **заверше́ние,** -я, completion; end, conclusion.
заверя́ть, -я́ю *imp.* of заве́рить.
заве́са, -ы, curtain; veil, screen. **заве́сить,** -е́шу *perf.* (*imp.* заве́шивать) cover; curtain, curtain off.
завести́, -еду́, -ёшь; -вёл, -а́ *perf.* (*imp.* заводи́ть) take, bring; leave, drop off; set up, start; acquire; institute, introduce; wind (up), crank; **~сь,** be; appear; be established, be set up; start.
заве́т, -а, behest, bidding, ordinance; Testament. **заве́тный,** cherished; intimate; secret.
заве́шивать, -аю *imp.* of заве́сить.
завеща́ние, -я, will, testament. **завеща́ть,** -а́ю, leave, bequeath; devise.
завзя́тый, inveterate, out-and-out downright; incorrigible.
завива́ть(ся, -а́ю(сь *imp.* of зави́ть(ся.
зави́вка, -и, waving; curling; wave.
зави́дно *impers.* + *dat.*; мне ~, I fee

envious. **зави́дный,** enviable. **зави́довать,** -дую *imp.* (*perf.* по~) + *dat.* envy.

за|визи́ровать, -рую *perf.*

завинти́ть, -нчу́ *perf.*, **зави́нчивать,** -аю *imp.* screw up; **~ся,** screw up.

зави́сеть, -и́шу *imp.*+от+*gen.* depend on; lie in the power of. **зави́симость,** -и, dependence; в зави́симости от, depending on, subject to. **зави́симый,** dependent.

зави́стливый, envious. **за́висть,** -и, envy.

завито́й; за́вит, -а́, -о, curled, waved. **завито́к,** -тка́, curl, lock; flourish; volute, scroll; tendril; helix. **зави́ть,** -вью́, -вьёшь; -и́л, -а́, -о *perf.* (*imp.* завива́ть) curl, wave; twist, wind; **~ся,** curl, wave, twine; curl, wave, one's hair; have one's hair waved.

завладева́ть, -а́ю *imp.*, **завладе́ть,** -е́ю *perf.*+*instr.* take possession of; seize, capture.

завлека́тельный, alluring; fascinating, captivating; attractive. **завлека́ть,** -а́ю *imp.*, **завле́чь,** -еку́, -ечёшь; -лёк, -ла́ *perf.* lure, entice; fascinate captivate.

заво́д[1], -а, factory; mill; works; plant; stud, studfarm.

заво́д[2], -а, winding up; winding mechanism. **заводи́ть(ся,** -ожу́(сь, -о́дишь(ся *imp.* of завести́(сь. **заво́дка,** -и, winding up; starting, cranking. **заводно́й,** clockwork, mechanical; winding, cranking, starting.

заво́дский, заводско́й, factory, works, mill; prefabricated; stud; *sb.* factory worker. **заводча́не,** -а́н *pl.* factory workers. **заво́дчик,** -а, manufacturer, mill-owner, factory owner.

завоева́ние, -я, winning; conquest; achievement, gain. **завоева́тель,** -я *m.* conqueror. **завоева́тельный,** aggressive; of aggression. **завоева́ть,** -ою́ю *perf.*, **завоёвывать,** -аю *imp.* conquer; win, gain; try to get.

завожу́ etc.: see заводи́ть, завози́ть.

заво́з, -а, delivery; carriage. **завози́ть,** -ожу́, -о́зишь *imp.* of завезти́.

завора́чивать(ся, -аю(сь *imp.* of завернýть(ся. **заворо́т**[1], -а, turn, turning; sharp bend. **за́ворот**[2], -а; ~ кишо́к, twisted intestines, volvulus.

заво́ю, etc.: see завы́ть.

завсегда́ *adv.* always. **завсегда́тай,** -я, habitué, frequenter.

за́втра, tomorrow. **за́втрак,** -а, breakfast; lunch. **за́втракать,** -аю *imp.* (*perf.* по~) have breakfast; have lunch. **за́втрашний,** tomorrow's; ~ день, tomorrow, the morrow; the (near) future.

за|вуали́ровать, -рую *perf.*

завыва́ть, -а́ю *imp.*, **завы́ть,** -во́ю *perf.* (begin to) howl.

завяза́ть, -яжу́, -я́жешь *perf.* (*imp.* завя́зывать), tie, tie up; knot; bind, bind up; start; **~ся,** start; arise; (of fruit) set. **завя́зка,** -и, string, lace, band; beginning, start; opening; plot.

за|вя́знуть, -ну; -я́з *perf.* **завя́зывать(ся,** -аю(сь *imp.* of завяза́ть(ся.

завя́лый, withered, faded; dead. **за|вя́нуть,** -ну; -я́л *perf.*

загада́ть, -а́ю *perf.*, **зага́дывать,** -аю *imp.* think of; plan ahead, look ahead; guess at the future; ~ зага́дку, ask a riddle. **зага́дка,** -и, riddle; enigma, mystery. **зага́дочный,** enigmatic, mysterious.

зага́р, -а, sunburn tan.

за|гаси́ть, -ашу́, -а́сишь *perf.* **за|га́снуть,** -ну *perf.*

загво́здка, -и, snag, obstacle; difficulty.

заги́б, -а, fold; bend; exaggeration; deviation. **загиба́ть(ся,** -а́ю(сь *imp.* of загну́ть(ся. **заги́бщик,** -а, deviationist.

за|гипнотизи́ровать, -рую *perf.*

загла́вие, -я, title; heading. **загла́вн|ый,** title; ~ая бу́ква, capital letter; ~ая роль, title-role, name-part.

загла́дить, -а́жу *perf.*, **загла́живать,** -аю *imp.* iron, iron out, press; make up for, make amends for; expiate; **~ся,** iron out, become smooth; fade.

за|гло́хнуть, -ну́; -гло́х *perf.*

заглуша́ть, -а́ю *imp.*, **за|глуши́ть,** -шу́ *perf.* drown, deaden, muffle; jam; choke; suppress, stifle; alleviate, soothe. **заглу́шка,** -и, choke, plug, stopper.

загляде́нье, -я, lovely sight. **загляде́ться, -яжу́сь** *perf.*, **загля́дываться, -аюсь** *imp.* на+*acc.* stare at; be lost in admiration of. **загля́дывать, -аю** *imp.*, **загляну́ть, -ну́, -нешь** *perf.* peep; glance; look in, drop in.

за́гнанный, driven, at the end of one's tether; tired out, exhausted, downtrodden, cowed. **загна́ть, -гоню́, -го́нишь; -а́л, -а́, -о** *perf.* (*imp.* загоня́ть) drive in, drive home; drive; exhaust; sell, flog.

загнива́ние, -я, rotting, putrescence; decay; suppuration. **загнива́ть, -а́ю** *imp.*, **загни́ть, -ию́, -иёшь; -и́л, -а́, -о** *perf.* rot; decay; fester.

загну́ть, -ну́, -нёшь *perf.* (*imp.* загиба́ть) turn up, turn down; bend, fold; crease; utter; **~ся,** turn up, stick up; turn down; turn up one's toes.

загова́ривать, -аю *imp.*, **заговори́ть, -рю́** *perf.* begin to talk; begin to speak; talk to death, tire out with talk; cast a spell over; protect with a charm (от+*gen.* against); ~ с+*instr.* speak to. **за́говор, -а,** plot, conspiracy; charm, spell. **загово́рщик, -а,** conspirator.

заголо́вок, -вка, title; heading; headline.

заго́н, -а, enclosure, pen; driving in; rounding up. **заго́нщик, -а,** beater. **загоня́ть**[1], -я́ю *imp.* of загна́ть. **загоня́ть**[2], -я́ю *perf.* tire out; work to death; grill.

загора́живать, -аю(сь *imp.* of загороди́ть.

загора́ть, -а́ю *imp.*, **загоре́ть, -рю́** *perf.* become sunburnt, brown, tan; (*sl.*) serve a sentence; **~ся,** catch fire; blaze, burn; break out, start; *impers.*+*dat.* become eager, want very much.

за́город, -а, suburbs; ~ом, in the suburbs.

загороди́ть, -рожу́, -ро́дишь *perf.* (*imp.* загора́живать), enclose, fence in; barricade; bar; obstruct, block. **загоро́дка, -и,** fence, enclosure.

за́городный, out-of-town; country; suburban.

загота́вливать, -аю *imp.*, **заготовля́ть, -я́ю** *imp.*, **загото́вить, -влю** *perf.* lay in; lay in a stock of, stockpile, store; prepare. **загото́вка, -и,** State procurement, purchase; laying in; stocking up, stockpiling; semi-finished product.

загради́тельный, defensive; barrage; mine-laying. **загради́ть, -ажу́** *perf.*, **загражда́ть, -а́ю** *imp.* block, obstruct; bar. **загражде́ние, -я,** blocking; obstruction; obstacle, barrier.

грани́ца, — **заграни́ца, -ы,** abroad, foreign parts. **заграни́чный,** foreign.

загреба́ть, -а́ю *imp.*, **загрести́, -ебу́, -ебёшь; -ёб, -ла́** *perf.* rake up, gather; rake in.

загри́вок, -вка, withers; nape (of the neck).

за|гримирова́ть(ся, -ру́ю(сь *perf.*

загроможда́ть, -а́ю *imp.*, **загромозди́ть, -зжу́** *perf.* block up, encumber; pack, cram; overload.

загрубе́лый, coarsened, callous. **за|грубе́ть, -е́ю** *perf.*

загружа́ть, -а́ю *imp.*, **за|грузи́ть, -ужу́, -у́зишь** *perf.* load; overload; feed; keep fully occupied; **~ся**+*instr.* load up with, take on. **загру́зка, -и,** loading, feeding; charge, load, capacity.

за|грунтова́ть, -ту́ю *perf.*

загрусти́ть, -ущу́ *perf.* grow sad.

загрязне́ние, -я, soiling; pollution; contamination. **за|грязни́ть, -ню́** *perf.*, **загрязня́ть, -я́ю** *imp.* soil, make dirty; contaminate, pollute; **~ся,** make oneself dirty, become dirty; be polluted.

загс, -а *abbr.* (отде́л) за́писи а́ктов гражда́нского состоя́ния, registry office.

загуби́ть, -блю́, -бишь *perf.* ruin; squander, waste.

за|гудрони́ровать, -рую *perf.*

загуля́ть, -я́ю *perf.*, **загу́ливать, -аю** *imp.* take to drink.

за|густе́ть, -е́ет *perf.* thicken, grow thick.

зад, -а (-у), *loc.* -у́; *pl.* -ы́, back; hindquarters; buttocks, seat; croup, rump; *pl.* back-yard(s); бить ~ом, kick; ~ом наперёд, back to front.

зада́бривать, -аю *imp.* of задо́брить.

задава́ть(ся, -даю́сь *imp.* of зада́ть(ся.

за|дави́ть, -влю́, -вишь *perf.* crush; run over, knock down.

задади́м, etc., за́дал, etc., зада́м, etc.: see зада́ть.
зада́ние, -я, task, job; commission, assignment.
зада́ривать, -аю *imp.*, **задари́ть**, -рю́ -ришь *perf.* load with presents; bribe.
зада́тки, -тков *pl.* instincts, inclinations.
зада́ток, -тка, deposit, advance.
зада́ть, -а́м, -а́шь, -а́ст, -ади́м; за́дал, -а́, -о *perf.* (*imp.* задава́ть) set; give; put; ~ вопро́с, ask a question; ~ тя́гу, take to one's heels; я ему́ зада́м! I'll give him what-for!; **~ся**, turn out well; work out, succeed; ~ся мы́слью, це́лью, set oneself, make up one's mind. **зада́ча**, -и, problem, sum; task; mission.
задвига́ть, -а́ю *imp.*, **задви́нуть**, -ну *perf.* bolt; bar; close; push, slide; ~ задви́жку, shoot a bolt; ~ за́навес, draw a curtain; **~ся**, shut; slide. **задви́жка**, -и, bolt; catch, fastening; slide-valve. **задвижно́й**, sliding.
задво́рки, -рок *pl.* back-yard; back parts; out-of-the-way place, backwoods.
задева́ть, -а́ю *imp.* of заде́ть.
заде́лать, -аю *perf.*, **заде́лывать**, -аю *imp.* do up; block up, close up; wall up; stop (up). **заде́лка**, -и, doing up; blocking up, stopping up.
заде́ну, etc.: see заде́ть. **задёргивать**, -аю *imp.* of задёрнуть. **за|деревене́ть**, -е́ю *perf.*
задержа́ние, -я, detention, arrest; retention; suspension. **задержа́ть**, -жу́, -жишь *perf.*, **заде́рживать**, -аю *imp.* detain; delay; withhold, keep back; retard; arrest; ~ дыха́ние, hold one's breath; **~ся**, stay too long; linger.
задёрнуть, -ну *perf.* (*imp.* задёргивать), pull; draw; cover; curtain off.
задеру́, etc.: see задра́ть.
заде́ть, -е́ну *perf.* (*imp.* задева́ть), touch, brush (against), graze; offend, wound; catch (against), catch on; ~ за живо́е, touch on the raw.
зади́ра, -ы *m.* and *f.* bully; trouble-maker. **задира́ть(ся**, -а́ю(сь *imp.* of задра́ть(ся. **зади́ристый**, provocative, pugnacious; cocky, pert.
за́дн|ий, back, rear; hind; дать ~ий ход, back, reverse; ~яя мысль, ulterior motive; ~ий план, background; ~ий прохо́д, anus, back passage. **за́дник**, -а, back; back drop.
задо́брить, -рю *perf.* (*imp.* зада́бривать) cajole; coax; win over.
задо́к, -дка́, back.
задо́лго *adv.* long before.
за|должа́ть, -а́ю *perf.*; **~ся**, run into debt. **задо́лженность**, -и, debts; liabilities.
задо́р, -а, fervour, ardour; enthusiasm; passion; temper. **задо́рный**, provocative; fervent, ardent; impassioned; quick-tempered.
задохну́ться, -ну́сь, -нёшься; -о́хся or -у́лся *perf.* (*imp.* задыха́ться) suffocate; choke; pant; gasp for breath.
за|дра́ть, -деру́, -дерёшь; -а́л, -а́, -о *perf.* (*imp.* also задира́ть) tear to pieces, kill; lift up, stretch up; break, split; provoke, insult; ~ нос, put on airs; **~ся**, break; split; ride up.
задрема́ть, -млю́, -млешь *perf.* doze off, begin to nod.
задува́ть, -а́ю *imp.* of заду́ть.
заду́мать, -аю *perf.*, **заду́мывать**, -аю *imp.* plan; intend; think of; conceive the idea (of); **~ся**, become thoughtful, pensive; meditate; ponder. **заду́мчивость**, -и, thoughtfulness; reverie. **заду́мчивый**, thoughtful, pensive.
заду́ть, -у́ю *perf.* (*imp.* задува́ть) blow out; blow in; begin to blow.
задуше́вный, sincere; cordial; intimate; ~ разгово́р, heart-to-heart talk.
за|души́ть, -ушу́, -у́шишь *perf.* **зады́** etc.: see зад.
задыха́ться, -а́юсь *imp.* of задохну́ться
заеда́ние, -я, jamming. **заеда́ть**, -а́ю *imp.* of зае́сть. **зади́м**, etc.: see зае́сть.
зае́зд, -а, calling in; lap, round, heat. **зае́здить**, -зжу *perf.* override; wear out; work too hard. **заезжа́ть**, -а́ю *imp.* of зае́хать. **зае́зженный**, hackneyed, trite; worn out. **зае́зж|ий**, visiting; ~ий двор, wayside inn; ~ая тру́ппа, touring company.
заём, за́йма, loan. **заёмный**, loan. **заёмщик**, -а, **-щица**, -ы, borrower, debtor.

заéсть, -éм, -éшь, -éст, -едúм *perf.* (*imp.* заедáть) torment, oppress; jam; foul; +*instr.* take with.

заéхать, -éду *perf.* (*imp.* заезжáть) call in; enter, ride in, drive in; land oneself; reach; +за+*acc.* go beyond, go past; +за+*instr.* call for, fetch.

за|жáрить(ся, -рю(сь *perf.*

зажáть, -жмý, -жмёшь *perf.* (*imp.* зажимáть) squeeze; press; clutch; grip; suppress.

зажéчь, -жгý, -жжёшь; -жёг, -жглá *perf.* (*imp.* зажигáть) set fire to; kindle; light; strike; inflame; **~ся,** catch fire; light up; flame up.

заживáть(ся, -áю(сь *imp.* of зажúть(ся. **заживúть, -влю́** *perf.*, **заживля́ть, -я́ю** *imp.* heal. **зáживо** *adv.* alive.

заживý, etc.: see зажúть.

зажигáлка, -и, lighter; incendiary. **зажигáтельн|ый,** inflammatory; incendiary; ~ая свечá, sparking-plug. **зажигáть(ся, -áю(сь** *imp.* of зажéчь(ся.

зажúм, -а, clamp; clutch; clip; (screw) terminal; suppression, clamping down. **зажимáть, -áю** *imp.* of зажáть. **зажúмистый,** strong, powerful; tight-fisted, stingy. **зажимнóй,** tight-fisted. **зажúмщик, -а,** suppressor.

зажúточность, -и, prosperity; easy circumstances. **зажúточный,** well-to-do; prosperous. **зажúть, -ивý, -ивёшь; -ил, -á, -о** *perf.* (*imp.* заживáть) heal; close up; begin to live; **~ся,** live to a great age; live too long.

зажмý, etc.: see зажáть. **за|жмýриться, -рюсь** *perf.*

зазеленéть, -éет *perf.* turn green.

заземлéние, -я, earthing; earth. **заземлúть, -лю́** *perf.*, **заземля́ть, -я́ю** *imp.* earth.

зазнавáться, -наю́сь, -наёшься *imp.*, **зазнáться, -áюсь** *perf.* give oneself airs, become conceited.

зазýбренный, notched, jagged, serrated. **зазýбрина, -ы,** notch, jag. **за|зубрúть**[1], **-рю́** *perf.*

за|зубрúть[2], **-рю́, -ýбрúшь** *perf.*

заúгрывать, -аю *imp.* make advances; flirt.

заúка, -и *m.* and *f.* stammerer, stutterer.

заикáние, -я, stammer, stutter; stammering, stuttering. **заикáться, -áюсь** *imp.*, **заикнýться, -нýсь, -нёшься** *perf.* stammer, stutter; +о+*prep.* hint at, mention, touch on.

заимообрáзно *adv.* on credit, on loan.

заúмствование, -я, borrowing, adoption. **заúмствованн|ый,** borrowed, taken over; ~ое слóво, loan-word. **заúмствовать, -твую** *perf.* and *imp.* (*perf.* also по~) borrow, take over, adopt.

заинтересóванный, interested, concerned. **заинтересовáть, -сýю** *perf.*, **заинтересóвывать, -аю** *imp.* interest; excite the curiosity of; **~ся**+*instr.* become interested in, take an interest in.

заúскивать, -аю *imp.* make up (to), ingratiate oneself.

зайдý, etc.: see зайтú. **займý,** etc.: see заня́ть.

зайтú, -йдý, -йдёшь; зашёл, -шлá *perf.* (*imp.* заходúть) call; look in, drop in; go go on; set; wane; +в+*acc.* get to, reach; +за+*acc.* go behind, turn; +за+*instr.* call for, go for, fetch.

зáйца, etc.: see зáяц. **зáйчик, -а,** dear little hare; reflection of sunlight. **зайчúха, -и,** doe (of hare). **зайчóнок, -нка;** *pl.* -чáта, -чáт, leveret.

закабалúть, -лю́ *perf.*, **закабаля́ть, -я́ю** *imp.* enslave.

закавкáзский, Trans-Caucasian.

закады́чный, intimate, bosom.

закáз, -а, order; prohibition; на ~, to order. **заказáть, -ажý, -áжешь** *perf.*, **закáзывать, -аю** *imp.* order; reserve, book. **закáзник, -а,** reserve; preserve. **заказн|óй,** made to order, made to measure, bespoke; registered; ~óе (письмó), registered letter. **закáзчик, -а,** customer, client.

закáл, -а, temper, tempering; stamp, cast; strength of character, backbone. **закалённый,** tempered, hardened, hard; seasoned, tough; fully trained. **закáливать, -аю** *imp.*, **закалúть, -лю́** *perf.* (*imp.* also закаля́ть) temper; harden, case-harden; harden off. **закáлка, -и** tempering, hardening; temper, calibre.

закáлывать, -аю *imp.* of заколóть. **закаля́ть,** -я́ю *imp.* of закали́ть. **закáнчивать(ся,** -аю(сь *imp.* of закóнчить(ся.

закáпать, -аю *perf.*, **закáпывать**[1], -аю *imp.* begin to drip; rain, fall in drops; pour in drops; spot, spatter.

закáпывать[2]**(ся,** -аюсь *imp.* of закопáть(ся.

закáт, -а, setting; sunset; decline; на ~е, at sunset; на ~е дней, in one's declining years. **закатáть,** -áю *perf.*, **закáтывать**[1], -аю *imp.* begin to roll; roll up; roll out; ~ в тюрьмý, throw into prison. **закати́ть,** -ачý, -áтишь *perf.*, **закáтывать**[2], -аю *imp.* roll; **~ся** roll; set; wane; vanish, disappear; go off; ~ся смéхом, burst out laughing. **закáтный,** sunset.

заквáсить, -áшу *perf.*, **заквáшивать,** -аю *imp.* ferment; leaven. **заквáска,** -и, ferment; leaven.

закидáть, -áю *perf.*, **заки́дывать**[1], -аю *imp.* shower; cover up; fill up; spatter, bespatter; ~ вопрóсами, ply with questions; ~ гря́зью, fling mud at.

заки́дывать[2], -аю *imp.*, **заки́нуть.** -ну *perf.* throw; throw out, away; fling, cast, toss.

закипáть, -áет *imp.*, **закипéть,** -пи́т *perf.* begin to boil; boil, simmer; be in full swing.

закисáть, -áю *imp.*, **заки́снуть,** -ну; -и́с. -ла *perf.* turn sour; become apathetic. **зáкись,** -и, oxide, protoxide; ~ азóта, nitrous oxide.

заклáд, -а. pawn; pledge; mortgage; bet, wager; би́ться об ~, bet, wager; в ~е, in pawn. **заклáдка,** -и, laying laying down; batch, charge; bookmark. **закладнáя** *sb.* mortgage. **закладнóй,** mortgage; pawn. **заклáдывать,** -аю *imp.* of заложи́ть.

заклéивать, -аю *imp.*, **заклéить,** -éю *perf.* glue up; stick up; seal; **~ся,** stick.

за|клейми́ть, -млю *perf.*

заклепáть, -áю *perf.*, **заклёпывать,** -аю *imp.* rivet. **заклёпка,** -и, rivet; riveting.

заклинáние, -я, incantation; spell, charm; exorcism. **заклинáтель.** -я *m.* exorcist; ~ змей, snake-charmer

заклинáть, -áю *imp.* conjure; invoke; exorcize; adjure, entreat.

заключáть, -áю *imp.*, **заключи́ть,** -чý *perf.* conclude; end; infer; enter into; contain; enclose; comprise; confine. **заключáться,** -áется, consist; lie, be; be contained. **заключéние,** -я conclusion; end; inference; resolution, decision; confinement, detention. **заключённый** *sb.* prisoner convict. **заключи́тельный,** final concluding.

закля́тие, -я, oath, pledge. **закля́тый,** sworn, inveterate; enchanted, bewitched.

заковáть, -кую, -куёшь *perf.*, **закóвывать,** -аю *imp.* chain; shackle, put in irons.

заколáчивать, -аю *imp.* of заколоти́ть.

заколдóванный, bewitched, enchanted; spellbound; ~ круг, vicious circle. **заколдовáть,** -дýю *perf.* bewitch, enchant; lay a spell on.

закóлка, -и, hairpin; hair-grip; hair-slide.

заколоти́ть, -лочý, -лóтишь *perf.* (*imp.* заколáчивать) board up; nail up; knock in, drive in; beat the life out of, knock insensible.

за|колóть, -олю́, -óлешь *perf.* (*imp.* also закáлывать) stab, spear, stick; kill; pin, pin up; fasten; (*impers.*) у меня́ заколóло в бокý, I have a stitch in my side; **~ся,** stab oneself.

закóн, -а, law; ~ бóжий, scripture, divinity. **законнорождённый,** legitimate. **закóнный,** lawful, legal; legitimate, rightful.

законо- in *comb.* law, legal. **законовéдение,** -я, law, jurisprudence. **~дáтельный,** legislative. **~мéрность,** -и, regularity, normality. **~мéрный,** regular, natural. **~положéние,** -я, statute. **~проéкт,** -а, bill.

за|конопáтить, -áчу *perf.* **за|консерви́ровать,** -рую *perf.* **за|конспекти́ровать,** -рую *perf.* **за|контрактовáть(ся,** -тýю(сь *perf.*

закóнченность, -и, finish; completeness. **закóнченный,** finished; complete; consummate. **закóнчить,** -чу *perf.* (*imp.* закáнчивать), end, finish; **~ся,** end, finish; come to an end.

закопа́ть, -а́ю *perf.* (*imp.* зака́пывать) begin to dig; bury; **~ся**, begin to rummage; bury oneself; dig (oneself) in.
закопте́лый, sooty, smutty; smoke-grimed. **за|копте́ть**, **-ти́т** *perf.* **за|копти́ть**, -пчу́ *perf.*
азкорене́лый, deep-rooted; ingrained; inveterate.
зако́рки, -рок *pl.* back, shoulders.
закосне́лый, deep-rooted; incorrigible, inveterate. **за|косне́ть**, -е́ю *perf.*
закостене́лый, ossified; stiff.
закоу́лок, -лка, back street, alley, passage; secluded corner, nook; знать все закоу́лки, know all the ins and outs.
закочене́лый, numb with cold. **за|кочене́ть**, -е́ю *perf.*
закра́дываться, -аюсь *imp.* of закра́сться. **закра́ивать**, -аю *imp.* of закрои́ть.
закра́сить, -а́шу *perf.* (*imp.* закра́шивать) paint over, paint out.
закра́сться, -аду́сь, -адёшься *perf.* (*imp.* закра́дываться) steal in, creep in.
закра́шивать, -аю *imp.* of закра́сить.
закре́па, -ы, catch; fastener. **закрепи́тель**, -я *m.* fastener; fixative, fixing agent, fixer. **закрепи́ть**, -плю́ *perf.*, **закрепля́ть**, -я́ю *imp.* fasten, secure; make fast; fix; consolidate; +за+ *instr.* allot to, assign to; appoint to, attach to; ~ за собо́й secure; **~ся**, на+*acc.* consolidate one's hold on.
закрепости́ть -ощу́ *perf.* **закрепоща́ть**, -а́ю *imp.* enslave; make a serf of. **закрепоще́ние**, -я, enslavement; slavery, serfdom.
закрича́ть, -чу́ *perf.* cry out; begin to shout; give a shout.
закрои́ть, -ою́ *perf.* (*imp.* закра́ивать) cut out; groove. **закро́й**, -я, cutting out; cut, style; groove. **закро́йный**, cutting, cutting-out. **закро́йщик**, -а, cutter.
за́кром, -а; *pl.* -а́, corn-bin.
закро́ю, etc.: see закры́ть. **закрою́**, etc.: see закрои́ть.
закругле́ние, -я, rounding, curving; curve; curvature; well-rounded period.
закруглённый; -ён, -а́, rounded; well-rounded. **закругли́ть**, -лю́ *perf.*, **закругля́ть**, -я́ю *imp.* make round; round off; **~ся**, become round.
закружи́ться, -ужу́сь, -у́жи́шься *perf.* begin to whirl, begin to go round; be in a whirl.
за|крути́ть, -учу́, -у́тишь *perf.*, **закру́чивать**, -аю *imp.* twist, twirl, whirl round; wind round; roll; turn; screw in; turn the head of; **~ся**, twist twirl, whirl; wind round; begin to whirl.
закрыва́ть, -а́ю *imp.* **закры́ть**, -ро́ю *perf.* close, shut; shut off, turn off; close down, shut down; cover; **~ся**, close, shut; end; close down; cover oneself, take cover; find shelter, shelter. **закры́тие**, -я, closing; shutting; closing down; shelter, cover. **закры́т|ый**, closed, shut; private; ~ое голосова́ние, secret ballot; ~ое заседа́ние, private meeting; closed session; ~ое мо́ре, inland sea; ~ое пла́тье, high-necked dress; ~ый просмо́тр, private view.
закули́сный, behind the scenes; secret; underhand, under-cover.
закупа́ть, -а́ю *imp.*, **закупи́ть**, -плю́, -пишь *perf.* buy up; lay in; stock up with; bribe. **заку́пка**, -и, purchase. **закупно́й**, bought, purchased.
заку́поривать, -аю *imp.*, **заку́порить**, -рю *perf.* cork; stop up; plug, clog; shut up; coop up. **заку́порка**, -и, corking; embolism, thrombosis.
заку́почный, purchase. **заку́пщик**, -а, **-щица** -ы, purchaser; buyer.
заку́ривать, -аю *imp.*, **закури́ть**, -рю́, -ришь *perf.* light; light up; begin to smoke.
закуси́ть, -ушу́, -у́сишь *perf.*, **заку́сывать**, -аю *imp.* have a snack have a bite; +*instr.* have a bit of; ~ удила́, take the bit between one's teeth. **заку́ска**, -и, hors-d'oeuvre; appetizer, snack, titbit. **заку́сочная** *sb.* snack-bar.
за|ку́тать, -аю *perf.*, **заку́тывать**, -аю *imp.* wrap up muffle; tuck up; **~ся**, wrap oneself up.
зал, -а, hall, room; ~ ожида́ния, waiting-room.
зала́вок. -вка, chest, locker.

залёг, etc.: see зале́чь. **залега́ние** -я, bedding; bed, seam. **залега́ть**, -а́ю *imp.* of зале́чь.

за|ледене́ть, -е́ю *perf.*

залежа́лый, stale, long unused. **залежа́ться**, -жу́сь *perf.*, **залёживаться**, -аюсь *imp.* lie too long; lie idle a long time; find no market; become stale. **за́лежь**, -и, deposit, bed, seam; stale goods.

залеза́ть, -а́ю *imp.*, **зале́зть**, -зу; -е́з, *perf.* climb, climb up; get in; creep in; ~ в долги́, run into debt.

за|лепи́ть, -плю́, -пишь *perf.*, **залепля́ть**, -я́ю *imp.* paste up, paste over; glue up, stick up.

залета́ть, -а́ю *imp.*, **залете́ть**, -ечу́ *perf.* fly; +в+*acc.* fly into; land at; +за+*acc.* fly over, fly beyond. **залётн|ый**, flown in; ~ая пти́ца, bird of passage.

зале́чивать, -аю *imp.*, **залечи́ть**, -чу́, -чишь *perf.* heal, cure; **~ся**, heal, heal up.

зале́чь, -ля́гу, -ля́жешь; залёг, -ла́ *perf.* (*imp.* залега́ть) lie down; lie low; lie in wait; lie, be deposited; take root, become ingrained; become blocked.

зали́в, -а, bay; gulf; creek, cove. **залива́ть**, -а́ю *imp.*, **зали́ть**, -лью́, -льёшь; за́лил, -а́, -о *perf.* flood, inundate; quench, extinguish, put out; lay, spread; stop holes in; +*instr.* pour over, spill on; ~ ска́терть черни́лами spill ink on the tablecloth; ~ ту́шью, ink in; **~ся**, be flooded; pour, spill; +*instr.* break into, burst into; ~ся слеза́ми, burst into tears, dissolve in tears.

зало́г, -а deposit; pledge; security, mortgage; token; voice. **заложи́ть**, -жу́, -жишь *perf.* (*imp.* закла́дывать) lay; put; mislay; pile up, heap up; block up; pawn, mortgage; harness; lay in, store, put by. **зало́жник**, -а, hostage.

залп, -а, volley, salvo; ~ом, without pausing for breath, at one gulp.

залью́, etc.: see зали́ть. **заля́гу**, etc.: see зале́чь.

зам, -а *abbr.* замести́тель, assistant, deputy. **зам-** *abbr.* in *comb.* of замести́тель assistant, deputy; vice-. **замдире́ктора**, deputy director; vice-principal, assistant head. **~мини́стра**, deputy minister. **~председа́теля**, vice-chairman.

за|ма́зать, -а́жу *perf.*, **зама́зывать**, -аю *imp.* paint over; efface; slur over; putty; daub, smear; soil; **~ся**, smear oneself; get dirty. **зама́зка**, -и, putty, paste, cement; puttying.

зама́лчивать, -аю *imp.* of замолча́ть.

зама́нивать, -аю *imp.*, **замани́ть**, -ню́, -нишь *perf.* entice, lure; attract; decoy. **зама́нчивость**, -и, allurements. **зама́нчивый**, tempting, alluring.

за|мара́ть(ся, -а́ю(сь *perf.* **за|марино-ва́ть**, -ну́ю *perf.*

замаскиро́ванный, masked; disguised; concealed. **за|маскирова́ть**, -ру́ю *perf.*, **замаскиро́вывать**, -аю *imp.* mask; disguise; camouflage; conceal; **~ся**, disguise oneself.

зама́х, -а, threatening gesture. **замахива́ться**, -аюсь *imp.*, **замахну́ться**, -ну́сь, -нёшься *perf.* threaten; +*instr.* raise threateningly; ~ руко́й на+*acc.* life one's hand against.

зама́чивать, -аю *imp.* of замочи́ть.

зама́щивать, -аю *imp.* of замости́ть.

замедле́ние, -я, slowing down, deceleration; delay. **заме́дленный**, retarded, delayed. **заме́длить**, -лю *perf.*, **замедля́ть**, -я́ю *imp.* slow down, retard; reduce, slacken; delay; hold back; be slow (to), be long (in); **~ся**, slow down; slacken, grow slower.

замёл, etc.: see замести́.

заме́на, -ы, substitution; replacement; commutation; substitute. **замени́мый**, replaceable. **замени́тель**, -я *m.* (+*gen.*) substitute (for). **замени́ть**, -ню́, -нишь *perf.*, **заменя́ть**, -я́ю *imp.* replace; take the place of; be a substitute for.

замере́ть, -мру́ -мрёшь; за́мер, -ла́, -о *perf.* (*imp.* замира́ть) stand still; freeze, be rooted to the spot; die down, die away; die.

замерза́ние, -я, freezing. **замерза́ть**, -а́ю *imp.*, **за|мёрзнуть**, -ну *perf.* freeze, freeze up; freeze to death.

заме́рить, -рю *perf.* (*imp.* замеря́ть) measure, gauge. **заме́рн|ый**, gauge,

measuring; ~ая ре́йка, dip-stick, gauge rod.
за́мертво *adv.* like one dead, in a dead faint.
замеря́ть, -я́ю *imp.* of заме́рить.
замеси́ть, -ешу́, -е́сишь *perf.* (*imp.* заме́шивать), knead.
замести́ -ету́, -етёшь; -мёл, -á *perf.* (*imp.* замета́ть) sweep up; cover; ~ следы́ cover one's traces.
замести́тель, -я *m.*, **~ница**, -ы, substitute; assistant, deputy, vice-. **замести́ть**, -ещу́ *perf.* (*imp.* замеща́ть), replace, be substitute for; deputize for, act for; serve in place of.
замета́ть[1], -а́ю *imp.* of замести́.
замета́ть[2], -а́ю *perf.* (*imp.* замётывать) tack, baste.
заме́тить, -е́чу *perf.* (*imp.* замеча́ть) notice; take notice of, make a note of; remark, observe. **заме́тка**, -и, paragraph; mark; note. **заме́тный**, noticeable; appreciable; outstanding.
замётывать, -аю *imp.* of замета́ть[2].
замеча́ние, -я, remark, observation; reprimand, reproof. **замеча́тельный**, remarkable; splendid, wonderful. **замеча́ть**, -а́ю *imp.* of заме́тить. **заме́ченный**, discovered; noticed; detected.
замеша́тельство, -а, confusion; embarrassment. **замеша́ть**, -а́ю *perf.*, **заме́шивать**, -аю *imp.* mix up, entangle; **~ся**, become mixed up, become entangled; mix, mingle. **заме́шивать**, -аю *imp.* of замеси́ть, замеша́ть.
заме́шка, -и delay. **заме́шкаться**, -аюсь *perf.* linger, loiter.
замеща́ть, -а́ю *imp.* of замести́ть. **замеще́ние**, -я, substitution; filling.
замина́ть, -а́ю *imp.* of замя́ть. **зами́нка**, -и, hitch; hesitation.
замира́ние, -я, dying out, dying down; sinking. **замира́ть**, -а́ю *imp.* of замере́ть.
за́мкнутость, -и, reserve, reticence. **за́мкнутый**, reserved; closed, exclusive. **замкну́ть**, -ну, -нёшь *perf.* (*imp.* замыка́ть) lock; close; **~ся**, close; shut oneself up; become reserved; ~ся в себя́, shrink into oneself.
замну́, etc.: see замя́ть.
за́мок[1], -мка, castle.
замо́к[2], -мка́, lock; padlock; keystone; bolt; clasp, clip; запере́ть на ~, lock; под замко́м, under lock and key.
замо́лвить, -влю *perf.*; ~ слове́чко, put in a word.
замолка́ть, -а́ю *imp.*, **замо́лкнуть**, -ну; -мо́лк *perf.* fall silent; stop, cease.
замолча́ть, -чу́ *perf.* (*imp.* зама́лчивать) fall silent; cease corresponding; keep silent about, hush up.
замора́живание, -я, freezing; chilling, refrigeration; congealing; quenching. **замора́живать**, -аю *imp.*, **заморо́зить**, -ро́жу *perf.* freeze; refrigerate; ice, chill. **заморо́женный**, frozen; iced.
за́морозки, -ов *pl.* (slight) frosts.
замо́рский, overseas.
замо́рыш, -а, weakling, puny creature; runt.
за|мости́ть, -ощу́ *perf.* (*imp.* also зама́щивать) pave.
за|мочи́ть, -чу́, -чишь *perf.* (*imp.* also зама́чивать) wet; soak; ret.
замо́чн|ый, lock; ~ая сква́жина, keyhole.
замру́, etc.: see замере́ть.
за́муж *adv.*; вы́йти ~ (за+*acc.*) marry; вы́дать ~ за+*acc.* marry (off) to. **за́мужем** *adv.* married (за+*instr.* to). **заму́жество**, -а, marriage.
замурова́ть, -ру́ю *perf.*, **замуро́вывать**, -аю *imp.* brick up; wall up; immure.
за|мути́ть(ся, -учу́(сь, -у́тишь(ся *perf.*
заму́чивать, -аю *imp.*, **за|му́чить**, -чу *perf.* torment; wear out; plague the life out of, bore to tears. **за|му́читься**, -чусь *perf.*
за́мша, -и, suede; chamois leather, shammy.
замыка́ние, -я, locking, closing; closure; short circuit, shorting. **замыка́ть(ся**, -а́ю(сь *imp.* of замкну́ть(ся. **замыка́ющ|ий**; идти́ ~им, bring up the rear.
за́мысел, -сла, project, plan; design, scheme; idea. **замы́слить**, -лю *perf.*, **замышля́ть**, -я́ю *imp.* plan; contemplate, intend, think of. **замыслова́тый**, intricate, complicated.
замя́ть, -мну, -мнёшь *perf.* (*imp.* замина́ть) hush up, stifle, smother;

suppress; put a stop to; distract attention from; **~ся**, falter; stumble; stop short.

за́навес, -а, **занаве́ска**, -и, curtain. **занаве́сить**, -е́шу *perf.*, **занаве́шивать**, -аю *imp.* curtain; hang; cover.

за|неме́ть, -е́ю *perf.*

занесённый сне́гом, snowbound. **занести́**, -су́, -сёшь; -ёс, -ла́ *perf.* (*imp.* заноси́ть) bring; leave, drop; raise, lift; note down, put down, enter; cover with snow, sand, etc.; ~ в протоко́л, place on record, record in the minutes; **~сь**, be carried away.

занима́тельный, entertaining, diverting; absorbing. **занима́ть**, -а́ю *imp.* (*perf.* заня́ть) occupy; interest; engage, secure; take, take up; borrow; **~ся** + *instr.* be occupied with, be engaged in; work at, work on; study; busy oneself with; devote oneself to.

зано́за, -ы, splinter. **занози́ть**, -ожу́ *perf.* get a splinter in.

зано́с, -а, drift, accumulation; raising lifting; skid, skidding. **заноси́ть(ся**, -ошу́(сь, -о́сишь(ся *imp.* of занести́(сь. **зано́сный**, alien, foreign, imported. **зано́счивый**, arrogant, haughty.

за|нумерова́ть, -ру́ю *perf.*

заня́тие, -я, occupation; pursuit; *pl.* studies, work. **заня́тный**, entertaining, amusing; interesting. **за́нято** *adv.* engaged, number engaged. **занято́й**, busy. **за́нятый**; -нят, -а́, -о, occupied taken; engaged; employed; busy. **заня́ть(ся**, займу́(сь, -мёшь(ся; за́нял(ся, -а́(сь, -о(сь *perf.* of занима́ть(ся.

заодно́ *adv.* in concert; at one; at the same time.

заострённый, pointed, sharp. **заостри́ть**, -рю́ *perf.*, **заостря́ть**, -я́ю *imp.* sharpen; stress, emphasize; **~ся**, grow sharp; become pointed.

заочник, -а, **-ница**, -ы student taking correspondence course. **зао́чно** *adv.* in one's absence; by correspondence course. **зао́чн|ый**; ~ый курс, correspondence course; ~ое обуче́ние, postal tuition; ~ый пригово́р, judgment by default.

за́пад, -а, west; the West, the Occident. **за́падный**, west, western; westerly.

западня́, -и́; *gen. pl.* -не́й, trap; pitfall, snare.

запа́здывать, -аю *imp.* of запозда́ть.

запа́ивать, -аю *imp.* of запая́ть. **запа́йка**, soldering; sealing (off), seal.

за|пакова́ть, -ку́ю *perf.*, **запако́вывать**, -аю, *imp.* pack; wrap up, do up.

за|па́костить, -ощу *perf.*

запа́л, -а, ignition; fuse; detonator. **запа́ливать**, -аю *imp.*, **запали́ть**, -лю́, light, ignite, kindle; set fire to. **запа́льн|ый**, ignition; detonating; ~ая свеча́, (sparking-)plug. **запа́льчивый**, quick-tempered.

запа́с, -а, reserve; stock, supply; hem; *pl.* turnings; вы́пустить ~, let out; отложи́ть про ~, put by; про ~, for an emergency; прове́рить ~, take stock; ~ слов, vocabulary. **запаса́ть**, -а́ю *imp.*, **запасти́**, -су́, -сёшь; -а́с, -ла́ *perf.* stock, store; lay in a stock of; **~ся**, +*instr.* provide oneself with; stock up with; arm oneself with. **запа́сливый**, thrifty; provident. **запа́сник**, -а, **запасно́й** *sb.* reservist. **запасно́й, запа́сный**, spare; reserve; ~ вы́ход, emergency exit; ~ путь, siding.

за́пах[1], -а (-у), smell.

запа́х[2], -а, wrapover. **запа́хивать**, -аю *imp.*, **запахну́ть**[2], -ну́, -нёшь *perf.* wrap up; **~ся**, wrap (oneself) up.

запа́хнуть[1], -ну; -а́х *perf.* begin to smell.

за|па́чкать, -аю *perf.*

запа́шка, -и, ploughing in, ploughing up; plough-land, arable land.

запая́ть, -я́ю *perf.* (*imp.* запа́ивать) solder; seal, seal off.

запе́в, -а, solo part. **запева́ла**, -ы *m.* singer of solo part; leader of chorus; leader, instigator. **запева́ть**, -а́ю *imp.* (*perf.* запе́ть) lead the singing, set the tune.

запека́нка, -и, baked pudding, baked dish; spiced brandy. **запека́ть(ся**, -а́ю *imp.* of запе́чь(ся. **запеку́** etc.: see запе́чь.

за|пелена́ть, -а́ю *perf.*

запере́ть. -пру́, -прёшь; за́пер, -ла́, -ло

perf. (*imp.* запира́ть) lock; lock in; shut up; bar; block up; ~ на засо́в bolt; **~ся,** lock oneself in; shut (oneself) up; +в+*prep.* refuse to admit, refuse to speak about.
запе́ть, -пою́, -поёшь *perf.* (*imp.* запева́ть) begin to sing; ~ друго́е, change one's tune; ~ пе́сню, strike up a song; plug a song.
запеча́тать, -аю *perf.*, **запеча́тывать,** -аю *imp.* seal. **запечатлева́ть,** -а́ю *imp.* **запечатле́ть,** -е́ю *perf.* imprint, impress, engrave; **~ся,** imprint, stamp, impress, itself.
запе́чь, -еку́, -ечёшь; -пёк, -ла́ *perf.* (*imp.* запека́ть) bake; **~ся,** bake; become parched; clot, coagulate.
запива́ть, -а́ю *imp.* of запи́ть.
запина́ться, -а́юсь *imp.* of запну́ться. **запи́нка,** -и, hesitation; без запи́нки, smoothly.
запира́тельство, -а, denial, disavowal. **запира́ть(ся,** -а́ю(сь *imp.* of запере́ть(ся.
записа́ть, -ишу́, -и́шешь *perf.* **запи́сывать,** -аю *imp.* note, make a note of, take notes; take down; record; enter, register, enrol; make over (to); begin to write, begin to correspond; **~ся,** register, enter one's name, enrol; ~ся в клуб, join a club; ~ся к врачу́, make an appointment with the doctor. **запи́ска,** -и, note; minute, memorandum; *pl.* notes; memoirs; transactions. **записн|о́й,** note, writing; regular; inveterate; ~а́я кни́жка, notebook. **за́пись,** -и, writing down; recording; registration; entry, record; deed.
запи́ть, -пью́, -пьёшь; за́пи́л, -а́, -о *perf.* (*imp.* запива́ть) begin drinking, take to drink; wash down (with), take (with).
запиха́ть, -а́ю *perf.*, **запи́хивать,** -аю *imp.*, **запихну́ть,** -ну́, -нёшь *perf.* push in, cram in.
запишу́, etc.: see записа́ть.
запла́канный, tear-stained; in tears. **запла́кать,** -а́чу *perf.* begin to cry.
за|плани́ровать, -рую *perf.*
запла́та, -ы, patch. **запла́танный,** patched, mended.
за|плати́ть, -ачу́, -а́тишь *perf.* pay; +за+*acc.* pay for; ~ по счёту, settle an account.
запла́чу, etc.: see запла́кать. **заплачу́**: see заплати́ть.
запле́сневелый, mouldy, mildewed. **за|пле́сневеть,** -веет *perf.*
заплести́, -ету́, -етёшь; -ёл, -а́ *perf.*, **заплета́ть,** -а́ю *imp.* plait, braid; **~сь,** stumble; be unsteady in one's gait; falter.
за|пломбирова́ть, -ру́ю *perf.*
заплы́в, -а, heat, round. **заплыва́ть,** -а́ю *imp.*, **заплы́ть,** -ыву́, -ывёшь; -ы́л, -а́, -о *perf.* swim in, sail in; swim out, sail out; be swollen, be bloated.
запну́ться, -ну́сь, -нёшься *perf.* (*imp.* запина́ться) hesitate; stumble, halt; stammer; ~ ного́й, trip (up).
запове́дник, -а, reserve; preserve; госуда́рственный ~, national park. **запове́дный,** prohibited; ~ лес, forest reserve. **за́поведь,** -и, precept; commandment.
запода́зривать, -аю *imp.*, **заподо́зрить,** -рю *perf.* suspect (в+*prep.* of); be suspicious of.
запо́ем: see запо́й.
запозда́лый, belated; late; delayed. **запозда́ть,** -а́ю *perf.* (*imp.* запа́здывать) be late.
запо́й, -я, hard drinking; alcoholism; кури́ть запо́ем, smoke like a chimney; пить запо́ем, have bouts of heavy drinking. **запо́йный** *adj.*; ~ пья́ница, chronic drunk; old soak.
заполза́ть, -а́ю, **заползти́,** -зу́, -зёшь; -о́лз, -зла́, creep in, creep under; crawl in, crawl under.
запо́лнить, -ню *perf.*, **заполня́ть,** -я́ю *imp.* fill (in, up).
заполя́рный, polar; trans-polar. **заполя́рье,** -я, polar regions.
запомина́ть, -а́ю *imp.*, **запо́мнить,** -ню *perf.* remember, keep in mind; memorize; **~ся,** be retained in memory, stay in one's mind. **запомина́ющ|ий;** ~ее устро́йство, (computer) memory.
за́понка, -и, cuff-link; (collar-)stud.
запо́р, -а, bolt; lock; closing, locking, bolting; constipation; на ~е, locked, bolted.

запороши́ть, -ши́т *perf.* powder, dust, scatter.
запоте́лый, misted, dim. **за|поте́ть**, -е́ет *perf.* mist over.
запою́, etc.: see запе́ть.
заправи́ла, -ы, boss. **запра́вить**, -влю *perf.*, **заправля́ть**, -я́ю *imp.* insert, tuck in; prepare, set up; fuel, refuel, fill up; season, dress flavour; mix in; ~ ла́мпу, trim a lamp; заправля́ть дела́ми, boss the show; **~ся**, refuel. **запра́вка**, -и, refuelling, filling; servicing, setting up; seasoning, dressing, flavouring.
запра́шивать, -аю *imp.* of запроси́ть.
запре́т, -а, prohibition, ban; под ~ом, banned, prohibited. **запрети́тельный**, prohibitive. **запрети́ть**, -ещу́ *perf.*, **запреща́ть**, -а́ю *imp.* prohibit, forbid, ban. **запре́тный**, forbidden, prohibited. **запреще́ние**, -я, prohibition; distraint. **запрещённый**, forbidden, illicit.
за|прихо́довать, -дую *perf.* **за|программи́ровать**, -рую *perf.*
запроки́дывать, -аю *imp.*, **запроки́нуть**, -ну *perf.* throw back; **~ся**, throw oneself back; fall back, sink back.
запро́с, -а, inquiry; overcharging; *pl.* requirements, needs. **запроси́ть**, -ошу́, -о́сишь *perf.* (*imp.* запра́шивать), inquire; inquire of, question; ask (a high price).
за́просто *adv.* without ceremony, without formality.
за|протоколи́ровать, -рую *perf.* **запрошу́**, etc.: see запроси́ть. **запру́**, etc.: see запере́ть.
запру́да, -ы, dam, weir; mill-pond. **за|пруди́ть**, -ужу́, -у́дишь *perf.*, **запру́живать**, -аю *imp.* block; dam; fill to overflowing, cram, jam.
запряга́ть, -а́ю *imp.* of запря́чь. **запрягу́**, etc.: see запря́чь. **запря́жка**, -и, harnessing; harness, team.
запря́тать(ся, -я́чу(сь *perf.*, **запря́тывать(ся**, -аю(сь *imp.* hide.
запря́чь, -ягу́, -яжёшь; -я́г, -ла́ *perf.* (*imp.* запряга́ть) harness; yoke.
запу́ганный, cowed, intimidated, broken-spirited. **запуга́ть**, -а́ю *perf.*, **запу́гивать**, -аю *imp.* cow, intimidate.
запуска́ть, -а́ю *imp.*, **запусти́ть**, -ущу́, -у́стишь *perf.* thrust (in), push (in), dig (in); start, start up; launch; (+*acc.* or *instr.*) throw, fling; neglect, let go. **запусте́лый**, neglected; desolate. **запусте́ние**, -я, neglect; desolation.
запу́танный, tangled; intricate, involved, knotty. **за|пу́тать**, -аю *perf.*, **запу́тывать**, -аю *imp.* tangle; confuse; complicate; muddle; involve; **~ся**, get tangled, get entangled; be involved, get involved; become complicated.
запу́щенный, neglected. **запущу́**, etc.: see запусти́ть.
запча́сть, -и; *gen. pl.* -е́й *abbr.* запасна́я часть, spare part, spare.
за|пыли́ть(ся, -лю́(сь *perf.*
запыха́ться, -а́юсь *perf.* be out of breath.
запью́, etc.: see запи́ть.
запя́стье, -я, wrist; bracelet.
запята́я *sb.* comma; difficulty, snag.
за|пятна́ть, -а́ю *perf.*
зараба́тывать, -аю *imp.*, **зарабо́тать**, -аю *perf.* earn; start (up), begin to work; **~ся**, overwork. **за́работн|ый**; ~ая пла́та, wages; pay, salary. **за́работок**, -тка, earnings.
заража́ть, -а́ю *imp.*, **зарази́ть**, -ажу́ *perf.* infect; **~ся**+*instr.* be infected with, catch. **зара́за**, -ы, infection, contagion; pest, plague. **зарази́тельный**, infectious; catching. **зара́зный**, infectious, contagious; *sb.* infectious case.
зара́нее *adv.* beforehand; in good time; in advance.
зараста́ть, -а́ю *imp.*, **зарасти́**, -ту́, -тёшь; -ро́с, -ла́ *perf.* be overgrown; heal, skin over.
за́рево, -а glow.
за|регистри́ровать(ся, -и́рую(сь *perf.* **за|регули́ровать**, -рую *perf.*
заре́з, -а (-у), disaster; до ~у, desperately, badly, urgently. **за|ре́зать**, -е́жу *perf.* kill, knife; slaughter; **~ся**, cut one's throat.
зарека́ться, -а́юсь *imp.* of заре́чься.
зарекомендова́ть, -ду́ю *perf.*; ~ себя́, show oneself, present oneself; +*instr.* prove oneself, show oneself, to be.
заре́чься, -еку́сь, -ечёшься; -ёкся, -екла́сь *perf.* (*imp.* зарека́ться) +*inf.*

renounce; swear off, promise to give up.
за|ржа́веть, -еет *perf.* **заржа́вленный**, rusty.
зарисова́ть, -су́ю *perf.*, **зарисо́вывать**, -аю *imp.* sketch. **зарисо́вка**, -и, sketching; sketch.
зарни́ца, -ы, summer lightning.
зароди́ть, -ожу́ *perf.*, **зарожда́ть**, -а́ю *imp.* generate, engender; **~ся**, be born; arise. **заро́дыш**, -а, foetus; bud; embryo, germ. **заро́дышевый**, embryonic. **зарожде́ние**, -я, conception; origin.
заро́к, -а, (solemn) promise, vow, pledge, undertaking.
заро́с, etc.: see зарасти́. **за́росль**, -и, thicket; brushwood.
заро́ю, etc.: see зары́ть.
зарпла́та, -ы *abbr.* за́работная пла́та, wages; pay; salary.
заруба́ть, -а́ю *imp.* of заруби́ть.
зарубе́жный, foreign.
заруби́ть, -блю́, -бишь *perf.* (*imp.* заруба́ть, -а́ю) kill, cut down; notch, cut in. **зару́бка**, -и notch, incision.
за|румя́нить(ся, -ню(сь *perf.*
заруча́ться, -а́юсь *imp.*, **заручи́ться**, -учу́сь *perf.* + *instr.* secure. **зару́чка**, -и, pull, protection.
зарыва́ть, -а́ю *imp.*, **зары́ть** -ро́ю *perf.* bury; **~ся**, bury oneself; dig in.
заря́, -и́; *pl.* зо́ри, зо́рь, dawn, daybreak; sunset, nightfall; reveille, retreat.
заря́д, -а, charge; cartridge; fund, supply. **заряди́ть**, -яжу́, -я́ди́шь *perf.*, **заряжа́ть**, -а́ю *imp.* load; charge; stoke; **~ся**, be loaded; be charged. **заря́дка**, -и, loading; charging; exercises, drill. **заряжа́ющий** *sb.* loader.
заса́да, -ы, ambush. **засади́ть**, -ажу́, -а́дишь *perf.*, **заса́живать**, -аю *imp.* plant; plunge, drive; shut in, confine; keep in; set (за + *acc.* to); ~ (в тюрьму́), put in prison, lock up. **заса́дка**, -и, planting. **заса́живаться**, -аюсь *imp.* of засе́сть.
заса́ливать[1], -аю *imp.* of засоли́ть.
заса́ливать[2], -аю *imp.*, **заса́лить**, -лю *perf.* soil, make greasy.
заса́сывать, -аю *imp.* of засоса́ть.
заса́харенный, candied, crystallized.
засвети́ть, -ечу́, -е́тишь *perf.* light; **~ся**, light up. **за́светло** *adv.* before nightfall, before dark.
за|свиде́тельствовать, -твую *perf.*
засе́в, -а, sowing; seed, seed-corn; sown area. **засева́ть**, -а́ю *imp.* of засе́ять.
заседа́ние, -я, meeting; session, sitting; conference. **заседа́тель**, -я *m.* assessor. **заседа́ть**, -а́ю *imp.* sit, meet, be in session.
засе́ивать, -аю *imp.* of засе́ять. **засе́к**, etc.: see засе́чь. **засека́ть**, -а́ю *imp.* of засе́чь.
засекре́тить, -ре́чу *perf.*, **засекре́чивать**, -аю *imp.* classify; restrict; make secret; clear, give access to secret material. **засекре́ченный**, classified; cleared; hush-hush, secret.
засеку́, etc.: see засе́чь. **засе́л**, etc.: see засе́сть.
заселе́ние, -я, settlement; colonization. **заселённый**; -ён, -ена́, populated, inhabited. **засели́ть**, -лю́ *perf.*, **заселя́ть**, -я́ю *imp.* settle; colonize; populate; occupy.
засе́сть, -ся́ду; -се́л *perf.* (*imp.* заса́живаться), sit down (за + *acc.* to); sit firm, sit tight; settle, ensconce oneself; lodge in, stick in.
засе́чка, -и, notch, indentation, mark; intersection; fix; serif. **засе́чь**, -еку́, -ечёшь; -е́к, -ла́ *perf.* (*imp.* засека́ть) flog to death; notch; intersect; locate; fix.
засе́ять, -е́ю *perf.* (*imp.* засева́ть, засе́ивать) sow.
засиде́ться, -ижу́сь *perf.*, **заси́живаться**, -аюсь *imp.* sit too long, stay too long; sit up late; stay late. **заси́женный**, fly-specked, flyblown.
за|силосова́ть, -су́ю *perf.*
заси́лье, -я, dominance, sway.
засла́ть, зашлю́, -шлёшь *perf.* (*imp.* засыла́ть) send.
засло́н, -а, screen; barrier, road-block; (furnace, oven) door. **заслони́ть**, -оню́ *perf.*, **заслоня́ть**, -я́ю *imp.* cover; shield, screen; hide, push into the background. **засло́нка**, -и, (stove-)lid; damper; slide; baffle-plate; (furnace, oven) door.
заслу́га, -и, merit, desert; service. **заслу́женный**, **заслужённый**, deserved,

merited; meritorious, of merit, distinguished; Honoured; time-honoured, good old. **заслу́живать,** -аю *imp.*, **заслужи́ть,** -ужу́, -у́жишь *perf.* deserve, merit; win, earn; +*gen.* be worthy or deserving of.

заслу́шать, -аю *perf.*, **заслу́шивать,** -аю *imp.* listen to, hear; **~ся** (+*gen.*) listen spellbound (to).

засме́ивать, -аю *imp.*, **засмея́ть** -ею́, -еёшь *perf.* ridicule; **~ся,** begin to laugh; burst out laughing.

засмоли́ть, -лю́ *perf.* tar, pitch.

засну́ть, -ну́, -нёшь *perf.* (*imp.* засыпа́ть) go to sleep, fall asleep, die down.

засо́в, -а, bolt, bar.

засо́вывать, -аю *imp.* of засу́нуть.

засо́л, -а, salting, pickling. **засоли́ть,** -олю́, -о́ли́шь *perf.* (*imp.* заса́ливать), salt, corn, pickle. **засо́лка,** -и, salting, pickling; brine, pickle.

засоре́ние, -я, littering; pollution, contamination; obstruction, clogging up. **засори́ть,** -рю́ *perf.*, **засоря́ть,** -я́ю *imp.* litter; get dirt into; clog, block up, stop.

засосать, -осу́, -осёшь *perf.* (*imp.* заса́сывать) suck in engulf, swallow up.

за|со́хнуть, -ну; -со́х *perf.* (*imp.* also засыха́ть), dry, dry up; wither.

за́спанный, sleepy.

заста́ва, -ы, gate, gates; barrier; picket, picquet; outpost; пограни́чная ~, frontier post.

застава́ть, -таю́, -таёшь *imp.* of **заста́ть.**

заста́вить[1], -влю *perf.*, **заставля́ть,** -я́ю *imp.* cram, fill; block up, obstruct.

заста́вить[2], -влю *perf.*, **заставля́ть,** -я́ю *imp.* make; compel, force.

заста́иваться, -ается *imp.* of застоя́ться. **заста́ну,** etc.: see заста́ть.

застаре́лый, chronic; rooted.

заста́ть, -а́ну *perf.* (*imp.* застава́ть) find; catch.

застёгивать, -аю *imp.*, **застегну́ть,** -ну́, -нёшь *perf.* fasten, do up; button up, hook up. **застёжка,** -и, fastening; clasp, buckle; hasp; ~-мо́лния, zip fastener, zip.

застекли́ть, -лю́ *perf.*, **застекля́ть,** -я́ю *imp.* glaze, fit with glass.

застелю́, etc.: see застла́ть.

засте́нчивый, shy.

застига́ть, -а́ю *imp.*, **засти́гнуть, засти́чь,** -и́гну; -сти́г *perf.* catch; take unawares.

застила́ть, -а́ю *imp.* of застла́ть. **засти́лка,** -и, covering; floor-covering.

засти́чь: see засти́гнуть.

застла́ть, -телю́, -те́лешь *perf.* (*imp.* застила́ть) cover; spread over; cloud; ~ ковро́м, carpet.

засто́й, -я, stagnation; standstill; depression. **засто́йный,** stagnant; sluggish, immobile.

засто́льн|ый, table-; ~ая речь, after-dinner speech.

за|сто́порить, -рю *perf.*

застоя́ться. -и́тся *perf.* (*imp.* заста́иваться) stagnate, stand too long, get stale.

застра́ивать. -аю *imp.* of застро́ить.

застрахо́ванный, insured. **за|страхова́ть,** -ху́ю *perf.*, **застрахо́вывать,** -аю *imp.* insure (от+*gen.* against).

застрева́ть, -а́ю *imp.* of застря́ть.

застрели́ть, -елю́, -е́лишь *perf.* shoot (dead); **~ся,** shoot oneself; blow one's brains out. **застре́льщик,** -а, pioneer, leader.

застро́ить, -о́ю *perf.* (*imp.* застра́ивать) build over, build on, build up. **застро́йка,** -и, building.

застря́ть, -я́ну *perf.* (*imp.* застрева́ть), stick; get stuck; be held up; be bogged down.

за|студене́ть, -е́ет *perf.*

застуди́ть, -ужу́, -у́дишь *perf.*, **засту́живать,** -аю *imp.* expose to cold, chill; **~ся,** catch cold.

за́ступ, -а, spade.

заступа́ться, -а́юсь *imp.*, **заступи́ться,** -плю́сь, -пишься *perf.* +за+*acc.* stand up for, take the part of; plead for. **засту́пник,** -а, defender; protector. **засту́пничество,** -а, protection; intercession, defence.

застыва́ть, -а́ю *imp.*, **засты́ть,** -ы́ну *perf.* congeal; thicken, harden, set; become stiff; freeze; be petrified, be paralysed. **засты́лый,** congealed; stiff.

засу́нуть, -ну *perf.* (*imp.* засо́вывать) thrust in, push in, shove in; stuff in; tuck in.
за́суха, -и, drought.
засу́чивать, -аю *imp.*, **засучи́ть**, -чу́, -чишь *perf.* roll up.
засу́шивать, -аю *imp.*, **засуши́ть**, -шу́, -шишь *perf.* dry up, shrivel. **засу́шливый.** arid, dry, drought.
засыла́ть -а́ю *imp.* of засла́ть.
засы́пать[1], -плю *perf.*, **засыпа́ть**, -а́ю *imp.* fill up, fill in; cover, strew; put in, add; ~ вопро́сами, bombard with questions.
засыпа́ть[2](**ся**, -а́ю(сь *imp.* of засну́ть, засы́пать(ся.
засы́паться, -плюсь *perf.* (*imp.* засыпа́ться) be caught; come to grief, slip up; fail an examination.
засы́пка, -и filling; backfilling; filling up, charging; covering, strewing; putting in.
засыха́ть, -а́ю *imp.* of засо́хнуть. **зася́ду**, etc.: see засе́сть.
затаённый; -ён, -ена́, secret; repressed, suppressed. **зата́ивать**, -аю *imp.*, **затаи́ть**, -аю́ *perf.* suppress, repress; conceal; harbour, cherish; ~ дыха́ние, hold one's breath; ~ оби́ду, nurse a grievance, bear a grudge.
зата́лкивать, -аю *imp.* of затолка́ть. **зата́пливать**, -аю *imp.* of затопи́ть. **зата́птывать**, -аю *imp.* of затопта́ть.
зата́сканный, worn; threadbare; hackneyed, trite. **затаска́ть**, -а́ю *perf.*, **зата́скивать**[1], -аю *imp.* wear out; make hackneyed, make trite; drag about; ~ по суда́м, drag through the courts; **~ся**, wear (out), get dirty or threadbare with use.
зата́скивать[2], -аю *imp.*, **затащи́ть**, -щу́, -щишь *perf.* drag in; drag off, drag away.
затвердева́ть, -а́ет *imp.*, **за|тверде́ть**, -е́ет *perf.* harden, become hard; set; solidify; freeze. **затверде́вший**, **затверде́лый**, hardened; solidified, set, congealed. **затверде́ние**, -я, hardening; induration, callosity; callus.
за|тверди́ть, -ржу́ *perf.*
затво́р, -а, bolt, bar; lock; breech-block; shutter; water-gate, flood-gate.
затвори́ть, -рю́, -ришь *perf.*, **затворя́ть**, -я́ю *imp.* shut, close; **~ся**, shut oneself up, lock oneself in. **затво́рник**, -а, hermit, anchorite, recluse.
затева́ть, -а́ю *imp.* of зате́ять. **зате́йливый**, ingenious; intricate, involved; original.
затёк, etc.: see зате́чь. **затека́ть**, -а́ет *imp.* of зате́чь.
зате́м *adv.*, then, after that, next; for that reason; ~ что, because, since, as.
затемне́ние, -я, darkening, obscuring; blacking out; black-out; fade-out.
затемни́ть, -ню́ *perf.*, **затемня́ть**, -я́ю *imp.* darken, obscure; black out. **за́темно** *adv.* before dawn.
затере́ть, -тру́, -трёшь; -тёр *perf.* (*imp.* затира́ть) rub out; block, jam; су́дно затёрло льда́ми, the ship was ice-bound.
зате́рянный, lost; forgotten, forsaken.
затеря́ть, -я́ю *perf.* lose, mislay; **~ся**, be lost; be mislaid; be forgotten.
зате́чь -ечёт, -еку́т; -тёк, -кла́ *perf.* (*imp.* затека́ть) pour, flow; leak; swell up; become numb.
зате́я, -и, undertaking, enterprise, venture; escapade; joke. **зате́ять**, -е́ю *perf.* (*imp.* затева́ть) undertake, venture; organize; ~ дра́ку, start a fight.
затира́ть, -а́ю *imp.* of затере́ть.
затиха́ть, -а́ю *imp.*, **зати́хнуть**, -ну; -ти́х *perf.* die down, abate; die away, fade; become quiet. **зати́шье**, я, calm; lull; sheltered corner; backwater.
заткну́ть, -ну́, -нёшь *perf.* (*imp.* затыка́ть) stop up; plug; stick, thrust; ~ про́бкой, cork.
затмева́ть, -а́ю *imp.*, **затми́ть**, -ми́шь *perf.* darken, obscure; eclipse; overshadow. **затме́ние**, -я, eclipse; darkening; black-out.
зато́, *conj.* but then, but on the other hand.
затова́ренность, -и, **затова́ривание**, -я, overstocking; glut.
затолка́ть, -а́ю *perf.* (*imp.* зата́лкивать) jostle.
зато́н, -а, backwater; boat-yard. **затону́ть**, -о́нет *perf.* sink, be submerged.

затопи́ть[1], -плю́, -пишь *perf.* (*imp.* зата́пливать) light; turn on the heating.
затопи́ть[2], -плю́, -пишь *perf.*, **затопля́ть**, -я́ю *imp.* flood, submerge; sink, scuttle.
затопта́ть, -пчу́, -пчешь *perf.* (*imp.* зата́птывать) trample, trample down; trample underfoot.
зато́р, -а, obstruction, block, jam; congestion.
за|тормози́ть, -ожу́ *perf.*
заточа́ть, -а́ю *imp.*, **заточи́ть**, -чу́ *perf.* confine, shut up; incarcerate, imprison. **заточе́ние**, -я, confinement; incarceration, captivity.
за|трави́ть, -влю́, -вишь *perf.*, **затра́вливать**, -аю *imp.* hunt down, bring to bay; persecute, harass, harry; badger.
затра́гивать, -аю *imp.* of затро́нуть.
затра́та, -ы, expense; outlay. **затра́тить**, -а́чу *perf.*, **затра́чивать**, -аю *imp.* expend, spend.
затре́бовать, -бую *perf.* request, require; ask for.
затро́нуть, -ну *perf.* (*imp.* затра́гивать) affect; touch, graze; touch on.
затрудне́ние, -я, difficulty. **затрудни́тельный**, difficult; embarrassing. **затрудни́ть**, -ню́ *perf.*, **затрудня́ть**, -я́ю *imp.* trouble; cause trouble to; embarrass; make difficult; hamper; **~ся**, be in difficulties; +*inf.* or *instr.* find difficulty in.
затума́нивать, -ает *imp.*, **за|тума́нить** -ит *perf.* befog; cloud, dim, obscure.
за|тупи́ть, -плю́, -пишь *perf.*
за|тушева́ть, -шу́ю *perf.*, **затушёвывать**, -аю *imp.* shade; conceal; draw a veil over.
за|туши́ть, -шу́, -шишь *perf.* put out, extinguish; suppress.
за́тхлый, musty, mouldy; stuffy, close; stagnant.
затыка́ть, -а́ю *imp.* of заткну́ть.
заты́лок, -лка, back of the head; occiput; scrag scrag-end. **заты́лочный**, occipital.
затя́гивать, -аю *imp.*, **затяну́ть**, -ну́, -нешь *perf.* tighten; lace up; cover; close, heal; drag out, draw out, spin out; **~ся**, lace oneself up; be covered; close, skin over; be delayed; linger; be drawn out, drag on; inhale. **затя́жка**, -и, inhaling; prolongation; dragging on; drawing out; delaying, putting off; lagging. **затяжно́й**, long-drawn-out; lingering.
зауны́вный, mournful, doleful.
зауря́дный, ordinary, commonplace; mediocre.
заусе́нец, -нца, **заусе́ница**, -ы, agnail, hangnail, wire-edge, burr.
за|фарширова́ть, -ру́ю *perf.* **за|фикси́ровать**, -рую *perf.* **за|фрахтова́ть**, -ту́ю *perf.*
захва́т, -а, seizure, capture; usurpation; clamp claw. **захвати́ть**, -ачу́, -а́тишь *perf.* **захва́тывать**, -аю *imp.* take; seize, capture; carry away; thrill, excite; catch; у меня́ захвати́ло дух it took my breath away. **захва́тнический**, predatory; aggressive. **захва́тчик**, -а, invader; aggressor. **захва́тывающий**, gripping; ~ дух, breath-taking.
захвора́ть -а́ю *perf.* fall ill, be taken ill.
за|хире́ть -е́ю *perf.*
захлебну́ться -ну́сь, -нёшься *perf.*, **захлёбываться**, -аюсь *imp.* choke (от +*gen.* with).
захлестну́ть, -ну́, -нёшь *perf.* **захлёстывать**, -аю *imp.* flow over, swamp, overwhelm; overflow.
захло́пнуть, -ну *perf.*, **захло́пывать**, -аю *imp.* slam, bang; **~ся**, slam (to) bang (to), shut with a bang.
захо́д, -а setting, sunset; stopping, calling, putting in. **заходи́ть** -ожу́, -о́дишь *imp.* of зайти́. **захо́жий**, newly-arrived.
захолу́стный, remote, out-of-the-way, provincial. **захолу́стье**, -я, backwoods; godforsaken hole.
за|хорони́ть, -ню́ -нишь *perf.* **за|хоте́ть(ся**, -очу́(сь, -о́чешь(ся, -оти́м(ся *perf.*
захуда́лый. impoverished, poor, shabby; emaciated.
зацвести́, -етёт; -вёл -а́ *perf.*, **зацвета́ть**, -а́ет *imp.* burst into flower come into bloom.
зацепи́ть, -плю́, -пишь *perf.*, **зацепля́ть**, -я́ю *imp.* hook; engage; sting; catch (за+*acc.* on); **~ся** за+*acc.* catch on; catch hold of. **заце́пка**, -и, catch, hook,

peg; hooking; hitch, catch; pull, protection.

зачасту́ю *adv.* often, frequently.

зача́тие, -я, conception. **зача́ток, -тка,** embryo; rudiment; beginning, germ. **зача́точный,** rudimentary. **зача́ть, -чну́ -чнёшь; -ча́л, -а́, -о** *perf.* (*imp.* зачина́ть) conceive; begin.

за|ча́хнуть -ну; -ча́х *perf.* **зачёл,** etc.: see заче́сть.

заче́м *adv.* why; what for. **заче́м-то** *adv.* for some reason.

зачёркивать, -аю *imp.*, **зачеркну́ть, -ну, -нёшь** *perf.* cross out, strike out; delete.

за|черни́ть -ню́ *perf.*

зачерпну́ть -ну́ -нёшь *perf.*, **зачёрпывать, -аю** *imp.* scoop up; ladle; draw up.

зачерстве́лый, stale; hard-hearted. **за|черстве́ть, -е́ет** *perf.*

заче́сть, -чту́, -чтёшь; -чёл -чла́ *perf.* (*imp.* зачи́тывать) take into account, reckon as credit. **зачёт, -а,** reckoning; instalment; test; в ~ пла́ты in payment, on account; получи́ть сдать ~ по+*dat.* pass a test in; поста́вить ~ по+*dat.* pass in. **зачётн|ый; ~ая** квита́нция, receipt; **~ая** кни́жка, (student's) record book.

за|чехли́ть, -лю́ *perf.*

зачина́тель, -я *m.* founder, author. **зачина́ть, -а́ю** *imp.* of зача́ть. **зачи́нщик, -а,** instigator, ringleader.

зачи́слить -лю *perf.*, **зачисля́ть, -я́ю** *imp.* include; enter; enrol, enlist; **~ся,** join, enter.

зачи́тывать, -аю *imp.* of заче́сть. **зачну́,** etc.: see зача́ть. **зачту́,** etc.: see заче́сть. **зашёл,** etc.: see зайти́.

зашива́ть, -а́ю *imp.* **заши́ть -шью́, -шьёшь** *perf.* sew up; suture; put stitches in.

зашифро́ванный encoded, in cipher. **за|шифрова́ть -ру́ю** *perf.* **зашифро́вывать, -аю** *imp.* encipher, encode.

зашлю́ etc : see засла́ть.

за|шнурова́ть, -ру́ю *perf*, **зашнуро́вывать -аю** *imp.* lace up.

за|шпаклева́ть, -лю́ю *perf.* **за|штемпелева́ть, -лю́ю** *perf.* **за|што́пать, -аю** *perf.* **за|штрихова́ть -ху́ю** *perf.* **зашью́,** etc.: see заши́ть.

зашипну́ть, -ну́ -нёшь *perf.*, **защи́пывать -аю** *imp* pinch, nip, tweak; take; curl; punch.

защи́та, -ы, defence; protection; the defence. **защити́ть, -ищу́** *perf.*, **защища́ть, -а́ю** *imp.* defend, protect; stand up for.

заяви́ть, -влю́, -вишь *perf.*, **заявля́ть, -я́ю** *imp.* announce, declare; claim; show, attest; **~ся,** appear, turn up. **зая́вка, -и,** claim; demand, request. **заявле́ние, -я,** statement, declaration; application.

зая́длый, inveterate, confirmed.

за́яц, за́йца, hare; stowaway; gate-crasher; е́хать за́йцем, travel without a ticket. **за́ячий,** hare, hare's; ~ щаве́ль, wood-sorrel.

зва́ние, -я, calling, profession; rank; title. **зва́ный,** invited; ~ ве́чер, guest-night; ~ гость, guest; ~ обе́д, banquet, dinner, dinner-party. **зва́тельный,** vocative. **звать,** зову́, -вёшь; звал, -а́, -о *imp.* (*perf.* по~) call; ask, invite; как вас зову́т? what is your name?; **~ся,** be called.

звезда́, -ы́; *pl.* звёзды, star. **звёздный,** star; starry; starlit; stellar. **звездообра́зный,** star-shaped; radial; stellate. **звездочёт, -а,** astrologer. **звёздочка, -и,** little star; asterisk.

звене́ть, -ню́ *imp.* ring; +*instr.* jingle, clink.

звено́, -а́; *pl.* зве́нья, -ьев, link; bond; team, group, section, flight; unit; component, element; network. **звеньево́й** *sb.* team leader; section leader.

звери́нец, -нца, menagerie. **звери́ный,** wild-animal, wild-beast. **зверобо́й,** hunter, sealer. **зверово́дство, -а,** fur farming, fur breeding. **зверело́в, -а,** trapper. **зве́рски** *adv.* brutally, bestially; terribly, awfully. **зве́рский,** brutal, bestial; terrific, tremendous. **зве́рство, -а,** brutality; atrocity. **зве́рствовать, -твую** *imp.* commit atrocities. **зверь, -я;** *pl.* -и, -е́й *m.* wild animal, wild beast; brute. **зверьё, -я́,** wild animals; wild beasts.

звон, -а, ringing; ringing sound, chime,

peal, chink, clink. **звонить, -ню** *imp.* (*perf.* по~) ring; ring up; ~ в колокола, ring the bells; ~ кому-нибудь (по телефону), ring somebody up, telephone to somebody; вы не туда звоните, you've got the wrong number; звонят, the telephone's ringing; there's somebody at the door; **~ся,** ring the (door-)bell, ring. **звонк|ий; -нок, -нка, -о,** ringing, clear; voiced; ~ая монета, hard cash, coin. **звонок, -нка,** bell; ~ по телефону, (telephone) call. **звонче, звончее,** *comp.* of звонкий, звонко.

звук, -а, sound; ни ~а, not a sound.

звуко- in *comb.* sound. **звукозапись,** -и, sound recording. **~изоляция, -и,** sound-proofing. **~непроницаемый,** sound-proof. **~подражательный,** onomatopoeic. **~проводный,** sound-conducting. **~сниматель, -я** *m.* pick-up. **~улавливатель, -я** *m.* sound locator. **~частотный,** audio, audio-frequency.

звуковой, sound; audio; acoustical, acoustic. **звучание, -я,** sound vibration; phonation. **звучать, -чит** *imp.* be heard; sound; *+instr.* express, convey; ~ искренно, ring true. **звучный; -чен, -чна, -о,** sonorous.

звяканье, -я, jingling; tinkling. **звякать, -аю** *imp*, **звякнуть, -ну** *perf.* (*+instr.*) jingle; tinkle.

здание, -я, building.

здесь *adv.* here; at this point; in this. **здешний,** local; не ~, a stranger here.

здороваться, -аюсь *imp.* (*perf.* по~) exchange greetings; ~ за руку, shake hands. **здорово** *adv.* splendidly, magnificently; well done! fine! **здоровый,** healthy, strong; well; health-giving, wholesome, sound. **здоровье, -я,** health; за ваше ~! your health!; как ваше ~? how are you? **здравица, -ы,** toast. **здравница, -ы,** sanatorium.

здраво *adv.* soundly; sensibly.

здраво- in *comb.* health; sound, sensible. **здравомыслящий,** sensible, judicious. **~охранение, -я,** public health; health service. **~охранительный,** public-health.

здравпункт, -а, medical post, medical centre. **здравствовать, -твую** *imp.* be healthy; thrive, prosper; здравствуй(те), how do you do?; good morning, afternoon, evening; да здравствует! long live! **здрав|ый,** sensible; healthy; в ~ом уме, in one's right mind; ~ый смысл, common sense.

зев, -а, pharynx; jaws. **зевака, -и** *m.* and *f.* idler, gaper. **зевать, -аю** *imp.*, **зевнуть, -ну, -нёшь** *perf.* (*perf.* also про~) yawn; gape; miss, let slip, lose. **зевок, -вка, зевота, -ы,** yawn.

зеленеть, -еет *imp.* (*perf.* по~) turn green, go green; show green. **зелен|ой;** ~ая лавка, greengrocer's. **зеленоватый,** greenish. **зелён|ый;** зелен, -а, -о, green; ~ый лук, spring onions; ~ая улица, go, green light. **зелень, -и,** green; greenery, vegetation; greens; vegetables.

земле- in *comb.* land; earth. **землеведение, -я,** physical geography. **~владелец, -льца,** landowner. **~делец, -льца,** farmer. **~делие, -я,** farming, agriculture. **~дельческий,** agricultural. **~коп, -а,** navvy. **~мер, -а,** land-surveyor. **~мерный,** surveying, surveyor's. **~ройный,** earth-moving, excavating. **~трясение, -я,** earthquake. **~черпалка, -и,** mechanical dredger, bucket dredger. **~черпание, -я,** dredging.

землистый, earthy; sallow. **земля, -и,** *acc.* -ю; *pl.* -и, земель, -ям, earth; land; soil. **земляк, -а,** fellow-countryman. **земляника, -и,** strawberries; wild strawberries. **землянка, -и,** dug-out; mud hut. **землян|ой,** earthen; earth; earthy; ~ая груша, Jerusalem artichoke. **землячка, -и,** country-woman. **земной,** earthly; terrestrial; ground; mundane; ~ шар, the globe.

зенит, -а, zenith. **зенитный,** zenith; anti-aircraft.

зеркало, -а; *pl.* -а, looking-glass; mirror; reflector. **зеркальн|ый,** mirror; looking-glass; reflecting; smooth; plate, plate-glass; ~ое изображение, mirror image.

зернист|ый, granular, granulated; grainy; ~ая икра, unpressed caviare.

зерно, -а; *pl.* зёрна, зёрен, grain; seed;

kernel, core; corn; ко́фе в зёрнах, coffee beans. **зернови́дный,** granular. **зерново́й,** grain, corn, seed. **зерновы́е** *sb. pl.* cereals; grain crop. **зерносовхо́з,** -а *abbr.* State grain farm. **зернохрани́лище,** -а, granary.

зерца́ло, -а, looking-glass; *pl.* breastplate.

зима́, -ы́, *acc.* -у; *pl.* -ы, winter. **зи́мний,** winter, wintry. **зимова́ть,** -му́ю *imp.* (*perf.* пере~, про~) winter, spend the winter; hibernate. **зимо́вка,** -и, wintering, winter stay; hibernation; polar station. **зимо́вщик,** -а, winterer. **зимо́вье,** -я, winter quarters. **зимо́й** *adv.* in winter. **зимосто́йкий,** hardy.

зия́ние, -я, gaping, yawning; gap; hiatus. **зия́ть,** -я́ет *imp.* gape, yawn.

злак, -а, grass; cereal. **зла́ковый,** grassy, herbaceous; cereal, grain.

зле́йший *superl.* of злой; ~ враг, worst enemy. **злить,** злю *imp.* (*perf.* обо~, о~, разо~) anger; irritate; **~ся,** be angry, be in a bad temper; rage. **зло,** -а; *gen. pl.* зол, evil; harm; misfortune, disaster; malice, spite; vexation. **зло** *adv.* maliciously, spitefully.

зло- in *comb.*, evil, harm, malice; wicked, malicious; bad-tempered. **злове́щий,** ominous, ill-omened. **~во́ние,** -я, stink, stench. **~во́нный,** fetid, stinking. **~вре́дный,** pernicious; noxious. **~ка́чественный,** malignant; pernicious. **~наме́ренный,** ill-intentioned. **~па́мятный,** rancorous, unforgiving. **~полу́чный,** unlucky, ill-starred. **~ра́дный,** malevolent, gloating. **~сло́вие,** -я, malicious gossip; backbiting. **~умы́шленник,** -а, malefactor, criminal; plotter. **~умы́шленный,** with criminal intent. **~язы́чие,** -я, slander, backbiting. **~язы́чный,** slanderous.

зло́ба, -ы, malice; spite; anger; ~ дня, topic of the day, latest news. **зло́бный,** malicious, spiteful; bad-tempered. **злободне́вн|ый,** topical; ~ые вопро́сы, burning issues, topics of the day. **злоде́й,** -я, villain; scoundrel. **злоде́йский,** villainous. **злоде́йство,** -а, villainy; crime, evil deed. **злодея́ние,** -я, crime, evil deed. **злой;** зол, зла, evil; bad; wicked; malicious; malevolent; vicious; bad-tempered; savage; dangerous; severe, cruel; bad, nasty; зла́я соба́ка, beware of the dog. **зло́стн|ый,** malicious; conscious, intentional; persistent, hardened; ~ное банкро́тство, fraudulent bankruptcy. **злость,** -и, malice, spite; fury. **злоупотреби́ть,** -блю́ *perf.*, **злоупотребля́ть,** -я́ю *imp.* + *instr.* abuse. **злоупотребле́ние,** -я, + *instr.* abuse of; ~ дове́рием, breach of confidence.

змеи́ный, snake; snake's; cunning, crafty; wicked. **змеи́стый,** serpentine; sinuous. **змей,** -я, snake; dragon; kite. **змея́,** -и́; *pl.* -и, snake. **змий,** -я, serpent, dragon.

знак, -а, sign; mark; token, symbol; omen; signal; ~и препина́ния, punctuation marks; ~и разли́чия, insignia, badges of rank.

знако́мить, -млю *imp.* (*perf.* о~, по~), acquaint; introduce; **~ся,** become acquainted, acquaint oneself; get to know; introduce oneself; study, investigate; +с+*instr.* meet, make the acquaintance of. **знако́мство,** -а, acquaintance; (circle of) acquaintances; knowledge (с+*instr.* of). **знако́м|ый,** familiar; быть ~ым с+*instr.* be acquainted with, know; **~ый, ~ая,** *sb.* acquaintance, friend.

знамена́тель, -я *m.* denominator; привести́ к одному́ знамена́телю, reduce to a common denominator. **знамена́тельный,** significant, important; principal. **зна́мение,** -я, sign. **знамени́тость,** -и, celebrity. **знамени́тый,** celebrated, famous, renowned; outstanding, superlative. **знаменова́ть,** -ну́ю *imp.* signify, mark. **знамено́сец,** -сца, standard-bearer. **зна́мя,** -мени; *pl.* -мёна *n.* banner; flag; standard.

зна́ние, -я, knowledge; *pl.* learning; accomplishments; со зна́нием де́ла, capably, competently.

зна́тный; -тен, -тна́, -о, distinguished; outstanding, notable; noble, aristocratic; splendid.

знато́к, -а́, expert; connoisseur. **знать,** -а́ю *imp.* know; дать ~, inform, let know; да́йте мне ~ о вас, let me hear from you; дать себе́ ~, make itself felt; ~ в лицó, know by sight; ~ мéру, know where to stop; ~ себé цéну, know one's own value; ~ толк в +*prep*. be knowledgeable about; **~ся,** associate.

значéние, -я, meaning; significance; importance; value. **знáчит,** so, then; that means. **значи́тельный,** considerable, sizeable; important; significant; meaningful. **знáчить, -чу** *imp*. mean; signify; have significance, be of importance; **~ся,** be; be mentioned, appear. **значóк, -чкá,** badge; mark.

знáющий, expert; learned, erudite; knowledgeable; well-informed.

знobи́ть, -и́т *imp., impers.*+*acc.*; меня́, etc., знобит, I feel shivery, feverish.

зной, -я, intense heat. **знóйный,** hot, sultry; burning.

зов, -а (-у), call, summons; invitation. **зову́,** etc.: see звать.

зóдческий, architecture, architectural. **зóдчество, -а,** architecture. **зóдчий** *sb*. architect.

зол: see зло, злой.

золá -ы́, ashes, cinders.

золóвка, -и, sister-in-law, husband's sister.

золоти́стый, golden. **золоти́ть, -очу́** *imp*. (*perf*. вы́~, по~) gild. **зóлото, -а,** gold. **золот|óй,** gold; golden; ~óе дно, gold-mine; ~óй запáс, gold reserves; ~óй песóк, gold-dust; ~ы́е прóмыслы, gold-fields. **золотонóсный,** auriferous; gold-bearing.

золоту́ха, -и, scrofula. **золоту́шный,** scrofulous.

золочéние, -я, gilding. **золочёный,** gilt, gilded.

зóна, -ы, zone; region; band, belt. **зонáльный,** zonal, zone; regional.

зонд, -а, probe; bore; sonde. **зонди́ровать, -рую** *imp*. sound, probe.

зонт, -á, umbrella; awning. **зóнтик, -а,** umbrella; sunshade; umbel. **зóнтичный,** umbellate, umbelliferous.

зоóлог, -а, zoologist. **зоологи́ческий,** zoological. **зоолóгия, -и,** zoology. **зоопáрк, -а.** zoo, zoological gardens.

зóри, etc.: see заря́.

зóркий; -рок, -ркá, -о, sharp-sighted; perspicacious, penetrating; vigilant.

зрачóк, -чкá, pupil.

зрéлище -а, sight; spectacle; show; pageant.

зрéлость, -и, ripeness; maturity; аттестáт зрéлости, school-leaving certificate. **зрéлый;** зрел, -á, -о, ripe, mature.

зрéние, -я, sight, eyesight, vision; обмáн зрéния, optical illusion; пóле зрéния, field of vision, field of view; тóчка зрéния, point of view; у́гол зрéния, viewing angle, camera angle.

зреть, -éю *imp*. (*perf*. со~) ripen; mature.

зри́мый, visible. **зри́тель, -я** *m*. spectator, observer; onlooker; *pl*. audience. **зри́тельный,** visual; optic; ~ зал, hall, auditorium.

зря *adv*. to no purpose, for nothing, in vain.

зря́чий, sighted, seeing.

зуб, -а; *pl*. -ы or -бья, -óв or -бьев, tooth; cog. **зубáстый,** large-toothed; sharp-tongued. **зубéц, -бцá,** tooth, cog, tine; blip. **зуби́ло, -а,** chisel. **зубнóй,** dental; tooth; ~ врач, dentist. **зубоврачéбный,** dentists', dental; ~ кабинéт, dental surgery. **зубоврачевáние, -я,** dentistry. **зубóк, -бкá;** *pl*. -бки́, tooth; cog; clove. **зубоскáл, -а,** scoffer. **зубочи́стка, -и,** toothpick.

зубр, -а, (European) bison, aurochs; die-hard.

зубри́ть[1], -рю́ *imp*. (*perf*. за~) notch, serrate.

зубри́ть[2], -рю́, зу́бри́шь *imp*. (*perf*. вы́~, за~) cram, learn by rote.

зубчáтка, -и, sprocket; gear-wheel, gear; rack-wheel. **зубчáтый,** toothed, cogged; gear, gear-wheel; serrate, serrated, jagged, indented.

зуд, -а, itch. **зудá, -ы́** *m*. and *f*. bore. **зудéть, -и́т,** itch.

зы́бкий; -бок, -бкá, -о, unsteady, shaky; unstable, shifting; vacillating. **зыбу́ч|ий,** unsteady, unstable, shifting; ~ие пески́, quicksands. **зыбь, -и;** *gen. pl*. -éй, ripple rippling.

зы́чный, loud, stentorian.

зэ *n. indecl.* the letter з.
зя́бкий, chilly, sensitive to cold.
зя́блик, -а, chaffinch.
зя́блый, frozen; damaged by frost.
зя́бнуть, -ну; зяб *imp.* suffer from cold, feel the cold.
зять, -я; *pl.* -тья́, -тьёв, son-in-law; brother-in-law, sister's husband.

И, Й

и *n. indecl.* the letter и; и с кра́ткой, и кра́ткое, the letter й.
и *conj.* and; and so; even; just; too, as well; (with *neg.*) either; в то́м-то и де́ло, that's just it, that's the whole point; и .. и, both .. and; и он не знал, he didn't know either; и про́чее, и так да́лее, etc., etcetera, and so on and so forth; и тому́ подо́бное, and the like; и тот и друго́й, both.
и́бо *conj.* for; because, since.
и́ва, -ы, willow. **ивня́к,** -а́, osier-bed; osiers, osier. **и́вовый,** willow.
и́волга, -и, oriole.
игла́, -ы́; *pl.* -ы, needle; thorn; spine; quill.
и́го, -а, yoke.
иго́лка, -и, needle. **иго́лочка,** -и *dim.*; с иго́лочки, brand-new, spick and span. **иго́льник,** -а, needle-case. **иго́льный,** needle, needle's. **иго́льчатый,** needle-shaped; acicular; needle.
иго́рный, gaming, gambling. **игра́,** -ы́; *pl.* -ы, play, playing; game; hand; turn, lead; ~ приро́ды, sport, freak (of nature); ~ слов, pun. **игра́льн|ый,** playing; ~ые ко́сти, dice. **игра́ть,** -а́ю *imp.* (*perf.* сыгра́ть) play; act; ~ в+*acc.* play (game); ~ на+*prep.* play (an instrument), play on; +*instr.* or с+*instr.* play with, toy with, trifle with; ~ в билья́рд, на билья́рде, play billiards; э́то не игра́ет ро́ли, it is of no importance, of no significance. **игри́вый,** playful. **игри́стый,** sparkling. **игро́к,** -а́, player; gambler. **игру́шечный,** toy. **игру́шка,** -и, toy; plaything.
иде́йность, -и, principle, integrity; ideological content. **иде́йный,** high-principled; acting on principle; ideological.
идёт, etc.: see идти́.
иде́я, -и, idea; notion, concept; счастли́вая ~, happy thought.
идио́т, -а, idiot, imbecile. **идиоти́зм,** -а, idiocy, imbecility. **идиоти́ческий, идио́тский,** idiotic, imbecile.
идти́, итти́, иду́, идёшь; шёл, шла *imp.* (*perf.* пойти́) go; come; go round; run, work; pass; go on, be in progress; be on, be showing; fall; + в + *nom.-acc.* become; + в + *acc.* be used for, go for; + (к +) *dat.* suit, become; + на + *acc.* enter; go to make, go on; + о + *prep.* be about; + *instr.* or с + *gen.* play, lead, move; ей идёт тридца́тый год, she is in her thirtieth year; ~ в лётчики, become a flyer; ~ в лом, go for scrap; ~ на сме́ну+*dat.* take the place of, succeed; ~ ферзём, move the queen; ~ с черве́й, lead a heart; хорошо́ ~, be selling well, be going well; шли го́ды, years passed; э́та шля́па ей не идёт, that hat doesn't suit her.
иере́й, -я, priest. **иере́йство,** -а, priesthood.
иждиве́нец, -нца, **-ве́нка,** -и, dependant. **иждиве́ние,** -я, maintenance; means, funds; на иждиве́нии, at the expense of; жить на своём иждиве́нии, keep oneself; жить на иждиве́нии роди́телей, live on one's parents. **иждиве́нчество,** -а, dependence.
из, изо *prep.* + *gen.* from, out of, of; вы́йти из до́ма, go out, leave the house; изо всех сил, with all one's might; из достове́рных исто́чников,

from reliable sources, on good authority; ло́жки из серебра́, silver spoons; обе́д из трёх блюд, a three-course dinner; оди́н из ста, one in a hundred.

из-, изо-, изъ-, ис-, *vbl. pref.* indicating motion outwards; action over entire surface of object, in all directions; expenditure of instrument or object in course of action; continuation or repetition of action to extreme point; exhaustiveness of action.

изба́, -ы́; *pl.* -ы, izba; ~-чита́льня, village reading-room.

избави́тель, -я *m.* deliverer. **изба́вить,** -влю *perf.*, **избавля́ть,** -я́ю *imp.* save, deliver; изба́ви Бог! God forbid; **~ся,** be saved, escape; ~ся от, get rid of; get out of. **избавле́ние,** -я, deliverance.

избало́ванный, spoilt. **из|балова́ть,** -лу́ю *perf.*, **избало́вывать,** -аю *imp.* spoil.

изба́ч, -а́, village librarian.

избега́ть, -а́ю *imp.*, **избе́гнуть,** -ну; -бе́г(нул) *perf.*, **избежа́ть,** -егу́ *perf.*+*gen.* or *inf.* avoid; shun, escape, evade. **избежа́ние,** -я; во ~+*gen.* (in order) to avoid.

изберу́, etc.: see избра́ть.

избива́ть, -а́ю *imp.* of изби́ть. **избие́ние,** -я, slaughter, massacre; beating, beating-up.

избира́тель, -я *m.*, **~ница,** -ы, elector, voter. **избира́тельн|ый,** electoral; election; selective; ~ый бюллете́нь, voting-paper, ballot-paper; ~ая у́рна, ballot-box; ~ый уча́сток, polling station. **избира́ть,** -а́ю *imp.* of избра́ть.

изби́тый, beaten, beaten up; hackneyed, trite. **изби́ть,** изобью́, -бьёшь *perf.* (*imp.* избива́ть) beat unmercifully, beat up; slaughter, massacre; wear down, ruin.

избра́ние, -я, election. **и́збранн|ый,** selected; select; **~ые** *sb. pl.* the élite. **избра́ть,** -беру́, -берёшь; -а́л, -а́, -о *perf.* (*imp.* избира́ть) elect; choose.

избу́шка, -и, small hut.

избы́ток, -тка, surplus, excess; abundance, plenty. **избы́точный,** surplus; abundant, plentiful.

извая́ние, -я, statue, sculpture. **изва́ять,** -я́ю *perf.*

изве́дать, -аю *perf.*, **изве́дывать,** -аю *imp.* come to know, learn the meaning of.

изведу́, etc., **извёл,** etc.: see извести́.

и́зверг, -а, monster. **изверга́ть,** -а́ю *imp.*, **изве́ргнуть,** -ну; -е́рг *perf.* disgorge; eject; throw out; excrete; expel; **~ся,** erupt. **изверже́ние,** -я, eruption; ejection, expulsion; excretion.

изверну́ться, -ну́сь, -нёшься *perf.*, **извёртываться,** -аюсь *imp.* (*imp.* also изворачиваться) dodge, take evasive action; be evasive.

извести́, -еду́, -едёшь; -ёл, -ела́ *perf.* (*imp.* изводи́ть) use (up); waste; destroy, exterminate; exhaust; torment.

изве́стие, -я, news; information; intelligence; *pl.* proceedings, transactions. **извести́ть,** -ещу́ *perf.* (*imp.* извеща́ть) inform, notify.

извёстка, -и, lime. **известкова́ть,** -ку́ю *perf.* and *imp.* lime. **известко́вый,** lime; limestone; calcareous.

изве́стно, it is (well) known; of course, certainly; как ~, as everybody knows; наско́лько мне ~, as far as I know. **изве́стность,** -и, fame, reputation; repute; notoriety. **изве́стн|ый,** known; well-known, famous; notorious; certain; в ~ых слу́чаях, in certain cases.

известня́к, -а́, limestone. **и́звесть,** -и, lime.

извеща́ть, -а́ю *imp.* of извести́ть. **извеще́ние,** -я, notification, notice; advice.

изви́в, -а, winding, bend. **извива́ть,** -а́ю *imp.* of изви́ть; **~ся,** coil; wriggle, writhe; twist, wind; meander. **изви́лина,** -ы, bend, twist, winding; convolution. **изви́листый,** winding; tortuous; sinuous; meandering.

извине́ние, -я, excuse; apology; pardon. **извини́тельный,** excusable, pardonable; apologetic. **извини́ть,** -ню́ *perf.*, **извиня́ть,** -я́ю *imp.* excuse; извини́те (меня́), I beg your pardon, excuse me, (I'm) sorry; извини́те, что я опозда́л, sorry I'm late; **~ся,** apologize; make excuses, excuse oneself; извиня́юсь, I

apologize, (I'm) sorry; извините́сь за меня́, present my apologies, make my excuses.
изви́ть, изовью́, -вьёшь; -и́л, -á, -o *perf.* (*imp.* извива́ть) coil, twist, wind; **~ся,** coil; writhe, twist.
извлека́ть, -а́ю *imp.*, **извле́чь,** -еку́, -ечёшь; -ёк, -ла́ *perf.* extract; derive, elicit; extricate; ~ уро́к из, learn a lesson from. **извлече́ние,** -я, extraction; extract, excerpt.
извне́ *adv.* from outside.
изводи́ть, -ожу́, -о́дишь *imp.* of извести́.
изво́зчик, -а, cabman, cabby; carrier, carter, drayman; cab.
изво́лить, -лю *imp.*+*inf.* or *gen.* wish, desire; + *inf.* deign, be pleased; изво́льте, if you wish; all right; with pleasure.
извора́чиваться, -аюсь *imp.* of изверну́ться. **изворо́т,** -а, bend, twist; *pl.* tricks, wiles. **изворо́тливый,** resourceful, artful; wily, shrewd.
извратить, -ащу́ *perf.*, **извраща́ть,** -а́ю *imp.* distort; pervert; misinterpret, misconstrue. **извраще́ние,** -я, perversion; misinterpretation, distortion. **извращённый,** perverted, unnatural.
изга́дить, -а́жу *perf.* befoul, soil; spoil, make a mess of.
изги́б, -а, bend, twist; winding; inflexion, nuance. **изгиба́ть(ся,** -а́ю(сь *imp.* of изогну́ть(ся.
изгла́дить, -а́жу *perf.*, **изгла́живать,** -аю *imp.* efface, wipe out, blot out.
изгна́ние, -я, banishment; expulsion; exile. **изгна́нник,** -а, exile. **изгна́ть,** -гоню́, -го́нишь; -а́л, -á, -o *perf.* (*imp.* изгоня́ть) banish, expel; exile; oust, do away with.
изголо́вье. -я, bed-head; bedside; служи́ть изголо́вьем, serve as a pillow.
изголода́ться, -а́юсь, be famished, starve; +по+*dat.* thirst for, yearn for.
изгоню́, etc.: see изгна́ть. **изгоня́ть,** -я́ю *imp.* of изгна́ть.
и́згородь, -и, fence, hedge.
изготавливать, -аю *imp.*, **изгото́вить,** -влю *perf.*, **изготовля́ть,** -я́ю *imp.* make, manufacture, produce; prepare; cook; **~ся,** get ready, make ready.
изгото́вка, -и, **изготовле́ние,** -я making, manufacture, production; preparation.
издава́ть, -даю́, -даёшь *imp.* of изда́ть.
и́здавна *adv.* from time immemorial; for a very long time.
издади́м, etc.: see изда́ть.
издалека́, издалёка, и́здали *advs.* from afar, from far away, from a distance.
изда́ние, -я, publication; edition; promulgation. **изда́тель,** -я *m.*, **~ница,** -ы, publisher. **изда́тельство,** -а, publishing house, press, publisher's. **изда́ть,** -а́м, -а́шь, -а́ст -ади́м; -а́л, -á, -o *perf.* (*imp.* издава́ть) publish; promulgate; issue; produce emit; let out, utter; **~ся,** be published.
издева́тельский, mocking. **издева́тельство,** -а, mocking, scoffing; mockery; taunt, insult. **издева́ться,** -а́юсь *imp.* (+над+*instr.*) mock, scoff, (at). **издёвка** -и, taunt, insult.
изде́лие, -я make, work; article; *pl.* wares.
издержа́ть, -жу́, -жишь *perf.* spend; **~ся,** spend all one's money; be spent up. **издéржки,** -жек *pl.* expenses; costs; cost.
издеру́, etc.: see изодра́ть. **издира́ть,** -а́ю *imp.* of изодра́ть.
из|до́хнуть, -ну; -до́х *perf.*, **издыха́ть,** -а́ю *imp.* die; peg out, kick the bucket. **издыха́ние,** -я; после́днее ~, last breath, last gasp.
из|жа́рить(ся -рю(сь *perf.*
изжива́ть -а́ю *imp.*, **изжи́ть,** -иву́, -вёшь; -и́л, -á, -o *perf.* overcome, get over: eliminate, get rid of.
изжо́га. -и, heartburn.
из-за *prep.*+*gen.* from behind, from beyond; because of, through; жени́ться ~ де́нег, marry for money.
излага́ть, -а́ю *imp.* of изложи́ть.
изла́мывать, -аю *imp.* of излома́ть.
излече́ние, -я, treatment; recovery cure. **изле́чивать,** -аю *imp.*, **излечи́ть,** -чу́, -чишь, cure; **~ся,** be cured, make a complete recovery; +от+*gen.* rid oneself of, shake off.
излива́ть, -а́ю *imp.*, **изли́ть,** изолью́, -льёшь; -и́л, -á, -o *perf.* pour out, give

vent to; ~ ду́шу, unbosom oneself; unburden one's heart.

изли́шек, -шка, surplus; remainder; excess; с изли́шком, enough and to spare. **изли́шество**, -а, excess; over-indulgence. **изли́шний**; -шен, -шня, superfluous; excessive; unnecessary.

излия́ние, -я, outpouring, outflow, effusion, discharge.

изловчи́ться, -чу́сь *perf.* contrive, manage.

изложе́ние, -я, exposition; account. **изложи́ть**, -жу́, -жишь *perf.* (*imp.* излага́ть) expound, state; set forth; word, draft; ~ на бума́ге commit to paper.

изло́м, -а, break, fracture; sharp bend; salient point. **изло́манный**, broken, fractured; winding, tortuous; worn out. **излома́ть**, -а́ю *perf.* (*imp.* изла́мывать) break; smash; wear out; warp, corrupt.

излуча́ть, -а́ю *imp.* radiate, emit; **~ся**, be emitted, be radiated; emanate. **излуче́ние**, -я radiation; emanation.

излу́чина, -ы, bend, curve, meander. **излу́чистый**, winding, meandering.

излю́бленный, favourite.

из|ма́зать, -а́жу *perf.*, dirty, smear all over; use up; **~ся**, get dirty, smear oneself all over.

из|мара́ть, -а́ю *perf.* **из|мельча́ть**, -а́ю *perf.* **из|мельчи́ть**, -чу́ *perf.*

изме́на, -ы, betrayal; treachery, treason; infidelity.

измене́ние, -я, change, alteration; inflexion. **измени́ть**[1], -ню́, -нишь *perf.* (*imp.* изменя́ть) change, alter; **~ся**, change, alter; vary; ~ся в лице́, change countenance.

измени́ть[2], -ню́, -нишь *perf.* (*imp.* изменя́ть) + *dat.* betray; be unfaithful to; fail. **изме́нник**, -а, traitor **изме́ннический**, treacherous, traitorous.

изме́нчивый, changeable; inconstant, fickle. **изменя́емый**, variable. **изменя́ть(ся**, -я́ю(сь *imp.* of измени́ть(ся.

измере́ние, -я, measurement, measuring; mensuration; sounding, fathoming; metering, gauging; taking; dimension. **измери́мый**, measurable. **измери́тель**, -я *m.* gauge, meter; index. **измери́тельный**, measuring; standard. **изме́рить**, -рю *perf.*, **измеря́ть**, -я́ю *imp.* measure, gauge; sound; survey.

изможде́нный; -ён, -ена́, emaciated; worn out.

и́зморозь, -и, hoar-frost; rime.

изму́чать, -аю *perf.*, **изму́чивать**, -аю *imp.*, **из|му́чить**, -чу *perf.* torment; tire out, exhaust; **~ся**, be tired out, be exhausted. **изму́ченный**, worn out, tired out.

измы́слить, -лю *perf.*, **измышля́ть**, -я́ю *imp.* fabricate, invent; contrive. **измышле́ние**, -я, fabrication, invention.

измя́тый, crumpled, creased; haggard, jaded. **из|мя́ть(ся**, изомну́(сь, -нёшь(ся *perf.*

изна́нка, -и, wrong side; under side; reverse; seamy side. изна́ночн|ый; ~ая пе́тля, purl (stitch).

из|наси́ловать, -лую *perf.* rape, assault, violate.

изна́шивание, -я, wear (and tear). **изна́шивать(ся**, -аю(сь *imp.* of износи́ть(ся.

изне́женный, pampered; delicate; soft, effete; effeminate. **изне́живать**, -аю *imp.*, **изне́жить**, -жу *perf.* pamper, coddle; make effeminate; **~ся**, go soft, grow effete; become effeminate.

изнемога́ть, -а́ю *imp.*, **изнемо́чь**, -огу́, -о́жешь; -о́г, -ла́ *perf.* be exhausted, be dead tired. **изнеможе́ние**, -я exhaustion. **изнеможённый**; -ён, -а́, exhausted.

изно́с, -а (-у), wear; wear and tear; deterioration; не знать ~у, wear well, stand hard wear. **износи́ть**, -ошу́, -о́сишь *perf.* (*imp.* изна́шивать) wear out; **~ся**, wear out; be used up, be played out; age (prematurely). **изно́шенный**, worn out; threadbare; worn; aged.

изно́ю, etc.: see изны́ть.

изнуре́ние, -я, exhaustion; emaciation. **изнурённый**; -ён, -ена́, exhausted, worn out; jaded; ~ го́лодом, faint with hunger. **изнури́тельный**, exhausting. **изнури́ть**, -рю́ *perf.*, **изнуря́ть**, -я́ю *imp.* exhaust, wear out.

изнутри́ *adv.* from inside, from within.

изнывáть, -áю *imp.*, **изны́ть,** -нóю *perf.* languish, be exhausted; ~ от жáжды, be tormented by thirst; ~ по + *dat.* pine for.

изо: see из. **изо-**[1]: see из-. **изо-**[2], iso-.

изоби́лие, -я, abundance, plenty, profusion. **изоби́ловать,** -лует *imp.* + *instr.* abound in, be rich in. **изоби́льный,** abundant; + *instr.* abounding in.

изобличáть, -áю *imp.*, **изобличи́ть,** -чý *perf.* expose; unmask; reveal, show. **изобличéние,** -я, exposure; conviction. **изобличи́тельн|ый,** damning; ~ые докумéнты, documentary evidence.

изобрести́, -етý, -етёшь; -ёл, -á *perf.*, **изобретáть,** -áю *imp.* invent; devise, contrive. **изобретáтель,** -я *m.* inventor. **изобретáтельный,** inventive; resourceful. **изобретéние,** -я, invention.

изображáть, -áю *imp.*, **изобрази́ть,** -ажý *perf.* represent, depict, portray (+*instr.* as); imitate, take off; ~ из себя́ + *acc.* make oneself out to be, represent oneself as; **~ся,** appear, show itself. **изображéние,** -я, image; representation; portrayal; imprint. **изобрази́тельн|ый,** graphic; decorative; ~ые искýсства, fine arts.

изобью́, etc.: see изби́ть. **изовью́,** etc.: see изви́ть.

изóгнутый, bent, curved; winding. **изогнýть(ся,** -нý(сь, -нёшь(ся *perf.* (*imp.* изгибáть(ся) bend, curve.

изóдранный, tattered. **изодрáть,** издерý, -лерёшь; -áл, -á, -о *perf.* (*imp.* издирáть) tear to pieces; scratch all over.

изолгáться, -лгýсь, -лжёшься; -áлся, -áсь, -ось *perf.* become a hardened liar.

изоли́рованный, isolated; separate; insulated. **изоли́ровать,** -рую *perf.* and *imp.* isolate; quarantine; insulate. **изолирóвка,** -и, insulation; insulating tape.

изолью́, etc.: see изли́ть.

изоля́тор, -а insulator; isolation ward; solitary confinement cell. **изоля́ция,** -и, isolation; quarantine; insulation.

изомнý(сь, etc.: see измя́ть.

изóрванный, tattered, torn. **изорвáть,** -вý, -вёшь; -áл, -á, -о *perf.* tear, tear to pieces; **~ся,** be in tatters.

изотрý, etc.: see истерéть.

изощрённый; -рён, -á, refined; keen. **изощри́ть,** -рю́ *perf.*, **изощря́ть,** -я́ю *imp.* sharpen; cultivate, refine, develop; **~ся,** acquire refinement; excel.

из-под *prep.* + *gen.* from under; from near; from; буты́лка ~ молокá, milk-bottle.

изразéц, -зцá, tile. **изразцóвый,** tile; tiled.

из|расхóдовать(ся, -дую(сь *perf.*

и́зредка *adv.* now and then; occasionally; from time to time.

изрéзанный, cut up; indented, rugged. **изрéзать,** -éжу *perf.*, **изрéзывать,** -аю *imp.* cut up; cut to pieces; indent.

изрекáть, -áю *imp.*, **изрéчь,** -екý, -ечёшь; -ёк, -лá *perf.* speak solemnly; utter. **изречéние,** -я, apophthegm, dictum, saying.

изрóю, etc.: see изры́ть.

изрубáть, -áю *imp.*, **изруби́ть,** -блю́, -бишь *perf.* cut (up); chop, chop up, mince; cut down, cut to pieces.

изругáть, -áю *perf.* abuse, swear at, curse.

изрывáть, -áю *imp.*, **изры́ть,** -рóю *perf.* dig up, tear up, plough up. **изры́тый,** pitted; cratered; torn up.

изря́дно *adv.* fairly, pretty; tolerably. **изря́дный,** fair, handsome; fairly large.

изувéчивать, -аю *imp.*, **изувéчить,** -чу *perf* maim, mutilate.

изуми́тельный amazing astounding. **изуми́ть** -млю́ *perf.* **изумля́ть** -я́ю *imp.* amaze astonish; **~ся,** be amazed. **изумлéние,** -я, amazement. **изумлённый;** -лён, -á, amazed, astonished; dumbfounded.

изумрýд, -а, emerald.

изурóдованный, maimed, mutilated; disfigured. **из|урóдовать,** -дую *perf.*

изучáть, -áю *imp.*, **изучи́ть,** -чý, -чишь *perf.* learn, study; master; come to know (very well). **изучéние,** -я, study.

изъ-: see из-.

изъéздить, -зжу *perf.* travel all over; wear out. **изъéзженный,** much-travelled, well-worn; rutted.

изъяви́тельн|ый; ~ое наклоне́ние, indicative (mood). **изъяви́ть,** -влю́, -вишь *perf.*, **изъявля́ть,** -я́ю *imp.* express; ~ согла́сие, give consent. **изъявле́ние** -я, expression.

изъя́н -а (-у), defect, flaw.

изъя́тие -я withdrawal; removal; exception. **изъя́ть,** изыму́, -мешь *perf.* **изыма́ть,** -а́ю *imp.* withdraw; remove; confiscate.

изыска́ние, -я investigation, research; prospecting; survey. **изы́сканный,** refined; recherché. **изыска́тель,** -я *m.* project surveyor; prospector. **изыска́ть** -ыщу́, -ы́щешь *perf.*, **изы́скивать,** -аю *imp.* search (successfully) for, search out; (try to) find; prospect for.

изю́м, -а (-у), raisins; sultanas. **изю́мина,** -ы, raisin. **изю́минка,** -и, zest, go, spirit; sparkle; с изю́минкой, spirited, piquant.

изя́щество, -а, elegance, grace. **изя́щный**, elegant graceful.

ика́ние, -я, hiccupping. **ика́ть,** -а́ю *imp.*, **икну́ть,** -ну́, -нёшь *perf.* hiccup.

ико́на, -ы, icon. **иконогра́фия,** -и, iconography; portraiture, portraits. **иконопи́сец**, -сца icon-painter. **ико́нопись,** -и, icon-painting.

ико́та, -ы, hiccup, hiccups.

икра́[1], -ы́, (hard) roe; spawn; caviare; pâté, paste.

икра́[2], -ы́; *pl* -ы, calf.

икс, -а, (letter) x.

ил, -а, silt, mud, ooze; sludge.

и́ли, иль, *conj.* or; ~ . . ~, either . . or.

и́листый, muddy, silty, oozy.

иллюзиони́ст, -а illusionist; conjurer, magician. **иллю́зия,** -и, illusion. **иллюзо́рный**, illusory.

иллюмина́тор, -а, porthole.

иллюстри́рованный, illustrated. **иллюстри́ровать,** -рую *perf.* and *imp.* illustrate.

иль: see и́ли. **им:** see он, они́, оно́.

им. *abbr.* и́мени, named after.

и́мени, etc.: see и́мя.

име́ние, -я, estate; property, possessions.

имени́ны, -и́н *pl.* name-day (party). **имени́тельный,** nominative. **и́менно** *adv.* namely; to wit, viz.; just, exactly, precisely; to be exact; вот ~! exactly! precisely! **именно́й**, named, nominal; bearing the owner's name; inscribed, autographed; name. **именова́ть,** -ну́ю *imp.* (*perf.* на~) name; **~ся**+*instr.* be called; be termed. **имену́емый,** called.

име́ть, -е́ю *imp.* have; ~ в виду́, bear in mind, think of, mean; ~ де́ло с+*instr.* have dealings with, have to do with; ~ значе́ние, be of importance, matter; ~ ме́сто, take place; **~ся,** be; be present, be available.

и́ми: see они́.

импера́тор, -а, emperor. **импера́торский,** imperial. **императри́ца,** -ы, empress. **импе́рия,** -и, empire.

импони́ровать, -рую *imp.*+*dat.* impress.

иму́щественный, property. **иму́щество,** -а, property, belongings; stock; stores, equipment. **иму́щий,** propertied; well off, wealthy.

и́мя, и́мени; *pl.* имена́, -ён *n.* name; first name, Christian name; reputation; noun; во ~ + *gen.* in the name of; ~ прилага́тельное, adjective; ~ существи́тельное, substantive, noun; ~ числи́тельное numeral; от и́мени +*gen.* on behalf of; по и́мени, by name; in name, nominally; Теа́тр и́мени Го́рького, the Gorky Theatre.

ин- *abbr.* in *comb.* of иностра́нный, foreign. **инвалю́та,** -ы, foreign currency. **инотде́л,** -а, foreign department.

и́на́че *adv.* differently, otherwise; так и́ли ~, in either case, in any event, at all events; *conj.* otherwise, or, or else.

инвали́д, -а, disabled person; invalid. **инвали́дность,** -и, disablement, disability.

инвента́рн|ый, inventory, stock; ~ая о́пись, inventory. **инвента́рь,** -я *m.* stock; equipment, appliances; inventory.

инде́ец, -е́йца, (American) Indian. **инде́йка,** -и; *gen. pl.* -е́ек, turkey (-hen). **инде́йский,** (American) Indian; ~ пету́х, turkey-cock. **индиа́нка,** -и, Indian; American Indian. **инди́ец,** -и́йца, Indian. **инди́йский,** Indian.

инду́с, -а, **инду́ска**, -и Hindu. **инду́сский**, Hindu.
индю́к, -а́, **индю́шка** -и, turkey.
и́ней, -я, hoar-frost, rime.
ине́ртность, -и, inertness, inertia; sluggishness, inaction, passivity. **ине́ртный**, inert; passive; sluggish, inactive. **ине́рция**, -и, inertia.
инжене́р, -а, engineer; ~-меха́ник, mechanical engineer; ~-строи́тель, civil engineer. **инжене́рн|ый**, engineering; ~ые войска́, Engineers; ~ое де́ло, engineering.
ин-ква́рто *n. indecl.* quarto.
инкруста́ция, -и, inlaid work, inlay. **инкрусти́ровать**, -рую *perf.* and *imp.* inlay.
ино- in *comb.* other, different; hetero-. **иногоро́дн|ый**, of, from, for, another town. **~зе́мец**, -мца, foreigner. **~зе́мный**, foreign. **~ро́дец**, -дца, non-Russian. **~ро́дный**, foreign. **~сказа́ние**, -я, allegory. **~сказа́тельный**, allegorical. **~стра́нец**, -нца, **~стра́нка**, -и; *gen. pl.* -нок, foreigner. **~стра́нный**, foreign. **~язы́чный**, speaking, belonging to, another language; non-native, foreign.
иногда́ *adv.* sometimes.
ино́й, different; other; some; ~ раз, sometimes; ины́ми слова́ми, in other words.
и́нок, -а, monk. **и́нокиня**, -и, nun.
ин-окта́во *n. indecl.* octavo.
инотде́л: see ин-.
и́ноходь, -и amble.
инспе́кция, -и inspection; inspectorate.
институ́т, -а, institution; institute; young ladies' boarding school. **институ́тка** -и, boarding-school miss; innocent unsophisticated girl.
инструкти́ровать, -рую *perf.* and *imp.* (*perf.* also про~), instruct, give instructions to; brief. **инстру́кция**, -и, instructions; directions.
инструме́нт, -а, instrument; tool, implement; tools, implements.
инсцени́ровать, -рую *perf.* and *imp.* dramatize, adapt; stage. **инсцениро́вка**, -и, dramatization, adaptation; pretence, act.
интеллиге́нт, -а, intellectual, member of intelligentsia. **интеллиге́нтный**, cultured, educated. **интеллиге́нтский**, dilettante. **интеллиге́нция**, -и, intelligentsia.
интенда́нт, -а, commissary, quartermaster.
интере́с, -а, interest. **интере́сный**, interesting; striking, attractive. **интересова́ть**, -су́ю *imp.* interest; **~ся**, be interested (+ *instr.* in).
интерна́т -а, boarding-school.
интри́га -и, intrigue; plot.
инфа́ркт, -а, infarct; coronary (thrombosis), heart attack.
инфля́ция -и, inflation.
ин-фо́лио *n. indecl.* folio.
и.о. *abbr.* исполня́ющий обя́занности, acting.
ио́д, etc.: see йод.
и пр. *abbr.* и про́чее, etc. etcetera; and so on; и про́чие, *et al.*, and Co.
ирла́ндец, -дца, Irishman. **ирла́ндка**, -и, Irishwoman. **ирла́ндский**, Irish.
ис-: see из-.
ИСЗ (*ieszé*) *abbr.* иску́сственный спу́тник Земли́, artificial Earth satellite, sputnik.
иск, -а, suit action.
искажа́ть -а́ю *imp.*, **искази́ть**, -ажу́ *perf.* distort, pervert, twist; misrepresent. **искаже́ние**, -я distortion, perversion. **искажённый**; -ён, -ена́, distorted, perverted.
искале́ченный, crippled, maimed. **искале́чивать**, -аю *imp.*, **ис|кале́чить**, -чу *perf.* cripple, maim; break, damage; **~ся**, become a cripple; be crippled.
иска́ние, -я, search, quest; *pl.* strivings.
иска́тель, -я *m.* seeker; searcher; view-finder; selector; scanner. **иска́ть**, ищу́, и́щешь *imp.* (+*acc.* or *gen.*) seek, look for, search for.
исключа́ть, -а́ю *imp.*, **исключи́ть**, -чу́ *perf.* exclude; eliminate; expel; dismiss; rule out. **исключа́я**, *prep.*+*gen.* except, excepting, with the exception of; ~ прису́тствующих, present company excepted. **исключе́ние**, -я, exception; exclusion; expulsion; elimination; за исключе́нием+*gen.* with the exception of. **исключи́тельно** *adv.*

exceptionally; exclusively, solely; exclusive. **исключи́тельный,** exceptional; exclusive, sole; excellent.

исковéрканный, corrupt, corrupted; broken; spoilt. **ис|ковéркать, -аю** *perf.*

исколеси́ть, -ешу́ *perf.* travel all over.

ис|кóмкать, -аю *perf.*

ископáемое *sb.* mineral; fossil. **ископáемый,** fossilized fossil.

искоренéние, -я, eradication. **искорени́ть, -ню́** *perf.*, **искореня́ть -я́ю** *imp.* eradicate.

и́скоса *adv.* sideways sidelong; askance.

и́скра -ы spark; flash glimmer.

и́скренний, sincere candid. **и́скренно** *adv.* sincerely; candidly. **и́скренность,** -и, sincerity; candour.

искриви́ть, -влю́ *perf.*, **искривля́ть,** -я́ю *imp.* bend; curve; distort, twist, warp. **искривлéние, -я,** bend; distortion, warping.

искри́стый, sparkling. **искри́ть,** -и́т *imp.* spark; **~ся** sparkle; scintillate. **искровóй** spark.

ис|кромсáть, -áю *perf.* **ис|кроши́ть(ся,** -шу́(сь, -шись(ся *perf.*

ис|купáть[1]**(ся, -áю(сь** *perf.*

искупáть[2], -áю *imp.*, **искупи́ть, -плю́,** -пишь *perf.* expiate, atone for; make up for, compensate for. **искупи́тель,** -я *m.* redeemer. **искуплéние, -я,** redemption, expiation, atonement.

искуси́ть, -ушу́ *perf.* of искушáть.

иску́сный, skilful; expert. **иску́сственный,** artificial; synthetic; feigned, pretended. **иску́сство, -а,** art; craftsmanship, skill.

искушáть, -áю *imp.* (*perf.* искуси́ть), tempt; seduce. **искушéние, -я,** temptation, seduction. **искушённый;** -ён, -енá, experienced; tested.

ИСЛ (*iesél*) *abbr.* иску́сственный спу́тник Луны́, artificial Moon satellite, sputnik.

ис|пáкостить, -ощу *perf.*

испáнец, -нца, испáнка, -и, Spaniard. **испáнский,** Spanish.

испарéние, -я, evaporation; *pl.* fumes. **испáрина, -ы,** perspiration. **испари́тель,** -я *m.* evaporator; vaporizer. **испари́ть, -рю́** *perf.*, **испаря́ть, -я́ю** *imp.* evaporate, volatilize; exhale; **~ся,** evaporate, vaporize; be evaporated.

ис|пáчкать, -аю *perf.* **ис|пéчь,** -еку́, -ечёшь *perf.*

испещрённый; -рён, -ренá, speckled. **испещри́ть,** -рю́ *perf.*, **испещря́ть,** -я́ю *imp.* speckle, spot; mark all over, cover.

исписáть, -ишу́, -и́шешь *perf.*, **испи́сывать,** -аю *imp.* cover, fill, with writing; use up.

испитóй, haggard, gaunt; hollow-cheeked.

исповéдовать, -дую *perf.* and *imp.* confess; profess; **~ся,** confess; make one's confession; +в+*prep.* unburden oneself of, acknowledge. **и́споведь, -и,** confession.

исподлóбья *adv.* sullenly, distrustfully.

исподтишкá *adv.* in an underhand way; on the quiet, on the sly; смея́ться ~, laugh in one's sleeve.

испокóн векóв, вéку: see век.

исполи́н, -а, giant. **исполи́нский,** gigantic.

исполкóм, -а *abbr.* исполни́тельный комитéт, executive committee. **исполнéние,** -я, fulfilment, execution, discharge; performance; привести́ в ~, carry out, execute. **исполни́мый,** feasible, practicable. **исполни́тель,** -я *m.*, **-тельница,** -ы, executor; performer. **исполни́тельный,** executive; assiduous, careful, attentive; ~ лист, writ, court order. **испóлнить,** -ню *perf.*, **исполня́ть,** -я́ю *imp.* carry out, execute; fulfil; perform; ~ обещáние, keep a promise; ~ прóсьбу, grant a request; **~ся,** be fulfilled; *impers.* (+*dat.*); ему́ испóлнилось семь лет, he is seven years old; испóлнилось пять лет с тех пор, как, it is five years since, five years have passed since. **исполня́ющий;** ~ обя́занности+*gen.* acting.

испóльзование, -я, utilization. **испóльзовать,** -зую *perf.* and *imp.* make (good) use of, utilize; turn to account.

ис|пóртить(ся, -рчу(сь *perf.* **испóрченность,** -и, depravity. **испóрченный,** depraved; corrupted; spoiled; bad, rotten.

исправи́тельный, correctional; corrective; ~ дом, reformatory. **испра́вить**, -влю *perf.* **исправля́ть**, -я́ю *imp.* rectify, correct, emendate; repair, mend; reform, improve, amend; **~ся**, improve, reform. **исправле́ние**, -я, correcting; repairing; improvement; correction; emendation. **испра́вленный**, improved, corrected; revised; reformed. **испра́вник**, -а, district police superintendent. **испра́вность**, -и, good repair, good condition; punctuality; preciseness; meticulousness. **испра́вный**, in good order; punctual; precise; meticulous.

ис|про́бовать, -бую *perf.*

испу́г, -а (-у), fright; alarm. **испу́ганный**, frightened, scared, startled.

ис|пуга́ть(ся, -а́ю(сь *perf.*

испуска́ть, -а́ю *imp.*, **испусти́ть**, -ущу́, -у́стишь *perf.* emit, let out; utter; ~ вздох, heave a sigh; ~ дух, breathe one's last.

испыта́ние, -я, test, trial; ordeal; examination. **испы́танный**, tried, well-tried; tested. **испыта́тельный**, test, trial; examining; experimental; probationary. **испыта́ть**, -а́ю *perf.*, **испы́тывать**, -аю *imp.* test; try; feel, experience.

и́ссера- in *comb.* grey-, greyish.

и́ссиня- in *comb.* blue-, bluish.

иссле́дование, -я, investigation; research; analysis; exploration; paper; study. **иссле́дователь**, -я *m.* researcher; investigator; explorer. **иссле́довательский**, research. **иссле́довать**, -дую *perf.* and *imp.* investigate, examine; research into; explore, analyse.

и́сстари *adv.* from of old; так ~ ведётся, it is an old custom.

исступле́ние, -я, frenzy, transport. **исступлённый**, frenzied; ecstatic.

иссуша́ть -а́ю *imp.*, **иссуши́ть**, -шу́, -шишь *perf.* dry up; consume, waste.

иссяка́ть -а́ет *imp.*, **исся́кнуть**, -нет; -я́к *perf.* run dry, dry up; run low fail.

иста́сканный, worn out; threadbare; worn; haggard. **истаска́ть**, -а́ю *perf.*, **иста́скивать**, -аю *imp.* wear out; **~ся**, wear out; be worn out.

истека́ть, -а́ет *imp.* of исте́чь. **исте́кший**, past, last; preceding, previous.

истере́ть, изотру́, -трёшь; истёр *perf.* (*imp.* истира́ть) grate; wear away, wear down; **~ся**, wear out; wear away, be worn away.

исте́рзанный, tattered, lacerated; tormented.

исте́рик, -а, **истери́чка**, -и, hysterical subject. **исте́рика**, -и, hysterics. **истери́чный**, hysterical. **истери́я**, -и, hysteria.

исте́ц, -тца́, **исти́ца**, -ы, plaintiff; petitioner.

истече́ние, -я, outflow; expiry, expiration; ~ кро́ви, haemorrhage. **исте́чь**, -ечёт; -тёк, -ла́ *perf.* (*imp.* истека́ть) flow out; elapse; expire.

и́стина, -ы, truth. **и́стинный**, true.

истира́ние, -я, abrasion. **истира́ть(ся**, -а́юсь *imp.* of истере́ть(ся.

исти́ца: see исте́ц.

истлева́ть. -а́ю *imp.*, **истле́ть**, -е́ю *perf.* rot, decay; be reduced to ashes, smoulder away.

исто́к, -а, source.

истолкова́ть, -ку́ю *perf.*, **истолко́вывать**, -аю *imp.* interpret expound; comment on.

ис|толо́чь, -лку́, -лчёшь; -ло́к, -лкла́ *perf.*

исто́ма, -ы, lassitude; languor. **ис|томи́ть**, -млю́ *perf.*, **истомля́ть**, -я́ю *imp.* exhaust, weary; **~ся**, be exhausted, be worn out; be weary. **истомлённый**; -ён, -ена́, exhausted, tired out, worn out.

истопни́к, -а́, stoker, boilerman.

исторга́ть, -а́ю *imp.*, **исто́ргнуть**, -ну; -о́рг *perf.* throw out, expel; wrest, wrench; force, extort.

исто́рик, -а, historian. **истори́ческий**, historical; historic. **истори́чный**, historical. **исто́рия**, -и, history; story; incident, event; заба́вная ~, a funny thing.

исто́чник, -а, spring; source.

истоща́ть, -а́ю *imp.*, **истощи́ть**, -щу́ *perf.* exhaust; drain, sap; deplete; emaciate. **истоще́ние**, -я, emaciation; exhaustion; depletion. **истощённый**; -ён, -ена́, emaciated; exhausted.

ис|тра́тить, -а́чу *perf.*

истреби́тель, -я *m.* destroyer; fighter.

истреби́тельный, destructive; fighter. **истреби́ть,** -блю́ *perf.*, **истребля́ть,** -я́ю *imp.* destroy; exterminate, extirpate.
истрёпанный, torn, frayed; worn. **ис|трепа́ть,** -плю́, -плешь *perf.*
истука́н, -а, idol, image.
ис|тупи́ть, -плю́, -пишь *perf.*
и́стый, true genuine.
истяза́ние, -я, torture. **истяза́ть,** -а́ю *imp.* torture.
исхо́д, -а, outcome, issue; end; Exodus; на ~е, nearing the end, coming to an end; на ~е дня, towards evening. **исходи́ть,** -ожу́, -о́дишь *imp.* (+из or от +*gen.*) issue (from), come (from); emanate (from); proceed (from), base oneself (on). **исхо́дный,** initial, original, starting; departure, of departure.
исхуда́лый, emaciated, wasted. **исхуда́ть,** -а́ю *perf.* grow thin, become wasted.
исцеле́ние, -я, healing, cure; recovery. **исцели́мый,** curable. **исцели́ть,** -лю́ *perf.*, **исцеля́ть,** -я́ю *imp.* heal, cure.
исчеза́ть, -а́ю *imp.*, **исче́знуть,** -ну; -е́з *perf.* disappear, vanish. **исчезнове́ние,** -я, disappearance.
и́счерна- in *comb.* blackish, very dark.
исче́рпать, -аю *perf.*, **исче́рпывать,** -аю *imp.* exhaust, drain; settle, conclude. **исче́рпывающий,** exhaustive.
исчисле́ние, -я, calculation; calculus. **исчи́слить,** -лю *perf.*, **исчисля́ть,** -я́ю *imp.* calculate, compute; estimate. **исчисля́ться,** -я́ется *imp.*+*instr.* or в+*acc.* amount to, come to; be calculated at.
ита́к *conj.* thus; so then; and so.
италья́нец, -нца, **италья́нка,** -и, Italian. **италья́нск|ий,** Italian; ~ая забасто́вка, sit-down strike, working to rule, go-slow.
и т.д. *abbr.* и так да́лее, etc., and so on.
ито́г, -а, sum; total; result, upshot. **итого́** (*-vo*) *adv.* in all, altogether. **ито́говый,** total, final.
и т.п. *abbr.* и тому́ подо́бное, etc., and so on.
ИТР (*iteér*) *abbr.* инжене́рно-техни́ческие рабо́тники, engineering and technical staff.
итти́: see идти́.
иуде́й, -я, **иуде́йка,** -и, Jew. **иуде́йский,** Judaic.
их: see они́. **их, и́хний,** their, theirs.
ихтиоза́вр, -а, ichthyosaurus. **ихтиоло́гия,** -и, ichthyology.
иша́к, -а́, donkey, ass; hinny.
ище́йка, -и, bloodhound; police dog; sleuth.
ищу́, etc.: see иска́ть.
ию́ль, -я *m.* July. **ию́льский,** July.
ию́нь, -я *m.* June. **ию́ньский,** June.
й *letter*: see и.
йог (*yo-*), -а, Yogi.
йод (*yo-*), -а, iodine.
йо́та (*yo-*), -ы, iota.

К

к *letter*: see ка.
к, ко *prep.*+*dat.* to, towards; by; for; on; on the occasion of; к лу́чшему, for the better; к (не)сча́стью, (un)fortunately, (un)luckily; к пе́рвому января́, by the first of January; к сро́ку, on time; к тому́ вре́мени, by then, by that time; к тому́ же, besides, moreover; к чему́? what for? лицо́м к лицу́, face to face; ни к чему́, no good, no use.
к. *abbr.* ко́мната, room; копе́йка, copeck.
ка *n. indecl.* the letter к.
-ка *part.* modifying force of imper. or expressing decision or intention; да́йте-ка пройти́, let me pass, please; скажи́-ка мне, do tell me.
каба́к, -а́, tavern, drinking-shop; pub.
кабала́, -ы́, servitude, bondage. **кабали́ть,** -лю́ *imp.* enslave.

кабáн, -á wild boar.
кабачóк[1], -чкá *dim.* of кабáк.
кабачóк[2], -чкá, vegetable marrow.
кáбель, -я *m.* cable. **кáбельный** *adj.* **кáбельтов**, -а, cable, hawser; cable's length.
каби́на, -ы, cabin; booth; cockpit; cab. **кабинéт**, -а, study; consulting-room, surgery; room, classroom, laboratory, office; cabinet. **кабинéтский**, cabinet.
каблýк, -á, heel. **каблучóк**, -чкá heel; ogee; ~-шпи́лька stiletto heel.
каботáж, -а, cabotage; coastal shipping. **каботáжник**, -а, coaster. **каботáжный**, cabotage; coastal, coasting, coastwise.
кавалéр, -а, knight; partner, gentleman. **кавалергáрд**, -а, horse-guardsman. **кавалери́йский**, cavalry. **кавалери́ст**, -а, cavalryman. **кавалéрия**, -и, cavalry.
кáверза, -ы, chicanery; mean trick, dirty trick. **кáверзный**, tricky, ticklish.
кавкáзец, -зца, **кавкáзка**, -и, Caucasian. **кавкáзский**, Caucasian.
кавы́чки, -чек *pl.* inverted commas, quotation marks; откры́ть ~, quote; закры́ть ~, unquote.
кадéт[1], -а, cadet. **кадéтский**, cadet; ~ кóрпус, military school.
кадéт[2], -а, *abbr.* конституциóнный демокрáт, Cadet, Kadet.
кáдка, -и, tub, vat.
кадр, -а, frame, still; close-up; cadre; *pl.* establishment; staff; personnel; specialists, skilled workers. **кадрови́к**, -а, member of permanent establishment, professional body, etc. **кáдровый**, regular; experienced, skilled; trained.
кады́к, -á, Adam's apple.
каёмка, -и, (narrow) border, (narrow) edging. **каёмчатый** with a border.
каждоднéвный, daily, everyday. **кáждый**, each, every; *sb.* everybody, everyone.
кáжется, etc.: see казáться.
казáк, -á; *pl.* -аки́, -áкóв, **казáчка**, -и, Cossack.
казáрма, -ы, barracks; barrack.
казáться, кажýсь, кáжешься *imp.* (*perf.* по~), seem, appear; *impers.* кáжется, казáлось, apparently; казáлось бы, it would seem, one would think; +*dat.* мне кáжется, it seems to me; I think.
казáцкий, казáчий, Cossack. **казáчка**: see казáк. **казачóк**, -чкá, page, boy.
казённый, State; government; fiscal; public; bureaucratic, formal; banal, undistinguished, conventional; ~ язы́к, official jargon; на ~ счёт, at the public expense. **казнá**, -ы́, Exchequer, Treasury; public purse; the State; money, property. **казначéй**, -я, treasurer, bursar; paymaster; purser.
казни́ть, -ню́ *perf.* and *imp.* execute, put to death; punish, chastise; castigate. **казнь**, -и, execution.
каймá, -ы́; *gen. pl.* каём, border, edging; hem, selvage.
как *adv.* how; what; all of a sudden, all at once; вот ~! not really! you don't say!; ~ вы дýмаете? what do you think?; ~ вы поживáете? how are you?; ~ делá? how are you getting on?; ~ его зовýт? what is his name? what is he called?; ~ есть, complete(ly), utter(ly); ~ же, naturally, of course; ~ же так? how is that?; ~ ни, however; ~-никáк, nevertheless, for all that; он ~ есть дурáк, he's a complete fool. **как** *conj.* as; like; when; since; + *neg.* but, except, than; бýдьте ~ дóма, make yourself at home; в то врéмя ~, while, whereas; ~ вдруг, when suddenly; **~ мóжно, ~ нельзя́**, + *comp.* as . . as possible; ~ мóжно скорée, as soon as possible; ~ нельзя́ лýчше, as well as possible; ~ нарóчно, as luck would have it; ~ . ., так и, both . . and; ~ тóлько, as soon as, when; мéжду тем, ~, while, whereas; я ви́дел, ~ онá ушлá, I saw her go. **как бýдто** *conj.* as if, as though; *part.* apparently, it would seem. **как бы**, how; as if, as though; как бы . . не, what if, supposing; боюсь, как бы он нé был в дурнóм настроéнии, I am afraid he may be in a bad temper; как бы не так! not likely, certainly not; как бы . . ни, however. **кáк-либо** *adv.* somehow. **кáк-нибудь** *adv.* somehow; in some way or other; anyhow; some time.

как раз *adv.* just, exactly. **как-то** *adv.* somehow; once, one day.
како́в *m.*, **какова́** *f.*, **каково́** *n.*, **каковы́** *pl. pron.* what, what sort (of); ~ он? what is he like? ~ он собо́й? what does he look like?; пого́да-то какова́! what weather! **каково́** *adv.* how. **како́й** *pron.* what; (such) as; which; ~ . . ни, whatever, whichever; каки́м о́бразом? how?; ~ тако́й? which (exactly)?; како́е там, nothing of the kind, quite the contrary. **како́й-либо, како́й-нибудь** *pron.* some; any; only. **како́й-то** *pron.* some; a; a kind of; something like.
как раз, ка́к-то: see как.
каланча́, -и́, watch-tower.
кале́ка, -и *m.* and *f.* cripple.
кале́ние, -я, incandescence.
кале́чить, -чу *imp.* (*perf.* ис~, по~) cripple, maim, mutilate; twist, pervert; **~ся**, become a cripple, be crippled.
кали́бр, -а, calibre; bore; gauge.
ка́лий, -я, potassium.
кали́тка, -и, wicket, (wicket-)gate.
кало́ша, -и, galosh.
ка́лька, -и, tracing-paper; tracing; calque.
ка́льций, -я, calcium.
ка́мбала, -ы, flat-fish; plaice; flounder.
камени́стый, stony, rocky. **каменно-уго́льный**, coal; ~ бассе́йн, coal-field. **ка́менн|ый**, stone; rock; stony; hard, immovable; ~ый век, Stone Age; ~ая соль, rock-salt; ~ у́голь, coal. **каменоло́мня**, -и; *gen. pl.* -мен, quarry. **ка́менщик**, -а, (stone)mason; brick-layer. **ка́мень**, -мня; *pl.* -мни, -мне́й *m.* stone.
ка́мера, -ы, chamber; compartment; cell, ward; camera; inner tube, (foot-ball) bladder; ~ хране́ния (багажа́), cloak-room, left-luggage office. **ка́мерный**, chamber. **камерто́н**, -а, tuning-fork.
ками́н, -а, fireplace; fire.
камо́рка, -и, closet, cell, very small room.
кампа́ния, -и campaign; cruise.
камфара́, -ы́, camphor.
камы́ш, -а́, reed, rush; cane.
кана́ва, -ы, ditch; gutter; drain; trench; inspection pit.
кана́дец, -дца, **кана́дка**, -и, Canadian. **кана́дский**, Canadian.
кана́л, -а, canal; channel; duct; bore. **канализа́ция**, -и, sewerage sewerage system; drainage; underground cable system.
канаре́ечный, canary; canary-coloured. **канаре́йка**, -и, canary.
кана́т, -а, rope; cable, hawser. **канато-хо́дец**, -дца, rope-walker.
канва́, -ы, canvas; groundwork; out-line, design. **канво́вый**, canvas.
кандалы́, -о́в *pl.* shackles, fetters, irons.
кани́кулы, -ул *pl.* vacation; holidays. **каникуля́рный**, holiday.
кани́стра, -ы, can, canister.
канифо́ль, -и, rosin.
каноне́рка, -и, gunboat. **канони́р**, -а, gunner.
кант, -а, edging, piping; welt; mount. **кантова́ть**, -ту́ю *imp.* (*perf.* о~) border, pipe; mount.
кану́н, -а, eve; vigil, watch-night.
ка́нуть, -ну *perf.* drop, sink; ~ в ве́чность, sink into oblivion; как в во́ду ~, vanish into thin air, disappear without trace.
канцеля́рия, -и, office. **канцеля́рск|ий**, office; clerical; ~ие принадле́жности, stationery. **канцеля́рщина**, office--work; red tape.
ка́нцлер, -а, chancellor.
ка́пать, -аю or -плю *imp.* (*perf.* ка́пнуть на~) drip, drop; trickle, dribble; fall in drops; pour out in drops; +*instr.* spill. **ка́пелька**, -и, small drop, droplet; a little; a bit, a grain, a whit; ~ росы́, dew-drop.
капельме́йстер, -а, conductor; band-master.
ка́пельный, drip, drop, drip-feed, trickle; tiny.
капита́л, -а, capital. **капиталисти́ческий**, capitalist, capitalistic. **капита́льный**, capital; main, fundamental; most important; ~ ремо́нт, capital repairs, major overhaul.
капита́н, -а, captain; master, skipper.
капите́ль, -и, capital; small caps.

капка́н, -а, trap. **капка́нный**, trap; trapping.
ка́пля, -и; *gen. pl.* -пель, drop; bit, scrap; ни ка́пли, not a bit, not a scrap, not a whit; по ка́пле drop by drop. **ка́пнуть**, -ну *perf.* of ка́пать.
ка́пор, -а, hood, bonnet.
капо́т, -а, hood cowl, cowling; bonnet; (loose) dressing-gown, house-coat.
капу́ста, -ы, cabbage.
капюшо́н, а, hood.
ка́ра, -ы, punishment, retribution.
кара́бкаться, -аюсь *imp.* (*perf.* вс~) clamber, scramble up.
карава́й, -я, round loaf, cob; pudding.
карава́н, -а, caravan; convoy.
кара́куль, -я *m.* karakul, Persian lamb.
кара́куля, -и, scrawl, scribble.
карамбо́ль, -я *m.* cannon.
караме́ль, -и, caramel; caramels. **караме́лька**, -и, caramel.
каранда́ш, -а́, pencil.
карапу́з, -а, chubby little fellow.
кара́сь, -я́ *m.* crucian carp.
кара́тельный, punitive. **кара́ть**, -а́ю *imp.* (*perf.* по~) punish, chastise.
карау́л, -а, guard; watch; ~! help!; нести́ ~, be on guard. **карау́лить**, -лю *imp.* guard; watch for, lie in wait for. **карау́льный**, guard; *sb.* sentry, sentinel, guard.
карбюра́тор, -а, carburettor.
каре́л, -а, **каре́лка**, -и, Karelian. **каре́льск|ий**, Karelian; ~ая берёза, Karelian birch.
каре́та, -ы, carriage, coach; ~ ско́рой по́мощи, ambulance.
ка́рий, brown; hazel.
карикату́ра, -ы, caricature; cartoon.
карка́с, -а, frame; framework.
ка́ркать, -аю *imp.*, **ка́ркнуть**, -ну *perf.* (*perf.* also на~) caw, croak.
ка́рлик, -а, **ка́рлица**, -ы, dwarf; pygmy. **ка́рликовый**, dwarf, dwarfish; pygmy.
карма́н, -а, pocket. **карма́нный** *adj.* pocket; ~ вор, pickpocket.
карни́з, -а, cornice; ledge.
ка́рта, -ы, map; chart; (playing-)card.
карта́вить, -влю *imp.* burr. **карта́вость**, -и, burr. **карта́вый**, burring.
ка́ртер, -а, gear casing, crank-case.
карте́чь, -и, case-shot, grape-shot; buckshot.
карти́на, -ы, picture; scene. **карти́нка**, -и, picture; illustration. **карти́нный**, picturesque; picture.
карто́н, -а, cardboard, pasteboard; cartoon. **карто́нка**, -и, cardboard box; hat-box, bandbox.
картоте́ка, -и, card-index.
карто́фелина, -ы, potato. **карто́фель**, -я (-ю) *m.* potatoes; potato (-plant). **карто́фельн|ый**, potato; ~ая запека́нка, shepherd's pie; ~ый крахма́л, potato flour; ~ое пюре́, mashed potatoes.
ка́рточка, -и, card; season ticket; photograph; ~ вин, wine-list; ~ ку́шаний, menu, bill of fare. **ка́рточный**, card; ~ до́мик, house of cards.
карто́шка, -и, potatoes; potato.
карту́з, -а́, (peaked) cap.
карусе́ль, -и, roundabout, merry-go-round.
ка́рцер, -а, cell, lock-up.
карье́р[1], -а, full gallop.
карье́р[2], -а, quarry; sand-pit.
каса́ние, -я, contact. **каса́тельная** *sb.* tangent. **каса́ться**, -а́юсь *imp.* (*perf.* косну́ться) + *gen.* or до + *gen.* touch; touch on; concern, relate to; что каса́ется, as to, as regards, with regard to.
ка́ска, -и, helmet.
каспи́йский, Caspian.
ка́сса, -ы, till; cash-box; booking-office; box-office; cash-desk; cash; case; ~-автома́т, slot-machine, ticket-machine; ~ взаимопо́мощи, benefit fund, mutual aid fund, friendly society.
кассе́та, -ы, cassette; plate-holder.
касси́р, -а, **касси́рша**, -и, cashier. **ка́ссовый**, cash; box-office; ~ аппара́т, cash register; ~ счёт, cash-account; ~ успе́х, box-office success.
кастра́т, -а, eunuch. **кастра́ция**, -и, castration. **кастри́ровать**, -рую *perf.* and *imp.* castrate, geld.
кастрю́ля, -и, saucepan.
ката́ние, -я, rolling; driving; ~ верхо́м, riding; ~ на коньках, skating; ~ с гор, tobogganing.

катáть, -áю *imp.* (*perf.* вы́~, с~) roll; wheel, trundle; drive, take for a drive, take out; roll out; mangle; **~ся,** roll, roll about; go for a drive; ~ся верхóм ride, go riding; ~ся на конькáх, skate, go skating; ~ся сó смеху, split one's sides.

катастрóфа, -ы, catastrophe, disaster; accident, crash.

катафáлк, -а, catafalque; hearse.

кáтер, -а; *pl.* **-á,** cutter; boat, motor-boat, launch.

кати́ть, -ачу́ -áтишь *imp.* bowl along, rip, tear; **~ся,** rush, tear; flow, stream, roll; ~ся пóд гору, go downhill; ~ся с горы́, slide downhill; кати́сь, кати́тесь, get out! clear off! **катóк, -тка́,** skating-rink; roller; mangle.

кáторга, -и, penal servitude, hard labour. **каторжáнин, -а,** convict, ex-convict. **кáторжник, -а,** convict. **кáторжн|ый,** penal, convict; ~ые рабóты, hard labour; drudgery.

катýшка, -и, reel, bobbin; spool; coil.

каучýк, -а, rubber.

кафé *n. indecl.* café.

кáфедра, -ы, pulpit; rostrum, platform; chair; department.

качáлка, -и, rocking-chair; конь-~, rocking-horse. **качáние, -я,** rocking, swinging, swing; pumping. **качáть, -áю** *imp.* (*perf.* качнýть) + *acc.* or *instr.* rock, swing; shake; lift up, chair; pump; **~ся,** rock, swing; roll, pitch; reel, stagger. **качéли, -ей** *pl.* swing.

кáчественный, qualitative; high-quality.

кáчество, -а, quality; в кáчестве + *gen.* as, in the capacity or character of; вы́играть ~, потеря́ть ~, gain, lose, by an exchange.

кáчка, -и, rocking; tossing.

качнýть(ся, -нý(сь, -нёшь(ся *perf.* of качáть(ся. **качý,** etc.: see кати́ть.

кáша -и, kasha; gruel, porridge; заварúть кáшу, start something, stir up trouble. **кашевáр, -а,** cook.

кáшель, -шля *m.* cough. **кáшлянуть, -ну** *perf.*, **кáшлять, -яю** *imp.* cough; have a cough.

кашнé *n. indecl.* scarf, muffler.

каштáн, -а, chestnut. **каштáновый,** chestnut.

каю́та, -ы, cabin, stateroom. **каю́т-компáния, -и,** wardroom; passengers' lounge.

кáющийся, repentant, contrite, penitent. **кáяться,** кáюсь *imp.* (*perf.* по~, рас~) repent; confess; кáюсь, I am sorry to say, I (must) confess.

кв. *abbr.* квадрáтный, square; квартúра, flat, apartment.

КВ (*kavé*) *abbr.* корóткие вóлны, short waves, коротковóлновый, short-wave.

квадрáт, -а, square; quad; в квадрáте, squared; возвести́ в ~, square. **квадрáтный,** square; quadratic. **квадратýра, -ы,** squaring; quadrature.

квáканье, -я, croaking. **квáкать, -аю** *imp.*, **квáкнуть, -ну** *perf.* croak.

квалифици́рованный, qualified; skilled, trained, specialized. **квалифици́ровать, -рую** *perf.* and *imp.* qualify; check, test.

квант, -а. квáнта, -ы, quantum.

квартáл, -а, block; quarter. **квартáльный,** quarterly; *sb.* police officer.

квартúра, -ы, flat; lodging(s); apartment(s); quarters, billets. **квартирáнт, -а, -рáнтка, -и,** lodger; tenant. **квартúрн|ый;** ~ая плáта, **квартплáта, -ы,** rent.

кварц, -а, quartz.

квас, -а (-у); *pl.* ~ы́, kvass. **квáсить, -áшу** *imp.* sour; ferment; pickle; leaven. **квасцóвый,** alum. **квасцы́, -óв** *pl.* alum. **квáшен|ый,** sour, fermented; ~ая капýста, sauerkraut.

квéрху *adv.* up, upwards.

квит, квúты, quits.

квитáнция, -и, receipt. **квитóк, -ткá,** ticket, check.

квт *abbr.* киловáтт, kilowatt; **квт-ч,** kilowatt-hour.

кг *abbr.* килогрáмм, kilogram.

КГБ (*kagebé*) *abbr.* Комитет государственной безопáсности, State Security Committee.

КДП (*kadepé*) *abbr.* командно-диспéтчерский пункт, control tower.

кегль, -я *m.* point size, body size.

кéгля, -и, skittle.

кедр, -а, cedar. **кедрóвый,** cedar.

кéды, -ов *pl.* sports boots, sneakers.

кекс, -а, cake; fruit-cake.

ке́лья, -и; *gen. pl.* -лий, cell.
кем: see кто.
ке́мпинг, кэ́мпинг, -а, camping site, tourist camp.
кенгуру́ *m. indecl.* kangaroo.
ке́пка, -и, cap, cloth cap.
керога́з, -а, oil pressure stove. **кероси́н, -а**, paraffin, kerosene. **кероси́нка, -и**, oil-stove.
ке́та, -ы, Siberian salmon. **ке́тов|ый**; ~ая икра́, red caviare.
киберне́тика, -и, cybernetics. **кибернети́ческий**, cybernetic.
киби́тка, -и, kibitka, covered wagon; nomad tent.
кива́ть, -а́ю *imp.*, **кивну́ть, -ну́, -нёшь** *perf.* (голово́й) nod, nod one's head; (+на+*acc.*) motion (to). **кивóк, -вка́**, nod.
кида́ть, -а́ю *imp.* (*perf.* ки́нуть) throw, fling, cast; **~ся**, throw oneself, fling oneself; rush; + *instr.* throw, fling, shy.
кий, -я́: *pl.* -и́, -ёв, (billiard) cue.
килев|о́й, keel; ~а́я ка́чка, pitching. **киль, -я** *m.* keel; fin. **кильва́тер, -а**, wake.
ки́лька, -и, sprat.
кинжа́л, -а, dagger.
кино́ *n. indecl.* cinema.
кино- in *comb.* film-, cine-. **киноаппара́т, -а**, cinecamera. **~арти́ст, -а**, **~арти́стка, -и**, film actor, actress. **~ателье́** *n. indecl.* film studio. **~журна́л, -а**, news-reel. **~звезда́, -ы́**, film-star. **~зри́тель, -я** *m.* film-goer. **~карти́на, -ы**, film, picture. **~опера́тор, -а**, camera-man. **~плёнка, -и**, film. **~режиссёр, -а** film director. **~хро́ника -и**, news-reel.
ки́нуть(ся, -ну(сь *perf.* of кида́ть(ся.
кио́ск, -а, kiosk, stall, stand.
ки́па -ы, pile stack; pack, bale.
кипари́с, -а, cypress.
кипе́ние, -я, boiling. **кипе́ть, -плю́** *imp.* (*perf.* вс~) boil, seethe; рабо́та кипе́ла, work was in full swing. **кипу́чий**, boiling, seething; ebullient, turbulent. **кипяти́льник, -а**, kettle, boiler. **кипяти́льный**, boiling, boiler. **кипяти́ть, -ячу́** *imp.* (*perf.* вс~) boil; **~ся**, boil; get excited, be enraged, be in a rage. **кипято́к, -тка́**, boiling water. **кипячёный**, boiled.
кирка́, -и́, pickaxe pick.
кирпи́ч -а́ brick; bricks; 'no-entry' sign. **кирпи́чный**, brick; brick-red; ~ заво́д, brickworks, brick-field brick-yard.
кисе́йный, muslin.
кисе́т, -а tobacco-pouch.
кисея́, -и́ muslin.
ки́ска, -и, pussy.
кислоро́д, -а, oxygen. **кислота́, -ы́**; *pl.* -ы, acid; sourness, acidity. **кисло́тный**, acid. **ки́сл|ый**, sour; acid; ~ая капу́ста, sauerkraut. **ки́снуть, -ну**; **кис** *imp.* (*perf.* про~) turn sour, go sour; mope.
ки́сточка, -и, brush; tassel. **кисть, -и**; *gen. pl.* -е́й, cluster, bunch; brush; tassel; hand.
кит -а́, whale.
кита́ец -а́йца; *pl.* -цы, -цев, **китая́нка, -и**, Chinese. **кита́йка, -и**, nankeen. **кита́йск|ий** Chinese; ~ая тушь, Indian ink.
китобо́й, -я, whaler, whaling ship. **кито́вый**, whale; ~ ус, whalebone. **китобо́йный**, whaling. **китообра́зный**, cetacean.
кичи́ться, -чу́сь *imp.* plume oneself; strut. **кичли́вость, -и**, conceit; arrogance. **кичли́вый**, conceited, arrogant, haughty, strutting.
кише́ть, -ши́т *imp.* swarm, teem.
кише́чник, -а, bowels, intestines. **кише́чный**, intestinal. **кишка́, -и́**, gut, intestine; hose.
кишмя́ *adv.*; ~ кише́ть, swarm.
кл. *abbr.* класс, class form.
к.л. *abbr.* како́й-либо, some.
клавеси́н, -а harpsichord. **клавиату́ра, -ы**, keyboard. **кла́виш, -а, кла́виша, -ы** key. **кла́вишн|ый**; ~ые инструме́нты keyboard instruments.
клад, -а, treasure.
кла́дбище, -а, cemetery, graveyard, churchyard.
кла́дка, -и, laying; masonry, walling. **кладова́я** *sb.* pantry, larder; store-room. **кладовщи́к, -а́**, storeman; shopman. **кладу́**, etc.: see класть. **кла́дчик, -а**, bricklayer.

кла́няться, -яюсь *imp.* (*perf.* поклони́ться)+*dat.* bow to; greet; send, convey greetings; humble oneself; go cap in hand to.
кла́пан, -а, valve; vent; flap.
кларне́т, -а clarinet.
класс, -а, class; form; class-room; *pl.* hopscotch. **кла́ссн|ый** class; class-room; high-class; first-class; ~ый ваго́н, passenger coach; ~ая доска́, blackboard; ~ая каю́та, private cabin. **кла́ссовый,** class.
класть, -аду́, -адёшь; -ал *imp.* (*perf.* положи́ть, сложи́ть) lay; put; place; construct, build.
клева́ть, клюю́, клюёшь *imp.* (*perf.* клю́нуть) peck; bite; ~ но́сом, nod.
кле́вер, -а; *pl.* -а́, clover.
клевета́, -ы́, slander; calumny, aspersion; libel. **клевета́ть,** -ещу́, -е́щешь *imp.* (*perf.* на~)+на+*acc.* slander, calumniate; libel. **клеветни́к,** -а́, **-ни́ца,** -ы, slanderer. **клеветни́ческий,** slanderous; libellous, defamatory.
клеево́й, glue; adhesive; size. **клеёнка,** -и, oilcloth; oilskin. **кле́ить,** -е́ю *imp.* (*perf.* с~) glue; gum; paste; stick; **~ся,** stick; become sticky; get on, go well. **клей,** -я (-ю), *loc.* -ю́, glue, adhesive, gum; size. **кле́йкий,** sticky.
клеймёный, branded. **клейми́ть,** -млю́ *imp.* (*perf.* за~) brand; stamp; stigmatize. **клеймо́,** -а́; *pl.* -а, brand; stamp; mark.
кле́мма, -ы clamp, clip; terminal.
клён, -а, maple.
клёпаный, riveted. **клепа́ть,** -а́ю *imp.* rivet.
кле́тка, -и, cage; coop; hutch; square; check; cell. **кле́точка,** -и, cellule. **кле́точный,** cage; cell, cellular. **клетча́тка,** -и, cellulose. **кле́тчатый,** checked; squared; cellular.
клёш, -а, flare; брю́ки ~, bell-bottoms; ю́бка ~, flared skirt.
клешня́ -и́; *gen. pl.* -е́й, claw.
кле́щи́, -е́й *pl.* pincers, tongs; pincer-movement.
клие́нт, -а, client; customer. **клиенту́ра,** -ы, clientèle.
клик -а cry, call. **кли́кать,** -и́чу *imp.*, **кли́кнуть,** -ну *perf.* call, hail; honk.
клин, -а; *pl.* -нья, -ньев, wedge; quoin; gore; gusset; field. **клино́к,** -нка́, blade. **кли́нопись,** -и, cuneiform.
кли́рос, -а, choir.
клич, -а, call. **кли́чка,** -и, name; alias; nickname. **кли́чу,** etc.: see кли́кать.
клок, -а́; *pl.* -о́чья, -ьев or -и́, -о́в, rag, shred; tuft; ~ се́на, wisp of hay.
кло́кот, -а, bubbling; gurgling. **клокота́ть,** -о́чет *imp.* bubble; gurgle; boil up.
клони́ть, -ню́, -нишь *imp.* bend; incline; +к+*dat.* lead; drive at; **~ся,** bow, bend; +к+*dat.* near, approach, lead up to, head for; день клони́лся к ве́черу, the day was declining.
клоп, -а́, bug.
кло́ун, -а clown.
клочо́к, -чка́, scrap, shred, wisp; plot. **кло́чья,** etc.: see клок.
клуб, -а; *pl.* -ы́, puff; ~ы́ пы́ли, clouds of dust.
клу́бень, -бня *m.* tuber.
клуби́ться, -и́тся *imp.* swirl; wreathe, curl.
клубни́ка, -и, strawberry; strawberries. **клубни́чный,** strawberry.
клубо́к, -бка́, ball; tangle, mass; ~ в го́рле, lump in the throat.
клу́мба, -ы, (flower-)bed.
клык -а́, fang; tusk; canine (tooth).
клюв, -а, beak.
клю́ква, -ы, cranberry; cranberries; разве́систая ~, traveller's tale, tall story.
клю́нуть, -ну *perf.* of клева́ть.
ключ[1], -а́, key; clue; keystone; clef; wrench, spanner; запере́ть на ~, lock.
ключ[2], -а́, spring; source; бить ~о́м, spout, jet; be in full swing.
ключево́й, key; ~ знак, clef; ~ ка́мень, keystone. **ключи́ца,** -ы, collar-bone, clavicle.
клю́шка, -и, (hockey) stick; (golf-)club.
клюю́, etc.: see клева́ть.
кля́кса, -ы, blot, smudge.
кляну́, etc.: see клясть.
кля́нчить, -чу *imp.* (*perf.* вы́~) beg.
клясть, -яну́, -янёшь; -ял, -а́, -о *imp.* curse; **~ся** (*perf.* по~ся) swear, vow. **кля́тва,** -ы, oath, vow; дать кля́тву,

take an oath. **кля́твенный**, sworn, on oath.

км *abbr*. киломе́тр, kilometre.

к.-н. *abbr*. како́й-нибудь, some, any.

кни́га, -и, book.

книго- in *comb*. book, biblio-. **книгове́дение**[1], -я, bibliography. **~ведéние**[2], -я, book-keeping. **~держа́тель, -я** *m*. book-end. **~е́д, -а**, bookworm. **~изда́тель, -я** *m*. publisher. **~люб, -а**, bibliophile, book-lover. **~храни́лище, -а**, library; book-stack; book-storage, shelving.

кни́жечка, -и, booklet. **кни́жка, -и**, book; note-book; bank-book. **кни́жн|ый**, book; ~ая по́лка, bookshelf; ~ый червь, bookworm; ~ый шкаф, bookcase.

кни́зу *adv*. downwards.

кно́пка, -и, drawing-pin; press-stud; (push-)button, knob.

КНР (*kaenér*) *abbr*. Кита́йская Наро́дная Респу́блика, Chinese People's Republic.

кнут, -а́, whip; knout.

княги́ня, -и, princess. **кня́жество, -а**, principality. **княжна́, -ы́**; *gen*. *pl*. -жо́н, princess. **князь, -я**; *pl*. -зья́, -зе́й *m*. prince.

ко: see к *prep*.

кобура́, -ы́, holster.

кобы́ла, -ы, mare; (vaulting-)horse. **кобы́лка, -и**, filly; bridge.

ко́ваный, forged; hammered; wrought; iron-bound, iron-tipped; terse.

кова́рный, inisidious, crafty; perfidious, treacherous. **кова́рство, -а**, insidiousness, craftiness; perfidy, treachery.

кова́ть, кую́, -ёшь *imp*. (*perf*. под~) forge; hammer; shoe.

ковёр, -вра́, carpet; rug; ~-самолёт, magic carpet.

кове́ркать, -аю *imp*. (*perf*. ис~) distort, mangle, mispronounce; spoil, ruin.

ко́вка, -и, forging; shoeing. **ко́вкий**; -вок, -вка́, -вко, malleable, ductile.

коври́га, -и, loaf. **коври́жка, -и**, honey-cake, gingerbread.

ковш, -а́, scoop, ladle, dipper; bucket.

ковы́ль, -я *m*. feather-grass.

ковыля́ть, -я́ю *imp*. hobble; stump; toddle.

ковырну́ть, -ну́, -нёшь *perf*., **ковыря́ть, -я́ю** *imp*. dig into; tinker, potter; +в+*prep*. pick; pick at; ~ в зуба́х, pick one's teeth; **~ся**, rummage; tinker, potter.

когда́ *adv*. when; ~ . ., ~, sometimes . ., sometimes; ~ (бы) ни, whenever; ~ как, it depends; *conj*. when; while, as; if; ~ так, if so, if that is the case. **когда́-либо, когда́-нибудь** *advs*. som[illegible] time, some day; ever. **ког**[illegible] once, at one time; at so[illegible] merly; some day, some time.

кого́: see кто.

ко́готь, -гтя; *pl*. -гти, -гте́й *m*. claw; talon; показа́ть свои́ ко́гти, show one's teeth.

ко́декс, -а, code; codex.

ко́е-где́ *adv*. here and there, in places. **ко́е-ка́к** *adv*. anyhow; somehow (or other), just. **ко́е-како́й** *pron*. some. **ко́е-кто́, -кого́** *pron*. somebody; some people. **ко́е-что́, -чего́** *pron*. something; a little.

ко́жа, -и, skin, hide; leather; peel, rind; epidermis. **кожа́н, -а́**, leather coat. **ко́жанка, -и**, leather jacket, leather coat. **ко́жаный**, leather. **коже́венный**, leather; tanning, leather-dressing; ~ заво́д, tannery. **коже́вник, -а**, tanner, leather-dresser, currier. **ко́жица, -ы**, thin skin; film, pellicle; peel, skin. **ко́жный**, skin; cutaneous. **кожура́, -ы́**, rind, peel, skin.

коза́, -ы́; *pl*. -ы, she-goat, nanny-goat. **козёл, -зла́**, goat; he-goat, billy-goat. **козеро́г, -а**, ibex; Capricorn. **ко́зий**, goat; ~ пух, angora. **козлёнок, -нка**; *pl*. -ля́та, -ля́т, kid. **козло́вый**, goat-skin.

ко́злы, -зел *pl*. (coach-)box; trestle(s); saw-horse.

ко́зни, -ей *pl*. machinations, intrigues.

козырёк, -рька́, peak; eye-shade; взять под ~+*dat*. salute.

козырно́й, trump, of trumps. **козырну́ть, -ну́, -нёшь** *perf*., **козыря́ть, -я́ю** *imp*. lead trumps; trump; play one's trump card; salute. **ко́зырь, -я**; *pl*. -и, -е́й *m*. trump; откры́ть свои́ ко́зыри, lay one's cards on the table.

[illegible] *gen. pl.* ко́ек, berth, bunk; [illegible]к; bed.

[illegible], -а, whooping-cough.

[illegible], coke.

[illegible]; *pl.* -лья, -ьев, stake, picket; ни [illegible]ни двора́, neither house nor home.

[illegible]**а**, -ы, retort.

[illegible]**баса́**, -ы́; *pl.* -ы, sausage.

[illegible]**лго́тки**, -ток *pl.* tights.

[illegible]**олдовство́**, -а́, witchcraft, sorcery, magic. **колду́н**, -а́, sorcerer, magician, wizard. **колду́нья**, -и; *gen. pl.* -ний, witch, sorceress.

колеба́ние, -я, oscillation, vibration; fluctuation, variation; hesitation; wavering, vacillation. **колеба́тельный**, oscillatory, vibratory. **колеба́ть**, -е́блю *imp.* (*perf.* по~) shake; **~ся**, oscillate, vibrate, swing; shake; fluctuate, vary; hesitate; waver.

коленко́р, -а, calico. **коленко́ровый**, calico.

коле́но, -а; *pl.* -и or -а or -нья, -ей or -лен or -ньев, knee; joint, node; bend; elbow, crank; по ~, по коле́ни knee-deep, up to one's knees; стать на коле́ни, kneel (down); стоя́ть на коле́нях, be kneeling, be on one's knees. **коле́нчатый**, crank, cranked; bent, elbow; ~ вал, crankshaft.

коле́сник, -а, wheelwright. **колесни́ца**, -ы, chariot. **колёсный**, wheel; wheeled. **колесо́**, -а́; *pl.* -ёса, wheel.

коле́чко, -а, ringlet.

колея́, -и́, rut; track, gauge.

коли́чественн|ый, quantitative; ~ое числи́тельное, cardinal number. **коли́чество**, -а, quantity, amount; number.

ко́лкий; -лок, -лка́, -о, prickly; sharp, biting, caustic.

колле́га, -и, colleague. **коллегиа́льный**, joint, collective; corporate. **колле́гия**, -и, board; college. **колле́жский**, collegiate; ~ асе́ссор, регистра́тор, секрета́рь, сове́тник (8th, 14th, 10th, 6th grade: see чин).

колли́зия, -и, clash, conflict, collision.

коло́да, -ы, block; log; pack (of cards).

коло́дезный, well; well-deck. **коло́дец**, -дца, well; shaft.

коло́дка, -и, last; block, chock.

ко́локол, -а; *pl.* -а́, -о́в, bell. **колоко́льный**, bell; ~ звон, peal, chime. **колоко́льня**, -и, bell-tower. **колоко́льчик**, -а, small bell; handbell; campanula, harebell.

коло́нка, -и, geyser; (street) fountain; stand-pipe; column; бензи́новая ~, petrol pump. **коло́нна**, -ы, column. **коло́нный**, columned. **колонти́тул**, -а, running title, catchword. **колонци́фра**, -ы, page number, folio.

колори́т, -а, colouring, colour. **колори́тный**, colourful, picturesque, graphic.

ко́лос, -а; -о́сья, -ьев, ear, spike. **колоси́ться**, -и́тся *imp.* form ears.

колосники́, -о́в *pl.* fire-bars; grate; flies.

колоти́ть, -очу́, -о́тишь *imp.* (*perf.* по~) beat; batter, pound; thrash, drub; break, smash; shake; **~ся**, pound, thump; shake; +о+*acc.* beat, strike, against.

коло́ть[1], -лю́, -лешь *imp.* (*perf.* рас~), break, chop, split; ~ оре́хи, crack nuts.

коло́ть[2], -лю́, -лешь *imp.* (*perf.* за~, кольну́ть) prick; stab; sting; taunt; slaughter; **~ся**, prick.

колпа́к, -а́, cap; lamp-shade; hood, cover, cowl.

колу́н, -а́, axe, chopper.

колхо́з, -а *abbr.* коллекти́вное хозя́йство, collective farm.

колыбе́ль, -и, cradle.

колыха́ть, -ы́шу *imp.*, **колыхну́ть**, -ну́, -нёшь *perf.* sway, rock; **~ся**, sway, heave; flutter, flicker.

ко́лышек, -шка, peg.

кольну́ть, -ну́, -нёшь *perf.* of коло́ть.

кольцева́ть, -цу́ю *imp.* (*perf.* о~) ring. **кольцево́й**, annular; circular. **кольцо́**, -а́; *pl.* -а, -ле́ц, -льцам ring; hoop.

колю́ч|ий, prickly; thorny; sharp, biting; ~ая про́волока barbed wire. **колю́чка**, -и, prickle; thorn; quill; burr.

коля́ска, -и, carriage; pram; side-car.

ком, -а; *pl.* -мья, -ьев, lump; ball; clod.

ком: see кто.

ком- *abbr.* in *comb.* of коммунисти́ческий, Communist; команди́р, commander; кома́ндный, command. **комба́т**, -а, battalion commander. **~ди́в**,

-а, divisional commander. **~интéрн,** -а, Comintern. **~пáртия,** -и, Communist Party. **~сомóл,** -а, Komsomol, Young Communist League. **~сомóлец,** -льца, **-óлка,** -и, member of Komsomol.

кома́нда, -ы, command; order; party, detachment; crew; ship's company, team. **команди́р,** -а, commander, commanding officer; captain. **командирова́ть,** -ру́ю *perf.* and *imp.* post, send, dispatch on mission, on official business. **командиро́вка,** -и, posting, dispatching; mission, commission, business trip; warrant authority. **командиро́вочн|ый** *adj.*; ~ые де́ньги, travelling allowance; **~ые** *sb. pl.* travelling allowance, expenses. **кома́нди|ый,** command; commanding; control; ~ая вы́шка, control tower; -ый пункт, command post; ~ый соста́в, officers; executive (body). **кома́ндование,** -я, commanding; command; headquarters. **кома́ндовать,** -дую *imp.* (*perf.* с~) give orders; be in command; +*instr* command; +*instr.* or над+*instr.* order about; +над+*instr.* command. **кома́ндующий** *sb.* commander.

кома́р, -а́, mosquito.

комбина́т, -а, industrial complex; combine; training centre. **комбина́ция,** -и, combination; merger; scheme, system; manoeuvre; combinations, slip. **комбинезо́н,** -а, overalls, boiler suit. **комбини́ровать,** -рую *imp.* (*perf.* с~) combine.

коменда́нт, -а, commandant; manager; warden; superintendent. **комендату́ра,** -ы, commandant's office.

коми́зм, -а, humour; the funny side, the comic element; the comic. **ко́мик,** -а, comic actor; comedian, funny man. **ко́микс,** -а, comic, comic strip, comic book; *pl.* the funnies.

комисса́р, -а, commissar. **комиссариа́т,** -а, ministry department.

комиссионе́р, -а, (commission-)agent, factor, broker. **комиссио́нн|ый,** commission; committee, board; ~ый магази́н, second-hand shop; **~ые** *sb.* commission. **коми́ссия,** -и, commission; committee board.

комите́т, -а, committee.

коми́ческий, comic; comical, funny. **коми́чный,** comical, funny.

ко́мкать, -аю *imp.* (*perf.* ис~, с~) crumple; make a hash of, muff.

коммента́рий, -я, commentary; *pl.* comment. **комменти́ровать,** -рую *perf.* and *imp.* comment (on).

коммерса́нт, -а, merchant; business man. **комме́рция,** -и, commerce, trade. **комме́рческий,** commercial, mercantile.

комму́на, -ы, commune. **коммуна́льн|ый,** communal; municipal; ~ые услу́ги, public utilities. **коммуна́р,** -а, Communard.

коммута́тор, -а, commutator; switchboard.

ко́мната, -ы, room. **ко́мнатный,** room; indoor.

комо́д, -а, chest of drawers.

комо́к, -мка́, lump; ~ не́рвов, bundle of nerves.

компа́ния, -и, company. **компаньо́н,** -а, **-о́нка,** -и, companion; partner.

компенса́ция, -и, compensation. **компенси́ровать,** -рую, *perf.* and *imp.* compensate; indemnify; equilibrate.

ко́мплексный, complex, compound, composite; combined; over-all, all-in; ~ обе́д, table d'hôte dinner. **компле́кт,** -а, complete set; complement; specified number; ~ белья́, bed-clothes. **компле́ктный,** complete, **комплектова́ть,** -ту́ю *imp.* (*perf.* с~, у~) complete; replenish; bring up to strength, (re)man. **компле́кция,** -и. build; constitution.

компози́тор, -а, composer. **компози́ция,** -и, composition.

компо́стер, -а, punch. **компости́ровать,** -рую *imp.* (*perf.* про~) punch.

компромети́ровать, -рую *imp.* (*perf.* с~) compromise. **компроми́сс,** -а, compromise.

кому́: see кто.

конве́йер, -а, conveyor.

конве́рт, -а, envelope; sleeve.

конвои́р, -а, escort. **конвои́ровать,**

-рую *imp.* escort, convoy. **конво́й, -я,** escort, convoy.

конденса́тор, -а, capacitor; condenser.

конди́терская *sb.* confectioner's, sweet-shop, cake-shop.

кондиционе́р, -а, air-conditioning plant. **кондицио́нный,** air-conditioning.

конду́ктор, -а; *pl.* -á, **-торша,** -и, conductor; guard.

коневóдство, -а, horse-breeding. **коневóдческий,** horse-breeding. **конёк,** -нькá *dim.* of конь; hobby-horse, hobby.

коне́ц, -нцá, end; distance, way; в концé концóв, in the end, after all; в óба концá, there and back; в оди́н ~, one way; и концы́ в вóду, and nobody any the wiser; оди́н ~, it comes to the same thing in the end; своди́ть концы́ с концáми, make (both) ends meet; со всех концóв, from all quarters. **коне́чно** *adv.* of course, certainly; no doubt. **коне́чность,** -и, extremity. **коне́чн|ый,** final, last; ultimate; terminal; finite; ~ая останóвка, ~ая стáнция, terminus.

кони́на, -ы, horse-meat.

кони́ческий, conic, conical.

конкуре́нт, -а, competitor. **конкуре́нция,** -и, competition; вне конкуре́нции, *hors concours*. **конкури́ровать,** -рую *imp.* compete. **кóнкурс,** -а, competition; вне ~а, *hors concours*. **кóнкурсный,** competitive.

кóнник, -а, cavalryman. **кóнница,** -ы, cavalry; horse. **конногвардéец,** -éйца, horse-guardsman; life-guard. **коннозавóдство,** -а, horse-breeding; stud, stud-farm. **кóнный,** horse; mounted; equestrian; ~ завóд, stud.

конопáтить, -áчу *imp.* (*perf.* за~) caulk.

коноплá, -и́, hemp.

консервáция, -и, conservation; temporary closing-down. **консерви́ровать,** -рую *perf.* and *imp.* (*perf.* also за~), preserve; can, tin, bottle, pot; close down temporarily. **консе́рвн|ый,** preserving; ~ая бáнка, tin; can. **консе́рвы,** -ов *pl.* tinned goods; goggles.

конси́лиум, -а, consultation.

консóль, -и, console; cantilever; pedestal.

конспе́кт, -а, synopsis, summary, abstract, précis. **конспекти́вный,** concise, summary. **конспекти́ровать,** -рую *imp.* (*perf.* за~, про~) make an abstract of.

конспирати́вный, secret, clandestine.

констатáция, -и, ascertaining; verification, establishment. **констати́ровать,** -рую *perf.* and *imp.* ascertain; verify, establish; certify.

конструкти́вный, structural; constructional; constructive. **констру́ктор,** -а, designer, constructor. **констру́кция,** -и, construction; structure; design.

консультáция, -и, consultation; advice; advice bureau; clinic, surgery; tutorial; supervision. **консульти́ровать,** -рую *imp.* (*perf.* про~) advise; act as tutor (to); +с+*instr.* consult; **~ся,** have a consultation; obtain advice; +с+*instr.* be a pupil of; consult.

контáкт, -а, contact; touch. **контáктный,** contact; ~ рельс, live rail.

контóра, -ы, office. **контóрск|ий,** office; -ая кни́га, account-book, ledger. **контóрщик,** -а, clerk.

контр- in *comb.* counter-.

контрабáс, -а, double-bass.

контрагéнт, -а, contracting party; subcontractor. **контрáкт,** -а, contract. **контрактовáть,** -тýю *imp.* (*perf.* за~) contract for; engage; **~ся,** contract, undertake.

контрамáрка, -и, complimentary ticket.

контрапу́нкт, -а, counterpoint. **контрапункти́ческий, контрапу́нктный,** contrapuntal.

контрáст, -а, **контрáстность,** -и, contrast.

контрибу́ция, -и, indemnity; contribution.

контрнаступлéние, -я, counter-offensive.

контролёр, -а, inspector; ticket-collector. **контроли́ровать,** -рую *imp.* (*perf.* про~) check; inspect. **контрóль,** -я *m.* control; check, checking; inspection; inspectors. **контрóльн|ый,** control; check; monitoring; reference; ~ая вы́шка, conning-tower.

контрразве́дка, -и, counter-intelligence; security service, secret service.
контý́женный, contused, bruised; shell-shocked. **контý́зить, -ý́жу** *perf.* contuse, bruise; shell-shock. **контý́зия, -и,** contusion; shell-shock.
ко́нтур, -а, contour, outline; circuit.
конура́, -ы́, kennel.
ко́нус, -а, cone. **конусообра́зный,** conical.
конфекцио́н, -а, ready-made clothes shop, department.
конфе́та, -ы, sweet, chocolate.
конфу́з, -а, discomfiture, embarrassment. **конфу́зить, -у́жу** *imp.* (*perf.* с~) confuse, embarrass; place in an awkward or embarrassing position; **~ся,** feel awkward or embarrassed; be shy. **конфу́зливый,** bashful; shy. **конфу́зный,** awkward, embarrassing.
концентра́т, -а, concentrate **концентрацио́нный,** concentration. **концентра́ция -и,** concentration. **концентри́ровать, -рую** *imp.* (*perf.* с~) concentrate; mass.
конце́рт, -а concert; recital; concerto. **концерта́нт, -а, -а́нтка, -и** performer. **концертме́йстер, -а,** first violin; leader; soloist; accompanist. **конце́ртный,** concert.
концла́герь, -я *m. abbr.* концентрацио́нный ла́герь, concentration camp.
концо́вка, -и, tail-piece; colophon; ending.
конча́ть, -а́ю *imp.*, **ко́нчить, -чу** *perf.* finish; end; +*inf.* stop; **~ся,** end, finish; come to an end; be over; expire. **ко́нчен|ый,** finished; decided, settled; всё ~о, it's all over; it's all up. **ко́нчик, -а,** tip; point. **кончи́на, -ы,** decease, demise; end.
конь, -я́; *pl.* **-и, -е́й,** horse; vaulting-horse; knight; ~-кача́лка, rocking-horse. **коньки́, -о́в** *pl.* skates; ~ на ро́ликах, roller skates. **конькобе́жец, -жца,** skater. **конькобе́жный,** skating. **ко́нюх, -а,** groom, stable-boy. **коню́шня, -и;** *gen. pl.* **-шен,** stable.
копа́ть -а́ю *imp.* (*perf.* копну́ть, вы́~) dig; dig up dig out; **~ся,** rummage; root; dawdle.
копе́ечный, worth, costing, a copeck; cheap; petty, trifling. **копе́йка, -и,** copeck.
ко́пи, -ей *pl.* mines.
копи́лка, -и, money-box.
копи́рка, -и, carbon paper copying paper. **копирова́льный,** copying. **копи́ровать, -рую** *imp.* (*perf.* с~) copy; imitate, mimic. **копиро́вка, -и,** copying. **копиро́вщик, -а, -щица, -ы,** copyist.
копи́ть, -плю́, -пишь *imp.* (*perf.* на~) save (up); accumulate, amass; store up; **~ся,** accumulate.
ко́пия, -и, copy; duplicate; replica.
копна́, -ы́; *pl.* **-ы, -пён,** shock, stook; heap, pile; ~ се́на, hay-cock. **копни́ть, -ню́** *imp.* (*perf.* с~) shock, stook; cock.
копну́ть, -ну́, -нёшь *perf.* of копа́ть.
ко́поть, -и, soot; lamp-black.
копоши́ться, -шу́сь *imp.* swarm; potter (about).
копте́ть -и́т *imp.* (*perf.* за~) be covered with soot; smoke. **копти́лка, -и,** oil-lamp. **копти́ть, -пчу́** *imp.* (*perf.* за~, на~) smoke, (smoke-)cure; blacken with smoke; cover with soot. **копче́ние, -я,** smoking, curing; smoked foods. **копчёный,** smoked, cured.
копы́тный, hoof; hoofed, ungulate. **копы́то, -а,** hoof.
копьё, -я́; *pl.* **-я, -пий,** spear, lance. **копьеви́дный,** lanceolate.
кора́, -ы́, bark, rind; cortex; crust.
корабе́льный, ship's, ship; marine, naval. **корабе́льщик, -а,** shipwright. **кораблевожде́ние, -я,** navigation. **кораблекруше́ние, -я,** shipwreck. **кораблестрое́ние, -я,** shipbuilding. **кораблестрои́тель, -я** *m.* shipbuilder, naval architect. **кора́бль, -я́** *m.* ship, vessel; nave.
корево́й, measles.
коре́ец, -е́йца, корея́нка, -и, Korean. **коре́йский,** Korean.
корена́стый, thickset, stocky. **корени́ться, -и́тся** *imp.* be rooted. **коренн|о́й,** radical, fundamental; ~о́й жи́тель, native; ~о́й зуб, molar; ~а́я ло́шадь, shaft-horse; ~о́е населе́ние, indigenous population. **ко́рень, -рня;** *pl.* **-и, -е́й** *m.* root; radical. **коре́нья,**

-ьев *pl.* root vegetables. **корешо́к,** -шка́, rootlet; root; back, spine; counterfoil; pal, mate.
корея́нка: see коре́ец.
корзи́на, -ы, **корзи́нка,** -и, basket. **корзи́нный,** basket.
кори́нка, -и, currants.
кори́ца, -ы, cinnamon.
кори́чневый, brown.
ко́рка, -и, crust; rind, peel; scab.
корм, -а (-у), *loc.* -у́; *pl.* -а́, fodder, food, feed; forage.
корма́, -ы, stern, poop.
корми́лец, -льца, bread-winner; benefactor. **корми́лица,** -ы, wet-nurse; benefactress. **корми́ть,** -млю́, -мишь *imp.* (*perf.* на~, по~, про~) feed; keep, maintain; **~ся,** eat, feed; +*instr.* live on, make a living by. **кормле́ние,** -я, feeding. **кормов|о́й**[1], fodder, forage; ~а́я свёкла, mangel-wurzel.
кормово́й[2], stern, poop; after.
корневи́ще, -а, rhizome. **корнево́й,** root; radical. **корнепло́ды,** -ов, root-crops.
корнишо́н, -а, gherkin.
коро́бить, -блю *imp.* (*perf.* по~) warp; jar upon, grate upon; **~ся** (*perf.* also с~ся) warp, buckle.
коро́бка, -и, box, case; ~ скоросте́й, gear-box.
коро́ва, -ы, cow. **коро́в|ий,** cow, cow's; ~ье ма́сло, butter. **коро́вник,** -а, cow-shed.
короле́ва, -ы, queen. **короле́вич,** -а, king's son. **короле́вна,** -ы, king's daughter. **короле́вский,** royal; king's; regal, kingly. **короле́вство,** -а, kingdom. **королёк,** -лька́, petty king, kinglet; gold-crest; blood-orange. **коро́ль,** -я́ *m.* king.
коромы́сло, -а, yoke; beam; rocking shaft, rocker (arm); balance arm.
коро́на, -ы, crown; coronet; corona. **коро́нка,** -и, crown. **коро́нный,** crown, of state. **коронова́ть,** -ну́ю *perf.* and *imp.* crown.
коросте́ль, -я *m.* corncrake.
корота́ть, -а́ю *imp.* (*perf.* с~) while away, pass. **коро́тк|ий;** ко́ро́ток, -тка́, ко́ро́тко́, ко́ро́тки́, short; brief; close, intimate; ~ая распра́ва, short shrift; на ~ой ноге́, on intimate terms. **ко́ротко** *adv.* briefly; intimately; ~ говоря́, in short. **коротково́лновый,** short-wave. **коро́че,** *comp.* of коро́ткий, ко́ротко.
корпе́ть, -плю́ *imp.* sweat, pore (над+*instr.* over).
ко́рпус, -а́; *pl.* -ы, -ов or -а́, -о́в, corps; services high school; building; hull; housing, frame, case; long primer; body; trunk, torso; length.
корректи́в, -а, amendment, correction. **корректи́ровать,** -рую *imp.* (*perf.* про~, с~) correct, read, edit. **корре́ктный,** correct, proper. **корре́ктор,** -а; *pl.* -а́, proof-reader, corrector. **корректу́ра,** -ы, proof-reading; proof.
корт, -а, (tennis-)court.
ко́ртик, -а, dirk.
ко́рточки, -чек *pl.*; сесть на ~, сиде́ть на ко́рточках, squat.
корчева́ть, -чу́ю *imp.* grub up, root out. **корчёвка,** -и, grubbing up, rooting out.
ко́рчить, -чу *imp.* (*perf.* с~) contort; *impers.* convulse; make writhe; ~ грима́сы, ро́жи, make faces, pull faces; ~ дурака́, play the fool; ~ из себя́, pose as; **~ся,** writhe.
ко́ршун, -а, kite.
коры́стный, mercenary. **корыстолюби́вый,** self-interested, mercenary. **корыстолю́бие,** -я, self-interest, cupidity. **коры́сть,** -и, cupidity, avarice; profit, gain.
коры́то, -а, trough; wash-tub.
корь, -и, measles.
коря́вый, rough, uneven; gnarled; clumsy, uncouth; pock-marked.
коса́[1], -ы́, *acc.* -у; *pl.* -ы, plait, tress, braid.
коса́[2], -ы́, *acc.* ко́су; *pl.* -ы, spit.
коса́[3], -ы́, *acc.* ко́су́; *pl.* -ы, scythe. **коса́рь,** -я́ *m.* mower, hay-maker.
ко́свенн|ый, indirect; oblique; ~ые ули́ки, circumstantial evidence.
коси́лка, -и, mower, mowing-machine. **коси́ть**[1], кошу́, ко́сишь *imp.* (*perf.* с~) mow; cut; mow down
коси́ть[2], кошу́ *imp.* (*perf.* по~, с~)

squint; be crooked; **~ся**, slant; look sideways; look askance.
косица, -ы, lock; pigtail.
косматый, shaggy.
космическ|ий, cosmic; space; ~ое пространство, (outer) space. **космодром**, -а, spacecraft launching-site. **космонавт**, -а, **-навтка**, -и, cosmonaut, astronaut. **космос**, -а, cosmos; (outer) space.
коснеть, -ею *imp.* (*perf.* за~) stagnate; stick. **косноязычный**, tongue-tied.
коснуться, -нусь, -нёшься *perf.* of касаться.
косный, inert, sluggish; stagnant.
косо *adv.* slantwise, aslant, askew; sidelong, obliquely. **косоглазие**, -я, squint, cast. **косоглазый**, cross-eyed, squint-eyed. **косогор**, -а, slope, hillside. **косой**; кос, -а -о, slanting; oblqiue; sloping; sidelong; squinting, cross-eyed; скроенный по ~ cut on the cross. **косолапый**, pigeon-toed; clumsy, awkward.
костёр -тра, bonfire; camp-fire.
костистый, **костлявый**, bony; **костный**, bone, bony, osseous. **косточка**, -и, *dim.* of кость; bone; kernel, stone, pip.
костыль, -я *m.* crutch; tail skid.
кость, -и, *loc.* -и; *pl.* -и, -ей, bone; die; играть в кости, dice.
костюм, -а, dress, clothes; suit; costume, coat and skirt; английский ~, tailor-made (coat and skirt). **костюмированный**, in costume; fancy-dress. **костюмн|ый** *adj.*; ~ая пьеса, period play, costume play.
костяк, -а, skeleton; backbone. **костяной**, bone; ivory.
косынка, -и, (three-cornered) head-scarf, shawl.
кот, -а, tom-cat.
котёл, -тла, boiler; copper, cauldron. **котелок**, -лка, pot; mess-tin; bowler (hat); head. **котельная** *sb.* boiler-room, boiler-house.
котёнок, -нка; *pl.* -тята, -тят, kitten. **котик**, -а, fur-seal; sealskin. **котиковый**, sealskin.
котлета, -ы, rissole croquette; отбивная ~, cutlet, chop.
котлован, -а, foundation pit, excavation. **котловина**, -ы, basin, hollow; trough.
котомка, -и, knapsack.
который, *pron.* which, what; who; that; в котором часу, (at) what time; которые . ., которые, some . ., some; ~ раз, how many times; ~ час? what time is it? **который-либо**, **который-нибудь** *prons.* some; one or other.
котята, etc.: see котёнок.
кофе *m. indecl.* coffee. **кофеин**, -а, caffeine. **кофейник**, -а, coffee-pot. **кофейный**, coffee. **кофемолка**, coffee-mill, coffee-grinder.
кофта, -ы, **кофточка**, -и, blouse.
кочан, -а or -чна (cabbage-)head.
кочевать, -чую *imp.* lead a nomadic life; rove, wander; migrate. **кочёвка**, -и, nomad camp; wandering, migration; nomadic existence. **кочевник**, -а, nomad. **кочевой**, nomadic; migratory. **кочевье**, -я; *gen. pl.* -вий, nomad encampment; nomad territory.
кочегар, -а, stoker, fireman. **кочегарка**, -и, stokehold, stokehole.
коченеть, -ею *imp.* (*perf.* за~, о~) grow numb; stiffen.
кочерга, -и; *gen. pl.* -рёг poker.
кочерыжка, -и. cabbage-stalk.
кочка, -и, hummock; tussock. **кочковатый**, hummocky, tussocky.
кошачий, cat, cat's; catlike; feline; ~ концерт, caterwauling; hooting, barracking.
кошелёк, -лька, purse.
кошка, -и, cat; grapnel, drag; *pl.* climbing-irons; cat(-o'-nine-tails).
кошмар, -а, nightmare. **кошмарный**, nightmarish; horrible, awful.
кошу, etc.: see косить.
кощунственный, blasphemous. **кощунство**, -а, blasphemy.
КП (*kapé*) *abbr.* командный пункт, Command Post; Коммунистическая партия, Communist Party. **КПСС**, (*kapeesés*) *abbr.* Коммунистическая партия Советского Союза, Communist Party of the Soviet Union, C.P.S.U.
краденый, stolen. **краду**, etc.: see красть. **крадучись** *adv.* stealthily, furtively.

краеве́дение, -я, regional studies. **краеуго́льный**; ~ ка́мень, corner-stone.

кра́жа, -и, theft; ~ со взло́мом, burglary.

край, -я (-ю), *loc.* -ю́; *pl.* -я́ -ёв, edge; brim; brink; land, country; territory, region; side (of meat); в чужи́х края́х, in foreign parts; на краю́ све́та, at the world's end; че́рез ~, overmuch, beyond measure. **кра́йне** *adv.* extremely. **кра́йний**, extreme; last; uttermost; outside, wing. **кра́йность**, -и, extreme; extremity.

крал, etc : see красть.

кран, -а, tap, cock, faucet; crane.

крапи́ва, -ы, nettle. **крапи́вница**, -ы, nettle-rash. **крапи́вный**, nettle.

кра́пина, -ы, **кра́пинка**, -и, speck, spot. **краплёный**, marked.

краса́вец, -вца, handsome man; Adonis. **краса́вица**, -ы, beauty. **краси́вость**, -и, (mere) prettiness. **краси́вый**, beautiful; handsome; fine.

краси́льный, dye, dyeing. **краси́льня**, -и; *gen. pl.* -лен, dye-house, dye-works. **краси́льщик**, -а, dyer. **краси́тель**, -я *m.* dye, dye-stuff. **кра́сить**, -а́шу *imp.* (*perf.* вы́~, о~, по~) paint; colour; dye; stain; **~ся**, (*perf.* на~) make up. **кра́ска**, -и, paint, dye; colour; painting, colouring, dyeing; (printer's) ink.

красне́ть, -е́ю *imp.* (*perf.* по~) blush; redden, grow red; show red; colour; **~ся**, show red.

красно- in *comb.* red; beautiful. **красноарме́ец**, -е́йца, Red Army man. **~арме́йский**, Red-Army. **~ва́тый**, reddish. **~гварде́ец**, -е́йца, Red Guard. **~дере́вец**, -вца, **~дере́вщик**, -а, cabinet-maker. **~знамённый**, Red-Banner. **~ко́жий**, red-skinned; *sb.* redskin. **~речи́вый**, eloquent; expressive. **~ре́чие**, -я, eloquence; oratory.

краснота́, -ы, redness; red spot. **кра́сн|ый**; -сен, -сна́, -о, red; beautiful; fine; of high quality or value; ~ое де́рево, mahogany; ~ый лес, coniferous forest; ~ая строка́, (first line of) new paragraph; ~ый у́гол, place of honour; ~ый уголо́к, Red Corner.

красова́ться, -су́юсь *imp.* (*perf.* по~) stand in beauty; show off; + *instr.* flaunt. **красота́**, -ы́; *pl.* -ы, beauty. **кра́сочный**, paint; ink; colourful, (highly) coloured.

красть, -аду́, -адёшь; крал *imp.* (*perf.* у~), steal; **~ся**, steal, creep, sneak.

кра́тк|ий; -ток, -тка́, -о, short; brief; concise; ~ое содержа́ние, summary. **кра́тко** *adv.* briefly. **кратковре́менный**, short, brief; short-lived; transitory. **краткосро́чный**, short-term; short-dated.

кра́тное *sb.* multiple. **кра́тный**, divisible without remainder.

кратча́йший *superl.* of кра́ткий. **кра́тче** *comp.* of кра́ткий, кра́тко.

крах, -а, crash; failure.

крахма́л, -а, starch. **крахма́лить**, -лю *imp.* (*perf.* на~) starch. **крахма́льный**, starched.

кра́ше, *comp.* of краси́вый, краси́во.

кра́шеный, painted; coloured; dyed; made up, wearing make-up. **кра́шу**, etc.: see кра́сить.

краю́ха, -и, hunk, thick slice.

креди́тка, -и, bank-note. **креди́тный**, credit, on credit; ~ биле́т, bank-note. **кредитоспосо́бный**, solvent.

кре́йсер, -а; *pl.* -а́, -о́в, cruiser. **кре́йсерский**, cruiser, cruising. **крейси́ровать**, -рую *imp.* cruise.

крем, -а, cream.

креме́нь, -мня́ *m.*, **кремешо́к**, -шка́, flint.

кремлёвский, Kremlin. **кремль**, -я́ *m.* citadel; Kremlin.

кремнёв|ый, flint; silicon; siliceous; ~ое ружьё, flint-lock. **кремнезём**, -а, silica. **кре́мний**, -я, silicon. **кремни́стый**, siliceous; stony.

кре́мовый, cream; cream-coloured.

крен, -а, list, heel; bank. **крени́ть**, -ню́ *imp.* (*perf.* на~) heel; bank; **~ся**, heel over, lis ; bank.

креп, -а, crêpe; crape.

крепи́ть, -плю́ *imp.* strengthen; support, shore up, timber; make fast, hitch, lash; furl; constipate, make costive; **~ся**, hold out. **кре́пк|ий**; -пок, -пка́, -о, strong; sound; sturdy, robust; firm; ~ий моро́з, hard frost; ~ие напи́тки, spirits; ~ое сло́во, словцо́, swear-word, curse. **кре́пко** *adv.* strongly; firmly; soundly. **крепле́ние,** -я, strengthening; fastening; binding; timbering, shoring up; lashing, furling.

кре́пнуть, -ну; -еп *imp.* (*perf.* о~) get stronger.

крепостни́чество, -а, serfdom. **крепостн|о́й,** serf; ~о́е пра́во serfdom; **~о́й** *sb.* serf.

кре́пость, -и fortress; strength. **крепча́ть,** -а́ет *imp.* (*perf.* по~) strengthen; get stronger, get harder, get up. **кре́пче,** *comp.* of кре́пкий, кре́пко.

кре́сло, -а; *gen. pl.* -сел, arm-chair, easy-chair; stall.

крест, -а́ cross; поста́вить ~ на+ *prep.* give up for lost. **крести́ны,** -и́н *pl.* christening. **крести́ть,** крещу́, -е́стишь *perf.* and *imp.* (*perf.* also о~, пере~) baptize, christen; nickname; make sign of the cross over; **~ся,** cross oneself; be baptized, be christened. **крест-на́крест** *adv.* crosswise. **кре́стник,** -а, **кре́стница,** -ы, god-child. **кре́стн|ый;** ~ая (мать), godmother; ~ый оте́ц, godfather. **кресто́вый,** of the cross; ~ похо́д, crusade. **крестоно́сец,** -сца, crusader. **крестообра́зный** cruciform.

крестья́нин, -а; *pl.* -я́не -я́н, **крестья́нка,** -и, peasant. **крестья́нский,** peasant. **крестья́нство,** -а, peasants, peasantry.

креще́ние, -я, baptism, christening; Epiphany. **крещён|ый;** -ён, -ена́, baptized; *sb.* Christian. **крещу́,** etc.: see крести́ть.

крива́я *sb.* curve. **кривизна́,** -ы́, crookedness; curvature. **криви́ть,** -влю́ *imp.* (*perf.* по~, с~) bend distort; ~ душо́й, go against one's conscience; **~ся,** become crooked or bent; make a wry face. **кривля́ка,** -и, *m.* and *f.* poseur; affected person. **кривля́нье,** -я affectation. **кривля́ться,** -я́юсь *imp.* be affected give oneself airs.

кри́во- in *comb.* curved, crooked; one-sided. **кривобо́кий,** lopsided. **~гла́зый** blind in one eye, one-eyed. **~лине́йный,** curvilinear. **~но́гий,** bandy-legged, bow-legged. **~то́лки,** -ов *pl.* false rumours. **~ши́п,** -а, crank; crankshaft.

криво́й; крив, -а́, -о, crooked; curved; one-eyed.

крик, -а, cry, shout; *pl.* clamour, outcry. **крикли́вый,** clamorous, shouting; bawling; loud; penetrating; blatant. **кри́кнуть,** -ну *perf.* of крича́ть. **крику́н,** -а́, shouter, bawler; babbler.

кри́тик, -а, critic. **кри́тика,** -и, criticism; critique. **критикова́ть,** -ку́ю *imp.* criticize. **крити́ческий,** critical.

крича́ть, -чу́ *imp.* (*perf.* кри́кнуть) cry, shout; yell, scream. **крича́щий,** loud; blatant.

кров, -а roof; shelter; лишённый ~а homeless.

крова́вый, bloody.

крова́ть, -и, bed; bedstead.

кро́вельный, roof, roofing.

кровено́сный, blood-; circulatory. **крови́нка,** -и, drop of blood.

кро́вля, -и; *gen. pl.* -вель, roof.

кро́вн|ый, blood; thoroughbred; vital, deep, intimate; deadly; ~ая месть, blood-feud.

крово- in *comb.* blood, sangui-, haemo-. **кровожа́дный,** bloodthirsty. **~излия́ние,** -я, haemorrhage. **~обраще́ние,** -я, circulation. **~подтёк,** -а, bruise. **~проли́тие,** -я, bloodshed. **~проли́тный,** bloody; sanguinary. **~со́с,** -а, vampire bat; blood-sucker. **~тече́ние,** -я, bleeding; haemorrhage. **~точи́вость,** -и, haemophilia. **~точи́ть,** -чи́т *imp.* bleed. **~ха́ркание,** -я, spitting of blood; haemoptysis.

кровь, -и, *loc.* -и́, blood. **кровяно́й,** blood.

крои́ть, крою́ *imp.* (*perf.* с~) cut, cut out. **кро́йка,** -и, cutting out.

кро́лик, -а, rabbit. **кролиководство,** -а, rabbit-breeding. **кро́ликовый, кро́личий,** rabbit.

кроль, -я *m.* crawl (-stroke).

крольча́тник, -а, rabbit-hutch; rabbit farm. **крольчи́ха,** -и she-rabbit, doe.

кро́ме *prep.*+*gen.* except; besides, in addition to; ~ того́, besides, moreover, furthermore; ~ шу́ток, joking apart.

кро́мка, -и edge; selvage; rim brim.

кромса́ть, -а́ю *imp.* (*perf.* ис~) cut up carelessly, hack to pieces; shred.

кро́на, -ы crown top.

кронште́йн, -а, bracket; corbel.

кропотли́вый painstaking; minute; laborious; precise.

кросс, -а, cross-country race. **кроссме́н, -а**, competitor in cross-country race(s).

крот, -а́, mole moleskin.

кро́ткий; -ток, -тка́, -тко, meek, gentle; mild. **кро́тость, -и**, gentleness; mildness. meekness.

кроха́, -и́, *acc.* -у; *pl.* -и, -ох, -а́м, crumb. **кро́хотный, кро́шечный**, tiny, minute. **кро́шево, -а**, hash; medley. **кроши́ть, -шу́, -шишь** *imp.* (*perf.* ис~, на~, рас~) crumble; chop, hack; hack to pieces; + *instr.* drop crumbs of; **~ся**, crumble; break up small. **кро́шка, -и**, crumb; a bit.

круг, -а (-у), *loc.* -у́; *pl.* -и́, circle; ring; circuit, lap; sphere range compass; на ~, on average, taking it all round. **круглосу́точный.** round-the-clock, twenty-four-hour. **кру́гл|ый**; кругл, -а́ -о, round; complete utter, perfect; ~ый год all the year round; ~ый, ~ая сирота́, (complete) orphan; ~ые су́тки day and night. **кругов|о́й** circular; all-round; cyclic; ~а́я пору́ка, mutual responsibility guarantee; ~а́я чаша loving-cup. **кругозо́р, -а**, prospect; outlook horizon, range of interests. **круго́м** *adv.* round, around; round about; completely entirely; *prep.*+*gen.* round, around. **кругооборо́т, -а**, circulation. **кругосве́тный**, round-the-world.

кружевно́й lace; lacy. **кру́жево, -а**; *pl.* -а́ -ев -а́м. lace.

кружи́ть, -ужу́, -у́жи́шь *imp.* whirl, spin round; circle; wander; **~ся**, whirl spin round, go round.

кру́жка, -и, mug; tankard; collecting-box.

кру́жный. roundabout, circuitous. **кружо́к** -жка́, circle, society, group; disc; washer.

круи́з, -а cruise.

крупа́. -ы́; *pl.* -ы groats; sleet. **крупи́нка -и**, grain. **крупи́ца. -ы** grain, fragment, atom. **крупно-** in *comb.* large, coarse, macro-, megalo. **кру́пный**, large, big; large-scale; coarse; important; serious; prominent, outstanding; ~ый план, close-up; ~ый разгово́р, high words; ~ый шаг, coarse pitch; ~ым ша́гом, at a round pace. **крупча́тка, -и**, finest (white) flour. **крупча́тый**, granular.

крутизна́, -ы́, steepness; steep slope.

крути́льный, torsion torsional; doubling. **крути́ть, -учу́, -у́тишь** *imp.* (*perf.* за~, с~) twist, twirl; roll; turn, wind; whirl; **~ся**, turn, spin, revolve; whirl; be in a whirl.

кру́то *adv.* steeply; suddenly; abruptly, sharply; sternly, severely; drastically; thoroughly. **крут|о́й**; крут, -а́, -о, steep; sudden; abrupt, sharp; stern, severe; drastic; thick; well-done; ~о́е яйцо́, hard-boiled egg. **кру́ча, -и**, steep slope, cliff. **кру́че**, *comp.* of крутой кру́то.

кручу́, etc.: see крути́ть.

круше́ние, -я, wreck; crash; ruin; collapse.

крыжо́венный, gooseberry. **крыжо́вник, -а**, gooseberries; gooseberry bush.

крыла́тый, winged. **крыло́, -а́**; *pl.* -лья, -льев, wing; sail, vane; splashboard, mudguard.

крыльцо́, -а́; *pl.* -а, -ле́ц, -ца́м, porch; (front, back) steps.

кры́мский, Crimean.

кры́са, -ы, rat. **крысоло́в, -а**, rat-catcher. **крысоло́вка, -и**, rat-trap.

кры́тый, covered. **крыть** кро́ю *imp.* cover; roof; coat; trump; **~ся**, be, lie; be concealed. **кры́ша, -и**, roof. **кры́шка, -и**, lid; cover.

крюк, -а́ (-у); *pl.* -ки́, -ко́в or -ю́чья, -чьев, hook; detour. **крючкова́тый**, hooked. **крючо́к**, -чка́, hook; hitch, catch.

кря́ду *adv.* in succession running.

кряж, -а, ridge.

кря́кать, -аю *imp.* **кря́кнуть, -ну** *perf.* quack; grunt.

кряхте́ть, -хчу́ *imp.* groan.

кста́ти *adv.* to the point, to the purpose; opportunely; at the same time, incidentally; by the way.

кто, кого́, кому́, кем, ком *pron* who; anyone, anybody; кому́ как, tastes differ; ~ (бы) ни whoever, whosoever; ~ идёт? who goes there?; ~ кого́? who will win, who will come out on top?; ~ . . ~, some . . others; ~ куда́, in all directions; ~ что лю́бит, tastes differ. **кто́-либо, кто́-нибудь** *pron*. anyone, anybody; someone, somebody. **кто́-то** *pron*. someone, somebody.

куб, -а; *pl*. -ы́. cube; cubic metre; boiler, water-heater, urn; still; vat; в ~е, cubed.

куб, *abbr*. кубический, cubic.

ку́барем *adv*. head over heels; headlong.

кубату́ра, -ы, cubic content. **ку́бик**, -а, brick, block; cubic centimetre.

куби́нец, -нца **куби́нка**, -и, Cuban. **куби́нский**, Cuban.

куби́ческий, cubic, cubical; cube.

ку́бовый, indigo

ку́бок, -бка, goblet, bowl, beaker; cup; встре́ча на ~, cup-tie.

кубоме́тр, -а cubic metre.

кувши́н -а jug; pitcher. **кувши́нка**, -и, water-lily.

кувырка́ться, -а́юсь *imp*., **кувыркну́ться**, -ну́сь *perf*. turn somersaults, go head over heels **кувырко́м** *adv*. head over heels; topsy-turvy.

куда́ *adv*. where, where to; what for; +*comp*. much far; ~ (бы) ни wherever; ~ бы то ни́ было, anywhere; ~ лу́чше, much better; хоть ~, fine, excellent. **куда́-либо, куда́-нибудь** *adv*. anywhere, somewhere. **куда́-то** *adv*. somewhere.

куда́хтанье, -я, cackling, clucking. **куда́хтать**, -хчу *imp*. cackle, cluck.

ку́дри, -е́й *pl*. curls. **кудря́в|ый**, curly; curly-headed; leafy, bushy; flowery, florid, ornate; ~ая капу́ста, curly kale. **кудря́шки**, -шек *pl*. ringlets.

кузне́ц, -а́ smith blacksmith. **кузне́чик**, -а, grasshopper. **кузне́чный**, blacksmith's; ~ мех, bellows; ~ мо́лот, sledge-hammer. **ку́зница**, -ы, forge, smithy.

ку́зов, -а; *pl*. -а́ basket; body.

кукаре́кать, -ает *imp*., **кукаре́кнуть**, -нет *perf*. (*perf*. also про~) crow. **кукареку́**, cock-a-doodle-doo.

ку́киш, -а fico, fig.

ку́кла, -ы, doll; puppet; теа́тр ку́кол, puppet theatre.

кукова́ть, -ку́ю *imp*. (*perf*. про~) cuckoo.

ку́колка, -и, dolly; chrysalis, pupa. **ку́кольник**, -а, puppeteer. **ку́кольный**, doll's; doll-like; puppet.

кукуру́за, -ы, maize. Indian corn.

куку́шка, -и, cuckoo.

кула́к, -а́, fist; striking force; kulak. **кула́цкий**, kulak, kulak's. **кула́чный**, fist.

кулёк, -лька́, bag.

кули́к, -а́, sandpiper.

кули́сы -и́с, wings; за кули́сами, behind the scenes.

кули́ч, -а́, Easter cake.

кулуа́ры, -ов *pl* lobby.

культ- *abbr*. in *comb*. of культу́рно-, культу́рный, cultural, educational, recreational. **культотде́л**, -а, Cultural Section. **~похо́д**, -а, cultural crusade; cultural outing. **~рабо́та**, -ы, cultural and educational work.

культу́ра, -ы, culture; standard, level; cultivation, growing; **культу́рно** *adv*. in a civilized manner. **культу́рность**, -и, (level of) culture. **культу́рный**, cultured; cultivated; cultural.

культя́, -и́, **культя́пка**, -и, stump.

кум, -а; *pl*. -мовья́, -ьёв, **кума́**, -ы́, god-parent of one's child.

кума́ч, -а́, red cotton.

куми́р, -а, idol.

кумы́с, -а, koumiss.

ку́ний, marten, marten-fur. **куни́ца**, -ы, marten.

купа́льный, bathing, swimming. **купа́льня**, bathing-place. **купа́льщик**, -а, -щица, -ы, bather. **купа́ть**, -а́ю *imp*. (*perf*. вы~ ис~) bathe; bath; **~ся**, bathe; take a bath.

купе́ *n. indecl*. compartment.

купе́ц, -пца́, merchant. **купе́ческий**, merchant, mercantile. **купе́чество**, -а, merchant class. **купи́ть**, -плю́, -пишь *perf*. (*imp*. покупа́ть) buy. **ку́пля**, -и, buying, purchase.

ку́пол, -а; *pl*. -а́, cupola, dome.

купо́н, -а, coupon.
купоро́с, -а, vitriol.
купчи́ха, -и, merchant's wife; woman of merchant class.
кура́нты, -ов *pl.* chiming clock; chimes.
курга́н, -а, barrow; tumulus.
куре́ние, -я, smoking; incense. **кури́льница**, -ы, censer; incense-burner. **кури́льщик**, -а, **-щица**, -ы, smoker.
кури́н|ый, hen's; chicken's.
кури́тельн|ый, smoking; ~ая бума́га, cigarette paper. **кури́ть**, -рю́, -ришь *imp.* (*perf.* по~) smoke; distil; +*acc.* or *instr.* burn; **~ся**, burn; smoke; +*instr.* produce, emit.
ку́рица, -ы; *pl.* ку́ры, кур, hen, chicken.
курно́сый, snub; snub-nosed.
куро́к, -рка́, cock, cocking-piece; взвести́ ~, cock a gun; спусти́ть ~, pull the trigger.
куропа́тка, -и, partridge; ptarmigan.
куро́рт, -а, health-resort; spa.
курс, -а, course; policy; year; rate (of exchange). **курса́нт**, -а, student.
курси́в, -а, italics; ~ом in italics. **курси́вный**, italic.
курси́ровать, -рую *imp.* ply.
курси́стка, -и, woman student.
ку́ртка, -и, jacket.
курча́виться, -ится *imp.* curl. **курча́вый**, curly; curly-headed.
ку́ры, etc.: see ку́рица.
курьёз, -а, a funny thing; для ~а, ра́ди ~а, for a joke, for amusement. **курьёзный**, curious; funny.
курье́р, -а, messenger; courier. **курье́рский**, fast, express.
куря́тина, -ы chicken. **куря́тник**, -а, hen-house, hen-coop.
куря́щий, *sb.* smoker; ваго́н для куря́щих smoking-carriage, smoker.
куса́ть, -а́ю *imp.* bite; sting; **~ся**, bite; bite one another.
кусково́й, in lumps; lump. **кусо́к**, -ска́, piece, bit; slice; lump; cake.
куст, -а́, bush, shrub. **куста́рник**, -а, shrubbery; bush, shrub; bushes, shrubs.
куста́рн|ый hand-made, home-made; handicrafts; amateurish, primitive; ~ая промы́шленность, cottage industry. **куста́рь**, -я́ *m.* handicraftsman.
ку́тать, -аю *imp.* (*perf.* за~) wrap up, muffle up; **~ся**, muffle oneself up.
кутёж, -а́, drinking-bout; drunken revel, binge. **кутерьма́**, -ы́, commotion, stir, bustle. **кути́ть**, кучу́, ку́тишь *imp.*, **кутну́ть**, -ну́, -нёшь *perf.* drink, carouse; go on a binge, the spree.
куха́рка, -и, cook. **ку́хня**, -и; *gen. pl.* -хонь, kitchen; cook-house; cooking, cuisine. **ку́хонн|ый**, kitchen; ~ая посу́да, kitchen utensils.
ку́цый, tailless; bob-tailed; short; limited, abbreviated.
ку́ча, -и, heap, pile; heaps, piles, lots. **кучево́й**, cumulus.
ку́чер, -а; *pl.* -а́, coachman, driver. **кучерско́й**, coachman's.
ку́чка, -и, small heap; small group. **ку́чный**, closely-grouped.
кучу́: see кути́ть.
куша́к, -а́ sash; (plaited) girdle; belt.
ку́шанье, -я, food; dish **ку́шать**, -аю *imp.* (*perf.* по~, с~) eat, take, have.
куше́тка, -и, couch, chaise-longue.
кую́, etc.: see кова́ть.
кэ́мпинг: see ке́мпинг.
кюве́т, -а, ditch, drain; tray, dish, bath.

Л

л *letter*: see эль.
л. *abbr.* лист, sheet.
л *abbr.* литр, litre.
лабора́нт, -а, **-а́нтка**, -и, laboratory assistant. **лаборато́рия**, -и, laboratory. **лаборато́рный**, laboratory.

лави́на, -ы, avalanche.
ла́вка, -и, bench; shop. **ла́вочка,** -и, small shop. **ла́вочник,** -а, **-ница,** -ы, shopkeeper, retailer.
лавр, -а, bay-tree, laurel; *pl.* laurels.
ла́вра, -ы, monastery.
ла́вро́вый, laurel, bay; ~ **вено́к,** laurel wreath, laurels.
ла́герник, -а, inmate of camp. **ла́герн|ый,** camp; ~ая жизнь, nomad existence; ~ый сбор, annual camp.
ла́герь, -я; *pl.* -я́ or -и, -е́й or -ей *m.* camp.
лад, -а (-у), *loc.* -у́; -ы́, -о́в, harmony, concord; manner, way; stop, fret key, stud; в ~, не в ~, in, out of, tune; идти́ на ~ go well, be successful; на свой ~, in one's own way, after one's own fashion; не в ~а́х, at odds at variance; они́ не в ~а́х, they don't get on.
ла́дан, -а, incense; дыша́ть на ~, have one foot in the grave.
ла́дить, ла́жу *imp.* get on, be on good terms; **~ся,** go well, succeed. **ла́дно** *adv.* harmoniously; well; all right; very well! **ла́дный,** fine, excellent; harmonious.
ладо́нный, palmar. **ладо́нь,** -и, palm.
ладья́[1], -ьи́, rook, castle.
ладья́[2], -ьи́, boat, barge.
ла́жу, etc.: see ла́дить, ла́зить.
лазаре́т, -а, field hospital; sick quarters; sick-bay; infirmary.
ла́зать: see ла́зить. **лазе́йка,** -и, hole, gap; loop-hole.
ла́зер, -а, laser.
ла́зить, ла́жу, **ла́зать,** -аю *imp.* climb, clamber; +в+*acc.* climb into, get into.
лазу́рный, sky-blue, azure. **лазу́рь,** -и, azure.
лазу́тчик, -а, scout; spy.
лай, -я, bark, barking. **ла́йка**[1], -и, (Siberian) husky, laika.
ла́йка[2], -и, kid. **ла́йковый,** kid; kidskin.
ла́йнер, -а, liner air-liner.
лак, -а (-у), varnish, lacquer.
лака́ть, -а́ю *imp.* (*perf.* вы~) lap.
лаке́й, -я, footman, man-servant; lackey, flunkey. **лаке́йский,** man-servant's; servile.
лакиро́ванн|ый, varnished, lacquered; ~ая ко́жа, patent leather. **лакирова́ть,** -ру́ю *imp.* (*perf.* от~), varnish; lacquer. **лакиро́вка,** -и, varnishing, lacquering; varnish; gloss, polish.
ла́кмус, -а, litmus. **ла́кмусов|ый,** litmus; ~ая бума́га, litmus paper.
ла́ков|ый, varnished, lacquered; ~ая ко́жа, patent leather.
ла́комить, -млю *imp.* (*perf.* по~) regale, treat; **~ся**+*instr.* treat oneself to. **ла́комка,** -и *m.* and *f.* gourmand; lover of sweet things. **ла́комство,** -а, delicacy; *pl.* dainties, sweet things. **ла́комый,** dainty, tasty; +до, fond of, partial to.
ла́мпа, -ы, lamp; valve, tube. **ла́мпочка,** -и, lamp; bulb; light.
ландша́фт, -а, landscape.
ла́ндыш, -а, lily of the valley.
лань, -и, fallow deer; doe.
ла́па, -ы, paw; tenon, dovetail; fluke; (*sl.*) bribe; попа́сть в ла́пы к+*dat.*, fall into the clutches of.
ла́поть, -птя; *pl.* -и, -е́й *m.* bast shoe, bast sandal.
ла́пчатый, palmate; web-footed.
лапша́, -и́, noodles; noodle soup.
ларёк, -рька́ stall. **ларёчник,** -а, stall-keeper. **ларь,** -я́ *m.* chest, coffer; bin; stall.
ла́ска, -и, caress, endearment; kindness. **ласка́тельн|ый,** caressing; affectionate; ~ое и́мя, pet name. **ласка́ть,** -а́ю, *imp.* caress, fondle, pet; comfort, console; **~ся**+к+*dat.* make up to; snuggle up to; coax; fawn upon. **ла́сковый,** affectionate, tender.
ла́стик, -а, (india-)rubber, eraser.
ла́сточка, -и, swallow.
лату́к, -а, lettuce.
лату́нный, brass. **лату́нь,** -и, brass.
ла́ты, лат *pl.* armour.
лат́ынь, -и, Latin.
латы́ш, -а́ **латы́шка,** -и, Lett, Latvian. **латы́шский**, Lettish, Latvian.
лауреа́т, -а, prize-winner.
лафе́т, -а, gun-carriage.
ла́цкан, -а, lapel.
лачу́га, -и, hovel, shack.
ла́ять, ла́ю *imp.* bark; bay.
лба, etc.: see лоб.

лганьё, -я́, lying. **лга́ть**, лгу, лжёшь; лгал, -á, -o *imp.* (*perf.* на~, со~) lie; tell lies; +на+*acc.* slander. **лгун**, -á, **лгу́нья**, -и, liar.

ЛГУ (*elgeú*) *abbr.* Ленингра́дский госуда́рственный университе́т, Leningrad State University.

лебедёнок, -нка; *pl.* -дя́та, -дя́т, cygnet. **лебеди́ный**, swan, swan's. **лебёдка**, -и, swan, pen; winch, windlass. **ле́бедь**, -я; *pl.* -и, -е́й *m.* swan, cob.

лебези́ть, -ежу́ *imp.* fawn, cringe.

лев, льва, lion.

левко́й, -я, stock.

лево- in *comb.* left, left-hand; laevo-. **левобере́жный**. left-bank. **левша́**, -и́; *gen. pl.* -е́й *m.* and *f.* left-handed person, left-hander, southpaw. **ле́в|ый** *adj.* left; left-hand; port; left-wing; -ая сторона́, left-hand side, near side, wrong side.

лёг, etc.: see лечь.

лёгк|ий; -гок -гка́, лёгки́, light; easy; slight, mild; ~ая атле́тика, field and track events; лёгок на поми́не, talk of the devil!; у него́ ~ая рука́, he brings luck. **легко́** *adv.* easily, lightly, slightly.

легко- in *comb.* light, light-weight; easy, easily, readily. **легкове́рие**, -я, credulity, gullibility. **~ве́рный**, credulous, gullible. **~ве́с**, -а, **~ве́сный**, light-weight. **~ву́шка**, -и, (private) car. **~мы́сленный**, light-minded; thoughtless, careless, irresponsible; flippant, frivolous, superficial. **~мы́слие**, -я, flippancy, frivolity, levity.

легков|о́й; ~о́й автомоби́ль, ~а́я маши́на, (private) car. **лёгкое** *sb.* lung; lights. **лёгкость**, -и, lightness; easiness. **лего́нько** *adv.* slightly; gently. **лёгочный**, lung, pulmonary. **ле́гче** *comp.* of лёгкий, легко́.

лёд, льда (-у), *loc.* -у, ice. **ледене́ть**, -е́ю *imp.* (*perf.* за~, о~) freeze; grow numb with cold. **ледене́ц**, -нца́, fruit-drop. **ледени́стый**, frozen; icy. **ледени́ть**, -и́т *imp.* (*perf.* о~) freeze; chill. **леденя́щий**, chilling, icy.

ле́дник[1], -а, ice-house; ice-box; ваго́н -~, refrigerator van. **ледни́к**[2], -á, glacier. **леднико́вый**, glacial; glacier; ice; refrigerator; ~ пери́од, Ice Age.

ледоко́л, -а, ice-breaker. **ледору́б**, -а, ice-axe. **ледян|о́й**, ice; icy; ice-cold; ~а́я гора́, tobogganing run, ice slope; iceberg.

лежа́ть, -жу́ *imp.* lie; be, be situated. **лежа́чий**, lying (down); ~ больно́й, bed-patient.

ле́звие, -я, (cutting) edge; blade.

лезть, -зу; лез *imp.* (*perf.* по~), climb; clamber, crawl; make one's way; come on, keep on; creep, get, go; fall out; come to pieces; ~ в пе́тлю, stick one's neck out; ~ на́ стену, climb up the wall; не ~ за сло́вом в карма́н, not be at a loss for words.

ле́йка, -и, watering-can; pourer; funnel.

лейтена́нт, -а, lieutenant.

лека́рственный, medicinal. **лека́рство**, -а, medicine, drug.

ле́ксика, -и, vocabulary. **лексико́н**, -а, lexicon; vocabulary. **лекси́ческий**, lexical.

ле́ктор, -а, lecturer. **лекцио́нный**, lecture. **ле́кция**, -и, lecture; чита́ть ле́кцию, lecture, deliver a lecture.

леле́ять, -е́ю *imp.* (*perf.* вз~) cherish, foster; coddle, pamper.

лён, льна, flax.

лени́вый, lazy, idle; sluggish. **лени́ться**, -ню́сь, -нишься *imp.* (*perf.* по~) be lazy, be idle; +*inf.* be too lazy to.

ле́нта, -ы, ribbon; band; tape; film; belt; track.

лентя́й, -я, **-я́йка**, -и, lazy-bones; sluggard. **лентя́йничать**, -аю *imp.* be lazy, be idle, loaf. **лень**, -и, laziness, idleness; indolence; ей ~ встать, she is too lazy to move.

лепесто́к, -тка́, petal.

ле́пет, -а, babble; prattle. **лепета́ть**, -ечу́, -е́чешь *imp.* (*perf.* про~) babble, prattle.

лепёшка, -и, scone; tablet, lozenge, pastille.

лепи́ть, -плю́, -пишь *imp.* (*perf.* вы́~, за~, на~, с~) model, fashion; mould; stick; **~ся**, cling; crawl. **ле́пка**, -и, modelling. **лепн|о́й**, modelled, moulded; ~о́е украше́ние, stucco moulding.

лес, -а (-у), *loc.* -у́; *pl.* -а́, forest, wood,

woods; timber; *pl.* scaffold, scaffolding.
ле́са́, -ы́ or -ы; *pl.* лёсы, fishing-line.
леси́стый, wooded, forest, woodland.
лесни́к, -а́, forester; gamekeeper. **лесни́чество**, -а, forestry area. **лесни́чий** *sb.* forestry officer; forest warden; gamekeeper. **лесно́й**, forest, forestry; timber.
лесо- in *comb.* forest, forestry; timber wood. **лесово́дство**, -а, forestry. **~загото́вка**, -и, logging, lumbering. **~защи́тный**, forest-protection. **~насажде́ние**, -я, afforestation; (forest) plantation. **~пи́лка**, -и, **~пи́льня**, -и; *gen. pl.* -лен, sawmill. **~ру́б**, -а, woodcutter, logger. **~спла́в**, -а, (timber)-rafting. **~сте́пь**, -и, partially wooded steppe. **~ту́ндра**, -ы, forest-tundra.
ле́стница, -ы, stairs, staircase; ladder; steps. **ле́стничн|ый**; ~ая клётка, (stair-)well.
ле́стный, flattering; complimentary. **лесть**, -и, flattery; adulation.
лёт, -а, *loc.* -у́, flight, flying; на ~у́, in the air, on the wing; hurriedly, in passing.
лета́, лет *pl.* years; age; в ~х, elderly, getting on (in years); на ста́рости лет, in one's old age; прошло́ мно́го лет, many years passed; ско́лько вам лет? how old are you? сре́дних лет, middle--aged.
лета́тельный, flying. **лета́ть**, -а́ю *imp.*, **лете́ть**, лечу́ *imp.* (*perf.* полете́ть) fly; rush, tear; fall, drop.
ле́тний, summer. **ле́тник**, -а, annual.
лётный, flying, flight; ~ соста́в, air-crew.
ле́то, -а; *pl.* -а́, summer; *pl.* years. **ле́том** *adv.* in summer.
летопи́сец, -сца, chronicler, annalist. **ле́топись** -и, chronicle, annals.
летосчисле́ние, -я, (system of) chronology; era.
лету́н, -а́, **лету́нья**, -и, flyer; rolling stone, drifter. **лету́ч|ий**, flying; passing, ephemeral; brief; volatile; ~ий листо́к, leaflet; ~ий ми́тинг, emergency meeting, extraordinary meeting, impromptu meeting; ~ая мышь, bat; hurricane lamp. **лету́чка**, -и, leaflet; emergency meeting; mobile detachment, road patrol; mobile dressing station. **лётчик**, -а, **-чица**, -ы, pilot; aviator, flyer; ~-испыта́тель, test pilot.
лече́бница, -ы, clinic, hospital. **лече́бный**, medical; medicinal. **лече́ние**, -я, (medical) treatment; cure. **лечи́ть**, -чу́, -чишь *imp.* treat (от, for); **~ся**, be given, have, treatment (от, for); +*instr.* take a course of.
лечу́, etc.: see лете́ть, лечи́ть.
лечь, ля́гу, ля́жешь; лёг, -ла́ *perf.* (*imp.* ложи́ться) lie, lie down; go to bed, turn in; +на+*acc.* fall on, rest on, lie on.
лещ, -а́, bream.
лже- in *comb.* false, pseudo-, mock-. **лженау́ка**, -и, pseudo-science. **~свиде́тель**, -я *m.*, **~ница**, -ы, perjuror, perjured witness. **~свиде́тельство**, -а, false witness. **~уче́ние**, -я, false doctrine.
лжец, -а́, liar. **лжи́вый**, lying; mendacious; false, deceitful.
ли, **ль** *interrog. part.* and *conj.* whether, if; ли, . . ли, whether . . or; ра́но ли, по́здно ли, sooner or later.
ли́бо *conj.* or; ~ . . ~, either, . . or.
ли́вень, -вня *m.* heavy shower, downpour, rainstorm; cloud-burst; hail.
ливре́йный, livery, liveried. **ливре́я**, -и, livery.
ли́га, -и, league.
ли́дер, -а, leader; flotilla leader. **ли́дерство**, -а, leadership; first place, lead.
лиди́ровать, -рую *perf.* and *imp.* be in the lead.
лиза́ть, лижу́, -ешь *imp.*, **лизну́ть**, -ну́, -нёшь *perf.* lick.
лик, -а, face.
ликёр, -а, liqueur.
ликова́ние, -я, rejoicing, exultation, triumph. **ликова́ть**, -ку́ю *imp.* rejoice, exult, triumph.
лиле́йный, lily-white; liliaceous. **ли́лия**, -и, lily.
лило́вый, mauve, violet.
лима́н, -а, estuary.
лимо́н, -а, lemon. **лимо́нн|ый**, lemon; ~ая кислота́, citric acid.
лингви́ст, -а, linguist. **лингви́стика**, -и,

linguistics. **лингвистúческий,** linguistic.
линéйка, -и, ruler; rule; line. **линéйный,** linear, line; of the line; ~ корáбль, battleship.
лúнза, -ы, lens.
лúния, -и, line. **линóваный,** lined, ruled. **линовáть,** -нýю *imp.* (*perf.* на~) rule.
линогравю́ра, -ы, linocut.
линю́чий, liable to fade not fast. **линя́лый,** faded, discoloured; moulted. **линя́ть,** -я́ет *imp.* (*perf.* вы́~ по~, с~) fade, lose colour; run; cast the coat, skin; shed hair; moult; slough.
лúпа, -ы, lime(-tree).
лúпкий; -пок, -пкá, -о, sticky, adhesive. **лúпнуть,** -ну; лип *imp.* stick, adhere.
липня́к, -á, lime-grove. **лúповый,** lime, linden.
лúра, -ы, lyre. **лúрик,** -а, lyric poet. **лúрика,** -и, lyric poetry. **лирúческий,** lyric; lyrical. **лирúчный,** lyrical.
лисá, -ы́; *pl.* -ы, fox. **лисёнок,** -нка; *pl.* -ся́та, -ся́т, fox-cub. **лúсий,** fox, fox's. **лисúца,** -ы, fox.
лист, -а; *pl.* -ы́ or -ья, -óв or -ьев, leaf; sheet; quire; page; form; certificate; в ~, in folio; игрáть с ~á, play at sight; корректýра в ~áх, page-proofs. **листáть,** -áю *imp.* leaf through, turn over the pages of. **листвá,** -ы́, leaves, foliage. **лúственный,** deciduous. **листóвка,** -и, leaflet. **листовóй,** sheet, plate; leaf. **листóк,** -ткá, *dim.* of лист; leaflet; form, pro-forma. **листопáд,** -а, fall of the leaf.
лит- *abbr.* in *comb.* of литератýра, -тýрный, literature literary.
литéйная *sb.* foundry, smelting-house. **литéйный,** founding, casting. **литéйщик,** -а, founder.
лúтера, -ы, type, letter. **литерáтор,** -а, literary man, man of letters. **литератýра,** -ы, literature. **литератýрн|ый,** literary; ~ое воровствó, plagiarism.
лúтий, -я, lithium.
литóвец, -вца, **литóвка,** -и, Lithuanian. **литóвский,** Lithuanian.
литóй, cast. **лить,** лью, льёшь; лил, -á, -о *imp.* (*perf.* с~) pour; shed, spill; found, cast, mould. **литьё,** -я́ founding, casting, moulding; castings, mouldings. **лúться,** льётся; лúлся, -áсь, лúлóсь *imp.* flow; stream, pour.
лиф, -а, bodice. **лúфчик,** -а, bodice; bra.
лихáч, -á, (driver of) smart cab; reckless driver, road-hog. **лихóй**[1]; лих, -á, -о, dashing, spirited.
лихóй[2]; лих, -á, -о, лúхú, evil.
лихорáдка, -и, fever. **лихорáдочный,** feverish.
лицевáть, -цýю *imp.* (*perf.* пере~) turn. **лицев|óй,** facial; exterior; ~áя рýкопись, illuminated manuscript; ~áя пéтля, plain (stitch); ~áя сторонá, facade, front; right side; obverse.
лицемéр, -а, hypocrite, dissembler. **лицемéрие,** -я, hypocrisy, dissimulation. **лицемéрный,** hypocritical.
лицó, -á; *pl.* -а, face; exterior; right side; person; быть к лицý+*dat.*, suit, become; befit; в лицé+*gen.* in the person of; знать в ~, know by sight; ~м к лицý, face to face; на нём лицá нет, he looks awful; невзирáя на лúца, without respect of persons; от лицá+*gen.*, in the name of, on behalf of; сказáть в ~+*dat.* say to his, etc., face; черты́ лицá, features. **личúна,** -ы, mask; guise; escutcheon, key-plate. **личúнка,** -и, larva, grub; maggot. **лúчно** *adv.* personally, in person. **личнóй,** face; facial. **лúчность,** -и, personality; person, individual; *pl.* personalities, personal remarks. **лúчный,** personal; individual; private; ~ секретáрь, private secretary; ~ состáв, staff, personnel.
лишáй, -я, lichen; herpes; опоя́сывающий ~, shingles. **лишáйник,** -а, lichen.
лишáть(ся, -áю(сь *imp.* of лишúть(ся.
лúшек, -шка (-у), surplus; с лúшком, odd, and more, just over.
лишéнец, -нца, disfranchised person. **лишéние,** -я, deprivation; privation, hardship; ~ граждáнских прав, disfranchisement. **лишённый;** -ён, -енá+*gen.* lacking in, devoid of. **лишúть,** -шý *perf.* (*imp.* лишáть)+*gen.* deprive of; ~ себя́ жúзни, take one's own life; ~**ся**+*gen.* lose, be deprived of. **лúшн|ий,** superfluous; unnecessary;

left over; spare, odd; ~ раз, once more; с ~им, odd, and more.
лишь *adv.* only; *conj.* as soon as; ~ бы, if only, provided that; ~ (то́лько), as soon as.
лл. *abbr.* листы́, sheets.
лоб, лба, *loc.* лбу, forehead; brow.
ло́бзик, -а, fret-saw.
ло́бн|ый, frontal; front; ~ое ме́сто, place of execution. **лобово́й,** frontal, front.
лове́ц, -ца́, fisherman; hunter. **лови́ть,** -влю́, -вишь *imp.* (*perf.* пойма́ть) catch, try to catch; ~ на сло́ве, take at his, etc. word; ~ ста́нцию, try to pick up a (radio-)station.
ло́вкий; -вок -вка́, -о, adroit, dexterous, deft; cunning, smart; comfortable. **ло́вкость,** -и, adroitness, dexterity, deftness; cunning, smartness.
ло́вля, -и; *gen. pl.* -вель, catching, hunting; fishing-ground. **лову́шка,** -и, snare trap.
ло́вче, *comp.* of ло́вкий.
ло́говище, -а, **ло́гово,** -а, den, lair.
логопе́д, -а, speech therapist. **логопе́дия,** -и, speech therapy.
ло́дка, -и, **ло́дочка,** -и, boat. **ло́дочник,** -а boatman. **ло́дочный,** boat, boat-.
ло́дырничать, -аю *imp.* loaf, idle about. **ло́дырь,** -я *m.* loafer, idler.
ло́жа, -и, box; (masonic) lodge.
ложби́на, -ы, hollow.
ло́же, -а, couch; bed; channel; gun-stock.
ложи́ться, -жу́сь *imp.* of лечь.
ло́жка, -и, spoon; spoonful.
ло́жн|ый, false, erroneous; sham, dummy. **ложь,** лжи, lie, falsehood.
лоза́, -ы́; *pl.* -ы, vine. **лозня́к,** -а́, willow withy.
ло́зунг, -а, slogan, catchword; watchword; pass-word.
ло́кон, -а, lock, curl, ringlet.
локотни́к, -а́, (chair-, sofa-)arm. **ло́коть,** -ктя; *pl.* -и, -е́й *m.* elbow.
лом, -а; *pl.* -ы, -о́в, crowbar; scrap, waste. **ло́маный,** broken. **лома́ть,** -а́ю *imp.* (*perf.* по~, с~) break; fracture; rack, cause to ache; ~ ка́мень, quarry stone; ~ ру́ки, wring one's hands; ~ себе́ го́лову, rack one's brains; меня́ всего лома́ло, I was aching all over; **~ся,** break; crack; pose, put on airs; make difficulties, be obstinate.
ломба́рд, -а, pawnshop. **ломба́рдн|ый;** ~ная квита́нция pawn-ticket.
ло́мберный; ~ стол, card-table.
ломи́ть, ло́мит *imp.* break; break through, rush; *impers.* cause to ache; у меня ло́мит спи́ну my back aches; **~ся,** be (near to) breaking; +в+*acc.* force; + от + *gen.* be bursting, crammed, loaded, with. **ло́мка,** -и, breaking; *pl.* quarry. **ло́мкий;** -мок, -мка́, -о, fragile, brittle.
ломов|о́й, dray, draught; ~о́й изво́зчик, drayman, carter; ~а́я ло́шадь, cart-horse dray-horse, draught-horse.
ломо́та, -ы, ache (in one's bones).
ломо́ть, -мтя́; *pl.* -мти́ *m.* large slice, round; hunk chunk. **ло́мтик,** -а, slice.
ло́но, -а bosom, lap.
лопа́рь, -я́ *m.*, **лопа́рка,** -и, Lapp, Laplander. **лопа́рский,** Lapp Lappish.
ло́пасть, -и; *pl.* -и, -е́й, blade; fan, vane; paddle; lamina; ~ о́си axle-tree.
лопа́та, -ы, spade; shovel. **лопа́тка,** -и, shoulder-blade; shovel; trowel; blade.
ло́паться, -аюсь *imp.*, **ло́пнуть,** -ну *perf.* burst; split, crack; break; fail, be a failure; go bankrupt, crash.
лопоу́хий, lop-eared.
лопу́х, -а́, burdock.
лоси́на, -ы elk-skin, chamois leather; elk-meat; (*pl.*) buckskins. **лоси́ный,** elk, elk-.
лоск, -а (-у) lustre. gloss, shine.
лоску́т, -а́; *pl.* -ы́ or -ья, -о́в or -ьев rag, shred, scrap. **лоску́тн|ый,** scrappy; made of scraps, patchwork; ~ое одея́ло, patchwork quilt.
лосни́ться, -ню́сь *imp.* be glossy, shine.
лососи́на, -ы, salmon. **ло́со́сь,** -я *m.* salmon.
лось, -я; *pl.* -и, -е́й *m.* elk.
лосьо́н, -а, lotion.
лот, -а, lead, plummet.
лотере́йный, lottery, raffle. **лотере́я,** -и, lottery, raffle.
лото́к, -тка́, hawker's stand; hawker's tray; chute; gutter; trough. **лото́чник,** -а, **-ница,** -ы, hawker.

лоха́нка, -и, лоха́нь, -и, (wash-)tub. **лохма́тить,** -а́чу *imp.* (*perf.* раз~) tousle, ruffle; **~ся,** become tousled, be dishevelled. **лохма́тый,** shaggy(-haired); dishevelled tousled.

лохмо́тья, -ьев *pl.* rags.

ло́цман -а pilot; pilot-fish.

лошади́н|ый, horse; equine; ~ая си́ла, horsepower. **лоша́дка, -и,** (small) horse; hobby-horse; rocking-horse. **ло́шадь, -и;** *pl.* -и, -е́й, *instr.* -дьми́ or -дя́ми, horse.

лощёный, glossy, polished.

лощи́на, -ы, hollow, depression.

лощи́ть, -щу́ *imp.* (*perf.* на~), polish; gloss, glaze.

л.с. *abbr.* лошади́ная си́ла, horsepower.

луб, -а, bast. **лубо́к,** -бка́, splint; wood-block; popular print. **лубо́чн|ый;** ~ карти́нка, popular print.

луг, -а, *loc.* -у́; *pl.* -а́, meadow.

луди́ть, лужу́, лу́дишь *imp.* (*perf.* вы́~, по~) tin.

лу́жа, -и, puddle, pool.

лужа́йка, -и, grass-plot, lawn, (forest-) glade.

луже́ние, -я, tinning. **лужёный,** tinned, tin-plate. **лужу́,** etc.: see луди́ть.

лу́за, -ы, pocket.

лук[1], -а (-у), onions; зелёный лук, spring onions.

лук[2], -а, bow.

лука́вить, -влю *imp.* (*perf.* с~), be cunning. **лука́вство,** -а, craftiness slyness. **лука́вый,** crafty, sly, cunning; arch.

лу́ковица, -ы, onion; bulb; onion dome. **лу́ковичный,** onion-shaped; bulbous.

лукомо́рье, -я, cove, bay.

луна́, -ы́; *pl.* -ы, moon. **луна́тик,** -а, sleep-walker, somnambulist.

луко́шко, -а; *pl.* -и, punnet, bast basket.

лу́нка, -и, hole; socket, alveolus.

лу́нник, -а, moon-rocket. **лу́нн|ый,** moon; lunar; ~ый ка́мень, moonstone; ~ая ночь, moonlight night; ~ый свет, moonlight.

лу́па, -ы, magnifying-glass.

лупи́ть, -плю́ -пишь *imp.* (*perf.* об~, с~) peel (off); bark; fleece; **~ся,** peel (off), scale; come off, chip.

луч, -а́, ray; beam. **лучево́й,** ray, beam; radial, radiating; radiation. **лучеза́рный,** radiant, resplendent. **лучеиспуска́ние,** -я, radiation. **лучепреломле́ние,** -я, refraction.

лучи́на, -ы, spill; chip; splinter.

лучи́стый, radiant; radial.

лу́чше, better; ~ всего́, ~ всех, best of all; нам ~ верну́ться, we had better go back; тем ~, so much the better. **лу́чш|ий,** better; best; в ~ем слу́чае, at best; всего́ ~его! all the (very) best! к ~ему, for the better.

лущёный; -ён, -ена́, hulled, shelled, husked. **лущи́ть,** -щу́ *imp.* (*perf.* об~) shell, husk, hull, pod.

лы́жа, -и, ski; snow-shoe. **лы́жник,** -а, skier. **лы́жный,** ski, skiing; ~ спорт, skiing. **лыжня́,** -и́, ski-track.

лы́ко -а, bast, bass.

лысе́ть -е́ю *imp.* (*perf.* об~, по~) grow bald. **лы́сина,** -ы, bald spot, bald patch; blaze, star, patch. **лы́сый;** лыс, -а́, -о, bald.

ль: see ли.

льва, etc.: see лев. **львёнок** -нка; *pl.* львя́та, -я́т, lion-cub. **льви́ный,** lion, lion's; ~ зев, snapdragon. **льви́ца,** -ы, lioness.

льго́та, -ы, privilege; advantage. **льго́тн|ый,** privileged; favourable; ~ый биле́т, complimentary ticket, free ticket; на ~ых усло́виях, on easy terms.

льда, etc.: see лёд. **льди́на,** -ы, block of ice; ice-floe. **льди́нка,** -и, piece of ice. **льди́стый,** icy; ice-covered.

льна, etc.: see лён. **льново́дство,** -а, flax-growing. **льнопряде́ние,** -я, flax-spinning. **льнопряди́льный,** flax-spinning. **льнопряди́льня,** -и; *gen. pl.* -лен, flax-mill.

льнуть, -ну, -нёшь *imp.* (*perf.* при~)+ к+*dat.* cling to, stick to; have a weakness for; make up to, try to get in with.

льняно́й, flax, flaxen; linen; linseed.

льсте́ц, -а́, flatterer. **льсти́вый,** flattering; smooth-tongued. **льстить,** льщу *imp.* (*perf.* по~)+*dat.* flatter; gratify;

+ *acc.* delude; **~ся,** + на + *acc.* be tempted by.
лью, etc.: see лить.
ЛЗС (*elzeés*) *abbr.* лесозащи́тная ста́нция, Forest-protection Station.
любе́зность, -и, courtesy; politeness, civility; kindness; compliment. **любе́зн|ый,** courteous; polite; obliging; kind, amiable.
люби́мец, -мца, **-мица,** -ы, pet, favourite. **люби́мый,** beloved, loved; favourite. **люби́тель,** -я *m.*, **-ница,** -ы, lover; amateur. **люби́тельский,** amateur; amateurish; choice. **люби́ть,** -блю́, -бишь *imp.* love; like, be fond of; need, require.
любова́ться, -бу́юсь *imp.* (*perf.* по~) admire; feast one's eyes (на+*acc.* on).
любо́вник, -а, lover. **любо́вница,** -ы, mistress. **любо́вный,** love-; loving.
любо́вь, -бви́, *instr.* -бо́вью, love.
любозна́тельный, of an inquiring turn of mind, desirous of knowledge.
любо́й, any; either; *sb.* anyone, anybody.
любопы́тный, curious; inquisitive; prying; interesting. **любопы́тство,** -а, curiosity. **любопы́тствовать,** -твую *imp.* (*perf.* по~) be curious.
лю́бящий, loving, affectionate; ~ вас, yours affectionately.
лю́ди, -е́й, -ям, -дьми́, -ях *pl.* people; men; servants; в ~, away from home; на лю́дях, in the presence of others, in company. **лю́дный,** populous; crowded. **людое́д,** -а, cannibal; ogre. **людско́й,** human; servants'.
люк, -а. hatch, hatchway; trap.
лю́лька, -и, cradle.
лю́стра, -ы, chandelier.
лю́тик, -а, buttercup.
лю́тый; лют, -á, -о, ferocious, fierce, cruel.
ля *n. indecl.* A; lah.
ляга́ть, -а́ю *imp.*, **лягну́ть,** -ну́, -нёшь *perf.* kick; **~ся,** kick.
ля́гу, etc.: see лечь.
лягуша́тник, -а, paddling-pool. **лягу́шка,** -и, frog.
ля́жка, -и, thigh, haunch.
ля́згать, -аю *imp.* clank, clang; +*instr.* rattle, clatter; он ля́згал зуба́ми, his teeth were chattering.
ля́мка, -и, strap; тяну́ть ля́мку, toil, sweat, drudge.
ля́пис, -а, silver nitrate, lunar caustic.
ля́псус, -а blunder; slip (of the tongue, of the pen).

М

м *letter*: see эм.
м. *abbr.* мину́та, minute; мыс, cape.
м *abbr.* метр, metre.
мавзоле́й, -я, mausoleum.
мавр, -а **маврита́нка,** -и, Moor. **маврита́нский,** Moorish; Moresque; Mauretanian.
магази́н, -а, shop; store; depot; magazine. **магази́нный** *adj.*; ~ вор, shop-lifter.
магисте́рский, master's. **маги́стр,** -а, (holder of) master's degree; head of knightly or monastic order.
магистра́ль, -и, main; main line, main road.
маги́ческий, magic, magical. **ма́гия,** -и, magic.
ма́гний, -я, magnesium.
магни́т, -а, magnet. **магни́тный** magnetic. **магнитофо́н,** -а, tape-recorder. **магнитофо́нн|ый;** ~ая за́пись, tape-recording.
мада́м *f. indecl.* madam, madame; governess; dressmaker.
мадемуазе́ль, -и, mademoiselle; governess.
мадья́р, -а; *p*. -ы, -я́р, **мадья́рка,** -и, Magyar, Hungarian. **мадья́рский,** Magyar.
мажо́р, -а, major (key); cheerful mood,

good spirits. **мажо́рный,** major; cheerful.

ма́заный, dirty, soiled; cob, daub, clay. **ма́зать,** ма́жу *imp.* (*perf.* вы́~, за~, из~, на~, по~, про~) oil, grease, lubricate; smear, spread; soil, dirty; daub; miss; **~ся,** get dirty; soil; make up. **мазо́к,** -зка́, touch, dab; smear; miss. **мазу́т,** -а, crude oil, fuel oil. **мазь,** -и, ointment; grease.

маис, -а, maize. **маисов|ый;** ~ая ка́ша, polenta.

май, -я, May.

ма́йка, -и, (sleeveless) vest.

ма́йский, May; May-day; ~ жук, cockchafer.

мак, -а (-у), poppy; poppy-seeds.

мака́ть, -а́ю *imp.* (*perf.* макну́ть) dip.

маке́т, -а, model; dummy.

макну́ть, -ну́, -нёшь, *perf.* of мака́ть.

ма́ковка, -и, poppy-head; crown; cupola. **ма́ковый,** poppy; poppy-seed.

максима́льный, maximum. **ма́ксимум,** -а, maximum; at most.

маку́шка, -и, top, summit; crown.

мал, etc.: see ма́лый.

малева́ть, -лю́ю *imp.* (*perf.* на~) paint.

мале́йший, least, slightest. **ма́ленький,** little; small; slight; young.

мали́на, -ы, raspberries; raspberry-bush, raspberry-cane; raspberry tea. **мали́нник,** -а, raspberry-bushes. **мали́новый,** raspberry; crimson.

ма́ло *adv.* little, few; not enough; ~ кто, few (people); ~ ли что! what does it matter? ~ ли что мо́жет случи́ться, who knows what may happen? anything may happen; ~ того́, moreover; ~ того́ что . ., not only . ., it is not enough that . .; э́того ма́ло, this is not enough.

мало- in *comb.* (too) little, small-, low-, under-. **малова́жный,** of little importance, insignificant. **~вероя́тный,** unlikely, improbable. **~ве́сный,** light, light-weight. **~во́дье,** -я, shortage of water. **~во́льтный,** low-voltage. **~гра́мотный,** semi-literate; crude, ignorant. **~достове́рный,** improbable; not well-founded. **~ду́шие,** -я, faint-heartedness, cowardice. **~ду́шный,** faint-hearted, cowardly. **~заме́тный,** barely visible, hardly noticeable; ordinary, undistinguished. **~земе́лье,** -я, shortage of (arable) land. **~земе́льный,** without enough (arable) land; land-hungry. **~иму́щий,** needy, indigent, poor. **~кро́вие,** -я, anaemia. **~кро́вный,** anaemic. **~ле́тний,** young; juvenile; minor, under age. **~ле́тство,** -а, infancy; nonage, minority. **~лю́дный,** not crowded, unfrequented; poorly attended; thinly populated. **~ро́слый,** undersized, stunted. **~содержа́тельный,** empty, shallow. **~сро́чный,** short-term. **~употреби́тельный,** infrequent, rarely used. **~це́нный,** of little value. **~чи́сленный,** small (in number), few.

мало-ма́льски *adv.* in the slightest degree; at all. **малома́льский,** slightest, most insignificant. **мало-пома́лу** *adv.* little by little, bit by bit.

ма́л|ый; мал, -а́, little, (too) small; без ~ого, almost, all but; са́мое ~ое, at the least; с ~ых лет, from childhood; *sb.* fellow, chap; lad, boy. **малы́ш,** -а́, child, kiddy; little boy. **ма́льчик,** -а, boy, lad; child; apprentice. **мальчико́вый,** boy's, boys'. **мальчи́шеский,** boyish; childish, puerile. **мальчи́шка,** -и, *m.* urchin, boy. **мальчуга́н,** -а, little boy. **малю́тка,** -и *m.* and *f.* baby, little one.

ма́ма, -ы, mother, mummy, mamma. **мама́ша,** -и, **ма́менька,** -и, mummy, mamma. **ма́менькин, ма́мин,** mother's.

ма́монт, -а, mammoth.

мандари́н, -а, mandarin, tangerine.

манда́т, -а, warrant; mandate, credentials. **манда́тн|ый,** mandate, mandated; ~ая систе́ма голосова́ния, card-vote system.

манёвр, -а, manoeuvre; shunting. **манёвренный,** manoeuvre, manoeuvring, manoeuvrable; shunting, switching. **маневри́ровать,** -рую *imp.* (*perf.* с~) manoeuvre; shunt; +*instr.* make good use of, use to advantage. **маневро́вый,** shunting.

мане́ж, -а, riding-school; manège. **мане́жик,** -а, play-pen.

манеке́н, -а, lay figure; dummy; mannequin. **манеке́нщик,** -а, **-щица,** -ы, model, mannequin.

мане́р, -а, **мане́ра,** -ы, manner, way; style. **мане́рный,** affected; precious.

манже́та, -ы, cuff.

маникю́рша, -и, manicurist.

манипули́ровать, -рую *imp.* manipulate. **манипуля́ция,** -и, manipulation; machination, intrigue.

мани́ть, -ню́, -нишь *imp.* (*perf.* по~) beckon; attract; lure, allure.

манифе́ст, -а, manifesto. **манифеста́нт,** -а, demonstrator. **манифеста́ция,** -и, demonstration. **манифести́ровать,** -рую *imp.* demonstrate.

мани́шка, -и, false shirt-front, dickey.

ма́ния, -и, mania; passion, craze; ~ вели́чия megalomania.

манки́ровать, -рую *perf.* and *imp.* be absent; +*instr.* neglect; +*dat.* be impolite to.

ма́нн|ый: ~ая ка́ша, ~ая крупа́, semolina.

мано́метр, -а, pressure-gauge manometer.

ма́нтия, -и, cloak; mantle; robe, gown.

мануфакту́ра, -ы, manufacture; textiles; workshop; (textile) mill.

мара́тель, -я *m.* dauber; scribbler. **мара́ть,** -а́ю *imp.* (*perf.* вы́~, за~, из~, на~) soil, stain; daub; scribble; cross out, strike out; **~ся,** get dirty; soil one's hands.

марафо́нский бег, Marathon.

ма́рганец, -нца manganese.

маргари́тка, -и, daisy.

марино́ванный, pickled. **маринова́ть,** -ну́ю *imp.* (*perf.* за~), pickle, marinate; delay, hold up, shelve.

марионе́тка, -и, puppet, marionette. **марионе́точный,** puppet, marionette.

ма́рка, -и, stamp; mark; counter; brand, make; trade-mark; grade, sort; name, reputation.

ма́ркий, easily soiled. **маркирова́ть,** -ру́ю *perf.* and *imp.* mark.

ма́рлевый, gauze. **ма́рля,** -и, gauze; butter muslin, cheesecloth.

мармела́д, -а, fruit jellies. **мармела́дка,** -и, fruit jelly.

мармори́ровать, -рую *perf.* and *imp.* marble.

Марс, -а Mars. **марсиа́нин,** -а; *pl.* -а́не, -а́н. **марсиа́нка,** -и, Martian. **марсиа́нский,** Martian.

март, -а, March. **ма́ртовский,** March.

марты́шка, -и, marmoset; monkey.

марширова́ть, -ру́ю *imp.* march; ~ на ме́сте mark time. **марширо́вка,** -и, marching.

маршру́т, -а, route, itinerary. **маршру́тка, -и, маршру́тное такси́,** fixed-route taxi.

ма́ска, -и, mask. **маскара́д,** -а masked ball; masquerade. **маскирова́ть,** -ру́ю *imp.* (*perf.* за~) mask, disguise; camouflage. **маскиро́вка,** -и, masking, disguise; camouflage. **маскиро́вщик,** -а, camouflage expert.

ма́сленица, -ы, Shrovetide; carnival. **маслёнка,** -и, butter-dish; oil-can. **ма́слен|ый,** buttered; oiled, oily; unctuous; ~ая неде́ля, Shrove-tide. **масли́на,** -ы olive. **ма́слить,** -лю *imp.* (*perf.* на~, по~) butter; oil, grease. **ма́сло,** -а; *pl.* -а́, ма́сел, -сла́м, butter; oil; oil paints, oils; как по ма́слу, swimmingly. **маслобо́йка,** -и, churn; oil press. **маслобо́йный** завод, **маслобо́йня,** -и; *gen. pl.* -о́ен, **маслозаво́д,** -а, creamery; dairy; oil-mill. **масломе́р,** -а, oil gauge; dipstick. **маслянис́тый,** oily. **ма́сляный,** oil; butter.

ма́сса, -ы, mass; paste, pulp; a lot, lots.

масси́в, -а, massif; expanse, tract. **масси́вный,** massive.

массо́вка, -и, mass meeting; outing; crowd scene. **ма́ссов|ый,** mass; popular; bulk; ~ая поста́вка, bulk delivery; ~ые сце́ны, crowd scenes.

маста́к, -а́, expert, past master. **ма́стер,** -а; *pl.* -а́, **мастери́ца,** -ы, foreman, forewoman; master craftsman, skilled worker; expert, master; ~ на все ру́ки, Jack of all trades. **мастери́ть,** -рю́ *imp.* (*perf.* с~) make, build construct. **мастерска́я** *sb.* workshop; shop; studio. **мастерско́й,** masterly. **мастерство́,** -а́, trade, craft; skill, craftsmanship.

масти́ка, -и, mastic; putty; floor-polish.

масти́тый, venerable.

масть, -и; *pl.* -и -е́й, colour; suit; ходи́ть в ~, follow suit.
масшта́б, -а, scale. **масшта́бность**, -и, (large) scale, range, dimensions.
мат, -а, checkmate, mate; объяви́ть ~, mate, checkmate.
материа́л, -а, material; stuff. **материа́льный**, material; physical; financial, pecuniary, economic.
матери́к, -а́, continent; mainland; subsoil. **материко́вый**, continental.
матери́нский, maternal, motherly. **матери́нство**, -а, maternity, motherhood.
мате́рия, -и, material, cloth, stuff; matter; pus; subject, topic.
ма́тка, -и, uterus, womb; female, queen; (submarine) tender, depot ship.
ма́тов|ый, matt; dull; suffused; ~ое стекло́, frosted glass.
матра́с, -а, **матра́ц**, -а, mattress.
ма́трица, -ы, matrix; die, mould.
матро́с, -а, sailor seaman. **матро́ска**, -и, sailor's wife; sailor's blouse, sailor blouse. **матро́сский**, sailor's, sailors', seaman's, seamen's; ~ воро́тник, sailor collar.
ма́тушка, -и, mother; priest's wife.
матч, -а, match.
мать, ма́тери, *instr.* -рью; *pl.* -тери -ре́й, mother.
мах, -а (-у), swing, stroke; дать ~у, let a chance slip, make a blunder; одни́м ~ом, at one stroke, in a trice; с ~у, rashly, without thinking. **маха́ть**, машу́ ма́шешь *imp.*, **махну́ть**, -ну́, -нёшь *perf.* + *instr.* wave; brandish; wag; flap; go travel; rush, leap jump. **махови́к**, -а́, fly-wheel. **махов|о́й**; ~о́е колесо́, fly-wheel; ~ы́е пе́рья, wing-feathers.
ма́хонький, very little, small, tiny.
махро́в|ый, double; double-dyed, dyed-in-the-wool; terry; ~ая ткань, terry towelling.
ма́чеха, -и, stepmother.
ма́чта, -ы, mast.
маши́на, -ы, machine; mechanism; engine; (motor) vehicle; car; bicycle; train. **машина́льный**, mechanical; automatic, absent-minded; machine-like. **машинизи́ровать**, -рую *perf.* and *imp.* mechanize. **машини́ст**, -а, operator, engineer; engine-driver; scene-shifter. **машини́стка**, -и, typist.
маши́нка, -и, machine; typewriter; sewing-machine; clippers. **маши́нно-тра́кторн|ый**; ~ая ста́нция, machine and tractor station. **маши́нн|ый**, machine, engine; mechanical, mechanized; power-driven; ~ое бюро́ typing office, typing agency; ~ый зал, engine-room; machine-room. **машинопи́сный**, typewritten; ~ текст, typescript. **маши́нопись**, -и, typewriting; typescript. **машинострое́ние**, -я, mechanical engineering, machine-building.
мая́к, -а́ lighthouse; beacon.
ма́ятник, -а, pendulum. **ма́ять**, ма́ю *imp.* wear out, exhaust, weary; **~ся**, suffer, languish; loaf, loiter about.
мая́чить, -чу *imp.* loom, loom up; appear indistinctly.
МБР (*embeér*) *abbr.* межконтинента́льная баллисти́ческая раке́та, intercontinental ballistic missile.
МБТ (*embeté*) *abbr.* Междунаро́дное бюро́ труда́ I.L.O.
МВТ (*emveté*) *abbr.* министе́рство вне́шней торго́вли, Ministry of Foreign Trade.
мг *abbr.* миллигра́мм, milligram.
мгла, -ы, haze; mist; gloom, darkness. **мгли́стый** hazy.
мгнове́ние, -я, instant, moment. **мгнове́нный**, instantaneous, momentary.
МГУ (*emgeú*), Моско́вский госуда́рственный университе́т, Moscow State University.
ме́бель, -и, furniture. **ме́бельщик**, -а, upholsterer; furniture-dealer. **меблиро́ванный**, furnished. **меблирова́ть**, -ру́ю *perf.* and *imp.* furnish. **меблиро́вка**, -и, furnishing; furniture.
мег-, **мега-**, mega-, meg-. **мегава́тт**, -а; *gen. pl.* -атт, megawatt. **~ге́рц**, -а, megacycle. **мего́м**, -а, megohm. **~то́нна**, -ы, megaton.
мёд, -а (-у), *loc.* -ý; *pl.* -ы́, honey; mead.
мед- *abbr.* in *comb.* of медици́нский, of medicine, medical. **медву́з**, -а, Medical School, School of Medicine. **~осмо́тр**, -а, medical examination.

~пу́нкт, -а, first aid post, medical station; surgery. **~сестра́**, -ы́, (hospital) nurse.

медве́дица, -ы, she-bear; Bear, Ursa. **медве́дь**, -я *m.* bear. **медве́жий**, bear bear's; bearskin; bear-like. **медвежо́нок**, -нка; *pl.* -жа́та, -жа́т, bear-cub.

медеплави́льный, copper-smelting.

ме́дик, -а, medical student; doctor. **медикаме́нт**, -а, medicine; *pl.* medical supplies. **медици́на**, -ы, medicine. **медици́нск|ий**, medical; ~ое обслу́живание, medical attendance, medical care; ~ий пункт, dressing-station, first-aid post. **меди́чка**, -и medical student.

ме́дленно *adv.* slowly. **ме́дленный**, slow. **медли́тельный**, sluggish; slow, tardy. **ме́длить**, -лю *imp.* linger; tarry; be slow.

ме́дник, -а, coppersmith; tinker. **ме́дный**, copper; brass, brazen; cupric, cuprous.

медо́вый honey; honeyed; ~ ме́сяц, honeymoon.

меду́за, -ы, jellyfish, medusa.

медь, -и, copper.

меж *prep.*+*instr.* between.

меж- in *comb.* inter-; between. **межгалакти́ческий**, intergalactic. **~континента́льный**, intercontinental. **~плане́тный** interplanetary.

межа́, -и́; *pl.* -и, меж, -а́м, boundary; boundary-strip.

междоме́тие, -я, interjection.

ме́жду *prep.* + *instr.* between; among, amongst; ~ на́ми (говоря́), between ourselves, between you and me; ~ про́чим incidentally, by the way; ~ тем meanwhile; all the same; ~ тем как, while, whereas.

между- in *comb.*, inter-, between. **междугоро́дный**, inter-urban, inter-city; ~-горо́дный телефо́н, trunk-line. **~наро́дный**, international.

мезони́н, -а, attic (storey); mezzanine (floor).

мел -а, *loc.* -у́, chalk; whiting; whitewash.

мёл, etc.: see мести́.

меле́ть, -е́ет *imp.* (*perf.* об~) grow shallow.

мели́ть, -лю́ *imp.* (*perf.* на~) chalk.

ме́лк|ий; -лок, -лка́, -о, small; shallow; shallow-draught; fine; petty, small-minded; ~ая таре́лка, flat plate. **ме́лко** *adv.* fine, small.

мелко- in *comb.* small; fine, finely; petty; shallow. **мелкобуржуа́зный**, petty-bourgeois. **~во́дный**, shallow. **~во́дье**, -я, shallow water; shallow. **~зерни́стый**, fine-grained, small-grained. **~со́бственнический**, of small property holders.

мело́к, -лка́, chalk.

ме́лочность, -и, pettiness, small-mindedness, meanness. **ме́лочный** petty, trifling; paltry; small-minded. **ме́лочь**, -и; *pl.* -и -е́й, small items; small fry; small coin; (small) change; *pl.* minutiae; trifles, trivialities.

мель, -и, *loc.* -и́, shoal; bank; на мели́, aground; on the rocks in low water; сесть на ~, run aground.

мелька́ть, -а́ю *imp.*, **мелькну́ть**, -ну́, -нёшь *perf.* be glimpsed fleetingly; flash, gleam (for a moment). **ме́льком** *adv.* in passing; for a moment.

ме́льник, -а, miller. **ме́льница**, -ы, mill. **ме́льничный**, mill; ~ лото́к, mill-race.

мельча́йший *superl.* of ме́лкий. **мельча́ть**, -а́ю *imp.* (*perf.* из~) grow shallow; become small(er): become petty. **ме́льче** *comp.* of ме́лкий, ме́лко. **мельчи́ть**, -чу́ *imp.* (*perf.* из~, раз~) crush, crumble; pulverize; grind mill; reduce size or significance of. **мелюзга́**, -и, small fry.

мелю́ etc.: see моло́ть.

мембра́на, -ы, membrane; diaphragm.

ме́на, -ы, exchange, barter.

менажёр, -а, **ме́неджер**, -а, manager. **менажи́ровать**, -рую *imp.* manage, be manager of.

ме́нее *adv.* less; ~ всего́, least of all; тем не ~, none the less, all the same.

мензу́рка, -и, measuring-glass; graduated measure.

меново́й, exchange barter.

ме́ньше, smaller; less. **ме́ньш|ий**, lesser, smaller; younger; по ~ей ме́ре, at least; са́мое ~ее, at the least. **меньшинство́**. -а, minority.

меня́: see я *pron.*

меня́ть, -я́ю *imp*. (*perf*. об~, по~) change; exchange; **~ся**, change; +*instr*. exchange.

ме́ра, -ы measure; в ме́ру, fairly, moderately; в ме́ру+*gen*. to the extent of; по ме́ре возмо́жности, as far as possible; по ме́ре того́, как, (in proportion) as; не в ме́ру, сверх ме́ры, чрез ме́ру, excessively, immoderately.

мере́жка, -и, hem-stitching, open-work.

мере́щиться, -щусь *imp*. (*perf*. по~) seem, appear; appear dimly, glimmer.

мерза́вец, -вца, blackguard, scoundrel. **ме́рзкий**; -зок, -зка́, -о, disgusting, loathsome; abominable foul.

мерзлота́, -ы́; ве́чная ~, permafrost. **мёрзлый**, frozen, congealed. **мёрзнуть**, -ну; мёрз *imp*. (*perf*. за~) freeze.

ме́рзость, -и, vileness, loathsomeness; loathsome thing, nasty thing; abomination.

мери́ло, -а, standard, criterion. **мери́льный**, measuring.

ме́рить, -рю *imp*. (*perf*. по~, с~) measure; try on; **~ся**+*instr*. measure. **ме́рка**, -и, measure.

ме́ркнуть, -нет; ме́рк(нул) *imp*. (*perf*. по~) grow dark, grow dim; fade.

ме́рный, measured; rhythmical; measuring. **мероприя́тие**, -я, measure.

ме́ртвенный, deathly, ghastly. **мертве́ть**, -е́ю *imp*. (*perf*. о~, по~) grow numb; mortify; be benumbed. **мертве́ц**, -а́, corpse, dead man. **мертве́цкая** *sb*. mortuary, morgue. **мёртв|ый**; мёртв, -а́, мёртво́, dead; ~ая зыбь, swell; ~ая пе́тля, loop; noose; спать ~ым сном, sleep like the dead.

мерца́ть, -а́ет *imp*. twinkle; shimmer, glimmer; flicker.

ме́сиво, -а, mash; medley; jumble. **меси́ть**, мешу́, ме́сишь *imp*. (*perf*. с~) knead.

места́ми *adv*. here and there, in places. **месте́чко**, -а; *pl*. -и -чек, small town.

мести́, мету́, -тёшь; мёл, -а́ *imp*. sweep; whirl; метёт, there is a snow-storm.

местко́м, -а *abbr*. local (trade-union) committee. **ме́стность**, -и, locality, district; area; ground, country, terrain. **ме́стный**, local; localized; locative. **-ме́стный** in *comb*. -berth, -seater, -place. **ме́сто**, -а; *pl*. -а́, place; site; seat; berth; space, room; post, situation, job; passage; piece of luggage; *pl*. the provinces, the country; без ме́ста, out of work; име́ть ~, take place; ~ де́йствия, scene (of action); на ме́сте преступле́ния, in the act, red-handed; не к ме́сту, out of place; ни с ме́ста! don't move! stay where you are! **местожи́тельство**, -а, (place of) residence; без определённого местожи́тельства of no fixed abode. **местоиме́ние**, -я, pronoun. **местоиме́нный**, pronominal. **местонахожде́ние**, -я, location, whereabouts. **местопребыва́ние**, -я, abode, residence. **месторожде́ние**, -я, birthplace; deposit, bed; layer; ~ у́гля, coal-field.

месть, -и, vengeance, revenge.

ме́сяц, -а, month; moon. **ме́сячный**, monthly.

мета́лл, -а, metal. **металли́ст**, -а, metal-worker. **металли́ческий**, metal, metallic. **металлоло́м**, -а, scrap (-metal).

мета́ние, -я, throwing, casting, flinging; ~ копья́, throwing the javelin. **мета́тель**, -я *m*. thrower. **мета́ть**[1], мечу́, ме́чешь *imp*. (*perf*. метну́ть) throw, cast, fling; ~ банк, keep the bank; ~ икру́, spawn; **~ся**, rush about; toss (and turn).

мета́ть[2], -а́ю *imp*. (*perf*. на~, с~) tack, baste.

метёлка, -и, whisk; panicle.

мете́ль, -и, snow-storm; blizzard.

метео- *abbr*. in *comb*. of метеорологи́ческий, meteorological; weather-. **метеосво́дка**, -и, weather report. **~слу́жба**, -ы, weather service. **~ста́нция**, weather-station. **~усло́вия**, weather conditions.

метеорологи́ческ|ий, meteorological; ~ая сво́дка, weather report.

ме́тить[1], ме́чу *imp*. (*perf*. на~, по~) mark.

ме́тить[2], ме́чу *imp*. (*perf*. на~) aim; +в+*acc*. *pl*. aim at, aspire to; + в or на+*acc*. drive at, mean.

ме́тка, -и, marking, mark.
ме́ткий; -ток, -тка́, -о, well-aimed, accurate. **ме́ткость, -и,** marksmanship; accuracy; neatness, pointedness
метла́, -ы́; *pl.* мётлы, -тел, broom.
метну́ть, -ну́, -нёшь *perf.* of мета́ть[1].
ме́тод, -а. method. **мето́дика, -и,** method(s), system; principles; methodology. **методи́ческий,** methodical, systematic. **методи́чный,** methodical, orderly.
метр, -а, metre. **метра́ж, -а,** metric area; length in me res.
ме́трика, -и, birth-certificate. **метри́ческ|ий**[1]; ~ая кни́га, register of births deaths and marriages; ~ое свиде́тельство, birth-certificate.
метри́ческий[2], metric; metrical.
метро́ *n. indecl.* Metro; underground; на ~, by Metro, by underground.
мету́, etc.: see мести́.
ме́тче *comp.* of ме́ткий.
мех[1], -а, *loc.* -у́; *pl.* -а́, fur; на ~у́, fur-lined.
мех[2], -а; *pl.* -и́, wine-skin, water-skin; *pl.* bellows.
механиза́ция, -и, mechanization. **механи́зм, -а,** mechanism; gear, gearing; *pl.* machinery. **меха́ник, -а,** mechanic. **меха́ника, -и,** mechanics; trick; knack. **механи́ческий,** mechanical; power-driven; of mechanics; mechanistic; ~ моме́нт, momentum; ~ цех, machine shop. **механи́чный,** mechanical, automatic.
мехово́й, fur. **меховщи́к, -а́,** furrier.
меч, -а́, sword.
ме́ченый, marked; labelled, tagged; ~ а́том, tracer, tracer element.
мече́ть, -и, mosque.
мечта́, -ы́, dream, day-dream. **мечта́тельный,** dreamy. **мечта́ть, -а́ю** *imp.* dream.
ме́чу, etc.: see ме́тить. **мечу́,** etc.: see мета́ть.
меша́лка, -и, mixer, stirrer.
меша́ть[1], -а́ю *imp.* (*perf.* по~)+*dat.* hinder, impede, hamper; prevent; disturb; не меша́ло бы+*inf.*, it would be advisable to, it would not be a bad thing to.
меша́ть[2], -а́ю *imp.* (*perf.* по~, с~), stir; agitate; mix, blend, confuse, mix up; **~ся** (в+*acc.*) interfere (in), meddle (with).
ме́шкать, -аю *imp.* linger, delay; loiter.
мешкова́тый, baggy; awkward, clumsy. **мешкови́на, -ы,** sacking, hessian.
мешо́к, -шка́, bag; sack; clumsy fellow.
мещани́н, -а; *pl.* -а́не, -а́н, petty bourgeois; Philistine. **меща́нский,** lower-middle-class; bourgeois, vulgar, narrow-minded; Philistine. **меща́нство, -а,** petty bourgeoisie, lower middle class; philistinism, vulgarity, narrow-mindedness.
ми, *n. indecl.* E; me.
миг, -а. moment, instant.
мига́ть, -а́ю *imp.*, **мигну́ть, -ну́, -нёшь** *perf.* blink; wink, twinkle; +*dat.* wink at.
ми́гом *adv.* in a flash; in a jiffy.
МИД, мид, -а *abbr.* Министе́рство иностра́нных дел, Ministry for Foreign Affairs, Foreign Office, State Department.
мизе́рный, scanty, wretched.
мизи́нец, -нца, little finger; little toe.
микро- micro-; small. **микроавто́бус, -а,** minibus. **~ампе́р, -а,** microampere. **~органи́зм, -а,** micro-organism. **~ско́п, -а,** microscope. **~скопи́ческий, ~скопи́чный,** microscopic. **~фо́н, -а,** microphone.
микро́н, -а, micron.
миксту́ра, -ы, medicine, mixture.
ми́ленький, pretty; nice; sweet; dear, darling.
милицион́ер, -а, militiaman, policeman. **мили́ция, -и,** militia, police force.
миллиа́рд, -а, milliard, a thousand millions. **миллиарде́р, -а,** multi-millionaire. **миллио́н, -а,** million. **миллионе́р, -а,** millionaire. **миллио́нный,** millionth; worth, numbered in, millions.
милосе́рдие, -я, mercy, charity; сестра́ милосе́рдия, (hospital) nurse. **милосе́рдный,** merciful, charitable.
ми́лостив|ый, gracious, kind; ~ый госуда́рь, sir; (Dear) Sir; ~ая госуда́рыня, madam; (Dear) Madam. **ми́лостыня, -и,** alms. **ми́лость, -и,** favour, grace; mercy; charity; ва́ша

~, your worship; ми́лости про́сим! welcome!; you are always welcome; come and see us. **ми́лочка, -и,** dear, darling. **ми́лый;** мил, -á, -о, nice; kind; sweet, lovable; dear, darling.

ми́ля, -и, mile.

ми́мика, -и, (facial) expression; miming.

ми́мо *adv.* and *prep.+gen.* by, past. **мимоéздом** *adv.* in passing. **мимолётный,** fleeting, transient. **мимохо́дом** *adv.* in passing.

мин. *abbr.* мину́та, minute.

ми́на[1], -ы, mine; bomb; rocket.

ми́на[2], -ы, expression; face, countenance.

миндалеви́дн|ый, almond-shaped. **минда́лина,** -ы, almond; tonsil. **минда́ль,** -я́ *m.* almond(-tree); almonds. **минда́льн|ый,** almond; ~ое печéнье, macaroon.

минера́л, -а, mineral. **минерало́гия,** -и, mineralogy. **минера́льный,** mineral.

минима́льный, minimum. **ми́нимум,** -а, minimum; at the least.

министéрский, ministerial. **министéрство,** -а, ministry. **мини́стр,** -а, minister.

минова́ть, -ну́ю *perf.* and *imp.* pass, pass by, pass over; be over, be past; *impers.+dat* escape, avoid; тебé э́того не ~, you can't escape it.

миномёт, -а, mortar. **миноно́сец,** -сца, torpedo-boat.

мино́р, -а, minor (key); blues.

мину́вш|ий, past; **~ее** *sb.* the past.

ми́нус, -а, minus; defect, shortcoming. **ми́нусовый,** negative.

мину́та, minute. **мину́тный,** minute; momentary; transient, ephemeral, brief.

мину́ть, -нешь; ми́ну́л *perf.* pass; pass by; be over, be past; ему́ ми́нуло два́дцать лет, he is turned twenty.

мир[1], -а; *pl.* -ы́, world; universe; mir, village community.

мир[2], -а, peace. **мири́ть,** -рю́ *imp.* (*perf.* по~, при~) reconcile; **~ся,** be reconciled, make it up; reconcile oneself (с + *instr.* to). **ми́рный,** peace; peaceful; peaceable.

мировоззрéние, -я, (world-)outlook; philosophy. **миров|о́й,** world; **~а́я** держа́ва, world power.

миролюби́вость, -и, peaceable disposition. **миролюби́вый,** peace-loving, peaceful.

ми́ска, -и, basin, bowl, tureen.

ми́ссия, -и, mission; legation.

мистéрия, -и, mystery(-play).

ми́стика, -и, mysticism.

мистификáтор, -а, hoaxer. **мистифика́ция,** -и, hoax, leg-pull.

мисти́ческий, mystic, mystical.

ми́тинг, -а, mass meeting. **митингова́ть,** -гу́ю *imp.* hold a mass meeting; discuss endlessly.

миф, -а, myth. **мифи́ческий,** mythical. **мифологи́ческий,** mythological. **мифоло́гия,** -и, mythology.

мишéнь, -и, target.

ми́шка, -и, bear; Teddy bear.

мишура́, -ы́, tinsel; tawdriness, show. **мишу́рный,** tinsel; trumpery, tawdry.

МК (*emka*) *abbr.* мéстный комитéт, local committee, mestkom.

мл. *abbr.* мла́дший, junior.

млд. *abbr.* миллиа́рд, milliard.

млн. *abbr.* миллио́н, million.

младéнец, -нца, baby; infant. **младéнческий,** infantile. **младéнчество,** -а, infancy, babyhood. **мла́дший,** younger; youngest; junior; ~ кома́ндный соста́в, non-commissioned officers; ~ офицéрский соста́в, junior officers.

млекопита́ющие *sb. pl.* mammals. **млéчный,** milk; lactic; ~ Путь, Milky Way, Galaxy.

мм *abbr.* миллимéтр, millimetre.

мне: see я *pron.*

мнéние, -я opinion; по моему́ мнéнию in my opinion.

мни́мый, imaginary; sham, pretended. **мни́тельный,** hypochondriac; mistrustful, suspicious. **мнить,** мню *imp.* think, imagine; мно́го мнить о себé, think much of oneself.

мно́г|ий, much; many; **~ие** *sb.* many (people); **~ое** *sb.* much, a great deal, many things; во мно́гом, in many respects. **мно́го** *adv.* + *gen.* much; many; a great deal; a lot of; ~ лу́чше, much better; на ~ by far; ни ~ ни ма́ло, neither more nor less (than), no less (than).

много- in *comb.* many-, poly-, multi-, multiple-. **многобо́жие,** -я, polytheism. **~бо́рец,** -рца, competitor in combined event; all-rounder. **~бо́рье,** -я, combined event, combined competition. **~бра́чие,** -я, polygamy. **~вeково́й,** centuries-old. **~во́дный,** full, in spate; well-watered, abounding in water. **~гра́нник,** -а, polyhedron. **~гра́нный,** polyhedral; many-sided. **~де́тный,** having many children. **~же́нец,** -нца, polygamist. **~жёнство,** -а, polygamy. **~значи́тельный,** significant. **~зна́чный,** multi-digit; polysemantic. **~каска́дный,** multi-stage. **~кра́тный,** repeated, reiterated; multiple; frequentative, iterative. **~ле́тний,** lasting, living, many years; of many years' standing; perennial. **~ле́тник,** -а, perennial. **~лю́дный,** populous; crowded. **~му́жие,** -я, polyandry. **~национа́льный,** multi-national. **~обеща́ющий,** promising, hopeful; significant. **~обра́зие,** -я, variety, diversity. **~обра́зный,** varied, diverse. **~семе́йный,** having a large family. **~сло́вный,** verbose, prolix. **~сло́жный,** complex, complicated; polysyllabic. **~сло́йный,** multi-layer; multi-ply; ~сло́йная фане́ра, plywood. **~сторо́нний,** polygonal; multi-lateral; many-sided, versatile. **~ступе́нчатый,** multistage. **~тира́жка,** -и, factory newspaper; house organ. **~то́мный,** in many volumes. **~то́чие,** -я, dots, omission points. **~уважа́емый,** respected; Dear. **~уго́льник,** -а, polygon. **~уго́льный,** polygonal. **~цве́тный,** many-coloured, multi-coloured; polychromatic; multiflorous, floribunda. **~чи́сленный,** numerous. **~чле́н,** -а, polynomial. **~эта́жный,** multi-storey, many-storeyed. **~язы́чный,** polyglot; multi-lingual.

мно́жественный, plural. **мно́жество,** -а, great number; value; set; aggregate; great quantities; multitude. **мно́жимое** *sb.* multiplicand. **мно́житель,** -я, *m.* multiplier; factor. **мно́жить,** -жу *imp.* (*perf.* по~, у~) multiply; increase, augment; **~ся,** multiply, increase.

мной, etc.: see я *pron.* **мог,** etc.: see мочь. **мну,** etc.: see мять.

моги́ла, -ы, grave. **моги́льник,** -а, burial ground, cemetery. **моги́льн|ый,** grave; of the grave; sepulchral; ~ая плита́, tombstone, gravestone, headstone. **моги́льщик,** -а, grave-digger.

могу́, etc.: see мочь. **могу́чий,** mighty, powerful. **могу́щественный,** powerful. **могу́щество,** -а, power, might.

мо́да, -ы, fashion, vogue.

моделúровать, -рую *perf.* and *imp.* design. **моде́ль,** -и, model; pattern. **модельéр,** -а, dress-designer. **моде́льный,** model; fashionable.

моди́стка, -и, milliner; modiste. **мо́дный;** -ден, -дна́, -о, fashionable, stylish; fashion.

мо́жет: see мочь.

можжевéльник, -а, juniper.

мо́жно, one may, one can; it is permissible; it is possible; как ~+*comp.* as . . as possible; как ~ лу́чше, as well as possible, to the best of one's abilities; как ~ скоре́е, as soon as possible.

мозг, -а (-у), *loc.* -у́; *pl.* -и́, brain; marrow; шевели́ть ~а́ми, use one's head. **мозгови́тый,** brainy. **мозгово́й,** cerebral; brain.

мозо́листый, calloused; horny. **мозо́ль,** -и, corn; callus, callosity.

мой, моего́ *m.*, **моя́,** мое́й *f.*, **моё,** моего́ *n.*, **мои́,** -и́х *pl. pron.* my; mine; по-мо́ему, in my opinion, I think; in my way; as I wish, as I think right.

МОК, -а *abbr.* Междунаро́дный олимпи́йский комитéт, International Olympics Committee.

мо́кнуть, -ну; мок *imp.* get wet, get soaked; soak. **мокрова́тый,** moist, damp. **мокро́та**[1], -ы, phlegm. **мокрота́**[2], -ы́, humidity, damp. **мо́крый,** wet, damp; soggy.

мол, -а, *loc.* -у́, mole, pier.

молва́, -ы́, rumour, talk. **мо́лвить,** -влю *perf.* and *imp.* utter; say.

моле́ние, -я, prayer; entreaty, supplication. **моли́тва,** -ы, prayer. **моли́ть,** -лю́, -лишь *imp.* pray; entreat, supplicate, beg (о+*prep.* for); **~ся** (*perf.* по~ся) pray, offer prayers; say one's prayers; +на+*acc.* idolize.

мо́лкнуть, -ну; молк *imp*. fall silent.
молниено́сн|ый, lightning; ~ая война́, blitzkrieg. **молниеотво́д**, -а, lightning-conductor. **мо́лния**, -и, lightning; zip (-fastener); (телегра́мма-)~, express telegram.
молодёжь, -и, youth, young people; the younger generation. **молоде́ть**, -е́ю *imp*. (*perf*. по~), get younger, look younger. **молоде́ц**, -дца́, fine fellow; brick; ~! well done! good man!; вести́ себя́ молодцо́м, put up a good show. **молоде́цкий**, dashing, spirited. **молодня́к**, -а́, saplings; young animals; youth, young people. **молод|о́й**; мо́лод, -а́, -о, young, youthful; ~о́й карто́фель, new potatoes; ~о́й ме́сяц, new moon; **~о́й** *sb*. bridegroom; **~а́я** *sb*. bride; **~ы́е** *sb*. *pl*. young couple, newly-weds. **мо́лодость**, -и, youth; youthfulness. **моложа́вый**, young-looking; име́ть ~ вид, look young for one's age. **моло́же** *comp*. of молодо́й.
молоко́, -а́, milk. **молокосо́с**, -а, greenhorn, raw youth.
мо́лот, -а, hammer. **молоти́лка**, -и, threshing-machine. **молоти́ть**, -очу́, -о́тишь *imp*. (*perf*. с~) thresh; hammer. **молото́к**, -тка́, hammer.
мо́лотый, ground. **моло́ть**, мелю́, ме́лешь *imp*. (*perf*. с~) grind, mill; ~ вздор, talk nonsense, talk rot.
молотьба́, -ы́, threshing. **моло́ченный**, threshed.
моло́чник, -а, milk-jug, milk-can; milkman. **моло́чница**, -ы, milkwoman, milk-seller. **моло́чн|ый**, milk; dairy; milky; lactic; ~ый брат, foster-brother; ~ое стекло́, frosted glass, opal glass; ~ое хозя́йство, dairy-farm(ing); **~ая** *sb*. dairy; creamery.
мо́лча *adv*. silently, in silence. **молчали́вый**, silent, taciturn; tacit, unspoken. **молча́ние**, -я, silence. **молча́ть**, -чу́ *imp*. be silent, keep silence.
моль, -и, (clothes-)moth.
мольба́, -ы́, entreaty, supplication.
мольбе́рт, -а, easel.
моме́нт, -а, moment; instant; feature, element, factor. **момента́льно** *adv*. in a moment, instantly. **момента́льный**, instantaneous; ~ сни́мок, snap(shot). **моме́нтами** *adv*. now and then.
монасты́рь, -я́ *m*. monastery; convent. **мона́х**, -а, monk; friar. **мона́хиня**, -и, nun. **мона́шеский**, monastic; monkish.
моне́та, -ы, coin; приня́ть за чи́стую моне́ту, take at face value, take in good faith. **моне́тный**, monetary; ~ двор mint.
моноли́т, -а, monolith. **моноли́тность**, -и, monolithic character; solidity. **моноли́тный**, monolithic; massive, united.
моното́нный, monotonous.
монта́ж, -а́, assembling, mounting, installation; montage; editing, cutting; arrangement. **монта́жник**, -а, rigger, erector, fitter. **монтёр**, -а, fitter, maintenance man, mechanic. **монти́ровать**, -рую *imp*. (*perf*. с~) mount; install, fit; erect; edit, cut.
мор, -а, pestilence, plague.
мора́ль, -и, moral; morals, ethics. **мора́льн|ый**, moral; ethical; ~ое состоя́ние, morale.
морга́ть, -а́ю *imp*., **моргну́ть**, -ну́, -нёшь *perf*. blink; wink.
мо́рда, -ы, snout, muzzle; face, (ugly) mug.
мо́ре, -я; *pl*. -я́, -е́й, sea; в откры́том мо́ре, on the open sea; за́ морем, oversea(s).
море́на, -ы, moraine.
морепла́вание, -я, navigation; voyaging. **морепла́ватель**, -я *m*. navigator, seafarer. **морепла́вательный**, nautical, navigational. **мореход**, -а, seafarer.
морж, -а́, **моржи́ха**, -и, walrus; all-the-year-round swimmer. **моржо́вый**, walrus, walrus-hide.
Мо́рзе, Morse; а́збука ~, Morse code. **морзя́нка**, -и, Morse code.
мори́ть, -рю́ *imp*. (*perf*. по~, у~), exterminate; exhaust, wear out; ~ го́лодом, starve.
морко́вка, -и, carrot. **морко́вный**, carrot; carroty. **морко́вь**, -и, carrots.
моро́женое *sb*. ice-cream, ice. **моро́женый**, frozen, chilled. **моро́з**, -а, frost; *pl*. intensely cold weather. **моро́зить**, -о́жу, freeze. **моро́зный**, frost, frosty. **морозоусто́йчивый**, frost-resistant, hardy.

моросить, -ит *imp.* drizzle.

морс, -а, fruit-juice, fruit syrup; fruit drink.

морск|ой, sea; maritime; marine, nautical; shipping; naval; ~ой волк, old salt; ~ая звезда, starfish; ~ой конёк, sea-horse; ~ая пенка, meerschaum; ~ая пехота, marines; ~ой разбойник, pirate; ~ая свинья, porpoise; ~ой флот navy, fleet.

морфология, -и, morphology; accidence.

морщина, -ы, wrinkle; crease. **морщинистый**, wrinkled, lined; creased. **морщить**[1], -щу *imp.* (*perf.* на~, по~, с~) wrinkle; pucker; ~ лоб, knit one's brow; **~ся**, make a wry face; knit one's brow; wince; crease, wrinkle. **морщить**[2], -ит *imp.* crease; ruck up.

моряк, -а sailor seaman.

московск|ий, Moscow of Moscow.

мост, моста (-у), *loc.* -у; *pl.* -ы, bridge. **мостик**, -а, bridge. **мостить**, -ощу *imp.* (*perf.* вы~, за~, на~) pave; lay. **мостки**, -ов *pl.* planked footway, board-walk; wooden platform. **мостовая** *sb.* roadway; pavement. **мостовой**, bridge.

мотальный, winding. **мотать**[1], -аю *imp.* (*perf.* мотнуть, на~) wind, reel; shake.

мотать[2], -аю *imp.* (*perf.* про~) squander.

мотаться, -аюсь *imp.* dangle; wander; rush about; ~ по свету, knock about the world.

мотив, -а motive; reason; tune; motif. **мотивировать**, -рую *perf.* and *imp.* give reasons for, justify. **мотивировка**, -и reason(s); motivation; justification.

мотнуть, -ну, -нёшь *perf.* of мотать.

мото- in *comb.*, motor-, engine-; motor--cycle; motorized. **мотогонки**, -нок *pl.* motor-cycle races. **~дрезина**, -ы, (rail) motor-trolley. **~дром**, -а, motor--cycle race-track. **~кросс**, -а, motocross. **~пед**, -а, moped. **~пехота**, -ы, motorized infantry. **~роллер**, -а, (motor-)scooter. **~цикл**, -а, **~циклет**, -а, motor-cycle.

мотовской, wasteful, extravagant. **мотовство**, -а, wastefulness, extravagance, prodigality.

моток, -тка, skein, hank.

мотор, -а, motor, engine. **моторист**, -а, motor-mechanic. **моторка**, -и, motor-boat. **моторный**, motor; engine.

мотыга, -и hoe, mattock. **мотыжить**, -жу *imp.* hoe.

мотылёк, -лька, butterfly, moth.

мох, мха or моха, *loc.* мху; *pl.* мхи, мхов, moss. **мохнат|ый**, hairy, shaggy; ~ое полотенце, Turkish towel.

моцион, -а, exercise.

моча, -и, urine; water.

мочалка, -и, wisp of bast. **мочало**, -а, bast bass.

мочевина, -ы, urea. **мочевой**, urinary; uric; ~ пузырь, bladder. **моченный**, wetted; steeped; soused. **мочёный**, soaked, steeped. **мочить**, -чу, -чишь *imp.* (*perf.* за~, на~), wet, moisten; soak; steep, macerate; **~ся** (*perf.* по~ся) urinate, make water.

мочь, могу, можешь; мог, -ла *imp.* (*perf.* с~), be able; может (быть), perhaps, maybe; не могу знать, I don't know. **мочь**, -и, power, might; во всю ~, изо всей мочи, что есть мочи, with all one's might, with might and main.

мошенник, -а, rogue, scoundrel; swindler. **мошенничать**, -аю *imp.* (*perf.* с~) play the rogue, cheat, swindle. **мошеннический**, rascally, swindling.

мошка, -и, midge. **мошкара**, -ы, (swarm of) midges.

мощёный, paved.

мощность, -и, power; capacity, rating; output. **мощный**; -щен, -щна, -о, powerful; vigorous.

мощу, etc.: see мостить.

мощь, -и, power, might.

мою, etc.: see мыть. **моющий**, washing; detergent.

мрак, -а, darkness, gloom. **мракобес**, -а, obscurantist. **мракобесие**, -я, obscurantism.

мрамор, -а, marble; marbled; marmoreal.

мрачнеть, -ею *imp.* (*perf.* по~), grow

dark; grow gloomy. **мра́чный,** dark, sombre; gloomy, dismal.

мсти́тель -я *m.* avenger. **мсти́тельный,** vindictive. **мстить,** мщу *imp.* (*perf.* ото~) take vengeance on, revenge oneself; +за+*acc.* avenge.

МТС (*emteés*) *abbr.* маши́нно-тра́кторная ста́нция, agricultural-machinery pool.

мудрёный; -рён -а́, strange queer odd; difficult, abstruse, complicated; не мудрено́ что, no wonder (that). **мудре́ц,** -а́, sage, wise man. **мудри́ть** -рю́ *imp.* (*perf.* на~, с~) subtilize, complicate matters unnecessarily. **му́дрость,** -и, wisdom. **му́дрый;** -др, -а́, -о, wise, sage.

муж, -а; *pl.* -жья́ or -и́, husband; man. **мужа́ть,** -а́ю *imp.* grow up; mature, ripen; grow strong; **~ся,** take heart, take courage. **мужеподо́бный,** mannish; masculine. **му́жеский,** male; masculine. **му́жественный,** manly, steadfast. **му́жество,** -а, courage, fortitude.

мужи́к, -а́, moujik, muzhik; peasant; man, fellow.

мужск|о́й, masculine; male; ~о́й род, masculine gender; ~а́я шко́ла, boys' school. **мужчи́на,** -ы, man.

музе́й -я, museum.

му́зыка, -и, music; instrumental music; band; business, affair. **музыка́льность,** -и, melodiousness; musical talent. **музыка́льный,** musical. **музыка́нт,** -а, musician.

му́ка[1], -и, torment; torture; suffering; pangs, throes.

мука́[2], -и́, meal; flour. **мукомо́л,** -а, miller.

мультиплика́тор, -а, multiplier; multiplying camera; animator, animated-cartoon artist. **мультипликацио́нный,** cartoon, animated-cartoon. **мультипликáция,** -и, **мультфи́льм,** -а, cartoon film.

мунди́р, -а (full-dress) uniform; карто́фель в ~е, baked potatoes, jacket-potatoes.

мундшту́к, -а́, mouthpiece; cigarette-holder, cigar-holder; curb.

МУР, -а *abbr.* Моско́вский уголо́вный ро́зыск, Moscow C.I.D.

муравé́й, -вья́, ant. **мураве́йник,** -а, ant-hill; ant-bear. **мура́шка,** -и, small ant; мура́шки по спине́ бе́гают, it sends a shiver down one's spine.

мурлы́кать, -ы́чу or -каю *imp.* purr; hum.

муска́т, -а, nutmeg; muscat, muscatel. **муска́тный;** ~ оре́х, nutmeg; ~ цвет, mace.

му́скул. -а, muscle. **му́скулистый,** muscular, sinewy, brawny. **му́скульный,** muscular.

му́сор, -а, refuse; sweepings, dust; rubbish; garbage; debris. **му́сорн|ый;** ~ая пово́зка, dust-cart; ~ая сва́лка, rubbish heap; ~ый я́щик, dustbin. **мусоропрово́д,** -а, refuse chute.

муссо́н, -а, monsoon.

мути́ть, мучу́, му́ти́шь *imp.* (*perf.* вз~, за~, по~) trouble, make muddy; stir up, upset; dull, make dull; **~ся,** grow turbid, muddy, dull; dim. **мутне́ть,** -е́ет *imp.* (*perf.* по~) grow or become turbid, muddy, dull. **му́тность,** -и, turbidity; dullness. **му́тный;** -тен, -тна́, -о, turbid, troubled; dull, dulled, lack-lustre; confused.

му́фта, -ы, muff; sleeve, coupling, clutch; ~ сцепле́ния, clutch.

му́ха, -и, fly. **мухомо́р,** -а, fly-agaric, toadstool.

муче́ние, -я, torment, torture. **му́ченик,** -а, **му́ченица,** -ы, martyr. **мучи́тель,** -я *m.* torturer; tormentor. **му́чить,** -чу *imp.* (*perf.* за~, из~) torment; worry, harass; **~ся,** torment oneself; worry, feel unhappy; suffer agonies; ~ся от бо́ли, be racked with pain.

мучни́стый, farinaceous, starchy; mealy, floury. **мучно́й,** flour, meal; farinaceous, starchy; **~о́е** *sb.* starchy foods.

мха, etc.: see мох.

МХАТ, -а, **МХТ** (*emkhaté*) *abbr.* Моско́вский худо́жественный (академи́ческий) теа́тр, Moscow Arts Theatre.

мчать, мчу *imp.* rush along, whirl along; **~ся,** rush, race, tear along.

мши́стый, mossy.

мщу, etc.: see мстить.

мы, нас, нам, на́ми, нас *pron.* we; мы с ва́ми, мы с тобо́й, you and I.

мы́лить, -лю *imp.* (*perf.* на~) soap,

lather; **~ся,** soap oneself; lather, make a lather. **мы́лкий,** lathering easily; soapy. **мы́ло,** -а; *pl.* -á, soap; foam, lather. **мыловаре́ние,** -я, soap-boiling, soap-making. **мылова́ренный,** soap-making; ~ заво́д, soap works. **мы́льница,** -ы, soap-dish; soap-box. **мы́льн|ый,** soap, soapy; ~ый ка́мень, soapstone; ~ые хло́пья, soap-flakes.

мыс, -а cape, promontory.

мы́сленный, mental. **мы́слимый,** conceivable, thinkable. **мысли́тель** -я *m.* thinker. **мысли́тельный,** intellectual; thought, of thought. **мы́слить,** -лю *imp.* think; reason; conceive. **мысль,** -и, thought; idea. **мы́слящий,** thinking.

мыть, мо́ю *imp.* (*perf.* вы́~, по~) wash; **~ся,** wash (oneself); ~ся в ва́нне, have a bath; ~ся под ду́шем, take a shower.

мыча́ть, -чу́ *imp.* (*perf.* про~) low, moo; bellow; mumble.

мышело́вка, -и, mousetrap.

мы́шечный, muscular.

мышле́ние, -я, thinking, thought.

мы́шца, -ы, muscle.

мышь, -и; *gen. pl.* -е́й, mouse. **мышья́к,** -á (-у́), arsenic.

мя́гк|ий; -гок, -гка́, -о, soft; mild; gentle; ~ий ваго́н, 'soft-class' carriage, sleeping-car, sleeper; ~ий знак, soft sign, the letter ь; ~ое кре́сло, easy-chair; ~ий хлеб, new bread. **мя́гко** *adv.* softly; mildly; gently. **мя́гче,** *comp.* of мя́гкий, мя́гко. **мя́киш,** -а, soft part (of loaf), crumb. **мя́кнуть,** -нет; мяк *imp.* (*perf.* раз~) soften, become soft. **мя́коть,** -и, fleshy part, flesh; pulp.

мя́млить, -лю *imp.* (*perf.* про~), mumble; vacillate; procrastinate.

мяси́стый, fleshy; meaty; pulpy. **мясни́к,** -á, butcher. **мясн|о́й,** meat; ~ы́е консе́рвы, tinned meat; ~а́я *sb.* butcher's (shop). **мя́со,** -а, flesh; meat; beef. **мясору́бка,** -и, mincer.

мя́та, -ы, mint; peppermint.

мяте́ж, -á, mutiny, revolt. **мяте́жник,** -а, mutineer, rebel. **мяте́жный,** rebellious, mutinous; restless; stormy.

мя́тный, mint, peppermint.

мя́тый, crushed; rumpled, crumpled; ~ пар, exhaust steam. **мять,** мну, мнёшь *imp.* (*perf.* из~, раз~, с~) work up; knead; crumple, rumple; **~ся,** become crumpled; get creased, get crushed; crush (easily); hesitate, vacillate, hum and haw.

мяу́кать, -аю *imp.* mew, miaow.

мяч, -á, **мя́чик,** -а, ball.

Н

н *letter*: see эн.

на *prep.* I. +*acc.* on; on to, to, into; at; till, until; for; by; ко́мната на двои́х, a room for two; коро́че на дюйм, shorter by an inch, an inch shorter; на беду́, unfortunately; на вес, by weight; на друго́й день, (the) next day; на́ зиму, for the winter; на Но́вый год, on New Year's Day; на рубль ма́рок, a rouble's worth of stamps; на се́вер от, (to the) north of; на со́лнце, in the sun; на чёрный день, for a rainy day; на что э́то вам ну́жно? what do you want it for? на э́тот раз, this time, for this once; отложи́ть на за́втра, put off till tomorrow; перевести́ на, translate into; сесть на, get on, get in, go on board. II. +*prep.* on, upon; in; at; жа́рить на ма́сле, fry (in butter); игра́ть на роя́ле, play the piano; на ва́те, padded; на дворе́, на у́лице, out of doors; на его́ па́мяти, within his recollection; на кани́кулах, during the holidays, in the holidays; на конце́рте, at a concert; на лету́, in flight; на лю́дях, in public; на мои́х глаза́х, in my presence; на́ море, at sea; на рабо́те, at work; на э́тих днях, one of these days; на э́той неде́ле, this week; рабо́тать на не́фти, run on oil.

на *part.* here; here you are; here, take it.

на- *pref.* I. of *vbs.*, forms the perfective aspect; indicates direction on to, action applied to a surface, or to a certain quantity or number, or continued to sufficiency, excess, or the point of satisfaction or exhaustion. II. of *sbs.* and *adjs.* on. III. of *advs.* extremely, very.

наб. *abbr.* на́бережная, embankment, quay.

наба́вить, -влю *perf.*, **набавля́ть, -я́ю** *imp.* add; add to, increase, raise. **наба́вка, -и**, adding, addition, increase, rise. **наба́вочный**, extra, additional.

набалда́шник, -а, knob.

на|бальзами́ровать, -рую *perf.*

наба́т, -а, alarm, alarm-bell; бить в ~, sound the alarm, raise an alarm.

набе́г, -а, raid, foray. **набега́ть, -а́ю** *imp.*, **набежа́ть, -егу́** *perf.* run against, run into; come running, pour in; spring up; *impers.* pucker, wrinkle.

набекре́нь *adv.* on one side, over one ear.

на|бели́ть(ся, -елю́(сь, -е́ли́шь(ся *perf.*

на́бело *adv.*; переписа́ть ~, make a fair copy of.

на́бережная *sb.* embankment, quay.

наберу́, etc.: see набра́ть.

набива́ть(ся, -а́ю(сь *imp.* of наби́ть(ся. **наби́вка, -и**, stuffing, padding, packing; (textile) printing. **набивно́й**, printed.

набира́ть(ся, -а́ю(сь *imp.* of набра́ть(ся.

наби́т|ый, packed, stuffed, filled; crowded; битко́м ~, crammed, packed out; ~ый дура́к, utter fool. **наби́ть, -бью́, -бьёшь** *perf.* (*imp.* набива́ть), stuff, pack, fill; break to pieces, smash; kill, bag; print; beat, hammer, drive, knock; ~ оско́мину, set the teeth on edge; ~ ру́ку, get one's hand in, become skilled; ~ це́ну, put up the price; bid up; **~ся**, crowd in; be crowded; +*dat.* impose or force oneself on.

наблюда́тель, -я *m.* observer; spectator. **наблюда́тельность, -и**, (power of) observation. **наблюда́тельный**, observant; observation. **наблюда́ть, -а́ю** *imp.* observe, watch; +за+*instr.* take care of, look after; supervise, superintend, control. **наблюде́ние, -я**, observation; supervision, superintendence, control.

на́божный, devout, pious.

набо́йка, -и, print; printed fabric; printed pattern; (rubber, etc.) heel.

на́бок *adv.* on one side, crooked.

наболе́вший, sore, painful; ~ вопро́с, burning question, pressing problem. **наболе́ть, -е́ет** *perf.* ache, be painful.

набо́р, -а, recruiting, enlisting, engaging; collection, set; setting up, composing; matter set up; metal plaques, (horse-) brasses; ~ слов, mere verbiage. **набо́рная** *sb.* composing-room. **набо́рщик, -а**, compositor.

набра́сывать(ся, -аю(сь *imp.* of наброса́ть, набро́сить(ся.

набра́ть, -беру́, -берёшь; -а́л, -а́, -о *perf.* (*imp.* набира́ть), gather, collect, assemble; enlist, engage; compose, set up; ~ высоту́, gain height; ~ но́мер, dial a number; ~ ско́рость, pick up speed, gather speed; **~ся**, assemble, collect; +*gen.* find, acquire, pick up; ~ся сме́лости, pluck up courage.

набрести́, -еду́, -дёшь; -ёл, -ела́ *perf.*+на+*acc.* come across, hit upon.

наброса́ть, -а́ю *perf.* (*imp.* набра́сывать) throw, throw down; sketch, outline; jot down. **набро́сить, -о́шу** *perf.* (*imp.* набра́сывать) throw; **~ся**, throw oneself, fling oneself; ~ся на, attack, assail. **набро́сок, -ска**, sketch, outline, (rough) draft.

набуха́ть, -а́ет *imp.*, **набу́хнуть, -нет; -у́х** *perf.* swell.

набью́, etc.: see наби́ть.

наважде́ние, -я, delusion, hallucination.

на|ва́ксить, -кшу *perf.*

нава́ливать, -аю *imp.*, **навали́ть, -лю́, -лишь** *perf.* heap, pile up; put on top; load overload; **~ся**, lean, bring one's weight to bear; +на+*acc.* fall (up)on. **нава́лка, -и**, loading; list, listing; в нава́лку, in bulk, loose. **нава́лом** *adv.* in bulk, loose.

на|валять, -яю *perf.*
навар, -а, fat; goodness. **наваристый, наварный**, rich and nourishing. **наваривать**, -аю *imp.*, **наварить**, -рю, -ришь *perf.* weld (on); boil, cook. **наварной**, welded.
навевать, -аю *imp.* of навеять.
наведаться, -аюсь *perf.*, **наведываться**, -аюсь *imp.* call, look in.
наведение, -я, laying, laying on; placing; induction; ~ справок, making inquiries; ~ порядка, putting in order.
наведу, etc.: see навести.
навезти, -зу, -зёшь; -вёз, -ла *perf.* (*imp.* навозить) cart, bring in; + на + *acc.* drive against, drive into.
навеивать, -аю, *imp.* of навеять.
навек, навеки *adv.* for ever, for good.
навёл, etc.: see навести.
наверно, наверное *adv.* probably, most likely; certainly, for sure. **наверняка** *adv.* certainly, for sure; safely; держать пари ~, bet on a certainty.
наверстать, -аю *perf.*, **навёрстывать**, -аю *imp.* make up for, compensate for.
наверх *adv.* up, upwards; upstairs; to the top. **наверху** *adv.* above; upstairs.
навес, -а, awning, roof, canopy; penthouse; (open) shed; car-port.
навеселе *adv.* merry, a bit tight.
навесистый, overhanging, jutting. **навесить**, -ешу *perf.* (*imp.* навешивать) hang, hang up. **навеска**, -и, hanging; hinge. **навесн|ой**, hanging; ~ая дверь, hinged door.
навести, -еду, -едёшь; -вёл, -а *perf.* (*imp.* наводить) direct, lead; aim; cover, coat; cover with, spread; introduce, bring, produce; make; cause; ~ красоту, make up; ~ справку, make inquiries.
навестить, -ещу *perf.* (*imp.* навещать) visit, call on.
наветренный, windward, exposed to the wind.
навечно *adv.* for ever; in perpetuity.
навешать, -аю *perf.*, **навешивать**[1], -аю *imp.* hang, hang out; weigh out.
навешивать[2], -аю *imp.* of навесить.
навещать, -аю *imp.* of навестить.
навеять, -ею *perf.* (*imp.* навевать, навеивать) blow; cast, bring, bring about; winnow.
навзничь *adv.* backwards, on one's back.
навзрыд *adv.*; плакать ~, sob.
нависать, -ает *imp.*, **нависнуть**, -нет; -вис *perf.* hang, overhang, hang over; threaten, impend. **навислый, нависший**, beetling, overhanging.
навлекать, -аю *imp.*, **навлечь**, -еку, -ечёшь; -ёк, -ла *perf.* bring, draw, call down; incur.
наводить, -ожу, -одишь *imp.* of навести; наводящий вопрос, leading question. **наводка**, -и, aiming, directing; applying.
наводнение, -я, flood. **наводнить**, -ню *perf.*, **наводнять**, -яю *imp.* flood; inundate.
навожу: see навозить. **навожу**: see навозить.
навоз, -а (-у) dung, manure, muck. **навозить**[1], -ожу *imp.* (*perf.* у~) manure. **навозн|ый**, dung-, muck-; ~ая куча, dunghill.
навозить[2], -ожу, -озишь *imp.* of навезти.
наволока, -и, **наволочка**, -и, pillow-case.
навострить, -рю *perf.* sharpen; prick up; ~ лыжи, clear off, clear out; **~ся**, train oneself, grow skilful, become good.
на|вощить, -щу *perf.*
на|врать, -ру, -рёшь; -ал, -а, -о *perf.* tell lies, romance; talk nonsense; + в + *prep.* make a mistake (mistakes) in; get wrong.
навредить, -ежу *perf.* + *dat.* harm.
навсегда *adv.* for ever, for good; раз ~, once (and) for all.
навстречу *adv.* to meet; идти ~, go to meet; meet half-way; compromise with; consider sympathetically.
навыворот *adv.* inside out; back to front.
навык, -а, habit; knack; experience, skill.
навыкат(е *adv.* protuberant, bulging.
навылет *adv.* right through.
навынос *adv.* to take away; for consumption off the premises, off-licence.

навы́пуск *adv.* worn outside.
навы́тяжку *adv.*; стоя́ть ~, stand at attention.
навью́чивать, -аю *imp.*, **на|вью́чить,** -чу *perf.* load.
навяза́ть[1], -áет *imp.*, **навя́знуть,** -нет; -я́з *perf.* stick; э́то навя́зло у меня́ в зуба́х, I'm sick and tired of it.
навяза́ть[2], -яжу́, -я́жешь *perf.*, **навя́зывать** -аю *imp.* tie, fasten; knit; thrust, force, foist, press; **~ся,** thrust oneself, intrude; be importunate. **навя́зчив|ый,** importunate, intrusive; persistent; ~ая иде́я, fixed idea, obsession.
нагада́ть, -а́ю *perf.* predict, foretell.
на|га́дить, -а́жу *perf.*
нага́йка, -и, whip; riding-crop.
нага́н, -а, revolver.
нага́р, -а, snuff, scale.
нагиба́ть(ся, -а́ю(сь *imp.* of нагну́ть(ся.
нагишо́м *adv.* stark naked.
нагла́зник, -а, blinker; eye-shade, patch.
нагле́ц, -а́, impudent fellow. **на́глость,** -и, impudence, insolence, effrontery.
на́глухо *adv.* tightly, hermetically.
нагля́дн|ый, clear, graphic; visual; ~ые посо́бия, visual aids; ~ый уро́к, object-lesson.
нагна́ть, -гоню́, -го́нишь; -а́л, -а́, -о *perf.* (*imp.* нагоня́ть) overtake, catch up (with); drive; inspire, arouse, cause.
нагнести́, -ету́, -етёшь *perf.*, **нагнета́ть,** -а́ю *imp.* compress; supercharge. **нагнета́тель,** -я *m.* supercharger.
на́глый; -гл, -а́, -о, impudent, insolent, impertinent; bold-faced, brazen.
нагное́ние, -я, suppuration. **нагнои́ться,** -и́тся *perf.* fester, suppurate.
нагну́ть, -ну́, -нёшь *perf.* (*imp.* нагиба́ть) bend; **~ся,** bend, stoop.
нагова́ривать, -аю *imp.*, **наговори́ть,** -рю́ *perf.* slander, calumniate; talk a lot of, say a lot (of); record; ~ пласти́нку, make a record; **~ся,** talk oneself out.
наго́й; наг, -а́, -о, naked; bare.
на́голо́ *adv.* naked, bare; остри́женный на́голо, close-cropped; с ша́шками наголо́, with drawn swords.
нагоня́й, -я, scolding, telling-off. **нагоня́ть,** -я́ю *imp.* of нагна́ть.
нагора́живать, -аю *imp.* of нагороди́ть.
нагора́ть, -а́ет *imp.*, **нагоре́ть,** -ри́т *perf.* gutter; be consumed; *impers.*+ *dat.*, catch it, be scolded; ему́ за э́то нагоре́ло, he was told off for it.
наго́рн|ый, upland, mountain; mountainous; ~ая про́поведь, Sermon on the Mount.
нагороди́ть, -ожу́, -о́ди́шь *perf.* (*imp.* нагора́живать) pile up; erect, build; ~ вздо́р(а), talk a lot of nonsense.
нагота́, -ы́, nakedness, nudity, bareness.
нагота́вливать, -аю *imp.*, **наготóвить,** -влю *perf.* get in, lay in; prepare. **наготóве,** *adv.* in readiness, ready.
награ́бить, -блю *perf.* amass by dishonest means; acquire as loot.
награ́да, -ы, reward; award; decoration; prize. **награди́ть,** -ажу́ *perf.*, **награжда́ть,** -а́ю *imp.* reward; decorate; award prize to. **наградны́е** *sb. pl.* bonus. **награжде́ние,** -я, rewarding; award, decoration.
нагрева́тельный, heating. **нагрева́ть,** -а́ю *imp.*, **нагре́ть,** -е́ю *perf.* warm, heat; **~ся,** get hot, warm up.
на|гримирова́ть, -ру́ю *perf.*
нагроможда́ть, -а́ю *imp.*, **на|громозди́ть,** -зжу́ *perf.* heap up, pile up.
на|груби́ть, -блю́ *perf.* **на|грубия́нить,** -ню *perf.*
нагру́дник, -а, bib; breastplate. **нагру́дный,** breast; pectoral; ~ крест, pectoral cross.
нагружа́ть, -а́ю *imp.*, **на|грузи́ть,** -ужу́, -у́зишь *perf.* load, burden; **~ся,** load oneself, burden oneself. **нагру́зка,** -и, loading; load; work; commitments, obligation(s).
на|грязни́ть, -ню́ *perf.*
нагря́нуть, -ну *perf.* appear unexpectedly; + на + *acc.* descend on, take unawares.
над, надо *prep.*+*instr.* over, above; on, at; ~ голово́й, overhead; рабо́тать ~ диссерта́цией, be working on a dissertation; смея́ться над, laugh at.
над-, надо-. I. *vbl. pref.* indicating increase, addition; incomplete or partial action, superficiality, slightness. II. *pref.* of nouns and adjs., over-, super-

above-. **надво́дный,** above-water, surface-. **~гро́бие, -я,** epitaph. **~гро́бный,** on or over a grave. **~ду́в,** -а, supercharge, boost; pressurization. **~зе́мный,** above-ground; surface-. **~по́чечник,** -а, adrenal (gland). **~по́чечный,** adrenal.

надави́ть, -влю́, -вишь *perf.*, **нада́вливать,** -аю *imp.* press; squeeze out; crush.

надба́вить, -влю *perf.*, **надбавля́ть,** -я́ю *imp.* add; add to, increase, raise. **надба́вка,** -и, addition, increase; rise.

надвига́ть, -а́ю *imp.*, **надви́нуть,** -ну *perf.* move, pull, push; **~ся,** approach, advance, draw near.

на́двое *adv.* in two; ambiguously.

надво́рный; ~ сове́тник, Court Councillor (7th grade: see чин).

надёванный, worn, used. **надева́ть,** -а́ю *imp.* of наде́ть.

наде́жда, -ы, hope; в наде́жде+*inf.* or на+*acc.* in the hope of. **надёжный,** reliable, trustworthy, safe.

наде́л, -а, allotment.

наде́лать, -аю *perf.* make; cause; do.

надели́ть, -лю́, -лишь *perf.*, **наделя́ть,** -я́ю *imp.* endow, provide; allot to, give to.

наде́ть, -е́ну *perf.* (*imp.* надева́ть) put on.

наде́яться, -е́юсь *imp.* (*perf.* по~) hope, expect; rely.

надзира́тель, -я *m.* overseer, supervisor, superintendent; (police) inspector. **надзира́ть,** -а́ю *imp.*+за+*instr.* supervise, superintend, oversee. **надзо́р,** -а, supervision; surveillance; inspectorate.

надла́мывать(ся, -аю(сь *imp.* of надломи́ть(ся.

надлежа́щ|ий, fitting, proper, appropriate; ~им о́бразом, properly. **надлежи́т;** -жа́ло *impers.*+*dat.* it is necessary, required; ~ яви́ться в де́сять часо́в, you are required to present yourself at ten o'clock; ~ э́то сде́лать, it must be done.

надло́м, -а, break; fracture; crack; breakdown, crack-up. **надломи́ть,** -млю́, -мишь *perf.* (*imp.* надла́мывать) break; fracture; crack; break down; **~ся,** break, crack break down. **надло́мленный,** broken, cracked.

надме́нный, haughty, arrogant, supercilious.

на днях *adv.* one of these days; the other day, recently, lately.

на́до[1], **на́добно** (+*dat.*) it is necessary; I (etc.) must, ought to; I (etc.) need; так ему́ и ~, serve him right!; ~ быть, probably. **на́добность,** -и necessity need; в слу́чае на́добности, in case of need.

надо[2]: see над. **надо-**: see над-.

надоеда́ть, -а́ю *imp.*, **надое́сть,** -е́м, -е́шь, -е́ст, -еди́м *perf.* + *dat.* bore, bother, pester, plague; annoy. **надое́дливый,** boring, tiresome.

надо́лго *adv.* for a long time, for long.

надорва́ть, -ву́ -вёшь; -а́л, -а́, -о *perf.* (*imp.* надрыва́ть) tear; strain, overtax; ~**ся,** tear; overstrain oneself, rupture oneself.

надоу́мить, -млю *perf.*, **надоу́мливать,** -аю *imp.* advise, suggest an idea to.

надошью́, etc.: see надши́ть.

надписа́ть, -ишу́, -и́шешь *perf.*, **надпи́сывать,** -аю *imp.* inscribe, write. **на́дпись,** -и, inscription; notice; writing, legend; superscription, address.

надре́з, -а, cut, incision; notch. **надре́зать,** -е́жу *perf.*, **надреза́ть,** -а́ю *imp.*, **надре́зывать,** -аю *imp.* make an incision in.

надруга́тельство, -а, outrage. **надруга́ться,** -а́юсь *perf.*+над+*instr.* outrage, insult, abuse.

надры́в, -а, tear; strain; breakdown; outburst. **надрыва́ть(ся,** -а́ю(сь *imp.* of надорва́ть(ся. **надры́вный,** violent, hysterical; heartrending.

надсмо́тр, -а, supervision; surveillance. **надсмо́трщик,** -а, **-щица,** -ы, overseer; supervisor.

надста́вить, -влю *perf.*, **надставля́ть,** -я́ю *imp.* lengthen. **надста́вка,** -и, lengthening; piece put on.

надстра́ивать, -аю *imp.*, **надстро́ить,** -о́ю *perf.* build on top; extend upwards. **надстро́йка,** -и, building upwards; superstructure.

надува́ла, -ы *m.* and *f.* swindler, cheat. **надува́тельство,** -а, swindle, cheating, trickery. **надува́ть(ся,** -а́ю(сь *imp.* of наду́ть(ся. **надувно́й,** pneumatic, inflatable.

наду́манный, far-fetched, artificial, invented. **наду́мать,** -аю *perf.*, **наду́мывать,** -аю *imp.* make up one's mind; think up, make up.

наду́тый, swollen, inflated; haughty; sulky. **наду́ть,** -у́ю *perf.* (*imp.* надува́ть) inflate, blow up; puff out; dupe, swindle; ~ гу́бы, pout; **~ся,** fill out, swell out; be puffed up; pout, sulk.

наду́шенный, scented, perfumed. **на|души́ть(ся,** -ушу́(сь, -у́шишь(ся *perf.*

надшива́ть, -а́ю *imp.*, **надши́ть,** -дошью́, -дошьёшь *perf.* lengthen; sew on.

на|дыми́ть, -млю́ *perf.* **наеда́ться,** -а́юсь *imp.* of нае́сться.

наедине́ *adv.* privately, alone.

нае́зд, -а, flying visit; raid. **нае́здить,** -зжу *perf.*, **нае́зживать,** -аю *imp.* travel, cover; travel over; make by driving; break in. **нае́здник,** -а, horseman, rider; jockey. **нае́здница,** -ы, horsewoman, rider. **наезжа́ть,** -а́ю *imp.* of нае́здить, нае́хать; pay occasional visits. **нае́зженный,** well-travelled. **нае́зжий,** newly-arrived.

наём, на́йма, hire, hiring; renting; взять в ~ rent; сдать в ~ let. **наёмник,** -а, hireling; mercenary. **наёмный,** hired, rented. **наёмщик,** -а, tenant, lessee.

нае́сться, -е́мся, -е́шься, -е́стся, -еди́мся *perf.* (*imp.* наеда́ться) eat one's fill; stuff oneself.

нае́хать, -е́ду *perf.* (*imp.* наезжа́ть) come down arrive unexpectedly; +на +*acc.* run into, collide with.

нажа́ть[1], -жму́, -жмёшь *perf.* (*imp.* нажима́ть) press; squeeze; press on; put pressure (on).

нажа́ть[2], -жну́, -жнёшь *perf.* (*imp.* нажина́ть) reap harvest.

нажда́к, -а́, emery. **нажда́чн|ый;** ~ая бума́га, emery paper.

нажи́ва, -ы, profit, gain.

нажива́ть(ся, -а́ю(сь *imp.* of нажи́ть(ся. **наживно́й,** that may be acquired.

нажи́м, -а, pressure; clamp. **нажима́ть,** -а́ю *imp.* of нажа́ть[1]. **нажи́мистый,** exacting. **нажимно́й, нажи́мный,** pressure.

нажина́ть, -а́ю *imp.* of нажа́ть[2].

нажи́ть, -иву́, -ивёшь; на́жил, -а́, -о *perf.* (*imp.* нажива́ть) acquire, gain; contract, incur; ~ враго́в, make enemies; **~ся;** -жи́лся, -а́сь, get rich, make a fortune.

нажму́, etc.: see нажа́ть[1]. **нажну́,** etc.: see нажа́ть[2].

наза́втра *adv.* (the) next day.

наза́д *adv.* back, backwards; (тому) ~, ago. **назади́** *adv.* behind.

назва́ние, -я, name; title. **назва́ный,** adopted; sworn. **назва́ть,** -зову́, -зовёшь; -а́л, -а́, -о *perf.* (*imp.* называ́ть) call, name; invite; **~ся,** be called; call oneself; give one's name.

назём, -а, dung.

назе́мный, ground, surface. **на́земь** *adv.* to the ground.

назида́ние, -я, edification. **назида́тельный,** edifying.

на́зло́ *adv.* out of spite; to spite.

назнача́ть, -а́ю *imp.*, **назна́чить,** -чу *perf.* appoint; nominate; fix, set; prescribe.

назову́, etc.: see назва́ть.

назо́йливый, importunate, persistent; tiresome.

назрева́ть, -а́ет *imp.*, **назре́ть,** -е́ет *perf.* ripen, mature; become urgent, imminent, inevitable.

назубо́к *adv.*; знать ~, know by heart.

называ́емый; так ~, so-called. **называ́ть(ся** -а́ю(сь *imp.* of назва́ть(ся; что называ́ется, as they say.

наи- *pref.* used with comparatives and superlatives to signify the very highest degree. **наибо́лее** *adv.* (the) most. **~бо́льший,** greatest, biggest; ~бо́льший о́бщий дели́тель, highest common factor. **~вы́сший,** highest. **~лу́чший,** best. **~ме́нее** *adv.* (the) least. **~ме́ньший,** least, smallest; ~ме́ньшее о́бщее кра́тное, lowest common multiple. **~па́че** *adv.* most of all, especially. **~ху́дший,** worst.

наи́гранный, put on, assumed; forced. **наигра́ть,** -а́ю *perf.*, **наи́грывать,** -аю *imp.* win; play, strum, pick out; ~

пласти́нку, make a recording. **на́игрыш,** -а, folk-tune; artificiality, staginess.

наизна́нку *adv.* inside out.

наизу́сть *adv.* by heart.

наименова́ние, -я, name; title. **на|именова́ть,** -ну́ю *perf.*

наискосо́к, на́искось *adv.* obliquely, diagonally, aslant.

найти́е, -я, inspiration; influence; по найти́ю, instinctively, by intuition.

найдёныш, -а, foundling.

наймит, -а, hireling.

найму, etc.: see наня́ть.

найти́, -йду́, -йдёшь; нашёл, -шла́, -шло́ *perf.* (*imp.* находи́ть) find; find out, discover; gather, collect; +на+*acc.* come across, come over, come upon; **~сь,** be found; be, be situated; turn up; rise to the occasion, find the right thing (to do, say, etc.); не ~сь, be at a loss.

нака́з, -а, order, instructions; mandate. **наказа́ние,** -я, punishment. **наказа́ть,** -ажу́, -а́жешь *perf.*, **нака́зывать,** -аю *imp.* punish; order, tell. **наказу́емый,** punishable.

нака́л, -а, heating; incandescence, (white-)heat. **накалённый,** heated; red-hot, white-hot; incandescent; strained, tense. **нака́ливать,** -аю *imp.*, **накали́ть,** -лю́ *perf.*, **накаля́ть,** -я́ю *imp.* heat; make red-hot, white-hot; strain, make tense; **~ся,** glow, become incandescent; heat up; become strained, become tense.

нака́лывать(ся, -аю(сь *imp.* of наколо́ть(ся.

накану́не *adv.* the day before; *prep.*+*gen.* on the eve of the day before.

на|ка́пать, -аю *perf.* (*imp.* нака́пывать) pour out (drop by drop), measure out; +*instr.* spill.

нака́пливать(ся, -аю(сь *imp.* of накопи́ть(ся. **нака́пывать,** -аю *imp.* of нака́пать. **на|ка́ркать,** -аю *perf.*

накача́ть, -а́ю *perf.*, **нака́чивать** -аю *imp.* pump; pump up; **~ся,** get tight.

наки́д, -а, loop; made stitch. **накида́ть,** -а́ю *perf.*, **наки́дывать,** -аю *imp.* throw, throw down. **наки́дка,** -и, cloak, cape; wrap; pillow-cover; increase, extra charge. **наки́нуть,** -ну *perf.*, **наки́дывать,** -аю *imp.* throw; throw on, slip on; **~ся,** throw oneself, fling oneself; ~ся на, attack, assail.

накипа́ть, -а́ет *imp.*, **накипе́ть,** -пи́т *perf.* form a scum, form a scale; boil up. **на́кипь,** -и, scum; scale, fur, deposit.

накла́дка, -и, bracket; hair-piece, wig; appliqué. **накладна́я** *sb.* invoice, way-bill. **накладн|о́й,** laid on; false; ~о́е зо́лото, rolled gold; ~о́й карма́н, patch pocket; ~о́е серебро́, plated silver, (silver) plate; ~ы́е расхо́ды, overheads. **накла́дывать,** -аю *imp.* of наложи́ть.

на|клевета́ть, -ещу́, -е́щешь *perf.* **наклёвываться,** -ается *imp.* of наклю́нуться.

накле́ивать, -аю *imp.*, **накле́ить,** -е́ю *perf.* stick on, paste on. **накле́йка,** -и, sticking (on, up); label; patch.

наклепа́ть, -а́ю *perf.*, **наклёпывать,** -аю *imp.* rivet; make roughly, knock together.

накло́н, -а, slope, inclination, incline; bend. **наклоне́ние,** -я, inclination; mood. **наклони́ть,** -ню́, -нишь *perf.* **наклоня́ть,** -я́ю *imp.* incline, bend; **~ся,** stoop, bend; bow. **накло́нность,** -и, learning, inclination, propensity. **накло́нный,** inclined, sloping.

наклю́нуться, -нется *perf.* (*imp.* наклёвываться) peck its way out of the shell; turn up.

накова́льня, -и anvil.

нако́жный, cutaneous, skin.

нако́лка, -и, pinning, sticking; (pinned-on) ornament for hair; tattooing, tattoo. **наколо́ть**[1], -лю́, -лешь *perf.* (*imp.* нака́лывать) prick; pin; stick; **~ся,** prick oneself.

наколо́ть[2], -лю́, -лешь *perf.* (*imp.* нака́лывать) chop. split.

наконе́ц *adv.* at last; in the end; finally. **наконе́чник,** -а, tip, point. **наконе́чный,** final; on the end.

на|копи́ть, -плю́, -пишь *perf.*, **накопля́ть,** -я́ю *imp.* (*imp.* also нака́пливать) accumulate, amass, pile up, store; **~ся,** accumulate. **накопле́ние,** -я, accumulation; storage; build-up;

~ да́нных, data storage; (computer) memory.

на|копти́ть, -пчу́ *perf.* **на|корми́ть**, -млю́, -мишь *perf.*

накра́пывать, -ает *imp.* spit, drizzle.

накра́сить, -а́шу *perf.* (*imp.* накра́шивать) paint; make up. **на|кра́ситься**, -а́шусь *perf.*

на|крахма́лить, -лю *perf.* **накра́шивать**, -аю, *imp.* of накра́сить.

на|крени́ть, -ню́ *perf.* **накрени́ться**, -ни́тся *perf.*, **накреня́ться**, -я́ется *imp.* tilt; list, take a list, heel.

на́крепко *adv.* fast, tight; strictly.

на́крест *adv.* crosswise.

накрича́ть, -чу́ *perf.* (+на+*acc.*) shout (at).

на|кроши́ть, -шу́, -шишь *perf.* **накро́ю**, etc.: see накры́ть.

накрути́ть, -учу́, -у́тишь *perf.*, **накру́чивать**, -аю *imp.* wind, twist.

накрыва́ть, -а́ю *imp.*, **накры́ть**, -ро́ю *perf.* cover; catch; ~ (на) стол, lay the table; ~ на ме́сте, catch red-handed; **~ся**, cover oneself.

накупа́ть, -а́ю *imp.*, **накупи́ть**, -плю́, -пишь *perf.* buy up.

наку́ренный, smoky, smoke-filled. **накури́ть**, -рю́, -ришь *perf.* fill with smoke; distil.

налага́ть, -а́ю *imp.* of наложи́ть.

нала́дить, -а́жу *perf.* **нала́живать**, -аю *imp.* regulate, adjust; tune; repair; organize; **~ся**, come right; get going.

на|лга́ть, -лгу́, -лжёшь; -а́л, -а́, -о *perf.*

нале́во *adv.* to the left; on the side.

налёг, etc.: see нале́чь. **налега́ть**, -а́ю *imp.* of нале́чь.

налегке́ *adv.* lightly dressed; without luggage.

на|лепи́ть, -плю́, -пишь *perf.*

налёт, -а, raid, swoop; flight; thin coating, bloom, patina; touch, shade; с ~а, suddenly, without warning or preparation, just like that. **налета́ть**[1] -а́ю *perf.* have flown. **налета́ть**[2], -а́ю *imp.*, **налете́ть**, -лечу́ *perf.* swoop down; come flying; spring up; +на+*acc.* fly or drive into, run into. **налётчик**, -а, raider, robber.

нале́чь, -ля́гу, -ля́жешь; -лёг, -ла́ *perf.* (*imp.* налега́ть) lean, apply one's weight, lie; apply oneself; +на+*acc.* put one's weight behind.

налжёшь, etc.: see налга́ть.

нали́в, -а, pouring in; ripening, swelling. **налива́ть(ся**, -а́ю(сь *imp.* of нали́ть(ся. **нали́вка**, -и, (fruit-flavoured) liqueur. **наливн|о́й**, ripe, juicy; for carriage of liquids; overshot; ~о́й док, wet dock; ~о́е су́дно, tanker.

на|линова́ть, -ну́ю *perf.*

налипа́ть, -а́ет *imp.*, **нали́пнуть**, -нет; -и́п *perf.* stick.

налито́й, plump, juicy; ~ кро́вью, bloodshot. **нали́ть**, -лью́, -льёшь; на́ли́л, -а́, -о *perf.* (*imp.* налива́ть) pour (out). fill; pour on; **~ся**; -и́лся́, -а́сь, -и́ло́сь, pour in, run in; ripen, swell.

налицо́ *adv.* present, manifest; available, on hand.

нали́чие, -я, presence. **нали́чность**, -и, presence; amount on hand; cash, ready money. **нали́чн|ый** on hand, in hand, available; cash; ~ые (де́ньги), cash, ready money.

наловчи́ться, -чу́сь *perf.* become skilful.

нало́г, -а, tax. **нало́говый**, tax. **налогоплате́льщик**, -а, taxpayer. **нало́женн|ый**; ~ым платежо́м, C.O.D.

наложи́ть, -жу́, -жишь *perf.* (*imp.* накла́дывать, налага́ть) lay (in, on), put (in, on); apply; impose; ~ отпеча́ток, leave traces; ~ штраф, impose a fine; ~ на себя́ ру́ки, lay hands on oneself, commit suicide.

на|лощи́ть, -щу́ *perf.* **налью́**, etc.: see нали́ть.

налюбова́ться, -бу́юсь *perf.*+*instr.* or на+*acc.*, gaze one's fill at, admire (sufficiently).

наля́гу, etc.: see нале́чь.

нам, etc.: see мы.

на|ма́зать, -а́жу *perf.*, **нама́зывать**, -аю *imp.* oil, grease; smear, spread; daub; **~ся**, make up.

на|малева́ть, -лю́ю *perf.* **на|мара́ть**, -а́ю *perf.* **на|ма́слить**, -лю *perf.* **нама́тывать**, -аю *imp.* of намота́ть.

нама́чивать, -аю *imp.* of намочи́ть.

наме́дни *adv.* the other day, recently.

намёк, -а, hint. **намека́ть**, -а́ю *imp.*,

намекну́ть, -ну́, -нёшь *perf.* hint, allude.
на|мели́ть, -лю́ *perf.*
намерева́ться, -а́юсь *imp.*+*inf.* intend to, mean to, be about to. **наме́рен** *predic.*; я ~+*inf.* I intend to, I mean to; что она́ ~а сде́лать? what is she going to do? **наме́рение**, -я, intention, purpose. **наме́ренный**, intentional, deliberate.
на|мета́ть, -а́ю *perf.* **на|ме́тить**[1], **-е́чу** *perf.*
наме́тить[2], -е́чу *perf.* (*imp.* намеча́ть) plan, project; outline; nominate, select; **~ся**, be outlined, take shape. **намётка**[1], -и, draft, preliminary outline.
намётка[2], -и, tacking, basting; tacking thread.
намеча́ть(ся, -а́ю(сь *imp.* of наме́тить(ся.
намно́го *adv.* much, far.
намока́ть, -а́ю *imp.*, **намо́кнуть**, -ну *perf.* get wet.
намо́рдник, -а, muzzle.
на|мо́рщить(ся, -щу(сь *perf.* **на|мости́ть**, -ощу́ *perf.*
на|мота́ть, -а́ю *perf.* (*imp.* also нама́тывать) wind, reel.
на|мочи́ть, -очу́, -о́чишь *perf.* (*imp.* also нама́чивать) wet; soak, steep; splash, spill.
намы́в, -а, alluvium. **намывно́й**, alluvial. **намы́ливать**, -аю *imp.*, **на|мы́лить**, -лю *perf.* soap. **намы́ть**, -мо́ю *perf.* wash; wash down, wash up.
нанести́, -су́, -сёшь; -ёс, -ла́ *perf.* (*imp.* наноси́ть) carry, bring; draw, plot; cause, inflict; ~ оскорбле́ние, insult; ~ уда́р+*dat.* deal a blow; hit, punch, strike; ~ уще́рб, damage.
на|низа́ть, -ижу́, -и́жешь *perf.*, **нани́зывать**, -аю *imp.* string, thread.
нанима́тель, -я *m.* tenant; employer. **нанима́ть(ся**, -а́ю(сь *imp.* of наня́ть(ся.
нано́с, -а, alluvial deposit; drift. **наноси́ть**, -ошу́, -о́сишь *imp.* of нанести́. **нано́сный**, alluvial; alien, borrowed.
наня́ть, найму́, -мёшь; на́нял, -а́, -о *perf.* (*imp.* нанима́ть) hire, engage; rent; **~ся**, get a job, get work.
наоборо́т *adv.* on the contrary; back to front; the other, the wrong way (round); и ~, and vice versa.
наобу́м *adv.* without thinking, at random.
нао́тмашь *adv.* with a wild swing (of the hand), violently, full.
наотре́з *adv.* flatly, point-blank.
напада́ть, -а́ю *imp.* of напа́сть. **напада́ющий** *sb.* forward. **нападе́ние**, -я, attack; forwards. **напа́дки**, -док *pl.* attacks, accusations.
на|па́костить, -ощу *perf.*
напа́рник, -а, co-driver, fellow-worker; team-mate; mate.
напа́сть, -аду́, -адёшь; -а́л *perf.* (*imp.* напада́ть) на+*acc.* attack; descend on; grip, seize, come over; come upon, come across. **напа́сть**, -и, misfortune, disaster.
на|па́чкать, -аю *perf.*
напе́в, -а, melody, tune. **напева́ть**, -а́ю *imp.* of напе́ть. **напе́вный**, melodious.
наперебо́й, **наперере́в** *adv.* interrupting, vying with, one another.
напере́д *adv.* in advance, beforehand.
напереко́р *adv.* + *dat.* in defiance of, counter to.
наперерв: see наперебо́й.
напёрсток, -тка, thimble.
на|пе́рчить, -чу *perf.*
напе́ть, -пою́, -поёшь *perf.* (*imp.* напева́ть) sing; hum, croon; ~ пласти́нку, make a record.
на|печа́тать(ся, -аю(сь *perf.* **напива́ться**, -а́юсь *imp.* of напи́ться.
напи́лок, -лка, **напи́льник**, -а, file.
на|писа́ть, -ишу́, -и́шешь *perf.*
напи́ток, -тка, drink, beverage. **напи́ться**, -пью́сь, -пьёшься; -и́лся, -а́сь, -и́ло́сь *perf.* (*imp.* напива́ться) quench one's thirst, drink; get drunk.
напиха́ть, -а́ю *perf.*, **напи́хивать**, -аю *imp.* cram, stuff.
на|плева́ть, -люю́, -люёшь *perf.*; ~! to hell with it! who cares?
наплե́чник, -а, shoulder-strap. **напле́чный**, shoulder-.
наплы́в, -а, flow, influx; accumulation; dissolve; canker.

наплюю́ etc.: see наплева́ть.
напова́л *adv.* outright on the spot.
наподо́бие *prep.*+*gen.* like, not unlike.
на|пои́ть, -ою́, -о́ишь *perf.*
напока́з *adv.* for show; выставля́ть ~, display; show off.
наполне́ние, -я, filling; inflation. **напо́лнитель, -я** *m.* filler. **напо́лнить(ся, -ню(сь** *perf.*, **наполня́ть(ся, -я́ю(сь** *imp.* fill.
наполови́ну *adv.* half.
напомина́ние, -я, reminder. **напомина́ть, -а́ю** *imp.*, **напо́мнить, -мню** *perf.* remind.
напо́р, -а, pressure. **напо́ристость, -и,** energy; push, go. **напо́ристый,** energetic, pushing. **напо́рный,** pressure.
напо́ртить, -рчу *perf.* spoil; damage; +*dat.* injure, harm.
напосле́док *adv.* in the end; after all.
напою́, etc.: see напе́ть, напои́ть.
напр. *abbr.* наприме́р, for example.
напра́вить, -влю *perf.*, **направля́ть, -я́ю** *imp.* direct; aim; send; refer; sharpen, whet; organize; **~ся,** make (for), go (towards); get going, get under way. **напра́вка, -и,** setting, whetting. **направле́ние, -я,** direction; trend, tendency, turn; order, warrant, directive; action, effect; sector. **напра́вленный,** purposeful, unswerving; directional. **направля́ющая** *sb.* guide. **направля́ющий,** guiding, guide; leading.
напра́во *adv.* to the right, on the right.
напра́сно *adv.* vainly, in vain, to no purpose, for nothing; wrong, unjustly, mistakenly. **напра́сный,** vain, idle; unfounded, unjust.
напра́шиваться, -аюсь *imp.* of напроси́ться.
наприме́р, for example, for instance.
на|прока́зить, -а́жу *perf.* **на|прока́зничать, -аю** *perf.*
напрока́т *adv.* for hire, on hire; взять ~, hire.
напролёт *adv.* through, without a break; всю ночь ~, all night long.
напроло́м *adv.* straight, regardless of obstacles; идти́ ~, push one's way through.
на|проро́чить, -чу *perf.*
напроси́ться, -ошу́сь, -о́сишься *perf.* (*imp.* напра́шиваться) thrust oneself, force oneself; suggest itself; ~ на, ask for, invite; ~ на комплиме́нты, fish for compliments.
напро́тив *adv.* opposite; on the contrary; + *dat.* against, to spite. **напро́тив** *prep.*+*gen.* opposite.
напру́живать, -аю *imp.*, **напру́жить, -жу** *perf.* strain; tense; **~ся,** become tense, become taut.
напряга́ть(ся, -а́ю(сь *imp.* of напря́чь(ся. **напряже́ние, -я,** tension; effort, exertion, strain; stress; voltage; ~ смеще́ния, grid bias. **напряжённый,** tense, strained; intense; intensive.
напрями́к *adv.* straight, straight out.
напря́чь, -ягу́, -яжёшь; -я́г, -ла́ *perf.* (*imp.* напряга́ть) tense, strain; **~ся,** exert oneself, strain oneself; become tense.
на|пуга́ть(ся, -а́ю(сь *perf.* **на|пу́дрить(ся, -рю(сь** *perf.*
на́пуск, -а, letting in; slipping, letting loose; bloused or loosely hanging part.
напуска́ть, -а́ю *imp.*, **напусти́ть, -ущу́, -у́стишь** *perf.* let in, admit; let loose, slip; ~ на себя́, affect, put on, assume; **~**ся+на+*acc.* fly at, go for. **напускно́й,** assumed, put on, artificial.
напу́тать, -аю *perf.* (*imp.* напу́тывать) + в + *prep.* make a mess of, make a hash of; confuse. get wrong.
напу́тственный, parting, farewell. **напу́тствие, -я,** parting words, farewell speech.
напу́тывать, -аю *imp.* of напу́тать.
напуха́ть, -а́ет *imp.*, **напу́хнуть, -нет** *perf.* swell (up).
на|пыли́ть, -лю́ *perf.*
напы́щен|ный, pompous, bombastic, high-flown.
напью́сь, etc.: see напи́ться.
наравне́ *adv.* level, keeping pace; equally; on an equal footing.
нараспа́шку *adv.* unbuttoned; у него́ душа́ ~, he wears his heart on his sleeve.
нараспе́в *adv.* in a sing-song (way).
нараста́ние, -я, growth, accumulation; build-up. **нараста́ть, -а́ет** *imp.*, **нара-**

сти́, -тёт; -рос, -ла́ *perf.* grow, form; increase, swell; accumulate.

нарасхва́т *adv.* very quickly, like hot cakes; раскупа́ться ~, be in great demand.

нарва́ть[1], -рву́, -рвёшь; -а́л, -а́, -о *perf.* (*imp.* нарыва́ть) pick; tear up.

нарва́ть[2], -вёт; -а́л, -а́, -о *perf.* (*imp.* нарыва́ть) gather, come to a head.

нарва́ться, -ву́сь, -вёшься; -а́лся, -ала́сь, -а́ло́сь *perf.* (*imp.* нарыва́ться)+на+*acc.* run into, run up against.

наре́з, -а, thread, groove; rifling; plot. **наре́зать**, -е́жу *perf.*, **нареза́ть**, -а́ю *imp.* cut, cut up, slice, carve; thread, rifle; allot, parcel out. **наре́зка**, -и, cutting, slicing; thread, rifling. **нарезно́й**, rifled.

нарека́ние, -я, censure.

наре́чие[1], -я, dialect.

наре́чие[2], -я, adverb. **наре́чный**, adverbial.

на|рисова́ть, -су́ю *perf.*

нарица́тельн|ый, nominal; и́мя ~ое, common noun; ~ая сто́имость, face value, nominal value.

нарко́з, -а, anaesthesia; narcosis; anaesthetic. **наркома́н**, -а, -**ма́нка**, -и, drug addict. **наркома́ния**, -и, drug addiction.

наро́д, -а (-у), people.

народи́ться, -ожу́сь *perf.* (*imp.* нарожда́ться) be born; come into being, arise.

наро́дник, -а, narodnik, populist. **наро́днический** populist. **наро́дность**, -и, nationality; people; national character. **наро́дный**, national; folk; popular; people's. **народонаселе́ние**, -я population.

нарожда́ться, -а́юсь *imp.* of народи́ться. **нарожде́ние**, -я, birth, springing up.

наро́с, etc.: see нарасти́. **наро́ст**, -а, outgrowth, excrescence; burr, tumour; incrustation, scale.

нарочи́тый, deliberate, intentional. **наро́чно** *adv.* on purpose, purposely, deliberately; for fun, jokingly. **на́рочный** *sb.* courier; express messenger, special messenger; с ~м, express delivery.

на́рты, нарт *pl.*, **на́рта**, -ы. sledge.

нару́жно *adv.* outwardly, on the surface. **нару́жность**, -и, exterior, (outward) appearance. **нару́жный**, external, exterior, outward; for external use only, not to be taken. **нару́жу** *adv.* outside, out.

на|румя́нить(ся, -ню(сь *perf.*

нару́чник, -а, handcuff, manacle. **нару́чн|ый**: ~ые часы́, wrist-watch.

наруше́ние, -я, breach; infringement, violation; offence. **наруши́тель**, -я *m.* transgressor, infringer, violator; ~ грани́цы illegal entrant. **нару́шить**, -шу *perf.*, **наруша́ть**, -а́ю *imp.* break; disturb, infringe, violate, transgress.

на́ры, нар *pl.* plank-bed.

навы́в, -а, abscess, boil. **нарыва́ть(ся**, -а́ю(сь *imp.* of нарва́ть(ся.

наря́д[1], -а, order warrant; duty; detail.

наря́д[2], -а, attire, apparel, dress. **наряди́ть**, -яжу́ *perf.* (*imp.* наряжа́ть) dress array; dress up; **~ся**, dress up, array oneself. **наря́дный**, well-dressed, elegant, smart.

наряду́ *adv.* alike, equally; side by side; ~ с э́тим, at the same time.

наряжа́ть(ся, -а́ю(сь *imp.* of наряди́ть(ся. **нас**: see мы.

насади́ть, -ажу́, -а́дишь *perf.*, **насажда́ть**, -а́ю *imp.* (*imp.* also наса́живать) plant; seat; propagate; implant, inculcate; set fix, stick, pin. **наса́дка**, -и, setting, fixing, putting on; hafting; bait; nozzle, mouthpiece. **насажа́ть**, -а́ю *perf.* (*imp.* наса́живать) plant, seat. **насажде́ние**, -я, planting; plantation stand, wood; spreading, dissemination, propagation. **наса́живать**, -аю *imp.* of насади́ть, насажа́ть.

наса́ливать, -аю *imp.* of насоли́ть.

наса́сывать, -аю *imp.* of насоса́ть.

насви́стывать, -аю *imp.* whistle.

наседа́ть, -а́ю *imp.* (*perf.* насе́сть) press; settle, collect. **насе́дка**, -и, sitting hen.

насека́ть, -а́ю *imp.* of насе́чь. **насеко́мое** *sb.* insect. **насеку́**, etc.: see насе́чь.

населе́ние, -я, population, inhabitants; settling, peopling. **населённость**, -и, density of population. **населённый**, populated, settled, inhabited; thickly populated, populous; ~ пункт, settlement; inhabited place; built-up area. **насели́ть, -лю́** *perf.*, **населя́ть, -я́ю** *imp.* settle, people, inhabit. **насе́льник, -а**, inhabitant.

насе́ст, -а, roost, perch. **насе́сть, -ся́ду, -се́л** *perf.* of наседа́ть.

насе́чка, -и, incision, cut; notch; inlay. **насе́чь, -еку́, -ечёшь; -е́к, -ла́** *perf.* (*imp.* насека́ть) cut; cut up; incise; damascene.

насиде́ть, -ижу́ *perf.*, **наси́живать, -аю** *imp.* hatch; warm. **наси́женн|ый**, long occupied; ~ое ме́сто, old haunt, old home.

наси́лие, -я, violence, force, aggression. **наси́ловать, -лую** *imp.* (*perf.* из~) coerce constrain; rape. **наси́лу** *adv.* with difficulty, hardly. **наси́льник, -а**, aggressor, user of violence, violator. **наси́льно** *adv.* by force, forcibly. **наси́льственный**, violent, forcible.

наска́кивать, -аю *imp.* of наскочи́ть.

на|сканда́лить, -лю *perf.*

наскво́зь *adv.* through, throughout.

наско́лько *adv.* how much? how far?; as far as, so far as.

на́скоро *adv.* hastily hurriedly.

наскочи́ть, -очу́, -о́чишь *perf.* (*imp.* наска́кивать) + на + *acc.* run into, collide with; fly at.

наскреба́ть -а́ю *imp.*, **наскрести́, -ебу́, -ебёшь; -ёб, -ла́** *perf.* scrape up, scrape together.

наску́чить, -чу *perf.* bore.

наслади́ть, -ажу́ *perf.*, **наслажда́ть, -а́ю** *imp.* delight, please; **~ся**, enjoy, take pleasure, delight. **наслажде́ние, -я**, delight pleasure, enjoyment.

насла́иваться, -а́ется *imp.* of наслои́ться.

насле́дие, -я, legacy; heritage. **на|следи́ть, -ежу́** *perf.* **насле́дник, -а**, heir, legatee; successor. **насле́дница, -ы**, heiress. **насле́дный**, next in succession; ~ принц, crown prince. **насле́дование, -я**, inheritance, succession. **насле́довать, -дую** *perf.* and *imp.* (*perf.* also у~) inherit, succeed to. **насле́дственный**, hereditary, inherited. **насле́дство, -а**, inheritance, legacy; heritage.

наслое́ние, -я, stratification; stratum, layer, deposit. **наслои́ться, -ои́тся** *perf.* (*imp.* насла́иваться) form a layer or stratum, be deposited.

наслы́шаться, -шусь *perf.* have heard a lot. **наслы́шка, -и**: по наслы́шке, by hearsay.

на́смерть *adv.* to death; to the death.

насмеха́ться, -а́юсь *imp.* jeer, gibe; + над + *instr.* ridicule. **на|смеши́ть, -шу́** *perf.* **насме́шка, -и**, mockery, ridicule; gibe. **насме́шливый**, mocking, derisive; sarcastic.

на́сморк, -а, cold in the head.

насмотре́ться, -рю́сь, -ри́шься *perf.* see a lot; ~ на, see enough of, have looked enough at.

насоли́ть, -олю́, -о́ли́шь *perf.* (*imp.* наса́ливать) salt, pickle; oversalt; annoy, spite, injure.

на|сори́ть, -рю́ *perf.*

насо́с, -а, pump. **насоса́ть, -осу́, -осёшь** *perf.* (*imp.* наса́сывать) pump; suck; **~ся**, suck one's fill; drink oneself drunk. **насо́сный**, pumping.

на́спех *adv.* hastily.

на|спле́тничать, -аю *perf.* **настава́ть, -таёт** *imp.* of наста́ть.

настави́тельный, edifying, instructive.

наста́вить[1], **-влю** *perf.* (*imp.* наставля́ть) edify; exhort, admonish.

наста́вить[2], **-влю** *perf.* (*imp.* наставля́ть) lengthen; add, add on; aim, point; set up, place. **наста́вка, -и**, addition.

наставле́ние, -я, exhortation, admonition; directions, instructions, manual.

наставля́ть -я́ю *imp.* of наста́вить.

наста́вник, -а, tutor, teacher, mentor; кла́ссный ~, form-master. **наста́вничество**, a, tutorship, tutelage.

наставно́й, lengthened; added.

наста́ивать(ся, -аю(сь *imp.* of настоя́ть(ся.

наста́ть, -а́нет *perf.* (*imp.* настава́ть) come, begin, set in.

на́стежь *adv.* wide, wide open.

настелю́, etc.: see настла́ть.

насте́нн|ый, hanging; ~ые часы́, wall-clock.

настига́ть, -а́ю *imp.*, **насти́гнуть**, **насти́чь**, -и́гну; -и́г *perf.* catch up with, overtake.

насти́л, -а, flooring, planking. **настила́ть**, -а́ю *imp.* of настла́ть.

насти́чь: see настига́ть.

настла́ть, -телю́, -те́лешь *perf.* (*imp.* настила́ть) lay, spread.

насто́й, -я, infusion; (fruit-flavoured) liqueur, cordial. **насто́йка**, -и, (fruit-flavoured) liqueur, cordial.

насто́йчивый, persistent; urgent, insistent.

насто́лько *adv.* so, so much; ~, наско́лько, as much as.

насто́льник, -а, table-lamp, desk-lamp. **насто́льный**, table, desk; for constant reference, in constant use.

насторá́живать, -аю *imp.*, **насторожи́ть**, -жу́ *perf.* set; prick up, strain; **~ся**, prick up one's ears. **настороже́** *adv.* on the alert, on one's guard. **насторо́женный**; -ен, -енна, **насторожённый**; -ён, -ена́ or -ённа, guarded; alert.

настоя́ние, -я, insistence. **настоя́тельный**, persistent, insistent; urgent, pressing. **настоя́ть**¹, -ою́ *perf.* (*imp.* наста́ивать) insist.

настоя́ть², -ою́ *perf.* (*imp.* наста́ивать) brew, draw, infuse; **~ся**, draw, stand; stand a long time.

настоя́щее *sb.* the present. **настоя́щий** (the) present, this; real, genuine.

настра́ивать(ся, -аю(сь *imp.* of настро́ить(ся.

настри́г, -а, shearing, clipping; clip. **настри́чь**, -игу́, -ижёшь; -и́г *perf.* shear, clip.

на́строго *adv.* strictly.

настрое́ние, -я, mood, temper, humour; ~ умо́в, public feeling, general mood. **настро́ить**, -о́ю *perf.* (*imp.* настра́ивать) tune, tune in; dispose, incline; incite; **~ся**, dispose oneself, incline, settle; make up one's mind. **настро́йка**, -и, tuning; tuning in; tuning signal. **настро́йщик**, -а, tuner.

на|строчи́ть, -чу́ *perf.*

настря́пать, -аю *perf.* cook; cook up.

наступа́тельный, offensive; aggressive. **наступа́ть**¹, -а́ю *imp.* of наступи́ть¹.

наступа́ть², -а́ет *imp.* of наступи́ть². **наступа́ющий**, coming, beginning.

наступа́ющий *sb.* attacker.

наступи́ть¹, -плю́, -пишь *perf.* (*imp.* наступа́ть) tread, step; attack; advance.

наступи́ть², -у́пит *perf.* (*imp.* наступа́ть) come, set in; fall; наступи́ла ночь, night had fallen; наступи́ла тишина́, silence fell. **наступле́ние**¹, -я, coming, approach; с ~м но́чи, at nightfall.

наступле́ние², -я, offensive, attack.

насу́питься, -плюсь *perf.*, **насу́пливаться**, -аюсь *imp.* frown, knit one's brows.

на́сухо *adv.* dry. **насу́шивать**, -аю *imp.*, **насуши́ть**, -шу́, -шишь *perf.* dry.

насу́щность, -и, urgency. **насу́щный**, urgent, vital, essential; хлеб ~, daily bread.

насчёт *prep.*+*gen.* about, concerning; as regards. **насчита́ть**, -а́ю *perf.*, **насчи́тывать**, -аю *imp.* count; hold, contain; **~ся**+*gen.* number.

насы́пать, -плю *perf.*, **насыпа́ть**, -а́ю *imp.* pour in, pour on; fill; spread, scatter; raise, heap up. **насы́пка**, -и, pouring; filling. **насыпно́й**, bulk; piled up; ~ холм, artificial mound. **на́сыпь**, -и, embankment.

насы́тить, -ы́щу *perf.*, **насыща́ть**, -а́ю *imp.* sate, satiate; saturate, impregnate; **~ся**, be full, be sated; be saturated. **насы́щенный**, saturated; rich, concentrated.

нася́ду, etc.: see насе́сть.

ната́лкивать(ся, -аю(сь *imp.* of натолкну́ть(ся. **ната́пливать**, -аю *imp.* of натопи́ть.

натаска́ть, -а́ю *perf.*, **ната́скивать**, -аю *imp.* train; coach, cram; bring in, lay in; fish out, drag out, fetch out.

натвори́ть, -рю́ *perf.* do, get up to.

натере́ть, -тру́, -трёшь; -тёр *perf.* (*imp.* натира́ть) rub on, rub in; polish; chafe, rub; grate; **~ся**, rub oneself.

натерпе́ться, -плю́сь, -пишься *perf.* have suffered much, have gone through a great deal.

натира́ть(ся, -а́ю(сь *imp.* of натере́ть(ся.

на́тиск, -а, onslaught, charge, onset; pressure; impress, impression. **нати́скать,** -аю *perf.* impress; cram in; shove, push about.

наткну́ться, -ну́сь, -нёшься *perf.* (*imp.* натыка́ться) + на + *acc.* run against, run into; strike, stumble on, come across.

натолкну́ть, -ну́, -нёшь *perf.* (*imp.* ната́лкивать) push; lead; ~ на, suggest; **~ся,** run against, run across.

натопи́ть, -плю́, -пишь *perf.* (*imp.* ната́пливать) heat, heat up; stoke up; melt.

на|точи́ть, -чу́, -чишь *perf.*

натоща́к *adv.* on an empty stomach.

натр, а, natron, soda; е́дкий ~, caustic soda.

натрави́ть, -влю́, -вишь *perf.*, **натра́вливать,** -аю *imp.*, **натравля́ть,** -я́ю *imp.* set (on); stir up; etch; exterminate (by poison).

натрениро́ванный, trained. **на|тренирова́ть(ся,** -ру́ю(сь *perf.*

на́трий, -я, sodium.

нату́га, -и, effort, strain. **на́туго** *adv.* tight, tightly. **нату́жный,** strained, forced.

нату́ра, -ы, nature; kind; model; на нату́ре, on location; плати́ть нату́рой, pay in kind; с нату́ры, from life. **натура́льно** *adv.* naturally, of course. **натура́льный**, natural; real, genuine; in kind; ~ обме́н, barter. **нату́рный,** life, from life; on location. **нату́рщик,** -а, **-щица,** -ы, artist's model.

натыка́ть(ся, -а́ю(сь *imp.* of наткну́ть(ся.

натюрмо́рт, -а, still life.

натя́гивать, -аю *imp.*, **натяну́ть,** -ну́, -нешь *perf.* stretch; draw; pull tight, tauten; pull on; **~ся,** stretch. **натя́жка,** -и, stretching, straining; tension; stretch; допусти́ть натя́жку, stretch a point; с натя́жкой, by stretching a point, at a pinch. **натяжно́й,** tension. **натя́нутость,** -и, tension. **натя́нутый,** tight; strained, forced.

науга́д *adv.* at random; by guesswork.

нау́ка, -и, science; learning, scholarship; study; lesson. **наукообра́зный,** scientific; pseudo-scientific.

наутёк *adv.*: пусти́ться ~, take to one's heels, take to flight.

нау́тро *adv.* (the) next morning.

на|учи́ть, -чу́, -чишь *perf.*

нау́чн|ый, scientific; ~ая фанта́стика, science fiction.

нау́шник, -а, ear-flap, ear-muff; ear-phone, head-phone; informer, tale-bearer. **нау́шничать,** -аю *imp.* tell tales, inform.

нафтали́н, -а (-у), naphthalene. **нафтали́новый,** naphthalene; ~ ша́рик, moth-ball.

наха́л, -а, **-ха́лка,** -и, impudent creature brazen creature; lout, hussy. **наха́льный,** impudent, impertinent, cheeky; brazen, bold-faced. **наха́льство,** -а, impudence, effrontery.

нахвата́ть, -а́ю *perf.*, **нахва́тывать,** -аю *imp.* pick up, get hold of, come by; **~ся**+*gen.* pick up, get a smattering of.

нахле́бник, -а, parasite, hanger-on; boarder, paying guest.

нахлобу́чивать, -аю *imp.*, **нахлобу́чить,** -чу *perf.* pull down; + *dat.* tell off, dress down. **нахлобу́чка,** -и, telling-off, dressing-down.

нахлы́нуть, -нет *perf.* well up; surge; flow, gush; crowd.

нахму́ренный, frowning, scowling. **на|хму́рить(ся,** -рю(сь *perf.*

находи́ть(ся, -ожу́(сь, -о́дишь(ся *imp.* of найти́(сь. **нахо́дка,** -и, find; godsend. **нахо́дчивый,** resourceful, ready, quick-witted.

на|холоди́ть, -ожу́ *perf.*

нацеди́ть, -ежу́, -е́дишь *perf.*, **наце́живать,** -аю *imp.* strain.

наце́ливать, -аю *imp.*, **на|це́лить,** -лю *perf.* aim, level, direct; **~ся,** aim, take aim.

наце́нка, -и, extra, addition; additional charge.

национализи́ровать, -рую *perf.* and *imp.* nationalize. **националисти́ческий,** nationalist, nationalistic. **национа́льность,** -и, nationality; ethnic group; national character. **национа́льный,** national. **на́ция,** -и, nation. **нацме́н,** -а, **-ме́нка,** -и *abbr.* member of national minority. **нацменьшинство́,** -а́; *pl.* -а *abbr.* national minority.

на|чади́ть, -ажу́ *perf.*

нача́ло, -а, beginning, start; origin, source; principle, basis; command, authority; **для нача́ла,** to start with; с нача́ла, at, from, the beginning. **нача́льник,** -а, head, chief; superior boss. **нача́льный,** initial, first; primary. **нача́льственный,** overbearing, domineering. **нача́льство,** -а, the authorities; command, direction; head, boss. **нача́льствование,** -я, command. **нача́льствовать,** -твую *imp.* be in command; + над + *instr.* command. **нача́тки,** -ков *pl.* rudiments, elements. **нача́ть,** -чну́, -чнёшь; на́чал, -а́, -о *perf.* (*imp.* начина́ть) begin, start; **~ся,** begin, start.

начеку́ *adv.* on the alert, ready.

на|черни́ть, -ню́ *perf.* **на́черно** *adv.* roughly, in rough.

начерта́ние, -я, tracing; outline. **начерта́тельн|ый;** ~ая геоме́трия, descriptive geometry. **начерта́ть,** -а́ю *perf.* trace, inscribe. **на|черти́ть,** -рчу́, -ртишь *perf.*

начина́ние, -я, undertaking; project; initiative. **начина́тель,** -я *m.*, **-тельница,** -ы, originator, initiator. **начина́тельный,** inchoative, inceptive. **начина́ть(ся,** -а́юсь *imp.* of нача́ть(ся. **начина́ющий** *sb.* beginner. **начина́я с** *prep.*+*gen.* as from, starting with.

начи́нивать, -аю *imp.*, **начини́ть**[1], -ню́, -нишь *perf.* mend; sharpen.

начини́ть[2], -ню́ *perf.*, **начиня́ть,** -я́ю *imp.* stuff, fill. **начи́нка,** -и, stuffing, filling.

начисле́ние, -я, extra charge, supplement, addition. **начи́слить,** -лю *perf.*, **начисля́ть,** -я́ю *imp.* add.

начи́стить, -и́щу *perf.* (*imp.* начища́ть) clean; polish, shine; peel. **на́чисто** *adv.* flatly, decidedly; openly, frankly; переписа́ть ~, make a clean copy (of). **начистоту́, начисту́ю** *adv.* openly, frankly.

начи́танность, -и, learning, erudition; wide reading. **начи́танный,** well-read **начита́ть,** -а́ю *perf.* have read; **~ся,** have read (too) much, have read enough.

начища́ть, -а́ю *imp.* of начи́стить.

наш, -его *m.*, **на́ша,** -ей *f.*, **на́ше,** -его *n.*, **на́ши,** -их *pl.*, *pron.* our, ours; ~а взяла́, we've won; ~его (after *comp.*) than we (have, etc.); ~и, our (own) people; оди́н из ~их, one of us; служи́ть, угожда́ть, и ~им и ва́шим, run with the hare and hunt with the hounds.

нашаты́рный; ~ спирт, ammonia. **нашаты́рь,** -я́ *m.* sal-ammoniac; ammonia.

нашёл, etc.: see найти́.

нашепта́ть, -пчу́, -пчешь *perf.*, **нашёптывать,** -аю *imp.* whisper; cast a spell.

наше́ствие, -я, invasion.

нашива́ть, -а́ю *imp.*, **наши́ть,** -шью́, -шьёшь *perf.* sew on. **наши́вка,** -и, stripe, chevron; tab. **нашивно́й,** sewn on; ~ карма́н, patch pocket.

нашинкова́ть, -ку́ю *perf.*, **нашинко́вывать,** -аю *imp.* shred, chop.

нашпи́ливать, -аю *imp.*, **нашпи́лить,** -лю *perf.* pin on.

нашлёпать, -аю *imp.* slap.

нашуме́ть, -млю *perf.* make a din; cause a sensation.

нашью́, etc.: see наши́ть.

нащу́пать, -аю *perf.*, **нащу́пывать,** -аю *imp.* grope for, fumble for, feel (about) for; grope one's way to, find by groping.

на|электризова́ть, -зу́ю *perf.*

на|я́бедничать, -аю *perf.*

наяву́ *adv.* awake; in reality; сон ~, waking dream.

не *part.* not; не раз, more than once.

не- *pref.* un-, in-, non-, mis-, dis-; -less; not. **неаккура́тный,** careless, inaccurate; unpunctual; untidy. **небезопа́сный,** unsafe. **небезразли́чный,** not indifferent. **небезызве́стн|ый,** not unknown; notorious; well-known; ~о, что, it is no secret that; нам ~о, we are not unaware. **небезынтере́сный,** not without interest.

небеса́, etc.: see не́бо[2]. **небе́сный,** heavenly, of heaven; celestial.

не-. небесполе́зный, of some use, useful. **неблагода́рный,** ungrateful, thankless. **неблагожела́тельный,**

malevolent, ill-disposed. **неблагозву́чие, -я,** disharmony, dissonance. **неблагозву́чный,** inharmonious, discordant. **неблагонадёжный,** unreliable. **неблагополу́чие, -я,** trouble. **неблагополу́чный,** unsuccessful, bad, unfavourable. **неблагопристо́йный,** obscene, indecent, improper. **неблагоразу́мный,** imprudent, ill-advised, unwise. **неблагоро́дный,** ignoble, base.

нёбный, palatal, palatine. **нёбо**[1], -а, palate.

не́бо[2], -а; *pl.* -беса́, -бе́с, sky; heaven.

не-. **небога́тый,** of modest means, modest. **небольшо́й,** small, not great; с небольши́м, a little over.

небосво́д -а, firmament, vault of heaven. **небосклóн,** -а, horizon. **небоскрёб,** -а, skyscraper.

небо́сь *adv.* I dare say; probably, very likely; I suppose.

не-. **небре́жничать,** -аю *imp.* be careless. **небре́жный,** careless, negligent; slipshod; offhand. **небыва́лый,** unprecedented; fantastic, imaginary; inexperienced. **небыли́ца,** -ы, fable, cock-and-bull story. **небытие́,** -я́, non-existence. **небью́щийся,** unbreakable. **нева́жно** *adv.* not too well, indifferently. **нева́жный,** unimportant, insignificant; poor, indifferent. **невдалеке́** *adv.* not far away. **неве́дение,** -я, ignorance. **неве́домо** *adv.* God (only) knows. **неве́домый,** unknown; mysterious. **неве́жа,** -и *m.* and *f.* boor, lout. **неве́жда,** -ы, *m.* and *f.* ignoramus. **неве́жественный,** ignorant. **неве́жество,** -а, ignorance; rudeness, bad manners, discourtesy. **неве́жливый,** rude, impolite, ill-mannered. **невели́кий;** -и́к, -а́, -и́ко́, small, short; slight, insignificant. **неве́рие,** -я, unbelief, atheism; lack of faith, scepticism. **неве́рный;** -рен, -рна́, -о, incorrect, wrong; inaccurate, uncertain, unsteady; false; faithless, disloyal; unfaithful; Фома́ ~, doubting Thomas. **невероя́тный,** improbable, unlikely; incredible, unbelievable. **неве́рующий,** unbelieving; *sb.* unbeliever, atheist. **невесёлый,** joyless, sad. **невесо́мость,** -и, weightlessness. **невесо́мый,** weightless; imponderable, insignificant.

неве́ста, -ы, fiancée; bride. **неве́стка,** -и, daughter-in-law; brother's wife, sister-in-law.

не-. **невзго́да,** -ы, adversity, misfortune. **невзира́я на** *prep.*+*acc.* in spite of; regardless of. **невзнача́й** *adv.* by chance, unexpectedly. **невзра́чный,** unattractive, plain. **невзыска́тельный,** unexacting, undemanding. **не́видаль,** -и, wonder, prodigy. **неви́данный,** unprecedented, unheard of; mysterious. **неви́димый,** invisible. **неви́дящий,** unseeing. **неви́нность,** -и, innocence. **неви́нный,** innocent. **невино́вный,** innocent, not guilty. **невку́сный,** tasteless, unappetizing, not nice. **невменя́емый,** irresponsible, not responsible; beside oneself. **невмеша́тельство,** -а, non-intervention; non-interference. **невмоготу́, невмо́чь** *advs.* unbearable, unendurable, too much (for). **невнима́ние,** -я, inattention; carelessness; lack of consideration. **невнима́тельный,** inattentive, thoughtless. **невня́тный,** indistinct, incomprehensible.

не́вод, -а, seine, seine-net.

не-. **невозврати́мый, невозвра́тный,** irrevocable, irrecoverable. **невозвраще́нец,** -нца, defector. **невозде́ланный,** untilled, waste. **невозде́ржанный, невозде́ржный,** intemperate; incontinent; uncontrolled, unrestrained. **невозмо́жный,** impossible; insufferable. **невозмути́мый,** imperturbable; calm, unruffled.

нево́лить, -лю *imp.* (*perf.* при~) force, compel. **нево́льник,** -а, **-ница,** -ы, slave. **нево́льно** *adv.* involuntarily; unintentionally. **нево́льный,** involuntary; unintentional; forced; ~ная поса́дка, forced landing. **нево́ля,** -и, bondage, captivity; necessity.

не-. **невообрази́мый,** unimaginable, inconceivable. **невооружён|ный,** unarmed; ~ным гла́зом, with the naked eye. **невоспи́танность,** -и, ill breeding, bad manners. **невоспи́танный,** ill-bred. **невоспламеня́емый** not inflammable, non-flam. **невосприи́мчивый,** unreceptive; immune. **невпопа́д** *adv.* out of place; irrelevant, inopportune.

невралги́ческий, neuralgic. **невралги́я,** -и, neuralgia.

невреди́мый, safe, unharmed, uninjured.

неври́т, -а, neuritis. **невро́з,** -а, neurosis. **неврологи́ческий,** neurological. **невроло́гия,** -и, neurology. **невроти́ческий,** neurotic.

не-. неврyче́ние, -я, non-delivery. **невы́года,** -ы, disadvantage, loss. **невы́годный,** disadvantageous, unfavourable; unprofitable, unremunerative. **невы́держанный,** lacking self-control; unmatured. **невыноси́мый,** unbearable, insufferable, intolerable. **невыполне́ние,** -я, non-fulfilment, non-compliance. **невыполни́мый,** impracticable. **невырази́мый,** inexpressible, unmentionable. **невысо́кий;** -со́к, -а́, -о́ко́, not high, low; not tall, short. **невы́ясненный,** obscure, uncertain. **невя́зка,** -и, discrepancy.

не́га, -и, luxury; bliss, delight; voluptuousness.

негашён|ый, unslaked; ~ая и́звесть, quicklime.

не́где *adv.* there is nowhere.

не-. неги́бкий; -бок, -бка́, -о. inflexible, stiff. **негла́сный** secret. **неглубо́кий;** -о́к, -а́, -о, rather shallow; superficial. **неглу́п|ый;** -у́п, -а́, -о, sensible, quite intelligent; он ~, he is no fool. **него́дник,** -а, reprobate, scoundrel good-for-nothing. **него́дный;** -ден, -дна́, -о, unfit, unsuitable; worthless. **негодова́ние,** -я, indignation. **негодова́ть,** -ду́ю *imp.* be indignant. **негоду́ющий,** indignant. **негодя́й,** -я. scoundrel, rascal. **негостеприи́мный,** inhospitable.

негр, -а, Negro.

негра́мотность, -и, illiteracy. **негра́мотный,** illiterate.

негритёнок, -нка; *pl.* -тя́та, -тя́т, Negro child. **негритя́нка,** -и, Negress. **негритя́нский, не́грский,** Negro.

не-. неда́вний, recent. **неда́вно** *adv.* recently. **недалёкий;** -ёк, -а́, -ёко́, not far away, near; short; not bright, dull-witted. **недалёко́** *adv.* not far, near. **неда́ром** *adv.* not for nothing, not without reason, not without purpose. **недви́жимость.** -и, real property, real estate. **недви́жимый,** immovable; motionless. **недвусмы́сленный,** unequivocal. **недействи́тельный,** ineffective, ineffectual; invalid, null and void. **недели́мый,** indivisible.

неде́льный, of a week, week's. **неде́ля,** -и, week.

не-. недёшево *adv.* not cheap(ly), dear(ly). **недоброжела́тель,** -я *m.* ill-wisher. **недоброжела́тельность,** -и, **недоброжела́тельство,** -а, hostility, ill-will, malevolence. **недоброжела́тельный,** ill-disposed, hostile, malevolent. **недоброка́чественный,** of poor quality, low-grade; bad. **недобросо́вестный,** unscrupulous; not conscientious, careless. **недо́брый;** -о́бр, -бра́, -о, unkind, unfriendly; bad; evil, wicked. **недове́рие,** -я, distrust; mistrust; lack of confidence. **недове́рчивый,** distrustful, not confident, mistrustful. **недове́с,** -а, short weight. **недово́льный** dissatisfied, discontented, displeased; *sb.* malcontent. **недово́льство,** -а, dissatisfaction, discontent, displeasure. **недога́дливый,** slow-witted. **недогляде́ть,** -яжу́ *perf.* overlook; take insufficient care of. **недоеда́ние** -я, malnutrition. **недоеда́ть,** -а́ю *imp.* be undernourished, be underfed, not eat enough. **недозво́ленный,** unlawful; illicit.

недои́мка, -и, arrears. **недои́мочность,** -и, non-payment. **недои́мщик,** -а, defaulter, person in arrears.

не-. недо́лг|ий; -лог, -лга́, -о short, brief; вот и вся ~а́, that's all there is to it. **недо́лго** *adv.* not long. **недолгове́чный,** short-lived, ephemeral. **недоме́р,** -а, short measure. **недоме́рок,** -рка, undersized object; small size. **недомога́ние,** -я, indisposition. **недомога́ть,** -а́ю *imp.* be unwell, be indisposed. **недомо́лвка,** -и, reservation, omission. **недомы́слие,** -я, thoughtlessness. **недоно́сок,** -ска, premature child. **недоно́шенный,** premature. **недооце́нивать,** -аю *imp.*, **недооцени́ть,** -ню́, -нишь *perf.* underestimate, underrate. **недооце́нка,** -и, underestimation. **недопроизво́дство,** -а, underproduction. **недопусти́мый,** inadmissible, intolerable. **недоразуме́ние,** -я, misunderstanding. **недорого́й,** -до́рог, -á, -о, not dear, inexpensive; reasonable, modest. **недоро́д,** -а, crop failure, bad harvest. **недосмо́тр,** -а, oversight. **недосмотре́ть,** -рю́ -ришь *perf.* overlook, miss; take insufficient care. **недоспа́ть,** -плю́; -а́л, -á, -о *perf.* (*imp.* недосыпа́ть) not have enough sleep.

недостава́ть, -таёт *imp.*, **недоста́ть,** -а́нет *perf. impers.* be missing, be lacking, be wanting. **недоста́ток,** -тка, shortage, lack, deficiency, want; shortcoming, defect. **недоста́точно** *adv.* insufficiently, not enough. **недоста́точный,** insufficient, inadequate; ~ глаго́л, defective verb. **недоста́ча,** -и, lack, shortage, deficit.

не-. недостижи́мый, unattainable. **недостове́рный,** not authentic, doubtful, apocryphal. **недосто́йный,** unworthy. **недосту́пный,** inaccessible. **недосу́г,** a, lack of time, being too busy; за ~ом for lack of time. **недосчита́ться,** -а́юсь *perf.* **недосчи́тываться,** -аюсь *imp.* miss, find missing, be short (of). **недосыпа́ть,** -а́ю *imp.* of недоспа́ть. **недосяга́емый,** unattainable. **недотро́га,** -и *m.* and *f.* touch-me-not person; *f.* mimosa.

недоумева́ть, -а́ю *imp.* be puzzled, be at a loss, be bewildered. **недоуме́ние,** -я, perplexity, bewilderment. **недоуме́нный,** puzzled, perplexed.

не-. недоу́чка, -и *m.* and *f.* half-educated person. **недохва́тка,** -и, shortage, lack. **недочёт,** a, deficit, shortage; shortcoming, defect.

не́дра, недр *pl.* depths, heart, bowels; бога́тство недр, mineral wealth.

не-. недре́млющий, unsleeping, watchful, vigilant. **не́друг,** -а, enemy. **недружелю́бный,** unfriendly.

неду́г, a, illness, disease.

недурно́й, not bad; not bad-looking.

недю́жинный, out of the ordinary, outstanding, exceptional.

не-. неесте́ственный, unnatural. **нежда́нно** *adv.* unexpectedly; ~-нега́данно, quite unexpectedly. **нежда́нный,** unexpected, unlooked-for. **нежела́ние,** -я, unwillingness, disinclination. **нежела́тельный,** undesirable, unwanted. **нежена́тый,** unmarried.

не́женка, -и *m.* and *f.* mollycoddle.

нежило́й, uninhabited; not habitable.

не́жить, -жу *imp.* pamper; indulge; caress; **~ся,** luxuriate, bask. **не́жничать,** -аю *imp.* bill and coo; be soft, be over-indulgent. **не́жность,** -и, tenderness; delicacy; *pl.* endearments, display of affection, compliments, flattery. **не́жный,** tender; delicate; affectionate.

не-. незабве́нный, unforgettable. **незабу́дка,** -и, forget-me-not. **незабыва́емый,** unforgettable. **незаве́ренный,** uncertified. **незави́симо** *adv.* independently; ~ от, irrespective of. **незави́симый,** independent; sovereign. **незави́сящ|ий;** по ~им от нас обстоя́тельствам, owing to circumstances beyond our control. **незада́ча,** -и, ill luck, bad luck. **незада́чливый,** unlucky; luckless. **незадо́лго** *adv.* not long. **незако́нный,** illegal, illicit, unlawful; illegitimate. **незако́нченный,** unfinished incomplete. **незамени́мый,** irreplaceable, indispensable. **незамерза́ющ|ий,** ice-free; anti-freeze; ~ая смесь, anti-freeze. **незаме́тно** *adv.* imperceptibly, insensibly. **незаме́тный,** imperceptible; inconspicuous, insignificant. **незаму́жняя,** unmarried. **незамыслова́тый,** simple, uncomplicated. **незапа́мятный,** immemorial. **незапя́тнанный,** unstained, unsullied. **незара́зный,** non-contagious. **незаслу́женный,** unmerited, undeserved. **незастро́енный,** not built on, undeveloped; vacant. **незате́йливый,** simple, plain; modest. **незауря́дный,** uncommon, outstanding out of the ordinary.

не́зачем *adv.* there is no need; it is useless, pointless, no use.

не-. незащищённый, unprotected. **нezва́ный,** uninvited. **нездоро́виться,** -ится *imp. impers.*; мне нездоро́вится, I don't feel well, I am not well. **нездоро́вый,** unhealthy, sickly; morbid; unwholesome; unwell. **нездоро́вье,** -я, indisposition; ill health. **неземно́й,** not of the earth; unearthly. **незло́бивый,** gentle, mild, forgiving. **незнако́мец,** -мца, **незнако́мка,** -и, stranger. **незнако́мый,** unknown, unfamiliar; unacquainted. **незна́ние,** -я, ignorance. **незна́чащий, незначи́тельный** insignificant. unimportant, of no consequence. **незре́лый,** unripe, immature. **незри́мый,** invisible. **незы́блемый,** unshakable, stable, firm. **неизбе́жный** inevitable, unavoidable, inescapable. **неизве́данный,** unknown, unexplored; not experienced before.

неизве́стное *sb.* unknown quantity. **неизве́стность,** -и, uncertainty; ignorance; obscurity. **неизве́стный,** unknown; *sb.* stranger, unknown.

не-. неизглади́мый, indelible, uneffaceable. **неи́зданный,** unpublished. **неизлечи́мый,** incurable. **неизме́нный,** unchanged, unchanging; devoted, true. **неизменя́емый,** invariable, unalterable. **неизмери́мый,** immeasurable, immense. **неизу́ченный,** unstudied; obscure, unknown; unexplored. **неиме́ние,** -я, lack, want; absence; за ~м+*gen.* for want of **неимове́рный,** incredible, unbelievable. **неиму́щий,** indigent needy, poor. **неи́скренний,** insincere; false. **неиску́сный,** unskilful, inexpert. **неискушённый,** inexperienced, innocent, unsophisticated. **неисполне́ние,** -я, non-performance, non-observance, non-execution. **неисполни́мый,** impracticable, unrealizable. **неисправи́мый,** incorrigible; irremediable, irreparable. **неиспра́вность,** -и, disrepair, fault, defect; carelessness. **неиспра́вный,** out of order, faulty, defective; careless. **неиссле́дованный,** unexplored, uninvestigated. **неисся-ка́емый,** inexhaustible. **неи́стовство,** -а, fury, frenzy; violence; savagery, atrocity. **неи́стовый,** furious, frenzied, uncontrolled. **неистощи́мый, неисчерпа́емый,** inexhaustible. **неисчисли́мый,** innumerable, incalculable.

нейло́н, -а, **нейло́новый,** nylon.

нейро́н, -а, neuron.

нейтрализа́ция, -и, neutralization. **нейтрализова́ть,** -зу́ю *perf.* and *imp.* neutralize. **нейтралите́т,** -а, **нейтра́льность,** -и, neutrality. **нейтра́льный,** neutral. **нейтри́но,** -а, neutrino. **нейтро́н,** -а, neutron.

неквалифици́рованный, unskilled; unqualified.

не́кий *pron.* a certain, some.

не́когда[1] *adv.* once, long ago, in the old days.

не́когда[2] *adv.* there is no time; мне ~, I have no time.

не́кого (*-vo*), не́кому, не́кем, не́ о ком *pron.* (with separable *pref.*), there is nobody.

неколеби́мый, unshakeable.

некомпете́нтный, not competent, unqualified.

не́котор|ый *pron.* some; ~ым о́бразом, somehow, in a way; **~ые** *sb. pl.* some, some people.

некраси́вый, plain, ugly, unsightly, unpleasant.

некро́з, -а, necrosis. **некроло́г,** -а, obituary (notice). **некрома́нтия,** -и, necromancy; telling fortunes.

некры́тый, roofless.

некста́ти *adv.* malapropos, unseasonably, at the wrong time, out of place.

не́кто *pron.* somebody; one, a certain.

не́куда *adv.* there is nowhere.

не-. некульту́рный, uncivilized, uncultured; uncultivated; barbarous, ill-mannered, uncouth, boorish. **некуря́щий** *sb.* non-smoker. **нела́дн|ый,** wrong; здесь что́-то ~о, something is wrong here; будь он ~ен! blast him! **нелады́,** -о́в *pl.* discord, disagreement; trouble, something wrong. **нелега́льный,** illegal. **нелега́льщина,** -ы, illegal literature, illegal activity. **нелёгкая** *sb.* the devil, the deuce. **нелёгкий,** difficult, not easy; heavy, not light. **неле́пость,** -и, absurdity, nonsense. **неле́пый,** absurd, ridiculous. **нело́вк|ий,** awkward, clumsy, gauche; uncomfortable, embarrassing; мне ~о, I'm uncomfortable. **нело́вко** *adv.* awkwardly, uncomfortably. **нело́вкость,** -и, awkwardness, gaucherie, clumsiness; blunder.

нельзя́ *adv.* it is impossible, it is not allowed; one ought not, one should not, one can't; здесь кури́ть ~, smoking is not allowed here; как ~ лу́чше, in the best possible way.

не-. **нелюбе́зный**, ungracious; discourteous. **нелюби́мый**, unloved. **нелюди́м**, -а **нелюди́мка**, -и, unsociable person. **нелюди́мый**, unsociable; unpeopled lonely. **нема́ло** *adv*. not a little, not a few; a considerable amount or number. **немалова́жный**, of no small importance. **нема́лый**, no small, considerable. **неме́дленно** *adv*. immediately, at once, without delay. **неме́дленный**, immediate.

неме́ть, -е́ю *imp*. (*perf*. за~, о~) become dumb; grow numb. **не́мец**, -мца, German. **неме́цк|ий**, German; ~ая овча́рка, Alsatian.

неми́лость, -и, disgrace, disfavour.

немину́емый, inevitable, unavoidable.

не́мка, -и, German.

немно́г|ий, a little; not much; (a) few; **~ие** *sb. pl*. few, a few. **немно́го** *adv*. a little; some, not much; a few; somewhat, slightly. **немногосло́вный**, laconic, brief, terse. **немно́жко** *adv*. a little, a bit, a trifle.

немну́щийся, uncrushable, crease-resistant.

нем|о́й; нем, -á, -о, dumb, mute, (utterly) silent; ~а́я а́збука, deaf-and-dumb alphabet; ~о́й согла́сный, voiceless consonant; ~о́й фильм, silent film. **немота́**, -ы́, dumbness.

не́мощный, feeble, ill, sick. **не́мощь**, -и, sickness; feebleness, infirmity.

немудрёный, simple, easy; немудрено́, no wonder.

ненави́деть, -и́жу *imp*. hate, detest, loathe. **ненави́стник**, -а, hater. **ненави́стный**, hated, hateful. **не́нависть**, -и, hatred.

не-. **ненагля́дный**, dear, beloved. **ненадёжный**, insecure; unreliable, untrustworthy. **нена́добность**, -и, uselessness **ненадо́лго** *adv*. for a short time, not for long. **ненападе́ние**, -я, non-aggression. **ненаруши́мый**, inviolable. **ненаси́лие**, -я, non-violence. **нена́стный**, bad, foul, rainy. **нена́стье**, -я, bad weather, wet weather. **ненастоя́щий**, artificial, imitation, counterfeit. **ненасы́тный**, insatiable. **нену́жный**, unnecessary, superfluous.

нео- *pref*. neo-. **неозо́йский**, neozoic. **~классици́зм**, -а, neo-classicism, **~колониали́зм**, -а, neo-colonialism. **~фаши́стский**, neo-fascist. **~фи́т**, -а, neophyte.

не-. **необду́манный**, thoughtless, hasty, precipitate. **необеспе́ченный**, without means, unprovided for, not provided (with). **необита́емый**, uninhabited; ~ **о́стров**, desert island. **необозна́ченный**, not indicated, not marked. **необозри́мый**, boundless, immense, **необосно́ванный**, unfounded, groundless. **необрабо́танный**, uncultivated, untilled; raw, crude; unpolished, untrained. **необразо́ванный**, uneducated. **необу́зданный**, unbridled, ungovernable. **необу́ченный**, untrained.

необходи́мость, -и, necessity; по необходи́мости, of necessity, perforce. **необходи́мый**, necessary, essential.

не-. **необъясни́мый**, inexplicable, unaccountable. **необъя́тный**, immense, unbounded. **необыкнове́нный**, unusual, uncommon. **необыча́йный**, extraordinary, exceptional, unaccustomed. **необы́чный**, unusual singular. **необяза́тельный**, optional. **неограни́ченный**, unlimited, absolute. **неоднокра́тно** *adv*. repeatedly, more than once. **неоднокра́тный**, repeated. **неодобре́ние**, -я, disapproval. **неодобри́тельный**, disapproving. **неодушевлённый**, inanimate.

неожи́данность, -и, unexpectedness, suddenness; surprise. **неожи́данный**, unexpected, sudden.

не-. **неоконча́тельный**, inconclusive. **неоко́нченный**, unfinished. **неопису́емый**, indescribable. **неопла́тный**, that cannot be repaid; insolvent. **неопла́ченный**, unpaid. **неопра́вданный**, unjustified, unwarranted. **неопределённый**, indefinite, indeterminate; infinitive; vague, uncertain. **неопредели́мый**, indefinable. **неопровержи́мый**, irrefutable; incontestable. **неопря́тный**, slovenly, untidy, sloppy. **неопублико́ванный**, unpublished. **нео́пытность**, -и, inexperience. **нео́пытный**, inexperienced. **неосведомлённый,** ill-informed. **неосéдлый,** nomadic. **неослáбный,** unremitting, unabated, untiring. **неосмотри́тельный,** imprudent, incautious; indiscreet. **неосновáтельный,** unfounded, unwarranted; frivolous. **неоспори́мый,** unquestionable, incontestable, indisputable. **неосторóжный,** careless, imprudent, indiscreet, incautious. **неосуществи́мый,** impracticable, unrealizable. **неосязáмый,** intangible. **неотврати́мый,** inevitable. **неотвя́зный, неотвя́зчивый,** importunate; obsessive. **неотёсанный,** rough, undressed; unpolished, uncouth.

нéоткуда *adv.* there is nowhere; there is no reason; мне ~ это получи́ть, there is nowhere I can get it from.

не-. неотлóжн|ый, urgent, pressing; ~ая пóмощь, first aid. **неотлу́чно** *adv.* constantly, continually, unremittingly; permanent. **неотлу́чный,** continual, constant, permanent. **неотрази́мый,** irresistible; incontrovertible, irrefutable. **неотсту́пный,** persistent, importunate. **неотъéмлемый,** inalienable; inseparable, integral. **неохóта,** -ы, reluctance. **неохóтно** *adv.* reluctantly; unwillingly. **неоцени́мый,** inestimable, invaluable. **неощути́мый,** imperceptible. **непáрный,** odd. **непарти́йный,** non-party; unbefitting a member of the (Communist) Party. **непереводи́мый,** untranslatable. **непередавáемый,** incommunicable, inexpressible. **неперехóдный,** intransitive. **непечáтный,** unprintable.

неплатёж, -ежá, non-payment. **неплатёжеспосóбный,** insolvent. **неплатéльщик,** -а, defaulter; person in arrears.

не-. неплодорóдный, infertile. **неплóхо** *adv.* not badly, quite well. **неплохóй,** not bad, quite good. **непобеди́мый,** invincible; unbeatable. **неповиновéние,** -я, insubordination, disobedience. **неповорóтливый,** clumsy, awkward; sluggish, slow. **неповтори́мый,** inimitable, unique. **непогóда,** -ы, bad weather. **непогреши́мый,** infallible. **неподалёку** *adv.* not far (away). **неподáтливый,** stubborn, intractable, unyielding. **неподви́жный,** motionless, immobile, immovable; fixed, stationary. **неподдéльный,** genuine; sincere, unfeigned. **неподку́пный,** incorruptible, unbribable. **неподражáемый,** inimitable. **неподходя́щий,** unsuitable, inappropriate. **непокóйный,** troubled, disturbed, restless. **непоколеби́мый,** unshakable, steadfast. **непокóрный,** recalcitrant, unruly, insubordinate. **непокры́тый,** uncovered, bare.

не-. неполáдки, -док *pl.* defects. **неполноцéнность,** -и; кóмплекс неполноцéнности, inferiority complex. **неполноцéнный,** defective, imperfect; inadequate. **непóлный,** incomplete; defective; not quite, not (a) full. **непомéрный,** excessive, inordinate. **непонимáние,** -я, incomprehension, lack of understanding. **непоня́тливый,** slow-witted, stupid, dull. **непоня́тный,** unintelligible, incomprehensible. **непоправи́мый,** irreparable, irremediable. **непоря́док,** -дка, disorder. **непоря́дочный,** dishonourable. **непосвящённый,** uninitiated. **непосéда,** -ы, *m.* and *f.* fidget, restless person. **непоси́льный,** beyond one's strength, excessive. **непослéдовательный,** inconsistent; inconsequent. **непослушáние,** -я, disobedience. **непослу́шный,** disobedient, naughty. **непосрéдственный,** immediate, direct; spontaneous; ingenuous. **непостижи́мый,** incomprehensible. **непостоя́нный,** inconstant, changeable. **непостоя́нство,** -а, inconstancy. **непотопля́емый,** unsinkable. **непотрéбный,** obscene, indecent; useless; bad. **непочáтый,** untouched, not begun; ~ край, у́гол, a lot, a wealth, no end. **непочтéние,** -я, disrespect. **непочти́тельный,** disrespectful.

не-. непрáвда, -ы, untruth, falsehood, lie. **неправдоподóбие,** -я, improbability, unlikelihood. **неправдоподóбный,** improbable, unlikely, implausible. **непрáвильно** *adv.* wrong; irregularly; incorrectly; erroneously. **непрáвильность,** -и, irregularity; anomaly; incorrectness. **непрáвильн|ый,** irregular; anomalous; incorrect, erroneous, wrong, mistaken; ~ая дробь, improper fraction. **неправомо́чный,** incompetent; not entitled. **неправоспосо́бный,** disqualified. **неправота́, -ы́,** error; injustice. **непра́вый,** wrong, mistaken; unjust. **непракти́чный,** unpractical. **непревзойдённый,** unsurpassed, matchless. **непредви́денный,** unforeseen. **непредубеждённый,** unprejudiced. **непредусмо́тренный,** unforeseen; unprovided for. **непредусмотри́тельный,** improvident, short-sighted. **непреклонный,** inflexible, unbending; inexorable, adamant. **непрело́жный** immutable, unalterable; indisputable.

не-. непреме́нно *adv.* without fail; certainly; absolutely. **непреме́нный,** indispensable, necessary; ~ секрета́рь, permanent secretary. **непреодоли́мый,** insuperable, insurmountable; irresistible. **непреры́вно** *adv.* uninterruptedly, continuously. **непреры́вный,** uninterrupted, unbroken; continuous. **непреста́нный,** incessant, continual. **неприве́тливый,** unfriendly, ungracious; bleak. **непривлека́тельный,** unattractive. **неприві́чный,** unaccustomed, unwonted, unusual. **непригля́дный,** unattractive, unsightly. **непригодный,** unfit, unserviceable, useless; ineligible. **неприе́млемый,** unacceptable. **неприкоснове́нность, -и,** inviolability, immunity. **неприкоснове́нный,** inviolable; to be kept intact; reserve, emergency. **неприкра́шенный,** plain, unadorned, unvarnished. **неприли́чный,** indecent, improper; unseemly, unbecoming. **неприменимый,** inapplicable. **непримири́мый,** irreconcilable. **непринуждённый,** unconstrained; natural, relaxed, easy; spontaneous. **неприспосо́бленный,** unadapted; maladjusted. **непристо́йный,** obscene, indecent. **непристу́пный,** inaccessible, impregnable; unapproachable, haughty. **непритво́рный** unfeigned. **непритяза́тельный. неприхотли́вый,** modest, unpretentious, simple, plain. **неприя́зненный,** hostile, inimical. **неприя́знь, -и,** hostility, enmity. **неприя́тель, -я** *m.* enemy. **неприя́тельский,** hostile, enemy. **неприя́тный,** unpleasant, disagreeable; annoying, troublesome; obnoxious.

не-. непрове́ренный, unverified, unchecked. **непроводни́к, -а́,** non-conductor. **непроводя́щий,** non-conducting. **непрогля́дный,** impenetrable; pitch-dark. **непродолжи́тельный,** short, short-lived. **непроду́манный,** rash, unconsidered. **непрое́зжий** impassable. **непрозра́чный,** opaque. **непроизводи́тельный,** unproductive; wasteful. **непроизво́льный,** involuntary. **непрола́зный,** impassable, impenetrable. **непромока́емый,** waterproof. **непроница́емый,** impenetrable, impervious; inscrutable; +для+*gen.* proof against. **непрости́тельный,** unforgivable, unpardonable, inexcusable. **непроходи́мый,** impassable; complete, utter, hopeless. **непро́чный**; -чен, -чна́, -о, fragile flimsy; precarious, unstable; not durable.

не прочь *predic.* not averse; я ~ пойти́ туда́, I wouldn't mind going there.

не-. непро́шеный, uninvited, unasked (-for). **неработоспосо́бный,** incapacitated, disabled. **нерабо́чий**; ~ день, day off, free day. **нера́венство, -а,** inequality, disparity. **неравноме́рный,** uneven, irregular. **нера́вный,** unequal. **нерадивый,** negligent, indolent, careless, remiss. **неразбери́ха, -и,** muddle, confusion. **неразбо́рчивый,** not fastidious; unscrupulous; illegible. **неразвито́й**; -ра́звит, -а́, -о, undeveloped; backward. **неразгово́рчивый** taciturn, not talkative. **неразделимый, неразде́льный,** indivisible, inseparable. **неразличи́мый,** indistinguishable. **неразлу́чный,** inseparable. **неразрешённый,** unsolved; forbidden, prohibited. **неразреши́мый,** insoluble. **неразры́вный,** indissoluble, inseparable. **неразу́мный,** unwise, unreasonable. **нерасположе́ние, -я,** dislike; disinclination. **нерасполо́женный,** ill-disposed; unwilling, disinclined. **нераствори́мый,** insoluble. **нерасчётливый,** extravagant, wasteful; improvident.

нерв, -а, nerve; гла́вный ~, nerve--centre. **нерви́ческий,** nervous. **нервнобольно́й** *sb.* neurotic, nervous case. **не́рвный;** -вен, -вна́, -о, nervous; neural; irritable, highly strung; ~ у́зел, ganglion. **нерво́зный,** nervy, irritable, excitable. **нервю́ра,** -ы, rib.

не-. нереа́льный, unreal; unrealistic. **нере́дкий;** -док, -дка́, -о, not infrequent, not uncommon. **нере́дко** *adv.* not infrequently. **нереши́мость,** -и, **нереши́тельность,** -и, indecision; irresolution. **нереши́тельный,** indecisive, irresolute, undecided. **нержаве́ющ|ий,** rustless; ~ая сталь, stainless steel. **неро́вный;** -вен, -вна́, -о, uneven, rough; unequal, irregular. **нерукотво́рный,** not made with hands. **неруши́мый,** inviolable, indestructible, indissoluble.

неря́ха, -и *m.* and *f.* sloven; slattern, slut. **неря́шливый,** slovenly, untidy, slatternly; careless, slipshod.

не-. несбы́точн|ый, unrealizable; ~ые мечты́, castles in the air; ~ые наде́жды, vain hopes. **несваре́ние,** -я; ~ желу́дка, indigestion. **несве́жий;** -е́ж, -а́, not fresh; stale; tainted; weary, washed-out. **несвоевре́менный,** ill--timed, inopportune; overdue, not at the right time. **несво́йственный,** not characteristic, unusual, unlike. **несвя́зный,** disconnected, incoherent. **несгиба́емый,** unbending, inflexible. **несгово́рчивый,** intractable, hard to handle. **несгора́емый,** fireproof; ~ шкаф, safe.

несессе́р, -а, dressing-case.

нескла́дный, incoherent; ungainly, awkward; absurd.

несклоня́емый, indeclinable.

не́сколько, -их *pron.* some, several; a number a few; *adv.* somewhat, a little, rather.

не-. нескончáемый, interminable, never-ending. **нескро́мный;** -мен, -мна́, -о, immodest; vain; indelicate, tactless, indiscreet. **несло́жный,** simple. **неслы́ханный,** unheard of, unprecedented. **неслы́шный** inaudible; noiseless. **несме́тный,** countless, incalculable, innumerable. **несмина́емый,** uncrushable, crease-resistant. **несмолка́емый,** ceaseless, unremitting.

несмотря́ на *prep.*+*acc.* in spite of, despite notwithstanding.

не-. несно́сный, intolerable, insupportable, unbearable. **несоблюде́ние,** -я, non-observance. **несовершеннолéтие,** -я, minority. **несовершеннолéтний,** under age; *sb.* minor. **несоверше́нный,** imperfect, incomplete; imperfective. **несовмести́мость,** -и, incompatibility. **несовмести́мый,** incompatible. **несогла́сие,** disagreement, difference; discord, variance; refusal. **несогла́сный,** not agreeing; inconsistent, incompatible; discordant; not consenting. **несогласова́ние,** -я, non-agreement. **несогласо́ванный,** uncoordinated, not concerted. **несозна́тельный,** irresponsible. **несоизмери́мый,** incommensurable. **несокруши́мый,** indestructible; unconquerable. **несо́лоно:** уйти́ ~ хлеба́вши, get nothing for one's pains, go away empty-handed. **несомне́нно** *adv.* undoubtedly, doubtless, beyond question. **несомне́нный,** undoubted, indubitable, unquestionable. **несообра́зный,** incongruous, incompatible; absurd. **несоотве́тствие,** -я, disparity, incongruity. **несоразме́рный,** disproportionate. **несостоя́тельный,** insolvent, bankrupt; not wealthy, of modest means; groundless, unsupported. **неспе́лый,** unripe. **неспоко́йный,** restless; uneasy. **неспосо́бный,** dull, not able; incapable, not competent. **несправедли́вый,** unjust, unfair; incorrect, unfounded. **неспроста́** *adv.* not without purpose; with an ulterior motive. **несравне́нно** *adv.* incomparably, matchlessly; far, by far. **несравне́нный;** -е́нен, -е́нна, incomparable, matchless. **несравни́мый,** not comparable; incomparable, unmatched. **нестерпи́мый,** unbearable, unendurable.

нести́, -су́, -сёшь; нёс, -ла́ *imp.* (*perf.* по~, с~) carry; bear; bring, take; support; suffer; incur; perform; talk; lay; *impers.*+*instr.* stink of, reek of; **~сь,** rush, tear, fly; float, drift, be carried; skim; spread, be diffused; lay, lay eggs.

не-. нестóйкий, unstable. **нестроевúк,** -á, non-combatant. **нестроевóй,** non-combatant. **нестрóйный;** -óен, -ойнá, -о, discordant, dissonant; disorderly; clumsily built. **несудохóдный,** unnavigable. **несущéственный,** immaterial, inessential.

несý, etc.: see нестú. **несýщий,** supporting, carrying, bearing, lifting.

несхóдный, unlike, dissimilar; unreasonable.

несчастлúвец, -вца, **~вица,** -ы, unlucky person; unfortunate. **несчастлúвый,** unfortunate, unlucky; unhappy. **несчáстный,** unhappy, unfortunate, unlucky; *sb.* wretch, unfortunate. **несчáстье,** -я, misfortune; accident; к несчáстью, unfortunately.

несчётный, innumerable, countless.

нет *part.* no, not; nothing; ~ да ~, ~ как ~, absolutely not; свестú на ~, bring to naught; ~-~ да и, from time to time, every now and then. **нет, нéту,** there is not, there are not.

не-. нетактúчный, tactless. **нетвёрдый;** -ёрд, -á, -о, unsteady, shaky; not firm. **нетерпелúвый,** impatient. **нетерпéние,** -я, impatience. **нетерпúмый,** intolerable, intolerant. **нетóчный;** -чен, -чнá, -о, inaccurate, inexact. **нетрéбовательный,** not exacting, undemanding; unpretentious. **нетрéзвый,** drunk, intoxicated. **нетрóнутый,** untouched; chaste, virginal. **нетрудовóй;** ~ дохóд, unearned income. **нетрудоспосóбность,** -и, disablement, disability.

нéтто *indecl. adj.* and *adv.* net, nett.

нéту: see нет.

не-. неубедúтельный, unconvincing. **неуважéние,** -я, disrespect. **неуважúтельный,** inadequate; disrespectful. **неувéренный,** uncertain; hesitant; ~ в себé, diffident. **неувядáемый, неувядáющий,** unfading, eternal, immortal. **неувя́зка,** -и, lack of co-ordination; misunderstanding. **неугасúмый,** inextinguishable, unquenchable; never extinguished. **неугомóнный,** restless; unsleeping, indefatigable. **неудáча,** -и, failure. **неудáчливый,** unlucky. **неудáчник,** -а, **-ница,** -ы, unlucky person, failure. **неудáчный,** unsuccessful, unfortunate. **неудержúмый,** irrepressible. **неудóбный,** uncomfortable; inconvenient, awkward, embarrassing. **неудóбство,** -а, discomfort, inconvenience, embarrassment. **неудовлетворéние,** -я, dissatisfaction. **неудовлетворённый,** dissatisfied, discontented. **неудовлетворúтельный,** unsatisfactory. **неудовóльствие,** -я, displeasure.

неужéли? *part.* indeed? really? surely not?; ~ он так дýмает? does he really think that?

не-. неузнавáемый, unrecognizable. **неуклóнный,** steady, steadfast; undeviating, unswerving, strict. **неуклю́жий,** clumsy, awkward. **неукротúмый,** ungovernable, untamable. **неукрощённый;** -ён, -á, untamed. **неуловúмый,** elusive, difficult to catch; imperceptible, subtle. **неумéлый,** unskilful; clumsy. **неумéренный,** immoderate; excessive. **неумéстный,** inappropriate; out of place, misplaced; irrelevant. **неумолúмый,** implacable, inexorable. **неумы́шленный,** unintentional.

не-. неуплáта, -ы, non-payment. **неупотребúтельный,** not in use, not current. **неуравновéшенный,** unbalanced. **неурожáй,** -я, bad harvest, crop failure. **неурóчный,** untimely, unseasonable, inopportune. **неуря́дица,** -ы, disorder, mess; squabbling, squabble. **неуспевáемость,** -и, poor progress. **неуспевáющий,** not making satisfactory progress. **неуспéх,** -а, failure, ill success. **неустóйка,** -и, forfeit, penalty; failure. **неустóйчивый,** unstable; unsteady. **неустрашúмый,** fearless, intrepid. **неустýпчивый,** unyielding, uncompromising. **неусы́пный,** vigilant, unremitting. **неутéшный,** inconsolable, disconsolate. **неутолúмый,** unquenchable; unappeasable; insatiable. **неутомúмый,** tireless, indefatigable. **нéуч,** -а, ignoramus. **неучтúвый,** discourteous, impolite. **неуязвúмый,** invulnerable; unassailable.

неф, -а, nave.
нефри́т, -а, jade.
нефте- in *comb.* oil, petroleum. **нефтево́з,** -а, tanker. **~но́сный,** oil-bearing. **~перего́нный заво́д,** oil refinery. **~прово́д,** -а, (oil) pipeline. **~проду́кты,** -ов *pl.* petroleum products. **~хими́ческий,** petrochemical.
нефть, -и, oil, petroleum; ~-сырéц, crude oil. **нефтян|о́й,** oil, petroleum; oil-fired; ~о́е покрыва́ло, ~а́я плёнка, oil-slick.
не-. **нехва́тка,** -и shortage, deficiency. **нехорошо́** *adv.* badly. **нехоро́ш|ий;** -о́ш, -а́, bad; ~о́, it is bad, it is wrong; как ~о́! what a shame!; чу́вствовать себя́ ~о́, feel unwell. **не́хотя** *adv.* reluctantly, unwillingly; unintentionally. **нецелесообра́зн|ый,** inexpedient; purposeless, pointless; ~ая тра́та, waste. **нецензу́рный,** unprintable. **нечáянный,** unexpected; accidental; unintentional.
не́чего, не́чему, -чем, не́ о чем *pron.* (with separable *pref.*), (there is) nothing; it's no good, it's no use; there is no need; ~ де́лать, there is nothing to be done; it can't be helped; ~ сказа́ть! well, really! well, I must say!; от ~ де́лать, for want of something better to do, idly.
нечелове́ческий, inhuman, superhuman.
нечести́вый, impious, profane. **нечéстно** *adv.* dishonestly, unfairly. **нечéстный,** dishonest, unfair.
не́чет, -а odd number. **нечётный,** odd.
нечистопло́тный, dirty; slovenly; unscrupulous. **нечистота́,** -ы́; *pl.* -о́ты, -о́т, dirtiness, dirt, filth; *pl.* sewage. **нечи́стый;** -и́ст, -а́, -о, dirty, unclean; impure; adulterated; careless, inaccurate; dishonourable, dishonest; *sb.* the evil one, the devil. **не́чисть,** -и, evil spirits; scum, vermin.
нечленоразде́льный, inarticulate.
не́что *pron.* something.
не-. **нешу́точн|ый,** grave, serious; ~ое де́ло, no joke, no laughing matter. **неща́дный,** merciless, pitiless. **неевкли́дов,** non-Euclidean. **нея́вка,** -и, non-appearance, failure to appear, absence. **неядови́тый,** non-poisonous, non-toxic. **нея́ркий,** not bright; not vivid, not striking; dull, subdued. **нея́сный;** -сен, -сна́, -о, not clear; vague, obscure.
НЗ (*enzé*) *abbr.* неприкоснове́нный запа́с, emergency ration.
ни *part.* not a; ни оди́н (одна́, одно́), not one, not a single; (with *prons.* and *pronominal advs.*) -ever; как . . ни, however; кто . . ни, whoever; что . . ни, whatever; како́й ни на есть, any whatsoever. **ни,** *conj.*; ни . . ни, neither . . nor; ни за что ни про что, for no reason, without rhyme or reason; ни ры́ба ни мя́со, neither fish, flesh, nor good red herring; ни с того́, ни с сего́, all of a sudden, for no apparent reason; ни то ни сё, neither one thing nor the other.
ни́ва, -ы, cornfield, field.
нивели́р, -а, level. **нивели́ровать,** -рую *perf.* and *imp.* level; survey, contour. **нивелиро́вщик,** -а, surveyor.
нигде́ *adv.* nowhere.
нидерла́ндец, -дца; *gen. pl.* -дцев, Dutchman. **нидерла́ндка,** -и, Dutchwoman. **нидерла́ндский,** Dutch.
нижа́йший, lowest, humblest; very low, very humble. **ни́же** *adj.* lower, humbler; *adv.* below; *prep.* + *gen.* below, beneath. **нижеподписа́вшийся,** (the) undersigned. **нижесле́дующий,** following. **нижестоя́щий,** subordinate. **нижеупомя́нутый,** (the) undermentioned. **ни́жн|ий,** lower, under-; ~ее бельё, underclothes; ~ий эта́ж, ground floor. **низ,** -а (-у), *loc.* -у́; *pl.* -ы́, bottom; ground floor; *pl.* lower classes; low notes.
низ-, нис-, *vbl. pref.* down, downward(s).
низа́ть, нижу́, ни́жешь *imp.* (*perf.* на~), string, thread.
низверга́ть, -а́ю *imp.*, **низве́ргнуть,** -ну; -ерг *perf.* precipitate; throw down, overthrow; **~ся,** crash down; be overthrown. **низверже́ние,** -я, overthrow.
низи́на, -ы, depression, hollow. **ни́зкий;** -зок, -зка́, -о, low; humble; base, mean. **ни́зко** *adv.* low; basely, meanly, despicably. **низкопокло́нник,** -а, toady, crawler. **низкопокло́нничать,**

-аю *imp.* crawl, cringe, grovel. **низкопоклóнство, -а,** obsequiousness, cringing, servility. **низкопрóбный,** base; low-grade; inferior. **низкорóслый,** undersized, stunted, dwarfish. **низкосóртный,** low-grade, of inferior quality.

нúзменность, -и, lowland; baseness. **нúзменный,** low-lying; low, base, vile.

низовóй, lower; down-stream, from lower down the Volga; local. **низóвье, -я;** *gen. pl.* -ьев, the lower reaches; низóвья Вóлги, the lower Volga. **нúзость, -и,** lowness; baseness, meanness. **нúзш|ий,** lower, lowest; ~ее образовáние, primary education; ~ий сорт, inferior quality.

НИИ (*nií*) *abbr.* наýчно-исслéдовательский инститýт, scientific research institute.

никáк *adv.* by no means, in no way. **никакóй** *pron.* no; no . . whatever.

нúкель, -я *m.* nickel.

никéм: see никтó. **никогдá** *adv.* never. **ник|óй,** no; ~óим óбразом, by no means, in no way. **никтó, -когó, -комý, -кéм,** ни о кóм *pron.* (with separable *pref.*) nobody, no one. **никудá,** nowhere; ~ не годúтся, (it) is worthless, (it) is no good at all, (it) won't do. **никудышный,** useless, worthless, good-for-nothing. **никчёмный,** pointless, useless; no good. **нимáло** *adv.* not at all, not in the least.

нимб, -а, halo, nimbus.

нúмфа, -ы, nymph; pupa. **нимфомáнка, -и,** nymphomaniac.

ниоткýда *adv.* from nowhere; not from anywhere.

нипочём *adv.* it is nothing; for nothing, dirt cheap; never, in no circumstances.

нúппель, -я; *pl.* -я́ *m.* nipple.

НИС *abbr.* наýчно-исслéдовательская стáнция, scientific research station.

нис-: see низ-.

нискóлько *adv.* not at all, not in the least.

ниспровергáть, -áю *imp.*, **ниспровéргнуть, -ну;** -ерг *perf.* overthrow, overturn. **ниспровержéние, -я,** overthrow.

нисходя́щий, descending, of descent; falling.

нúтка, -и, thread; string; до нúтки, to the skin; на живýю нúтку, hastily, carelessly, anyhow. **нúточка, -и,** thread. **нúточный,** thread; spinning.

нитро- in *comb.* nitro-. **нитробензóл, -а,** nitrobenzene. **~глицерúн, -а,** nitroglycerine. **~клетчáтка, -и,** nitrocellulose.

нúтчатый, filiform. **нить, -и,** thread; filament; suture; (путевóдная) ~ clue. **нитянóй, нúтяный,** cotton, thread.

ничегó, etc.: see ничтó. **ничегó** *adv.* all right; so-so, passably, not too badly; as *indecl. adj.* not bad, passable. **ничéй, -чья́, -чьё** *pron.* nobody's, no-one's; ничья́ земля́, no man's land. **ничья́** *sb.* draw, drawn game; tie; dead heat.

ничкóм *adv.* face downwards, prone.

ничтó, -чегó, -чемý, -чéм, ни о чём *pron.* (with separable *pref.*) nothing; naught; nil; ничегó! that's all right! it doesn't matter, never mind! **ничтóжество, -а,** nonentity, nobody; nothingness. **ничтóжный,** insignificant; paltry, worthless.

ничýть *adv.* not at all, not in the least, not a bit.

ничьё, etc.: see ничéй.

нúша, -и, niche, recess; bay.

нúщенка, -и, beggar-woman. **нúщенский,** beggarly. **нúщенствовать, -твую** *imp.* beg, be a beggar; be destitute. **нищетá, -ы́,** destitution, indigence, poverty; beggars, the poor. **нúщий;** нищ, -á, -е, destitute, indigent, poverty-stricken, poor; *sb.* beggar, mendicant, pauper.

НК (*enká*) *abbr.* Нарóдный комиссáр, Нарóдный комиссариáт, Peoples' Commissar(iat); натурáльный каучýк, natural rubber; наýчный комитéт, scientific committee. **НКВД** (*enkavedé*) *abbr.* Нарóдный комиссариáт внýтренних дел, People's Commissariat for Internal Affairs.

но *conj.* but; still, nevertheless; as *sb.*, snag, difficulty.

но *int.* gee up!

н.о., НО *abbr.* Национáльный óкруг, National Area.

нова́тор, -а, innovator. **нова́торство**, -а, innovation.
нове́йший, newest, latest.
нове́лла, -ы, short story. **новелли́ст**, -а, short-story writer.
но́веньк|ий, brand-new; **~ий**, **~ая** *sb.* new boy, new girl.
новизна́, -ы́, novelty; newness. **нови́нка**, -и, novelty. **новичо́к**, -чка́, novice, beginner, tyro; new recruit; new boy, new girl.
новo- in *comb.* new, newly; recent, recently; modern. **новобра́нец**, -нца, new recruit. **~бра́чный** *sb.* bridegroom; **~бра́чная** *sb.* bride; **~бра́чные** *sb. pl.* newly-weds. **~введе́ние**, -я, innovation. **~го́дний**, new year's, new-year. **~зела́ндец**, -дца; *gen. pl.* -дцев, **~зела́ндка**, -и, New Zealander. **~зела́ндский**, New Zealand. **~лу́ние**, -я, new moon. **~мо́дный**, up-to-date, fashionable; newfangled. **~прибы́вший**, newly-arrived; *sb.* newcomer. **~сёл**, -а, **~сёлка**, -и, new settler. **~се́лье**, -я, new home; house-warming.
но́вость, -и, news; novelty. **но́вшество**, -а, innovation, novelty. **но́вый**; нов, -á, -о, new, novel, fresh; modern, recent; ~ год New Year's Day. **новь**, -и, virgin soil.
нога́, -и́, *acc.* но́гу; *pl.* но́ги, нога́м, foot, leg; без (за́дних) ног, dead beat; встать с ле́вой ноги́, get out of bed on the wrong side; дать но́гу, get in step; идти́ в но́гу с + *instr.*, keep in step with; на коро́ткой ноге́ с + *instr.* intimate with, on good terms with; на широ́кую (большу́ю, ба́рскую) но́гу, in style, like a lord; протяну́ть но́ги, turn up one's toes; сбить с ног, knock down; сби́ться с ноги́, get out of step; со всех ног, as fast as one's legs will carry one; стать на́ ноги, стоя́ть на нога́х, stand on one's own feet.
ного́ток, -тка́, nail; *pl.* marigold. **но́готь**, -гтя; *pl.* -и *m.* finger-nail, toe-nail.
нож, -á, knife; на ~áх, at daggers drawn. **ножев|о́й**, knife; ~ы́е изде́лия, ~о́й това́р, cutlery; ~о́й ма́стер, cutler.
но́жка, -и, small foot or leg; leg; stem, stalk.
но́жницы, -иц *pl.* scissors, shears.
ножно́й, foot, pedal, treadle.
но́жны, -жен *pl.* sheath, scabbard.
ножо́вка, -и, saw, hacksaw.
ножо́вщик, -а, cutler.
ноздрева́тый, porous, spongy. **ноздря́**, -и́; *pl.* -и, -е́й, nostril.
нока́ут, -а, knock-out. **нокаути́рованный**, knocked out. **нокаути́ровать**, -рую *perf.* and *imp.* knock out.
нолево́й, **нулево́й**, zero. **ноль**, -я́, **нуль**, -я́ *m.* nought, zero, nil, love; cipher; абсолю́тный ~, absolute zero; в семна́дцать ~-~, at seventeen hundred hours, at five p.m.
но́мер, -а; *pl.* -á, number; size; (hotel-) room; item, turn; trick. **номера́тор**, etc.: see нумера́тор, etc. **номерно́й** *sb.* floor waiter, hotel servant. **номеро́к**, -рка́, tag; label, ticket; small room.
номина́л, -а, face value. **номина́льный**, nominal; rated, indicated.
нора́, -ы́; *pl.* -ы, burrow, hole; lair, form.
норве́жец, -жца, **норве́жка**, -и, Norwegian. **норве́жский**, Norwegian.
норд, -а, north, north wind. **норд-ве́ст**, -а, north-west, north-wester. **норд-о́ст**, -а north-east, north-easter.
но́рка, -и, mink.
но́рма, -ы, standard, norm; rate; ~ вре́мени, time limit. **нормализа́ция**, -и, standardization. **нормализова́ть**, -зу́ю *perf.* and *imp.* standardize. **норма́льный**, normal; standard. **нормати́в**, -а, norm, standard. **нормирова́ние**, -я, **нормиро́вка**, -и, regulation, normalization; rate-fixing. **нормирова́ть**, -ру́ю *perf.* and *imp.* regulate, standardize, normalize. **нормиро́вщик**, -а -щица, -ы, rate-fixer, rate-setter.
нос, -а (-у), *loc.* -у́; *pl.* -ы́, nose; beak; bow, prow; на ~у́, near (at hand), imminent; оста́вить с ~ом, dupe, make a fool of; пове́сить ~, be crestfallen, be discouraged. **но́сик**, -а, (small) nose; toe; spout.
носи́лки, -лок *pl.* stretcher; litter; hand-barrow. **носи́льщик**, -а, porter. **носи́тель**, -я *m.*, **-тельница**, -ы, bearer;

carrier; vehicle. **носи́ть,** -ошу́, -о́сишь *imp.* carry, bear; wear; ~ на рука́х, make much of, make a fuss of, spoil; **~ся,** rush, tear along, fly; float, drift, be carried; wear; + с + *instr.* make much of, make a fuss of. **но́ска,** -и, carrying, bearing, wearing; laying. **но́ский,** hard-wearing, durable; laying, that lays well.

носово́й, of or for the nose; nasal; bow, fore; ~ плато́к, (pocket) handkerchief. **носо́к,** -ска́, little nose; toe; sock. **носоро́г,** -а, rhinoceros.

НОТ, -а *abbr.* нау́чная организа́ция труда́, scientific organization of labour; work study.

но́та, -ы, note; *pl.* music. **нота́ция,** -и, notation; lecture, reprimand.

ночева́ть, -чу́ю *imp.* (*perf.* пере~), spend the night. **ночёвка,** -и, spending the night. **ночле́г,** -а, shelter for the night, a night's lodging; passing the night. **ночле́жка,** -и, **ночле́жный дом,** doss-house, common lodging-house. **ночни́к,** -а́, night-light. **ночн|о́й,** night, nocturnal; ~а́я ба́бочка, moth; ~а́я руба́шка, nightdress, nightgown, nightshirt; ~о́й сто́лик, bedside table; ~ы́е ту́фли, bedroom slippers. **ночь,** -и, *loc.* -и́; *gen. pl.* -е́й, night; глуха́я ~, dead of night. **но́чью** *adv.* at night, by night.

но́ша, -и, burden. **но́шеный,** in use, worn; part-worn, second-hand.

но́ю, etc.: see ныть.

ноя́брь, -я́ *m.* November. **ноя́брьский,** November.

нрав, -а, disposition, temper; *pl.* manners, customs, ways; по ~у, to one's taste, pleasing. **нра́виться,** -влюсь *imp.* (*perf.* по~), + *dat.* please; мне нра́вится, I like. **нравоуче́ние,** -я, moralizing, moral lecture; moral. **нравоучи́тельный,** edifying. **нра́вственность,** -и, morality, morals. **нра́вственный,** moral.

н. ст. *abbr.* но́вый стиль, New Style.

ну, *int.* and *part.* well, well then; what?; really; what a . . !, there's a . .!; а ну́ + *gen.*, to hell with; (да) ну? not really?; ну́ как+*future*, suppose, what if?

ну́дный, tedious, boring.

нужда́, -ы́; *pl.* -ы, want, straits; need; indigence; necessity; call of nature; нужды́ нет, never mind, it doesn't matter. **нужда́ться,** -а́юсь *imp.* be in want, be poor, be hard up; +в+*prep.* need, require, want. **ну́жник,** -а, lavatory, public convenience, latrine. **ну́жн|ый;** -жен, -жна́, -о, ну́жны́, necessary, requisite; **~о,** it is necessary; +*dat.* I, etc., must, ought to, should, need.

нуклейновый, nucleic.

нулево́й, нуль: see нолево́й, ноль.

нумера́тор, ном-, -а, numberer, numbering machine; annunciation. **нумера́ция, ном-,** -и, numeration; numbering. **нумерова́ть, ном-,** -ру́ю *imp.* (*perf.* за~, про~) number.

нутро́, -а́, inside, interior; core, kernel; instinct(s), intuition; всем ~м, with one's whole being, completely; по нутру́+*dat.*, to the liking of. **нутряно́й** internal.

НЧ (*enché*) *abbr.* ни́зкая частота́, низкочасто́тный, low(-)frequency.

ны́не *adv.* now; today. **ны́нешний,** the present, this; today's. **ны́нче** *adv.* today; now.

нырну́ть, -ну́, -нёшь *perf.*, **ныря́ть,** -я́ю *imp.* dive, plunge; duck. **ныро́к,** -рка́, dive, plunge; duck, ducking; diver. **ныря́ло,** -а, plunger.

ны́тик, -а, whiner, moaner. **ныть,** но́ю *imp.* ache; whine, moan. **нытьё,** -я́, whining, moaning.

н.э. *abbr.* на́шей э́ры, A.D.

нюх, -а, scent; nose, flair. **ню́хательный** таба́к, snuff. **ню́хать,** -аю *imp.* (*perf.* по~) smell, sniff; ~ таба́к, take snuff.

ня́нчить, -чу *imp.* nurse, look after; dandle; **~ся** с+*instr.* be nurse to, act as nurse to; fuss over, make a fuss of. **ня́нька,** -и, nanny. **ня́ня,** -и, (children's) nurse, nanny; hospital nurse.

О

о *n. indecl.* the letter о.
о, об, обо *prep.* I. +*prep.* of, about, concerning; on; with, having; стол о трёх нóжках, a three-legged table. II. +*acc.* against; on, upon; бок ó бок, side by side; оперéться о стéну, lean against the wall; рукá óб руку, hand in hand; споткнýться о кáмень, stumble against a stone. III. +*acc.* or *prep.* on, at, about; об э́ту пóру, about this time; о зарé, about dawn.
о *int.* oh!
о. *abbr.* óстров, island, isle.
о-, об-, обо-, объ, *vbl. pref.* indicates transformation, process of becoming, action applied to entire surface of object or to series of objects.
об: see о *prep.*
об-, обо- объ- *vbl. pref.* = о-, or indicates action or motion about an object.
óба обóих *m.* and *n.*, **óбе,** обéих *f.* both; обéими рукáми, with both hands; very willingly, readily; смотрéть в óба, keep one's eyes open, be on one's guard.
обагри́ть, -рю́ *perf.*, **обагря́ть,** -я́ю *imp.* crimson, incarnadine; ~ крóвью, stain with blood; ~ рýки в крови́, steep one's hands in blood; **~ся,** be crimsoned; ~ся (крóвью), be stained with blood.
обалдевáть, -áю *imp.*, **обалдéть,** -éю *perf.* go crazy; become dulled; be stunned.
обанкрóтиться, -óчусь *perf.* go bankrupt.
обая́ние, -я, fascination, charm. **обая́тельный,** fascinating, charming.
обвáл, -а, fall, falling, crumbling; collapse; caving-in; landslide; (снéжный) ~, avalanche. **обвáливать(ся,** -аю(сь *imp.* of обвали́ть(ся, обваля́ть. **обвáлистый,** liable to fall, liable to cave in. **обвали́ть,** -лю́, -лишь *perf.* (*imp.* обвáливать) cause to fall, cause to collapse; crumble; heap round; **~ся,** fall, collapse, cave in; crumble.
обваля́ть, -я́ю *perf.* (*imp.* обвáливать) roll; ~ в сухаря́х, roll in bread-crumbs.
обвáривать, -аю *imp.*, **обвари́ть,** -рю́, -ришь *perf.* pour boiling water over; scald; **~ся,** scald oneself.
обведý, etc.: see обвести́. **обвёл,** etc.: see обвести́. **об|венчáть(ся,** -áю(сь *perf.*
обвернýть, -нý, -нёшь *perf.*, **обвёртывать,** -аю *imp.* wrap, wrap up.
обвéс, -а, short weight. **обвéсить,** -éшу *perf.* (*imp.* обвéшивать) give short weight (to); cheat in weighing.
обвести́, -едý, -едёшь; -ёл, -елá *perf.* (*imp.* обводи́ть) lead round, take round; encircle; surround; outline; dodge, get past; deceive, fool, cheat; ~ взóром, глазáми, look round (at), take in; ~ вокрýг пáльца, twist round one's little finger.
обвéтренный, weather-beaten; chapped.
обветшáлый, decrepit, decayed; dilapidated. **об|ветшáть,** -áю *perf.*
обвéшивать, -аю *imp.* of обвéсить.
обвивáть(ся, -áю(сь *imp.* of обви́ть(ся.
обвинéние, -я, charge, accusation; prosecution; вы́нести ~ в+*prep.* find guilty of. **обвини́тель,** -я *m.* accuser; prosecutor. **обвини́тельн|ый,** accusatory; ~ый акт, indictment; ~ый пригов́ор, verdict of guilty; ~ая речь, speech for the prosecution. **обвини́ть,** -ню́ *perf.*, **обвиня́ть,** -я́ю *imp.* prosecute, indict; + в + *prep.* accuse of, charge with. **обвиня́емый** *sb.* the accused; defendant.
обвисáть, -áет *imp.*, **обви́снуть,** -нет; -ви́с *perf.* sag; hang, droop; grow flabby. **обви́слый,** flabby; hanging, drooping.
обви́ть, обовью́, обовьёшь; обви́л, -á, -о *perf.* (*imp.* обвивáть) wind round, entwine; **~ся,** wind round, twine oneself round.
обвóд, -а, enclosing, surrounding; outlining. **обводи́ть,** -ожý, -óдишь *imp.* of обвести́.

обводне́ние, -я, irrigation; filling up. **обводни́тельный**, irrigation. **обводни́ть**, -ню́ *perf.*, **обводня́ть**, -ня́ю *imp.* irrigate; fill with water.

обво́дный, bypass, leading round.

обвора́живать, -аю *imp.*, **обворожи́ть**, -жу́ *perf.* charm, fascinate, enchant. **обворожи́тельный**, charming, fascinating, enchanting.

обвяза́ть, -яжу́, -я́жешь *perf.*, **обвя́зывать**, -аю *imp.* tie round; edge; **~ся** + *instr.* tie round oneself.

обгла́дывать, -аю *imp.*, **обглода́ть**, -ожу́, -о́жешь *perf.* pick, gnaw (round). **обгло́док**, -дка, bare bone.

обго́н, -а, passing. **обгоня́ть**, -я́ю *imp.* of обогна́ть.

обгора́ть, -а́ю *imp.*, **обгоре́ть**, -рю́ *perf.* be burnt, be scorched. **обгоре́лый**, burnt, charred, scorched.

обдава́ть, -даю́, -даёшь *imp.*, **обда́ть**, -а́м, -а́шь, -а́ст, -ади́м; о́бдал, -а́, -о *perf.* + *instr.* pour over, cover with; overcome overwhelm, with; **~ся** + *instr.* pour over oneself.

обде́лать, -аю *perf.* (*imp.* обде́лывать), finish; cut polish, set; manage, arrange; cheat.

обдели́ть, -лю́, -лишь *perf.* (*imp.* обделя́ть) + *instr.* do out of one's (fair) share of.

обде́лывать, -аю *imp.* of обде́лать. **обделя́ть**, -я́ю *imp.* of обдели́ть.

обдеру́, etc.: see ободра́ть. **обдира́ть**, -аю *imp.* of ободра́ть. **обди́рка** -и, peeling; hulling, shelling; skinning, flaying; groats. **обди́рный**, peeled, hulled.

обдува́ла, -ы *m.* and *f.* cheat, trickster. **обдува́ть**, -а́ю *imp.* of обду́ть.

обду́манно *adv.* after careful consideration, deliberately. **обду́манный**, deliberate, well-considered, well-weighed, carefullv-thought-out. **обду́мать**, -аю *perf.*, **обду́мывать**, -аю *imp.* consider, think over, weigh.

обду́ть, -у́ю *perf.* (*imp.* обдува́ть) blow on, blow round; cheat, fool, dupe.

о́бе: see о́ба. **обега́ть**, -а́ю *imp.* of обежа́ть. **обегу́**, etc.: see обежа́ть.

обе́д, -а, dinner; пе́ред ~ом, in the morning; по́сле ~а, in the afternoon.

обе́дать, -аю *imp.* (*perf.* по~) have dinner, dine. **обе́денный**, dinner; ~ переры́в, dinner hour.

обедне́вший, **обедне́лый**, impoverished. **обедне́ние**, -я, impoverishment. **о|бедне́ть**, -е́ю *perf.*, **обедни́ть**, -ню́ *perf.*, **обедня́ть**, -я́ю *imp.* impoverish.

обе́дня, -и; *gen. pl.* -ден, mass.

обежа́ть, -егу́ *perf.* (*imp.* обега́ть) run round; run past; outrun, pass.

обезбо́ливание, -я, anaesthetization. **обезбо́ливать**, -аю *imp.*, **обезбо́лить**, -лю *perf.* anaesthetize.

обезвре́дить, -е́жу *perf.*, **обезвре́живать**, -аю *imp.* render harmless; neutralize.

обездо́ленный, deprived; unfortunate, hapless. **обездо́ливать**, -аю *imp.*, **обездо́лить**, -лю *perf.* deprive of one's share.

обеззара́живать, -аю *imp.*, **обеззара́зить**, -а́жу *perf.* disinfect. **обеззара́живающий**, disinfectant.

обезли́ченный, depersonalized; generalized, reduced to a standard; mechanical. **обезли́чивать**, -аю *imp.*, **обезли́чить**, -чу *perf.* deprive of individuality, depersonalize; do away with personal responsibility for. **обезли́чка**, -и, lack of personal responsibility.

обезобра́живать, -аю *imp.*, **о|безобра́зить**, -а́жу *perf.* disfigure, mutilate.

обезопа́сить, -а́шу *perf.* secure, make safe; **~ся**, secure oneself.

обезору́живание, -я, disarmament. **обезору́живать**, -аю *imp.*, **обезору́жить**, -жу *perf.* disarm.

обезу́меть, -ею *perf.* lose one's senses, lose one's head; ~ от испу́га, become panic-stricken.

обезья́на, -ы, monkey; ape. **обезья́ний**, monkey; simian; ape-like. **обезья́нник**, -а, monkey-house. **обезья́нничать**, -аю *imp.* (*perf.* с~) ape.

обели́ть, -лю́ *perf.*, **обеля́ть**, -я́ю *imp.* vindicate, prove the innocence of; clear of blame; whitewash; **~ся**, vindicate oneself, prove one's innocence.

оберега́ть, -а́ю *imp.*, **обере́чь**, -егу́, -ежёшь; -рёг, -ла́ *perf.* guard; protect; **~ся**, guard oneself, protect oneself.

оберну́ть, -ну́, -нёшь *perf.*, **обёртывать, -аю** *imp.* (*imp.* also обора́чивать) wind, twist; wrap up; turn; turn over; ~ кни́гу, jacket a book; cover a book; **~ся,** turn, turn round; turn out; come back; manage, get by; +*instr.* or в+ *acc.* turn into; ~ся лицо́м к, turn towards. **обёртка, -и,** wrapper; envelope; (dust-)jacket, cover. **обёрточн|ый,** wrapping; ~ая бума́га, brown paper, wrapping paper.

оберу́, etc.: see обобра́ть.

обескура́живать, -аю *imp.*, **обескура́жить, -жу** *perf.* discourage; dismay.

обескро́вить, -влю *perf.*, **обескро́вливать, -аю** *imp.* drain of blood, bleed white; render lifeless. **обескро́вленный,** bloodless; pallid, anaemic, lifeless.

обеспе́чение, -я, securing, guaranteeing; ensuring; providing, provision; guarantee; security; safeguard(s); protection. **обеспе́ченность, -и,** security; +*instr.* being provided with, provision of. **обеспе́ченный,** well-to-do; well provided for. **обеспе́чивать, -аю** *imp.*, **обеспе́чить, -чу** *perf.* provide for; secure, guarantee; ensure, assure; safeguard, protect; + *instr.* provide with guarantee supply of.

о|беспоко́ить(ся, -о́ю(сь *perf.*

обесси́леть, -ею *perf.* grow weak, lose one's strength; collapse, break down. **обесси́ливать, -аю** *imp.*, **обесси́лить, -лю** *perf.* weaken.

о|бессла́вить, -влю *perf.*

обессме́ртить, -рчу *perf.* immortalize.

обесцве́тить, -е́чу *perf.*, **обесцве́чивать, -аю** *imp.* fade, deprive of colour; make colourless, tone down; **~ся,** fade; become colourless.

обесце́нение, -я, depreciation; loss of value. **обесце́нивать, -аю** *imp.*, **обесце́нить, -ню** *perf.* depreciate, cheapen; **~ся,** depreciate, lose value.

о|бесче́стить, -е́щу *perf.*

обе́т, -а, vow, promise. **обетова́нный,** promised. **обеща́ние, -я,** promise; дать ~, give a promise, give one's word; сдержа́ть ~, keep a promise, keep one's word. **обеща́ть, -а́ю** *perf.* and *imp.* (*perf.* also по~) promise.

обжа́лование, -я, appeal. **обжа́ловать, -лую** *perf.* appeal against, lodge a complaint against.

обже́чь, обожгу́ обожжёшь; обжёг, обожгла́ *perf.*, **обжига́ть, -а́ю** *imp.* burn; scorch; bake; fire, calcine; sting; **~ся,** burn oneself; scald oneself; burn one's fingers; ~ся крапи́вой, be stung by a nettle. **обжига́тельн|ый,** glazing; baking; roasting; ~ая печь, kiln.

обжо́ра, -ы *m.* and *f.* glutton, gormandizer. **обжо́рливый,** gluttonous. **обжо́рство, -а,** gluttony.

обзаведе́ние, -я, providing, fitting out; establishment; fittings, appointments; bits and pieces. **обзавести́сь, -еду́сь, -едёшься; -вёлся, -ла́сь** *perf.*, **обзаводи́ться, -ожу́сь, -о́дишься** *imp.*+ *instr.* provide oneself with; set up.

обзову́, etc.: see обозва́ть.

обзо́р, -а, survey, review.

обзыва́ть, -а́ю *imp.* of обозва́ть.

обива́ть, -а́ю *imp.* of оби́ть. **оби́вка, -и,** upholstering; upholstery.

оби́да, -ы, offence, injury, insult; annoying thing, nuisance; не в оби́ду будь ска́зано, no offence meant; не дать себя́ в оби́ду, stand up for one-self. **оби́деть, -и́жу** *perf.*, **обижа́ть, -а́ю** *imp.* offend; hurt, wound; му́хи не оби́дит, he would not harm a fly; **~ся,** take offence, take umbrage; feel hurt; ~ся на+*acc.* resent; не обижа́йтесь, don't be offended. **оби́дный,** offensive; annoying, tiresome; мне оби́дно, I feel hurt, it pains me; оби́дно, it is a pity, it is a nuisance. **оби́дчивый,** touchy, sensitive. **оби́женный,** offended, hurt, aggrieved.

оби́лие, -я, abundance, plenty. **оби́льный,** abundant, plentiful; +*instr.* rich in.

обиня́к, -а́, circumlocution; hint, evasion; без ~о́в, plainly, in plain terms; говори́ть ~а́ми, beat about the bush.

обира́ть, -а́ю *imp.* of обобра́ть.

обита́емый, inhabited. **обита́тель, -я** *m.* inhabitant; resident; inmate. **обита́ть, -а́ю** *imp.* live, dwell, reside.

оби́ть, обобью́, -ьёшь *perf.* (*imp.* **обива́ть**) upholster, cover; knock off knock down; ~ гвоздя́ми, stud; ~ желе́зом, bind with iron.

обихо́д, -а, custom, (general) use, practice; в дома́шнем ~е, in domestic use, in the household. **обихо́дный**, everyday.

обката́ть, -а́ю *perf.*, **обка́тывать**, -аю *imp.* roll; roll smooth; run in. **обка́тка**, -и, running in.

обкла́дка, -и, facing; ~ дёрном, turfing. **обкла́дывать(ся**, -аю(сь *imp.* of обложи́ть(ся.

обко́м, -а *abbr.* областно́й комите́т, regional committee.

обкра́дывать, -аю *imp.* of обокра́сть.

обл. *abbr.* о́бласть, oblast, region.

обла́ва, -ы, raid swoop; round-up; cordon, cordoning off; battue.

облага́емый, taxable. **облага́ть(ся**, -а́ю(сь *imp.* of обложи́ть(ся; ~ся нало́гом, be liable to tax, be taxable.

облагора́живать, -аю *imp.*, **облагоро́дить**, -о́жу *perf.* ennoble.

облада́ние, -я, possession. **облада́тель**, -я *m.* possessor. **облада́ть**, -а́ю *imp.* + *instr.* possess, be possessed of; ~ пра́вом, have the right; ~ хоро́шим здоро́вьем, enjoy good health.

о́блако, -а; *pl.* -а́, -о́в, cloud.

обла́мывать(ся, -аю(сь *imp.* of облома́ть(ся, обломи́ться.

обласка́ть, -а́ю *perf.* treat with affection, show much kindness or consideration to.

областно́й, oblast; provincial; regional; dialectal. **о́бласть**, -и; *gen. pl.* -е́й, oblast, province; region; district; belt; tract; field, sphere, realm, domain.

обла́тка, -и, wafer; capsule; paper seal.

о́блачко, -а; *pl.* -а́, -о́в *dim.* of о́блако. **о́блачность**, -и, cloudiness; cloud. **о́блачный**, cloudy.

облёг, etc.: see обле́чь. **облега́ть**, -а́ет *imp.* of обле́чь. **облега́ющий**, tight-fitting.

облегча́ть, -а́ю *imp.*, **облегчи́ть**, -чу́ *perf.* lighten; relieve; alleviate, mitigate; commute; facilitate. **облегче́ние**, -я, relief.

обледене́лый, ice-covered. **обледене́ние**, я, icing over; пери́од обледене́ния, Ice Age. **обледене́ть**, -е́ет *perf.* ice over, become covered with ice.

облеза́ть, -а́ет *imp.*, **обле́зть**, -зет; -ле́з *perf.* come out, fall out, come off; grow bare, grow mangy; peel off. **обле́злый**, shabby, bare; mangy.

облека́ть(ся, -а́ю(сь *imp.* of обле́чь[2]-(ся. **облеку́**, etc.: see обле́чь[2].

обле́ниваться, -аюсь *imp.*, **облени́ться**, -ню́сь, -нишься *perf.* grow lazy, get lazy.

облепи́ть, -плю́, -пишь *perf.*, **облепля́ть**, -я́ю *imp.* stick to, cling to; surround, throng round; paste all over, plaster.

облета́ть, -а́ю *imp.*, **облете́ть**, -лечу́, fly (round); spread (round, all over); fall.

обле́чь[1], -ля́жет; -лёг, -ла́ *perf.* (*imp.* облега́ть) cover, surround, envelop; fit tightly.

обле́чь[2], -еку́, -ечёшь; -ёк, -кла́ *perf.* (*imp.* облека́ть) clothe, invest; wrap, shroud; **~ся**, clothe oneself, dress oneself; + *gen.* take the form of, assume the shape of.

облива́ние, -я, spilling over, pouring over; shower-bath; sponge-down. **облива́ть(ся**, -а́ю(сь *imp.* of обли́ть(ся; се́рдце у меня́ кро́вью облива́ется, my heart bleeds. **обли́вка**, -и, glazing; glaze. **обливно́й**, glazed.

облига́ция, -и, bond, debenture.

обли́занный, smooth. **облиза́ть**, -ижу́, -и́жешь *perf.*, **обли́зывать**, -аю *imp.* lick (all over); lick clean; **~ся**, smack one's lips; lick itself.

о́блик, -а, look, aspect, appearance; cast of mind, temper.

облиспolко́м, -а *abbr.* областно́й исполни́тельный комите́т, regional executive committee.

о́бли́тый; о́бли́т, -а́, -о, covered, enveloped; ~ све́том луны́, bathed in moonlight. **обли́ть**, оболью́, -льёшь; о́бли́л, -ила́, -о *perf.* (*imp.* облива́ть) pour, sluice, spill; glaze; **~ся**, sponge down, take a shower; pour over oneself, spill over oneself; ~ся по́том, be bathed in sweat; ~ся слеза́ми, melt into tears.

облицева́ть, -цу́ю *perf.*, **облицо́вывать,** -аю *imp.* face, revet. **облицо́вка,** -и, facing, revetment; lining, coating.

облича́ть, -а́ю *imp.*, **обличи́ть,** -чу́ *perf.* expose, unmask, denounce; reveal, display, manifest; point to. **обличе́ние,** -я, exposure, unmasking, denunciation. **обличи́тельн|ый,** denunciatory; ~ая речь, ~ая статья́, diatribe, tirade.

обложе́ние, -я, taxation; assessment, rating. **обложи́ть,** -жу́, -жишь *perf.* (*imp.* обкла́дывать, облага́ть) put round; edge; surface, face; cover; surround; close round, corner; assess; круго́м обложи́ло (не́бо), the sky is completely overcast; ~ ме́стным нало́гом, rate; ~ нало́гом tax; обложи́ло язы́к, the tongue is furred; **~ся**+*instr.* put round oneself, surround oneself with. **обло́жка,** -и, (dust-)cover; folder.

облока́чиваться, -аюсь *imp.*, **облокоти́ться,** -очу́сь, -о́тишься *perf.* на + *acc.* lean one's elbows on.

обло́м, -а, breaking off; break; profile. **облома́ть,** -а́ю *perf.* (*imp.* обла́мывать) break off; make yield; **~ся,** break off, snap. **обломи́ться,** -ло́мится *perf.* (*imp.* обла́мываться) break off. **обло́мок,** -мка, fragment; debris, wreckage.

об|лупи́ть, -плю́, -пишь *perf.*, **облу́пливать,** -аю *imp.* peel; shell; fleece; **~ся,** peel, peel off, scale; come off, chip. **облу́пленный,** chipped.

облучи́ть, -чу́ *perf.*, **облуча́ть,** -а́ю *imp.* irradiate. **облуче́ние,** -я, irradiation.

об|лущи́ть, -щу́ *perf.* **об|лысе́ть,** -е́ю *perf.*

облюбова́ть, -бу́ю *perf.*, **облюбо́вывать,** -аю *imp.* pick, choose, select.

обля́жет, etc.: see обле́чь[1].

обма́зать, -а́жу *perf.*, **обма́зывать,** -аю *imp.* coat; putty; soil, besmear; **~ся**+*instr.* besmear oneself with, get covered with. **обма́зка,** -и, coating, puttying.

обма́кивать, -аю *imp.*, **обмакну́ть,** -ну́, -нёшь *perf.* dip.

обма́н, -а, fraud, deception; illusion; ~ зре́ния, optical illusion. **обма́нный,** fraudulent, deceitful. **обману́ть,** -ну́, -нешь *perf.*, **обма́нывать,** -аю *imp.* deceive; cheat, swindle; betray, disappoint; **~ся,** be deceived, be disappointed. **обма́нчивый,** deceptive, delusive. **обма́нщик,** -а, deceiver; cheat, fraud.

обма́тывать(ся, -аю(сь *imp.* of обмота́ть(ся.

обма́хивать, -аю *imp.*, **обмахну́ть,** -ну́, -нёшь *perf.* brush off, dust (off); fan; **~ся,** fan oneself.

обмёл, etc.: see обмести́.

обмеле́ние, -я, shallowing, shoaling. **об|меле́ть,** -е́ет *perf.* become shallow, shoal; run aground.

обме́н -а, exchange, interchange; barter; в ~ за+*acc.* in exchange for; ~ веще́ств, metabolism; ~ мне́ниями, exchange of opinions. **обме́нивать,** -аю *imp.*, **обмени́ть,** -ню́, -нишь *perf.*, **об|меня́ть,** -я́ю *perf.* exchange; barter; swop; **~ся**+*instr.* exchange; обменя́ться впечатле́ниями, compare notes. **обме́нный,** exchange; metabolic.

обме́р, -а, measurement; false measure.

обмере́ть, обомру́, -рёшь; о́бмер, -ла́, -ло *perf.* (*imp.* обмира́ть) faint; ~ от у́жаса, be horror-struck; я о́бмер, my heart stood still.

обме́ривать, -аю *imp.*, **обме́рить,** -рю *perf.* measure; cheat in measuring, give short measure (to); **~ся,** make a mistake in measuring.

обмести́, -ету́, -етёшь; -мёл, -а́ *perf.*, **обмета́ть**[1], -а́ю *imp.* sweep off, dust.

обмета́ть[2], -ечу́ or -а́ю, -е́чешь or -а́ешь *perf.* (*imp.* обмётывать) oversew, overcast, whip; blanket-stitch.

обмету́, etc.: see обмести́. **обмётывать,** -аю *imp.* of обмета́ть. **обмира́ть,** -а́ю *imp.* of обмере́ть.

обмозгова́ть, -гу́ю *perf.*, **обмозго́вывать,** -аю *imp.* think over, turn over (in one's mind).

обмола́чивать, -аю *imp.* of обмолоти́ть.

обмо́лвиться, -влюсь *perf.* make a slip of the tongue; +*instr.* say, utter. **обмо́лвка,** -и, slip of the tongue.

обмоло́т, -а, threshing. **обмолоти́ть,**

-лочу́ -ло́тишь *perf.* (*imp.* обмола́чивать) thresh.

обмора́живать, -аю *imp.*, **обморо́зить,** -ро́жу *perf.* expose to frost subject to frost-bite, get frost-bitten; я обморо́зил себе́ ру́ки, I have got my hands frost-bitten; **~ся,** suffer frost-bite, be frost-bitten. **обморо́женный,** frost-bitten.

о́бморок, -а, fainting-fit, swoon; syncope.

обмота́ть, -а́ю *perf.* (*imp.* обма́тывать) wind round; **~ся**+*instr.* wrap oneself in. **обмо́тка,** -и, winding; lagging; taping; *pl.* puttees, leg-wrappings.

обмо́ю, etc.: see обмы́ть.

обмундирова́ние, -я, **обмундиро́вка,** -и, fitting out (with uniform), issuing of uniform; uniform. **обмундирова́ть,** -ру́ю *perf.*, **обмундиро́вывать,** -аю *imp.* fit out (with uniform), issue with clothing; **~ся,** fit oneself out; draw uniform. **обмундиро́вочный;** ~ые де́ньги, uniform allowance.

обмыва́ние, -я, bathing, washing. **обмыва́ть,** -а́ю *imp.*, **обмы́ть,** -мо́ю *perf.* bathe, wash; sponge down; **~ся,** wash, bathe; sponge down.

обмяка́ть, -а́ю *imp.*, **обмя́кнуть,** -ну; -мя́к *perf.* become soft; go limp, become flabby.

обнадёживать, -аю *imp.*, **обнадёжить,** -жу *perf.* give hope to, reassure.

обнажа́ть, -а́ю *imp.*, **обнажи́ть,** -жу́ *perf.* bare, uncover; unsheathe; lay bare, reveal. **обнажённый;** -ён, -ена́, naked, bare; nude.

обнаро́дование, -я, publication, promulgation. **обнаро́довать,** -дую *perf.* and *imp.* publish, promulgate.

обнару́жение, -я, disclosure; displaying, revealing; discovery; detection. **обнару́живать,** -аю *imp.*, **обнару́жить,** -жу *perf.* disclose; display; reveal, betray; discover, bring to light; detect; **~ся,** be revealed, come to light.

обнести́, -су́, -сёшь; -нёс, -ла́ *perf.* (*imp.* обноси́ть) enclose; +*instr.* serve round, pass round; pass over, leave out; меня́ обнесли́ вино́м, I have not been offered wine; ~ и́згородью, fence (in); ~ пери́лами, rail in, rail off.

обнима́ть(ся, -а́ю(сь *imp.* of обня́ть(ся.

обниму́, etc.: see обня́ть.

обнища́лый, impoverished; beggarly. **обнища́ние,** -я, impoverishment.

обнови́ть, -влю́ *perf.*, **обновля́ть,** -я́ю *imp.* renovate; renew; re-form; repair, restore; use or wear for the first time; **~ся,** revive, be restored. **обно́вка,** -и, new acquisition, new toy; new dress. **обновле́ние,** -я, renovation, renewal.

обноси́ть, -ошу́, -о́сишь *imp.* of обнести́; **~ся,** have worn out one's clothes; be out at elbow. **обно́ски,** -ов *pl.* old clothes, cast-offs.

обню́хать, -аю *perf.*, **обню́хивать,** -аю *imp.* smell, sniff at.

обня́ть, -ниму́, -ни́мешь; о́бнял, -а́, -о *perf.* (*imp.* обнима́ть) embrace; clasp in one's arms; take in; ~ взгля́дом, survey; ~ умо́м, comprehend, take in; **~ся,** embrace; hug one another.

обо: see о *prep.* **обо-:** see о-.

обобра́ть, оберу́, -рёшь; обобра́л, -а́, -о *perf.* (*imp.* обира́ть) rob; clean out; pick; gather all of.

обобща́ть, -а́ю *imp.*, **обобщи́ть,** -щу́ *perf.* generalize. **обобще́ние,** -я, generalization. **обобществи́ть,** -влю́ *perf.*, **обобществля́ть,** -я́ю *imp.* socialize; collectivize. **обобществле́ние,** -я, socialization; collectivization.

обобью́, etc.: see оби́ть. **обовью́,** etc.; see обви́ть.

обогати́ть, -ащу́ *perf.*, **обогаща́ть,** -а́ю *imp.* enrich; concentrate; **~ся,** become rich; enrich oneself. **обогаще́ние,** -я, enrichment; concentration.

обогна́ть, обгоню́, -о́нишь; обогна́л, -а́, -о *perf.* (*imp.* обгоня́ть) pass, leave behind; outstrip, outdistance.

обогну́ть -ну́, -нёшь *perf.* (*imp.* огиба́ть) round, skirt; double; bend round.

обогре́в, -а, heating. **обогрева́ние,** -я, heating, warming. **обогрева́тель,** -я *m.* heater. **обогрева́ть,** -а́ю *imp.*, **обогре́ть,** -е́ю *perf.* heat, warm; **~ся,** warm oneself; warm up.

о́бод, -а; *pl.* -о́дья, -ьев, rim; felloe.

ободо́к, -дка́, thin rim, narrow border; fillet.
ободра́нец, -нца, ragamuffin, ragged fellow. **обо́дранный,** ragged. **ободра́ть,** обдеру́, -рёшь; -а́л, -а́, -о *perf.* (*imp.* обдира́ть) strip; skin, flay; peel; fleece.
ободре́ние, -я encouragement, reassurance. **ободри́тельный,** encouraging, reassuring. **ободри́ть,** -рю́ *perf.*, **ободря́ть,** -я́ю *imp.* cheer up; encourage, reassure; **~ся,** cheer up, take heart.
обожа́ние, -я, adoration. **обожа́тель,** -я *m.* adorer; admirer. **обожа́ть,** -а́ю *imp.* adore, worship.
обожгу́, etc.: see обже́чь.
обожестви́ть, -влю́ *perf.*, **обожествля́ть,** -я́ю *imp.* deify; worship, idolize. **обожествле́ние,** -я, deification, worship.
обожжённый; -ён, -ена́, burnt, scorched; scalded; stung.
обо́з, -а, string of carts, string of sledges; transport; collection of vehicles.
обозва́ть, обзову́, -вёшь; -а́л, -а́, -о *perf.* (*imp.* обзыва́ть) call; call names; ~ дурако́м, call a fool.
обозлённый; -ён, -а́, angered; embittered. **обо|зли́ть,** -лю́ *perf.*, **о|зли́ть,** -лю́ *perf.* enrage, anger; embitter; **~ся,** get angry, grow angry.
обознача́ть, -а́ю *imp.*, **обозна́чить,** -чу *perf.* mean; mark; reveal; emphasize; **~ся,** appear, reveal oneself. **обозначе́ние,** -я, marking; sign, symbol.
обо́зник, -а, driver.
обозрева́тель, -я *m.* reviewer, observer; columnist; полити́ческий ~, political correspondent. **обозрева́ть,** -а́ю *imp.*, **обозре́ть,** -рю́ *perf.* survey; view; look round; (pass in) review. **обозре́ние,** -я, surveying, viewing; looking round; survey; review; revue. **обозри́мый,** visible.
обо́и, -ев *pl.* wall-paper.
обо́йма, -ы; *gen. pl.* -о́йм, cartridge-clip.
обойти́, -йду́, -йдёшь; -ошёл, -ошла́ *perf.* (*imp.* обходи́ть) go round, pass; make the round of, go (all) round; avoid; leave out; pass over; ~ молча́нием, pass over in silence; **~сь,** cost, come to; manage, make do; turn out, end; +с+*instr.* treat.
обо́йщик, -а, upholsterer.
обокра́сть, обкраду́, -дёшь *perf.* (*imp.* обкра́дывать) rob.
оболо́чка, -и, casing; membrane; cover, envelope, jacket; shell; coat.
обо́лтус, -а, blockhead, booby.
обольсти́тель, -я *m.* seducer. **обольсти́тельный,** seductive, captivating. **обольсти́ть,** -льщу́ *perf.*, **обольща́ть,** -а́ю *imp.* captivate; seduce. **обольще́ние,** -я, seduction; delusion.
оболью́, etc.: see обли́ть.
обомле́ть, -е́ю *perf.* be stupefied, be stunned.
обомру́, etc.: see обмере́ть.
обомше́лый, moss-grown.
обоня́ние, -я, (sense of) smell. **обоня́тельный,** olfactory. **обоня́ть,** -я́ю *imp.* smell.
обопру́, etc.: see оперéть.
обора́чиваемость, -и, turnover. **обора́чивать(ся,** -аюсь *imp.* of оберну́ть(ся, обороти́ть(ся.
оборва́нец, -нца, ragamuffin, ragged fellow. **обо́рванный,** torn, ragged. **оборва́ть,** -ву́, -вёшь; -а́л, -а́, -о *perf.* (*imp.* обрыва́ть) tear off, pluck; strip; break; snap; cut short, interrupt; **~ся,** break; snap; fall; come away; stop suddenly, stop short.
обо́рка, -и, frill, flounce.
оборо́на, -ы, defence; defences. **оборони́тельный,** defensive. **оборони́ть,** -ню́ *perf.*, **обороня́ть,** -я́ю *imp.* defend; **~ся,** defend oneself. **оборо́нный,** defence, defensive. **обороноспосо́бность,** -и, defence potential.
оборо́т, -а, turn; revolution, rotation; circulation; turnover; back; ~ ре́чи, (turn of) phrase; locution; смотри́ на ~е, P.T.O., please turn over; see other side. **оборо́тистый,** resourceful. **обороти́ть,** -рочу́, -ро́тишь *perf.* (*imp.* обора́чивать) turn; **~ся,** turn (round); + *instr.* or в + *acc.* turn into. **оборо́тливый,** resourceful. **оборо́тн|ый,** circulating, working; turn-round; reverse; **~ый** капита́л, working

capital; ~ая сторона́, reverse side; verso; э ~ое, the letter э.

обору́дование, -я, equipping; equipment. **обору́довать**, -дую *perf.* and *imp.* equip, fit out; manage, arrange.

обо́рыш, -а, left-over, remnant.

обоснова́ние, -я, basing; basis, ground. **обосно́ванный**, well-founded, well-grounded. **обоснова́ть**, -ную, -нуёшь *perf.*, **обосно́вывать**, -аю *imp.* ground, base; substantiate; **~ся**, settle down.

обосо́бить, -блю *perf.*, **обособля́ть**, -я́ю *imp.* isolate; **~ся**, stand apart; keep aloof. **обособле́ние**, -я, isolation. **обосо́бленный**, isolated, solitary.

обостре́ние, я, aggravation, exacerbation. **обострённый**, keen; strained, tense; sharp, pointed. **обостри́ть**, -рю́ *perf.*, **обостря́ть**, -я́ю *imp.* sharpen, intensify; strain; aggravate, exacerbate; **~ся**, become sharp, become pointed; become keener, become more sensitive; become strained; be aggravated; become acute.

оботру́, etc.: see обтере́ть.

обо́чина, -ы, verge; shoulder, edge, side.

обошёл, etc.: see обойти́. **обошью́**, etc.: see обши́ть.

обою́дность, -и, mutuality, reciprocity. **обою́дный**, mutual, reciprocal. **обоюдоо́стрый**, double-edged, two-edged.

обраба́тывать, -аю *imp.*, **обрабо́тать**, -аю *perf*, till, cultivate; work, work up; treat, process; machine; polish, perfect; work upon, win round. **обраба́тывающ|ий**; ~ая промы́шленность, manufacturing industry. **обрабо́тка**, -и, working (up); treatment, processing; cultivation.

об|ра́довать(ся, -дую(сь *perf.*

о́браз, -а, shape, form; appearance; image; type; figure; mode, manner; way; icon; гла́вным ~ом, mainly, chiefly, largely; **каки́м** ~ом? how?; ~ де́йствий, line of action, policy; ~ жи́зни, way of life; ~ мы́слей, way of thinking; ~ правле́ния, form of government; таки́м ~ом, thus. **образе́ц**, -зца́, model; pattern; example; specimen, sample. **о́бразный**, picturesque, graphic; figurative; employing images. **образова́ние**, -я, formation; education. **образо́ванный**, educated. **образова́тельный**, educational. **образова́ть**, -зу́ю *perf.* and *imp.*, **образо́вывать**, -аю *imp.* form; make (up); organize; educate; **~ся**, form; arise; turn out well.

образу́мить, -млю *perf.* bring to reason; make listen to reason; **~ся**, come to one's senses, see reason.

образу́ющая *sb.* generatrix.

образцо́вый, model; exemplary. **обра́зчик**, -а, specimen, sample; pattern.

обра́мить, -млю *perf.*, **обрамля́ть**, -я́ю *imp.* frame. **обрамле́ние**, -я, framing; frame; setting.

обраста́ть, -а́ю *imp.*, **обрасти́**, -ту́, -тёшь; -ро́с, -ла́ *perf.* be overgrown; be covered, surrounded, cluttered; +*instr.* acquire, accumulate.

обрати́м|ый, reversible, convertible; ~ая валю́та, convertible currency.

обрати́ть, -ащу́ *perf.*, **обраща́ть**, -а́ю *imp.* turn; convert; ~ в бе́гство, put to flight; ~ внима́ние на+*acc.* pay attention to, take notice of, notice; call, draw, attention to; ~ на себя́ внима́ние, attract attention (to oneself); ~ в шу́тку, turn into a joke; **~ся**, turn; revert; appeal; apply; accost, address; circulate; + в + *acc.* turn into, become; + с + *instr.* treat; handle, manage; ~ся в бе́гство, take to flight; ~ся в слух, be all ears; prick up one's ears. **обра́тно**, *adv.* back; backwards; conversely; inversely; ~ пропорциона́льный, inversely proportional; туда́ и ~, there and back.

обра́тн|ый, reverse; return; opposite; inverse; в ~ую сто́рону, in the opposite direction; ~ый а́дрес, sender's address, return address; ~ая вспы́шка, back-firing; ~ой по́чтой, by return (of post); ~ый уда́р, backfire; ~ый ход, reverse motion, back stroke. **обраще́ние**, -я, appeal, address; conversion; circulation; manner; (+с+*instr.*) treatment (of); handling (of), use (of).

об|ревизова́ть, -зу́ю *perf.*

обре́з, -а, edge, side; sawn-off gun; в ~ +*gen.* only just enough; де́нег у меня́ в ~, I haven't a penny to spare. **обре́зать**, -е́жу *perf.*, **обреза́ть**, -а́ю *imp.*

cut; cut off; clip trim; pare; prune; bevel; circumcise; cut short, snub; **~ся,** cut oneself. **обре́зок,** -зка, scrap; remnant; *pl.* ends; clippings.

обрека́ть, -а́ю *imp.* of обре́чь. **обреку́,** etc.: see обре́чь. **обрёл,** etc.: see обрести́.

обремени́тельный, burdensome, onerous. **о|бремени́ть,** -ню́ *perf.*, **обременя́ть,** -я́ю *imp.* burden.

обрести́, -ету́, -етёшь; -рёл, -а́ *perf.*, **обрета́ть,** -а́ю *imp.* find. **обрета́ться,** -а́юсь *imp.* be; live.

обрече́ние, -я, doom. **обречённый,** doomed. **обре́чь,** -еку́, -ечёшь; -ёк, -ла́ *perf.* (*imp.* обрека́ть) condemn, doom.

обрисова́ть, -су́ю *perf.*, **обрисо́вывать,** -аю *imp.* outline, delineate, depict; **~ся,** appear (in outline), take shape.

обро́к, -а, quit-rent.

оброни́ть, -ню́, -нишь *perf.* drop; let drop, let fall.

обро́с, etc : see обрасти́. **обро́сший,** overgrown.

обруба́ть, -а́ю *imp.*, **обруби́ть,** -блю́ -бишь *perf.* chop off; lop off, cut off; dock; hem seam. **обру́бок,** -бка, stump.

об|руга́ть, -а́ю *perf.*

о́бруч, -а; *pl.* -и, -е́й, hoop. **обруча́льн|ый,** engagement, betrothal; ~ое кольцо́, betrothal ring, wedding-ring. **обруча́ть,** -а́ю *imp.*, **обручи́ть,** -чу́, betroth; **~ся**+с+*instr.* become engaged to. **обруче́ние,** -я, betrothal.

обру́шивать, -аю *imp.*, **об|ру́шить,** -шу *perf.* bring down, rain down; **~ся,** come down, collapse, cave in; +на+*acc.* beat down on; come down on, fall on, pounce on.

обры́в -а, precipice; break, rupture. **обрыва́ть(ся,** -а́ю(сь *imp.* of оборва́ть(ся. **обры́вистый,** steep, precipitous; abrupt. **обры́вок,** -вка, scrap; snatch.

обры́згать, -аю *perf.*, **обры́згивать,** -аю *imp.*, **обры́знуть,** -ну *perf.* splash, spatter; sprinkle.

обрю́зглый, обрю́згший, fat and flabby.

обря́д, -а, rite, ceremony. **обря́дный, обря́довый,** ritual, ceremonial.

обслу́живание, -я, service; servicing, maintenance; бытово́е ~, consumer service(s); медици́нское ~, medical attendance, medical care. **обслу́живать,** -аю *imp.*, **обслужи́ть,** -жу́, -жишь *perf.* serve, attend to; service; mind, operate; обслу́живающий персона́л, staff; assistants, attendants.

обсле́дование, -я, inspection; inquiry; investigation. **обсле́дователь,** -я *m.* inspector, investigator. **обсле́довать,** -дую *perf.* and *imp.* inspect; investigate; examine.

обсо́хнуть, -ну; -о́х *perf.* (*imp.* обсыха́ть) dry, dry up.

обста́вить, -влю *perf.*, **обставля́ть,** -я́ю *imp.* surround, encircle; furnish; arrange; organize; **~ся,** establish oneself, furnish one's home. **обстано́вка,** -и, furniture; décor; situation, conditions; environment; set-up.

обстоя́тельный, thorough, reliable; detailed, circumstantial. **обстоя́тельственный,** adverbial. **обстоя́тельство,** -а, circumstance; adverbial modifier, adverb, adverbial phrase. **обстоя́ть,** -ои́т *imp.* be; get on go; как обстои́т де́ло? how is it going? how are things going?

обстра́гивать, -аю *imp.* of обстрога́ть. **обстра́ивать(ся,** -аю(сь *imp.* of обстро́ить(ся.

обстре́л, -а, firing, fire; под ~ом, under fire. **обстре́ливать,** -аю *imp.*, **обстреля́ть,** -я́ю *perf.* fire at, fire on; bombard; **~ся,** become seasoned (in battle), receive one's baptism of fire. **обстре́лянный,** seasoned, experienced.

обстрога́ть, -а́ю, **обструга́ть,** -а́ю *perf.* (*imp.* обстра́гивать) plane; whittle.

обстро́ить, -о́ю *perf.* (*imp.* обстра́ивать), build up, build round; **~ся,** be built; spring up; build for oneself.

обструга́ть: see обстрога́ть.

обступа́ть, -а́ет *imp.*, **обступи́ть,** -у́пит *perf.* surround; cluster round.

обсуди́ть, -ужу́, -у́дишь *perf.*, **обсужда́ть,** -а́ю *imp.* discuss; consider. **обсужде́ние,** -я, discussion.

обсчита́ть, -а́ю *perf.*, **обсчи́тывать,** -аю *imp.* cheat (in reckoning); **~ся,** make a mistake (in counting), miscalculate;

вы обсчита́лись на шесть копе́ек, you were six copecks out.

обсы́пать, -плю *perf.* **обсыпа́ть,** -а́ю *imp.* strew; sprinkle.

обсыха́ть, -а́ю *imp.* of обсо́хнуть. **обта́чивать,** -аю *imp.* of обточи́ть.

обтека́емый, streamlined, streamline. **обтека́тель,** -я *m.* fairing, cowling.

обтере́ть, оботру́, -трёшь; обтёр *perf.* (*imp.* обтира́ть) wipe; wipe dry; rub; **~ся,** wipe oneself dry, dry oneself; sponge down.

обтерпе́ться, -плю́сь, -пишься *perf.* become acclimatized, get used.

о(б)теса́ть, -ешу́, -е́шешь *perf.*, **о(б)тёсывать,** -аю *imp.* square; rough-hew; dress, trim; lick into shape.

обтира́ние, -я, sponge-down; lotion. **обтира́ть(ся,** -а́ю(сь *perf.* of обтере́ть(ся.

обточи́ть, -чу́, -чишь *perf.* (*imp.* обта́чивать) grind; turn, machine, round off. **обто́чка,** -и, turning, machining, rounding off.

обтрёпанный, frayed; shabby. **обтрепа́ть.** -плю́, -плешь *perf.* fray; **~ся,** fray become frayed; get shabby.

обтя́гивать, -аю *imp.*, **обтяну́ть,** -ну́, -нешь *perf.* cover; fit close. fit tight. **обтя́жка,** -и, cover; skin; в обтя́жку, close-fitting.

обува́ть(ся, -а́ю(сь *imp.* of обу́ть(ся. **обу́вка,** -и, boots, shoes. **обувно́й,** shoe. **о́бувь,** -и, footwear; boots, shoes.

обу́гливание, -я, carbonization. **обу́гливать,** -аю *imp.*, **обу́глить,** -лю *perf.* char; carbonize; **~ся,** char, become charred.

обу́живать, -аю *imp.* of обу́зить.

обу́за, -ы, burden, encumbrance.

обузда́ть, -а́ю *perf.*, **обу́здывать,** -аю *imp.* bridle, curb; restrain, control.

обу́зить, -у́жу *perf.* (*imp.* обу́живать) make too tight, too narrow.

обурева́емый, possessed; +*instr.* a prey to. **обурева́ть,** -а́ет *imp.* shake; grip. possess.

обусло́вить, -влю *perf.*, **обусло́вливать,** -аю *imp.* cause, bring about; +*instr.* make conditional on, limit by; **~ся**+ *instr.* be conditioned by, be conditional on; depend on.

обу́тый, shod. **обу́ть,** -у́ю *perf.* (*imp.* обува́ть) put boots, shoes, on; provide with boots, shoes; **~ся,** put on one's boots shoes.

о́бу́х, -а or -а́, butt, back.

обуча́ть, -а́ю *imp.*, **об|учи́ть,** -чу́, -чишь *perf.* teach; train, instruct; **~ся** + *dat.* or *inf.* learn. **обуче́ние,** -я, teaching; instruction, training.

обхва́т, -а girth; в ~е, in circumference. **обхвати́ть,** -ачу́, -а́тишь *perf.*, **обхва́тывать,** -аю *imp.* embrace; clasp.

обхо́д, -а, round; beat; roundabout way; bypass; evasion, circumvention. **обходи́тельный,** amiable; courteous; pleasant. **обходи́ть(ся,** -ожу́(сь, -о́дишь(ся *imp.* of обойти́(сь. **обхо́дный,** roundabout, circuitous; ~ путь, detour. **обхожде́ние,** -я, manners; treatment; behaviour.

обша́ривать, -аю *imp.*, **обша́рить,** -рю *perf.* rummage through, ransack.

обшива́ть, -а́ю *imp.* of обши́ть. **обши́вка,** -и, edging, bordering; trimming, facing; boarding, panelling; sheathing; plating; ~ фане́рой, veneering.

обши́рный, extensive; spacious; vast.

обши́ть, обошью́, -шьёшь *perf.* (*imp.* обшива́ть) edge, border; sew round; trim, face; fit out make outfit(s) for; plank; panel; sheathe, plate.

обшла́г, -а́; *pl.* -а́, -о́в, cuff.

обща́ться, -а́юсь *imp.* associate, mix.

обще- in *comb.* common(ly), general(ly). **общедосту́пный**, moderate in price; popular. **~жи́тие,** -я, hostel; community; communal life. **~изве́стный,** well-known, generally known; notorious. **~наро́дный,** general, national, public; ~наро́дный пра́здник, public holiday. **~образова́тельный**, general, of general education. **~при́нятый,** generally accepted. **~сою́зный,** All-Union. **~употреби́тельный,** in general use. **~челове́ческий,** common to all mankind; human; universal, general, ordinary.

общéние, -я, intercourse; relations, links; ли́чное ~, personal contact.
общéственник, -а, **-ица**, -ы, public-spirited person. **общéственность**, -и, (the) public; public opinion; community; communal organizations; дух общéственности, public spirit. **общéственн|ый**, social, public; voluntary, unpaid, amateur; на ~ых нача́лах, voluntary, unpaid; ~ые нау́ки social sciences; ~ое пита́ние, public catering. **óбщество**, -а, society; association; company.
óбщ|ий, general; common; в ~ем, on the whole, in general, in sum; ~ий итóг, ~ая сýмма, sum total. **общи́на**, -ы, community; commune. **óбщи́нный**, communal; common.
об|щипа́ть, -плю́, -плешь *perf*.
общи́тельный, sociable. **óбщность**, -и, community.
объ-: see о-, об-.
объеда́ть(ся, -а́ю(сь *imp*. of объéсть(ся.
объединéние, -я, unification; merger; union, association. **объединённый**; -ён, -а́, united. **объедини́тельный**, unifying, uniting. **объедини́ть**, -ню́ *perf*., **объединя́ть**, -я́ю *imp*. unite; join; pool. combine; **~ся** unite.
объéдки, -ов *pl*. leavings, leftovers, scraps.
объéздить, -зжу, -здишь *perf*. (*imp*. объезжа́ть) travel over; break in. **объезжа́ть**, -а́ю *imp*. of объéздить, объéхать. **объéзжий**, roundabout, circuitous.
объéкт, -а, object; objective; establishment, works **объекти́в**, -а, objective, lens. **объекти́вный**, objective; unbiassed.
объём. -а volume; bulk, size, capacity. **объёмистый**, voluminous, bulky. **объёмный**, by volume, volumetric.
объéсть, -éм -éшь, -éст, -еди́м *perf*. (*imp*. объеда́ть), gnaw (round), nibble; **~ся**, overeat.
объéхать -éду *perf*. (*imp*. объезжа́ть) drive round; go round; go past, skirt; visit, make the round of; travel over.
объяви́ть, -влю́, -вишь *perf*., **объявля́ть**, -я́ю *imp*. declare, announce; publish, proclaim; advertise; **~ся**, turn up, appear; + *instr*. announce oneself, declare oneself. **объявлéние**, -я, declaration, announcement; notice; advertisement.
объяснéние, -я, explanation; ~ в любви́, declaration of love. **объясни́мый**, explicable, explainable. **объясни́тельный**, explanatory. **объясни́ть**, -ню́ *perf*., **объясня́ть**, -я́ю *imp*. explain; **~ся**, explain oneself; become clear, be explained; speak, make oneself understood; +с+*instr*. have a talk with; have it out with; + *instr*. be explained, accounted for, by.
объя́тие, -я, embrace.
обыва́тель, -я *m*. man in the street; inhabitant, resident. **обыва́тельский**, commonplace; of the local inhabitants; narrow-minded.
обыгра́ть, -а́ю *perf*., **обы́грывать**, -аю *imp*. beat; win; use with effect, play up; turn to advantage, turn to account.
обы́денный, ordinary, usual; commonplace, everyday.
обыкновéние, -я, habit, wont; имéть ~ +*inf*. be in the habit of; по обыкновéнию, as usual. **обыкновéнно** *adv*. usually as a rule. **обыкновéнный**, usual; ordinary; commonplace; everyday.
óбыск, -а, search. **обыска́ть**, -ыщу́, -ы́щешь *perf*. **обы́скивать**, -аю *imp*. search.
обы́чай, -я, custom; usage. **обы́чно** *adv*. usually, as a rule. **обы́чный**, usual, ordinary.
обя́занность, -и, duty; responsibility; исполня́ющий обя́занности, acting. **обя́занный**, (+*inf*.) obliged, bound; +*dat*. obliged to, indebted to (+*instr*. for). **обяза́тельно** *adv*. without fail; он ~ там бýдет, he is sure to be there, he is bound to be there. **обяза́тельный**, obligatory; compulsory; binding; obliging, kind. **обяза́тельство**, -а, obligation; engagement; *pl*. liabilities; взять на себя́ ~, pledge oneself, undertake. **обяза́ть**, -яжý, -я́жешь *perf*., **обя́зывать**, -аю *imp*. bind; commit; oblige; **~ся**, bind oneself, pledge oneself, undertake; не хочý

ни перед кем обя́зываться, I do not want to be beholden to anybody.
ОВ (*ové*) *abbr.* отравля́ющее вещество́, poison, poisonous material; war gas.
овдове́вший, widowed. **овдове́ть,** -е́ю *perf.* become a widow, widower.
ове́н, овна́, Aries, the Ram.
овёс, овса́, oats.
ове́чий, sheep, sheep's. **ове́чка,** -и *dim.* of овца́; lamb, harmless person, gentle creature.
ови́н, -а, barn.
овладева́ть, -а́ю *imp.*, **овладе́ть,** -е́ю *perf.* + *instr.* take possession of; master; seize; ~ собо́й, get control of oneself, regain self-control. **овладе́ние,** -я, mastery; mastering.
о-во *abbr.* о́бщество, society.
о́вод, -а; *pl.* -ы or -а́, о́водо́в, gadfly.
о́вощ, -а; *pl.* -и, -е́й, vegetable, vegetables. **овощно́й,** vegetable; ~ магази́н, greengrocer's, greengrocery.
овра́г, -а, ravine, gully.
овся́нка, -и, oatmeal; porridge. **овсяно́й,** oat, of oats. **овся́н|ый,** oat, oatmeal; ~ая крупа́, (coarse) oatmeal.
овца́, -ы́; *pl.* -ы, ове́ц, о́вцам, sheep; ewe. **овцево́дство,** -а, sheep-breeding. **овча́р,** -а, shepherd. **овча́рка,** -и, sheep-dog. **овчи́на,** -ы, sheepskin. **овчи́нный,** sheepskin.
ога́рок, -рка, candle-end.
огиба́ть, -а́ю *imp.* of обогну́ть.
ОГИ́З, -а *abbr.* Объедине́ние госуда́рственных изда́тельств, Central State Publishing House.
оглавле́ние, -я, table of contents.
огласи́ть, -ашу́ *perf.*, **оглаша́ть,** -а́ю *imp.* proclaim; announce; divulge, make public; fill (with sound); **~ся,** resound, ring. **огла́ска,** -и, publicity; получи́ть огла́ску, be given publicity. **оглаше́ние,** -я, proclaiming, publication; не подлежи́т оглаше́нию, confidential, not for publication.
огло́бля, -и; *gen. pl.* -бель, shaft.
о|гло́хнуть, -ну; -о́х *perf.*
оглуша́ть, -а́ю *imp.*, **о|глуши́ть,** -шу́ *perf.* deafen; stun. **оглуши́тельный,** deafening.
огляде́ть, -яжу́ *perf.*, **огля́дывать,** -аю *imp.*, **огляну́ть,** -ну́, -нешь *perf.* look round; look over, examine, inspect; **~ся,** look round, look about; look back; turn to look; adapt oneself, become acclimatized. **огля́дка,** -и, looking round, looking back; care, caution; бежа́ть без огля́дки, run for one's life.
огнево́й, fire; fiery; igneous. **огнемёт,** -а, flame-thrower. **о́гненный,** fiery. **огнеопа́сный,** inflammable. **огнеприпа́сы,** -ов *pl.* ammunition. **огнесто́йкий,** fire-proof, fire-resistant. **огнестре́льн|ый;** ~ое ору́жие, firearm(s). **огнетуши́тель,** -я *m.* fire-extinguisher. **огнеупо́рн|ый,** fire-resistant, fire-proof; refractory; ~ая гли́на, fire-clay; ~ый кирпи́ч, fire-brick.
ого́ (*oho*) *int.* oho!
огова́ривать, -аю *imp.*, **оговори́ть,** -рю́ *perf.* slander; stipulate (for); fix, agree on; **~ся,** make a reservation, make a proviso; make a slip (of the tongue); я оговори́лся, it was a slip of the tongue. **огово́р,** -а, slander. **огово́рка,** -и, reservation, proviso; slip of the tongue; без огово́рок, without reserve.
оголённый, bare, nude; uncovered, exposed. **оголи́ть,** -лю́ *perf.* (*imp.* оголя́ть) bare; strip, uncover; **~ся,** strip, strip oneself; become exposed.
оголте́лый, wild, frantic; frenzied; unbridled.
оголя́ть(ся, -я́ю(сь *imp.* of оголи́ть(ся.
огонёк, -нька́, (small) light; zest, spirit.
ого́нь, огня́ *m.* fire; firing; light.
огора́живать, -аю *imp.*, **огороди́ть,** -рожу́, -ро́ди́шь *perf.* fence in, enclose; **~ся,** fence oneself in. **огоро́д,** -а, kitchen-garden; market-garden. **огоро́дник,** -а market-gardener. **огоро́дничество,** -а, market-gardening. **огоро́дный,** kitchen-garden, market-garden.
огоро́шить, -шу *perf.* take aback, dumbfound; startle.
огорча́ть, -а́ю *imp.*, **огорчи́ть,** -чу́ *perf.* grieve, distress, pain; **~ся,** grieve; distress oneself, be distressed, be pained. **огорче́ние,** -я, grief, affliction; chagrin. **огорчи́тельный,** distressing.

ОГПУ′ *abbr.* Объединённое государственное политическое управление, OGPU.

о|гра́бить, -блю *perf.* **ограбле́ние, -я,** robbery; burglary.

огра́да, -ы, fence. **огради́ть, -ажу́** *perf.*, **огражда́ть, -а́ю** *imp.* guard, protect; enclose, fence in; **~ся,** defend oneself, protect oneself, guard oneself.

ограниче́ние, -я, limitation, restriction. **ограни́ченный,** limited, narrow. **ограни́чивать, -аю** *imp.*, **ограни́чить, -чу** *perf.* limit, restrict, cut down; **~ся** + *instr.* limit oneself to, confine oneself to; be limited, be confined, to.

огро́мный, huge; vast; enormous.

огрубе́лый, coarse, hardened, rough. **о|грубе́ть, -е́ю** *perf.*

огрыза́ться, -а́юсь *imp.*, **огрызну́ться, -ну́сь, -нёшься** *perf.* snap (на + *acc.* at).

огры́зок, -зка, bit, end; stub, stump.

огу́зок, -зка, rump.

огу́лом *adv.* all together; wholesale, indiscriminately. **огу́льно** *adv.* without grounds. **огу́льный,** wholesale, indiscriminate; unfounded, groundless.

огуре́ц, -рца́, cucumber.

одарённый, gifted, talented. **ода́ривать, -аю** *imp.*, **одари́ть, -рю́** *perf.*, **одаря́ть, -я́ю** *imp.* give presents (to); + *instr.* endow with.

одева́ть(ся, -а́ю(сь *imp.* of оде́ть(ся.

оде́жда, -ы, clothes; garments; clothing; revetment; surfacing.

одеколо́н, -а, eau-de-Cologne.

одели́ть, -лю́ *perf.*, **оделя́ть, -я́ю** *imp.* (+ *instr.*) present (with); endow (with).

оде́ну, etc.: see оде́ть. **одёргивать, -аю** *imp.* of одёрнуть.

одеревене́лый, numb; lifeless. **о|деревене́ть, -е́ю** *perf.*

одержа́ть, -жу́, -жишь *perf.*, **оде́рживать, -аю** *imp.* gain, win; ~ верх, gain the upper hand, prevail. **одержи́мый,** possessed.

одёрнуть, -ну *perf.* (*imp.* одёргивать) pull down, straighten; call to order; silence.

оде́тый, dressed; clothed. **оде́ть, -е́ну** *perf.* (*imp.* одева́ть) dress; clothe; **~ся,** dress (oneself); + в + *acc.* put on.

одея́ло, -а, blanket; coverlet. **одея́ние, -я,** garb, attire.

оди́н, одного́, **одна́,** одно́й, **одно́,** одного́; *pl.* **одни́,** одни́х *num.* one; a, an; a certain; alone; only; by oneself; nothing but; same; в оди́н го́лос, with one voice, with one accord; все до одного́, (all) to a man; мне э́то всё одно́, it is all one to me; одни́ . ., други́е, some . ., others; оди́н за други́м, one after the other; оди́н и тот же, one and the same; одно́ и то же, the same thing; оди́н на оди́н in private, tête-à-tête; face to face; одни́ но́жницы, one pair of scissors; оди́н раз, once; одни́м сло́вом in a word, in short; по одному́, one by one, one at a time; in single file.

одина́ково *adv.* equally. **одина́ковый,** identical, the same, equal. **одина́рный,** single.

оди́ннадцатый, eleventh. **оди́ннадцать, -и,** eleven.

одино́кий, solitary; lonely; single. **одино́чество, -а,** solitude; loneliness. **одино́чка, -и** *m.* and *f.* (one) person alone; в одино́чку, alone, on one's own; мать-~, unmarried mother; по одино́чке, one by one. **одино́чкой** *adv.* alone, by oneself, by itself. **одино́чн|ый,** individual; one-man; single; ~ое заключе́ние, solitary confinement. **одино́чник, -а** individual competitor; skiff.

одио́зный, odious.

одича́лый, wild, gone wild. **одича́ние, -я,** running wild. **о|дича́ть, -а́ю** *perf.*

одна́жды *adv.* once; one day; once upon a time; ~ у́тром, ~ ве́чером, ~ но́чью, one morning, evening, night.

одна́ко *conj.* however; but; though; *int.* you don't say so! not really!

одно- in *comb.* single, one; uni-, mono-, homo-. **однобо́кий,** one-sided. **~бо́ртный,** single-breasted. **~вре́ме́нно** *adv.* simultaneously, at the same time. **~го́док, -дка, ~го́дка, -и,** person of the same age (с + *instr.* as). **~дне́вный,** one-day. **~зву́чный,** monotonous. **~зна́чащий,** synonymous; monosemantic. **~зна́чный,** synonymous; monosemantic; simple; one-digit. **~имён-**

ный, of the same name; eponymous. **~-кла́ссник,** class mate. **~клёточный,** unicellular. **~коле́йный,** single-track. **~кра́тный,** single; ~ кра́тный вид, momentary aspect. **~ле́тний,** one-year; annual. **~ле́тник,** -а, annual. **~лето́к,** -тка, **~ле́тка,** -и, (person) of the same age (с+*instr.* as). **~ме́стный,** for one (person); single-seater. **~мото́рный,** single-engined. **~обра́зие,** -я, **~обра́зность,** -и, monotony. **~обра́зный,** monotonous. **~-по́люсный,** unipolar. **~пу́тка,** -и, single-track railway. **~пу́тный,** one-way. **~ро́дность,** -и, homogeneity, uniformity. **~ро́дный,** homogeneous, uniform; similar. **~сло́жный,** monosyllabic; terse, abrupt. **~сло́йный,** single-layer; one-ply, single-ply. **~сторо́нний,** one-sided; unilateral; one-way; one-track. **~та́ктный,** one-stroke; single-cycle. **~ти́пный,** of the same type; of the same kind. **~то́мник,** one-volume edition. **~то́мный,** one-volume. **~фами́лец,** -льца, person of the same surname. **~цве́тный,** one-colour; monochrome. **~эта́жный,** single-stage; one-storeyed. **~я́русный,** single-tier, single-deck; single-layer.

одобре́ние, -я, approval. **одобри́тельный,** approving. **одо́брить,** -рю *perf.*, **одобря́ть,** -я́ю *imp.* approve of, approve.

одолева́ть, -а́ю *imp.*, **одоле́ть,** -е́ю *perf.* overcome, conquer; master, cope with.

одолжа́ть, -а́ю *imp.*, **одолжи́ть,** -жу́ *perf.* lend; +у+*gen.* borrow from; **~ся,** be obliged, be beholden; borrow, get into debt. **одолже́ние,** -я, favour, service.

одома́шненный, domesticated. **одома́шнивать,** -аю *imp.*, **одома́шнить,** -ню *perf.* domesticate, tame.

о|дряхле́ть, -е́ю *perf.*

одува́нчик, -а dandelion.

оду́маться, -аюсь *perf.*, **оду́мываться,** -аюсь *imp.* change one's mind; think better of it; have time to think.

одура́чивать, -аю *imp.*, **о|дура́чить,** -чу *perf.* fool, make a fool of.

одуре́лый, stupid. **одуре́ние,** -я, stupefaction, torpor. **о|дуре́ть,** -е́ю *perf.*

одурма́нивать, -аю *imp.*, **о|дурма́нить,** -ню *perf.* stupefy. **о́дурь,** -и, stupefaction, torpor. **одуря́ть,** -я́ю *imp.* stupefy; одуря́ющий за́пах, overpowering scent.

одухотворённый, inspired; spiritual. **одухотвори́ть,** -рю́ *perf.*, **одухотворя́ть,** -я́ю *imp.* inspire.

одушеви́ть, -влю́ *perf.*, **одушевля́ть,** -я́ю *imp.* animate; **~ся,** be animated. **одушевле́ние,** -я, animation. **одушевлённый,** animated; animate.

оды́шка, -и, shortness of breath; страда́ть оды́шкой, be short-winded.

ожере́лье, -я, necklace.

ожесточа́ть, -а́ю *imp.*, **ожесточи́ть,** -чу́ *perf.* embitter, harden; **~ся,** become embittered, become hard. **ожесточе́ние,** -я, **ожесточённость,** -и, bitterness; hardness. **ожесточённый,** bitter, embittered; hard.

ожива́ть, -а́ю *imp.* of ожи́ть.

оживи́ть, -влю́ *perf.*, **оживля́ть,** -я́ю *imp.* revive; enliven, vivify, animate; **~ся,** become animated, liven up. **оживле́ние,** -я, animation, gusto; reviving; enlivening. **оживлённый,** animated, lively.

ожида́ние, -я, expectation; waiting; в ожида́нии, expecting; +*gen.* pending; про́тив ожида́ния, unexpectedly; сверх ожида́ния, beyond expectation. **ожида́ть,** -а́ю *imp.*+*gen.* wait for; expect, anticipate.

ожире́ние, -я, obesity. **о|жире́ть,** -е́ю *perf.*

ожи́ть, -иву́, -ивёшь; о́жил, -а́, -о *perf.* (*imp.* ожива́ть) come to life, revive.

ожо́г, -а, burn, scald.

оз. *abbr.* о́зеро, lake.

о|забо́тить, -о́чу *perf.*, **озабо́чивать,** -аю *imp.* trouble, worry; cause anxiety to; **~ся** + *instr.* attend to, see to. **озабо́ченность,** -и, preoccupation; anxiety. **озабо́ченный,** preoccupied; anxious, worried.

озагла́вить, -лю *perf.*, **озагла́вливать,** -аю *imp.* entitle, call; head.

озада́ченный, perplexed, puzzled. **озада́чивать,** -аю *imp.*, **озада́чить,** -чу *perf.* perplex, puzzle; take aback.

озари́ть, -рю́ *perf.*, **озаря́ть,** -я́ю *imp.*

light up, illuminate; их озари́ло, it dawned on them; **~ся,** light up.
озвере́лый, brutal; brutalized. **о|звере́ть, -е́ю** *perf.*
озву́ченный фильм, sound film.
оздорови́тельный, sanitary. **оздорови́ть, -влю́** *perf.*, **оздоровля́ть, -я́ю** *imp.* render (more) healthy; improve sanitary conditions of.
озелени́ть, -ню́ *perf.*, **озеленя́ть, -я́ю** *imp.* plant (with trees, grass, etc.).
озёрный, lake; ~ райо́н, lake district.
о́зеро, -а; *pl.* озёра, lake.
ози́мые *sb.* winter crops. **ози́мый,** winter. **о́зимь, -и,** winter crop.
озира́ться, -а́юсь *imp.* look round; look back.
о|зли́ть(ся: see обозли́ть(ся.
озло́бить, -блю *perf.*, **озлобля́ть, -я́ю** *imp.* embitter; **~ся,** grow bitter, be embittered. **озлобле́ние, -я,** bitterness, animosity. **озло́бленный,** embittered, bitter; angry.
о|знако́мить, -млю *perf.*, **ознакомля́ть, -я́ю** *imp.* с+*instr.* acquaint with; **~ся** с+*instr.* familiarize oneself with.
ознаменова́ние, -я, marking, commemoration; в ~+*gen.* to mark, to commemorate, in commemoration of. **ознаменова́ть, -ну́ю** *perf.*, **ознамено́вывать, -аю** *imp.* mark, commemorate; celebrate.
означа́ть, -а́ет *imp.* mean, signify, stand for. **озна́ченный,** aforesaid.
озно́б, -а, shivering, chill.
озорни́к, -а́, naughty child, mischievous child; rowdy person. **озорнича́ть, -а́ю** *imp.* (*perf.* с~) be naughty, get up to mischief. **озорно́й,** naughty, mischievous; rowdy. **озорство́, -а́,** naughtiness, mischief.
озя́бнуть, -ну; озя́б *perf.* be cold, be freezing.
ой *int.* oh.
ок. *abbr.* о́коло, about.
оказа́ть, -ажу́, -а́жешь *perf.* (*imp.* ока́зывать) render, show; ~ влия́ние на+*acc.* influence, exert influence on; ~ де́йствие, have an effect, take effect; ~ предпочте́ние, show preference; ~ услу́гу, do a service, do a good turn; ~ честь, do honour; **~ся,** turn out, prove; find oneself, be found.
ока́зия, -и, opportunity; unexpected happening, funny thing.
ока́зывать(ся, -аю(сь *imp.* of оказа́ть(ся.
окайми́ть, -млю́ *perf.*, **окаймля́ть, -я́ю** *imp.* border, edge.
окамене́лость, -и, fossil. **окамене́лый,** fossil; fossilized; petrified. **о|камене́ть, -е́ю** *perf.*
о|кантова́ть, -ту́ю *perf.* **окanто́вка, -и,** mount; edge.
ока́нчивать(ся, -аю(сь *imp.* of око́нчить(ся. **ока́пывать(ся, -аю(сь** *imp.* of окопа́ть(ся.
окая́нный, damned, cursed.
океа́н, -а. ocean. **океа́нский,** ocean; oceanic; ocean-going; ~ парохо́д, ocean liner.
оки́дывать, -аю *imp.*, **оки́нуть, -ну** *perf.* cast round; ~ взгля́дом, take in at a glance, glance over.
о́кисел, -сла, oxide. **окисле́ние, -я,** oxidation. **окисли́ть, -лю́** *perf.*, **окисля́ть, -я́ю** *imp.* oxidize; **~ся,** oxidize.
о́кись, -и, oxide.
оккупа́нт, -а, invader; *pl.* occupying forces, occupiers. **оккупа́ция, -и,** occupation. **оккупи́ровать, -рую** *perf.* and *imp.* occupy.
окла́д, -а, salary scale; (basic) pay; tax(-rate); metal overlay, setting.
оклевета́ть, -ещу́, -е́щешь *perf.* slander, calumniate, defame.
окле́ивать, -аю *imp.*, **окле́ить, -е́ю** *perf.* cover; glue over, paste over; ~ обо́ями, paper.
окно́, -а́; *pl.* о́кна, window; port; gap; aperture; interval, free period.
о́ко, -а; *pl.* о́чи, оче́й, eye; в мгнове́ние о́ка, in the twinkling of an eye.
окова́ть, окую́, -ёшь *perf.*, **око́вывать, -аю** *imp.* bind; fetter, shackle. **око́вы, око́в** *pl.* fetters.
окола́чиваться, -аюсь *imp.* lounge about, kick one's heels.
околдова́ть, -ду́ю *perf.*, **околдо́вывать, -аю** *imp.* bewitch, entrance, enchant.
околева́ть, -а́ю *imp.*, **околе́ть, -е́ю** *perf.* die. **околе́лый,** dead.

о́коло *adv.* and *prep.* + *gen.* by; close (to), near; around; about; где́-нибудь ~, hereabouts, somewhere here; ~ э́того, ~ того́, thereabouts.
око́лыш, -а, cap-band.
око́льн|ый, roundabout; ~ым путём, in a roundabout way.
о|кольцева́ть, -цу́ю *perf.*
око́нный, window; ~ переплёт, sash.
оконча́ние, -я, end; conclusion, termination; ending; ~ сле́дует, to be concluded. **оконча́тельно** *adv.* finally, definitively; completely. **оконча́тельный,** final; definitive, decisive. **око́нчить, -чу** *perf.* (*imp.* ока́нчивать) finish, end; **~ся,** finish, end, terminate; be over.
око́п, -а, trench; entrenchment. **окопа́ть, -а́ю** *perf.* (*imp.* ока́пывать) dig up, dig round; **~ся,** entrench oneself, dig in. **око́пн|ый,** trench; ~ая война́, trench warfare.
о́корок, -а; *pl.* -а́, -о́в, ham, gammon; leg.
окостенева́ть, -а́ю *imp.*, **окостене́ть, -е́ю** *perf.* ossify; stiffen. **окостене́лый,** ossified; stiff.
окочене́лый, stiff with cold. **о|кочене́ть, -е́ю** *perf.*
око́шечко, -а, око́шко, -а, (small) window; opening.
окра́ина, -ы, outskirts, outlying districts; borders, marches.
о|кра́снть, -а́шу *perf.*, **окра́шивать, -аю** *imp.* paint, colour; dye; stain. **окра́ска, -и,** painting; colouring; dyeing, staining; coloration; tinge, tint, touch, slant.
о|кре́пнуть, -ну *perf.* **о|крести́ть(ся, -ещу́(сь, -е́стишь(ся** *perf.*
окре́стность, -и, environs; neighbourhood, vicinity. **окре́стный,** neighbouring, surrounding.
о́крик, -а, hail, call; cry, shout. **оклрикивать, -аю** *imp.*, **окри́кнуть, -ну** *perf.* hail, call, shout to.
окрова́вленный, blood-stained, bloody.
окро́шка, -и, okroshka; hotch-potch, jumble.
о́круг, -а, okrug; region, district; circuit. **окру́га, -и,** neighbourhood **округлённый; -лён, -а́,** rounded. **округли́ть, -лю́** *perf.*, **округля́ть, -я́ю** *imp.* round; round off; express in round numbers; **~ся,** become rounded; be expressed in round numbers. **окру́глый,** rounded, roundish. **окружа́ть, -а́ю** *imp.*, **окружи́ть, -жу́** *perf.* surround; encircle. **окружа́ющ|ий,** surrounding; ~ая среда́, environment; **~ее** *sb.* environment; **~ие** *sb. pl.* associates; entourage. **окруже́ние, -я.** encirclement; surroundings; environment; milieu; в окруже́нии + *gen.* accompanied by; surrounded by, in the midst of. **окружн|о́й,** okrug, district, circuit; circle; ~а́я желе́зная доро́га, circle line. **окру́жность, -и,** circumference; circle; neighbourhood; на три ми́ли в окру́жности, within a radius of three miles, for three miles round. **окру́жный,** neighbouring.
окрыли́ть, -лю́ *perf.*, **окрыля́ть, -я́ю** *imp.* inspire, encourage.
окта́н, -а, octane. **окта́нов|ый,** octane; ~ое число́, octane rating.
октя́брь, -я́ *m.* October. **октя́брьский,** October.
окуна́ть, -а́ю *imp.*, **окуну́ть, -ну́, -нёшь** *perf.* dip; **~ся,** dip; plunge; become absorbed, become engrossed.
о́кунь, -я; *pl.* -и, -е́й *m.* perch.
окупа́ть, -а́ю *imp.*, **окупи́ть, -плю́, -пишь** *perf.* compensate, repay, make up for; **~ся,** be compensated, be repaid, pay for itself; pay; be justified, be requited, be rewarded.
оку́ривание, -я, fumigation. **оку́ривать, -аю** *imp.*, **окури́ть, -рю́, -ришь** *perf.* fumigate. **оку́рок, -рка,** cigarette-end; (cigar-)stub.
оку́тать, -аю *perf.*, **оку́тывать, -аю** *imp.* wrap up; shroud, cloak; **~ся,** wrap up; be shrouded be cloaked.
оку́чивать, -аю *imp.*, **оку́чить, -чу** *perf.* earth up.
ола́дья, -и; *gen. pl.* -ий, fritter; girdle scone, drop-scone.
оледене́лый, frozen. **о|ледене́ть, -е́ю** *perf.* **о|ледени́ть, -и́т** *perf.*
оле́н|ий, deer, deer's; reindeer; hart, hart's; ~ий мох, reindeer moss; ~ьи рога́, antlers. **оле́нина, -ы,** venison.

оле́нь, -я *m.* deer; reindeer; (*sl.*) simpleton, greenhorn.
оли́ва, -ы, olive. **оли́вковый,** olive; olive(-coloured).
олимпиа́да, -ы olympiad; competition. **олимпи́йск|ий,** Olympic; Olympian; ~ие и́гры, Olympic games, Olympics. **олимпи́ец,** -и́йца, **олимпи́йка,** -и, contestant in Olympic games.
оли́фа, -ы, drying oil.
олицетворе́ние, -я, personification; embodiment. **олицетворённый;** -рён, -а́, personified. **олицетвори́ть,** -рю́ *perf.*, **олицетворя́ть,** -я́ю *imp.* personify, embody.
о́лово, -а tin. **оловя́нн|ый,** tin; stannic; ~ая посу́да, tinware; pewter; ~ая фо́льга, tinfoil.
ом, -а, ohm.
омерзе́ние, -я, loathing. **омерзе́ть,** -е́ю *perf.* become loathsome. **омерзи́тельн|ый** loathsome, sickening; ~ое настрое́ние, foul mood.
омертве́лость, -и, stiffness, numbness; necrosis, mortification. **омертве́л|ый,** stiff, numb; necrotic; ~ая ткань dead tissue. **омертве́ние,** -я, necrosis. **о|мертве́ть,** -е́ю *perf.*
омоложе́ние, -я, rejuvenation.
омо́ним, -а, homonym.
омо́ю, etc.: see омы́ть.
омрача́ть, -а́ю *imp.*, **омрачи́ть,** -чу́ *perf.* darken, cloud, overcloud; **~ся,** become darkened, become clouded.
о́мут, -а, pool; whirlpool; whirl, maelstrom.
омыва́ть, -а́ю *imp.*, **омы́ть,** омо́ю *perf.* wash; wash away, wash out; wash down; **~ся,** be washed.
он, его́, ему́, им, о нём *pron.* he. **она́,** её, ей, ей (е́ю), о ней *pron.* she.
онда́тра, -ы musk-rat, musquash. **онда́тровый,** musquash.
онеме́лый, dumb; numb. **о|неме́ть,** -е́ю *perf.*
они́, их, им, и́ми, о них *pron.* they. **оно́,** его́, ему́ им, о нём *pron.* it; this, that.
ОНО *abbr.* отде́л наро́дного образова́ния, (local) education department.
ОО'Н *abbr.* Организа́ция объединённых на́ций, U.N.(O.), United Nations (Organisation). **оо́новский,** United Nations.
опада́ть, -а́ет *imp.* of опа́сть. **опада́ющий,** deciduous.
опа́здывать, -аю *imp.* of опозда́ть.
опа́ла, -ы, disgrace, disfavour.
о|пали́ть, -лю́ *perf.*
опа́ловый, opal; opaline.
опа́лубка, -и, shuttering, casing.
опаса́ться, -а́юсь *imp.*+*gen.* fear, be afraid of; +*gen.* or *inf.* beware (of); avoid, keep off. **опасе́ние,** -я, fear; apprehension; misgiving(s). **опа́сливый,** cautious; wary.
опа́сность, -и, danger; peril. **опа́сный,** dangerous, perilous.
опа́сть, -адёт *perf.* (*imp.* опада́ть) fall, fall off; subside, go down.
опе́ка, -и, guardianship, tutelage; trusteeship; guardians, trustees; care; surveillance. **опека́емый** *sb.* ward. **опека́ть,** -а́ю *imp.* be guardian of; take care of, watch over. **опеку́н,** -а́, **-у́нша,** -и, guardian; tutor; trustee.
операти́вность, -и, drive, energy. **операти́вный,** energetic; efficient; executive; operative, surgical; operation(s) operational; strategical. **опера́тор,** -а, operator; cameraman; (computer) instruction. **опера́торная** *sb.* management and control centre. **операцио́нн|ый,** operating; surgical; ~ая *sb.* operating theatre. **опера́ция,** -и, operation.
опереди́ть, -режу́ *perf.*, **опережа́ть,** -а́ю *imp.* outstrip, leave behind; forestall.
опере́ние, -я, plumage. **оперённый;** -ён, -а́, feathered.
опере́тта, -ы, **-е́тка,** -и, musical comedy, operetta.
опере́ть, обопру́, -прёшь; опёр, -ла́ *perf.* (*imp.* опира́ть)+о+*acc.* lean against; **~ся,** на or о+*acc.* lean on, lean against.
опери́ровать, -рую *perf.* and *imp.* operate on; operate, act; + *instr.* operate with; use, handle.
опери́ть, -рю́ *perf.* (*imp.* оперя́ть) feather; adorn with feathers; **~ся,** be fledged; stand on one's own feet.

о́перный, opera; operatic; ~ теа́тр, opera-house.
оперуполномо́ченный, *sb*. C.I.D. officer; security officer.
опершись на + *acc*. leaning on.
оперя́ть(ся, -я́ю(сь *imp*. of опери́ть(ся.
о|**печа́лить(ся,** -лю(сь *perf*.
опеча́тать, -аю *perf*. (*imp*. опеча́тывать) seal up.
опеча́тка, -и, misprint; спи́сок опеча́ток, errata.
опеча́тывать, -аю *imp*. of опеча́тать.
опе́шить, -шу *perf*. be taken aback.
опи́вки, -вок *pl*. dregs.
опи́лки, -лок *pl*. sawdust; (metal) filings.
опира́ть(ся, -а́ю(сь *imp*. of опере́ть(ся.
описа́ние, -я, description; account. **опи́санный**, circumscribed. **описа́тельный,** descriptive. **описа́ть,** -ишу́ -и́шешь *perf*. **опи́сывать,** -аю *imp*. describe; list inventory; circumscribe; distrain; **~ся,** make a slip of the pen. **о́пись,** -и, list, schedule; inventory.
опла́кать, -а́чу *perf*., **опла́кивать,** -аю *imp*. mourn for; bewail, deplore.
опла́та, -ы, pay, payment; remuneration. **оплати́ть,** -ачу́, -а́тишь *perf*., **опла́чивать**, -аю *imp*. pay for. pay; ~ расхо́ды, meet the expenses, foot the bill; ~ счёт, settle the account, pay the bill. **опла́ченн|ый,** paid; с ~ым отве́том, reply-paid.
опла́чу, etc.: see опла́кать. **оплачу́,** etc.: see оплати́ть.
оплева́ть, -люю́, -люёшь *perf*., **оплёвывать,** -аю *imp*. spit on; humiliate.
оплеу́ха, -и, slap in the face.
о|**плеши́веть,** -ею *perf*.
оплодотворе́ние, -я, impregnation, fecundation; fertilization. **оплодотвори́тель,** -я *m*. fertilizer. **оплодотвори́ть,** -рю́ *perf*., **оплодотворя́ть,** -я́ю *imp*. impregnate, fecundate; fertilize.
о|**пломбирова́ть,** -ру́ю *perf*.
опло́т, -а, stronghold, bulwark.
опло́шность, -и, blunder, oversight. **опло́шный,** mistaken, blundering.
оплюю́, etc.: see оплева́ть.
оповести́ть, -ещу́ *perf*., **оповеща́ть,** -а́ю *imp*. notify, inform. **оповеще́ние,** -я, notification; warning.
о|**пога́нить,** -ню *perf*.
опозда́вший *sb*. late-comer. **опозда́ние,** -я, being late, lateness; delay; без опозда́ния, on time; с ~м на де́сять мину́т, ten minutes late. **опозда́ть,** -а́ю *perf*. (*imp*. опа́здывать) be late; be overdue; be slow.
опознава́тельный, distinguishing; ~ знак, landmark, beacon; marking. **опознава́ть,** -наю́, -наёшь *imp*., **опозна́ть,** -а́ю *perf*. identify. **опозна́ние,** -я, identification.
опозо́рение, -я, defamation. о|**позо́рить(ся,** -рю(сь *perf*.
ополза́ть, -а́ет *imp*., **оползти́,** -зёт; -о́лз, -ла́ *perf*. slip, slide. **о́ползень,** -зня *m*. landslide, landslip.
ополча́ться, -а́юсь *imp*., **ополчи́ться,** -чу́сь *perf*. take up arms; be up in arms; + на + *acc*. fall on, attack. **ополче́нец,** -нца, militiaman. **ополче́ние,** -я, militia; irregulars, levies.
опо́мниться, -нюсь *perf*. come to one's senses, collect oneself.
опо́р, -а; во весь ~, at full speed, at top speed, full tilt.
опо́ра, -ы, support; bearing; pier; buttress; то́чка опо́ры, fulcrum, bearing.
опора́жнивать, -аю *imp*. of опоро́жни́ть.
опо́рн|ый, support, supporting, supported; bearing; ~ый прыжо́к, vault; ~ый пункт, strong point; ~ая то́чка, fulcrum.
опоро́жни́ть, -ню́ or -ню *perf*., **опорожня́ть,** -я́ю *imp*. (*imp*. also опора́жнивать) empty; drain.
о|**пороси́ться,** -и́тся *perf*. о|**поро́чить,** -чу *perf*.
опохмели́ться, -лю́сь *perf*., **опохмеля́ться,** -я́юсь *imp*. take a hair of the dog that bit you.
опо́шлить, -лю *perf*., **опошля́ть,** -я́ю *imp*. vulgarize, debase.
опоя́сать, -я́шу *perf*., **опоя́сывать,** -аю *imp*. gird on; girdle.
оппозицио́нный, opposition, in opposition; antagonistic, of opposition. **оппози́ция**, -и, opposition.
опра́ва, -ы, setting, mounting; case; rim.
оправда́ние, -я, justification; excuse;

acquittal, discharge. **оправдательный** приговор, verdict of not guilty. **оправдать,** -аю *perf.*, **оправдывать,** -аю *imp.* justify, warrant; vindicate; authorize; excuse; acquit, discharge; **~ся,** justify oneself; vindicate oneself; be justified.

оправить, -влю *perf.*, **оправлять,** -яю *imp.* put in order, set right adjust; set, mount; **~ся,** put one's dress in order; recover; +от+*gen.* get over.

опрашивать, -аю *imp.* of опросить.

определение, -я, definition; determination; decision; attribute. **определённый,** definite; determinate; fixed; certain. **определимый,** definable. **определить,** -лю *perf.*, **определять,** -яю *imp.* define; determine; fix, appoint; allot, assign; ~ на службу, appoint; **~ся,** be formed; take shape; be determined; obtain a fix, find one's position.

опровергать, -аю *imp.*, **опровергнуть,** -ну; -верг *perf.* refute, disprove. **опровержение,** -я, refutation; disproof; denial.

опрокидн|ой, tipping, tip-up. **опрокидывать,** -аю *imp.*, **опрокинуть,** -ну *perf.* overturn; upset; topple; overthrow; overrun; refute; knock back; **~ся,** overturn; topple over, tip over, tip up; capsize.

опрометчивый, precipitate, rash, hasty, unconsidered. **опрометью** *adv.* headlong.

опрос, -а, interrogation; (cross-)examination; referendum; (opinion) poll. **опросить,** -ошу -осишь *perf.* (*imp.* опрашивать) interrogate, question; (cross-)examine. **опросный,** interrogatory; ~ лист, questionnaire.

опротиветь, -ею *perf.* become loathsome, become repulsive.

опрыскать, -аю *perf.*, **опрыскивать,** -аю *imp.* sprinkle; spray. **опрыскиватель,** -я *m.* sprinkler, spray(er).

опрятный, neat, tidy.

оптик, -а, optician. **оптика,** -и, optics; optical instruments. **оптический,** optic, optical; ~ обман, optical illusion.

оптовый. wholesale. **оптом** *adv.* wholesale; ~ и в розницу, wholesale and retail.

опубликование, -я, publication; promulgation. **о|публиковать,** -кую *perf.*, **опубликовывать,** -аю *imp.* publish; promulgate.

опускать(ся, -аю(сь *imp.* of опустить(ся.

опускн|ой, movable; ~ая дверь, trap-door.

опустелый, deserted. **о|пустеть,** -еет *perf.*

опустить, -ущу, -устишь *perf.* (*imp.* опускать) lower; let down; turn down; omit; ~ глаза, look down; ~ голову, hang one's head; ~ руки, lose heart; ~ шторы, draw the blinds; **~ся,** lower oneself; sink; fall; go down; let oneself go, go to pieces.

опустошать, -аю *imp.*, **опустошить,** -шу *perf.* devastate, lay waste, ravage. **опустошение,** -я, devastation, ruin. **опустошительный,** devastating.

опутать, -аю *perf.*, **опутывать,** -аю *imp.* enmesh, entangle; ensnare.

опухать, -аю *imp.*, **о|пухнуть,** -ну; опух *perf.* swell, swell up. **опухлый,** swollen. **опухоль,** -и, swelling; tumour.

опущу, etc.: see опустить.

опыление, -я, pollination. **опылить,** -лю *perf.*, **опылять,** -яю *imp.* pollinate.

опыт, -а, experience; experiment; test, trial; attempt. **опытный,** experienced; experimental.

опьянелый, intoxicated. **опьянение,** -я, intoxication. **о|пьянеть,** -ею *perf.* **о|пьянить,** -ит *perf.*, **опьянять,** -яет *imp.* intoxicate, make drunk. **опьяняющий,** intoxicating.

опять *adv.* again.

орава, -ы, crowd, horde.

оранжевый, orange. **оранжерейный,** hothouse, greenhouse. **оранжерея,** -и, hothouse, greenhouse, conservatory.

оратор, -а, orator, (public) speaker. **ораторский,** orator's, speaker's; oratorical. **ораторствовать,** -твую *imp.* orate, harangue, speechify.

орать, ору, орёшь *imp.* bawl, yell.

орбита, -ы, orbit; (eye-)socket; вывести на орбиту, put into orbit; ~ влияния, sphere of influence.

орг- *abbr.* in *comb.* organization, organizational.

о́рган[1], -а, organ; organization; unit, element; department, body; исполни́тельный ~, executive; agency. **орга́н**[2], -а, organ. **организа́тор**, -а, organizer. **организацио́нный**, organization, organizational. **организа́ция**, -и, organization; ~ Объединённых На́ций, United Nations Organisation. **организо́ванный**, organized; orderly, disciplined. **организова́ть**, -зу́ю *perf.* and *imp.* (*perf.* also с~) organize; **~ся**, be organized; organize. **органи́ческий**, **органи́чный**, organic.

о́ргия, -и, orgy.

орда́, -ы́; *pl.* -ы, horde.

о́рден, -а; *pl.* -а́, order. **орденоно́сец**, -сца, holder of an order or decoration. **орденоно́сный**, decorated with an order.

о́рдер, -а; *pl.* -а́, order; warrant; writ.

ордина́рец, -рца, orderly; batman.

ордина́тор, -а, house-surgeon. **ордина-ту́ра**, -ы, house-surgeon's appointment; clinical studies.

орды́нский, of the (Tartar) horde(s).

орёл, орла́, eagle; ~ или ре́шка? heads or tails?

орео́л, -а, halo, aureole.

оре́х, -а, nut, nuts; nut-tree; walnut. **оре́ховый**, nut; walnut. **оре́шник**, -а, hazel; hazel-thicket.

оригина́л, -а, original; eccentric, oddity. **оригина́льный**, original.

ориента́ция, -и, orientation (на+*acc.* towards); understanding, grasp (в+*prep.* of). **ориенти́р**, -а, landmark; reference point, guiding line. **ориенти́рование**, -я, orienteering. **ориенти́роваться**, -аюсь *perf.* and *imp.* orient oneself; find, get, one's bearings; +на +*acc.* head for, make for; aim at. **ориентиро́вка**, -и, orientation. **ориентиро́вочный**, serving for orientation, position-finding; tentative; provisional; rough approximate.

орли́ный, eagle's, eagle; aquiline. **орли́ца**, -ы, female eagle.

орна́мент, -а, ornament; ornamental design; plaster cast.

оробе́лый, timid; frightened. **о|робе́ть**, -е́ю *perf.*

ороси́тельный, irrigation. **ороси́ть**, -ошу́ *perf.*, **ороша́ть**, -а́ю *imp.* irrigate. **ороше́ние**, -я, irrigation; поля́ ороше́ния, sewage farm.

ору́, etc.: see ора́ть.

ору́дие, -я, instrument; implement; tool; gun. **оруди́йный**, gun. **ору́довать**, -дую *imp.*+*instr.* handle; be active in; run; он там всем ору́дует, he bosses the whole show. **оруже́й-н|ый**, arms; gun; ~ый заво́д, arms factory; ~ая пала́та, armoury. **ору́жие**, -я, arm, arms; weapons.

орфографи́ческ|ий, orthographic, orthographical; ~ая оши́бка, spelling mistake. **орфогра́фия**, -и, orthography, spelling.

оса́, -ы́; *pl.* -ы, wasp.

оса́да, -ы, siege. **осади́ть**[1], -ажу́ *perf.* (*imp.* осажда́ть) besiege, lay siege to; beleaguer; ~ вопро́сами, ply with questions; ~ про́сьбами, bombard with requests.

осади́ть[2], -ажу́, -а́дишь *perf.* (*imp.* осажда́ть) precipitate.

осади́ть[3], -ажу́, -а́дишь *perf.* (*imp.* оса́живать) check, halt; force back; rein in; put in his (her) place; take down a peg.

оса́дн|ый, siege; ~ое положе́ние, state of siege.

оса́док, -дка, sediment; precipitate; fall-out; after-taste; *pl.* precipitation, fall-out. **оса́дочный**, precipitation; sedimentary.

осажда́ть, -а́ю *imp.* of осади́ть. **осажда́ться**, -а́ется *imp.* fall; be precipitated, fall out.

оса́живать, -аю *imp.* of осади́ть. **осажу́**: see осади́ть.

оса́нистый, portly. **оса́нка**, -и, carriage, bearing.

осва́ивать(ся, -аю(сь *imp.* of осво́ить(ся.

осведоми́тель, -я *m.* informer. **осведоми́тельный**, informative; information. **осве́домить**, -млю *perf.*, **осведомля́ть**, -я́ю *imp.* inform; **~ся** о+*prep.* inquire about, ask after. **осведомле́ние**, -я, informing, notification. **осведомлённость**, -и, knowledge, information. **осведомлённый**, well-informed, knowledgeable; conversant, versed.

освежа́ть, -а́ю *imp.*, **освежи́ть**, -жу́ *perf.* refresh; freshen; air; revive. **освежи́тельный**, refreshing.

освети́тельный, lighting, illuminating. **освети́ть**, -ещу́ *perf.*, **освеща́ть**, -а́ю *perf.* light; light up; illuminate, illumine; throw light on; **~ся**, light up, brighten; be lighted. **освеще́ние**, -я, light, lighting illumination. **освещённый**; -ён, -а́, lit; ~ луно́й, moonlit.

о|свиде́тельствовать, -твую *perf.*

освиста́ть, -ищу́, -и́щешь *perf.*, **осви́стывать**, -аю *imp.* hiss (off); boo, hoot; greet with catcalls.

освободи́тель, -я *m.* liberator. **освободи́тельный**, liberation, emancipation. **освободи́ть**, -ожу́ *perf.*, **освобожда́ть**, -а́ю *imp.* free, liberate; release, set free; emancipate; dismiss; vacate; clear, empty; **~ся**, free oneself; become free. **освобожде́ние**, -я, liberation; release; emancipation; discharge; dismissal; vacation. **освобождённый**; -ён, -а́, freed, free; exempt; ~ от нало́га, tax-free.

освое́ние, -я, assimilation, mastery, familiarization; reclamation, opening up. **housеосво́ить**, -о́ю *perf.* (*imp.* осва́ивать) assimilate, master; cope with; become familiar with; acclimatize; **~ся**, familiarize oneself; feel at home.

о|святи́ть, -ящу́ *perf.* **освящённый**; -ён, -ена́, consecrated; sanctified, hallowed; обы́чай, ~ века́ми, time-honoured custom.

осево́й, axle; axis; axial.

оседа́ние, -я, settling, subsidence; settlement. **оседа́ть**, -а́ю *imp.* of осе́сть.

осёдланный, saddled. **о|седла́ть**, -а́ю *perf.*, **осёдлывать**, -аю *imp.* saddle.

осе́длый, settled.

осека́ться, -а́юсь *imp.* of осе́чься.

осёл, -сла́, donkey; ass.

осело́к, -лка́, touchstone; hone, whetstone, oil-stone.

осени́ть, -ню́ *perf.* (*imp.* осеня́ть) cover; overshadow; shield; dawn upon, strike; **~ся** кресто́м, cross oneself.

осе́нний, autumn, autumnal. **о́сень**, -и, autumn. **о́сенью** *adv.* in autumn.

осеня́ть(ся, -я́ю(сь *imp.* of осени́ть(ся.

осерди́ться, -ржу́сь, -рдишься *perf.* (+на+*acc.*) become angry (with).

осеребри́ть, -ри́т *perf.* silver (over).

осе́сть, ося́ду; осе́л *perf.* (*imp.* оседа́ть) settle; subside; sink; form a sediment.

осётр, -а́, sturgeon. **осетри́на**, -ы, sturgeon. **осетро́вый**, sturgeon, sturgeon's.

осе́чка, -и, misfire. **осе́чься**, -еку́сь, -ечёшься *perf.* (*imp.* осека́ться) misfire; stop short, break (off).

оси́ливать, -аю *imp.*, **оси́лить**, -лю *perf.* overpower; master; manage.

оси́на, -ы, aspen. **оси́новый**, aspen.

оси́ный, wasp, wasp's; hornets'.

оси́плый, hoarse, husky. **о|си́пнуть**, -ну; оси́п *perf.* get hoarse, grow hoarse.

осироте́лый, orphaned. **осироте́ть**, -е́ю *perf.* be orphaned.

оска́ливать, -аю *imp.*, **о|ска́лить**, -лю *perf.*; ~ зу́бы, ~ся, show one's teeth, bare one's teeth.

о|сканда́лить(ся, -лю(сь *perf.*

оскверне́ние, -я, defilement; profanation. **оскверни́ть**, -ню́ *perf.*, **оскверня́ть**, -я́ю *imp.* profane; defile.

оскла́биться, -блюсь *perf.* grin.

оско́лок, -лка, splinter; fragment. **оско́лочный** *adj.* splinter; fragmentation.

оско́мина, -ы, bitter taste (in the mouth); наби́ть оско́мину, set the teeth on edge. **оско́мистый**, sour, bitter.

оскорби́тельный, insulting, abusive. **оскорби́ть**, -блю́ *perf.*, **оскорбля́ть**, -я́ю *imp.* insult; offend; **~ся**, take offence; be offended, be hurt. **оскорбле́ние**, -я, insult; ~ де́йствием, assault and battery. **оскорблённ|ый**; -ён, -а́, offended, insulted; ~ая неви́нность, outraged innocence.

ослабева́ть, -а́ю *imp.*, **о|слабе́ть**, -е́ю *perf.* weaken, become weak; slacken; abate. **ослабе́лый**, weakened, enfeebled. **осла́бить**, -блю *perf.*, **ослабля́ть**, -я́ю *imp.* weaken; slacken, relax; loosen. **ослабле́ние, -я,** weakening; slackening, relaxation.

ослепи́тельный, blinding, dazzling. **ослепи́ть,** -плю́ *perf.*, **ослепля́ть,** -я́ю *imp.* blind, dazzle. **ослепле́ние,** -я, blinding, dazzling; blindness. **о|сле́пнуть,** -ну; -еп *perf.*

осли́ный, donkey; ass's, asses'; asinine. **осли́ца,** -ы, she-ass.

осложне́ние, -я, complication. **осложни́ть,** -ню́ *perf.*, **осложня́ть,** -я́ю *imp.* complicate; **~ся,** become complicated.

ослуша́ние, -я, disobedience. **ослу́шаться,** -аюсь *perf.*, **ослу́шиваться,** -аюсь *imp.* disobey.

ослы́шаться, -шусь *perf.* mishear. **ослы́шка,** -и, mishearing, mistake of hearing.

осма́тривать(ся, -аю(сь *imp.* of осмотре́ть(ся. **осме́ивать,** -аю *imp.* of осмея́ть.

о|смеле́ть, -е́ю *perf.* **осме́ливаться,** -аюсь *imp.*, **осме́литься,** -люсь *perf.* dare; beg to, take the liberty of.

осмея́ть, -ею́, -еёшь *perf.* (*imp.* осме́ивать) mock, ridicule.

о|смоли́ть, -лю́ *perf.*

осмо́тр, -а, examination, inspection. **осмотре́ть,** -рю́, -ришь *perf.* (*imp.* осма́тривать) examine, inspect; look round, look over; **~ся,** look round; take one's bearings, see how the land lies. **осмотри́тельный,** circumspect. **осмо́трщик,** -а, inspector.

осмы́сленный, sensible, intelligent. **осмы́сливать,** -аю *imp.*, **осмы́слить,** -лю *perf.*, **осмысля́ть,** -я́ю *imp.* interpret, give a meaning to; comprehend.

оснасти́ть, -ащу́ *perf.*, **оснаща́ть,** -а́ю *imp.* rig; fit out, equip. **осна́стка,** -и, rigging. **оснаще́ние,** -я, rigging; fitting out; equipment.

осно́ва, -ы, base, basis, foundation; *pl.* principles, fundamentals; на осно́ве + *gen.* on the basis of; положи́ть в осно́ву, take as a principle. **основа́ние,** -я, founding, foundation; base; basis; ground, reason; на како́м основа́нии? on what grounds?; разру́шить до основа́ния, raze to the ground. **основа́тель,** -я *m.* founder. **основа́тельный,** well-founded; just; solid, sound; thorough; bulky. **основа́ть,** -ную́, -нуёшь *perf.*, **осно́вывать,** -аю *imp.* found; base; **~ся,** settle; base oneself; be founded, be based. **основно́й,** fundamental, basic; principal main; primary; в основно́м, in the main, on the whole. **основополо́жник,** -а, founder, initiator.

осо́ба, -ы, person, individual, personage. **осо́бенно** *adv.* especially; particularly; unusually; не ~, not very, not particularly; not very much. **осо́бенность,** -и, peculiarity; в осо́бенности, especially, in particular; (more) particularly. **осо́бенный,** special particular, peculiar; ничего́ осо́бенного, nothing in particular; nothing (very) much. **особня́к,** -а́, private residence; detached house. **особняко́м** *adv.* by oneself. **осо́бо** *adv.* apart, separately; particularly, especially. **осо́бый,** special; particular; peculiar.

ОТС (*ote-és*) *abbr.* областна́я трансляцио́нная сеть, regional broadcasting network.

осознава́ть, -наю́, -наёшь *imp.*, **осозна́ть,** -а́ю *perf.* realize.

осо́ка, -и sedge.

о́спа, -ы, smallpox; pock-marks; vaccination marks.

оспа́ривать, -аю *imp.*, **оспо́рить,** -рю *perf.* dispute, question; challenge, contest; contend for.

о|срами́ть(ся, -млю́(сь *perf.* **остава́ться,** -таю́сь, -таёшься *imp.* of оста́ться.

оста́вить, -влю *perf.*, **оставля́ть,** -я́ю *imp.* leave; abandon, give up; reserve, keep; ~ в поко́е, leave alone, let alone; ~ за собо́й пра́во, reserve the right; ~ь(те)! stop it! stop that! lay off!

остальн|о́й the rest of; в ~о́м, in other respects; **~о́е** *sb.* the rest; **~ы́е** *sb.* the others.

остана́вливать(ся, -аю(сь *imp.* of останови́ть(ся.

оста́нки, -ов *pl.* remains.

остано́в, -а, stop, stopper, ratchet-gear. **останови́ть,** -влю́, -вишь *perf.* (*imp.* остана́вливать) stop; interrupt; pull up, restrain; check; direct, concentrate; **~ся,** stop, come to a stop, come to a halt; stay, put up; + на + *prep.*

dwell on; settle on, rest on. **остано́вка,** stop; stoppage; hold-up; ~ за ва́ми, you are holding us up.

оста́ток, -тка, remainder; rest; residue; remnant; residuum; balance; *pl.* remains; leavings; leftovers. **оста́точный,** residual, remaining. **оста́ться,** -а́нусь *perf.* (*imp.* остава́ться) remain; stay; be left, be left over; за ним оста́лось пять рубле́й, he owes five roubles; ~ в живы́х, survive, come through; ~ на́ ночь, stay the night; *impers.* it remains, it is necessary; нам не остаётся ничего́ друго́го, как, there is nothing for us to do but, we have no choice but.

о|**стекленеть,** -е́ет *perf.* **остекли́ть,** -лю́ *perf.*, **остекля́ть,** -я́ю *imp.* glaze.

остепени́ться, -ню́сь *perf.*, **остепеня́ться,** -я́юсь *imp.* settle down; become staid, become respectable; mellow.

остерега́ть, -а́ю *imp.*, **остере́чь,** -регу́, -режёшь; -рёг, -ла́ *perf.* warn, caution; **~ся** (+*gen.*) beware (of); be careful (of), be on one's guard (against).

о́стов, -а, frame, framework; shell; hull; skeleton.

остолбене́лый, dumbfounded. о|**столбене́ть,** -е́ю *perf.*

осторо́жно *adv.* carefully; cautiously; guardedly; ~! with care; look out! **осторо́жность,** -и, care, caution; prudence. **осторо́жный,** careful, cautious; prudent.

острига́ть(ся, -а́ю(сь *imp.* of остри́чь-(ся.

остриё, -я́ point; spike; (cutting) edge.

остри́ть[1], -рю́ *imp.* sharpen, whet.

остри́ть[2], -рю́ *imp.* (*perf.* с~) be witty.

о|**стри́чь,** -игу́, -ижёшь; -и́г *perf.* (*imp.* also острига́ть) cut, clip; **~ся,** cut one's hair; have one's hair cut.

остро- in *comb.* sharp, pointed. **остроглазый,** sharp-sighted, keen-eyed. **~коне́чный,** pointed. **~ли́ст,** -а, holly. **~но́сый,** sharp-nosed; pointed, tapered. **~сло́в,** -а, wit. **~уго́льный,** acute-angled. **~у́мие,** -я, wit. **~у́мный,** witty.

о́стров, -а; *pl.* -а́, island; isle. **острово́й,** island; insular. **острово́к,** -вка́, islet; ~ безопа́сности, (traffic) island.

остро́та[1], -ы, witticism, joke. **острота́**[2], -ы́, sharpness; keenness; acuteness; pungency, poignancy.

о́стр|ый; остр, -а́, -о, sharp; pointed; acute; keen; ~ое положе́ние, critical situation; ~ый сыр, strong cheese; ~ый у́гол, acute angle. **остря́к,** -а́, wit.

о|**студи́ть,** -ужу́, -у́дишь *perf.*, **остужа́ть,** -а́ю *imp.* cool.

оступа́ться, -а́юсь *imp.*, **оступи́ться,** -плю́сь, -пишься *perf.* stumble.

остыва́ть, -а́ю *imp.*, **осты́ть,** -ы́ну *perf.* get cold; cool, cool down.

осуди́ть, -ужу́, -у́дишь *perf.*, **осужда́ть,** -а́ю *imp.* condemn, sentence; convict; censure, blame. **осужде́ние,** -я, censure, condemnation; conviction. **осуждённый;** -ён, -а́, condemned, convicted; *sb.* convict, convicted person.

осу́нуться, -нусь *perf.* grow thin, get pinched-looking.

осуша́ть, -а́ю *imp.*, **осуши́ть,** -шу́, -шишь *perf.* drain; dry. **осуше́ние,** -я, drainage. **осуши́тельный,** drainage.

осуществи́мый practicable, realizable, feasible. **осуществи́ть,** -влю́ *perf.*, **осуществля́ть,** -я́ю *imp.* realize, bring about; accomplish, carry out; implement; **~ся,** be fulfilled, come true. **осуществле́ние,** -я, realization; accomplishment; implementation.

осчастли́вить, -влю *perf.*, **осчастли́вливать,** -аю *imp.* make happy.

осы́пать, -плю *perf.*, **осыпа́ть,** -а́ю *imp.* strew; shower; heap; pull down, knock down; ~ уда́рами, rain blows on; **~ся,** crumble; fall. **о́сыпь,** -и, scree.

ось, -и; *gen. pl.* -е́й, axis; axle; spindle; pin.

ося́ду, etc.: see осе́сть.

осяза́емый, tangible; palpable. **осяза́ние,** -я, touch. **осяза́тельный,** tactile, tactual; tangible, palpable, sensible. **осяза́ть,** -а́ю *imp.* feel.

от, ото *prep.*+*gen.* from; of; for; against; бли́зко от го́рода, near the town; вре́мя от вре́мени, from time to time; день ото дня, from day to day; дрожа́ть от стра́ха, tremble with fear; застрахова́ть от огня́, insure against fire; ключ от две́ри, door-key; на се́вер от Ленингра́да, north of Leningrad; от всей души́, with all one's heart; от и́мени+*gen.*, on behalf of; от нача́ла до конца́, from beginning to end; от ра́дости, for joy; письмо́ от пе́рвого а́вгуста, letter of the first of August; рабо́чий от станка́, machine operative; сре́дство от, a remedy for; сын от пре́жнего бра́ка, a son by a previous marriage; умере́ть от го́лода die of hunger; це́ны от рубля́ и вы́ше, prices from a rouble upwards.

от-, ото-, отъ- *vbl. pref.* indicating completion of action or task, fulfilment of duty or obligation; action or motion away from a point; action continued through a certain time; (with verbs reflexive in form) action of negative character, cancelling or undoing of a state, omission, etc.

ота́пливать, -аю *imp.* of отопи́ть.

отба́вить, -влю *perf.*, **отбавля́ть,** -я́ю *imp.* take away; pour off; хоть отбавля́й more than enough.

отбега́ть, -а́ю *imp.*, **отбежа́ть,** -егу́ *perf.* run off.

отберу́, etc.: see отобра́ть.

отбива́ть(ся, -а́ю(сь *imp.* of отби́ть(ся. **отби́вка,** -и, marking out, delineation; whetting, sharpening.

отбивн|о́й; ~а́я котле́та, cutlet, chop.

отбира́ть, -а́ю *imp.* of отобра́ть.

отби́тие, -я, repulse; repelling. **отби́ть,** отобью́, -ёшь *perf.* (*imp.* отбива́ть) beat off, repulse, repel; parry; take; win over; break off, knock off; knock up; damage by knocks or blows; whet, sharpen; **~ся,** break off; drop behind, straggle; + от + *gen.* defend oneself against; repulse, beat off; ~ся от рук, get out of hand.

от|бла́говестить, -ещу *perf.*

о́тблеск, -а, reflection.

отбо́й, -я (-ю), repulse, repelling; retreat; ringing off; бить ~, beat a retreat; дать ~, ring off; ~ возду́шной трево́ги, the all-clear; ~ мяча́, return; отбо́ю нет от, there is no getting rid of.

отбо́р, -а, selection. **отбо́рный,** choice, select(ed); picked. **отбо́рочн|ый,** selection; ~ая коми́ссия, selection board; ~ое соревнова́ние, knock-out competition.

отбра́сывать, -аю *imp.*, **отбро́сить,** -о́шу *perf.* throw off; cast away; throw back, thrust back, hurl back; give up, reject, discard; ~ тень, cast a shadow. **отбро́с,** -а, garbage, refuse; offal.

отбыва́ть, -а́ю *imp.*, **отбы́ть,** -бу́ду; о́тбыл, -а́, -о *perf.* depart, leave; serve, do; ~ наказа́ние, serve one's sentence, do time.

отва́га, -и, courage, bravery.

отва́дить, -а́жу *perf.*, **отва́живать,** -аю *imp.* scare away; +от+*gen.* break of, cure of.

отва́живаться, -аюсь *imp.*, **отва́житься,** -жусь *perf.* dare, venture; have the courage. **отва́жный,** courageous, brave.

отва́л, -а, mould-board; dump, slag-heap; putting off, pushing off, casting off; до ~а, to satiety; нае́сться до ~а, eat one's fill, stuff oneself. **отва́ливать,** -аю *imp.*, **отвали́ть,** -лю́, -лишь *perf.* heave off; push aside; put off, push off, cast off; fork out, stump up.

отва́р, -а, broth; decoction. **отва́ривать,** -аю *imp.*, **отвари́ть,** -рю́, -ришь *perf.* boil. **отварно́й,** boiled.

отве́дать, -аю *perf.* (*imp.* отве́дывать), taste, try.

отведённый, allotted. **отведу́,** etc.: see отвести́.

отве́дывать, -аю *imp.* of отве́дать.

отвезти́, -зу́, -зёшь; -вёз, -ла́ *perf.* (*imp.* отвози́ть) take, take away; cart away.

отвёл, etc.: see отвести́.

отверга́ть, -а́ю *imp.*, **отве́ргнуть,** -ну; -ве́рг *perf.* reject, turn down; repudiate; spurn.

отвердева́ть, -а́ет *imp.*, **отверде́ть,** -е́ет *perf.* harden. **отверде́лость,** -и, hardening; callus. **отверде́лый,** hardened.

отве́рженец, -нца, outcast. **отве́рженный,** outcast.

отверну́ть, -ну́, -нёшь *perf.* (*imp.* отвёртывать, отвора́чивать) turn away, turn aside; turn down; turn on; unscrew; screw off, twist off; **~ся,** turn away, turn aside; come on; come unscrewed.

отве́рстие, -я, opening, aperture, orifice; hole; slot.

отверте́ть, -рчу́, -ртишь *perf.* (*imp.* отвёртывать) unscrew; screw off, twist off; **~ся,** come unscrewed; get off; get out, wriggle out. **отвёртка,** -и, screwdriver.

отвёртывать(ся, -аю(сь *imp.* of отверну́ть(ся, отверте́ть(ся.

отве́с, -а, plumb plummet; slope. **отве́сить,** -е́шу *perf.* (*imp.* отве́шивать) weigh out. **отве́сно** *adv.* plumb; sheer. **отве́сный** perpendicular, sheer.

отвести́, -еду́, -едёшь; -вёл, -а́ *perf.* (*imp.* отводи́ть) lead, take, conduct; draw aside, take aside; deflect; draw off; reject; challenge; allot, assign; ~ глаза́, look aside, look away; ~ глаза́ от, take one's eyes off; ~ ду́шу, unburden one's heart; ~ обвине́ние, justify oneself.

отве́т, -а, answer, reply, response; responsibility; быть в отве́те (за), be answerable (for).

ответви́ться, -и́тся *perf.*, **ответвля́ться,** -я́ется *imp.* branch off. **ответвле́ние,** -я, branch, offshoot; branch pipe; tap, shunt.

отве́тить, -е́чу *perf.*, **отвеча́ть,** -а́ю *imp.* answer, reply; + на + *acc.* return; + за + *acc.* answer for, pay for. **отве́тный,** given in answer answering. **отве́тственность,** -и, responsibility; привле́чь к отве́тственности, call to account, bring to book. **отве́тственный,** responsible; crucial; ~ реда́ктор, editor-in-chief. **отве́тчик,** -а, defendant, respondent; bearer of responsibility.

отве́шивать, -аю *imp.* of отве́сить. **отве́шу,** etc.: see отве́сить.

отви́ливать, -аю *imp.*, **отвильну́ть,** -ну́, -нёшь *perf.* dodge.

отвинти́ть, -нчу́ *perf.*, **отви́нчивать,** -аю *imp.* unscrew; **~ся,** unscrew, come unscrewed.

отвиса́ть, -а́ет *imp.*, **отви́снуть,** -нет; -и́с *perf.* hang down, sag. **отви́сл|ый,** hanging, baggy; с ~ыми уша́ми, lop-eared.

отвлека́ть, -а́ю *imp.*, **отвле́чь,** -еку́, -ечёшь; -влёк, -ла́ *perf.* distract, divert; draw away attention of; **~ся,** be distracted; become abstracted. **отвлече́ние,** -я, abstraction; distraction. **отвлечённый** abstract.

отво́д, -а, taking aside; deflection; diversion; leading, taking, conducting; withdrawal; rejection; challenge; allotment, allocation; tap, tapping. **отводи́ть,** -ожу́, -о́дишь *imp.* of отвести́. **отво́дка,** -и, branch; diversion; shifting device, shifter. **отво́док,** -дка, cutting, layer.

отвоева́ть, -ою́ю *perf.*, **отвоёвывать,** -аю *imp.* win back, reconquer; fight, spend in fighting; finish fighting, finish the war.

отвози́ть, -ожу́, -о́зишь *imp.* of отвезти́. **отвора́чивать(ся,** -аю(сь *imp.* of отверну́ть(ся.

отвори́ть, -рю́, -ришь *perf.* (*imp.* отворя́ть) open; **~ся,** open.

отворо́т, -а, lapel flap; top.

отворя́ть(ся, -я́ю(сь *imp.* of отвори́ть(ся. **отвою́ю,** etc.: see отвоева́ть.

отврати́тельный, отвра́тный, repulsive, disgusting, loathsome; abominable. **отврати́ть,** -ащу́ *perf.*, **отвраща́ть,** -а́ю *imp.* avert, stave off; deter, stay the hand of. **отвраще́ние,** aversion, disgust, repugnance; loathing.

отвяза́ть, -яжу́ -я́жешь *perf.*, **отвя́зывать,** -аю *imp.* untie unfasten; untether; **~ся,** come untied, come loose; + от + *gen.* get rid of, shake off, get shut of; leave alone, leave in peace; stop nagging at; отвяжи́сь от меня́! leave me alone!

отвыка́ть, -а́ю *imp.*, **отвы́кнуть,** -ну; -вы́к *perf.* + от or *inf.* break oneself of, give up; lose the habit of; grow out of.

отгада́ть, -а́ю *perf.*, **отга́дывать,** -аю *imp.* guess. **отга́дка.** -и, answer. **отга́дчик,** -а, guesser, solver, diviner.

отгиба́ть(ся, -а́ю(сь *imp.* of отогну́ть(ся.

отглаго́льный, verbal.

отгла́дить, -а́жу *perf.*, **отгла́живать,** -аю *imp.* iron (out).

отгова́ривать, -аю *imp.* **отговори́ть,** -рю́ *perf.* dissuade; talk out of; **~ся** +

instr. plead, excuse oneself on the ground of. **отгово́рка,** -и, excuse, pretext.
отголо́сок, -ска echo.
отго́н, -а, driving off; distillation; distillate. **отго́нка,** -и, driving off; distillation. **отго́нн|ый;** ~ые па́стбища, distant pastures. **отгоня́ть,** -я́ю *imp.* of отогна́ть.
отгора́живать, -аю *imp.,* **отгороди́ть,** -ожу́, -о́дишь *perf.* fence off; partition off, screen off; **~ся** fence oneself off; shut oneself off, cut oneself off.
отгрыза́ть, -а́ю *imp.,* **отгры́зть,** -зу́, -зёшь *perf.* gnaw off, bite off.
отдава́ть[1]**(ся,** -даю́(сь *imp.* of отда́ть(ся. **отдава́ть**[2], -аёт *imp. impers.* + *instr.* taste of; smell of; smack of; от него́ отдаёт во́дкой, he reeks of vodka.
отдави́ть, -влю́, -вишь *perf.* crush; ~ но́гу + *dat.* tread on the foot of.
отдале́ние, -я, removal; estrangement; distance; держа́ть в отдале́нии, keep at a distance. **отдалённость,** -и, remoteness. **отдалённый,** distant, remote. **отдали́ть,** -лю́ *perf.,* **отдаля́ть,** -я́ю *imp.* remove; estrange, alienate; postpone, put off; **~ся,** move away; digress.
отда́ние, -я giving back returning. **отда́ть,** -а́м, -а́шь, -а́ст, -ади́м; о́тдал, -а́, -о *perf.* (*imp.* отдава́ть) give back, return; give; give up, devote; give in marriage, give away; put, place; make; sell, let have; recoil, kick; let go; cast off; ~ в шко́лу, send to school; ~ до́лжное + *dat.* render his due to; ~ под суд, prosecute; ~ прика́з, issue an order, give orders; ~ честь + *dat.* salute; **~ся,** give oneself (up); devote oneself; resound; reverberate; ring. **отда́ча,** -и, return; payment, reimbursement; letting go, casting off; efficiency, performance; output; recoil, kick.
отде́л, -а, department; section, part.
отде́лать, -аю *perf.* (*imp.* отде́лывать) finish, put the finishing touches to; trim; **~ся** + от + *gen.* get rid of, finish with; + *instr.* escape with, get off with.
отделе́ние, -я, separation; department, branch; compartment; section; part; ~ шка́фа, pigeon-hole. **отделённый,** section; *sb.* section commander. **отделе́нский, отделе́нческий,** department(al), branch. **отдели́мый,** separable. **отдели́ть,** -елю́, -е́лишь *perf.* (*imp.* отделя́ть) separate part; detach; separate off; cut off; **~ся,** separate, part; detach oneself, itself; get detached; come apart; come off.
отде́лка, -и, finishing; trimming; finish, decoration. **отде́лывать(ся,** -аю(сь *imp.* of отде́лать(ся.
отде́льно, separately; apart. **отде́льность,** -и; в отде́льности, taken separately, individually. **отде́льный,** separate, individual; independent. **отделя́ть(ся,** -я́ю(сь *imp.* of **отдели́ть(ся.**
отдёргивать, -аю *imp.,* **отдёрнуть,** -ну *perf.* draw aside, pull aside; draw back, pull back; jerk back.
отдеру́, etc.: see отодра́ть. **отдира́ть,** -а́ю *imp.* of отодра́ть.
отдохну́ть, -ну́, -нёшь *perf.* (*imp.* отдыха́ть) rest; have a rest, take a rest.
отду́шина, -ы, air-hole, vent; safety-valve. **отду́шник,** -а, air-hole, vent.
о́тдых, -а, rest; relaxation; holiday. **отдыха́ть,** -а́ю *imp.* (*perf.* отдохну́ть), be resting; be on holiday. **отдыха́ющий** *sb.* holiday-maker.
отдыша́ться, -шу́сь, -шишься *perf.* recover one's breath.
отека́ть, -а́ю *imp.* of отёчь. **о|тели́ться,** -е́лится *perf.* **отеса́ть,** etc.: see обтеса́ть.
оте́ц, отца́, father. **оте́ческий,** fatherly, paternal. **оте́чественн|ый,** home, native; ~ая промы́шленность, home industry; Вели́кая ~ая война́, Great Patriotic War. **оте́чество,** -а, native land, fatherland, home country.
отёчь, -еку́, -ечёшь; отёк, -ла́ *perf.* (*imp.* отека́ть) swell, become swollen; gutter.
отжива́ть, -а́ю *imp.,* **отжи́ть,** -иву́, -ивёшь; о́тжил, -а́, -о *perf.* become obsolete; become outmoded; ~ свой век have had one's day; go out of fashion. **отжи́вший,** obsolete; outmoded.
о́тзвук, -а, echo.

о́тзыв[1], -а, opinion, judgement; reference; testimonial; review; reply, response; похва́льный ~, honourable mention. **отзы́в**[2], -а, recall. **отзыва́ть(ся**, -а́ю(сь *imp.* of отозва́ть(ся. **отзывн|о́й**; ~ы́е гра́моты, letters of recall. **отзы́вчивый**, responsive.

отка́з, -а, refusal; denial; repudiation; rejection; renunciation, giving up; failure; natural; де́йствовать без ~а, run smoothly; получи́ть ~, be refused, be turned down; по́лный до ~а, full to capacity, cram-full. **отказа́ть**, -ажу́, -а́жешь *perf.*, **отка́зывать**, -аю *imp.* fail, break down; (+*dat.* в+*prep.*) refuse, deny; + *dat.* от + *gen.* dismiss discharge; ~ от до́ма, forbid the house; **~ся** (+ от + *gen.* or + *inf.*) refuse, decline; turn down; retract; renounce, give up; relinquish, abdicate; ~ся от свое́й по́дписи, repudiate one's signature; ~ся служи́ть, be out of order.

отка́лывать(ся, -аю(сь *imp.* of отколо́ть(ся. **отка́пывать**, -аю *imp.* of откопа́ть. **отка́рмливать**, -аю *imp.* of откорми́ть.

откати́ть, -ачу́, -а́тишь *perf.*, **отка́тывать**, -аю *imp.* roll away; **~ся**, roll away; roll back, be forced back.

откача́ть, -а́ю *perf.*, **отка́чивать**, -аю *imp.* pump out; resuscitate, give artificial respiration to.

отка́шливаться, -аюсь *imp.*, **отка́шляться**, -яюсь *perf.* clear one's throat.

откидно́й, folding, collapsible. **отки́дывать**, -аю *imp.*, **отки́нуть**, -ну *perf.* turn back, fold back; throw aside; cast away.

откла́дывать, -аю *imp.* of отложи́ть.

откла́няться, -яюсь *perf.* take one's leave.

откле́ивать, -аю *imp.*, **откле́ить**, -е́ю *perf.* unstick; **~ся**, come unstuck.

о́тклик, -а, response; comment; echo; repercussion. **отклика́ться**, -а́юсь *imp.*, **откли́кнуться**, -нусь *perf.* answer, respond.

отклоне́ние, -я, deviation; divergence; declining refusal; deflection, declination; error; diffraction; ~ в сто́рону, deviation; ~ от те́мы digression.

отклони́ть, -ню́, -нишь *perf.*, **отклоня́ть**, -я́ю *imp.* deflect; decline; **~ся**, deviate; diverge; swerve.

отключа́ть, -а́ю *imp.*, **отключи́ть**, -чу́ *perf.* cut off, disconnect.

отколоти́ть, -очу́, -о́тишь *perf.* knock off; beat up, thrash, give a good hiding.

отколо́ть, -лю́, -лешь *perf.* (*imp.* отка́лывать) break off; chop off; unpin; **~ся**, break off; come unpinned, come undone; break away, cut oneself off.

откопа́ть, -а́ю *perf.* (*imp.* отка́пывать) dig out; exhume, disinter; dig up, unearth.

откорми́ть, -млю́, -мишь *perf.* (*imp.* отка́рмливать) fatten, fatten up. **отко́рмленный**, fat, fatted, fattened.

отко́с, -а, slope; пусти́ть под отко́с, derail.

открепи́ть, -плю́ *perf.*, **открепля́ть**, -я́ю *imp.* unfasten, untie; **~ся**, become unfastened.

открове́ние, -я, revelation. **открове́нничать**, -аю *imp.* be candid, be frank; open one's heart. **открове́нный**, candid, frank; blunt, outspoken; open, unconcealed; revealing. **откро́ю**, etc.: see открыть.

открути́ть, -учу́, -у́тишь *perf.*, **откру́чивать**, -аю *imp.* untwist, unscrew; **~ся**, come untwisted; + от + *gen.* get out of.

открыва́ть, -а́ю *imp.*, **откры́ть**, -ро́ю *perf.* open; uncover, reveal, bare; discover; turn on; ~ па́мятник, unveil a monument; **~ся**, open; come to light, be revealed; confide. **откры́тие**, -я, discovery; revelation; opening; inauguration; unveiling. **откры́тка**, -и, postcard. **откры́то**, openly. **откры́т|ый**, open; на ~ом во́здухе, под ~ым не́бом, out of doors, in the open air; ~ое заседа́ние, public sitting; ~ое письмо́ postcard; open letter.

отку́да *adv.* whence; where from; from which; ~ вы об э́том зна́ете? how do you come to know about that?; ~ ни возьми́сь, quite unexpectedly, suddenly. **отку́да-либо, -нибудь**, from somewhere or other. **отку́да-то**, from somewhere.

отку́поривать -аю *imp.*, **отку́порить,** -рю *perf.* uncork; open. **отку́порка,** -и, opening, uncorking.

откуси́ть -ушу́, -у́сишь *perf.*, **отку́сывать,** -аю *imp.* bite off; snap off, nip off.

отлага́тельство, -а, delay; procrastination; де́ло не те́рпит отлага́тельства, the matter is urgent. **отлага́ть(ся,** -а́юсь *imp.* of отложи́ть(ся.

от|лакирова́ть, -ру́ю *perf.* **отла́мывать,** -аю *imp.* of отлома́ть, отломи́ть.

отлежа́ть, -жу́ *perf.*, **отлёживать,** -аю *imp.*; я отлежа́л но́гу, my foot has gone to sleep.

отлепи́ть, -плю́, -пишь *perf.*, **отлепля́ть,** -я́ю *imp.* unstick, take off; **~ся,** come unstuck, come off.

отлёт, -а, flying away; departure; на ~е, on the point of departure, about to leave; in one's outstretched hand; (standing) by itself. **отлета́ть,** -а́ю *imp.*, **отлете́ть,** -лечу́ *perf.*, fly, fly away, fly off; vanish; rebound, bounce back; come off, burst off.

отли́в, -а, ebb, ebb-tide; tint; play of colours; с золоты́м ~ом, shot with gold. **отлива́ть,** -а́ю *imp.*, **отли́ть,** отолью́; о́тли́л, -а́, -о *perf.* pour off; pump out; cast, found; (no *perf.*) + *instr.* be shot with. **отли́вка,** -и, casting founding; cast, ingot, moulding. **отливно́й,** cast, casting; founded, moulded.

отлича́ть, -а́ю *imp.*, **отличи́ть,** -чу́ *perf.* distinguish; single out; ~ одно́ от друго́го tell one (thing) from another; **~ся,** distinguish oneself, excel; differ; + *instr.* be notable for. **отли́чие,** -я, difference; distinction; в ~ от, unlike, as distinguished from, in contradistinction to; знак отли́чия, order, decoration; с отли́чием, with honours. **отли́чник,** -а, outstanding student, worker, etc. **отличи́тельный,** distinctive; distinguishing. **отли́чно** *adv.* excellently; perfectly; extremely well. **отли́чный,** different; excellent; perfect; extremely good.

отло́гий, sloping. **отло́гость,** -и, slope. **отло́же,** *comp.* of отло́гий.

отложе́ние, -я, sediment, precipitation; deposit. **отложи́ть,** -ожу́, -о́жишь *perf.* (*imp.* откла́дывать, отлага́ть) put aside, set aside; put away, put by; put off, postpone; adjourn; turn back, turn down; unharness; deposit; **~ся,** detach oneself, separate; deposit, be deposited. **отложно́й** воротни́к, turn-down collar.

отлома́ть, -а́ю, **отломи́ть,** -млю́, -мишь *perf.* (*imp.* отла́мывать) break off.

отлуча́ть, -а́ю *imp.*, **отлучи́ть,** -чу́ *perf.* separate, remove; ~ (от це́ркви), excommunicate; **~ся,** absent oneself. **отлу́чка,** -и, absence; быть в отлу́чке, be absent, be away.

отлы́нивать, -аю *imp.*+от+*gen.* shirk.

отма́лчиваться, -аюсь *imp.* of отмолча́ться.

отма́хивать, -аю *imp.*, **отмахну́ть,** -ну́, -нёшь *perf.* brush off; wave away; **~ся** от + *gen.* brush off; brush aside.

отмежева́ться, -жу́юсь *perf.*, **отмежёвываться,** -аюсь *imp.* от + *gen.* dissociate oneself from; refuse to acknowledge.

о́тмель, -и, bar, (sand-)bank; shallow.

отме́на, -ы, abolition; abrogation, repeal, revocation; cancellation, countermand. **отмени́ть,** -ню́, -нишь *perf.*, **отменя́ть,** -я́ю *imp.* abrogate, repeal, revoke, rescind; abolish; cancel, countermand; disaffirm.

отмере́ть, отомрёт; о́тмер, -ла́, -ло *perf.* (*imp.* отмира́ть) die off; die out, die away.

отме́ривать, -аю *imp.*, **отме́рить,** -рю *perf.*, **отмеря́ть,** -я́ю *imp.* measure off.

отмести́, -ету́, -етёшь; -ёл, -а́ *perf.* (*imp.* отмета́ть) sweep aside.

отме́стка, -и, revenge.

отмета́ть, -а́ю *imp.* of отмести́.

отме́тина, -ы, mark, notch; star, blaze.

отме́тить, -е́чу *perf.*, **отмеча́ть,** -а́ю *imp.* mark, note; make a note of; point to, mention, record; celebrate, mark by celebration; **~ся,** sign one's name; sign out. **отме́тка,** -и, note; mark; blip. **отме́тчик,** -а, marker.

отмира́ние, -я, dying off; dying away,

fading away, withering away. **отмира́ть,** -а́ет *imp.* of отмере́ть.

отмолча́ться, -чу́сь *perf.* (*imp.* отма́лчиваться) keep silent, say nothing.

отмора́живать, -аю *imp.*, **отморо́зить,** -о́жу *perf.* injure by frost-bite. **отморо́жение,** -я, frost-bite. **отморо́женный,** frost-bitten.

отмо́ю, etc.: see отмы́ть.

от|мсти́ть, -мщу *perf.* **отмще́ние,** -я, vengeance.

отмыва́ть, -а́ю *imp.*, **отмы́ть,** -мо́ю *perf.* wash clean; wash off, wash away; **~ся,** wash oneself clean; come out, come off.

отмы́чка, -и, picklock; master-key.

отне́киваться, -аюсь *imp.* refuse.

отнести́, -су́, -сёшь; -нёс, -ла́ *perf.* (*imp.* относи́ть) take; carry away, carry off; ascribe, attribute, refer; **~сь** к + *dat.* treat; regard; apply to; concern, have to do with; date from; э́то к де́лу не отно́сится, that's beside the point, that is not relevant.

отнима́ть(ся, -а́ю(сь *imp.* of отня́ть(ся.

относи́тельно *adv.* relatively; *prep.* + *gen.* concerning, about, with regard to. **относи́тельность,** -и, relativity. **относи́тельн|ый,** relative; ~ое местоиме́ние, relative pronoun. **относи́ть**[1]**(ся,** -ошу́(сь, -о́сишь(ся *imp.* of отнести́(сь. **относи́ть**[2], -ошу́, -о́сишь *perf.* stop wearing. **отноше́ние,** -я, attitude; treatment; relation; respect; ratio; letter, memorandum; *pl.* relations; terms; в не́которых отноше́ниях, in some respects; в отноше́нии +*gen.* по отноше́нию к + *dat.*, with respect to, with regard to; в прямо́м (обра́тном) отноше́нии, in direct (inverse) ratio; не име́ть отноше́ния к+ *dat.*, bear no relation to, have nothing to do with.

отны́не *adv.* henceforth, henceforward.

отня́тие, -я, taking away; amputation. **отня́ть,** -ниму́, -ни́мешь; о́тнял, -а́, -о *perf.* (*imp.* отнима́ть) take (away); amputate; ~ от груди́, wean; ~ три от шести́, take three away from six; э́то о́тняло у меня́ три часа́, it took me three hours; **~ся,** be paralysed; у него́ отняла́сь пра́вая рука́, he has lost the use of his right arm.

ото: see от. **ото-:** see от-.

отобража́ть, -а́ю *imp.*, **отобрази́ть,** -ажу́ *perf.* reflect; represent. **отображе́ние,** -я, reflection; representation.

отобра́ть, отберу́, -рёшь; отобра́л, -а́, -о *perf.* (*imp.* отбира́ть) take (away); seize; select, pick out.

отобью, etc.: see отби́ть.

отовсю́ду *adv.* from everywhere.

отогна́ть, отгоню́, -о́нишь; отогна́л, -а́, -о *perf.* (*imp.* отгоня́ть) drive away, off; keep off; distil (off).

отогну́ть, -ну́, -нёшь *perf.* (*imp.* отгиба́ть) bend back; flange; **~ся,** bend back.

отогрева́ть, -а́ю *imp.*, **отогре́ть,** -е́ю *perf.* warm; **~ся,** warm oneself.

отодвига́ть, -а́ю *imp.*, **отодви́нуть,** -ну *perf.* move aside; put off, put back; **~ся,** move aside.

отодра́ть, отдеру́, -рёшь; отодра́л, -а́, -о *perf.* (*imp.* отдира́ть) tear off, rip off; flog.

отож(д)естви́ть, -влю́ *perf.*, **отож(д)ествля́ть,** -я́ю *imp.* identify.

отожжённый; -ён -а́, annealed.

отозва́ть, отзову́, -вёшь; отозва́л, -а́, -о *perf.* (*imp.* отзыва́ть) take aside; recall; **~ся** на + *acc.* answer; respond to; о+*acc.* speak of; на+*acc.* or *prep.* tell on; have an effect on.

отойти́, -йду́, -йдёшь; отошёл, -шла́ *perf.* (*imp.* отходи́ть) move away; move off; leave, depart; withdraw; recede; fall back; digress, diverge; come out, come away, come off; recover; come to oneself, come round; pass, go; be lost.

отолью́, etc.: see отли́ть. **отомрёт,** etc.: see отмере́ть. **ото|мсти́ть,** -мщу́ *perf.*

отопи́тельный, heating. **отопи́ть,** -плю́, -пишь *perf.* (*imp.* ота́пливать) heat. **отопле́ние,** -я, heating.

отопру́, etc.: see отпере́ть. **отопью́,** etc.: see отпи́ть.

ото́рванность, -и, detachment, isolation; loneliness. **ото́рванный,** cut off, isolated, out of touch. **оторва́ть,** -ву́, -вёшь *perf.* (*imp.* отрыва́ть) tear off;

tear away; **~ся,** come off, be torn off; be cut off, lose touch, lose contact; break away; tear oneself away; ~ся от земли́, take off.

оторопéлый, dumbfounded. **оторопéть,** -éю *perf.* be struck dumb.

отослáть, -ошлю́, -ошлёшь *perf.* (*imp.* отсылáть) send (off), dispatch; send back; + к + *dat.* refer to.

отошёл, etc.: see отойти́. **отошлю́,** etc.: see отослáть.

отощáлый, emaciated. **о|тощáть,** -áю *perf.*

отпадáть, -áет *imp.* of **отпáсть. отпадéние,** -я, falling away; defection.

от|пари́ровать, -рую *perf.* **отпáрывать,** -аю *imp.* of отпорóть.

отпáсть, -адёт *perf.* (*imp.* отпадáть) fall off, drop off; fall away; defect, drop away; pass, fade.

отперéть, отопрý, -прёшь; óтпер, -лá, -ло *perf.* (*imp.* отпирáть) unlock; open; **~ся,** open; + от + *gen.* deny; disown.

отпéтый, arrant, inveterate.

от|печáтать, -аю *perf.*, **отпечáтывать,** -аю *imp.* print (off); type (out); imprint; unseal, open (up); **~ся,** leave an imprint; be printed. **отпечáток,** -тка, imprint, print; impress.

отпивáть, -áю *imp.* of отпи́ть.

отпи́ливать, -аю *imp.*, **отпили́ть,** -лю́, -лишь *perf.* saw off.

отпирáтельство, -а, denial, disavowal. **~пирáть(ся,** -áю(сь *imp.* of отперéть(ся.

отпи́ть, отопью́, -пьёшь; óтпил, -á, -о *perf.* (*imp.* отпивáть) sip, take a sip of.

отпи́хивать, -аю *imp.*, **отпихнýть,** -нý, -нёшь *perf.* push off; shove aside.

отплáта, -ы, repayment. **отплати́ть,** -ачý, -áтишь *perf.*, **отплáчивать,** -аю *imp.* + *dat.* pay back, repay, requite; ~ той же монéтой, pay back in his own coin.

отплывáть, -áю *imp.*, **отплы́ть,** -ывý, -ывёшь; -ы́л, -á, -о *perf.* sail, set sail; swim off. **отплы́тие,** -я, sailing, departure.

óтповедь, -и, reproof, rebuke.

отползáть, -áю *imp.* **отползти́,** -зý, -зёшь; -óлз, -лá, *perf.* crawl away.

от|полировáть, -рýю *perf.* **от|полоскáть,** -ощý *perf.*

отпóр, -а, repulse; rebuff; встрéтить ~, meet with a rebuff; дать ~, repulse.

отпорóть[1], -рю́, -решь *perf.* (*imp.* отпáрывать) rip off, rip out.

отпорóть[2], -рю́, -решь *perf.* flog, thrash, give a thrashing.

отправи́тель, -я *m.* sender. **отпрáвить,** -влю *perf.*, **отправля́ть,** -я́ю *imp.* send, forward, dispatch; **~ся,** set out, set off, start; leave, depart. **отпрáвка,** -и, sending off, forwarding, dispatch. **отправлéние,** -я, sending; departure; exercise, performance; ~ обязанностей, performance of one's duties. **отправн|óй;** ~óй пункт, ~áя тóчка, starting-point.

от|прáздновать, -ную *perf.*

отпрáшиваться, -аюсь *imp.*, **отпроси́ться,** -ошýсь, -óсишься *perf.* ask for leave, get leave.

отпры́гивать, -аю *imp.*, **отпры́гнуть,** -ну *perf.* jump back, spring back; jump aside, spring aside; bounce back.

óтпрыск, -а, offshoot, scion.

отпрягáть, -áю *imp.* of отпря́чь.

отпря́дывать, -аю *imp.*, **отпря́нуть,** -ну *perf.* recoil, start back.

отпря́чь, -ягý, -яжёшь; -я́г, -лá *perf.* (*imp.* отпрягáть) unharness.

отпýгивать, -аю *imp.*, **отпугнýть,** -нý, -нёшь *perf.* frighten off, scare away.

óтпуск, -а, *loc.* -ý; *pl.* -á, leave, holiday(s); furlough; issue, delivery, distribution; tempering, drawing; в ~е, в ~ý, on leave; ~ по болéзни, sick-leave. **отпускáть,** -áю *imp.*, **отпусти́ть,** -ущý, -ýстишь *perf.* let go, let off; let out; set free; release; give leave (of absence); relax, slacken; (let) grow; issue, give out; serve; assign, allot; remit; forgive; temper, draw; ~ шýтку, crack a joke. **отпускни́к,** -á, person on leave, holiday-maker; soldier on leave. **отпускн|óй,** holiday; leave; on leave; ~ы́е дéньги, holiday pay; ~áя ценá, (wholesale) selling price. **отпущéние,** -я, remission; козёл отпущéния, scapegoat. **отпýщенник,** -а, freedman.

отрабáтывать, -аю *imp.*, **отрабóтать,** -аю *perf.* work off; work (for); finish work; finish working on; master. **от-рабо́танный,** worked out; waste, spent, exhaust.

отра́ва, -ы, poison; bane. **отрави́тель,** -я *m.* poisoner. **отрави́ть,** -влю́, -вишь *perf.*, **отравля́ть,** -я́ю *imp.* poison; **~ся,** poison oneself.

отра́да, -ы, joy, delight; comfort. **от-ра́дный,** gratifying, pleasing; comforting.

отража́тель, -я *m.* reflector; scanner; ejector. **отража́тельный,** reflecting, deflecting; reverberatory. **отража́ть,** -а́ю *imp.*, **отрази́ть,** -ажу́ *perf.* reflect; repulse, repel, parry; ward off; **~ся,** be reflected; reverberate; + на + *prep.* affect, tell on.

отраслево́й, branch. **о́трасль,** -и, branch.

отраста́ть, -а́ет *imp.*, **отрасти́,** -тёт; отро́с, -ла́ *perf.* grow. **отрасти́ть,** -ащу́ *perf.*, **отра́щивать,** -аю *imp.* (let) grow.

от|реаги́ровать, -рую *perf.* **от|регу-ли́ровать,** -рую *perf.* **от|редакти́ро-вать,** -рую *perf.*

отре́з, -а, cut; length; ~ на пла́тье, dress-length. **отре́зать,** -е́жу *perf.*, **отреза́ть,** -а́ю *imp.* cut off; divide, apportion; snap.

о|трезве́ть, -е́ю *perf.* **отрезви́тельный,** sobering. **отрезви́ть,** -влю́, -вишь *perf.*, **отрезвля́ть,** -я́ю *imp.* sober; **~ся,** become sober, sober up. **отрезвле́ние,** -я, sobering (up).

отрезно́й, cutting; tear-off, cut-off. **отре́зок,** -зка, piece, cut; section; portion; segment; ~ вре́мени, period, space of time.

отрека́ться, -а́юсь *imp.* of отре́чься. **от|рекомендова́ть(ся,** -а́ю(сь *perf.* **отрёкся,** etc.: see отре́чься. **от|ре-монти́ровать,** -рую *perf.* **от|репети́-ровать,** -рую *perf.*

отре́пье, -я, **отре́пья,** -ьев *pl.* rags.

от|реставри́ровать, -и́рую *perf.*

отрече́ние, -я, renunciation; ~ от пре-сто́ла, abdication. **отре́чься,** -еку́сь, -ечёшься *perf.* (*imp.* отрека́ться) renounce, disavow, give up.

отреша́ть -а́ю *imp.*, **отреши́ть,** -шу́ *perf.* release; dismiss, suspend; **~ся,** renounce, give up; get rid of. **отрешён-ность,** -и, estrangement, aloofness.

отрица́ние, -я, denial; negation. **отри-ца́тельный,** negative; bad, unfavourable. **отрица́ть,** -а́ю *imp.* deny; disclaim.

отро́г, -а, spur.

отро́дье, -я, race, breed, spawn.

отро́с, etc.: see отрасти́. **отро́сток,** -тка, shoot, sprout; branch, extension; appendix.

о́троческий, adolescent. **о́трочество,** -а, adolescence.

отруба́ть, -а́ю *imp.* of отруби́ть.

о́труби, -ей *pl.* bran.

отруби́ть, -блю́, -бишь *perf.* (*imp.* отруба́ть) chop off; snap back.

от|руга́ть, -а́ю *perf.*

отры́в, -а, tearing off; alienation, isolation; loss of contract, estrangement; без ~а от произво́дства, while remaining at work; в ~е от + *gen.*, out of touch with; ~ (от земли́), take-off. **отрыва́ть(ся,** -а́ю(сь *imp.* of отор-ва́ть(ся. **отры́вистый,** jerky, abrupt; curt. **отрывно́й,** detachable, tear-off. **отры́вок,** -вка, fragment, except; passage. **отры́вочный,** fragmentary, scrappy.

отры́жка, -и, belch; belching, eructation; survival, throw-back.

от|ры́ть, -ро́ю *perf.*

отря́д, -а, detachment; order. **отряди́ть,** -яжу́ *perf.*, **отряжа́ть,** -а́ю *imp.* detach, detail, tell off.

отря́хивать, -аю *imp.*, **отряхну́ть,** -ну́, -нёшь *perf.* shake down, shake off; **~ся,** shake oneself down.

от|салютова́ть, -ту́ю *perf.*

отса́сывание, -я, suction. **отса́сыва-тель,** -я *m.* suction pump. **отса́сывать,** -аю *imp.* of отсоса́ть.

о́тсве́т, -а, reflection; reflected light. **отсве́чивать,** -аю *imp.* be reflected; + *instr.* shine with, reflect.

отсебя́тина, -ы, words of one's own; ad-libbing.

отсе́в, -а sifting, selection; siftings, residue. **отсева́ть(ся,** -а́ю(сь, **отсе́и-вать(ся,** -аю(сь *imp.* of отсе́ять(ся. **отсе́вки,** -ов *pl.* siftings, residue.

отсе́к, -а, compartment. **отсека́ть,** -а́ю

imp., **отсéчь,** -екý, -ечёшь; -сéк, -лá *perf.* sever, chop off, cut off. **отсечéние,** -я, cutting off, severance; дать гóлову на ~, stake one's life. **отсéчка, -и,** cut-off.

отсéять, -éю *perf.* (*imp.* отсевáть, отсéивать) sift, screen; eliminate; **~ся,** fall out, fall off; fall away, drop out.

отскáкивать, -аю *imp.*, **отскочи́ть,** -чý, -чишь *perf.* jump aside, jump away; rebound, bounce back; come off, break off.

отслýживать, -аю *imp.*, **отслужи́ть,** -жý, -жишь *perf.* serve; serve one's time; have served its turn, be worn out.

отсовéтовать, -тую *perf.* + *dat.* dissuade.

отсосáть, -осý, -осёшь *perf.* (*imp.* отсáсывать) suck off, draw off; filter by suction.

отсрóчивать, -аю *imp.*, **отсрóчить,** -чу *perf.* postpone, delay, defer; adjourn; extend (date of). **отсрóчка,** -и, postponement, delay, deferment; adjournment; respite; extension.

отставáние, -я, lag; lagging behind. **отставáть,** -таю, -аёшь *imp.* of отстáть.

отстáвить, -влю *perf.*, **отставля́ть** -яю *imp.* set aside, put aside; dismiss, discharge; rescind; ~! as you were! **отстáвка,** -и, dismissal, discharge; resignation; retirement; в отстáвке, retired, in retirement; вы́йти в отстáвку, resign, retire. **отставнóй** retired.

отстáивать(ся, -аю(сь *imp.* of отстоя́ть(ся.

отстáлость, -и, backwardness. **отстáлый,** backward. **отстáть,** -áну *perf.* (*imp.* отставáть) fall behind, drop behind; lag behind; be backward, be retarded; be behind(hand); be left behind, become detached; lose touch; break (off); break oneself; be slow; come off; ~ на полчасá, be half an hour late; ~ от, break oneself of, give up; leave alone.

от|стегáть, -áю *perf.*

отстёгивать, -аю *imp.*, **отстегнýть,** -нý, -нёшь *perf.* unfasten, undo; unbutton; **~ся,** come unfastened, come undone.

отстóй, -я, sediment, deposit. **отстóйник,** -а, settling tank; sedimentation tank; cesspool.

отстоя́ть[1], -ою́ *perf.* (*imp.* отстáивать) defend, save; stand up for; ~ свои́ правá, assert one's rights. **отстоя́ть**[2], -ои́т *imp.* be . . away; стáнция отстои́т от цéнтра гóрода на два киломéтра, the station is two kilometres from the town centre. **отстоя́ться,** -ои́тся *perf.* (*imp.* отстáиваться) settle; precipitate; become stabilized, become fixed.

отстрáивать(ся, -аю(сь *imp.* of отстрóить(ся.

отстранéние, -я, pushing aside; dismissal, discharge. **отстрани́ть,** -ню́ *perf.*, **отстраня́ть**, -я́ю *imp.* push aside, lay aside; dismiss, discharge, remove; suspend; **~ся,** move away; keep out of the way, keep aloof; ~ся от, dodge; relinquish.

отстрéливаться, -аюсь *imp.*, **отстреля́ться,** -я́юсь *perf.* fire back.

отстригáть, -áю *imp.*, **отстри́чь,** -игý, -ижёшь; -ри́г *perf.* cut off, clip.

отстрóить, -óю *perf.* (*imp.* отстрáивать), complete the construction of, finish building; build up; **~ся,** finish building; be built up.

отступáть, -áю *imp.*, **отступи́ть,** -плю́, -пишь *perf.* step back; recede; retreat, fall back; back down; ~ от + *gen.* go back on; give up; swerve from, deviate from; **~ся** от + *gen.* give up, renounce; go back on. **отступлéние,** -я, retreat; deviation; digression. **отстýпник,** -а, apostate; recreant. **отступн|óй;** ~ы́е дéньги, **~óе** *sb.* indemnity, compensation. **отступя́** *adv.* (farther) off, away (от + *gen.* from).

отсýтствие, -я absence; lack, want; за ~м + *gen.*, in the absence of; for lack of, for want of; находи́ться в отсýтствии, be absent. **отсýтствовать,** -твую *imp.* be absent; default. **отсýтствующий,** absent; *sb.* absentee.

отсчитáть, -áю *perf.*, **отсчи́тывать,** -аю *imp.* count off, count out; read off.

отсылáть, -áю *imp.* of отослáть. **отсы́лка,** -и, dispatch; reference; ~ дéнег, remittance.

отсы́пать, -плю *perf.*, **отсыпáть,** -áю

imp. pour off; measure off; **~ся,** pour out.
отсыре́лый, damp. **от|сыре́ть,** -е́ет *perf.*
отсю́да *adv.* from here; hence; from this.
отта́ивать, -аю *imp.* of отта́ять.
отта́лкивание, -я, repulsion. **отта́лкивать,** -аю *imp.* of оттолкну́ть. **отта́лкивающий,** repulsive, repellent.
отта́чивать, -аю *imp.* of отточи́ть.
отта́ять, -а́ю *perf.* (*imp.* отта́ивать) thaw out.
оттени́ть, -ню́ *perf.*, **оттеня́ть,** -я́ю *imp.* shade, shade in; set off, make more prominent. **отте́нок,** -нка, shade, nuance; tint, hue.
о́ттепель, -и, thaw.
оттесни́ть, -ню́ *perf.*, **оттесня́ть,** -я́ю *imp.* drive back, press back; push aside, shove aside.
оттого́ (-*vo*) *adv.* that is why; ~, что, because.
о́ттиск, -а, impression; off-print, reprint.
оттолкну́ть, -ну́, -нёшь *perf.* (*imp.* отта́лкивать) push away, push aside; antagonize, alienate; **~ся,** push off.
оттопы́ренный, protruding, sticking out. **оттопы́ривать,** -аю *imp.*, **оттопы́рить,** -рю *perf.* stick out; ~ губы, pout; **~ся,** protrude, stick out; bulge.
отточи́ть, -чу́, -чишь *perf.* (*imp.* отта́чивать) sharpen, whet.
отту́да *adv.* from there.
оття́гивать, -аю *imp.*, **оттяну́ть,** -ну́, -нешь *perf.* draw out, pull away; draw off; delay. **оття́жка,** -и, delay, procrastination; guy-rope; strut, brace, stay.
отупе́лый, stupefied, dulled. **отупе́ние,** -я, stupefaction, dullness, torpor. **о|тупе́ть,** -е́ю *perf.* grow dull, sink into torpor.
от|утю́жить, -жу *perf.*
отуча́ть, -а́ю *imp.*, **отучи́ть,** -чу́, -чишь *perf.* break (of); **~ся,** break oneself (of).
от|футбо́лить, -лю *perf.*, **отфутбо́ливать,** -аю *imp.* pass on; send from pillar to post.
отха́ркать, -аю *perf.*, **отха́ркивать,** -аю *imp.* expectorate. **отха́ркивающ|ий** *adj.*; ~ее (сре́дство), expectorant.
отхлебну́ть, -ну́, -нёшь *perf.*, **отхлёбывать,** -аю *imp.* sip, take a sip of; take a mouthful of.
отхлы́нуть, -нет *perf.* flood back, rush back, rush away.
отхо́д, -а, departure, sailing; withdrawal, retirement, falling back; ~ от, deviation from; break with. **отходи́ть,** -ожу́, -о́дишь *imp.* of отойти́. **отхо́дчивый,** not bearing grudges. **отхо́ды,** -ов *pl.* waste; siftings, screenings; tailings.
отцвести́, -ету́, -етёшь; -ёл, -а́ *perf.*, **отцвета́ть,** -а́ю *imp.* finish blossoming, fade.
отцепи́ть, -плю́, -пишь *perf.*, **отцепля́ть,** -я́ю *imp.* unhook; uncouple; **~ся,** come unhooked, come uncoupled; + от + *gen.* leave alone. **отце́пка,** -и uncoupling.
отцо́вский, father's; paternal. **отцо́вство,** -а, paternity.
отча́иваться, -аюсь *imp.* of отча́яться.
отча́ливать, -аю *imp.*, **отча́лить,** -лю *perf.* cast off; push off.
отча́сти *adv.* partly.
отча́яние, -я, despair. **отча́янный,** despairing; desperate; daredevil. **отча́яться,** -а́юсь *perf.* (*imp.* отча́иваться) despair.
отчего́ (-*vo*) *adv.* why. **отчего́-либо, -нибудь** *adv.* for some reason or other. **отчего́-то** *adv.* for some reason.
от|чека́нить, -ню *perf.*
о́тчество, -а, patronymic; как его́ по о́тчеству? what is his patronymic?
отчёт, -а, account; дать ~ в + *prep.*, give an account of; report on; отда́ть себе́ ~ в + *prep.* be aware of, realize. **отчётливый,** distinct; precise; intelligible, clear. **отчётность,** -и, book-keeping; accounts. **отчётный** *adj.*; ~ год, financial year, current year; ~ докла́д, report.
отчи́зна, -ы, country, native land; fatherland. **о́тчий,** paternal. **о́тчим,** -а, step-father.
отчисле́ние, -я, deduction; assignment;

dismissal. **отчи́слить, -лю** *perf.*, **отчисля́ть, -я́ю** *imp.* deduct; assign; dismiss.

отчитáть, -áю *perf.*, **отчи́тывать, -аю** *imp.* scold, read a lecture, tell off; **~ся,** report back; + в + *prep.* give an account of, report on.

отчуди́ть, -ужу́ *perf.*, **отчуждáть, -áю** *imp.* alienate; estrange. **отчуждéние, -я,** alienation; estrangement.

отшатну́ться, -ну́сь, -нёшься *perf.*, **отшáтываться, -аюсь** *imp.* start back, recoil; + от + *gen.* give up, forsake, break with.

отшвы́ривать, -аю *imp.*, **отшвырну́ть, -ну́, -нёшь** *perf.* fling away; throw off.

отшéльник, -а, hermit, anchorite; recluse.

от|шлифовáть, -фу́ю *perf.* **от|штукату́рить, -рю** *perf.*

отшути́ться, -учу́сь, -у́тишься *perf.*, **отшу́чиваться, -аюсь** *imp.* reply with a joke; laugh it off.

отщепéнец, -нца, renegade.

отъ-: see от-.

отъéзд, -а, departure. **отъезжáть, -áю** *imp.*, **отъéхать, -éду** *perf.* drive off, go off. **отъéзжий,** distant.

отъя́вленный, thorough; inveterate.

отыгрáть, -áю *perf.*, **оты́грывать, -аю** *imp.* win back; **~ся,** win, get, back what one has lost; get one's own back, get one's revenge.

отыскáть, -ыщу́, -ы́щешь *perf.*, **оты́скивать, -аю** *imp.* find; track down, run to earth; look for, try to find; **~ся,** turn up, appear.

офицéр, -а, officer. **офицéрский,** officer's, officers'. **офицéрство, -а,** officers; commissioned rank.

официáльный, official.

официáнт, -а, waiter. **официáнтка, -и,** waitress.

официóз, -а, semi-official organ (of the press). **официóзный,** semi-official.

оформи́тель, -я *m.* decorator, stage-painter. **офóрмить, -млю** *perf.*, **оформля́ть, -я́ю** *imp.* get up, mount, put into shape; register officially, legalize; ~ пьéсу, stage a play; **~ся,** take shape; be registered; legalize one's position; be taken on the staff, join the staff. **оформлéние, -я,** get-up; mounting, staging; registration, legalization.

ох *int.* oh! ah!

охáпка, -и, armful; взять в охáпку, take in one's arms.

о|характеризовáть, -зу́ю *perf.*

óхать, -аю *imp.* (*perf.* óхнуть) moan, groan; sigh.

охвáт, -а, scope, range; inclusion; outflanking, envelopment. **охвати́ть, -ачу́, -áтишь** *perf.*, **охвáтывать, -аю** *imp.* envelop; enclose; grip, seize; comprehend, take in; outflank; + *instr.* draw into, involve in. **охвáченный,** seized, gripped; ~ у́жасом, terror-stricken.

охладевáть, -áю *imp.*, **охладéть, -éю** *perf.* grow cold. **охладéлый,** cold; grown cold. **охлади́тельный,** cooling, cool. **охлади́ть, -ажу́** *perf.*, **охлаждáть, -áю** *imp.* cool, chill; refrigerate, freeze; **~ся,** become cool, cool down. **охлаждáющ|ий,** cooling, refrigerating; ~ая жи́дкость, coolant. **охлаждéние, -я,** cooling, chilling; refrigerating, freezing; coolness; с возду́шным ~м, air-cooled.

о|хмелéть, -éю *perf.* **óхнуть, -ну** *perf.* of óхать.

охóта[1]**, -ы,** hunt, hunting; chase.

охóта[2]**, -ы,** desire, wish; inclination.

охóтиться, -óчусь *imp.* hunt. **охóтник**[1]**, -а,** hunter; sportsman.

охóтник[2]**, -а,** volunteer; + до + *gen.*, or + *inf.* lover of, enthusiast for.

охóтничий, hunting; sporting, shooting.

охóтно *adv.* willingly, gladly, readily.

óхра, -ы, ochre.

охрáна, -ы, guarding; protection; conservation, preservation; guard. **охрани́ть, -ню́** *perf.*, **охраня́ть, -я́ю** *imp.* guard, protect; preserve. **охрáнка, -и,** secret police. **охрáнн|ый,** guard, protection; ~ая грáмота, ~ый лист, safe-conduct, pass.

охри́плый, охри́пший, hoarse, husky. **о|хри́пнуть, -ну; охри́п** *perf.* become hoarse.

о|хромéть, -éю *perf.*

о|цара́пать(ся, -аю(сь *perf.*

оцéнивать, -аю *imp.*, **оцени́ть, -ню́,**

-нишь *perf.* estimate, evaluate; appraise; appreciate. **оцéнка,** -и, estimation, evaluation; appraisal; estimate; appreciation. **оцéнщик,** -а, valuer.

оцепенéлый, torpid, benumbed. **о|цепенéть,** -éю *perf.*

оцепúть, -плю́, -пишь *perf.*, **оцеплять,** -яю *imp.* surround; cordon off. **оцеплéние,** -я, surrounding; cordoning off; cordon.

оцинкóванный, galvanized.

очáг, -á, hearth; centre, seat; focus; nidus; домáшний ~, hearth, home; ~ зарáзы, nidus of infection; ~ землетрясéния, focus of earthquake; ~ сопротивлéния, pocket of resistance.

очаровáние, -я, charm, fascination. **очаровáтельный,** charming, fascinating. **очаровáть,** -ру́ю *perf.*, **очарóвывать,** -аю, charm, fascinate.

очевúдец, -дца, eye-witness. **очевúдно** *adv.* obviously, evidently. **очевúдный,** obvious, evident, manifest, patent.

óчень *adv.* very; very much.

очередн|óй, next; next in turn; periodic, periodical; recurrent; usual, regular; routine; ~áя задáча, immediate task; ~óй óтпуск, usual holiday. **óчередь,** -и; *gen. pl.* -éй, turn; queue, line; burst, salvo; на óчереди, next (in turn); по óчереди, in turn, in order, in rotation; в пéрвую ~, in the first place, in the first instance; ~ за вáми, it is your turn; стоять в óчереди (за + *instr.*), queue (for), stand in line (for).

óчерк, -а, essay, sketch, study; outline.

о|чернúть, -ню́ *perf.*

очерствéлый, hardened, callous. **о|черствéть,** -éю *perf.*

очертáние, -я, outline(s), contour(s). **очертúть,** -рчу́, -ртишь *perf.*, **очéрчивать,** -аю *imp.* outline, trace.

очёски, -ов *pl.* combings; flocks.

очéчник, -а spectacle case.

óчи, etc.: see óко.

очúнивать, -аю *imp.*, **о|чинúть,** -ню́, -нишь *perf.* sharpen, point.

очистúтельный, purifying, cleansing. **о|чúстить,** -ищу *perf.*, **очищáть,** -áю *imp.* clean; cleanse, purify; refine; rectify; clear; free; peel; **~ся,** clear oneself; become clear (от + *gen.* of).

очúстка, -и, cleaning; cleansing, purification; refinement, rectification; clearance; freeing; mopping up; для очúстки сóвести, for conscience sake. **очúстки,** -ов *pl.* peelings. **очищéние,** -я, cleansing; purification.

очкú, -óв *pl.* glasses, spectacles. **очкó,** -á; *gen. pl.* -óв, pip; point; hole. **очкóв|ый**[1]; ~ая систéма, points system. **очкóв|ый**[2]; ~ая змея́, cobra.

очну́ться, -ну́сь, -нёшься *perf.* wake, wake up; come to (oneself), regain consciousness.

óчн|ый; ~ое обучéние, internal courses; ~ая стáвка, confrontation.

очутúться, -у́тишься *perf.* find oneself; come to be.

о|швартовáть, -ту́ю *perf.*

ошéйник, -а, collar.

ошеломúтельный, stunning. **ошеломúть,** -млю́ *perf.*, **ошеломлять,** -яю *imp.* stun. **ошеломлéние,** -я, stupefaction.

ошибáться, -áюсь *imp.*, **ошибúться,** -бу́сь, -бёшься; -úбся *perf.* be mistaken, make a mistake, make mistakes; be wrong; err, be at fault. **ошúбка,** -и, mistake; error; blunder; по ошúбке, by mistake. **ошúбочный,** erroneous, mistaken.

ошпáривать, -аю *imp.*, **о|шпáрить,** -рю *perf.* scald.

о|штрафовáть, -фу́ю *perf.* **о|штукату́рить,** -рю *perf.* **о|щенúться,** -úтся *perf.*

ощетúниваться, -ается *imp.*, **о|щетúниться,** -нится *perf.* bristle (up).

о|щипáть, -плю́, -плешь *perf.*, **ощúпывать,** -аю *imp.* pluck.

ощу́пать, -аю *perf.*, **ощу́пывать,** -аю *imp.* feel, touch; grope about. **óщупь,** -и; на ~, to the touch; by touch; идтú на ~, grope one's way, feel one's way. **óщупью** *adv.* gropingly, fumblingly; by touch; blindly; идтú ~, grope one's way, feel one's way; искáть ~, grope for.

ощутúмый, ощутúтельный, perceptible, tangible, palpable; appreciable. **ощутúть,** -ущу *perf.*, **ощущáть,** -áю *imp.* feel, sense, experience. **ощущéние,** -я, sensation; feeling, sense.

П

п *letter*: see пэ.
па *n. indecl.* step, *pas.*
па́ва, -ы, peahen.
павильо́н, -а, pavilion; film studio.
павли́н, -а, peacock.
па́водок, -дка, (sudden) flood, freshet.
па́вш|ий, fallen; ~ие в бою́, (those) who fell in action.
па́губа, -ы, ruin, destruction; bane. **па́губный**, pernicious, ruinous; baneful; fatal.
па́даль, -и, carrion.
па́дать, -аю *imp.* (*perf.* пасть, упа́сть) fall; sink; drop; decline; fall out, drop out; die; ~ ду́хом, lose heart, lose courage; ~ от уста́лости, be ready to drop. **па́дающ|ий**, falling; incident; incoming; ~ие звёзды, shooting stars. **паде́ж**, -а́, case. **паде́ние**, -я, fall; drop, sinking; degradation; slump; incidence; dip. **па́дкий** на + *acc.* or до + *gen.* having a weakness for; susceptible to; greedy for. **паду́чий**, falling; ~ая (боле́знь), falling sickness, epilepsy.
па́дчерица, -ы, step-daughter.
па́дш|ий, fallen; ~ие *sb. pl.* the fallen.
паёк, пайка́, ration.
па́зуха, -и, bosom; sinus; axil; за па́зухой, in one's bosom.
пай, -я; *pl.* -и́, -ёв, share. **па́йщик**, -а, shareholder.
пак, -а, pack-ice.
паке́т, -а, parcel, package; packet; (official) letter; paper bag.
па́кля, -и tow; oakum.
пакова́ть, -ку́ю *imp.* (*perf.* за~, у~) pack.
па́костить, -ощу *imp.* (*perf.* за~, ис~, на~) soil, dirty; spoil, mess up; + *dat.* play dirty tricks on. **па́костный**, dirty, mean, foul; nasty. **па́кость**, -и, filth; dirty trick, nasty trick; obscenity, dirty word.
пакт, -а, pact; ~ догово́ра, covenant; ~ о ненападе́нии, non-aggression pact.
паланти́н -а (fur) stole, cape.
пала́та, -ы, ward; chamber, house; hall; *pl.* palace; Оруже́йная ~, Armoury; ~ мер и весо́в, Board of Weights and Measures; ~ о́бщин, House of Commons; торго́вая ~, Chamber of Commerce. **пала́тка**, -и, tent; marquee; stall, booth; в ~х, under canvas. **пала́тн|ый**, ward; ~ая сестра́, (ward) sister. **пала́точный**, tent; tented, of tents.
пала́ч, -а́, hangman; executioner; butcher.
па́лец, -льца, finger; toe; pin, peg; cam, cog, tooth; знать как свой пять па́льцев, have at one's finger-tips; он па́льцем никого́ не тро́нет, he wouldn't lay a finger on anybody; he wouldn't harm a fly; ~ о ~ не уда́рить, not lift a finger; смотре́ть сквозь па́льцы на + *acc.*, wink at, shut one's eyes to.
палиса́д, -а, paling; palisade, stockade. **палиса́дник**, -а, (small) front garden.
палиса́ндр, -а, rosewood.
пали́тра, -ы, palette.
пали́ть[1], -лю́ *imp.* (*perf.* о~, с~) burn; scorch.
пали́ть[2], -лю́ *imp.* (*perf.* вы́~, пальну́ть) fire, shoot.
па́лка, -и, stick; walking-stick, cane; staff; из-под па́лки, under the lash, under duress; ~ о двух конца́х, double-edged weapon.
пало́мник, -а, pilgrim. **пало́мничество**, -а, pilgrimage.
па́лочка, -и, stick; bacillus; дирижёрская ~, (conductor's) baton. **па́лочковый**, bacillary. **па́лочный**, stick, cane.
па́луба, -ы, deck. **па́лубный**; ~ груз, deck cargo.
пальба́, -ы́, fire, cannonade.
па́льма, -ы, palm(-tree). **па́льмов|ый**, palm; ~ая ветвь, olive-branch; ~ое де́рево, box-wood.
пальну́ть, -ну́, -нёшь *perf.* of пали́ть.
пальто́ *n. indecl.* (over)coat; topcoat.
паля́щий, burning, scorching.
па́мятник, -а, monument; memorial;

tombstone. **па́мятн|ый,** memorable; memorial; ~ая кни́жка, notebook, memorandum book. **па́мять,** -и, memory; recollection, remembrance; mind, consciousness; без па́мяти, unconscious; на ~, by heart; по па́мяти, from memory; подари́ть на ~, give as a keepsake.

пана́ма, -ы, **пана́мка,** -и, Panama (hat).

пане́ль, -и, pavement, footpath; panel(ling), wainscot(ing). **пане́льн|ый,** panelling; ~ая обши́вка, panelling, wainscot.

па́ника, -и, panic. **паникёр,** -а, panic-monger, scaremonger, alarmist.

панихи́да, -ы, office for the dead; requiem; гражда́нская ~, (civil) funeral. **панихи́дный,** requiem; funereal.

пани́ческий, panic; panicky.

панно́ *n. indecl.* panel.

пансио́н, -а, boarding-school; boarding-house; board and lodging; ко́мната с ~ом, room and board. **пансиона́т,** -а, living in; holiday hotel. **пансионе́р,** -а, boarder; guest.

панталo̍ны, -о́н *pl.* trousers; knickers, panties.

панте́ра, -ы, panther.

пантоле́ты, -ле́т *pl.* open sandals.

па́па[1], -ы *m.* pope.

па́па[2], -ы *m.*, **папа́ша,** -и *m.* daddy; papa.

папиро́са, -ы, (Russian) cigarette. **папиро́сн|ый** *adj.*; ~ая бума́га, rice-paper.

па́пка, -и, file; document case, folder; cardboard, pasteboard.

па́поротник, -а, fern.

па́пский, papal. **па́пство,** -а, papacy.

пар[1], -а (-у), *loc.* -у́; *pl.* -ы́, steam; exhalation; на всех пара́х, full steam ahead, at full speed.

пар[2], -а, *loc.* -у́; *pl.* -ы́, fallow.

па́ра, -ы, pair, couple; (two-piece) suit.

пара́граф, -а, paragraph.

пара́д, -а, parade; review. **пара́дность,** -и, magnificence; ostentation. **пара́дн|ый,** parade; gala; main, front; ~ая дверь, front door; ~ые ко́мнаты, state rooms, (suite of) reception rooms; ~ый подъе́зд, main entrance; ~ая фо́рма, full dress (uniform).

парализо́ванный, paralysed. **парализова́ть,** -зу́ю *perf.* and *imp.* paralyse. **парали́ч,** -а́, paralysis, palsy. **парали́чный,** paralytic.

паралле́ль, -и, parallel. **паралле́льн|ый,** parallel; ~ые бру́сья, parallel bars.

пара́ф, -а, flourish; initials. **парафи́ровать,** -рую *perf.* and *imp.* initial.

паре́ние, -я, soaring.

па́рень, -рня; *gen. pl.* -рне́й *m.* boy, lad; chap, fellow.

пари́ *n. indecl.* bet; держа́ть ~, bet, lay a bet.

парижа́нин, -а; *pl.* -а́не, -а́н, **парижа́нка,** -и, Parisian. **Пари́жский,** Parisian.

пари́к, -а́, wig. **парикма́хер,** -а, barber; hairdresser. **парикма́херская** *sb.* barber's, hairdresser's.

пари́ровать, -и́рую *perf.* and *imp.* (*perf.* also от~) parry, counter.

парите́т, -а, parity. **парите́тн|ый;** на ~ых нача́лах, on a par, on an equal footing.

пари́ть[1], -рю́ *imp.* soar, swoop, hover.

па́рить[2], -рю *imp.* steam, induce sweating in; stew; *impers.* па́рит it is sultry; **~ся** (*perf.* по~ся), steam, sweat; stew.

парк, -а, park; yard, depot; fleet; stock; pool; ваго́нный ~, rolling-stock.

па́рка, -и, steaming; stewing.

парке́т, -а, parquet.

па́ркий, steamy.

парла́мент, -а, parliament. **парламента́рный,** parliamentarian. **парламентёр,** -а, envoy; bearer of flag of truce. **парламентёрский;** ~ флаг, flag of truce. **парла́ментский,** parliamentary; ~ зако́н, Act of Parliament.

парни́к, -а́, hot bed, seed-bed; frame. **парнико́в|ый** *adj.*; ~ые расте́ния, hothouse plants.

парни́шка, -и, boy, lad.

парн|о́й, fresh; steamy; ~о́е молоко́, milk fresh from the cow. **па́рный**[1], steamy.

па́рный[2], pair; forming a pair; twin; pair-horse.

паро- in *comb.* steam-. **парово́з,** -а, (steam-)engine, locomotive. **~во́зник,** -а, engine-driver, engineer. **~во́зный,**

engine. **~выпускнóй,** exhaust. **~непроницáемый,** steam-tight, steam-proof. **~обрáзный,** vaporous. **~прóвод,** -а, steam-pipe. **~силовóй,** steam-power. **~хóд,** -а, steamer; steamship. **~хóдный,** steam; steamship; ~хóдное óбщество, steamship company. **~хóдство,** -а, steam-navigation; steamship-line.

паров|óй, steam; steamed; ~áя машúна, steam-engine; ~óе отоплéние, steam heating; central heating.

парóль, -я *m.* password, countersign.

парóм, -а, ferry(-boat). **парóмщик,** -а, ferryman.

парóсский, Parian.

парт- *abbr.* in *comb.* Party. **партактúв,** -а, Party activists. **~билéт,** -а, Party (membership) card. **~кабинéт,** -а, Party educational centre. **~кóм,** -а, Party committee. **~óрг,** -а, Party organizer. **~организáция,** -и, Party organization. **~съéзд,** -а, Party congress.

пáрта, -ы, (school) desk.

партéр, -а, stalls; pit.

партúец, -йица, Party member.

партизáн, -а; *gen. pl.* -áн, partisan; guerilla. **партизáнск|ий,** partisan, guerilla; unplanned, haphazard; ~ая войнá, guerilla warfare; ~ое движéние, Resistance (movement).

партúйка, -и, Party member. **партúйность,** -и, Party membership; Party spirit, Party principles. **партúйный,** party, Party; *sb.* Party member.

партитýра, -ы, score.

пáртия, -и, party; group; batch; lot; consignment; game, set; part.

партнёр, -а, partner.

пáрус, -а; *pl.* -á, -óв, sail; идтú под ~áми, sail, be under sail; на всех ~áх, in full sail; поднять ~á, set sail. **парусúна,** -ы, canvas, sail-cloth; duck. **пáрусник,** -а, sailing vessel. **пáрусный,** sail; ~ спорт, sailing.

парчá, -ú; *gen. pl.* -éй, brocade. **парчевóй, парчóвый,** brocade.

парящ|ий, soaring, hovering; ~ая машúна, hovercraft.

пáсека, -и, apiary, beehive. **пáсечный** *adj.* beekeeper's, beekeeping.

пасётся: see пастúсь.

пáсмурный, dull, cloudy; overcast; gloomy, sullen.

пасовáть, -сýю *imp.* (*perf.* с~) pass; be unable to cope (with), give up, give in.

пáспорт, -а; *pl.* -á, passport; registration certificate.

пассáж, -а, passage; arcade.

пассажúр, -а, passenger. **пассажúрск|ий,** passenger; ~ое движéние, passenger services.

пáста, -ы, paste.

пáстбище, -а, pasture.

пастернáк, -а, parsnip.

пастú, -сý, -сёшь; пас, -лá *imp.* graze, pasture; shepherd, tend.

пастúсь, -сётся; пáсся, -лáсь *imp.* graze; browse. **пастýх,** -á, shepherd; herdsman. **пастýшеский,** shepherd's, herdsman's; pastoral. **пастушóк,** -шкá, shepherd. **пастýшка,** -и, shepherdess.

пасть, -и, mouth; jaws.

пасть, падý, -дёшь; пал *perf.* of пáдать.

пáсха, -и, Easter; Passover.

пáсынок, -нка, stepson, stepchild; outcast.

пат, -а, stalemate.

патетúческий, патетúчный, pathetic.

патефóн, -а, (portable) gramophone.

пáтока, -и, treacle; syrup. **пáточный,** treacle; treacly.

патрóн, -а, cartridge; chuck, holder; lamp-socket lamp-holder; pattern.

патронáж, -а, patronage; home health service. **патронáжн|ый;** ~ая сестрá, health visitor, district nurse.

патрóнка, -и, pattern.

патрóнный, cartridge.

патрýль, -я́ *m.* patrol.

пáуза, -ы, pause; interval; rest.

паýк, -á, spider. **паутúна,** -ы, cobweb, spider's web; gossamer; web. **паýчий,** spider, spider's.

пáфос, -а, (excessive) feeling; zeal, enthusiasm; spirit.

пах, -а, *loc.* -ý, groin.

пáханый, ploughed. **пáхарь,** -я *m.* ploughman. **пахáть,** пашý, пáшешь *imp.* (*perf.* вс~) plough, till.

па́хнуть[1], -ну; пах *imp.* + *instr.* smell of; reek of; savour of, smack of.

пахну́ть[2], -нёт *perf.* puff, blow.

па́хота, -ы, ploughing, tillage. **па́хотный**, arable.

паху́чий, odorous, strong-smelling.

па́чка, -и, bundle; batch; packet, pack; tutu.

па́чкать, -аю *imp.* (*perf.* за~, ис~, на~) dirty, soil, stain, sully; daub. **пачкотня́**, -и́, daub. **пачку́н**, -а́, sloven; dauber.

пашу́, etc.: see паха́ть. **па́шня**, -и; *gen. pl.* -шен, ploughed field.

паште́т, -а, pie; pâté.

па́юсн|ый; ~ая икра́, pressed caviare.

пая́льник, -а, soldering iron. **пая́льн|ый**, soldering; ~ая ла́мпа, blow-lamp. **пая́льщик**, -а, tinman, tinsmith. **па́янный**, soldered. **пая́ть**, -я́ю *imp.* solder.

пая́ц, -а, clown.

певе́ц, -вца́, **певи́ца**, -ы, singer. **певу́чий**, melodious. **пе́вч|ий**, singing; ~ая пти́ца, song-bird; *sb.* chorister.

пе́гий, skewbald, piebald.

пед- *abbr.* in *comb.* of педагоги́ческий, pedagogic(al); teachers'; education, educational. **педву́з**, -а, **~институ́т**, -а, (teachers') training college. **~ку́рсы**, -ов *pl.* teachers' training courses. **~сове́т**, -а, staff-meeting. **~фа́к**, -а, education department.

педаго́г, -а, teacher; pedagogue, educationist. **педаго́гика**, -и, pedagogy, pedagogics. **педагоги́ческий**, pedagogical; educational; ~ институ́т, (teachers') training college; ~ факульте́т, education department.

педа́ль, -и, pedal; treadle. **педа́льный**, pedal.

пейза́ж, -а, landscape; scenery. **пейзажи́ст**, -а, landscape painting.

пёк: see печь. **пека́рный**, baking, bakery. **пека́рня**, -и; *gen. pl.* -рен, bakery, bakehouse. **пе́карь**, -я; *pl.* -я́, -е́й *m.* baker. **пе́кло**, -а, scorching heat; hell-fire. **пеку́**, etc.: see печь.

пелена́ -ы́; *gen. pl.* -лён, shroud. **пелена́ть**, -а́ю *imp.* (*perf.* за~, с~) swaddle; put nappy on, change.

пе́ленг, -а, bearing. **пеленга́тор**, -а, direction finder. **пеленгова́ть**, -гу́ю *perf.* and *imp.* take the bearings of.

пелёнка, -и, napkin, nappy; *pl.* swaddling-clothes; с пелёнок, from the cradle.

пе́мза, -ы, pumice(-stone). **пе́мзовый**, pumice.

пе́на, -ы, foam, spume; scum; froth, head; lather; (мы́льная) ~, soapsuds.

пена́л, -а, pencil-box, pencil-case.

пе́ние, -я, singing; ~ петуха́, crowing.

пе́нист|ый, foamy; frothy; ~ое вино́, sparkling wine. **пе́нить**, -ню *imp.* (*perf.* вс~) froth; **~ся**, foam, froth.

пе́нка, -и, skin; (морска́я) ~, meerschaum. **пе́нковый**, meerschaum. **пенопла́ст**, -а, plastic foam, cellular plastic. **пенопластма́сса**, -ы, expanded plastic. **пеностекло́**, -а́, fibreglass.

пенсионе́р, -а, pensioner. **пенсио́нный**, pension. **пе́нсия**, -и, pension; ~ по инвали́дности, disability pension; ~ по ста́рости, old-age pension.

пенсне́ *n. indecl.* pince-nez.

пень, пня *m.* stump, stub.

пенька́, -и́, hemp. **пенько́вый**, hempen.

пе́ня, -и, fine. **пеня́ть**, -я́ю *imp.* (*perf.* по~) + *dat.* reproach; + на + *acc.* blame.

пе́пел, -пла, ash, ashes. **пепели́ще**, -а, site of fire; (hearth and) home; родно́е ~, old home. **пе́пельница**, -ы, ashtray. **пе́пельный**, ashy.

пер. *abbr.* переу́лок, Street, Lane.

перве́йший, the first, the most important; first-class. **пе́рвенец**, -нца, first-born; first of its kind. **пе́рвенство**, -а, first place; championship; ~ по футбо́лу, football championship. **пе́рвенствова́ть**, -твую or -тву́ю *imp.* take first place; take precedence, take priority. **перви́чный**, primary; initial.

перво- in *comb.* first, primary; prime, top; newly, just; archi-, archaeo-, proto-; prim(o)-. **первобы́тный**, primitive; primordial; primeval; pristine. **~зда́нный**, primordial; primitive, primary. **~-исто́чник**, -а, primary source; origin. **~катего́рник**, -а, first-rank player. **~кла́ссный,** first-class, first-rate. **~ку́рсник,** -а, first-year student, freshman. **~ма́йский,** May-day. **~нача́льно** *adv.* originally. **~нача́льный,** original; primary; initial; prime; elementary. **~о́браз,** -а, prototype, original; protoplast. **~очередно́й, ~очерёдный,** first and foremost, immediate. **~печа́тный,** early printed, incunabular; first printed, first-edition; ~печа́тные кни́ги, incunabula. **~причи́на,** -ы, first cause. **~разря́дный,** first-class, first-rank. **~ро́дный,** first-born; primal original. **~рождённый,** first-born. **~со́ртный,** best-quality; first-class, first-rate. **~степе́нный,** paramount, of the first order.

пе́рвое *sb.* first course. **пе́рво-на́перво** *adv.* first of all. **пе́рв|ый,** first; former; earliest; быть ~ым, идти́ ~ым come first, lead; ~ое де́ло, ~ым де́лом, first of all, first thing; с ~ого ра́за, from the first.

перга́мент -а, parchment; greaseproof paper. **перга́ментный,** parchment; parchment-like; greaseproof.

пере-, *vbl. pref.* indicating action across or through something; repetition of action; superiority, excess, etc.; extension of action to encompass many or all objects or cases of a given kind; division into two or more parts; reciprocity of action; trans-, re-, over-, out-.

переадресова́ть, -су́ю *perf.*, **переадресо́вывать,** -аю *imp.* re-address.

перебега́ть, -а́ю *imp.*, **перебежа́ть,** -бегу́ *perf.* cross; run across; desert, go over. **перебе́жка,** -и, bound, rush; re-run. **перебе́жчик,** -а, deserter; turncoat.

перебе́ливать, -аю *imp.*, **перебели́ть,** -елю́, -е́ли́шь *perf.* re-whitewash; make a fair copy of.

переберу́, etc.: see перебра́ть.

перебива́ть(ся, -а́ю(сь *imp.* of переби́ть(ся. **переби́вка,** -и, re-upholstering.

перебира́ть(ся, -а́ю(сь *imp.* of перебра́ть(ся.

переби́ть, -бью -бьёшь *perf.* (*imp.* перебива́ть) interrupt; intercept; kill, slay, slaughter; beat; beat up again; break; re-upholster; **~ся,** break; make ends meet; get by. **перебо́й,** interruption, intermission; stoppage, hold-up; irregularity; misfire. **перебо́йный,** interrupted, intermittent.

перебо́рка, -и, sorting out; re-assembly; partition; bulkhead.

переборо́ть, -рю́, -решь *perf.* overcome; master.

переборщи́ть, -щу́ *perf.* go too far; overdo it.

перебра́нка, -и, wrangle squabble.

перебра́сывать(ся, -аю(сь *imp.* of перебро́сить(ся.

перебра́ть, -беру́, -берёшь; -а́л, -а́, -о *perf.* (*imp.* перебира́ть) sort out, pick over; look through, look over; turn over; turn over in one's mind; finger; dismantle and re-assemble; reset; take in excess; score more than enough; **~ся,** get over, cross; move.

перебро́сить, -о́шу *perf.* (*imp.* перебра́сывать) throw over; transfer; **~ся,** fling oneself; spread; + *instr.* throw to one another; ~ся не́сколькими слова́ми, exchange a few words. **перебро́ска,** -и, transfer.

перебью́, etc.: see переби́ть.

перева́л, -а, passing, crossing; pass. **перева́ливать,** -аю *imp.*, **перевали́ть,** -лю́, -лишь *perf.* transfer, shift; cross, pass; *impers.* перевали́ло за́ полночь, it is past midnight; ей перевали́ло за́ сорок, she's turned forty, she's over forty; **~ся,** waddle.

перева́ривать, -аю *imp.*, **перевари́ть,** -рю́, -ришь *perf.* boil again; reheat; overdo, overcook; digest; swallow, bear, stand.

переведу́, etc.: see перевести́.

перевезти́, -зу́, -зёшь; -вёз, -ла́ *perf.* (*imp.* перевози́ть) take across, put across; transport, convey; (re)move.

переверну́ть, -ну́, -нёшь *perf.*, **перевёртывать,** -аю *imp.* (*imp.* also перевора́чивать) turn (over); overturn, upset; turn inside out; ~ вверх дном, turn upside-down; **~ся,** turn (over).

переве́с, -а, preponderance; predominance; advantage, superiority; с ~ом в пять голосо́в, with a majority of five votes. **переве́сить,** -е́шу *perf.* (*imp.*

перевéшивать) re-weigh, weigh again; outweigh, outbalance; tip the scales; hang somewhere else.

перевести́, -веду́, -ведёшь; -вёл, -á, *perf.* (*imp.* переводи́ть), take across; transfer move, switch, shift; translate; convert, express; transfer, copy; ~ дух, take breath; ~ часы́ вперёд (наза́д), put a clock forward (back); **~сь,** be transferred; come to an end, run out; become extinct; у меня́ перевели́сь де́ньги, my money ran out, I was spent up.

перевéшивать, -аю *imp.* of перевéсить. **перевира́ть,** -а́ю *imp.* of перевра́ть.

перево́д, -а (-у), transfer, move, switch, shift; translation; version; conversion; spending, using up, waste; нет ~у + *dat.*, there is no shortage of, there is an inexhaustible supply of. **переводи́ть(ся,** -ожу́(сь, -о́дишь(ся *imp.* of перевести́(сь. **переводн|о́й,** transfer; ~а́я бума́га, carbon paper, transfer paper; ~а́я карти́нка, transfer. **перево́дный,** transfer; translated. **перево́дчик,** -а, translator; interpreter.

перево́з, -а, transporting, conveyance; crossing; ferry. **перевози́ть,** -ожу́, -о́зишь *imp.* of перевезти́. **перево́зка,** -и conveyance, carriage. **перево́зчик,** -а, ferryman; boatman; carrier, carter, removal man.

перевооружа́ть, -а́ю *imp.*, **перевооружи́ть,** -жу́ *perf.* rearm; **~ся,** rearm. **перевооруже́ние,** -я, rearmament.

перевоплоти́ть, -лощу́ *perf.*, **перевоплоща́ть,** -а́ю *imp.* reincarnate; transform; **~ся,** be reincarnated; transform oneself, be transformed. **перевоплоще́ние,** -я, reincarnation; transformation.

перевора́чивать(ся, -аю(сь *imp.* of переверну́ть(ся. **переворо́т,** -а, revolution; overturn; cataclysm; госуда́рственный ~, coup d'état.

перевоспита́ние, -я, re-education. **перевоспита́ть,** -а́ю *perf.*, **перевоспи́тывать,** -аю *imp.* re-educate.

перевра́ть, -ру́, -рёшь; -а́л, -á, -о *perf.* (*imp.* перевира́ть) garble, confuse; misinterpret; misquote.

перевыполне́ние, -я, over-fulfilment. **перевы́полнить,** -ню *perf.*, **перевыполня́ть,** -я́ю *imp.* over-fulfil.

перевяза́ть, -яжу́, -я́жешь *perf.*, **перевя́зывать,** -аю *imp.* dress, bandage; tie up, cord; tie again, re-tie; knit again. **перевя́зка,** -и, dressing, bandage. **перевя́зочный;** ~ материа́л, dressing; ~ пункт, dressing station. **пе́ревязь,** -и, cross-belt, shoulder-belt; sling.

переги́б, -а, bend, twist; fold; exaggeration; допусти́ть ~ в + *prep.*, carry too far. **перегиба́ть(ся,** -а́ю(сь *imp.* of перегну́ть(ся.

перегля́дываться, -аюсь *imp.*, **переглянуться,** -ну́сь, -нешься *perf.* exchange glances.

перегна́ть, -гоню́, -го́нишь; -а́л, -á, -о *perf.* (*imp.* перегоня́ть) outdistance, leave behind; overtake, surpass; drive; ferry; distil, sublimate.

перегно́й, -я, humus.

перегну́ть, -ну́, -нёшь *perf.* (*imp.* перегиба́ть) bend; ~ па́лку, go too far; **~ся,** bend; lean over.

перегова́ривать, -аю *imp.* **переговори́ть,** -рю́ *perf.* talk, speak; silence, out-talk; + о + *prep.* talk over, discuss; **~ся** (с + *instr.*) exchange remarks (with). **перегово́р,** -а, (telephone) call, conversation; *pl.* negotiations, parley; вести́ ~ы, negotiate, conduct negotiations, parley. **перегово́рн|ый** *adj.*; ~ая бу́дка, call-box, telephone booth; ~ый пункт, public call-boxes; trunk-call office.

перего́н, -а, driving; stage. **перего́нка,** -и, distillation. **перего́нный,** distilling, distillation; ~ заво́д, distillery; ~ куб, still. **перегоню́,** etc.: see перегна́ть. **перегоня́ть,** -я́ю *imp.* of перегна́ть.

перегора́живать, -аю *imp.* of перегороди́ть.

перегора́ть, -а́ет *imp.*, **перегоре́ть,** -ри́т *perf.* burn out, fuse; burn through; rot through.

перегороди́ть, -рожу́, -ро́ди́шь *perf.* (*imp.* перегора́живать) partition off; block. **перегоро́дка,** -и, partition; baffle (plate). **перегоро́женный,** partitioned off; blocked.

перегре́в, -а, overheating; superheating.

перегрева́ть, -а́ю *imp.*, **перегре́ть, -е́ю** *perf.* overheat; **~ся,** overheat; burn, burn out, get burned.

перегружа́ть, -а́ю *imp.*, **перегрузи́ть,** -ужу́, -у́зишь *perf.* overload; transfer, trans-ship; overwork. **перегру́зка, -и,** overload; overwork; transfer; reloading.

перегрыза́ть, -а́ю *imp.*, **перегры́зть,** -зу́, -зёшь; -гры́з *perf.* gnaw through, bite through; **~ся,** fight; quarrel, wrangle.

пе́ред, пе́редо, пред, пре́до, *prep.* + *instr.* before; in front of; in the face of; to; compared to, in comparison with; извини́ться ~, apologize to. **перёд,** пе́реда; *pl.* -а́, front, forepart.

передава́ть, -даю́, -даёшь *imp.*, **переда́ть,** -а́м, -а́шь, -а́ст, -ади́м; пе́редал, -а́, -о *perf.* pass, hand, hand over; hand down; make over; tell; communicate; transmit, convey; pay too much, give too much; вы пе́редали три рубля́, you have paid three roubles too much; ~ де́ло в суд, take a matter to court, sue; ~ приве́т, convey one's greetings, send one's regards; переда́й(те) им приве́т, remember me to them; **~ся,** pass; be transmitted; be communicated; be inherited; + *dat.* go over to. **переда́точн|ый;** ~ый механи́зм, drive, driving mechanism, transmission; ~ое число́, gear ratio. **переда́тчик,** -а, transmitter, sender; conductor. **переда́ча,** -и, passing; transmission; communication; broadcast; drive; gear, gearing; transfer

передвига́ть, -а́ю *imp.*, **передви́нуть,** -ну *perf.* move, shift; ~ часы́ вперёд (наза́д), put the clock forward (back); ~ сро́ки экза́менов change the date of examinations; **~ся,** move, shift; travel. **передвиже́ние,** -я, movement, moving; conveyance; travel; сре́дства передвиже́ния, means of transport. **передви́жка,** -и, movement; moving; travel; in *comb.*, travelling, itinerant; библиоте́ка-~, travelling library, mobile library; теа́тр-~, strolling players. **передвижно́й,** movable, mobile; travelling, itinerant.

переде́л, -а, re-partition; re-division, redistribution; re-allotment.

переде́лать, -аю *perf.*, **переде́лывать,** -аю *imp.* alter; change; refashion, recast; do. **переде́лка,** -и, alteration; adaptation; отда́ть в переде́лку, have altered; попа́сть в переде́лку, get into a pretty mess.

передёргивать(ся, -аю(сь *imp.* of передёрнуть(ся.

передержа́ть, -жу́, -жишь *perf.*, **переде́рживать,** -аю *imp.* keep too long; overdo; overcook; overexpose. **переде́ржка,** -и, overexposure.

передёрнуть, -ну *perf.* (*imp.* передёргивать) pull aside, pull across; cheat; distort, misrepresent; ~ фа́кты, juggle with facts; **~ся,** flinch, wince.

пере́дний, front, fore; anterior; first, leading; ~ план, foreground. **пере́дник,** -а, apron; pinafore. **пере́дняя** *sb.* ante-room; (entrance) hall, lobby.

пе́редо: see пе́ред. **передови́к,** -а́, peredovik, leader; standard-bearer, pioneer; leader-writer. **передови́ца,** -ы, leading article, leader; editorial. **передов|о́й,** forward; advanced; foremost; ~ы́е взгля́ды, advanced views; ~о́й отря́д, advanced detachment; vanguard; ~а́я (статья́), leading article, leader; editorial.

передохну́ть, -ну́, -нёшь *perf.* pause for breath, take a breather.

передра́знивать, -аю *imp.*, **передразни́ть,** -ню́, -нишь *perf.* take off, mimic.

передря́га, -и, scrape, tight corner; unpleasantness.

переду́мать, -аю *perf.*, **переду́мывать,** -аю *imp.* change one's mind, think better of it; do a lot of thinking.

передышка, -и, respite, breathing-space.

переезд, -а, crossing; removal. **переезжа́ть,** -а́ю *imp.*, **перее́хать,** -е́ду *perf.* cross; run over, knock down; move, remove.

пережа́ренный, overdone; burnt. **пережа́ривать,** -аю *imp.*, **пережа́рить,** -рю *perf.* overdo, overcook.

пережда́ть, -жду́, -ждёшь; -а́л, -а́, -о *perf.* (*imp.* пережида́ть) wait; wait through, wait for the end of.

пережёвывать, -аю *imp.* masticate, chew; repeat over and over again.

переживáние, -я, experience. **переживáть** -áю *imp*. of пережи́ть.
пережидáть, -áю *imp*. of переждáть.
пережитóе *sb*. the past. **пережи́ток**, -тка, survival; vestige. **пережи́ть**, -иву́ -ивёшь; пéрежил, -á, -о *perf*. (*imp*. переживáть) live through; experience; go through; endure, suffer; outlive, outlast, survive.
перезаряди́ть, -яжу́, -я́ди́шь *perf*., **перезаряжáть**, -áю *imp*. re-charge, reload. **перезаря́дка**, -и, re-charging, reloading.
перезвóн, -а ringing, chime.
пере|зимовáть, -му́ю *perf*.
перезревáть, -áю *imp*., **перезрéть**, -éю *perf*. become overripe; be past one's prime. **перезрéлый**, overripe; past one's first youth, past one's prime.
переизбирáть, -áю *imp*., **переизбрáть**, -беру́, -берёшь; -брáл, -á, -о *perf*. re-elect. **переизбрáние**, -я, re-election.
переиздавáть, -даю́, -даёшь *imp*., **переиздáть**, -áм, -áшь, -áст, -ади́м; -áл, -á, -о *perf*. republish, reprint. **переиздáние**, -я, re-publication; new edition, reprint.
переименовáть, -ну́ю *perf*., **переимено́вывать**, -аю *imp*. rename.
переймý, etc.: see переня́ть.
перейти́, -йду́, -йдёшь; перешёл, -шлá *perf*. (*imp*. переходи́ть) cross; get across, get over, go over; pass; turn (в + *acc*. to, into); ~ в наступлéние, go over to the offensive; ~ грани́цу, cross the frontier; ~ из рук в ру́ки, change hands; ~ на другу́ю рабóту, change one's job; ~ чéрез мост, cross a bridge.
перекáрмливать, -аю *imp*. of перекорми́ть.
переквалификáция, -и, training for a new profession; re-training. **переквалифици́роваться**, -руюсь *perf*. and *imp*. change one's profession; retrain.
перекиднóй; ~ мóстик, footbridge, gangway. **переки́дывать**, -аю *imp*., **переки́нуть**, -ну *perf*. throw over; **~ся**, leap; spread; go over, defect; ~ся словáми, exchange a few remarks.
перекисáть, -áет *imp*., **переки́снуть**, -нет *perf*. turn sour, go sour. **пéрекись**, -и, peroxide.
перекла́дина, -ы, cross-beam cross-piece, transom; joist; horizontal bar.
перекла́дывать, -аю *imp*. of переложи́ть.
перекликáться, -áюсь *imp*., **перекли́кнуться**, -нусь *perf*. call to one another. **перекли́чка**, -и, roll-call, call-over; hook-up.
переключáтель, -я *m*. switch. **переключáть**, -áю *imp*., **переключи́ть**, -чу́ *perf*. switch, switch over; **~ся**, switch (over).
перековáть, -кую́, -куёшь *perf*., **перекóвывать**, -аю *imp*. re-shoe; re-forge; hammer out, beat out.
переколоти́ть, -лочу́, -лóтишь *perf*. break, smash.
перекорми́ть, -млю́, -мишь *perf*. (*imp*. перекáрмливать) overfeed, surfeit; feed.
перекоси́ть, -ошу́, -óсишь *perf*. warp; distort; **~ся**, warp, be warped; become distorted.
перекочевáть, -чу́ю *perf*., **перекочёвывать**, -аю *imp*. migrate move on.
перекóшенный, distorted, twisted.
перекрáивать, -аю *imp*. of перекрои́ть.
перекрáсить, -áшу *perf*., **перекрáшивать**, -аю *imp*. (re-)colour, (re-)paint; (re-)dye; **~ся**, change colour; turn one's coat.
пере|крести́ть, -ещу́, -éстишь *perf*., **перекрéщивать**, -аю *imp*. cross; **~ся**, cross, intersect; cross oneself. **перекрёстн|ый**, cross; ~ый допрóс, cross-examination; ~ый огóнь, cross-fire; ~ая ссы́лка, cross-reference. **перекрёсток**, -тка, cross-roads, crossing.
перекри́кивать, -аю *imp*., **перекричáть**, -чу́ *perf*. out-shout, outroar; shout down.
перекрои́ть, -ою́ *perf*. (*imp*. перекрáивать) cut out again; rehash; reshape.
перекрывáть, -áю *imp*., **перекры́ть**, -рóю *perf*. re-cover; exceed; ~ рекóрд, break a record.
перекую́, etc.: see перековáть.
перекупáть, -áю *imp*., **перекупи́ть**, -плю́, -пишь *perf*. buy; buy up; buy

secondhand. **перекупщик**, -а, second-hand dealer.

перекусить, -ушу, -усишь *perf.*, **перекусывать**, -аю *imp.* bite through; have a bite, have a snack.

перелагать, -аю *imp.* of переложить.

переламывать, -аю *imp.* of переломить.

перелезать, -аю *imp.* **перелезть**, -зу; -ез *perf.* climb over, get over.

перелёт, -а, migration; flight. **перелетать**, -аю *imp.*, **перелететь**, -лечу *perf.* fly over, fly across; overshoot the mark. **перелётн|ый**, migratory; ~ая птица, bird of passage.

переливание, -я, decanting; transfusion; ~ крови, blood transfusion. **переливать**, -аю *imp.* of перелить. **переливаться**, -ается *imp.* of перелиться play; modulate. **переливчатый**, iridescent; shot; modulating.

перелистать, -аю *perf.*, **перелистывать**, -аю *imp.* turn over, leaf through; look through glance at.

перелить, -лью, -льёшь; -ил, -а, -о *perf.* (*imp.* переливать) pour; decant; let overflow; transfuse. **перелиться**, -льётся; -лился, -лилась, -лилось *perf.* (*imp.* переливаться) flow; overflow, run over.

пере|лицевать, -цую *perf.*, **перелицовывать**, -аю *imp.* turn; have turned.

переложение, -я, arrangement. **переложить**, -жу, -жишь *perf.* (*imp.* перекладывать, перелагать) put somewhere else; shift, move; transfer; interlay; re-set, re-lay; put in too much; put, set arrange; transpose; ~ в стихи, put into verse; ~ на музыку, set to music.

перелом, -а break, breaking; fracture; turning-point, crisis; sudden change; на ~е+*gen.*, on the eve of. **переломать**, -аю *perf.* break; **~ся**, break, be broken. **переломить**, -млю, -мишь *perf.* (*imp.* переламывать) break in two; break; fracture; master; ~ себя, master oneself, restrain one's feelings. **переломный**; ~ момент, critical moment, crucial moment.

перелью, etc.: see перелить. **перемалывать**, -аю *imp.* of перемолоть.

переманивать, -аю *imp.*, **переманить**, -ню -нишь *perf.* win over; entice.

перемежаться, -ается *imp.* alternate; перемежающаяся лихорадка, intermittent fever.

перемелю, etc.: see перемолоть.

перемена, -ы, change, alteration; change (of clothes); interval, break. **переменить**, -ню, -нишь *perf.*, **переменять**, -яю *imp.* change; **~ся**, change. **переменный**, variable, changeable; ~ ток, alternating current. **переменчивый** changeable.

переместить, -мещу *perf.* (*imp.* перемещать) move; transfer; **~ся**, move.

перемешать, -аю *perf.*, **перемешивать**, -аю *imp.* mix, intermingle; mix up; confuse; **~ся**, get mixed; get mixed up.

перемещать(ся, -аю(сь *imp.* of переместить(ся. **перемещение**, -я, transference, shift; displacement; dislocation; travel. **перемещённ|ый**, displaced; ~ые лица, displaced persons.

перемигиваться, -аюсь *imp.*, **перемигнуться**, -нусь, -нёшься *perf.* wink at each other; + с + *instr.* wink at.

перемирие, -я, armistice, truce.

перемогать, -аю *imp.* (try to) overcome; **~ся**, struggle (against illness, tears, etc.).

перемолоть, -мелю, -мелешь *perf.* (*imp.* перемалывать) grind, mill; pulverize.

перемывать, -аю *imp.*, **перемыть**, -мою *perf.* wash (up) again.

перенапрягать, -аю *imp.*, **перенапрячь**, -ягу, -яжёшь; -яг, -ла *perf.* overstrain; **~ся**, overstrain oneself.

перенаселение, -я, overpopulation. **перенаселённый**; -лён, -а, overpopulated; overcrowded. **перенаселить**, -лю *perf.*, **перенаселять**, -яю *imp.* overpopulate; overcrowd.

перенести, -су, -сёшь; -нёс, -ла *perf.* (*imp.* переносить) carry, move, take; transport; transfer; carry over; take over; put off, postpone; endure, bear, stand; **~сь**, be carried; be borne; be carried away.

перенимать, -аю *imp.* of перенять.

перенос, -а, transfer; transportation; division of words; знак ~а, hyphen.

переноси́мый, bearable, endurable. **переноси́ть(ся,** -ошу́(сь, -óсишь(ся *imp.* of перенести́(сь.

перенóсица, -ы, bridge (of the nose).

перенóска, -и, carrying over; transporting; carriage. **перенóсный,** portable; figurative, metaphorical.

пере|ночевáть, -чу́ю *perf.* **переношу́,** etc.: see переноси́ть.

переня́ть, -ейму́, -еймёшь; пéренял, -á, -о *perf.* (*imp.* перенимáть) imitate, copy; adopt.

переобору́довать, -дую *perf.* and *imp.* re-equip.

переосвидéтельствовать, -твую *perf.* and *imp.* re-examine.

переоцéнивать, -аю *imp.,* **переоцени́ть,** -ню́, -нишь *perf.* overestimate, overrate; revalue, reappraise. **переоцéнка,** -и, overestimation; revaluation, reappraisal.

перепáчкать, -аю *perf.* dirty, make dirty; **~ся,** get dirty.

пéрепел, -á; *pl.* -á, **перепёлка,** -и, quail.

перепечáтать, -аю *perf.,* **перепечáтывать,** -аю *imp.* reprint; type (out). **перепечáтка,** -и, reprinting; reprint.

перепи́ливать, -аю *imp.,* **перепили́ть,** -лю́, -лишь *perf.* saw in two.

переписáть, -ишу́, -и́шешь *perf.,* **перепи́сывать,** -аю *imp.* copy; type; re--write; list, make a list of. **перепи́ска,** -и, copying; typing; correspondence; letters; быть в перепи́ске с+*instr.* be in correspondence with. **перепи́счик,** -а, **-чица,** -ы, copyist; typist. **перепи́сываться,** -аюсь *imp.* correspond. **пéрепись,** -и, census; inventory.

перепла́вить, -влю *perf.,* **переплавля́ть,** -я́ю *imp.* smelt.

переплáта, -ы, overpayment; surplus. **переплати́ть,** -ачу́, -áтишь *perf.,* **переплáчивать,** -аю *imp.* overpay, pay too much.

переплести́, -лету́, -летёшь; -лёл, -á *perf.,* **переплетáть,** -áю *imp.* bind; interlace, interknit; re-plait; **~ся,** interlace, interweave; get mixed up. **переплёт,** -а, binding; cover; transom; caning; mess, scrape. **переплётная** *sb.* bindery; bookbinder's. **переплётчик,** -а, bookbinder.

переплывáть, -áю *imp.,* **переплы́ть,** -ыву́, -ывёшь; -ы́л, -á, -о *perf.* swim (across); sail across, row across, cross.

переподготáвливать, -аю *imp.,* **переподготóвить,** -влю *perf.* re-train; give further training. **переподготóвка,** -и, further training; re-training; ку́рсы по переподготóвке, refresher courses.

переползáть, -áю *imp.,* **переползти́,** -зу́, -зёшь; -óлз, -лá *perf.* crawl across; creep across.

переполнéние, -я, overfilling; overcrowding. **перепóлненный,** overcrowded, too full, overfull. **перепóлнить,** -ню *perf.,* **переполня́ть,** -я́ю *imp.* overfill; overcrowd; **~ся,** be overflowing; be overcrowded.

переполóх, -а, alarm; commotion, rumpus. **переполоши́ть,** -шу́ *perf.* alarm; arouse, alert; **~ся,** take alarm, became alarmed.

перепóнка, -и, membrane; web. **перепóнчатый,** membranous; webbed; web-footed.

перепрáвить, -влю *perf.,* **переправля́ть,** -я́ю *imp.* convey, transport; take across; forward; correct; **~ся,** cross, get across.

перепродавáть, -даю́, -даёшь *imp.,* **перепродáть,** -áм, -áшь, -áст, -ади́м; -прóдáл, -á, -о *perf.* re-sell. **перепродáжа,** -и, re-sale.

перепроизвóдство, -а, overproduction.

перепры́гивать, -аю *imp.,* **перепры́гнуть,** -ну *perf.* jump, jump over.

перепу́г, -а (-у), fright. **перепугáть,** -áю *perf.* frighten, give a fright, give a turn; **~ся,** get a fright.

пере|пу́тать, -аю *perf.,* **перепу́тывать,** -аю *imp.* entangle; confuse, mix up, muddle up.

перепу́тье, -я, cross-roads.

перерабáтывать, -аю *imp.,* **переработáть,** -аю *perf.* work up, make; convert; treat; re-make; recast, re-shape; process; work overtime; overwork; **~ся,** overwork.

перераспределéние, -я, redistribution. **перераспредели́ть,** -лю́ *perf.,* **перераспределя́ть,** -я́ю *imp.* redistribute.

перерастáние, -я, outgrowing; escalation; growing (into), development (into). **перераста́ть,** -а́ю *imp.*, **пере-расти́,** -ту́, -тёшь; -ро́с, -ла́ *perf.* outgrow, overtop; outstrip; be too old (for); + в + *acc.* grow into, develop into, turn into.

перерасхо́д, -а, over-expenditure; overdraft. **перерасхо́довать,** -дую *perf.* and *imp.* overspend, expend too much of; overdraw.

перерасчёт, -а, recalculation, recomputation.

перерва́ть, -ву́, -вёшь; -а́л, -а́, -о *perf.* (*imp.* перерыва́ть) break, tear asunder; **~ся,** break, come apart.

перерегистра́ция, -и, re-registration. **перерегистри́ровать,** -рую *perf.* and *imp.* re-register.

перере́зать, -е́жу *perf.*, **перереза́ть,** -а́ю *imp.*, **перере́зывать,** -аю *imp.* cut; cut off; cut across; break; kill, slaughter.

перереша́ть, -а́ю *imp.*, **перереши́ть,** -шу́ *perf.* re-solve; decide differently; change one's mind, reconsider one's decision.

перероди́ть, -ожу́ *perf.*, **перерожда́ть,** -а́ю *imp.* regenerate; **~ся,** be re-born; be regenerated; degenerate. **перерожде́ние,** -я, regeneration; degeneration.

перeróс, etc.: see перерасти́. **перeró́ю,** etc.: see переры́ть.

переруба́ть, -а́ю *imp.*, **перерубить,** -блю́, -бишь *perf.* chop in two; cut up, chop up.

переры́в, -а, interruption; interval, break, intermission; с ~ами, off and on.

перерыва́ть[1]**(ся,** -а́ю(сь *imp.* of перерва́ть(ся.

перерыва́ть[2], -а́ю *imp.*, **переры́ть,** -ро́ю *perf.* dig up; rummage through, search thoroughly.

пересади́ть, -ажу́, -а́дишь *perf.*, **переса́живать,** -аю *imp.* transplant; graft; seat somewhere else; make change, help change; ~ че́рез + *acc.* help across. **переса́дка,** -и, transplantation; grafting; change, changing.

переса́живаться, -аюсь *imp.* of пересе́сть. **переса́ливать,** -аю *imp.* of пересоли́ть. **пересека́ть(ся,** -а́ю(сь *imp.* of пересе́чь(ся.

переселе́нец, -нца, settler; migrant, emigrant; immigrant. **переселе́ние,** -я, migration, emigration; immigration, resettlement; move, removal. **пересели́ть,** -лю́ *perf.*, **переселя́ть,** -я́ю *imp.* move; transplant; resettle; **~ся,** move; migrate.

пересе́сть, -ся́ду *perf.* (*imp.* переса́живаться) change one's seat; change, change trains, etc.

пересече́ние, -я, crossing, intersection. **пересе́чь,** -секу́, -сечёшь; -се́к, -ла́ *perf.* (*imp.* пересека́ть) cross; traverse; intersect; cut, cut up; **~ся,** cross, intersect.

переси́ливать, -аю *imp.*, **переси́лить,** -лю *perf.* overpower; overcome, master.

переска́з, -а, (re)telling; exposition. **пересказа́ть,** -ажу́, -а́жешь *perf.*, **переска́зывать,** -аю *imp.* tell, retell; expound; retail, relate.

переска́кивать, -аю *imp.*, **перескочи́ть,** -чу́, -чишь *perf.* jump (over), vault (over); skip (over).

пересла́ть, -ешлю́, -шлёшь *perf.* (*imp.* пересыла́ть) send; remit; send on, forward.

пересма́тривать, -аю *imp.*, **пересмотре́ть,** -трю́, -тришь *perf.* revise; reconsider; review. **пересмо́тр,** -а, revision; reconsideration; review; re--trial.

пересоли́ть, -олю́, о́ли́шь *perf.* (*imp.* переса́ливать) put too much salt in, over-salt; exaggerate, overdo it.

пересо́хнуть, -нет; -о́х *perf.* (*imp.* пересыха́ть) dry up, become parched; dry out.

переспа́ть, -плю́; -а́л, -а́, -о *perf.* oversleep; spend the night; ~ с + *instr.* sleep with.

переспе́лый, overripe.

переспо́рить, -рю *perf.* out-argue, defeat in argument.

переспра́шивать, -аю *imp.*, **переспроси́ть,** -ошу́, -о́сишь *perf.* ask again; ask to repeat.

перессо́риться, -рюсь *perf.* quarrel, fall out.

перестава́ть, -таю́, -таёшь *imp.* of переста́ть.

переста́вить, -влю *perf.*, **переставля́ть**, -я́ю *imp.* move, shift; re-arrange; transpose; ~ часы́ вперёд (наза́д), put the clock forward (back).
перестара́ться, -а́юсь *perf.* overdo it, try too hard.
переста́ть, -а́пу *perf.* (*imp.* перестава́ть) stop, cease.
перестрада́ть, -а́ю *perf.* have suffered, have gone through.
перестра́ивать(ся, -аю(сь *imp.* of перестро́ить(ся.
перестре́лка, -п, exchange of fire; firing; skirmish. **перестреля́ть**, -я́ю *perf.* shoot (down).
перестро́ить, -о́ю *perf.* (*imp.* перестра́ивать) rebuild, reconstruct; re-design, refashion, reshape; reorganize; retune; **~ся**, re-form; reorganize oneself; switch over, retune (на+*acc.* to). **перестро́йка**, -и, rebuilding, reconstruction; reorganization; retuning.
переступа́ть, -а́ю *imp.*, **переступи́ть**, -плю́, -пишь *perf.* step over; cross; overstep; ~ с ноги́ на́ ногу, shuffle one's feet.
пересу́ды, -ов *pl.* gossip.
пересчита́ть, -а́ю *perf.*, **пересчи́тывать**, -аю *imp.* (*perf.* also перече́сть) re-count; count; + на + *acc.* convert to, express in terms of.
пересыла́ть, -а́ю *imp.* of пересла́ть. **пересы́лка**, -и, sending, forwarding; ~ беспла́тно, post free; carriage paid; сто́имость пересы́лки, postage. **пересы́льный**, transit.
пересыха́ть, -а́ет *imp.* of пересо́хнуть. **пересяду**, etc.: see пересе́сть. **перета́пливать**, -аю *imp.* of перетопи́ть.
перета́скивать, -аю *imp.*, **перетащи́ть**, -щу́, -щишь *perf.* drag (over, through); move, remove.
перетере́ть, -тру́, -трёшь; -тёр *perf.*, **перетира́ть**, -а́ю *imp.* wear out, wear down; grind; wipe, dry; **~ся**, wear out, wear through.
перетопи́ть, -плю́, -пишь *perf.* (*imp.* перета́пливать) melt.
перетру́, etc.: see перетере́ть.
перетя́гивание, -я; ~ кана́та, tug-of-war. **перетя́гивать**, -аю *imp.*, **перетяну́ть**, -ну́, -нешь *perf.* pull, draw; attract, win over; outbalance, outweigh; ~ на свою́ сто́рону, win over.
переу́лок, -лка, narrow street; cross-street; lane, passage.
переустро́йство, -а, reconstruction, reorganization.
переутоми́ть, -млю́ *perf.*, **переутомля́ть**, -я́ю *imp.* overtire, overstrain; overwork; **~ся**, overtire oneself, overstrain oneself; overwork; be run down. **переутомле́ние**, -я, overstrain; overwork.
переформирова́ть, -ру́ю *perf.*, **переформиро́вывать**, -аю *imp.* re-form.
перехвати́ть, -ачу́, -а́тишь *perf.*, **перехва́тывать**, -аю *imp.* intercept, catch; snatch a bite (of); borrow; go too far, overdo it. **перехва́тчик**, -а, interceptor.
перехитри́ть, -рю́ *perf.* outwit, overreach.
перехо́д, -а, passage, transition; crossing; day's march; going over, conversion. **переходи́ть**, -ожу́, -о́дишь *imp.* of перейти́. **перехо́дный**, transitional; transitive; transient. **переходя́щий**, transient, transitory; intermittent; brought forward, carried over; ~ ку́бок, challenge cup.
пе́рец, -рца, pepper.
перечёл, etc.: see перече́сть.
пе́речень, -чня *m.* list, enumeration.
перечёркивать, -аю *imp.*, **перечеркну́ть**, -ну́, -нёшь *perf.* cross out, cancel.
перече́сть, -чту́, -чтёшь; -чёл, -чла́ *perf.*: see пересчита́ть, перечита́ть.
перечисле́ние, -я, enumeration; list; transfer, transferring. **перечи́слить**, -лю *perf.*, **перечисля́ть**, -я́ю *imp.* enumerate, list; transfer.
перечита́ть, -а́ю *perf.*, **перечи́тывать**, -аю *imp.* (*perf.* also перече́сть) re-read.
пере́чить, -чу *imp.* contradict; cross, go against.
пе́речница, -ы, pepper-pot. **пе́речн|ый**, pepper; ~ая мя́та, peppermint.
перечту́, etc.: see перече́сть. **пере́чу**, etc.: see пере́чить.
переша́гивать, -аю *imp.*, **перешагну́тв**, -ну́, -нёшь *perf.* step over; ~ иоро́г, cross the threshold.
перешеек, -е́йка, isthmus, neck.

перешёл, etc.: see перейтѝ.
перешёптываться, -аюсь *imp.* whisper (together), exchange whispers.
перешивáть, -áю *imp.*, **перешѝть,** -шью́, -шьёшь *perf.* alter; have altered. **перешѝвка,** -и, altering, alteration.
перешлю́, etc.: see переслáть.
перещеголя́ть, -я́ю *perf.* outdo, surpass.
переэкзаменовáть, -ну́ю *perf.*, **переэкзаменóвывать,** -аю, re-examine; **~ся,** take an examination again.
перѝла, -ил *pl.* rail, railing(s); handrail; banisters.
перѝна, -ы, feather-bed.
перѝод, -а, period. **периóдика,** -и, periodicals, journals. **периодѝческ|ий,** periodic; periodical; recurring, recurrent; ~ая дробь, recurring decimal.
пéристо-кучевóй, cirro-cumulus. **пéрист|ый,** feathery; plumose; pinnate; ~ые облакá, fleecy clouds; cirrus.
перифéрия, -и, periphery; the provinces; outlying districts.
перл, -а, pearl. **перламу́тр,** -а, mother-of-pearl, nacre. **перламу́тров|ый;** ~ая пу́говица, pearl button. **перлóв|ый;** ~ая крупá, pearl barley.
перманéнт, -а, permanent wave, perm. **перманéнтный,** permanent.
пернáтый, feathered. **пернáтые** *sb. pl.* birds. **перó,** -á; *pl.* пéрья, -ьев, feather; pen; fin; blade, paddle. **перочѝнный** нож, нóжик, penknife.
перрóн, -а, platform.
перс, -а, Persian. **персѝдский,** Persian.
пéрсик, -а, peach.
персия́нин, -а; *pl.* -я́не, -я́н, **персия́нка,** -и, Persian.
персóна, -ы, person; сóбственной персóной, in person. **персонáж,** -а, character; personage. **персонáл,** -а, personnel, staff. **персонáльный,** personal; individual; ~ состáв, staff, personnel.
перспектѝва, -ы, perspective; vista; prospect; outlook. **перспектѝвный,** perspective; prospective, forward-looking; long-term; having prospects, promising.
перст, -á, finger. **пéрстень,** -тня *m.* ring; signet-ring.
перфокáрта, -ы, punched card.
пéрхоть, -и, dandruff, scurf.
перцóвый, pepper.
перчáтка, -и, glove; gauntlet.
перчѝнка, -и, peppercorn. **пéрчить,** -чу *imp.* (*perf.* на~, по~) pepper.
першѝть, -ѝт *imp. impers.*; у меня́ першѝт в гóрле, I have a tickle in my throat.
пёс, пса, dog.
пéсенник, -а, song-book; (choral) singer; song-writer. **пéсенный,** song; of songs.
песéц, -сцá, (polar) fox.
пёсий, dog; dog's, dogs'; пёсья звездá, dog-star, Sirius.
песнь, -и; *gen. pl.* -ей, song; canto, book; ~ пéсней, Song of Songs. **пéсня,** -и; *gen. pl.* -сен, song; air.
песóк, -скá (-у́), sand; *pl.* sands, stretches of sand. **песóчница,** -ы, sand-box; sand-pit. **песóчн|ый,** sand; sandy; short; ~ое печéнье, ~ое тéсто, shortbread; ~ые часы́, sand-glass, hourglass.
пест, -á, pestle. **пéстик,** -а, pistil; pestle.
пестротá, -ы́, variegation, diversity of colours; mixed character. **пёстрый,** motley, variegated, many-coloured, particoloured; colourful.
песчáник, -а, sandstone. **песчáный,** sand, sandy. **песчѝнка,** -и, grain of sand.
петáрда, -ы, petard; squib, cracker.
петлѝца, -ы, buttonhole; tab. **пéтля,** -и; *gen. pl.* -тель, loop; noose; button-hole; stitch; hinge.
петру́шка[1], -и, parsley.
петру́шка[2], -и, *m.* Punch; *f.* Punch-and-Judy show; foolishness, absurdity.
пету́х, -á, cock; встать с ~áми, be up with the lark; **~-боéц,** fighting-cock. **пету́ший, петушѝный,** cock, cock's. **петушóк,** -шкá, cockerel.
петь, пою́, поёшь *imp.* (*perf.* про~, с~) sing; chant, intone; crow; ~ вполгóлоса, hum.
пехóта, -ы, infantry, foot. **пехотѝнец,** -нца, infantryman. **пехóтный,** infantry.
печáлить, -лю *imp.* (*perf.* о~) grieve,

sadden; **~ся,** grieve, be sad. **печа́ль,** -и, grief, sorrow. **печа́льный,** sad, mournful, sorrowful; sorry, bad.

печа́тание, -я, printing. **печа́тать,** -аю *imp.* (*perf.* на~, от~), print; type; **~ся,** write, be published; be at the printer's. **печа́тка,** -и, signet, seal, stamp. **печа́тн|ый,** printing; printer's; printed; ~ые бу́квы, block letters, block capitals; ~ая кра́ска, printer's ink; ~ый лист, quire, sheet; ~ый стано́к, printing-press. **печа́ть,** -и, seal, stamp; print; printing; type; press.

пече́ние, -я, baking.

печёнка, -и, liver.

печёный, baked.

пе́чень, -и, liver.

пече́нье, -я, pastry; biscuit; cake. **пе́чка,** -и, stove. **печно́й,** stove; oven; furnace; kiln. **печь,** -и, *loc.* -и́; *gen. pl.* -е́й, stove; oven; furnace, kiln. **печь,** пеку́, -чёшь; пёк, -ла́ *imp.* (*perf.* ис~) bake; scorch, parch; **~ся,** bake; broil.

пешехо́д, -а, pedestrian. **пешехо́дн|ый,** pedestrian; foot-; ~ая доро́жка, ~ая тропа́, footpath; ~ый мост, foot-bridge. **пе́шечный,** pawn, pawn's. **пе́ший,** pedestrian; unmounted, foot. **пе́шка,** -и, pawn. **пешко́м** *adv.* on foot.

пеще́ра, -ы, cave, cavern; grotto. **пеще́ристый,** cavernous. **пеще́рник,** -а, caver, pot-holer. **пеще́рный,** cave; ~ челове́к, caveman, cave-dweller.

пиани́но *n. indecl.* (upright) piano.

пивна́я *sb.* alehouse; pub. **пивн|о́й,** beer; ~ы́е дро́жжи, brewer's yeast. **пи́во,** -а, beer, ale. **пивова́р,** -а, brewer.

пиджа́к, -а́, jacket, coat. **пиджа́чн|ый;** ~ый костю́м, ~ая па́ра, (lounge-) suit.

пижа́ма, -ы, pyjamas.

пик, -а, peak; часы́ ~, rush-hour.

пи́ка, -и, pike, lance.

пика́нтный, piquant; spicy; savoury.

пика́п, -а, pick-up (van).

пике́ *n. indecl.* dive.

пике́т, -а, picket; piquet. **пике́тчик,** -а, picket.

пи́ки, пик *pl.* spades.

пики́рование, -я, dive, diving. **пики́ровать,** -рую *perf.* and *imp.* (*perf.* also с~) dive.

пики́роваться, -руюсь *imp.* exchange caustic remarks, cross swords. **пики́ровка,** -и, altercation, slanging-match.

пикиро́вщик, -а, dive-bomber. **пики́рующий,** diving; ~ бомбардиро́вщик, dive-bomber.

пи́кнуть, -ну *perf.* squeak, let out a squeak; make a sound.

пи́ковый, of spades; awkward, unfavourable.

пила́, -ы́; *pl.* -ы, saw; nagger. **пилёный,** sawed, sawn; ~ са́хар, lump sugar. **пили́ть,** -лю́, -лишь *imp.* saw; nag (at). **пи́лка,** -и, sawing; fret-saw; nail-file. **пилообра́зный,** serrated, notched.

пило́тка, -и, forage-cap.

пилоти́ровать, -рую *imp.* pilot. **пилоти́руемый,** manned.

пилю́ля, -и, pill.

пина́ть, -а́ю *imp.* (*perf.* пну́ть) kick. **пино́к,** -нка́, kick.

пинце́т, -а, pincers, tweezers.

пио́н, -а, peony.

пионе́р, -а, pioneer. **пионе́рский,** pioneer.

пир, -а, *loc.* -у́; *pl.* -ы́, feast, banquet. **пирова́ть,** -ру́ю *imp.* feast; celebrate.

пиро́г, -а́, pie; tart. **пиро́жное** *sb.* pastries; cake, pastry. **пирожо́к,** -жка́, patty, pastry, pie.

пиру́шка, -и, party, celebration. **пи́ршество,** -а, feast, banquet; celebration.

писа́ка, -и *m.* and *f.* scribbler, quill-driver, pen-pusher. **пи́сан|ый,** written, manuscript; ~ая краса́вица, as pretty as a picture. **пи́сарь,** -я; *pl.* -я́ *m.* clerk. **писа́тель,** -я *m.*, **писа́тельница,** -ы, writer, author. **писа́ть,** пишу́, пи́шешь *imp.* (*perf.* на~) write; paint; ~ ма́слом, paint in oils; **~ся,** be written, be spelt. **писе́ц,** -сца́, clerk; scribe.

писк, -а, squeak, cheep, chirp, peep. **пискли́вый, писклявый,** squeaky. **пи́скнуть,** -ну *perf.* of пища́ть.

пистоле́т, -а, pistol; gun; ~-пулемёт, sub-machine gun.

писто́н, -а, (percussion-)cap; piston; hollow rivet.

писчебума́жный, writing-paper; stationery; ~ магази́н, stationer's (shop). **пи́сч|ий,** writing; ~ая бума́га, writing paper. **пи́сьменно** *adv.* in writing. **пи́сьменн|ый,** writing, written; в ~ом ви́де, в ~ой фо́рме, in writing; ~ый знак, letter; ~ый стол, writing-table, desk. **письмо́,** -а́; *pl.* -а, -сем, letter; writing; script; hand(-writing). **письмоно́сец,** -сца, postman.

пита́ние, -я, nourishment, nutrition; feeding; feed. **пита́тельн|ый,** nourishing, nutritious; alimentary; feed, feeding; ~ая среда́, culture medium; breeding-ground. **пита́ть,** -а́ю *imp.* (*perf.* на~) feed; nourish; sustain; supply; **~ся,** be fed, eat; + *instr.* feed on, live on.

пи́терский, of St. Petersburg.

пито́мец, -мца, foster-child, nursling; charge; pupil; alumnus. **пито́мник,** -а, nursery.

пить, пью, пьёшь; пил, -а́, -о *imp.* (*perf.* вы́~) drink; have, take; мне хо́чется ~, я хочу́ ~, I am thirsty. **питьё,** -я́, drinking; drink, beverage. **питьев|о́й,** drinkable; ~а́я вода́, drinking-water.

пи́хта, -ы, (silver) fir.

пи́чкать, -аю *imp.* (*perf.* на~) stuff, cram.

пи́шущ|ий, writing; ~ая маши́нка, typewriter.

пи́ща, -и, food.

пища́ть, -щу́ *imp.* (*perf.* пи́скнуть) squeak; cheep, peep; whine; sing.

пищеваре́ние, -я, digestion; расстро́йство пищеваре́ния, indigestion. **пищево́д,** -а, oesophagus, gullet. **пищев|о́й,** food; ~ы́е проду́кты, foodstuffs; foods; eatables.

пия́вка, -и, leech.

ПКиО (*pekeió*) *abbr.* парк культу́ры и о́тдыха, Park of Culture and Rest.

пл. *abbr.* пло́щадь, Square.

пла́вание, -я, swimming; sailing; navigation; voyage; су́дно да́льнего пла́вания, ocean-going ship. **пла́вательный,** swimming, bathing; ~ бассе́йн, swimming-bath, pool. **пла́вать,** -аю *imp.* swim; float; sail. **плавба́за,** -ы, depot ship, factory ship, factory trawler.

плави́льник, -а, crucible. **плави́льный,** melting, smelting; fusion. **плави́льня,** -и, foundry. **плави́льщик,** -а, founder, smelter. **пла́вить,** -влю *imp.* (*perf.* рас~) melt, smelt; fuse; **~ся,** melt; fuse. **пла́вка**, -и, fusing; fusion.

пла́вки, -вок *pl.* bathing trunks.

пла́вк|ий, fusible; fuse; ~ая вста́вка, ~ий предохрани́тель, ~ая про́бка, fuse. **плавле́ние,** -я, melting, fusion. **пла́вленый** сыр, processed cheese.

плавни́к, -а́, fin; flipper. **пла́вный,** smooth, flowing; liquid. **плаву́ч|ий,** floating; buoyant; ~ая льди́на, ice-floe; ~ий мая́к, lightship, floating light; ~ий рыбозаво́д, factory ship.

плагиа́т, -а, plagiarism. **плагиа́тор,** -а, plagiarist.

плака́т, -а, poster, bill; placard. **плакати́ст,** -а, poster artist.

пла́кать, -а́чу *imp.* cry, weep; cry for, weep for; mourn; ~ навзры́д, sob; **~ся,** complain, lament; + на + *acc.* complain of; lament, bewail, bemoan.

плакирова́ть, -ру́ю *perf.* and *imp.* plate. **плакиро́вка,** -и, plating.

пла́кса, -ы, cry-baby. **плакси́вый,** whining; piteous, pathetic. **плаку́чий,** weeping.

пла́менность, -и, ardour. **пла́менный,** flaming, fiery; ardent, burning. **пла́мя,** -мени *n.* flame; fire, blaze.

план, -а, plan; scheme; plane.

планёр, -а, glider. **планери́зм,** -а, gliding. **планери́ст,** -а, glider-pilot. **планёрный,** gliding; ~ спорт, gliding.

плане́та, -ы, planet. **плане́тный,** planetary.

плани́рование[1], -я, planning.

плани́рование[2], -я, gliding; glide.

плани́ровать[1], -рую *imp.* (*perf.* за~) plan.

плани́ровать[2], -рую *imp.* (*perf.* с~), glide, glide down.

пла́нка, -и, lath, slat.

пла́новый, planned, systematic; planning. **планоме́рный,** systematic, planned, balanced, regular.

планше́т, -а, plane-table; map-case.

пласт, -а́, layer; sheet; course; stratum, bed. **пласти́на,** -ы, plate. **пласти́нка,** -и, plate; (gramophone) record, disc.

пласти́ческий, plastic. **пласти́чность,** -и, plasticity. **пласти́чный,** plastic; supple, pliant; rhythmical; fluent, flowing. **пластма́сса,** -ы, plastic. **пластма́ссовый,** plastic.

пла́та, -ы, pay; salary; payment, charge; fee; fare. **платёж,** -а́, payment. **платёжеспосо́бный,** solvent. **платёжный,** payment; pay. **плате́льщик,** -а, payer.

пла́тина, -ы, platinum. **пла́тиновый,** platinum.

плати́ть, -ачу́, -а́тишь *imp.* (*perf.* за∼, у∼) pay; + *instr.* pay back, return; **∼ся** (*perf.* по∼ся) за + *acc.* pay for. **пла́тный,** paid; requiring payment, chargeable; paying.

плато́к, -тка́, shawl; head-scarf; handkerchief.

платфо́рма, -ы, platform; truck.

пла́тье, -я; *gen. pl.* -ьев, clothes, clothing; dress; gown, frock. **платяно́й,** clothes; ∼ шкаф, wardrobe.

плафо́н, -а, ceiling; lamp shade, ceiling light; bowl.

плац, -а, *loc.* -у́, parade-ground. **плацда́рм,** -а, bridgehead, beach-head; base; springboard.

плацка́рта, -ы, reserved-seat ticket.

плач, -а, weeping, crying; wailing; keening; lament. **плаче́вный,** mournful, sad; sorry; lamentable, deplorable. **пла́чу,** etc.: see пла́кать.

плачу́, etc.: see плати́ть.

плашмя́ *adv.* flat, prone.

плащ, -а́, cloak; raincoat; waterproof cape.

плева́тельница, -ы, spittoon. **плева́ть,** плюю́, плюёшь *imp.* (*perf.* на∼, плю́нуть) spit; ∼ в потоло́к, idle, fritter away the time; *impers.* + *dat.*; мне ∼, I don't give a damn, I don't care a rap (на + *acc.* about); **∼ся,** spit. **плево́к,** -вка́, spit, spittle.

плеври́т, -а, pleurisy.

плед, -а, rug; plaid.

плёл, etc.: see плести́.

племенно́й, tribal; pedigree. **пле́мя,** -мени; *pl.* -мена́, -мён *n.* tribe; breed; stock. **племя́нник,** -а, nephew. **племя́нница,** -ы, niece.

плен, -а, *loc.* -у́, captivity.

плена́рный, plenary.

плени́тельный, captivating, fascinating, charming. **плени́ть,** -ню́ *perf.* (*imp.* пленя́ть) take prisoner take captive; captivate, fascinate, charm; **∼ся,** be captivated, be fascinated.

плёнка, film; pellicle.

пле́нник, -а, prisoner, captive. **пле́нный,** captive.

плёночный, film; filmy.

пленя́ть(ся, -я́ю(сь *imp.* of плени́ть(ся.

пле́сенный, mouldy, musty. **пле́сень,** -и, mould.

плеск, -а, splash, plash, lapping. **плеска́тельный** бассе́йн, paddling pool. **плеска́ть,** -ещу́, -е́щешь *imp.* (*perf.* плесну́ть) splash, plash; lap; **∼ся,** splash; lap.

пле́сневеть, -еет *imp.* (*perf.* за∼), go mouldy, grow musty.

плесну́ть, -ну́, -нёшь *perf.* of плеска́ть.

плести́, -ету́, -етёшь; плёл, -а́ *imp.* (*perf.* с∼) plait, braid; weave; tat; spin; net; ∼ вздор, ∼ чепуху́, talk rubbish; **∼сь,** drag oneself along; trudge; ∼сь в хвосте́, lag behind. **плете́ние,** -я, plaiting, braiding; wickerwork. **плетёнка,** -и, (wicker) mat, basket; hurdle. **плетён|ый,** woven; wattled; wicker. **плете́нь,** -тня *m.* hurdle; wattle fencing. **плётка,** -и, **плеть,** -и; *gen. pl.* -е́й, lash.

пле́чико, -а; *pl.* -и, -ов, shoulder-strap; *pl.* coat-hanger; padded shoulders. **плечи́стый,** broad-shouldered. **плечо́,** -а́; *pl.* -и, -а́м, shoulder; arm.

плеши́веть, -ею *imp.* (*perf.* о∼) grow bald. **плеши́вый,** bald. **плеши́на,** -ы, **плешь,** -и, bald patch; bare patch.

плещу́, etc.: see плеска́ть.

пли́нтус, -а, plinth; skirting-board.

плис, -а, velveteen. **пли́совый,** velveteen.

плиссиро́ванный, pleated. **плиссирова́ть,** -ру́ю *imp.* pleat.

плита́, -ы́; *pl.* -ы plate, slab; flag(stone); stove, cooker; моги́льная ∼, gravestone, tombstone. **пли́тка,** -и, tile; (thin) slab; stove, cooker; ∼

шоколáда, bar, block, of chocolate. **плúточный**, tile, of tiles; ~ пол, tiled floor.

пловéц, -вцá, **пловчúха**, -и, swimmer. **пловýчий**, floating; buoyant.

плод, -á, fruit; **приносить** ~ы́, bear fruit. **плодúть**, -ожý *imp.* (*perf.* рас~) produce, procreate; engender; **~ся**, multiply; propagate. **плóдный**, fertile; fertilized.

плодо- in *comb.* fruit-. **плодовúтый**, fruitful, prolific; fertile. **~вóдство**, -а, fruit-growing. **~нóсный**, fruit-bearing, fruitful. **~овощнóй**, fruit and vegetable. **~рóдный**, fertile. **~смéн|ый**; ~смéнная систéма, rotation of crops. **~твóрный**, fruitful.

плóмба, -ы, stamp, seal; stopping; filling. **пломбировáть**, -рýю *imp.* (*perf.* за~, о~) seal; stop, fill.

плóский; -сок, скá, -о, flat; plane; trivial, tame.

плóско- in *comb.* flat. **плоскогóрье**, -я, plateau; tableland. **~грýдый**, flat-chested. **~гýбцы**, -ев *pl.* pliers. **~дóнный**, flat-bottomed. **~стóпие**, -я, flat feet.

плóскость, -и; *gen. pl.* -éй, flatness; plane; platitude, triviality.

плот, -á, raft.

плотúна, -ы, dam; weir; dike, dyke.

плóтник, -а, carpenter, joiner.

плóтно *adv.* close(ly), tight(ly). **плóтность**, -и, thickness; compactness; solidity, strength; density. **плóтный**; -тен, -тнá, -о, thick; compact; dense; solid, strong; thickset, solidly built; tightly-filled; square, hearty.

плотоя́дный, carnivorous; lustful.

плоть -и flesh

плóхо *adv.* badly; ill; bad; ~ кóнчить, come to a bad end; чýвствовать себя́ ~, feel unwell, feel bad; *sb.* bad mark. **плоховáтый**, rather bad, not too good. **плохóй**, bad; poor.

площáдка, -и, area, (sports) ground, playground; site; landing; platform. **плóщадь**, -и; *gen. pl.* -éй, area; space; square.

плóще, *comp.* of плóский.

плуг, -а; *pl*, -ú, plough.

плут, -á, cheat, swindler, knave; rogue. **плутовáтый**, cunning. **плутовáть**, -тýю *imp.* (*perf.* с~) cheat, swindle. **плутовскóй**, knavish; roguish, mischievous; picaresque.

плыть, -ывý, -ывёшь; плыл, -á, -о *imp.* swim; float; drift; sail; ~ стóя, tread water.

плю́нуть, -ну *perf.* of плевáть.

плюс, -а, plus; advantage.

плюш, -а, plush. **плю́шевый**, plush; plush-covered.

плющ, -á, ivy.

плюю́, etc.: see плевáть.

пляж, -а, beach.

плясáть, -яшý, -я́шешь *imp.* (*perf.* с~) dance. **пля́ска**, -и, dance; dancing. **плясов|óй**, dancing; **~áя** *sb.* dance tune, dancing song. **плясýн**, -á, **плясýнья**, -и; *gen. pl.* -ий, dancer.

пневмáтик, -а, pneumatic tyre. **пневматúческий**, pneumatic.

пнуть, пну, пнёшь *perf.* of пинáть.

пня, etc.. see пень.

по *prep.* I. + *dat.* on; along; round, about; by; over; according to; in accordance with; for; in: at; by (reason of); on account of; from; жить по срéдствам, live within one's means; идтú по следáм + *gen.* follow in the track(s) of; идтú по травé, walk on the grass; лýчший по кáчеству, better in quality; передáть по рáдио, broadcast; по áдресу + *gen.*, to the address of; по вóздуху, by air; по дéлу, on business; по úмени, by name; по любвú, for love; по мáтери, on the mother's side; по ошúбке, by mistake; по положéнию, by one's position; ex officio; по понедéльникам, on Mondays; по пóчте, by post; по прáву, by right, by rights; по происхождéнию, by descent, by origin; по профéссии, by profession; по рáдио, over the radio; по рассéянности, from absent-mindedness; по утрáм, in the mornings; товáрищ по шкóле, school-fellow; тоскá по дóму, по рóдине, homesickness; чемпиóн по шáхматам, chess champion. II. + *dat.* or *acc.* of cardinal number, forms distributive number; пó два, пó двое, in twos, two by two; по пять рублей шту́ка, at five roubles each; по рублю́ шту́ка, one rouble each; по ча́су в день, an hour a day. III. + *acc.* to, up to; for, to get; идти́ по грибы́, go to get mushrooms; по пе́рвое сентября́, up to (and including) the first of September; по по́яс, up to the waist; по ту сто́рону, on that side. IV. + *prep.* on, (immediately) after; for; носи́ть тра́ур по, be in mourning for; по нём, to his liking; по прибы́тии, on arrival.

по-[1] *vbl. pref.* forms the perfective aspect; indicates action of short duration or incomplete or indefinite character, and action repeated at intervals or of indeterminate duration.

по-[2] *pref.* I. in *comb.* with dative case of adjectives, or with adverbs ending in -и, indicates manner of action, conduct, etc., use of a named language, or accordance with the opinion or wish of; говори́ть по-ру́сски, speak Russian; жить по-ста́рому, live in the old style; по-мо́ему, in my opinion. II. in *comb.* with adjectives and nouns, indicates situation along or near something. **пово́лжский,** situated on the Volga. **пово́лжье,** -я, the Volga region. **помо́ры,** -ов *pl.* native Russian inhabitants of White-Sea coasts. **помо́рье,** -я, seaboard, coastal region. III. in *comb.* with comparative of adjectives indicates a smaller degree of comparison, slightly more (or less) ...; поме́ньше, a little less; помоло́же, rather younger.

по|багрове́ть, -е́ю *perf.*

поба́иваться, -аюсь *imp.* be rather afraid.

побе́г[1], -а, flight; escape.

побе́г[2], -а, sprout, shoot; sucker; set; graft.

побегу́шки; быть на побегу́шках у + *gen.* run errands for; be at the beck and call of.

побе́да, -ы, victory. **победи́тель,** -я *m.* victor, conqueror; winner. **победи́ть,** -и́шь *perf.* (*imp.* побежда́ть) conquer, vanquish; defeat; master, overcome. **побе́дный** **победоно́сный,** victorious, triumphant.

побежда́ть, -а́ю *imp.* of победи́ть.

по|беле́ть, -е́ю *perf.* **по|бели́ть,** -лю́, -е́ли́шь *perf.*

побере́жный, coastal. **побере́жье,** -я, (sea-)coast, seaboard, littoral.

по|беспоко́ить(ся, -о́ю(сь *perf.*

побира́ться, -а́юсь *imp.* beg; live by begging.

по|би́ть(ся, -бью́(сь, -бьёшь(ся *perf.* **по|благодари́ть,** -рю́ *perf.*

побла́жка, -и, indulgence.

по|бледне́ть, -е́ю *perf.* **по|блёкнуть,** -ну; -блёк *perf.*

побли́зости *adv.* near at hand, hereabouts.

по|божи́ться, -жу́сь, -жи́шься *perf.*

побо́и, -ев *pl.* beating, blows. **побо́ище,** -а, slaughter, carnage; bloody battle.

побо́рник, -а, champion, upholder, advocate. **поборо́ть,** -рю́, -решь *perf.* overcome; fight down; beat.

побо́чн|ый, secondary, accessory; collateral; ~ый проду́кт, by-product; ~ая рабо́та, side-line; ~ый сын, natural son.

по|брани́ться, -ню́сь *perf.*

по|брата́ться, -а́юсь *perf.* **по-бра́тски** *adv.* like a brother; fraternally. **побрати́мы,** -ов *pl.* twin cities.

по|бре́згать, -аю *perf.* **по|бри́ть(ся,** -бре́ю(сь *perf.*

побуди́тельный, stimulating. **побуди́ть,** -ужу́ *perf.*, **побужда́ть.** -а́ю *imp.* induce, impel, prompt, spur. **побужде́ние,** -я, motive; inducement; incentive.

побыва́ть, -а́ю *perf.* have been, have visited; look in, visit. **побы́вка,** -и, leave, furlough; прие́хать на побы́вку, come on leave. **побы́ть,** -бу́ду, -дешь; по́был, -а́, -о *perf.* stay (for a short time).

побью́(сь, etc.: see поби́ть(ся.

пова́дить, -а́жу *perf.*, **пова́живать,** -аю *imp.* accustom; train; **~ся,** get into the habit (of). **пова́дка,** -и, habit.

по|вали́ть(ся, -лю́(сь, -лишь(ся *perf.*

пова́льно *adv.* without exception. **пова́льный,** general, mass; epidemic.

по́вар, -а; *pl.* -а́, cook, chef. **пова́ренный,** culinary; cookery, cooking.

по-ва́шему *adv.* in your opinion; as you wish.
поведе́ние, -я, conduct, behaviour.
поведу́, etc.: see повести́. **по|везти́, -зу́, -зёшь; -вёз, -ла́** *perf.* **повёл,** etc.: see повести́.
повелева́ть, -а́ю *imp.*+*instr.* command, rule; + *dat.* enjoin. **повеле́ние, -я,** command, injunction. **повели́тельный,** imperious, peremptory; authoritative; imperative.
по|венча́ть(ся, -а́ю(сь *perf.*
поверга́ть, -а́ю *imp.*, **пове́ргнуть, -ну; -ве́рг** *perf.* throw down; lay low; plunge.
пове́ренная *sb.* confidante. **пове́ренный** *sb.* attorney; confidant; ~ в дела́х, chargé d'affaires. **пове́рить, -рю** *perf.* (*imp.* поверя́ть) believe; check, verify; confide, entrust. **пове́рка, -и,** check-up, check; verification; proof; roll-call; ~ вре́мени, time-signal.
поверну́ть, -ну́, -нёшь *perf.*, **повёртывать, -аю** *imp.* (*imp.* also повора́чивать) turn; change; **~ся,** turn; ~ся спино́й к + *dat.* turn one's back on.
пове́рх *prep.*+*gen.* over, above. **пове́рхностн|ый,** surface, superficial; shallow; perfunctory; ~ое унаво́живание, top dressing. **пове́рхность, -и** surface.
пове́рье, -я; *gen. pl.* **-ий,** popular belief, superstition. **поверя́ть, -я́ю** *imp.* of пове́рить.
по|веселе́ть, -е́ю *perf.* **пове́сить(ся, -ве́шу(сь** *perf.* of ве́шать(ся.
повествова́ние, -я narrative, narration. **повествова́телный,** narrative. **повествова́ть, -тву́ю** *imp.* + о + *prep.* narrate, recount, relate, tell about.
по|вести́, -еду́, -едёшь; -вёл, -а́ *perf.* (*imp.* also поводи́ть) + *instr.* move; ~ бровя́ми, raise one's eyebrows.
пове́стка, -и, notice, notification; summons; writ; signal; last post; ~ (дня), agenda.
по́весть, -и; *gen. pl.* **-е́й,** story, tale.
пове́трие, -я, epidemic; infection.
пове́шу, etc.: see пове́сить. **по|вздо́рить, -рю** *perf.*
повива́льн|ый, obstetric; ~ая ба́бка, midwife.
по|вида́ть(ся, -а́ю(сь *perf.* **по|вини́ться, -ню́сь** *perf.*
пови́нность, -и, duty, obligation; во́инская ~, conscription. **пови́нный,** guilty; obliged, bound.
повинова́ться, -ну́юсь *perf.* and *imp.* obey. **повинове́ние, -я,** obedience.
повиса́ть, -а́ю *imp.*, **по|ви́снуть, -ну; -ви́с** *perf.* hang on; hang down, droop; hang; ~ в во́здухе, hang in mid-air.
по|влажне́ть, -е́ет *perf.*
повле́чь, -еку́, -ечёшь; -ёк, -ла́ *perf.* drag; pull behind one; ~ (за собо́й), entail, bring in its train.
по|влия́ть, -я́ю *perf.*
по́вод[1], **-а,** occasion, cause, ground; по ~у+*gen.* a propos of, as regards, concerning.
по́вод[2], **-а,** *loc.* **-у́;** *pl.* **-о́дья, -ьев,** rein; быть на ~у́ у + *gen.* be under the thumb of. **поводи́ть, -ожу́, -о́дишь** *imp.* of повести́. **поводо́к, -дка́,** rein; lead.
пово́зка, -и, cart; vehicle, conveyance; (unsprung) carriage.
пово́лжский, пово́лжье: see по-[2] II.
повора́чивать(ся, -аю(сь *imp.* of поверну́ть(ся, повороти́ть(ся; повора́чивайся, -айтесь! get a move on! look sharp! look lively!
по|ворожи́ть, -жу́ *perf.*
поворо́т, -а, turn, turning; bend; turning-point. **повороти́ть(ся, -рочу́(сь -ро́тишь(ся** *perf.* (*imp.* повора́чивать(ся) turn. **поворо́тливый,** nimble, agile, quick; manoeuvrable. **поворо́тный,** turning; rotary, rotating; revolving; ~ круг, turntable; ~ мост, swing bridge; ~ пункт, turning point.
по|вреди́ть, -ежу́ *perf.*, **повређда́ть, -а́ю** *imp.* damage; injure, hurt; **~ся,** be damaged; be injured, be hurt. **поврежде́ние, -я,** damage, injury.
повремени́ть, -ню́ *perf.* wait a little; + с + *instr.* linger over, delay. **повреме́нный,** periodic, periodical; by time.
повседне́вно *adv.* daily, every day. **повседне́вный,** daily; everyday.
повсеме́стно *adv.* everywhere, in all parts. **повсеме́стный,** universal, general.

повста́нец, -нца, rebel, insurgent, insurrectionist. **повста́нческий,** rebel; insurgent.

повсю́ду *adv.* everywhere.

повторе́ние, -я, repetition; reiteration. **повтори́тельный,** repeated; revision. **повтори́ть,** -рю́ *perf.*, **повторя́ть,** -я́ю *imp.* repeat; **~ся,** repeat oneself; be repeated; recur. **повто́рный,** repeated; recurring.

повы́сить, -ы́шу *perf.*, **повыша́ть,** -а́ю *imp.* raise, heighten; promote, prefer, advance; ~ вдвое́, втрое́, double, treble; ~ го́лос, ~ тон, raise one's voice; **~ся,** rise; improve; be promoted, receive advancement. **повыше́ние,** -я, rise, increase; advancement, promotion. **повы́шенн|ый,** heightened, increased; ~ое настрое́ние, state of excitement; ~ая температу́ра, high temperature.

повяза́ть, -яжу́, -я́жешь *perf.*, **повя́зывать,** -аю *imp.* tie. **повя́зка,** -и, band, bandeau, fillet; bandage.

по|гада́ть, -а́ю *perf.*

пога́нец, -нца, swine; scoundrel. **пога́нить,** -ню *imp.* (*perf.* о~) pollute, defile. **пога́нка,** -и, toadstool. **пога́ный,** foul; unclean; filthy, vile; ~ гриб, toadstool, poisonous mushroom.

погаса́ть, -а́ю *imp.*, **по|га́снуть,** -ну *perf.* go out, be extinguished. **по|гаси́ть,** -ашу́, -а́сишь *perf.* **погаша́ть,** -а́ю *imp.* liquidate, cancel. **пога́шенный,** used, cancelled, cashed.

погиба́ть, -а́ю *imp.*, **по|ги́бнуть,** -ну; -ги́б *perf.* perish; be lost. **поги́бель,** -и, ruin, perdition. **поги́бельный,** ruinous, fatal. **поги́бший,** lost; ruined; killed; число́ поги́бших, death-roll.

по|гла́дить, -а́жу *perf.*

поглоти́ть, -ощу́, -о́тишь *perf.*, **поглоща́ть,** -а́ю *imp.* swallow up; take up; absorb.

по|глупе́ть, -е́ю *perf.*

по|гляде́ть(ся, -яжу́(сь *perf.* **погля́дывать,** -аю *imp.* glance; look from time to time; + за + *instr.* keep an eye on.

погна́ть, -гоню́, -го́нишь; -гна́л, -а́, -о *perf.* drive; begin to drive; **~ся** за + *instr.* run after; start in pursuit of, give chase to; strive for, strive after.

по|гну́ть(ся, -ну́(сь, -нёшь(ся *perf.* **по|гнуша́ться,** -а́юсь *perf.*

поговóрка, -и, saying, proverb; byword.

пого́да, -ы, weather.

погоди́ть, -ожу́ *perf.* wait a little, wait a bit; немно́го погодя́, a little later.

поголо́вно *adv.* one and all; to a man. **поголо́вный,** general, universal; capitation, poll. **поголо́вье,** -я, head, number.

по|голубе́ть, -е́ет *perf.*

пого́н, -а; *gen. pl.* -о́н, shoulder-strap; (rifle-)sling.

пого́нщик, -а, driver. **погоню́,** etc.: see погна́ть. **пого́ня,** -и, pursuit, chase. **погоня́ть,** -я́ю *imp.* urge on, drive.

погора́ть, -а́ю *imp.*, **погоре́ть,** -рю́ *perf.* burn down; be burnt out; lose everything in a fire. **погоре́лец,** -льца, one who has been burnt out.

пограни́чник, -а, frontier guard. **пограни́чн|ый,** frontier; boundary; ~ая полоса́, border; ~ая стра́жа, frontier guards.

по́греб, -а; *pl.* -а́, cellar. **погреба́льн|ый,** funeral; ~ая колесни́ца, hearse. **погреба́ть,** -а́ю *imp.* of погрести́. **погребе́ние,** -я, burial.

погрему́шка, -и, rattle.

погрести́[1], -ебу́, -ебёшь; -рёб, -ла́ *perf.* (*imp.* погреба́ть) bury.

погрести́[2], -ебу́, -ебёшь; -рёб, -ла́ *perf.* row for a while.

погре́ть, -е́ю *perf.* warm; **~ся,** warm oneself.

погреша́ть, -а́ю *imp.*, **по|греши́ть,** -шу́ *perf.* sin; err. **погре́шность,** -и, error, mistake, inaccuracy.

по|грози́ть(ся, -ожу́(сь *perf.* **по|грубе́ть,** -е́ю *perf.*

погружа́ть, -а́ю *imp.*, **по|грузи́ть,** -ужу́, -у́зишь *perf.* load; ship; dip, plunge, immerse; submerge; duck; **~ся,** sink, plunge; submerge, dive; be plunged, absorbed, buried, lost. **погруже́ние,** -я, sinking, submergence; immersion; dive, diving. **погру́зка,** -и, loading; shipment.

погряза́ть, -а́ю *imp.*, **по|гря́знуть,** -ну; -я́з *perf.* be bogged down, be stuck.

по|губи́ть, -блю́, -бишь *perf.* **по|гуля́ть,** -я́ю *perf.* **по|густе́ть,** -е́ет *perf.*

под, подо *prep.* I. + *acc.* or *instr.* under; near, close to; быть ~ ружьём, be under arms; взять по́д руку + *acc.* take the arm of; ~ ви́дом + *gen.* under the guise of; по́д гору, down hill; ~ замко́м, under lock and key; ~ землёй, underground; ~ Москво́й, in the neighbourhood of Moscow; ~ руко́й, (close) at hand, to hand. II. + *instr.* occupied by, used as; (meant, implied) by; in, with; говя́дина ~ хре́ном, beef with horse-radish; по́ле ~ карто́фелем potato-field. III. + *acc.* towards; on the eve of; to (the accompaniment of); in imitation of; on; for, to serve as; ему ~ пятьдеся́т (лет), he is getting on for fifty; ~ аплодисме́нты, to applause; ~ ве́чер, towards evening; подде́лка ~ же́мчуг, fake pearls; ~ дикто́вку, from dictation; ~ зву́ки му́зыки, to the sound of music; ~ коне́ц, towards the end; ~ Но́вый год, on New Year's Eve; шу́ба ~ ко́тик, imitation sealskin coat.

под-, подо-, подъ-. I. *vbl. pref.* indicating action from beneath or affecting lower part of something, motion upwards or towards a point, slight or insufficient action or effect, supplementary action, underhand action. II. *pref.* of nouns and adjs., under-, sub-.

подава́льщик, -а, waiter; supplier. **подава́льщица,** -ы, waitress. **подава́ть(ся,** -даю́(сь, -даёшь(ся *imp.* of пода́ть(ся.

подави́ть, -влю́, -вишь *perf.*, **подавля́ть,** -я́ю *imp.* suppress, put down; repress; depress; crush, overwhelm. **по|дави́ться,** -влю́сь, -вишься *perf.* **подавле́ние,** -я, suppression; repression. **пода́вленность,** -и, depression; blues. **пода́вленный,** suppressed; depressed, dispirited. **подавля́ющ|ий,** overwhelming; overpowering; ~ее большинство́, overwhelming majority.

пода́вно *adv.* much less, all the more.

пода́льше *adv.* a little further.

по|дари́ть, -рю́, -ришь *perf.* **пода́рок,** -рка, present gift.

пода́тель, -я *m.* bearer; ~ проше́ния, petitioner. **пода́тливый,** pliant, pliable; complaisant. **по́дать,** -и; *gen. pl.* -е́й, tax duty, assessment. **пода́ть,** -а́м, -а́шь, -а́ст, -ади́м; по́дал, -а́, -о *perf.* (*imp.* подава́ть) serve; give; put, move, turn; put forward, present, hand in; display; обе́д по́дан, dinner is served; ~ в отста́вку, send in one's resignation; ~ в суд на + *acc.*, bring an action against; ~ го́лос, vote; ~ жа́лобу, lodge a complaint; ~ заявле́ние, hand in an application; ~ мяч, serve; ~ ру́ку, hold out one's hand; ~ телегра́мму, send a telegram; **~ся,** move; give way, yield; cave in, collapse; + на + *acc.* make for, set out for; ~ся в сто́рону, move aside; ~ся наза́д, draw back. **пода́ча,** -и, giving, presenting; service, serve; feed, supply; introduction; ~ голосо́в, voting. **пода́чка,** -и, (charitable) gift; pittance. **подаю́,** etc.: see подава́ть. **подая́ние,** -я, charity, alms; dole.

подбега́ть, -а́ю *imp.*, **подбежа́ть,** -егу́ *perf.* run up, come running up.

подбива́ть, -а́ю *imp.* of подби́ть. **подби́вка,** -и, lining; re-soling.

подберу́, etc.: see подобра́ться. **подбира́ть(ся,** -а́ю(сь *imp.* of подобра́ть(ся.

подби́тый, bruised; lined; padded; ~ глаз, black eye. **подби́ть,** -добью́, -добьёшь *perf.* (*imp.* подбива́ть), line; pad, wad; re-sole; injure, bruise; put out of action, knock out, shoot down; incite, instigate.

подбодри́ть, -рю́ *perf.*, **подбодря́ть,** -я́ю *imp.*, cheer up, encourage; **~ся,** cheer up, take heart.

подбо́йка, -и, lining; re-soling.

подбо́р, -а, selection, assortment; в ~ run on; (как) на ~, choice, well-matched.

подборо́док, -дка, chin.

подбоче́ниваться, -аюсь *imp.*, **подбоче́ниться,** -нюсь *perf.* place one's arms akimbo. **подбоче́нившись** *adv.* with arms akimbo, with hands on hips.

подбра́сывать, -аю *imp.*, **подбро́сить,** -ро́шу *perf.* throw up, toss up; throw in, throw on; abandon, leave surreptitiously.

подва́л, -а, cellar; basement; (article appearing at) foot of page. **подва́льный,** basement, cellar.

подведу́, etc.: see подвести́.

подвезти́, -зу́, -зёшь; -вёз, -ла́ *perf.* (*imp.* подвози́ть) bring, take; give a lift.

подвене́чн|ый, wedding; ~ое пла́тье, wedding-dress.

подверга́ть, -а́ю *imp.*, **подве́ргнуть,** -ну; -ве́рг *perf.* subject; expose; ~ опа́сности, expose to danger; ~ сомне́нию, call in question. **подве́рженный** subject, liable; susceptible.

подве́сить, -е́шу *perf.* (*imp.* подве́шивать) hang up, suspend; **~ся,** hang, be suspended. **подвесно́й,** hanging, suspended, pendant; overhead; suspension; ~ дви́гатель, мото́р, outboard motor, engine.

подвести́, -еду́, -едёшь; -вёл, -а́ *perf.* (*imp.* подводи́ть) lead up, bring up; place (under); bring under, subsume; put together; let down; ~ ито́ги, reckon up; sum up; ~ фунда́мент, underpin.

подве́шивать(ся, -аю(сь *imp.* of подве́сить(ся.

по́двиг, -а, exploit, feat; heroic deed.

подвига́ть(ся, -а́ю(сь *imp.* of подви́нуть(ся.

подвижно́й, mobile; movable; travelling; lively; agile; ~ соста́в, rolling-stock. **подви́жный,** mobile; lively; agile.

подвиза́ться, -а́юсь *imp.* (в or на + *prep.*) work (in), make a career (in).

подви́нуть, -ну *perf.* (*imp.* подвига́ть) move; push; advance, push forward; **~ся,** move; advance, progress.

подвла́стный + *dat.* subject to; under the jurisdiction of.

подво́да, -ы, cart. **подводи́ть,** -ожу́, -о́дишь *imp.* of подвести́.

подво́дник, -а, submariner. **подво́дн|ый,** submarine; underwater; ~ая скала́ reef.

подво́з, -а, transport; supply. **подвози́ть,** -ожу́, -о́зишь *imp.* of подвезти́.

подворо́тня, -и; *gen. pl.* -тен, gateway.

подво́х, -а, trick.

подвы́пивший, a bit tight.

подвяза́ть, -яжу́, -я́жешь *perf.*, **подвя́зывать,** -аю *imp.* tie up; keep up. **подвя́зка,** -и, garter; suspender.

подгиба́ть(ся, -а́ю(сь *imp.* of подогну́ть(ся.

подгляде́ть, -яжу́ *perf.*, **подгля́дывать,** -аю *imp.* peep; spy, watch furtively.

подгова́ривать, -аю *imp.*, **подговори́ть,** -рю́ *perf.* put up, incite, instigate.

подголо́сок, -ска, second part, supporting voice; yes-man.

подгоню́, etc.: see подогна́ть. **подгоня́ть,** -я́ю *imp.* of подогна́ть.

подгора́ть, -а́ет *imp.*, **подгоре́ть,** -ри́т *perf.* get a bit burnt. **подгоре́лый,** slightly burnt.

подготови́тельный, preparatory. **подгото́вить,** -влю *perf.*, **подготовля́ть,** -я́ю *imp.* prepare; ~ по́чву, pave the way; **~ся,** prepare, get ready. **подгото́вка,** -и, preparation, training; grounding, schooling. **подгото́вленность,** -и, preparedness.

поддава́ться, -даю́сь, -даёшься *imp.* of подда́ться.

подда́кивать, -аю *imp.* agree, assent.

по́дданный *sb.* subject; national. **по́дданство,** -а, citizenship, nationality. **подда́ться,** -а́мся, -а́шься, -а́стся, -адимся; -а́лся, -ла́сь *perf.* (*imp.* поддава́ться) yield, give way, give in; не ~ описа́нию, beggar description.

подде́лать, -аю *perf.*, **подде́лывать,** -аю *imp.* counterfeit, falsify, fake; forge; fabricate. **подде́лка,** -и, falsification; forgery; counterfeit; imitation, fake; ~ под же́мчуг, artificial pearls. **подде́льный,** false, counterfeit; forged; sham, spurious.

поддержа́ние, -я, maintenance, support. **поддержа́ть,** -жу́, -жишь *perf.*, **подде́рживать,** -аю *imp.* support; back up, second; keep up, maintain; bear; ~ поря́док, maintain order. **подде́ржка,** -и, support; encouragement, backing; seconding; prop, stay; при подде́ржке + *gen.* with the support of.

поддра́знивать, -аю *imp.*, **поддразни́ть,** -ню́, -нишь *perf.* tease (slightly).
поддува́ло, -а, ash-pit.
по|де́йствовать, -твую *perf.*
поде́лать, -аю *perf.* do; ничего́ не поде́лаешь, it can't be helped, there's nothing to be done about it.
по|дели́ть(ся, -лю́(сь, -лишь(ся *perf.*
поде́лка, -и, *pl.* small (hand-made) articles.
подело́м *adv.*; ~ ему́ (etc.), it serves him (etc.) right.
подённо *adv.*, **подённый,** by the day; подённая опла́та, payment by the day. **подёнщик,** -а, day-labourer, workman hired by the day. **подёнщица,** -ы, daily, char.
подёргивание, -я, twitch, twitching; jerk. **подёргиваться,** -аюсь *imp.* twitch.
подёржанный, second-hand.
подёрнуть, -нет *perf.* cover, coat; **~ся,** be covered.
подеру́, etc.: see подра́ть. **по|дешеве́ть,** -е́ет *perf.*
поджа́ривать(ся, -аю(сь *imp.*, **поджа́рить(ся,** -рю(сь *perf.* fry, roast, grill; brown, toast. **поджа́ристый,** brown, browned; crisp.
поджа́рый, lean, wiry, sinewy.
поджа́ть, -дожму́, -дожмёшь *perf.* (*imp.* поджима́ть) draw in, draw under; ~ гу́бы, purse one's lips; ~ хвост, have one's tail between one's legs.
поджёчь, -дожгу́, -ожжёшь; -жёг, -дожгла́ *perf.*, **поджига́ть,** -а́ю *imp.* set fire to, set on fire; burn. **поджига́тель,** -я *m.* incendiary; instigator; ~ войны́, warmonger. **поджига́тельский,** inflammatory.
поджида́ть, -а́ю *imp.* (+ *gen.*) wait (for); lie in wait (for).
поджима́ть, -а́ю *imp.* of поджа́ть.
поджо́г, -а, arson.
подзаголо́вок, -вка, subtitle, sub-heading.
подзадо́ривать, -аю *imp.*, **подзадо́рить,** -рю *perf.* egg on, set on.
подзащи́тный *sb.* client.
подземе́лье, -я; *gen. pl.* -лий, cave; dungeon. **подзе́мка,** -и, underground, tube. **подзе́мный,** underground, subterranean.
подзо́рн|ый; ~ая труба́, telescope.
подзову́, etc.: see подозва́ть. **подзыва́ть,** -а́ю *imp.* of подозва́ть.
подиви́ть, -влю́ *perf.* astonish, amaze. **по|диви́ться,** -влю́сь *perf.*
подка́пывать(ся, -аю(сь *imp.* of подкопа́ть(ся.
подкарау́ливать, -аю *imp.*, **подкарау́лить,** -лю *perf.* be on the watch (for), lie in wait (for); catch.
подка́рмливать, -аю *imp.* of подкорми́ть.
подкати́ть, -ачу́, -а́тишь *perf.*, **подка́тывать,** -аю *imp.* roll up, drive up; roll.
подка́шивать(ся, -аю(сь *imp.* of подкоси́ть(ся.
подки́дывать, -аю *imp.*, **подки́нуть,** -ну *perf.* throw up, toss up; throw in, throw on; abandon. **подки́дыш,** -а, foundling.
подкла́дка, -и, lining; на шёлковой подкла́дке, silk-lined. **подкла́дочный,** lining. **подкла́дывать,** -аю *imp.* of подложи́ть.
подкле́ивать, -аю *imp.*, **подкле́ить,** -е́ю *perf.* glue, paste; glue up, paste up; stick together, mend. **подкле́йка,** -и, glueing, pasting; sticking.
подко́ва, -ы, (horse-)shoe. **под|кова́ть,** -кую, -ёшь *perf.*, **подко́вывать,** -аю *imp.* shoe.
подко́жный, subcutaneous, hypodermic.
подкоми́ссия, -и, **подкомите́т,** -а, subcommittee.
подко́п, -а, undermining; underground passage; intrigue, underhand plotting. **подкопа́ть,** -а́ю *perf.* (*imp.* подка́пывать), undermine, sap; **~ся** под + *acc.* undermine, sap; burrow under; intrigue against.
подкорми́ть, -млю́, -мишь *perf.* (*imp.* подка́рмливать) top-dress, give a top-dressing; feed up. **подко́рмка,** -и, top-dressing.
подкоси́ть, -ошу́, -о́сишь *perf.* (*imp.* подка́шивать) cut down; fell, lay low; **~ся,** give way, fail one.
подкра́дываться, -аюсь *imp.* of подкра́сться.

подкра́сить, -а́шу *perf.* (*imp.* подкра́шивать), touch up; tint, colour; **~ся,** make up lightly.
подкра́сться, -аду́сь, -адёшься *perf.* (*imp.* подкра́дываться) steal up, sneak up.
подкра́шивать(ся, -аю(сь *imp.* of подкра́сить(ся. **подкра́шу,** etc.: see подкра́сить.
подкрепи́ть, -плю́ *perf.*, **подкрепля́ть,** -я́ю *imp.* reinforce; support; back; confirm, corroborate; fortify recruit the strength of; **~ся,** fortify oneself. **подкрепле́ние,** -я, confirmation, corroboration; sustenance; reinforcement.
по́дкуп, -а, bribery. **подкупа́ть,** -а́ю *imp.*, **подкупи́ть,** -плю́, -пишь *perf.* bribe; suborn; win over.
подла́диться, -а́жусь *perf.*, **подла́живаться** -аюсь *imp.* + к + *dat.* adapt oneself to, fit in with; humour; make up to.
подла́мываться, -ается *imp.* of подломи́ться.
по́дле *prep.* + *gen.* by the side of, beside.
подлежа́ть, -жу́ *imp.* + *dat.* be liable to, be subject to; не подлежи́т сомне́нию, it is beyond doubt; unquestionably. **подлежа́щее** *sb.* subject. **подлежа́щий** + *dat.* liable to, subject to; не ~ оглаше́нию, confidential, private; off the record.
подлеза́ть, -а́ю *imp.*, **подле́зть,** -зу; -е́з *perf.* crawl (under), creep (under).
подле́ц, -а́, scoundrel, villain.
подлива́ть, -а́ю *imp.* of подли́ть. **подли́вка,** -и, sauce, dressing; gravy. **подливн|о́й;** ~о́е колесо́ undershot wheel.
подли́за, -ы *m.* and *f.* lickspittle, toady. **подлиза́ться,** -ижу́сь, -и́жешься *perf.*, **подли́зываться,** -аюсь *imp.* + к + *dat.* make up to, suck up to; wheedle.
по́длинник, -а, original. **по́длинно** *adv.* really; genuinely. **по́длинн|ый,** genuine; authentic; original; true, real; с ~ым ве́рно, certified true copy.
подли́ть, -долью́, -дольёшь; по́длил, -а́, -о *perf.* (*imp.* подлива́ть) pour; add; ~ ма́сла в ого́нь, add fuel to the flames.
подло́г, -а, forgery.
подложи́ть, -жу́, -жишь *perf.* (*imp.* подкла́дывать) add; + под + *acc.* lay under; line.
подло́жный, false, spurious; counterfeit, forged.
подломи́ться, -о́мится *perf.* (*imp.* подла́мываться) break; give way under one.
по́длость, -и, meanness, baseness; mean trick, low trick.
подлу́нный, sublunar.
по́длый; подл, -а́, -о, mean, base, ignoble.
подма́зать, -а́жу *perf.*, **подма́зывать,** -аю *imp.* grease, oil; paint; give bribes, grease palms.
подманда́тный, mandated.
подмасте́рье, -я; *gen. pl.* -ьев *m.* apprentice.
подме́н, -а, **подме́на,** -ы, replacement. **подме́нивать,** -аю *imp.*, **подмени́ть,** -ню́, -нишь *perf.*, **подменя́ть,** -я́ю *imp.* replace.
подмести́, -ету́, -етёшь; -мёл, -а́ *perf.*, **подмета́ть**[1], -а́ю *imp.* sweep.
подмета́ть[2], -а́ю *perf.* (*imp.* подмётывать) baste, tack.
подме́тить, -е́чу *perf.* (*imp.* подмеча́ть) notice.
подмётка, -и, sole.
подмётывать, -аю *imp.* of подмета́ть[2]. **подмеча́ть,** -а́ю *imp.* of подме́тить.
подмеша́ть, -а́ю *perf.*, **подме́шивать,** -аю *imp.* mix in, stir in.
подми́гивать, -аю *imp.*, **подмигну́ть,** -ну́, -нёшь *perf.* + *dat.* wink at.
подмо́га, -и, help, assistance; идти́ на подмо́гу, lend a hand.
подмока́ть, -а́ет *imp.*, **подмо́кнуть,** -нет; -мо́к *perf.* get damp, get wet.
подмора́живать, -ает *imp.*, **подморо́зить,** -зит *perf.* freeze. **подморо́женный,** frost-bitten, frozen.
подмо́стки, -ов *pl.* scaffolding, staging; stage.
подмо́ченный, damp; tarnished, tainted, blemished.
подмы́в, -а, washing away, undermining. **подмыва́ть,** -а́ю *imp.*, **подмы́ть,** -о́ю *perf.* wash; wash away, undermine; его́ так и подмыва́ет, he feels

an urge (to), he can hardly help (doing).
подмы́шка, -и, armpit. **подмы́шник**, -а, dress-protector.
поднево́льный, dependent; subordinate; forced.
поднести́, -су́, -сёшь; -ёс, -ла́ *perf.* (*imp.* подноси́ть) present; take, bring.
поднима́ть(ся, -а́ю(сь *imp.* of подня́ть-(ся.
поднови́ть, -влю́ *perf.*, **подновля́ть**, -я́ю *imp.* renew, renovate.
подно́жие, -я, foot; pedestal. **подно́жка**, -и, step; running-board. **подно́жный**; ~ корм, pasture.
подно́с, -а, tray; salver. **подноси́ть**, -ошу́, -о́сишь *imp.* of поднести́. **подноше́ние**, -я, giving; present, gift.
подня́тие, -я, raising; rise; rising. **подня́ть**, -ниму́, -ни́мешь; по́днял, -а́, -о *perf.* (*imp.* поднима́ть, подыма́ть) raise; lift (up); hoist; pick up; rouse, stir up; open up; improve, enhance; ~ на́ смех, hold up to ridicule; ~ пе́тли, pick up stitches; ~ ору́жие, take up arms; ~ целину́, break fresh ground; open up virgin lands; **~ся**, rise; go up; get up; climb, ascend; arise; break out, develop; improve; recover.
подо: see под. **подо-**: see под-.
подоба́ть, -а́ет *imp.* be becoming, be fitting. **подоба́ющий**, proper, fitting.
подо́бие, -я, likeness; similarity. **подо́бн|ый**, like, similar; и тому́ ~ое, and the like, and so on, and such like; ничего́ ~ого! nothing of the sort!
подобостра́стие, -я, servility. **подобостра́стный**, servile.
подобра́ть, -дберу́, -дберёшь; -бра́л, -а́, -о *perf.* (*imp.* подбира́ть) pick up; tuck up, put up; select, pick; **~ся**, steal up, approach stealthily; make oneself tidy.
подобью́, etc.: see подби́ть.
подогна́ть, -дгоню́, -дго́нишь; -а́л, -а́, -о *perf.* (*imp.* подгоня́ть), drive; drive on, urge on, hurry; adjust, fit.
подогну́ть, -ну́, -нёшь *perf.* (*imp.* подгиба́ть) tuck in; bend under; **~ся**, bend.
подогрева́ть -а́ю *imp.*, **подогре́ть**, -е́ю *perf.* warm up, heat up; arouse.
пододвига́ть, -а́ю *imp.*, **пододви́нуть**, -ну *perf.* move up, push up.
пододея́льник, -а, quilt cover, blanket cover; top sheet.
подожгу́, etc.: see подже́чь.
подожда́ть, -ду́, -дёшь; -а́л, -а́, -о *perf.* wait (+ *gen.* or *acc.* for).
подожму́, etc.: see поджа́ть.
подозва́ть, -дзову́, -дзовёшь; -а́л, -а́, -о *perf.* (*imp.* подзыва́ть) call up; beckon.
подозрева́емый, suspected; suspect. **подозрева́ть**, -а́ю *imp.* suspect. **подозре́ние**, -я, suspicion. **подозри́тельный**, suspicious; suspect; shady, fishy.
по|дои́ть, -ою́, -о́ишь *perf.* **подо́йник**, -а milk-pail.
подойти́, -йду́, -йдёшь; -ошёл, -шла́ *perf.* (*imp.* подходи́ть) approach; come up, go up; + *dat.* do for; suit, fit.
подоко́нник, -а, window-sill.
подо́л, -а, hem; lower part, lower slopes, foot.
подо́лгу *adv.* for a long time; for ages; for hours (etc.) together.
подолью́, etc.: see подли́ть.
подо́нки, -ов *pl.* dregs; scum.
подоплёка, -и, underlying cause, hidden motive.
подопру́, etc.: see подпере́ть.
подо́пытный, experimental; ~ кро́лик, guinea-pig.
подорва́ть -рву́, -рвёшь; -а́л, -а́, -о *perf.* (*imp.* подрыва́ть) undermine, sap; damage severely; blow up; blast.
по|дорожа́ть, -а́ет *perf.*
подоро́жник. -а, plantain; provisions for a journey. **подоро́жный**, on the road; along the road; ~ столб, milestone.
подосла́ть, -ошлю́, -ошлёшь *perf.* (*imp.* подсыла́ть) send (secretly).
подоспева́ть, -а́ю *imp.* **подоспе́ть**, -е́ю *perf.* arrive, appear (at the right moment).
подостла́ть, -дстелю́, -дсте́лешь *perf.* (*imp.* подстила́ть) lay underneath.
подотде́л, -а, section, subdivision.
подотру́, etc.: see подтере́ть.
подотчётный accountable; on account.
по|до́хнуть, -ну *perf.* (*imp.* also подыха́ть) die; peg out, kick the bucket.

подохо́дный; ~ нало́г, income-tax.
подо́шва, -ы, sole; foot; base.
подошёл, etc.: see подойти́. **подошлю́**, etc.: see подосла́ть. **подошью́**, etc.: see подши́ть. **подпада́ть**, -а́ю *imp.* of подпа́сть. **подпа́ивать**, -аю *imp.* of подпои́ть.
подпа́сть, -аду́, -адёшь; -а́л *perf.* (*imp.* подпада́ть) под + *acc.* fall under; ~ под влия́ние + *gen.* fall under the influence of.
подпева́ла, -ы *m.* and *f.* yes-man.
подпере́ть, -допру́; -пёр *perf.* (*imp.* подпира́ть) prop up.
подпи́ливать, -аю *imp.*, **подпили́ть**, -лю́, -лишь *perf.* saw; saw a little off; file, file down. **подпи́лок**, -лка, file.
подпира́ть, -а́ю *imp.* of подпере́ть.
подписа́вший *sb.* signatory. **подписа́ние**, -я, signing, signature. **подписа́ть**, -ишу́, -и́шешь *perf.*, **подпи́сывать**, -аю *imp.* sign; write underneath, add; **~ся**, sign; subscribe. **подпи́ска**, -и, subscription; engagement, written undertaking; signed statement. **подписно́й**, subscription; ~ лист, subscription list. **подпи́счик**, -а, subscriber. **по́дпись**, -и, signature; caption; inscription; за ~ю + *gen.* signed by; за ~ю и печа́тью, signed and sealed.
подпои́ть, -ою́, -о́ишь *perf.* (*imp.* подпа́ивать) make tipsy.
подполко́вник, -а, lieutenant-colonel.
подпо́лье, -я, cellar; underground. **подпо́льный**, under the floor; underground.
подпо́ра, -ы, **подпо́рка**, -и, prop, support; brace, strut.
подпры́гивать, -аю *imp.*, **подпры́гнуть**, -ну *perf.* leap up, jump up.
подпуска́ть, -а́ю *imp.*, **подпусти́ть**, -ущу́, -у́стишь *perf.* allow to approach; add in; get in, put in; ~ шпи́льку, sting.
подража́ние, -я, imitation. **подража́ть**, -а́ю *imp.* imitate.
подразде́л, -а, subsection. **подразделе́ние**, -я, subdivision; sub-unit. **подразделИ́ть**, -лю́ *perf.*, **подразделя́ть**, -я́ю, subdivide.
подразумева́ть, -а́ю *imp.* imply, mean; **~ся**, be implied, be meant, be understood.
подраста́ть, -а́ю *imp.*, **подрасти́**, -ту́, -тёшь; -ро́с, -ла́ *perf.* grow.
по|дра́ть(ся, -деру́(сь, -дерёшь(ся, -а́л(ся, -ла́(сь, -о́(сь or -ось *perf.*
подре́зать, -е́жу *perf.*, **подреза́ть**, -а́ю *imp.* cut; clip, trim; prune, lop; + *gen.* cut (off) more of.
подро́бно *adv.* minutely, in detail; at (great) length. **подро́бность**, -и, detail; minuteness. **подро́бный**, detailed, minute.
подровня́ть, -я́ю *perf.* level, even; trim.
подро́с, etc.: see подрасти́. **подро́сток**, -тка, adolescent; teenager; youth, young girl.
подро́ю, etc.: see подры́ть.
подруба́ть[1], -а́ю *imp.*, **подруби́ть**, -блю́, -бишь *perf.* chop down; cut short(er); hew.
подруба́ть[2], -а́ю *imp.*, **подруби́ть**, -блю́, -бишь *perf.* hem.
подру́га, -и, friend. **по-дру́жески** *adv.* in a friendly way; as a friend. **по|дружи́ться**, -жу́сь *perf.*
подру́ливать, -аю *imp.*, **подрули́ть**, -лю́ *perf.* taxi up.
подру́чный, at hand, to hand; improvised, makeshift; *sb.* assistant, mate.
подры́в, -а, undermining; injury, blow, detriment.
подрыва́ть[1], -а́ю *imp.* of подорва́ть.
подрыва́ть[2], -а́ю *imp.*, **подры́ть**, -ро́ю *perf.* undermine, sap. **подрывно́й**, blasting, demolition; undermining, subversive.
подря́д *adv.* in succession; running; on end.
подря́д, -а, contract. **подря́дный**, (done by) contract. **подря́дчик**, -а, contractor.
подса́живаться, -аюсь *imp.* of подсе́сть.
подсве́чник, -а, candlestick.
подсе́сть, -ся́ду; -се́л *perf.* (*imp.* подса́живаться) sit down, take a seat (к + *dat.* by, near, next to).
под|сини́ть, -ню́ *perf.*
подсказа́ть, -ажу́, -а́жешь *perf.*, **подска́зывать**, -аю *imp.* prompt; suggest.
подска́зка, -и, prompting.

подска́кивать, -аю *imp.*, **подскочи́ть,** -чу́, -чишь *perf.* jump (up), leap up, soar; run up, come running.
подслепова́тый, weak-sighted.
подслу́шать, -аю *perf.*, **подслу́шивать,** -аю *imp.* overhear; eavesdrop, listen.
подсма́тривать, -аю *imp.* of подсмотре́ть.
подсме́иваться, -аюсь *imp.* над + *instr.* laugh at, make fun of.
подсмотре́ть, -рю́, -ришь *perf.* (*imp.* подсма́тривать) spy (on).
подсне́жник, -а, snowdrop.
подсо́бный, subsidiary, supplementary; secondary; auxiliary; accessory.
подсо́вывать, -аю *imp.* of подсу́нуть.
подсозна́ние, -я, subconscious (mind). **подсозна́тельный,** subconscious.
подсо́лнечник, -а, sunflower. **подсо́лнечн|ый,** sunflower; ~ое ма́сло, sunflower(-seed) oil. **подсо́лнух,** -а, sunflower; sunflower seed.
подсо́хнуть, -ну *perf.* (*imp.* подсыха́ть) get dry, dry out a little.
подспо́рье, -я, help, support.
подста́вить, -влю *perf.*, **подставля́ть,** -я́ю *imp.* put (under), place (under); bring up, put up; hold up; expose, lay bare; substitute; ~ но́жку + *dat.* trip up. **подста́вка,** -и, stand; support, rest, prop. **подставн|о́й,** false; substitute; ~о́е лицо́, dummy, figure-head.
подстака́нник, -а, glass-holder.
подстелю́, etc.: see подостла́ть.
подстерега́ть, -а́ю *imp.*, **подстере́чь,** -егу́, -ежёшь; -рёг, -ла́ *perf.* be on the watch for, lie in wait for.
подстила́ть, -а́ю *imp.* of подостла́ть. **подсти́лка,** -и, bedding; litter.
подстра́ивать, -аю, *imp.* of подстро́ить.
одстрека́тель, -я *m.* instigator. **подпстрека́тельство,** -а, instigation, incitement, setting-on. **подстрека́ть,** -а́ю *imp.*, **подстрекну́ть,** -ну́, -нёшь *perf.* instigate, incite, set on; excite.
подстре́ливать, -аю *imp.*, **подстрели́ть,** -лю́, -лишь *perf.* wound; wing.
подстрига́ть, -а́ю *imp.*, **подстри́чь,** -игу́, -ижёшь; -и́г *perf.* cut; clip, trim; prune; **~ся,** trim one's hair; have a hair-cut, a trim.
подстро́ить, -о́ю *perf.* (*imp.* подстра́ивать) build on; tune (up); arrange, contrive.
подстро́чн|ый, interlinear; literal, word-for-word; ~ое примеча́ние, footnote.
по́дступ, -а, approach. **подступа́ть,** -а́ю *imp.* **подступи́ть,** -плю́, -пишь *perf.* approach, come up, come near; **~ся** к + *dat.* approach.
подсуди́мый *sb.* defendant; the accused. **подсу́дн|ый** + *dat.* under the jurisdiction of, within the competence of; ~ое де́ло, punishable offence.
подсу́нуть, -ну *perf.* (*imp.* подсо́вывать), put, thrust, shove; slip, palm off.
подсчёт, -а, calculation; count. **подсчита́ть,** -а́ю *perf.*, **подсчи́тывать,** -аю, count (up); calculate.
подсыла́ть, -а́ю *imp.* of подосла́ть.
подсыха́ть, -а́ю *imp.* of подсо́хнуть.
подся́ду, etc.: see подсе́сть. **подта́лкивать,** -аю *imp.* of подтолкну́ть.
подтасова́ть, -су́ю *perf.*, **подтасо́вывать,** -аю *imp.* shuffle unfairly; garble, juggle with.
подта́чивать, -аю *imp.* of подточи́ть.
подтверди́тельный, confirmatory; of acknowledgement. **подтверди́ть,** -ржу́ *perf.*, **подтвержда́ть,** -а́ю *imp.* confirm; corroborate, bear out; ~ получе́ние + *gen.* acknowledge receipt of. **подтвержде́ние,** -я, confirmation, corroboration; acknowledgement.
подтёк, -а, bruise. **подтека́ть,** -а́ет *imp.* of подте́чь; leak, be leaking.
подтере́ть, -дотру́, -дотрёшь; подтёр *perf.* (*imp.* подтира́ть) wipe, wipe up.
подте́чь, -ечёт; -тёк, -ла́ *perf.* (*imp.* подтека́ть) под + *acc.* flow under, run under.
подтира́ть, -а́ю *imp.* of подтере́ть.
подтолкну́ть, -ну́, -нёшь *perf.* (*imp.* подта́лкивать) push, nudge; urge on.
подточи́ть, -чу́, -чишь *perf.* (*imp.* подта́чивать) sharpen slightly, give an edge (to); eat away, gnaw; undermine.
подтру́нивать, -аю *imp.*, **подтруни́ть,** -ню́ *perf.* над + *instr.* chaff, tease.
подтя́гивать, -аю *imp.*, **подтяну́ть,** -ну́, -нешь *perf.* tighten; pull up, haul up; bring up move up; take in hand, chase

up; **~ся**, tighten one's belt, etc.; pull oneself up; move up, move in; pull oneself together, take oneself in hand. **подтя́жки**, -жек *pl.* braces, suspenders. **подтя́нутый**, smart.

по|ду́мать, -аю *perf.* think; think a little, think for a while. **поду́мывать**, -аю *imp.* + *inf.* or о + *prep.* think of, think about.

по|ду́ть, -у́ю *perf.*

поду́чивать, -аю *imp.*, **подучи́ть**, -чу́, -чишь *perf.* + *acc.* study, learn; + *acc.* and *dat.* instruct in; **~ся** (+ *dat.*) learn.

поду́шка, -и, pillow; cushion.

подхали́м, -а *m.* toady, lickspittle. **подхали́мничать**, -аю *imp.* toady. **подхали́мство**, -а, toadying, grovelling.

подхвати́ть, -ачу́, -а́тишь *perf.*, **подхва́тывать**, -аю *imp.* catch (up), pick up, take up; ~ пе́сню, take up, join in, a song.

подхо́д, -а, approach. **подходи́ть**, -ожу́, -о́дишь *imp.* of подойти́. **подходя́щий**, suitable, proper, appropriate.

подцепи́ть, -плю́, -пишь *perf.*, **подцепля́ть**, -я́ю *imp.* hook on, couple on; pick up.

подча́с *adv.* sometimes, at times.

подчёркивать, -аю *imp.*, **подчеркну́ть**, -ну́, -нёшь *perf.* underline; emphasize.

подчине́ние, -я, subordination; submission, subjection. **подчинённый**, subordinate; tributary; *sb.* subordinate. **подчини́ть**, -ню́ *perf.*, **подчиня́ть**, -я́ю, subordinate, subject; place (under); **~ся** + *dat.* submit to, obey.

подше́фный, aided, assisted; + *dat.* under the patronage of, sponsored by.

подшива́ть, -а́ю *imp.* of подши́ть. **подши́вка**, -и, hemming; lining; soling; hem, facing; filing, file.

подши́пник, -а, bearing.

подши́ть, -дошью́, -дошьёшь *perf.* (*imp.* подшива́ть) hem, line, face; sole; sew underneath; file.

подшути́ть, -учу́, -у́тишь *perf.*, **подшу́чивать**, -аю *imp.* над + *instr.* chaff, mock; play a trick on.

подъ-: see под-. **подъеду**, etc.: see подъе́хать.

подъе́зд, -а, porch, entrance, doorway; approach, approaches. **подъездн|о́й**, approach; ~а́я алле́я, drive; ~а́я доро́га, access road; **~**о́й путь, spur (track). **подъе́здный**, entrance. **подъезжа́ть**, -а́ю *imp.* of подъе́хать.

подъём, -а, lifting; raising; hoisting; ascent; climb; rise; upward slope; development; élan; enthusiasm, animation; instep; reveille; тяжёл (лёгок) на ~, slow (quick) off the mark, (not) easily persuaded to go somewhere. **подъёмник**, -а, lift, elevator, hoist; jack. **подъёмн|ый**, lifting; ~ые де́ньги, removal allowance; travelling expenses; ~ кран, crane, jenny, derrick; ~ маши́на, lift; ~ мост, drawbridge; **~ые** *sb. pl.* removal allowance, travelling expenses.

подъе́хать, -е́ду *perf.* (*imp.* подъезжа́ть) drive up, draw up; call; get round.

подыма́ть(ся, -а́ю(сь *imp.* of подня́ть(ся.

подыска́ть, -ыщу́, -ы́щешь *perf.*, **поды́скивать**, -аю *imp.* seek (out), (try to) find.

подыто́живать, -аю *imp.*, **подыто́жить**, -жу *perf.* sum up.

подыха́ть, -а́ю *imp.* of подо́хнуть.

подыша́ть, -шу́, -шишь *perf.* breathe; ~ све́жим во́здухом, have, get, a breath of fresh air.

поеда́ть, -а́ю *imp.* of пое́сть.

поеди́нок, -нка, duel; single combat.

по́езд, -а; *pl.* -а́, train; convoy, procession; ~ом, by train. **пое́здка**, -и, journey; trip, excursion, outing, tour. **поездн|о́й**, train; ~а́я брига́да, train crew.

пое́сть. -е́м, -е́шь, -е́ст, -еди́м; -е́л *perf.* (*imp.* поеда́ть) eat, eat up; have a bite to eat.

по|е́хать, -е́ду *perf.* go; set off, depart.

по|жале́ть, -е́ю *perf.*

по|жа́ловать(ся, -лую(сь *perf.* **пожа́луй** *adv.* perhaps; very likely; it may be. **пожа́луйста** *part.* please; certainly! by all means! with pleasure!; not at all, don't mention it.

пожáр, -а, fire; conflagration. **пожáрка**, -и, fire-station. **пожáрник**, -а, **пожáрный** *sb.* fireman. **пожáрн|ый**, fire; ~ая комáнда, fire-brigade; ~ая лéстница, fire-escape; ~ая машúна, fire-engine.

пожáтие, -я; ~ рýки, handshake. **пожáть**[1], -жмý, -жмёшь *perf.* (*imp.* пожимáть) press, squeeze; ~ рýку + *dat.*, shake hands with; ~ плечáми, shrug one's shoulders; **~ся**, shrink; huddle up, hug oneself.

пожáть[2], -жнý, -жнёшь *perf.* (*imp.* пожинáть) reap.

пожелáние, -я, wish, desire. **по|желáть**, -áю *perf.*

пожелтéлый, yellowed; gone yellow. **по|желтéть**, -éю *perf.*

по|женúть, -нió, -нишь *perf.* **поженúться**, -жéнимся *perf.* get married

пожéртвование, -я, donation; sacrifice. **по|жéртвовать**, -твую *perf.*

поживáть, -áю *imp.* live; как (вы) поживáете? how are you (getting on)?; стáли онú жить-~ да добрá наживáть, they lived happily ever after. **поживúться**, -влюсь *perf.* (+ *instr.*) profit (by), live (off). **пожúвший**, experienced. **пожилóй**, middle-aged; elderly.

пожимáть(ся, -áю(сь *imp.* of пожáть[1]-(ся. **пожинáть**, -áю *imp.* of пожáть[2]. **пожирáть**, -áю *imp.* of пожрáть.

пожúтки, -ов *pl.* belongings, things; goods and chattels; со всéми пожúтками, bag and baggage.

пожмý, etc.: see пожáть[1]. **пожнý**, etc.: see пожáть[2].

пожрáть, -рý, -рёшь; -áл, -á, -о *perf.* (*imp.* пожирáть) devour.

пóза, -ы, pose; attitude, posture.

по|забóтиться, -óчусь *perf.* **по|завúдовать**, -дую *perf.* **по|зáвтракать**, -аю *perf.*

позавчерá *adv.* the day before yesterday.

позадú *adv.* and *prep.* + *gen.* behind.

по|заúмствовать, -твую *perf.* **по|звáть**, -зовý, -зовёшь; -áл, -á, -о *perf.*

позволéние, -я, permission, leave; с вáшего позволéния, with your permission, by your leave; с позволéния сказáть, if one may say so. **позволúтельный**, permissible. **позвóлить**, -лю *perf.*, **позволя́ть**, -я́ю *imp.* + *dat.* or *acc.* allow, permit; ~ себé поéздку в Парúж, be able to afford a trip to Paris; позвóль(те), allow me; excuse me.

по|звонúть(ся, -нió(сь *perf.*

позвонóк, -нкá, vertebra. **позвонóчник**, -а, spine, backbone; spinal column. **позвонóчн|ый**, spinal, vertebral; vertebrate; **~ые** *sb. pl.* vertebrates.

позднéее *adv.* later. **позднéйший**, latest. **пóздний**, late; пóздно, it is late.

пóздно *adv.* late.

по|здорóваться, -аюсь *perf.* **поздрáвить**, -влю *perf.*, **поздравля́ть**, -я́ю *imp.* с + *instr.* congratulate on; ~ с днём рождéния, wish many happy returns. **поздравлéние**, -я, congratulation.

по|зеленéть, -éет *perf.*

поземéльный, land; ~ налóг, land-tax.

пóзже *adv.* later (on).

позициóнн|ый, positional, position; static; ~ая войнá, trench warfare.

позúция, -и, position; stand; заня́ть позúцию, take one's stand.

познавáемый, cognizable, knowable. **познавáтельный**, cognitive. **познавáть**, -наió, -наёшь *imp.* of познáть. **познавáться**, -наióсь, -наёшься *imp.* become known, be recognized.

по|знакóмить(ся, -млю(сь *perf.*

познáние, -я, cognition; *pl.* knowledge.

познáть, -áю *perf.* (*imp.* познавáть) get to know, become acquainted with.

позолóта, -ы, gilding, gilt. **по|золотúть**, -лочý *perf.*

позóр, -а, shame, disgrace; infamy, ignominy. **позóрить**, -рю *imp.* (*perf.* о~) disgrace; **~ся**, disgrace oneself. **позóрный**, shameful, disgraceful; infamous, ignominious.

позы́в, -а, urge, call; inclination. **позывн|óй**, call; ~óй сигнáл, ~ы́е *sb. pl.*, call sign.

поимённо *adv.* by name; вызывáть ~, call over, call the roll of. **поимённый**, nominal; ~ спúсок, list of names.

пóиски, -ов *pl.* search; в пóисках + *gen.* in search of, in quest of.

поúстине *adv.* indeed, in truth.

пои́ть, пою́, пои́шь *imp.* (*perf.* на~) give something to drink; water.
пойду́, etc.: see пойти́.
по́йло, -а, swill, mash.
пойма́ть, -а́ю *perf.* of лови́ть. **пойму́,** etc.: see поня́ть.
пойти́, -иду́, -йдёшь; пошёл, -шла́ *perf.* of идти́, ходи́ть; go, walk; begin to walk; + *inf.* begin; + в + *acc.* take after; пошёл! off you go! I'm off; пошёл вон! be off! get out!; (так) не пойдёт, that won't work, that won't wash; э́то ей не пойдёт, it won't suit her.
пока́ *adv.* for the present, for the time being; ~ что, in the meanwhile. **пока́** *conj.* while; ~ не, until, till.
пока́з, -а, showing, demonstration. **показа́ние,** -я, testimony, evidence; deposition; affidavit; reading. **показа́тель,** -я *m.* index, exponent; showing. **показа́тельный,** significant; instructive revealing; model; demonstration; exponential; ~ суд, show-trial. **показа́ть,** -ажу́, -а́жешь *perf.*, **пока́зывать,** -аю *imp.* show; display, reveal; register, read; testify, give evidence; + на + *acc.* point at, point to; ~ вид, pretend; ~ лу́чшее вре́мя, clock (make) the best time; ~ на дверь + *dat.* show the door (to). **по|каза́ться,** -ажу́сь, -а́жешься *perf.*, **пока́зываться,** -аюсь *imp.* show oneself (itself); come in sight; appear; seem. **показно́й,** for show; ostentatious.
по-како́вски *adv.* in what language?
по|кале́чить(ся, -чу(сь *perf.*
пока́мест *adv.* and *conj.* for the present; while; meanwhile.
по|кара́ть, -а́ю *perf.*
пока́тость, -и, slope, incline. **пока́тый,** sloping; slanting.
покача́ть, -а́ю *perf.* rock, swing; ~ голово́й, shake one's head. **пока́чивать,** -аю, rock slightly; **~ся,** rock; swing; stagger, totter. **покачну́ть,** -ну́, -нёшь, shake; rock; **~ся,** sway, totter, lurch.
покая́ние, -я, confession; penitence, repentance. **покая́нный,** penitential. **по|ка́яться,** -а́юсь *perf.*
поквита́ться, -а́юсь *perf.* be quits; get even.
покида́ть, -а́ю *imp.*, **поки́нуть,** -ну *perf.* leave; desert, abandon, forsake. **поки́нутый,** deserted; abandoned.
покла́дистый, complaisant, obliging; easy to get on with.
покла́жа, -и, load; baggage, luggage.
поклёп, -а, slander, calumny.
покло́н, -а, bow; greeting; переда́ть мой ~ + *dat.* remember me to, give my regards to; посла́ть ~, send one's compliments, one's kind regards. **поклоне́ние,** -я, worship. **поклони́ться,** -ню́сь -ни́шься *perf.* of кла́няться. **покло́нник,** -а, admirer; worshipper. **поклоня́ться,** -я́юсь *imp.* + *dat.* worship.
по|кля́сться, -яну́сь, -нёшься; -я́лся, -ла́сь *perf.*
поко́иться, -о́юсь *imp.* rest. repose, be based; lie. **поко́й,** -я, rest, peace; room, chamber. **поко́йник,** -а, the deceased. **поко́йн|ый,** calm, quiet; comfortable; restful; ~ой но́чи! good night!
по|колеба́ть(ся, -е́блю(сь *perf.*
поколе́ние, -я, generation.
по|колоти́ть(ся, -очу́(сь, -о́тишь(ся *perf.*
поко́нчить, -чу *perf.* с + *instr.* finish; finish with, have done with; put an end to, do away with; ~ с собо́й, commit suicide; с э́тим поко́нчено, that's done with.
покоре́ние, -я, subjugation, subdual; conquest. **покори́ть;** -рю́ *perf.* (*imp.* покоря́ть) subjugate, subdue; conquer; **~ся,** submit, resign oneself.
по|корми́ть(ся, -млю́(сь, -ми́шь(ся *perf.*
поко́рно *adv.* humbly; submissively, obediently.
по|коро́бить(ся, -блю(сь *perf.* **покоро́бленный,** warped.
покоря́ть(ся, -я́ю(сь *imp.* of покори́ть(ся.
поко́с, -а, mowing, haymaking; meadow (-land); второ́й ~, aftermath.
покоси́вшийся, rickety, crazy, ramshackle; leaning. **по|коси́ть(ся,** -ошу́(сь *perf.*

покра́жа, -и, theft; stolen goods.
по|кра́сить, -а́шу *perf.* **покра́ска**, -и, painting, colouring.
по|краснéть, -éю *perf.* **по|красова́ться**, -су́юсь *perf.* **по|крепча́ть**, -а́ет *perf.* **по|криви́ть(ся**, -влю́(сь *perf.*
покри́кивать, -аю *imp.* shout (на + *acc.* at).
покро́в, -а, cover; covering; pall; cloak, shroud; protection. **покрови́тель**, -я *m.*, **покрови́тельница**, -ы, patron; sponsor. **покрови́тельственный**, protective; condescending, patronizing. **покрови́тельство**, -а, protection, patronage. **покрови́тельствовать**, -твую *imp.* + *dat.* protect, patronize.
покро́й, -я, cut.
покроши́ть, -шу́, -шишь *perf.* crumble; mince, chop.
покрыва́ло, -а, cover; bedspread, counterpane; shawl; veil. **покрыва́ть**, -а́ю *imp.*, **по|кры́ть**, -ро́ю *perf.* cover; coat; roof; drown; shield, cover up for; hush up; discharge, pay off; **~ся**, cover oneself; get covered. **покры́тие**, -я, covering; surfacing; discharge, payment. **покры́шка**, -и, cover, covering; outer cover.
покупа́тель, -я *m.* buyer, purchaser; customer, client. **покупа́тельный**, purchasing. **покупа́ть**, -а́ю *imp.* of купи́ть. **поку́пка**, -и, buying; purchasing; purchase. **покупн|о́й**, bought, purchased; purchase, purchasing; ~а́я цена́, purchase-price.
по|кури́ть, -рю́, -ришь *perf.*, **поку́ривать**, -аю *imp.* smoke a little; have a smoke.
по|ку́шать, -аю *perf.*
пол[1], -а (-у), *loc.* -у́; *pl.* -ы́, floor.
пол[2], -а, sex.
пол-[1] in *comb.* with noun in *gen.*, in oblique cases usu. полу-, half. **полве́ка**, half a century. **~го́да**, half a year, six months. **~доро́ги**, half-way. **~дю́жины**, half a dozen. **~миллио́на**, half a million. **~мину́ты**, half a minute. **~цены́**, half price. **~часа́**, half an hour.
пол-[2] *abbr.* in *comb.* of полномо́чный, plenipotentiary. **полпре́д**, -а, (ambassador) plenipotentiary. **~пре́дство**, -а, embassy.
пола́, -ы́; *pl.* -ы, skirt, flap; из-под полы́, on the sly, under cover.
полага́ть, -а́ю *imp.* suppose, think, believe; lay, place. **полага́ться**, -а́юсь *imp.* of положи́ться; полага́ется *impers.* one is supposed to; + *dat.* it is due to; нам э́то полага́ется, it is our due, we have a right to it; не полага́ется, it is not done; так полага́ется, it is the custom.
пола́дить, -а́жу *perf.* come to an understanding; get on good terms.
по|ла́комить(ся, -млю(сь *perf.*
по́лдень, -дня or -лу́дня *m.* noon, midday; south. **полдне́вный** *adj.*
по́ле, -я; *pl.* -я́, field; ground; margin; brim; ~ де́ятельности, sphere of action. **полев|о́й**, field; ~ы́е цветы́, wild flowers; ~о́й шпат, feldspar.
поле́зн|ый, useful; helpful; good, wholesome; effective; ~ая нагру́зка, payload.
по|ле́зть, -зу; -ле́з *perf.*
поле́мика, -и, controversy, dispute; polemics. **полемизи́ровать**, -рую *imp.* argue, debate, engage in controversy. **полеми́ческий**, controversial; polemical.
по|лени́ться, -ню́сь, -нишься *perf.*
поле́но, -а; *pl.* -е́нья, -ьев, log.
поле́сье, -я, woodlands, wooded region.
полёт, -а, flight; flying; вид с пти́чьего ~а, bird's-eye view. **по|лете́ть**, -лечу́ *perf.*
по́лзать, -аю *indet. imp.*, **ползти́**, -зу́, -зёшь; полз, -ла́ *det. imp.* crawl, creep; ooze; spread; fray, ravel; slip, slide, collapse. **ползу́ч|ий**, creeping; ~ие расте́ния, creepers.
поли- in *comb.* poly-.
поли́ва, -ы, glaze. **полива́ть(ся**, -а́ю(сь *imp.* of поли́ться. **поли́вка**, -и, watering.
полиграфи́ст, -а, printing-trades worker. **полиграфи́ческ|ий**, printing-trades; ~ая промы́шленность, printing industry. **полиграфи́я**, -и, printing.
полиго́н, -а, range.
поликли́ника, -и, polyclinic; outpatients' (department).

полиня́лый, faded, discoloured. **по|линя́ть,** -я́ет *perf.*

полирова́льн|ый, polishing; ~ая бума́га, sandpaper. **полирова́ть,** -ру́ю *imp.* (*perf.* от~) polish. **полиро́вка,** -и, polishing; polish. **полиро́вочный,** polishing; buffing. **полиро́вщик,** -а, polisher.

полит- *abbr.* in *comb.* of полити́ческий, political. **политбюро́** *n. indecl.* Politbureau. **~гра́мота,** -ы, elementary political education. **~заключённый** *sb.* political prisoner. **~кружо́к,** -жка́, political study circle. **~просве́т,** -а, political education. **~рабо́тник,** -а, political worker.

полите́хник, -а, polytechnic student. **полите́хникум,** -а, polytechnic. **политехни́ческий,** polytechnic, polytechnical.

поли́тика, -и, policy; politics. **полити́ческий,** political.

поли́ть, -лью́, -льёшь; по́ли́л, -а́, -о *perf.* (*imp.* полива́ть) pour on, pour over; ~ (водо́й) water; **~ся** + *instr.* pour over oneself.

полице́йский, police; *sb.* policeman. **поли́ция,** -и, police.

поли́чн|ое *sb.*; с ~ым, red-handed.

полк, -а́, *loc.* -у́, regiment.

по́лка[1], -и, shelf; berth.

по́лка[2], -и, weeding.

полко́вник, -а, colonel. **полково́дец,** -дца, commander; general. **полково́й,** regimental.

полне́ть, -е́ю *imp.* (*perf.* по~) put on weight, fill out.

по́лно *adv.* that's enough! that will do! stop it! ~ ворча́ть! stop grumbling.

полно- in *comb.* full; completely. **полновла́стный,** sovereign. **~кро́вный,** full-blooded. **~лу́ние,** -я, full moon. **~метра́жный,** full-length. **~пра́вный,** enjoying full rights; competent; ~пра́вный член, full member. **~сбо́рный,** prefabricated. **~це́нный,** of full value.

полномо́чие, -я, authority, power; plenary powers; commission; proxy; *pl.* terms of reference; credentials; дать полномо́чия + *dat.* empower, commission; превы́сить полномо́чия, exceed one's commission. **полномо́чный,** plenipotentiary.

по́лностью *adv.* fully, in full; completely, utterly. **полнота́,** -ы́, fullness, completeness; plenitude; stoutness, corpulence, plumpness.

по́лночь, -л(у́)ночи, midnight; north; за ~, after midnight.

по́лн|ый; -лон, -лна́, по́лно́, full; complete; entire, total; absolute; stout, portly; plump; в ~ом соста́ве, in full force; in a body; ~ым го́лосом, at the top of one's voice; ~ы́м-полно́, chock-full, cram-full; ~ый сбор, full house; ~ое собра́ние сочине́ний, complete works; ~ый стенографи́ческий отчёт, verbatim record.

полови́к, -а́, mat, matting; door-mat.

полови́на, -ы, half; middle; два с полови́ной, two and a half; ~ (две́ри), leaf; ~ шесто́го, half-past five. **полови́нка,** -и, half; leaf. **полови́нчатый,** halved; half-and-half; half-hearted; undecided; indeterminate.

полово́й[1], floor.

полово́й[2], sexual.

по́лог, -а, curtains; cover, blanket.

поло́гий, gently sloping.

положе́ние, -я, position; whereabouts; posture; attitude; condition, state; situation; status, standing; circumstances; regulations, statute; thesis; tenet; clause, provisions; быть на высоте́ положе́ния, rise to the situation; по положе́нию, according to the regulations. **поло́женный,** agreed; determined. **поло́жим,** let us assume; suppose; though, even if. **положи́тельный,** positive; affirmative; favourable; complete, absolute; practical. **положи́ть,** -жу́, -жишь *perf.* (*imp.* класть) put, place; lay (down); decide; agree; propose, offer; fix; **~ся** (*imp.* полага́ться) rely, count; pin one's hopes.

по́лоз, -а; *pl.* -о́зья, -ьев, runner.

по|лома́ть(ся, -а́ю(сь *perf.* **поло́мка,** -и, breakage.

полоса́, -ы́, *acc.* по́лосу́; *pl.* по́лосы, -ло́с, -а́м, stripe, streak; strip; band;

region; zone, belt; period; phase; spell, run. **полоса́тый**, striped, stripy.

полоска́ние, -я, rinse, rinsing; gargle, gargling. **полоска́тельница**, -ы, slop--basin. **полоска́ть**, -ощу́, -о́щешь *imp.* (*perf.* вы́~, от~, про~) rinse; ~ го́рло, gargle; **~ся**, paddle; flap.

по́лость[1], -и; *gen. pl.* -е́й, cavity.

по́лость[2], -и; *gen. pl.* -е́й, carriage-rug.

полоте́нце, -а; *gen. pl.* -нец, towel.

полотёр, -а, floor-polisher.

поло́тнище, -а, width; panel. **полотно́**, -а́; *pl.* -а, -тен, linen; canvas. **полотня́ный**, linen.

поло́ть, -лю́, -лишь *imp.* (*perf.* вы́~) weed.

полоши́ть, -шу́ *imp.* (*perf.* вс~) agitate, alarm; **~ся**, take alarm, take fright.

полощу́, etc.: see полоска́ть.

полти́на, -ы, **полти́нник**, -а, fifty copecks; fifty-copeck piece.

полтора́, -лу́тора *m.* and *n.*, **полторы́**, -лу́тора *f.* one and a half. **полтора́ста**, полу́т-, a hundred and fifty.

полу-[1]: see пол-[1].

полу-[2] in *comb.* half-, semi-, demi-. **полуботи́нок**, -нка; *gen. pl.* -нок, shoe. **~го́дие**, -я, six months, half a year. **~годи́чный**, six months', lasting six months. **~годова́лый**, six-month-old. **~-годово́й**, half-yearly, six-monthly. **~гра́мотный**, semi-literate. **~гу́сеничный**, half-track. **~защи́та**, -ы, half-backs; центр ~защи́ты, centre half. **~защи́тник**, -а, half-back. **~круг**, -а, semicircle. **~кру́глый**, semicircular. **~ме́ра**, -ы, half-measure. **~ме́сяц**, -а, crescent (moon). **~оборо́т**, -а, half--turn. **~о́стров**, -а, peninsula. **~откры́тый**, half-open; ajar. **~официа́льный**, semi-official. **~подва́льный**, semi-basement. **~проводни́к**, -а́, semi-conductor, transistor. **~проводнико́вый**, transistor, transistorized. **~со́нный**, half-asleep; dozing. **~ста́нок**, -нка, halt. **~то́нка**, -и, half-ton lorry. **~тьма́**, -ы, semi-darkness; twilight, dusk. **~фабрика́т**, -а, semi--finished product, convenience food. **~фина́л**, -а, semi-final. **~ша́рие**, -я, hemisphere. **~шу́бок**, -бка, sheepskin coat.

полу́да, -ы, tinning. **по|луди́ть**, -ужу́, -у́дишь *perf.*

полу́денный, midday.

полу́торка, -и, thirty-hundredweight lorry.

получа́тель, -я *m.* recipient. **получа́ть**, -а́ю *imp.*, **получи́ть**, -чу́, -чишь *perf.* get, receive, obtain; **~ся**, come, arrive, turn up; turn out, prove, be; из э́того ничего́ не получи́лось, nothing came of it; результа́ты получи́лись нева́жные, the results are poor. **получе́ние**, -я, receipt. **полу́чка**, -и, receipt; pay(-packet).

полу́чше *adv.* rather better, a little better.

по́лчище, -а, horde; mass, flock.

полынн|ый, wormwood; ~ая во́дка, absinthe. **полы́нь**, -и, wormwood.

по|лысе́ть, -е́ю *perf.*

по́льза, -ы, use; advantage, benefit, profit; в по́льзу + *gen.* in favour of, on behalf of. **по́льзование**, -я, use. **по́льзоваться**, -зуюсь *imp.* (*perf.* вос~) + *instr.* make use of, utilize; profit by; enjoy; take advantage of, ~ дове́рием + *gen.* enjoy the confidence of; ~ креди́том, be credit-worthy; ~ слу́чаем, take the opportunity; ~ уваже́нием, be held in respect.

по́лька, -и, Pole; polka. **по́льский**, Polish; *sb.* polonaise.

по|льсти́ть(ся, -льщу́(сь *perf.* **полью́**, etc.: see поли́ть.

полюби́ть, -блю́, -бишь *perf.* come to like, take to; fall in love with.

по|любова́ться, -бу́юсь *perf.*

полюбо́вный, amicable.

по|любопы́тствовать, -твую *perf.*

по́люс, -а, pole.

поля́к, -а, Pole.

поля́на, -ы, glade, clearing.

поля́рник, -а, polar explorer, member of polar expedition. **поля́рн|ый**, polar, arctic; diametrically opposed; ~ая звезда́, pole-star; (се́верное) ~ое сия́ние, aurora borealis, Northern Lights.

пом- *abbr.* in *comb.* of помо́щник, assistant. **помбу́х**, -а, assistant accountant. **~дире́ктор**, -а, assistant manager. **~нáч,** -а, assistant chief, assistant head.

помáда, -ы, pomade; lipstick.

по|мáзать(ся, -áжу(сь *perf.* **помазóк,** -зкá small brush.

помалéньку *adv.* gradually, little by little; gently; in a small way, modestly; tolerably, so-so.

помáлкивать, -аю *imp.* hold one's tongue, keep mum.

по|манúть, -ню́, -нишь *perf.*

помáрка, -и, blot; pencil mark; correction.

по|мáслить, -лю *perf.*

помахáть, -машу́, -мáшешь *perf.*, **помáхивать,** -аю *imp.* + *instr.* wave; brandish, swing; wag.

помéньше, somewhat smaller, rather smaller, a little smaller; somewhat less, a little less, rather less.

по|менять(ся, -я́ю(сь *perf.* **по|мерéщиться,** -щу́сь *perf.* **по|мéрить-(ся,** -рю(сь *perf.* **по|мéркнуть,** -нет; -мéрк(нул) *perf.*

помертвéлый, deathly pale. **по|мертвéть,** -éю *perf.*

поместúтельный, roomy; capacious; spacious. **поместúть,** -ещу́ *perf.* (*imp.* помещáть), lodge, accommodate; put up; place, locate; invest; ~ статью́, publish an article; **~ся,** lodge; find room; put up; go in. **помéстье,** -я; *gen. pl.* -тий, -тьям estate.

пóмесь, -и, cross-breed, hybrid; cross; mongrel; mixture, hotch-potch.

помéсячный, monthly.

помёт, -а, dung, excrement; droppings; litter, brood, farrow.

помéта, -ы, mark, note. **по|мéтить,** -éчу *perf.* (*imp.* also помечáть) mark; date; ~ гáлочкой, tick.

помéха, -и, hindrance; obstacle; encumbrance; *pl.* interference; быть (служúть) помéхой + *dat.* hinder, impede, stand in the way of. **помехоустóйчивый,** anti-static, anti-interference

помечáть, -áю *imp.* of помéтить.

помéшанный, mad, crazy; insane; *sb.* madman, madwoman. **помешáтельство,** -а, madness, craziness; lunacy, insanity; craze. **по|мешáть,** -áю *perf.*

помешáться, -áюсь *perf.* go mad, go crazy.

помéшивать, -аю *imp.* stir slowly.

помещáть, -áю *imp.* of поместúть. **помещáться,** -áюсь *imp.* of поместúться; be; be located, be situated; be housed; be accommodated, find room; в э́тот стадиóн помещáются сéмьдесят ты́сяч человéк, this stadium holds seventy thousand people. **помещéние,** -я, premises; apartment, room, lodging; placing, location; investment; жилóе ~, housing, living accommodation. **помéщик,** -а, landowner, landlord. **помéщичий,** landowner's; ~ дом, manor-house, gentleman's residence.

помидóр, -а, tomato.

помúлование, -я, forgiveness, pardon. **помúловать,** -лую *perf.* forgive, pardon.

помúмо *prep.* + *gen.* apart from; besides; without the knowledge of, unbeknown to.

помúн, -а (-у), mention; лёгок на ~е, talk of the devil. **поминáть,** -áю *imp.* of помяну́ть; не ~ лúхом, remember kindly; not bear a grudge against; поминáй как звáли, he (etc.) has vanished into thin air; ~ добрóм, speak well of. **помúнки,** -нок *pl.* funeral repast.

по|мирúть(ся, -рю́(сь *perf.*

пóмнить, -ню *imp.* remember.

помножáть, -áю *imp.*, **по|мнóжить,** -жу *perf.* multiply; ~ два нá три, multiply two by three.

помогáть, -áю *imp.* of помóчь.

по-мóему *adv.* I think; in my opinion; to my mind, to my way of thinking; as I (would) wish, as I would have it.

помóи, -ев *pl.* slops. **помóйка,** -и; *gen. pl.* -óек dustbin; rubbish heap, rubbish dump; cesspit. **помóйн|ый,** slop; ~ое ведрó, slop-pail.

помóл, -а, grinding, milling; grist.

помóлвка, -и, betrothal, engagement.

по|молúться, -лю́сь, -лишься *perf.* **по|молодéть,** -éю *perf.*

помолчáть, -чу́ *perf.* be silent for a time, pause.

помóр, помóрский, etc.: see по-[2] II.

по|мори́ть, -рю́ *perf.* **по|мо́рщиться,** -щусь *perf.*

помо́ст, -а, dais; platform, stage, rostrum; scaffold.

по|мочи́ться, -чу́сь, -чишься *perf.*

помо́чь, -огу́, -о́жешь; -о́г, -ла́ *perf.* (*imp.* помога́ть) help, aid, assist; relieve, bring relief. **помо́щник,** -а, **помо́щница,** -ы, assistant, mate; help, helper, helpmeet. **по́мощь,** -и, help, aid, assistance; relief; без посторо́нней по́мощи, unaided, single-handed; на ~! help!; пода́ть ру́ку по́мощи, lend a hand, give a helping hand; при по́мощи, с по́мощью, + *gen.* with the help of, by means of.

помо́ю, etc.: see помы́ть.

по́мпа, -ы, pump.

по|мрачне́ть, -е́ю *perf.*

по|мути́ть(ся, -учу́(сь, -у́ти́шь(ся *perf.* **помутне́ние,** -я, dimness, dullness, clouding. **по|мутне́ть,** -е́ет *perf.*

помча́ться, -чу́сь *perf.* dash, rush, tear; dart off.

помыка́ть, -а́ю *imp.* + *instr.* order about.

по́мысел, -сла, intention, design; thought.

по|мы́ть(ся, -мо́ю(сь *perf.*

помяну́ть, -ну́ -нешь *perf.* (*imp.* помина́ть) mention; remember in one's prayers; помяни́ моё сло́во, mark my words.

помя́тый, crushed; flabby, baggy. **по|мя́ться,** -мнётся *perf.*

по|наде́яться, -е́юсь *perf.* count, rely.

пона́добиться, -блюсь *perf.* become necessary, be needed; е́сли пона́добится, if necessary.

понапра́сну *adv.* in vain.

понаслы́шке *adv.* by hearsay.

по-настоя́щему *adv.* in the right way, properly, truly.

понево́ле *adv.* willynilly; against one's will.

понеде́льник, -а, Monday. **понеде́льный,** weekly.

понемно́гу, понемно́жку *adv.* little by little; a little.

по|нести́(сь, -су́(сь, -сёшь(ся; -нёс(ся, -ла́(сь *perf.*

понижа́ть, -а́ю *imp.*, **пони́зить,** -ни́жу *perf.* lower; reduce; **~ся,** fall, drop, go down, fall off. **пониже́ние,** -я, fall, drop; lowering; reduction.

поника́ть, -а́ю *imp.*, **по|ни́кнуть,** -ну; -ни́к *perf.* droop, flag, wilt; ~ голово́й, hang one's head.

понима́ние, -я, understanding; comprehension; interpretation, conception.

понима́ть, -а́ю *imp.* of поня́ть.

по-но́вому *adv.* in a new fashion; нача́ть жить ~, begin a new life, turn over a new leaf.

поно́с, -а, diarrhoea.

поноси́ть[1], -ошу́, -о́сишь *perf.* carry; wear.

поноси́ть[2], -ошу́, -о́сишь *imp.* abuse, revile. **поно́сный,** abusive, defamatory.

поно́шенный, worn; shabby, threadbare.

по|нра́виться, -влюсь *perf.*

понто́н, -а, pontoon; pontoon bridge. **понто́нный,** pontoon.

понуди́тельный, compelling, pressing; coercive. **пону́дить,** -у́жу *perf.* **понужда́ть,** -а́ю *imp.* force, compel, coerce; impel.

понука́ть, -а́ю *imp.* urge on.

пону́рить, -рю *perf.*; ~ го́лову, hang one's head. **пону́рый,** downcast, depressed.

по|ню́хать, -аю *perf.* **поню́шка,** -и; ~ табаку́, pinch of snuff.

поня́тие, -я, concept, conception; notion, idea. **поня́тливость,** -и, comprehension, understanding. **поня́тливый,** bright, quick. **поня́тн|ый,** understandable; clear, intelligible; perspicuous; ~о, of course, naturally; ~о? (do you) see? is that clear?; ~но! I see; I understand; quite! **поня́ть,** пойму́, -мёшь; по́нял, -а́, -о *perf.* (*imp.* понима́ть) understand, comprehend; realize.

по|обе́дать, -аю *perf.* **по|обеща́ть,** -а́ю *perf.*

поо́даль *adv.* at some distance, a little way away.

поодино́чке *adv.* one by one, one at a time.

поочерёдно *adv.* in turn, by turns.

поощре́ние, -я, encouragement; incentive, spur. **поощри́ть,** -рю́ *perf.*, **поощря́ть,** -я́ю *imp.* encourage.

поп, -а́, priest.
попада́ние, -я, hit. **попада́ться, -а́ю(сь** *imp.* of попа́сть(ся.
попадья́, -и́, priest's wife.
попа́ло: see попа́сть. **по|па́риться, -рюсь** *perf.*
попа́рно *adv.* in pairs, two by two.
попа́сть, -аду́, -адёшь; -а́л *perf.* (*imp.* попада́ть) + в + *acc.* hit; get to, get into, find oneself in; + на + *acc.* hit upon, come on; не туда́ ~, get the wrong number; ~ в плен, be taken prisoner; ~ в цель, hit the target; ~ на по́езд, catch a train; ~ на рабо́ту, land a job; **~ся,** be caught; find oneself; turn up; пе́рвый попа́вшийся, the first person one happens to meet; ~ся на у́дочку, swallow the bait; что попадётся, anything. **попа́ло** with *prons.* and *advs.*; где ~, anywhere; как ~, anyhow; helter-skelter; что ~, the first thing to hand.
по|пеня́ть, -я́ю *perf.*
поперёк *adv.* and *prep.* + *gen.* across; вдоль и ~, far and wide; знать вдоль и ~, know inside out, know the ins and outs of; стать ~ го́рла + *dat.* stick in the throat of; стоя́ть ~ доро́ги + *dat.* be in the way of.
попереме́нно *adv.* in turn, by turns.
попере́чник, -а, diameter. **попере́чн|ый,** transverse, diametrical, cross; dihedral; ~ый разре́з, ~ое сече́ние, cross-section.
по|пе́рчить, -чу *perf.*
попече́ние, -я, care; charge; быть на попече́нии + *gen.*, be under the charge of, be left to the care of. **попечи́тель, -я** *m.* guardian, trustee.
попира́ть, -а́ю *imp.* (*perf.* попра́ть) trample on; flout.
поплавко́в|ый, float; ~ая ка́мера, float chamber. **поплаво́к, -вка́,** float; floating restaurant.
попла́кать, -а́чу *perf.* cry a little; shed a few tears.
по|плати́ться, -чу́сь, -тишься *perf.*
попо́йка, -и, drinking-bout.
попола́м *adv.* in two, in half; half-and-half; fifty-fifty.
поползнове́ние, -я, feeble impulse; half-formed intention, half a mind; pretension(s).
пополне́ние, -я, replenishment; re-stocking; re-fuelling; reinforcement.
по|полне́ть, -е́ю *perf.* **попо́лнить, -ню** *perf.*, **пополня́ть, -я́ю** *imp.* replenish, supplement, fill up; re-stock; re-fuel; reinforce.
попол́удни *adv.* in the afternoon, p.m.
пополу́ночи *adv.* after midnight, a.m.
попо́на, -ы, horse-cloth.
поправи́мый, reparable, remediable.
попра́вить, -влю *perf.*, **поправля́ть, -я́ю** *imp.* mend, repair; correct, set right, put right; adjust, set straight, tidy; improve, better; ~ приче́ску, tidy one's hair; **~ся,** correct oneself; get better, recover; put on weight; look better; improve. **попра́вка, -и,** correction, amendment; mending, repairing; adjustment; recovery.
попра́ть; -а́л *perf.* of попира́ть.
по-пре́жнему *adv.* as before; as usual.
попрёк, -а, reproach. **попрека́ть, -а́ю** *imp.*, **попрекну́ть, -ну́, -нёшь** *perf.* reproach.
по́прище, -а, field; walk of life, profession career.
по|про́бовать, -бую *perf.* **по|проси́ть(ся, -ошу́(сь, -о́сишь(ся** *perf.*
по́просту *adv.* simply; without ceremony.
попроша́йка, -и *m.* and *f.* cadger; beggar. **попроша́йничать, -аю** *imp.* beg; cadge.
попуга́й, -я, parrot.
популя́рность, -и, popularity. **популя́рный,** popular.
попусти́тельство, -а, connivance; toleration; tolerance.
по-пусто́му, по́пусту *adv.* in vain, to no purpose.
попу́тно *adv.* at the same time; in passing; incidentally. **попу́тный,** accompanying; following; passing; incidental; ~ ве́тер, fair wind. **попу́тчик, -а,** fellow-traveller.
попыта́ть, -а́ю *perf.* try; ~ сча́стья, try one's luck. **по|пыта́ться, -а́юсь** *perf.* **попы́тка, -и,** attempt, endeavour.
по|пя́титься, -я́чусь *perf.* **попя́тный,**

backward; идтѝ на ~, go back on one's word.
порá, -ы́, *acc.* -у; *pl.* -ы, пор, -áм, time, season; it is time; в (сáмую) пóру, opportunely, at the right time; давнó ~, it is high time; до поры́ до врéмени, for the time being; до какѝх пор? till when? till what time? how long?; до сих пор, till now, up to now, so far; hitherto; на пéрвых ~х, at first; с какѝх пор? с котóрых пор? since when?
поработѝть, -ощý *perf.*, **порабощáть,** -áю *imp.* enslave. **порабощéние, -я,** enslavement.
по|рáдовать(ся, -дую(сь *perf.*
поражáть, -áю *imp.*, **по|разѝть, -ажý** *perf.* rout; hit; strike; defeat; affect; stagger, startle; **~ся,** be astounded, be startled; be staggered. **поражéнец,** -нца defeatist. **поражéние, -я,** defeat; hitting, striking; affection; lesion; ~ в правáх, disfranchisement. **поражéнчество,** -а, defeatism. **поразѝтельный,** striking; staggering, startling.
порáнить, -ню *perf.* wound; injure; hurt.
порвáть -вý, -вёшь; -вáл, -á, -о *perf.* (*imp.* порывáть) tear (up); break, break off; **~ся,** tear; break (off); snap; be broken off.
по|редéть, -éет *perf.*
порéз, -а, cut. **порéзать, -éжу** *perf.* cut; kill, slaughter; **~ся,** cut oneself.
порéй, -я, leek.
по|рекомендовáть, -дýю *perf.* **по|ржáветь, -еет** *perf*.
пóристый, porous.
порицáние, -я, censure; reproof, reprimand; blame; общéственное ~, public censure. **порицáтельный,** disapproving; reproving. **порицáть, -áю** *imp.* blame; censure.
пóровну *adv.* equally, in equal parts.
порóг, -а, threshold; rapids.
порóда, -ы, breed, race, strain, species, stock; kind. sort, type; breeding; rock; layer, bed, stratum; matrix. **порóдистый,** thoroughbred. pedigree. **породѝть, -ожý** *perf.* (*imp.* порождáть) give birth to, beget; raise, generate, engender, give rise to.
породнённ|ый; ~ые горoдá, twin cities.
по|роднѝть(ся, -ню́(сь *perf.* **порóдность, -и,** race, breed; stock, strain. **порóдный,** pedigree.
порождáть, -áю *imp.* of породѝть.
порóжний, empty.
пóрознь *adv.* separately, apart.
порóй, порóю *adv.* at times, now and then.
порóк, -а, vice; defect; flaw, blemish; ~ сéрдца, heart-disease.
поросёнок, -нка; *pl.* -сята, -сят, piglet; sucking-pig. **поросѝться, -ѝтся** *imp.* (*perf.* о~) farrow.
пóросль, -и, suckers, shoots; young wood.
порóть¹, -рю́, -решь *imp.* (*perf.* вы́~) flog, thrash; whip, lash.
порóть², -рю́, -решь *imp.* (*perf.* рас~), undo, unpick; rip (out); ~ вздор, ерундý, чушь, talk rot, talk nonsense; ~ горя́чку, be in a frantic hurry; **~ся,** come unstitched, come undone.
пóрох, -а (-у); *pl.* ~á, gunpowder, powder; он ~а не вы́думает, he'll never set the Thames on fire. **пороховóй,** powder; ~ пóгреб, ~ склад, powder-magazine.
порóчить, -чу *imp.* (*perf.* о~) discredit; bring into disrepute; defame, denigrate, blacken, smear. **порóчный,** vicious, depraved; wanton; faulty, defective, fallacious.
порошóк, -шкá powder.
порт, -а, *loc.* -ý; *pl.* -ы, -óв, port; harbour; dockyard.
пóртить, -чу *imp.* (*perf.* ис~), spoil, mar; damage; corrupt; **~ся,** deteriorate; go bad; decay, rot; get out of order; be corrupted, become corrupt.
портнѝха, -и, dressmaker, tailor. **портнóвский,** tailor's, tailoring. **портнóй** *sb.* tailor.
портовѝк, -á, docker. **портóвый,** port, harbour; ~ рабóчий, docker.
портрéт, -а portrait; likeness.
портсигáр, -а, cigarette-case, cigar-case.
портфéль, -я *m.* brief-case; portfolio.
портьéра, -ы, curtain(s), portière.
портя́нка, -и, foot-binding, puttee.
порýганный, profaned, desecrated; outraged. **поругáть, -áю** *perf.* scold,

swear at; **~ся**, curse, swear; fall out, quarrel.

пору́ка, -и, bail; guarantee; surety; на пору́ки, on bail.

по-ру́сский *adv.* (in) Russian; говори́ть ~, speak Russian.

поруча́ть, -а́ю *imp.* of поручи́ть. **пору-че́нец**, -нца, special messenger. **поруче́ние**, -я, commission, errand; message; mission.

по́ручень, -чня *m.* handrail.

пору́чик, -а, lieutenant.

поручи́ть, -чу́, -чишь *perf.* (*imp.* поруча́ть) charge, commission; entrust; instruct.

поручи́ться, -чу́сь, -чишься *perf.* of руча́ться.

порха́ть, -а́ю *imp.*, **порхну́ть**, -ну́, -нёшь *perf.* flutter, flit; fly about.

порцио́н, -а, ration. **порцио́нный**, à la carte. **по́рция**, -и, portion; helping.

по́рча, -и, spoiling; damage; wear and tear.

по́ршень, -шня *m.* piston; plunger. **поршнев|о́й**, piston, plunger; reciprocating; ~о́е кольцо́ piston ring.

поры́в[1], -а, gust; rush; fit; uprush, upsurge; impulse.

поры́в[2], -а, breaking, snapping. **порыва́ть(ся**[1], -а́ю(сь *imp.* of порва́ть(ся.

порыва́ться[2], -а́юсь *imp.* make jerky movements; try, endeavour, strive. **поры́висто** *adv.* fitfully, by fits and starts. **поры́вистый**, gusty; jerky; impetuous, violent; fitful.

поря́дковый, ordinal. **поря́дком** *adv.* pretty, rather; properly, thoroughly. **поря́док**, -дка (-у), order; sequence; manner, way; procedure; *pl.* customs, usages, observances; в обяза́тельном поря́дке, without fail; всё в поря́дке, everything is all right, it's all in order; в спе́шном поря́дке, quickly, in haste; не в поря́дке, out of order; по поря́дку, in order, in succession; ~ дня, agenda, order of business, order of the day. **поря́дочно** *adv.* decently; honestly; respectably; fairly, pretty; a fair amount; fairly well, quite decently. **поря́дочный**, decent; honest; respectable; fair, considerable.

пос. *abbr.* посёлок, settlement, housing estate.

посади́ть, -ажу́, -а́дишь *perf.* of сади́ть, сажа́ть. **поса́дка**, -и, planting; embarkation; boarding; landing; seat. **поса́дочн|ый**, planting; landing; ~ые огни́, flare-path; ~ фа́ры, landing lights.

посажу́, etc.: see посади́ть. **по|са́харить**, -рю *perf.* **по|сва́тать(ся**, -аю(сь *perf.* **по|свеже́ть**, -е́ет *perf.* **по|свети́ть**, -ечу́, -е́тишь *perf.* **по|светле́ть**, -е́ет *perf.*

по́свист, -а, whistle; whistling. **посви́стывать**, -аю *imp.* whistle.

по-сво́ему *adv.* (in) one's own way.

посвяти́ть, -ящу́ *perf.*, **посвяща́ть**, -а́ю *imp.* devote, give up; dedicate; initiate, let in; ordain, consecrate. **посвяще́ние**, -я, dedication; initiation; consecration, ordination.

посе́в, -а, sowing; crops. **посевн|о́й**, sowing; ~а́я пло́щадь, sown area, area under crops.

по|седе́ть, -е́ю *perf.* **посе́кся**, etc.: see посе́чься.

поселе́нец, -нца, settler; deportee, exile. **поселе́ние**, -я, settling, settlement; deportation, exile. **по|сели́ть**, -лю́ *perf.*, **поселя́ть**, -я́ю *imp.* settle; lodge; inspire, arouse, engender; **~ся**, settle, take up residence, make one's home. **посёлок**, -лка, settlement; housing estate.

посеребрённый; -рён, -а́, silver-plated; silvered. **по|серебри́ть**, -рю́ *perf.*

по|сере́ть, -е́ю *perf.*

посети́тель, -я *m.* visitor; caller; guest. **посети́ть**, -ещу́ *perf.* (*imp.* посеща́ть) visit; call on; attend.

по|се́товать, -тую *perf.* **по|се́чься**, -ечётся, -еку́тся; -се́кся, -ла́сь *perf.*

посеща́емость, -и, attendance, (number of) visitors. **посеща́ть**, -а́ю *imp.* of посети́ть. **посеще́ние**, -я, visiting; visit.

по|се́ять, -е́ю *perf.*

поси́льн|ый, within one's powers.

посине́лый, gone blue. **по|сине́ть**, -е́ю *perf.*

по|скака́ть, -ачу́, -а́чешь *perf.*

поскользну́ться, -ну́сь, -нёшься *perf.* slip.
поско́льку *conj.* as far as, as much as, (in) so far as; since.
по|скро́мничать, -аю *perf.* **по|скупи́ться**, -плю́сь *perf.*
посла́нец, -нца, messenger, envoy. **посла́ние**, -я, message; epistle. **посла́нник**, -а, envoy, minister. **посла́ть**, -шлю́, -шлёшь *perf.* (*imp.* посыла́ть) send, dispatch; move, thrust; ~ за до́ктором, send for the doctor; ~ по по́чте, post.
по́сле *adv.* and *prep.* + *gen.* after; afterwards, later (on); since; ~ всего́, after all, when all is said and done; ~ всех, last (of all).
по́сле- in *comb.* post-; after-. **послевое́нный**, post-war. **~за́втра** *adv.* the day after tomorrow. **~обе́денный**, after-dinner. **~родово́й**, post-natal. **~сло́вие**, epilogue; concluding remarks. **~уда́рный**, post-tonic.
после́дн|ий, last; final; recent; latest; latter; (в) ~ее вре́мя, за ~ее вре́мя, lately recently; (в) ~ий раз, for the last time; до ~его вре́мени, until very recently; ~яя ка́пля, the last straw; ~яя мо́да, the latest fashion. **после́дователь**, -я *m.* follower. **после́довательный**, successive, consecutive; consistent, logical. **по|сле́довать**, -дую *perf.* **после́дствие**, -я consequence, sequel; after-effect. **после́дующий**, subsequent, succeeding, following, ensuing; consequent.
посло́вица, -ы, proverb, saying. **посло́вичный**, proverbial.
по|служи́ть, -жу́, -жишь *perf.* **послужно́й**, service; ~ спи́сок, service record.
послуша́ние, -я, obedience. **по|слу́шать(ся**, -аю(сь *perf.* **послу́шный**, obedient, dutiful.
по|слы́шаться, -шится *perf.*
посма́тривать, -аю *imp.* look from time to time (at), glance occasionally.
посме́иваться, -аюсь *imp.* chuckle, laugh softly.
посме́ртный, posthumous.
по|сме́ть, -е́ю *perf.*
посме́шище, -а, laughing-stock, butt. **посмея́ние**, -я, mockery, ridicule. **посмея́ться**, -ею́сь, -еёшься *perf.* laugh; + над + *instr.* laugh at, ridicule, make fun of.
по|смотре́ть(ся, -рю́(сь, -ришь(ся *perf.*
посо́бие, -я, aid, help, relief, assistance; allowance, benefit; textbook; (educational) aid; *pl.* teaching equipment; уче́бные посо́бия, educational supplies. **посо́бник**, -а, accomplice; abettor.
по|сове́товать(ся, -тую(сь *perf.* **по|соде́йствовать**, -твую *perf.*
посо́л, -сла́, ambassador.
по|соли́ть, -олю́, -о́ли́шь *perf.*
посо́льский, ambassadorial, ambassador's; embassy. **посо́льство**, -а, embassy.
поспа́ть, -сплю́; -а́л, -а́, -о *perf.* sleep; have a nap.
поспева́ть[1], -а́ет *imp.*, **по|спе́ть**[1], -е́ет *perf.* ripen; be done, be ready.
поспева́ть[2], -а́ю *imp.*, **поспе́ть**[2], -е́ю *perf.* have time; be in time (к + *dat.*, на + *acc.* for); + за + *instr.* keep up with, keep pace with; не ~ к по́езду, miss the train; ~ на по́езд, catch the train.
по|спеши́ть, -шу́ *perf.* **поспе́шно** *adv.* in a hurry, hurriedly, hastily. **поспе́шный**, hasty, hurried.
по|спо́рить, -рю *perf.* **по|спосо́бствовать**, -твую *perf.*
посреди́ *adv.* and *prep.* + *gen.* in the middle (of), in the midst (of). **посреди́не** *adv.* in the middle. **посре́дник**, -а, mediator, intermediary; go-between; middleman; umpire. **посре́дничество**, -а, mediation. **посре́дственно** *adv.* so-so, (only) fairly well; fair; satisfactory. **посре́дственность**, -и, mediocrity. **посре́дственный**, mediocre, middling; fair, satisfactory. **посре́дством** *prep.* + *gen.* by means of; by dint of; with the aid of.
по|ссо́рить(ся, -рю(сь *perf.*
пост[1], -а́, *loc.* -у́, post; занима́ть ~, occupy a post; на ~у́, at one's post; on one's beat; on point-duty.
пост[2], -а́, *loc.* -у́, fasting; abstinence; fast.
по|ста́вить[1], -влю *perf.*
поста́вить[2], -влю *perf.*, **поставля́ть**, -я́ю

imp. supply, purvey. **поста́вка, -и,** supply; delivery. **поставщи́к, -а́,** supplier, purveyor, provider; caterer; outfitter.

постана́вливать, -аю *imp.*, **постанови́ть, -влю́,** -вишь *perf.* (*imp.* also постановля́ть) decree, enact, ordain; decide, resolve.

постано́вка, -и, staging, production; arrangement, organization; putting, placing, setting; erection, raising; ~ го́лоса, voice training; ~ па́льцев, fingering.

постановле́ние, -я, decree, enactment; decision, resolution. **постановля́ть,** -я́ю *imp.* of постанови́ть.

постано́вочный, stage, staging, production. **постано́вщик,** -а, producer, stage-manager; (film) director.

по|стара́ться, -а́юсь *perf.*

по|старе́ть, -е́ю *perf.* **по-ста́рому** *adv.* as before; as of old.

посте́ль, -и, bed; bottom. **посте́льн|ый,** bed; ~ое бельё, bed-clothes; ~ режи́м, confinement to bed. **постелю́,** etc.: see постла́ть.

постепе́нно *adv.* gradually, little by little. **постепе́нный,** gradual.

по|стесня́ться, -я́юсь *perf.*

постига́ть, -а́ю *imp.* of пости́чь. **пости́гнуть:** see пости́чь. **постиже́ние,** -я comprehension, grasp. **постижи́мый,** comprehensible.

постила́ть, -а́ю *imp.* of постла́ть. **пости́лка,** -и, spreading, laying; bedding; litter.

пости́чь, пости́гнуть, -и́гну; -и́г(нул) *perf.* (*imp.* постига́ть) comprehend, grasp; befall.

по|стла́ть, -стелю́, -сте́лешь *perf.* (*imp.* also постила́ть) spread, lay; ~ посте́ль, make a bed.

по́стн|ый, lenten; lean; glum; ~ое ма́сло, vegetable oil.

посто́й, -я, billeting, quartering.

посто́льку *conj.* to the same extent, to the same degree; (so).

по|сторони́ться, -ню́сь, -ни́шься *perf.* **посторо́нн|ий,** strange; foreign; extraneous, outside; *sb.* stranger, outsider; ~им вход запрещён, no admission; private.

постоя́нно *adv.* constantly, continually, perpetually, always. **постоя́нн|ый,** permanent; constant; continual; invariable; steadfast, unchanging; ~ый а́дрес, permanent address; ~ая (величина́), constant; ~ый ток, direct current. **постоя́нство,** -а, constancy; permanency.

по|стоя́ть -ою́ *perf.* stand, stop; + за + *acc.* stand up for.

пострада́вший *sb.* victim. **по|страда́ть,** -а́ю *perf.*

построе́ние, -я, construction; building; formation. **по|стро́ить(ся,** -ро́ю(сь *perf.* **постро́йка,** -и, building; erection, construction; building-site.

постро́мка, -и, trace; strap.

поступа́тельный, progressive, forward, advancing. **поступа́ть** -а́ю *imp.*, **поступи́ть,** -плю́, -пишь *perf.* act; do; come through, come in, be received; + в or на + *acc.* enter, join, go to, go into; + с + *instr.* treat, deal with; ~ в прода́жу, be on sale, come on the market; ~ в шко́лу, go to school, start school; поступи́ла жа́лоба, a complaint has been received; **~ся** + *instr.* waive, forgo; give up. **поступле́ние,** -я, entering, joining; receipt; entry. **посту́пок,** -пка, action; act, deed; *pl.* conduct, behaviour. **по́ступь,** -и, gait; step, tread.

по|стуча́ть(ся, -чу́(сь *perf.*

по|стыди́ться, -ыжу́сь *perf.* **посты́дный,** shameful.

посу́да, -ы, crockery; plates and dishes; service; ware; utensils; vessel, crock. **посу́дн|ый,** china; dish; ~ое полоте́нце, tea-towel; ~ый шкаф, dresser, china-cupboard.

по|сули́ть, -лю́ *perf.*

посу́точный, 24-hour, round-the-clock; by the day.

посчастли́виться, итсся *perf.* *impers.* (+ *dat.*) turn out well, go well (for); ей посчастли́вилось + *inf.* she had the luck to, she was lucky enough to.

посчита́ть, -а́ю *perf.* count (up). **по|счита́ться,** -а́юсь *perf.*

посыла́ть, -а́ю *imp.* of посла́ть. **посы́лка,** -и, sending; parcel, package;

errand; premise. **посы́лочный,** parcel. **посы́льный** *sb.* messenger.

посы́пать, -плю, -плешь *perf.*, **посыпа́ть,** -а́ю *imp.* strew; sprinkle; powder.

посяга́тельство, -а, encroachment; infringement. **посяга́ть,** -а́ю *imp.*, **посягну́ть,** -ну́, -нёшь *perf.* encroach, infringe; make an attempt (на + *acc.* on).

пот, -а (-у), *loc.* -у́; *pl.* -ы́, sweat, perspiration.

потаённый **потайно́й,** secret.

по-тво́ему *adv.* in your opinion; as you wish; as you advise; пусть бу́дет ~, have it your own way; just as you think.

потака́ть, -а́ю *imp.* + *dat.* indulge, pander to.

потасо́вка, -и, brawl, fight; hiding, beating.

потво́рствовать, -твую *imp.* (+ *dat.*) be indulgent (towards), connive (at), pander (to).

потёмки, -мок *pl.* darkness. **по|темне́ть,** -е́ет *perf.*

по|тепле́ть, -е́ет *perf.*

потерпе́вший *sb.* victim; survivor. **по|терпе́ть,** -плю́ -пишь *perf.*

поте́ря, -и, loss; waste; *pl.* losses, casualties. **по|теря́ть(ся,** -я́ю(сь *perf.*

по|тесни́ть, -ню́ *perf.* **по|тесни́ться,** -ню́сь *perf.*; make room; sit closer, stand closer, squeeze up, move up.

поте́ть, -е́ю *imp.* (*perf.* вс~, за~) sweat, perspire; mist over, steam up; (+ над + *instr.*) sweat, toil (over).

поте́ха, -и, fun, amusement. **по|те́шить(ся,** -шу(сь *perf.* **поте́шный,** funny amusing.

потира́ть, -а́ю *imp.* rub.

потихо́ньку *adv.* noiselessly, softly; secretly, by stealth, on the sly; slowly.

по́тн|ый; -тен, -тна́, -тно, sweaty, damp with perspiration; misty, steamed up; ~ые ру́ки, clammy hands.

пото́к, -а, stream; flow; torrent; flood; production line; group; поток маши́н, traffic flow.

потоло́к, -лка́, ceiling.

по|толсте́ть, -е́ю *perf.*

пото́м *adv.* afterwards; later (on); then, after that. **пото́мок,** -мка, descendant; scion; offspring, progeny. **пото́мство,** -а, posterity, descendants.

потому́ *adv.* that is why; ~ что *conj.* because, as.

по|тону́ть, -ну́, -нешь *perf.* **пото́п,** -а, flood, deluge. **по|топи́ть,** -плю́, -пишь *perf.*, **потопля́ть,** -я́ю *imp.* sink. **потопле́ние,** -я, sinking.

по|топта́ть, -пчу́, -пчешь *perf.* **по|тороп́ить(ся** -плю́(сь, -пишь(ся *perf.*

пото́чн|ый, continuous; production-line; ~ая ли́ния, production line; ма́ссовое ~ое произво́дство, mass production.

по|тра́тить, -а́чу *perf.*

потреби́тель, -я *m.* consumer, user. **потреби́тельск|ий,** consumer; consumer's, consumers'; ~ие това́ры, consumer goods. **потреби́ть,** -блю́ *perf.*, **потребля́ть,** -я́ю *imp.* consume, use. **потребле́ние,** -я, consumption, use. **потре́бность,** -и, need, want, necessity, requirement. **потре́бный,** necessary, required, requisite. **по|тре́бовать(ся,** -бую(сь *perf.*

по|трево́жить(ся, -жу(сь *perf.*

потрёпанный, shabby; ragged, tattered; battered; worn, seedy. **по|трепа́ть(ся,** -плю́(сь, -плешь(ся *perf.*

по|тре́скаться, -ается *perf.* **потре́скивать,** -ает *imp.* crackle.

потроха́, -о́в *pl.* giblets; pluck. **потроши́ть,** -шу́ *imp.* (*perf.* вы́~) disembowel, clean; draw.

потруди́ться, -ужу́сь, -у́дишься *perf.* take some pains do some work; take the trouble.

потряса́ть, -а́ю *imp.*, **потрясти́,** -су́, -сёшь; -я́с, -ла́ *perf.* shake; rock; stagger, stun; + *acc.* or *instr.* brandish, shake; ~ кулако́м, shake one's fist. **потряса́ющий** staggering, stupendous, tremendous.

поту́га, -и, muscular contraction; *pl.* labours vain attempts; родовы́е поту́ги, labour.

поту́пить -плю *perf.*, **потупля́ть,** -я́ю *imp.* lower cast down; **~ся,** look down, cast down one's eyes.

потускне́лый, tarnished; lack-lustre. **по|тускне́ть,** -е́ет *perf.*
потуха́ть, -а́ет *imp.*, **по|ту́хнуть,** -нет, -у́х *perf.* go out; die out. **поту́хший,** extinct; lifeless, lack-lustre.
по|туши́ть, -шу́, -шишь *perf.* **по|тяга́ться,** -а́юсь *perf.*
потя́гиваться, -аюсь *imp.*, **по|тяну́ться,** -ну́сь, -нешься *perf.* stretch oneself. **по|тяну́ть,** -ну́, -нешь *perf.*
по|у́жинать, -аю *perf.* **по|умне́ть,** -е́ю *perf.*
поучи́тельный, instructive.
похвала́, -ы́, praise. **по|хвали́ть(ся,** -лю́(сь, -лишь(ся *perf.* **похвальба́,** -ы́, bragging, boasting. **похва́льный,** praiseworthy, laudable, commendable; laudatory.
по|хва́стать(ся, -аю(сь *perf.*
похити́тель, -я *m.* kidnapper; abductor; thief. **похи́тить,** -хи́щу *perf.*, **похища́ть,** -а́ю *imp.* kidnap; abduct, carry off; steal. **похище́ние,** -я, theft; kidnapping; abduction.
похлёбка, -и, broth, soup.
по|хлопота́ть, -очу́, -о́чешь *perf.*
похме́лье, -я, hangover.
похо́д, -а, campaign; march; cruise; (long) walk, hike; outing, excursion; вы́ступить в ~, take the field; set out; на ~е, on the march.
по|хода́тайствовать, -твую *perf.*
походи́ть, -ожу́, -о́дишь *imp.* на + *acc.* be like, look like, resemble.
похо́дка, -и, gait, walk, step. **похо́дн|ый,** mobile, field; marching, cruising; ~ая крова́ть, camp-bed; ~ая ку́хня, mobile kitchen, field kitchen; ~ый мешо́к, kit-bag; ~ый поря́док, marching order; ~ая ра́ция, walkie-talkie. **похожде́ние,** -я, adventure, escapade.
похо́жий, similar, alike; ~ на, like.
по|хорони́ть, -ню́, -нишь *perf.* **похоро́нный,** funeral. **по́хороны,** -ро́н *pl.* funeral; burial.
по|хороше́ть, -е́ю *perf.*
по́хоть, -и, lust.
по|худе́ть, -е́ю *perf.*
по|целова́ть(ся, -лу́ю(сь *perf.* **поцелу́й,** -я, kiss.
по|церемо́ниться, -нюсь *perf.*
по́чва, -ы, soil, earth; ground; basis, footing. **по́чвенный,** soil, ground; ~ покро́в, top-soil.
почём *adv.* how much; how; ~ знать? who can tell? how is one to know?; ~ сего́дня я́блоки? how much are apples today?; ~ я зна́ю? how should I know?
почему́ *adv.* why; (and) so, that's why. **почему́-либо, -нибудь** *advs.* for some reason or other. **почему́-то** *adv.* for some reason.
о́черк, -а, hand(writing).
почерне́лый, blackened, darkened. **по|-пчерне́ть,** -е́ю *perf.*
почерпа́ть, -а́ю *imp.*, **почерпну́ть,** -ну, -нёшь *perf.* get, draw, scoop up; pick up.
по|черстве́ть, -е́ю *perf.* **по|чеса́ть(ся,** -ешу́(сь, -е́шешь(ся *perf.*
по́честь, -и, honour. **почёт,** -а, honour; respect, esteem. **почётный,** honoured, respected, esteemed; of honour; honourable; honorary; ~ карау́л, guard of honour.
по́чечный, renal; kidney.
почива́ть, -а́ю *imp.* of почи́ть.
почи́н, -а, initiative; beginning, start.
по|чини́ть, -ню́, -нишь *perf.*, **починя́ть,** -я́ю *imp.* repair, mend. **почи́нка,** -и, repairing, mending.
по|чи́стить(ся, -и́щу(сь *perf.*
почита́ние, -я, honouring; respect, esteem. **почита́ть**[1], -а́ю *imp.* honour, respect, esteem; revere; worship.
почита́ть[2], -а́ю *perf.* read for a while, look at.
почи́ть, -и́ю *perf.* (*imp.* почива́ть) rest, take one's rest; pass away; ~ на ла́врах, rest on one's laurels.
по́чка[1], -и, bud.
по́чка[2], -и, kidney.
по́чта, -ы, post, mail; post-office. **почтальо́н,** -а, postman. **почтальо́нша,** -и, postwoman. **почта́мт,** -а, (head) post-office.
почте́ние, -я, respect; esteem; deference. **почте́нный,** honourable; respectable, estimable; venerable; considerable.
почти́ *adv.* almost, nearly.
почти́тельный, respectful, deferential; considerable. **почти́ть,** -чту́ *perf.* honour.

почтóв|ый, post, mail; postal; ~ая карéта, stage coach, mail; ~ая кáрточка, postcard; ~ый перевóд, postal order; ~ый пóезд, mail (train); ~ый ящик, letter-box.

по|чýдиться, -ишься *perf.* **по|шабáшить,** -шу *perf.*

пошатнýть, -нý -нёшь *perf.* shake; **~ся,** shake; totter, reel, stagger; be shaken.

по|шевели́ть(ся, -елю́(сь, -éлишь(ся *perf.* **пошёл,** etc.: see пойти́.

поши́вка, -и, sewing. **поши́вочный,** sewing.

пóшлина, -ы, duty; customs.

пóшлость, -и, vulgarity, commonness; triviality; triteness, banality. **пóшлый,** vulgar, common; commonplace, trivial; trite, banal. **пошля́к,** -á, vulgarian, Philistine.

поштýчно *adv.* by the piece. **поштýчный,** by the piece; piece-work.

по|шути́ть, -учý, -ýтишь *perf.*

пощáда, -ы, mercy. **по|щади́ть,** -ажý *perf.*

по|щекотáть, -очý, -óчешь *perf.*

пощёчина, -ы box on the ear; slap in the face.

по|щýпать, -аю *perf.*

поэ́зия, -и, poetry. **поэ́ма,** -ы, poem. **поэ́т,** -а, poet. **поэти́ческий,** poetic, poetical.

поэ́тому *adv.* therefore, and so.

пою́, etc.: see петь, пои́ть.

появи́ться, -влю́сь, -вишься *perf.*, **появля́ться,** -я́юсь *imp.* appear; show up; emerge. **появлéние,** -я, appearance.

пóяс, -а; *pl.* -á, belt; girdle; waist-band; waist; zone; по ~, up to the waist, waist-deep, waist-high.

пояснéние, -я, explanation, elucidation. **поясни́тельный,** explanatory. **поясни́ть,** -ню́ *perf.* (*imp* поясня́ть) explain, elucidate.

поясни́ца, -ы, small of the back. **поясн|óй,** waist; to the waist, waist-high; zone, zonal; ~áя вáнна, hip-bath.

поясня́ть, -я́ю *imp.* of поясни́ть.

пр. *abbr.* проéзд, passage, thoroughfare; проспéкт, Prospect, avenue; прóчие, (the) others.

пра- *pref.* original, first, oldest; great-. **прабáбушка,** -и, great-grandmother. **прáвнук,** -а, great-grandson. **прáвнучка,** -и, great-granddaughter. **прáдед,** -а, great-grandfather; *pl.* ancestors, forefathers. **~дéдовский,** great-grandfather's; ancestral; ancient. **~дéдушка,** -и *m.* great-grandfather. **прáотец,** -тца, forefather. **~прáдед,** -а, great-great-grandfather. **~роди́тель,** -я *m.* primogenitor; forefather. **~язы́к,** -á, parent language.

прáвда, -ы, (the) truth; true; justice; всéми ~ми и непрáвдами, by fair means or foul, by hook or by crook; э́то ~, that's true. **правди́вый,** true; truthful; honest, upright. **правдоподóбный,** probable, likely; plausible.

прáвило, -а, rule; regulation; principle; взять за ~, положи́ть за ~, make it a rule; взять себé за ~, make a point of; как ~, as a rule; прáвила ýличного движéния, traffic regulations.

прáвильно *adv.* rightly; correctly; regularly. **прáвильн|ый,** right, correct; regular; rectilinear, rectilineal; ~о! that's right! exactly!

прави́тельственный, government, governmental. **прави́тельство,** -а, government. **прáвить**[1], -влю + *instr.* rule, govern; drive.

прáвить[2], -влю *imp.* correct; ~ корректýру, read proofs, correct proofs. **прáвка,** -и, correcting; (proof-)reading.

правлéние, -я, board, governing body; administration, management; governing, government.

прáвленый, corrected.

прáвнук, ~внучка: see пра-.

прáво, -а; *pl.* -á, law; right; (води́тельские) правá, driving licence; на правáх + *gen.* in the capacity, character, or position of; на правáх рýкописи, all rights reserved; ~ гóлоса, the vote, suffrage.

прáво *adv.* really, truly, indeed.

право-[1] in *comb.* law; right. **правовéд,** -а, jurist; law-student. **~вéдение,** -я, jurisprudence. **~вéрный,** orthodox; *sb.* true believer, Moslem. **~мéрный,**

lawful, rightful. **~мóчие**, -я, competence. **~мóчный**, competent, authorized. **~нарушéние**, -я, infringement of the law, offence. **~нарушíтель**, -я *m*. offender, delinquent. **~писáние**, -я, spelling, orthography. **~слáвный**, orthodox; *sb*. member of Orthodox Church. **~сýдие**, -я, justice.

право-[2] in *comb*. right, right-hand. **правобережный**, on the right bank right-bank. **~сторóнний**, right; right-hand. **~флангóвый**, right-flank, right-wing.

правовóй, legal, of the law; lawful, rightful.

правотá, -ы́, rightness; innocence.

прáвый[1], right; right-hand; right-wing

прáв|ый[2]; прав, -á, -о, right, correct; righteous, just; innocent not guilty; ~ое дéло, a just cause.

прáвящий, ruling.

прáдед, etc.: see пра-.

прáздник, -а, (public) holiday; feast; festival; festive occasion. **прáзднование**, -я, celebration. **прáздновать** -ную *imp*. (*perf*. от~) celebrate. **прáздность**, -и, idleness, inactivity; emptiness. **прáздный**, idle; inactive; empty; vain, useless.

прáктика, -и, practice; practical work; на прáктике, in practice. **практиковáть**, -кýю *imp*. practise; apply in practice; **~ся** (*perf*. на~ся) practise; be used, be practised; + в + *prep*. have practice in. **прáктикум**, -а, practical work. **практи́ческий**, **практи́чный**, practical.

прáотец: see пра-.

прáпорщик, -а, ensign.

прапрáдед, etc.: see пра-.

прах, -а, dust; ashes, remains; пойти́ ~ом, go to rack and ruin.

прáчечная *sb*. laundry; wash-house. **прáчка**, -и, laundress.

праязы́к: see пра-.

пре- *pref*. I. of verbs, indicating action in extreme degree or superior measure; sur-, over-, out-. II. of adjs. and advs., indicating superlative degree; very, most, exceedingly.

пребывáние, -я, stay; residence; tenure, period; ~ в дóлжности, ~ на постý, tenure of office, period in office. **пребывáть**, -áю *imp*. be; reside; ~ в невéдении, be in the dark; ~ в отсýтствии, be absent; ~ у влáсти, be in power.

превзойти́, -йдý, -йдёшь; -ошёл, -шлá *perf*. (*imp*. превосходи́ть) surpass; excel; ~ самогó себя́, surpass oneself; ~ чи́сленностью, outnumber.

превозмогáть -áю *imp*., **превозмóчь**, -огý, -óжешь; -óг, -лá *perf*. overcome, surmount.

превознести́, -сý, -сёшь; -ёс, -лá *perf*., **превозноси́ть**, -ошý, -óсишь *imp*. extol, praise.

превосходи́тельство, -а, Excellency. **превосходи́ть**, -ожý, -óдишь *imp*. of превзойти́. **превосхóдн|ый**, superlative; superb, outstanding, excellent; superior; ~ая стéпень, superlative (degree). **превосходя́щий**, superior.

преврати́ть, -ащý *perf*., **превращáть**, -áю *imp*. convert, turn, reduce; transmute; **~ся**, turn, change. **преврáтно** *adv*. wrongly; ~ истолковáть, misinterpret; ~ поня́ть, misunderstand. **преврáтный**, wrong, false; changeful, inconstant, perverse. **превращéние** -я, transformation, conversion; transmutation; metamorphosis.

превы́сить, -ы́шу *perf*., **превышáть**, -áю *imp*. exceed. **превышéние**, -я, exceeding, excess.

прегрáда, -ы, obstacle; bar, barrier. **прегради́ть**, -ажý *perf*., **преграждáть**, -áю *imp*. bar, obstruct, block.

пред *prep*. + *instr*.: see пéред.

пред-[1], **предъ-** *pref*. pre-, fore-, ante-.

пред-[2] *abbr*. in *comb*. of председáтель, chairman.

-прéд, -а, *abbr*. in *comb*. of представи́тель, representative, spokesman.

предавáть(ся, -даю́(сь, -даёшь(ся *imp*. of предáть(ся.

предáние, -я, legend; tradition; handing over, committal. **прéданность**, -и, devotion; faithfulness; loyalty. **прéданный**, devoted, faithful. **предáтель**, -я *m*. traitor; betrayer. **предáтельский**, traitorous; perfidious; treacherous. **предáтельство**, -а, treachery, betrayal, perfidy. **предáть**, -áм, -áшь,

-áст, -адим; прéдал, -á, -о *perf.* (*imp.* предавáть) hand over, commit; betray; ~ забвéнию, bury in oblivion; ~ землé, commit to the earth; ~ судý, bring to trial; **~ся** give oneself up, abandon oneself; give way, indulge; + *dat.* go over to. put oneself in the hands of.

предаю, etc.: see предавáть.

предварúтельн|ый, preliminary; prior; по ~ому соглашéнию by prior arrangement; ~ое заключéние, detention before trial; ~ая продáжа билéтов, advance sale of tickets, advance booking. **предварúть,** -рю *perf.*, **предварять,** -яю *imp.* forestall, anticipate; forewarn inform beforehand.

предвéстник, -а, forerunner. precursor; herald, harbinger; presage, portent. **предвещáть,** -áю *imp.* foretell; herald, presage, portend; это предвещáет хорóшее, this augurs well.

предвзятый, preconceived; prejudiced, biased.

предвúдеть. -úжу *imp.* foresee; **~ся** be foreseen; be expected.

предвкусúть, -ушý, -ýсишь *perf.*, **предвкушáть,** -áю *imp.* look forward to, anticipate (with pleasure).

предводúтель, -я *m.* leader. **предводúтельствовать,** -твую *imp.* + *instr.* lead.

предвоéнный pre-war.

предвосхúтить -úщу *perf.*, **предвосхищáть,** -áю *imp.* anticipate.

предвы́борный, (pre-)election.

предгóрье, -я, foothills.

предéл, -а, limit; bound. boundary; end; *pl.* range; положúть ~ + *dat.* put an end to terminate. **предéльн|ый,** boundary; limiting; maximum; utmost; critical; saturated; ~ый вóзраст, age-limit; ~ое напряжéние, breaking load, maximum stress; ~ая скóрость, maximum speed; ~ый срок time-limit deadline.

предзнаменовáние, -я, omen, augury. **предзнаменовáть,** -нýю *imp.* bode, augur, portend.

предислóвие, -я, preface, foreword.

предлагáть, -áю *imp.* of предложúть.

предлóг[1], -а, pretext; под ~ом + *gen.* on the pretext of.

предлóг[2], -а, preposition.

предложéние[1], -я, sentence; clause; proposition.

предложéние[2], -я, offer; proposition; proposal; motion; suggestion; supply; внестú ~, move, introduce, put down, a motion; сдéлать ~ + *dat.* make an offer to; propose to; спрос и ~, supply and demand. **предложúть,** -жý, -жишь *perf.* (*imp.* предлагáть) offer; propose; suggest; put, set, propound; order, require; ~ резолю́цию, move a resolution.

предлóжный, prepositional.

предмéт, -а, object; article, item; subject; topic, theme; (*pl.*) goods; на сей ~, to this end, with this object; ~ спóра, point at issue; ~ы пéрвой необходúмости, necessities. **предмéтный,** object; ~ каталóг, subject catalogue; ~ стóлик stage; ~ урóк, object-lesson.

предназначáть, -áю *imp.*, **предназнáчить,** -чу *perf.* destine, intend, mean; earmark, set aside. **предназначéние,** -я earmarking; destiny.

преднамéренный, premeditated; aforethought; deliberate.

прéдо: see пéред.

прéдок, -дка, forefather, ancestor; *pl.* forebears.

предостáвить, -влю *perf.*, **предоставлять,** -яю *imp.* grant; leave; give; ~ в его распоряжéние, put at his disposal; ~ прáво, concede a right; ~ слóво + *dat.* give the floor to, call on to speak.

предостерегáть, -áю *imp.*, **предостерéчь,** -егý, -ежёшь; -ёг, -лá *perf.* warn, caution. **предостережéние,** -я, warning, caution. **предосторóжность,** -и, caution; precaution; мéры предосторóжности, precautionary measures.

предосудúтельный, wrong, reprehensible, blameworthy.

предотвратúть, -ащý *perf.*, **предотвращáть.** -áю *imp.* avert, prevent; ward off, stave off.

предохранéние, -я, protection; preservation. **предохранúтель,** -я *m.* guard;

safety device, safety-catch; fuse. **предохранíтельн|ый,** preservative; preventive; safety; protective; ~ый клáпан, safety-valve; ~ая корóбка, fuse-box. **предохранúть,** -ню́ *perf.*, **предохранять,** -яю *imp.* preserve, protect.

предписáние, -я, order, injunction; *pl.* directions, instructions; prescription; соглáсно предписáнию, by order. **предписáть,** -ишу́, -и́шешь *perf.*, **предпи́сывать,** -аю *imp.* order, direct, instruct; prescribe.

предполагáемый, supposed, conjectural. **предполагáть,** -áю *imp.*, **предположи́ть,** -ожу́, -óжишь *perf.* suppose, assume; conjecture, surmise; intend, propose; contemplate; presuppose; **предполагáется** *impers.* it is proposed, it is intended. **предположéние** -я, supposition, assumption; intention. **предположи́тельно** *adv.* supposedly, presumably; probably. **предположи́тельный**, conjectural; hypothetical.

предпослéдний, penultimate, last but one, next to the last.

предпосы́лка, -и, prerequisite, pre-condition; premise.

предпочéсть, -чту́, -чтёшь; -чёл, -чла́ *perf.*, **предпочитáть,** -áю *imp.* prefer; я предпочёл бы, I would rather. **предпочтéние,** -я, preference. **предпочти́тельный,** preferable.

предприи́мчивость, -и, enterprise. **предприи́мчивый,** enterprising.

предпринимáтель, -я *m.* owner; employer; entrepreneur; contractor. **предпринимáтельство,** -а, business undertakings; свобóдное ~, free enterprise. **предпринимáть,** -áю *imp.*, **предприня́ть,** -иму́, -и́мешь; -и́нял, **-á,** -о *perf.* undertake; ~ атáку, launch an attack; ~ шаги́, take steps. **предприя́тие,** -я, undertaking, enterprise; business; concern; works; рискóванное ~, venture risky undertaking

предрасположéние, -я, predisposition. **предрасполóженный,** predisposed.

предрассу́док, -дка, prejudice.

предрешáть, -áю *imp.* **предреши́ть,** -шу́ *perf.* decide beforehand; predetermine.

председáтель, -я *m.* **председáтельница,** -ы, chairman. **председáтельск|ий,** chairman's; ~ое крéсло, the chair. **председáтельствовать,** -твую *imp.* preside, be in the chair.

предсказáние, -я, prediction, forecast, prophecy; prognostication. **предсказáтель,** -я *m.* foreteller, forecaster; soothsayer. **предсказáть,** -ажу́ -áжешь *perf.*, **предскáзывать,** -аю *imp.* foretell, predict; forecast, prophesy.

предсмéртный, dying; ~ час, one's last hour.

представи́тель, -я *m.* representative; spokesman; specimen. **представи́тельный,** representative; imposing. **представи́тельство,** -а, representation; representatives; delegation.

представáть, -таю́, -таёшь *imp.* of предстáть.

предстáвить, -влю *perf.*, **представля́ть,** -я́ю *imp.* present; produce, submit; introduce; recommend, put forward; display; perform; play; represent; ~ себé, imagine, fancy, picture, conceive; представля́ть собóй, represent, be; constitute; **~ся,** present itself, occur, arise; seem; introduce oneself; + *instr.* pretend to be, pass oneself off as. **представлéние**, -я, presentation, introduction; declaration statement; representation; performance; idea, notion, conception.

предстáть -áну *perf.* (*imp.* представáть), appear; ~ пéред судóм, appear in court.

предстоя́ть, -ои́т *imp.* be in prospect, lie ahead, be at hand; мне предстои́т пойти́ тудá, I shall have to go there. **предстоя́щий,** coming, forthcoming; impending, imminent.

предтéча, -и *m.* and *f.* forerunner, precursor; Иоáнн ~, John the Baptist.

предубеждéние, -я, prejudice, bias.

предугадáть, -áю *perf.*, **предугáдывать,** -аю *imp.* guess; foresee.

предупреди́тельность, -и, courtesy; attentiveness. **предупреди́тельный**, preventive, precautionary; courteous, attentive; obliging. **предупреди́ть,** -ежу́ *perf.*, **предупреждáть,** -áю *imp.*

notify in advance, let know beforehand; warn; give notice; prevent, avert; anticipate, forestall. **предупрежде́ние,** -я, notice; notification; warning, caution; prevention; anticipation; forestalling.

предусма́тривать, -аю *imp.*, **предусмотре́ть,** -рю́, -ришь *perf.* envisage, foresee; provide for, make provision for. **предусмотри́тельный,** prudent; provident; far-sighted.

предчу́вствие, -я, presentiment; foreboding, misgiving, premonition. **предчу́вствовать** -твую *imp.* have a presentiment (about) have a premonition of.

предше́ственник, -а, predecessor; forerunner, precursor. **предше́ствовать,** -твую *imp.* + *dat.* go in front of; precede.

предъ-: see пред-[1].

предъяви́тель -я *m.* bearer; а́кция на предъяви́теля, ordinary share. **предъяви́ть,** -влю́, -вишь *perf.*, **предъявля́ть,** -я́ю *imp* show, produce, present; bring, bring forward; ~ иск к + *dat.* bring suit against; ~ обвине́ние + *dat.* charge; ~ пра́во на + *acc.* lay claim to.

предыду́щ|ий previous, preceding; **~ее** *sb* the foregoing.

пре́емник -а, successor. **пре́емственность,** -и succession; continuity.

пре́жде *adv.* before; first; formerly, in former times; ~ чем, before; *prep.* + *gen* before; ~ всего́, first of all, to begin with; first and foremost. **преждевре́менный,** premature, untimely. **пре́жний,** previous, former.

президе́нт, -а, president. **президе́нтский,** presidential. **прези́диум,** -а, presidium.

презира́ть, -а́ю *imp* despise hold in contempt; disdain scorn. **презре́ние,** -я, contempt; scorn. **презре́нный,** contemptible, despicable **презри́тельный,** contemptuous scornful.

преиму́щественно *adv.* mainly, chiefly, principally. **преиму́щественный,** main, principal primary prime; preferential; priority **преиму́щество,** -а, advantage; preference; по преиму́ществу for the most part, chiefly.

преклоне́ние, -я, admiration, worship.

преклони́ть, -ню́ *perf.*, **преклоня́ть,** -я́ю *imp.* bow bend; ~ го́лову, bow; ~ коле́на genuflect kneel; **~ся** bow down; + *dat.* or перед + *instr.* admire, worship. **преклóнный;** ~ во́зраст old age; declining years.

прекра́сно *adv.* excellently; perfectly well. **прекра́сный,** beautiful; fine; excellent, capital first-rate; в оди́н ~ день, one fine day; ~ пол, the fair sex.

прекрати́ть, -ащу́ *perf.*, **прекраща́ть,** -а́ю *imp.* stop, cease discontinue; put a stop to, end; break off sever, cut off; ~ войну́ end the war; ~ подпи́ску, discontinue a subscription, stop subscribing; **~ся**, cease, end.

преле́стный charming, delightful lovely. **пре́лесть,** -и, charm fascination.

преломи́ть, -млю́, -мишь *perf.*, **преломля́ть,** -я́ю *imp.* refract; **~ся,** be refracted. **преломле́ние** -я, refraction.

пре́лый, fusty, musty; rotten. **прель,** -и, mouldiness, mould, rot.

прельсти́ть, -льщу́ *perf.*, **прельща́ть,** -а́ю *imp.* attract; lure, entice; **~ся**, be attracted; be tempted; fall (+ *instr.* for)

премиа́льн|ый, bonus; prize; **~ые** *sb. pl.* bonus.

преми́нуть, -ну *perf.* with *neg.* (not) fail.

премирова́ть, -ру́ю *perf.* and *imp.* award a prize to; give a bonus. **пре́мия,** -и, prize; bonus; bounty, gratuity; premium.

премье́р, -а, prime minister; leading actor, lead. **премье́ра,** -ы, première, first performance. **премье́рша,** -и, leading lady, lead.

пренебрега́ть, -а́ю *imp.*, **пренебре́чь,** -егу́, -ежёшь; -ёг, -ла́ *perf.* + *instr.* scorn despise; neglect, disregard. **пренебреже́ние,** -я, scorn, contempt, disdain; neglect, disregard. **пренебрежи́тельный,** scornful; slighting; disdainful.

пре́ния -ий *pl.* debate; discussion; pleadings; вы́ступить в ~х, take part in a discussion.

преоблада́ние, -я, predominance. **преоблада́ть, -áет** *imp.* predominate; prevail.

преобража́ть, -áю *imp.* **преобрази́ть, -ажý,** transform. **преображе́ние, -я,** transformation; Transfiguration. **преобразова́ние, -я,** transformation; reform; reorganization. **преобразова́ть, -зýю** *perf.*, **преобразóвывать, -аю** *imp.* transform; reform, reorganize.

преодолева́ть, -áю *imp.*, **преодоле́ть, -éю** *perf.* overcome, get over, surmount.

препара́т, -а, preparation.

препина́ние, -я; знáки препинáния, punctuation marks.

препира́тельство, -а, altercation, wrangling squabbling. **препира́ться, -áюсь** *imp.* wrangle, squabble.

преподава́ние, -я, teaching, tuition, instruction. **преподава́тель, -я** *m.*, **-ница, -ы,** teacher; lecturer, instructor. **преподава́тельский,** teaching; teacher's, teachers'; ~ состáв, (teaching) staff. **преподава́ть, -даю́, -даёшь** *imp.* teach.

преподнести́, -сý, -сёшь -ёс, -лá *perf.*, **преподноси́ть, -ошý, -óсишь,** present with, make a present of.

препроводи́тельный, accompanying. **препроводи́ть, -вожý, -вóдишь** *perf.*, **препровожда́ть, -áю** *imp.* send, forward, dispatch.

препя́тствие, -я, obstacle, impediment, hindrance; hurdle; скáчки (бег) с препя́тствиями, steeplechase; hurdle-race, obstacle-race. **препя́тствовать, -твую** *imp.* (*perf.* вос~) + *dat.* hinder, impede hamper; stand in the way of.

прерва́ть, -вý, -вёшь; -áл, -á, -о *perf.* (*imp.* прерывáть) interrupt; break off; cut off, sever; cut short; нас прервáли we've been cut off; **~ся,** be interrupted; be broken off; break down; break.

пререка́ние, -я, altercation, argument, wrangle. **препека́ться, -áюсь** *imp.* argue, wrangle, dispute.

прерыва́ть(ся, -áю(сь *imp.* of прервáть(ся.

пресека́ть, -áю *imp.*, **пресе́чь, -екý, -ечёшь; -ёк, -еклá** *perf.* stop, cut short; put an end to; ~ в кóрне, nip in the bud; **~ся,** stop; break.

пресле́дование, -я, pursuit, chase; persecution, victimization; prosecution. **пресле́довать, -дую** *imp.* pursue, chase, be after; haunt; persecute, torment; victimize; prosecute.

пресловýтый, notorious.

пресмыка́ться, -áюсь *imp.* grovel, cringe; creep, crawl. **пресмыка́ющееся** *sb.* reptile.

пре́сный, fresh; unsalted; unleavened; flavourless, tasteless; insipid, vapid, flat.

престаре́лый, aged; advanced in years.

престо́л, -а, throne; altar.

преступле́ние, -я crime, offence; felony; transgression. **престýпник, -а,** criminal, offender delinquent; felon; воéнный ~, war criminal. **престýпность, -и,** criminality; crime, delinquency. **престýпный,** criminal; felonious.

пресы́титься, -ы́щусь *perf.*, **пресыща́ться, -áюсь** *imp.* be satiated, be surfeited. **пресыще́ние, -я,** surfeit, satiety.

претвори́ть, -рю́ *perf.*, **претворя́ть, -я́ю** *imp* (в + *acc.*) turn, change, convert; ~ в жизнь, put into practice, realize, carry out; **~ся** в + *acc.* turn into, become; ~ в жизнь, be realized, come true.

претенде́нт, -а, claimant; aspirant; candidate; pretender. **претендова́ть, -дýю** *imp.* на + *acc.* claim, lay claim to; have pretensions to; aspire to. **прете́нзия, -и,** claim; pretension; быть в претéнзии на + *acc.* have a grudge, a grievance, against; bear a grudge.

претерпева́ть, -áю *imp.*, **претерпе́ть, -плю́, -пишь** *perf.* undergo; suffer, endure.

преувеличе́ние, -я, exaggeration; overstatement. **преувели́чивать, -аю** *imp.*, **преувели́чить, -чу** *perf.* exaggerate; overstate.

преуменьша́ть, -áю *imp.*, **преуме́ньшить, -éньшу** *perf.* underestimate; minimize; belittle; understate.

преуспева́ть, -áю *imp.*, **преуспе́ть, -éю** *perf.* succeed be successful; thrive, prosper, flourish.

преходя́щий, transient.

при *prep.* + *prep.* by, at; in the presence of; attached to, affiliated to, under the auspices of; with; about; on; for, notwithstanding; in the time of, in the days of; under; during; when, in case of; би́тва ~ Бородине́, the battle of Borodino; ~ всём том, with it all, moreover; for all that; ~ де́тях, in front of the children; ~ дневно́м све́те, by daylight; ~ доро́ге, by the road(-side); ~ Ива́не Гро́зном, in the reign of Ivan the Terrible; under Ivan the Terrible; при мне, in my presence; ~ перехо́де че́рез у́лицу, when crossing the street; ~ Пу́шкине, in Pushkin's day; ~ слу́чае, when the occasion arises; ~ све́те ла́мпы, by lamplight; у него́ не́ было ~ себе́ де́нег, he had no money on him.

при-. I. *vbl. pref.* indicating action or motion continued to a given terminal point; action of attaching or adding; direction of action towards speaker or from above downward; incomplete or tentative action; exhaustive action; action to an accompaniment. II. *pref.* of nouns and adjs., indicating juxtaposition or proximity.

приба́вить, -влю *perf.*, **прибавля́ть,** -я́ю, add, put on; increase, augment; exaggerate, lay it on (thick); ~ (в ве́се), put on weight; ~ хо́ду, put on speed; ~ ша́гу, mend one's pace; **~ся,** increase; rise; wax; день приба́вился, the days are getting longer, are drawing out. **приба́вка,** -и, addition, augmentation; increase, supplement, rise. **прибавле́ние,** -я, addition, augmentation; supplement, appendix. **приба́вочный,** additional; surplus.

прибега́ть[1], -а́ю *imp.* of прибежа́ть.

прибега́ть[2], -а́ю *imp.*, **прибе́гнуть,** -ну; -бе́г *perf.* + к + *dat.* resort to, fall back on.

прибежа́ть, -егу́ *perf.* (*imp.* прибега́ть) come running, run up.

прибе́жище, -а, refuge; после́днее ~, last resort.

приберега́ть, -а́ю *imp.*, **прибере́чь,** -егу́, -ежёшь; -ёг, -ла́ *perf.* save (up), reserve.

приберу́, etc.: see прибра́ть. **прибива́ть,** -а́ю *imp.* of приби́ть. **прибира́ть,** -а́ю *imp.* of прибра́ть.

приби́ть, -бью́, -бьёшь *perf.* (*imp.* прибива́ть), nail, fix with nails; lay, flatten; drive, carry; beat up.

приближа́ть, -а́ю *imp.*, **прибли́зить,** -и́жу *perf.* bring nearer, move nearer; hasten, advance; **~ся,** approach, draw near; draw (come) nearer.

прибо́й, -я, surf, breakers.

прибо́р, -а, instrument, device, apparatus, appliance, gadget; set, service, things; fittings; бри́твенный ~, shaving things; ча́йный ~, tea-service, tea-things. **прибо́рн|ый,** instrument; ~ая доска́, dash-board, instrument panel.

прибра́ть, -беру́, -берёшь; -а́л, -а́, -о *perf.* (*imp.* прибира́ть) tidy (up), clear up, clean up; put away; ~ ко́мнату, do (out) a room; ~ посте́ль, make a bed.

прибре́жн|ый, coastal; littoral, riverside; riparian; ~ые острова́, off-shore islands.

прибыва́ть, -а́ю *imp.*, **прибы́ть,** -бу́ду; при́был, -а́, -о *perf.* arrive; get in; increase, grow; rise, swell; wax. **при́быль,** -и, profit, gain; return; increase, rise. **при́быльный,** profitable, lucrative. **прибы́тие,** -я, arrival.

прибью́, etc.: see приби́ть.

прива́л -а, halt, stop; stopping-place.

приведу́, etc.: see привести́.

привезти́, -зу́, -зёшь; -ёз, -ла́ (*imp.* привози́ть), bring.

привере́дливый, fastidious, squeamish, hard to please. **привере́дничать,** -аю *imp.* be hard to please, be fastidious, be squeamish.

приве́рженец, -нца, adherent; follower. **приве́рженный,** attached, devoted.

приве́сить, -е́шу *perf.* (*imp.* приве́шивать) hang up, suspend.

привести́, -еду́, -едёшь; -ёл, -а́ *perf.* (*imp.* приводи́ть) bring; lead; take; reduce; adduce, cite; + к + *dat.* lead to, bring to, conduce to, result in; + в + *acc.* put in(to), set; ~ в движе́ние, в де́йствие set in motion, set going; ~ в изумле́ние, astonish, astound; ~ в исполне́ние, execute, carry out; ~ в отча́яние, drive to despair; ~ в поря́док, put in order, tidy (up); arrange, fix; ~ в у́жас, horrify.

приве́т, -а, greeting(s); regards; переда́йте ~ + *dat*. remember me to, my regards to; с серде́чным ~ом, yours sincerely. **приве́тливость**, -и, affability; cordiality. **приве́тливый**, cordial, friendly; affable. **приве́тствие**, -я, greeting, salutation; speech of welcome. **приве́тствовать**, -твую *perf*. and *imp*. greet, salute, hail; welcome; ~ сто́я, give a standing ovation (to).

приве́шивать, -аю *imp*. of приве́сить.

прививá́ть(ся, -а́ю(сь, -а́ешь(ся *imp*. of приви́ть(ся. **приви́вка**, -и, inoculation; vaccination; grafting, graft.

привиде́ние, -я, ghost, spectre; apparition. **при|ви́деться**, -дится *perf*.

привилегиро́ванн|ый, privileged; ~ая а́кция, preference share. **привиле́гия**, -и, privilege.

привинти́ть, -нчу́ *perf*., **приви́нчивать**, -аю *imp*. screw on.

приви́ть, -вью́, -вьёшь; -и́л, -а́, -о *perf*. (*imp*. прививá́ть) inoculate, vaccinate; graft; implant; inculcate; cultivate, foster; ~ о́спу + *dat*. vaccinate; **~ся**, take; become established, find acceptance, catch on.

при́вкус, а, after-taste; smack.

привлека́тельный, attractive. **привлека́ть**, -а́ю *imp*., **привле́чь**, -еку́, -ечёшь; -ёк, -ла́ *perf*. attract; draw; draw in, win over; have up; ~ внима́ние, attract attention; ~ к суду́, sue, take to court; prosecute; put on trial.

приво́д, -а, drive, driving-gear. **приводи́ть**, -ожу́, -о́дишь *imp*. of привести́. **приводно́й**, driving.

привожу́, etc.: see приводи́ть, привози́ть.

приво́з, -а, bringing, supply; importation; import. **привози́ть**, -ожу́, -о́зишь *imp*. of привезти́. **привозно́й**, **приво́зный**, imported.

приво́льный, free.

привстава́ть, -таю́, -таёшь *imp*., **привста́ть**, -а́ну *perf*. half-rise; rise, stand up.

привыка́ть, -а́ю *imp*., **привы́кнуть**, -ну; -ы́к *perf*. get used, get accustomed; get into the habit, get into the way. **привы́чка**, -и, habit. **привы́чный**, habitual, usual, customary; accustomed, used; of habit.

привью́, etc.: see приви́ть.

привя́занность, -и, attachment; affection. **привя́занный**, attached. **привяза́ть**, -яжу́, -я́жешь *perf*., **привя́зывать**, -аю *imp*. attach; tie, bind, fasten, secure, tether; **~ся**, become attached; attach oneself; + к + *dat*. pester, bother. **привязно́й**, fastened, secured, tethered. **привя́зчивый**, importunate, insistent, annoying; affectionate; susceptible. **при́вязь**, -и, tie; lead, leash; tether.

пригласи́ть, -ашу́ *perf*., **приглаша́ть**, -а́ю *imp*. invite, ask; call (in); ~ на обе́д, ask to dinner. **приглаше́ние**, -я, invitation; offer.

пригляде́ться, -яжу́сь *perf*., **пригля́дываться**, -аюсь *imp*. look closely; + к + *dat*. scrutinize, examine; get used to, get accustomed to.

пригна́ть, -гоню́, -го́нишь; -а́л, -а́, -о *perf*. (*imp*. пригоня́ть) drive in, bring in; fit, adjust.

пригова́ривать[1], -аю *imp*. keep saying, keep (on) repeating.

пригова́ривать[2], -аю *imp*., **приговори́ть**, -рю́ *perf*. sentence, condemn.

пригоди́ться, -ожу́сь *perf*. prove useful; be of use; come in useful come in handy. **приго́дный**, fit, suitable, good; useful. **приго́жий**, fine.

пригоня́ть, -я́ю *imp*. of пригна́ть.

пригора́ть, -а́ет *imp*., **пригоре́ть**, -ри́т *perf*. be burnt. **пригоре́лый**, burnt.

при́город, -а, suburb. **при́городный**, suburban.

приго́рок, -рка, hillock, knoll.

при́горшня, -и, *gen. pl*. -ей, handful.

приготови́тельный, preparatory. **пригото́вить**, -влю *perf*., **приготовля́ть**, -я́ю *imp*. prepare, cook, ~ роль, learn a part; **~ся**, prepare; prepare oneself. **приготовле́ние**, -я, preparation.

пригрева́ть, -а́ю *imp*. of пригре́ть. **при|гре́зиться**, -е́жусь *perf*.

пригре́ть, -е́ю *perf.* (*imp.* пригрева́ть) warm; cherish.
при|грози́ть, -ожу́ *perf.*
придава́ть, -даю́, -даёшь *imp.*, **прида́ть,** -а́м, -а́шь, -а́ст, -ади́м; при́дал, -а́, -о *perf.* add; increase, strengthen; give, impart; attach; ~ значе́ние + *dat.* attach importance to. **прида́ча,** -и, adding; addition, supplement; в прида́чу, into the bargain, in addition.
придвига́ть, -а́ю *imp.* **придви́нуть,** -ну *perf.* move up, draw up; **~ся,** move up, draw near.
придво́рный, court; *sb.* courtier.
приде́лать, -аю *perf.*, **приде́лывать,** -аю *imp.* fix, attach.
приде́рживаться, -аюсь *imp.* hold on, hold; + *gen.* hold to, keep to; stick to, adhere to; ~ пра́вой стороны́, keep to the right; ~ мне́ния, be of the opinion.
придеру́сь, etc.: see придра́ться. **придира́ться,** -а́юсь *imp.* of придра́ться. **приди́рка,** -и, cavil, captious objection; fault-finding; carping. **приди́рчивый,** niggling; captious.
придоро́жный, roadside wayside.
придра́ться, -деру́сь, -дерёшься; -а́лся, -а́сь, -а́ло́сь *perf.* (*imp.* придира́ться) find fault, cavil carp; seize; ~ к слу́чаю, seize an opportunity.
приду́, etc.: see прийти́.
приду́мать, -аю *perf.*, **приду́мывать,** -аю *imp.* think up, devise, invent; think of.
придыха́тельное *sb.* aspirate.
прие́ду, etc.; see прие́хать. **прие́зд,** -а, arrival, coming. **приезжа́ть,** -а́ю *imp.* of прие́хать. **прие́зжий,** newly arrived; *sb.* newcomer; visitor.
приём, -а, receiving; reception; surgery; welcome; admittance; dose; go; motion, movement; method, way, mode; device, trick; hold, grip; в оди́н ~, at one go. **прие́млемый,** acceptable; admissible. **приёмная** *sb.* waiting-room; reception room. **приёмник,** -а, radio, wireless, receiver. **приёмн|ый,** receiving; reception; entrance; foster, adoptive, adopted; ~ый день, visiting day; ~ая коми́ссия, selection board; ~ая мать, foster-mother; ~ые часы́, (business) hours; surgery (hours); ~ый экза́мен, entrance examination.
приёмо-передаю́щий, two-way. **приёмщик,** -а, inspector, examiner. **приёмочный,** inspection, examining.
прие́хать, -е́ду *perf.* (*imp.* приезжа́ть) arrive, come.
прижа́ть, -жму́, -жмёшь *perf.* (*imp.* прижима́ть) press; clasp; **~ся,** press oneself; cuddle up, snuggle up, nestle up.
приже́чь, -жгу́, -жжёшь; -жёг, -жгла́ *perf.* (*imp.* прижига́ть) cauterize, sear.
прижива́лка, -и, **прижива́льщик,** -а, dependant; hanger-on, sponger, parasite.
прижига́ние, -я, cauterization. **прижига́ть,** -а́ю *imp.* of приже́чь.
прижима́ть(ся, -а́ю(сь *imp.* of прижа́ть(ся. **прижи́мистый,** tight-fisted, stingy. **прижму́,** etc.: see прижа́ть.
приз, -а; *pl.* -ы́, prize.
призаду́маться, -аюсь *perf.*, **призаду́мываться,** -аюсь *imp.* become thoughtful, become pensive.
призва́ние, -я, vocation, calling; по призва́нию, by vocation. **призва́ть,** -зову́, -зовёшь; -а́л, -а́, -о *perf.* (*imp.* призыва́ть) call, summon; call upon, appeal to; call up; **~ся,** be called up.
призе́мистый, stocky, squat; thickset.
приземле́ние, -я, landing, touch-down.
приземли́ться, -лю́сь *perf.*, **приземля́ться,** -я́юсь *imp.* land, touch down.
призёр, -а, **призёрша,** -и, prizewinner.
признава́ть, -наю́, -наёшь *imp.*, **призна́ть,** -а́ю *perf.* recognize; spot, identify; admit, own, acknowledge; deem vote; (не) ~ себя́ вино́вным, plead (not) guilty; **~ся,** confess, own; ~ся (сказа́ть), to tell the truth. **при́знак,** -а, sign, symptom; indication. **призна́ние,** -я, confession, declaration; admission, acknowledgement; recognition. **при́знанный,** acknowledged, recognized. **призна́тельный,** grateful.
призову́, etc.: see призва́ть.
при́зрак, -а, spectre, ghost, phantom, apparition. **при́зрачный,** spectral, ghostly, phantasmal; illusory, imagined
призы́в, -а, call, appeal; slogan; call-up, conscription. **призыва́ть(ся,** -а́ю(сь

imp. of призва́ть(ся. **призывно́й,** conscription; ~ во́зраст, military age; *sb.* conscript.

при́иск, -а, mine; золоты́е ~и, gold--field(s).

прийти́, приду́, -дёшь; пришёл, -шла́ *perf.* (*imp.* приходи́ть) come; arrive; ~ в себя́, come round, regain consciousness; ~ в у́жас, be horrified; ~ к концу́, come to the end; ~ к заключе́нию, come to the conclusion, arrive at a conclusion; **~сь** + по + *dat.* fit; suit; + на + *acc.* fall on; *impers.* + *dat.* have to; happen (to), fall to the lot (of); + на + *acc.* or с + *gen.* be owing to from; нам пришло́сь верну́ться в Москву́, we had to return to Moscow; как придётся, anyhow, at haphazard.

прика́з, -а, order, command; order of the day; office, department. **приказа́ние,** -я, order, command, injunction. **приказа́ть,** -ажу́, -а́жешь *perf.*, **прика́зывать,** -аю *imp.* order, command; give orders, direct.

прика́лывать, -аю *imp.* of приколо́ть. **прикаса́ться,** -а́юсь *imp.* of прикосну́ться.

прики́дывать, -аю *imp.*, **прики́нуть,** -ну *perf.* throw in, add; weigh; estimate; calculate, reckon; **~ся** + *instr.* pretend (to be), feign; ~ся больны́м, pretend to be ill, feign illness.

прикла́д[1], -а, butt.

прикла́д[2], -а, trimmings, findings. **прикладно́й,** applied. **прикла́дывать(ся,** -аю(сь *imp.* of приложи́ть(ся.

прикле́ивать, -аю *imp.*, **прикле́ить,** -е́ю *perf.* stick; glue; paste; affix; **~ся,** stick, adhere.

приключа́ться, -а́ется *imp.*, **приключи́ться,** -и́тся *perf.* happen, occur. **приключе́ние,** -я, adventure. **приключе́нческий,** adventure.

прикова́ть, -кую́, -куёшь *perf.*, **прико́вывать,** -аю *imp.* chain; rivet.

прико́л, -а, stake; на ~е, laid up, idle.

прикола́чивать, -аю *imp.*, **приколоти́ть,** -очу́, -о́тишь *perf.* nail, fasten with nails; beat up.

приколо́ть, -лю́, -лешь *perf.* (*imp.* прика́лывать) pin, fasten with a pin; stab, transfix.

прикомандирова́ть, -ру́ю *perf.*, **прикомандиро́вывать,** -аю *imp.* attach, second.

прикоснове́ние, -я, touch, contact; concern. **прикоснове́нный,** concerned, involved, implicated (к + *dat.* in).
прикосну́ться, -ну́сь, -нёшься *perf.* (*imp.* прикаса́ться) к + *dat.* touch.

прикра́сить, -а́шу *perf.*, **прикра́шивать,** -аю *imp.* embellish, embroider.

прикрепи́ть, -плю́ *perf.*, **прикрепля́ть,** -я́ю *imp.* fasten, attach. **прикрепле́ние,** -я, fastening; attachment; registration.

прикрыва́ть, -а́ю *imp.*, **прикры́ть,** -ро́ю *perf.* cover; screen; protect, shelter, shield; cover up, conceal; close down, wind up; **~ся,** cover oneself; close down, go out of business; + *instr.* use as cover, take refuge in, shelter behind.

прику́ривать, -аю *imp.*, **прикури́ть,** -рю́, -ришь *perf.* get a light; light a cigarette from another.

прику́с, -а, bite. **прикуси́ть,** -ушу́, -у́сишь *perf.*, **прику́сывать,** -аю *imp.* bite; ~ язы́к, hold one's tongue, keep one's mouth shut.

прила́вок, -вка, counter; рабо́тник прила́вка, counter-hand; (shop) assistant.

прилага́тельн|ый, adjective; **~ое** *sb.* adjective. **прилага́ть,** -а́ю *imp.* of приложи́ть.

прила́дить, -а́жу *perf.*, **прила́живать.** -аю *imp.* fit, adjust.

приласка́ть, -а́ю *perf.* caress, fondle, pet; **~ся,** snuggle up, nestle up.

прилега́ть, -а́ет *imp.* (*perf.* приле́чь) к + *dat.* fit; adjoin, be adjacent to, border (on). **прилега́ющий,** close-fitting, tight-fitting; adjoining, adjacent, contiguous.

прилежа́ние, -я, diligence, industry; application. **приле́жный,** diligent, industrious, assiduous.

прилепи́ть(ся, -плю́(сь, -пишь(ся *perf.*, **прилепля́ть(ся,** -я́ю(сь *imp.* stick.

прилёт, -а, arrival. **прилета́ть,** -а́ю *imp.*, **прилете́ть,** -ечу́ *perf.* arrive, fly in; fly, come flying.

прилéчь, -лягу, -ляжешь; -ёг, -глá *perf.* (*imp.* прилегáть) lie down; be laid flat; + к + *dat.* fit.

прилив, -а, flow, flood; rising tide; surge, influx; congestion; ~ крóви, rush of blood; ~ энéргии, burst of energy. **приливáть,** -áет *imp.* of прилить. **приливный,** tidal.

прилипáть, -áет *imp.*, **прилипнуть,** -нет; -лип *perf.* stick, adhere. **прилипчивый,** sticking, adhesive; clinging; not to be shaken off; tiresome; catching

прилить, -льёт; -ил, -á, -о *perf.* (*imp.* приливáть) flow; rush.

прилúчие, -я, decency, propriety; decorum. **прилúчный,** decent; proper, decorous, seemly; tolerable, fair.

приложéние, -я, application; affixing; enclosure; supplement; appendix; schedule, exhibit; apposition. **приложить,** -жý, -жишь *perf.* (*imp.* приклáдывать, прилагáть) put; apply; affix; add, join; enclose; ~ все старáния, do one's best, try one's hardest; **~ся,** take aim; + *instr.* put, apply; + к + *dat.* kiss.

прилуниться, -нюсь *perf.* land on the moon.

прильёт, etc.: see прилить. **при|льнýть,** -нý, -нёшь *perf.* **прилягу,** etc.: see прилéчь.

примáнивать, -аю *imp.*, **приманить,** -ню, -нишь *perf.* lure; entice, allure. **примáнка,** -и, bait, lure; enticement, allurement.

применéние, -я, application; employment, use. **применить,** -ню, -нишь *perf.*, **применять,** -яю *imp.* apply; employ, use; ~ на прáктике, put into practice; **~ся,** adapt oneself, conform.

примéр, -а, example; instance; model; не в ~ + *dat.* unlike; + *comp.* far more, by far; подавáть ~, set an example; привести в ~, cite as an example.

при|мéрить, -рю *perf.* (*imp.* also примерять) try on; fit. **примéрка,** -и, trying on; fitting.

примéрно *adv.* in exemplary fashion; approximately, roughly. **примéрный,** exemplary, model; approximate, rough.

примерять, -яю *imp.* of примéрить.

примесь, -и, admixture; dash; без примесей, unadulterated.

примéта, -ы, sign, token; mark. **примéтный,** perceptible, visible, noticeable; conspicuous, prominent.

примечáние, -я, note, footnote; *pl.* comments.

примешáть, -áю *perf.*, **примéшивать,** -аю *imp.* add, mix in.

приминáть, -áю *imp.* of примять.

примирéние, -я, reconciliation. **примирéнчество,** -а, appeasement, compromise. **примиримый,** reconcilable. **примиритель,** -я *m.* reconciler, conciliator, peace-maker. **примирительный,** conciliatory. **при|мирить,** -рю *perf.*, **примирять,** -яю *imp.* reconcile; conciliate; **~ся,** be reconciled, make it up; + с + *instr.* reconcile oneself to, put up with.

примкнýть, -нý, -нёшь *perf.* (*imp.* примыкáть) join; fix, attach.

примнý, etc.: see примять.

примóрский, seaside; maritime. **примóрье,** -я, seaside; littoral.

примóчка, -и, wash, lotion.

примý, etc.: see принять.

примчáться, -чýсь *perf.* come tearing along.

примыкáние, -я, contiguity; agglutination. **примыкáть,** -áю *imp.* of примкнýть; + к + *dat.* adjoin, abut on, border on. **примыкáющий,** affiliated.

примять, -мнý, -мнёшь *perf.* (*imp.* приминáть) crush, flatten; trample down.

принадлежáть, -жý *imp.* belong. **принадлéжность,** -и, belonging; membership; *pl.* accessories, appurtenances; equipment; outfit, tackle.

при|невóлить, -лю *perf.*

принести, -сý, -сёшь *perf.* (*imp.* приносить) bring; fetch; bear, yield; bring in; ~ в жéртву, sacrifice; ~ пóльзу, be of use, be of benefit.

принимáть(ся, -áю(сь *imp.* of принять(ся; принимáющая сторонá, host country.

принорáвливать, -аю *imp.*, **приноровить,** -влю *perf.* fit, adapt, adjust;

~ся, adapt oneself, accommodate oneself.

приноси́ть, -ошу́, -о́сишь *imp.* of принести́. **приноше́ние,** -я, gift, offering.

принуди́тельн|ый, compulsory; forced, coercive; ~ые рабо́ты, forced labour, hard labour. **принý́дить,** -у́жу *perf.*, **принужда́ть,** -а́ю *imp.* force, compel, coerce, constrain. **принужде́ние,** -я, compulsion, coercion, constraint; duress. **принуждённый,** constrained, forced.

при́нцип, -а, principle. **принципиа́льно** *adv.* on principle; in principle. **принципиа́льный,** of principle; in principle; general.

приня́тие, -я, taking; taking up, assumption; acceptance, adoption; admission, admittance. **при́нято,** it is accepted, it is usual; не ~, it is not done. **приня́ть,** -иму́, -и́мешь; при́нял, -а́, -о *perf.* (*imp.* принима́ть) take; accept; take up; take over; pass, approve; admit; receive; + за + *acc.* take for; ~ ва́нну, take (have) a bath; ~ в шко́лу, admit to, accept for, a school; ~ зако́н, pass a law; ~ лека́рство, take medicine; ~ ме́ры, take measures; ~ резолю́цию, pass, adopt, carry a resolution; ~ уча́стье, take part; **~ся,** begin; start; take; take root, strike root; + за + *acc.* take in hand; set to, get down to; ~ за рабо́ту, set to work.

приободри́ть, -рю́ *perf.*, **приободря́ть,** -я́ю *imp.* cheer up, encourage, hearten; **~ся,** cheer up.

приобрести́, -ету́, -етёшь; -рёл, -а́ *perf.*, **приобрета́ть,** -а́ю *imp.* acquire, gain. **приобрете́ние,** -я, acquisition; gain; bargain, find.

приобща́ть, -а́ю *imp.*, **приобщи́ть,** -щу́ *perf.* join, attach, unite; ~ к де́лу, file, **~ся** к + *dat.* join in.

приозёрный, lakeside, lakeland.

приостана́вливать, -аю *imp.* **приостанови́ть,** -влю́, -вишь *perf.* stop, suspend, check; **~ся,** halt, stop, pause. **приостано́вка,** -и, halt, check, stoppage, suspension.

приотвори́ть, -рю́, -ришь *perf.*, **приотворя́ть,** -я́ю *imp.* open slightly, half-open, set ajar.

припа́док, -дка, fit; attack; paroxysm.

припаса́ть, -а́ю *imp.*, **припасти́,** -су́ -сёшь; -а́с, -ла́ *perf.* store, lay in, lay up. **припа́сы,** -ов *pl.* stores, supplies; provisions; munitions.

припе́в, -а, refrain, burden.

приписа́ть, -ишу́, -и́шешь *perf.*, **припи́сывать,** -аю *imp.* add; attribute, ascribe; put down, impute. **припи́ска,** -и, addition; postscript; codicil.

припла́та, -ы, extra pay; additional payment. **приплати́ть,** -ачу́, -а́тишь *perf.* **припла́чивать,** -аю *imp.* pay in addition.

припло́д, -а, issue, increase.

приплыва́ть, -а́ю *imp.*, **приплы́ть,** -ыву́, -ывёшь; -ы́л, -а́, -о *perf.* swim up, sail up.

приплю́снуть, -ну *perf.*, **приплю́щивать,** -аю *imp.* flatten.

приподнима́ть, -а́ю *imp.*, **приподня́ть,** -ниму́, -ни́мешь; -о́днял, -а́, -о *perf.* raise (a little); **~ся,** raise oneself (a little), rise.

припо́й, -я, solder.

припомина́ть, -а́ю *imp.*, **припо́мнить,** -ню *perf.* remember, recollect, recall; + *dat.* remind.

припра́ва, -ы, seasoning, flavouring; relish, condiment, dressing. **припра́вить,** -влю *perf.*, **приправля́ть,** -я́ю *imp.* season, flavour, dress.

припря́тать, -я́чу *perf.*, **припря́тывать,** -аю *imp.* secrete, put by.

припу́гивать, -аю *imp.*, **припугну́ть,** -ну́, -нёшь *perf.* intimidate, scare.

при́пуск, -а, allowance, margin.

прираба́тывать, -аю *imp.*, **прирабо́тать,** -аю *perf.* earn . . extra, earn in addition. **при́работок,** -тка, supplementary earnings, additional earnings.

прира́внивать, -аю *imp.*, **приравня́ть,** -я́ю *perf.* equate, place on the same footing; compare (к + *dat.* to).

прираста́ть, -а́ю *imp.*, **прирасти́,** -тёт; -ро́с, -ла́ *perf.* adhere; take; increase; accrue; ~ к ме́сту, be rooted to the spot.

прире́чный, riverside.

приро́да, -ы, nature; character. **приро́дный,** natural; native; born, by birth;

inborn, innate. **прирождённый**, inborn, innate; born.

приро́с, etc.: see прирасти́. **приро́ст**, -а, increase, growth.

приуча́ть, -а́ю *imp.*, **приручи́ть**, -чу́ *perf.* tame; domesticate. **прируче́ние**, -я, taming, domestication.

приса́живаться, -аюсь *imp.* of присе́сть.

присва́ивать, -аю *imp.*, **присво́ить**, -о́ю *perf.* appropriate; give, award, confer; ~ и́мя + *dat.* and *gen.* name after.

приседа́ть, -а́ю *imp.*, **присе́сть**, -ся́ду *perf.* (*imp.* also приса́живаться) sit down, take a seat; squat; cower; bend the knees (in walking).

прискака́ть, -ачу́, -а́чешь *perf.* come galloping, arrive at a gallop; rush, tear.

приско́рбный, sorrowful, regrettable, lamentable.

присла́ть, -ишлю́, -ишлёшь *perf.* (*imp.* присыла́ть) send, dispatch.

прислони́ть(ся, -оню́(сь, -о́нишь(ся *perf.*, **прислоня́ть(ся**, -я́ю(сь *imp.* lean, rest (к + *dat.* against).

прислу́га, -и, maid, servant; servants, domestics; crew. **прислу́живать**, -аю *imp.* (к + *dat.*) wait (upon); **~ся** к + *dat.* fawn upon, cringe to.

прислу́шаться, -аюсь *perf.*, **прислу́шиваться**, -аюсь *imp.* listen; + к + *dat.* listen to; heed, pay attention to; get used to (the sound of), cease to notice.

присма́тривать, -аю *imp.*, **присмотре́ть**, -рю́, -ришь *perf.* look for, find; + за + *instr.* look after, keep an eye on; supervise, superintend; ~ за ребёнком, mind the baby; **~ся** (к + *dat.*) look closely (at); get accustomed, get used (to).

при|сни́ться, -ню́сь *perf.*

присовокупи́ть, -плю́ *perf.*, **присовокупля́ть**, -я́ю *imp.* add; attach.

присоедине́ние -я, joining; addition; annexation; connection. **присоедини́ть**, -ню́ *perf.* **присоединя́ть**, -я́ю *imp.* join; add; annex; connect; **~ся** к + *dat.* join; associate oneself with; ~ к мне́нию, subscribe to an opinion.

приспосо́бить, -блю *perf.*, **приспособля́ть**, -я́ю *imp.* fit, adjust, adapt, accommodate; **~ся**, adapt oneself, accommodate oneself. **приспособле́ние**, -я, adaptation, accommodation; device, contrivance; appliance, gadget. **приспосо́бленность**, -и, fitness, suitability. **приспособля́емость**, -и, adaptability.

при́став, -а; *pl.* -а́ or -ы, police officer police sergeant.

пристава́ть, -таю́, -таёшь *imp.* of приста́ть.

приста́вить, -влю *perf.* (*imp.* приставля́ть) к + *dat.* put, place, set to, against; lean against; add to; appoint to look after.

приста́вка, -и, prefix.

приставля́ть, -я́ю *imp.* of приста́вить. **приставн|о́й**, added, attached; **~а́я** ле́стница, step-ladder.

при́стальный, fixed, intent.

при́стань, -и; *gen. pl.* -е́й, landing-stage, jetty; pier; wharf; refuge; haven.

приста́ть, -а́ну *perf.* (*imp.* пристава́ть) stick, adhere; attach oneself; pester, bother, badger; put in, come alongside.

пристёгивать, -аю *imp.*, **пристегну́ть**, -ну́, -нёшь *perf.* fasten. **пристежно́й**; ~ воротничо́к, separate collar.

пристра́ивать(ся, -аю(сь *imp.* of **пристро́ить(ся**.

пристра́стие, -я, weakness, predilection, passion; partiality, bias. **пристра́стный** partial, biased.

пристро́ить, -о́ю *perf.* (*imp.* пристра́ивать), add, build on; place, settle, fix up; **~ся**, be placed be settled, be fixed up, get a place; join up form up. **пристро́йка**, -и, annexe, extension; outhouse; lean-to.

при́ступ, -а, assault, storm; fit, attack; bout, touch; access approach. **приступа́ть**, -а́ю *imp* **приступи́ть**, -плю́, -пишь *perf.* к + *dat.* set about, start; get down to; approach; importune, pester. **присту́пок**, -пка, step.

при|стыди́ть, -ыжу́ *perf.* **пристыжённый**; -жён, -а́ ashamed.

при|стыкова́ться, -ку́ется *perf.*

пристя́жка, -и, **пристяжна́я** *sb.* trace-horse, outrunner.

присуди́ть, -ужу́, -ýдишь *perf.*, **присужда́ть,** -áю *imp.* sentence, condemn; award; confer; ~ к штрáфу, fine, impose a fine on. **присуждéние,** -я, awarding, adjudication; conferment.

присýтственн|ый; ~ое мéсто government office. **присýтствие** -я, presence; attendance; government office; ~ дýха, presence of mind. **присýтствовать,** -твую, be present, attend. **присýтствующ|ий,** present; **~ие** *sb.* those present, present company.

присýщий, inherent; characteristic, distinctive.

присыла́ть, -áю *imp.* of присла́ть.

присяга, -и, oath; привести́ к присяге, swear in, administer the oath to. **присяга́ть,** -áю *imp.*, **присягнýть,** -нý, -нёшь *perf.* take one's oath, swear; ~ в вéрности, swear allegiance.

прися́ду, etc.: see присéсть.

прися́жный, sworn; born, inveterate; ~ заседа́тель, juror, juryman; ~ повéренный, barrister.

прита́йться, -аюсь *perf.* hide, conceal oneself.

притáскивать, -аю *imp*., **притащи́ть,** -ащý, -áщишь *perf.* bring, drag, haul; **~ся** drag oneself.

притвори́ться, -рю́сь *perf.*, **притворя́ться,** -я́юсь *imp.* + *instr.* pretend to be; feign; sham; ~ больны́м, pretend to be ill, feign illness. **притвóрный,** pretended, feigned, sham. **притвóрство,** -а, pretence, sham. **притвóрщик,** -а, sham; dissembler, hypocrite.

притека́ть, -áю *imp.* of притéчь.

притеснéние, -я, oppression. **притесни́ть,** -ню́ *perf.*, **притесня́ть,** -я́ю *imp.* oppress.

притéчь, -ечёт, -екýт; -ёк, -лá *perf.* (*imp.* притека́ть) flow in, pour in.

притиха́ть, -áю *imp.*, **прити́хнуть,** -ну; -и́х *perf.* quiet down, grow quiet, hush

притóк, -а, tributary; flow, influx; intake.

притóм *conj.* (and) besides.

притóн, -а, den, haunt.

при́торный, sickly-sweet, luscious, cloying.

притра́гиваться, -аюсь *imp.*, **притрóнуться,** -нусь *perf.* touch.

притупи́ть, -плю́, -пишь *perf.*, **притупля́ть,** -я́ю *imp.* blunt, dull; deaden; **~ся,** become blunt, lose its edge; become dull.

при́тча, -и, parable.

притяга́тельный, attractive, magnetic.

притя́гивать, -аю *imp.* of притянýть.

притяжа́тельный, possessive.

притяжéние, -я, attraction; земнóе ~, gravity.

притяза́ние, -я, claim, pretension. **притяза́ть,** -áю *imp.* на + *acc.* lay claim to, have pretensions to.

притя́нутый: ~ зá уши, зá волосы, far-fetched. **притянýть,** -нý -нешь *perf.* (*imp.* притя́гивать) draw, attract; drag (up), pull (up).

приурóчивать, -аю *imp.*, **приурóчить,** -чу *perf.* к + *dat.* time for, time to coincide with.

приуса́дебный; ~ учáсток, individual holding (in kolkhoz), personal plot.

приуча́ть, -áю *imp.*, **приучи́ть,** -чý, -чишь *perf.* accustom; train, school.

прихва́рывать, -аю *imp.*, **прихворнýть,** -нý, -нёшь *perf.* be unwell, be indisposed.

при́хвостень, -тня *m.* hanger-on.

прихлеба́тель, -я *m.* sponger, parasite.

прихóд, -а, coming, arrival; advent; receipts; parish; ~ и расхóд, credit and debit. **приходи́ть(ся,** -ожý(сь, -óдишь(ся *imp.* of прийти́(сь. **прихóдный,** receipt. **прихóдовать,** -дую *imp.* (*perf.* за~) credit. **приходя́щ|ий,** non-resident; ~ий больнóй, out-patient; ~ая домрабóтница, daily (maid), char(woman).

прихотли́вый, capricious, whimsical; fanciful, intricate. **при́хоть,** -и, whim, caprice, fancy.

прихра́мывать, -аю, limp (slightly).

прицéл, -а, sight; aiming. **прицéливаться,** -аюсь *imp.*, **прицéлиться,** -люсь *perf.* aim, take aim.

прицéниваться, -аюсь *imp.*, **прицени́ться,** -ню́сь, -нишься (к + *dat.*) ask the price (of).

прицéп, -а, trailer. **прицепи́ть,** -плю́, -пишь *perf.*, **прицепля́ть,** -я́ю *imp.* hitch, hook on; couple; **~ся** к + *dat.*

stick to, cling to; pester; nag at. **прицéпка, -и,** hitching, hooking on; coupling; trailer; pestering; nagging. **прицепнóй**; ~ вагóн, trailer.

причáл, -а, mooring, making fast; mooring line; berth, moorings. **причáливать, -аю** *imp.*, **причáлить, -лю** *perf.* moor.

причáстие[1], **-я,** participle. **причáстие**[2], -я, communion.

причáстный[1], participial. **причáстный**[2], participating, concerned; involved; accessary, privy.

причём *conj.* moreover, and; while. **причём** *adv.* why? what for?; а ~ же я тут? what has it to do with me?

причесáть, -ешý, -éшешь *perf.*, **причёсывать, -аю** *imp.* brush, comb; do the hair (of); **~ся,** do one's hair, have one's hair done. **причёска, -и,** hair-do, hair-style; haircut.

причи́на, -ы, cause; reason. **причини́ть, -ню́** *perf.*, **причиня́ть, -я́ю** *imp.* cause; occasion.

причи́слить, -лю *perf.*, **причисля́ть, -я́ю** *imp.* reckon, number, rank (к + *dat.* among); add on; attach.

причитáние, -я, lamentation.

причитáться, -áется *imp.* be due; вам причитáется два рубля́, there is two roubles due to you, you have two roubles to come; с вас причитáется два рубля́, you have two roubles to pay.

причýда, -ы, caprice, whim, fancy; oddity, vagary.

при|чýдиться, -ится *perf.*

причýдливый, odd, queer; fantastic; capricious, whimsical.

при|швартовáть, -тýю *perf.* **пришёл,** etc.: see прийти́.

приши́бленный, crest-fallen, dejected.

пришивáть, -áю *imp.*, **приши́ть, -шью́, -шьёшь** *perf.* sew on, attach; nail (on).

пришлю́, etc.: see прислáть.

пришпóривать, -аю *imp.*, **пришпóрить, -рю** *perf.* spur (on).

прищеми́ть, -млю́ *perf.*, **прищемля́ть, -я́ю** *imp.* pinch, squeeze.

прищéпка, -и, прищéпок, -пка, clothes-peg.

прищýриваться, -аюсь *imp.*, **прищýриться, -рюсь** *perf.* screw up one's eyes.

прию́т, -а, asylum, orphanage; shelter, refuge. **приюти́ть, -ючý** *perf.* shelter, give refuge; **~ся,** take shelter.

прия́тель, -я *m.*, **прия́тельница, -ы,** friend. **прия́тельский,** friendly, amicable. **прия́тный,** nice, pleasant, agreeable, pleasing; ~ на вкус, nice, palatable, tasty.

про *prep.* + *acc.* about; for; ~ себя́, to oneself.

про-[1] *vbl. pref.* indicating action through, across, or past object; action continued throughout given period of time; overall or exhaustive action or effect; loss or failure.

про-[2] *pref.* of nouns and adjs., pro-.

прóба, -ы, trial, test; try-out; assay; hallmark; sample; standard, measure of fineness of gold; зóлото 96-óй прóбы, 24-carat gold, pure gold.

пробéг, -а, run; race; mileage, distance. **пробегáть, -áю** *imp.*, **пробежáть, -егý** *perf.* run; cover; pass, run past, run by; run through; run along, run over.

пробéл, -а, blank, gap; hiatus; lacuna; deficiency, flaw.

проберý, etc.: see пробрáть. **пробивáть(ся, -áю(сь** *imp.* of проби́ть(ся. **пробирáть(ся, -áю(сь** *imp.* of пробрáть(ся.

проби́рка, -и, test-tube. **проби́рный,** test, assay; ~ое клеймó, hallmark. **проби́ровать, -рую** *imp.* test, assay.

про|би́ть, -бью́, -бьёшь *perf.* (*imp.* also пробивáть) make a hole in; hole, pierce; punch; strike; **~ся,** fight, force, make, one's way through; break through, strike through.

прóбка, -и, cork; stopper; plug; fuse; (traffic) jam, blockage, congestion. **прóбковый,** cork; ~ пóяс, life-belt, life-jacket.

прóблеск, -а, flash; gleam, ray.

прóбный, trial, test, experimental; hall-marked; ~ кáмень, touchstone. **прóбовать, -бую** *imp.* (*perf.* ис~, по~), try; attempt, endeavour; test; taste, feel.

пробóина, -ы, hole.

проболта́ться, -а́юсь *perf.* blab, let out a secret; hang about.

пробо́р, -а, parting; де́лать (себе́) ~, part one's hair.

про|бормота́ть, -очу́, -о́чешь *perf.*

пробра́ть, -беру́, -берёшь; -а́л, -а́, -о *perf.* (*imp.* пробира́ть) go through; scold, rate; clear, weed; **~ся,** make one's way; force one's way; steal (through); ~ о́щупью, feel one's way.

пробу́ду, etc.: see пробы́ть.

про|буди́ть, -ужу́, -у́дишь *perf.*, **пробужда́ть,** -а́ю *imp.* wake (up); awaken, rouse, arouse; **~ся,** wake, wake up. **пробужде́ние,** -я, waking (up), awakening.

про|бура́вить, -влю *perf.*, **пробура́вливать,** -аю *imp.* bore (through), drill.

про|бурча́ть, -чу́ *perf.*

пробы́ть, -бу́ду; про́бы́л, -а́, -о *perf.* remain, stay; be.

пробью́, etc.: see пробить.

прова́л, -а, failure; flop; downfall; gap; funnel. **прова́ливать,** -аю *imp.*, **провали́ть,** -лю́, -лишь *perf.* cause to fall in, bring down; ruin, make a mess of; reject, fail; **~ся,** collapse; fall in, come down; fall through; fail; disappear, vanish.

прова́нск|ий, Provençal; ~ое ма́сло, olive oil.

прове́дать, -аю *perf.*, **прове́дывать,** -аю *imp.* come to see, call on; find out, learn.

провезти́, -зу́, -зёшь; -ёз, -ла́ *perf.* (*imp.* провози́ть) convey, transport; smuggle (through, in, out); bring.

прове́рить, -рю *perf.* **проверя́ть,** -я́ю *imp.* check, check up on; verify; audit; control; test; ~ биле́ты, examine tickets; ~ тетра́ди, correct exercise-books. **прове́рка,** -и, checking, check; examination; verification; control; testing.

про|вести́, -еду́, -едёшь; -ёл, -а́ *perf.* (*imp.* also проводи́ть) lead, take; pilot; build; install; carry out, carry on; conduct, hold; carry through; carry; pass; advance, put forward; draw; spend; + *instr.* pass over, run over; ~ в жизнь, put into effect, put into practice; ~ водопрово́д, lay on water; ~ вре́мя, pass the time; ~ черту́, draw a line; хорошо́ ~ вре́мя, have a good time.

прове́тривать, -аю *imp.*, **прове́трить,** -рю *perf.* air; ventilate.

про|ве́ять, -е́ю *perf.*

провиде́ние, -я, Providence. **прови́деть,** -и́жу *imp.* foresee.

прови́зия, -и, provisions.

провизо́рный, preliminary, provisional; temporary.

провини́ться, -ню́сь *perf.* be guilty; do wrong; ~ пе́ред + *instr.* wrong.

провинциа́льный, provincial. **прови́нция,** -и, province; the provinces.

про́вод, -а; *pl.* -а́, wire, lead, conductor. **проводи́мость,** -и, conductivity; conductance. **проводи́ть**[1], -ожу́, -о́дишь *imp.* of провести́; conduct, be a conductor.

проводи́ть[2], -ожу́, -о́дишь *perf.* (*imp.* провожа́ть) accompany; see off; ~ глаза́ми, follow with one's eyes; ~ домо́й, see home.

прово́дка, -и, leading, taking; building; installation; wiring, wires.

проводни́к[1], -а́, guide; conductor, guard.

проводни́к[2], -а́, conductor; bearer; transmitter. **проводно́й,** wire, line.

про́воды, -ов *pl.* seeing off, send-off. **провожа́тый** *sb.* guide, escort. **провожа́ть,** -а́ю *imp.* of проводи́ть.

прово́з, -а, carriage, conveyance, transport.

провозгласи́ть, -ашу́ *perf.*, **провозглаша́ть,** -а́ю *imp.* proclaim, declare; announce; + *instr.* proclaim, hail as; ~ тост, propose a toast. **провозглаше́ние,** -я, proclamation; declaration.

провози́ть, -ожу́, -о́зишь *imp.* of провезти́.

провока́тор, -а, agent provocateur; instigator, provoker. **провокацио́нный,** provocative. **провока́ция,** -и, provocation.

про́волока, -и, wire. **про́волочн|ый,** wire; ~ая сеть, wire netting.

прово́рный, quick, swift, prompt; agile, nimble, adroit, dexterous. **прово́рство,** -а, quickness, swiftness; agility, nimbleness, adroitness, dexterity.

провоци́ровать, -рую *perf.* and *imp.* (*perf.* also с~) provoke.

про|вя́лить, -лю *perf.*

прогада́ть, -а́ю *perf.*, **прога́дывать,** -аю *imp.* miscalculate.

прога́лина, -ы, glade; (clear) space.

прогла́тывать, -аю *imp.*, **проглоти́ть,** -очу́, -о́тишь *perf.* swallow.

проглядéть, -яжу́ *perf.*, **прогля́дывать**[1], -аю *imp.* overlook, miss; look through, glance through. **прогляну́ть,** -я́нет *perf.*, **прогля́дывать**[2], -ает *imp.* show, show through, peep out, peep through, appear.

прогна́ть, -гоню́, -го́нишь; -а́л, -а́, -о *perf.* (*imp.* прогоня́ть) drive away; banish; drive; sack, fire.

про|гневи́ть, -влю́ *perf.*

прогнива́ть, -а́ет *imp.*, **прогни́ть,** -ниёт; -и́л, -а́, -о *perf.* rot through, be rotten.

прогно́з, -а, prognosis; (weather) forecast. **прогнози́рование,** -я, forecasting. **прогнози́ст,** -а, forecaster.

проголода́ться, -а́юсь *perf.* get hungry, grow hungry.

про|голосова́ть, -су́ю *perf.* **прогоня́ть,** -я́ю *imp.* of прогна́ть.

прогора́ть, -а́ю *imp.*, **прогорéть,** -рю́ *perf.* burn; burn out; get burnt; go bankrupt, go bust.

прого́рклый, rancid, rank.

програ́мма, -ы, programme; schedule; syllabus, curriculum. **программи́ровать,** -рую *imp.* (*perf.* за~), programme.

прогрéв, -а, warming up. **прогрева́ть,** -а́ю *imp.*, **прогрéть,** -éю *perf.* heat, warm thoroughly; warm up; **~ся,** get warmed through, get thoroughly warmed; warm up.

про|гремéть, -млю́ *perf.* **про|грохота́ть,** -очу́, -о́чешь *perf.*

прогрыза́ть, -а́ю *imp.*, **прогры́зть,** -зу́, -зёшь; -ы́з *perf.* gnaw through.

про|гудéть, -гужу́ *perf.*

прогу́л, -а, absence (from work); absenteeism. **прогу́ливать,** -аю *imp.*, **прогуля́ть,** -я́ю *perf.* be absent from work; miss; take for a walk, walk; ~ уро́ки, play truant; **~ся,** stroll, saunter; take a walk. **прогу́лка,** -и, walk, stroll; ramble; outing. **прогу́льщик,** -а, absentee, truant.

прод- *abbr.* in *comb.* of продово́льственный, food-, provision-. **продма́г,** -а, grocery; provision-shop. **~пу́нкт,** -а, food centre. **~това́ры,** -ов *pl.* food products.

продава́ть, -даю́, -даёшь *imp.*, **прода́ть,** -а́м, -а́шь, -а́ст, -ади́м; про́дал, -а́, -о *perf.* sell. **продава́ться,** -даётся *imp.* be for sale; sell. **продавéц,** -вца́, seller, vendor; salesman; shop-assistant. **продавщи́ца,** -ы, seller, vendor; saleswoman; shop-assistant, shop-girl. **прода́жа,** -и, sale, selling. **прода́жный,** for sale, to be sold; mercenary, venal.

продвига́ть, -а́ю *imp.*, **продви́нуть,** -ну *perf.* move forward, push forward; promote, further, advance; **~ся,** advance; move on, move forward; push on, push forward, forge ahead; be promoted.

про|деклами́ровать, -рую *perf.*

продéлать, -аю *perf.*, **продéлывать,** -аю *imp.* do, perform, accomplish. **продéлка,** -и, trick; prank, escapade.

продёргивать, -аю *imp.* of продёрнуть.

продержа́ть, -жу́, -жишь *perf.* hold; keep; **~ся,** hold out.

продёрнуть, -ну, -нешь *perf.* (*imp.* продёргивать) pass, run; put through; criticize, pull to pieces; ~ **ни́тку** в иго́лку, thread a needle.

продешеви́ть, -влю́ *perf.* sell too cheap.

про|диктова́ть, -ту́ю *perf.*

продлева́ть, -а́ю *imp.*, **продли́ть,** -лю́ *perf.* extend, prolong. **продлéние,** -я, extension, prolongation. **про|дли́ться,** -и́тся *perf.*

продово́льственн|ый, food, provision; ~ая ка́рточка, ration book, ration card; ~ый магази́н, grocery, provision shop. **продово́льствие,** -я, food, food-stuffs; provisions.

продолгова́тый, oblong.

продолжа́тель, -я *m.* continuer, successor. **продолжа́ть,** -а́ю *imp.*, **продо́лжить,** -жу *perf.* continue, go on (with), proceed (with); extend, prolong; **~ся,** continue, last, go on, be in progress. **продолжéние,** -я, continuation; sequel;

extension, prolongation; в ~ + *gen.* in the course of, during, for, throughout; ~ сле́дует, to be continued. **продолжи́тельность,** -и, duration, length. **продолжи́тельный,** long; prolonged, protracted.

продо́льный, longitudinal, lengthwise, linear.

продро́гнуть, -ну; -о́г *perf.* be chilled to the marrow, be half frozen.

проду́кт, -а, product; produce; provisions, food-stuffs. **продукти́вно** *adv.* productively; to good effect, with a good result. **продукти́вность,** -и, productivity. **продукти́вный,** productive; fruitful. **продукто́вый,** food, provision; ~ магази́н, grocery, food-shop.

проду́кция, -и, production, output.

проду́мать, -аю *perf.,* **проду́мывать,** -аю *imp.* think over; think out.

продыря́вить, -влю *perf.* make a hole in, pierce.

продю́с(с)ер, -а, (film) producer.

проеда́ть, -а́ю *imp.* of прое́сть. **прое́ду,** etc.: see прое́хать.

прое́зд, -а, passage, thoroughfare; journey; ~а нет, no thoroughfare. **прое́здить,** -зжу *perf.* (*imp.* проезжа́ть) spend on a journey, spend in travelling; spend travelling (driving, riding). **проездн|о́й,** travelling; ~о́й биле́т, ticket; ~а́я пла́та, fare; **~ы́е** *sb.* travelling expenses. **прое́здом** *adv.* en route, in transit, while passing through. **проезжа́ть,** -а́ю *imp.* of прое́здить, прое́хать. **прое́зж|ий,** passing (by); ~ая доро́га, highway, thoroughfare; **~ий** *sb.* passer-by.

прое́кт, -а, project, scheme, design; draft; ~ догово́ра, draft treaty; ~ резолю́ции, draft resolution. **проекти́ровать,** -рую *imp.* (*perf.* за~, с~) project; plan, design. **прое́ктный,** planning, designing; planned. **прое́ктор,** -а, projector.

проекцио́нный; ~ фона́рь, projector. **прое́кция,** -и, projection.

прое́сть, -е́м, -е́шь, -е́ст, -еди́м; -е́л *perf.* (*imp.* проеда́ть) eat through, corrode; spend on food.

прое́хать, -е́ду *perf.* (*imp.* проезжа́ть) pass by, through; drive by, through; ride by, through; go past, pass; go, do, make, cover.

прожа́ренный, well-done.

проже́ктор, -а; *pl.* -ы or -а́, searchlight; floodlight.

проже́чь, -жгу́, -жжёшь; -жёг, -жгла́ *perf.* (*imp.* прожига́ть) burn; burn through.

прожива́ть, -а́ю *imp.* of прожи́ть. **прожига́ть,** -а́ю *imp.* of проже́чь.

прожи́точный, enough to live on; ~ ми́нимум, living wage. **прожи́ть,** -иву́, -ивёшь; -о́жи́л, -а́, -о *perf.* (*imp.* прожива́ть) live; spend; run through.

прожо́рливый, voracious, gluttonous.

про́за, -ы, prose. **прозаи́ческий,** prose; prosaic; prosy.

прозва́ние, -я, **про́звище,** -а, nickname. **прозва́ть,** -зову́, -зовёшь; -а́л, -а́, -о *perf.* (*imp.* прозыва́ть) nickname, name.

про|зева́ть, -а́ю *perf.* **про|зимова́ть,** -му́ю *perf.* **прозову́,** etc.: see прозва́ть.

прозоде́жда, -ы *abbr.* working clothes; overalls.

прозорли́вый, sagacious; perspicacious.

прозра́чный, transparent; limpid, pellucid.

прозыва́ть, -а́ю *imp.* of прозва́ть.

прозяба́ние, -я, vegetation. **прозяба́ть,** -а́ю *imp.* vegetate.

проигра́ть, -а́ю *perf.,* **прои́грывать,** -аю *imp.* lose; play; **~ся,** lose everything, gamble away all one's money. **прои́грыватель,** -я *m.* record-player. **про́игрыш,** -а, loss.

произведе́ние, -я, work; production; product. **произвести́,** -еду́, -едёшь; -ёл, -а́ *perf.,* **производи́ть,** -ожу́, -о́дишь *imp.* make; carry out; execute; produce; cause; effect; give birth to; + в + *acc./nom. pl.* promote to (the rank of); ~ впечатле́ние, make an impression, create an impression; ~ на свет, bring into the world. **производи́тельность,** -и, productivity, output; productiveness. **производи́тельный,** productive; efficient. **произво́дн|ый,** derivative, derived; ~ое сло́во, derivative. **произво́дственный,** industrial;

production; commercial; ~ стаж, industrial experience, industrial work record. **произво́дство,** -а, production, manufacture; factory, works; carrying out, execution.

произво́л, -а, arbitrariness; arbitrary rule; оста́вить на ~ судьбы́, leave to the mercy of fate; чини́ть ~, impose arbitrary rule. **произво́льный,** arbitrary.

произнести́, -су́, -сёшь; -ёс, -ла́ *perf.*, **произноси́ть,** -ошу́, -о́сишь *imp.* pronounce; articulate; say, utter; ~ речь, deliver a speech. **произноше́ние,** -я, pronunciation; articulation.

произойти́, -ойдёт; -ошёл, -шла́ *perf.* (*imp.* происходи́ть) happen, occur, take place; spring, arise, result; come, descend, be descended.

про|инструкти́ровать, -рую *perf.*

про́иски, -ов *pl.* intrigues; machinations, schemes, underhand plotting.

проистека́ть, -а́ет *imp.*, **происте́чь,** -ечёт; -ёк, -ла́ *perf.* spring, result; stem.

происходи́ть, -ожу́, -о́дишь *imp.* of произойти́; go on, be going on. **происхожде́ние,** -я, origin; provenance; parentage, descent, extraction, birth; по происхожде́нию, by birth.

происше́ствие, -я, event, incident, happening, occurrence; accident.

пройти́, -йду́, -йдёшь; -ошёл, -шла́ *perf.* (*imp.* проходи́ть) pass; go; go past, go by, elapse; do, cover; be over; pass off, abate, let up; go off; take, study, learn; go through, get through; fall; ~ в + *acc.* or *acc.*/*nom. pl.*, become, be made; be taken on; ему́ э́то да́ром не пройдёт, he will have to pay for it; ~ ми́мо, pass by, go by, go past; overlook, disregard; ~ че́рез, pass, get through; э́то не пройдёт, it won't work; **~сь,** walk up and down; take a stroll, a walk; dance.

прок, -а (-у), use, benefit.

прокажённый *sb.* leper. **прока́за**[1], -ы, leprosy.

прока́за[2], -ы, mischief, prank, trick. **прока́зить,** -а́жу *imp.*, **прока́зничать,** -аю *imp.* (*perf.* на~) be up to mischief, play pranks. **прока́зник,** -а, mischievous child.

прока́лывать, -аю *imp.* of проколо́ть.

прока́т, -а, hire.

прокати́ться, -ачу́сь, -а́тишься *perf.* roll; go for a drive, go for a run.

прока́тный, rolling; rolled; ~ стан, rolling-mill.

прокипяти́ть, -ячу́ *perf.* boil; boil thoroughly.

прокиса́ть, -а́ет *imp.*, **про|ки́снуть,** -нет *perf.* turn (sour).

прокла́дка, -и, laying; building, construction; washer, gasket; packing. **прокла́дывать,** -аю *imp.* of проложи́ть.

проклама́ция, -и, proclamation, leaflet.

проклина́ть, -а́ю *imp.*, **прокля́сть,** -яну́, -янёшь; -о́клял, -а́, -о *perf.* curse, damn; swear at. **прокля́тие,** -я, curse; damnation, perdition; imprecation. **прокля́тый;** -я́т, -а́, -о, accursed, damned; damnable, confounded.

проколо́ть, -лю́, -лешь *perf.* (*imp.* прока́лывать) prick, pierce; perforate; run through.

про|компости́ровать, -рую *perf.* **про|конопа́тить,** -а́чу *perf.* **про|конспекти́ровать,** -рую *perf.* **про|консульти́ровать(ся,** -рую(сь *perf.* **про|контроли́ровать,** -рую *perf.*

прoко́рм, -а, nourishment, sustenance.

про|корми́ть(ся, -млю́(сь, -мишь(ся *perf.*

про|корректи́ровать, -рую *perf.*

прокра́дываться, -аюсь *imp.*, **прокра́сться,** -аду́сь, -адёшься *perf.* steal in.

про|кукаре́кать, -ает *perf.* **про|кукова́ть,** -ку́ю *perf.*

прокуро́р, -а, public prosecutor; procurator; investigating magistrate.

прокути́ть, -учу́, -у́тишь *perf.*, **проку́чивать,** -аю *imp.* squander, dissipate; go on the spree, go on the binge.

пролага́ть, -а́ю *imp.* of проложи́ть.

пролега́ть, -а́ет *imp.* lie, run.

про́лежень, -жня *m.* bedsore.

пролеза́ть, -а́ю *imp.*, **проле́зть,** -зу; -ле́з *perf.* get through, climb through; get in, worm oneself in.

про|лепета́ть, -ечу́, -е́чешь *perf.*

пролёт, -а span; stair-well; bay.

пролета́рий, -я, proletarian; пролета́рии всех стран, соединя́йтесь! workers of the world, unite! **пролета́рский,** proletarian.

пролета́ть, -а́ю *imp.*, **пролете́ть,** -ечу́ *perf.* fly; cover; fly by, fly past, fly through; flash, flit.

проли́в, -а, strait, sound. **пролива́ть,** -а́ю *imp.*, **проли́ть,** -лью́, -льёшь; -о́лил, -а́, -о *perf.* spill, shed; ~ свет на + *acc.* throw light on; shed light on.

проложи́ть, -жу́, -жишь *perf.* (*imp.* прокла́дывать, пролага́ть) lay; build, construct; interlay; insert; interleave; ~ доро́гу, build a road; pave the way, blaze a trail; ~ себе́ доро́гу, carve one's way.

проло́м, -а, breach, break; gap; fracture. **пролома́ть,** -а́ю *perf.* break, break through.

пролью́, etc.: see проли́ть.

пром- *abbr.* in *comb.* of промы́шленный; industrial. **промтова́ры,** -ов *pl.* manufactured goods. **~финпла́н,** -а, industrial and financial plan.

про|ма́зать, -а́жу *perf.* **прома́тывать-(ся,** -аю(сь *imp.* of промота́ть(ся.

про́мах, -а, miss; slip, blunder. **прома́хиваться,** -аюсь *imp.*, **промахну́ться,** -ну́сь, -нёшься *perf* miss; miss the mark; miscue; be wide of the mark, make a mistake, miss an opportunity.

прома́чивать, -аю *imp.* of промочи́ть.

промедле́ние, -я, delay; procrastination. **проме́длить,** -лю *perf.* delay, dally; procrastinate.

промежу́ток, -тка, interval; space. **промежу́точный,** intermediate; intervening; interim.

промелькну́ть, -ну́, -нёшь *perf.* flash; flash past, fly by; be perceptible, be discernible.

проме́нивать, -аю *imp.*, **променя́ть,** -я́ю *perf.* exchange, trade, barter; change.

промерза́ть, -а́ю *imp.*, **промёрзнуть,** -ну; -ёрз *perf.* freeze through. **промёрзлый,** frozen.

промока́тельн|ый: ~ая бума́га, blotting-paper. **промока́ть,** -а́ю *imp.*, **промо́кнуть,** -ну; -мо́к *perf.* get soaked, get drenched.

промо́лвить, -влю *perf.* say, utter.

про|мота́ть, -а́ю *perf.* (*imp.* also прома́тывать) squander; **~ся,** run through one's money.

промочи́ть, -чу́, -чишь *perf.* (*imp.* прома́чивать) get wet (through); soak, drench; ~ но́ги, get one's feet wet.

промо́ю, etc.: see промы́ть.

промча́ться, -чу́сь *perf.* tear, dart, rush (by, past, through); fly.

промыва́ние, -я, washing (out, down); bathing; irrigation. **промыва́ть,** -а́ю *imp.* of промы́ть.

про́мысел, -сла, trade business; *pl.* works; го́рный ~, mining; охо́тничий ~, hunting, trapping; ры́бный ~, fishing, fishery. **промысло́в|ый,** producers'; business; hunters', trappers'; game; ~ая коопера́ция, producers' cooperative.

промы́ть, -мо́ю *perf.* (*imp.* промыва́ть) wash well, wash thoroughly; bathe, irrigate; wash; scrub; ~ мозги́ + *dat.* brain-wash.

про|мыча́ть, -чу́ *perf.*

промы́шленник, -а, manufacturer, industrialist. **промы́шленность,** -и, industry. **промы́шленный,** industrial.

про|мя́млить, -лю *perf.*

пронести́, -су́, -сёшь; -ёс, -ла́ *perf.* (*imp.* проноси́ть) carry; carry by, past, through; pass (over), be over, be past; **~сь,** rush by, past, through; scud (past); fly; be carried, spread; пронёсся слух, there was a rumour.

пронза́ть, -а́ю *imp.*, **пронзи́ть,** -нжу́ *perf.* pierce, run through, transfix. **пронзи́тельный,** penetrating; piercing; shrill, strident.

пронза́ть, -ижу́ -и́жешь *perf.*, **прони́зывать,** -аю *imp.* pierce; permeate, penetrate; run through. **прони́зывающий,** piercing, penetrating.

проника́ть, -а́ю *imp.*, **прони́кнуть,** -ну́; -и́к *perf.* penetrate; percolate; run through; **~ся,** be imbued, be filled. **проникнове́ние,** -я, penetration; feeling; heartfelt conviction. **проникнове́нный,** full of feeling; heartfelt.

прони́кнутый + *instr.* imbued with, instinct with, full of.
проница́емый, permeable, pervious.
проница́тельный, penetrating; perspicacious; acute, shrewd.
проноси́ть(ся, -ошу́(сь, -о́сишь(ся *imp.* of пронести́(сь. **про|нумерова́ть,** -ру́ю *perf.*
проны́рливый, pushful, pushing.
проню́хать, -аю *perf.*, **проню́хивать,** -аю *imp.* smell out, nose out, get wind of.
прообраз, -а, prototype.
пропада́ть, -а́ю *imp.* of пропа́сть. **пропа́жа,** -и, loss; lost object, missing thing.
пропа́лывать, -аю *imp.* of прополо́ть.
про́пасть, -и, precipice; abyss; a mass, masses.
пропа́сть, -аду́, -адёшь *perf.* (*imp.* пропада́ть) be missing; be lost; disappear, vanish; be done for, die; be wasted; мы пропа́ли, we're lost, we're done for; ~ бе́з вести, be missing.
пропека́ть(ся, -а́ю(сь *imp.* of пропе́чь(ся. **про|пе́ть,** -пою́, -поёшь *perf.*
пропе́чь, -еку́, -ечёшь; -ёк, -ла́ *perf.* (*imp.* пропека́ть) bake well, bake thoroughly; **~ся**, bake well; get baked through.
пропива́ть, -а́ю *imp.* of пропи́ть.
прописа́ть, -ишу́, -и́шешь *perf.*, **прописывать,** -аю *imp.* prescribe; register; **~ся**, register. **пропи́ска,** -и, registration; residence permit. **прописн|о́й,** capital; commonplace, trivial; ~ая бу́ква, capital letter; ~ая и́стина, truism. **про́пись,** -и, copy; copy-book maxim. **про́писью** *adv.* in words, in full; писа́ть ци́фры ~, write out figures in words.
пропита́ние, -я, subsistence, sustenance, food; зарабо́тать себе́ на ~, earn one's living. **пропита́ть,** -а́ю *perf.*, **пропи́тывать,** -аю *imp.* impregnate, saturate; soak, steep; keep, provide for; **~ся**, be saturated, be steeped; keep oneself.
пропи́ть, -пью́, -пьёшь; -о́пил, -а́, -о *perf.* (*imp.* пропива́ть) spend on drink, squander on drink.
проплы́в, -а, (swimming) race, heat.
проплыва́ть, -а́ю *imp.*, **проплы́ть,** -ыву́, -ывёшь; -ы́л, -а́, -о *perf.* swim, swim by, past, through; sail by, past, through; float; drift by, past, through; ~ стометро́вку, swim the hundred metres.
пропове́довать, -дую *imp.* preach; advocate. **про́поведь,** -и, sermon; homily; preaching, advocacy; наго́рная ~, Sermon on the Mount.
пропо́лка, -и, weeding. **прополо́ть,** -лю́, -лешь *perf.* (*imp.* пропа́лывать) weed.
про|полоска́ть, -ощу́, -о́щешь *perf.*
пропорциона́льный, proportional, proportionate. **пропо́рция,** -и, proportion; ratio.
про́пуск, -а; *pl.* -а́ or -и, -о́в or -ов, pass, permit; password; admission; omission, lapse; absence, non-attendance; blank, gap. **пропуска́ть,** -а́ю *imp.*, **пропусти́ть,** -ущу́, -у́стишь *perf.* let pass, let through; let in, admit; absorb; pass; omit, leave out; skip; miss; let slip; ~ ми́мо уше́й, pay no heed to, turn a deaf ear to; не пропуска́ть воды́, be waterproof; пропуска́ть во́ду, leak. **пропускн|о́й;** ~а́я бума́га, blotting-paper; ~о́й свет, transmitted light; ~а́я спосо́бность, capacity.
пропью́, etc.: see пропи́ть.
прораба́тывать, -аю *imp.*, **прорабо́тать,** -аю *perf.* work, work through; work at, study; get up; slate, pick holes in. **прорабо́тка,** -и, study, studying, getting up; slating.
прораста́ть, -а́ет *imp.*, **прорасти́,** -тёт; -ро́с, -ла́ *perf.* germinate, sprout, shoot.
прорва́ть, -ву́, -вёшь; -а́л, -а́, -о *perf.* (*imp.* прорыва́ть) break through; tear, make a hole in; burst; ~ блока́ду, run the blockade; **~ся**, burst open, break; tear; break out break through.
про|реаги́ровать, -рую *perf.*
проре́з, -а, cut; slit, notch, nick. **про|ре́зать,** -е́жу *perf.*, **прореза́ть,** -а́ю *imp.* (*imp.* also проре́зывать) cut through; **~ся**, be cut, come through.
прорези́нивать, -аю *imp.*, **прорези́нить** -ню *perf.* rubberize.

прорéзывать(ся, -аю(сь *imp.* of прорéзать(ся. **про|репетúровать,** -рую *perf.*

прорéха, -и, rent, tear, slit; fly, flies; gap deficiency.

про|рецензúровать, -рую *perf.*

пророк, -а, prophet.

порóс, etc.: see прорасти́.

проронúть, -ню́, -нишь *perf.* utter, breathe, drop.

пророческий. prophetic, oracular. **пророчество,** -а prophecy. **пророчить,** -чу *imp.* (*perf.* на~) prophesy; predict.

пророю, etc.: see проры́ть.

прорубáть, -áю *imp.*, **прорубúть,** -блю́, -бишь *perf.* cut through, hack through; break. **прóрубь,** -и, ice-hole.

прорыв, -а, break; break-through, breach; hitch, hold-up· ликвидúровать ~, put things right; пóлный ~, breakdown. **прорывáть**[1]**(ся,** -áю(сь *imp.* of прорвáть(ся.

прорывáть[2], -áю *imp.*, **проры́ть,** -рóю *perf.* dig through; **~ся,** dig one's way through, tunnel through.

просáчиваться, -áется *imp.* of просочúться.

просвéрливать, -аю *imp.*, **про|сверлúть,** -лю́ *perf.* drill, bore; perforate, pierce.

просвéт, -а, (clear) space; shaft of light; ray of hope; aperture, opening. **просветúтельный,** educational; cultural. **просветúтельство,** -а, educational activities, cultural activities. **просветúть**[1], -ещу́ *perf.* (*imp.* просвещáть) educate; enlighten.

просветúть[2], -ечу́, -éтишь *perf.* (*imp.* просвéчивать) X-ray.

просветлéние, -я, clearing up; brightening (up); clarity, lucidity. **просветлённый,** clear, lucid. **про|светлéть,** -éет *perf.*

просвéчивание -я, fluoroscopy; radioscopy. **просвéчивать.** -аю *imp.* of просветúть; be translucent; be visible; show, appear, shine.

просвещáть, -áю *imp.* of просветúть.

просвещéние, -я, enlightenment; education, instruction; нарóдное ~, public education. **просвещённый,** enlightened; educated, cultured.

прóседь, -и, streak(s) of grey; вóлосы с ~ю, greying hair, hair touched with grey.

просéивать, -аю *imp.* of просéять.

прóсека, -и, cutting, ride.

просёлок, -лка, country road, cart-track.

просéять, -éю *perf.* (*imp.* просéивать) sift, riddle, screen.

про|сигнализúровать, -рую *perf.*

просидéть, -ижу́ *perf.*, **просúживать,** -аю *imp.* sit; ~ всю ночь, sit up all night.

просúтель, -я *m.* applicant; suppliant; petitioner. **просúтельный,** pleading. **просúть,** -ошу́, -óсишь *imp.* (*perf.* по~) ask; beg; plead, intercede; invite; прóсят не курúть, no smoking, please; **~ся,** ask; apply.

просиять, -я́ю *perf.* brighten; begin to shine; beam, light up.

проскáкивать, -аю *imp.* of проскочúть.

проскáльзывать -аю *imp.*, **проскользнýть,** -ну́, -нёшь *perf.* slip in, creep in; ~ мúмо, slip past.

проскочúть, -чу́, -чишь *perf.* (*imp.* проскáкивать) rush, tear; slip through; slip in, creep in.

про|слáбить, -бит *perf.*

прослáвить, -влю *perf.*, **прославля́ть,** -я́ю *imp.* glorify; bring fame to; make famous; **~ся,** become famous, be renowned. **прослáвленный,** famous, renowned, celebrated, illustrious.

проследúть, -ежу́ *perf.* track (down); trace.

прослезúться, -ежу́сь *perf.* shed a tear, a few tears.

прослоúть, -ою́ *perf.* layer; sandwich. **прослóйка,** -и, layer, stratum; seam, streak.

про|слу́шать, -аю *perf.*, **прослу́шивать,** -аю *imp.* hear; listen to; miss, not catch.

про|слы́ть, -ыву́, -ывёшь; -ы́л, -á, -о *perf.*

просмáтривать, -аю *imp.*, **просмотрéть,** -рю́, -ришь *perf.* look over, look through; glance over, glance through; survey; view; run over; overlook miss. **просмóтр,** -а, survey; view, viewing;

examination; закры́тый ~, private view; предвари́тельный ~, preview.

проснýться, -нýсь, -нёшься *perf.* (*imp.* просыпáться) wake up, awake.

прóсо, -а millet.

просóвывать(ся, -аю(сь *imp.* of просýнуть(ся.

про|сóхнуть, -ну; -óх *perf.* (*imp.* also просыхáть) get dry, dry out. **просóхший**, dried.

просочи́ться, -и́тся *perf.* (*imp.* просáчиваться) percolate; filter; leak, ooze; seep out; filter through, leak out.

проспáть, -плю́; -áл, -á, -о *perf.* (*imp.* просыпáть) sleep (for, through); oversleep; miss.

проспéкт, -а, avenue.

проспóрить, -рю *perf.* lose, lose a bet; argue.

про|спрягáть, -áю *perf.*

просрóчен|ный, overdue; out of date, expired; пáспорт ~ the passport is out of date. **просрóчивать**, -аю *imp.*, **просрóчить**, -чу *perf.* allow to run out; be behind with; overstay; ~ óтпуск, overstay one's leave. **просрóчка**, -и, delay; expiration of time limit.

простáк, -á, simpleton. **простéйший** *superl.* of простóй.

простéнок, -нка, pier; partition.

простерéться, -трётся; -тёрся *perf.*, **простирáться**, -áется *imp.* stretch, extend.

прости́тельный, pardonable, excusable, justifiable. **прости́ть**, -ощý *perf.* (*imp.* прощáть) forgive, pardon; excuse; **~ся** (с + *instr.*) say goodbye (to), take (one's) leave (of), bid farewell.

прóсто *adv.* simply; ~ так, for no particular reason.

просто- in *comb.* simple; open; mere. **простоволóсый**, bare-headed, with head uncovered. **~дýшный**, open-hearted; simple-hearted, simple-minded; ingenuous, artless. **~квáша**, -и, (thick) sour milk, yoghurt. **~люди́н**, -а, man of the common people. **~нарóдный**, of the common people. **~рéчие**, -я, popular speech; в ~рéчии, colloquially. **~рéчный**, popular, of popular speech. **~сердéчный**, simple-hearted; frank; open.

простóй, -я, standing idle, enforced idleness; stoppage.

прост|óй, simple; easy; ordinary; plain; unaffected, unpretentious; mere; ~ы́м глáзом, with the naked eye; ~ы́е лю́ди, ordinary people; homely people; ~óй нарóд, the common people; ~óе предложéние, simple sentence; ~óе числó, prime number. **прóсто-нáпросто** *adv.* simply.

простóр, -а, spaciousness; space, expanse; freedom, scope; elbow-room; дать ~, give scope, free range, full play. **простóрн|ый**, spacious, roomy; ample; здесь ~о, there is plenty of room here.

простотá, -ы́, simplicity.

пространный, extensive, vast; diffuse; verbose. **прострáнственный**, spatial. **прострáнство**, -а, space; expanse; area.

прострéл, -а, lumbago. **прострéливать**, -аю *imp.*, **прострели́ть**, -лю́, -лишь *perf.* shoot through.

прострётся, etc.: see простерéться.

про|строчи́ть, -очý, -óчишь *perf.*

простýда, -ы, cold; chill. **простуди́ть**, -ужý, -ýдишь *perf.*, **простужáть**, -áю *imp.* let catch cold; **~ся**, catch (a) cold, a chill.

простýпок, -пка, fault; misdemeanour.

просты́нн|ый, sheet; ~ое полотнó, sheeting. **простыня́** -и́; *pl.* прóстыни, -ы́нь, -ня́м, sheet.

просты́ть, -ы́ну *perf.* get cold; cool; catch cold.

просýнуть, -ну *perf.* (*imp.* просóвывать) push, shove, thrust; **~ся**, push through, force one's way through.

просýшивать, -аю *imp.*, **просуши́ть**, -шý, -шишь *perf.* dry (thoroughly, properly); **~ся**, dry, get dry. **просýшка**, -и, drying.

просуществовáть, -твýю *perf.* exist; last, endure.

просчитáться, -áюсь *perf.*, **просчи́тываться**, -аюсь *imp.* miscalculate.

прóсып -а (-у); без ~у, without waking, without stirring.

просы́пать, -плю *perf.*, **просыпáть**[1], -áю *imp.* spill; **~ся**, spill, get spilt; fail, be ploughed.

просыпа́ть², -а́ю *imp.* of проспа́ть. **просыпа́ться**, -а́юсь *imp.* of просну́ться. **просыха́ть**, -а́ю *imp.* of просо́хнуть.

про́сьба, -ы, request; application, petition; ~ не кури́ть, no smoking, please; у меня́ к вам ~, I have a favour to ask you.

прота́лкивать, -аю *imp.* of протолкну́ть. **прота́пливать**, -аю *imp.* of протопи́ть.

прота́скивать, -аю *imp.*, **протащи́ть**, -щу́, -щишь *perf.* pull, drag, trail.

проте́з, -а, artificial limb; (artificial) aid; prosthesis, prosthetic appliance; зубно́й ~, false teeth, denture; слухово́й ~, hearing aid. **проте́зный**, prosthetic.

протека́ть, -а́ет *imp.* of проте́чь. **протёкший**, past, last.

проте́кция, -и, patronage, influence.

протере́ть, -тру́, -трёшь; -тёр *perf.* (*imp.* протира́ть) wipe (over); wipe dry; rub (through).

проте́чь, -ечёт; -тёк, -ла́ *perf.* (*imp.* протека́ть) flow, run; leak; ooze, seep; elapse, pass; take its course.

про́тив *prep.* + *gen.* against; opposite; facing; contrary to, as against; in proportion to, according to; име́ть что́-нибудь ~, have something against, mind, object; ничего́ не име́ть ~, not mind, not object.

про́тивень, -вня *m.* dripping-pan; meat-tin; girdle, griddle.

проти́виться, -влюсь *imp.* (*perf.* вос~) + *dat.* oppose; resist, stand up against. **проти́вник**, -а, opponent, adversary, antagonist; the enemy. **проти́вно** *prep.* + *dat.* against; contrary to. **проти́вн|ый**¹, opposite; contrary; opposing, opposed; в ~ом слу́чае, otherwise; ~ый ве́тер, contrary wind, head wind. **проти́вный**², nasty, offensive, disgusting; unpleasant, disagreeable; мне проти́вно, I am disgusted.

противо- in *comb.* anti-, contra- counter-. **противове́с**, -а, counterbalance, counterpoise. **~возду́шный**, anti-aircraft. **~га́з**, -а, gas-mask, respirator. **~га́зовый**, anti-gas. **~де́йствие**, -я, opposition, counteraction. **~де́йствовать**, -твую *imp.* + *dat.* oppose, counteract. **~есте́ственный**, unnatural. **~зако́нный**, unlawful; illegal. **~зача́точный**, contraceptive. **~лежа́щий**, opposite. **~обще́ственный**, anti-social. **~пожа́рный**, fire-fighting, fire-prevention. **~поло́жность**, -и, opposition; contrast; opposite, antithesis; пряма́я ~поло́жность, exact opposite. **~поло́жный**, opposite; opposed, contrary. **~поста́вить**, -влю *perf.*, **~поставля́ть**, -я́ю *imp.* oppose; contrast, set off. **~раке́та**, -ы, anti-missile missile. **~раке́тный**, anti-missile. **~речи́вый**, contradictory; discrepant, conflicting. **~ре́чие**, -я, contradiction; inconsistency; conflict, clash. **~ре́чить**, -чу *imp.* + *dat.* contradict; be at variance with, conflict with, be contrary to, run counter to. **~стоя́ть**, -ою́ *imp.* + *dat.* resist, withstand. **~та́нковый**, anti-tank. **~хими́ческий**, anti-gas. **~я́дие**, -я, antidote.

протира́ть, -а́ю *imp.* of протере́ть. **проти́рка**, -и, cleaning rag.

проткну́ть, -ну́, -нёшь *perf.* (*imp.* протыка́ть) pierce; transfix; spit, skewer.

протоко́л, -а, minutes, record of proceedings; report; statement; charge-sheet; protocol; вести́ ~, take, record, the minutes; занести́ в ~, enter in the minutes. **протоколи́ровать**, -рую *perf.* and *imp.* (*perf.* also за~) minute, record. **протоко́льный**, of protocol; exact, factual.

протолкну́ть, -ну́, -нёшь *perf.* (*imp.* прота́лкивать) push through.

протопи́ть, -плю́, -пишь *perf.* (*imp.* прота́пливать) heat (thoroughly).

проторённ|ый, beaten, well-trodden; ~ая доро́жка, beaten track.

прото́чный, flowing, running.

про|тра́лить, -лю *perf.* **протру́**, etc.: see протере́ть. **про|труби́ть**, -блю́ *perf.*

протуха́ть, -а́ет *imp.*, **проту́хнуть**, -нет; -у́х *perf.* become foul, become rotten; go bad. **проту́хший**, foul, rotten; bad, tainted.

протыка́ть, -а́ю *imp.* of проткну́ть.

протя́гивать, -аю *imp.*, **протяну́ть**, -ну́, -нешь *perf.* stretch; extend; stretch out, hold out; reach out; protract; drawl out; last; **~ся,** stretch out; reach out; extend, stretch, reach; last, go on. **протяже́ние, -я,** extent, stretch; distance, expanse, area; space; на всём протяже́нии + *gen.* along the whole length of, all along; на протяже́нии, during, for the space of. **протяжённость,** -и, extent, length. **протя́жность,** -и, slowness; ~ ре́чи, drawl. **протя́жный,** long-drawn-out; drawling.

проу́чивать, -аю *imp.*, **проучи́ть,** -чу́, -чишь *perf.* study, learn (up); teach a lesson, punish.

проф. *abbr.* профе́ссор, professor.

проф- *abbr.* in *comb.* of профессиона́льный, professional, occupational; профсою́зный, trade-union. **профбиле́т,** -а, trade-union card. **~боле́знь,** -и occupational disease. **~ко́м,** -а, trade-union commitee. **~о́рг,** -а, trade-union organizer. **~ориента́ция,** -и, vocational guidance. **~рабо́тник,** -а trade-union official. **~сою́з,** -а, trade union. **~сою́зный,** trade-union. **~техучи́лище,** -а, technical college. **~техшко́ла,** -ы, trade school. **~шко́ла,** -ы, trade-union school.

профа́н, -а, layman; ignoramus.

профессиона́льный, professional; occupational; ~ сою́з, trade union. **профе́ссия,** -и, profession, occupation, trade.

про́филь, -я *m.* profile; side-view; outline; section; type.

прохла́да, -ы, coolness, cool. **прохлади́тельный,** refreshing, cooling. **прохла́дный,** cool, fresh.

прохо́д, -а (-у) passage; passageway; gangway, aisle; duct; пра́во ~а, right of way; ~а нет, no thoroughfare. **проходи́мец,** -мца, rogue, rascal. **проходи́мый,** passable. **проходи́ть,** -ожу́, -о́дишь *imp.* of пройти́. **прохо́дка,** -и, going through, getting through; tunnelling, driving. **проходно́й,** of passage; through, communicating. **прохо́жий,** passing, in transit; *sb.* passer-by.

процвета́ние, -я, prosperity, well-being; flourishing, thriving. **процвета́ть,** -а́ю *imp.* prosper, flourish, thrive.

процеди́ть, -ежу́, -е́дишь *perf.* (*imp.* проце́живать) filter, strain; ~ сквозь зу́бы, mutter, mumble.

процеду́ра, -ы, procedure; treatment; лече́бные процеду́ры, medical treatment.

проце́живать, -аю *perf.* of процеди́ть.

проце́нт, -а, percentage; per cent; interest; сто ~ов, a hundred per cent.

проце́сс, -а, process; trial; legal action, legal proceedings; lawsuit; cause, case. **проце́ссия,** -и, procession. **процессуа́льный,** trial; legal.

про|цити́ровать, -рую *perf.*

прочёска, -и, screening; combing.

проче́сть, -чту́, -чтёшь; -чёл, -чла́ *perf.* of чита́ть.

про́ч|ий, other; и ~ее, etc., etcetera, and so on; ме́жду ~им, incidentally, by the way; **~ие** *sb.* (the) others.

прочи́стить, -и́щу *perf.* (*imp.* прочища́ть) clean; cleanse thoroughly.

про|чита́ть, -а́ю *perf.*, **прочи́тывать,** -аю *imp.* read (through).

прочища́ть, -а́ю *imp.* of прочи́стить.

про́чно *adv.* firmly, soundly, solidly, well. **про́чн|ый;** -чен, -чна́, -о, firm, sound, stable, solid; durable, lasting; enduring; ~ая кра́ска, fast colour.

прочте́ние, -я, reading; reciting; giving, delivering. **прочту́,** etc.; see проче́сть.

прочу́вствовать, -твую *perf.* feel; feel deeply, acutely, keenly; experience, go through; get the feel of.

прочь *adv.* away, off; averse to; (поди́) ~! go away! be off!; (пошёл) ~ отсю́да! get out of here!; ~ с доро́ги! get out of the way!; ру́ки ~! hands off!; я не прочь, I have no objection, I am not averse to, I am quite willing.

проше́дш|ий, past; last; **~ее** *sb.* the past. **прошёл,** etc.: see пройти́.

проше́ние, -я, application, petition.

прошепта́ть, -пчу́, -пчешь *perf.* whisper.

проше́ствие, -я; по проше́ствии + *gen.* after the lapse of, after the expiration of.

прошива́ть, -а́ю *imp.*, **проши́ть,** -шью́, -шьёшь *perf.* sew, stitch. **проши́вка,** -и, insertion.

прошлогóдний, last year's. **прóшл|ый**, past; of the past; bygone, former; last; в ~ом годý, last year; **~ое** *sb.* the past.

прошмáнивать, -аю *imp.*, **про|шмонáть**, -áю *perf.*, **про|шмонúть**, -нó, -нишь *perf.* (*sl.*) search, frisk.

про|шнуровáть, -рýю *perf.* **про|штудúровать**, -рую *perf.* **прошьó**, etc.: see прошúть.

прощáй(те), goodbye; farewell. **прощáльный**, parting; farewell. **прощáние**, -я, farewell; parting, leave-taking. **прощáть(ся**, -áю(сь *imp.* of простúть(ся.

прóще, simpler, plainer, easier.

прощéние, -я, forgiveness, pardon; прошý прощéния, I beg your pardon; (I'm) sorry.

прощýпать, -аю *perf.*, **прощýпывать**, -аю *imp.* feel; detect; sound (out).

про|экзаменовáть, -нýю *perf.*

проявúтель, -я *m.* developer. **проявúть**, -влю́, -вишь *perf.*, **проявля́ть**, -я́ю *imp.* show, display, manifest, reveal; develop.

проя́снеть[1], -еет *perf.* clear; проя́снело, it cleared up. **прояснéть**[2], -éет *perf.* brighten (up). **прояснúться**, -úтся *perf.*, **проясня́ться**, -я́ется *imp.* clear, clear up.

пруд, -á, *loc.* -ý, pond. **прудúть**, -ужý, -ýдишь *imp.* (*perf.* за~) dam. **прудовóй**, pond.

пружúна, -ы, spring. **пружúнистый**, springy, elastic. **пружúнка**, -и, mainspring; hairspring. **пружúнный**, spring.

прусáк, -á, cockroach.

пруссáк, -á **пруссáчка**, -и, Prussian. **прýсский**, Prussian.

прут, -а or -á; *pl.* -тья twig; switch; rod.

пры́галка, -и, skipping-rope. **пры́гать**, -аю *imp.*, **пры́гнуть**, -ну *perf.* jump, leap, spring; bound; hop; bounce; ~ со скакáлкой, skip; ~ с упóром, vault; ~ с шестóм, pole-vault. **прыгýн**, -á, **прыгýнья**, -и; *gen. pl.* -ний, jumper. **прыжóк**, -жкá, jump; leap, spring; caper; прыжкú, jumping; прыжкú в вóду, diving; ~ в высотý, high jump; ~ в длинý, long jump; ~ с мéста, standing jump; ~ с разбéга, running jump; ~ с упóром, vault, vaulting; ~ с шестóм, pole-vault.

пры́скать, -аю *imp.*, **пры́снуть**, -ну *perf.* spurt, gush; ~ на or в + *acc.* spray, sprinkle; ~ (сó смеху) burst out laughing.

пры́ткий, quick, lively, sharp. **прыть**, -и, speed; quickness, liveliness, go.

прыщ, -á, **пры́щик**, -а, pimple; pustule, **прыщáвый**, pimply, pimpled.

прядéние, -я, spinning. **пря́деный**, spun. **прядúльный**, spinning. **прядúльня**, -и; *gen. pl.* -лен, (spinning-) mill. **прядúльщик**, -а, spinner. **прядý**, etc.: see прясть. **прядь**, -и, lock; strand. **пря́жа**, -и, yarn, thread.

пря́жка, -и, buckle, clasp.

пря́лка, -и, distaff; spinning-wheel.

прямáя *sb.* straight line; по прямóй, on the straight. **пря́мо** *adv.* straight; straight on; directly; frankly, openly, bluntly; really.

прямо- in *comb.* straight-; direct; ortho-, rect(i)-, right. **прямодýшие**, -я, directness, frankness, straightforwardness. **~дýшный**, direct, frank, straightforward. **~кры́лый**, orthopterous. **~линéйный**, rectilinear; straightforward, forthright. **~слóйный**, straight-grained. **~угóльник**, -а, rectangle. **~угóльный**, right-angled, rectangular.

прямóй; -ям, -á, -о, straight; upright, erect; through; direct; straightforward; real.

пря́ник, -а, spice cake; gingerbread; honey-cake. **пря́ничный**, gingerbread.

пря́ность, -и, spice; spiciness. **пря́ный**, spicy; heady.

прясть, -ядý, -ядёшь; -ял, -я́лá, -о *imp.* (*perf.* с~) spin.

пря́тать, -я́чу *imp.* (*perf.* с~) hide, conceal; **~ся**, hide, conceal oneself. **пря́тки**, -ток *pl.* hide-and-seek.

пря́ха, -и, spinner.

пса, etc.: see пёс.

псалóм, -лмá, psalm. **псалóмщик**, -а, (psalm-)reader; sexton.

псевдонúм, -а, pseudonym; pen-name.

псих, -а, madman, lunatic, crank. **псúхика**, -и, state of mind; psyche; psychology. **психúческий**, mental, psychical. **психо́з**, -а, psychosis. **психопа́т**, -а, psychopath; lunatic.

птене́ц, -нца́, nestling; fledgeling. **пти́ца**, -ы, bird; ва́жная ~, big noise; дома́шняя ~, poultry. **птицево́д**, -а, poultry-farmer, poultry-breeder. **пти́ч|ий**, bird, bird's, poultry; вид с ~ьего полёта, bird's-eye view; ~ий двор, poultry-yard. **пти́чка**, -и, bird.

ПТО (*peteó*) *abbr*. профессиона́льно-техни́ческое обуче́ние, technical education.

ПТУ (*peteú*) *abbr*. профтехучи́лище, профессиона́льно-техни́ческое учи́лище, technical college.

пу́блика, -и, public; audience. **публика́ция**, -и, publication; notice, advertisement. **публикова́ть**, -ку́ю *imp*. (*perf*. о~) publish. **публици́стика**, -и, social and political journalism; writing on current affairs. **публи́чно** *adv*. publicly; in public; openly. **публи́чность**, -и publicity. **публи́чный**, public.

пу́гало, -а, scarecrow. **пу́ганый**, scared, frightened. **пуга́ть**, -а́ю *imp*. (*perf*. ис~, на~) frighten, scare; intimidate; + *instr*. threaten with; **~ся** (+ *gen*.) be frightened (of), be scared (of); take fright (at); shy (at). **пуга́ч**, -а́, toy pistol; screech owl. **пугли́вый**, fearful, timorous; timid. **пугну́ть**, -ну́, -нёшь *perf*. scare, frighten; give a fright.

пу́говица, -ы, **пу́говка**, -и, button.

пуд, -а; *pl*. -ы́, pood (= 16·3 kg). **пудово́й, пудо́вый**, one pood in weight.

пу́дра, -ы powder. **пу́дреный**, powdered. **пу́дрить**, -рю *imp*. (*perf*. на~) powder; **~ся**, powder one's face, use powder.

пуза́тый, big-bellied, pot-bellied.

пузырёк, -рька́, phial, vial; bubble; bleb. **пузы́рь**, -я́ *m*. bubble; blister; bladder.

пук, -а; *pl*. -и́, bunch, bundle; tuft; wisp.

пулево́й, bullet. **пулемёт**, -а, machine-gun. **пулемётный**, machine-gun. **пулемётчик**, -а, machine-gunner. **пулесто́йкий**, bullet-proof.

пульс, -а, pulse. **пу́льсар**, -а, pulsar. **пульси́ровать**, -рует *imp*. pulse, pulsate; beat, throb.

пульт, -а, desk, stand; control panel.

пу́ля, -и, bullet.

пункт, -а, point; spot; post; centre; item; plank; по всем ~ам, at all points. **пункти́р**, -а, dotted line. **пункти́рный**, dotted, broken.

пунцо́вый, crimson.

пуп, -а́, navel; umbilicus; ~ земли́, hub of the universe. **пупови́на**, -ы, umbilical cord. **пупо́к**, -пка́, navel; gizzard. **пупо́чный**, umbilical.

пурга́ -и́, snow-storm, blizzard.

пу́рпур, -а, purple, crimson. **пурпу́рный, пурпу́ровый**, purple, crimson.

пуск, -а, starting (up); setting in motion. **пуска́й**: see пусть. **пуска́ть(ся**, -а́ю(сь *imp*. of пусти́ть(ся. **пусков|о́й**, starting; initial; ~а́я площа́дка, (rocket-)launching platform.

пусте́ть, -е́ет *imp*. (*perf*. о~) empty; become deserted.

пусти́ть, пущу́, пу́стишь *perf*. (*imp*. пуска́ть) let go; set free; let in, allow to enter; let, allow, permit; start; set, put; send; set in motion, set going, set working; throw, shy; put forth, put out; не ~, keep out; ~ во́ду, turn on the water; ~ в ход, start, launch, set going, set in train; ~ ко́рни, take root; ~ ростки́, shoot, sprout; ~ слух, start, spread, a rumour; ~ фейерве́рк, let off fireworks; **~ся**, set out; start; begin; ~ся в путь, set out, get on one's way.

пустобрёх, -а, chatterbox, windbag.

пустова́ть, -ту́ет *imp*. be empty, stand empty; lie fallow. **пуст|о́й**; -ст, -а́, -о, empty; void; tenantless, vacant, uninhabited; deserted; idle; shallow; futile, frivolous; vain, ungrounded; ~о́е ме́сто, blank space; ~а́я отгово́рка, lame excuse, hollow pretence; ~ы́е слова́, mere words; ~о́й чай, just tea. **пустота́**, -ы́; pl. -ы, emptiness; void; vacuum; shallowness; futility, frivolousness. **пустоте́лый**, hollow.

пусты́нник, -а, hermit, anchorite. **пусты́нный**, uninhabited; deserted; ~ о́стров, desert island. **пу́стынь**, -и,

hermitage, monastery. **пусты́ня, -и,** desert, wilderness. **пусты́рь, -я** *m.* waste land; vacant plot; desolate area.
пусты́шка, -и, blank; hollow object; (baby's) dummy; empty-headed person.
пусть, пуска́й *part.* let; all right, very well; though, even if; ~ бу́дет так, so be it; ~ x ра́вен 3, let $x = 3$.
пустя́к, -а́, trifle; bagatelle. **пустяко́вый,** trifling, trivial.
пу́таница, -ы, muddle, confusion; mess, tangle. **пу́таный,** muddled, confused; tangled; confusing; muddle-headed. **пу́тать, -аю** *imp.* (*perf.* за~, пере~, с~) tangle; confuse; muddle; mix up; **~ся,** get tangled; get confused; get muddled; get mixed up.
путёвка, -и, pass, authorization; permit; проси́ть путёвку в санато́рий, apply for a place in a sanatorium.
путеводи́тель, -я *m.* guide, guide-book. **путево́дн|ый,** guiding; ~ая звезда́, guiding star; lodestar. **путев|о́й,** travelling, itinerary; ~а́я ка́рта, road-map; ~а́я ско́рость, ground-speed. **путём** *prep.* + *gen.* by means of, by dint of. **путепрово́д, -а,** overpass; underpass; bridge. **путеше́ственник, -а,** traveller. **путеше́ствие, -я,** journey; trip; voyage; cruise; *pl.* travels. **путеше́ствовать, -твую** *imp.* travel; voyage. **путь, -и́,** *instr.* -ём, *prep.* -и́, way; track; path; road; course; journey; voyage; passage, duct; means; use, benefit; во́дный ~, water-way; в пути́, en route, on one's way; в четырёх днях пути́ от, four days' journey from; ми́рным путём, amicably, peaceably; морски́е пути́, shipping-routes, sea-lanes; нам с ва́ми по пути́, we are going the same way; на обра́тном пути́, on the way back; пойти́ по пути́ + *gen.* take, follow, the path of; по пути́, on the way; пути́ сообще́ния, communications; стоя́ть на пути́, be in the way.
пух, -а (-у), *loc.* -у́, down; fluff; разби́ть в ~ и прах, put to complete rout.
пу́хл|ый; -хл, -а́, -о, chubby, plump.
пу́хнуть, -ну; пух *imp.* (*perf.* вс~, о~) swell.
пухови́к, -а́, feather-bed; down quilt; eiderdown. **пухо́вка, -и,** powder-puff. **пухо́вый,** downy.
пучегла́зый, goggle-eyed.
пучи́на, -ы, gulf, abyss; the deep.
пучо́к, -чка́, bunch, bundle; tuft, fascicle; wisp.
пу́шечен|ый, gun, cannon; ~ое мя́со, cannon-fodder.
пуши́нка, -и, bit of fluff; ~ сне́га, snow-flake. **пуши́стый,** fluffy, downy.
пу́шка, -и, gun, cannon.
пушни́на, -ы, furs, fur-skins, pelts. **пушно́й,** fur; fur-bearing; ~ зверь, fur-bearing animals.
пу́ще *adv.* more; ~ всего́, most of all.
пущу́, etc.: see пусти́ть.
пчела́, -ы́; *pl.* -ёлы, bee. **пчели́ный,** bee, bees', of bees; ~ воск, beeswax. **пчелово́д, -а,** bee-keeper, bee-master, apiarist. **пче́льник, -а,** apiary.
пшени́ца, -ы, wheat. **пшени́чный,** wheaten, wheat.
пшённый, millet. **пшено́, -а́,** millet.
пыл, -а (-у), *loc.* -у́, heat, ardour, passion. **пыла́ть, -а́ю** *imp.* blaze, flame; burn; glow.
пылеви́дный, powdered, pulverized. **пылесо́с, -а,** vacuum cleaner. **пылесо́сить, -сю** *imp.* vacuum(-clean). **пыли́нка, -и,** speck of dust. **пыли́ть, -лю́** *imp.* (*perf.* за~, на~) raise a dust, raise the dust; cover with dust, make dusty; **~ся,** get dusty, get covered with dust.
пы́лкий, ardent, passionate; fervent; fervid. **пы́лкость, -и,** ardour, passion; fervency.
пыль, -и, *loc.* -и́, dust. **пы́льн|ый;** -лен, -льна́, -о, dusty; ~ый котёл, dust-bowl; ~ая тря́пка, duster. **пыльца́, -ы́,** pollen.
пыта́ть, -а́ю *imp.* torture, torment. **пыта́ться, -а́юсь** *imp.* (*perf.* по~) try. **пы́тка, -и,** torture, torment. **пытли́вый,** inquisitive searching.
пы́хать, пы́шет *imp.* blaze.
пыхте́ть, -хчу́ *imp.* puff, pant.
пы́шет: see пы́хать.
пы́шка, -и, bun; doughnut; chubby child; plump woman.

пышность, -и, splendour, magnificence. **пышный**; -шен, -шна́, шно, splendid, magnificent; fluffy, light; luxuriant.
пьексы, -с *pl.* ski boots.
пьеса, -ы, play; piece.
пью, etc.: see пить.
пьяне́ть, -е́ю *imp.* (*perf.* о~) get drunk. **пьяни́ть**, -ни́т *imp.* (*perf.* о~) intoxicate, make drunk; go to one's head. **пья́ница**, -ы *m.* and *f.* drunkard; tippler, toper. **пья́нство**, -а, drunkenness; hard drinking. **пья́нствовать**, -твую *imp.* drink hard, drink heavily. **пья́ный**, drunk; drunken; tipsy, tight; intoxicated; heady, intoxicating.
пэ *n. indecl.* the letter п.
пюпи́тр, -а, desk; reading-desk; music-stand.
пюре́ *n. indecl.* purée.
пядь, -и; *gen. pl.* -е́й, span; ни пя́ди, not an inch.
пя́льцы, -лец *pl.* tambour; embroidery frame.
пята́, -ы́; *pl.* -ы, -а́м, heel.
пята́к, -а́, **пятачо́к**, -чка́, five-copeck piece. **пятёрка**, -и, five; figure 5; No. 5; group of five; five-rouble note.
пя́теро, -ы́х, five.
пяти- in *comb.* five; penta-. **пятибо́рье**, -я, pentathlon. **~гла́вый**, five-headed; five-domed. **~десятиле́тие**, -я, fifty years; fiftieth anniversary; fiftieth birthday. **~деся́тница**, -ы, Pentecost. **~деся́тый**, fiftieth; ~деся́тые го́ды, the fifties. **~кла́ссник**, -а, -**ница**, -ы, **~кла́шка**, -и *m.* and *f.* class-five pupil. **~кни́жие**, -я, Pentateuch. **~коне́чный**, five-pointed. **~кра́тный**, fivefold, quintuple. **~ле́тие**, -я, five years; fifth anniversary. **~ле́тка**, -и, five years; five-year plan; five-year-old. **~со́тенный**, five-hundred-rouble. **~сотле́тие**, -я, five centuries; quincentenary. **~со́тый**, five-hundredth. **~сто́пный**, pentameter. **~то́нка**, -и, five-ton lorry. **~ты́сячный**, five-thousandth. **~уго́льник**, -а, pentagon. **~уго́льный**, pentagonal.
пя́тка, -и, heel.
пятна́дцатый, fifteenth. **пятна́дцать**, -и, fifteen.
пятна́ть, -а́ю *imp.* (*perf.* за~) spot, stain, smirch; tig, catch. **пятна́шки**, -шек *pl.* tag, tig. **пятни́стый**, spotted, dappled.
пя́тница, -ы, Friday.
пятно́, -а́; *pl.* -а, -тен, stain; spot; patch; blot; stigma, blemish; роди́мое ~, birth-mark.
пято́к, -тка́, five. **пя́тый**, fifth. **пять**, -и́, *instr.* -ью, five. **пятьдеся́т**, -и́десяти, *instr.* -ью́десятью, fifty. **пятьсо́т**, -тисо́т, -тиста́м, five hundred. **пя́тью** *adv.* five times.

Р

р *letter*: see эр.
р. *abbr.* река́, river; рубль, rouble.
р *abbr.* рентге́н, roentgen.
раб, -а́, slave, bondsman.
раб- *abbr.* in *comb.* of рабо́чий, worker. **рабко́р**, -а, Workers' Correspondent. **~селько́р**, -а, Workers' and Rural Correspondent. **~си́ла**, -ы, manpower, labour force.
раба́, -ы́, slave; bondswoman. **рабовладе́лец**, -льца, slave-owner. **рабовладе́льческий**, slave-owning. **раболе́пие**, -я, servility. **раболе́пный**, servile. **раболе́пствовать**, -твую, cringe, fawn.
рабо́та, -ы, work; labour; job, employment; working; functioning, running; workmanship. **рабо́тать**, -аю *imp.* work; run, function; be open; + *instr.* work, operate; не ~, not work, be out of order; ~ над + *instr.* work at, work on. **рабо́тник**, -а, **рабо́тница**, -ы, worker; workman; hand, labourer. **рабо́тный**, working; ~ дом, workhouse. **работоспосо́бность**, -и, capa-

city for work, efficiency. **работоспосо́бный,** able-bodied, efficient. **работя́щий,** hardworking, industrious. **рабо́чий** *sb.* worker; working man; workman; hand, labourer. **рабо́ч|ий,** worker's; work; working; working-class; driving; ~ее движе́ние, working-class movement, labour movement; ~ий день, working day; ~ее колесо́, driving wheel; ~ая ло́шадь, draught-horse; ~ие ру́ки, hands; ~ая си́ла, manpower, labour force; labour.

ра́бский, slave; servile. **ра́бство,** -а, slavery, servitude.

равви́н, -а, rabbi.

ра́венство, -а, equality; знак ра́венства, equals sign. **равне́ние,** -я, dressing, alignment; ~ напра́во! eyes right! **равни́на,** -ы, plain. **равни́нный,** plain; level, flat.

равно́ *adv.* alike; equally; ~ как, as well as; and also, as also. **равно́** *predic.*: see ра́вный.

равно- in *comb.* equi-, iso-. **равнобе́дренный,** isosceles. **~ве́сие,** -я, equilibrium; balance, equipoise; привести́ в ~ве́сие, balance. **~-де́йствующая** *sb.* resultant force. ~**де́нствие,** -я, equinox. **~ду́шие,** -я, indifference. **~ду́шный,** indifferent. **~зна́чащий, ~зна́чный,** equivalent, equipollent. **~ме́рный,** even; uniform. **~-отстоя́щий,** equidistant. **~пра́вие,** -я, equality of rights. **~пра́вный,** equal in rights, having equal rights. **~си́льный,** of equal strength; equal, equivalent, tantamount. **~сторо́нний,** equilateral. **~уго́льный,** equiangular. **~це́нный,** of equal value, of equal worth; equivalent.

ра́вн|ый; -вен, -вна́, equal; на ~ых, as equals, on an equal footing; при про́чих ~ых усло́виях, other things being equal; ~ым о́бразом, equally, likewise; **равно́** *predic.* make(s), equals; всё ~о́, it is all the same, it makes no difference; all the same; мне всё ~о́, I don't mind, it's all the same to me; не всё ли ~о́? what difference does it make? what does it matter? **равня́ть,** -я́ю *imp.* (*perf.* с~) make even; treat equally; + с + *instr.* compare with, treat as equal to; ~ счёт, equalize; **~ся,** compete, compare; be equal; be equivalent, be tantamount; dress; + *dat.* equal, amount to; + с + *instr.* compete with, match.

рад, -а, -о *predic.* glad.

ра́ди *prep.* + *gen.* for the sake of; чего́ ~? what for?

ра́диевый, radium. **ра́дий,** -я, radium.

ра́дио *n. indecl.* radio, wireless; radio set; переда́ть по~, broadcast; слу́шать ~, listen in.

радио- in *comb.*, radio-; radioactive. **радиоакти́вность,** -и, radioactivity. **~акти́вный,** radioactive. **~аппара́т,** -а, radio set. **~веща́ние,** -я, broadcasting. **~веща́тельный,** broadcasting. **~гра́мма,** -ы, radiogram; wireless message. **~зо́нд,** -а, radiosonde. **радио́лог,** -а, radiologist. **~логи́ческий,** radiological. **~ло́гия,** -и, radiology. **~лока́тор,** -а, radar (set). **~люби́тель** -я *m.* radio amateur, ham. **~мая́к,** -а, radio beacon. **~переда́тчик,** -а, transmitter. **~переда́ча,** -и, transmission, broadcast. **~перекли́чка,** -и, radio hook-up. **~приёмник,** -а, receiver radio (set). **~свя́зь,** -и, radio communication, radio link. **~слу́шатель,** -я *m.* listener. **~ста́нция,** -и, radio station, set. **~те́хника,** -и, radio-engineering. **~фици́ровать,** -рую *perf.* and *imp.* instal radio in, equip with radio. **~хими́ческий,** radiochemical. **~хи́мия,** -и, radiochemistry. **~электро́ника,** -и, radio-electronics.

радио́ла, -ы, radiogram.

ради́ровать, -рую *perf.* and *imp.* radio.

ра́довать, -дую *imp.* (*perf.* об~, по~) gladden, make glad, make happy; **~ся,** be glad, be happy, rejoice. **ра́достный,** glad, joyous, joyful. **ра́дость,** -и, gladness, joy; от ра́дости, for joy, with joy; с ~ю, with pleasure, gladly.

ра́дуга, -и, rainbow. **ра́дужн|ый,** iridescent, opalescent, rainbow-coloured; cheerful; optimistic; ~ая оболо́чка, iris.

раду́шие, -я, cordiality. **раду́шный,** cordial; ~ приём, hearty welcome.

раёк, райка́, gallery; gods.

ражу́, etc.: see рази́ть.
раз, -а, *pl.* -ы́, раз, time, occasion; one; в друго́й ~, another time, some other time; в са́мый ~, at the right moment, just right; ещё ~, (once) again, once more; как ~, just, exactly; как ~ то, the very thing; на э́тот ~, this time, on this occasion, (for) this once; не ~, more than once; time and again; ни ~у, not once, never; оди́н ~, once; ~ навсегда́, once (and) for all. **раз** *adv.* once, one day. **раз** *conj.* if; since; ~ так, in that case.
раз-, разо-, разъ-, рас- *vbl. pref.* indicating division into parts; distribution; action in different directions; action in reverse; termination of action or state; intensification of action; dis-, un-.
разба́вить, -влю *perf.,* **разбавля́ть,** -я́ю *imp.* dilute.
разбаза́ривание, -я, squandering; sell-out. **разбаза́ривать,** -аю *imp.,* **разбаза́рить,** -рю *perf.* squander, waste; (*sl.*) sell (government property).
разба́лтывать(ся, -аюсь *imp.* of разболта́ть(ся.
разбе́г, -а (-у), run, running start; прыжо́к с разбе́га (-е́гу), running jump. **разбега́ться,** -а́юсь *imp.,* **разбежа́ться,** -егу́сь *perf.* take a run, run up; scatter, disperse; be scattered; у меня́ разбежа́лись глаза́, I was dazzled.
разберу́, etc.: see разобра́ть.
разбива́ть(ся, -а́ю(сь *imp.* of разби́ть(ся. **разби́вка,** -и, laying out; spacing (out).
разбинтова́ть, -ту́ю *perf.,* **разбинто́вывать,** -аю *imp.* unbandage remove a bandage from; **~ся,** remove one's bandage(s); come off, come undone; come unbandaged, lose its bandage.
разбира́тельство, -а, examination, investigation. **разбира́ть,** -а́ю *imp.* of разобра́ть; be particular; не разбира́я, indiscriminately; **~ся** *imp.* of разобра́ться.
разби́ть, -зобью́, -зобьёшь *perf.* (*imp.* разбива́ть) break; smash; break up, break down; divide (up), split; damage; fracture; beat, defeat; lay out, mark out; space (out); **~ся,** break, get broken, get smashed; hurt oneself badly; smash oneself up. **разби́тый,** broken; jaded.
раз|бла́говестить, -ещу *perf.* **раз|богате́ть,** -е́ю *perf.*
разбо́й, -я, robbery, brigandage. **разбо́йник,** -а, robber, brigand, bandit. **разбо́йнич|ий,** robber; thieves'; ~ья ша́йка, gang of robbers.
разболе́ться[1], -ли́тся *perf.* ache; у меня́ разболе́лась голова́, I've got a (bad) headache.
разболе́ться[2], -е́юсь *perf.* become ill, lose one's health.
разболта́ть[1], -а́ю *perf.* (*imp.* разба́лтывать) divulge, let out, give away.
разболта́ть[2], -а́ю *perf.* (*imp.* разба́лтывать) shake up, stir up; loosen; **~ся,** mix; come loose, work loose; get slack, get out of hand.
разбомби́ть, -блю́ *perf.* bomb, destroy by bombing.
разбо́р, -а (-у), analysis; parsing; criticism, critique; selectiveness, discrimination; investigation; stripping, dismantling; buying up; sorting out; sort, quality; без ~у (-а) indiscriminately. **разбо́рный,** collapsible. **разбо́рчивость,** -и, legibility; scrupulousness; fastidiousness. **разбо́рчивый,** legible; scrupulous; fastidious, exacting; discriminating.
разбра́сывать, -аю *imp.* of разброса́ть.
разбреда́ться, -а́ется *imp.,* **разбрести́сь,** -едётся; -ёлся, -ла́сь *perf.* disperse; straggle. **разбро́д,** -а, disorder.
разбро́санный, sparse, scattered; straggling; disconnected, incoherent. **разброса́ть,** -а́ю *perf.* (*imp.* разбра́сывать) throw about; scatter, spread, strew.
раз|буди́ть, -ужу́, -у́дишь *perf.*
разбуха́ние, -я, swelling; ~ шта́та, over-staffing. **разбуха́ть,** -а́ет *imp.,* **разбу́хнуть,** -нет; -бу́х *perf.* swell.
разбушева́ться, -шу́юсь *perf.* fly into a rage; blow up; run high.
разва́л, -а, breakdown, disintegration, disruption; disorganization. **развáливать,** -аю *imp.,* **развали́ть,** -лю́, -лишь *perf.* pull down; break up; mess up; **~ся,** collapse; go to pieces, fall to pieces; fall down, tumble down; break

down; sprawl, lounge. **развáлина**, -ы, ruin; wreck; грýда развáлин, a heap of ruins.

разварнóй boiled soft.

рáзве *part*. really?; ~ вы не знáете? don't you know?; ~ (тóлько), ~ (что), only; perhaps; except that, only. **рáзве** *conj*. unless.

развевáться, -áется *imp*. fly, flutter.

развед- *abbr*. in *comb*. of развéдывательный, reconnaissance; intelligence. **разведгрýппа**, -ы, reconnaissance party. **~óрган**, -а, intelligence agency; reconnaissance unit. **~свóдка**, -и, intelligence summary. **~слýжба**, -ы, intelligence service.

развéдать, -аю *perf*. (*imp*. развéдывать) find out; investigate; reconnoitre; prospect.

разведéние, -я, breeding, rearing; cultivation.

разведённ|ый, divorced; **~ый**, **~ая** *sb*. divorcee.

развéдка, -и, intelligence; secret service, intelligence service; reconnaissance; prospecting; идтú в развéдку, reconnoitre. **развéдочный**, prospecting, exploratory.

разведý, etc.: see развестú.

развéдчик, -а, intelligence officer; scout; prospector. **развéдывать**, -аю *imp*. of развéдать.

развезтú, -зу, -зёшь; -ёз, -лá *perf*. (*imp*. развозúть), convey, transport; deliver; exhaust, wear out; make impassable, make unfit for traffic.

развéивать(ся, -аю(сь *imp*. of развéять(ся. **развёл**, etc.: see развестú.

развенчáть, -áю *perf*., **развéнчивать**, -аю *imp*. dethrone; debunk.

развёрнутый, extensive, large-scale, all-out; detailed; deployed, extended. **развернýть**, -нý, -нёшь *perf*. (*imp*. развёртывать, разворáчивать) unfold, unwrap, open; unroll; unfurl; deploy; expand; develop; turn, swing; scan; show, display; **~ся**, unfold, unroll, come unwrapped; deploy; develop; spread; expand; turn, swing.

разверстáть, -áю *perf*., **развёрстывать**, -аю *imp*. distribute, allot, apportion.

развёрстка, allotment, apportionment; distribution.

развёртывать(ся, -аю(сь *imp*. of развернýть(ся.

развéс, -а, weighing out.

раз|веселúть, -лю *perf*. cheer up, amuse; **~ся**, cheer up.

развéсистый, branchy, spreading. **развéсить**[1], -éшу *perf*. (*imp*. развéшивать) spread; hang (out).

развéсить[2], -éшу *perf*. (*imp*. развéшивать) weigh out. **развеснóй**, sold by weight.

развестú, -едý, -едёшь; -ёл, -á *perf*. (*imp*. разводúть), take, conduct; part, separate; divorce; dilute; dissolve; start; breed, rear; cultivate; ~ мост, raise a bridge, swing a bridge open; ~ огóнь, light a fire; **~сь**, be divorced; breed, multiply.

разветвúться, -вúтся *perf*. **разветвля́ться**, -я́ется *imp*. branch; fork; ramify. **разветвлéние**, -я, branching, ramification, forking; branch; fork.

развéшать, -аю *perf*., **развéшивать**, -аю *imp*. hang.

развéшивать, -аю *imp*. of развéсить, развéшать. **развéшу**, etc.: see развéсить.

развéять, -éю *perf*. (*imp*. развéивать) scatter, disperse; dispel; destroy; **~ся**, disperse; be dispelled.

развивáть(ся, -áю(сь *imp*. of развúть(ся.

развинтúть, -нчý *perf*., **развúнчивать**, -аю *imp*. unscrew. **развúнченный**, unstrung; unsteady, lurching.

развúтие, -я, development; evolution; progress; maturity. **развитóй**; рáзвит, -á, -о, developed; mature, adult. **развúть**, -зовью; зовьёшь; -úл, -á, -о *perf*. (*imp*. развивáть) develop; unwind, untwist; **~ся**, develop.

развлекáть, -áю *imp*., **развлéчь**, -екý, -ечёшь; -ёк, -лá *perf*. entertain, amuse; divert; **~ся**, have a good time; amuse oneself; be diverted, be distracted.

развóд, -а, divorce. **разводúть(ся**, -ожý(сь, -óдишь(ся *imp*. of развестú(сь. **развóдка**, -и, separation.

разводно́й; ~ ключ, adjustable spanner, monkey-wrench; ~ мост, drawbridge, swing bridge.

развози́ть, -ожу́, -о́зишь *imp.* of развезти́.

разволнова́ться, -ну́ю(сь *perf.* get excited, be agitated.

развора́чивать(ся, -аю(сь *imp.* of развернý́ть(ся.

раз|вороши́ть, -шу́ *perf.*

развра́т, -а, debauchery, depravity, dissipation. **разврати́ть**, -ащу́ *perf.* **развраща́ть**, -а́ю *imp.* debauch, corrupt; deprave. **развра́тничать**, -аю *imp.* indulge in debauchery, lead a depraved life. **развра́тный**, debauched, depraved, profligate; corrupt. **развращённый**; -ён, -а́, corrupt.

развяза́ть, -яжу́, -я́жешь *perf.*, **развя́зывать**, -аю *imp.* untie, unbind, undo; unleash; **~ся**, come untied, come undone; ~ся с + *instr.* rid oneself of, have done with. **развя́зка**, -и, dénouement; outcome, issue, upshot; (motorway) junction; де́ло идёт к развя́зке, things are coming to a head. **развя́зный**, familiar; free-and-easy.

разгада́ть, -а́ю *perf.*, **разга́дывать**, -аю *imp.* solve, guess, puzzle out, make out; ~ сны, interpret dreams; ~ шифр, break a cipher. **разга́дка**, -и, solution.

разга́р, -а, height, peak, climax; в по́лном ~е, in full swing; в ~е ле́та, in the height of summer.

разгиба́ть(ся, -а́ю(сь *imp.* of разогну́ться.

разглаго́льствовать, -твую *imp.* hold forth, expatiate.

разгла́дить, -а́жу *perf.*, **разгла́живать**, -аю *imp.* smooth out; iron out, press.

разгласи́ть, -ашу́ *perf.*, **разглаша́ть**, -а́ю *imp.* divulge, give away, let out; + о + *prep.* spread, broadcast; herald, trumpet. **разглаше́ние**, -я, divulging, disclosure.

разгляде́ть, -яжу́ *perf.*, **разгля́дывать**, -аю *imp.* make out, discern, descry; examine closely, scrutinize.

разгне́ванный, angry. **разгне́вать**, -аю, *perf.* anger, incense. **раз|гне́ваться**, -аюсь *perf.*

разгова́ривать, -аю *imp.* talk, speak, converse. **разгово́р**, -а (-у), talk, conversation. **разгово́рник**, -а, phrase-book. **разгово́рный**, colloquial; conversational. **разгово́рчивый**, talkative, loquacious.

разго́н, -а, dispersal; breaking up; run, running start; distance; space. **разго́нистый**, widely-spaced. **разгоня́ть(ся**, -я́ю(сь *imp.* of разогна́ть(ся.

разгора́живать, -аю *imp.* of разгороди́ть.

разгора́ться, -а́юсь *imp.*, **разгоре́ться**, -рю́сь *perf.* flame up, flare up; flush; стра́сти разгоре́лись, feeling ran high, passions rose.

разгороди́ть, -ожу́, -о́ди́шь *perf.* (*imp.* разгора́живать) partition off.

раз|горячи́ть(ся, -чу́(сь *perf.*; ~ся от вина́, be flushed with wine.

разгра́бить, -блю *perf.* plunder, pillage, loot. **разграбле́ние**, -я, plunder, pillage; looting.

разграниче́ние, -я, demarcation, delimitation; differentiation. **разграни́чивать**, -аю *imp.*, **разграни́чить**, -чу *perf.* delimit, demarcate; differentiate, distinguish.

раз|графи́ть, -флю́ *perf.*, **разграфля́ть**, -я́ю *imp.* rule, square. **разграфле́ние**, -я, ruling.

разгреба́ть, -а́ю *imp.*, **разгрести́**, -ебу́, -ебёшь; -ёб, -ла́ *perf.* rake (away), shovel (away).

разгро́м, -а, rout, crushing defeat; knock-out blow; havoc, devastation. **разгроми́ть**, -млю́ *perf.* rout, defeat.

разгружа́ть, -а́ю *imp.*, **разгрузи́ть**, -ужу́, -у́зи́шь *perf.* unload; relieve; **~ся**, unload; be relieved. **разгру́зка**, -и, unloading; relief, relieving.

разгрыза́ть, -а́ю *imp.*, **раз|гры́зть**, -зу́ -зёшь; -ы́з *perf.* crack; bite through.

разгу́л, -а, revelry, debauch; raging; (wild) outburst. **разгу́ливать**, -аю *imp.* stroll about, walk about. **разгу́ливаться**, -аюсь *imp.*, **разгуля́ться**, -а́юсь *perf.* spread oneself; have free scope; wake up, be wide awake; clear up; improve. **разгу́льный**, loose, wild, rakish.

раздава́ть(ся, -даю́(сь, -даёшь(ся *imp.* of разда́ть(ся.

раз|дави́ть, -влю́, -вишь *perf.* **раздáвливать,** -аю *imp.* crush; squash; run down, run over; overwhelm.

раздáть, -áм, -áшь, -áст, -адим; рóз- or раздáл, -á, -о *perf.* (*imp.* раздавáть) distribute, give out, serve out, dispense; **~ся,** be heard; resound; ring out; make way; stretch, expand; put on weight. **раздáча,** -и, distribution. **раздаю́,** etc.: see раздавáть.

раздвáивать(ся, -аю(сь *imp.* of раздвоúться.

раздвигáть, -áю *imp.*, **раздви́нуть,** -ну *perf.* move apart, slide apart; draw back; ~ стол, extend a table; **~ся,** move apart, slide apart; be drawn back; зáнавес раздви́нулся, the curtain rose. **раздвижнóй,** expanding; sliding; extensible.

раздвоéние, -я, division into two; bifurcation; ~ ли́чности, split personality. **раздвóенный, раздвоённый,** forked; bifurcated; cloven; split. **раздвои́ть,** -ою́ *perf.* (*imp.* раздвáивать), divide into two; bisect; **~ся,** bifurcate, fork; split, become double.

раздевáлка, -и, **раздевáльня,** -и; *gen. pl.* -лен, cloakroom. **раздевáть(ся,** -áю(сь *imp.* of раздéть(ся.

раздéл, -а, division; partition; allotment; section, part.

раздéлаться, -аюсь *perf.* + с + *instr.* finish with, be through with; settle accounts with; pay off; get even with.

разделéние, -я, division; ~ трудá, division of labour. **раздели́мый,** divisible. **раз|дели́ть,** -лю́, -лишь *perf.*, **разделя́ть,** -я́ю *imp.* divide; separate, part; share; **~ся,** divide; be divided; be divisible; separate, part. **раздéльный,** separate; clear, distinct.

раздéну, etc.: see раздéть. **раздеру́,** etc.: see разодрáть.

раздéть, -дéну *perf.* (*imp.* раздевáть) undress; **~ся,** undress (oneself), strip; take off one's coat, one's things.

раздирáть, -áю *imp.* of разодрáть. **раздирáющий** (ду́шу), heart-rending, harrowing.

раздобывáть, -áю *imp.*, **раздобы́ть,** -бу́ду *perf.* get, procure, come by, get hold of.

раздóлье, -я, expanse; freedom, liberty. **раздóльный,** free.

раздóр, -а, discord, dissension; сéять ~, breed strife, sow discord.

раздосáдовать, -дую *perf.* vex.

раздражáть, -áю *imp.*, **раздражи́ть,** -жу́ *perf.* irritate; annoy, exasperate, put out; **~ся,** lose one's temper, get annoyed; get irritated; become inflamed. **раздражéние,** -я, irritation; в раздражéнии, in a temper. **раздражи́тельный,** irritable; short-tempered.

раздразни́ть, -ню́, -нишь *perf.* tease; arouse, stimulate.

раз|дроби́ть, -блю́ *perf.*, **раздробля́ть,** -я́ю *imp.* break; smash to pieces, splinter; turn, convert, reduce. **раздрóбленный, раздроблённый,** shattered; small-scale; fragmented.

раздувáть(ся, -áю(сь *imp.* of разду́ть(ся.

разду́мать, -аю *perf.*, **разду́мывать,** -аю *imp.* change one's mind; + *inf.* decide not to; ponder, consider; hesitate; не разду́мывая, without a moment's thought. **разду́мье,** -я, meditation; thought, thoughtful mood; hesitation; в глубóком ~, deep in thought.

разду́ть, -у́ю *perf.* (*imp.* раздувáть), blow; fan; blow out; exaggerate; whip up; inflate, swell; blow about; **~ся,** swell.

разевáть, -áю *imp.* of рази́нуть.

разжáлобить, -блю *perf.* move (to pity).

разжáловать, -лую *perf.* degrade, demote.

разжáть, -зожму́, -мёшь *perf.* (*imp.* разжимáть) unclasp, open; release, unfasten, undo.

разжевáть, -жую́ -жуёшь *perf.*, **разжёвывать,** -аю *imp.* chew, masticate; chew over.

разжéчь, -зожгу́, -зожжёшь; -жёг, -зожглá *perf.*, **разжигáть,** -áю *imp.* kindle; rouse, stir up.

разжимáть, -áю *imp.* of разжáть. **раз|жирéть,** -éю *perf.*

рази́нуть, -ну *perf.* (*imp.* разевáть) open; ~ **рот,** gape; **рази́нув рот,**

open-mouthed. **разиня**, -и *m.* and *f.* scatter-brained person.

разительный, striking. **разить**, ражу *imp.* (*perf.* по~) strike.

разлагать(ся, -аю(сь *imp.* of разложить(ся.

разлад, -а, discord, dissension; disorder.

разламывать(ся, -аю(сь *imp.* of разломать(ся, разломить(ся. **разлёгся**, etc.: see разлечься.

разлезаться, -ается *imp.*, **разлезться**, -зется; -лезся *perf.* come to pieces; come apart, fall apart.

разлениться, -нюсь, -нишься *perf.* get very lazy, sink into sloth.

разлетаться, -аюсь *imp.*, **разлететься**, -лечусь *perf.* fly away; fly about, scatter; shatter; vanish, be shattered; fly, rush; rush up.

разлечься, -лягусь; -лёгся, -глась *perf.* stretch out; sprawl.

разлив, -а, bottling; flood; overflow. **разливать**, -аю *imp.*, **разлить**, -золью, -зольёшь; -ил, -а, -о *perf.* pour out; spill; flood (with), drench (with); **~ся**, spill; overflow, flood; spread. **разливка**, -и, bottling. **разливн|ой**, on tap, on draught; ~ое вино, wine from the wood. **разлитие**, -я, flooding.

различать, -аю *imp.*, **различить**, -чу *perf.* distinguish; tell the difference; discern, make out; **~ся**, differ. **различие**, -я, distinction; difference; знаки различия, badges of rank. **различительный**, distinctive, distinguishing. **различный**, different; various, diverse.

разложение, -я, breaking down; decomposition; decay; putrefaction; demoralization, corruption; disintegration; expansion; resolution. **разложить**, -жу, -жишь *perf.* (*imp.* разлагать, раскладывать) put away; lay out; spread (out); distribute, apportion; break down; decompose; expand; resolve; demoralize, corrupt; ~ костёр, make a fire; ~ся, decompose; rot, decay; become demoralized; be corrupted; disintegrate, crack up, go to pieces.

разлом, -а, breaking; break. **разломать**, -аю, **разломить**, -млю, -мишь *perf.* (*imp.* разламывать) break, break to pieces; pull down; **~ся**, break to pieces.

раз|лохматить, -ачу *perf.*

разлука, -и, separation; parting. **разлучать**, -аю *imp.*, **разлучить**, -чу *perf.* separate, part, sever; **~ся**, separate, part.

разлюбить, -блю, -бишь *perf.* cease to love, stop loving; stop liking, no longer like.

разлягусь, etc.: see разлечься.

размазать, -ажу *perf.*, **размазывать**, -аю *imp.* spread, smear.

размалывать, -аю *imp.* of размолоть. **разматывать**, -аю *imp.* of размотать.

размах, -а (-у), sweep; swing; span; amplitude; scope, range, scale. **размахивать**, -аю *imp.* + *instr.* swing; brandish; ~ руками, gesticulate. **размахиваться**, -аюсь *imp.*, **размахнуться**, -нусь, -нёшься *perf.* swing one's arm. **размашистый**, sweeping.

размежевание, -я, demarcation, delimitation. **размежевать**, -жую *perf.*, **размежёвывать**, -аю *imp.* divide out, delimit; **~ся**, fix one's boundaries; delimit functions or spheres of action.

размёл, etc.: see размести.

размельчать, -аю *imp.*, **раз|мельчить**, -чу *perf.* crumble, crush, pulverize.

размелю, etc.: see размолоть.

размен, -а, exchange; changing. **разменивать**, -аю *imp.*, **разменять**, -яю *perf.* change; **~ся** + *instr.* exchange; dissipate. **размені|ый**, exchange; ~ая монета, (small) change.

размер, -а, dimension(s); size; measurement; rate, amount; scale, extent; metre; measure; (*pl.*) proportions. **размеренный**, measured. **размерить**, -рю *perf.*, **размерять**, -яю *imp.* measure off; measure.

размести, -ету, -етёшь; -мёл, -а *perf.* (*imp.* разметать) sweep clear; clear; sweep away.

разместить, -ещу *perf.* (*imp.* размещать) place, accommodate; quarter; stow; distribute; **~ся**, take one's seat.

разметать, -аю *imp.* of размести.

размéтить, -éчу *perf.*, **размечáть**, -áю *imp.* mark.

размешáть, -áю *perf.*, **размéшивать**, -аю *imp.* stir (in).

размещáть(ся, -áю(сь *imp.* of разместить(ся. **размещéние**, -я, placing; accommodation; distribution, disposal, allocation; investment. **размещý**, etc.: see разместить.

разминáть(ся, -áю(сь *imp.* of размять(ся.

разминýться, -нýсь, -нёшься *perf.* pass (one another); cross; + *c* + *instr.* pass; miss.

размножáть, -áю *imp.*, **размнóжить**, -жу *perf.* multiply, manifold, duplicate; breed, rear; **~ся**, propagate itself; breed; spawn.

размозжить, -жý *perf.* smash.

размóлвка, -и, tiff, disagreement.

размолóть, -мелю, -мéлишь *perf.* (*imp.* размáлывать) grind.

размораживать, -áю *imp.*, **разморóзить**, -óжу *perf.* unfreeze, defreeze, defrost; **~ся**, unfreeze; become defrozen, defrosted.

размотáть, -áю *perf.* (*imp.* размáтывать) unwind, unreel; squander.

размывáть, -áет *imp.*, **размыть**, -óет *perf.* wash away; erode.

размышлéние, -я, reflection; meditation, thought. **размышлять**, -яю *imp.* reflect, ponder; think (things) over.

размягчáть, -áю *imp.*, **размягчить**, -чý *perf.* soften; **~ся**, soften, grow soft. **размягчéние**, -я, softening.

размякáть, -áю *imp.*, **раз|мякнуть**, -ну; -мяк *perf.* soften, become soft.

раз|мять, -зомнý, -зомнёшь *perf.* (*imp.* also разминáть) knead; mash; **~ся**, soften, grow soft; stretch one's legs; limber up, loosen up.

разнáшивать, -аю *imp.* of разносить.

разнести, -сý, -сёшь; -ёс, -лá *perf.* (*imp.* разносить) carry, convey; take round, deliver; spread; enter, note down; smash, break up, destroy; blow up; scatter, disperse; *impers.* make puffy, swell, blow out; меня разнеслó, I've got very fat.

разнимáть, -áю *imp.* of разнять.

рáзниться, -нюсь *imp.* differ. **рáзница**, -ы, difference; disparity; какáя ~? what difference does it make?

рáзно- in *comb.* different, vari-, hetero-. **разнобóй**, -я, lack of co-ordination; difference, disagreement. **~вéс**, -а, (set of) weights. **~видность**, -и variety. **~глáсие**, -я, difference, disagreement; discrepancy. **~голóсый**, discordant. **~калиберный**, of different calibres; mixed, heterogeneous. **~мыслие**, -я, difference of opinions. **~образие**, -я, variety, diversity; для ~образия, for a change. **~образить**, -áжу *imp.* vary, diversify. **~образный**, various, varied, diverse. **~рабóчий** *sb.* unskilled labourer. **~речивый**, contradictory, conflicting. **~рóдный**, heterogeneous. **~склоняемый**, irregularly declined. **~сторóнний**, many-sided; versatile; all-round; scalene. **~харáктерный**, diverse, varied. **~цвéтный**, of different colours; many-coloured, variegated, motley. **~чтéние**, -я, variant reading. **~шёрстный**, **~шёрстый**, with coats of different colours; mixed, ill-assorted. **~язычный**, polyglot.

разносить[1], -ошý, -óсишь *perf.* (*imp.* разнáшивать) break in, wear in; **~ся**, become comfortable with wear.

разносить[2], -ошý, -óсишь *imp.* of разнести. **разнóска**, -и, delivery. **разнóсн|ый**, delivery; abusive; ~ые словá, swear-words.

рáзность, -и, difference; diversity.

разнóсчик, -а, pedlar, hawker.

разношý, etc.: see разносить.

разнýзданный, unbridled, unruly.

рáзн|ый, different, differing; various, diverse; **~ое** *sb.* different things; various matters, any other business.

разнять, -нимý, -нимешь; рóз- or разнял -á, -о *perf.* (*imp.* разнимáть) take to pieces, dismantle, disjoint; part, separate.

разо-: see раз-.

разоблачáть, -áю *imp.*, **разоблачить**, -чý *perf.* expose, unmask. **разоблачéние**, -я, exposure, unmasking.

разобрáть, -зберý, -рёшь; -áл, -á, -о *perf.* (*imp.* разбирáть) take; take to pieces, strip, dismantle; buy up; sort out; investigate, look into; analyse, parse; make out, understand; ничегó нельзя́ ~, one can't make head or tail of it; **~ся**, sort things out; + в + *prep.* investigate, look into; understand.

разобщáть, -áю *imp.*, **разобщи́ть, -**щу́ *perf.* separate; estrange, alienate; disconnect, uncouple, disengage. **разобщéние, -**я, disconnection, uncoupling. **разобщённо** *adv.* apart, separately.

разобью́, etc.: see разби́ть. **разовью́,** etc.: see разви́ть.

разогнáть, -згоню́, -óнишь; -гнáл, -á, -о *perf.* (*imp.* разгоня́ть) scatter, drive away; disperse; dispel; drive fast, race; space; **~ся,** gather speed, gather momentum.

разогну́ть, -ну́, -нёшь *perf.* (*imp.* разгибáть), unbend, straighten; **~ся,** straighten (oneself) up.

разогревáть, -áю *imp.*, **разогрéть, -**éю *perf.* warm up; **~ся,** warm up, grow warm.

разодéть(ся, -éну(сь *perf.* dress up.

разодрáть, -здеру́, -рёшь; -áл, -á, -о *perf.* (*imp.* раздирáть) tear (up); lacerate, harrow.

разожгу́, etc.: see разжéчь. **разожму́,** etc.: see разжáть.

разо|зли́ть, -лю́ *perf.* anger, enrage; **~ся,** get angry, fly into a rage.

разойти́сь, -йду́сь, -йдёшься; -ошёлся, -ошлáсь *perf.* (*imp.* расходи́ться) go away; break up, disperse; branch off, diverge; radiate; differ, be at variance, conflict; part, separate, be divorced; dissolve, melt; be spent; be sold out; be out of print; gather speed; be carried away.

разолью́, etc.: see разли́ть.

рáзом *adv.* at once, at one go.

разомну́, etc.: see размя́ть.

разорвáть, -ву́, -вёшь; -áл, -á, -о *perf.* (*imp.* разрывáть) tear; break (off), sever; blow up, burst; **~ся,** tear, become torn; break, snap; blow up, burst; explode, go off.

разорéние, -я, ruin; destruction, havoc. **разори́тельный,** ruinous; wasteful. **разори́ть, -**рю́ *perf.* (*imp.* разоря́ть) ruin, bring to ruin; destroy, ravage; **~ся,** ruin oneself, be ruined.

разоружáть, -áю *imp.*, **разоружи́ть,** -жу́ *perf.* disarm; **~ся,** disarm. **разоружéние, -**я, disarmament.

разоря́ть(ся, -я́ю(сь *imp.* of разори́ть(ся.

разослáть, -ошлю́, -ошлёшь *perf.* (*imp.* рассылáть) send round, distribute, circulate; send out, dispatch.

разостлáть, расстели́ть, -стелю́, -тéлешь *perf.* (*imp.* расстилáть) spread (out); lay; **~ся,** spread.

разотру́, etc.: see растерéть.

разочаровáние, -я, disappointment. **разочарóванный,** disappointed, disillusioned. **разочаровáть, -**ру́ю *perf.*, **разочарóвывать, -**аю *imp.* disappoint, disillusion, disenchant; **~ся,** be disappointed, be disillusioned.

разочту́, etc.: see расчéсть. **разошёлся,** etc.: see разойти́сь. **разошлю́,** etc.: see разослáть. **разошью́,** etc.: see расши́ть.

разрабáтывать, -аю *imp.*, **разрабóтать,** -аю *perf.* cultivate; work, exploit; work out, work up; develop; elaborate. **разрабóтка, -**и, cultivation; working, exploitation; working out, working up; elaboration; field; pit, working, quarry.

разражáться, -áюсь *imp.*, **разрази́ться,** -ажу́сь *perf.* break out; burst out; ~ смéхом, burst out laughing.

разрастáться, -áется *imp.*, **разрасти́сь,** -тётся; -рóсся, -лáсь *perf.* grow, grow up; grow thickly; spread.

разрежённ|ый; -ён, -á, rarefied, rare; ~ое прострáнство, vacuum.

разрéз, -а, cut; slit, slash; section; point of view; в ~е + *gen.* from the point of view of, in the context of; в э́том ~е, in this connection. **разрéзать, -**éжу *perf.*, **разрезáть, -**áю *imp.* cut; slit. **разрезнóй,** cutting; slit, with slits; ~ нож, paper-knife.

разрешáть, -áю *imp.*, **разреши́ть, -**шу́ *perf.* (+ *dat.*) allow, permit; authorize; (+ *acc.*) release, absolve; solve; settle; разреши́те пройти́, let me pass; do you mind letting me pass?; **~ся,** be allowed; be solved; be settled;

~ся от бре́мени, be delivered of; кури́ть не разреша́ется, no smoking. **разреше́ние**, -я, permission; authorization, permit; solution; settlement. **разреши́мый**, solvable.

разро́зненный, uncoordinated; odd; incomplete, broken.

разро́сся, etc.: see разрасти́сь. **разро́ю**, etc.: see разры́ть.

разруба́ть, -а́ю *imp.*, **разруби́ть**, -блю́, -бишь *perf.* cut, cleave; hack; chop.

разру́ха, -и, ruin, collapse. **разруша́ть**, -а́ю *imp.*, **разру́шить**, -шу *perf.* destroy; demolish, wreck; ruin; frustrate, blast, blight; **~ся**, go to ruin, collapse. **разруше́ние**, -я, destruction. **разруши́тельный**, destructive.

разры́в, -а, breach; break; gap; rupture, severance; burst, explosion. **разрыва́ть**[1](**ся**, -а́ю(сь *imp.* of разорва́ть(ся.

разрыва́ть[2], -а́ю *imp.* of разры́ть.

разрывно́й, explosive, bursting.

разры́ть, -ро́ю *perf.* (*imp.* разрыва́ть) dig (up); turn upside down, rummage through.

раз|рыхли́ть, -лю́ *perf.*, **разрыхля́ть**, -я́ю *imp.* loosen; hoe.

разря́д[1], -а, category, rank; sort; class, rating.

разря́д[2], -а, discharge. **разряди́ть**, -яжу́, -я́дишь *perf.* (*imp.* разряжа́ть) unload; discharge; space out; **~ся**, run down; clear, ease. **разря́дка**, -и, spacing (out); discharging; unloading; ~ напряжённости, lessening of tension, détente.

разря́дник, -а, **-ница**, -ы, ranking player or competitor.

разряжа́ть(ся, -а́ю(сь *imp.* of разряди́ть(ся.

разубеди́ть, -ежу́ *perf.*, **разубежда́ть**, -а́ю *imp.* dissuade; **~ся**, change one's mind, change one's opinion.

разува́ться, -а́юсь *imp.* of разу́ться.

разуве́рить, -рю *perf.*, **разуверя́ть**, -я́ю *imp.* dissuade, undeceive; + в + *prep.* argue out of; **~ся** (в + *prep.*) lose faith (in), cease to believe.

разузнава́ть, -наю́, -наёшь *imp.*, **разузна́ть**, -а́ю *perf.* (try to) find out; make inquiries.

разукра́сить, -а́шу *perf.*, **разукра́шивать**, -аю *imp.* adorn, decorate, embellish.

разукрупни́ть(ся, -ню́(сь *perf.*, **разукрупня́ть(ся**, -я́ю(сь *imp.* break up into smaller units.

ра́зум, -а, reason; mind, intellect; у него́ ум за ~ зашёл, he is (was) at his wit's end. **разуме́ться**, -е́ется *imp.* be understood, be meant; (само́ собо́й) разуме́ется, of course; it stands to reason, it goes without saying. **разу́мный**, possessing reason; judicious, intelligent; sensible; reasonable; wise.

разу́ться, -у́юсь *perf.* (*imp.* разува́ться), take off one's shoes.

разу́чивать, -аю *imp.*, **разучи́ть**, -чу́ -чишь *perf.* study; learn (up). **разу́чиваться**, -аюсь *imp.*, **разучи́ться**, -чу́сь, -чишься *perf.* forget (how to).

разъ-: see раз-.

разъеда́ть, -а́ет *imp.* of разъе́сть.

разъедини́ть, -ню́ *perf.*, **разъединя́ть**, -я́ю *imp.* separate, disunite; disconnect; нас разъедини́ли, we were cut off.

разъе́дусь, etc.: see разъе́хаться.

разъе́зд, -а, departure; dispersal; passing loop, siding (track); mounted patrol; travelling (about), journeys. **разъездно́й**, travelling. **разъезжа́ть**, -а́ю *imp.* drive about, ride about; travel, wander; **~ся** *imp.* of разъе́хаться.

разъе́сть, -е́ст, -едя́т; -е́л *perf.* (*imp.* разъеда́ть) eat away; corrode.

разъе́хаться, -е́дусь *perf.* (*imp.* разъезжа́ться) depart; disperse; separate; (be able to) pass; pass one another, miss one another; slide apart.

разъярённый; -ён, -а́, furious, in a furious temper, frantic with rage. **разъяри́ть**, -рю́ *perf.*, **разъяря́ть**, -я́ю *imp.* infuriate, rouse to fury; **~ся**, get furious, become frantic with rage.

разъясне́ние, -я, explanation, elucidation; interpretation. **разъясни́тельный**, explanatory, elucidatory.

разъя́сниваться, -а́ется *imp.*, **разъя́сниться**, -ится *perf.* clear (up).

разъясни́ть, -ню́ *perf.*, **разъясня́ть**, -я́ю, *imp.* explain, elucidate; interpret; **~ся**, become clear, be cleared up.

разыгра́ть, -а́ю *perf.*, **разы́грывать**, -аю *imp.* play (through); perform; draw; raffle; play a trick on; **~ся**, rise, get up; run high.

разыска́ть, -ыщу́, -ы́щешь *perf.* find. **разы́скивать**, -аю *imp.* look for, search for; **~ся**, be wanted.

рай, -я, *loc.* -ю́, paradise; garden of Eden.

рай- *abbr.* in *comb.* of райо́нный, district. **райко́м**, -а, district committee. **~сове́т**, -а, district soviet.

райо́н, -а, region; area; zone; (administrative) district. **райо́нный**, district.

ра́йский, heavenly.

рак, -а, crawfish, crayfish; cancer, canker; Crab; Cancer.

ракéта[1], -ы, **ракéтка**, -и, racket.

ракéта[2], -ы, rocket; ballistic missile; flare; ~-носи́тель, carrier rocket. **ракéтный**, rocket; jet.

ра́ковина, -ы, shell; sink.

ра́ковый, cancer; cancerous.

ра́ма, -ы, frame; chassis, carriage; вста́вить в ра́му, frame. **ра́мка**, -и, frame; *pl.* framework, limits; в ра́мке, framed.

ра́мпа, -ы, footlights.

ра́на, -ы, wound. **ранéние**, -я, wounding; wound, injury. **ра́неный**, wounded; injured.

ра́нец, -нца, knapsack, haversack; satchel.

ра́нить, -ню *perf.* and *imp.* wound; injure.

ра́нний, early. **ра́но** *predic.* it is (too) early. **ра́но** *adv.* early; ~ и́ли по́здно, sooner or later. **ра́ньше** *adv.* earlier; before; formerly; first (of all).

рапи́ра, -ы, foil. **рапири́ст**, -а, **рапири́стка**, -и, fencer.

ра́порт, -а, report. **рапортова́ть**, -ту́ю *perf.* and *imp.* report.

рас-: see раз-. **раска́иваться**, -аюсь *imp.* of раска́яться.

раскалённый; -ён, -а́, scorching, burning hot; incandescent. **раскали́ть**, -лю́ *perf.* (*imp.* раскаля́ть) make very hot, make red-hot, white-hot; **~ся**, heat up, glow, become red-hot, white-hot.

раска́лывать(ся, -аю(сь *imp.* of расколо́ть(ся. **раскаля́ть(ся**, -я́ю(сь *imp.* of раскали́ть(ся. **раска́пывать**, -аю *imp.* of раскопа́ть.

раска́т, -а, roll, peal. **раската́ть**, -а́ю *perf.*, **раска́тывать**, -аю *imp.* roll, roll out, smooth out, level; drive, ride, (about). **раска́тистый**, rolling, booming. **раскати́ться**, -ачу́сь, -а́тишься *perf.*, **раска́тываться**, -аюсь *imp.* gather speed; roll away; peal, boom.

раскача́ть, -а́ю *perf.*, **раска́чивать**, -аю *imp.* swing; rock; loosen, shake loose; shake up, stir up; **~ся**, swing, rock; shake loose; bestir oneself.

раска́яние, -я, repentance, remorse.

рас|ка́яться, -а́юсь *perf.* (*imp.* also раска́иваться) repent.

расквита́ться, -а́юсь *perf.* settle accounts; get even, be quits.

раски́дывать, -аю *imp.*, **раски́нуть**, -ну *perf.* stretch (out); spread; scatter; set up, pitch; ~ умо́м, ponder, think things over, consider; **~ся**, spread out, lie; sprawl.

раскла́дка, -и, laying; putting up; allotment. **раскладн|о́й**, folding; ~а́я крова́ть, camp-bed. **раскладу́шка**, -и, camp-bed. **раскла́дывать**, -аю *imp.* of разложи́ть.

раскла́няться, -яюсь *perf.* bow; exchange bows; take leave.

раскле́ивать, -аю *imp.*, **раскле́ить**, -е́ю *perf.* unstick; stick (up), paste (up); **~ся**, come unstuck; fall through, fail to come off; feel seedy, be off colour.

расклёшенный, flared.

раско́л, -а, split, division; schism; dissent. **рас|коло́ть**, -лю́, -лешь *perf.* (*imp.* also раска́лывать) split; chop; break; disrupt, break up; **~ся**, split; crack, break. **раско́льник**, -а, dissenter, schismatic. **раско́льнический**, dissenting, schismatic.

раскопа́ть, -а́ю *perf.* (*imp.* раска́пывать) dig up, unearth, excavate. **раско́пка**, -и, digging up; *pl.* excavation, excavations.

раско́сый, slanting, slant.

раскраду́, etc.: see раскра́сть. **раскра́дывать**, -аю *imp.* of раскра́сть. **раскра́ивать**, -аю *imp.* of раскрои́ть.

раскра́сить, -а́шу *perf.* (*imp.* раскра́шивать) paint, colour. **раскра́ска**, -и, painting, colouring; colours, colour scheme.

раскрасне́ться, -е́юсь *perf.* flush, go red.

раскра́сть, -аду́, -адёшь *perf.* (*imp.* раскра́дывать) loot, clean out.

раскра́шивать, -аю *imp.* of раскра́сить.

раскрепости́ть, -ощу́ *perf.*, **раскрепоща́ть**, -а́ю *imp.* set free, liberate, emancipate. **раскрепоще́ние**, -я, liberation, emancipation.

раскритикова́ть, -ку́ю *perf.* criticize harshly, slate.

раскрои́ть, -ою́ *perf.* (*imp.* раскра́ивать) cut out; cut open.

рас|кроши́ть(ся, -шу́(сь, -шишь(ся *perf.* **раскро́ю**, etc.: see раскры́ть.

раскрути́ть, -учу́, -у́тишь *perf.*, **раскру́чивать**, -аю *imp.* untwist, undo; **~ся**, come untwisted, come undone.

раскрыва́ть, -а́ю *imp.*, **раскры́ть**, -о́ю *perf.* open; expose, bare; reveal, disclose, lay bare; discover; **~ся**, open; uncover oneself; come out, come to light, be discovered.

раскупа́ть, -а́ет *imp.*, **раскупи́ть**, -у́пит *perf.* buy up.

раску́поривать, -аю *imp.*, **раску́порить**, -рю *perf.* uncork, open.

раскуси́ть, -ушу́, -у́сишь *perf.*, **раску́сывать**, -аю *imp.* bite through; get to the core of; see through.

раску́тать, -аю *perf.* unwrap.

ра́совый, racial.

распа́д, -а, disintegration, break-up; collapse; decomposition. **распада́ться**, -а́ется *imp.* of распа́сться.

распакова́ть, -ку́ю *perf.*, **распако́вывать**, -аю *imp.* unpack; **~ся**, unpack; come undone.

распа́рывать(ся, -аю(сь *imp.* of распоро́ть(ся.

распа́сться, -адётся *perf.* (*imp.* распада́ться) disintegrate, fall to pieces; break up; collapse; decompose, dissociate.

распаха́ть, -ашу́, -а́шешь *perf.*, **распа́хивать**[1], -аю *imp.* plough up.

распа́хивать[2], -аю *imp.*, **распахну́ть**, -ну́, -нёшь *perf.* open (wide); fling open, throw open; **~ся**, open; fly open, swing open; throw open one's coat.

распая́ть, -я́ю *perf.* unsolder; **~ся**, come unsoldered.

распева́ть, -а́ю *imp.* sing.

распеча́тать, -аю *perf.*, **распеча́тывать**, -аю *imp.* open; unseal.

распи́вочн|ый, for consumption on the premises; **~ая** *sb.* tavern, bar.

распи́ливать, -аю *imp.*, **распили́ть**, -лю́, -лишь *perf.* saw up.

расписа́ние, -я, time-time, schedule. **расписа́ть**, -ишу́, -и́шешь *perf.*, **распи́сывать**, -аю *imp.* enter; assign allot; paint; decorate; **~ся**, sign; register one's marriage; + в + *prep.* sign for; acknowledge; testify to. **распи́ска**, -и, receipt. **расписно́й**, painted, decorated.

рас|пла́вить, -влю *perf.*, **расплавля́ть**, -я́ю *imp.* melt, fuse. **расплавле́ние**, -я, melting, fusion.

распла́каться, -а́чусь *perf.* burst into tears.

распласта́ть, -а́ю *perf.* spread; flatten; split, divide into layers; **~ся**, sprawl.

распла́та, -ы, payment; retribution; час распла́ты, day of reckoning. **расплати́ться**, -ачу́сь, -а́тишься *perf.*, **распла́чиваться**, -аюсь *imp.* (+ с + *instr.*) pay off; settle accounts, get even; + за + *acc.* pay for.

расплеска́ть(ся), -ещу́(сь), -е́шешь(ся) *perf.*, **расплёскивать(ся)**, -аю(сь) *imp.* spill.

расплести́, -ету́, -етёшь; -ёл, -а́ *perf.*, **расплета́ть**, -а́ю *imp.* unplait; untwine, untwist, undo; **~сь**, come unplaited, come undone; untwine, untwist.

рас|плоди́ть(ся, -ожу́(сь *perf.*

расплыва́ться, -а́ется *imp.*, **расплы́ться**, -ывётся; -ы́лся, -а́сь *perf.* run; spread. **расплы́вчатый**, dim, indistinct; diffuse, vague.

расплю́щивать, -аю *imp.*, **расплю́щить**, -щу *perf.* flatten out, hammer out.

распну́, etc.: see распя́ть.

распознава́емый, recognizable, identifiable. **распознава́ть**, -наю́, -наёшь *imp.*, **распозна́ть**, -а́ю *perf.* recognize, identify; distinguish; diagnose.

располагáть, -áю *imp.* (*perf.* расположи́ть) + *instr.* dispose of, have at one's disposal, have available; не ~ врéменем, have no time to spare. **располагáться,** -áюсь *imp.* of расположи́ться. **располагáющий,** prepossessing.

расползáться, -áется *imp.*, **расползти́сь,** -зётся; -óлзся, -злáсь *perf.* crawl, crawl away; ravel out; give (at the seams).

расположéние, -я, disposition; arrangement; situation, location; inclination; tendency, propensity; bias, penchant; favour, liking; sympathies; mood, humour. **располóженный,** well-disposed; disposed, inclined, in the mood; я не óчень располóжен сегóдня рабóтать, I don't feel much like working today. **расположи́ть,** -жý, -жишь *perf.* (*imp.* располагáть) dispose; arrange, set out; win over, gain; **~ся,** settle down; compose oneself, make oneself comfortable.

рас|порóть, -рю́, -решь *perf.* (*imp.* also распáрывать) unpick, undo, rip; **~ся,** rip, come undone.

распоряди́тель, -я *m.* manager. **распоряди́тельность,** -и, good management; efficiency; отсýтствие распоряди́тельности, mismanagement. **распоряди́тельный,** capable; efficient; active. **распоряди́ться,** -яжýсь *perf.*, **распоряжáться,** -áюсь *imp.* order, give orders; see; + *instr.* manage, deal with, dispose of. **распоря́док,** -дка, order; routine; прáвила внýтреннего распоря́дка на фáбрике, factory regulations. **распоряжéние,** -я, order; instruction, direction; disposal, command; быть в распоряжéнии + *gen.* be at the disposal of; до осóбого распоряжéния, until further notice.

распрáва, -ы, punishment, execution; violence; reprisal; кровáвая ~, massacre, butchery.

распрáвить, -влю *perf.*, **расправля́ть,** -я́ю *imp.* straighten; smooth out; spread, stretch; ~ кры́лья, spread one's wings.

распрáвиться, -влюсь *perf.*, **расправля́ться,** -я́юсь *imp.* c + *instr.* deal with, make short work of; give short shrift to.

распределéние, -я, distribution; allocation, assignment. **распредели́тель,** -я *m.* distributor; retailer. **распредели́тельный,** distributive, distributing; ~ щит, switchboard. **распредели́ть,** -лю́ *perf.*, **распределя́ть,** -я́ю *imp.* distribute; allocate, allot, assign; ~ своё врéмя, allocate one's time.

распродавáть, -даю́, -даёшь *imp.*, **распродáть,** -áм, -áшь, -áст, -ади́м; -óдал, -á, -о *perf.* sell off; sell out. **распродáжа,** -и, sale; clearance sale.

распростёрт|ый, outstretched; prostrate, prone; с ~ыми объя́тиями, with open arms.

распрости́ться, -ощýсь *perf.*, **распрощáться,** -áюсь *perf.* take leave, bid farewell.

распространéние, -я, spreading, diffusion; dissemination; circulation. **распространённый;** -ён, -á, widespread, prevalent. **распространи́ть,** -ню́ *perf.*, **распространя́ть,** -я́ю *imp.* spread; give currency to; diffuse; disseminate, propagate; popularize; extend; give off, give out; **~ся,** spread; extend; apply; enlarge, expatiate, dilate (о + *prep.* on).

распрощáться, etc.: see распрости́ться.

рáспря, -и; *gen. pl.* -ей, quarrel, feud.

распрягáть, -áю *imp.*, **распря́чь,** -ягý, -яжёшь; -я́г, -лá *perf.* unharness.

распускáть, -áю *imp.*, **распусти́ть,** -ущý, -ýстишь *perf.* dismiss; dissolve; disband; let out; relax; let get out of hand; spoil; dissolve; melt; spread; ~ вóлосы, loosen one's hair; ~ на кани́кули, dismiss for the holidays; **~ся,** open, come out; come loose; dissolve; melt; get out of hand; let oneself go.

распýтать, -аю *perf.* (*imp.* распýтывать) disentangle, untangle; unravel; untie, loose; puzzle out.

распýтица, -ы, season of bad roads; slush.

распýтный, dissolute, dissipated, debauched.

распýтывать, -аю *imp.* of распýтать.

распу́тье, -я, crossroads; parting of the ways.
распуха́ть, -а́ю *imp.*, **распу́хнуть**, -ну; -у́х *perf.* swell (up).
распу́щенный, undisciplined; spoilt; dissolute, dissipated.
распыле́ние, -я, dispersion, scattering; spraying; atomization. **распыли́тель**, -я *m.* spray, atomizer. **распыли́ть**, -лю́ *perf.*, **распыля́ть**, -я́ю *imp.* spray; atomize; pulverize; disperse, scatter; **~ся**, disperse, get scattered.
распя́тие, -я, crucifixion; crucifix, cross. **распя́ть**, -пну́, -пнёшь *perf.* crucify.
расса́да, -ы, seedlings. **рассади́ть**, -ажу́, -а́дишь *perf.*, **расса́живать**, -аю *imp.* plant out, transplant; seat, offer seats; separate, seat separately.
расса́живаться, -ается *imp.* of рассе́сться. **расса́сываться**, -ается *imp.* of рассоса́ться.
рассвести́, -етёт; -ело́ *perf.*, **рассвета́ть**, -а́ет *imp.* dawn; рассвета́ет, day is breaking; соверше́нно рассвело́, it is (was) broad daylight. **рассве́т**, -а, dawn, daybreak.
рас|свирепе́ть, -е́ю *perf.*
расседла́ть, -а́ю *perf.* unsaddle.
рассе́ивание, -я, dispersion; dispersal, scattering, dissipation. **рассе́ивать(ся**, -аю(сь *imp.* of рассе́ять(ся.
рассека́ть, -а́ю *imp.* of рассе́чь.
расселе́ние, -я, settling, resettlement; separation.
рассе́лина, -ы, cleft, fissure; crevasse.
рассели́ть, -лю́ *perf.*, **расселя́ть**, -я́ю *imp.* settle, resettle; separate, settle apart.
рас|серди́ть(ся, -жу́(сь, -рдишь(ся *perf.* **рассе́рженный**, angry.
рассе́сться, -ся́дусь *perf.* (*imp.* расса́живаться) take seats; sprawl.
рассе́чь, -еку́, -ечёшь; -е́к, -ла́ *perf.* (*imp.* рассека́ть) cut, cut through; cleave.
рассе́янность, -и, absent-mindedness, distraction; diffusion; dispersion; dissipation. **рассе́янный**, absent-minded; diffused; scattered, dispersed; dissipated; ~ свет, diffused light. **рассе́ять**, -е́ю *perf.* (*imp.* рассе́ивать) sow, broadcast; place at intervals, dot about; disperse, scatter; dispel; **~ся**, disperse, scatter; clear, lift; divert oneself, have some distraction.
расска́з, -а, story, tale; account, narrative. **рассказа́ть**, -ажу́, -а́жешь *perf.*, **расска́зывать**, -аю *imp.* tell, narrate, recount. **расска́зчик**, -а, story-teller, narrator.
рассла́бить, -блю *perf.*, **расслабля́ть**, -я́ю *imp.* weaken, enfeeble; enervate. **расслабле́ние**, -я, weakening, enfeeblement; relaxation.
рассла́ивать(ся, -аю(сь *imp.* of рас-слои́ть(ся.
рассле́дование, -я, investigation, examination; inquiry; произвести́ ~ + *gen.* hold an inquiry into. **рассле́довать**, -дую *perf.* and *imp.* investigate, look into, hold an inquiry into.
расслое́ние, -я, stratification; exfoliation. **расслои́ть**, -ою́ *perf.* (*imp.* рас-сла́ивать), divide into layers, stratify; **~ся**, become stratified; exfoliate, flake off.
рассль́ышать, -шу *perf.* catch.
рассма́тривать, -аю *imp.* of рассмо-тре́ть; examine, scrutinize; regard as, consider.
рас|смеши́ть, -шу́ *perf.*
рассмея́ться, -ею́сь, -еёшься *perf.* burst out laughing.
рассмотре́ние, -я, examination, scrutiny; consideration; предста́вить па ~, submit for consideration. **рассмотре́ть**, -рю́, -ришь *perf.* (*imp.* рассма́тривать) examine, consider; descry, discern, make out.
рассова́ть, -сую́, -суёшь *perf.*, **рассо́вывать**, -аю *imp.* по + *dat.* shove into, stuff into.
рассо́л, -а (-у), brine; pickle.
рассо́риться, -рюсь *perf.* с + *instr.* fall out with, quarrel with.
рас|сортирова́ть, -ру́ю *perf.*, **рассортиро́вывать**, -аю *imp.* sort out.
рассоса́ться, -сётся *perf.* (*imp.* рас-са́сываться) resolve.
рассо́хнуться, -нется; -о́хся *perf.* (*imp.* рассыха́ться) warp, crack, shrink.
расспра́шивать, -аю *imp.*, **расспроси́ть**, -ошу́, -о́сишь *perf.* question; make inquiries of.

рассро́чить, -чу *perf.* spread (over), divide into instalments. **рассро́чка**, -и, instalment; в рассро́чку, in instalments, by instalments.
расстава́ние, -я, parting. **расстава́ться**, -таю́сь, -таёшься *imp.* of расста́ться.
расста́вить, -влю *perf.*, **расставля́ть**, -я́ю *imp.*, **расстана́вливать**, -аю *imp.* place, arrange, post; move apart, set apart; let out; ~ часовы́х, post sentries. **расстано́вка**, -и, placing; arrangement; pause; spacing; говори́ть с расстано́вкой, speak slowly and deliberately.
расста́ться, -а́нусь *perf.* (*imp.* расстава́ться) part; separate; + с + *instr.* leave; give up.
расстёгивать, -аю *imp.*, **расстегну́ть**, -ну́, -нёшь *perf.* undo, unfasten; unbutton; unhook, unclasp, unbuckle; **~ся**, come undone; undo one's coat.
расстели́ть(ся, etc.: see разостла́ть(ся. **расстила́ть(ся**, -а́ю(сь) *imp.* of разостла́ть(ся.
расстоя́ние, -я, distance, space, interval; на далёком расстоя́нии, a long way off, in the far distance.
расстра́ивать(ся, -аю(сь *imp.* of расстро́ить(ся.
расстре́л, -а, execution, shooting. **расстре́ливать**, -аю *imp.*, **расстреля́ть**, -я́ю *perf.* shoot.
расстро́енный, disordered, deranged; upset; out of tune. **расстро́ить**, -о́ю *perf.* (*imp.* расстра́ивать) upset; thwart, frustrate; put out; disorder, derange; disturb; throw into confusion; unsettle; put out of tune; ~ ряды́ проти́вника, break the enemy's ranks; **~ся**, be frustrated; be shattered; be upset, be put out; get out of tune; fall into confusion, fall apart; fall through. **расстро́йство**, -а, disorder, disarray; derangement; confusion; frustration; discomposure; ~ желу́дка, indigestion; diarrhoea.
расступа́ться, -а́ется *imp.*, **расступи́ться**, -у́пится *perf.* part, make way.
расстыкова́ться, -ку́ется *perf.* disengage, cast off. **расстыко́вка**, -и, disengagement, casting off.
рассуди́тельность, -и, reasonableness; good sense. **рассуди́тельный**, reasonable; sober-minded; sensible. **рассуди́ть**, -ужу́, -у́дишь *perf.* judge, arbitrate; think, consider; decide. **рассу́док**, -дка, reason; intellect, mind; good sense. **рассужда́ть**, -а́ю *imp.* reason; deliberate; debate; argue; + о + *prep.* discuss. **рассужде́ние**, -я, reasoning; discussion, debate; argument; без рассужде́ний, without arguing.
рассую́, etc.: see рассова́ть.
рассчи́танный, calculated, deliberate; meant, intended, designed. **рассчита́ть**, -а́ю *perf.*, **рассчи́тывать**, -аю *imp.*, **расче́сть**, разочту́, -тёшь; расчёл, разочла́ *perf.* calculate; compute; rate; count, reckon; expect, hope; rely, depend; **~ся**, settle accounts, reckon.
рассыла́ть, -а́ю *imp.* of разосла́ть. **рассы́лка**, -и, delivery, distribution. **рассы́льный** *sb.* messenger; delivery man.
рассы́пать, -плю *perf.*, **рассыпа́ть**, -а́ю *imp.* spill; strew, scatter; **~ся**, spill, scatter; spread out, deploy; crumble; go to pieces, disintegrate; be profuse; ~ся в похвала́х + *dat.* shower praises on. **рассыпно́й**, (sold) loose. **рассы́пчатый**, friable; short, crumbly; floury.
рассыха́ться, -а́ется *imp.* of рассо́хнуться. **расся́дусь**, etc.: see рассе́сться. **раста́лкивать**, -аю *imp.* of растолка́ть. **раста́пливать(ся**, -аю(сь *imp.* of растопи́ть(ся. **раста́птывать**, -аю *imp.* of растопта́ть.
растаска́ть, -а́ю *perf.*, **раста́скивать**, -аю *imp.*, **растащи́ть**, -щу́, -щишь *perf.* pilfer, filch.
раста́чивать, -аю *imp.* of расточи́ть. **растащи́ть**: see растаска́ть. **рас|та́ять**, -а́ю *perf.*
раство́р[2], -а, (extent of) opening, span.
раство́р[1], -а, solution; mortar. **раствори́мый**, soluble. **раствори́тель**, -я *m.* solvent. **раствори́ть**[1], -рю́ *perf.* (*imp.* растворя́ть) dissolve; mix; **~ся**, dissolve.
раствори́ть[2], -рю́, -ришь *perf.* (*imp.* растворя́ть) open; **~ся**, open.

растворя́ть(ся, -я́ю(сь *imp.* of раствори́ть(ся. **растекáться**, -áется *imp.* of растéчься.

растéние, -я, plant.

растерéть, разотрý, -трёшь; растёр *perf.* (*imp.* растирáть) grind; pound; triturate; spread; rub; massage; **~ся**, rub oneself briskly.

растерзáть, -áю *perf.*, **растéрзывать**, -аю *imp.* tear to pieces; lacerate, harrow.

растéрянность, -и, confusion, perplexity, dismay. **растéрянный**, confused, perplexed, dismayed. **растеря́ть**, -я́ю *perf.* lose; **~ся**, get lost; lose one's head, get confused.

растéчься, -ечётся, -екýтся; -тёкся, -лáсь *perf.* (*imp.* растекáться) spill; run; spread.

расти́, -тý, -тёшь; рос, -лá *imp.* grow; increase; grow up; advance, develop.

растирáние, -я, grinding; rubbing, massage. **растирáть(ся**, -áю(сь *imp.* of растерéть(ся.

расти́тельность, -и, vegetation; hair. **расти́тельный**, vegetable. **расти́ть**, ращý *imp.* raise, bring up; train; grow, cultivate.

растолкáть, -áю *perf.* (*imp.* растáлкивать) push apart; shake. **растолкнýть**, -нý, -нёшь *perf.* part forcibly, push apart.

растолковáть, -кýю *perf.*, **растолкóвывать**, -аю *imp.* explain, make clear.

рас|толóчь, -лкý, -лчёшь; -лóк, -лклá *perf.*

растолстéть, -éю *perf.* put on weight, grow stout.

растопи́ть[1], -плю́, -пишь *perf.* (*imp.* растáпливать) melt; thaw; **~ся**, melt.

растопи́ть[2], -плю́, -пишь *perf.* (*imp.* растáпливать) light, kindle; **~ся**, begin to burn. **растóпка**, -и, lighting; kindling, firewood.

растоптáть, -пчý, -пчешь *perf.* (*imp.* растáптывать) trample, stamp on, crush.

расторгáть, -áю *imp.*, **растóргнуть**, -ну; -óрг *perf.* cancel, dissolve annul, abrogate. **расторжéние**, -я, cancellation, dissolution, annulment, abrogation.

растóропный, quick, prompt, smart; efficient.

расточáть, -áю *imp.*, **расточи́ть**[1], -чý *perf.* waste, squander dissipate; lavish, shower. **расточи́тельный**, extravagant, wasteful.

расточи́ть[2], -чý, -чишь *perf.* (*imp.* растáчивать) bore, bore out.

растрави́ть, -влю́, -вишь *perf.*, **растравля́ть**, -я́ю *imp.* irritate.

растрáта, -ы, spending; waste, squandering; embezzlement. **растрáтить**, -áчу *perf.*, **растрáчивать**, -аю *imp.* spend; waste, squander, dissipate; fritter away; embezzle. **растрáтчик**, -а, embezzler.

растрёпанный, tousled, dishevelled; tattered. **рас|трепáть**, -плю́, -плешь *perf.* disarrange; tousle, dishevel; tatter, tear; **~ся**, get tousled; be dishevelled; get tattered.

растрéскаться, -ается *perf.*, **растрéскиваться**, -ается *imp.* crack, chap.

растрóгать, -аю *perf.* move, touch; **~ся**, be moved.

растя́гивать, -аю *imp.*, **растянýть**, -нý, -нешь *perf.* stretch (out); strain, sprain; prolong, drag out; ~ себé мы́шцу, pull a muscle; **~ся**, stretch; lengthen; be prolonged, drag out; stretch oneself out, sprawl; measure one's length, fall flat. **растяжéние**, -я, tension; stretch, stretching; strain, sprain. **растяжи́мость**, -и, stretchability; tensility; extensibility. **растяжи́мый**, tensile; extensible; stretchable. **растя́нутый**, stretched; long-winded, prolix.

рас|фасовáть, -сýю *perf.*

расформировáние, -я, breaking up; disbandment. **расформировáть**, -рýю *perf.*, **расформирóвывать**, -аю *imp.* break up; disband.

расхáживать, -аю *imp.* walk about; pace up and down; ~ по кóмнате, pace the floor.

расхвáливать, -аю *imp.*, **расхвали́ть**, -лю́, -лишь *perf.* lavish, shower, praises on.

расхвáрываться, -аюсь *imp.* of расхворáться.

расхвата́ть, -а́ю *perf.*, **расхва́тывать**, -аю *imp.* seize on, buy up.
расхвора́ться, -а́юсь *perf.* (*imp.* расхва́рываться) fall (seriously) ill.
расхити́тель, -я *m.* plunderer. **расхи́тить**, -и́щу *perf.*, **расхища́ть**, -а́ю *imp.* plunder, misappropriate. **расхище́ние**, -я, plundering, misappropriation.
расхля́банный, loose; unstable; lax, undisciplined.
расхо́д, -а, expenditure; consumption; outlay; expense; *pl.* expenses, outlay, cost; списа́ть в ~, write off. **расходи́ться**, -ожу́сь, -о́дишься *imp.* of разойти́сь. **расхо́дование**, -я, expense, expenditure. **расхо́довать**, -дую *imp.* (*perf.* из~) spend, expend; use up, consume; **~ся**, spend money; be spent, be consumed. **расхожде́ние**, -я, divergence; ~ во мне́ниях, difference of opinion.
расхола́живать, -аю *imp.*, **расхолоди́ть**, -ожу́ *perf.* damp the ardour of.
расхоте́ть, -очу́, -о́чешь, -оти́м *perf.* cease to want, no longer want.
расхохота́ться, -очу́сь, -о́чешься *perf.* burst out laughing.
расцара́пать, -аю *perf.* scratch (all over).
расцвести́, -ету́, -етёшь; -ёл, -а́ *perf.*, **расцвета́ть**, -а́ю *imp.* blossom, come into bloom; flourish. **расцве́т**, -а, bloom, blossoming (out); flourishing; flowering, heyday; в ~е сил, in the prime of life, in one's prime.
расцве́тка, -и, colours; colouring.
расце́нивать, -аю *imp.*, **расцени́ть**, -ню́, -нишь *perf.* estimate, assess, value; rate; consider, think. **расце́нка**, -и, valuation; price; (wage-)rate.
расцепи́ть, -плю́, -пишь *perf.*, **расцепля́ть**, -я́ю *imp.* uncouple, unhook; disengage, release. **расцепле́ние**, -я, uncoupling, unhooking; disengaging, release.
расчеса́ть, -ешу́, -е́шешь *perf.* (*imp.* расчёсывать) comb; scratch. **расчёска**, -и, comb.
расче́сть, etc.: see рассчита́ть. **расчёсывать**, -аю *imp.* of расчеса́ть.
расчёт[1], -а, calculation; computation; estimate, reckoning; gain, advantage; settling, settlement; dismissal, discharge; быть в ~е, be quits, be even; дать ~ + *dat.* dismiss, sack; не принима́ть в ~, leave out of account; приня́ть в ~, take into consideration. **расчётливый**, economical, thrifty; careful. **расчётный**, calculation, computation, reckoning; pay; accounts; rated, calculated, designed; ~ день, pay-day; ~ отде́л, accounts department.
расчи́стить, -и́щу *perf.*, **расчища́ть**, -а́ю *imp.* clear; **~ся**, clear. **расчи́стка**, -и, clearing.
расчлене́ние, -я, dismemberment; partition. **рас|члени́ть**, -ню́ *perf.*, **расчленя́ть**, -я́ю *imp.* dismember; partition; break up, divide.
расшата́ть, -а́ю *perf.*, **расша́тывать**, -аю *imp.* shake loose, make rickety; shatter, impair; **~ся**, get loose, get rickety; go to pieces, crack up.
расшеве́ливать, -аю *imp.*, **расшевели́ть**, -лю́, -е́ли́шь *perf.* stir, shake; rouse.
расшиба́ть, -а́ю *imp.*, **расшиби́ть**, -бу́, -бёшь; -и́б *perf.* break up, smash to pieces; hurt; knock, stub; **~ся**, hurt oneself, knock oneself; ~ся в лепёшку, go flat out.
расшива́ть, -а́ю *imp.* of расши́ть. **расшивно́й**, embroidered.
расшире́ние, -я, broadening, widening; expansion; extension; dilation, dilatation; distension. **расши́рить**, -рю *perf.*, **расширя́ть**, -я́ю *imp.* broaden, widen; enlarge; expand; extend; **~ся**, broaden, widen, gain in breadth; extend; expand, dilate.
расши́ть, разошью́, -шьёшь *perf.* (*imp.* расшива́ть) embroider; undo, unpick.
расшифрова́ть, -ру́ю *perf.*, **расшифро́вывать**, -аю *imp.* decipher, decode; interpret.
расшнурова́ть, -ру́ю *perf.*, **расшнуро́вывать**, -аю *imp.* unlace, undo.
расще́дриться, -рюсь *perf.* be generous, turn generous.
расще́лина, -ы, cleft, crevice, crack.
расще́п, -а, split. **расщепи́ть**, -плю́ *perf.*, **расщепля́ть**, -я́ю *imp.* split; splinter; break up; **~ся**, split, splinter. **расщепле́ние**, -я, splitting; splintering;

fission; break-up, disintegration; ~ ядра́, nuclear fission. **расщепля́емый, расщепля́ющийся,** fissile, fissionable.

ратифици́ровать, -рую *perf.* and *imp.* ratify.

рационализа́тор, -а, efficiency expert. **рационализа́торский,** rationalization. **рационализа́ция,** -и, rationalization, improvement. **рационализи́ровать,** -рую *perf.* and *imp.* rationalize, improve. **рациона́льный,** rational; efficient.

ра́ция, -и, portable radio transmitter; walkie-talkie.

РВ (*ervé*) *abbr.* радиоакти́вные вещества́, radioactive substances.

рвану́ться, -ну́сь, -нёшься *perf.* dart, rush, dash.

рва́ный, torn; lacerated. **рвать**[1], рву, рвёшь; рвал, -а́, -о *imp.* tear; rend; rip; pull out, tear out; pick, pluck; blow up; break off, sever; ~ и мета́ть, rant and rave; **~ся,** break; tear; burst, explode; strive; be eager, be bursting; ~ с при́вязи, strain at the leash.

рвать[2], рвёт; рва́ло *imp.* (*perf.* вы́ ~) *impers.* vomit, be sick, throw up.

рве́ние, -я, zeal, fervour, ardour.

рво́та, -ы, vomiting; retching; vomit. **рво́тн|ый,** emetic; **~ое** *sb.* emetic.

ре *n. indecl.* D; ray.

реаги́ровать, -рую *imp.* (*perf.* от~, про~) react; respond.

реакти́вный, reactive; jet, jet-propelled; rocket; ~ самолёт, jet (plane). **реа́ктор,** -а, reactor, pile.

реакционе́р, -а, reactionary. **реакцио́нный,** reactionary. **реа́кция,** -и, reaction.

реа́льность, -и, reality; practicability. **реа́льный,** real; realizable, practicable, workable; realistic; practical.

ребёнок, -нка; *pl.* ребя́та, -я́т and де́ти, -е́й, child; infant.

ребро́, -а́; *pl.* рёбра, -бер, rib; fin; edge, verge; поста́вить вопро́с ~м, put a question point-blank.

ребя́та, -я́т *pl.* children; boys, lads. **ребя́ческий,** child's; childish; infantile, puerile. **ребя́чество,** -а, childishness, puerility. **ребя́чий,** childish. **ребя́читься,** -чусь *imp.* behave like a child.

рёв, -а, roar; bellow, howl.

рев- *abbr* in *comb.* of революцио́нный, revolutionary; ревизио́нный, inspection. **ревко́м,** -а, revolutionary committee. **~коми́ссия,** -и, Inspection Board.

рева́нш, -а, revenge; return match.

реве́ть, -ву́, -вёшь *imp.* roar; bellow; howl.

ревизио́нный, inspection; auditing. **реви́зия,** -и, inspection; audit; revision. **ревизова́ть,** -зу́ю *perf.* and *imp.* (*perf.* also об~) inspect; revise. **ревизо́р,** -а, inspector.

ревни́вый, jealous. **ревнова́ть,** -ну́ю *imp.* (*perf.* при~) be jealous. **ре́вностный,** zealous, earnest, fervent. **ре́вность,** -и, jealousy; zeal, earnestness, fervour.

революционе́р, -а, revolutionary. **революцио́нный,** revolutionary. **револю́ция,** -и, revolution.

регистра́тор, -а, registrar. **регистрату́ра,** -ы, registry. **регистра́ция,** registration. **регистри́ровать,** -рую *perf.* and *imp.* (*perf.* also за~), register, record; **~ся,** register; register one's marriage.

регла́мент, -а, regulations; standing orders; time-limit; установи́ть ~, agree on procedure. **регламента́ция,** -и, regulation. **регламенти́ровать,** -рую *perf.* and *imp.* regulate.

регули́рование, -я, regulation, control; adjustment. **регули́ровать,** -рую *imp.* (*perf.* за~, от~, у~) regulate; control; adjust, tune. **регулиро́вщик,** -а, traffic controller; man on point duty.

ред- *abbr.* in *comb.* of редакцио́нный, editorial. **редколле́гия,** -и, editorial board. **~отде́л,** -а, editorial department. **~сове́т,** -а, editorial committee.

-ред *abbrev.* in *comb.* of реда́ктор, editor.

редакти́рование, -я, editing. **редакти́ровать,** -рую *imp.* (*perf.* от~) edit, be editor of; word. **реда́ктор,** -а, editor; гла́вный ~, editor-in-chief; ~ отде́ла, sub-editor. **реда́кторский,** editorial. **редакцио́нн|ый,** editorial, editing; ~ая коми́ссия, drafting committee. **реда́кция,** -и, editorial staff;

editorial office; editing; wording; под редáкцией + *gen.* edited by.
редéть, -éет *imp.* (*perf.* по~) thin, thin out.
реди́с, -а, radishes. **реди́ска, -и,** radish.
рéдкий; -док, -дкá, -о, thin; sparse; rare; uncommon. **рéдко** *adv.* sparsely; far apart; rarely, seldom. **рéдкость, -и,** rarity; curiosity, curio.
рéдька, -и, black radish.
реéстр, -а, list, roll, register.
режи́м, -а, régime; routine; procedure; regimen; mode of operation; conditions; rate; ~ питáния, diet.
режиссёр, -а, producer; director. **режисси́ровать, -рую** *imp.* produce; direct.
рéжущий, cutting, sharp. **рéзать, рéжу** *imp.* (*perf.* за~, про~, с~) cut; slice; carve; engrave; pass close to, shave; cut into; kill, slaughter, knife; speak bluntly; **~ся,** be cut, come through; gamble.
резви́ться, -влю́сь *imp.* sport, gambol, play. **рéзвый,** frisky, playful, sportive.
резервуáр, -а, reservoir, vessel, tank.
резéц, -зцá, cutter; cutting tool; chisel; incisor.
рези́на, -ы, rubber. **рези́нка, -и,** rubber; (piece of) elastic. **рези́нов|ый,** rubber; elastic; ~ые сапоги́, gum-boots.
рéзкий, sharp; harsh; abrupt; shrill.
резнóй, carved, fretted. **резня́, -и́,** slaughter, butchery, carnage.
результáт, -а, result, outcome. **результати́вный,** resulting.
резьбá, -ы́, carving, fretwork.
рейд[1], -а, roads, roadstead.
рейд[2], -а, raid.
рейнвéйн, -а (-у), hock. **рéйнский,** Rhine, Rhenish.
рейс, -а, trip, run; voyage, passage; flight.
рекá, -и́, *acc.* рéку́; *pl.* -и, рéкáм, river.
реквизи́т, -а, properties, props.
реклáма, -ы, advertising, advertisement; publicity. **реклами́ровать, -рую** *perf.* and *imp.* advertise, publicize, push. **реклáмный,** publicity.
рекомендáтельн|ый, of recommendation; ~ое письмó, letter of introduction. **рекомендáция, -и,** recommendation; reference. **рекомендовáть, -дýю** *perf.* and *imp.* (*perf.* also от~, по~) recommend; speak well for; advise; **~ся,** introduce oneself; be advisable.
реконструи́ровать, -рую *perf.* and *imp.* reconstruct.
рекóрд, -а, record; поби́ть ~, break, beat, a record. **рекóрдный,** record, record-breaking. **рекордсмéн, -а, -éнка, -и,** record-holder.
религиóзный, religious; of religion; pious. **рели́гия, -и,** religion.
рельéф, -а, relief. **рельéфно** *adv.* boldly. **рельéфный,** relief; raised, embossed, bold.
рельс, -а, rail; сойти́ с ~ов, be derailed, go off the rails. **рéльсовый,** rail, railway.
ремáрка, -и, stage direction.
ремéнь, -мня́ *m.* strap; belt; thong.
ремéсленник, -а, artisan, craftsman; hack. **ремéсленничество, -а,** workmanship, craftsmanship; hack-work.
ремéсленн|ый, handicraft; trade; mechanical; stereotyped; ~ое учи́лище, trade school. **ремеслó, -á;** *pl.* -ёсла, -ёсел, handicraft; trade; profession.
ремóнт, -а, repair, repairs; maintenance. **ремонти́ровать, -рую** *perf.* and *imp.* (*perf.* also от~), repair; refit, recondition, overhaul. **ремóнтный,** repair, repairing.
рéнта, -ы, rent; income. **рентáбельный,** paying, profitable.
рентгéн, -а, X-rays; roentgen. **рентгенизи́ровать, -рую** *perf.* and *imp.* X-ray. **рентгéновский,** X-ray. **рентгенóлог, -а,** radiologist. **рентгенолóгия, -и,** radiology.
реомю́р, -а, Réaumur.
рéпа, -ы, turnip.
репети́ровать, -рую *imp.* (*perf.* от~, про~, с~) rehearse; coach. **репети́тор, -а,** coach. **репети́ция, -и,** rehearsal; repeater mechanism; часы́ с репети́цией, repeater.
рéплика, -и, rejoinder, retort; cue.
репортёр, -а, reporter.
репродýктор, -а, loud-speaker.
респýблика, -и, republic.

рессóра, -ы, spring. **рессóрный**, spring; sprung.
реставрáция, -и, restoration. **реставри́ровать**, -рую *perf.* and *imp.* (*perf.* also от~) restore.
ресторáн, -а, restaurant.
рети́вый, zealous, ardent.
ретировáться, -рýюсь *perf.* and *imp.* retire, withdraw; make off.
ретранслятор, -а, (radio-)relay. **ретрансляция**, -и, relaying, retransmission.
ретроракéта, -ы, retro-rocket.
реферáт, -а, synopsis, abstract; paper, essay.
рецензéнт, -а, reviewer. **рецензи́ровать**, -рую *imp.* (*perf.* про~) review, criticize. **рецéнзия**, -и, review; notice.
рецéпт, -а, prescription; recipe; method, way, practice.
рециди́в, -а, recurrence; relapse; repetition. **рецидиви́ст**, -а, recidivist.
речевóй, speech; vocal.
рéчка, -и, river. **речнóй**, river; riverine; fluvial; ~ вокзáл, river-steamer and water-bus station; ~ трамвáй, water-bus.
речь, -и; *gen. pl.* -éй, speech; enunciation, way of speaking; language; discourse; oration; address; вы́ступить с ~ю, make a speech; не об э́том ~, that's not the point; об э́том не мóжет быть и рéчи, it is out of the question; о чём ~? what are you talking about? what is it all about?; ~ идёт о том . ., the question is . . .
решáть(ся, -áю(сь *imp.* of реши́ть(ся. **решáющий**, decisive, deciding; key, conclusive. **решéние**, -я, decision; decree, judgement; verdict; solution, answer; вы́нести ~, pass a resolution.
решётка, -и, grating; grille, railing; lattice; trellis; fender, (fire)guard; (fire)-grate; tail; орёл или ~ (рéшка)? heads or tails? **решетó**, -á; *pl.* -ёта, sieve. **решётчатый**, lattice, latticed; trellised.
реши́мость, -и, resolution, resoluteness; resolve. **реши́тельно** *adv.* resolutely; decidedly, definitely; absolutely; ~ всё равнó, it makes no difference whatever. **реши́тельность**, -и, resolution, determination, firmness. **реши́тельный**, resolute, determined; decided; firm; definite; decisive; crucial; absolute. **реши́ть**, -шý *perf.* (*imp.* решáть) decide, determine; make up one's mind; solve, settle; **~ся**, make up one's mind, resolve; bring oneself; + *gen.* lose, be deprived of.
рéшка: see решётка.
ржáветь, -еет *imp.* (*perf.* за~, по~), rust. **ржáвчина**, -ы, rust; mildew. **ржáвый**, rusty.
ржанóй, rye.
ржать, ржу, ржёшь *imp.* neigh.
ри́га, -и, (threshing-)barn.
ри́млянин, -а; *pl.* -яне, -ян, **ри́млянка**, -и, Roman. **ри́мск|ий**, Roman; пáпа ~ий, pope; ~ие ци́фры, Roman numerals.
ри́нуться, -нусь *perf.* rush, dash, dart.
рис, -а (-у), rice.
риск, -а, risk; hazard; пойти́ на ~, run risks, take chances. **рискóванный**, risky; risqué. **рисковáть**, -кýю *imp.* run risks, take chances; + *instr.* or *inf.* risk, take the risk of.
рисовáние, -я, drawing. **рисовáть**, -сýю *imp.* (*perf.* на~) draw; paint, depict, portray; **~ся**, be silhouetted; appear, present oneself; pose, act.
ри́сов|ый, rice; ~ая кáша, rice pudding; boiled rice.
рисýнок, -нка, drawing; illustration; figure; pattern, design; outline; draughtsmanship.
риф, -а, reef.
ри́фма, -ы, rhyme. **рифмовáть**, -мýю *imp.* (*perf.* с~) rhyme; **~ся**, rhyme. **рифмóвка**, -и, rhyming (system).
р-н *abbr.* райóн, district.
РНК (*erenká*) *abbr.* рибонуклеи́новая кислотá, RNA, ribonucleic acid.
робéть, -éю *imp.* (*perf.* о~) be timid; be afraid, quail. **рóбкий**; -бок, -бкá, -о, timid, shy. **рóбость**, -и, timidity, shyness. **рóбче**, *comp.* of рóбкий.
ров, рва, *loc.* -у, ditch.
ровéсник, -а, coeval. **рóвно** *adv.* regularly, evenly; exactly; sharp; absolutely; just as, exactly like; ~ в час, at one sharp, on the stroke of one; ~ ничегó, absolutely nothing, nothing at all. **рóвный**, flat; even; level; regular;

equable; exact; equal. **ровня́, ро́вни́** *m.* and *f.* equal; match. **ровня́ть, -я́ю** *imp.* (*perf.* с~) even, level; ~ с землёй, raze to the ground.

рог, -а; *pl.* -á, -óв, horn; antler; bugle. **рога́тый,** horned. **рогови́ца, -ы,** cornea. **роговóй,** horn; horny; horn-rimmed.

рогóжа, -и, bast mat(ting).

род, -а (-у), *loc.* -ý; *pl.* -ы́, family, kin, clan; birth, origin, stock; generation; genus; sort, kind; без ~у, без пле́мени, without kith or kin; в э́том ~е, of this sort, of the kind; ей де́сять лет от ~у, she is ten years old; он своего́ ~а ге́ний, he is a genius in his (own) way; ~ом, by birth; своего́ ~а, a kind of, a sort of; челове́ческий ~, mankind, the human race. **роди́льный,** maternity; puerperal. **ро́дина, -ы,** native land, mother country; home, homeland. **ро́динка, -и,** birth-mark. **роди́тель, -я** *m.* father; **~ница, -ы,** mother; **роди́тели, -ей** *pl.* parents. **роди́тельный,** genitive. **роди́тельский,** parental, parents'; paternal. **роди́ть,** рожу́, -и́л, -ила́, -о *perf.* and *imp.* (*imp.* also рожа́ть, рожда́ть), bear; give birth to; give rise to; **~ся,** be born; arise, come into being; spring up, thrive.

родни́к, -á, spring. **роднико́вый,** spring.

родни́ть, -ни́т (*perf.* по~) make related, link; make similar, make alike; **~ся,** become related, be linked. **родн|о́й,** own; native; home; ~о́й брат, brother; ~о́й язы́к, mother tongue; **~ы́е** *sb.* relations, relatives, family. **родня́, -и́,** relation(s), relative(s); kinsfolk. **родово́й,** clan, tribal; ancestral; generic; gender. **родонача́льник, -а,** ancestor, forefather; father. **родосло́вн|ый,** genealogical; **~ая** *sb.* genealogy, pedigree. **ро́дственник, -а,** relation, relative. **ро́дственный,** kindred, related; allied; cognate; familiar, intimate. **родство́, -á,** relationship, kinship; relations, relatives. **ро́ды, -ов** *pl.* birth; childbirth, delivery; labour.

ро́жа[1], -и, erysipelas.

ро́жа[2], -и, mug; строи́ть ро́жи, pull faces.

рожа́ть, -а́ю, рожда́ть(ся, -а́ю(сь *imp.* of роди́ть(ся. **рожда́емость, -и,** birth-rate. **рожде́ние, -я,** birth; birthday. **рождённый; -ён, -á,** born. **рождество́, -á,** Christmas.

рожь, ржи, rye.

ро́за, -ы, rose; rose-bush, rose-tree; rose window.

ро́зга, -и; *gen. pl.* -зог, birch.

ро́здал, etc.: see разда́ть.

ро́зница, -ы, retail; в ~у, retail. **ро́зничный,** retail. **ро́зно** *adv.* apart, separately. **рознь, -и,** difference; dissension.

ро́знял, etc.: see разня́ть.

ро́зовый, pink; rose-coloured; rosy; rose.

ро́зыгрыш, -а, draw; drawing; drawn game; playing off; tournament, competition, championship.

ро́зыск, -а, search; inquiry; investigation.

рои́ться, -и́тся, swarm. **рой, -я,** *loc.* -ю́; *pl.* -и́, -ёв, swarm.

рок, -а, fate.

рокирова́ть(ся, -ру́ю(сь *perf.* and *imp.* castle. **рокиро́вка, -и,** castling.

РОКК, -а *abbr.* Росси́йское О́бщество Кра́сного Креста́, Russian Red Cross.

рокова́й, fateful; fated; fatal.

ро́кот, -а, roar, rumble. **рокота́ть,** -о́чет *imp.* roar, rumble.

ро́лик, -а, roller; castor; *pl.* roller skates. **ро́ллер, -а,** scooter.

роль, -и; *gen. pl.* -е́й, role, part.

ром, -а (-у), rum.

рома́н, -а, novel; romance; love affair. **романи́ст, -а,** novelist.

рома́нс, -а, song; romance.

рома́шка, -и, рома́шковый, camomile.

роня́ть, -я́ю *imp.* (*perf.* урони́ть) drop, let fall; shed; lower, injure, discredit.

ро́пот, -а, murmur, grumble. **ропта́ть,** -пщу́, -пщешь *imp.* murmur, grumble.

рос, etc.: see расти́.

роса́, -ы́; *pl.* -ы, dew. **роси́стый,** dewy.

роско́шный, luxurious, sumptuous; luxuriant; splendid. **ро́скошь, -и,** luxury; luxuriance; splendour.

ро́слый, tall, strapping.

ро́спись, -и, list, inventory; painting(s), mural(s).
ро́спуск, -а, dismissal; disbandment; breaking up.
росси́йский, Russian.
ро́сказни, -ей *pl.* old wives' tales, cock-and-bull stories.
ро́ссыпь, -и, scattering, *pl.* deposit; ~ю, in bulk, loose.
рост, -а (-у), growth; increase, rise; height, stature; во весь ~, upright, straight; ~ом, in height.
ростовщи́к, -а́, usurer, money-lender.
росто́к, -тка́, sprout, shoot; пусти́ть ростки́, sprout, put out shoots.
ро́счерк, -а, flourish, одни́м ~ом пера́, with a stroke of the pen.
рот, рта (рту), *loc.* рту, mouth.
ро́та, -ы, company.
рота́тор, -а, duplicator. **ротацио́нн|ый,** rotary; ~ая маши́на, rotary press. **рота́ция,** -и, rotary press.
ро́тный, company; *sb.* company commander.
ротозе́й, -я, **-зе́йка,** -и, gaper, rubberneck; scatter-brain. **ротозе́йство,** -а, carelessness, absent-mindedness.
ро́ща, -и, **ро́щица,** -ы, grove.
ро́ю, etc.: see рыть.
роя́ль, -я *m.* (grand) piano; игра́ть на роя́ле, play the piano.
РСФСР (*eresefesér*) *abbr.* Росси́йская Сове́тская Федерати́вная Социалисти́ческая Респу́блика, Russian Soviet Federative Socialist Republic.
рту́тный, mercury, mercurial. **ртуть,** -и, mercury; quicksilver.
руба́нок, -нка, plane.
руба́шка, -и, shirt; ночна́я ~, night-shirt, nightgown, nightdress.
рубе́ж, -а́, boundary, border(line), frontier; line; за ~о́м, abroad.
рубе́ц, -бца́, scar, cicatrice; weal; hem; seam; tripe.
руби́н, -а, ruby. **руби́новый,** ruby; ruby-coloured.
руби́ть, -блю́, -бишь *imp.* (*perf.* с~) fell; hew, chop, hack; mince, chop up; build (of logs), put up, erect.
ру́бище, -а, rags, tatters.
ру́бка[1], -и, felling; hewing, hacking; chopping; mincing.
ру́бка[2], -и, deck house, deck cabin; **боева́я** ~, conning-tower; рулева́я ~, wheelhouse.
рублёвка, -и, one-rouble note. **рублёвый,** (one-)rouble.
ру́блен|ый, minced, chopped; log, of logs; ~ые котле́ты, rissoles; ~ое мя́со, mince, minced meat, hash.
рубль, -я́ *m.* rouble.
ру́брика, -и, rubric, heading; column.
ру́бчатый, ribbed. **ру́бчик,** -а, scar, seam, rib.
ру́гань, -и, abuse, bad language, swearing. **руга́тельн|ый,** abusive; ~ые слова́, bad language, swear-words. **руга́тельство,** -а, oath, swear-word.
руга́ть, -а́ю *imp.* (*perf.* вы́~, об~, от~) curse, swear at; abuse; tear to pieces; criticize severely; **~ся,** curse, swear, use bad language; swear at, abuse, one another.
руда́, -ы́; *pl.* -ы, ore. **рудни́к,** -а́, mine, pit. **рудни́чный,** mine, pit; mining; ~ газ, fire-damp. **рудоко́п,** -а, miner.
руже́йный, rifle, gun; ~ вы́стрел, rifle-shot. **ружьё,** -ья́; *pl.* -ья, -жей, -ьям, gun, rifle.
рука́, -и́, *acc.* -у; *pl.* -и, рук, -а́м, hand; arm; в со́бственные ру́ки, personal; игра́ть в четы́ре руки́, play duets; идти́ по́д руку с + *instr.*, walk arm in arm with; маха́ть руко́й, wave one's hand; махну́ть руко́й на + *acc.* give up as lost; на ско́рую ру́ку, hastily; extempore; не поднима́ется ~ + *inf.* one cannot bring oneself to; под руко́й, at hand; по рука́м! done! it's a bargain!; приложи́ть ру́ку, append one's signature; рука́ми не тро́гать! (please) don't touch!; ру́ки вверх! hands up; ру́ки прочь! hands off!; руко́й пода́ть, a stone's throw away; у вас на ~х, on you; чёткая ~, a clear hand; э́то мне на́ руку, that suits me.
рука́в, -а́; *pl.* -а́, -о́в sleeve; branch, arm; hose; пожа́рный ~, fire-hose.
рукави́ца, -ы, mitten; gauntlet.
руководи́тель, -я *m.* leader; manager; instructor; guide. **руководи́ть,** -ожу́ *imp.* + *instr.* lead; guide; direct, manage. **руково́дство,** -а, leadership; guidance; direction; guide; handbook,

manual; instructions; leaders; governing body. **руково́дствоваться,** -твуюсь + *instr.* follow; be guided by, be influenced by. **руководя́щ|ий,** leading; guiding; ~ая статья́, leader; ~ий комите́т, steering committee.

рукоде́лие, -я, needlework; *pl.* hand-made goods.

рукомо́йник, -а, wash-stand.

рукопа́шн|ый, hand-to-hand; **~ая** *sb.* hand-to-hand fighting.

рукопи́сный, manuscript. **ру́копись,** -и, manuscript.

рукоплеска́ние, -я, applause. **рукоплеска́ть,** -ещу́, -е́щешь *imp.* + *dat.* applaud, clap.

рукопожа́тие, -я, handshake; обменя́ться рукопожа́тиями, shake hands.

рукоя́тка, -и, handle; hilt; haft, helve; shaft; grip.

рулев|о́й, steering; ~о́е колесо́, steering wheel; *sb.* helmsman, man at the wheel.

руле́тка, -и, tape-measure; roulette.

рули́ть, -лю́ *imp.* (*perf.* вы́~) taxi.

руль, -я́ *m.* rudder; helm; (steering-)-wheel; handlebar.

румы́н, -а; *gen. pl.* -ы́н, **румы́нка,** -и, Rumanian. **румы́нский,** Rumanian.

румя́на, -я́н *pl.* rouge. **румя́нец,** -нца, (high) colour; flush; blush. **румя́нить,** -ню *imp.* (*perf.* за~, на~) redden, bring colour to; rouge; brown; **~ся,** redden; glow; flush; use rouge, put on rouge. **румя́ный,** rosy, ruddy; brown.

ру́пор, -а, megaphone, speaking-trumpet; loud-hailer; mouthpiece.

руса́лка, -и, mermaid. **руса́лочий,** mermaid, mermaid's.

ру́сский, Russian; *sb.* Russian.

ру́сый, light brown.

ру́хлядь, -и, junk, lumber.

ру́хнуть, -ну *perf.* crash down; fall heavily; crash (to the ground).

руча́тельство, -а, guarantee; с ~м, warranted, guaranteed. **руча́ться,** -а́юсь *imp.* (*perf.* поручи́ться) answer, vouch; + за + *acc.* warrant, guarantee, certify.

руче́й, -чья́, stream, brook.

ру́чка, -и, handle; (door-)knob; (chair-)-arm; penholder. **ручн|о́й,** hand; arm; manual; hand-made; tame; ~ы́е часы́, wrist-watch.

ру́шить, -у *imp.* (*perf.* об~) pull down; **~ся,** fall, fall in; collapse.

ры́ба, -ы, fish; *pl.* Pisces. **рыба́к,** -а́, fisherman. **рыба́лка,** -и, fishing. **рыба́цкий, рыба́чий,** fishing. **ры́бий,** fish; fishlike, fishy; ~ жир, cod-liver oil. **ры́бн|ый,** fish; ~ые консе́рвы, tinned fish. **рыбо́лов,** -а, fisherman; angler. **рыболо́вный,** fishing.

рыво́к, -вка́, jerk; dash, burst, spurt.

рыда́ние, -я, sobbing, sobs. **рыда́ть,** -а́ю *imp.* sob.

ры́жий; рыж, -а́, -е, red, red-haired; ginger; chestnut; reddish-brown, brown with age; gold. **ры́жики,** -ов *pl.* (*sl.*) gold watch.

ры́ло, -а, snout; mug.

ры́нок, -нка, market; market-place. **ры́ночный,** market.

рыса́к, -а́, trotter.

ры́сий, lynx.

рыси́стый, trotting. **рыси́ть,** -и́шь *imp.* trot. **рысь**[1], -и, *loc.* -и́, trot; ~ю, на рыся́х, at a trot.

рысь[2], -и, lynx.

ры́твина, -ы, rut, groove. **рыть,** ро́ю *imp.* (*perf.* вы́~, от~) dig; rummage about (in), ransack, burrow in; **~ся,** dig; rummage.

рыхли́ть, -лю́ *imp.* (*perf.* вз~, раз~) loosen, make friable. **ры́хлый;** -л, -а́, -о, friable; loose; porous; pudgy, podgy.

ры́царский, knightly; chivalrous. **ры́царь,** -я *m.* knight.

рыча́г, -а́ lever.

рыча́ть, -чу́ *imp.* growl, snarl.

рья́ный, zealous, ardent.

РЭС *abbr.* райо́нная электроста́нция, Regional power station.

рю́мка, -и, wineglass.

ряби́на[1], -ы, rowan. mountain ash; service(-tree); rowan-berry.

ряби́на[2], -ы, pit, pock. **ряби́ть,** -и́т *imp.* ripple; *impers.* у меня́ ряби́т в глаза́х, I am dazzled. **рябо́й,** pitted, pock-marked; speckled. **ря́бчик,** -а, hazel-hen, hazel grouse. **рябь,** -и, ripple, ripples; dazzle.

ря́вкать, -аю *imp.*, **ря́вкнуть,** -ну *perf.* bellow, roar.

ряд, -а (-у), *loc.* -ý; *pl.* -ы́, row; line; file, rank; series; number; из ~а вон выходя́щий, outstanding, exceptional, out of the common run; пе́рвый ~ front row; после́дний ~, back row; стоя́ть в одно́м ~ý с + *instr.* rank with. **рядово́й,** ordinary common; ~ соста́в, rank and file; men, other ranks; *sb.* private. **ря́дом** *adv.* alongside; near, close by, next door; + с + *instr.* next to.

ря́са, -ы cassock.

С

с *letter*: see эс.

с, со *prep.* I. + *gen.* from; since; off; for, with; on; by; дово́льно с тебя́! that's enough from you!; перево́д с ру́сского, translation from Russian; с большо́й бу́квы, with a capital letter; сда́ча с рубля́ change for a rouble; с ле́вой стороны́ on the left-hand side; с одно́й стороны́ с друго́й стороны́, on the one hand, on the other hand; со сна, just up, half awake; со стыда́, for shame, with shame; с пе́рвого взгля́да, at first sight; с ра́дости, for joy; с утра́, since morning. II. + *acc.* about; the size of; ма́льчик с па́льчик, Tom Thumb; на́ша до́чка ро́стом с ва́шу, our daughter is about the same height as yours; с неде́лю for about a week. III. + *instr.* with; and; мы с ва́ми, you and I; получи́ть с пе́рвой по́чтой, receive by the first post; что с ва́ми? what is the matter with you? what's up?

с. *abbr.* се́вер, N.; село́, village; страни́ца, page.

с-, со-, съ- *vbl. pref.* indicating perfective aspect; unification, joining, fastening; accompaniment, participation; comparison; copying; removal; movement away (from), to one side, downwards, down (from), off, there and back, directed to a point or centre; action in concert.

СА (*esá*) *abbr.* Сове́тская А́рмия, Soviet Army.

са́бельный, sabre. **са́бля,** -и; *gen. pl.* -бель, sabre; (cavalry) sword.

саботи́ровать, -рую *perf.* and *imp.* sabotage.

са́ван, -а, shroud; blanket.

с|агити́ровать, -рую *perf.*

сад, -а, *loc.* -ý; *pl.* -ы́, garden, gardens. **сади́ть,** сажу́, са́дишь *imp.* (*perf.* по~) plant. **сади́ться,** сажу́сь, *imp.* of сесть. **садо́вник,** -а, **-ница,** -ы, gardener. **садово́дство**, -а, gardening; horticulture; nursery; garden(s). **садо́вый,** garden; cultivated.

са́жа, -и, soot.

сажа́ть, -а́ю *imp.* (*perf.* посади́ть) plant; seat; set put; ~ в тюрьму́, put in prison, imprison, jail; ~ под аре́ст, put under arrest. **са́женец,** -нца, seedling; sapling.

са́жень, -и; *pl.* -и, -жен or -же́не́й, sazhen (2·13 metres).

сажу́, etc.: see сади́ть.

са́йка, -и, roll.

с|акти́ровать, -рую *perf.*

сала́зки, -зок *pl.* sled, toboggan.

сала́т, -а (-у), lettuce; salad. **сала́тник,** -а, **сала́тница,** -ы, salad-dish, salad--bowl.

са́ло, -а, fat, lard; suet; tallow.

салфе́тка, -и, napkin, serviette.

са́льный, greasy; fat; tallow; obscene, bawdy.

салю́т, -а, salute. **салютова́ть,** -ту́ю *perf.* and *imp.* (*perf.* also от~) + *dat.* salute.

сам, -ого́ *m.*, **сама́,** -о́й, *acc.* -оё *f.*, **само́,** -ого́ *n.*, **са́ми,** -и́х *pl.*, *pron.* -self, -selves; myself, etc., ourselves, etc.; она́ — ~а́ доброта́ she is kindness itself; ~ по себе́, in itself; by oneself, unassisted; ~ собо́й, of itself, of its own accord; ~о́ собо́й (разуме́ется), of course; it goes without saying.

са́мбо *n. indecl. abbr.* самозащи́та без ору́жия, unarmed combat.

саме́ц, -мца́, male. **са́мка**, -и, female.

само- *perf.* self-, auto-. **самобы́тный**, original, distinctive. **~внуше́ние**, -я, auto-suggestion. **~возгора́ние**, -я, spontaneous combustion. **~во́льный**, wilful, self-willed; unauthorized; unwarranted. **~движущийся**, self-propelled. **~де́лка**, -и, home-made. **~де́льный**, home-made; self-made. **~держа́вие**, -я. autocracy. **~держа́вный**, autocratic. **~де́ятельность**, -и, amateur work, amateur performance; initiative. **~дово́льный**, self-satisfied, smug, complacent. **~ду́р**, -а, petty tyrant; self-willed person. **~ду́рство**, -а, petty tyranny, obstinate wilfulness. **~забве́ние**, -я, selflessness. **~забве́нный**, selfless. **~защи́та**, -ы, self-defence. **~зва́нец** -нца, impostor, pretender. **~зва́нство**, -а, imposture. **~ка́т**, -а, scooter; bicycle. **~кри́тика**, -и, self-criticism. **~люби́вый**, proud; touchy. **~любие** -я, pride self-esteem. **~мне́ние**, -я conceit, self-importance. **~наде́янный**, presumptuous. **~облада́ние**, -я, self-control, self-possession; composure. **~обма́н**, -а, self-deception. **~оборо́на**, -ы, self-defence. **~образова́ние**, -я, self-education. **~обслу́живание**, -я, self-service. **~определе́ние**, -я, self-determination. **~опроки́дывающийся**, self-tipping; ~опроки́дывающийся грузови́к, tip-up lorry. **~отверже́ние**, -я, **~отве́рженность**, -и, selflessness. **~отве́рженный**, selfless, self-sacrificing. **~пи́шущий**, recording, registering; ~пи́шущее перо́ fountain-pen. **~поже́ртвование**, -я, self-sacrifice. **~пу́ск**, -а, self-starter. **~рекла́ма**, -ы, self-advertisement. **~ро́дный**, native. **~ро́док**, -дка, nugget; rough diamond. **~сва́л**, -а tip-up lorry. **~-созна́ние**, -я, self-consciousness. **~сохране́ние**, -я, self-preservation. **~стоя́тельно** *adv.* independently; on one's own. **~стоя́тельность**, -и, independence. **~стоя́тельный**, independent. **~су́д**, -а, lynch law, mob law. **~тёк**, -а, drift. **~тёком** *adv.* by gravity; haphazard of its own accord; идти́ ~тёком, drift. **~уби́йственный**, suicidal. **~уби́йство**, -а, suicide. **~уби́йца**, -ы *m.* and *f.* suicide. **~уве́ренность**, -и, self-confidence, self-assurance. **~уве́ренный**, self-confident, self-assured; cocksure. **~униже́ние**, -я, self-abasement, self-disparagement. **~управле́ние**, -я, self-government; local authority. **~управля́ющийся**, self-governing. **~упра́вный**, arbitrary. **~упра́вство**, -а, arbitrariness. **~учи́тель**, -я *m.* self-instructor, manual. **~у́чка**, -и *m.* and *f.* self-taught person. **~хо́дный**, self-propelled. **~чу́вствие**, -я, general state; как ва́ше ~чу́вствие? how do you feel?

самова́р, -а, samovar.

самолёт, -а, aeroplane, aircraft, plane.

самоцве́т, -а, semi-precious stone.

са́м|ый *pron.* (the) very (the) right; (the) same; (the) most; в ~ое вре́мя, at the right time; в ~ом де́ле, indeed; в ~ом де́ле? indeed? really?; в ~ый раз, just right; на ~ом де́ле, actually, in fact; ~ый глу́пый, the stupidest, the most stupid; ~ые пустяки́, the merest trifles; с ~ого нача́ла, from the very beginning, right from the start; с ~ого утра́, ever since the morning, since first thing.

сан, -а, dignity, office.

сан- *abbr.* in *comb.* of санита́рный, medical, hospital; sanitary. **санвра́ч**, -а́, medical officer of health; sanitary inspector. **~по́езд**, -а, hospital train, ambulance train. **~пу́нкт**, -а, medical centre; dressing-station, aid-post. **~у́зел**, -зла, sanitary arrangements. **~ча́сть**, -и, medical unit.

са́ни, -е́й *pl.* sledge, sleigh.

санита́р, -а, medical orderly, hospital orderly, male nurse; stretcher-bearer. **санитари́я**, -и, hygiene, public health. **санита́рка**, -и, nurse. **санита́рн|ый**, medical; hospital; (public) health; sanitary; ~ый автомоби́ль, ~ая каре́та, ~ая маши́на, ambulance; ~ый у́зел, sanitary arrangements.

са́нки, -нок *pl.* sledge; toboggan. **са́нный**, sledge, sleigh; ~ путь, sleigh-road. **са́ночник**, -а, tobogganist.

сантиме́тр, -а, centimetre; tape-measure, ruler.

сапёр, -а, sapper; pioneer. **сапёрный**, sapper, pioneer; engineer.

сапо́г, -а́; *gen. pl* -о́г boot; top-boot, jackboot. **сапо́жник**, -а, shoemaker, bootmaker; cobbler. **сапо́жный**, boot, shoe.

сапфи́р, -а sapphire.

сара́й, -я, shed; barn, barrack.

саранча́, -и́ locust; locusts.

сарафа́н, -а, sarafan; pinafore dress, pinafore skirt.

сарде́лька, -и, small fat sausage; sardelle.

сатана́, -ы́ *m.* Satan. **сатани́нский**, satanic.

сати́н, -а, sateen. **сати́новый**, sateen.

сафья́н, -а, morocco. **сафья́новый**, morocco.

са́хар, -а (-у), sugar. **сахари́н**, -а, saccharine. **са́харистый**, sugary; saccharine. **са́харить**, -рю *imp.* (*perf.* по~) sugar, sweeten. **са́харница**, -ы, sugar-basin. **са́харн|ый**, sugar; sugary; ~ая голова́, sugar-loaf; ~ый заво́д, sugar-refinery; ~ый песо́к granulated sugar; ~ая пу́дра, castor sugar; ~ая свёкла, sugar-beet.

сачо́к, -чка́, net; landing net; butterfly-net.

сб. *abbr.* сбо́рник, collection.

сба́вить, -влю *perf.* **сбавля́ть**, -я́ю *imp.* take off, deduct; reduce; ~ в ве́се, lose weight; ~ газ, throttle down; ~ с цены́ reduce the price.

с|баланси́ровать, -рую *perf.*

сбе́гать[1], -аю *perf.* run; + за + *instr.* run for. **сбега́ть**[2], -а́ю *imp.*, **сбежа́ть**, -егу́ *perf.* run down (from); run away; disappear, vanish; **~ся**, come running; gather, collect

сберега́тельн|ый; ~ая ка́сса savings bank. **сберега́ть**, -а́ю *imp.*, **сбере́чь**, -егу́ -ежёшь; -ёг -гла́ *perf.* save; save up, put aside; preserve, protect. **сбереже́ние**, -я, economy; saving, preservation; savings. **сберка́сса**, -ы *abbr* savings bank.

сбива́ть, -а́ю *imp.*, **с|бить**, собью́, -бьёшь *perf.* bring down, knock down, throw down; knock off, dislodge; put out; distract; deflect; wear down, tread down; knock together; churn; beat up, whip, whisk; ~ с доро́ги, misdirect; ~ с ног, knock down; ~ с то́лку, muddle, confuse; ~ це́ну, beat down the price; **~ся**, be dislodged; slip; be deflected; go wrong; be confused; be inconsistent; ~ся в ку́чу, ~ся толпо́й, bunch, huddle; ~ся с доро́ги, ~ся с пути́, lose one's way, go astray; ~ся с ног, be run off one's feet; ~ся со счёта, lose count. **сби́вчивый**, confused, indistinct; inconsistent, contradictory. **сби́т|ый**; ~ые сли́вки, whipped cream.

сближа́ть, -а́ю *imp.*, **сбли́зить**, -и́жу *perf.* bring (closer) together, draw together; **~ся**, draw together, converge; become good friends. **сближе́ние**, -я, rapprochement; intimacy; approach, closing in.

сбо́ку *adv.* from one side; on one side; at the side.

сбор, -а, collection; dues; duty; charge(s), fee, toll; takings, returns; salvage; assemblage, gathering; course of instruction; быть в ~е, be assembled, be in session; ~ урожа́я, harvest. **сбо́рище**, -а, crowd, mob. **сбо́рка**, -и, assembling, assembly, erection; gather. **сбо́рник**, -а, collection; ~ пра́вил, code of rules. **сбо́рн|ый**, assembly; mixed, combined; that can be taken to pieces; prefabricated, sectional; detachable; ~ая кома́нда, combined team, representative team; picked team; scratch team; ~ый пункт, assembly point, rallying point. **сбо́рочный**, assembly; ~ цех, assembly shop. **сбо́рчатый**, gathered. **сбо́рщик**, -а, collector; assembler, fitter, mounter.

сбра́сывать(ся, -аю(сь *imp.* of **сбро́сить(ся**.

сбрива́ть, -а́ю *imp.*, **сбрить,** сбре́ю *perf.* shave off.
сброд, -а, riff-raff, rabble.
сброс, -а, fault, break. **сбро́сить,** -о́шу *perf.* (*imp.* сбра́сывать) throw down, drop; throw off; cast off, shed; throw away, discard; **~ся,** throw oneself down, leap (+ *gen.* off, from).
с|брошюрова́ть, -ру́ю *perf.*
сбру́я, -и, harness.
сбыва́ть, -а́ю *imp.*, **сбыть,** сбу́ду; сбыл, -а́, -о *perf.* sell, market; get rid of; dump; ~ с рук, get off one's hands; **~ся,** come true, be realized; happen; что сбу́дется с ней? what will become of her? **сбыт,** -а, sale; market. **сбытово́й,** selling, marketing.
СВ (*esvé*) *abbr.* сре́дние во́лны, medium waves; medium-wave.
св. *abbr.* свы́ше, over; свято́й, saint.
сва́дебный, wedding; nuptial. **сва́дьба,** -ы; *gen. pl.* -деб, wedding.
сва́ливать, -аю *imp.*, **с|вали́ть,** -лю́, -лишь *perf.* throw down, bring down; overthrow; lay low; heap up, pile up; abate; **~ся,** fall, fall down, collapse. **сва́лка,** -и, dump; scrap-heap, rubbish-heap; scuffle; вы́бросить на сва́лку, dump.
с|валя́ть, -я́ю *perf.* **сваля́ться,** -я́ется *perf.* get tangled, get matted.
сва́ривать, -аю *imp.*, **с|вари́ть,** -рю́, -ришь *perf.* boil; cook; weld; **~ся,** boil, cook; weld (together), unite. **сва́рка,** -и, welding.
сварли́вый, peevish; shrewish.
сварно́й, welded. **сва́рочный,** welding. **сва́рщик,** -а, welder.
сва́тать, -аю *imp* (*perf.* по~, со~) propose as a husband or wife; ask in marriage; **~ся** к + *dat.* or за + *acc.* ask, seek in marriage.
сва́я, -и, pile.
све́дение, -я piece of information; knowledge; attention, notice; report, minute; *pl.* information, intelligence; knowledge. **све́дущ|ий,** knowledgeable; versed experienced; ~ие ли́ца, experts, informed persons.
сведу́, etc.: see свести́.
свежезаморо́женный, fresh-frozen; chilled. **све́жесть,** -и, freshness; coolness. **свеже́ть,** -е́ет *imp.* (*perf.* по~) become cooler; freshen. **све́ж|ий;** -еж, -а́, fresh; ~ее бельё, clean underclothes; ~ие проду́кты, fresh food; ~ий хлеб, new bread.
свезти́, -зу́, -зёшь; свёз, -ла́ *perf.* (*imp.* свози́ть) take, convey; bring down, take down; take away, clear away.
свёкла, -ы, beet, beetroot.
свёкор, -кра, father-in-law. **свекро́вь,** -и, mother-in-law.
свёл, etc.: see свести́.
сверга́ть, -а́ю *imp.*, **све́ргнуть,** -ну; све́рг *perf.* throw down, overthrow. **сверже́ние,** -я, overthrow; ~ с престо́ла, dethronement.
све́рить, -рю *perf.* (*imp.* сверя́ть) collate; check.
сверка́ние, -я, sparkling, sparkle; twinkling, twinkle; glitter; glare. **сверка́ть,** -а́ю *imp.* sparkle, twinkle; glitter; gleam. **сверкну́ть,** -ну́, -нёшь *perf.* flash.
сверли́льный, drill, drilling; boring. **сверли́ть,** -лю́ *imp.* (*perf.* про~) drill; bore, bore through; nag, gnaw. **сверло́,** -а́, drill. **сверля́щий,** nagging, gnawing, piercing.
сверну́ть, -ну́, -нёшь *perf.* (*imp.* свёртывать, свора́чивать) roll, roll up; turn; reduce, contract, curtail, cut down; wind up; ~ ла́герь, break camp; ~ ше́ю + *dat.* wring the neck of; **~ся,** roll up, curl up; coil up; fold; curdle, coagulate, turn; contract.
све́рстник, -а, coeval, contemporary; мы с ним ~и, he and I are the same age.
свёрток, -тка, package, parcel, bundle. **свёртывание,** -я, rolling, rolling up; curdling, turning; coagulation; reduction, curtailment, cutting down, cuts. **свёртывать(ся,** -аю(сь *imp.* of сверну́ть(ся.
сверх *prep.* + *gen.* over, above on top of; beyond; over and above; in addition to; in excess of; ~ того́, moreover, besides.
сверх- in *comb.* super-, supra-, extra-, over-, preter-, hyper-. **сверхзвезда́,** -ы́, quasar. **~звуково́й,** supersonic. **~пла́новый,** over and above the plan.

~при́быль, -и, excess profit, excessive profit. **~проводни́к**, -а́, superconductor. **~секре́тный**, top secret. **~совреме́нный**, ultra-modern. **~уро́чный**, overtime; **~уро́чные** *sb. pl.* overtime. **~челове́к**, -а, superman. **~челове́ческий**, superhuman. **~шпио́н**, -а, super-spy. **~шта́тный**, supernumerary. **~ъесте́ственный**, supernatural, preternatural.

све́рху *adv.* from above; from the top; on the surface; ~ до́низу, from top to bottom.

сверчо́к, -чка́, cricket.

сверя́ть, -я́ю *imp.* of све́рить.

свес, -а, overhang. **све́сить**, -е́шу *perf.* (*imp.* све́шивать) let down, lower; dangle; weigh; **~ся**, hang over, overhang; lean over.

свести́, -еду́, -едёшь; -ёл, -а́ *perf.* (*imp.* своди́ть) take; take down; take away, lead off; remove, take out; bring together, put together; unite; reduce, bring; cramp, convulse; ~ дру́жбу, ~ знако́мство, make friends; ~ концы́ с конца́ми, make (both) ends meet; ~ на нет, bring to naught; ~ с ума́, drive mad; ~ счёты, settle accounts, get even; у меня́ свело́ но́гу, I've got cramp in the leg.

свет[1], -а (-у), light; daybreak; при ~е + *gen.* by the light of.

свет[2], -а (-у), world; society, beau monde.

света́ть, -а́ет *imp. impers.* dawn; ~а́ет, day is breaking, it is getting light. **светёлка**, -и, attic. **свети́ло**, -а, luminary. **свети́льный**, illuminating; ~ газ, coal-gas. **свети́ть**, -ечу́, -е́тишь *imp.* (*perf.* по~) shine; + *dat.* light; hold a light for, light the way for; **~ся**, shine, gleam. **светле́ть**, -е́ет *imp.* (*perf.* по~, про~) brighten; grow lighter; clear up, brighten up. **све́тлый**, light; bright; light-coloured; radiant, joyous; pure, unclouded; lucid, clear. **светля́к**, -а́, **светлячо́к**, -чка́, glow-worm; fire-fly.

свето- in *comb.* light, photo-. **светобоя́знь**, -и, photophobia. **~ко́пия**, -и, photostat; blueprint; photocopy. **~маскиро́вка**, -и, black-out. **~непроница́емый**, light-proof, light-tight, opaque. **~си́ла**, -ы, candlepower; rapidity, speed, focal ratio. **~фи́лтр**, -а, light filter; (colour) filter. **~фо́р**, -а, traffic light(s). **~чувстви́тельный**, photosensitive, light-sensitive, photographic, sensitized.

светов|о́й, light; lighting; luminous; ~о́й год, light-year; ~а́я рекла́ма, illuminated sign(s).

све́тский, society, fashionable; genteel, refined; temporal, lay, secular; ~ челове́к, man of the world, man of fashion.

светя́щийся, luminous, luminescent, fluorescent, phosphorescent. **свеча́**, -и́; *pl.* -и, -е́й, candle; taper; (sparking)-plug. **свече́ние**, -я, luminescence, fluorescence; phosphorescence. **све́чка**, -и, candle. **свечно́й**, candle; ~ ога́рок, candle-end. **свечу́**, etc.: see свети́ть.

с|ве́шать, -аю *perf.* **све́шивать(ся**, -аю(сь *imp.* of све́сить(ся. **свива́ть**, -а́ю *imp.* of свить.

свида́ние, -я, meeting; appointment; rendezvous; date; до свида́ния! goodbye!; назна́чить ~, make an appointment; make a date.

свиде́тель, -я *m.*, **-ница**, -ы, witness. **свиде́тельство**, -а, evidence; testimony; certificate; ~ о бра́ке, marriage certificate; ~ о прода́же, bill of sale. **свиде́тельствовать**, -твую *imp.* (*perf.* за~, о~) give evidence, testify; be evidence (of), show; witness; attest, certify; examine, inspect.

свина́рник -а, **свинарня**, -и, pigsty.

свине́ц, -нца́, lead.

свини́на, -ы, pork. **свин|о́й**, pig; pork; ~а́я ко́жа, pigskin; ~о́е са́ло, lard.

свинцо́в|ый. lead; leaden; lead-coloured; ~ые бели́ла, white lead.

свинья́, -и́; *pl.* -и, -е́й, -ям, pig, swine; hog; sow.

свире́ль, -и, (reed-)pipe.

свирепе́ть, -е́ю *imp.* (*perf.* рас~), grow fierce, grow savage. **свире́пствовать**, -твую *imp.* rage; be rife. **свире́пый**, fierce, ferocious, savage; violent.

свиса́ть, -а́ю *imp.*, **сви́снуть**, -ну; -ис *perf.* hang down, droop, dangle; trail.

свист, -а, whistle; whistling; singing, piping, warbling. **свиста́ть,** -ищу́, -и́щешь *imp.* whistle; sing, pipe, warble. **свисте́ть,** -ищу́ *imp.*, **сви́стнуть,** -ну *perf.* whistle; hiss. **свисто́к,** -тка́, whistle.

сви́та, -ы, suite; retinue; series, formation.

сви́тер, -а, sweater.

сви́ток, -тка roll, scroll. **с|вить,** совью́ совьёшь; -ил, -а́, -о *perf.* (*imp.* also свива́ть) twist, wind; **~ся,** roll up, curl up, coil.

свищ, -а́, flaw; (knot-)hole; fistula.

свищу́, etc.: see свиста́ть, свисте́ть.

свобо́да, -ы, freedom, liberty; на свобо́де, at leisure; at large, at liberty; ~ рук, a free hand; ~ сло́ва, freedom of speech. **свобо́дно** *adv.* freely; easily, with ease; fluently; loose, loosely. **свобо́дн|ый,** free; easy; vacant; spare; free-and-easy; loose, loose-fitting; flowing; ~ое вре́мя, free time time off; spare time; ~ый до́ступ, easy access; ~ый уда́р, free kick. **свободолюби́вый,** freedom-loving. **свободомы́слие,** -я, free-thinking. **свободомы́слящий,** free-thinking; *sb.* free-thinker.

свод, -а code; collection; arch, vault; ~ зако́нов, code of laws.

своди́ть, -ожу́, -о́дишь *imp.* of свести́.

сво́дка, -и, summary, résumé; report; communiqué; revise. **сво́дный,** composite combined; collated; step-; ~ брат, step-brother.

сво́дчатый, arched, vaulted.

своево́лие, -я, self-will, wilfulness. **своево́льный,** self-willed, wilful.

своевре́менно *adv.* in good time; opportunely. **своевре́менный,** timely, opportune; well-timed.

своенра́вие, -я, wilfulness, waywardness, capriciousness. **своенра́вный,** wilful, wayward, capricious.

своеобра́зие, -я originality; peculiarity. **своеобра́зный,** original; peculiar, distinctive.

свожу́ etc.: see своди́ть, свози́ть.

свози́ть, -ожу́ -о́зишь *imp.* of свезти́.

свой, своего́ *m.*, **своя́,** свое́й *f.*, **своё,** своего́ *n.*, **свои́,** свои́х *pl.*, *pron.* one's (own); my, his, her, its; our, your, their; доби́ться своего́, get one's own way; она́ сама́ не своя́, she is not herself; он не в своём уме́, he is not in his right mind. **сво́йственный,** peculiar, characteristic. **сво́йство,** -а, property, quality, attribute, characteristic.

сво́ра, -ы, leash, pair; pack; gang.

свора́чивать, -аю *imp.* of сверну́ть, свороти́ть. **с|ворова́ть,** -ру́ю *perf.*

свороти́ть, -очу́, -о́тишь *perf.* (*imp.* свора́чивать) dislodge, displace, shift; turn, swing; twist, dislocate.

свыка́ться, -а́юсь *imp.*, **свы́кнуться,** -нусь; -ы́кся *perf.* get used, accustom oneself.

свысока́ *adv.* haughtily; condescendingly. **свы́ше** *adv.* from above; from on high. **свы́ше** *prep.* + *gen.* over, more than; beyond.

свя́занный, constrained; combined, fixed; bound; coupled. **с|вяза́ть,** -яжу́, -я́жешь *perf.*, **свя́зывать,** -аю *imp.* tie together; tie, bind; connect, link; associate; **~ся,** get in touch, communicate; get involved, get mixed up. **связи́ст,** -а, **-и́стка,** -и, signaller; worker in communication services. **свя́зка,** -и, sheaf, bunch, bundle; chord; ligament; copula. **связно́й,** liaison, communication. **свя́зный,** connected, coherent. **связу́ющий,** connecting, linking; liaison. **связь,** -и, *loc.* -и́, connection; causation; link, tie, bond; liaison, association; communication(s); signals; tie, stay, brace, strut; coupling; *pl.* connections, contacts.

святи́лище, -а, sanctuary. **святи́тель,** -я *m.* prelate. **святи́ть,** -ячу́ *imp.* (*perf.* о~) consecrate; bless, sanctify. **свя́тки,** -ток *pl.* Christmas-tide. **свя́то** *adv.* piously; religiously; ~ бере́чь, treasure; ~ чтить, hold sacred. **свят|о́й;** -ят, -а́, -о holy; sacred; saintly; pious; **~о́й, ~а́я** *sb.* saint. **свяще́нник,** -а, priest. **свяще́нный,** holy; sacred. **свяще́нство,** -а, priesthood; priests.

с.г. *abbr.* сего́ го́да, of this year.

сгиб, -а, bend. **сгиба́емый,** flexible, pliable. **сгиба́ть,** -а́ю *imp.* of согну́ть.

сгла́дить, -а́жу *perf.*, **сгла́живать**, -аю *imp.* smooth out; smooth over, soften; **~ся**, smooth out, become smooth; be smoothed over, be softened; diminish, abate.

с|глупи́ть, -плю́ *perf.*

сгнива́ть, -а́ю *imp.*, **с|гнить**, -ию́, -иёшь; -ил, -а́, -о *perf.* rot, decay.

с|гноить -ою́ *perf.*

сгова́риваться, -аюсь *imp.*, **сговори́ться**, -рю́сь *perf.* come to an arrangement, reach an understanding; arrange; make an appointment. **сго́вор**, -а, agreement, compact, deal; betrothal. **сгово́рчивый**, compliant, complaisant, tractable.

сгон, -а, driving; herding, rounding-up. **сго́нка**, -и, rafting, floating. **сго́нщик**, -а, herdsman, drover; rafter. **сгоня́ть**, -я́ю *imp.* of согна́ть.

сгора́ние, -я, combustion; двигатель вну́треннего сгора́ния, internal-combustion engine. **сгора́ть**, -а́ю *imp.* of сгоре́ть.

с|го́рбить(ся, -блю(сь *perf.* **сго́рбленный**, crooked, bent; hunchbacked.

с|горе́ть, -рю́ *perf.* (*imp.* also сгора́ть) burn down; be burnt out, be burnt down; be burned be used up; burn; burn oneself out; ~ от стыда́, burn with shame. **сгоряча́** *adv.* in the heat of the moment; in a fit of temper.

с|гото́вить, -влю *perf.*

сгреба́ть, -а́ю *imp.*, **сгрести́**, -ебу́, -ебёшь; -ёб, -ла́ *perf.* rake up, rake together; shovel away, off.

сгружа́ть, -а́ю *imp.*, **сгрузи́ть**, -ужу́, -у́зишь *perf.* unload.

с|группирова́ть(ся, -ру́ю(сь *perf.*

сгусти́ть, -ущу́ *perf.*, **сгуща́ть**, -а́ю *imp.* thicken; condense; **~ся**, thicken; condense; clot. **сгу́сток**, -тка, clot. **сгуще́ние**, -я, thickening, condensation; clotting. **сгущённ|ый**; -ён, -а́, condensed; ~ое молоко́, condensed milk; evaporated milk.

сда́бривать, -аю *imp.* of сдо́брить.

сдава́ть, сдаю́, сдаёшь *imp.* of сдать; ~ экза́мен, take sit for, an examination; **~ся** *imp.* of сда́ться.

сдави́ть, -влю́, -вишь *perf.*, **сда́вливать**, -аю *imp.* squeeze. **сда́вленный**, squeezed; constrained.

сда́точн|ый, delivery; ~ая квита́нция, receipt. **сдать**, -ам, -ашь, -аст, -ади́м; -ал, -а́, -о *perf.* (*imp.* сдава́ть), hand over; pass; let, let out, hire out; give in change; surrender, yield, give up; deal; ~ бага́ж на хране́ние, deposit, leave, one's luggage; ~ экза́мен, pass an examination; **~ся**, surrender, yield. **сда́ча**, -и, handing over; letting out, hiring out; surrender; change; deal; дать сда́чи, give change; give as good as one gets.

сдвиг, -а, displacement; fault, dislocation; change, improvement. **сдвига́ть**, -а́ю *imp.*, **сдви́нуть**, -ну *perf.* shift, move, displace; move together, bring together; **~ся**, move, budge; come together. **сдвижно́й**, movable.

с|де́лать(ся, -аю(сь *perf.* **сде́лка**, -и, transaction; deal, bargain; agreement. **сде́льн|ый**, piece-work; ~ая рабо́та, piece-work. **сде́льщик**, -а, piece-worker. **сде́льщина**, -ы, piece-work.

сдёргивать, -аю *imp.* of сдёрнуть.

сде́ржанно *adv.* with restraint, with reserve. **сде́ржанный**, restrained, reserved. **сдержа́ть**, -жу́, -жишь *perf.*, **сде́рживать**, -аю *imp.* hold, hold back; hold in check, contain; keep back, restrain; keep; ~ сло́во, keep one's word.

сдёрнуть, -ну *perf.* (*imp.* сдёргивать) pull off.

сдеру́, etc.: see содра́ть. **сдира́ть**, -а́ю *imp.* of содра́ть.

сдо́ба, -ы, shortening; fancy bread, bun(s). **сдо́бн|ый**; -бен, -бна́, -о, rich, short; ~ая бу́лка, bun. **сдо́брить**, -рю *perf.* (*imp.* сда́бривать) flavour; spice; enrich.

с|до́хнуть, -нет; сдох *perf.* (*imp.* also сдыха́ть) die; croak, kick the bucket.

сдружи́ться, -жу́сь *perf.* become friends.

сдубли́рованный, bonded.

сдува́ть, -а́ю *imp.*, **сду́нуть**, -ну *perf.*, **сдуть**, -у́ю *perf.* blow away, blow off; crib.

сдыха́ть, -а́ет *imp.* of сдо́хнуть.

сеа́нс, -а, performance; showing, house; sitting.

себесто́имость, -и, prime cost; cost (price).
себя́, *dat., prep.* -бе́, *instr.* собо́й or -о́ю *refl. pron.* oneself; myself, yourself, himself, etc.; ничего́ себе́, not bad; собо́й, in appearance; так себе́, so-so; хоро́ш собо́й, good-looking, nice-looking.
сев, -а sowing.
се́вер -а, north. **се́率вернее** *adv.* + *gen.* northwards of, to the north of. **се́верн|ый,** north, northern; northerly; ~ый оле́нь, reindeer; ~ое сия́ние, northern lights, aurora borealis. **се́веро-восто́к,** -а, north-east. **се́веро-восто́чный,** north-east, north-eastern. **се́веро-за́пад,** -а, north-west. **се́веро-за́падный** north-west, north-western. **северя́нин,** -а; *pl.* -я́не, -я́н, northerner.
севооборо́т, -а, rotation of crops.
сего́: see сей. **сего́дня** (*-vo-*) *adv.* today; ~ ве́чером, this evening, tonight. **сего́дняшний,** of today, today's.
седе́льник, -а, saddler. **седе́льный,** saddle.
седе́ть, -е́ю *imp.* (*perf.* по~) go grey, turn grey. **седе́ющий,** grizzled, greying. **седина́,** -ы́; *pl.* -ы, grey hairs; grey streak.
седла́ть, -а́ю *imp.* (*perf.* о~) saddle. **седло́,** -а́; *pl.* сёдла, -дел, saddle. **седлови́на,** -ы, arch; saddle; col.
седоборо́дый, grey-bearded. **седовла́сый, седоволо́сый,** grey-haired. **седо́й;** сед, -á, -о, grey; hoary; grey-haired; flecked with white.
седо́к, -а́, fare, passenger; rider, horseman.
седьмо́й, seventh.
сезо́н, -а, season. **сезо́нник,** -а, seasonal worker. **сезо́нный,** seasonal.
сей, сего́ *m.*, **сия́,** сей *f.*, **сие́,** сего́ *n.*, **сии́,** сих *pl.*, *pron.* this; these; на сей раз, this time, for this once; сего́ ме́сяца, this month's; сию́ мину́ту, this (very) minute; at once, instantly.
сейча́с *adv.* now, at present, at the (present) moment; just, just now; presently, soon; straight away, immediately.
сек, etc.: see сечь.
сек. *abbr.* секу́нда, second.
секре́т, -а, secret; hidden mechanism; listening post; по ~у, secretly; confidentially, in confidence.
секрета́рский, secretarial; secretary's. **секрета́рша,** -и, **секрета́рь,** -я́ *m.* secretary.
секре́тно *adv.* secretly, in secret; secret, confidential; соверше́нно ~, top secret. **секре́тный,** secret; confidential; ~ сотру́дник, secret agent, under-cover agent. **сексо́т,** -а *abbr.* (*sl.*) prison informer, collaborator.
се́кта, -ы, sect. **секта́нт,** -а, sectarian, sectary. **секта́нтство,** -а, sectarianism.
секу́, etc.: see сечь.
секу́нда, -ы, second; сию́ секу́нду! (in) just a moment! **секунда́нт,** -а, second; second string. **секу́ндн|ый,** second; ~ая стре́лка, second hand. **секундоме́р,** -а, stop-watch.
секцио́нный, sectional. **се́кция,** -и, section.
селёдка, -и, herring. **селёдочный,** herring, of herring(s).
се́лезень, -зня *m.* drake.
селе́ние, -я, settlement, village.
сели́тра, -ы, saltpetre, nitre. **сели́трян|ый,** saltpetre; ~ая кислота́, nitric acid.
сели́ть, -лю́ *imp.* (*perf.* по~) settle; **~ся,** settle. **сели́тебный,** built-up; building, development. **сели́тьба,** -ы; *gen. pl.* -и́тьб, developed land; built-up area; settlement. **село́,** -а́; *pl.* сёла, village.
сель- *abbr.* in *comb.* of се́льский, village; country, rural. **селько́р,** -а, rural correspondent. **~ма́г,** -а, **~по́** *n. indecl.* village shop. **~сове́т,** -а, village soviet.
сельдь, -и; *pl.* -и, -е́й, herring. **сельдяно́й,** herring.
се́льск|ий, country, rural; village; ~ое хозя́йство, agriculture, farming. **сельскохозя́йственный,** agricultural, farming.
семафо́р, -а, semaphore; signal.
сёмга, -и, salmon; smoked salmon.
семе́йный, family; domestic; ~ челове́к, married man, family man. **семе́йство,** -а family.
се́мени, etc.: see се́мя.

семени́ть, -ню́ *imp.* mince.

семени́ться, -и́тся *imp.* seed. **семенни́к**, -а́, testicle; pericarp, seed-vessel; seed-plant. **семенно́й**, seed; seminal, spermatic.

семери́чный, septenary. **семёрка**, -и, seven; figure 7; No. 7; group of seven. **семерно́й**, sevenfold, septuple. **се́меро**, -ы́х, seven.

семе́стр, -а, term, semester. **семестро́вый**, terminal.

се́мечко, -а; *pl.* -и, seed; *pl.* sunflower seeds.

семидесятиле́тие, -я, seventy years; seventieth anniversary, birthday. **семидесятиле́тний**, seventy-year, seventy years'; seventy-year-old. **семидеся́т|ый**, seventieth; ~ые го́ды, the seventies. **семикра́тный**, sevenfold, septuple. **семиле́тка**, -и, seven-year school; seven-year plan; seven-year-old. **семиле́тний**, seven-year; septennial; seven-year-old; ~ ребёнок, child of seven, seven-year-old.

семинари́ст, -а, seminarist. **семина́рия**, -и, seminary; training college.

семисо́тый, seven-hundredth. **семиты́сячный**, seven-thousandth. **семиуго́льник**, -а, heptagon. **семиуго́льный**, heptagonal. **семна́дцатый**, seventeenth. **семна́дцать**, -и, seventeen. **семь**, -ми́, -мью́, seven. **се́мьдесят**, -ми́десяти, -мью́десятью, seventy. **семьсо́т**, -мисо́т, *instr.* -мьюста́ми, seven hundred. **се́мью** *adv.* seven times.

семья́, -и́; *pl.* -и, -е́й, -ям, family. **семьяни́н**, -а, family man.

се́мя, -мени; *pl.* -мена́, -мя́н, -мена́м, seed; semen, sperm.

се́ни, -е́й *pl.* (entrance-)hall; (enclosed) porch

сенно́й, hay. **се́но**, -а, hay. **сенова́л**, -а, hayloft, hay-mow. **сеноко́с**, -а mowing, haymaking; hayfield. **сенокоси́лка**, -и, mowing-machine. **сеноко́сный**, haymaking.

сенсацио́нный, sensational. **сенса́ция**, -и, sensation.

сентя́брь, -я́ *m.*, **сентя́брьский**, September.

се́ра, -ы, sulphur; brimstone; ear-wax.

серва́нт, -а, sideboard.

серви́з, -а, service, set. **сервирова́ть**, -ру́ю *perf.* and *imp.* serve; ~ стол, lay a table. **сервиро́вка**, -и, laying; serving, service.

серде́чник, -а, core. **серде́чность**, -и, cordiality; warmth. **серде́чный**, heart; of the heart; cardiac; cordial, hearty; heartfelt, sincere; warm, warm-hearted.

серди́тый, angry, cross; irate; strong.

серди́ть, -ржу́, -рдишь *imp.* (*perf.* рас~) anger, make angry; **~ся**, be angry, be cross. **се́рдце**, -а; *pl.* -а́, -де́ц, heart; в сердца́х, in anger, in a fit of temper; от всего́ се́рдца, from the bottom of one's heart, wholeheartedly. **сердцебие́ние**, -я, palpitation. **сердцеви́дный**, heart-shaped; cordate. **сердцеви́на**, -ы, core, pith, heart.

серебрёный, silver-plated. **серебри́стый**, silvery. **серебри́ть**, -рю́ *imp.* (*perf.* по~) silver, silver-plate; **~ся**, silver, become silvery. **серебро́**, -а́, silver. **сере́бряник**, -а, silversmith. **сере́брян|ый**, silver; ~ая сва́дьба, silver wedding.

середи́на, -ы, middle, midst; золота́я ~, golden mean. **середи́нный**, middle, mean, intermediate. **серёдка**, -и, middle, centre.

серёжка, -и, earring; catkin.

се́ренький, grey; dull, drab. **сере́ть**, -е́ю *imp.* (*perf.* по~), turn grey, go grey; show grey.

сержа́нт, -а, sergeant.

сери́йн|ый, serial; ~ое произво́дство, mass production. **се́рия**, -и, series; range; part.

се́рн|ый, sulphur; sulphuric; ~ая кислота́ sulphuric acid.

серова́тый, greyish. **сероглазый**, grey-eyed.

серп, -а́, sickle, reaping-hook; ~ луны́, crescent moon.

серпанти́н, -а, paper streamer; serpentine road.

серпови́дный, crescent(-shaped).

серсо́ *n. indecl.* hoop.

се́рый; сер, -а́, -о, grey; dull; drab; dim; ignorant, uncouth, uneducated.

серьга́, -и́; *pl.* -и, -рёг, earring.

серьёзно *adv.* seriously; earnestly; in earnest. **серьёзный,** serious; earnest; grave.
се́ссия, -и, session, sitting; conference, congress; term.
сестра́, -ы́; *pl.* сёстры, сестёр, сёстрам, sister.
сесть, ся́ду *perf.* (*imp.* сади́ться) sit down; alight, settle, perch; land; set; shrink; + на + *acc.* board, take, get on; ~ за рабо́ту, set to work; ~ на кора́бль, go on board, go aboard; ~ на ло́шадь, mount a horse; ~ на по́езд, board a train.
сетево́й, net, netting, mesh. **се́тка,** -и, net, netting; (luggage-)rack; string bag; grid; co-ordinates; scale.
се́товать, -тую *imp.* (*perf.* по~) complain; lament, mourn.
се́точный, net; grid. **сетча́тка,** -и, retina. **се́тчатый,** netted, network; reticular. **сеть,** -и, *loc.* -и́; *pl.* -и, -е́й, net; network; circuit, system.
сече́ние, -я, cutting; section. **сечь,** секу́, сечёшь; сек *imp.* (*perf.* вы́~) cut to pieces; beat, flog; **~ся** (*perf.* по~ся) split; cut.
се́ялка, -и, sowing-machine, seed drill. **се́яльщик,** -а, **се́ятель,** -я *m.* sower. **се́ять,** се́ю *imp.* (*perf.* по~) sow; throw about.
сжа́литься, -люсь *perf.* take pity (над + *instr.*) on.
сжа́тие, -я, pressing, pressure; grasp, grip; compression; condensation. **сжа́тость,** -и, compression; conciseness, concision. **сжа́тый,** compressed; condensed, compact; concise, brief.
с|жать[1], сожну́, -нёшь *perf.*
сжать[2], сожму́, -мёшь *perf.* (*imp.* сжима́ть) squeeze; compress; grip; clench; ~ зу́бы, grit one's teeth; **~ся,** tighten, clench; shrink, contract.
с|жечь, сожгу́, сожжёшь; сжёг, сожгла́ *perf.* (*imp.* also сжига́ть), burn; burn up, burn down; cremate.
сжива́ться, -а́юсь *imp.* of сжи́ться. **сжига́ть,** -а́ю *imp.* of сжечь.
сжим, -а, clip, grip, clamp. **сжима́емость,** -и, compressibility, condensability. **сжима́ть(ся** *imp.* of сжать[2](ся.
сжи́ться, -иву́сь, -ивёшься; -и́лся, -а́сь *perf.* (*imp.* сжива́ться) с + *instr.* get used to, get accustomed to.
с|жу́льничать, -аю *perf.*
сза́ди *adv.* from behind; behind; from the end; from the rear. **сза́ди** *prep.* + *gen.* behind.
сзыва́ть, -а́ю *imp.* of созва́ть.
си *n. indecl.* B; te.
сиби́рский, Siberian; ~ кедр, Siberian pine. **сибиря́к,** -а́, **сибиря́чка,** -и, Siberian.
сига́ра, -ы, cigar. **сигаре́та,** -ы, cigarette; small cigar. **сига́рка,** -и, (home-made) cigarette. **сига́рный,** cigar.
сигна́л, -а, signal. **сигнализа́ция,** -и, signalling. **сигнализи́ровать,** -рую *perf.* and *imp.* (*perf.* also про~) signal; give warning. **сигна́льный,** signal. **сигна́льщик,** -а, signaller, signal-man.
сиде́лка, -и (untrained) nurse, sick-nurse. **сиде́ние,** -я, sitting. **сиде́нье,** -я, seat. **сиде́ть,** -ижу́ *imp.* sit; be; fit; пла́тье хорошо́ сиди́т на ней, the dress fits her; ~ без де́ла, have nothing to do; ~ верхо́м, be on horseback; ~ (в тюрме́), be in prison; ~ на насе́сте, roost, perch. **си́дка,** -и (*sl.*) imprisonment. **сидя́чий,** sitting; sedentary; sessile.
сие́, etc.: see сей.
си́зый; сиз, -а́, -о, dove-coloured, (blue-)grey; bluish, blue.
сий: see сей.
си́ла, -ы, strength; force; power; energy; quantity, multitude; point, essence; *pl.* force(s); в си́ле, in force, valid; в си́лу + *gen.*, on the strength of, by virtue of, because of; име́ющий си́лу, valid; не по ~ам, beyond one's powers, beyond one's strength; свои́ми ~ами, unaided; си́лой, by force. **сила́ч,** -а́, strong man. **си́литься,** -люсь *imp.* try, make efforts. **силов|о́й,** power; of force; ~о́е по́ле, field of force; ~а́я ста́нция, power-station, power-house; ~а́я устано́вка power-plant.
сило́к, -лка́, noose, snare.
си́лос, -а, silo, silage. **силосова́ть,** -су́ю *perf.* and *imp.* (*perf.* also за~), silo, ensile.

си́льно *adv.* strongly, violently; very much, greatly; badly. **си́льный**; -лен or -лён, -льна́, -о, strong; powerful; intense, keen, hard; он не силён в языка́х, he is not good at languages; ~ моро́з, hard frost.

си́мвол, -а, symbol; emblem; ~ ве́ры, creed. **символизи́ровать**, -рую *imp.* symbolize. **символи́зм**, -а, symbolism. **символи́ческий**, symbolic.

симпатизи́ровать, -рую *imp.* + *dat.* be in sympathy with, sympathize with. **симпати́ческий**, sympathetic. **симпати́чный**, likeable, attractive, nice. **симпа́тия**, -и, liking; sympathy.

симули́ровать, -рую *perf.* and *imp.* simulate, feign, sham. **симуля́нт**, -а, malingerer, sham. **симуля́ция**, -и, simulation, pretence.

симфо́ния, -и, symphony; concordance.

синева́, -ы́, blue; ~ под глаза́ми, dark rings under the eyes. **синева́тый**, bluish. **синегла́зый**, blue-eyed. **сине́ть**, -е́ю *imp.* (*perf.* по~), turn blue, become blue; show blue. **си́ний**; синь, -ня́, -не, (dark) blue. **сини́льная** кислота́, prussic acid. **сини́ть**, -ню́ *imp.* (*perf.* под~) paint blue; blue.

сино́ним, -а, synonym. **синони́мика**, -и, synonymy; synonyms.

сино́птик, -а, **синопти́чка**, -и, weather-forecaster. **сино́птика**, -и, weather-forecasting.

си́нтез, -а, synthesis. **синтези́ровать**, -рую *perf.* and *imp.* synthesize. **синтети́ческий**, synthetic.

си́нус, -а sine; sinus.

синхрони́ст, -а, simultaneous interpreter.

синь[1], -и, blue. **синь**[2]: see си́ний. **си́нька**, -и blue, blueing; blue-print. **синя́к**, -а́, bruise; ~ (под гла́зом) black eye.

си́плый, hoarse, husky. **си́пнуть**, -ну; сип *imp.* (*perf.* о~) become hoarse, become husky.

сире́на, -ы, siren; hooter.

сире́невый, lilac(-coloured). **сире́нь**, -и, lilac.

сиро́п, -а, syrup.

сирота́, -ы́; *pl.* -ы *m.* and *f.* orphan. **сиротли́вый**, lonely. **сиро́тский**, orphan's, orphans'; ~ дом, orphanage.

систе́ма, -ы, system; type. **систематизи́ровать**, -рую *perf.* and *imp.* systematize. **система́тика**, -и, systematics; classification; taxonomy. **системати́ческий**, **системати́чный**, systematic; methodical.

си́тец -тца (-тцу), (cotton) print, (printed) cotton; chintz.

си́то, -а, sieve; screen; riddle.

си́тцевый, print, chintz; chintz-covered.

сия́: see сей.

сия́ние -я, radiance; halo. **сия́ть**, -я́ю *imp.* shine, beam; be radiant.

СКА (*ska*, *eská*) *m.* *indecl.* *abbr.* спорти́вный клуб а́рмии, Soviet Army Sports Club.

сказ, -а, tale, lay. **сказа́ние**, -я, story, tale, legend lay. **сказа́ть**, -ажу́, -а́жешь *perf.* (*imp.* говори́ть) say; speak; tell; как ~, how shall I put it?; ска́зано — сде́лано, no sooner said than done; так сказа́ть, so to say. **сказа́ться**, -ажу́сь -а́жешься *perf.*, **ска́зываться**, -аюсь *imp.* give notice, give warning; tell (on); declare oneself; ~ больны́м, report sick. **сказа́тель**, -я *m.* narrator, story-teller. **ска́зка**, -и, tale; story; fairy-tale; fib. **ска́зочник**, -а, story-teller. **ска́зочный**, fairy-tale; fabulous, fantastic; ~ая страна́, fairyland. **сказу́емое**, *sb.* predicate.

скака́лка, -и, skipping-rope. **скака́ть**, -ачу́, -а́чешь *imp.* (*perf.* по~) skip, jump; hop; gallop. **скаково́й**, race, racing. **скаку́н**, -а́, fast horse, race-horse.

скала́, -ы́; *pl.* -ы, rock face, crag; cliff; подво́дная ~, reef. **скали́стый**, rocky; precipitous.

ска́лить, -лю *imp.* (*perf.* о~); ~ зу́бы bare one's teeth; grin.

ска́лка, -и, rolling-pin.

скалола́з, -а, rock-climber. **скалола́зание**, -я, rock-climbing.

ска́лывать, -аю *imp.* of сколо́ть.

скаме́ечка, -и, footstool; small bench. **скаме́йка**, -и, bench. **скамья́**, -и́; *pl.* ска́мьи́, -е́й, bench; ~ подсуди́мых,

dock; со шко́льной скамьи́, straight from school.
сканда́л, -а, scandal; disgrace; brawl, rowdy scene. **скандали́ст**, -а, brawler; trouble-maker; rowdy. **сканда́лить**, -лю *imp*. (*perf*. на~, о~) brawl; kick up a row; shame; **~ся**, disgrace oneself; cut a poor figure. **сканда́льный**, scandalous; rowdy; scandal.
сканди́рование, -я scansion.
ска́пливать(ся, -аю(сь *imp*. of скопи́ть-(ся.
скарб, -а, goods and chattels, bits and pieces.
ска́ред, -а, **ска́реда**, -ы *m*. and *f*. miser. **ска́редничать**, -аю *imp*. be stingy. **ска́редный**, stingy, miserly, niggardly.
скат -а, slope, incline; pitch.
с|ката́ть, -а́ю *perf*. (*imp*. ска́тывать) roll (up); furl.
ска́терть, -и; *pl*. -и, -е́й. table-cloth; ~ью доро́га! good riddance!
скати́ть, -ачу́, -а́тишь *perf*., **ска́тывать**[1], -аю *imp*. roll down; **~ся**, roll down; slip, slide. **ска́тывать**[2], -аю *imp*. of ската́ть.
скафа́ндр, -а, diving-suit; space-suit.
ска́чка, -и, gallop, galloping. **ска́чки**, -чек *pl*. horse-race; races, race-meeting; ~ с препя́тствиями, steeple--chase, obstacle-race. **скачкообра́зный**, spasmodic; uneven. **скачо́к**, -чка́, jump, leap, bound.
ска́шивать, -аю *imp*. of скоси́ть.
сква́жина, -ы, slit, chink; bore-hole; well. **сква́жистый, сква́жный**, porous.
сквер, -а public garden; square.
скве́рно, badly; bad, poorly. **скверносло́вить**, -влю *imp*. use foul language. **скве́рный**, nasty, foul; bad.
сквози́ть, -и́т *imp*. be transparent, show light through; show through; сквози́т *impers*. there is a draught. **сквозно́й**, through; all-round; transparent; ~ ве́тер, draught. **сквозня́к**, -а́, draught. **сквозь** *prep*. + *gen*. through.
скворе́ц, -рца́, starling.
скеле́т, -а, skeleton.
ски́дка, -и, rebate, reduction, discount; allowance(s); со ски́дкой в + *acc*., with a reduction of, at a discount of. **ски́дывать**, -аю *imp*., **ски́нуть**, -ну *perf*. throw off, throw down; knock off.
ски́петр, -а, sceptre.
скипида́р, -а (-у), turpentine.
скирд, -а́; *pl*. -ы, **скирда́**, -ы́; *pl*. -ы, -а́м, stack, rick.
скиса́ть, -а́ю *imp*., **ски́снуть**, -ну; скис *perf*. go sour, turn (sour).
скита́лец, -льца, wanderer. **скита́льческий** wandering. **скита́ться**, -а́юсь *imp*. wander.
скиф, -а, Scythian. **ски́фский**, Scythian.
склад[1], -а, storehouse; depot; store.
склад[2], -а (-у), stamp, mould; turn; logical connection; ~ ума́, turn of mind, mentality.
скла́дка, -и, fold; pleat, tuck; crease; wrinkle.
скла́дно *adv*. smoothly, coherently.
складн|о́й, folding, collapsible; ~а́я крова́ть, camp-bed; ~а́я ле́стница, steps, step-ladder.
скла́дный; -ден, -дна, -о, well-knit, well-built; well-made; rounded, smooth, coherent.
скла́дочный, складско́й, storage, warehousing; скла́дочное ме́сто, store--room, lumber-room. box-room.
скла́дчатый, plicated, folded.
скла́дчина, -ы, clubbing; pooling; в скла́дчину, by clubbing together. **скла́дывать(ся**, -аю(сь *imp*. of сложи́ть(ся.
скле́ивать, -аю *imp*., **с|кле́ить**, -е́ю *perf*. stick together; glue together, paste together; **~ся**, stick together. **скле́йка**, -и, glueing, pasting, together.
склеп, -а, (burial) vault, crypt.
склепа́ть, -а́ю *perf*. **склёпывать**, -аю *imp*. rivet. **склёпка** -и riveting.
склó**ка**, -и, squabble; row.
склон, -а, slope; на ~е лет, in one's declining years. **склоне́ние** -я, inclination; declination; declension. **склони́ть**, -ню́, -нишь *perf*., **склоня́ть**, -я́ю *imp*. incline; bend, bow; win over, gain over; decline; **~ся**, bend, bow; give in, yield; decline, be declined. **скло́нность**, -и, inclination; disposition; susceptibility; bent, penchant. **скло́нный**; -нен, -нна́, -нно, inclined,

disposed, susceptible, given, prone. **склоня́емый** declinable.

склóчник, -а, squabbler, trouble-maker. **склóчный,** troublesome, trouble-making.

скля́нка, -и, phial; bottle; hour-glass; bell; шесть склянок six bells.

скобá, ы́; *pl.* -ы, -áм, cramp, clamp; staple; catch, fastening; shackle.

скóбель, -я *m.* spoke-shave, draw(ing)-knife.

скóбка, -и, *dim.* of скобá; bracket, (*pl.*) parenthesis, parentheses; в ~х, in brackets; in parenthesis, by the way, incidentally

скобли́ть, -облю́, -óбли́шь *imp.* scrape, plane.

скóбочн|ый, cramp, clamp staple, shackle; bracket; ~ая маши́на, stapler, stapling machine.

скóванность. -и, constraint. **скóванный,** constrained; locked, bound; ~ льдáми, ice-bound. **скова́ть,** скую́, скуёшь *perf.* (*imp.* скóвывать) forge; hammer out; chain; fetter, bind; pin down, hold, contain; lock; лёд сковáл рéку, the river is ice-bound.

сковородá, -ы́; *pl.* скóвороды, -рóд, -áм, **сковорóдка, -и** frying-pan.

скóвывать, -аю *imp* of сковáть.

сколáчивать, -аю *imp.*, **сколоти́ть,** -очу́, -óтишь *perf.* knock together; knock up; put together.

сколóть, -лю́, -лешь *perf.* (*imp.* скáлывать) split off chop off; pin together.

скольжéние, -я, sliding, slipping; glide; ~ на крылó, side-slip. **скользи́ть,** -льжу́ *imp.*, **скользну́ть,** -ну́, -нёшь *perf.* slide; slip; glide. **скóльзкий;** -зок, -зкá, -о, slippery. **скользя́щий,** sliding; ~ у́зел, slip-knot.

скóлько *adv.* how much; how many; as far as, so far as; ~ вам лет? how old are you?; ~ врéмени? what time is it? how long?; ~ раз? how many times? **скóлько-нибудь** *adv.* any.

с|**комáндовать,** -дую *perf.* с|**комбини́ровать,** -рую *perf.* с|**кóмкать,** -аю *perf.* с|**комплектовáть,** -ту́ю *perf.* с|**компрометúровать,** -рую *perf.*

сконфу́женный, embarrassed, confused, abashed, disconcerted. с|**конфу́зить-(ся,** -у́жу(сь *perf.*

с|**концентри́ровать,** -рую *perf.*

скончáние, -я, end; passing, death. **скончáться,** -áюсь *perf.* pass away, die.

с|**копи́ровать,** -рую *perf.*

скопи́ть, -плю́, -пишь *perf.* (*imp.* скáпливать) save, save up; amass pile up; **~ся,** accumulate, pile up; gather, collect. **скоплéние, -я,** accumulation; crowd; concentration, conglomeration.

с|**копни́ть,** -ню́ *perf.* **скóпом** *adv.* in a crowd, in a bunch, en masse.

скорбéть, -блю́ *imp.* grieve, mourn, lament. **скóрбный,** sorrowful, mournful, doleful. **скорбь, -и;** *pl.* -и, -éй, sorrow, grief.

скорéе, скорéй *comp.* of скóро, скóрый; *adv.* rather, sooner; как мóжно ~, as soon as possible; ~ всегó, most likely, most probably.

скорлупá, -ы́; *pl.* -ы, shell.

скорня́жн|ый, fur, fur-dressing; ~ое дéло, fur-trade, furrier's art; ~ый товáр, furs. **скорня́к, -á,** furrier, fur-dresser.

скóро *adv.* quickly, fast; soon.

скоро- in *comb.* quick-, fast-. **скоровáрка, -и,** pressure-cooker. **~говóрка,** -и, patter; tongue-twister. **~ду́м,** -а, quick-witted person. **~пи́сный,** cursive. **скóропись, -и,** cursive; shorthand. **~подъёмность,** -и, rate of climb. **~пóртящийся,** perishable. **~пости́жный,** sudden. **~спéлый,** early; fast-ripening; premature; hasty. **~стрéльный,** rapid-firing, quick-firing. **~сшивáтель,** -я *m.* loose-leaf binder; folder, file. **~тéчный,** transient, short-lived; ~тéчная чахóтка, galloping consumption. **~хóд,** -а, runner, messenger; fast runner; high-speed skater.

с|**корóбиться,** -ится *perf.*

скоростни́к, -á, high-speed worker, performer. **скоростнóй,** high-speed; ~ автóбус, express bus. **скóрость,** -и; *gen. pl.* -éй, speed; velocity; rate; в скóрости, soon, in the near future; корóбка скоростéй, gear-box.

с|**коротáть,** -áю *perf.*

скорпио́н, -а, scorpion; Scorpio.
с|корректи́ровать, -рую *perf.* **с|ко́рчить(ся,** -чу(сь *perf.*
ско́р|ый; скор, -а́, -о, quick, fast; rapid; near; short; forthcoming; в ~ом бу́дущем, in the near future; в ~ом вре́мени, shortly, before long; на ~ую ру́ку, off-hand, in a rough-and-ready way; ~ый по́езд, fast train, express; ~ая по́мощь, first aid; ambulance service.
скос, -а, mowing. **с|коси́ть**[1], -ошу́, -о́сишь *perf.* (*imp.* also ска́шивать) mow.
с|коси́ть[2], -ошу́ *perf.* (*imp.* also ска́шивать) squint; be drawn to one side; cut on the cross.
скот, -а́, **скоти́на,** -ы, cattle; livestock; beast, swine. **ско́тник,** -а, herdsman; cowman. **ско́тный,** cattle, livestock; ~ двор, cattle-yard, farmyard.
ското- in *comb.* cattle. **скотобо́йня,** -и; *gen. pl.* -о́ен, slaughter-house. **~во́д,** -а, cattle-breeder, stock-breeder. **~во́дство,** -а, cattle-raising, stock-breeding. **~кра́дство,** -а, cattle-stealing. **~приго́нный** двор, stock-yard. **~промы́шленник,** -а, cattle-dealer. **~сбра́сыватель,** -я *m.* cow-catcher.
ско́тский, cattle; brutal, brutish, bestial. **ско́тство,** -а, brutish condition; brutality, bestiality.
скра́сить, -а́шу *perf.*, **скра́шивать,** -аю *imp.* smooth over; relieve, take the edge off; improve.
скребо́к, -бка́, scraper. **скребу́,** etc.: see скрести́.
скре́жет, -а, grating; gnashing, grinding. **скрежета́ть,** -ещу́, -е́щешь *imp.* grate, grit; + *instr.* scrape, grind, gnash.
скре́па, -ы, tie, clamp, brace; counter-signature, authentication.
скре́пер, -а, scraper.
скрепи́ть, -плю́ *perf.*, **скрепля́ть,** -я́ю *imp.* fasten (together), make fast; pin (together); clamp, brace; countersign, authenticate, ratify; скрепя́ се́рдце, reluctantly, grudgingly. **скре́пка,** -и, paper-clip. **скрепле́ние,** -я, fastening; clamping; tie, clamp.
скрести́, -ебу́, -ебёшь; -ёб, -ла́ *imp.* scrape; scratch, claw; **~сь,** scratch.
скрести́ть, -ещу́ *perf.*, **скре́щивать,** -аю *imp.* cross; interbreed; **~ся,** cross; clash; interbreed. **скреще́ние,** -я, crossing; intersection. **скре́щивание,** -я, crossing; interbreeding.
с|криви́ть(ся, -влю́(сь *perf.*
скрип, -а, squeak, creak. **скрипа́ч,** -а́, violinist; fiddler. **скрипе́ть,** -плю́ *imp.*, **скри́пнуть,** -ну *perf.* squeak, creak; scratch. **скрипи́чный,** violin; ~ ключ, treble clef. **скри́пка,** -и, violin, fiddle. **скрипу́чий,** squeaking, creaking; rasping, scratching.
с|крои́ть, -ою́ *perf.*
скро́мник, -а, modest man. **скро́мничать,** -аю *imp.* (*perf.* по~) be (too) modest. **скро́мность,** -и, modesty. **скро́мный;** -мен, -мна́, -о, modest.
скро́ю, etc.: see скрыть. **скрою́,** etc.: see скрои́ть.
скру́пул, -а, scruple. **скрупулёзный,** scrupulous.
с|крути́ть, -учу́, -у́тишь *perf.*, **скру́чивать,** -аю *imp.* twist; roll; bind, tie up.
скрыва́ть, -а́ю *imp.*, **скрыть,** -о́ю *perf.* hide, conceal; **~ся,** hide, go into hiding, be hidden; steal away, escape; disappear, vanish. **скры́тничать,** -аю *imp.* be secretive, be reticent. **скры́тный,** reticent, secretive. **скры́тый,** secret, concealed, hidden; latent.
скря́га, -и *m.* and *f.* miser. **скря́жничать,** -аю *imp.* pinch, scrape; be miserly.
ску́дный; -ден, -дна́, -о, scanty, poor; slender, meagre; scant; + *instr.* poor in, short of. **ску́дость,** -и, scarcity poverty.
ску́ка, -и, boredom, tedium.
скула́, -ы́; *pl.* -ы, cheek-bone. **скула́стый,** with high cheek-bones.
скули́ть, -лю́ *imp.* whine, whimper.
скупа́ть, -аю *imp.* of скупи́ть.
скупе́ц, -пца́, miser.
скупи́ть, -плю́, -пишь *perf.* (*imp.* скупа́ть) buy (up); corner.
скупи́ться, -плю́сь *imp.* (*perf.* по~), pinch, scrape, be stingy, be miserly; be sparing; + на + *acc.* stint, grudge; ~ на де́ньги, be close-fisted.

скупка, -и, buying (up); cornering.
скупо *adv.* sparingly. **скупой**; -п, -á, -о, stingy, miserly, niggardly; inadequate. **скупость**, -и, stinginess, miserliness, niggardliness.
скупщик, -а, buyer(-up); ~ краденого, fence.
скурвиться, -влюсь *perf.* (*sl.*) turn informer.
скутер, -а; *pl.* -á, outboard speed-boat.
скучать, -áю *imp.* be bored; + по + *dat.* or *prep.* miss, yearn for.
скученность, -и, density, congestion; ~ населения, overcrowding. **скученный**, dense, congested. **скучивать**, -аю *imp.*, **скучить**, -чу *perf.* crowd (together); **~ся**, flock, cluster; crowd together, huddle together.
скучный; -чен, -чнá, -о, boring, tedious, dull; bored; мне скучно, I'm bored.
с|кушать, -аю *perf.* **скую**, etc.: see сковать.
слабеть, -éю *imp.* (*perf.* о~) weaken, grow weak; slacken, drop. **слабина**, -ы́, slack; weak spot, weak point. **слабительн|ый**, laxative, purgative; **~ое** *sb.* purge. **слабить**, -ит *imp.* (*perf.* про~) purge, act as a laxative; *impers.* его слабит, he has diarrhoea.
слабо- in *comb.* weak, feeble, slight. **слабоволие**, -я, weakness of will. **~вольный**, weak-willed. **~душный**, faint-hearted. **~нервный**, nervy, nervous; neurasthenic. **~-развитый**, under-developed. **~сильный**, weak, feeble; low-powered. **~точный**, low-current, weak-current, low-power. **~умие**, -я, feeble-mindedness, imbecility; dementia. **~умный**, feeble-minded, imbecile. **~характерный**, characterless, of weak character.
слабый; -б, -á, -о, weak; feeble; slack, loose; poor.
слава, -ы, glory; fame; name, repute, reputation; rumour; на славу, wonderfully well, excellently, famously. **славить**, -влю *imp.* celebrate, hymn, sing the praises of; **~ся** (+ *instr.*) be famous, famed, renowned, (for); have a reputation (for). **славный**, glorious, famous, renowned; nice, splendid.
славянин, -а; *pl.* -яне, -ян, **славянка**, -и, Slav. **славянофил**, -а, Slavophil(e). **славянский**, Slav, Slavonic.
слагаемое *sb.* component, term, member. **слагать**, -áю *imp.* of сложить.
сладить, -áжу *perf.* с + *instr.* cope with, manage, handle; make, construct.
сладк|ий; -док, -дкá, -о, sweet; sugary, sugared, honeyed; ~кое мясо, sweetbread; **~ое** *sb.* sweet course. **сладострастник**, -а, voluptuary. **сладострастный**, voluptuous. **сладость**, -и, joy; sweetness; sweetening; *pl.* sweets.
слаженность, -и, co-ordination, harmony, order. **слаженный**, co-ordinated, harmonious, orderly.
сланец, -нца, shale, slate; schist. **сланцеватый**, **сланцевый**, shale; shaly, slaty, schistose.
сластёна *m.* and *f.* person with a sweet tooth. **сласть**, -и; *pl.* -и, -éй, delight, pleasure; *pl.* sweets, sweet things.
слать, шлю, шлёшь *imp.* send.
слащавый, sugary, sickly-sweet. **слаще** *comp.* of сладкий.
слева *adv.* from (the) left; on, to, the left; ~ направо, from left to right.
слёг, etc.: see слечь.
слегка *adv.* slightly; lightly, gently; somewhat.
след, следá (-у), *dat.* -у; *loc.* -ý; *pl.* -ы́, track; trail, footprint, footstep; trace, sign, vestige. **следить**[1], -ежý *imp.* + за + *instr.* watch; track; shadow; follow; keep up with; look after; keep an eye on. **следить**[2], -ежý *imp.* (*perf.* на~) leave traces, marks, footmarks, footprints. **следование**, -я, movement, proceeding. **следователь**, -я *m.* investigator. **следовательно** *adv.* consequently, therefore, hence. **следовать**, -дую *imp.* (*perf.* по~), I. + *dat.* or за + *instr.* follow; go after; comply with; result; go, be bound; поезд следует до Москвы́, the train goes to Moscow; II. *impers.* + *dat.* ought, should; be owing, be owed; вам следует + *inf.* you should, you ought to; как и следовало ожидать, as was to be expected; как следует, properly, well; as it should be; кудá следует, to the proper quarter; сколько с меня

сле́дует? how much do I owe (you)? **сле́дом** *adv.* (за + *instr.*) immediately after, behind, close behind. **следопы́т,** -а, pathfinder, tracker. **сле́дствен|ный,** investigation, inquiry; ~ая коми́ссия commission (committee) of inquiry. **сле́дствие**[1], -я, consequence, result. **сле́дствие**[2], -я, investigation. **сле́дующ|ий,** following, next; в ~ий раз, next time; на ~ей неде́ле, next week; ~им о́бразом, in the following way. **сле́жка,** -и, shadowing.

слеза́, -ы́; *pl.* -ёзы, -а́м, tear.

слеза́ть, -а́ю *imp.* of слезть.

слези́ться, -и́тся *imp.* water. **слезли́вый,** tearful, lachrymose. **слёзный,** tear; lachrymal; tearful, plaintive. **слезоточи́вый,** watering, running; lachrymatory; ~ газ, tear-gas.

слезть, -зу; слез *perf.* (*imp.* слеза́ть) climb down, get down; dismount; alight, get off; come off, peel.

слепе́нь, -пня́ *m.* gadfly horse-fly.

слепе́ц, -пца́. blind man. **слепи́ть**[1], -пи́т *imp.* blind; dazzle.

с|лепи́ть[2], -плю́, -пишь *perf.*, **слепля́ть,** -я́ю *imp.* stick together; mould, model.

сле́пнуть, -ну; слеп *imp.* (*perf.* о~) go blind, become blind. **сле́по** *adv.* blindly; indistinctly. **слеп|о́й;** -п, -а́, -о, blind; indistinct; **~ы́е** *sb. pl.* the blind.

сле́пок, -пка, cast.

слепота́, -ы́, blindness.

сле́сарь, -я; *pl.* -я́ or -и *m.* metal worker; locksmith.

слёт, -а, gathering, meeting; rally. **слета́ть,** -а́ю *imp.*, **слете́ть,** -ечу́ *perf.* fly down; fall down, fall off; fly away; **~ся,** fly together; congregate.

слечь, сля́гу, -я́жешь; слёг, -ла́ *perf.* take to one's bed.

сли́ва, -ы, plum; plum-tree.

слива́ть(ся, -а́ю(сь *imp.* of слить(ся. **сли́вки,** -вок *pl.* cream. **сли́вочник,** -а, cream-jug. **сли́вочн|ый,** cream; creamy; ~ое ма́сло, butter; ~ое моро́женое, ice-cream.

сли́зистый, mucous; slimy. **слизня́к,** -а́, slug. **слизь,** -и, mucus; slime.

с|линя́ть, -я́ет *perf.*

слипа́ться, -а́ется *imp.*, **сли́пнуться,** -нется; -и́пся *perf.* stick together.

сли́тно, together, as one word. **сли́ток,** -тка, ingot, bar. **с|лить,** солью́, -ьёшь; -ил, -а́, -о *perf.* (*imp.* also слива́ть) pour, pour out, pour off; fuse, merge, amalgamate; **~ся,** flow together; blend, mingle; merge, amalgamate.

слича́ть, -а́ю *imp.*, **сличи́ть,** -чу́ *perf.* collate; check. **сличе́ние,** -я, collation, checking. **сличи́тельный,** checking, check.

слия́ние, -я, confluence; blending, merging, amalgamation; merger.

сли́шком *adv.* too; too much.

слова́рный, lexical; lexicographic(al), dictionary. **слова́рь,** -я́ *m.* dictionary; glossary; vocabulary. **слове́сник,** -а, **-ница,** -ы, philologist; student of philology; (Russian) language and literature teacher. **слове́сность,** -и, literature; philology. **слове́сный,** verbal, oral; literary; philological. **сло́вник,** -а, glossary; word-list, vocabulary. **сло́вно** *conj.* as if; like, as. **сло́во,** -а; *pl.* -а́, word; speech; speaking; address; lay, tale; к сло́ву by the way, by the by; одни́м ~м, in a word. **сло́вом** *adv.* in a word, in short. **словообразова́ние,** -я, word-formation. **словохо́тливый,** talkative, loquacious. **словосочета́ние,** -я, word combination, word-group, phrase. **словоупотребле́ние,** -я, use of words, usage. **словцо́,** -а́, word; apt word, the right word; для кра́сного словца́, for effect, to display one's wit.

слог[1], -а, style.

слог[2], -а; *pl.* -и, -о́в, syllable. **слогово́й,** syllabic.

слое́ние, -я, stratification. **слоён|ый,** flaky; ~ое те́сто, puff pastry, flaky pastry.

сложе́ние, -я, adding; composition; addition; build, constitution. **сложи́ть,** -жу́, -жишь *perf.* (*imp.* класть, скла́дывать, слага́ть) put (together), lay (together); pile, heap, stack; add, add up; fold (up); make up, compose; take off, put down, set down; lay down; сложа́ ру́ки, with arms folded; idle; ~ ве́щи, pack pack up; ~ наказа́ние, remit a punishment; **~ся,**

form, turn out; take shape; arise; club together, pool one's resources. **сложносокращённ|ый,** acronymic; ~ое сло́во, acronym. **сло́жность, -и,** complication; complexity; в о́бщей сло́жности, all in all, in sum. **сло́жный; -жен, -жна́, -о,** compound; complex; multiple; complicated, intricate; ~ое сло́во, compound (word).

слои́стый, stratified; lamellar; flaky, foliated; schistose. **слои́ть, -ою́** *imp.* stratify; layer; make flaky. **слой, -я;** *pl.* -и́, -ёв, layer; stratum; coat, coating, film.

слом, -а, demolition, pulling down, breaking up; пойти́ на ~, be scrapped.

с|лома́ть(ся, -а́ю(сь *perf.* **сломи́ть, -млю́, -мишь** *perf.* break, smash; overcome; сломя́ го́лову, like mad, at breakneck speed; **~ся,** break.

слон, -а́, elephant; bishop. **слони́ха, -и,** she-elephant. **слоно́в|ый,** elephant; elephantine; ~ая кость, ivory.

слою́, etc.: see слои́ть.

слоня́ться, -я́юсь *imp.* loiter (about), mooch about.

слуга́, -и́; *pl.* -и *m.* man, (man)servant. **служа́нка, -и,** servant, maid. **слу́жащий** *sb.* employee; *pl.* staff. **слу́жба, -ы,** service; work; employment. **служе́бн|ый,** service; office; official; work; auxiliary; secondary; ~ый вход, staff entrance; ~ое вре́мя, office hours; ~ое де́ло, official business. **служе́ние, -я,** service, serving. **служи́ть -жу́, -жишь** *imp.* (*perf.* по~) serve; work, be employed, be; be used, do; be in use, do duty; + *dat.* devote oneself to; ~ доказа́тельством + *gen.* serve as evidence of; ~ при́знаком, indicate, be a sign of.

с|лука́вить, -влю *perf.* **с|лупи́ть, -плю́, -пишь** *perf.*

слух, -а, hearing; ear; rumour, hearsay; по ~у by ear. **слуха́ч, -а́,** monitor. **слухов|о́й,** acoustic, auditory, aural; ~о́й аппара́т, hearing aid; ~о́е окно́, dormer (window).

слу́чай, -я, incident, occurrence, event; case; accident; opportunity, occasion; chance; ни в ко́ем слу́чае, in no circumstances; по слу́чаю, secondhand; + *gen.* by reason of, on account of; on the occasion of. **случа́йно** *adv.* by chance, by accident, accidentally; by any chance. **случа́йность, -и,** chance; по счастли́вой случа́йности, by a lucky chance, by sheer luck. **случа́йн|ый,** accidental, fortuitous; chance; casual, incidental; ~ая встре́ча, chance meeting. **случа́ться, -а́ется** *imp.*, **случи́ться, -и́тся** *perf.* happen; come about, come to pass, befall; turn up, show up; что случи́лось? what has happened? what's up?

слу́шатель, -я *m.* hearer, listener; student; *pl.* audience. **слу́шать, -аю** *imp.* (*perf.* по~, про~), listen to; hear; attend lectures on; (я) слу́шаю! hello!; very well, very good; yes, sir; **~ся** + *gen.* obey, listen to.

слыть, -ыву́, -ывёшь; -ыл, -а́, -о *imp.* (*perf.* про~), have the reputation, be known, be said; pass (+ *instr.* or за + *acc.*, for).

слыха́ть *imp.*, **слы́шать, -шу** *imp.* (*perf.* у~) hear; notice; feel, sense. **слы́шаться, -шится** *imp.* (*perf.* по~) be heard, be audible. **слы́шимость, -и,** audibility. **слы́шимый,** audible. **слы́шно** *adv.* audibly. **слы́шный,** audible; **~но** *predic. impers.* (+ *dat.*) one can hear; it is said they say; нам никого́ не́ было ~но, we could not hear anyone; что ~? what news? any news?

слюда́, -ы́, mica. **слюдяно́й,** mica.

слюна́, -ы́; *pl.* -и -е́й, saliva; spit; *pl.* slobber, spittle. **слюня́вый,** dribbling, drivelling, slavering.

слягу, etc.: see слечь.

сля́котный, slushy. **сля́коть, -и,** slush.

см. *abbr.* смотри́, see, *vide.*

с.м. *abbr.* сего́ ме́сяца, this month's, of this month; inst

сма́зать, -а́жу *perf.*, **сма́зывать, -аю** *imp.* oil, lubricate; grease; smudge; rub over; slur over. **сма́зка, -и,** oiling, lubrication; oil, lubricant; greasing; grease. **сма́зочн|ый,** oil; lubricating; ~ое ма́сло, lubricating oil. **сма́зчик, -а,** greaser. **сма́зывание, -я,** oiling, lubrication; greasing; slurring over.

смак, -а (-у), relish, savour. **смакова́ть, -ку́ю** *imp.* relish, enjoy; savour.

с|маневри́ровать, -рую *perf*.
сма́нивать, -аю *imp*., **смани́ть**, -ню́, -нишь *perf*. entice, lure.
с|мастери́ть, -рю́ *perf*. **сма́тывать**, -аю *imp*. of смота́ть.
сма́хивать, -аю *imp*., **смахну́ть**, -ну́, -нёшь *perf*. brush away, off; flick away, off.
сма́чивать, -аю *imp*. of смочи́ть.
сме́жный, adjacent, contiguous, adjoining, neighbouring.
смека́лка, -и, native wit, mother wit; sharpness.
смёл, etc.: see смести́.
смеле́ть, -е́ю *imp*. (*perf*. о∼), grow bold, grow bolder. **сме́ло** *adv*. boldly; easily, with ease. **сме́лость**, -и, boldness, audacity, courage. **сме́лый**, bold, audacious, courageous, daring. **смельча́к**, -а́, bold spirit; daredevil.
смелю́, etc.: see смоло́ть.
сме́на, -ы, changing, change; replacement(s); relief; shift; change; идти́ на сме́ну + *dat*. take the place of, relieve; ∼ карау́ла, changing of the guard. **смени́ть**, -ню́, -нишь *perf*., **сменя́ть**[1], -я́ю *imp*. change; replace; relieve; succeed; **∼ся**, hand over; be relieved; take turns; + *instr*. give place to. **сме́нность**, -и, shift system; shiftwork. **сме́нн|ый**, shift; changeable; ∼ое колесо́, spare wheel. **сме́нщик**, -а, relief; *pl*. new shift. **сменя́емый**, removable, interchangeable. **сменя́ть**[2], -я́ю *perf*. exchange.
с|ме́рить, -рю *perf*.
смерка́ться, -а́ется *imp*., **сме́ркнуться**, -нется *perf*. get dark.
смерте́льно *adv*. mortally; extremely, terribly; ∼ уста́ть, be dead tired. **смерте́льный**, mortal, fatal, death; extreme, terrible. **сме́ртность**, -и, mortality, death-rate. **сме́ртн|ый**, mortal; death; deadly, extreme; ∼ая казнь, death penalty; capital punishment; ∼ый пригово́р, death sentence. **смерть**, -и; *gen*. *pl*. -е́й, death; decease; до́ сме́рти, to death; умере́ть свое́й сме́ртью, die a natural death; **∼ как** *adv*. awfully, terribly.
смерч, -а, whirlwind, tornado; waterspout; sandstorm.
смеси́тельный, mixing. **с|меси́ть**, -ешу́, -е́сишь *perf*.
смести́, -ету́, -етёшь -ёл, -а́ *perf*, (*imp*. смета́ть) sweep off, sweep (away).
смести́ть, -ещу́ *perf*. (*imp*. смеща́ть) displace; remove; move; dismiss; **∼ся**, change position, become displaced.
смесь, -и, mixture; blend, miscellany, medley.
сме́та, -ы, estimate.
смета́на, -ы, smetana sour cream.
с|мета́ть[1], -а́ю *perf*. (*imp*. also смётывать), tack (together).
смета́ть[2], -а́ю *imp*. of смести́.
сме́тливый, quick, sharp; resourceful.
сме́тный, estimated, budget, planned.
смету́, etc.: see смести́. **смётывать**, -аю *imp*. of смета́ть.
сметь, -е́ю *imp*. (*perf*. по∼) dare; have the right.
смех, -а (-у), laughter; laugh; ∼а ра́ди, for a joke, for fun. **смехотво́рный**, laughable, ludicrous, ridiculous.
сме́шанн|ый, mixed; combined; ∼ое акционе́рное о́бщество, joint-stock company. **с|меша́ть**, -а́ю *perf*., **сме́шивать**, -аю *imp*. mix, blend; lump together; confuse, mix up; **∼ся**, mix, (inter)blend, blend in; mingle; become confused, get mixed up. **смеше́ние**, -я, mixture, blending, merging; confusion, mixing up.
смеши́ть, -шу́ *imp*. (*perf*. на∼, рас∼) amuse, make laugh. **смешли́вость**, -и, risibility. **смешли́вый**, inclined to laugh, easily amused, given to laughing. **смешн|о́й**, funny; amusing; absurd, ridiculous, ludicrous; здесь нет ничего́ ∼о́го, there's nothing to laugh at, it is no laughing matter; **∼о́** *predic*. it is funny; it makes one laugh.
смешу́, etc.: see смеси́ть, смеши́ть.
смеща́ть(ся, -а́ю(сь *imp*. of смести́ть(ся. **смеще́ние**, -я, displacement, removal; shifting, shift; drift; bias.
смещу́, etc.: see смести́ть.
смея́ться, -е́юсь, -еёшься *imp*. laugh; + над + *instr*. laugh at, make fun of.
смире́ние, -я, humility, meekness. **смире́нный**, humble, meek. **смири́тельн|ый**; ∼ая руба́шка, straitjacket.
смири́ть, -рю́ *perf*., **смиря́ть**, -я́ю *imp*.

restrain subdue; humble; **~ся,** submit; resign oneself. **сми́рно** *adv.* quietly; ~! attention! **сми́рный,** quiet; submissive.

смогу́, etc.: see смочь.

смола́, -ы́; *pl.* -ы, resin; pitch, tar; rosin. **смолёный,** resined; tarred, pitched. **смоли́стый,** resinous. **смоли́ть,** -лю́ *imp.* (*perf.* вы́~, о~) resin; tar, pitch.

смолка́ть, -а́ю *imp.,* **смо́лкнуть,** -ну; -олк *perf.* fall silent be silent; cease.

смо́лоду *adv.* from one's youth.

с|молоти́ть, -очу́, -о́тишь *perf.* **с|моло́ть,** смелю́, смéлешь *perf.*

смоляно́й, pitch, tar, resin.

с|монти́ровать, -рую *perf.*

сморка́ть, -а́ю *imp.* (*perf.* вы́~) blow; **~ся,** blow one's nose.

сморо́дина, -ы, currants; currant (-bush). **сморо́динный,** currant.

смо́рщенный, wrinkled. **с|мо́рщить(ся,** -щу(сь *perf.*

смота́ть, -а́ю *perf.* (*imp.* сма́тывать) wind, reel; **~ся,** hurry (away); go, drop in.

смотр, -а *loc.* -у́; *pl.* -о́тры́, review, inspection; public showing; произвести́ ~ + *dat.*, inspect, review; ~ худо́жественной самодея́тельности, amateur arts festival. **смотре́ть,** -рю́, -ришь *imp.* (*perf.* по~) look; see; watch; look through; examine; review, inspect; + за + *instr.* look after; be in charge of, supervise; + в + *acc.*, на + *acc.* look on to, look over; + *instr.* look (like); смотри́(те)! mind! take care!; ~ за поря́дком, keep order; смотря́ it depends; смотря́ по, depending on, in accordance with; **~ся,** look at oneself. **смотри́тель,** -я *m.* supervisor; custodian keeper. **смотрово́й,** review; observation, inspection, sight.

смочи́ть, -чу́, -чишь *perf.* (*imp.* сма́чивать) damp, wet, moisten.

с|мочь, -огу́, -о́жешь; смог, -ла́ *perf.*

с|моше́нничать, -аю *perf.* **смо́ю,** etc.: see смыть.

смрад, -а, stink, stench. **смра́дный,** stinking.

смуглоли́цый, сму́глый; -гл, -а́, -о, dark-complexioned; swarthy.

с|мудри́ть, -рю́ *perf.*

сму́та, -ы, disturbance, sedition. **смути́ть,** -ущу́ *perf.,* **смуща́ть,** -а́ю *imp.* embarrass, confuse; disturb, trouble; **~ся,** be embarrassed, be confused. **сму́тн|ый,** vague; confused; dim; disturbed, troubled; ~ое вре́мя, Time of Troubles. **смутья́н,** -а, trouble-maker. **смуще́ние,** -я, embarrassment, confusion. **смущённый;** -ён, -а́ embarrassed, confused.

смыва́ть(ся, -а́ю(сь *imp.* of смыть(ся.

смыка́ть(ся, -а́ю(сь *imp.* of сомкну́ть(ся.

смысл, -а, sense; meaning; purport; point; в по́лном ~е сло́ва, in the full sense of the word; нет ~а, there is no sense, there is no point. **смы́слить,** -лю *imp.* understand. **смыслово́й,** sense, semantic; of meaning.

смыть, смо́ю *perf.* (*imp.* смыва́ть) wash off; wash away; **~ся,** wash off, come off; slip away, run away, disappear.

смы́чка, -и, union; linking.

смычо́к, -чка́ bow.

смышлёный, clever, bright.

смягча́ть -а́ю *imp.,* **смягчи́ть,** -чу́ *perf.* soften; mollify; ease, alleviate; assuage; palatalize; **~ся,** soften, become soft, grow softer; be mollified; relent, relax; grow mild; ease (off).

смяте́ние, -я, confusion, disarray; commotion; приводи́ть в ~, confuse, perturb. **с|мять(ся,** сомну́(сь, -нёшь(ся *perf.*

снабди́ть, -бжу́ *perf.,* **снабжа́ть,** -а́ю *imp.* + *instr.* supply with, furnish with, provide with. **снабже́ние,** -я, supply, supplying, provision.

сна́добье, -я; *gen. pl.* -ий, drug, concoction.

снару́жи *adv.* on the outside; from (the) outside.

снаря́д, -а, projectile, missile; shell; contrivance, machine, gadget; tackle, gear. **снаряди́ть,** -яжу́ *perf.,* **снаряжа́ть,** -а́ю *imp.* equip, fit out; **~ся,** equip oneself, get ready. **снаря́дн|ый,**

shell, projectile; ammunition; apparatus. **снаряжéние,** -я, equipment, outfit.

снасть, -и; *gen. pl.* -éй, tackle, gear; (*pl.*) rigging.

сначáла *adv.* at first, at the beginning; all over again.

снáшивать, -аю *imp.* of сносúть.

снег, -а (-у); *pl.* -á, snow.

снегúрь, -я, bullfinch.

снеговóй, snow. **снегоочистúтель,** -я *m.* snow-plough. **снегопáд,** -а, snowfall, fall of snow. **снегостýпы,** -ов *pl.* snow-shoes. **снегохóд,** -а, snow-tractor. **снегýрочка,** -и, Snow-maiden. **снежúнка,** -и, snow-flake. **снéжн|ый,** snow; snowy; ~ая бáба, snowman. **снежóк,** -жкá, light snow; snowball.

снестú[1], -сý, -сёшь; -ёс, -лá *perf.* (*imp.* сносúть) take; bring together, pile up; bring down, fetch down; carry away; blow off; take off; demolish, take down, pull down; bear endure, stand, put up with; **~сь,** communicate (с + *instr.* with).

с|нестú[2]**(сь,** -сý(сь, -сёшь(ся; снёс(ся, -слá(сь *perf.*

снижáть, -áю *imp.*, **снúзить,** -úжу *perf.* lower; bring down; reduce; **~ся,** descend; come down; lose height; fall, sink. **снижéние,** -я, lowering; reduction; loss of height.

снизойтú, -йдý, -йдёшь; -ошёл, -шлá *perf.* (*imp.* снисходúть) condescend, deign.

снúзу *adv.* from below; from the bottom; ~ дóверху, from top to bottom.

снимáть(ся, -áю(сь *imp.* of снять(ся.

снúмок, -мка, photograph; print.

снимý, etc.: see снять.

сниская, -ищý, -úщешь *perf.*, **снúскивать,** -аю *imp.* gain, get, win.

снисходúтельность, -и, condescension; indulgence, tolerance, leniency. **снисходúтельный,** condescending; indulgent, tolerant, lenient. **снисходúть,** -ожý, óдишь *imp.* of снизойтú. **снисхождéние,** -я, indulgence, leniency.

снúться, снюсь *imp.* (*perf.* при~) *impers.* + *dat.* dream; ей снúлось, she dreamed; мне снúлся сон, I had a dream.

снóва *adv.* again, anew, afresh.

сновидéние, -я, dream.

сноп, -á, sheaf; ~ лучéй, shaft of light. **сноповязáлка,** -и, binder.

сноровúстый, quick, smart, nimble, clever. **снорóвка,** -и, knack, skill.

снос, -а, demolition, pulling down; drift; wear. **сносúть**[1], -ошý, -óсишь *perf.* (*imp.* снáшивать) wear out.

сносúть[2]**(ся,** -ошý(сь, -óсишь(ся *imp.* of снестú(сь. **снóска,** -и, footnote.

снóсно *adv.* tolerably, so-so. **снóсный,** tolerable; fair, reasonable.

снотвóрн|ый, soporific; **~ые** *sb. pl.* sleeping-pills.

снохá, -ú; *pl.* -и, daughter-in-law.

сношéние, -я, intercourse; relations, dealings.

сношý, etc.: see сносúть.

снятие, -я, taking down; removal, lifting; raising; taking, making; ~ кóпии, copying. **снят|óй;** ~óе молокó, skim milk. **снять,** снимý, -úмешь; -ял, -á, -о *perf.* (*imp.* снимáть) take off; take down; gather in; remove; withdraw, cancel; take; make; photograph; ~ запрéт, lift a ban; ~ с рабóты, discharge, sack; ~ с учёта, strike off the register; ~ фильм, shoot, make, a film; **~ся,** come off; move off; have one's photograph taken; ~ с якоря, weigh anchor; get under way.

со: see **с** *prep.*

со- *pref.* I. of verbs, used instead of с- before и, й, о, before two or more consonants, and before single consonants followed by ь. II. forming *sbs.* and *adjs.*, со-, joint. **соáвтор,** -а, co-author, joint author. **~áвторство,** -а, co-authorship, joint authorship. **~брáт,** -а; *pl.* -ья, -ьев, colleague. **~владéлец,** -льца, joint owner, joint proprietor. **~владéние,** -я, joint ownership. **~вмéстно** *adv.* in common, jointly. **~вмéстный,** joint, combined; ~вмéстное обучéние, co-education; ~вмéстная рабóта, team-work. **~вóюющий,** co-belligerent. **согражданúн,** -а, *pl.* -áждане, -ан, fellow-citizen. **~доклáд,** -а, supplementary report, paper. **~жúтель,** -я *m.* room-mate, flat-mate; lover. **~жúтельница,** -ы, room-mate, flat-mate; mistress. **~жи́тельство,** -а, living together, lodging together; cohabitation. **~квартирáнт,** -а, co-tenant, sharer of flat or lodgings. **~наслéдник,** -а, co-heir. **~óбщник,** -а, accomplice, confederate. **~отéчественник,** -а, compatriot, fellow-countryman. **~племéнник,** -а, fellow-tribesman. **~подчинéние,** -я, co-ordination. **~предéльный,** contiguous. **~причáстность** -и, complicity, participation. **~рáтник,** -а, comrade-in-arms. **~служи́вец,** -вца, colleague, fellow-employee. **~существовáние,** -я, co-existence. **~умы́шленник,** -а, accomplice. **~учени́к,** -á, schoolfellow. **~члéн,** -а, fellow-member.

собáка, -и, dog; hound. **собáчий,** dog, dog's; canine. **собáчка,** -и little dog, doggie; trigger. **собáчник,** -а, dog-lover.

с|обезья́нничать, -аю *perf.*

соберý, etc.: see собрáть.

собéс, -а *abbr.* социáльное обеспечéние, social security (department).

собесéдник, -а, interlocutor, party to conversation, companion; он — забáвный ~, he is amusing to talk to, amusing company.

собирáние, -я, collecting, collection. **собирáтель,** -я *m.* collector. **собирáтельный,** collective. **собирáть(ся,** -áю(сь *imp.* of собрáться.

соблáзн, -а, temptation. **соблазни́тель,** -я *m.* tempter; seducer. **соблазни́тельница,** -ы, temptress. **соблазни́тельный,** tempting; alluring; seductive; suggestive, corrupting. **соблазни́ть,** -ню́ *perf.*, **соблазня́ть,** -я́ю *imp.* tempt; seduce, entice.

соблюдáть, -áю *imp.*, **со|блюсти́,** -юдý, -дёшь, -ю́л, -á *perf.* observe; keep (to), stick to. **соблюдéние,** -я, observance; maintenance.

собóй, собóю: see себя́.

соболéзнование, -я, sympathy, condolence(s). **соболéзновать,** -ную *imp.* + *dat.* sympathize with, condole with.

собóлий, соболи́ный, sable. **сóболь,** -я; *pl.* -и or -я́ *m.* sable.

собóр, -а, cathedral; council, synod, assembly. **собóрный,** cathedral; synod, council.

собрáние, -я, meeting; gathering; assembly; collection; ~ сочинéний, collected works. **сóбранный,** collected; concentrated. **собрáть,** -берý, -берёшь; -áл, -á, -о *perf.* (*imp.* собирáть), gather; collect; pick; assemble, muster; convoke, convene; mount; obtain, poll; prepare, make ready, equip; make gathers in, take in; **~ся,** gather, assemble, muster; be amassed; prepare, make ready, get ready; intend, be about, be going; + с + *instr.* collect; ~ся с дýхом, take a deep breath; pluck up one's courage; pull oneself together; ~ся с мы́слями, collect one's thoughts.

сóбственник, -а, owner, proprietor. **сóбственнический,** proprietary; proprietorial, possessive. **сóбственно** *adv.* strictly; ~ (говоря́), strictly speaking, properly speaking, as a matter of fact.

сóбственнорýчно *adv.* personally, with one's own hand. **собственнорýчн|ый,** done, made, written, with one's own hand(s); ~ая пóдпись, autograph.

сóбственность, -и, property; possession, ownership. **сóбственн|ый,** (one's) own; proper; true; natural; internal; в ~ые рýки, personal; и́мя ~ое, proper name; ~ой персóной, in person.

собы́тие, -я, event; текýщие собы́тия, current affairs.

собью́, etc.: see сбить.

сов- *abbr.* in *comb.* of совéт, soviet, Soviet, council; совéтский, Soviet. **совми́н,** -а, Council of Ministers. **~наркóм,** -а Council of People's Commissars. **~нархóз,** -а (Regional) Economic Council. **~хóз,** -а, Sovkhoz, State farm.

совá, -ы́; *pl.* -ы, owl.

совáть, сую́, -ёшь *imp.* (*perf.* сýнуть) thrust, shove, poke; **~ся,** push, push in; poke one's nose in, butt in.

совершáть, -áю *imp.* **соверши́ть,** -шý *perf.* accomplish; carry out; perform; commit, perpetuate; complete, conclude; **~ся,** happen; be accomplished, be completed. **совершéние,** -я, accomplishment, fulfilment; perpetration, commission. **соверше́нно** *adv.* perfectly; absolutely, utterly, completely, totally. **совершенноле́тие, -я,** majority. **совершенноле́тний,** of age. **соверше́нный**[1], perfect; absolute, utter, complete, total. **соверше́нный**[2], perfective. **соверше́нство, -а,** perfection. **соверше́нствовать,** -твую *imp.* (*perf.* у~) perfect; improve; **~ся** в + *instr.* perfect oneself in; pursue advanced studies in.

со́вестливый, conscientious. **со́вестно** *impers.* + *dat.* be ashamed; ему́ было ~, he was ashamed. **со́весть, -и,** conscience; по со́вести (говоря́), to be honest.

сове́т, -а, advice, counsel; opinion; council; conference; soviet, Soviet; ~ Безопа́сности, Security Council. **сове́тник, -а,** adviser; counsellor. **сове́товать,** -тую *imp.* (*perf.* по~) advise; **~ся** с + *instr.* consult, ask advice of, seek advice from. **советове́д, -а,** Sovietologist. **советóлог, -а,** Kremlinologist. **сове́тск|ий,** Soviet; of soviets; of the Soviet Union; ~ая власть, the Soviet regime; ~кий Сою́з, the Soviet Union. **сове́тчик, -а,** adviser, counsellor.

совеща́ние, -я, conference, meeting. **совеща́тельный,** consultative, deliberative. **совеща́ться, -а́юсь** *imp.* deliberate; consult; confer.

совлада́ть, -а́ю *perf.* с + *instr.* control, cope with.

совмести́мый, compatible. **совмести́тель, -я** *m.* person holding more than one office, combining jobs; pluralist. **совмести́ть, -ещу́** *perf.*, **совмеща́ть, -а́ю** *imp.* combine; **~ся,** coincide; be combined, combine.

сово́к, -вка́, shovel; scoop; dust-pan; садо́вый ~, trowel.

совокупи́ть, -плю́ *perf.*, **совокупля́ть, -я́ю** *imp.* combine, unite; **~ся,** copulate. **совокупле́ние, -я,** copulation. **сово́купно** *adv.* in common, jointly. **сово́купность, -и,** aggregate, sum total; totality. **сово́купный,** joint, combined, aggregate.

совпада́ть, -а́ет *imp.*, **совпа́сть, -адёт** *perf.* coincide; agree, concur, tally.

соврати́ть, -ащу́ *perf.* (*imp.* совраща́ть) pervert, seduce; **~ся,** go astray.

со|вра́ть, -вру́, -врёшь; -а́л, -а́, -о *perf.*

совраща́ть(ся, -а́юсь *imp.* of совратить(ся. **совраще́ние, -я,** perverting, seducing, seduction.

совреме́нник, -а, contemporary. **совреме́нность, -и,** the present (time); contemporaneity. **совреме́нный,** contemporary, present-day; modern; up-to-date; + *dat.* contemporaneous with, of the time of.

совру́, etc.: see соврать.

совсе́м *adv.* quite; entirely, completely, altogether; ~ не, not at all, not in the least.

совью́, etc.: see свить.

согла́сие, -я, consent; assent; agreement; accordance; accord; concord, harmony. **согласи́ть, -ашу́** *perf.* (*imp.* соглаша́ть) reconcile; **~ся,** consent; agree; concur. **согла́сно** *adv.* in accord, in harmony, in concord; *prep.* + *dat.* in accordance with; according to. **согла́сность, -и,** harmony harmoniousness. **согла́сн|ый**[1], agreeable (to); in agreement; concordant; harmonious; быть ~ым, agree (with). **согла́сн|ый**[2], consonant, consonantal; **~ое** *sb.* consonant.

согласова́ние, -я, co-ordination; concordance; agreement; concord. **согласо́ванность, -и** co-ordination; ~ во вре́мени, synchronization. **согласова́ть, -су́ю** *perf.*, **согласо́вывать, -аю** *imp.* co-ordinate; agree; make agree; **~ся,** accord; conform; agree.

соглаша́тель, -я *m.* appeaser; compromiser. **соглаша́тельский,** conciliatory. **соглаша́тельство, -а,** appeasement; compromise. **соглаша́ть(ся, -а́ю(сь** *imp.* of согласить(ся. **соглаше́ние, -я,** agreement; understanding; covenant.

соглашу́, etc.: see согласить.

согна́ть, сгоню́, сго́нишь; -а́л, -а́, -о *perf.* (*imp.* сгоня́ть), drive away; drive together, round up.

со|гну́ть, -ну́, -нёшь *perf.* (*imp.* also сгиба́ть) bend, curve, crook; **~ся,** bend (down), bow (down); stoop.

согрева́ть, -а́ю *imp.*, **согре́ть, -е́ю** *perf.*

warm, heat; **~ся,** get warm; warm oneself.

согрешéние, -я, sin, trespass. **со|греши́ть,** -шý *perf.*

содéйствие, -я, assistance, help; good offices. **содéйствовать,** -твую *perf.* and *imp.* (*perf.* also по~) + *dat.* assist, help; further, promote; make for, contribute to.

содержáние, -я, maintenance, upkeep; keeping; allowance; pay; content; matter, substance; contents; plot; table of contents; быть на содержáнии у + *gen.* be kept, supported, by. **содержáнка,** -и, kept woman. **содержáтельный,** rich in content; pithy, sapid. **содержáть,** -жý, -жишь *imp.* keep; maintain; support; have, contain; **~ся,** be kept; be maintained; be; be contained. **содержи́мое** *sb.* contents.

со|дрáть, сдерý, -рёшь; -áл, -á, -о *perf.* (*imp.* also сдирáть) tear off, strip off; fleece.

содрогáние, -я, shudder. **содрогáться,** -áюсь *imp.*, **содрогнýться,** -нýсь, -нёшься *perf.* shudder, shake, quake.

содрýжество, -а, concord; community, commonwealth.

сóевый, soya.

соединéние, -я, joining, conjunction, combination; joint, join, junction; compound; formation. **соединённый;** -ён, -á, united, joint. **соедини́тельный,** connective, connecting; copulative. **соедини́ть,** -ню́ *perf.*, **соединя́ть,** -я́ю *imp.* join, unite; connect, link; combine; ~ (по телефóну), put through; **~ся,** join, unite; combine.

сожалéние, -я, regret; pity; к сожалéнию, unfortunately. **сожалéть,** -éю *imp.* regret, deplore.

сожгý, etc.: see сжечь. **сожжéние,** -я, burning; cremation.

сожмý, etc.: see сжать[2]. **сожнý,** etc.: see сжать[1]. **созвáниваться,** -аюсь *imp.* of созвони́ться.

созвáть, -зовý, -зовёшь; -áл, -á, -о *perf.* (*imp.* сзывáть, созывáть) call together; call; invite; summon; convoke, convene.

созвéздие, -я, constellation.

созвони́ться, -ню́сь *perf.* (*imp.* созвáниваться) ring up; speak on the telephone.

созвýчие, -я, accord, consonance; assonance. **созвýчный,** harmonious; + *dat.* consonant with, in keeping with.

создавáть, -даю́, -даёшь *imp.*, **создáть,** -áм, -áшь, -áст, -адим; сóздáл, -á, -о *perf.* create; found, originate; set up, establish; **~ся,** be created; arise, spring up. **создáние,** -я, creation; making; work; creature. **создáтель,** -я *m.* creator; founder, originator.

созерцáние, -я, contemplation. **созерцáтельный,** contemplative, meditative. **созерцáть,** -áю *imp.* contemplate.

сознавáть, -наю́, -наёшь *imp.*, **сознáть,** -áю *perf.* be conscious of, realize; recognize, acknowledge; **~ся,** confess; plead guilty. **сознáние,** -я consciousness; recognition, acknowledgement; admission, confession; прийти́ в ~, recover consciousness; ~ дóлга, sense of duty. **сознáтельность,** -и, awareness, consciousness; intelligence, acumen; deliberation, deliberateness. **сознáтельный,** conscious; politically conscious; intelligent; deliberate.

созовý, etc.: see созвáть. **с|озорничáть,** -áю *perf.*

созревáть, -áю *imp.*, **со|зрéть,** -éю *perf.* ripen, mature; come to a head.

созы́в, -а, convocation; summoning, calling. **созывáть,** -áю *imp.* of созвáть.

соизвóлить, -лю *perf.*, **соизволя́ть,** -я́ю *imp.* deign, condescend, be pleased.

соизмери́мый, commensurable.

соискáние, -я, competition, candidacy. **соискáтель,** -я *m.*, **-ница,** -ы, competitor, candidate.

сойти́, -йдý, -йдёшь; сошёл, -шлá *perf.* (*imp.* сходи́ть), go down, come down; descend, get off, alight; leave; come off; pass, go off; + за + *acc.* pass for, be taken for; снег сошёл, the snow has melted; сойдёт и так, it will do (as it is); ~ с дорóги, get out of the way, step aside; ~ с умá, go mad, go out of one's mind; сошлó благополýчно, it

went off all right; **~сь,** meet; come together, gather; become friends; become intimate; agree; tally; ~сь харáктером, get on, hit it off.
сок, -а (-у), *loc.* -ý, juice; sap; в (пóлном) ~ý, in the prime of life. **соковыжимáлка,** -и, juicer, juice-extractor.
сóкол, -а, falcon.
сократúть, -ащý *perf.*, **сокращáть,** -áю *imp.* shorten; curtail; abbreviate; abridge; reduce, cut down; dismiss, discharge, lay off; cancel; **~ся,** grow shorter, get shorter; decrease, decline; cut down; be cancelled; contract. **сокращéние,** -я, shortening; abridgement; abbreviation; reduction, cutting down; curtailment; cancellation; contraction; ~ штáтов, staff reduction; уволúть по сокращéнию штáтов, dismiss as redundant. **сокращённ|ый,** brief; abbreviated; ~ое слóво, abbreviation.
сокровéнный, secret, concealed; innermost. **сокрóвище,** -а, treasure. **сокрóвищница,** -ы, treasure-house, treasury.
сокрушáть, -áю *imp.*, **сокрушúть,** -шý *perf.* shatter; smash; crush; distress, grieve; **~ся,** grieve, be distressed. **сокрушéние,** -я, smashing, shattering; grief, distress. **сокрушённый;** -ён, -á, grief-stricken. **сокрушúтельный,** shattering; crippling, withering, destructive.
сокры́тие, -я, concealment. **сокры́ть,** -рóю *perf.* conceal, hide, cover up; **~ся,** hide, conceal oneself.
со|лгáть, -лгý, -лжёшь; ~áл, -á, -о *perf.*
солдáт, -а; *gen. pl.* -áт, soldier. **солдáтский** soldier's; army.
солéние, -я, salting; pickling. **солёный;** сóлон, -á, -о, salt; salty; salted; pickled; corned; spicy; hot. **солéнье,** -я, salted food(s); pickles.
солидáрность, -и, solidarity; collective (joint) responsibility. **солидáрный,** at one, in sympathy; collective, joint, solidary. **солúдность,** -и, solidity; reliability. **солúдн|ый,** solid; strong, sound; reliable; respectable; sizeable; ~ый вóзраст, middle age; человéк ~ых лет, a middle-aged man.
солúст, -а, **солúстка,** -и, soloist.
солúть, -лю, сóлúшь *imp.* (*perf.* по~) salt; pickle, corn.
сóлнечн|ый, sun; solar; sunny; ~ый свет, sunlight, sunshine; ~ый удáр, sunstroke; ~ые часы́, sundial. **сóлнце** (-*on*-), -а, sun. **солнцепёк,** -а; на ~е, right in the sun, in the full blaze of the sun. **солнцестоя́ние,** -я, solstice.
соловéй, -вья́, nightingale. **соловьúный,** nightingale's.
сóлод, -а (-у), malt.
солóдка, -и, liquorice. **солодкóвый,** liquorice.
солóма, -ы, straw; thatch. **солóменн|ый,** straw; straw-coloured; ~ая вдовá, grass widow; ~ая кры́ша, thatch, thatched roof. **солóминка,** -и, straw.
сóлон, etc.: see солёный. **солонúна,** -ы, salted beef, corned beef. **солóнка,** -и, salt-cellar. **солончáк,** -á, saline soil; *pl.* salt marshes. **соль**[1], -и; *pl.* -и, -éй, salt.
соль[2], *n. indecl.* G; sol, soh.
сóльный, solo.
солью́, etc.: see слить.
соляно́й, соля́ный, salt, saline; соля́ная кислотá, hydrochloric acid.
сóмкнутый, close; ~ строй, close order. **сомкнýть,** -нý, -нёшь *perf.* (*imp.* смыкáть) close; **~ся,** close, close up.
сомневáться, -áюсь *imp.* doubt, have doubts; question; worry; не ~ в + *prep.* have no doubts of. **сомнéние,** -я, doubt; uncertainty; без сомнéния, without doubt, undoubtedly. **сомнúтельн|ый,** doubtful, questionable; dubious; equivocal; **~о,** it is doubtful, it is open to question.
сомнý, etc.: see смять.
сон, сна, sleep; dream; вúдеть во сне, dream, dream about. **сонлúвость,** -и, sleepiness, drowsiness; somnolence. **сонлúвый,** sleepy, drowsy; somnolent. **сóнный,** sleepy, drowsy; somnolent; slumberous; sleeping, soporific.
соображáть, -áю *imp.*, **сообразúть,** -ажý *perf.* consider, ponder, think out;

weigh; understand, grasp; think up, arrange; have a quick one, have a round of drinks. **сообрази́тельный,** quick-witted, quick, sharp, bright.

сообра́зный с + *instr.* conformable to, in conformity with, consistent with. **сообразова́ть,** -зу́ю *perf.* and *imp.* conform, make conformable; adapt; **~ся,** conform, adapt oneself.

сообща́ *adv.* together, jointly. **сообща́ть,** -а́ю *imp.,* **сообщи́ть,** -щу́ *perf.* communicate, report, announce; impart; + *dat.* inform of, tell that. **сообще́ние,** -я, communication report; information; announcement; connection.

сооруди́ть, -ужу́ *perf.,* **сооружа́ть,** -а́ю *imp.* build erect. **сооруже́ние,** -я, building; erection; construction; structure.

соотве́тственно *adv.* accordingly, correspondingly; *prep.* + *dat.* according to, in accordance with, in conformity with, in compliance with. **соотве́тственный,** corresponding. **соотве́тствие,** -я, accordance, conformity, correspondence. **соотве́тствовать,** -твую *imp.* correspond, conform, be in keeping. **соотве́тствующий,** corresponding; proper, appropriate, suitable.

сопе́рник, -а, rival. **сопе́рничать,** -аю *imp.* be rivals; compete, vie. **сопе́рничество,** -а, rivalry.

сопе́ть, -плю́ *imp.* breathe heavily; sniff; snuffle; huff and puff.

со́пка, -и, knoll, hill, mound.

сопли́вый, snotty.

сопостави́мый, comparable. **сопоста́вить,** -влю *perf.,* **сопоставля́ть,** -я́ю *imp.* compare. **сопоставле́ние,** -я, comparison.

соприкаса́ться, -а́юсь *imp.,* **соприкосну́ться,** -ну́сь, -нёшься *perf.* adjoin, be contiguous (to); come into contact. **соприкоснове́ние,** -я, contiguity; contact.

сопроводи́тель, -я *m.* escort. **сопроводи́тельный** accompanying. **сопроводи́ть,** -ожу́ *perf.,* **сопровожда́ть,** -а́ю *imp.* accompany; escort. **сопровожде́ние,** -я, accompaniment; escort.

сопротивле́ние, -я, resistance; opposition. **сопротивля́ться,** -я́юсь *imp.* + *dat.* resist, oppose.

сопу́тствовать, -твую *imp.* + *dat.* accompany.

сопью́сь, etc.: see спи́ться.

сор, -а (-у), litter, dust, rubbish.

сораз́мерить, -рю *perf.,* **соразмеря́ть,** -я́ю *imp.* proportion, balance, match. **соразме́рный,** proportionate, commensurate.

сорва́ть, -ву́, -вёшь; -а́л, -а́, -о *perf.* (*imp.* срыва́ть) tear off, away, down; break off; pick, pluck; get, extract; break; smash, wreck, ruin, spoil; vent; **~ся,** break away, break loose; fall, come down; fall through, fall to the ground, miscarry; ~ с ме́ста, dart off; ~ с пе́тель, come off its hinges.

с|организова́ть, -зу́ю *perf.*

соревнова́ние, -я, competition; contest; tournament; event; emulation. **соревнова́ться,** -ну́юсь *imp.* compete, contend. **соревну́ющийся** *sb.* competitor, contestant, contender.

сори́ть, -рю́ *imp.* (*perf.* на~) + *acc.* or *instr.* litter; throw about. **со́рн|ый,** dust, rubbish, refuse; ~ая трава́, weed, weeds. **сорня́к,** -а́, weed.

со́рок, -а́, forty.

соро́ка, -и, magpie.

сороков|о́й, fortieth; ~ы́е го́ды, the forties.

соро́чка, -и, shirt; blouse; shift.

сорт, -а; *pl.* -а́, grade, quality; brand; sort, kind, variety. **сортирова́ть,** -ру́ю *imp.* (*perf.* рас~) sort, assort, grade, size. **сортиро́вка,** -и, sorting, grading, sizing. **сортиро́вочный,** sorting; **~ая** *sb.* marshalling-yard. **сортиро́вщик,** -а, sorter. **со́ртность,** -и, grade, quality. **со́ртный,** of high quality. **сортово́й,** high-grade, of high quality.

соса́ть, -су́, -сёшь *imp.* suck.

со|сва́тать, -аю *perf.*

сосе́д, -а; *pl.* -и, neighbour. **сосе́дний,** neighbouring; adjacent, next; ~ дом, the house next door. **сосе́дский,** neighbours', neighbouring, next-door. **сосе́дство,** -а, neighbourhood, vicinity.

соси́ска, -и, sausage; frankfurter.

со́ска, -и, (baby's) dummy.

соска́кивать, -аю *imp.* of соскочи́ть.

соска́льзывать, -аю *imp.*, **соскользну́ть, -ну́, -нёшь** *perf.* slide down, glide down; slip off, slide off.
соскочи́ть, -чу́, -чишь *perf.* (*imp.* соска́кивать) jump off, leap off; jump down, leap down; come off; vanish suddenly.
соску́читься, -чусь *perf.* get bored, be bored; ~ по, miss.
сослага́тельный, subjunctive.
сосла́ть, сошлю́, -лёшь *perf.* (*imp.* ссыла́ть) exile, banish, deport; **~ся** на + *acc.* refer to, allude to; cite, quote; plead, allege.
сосло́вие, -я, estate; corporation, professional association.
сосна́, -ы́; *pl.* -ы, -сен, pine(-tree). **сосно́вый,** pine; deal.
соснуть, -ну́, -нёшь *perf.* have a nap.
сосо́к, -ска́, nipple, teat.
сосредото́ченность, -и, concentration. **сосредото́ченный,** concentrated. **сосредото́чивать, -аю** *imp.*, **сосредото́чить, -чу** *perf.* concentrate; focus; **~ся,** concentrate.
соста́в, -а, composition, make-up; structure; compound; staff; personnel; membership; strength; train; в ~е + *gen.* numbering, consisting of, amounting to; в по́лном ~е, with its full complement; in, at, full strength; in a body. **составúтель, -я** *m.* compiler, author. **соста́вить, -влю** *perf.*, **составля́ть, -я́ю** *imp.* put together; make (up); compose; draw up; compile; work out; form; construct; be, constitute; amount to, total; ~ в сре́днем, average; **~ся,** form, be formed, come into being. **составно́й,** compound, composite; sectional; component, constituent.
со|ста́рить(ся, -рю(сь *perf.*
состоя́ние, -я, state, condition; position; status; fortune; в состоя́нии + *inf.* able to, in a position to. **состоя́тельный,** solvent; well-off, well-to-do; well-grounded. **состоя́ть, -ою́** *imp.* be; + из + *gen.* consist of, comprise, be made up of; + в + *prep.* consist in, lie in, be; ~ в до́лжности + *gen.* occupy the post of. **состоя́ться, -ои́тся** *perf.* take place.
сострада́ние, -я, compassion, sympathy. **сострада́тельный,** compassionate, sympathetic.
с|остри́ть, -рю́ *perf.* **со|стря́пать, -аю** *perf.*
со|стыкова́ть, -у́ю *perf.*, **состыко́вывать, -аю** *imp.* dock; **~ся,** dock.
состяза́ние, -я, competition, contest; match; уча́стник состяза́ния, competitor. **состяза́ться, -а́юсь** *imp.* compete, contend.
сосу́д, -а, vessel.
сосу́лька, -и, icicle.
со|счита́ть, -а́ю *perf.* **сот;** see сто.
со|твори́ть, -рю́ *perf.*
со́тенная *sb.* hundred-rouble note.
со|тка́ть, -ку́, -кёшь; -а́л, -ала́, -о *perf.*
со́тня, -и; *gen. pl.* -тен, a hundred.
сотови́дный, honeycomb. **со́товый,** honeycomb; ~ мёд, honey in the comb.
сотру́, etc.: see стере́ть.
сотру́дник, -а, collaborator; employee, assistant, official; contributor. **сотру́дничать, -аю** *imp.* collaborate; + в + *prep.* contribute to. **сотру́дничество, -а,** collaboration; co-operation.
сотряса́ть, -а́ю *imp.*, **сотрясти́, -су́, -сёшь; -я́с, -ла́** *perf.* shake; **~ся,** shake, tremble. **сотрясе́ние, -я,** shaking; concussion.
со́ты, -ов *pl.* honeycomb; мёд в со́тах, honey in the comb.
со́тый, hundredth.
со́ус, -а (-у), sauce; gravy; dressing.
соуча́стие, -я, participation, taking part; complicity. **соуча́стник, -а,** partner; participant; accessory, accomplice.
соха́, -и́; *pl.* -и, (wooden) plough.
со́хнуть, -ну; сох *imp.* (*perf.* вы́~, за~, про~) dry, get dry; become parched; wither.
сохране́ние, -я, preservation; conservation; care, custody, charge, keeping; retention. **сохрани́ть, -ню́** *perf.*, **сохраня́ть, -я́ю** *imp.* preserve, keep; keep safe; retain, reserve; **~ся,** remain (intact); last out, hold out; be well preserved. **сохра́нность, -и,** safety, undamaged state; safe-keeping. **сохра́нный,** safe.

соц- *abbr.* in *comb.* of социа́льный, social; социалисти́ческий, socialist. **соцреали́зм,** -а, socialist realism. **~соревнова́ние,** -я, socialist emulation. **~стра́х,** -а, social insurance.

социа́л-демокра́т, -а, Social Democrat. **социа́л-демократи́ческий,** Social-Democratic. **социализа́ция,** -и, socialization. **социализи́ровать,** -рую *perf.* and *imp.* socialize. **социали́ст,** -а, socialist. **социалисти́ческий,** socialist. **социа́льн|ый,** social; ~ое обеспече́ние, social security; ~ое положе́ние, social status; ~ое страхова́ние, social insurance. **социо́лог,** -а, sociologist.

соч. *abbr.* сочине́ния, works.

сочета́ние, -я, combination. **сочета́ть,** -а́ю *perf.* and *imp.* combine; + с + *instr.* go with, harmonize with; match; ~ бра́ком, marry; **~ся,** combine; harmonize; match; ~ся бра́ком, be married.

сочине́ние, -я, composition; work; essay; co-ordination. **сочини́ть,** -ню́ *perf.*, **сочиня́ть,** -я́ю *imp.* compose; write; make up, fabricate.

сочи́ться, -и́тся *imp.* ooze (out), trickle; ~ кро́вью, bleed.

сочлени́ть, -ню́ *perf.*, **сочленя́ть,** -я́ю *imp.* join, couple.

со́чный; -чен, -чна́, -о, juicy; succulent; rich; lush.

сочту́, etc.: see счесть.

сочу́вственный, sympathetic. **сочу́вствие,** -я, sympathy. **сочу́вствовать,** -твую *imp.* + *dat.* sympathize with, feel for.

сошёл, etc.: see сойти́. **сошлю́,** etc.: see сосла́ть. **сошью́,** etc.: see сшить.

сощу́ривать, -аю *imp.*, **со|щу́рить,** -рю *perf.* screw up, narrow; **~ся,** screw up one's eyes; narrow.

сою́з[1], -а, union; alliance; agreement; league. **сою́з**[2], -а, conjunction. **сою́зник,** -а, ally. **сою́зный,** allied; of the (Soviet) Union.

СП (*espé*) *m. indecl. abbr.* Се́верный по́люс, North Pole.

спад, -а, slump, recession; abatement. **спада́ть,** -а́ет *imp.* of спасть.

спа́ивать, -аю *imp.* of спая́ть, споить.

спа́йка, -и, soldered joint; solidarity, unity.

с|пали́ть, -лю́ *perf.*

спа́льник, -а, sleeping-bag. **спа́льн|ый,** sleeping; ~ый ваго́н, sleeper, sleeping-car; ~ое ме́сто, berth, bunk. **спа́льня,** -и; *gen. pl.* -лен, bedroom; bedroom suite.

спа́ржа, -и, asparagus.

спартакиа́да, -ы, sports, sports meeting.

спа́рывать, -аю *imp.* of споро́ть.

спаса́ние, -я, rescuing, life-saving. **спаса́тельн|ый,** rescue, life-saving; ~ый круг, lifebuoy; ~ый по́яс, lifebelt; ~ая экспеди́ция, rescue party. **спаса́ть(ся,** -а́ю(сь *imp.* of спасти́(сь. **спасе́ние,** -я, rescuing, saving; rescue, escape; salvation. **спаси́бо,** thanks; thank you. **спаси́тель,** -я *m.* rescuer, saver; saviour. **спаси́тельный,** saving; of rescue, of escape; salutary.

с|пасова́ть, -су́ю *perf.*

спасти́, -су́, -сёшь; спас, -ла́ *perf.* (*imp.* спаса́ть) save; rescue; **~сь,** save oneself, escape; be saved.

спасть, -адёт *perf.* (*imp.* спада́ть) fall (down); abate.

спать, сплю; -ал, -а́, -о *imp.* sleep, be asleep; лечь ~, go to bed; пора́ ~, it is bedtime.

спа́янность, -и, cohesion, unity; solidarity. **спа́янный,** united. **спая́ть,** -я́ю *perf.* (*imp.* спа́ивать) solder together, weld; unite, knit together.

спекта́кль, -я *m.* performance.

спектр, -а, spectrum.

спекули́ровать, -рую *imp.* speculate; profiteer; gamble; + на + *prep.* gamble on, reckon on; profit by. **спекуля́нт,** -а, speculator, profiteer. **спекуля́ция,** -и, speculation; profiteering; gamble.

с|пелена́ть, -а́ю *perf.*

спелео́лог, -а, caver, pot-holer.

спе́лый, ripe.

сперва́ *adv.* at first; first.

спе́реди *adv.* in front at the front, from the front; *prep.* + *gen.* (from) in front of.

спёртый, close, stuffy.

спеси́вый, arrogant, haughty, lofty. **спесь,** -и, arrogance, haughtiness, loftiness.

спеть[1], -éет *imp.* (*perf.* по~) ripen.

с|петь[2], спою́, споёшь *perf.*

спец, -ецá; *pl.* -éцы́, -ев or -óв, *abbr.* specialist, expert, authority.

спец- *abbr.* in *comb.* of специа́льный, special. **спецкóр,** -а, special correspondent. **~кýрс,** -а, special course of lectures. **~одéжда,** -ы, working clothes, protective clothing; overalls.

специализи́роваться, -руюсь *perf.* and *imp.* specialize. **специали́ст,** -а, specialist, expert, authority. **специа́льность,** -и, speciality, special interest; profession; trade. **специа́льный,** special; specialist; ~ тéрмин, technical term.

специ́фика, -и, specific character. **специфи́ческий,** specific.

спецóвка, -и, protective clothing, working clothes; overall(s).

спеши́ть, -шý *imp.* (*perf.* по~), hurry, be in a hurry; make haste, hasten; hurry up; be fast.

спéшка, -и, hurry, haste, rush. **спéшн|ый,** urgent, pressing; ~ый закáз, rush order; ~ая пóчта, express delivery.

спивáться, -áюсь *imp.* of спи́ться.

с|пики́ровать, -рую *perf.*

спи́ливать, -аю *imp.*, **спили́ть,** -лю́, -лишь *perf.* saw down; saw off.

спинá, -ы́; *acc.* -у; *pl.* -ы, back. **спи́нка,** -и, back. **спиннóй,** spinal; ~ мозг, spinal cord; ~ хребéт, spinal column.

спирт, -а (-у), alcohol, spirit(s). **спиртн|óй,** spirituous; ~ы́е напи́тки, spirits; **~óе** *sb.* spirits. **спиртóвка,** -и, spirit-stove. **спиртовóй,** spirit, spirituous.

списáть, -ишý, -и́шешь *perf.*, **спи́сывать,** -аю *imp.* copy; crib; write off; **~ся,** exchange letters. **спи́сок,** -ска, list; roll; record; manuscript copy; ~ избирáтелей, voters' list, electoral roll; ~ уби́тых и рáненых, casualty list.

спи́ться, сопью́сь, -ьёшься; -и́лся, -áсь *perf.* (*imp.* спивáться) take to drink, become a drunkard.

спи́хивать, -аю *imp.*, **спихнýть,** -нý, -нёшь *perf.* push aside; push down.

спи́ца, -ы, knitting-needle; spoke.

спи́чечн|ый, match; ~ая корóбка, match-box. **спи́чка,** -и, match.

спишý etc.: see списáть.

сплав[1], -а, floating, rafting. **сплав**[2], -а, alloy. **сплáвить**[1], -влю *perf.*, **сплавля́ть**[1], -я́ю *imp.* float; raft; get rid of. **сплáвить**[2], -влю *perf.*, **сплавля́ть**[2], -я́ю *imp.* alloy; **~ся,** fuse, coalesce.

с|плани́ровать, -рую *perf.* **сплáчивать(ся,** -аю(сь *imp.* of сплоти́ть(ся.

сплёвывать, -аю *imp.* of сплю́нуть.

с|плести́, -етý, -етёшь; -ёл, -á *perf.*, **сплетáть,** -áю *imp.* weave; plait; interlace. **сплетéние,** -я, interlacing; plexus.

сплéтник, -а, **-ница,** -ы, gossip, scandalmonger. **сплéтничать,** -аю *imp.* (*perf.* на~) gossip, tittle-tattle; talk scandal. **сплéтня,** -и; *gen. pl.* -тен, gossip, scandal.

сплоти́ть, -очý *perf.* (*imp.* сплáчивать) join; unite, rally; ~ ряды́, close the ranks; **~ся,** unite, rally; close the ranks. **сплочённость,** -и, cohesion, unity. **сплочённый;** -ён, -á, united, firm; unbroken.

сплошнóй, solid; all-round, complete; unbroken, continuous; sheer, utter, unreserved. **сплошь** *adv.* all over; throughout; without a break; completely, utterly; without exception; ~ да ря́дом, nearly always; pretty often.

с|плутовáть, -тýю *perf.*

сплывáть, -áет *imp.*, **сплыть,** -ывёт; -ыл, -á, -о *perf.* sail down, float down; be carried away; overflow, run over; бы́ло да сплы́ло those were the days; it's all over; **~ся,** run (together), merge, blend.

сплю: see спать.

сплю́нуть, -ну *perf.* (*imp.* сплёвывать) spit; spit out.

сплю́щенный, flattened out. **сплю́щивать,** -аю *imp.*, **сплю́щить,** -щу *perf.* flatten; **~ся,** become flat.

с|плясáть, -яшý, -я́шешь *perf.*

сподви́жник, -а, comrade-in-arms.

споить, -ою́, -óишь *perf.* (*imp.* спáивать) accustom to drinking, make a drunkard of.

споко́йн|ый, quiet; calm, tranquil; placid, serene; composed; comfortable; ~ой но́чи! good night! **споко́йствие,** -я, quiet; tranquillity; calm, calmness; order; composure, serenity.
споласкивать, -аю *imp.* of сполосну́ть.
сполза́ть. -а́ю *imp.*, **сползти́,** -зу́, -зёшь; -олз, -ла́ *perf.* climb down; slip (down); fall away.
сполна́ *adv.* completely, in full.
сполосну́ть, -ну́, -нёшь *perf.* (*imp.* спола́скивать) rinse.
спор, -а (-у), argument; controversy; debate; dispute. **спо́рить,** -рю *imp.* (*perf.* по~) argue; dispute; debate; bet, have a bet. **спо́рный,** disputable, debatable, questionable; disputed, at issue; ~ вопро́с, moot point, vexed question; ~ мяч, jump ball; held ball.
споро́ть, -рю́, -решь *perf.* (*imp.* спа́рывать) rip off.
спорт, -а, sport sports; лы́жный ~, skiing; парашю́тный ~, parachute-jumping. **спорти́вн|ый,** sports; ~ый зал, gymnasium; ~ая площа́дка, sports ground, playing-field; ~ые состяза́ния, sports. **спортсме́н,** -а, **спортсме́нка,** -и, athlete player.
спо́рый; -ор, -а́, -о, successful, profitable; skilful, efficient.
спо́соб, -а, way, manner, method; mode; means; ~ употребле́ния directions for use; таки́м ~ом, in this way. **спосо́бность,** -и, ability, talent, aptitude, flair; capacity. **спосо́бный,** able; talented, gifted, clever; capable. **спосо́бствовать,** -твую *imp.* (*perf.* по~) + *dat.* assist; be conducive to, further, promote, make for.
споткну́ться, -ну́сь, -нёшься *perf.*, **спотыка́ться,** -а́юсь *imp.* stumble; get stuck, come to a stop.
спохвати́ться, -ачу́сь, -а́тишься *perf.*, **спохва́тываться,** -аюсь *imp.* remember suddenly.
спою́, etc.: see спеть, споить.
спра́ва *adv.* to the right.
справедли́вость, -и, justice; equity; fairness; truth, correctness. **справедли́вый.** just; equitable, fair; justified.
спра́вить, -влю *perf.*, **справля́ть,** -я́ю *imp.* celebrate. **спра́виться**[1], -влюсь *perf.* **справля́ться,** -я́юсь *imp.* с + *instr.* cope with, manage; deal with. **спра́виться**[2], -влюсь *perf.*, **справля́ться,** -я́юсь *imp.* ask, inquire; inform oneself; ~ в словаре́, consult a dictionary. **спра́вка,** -и, information; reference; certificate; навести́ спра́вку, inquire; наводи́ть спра́вку, make inquiries. **спра́вочник,** -а, reference-book, handbook, guide, directory. **спра́вочн|ый,** inquiry, information; ~ая кни́га, reference-book, handbook.
спра́шивать(ся, -аю(сь *imp.* of спроси́ть(ся. **с|провоци́ровать,** -рую *perf.* **с|проекти́ровать,** -рую *perf.*
спрос, -а (-у), demand; asking; без ~у, without asking leave, without permission; по́льзоваться (больши́м) ~ом, be in (great) demand; ~ на + *acc.* demand for, run on. **спроси́ть,** -ошу́, -о́сишь *perf.* (*imp.* спра́шивать) ask (for); inquire; ask to see; + с + *gen.* make answer for, make responsible for; **~ся,** ask permission.
спросо́нок *adv.* (being) only half-awake.
спры́гивать, -аю *imp.*, **спры́гнуть,** -ну *perf.* jump off, jump down.
спры́скивать, -аю *imp.*, **спры́снуть,** -ну *perf.* sprinkle.
спряга́ть, -а́ю *imp.* (*perf.* про~) conjugate; **~ся,** be conjugated. **спряже́ние,** -я, conjugation.
с|прясть, -яду́, -ядёшь; -ял, -я́ла́, -о *perf.* **с|пря́тать(ся,** -я́чу(сь *perf.*
спу́гивать, -аю *imp.*, **спугну́ть,** -ну́, -нёшь *perf.* frighten off, scare off.
спуртова́ть, -ту́ю *perf.* and *imp.* spurt.
спуск, -а, lowering, hauling down; descent; descending; landing; release; draining; slope. **спуска́ть,** -а́ю *imp.*, **спусти́ть,** -ущу́, -у́стишь *perf.* let down, lower; haul down; let go, let loose release; let out, drain; send out; go down; forgive, let off, let go, let pass; lose; throw away, squander; ~ кора́бль, launch a ship; ~ куро́к, pull the trigger; ~ пе́тлю, drop a stitch; ~ с це́пи, unchain; спустя́ рукава́, carelessly. **спускн|о́й,** drain; ~а́я труба, drain-pipe. **спусково́й,** trigger. **спустя́** *prep.* + *acc.* after; later; немно́го ~ not long after.

с|пу́тать(ся, -аю(сь *perf.*
спу́тник, -а, satellite, sputnik; (travelling) companion; fellow-traveller; concomitant.
спущу́, etc.: see спусти́ть.
спя́чка, -и, hibernation; sleepiness, lethargy.
ср. *abbr.* сравни́, compare, cf.; сре́дний, mean.
сравне́ние, -я, comparison; simile; по сравне́нию с + *instr.*, as compared with, as against.
сра́внивать, -аю *imp.* of сравни́ть, сравня́ть.
сравни́тельно *adv.* comparatively; ~ с + *instr.* compared with. **сравни́тельный,** comparative. **сравни́ть,** -ню́ *perf.* (*imp.* сра́внивать) compare; **~ся** с + *instr.* compare with, come up to, touch.
с|равня́ть, -я́ю *perf.* (*imp.* also сра́внивать) make even, make equal; level.
сража́ть, -а́ю *imp.*, **срази́ть,** -ажу́ *perf.* slay, strike down, fell; overwhelm, crush; **~ся,** fight, join battle. **сраже́ние,** -я, battle, engagement.
сра́зу *adv.* at once; straight away, right away.
срам, -а (-у), shame. **срами́ть,** -млю́ *imp.* (*perf.* о~) shame, put to shame; **~ся,** cover oneself with shame. **срамни́к,** -а́, shameless person. **срамно́й,** shameless. **срамота́,** -ы́, shame.
сраста́ние, -я, growing together; knitting. **сраста́ться,** -а́ется *imp.*, **срасти́сь,** -тётся; сро́сся, -ла́сь *perf.* grow together; knit.
сребролюби́вый, money-grubbing. **среброно́сный,** argentiferous.
среда́[1], -ы́; *pl.* -ы, environment, surroundings; milieu; habitat; medium; в на́шей среде́, in our midst, among us. **среда́**[2], -ы́, *acc.* -у; *pl.* -ы, -а́м or -ам, Wednesday. **среди́** *prep.* + *gen.* among, amongst; amidst; in the middle of; ~ бе́ла дня, in broad daylight.
средиземномо́рский, Mediterranean.
среди́на, -ы middle. **сре́дне** *adv.* middling, so-so. **средневеко́вый,** medieval. **средневеко́вье,** -я, the Middle Ages. **средневи́к,** -а́, middle-distance runner. **сре́дн|ий,** middle; medium; mean; average; middling; secondary; neuter; ~ие века́, the Middle Ages; ~яя величина́, mean value; ~ий па́лец, middle finger, second finger; **~ее** *sb.* mean, average; выше ~его, above (the) average.
сре́дство, -а, means; remedy; *pl.* means; resources; credits; жить не по сре́дствам, live beyond one's means.
срез, -а, cut; section; shear, shearing; slice, slicing. **с|ре́зать,** -е́жу *perf.* **среза́ть,** -а́ю *imp.* cut off; slice, cut, chop; fail, plough; **~ся,** fail, be ploughed.
с|репети́ровать, -рую *perf.*
срисова́ть, -су́ю *perf.*, **срисо́вывать,** -аю *imp.* copy.
с|рифмова́ть(ся, -му́ю(сь *perf.* **с|ровня́ть,** -я́ю *perf.*
сродство́, -а́, affinity.
срок, -а (-у), date; term; time, period; в ~, к ~у, in time to time.
сро́сся, etc.: see срасти́сь.
сро́чно *adv.* urgently; quickly. **сро́чность,** -и, urgency; hurry; что за ~? what's the hurry? **сро́чный,** urgent, pressing; at a fixed date; for a fixed period; periodic, routine; ~ зака́з, rush order.
сро́ю, etc.: see срыть.
сруб, -а, felling; framework. **руба́ть,** -а́ю *imp.*, **с|руби́ть,** -блю́, -бишь *perf.* fell, cut down; build (of logs).
срыв, -а, disruption; derangement, frustration; foiling, spoiling, ruining, wrecking; ~ перегово́ров, breaking-off of talks, breakdown in negotiations.
срыва́ть[1]**(ся,** -а́ю(сь *imp.* of сорва́ть(ся.
срыва́ть[2], -а́ю *imp.*, **срыть,** сро́ю *perf.* raze, level, to the ground.
сря́ду *adv.* running.
ссади́на, -ы, scratch, abrasion. **ссади́ть,** -ажу́, -а́дишь *perf.*, **сса́живать,** -аю *imp.* set down; help down, help to alight; put off, turn off.
ссо́ра, -ы, quarrel; falling-out; slanging-match; быть в ссо́ре, be on bad terms, have fallen out. **ссо́рить,** -рю *imp.* (*perf.* по~) cause to quarrel, embroil; **~ся,** quarrel, fall out.

СССР (*esesesér*) *abbr.* Сою́з Сове́тских Социалисти́ческих Респу́блик, U.S.S.R.
ссу́да, -ы, loan. **ссуди́ть**, -ужу́, -у́дишь *perf.*, **ссужа́ть**, -а́ю *imp.* lend, loan.
с|сучи́ть, -чу́, -у́чи́шь *perf.*
ссыла́ть(ся, -а́ю(сь *imp.* of сосла́ть(ся. **ссы́лка**[1], -и, exile, banishment; deportation. **ссы́лка**[2], -и, reference. **ссы́льный**, **ссы́льная** *sb.* exile.
ссы́пать, -плю *perf.*, **ссыпа́ть**, -а́ю *imp.* pour. **ссыпно́й** пункт, grain-collecting station.
ст. *abbr.* статья́, article; столе́тие, century.
стабилиза́тор, -а, stabilizer; tail-plane. **стабилизи́ровать**, -рую *perf.* and *imp.*, **стабилизова́ть**, -зу́ю *perf.* and *imp.* stabilize; **~ся**, become stable. **стаби́льный**, stable, firm; ~ учёбник, standard textbook.
ста́вень, -вня; *gen. pl.* -вней *m.*, **ста́вня**, -и; *gen. pl.* -вен, shutter.
ста́вить, -влю *imp.* (*perf.* по~) put, place, set; stand; station; put up, erect; install; put in; put on apply; present, stage; stake. **ста́вка**[1], -и, rate; stake; ~ зарпла́ты, rate of pay. **ста́вка**[2], -и, headquarters.
ста́вня: see ста́вень.
стадио́н -а, stadium.
ста́дия, -и, stage.
ста́дность, -и, herd instinct. **ста́дный**, gregarious. **ста́до**, -а; *pl.* -а́, herd, flock.
стаж, -а length of service; record; probation. **стажёр**, -а, probationer, houseman; trainee. **стажи́ровать(ся**, -рую(сь *imp.* go through period of training.
ста́ивать, -ает *imp.* of стая́ть.
ста́йер, -а, long-distance runner, stayer.
стака́н, -а, glass, tumbler beaker.
сталелите́йный, steel-founding, steel-casting; ~ заво́д, steel foundry. **сталеплави́льный**, steel-making; ~ заво́д, steel works. **сталепрока́тный**, (steel-)rolling; ~ стан, rolling-mill.
ста́лкивать(ся, -аю(сь *imp.* of столкну́ть(ся.
ста́ло быть *conj.* consequently, therefore, so.
сталь, -и, steel. **стально́й**, steel.
стаме́ска, -и, chisel.
стан[1] -а, figure, torso.
стан[2], -а, camp.
стан[3], -а, mill.
станио́ль, -я *m.* foil, tinfoil.
станко́вый, machine; mounted; (free-)standing. **станкострое́ние**, -я, machine-tool engineering.
станови́ться, -влю́сь, -вишься *imp.* of стать.
стано́к, -нка́, machine tool, machine; bench; mount, mounting.
ста́ну, etc.: see стать.
станцио́нный, station. **ста́нция**, -и, station.
ста́пель, -я; *pl.* -я́ *m.* stocks.
ста́птывать(ся, -аю(сь *imp.* of стопта́ть(ся.
стара́ние, -я, effort, endeavour, pains, diligence. **стара́тель**, -я *m.* prospector (for gold), (gold-)digger. **стара́тельность**, -и, application, diligence. **стара́тельный**, diligent, painstaking, assiduous. **стара́ться**, -а́юсь *imp.* (*perf.* по~) try, endeavour; take pains; make an effort.
старе́ть, -е́ю *imp.* (*perf.* по~ у~) grow old, age. **ста́рец**, -рца, elder, (venerable) old man; hermit **стари́к**, -а́, old man. **старина́**, -ы́, antiquity, olden times; antique(s); old man, old fellow. **стари́нный**, ancient; old; antique. **ста́рить**, -рю *imp.* (*perf.* со~) age, make old; **~ся**, age, grow old.
старо- in *comb.* old. **старове́р**, -а, Old Believer. **~да́вний**, ancient. **~жи́л**, -а, old inhabitant; old resident. **~заве́тный**, old-fashioned, conservative; antiquated. **~мо́дный**, old-fashioned, out-moded; out-of-date. **~печа́тный**; ~печа́тные кни́ги, early printed books. **~све́тский**, old-world; old-fashioned. **~славя́нский**, Old Slavonic.
ста́роста, -ы, head; senior; monitor; churchwarden. **ста́рость**, -и, old age.
старт, -а, start; на ~! on your marks! **ста́ртёр**, -а, starter. **стартова́ть**, -ту́ю *perf.* and *imp.* start. **ста́ртовый**, starting.
стару́ха, -и, old woman. **ста́рческ|ий**,

old man's; senile; ~ое слабоу́мие, senility, senile decay. **ста́рше,** *comp.* of ста́рый. **ста́рш|ий,** oldest, eldest; senior; superior; chief, head; upper, higher; ~ий адъюта́нт, adjutant; **~ие** *sb.* (one's) elders; **~ий** *sb.* chief; man in charge; кто здесь ~ий? who is in charge here? **старшина́,** -ы́ *m.* sergeant-major; petty officer; leader, senior representative doyen, foreman. **старшинство́,** -á, seniority; по старшинству́, by right of, in order of, seniority. **ста́рый;** -ар, -á, -о, old. **старьё,** -я́, old things, old clothes, old junk.

ста́скивать, -аю *imp.* of стащи́ть.

с|тасова́ть -су́ю *perf.*

стати́ст, -а, super, extra.

стати́стика, -и, statistics. **статисти́ческий,** statistical.

ста́тный, stately.

ста́тский, civil, civilian; State; ~ сове́тник, State Councillor (5th grade: see чин).

ста́туя, -и, statue.

стать, -а́ну *perf.* (*imp.* станови́ться) stand; take up position; stop, come to a halt; cost; suffice, do; begin, start; + *instr.* become, get, grow; + с + *instr.* become of happen to; не ~ *impers.* + *gen.* cease to be; disappear, be gone; его́ не ста́ло, he is no more; её отца́ давно́ не ста́ло, her father has been dead a long time; ~ в о́чередь, queue up; ~ в по́зу, strike an attitude; ~ на коле́ни, kneel; ~ на рабо́ту, begin work; часы́ ста́ли, the clock (has) stopped.

стать, -и; *gen. pl.* -е́й, need, necessity; physique, build; points; быть под ~, be well-matched; + *dat.* be like; с како́й ста́ти? why? what for?

ста́ться, -а́нется *perf.* happen; become; вполне́ мо́жет ~, it is quite possible.

статья́, -и́; *gen. pl.* -е́й, article; clause; item; matter, job; class, rating; э́то осо́бая ~, that is another matter.

стациона́р, -а, permanent establishment; hospital. **стациона́рный,** stationary; permanent, fixed; ~ больно́й, in-patient.

с|тача́ть, -а́ю *perf.*

ста́чечник, -а, striker. **ста́чка,** -и, strike.

с|тащи́ть, -щу́, -щишь *perf.* (*imp.* also ста́скивать) drag off, pull off; drag down; pinch, swipe, whip.

ста́я, -и, flock, flight; school, shoal; pack.

ста́ять, -а́ет *perf.* (*imp.* ста́ивать) melt.

ствол, -á, trunk; stem; bole, barrel; tube, pipe; shaft.

ство́рка, -и, leaf, fold; door, gate, shutter. **ство́рчатый,** folding; valved.

сте́бель, -бля; *gen. pl.* -бле́й *m.* stem, stalk. **стебе́льчатый,** stalky, stalk-like; ~ шов, feather-stitch.

стёганка, -и, quilted jacket. **стёган|ый,** quilted; ~ое одея́ло, quilt. **стега́ть**[1], -а́ю *imp.* (*perf.* вы́~) quilt.

стега́ть[2], -а́ю *imp.*, **стегну́ть,** -ну́ *perf.* (*perf.* also от~) whip, lash.

стежо́к, -жка́, stitch.

стёк, etc.: see стечь. **стека́ть(ся,** -а́ет(ся *imp.* of стечь(ся.

стеклене́ть, -е́ет *imp.* (*perf.* о~), become glassy. **стекло́,** -á; *pl.* -ёкла, -кол, glass; lens; (window-)pane.

стекло- in *comb.* glass. **стекловолокно́,** -á, glass fibre. **~ду́в,** -а, glass-blower. **~ма́сса,** -ы, molten glass. **~очисти́тель,** -я *m.* windscreen-wiper. **~пла́ст,** -а, fibreglass laminate. **~ре́з,** -а, glass-cutter. **~тка́нь,** -и, fibreglass.

стекля́нн|ый, glass; glassy; ~ый колпа́к, bell-glass, glass case; ~ая посу́да, glassware. **стеко́льный,** glass; vitreous. **стеко́льщик,** -а glazier.

стели́ть: see стлать.

стелла́ж, -á, shelves, shelving; rack, stand.

сте́лька, -и, insole, sock.

сте́льная коро́ва, cow in calf.

стелю́, etc.: see стлать.

с|темне́ть, -е́ет *perf.*

стена́, -ы́, *acc.* -у; *pl.* -ы, -а́м, wall. **стенгазе́та,** -ы, wall newspaper. **стенно́й,** wall; mural.

стеногра́мма, -ы, shorthand record. **стено́граф,** -а, **стенографи́ст,** -а, **стенографи́стка,** -и, stenographer, shorthand-writer. **стенографи́ровать,** -рую *perf.* and *imp.* take down in

shorthand. **стенографи́ческий,** shorthand. **стеногра́фия,** -и, shorthand, stenography.
сте́нопись, -и, mural.
степе́нный, staid, steady; middle-aged.
сте́пень, -и; *gen. pl.* -е́й, degree; extent; power.
степно́й, steppe. **степня́к,** -а́, steppe-dweller; steppe horse. **степь,** -и, *loc.* -и́; *gen. pl.* -е́й, steppe.
стерегу́, etc.: see стере́чь.
стере́ть, сотру́, сотрёшь; стёр *perf.* (*imp.* стира́ть) wipe off; rub out, erase; rub sore; grind down; **~ся,** rub off; fade; wear down; be effaced, be obliterated.
стере́чь, -регу́, -режёшь; -ёг, -ла́ *imp.* guard; watch (over); watch for.
сте́ржень, -жня *m.* pivot; shank, rod; core. **стержнево́й,** pivoted; ~ вопро́с, key question.
сте́рлядь, -и; *gen. pl.* -е́й, sterlet.
стерпе́ть, -плю́, -пишь *perf.* bear, suffer, endure.
стёртый, worn, effaced.
стесне́ние, -я, constraint. **стесни́тельный,** shy; inhibited; difficult, inconvenient. **с|тесни́ть,** -ню́ *perf.,* **стесня́ть,** -я́ю *imp.* constrain; hamper; inhibit. **с|тесни́ться,** -ню́сь *perf.,* **стесня́ться,** -я́юсь *imp.* (*perf.* also по~) + *inf.* feel too shy to, be ashamed to; (+ *gen.*) feel shy (of).
стече́ние, -я, confluence; ~ наро́да, concourse; ~ обстоя́тельств, coincidence. **стечь,** -чёт; -ёк, -ла́ *perf.* (*imp.* стека́ть) flow down; **~ся,** flow together; gather, throng.
стиль, -я *m.* style. **сти́льный,** stylish; period.
сти́мул, -а, stimulus. incentive. **стимули́ровать,** -рую *perf.* and *imp.* stimulate.
стипендиа́т, -а, grant-aided student. **стипе́ндия,** -и, grant.
стира́льный, washing.
стира́ть[1](ся, -а́ю(сь *imp.* of стере́ть(ся.
стира́ть[2], -а́ю *imp.* (*perf.* вы́~) wash, launder; **~ся,** wash. **сти́рка,** -и, washing, wash, laundering, laundry.
сти́скивать, -аю *imp.,* **сти́снуть,** -ну *perf.* squeeze; clench; hug.
стих, -а́, verse; line; *pl.* verses, poetry.
стиха́ть, -а́ю *imp.* of сти́хнуть.
стихи́йн|ый, elemental; spontaneous, uncontrolled; ~ое бе́дствие, disaster. **стихи́я,** -и, element.
сти́хнуть, -ну; стих *perf.* (*imp.* стиха́ть) abate, subside; die down; calm down.
стихове́дение, -я, prosody. **стихосложе́ние,** -я, versification; prosody. **стихотворе́ние,** -я, poem. **стихотво́рный,** in verse form; of verse; poetic; ~ разме́р, metre.
стлать (*sl-*), **стели́ть,** стелю́, сте́лешь *imp.* (*perf.* по~) spread; ~ посте́ль, make a bed; ~ ска́терть, lay the cloth; **~ся,** spread; drift, creep.
сто, ста; *gen. pl.* сот, a hundred.
стог, -а, *loc.* -у́; *pl.* -а́, stack, rick.
стогра́дусный, centigrade.
сто́имость, -и, cost; value. **сто́ить,** -о́ю *imp.* cost; be worth; be worthy of, deserve; не сто́ит, don't mention it; сто́ит, it is worth while; ~ то́лько + *inf.* one has only to.
стой: see стоя́ть.
сто́йка, -и, counter, bar; support, prop; stanchion, upright; strut; set; stand, stance. **сто́йкий,** firm; stable; persistent; steadfast, staunch, steady. **сто́йкость,** -и, firmness, stability; steadfastness, staunchness; determination.
сто́йло, -а, stall. **стоймя́** *adv.* upright.
сток, -а, flow; drainage, outflow; drain, gutter; sewer.
стол, -а́, table; desk; board; cooking, cuisine; department, section; office, bureau.
столб, -а́, post, pole, pillar, column. **столбене́ть,** -е́ю *imp.* (*perf.* о~) be rooted to the ground, be transfixed. **столбе́ц,** -бца́, column. **сто́лбик,** -а, column; style; double crochet, treble. **столбня́к,** -а́, stupor; tetanus. **столбово́й,** main, chief.
столе́тие, -я, century; centenary. **столе́тний,** of a hundred years; a hundred years old; ~ стари́к, centenarian.
столи́ца, -ы, capital; metropolis. **столи́чный,** capital; of the capital.

столкновéние, -я, collision; clash. **столкнýть,** -нý, -нёшь *perf.* (*imp.* стáлкивать) push off, push away; cause to collide, bring into collision; bring together; **~ся,** collide, come into collision; clash, conflict; + с + *instr.* run into, bump into.

столовáться, -лýюсь *imp.* have meals, board, mess. **столóвая** *sb.* dining-room; mess; canteen; dining-room suite. **столóвый,** table; dinner; feeding, catering, messing.

столп, -á, pillar, column.

столпи́ться, -и́тся *perf.* crowd.

столь *adv.* so. **стóлько** *adv.* so much, so many.

столя́р, -á, joiner, carpenter. **столя́рный,** joiner's, carpenter's.

стометрóвка, -и, (the) hundred metres; hundred-metre event.

стон, -а, groan, moan. **стонáть,** -нý, -нешь *imp.* groan, moan.

стоп! *int.* stop!; *indecl. adj.* stop.

стопá[1], -ы́; *pl.* -ы, foot.

стопá[2], -ы́; *pl.* -ы, goblet.

стопá[3], -ы́; *pl.* -ы, ream; pile, heap. **стóпка**[1], -и, pile, heap.

стóпка[2], -и, small glass.

стóпор, -а, stop, catch, pawl. **стóпорить,** -рю *imp.* (*perf.* за~) stop, lock; slow down, bring to a stop; **~ся,** slow down, come to a stop.

стопроцéнтный, hundred-per-cent.

стоп-сигнáл, -а, brake-light.

стоптáть, -пчý, -пчешь *perf.* (*imp.* стáптывать) wear down; trample; **~ся,** wear down, be worn down.

с|торговáть(ся, -гýю(сь *perf.*

стóрож, -а; *pl.* -á, watchman, guard. **сторожев|óй,** watch; ~áя бýдка, sentry-box; ~óй корáбль, escort vessel; ~óе сýдно, patrol-boat. **сторожи́ть,** -жý *imp.* guard, watch, keep watch over.

сторонá, -ы́, *acc.* стóрону; *pl.* стóроны, -рóн, -áм, side; quarter; hand; feature, aspect; part; party; land, place; parts; в сторонé, aside, aloof; в стóрону, aside; на чужóй сторонé, in foreign parts; по ту стóрону + *gen.* across; on the other, the far, side of; с моéй стороны́, for my part; с однóй стороны́, on the one hand; шýтки в стóрону, joking apart. **сторони́ться,** -ню́сь, -нишься *imp.* (*perf.* по~) stand aside, make way; + *gen.* shun, avoid. **сторóнний,** strange, foreign; detached; indirect. **сторóнник,** -а, supporter, adherent, advocate.

стóчн|ый, sewage, drainage; ~ые вóды, sewage; ~ая трубá, drainpipe, sewer.

стоя́к, -á, post, stanchion, upright; stand-pipe; chimney. **стоя́нка,** -и, stop; parking; stopping place, parking space; stand; rank; moorage; site; ~ запрещенá! no parking; ~ такси́, taxi-rank. **стоя́ть,** -ою́ *imp.* (*perf.* по~) stand; be; be situated, lie; continue; stay; be stationed; stop; have stopped, have come to a stop; + за + *acc.* stand up for; мои́ часы́ стоя́т, my watch has stopped; рабóта стои́т, work has come to a standstill; стóй(те)! stop! halt!; ~ во главé + *gen.* head, be at the head of; ~ лáгерем, be encamped, be under canvas; ~ на колéнях, kneel, be kneeling; ~ у влáсти, be in power, be in office; стоя́ла хорóшая погóда, the weather kept fine. **стоя́чий,** standing; upright, vertical; stagnant.

стóящий deserving; worth-while.

стр. *abbr.* страни́ца, page.

страдáлец, -льца, sufferer. **страдáние,** -я, suffering. **страдáтельный,** passive. **страдáть,** -áю or -рáжду *imp.* (*perf.* по~) suffer; be subject; be in pain; be weak, be poor; ~ за + *gen.* feel for; ~ по + *dat.* or *prep.* miss, long for, pine for; ~ от зубнóй бóли, have toothache.

стрáжа, -и, guard, watch; взять под стрáжу, take into custody; под стрáжей, under arrest, in custody; стоя́ть на стрáже + *gen.* guard.

странá, -ы́; *pl.* -ы, country; land; ~ свéта, cardinal point.

страни́ца, -ы, page.

стрáнник, -а, **стрáнница,** -ы, wanderer; pilgrim.

стра́нно *adv.* strangely, oddly. **стра́нность, -и,** strangeness; oddity, eccentricity, singularity. **стра́нн|ый; -а́нен, -анна́, -о,** strange; funny, odd, queer.
стра́нствие, -я, wandering, journeying, travelling. **стра́нствовать, -твую** *imp.* wander, journey, travel.
страстн|о́й, of Holy Week; **~а́я** пя́тница, Good Friday. **стра́стный; -тен, -тна́, -о** passionate; impassioned; ardent. **страсть, -и;** *gen. pl.* **-е́й,** passion; + к + *dat.* passion for; до стра́сти, passionately. **страсть** *adv.* awfully, frightfully; an awful lot, a terrific number.
стратоста́т, -а, stratosphere balloon.
стра́ус, -а, ostrich. **стра́усовый,** ostrich.
страх, -а (-у), fear; terror; risk, responsibility; на свой ~, at one's own risk; под ~ом сме́рти, on pain of death. **страх** *adv.* terribly.
страхка́сса, -ы, insurance office. **страхова́ние, -я,** insurance; ~ жи́зни, life insurance; ~ от огня́, fire insurance. **страхова́ть, -ху́ю** *imp.* (*perf.* за~) insure (от + *gen.* against); **~ся,** insure oneself. **страхо́вка, -и,** insurance; guarantee.
стра́шно *adv.* terribly, awfully. **стра́шн|ый; -шен, -шна́, -о,** terrible, awful, dreadful, frightful, fearful; terrifying, frightening; ~ый сон, bad dream.
стрекоза́, -ы́; *pl.* **-ы,** dragonfly.
стре́кот, -а, стрекотня́, -и́, chirr; rattle, chatter, clatter. **стрекота́ть, -очу́, -о́чешь** *imp.* chirr; rattle, chatter, clatter.
стрела́, -ы́; *pl.* **-ы,** arrow; shaft; dart; arm, boom, jib; derrick. **стреле́ц, -льца́,** Sagittarius. **стре́лка, -и,** pointer, indicator; needle; arrow; spit; points. **стрелко́вый,** rifle; shooting, fire; small-arms; infantry. **стрелови́дность, -и,** angle, sweep. **стрелови́дн|ый,** arrow-shaped; ~ое крыло́, swept-back wing. **стрело́к, -лка́,** shot; rifleman, gunner. **стре́лочник, -а,** pointsman. **стрельба́, -ы́;** *pl.* **-ы,** shooting, firing; shoot, fire. **стрельну́ть, -ну́, -нёшь** *perf.* fire, fire a shot; rush away. **стре́льчатый,** lancet; arched, pointed. **стре́ляный,** shot; used, fired, spent; that has been under fire. **стреля́ть, -я́ю** *imp.* shoot; fire; ~ глаза́ми, dart glances; make eyes; ~ кнуто́м, crack a whip.
стремгла́в *adv.* headlong.
стременно́й, stirrup.
стреми́тельный, swift, headlong; impetuous. **стреми́ться, -млю́сь** *imp.* strive; seek, aspire; try; rush, speed, charge. **стремле́ние, -я,** striving, aspiration. **стремни́на, -ы,** rapid, rapids; precipice.
стре́мя, -мени; *pl.* **-мена́, -мя́н, -а́м** *n.* stirrup. **стремя́нка, -и,** step-ladder, steps. **стремя́нный,** stirrup.
стреха́, -и́; *pl.* **-и,** eaves.
стрига́льщик, -а, shearer. **стри́женый,** short; short-haired, cropped; shorn, sheared; clipped. **стри́жка, -и.** hair-cut; cut; shearing; clipping. **стричь, -игу́, -ижёшь; -иг** *imp.* (*perf.* о~) cut, clip; cut the hair of; shear; cut into pieces; **~ся,** cut one's hair, have one's hair cut; wear one's hair short.
строга́ль, -я *m.*, **строга́льщик, -а,** plane operator, planer. **строга́льный,** planing; ~ резе́ц, planer cutter. **строга́ть, -а́ю** *imp.* (*perf.* вы́~) plane, shave.
стро́гий, strict; severe; stern. **стро́гость, -и,** strictness; severity; *pl.* strong measures.
строев|о́й, combatant; line; drill; **-а́я** слу́жба, combatant service. **строе́ние, -я,** building; structure; composition; texture.
строжа́йший, стро́же, *superl.* and *comp.* of стро́гий.
строи́тель, -я *m.* builder. **строи́тельн|ый,** building, construction; ~ое иску́сство, civil engineering; ~ая площа́дка, building site. **строи́тельство, -а,** building, construction; building site, construction site. **стро́ить, -о́ю** *imp.* (*perf.* по~) build; construct; make; formulate, express; base; draw up, form up; **~ся,** be built, be under construction; draw up, form up; стро́йся! fall in! **строй, -я,** *loc.* **-ю́;** *pl.* **-и** or **-и́, -ев** or **-ёв,** system; order; régime; structure; pitch; formation; service, commission. **стро́йка, -и,**

building, construction; building-site. **стро́йность, -и,** proportion; harmony; balance, order. **стро́йный; -о́ен, -ойна́, -о,** harmonious, well-balanced, orderly, well put together, well-proportioned, shapely.

строка́, -и́, *acc.* -о́ку́, *pl.* -и, -а́м, line; красная ~, break-line, new paragraph.

строп, -а, стро́па, -ы, sling; shroud line.

стропи́ло, -а, rafter, truss, beam.

стропти́в|ый, obstinate, refractory; **~ая** *sb.* shrew.

строфа́, -ы́; *pl.* -ы, -а́м, stanza, strophe.

строчёный, stitched; hem-stitched. **строчи́ть, -чу́, -о́чи́шь** *imp.* (*perf.* на~, про~) sew, stitch; back-stitch; scribble, dash off. **стро́чка, -и,** stitch; back-stitching; hem-stitching; line.

строчно́й, lower-case, small.

стро́ю, etc.: see стро́ить.

струг, -а, plane. **струга́ть, -а́ю** *imp.* (*perf.* вы́~) plane, shave. **стру́жка, -и,** shaving, filing.

струи́ться, -и́тся, *imp.* stream, flow.

струна́, -ы́; *pl.* -ы, string. **стру́нный,** stringed.

с|тру́сить, -у́шу *perf.*

стручко́вый, leguminous, podded; ~ перец, capsicum; ~ горо́шек, peas in the pod. **стручо́к, -чка́,** pod.

струя́, -и́; *pl.* -и, -уй, jet, spurt, stream; current; spirit; impetus.

стря́пать, -аю *imp.* (*perf.* со~) cook; cook up; concoct. **стряпня́, -и́,** cooking. **стряпу́ха, -и,** cook.

стря́хивать, -аю *imp.*, **стряхну́ть, -ну́, -нёшь** *perf.* shake off.

ст. ст. *abbr.* ста́рый стиль, Old Style.

студене́ть, -е́ет *imp.* (*perf.* за~) thicken, set. **студени́стый,** jelly-like.

студе́нт, -а, студе́нтка, -и, student. **студе́нческий,** student.

сту́день, -дня *m.* jelly; galantine; aspic.

студи́ец, -и́йца, студи́йка, -и, student. **студи́йный,** studio.

студи́ть, -ужу́, -у́дишь *imp.* (*perf.* о~) cool.

сту́дия, -и, studio, workshop; school.

стук, -а, knock; tap; thump; rumble; clatter. **сту́кать, -аю** *imp.*, **сту́кнуть, -ну** *perf.* knock; bang; tap; rap; hit, strike; **~ся**, knock (oneself), bang, bump.

стул, -а; *pl.* -лья, -льев, chair. **стульча́к, -а́,** (lavatory) seat. **сту́льчик, -а,** stool.

сту́па, -ы, mortar.

ступа́ть, -а́ю *imp.*, **ступи́ть, -плю́, -пишь** *perf.* step; tread; ступа́й(те)! be off! clear out! **ступе́нчатый,** stepped, graduated, graded; multi-stage. **ступе́нь, -и;** *gen. pl.* -е́не́й, step, rung; stage, grade, level, phase. **ступня́, -и́,** foot; sole.

стуча́ть, -чу́ *imp.* (*perf.* по~) knock; bang; tap; rap; chatter; hammer, pulse, thump, pound; **~ся в** + *acc.* knock at.

стушева́ться, -шу́юсь *perf.*, **стушёвываться, -аюсь** *imp.* efface oneself, retire to the background; be covered with confusion; shade off, fade out.

с|туши́ть, -шу́, -шишь *perf.*

стыд, -а́, shame. **стыди́ть, -ыжу́** *imp.* (*perf.* при~) shame, put to shame; **~ся** (*perf.* по~ся) be ashamed. **стыдли́вый,** bashful. **сты́дн|ый,** shameful; **~о!** shame! for shame!; **~о** *impers.* + *dat.* ему́ ~о, he is ashamed; как тебе́ не ~о! you ought to be ashamed of yourself!

стык, -а, joint; junction; meeting-point. **стыкова́ть, -ку́ю** *imp.* (*perf.* со~) join end to end; dock; **~ся** (*perf.* при~ся) dock. **стыко́вка, -и,** docking. **стыко́вочный,** docking.

сты́нуть, стыть, -ы́ну; стыл *imp.* cool; get cold; run cold; freeze.

сты́чка, -и, skirmish, clash; squabble.

стюарде́сса, -ы, stewardess; air hostess.

стя́гивать, -аю *imp.*, **стяну́ть, -ну́, -нешь** *perf.* tighten; pull together; gather, assemble; pull off; pinch, steal; **~ся,** tighten; gird oneself tightly; gather, assemble.

суббо́та, -ы, Saturday.

субсиди́ровать, -рую *perf.* and *imp.* subsidize. **субси́дия, -и,** subsidy, grant.

субъе́кт, -а, subject; self, ego; person, individual; character, type. **субъекти́вный,** subjective.

сувере́нный, sovereign.

сугли́нок, -нка, loam.

сугрóб, -а snowdrift.
сугу́бо *adv.* especially, particularly; exclusively.
суд, -á, court; law-court; trial, legal proceedings; the judges; the bench; judgement, verdict; пода́ть в ~ на + *acc.*, bring an action against; ~ че́сти, court of honour.
суда́, etc.: see суд, су́дно[1].
суда́к, -а, pike-perch.
суде́бный, judicial; legal; forensic. **суде́йский**, judge's; referee's, umpire's. **суде́йство**, -а, refereeing, umpiring; judging. **суди́мость**, -и, previous convictions, record. **суди́ть**, сужу́, су́дишь *imp.* judge; form an opinion; try; pass judgement; referee, umpire; foreordain; **~ся**, go to law.
су́дно[1], -а; *pl.* -дá, -óв, vessel, craft.
су́дно[2], -а; *gen. pl.* -ден, bed-pan.
судоводи́тель, -я *m.* navigator. **судовожде́ние**, -я, navigation. **судово́й**, ship's; marine.
судомо́йка, -и, kitchen-maid, scullery maid, washer-up; scullery.
судопроизво́дство, -а, legal proceedings.
су́дорога, -и, cramp, convulsion, spasm. **су́дорожный**, convulsive, spasmodic.
судострое́ние, -я, shipbuilding. **судострои́тельный**, shipbuilding. **судохо́дный**, navigable; shipping; ~ кана́л, ship canal.
судьба́, -ы́; *pl.* -ы, -деб, fate, fortune, destiny, lot; каки́ми судьба́ми? how do you come to be here?
судья́, -и́; *pl.* -и, -е́й, -ям *m.* judge; referee; umpire.
суеве́р, -а, superstitious person. **суеве́рие**, -я, superstition. **суеве́рный**, superstitious.
суета́, -ы́, bustle, fuss. **суети́ться**, -ечу́сь *imp.* bustle fuss. **суетли́вый**, fussy, bustling.
сужде́ние, -я, opinion: judgement.
су́женая *sb.* fiancée; intended (wife). **су́женый** *sb.* fiancé; intended (husband).
суже́ние, -я, narrowing; constriction.
су́живать, -аю *imp.*, **су́зить**, -у́жу *perf.* narrow, contract; make too narrow; **~ся**, narrow; taper.
сук, -á, *loc.* -у́; *pl.* су́чья, -ьев or -и́, -óв, bough; knot.
су́ка, -и, bitch. **су́кин** *adj.*; ~ сын, son of a bitch.
сукно́, -á; *pl.* -а, -кон, cloth; положи́ть под ~, shelve. **суко́нный**, cloth; rough, clumsy, crude.
сули́ть, -лю́ *imp.* (*perf.* по~), promise.
султа́н, -а, plume.
сума́, -ы́ bag; pouch.
сумасбро́д, -а, **сумасбро́дка**, -и, madcap. **сумасбро́дный**, wild, extravagant. **сумасбро́дство** -а, extravagance, wild behaviour. **сумасше́дш|ий**, mad; lunatic; **~ий** *sb.* madman, lunatic; **~ая** *sb.* madwoman, lunatic. **сумасше́ствие**, -я, madness, lunacy.
сумато́ха, -и, hurly-burly, turmoil; bustle; confusion, chaos.
сумбу́р, -а, confusion, chaos. **сумбу́рный**, confused, chaotic.
су́меречный, twilight; crepuscular. **су́мерки**, -рек *pl.* twilight, dusk; half-light.
суме́ть, -е́ю *perf.* + *inf.* be able to, manage to.
су́мка, -и, bag; handbag; shopping-bag; case; satchel; pouch.
су́мма, -ы, sum. **сумма́рный**, summary; total. **сумми́ровать**, -рую *perf.* and *imp.* sum up, total up; summarize.
су́мрак, -а, dusk, twilight; murk. **су́мрачный**, gloomy; murky; dusky.
су́мчатый, marsupial.
сунду́к, -á, trunk, box, chest.
су́нуть(ся, -ну(сь *perf.* of сова́ть(ся.
суп, -а (-у); *pl.* -ы́, soup.
суперобло́жка, -и, (book-)jacket, dust-cover.
супов|о́й, soup; ~а́я ло́жка, soup-spoon; ~а́я ми́ска, soup-tureen.
супру́г, -а, husband, spouse; *pl.* husband and wife, (married) couple. **супру́га**, -и, wife, spouse. **супру́жеск|ий**, conjugal, matrimonial; ~ая изме́на, infidelity. **супру́жество**, -а, matrimony, wedlock.
сургу́ч, -á, sealing-wax.
сурди́нка, -и mute; под сурди́нку, on the quiet, on the sly. **сурдока́мера**, -ы, sound-proof room.

суро́вость, -и, severity, sternness. **суро́в|ый,** severe, stern; rigorous; bleak; unbleached, brown; ~ое полотно́, crash; brown holland.
суро́к, -рка́, marmot.
суррога́т, -а, substitute.
су́слик, -а, ground-squirrel.
су́сло, -а, must; wort; grape-juice.
суста́в, -а, joint, articulation.
су́тки, -ток *pl.* twenty-four hours; a day (and a night); двое́ с полови́ной су́ток, sixty hours.
су́толока, -и, commotion, hubbub, hurly-burly.
су́точн|ый twenty-four-hour; daily; per diem; round-the-clock; ~ые де́ньги, **~ые** *sb.* per diem allowance.
суту́литься, -люсь *imp.* stoop. **суту́лый,** round-shouldered, stooping.
суть, -и, essence, main point; по су́ти де́ла, as a matter of fact, in point of fact; ~ де́ла, the heart of the matter.
суфлёр, -а, prompter. **суфлёрск|ий,** prompt; ~ая бу́дка, prompt-box. **суфли́ровать, -рую** *imp.* + *dat.* prompt.
суха́рь, -я́ *m.* rusk; *pl.* bread-crumbs. **су́хо** *adv* drily; coldly.
сухожи́лие, -я tendon, sinew.
сухо́й; сух, -а́, -о, dry; dried-up; arid; dried; withered; chilly, cold. **сухопу́тный,** land. **су́хость, -и** dryness, aridity; chilliness, coldness. **сухоща́вый,** lean, skinny.
сучи́ть, -чу́, су́чи́шь *imp.* (*perf.* с~) twist, spin; throw; roll out.
сучкова́тый, knotty; gnarled. **сучо́к, -чка́,** twig; knot.
су́ша, -и, (dry) land. **су́ше** *comp.* of сухо́й. **сушёный,** dried. **суши́лка, -и,** dryer; drying-room. **суши́льня, -и;** *gen. pl.* -лен, drying-room. **суши́ть, -шу́,** -шишь *imp.* (*perf.* вы́~) dry, dry out, dry up; **~ся,** dry, get dry.
суще́ственный, essential, vital; material; important. **существи́тельное** *sb.* noun, substantive. **существо́, -а́,** being, creature; essence. **существова́ние, -я,** existence **существова́ть, -тву́ю** *imp.* exist. **су́щий,** existing; real; absolute, utter, downright. **су́щность, -и,** essence; ~ де́ла, the point; в су́щности, in essence, at bottom; as a matter of fact.
сую́, etc.: see сова́ть. **с|фабрикова́ть, -ку́ю** *perf.* **с|фальши́вить, -влю** *perf.* **с|фантази́ровать, -рую** *perf.*
сфе́ра, -ы, sphere; realm; zone, area; ~ влия́ния, sphere of influence. **сфери́ческий,** spherical.
с|формирова́ть(ся, -ру́ю(сь *perf.* **с|формова́ть, -му́ю** *perf.* **с|формули́ровать, -рую** *perf.* **с|фотографи́ровать(ся, -рую(сь** *perf.*
с.-х. *abbr.* се́льское хозя́йство, agriculture.
схвати́ть, -ачу́, -а́тишь *perf.*, **схва́тывать, -аю** *imp.* (*imp.* also хвата́ть) seize; catch; grasp, comprehend; clamp together; **~ся,** snatch, catch; grapple, come to grips. **схва́тка, -и,** skirmish, fight, encounter; squabble; *pl.* contractions; fit, spasm; родовы́е схва́тки, labour.
схе́ма, -ы, diagram, chart; sketch, outline, plan; circuit. **схемати́ческий,** diagrammatic, schematic; sketchy, over-simplified. **схемати́чный,** sketchy, over-simplified.
с|хитри́ть, -рю́ *perf.*
схлы́нуть, -нет *perf.* (break and) flow back; break up, rush away; subside, vanish.
сход, -а, coming off, alighting; descent; gathering, assembly. **сходи́ть**[1]**(ся, -ожу́(сь, -о́дишь(ся** *imp.* of сойти́(сь. **с|ходи́ть**[2]**, -ожу́, -о́дишь** *perf.* go; + за + *instr.* go for, go to fetch. **схо́дка, -и,** gathering, assembly, meeting. **схо́дный;** -ден, -дна́, -о, similar; reasonable, fair. **схо́дня, -и;** *gen. pl.* -ей, (usu. *pl.*) gangway, gang-plank. **схо́дство, -а,** likeness, similarity, resemblance.
схола́стика, -и, scholasticism. **схоласти́ческий,** scholastic.
с|хорони́ть(ся, -ню́(сь, -нишь(ся *perf.*
сцеди́ть, -ежу́, -е́дишь *perf.*, **сце́живать, -аю** *imp.* strain off, pour off, decant.
сце́на, -ы, stage; scene. **сцена́рий, -я,** scenario; script; stage directions. **сценари́ст, -а,** script-writer. **сцени́ческ|ий,** stage; ~ая рема́рка, stage direction. **сцени́чный,** good theatre.

сцеп, -а, coupling; drawbar. **сцепи́ть,** -плю́, -пишь *perf.*, **сцепля́ть,** -я́ю *imp.* couple; **~ся,** be coupled; grapple, come to grips. **сце́пка,** -и, coupling. **сцепле́ние,** -я, coupling; adhesion; cohesion; accumulation, chain; clutch.

счастли́вец, -вца, **счастли́вчик,** -а, lucky man. **счастли́вица,** -ы, lucky woman. **счастли́в|ый;** сча́стли́в, happy; lucky, fortunate; successful; ~ая иде́я, happy thought; ~ого пути́, ~ого пла́вания, bon voyage, pleasant journey. **сча́стье,** -я, happiness; luck, good fortune.

счесть(ся, сочту́(сь, -тёшь(ся; счёл(ся, сочла́(сь *perf.* of счита́ть(ся. **счёт,** -а (-у), *loc.* -у́; *pl.* -а́, bill; account; counting, calculation, reckoning; score; expense; быть на хоро́шем ~у́, be in good repute, stand well; в два ~а, in two ticks, in two shakes; за ~ + *gen.*, at the expense of; на ~, on account; + *gen.* on the account, to the account, of; потеря́ть ~ + *dat.* lose count of. **счётн|ый,** counting, calculating, computing; accounts, accounting; ~ая лине́йка, slide-rule; ~ая маши́на, calculating machine. **счетово́д,** -а, accountant, book-keeper. **счетово́дство,** -а, accounting, book-keeping. **счётчик,** -а, **счётчица,** -ы, teller; counter; meter. **счёты,** -ов *pl.* abacus.

счи́стить, -ищу *perf.* (*imp.* счища́ть) clean off; clear away; **~ся,** come off, clean off.

счита́ть, -а́ю *imp.* (*perf.* со~, счесть) count; compute, reckon; consider, think; regard (as); **~ся** (*perf.* also по~ся) settle accounts; be considered, be thought, be reputed; be regarded (as); + с + *instr.* take into consideration; take into account, reckon with.

счища́ть(ся, -а́ю(сь *imp.* of счи́стить(ся.

сшиба́ть, -а́ю *imp.*, **сшиби́ть,** -бу́, -бёшь; сшиб *perf.* strike, hit, knock (off); ~ с ног knock down; **~ся,** collide; come to blows.

сшива́ть, -а́ю *imp.*, **с|шить,** сошью́, -ьёшь *perf.* sew; sew together, sew up. **сши́вка,** -и, sewing together.

съ- *vbl. pref.*: see с-.

съеда́ть, -а́ю *imp.* of съесть. **съедо́бный,** edible; eatable, nice.

съе́ду, etc.: see съе́хать.

съёживаться, -аюсь *imp.*, **съ|ёжиться,** -жусь *perf.* huddle up; shrivel, shrink.

съезд, -а, congress; conference, convention; arrival, gathering. **съе́здить,** -зжу *perf.* go, drive, travel.

съезжа́ть(ся, -а́ю(сь *imp.* of съе́хать(ся.

съел, etc.: see съесть.

съём, -а, removal. **съёмка,** -и, removal; survey, surveying; plotting; exposure; shooting. **съёмный,** detachable, removable. **съёмщик,** -а, **съёмщица,** -ы, tenant, lessee; surveyor.

съестн|о́й, food; ~ы́е припа́сы, **~о́е** *sb.* food supplies, provisions, eatables, food-stuffs. **съ|есть,** -ем, -ешь, -ест, -еди́м; съел *perf.* (*imp.* also съеда́ть).

съе́хать, -е́ду *perf.* (*imp.* съезжа́ть) go down; come down; move, remove; slip; **~ся,** meet; arrive, gather, assemble.

съ|язви́ть, -влю́ *perf.*

сы́воротка, -и, whey; serum. **сы́вороточный,** serum; serous.

сы́гранность, -и, team-work. **сыгра́ть,** -а́ю *perf.* of игра́ть; ~ на роя́ле, (*sl.*) be finger-printed; **~ся,** play (well) together, play as a team.

сын, -а; *pl.* сыновья́, -е́й or -ы́, -о́в, son. **сыно́вий, сыно́вний,** filial. **сыно́к,** -нка́, little son, little boy; sonny.

сы́пать, -плю *imp.* pour; strew; pour forth; **~ся,** fall; pour out, run out; scatter; fly; rain down; fray. **сыпно́й** тиф, typhus. **сыпу́ч|ий,** friable; free-flowing; shifting; ме́ры ~их тел, dry measures; ~ий песо́к, quicksand; shifting sand. **сыпь,** -и, rash, eruption.

сыр, -а (-у), *loc.* -у́; *pl.* -ы́, cheese.

сыре́ть, -е́ю *imp.* (*perf.* от~) become damp.

сыре́ц, -рца́, unfinished product, raw product; шёлк-~, raw silk.

сы́рный, cheese; cheesy. **сырова́р,** -а, cheese-maker. **сыроваре́ние,** -я, **сыроде́лие,** -я, cheese-making.

сыр|о́й; сыр, -а́, -о, damp; raw; uncooked; unfinished; green, unripe;

~а́я вода́, unboiled water; ~ы́е материа́лы, raw materials. **сы́рость,** -и, dampness, humidity. **сырьё,** -я́, raw material(s).

сыск, -а, investigation, detection. **сыска́ть,** сыщу́, сы́щешь *perf.* find; **~ся,** be found, come to light. **сыскно́й,** investigation.

сы́тный; -тен, -тна́, -о, satisfying, substantial, copious. **сы́тость,** -и, satiety, repletion. **сы́тый;** сыт, -а́, -о, satisfied, replete, full; fat; ~ по го́рло, full up; ~ скот, fat stock.

сыч, -а́, little owl.

сы́щик, -а, **сы́щица,** -ы, detective.

с|эконо́мить, -млю *perf.*

сюда́ *adv.* here.

сюже́т, -а, subject; plot; topic. **сюже́тный,** subject; based on, having, a theme.

сюрту́к, -а́, frock-coat.

сюсю́кать, -аю *imp.* lisp.

сяк *adv.*: see так. **сям** *adv.*: see там.

Т

т *letter*: see тэ.

т. *abbr.* това́рищ, Comrade; том, volume.

та: see тот.

таба́к, -а́ (-у́), tobacco; snuff. **табаке́рка,** -и, snuff-box. **таба́чн|ый,** tobacco; ~ого цве́та, snuff-coloured.

та́бель, -я; *pl.* -и, -ей or -я́, -е́й *m.* table, list, scale. **та́бельн|ый,** table; time; ~ые часы́, time-clock. **та́бельщик,** -а, **-щица,** -ы, timekeeper.

табле́тка, -и, tablet.

табли́ца, -ы, table; list; plate; ~ вы́игрышей, prize-list; табли́цы логари́фмов, logarithm tables; ~ Менделе́ева, periodic table; ~ умноже́ния, multiplication table. **табли́чный,** tabular; standard.

та́бор, -а, camp; gipsy encampment. **та́борный,** camp; gipsy.

табулягра́мма, -ы, tabulation, print-out. **табуля́тор,** -а, tabulator.

табу́н, -а́, herd.

табуре́т, -а, **табуре́тка,** -и, stool.

таврёный, branded. **тавро́,** -а́; *pl.* -а, -а́м, brand.

таёжник, -а, **-ница,** -ы, taiga dweller. **таёжный,** taiga.

таз, -а *loc.* -у́; *pl.* -ы́, basin; wash-basin; pelvis. **тазобе́дренный,** hip; ~ суста́в, hip-joint. **та́зовый,** pelvic.

таи́нственный, mysterious; enigmatic; secret; secretive. **таи́ть,** таю́ *imp.* hide, conceal; harbour; **~ся,** hide, be in hiding; lurk.

тайга́, -и́, taiga.

тайко́м *adv.* in secret, surreptitiously, by stealth; ~ от + *gen.* behind the back of.

тайм, -а, half; period of play.

та́йна, -ы, mystery; secret. **тайни́к,** -а́, hiding-place; *pl.* secret places, recesses. **тайнопи́сный,** cryptographic. **та́йнопись,** -и, cryptography, cryptogram. **та́йный,** secret; clandestine; privy; ~ **сове́тник,** Privy Councillor (3rd grade: see чин).

так *adv.* so; thus, in this way, like this; in such a way; as it should be; just like that; и ~, even so; as it is, as it stands; и ~ да́лее, and so on, and so forth; и ~ и сяк, this way and that; мы сде́лали ~, this is what we did, we did it this way; не ~, amiss, wrong; про́сто ~, ~ (то́лько), for no special reason, just for fun; ~ же, in the same way; ~ же . . как, as . . as; ~ и, simply, just; ~ и быть, all right, right you are; ~ и есть, I thought so!; ~ ему́ и на́до, serves him right; ~ и́ли ина́че, in any event, whatever happens; one way or another; ~ себе́, so-so, middling, not too good; что́-то бы́ло не совсе́м ~, something was amiss, something was not quite right; я ~ и забы́л, I clean forgot, I've gone and forgotten. **так** *conj.* then; so;

не сего́дня, ~ за́втра, if not today, then tomorrow; ~ как, as, since. **так** *part.* yes.

такела́ж, -а, rigging; tackle, gear. **такела́жник**, -а, rigger, scaffolder. **такела́жный**, rigging; scaffolding.

та́кже *adv.* also, too, as well.

таки, -таки *part.* after all; всё-~ nevertheless; опя́ть-~, again; та́к-~, after all, really.

тако́в *m.*, **-а́** *f.*, **-о́** *n.*, **-ы́** *pl.*, *pron.* such; все они́ ~ы́, they are all the same.

так|о́й *pron.* such; so; a kind of; в ~о́м слу́чае, in that case; кто он ~о́й? who is he?; ~о́й же, the same; ~и́м о́бразом, thus, in this way; что ~о́е? what's that? what did you say?; что э́то ~о́е? what is this? **тако́й-то** *pron.* so-and-so; such-and-such.

та́кса, -ы, fixed price, statutory price; tariff. **таксáтор**, -а, price-fixer; valuer. **такса́ция**, -и, price-fixing; valuation.

таксёр, -а, taxi-driver. **такси́**, *n. indecl.* taxi.

такси́ровать, -рую *perf.* and *imp.* fix the price of, value.

такси́ст, -а, taxi-driver. **таксомото́рный**, taxi. **таксомото́рщик**, -а, taxi-driver. **таксопа́рк**, -а, taxi depot, fleet of taxis.

такт, -а, time; measure; bar; stroke; tact.

та́к-таки: see таки.

такти́чность, -и, tact. **такти́чный**, tactful.

та́ктов|ый, time, timing; ~ая черта́, bar.

тала́нт, -а, talent, gift; talented man. **тала́нтливый**, talented, gifted.

та́лия, -и, waist.

тало́н, -а, **тало́нчик**, -а, coupon; stub.

та́л|ый, thawed, melted; ~ая вода́, melted snow; ~ый снег, slush.

там *adv.* there; и ~ и сям, here, there, and everywhere; ~ же, in the same place; ibid, *ibidem.*

тамада́, -ы *m.* master of ceremonies; toast-master.

та́мбур[1], -а, tambour; lobby; platform. **та́мбур**[2], -а, tambour-stitch, chain-stitch. **та́мбурный**, tambour; ~ шов, tambour-stitch; chain-stitch.

тамо́женный, customs. **тамо́жня**, -и, custom-house.

та́нгенс, -а, tangent. **тангенциа́льный**, tangential.

та́нец, -нца, dance; dancing.

та́нковый, tank, armoured.

танцева́льный, dancing; ~ ве́чер, dance. **танцева́ть**, -цу́ю *imp.* dance. **танцо́вщик**, -а, **танцо́вщица**, -ы (ballet) dancer. **танцо́р**, -а, **танцо́рка**, -и, dancer.

та́пка, -и, **та́почка**, -и, (heelless) slipper; sports shoe, gym shoe.

та́ра, -ы, packing, packaging; tare.

тарака́н, -а, cockroach, black-beetle.

тара́щить, -щу *imp.* (*perf.* вы́~); ~ глаза́, goggle.

таре́лка, -и, plate; disc; быть не в свое́й таре́лке, feel uneasy, feel unsettled, be not quite oneself. **таре́льчатый**, plate; disc.

таска́ть, -а́ю *imp.* drag, lug; carry; pull; take; drag off; pull out; pinch, swipe; wear; **~ся**, drag, trail; roam about, hang about.

тасова́ть, -су́ю *imp.* (*perf.* с~) shuffle. **тасо́вка**, -и, shuffle, shuffling.

ТАСС *abbr.* Телегра́фное аге́нтство Сове́тского Сою́за, Telegraph Agency of the Soviet Union.

тафта́, -ы́, taffeta.

тахта́, -ы́, divan, ottoman.

тача́ть, -а́ю *imp.* (*perf.* вы́~, с~) stitch.

та́чка, -и, wheelbarrow.

тащи́ть, -щу́, -щишь *imp.* (*perf.* вы́~ с~) pull; drag, lug; carry; take; drag off; pull out; pinch, swipe; **~ся**, drag oneself along; drag, trail.

та́яние, -я, thaw, thawing. **та́ять**, та́ю *imp.* (*perf.* рас~) melt; thaw; melt away, dwindle, wane; waste away.

тварь, -и, creature; creatures; wretch.

тверде́ть, -е́ет *imp.* (*perf.* за~) harden, become hard. **тверди́ть**, -ржу́ *imp.* (*perf.* вы́~, за~) repeat, say again and again; memorize, learn by heart. **твёрдо** *adv.* hard; firmly, firm. **твердоло́бый**, thick-skulled; diehard. **твёрд|ый**, hard; firm; solid; stable; steadfast; ~ый знак, hard sign, ъ;

~ое тéло, solid; ~ые цéны, fixed prices. **тверды́ня**, -и, stronghold.

твой, -егó *m.*, **твоя́**, -éй *f.*, **твоё**, -егó *n.*, **твои́**, -и́х *pl.* your, yours; **твои́** *sb. pl.* your people.

творéние, -я, creation, work; creature; being. **творéц**, -рцá, creator. **твори́тельный**, instrumental. **твори́ть**, -рю́ *imp.* (*perf.* со~) create; do; make; ~ чудесá, work wonders; **~ся**, happen, go on; что тут твори́тся? what is going on here?

твóрóг, -á (-ý) or -а (-у) curds; cottage cheese. **творóжный**, curd.

твóрческий, creative. **твóрчество**, -а, creation; creative work; works.

те: see тот.

т.е. *abbr.* то есть, that is, i.e.

теáтр, -а, theatre; stage; plays, dramatic works. **театрáл**, -а, theatre-goer, playgoer. **театрáльн|ый**, theatre; theatrical; stagy; ~ая кácca, box-office. **театровéдение**, -я, the theatre, theatre studies.

тебя́, etc.: see ты.

тéзис, -а, thesis; proposition, point.

тёзка, -и, namesake.

тёк: see течь.

текст, -а, text; words, libretto, lyrics.

тексти́ль, -я *m.* textiles. **тексти́льный**, textile. **тексти́льщик**, -а, **-щица**, -ы, textile worker.

текстуáльный, verbatim, word-for-word; textual.

текýчесть, -и, fluidity; fluctuation; instability. **текýчий**, fluid; fluctuating, unstable. **текýщ|ий**, current, of the present moment; instant; routine, ordinary; ~ий ремóнт, running repair(s), routine maintenance; ~ие собы́тия current affairs; ~ий счёт, current account; 6-го числá ~его мéсяца, the 6th inst.

теле- in *comb.* tele-; television. **телеательé** *n. indecl.* television maintenance workshop. **~ви́дение**, -я, television. **~визиóнный**, television, TV. **~ви́зор** -а, television (set). **~ви́к**, -á, telephoto lens. **~грáмма**, -ы, telegram, wire. **~грáф**, -а, telegraph (office). **~графи́ровать**, -рую *perf.* and *imp.* telegraph, wire. **~грáфный**, telegraph; telegraphic; ~грáфный столб, telegraph-pole. **~зри́тель**, -я *m.* (television) viewer. **~мóст**, -а, TV link or transmission by satellite. **~объекти́в**, -а, telephoto lens. **~пати́ческий**, telepathic. **~пáтия**, -и, telepathy. **~скóп**, -а, telescope. **~скопи́ческий**, telescopic. **~стáнция**, -и, television station. **~стýдия**, -и, television studio. **~управлéние**, -я, remote control. **~фóн**, -а, telephone; (telephone) number; (по)звони́ть по ~фóну + *dat.* telephone, ring up; ~фон-автомáт, automatic telephone; public telephone, call-box. **~фони́ровать**, -рую *perf.* and *imp.* telephone. **~фони́ст**, -а, **-и́стка**, -и, telephone operator. **~фони́я**, -и, telephony. **~фóнный**, telephone; ~фóнная кни́га, telephone directory; ~фóнная стáнция, telephone exchange; ~фóнная трýбка, receiver. **~фотогрáфия**, -и, telephotography. **~цéнтр**, -а, television centre.

телéга, -и, cart, waggon. **телéжка**, -и, small cart; handcart; bogie, trolley. **телéжный**, cart.

телёнок, -нка; *pl.* -я́та, -я́т, calf.

телéсн|ый, bodily; corporal; somatic; physical; corporeal; ~ое наказáние, corporal punishment; ~ого цвéта, flesh-coloured.

тели́ться, -ится *imp.* (*perf.* о~) calve. **тёлка**, -и, heifer.

тéло, -а; *pl.* -á, body; держáть в чёрном тéле, ill-treat, maltreat. **телогрéйка**, -и, quilted jacket, padded jacket. **телодвижéние**, -я, movement, motion; gesture. **телосложéние**, -я, build, frame. **телохрани́тель**, -я *m.* bodyguard. **тельня́шка**, -и, vest.

теля́та, etc.: see телёнок. **теля́тина**, -ы, veal. **теля́чий**, calf; veal.

тем *conj.* (so much) the; ~ лýчше, so much the better; ~ не мéнее, none the less, nevertheless.

тем: see тот, тьма.

тéма, -ы, subject; topic; theme. **темáтика**, -и, subject-matter; themes, subjects. **темати́ческий**, subject; thematic.

тембр, -а, timbre.

темне́ть, -е́ет *imp.* (*perf.* по~, с~) grow dark, become dark; darken; show dark; темне́ет, it gets dark, it is getting dark. **темни́ца,** -ы, dungeon. **темно́** *predic.* it is dark. **темноко́жий,** dark-skinned, swarthy. **темноси́ний,** dark blue. **темнота́,** -ы́, dark, darkness; ignorance; backwardness. **тёмный,** dark; obscure; vague; sombre; shady, fishy, suspicious; ignorant, benighted.

темп, -а, tempo; rate, speed, pace.

те́мпера, -ы distemper; tempera.

температу́ра, -ы, temperature; ~ кипе́ния, boiling-point; ~ замерза́ния, freezing-point.

те́мя, -мени *n.* crown, top of the head.

тенде́нция, -и, tendency; bias.

теневой тени́стый, shady.

те́ннис, -а, tennis. **теннисист,** -а, **-и́стка,** -и, tennis-player. **те́ннисн|ый,** tennis; ~ая площа́дка, tennis-court.

тент, -а, awning, canopy.

тень, -и, *loc.* -и́; *pl.* -и, -е́й, shade; shadow; phantom, ghost; particle, vestige, atom; suspicion.

тепе́решн|ий, present; в ~ее вре́мя, at the present time, nowadays. **тепе́рь** *adv.* now; nowadays, today.

тепле́ть, -е́ет *imp.* (*perf.* по~) get warm. **те́плиться,** -ится *imp.* flicker; glimmer. **тепли́ца,** -ы, greenhouse, hothouse, conservatory. **тепли́чный,** hothouse. **тепло́,** -а́, heat; warmth. **тепло́** *adv.* warmly; *predic.* it is warm.

тепло- in *comb.* heat; thermal; thermo-. **тепловоз,** -а, diesel locomotive. **~во́зный,** diesel. **~ёмкость,** -и, heat capacity, thermal capacity; heat. **~кро́вный,** warm-blooded. **~обме́н,** -а, heat exchange. **~прово́д,** -а, hot-water system. **~прово́дный,** heat-conducting. **~сто́йкий,** heat-proof, heat-resistant. **~те́хник,** -а, heating engineer. **~те́хника,** -и, heat engineering. **~хо́д,** -а, motor ship. **~центра́ль,** -и, heat and power station.

теплово́й, heat; thermal; ~ дви́гатель, heat-engine; ~ уда́р, heat-stroke; thermal shock. **теплота́,** -ы́, heat; warmth. **теплу́шка,** -и, heated railway van. **тёплый;** -пел, -пла́, тёпло́, warm; warmed, heated; cordial; kindly, affectionate; heartfelt.

терапе́вт, -а, therapeutist. **терапи́я,** -и, therapy.

теребить, -блю́ *imp.* (*perf.* вы́~), pull, pick; pull at, pull about; pester, bother.

тере́ть, тру, трёшь; тёр *imp.* rub; grate, grind; chafe; **~ся,** rub oneself; ~ся о + *acc.* rub against; ~ся о́коло + *gen.* hang about, hang around; ~ся среди́ + *gen.* mix with, hobnob with.

терза́ть, -а́ю *imp.* tear to pieces; pull about; torment, torture; **~ся** + *instr.* suffer; be a prey to.

тёрка, -и, grater.

те́рмин, -а, term. **терминоло́гия,** -и, terminology.

терми́ческий, thermic, thermal. **те́рмос,** -а, thermos (flask). **термоя́дерный,** thermonuclear.

тёрн, -а, **терно́вник,** -а, sloe, blackthorn. **терни́стый, терно́вый,** thorny, prickly.

терпели́вый, patient. **терпе́ние,** -я, patience; endurance, perseverance; запасти́сь ~м, be patient. **терпе́ть,** -плю́, -пишь *imp.* (*perf.* по~) suffer; undergo; bear, endure, stand; have patience; tolerate, put up with; вре́мя не те́рпит, there is no time to be lost, time is getting short; вре́мя те́рпит, there is plenty of time; ~ не могу́, I can't stand, I hate. **терпе́ться,** -пится *imp. impers.* + *dat.*; ему́ не те́рпится + *inf.* he is impatient to.

терпи́мость, -и, tolerance; indulgence.

терпи́мый, tolerant; indulgent, forbearing; tolerable, bearable, supportable.

те́рпкий; -пок, -пка́, -о, astringent; tart, sharp. **те́рпкость,** -и, astringency; tartness, sharpness, acerbity.

терра́са, -ы, terrace.

террито́рия, -и, territory, confines, grounds; area.

тёртый, ground; grated; hardened, experienced.

теря́ть, -я́ю *imp.* (*perf.* по~, у~) lose; shed; ~ в ве́се, lose weight; ~ из ви́ду, lose sight of; ~ си́лу, become invalid; **~ся,** get lost; disappear, vanish; fail, decline, decrease, weaken; become flustered; be at a loss; ~ся в догáдках, be at a loss.

тёс, -a (-y) boards, planks. **тесáть,** тешý, тéшешь *imp.* cut, hew; trim, square.

тесёмка, -и, tape, ribbon, lace, braid. **тесёмчатый,** ribbon, braid; ~ глист, tapeworm.

теснúть, -ню́ *imp.* (*perf.* по~, с~) press; crowd; squeeze, constrict; be too tight; **~ся,** press through, push a way through; move up, make room; crowd, cluster, jostle. **тéсно** *adv.* closely; tightly; narrowly. **теснотá, -ы́,** crowded state; narrowness; crush, squash. **тéсн|ый,** crowded, cramped; narrow; (too) tight; close; compact; hard, difficult; ~о, it is crowded, there is not enough room.

тесóвый, board, plank.

тéсто, -a, dough; pastry; paste.

тесть, -я *m.* father-in-law.

тесьмá, -ы́ tape, ribbon, lace, braid.

тéтерев, -a; *pl.* ~á, black grouse, blackcock. **тетёрка,** -и, grey hen.

тётка, -и, aunt.

тетрáдка, -и, **тетрáдь,** -и, exercise book; copy-book; part, fascicule.

тётя, -и; *gen. pl.* -ей, aunt.

тех- *abbr.* in *comb.* of технúческий, technical. **техмúнимум,** -a, minimum (technical) qualifications. **~персонáл,** -a, technical personnel. **~рéд,** -a, technical editor.

тéхник, -a, technician. **тéхника,** -и, machinery, technical equipment; technical devices; engineering; technology; technique, art. **тéхникум,** -a, technical college, technical school. **техни́ческий,** technical; engineering; maintenance; industrial; commercial -(grade); assistant, subordinate; ~ие услóвия, specifications.

течéние, -я, flow; course; current, stream; trend, tendency; вверх по течéнию, upstream.

течь, -чёт; тёк, -лá *imp.* flow; stream; pass; leak, be leaky.

тéшить, -шу *imp.* (*perf.* по~), amuse, entertain; gratify, please; **~ся** (+ *instr.*) amuse oneself (with), play (with).

тешý, etc.: see тесáть.

тёща, -и, mother-in-law.

тигр, -a, tiger. **тигрúца,** -ы, tigress. **тигрóвый,** tiger.

тúна, -ы, slime, mud; mire. **тúнистый,** slimy, muddy.

тип, -a, type. **типúчный,** typical. **типовóй,** standard; model; type. **типогрáфия,** -и, printing-house, press. **типогрáфск|ий,** typographical; printing, printer's; ~ая крáска, printer's ink.

тир, -a, shooting-range; shooting--gallery. **тирáж,** -á, draw; circulation; edition; вы́йти в тирáж, be drawn; have served one's turn, become redundant, be superannuated.

тирé *n. indecl.* dash.

тúскать, -аю *imp.*, **тúснуть,** -ну *perf.* press, squeeze; pull. **тискú,** -óв *pl.* vice; в тискáх + *gen.*, in the grip of, in the clutches of. **тиснéние,** -я, stamping, printing; imprint; design. **тиснёный,** stamped, printed.

тúтул, -a, title; title-page. **тúтульный,** title; ~ лист, title-page; ~ спúсок, itemized list. **титуля́рный,** titular; ~ совéтник, Titular Councillor (9th grade: see чин).

тиф, -a, *loc.* -ý, typhus; typhoid.

тúхий; тих, -á, -о, quiet; low, soft, faint; silent, noiseless; still; calm; gentle; slow, slow-moving; ~ ход, slow speed, slow pace. **тúхо** *adv.* quietly; softly; gently; silently, noiselessly; calmly; still; slowly. **тихоокеáнский,** Pacific. **тúше** *comp.* of тúхий, тúхо; тúше! quiet! silence! hush! gently! careful! **тишинá,** -ы́, quiet, silence; stillness; нарýшить тишинý, break the silence; соблюдáть тишинý, keep quiet.

ткáневый, tissue. **ткáный,** woven. **ткань,** -и, fabric, cloth; tissue; substance, essence. **ткать,** тку, ткёшь; -ал, -алá, -о *imp.* (*perf.* со~), weave. **ткáцкий,** weaver's, weaving; ~ станóк, loom. **ткач,** -a, **ткачúха,** -и, weaver.

ткнуть(ся, -у(сь, -ёшь(ся *perf.* of ты́кать(ся.

тле́ние, -я, decay, decomposition, putrefaction; smouldering. **тлеть**, -е́ет *imp.* rot, decay, decompose, putrefy; moulder; smoulder; **~ся**, smoulder.

тмин, -а (-у), caraway-seeds.

то *pron.* that; а не то́, or else, otherwise; (да) и то́, and even then and that; то́ есть, that is (to say); то и де́ло, every now and then. **то** *conj.* then; не то . ., не то, either . . or; whether . . or; half . ., half; не то, что́бы . ., но, it is (was) not that . ., (but); то . ., то, now . ., now; то ли . ., то ли, whether . . or; то тут, то там, now here, now there.

-то *part.* just, precisely, exactly; в то́м-то и де́ло, that's just it.

тобо́й: see ты.

тов. *abbr.* това́рищ, Comrade.

това́р, -а, goods; wares; article; commodity.

това́рищ, -а, comrade; friend; companion; colleague; person; assistant, deputy, vice-; ~ по рабо́те, colleague; mate; ~ по шко́ле, school-friend; ~ председа́теля, vice-president. **това́рищеск|ий**, comradely; friendly; communal; unofficial; с ~им приве́том, with fraternal greetings. **това́рищество**, -а, comradeship, fellowship; company; association, society.

това́рность, -и, marketability. **това́рный**, goods; freight; commodity; marketable; ~ ваго́н, goods truck; ~ скла́д, warehouse; ~ соста́в, goods train.

товаро- in *comb.* commodity; goods. **товарообме́н**, -а, barter, commodity exchange. **~оборо́т**, -а, (sales) turnover; commodity circulation. **~отправи́тель**, -я *m.* consignor, forwarder (of goods). **~получа́тель**, -я *m.* consignee.

тогда́ *adv.* then; ~ как, whereas, while. **тогда́шний**, of that time, of those days; the then.

того́: see тот.

тожде́ственный, identical, one and the same. **то́ждество**, -а, identity.

то́же *adv.* also, as well, too.

ток, -а (-у); *pl.* -и, current.

тока́рный, turning; ~ стано́к, lathe. **то́карь**, -я; *pl.* -я́, -е́й or -и, -ей *m.* turner, lathe operator.

толк, -а (-у), sense; understanding; use, profit; бе́з ~у, senselessly, wildly; to no purpose; знать ~ в + *prep.* know what's what in; be a good judge of; сбить с ~у, confuse, muddle; с ~ом, sensibly, intelligently.

толка́ть, -а́ю *imp.* (*perf.* толкну́ть) push, shove; jog; ~ ло́ктем, nudge; ~ ядро́, put the shot; **~ся**, jostle.

то́лки, -ов *pl.* talk; rumours, gossip.

толкну́ть(ся, -ну́(сь, -нёшь(ся *perf.* of толка́ть(ся.

толкова́ние, -я, interpretation; *pl.* commentary. **толкова́ть**, -ку́ю *imp.* interpret; explain; talk; say; ло́жно ~ misinterpret, misconstrue. **толко́вый**, intelligent, sensible; intelligible, clear; ~ слова́рь, defining dictionary. **то́лком** *adv.* plainly, clearly.

толкотня́, -и́, crush, scrum, squash; crowding.

толку́, etc.: see толо́чь.

толку́чий ры́нок second-hand market, junk-market. **толку́чка**, -и, crush, scrum, squash; crowded place; second-hand market.

толокно́, -а́, oatmeal.

толо́чь, -лку́, -лчёшь; -ло́к, -лкла́ *imp.* (*perf.* ис~, рас~) pound, crush.

толпа́, -ы́; *pl.* -ы, crowd; throng; multitude. **толпи́ться**, -и́тся *imp.* crowd; throng; cluster.

толсте́ть, -е́ю *imp.* (*perf.* по~) grow fat, get stout; put on weight. **толсти́ть**, -и́т *imp.* fatten; make look fat. **толстоко́жий**, thick-skinned; pachydermatous. **толстомо́рдый**, fat-faced. **то́лстый**; -а́, -о, fat; stout; thick; heavy. **толстя́к**, -а́, fat man; fat boy.

толчёный, pounded, crushed; ground.

толчёт, etc.: see толо́чь.

толчея́, -и́, crush, scrum, squash.

толчо́к, -чка́, push, shove; put; jolt, bump; shock, tremor; incitement, stimulus.

то́лща, -и, thickness; thick. **то́лще** *comp.* of то́лстый. **толщина́**, -ы́ thickness; fatness, stoutness.

то́лько *adv.* only, merely; solely; just; ~ что, just, only just; ~-~, barely; *conj.* only, but; (как) ~, (лишь) ~, as soon as; ~ бы, if only.

том, -а; *pl.* ~а́, volume. **то́мик,** -а small volume, slim volume.

томи́тельный, wearisome, tedious, wearing; tiresome, trying; agonizing. **томи́ть,** -млю́ *imp.* (*perf.* ис~), tire, wear, weary; torment; wear down; stew, steam, braise; **~ся,** pine; languish; be tormented. **томле́ние,** -я, languor. **томлённый,** stewed, steamed, braised. **то́мность,** -и, languor. **то́мный;** -мен, -мна́, -о, languid, languorous.

тон, -а; *pl.* -а́ or -ы, -о́в, tone; note; shade; tint; дурно́й ~, bad form; хоро́ший ~, good form. **тона́льность,** -и, key; tonality.

то́ненький, thin; slender, slim. **то́нкий;** -нок, -нка́, -о, thin; slender, slim; fine; delicate; refined; dainty; subtle; nice; keen; crafty, sly; ~ вкус, refined taste; ~ за́пах, delicate perfume; ~ знато́к, connoisseur; ~ слух, good ear; ~ сон, light sleep. **то́нкость,** -и, thinness; slenderness, slimness; fineness; subtlety; nice point; nicety.

тонне́ль: see тунне́ль.

тону́ть, -ну́, -нешь *imp.* (*perf.* по~ у~) sink; drown; go down; be lost, be hidden, be covered.

тонфи́льм, -а, sound film; (sound) recording.

то́ньше, *comp.* of то́нкий.

то́пать, -аю *imp.* (*perf.* то́пнуть) stamp; ~ ного́й, stamp one's foot.

топи́ть[1], -плю́, -пишь *imp.* (*perf.* по~, у~), sink; drown; wreck, ruin; **~ся,** drown oneself.

топи́ть[2], -плю́, -пишь *imp.* stoke; heat; melt (down); render; **~ся,** burn, be alight; melt. **то́пка,** -и, stoking; heating; melting (down); furnace, fire-box.

то́пкий, boggy, marshy, swampy.

то́пливн|ый, fuel; ~ая нефть, fuel oil. **то́пливо,** -а, fuel.

то́пнуть, -ну *perf.* of то́пать.

то́полевый, poplar. **то́поль,** -я; *pl.* -я́ or -и *m.* poplar.

топо́р, -а́, axe. **топо́рик,** -а, hatchet. **топори́ще,** -а, axe-handle. **топо́рный,** axe; clumsy, crude; uncouth.

то́пот, -а, tread; tramp; ко́нский ~, clatter of hooves. **топта́ть,** -пчу́, -пчешь *imp.* (*perf.* по~) trample (down); **~ся,** stamp; ~ся на ме́сте, mark time.

торг[1], -а, *loc.* -у́; *pl.* -и́, trading; bargaining, haggling; market; *pl.* auction.

торг[2], -а *abbr.* торго́вое учрежде́ние, trading organization. **торгова́ть,** -гу́ю *imp.* (*perf.* с~), trade, deal; bargain for; be open; + *instr.* sell; **~ся,** bargain, chaffer, haggle. **торго́вец,** -вца, merchant; trader, dealer; tradesman. **торго́вка,** -и, market-woman; stall-holder; street-trader. **торго́вля,** -и, trade, commerce. **торго́в|ый,** trade, commercial; mercantile; ~ое су́дно, merchant ship; ~ый флот, merchant navy. **торгпре́д,** -а *abbr.* trade representative. **торгпре́дство,** -а *abbr.* trade delegation.

торже́ственный, solemn; ceremonial; festive; gala. **торжество́,** -а́, celebration; triumph; exultation; *pl.* festivities, rejoicings. **торжествова́ть,** -тву́ю *imp.* celebrate; triumph, exult. **торжеству́ющий,** triumphant, exultant.

торможе́ние, -я, braking; deceleration; inhibition. **то́рмоз,** -а; *pl.* -а́ or -ы, brake; drag, hindrance, obstacle. **тормози́ть,** -ожу́ *imp.* (*perf.* за~) brake, apply the brake(s); hamper, impede, be a drag on; retard, damp; inhibit. **тормозно́й,** brake, braking.

тормоши́ть, -шу́ *imp.* pester, plague, worry, torment; bother.

торопи́ть, -плю́, -пишь *imp.* (*perf.* по~) hurry; hasten; press; **~ся,** hurry, be in a hurry; make haste. **торопли́вый,** hurried, hasty.

торт, -а, cake.

торф, -а, peat. **торфоболо́тный,** peat-moss. **торфяни́стый,** peaty. **торфян|о́й,** peat; ~о́е боло́то, peat-moss, peat-bog.

торча́ть, -чу́ *imp.* stick up, stick out; protrude, jut out; hang about. **торчко́м** *adv.* on end, sticking up.

торшéр, -а, standard lamp.
тоскá, -и́, melancholy; anguish; pangs; depression; boredom; nostalgia; ~ по, longing for, yearning for; ~ по рóдине, homesickness. **тоскли́вый,** melancholy; depressed, miserable; dull, dreary, depressing. **тосковáть,** -кýю *imp.* be melancholy, depressed, miserable; long, yearn, pine; ~ по, miss.
тост, -а, toast; toasted sandwich.
тот *m.*, **та** *f.*, **то** *n.*, **те** *pl. pron.* that; the former; he, she, it; the other; the opposite; the one; the same; the right; *pl.* those; в том слýчае, in that case; и томý подóбное, and so on, and so forth; и ~ и другóй, both; к томý же, moreover; на той сторонé, on the other side; не ~, the wrong; не ~, так другóй, if not one, then the other; ни с тогó ни с сегó, for no reason at all; without rhyme or reason; ни ~ ни другóй, neither; однó и то же, one and the same thing, the same thing over again; по ту стóрону + *gen.*, beyond, on the other side of; с тем, чтóбы, in order to, with a view to; on condition that, provided that; с тогó бéрега, from the other shore; тем врéменем, in the meantime; тогó и гляди́, any minute now; before you know where you are; тот, кто, the one who, the person who; э́то не та дверь, that's the wrong door. **тóтчас** *adv.* at once; immediately.
точи́лка, -и, steel, knife-sharpener; pencil-sharpener. **точи́ло, -а**, whetstone, grindstone. **точи́льный,** grinding, sharpening; ~ кáмень, whetstone, grindstone. **точи́льщик**, -а, (knife-) grinder. **точи́ть, -чý, -чишь** *imp.* (*perf.* вы́~, на~) sharpen; grind; whet, hone; turn; eat away, gnaw away; corrode; gnaw at, prey upon.
тóчка, -и, spot; dot; full stop; point; попáсть в тóчку, hit the nail on the head; ~ в тóчку, exactly; to the letter, word for word; ~ зрéния, point of view; ~ с запятóй, semicolon. **тóчно**[1] *adv.* exactly, precisely; punctually; ~ в час, at one o'clock sharp. **тóчно**[2] *conj.* as though, as if; like. **тóчность, -и**, punctuality; exactness; precision; accuracy; в тóчности, exactly, precisely; accurately; to the letter. **тóчн|ый; -чен, -чнá, -о**, exact, precise; accurate; punctual; ~ые наýки, exact sciences; ~ый прибóр precision instrument. **тóчь-в-тóчь** *adv.* exactly; to the letter; word for word.
тошни́ть, -и́т *imp. impers.*; меня́ тошни́т, I feel sick; меня́ от э́того тошни́т, it makes me sick, it sickens me. **тошнотá, -ы́**, sickness, nausea. **тошнотвóрный,** sickening, nauseating.
тощáть, -áю *imp.* (*perf.* о~), become thin, get thin. **тóщ|ий; тощ, -á, -е** gaunt, emaciated; scraggy skinny, scrawny; lean; empty; poor; ~ая пóчва, poor soil.
тпру *int.* whoa.
травá, -ы́; *pl.* **-ы**, grass; herb. **трави́нка,** -и, blade of grass.
трави́ть, -влю́, -вишь *imp.* (*perf.* вы́~, за~) poison; exterminate, destroy; etch; hunt; persecute, torment; badger; bait; worry the life out of. **травлéние, -я**, extermination, destruction; etching. **трáвленый,** etched. **трáвля,** -и, hunting; persecution, tormenting; badgering.
трáвма, -ы, trauma, injury; shock. **травмати́зм, -а**, traumatism; injuries.
травоя́дный, herbivorous. **травяни́стый,** grass; herbaceous; grassy; tasteless, insipid. **травянóй,** grass; herbaceous; herb; grassy.
трагéдия, -и, tragedy. **трáгик, -а**, tragic actor; tragedian. **траги́ческий, траги́чный,** tragic.
традициóнный, traditional. **тради́ция,** -и, tradition.
тракт, -а, high road, highway; route; channel.
трактáт, -а, treatise; treaty.
тракти́р, -а, inn, tavern. **тракти́рный,** inn. **тракти́рщик, -а, тракти́рщица,** -ы, innkeeper.
трактовáть, -тýю *imp.* interpret; treat, discuss. **трактóвка, -и**, treatment; interpretation.
трал, -а, trawl. **трáлить, -лю** *imp.* (*perf.* про~) trawl; sweep. **трáльщик,** -а, trawler; mine-sweeper.

трамбова́ть, -бу́ю *imp.* (*perf.* у~) ram, tamp. **трамбо́вка, -и**, ramming; rammer, beetle.

трамва́й, -я, tram-line; tram. **трамва́йный**, tram.

трампли́н, -а, spring-board; ski-jump; trampoline; jumping-off place.

транзи́стор, -а, transistor; transistor radio, transistor set. **транзи́сторный**, transistor; transistorized.

трансли́ровать, -рую *perf.* and *imp.* broadcast, transmit; relay. **трансля́тор, -а**, repeater. **трансляцио́нный**, transmission; broadcasting; relaying. **трансля́ция, -и**, broadcast, transmission; relay.

тра́нспорт, -а, transport; transportation, conveyance; consignment; train; supply ship; troopship. **транспорта́бельный**, transportable, mobile. **транспортёр, -а** conveyer; carrier. **транспорти́р, -а**, protractor. **транспорти́ровать**, -рую *perf.* and *imp.* transport. **тра́нспортник, -а**, transport worker; transport plane.

трансформа́тор, -а, transformer; quick-change artist; conjurer, illusionist.

транше́йный, trench. **транше́я, -и**, trench.

трап, -а, ladder; steps.

тра́пеза, -ы, (monastery) dining-table; meal; refectory. **тра́пезная** *sb.* refectory.

трапе́ция, -и trapezium; trapeze.

тра́сса, -ы, line, course, direction; route, road. **трасси́ровать**, -рую *perf.* and *imp.* mark out, trace. **трасси́рующий**, tracer.

тра́та, -ы, expenditure; expense; waste. **тра́тить**, -а́чу *imp.* (*perf.* ис~, по~) spend, expend; waste.

тра́улер, -а, trawler.

тра́ур, -а, mourning. **тра́урный**, mourning; funeral; mournful, sorrowful.

трафаре́т, -а, stencil; conventional pattern; cliché. **трафаре́тный**, stencilled; conventional, stereotyped; trite, hackneyed.

тра́чу, etc.: see **тра́тить**.

ТРД (*te-erdé*) *abbr.* турбореакти́вный дви́гатель, turbo-jet engine.

тре́бование, -я demand; request; claim; requirement, condition; requisition, order; *pl.* aspirations; needs. **тре́бовательный**, demanding, exacting; particular; requisition, order. **тре́бовать**, -бую *imp.* (*perf.* по~) send for, call, summon; + *gen.* demand, request, require; expect, ask; need, call for; **~ся**, be needed, be required; на э́то тре́буется мно́го вре́мени, it takes a lot of time; что и тре́бовалось доказа́ть, Q.E.D.

трево́га, -и, alarm; anxiety; uneasiness, disquiet; alert. **трево́жить**, -жу *imp.* (*perf.* вс~, по~) alarm; disturb; worry, trouble; interrupt; **~ся**, worry, be anxious, be alarmed, be uneasy; worry oneself, trouble oneself, put oneself out. **трево́жный**, worried, anxious uneasy, troubled; alarming, disturbing, disquieting; alarm.

тре́звенник, -а, teetotaller, abstainer. **трезве́ть**, -е́ю *imp.* (*perf.* о~), sober up, become sober.

трезво́н, -а, peal (of bells); rumours, gossip; row, shindy.

тре́звый; -зв, -а́, -о, sober; teetotal, abstinent.

тре́йлер, -а, trailer.

трель, -и, trill, shake; warble.

тре́нер -а, trainer, coach. **тре́нерский**, trainer's, training.

тре́ние, -я friction; rubbing; *pl.* friction.

тренирова́ть, -ру́ю *imp.* (*perf.* на~), train coach; **~ся**, train oneself; be in training. **трениро́вка, -и**, training, coaching. **трениро́вочный**, training; practice.

трепа́ть, -плю́, -плешь *imp.* (*perf.* ис~, по~ рас~) scutch, swingle; pull about; blow about; dishevel, tousle; tear; wear out; pat; его тре́плет лихора́дка he is feverish; **~ся**, tear, fray; wear out; flutter, blow about; go round; hang out; blather, talk rubbish; play the fool. **тре́пет, -а**, trembling, quivering; trepidation. **трепета́ть**, -пещу́, -пе́щешь *imp.* tremble; quiver;

flicker; palpitate. **тре́петный**, trembling; flickering; palpitating; anxious; timid.

треск, -а, crack, crash; crackle, crackling; noise, fuss.

треска́, -и́, cod.

тре́скаться[1], -ается *imp.* (*perf.* по~) crack; chap.

тре́скаться[2], -аюсь *imp.* of тре́снуться.

тре́ско́вый, cod.

трескотня́, -и́, crackle, crackling; chirring; chatter, blather. **трескучий**, crackling; highfaluting, high-flown; ~ моро́з, hard frost. **тре́снуть, -нет** *perf.* snap, crackle; crack; chap; **~ся** (*imp.* тре́скаться) + *instr.* bang.

трест, -а trust.

трете́йский, arbitration; ~ суд, arbitration tribunal.

тре́т|ий, -ья, -ье, third; в ~ьем часу́, between two and three; полови́на ~ьего, half past two; ~ьего дня, the day before yesterday; **~ье** *sb.* sweet (course).

трети́ровать, -рую *imp.* slight.

трети́чный, tertiary, ternary. **треть, -и**; *gen. pl.* -е́й, third. **тре́тье**, etc.: see тре́тий. **треуго́льник, -а**, triangle. **треуго́льный**, three-cornered, triangular.

трефо́вый, of clubs. **тре́фы**, треф *pl.* clubs.

трёх- in *comb.* three-, tri-. **трёхгоди́чный**, three-year. **~годова́лый**, three-year-old. **~голо́сный**, three-part. **~гра́нный**, three-edged; trihedral. **~дне́вный**, three-day; tertian. **~зна́чный**, three-digit, three-figure. **~колёсный**, three-wheeled. **~ле́тний**, three-year; three-year-old. **~ме́рный**, three-dimensional. **~ме́стный**, three-seater. **~ме́сячный**, three-month; quarterly; three-month-old. **~сло́жный**, trisyllabic. **~сло́йный**, three-layered; three-ply. **~со́тый**, three-hundredth. **~сторо́нний**, three-sided; trilateral; tripartite. **~то́нка, -и**, three-ton lorry. **~ходово́й**, three-way, three-pass; three-move. **~цве́тный**, three-coloured; tricolour; trichromatic. **~эта́жный**, three-storeyed.

треща́ть, -щу́ *imp.* crack; crackle; creak; chirr; crack up; jabber, chatter. **тре́щина, -ы**, crack, split; cleft, fissure; chap.

три, трёх -ём -емя́, -ёх, three.

трибу́на, -ы, platform, rostrum; **tribune**; stand.

тридцатиле́тний, thirty-year; thirty-year old. **тридца́тый**, thirtieth. **три́дцать, -и́**, *instr.* -ью́, thirty. **три́дцатью** *adv.* thirty times. **три́жды** *adv.* three times; thrice.

трико́ *n. indecl.* jersey, tricot stockinet; knitted fabric; tights; pants, knickers. **трико́вый**, jersey, tricot. **трикота́ж, -а**, jersey, tricot, stockinet; knitted fabric; knitted wear, knitted garments. **трикота́жный**, jersey, tricot; knitted.

трина́дцатый, thirteenth. **трина́дцать, -и**, thirteen. **трино́м, -а**, trinomial.

трио́ль, -и, triplet.

три́ппер, -а, gonorrhoea.

три́ста, трёхсо́т, -ёмста́м, -емяста́ми, -ёхста́х, three hundred.

тро́гательный, touching, moving, affecting. **тро́гать(ся, -аю(сь** *imp.* of тро́нуть(ся.

тро́е, -и́х *pl.* three. **троебо́рье, -я**, triathlon. **троекра́тный**, thrice-repeated. **трои́ть, -ою́** *imp.* treble; divide into three; **~ся**, be trebled; appear treble. **тро́ица, -ы**, Trinity; trio. **тро́ицын день**, Whit Sunday. **тро́йка, -и**, (figure) three; troika; No. 3; three-piece suit; three-man commission. **тройно́й**, triple, threefold, treble; three-ply. **тро́йственный**, triple; tripartite.

тролле́й, -я, trolley. **тролле́йбус, -а**, trolley-bus. **тролле́йбусный**, trolley-bus.

трон, -а, throne. **тро́нный**, throne.

тро́нуть, -ну *perf.* (*imp.* тро́гать) touch; disturb, trouble; move, affect; start; **~ся**, start, set out; go bad; be touched; be moved, be affected; be cracked.

тропа́, -ы́, path.

тро́пик, -а, tropic.

тропи́нка, -и, path.

тропи́ческий, tropical; ~ по́яс, torrid zone.

трос, -а, rope, cable, hawser.
тростни́к, -а́, reed, rush. **тростнико́вый**, reed.
тро́сточка, -и, **трость**, -и; *gen. pl.* -е́й, cane, walking-stick.
тротуа́р, -а, pavement.
трофе́й, -я, trophy; spoils (of war), booty; captured material. **трофе́йный**, captured.
троюро́дн|ый; ~ый брат, ~ая сестра́, second cousin.
тру etc.: see тере́ть.
труба́, -ы́; *pl.* -ы, pipe; conduit; chimney, flue; funnel, smoke-stack; trumpet; tube; duct. **труба́ч**, -а, trumpeter; trumpet-player. **труби́ть**, -блю́ *imp.* (*perf.* про~) blow, sound; blare; ~ в + *acc.* blow. **тру́бка**, -и, tube; pipe; fuse; (telephone) receiver. **тру́бный**, trumpet. **трубопрово́д**, -а, pipe-line; piping, tubing; manifold. **трубочи́ст**, -а, chimney-sweep. **тру́бочный**, pipe; ~ таба́к, pipe tobacco. **тру́бчатый**, tubular.
труд, -а́, labour; work; effort; *pl.* works; transactions; не сто́ит ~а́, it is not worth the trouble; с ~о́м, with difficulty, hardly. **труди́ться**, -ужу́сь, -у́дишься *imp.* toil, labour, work; trouble. **тру́дно** *predic.* it is hard, it is difficult. **тру́дность**, -и, difficulty; obstacle. **тру́дный**; -ден, -дна́, -о, difficult; hard; arduous; awkward; serious grave.
трудо- in *comb.* labour, work. **трудоде́нь**, -дня́ *m.* work-day (unit), labour-day (unit). **~люби́вый**, hard-working, industrious. **~лю́бие**, -я, industry, diligence. **~спосо́бность**, -и, ability to work, capacity for work. **~спосо́бный**, able-bodied; capable of working.
трудово́й, labour, work; working; earned; hard-earned; ~ стаж, working life. **трудя́щ|ийся**, working; **~иеся** *sb. pl.* the workers. **тру́женик**, -а **тру́женица** -ы, toiler. **тру́женический**, toiling; of toil.
труп -а, dead body, corpse; carcass. **тру́пный**, corpse; post-mortem; ptomaine.
тру́ппа, -ы, troupe company.
трус, -а, coward.
тру́сики, -ов *pl.* shorts; (swimming) trunks.
труси́ть[1], -ушу́ *imp.* trot along, jog along.
тру́сить[2], -у́шу *imp.* (*perf.* с~) be a coward; lose one's nerve; quail; be afraid, be frightened. **труси́ха**, -и, coward. **трусли́вый**, cowardly; faint-hearted, timorous; apprehensive. **тру́сость**, -и, cowardice.
трусы́, -о́в *pl.* shorts; trunks; pants.
трушу́, etc.: see труси́ть, тру́сить.
трущо́ба, -ы, godforsaken hole; slum.
трюк, -а, feat, stunt; trick. **трю́ковый**, trick.
трюм, -а, hold.
трюмо́ *n. indecl.* pier-glass.
тряпи́чный, rag; soft, spineless. **тря́пка**, -и, rag; duster; spineless creature; *pl.* finery, clothes. **тряпьё**, -я́, rags; clothes, things.
тряси́на, -ы, bog, swampy ground; quagmire. **тря́ска**, -и, shaking, jolting. **тря́ский**, shaky, jolty; bumpy. **трясти́**, -су́, -сёшь; -яс, -ла́ *imp.*, **тряхну́ть**, -ну́, -нёшь *perf.* (*perf.* also вы́~) shake; shake out; jolt; + *instr.* shake, swing, toss; **~сь**, shake; tremble, shiver; quake; bump along, jolt.
тсс *int.* sh! hush!
тт. *abbr.* това́рищи, Comrades; тома́, volumes.
туале́т, -а, dress; toilet; dressing; dressing-table; lavatory, cloak-room. **туале́тный** toilet; ~ сто́лик, dressing-table. **туале́тчик**, -а, **туале́тчица**, -ы, lavatory attendant, cloak-room attendant.
туберкулёз, -а, tuberculosis, consumption. **туберкулёзник**, -а, **-ница**, -ы, consumptive. **туберкулёзный**, tubercular, consumptive; tuberculosis.
ту́го *adv.* tight(ly), taut; with difficulty; ~ наби́ть, pack tight, cram; *predic. impers.* с деньга́ми у нас ~, we are in a tight spot financially, money is tight with us; ему́ ~ прихо́диться, he is in straits, he is in a spot. **туго́й**; туг, -а́, -о, tight; taut; tightly filled, tightly stuffed; blown up hard; close-fisted; difficult; ~ на́ ухо, hard of hearing. **тугопла́вкий**, refractory.

туда́ *adv.* there, thither; that way; to the right place; не ~! not that way!; ни ~ ни сюда́, neither one way nor the other; ~ и обра́тно, there and back.

ту́же, *comp.* of ту́го, туго́й.

тужу́рка, -и, (double-breasted) jacket.

туз, -а́, *acc.* -а́, ace; dignitary; big name

тузе́мец, -мца, **тузе́мка**, -и, native. **тузе́мный**, native, indigenous.

ту́ловище, -а, trunk; torso.

тулу́п, -а, sheepskin coat.

тума́н, -а (-у) fog; mist; haze. **тума́нить**, -ит *imp.* (*perf.* за~) dim, cloud, obscure; **~ся**, grow misty, grow hazy; be enveloped in mist; be befogged; grow gloomy, be depressed. **тума́нность**, -и, fog, mist; nebula; haziness, obscurity. **тума́нный**, foggy; misty; hazy; dull, lacklustre; obscure, vague.

ту́мба, -ы, post; bollard; pedestal. **ту́мбочка**, -и, bedside table.

тунея́дец, -дца, parasite, sponger. **тунея́дствовать**, -твую *imp.* be a parasite, sponge.

туни́ка, -и, tunic.

тунне́ль, -я *m.*, **тонне́ль**, -я *m.* tunnel; subway. **тунне́льный**, **тонне́льный**, tunnel; subway.

тупе́ть -е́ю *imp.* (*perf.* о~), become blunt; grow dull. **тупи́к**, -а́, blind alley, cul-de-sac, dead end; siding; impasse, deadlock; зайти́ в ~, reach a deadlock; поста́вить в ~, stump, nonplus. **тупи́ть**, -плю́, -пишь *imp.* (*perf.* за~, ис~) blunt; **~ся**, become blunt. **тупи́ца**, -ы *m.* and *f.* dolt, blockhead, dimwit. **тупо́й**; туп, -а́, -о, blunt; obtuse; dull; vacant, stupid, meaningless; slow; dim; blind, unquestioning. **ту́пость**, -и, bluntness; vacancy; dullness, slowness. **тупоу́мный**, dull, obtuse.

тур, -а, turn; round.

туре́цкий, Turkish; ~ бараба́н, big drum, bass drum.

тури́ст, -а, **-и́стка**, -и, tourist, hiker. **тури́стский**, tourist; ~ похо́д: see турпохо́д.

турне́ *n. indecl.* tour.

турни́к, -а́, horizontal bar.

турнике́т, -а, turnstile; tourniquet.

турни́р, -а, tournament.

ту́рок, -рка, Turk. **турча́нка**, -и, Turkish woman.

турпохо́д, -а *abbr.* тури́стский похо́д, walking-tour; tourist excursion; outing.

ту́склый, dim, dull; matt; tarnished; wan; lacklustre; colourless, tame. **тускне́ть**, -е́ет *imp.* (*perf.* по~), dim; grow dim, grow dull; tarnish; pale.

тут *adv.* here; now; ~ же, there and then. **ту́т-то** *adv.* just here; there and then.

ту́фля, -и, shoe; slipper.

ту́хлый; -хл, -а́, -о, rotten, bad. **ту́хнуть**[1], -нет; тух, go bad.

ту́хнуть[2], -нет; тух *imp.* (*perf.* по~) go out.

ту́ча, -и, cloud; storm-cloud; swarm, host. **тучево́й**, cloud.

ту́чный; -чен, -чна́, -чно, fat obese; rich, fertile; succulent.

туш, -а, flourish.

ту́ша, -и, carcass.

тушева́ть, -шу́ю *imp.* (*perf.* за~) shade. **тушёвка**, -и, shading.

тушёный, braised, stewed. **туши́ть**[1], -шу́, -шишь *imp.* (*perf.* с~) braise, stew.

туши́ть[2], -шу́, -шишь *imp.* (*perf.* за~, по~) extinguish, put out; suppress, stifle, quell.

тушу́ю, etc.: see тушева́ть. **тушь**, -и, Indian ink.

тща́тельность, -и, thoroughness, carefulness; care. **тща́тельный**, thorough, careful; painstaking.

тщеду́шный, feeble, frail, weak; puny.

тщесла́вие, -я, vanity, vainglory. **тщесла́вный**, vain, vainglorious.

тщета́, -ы́, vanity. **тще́тно** *adv.* vainly, in vain. **тще́тный**, vain, futile; unavailing.

ты, тебя́, -бе́, тобо́й, тебе́, you; thou; быть на ты с + *instr.*, be on intimate terms with.

ты́кать, ты́чу *imp.* (*perf.* ткнуть) poke; prod; jab; stick; ~ па́льцем, point; **~ся**, knock (в + *acc.* against, into); rush about, fuss about.

ты́ква, -ы, pumpkin; gourd.

тыл, -а (-у), *loc.* -у́; *pl.* -ы́, back; rear; the interior. **тылово́й,** rear; ~ го́спиталь, base hospital. **ты́льный,** back; rear.

тын, -а, paling; palisade, stockade.

ты́сяча, -и *instr.* -ей or -ью, thousand. **тысячеле́тие,** -я, a thousand years; millennium; thousandth anniversary. **тысячеле́тний,** thousand-year; millennial. **ты́сячный,** thousandth; of (many) thousands.

тычи́нка, -и stamen.

тьма[1], -ы, dark, darkness.

тьма[2], -ы; *gen. pl.* тем, ten thousand; host, swarm, multitude.

тэ *n. indecl.* the letter т.

ТЭЦ *f. indecl., abbr.* теплоэлектроцентра́ль, district-heating and power station.

тю́бик, -а, tube.

ТЮЗ *m. indecl., abbr.* теа́тр ю́ного зри́теля, young people's theatre.

тюк, -а́, bale, package.

тюле́невый, sealskin. **тюле́ний,** seal. **тюле́нь,** -я *m.* seal.

тюль, -я *m.* tulle.

тюльпа́н, -а, tulip.

тюни́ка, -и, over-skirt; 'romantic' tutu, long ballet dress.

тюре́мн|ый, prison; ~ое заключе́ние, imprisonment. **тюре́мщик,** -а, gaoler, warder; enslaver. **тюре́мщица,** -ы, wardress. **тюрьма́,** -ы́; *pl.* -ы, -рем, prison; jail gaol; imprisonment.

тю́ря, -и, (*sl.*) 'bread soup', sop(s), slops.

тюфя́к, -а́, mattress. **тюфя́чный,** mattress.

тя́га, -и, traction; locomotion; locomotives; thrust; draught; pull, attraction; thirst, craving; taste; дать тя́гу, take to one's heels. **тяга́ться,** -а́юсь *imp.* (*perf.* по~) measure one's strength (against); vie, contend; have a tug-of-war. **тяга́ч,** -а́, tractor.

тя́гостный, burdensome, onerous; painful, distressing. **тя́гость,** -и, weight, burden; fatigue. **тяготе́ние,** -я, gravity, gravitation; attraction, taste; bent, inclination. **тяготе́ть,** -е́ю *imp.* gravitate; be drawn, be attracted; ~ над, hang over, threaten. **тяготи́ть,** -ощу́ *imp.* burden, be a burden on; lie heavy on, oppress.

тягу́чий, malleable, ductile; viscous; slow leisurely, unhurried.

тя́жба, -ы, lawsuit; litigation; competition, rivalry.

тяжело́ *adv.* heavily; seriously, gravely; with difficulty. **тяжело́** *predic.* it is hard; it is painful; it is distressing; ему́ ~, he feels miserable, he feels wretched. **тяжелоатле́т,** -а, weight-lifter. **тяжелове́с,** -а, heavy-weight. **тяжелове́сный,** heavy; ponderous, clumsy. **тяжелово́з,** -а, heavy draught-horse; heavy lorry. **тяжёлый;** -ёл, -а́, heavy; hard; difficult; slow; severe; serious, grave, bad; seriously ill; painful; ponderous, unwieldy. **тя́жесть,** -и, gravity; weight; heavy object; heaviness; difficulty; severity. **тя́жкий,** heavy, hard; severe; serious, grave.

тяну́ть, -ну́, -нешь *imp.* (*perf.* по~) pull; draw; haul; drag; tug; drawl; drag out, protract, delay; weigh, weigh down; draw up; take in; extract; extort; *impers.* draw, attract; be tight; его́ тя́нет домо́й, he wants to go home; тя́нет в плеча́х, it feels tight across the shoulders; ~ жре́бий, draw lots; ~ на букси́ре, tow; **~ся,** stretch; extend; stretch out; stretch oneself; drag on; crawl; drift; move along one after another; last out, hold out; reach (out), strive (к + *dat.* after); + за + *instr.* try to keep up with, try to equal.

тяну́чка, -и, toffee, caramel.

У

у *n. indecl.* the letter у.
у *int.* oh.
у *prep.* + *gen.* by; at; with; from, of; belonging to; спроси́те у него́ о́ттиск, ask him to let you have an offprint; у вла́сти, in power; у воро́т, at the gate; у меня́ (есть), I have; у меня́ к вам ма́ленькая про́сьба, I have a small favour to ask of you; у нас, at our place, with us; in our country; у неё нет вре́мени, she has no time; у окна́, by the window; я за́нял де́сять рубле́й у сосе́да, I borrowed ten roubles from a neighbour.
у- *vbl. pref.* indicating movement away from a place, insertion in something, covering all over, reduction or curtailment, achievement of aim; and, with adjectival roots, forming verbs expressing comparative degree.
уба́вить, -влю *perf.*, **убавля́ть, -я́ю** *imp.* reduce, lessen, diminish; ~ в ве́се, lose weight.
у|баю́кать, -аю *perf.*, **убаю́кивать, -аю** *imp.* lull (to sleep); rock to sleep, sing to sleep.
убега́ть, -а́ю *imp.* of убежа́ть.
убеди́тельн|ый, convincing, persuasive, cogent; pressing; earnest; быть ~ым, carry conviction. **убеди́ть, -и́шь** *perf.* (*imp.* убежда́ть) convince; persuade; prevail on; **~ся,** be convinced; make certain, satisfy oneself.
убежа́ть, -егу́ *perf* (*imp.* убега́ть) run away, run off, make off; escape; boil over.
убежда́ть(ся, -а́ю(сь *imp.* of убеди́ть(ся. **убежде́ние, -я,** persuasion; conviction, belief. **убеждённость, -и,** conviction. **убеждённый; -ён, -а́,** convinced; persuaded; confirmed; staunch, stalwart.
убе́жище, -а, refuge, asylum; sanctuary; shelter; dug-out; иска́ть убе́жища, seek refuge seek sanctuary; пра́во убе́жища, right of asylum.
убелённый; -ён, -а́, whitened, white; ~ седи́нами, white-haired; ~ сединóй, white. **убели́ть, -и́т** *perf.* whiten.
уберега́ть, -а́ю *imp.*, **убере́чь, -регу́, -режёшь; -рёг, -гла́** *perf.* protect, guard, keep safe, preserve; **~ся** от + *gen.* protect oneself against, guard against.
уберу́, etc.: see убра́ть.
убива́ть(ся, -а́ю(сь *imp.* of уби́ть(ся. **уби́йственный,** deadly; murderous; killing. **уби́йство, -а,** murder, assassination. **уби́йца, -ы** *m.* and *f.* murderer; killer; assassin.
убира́ть(ся, -а́ю(сь *imp.* of убра́ть(ся; убира́йся! clear off! hop it! **убира́ющийся,** retractable.
уби́тый, killed; crushed, broken; *sb.* dead man. **уби́ть, убью́, -ьёшь** *perf.* (*imp.* убива́ть) kill; murder; assassinate; finish; break, smash; expend; waste; **~ся,** hurt oneself, bruise oneself; grieve.
убо́гий, wretched; poverty-stricken, beggardly; squalid; *sb.* pauper, beggar. **убо́жество, -а,** poverty; squalor; mediocrity; physical disability; infirmity.
убо́й, -я, slaughter; корми́ть на ~, fatten; feed up, stuff. **убо́йность, -и,** effectiveness, destructive power. **убо́йный,** killing, destructive, lethal; for slaughter.
убо́р, -а, dress, attire; головно́й ~, headgear, head-dress.
убо́ристый, close, small.
убо́рка, -и, harvesting, reaping, gathering in; picking; collection, removal; clearing up, tidying up. **убо́рная** *sb.* lavatory; public convenience; dressing-room. **убо́рочн|ый,** harvest, harvesting; ~ая маши́на, harvester. **убо́рщик, -а, убо́рщица, -ы,** cleaner. **убра́нство, -а,** furniture, appointments; decoration; attire. **убра́ть, уберу́, -рёшь; -а́л, -а́, -о** *perf.* (*imp.* убира́ть) remove; take away; kick out; sack; put away, store; harvest, reap, gather in; clear up, tidy up; decorate, adorn; ~ ко́мнату, do a room; ~ посте́ль, make a bed; ~ с доро́ги, put out of

the way; ~ со столá, clear the table; **~ся**, clear up, tidy up, clean up; clear off, clear out; attire oneself.

убывáть, -áю *imp.*, **убы́ть**, убýду; ýбыл, -á, -о *perf.* decrease, diminish; subside, fall, go down; wane; go away, leave. **ýбыль**, -и, diminution, decrease; subsidence; losses, casualties. **убы́ток**, -тка (-тку), loss; *pl.* damages. **убы́точно** *adv.* at a loss. **убы́точн|ый**, unprofitable; ~ая продáжа, sale at a loss.

убью́, etc.: see уби́ть.

уважáемый, respected, esteemed, honoured; dear. **уважáть**, -áю *imp.* respect, esteem. **уважéние**, -я, respect, esteem; с ~м, yours sincerely. **уважи́тельный**, valid, good; respectful, deferential.

увáриваться, -ается *imp.*, **увари́ться**, -áрится *perf.* be thoroughly cooked; boil down, boil away.

уведоми́тельн|ый, notifying, informing; ~ое письмó, letter of advice; notice. **увéдомить**, -млю *perf.*, **уведомля́ть**, -я́ю *imp.* inform, notify. **уведомлéние**, -я, information, notification.

уведý, etc.: see увести́.

увезти́, -зý, -зёшь; увёз, -лá *perf.* (*imp.* увози́ть) take (away); take with one; steal; abduct, kidnap.

увековéчивать, -аю *imp.*, **увековéчить**, -чу *perf.* immortalize; perpetuate.

увёл, etc.: see увести́.

увеличéние, -я, increase; augmentation; extension; magnification; enlargement. **увели́чивать**, -аю *imp.*, **увели́чить**, -чу *perf.* increase; augment; extend; enhance; magnify; enlarge; **~ся**, increase, grow, rise. **увеличи́тель**, -я *m.* enlarger. **увеличи́тельн|ый**, magnifying; enlarging; augmentative; ~ое стеклó, magnifying glass.

у|венчáть, -áю *perf.*, **увéнчивать**, -аю *imp.* crown; **~ся** be crowned.

уверéние, -я, assurance; protestation. **увéренность**, -и, confidence; certitude, certainty; в пóлной увéренности, in the firm belief, quite certain. **увéренный**, confident; sure; certain; бýдь(те) увéрен(ы)! you may be sure, you may rely on it. **увéрить**, -рю *perf.* (*imp.* уверя́ть) assure; convince, persuade; **~ся**, assure oneself, satisfy oneself; be convinced.

увернýться, -нýсь, -нёшься *perf.*, **увёртываться**, -аюсь *imp.* от + *gen.* dodge; evade. **увёртка**, -и, dodge, evasion; subterfuge; *pl.* wiles. **увёртливый**, evasive, shifty.

увертю́ра, -ы, overture.

уверя́ть(ся, -я́ю(сь *imp.* of увéрить(ся.

увеселéние, -я, amusement, entertainment. **увесели́тельн|ый**, amusement, entertainment; pleasure; ~ая поéздка, pleasure trip. **увеселя́ть**, -я́ю *imp.* amuse, entertain.

увéсистый, weighty; heavy.

увести́, -едý, -едёшь; -ёл, -á *perf.* (*imp.* уводи́ть) take (away); take with one; carry off, walk off with.

увéчить, -чу *imp.* maim, mutilate, cripple. **увéчный**, maimed, mutilated, crippled; *sb.* cripple. **увéчье**, -я, maiming, mutilation; injury.

увéшать, -аю *perf.*, **увéшивать**, -аю *imp.* hang, cover (+ *instr.* with).

увещáние, -я, exhortation, admonition. **увещáть**, -áю *imp.*, **увещевáть**, -áю *imp.* exhort, admonish.

у|видáть(ся, -áю(сь *perf.* **у|ви́деть(ся**, -и́жу(сь *perf.*

уви́ливать, -аю *imp.*, **увильнýть**, -нý, -нёшь *perf.* от + *gen.* dodge; evade, shirk; (try to) wriggle out of.

увлажни́ть, -ню́ *perf.*, **увлажня́ть**, -я́ю *imp.* moisten, damp, wet.

увлекáтельный, fascinating; absorbing. **увлекáть**, -áю *imp.*, **увлéчь**, -екý, -ечёшь; -ёк, -лá *perf.* carry along; carry away, distract; captivate, fascinate; entice, allure; **~ся**, be carried away; become keen; become mad (+ *instr.* about); become enamoured, fall (+ *instr.* for).

увóд, -а, taking away, withdrawal; carrying off; stealing. **уводи́ть**, -ожý, -óдишь *imp.* of увести́.

увожý, etc.: see уводи́ть, увози́ть.

увóз, -а, abduction; carrying off; свáдьба ~ом, elopement. **увози́ть**, -ожý, -óзишь *imp.* of увезти́.

увóлить, -лю *perf.*, **увольня́ть**, -я́ю *imp.* discharge, dismiss; retire; sack, fire; **~ся**, retire; resign, leave the service. **увольнéние**, -я, discharge, dismissal; retiring, pensioning off. **увольнúтельный**, discharge, dismissal; leave.

УВЧ (*uveché*) *abbr.* ультравысóкая частотá, ультравысокочастóтный, ultrahigh frequency, UHF.

увы́ *int.* alas!

увядáние, -я, fading, withering. **увядáть**, -áю *imp.* of увя́нуть. **увя́дший**, withered.

увязáть[1], -áю *imp.* of увя́знуть.

увязáть[2], -яжý -я́жешь *perf.* (*imp.* увя́зывать) tie up; pack up; co-ordinate; **~ся**, pack; tag along. **увя́зка**, -и, tying up, roping, strapping; co-ordination.

у|вя́знуть, -ну; -я́з *perf.* (*imp.* also увязáть) get bogged down, get stuck.

увя́зывать(ся, -аю(сь *imp.* of увязáть-(ся.

у|вя́нуть, -ну *perf.* (*imp.* also увядáть) fade, wither, wilt, droop.

угадáть, -áю *perf.*, **угáдывать**, -аю *imp.* guess (right).

угáр, -а, charcoal fumes; carbon monoxide (poisoning); ecstasy, intoxication. **угáрный**, full of fumes; ~ газ, carbon monoxide.

угасáть, -áет *imp.*, **у|гáснуть**, -нет; -áс *perf.* go out; die down.

угле- in *comb.* coal; charcoal; carbon. **углевóд**, -а, carbohydrate. **~водорóд**, -а, hydrocarbon. **~добы́ча**, -и, coal extraction. **~жжéние**, -я, charcoal burning. **~жóг**, -а, charcoal-burner. **~кислотá**, -ы́, carbonic acid; carbon dioxide. **~кúслый**, carbonate (of); ~кúслый аммóний, ammonium carbonate. **~рóд**, -а, carbon.

угловáтый, angular; awkward. **угловóй**, corner; angle; angular.

углубúть, -блю́ *perf.*, **углубля́ть**, -я́ю *imp.* deepen; make deeper; sink deeper; extend; **~ся**, deepen; become deeper; become intensified; go deep; delve deeply; become absorbed. **углублéние**, -я, hollow, depression, dip; draught; deepening; extending; intensification. **углублённый**, deepened; deep; profound; absorbed.

угнáть, угоню́, -óнишь; -áл, -á, -о *perf.* (*imp.* угоня́ть) drive away; send off, despatch; steal; **~ся** за + *instr.* keep pace with, keep up with.

угнетáтель, -я *m.* oppressor. **угнетáтельский**, oppressive. **угнетáть**, -áю *imp.* oppress; depress, dispirit. **угнетéние**, -я, oppression; depression. **угнетённ|ый**, oppressed; depressed; ~ое состоя́ние, low spirits, depression.

уговáривать, -аю *imp.*, **уговорúть**, -рю́ *perf.* persuade, induce; urge; talk into; **~ся**, arrange, agree. **уговóр**, -а (-у), persuasion; agreement compact.

угóда, -ы; в угóду + *dat.* to please. **угодúть**, -ожý *perf.*, **угождáть**, -áю *imp.* fall, get; bang; (+ *dat.*) hit; + *dat.* or на + *acc.* please, oblige. **угóдливый**, obsequious. **угóдно** *predic.* + *dat.*; как вам ~, as you wish, as you please; please yourself; что вам ~? what would you like? what can I do for you?; *part.* кто ~, anyone (you like), whoever you like; что ~, anything (you like), whatever you like. **угóдный**, pleasing, welcome.

ýгол, углá, *loc.* -ý, corner; angle; part of a room; place; из-за углá, (from) round the corner; on the sly; имéть свой ~, have a place of one's own; ~ зрéния, visual angle; point of view.

уголóвник, -а, **-ница**, -ы, criminal. **уголóвный**, criminal.

уголóк, -лкá, *loc.* -ý, corner.

ýголь, ýгля́; *pl.* ýгли, -ей or -éй *m.* coal; charcoal.

угóльник, -а, set square; angle iron, angle bracket. **угóльный**[1], corner.

ýгольный[2], coal; carbon; carbonic.

ýгольщик, -а, collier; coal-miner; coal-man; charcoal-burner.

угомонúть, -ню́ *perf.* calm down, pacify; **~ся**, calm down.

угóн, -а, driving away; stealing. **угоня́ть**, -я́ю *imp.* of угнáть.

угорáть, -áю *imp.*, **угорéть**, -рю́ *perf.* get carbon monoxide poisoning; be mad, be crazy. **угорéлый**; как ~, like a madman, like one possessed.

ýгорь[1], угря́ *m.* eel.

ýгорь[2], угря́ *m.* blackhead.

угости́ть, -ощу́ *perf.*, **угоща́ть,** -а́ю *imp.* entertain; treat. **угоще́ние,** -я, entertaining, treating; refreshments; fare.

угро́бить, -блю *perf.* (*sl.*) do in; ruin, wreck.

угрожа́ть, -а́ю *imp.* threaten. **угрожа́ющий,** threatening, menacing. **угро́за,** -ы, threat, menace.

угро́зыск, -а *abbr.* criminal investigation department.

угрызе́ние, -я, pangs; угрызе́ния со́вести, remorse.

угрю́мый, sullen, morose, gloomy.

уда́в, -а, boa, boa-constrictor.

удава́ться, удаётся *imp.* of уда́ться.

у|дави́ть(ся, -влю́(сь, -вишь(ся *perf.* **уда́вка,** -и, running knot, half hitch. **удавле́ние,** -я, strangling, strangulation.

удале́ние, -я, removal; extraction; sending away, sending off; moving off.

удали́ть, -лю́ *perf.* (*imp.* удаля́ть) remove; extract; send away; move away; **~ся,** move off, move away; leave, withdraw, retire.

удало́й, уда́лый; -а́л, -а́, -о, daring, bold. **у́даль, -и, удальство́,** -а́, daring, boldness.

удаля́ть(ся, -я́ю(сь *imp.* of удали́ть(ся.

уда́р, -а, blow; stroke; shock; attack; thrust; seizure; быть в ~е, be in good form; нанести́ ~, strike a blow; ~ гро́ма, thunder-clap. **ударе́ние,** -я, accent; stress; stress-mark; emphasis. **уда́ренный** stressed, accented. **уда́рить,** -рю *perf.*, **ударя́ть,** -я́ю *imp.* (*imp.* also бить) strike; hit; sound; beat; attack; set in; **~ся,** strike, hit; ~ся в бе́гство, break into a run; ~ся в слёзы, burst into tears. **уда́рник,** -а, **-ница,** -ы, shock-worker. **уда́рный,** percussive; percussion; shock; of shock-workers; urgent, rush. **ударопро́чный ударосто́йкий,** shockproof, shock-resistant.

уда́ться, -а́стся, -аду́тся; -а́лся, -ла́сь *perf.* (*imp.* удава́ться) succeed, be a success, turn out well, work. **уда́ча,** -и, good luck, good fortune; success. **уда́чный,** successful; felicitous, apt, good.

удва́ивать, -аю *imp.*, **удво́ить,** -о́ю *perf.* double, redouble; reduplicate. **удвое́ние,** -я, doubling; reduplication. **удво́енный,** doubled, redoubled; reduplicated.

уде́л, -а, lot, destiny; apanage; crown lands.

удели́ть, -лю́ *perf.* (*imp.* уделя́ть) spare, devote, give.

уде́льный[1], specific; ~ вес, specific gravity.

уде́льный[2], apanage, crown.

уделя́ть, -я́ю *imp.* of удели́ть.

у́держ, -у; без ~у, unrestrainedly, without restraint, uncontrollably. **удержа́ние,** -я, deduction; retention, keeping, holding. **удержа́ть,** -жу́, -жишь *perf.*, **уде́рживать,** -аю *imp.* hold, hold on to, not let go; keep, retain; hold back, keep back; restrain; keep down, suppress; deduct; ~ в па́мяти, bear in mind, retain in one's memory; **~ся,** hold one's ground, hold on, hold out; stand firm; keep one's feet; keep (from), refrain (from); мы не могли́ ~ся от сме́ха, we couldn't help laughing; ~ся от собла́зна, resist a temptation.

удеру́, etc.: see удра́ть.

удешеви́ть, -влю́ *perf.*, **удешевля́ть,** -я́ю *imp.* reduce the price of; **~ся,** become cheaper. **удешевле́ние,** -я, price-reduction.

удиви́тельный, astonishing, surprising, amazing; wonderful, marvellous; не удивительно, что, no wonder (that). **удиви́ть,** -влю́ *perf.*, **удивля́ть,** -я́ю *imp.* astonish, surprise, amaze; **~ся,** be astonished, be surprised, be amazed; marvel. **удивле́ние,** -я, astonishment, surprise, amazement; к моему́ удивле́нию, to my surprise; на ~, excellently, splendidly, marvellously.

удила́, -и́л *pl.* bit.

уди́лище, -а, fishing-rod. **уди́льщик,** -а, **-щица,** -ы, angler.

удира́ть, -а́ю *imp.* of удра́ть.

уди́ть ужу́, у́дишь *imp.* fish for; ~ рыбу, fish; **~ся,** bite.

удлине́ние, -я lengthening; extension. **удлини́ть,** -ню́ *perf.*, **удлиня́ть,** -я́ю *imp.* lengthen; extend, prolong; **~ся,**

become longer, lengthen; be extended, be prolonged.

удóбно *adv.* comfortably; conveniently. **удóбн|ый,** comfortable; cosy; convenient, suitable, opportune; proper, in order; ~ый слýчай, opportunity; ~о + *dat.* it is convenient for, it suits.

удобо- in *comb.* conveniently, easily, well. **удобовари́мый,** digestible. **~испо́лни́мый,** easy to carry out. **~обтекáемый,** streamlined. **~переноси́мый,** portable, easily carried. **~поня́тный,** comprehensible, intelligible. **~произноси́мый,** easy to pronounce. **~управля́емый,** easily controlled. **~усвоя́емый,** easily assimilated. **~читáемый,** legible, easy to read.

удобрéние, -я, fertilization, manuring; fertilizer. **удóбрить,** -рю *perf.,* **удобря́ть,** -я́ю *imp.* fertilize.

удóбство, -а, comfort; convenience; amenity; квартúра со всéми удóбствами, flat with all conveniences.

удовлетворéние, -я, satisfaction; gratification. **удовлетворённый;** -рён, -á, satisfied, contented. **удовлетвори́тельно** *adv.* satisfactorily; fair, satisfactory. **удовлетвори́тельный,** satisfactory. **удовлетвори́ть,** -рю́ *perf.,* **удовлетворя́ть,** -я́ю *imp.* satisfy; gratify; give satisfaction to; comply with; + *dat.* answer, meet; + *instr.* supply with, furnish with; ~ желáние, gratify a wish; ~ потрéбности, satisfy the requirements; ~ прóсьбу, comply with a request; **~ся,** content oneself; be satisfied.

удовóльствие, -я, pleasure; amusement. **у|довóльствоваться,** -твуюсь *perf.*

удóй, -я, milk-yield; milking. **удóйлив|ый,** yielding much milk; ~ая корóва, good milker.

удостáивать(ся, -аю(сь *imp.* of удостóить(ся.

удостоверéние, -я, certification, attestation; certificate; ~ ли́чности, identity card. **удостовéрить,** -рю *perf.,* **удостоверя́ть,** -я́ю *imp.* certify, attest, witness; ~ ли́чность + *gen.* prove the identity of, identify; **~ся,** make sure (в + *prep.* of), assure oneself.

удостóить, -óю *perf.* (*imp.* удостáивать) make an award to; + *gen.* award to, confer on; + *instr.* favour with, vouchsafe to; **~ся** + *gen.* receive, be awarded; be favoured with, be vouchsafed; be found worthy.

удосýживаться, -аюсь *imp.,* **удосýжиться,** -жусь *perf.* find time.

ýдочка, -и, (fishing-)rod.

удрáть, удерý, -ёшь; удрáл, -á, -о *perf.* (*imp.* удирáть) make off, clear out, run away.

удружи́ть, -жý *perf.* + *dat.* do a good turn.

удручáть, -áю *imp.,* **удручи́ть,** -чý *perf.* depress, dispirit. **удручённый;** -чён, -á, depressed, despondent.

удушáть, -áю *imp.,* **удуши́ть,** -шý, -шишь *perf.* smother, stifle, suffocate; asphyxiate. **удушéние,** -я, suffocation; asphyxiation. **удýшливый,** stifling, suffocating; asphyxiating. **удýшье,** -я, asthma; suffocation, asphyxia.

уединéние, -я, solitude; seclusion. **уединённый,** solitary, secluded; lonely. **уедини́ться,** -ню́сь *perf.,* **уединя́ться,** -я́юсь *imp.* retire, withdraw; seclude oneself.

уéзд, -а, uezd, District.

уезжáть, -áю *imp.,* **уéхать,** уéду *perf.* go away, leave, depart.

уж, -á, grass-snake.

уж *adv.* see ужé. **уж, ужé** *part.* to be sure, indeed, certainly; really.

у|жáлить, -лю *perf.*

ýжас, -а, horror, terror; *predic.* it is awful, it is terrible; ~ (как), awfully, terribly; ~ скóлько, an awful lot of. **ужасáть,** -áю *imp.,* **ужаснýть,** -нý, -нёшь *perf.* horrify, terrify; **~ся,** be horrified, be terrified. **ужáсно** *adv.* horribly, terribly; awfully; frightfully. **ужáсный,** awful, terrible, ghastly, frightful.

ýже, *comp.* of ýзкий.

ужé, уж *adv.* already; now; by now; ~ давнó, it's a long time ago; ~ не, no longer. **ужé** *part.*: see уж *part.*

ужéние, -я, fishing, angling.

ужесточáться, -áется *imp.* become, be made, stricter, tighter, more rigorous.

ужесточéние, -я, tightening up intensification; making stricter, more rigorous. **ужесточи́ть,** -чу́ *perf.* make stricter, make more rigorous; intensify, tighten (up).

ужива́ться, -а́юсь *imp.* of ужи́ться. **ужи́вчивый,** easy to get on with.

ужи́мка, -и, grimace.

у́жин, -а, supper. **у́жинать,** -аю *imp.* (*perf.* по~) have supper.

ужи́ться, -иву́сь, -ивёшься; -и́лся, -ла́сь *perf.* (*imp.* ужива́ться) get on.

ужу́: see уди́ть.

узаконéние, -я, legalization, legitimization; statute. **узакóнивать,** -аю *imp.*, **узакóнить,** -ню *perf.*, **узаконя́ть,** -я́ю *imp.* legalize, legitimize.

узда́, -ы́; *pl.* -ы, bridle.

у́зел, узла́, knot; bend, hitch; junction; centre; node; bundle, pack; нéрвный ~, nerve-centre, ganglion.

у́зк|ий; у́зок, узка́, -о, narrow; tight; limited; narrow-minded; ~ое мéсто, bottleneck. **узкоколéйка,** -и, narrow-gauge railway. **узкоколéйный,** narrow-gauge. **узкоплёночный,** 16-mm, sixteen-millimetre.

узлова́тый, knotty; nodose; gnarled. **узлов|óй,** junction; main, principal, central, key; ~а́я ста́нция, junction.

узнава́ть, -наю́, -наёшь *imp.*, **узна́ть,** -а́ю *perf.* recognize; get to know, become familiar with; learn, find out.

у́зник, -а, **у́зница,** -ы, prisoner.

узóр, -а, pattern, design. **узóрный,** pattern; patterned. **узóрчатый,** patterned.

у́зость, -и, narrowness; tightness.

у́зы, уз *pl.* bonds, ties.

уйду́, etc.: see уйти́. **уйму́,** etc.: see унять.

уйти́, уйду́, -дёшь; ушёл, ушла́ *perf.* (*imp.* уходи́ть) go away, leave, depart; escape, get away; evade; retire; sink; bury oneself; be used up, be spent; pass away, slip away; boil over; spill; ~ (вперёд), gain, be fast; на э́то уйдёт мнóго врéмени, it will take a lot of time; так вы далекó не уйдёте, you won't get very far like that; ~ на пéнсию, retire on a pension; ~ со сцéны, quit the stage; ~ с рабóты, leave work, give up work.

ука́з, -а, decree; edict, ukase. **указа́ние,** -я, indication, pointing out; instruction, direction. **ука́занный,** fixed, appointed, stated. **указа́тель,** -я *m.* indicator; marker; gauge; index; guide, directory; ~ направлéния, road-sign. **указа́тельн|ый,** indicating; demonstrative; ~ый па́лец, index finger, forefinger; ~ая стрéлка, pointer. **указа́ть,** -ажу́, -а́жешь *perf.*, **ука́зывать**, -аю *imp.* show; indicate; point; point out; explain; give directions; give orders. **ука́зка,** -и, pointer; orders; по чужóй ука́зке, at someone else's bidding.

ука́лывать, -аю *imp.* of уколóть.

уката́ть, -а́ю *perf.*, **ука́тывать**[1], -аю *imp.* roll, roll out; flatten; wear out, tire out; **~ся,** become smooth. **укати́ть,** -ачу́, -а́тишь *perf.*, **ука́тывать**[2], -аю *imp.* roll away; drive off; **~ся,** roll away.

укача́ть, -а́ю *perf.*, **ука́чивать,** -аю *imp.* rock to sleep; make sick.

УКВ (*ukavé*) *abbr.* ультракорóткие вóлны, ультракоротковóлновый, ultra-short waves, ultrashort-wave.

укла́д, -а, structure; form; organization, set-up; ~ жи́зни, style of life, mode of life; общéственно-экономи́ческий ~, social and economic structure. **укла́дка,** -и, packing; stacking, piling; stowing; laying; setting, set. **укла́дчик,** -а, packer; layer. **укла́дывать(ся**[1], -аю(сь *imp.* of уложи́ть(ся.

укла́дываться[2], -аюсь *imp.* of улéчься.

уклóн, -а, slope, declivity; inclination; incline; gradient; bias, tendency; deviation. **уклонéние,** -я, deviation; evasion; digression. **уклони́ст,** -а, deviationist. **уклони́ться,** -ню́сь, -ни́шься *perf.*, **уклоня́ться,** -я́юсь *imp.* deviate; + от + *gen.* turn, turn off, turn aside; avoid; evade. **уклóнчивый,** evasive.

уклю́чина, -ы, rowlock.

укóл, -а, prick; jab; injection; thrust. **уколóть,** -лю́, -лешь *perf.* (*imp.* ука́лывать) prick; sting, wound.

укомплектова́ние, -я, bringing up to strength. **укомплекто́ванный**, complete, at full strength. **у|комплектова́ть**, -ту́ю *perf.*, **укомплекто́вывать**, -аю *imp.* complete; bring up to (full) strength; man; + *instr.* equip with, furnish with.

уко́р, -а, reproach.

укора́чивать, -аю *imp.* of укороти́ть.

укорени́ть, -ню́ *perf.*, **укореня́ть**, -я́ю *imp.* implant, inculcate; **~ся**, take root, strike root.

укори́зна, -ы, reproach. **укори́зненный**, reproachful. **укори́ть**, -рю́ *perf.* (*imp.* укоря́ть) reproach (в + *prep.* with).

укороти́ть, -очу́ *perf.* (*imp.* укора́чивать) shorten.

укоря́ть, -я́ю *imp.* of укори́ть.

уко́с, -а, (hay-)crop.

укра́дкой *adv.* stealthily, by stealth, furtively. **украду́**, etc.: see укра́сть.

украи́нец, -нца, **украи́нка**, -и, Ukrainian. **украи́нский**, Ukrainian.

укра́сить, -а́шу *perf.* (*imp.* украша́ть) adorn, decorate, ornament; **~ся**, be decorated; adorn oneself.

у|кра́сть, -аду́, -дёшь *perf.*

украша́ть(ся, -а́ю(сь *imp.* of укра́сить(ся. **украше́ние**, -я, adorning; decoration; adornment, ornament.

укрепи́ть, -плю́ *perf.*, **укрепля́ть**, -я́ю *imp.* strengthen; reinforce; fix, make fast; fortify; consolidate; brace; enhance; **~ся**, become stronger; fortify one's position. **укрепле́ние**, -я, strengthening; reinforcement; consolidation; fortification; work. **укрепля́ющее** *sb.* tonic, restorative.

укро́мный, secluded, sheltered, cosy.

укро́п, -а (-у), dill.

укроти́тель, -я *m.* (animal-)tamer. **укроти́ть**, -ощу́ *perf.*, **укроща́ть**, -а́ю *imp.* tame; curb, subdue, check; **~ся**, become tame, be tamed; calm down, die down. **укроще́ние**, -я, taming.

укро́ю, etc.: see укры́ть.

укрупне́ние, -я, enlargement, extension; amalgamation. **укрупни́ть**, -ню́ *perf.*, **укрупня́ть**, -я́ю *imp.* enlarge, extend; amalgamate.

укрыва́тель, -я *m.* concealer, harbourer; ~ кра́деного, receiver (of stolen goods). **укрыва́тельство**, -а, concealment, harbouring; receiving. **укрыва́ть**, -а́ю *imp.*, **укры́ть**, -ро́ю *perf.* cover, cover up; conceal, harbour; give shelter (to); receive, act as receiver of; **~ся**, cover oneself; take cover; find shelter; escape notice. **укры́тие**, -я, cover; concealment; shelter.

у́ксус, -а (-у), vinegar.

уку́с, -а, bite; sting. **укуси́ть**, -ушу́ -у́сишь *perf.* bite; sting.

уку́тать, -аю *perf.*, **уку́тывать**, -аю *imp.* wrap up; **~ся** wrap oneself up.

укушу́, etc.: see укуси́ть.

ул. *abbr.* у́лица, street, road.

ула́вливать, -аю *imp.* of улови́ть.

ула́дить, -а́жу *perf.*, **ула́живать**, -аю *imp.* settle, arrange; reconcile.

ула́мывать, -аю *imp.* of улома́ть.

у́лей, у́лья, (bee)hive.

улета́ть, -а́ю *imp.*, **улете́ть**, улечу́ *perf.* fly, fly away; vanish. **улету́чиваться**, -аюсь *imp.*, **улету́читься**, -чусь *perf.* evaporate, volatilize; vanish, disappear.

уле́чься, уля́гусь, -я́жешься; улёгся, -гла́сь *perf.* (*imp.* укла́дываться) lie down; find room; settle; subside; calm down.

улизну́ть, -ну́, -нёшь *perf.* slip away, steal away.

ули́ка, -и, clue; evidence.

ули́тка, -и, snail.

у́лица, -ы, street; на у́лице, in the street; out of doors, outside.

улича́ть, -а́ю *imp.*, **уличи́ть**, -чу́ *perf.* establish the guilt of; ~ в + *prep.* catch out in.

у́личный, street.

уло́в, -а, catch, take, haul. **улови́мый**, perceptible; audible. **улови́ть**, -влю́, -вишь *perf.* (*imp.* ула́вливать) catch, pick up, locate; detect, perceive; seize. **уло́вка**, -и, trick, ruse, subterfuge.

уложе́ние, -я, code. **уложи́ть**, -жу́, -жишь *perf.* (*imp.* укла́дывать) lay; pack; stow; pile, stack; cover; set; ~ спать, put to bed; **~ся**, pack, pack up; go in; fit in; sink in; + в + *acc.* keep within, confine oneself to.

улома́ть, -а́ю (*imp.* ула́мывать) talk round, prevail on.

улуча́ть, -а́ю *imp.*, **улучи́ть,** -чу́ *perf.* find, seize, catch.
улучша́ть, -а́ю *imp.*, **улу́чшить,** -шу *perf.* improve; ameliorate; better; **~ся,** improve; get better. **улучше́ние,** -я, improvement; amelioration.
улыба́ться, -а́юсь *imp.*, **улыбну́ться,** -ну́сь, -нёшься *perf.* smile; + *dat.* appeal to. **улы́бка,** -и, smile.
ультра- in *comb.* ultra-. **ультравысо́кий,** ultra-high. **~звуково́й,** supersonic, ultrasonic. **~коро́ткий,** ultra-short. **~фиоле́товый,** ultra-violet.
уля́гусь, etc.: see уле́чься.
ум, -а́, mind, intellect; wits; head; свести́ с ~а́, drive mad; склад ~а́, mentality turn of mind; сойти́ с ~а́, go mad; go crazy.
умале́ние, -я, belittling, disparagement. **умали́ть,** -лю́ *perf.* (*imp.* умаля́ть) belittle, disparage; decrease, lessen.
умалишённый, mad, lunatic; *sb.* lunatic, madman, madwoman.
ума́лчивать, -аю *imp.* of умолча́ть.
умаля́ть, -я́ю *imp.* of умали́ть.
уме́лец, -льца, skilled workman, craftsman. **уме́лый,** able, skilful; capable; skilled. **уме́ние,** -я, ability, skill; know-how.
уменьша́ть, -а́ю *imp.*, **уме́ньши́ть,** -шу or -шу́ *perf.* reduce, diminish decrease, lessen; ~ расхо́ды, cut down expenditure; ~ ско́рость, slow down; **~ся,** diminish, decrease, drop, dwindle; abate. **уменьше́ние,** -я, decrease, reduction, diminution, lessening, abatement. **уменьши́тельный,** diminutive.
уме́ренность, -и, moderation. **уме́ренный,** moderate; temperate.
умере́ть, умру́, -рёшь; у́мер, -ла́, -о *perf.* (*imp.* умира́ть) die.
уме́рить, -рю *perf.* (*imp.* умеря́ть) moderate; restrain.
умертви́ть, -рщвлю́ *perf.*, **умерщвля́ть,** -я́ю *imp.* kill, destroy; mortify. **уме́рший,** dead; *sb.* the deceased. **умерщвле́ние,** -я, killiug, destruction; mortification.
умеря́ть, -я́ю *imp.* of уме́рить.
умести́ть, -ещу́ *perf.* (*imp.* умеща́ть) get in, fit in, find room for; **~ся,** go in, fit in, find room. **уме́стно** *adv.* appropriately; opportunely; to the point. **уме́стный,** appropriate; pertinent, to the point; opportune, timely.
уме́ть, -е́ю *imp.* be able, know how.
умеща́ть(ся, -а́ю(сь *imp.* of умести́ть(ся.
умиле́ние, -я, tenderness; emotion. **умили́тельный,** moving, touching, affecting. **умили́ть,** -лю́ *perf.*, **умиля́ть,** -я́ю *imp.* move, touch; **~ся,** be moved, be touched.
умира́ние, -я, dying. **умира́ть,** -а́ю *imp.* of умере́ть. **умира́ющий,** dying; *sb.* dying person.
умне́ть, -е́ю *imp.* (*perf.* по~) grow wiser. **у́мник,** -а, good boy; clever person. **у́мница,** -ы, good girl; *m.* and *f.* clever person. **у́мно́** *adv.* cleverly, wisely; sensibly.
умножа́ть, -а́ю *imp.*, **у|мно́жить,** -жу *perf.* multiply; increase; augment; **~ся,** increase, multiply. **умноже́ние,** -я, multiplication; increase, rise. **умно́житель,** -я *m.* multiplier.
у́мный; умён, умна́, у́мно́, clever, wise, intelligent; sensible. **умозаключа́ть,** -а́ю *imp.*, **умозаключи́ть,** -чу́ *perf.* deduce; infer, conclude. **умозаключе́ние,** -я, deduction; conclusion, inference.
умоли́ть, -лю́ *perf.* (*imp.* умоля́ть) move by entreaties.
у́молк, -у; без ~у, without stopping, incessantly. **умолка́ть,** -а́ю *imp.*, **умо́лкнуть,** -ну; -о́лк *perf.* fall silent; stop; cease. **умолча́ть,** -чу́ *perf.* (*imp.* ума́лчивать) pass over in silence, fail to mention, suppress.
умоля́ть, -я́ю *imp.* of умоли́ть; beg, entreat, implore, beseech. **умоля́ющий,** imploring, pleading.
умопомеша́тельство, -а, derangement, madness, insanity.
умори́тельный, incredibly funny, killing. **у|мори́ть,** -рю́ *perf.* kill; tire out, exhaust.
умо́ю, etc.: see умы́ть. **умру́,** etc.: see умере́ть.
у́мственный. mental, intellectual; ~ труд, brainwork.

умудри́ть, -рю́ *perf.*, **умудря́ть**, -я́ю *imp.* make wise, make wiser; **~ся**, contrive, manage.

умча́ть, -чу́ *perf.* whirl away, dash away; **~ся**, whirl away, dash away.

умыва́льная *sb.* lavatory, cloak-room. **умыва́льник**, -а, wash-stand, wash-basin. **умыва́льный**, wash, washing. **умыва́ть(ся**, -а́ю(сь *imp.* of умы́ть(ся.

у́мысел, -сла, design, intention; злой ~ evil intent; с у́мыслом, of set purpose.

умы́ть, умо́ю *perf.* (*imp.* умыва́ть) wash; **~ся**, wash (oneself).

умы́шленный, intentional, deliberate.

унаво́живать, -аю *imp.*, **у|наво́зить**, -о́жу *perf.* manure.

у|насле́довать, -дую *perf.*

унести́, -су́, -сёшь; -ёс, -ла́ *perf.* (*imp.* уноси́ть) take away; carry off, make off with; carry away, remove; **~сь**, whirl away; fly away, fly by; be carried (away).

универма́г, -а, *abbr.* department store. **универса́льн|ый**, universal; all-round; many-sided; versatile; multi-purpose, all-purpose; ~ магази́н, department store; ~ое сре́дство, panacea. **универса́м**, -а *abbr.* supermarket.

университе́т, -а, university. **университе́тский**, university.

унижа́ть, -а́ю *imp.*, **уни́зить**, -и́жу *perf.* humble. humiliate; lower, degrade; **~ся**, debase oneself, lower oneself, stoop. **униже́ние**, -я, humiliation, degradation, abasement. **уни́женный**, humble. **унижённый**, oppressed, degraded. **унизи́тельный**, humiliating, degrading.

унима́ть(ся, -а́ю(сь *imp.* of уня́ть(ся.

унита́з, -а, lavatory pan.

уничтожа́ть, -а́ю *imp.*, **уничто́жить**, -жу *perf.* destroy, annihilate; wipe out; exterminate, obliterate; abolish; do away with, eliminate; put an end to; crush. **уничтожа́ющий**, destructive, annihilating. **уничтоже́ние**, -я, destruction, annihilation; extermination, obliteration; abolition, elimination.

уноси́ть(ся, -ошу́(сь, -о́сишь(ся *imp.* of унести́(сь.

у́нтер, -а, **у́нтер-офице́р**, -а, non-commissioned officer.

унывáть, -а́ю *imp.* be depressed, be dejected. **уны́лый**, depressed, dejected, despondent, downcast; melancholy, doleful, cheerless. **уны́ние**, -я, depression, dejection, despondency.

уня́ть, уйму́, -мёшь; -я́л, -а́, -о *perf.* (*imp.* унима́ть) calm, soothe, pacify; stop, check; suppress; **~ся**, calm down; stop, abate, die down.

упа́док, -дка, decline; decay, collapse; decadence; depression; ~ ду́ха, depression. **упа́дочнический**, decadent. **упа́дочный**, depressive; decadent.

упаду́, etc.: see упа́сть.

у|пакова́ть, -ку́ю *perf.*, **упако́вывать**, -аю *imp.* pack (up); wrap (up), bale. **упако́вка**, -и, packing; wrapping, baling; package. **упако́вочный**, packing. **упако́вщик**, -а, packer.

упа́сть, -аду́, -адёшь *perf.* of па́дать.

упере́ть, упру́, -рёшь; -ёр *perf.*, **упира́ть**, -а́ю *imp.* rest, prop, lean (heavily): (*sl.*) pinch, steal; ~ глаза́ в + *acc.* fix one's eyes on; ~ на + *acc.* stress, insist on; **~ся**, rest, lean, prop oneself; resist; jib; dig one's heels in; + в + *acc.* come up against; run into.

упи́танный, well-fed; fattened; plump.

упла́та, -ы, payment, paying. **у|плати́ть**, -ачу́, -а́тишь *perf.*, **упла́чивать**, -аю *imp.* pay.

уплотне́ние, -я, compression; condensation; consolidation; sealing. **уплотни́ть**, -ню́ *perf.*, **уплотня́ть**, -я́ю *imp.* condense; consolidate, concentrate, compress; pack (in).

уплыва́ть, -а́ю *imp.*, **уплы́ть**, -ыву́, -ывёшь; -ы́л, -а́, -о *perf.* swim away; sail away, steam away; pass, elapse; be lost to sight; vanish, ebb.

уподо́биться, -блюсь *perf.*, **уподобля́ться**, -я́юсь *imp.* + *dat.* become like; be assimilated to. **уподобле́ние**, -я, likening, comparison; assimilation.

упое́ние, -я, ecstasy, rapture, thrill. **упоённый**, intoxicated, thrilled, in raptures. **упои́тельный**, intoxicating, ravishing.

уползáть, -áю *imp.*, **уползти́**, -зý, -зёшь; -óлз, -злá *perf.* creep away, crawl away.

уполномóченный *sb.* (authorized) agent, delegate, representative; proxy; commissioner. **уполномáчивать, уполномóчивать**, -аю *imp.*, **уполномóчить**, -чу *perf.* authorize, empower. **уполномóчие**, -я, authorization; authority; credentials.

упоминáние, -я, mention; reference; reminder. **упоминáть**, -áю *imp.*, **упомянýть**, -нý, -нешь *perf.* mention, refer to.

упóр, -а, rest, prop, support; stay, brace; в ~, point-blank; сдéлать ~ на + *acc.* or *prep.* lay stress on; смотрéть в ~ на + *acc.* stare straight at. **упóрный**, stubborn, unyielding, obstinate; dogged, persistent; sustained. **-упóрный** in *comb.* -resistant. **упóрство**, -а, stubbornness, obstinacy; doggedness, persistence. **упóрствовать**, -твую *imp.* be stubborn; persist (в + *prep.* in).

упорядочивать, -аю *imp.*, **упорядочить**, -чу *perf.* regulate, put in (good) order, set to rights.

употреби́тельный, (widely-)used; common, generally accepted, usual. **употреби́ть**, -блю́ *perf.*, **употребля́ть**, -я́ю *imp.* use; make use of; take. **употреблéние**, -я, use; usage; application; вы́йти из употреблéния, go out of use, fall into disuse; спóсоб употреблéния, directions for use.

управдéл, -а *abbr.* office manager, business manager. **управдóм**, -а *abbr.* manager (of block of flats), house manager. **управи́тель**, -я *m.* manager; bailiff, steward. **упрáвиться**, -влюсь *perf.*, **управля́ться**, -я́юсь *imp.* cope, manage; + с + *instr.* deal with. **управлéние**, -я management; administration; direction; control; driving, piloting, steering; government; authority, directorate, board; controls; под управлéнием + *gen.* conducted by; ~ автомоби́лем, driving; ~ на расстоя́нии, remote control; ~ по рáдио, radio control. **управля́емый** снаря́д, guided missile. **управля́ть**, -я́ю *imp.* + *instr.* manage, administer, direct, run; govern; be in charge of; control, operate; drive, pilot, steer, navigate; ~ веслóм, paddle. **управля́ющий**, control, controlling; *sb.* manager; bailiff, steward; ~ пóртом, harbour-master.

упражнéние, -я, exercise. **упражня́ть**, -я́ю *imp.* exercise, train; **~ся**, practise, train.

упразднéние, -я, abolition; cancellation, annulment. **упраздни́ть**, -ню́ *perf.*, **упраздня́ть**, -я́ю *imp.* abolish; cancel, annul.

упрáшивать, -аю *imp.* of упроси́ть.

упревáть, -áет *imp.* of упрéть.

упрёк, -а, reproach, reproof. **упрекáть**, -áю *imp.*, **упрекнýть**, -нý, -нёшь *perf.* reproach, reprove; accuse, charge.

у|прéть, -éет *perf.* (*imp.* also упревáть) stew.

упроси́ть, -ошý, -óсишь *perf.* (*imp.* упрáшивать) beg, entreat; prevail upon.

упрости́ть, -ощý *perf.* (*imp.* упрощáть) simplify; over-simplify; **~ся**, be simplified, get simpler.

упрóчивать, -аю *imp.*, **упрóчить** -чу *perf.* strengthen, consolidate; fix; secure; establish firmly; + за + *instr.* leave to; establish for, ensure for; **~ся**, be strengthened be consolidated; become firmer; be firmly established; establish oneself settle oneself; + за + *instr.* become attached to, stick to.

упрошý, etc.: see упроси́ть.

упрощáть(ся, -áю(сь *imp.* of упрости́ть(ся. **упрощéние**, -я, simplification. **упрощённый**; -щён, -á, simplified; over-simplified.

упрý, etc.: see уперéть.

упрýгий, elastic; resilient, flexible; springy. **упрýгость**, -и, elasticity; pressure, tension; spring, bound. **упрýже** *comp.* of упрýгий.

упря́жка, -и, harness, gear; team, relay. **упряжн|óй**, draught; ~áя лóшадь, draught-horse, carriage-horse. **ýпряжь**, -и, harness, gear.

упря́миться, -млюсь *imp.* be obstinate; persist. **упря́мство**, -а, obstinacy, stubbornness. **упря́мый**, obstinate, stubborn; persistent.

упря́тать, -я́чу *perf.*, **упря́тывать**, -аю *imp.* hide, conceal; put away, banish; **~ся**, hide.

упуска́ть, -а́ю *imp.*, **упусти́ть**, -ущу́, -у́стишь *perf.* let go, let slip, let fall; miss; lose; neglect; ~ и́з виду, lose sight of, overlook, fail to take account of. **упуще́ние**, -я, omission; slip; negligence.

ура́ *int.* hurrah.

уравне́ние, -я, equalization; equation. **ура́внивать**, -аю *imp.*, **уравня́ть**, -я́ю *perf.* equalize, make equal, make level; equate. **уравни́тельный**, equalizing, levelling. **уравнове́сить**, -е́шу *perf.*, **уравнове́шивать**, -аю *imp.* balance; equilibrate; counterbalance; neutralize. **уравнове́шенность**, -и, balance, steadiness, composure. **уравнове́шенный**, balanced, steady, composed.

урага́н, -а, hurricane; storm.

ура́н, -а, uranium; Uranus. **ура́новый**, uranium; uranic.

урва́ть, -ву́, -вёшь; -а́л, -а́, -о *perf.* (*imp.* урыва́ть) snatch, grab.

урегули́рование, -я, regulation; settlement, adjustment. **у|регули́ровать**, -рую *perf.*

уре́з, -а, reduction, cut. **уре́зать**, -е́жу *perf.*, **уреза́ть**, -а́ю, **уре́зывать**, -аю *imp.* cut off; shorten; cut down, reduce; axe.

у́рка, -и *m.* and *f.* (*sl.*) lag, convict, (non-political) prisoner.

у́рна, -ы, urn; ballot-box; refuse-bin, litter-bin.

у́ровень, -вня *m.* level; plane; standard; grade; gauge.

уро́д, -а, freak, monster; deformed person; ugly person; depraved person.

уроди́ться, -ожу́сь *perf.* ripen; grow; be born; + в + *acc.* take after.

уро́дливость, -и, deformity; ugliness. **уро́дливый**, deformed, misshapen; ugly; bad; abnormal; faulty; distorting, distorted. **уро́довать**, -дую *imp.* (*perf.* из~) deform, disfigure, mutilate; make ugly; distort. **уро́дство**, -а, deformity; disfigurement; ugliness; abnormality.

урожа́й, -я, harvest; crop, yield; abundance. **урожа́йность**, -и, yield; productivity. **урожа́йный**, harvest; productive, high-yield; ~ год, good year.

урождённый, née; inborn, born. **уроже́нец**, -нца, **урожéнка**, -и, native. **урожу́сь**: see уроди́ться.

уро́к, -а, lesson; homework; task.

уро́н, -а, losses, casualties; damage. **урони́ть**, -ню́, -нишь *perf.* of роня́ть.

уро́чный, fixed, agreed; usual, established.

УРС, -а *abbr.* управля́емый реакти́вный снаря́д, guided missile.

урыва́ть, -а́ю *imp.* of урва́ть. **уры́вками** *adv.* in snatches, by fits and starts; at odd moments. **уры́вочный**, fitful; occasional.

ус, -а; *pl.* -ы́, whisker; antenna; tendril; awn; *pl.* moustache.

усади́ть, -ажу́, -а́дишь *perf.*, **уса́живать**, -аю *imp.* seat, offer a seat; make sit down; set; plant; cover; ~ в тюрьму́, clap in prison. **уса́дьба**, -ы; *gen. pl.* -деб or -дьб, country estate, country seat; farmstead; farm centre. **уса́живаться**, -аюсь *imp.* of усе́сться.

уса́тый, moustached; whiskery; whiskered.

усва́ивать, -аю *imp.*, **усво́ить**, -о́ю *perf.* master; assimilate; adopt, acquire; imitate; pick up. **усвое́ние**, -я, mastering; assimilation; adoption.

усе́ивать, -аю *imp.* of усе́ять.

усе́рдие, -я, zeal; diligence. **усе́рдный**, zealous; diligent, painstaking.

усе́сться, уся́дусь; -е́лся *perf.* (*imp.* уса́живаться) take a seat; settle; set (to), settle down (to).

усе́ять, -е́ю *perf.* (*imp.* усе́ивать) sow; cover, dot, stud; litter, strew.

усиде́ть, -ижу́ *perf.* keep one's place, remain seated, sit still; hold down a job. **усидчивость**, -и, assiduity. **уси́дчивый**, assiduous; painstaking.

у́сик, -а, tendril; awn; runner; antenna; *pl.* small moustache.

усиле́ние, -я, strengthening; reinforcement; intensification; aggravation; amplification. **уси́ленный**, reinforced; intensified, increased; earnest, urgent, importunate; copious. **уси́ливать**, -аю *imp.*, **уси́лить,** -лю *perf.* intensify, increase, heighten; aggravate; amplify; strengthen, reinforce; **~ся,** increase, intensify; become stronger; become aggravated; swell, grow louder; make efforts, try. **уси́лие,** -я, effort; exertion. **усили́тель,** -я *m.* amplifier; booster. **усили́тельный,** amplifying; booster.

ускака́ть, -ачу́, -а́чешь *perf.* bound away; skip off; gallop off.

ускольза́ть, -а́ю *imp.*, **ускользну́ть,** -ну́, -нёшь *perf.* slip off; steal away; get away; disappear; escape; + от + *gen.* evade, avoid.

ускоре́ние, -я, acceleration; speeding-up. **ускори́тель,** -я, accelerator. **уско́рить,** -рю *perf.*, **ускоря́ть,** -я́ю *imp.* quicken; speed up, accelerate; hasten; precipitate; **~ся,** accelerate, be accelerated; quicken.

усла́вливаться: see усло́виться.

услади́ть, -ажу́ *perf.*, **услажда́ть,** -а́ю *imp.* delight, charm; soften, mitigate.

уследи́ть, -ежу́ *perf.* + за + *instr.* keep an eye on, mind; follow.

усло́вие, -я, condition; clause, term; stipulation, proviso; agreement; *pl.* conditions; усло́вия приёма, reception. **усло́виться,** -влюсь *perf.*, **усло́вливаться, усла́вливаться,** -аюсь *imp.* agree, settle; arrange, make arrangements. **усло́вленный,** agreed, fixed, stipulated. **усло́вность,** -и, convention, conventionality; conditional character. **усло́вный,** conditional; conditioned; conventional; agreed, prearranged; relative; theoretical; ~ знак, conventional sign.

усложне́ние, -я, complication. **усложни́ть,** -ню́ *perf.*, **усложня́ть,** -я́ю *imp.* complicate; **~ся,** become complicated.

услу́га, -и, service; good turn; *pl.* service(s), public utilities; оказа́ть услу́гу, do a service. **услу́живать,** -аю *imp.* **услужи́ть,** -жу́, -жишь *perf.* serve, act as a servant; + *dat.* do a service, do a good turn. **услу́жливый,** obliging.

услыха́ть, -ы́шу *perf.*, **у|слы́шать,** -ы́шу *perf.* hear; sense; scent.

усма́тривать, -аю *imp.* of усмотре́ть.

усмеха́ться, -а́юсь *imp.*, **усмехну́ться,** -ну́сь, -нёшься *perf.* smile; grin; sneer; smirk. **усме́шка,** -и, smile; grin; sneer.

усмире́ние, -я, pacification; suppression, putting down. **усмири́ть,** -рю́ *perf.*, **усмиря́ть,** -я́ю *imp.* pacify; calm, quieten; tame; suppress, put down.

усмотре́ние, -я, discretion, judgement; по усмотре́нию, at one's discretion, as one thinks best. **усмотре́ть,** -рю́, -ришь *perf.* (*imp.* усма́тривать) perceive, observe; see; regard, interpret.

усну́ть, -ну́, -нёшь *perf.* go to sleep, fall asleep.

усоверше́нствование, -я, perfecting; finishing, qualifying; advanced studies; improvement, refinement. **усоверше́нствованный,** improved; finished, complete. **у|соверше́нствовать(ся,** -твую(сь *perf.*

усомни́ться, -ню́сь *perf.* doubt.

усо́пший, (the) deceased.

успева́емость, -и, progress. **успева́ть,** -а́ю *imp.*, **успе́ть,** -е́ю *perf.* have time; manage; succeed, be successful. **успе́ется** *impers.* there is still time, there is no hurry. **успе́х,** -а, success; progress. **успе́шный,** successful.

успока́ивать, -аю *imp.*, **успоко́ить,** -о́ю *perf.* calm, quiet, soothe, tranquillize; reassure, set one's mind at rest; assuage, deaden; reduce to order, control; **~ся,** calm down; compose oneself; rest content; abate; become still; drop. **успока́ивающ|ий,** calming, soothing, sedative; ~ее сре́дство, sedative, tranquillizer. **успокое́ние,** -я, calming, quieting, soothing; calm; peace, tranquillity. **успокои́тельн|ый,** calming, soothing; reassuring; **~ое** *sb.* sedative, tranquillizer.

УССР (*u-esesér*) *abbr.* Украи́нская Сове́тская Социалисти́ческая Респу́блика, Ukrainian Soviet Socialist Republic.

уста́в, -а, regulations, rules, statutes; service regulations; rule; charter.

устава́ть, -таю́, -ёшь *imp.* of уста́ть; не устава́я, incessantly, uninterruptedly.

уста́вить, -влю *perf.*, **уставля́ть**, -я́ю *imp.* set, arrange, dispose; cover, fill, pile; direct, fix; **~ся**, find room, go in; fix one's gaze, stare; become fixed, become steady. **уста́вный**, regulation, statutory, prescribed.

уста́лость, -и, fatigue, tiredness, weariness. **уста́лый** tired, weary, fatigued.

устана́вливать, -аю *imp.*, **установи́ть**, -влю́, -вишь *perf.* place, put, set up; install, mount, rig up; adjust, regulate. set; establish; institute; fix, prescribe; secure obtain; determine; ascertain; **~ся**, take position, dispose oneself; be settled, be established; set in; be formed be fixed. **устано́вка**, -и, placing, putting, setting up, arrangement; installation; mounting, rigging; adjustment, regulation, setting; plant, unit; directions, directive. **установле́ние**, -я, establishment; statute; institution. **устано́вленный**, established, fixed, prescribed, regulation.

уста́ну, etc.: see уста́ть.

устарева́ть, -а́ю *imp.*, **у|старе́ть**, -е́ю *perf.* grow old; become obsolete; become antiquated, go out of date. **устаре́лый**, obsolete; antiquated, out of date.

уста́ть, -а́ну *perf.* (*imp.* устава́ть), become tired, tire; я уста́ла, I am tired.

у́стно *adv.* orally, by word of mouth. **у́стн|ый**, oral, verbal; ~ая речь, spoken language.

усто́й, -я, abutment, buttress, pier; foundation, support; *pl.* foundations, bases. **усто́йчивость**, -и, stability, steadiness, firmness; resistance. **усто́йчивый**, stable, steady, firm; settled; resistant (к + *dat.* to). **устоя́ть**, -ою́ *perf.* keep one's balance, keep one's feet; stand firm, stand one's ground; resist, hold out.

устра́ивать(ся, -аю(сь *imp.* of устро́ить(ся.

устране́ние, -я, removal, elimination, clearing. **устрани́ть**, -ню́ *perf.*, **устраня́ть**, -я́ю *imp.* remove; eliminate, clear; dismiss; **~ся**, resign, retire, withdraw.

устраша́ть, -а́ю *imp.*, **устраши́ть**, -шу́ *perf.* frighten; scare; **~ся**, be afraid; be frightened, be terrified. **устраша́ющий**, frightening; deterrent. **устраше́ние**, -я, frightening; fright, fear; сре́дство устраше́ния, deterrent.

устреми́ть, -млю́ *perf.*, **устремля́ть**, -я́ю *imp.* direct, fix; **~ся**, rush; head; be directed, be fixed, be concentrated; concentrate. **устремле́ние**, -я, rush; striving, aspiration. **устремлённость**, -и, tendency.

у́стрица, -ы, oyster. **у́стричный**, oyster.

устрое́ние, -я, arranging, organization. **устрои́тель**, -я *m.*, **-тельница**, -ы, organizer. **устро́ить**, -о́ю *perf.* (*imp.* устра́ивать) arrange, organize; establish; make; construct; cause, create; settle, order, put in order; place, fix up; get, secure; suit, be convenient; ~ на рабо́ту, find, fix up with, a job; ~ сканда́л, make a scene; **~ся**, work out; come right; manage, make arrangements; settle down, get settled; be found, get fixed up. **устро́йство**, -а, arrangement, organization; (mode of) construction; layout; apparatus, mechanism, device; structure, system.

усту́п, -а, shelf, ledge; terrace; bench. **уступа́ть**, -а́ю *imp.*, **уступи́ть**, -плю́, -пишь *perf.* yield; give in; cede; concede; let have, give up; be inferior; take off, knock off; ~ доро́гу, make way; ~ ме́сто, give up one's place, seat. **усту́пка**, -и, concession, compromise; reduction. **усту́пчатый**, ledged, stepped, terraced. **усту́пчивый**, pliant, pliable; compliant, tractable.

устыди́ться, -ыжу́сь *perf.* (+ *gen.*) be ashamed (of).

у́стье, -я; *gen. pl.* -ьев, mouth; estuary.

усугу́би́ть, -у́блю *perf.*, **усугубля́ть**, -я́ю *imp.* increase; intensify; aggravate, make worse.

усы́: see ус.

усынови́ть, -влю́ *perf.*, **усыновля́ть**, -я́ю *imp.* adopt. **усыновле́ние**, -я, adoption.

усы́пать, -плю *perf.*, **усыпа́ть**, -а́ю *imp.* strew, scatter; cover.

усыпи́тельный, soporific. **усыпи́ть**, -плю́ *perf.*, **усыпля́ть**, -я́ю *imp.* put to sleep; lull; weaken, undermine, neutralize; ~ боль, deaden pain.

усядусь, etc.: see усесться.
утаивать, -аю *imp.*, **утаить,** -аю *perf.* conceal; keep to oneself, keep secret; appropriate.
утаптывать, -аю *imp.* of утоптать.
утаскивать, -аю *imp.*, **утащить,** -щу -щишь *perf.* drag away, drag off; make off with.
утварь, -и, utensils, equipment.
утвердительный, affirmative. **утвердить,** -ржу *perf.*, **утверждать,** -аю *imp.* confirm; approve; sanction, ratify; establish; assert, maintain, hold, claim, allege. **утверждение,** -я, approval; confirmation; ratification; assertion, affirmation, claim, allegation; establishment.
утекать, -аю *imp.* of утечь.
утёнок, -нка; *pl.* утята, -ят, duckling.
утереть, утру, -рёшь; утёр *perf.* (*imp.* утирать) wipe; wipe off; wipe dry; ~ нос + *dat.* score off.
утерпеть, -плю, -пишь *perf.* restrain oneself.
утеря, -и, loss. **у|терять,** -яю *perf.*
утёс, -а, cliff, crag. **утёсистый,** steep, precipitous.
утечка, -и, leak, leakage; escape; loss, wastage, dissipation; ~ газа, escape of gas. **утечь,** -еку, -ечёшь; утёк, -ла *perf.* (*imp.* утекать) flow away; leak, escape; run away; pass, elapse, go by.
утешать, -аю *imp.*, **утешить,** -шу *perf.* comfort, console; **~ся,** console oneself. **утешение,** -я, comfort, consolation. **утешительный,** comforting, consoling.
утиль, -я *m.*, **утильсырьё,** -я, salvage; scrap; rubbish, refuse. **утильный,** scrap.
утиный, duck, duck's.
утирать(ся, -аю(сь *imp.* of утереть(ся.
утихать, -аю *imp.*, **утихнуть,** -ну; -их *perf.* abate, subside; cease, die away; slacken; drop; become calm, calm down.
утка, -и, duck; canard.
уткнуть, -ну, -нёшь *perf.* bury; fix; **~ся,** bury oneself; ~ся головой в подушку, bury one's head in the pillow.
утолить, -лю *perf.* (*imp.* утолять) quench, slake; satisfy; relieve, alleviate, soothe.
утолстить, -лщу *perf.*, **утолщать,** -аю *imp.* thicken, make thicker; **~ся,** thicken, become thicker. **утолщение,** -я, thickening; thickened part, bulge; reinforcement, rib, boss.
утолять, -яю *imp.* of утолить.
утомительный, tiresome; tedious; wearisome, tiring, fatiguing. **утомить,** -млю *perf.*, **утомлять,** -яю *imp.* tire, weary, fatigue; **~ся,** get tired. **утомление,** -я, tiredness, weariness, fatigue. **утомлённый,** tired, weary, fatigued.
у|тонуть, -ну, -нешь *perf.* (*imp.* also утопать) drown, be drowned; sink, go down.
утончённость, -и, refinement. **утончённый,** refined; exquisite, subtle.
утопать, -аю *imp.* of утонуть; roll, wallow. **у|топить(ся,** -плю(сь, -пишь(ся *perf.* **утопленник,** -а, drowned man.
утоптать, -пчу, -пчешь *perf.* (*imp.* утаптывать) trample down, pound.
уточнение, -я, more precise definition; amplification, elaboration. **уточнить,** -ню *perf.*, **уточнять,** -яю *imp.* define more precisely; amplify, elaborate.
утраивать, -аю *imp.* of утроить.
у|трамбовать, -бую *perf.*, **утрамбовывать,** -аю *imp.* ram, tamp; **~ся,** become flat, become level.
утрата, -ы, loss. **утратить,** -ачу *perf.*, **утрачивать,** -аю *imp.* lose.
утренний, morning, early. **утренник,** -а, morning performance, matinée; early-morning frost.
утрировать, -рую *perf.* and *imp.* exaggerate; overplay. **утрировка,** -и, exaggeration.
утро, -а or -а, -у or -у; *pl.* -а, -ам or -ам, morning.
утроба, -ы, womb; belly.
утроить, -ою *perf.* (*imp.* утраивать) triple, treble.
утром *adv.* in the morning; сегодня ~, this morning.
утру, etc.: see утереть, утро.
утрудить, -ужу *perf.*, **утруждать,** -аю *imp.* trouble, tire.

утю́г, -а́, iron. **утю́жить,** -жу *imp.* (*perf.* вы́~, от~) iron, press; smooth. **утю́жка,** -и, ironing, pressing.

ух *int.* oh, ooh, ah.

уха́, -и́, fish soup.

уха́б, -а, pot-hole. **уха́бистый,** full of pot-holes; bumpy.

уха́живать, -аю *imp.* за + *instr.* nurse, tend; look after; court; pay court to, make advances to.

у́хать, -аю *imp.* of у́хнуть.

ухвати́ть, -ачу́, -а́тишь *perf.*, **ухва́тывать,** -аю *imp.* catch, lay hold of; seize; grasp; **~ся** за + *acc.* grasp, lay hold of; set to, set about; seize; jump at; take up. **ухва́тка,** -и, grip; grasp; skill; trick; manner.

ухитри́ться, -рю́сь *perf.*, **ухитря́ться,** -я́юсь *imp.* manage, contrive.

ухло́пать, -аю *perf.*, **ухло́пывать,** -аю *imp.* squander, waste; (*sl.*) kill.

ухмы́лка, -и, smirk, grin. **ухмыльну́ться,** -ну́сь, -нёшься *perf.*, **ухмыля́ться,** -я́юсь *imp.* smirk, grin.

у́хнуть, -ну *perf.* (*imp.* у́хать) cry out; hoot; crash; bang; rumble; slip, fall; come a cropper; come to grief; drop; lose, squander, spend up.

у́хо, -а; *pl.* у́ши, уше́й, ear; ear-flap, ear-piece; lug, hanger; заткну́ть у́ши, stop one's ears; кра́ем ~а, with half an ear; по́ уши, up to one's eyes; слу́шать во все у́ши, be all ears; туго́й на́ ~, hard of hearing.

ухо́д[1], -а, + за + *instr.* care of; maintenance of; nursing, tending, looking after.

ухо́д[2], -а, going away, leaving, departure; withdrawal. **уходи́ть,** -ожу́, -о́дишь *imp.* of уйти́; stretch, extend.

ухудша́ть, -а́ю *imp.*, **уху́дшить,** -шу *perf.* make worse, aggravate; **~ся**, get worse.

уцеле́ть, -е́ю *perf.* remain intact, escape destruction; survive; escape.

уцепи́ть, -плю́, -пишь *perf.*, **уцепля́ть,** -я́ю *imp.* catch hold of, grasp, seize; **~ся** за + *acc.* catch hold of, grasp, seize; jump at.

уча́ствовать, -твую *imp.* take part, participate; have a share, hold shares. **уча́ствующий** *sb.* participant. **уча́стие,** -я, participation, taking part; share, sharing; sympathy, concern.

участи́ть, -ащу́ *perf.* (*imp.* учаща́ть) make more frequent, quicken; **~ся**, become more frequent, become more rapid.

уча́стливый, sympathetic. **уча́стник,** -а, participant, member; ~ состяза́ния, competitor. **уча́сток,** -тка, plot, strip; allotment; lot, parcel; part, section, portion; length; division; sector, area, zone, district; police district, police-station; field, sphere. **у́часть,** -и, lot, fate, portion.

учаща́ть(ся, -а́ю(сь *imp.* of участи́ть(ся. **учащённый**; -ён, -ена́, quickened; faster.

уча́щийся *sb.* student; pupil. **учёба,** -ы, studies; course; studying, learning; drill, training. **уче́бник,** -а, text-book; manual, primer. **уче́бн|ый**, educational; school; training, practice; ~ый год, academic year, school year; ~ые посо́бия, teaching equipment, teaching aids; ~ое су́дно, training-ship.

уче́ние, -я, learning; studies; apprenticeship; teaching, instruction; doctrine; exercise; *pl.* training. **учени́к,** -а́, **учени́ца,** -ы, pupil; student; learner; apprentice; disciple, follower. **учени́ческий,** pupil'(s); apprentice('s); unskilled; raw, crude, immature. **учени́чество,** -а, time spent as pupil or student; apprenticeship; rawness, immaturity. **учёность,** -и, learning, erudition. **учён|ый** learned, erudite; educated; scholarly; academic; scientific; trained, performing; ~ая сте́пень, (university) degree; **~ый** *sb.* scholar; scientist.

уче́сть, учту́, -тёшь; учёл, учла́ *perf.* (*imp.* учи́тывать) take stock of, make an inventory of; take into account, take into consideration; allow for; bear in mind; discount. **учёт,** -а, stock-taking; reckoning, calculation; taking into account; registration; discount, discounting; без ~а + *gen.*, disregarding; взять на ~, register. **учётн|ый,** registration; discount; ~ое отделе́ние, records section.

учи́лище, -а, school; (training) college.

у|чинить, -ню *perf.*, **учинять**, -яю *imp.* make; carry out, execute; commit.

учитель, -я; *pl.* -я *m.*, **учительница**, -ы, teacher. **учительск|ий**, teacher's, teachers'; **~ая** *sb.* staff-room.

учитывать, -аю *imp.* of учесть.

учить, учу, учишь *imp.* (*perf.* вы~, на~, об~) teach; be a teacher; learn, memorize; **~ся**, be a student; + *dat.* or *inf.* learn, study.

учредитель, -я *m.* founder. **учредительница**, -ы, foundress. **учредительн|ый**, constituent; ~ый акт, constituent act; ~ое собрание, constituent assembly. **учредить**, -ежу *perf.*, **учреждать**, -аю *imp.* found, establish, set up; introduce, institute **учреждение**, -я, founding, setting up; establishment; institution.

учтивый, civil, courteous, polite.

учту, etc.: see учесть.

учхоз, -а *abbr.* (school) experimental farm

ушёл, etc.: see уйти. **уши**, etc.: see ухо.

ушиб, -а, injury; knock; bruise, contusion. **ушибать**, -аю *imp.*, **ушибить**, -бу, -бёшь; ушиб *perf.* injure; bruise; hurt, shock; **~ся**, hurt oneself, give oneself a knock; bruise oneself.

ушко. -а; *pl.* -и, -ов, eye; lug; tab, tag; *pl.* pasta shells.

ушной, ear, aural.

ущелье, -я, ravine gorge. canyon.

ущемить, -млю *perf.*, **ущемлять**, -яю *imp.* pinch jam. nip; limit; encroach on; wound, hurt. **ущемление**, -я, pinching, jamming, nipping; limitation; wounding hurting.

ущерб, -а, detriment; loss; damage, injury; prejudice; на ~е, waning. **ущербный**, waning.

ущипнуть, -ну, -нёшь *perf.* of щипать.

уют, -а, cosiness, comfort. **уютный**, cosy comfortable.

уязвимый, vulnerable. **уязвить**. -влю *perf.*, **уязвлять**, -яю *imp.* wound, hurt.

уяснение, -я, explanation, elucidation.

уяснить, -ню *perf.* **уяснять**. -яю *imp.* understand, make out; explain.

Ф

ф *letter*: see эф.

фа *n. indecl.* F; fah.

фаб- *abbr.* in *comb.* of фабричный, factory, works. **фабзавком**, -а, factory and works committee. **~завместком**, -а, factory, plant, and local committee. **~завуч**, -а, factory industrial-training school. **~ком**, -а, works committee. **~мас**. -а, mass-production factory.

фабрика, -и, factory, mill, works. **фабрикант**, -а, manufacturer. **фабрикат**, -а, finished product, manufactured product. **фабриковать**, -кую *imp.* (*perf.* с~) manufacture, make, fabricate, forge. **фабричн|ый**, factory; industrial, manufacturing; factory-made; ~ая марка ~ое клеймо trade-mark.

фабула, -ы, plot, story.

фагот, -а, bassoon. **фаготист**, -а, bassoon-player.

фаза, -ы, phase; stage.

фазан, -а, **фазаниха**, -и, pheasant. **фазаний**, pheasant, pheasants'.

фазис, -а, phase. **фазный**, **фазовый**, phase.

факел, -а, torch, flare, flame. **факельный**, torch(-light). **факельщик**, -а, torch-bearer; incendiary.

факт, -а, fact; совершившийся ~, fait accompli. **фактически** *adv.* in fact, actually; practically, virtually, to all intents and purposes. **фактический**, actual; real; virtual.

фактура, -ы, invoice, bill; style, execution, texture; structure.

факультати́вный, optional. **факульте́т,** -а, faculty, department. **факульте́тский,** faculty.

фа́лда, -ы, tail, skirt.

фальсифика́тор, -а, falsifier, forger. **фальсифика́ция,** -и, falsification; forging; adulteration; forgery, fake, counterfeit. **фальсифици́ровать,** -рую *perf.* and *imp.* falsify; forge; adulterate. **фальши́вить,** -влю *imp.* (*perf.* с~) be a hypocrite, act insincerely; sing or play out of tune. **фальши́вка,** -и, forged document. **фальши́вый,** false; spurious; forged, fake; artificial, imitation; out of tune; hypocritical, insincere. **фальшь,** -и, deception, trickery; falsity; falseness; hypocrisy, insincerity.

фами́лия, -и, surname; family, kin. **фами́льный,** family. **фамилья́рничать,** -аю, be over-familiar, take liberties. **фамилья́рность,** -и, familiarity; liberty, liberties. **фамилья́рный,** (over-) familiar; unceremonious; off-hand, casual.

фане́ра, -ы, veneer; plywood. **фане́рный,** veneer, of veneer; plywood.

фантазёр, -а, dreamer, visionary. **фантази́ровать,** -рую *imp.* (*perf.* с~), dream, indulge in fantasies; make up, dream up; improvise. **фанта́зия,** -и, fantasy; fancy; imagination; whim; fabrication. **фанта́стика,** -и, fiction, fantasy; the fantastic; works of fantasy; нау́чная ~, science fiction. **фантасти́ческий, фантасти́чный,** fantastic; fabulous; imaginary.

фа́ра, -ы, headlight; поса́дочные фа́ры, landing lights.

фарао́н, -а, pharaoh; faro. **фарао́нов,** pharaoh's.

фарва́тер, -а, fairway, channel.

фармазо́н, -а, freemason.

фарт, -а, (*sl.*) luck, success.

фа́ртук, -а, apron; carriage-rug.

фарфо́р, -а, china; porcelain. **фарфо́ров|ый,** china; ~ая посу́да, china.

фарцева́ть, -цу́ю *imp.* speculate in currency. **фарцо́вщик,** -а, currency speculator.

фарш, -а, stuffing, force-meat; minced meat, sausage-meat. **фарширо́ванный,** stuffed. **фарширова́ть,** -ру́ю *imp.* (*perf.* за~) stuff.

фасова́ть, -су́ю *imp.* (*perf.* рас~) package, pre-pack. **фасо́вка,** -и, packaging, pre-packing.

фасо́ль, -и, kidney bean(s), French bean(s); haricot beans.

фасо́н, -а, cut; fashion; style; manner, way; держа́ть ~, show off, put on airs. **фасо́нистый,** fashionable, stylish. **фасо́нный,** fashioned, shaped; form, forming, shape, shaping.

фая́нс, -а, faience, pottery. **фая́нсовый,** pottery.

ФБР (*febeér*) *abbr.* Федера́льное бюро́ рассле́дований, F.B.I.

февра́ль, -я́ *m.* February. **февра́льский,** February.

фееpи́ческий, fairy-tale, magical.

фейерве́рк, -а, firework, fireworks.

фе́льдшер, -а; *pl.* -а́, **-шери́ца,** -ы, doctor's assistant; (partly-qualified) medical attendant; hospital attendant; trained nurse.

фельето́н, -а, feuilleton, feature.

фен, -а, (hair-)dryer.

фе́рзевый, queen's. **ферзь,** -я́ *m.* queen.

фе́рма[1], -ы, farm.

фе́рма[2], -ы, girder, truss. **фе́рменный,** lattice.

фетр, -а, felt. **фе́тровый,** felt.

фехтова́льный, fencing, of fencing. **фехтова́льщик,** -а, **-щица,** -ы, fencer. **фехтова́ние,** -я, fencing. **фехтова́ть,** -ту́ю *imp.* fence.

фе́я, -и, fairy.

фиа́лка, -и, violet.

фиброли́т, -а, chipboard.

фигаро́ *n. indecl.* bolero.

фигля́р, -а, (circus) acrobat; clown; mountebank; buffoon. **фигля́рить,** -рю, **фигля́рничать,** -аю **фигля́рствовать,** -твую *imp.* put on an act.

фигу́ра, -ы, figure; court-card; (chess-) -piece. **фигура́льный,** figurative, metaphorical; ornate, involved. **фигура́нт,** -а, figurant; super, extra. **фигури́ровать,** -и́рую *imp.* figure, appear. **фигури́ст,** -а, **-и́стка,** -и, figure-skater. **фигу́рка,** -и, figurine, statuette; figure. **фигу́рн|ый,** figured;

ornamented, patterned; figure; ~ое ката́ние, figure skating.

фи́зик, -а, physicist. **фи́зика**, -и, physics. **физио́лог**, -а, physiologist. **физиотерапе́вт**, -а, physiotherapist. **физи́ческ|ий**, physical; physics; ~ая культу́ра, physical culture; gymnastics. **физкульту́ра**, -ы *abbr.* P.T., gymnastics. **физкульту́рник**, -а, **-у́рница**, -ы *abbr.* gymnast, athlete. **физкульту́рный** *abbr.* gymnastic; athletic; sports; ~ зал, gymnasium.

фикс, -а, fixed price, fixed sum. **фикса́ж**, -а, fixing; fixer, fixing solution. **фикси́ровать**, -рую *perf.* and *imp.* (*perf.* also за~) fix; record, register.

фикти́вный, fictitious. **фи́кция**, -и, fiction.

филе́ *n. indecl.* sirloin; fillet; drawn-thread work, filet (lace). **филе́й**, -я, sirloin. **филе́йн|ый**, sirloin; filet-lace, drawn-thread; ~ая рабо́та, drawn-thread work, filet.

филиа́л, -а, branch. **филиа́льный**, branch.

фи́лин, -а, eagle-owl.

фили́стер, -а, philistine. **фили́стерский**, philistine. **фили́стерство**, -а, philistinism.

фило́лог, -а, philologist; student of language and literature. **филологи́ческий**, philological. **филоло́гия**, -и, philology, study of language and literature.

фило́н, -а, (*sl.*) shirker, lazy-bones. **фило́нить**, -ню *imp.* (*sl.*), loaf about, slack, shirk work.

фильм, -а, **фи́льма**, -ы, film.

фин- *abbr.* of фина́нсовый, financial, finance. **фининспе́ктор**, -а, financial officer. **~отде́л**, finance department.

фина́л, -а, finale; final. **фина́льный**, final.

фина́нсовый, financial. **фина́нсы**, -ов *pl.* finance, finances; money.

фи́ник, -а, date. **фи́никовый**, date.

фи́ниш, -а, finish; finishing post. **фи́нишный**, finishing.

фи́нка, -и, Finn; Finnish knife; Finnish cap; Finnish pony. **финля́ндский**, Finnish. **финн**, -а, Finn. **фи́нно-уго́рский**, Finno-Ugrian. **фи́нский**, Finnish.

финт, -а, feint.

фиоле́товый, violet.

фи́рма, -ы, firm; company; combine; large enterprise; trade name; appearance, guise.

фисгармо́ния, -и, harmonium.

фити́ль, -я́ *m.* wick; fuse.

флаг, -а, flag; под ~ом + *gen.* flying the flag of; under the guise of; приспу́щенные ~и, flags at half-mast; спусти́ть ~, lower a flag.

флако́н, -а, (scent-)bottle, flask.

флама́ндец, -дца, **флама́ндка**, -и, Fleming. **флама́ндский**, Flemish.

фле́йта, -ы, flute. **флейти́ст**, -а, **-и́стка**, -и, flautist. **фле́йтовый**, flute.

фле́ксия, -и, inflexion. **флекти́вный**, inflexional; inflected.

фли́гель, -я; *pl.* -я́ *m.* wing; pavilion, extension, annexe.

флот, -а, fleet; возду́шный ~, air force; aviation. **фло́тский**, naval; *sb.* sailor.

флю́гер, -а; *pl.* -а́, weather-vane, weathercock; pennant.

флюс[1], -а, gumboil, abscess.

флюс[2], -а; *pl.* -ы́, flux.

фля́га, -и, flask; water-bottle; (milk-) churn, milk-can. **фля́жка**, -и, flask.

фо́кус[1], -а, trick; conjuring trick.

фо́кус[2], -а, focus. **фокуси́ровать**, -рую *imp.* focus. **фокусиро́вка**, -и, focusing.

фо́кусник, -а, conjurer, juggler.

фо́кусный, focal.

фо́льга, -и, foil.

фо́мка, -и, (*sl.*) jemmy.

фон, -а, background.

фона́рик, -а, small lamp; torch, flashlight. **фона́рный**, lamp; ~ столб, lamp-post. **фона́рщик**, -а, lamplighter **фона́рь**, -я́ *m.* lantern; lamp; light; skylight; black eye, bruise.

фонд, -а, fund; stock; reserves, resources; stocks; foundation.

фонта́н, -а, fountain; stream; gusher.

форе́ль, -и, trout.

фо́рзац, -а, fly-leaf.

фóрма, -ы, form; shape; mould, cast; uniform; *pl.* contours; в пи́сьменной фóрме, in writing; в фóрме, in form; отли́ть в фóрму, mould, cast. **формáльный**, formal. **формáция**, -и, structure; stage; formation; stamp, mentality. **фóрменный**, uniform; regulation; formal; proper, regular, positive. **формировáние**, -я, forming; organization; unit, formation. **формировáть**, -рýю *imp.* (*perf.* с~) form; organize; shape; **~ся**, form, shape, develop. **формовáть**, -мýю *imp.* (*perf.* с~) form, shape; model; mould, cast. **формóвщик**, -а, moulder.

фóрмула, -ы, formula; formulation. **формули́ровать**, -рую *perf.* and *imp.* (*perf.* also с~) formulate. **формулирóвка**, -и, formulation; wording; formula. **формуля́р**, -а, record of service; log-book; library card; (*sl.*) dossier.

форси́рованный, forced; accelerated. **форси́ровать**, -рую *perf.* and *imp.* force; speed up.

фóрточка, -и, fortochka; small hinged (window-)pane; air vent.

фóто *n. indecl.* photo(graph).

фото- in *comb.*, photo-, photo-electric. **фотоаппарáт**, -а, camera. **~бумáга**, -и, photographic paper. **~гени́чный**, photogenic. **фотóграф**, -а, photographer. **~графи́ровать**, -рую *imp.* (*perf.* с~) photograph; **~графи́роваться**, be photographed, have one's photograph taken. **~графи́ческий**, photographic. **~грáфия**, -и, photography; photograph; photographer's studio. **~кóпия**, photocopy. **~лáмпа**, -ы, dark-room lamp; photoelectric cell. **~люби́тель**, -я *m.* amateur photographer. **~набóр**, -а, film-setting; photo-setting. **~объекти́в**, -а, (camera) lens. **~паннó** *n. indecl.* photo-mural; blow-up. **~репортёр**, -а, press photographer. **~хрóника**, -и, news in pictures. **~элемéнт**, -а, photoelectric cell.

фрáза, -ы, sentence; phrase. **фразёр**, -а, phrase-monger.

фрак, -а, tail-coat, dress coat, tails; evening dress.

фракциóнный, fractional; factional. **фрáкция**, -и, fraction; faction.

франкоязы́чный, Francophone.

франкмасóн, -а, freemason.

франт, -а, dandy. **франтовскóй**, dandyish, dandyfied. **франтовствó**, -á, dandyism.

францýженка, -и, Frenchwoman. **францýз**, -а, Frenchman. **францýзский**, French; ~ ключ, monkey-wrench.

фрахт, -а, freight. **фрахтовáть**, -тýю *imp.* (*perf.* за~) charter.

ФРГ (*fe-ergé*) *abbr.* Федерати́вная Респýблика Гермáнии, German Federal Republic.

фрéйлина, -ы, maid of honour.

френч, -а, service jacket.

фронт, -а; *pl.* -ы, -óв, front; стать во ~, stand to attention. **фронтови́к**, -á, front-line soldier. **фронтовóй**, front(-line).

фронтóн, -а, pediment.

фрукт, -а, fruit. **фруктóвый**, fruit; ~ сад, orchard.

фтор, -а, fluorine. **фтóристый**, fluorine; fluoride; ~ кáльций, calcium fluoride.

фу *int.* ugh! oh!

фугáс, -а, landmine. **фугáсный**, high-explosive.

фундáмент, -а, foundation, base; substructure; seating. **фундаментáльный**, fundamental; solid, sound; thorough(-going); main; basic.

фунди́рованный, funded, consolidated.

функциони́ровать, -рую *imp.* function. **фýнкция**, -и, function.

фунт, -а, pound. **фýнтик**, -а, paper bag, paper cone, screw of paper.

фурáж, -á, forage, fodder. **фурáжка**, -и, peaked cap, service cap, forage-cap.

фургóн, -а, van; estate car, station wagon; caravan; pantechnicon.

фурнитýра, -ы, accessories; parts, components; fittings.

фут, -а, foot; foot-rule. **футбóл**, -а, football, soccer. **футболи́ст**, -а, footballer. **футбóлить**, -лю *perf.* and *imp.* (*perf.* also от~) give, be given, the run-around. **футбо́лка,** -и, football jersey, sports shirt. **футбо́льный,** football: ~ мяч, football.

футля́р, -а case, container; sheath; cabinet; casing, housing.

фу́товый. one-foot.

футуроло́гия -и. futurology.

фуфа́йка, -и, jersey; sweater.

фы́ркать -аю *imp.*, **фы́ркнуть.** -ну *perf.* snort; chuckle; grouse, grumble.

Х

ха *n. indecl.* the letter х.

хаба́р, -а, **хабара́,** -ы́, bribe.

хавро́нья, -и, sow.

хала́т, -а, robe; dressing-gown; overall. **хала́тность,** -и, carelessnesss, negligence. **хала́тный,** careless, negligent.

халту́ра, -ы, pot-boiler; hackwork; money made on the side, extra earnings. **халту́рить,** -рю *imp.* do hackwork; earn a little extra. **халту́рщик,** -а, hack.

хам, -а, boor, lout. **ха́мский,** boorish, loutish. **ха́мство,** -а, boorishness, loutishness.

хан, -а, khan.

хандра́, -ы́, depression, dejection. **хандри́ть,** -рю́ *imp.* suffer from melancholy; be dejected, be depressed.

ханжа́, -и́, canting hypocrite, sanctimonious person. **ха́нжеский, ханжеско́й,** sanctimonious, hypocritical.

ха́нство, -а, khanate.

хара́ктер, -а, character; personality; nature; disposition; type. **характеризова́ть,** -зу́ю *perf.* and *imp.* (*perf.* also о~) describe; characterize, be characteristic of; **~ся,** be characterized. **характери́стика,** -и, reference; description. **характе́рный**[1], characteristic; typical; distinctive; character. **хара́ктерный**[2], of strong character, strong-willed; temperamental; quick-tempered.

ха́ркать, -аю *imp.*, **ха́ркнуть,** -ну *perf.* spit, hawk; ~ кро́вью, spit blood.

ха́ртия, -и, charter.

ха́ря, -и, mug, face.

ха́та, -ы, peasant hut.

ха́ять, ха́ю *imp.* run down; abuse; slate, slang, swear at, curse.

хвала́, -ы́, praise. **хвале́бный,** laudatory, eulogistic, complimentary. **хвалёный,** highly-praised, much-vaunted. **хвали́ть,** -лю́, -лишь *imp.* (*perf.* по~) praise, compliment; **~ся,** boast.

хва́стать(ся, -аю(сь *imp.* (*perf.* по~) boast, brag. **хвастли́вый,** boastful. **хвастовство́,** -а́, boasting, bragging. **хвасту́н,** -а́, boaster, braggart.

хвата́ть[1], -а́ю *imp.*, **хвати́ть,** -ачу́, -а́тишь *perf.* (*perf.* also схвати́ть) snatch, seize, catch hold of; grab, grasp; bite; hit, strike, knock; **~ся,** wake up (to), remember; + *gen.* realize the absence of; + за + *acc.* snatch at, clutch at, catch at; take up, try out; по́здно хвати́лись, you thought of it too late; ~ся за ум, come to one's senses.

хвата́ть[2], -а́ет *imp.*, **хвати́ть,** -а́тит *perf.*, *impers.* (+ *gen.*) suffice, be sufficient, be enough; last out; вре́мени не хвата́ло, there was not enough time; мне его́ не хвата́ет, I miss him; на сего́дня хва́тит, that will do for today, let's call it a day; у нас не хвата́ет денег, we haven't enough money; хва́тит! that will do! that's enough!; э́того ещё не хвата́ло! that's all we needed! that's the last straw!; э́того мне хва́тит на ме́сяц, this will last me a month. **хва́тка,** -и, grasp, grip, clutch; method, technique; skill. **хва́ткий,** strong; tenacious; skilful, crafty.

хво́йн|ый, coniferous; **~ые** *sb. pl.* conifers.
хвора́ть, -а́ю *imp.* be ill.
хво́рост, -а (-у), brushwood; straws. **хворости́на**, -ы, stick, switch. **хворостяно́й**, brushwood.
хвост, -а́, tail; end, tail-end; train; queue. **хво́стик**, -а, tail; с ~ом, and a bit; сто с ~ом, a hundred odd. **хвостово́й**, tail.
хво́я, -и, needle, needles; (coniferous) branch(es).
хи́жина, -ы, shack, hut, cabin.
хим- *abbr.* in *comb.* of хими́ческий, chemical. **химкомбина́т**, -а, chemical plant. **~проду́кты**, chemical products. **~чи́стка**, -и, dry-cleaning; dry-cleaner's.
химе́ра, -ы, chimera. **химери́ческий**, chimerical.
хи́мик, -а, chemist. **хими́ческ|ий**, chemical; ~ая война́ chemical warfare. **хи́мия**, и, chemistry.
хи́на, -ы, **хини́н**, -а quinine. **хи́нный**, cinchona.
хире́ть, -е́ю *imp.* (*perf.* за~), grow sickly; wither; decay.
хиру́рг, -а, surgeon. **хирурги́ческ|ий**, surgical; ~ая сестра́, theatre nurse, theatre sister. **хирурги́я**, -и, surgery.
хитре́ц, -а́, sly, cunning person. **хитри́ть**, -рю́ *imp.* (*perf.* с~) use cunning, be cunning, be crafty; dissemble. **хи́трость**, -и, cunning, craftiness; ruse, stratagem; skill, resource; intricacy, subtlety. **хи́трый**, cunning, sly, crafty, wily; skilful, resourceful; intricate, subtle; complicated.
хихи́кать, -аю *imp.*, **хихи́хнуть**, -ну *perf.* giggle, titter, snigger.
хище́ние, -я, theft; embezzlement, misappropriation. **хи́щник**, -а, predator, bird of prey, beast of prey; plunderer, despoiler. **хи́щнический**, predatory, rapacious; destructive; injurious. **хи́щн|ый**, predatory; rapacious, grasping, greedy; ~ые пти́цы, birds of prey.
хладаге́нт, -а, refrigerant; coolant. **хладнокро́вие**, -я, coolness, composure, presence of mind, sang-froid; сохраня́ть ~, keep one's head. **хладнокро́вный** cool, composed self-possessed. **хладосто́йкий**, cold-resistant; anti-freeze.
хлам, -а, rubbish, trash, lumber.
хлеб, -а; *pl.* -ы, -ов or -а́, -о́в, bread; loaf; grain, corn, cereal; ~-со́ль, bread and salt, hospitality. **хлеба́ть**, -а́ю *imp.*, **хлебну́ть**, -ну́, -нёшь *perf.* gulp down, drink down; eat; go through, experience. **хле́бный**, bread; baker's; grain, corn, cereal; rich, abundant; grain-producing.
хлебо- in *comb.*, bread; baking; grain. **хлебобу́лочный**, bread. **~загото́вка**, -и, grain-procurement. **~заво́д**, -а, (mechanized) bakery. **~пека́рня**, -и; *gen. pl.* -рен, bakery; bake-house. **~поста́вка**, grain delivery. **~ре́з**, -а, **~ре́зка**, -и, bread-cutter. **~ро́дный**, grain-growing; rich; ~ро́дный год, good year (for cereals).
хлев, -а, *loc.* -у́; *pl.* -а́, cow-house, cattle-shed, byre.
хлеста́ть, -ещу́, -е́щешь *imp.*, **хлестну́ть**, -ну́, -нёшь *perf.* lash; whip; beat (down), teem, pour; gush, spout.
хлоп *int.* bang! **хлоп**, -а, bang, clatter.
хло́пать -аю *imp.* (*perf.* хло́пнуть) bang; slap; ~ (в ладо́ши), clap, applaud.
хлопково́дство, -а, cotton-growing. **хло́пковый**, cotton.
хло́пнуть, -ну *perf.* of хло́пать.
хлопо́к[1], -пка́, clap.
хло́пок[2], -пка, cotton.
хлопота́ть, -очу́, -о́чешь *imp.* (*perf.* по~), busy oneself; bustle about; take trouble, make efforts; + о + *prep.* or за + *acc.* petition for, plead for, solicit for. **хлопотли́вый**, troublesome, bothersome; exacting; busy, bustling, restless. **хло́поты**, -о́т *pl.* trouble; efforts; pains.
хлопча́тка, -и, cotton. **хлопчатобума́жный**, cotton.
хло́пья. -ьев *pl.* flakes.
хлор, -а, chlorine. **хлорвини́ловый**, vinyl chloride. **хло́ристый**, **хло́рный**, chlorine; chloride; хло́рная и́звесть, chloride of lime. **хло́рка**, -и, bleaching powder, bleach liquor.
хлы́нуть, -нет *perf.* gush, pour; rush, surge.

хлыст, -á, whip, switch.

хмелевóд, -a, hop-grower. **хмелевóй,** hop. **хмелéть,** -éю *imp.* (*perf.* за~, о~) get tipsy, get tight. **хмель,** -я, *loc.* -ю́ *m.* hop, hops; drunkenness, tipsiness; во хмелю́, tipsy, tight. **хмельнóй**; -лён, -льнá, drunken, drunk; tipsy; intoxicating.

хму́рить, -рю *imp.* (*perf.* на~); ~ брóви, knit one's brows; **~ся,** frown; become gloomy; be overcast, be cloudy. **хму́рый,** gloomy, sullen; overcast, dull, cloudy; lowering.

хны́кать, -ы́чу or -аю *imp.* whimper, snivel; whine.

хóбот, -a, trunk, proboscis. **хоботóк,** -ткá, proboscis.

ход, -a (-у), *loc.* -у́; *pl.* -ы, -ов or -ы́ or -á, -óв, motion, movement; travel, going; speed, pace; procession; course, progress; work, operation, running; stroke; move; lead; gambit, manœuvre; entrance; passage, thoroughfare, covered way; wheel-base; runners; быть в ~у́, be in demand, be in vogue; дать зáдний ~, back, reverse; дать ~, set in motion, set going; знать все ~ы и вы́ходы, know all the ins and outs; на ~у́, in transit, on the move, without halting; in motion; in operation; пóлным ~ом, at full speed, in full swing; пусти́ть в ~, start, set in motion, set going; put into operation, put into service; три часá ~у, three hours' journey.

ходáтай, -я, intercessor, mediator. **ходáтайство** -a, petitioning; entreaty pleading; petition, application. **ходáтайствовать,** -твую *imp.* (*perf.* по~) petition, apply.

хóдики, -ов *pl.* wall-clock.

ходи́ть, хожу́, хóдишь *imp.* (*perf.* с~) walk; go; run; pass, go round; lead, play; move; sway, shake; + в + *prep.* be; wear; + за + *instr.* look after, take care of tend; ~ с пик, lead a spade; ~ ферзём, move one's queen. **хóдкий**; -док, -дкá, -о, fast; saleable, marketable; popular, in demand, sought after; current. **ходу́ли,** -ей *pl.* stilts. **ходу́льный,** stilted. **ходьбá,** -ы́, walking; walk; полчасá ходьбы́, half an hour's walk. **ходя́ч|ий,** walking; able to walk; popular; current; ~ая добродéтель, virtue personified; ~ая монéта, currency.

хозрасчёт, -a *abbr.* хозя́йственный расчёт, self-financing system. **хозя́ин,** -a; *pl.* -я́ева, -я́ев, owner, proprietor; master; boss; landlord; host; хозя́ева пóля, home team. **хозя́йка,** -и, owner; mistress; hostess; landlady; wife, missus. **хозя́йничать,** -аю *imp.* keep house; be in charge; play the master, take charge. **хозя́йственник,** -a, financial manager, economic manager. **хозя́йственный,** economic, of the economy; management; household; economical, thrifty. **хозя́йство,** -a, economy; management; housekeeping; equipment; farm, holding; домáшнее ~, housekeeping; сéльское ~, agriculture.

хоккеи́ст, -a, (ice-)hockey-player. **хоккéй,** -я, hockey, ice-hockey. **хоккéйный,** (ice-)hockey.

холестери́н, -a, cholesterol. **холестери́новый,** cholesteric.

холм, -á, hill. **холми́стый,** hilly.

хóлод, -a (-у); *pl.* -á, -óв, cold; coldness; cold spell, cold weather. **холоди́льник,** -a, refrigerator; cooler, condenser. **холоди́льный,** cooling; refrigerating, freezing. **холоди́ть,** -ожу́ *imp.* (*perf.* на~) cool, chill; produce feeling of cold. **хóлодно** *adv.* coldly. **хóлодность,** -и, coldness. **холóдн|ый**; хóлоден, -днá, -о, cold; inadequate, thin; ~ое ору́жие, side-arms, cold steel; **~ая** *sb.* cooler, lock-up.

холóп, -a, serf. **холóпий,** serf's, of serfdom, servile.

холостóй; хóлост, -á, unmarried, single; bachelor; idle, free; blank, dummy. **холостя́к,** -á, bachelor. **холостя́цкий,** bachelor.

холст, -á, canvas; coarse linen. **холщóвый,** canvas, (coarse) linen.

хому́т, -á, (horse-)collar; burden; clamp, clip.

хор, -a; *pl.* хóры́, choir; chorus.

хорвáт, -а, **хорвáтка,** -и, Croat. **хорвáтский,** Croatian.

хорёк, -рькá, polecat.

хорист, -а, member of choir or chorus. **хоровóд,** -а, round dance.

хоронить, -ню́, -нишь *imp.* (*perf.* за~, по~, с~) bury; hide, conceal; **~ся,** hide, conceal oneself.

хорóшенький, pretty; nice. **хорошéнько** *adv.* properly, thoroughly, well and truly. **хорошéть,** -éю *imp.* (*perf.* по~) grow prettier. **хорóший;** -óш, -á, -ó, good; nice; pretty, nice-looking; **хорошó** *predic.* it is good; it is nice, it is pleasant. **хорошó** *adv.* well; nicely; all right! very well!; good.

хóры, хор or -ов *pl.* gallery.

хотéние, -я, desire, wish. **хотéть,** хочу́, хóчешь, хоти́м *imp.* (*perf.* за~) wish; + *gen.* want; éсли хоти́те, perhaps; ~ пить, be thirsty; ~ сказáть, mean; **~ся** *impers.* + *dat.* want; мне хотéлось бы, I should like; мне хóчется, I want; мне хóчется спать, I am sleepy.

хоть *conj.* although; even if; *part.* at least, if only; for example, even; ~ бы, if only. **хотя́** *conj.* although, though; ~ бы, even if; if only.

хохлáтый, crested, tufted.

хóхот, -а, guffaw, loud laugh. **хохотáть,** -очу́, -óчешь *imp.* guffaw, laugh loudly.

хочу́, etc.: see хотéть.

храбрéц, -á, brave man. **храбри́ться,** -рю́сь, make a show of bravery; pluck up one's courage. **хрáбрость,** -и, bravery, courage. **хрáбрый,** brave, courageous, valiant.

храм, -а, temple, church.

хранéние, -я, keeping, custody; storage; conservation; кáмера хранéния, cloakroom, left-luggage office; сдать на ~, store, deposit, leave in a cloakroom. **храни́лище,** -а, storehouse, depository. **храни́тель,** -я *m.* keeper, custodian; repository; curator. **храни́ть,** -ню́ *imp.* keep; preserve, maintain; store; **~ся,** be, be kept; be preserved.

храпéть, -плю́ *imp.* snore; snort.

хребéт, -бтá, spine; back; (mountain) range; ridge; crest, peak. **хребтóвый,** spinal; range, ridge, crest.

хрен, -а (-у), horseradish. **хренóвый,** horseradish.

хрестомáтия, -и, reader.

хрип, -а, wheeze; hoarse sound. **хрипéть,** -плю́ *imp.* wheeze. **хри́плый;** -пл, -á, -о, hoarse, wheezing. **хри́пнуть,** -ну; хрип *imp.* (*perf.* о~) become hoarse, lose one's voice. **хрипотá,** -ы́, hoarseness.

христиани́н, -а; *pl.* -áне, -áн **христиáнка,** -и, Christian. **христиáнский,** Christian. **христиáнство,** -а, Christianity; Christendom. **Христóс,** -истá, Christ.

хром, -а, box-calf.

хромáть, -áю *imp.* limp, be lame; be poor, be shaky. **хромéть,** -éю *imp.* (*perf.* о~) go lame. **хромóй;** хром, -á, -о, lame, limping; game, gammy; shaky, rickety; *sb.* lame man, woman. **хромотá,** -ы́, lameness.

хрóник, -а, chronic invalid.

хрóника, -и, chronicle; news items; newsreel; historical film. **хроникáльный,** news; documentary.

хрони́ческий, chronic.

хронологи́ческий, chronological. **хронолóгия,** -и, chronology. **хронóметр,** -а, chronometer. **хронометрáж,** -а, time-study.

хру́пкий; -пок, -пкá, -о, fragile; brittle; frail; delicate. **хру́пкость,** -и, fragility; brittleness; frailness.

хруст, -а, crunch; crackle.

хрустáлик, -а, crystalline lens. **хрустáль,** -я́ *m.* cut glass; crystal. **хрустáльный,** cut-glass; crystal; crystal-clear.

хрустéть, -ущу́ *imp.*, **хру́стнуть,** -ну *perf.* crunch; crackle. **хрустя́щий,** crackling; crisp, crunchy; ~ картóфель, potato crisps.

хрю́кать, -аю *imp.*, **хрю́кнуть,** -ну *perf.* grunt.

хрящ[1], -á, cartilage, gristle.

хрящ[2], -á, gravel, shingle. **хрящевáтый**[2], **хрящевóй**[2], gravelly, shingly.

хрящевáтый[1], **хрящевóй**[1], cartilaginous, gristly.

худе́ть, -е́ю *imp.* (*perf.* по~) grow thin.
ху́до, -а, harm, ill; evil. **ху́до** *adv.* ill, badly.
худо́жественный, art, arts; artistic; aesthetic; ~ фильм, feature film. **худо́жество,** -а, art; artistry; *pl.* the arts. **худо́жник,** -а, artist.
худо́й[1]; худ, -а́, -о, thin, lean.
худо́й[2]; худ, -а́, -о, bad; full of holes; worn; tumbledown; ему́ ху́до, he feels bad; на ~ коне́ц, if the worst comes to the worst, at (the) worst.
худоща́вый, thin, lean.
ху́дший, *superl.* of худо́й, плохо́й, (the) worst. **ху́же,** *comp.* of худо́й, ху́до, плохо́й, пло́хо, worse.
хула́, -ы́, abuse, criticism.
хулига́н, -а, hooligan. **хулига́нить,** -ню *imp.* behave like a hooligan. **хулига́нство,** -а, hooliganism.
ху́тор, -а; *pl.* -а́, farm; farmstead; small village.
ХФ (*khafé*) *abbr.* холо́дный фронт, cold front.

Ц

ц *letter*: see цэ.
ца́пля, -и; *gen. pl.* -пель, heron.
цара́пать, -аю *imp.*, **цара́пнуть,** -ну *perf.* (*perf.* also на~, о~) scratch; scribble; **~ся,** scratch; scratch one another; scramble, scrabble. **цара́пина,** -ы, scratch; abrasion.
цари́зм, -а, tsarism. **цари́стский,** tsarist. **цари́ть,** -рю́ *imp.* be tsar; hold sway; reign, prevail. **цари́ца,** -ы, tsarina; queen. **ца́рский,** of the tsar, tsar's; royal; tsarist; regal, kingly. **ца́рство,** -а, kingdom, realm; reign; domain. **ца́рствование,** -я, reign. **ца́рствовать,** -твую *imp.* reign. **царь,** -я́ *m.* tsar; king, ruler.
цвести́, -ету́, -етёшь; -ёл, -а́ *imp.* flower, bloom, blossom; prosper, flourish; grow mouldy.
цвет[1], -а; *pl.* -а́, colour; ~ лица́, complexion.
цвет[2], -а (-у), *loc.* -у́; *pl.* -ы́, flower, cream, pick; blossom-time; prime; blossom; во ~е лет, in the prime of life; во ~е сил, at the height of one's powers; в цвету́, in blossom. **цветни́к,** -а́, flower-bed, flower-garden.
цветн|о́й, coloured; colour; non-ferrous; ~а́я капу́ста, cauliflower; ~ы́е мета́ллы, non-ferrous metals; ~о́е стекло́, stained glass; ~о́й фильм, colour-film.
цветово́дство, -а, flower-growing, floriculture.
цветов|о́й, colour; ~а́я слепота́, colour-blindness.
цвето́к, -тка́; *pl.* цветы́ or цветки́, -о́в, flower. **цвето́чный,** flower; ~ магази́н, flower-shop. **цвету́щий,** flowering, blossoming, blooming; prosperous, flourishing.
ЦВМ (*tseveém*) *abbr.* цифрова́я вычисли́тельная маши́на digital computer.
цеди́лка, -и, strainer, filter. **цеди́ть,** цежу́, це́дишь *imp.* strain, filter; percolate; mutter (through clenched teeth).
целе́бный, curative, healing.
целево́й, special; earmarked for a specific purpose. **целенапра́вленный,** purposeful. **целесообра́зный,** expedient. **целеустремлённый**; -ён, -ённа or -ена́, purposeful.
целико́м *adv.* whole; wholly, entirely.
целина́, -ы, virgin lands, virgin soil. **цели́нн|ый,** virgin; ~ые зе́мли, virgin lands.
цели́тельный, curative, healing, medicinal.
це́лить(ся, -лю(сь *imp.* (*perf.* на~), aim, take aim.
целко́вый *sb.* one rouble.

целова́ть, -лу́ю *imp.* (*perf.* по~) kiss; **~ся,** kiss.

це́лое *sb.* whole; integer. **целому́дренный,** chaste. **целому́дрие,** -я, chastity. **це́лостность,** -и, integrity. **це́лостный,** integral; entire, complete. **це́лый;** цел, -а́, -о, whole, entire; safe, intact.

цель, -и, target; aim, object, goal, end, purpose; с це́лью, with the object (of), in order to.

цельнометалли́ческий, all-metal. **це́льный;** -лен, -льна́, -о, of one piece, solid; entire; whole; integral; single; undiluted. **це́льность,** -и, wholeness, entirety, integrity.

цеме́нт, -а, cement. **цементи́ровать,** -рую *perf.* and *imp.* cement; case-harden.

цена́, -ы́, *acc.* -у; *pl.* -ы, price, cost; worth, value; цено́й + *gen.* at the price of, at the cost of; любо́й цено́й, at any price.

ценз, -а, qualification. **це́нзовый,** qualifying. **це́нзор,** -а, censor. **цензу́ра,** -ы, censorship.

цени́тель, -я *m.* judge, connoisseur, expert. **цени́ть,** -ню́, -нишь *imp.* value; assess; estimate; appreciate. **це́нник,** -а, price-list. **це́нность,** -и, value; price; importance; *pl.* valuables; values. **це́нный,** valuable; costly; precious; important.

центр, -а, centre. **центра́ль,** -и, main. **центра́льный,** central. **центробе́жный,** centrifugal.

цеп, -а́, flail.

цепене́ть, -е́ю *imp.* (*perf.* о~) freeze; be numbed; be rooted to the spot. **це́пкий,** tenacious, strong; prehensile; sticky, tacky, loamy; obstinate, persistent, strong-willed. **це́пкость,** -и, tenacity, strength; obstinacy, persistence. **цепля́ться,** -я́юсь *imp.* за + *acc.* clutch at, try to grasp; cling to; stick to.

цепн|о́й, chain; ~а́я реа́кция, chain reaction. **цепо́чка,** -и, chain; file, series.

цепь, -и, *loc.* -и́; *gen. pl.* -е́й, chain; row; series; range; line, file; succession; circuit; *pl.* chains, bonds.

церемо́ниться, -нюсь *imp.* (*perf.* по~) stand on ceremony; be (over-)considerate. **церемо́ния,** -и, ceremony; без церемо́ний, informally.

церковнославя́нский, Church Slavonic. **церко́вный,** church; ecclesiastical. **це́рковь,** -кви; *gen. pl.* -е́й, church.

цех, -а, *loc.* -у́; *pl.* -и or -а́, shop; section; guild, corporation.

цивилиза́ция, -и, civilization. **цивилизо́ванный,** civilized. **цивилизова́ть,** -зу́ю *perf.* and *imp.* civilize.

цигейка, -и, beaver lamb. **цигейковый,** beaver-lamb.

цикл, -а, cycle.

цико́рий, -я, chicory. **цико́рный,** chicory.

цили́ндр, -а, cylinder; drum; top hat. **цилиндри́ческий,** cylindrical.

цимба́лы, -а́л *pl.* cymbals.

цинга́, -и́, scurvy. **цинго́тный,** scurvy; scorbutic.

цинк, -а, zinc. **ци́нковый,** zinc.

цино́вка, -и, mat. **цино́вочный,** mat, of mats.

цирк, -а, circus. **цирково́й,** circus.

циркули́ровать, -рует *imp.* circulate. **ци́ркуль,** -я *m.* (pair of) compasses; dividers. **циркуля́р,** -а, circular.

цирю́льник, -а, barber.

цисте́рна, -ы, cistern, tank.

цитаде́ль, -и, citadel; bulwark, stronghold.

цита́та, -ы, quotation. **цити́ровать,** -рую *imp.* (*perf.* про~) quote.

ци́тра, -ы, zither.

ци́трус, -а, citrus. **ци́трусов|ый,** citrous; ~ые *sb. pl.* citrus plants.

цифербла́т, -а, dial, face.

ци́фра, -ы, figure; number, numeral. **цифров|о́й,** numerical, in figures; ~ы́е да́нные, figures.

ЦК (*tseká*) *abbr.* Центра́льный Комите́т, Central Committee.

цо́кать, -аю *imp.*, **цо́кнуть,** -ну *perf.* clatter, clang; click.

цо́коль, -я *m.* socle, plinth, pedestal. **цо́кольный,** plinth; ~ эта́ж, ground floor.

ЦРУ (*tse-erú*) *abbr.* Центра́льное разве́дывательное управле́ние, C.I.A.

ЦС (*tse-és*) *abbr.* Центра́льный сове́т, Central Soviet, Central Council.

ЦСУ (*tse-esú* or *-seú*) *abbr.* Центра́ль-

ное статисти́ческое управле́ние, Central Statistical Board.
цука́т, -а, candied fruit, candied peel.
цыга́н, -а; *pl.* -е, -а́н or -ы, -ов, **цыга́нка**, -и, gipsy. **цыга́нский**, gipsy.
цыплёнок, -нка; *pl.* -ля́та, -ля́т, chicken; chick.
цы́почки; на ~, на цы́почках, on tip-toe.
цэ *n. indecl.* the letter ц.

Ч

ч *letter*: see чэ.
ч. *abbr.* час, hour, (after numerals) o'clock; часть, part.
чад, -а (-у), *loc.* -у́, fumes, smoke. **чади́ть**, чажу́ *imp.* (*perf.* на~) smoke. **ча́дный**, smoky, smoke-laden; stupefied, stupefying.
чай, -я (-ю); *pl.* -и́, -ёв, tea.
чай *part.* probably, perhaps; no doubt; I suppose; after all.
ча́йка, -и; *gen. pl.* ча́ек, gull, sea-gull.
ча́йник, -а, teapot; kettle. **ча́йн|ый**, tea; ~ая посу́да, tea-service; ~ая ро́за, tea-rose. **чайхана́**, -ы́, tea-house.
чалма́, -ы́, turban.
ча́лый, roan.
чан, -а, *loc.* -у́; *pl.* -ы́, vat, tub, tank.
ча́рка, -и, cup, goblet, small glass.
چарова́ть, -ру́ю *imp.* bewitch; charm, captivate, enchant.
ча́ртерный, chartered.
час, -а (-у), with numerals -а́, *loc.* -у́; *pl.* -ы́, hour; hours, time, period; *pl.* guard-duty; ~, one o'clock; в два ~а́, at two o'clock; стоя́ть на ~а́х, stand guard; ~ы́ пик, rush-hour. **часо́вня**, -и; *gen. pl.* -вен, chapel. **часово́й** *sb.* sentry, sentinel, guard. **часов|о́й**, clock, watch; time; of one hour, an hour's; by the hour; one o'clock; ~о́й переры́в, an hour's interval; ~а́я пла́та, payment by the hour; ~о́й по́яс, time zone; ~а́я стре́лка, (hour-) hand. **часовщи́к**, -а́, watchmaker. **ча́сом** *adv.* sometimes, at times; by the way.
части́ца, -ы, small part, element; particle. **части́чно** *adv.* partly, partially. **части́чный**, partial.
ча́стность, -и, detail; в ча́стности, in particular. **ча́стн|ый**, private; personal; particular, individual; local; district; ~ая со́бственность, private property.
ча́сто *adv.* often, frequently; close, thickly. **частоко́л**, -а, paling, palisade. **частота́**, -ы́; *pl.* -ы, frequency. **часто́тный**, frequency. **часту́шка**, -и, ditty, folk-song. **ча́стый**; част, -а́, -о, frequent; close, close together; dense, thick; close-woven; quick, rapid; ~ гре́бень, fine-tooth comb.
часть, -и; *gen. pl.* -е́й, part; portion; section, department, side; sphere, field; share; unit; ча́сти ре́чи, parts of speech.
часы́, -о́в *pl.* clock, watch; нару́чные ~, ручны́е ~, wrist-watch.
ча́хлый, stunted; poor, sorry; weakly, sickly, puny. **ча́хнуть**, -ну; ча́х *imp.* (*perf.* за~) wither away; become weak, go into a decline. **чахо́тка**, -и, consumption. **чахо́точный**, consumptive; poor, sorry, feeble.
ча́ша, -и, cup, bowl; chalice; ~ весо́в, scale, pan. **ча́шка**, -и, cup; bowl; scale, pan.
ча́ща, -и, thicket.
ча́ще *comp.* of ча́сто, ча́стый; ~ всего́, most often, mostly.
ча́яние, -я, expectation; hope. **ча́ять**, ча́ю *imp.* hope, expect; think, suppose.
чва́ниться, -нюсь *imp.* (+ *instr.*) boast (of). **чва́нство**, -а, conceit, arrogance, pride.
чв-д (*chevedé*) *abbr.* челове́ко-де́нь, man-day. **чв-ч(ас)** *abbr.* челове́ко-ча́с, man-hour.

чего́: see что.
чей *m.*, **чья** *f.*, **чьё** *n.*, **чьи** *pl.*, *pron.* whose. **че́й-либо, че́й-нибудь,** anyone's. **че́й-то,** someone's.
чек, -а, cheque; check, bill; receipt.
Чека́ *f. indecl.*, or -и́, **ЧК** (*cheká*) *abbr.* Чрезвыча́йная Коми́ссия (по борьбе́ с контрреволю́цией, сабота́жем и спекуля́цией), Cheka.
чека́н, -а, stamp, die. **чека́нить,** -ню *imp.* (*perf.* вы́~, от~) mint, coin; stamp, engrave, emboss, chase; ~ слова́, enunciate words clearly; rap out; ~ шаг, step out. **чека́нный,** stamping, engraving, embossing; stamped, engraved, embossed, chased; precise, expressive, chiselled; ~ шаг, measured tread.
чёлка, -и, fringe; forelock.
чёлн, -а́; *pl.* чёлны́, dug-out canoe; boat. **челно́к,** -а́, dug-out canoe; shuttle.
челове́к, -а; *pl.* лю́ди; with numerals, *gen.* -ве́к, -ам, man, person, human being; (man-)servant, waiter.
человеко- in *comb.* man-, anthropo-. **челове́ко-де́нь,** -дня *m.* man-day. **~люби́вый,** philanthropic. **~лю́бие,** -я, philanthropy; humanity, humaneness. **~ненави́стнический,** misanthropic. **~обра́зный,** anthropomorphous; anthropoid. **челове́ко-ча́с,** -а; *pl.* -ы́, man-hour.
челове́чек, -чка, little man. **челове́ческий,** human; humane. **челове́чество,** -а, humanity, mankind. **челове́чий,** human. **челове́чный,** humane.
че́люсть, -и, jaw, jaw-bone; denture, dental plate, false teeth.
чем, чём: see что. **чем** *conj.* than; + *inf.* rather than, instead of; ~. ., тем . . + *comp.* the more . ., the more.
чемода́н, -а, suitcase.
чемпио́н, -а, **чемпио́нка,** -и, champion(s), title-holder(s). **чемпиона́т,** -а, championship.
чему́: see что.
чепуха́, -и́, nonsense, rubbish; trifle, triviality.
че́пчик, -а, cap; bonnet.
че́рви, -е́й, **че́рвы,** черв *pl.* hearts. **черво́нн|ый,** of hearts; red; ~ое зо́лото, pure gold; ~ый туз, ace of hearts.
червь, -я́; *pl.* -и, -е́й *m.* worm; maggot; bug, virus, germ. **червя́к,** -а́, worm; screw.
черда́к, -а́, attic, loft.
черёд, -а́, *loc.* -у́, turn; queue; идти́ свои́м ~о́м, take its course. **чередова́ние,** -я, alternation, interchange, rotation; (vowel) gradation, ablaut.
чередова́ть, -ду́ю *imp.* alternate; **~ся,** alternate, take turns.
че́рез, чрез *prep.* + *acc.* across; over; through; via; in; after; (further) on; every (other); ~ день, every other day, on alternate days; ~ полчаса́, in half an hour; ~ три киломе́тра, three kilometres further on; ~ ка́ждые три страни́цы, every four pages.
черёмуха, -и, bird cherry.
че́реп, -а; *pl.* -а́, skull, cranium.
черепа́ха, -и, tortoise; turtle; tortoiseshell. **черепа́ховый,** tortoise; turtle; tortoiseshell. **черепа́ший,** tortoise, turtle; very slow.
черепи́ца, -ы, tile. **черепи́чный,** tile; tiled.
черепо́к, -пка́, crock, potsherd, broken piece of pottery.
чересчу́р *adv.* too; too much.
чере́шневый, cherry; cherry-wood. **чере́шня,** -и; *gen. pl.* -шен, cherry; cherry-tree.
черке́с, -а, **черке́шенка,** -и, Circassian. **черке́сский,** Circassian.
черкну́ть, -ну́, -нёшь *perf.* scrape; leave a mark on; scribble, dash off.
черне́ть, -е́ю *imp.* (*perf.* по~) turn black, go black; show black. **черни́ка,** -и, bilberry, whortleberry. **черни́ла,** -и́л *pl.* ink. **черни́льница,** -ы, ink-pot ink-well. **черни́льный,** ink; ~ каранда́ш, indelible pencil. **черни́ть,** -ню́ *imp.* (*perf.* за~, на~, о~) blacken; paint black; slander. **черни́чный,** bilberry.
черно- in *comb.* black; unskilled; rough. **чёрно-бе́лый,** black-and-white. **черно-бу́рка,** -и, silver fox (fur). **~бу́рый.** dark-brown; ~бу́рая лиса́, silver fox,

~волосый, black-haired. **~глазый,** black-eyed. **~зём,** -а, chernozem, black earth. **~зёмный,** black-earth. **~кожий,** black, coloured; *sb.* Negro, black. **~морский,** Black-Sea. **~рабочий** *sb.* unskilled worker, labourer. **~слив,** -а (-у), prunes. **~смородинный,** blackcurrant.

черновик, -а, rough copy, draft. **черновой,** rough; draft, preparatory; heavy, dirty; crude. **чернота,** -ы, blackness; darkness. **чёрн|ый;** -рен, -рна, black; back; heavy, unskilled; ferrous; gloomy, melancholy; на ~ый день, for a rainy day; ~ый ворон, (*sl.*) Black Maria; ~ые металлы, ferrous metals; ~ый хлеб black bread, rye-bread; ~ый ход, back way, back door; **~ый** *sb.* Negro, black.

черпак, -а, scoop; bucket; grab. **черпалка,** -и, scoop; ladle. **черпать,** -аю *imp.*, **черпнуть,** -ну, -нёшь *perf.* draw; scoop, ladle; extract, derive.

черстветь, -ею *imp.* (*perf.* за~, о~, по~) grow stale, get stale; become hardened, grow callous. **чёрствый;** чёрств, -а, -о, stale; hard callous.

чёрт, -а; *pl.* черти, -ей, devil; the devil.

черта, -ы, line; boundary; trait, characteristic; в общих ~х, in general outline; в черте города, within the town boundary. **чертёж,** -а, drawing; blueprint, plan, scheme. **чертёжная** *sb.* drawing-office. **чертёжник,** -а, draughtsman. **чертёжный,** drawing. **чертить,** -рчу, -ртишь *imp.* (*perf.* на~) draw; draw up.

чёртов *adj.* devil's; devilish, hellish. **чертовский** devilish, damnable.

чёрточка, -и line; hyphen. **черчение,** -я, drawing. **черчу,** etc.: see чертить.

чесать, чешу, -шешь *imp.* (*perf.* по~) scratch; comb; card; **~ся,** scratch oneself; comb one's hair; у него руки чешутся + *inf.* he is itching to.

чеснок, -а (-у), garlic. **чесночный,** garlic.

чесотка, -и, scab; rash; mange; itch.

чествование, -я, celebration. **чествовать,** -твую *imp.* celebrate; honour. **честность,** -и, honesty, integrity. **честный;** -тен, -тна, -о, honest, upright. **честолюбивый,** ambitious. **честолюбие,** -я, ambition. **честь,** -и, *loc.* -и, honour; regard, respect; отдать ~ + *dat.* salute.

четверг, -а, Thursday. **четвереньки;** на ~, на четвереньках, on all fours, on hands and knees. **четвёрка,** -и, figure 4; No. 4; four; good. **четверо,** -ых four. **четвероног|ий,** four-legged; **~ое** *sb.* quadruped. **четверостишие,** -я, quatrain. **четвёртый,** fourth. **четверть,** -и; *gen. pl.* -ей, quarter; quarter of an hour; term; без четверти час, a quarter to one. **четвертьфинал,** -а, quarter-final.

чёткий; -ток, -тка, -о, precise; clear-cut; clear well-defined; legible; plain, distinct; articulate. **чёткость,** -и, precision; clarity, clearness, definition; legibility; distinctness.

чётный, even.

четыре, -рёх, -рьмя, -рёх, four. **четыреста,** -рёхсот, -ьмястами, -ёхстах, four hundred.

четырёх- in *comb.* four-, tetra-. **четырёхголосный,** four-part. **~гранник,** -а, tetrahedron. **~кратный,** fourfold. **~летие,** -я, four-year period; fourth anniversary. **~местный,** four-seater. **~моторный,** four-engined. **~сотый,** four-hundredth. **~стопный,** tetrameter. **~тактный,** four-stroke. **~угольник,** -а, square, quadrangle. **~угольный,** square, quadrangular. **~часовой,** four hours', four-hour; four-o'clock.

четырнадцатый, fourteenth. **четырнадцать,** -и, fourteen.

чех, -а, Czech.

чехарда, -ы, leap-frog.

чехлить, -лю *imp.* (*perf.* за~) cover. **чехол,** -хла, cover, case; loose cover.

чечевица, -ы, lentil; lens. **чечевичн|ый,** lentil; ~ая похлёбка, mess of pottage.

чешка, -и, Czech. **чешский,** Czech.

чешу, etc.: see чесать.

чешуйка, -и, scale. **чешуя,** -и, scales.

чиж, -а, **чижик,** -а, siskin.

чин, -а; *pl.* -ы, rank; any of fourteen grades (numbered from the top) of Tsarist Civil Service; official; rite, ceremony, order; быть в ~а́х, hold high rank, be of high rank.

чина́рик, -а, (*sl.*) cigarette end.

чини́ть[1], -ню́, -нишь *imp.* (*perf.* по~) repair, mend.

чини́ть[2], -ню́, -нишь *imp.* (*perf.* о~) sharpen.

чини́ть[3], -ню́ *imp.* (*perf.* у~) carry out, execute; cause; ~ препя́тствия + *dat.* put obstacles in the way of.

чино́вник, -а, civil servant; official, functionary; bureaucrat. **чино́внический, чино́вничий,** civil-service; bureaucratic.

чи́псы, -ов *pl.* chips.

чири́кать, -аю *imp.*, **чири́кнуть,** -ну *perf.* chirp.

чи́ркать, -аю *imp.*, **чи́ркнуть,** -ну *perf.* + *instr.* strike; ~ спи́чкой, strike a match.

чи́сленность, -и, numbers; strength. **чи́сленный,** numerical. **числи́тель,** -я *m.* numerator. **числи́тельное** *sb.* numeral. **чи́слить,** -лю *imp.* count, reckon; **~ся,** be; + *instr.* be reckoned, be on paper; be attributed; за ним чи́слится мно́го недоста́тков, he has many failings; ~ся больны́м, be on the sick-list; ~ся в спи́ске, be on the list. **число́,** -а́; *pl.* -а, -сел, number; date, day; в числе́ + *gen.* among; в том числе́, including; еди́нственное ~, singular; мно́жественное ~, plural; сего́дня восемна́дцатое ~, today is the eighteenth. **числово́й,** numerical.

чи́стильщик, -а, cleaner; ~ сапо́г, bootblack, shoeblack. **чи́стить,** чи́щу *imp.* (*perf.* вы́~, о~, по~) clean; brush, scour, sweep; peel, shell; purge; clear; dredge. **чи́стка,** -и, cleaning; purge; отда́ть в чи́стку, have cleaned, send to the cleaner's. **чи́сто** *adv.* cleanly, clean; purely, merely; completely. **чистов|о́й,** fair, clean; ~а́я ко́пия, ~о́й экземпля́р, fair copy, clean copy. **чистокро́вный,** thoroughbred, pure-blooded. **чистописа́ние,** -я, calligraphy, (hand)writing. **чистопло́тный,** clean; neat, tidy; decent. **чистосерде́чный,** frank, sincere, candid.

чистота́, -ы́, cleanness, cleanliness; neatness, tidiness; purity, innocence. **чи́ст|ый,** clean; neat; tidy; pure; unsullied; undiluted; clear; net; utter; mere, sheer; complete, absolute; на ~ом во́здухе, in the open air; ~ый вес, net weight; ~ые де́ньги, cash; ~ый лист, blank sheet; ~ая при́быль, clear profit; ~ая случа́йность, pure chance.

чита́емый, widely-read, popular. **чита́льный,** reading. **чита́льня,** -и; *gen. pl.* -лен, reading-room. **чита́тель,** -я *m.* reader. **чита́ть,** -а́ю *imp.* (*perf.* про~, проче́сть) read; recite, say; ~ ле́кции, lecture, give lectures; **~ся,** be legible; be visible, be discernible. **чи́тка,** -и, reading; reading through.

чих, -а, sneeze. **чиха́ть,** -а́ю *imp.*, **чихну́ть,** -ну́, -нёшь *perf.* sneeze, cough, splutter.

чи́ще, *comp.* of чи́сто, чи́стый.

чи́щу, etc.: see чи́стить.

ЧК: see **Чека́.**

член, -а, member; limb; term; part; article. **члене́ние,** -я, articulation. **члени́ть,** -ню́ *imp.* (*perf.* рас~) divide; articulate. **член(-)ко́р(р),** -а *abbr.*, **член-корреспонде́нт,** -а, **чл.-кор.** *abbr.* corresponding member, associate. **членоразде́льный,** articulate. **чле́нск|ий,** membership; ~ие взно́сы, membership fee, dues. **чле́нство,** -а, membership. **чл.-кор.**: see членко́рр.

чмо́кать, -аю *imp.*, **чмо́кнуть,** -ну *perf.* make smacking or sucking sound; kiss noisily; ~ губа́ми, smack one's lips.

чо́канье, -я, clinking of glasses. **чо́каться,** -аюсь *imp.*, **чо́кнуться,** -нусь *perf.* clink glasses.

чо́порный, prim, stiff; stuck-up, stand-offish.

чрева́тый + *instr.* fraught with, pregnant with. **чре́во,** -а, belly, womb. **чревовеща́ние,** -я, ventriloquism. **чревовеща́тель,** -я *m.* ventriloquist.

чрез: see че́рез. **чрезвыча́йн|ый,** extraordinary; special, extreme; ~ое положе́ние, state of emergency. **чрезме́рный,** excessive, inordinate, extreme.

чте́ние, -я, reading; reading-matter. **чтец**, -á, **чти́ца**, -ы, reader; reciter. **чти́во**, -а, reading-matter, trash.

чтить, чту *imp.* honour.

чти́ца: see чтец.

что, чего́, чему́, чем, о чём *pron.* what?; how?; why?; how much?; which, what, who; anything; в чём де́ло? what is the matter?; для чего́? what . . for? why?; е́сли ~ случи́тся, if anything happens; к чему́? why?; ~ ему́ до э́того? what does it matter to him?; ~ каса́ется меня́, as for me, as far as I am concerned; ~ с тобо́й? what's the matter (with you)?; я зна́ю, ~ вы име́ете в виду́, I know what you mean; **~ ж**, yes; all right, right you are; **~ за**, what? what sort of?; what (a) . . !; ~ за ерунда́! what (utter) nonsense! **что** *conj.* that. **что (бы) ни** *pron.* whatever, no matter what; во что бы то ни ста́ло, at whatever cost.

чтоб, что́бы *conj.* in order (to), so as; that; to; он сказа́л, что́бы вы к нему́ зашли́, he said you were to go and see him; он хо́чет, что́бы я сде́лал э́то сейча́с же, he wants me to do it at once. **что́-либо, что́-нибудь** *pron.* anything. **что́-то,** *pron.* something. **что́-то** *adv.* somewhat, slightly; somehow, for some reason.

чу́вственность, -и, sensuality. **чу́вственный**, sensual; perceptible, sensible. **чувстви́тельность**, -и, sensitivity, sensitiveness, sensibility; perceptibility; sentimentality; tenderness, feeling; (film) speed. **чувстви́тельный**, sensitive, susceptible; sensible, perceptible; sentimental; tender. **чу́вство**, -а, feeling; sense; senses; прийти́ в ~, come round, regain consciousness. **чу́вствовать**, -твую *imp.* feel; realize; appreciate, have a feeling for; **~ся**, be perceptible; make itself felt.

чугу́н, -á, cast iron. **чугу́нка**, -и, (cast-iron) pot; (cast-iron) stove; railway. **чугу́нный**, cast-iron.

чуда́к, -á, **чуда́чка**, -и, eccentric, crank. **чуда́ческий**, eccentric, extravagant. **чуда́чество**, -а, eccentricity, extravagance.

чудеса́, etc.: see чу́до. **чуде́сный**, miraculous; marvellous, wonderful.

чу́диться, -ишься *imp.* (*perf.* по~, при~), seem.

чу́дно *adv.* wonderfully, beautifully. **чудно́й**; -дён, -дна́, odd, strange. **чу́дный**, wonderful, marvellous; beautiful, lovely; magical. **чу́до**, -а; *pl.* -деса́, miracle; wonder, marvel. **чудо́вище**, -а, monster. **чудо́вищный**, monstrous; enormous. **чудоде́й**, -я, -де́йка, -и, miracle-worker. **чудоде́йственный**, miracle-working; miraculous. **чу́дом** *adv.* miraculously. **чудотво́рный**, miraculous, miracle-working.

чужби́на, -ы, foreign land, foreign country. **чужда́ться** -а́юсь *imp.* + *gen.* shun, avoid; stand aloof from, be untouched by. **чу́ждый**; -жд, -á, -о, alien (to); + *gen.* free from, devoid of, a stranger to. **чужезе́мец**, -мца, -зе́мка, -и, foreigner stranger. **чужезе́мный**, foreign. **чуж|о́й**, someone else's, another's, others'; strange, alien; foreign; на ~о́й счёт, at somebody else's expense; ~и́е края́, foreign lands; *sb.* stranger.

чула́н, -а, store-room, lumber-room; larder; built-in cupboard.

чуло́к, -лка́; *gen. pl.* -ло́к, stocking. **чуло́чн|ый**, stocking; ~ая вя́зка, stocking-stitch.

чум, -а, tent.

чума́, -ы́, plague.

чурба́н, -а, block, chock; blockhead. **чу́рка**, -и, block, lump.

чу́ткий; -ток, -тка́, -о, keen, sharp, quick; sensitive; sympathetic; tactful, delicate, considerate; ~ сон, light sleep. **чу́ткость**, -и, keeness, sharpness, quickness; delicacy, tact, consideration.

чу́точка, -и; ни чу́точки, not in the least; чу́точку, a little (bit), a wee bit.

чу́тче *comp.* of чу́ткий.

чуть *adv.* hardly, scarcely; just; a little, very slightly; ~ не, almost, nearly, all but; ~ свет, at daybreak, at first light; ~-чу́ть, a tiny bit.

чухо́нец, -нца, **чухо́нка**, -и, Finn. **чухо́нск|ий**, Finnish; ~ое ма́сло, butter.
чу́чело, -а, stuffed animal, stuffed bird; scarecrow.
чушь, -и, nonsense, rubbish.
чу́ять, чу́ю *imp.* scent, smell; sense feel.
чьё, etc.: see чей.
чэ *n. indecl.* the letter ч.

Ш

ша *n. indecl.* the letter ш.
ша́баш[1], -а, sabbath. **шаба́ш**[2], -а́, end of work, break; finish; ~! that's all! that's enough! that'll do! **шаба́шить**, -шу *imp.* (*perf.* по~) (*sl.*) knock off, stop work; take a break.
шабло́н, -а, template, pattern; mould, form; stencil; cliché; routine. **шабло́нный**, stencil, pattern; trite, banal; stereotyped; routine.
шаг, -а (-у), with numerals -а́, *loc.* -у́; *pl.* -и́, step; footstep; pace; stride. **шага́ть**, -а́ю *imp.*, **шагну́ть**, -ну́, -нёшь *perf.* step; walk, stride; pace; go, come; make progress. **ша́гом** *adv.* at walking pace, at a walk; slowly.
ша́йба, -ы, washer; puck.
ша́йка[1], -и, tub.
ша́йка[2], -и, gang, band.
шака́л, -а, jackal.
шала́нда, -ы, barge, lighter.
шала́ш, -а́, cabin, hut.
шали́ть, -лю́ *imp.* be naughty; play up, play tricks. **шаловли́вый**, naughty, mischievous, playful. **ша́лость**, -и, prank, game; *pl.* mischief, naughtiness. **шалу́н**, -а́, **шалу́нья**, -и; *gen. pl.* -ний, naughty child.
шаль, -и, shawl.
шальн|о́й, mad, crazy; wild; ~а́я пу́ля, stray bullet.
ша́мать, -аю *imp.* (*sl.*) scoff, eat.
ша́мкать, -аю *imp.* mumble, lisp.
шамо́вка, -и (*sl.*) grub, food.
шампа́нское *sb.* champagne.
шанда́л, -а, candlestick.
шанта́ж, -а́, blackmail. **шантажи́ровать**, -рую *imp.* blackmail.
ша́пка, -и, cap; banner headline. **ша́почка**, -и, cap.
шар, -а, with numerals -а́; *pl.* -ы́, sphere; ball; balloon; ballot; *pl.* (*sl.*) eyes; ~-зо́нд, sonde.
шара́хать, -аю *imp.*, **шара́хнуть**, -ну, hit; **~ся**, rush, dash; shy.
шарж, -а, caricature, cartoon. **шаржи́ровать**, -рую *imp.* caricature.
ша́рик, -а, ball; corpuscle. **ша́рико-в|ый**; ~ая (авто)ру́чка, ball-point pen; ~ый подши́пник, ball-bearing. **шарикоподши́пник**, -а, ball-bearing.
ша́рить, -рю *imp.* grope, feel, fumble; sweep.
ша́ркать, -аю *imp.*, **ша́ркнуть**, -ну *perf.* shuffle; scrape; ~ ного́й, click one's heels.
шарма́нка, -и, barrel-organ, street organ. **шарма́нщик**, -а, organ-grinder.
шарни́р, -а, hinge, joint.
шарова́ры, -а́р *pl.* (wide) trousers; bloomers.
шарови́дный, spherical, globular. **шарово́й**, ball; globular. **шарообра́зный**, spherical, globular.
шарф, -а, scarf.
шасси́ *n. indecl.* chassis; undercarriage.
шата́ть, -а́ю *imp.*, rock, shake; *impers.* его́ шата́ет, he is reeling, staggering; **~ся**, rock, sway; reel, stagger, totter; come loose, be loose; be unsteady; wander; loaf, lounge about. **шата́ющийся**, loose.
шатёр, -тра́, tent; marquee; tent-shaped roof or steeple.
ша́тия, -и (*sl.*) gang, band, crowd, mob.

шáткий, unsteady; shaky; loose; unstable, insecure; unreliable; vacillating.
шатрóвый, tent-shaped.
шатýн, -á, connecting-rod.
шáфер, -а; *pl.* -á, best man.
шафрáн, -а, saffron. **шафрáнный**, **шафрáновый**, saffron.
шах[1], -а, Shah.
шах[2], -а, check; ~ и мат, checkmate. **шахматист**, -а, chess-player. **шáхматн|ый**, chess; chess-board, chequered, check; ~ая пáртия, game of chess; в ~ом порядке, quincunx fashion. **шáхматы**, -ат *pl.* chess; chessmen.
шáхта, -ы, mine, pit; shaft. **шахтёр**, -а, miner. **шахтёрский**, miner's, miners'; mining. **шáхтный**, pit, mine.
шáшечница, -ы, draught-board, chess-board. **шáшка**[1], -и, draught; *pl.* draughts.
шáшка[2], -и, sabre, cavalry sword.
шашлы́к, -á, shashlik, kebab.
шва, etc.: see шов.
швáбра, -ы, mop, swab.
шваль, -и, rubbish; trash; riff-raff.
швартóв, -а, hawser; mooring-line; *pl.* moorings. **швартовáть**, -тýю *imp.* (*perf.* о~, при~) moor; **~ся**, moor, make fast.
швах, -а, weak, poor; bad; in a bad way.
швед, -а, **швéдка**, -и, Swede. **швéдский**, Swedish.
швéйн|ый, sewing; ~ая маши́на, sewing-machine; ~ая мастерскáя, dressmaker's.
швейцáр, -а, (hall-)porter, door-keeper, commissionaire.
щвейцáрец, -рца, **-цáрка**, -и, Swiss. **щвейцáрский**, Swiss.
швея́, -и́, seamstress, machinist.
швырнýть, -нý, -нёшь *perf.* **швыря́ть**, -яю *imp.* throw, fling, chuck, hurl; **~ся** + *instr.* throw; throw about, treat carelessly, muck about.
шевели́ть, -елю́, -éлишь *imp.*, **шевельнýть**, -нý, -нёшь *perf.* (*perf.* also по~), turn (over); (+ *instr.*) move, stir, budge; **~ся**, move, stir, budge.
шевpó *n. indecl.* kid.
шедéвр, -а, masterpiece, chef d'œuvre.
шёл: see идти́.
шéлест, -а rustle, rustling. **шелестéть**, -сти́шь *imp.* rustle.
шёлк, -а (-у), *loc.* -ý; *pl.* -á, silk. **шелкови́стый**, silk, silky. **шелкови́ца**, -ы, mulberry(-tree). **шелкови́чный**, mulberry; ~ червь, silkworm. **шёлковый**, silk.
шелохнýть, -нý, -нёшь *perf.* stir, agitate; **~ся**, stir, move.
шелухá, -и́, skin; peel, peelings; pod; scale. **шелуши́ть**, -шý, peel; shell; **~ся**, peel; peel off, flake off.
шепеля́вить, -влю *imp.* lisp. **шепеля́вый**, lisping; hissing.
шепнýть, -нý, -нёшь *perf.*, **шептáть**, -пчý, -пчешь *imp.* whisper; **~ся**, whisper (together). **шёпот**, -а, whisper. **шёпотом** *adv.* in a whisper.
шерéнга, -и, rank; file, column.
шероховáтый, rough; uneven; rugged.
шерсть, -и, wool, woollen; fleece; hair, coat. **шерстянóй**, wool, woollen.
шершáветь, -еет *imp.* become rough, get rough. **шершáвый**, rough.
шест, -á, pole; staff.
шéствие, -я, procession. **шéствовать**, -твую, walk in procession, process; march, pace, proceed.
шестёрка, -и, six; figure 6; No. 6; group of six.
шестерня́, -и́; *gen. pl.* -рён, gear-wheel, cogwheel, pinion.
шéстеро, -ы́х, six.
шести- in *comb.* six-, hexa-, sex(i)-. **шестигрáнник**, -а, hexahedron. **~днéвка**, -и, six-day (working) week. **~деся́тый**, sixtieth. **~клáссник** -а, **~клáссница**, -ы, sixth-class pupil. **~лéтний**, six-year; six-year-old. **~мéсячный**, six-month; six-month-old. **~сотлéтие**, -я, six hundred years; sexcentenary, six-hundredth anniversary. **~сóтый**, six-hundredth. **~угóльник**, -а, hexagon. **~угóльный**, hexagonal. **~часовóй**, six-hour; six-o'clock.
шестнадцатилéтний, sixteen-year; sixteen-year-old. **шестнáдцатый**, sixteenth. **шестнáдцать**, -и, sixteen.
шест|óй, sixth; однá ~áя, one-sixth.
шесть, -и́, *instr.* -ью six. **шестьдеся́т**,

-и́десяти, *instr.* -ью́десятью, sixty. **шестьсо́т**, -исо́т, -иста́м, -ьюста́ми, -иста́х, six hundred. **ше́стью** *adv.* six times.

шеф, -а, boss, chief; patron, sponsor. **ше́фский**, patronage, sponsorship, adoption; sponsored. **ше́фство**, -а, patronage, adoption. **ше́фствовать**, -твую *imp.* + над + *instr.* adopt; sponsor.

ше́я, -и neck; сиде́ть на ше́е у, be a burden to.

ши́ворот, -а, collar.

шика́рный, chic, smart, stylish; splendid, magnificent; done for effect.

ши́кать, -аю *imp.*, **ши́кнуть**, -ну *perf.* + *dat.* hiss, boo; + на + *acc.* hush, call 'sh' to.

ши́ло, -а; *pl.* -ья, -ьев, awl.

ши́на, -ы, tyre; splint.

шине́ль, -и, greatcoat, overcoat.

шинко́ванный, shredded, chopped. **шинкова́ть**, -ку́ю *imp.* shred, chop.

ши́нный tyre. **шиноремо́нтный**, tyre-repairing, tyre-maintenance.

шип, -а́, thorn, spine; spike, crampon, nail; pin; tenon.

шипе́ние, -я, hissing; sizzling; sputtering. **шипе́ть**, -плю́ *imp.* hiss; sizzle; fizz; sputter.

шипо́вник, -а, wild rose, dog-rose.

шипу́чий, sparkling; fizzy. **шипу́чка**, -и, fizzy drink. **шипя́щий**, sibilant.

ши́ре *comp.* of широ́кий, широ́ко́. **ширина́**, -ы́, width, breadth; gauge. **ши́рить**, -рю *imp.* extend, expand; **~ся**, spread, extend.

ши́рма, -ы, screen.

широ́к|ий; -о́к, -а́, -о́ко́. wide, broad; това́ры ~ого потребле́ния, consumer goods; ~ие ма́ссы, the broad masses; ~ое пла́тье, loose dress; ~ая пу́блика, the general public; ~ий экра́н, wide screen. **широ́ко́** *adv.* wide, widely, broadly; extensively, on a large scale; ~ смотре́ть на ве́щи, be broad-minded.

широко- in *comb.* wide-, broad-. **широковеща́ние**, -я, broadcasting. **~веща́тельный**, broadcasting. **~коле́йный**, broad-gauge. **~ко́стный**, big-boned. **~пле́чий**, broad-shouldered. **~по́лый**, wide-brimmed; full-skirted. **~форма́тный**, **~экра́нный**, wide-screen.

широта́, -ы́; *pl.* -ы, width, breadth; latitude. **широ́тный**, of latitude; latitudinal. **широча́йший** *superl.* of широ́кий. **ширпотре́б**, -а *abbr.* consumption; consumer goods. **ширь**, -и, (wide) expanse; во всю ~, to full width; to the full extent.

ши́тый, embroidered. **шить**, шью, шьёшь *imp.* (*perf.* с~) sew; make; embroider. **шитьё**, -я́, sewing, needlework; embroidery.

шифр, -а, cipher, code; press-mark; monogram. **шифро́ванный**, in cipher, coded. **шифрова́ть**, -ру́ю *imp.* (*perf.* за~) encipher, code. **шифро́вка**, -и, enciphering, coding; coded communication, communication in cipher.

шиш, -а́, fico, fig; nothing; ruffian, brigand; ни ~а́, damn all. **ши́шка**, -и, cone; bump; lump, knob; core; (*sl.*) big shot, big noise. **шишкова́тый**, knobby, knobbly; bumpy. **шишкови́дный**, cone-shaped. **шишконо́сный**, coniferous.

шкала́, -ы́; *pl.* -ы, scale; dial.

шкап: see шкаф.

шкату́лка, -и, box, casket, case.

шкаф, **шкап**, -а, *loc.* -у́; *pl.* -ы́, cupboard; wardrobe; dresser; кни́жный ~, bookcase; несгора́емый ~, safe. **шка́фчик**, -а, cupboard, locker.

шквал, -а, squall. **шква́листый**, squally.

шкет, -а, (*sl.*) boy; apprentice criminal.

шкив, -а; *pl.* -ы́, pulley; sheave.

шко́ла, -ы, school; ~-интерна́т, boarding-school. **шко́лить**, -лю *imp.* (*perf.* вы́~) train, discipline. **шко́льник**, -а, schoolboy. **шко́льница**, -ы, schoolgirl. **шко́льный**, school; ~ учи́тель, school-teacher, school-master.

шку́ра, -ы, skin, hide, pelt. **шку́рка**, -и, skin; rind; emery paper, sandpaper. **шку́рник**, -а, **-ница**, -ы, person who looks after number one. **шку́рный**, self-centred, selfish.

шла: see идти́.

шлагба́ум, -а, barrier; arm.

шлак, -а, slag; dross; cinder; clinker. **шлакобло́к**, -а, breeze-block. **шла́ковый**, slag.
шланг, -а, hose.
шлейф, -а, train.
шлем, -а, helmet.
шлёпать, -аю *imp*., **шлёпнуть**, -ну *perf*. smack, spank; shuffle; tramp; (*sl*.) shoot, execute by shooting; **~ся**, fall flat, plop down, plump down.
шли: see идти́.
шлифова́льный, polishing; grinding; abrasive. **шлифова́ть**, -фу́ю *imp*. (*perf*. от~) polish; grind; abrade. **шлифо́вка**, -и, polishing; grinding; polish.
шло: see идти́. **шлю́**, etc.: see слать.
шлюз, -а, lock, sluice, floodgate. **шлю́зный**, **шлюзово́й**, lock, sluice.
шлю́пка, -и, launch, boat.
шля́па, -ы, hat; hèlpless feeble creature; де́ло в шля́пе, it's in the bag. **шля́пка**, -и, hat, bonnet; head; cap. **шля́пник**, -а, **шля́пница**, -ы, milliner, hatter. **шля́пный**, hat.
шмель, -я́, bumble-bee.
шмон, -а, (*sl*.) search, frisking. **шмона́ть**, -а́ю *imp*., **шмони́ть**, -ню́, -нишь *perf*., **шмоня́ть**, -я́ю *imp*. (*perf*. also про~), (*sl*.) search, frisk.
шмы́гать, -аю *imp*., **шмыгну́ть**, -ыгну́, -ы́гнёшь *perf*. dart, rush, slip, sneak; + *instr*. rub, brush; ~ но́сом, sniff.
шнур, -а́, cord; lace; flex, cable. **шнурова́ть**, -ру́ю *imp*. (*perf*. за~, про~) lace up; tie. **шнуро́к**, -рка́, lace.
шныря́ть, -я́ю *imp*. dart about, run in and out.
шов, шва, seam; stitch; suture; joint; weld.
шокола́д, -а, chocolate. **шокола́дка**, -и, chocolate, bar of chocolate. **шокола́дный**, chocolate; chocolate-coloured.
шо́рох, -а, rustle.
шо́ры, шор *pl*. blinkers.
шоссе́ *n. indecl*. highway, main road; (made) road. **шоссе́йник**, -а, road-racer.
шотла́ндец, -дца, Scotsman, Scot. **шотла́ндка**[1], -и, Scotswoman. **шотла́ндка**[2], -и, tartan, plaid. **шотла́ндский**, Scottish, Scots.
шофёр, -а, **шофёрша**, -и, driver; chauffeur. **шофёрский**, driver's; driving.
шпа́га, -и, sword.
шпага́т, -а, cord; twine; string; splits.
шпаклева́ть, -лю́ю *imp*. (*perf*. за~) caulk; fill, stop, putty. **шпаклёвка**, -и, filling, puttying, stopping; putty.
шпа́ла, -ы, sleeper.
шпана́, -ы́ (*sl*.) hooligan(s), rowdy, rowdies; riff-raff, rabble; petty criminals.
шпарга́лка, -и, crib.
шпа́рить, -рю *imp*. (*perf*. о~) scald.
шпат, -а, spar.
шпиль, -я *m*. spire, steeple; capstan, windlass. **шпи́лька**, -и, hairpin; hat-pin; tack, brad; stiletto heel.
шпина́т, -а, spinach.
шпингале́т, -а, espagnolette, (vertical) bolt; catch, latch.
шпио́н, -а, spy. **шпиона́ж**, -а, espionage. **шпио́нить**, -ню *imp*. be a spy; spy (за + *instr*. on). **шпио́нский**, spy's; espionage.
шпо́ра, -ы, spur.
шприц, -а, syringe.
шпро́та, -ы, sprat; *pl*. smoked sprats in oil.
шпу́лька, -и, spool, bobbin.
шрам, -а, scar.
шрифт, -а; *pl*. -ы́, type, print; script; курси́вный ~, italic(s). **шрифтово́й**, type.
шт. *abbr*. штýка, item, piece.
штаб, -а; *pl*. -ы́, staff; headquarters.
шта́бель, -я; *pl*. -я́ *m*. stack, pile.
штаби́ст, -а, **штабни́к**, -а́, staff-officer. **штабно́й**, staff, headquarters.
штамп, -а, die, punch; stamp, impress; letter-head; cliché, stock phrase. **штампо́ванный**, punched, stamped, pressed; trite, hackneyed; stock, standard.
шта́нга, -и, bar, rod, beam; weight; crossbar. **штанги́ст**, -а, weight-lifter.
штани́шки, -шек *pl*. (child's) shorts. **штаны́**, -о́в, trousers.
штат[1], -а, State.
штат[2], -а, **шта́ты**, -ов *pl*. staff, establishment.

штати́в, -а, tripod, base, support, stand.
шта́тный, staff; established, permanent.
шта́тск|ий, civilian; ~ое (пла́тье), civilian clothes, mufti, civvies; **~ий** *sb.* civilian.
штемпелева́ть, -лю́ю *imp.* (*perf.* за~) stamp; frank, postmark. **ште́мпель,** -я; *pl.* -я́ *m.* stamp; почто́вый ~, postmark.
ште́псель, -я, *pl.* -я́ *m.* plug, socket. **ште́псельный,** plug, socket.
штиль, -я *m.* calm.
што́льня, -и; *gen. pl.* -лен, gallery.
што́пальный, darning. **што́паный,** darned. **што́пать,** -аю *imp.* (*perf.* за~) darn. **што́пка,** -и, darning; darn; darning wool, darning thread.
што́пор, -а, corkscrew; spin.
што́ра, -ы, blind.
шторм, -а, gale, storm.
штраф, -а, fine. **штрафба́т,** -а *abbr.* (*sl.*) penal battalion. **штрафно́й,** penal; penalty; ~ батальо́н, penal battalion; ~ уда́р, penalty kick. **штрафова́ть,** -фу́ю *imp.* (*perf.* о~) fine.
штрих, -а́, stroke; hatching; feature, trait. **штрихова́ть,** -ху́ю *imp.* (*perf.* за~) shade, hatch.
штуди́ровать, -рую *imp.* (*perf.* про~) study.
шту́ка, -и, item, one; piece; trick; thing; вот так ~! well, I'll be damned! в то́м-то и ~! that's just the point; пять штук яи́ц, five eggs.
штукату́р, -а, plasterer. **штукату́рить,** -рю *imp.* (*perf.* от~, о~) plaster, parget. **штукату́рка,** -и, plastering; plaster; facing, rendering; stucco. **штукату́рный,** plaster, stucco.
штурва́л, -а, (steering-)wheel, helm; controls. **штурва́льный,** steering, control; *sb.* helmsman, pilot.
штурм, -а, storm, assault.
шту́рман, -а; *pl.* -ы or -а́, navigator.
штурмова́ть, -му́ю *imp.* storm, assault. **штурмов|о́й,** assault; storming; ~а́я авиа́ция, ground-attack aircraft; ~а́я ле́стница, scaling-ladder; ~а́я полоса́, assault course. **штурмовщи́на,** -ы, rushed work, production spurt, sporadic effort.
шту́чн|ый, piece, by the piece; ~ый пол, parquet floor; ~ая рабо́та, piece-work; ~ый това́р, piece-goods.
штык, -а́, bayonet. **штыково́й,** bayonet.
штырь, -я́ *m.* pintle, pin.
шу́ба, -ы, winter coat, fur coat.
шу́лер, -а; *pl.* -а́, card-sharper, cheat. **шу́лерство,** -а, card-sharping, sharp practice.
шум, -а (-у), noise; din, uproar, racket; sensation, stir; мно́го ~у из-за ничего́, much ado about nothing; наде́лать ~у, cause a sensation. **шуме́ть,** -млю́ *imp.* make a noise; row, wrangle; make a stir; make a fuss; cause a sensation. **шу́мный;** -мен, -мна́, -о, noisy; loud; sensational. **шумови́к,** -а́, sound-effects man.
шумо́вка, -и, perforated spoon; skimmer.
шумов|о́й, sound, noise; ~ы́е эффе́кты, sound effects. **шумо́к,** -мка́, noise; под ~, under cover, on the quiet.
шу́рин, -а, brother-in-law.
шурша́ть, -шу́ *imp.* rustle, crackle.
шу́стрый; -тёр, -тра́, -о, smart, bright, sharp.
шут, -а́, fool; jester; buffoon, clown. **шути́ть,** -чу́, -тишь *imp.* (*perf.* по~) joke, jest; play, trifle; + над + *instr.* laugh at, make fun of. **шу́тка,** -и, joke, jest; trick; farce; без шу́ток, кро́ме шу́ток, joking apart; в шу́тку, as a joke, in jest; не на шу́тку, in earnest; сыгра́ть шу́тку с + *instr.* play a trick on. **шутли́вый,** humorous; joking, light-hearted. **шу́точн|ый,** comic; joking; де́ло не ~ое, it's no joke, no laughing matter. **шутя́** *adv.* for fun, in jest; easily, lightly.
шушу́каться, -аюсь *imp.* whisper together.
шху́на, -ы, schooner.
шью, etc.: see шить.

Щ

ща *n. indecl.* the letter щ.
щаве́ль, -я́ *m.* sorrel.
щади́ть, щажу́ *imp.* (*perf.* по~) spare; have mercy on.
щебёнка, -и, ще́бень, -бня *m.* gravel, crushed stone, ballast; road-metal.
ще́бет, -а, twitter, chirp. **щебета́ть,** -ечу́, -е́чешь *imp.* twitter, chirp.
щего́л, -гла́, goldfinch.
щёголь, -я *m.* dandy, fop. **щегольну́ть,** -ну́, -нёшь *perf.*, **щеголя́ть, -я́ю** *imp.* dress fashionably; strut about; + *instr.* show off, parade, flaunt. **щегольско́й,** foppish, dandified.
ще́дрость, -и, generosity. **ще́дрый;** -др, -á, -о, generous; lavish, liberal.
щека́, -и́, *acc.* щёку; *pl.* щёки, -а́м, cheek.
щеко́лда, -ы, latch, catch.
щекота́ть, -очу́, -о́чешь *imp.* (*perf.* по~) tickle. **щеко́тка, -и,** tickling, tickle. **щекотли́вый,** ticklish, delicate.
щёлкать, -аю *imp.*, **щёлкнуть, -ну** *perf.* crack; flick, fillip, flip; trill; + *instr.* click, snap, pop; он щёлкает зуба́ми, his teeth are chattering; ~ па́льцами, snap one's fingers.
щёлок, -а, lye, liquor. **щелочно́й,** alkaline. **щёлочь, -и;** *gen. pl.* -е́й, alkali.
щелчо́к, -чка́, flick, fillip; slight; blow.
щель, -и; *gen. pl.* -е́й, crack; chink; slit; fissure, crevice; slit trench; голосова́я ~, glottis.
щени́ться, -и́тся *imp.* (*perf.* о~) pup, whelp, cub. **щено́к,** -нка́; *pl.* -нки́, -о́в or -ня́та, -я́т, puppy, pup; whelp, cub.
щепа́, -ы́; *pl.* -ы, -а́м, **ще́пка, -и,** splinter, chip; kindling; худо́й как ще́пка, as thin as a rake. **щепа́ть,** -плю́, -плёшь *imp.* chip, chop.
щепети́льный, punctilious, correct; pernickety, fussy, finicky.
ще́пка: see щепа́.
щепо́тка, -и, щепо́ть, -и, pinch.
щети́на, -ы, bristle; stubble. **щети́нистый,** bristly, bristling. **щети́ниться,** -ится *imp.* (*perf.* о~) bristle. **щётка,** -и, brush; fetlock. **щёточный,** brush.
щёчный, cheek.
щи, щей or щец, щам, ща́ми *pl.* shchi, cabbage soup.
щи́колотка, -и, ankle.
щипа́ть, -плю́, -плешь *imp.*, **щипну́ть,** -ну́, -нёшь *perf.* (*perf.* also об~, о~, ущипну́ть) pinch, nip, tweak; sting, bite; burn; pluck; nibble; **~ся,** pinch.
щипко́м *adv.* pizzicato. **щипо́к,** -пка́, pinch, nip, tweak. **щипцы́,** -о́в *pl.* tongs, pincers, pliers; forceps. **щи́пчики,** -ов *pl.* tweezers.
щит, -á, shield; screen; sluice-gate; (tortoise-)shell; hoarding; board; panel; распредели́тельный ~, switchboard; ~ управле́ния, control panel. **щитови́дный,** thyroid. **щито́к,** -тка́, dashboard.
щу́ка, -и, pike.
щуп, -а, probe. **щу́пальце, -а;** *gen. pl.* -лец, tentacle; antenna. **щу́пать, -аю** (*perf.* по~) feel, touch; feel for; probe.
щу́плый; -пл, -á, -о, weak, puny, frail.
щу́рить, -рю *imp.* (*perf.* со~) screw up, narrow; **~ся,** screw up one's eyes; narrow.
щу́ч|ий, pike's; (как) по ~ьему веле́нью, of its own accord, as if by magic.

Э

э *n. indecl.*, **э оборо́тное,** the letter э.
эв *abbr.* электро́н-во́льт, electron volt, eV.
эвакуацио́нный, evacuation. **эвакуа́ция,** -и, evacuation. **эвакуи́рованный** *sb.* evacuee. **эвакуи́ровать,** -рую *perf.* and *imp.* evacuate.
ЭВМ (*eveém*) *abbrev.* of электро́нная вычисли́тельная маши́на, (electronic) computer.
эволюциони́ровать, -рую *perf.* and *imp.* evolve. **эволюцио́нный,** evolutionary. **эволю́ция,** -и, evolution; manœuvre.
эй *int.* hi! hey!
эква́тор, -а, equator. **экваториа́льный,** equatorial.
экз. *abbr.* экземпля́р, copy, specimen.
экза́мен, -а, examination, exam; вы́держать, сдать, ~, pass an examination. **экзаменова́ть,** -ну́ю *imp.* (*perf.* про~) examine; **~ся,** take an examination.
экземпля́р, -а, specimen, example; copy.
экипа́ж[1], -а, carriage.
экипа́ж[2], -а, crew; ship's company. **экипирова́ть,** -ру́ю *perf.* and *imp.* equip. **экипиро́вка,** -и, equipping; equipment.
эконо́м, -а, steward, housekeeper; economist. **эконо́мика,** -и, economics; economy. **эконо́мить,** -млю *imp.* (*perf.* с~) use sparingly, husband; save; economize. **экономи́ческий,** economic; economical. **экономи́чный,** economical. **эконо́мия,** -и, economy; saving. **эконо́мка,** -и, housekeeper. **эконо́мный,** economical; careful, thrifty.
экра́н, -а, screen; голубо́й ~, television (screen). **экраниза́ция,** -и, filming, screening; film version.
экскурса́нт, -а, tourist. **экскурсио́нный,** excursion. **экску́рсия,** -и, (conducted) tour; excursion, trip; outing; group, party (of tourists). **экскурсово́д,** -а, guide.
экспанси́вный, effusive, expansive, talkative.
экспеди́ровать, -рую *perf.* and *imp.* dispatch. **экспеди́ция,** -и, expedition; dispatch, forwarding; forwarding office.
экспе́рт, -а, expert. **эксперти́за,** -ы, (expert) examination, expert opinion; commission of experts.
эксплуата́тор, -а, exploiter. **эксплуатацио́нн|ый,** exploitational, operating; ~ые расхо́ды, running costs; ~ые усло́вия, working conditions. **эксплуата́ция,** -и, exploitation; utilization; operation, running. **эксплуати́ровать,** -рую *imp.* exploit; operate, run, work.
экспо́ *f. indecl.* Expo. **экспози́ция,** -и, lay-out; exposition; exposure. **экспона́т,** -а, exhibit. **экспони́ровать,** -рую *perf.* and *imp.* exhibit; expose. **экспоно́метр,** -а, exposure meter.
экспро́мт, -а, impromptu. **экспро́мтом** *adv.* impromptu; suddenly, without warning; игра́ть ~, improvise.
экстерн, -а, external student. **экстерна́т,** -а, extramural course(s).
э́кстра *indecl. adj.* highest, best; jolly good, splendid, smashing.
экстравага́нтный, extravagant, eccentric, bizarre, preposterous.
экстра(-)кла́сс, -а, first class; highest rating, qualification, standing, etc.
э́кстренн|ый, urgent; emergency; extra, special; ~ое заседа́ние, extraordinary session; ~ое изда́ние, ~ый вы́пуск, special edition; ~ые расхо́ды, unforeseen expenses.
эксцентри́чный, eccentric.
электризова́ть, -зу́ю *imp.* (*perf.* на~) electrify. **эле́ктрик,** -а, electrician. **электрифици́ровать,** -рую *perf.* and *imp.* electrify. **электри́ческий,** electric; ~ фона́рик, torch, flashlight. **электри́чество,** -а, electricity; electric light. **электри́чка,** -и, electric train.
электро- in *comb.* electro-, electric, electrical. **электробытово́й,** electrical.

\~во́з, -а, electric locomotive. **\~дви́гатель**, -я *m.* electric motor. **\~дина́мика**, -и, electrodynamics. **\~дугово́й**, electric-arc. **\~и́згородь**, -и, electric fence. **электро́лиз**, -а, electrolysis. **\~маши́нка**, -и, electric typewriter. **\~монтёр**, -а, electrician. **\~одея́ло**, -а, electric blanket. **\~подогрева́тель**, -я *m.* electric heater. **\~по́езд**, -а, electric train. **\~полотёр**, -а, electric floor-polisher. **\~прибо́р**, -а, electrical appliance. **\~про́вод**, -а; *pl.* -á, electric cable. **\~прово́дка**, -и, electric wiring. **\~прои́грыватель**, -я *m.* record-player. **\~сва́рка**, -и, electric welding. **\~ста́нция**, -и, power-station. **\~те́хник**, -а, electrical engineer. **\~те́хника**, -и, electrical engineering. **\~тя́га**, -и, electric traction. **\~шо́к**, -а, electric-shock treatment. **\~энцефалогра́мма**, -ы, (electro-)encephalogram. **\~энцефало́граф**, -а, (electro-)encephalograph.

электро́н, -а, electron. **электро́н-во́льт**, -а, **электроново́льт**, -а, electron volt, eV. **электро́ник**: see электро́нщик. **электро́ника**, -и, electronics.

электронно- in *comb.* electron, electronic. **электро́нно-вычисли́тельный**, electronic-computer. **\~лучево́й**, electron-beam, cathode-ray. **\~микроскопи́ческий**, electron-microscope.

электро́нный, electron; electronic.

электроново́льт: see электро́н-во́льт. **электро́нщик**, -а, **электро́ник**, -а, specialist in electronics.

элеме́нт, -а, element; cell; type, character. **элемента́рный**, elementary; simple.

эль *n. indecl.* the letter л.

эм *n. indecl.* the letter м.

эма́левый, enamel. **эмалиро́ванный**, enamelled. **эмалирова́ть**, -ру́ю *imp.* enamel. **эма́ль**, -и, enamel.

эмбле́ма, -ы, emblem; insignia.

эмбрио́н, -а, embryo.

эмигра́нт, -а, emigrant, émigré. **эмигра́ция**, -и, emigration.

эмпири́зм, -а, empiricism. **эмпи́рик**, -а, empiricist. **эмпири́ческий**, empiricist; empirical.

эн *n. indecl.* the letter н.

э́ндшпиль, -я *m.* end-game.

энерге́тика, -и, power engineering. **энерги́чный**, energetic, vigorous, forceful. **эне́ргия**, -и, energy; vigour, effort.

энерго- in *comb.* power, energy. **энерговооружённость**, -и, power capacity, power supply. **\~ёмкий**, power-consuming. **\~затра́та**, energy expenditure. **\~систе́ма**, -ы, electric power system.

эпиде́мия, -и, epidemic.

эпизо́д, -а, episode. **эпизоди́ческий**, episodic; occasional, sporadic.

эпопе́я, -и, epic.

эпо́ха, -и, epoch, age, era. **эпоха́льный**, epoch-making.

эр *n. indecl.* the letter р.

э́ра, -ы, era; до на́шей э́ры, B.C.; на́шей э́ры, A.D.

эрэ́с, -а *abbr.* реакти́вный снаря́д, missile.

эро́тика, -и, sensuality. **эроти́ческий**, **эроти́чный**, erotic, sensual.

эс *n. indecl.* the letter с.

эсе́р, -а *abbr.* S.R., Socialist Revolutionary. **эсе́ровский**, Socialist-Revolutionary.

эска́дра, -ы, squadron. **эска́дренный**, squadron; \~ миноно́сец, destroyer. **эскадри́льный**, squadron. **эскадри́лья**, -и; *gen. pl.* -лий, squadron. **эскадро́н**, -а, squadron, troop. **эскадро́нный**, squadron, troop.

эски́з, -а, sketch, study; draft, outline. **эски́зный**, sketch; sketchy; draft.

эскимо́ *n. indecl.* choc-ice.

эскимо́с, -а, **эскимо́ска**, -и, Eskimo. **эскимо́сский**, Eskimo.

эсми́нец, -нца *abbr.* эска́дренный миноно́сец, destroyer.

эстака́да, -ы, trestle, platform; trestle bridge; gantry; overpass; pier, boom.

эста́мп, -а, print, engraving, plate.

эстафе́та, -ы, relay race; baton.

эсте́тика, -и, aesthetics; design. **эстети́ческий**, aesthetic.

эстра́да, -ы, stage, platform; variety, music hall; арти́ст эстра́ды, music-hall artiste. **эстра́дный**, stage; variety; \~ конце́рт, variety show.

эта́ж, -а́, storey, floor. **этаже́рка, -и**, shelves; whatnot; stand. **эта́жность**, -и, number of floors.

э́так *adv*. so, thus; about, approximately. **э́такий**, such (a), what (a).

этало́н, -а, standard.

эта́п, -а, stage, phase; lap; halting-place; transport, shipment, of prisoners. **этапи́ровать**, -рую *imp*. ship, transport.

этике́тка, -и, label.

эти́ческий, **эти́чный**, ethical.

этни́ческий, ethnic.

э́то *part*. this (is), that (is), it (is). **э́тот** *m*., **э́та** *f*., **э́то** *n*., **э́ти** *pl*. *pron*. this, these.

этю́д, -а, study, sketch; étude; exercise; problem.

эф *n*. *indecl*. the letter ф.

эфе́с, -а, hilt, handle.

эфио́п, -а, **эфио́пка**, -и, Ethiopian. **эфио́пский**, Ethiopian.

эфи́р, -а, ether; air. **эфи́рн|ый**, ethereal; ether, ester; ~ое ма́сло, essential oil; volatile oil.

эффе́кт, -а, effect, impact; result, consequences; *pl*. effects. **эффекти́вный**, effective; efficient. **эффе́ктный**, effective; striking; done for effect.

эх *int*. eh! oh!

э́хо, -а, echo. **эхоло́т**, -а, echo-sounder. **эхолока́ция**, -и, echo location.

ЭЦВМ (*etseveém*) *abbr*. электро́нная цифрова́я вычисли́тельная маши́на, electronic digital computer.

эшафо́т, -а, scaffold.

эшело́н, -а, echelon; special train, troop-train.

Ю

ю *n*. *indecl*. the letter ю.

ю. *abbr*. юг, S., south.

ЮАР (*yuár*) *abbr*. Ю́жно-Африка́нская Респу́блика, Republic of South Africa.

юбиле́й, -я, anniversary; jubilee. **юбиле́йный**, jubilee.

ю́бка, -и, skirt. **ю́бочка**, -и, short skirt.

ювели́р, -а, jeweller. **ювели́рный**, jeweller's, jewellery; fine, intricate; ~ магази́н, jeweller's.

юг, -а, south; на ~е, in the south. **ю́го-восто́к**, -а, south-east. **ю́го-за́пад**, -а, south-west. **югосла́в**, -а, **югосла́вка**, -и, Yugoslav. **югосла́вский**, Yugoslav. **южа́нин**, -а; *pl*. -а́не, -а́н, **южа́нка**, -и, southerner. **ю́жный**, south, southern.

ю́мор, -а, humour. **юморе́ска**, -и, humoresque. **юмори́ст**, -а, humourist. **юмори́стика**, -и, humour. **юмористи́ческий**, humorous, comic, funny.

юнио́р, -а, **юнио́рка**, -и, junior; junior competitor, player, etc. **юнко́р**, -а *abbr*. young contributor, youth correspondent.

ю́ность, -и, youth. **ю́ноша**, -и *m*. youth. **ю́ношеский**, youthful. **ю́ношество**, -а, youth; young people. **ю́ный**; юн, -а́, -о, young; youthful.

юпи́тер, -а, floodlight.

юриди́ческ|ий, legal, juridical; ~ие нау́ки, jurisprudence, law; ~ий факульте́т, faculty of law. **юриско́нсульт**, -а, legal adviser. **юри́ст**, -а, legal expert, lawyer.

ю́ркий; -рок, -рка́, -рко, quick-moving, brisk; sharp, smart.

ю́рта, -ы, yurt, nomad's tent.

юсти́ция, -и, justice.

юти́ться, ючу́сь *imp*. huddle (together); take shelter.

ю́шка, -и (*sl*.) watery gruel; blood.

Я

я, *n. indecl.* the letter я.

я, меня́, мне, мной (-о́ю), (обо) мне *pron.* I.

я́беда, -ы *m.* and *f.*, **я́бедник**, -а, sneak, tell-tale; informer. **я́бедничать**, -аю *imp.* (*perf.* на~) inform, tell tales, sneak.

я́блоко, -а; *pl.* -и, -ок, apple; в я́блоках, dappled, dapple; глазно́е ~, eyeball. **я́блоневый**, **я́блонный**, **я́блочный**, apple. **я́блоня**, -и, apple-tree.

яви́ться, явлю́сь, я́вишься *perf.*, **явля́ться**, -я́юсь *imp.* appear; present oneself, report; turn up, arrive, show up; arise, occur; + *instr.* be, serve as. **я́вка**, -и, appearance, attendance, presence; secret rendez-vous; ~ обяза́тельна, attendance obligatory. **явле́ние**, -я, phenomenon; appearance; occurrence, happening; scene. **я́вный**, obvious, manifest, patent; overt, explicit. **я́вственный**, clear, distinct. **я́вствовать**, -твует, appear; be clear, be obvious; follow.

ягнёнок, -нка; *pl.* -ня́та, -я́т, lamb.

я́года, -ы, berry; berries.

я́годица, -ы, buttock, buttocks.

яд, -а (-у), poison; venom.

я́дерник, -а, **я́дерщик**, -а, nuclear physicist. **я́дерный**, nuclear.

ядови́тый, poisonous; venomous; toxic.

ядрёный, vigorous, healthy; bracing; sound, crisp, juicy. **ядро́**, -а́; *pl.* -а, я́дер, kernel, core; nucleus; main body; (cannon-)ball; shot. **ядро-толка́тель**, -я *m.* shot-putter.

я́зва, -ы, ulcer, sore. **я́звенн|ый**, ulcerous; ~ая боле́знь, ulcers. **я́звина**, -ы, large ulcer; indentation, pit. **язви́тельный**, caustic, biting, sarcastic. **язви́ть**, -влю́ *imp.* (*perf.* съ~), wound, sting; be sarcastic.

язы́к, -а́, tongue; clapper; language; англи́йский ~, English. **языка́стый**, sharp-tongued. **языкове́д**, -а, linguist, language specialist. **языкове́дение**, -я, **языкозна́ние**, -я, linguistics. **языково́й**, linguistic. **языко́вый**, tongue; lingual. **язычко́вый**, uvular; reed. **язы́чник**, -а, heathen, pagan. **язы́чный**, lingual. **язычо́к**, -чка́, tongue; uvula; reed; catch.

яи́чко, -а; *pl.* -и, -чек, egg; testicle. **яи́чник**, -а, ovary. **яи́чница**, -ы, fried eggs. **яйцеви́дный**, oval; oviform, ovoid, egg-shaped. **яйцо́**, -а́; *pl.* я́йца, яи́ц, egg; ovum.

я́кобы *conj.* as if, as though; *part.* supposedly, ostensibly, allegedly.

я́корн|ый, anchor; mooring; ~ая стоя́нка, anchorage. **я́корь**, -я; *pl.* -я́ *m.* anchor; armature.

ял, -а, whaleboat, whaler; yawl. **я́лик**, -а, skiff, dinghy; yawl. **я́личник**, -а, ferryman.

я́ма, -ы, pit, hole; depression, hollow; (*sl.*) fence.

ямщи́к, -а́, coachman.

янва́рский, January. **янва́рь**, -я́ *m.* January.

янта́рный, amber. **янта́рь**, -я́ *m.* amber.

япо́нец, -нца, **япо́нка**, -и, Japanese. **япо́нский**, Japanese; ~ лак, japan.

я́ркий; я́рок, ярка́, -о, bright; colourful, striking; vivid, graphic; ~ приме́р, striking example, glaring example.

ярлы́к, -а́, label; tag.

я́рмарка, -и, fair. **я́рмарочный**, fair, market.

ярмо́, -а́; *pl.* -а, yoke.

яровой, spring, spring-sown.

я́ростный, furious, fierce, savage, frenzied. **я́рость**, -и, fury, rage, frenzy.

я́рус, -а, circle; tier; layer.

я́рче *comp.* of я́ркий.

я́рый, vehement, fervent; furious, raging; violent.

я́сельный, creche, day-nursery.

я́сеневый, ash. **я́сень**, -я *m.* ash(-tree).

я́сли, -ей *pl.* manger, crib; creche, day nursery.

ясне́ть, -е́ет *imp.* become clear, clear. **я́сно** *adv.* clearly. **ясновиде́ние**, -я, clairvoyance. **ясновиде́ц**, -дца, **ясновиди́ца**, -ы, clairvoyant. **я́сный**; -я́сен, ясна́, -о, clear; bright; fine;

distinct; serene; plain; lucid; precise, logical.

я́ства, яств *pl.* viands, victuals.

я́стреб, -а; *pl.* -á, hawk. **ястреби́н|ый,** hawk; с ~ым взгля́дом, hawk-eyed. **ястребо́к,** -бка́, hawk; fighter (plane).

я́хта, -ы, yacht

яче́истый, cellular, porous. **яче́йка,** -и, **ячея́,** -и́, cell.

ячме́нный, barley. **ячме́нь**[1], -я́ *m.* barley.

ячме́нь[2], -я́ *m.* stye.

я́щерица -ы, lizard.

я́щик, -а, box, chest, case; cabinet; drawer; му́сорный ~, dustbin; откла́дывать в до́лгий ~, shelve, put off.

я́щур, -а, foot-and-mouth disease.

THE
POCKET OXFORD
ENGLISH–RUSSIAN
DICTIONARY

THE POCKET OXFORD ENGLISH–RUSSIAN DICTIONARY

COMPILED BY
NIGEL RANKIN
AND
DELLA THOMPSON

CLARENDON PRESS · OXFORD
1981

Oxford University Press, Walton Street, Oxford OX2 6DP
London Glasgow New York Toronto
Delhi Bombay Calcutta Madras Karachi
Kuala Lumpur Singapore Hong Kong Tokyo
Nairobi Dar es Salaam Cape Town
Melbourne Wellington
and associate companies in
Beirut Berlin Ibadan Mexico City

Published in the United States
by Oxford University Press, New York

© *Oxford University Press 1981*

All rights reserved. No part of this publication may be reproduced, stored in a retrieval system, or transmitted, in any form or by any means, electronic, mechanical, photocopying, recording, or otherwise, without the prior permission of Oxford University Press

British Library Cataloguing in Publication Data
The pocket Oxford English – Russian dictionary.
1. English language – Dictionaries – Russian
I. Rankin, Nigel II. Thompson, Della
491. 7'3'21 PG2640 79–40382
ISBN 0–19–864127–3

Typeset by William Clowes Ltd, Great Yarmouth
and Latimer Trend & Company Ltd, Plymouth
Printed and bound in Great Britain by
William Clowes (Beccles) Limited, Beccles and London

PREFACE

This dictionary forms a companion volume to the *Pocket Oxford Russian–English Dictionary* (1975), and is likewise designed primarily for English-speaking users who do not have an advanced knowledge of Russian.

For this reason, particular attention has been given to the provision of the inflected forms of nouns, pronouns, adjectives, and verbs wherever they occur as translations and are not within the group of regular forms defined in the Introduction (pp. vii–xi). The stressed syllable of every Russian word is shown, and changes of stress are also marked. Perfective and imperfective aspects are distinguished, and both are given wherever appropriate.

The English vocabulary is drawn from that of the smaller Oxford English dictionaries, and the Russian translations are based on the best bilingual and monolingual dictionaries and grammars published in the Soviet Union and elsewhere. The aim has been to meet the needs of as wide a range of users as possible, by providing a single alphabetical list of almost 30,000 words in the general, technical, colloquial, and idiomatic areas of the language.

PUBLISHER'S NOTE

The major part of this dictionary was compiled by Mr Nigel Rankin. After his death on 4 October 1979, the remaining work was undertaken by Miss Della Thompson, under the supervision of Dr John Sykes, Editor of the *Concise Oxford Dictionary* and of the *Pocket Oxford Dictionary*.

ACKNOWLEDGEMENTS

The Publisher takes this opportunity to thank Dr Jane Grayson, Mrs Vera Konnova-Stone, and Miss Helen Szamuely for valuable comments on the galley proofs; the late Professor R. Auty, Professor J. L. I. Fennell, Mr P. S. Falla, Mr I. P. Foote, Mrs Konnova-Stone, Professor A. E. Pennington, Miss Szamuely, and Professor M. C. C. Wheeler for useful remarks on a preliminary specimen of the dictionary; Mrs Jessie Coulson for a considerable amount of preliminary drafting done before her retirement; and Mr and Mrs A. Levtov for their valuable advice on contemporary Russian usage.

INTRODUCTION

NOTES ON THE USE OF THE DICTIONARY

General

In order to save space, several English words are sometimes included in one entry. They are printed in **bold type** and separated by full stops. Compounds and phrases within an entry are printed in *italics* and separated by semicolons. When a bold-type word is used in a compound or phrase, it is abbreviated to its first letter, e.g. **crash** . . . *c. landing*. A swung dash ~ stands for the preceding Russian word, e.g. **Georgian** . . . грузи́н, ~ка indicates грузи́нка; **sing** . . . петь *imp.*, про ~, с ~ *perf.* indicates пропе́ть, спеть. In giving grammatical forms a hyphen is often used to stand for the whole or a part of the preceding or following Russian word, e.g. **grey** . . . седо́й (сед, -á, -о) = седо́й (сед, седá, се́до); **come** . . . приходи́ть (-ожу́, -о́дишь) = приходи́ть (прихожу́, прихо́дишь); **prepare** . . . при-, под-, гото́вливаться = пригото́вливаться, подгото́вливаться. Superscript numbers are used to distinguish unrelated headwords spelt alike, and glosses may follow in brackets, e.g. **bank**[1] *n.* (*of river*), **bank**[2] *n.* (*econ.*).

The comma is used to show alternatives, e.g.

(i) **want** . . . хоте́ть + *gen.*, *acc.* means that the Russian verb may govern either the genitive or (less often) the accusative;

(ii) **classify** . . . классифици́ровать *imp.*, *perf.* means that the Russian verb is both imperfective and perfective.

The ampersand (&) also shows alternatives, e.g.

(i) **dilate** *v.t.* & *i.* . . . расширя́ть(ся) means that the Russian verb forms given cover both the transitive and the intransitive English verb;

(ii) **orphan** . . . сирота́ *m.* & *f.* means that the Russian noun can be treated as either masculine or feminine according to the sex of the person it denotes;

(iii) **move** . . . дви́гаться (-аюсь, -аешься & дви́жусь,

-жешься) shows alternative forms for the first and second persons singular present.

The double hyphen is used when a hyphenated word is split between two lines, to show that the hyphen is not simply the result of printing convention. Where the first part is abbreviated, the hyphen is not repeated, e.g. **red** . . . *r.-/handed.*

Stress

The stress of each Russian word is indicated by an acute accent over the vowel of the stressed syllable. It is not given for monosyllabic words, except those which bear the main stress in a phrase, e.g. **be** . . . не́ было; **year** . . . год о́т году; here, the stressed monosyllable and the next word are pronounced as one. The vowel ё has no stress-mark, since it is almost always stressed; when the stress falls elsewhere, this is shown, e.g. **three-ply** . . . трёхсло́йный. The presence of two stress-marks indicates that either of the marked syllables may be stressed, e.g. **decrease** . . . уме́ньши́ть = уме́ньшить or уменьши́ть. Changes of stress which take place in conjugation, or declension, or in the short forms of adjectives, are shown, e.g.

(i) **suggest** . . . предложи́ть (-жу́, -жишь). Here, the absence of a stress-mark on the second person singular indicates that the stress is on the preceding syllable: предло́жишь.

(ii) **begin** . . . нача́ть (-чну́, -чнёшь; на́чал, -а́, -о). When the stress of the two preceding forms is not identical as it is in (i), the final form takes the stress of the first of these: на́чало. Forms not shown at all, e.g. the rest of the conjugation of предложи́ть, and the rest of the future and the past plural of нача́ть, are stressed like the last form given: предло́жит etc., начнёт etc., на́чали.

(iii) **boring**[2] . . . ску́чный (-чен, -чна́, -чно) = (ску́чен, скучна́, ску́чно, ску́чны); where the ending (e.g. -чны here) is not given, the stress is the same as for the previous form.

(iv) **rain** . . . дождь (-дя́). The single form in brackets is the genitive (see *Declension* below), and all other forms have the same stressed syllable. If only one case-labelled form is given in the singular, it is an exception to the regular paradigm. For example, **leg**... нога́ (*acc.* -гу; *pl.* -ги, -г, -га́м); the other singular forms have end-stress, while the unmentioned plural forms follow the stress of the last form given: нога́ми, нога́х.

Nouns

Gender This can usually be deduced from the ending of the nominative singular: a final consonant or -й indicates a masculine noun, -а or -я or -ь a feminine, -е or -о a neuter. Gender is shown explicitly for masculine nouns in -а, -я, or -ь, neuter nouns in -мя, and indeclinable nouns. If a noun is given only as a plural form, the gender is shown where possible; otherwise, the genitive plural is shown. Nouns denoting persons are often given a masculine and a feminine translation, e.g. **teacher** . . . учи́тель, ~ница; **Cossack** . . . каза́к, -а́чка; these correspond to the sex of the person concerned.

Declension The declensions treated as regular here are exemplified on pp. 38–41, 44–5, 58–60, and 64–5 of B. O. Unbegaun's *Russian Grammar* (Clarendon Press, 1957). (Some of the points mentioned there have been regarded in this dictionary as irregularities.) When a single inflected form is added in brackets with no label of case or number, it is the genitive singular, e.g. **Indian** . . . инде́ец (-е́йца), and all other inflected cases have the genitive stem. Apart from changes in stress (see *Stress* above), the following irregularities are among those indicated:

(i) The 'mobile vowel' in masculine nouns, e.g. **stub** . . . оку́рок (-рка).

(ii) The alternative genitive singular in -у or -ю of masculine nouns, e.g. **cheese** . . . сыр (-а(у)), i.e. сы́ра or сы́ру. For nouns denoting a substance, a number of objects, or a collective unit, the -у/-ю form has partitive value; with other nouns, it is used only in some set phrases.

(iii) The prepositional singular of masculine nouns, when ending in -у́ (or -ю́) after в or на. Here the term *locative* is used, e.g. **shore** . . . бе́рег (*loc.* -у́).

(iv) Substantivized adjectives are followed by *sb.* to show that they retain the adjectival declension.

Adjectives

The declensions treated as regular here are exemplified on pp. 96–8 and 131–5 of B. O. Unbegaun's *Russian Grammar* (Clarendon Press, 1957). The short forms of adjectives are shown when they are irregular, when the stress moves (see *Stress* above), and for all adjectives in -нный or -нний, e.g. **sickly** . . . боле́зненный (-ен, -енна); **sincere** . . . и́скренний (-нен, -нна, -нно & -нне).

Verbs

The conjugations treated as regular here are exemplified in B. O. Unbegaun's *Russian Grammar* (Clarendon Press, 1957): verbs in -ать, -еть, and -ять on p. 195, those in -ить on p. 198, those in -нуть on p. 192, and those in -овать on p. 197. Persons and tenses treated as irregular, and changes of stress in conjugation, are shown in brackets, e.g. **come** . . . приходи́ть (-ожу́, -о́дишь) *imp.*, прийти́ (приду́, -дёшь; пришёл, -шла́) *perf.* The first two forms in brackets are the first and second persons singular of the present or future tense; other persons and the past tense follow where necessary. Each verb is labelled with its aspect. The case construction is shown for transitive verbs *not* followed by the accusative.

The conjugation of быть is given only under *be*. Irregularities of imperative, participial, and gerundial forms are not usually shown.

The following changes in the first person singular of the present or future tense of verbs in -ить are treated as regular:

(i) insertion of л after a stem in -б, -в, -м, -п, or -ф, e.g. **add** . . . доба́вить: доба́влю, доба́вишь.

(ii) change of д or з to ж, к or т to ч, с or х to ш, ск or ст to щ, e.g. **annoy** . . . досади́ть: досажу́, досади́шь; **answer** . . . отве́тить: отве́чу, отве́тишь; **paint** . . . кра́сить: кра́шу, кра́сишь; **clean** . . . чи́стить: чи́щу, чи́стишь.

The reflexive suffix -ся or -сь is placed in brackets when the verb may be used with or without it, usually as an intransitive or a transitive verb respectively, e.g. **open** *v.t.* & *i.* открывáть(ся) *imp.*, откры́ть(ся) (-рóю(сь), -рóешь(ся)).

ABBREVIATIONS
USED IN THE DICTIONARY

abbr. abbreviation
abs. absolute
acc. accusative
adj. adjective
adv. adverb
aeron. aeronautics
agr(ic). agriculture
anat. anatomy
approx. approximately
archaeol. archaeology
arch(it). architecture
astron. astronomy
attrib. attributive
aux. auxiliary
Bibl. Biblical
biol. biology
bot. botany
chem. chemistry
cin. cinema
coll. colloquial
collect. collective(ly)
comb. combination
comm. commerce
comp. comparative, complement
conj. conjunction
cul. culinary
dat. dative
demonstr. demonstrative
derog. derogatory
det. determinate
dim. diminutive
dipl. diplomacy
eccl. ecclesiastical
econ. economics
electr. electrical
electron. electronics
emph. emphatic
ent. entomology
esp. especially
euphem. euphemism
f. feminine
fig. figurative
fut. future
gen. genitive
geog. geography
geol. geology
geom. geometry
gram. grammar
hist. history
hort. horticulture
i. intransitive
imp. imperfective
imper. imperative
impers. impersonal
inc. including
indecl. indeclinable
indet. indeterminate
inf. infinitive
instr. instrumental
interj. interjection
interrog. interrogative

journ. journalism
leg. legal
ling. linguistics
lit. literary
loc. locative
m. masculine
math. mathematics
med. medicine
meteorol. meteorology
mil. military
min. mineralogy
mus. music
myth. mythology
n. noun
naut. nautical
neg. negative
neut. neuter
nom. nominative
obl. oblique
opp. opposed
orn. ornithology
parl. parliamentary
perf. perfective
pers. person
phon. phonetics
phot. photography
phys. physics
pl. plural
poet. poetical
polit. politics
poss. possessive
predic. predicative
pref. prefix
prep. preposition(al)
pres. present
print. printing
pron. pronoun
psych. psychology
refl. reflexive
relig. religion
rly. railway
sb. substantive
s.b. somebody
sing. singular
sl. slang
s.o. someone
s.th. something
superl. superlative
surg. surgery
t. transitive
tech. technical
tel. telephone
theat. theatre
theol. theology
trigon. trigonometry
univ. university
usu. usually
v. verb
v.abs. verb absolute
var. various
v.aux. verb auxiliary
vet. veterinary
v.i. verb intransitive
voc. vocative
v.t. verb transitive
zool. zoology
~ see Introduction, p.vii

A

A *n.* (*mus.*) ля *neut.indecl.*; *from A to Z*, с начáла до концá.

a, an *indef. article, not translated*; *adj.* одúн, нéкий, какóй-то; *fifty miles an hour*, пятьдесят миль в час; *twice a week*, два рáза в недéлю.

aback *adv.*: *take a.*, поражáть *imp.*, поразúть *perf.*; застúгнуть *perf.* врасплóх.

abacus *n.* счёты *m.pl.*

abandon *v.t.* (*leave*) оставлять *imp.*, остáвить *perf.*; (*desert*) покидáть *imp.*, покúнуть *perf.*; (*give up*) бросáть *imp.*, брóсить *perf.*; *a. oneself to*, предавáться (-даюсь, -даёшься) *imp.*, предáться (-áмся, -áшься, -áстся, -адúмся; -áлся, -алáсь) *perf.*+*dat.* **abandoned** *adj.* забрóшенный, покúнутый; (*profligate*) распýтный. **abandonment** *n.* (*action*) оставлéние; (*state*) забрóшенность.

abase *v.t.* унижáть *imp.*, унúзить *perf.* **abasement** *n.* унижéние.

abate *v.i.* (*lessen*) уменьшáться *imp.*, умéньшúться *perf.*; (*weaken*) слабéть *imp.*, о~ *perf.*; (*calm*) успокáиваться *imp.*, успокóиться *perf.*; (*die down*) затихáть *imp.*, затúхнуть (-х) *perf.* **abatement** *n.* уменьшéние.

abattoir *n.* скотобóйня (*gen.pl.* -óен).

abbess *n.* аббатúса. **abbey** *n.* аббáтство. **abbot** *n.* аббáт.

abbreviate *v.t.* сокращáть *imp.*, сократúть (-ащý, -атúшь) *perf.* **abbreviation** *n.* сокращéние.

ABC *abbr.* áзбука, алфавúт.

abdicate *v.i.* отрекáться *imp.*, отрéчься (-екýсь, -ечёшься; -ёкся, -еклáсь) *perf.* от престóла. **abdication** *n.* отречéние (от престóла).

abdomen *n.* брюшнáя пóлость (*pl.* -ти, -тéй); (*entom.*) брюшкó (*pl.* -кú, -кóв). **abdominal** *adj.* брюшнóй.

abduct *v.t.* насúльно увозúть (-ожý, -óзишь) *imp.*, увезтú (увезý, -зёшь; увёз, -лá) *perf.* **abduction** *n.* насúльственный увóз.

aberration *n.* аберрáция; (*mental*) помрачéние умá.

abet *v.t.* подстрекáть *imp.*, подстрекнýть *perf.* (к совершéнию преступлéния *etc.*); содéйствовать *imp.*, *perf.* совершéнию (преступлéния *etc.*).

abhor *v.t.* питáть *imp.* отвращéние к+*dat.*; (*hate*) ненавúдеть (-úжу, -úдишъ) *imp.* **abhorrence** *n.* отвращéние. **abhorrent** *adj.* отвратúтельный.

abide *v.t.* (*tolerate*) выносúть (-ошý, -óсишь) *imp.*, вы́нести (-су, -сешь; -с) *perf.*; *v.i.* (*remain*) оставáться (-таюсь, -таёшься) *imp.*, остáться (-áнусь, -áнешься) *perf.*; *a. by*, (*promise etc.*) выполнять *imp.*, вы́полнить *perf.*

ability *n.* спосóбность, умéние.

abject *adj.* (*miserable*) жáлкий (-лок, -лкá, -лко); (*low*) нúзкий (-зок, -зкá, -зко); (*craven*) малодýшный.

abjure *v.t.* отрекáться *imp.*, отрéчься (-екýсь, -ечёшься; -ёкся, -еклáсь) *perf.* от+*gen.*

ablative *n.* аблятúв.

ablaze *predic.*: *be a.*, горéть (-рúт) *imp.*; сверкáть *imp.*

able *adj.* спосóбный, умéлый; (*talented*) талáнтливый; *be a. to*, мочь (могý, мóжешь; мог, -лá) *imp.*, с~ *perf.*; быть в состоя́нии; (*know how to*) умéть *imp.*, с~ *perf.*

abnormal *adj.* ненормáльный. **abnormality** *n.* ненормáльность.

aboard *adv.* на борт(ý); (*train*) на пóезд(е).

abolish *v.t.* отменять *imp.*, отменúть (-ню́, -нишь) *perf.*; уничтожáть *imp.*, уничтóжить *perf.* **abolition** *n.* отмéна; уничтожéние.

abominable *adj.* отврати́тельный; (*bad*) ужа́сный. **abomination** *n.* отвраще́ние; (*also object of a.*) ме́рзость.
aboriginal *adj.* иско́нный, коренно́й; *n.* абориге́н, коренно́й жи́тель *m.* **aborigines** *n.* абориге́ны *m.pl.*, коренны́е жи́тели *m.pl.*
abort *v.i.* (*med.*) выки́дывать *imp.*, вы́кинуть *perf.*; *v.t.* (*terminate*) прекраща́ть *imp.*, прекрати́ть (-ащу́, -ати́шь) *perf.*; обрыва́ть *imp.*, оборва́ть (-ву́, -вёшь; оборва́л, -а́, -о) *perf.* **abortion** *n.* або́рт, вы́кидыш. **abortive** *adj.* неуда́вшийся, безуспе́шный.
abound *v.i.* быть в большо́м коли́честве; *a. in*, изоби́ловать *imp.* + *instr.*; *a. with*, кише́ть (-ши́т) *imp.* + *instr.*
about *adv.*, *prep.* о́коло + *gen.*; (*concerning*) о + *prep.*, насчёт + *gen.*; (*up and down*) по + *dat.*; *be a. to*, собира́ться *imp.*, собра́ться (соберу́сь, -рёшься; собра́лся, -ала́сь, -а́ло́сь) *perf.* + *inf.*
above *adv.* наверху́; (*higher up*) вы́ше; *from a.*, све́рху; свы́ше; *prep.* над + *instr.*; (*more than*) свы́ше + *gen.*; *a.-board* че́стный (-тен, -тна́, -тно), прямо́й (прям, -а́, -о); *a.-mentioned*, вышеупомя́нутый.
abrasion *n.* стира́ние, истира́ние; (*wound*) ссади́на. **abrasive** *adj.* абрази́вный; *n.* абрази́в, шлифова́льный материа́л.
abreast *adv.* (*in line*) в ряд, ря́дом; (*on a level*) в у́ровень.
abridge *v.t.* сокраща́ть *imp.*, сократи́ть (-ащу́, -ати́шь) *perf.* **abridgement** *n.* сокраще́ние.
abroad *adv.* за грани́цей, за грани́цу; *from a.*, из-за грани́цы.
abrupt *adj.* (*steep*) обры́вистый, круто́й (крут, -а́, -о, кру́ты́); (*sudden*) внеза́пный; (*manner*) ре́зкий (-зок, -зка́, -зко).
abscess *n.* абсце́сс, нары́в, гнойни́к (-а́).
abscond *v.i.* скрыва́ться *imp.*, скры́ться (-ро́юсь, -ро́ешься) *perf.*; бежа́ть (бегу́, бежи́шь) *imp.*, *perf.*
absence *n.* отсу́тствие; (*temporary*) отлу́чка; (*from work*) нея́вка, невы́ход, на рабо́ту; *a. of mind*, рассе́янность. **absent** *adj.* отсу́тствующий; в отлу́чке; *be a.*, отсу́тствовать *imp.*; *a.-minded*, рассе́янный (-ян, -янна); *v.t.*: *a. oneself*, отлуча́ться *imp.*, отлучи́ться *perf.* **absentee** *n.* отсу́тствующий *sb.*; (*habitual*) прогу́льщик, -ица. **absenteeism** *n.* прогу́л, абсентеи́зм.
absolute *adj.* абсолю́тный; (*complete*) по́лный (-лон, -лна́, по́лно́), соверше́нный (-нен, -нна); (*unrestricted*) безусло́вный, неограни́ченный (-ен, -енна); (*pure*) чи́стый (чист, -а́, -о, чи́сты́); *a. alcohol*, чи́стый спирт (-а(у), *loc.* -е & -у́); *a. pitch*, (*of sound*) абсолю́тная высота́; (*in person*) абсолю́тный слух; *a. proof*, несомне́нное доказа́тельство; *a. zero*, абсолю́тный нуль (-ля́) *m.*
absolution *n.* отпуще́ние грехо́в. **absolve** *v.t.* проща́ть *imp.*, прости́ть *perf.*
absorb *v.t.* (*take in*) впи́тывать *imp.*, впита́ть *perf.*; (*swallow*, *also fig.*) поглоща́ть *imp.*, поглоти́ть (-ощу́, -о́тишь) *perf.*; (*suck in*) вса́сывать *imp.*, всоса́ть (-су́, -сёшь) *perf.*; (*tech.*) абсорби́ровать *imp.*, *perf.*; (*engross*) захва́тывать *imp.*, захвати́ть (-ачу́, -а́тишь) *perf.* **absorbed** *adj.* поглощённый (-ён, -ена́), захва́ченный (-ен). **absorbent** *adj.* вса́сывающий; поглоща́ющий. **absorption** *n.* впи́тывание; вса́сывание; поглоще́ние; абсо́рбция; (*mental*) погружённость.
abstain *v.i.* возде́рживаться *imp.*, воздержа́ться (-жу́сь, -жишься) *perf.* (from, от + *gen.*). **abstemious** *adj.* возде́ржанный (-ан, -анна). **abstention** *n.* воздержа́ние; (*from vote*) уклоне́ние, отка́з, от голосова́ния; (*person*) воздержа́вшийся *sb.* **abstinence** *n.* воздержа́ние; (*total a.*) тре́звость. **abstinent** *adj.* возде́ржанный (-ан, -анна).
abstract *adj.* абстра́ктный, отвлечённый (-ён, -ённа); *n.* конспе́кт, рефера́т; *in the a.*, абстра́ктно, отвлечённо; (*journal of*) *abstract*(*s*), реферати́вный журна́л; *v.t.* (*steal*) похища́ть *imp.*, похи́тить (-и́щу, -и́тишь) *perf.*; красть (-аду́, -адёшь; -ал) *imp.*, у~ *perf.*; (*make a. of*) рефери́ровать *imp.*, *perf.*, конспекти́ровать *imp.*, за~, про~ *perf.* **abstracted** *adj.* погружённый (-ён, -ена́) в мы́сли, рассе́янный (-ян,

-янна). **abstraction** *n.* абстра́кция, отвлечённость; (*abstractedness*) погружённость в мы́сли, рассе́янность; (*theft*) похище́ние, кра́жа.
absurd *adj.* неле́пый, абсу́рдный. **absurdity** *n.* неле́пость, абсу́рд(ность).
abundance *n.* (из)оби́лие. **abundant** *adj.* (из)оби́льный.
abuse *v.t.* (*revile*) руга́ть *imp.*, вы́~, об~, от~ *perf.*; брани́ть *imp.*, вы́~ *perf.*; (*misuse*) злоупотребля́ть *imp.*, злоупотреби́ть *perf.* **abuse** *n.* (*curses*) брань, ру́гань, руга́тельства *neut.pl.*; (*misuse*) злоупотребле́ние. **abusive** *adj.* оскорби́тельный, бра́нный.
abut *v.i.* примыка́ть *imp.* (on, к + *dat.*). **abutment** *n.* (берегово́й) усто́й.
abysmal *adj.* бездо́нный (-нен, -нна); (*bad*) ужа́сный. **abyss** *n.* бе́здна, про́пасть. **abyssal** *adj.* абисса́льный.
acacia *n.* ака́ция.
academic *adj.* академи́ческий, университе́тский; (*abstract*) академи́чный. **academician** *n.* акаде́мик. **academy** *n.* акаде́мия; уче́бное заведе́ние.
accede *v.i.* вступа́ть *imp.*, вступи́ть (-плю́, -пишь) *perf.* (to, в, на, + *acc.*); (*assent*) соглаша́ться *imp.*, согласи́ться *perf.*
accelerate *v.t.* & *i.* ускоря́ть(ся) *imp.*, уско́рить(ся) *perf.*; *v.i.* ускоря́ть *imp.*, уско́рить *perf.* ход. **acceleration** *n.* ускоре́ние. **accelerator** *n.* ускори́тель *m.*; (*pedal*) акселера́тор.
accent *n.* акце́нт; (*stress*) ударе́ние, знак ударе́ния; *v.t.* де́лать *imp.*, с~ *perf.* ударе́ние на + *acc.*; ста́вить *imp.*, по~ *perf.* зна́ки ударе́ния над + *instr.* **accentuate** *v.t.* подчёркивать *imp.*, подчеркну́ть *perf.* **accentuation** *n.* подчёркивание.
accept *v.t.* принима́ть *imp.*, приня́ть (приму́, -мешь; при́нял, -а́, -о) *perf.*; (*agree*) соглаша́ться *imp.*, согласи́ться *perf.* **acceptable** *adj.* прие́млемый; (*pleasing*) уго́дный. **acceptance** *n.* приня́тие. **acceptation** *n.* при́нятое значе́ние. **accepted** *adj.* (обще)при́нятый.
access *n.* до́ступ; (*attack*) при́ступ. **accessary** *n.* (*after the fact*) соуча́стник, -ица (преступле́ния по́сле собы́тия). **accessible** *adj.* досту́пный. **accession** *n.* вступле́ние, восше́ствие (на престо́л); (*acquisition*) приобрете́ние. **accessories** *n.* принадле́жности *f.pl.* **accessory** *adj.* доба́вочный, вспомога́тельный.
accidence *n.* морфоло́гия.
accident *n.* (*chance*) слу́чай, случа́йность; (*mishap*) несча́стный слу́чай; (*crash*) ава́рия, катастро́фа; *by a.*, случа́йно. **accidental** *adj.* случа́йный; *n.* (*mus.*) знак альтера́ции.
acclaim *v.t.* приве́тствовать *imp.* (*in past also perf.*); *n.* приве́тствие.
acclimatization *n.* акклиматиза́ция. **acclimatize** *v.t.* акклиматизи́ровать *imp.*, *perf.*
accommodate *v.t.* помеща́ть *imp.*, помести́ть *perf.*; размеща́ть *imp.*, размести́ть *perf.* **accommodating** *adj.* услу́жливый. **accommodation** *n.* помеще́ние; (*lodging*) жильё; *a. ladder*, нару́жный трап.
accompaniment *n.* сопровожде́ние; (*mus.*) аккомпанеме́нт. **accompanist** *n.* аккомпаниа́тор. **accompany** *v.t.* сопровожда́ть *imp.*, сопроводи́ть *perf.*; (*mus.*) аккомпани́ровать *imp.* + *dat.*
accomplice *n.* соо́бщник, -ица, соуча́стник, -ица.
accomplish *v.t.* соверша́ть *imp.*, соверши́ть *perf.* **accomplished** *adj.* завершённый (-ён, -ена́); (*skilled*) превосхо́дный. **accomplishment** *n.* выполне́ние, заверше́ние; *pl.* досто́инства *neut.pl.*, соверше́нства *neut.pl.*
accord *n.* согла́сие; *of one's own a.*, доброво́льно; *of its own a.*, сам собо́й, сам по себе́; *with one a.*, единогла́сно, единоду́шно. **accordance** *n.*: *in a. with*, в соотве́тствии с + *instr.*, согла́сно + *dat.*, с + *instr.* **according** *adv.*: *a. to*, по + *dat.*, соотве́тственно + *dat.*, с + *instr.*; *a. to him*, по его́ слова́м. **accordingly** *adv.* соотве́тственно.
accordion *n.* гармо́ника, аккордео́н.
account *n.* счёт (-а(у); *pl.* -а́); расчёт; отчёт; (*description, narrative*) описа́ние, расска́з; *call to a.*, призыва́ть *imp.*, призва́ть (-зову́, -зовёшь; призва́л, -а́, -о) *perf.* к отве́ту; *keep a. of*, вести́ (веду́, -дёшь; вёл, -а́) *imp.*

счёт + *dat.*; *not on any a., on no a.*, ни в ко́ем слу́чае; *on a.*, в счёт причита́ющейся су́ммы; *on a. of*, из-за + *gen.*, по причи́не + *gen.*; *settle accounts with*, своди́ть (-ожу́, -о́дишь) *imp.*, свести́ (сведу́, -дёшь; свёл, -а́) *perf.* счёты с + *instr.*; *take into a.*, принима́ть *imp.*, приня́ть (приму́, -мешь; при́нял, -а́, -о) *perf.* во внима́ние, в расчёт; *turn to (good) a.*, обраща́ть *imp.*, обрати́ть (-ащу́, -ати́шь) *perf.* в свою́ по́льзу; *v.i.*: *a. for*, объясня́ть *imp.*, объясни́ть *perf.* **accountable** *adj.* отве́тственный (-ен, -енна), подотчётный. **accountancy** *n.* бухгалте́рия. **accountant** *n.* бухга́лтер.

accredited *adj.* аккредито́ванный (-ан).

accretion *n.* прираще́ние, приро́ст.

accrue *v.i.* нараста́ть *imp.*, нарасти́ (-тёт; наро́с, -ла́) *perf.*; *accrued interest*, наро́сшие проце́нты *m.pl.*

accumulate *v.t.* & *i.* нака́пливать(ся) *imp.*, копи́ть(ся) (-плю́, -пит(ся)) *imp.*, на~ *perf.*; *v.i.* ска́пливаться *imp.*, скопи́ться (-ится) *perf.* **accumulation** *n.* накопле́ние, скопле́ние. **accumulator** *n.* аккумуля́тор.

accuracy *n.* то́чность, ме́ткость. **accurate** *adj.* то́чный (-чен, -чна́, -чно), ме́ткий (-ток, -тка́, -тко).

accursed *adj.* прокля́тый.

accusation *n.* обвине́ние. **accusative** *adj.* (*n.*) вини́тельный (паде́ж (-а́)). **accuse** *v.t.* обвиня́ть *imp.*, обвини́ть *perf.* (of, в + *prep.*); *the accused*, обвиня́емый *sb.*, подсуди́мый *sb.*

accustom *v.t.* приуча́ть *imp.*, приучи́ть (-чу́, -чишь) *perf.* (to, к + *dat.*). **accustomed** *adj.* привы́чный, обы́чный; *be, get, a.*, привыка́ть *imp.*, привы́кнуть (-к) *perf.* (to, к + *dat.*).

ace *n.* туз (-а́); (*airman*) ас.

acetic *adj.* у́ксусный. **acetylene** *n.* ацетиле́н; *adj.* ацетиле́новый.

ache *n.* боль; *v.i.* боле́ть (-ли́т) *imp.*

achieve *v.t.* достига́ть *imp.*, дости́чь & дости́гнуть (-и́гну, -и́гнешь; -и́г) *perf.* + *gen.*; добива́ться *imp.*, доби́ться (-бью́сь, -бьёшься) *perf.* + *gen.* **achievement** *n.* достиже́ние.

acid *n.* кислота́; *adj.* ки́слый (-сел, -сла́, -сло). **acidity** *n.* кислота́, кисло́тность.

acknowledge *v.t.* (*admit*) признава́ть (-наю́, -наёшь) *imp.*, призна́ть *perf.*; сознава́ть (-наю́, -наёшь) *imp.*, созна́ть *perf.*; (*express gratitude*) благодари́ть *imp.*, по~ *perf.* за + *acc.*; (*a. receipt of*) подтвержда́ть *imp.*, подтверди́ть *perf.* получе́ние + *gen.* **acknowledgement** *n.* призна́ние; благода́рность; подтвержде́ние; *in a. of*, в знак благода́рности за + *acc.*

acme *n.* верши́на, верх (*pl.* -и́), вы́сшая то́чка.

acne *n.* прыщи́ *m.pl.*

acorn *n.* жёлудь (*pl.* -ди, -де́й) *m.*

acoustic *adj.* (*of sound*) акусти́ческий, звуково́й; (*of hearing*) слухово́й; (*sound-absorbing*) звукопоглоща́ющий. **acoustics** *n.* аку́стика.

acquaint *v.t.* знако́мить *imp.*, по~ *perf.*; ознакомля́ть *imp.*, ознако́мить *perf.* **acquaintance** *n.* знако́мство; (*person*) знако́мый *sb.* **acquainted** *adj.* знако́мый.

acquiesce *v.i.* (мо́лча) соглаша́ться *imp.*, согласи́ться *perf.* **acquiescence** *n.* (молчали́вое, неохо́тное) согла́сие. **acquiescent** *adj.* (молчали́во) соглаша́ющийся.

acquire *v.t.* приобрета́ть *imp.*, приобрести́ (-ету́, -етёшь; -ёл, -ела́) *perf.*; (*habit etc.*) усва́ивать *imp.*, усво́ить *perf.* **acquired** *adj.* приобретённый (-ён, -ена́); *a. taste*, благоприобре́тенный вкус. **acquisition** *n.* приобрете́ние. **acquisitive** *adj.* жа́дный (-ден, -дна́, -дно).

acquit *v.t.* опра́вдывать *imp.*, оправда́ть *perf.*; *a. oneself*, вести́ (веду́, -дёшь; вёл, -а́) *imp.* себя́. **acquittal** *n.* оправда́ние.

acre *n.* акр; *pl.* зе́мли (-ме́ль, -млям) *f.pl.*, поме́стье. **acreage** *n.* пло́щадь в а́крах.

acrid *adj.* о́стрый (остр & остёр, остра́, о́стро́), е́дкий (е́док, едка́, е́дко). **acridity** *n.* острота́, е́дкость.

acrimonious *adj.* язви́тельный, жёлчный.

acrobat *n.* акроба́т. **acrobatic** *adj.* акробати́ческий. **acrobatics** *n.* акроба́тика.

acronym *n.* акро́ним, аббревиату́ра.

across *adv.*, *prep.* чéрез + *acc.*; поперёк (+*gen.*); (*to, on, other side*) на, по, ту стóрону (+*gen.*), на той стороне́ (+*gen.*); (*crosswise*) крест-нáкрест.
acrylic *adj.* акри́ловый.
act *n.* (*deed*) акт, постýпок (-пка); (*law*) закóн; (*of play*) дéйствие; *Acts*, Дея́ния *neut.pl.* апóстолов; *v.i.* поступáть *imp.*, поступи́ть (-плю́, -пишь) *perf.*; дéйствовать *imp.*, по~ *perf.*; *v.t.* игрáть *imp.*, сыгрáть *perf.* **acting** *n.* игрá на сце́не; *adj.* исполня́ющий обя́занности + *gen.* **action** *n.* дéйствие, постýпок (-пка); (*leg.*) иск, (судéбный) процéсс; (*battle*) бой (*loc.* бою́). **active** *adj.* акти́вный, дéятельный, энерги́чный; *a. service*, действи́тельная слýжба; *a. voice*, действи́тельный залóг. **activity** *n.* дéятельность; акти́вность; *pl.* дéятельность. **actor** *n.* актёр. **actress** *n.* актри́са.
actual *adj.* действи́тельный, факти́ческий. **actuality** *n.* действи́тельность. **actually** *adv.* на сáмом дéле, факти́чески.
actuate *v.t.* приводи́ть (-ожý, -óдишь) *imp.*, привести́ (приведý, -дёшь; привёл, -á) *perf.* в движе́ние.
acuity *n.* остротá.
acute *adj.* óстрый (остр & остёр, острá, óстрó); (*penetrating*) проницáтельный; *a. accent*, акýт.
A.D. *abbr.* н. э. (нáшей э́ры).
adamant *adj.* непреклóнный (-нен, -нна).
adapt *v.t.* приспосабля́ть *imp.*, приспосóбить *perf.*; (*for stage etc.*) инсцени́ровать *imp.*, *perf.*; *a. oneself*, приспосабля́ться *imp.*, приспосóбиться *perf.*; применя́ться *imp.*, приме ни́ться (-ню́сь, -нишься) *perf.* **adaptable** *adj.* приспосабля́ющийся. **adaptation** *n.* приспособле́ние, адаптáция, передéлка; инсцениро́вка.
add *v.t.* прибавля́ть *imp.*, прибáвить *perf.*; добавля́ть *imp.*, добáвить *perf.*; *a. together*, склáдывать *imp.*, сложи́ть (-жý, -жишь) *perf.*; *a. up to*, сводиться (-ится) *imp.*, свести́сь (сведётся; свёлся, -лáсь) *perf.* к + *dat.* **addenda** *n.* дополне́ния *neut.pl.*, приложе́ния *neut.pl.*
adder *n.* гадю́ка.
addict *n.* (*drug a.*) наркомáн, ~ка. **addicted** *adj.*: *be a. to*, быть рабóм + *gen.*; *a. to drink*, предаю́щийся пья́нству. **addiction** *n.* пáгубная привы́чка; (*to drugs*) наркомáния.
addition *n.* прибавле́ние, добавле́ние; дополне́ние; (*math.*) сложе́ние; *in a.*, вдобáвок, крóме тогó, к томý же. **additional** *adj.* добáвочный, дополни́тельный. **additive** *n.* добáвка.
address *n.* áдрес (*pl.* -á); (*speech*) обращéние, речь; *v.t.* адресовáть *imp.*, *perf.*; (*apply*) обращáться *imp.*, обрати́ться (-ащýсь, -ати́шься) *perf.* к + *dat.*; *a. a meeting*, выступáть *imp.*, вы́ступить *perf.* с ре́чью на собрáнии. **addressee** *n.* адресáт.
adept *n.* знатóк (-á), экспéрт; *adj.* свéдущий.
adequacy *n.* адеквáтность, достáточность. **adequate** *adj.* адеквáтный, достáточный.
adhere *v.i.* прилипáть *imp.*, прили́пнуть (-нет; прили́п) *perf.* (to, к + *dat.*); (*fig.*) придéрживаться *imp.* + *gen.* **adherence** *n.* привéрженность, вéрность. **adherent** *n.* привéрженец (-нца); послéдователь *m.*, ~ница. **adhesion** *n.* прилипáние, склéивание. **adhesive** *adj.* ли́пкий (-пок, -пкá, -пко), клéйкий; *n.* клей (-éя(ю), *loc.* -ею́; *pl.* -éи).
adjacent *adj.* смéжный, сосéдний.
adjectival *adj.* адъекти́вный. **adjective** *n.* (и́мя *neut.*) прилагáтельное *sb.*
adjoin *v.t.* прилегáть *imp.* к + *dat.*
adjourn *v.t.* отклáдывать *imp.*, отложи́ть (-жý, -жишь) *perf.*; *v.i.* объявля́ть *imp.*, объяви́ть (-влю́, -вишь) *perf.* переры́в; (*to another place*) переходи́ть (-ожý, -óдишь) *imp.*, перейти́ (перейдý, -дёшь; перешёл, -шлá) *perf.*
adjudicate *v.i.* выноси́ть (-ошý, -óсишь) *imp.*, вы́нести (-су, -сешь; -с) *perf.* (судéбное, арбитрáжное) решéние; разрешáть *imp.*, разреши́ть *perf.* спор; рассмáтривать *imp.*, рассмотрéть (-рю́, -ришь) *perf.* дéло.
adjust *v.t.* & *i.* приспосабля́ть(ся) *imp.*, приспосóбить(ся) *perf.*; *v.t.* пригоня́ть *imp.*, пригнáть (-гоню́, -гóнишь;

пригна́л, -а́, -о) *perf.*; (*regulate*) регули́ровать *imp.*, от~ *perf.* **adjustable** *adj.* регули́руемый; *a. spanner*, разводно́й ключ (-а́). **adjustment** *n.* регули́рование, регулиро́вка, подго́нка.

adjutant *n.* адъюта́нт.

administer *v.t.* (*manage*) управля́ть *imp.* + *instr.*; (*dispense*) отправля́ть *imp.*; (*give*) дава́ть (даю́, даёшь) *imp.*, дать (дам, дашь, даст, дади́м; дал, -а́, да́ло́, -и) *perf.* **administration** *n.* администра́ция, управле́ние; (*government*) прави́тельство. **administrative** *adj.* администрати́вный, управле́нческий. **administrator** *n.* администра́тор.

admirable *adj.* похва́льный; (*excellent*) замеча́тельный.

admiral *n.* адмира́л. **Admiralty** *n.* адмиралте́йство.

admiration *n.* любова́ние, восхище́ние. **admire** *v.t.* любова́ться *imp.*, по~ *perf.* + *instr.*, на + *acc.*; восхища́ться *imp.*, восхити́ться (-ищу́сь, -ити́шься) *perf.* + *instr.* **admirer** *n.* покло́нник.

admissible *adj.* допусти́мый, прие́млемый. **admission** *n.* до́ступ, впуск, вход; (*confession*) призна́ние. **admit** *v.t.* впуска́ть *imp.*, впусти́ть (-ущу́, -у́стишь) *perf.*; (*allow*) допуска́ть *imp.*, допусти́ть (-ущу́, -у́стишь) *perf.*; (*accept*) принима́ть *imp.*, приня́ть (приму́, -мешь; при́нял, -а́, -о) *perf.*; (*confess*) признава́ть (-наю́, -наёшь) *imp.*, призна́ть *perf.* **admittance** *n.* до́ступ. **admittedly** *adv.* призна́ться.

admixture *n.* при́месь.

adolescence *n.* ю́ность. **adolescent** *adj.* подро́стковый; *n.* подро́сток (-тка).

adopt *v.t.* (*child*) усыновля́ть *imp.*, усынови́ть *perf.*; (*thing*) усва́ивать *imp.*, усво́ить *perf.*; (*approve*) принима́ть *imp.*, приня́ть (приму́, -мешь; при́нял, -а́, -о) *perf.* **adopted, adoptive** *adj.* приёмный. **adoption** *n.* усыновле́ние; приня́тие.

adorable *adj.* восхити́тельный, преле́стный. **adoration** *n.* обожа́ние. **adore** *v.t.* обожа́ть *imp.* **adorer** *n.* обожа́тель *m.*

adorn *v.t.* украша́ть *imp.*, укра́сить *perf.* **adornment** *n.* украше́ние.

adroit *adj.* ло́вкий (-вок, -вка́, -вко, ло́вки́).

adult *adj.*, *n.* взро́слый (*sb.*).

adulterate *v.t.* фальсифици́ровать *imp.*, *perf.* **adulteration** *n.* фальсифика́ция.

adultery *n.* адюльте́р, небра́чная связь.

advance *n.* (*going forward*) продвиже́ние (вперёд); (*progress*) прогре́сс; (*mil.*) наступле́ние; (*rise*) повыше́ние; (*of pay etc.*) ава́нс; (*loan*) ссу́да; *in a.*, зара́нее, вперёд; ава́нсом; *make advances to*, уха́живать *imp.* за + *instr.*; *a. information*, предвари́тельные све́дения *neut.pl.*; *a. copy*, сигна́льный экземпля́р; *v.i.* (*go forward*) продвига́ться *imp.*, продви́нуться *perf.* вперёд; идти́ (иду́, идёшь; шёл, шла) *imp.* вперёд; (*mil.*) наступа́ть *imp.*; *v.t.* продвига́ть *imp.*, продви́нуть *perf.*; (*put forward*) выдвига́ть *imp.*, вы́двинуть *perf.*; (*promote*) повыша́ть *imp.*, повы́сить *perf.*; (*pay in advance*) выпла́чивать *imp.*, вы́платить *perf.* ава́нсом. **advanced** *adj.* передово́й, продви́нутый; *a. in years*, престаре́лый; *a. studies*, вы́сший курс. **advancement** *n.* продвиже́ние, повыше́ние.

advantage *n.* преиму́щество; (*profit*) вы́года, по́льза; *take a. of*, по́льзоваться *imp.*, вос~ *perf.* + *instr.*; *to a.*, вы́годно, хорошо́; в вы́годном све́те; *to the best a.*, в са́мом вы́годном све́те. **advantageous** *adj.* вы́годный.

adventure *n.* приключе́ние; *a. story*, приключе́нческий рома́н. **adventurer** *n.* авантюри́ст. **adventuress** *n.* авантюри́стка. **adventurous** *adj.* (*rash*) риско́ванный (-ан, -анна); (*enterprising*) предприи́мчивый.

adverb *n.* наре́чие. **adverbial** *adj.* наре́чный, обстоя́тельственный.

adversary *n.* проти́вник. **adverse** *adj.* неблагоприя́тный; *a. winds*, проти́вные ве́тры *m.pl.* **adversity** *n.* несча́стье.

advert *abbr.* объявле́ние, рекла́ма. **advertise** *v.t.* реклами́ровать *imp.*, *perf.*; афиши́ровать *imp.*, *perf.*; *v.i.* помеща́ть *imp.*, помести́ть *perf.*, дава́ть (даю́, даёшь) *imp.*, дать (дам, дашь, даст, дади́м; дал, -а́, да́ло́, -и) *perf.* объявле́ние (for, о + *prep.*). **advertisement** *n.* объявле́ние, рекла́ма.

advice *n.* совéт; (*specialist*) консультáция; (*notice*) авизо; *a piece, word of a.*, совéт. **advisability** *n.* желáтельность. **advisable** *adj.* рекомендýемый, желáтельный. **advise** *v.t.* совéтовать *imp.*, по~ *perf.* + *dat.* & *inf.*; рекомендовáть *imp.*, *perf.*, по~ *perf.* + *acc.* & *inf.*; (*notify*) уведомля́ть *imp.*, уведóмить *perf.* **advisedly** *adv.* обдýманно, намéренно. **adviser** *n.* совéтник, -ица; консультáнт; *legal a.*, юрискóнсульт; *medical a.*, врач (-á). **advisory** *adj.* совещáтельный; консультати́вный.

advocacy *n.* (*profession*) адвокатýра; (*support*) пропагáнда. **advocate** *n.* адвокáт; сторóнник; *v.t.* пропаганди́ровать *imp.*; выступáть *imp.*, вы́ступить *perf.* в защи́ту + *gen.*

aerial *n.* антéнна; *adj.* воздýшный.

aero- *in comb.* авиа-, аэро-, воздухо-. **aerodrome** *n.* аэродрóм. **aerodynamics** *n.* аэродинáмика. **aero-engine** *n.* авиациóнный дви́гатель *m.* **aeronautical** *adj.* авиациóнный. **aeroplane** *n.* самолёт. **aerosol** *n.* аэрозóль *m.*

aesthetic *adj.* эстети́ческий.

affable *adj.* привéтливый. **affability** *n.* привéтливость.

affair *n.* (*business*) дéло (*pl.* -лá); (*love*) ромáн.

affect *v.t.* дéйствовать *imp.*, по~ *perf.* на + *acc.*; влия́ть *imp.*, по~ *perf.* на + *acc.*; (*touch*) трóгать *imp.*, трóнуть *perf.*; затрáгивать *imp.*, затрóнуть *perf.*; (*concern*) касáться *imp.* + *gen.*; *it doesn't a. me*, э́то меня́ не касáется. **affectation** *n.* притвóрство, жемáнство. **affected** *adj.* притвóрный, жемáнный (-нен, -нна). **affecting** *adj.* трóгательный. **affection** *n.* привя́занность, любóвь (-бви́, *instr.* -бóвью); (*malady*) болéзнь. **affectionate** *adj.* лю́бящий, нéжный (-жен, -жнá, -жно, нéжны́), лáсковый.

affiliate *v.t.* & *i.* присоединя́ть(ся) *imp.*, присоедини́ть(ся) *perf.* как филиáл, отделéние. **affiliated** *adj.* филиáльный. **affiliation** *n.* присоединéние как филиáл; (*of child*) установлéние отцóвства + *gen.*

affinity *n.* (*relationship*) родствó; (*resemblance*) схóдство, бли́зость; (*attraction*) увлечéние.

affirm *v.t.* утверждáть *imp.*; *v.i.* торжéственно заявля́ть *imp.*, заяви́ть (-влю́, -вишь) *perf.* **affirmation** *n.* заявлéние. **affirmative** *adj.* утверди́тельный.

affix *v.t.* прикрепля́ть *imp.*, прикрепи́ть *perf.*; *n.* áффикс.

afflict *v.t.* огорчáть *imp.*, огорчи́ть *perf.*; причиня́ть *imp.*, причини́ть *perf.* страдáния + *dat.* **affliction** *n.* огорчéние.

affluence *n.* богáтство. **affluent** *adj.* богáтый; *a. society*, богатéющее óбщество.

afford *v.t.* позволя́ть *imp.*, позвóлить *perf.* себé; быть в состоя́нии + *inf.*; (*supply*) предоставля́ть *imp.*, предостáвить *perf.*; доставля́ть *imp.*, достáвить *perf.*; *I can't afford it*, мне э́то не по срéдствам, не по кармáну.

afforest *v.t.* засáживать *imp.*, засади́ть (-ажý, -áдишь) *perf.* лéсом; облеси́ть *perf.* **afforestation** *n.* лесонасаждéние, облесéние.

affront *n.* (публи́чное) оскорблéние, оби́да; *v.t.* оскорбля́ть *imp.*, оскорби́ть *perf.*

afoot *adv.*: *set a.*, пускáть *imp.*, пусти́ть (пущý, пýстишь) *perf.* в ход.

aforesaid *adj.* вышеупомя́нутый. **aforethought** *adj.* преднамéренный (-ен, -енна).

afraid *predic.*: *be a.*, боя́ться (бою́сь, бои́шься) *imp.*

afresh *adv.* снóва.

after *adv.* впослéдствии; пóсле, потóм; *prep.* пóсле + *gen.*, спустя́ + *acc.*; за + *acc.*, *instr.*; *a. all*, в концé концóв; *day a. day*, день за днём; *long a. midnight*, далекó за пóлночь.

after- *in comb.* после-. **afterbirth** *n.* послéд. **after-dinner** *adj.* послеобéденный. **aftermath** *n.* послéдствия *neut. pl.* **afternoon** *n.* вторáя полови́на дня; *in the a.*, днём, пополýдни. **afterthought** *n.* запоздáлая мысль.

afterwards *adv.* впослéдствии; потóм, пóзже.

again *adv.* опя́ть; (*once more*) ещё раз; (*anew*) снóва.

against *prep.* (*opposed to*) про́тив + *gen.*; (*a. background of*) на фо́не + *gen.*
agate *n.* ага́т.
age *n.* во́зраст; (*period*) век (на веку́; *pl.* -а́), эпо́ха; *v.t.* ста́рить *imp.*, со~ *perf.*; *v.i.* старе́ть *imp.*, по~ *perf.*; ста́риться *imp.*, со~ *perf.* **aged** *adj.* ста́рый (стар, -а́, ста́ро́), престаре́лый.
agency *n.* аге́нтство; (*mediation*) посре́дничество; *by, through, the a. of*, посре́дством, при по́мощи, при соде́йствии, + *gen.* **agenda** *n.* пове́стка дня. **agent** *n.* аге́нт.
agglomerate *n.* агломера́т. **agglomeration** *n.* скопле́ние, агломера́ция.
agglutination *n.* агглютина́ция. **agglutinative** *adj.* агглютинати́вный.
aggravate *v.t.* ухудша́ть *imp.*, уху́дшить *perf.*; (*annoy*) раздража́ть *imp.*, раздражи́ть *perf.* **aggravation** *n.* ухудше́ние; раздраже́ние.
aggregate *adj.* совоку́пный; *n.* совоку́пность, агрега́т; *in the a.*, в совоку́пности, в це́лом.
aggression *n.* агре́ссия; агресси́вность. **aggressive** *adj.* агресси́вный. **aggressor** *n.* агре́ссор.
aggrieved *adj.* оби́женный (-ен).
aghast *predic.* поражён (-а́) у́жасом; в у́жасе (at, от + *gen.*).
agile *adj.* прово́рный. **agility** *n.* прово́рство.
agitate *v.t.* волнова́ть *imp.*, вз~ *perf.*; *v.i.* агити́ровать *imp.* **agitation** *n.* волне́ние; агита́ция.
agnostic *n.* агно́стик; *adj.* агности́ческий. **agnosticism** *n.* агностици́зм.
ago *adv.* (тому́) наза́д; *long a.*, давно́.
agonizing *adj.* мучи́тельный. **agony** *n.* мучи́тельная боль; (*of death*) аго́ния.
agrarian *adj.* агра́рный, земе́льный.
agree *v.i.* соглаша́ться *imp.*, согласи́ться *perf.*; усла́вливаться *imp.*, усло́виться *perf.* (on, о + *prep.*); (*reach agreement*) догова́риваться *imp.*, договори́ться *perf.*; (*gram.*) согласова́ться *imp.*, *perf.* **agreeable** *adj.* согла́сный; (*pleasing*) прия́тный. **agreed** *adj.* согласо́ванный (-ан), усло́вленный (-ен). **agreement** *n.* согла́сие, соглаше́ние, догово́р; (*gram.*) согласова́ние; *in a.*, согла́сен (-сна).
agricultural *adj.* сельскохозя́йственный, земледе́льческий. **agriculture** *n.* се́льское хозя́йство, земледе́лие; (*science*) агроно́мия.
aground *predic.* на мели́; *adv.*: *run a.*, сади́ться *imp.*, сесть (ся́ду, -дешь; сел) *perf.* на мель.
ague *n.* маляри́я.
ahead *adv.* (*forward*) вперёд; (*in front*) впереди́; *a. of time*, досро́чно.
aid *v.t.* помога́ть *imp.*, помо́чь (-огу́, -о́жешь; -о́г, -огла́) *perf.* + *dat.*; *n.* по́мощь; (*teaching*) посо́бие; *in a. of*, в по́льзу + *gen.*; *come to the a. of*, прийти́ (приду́, -дёшь; пришёл, -шла́) *perf.* на по́мощь к + *dat.* **aide-de-camp** *n.* адъюта́нт (генера́ла).
aileron *n.* элеро́н.
ailing *adj.* (*ill*) больно́й (-лен, -льна́); (*sickly*) хи́лый (хил, -а́, -о).
ailment *n.* неду́г.
aim *n.* (*aiming*) прице́л; (*purpose*) цель, намере́ние; *v.i.* це́лить(ся) *imp.*, на~ *perf.* (at, в + *acc.*); прице́ливаться *imp.*, прице́литься *perf.* (at, в + *acc.*); (*also fig.*) ме́тить *imp.*, на~ *perf.* (at, в + *acc.*); *v.t.* наце́ливать *imp.*, наце́лить *perf.*; (*also fig.*) наводи́ть (-ожу́, -о́дишь) *imp.*, навести́ (наведу́, -дёшь; навёл, -а́) *perf.* **aimless** *adj.* бесце́льный.
air *n.* во́здух; (*look*) вид; (*mus.*) пе́сня (*gen.pl.* -сен), мело́дия; *by a.*, самолётом; *change of a.*, переме́на обстано́вки; *on the a.*, по ра́дио; *attrib.* возду́шный; *v.t.* (*ventilate*) прове́тривать *imp.*, прове́трить *perf.*; (*make known*) выставля́ть *imp.*, вы́ставить *perf.* напока́з; заявля́ть *imp.*, заяви́ть (-влю́, -вишь) *perf.* во всеуслы́шание.
air- *in comb.* **airborne** *adj.* (*mil.*) возду́шно-деса́нтный; *predic.* в во́здухе. **air-conditioning** *n.* кондициони́рование во́здуха. **air-cooled** *adj.* с возду́шным охлажде́нием. **aircraft** *n.* самолёт; (*collect.*) самолёты *m.pl.*, авиа́ция. **aircraft-carrier** *n.* авиано́сец (-сца). **air force** *n.* ВВС (вое́нно-возду́шные си́лы) *f.pl.* **air hostess** *n.* стюарде́сса. **airless** *adj.* (*stuffy*) ду́ш-

ный (-шен, -шна́, -шно); безвозду́шный. **air-lift** *n.* возду́шные перево́зки *f.pl.*; *v.t.* перевози́ть (-ожу́, -о́зишь) *imp.*, перевезти́ (перевезу́, -зёшь; перевёз, -ла́) *perf.* по во́здуху. **airline** *n.* авиали́ния. **airlock** *n.* возду́шная про́бка. **air mail** *n.* а́виа(по́чта). **airman** *n.* лётчик. **airport** *n.* аэропо́рт (*loc.* -у́). **airship** *n.* дирижа́бль *m.* **airspeed** *n.* возду́шная ско́рость. **airstrip** *n.* лётная полоса́ (*acc.* полосу́; *pl.* -осы, -о́с, -оса́м). **airtight** *adj.* непроница́емый для во́здуха. **airworthy** *adj.* приго́дный к полёту.

aisle *n.* боково́й неф; (*passage*) прохо́д.

alabaster *n.* алеба́стр.

alacrity *n.* жи́вость; (*readiness*) гото́вность.

alarm *n.* трево́га; *v.t.* трево́жить *imp.*, вс~ *perf.*; *a. clock*, буди́льник. **alarming** *adj.* трево́жный. **alarmist** *n.* паникёр; *adj.* паникёрский.

alas *interj.* увы́!

albatross *n.* альбатро́с.

albino *n.* альбино́с.

album *n.* альбо́м.

alchemist *n.* алхи́мик. **alchemy** *n.* алхи́мия.

alcohol *n.* алкого́ль *m.*, спирт (-а(у), *loc.* -е & -у́); спиртны́е напи́тки *m.pl.* **alcoholic** *adj.* алкого́льный, спиртно́й; *n.* алкого́лик, -и́чка.

alcove *n.* алько́в, ни́ша.

alder *n.* ольха́.

alderman *n.* о́лдермен.

ale *n.* пи́во, эль *m.*

alert *adj.* бди́тельный, живо́й (жив, -а́, -о); *predic.* на стороже́; *n.* трево́га; *v.t.* предупрежда́ть *imp.*, предупреди́ть *perf.*

algebra *n.* а́лгебра. **algebraic** *adj.* алгебраи́ческий. **algorithm** *n.* алгори́тм.

alias *adv.* ина́че (называ́емый); *n.* кли́чка, вы́мышленное и́мя *neut.*

alibi *n.* а́либи *neut.indecl.*

alien *n.* иностра́нец (-нца), -нка; *adj.* иностра́нный, чужо́й, чу́ждый (чужд, -а́, -о). **alienate** *v.t.* отчужда́ть *imp.*; отдаля́ть *imp.*, отдали́ть *perf.* **alienation** *n.* отчужде́ние, охлажде́ние; (*insanity*) умопомеша́тельство. **alienist** *n.* психиа́тр.

alight[1] *v.i.* сходи́ть (-ожу́, -о́дишь) *imp.*, сойти́ (сойду́, -дёшь; сошёл, -шла́) *perf.*; (*come down*) сади́ться *imp.*, сесть (ся́ду, -дешь; сел) *perf.*; (*dismount*) спе́шиваться *imp.*, спе́шиться *perf.*

alight[2] *predic.* зажжён (-а́); *be a.*, горе́ть (-ри́т) *imp.*; (*shine*) сия́ть *imp.*

align *v.t.* располага́ть *imp.*, расположи́ть (-жу́, -жишь) *perf.* по одно́й ли́нии; ста́вить *imp.*, по~ *perf.* в ряд. **alignment** *n.* выра́внивание, равне́ние.

alike *predic.* похо́ж, одина́ков; *adv.* одина́ково, то́чно так же.

alimentary *adj.* пищево́й; *a. canal*, пищевари́тельный кана́л.

alimony *n.* алиме́нты *m.pl.*

alive *predic.* жив (-а́, -о), в живы́х; (*brisk*) бодр (-а́, -о); *a. with*, киша́щий *+instr.*

alkali *n.* щёлочь (*pl.* -чи, -че́й). **alkaline** *adj.* щелочно́й.

all *adj.* весь (вся, всё; все); вся́кий; *n.* всё, все *pl.*; *adv.* всеце́ло, целико́м, по́лностью; совсе́м, соверше́нно; *a. along*, всё вре́мя; *a. but*, почти́, едва́ не; *a. in*, кра́йне утомлён (-а́), совсе́м без сил; *a.-in wrestling*, борьба́, допуска́ющая любы́е приёмы; *a. over*, повсю́ду; *a. right*, хорошо́, ла́дно; (*satisfactory*) так себе́; непло́х (-а́, -о); *a.-round*, разносторо́нний (-нен, -ння); *a. the same*, всё равно́; *in a.*, всего́; *love a.*, по нулю́; *two, etc., a.*, по́ два и т.д.; *not at a.*, ниско́лько; *on a. fours*, на четвере́ньках.

allay *v.t.* облегча́ть *imp.*, облегчи́ть *perf.*; успока́ивать *imp.*, успоко́ить *perf.*; утоля́ть *imp.*, утоли́ть *perf.*

allegation *n.* заявле́ние, утвержде́ние. **allege** *v.t.* заявля́ть *imp.*, заяви́ть (-влю́, -вишь) *perf.*; утвержда́ть *imp.* **allegedly** *adv.* я́кобы.

allegiance *n.* ве́рность.

allegorical *adj.* аллегори́ческий, иносказа́тельный. **allegory** *n.* аллего́рия, иносказа́ние.

allegretto *adv.* (*n.*) аллегре́тто (*neut. indecl.*). **allegro** *adv.* (*n.*) алле́гро (*neut.indecl.*).

allergic *adj*. аллерги́ческий. **allergy** *n*. аллерги́я.
alleviate *v.t*. облегча́ть *imp*., облегчи́ть *perf*.; смягча́ть *imp*., смягчи́ть *perf*. **alleviation** *n*. облегче́ние, смягче́ние.
alley *n*. переу́лок (-лка), прохо́д.
alliance *n*. сою́з. **allied** *adj*. сою́зный.
alligator *n*. аллига́тор.
alliterate *v.i*. аллитери́ровать *imp*. **alliteration** *n*. аллитера́ция.
allocate *v.t*. распределя́ть *imp*., распредели́ть *perf*.; ассигнова́ть *imp*., *perf*. **allocation** *n*. распределе́ние; ассигнова́ние.
allot *v.t*. предназнача́ть *imp*., предназна́чить *perf*.; распределя́ть *imp*., распредели́ть *perf*.; отводи́ть (-ожу́, -о́дишь) *imp*., отвести́ (отведу́, -дёшь; отвёл, -а́) *perf*.; выделя́ть *imp*., вы́делить *perf*. **allotment** *n*. выделе́ние; (*plot of land*) уча́сток (-тка).
allow *v.t*. позволя́ть *imp*., позво́лить *perf*.; разреша́ть *imp*., разреши́ть *perf*.; допуска́ть *imp*., допусти́ть (-ущу́, -у́стишь) *perf*.; *a. for*, принима́ть *imp*., приня́ть (приму́, -мешь; при́нял, -а́, -о) *perf*. во внима́ние, в расчёт; учи́тывать *imp*., уче́сть (учту́, -тёшь; учёл, учла́) *perf*. **allowance** *n*. (*financial*) содержа́ние, посо́бие; (*expenses*) де́ньги (-нег, -ньга́м) *pl*. на расхо́ды; (*deduction, also fig*.) ски́дка; *make allowance(s) for*, принима́ть *imp*., приня́ть (приму́, -мешь; при́нял, -а́, -о) *perf*. во внима́ние, в расчёт; де́лать *imp*., с~ *perf*. ски́дку на + *acc*.
alloy *n*. сплав; *v.t*. сплавля́ть *imp*., спла́вить *perf*.
allude *v.i*. ссыла́ться *imp*., сосла́ться (сошлю́сь, -лёшься) *perf*. (to, на + *acc*.); намека́ть *imp*., намекну́ть *perf*. (to, на + *acc*.).
allure *v.t*. зама́нивать *imp*., замани́ть (-ню́, -нишь) *perf*.; завлека́ть *imp*., завле́чь (-еку́, -ечёшь; -ёк, -екла́) *perf*. **allurement** *n*. приманка. **alluring** *adj*. зама́нчивый, завлека́тельный, соблазни́тельный.
allusion *n*. ссы́лка, намёк.
alluvial *adj*. аллювиа́льный, нано́сный.
ally *n*. сою́зник; *v.t*. соединя́ть *imp*., соедини́ть *perf*.
almanac *n*. календа́рь (-ря́) *m*.
almighty *adj*. всемогу́щий (-щ).
almond *n*. (*tree*; *pl. collect*.) минда́ль (-ля́) *m*.; (*nut*) минда́льный оре́х; *attrib*. минда́льный.
almost *adv*. почти́, едва́ (ли) не, чуть (бы́ло) не.
alms *n*. ми́лостыня; *a.-house*, богаде́льня (*gen.pl*. -лен).
aloe(s) *n*. ало́э *neut.indecl*.
aloft *adv*. наве́рх(у́).
alone *predic*. оди́н (одна́, одно́; одни́); одино́к; *adv*. то́лько; сам по себе́; *a. with*, наедине́ с + *instr*.; *leave a*., оставля́ть *imp*., оста́вить *perf*. в поко́е; *let a*., не говоря́ уже́ о + *prep*.
along *prep*. по + *dat*., вдоль + *gen*., вдоль по + *dat*.; *adv*. (*onward*) да́льше, вперёд; (*with oneself*) с собо́й; *all a*., всё вре́мя; *a. with*, вме́сте с + *instr*. **alongside** *adv*., *prep*. ря́дом (с + *instr*.), бок о́ бок (с + *instr*.).
aloof *predic*., *adv*. (*apart*) в стороне́, вдали́; (*distant*) хо́лоден (-дна́, -дно, хо́лодны́), равноду́шен (-шна).
aloud *adv*. вслух, гро́мко.
alphabet *n*. алфави́т, а́збука. **alphabetical** *adj*. алфави́тный.
alpine *adj*. альпи́йский.
already *adv*. уже́.
also *adv*. та́кже, то́же.
altar *n*. алта́рь (-ря́) *m*.; *a.-piece*, запресто́льный о́браз (*pl*. -а́).
alter *v.t*. переде́лывать *imp*., переде́лать *perf*.; *v.t*. & *i*. изменя́ть(ся) *imp*., измени́ть(ся) (-ню́(сь), -нишь(ся)) *perf*. **alteration** *n*. переде́лка; переме́на; измене́ние.
altercation *n*. препира́тельство.
alternate *adj*. череду́ющийся, перемежа́ющийся; *v.t*. & *i*. чередова́ть(ся) *imp*.; *alternating current*, переме́нный ток; *on a. days*, че́рез день. **alternation** *n*. чередова́ние. **alternative** *n*. альтернати́ва; *adj*. альтернати́вный.
although *conj*. хотя́.
altimeter *n*. альтиме́тр, высотоме́р. **altitude** *n*. высота́ (*pl*. -о́ты). **alto** *n*. альт (-а́); контра́льто *f*. & *neut. indecl*.; *attrib*. альто́вый; контра́льтовый.

altogether *adv.* (*fully*) совсе́м; (*in total*) всего́; (*wholly*) всеце́ло.
alum *n.* квасцы́ *m.pl.* **aluminium** *n.* алюми́ний; *attrib.* алюми́ниевый.
always *adv.* всегда́; (*constantly*) постоя́нно.
a.m. *abbr.* до полу́дня.
amalgamate *v.t.* & *i.* амальгами́ровать(ся) *imp.*, *perf.*; объединя́ть(ся) *imp.*, объедини́ть(ся) *perf.* **amalgamation** *n.* амальгами́рование; объедине́ние.
amanuensis *n.* перепи́счик, -ица.
amass *v.t.* копи́ть (-плю́, -пишь) *imp.*, на~ *perf.*
amateur *n.* люби́тель *m.*, ~ница; *adj.* самоде́ятельный, люби́тельский. **amateurish** *adj.* люби́тельский.
amatory *adj.* любо́вный.
amaze *v.t.* удивля́ть *imp.*, удиви́ть *perf.*; изумля́ть *imp.*, изуми́ть *perf.* **amazement** *n.* удивле́ние, изумле́ние. **amazing** *adj.* удиви́тельный, изуми́тельный.
ambassador *n.* посо́л (-сла́). **ambassadorial** *adj.* посо́льский.
amber *n.* янта́рь (-ря́) *m.*; *adj.* янта́рный; (*coloured*) жёлтый (жёлт, -а́, жёлто́). **ambergris** *n.* а́мбра.
ambidextrous *adj.* одина́ково свобо́дно владе́ющий обе́ими рука́ми.
ambiguity *n.* двусмы́сленность. **ambiguous** *adj.* двусмы́сленный (-ен, -енна).
ambition *n.* честолю́бие. **ambitious** *adj.* честолюби́вый.
amble *v.i.* (*horse*) бе́гать *indet.*, бежа́ть (-жи́т) *det.* и́ноходью; (*ride*) е́здить *indet.*, е́хать (е́ду, е́дешь) *det.* верхо́м на инохо́дце; (*on foot*) ходи́ть (хожу́, хо́дишь) *indet.*, идти́ (иду́, идёшь; шёл, шла) *det.* нетороплй́вым ша́гом; *n.* и́ноходь.
ambrosia *n.* амбро́зия.
ambulance *n.* каре́та ско́рой по́мощи; ско́рая по́мощь; *air a.*, санита́рный самолёт.
ambush *n.* заса́да; *v.t.* напада́ть *imp.*, напа́сть (-аду́, -адёшь; -а́л) *perf.* из заса́ды на + *acc.*; устра́ивать *imp.*, устро́ить *perf.* заса́ду на + *acc.*
ameliorate *v.t.* & *i.* улучша́ть(ся) *imp.*, улу́чшить(ся) *perf.* **amelioration** *n* улучше́ние.
amen *interj.* ами́нь!
amenable *adj.* усту́пчивый, сгово́рчивый (to, + *dat.*).
amend *v.t.* исправля́ть *imp.*, испра́вить *perf.*; вноси́ть (-ошу́, -о́сишь) *imp.*, внести́ (внесу́, -сёшь; внёс, -ла́) *perf.* измене́ния, попра́вки, в + *acc.* **amendment** *n.* попра́вка, исправле́ние, поправле́ние. **amends** *n.*: *make a. for*, загла́живать *imp.*, загла́ди́ть *perf.*
amenities *n.* пре́лести *f.pl.*, удо́бства *neut.pl.*
American *adj.* америка́нский; *n.* америка́нец (-нца), -нка. **Americanism** *n.* американи́зм. **Americanization** *n.* американиза́ция. **Americanize** *v.t.* американизи́ровать *imp.*, *perf.*
amethyst *n.* амети́ст.
amiability *n.* любе́зность. **amiable** *adj.* любе́зный. **amicability** *n.* дружелю́бие. **amicable** *adj.* дружелю́бный.
amid(st) *prep.* среди́ + *gen.*
amiss *adv.* ду́рно, пло́хо; *take it a.*, обижа́ться *imp.*, оби́деться (-и́жусь, -и́дишься) *perf.*
amity *n.* дру́жественные отноше́ния *neut.pl.*
ammonia *n.* аммиа́к; (*liquid a.*) нашаты́рный спирт (-а(у), *loc.* -е & -у́). **ammoniac(al)** *adj.* аммиа́чный.
ammunition *n.* боеприпа́сы *m.pl.*, снаря́ды *m.pl.*, патро́ны *m.pl.*, дробь.
amnesty *n.* амни́стия; *v.t.* амністи́ровать *imp.*, *perf.*
among(st) *prep.* среди́ + *gen.*, ме́жду + *instr.*
amoral *adj.* амора́льный.
amorous *adj.* влю́бчивый; (*in love*) влюблённый (-ён, -ена́).
amorphous *adj.* амо́рфный, безфо́рменный (-ен, -енна).
amortization *n.* амортиза́ция. **amortize** *v.t.* амортизи́ровать *imp.*, *perf.*
amount *n.* коли́чество; *v.i.*: *a. to*, составля́ть *imp.*, соста́вить *perf.*; равня́ться *imp.* + *dat.*; быть равноси́льным + *dat.*
ampere *n.* ампе́р (*gen.pl.* -р).
amphibian *n.* амфи́бия. **amphibious** *adj.* земново́дный.

amphitheatre *n.* амфитеа́тр.
ample *adj.* (*enough*) (вполне́) доста́точный; (*abundant*) оби́льный; (*spacious*) обши́рный. **amplification** *n.* усиле́ние. **amplifier** *n.* усили́тель *m.* **amplify** *v.t.* (*strengthen*) уси́ливать *imp.*, уси́лить *perf.*; (*enlarge*) расширя́ть *imp.*, расши́рить *perf.* **amplitude** *n.* обши́рность, просто́р. **amply** *adv.* доста́точно.
ampoule *n.* а́мпула.
amputate *v.t.* ампути́ровать *imp.*, *perf.* **amputation** *n.* ампута́ция.
amuse *v.t.* забавля́ть *imp.*; развлека́ть *imp.*, развле́чь (-еку́, -ечёшь; -ёк, -екла́) *perf.*; увеселя́ть *imp.* **amusement** *n.* заба́ва, развлече́ние, увеселе́ние; *pl.* аттракцио́ны *m.pl.* **amusing** *adj.* заба́вный; (*funny*) смешно́й (-шо́н, -шна́).
anachronism *n.* анахрони́зм. **anachronistic** *adj.* анахрони́чный, -ческий.
anaemia *n.* малокро́вие, анеми́я. **anaemic** *adj.* малокро́вный, анеми́чный, -ческий.
anaesthesia *n.* анестези́я, обезбо́ливание. **anaesthetic** *n.* анестези́рующее, обезбо́ливающее; сре́дство; *adj.* анестези́рующий, обезбо́ливающий. **anaesthetist** *n.* наркотиза́тор. **anaesthetize** *v.t.* анестези́ровать *imp.*, *perf.*; обезбо́ливать *imp.*, обезбо́лить *perf.*
anagram *n.* анагра́мма.
anal *adj.* ана́льный.
analogical *adj.* аналоги́ческий. **analogous** *adj.* аналоги́чный. **analogue** *n.* ана́лог; *a. computer*, анало́говая вычисли́тельная маши́на, АВМ. **analogy** *n.* анало́гия.
analyse *v.t.* анализи́ровать *imp.*, *perf.*; (*gram.*) разбира́ть *imp.*, разобра́ть (разберу́, -рёшь; разобра́л, -а́, -о) *perf.* **analysis** *n.* ана́лиз; разбо́р. **analyst** *n.* анали́тик; психоанали́тик. **analytical** *adj.* аналити́ческий.
anarchism *n.* анархи́зм. **anarchist** *n.* анархи́ст, ~ка; *adj.* анархи́стский. **anarchy** *n.* ана́рхия.
anastigmatic *adj.* анастигмати́ческий.
anatomical *adj.* анатоми́ческий. **anatomist** *n.* ана́том. **anatomy** *n.* анато́мия.
ancestor *n.* пре́док (-дка), прароди́тель *m.* **ancestral** *adj.* родово́й, насле́дственный. **ancestress** *n.* прароди́тельница. **ancestry** *n.* происхожде́ние; пре́дки *m.pl.*, прароди́тели *m.pl.*
anchor *n.* я́корь (*pl.* -ря́) *m.*; *v.t.* ста́вить *imp.*, по~ *perf.* на я́корь; *v.i.* станови́ться (-влю́сь, -вишься) *imp.*, стать (ста́ну, -нешь) *perf.* на я́корь. **anchorage** *n.* я́корная стоя́нка.
anchovy *n.* анчо́ус.
ancient *adj.* анти́чный, дре́вний (-вен, -вня), стари́нный.
and *conj.* и, а; с + *instr.*; *you and I*, мы с ва́ми; *my wife and I*, мы с жено́й.
andante *adv.* (*n.*) анда́нте (*neut.indecl.*).
anecdotal *adj.* анекдоти́ческий. **anecdote** *n.* анекдо́т.
anemometer *n.* анемо́метр, ветроме́р.
anemone *n.* анемо́н, ве́треница.
aneroid (barometer) *n.* анеро́ид, баро́метр-анеро́ид.
anew *adv.* сно́ва.
angel *n.* а́нгел. **angelic** *adj.* а́нгельский.
anger *n.* гнев; *v.t.* серди́ть (-ржу́, -рдишь) *imp.*, рас~ *perf.*
angle[1] *n.* у́гол (угла́); (*fig.*) то́чка зре́ния.
angle[2] *v.i.* уди́ть (ужу́, у́дишь) *imp.* ры́бу. **angler** *n.* рыболо́в. **angling** *n.* уже́ние.
angrily *adv.* серди́то, гне́вно. **angry** *adj.* серди́тый, гне́вный (-вен, -вна́, -вно); (*inflamed*) воспалённый (-ён, -ена́).
anguish *n.* страда́ние, боль. **anguished** *adj.* страда́ющий.
angular *adj.* углово́й; (*sharp*) углова́тый.
aniline *adj.* анили́новый.
animal *n.* живо́тное *sb.*; зверь (*pl.* -ри, -ре́й) *m.*; *adj.* живо́тный. **animate** *adj.* живо́й (жив, -а́, -о). **animated** *adj.* оживлённый (-ён, -ена́), живо́й (жив, -а́, -о); воодушевлённый (-ён, -ена́); (*film*) мультипликацио́нный; *a. cartoon*, мультфи́льм. **animation** *n.* оживле́ние, жи́вость, воодушевле́ние.
animosity, animus *n.* вражде́бность, неприя́знь.
aniseed *n.* ани́совое се́мя *neut.*
ankle *n.* лоды́жка, щи́колотка; *a. socks*,

коро́ткие носки́ *m.pl.* **anklet** *n.* ножно́й брасле́т.

annals *n.* ле́топись, анна́лы *m.pl.* **annalist** *n.* летопи́сец (-сца).

annex *v.t.* аннекси́ровать *imp.*, *perf.*; присоединя́ть *imp.*, присоедини́ть *perf.*; прилага́ть *imp.*, приложи́ть (-жу́, -жишь) *perf.* **annexation** *n.* анне́ксия; присоедине́ние. **annexe** *n.* (*building*) пристро́йка; дополне́ние.

annihilate *v.t.* уничтожа́ть *imp.*, уничто́жить *perf.* **annihilation** *n.* уничтоже́ние.

anniversary *n.* годовщи́на.

annotate *v.t.* аннoти́ровать *imp.*, *perf.* **annotated** *adj.* снабжённый (-ён, -ена́) примеча́ниями, коммента́риями. **annotation** *n.* примеча́ние, коммента́рий, аннота́ция.

announce *v.t.* объявля́ть *imp.*, объяви́ть (-влю́, -вишь) *perf.*; (*declare*) заявля́ть *imp.*, заяви́ть (-влю́, -вишь) *perf.*; (*radio*) сообща́ть *imp.*, сообщи́ть *perf.*; (*guest*) докла́дывать *imp.*, доложи́ть (-жу́, -жишь) *perf.* о + *prep.* **announcement** *n.* объявле́ние; сообще́ние. **announcer** *n.* ди́ктор.

annoy *v.t.* досажда́ть *imp.*, досади́ть *perf.*; раздража́ть *imp.*, раздражи́ть *perf.*; *I was annoyed*, мне бы́ло доса́дно. **annoyance** *n.* доса́да, раздраже́ние; (*nuisance*) неприя́тность. **annoying** *adj.* доса́дный.

annual *adj.* ежего́дный, годово́й, годи́чный; (*bot.*) однолетний; *n.* ежего́дник; одноле́тник. **annually** *adv.* ежего́дно. **annuity** *n.* (ежего́дная) ре́нта.

annul *v.t.* аннули́ровать *imp.*, *perf.* **annulment** *n.* аннули́рование.

Annunciation *n.* Благове́щение.

anode *n.* ано́д.

anodyne *n.* болеутоля́ющее сре́дство.

anoint *v.t.* пома́зывать *imp.*, пома́зать (-а́жу, -а́жешь) *perf.*

anomalous *adj.* анома́льный. **anomaly** *n.* анома́лия.

anon. *abbr.*, **anonymous** *adj.* анони́мный. **anonymity** *n.* анони́мность.

another *adj.*, *pron.* друго́й; *a.* (*one*), ещё (оди́н); *ask me a.*, почём я зна́ю? *in a. ten years*, ещё че́рез де́сять лет; *many a.*, мно́гие други́е.

answer *n.* отве́т; *v.t.* отвеча́ть *imp.*, отве́тить *perf.* + *dat.*, на + *acc.*; *a. back*, дерзи́ть *imp.*, на~ *perf.* + *dat.*; *a. for*, руча́ться *imp.*, поручи́ться (-чу́сь, -чишься) *perf.* за + *acc.*; *a. the door*, отворя́ть *imp.*, отвори́ть (-рю́, -ришь) *perf.* дверь на звоно́к, на стук. **answerable** *adj.* отве́тственный (-ен, -енна).

ant *n.* мураве́й (-вья́); *a.-eater*, муравье́д; *a.-hill*, мураве́йник.

antagonism *n.* антагони́зм, вражда́. **antagonist** *n.* антагони́ст, проти́вник. **antagonistic** *adj.* антагонисти́ческий, вражде́бный. **antagonize** *v.t.* порожда́ть *imp.*, породи́ть *perf.* антагони́зм, вражду́, у + *gen.*

antarctic *adj.* антаркти́ческий; *n.* Анта́рктика.

antecedent *n.* антецеде́нт; *pl.* про́шлое *sb.*; *adj.* антецеде́нтный; предше́ствующий, предыду́щий.

antechamber *n.* пере́дняя *sb.*, прихо́жая *sb.*

antedate *v.t.* дати́ровать *imp.*, *perf.* за́дним число́м; (*precede*) предше́ствовать *imp.* + *dat.*

antediluvian *adj.* допото́пный.

antelope *n.* антило́па.

antenatal *adj.* до рожде́ния.

antenna *n.* (*ent.*) у́сик, щу́пальце (*gen. pl.* -лец & -льцев); (*also radio*) анте́нна.

anterior *adj.* пере́дний; *a. to*, предше́ствующий + *acc.*

anteroom *n.* пере́дняя *sb.*

anthem *n.* гимн.

anthology *n.* антоло́гия.

anthracite *n.* антраци́т; *adj.* антраци́товый.

anthropoid *adj.* человекообра́зный; *n.* антропо́ид. **anthropological** *adj.* антропологи́ческий. **anthropologist** *n.* антропо́лог. **anthropology** *n.* антрополо́гия.

anti- *in comb.* анти-, противо-. **anti-aircraft** *adj.* противовозду́шный, зени́тный. **antibiotic** *n.* антибио́тик. **antibody** *n.* антите́ло (*pl.* -ла́). **Antichrist** *n.* анти́христ. **anticlimax** *n.* неосуществлённые ожида́ния *neut.pl.*, антиклимакс. **anticyclone** *n.* антициклон. **antidote** *n.* противоядие. **anti-Fascist** *n.* антифашист, ~ка; *adj.* антифашистский. **antifreeze** *n.* антифриз, хладностойкий состав. **antihero** *n.* антигерой. **antimatter** *n.* антивещество. **anti-missile missile** *n.* антиракета. **antipathetic** *adj.* антипатичный. **antipathy** *n.* антипатия. **antipodes** *n.* антипод; диаметрально противоположная точка. **anti-Semite** *n.* антисемит, ~ка. **anti-Semitic** *adj.* антисемитский. **anti-Semitism** *n.* антисемитизм. **antiseptic** *adj.* антисептический; *n.* антисептик. **anti-submarine** *adj.* противолодочный. **anti-tank** *adj.* противотанковый. **antithesis** *n.* антитеза; (*opposition*) противоположность. **antithetical** *adj.* антитетический; противоположный.

anticipate *v.t.* ожидать *imp.* + *gen.*; (*with pleasure*) предвкушать *imp.*, предвкусить (-ушу, -усишь) *perf.*; (*forestall*) предупреждать *imp.*, предупредить *perf.* **anticipation** *n.* ожидание; предвкушение; предупреждение.

antics *n.* выходки *f.pl.*, шалости *f.pl.*

antimony *n.* сурьма.

antiquarian *adj.* антикварный; *n.*, **antiquary** *n.* антиквар. **antiquated** *adj.* устарелый. **antique** *adj.* старинный; *n.* антик; *pl.* старина. **antiquity** *n.* древность, старина; *pl.* древности *f.pl.*

antler *n.* олений рог (*pl.* -а).

anus *n.* задний проход.

anvil *n.* наковальня (*gen.pl.* -лен).

anxiety *n.* беспокойство, тревога, озабоченность. **anxious** *adj.* беспокойный, тревожный, озабоченный (-ен, -енна); *be a.*, беспокоиться *imp.*; тревожиться *imp.*

any *adj.*, *pron.* какой-нибудь; сколько-нибудь; всякий, любой; кто-нибудь, что-нибудь; (*with neg.*) никакой, ни один; нисколько; никто, ничто; *adv.* сколько-нибудь; (*with neg.*) нисколько, ничуть. **anybody, anyone** *pron.* кто-нибудь; всякий, любой; (*with neg.*) никто. **anyhow** *adv.* как-нибудь; кое-как; (*with neg.*) никак; *conj.* во всяком случае; всё же, всё равно. **anyone** *see* **anybody**. **anything** *pron.* что-нибудь; всё (что угодно); (*with neg.*) ничего. **anyway** *adv.* во всяком случае; как бы то ни было. **anywhere** *adv.* где, куда, откуда, угодно; (*with neg.*, *interrog.*) где-, куда-, откуда-нибудь.

aorta *n.* аорта.

apart *adv.* (*aside*) в стороне, в сторону; (*separately*) раздельно, врозь; (*into pieces*) на части; *a. from*, кроме + *gen.*, не считая + *gen.*; *take a.*, разбирать *imp.*, разобрать (разберу, -рёшь; разобрал, -а, -о) *perf.* (на части); *tell a.*, различать *imp.*, различить *perf.*; отличать *imp.*, отличить *perf.* друг от друга.

apartheid *n.* апартеид.

apartments *n.* меблированные комнаты *f.pl.*

apathetic *adj.* апатичный. **apathy** *n.* апатия, безразличие.

ape *n.* обезьяна; *v.t.* обезьянничать *imp.*, с~ *perf.* с + *gen.*

aperient *adj.* слабительный; *n.* слабительное *sb.*

aperture *n.* отверстие.

apex *n.* вершина.

aphorism *n.* афоризм. **aphoristic** *adj.* афористичный, -ческий.

apiarist *n.* пчеловод. **apiary** *n.* пасека, пчельник.

apiece *adv.* (*persons*) на каждого; (*things*) за штуку; (*amount*) по + *dat. or acc. with* 2, 3, 4, 90, 100, *etc.*

Apocalypse *n.* Апокалипсис. **apocalyptic** *adj.* апокалиптический.

Apocrypha *n.* апокрифы *m.pl.* **apocryphal** *adj.* апокрифичный, -ческий.

apogee *n.* апогей.

apologetic *adj.* извиняющийся; *be a.*, извиняться *imp.*; *feel a.*, чувствовать *imp.* свою вину. **apologetics** *n.* апологетика. **apologia** *n.* апология. **apologize** *v.i.* извиняться *imp.*, извиниться *perf.* (to, перед + *instr.*; for, за + *acc.*). **apology** *n.* извинение; *a. for*, жалкое подобие + *gen.*

apoplectic *adj.* апоплексический. **apoplexy** *n.* апоплексия.

apostasy *n.* (веро)отступничество. **apostate** *n.* (веро)отступник, -ица; *adj.* (веро)отступнический.

apostle *n.* апо́стол. **apostolic** *adj.* апо́стольский.

apostrophe *n.* апостро́ф.

apotheosis *n.* апофео́з, прославле́ние.

appal *v.t.* ужаса́ть *imp.*, ужасну́ть *perf.* **appalling** *adj.* ужаса́ющий, ужа́сный.

apparatus *n.* аппара́т; прибо́р; (*gymnastic*) гимнасти́ческие снаря́ды *m.pl.*

apparel *n.* одея́ние.

apparent *adj.* (*seeming*) ви́димый; (*manifest*) очеви́дный, я́вный; *heir a.*, прямо́й насле́дник. **apparently** *adv.* ка́жется, по-ви́димому; очеви́дно.

apparition *n.* виде́ние, при́зрак.

appeal *n.* (*request*) призы́в, воззва́ние, обраще́ние; (*leg.*) апелля́ция, обжа́лование; (*attraction*) привлека́тельность; *a. court*, апелляцио́нный суд (-а́); *v.i.* (*request*) взыва́ть *imp.*, воззва́ть (-зову́, -зовёшь) *perf.* (to, к + *dat.*; for, о + *prep.*); обраща́ться *imp.*, обрати́ться (-ащу́сь, -ати́шься) *perf.* (с призы́вом); (*leg.*) апелли́ровать *imp.*, *perf.*; *a. against*, обжа́ловать *perf.*; *a. to*, (*attract*) привлека́ть *imp.*, привле́чь (-еку́, -ечёшь; -ёк, -екла́) *perf.*

appear *v.i.* появля́ться *imp.*, появи́ться (-влю́сь, -ви́шься) *perf.*; выступа́ть *imp.*, вы́ступить *perf.*; (*seem*) каза́ться (кажу́сь, -жешься) *imp.*, по~ *perf.* **appearance** *n.* появле́ние, выступле́ние; (*aspect*) вид, нару́жность; (*pl.*) ви́димость.

appease *v.t.* умиротворя́ть *imp.*, умиротвори́ть *perf.* **appeasement** *n.* умиротворе́ние.

appellant *n.* апелля́нт. **appellate** *adj.* апелляцио́нный.

append *v.t.* прилага́ть *imp.*, приложи́ть (-жу́, -жишь) *perf.*; прибавля́ть *imp.*, приба́вить *perf.* **appendicitis** *n.* аппендици́т. **appendix** *n.* приложе́ние, прибавле́ние; (*anat.*) аппе́ндикс.

appertain *v.i.*: *a. to*, принадлежа́ть (-жи́т) *imp.* + *dat.*; относи́ться (-ится) *imp.* + *dat.*

appetite *n.* аппети́т. **appetizing** *adj.* аппети́тный.

applaud *v.t.* аплоди́ровать *imp.* + *dat.*; рукоплеска́ть (-ещу́, -е́щешь) *imp.* + *dat.* **applause** *n.* аплодисме́нты *m.pl.*, рукоплеска́ние.

apple *n.* я́блоко (*pl.* -ки); *adj.* я́блочный; *a. charlotte*, шарло́тка; *a.-tree*, я́блоня.

appliance *n.* приспособле́ние, прибо́р. **applicable** *adj.* примени́мый. **applicant** *n.* пода́тель *m.*, ~ница, заявле́ния; проси́тель *m.*, ~ница; кандида́т. **application** *n.* (*use*) примене́ние, приложе́ние; (*putting on*) накла́дывание; (*request*) заявле́ние. **applied** *adj.* прикладно́й. **appliqué** *n.* апплика́ция. **apply** *v.t.* (*use*) применя́ть *imp.*, примени́ть (-ню́, -нишь) *perf.*; прилага́ть *imp.*, приложи́ть (-жу́, -жишь) *perf.*; (*put on*) накла́дывать *imp.*, наложи́ть (-жу́, -жишь) *perf.*; *v.i.* (*request*) обраща́ться *imp.*, обрати́ться (-ащу́сь, -ати́шься) *perf.* с про́сьбой (for, о + *prep.*); подава́ть (-даю́, -даёшь) *imp.*, пода́ть (-а́м, -а́шь, -а́ст, -ади́м; по́дал, -а́, -о) *perf.* заявле́ние.

appoint *v.t.* назнача́ть *imp.*, назна́чить *perf.* **appointment** *n.* назначе́ние; (*office*) до́лжность, пост (-а́, *loc.* -у́); (*meeting*) свида́ние.

apposite *adj.* уме́стный. **apposition** *n.* приложе́ние; *in a.*, прило́женный (-ен).

appraisal *n.* оце́нка. **appraise** *v.t.* оце́нивать *imp.*, оцени́ть (-ню́, -нишь) *perf.*

appreciable *adj.* ощути́мый, ощути́тельный. **appreciate** *v.t.* цени́ть (-ню́, -нишь) *imp.*; (пра́вильно) оце́нивать *imp.*, оцени́ть (-ню́, -нишь) *perf.*; *v.i.* повыша́ться *imp.*, повы́ситься *perf.* **appreciation** *n.* (*estimation*) оце́нка; (*recognition*) призна́тельность; (*rise in value*) повыше́ние це́нности, цены́. **appreciative** *adj.* призна́тельный (of, за + *acc.*).

apprehend *v.t.* (*arrest*) аресто́вывать *imp.*, арестова́ть *perf.*; (*understand*) понима́ть *imp.*, поня́ть (пойму́, -мёшь; по́нял, -а́, -о) *perf.*; (*anticipate*) опаса́ться *imp.* + *gen.*, *inf.* **apprehension** *n.* аре́ст; опасе́ние. **apprehensive** *adj.* опаса́ющийся.

apprentice *n.* учени́к (-а́), подмасте́рье (*gen.pl.* -в) *m.*; *v.t.* отдава́ть (-даю́, -даёшь) *imp.*, отда́ть (-а́м, -а́шь, -а́ст, -ади́м; о́тдал, -а́, -о) *perf.* в уче́ние.

apprenticeship *n.* учени́чество; обуче́ние.
appro. *abbr.*: *on a.*, на про́бу.
approach *v.t.* подходи́ть (-ожу́, -о́дишь) *imp.*, подойти́ (подойду́, -дёшь; подошёл, -шла́) *perf.* к + *dat.*; приближа́ться *imp.*, прибли́зиться *perf.* к + *dat.*; (*apply to*) обраща́ться *imp.*, обрати́ться (-ащу́сь, -ати́шься) *perf.* к + *dat.*; *n.* приближе́ние; подхо́д, подъе́зд, по́дступ.
approbation *n.* одобре́ние.
appropriate *adj.* подходя́щий, соотве́тствующий; *v.t.* присва́ивать *imp.*, присво́ить *perf.*; (*assign money*) ассигнова́ть *imp.*, *perf.* **appropriation** *n.* присвое́ние, присво́енное *sb.*; ассигнова́ние.
approval *n.* одобре́ние; утвержде́ние. **approve** *v.t.* утвержда́ть *imp.*, утверди́ть *perf.*; *v.t.* & *i.* (*a. of*) одобря́ть *imp.*, одо́брить *perf.*
approximate *adj.* приблизи́тельный; *v.i.* приближа́ться *imp.* (to, к + *dat.*). **approximation** *n.* приближе́ние.
apricot *n.* абрико́с.
April *n.* апре́ль *m.*; *attrib.* апре́льский.
apron *n.* пере́дник; (*theatre*) авансце́на; (*airfield*) площа́дка.
apropos *adv.* кста́ти; *a. of*, по по́воду + *gen.*; относи́тельно + *gen.*; что каса́ется + *gen.*
apse *n.* апси́да.
apt *adj.* (*suitable*) уда́чный; (*quick*) спосо́бный; (*inclined*) скло́нный (-о́нен, -о́нна́, -о́нно). **aptitude** *n.* спосо́бность.
aqualung *n.* акваланг. **aquamarine** *n.* аквамари́н. **aquarium** *n.* аква́риум. **Aquarius** *n.* Водоле́й. **aquatic** *adj.* водяно́й, во́дный. **aqueduct** *n.* акведу́к. **aqueous** *adj.* во́дный; (*watery*) водяни́стый.
aquiline *adj.* орли́ный.
Arab *n.* (*person*) ара́б, ~ка; (*horse*) ара́бская ло́шадь (*pl.* -ди, -де́й, *instr.* -дьми́); *adj.* ара́бский. **arabesque** *n.* арабе́ска. **Arabic** *adj.* ара́бский.
arable *adj.* па́хотный.
arbitrary *adj.* произво́льный. **arbitrate** *v.i.* де́йствовать *imp.* в ка́честве трете́йского судьи́. **arbitration** *n.* арбитра́ж, трете́йское реше́ние. **arbitrator** *n.* арби́тр, трете́йский судья́ (*pl.* -дьи, -де́й, -дьям) *m.*
arbor *n.* вал (*loc.* -у́; *pl.* -ы́), шпи́ндель *m.*
arboreal *adj.* древе́сный; (*living in trees*) обита́ющий на дере́вьях. **arbour** *n.* бесе́дка.
arc *n.* дуга́ (*pl.* -ги); *a. lamp*, дугова́я ла́мпа. **arcade** *n.* арка́да, пасса́ж. **arch**[1] *n.* а́рка, свод, дуга́ (*pl.* -ги); *v.t.* & *i.* выгиба́ть(ся) *imp.*, вы́гнуть(ся) *perf.*; изгиба́ть(ся) *imp.*, изогну́ть(ся) *perf.*
arch[2] *adj.* игри́вый.
archaeological *adj.* археологи́ческий. **archaeologist** *n.* архео́лог. **archaeology** *n.* археоло́гия.
archaic *adj.* архаи́чный. **archaism** *n.* архаи́зм.
archangel *n.* арха́нгел.
archbishop *n.* архиепи́скоп. **archdeacon** *n.* архидиа́кон.
archducal *adj.* эрцге́рцогский. **archduchess** *n.* эрцгерцоги́ня. **archduchy** *n.* эрцге́рцогство. **archduke** *n.* эрцге́рцог.
archer *n.* стрело́к (-лка́) из лу́ка. **archery** *n.* стрельба́ из лу́ка.
archipelago *n.* архипела́г.
architect *n.* архите́ктор, зо́дчий *sb.* **architectural** *adj.* архитекту́рный. **architecture** *n.* архитекту́ра.
archives *n.* архи́в. **archivist** *n.* архива́риус, архиви́ст.
archway *n.* прохо́д под а́ркой, сво́дчатый прохо́д.
arctic *adj.* аркти́ческий; *n.* А́рктика.
ardent *adj.* горя́чий (-ч, -ча́), пы́лкий (-лок, -лка́, -лко). **ardour** *n.* пыл (-а(у), *loc.* -у́), пы́лкость, рве́ние.
arduous *adj.* тру́дный (-ден, -дна́, -дно).
area *n.* (*extent*) пло́щадь (*pl.* -ди, -де́й); (*region*) райо́н, зо́на.
arena *n.* аре́на.
argon *n.* арго́н.
arguable *adj.* утвержда́емый, доказу́емый; (*disputed*) спо́рный. **argue** *v.t.* (*try to prove*) аргументи́ровать *imp.*, *perf.*; (*maintain*) утвержда́ть *imp.*; (*prove*) дока́зывать *imp.*; *v.i.* (*dispute*) спо́рить *imp.*, по~ *perf.* **argument** *n.*

аргумéнт, дóвод; (*dispute*) спор. **argumentative** *adj.* лю́бящий спóрить.

arid *adj.* сухóй (сух, -á, -о), безвóдный. **aridity** *n.* сýхость.

Aries *n.* Овéн (Овнá).

arise *v.i.* возникáть *imp.*, возни́кнуть (-к) *perf.*; происходи́ть (-ит) *imp.*, произойти́ (-ойдёт; -ошёл, -ошлá) *perf.*

aristocracy *n.* аристокрáтия. **aristocrat** *n.* аристокрáт, ~ка. **aristocratic** *adj.* аристократи́ческий, -чный.

arithmetic *n.* арифмéтика. **arithmetical** *adj.* арифмети́ческий. **arithmetician** *n.* арифмéтик.

ark *n.* (Нóев) ковчéг.

arm[1] *n.* (*of body*) рукá (*acc.* -ку; *pl.* -ки, -к, -кáм); (*of sea*) морскóй зали́в; (*of chair*) рýчка; (*of river*) рукáв (-á; *pl.* -á); (*of tree*) большáя ветвь (*pl.* -ви, -вéй); *a. in a.*, пóд руку; *at a.'s length*, (*fig.*) на почти́тельном расстоя́нии; *with open arms*, с распростёртыми объя́тиями.

arm[2] *n.* (*mil.*) род войск; *pl.* (*weapons*) орýжие; *pl.* (*coat of a.*) герб (-á); *v.t.* вооружáть *imp.*, вооружи́ть *perf.* **armaments** *n.* вооружéния *neut.pl.* **armature** *n.* арматýра.

armchair *n.* крéсло (*gen.pl.* -сел). **armful** *n.* охáпка. **armhole** *n.* прóйма.

armistice *n.* переми́рие.

armorial *adj.* гéрбовый, геральди́ческий. **armour** *n.* (*hist.*) доспéхи *m.pl.*; броня́; (*vehicles, collect.*) бронеси́лы *f.pl.* **armoured** *adj.* бронирóванный (-ан), броневóй; (*vehicles etc.*) бронетáнковый, броне-; *a. car*, броневи́к (-á), бронеавтомоби́ль *m.*; *a. forces*, бронетáнковые войскá *neut. pl.*, бронеси́лы *f.pl.* **armourer** *n.* оружéйник. **armoury** *n.* арсенáл, склад орýжия.

armpit *n.* подмы́шка.

army *n.* áрмия; *adj.* армéйский.

aroma *n.* аромáт. **aromatic** *adj.* аромати́чный.

around *adv.* кругóм, вокрýг; *prep.* вокрýг + *gen.*; *all a.*, повсю́ду.

arouse *v.t.* пробуждáть, буди́ть (бужý, бýдишь) *imp.*, про~ *perf.*; возбуждáть *imp.*, возбуди́ть *perf.*

arraign *v.t.* привлекáть *imp.*, привлéчь (-екý, -ечёшь; -ёк, -еклá) *perf.* к судý. **arraignment** *n.* привлечéние к судý.

arrange *v.t.* (*put in order*) приводи́ть (-ожý, -óдишь) *imp.*, привести́ (приведý, -дёшь; привёл, -á) *perf.* в поря́док; расставля́ть *imp.*, расстáвить *perf.*; (*plan*) устрáивать *imp.*, устрóить *perf.*; (*mus.*) аранжи́ровать *imp.*, *perf.*; *v.i.*: *a. for*, услáвливаться *imp.*, условиться *perf.* о + *prep.*; *a. to*, уговáриваться *imp.*, уговори́ться *perf.* + *inf.* **arrangement** *n.* расположéние; устрóйство; (*agreement*) соглашéние; (*mus.*) аранжирóвка; *pl.* приготовлéния *neut.pl.*

array *v.t.* наряжáть *imp.*, наряди́ть (-яжý, -я́дишь) *perf.*; (*marshal*) стрóить *imp.*, вы́~ *perf.*; *n.* наря́д; (*series*) совокýпность.

arrears *n.* задóлженность, недои́мка.

arrest *v.t.* арестóвывать *imp.*, арестовáть *perf.*; задéрживать *imp.*, задержáть (-жý, -жишь) *perf.*; (*attention*) прикóвывать *imp.*, приковáть (-кую́, -куёшь) *perf.*; *n.* арéст, задержáние.

arrival *n.* прибы́тие, приéзд; (*new a.*) вновь прибы́вший *sb.*; (*child*) новорождённый *sb.* **arrive** *v.i.* прибывáть *imp.*, прибы́ть (прибудý, -дешь; при́был, -á, -о) *perf.*; приезжáть *imp.*, приéхать (-éду, -éдешь) *perf.*; (*succeed*) доби́ться (-бью́сь, -бьёшься) *perf.* успéха.

arrogance *n.* высокомéрие, кичли́вость. **arrogant** *adj.* высокомéрный, кичли́вый.

arrow *n.* стрелá (*pl.* -лы); (*pointer etc.*) стрéлка. **arrowhead** *n.* наконéчник стрелы́.

arsenal *n.* арсенáл.

arsenic *n.* мышья́к (-á); *adj.* мышьякóвый.

arson *n.* поджóг.

art *n.* искýсство; *pl.* гуманитáрные наýки *f.pl.*; *adj.* худóжественный.

arterial *adj.* (*anat.*) артериáльный; магистрáльный; *a. road*, магистрáль. **artery** *n.* (*anat.*) артéрия; магистрáль.

artesian *adj.* артезиáнский.

artful *adj.* хи́трый (-тёр, -трá, хи́трó), лóвкий (-вок, -вкá, -вко, лóвки́).

arthritic *adj.* артрити́ческий. **arthritis** *n.* артри́т.
artichoke *n.* артишо́к; (*Jerusalem a.*) земляна́я гру́ша.
article *n.* (*literary*) статья́ (*gen.pl.* -те́й); (*clause*) пункт; (*thing*) предме́т; (*gram.*) арти́кль *m.*, член; *v.t.* отдава́ть (-даю́, -даёшь) *imp.*, отда́ть (-а́м, -а́шь, -а́ст, -ади́м; о́тдал, -а́, -о) *perf.* в уче́ние.
articulate *adj.* членоразде́льный, я́сный (я́сен, ясна́, я́сно, я́сны́); *v.t.* произноси́ть (-ошу́, -о́сишь) *imp.*, произнести́ (-есу́, -есёшь; -ёс, -есла́) *perf.*; артикули́ровать *imp.* **articulated** *adj.* сочленённый (-ён, -ена́). **articulation** *n.* артикуля́ция; сочлене́ние.
artifice *n.* хи́трость, (иску́сная) вы́думка. **artificer** *n.* (вое́нный) те́хник. **artificial** *adj.* иску́сственный (-ен(ен), -енна).
artillery *n.* артилле́рия; *adj.* артиллери́йский. **artilleryman** *n.* артиллери́ст.
artisan *n.* реме́сленник.
artist *n.* худо́жник; арти́ст. **artiste** *n.* арти́ст, ~ка. **artistic** *adj.* худо́жественный (-ен, -енна); артисти́ческий.
artless *adj.* бесхи́тростный, простоду́шный.
Aryan *n.* ари́ец (-и́йца), ари́йка; *adj.* ари́йский.
as *adv.* как; *conj.* (*time*) когда́; в то вре́мя как; (*cause*) так как; (*manner*) как; (*concession*) как ни; *rel.pron.* како́й; кото́рый; что; *as . . . as*, так (же)... как; *as for, to*, относи́тельно + *gen.*; что каса́ется + *gen.*; *as if*, как бу́дто; *as it were*, ка́к бы; так сказа́ть; *as soon as*, как то́лько; *as well*, та́кже; то́же.
asbestos *n.* асбе́ст; *adj.* асбе́стовый.
ascend *v.t.* поднима́ться *imp.*, подня́ться (-ниму́сь, -ни́мешься; -я́лся́, -яла́сь) *perf.* на + *acc.*; всходи́ть (-ожу́, -о́дишь) *imp.*, взойти́ (взойду́, -дёшь; взошёл, -шла́) *perf.* на + *acc.*; *v.i.* возноси́ться (-ошу́сь, -о́сишься) *imp.*, вознести́сь (-есу́сь, -есёшься; -ёсся, -есла́сь) *perf.* **ascendancy** *n.* доминиру́ющее влия́ние (over, на + *acc.*).
ascendant *adj.* восходя́щий. **Ascension** *n.* (*eccl.*) Вознесе́ние. **ascent** *n.* восхожде́ние (of, на + *acc.*).
ascertain *v.t.* устана́вливать *imp.*, установи́ть (-влю́, -вишь) *perf.*
ascetic *adj.* аскети́ческий; *n.* аске́т. **asceticism** *n.* аскети́зм.
ascribe *v.t.* припи́сывать *imp.*, приписа́ть (-ишу́, -и́шешь) *perf.* (to, + *dat.*). **ascription** *n.* припи́сывание.
asepsis *n.* асе́птика. **aseptic** *adj.* асепти́ческий.
asexual *adj.* беспо́лый.
ash[1] *n.* (*tree*) я́сень *m.*
ash[2], **ashes** *n.* зола́, пе́пел (-пла); (*human remains*) прах. **ashtray** *n.* пе́пельница.
ashamed *predic.*: *he is a.*, ему́ сты́дно; *be, feel, a. of*, стыди́ться *imp.*, по ~ *perf.* + *gen.*
ashen[1] *adj.* (*of tree*) я́сеневый.
ashen[2] *adj.* (*of ash*[2]) пе́пельный; (*pale*) мёртвенно-бле́дный.
ashore *adv.* на бе́рег(у́).
Asian, Asiatic *adj.* азиа́тский; *n.* азиа́т, ~ка.
aside *adv.* в сто́рону, в стороне́; *n.* слова́ *neut.pl.*, произноси́мые в сто́рону.
asinine *adj.* осли́ный; (*stupid*) глу́пый (глуп, -а́, -о).
ask *v.t.* (*inquire of*) спра́шивать *imp.*, спроси́ть (-ошу́, -о́сишь) *perf.*; (*request*) проси́ть (-ошу́, -о́сишь) *imp.*, по ~ *perf.* (for, *acc.*, *gen.*, о + *prep.*); (*invite*) приглаша́ть *imp.*, пригласи́ть *perf.*; (*demand*) тре́бовать *imp.* + *gen.* (of, от + *gen.*); *a. after*, осведомля́тьея *imp.*, осве́домиться *perf.* о + *prep.*; *a. a question*, задава́ть (-даю́, -даёшь) *imp.*, зада́ть (-а́м, -а́шь, -а́ст, -ади́м; за́дал, -а́, -о) *perf.* вопро́с; *you can have it for the asking*, сто́ит то́лько попроси́ть.
askance *adv.* ко́со, с подозре́нием.
askew *adv.* кри́во.
asleep *predic., adv.*: *be a.*, спать (сплю, спишь; спал, -а́,-о) *imp.*; *fall a.*, засыпа́ть *imp.*, засну́ть *perf.*; *my foot's a.*, нога́ затекла́.
asp *n.* а́спид.
asparagus *n.* спа́ржа.

aspect *n.* аспéкт, вид (-а(у), на видý), сторонá (*acc.* -ону; *pl.* -оны, -óн, -онáм).
aspen *n.* осúна.
asperity *n.* рéзкость.
aspersion *n.* клеветá.
asphalt *n.* асфáльт; *adj.* асфáльтовый; *v.t.* асфальтúровать *imp., perf.*
asphyxia *n.* асфúксия, удýшье. **asphyxiate** *v.t.* удушáть *imp.*, удушúть (-шý, -шишь) *perf.*
aspic *n.* заливнóе *sb.*; *in a.*, заливнóй.
aspirant *n.* претендéнт. **aspirate** *n.* придыхáтельный *sb.* **aspiration** *n.* (*ling.*) придыхáние; (*desire*) стремлéние. **aspire** *v.i.* стремúться *imp.* (to, к + *dat.*).
aspirin *n.* аспирúн; (*tablet*) таблéтка аспирúна.
ass *n.* осёл (ослá).
assail *v.t.* нападáть *imp.*, напáсть (-адý, -адёшь; -áл) *perf.* на + *acc.*; (*with questions*) забрáсывать *imp.*, забросáть *perf.* вопрóсами. **assailant** *n.* нападáющий *sb.*
assassin *n.* (наёмный, -ная) убúйца *m., f.* **assassinate** *v.t.* (веролóмно) убивáть *imp.*, убúть (убью, убьёшь) *perf.* **assassination** *n.* (предáтельское) убúйство.
assault *n.* нападéние; (*mil.*) штурм; (*rape*) изнасúлование; *a. and battery*, оскорблéние дéйствием; *v.t.* нападáть *imp.*, напáсть (-адý, -адёшь; -áл) *perf.* на + *acc.*; штурмовáть *imp.*; насúловать *imp.*, из ~ *perf.*
assay *n.* прóба; *v.t.* производúть (-ожý, -óдишь) *imp.*, произвестú (-едý, -едёшь; -ёл, -елá) *perf.* анáлиз + *gen.*; прóбовать *imp.*, по ~ *perf.*
assemblage *n.* сбор, собирáние. **assemble** *v.t.* собирáть *imp.*, собрáть (соберý, -рёшь; собрáл, -á, -о) *perf.*; (*machine*) монтúровать *imp.*, с ~ *perf.*; *v.i.* собирáться *imp.*, собрáться (-берётся; собрáлся, -алáсь, -áлóсь) *perf.* **assembly** *n.* собрáние, ассамблéя; (*of machine*) сбóрка.
assent *v.i.* соглашáться *imp.*, соглaсúться *perf.* (to, на + *acc.*, *inf.*); *n.* соглáсие; (*royal*) сáнкция.
assert *v.t.* утверждáть *imp.*; *a. oneself*, отстáивать *imp.*, отстоя́ть (-ою, -оишь) *perf.* свои́ правá. **assertion** *n.* утверждéние. **assertive** *adj.* настóйчивый, самонадéянный (-ян, -янна).
assess *v.t.* (*amount*) определя́ть *imp.*, определúть *perf.*; (*tax*) облагáть *imp.*, обложúть (-жý, -жишь) *perf.* налóгом; (*value*) оцéнивать *imp.*, оценúть (-ню́, -нишь) *perf.* **assessment** *n.* определéние; обложéние; оцéнка.
asset *n.* цéнное кáчество; блáго; *pl.* имýщество; *assets and liabilities*, актúв и пассúв.
assiduity *n.* прилежáние, усéрдие. **assiduous** *adj.* прилéжный, усéрдный.
assign *v.t.* назначáть *imp.*, назнáчить *perf.*; ассигновáть *imp.*, *perf.*; *n.*: *heirs and assigns*, наслéдники и правопреéмники *m.pl.* **assignation** *n.* (*meeting*) услóвленная встрéча, свидáние. **assignment** *n.* (*task*) задáние; (*mission*) командирóвка.
assimilate *v.t.* ассимилúровать *imp.*, *perf.*; усвáивать *imp.*, усвóить *perf.* **assimilation** *n.* ассимиля́ция; усвоéние.
assist *v.t.* помогáть *imp.*, помóчь (-огý, -óжешь; -óг, -оглá) *perf.* + *dat.*; содéйствовать *imp.*, *perf.* + *dat.* **assistance** *n.* пóмощь, содéйствие. **assistant** *n.* помóщник, ассистéнт.
assizes *n.* выезднáя сéссия судá.
associate *v.t.* ассоциúровать *imp.*, *perf.*; *v.i.* присоединя́ться *imp.*, присоединúться *perf.* (with, к + *dat.*); общáться *imp.* (with, с + *instr.*); *n.* (*colleague*) коллéга *m.*; (*subordinate member*) млáдший член, член-корреспондéнт. **association** *n.* óбщество, ассоциáция; присоединéние; *A. football*, футбóл.
assonance *n.* ассонáнс.
assorted *adj.* подóбранный (-ан). **assortment** *n.* ассортимéнт.
assuage *v.t.* успокáивать *imp.*, успокóить *perf.*; смягчáть *imp.*, смягчúть *perf.*
assume *v.t.* (*accept*) принимáть *imp.*, приня́ть (примý, -мешь; прúнял, -á, -о) *perf.*; (*pretend*) напускáть *imp.*, напустúть (-ущý, -ýстишь) *perf.* на себя́; (*suppose*) предполагáть *imp.*,

предположи́ть (-ожу́, -о́жишь) *perf.*; *assumed name*, вы́мышленное и́мя *neut.* **assumption** *n.* приня́тие на себе́; (*pretence*) притво́рство; (*supposition*) предположе́ние, допуще́ние; (*eccl., the A.*) Успе́ние.

assurance *n.* увере́ние; (*self-a.*) самоуве́ренность; (*insurance*) страхова́ние. **assure** *v.t.* уверя́ть *imp.*, уве́рить *perf.*; гаранти́ровать *imp., perf.*; (*insure*) страхова́ть *imp.*, за~ *perf.* (against, от+*gen.*). **assuredly** *adv.* несомне́нно.

aster *n.* а́стра.

asterisk *n.* звёздочка.

astern *adv.* позади́, наза́д.

asteroid *n.* астеро́ид.

asthma *n.* а́стма. **asthmatic** *adj.* астмати́ческий.

astigmatic *adj.* астигмати́ческий. **astigmatism** *n.* астигмати́зм.

astir *predic., adv.* (*in motion*) в движе́нии; (*out of bed*) на нога́х; (*excited*) в возбужде́нии.

astonish *v.t.* удивля́ть *imp.*, удиви́ть *perf.* **astonishing** *adj.* удиви́тельный. **astonishment** *n.* удивле́ние.

astound *v.t.* изумля́ть *imp.*, изуми́ть *perf.* **astounding** *adj.* изуми́тельный.

astrakhan *n.* кара́куль *m.*

astral *adj.* астра́льный, звёздный.

astray *adv.*: *go a.*, сбива́ться *imp.*, сби́ться (собью́сь, собьёшься) *perf.* с пути́; *lead a.*, сбива́ть *imp.*, сбить (собью́, собьёшь) *perf.* с пути́.

astride *adv.* расста́вив но́ги; верхо́м (of, на+*prep.*); *prep.* верхо́м на+*prep.*

astringent *adj.* вя́жущий; *n.* вя́жущее сре́дство.

astro- *in comb.* астро-, звездо-. **astrologer** *n.* астро́лог. **astrological** *adj.* астрологи́ческий. **astrology** *n.* астроло́гия. **astronaut** *n.* астрона́вт. **astronomer** *n.* астроно́м. **astronomical** *adj.* астрономи́ческий. **astronomy** *n.* астроно́мия. **astrophysical** *adj.* астрофизи́ческий. **astrophysics** *n.* астрофи́зика.

astute *adj.* проница́тельный; (*crafty*) хи́трый (-тёр, -тра́, хи́тро́).

asunder *adv.* (*apart*) врозь; (*in pieces*) на ча́сти.

asylum *n.* психиатри́ческая больни́ца; (*refuge*) убе́жище.

asymmetrical *adj.* асимметри́чный. **asymmetry** *n.* асимметри́я.

at *prep.* (*position, condition*) на+*prep.*, в+*prep.*, у+*gen.*; (*time, direction*) на+*acc.*, в+*acc.*; with verbs etc.: see verbs etc., e.g. *look* смотре́ть (at, на+*acc.*); *at all*, вообще́; *not at all*, совсе́м не; *at first*, снача́ла, сперва́; *at home*, до́ма; *at last*, наконе́ц; *at least*, по кра́йней ме́ре; *at most*, са́мое бо́льшее; *at night*, но́чью; *at once*, (*immediately*) сра́зу; (*at the same time*) одновре́ме́нно; *at present*, в настоя́щее вре́мя; *at that*, на том; (*moreover*) к тому́ же; *at work*, (*working*) за рабо́той; (*at place of work*) на рабо́те.

atheism *n.* атеи́зм. **atheist** *n.* атеи́ст, ~ка. **atheistic** *adj.* атеисти́ческий.

athlete *n.* атле́т; легкоатле́т, ~ка; спортсме́н, ~ка. **athletic** *adj.* атлети́ческий. **athletics** *n.* (лёгкая) атле́тика.

atlas *n.* а́тлас.

atmosphere *n.* атмосфе́ра. **atmospheric** *adj.* атмосфе́рный. **atmospherics** *n.* атмосфе́рные поме́хи *f.pl.*

atom *n.* а́том; *a. bomb*, а́томная бо́мба. **atomic** *adj.* а́томный.

atone *v.i.* искупа́ть *imp.*, искупи́ть (-плю́, -пишь) *perf.* (for, +*acc.*). **atonement** *n.* искупле́ние.

atrocious *adj.* отврати́тельный, ужа́сный. **atrocity** *n.* зве́рство, у́жас.

atrophy *n.* атрофи́я, притупле́ние; *v.i.* атрофи́роваться *imp., perf.*

attach *v.t.* (*fasten*) прикрепля́ть *imp.*, прикрепи́ть *perf.*; (*fig.*) привя́зывать *imp.*, привяза́ть (-яжу́, -я́жешь) *perf.*; (*second*) прикомандиро́вывать *imp.*, прикомандирова́ть *perf.*; (*attribute*) придава́ть (-даю́, -даёшь) *imp.*, прида́ть (-а́м, -а́шь, -а́ст, -ади́м; при́дал, -а́, -о) *perf.* **attaché** *n.* атташе́ *m.indecl.* **attachment** *n.* прикрепле́ние; привя́занность; *pl.* принадле́жности *f.pl.*

attack *v.t.* напада́ть *imp.*, напа́сть (-аду́, -адёшь; -а́л) *perf.* на+*acc.*; *n.* нападе́ние; (*mil. also*) ата́ка; (*of illness*) припа́док (-дка).

attain *v.t.* достига́ть *imp.*, дости́чь & дости́гнуть (-и́гну, -и́гнешь; -и́г) *perf.*

+*gen.*, до+*gen.*; *a. the age of*, доживáть *imp.*, дожи́ть (-иву́, -ивёшь; до́жил, -á, -о) *perf.* до+*gen.* **attainment** *n.* достижéние.

attar (of roses) *n.* рóзовое мáсло.

attempt *v.t.* пытáться *imp.*, по~ *perf.*+*inf.*; прóбовать *imp.*, по~ *perf.*+*inf.*; *n.* попы́тка; (*on the life of*) покушéние (на жизнь+*gen.*); *make an a. on the life of*, покушáться *imp.*, покуси́ться *perf.* на жизнь+*gen.*

attend *v.i.* занимáться *imp.*, заня́ться (займу́сь, -мёшься; -я́лся́, -ялáсь) *perf.* (to, +*instr.*); (*be present*) присýтствовать *imp.* (at, на+*prep.*); *v.t.* (*accompany*) сопровождáть *imp.*, сопроводи́ть *perf.*; (*serve*) обслу́живать *imp.*, обслужи́ть (-жу́, -жишь) *perf.*; (*visit*) посещáть *imp.*, посети́ть (-ещу́, -ети́шь) *perf.* **attendance** *n.* (*presence*) присýтствие; посещáемость; обслу́живание. **attendant** *adj.* сопровождáющий; *n.* (*escort*) провожáтый *sb.*

attention *n.* внимáние; *pay a. to*, обращáть *imp.*, обрати́ть (-ащу́, -ати́шь) *perf.* внимáние на+*acc.*; *interj.* (*mil.*) сми́рно! **attentive** *adj.* внимáтельный; (*polite*) вéжливый.

attenuated *adj.* утончённый (-ён, -енá). **attenuation** *n.* утончéние.

attest *v.t.* заверя́ть *imp.*, завéрить *perf.*; свидéтельствовать *imp.*, за~ *perf.*

attic *n.* мансáрда, чердáк (-á); (*storey*) мезони́н.

attire *v.t.* наряжáть *imp.*, наряди́ть (-яжу́, -я́дишь) *perf.*; *n.* наря́д.

attitude *n.* (*posture*) пóза; (*opinion*) отношéние (towards, к+*dat.*); (*a. of mind*) склад умá.

attorney *n.* повéренный *sb.*; *by a.*, чéрез повéренного; *power of a.*, довéренность; *A.-General*, генерáльный аттóрней.

attract *v.t.* притя́гивать *imp.*, притяну́ть (-ну́, -нешь) *perf.*; прельщáть *imp.*, прельсти́ть *perf.*; привлекáть *imp.*, привлéчь (-екý, -ечёшь; -ёк, -еклá) *perf.* **attraction** *n.* притяжéние; привлекáтельность; (*entertainment*) аттракциóн. **attractive** *adj.* привлекáтельный, притягáтельный.

attribute *v.t.* припи́сывать *imp.*, приписáть (-ишу́, -и́шешь) *perf.*; *n.* (*object*) атрибýт; (*quality*) свóйство; (*gram.*) определéние. **attribution** *n.* припи́сывание. **attributive** *adj.* атрибути́вный, определи́тельный.

attrition *n.* истирáние; *war of a.*, войнá на истощéние.

aubergine *n.* баклажáн.

auburn *adj.* каштáнового цвéта, рыжевáтый.

auction *n.* аукциóн; *v.t.* продавáть (-даю́, -даёшь) *imp.*, продáть (-áм, -áшь, -áст, -ади́м; прóдал, -á, -о) *perf.* с аукциóна. **auctioneer** *n.* аукциони́ст.

audacious *adj.* (*bold*) смéлый (смел, -á, -о); (*impudent*) дéрзкий (-зок, -зкá, -зко). **audacity** *n.* смéлость; дéрзость.

audibility *n.* слы́шимость. **audible** *adj.* слы́шный (-шен, -шнá, -шно). **audience** *n.* пýблика, аудитóрия; (радио) слýшатели *m.pl.*, (теле)зри́тели *m.pl.*; (*interview*) аудиéнция. **audit** *n.* провéрка счетóв, реви́зия; *v.t.* проверя́ть *imp.*, провéрить *perf.* (счетá+*gen.*). **audition** *n.* прóба; *v.t.* & *i.* устрáивать *imp.*, устрóить *perf.* прóбу+*gen.* **auditor** *n.* ревизóр. **auditorium** *n.* зри́тельный зал, аудитóрия. **auditory** *adj.* слуховóй.

auger *n.* бурáв (-á), сверлó (*pl.* свёрла).

augment *n.* увели́чивать *imp.*, увели́чить *perf.*; прибавля́ть *imp.*, прибáвить *perf.*+*gen.* **augmentation** *n.* увеличéние, прибáвка. **augmentative** *adj.* увеличи́тельный.

augur *v.t.* & *i.* предвещáть *imp.*

August *n.* áвгуст; *attrib.* áвгустовский; **august** *adj.* вели́чественный (-ен, -енна).

aunt *n.* тётя (*gen.pl.* -тей), тётка. **auntie** *n.* тётушка.

aureole *n.* ореóл.

auriferous *adj.* золотонóсный.

aurochs *n.* тур.

aurora *n.* аврóра; *a. borealis*, сéверное сия́ние.

auspices *n.* покрови́тельство. **auspicious** *adj.* благоприя́тный.

austere *adj.* стрóгий (строг, -á, -о), сурóвый. **austerity** *n.* стрóгость, сурóвость.

austral *adj.* ю́жный.

Australian *n.* австрали́ец (-и́йца), -и́йка; *adj.* австрали́йский.

Austrian *n.* австри́ец (-и́йца), -и́йка; *adj.* австри́йский.

authentic *adj.* (*genuine*) по́длинный (-нен, -нна), аутенти́чный; (*reliable*) достове́рный. **authenticate** *v.t.* удостоверя́ть *imp.*, удостове́рить *perf.*; устана́вливать *imp.*, установи́ть (-влю́, -вишь) *perf.* по́длинность + *gen.* **authenticity** *n.* по́длинность, аутенти́чность; достове́рность.

author, authoress *n.* а́втор, писа́тель *m.*, ~ница.

authoritarian *adj.* авторита́рный; *n.* сторо́нник авторита́рной вла́сти. **authoritative** *adj.* авторите́тный. **authority** *n.* (*power*) власть (*pl.* -ти, -те́й), полномо́чие; (*evidence*) авторите́т; (*source*) авторите́тный исто́чник. **authorize** *v.t.* (*action*) разреша́ть *imp.*, разреши́ть *perf.*; (*person*) уполномо́чивать *imp.*, уполномо́чить *perf.*

authorship *n.* а́вторство.

auto- *in comb.* авто-. **autobiographer** *n.* автобио́граф. **autobiographical** автобиографи́ческий. **autobiography** *n.* автобиогра́фия. **autoclave** *n.* автокла́в. **autocracy** *n.* автокра́тия. **autocrat** *n.* автокра́т. **autocratic** *adj.* автократи́ческий. **autograph** *n.* авто́граф; *adj.* напи́санный руко́й а́втора; *v.t.* писа́ть (пишу́, -шешь) *imp.*, на~ *perf.* авто́граф в + *prep.*, на + *prep.* **automatic** *adj.* автомати́ческий; *n.* автомати́ческий пистоле́т. **automation** *n.* автоматиза́ция. **automaton** *n.* автома́т. **autonomous** *adj.* автоно́мный. **autonomy** *n.* автоно́мия. **autopilot** *n.* автопило́т. **autopsy** *n.* вскры́тие тру́па; ауто́псия. **autosuggestion** *n.* самовнуше́ние.

autumn *n.* о́сень. **autumn(al)** *adj.* осе́нний.

auxiliary *adj.* вспомога́тельный; *n.* помо́щник, -ица; (*gram.*) вспомога́тельный глаго́л; *pl.* вспомога́тельные войска́ *neut.pl.*

avail *n.*: *of no a.*, бесполе́зен (-зна); *to no a.*, напра́сно; *v.t.*: *a. oneself of*, по́льзоваться *imp.*, вос~ *perf.* + *instr.*

available *adj.* досту́пный, нали́чный; *predic.* налицо́, в нали́чии.

avalanche *n.* лави́на.

avarice *n.* жа́дность. **avaricious** *adj.* жа́дный (-ден, -дна́, -дно).

avenge *v.t.* мстить *imp.*, ото~ *perf.* за + *acc.* **avenger** *n.* мсти́тель *m.*

avenue *n.* (*of trees*) алле́я; (*wide street*) проспе́кт; (*approach*) путь (-ти́, -тём) *m.*

aver *v.t.* утвержда́ть *imp.*; заявля́ть *imp.*, заяви́ть (-влю́, -вишь) *perf.*

average *n.* сре́днее число́ (*pl.* -ла, -сел, -слам), сре́днее *sb.*; *on an, the, a.*, в сре́днем; *adj.* сре́дний; *v.t.* составля́ть *imp.* в сре́днем; де́лать *imp.* в сре́днем.

averse *adj.* нерасполо́женный (-ен), нескло́нный (-нен, -нна́, -нно); *not a. to*, не прочь + *inf.*, не про́тив + *gen.* **aversion** *n.* отвраще́ние. **avert** *v.t.* (*ward off*) предотвраща́ть *imp.*, предотврати́ть (-ащу́, -ати́шь) *perf.*; (*turn away*) отводи́ть (-ожу́, -о́дишь) *imp.*, отвести́ (отведу́, -дёшь; отвёл, -а́) *perf.*

aviary *n.* пти́чник.

aviation *n.* авиа́ция. **aviator** *n.* лётчик.

avid *adj.* а́лчный, жа́дный (-ден, -дна́, -дно). **avidity** *n.* а́лчность, жа́дность.

avoid *v.t.* избега́ть *imp.*, избежа́ть (-егу́, -ежи́шь) *perf.* + *gen.*; уклоня́ться *imp.*, уклони́ться (-ню́сь, -нишься) *perf.* от + *gen.* **avoidance** *n.* избежа́ние, уклоне́ние.

avoirdupois *n.* эвердьюпо́йс.

avowal *n.* призна́ние.

await *v.t.* ждать (жду, ждёшь; ждал, -а́, -о) *imp.* + *gen.*; *to a. arrival*, до востре́бования.

awake *predic.*: *be a.*, не спать (сплю, спишь) *imp.*; *be a. to*, понима́ть *imp.*; *stay a.*, бо́дрствовать *imp.* **awake(n)** *v.t.* пробужда́ть *imp.*, пробуди́ть (-ужу́, -у́дишь) *perf.*; *v.i.* просыпа́ться *imp.*, просну́ться *perf.*

award *v.t.* присужда́ть *imp.*, присуди́ть (-ужу́, -у́дишь) *perf.*; награжда́ть *imp.*, награди́ть *perf.*; *n.* (*prize*) награ́да, пре́мия; (*decision*) присужде́ние.

aware *predic.*: *be a. of*, сознава́ть (-аю́, -аёшь) *imp.* + *acc.*; знать *imp.* + *acc.*

away *adv.* прочь; *far a.* (*from*), далеко́ (от+*gen.*); *a. game*, игра́ (*pl.* -ры) на чужо́м по́ле; *a. team*, кома́нда госте́й.

awe *n.* благогове́йный страх; *stand in a. of*, испы́тывать *imp.* благогове́йный тре́пет пе́ред+*instr.*; *v.t.* внуша́ть *imp.*, внуши́ть *perf.* (благогове́йный) страх+*dat.*; *a.-struck*, преиспо́лненный (-ен) благогове́йного стра́ха, благогове́ния. **awful** *adj.* ужа́сный, стра́шный (-шен, -шна́, -шно, стра́шны́). **awfully** *adv.* ужа́сно, о́чень, стра́шно.

awkward *adj.* нело́вкий (-вок, -вка́, -вко). **awkwardness** *n.* нело́вкость.

awl *n.* ши́ло (*pl.* -лья, -льев).

awning *n.* наве́с, тент.

awry *adv.* кри́во, на́бок; *go a.*, провали́ться (-ится) *perf.*

axe *n.* топо́р (-а́); *v.t.* уре́зывать, уреза́ть *imp.*, уре́зать (-е́жу, -е́жешь) *perf.*

axial *adj.* осево́й.

axiom *n.* аксио́ма. **axiomatic** *adj.* аксиомати́ческий.

axis, axle *n.* ось (*pl.* о́си, осе́й).

ay *interj.* да!; *n.* положи́тельный отве́т; (*in vote*) го́лос (*pl.* -а́) „за"; *the ayes have it*, большинство́ „за".

azure *n.* лазу́рь; *adj.* лазу́рный.

B

B *n.* (*mus.*) си *neut.indecl.* **B.A.** *abbr.* бакала́вр.

babble *n.* (*voices*) болтовня́; (*water*) журча́ние; *v.i.* болта́ть *imp*; журча́ть (-чи́т) *imp.*

babel *n.* галдёж (-а́); *tower of B.*, столпотворе́ние вавило́нское.

baboon *n.* павиа́н.

baby *n.* младе́нец (-нца); *b.-sitter*, приходя́щая ня́ня; *adj.* ма́лый (мал, -а́, ма́ло́, -ы́), де́тский. **babyish** *adj.* ребя́ческий.

Bacchanalia *n.* вакхана́лия. **Bacchanalian** *adj.* вакхи́ческий. **Bacchante** *n.* вакха́нка.

bachelor *n.* холостя́к (-а́); (*degree-holder*) бакала́вр; *adj.* холосто́й (-ост).

bacillus *n.* баци́лла.

back *n.* (*of body*) спина́ (*acc.* -ну; *pl.* -ны); (*rear*) за́дняя часть (*pl.* -ти, -те́й); (*reverse*) оборо́т; (*of book*) корешо́к (-шка́); (*of seat*) спи́нка; (*sport*) защи́тник; *adj.* за́дний; (*overdue*) просро́ченный (-ен); *v.t.* подде́рживать *imp.*, поддержа́ть (-жу́, -жишь) *perf.*; *v.i.* пя́титься *imp.* по~ *perf.*; отступа́ть *imp.*, отступи́ть (-плю́, -пишь) *perf.*; *b. down*, уступа́ть *imp.*, уступи́ть (-плю́, -пишь) *perf.*; *b. out*, уклоня́ться *imp.*, уклони́ться (-ню́сь, -ни́шься) *perf.* (of, от+*gen.*). **backbiter** *n.* клеветни́к (-а́). **backbiting** *n.* клевета́. **backbone** *n.* позвоно́чник; (*support*) гла́вная опо́ра; (*firmness*) твёрдость хара́ктера. **backer** *n.* лицо́ (*pl.* -ца), субсиди́рующее и́ли подде́рживающее предприя́тие; сторо́нник. **background** *n.* фон, за́дний план; (*person's*) воспита́ние, происхожде́ние, окруже́ние. **backside** *n.* зад (*loc.* -у́; *pl.* -ы́). **backslider** *n.* ренега́т, рецидиви́ст. **backward** *adj.* отста́лый; *adv.* наза́д. **backwash** *n.* отка́т (воды́). **backwater** *n.* за́водь, зато́н.

bacon *n.* бе́кон, груди́нка.

bacterium *n.* бакте́рия.

bad *adj.* плохо́й (плох, -а́, -о, пло́хи́); (*food etc.*) испо́рченный (-ен); (*language*) гру́бый (груб, -а́, -о); *b. taste*, безвку́сица.

badge *n.* значо́к (-чка́), эмбле́ма.

badger *n.* барсу́к (-а́); *v.t.* пристава́ть (-таю́, -таёшь) *imp.*, приста́ть (-а́ну,

-áнешь) *perf.* к + *dat.*; трави́ть (-влю́, -вишь) *imp.*, за~ *perf.*

badly *adv.* пло́хо; (*very much*) о́чень, си́льно.

baffle *v.t.* ста́вить *imp.*, по~ *perf.* в тупи́к; приводи́ть (-ожу́, -о́дишь) *imp.*, привести́ (-еду́, -едёшь; привёл, -а́) *perf.* в недоуме́ние; *n.* экра́н.

bag *n.* мешо́к (-шка́), су́мка; *v.t.* (*game*) убива́ть *imp.*, уби́ть (убью́, убьёшь) *perf.*; *v.i.* (*clothes*) сиде́ть (сиди́т) *imp.*, сесть (ся́дет; сел) *perf.* мешко́м.

baggage *n.* бага́ж (-а́(у́)); *adj.* бага́жный.

baggy *adj.* мешкова́тый.

bagpipe *n.* волы́нка. **bagpiper** *n.* волы́нщик.

bail[1] *n.* (*security*) поручи́тельство, зало́г; (*surety*) поручи́тель *m.*, -ница; *v.t.* (*b. out*) брать (беру́, -рёшь; брал, -а́, -о) *imp.*, взять (возьму́, -мёшь; взял, -а́, -о) *perf.* на пору́ки.

bail[2] *n.* (*cricket*) перекла́дина воро́т.

bail[3], **bale**[2] *v.t.* выче́рпывать *imp.*, вы́черпнуть *perf.* (во́ду из + *gen.*); *b. out*, *v.i.* выбра́сываться *imp.*, вы́броситься *perf.* с парашю́том. **bailer** *n.* черпа́к (-а́).

bait *n.* нажи́вка; прима́нка (*also fig.*); (*fig.*) собла́зн; *v.t.* (*torment*) трави́ть (-влю́, -вишь) *imp.*, за~ *perf.*

baize *n.* ба́йка.

bake *v.t.* печь (пеку́, печёшь; пёк, -ла́) *imp.*, ис~ *perf.*; (*bricks*) обжига́ть *imp.*, обже́чь (обожгу́, -жжёшь; обжёг, обожгла́) *perf.* **baker** *n.* пе́карь *m.*, бу́лочник. **bakery** *n.* пека́рня (*gen.pl.* -рен), бу́лочная *sb.* **baking** *n.* пече́ние, вы́печка.

balance *n.* (*scales*) весы́ *m.pl.*; (*equilibrium*) равнове́сие; (*econ.*) бала́нс; (*remainder*) оста́ток (-тка); *b. sheet*, бала́нс; *v.t.* уравнове́шивать *imp.*, уравнове́сить *perf.*; (*econ.*) баланси́ровать *imp.*, с~ *perf.*

balcony *n.* балко́н.

bald *adj.* лы́сый (лыс, -а́, -о), плеши́вый; *b. patch*, лы́сина.

baldness *n.* плеши́вость.

bale[1] *n.* (*bundle*) тюк (-а́), ки́па; *v.t.* укла́дывать *imp.*, уложи́ть (-жу́, -жишь) *perf.* в тюки́, ки́пы.

bale[2] *see* **bail**[3].

baleful *adj.* па́губный, мра́чный (-чен, -чна́, -чно).

balk *n.* ба́лка; (*hindrance*) препя́тствие; *v.t.* препя́тствовать *imp.*, вос~ *perf.* + *dat.*

ball[1] *n.* (*sphere*) мяч (-а́), шар (-а́ *with 2, 3, 4*; *pl.* -ы́), клубо́к (-бка́); *b. and socket*, шарово́й шарни́р; *b.-bearing*, шарикоподши́пник; *b.-point* (*pen*), ша́риковая ру́чка.

ball[2] *n.* (*dancing*) бал (*loc.* -у́; *pl.* -ы́).

ballad, ballade (*mus.*) *n.* балла́да.

ballast *n.* балла́ст (-а); *v.t.* грузи́ть (-ужу́, -у́зи́шь) *imp.*, за~, на~ *perf.* балла́стом.

ballerina *n.* балери́на.

ballet *n.* бале́т; *b.-dancer*, арти́ст, ~ка, бале́та, танцо́вщик, -ица.

balloon *n.* возду́шный шар (-а́ *with 2, 3, 4*; *pl.* -ы́); *v.i.* раздува́ться *imp.*, разду́ться (-у́ется) *perf.*

ballot *n.* голосова́ние, баллотиро́вка; *b.-paper*, избира́тельный бюллете́нь *m.*; *v.i.* голосова́ть *imp.*, про~ *perf.*

ballyhoo *n.* шуми́ха.

balm *n.* бальза́м. **balmy** *adj.* (*fragrant*) души́стый; (*crazy*) тро́нутый.

baluster *n.* баля́сина. **balustrade** *n.* балюстра́да.

bamboo *n.* бамбу́к.

bamboozle *v.t.* одура́чивать *imp.*, одура́чить *perf.*

ban *n.* запре́т, запреще́ние; *v.t.* запреща́ть *imp.*, запрети́ть (-ещу́, -ети́шь) *perf.*

banal *adj.* бана́льный.

banana *n.* бана́н.

band *n.* (*strip*) обо́д (*pl.* обо́дья, -ьев), тесьма́, поло́ска, кайма́ (*gen.pl.* каём); (*of people*) гру́ппа; (*mus.*) орке́стр; (*radio*) полоса́ (*acc.* по́лосу; *pl.* -осы, -о́с, -оса́м) часто́т; *v.i.*: *b. together*, объединя́ться *imp.*, объедини́ться *perf.*

bandage *n.* бинт (-а́), повя́зка; *v.t.* бинтова́ть *imp.*, за~ *perf.*

bandeau *n.* повя́зка, ободо́к (-дка́).

bandit *n.* банди́т.

bandoleer *n.* патронта́ш.

bandy *v.t.* (*throw about*) перебра́сываться *imp.*, перебро́ситься *perf.* + *instr.*

bandy-legged *adj.* кривоно́гий.

bane *n.* (*ruin*) ги́бель; (*poison*; *fig.*) отра́ва. **baneful** *adj.* ги́бельный, ядови́тый.

bang *n.* (*blow*) (си́льный) уда́р; (*noise*) (гро́мкий) стук; (*of gun*) вы́стрел; *v.t.* ударя́ть *imp.*, уда́рить *perf.*; хло́пать *imp.*, хло́пнуть *perf.*; стуча́ть (-чу́, -чи́шь) *imp.*, сту́кнуть *perf.*

bangle *n.* брасле́т.

banish *v.t.* изгоня́ть *imp.*, изгна́ть (-гоню́, -го́нишь; изгна́л, -а́, -о) *perf.*; высыла́ть *imp.*, вы́слать (вы́шлю, -шлешь) *perf.* **banishment** *n.* изгна́ние, вы́сылка, ссы́лка.

banister *n.* пери́ла *neut.pl.*

banjo *n.* банджо́ *neut.indecl.*

bank[1] *n.* (*of river*) бе́рег (*loc.* -у́; *pl.* -а́); (*in sea*) о́тмель; (*of earth*) вал (*loc.* -у́; *pl.* -ы́); (*aeron.*) крен; *v.t.* сгреба́ть *imp.*, сгрести́ (-ебу́, -ебёшь; сгрёб, -ла́) *perf.* в ку́чу.

bank[2] *n.* (*econ.*) банк, фонд; *b. holiday*, устано́вленный пра́здник; *v.i.* (*keep money*) держа́ть (-жу́, -жишь) *imp.* де́ньги (в ба́нке); *v.t.* (*put in bank*) класть (кладу́, -дёшь; клал) *imp.*, положи́ть (-жу́, -жишь) *perf.* в банк; *b. on*, полага́ться *imp.*, положи́ться (-жу́сь, -жишься) *perf.* на + *acc.*

bankrupt *n.* банкро́т; *adj.* обанкро́тившийся; *v.t.* доводи́ть (-ожу́, -о́дишь) *imp.*, довести́ (-еду́, -едёшь; -ёл, -ела́) *perf.* до банкро́тства. **bankruptcy** *n.* банкро́тство.

banner *n.* зна́мя (*pl.* -ёна) *neut.*, флаг; *b. headline*, ша́пка.

bannister *see* **banister.**

banquet *n.* банке́т, пир (*loc.* -у́; *pl.* -ы́).

bantam *n.* бента́мка. **bantamweight** *n.* легча́йший вес.

banter *n.* подшу́чивание; *v.i.* шути́ть (шучу́, шу́тишь) *imp.*

baptism *n.* креще́ние. **baptize** *v.t.* крести́ть (-ещу́, -е́стишь) *imp.*, о~ *perf.*

bar *n.* (*beam*) брус (*pl.* -ья, -ьев), полоса́ (*acc.* по́лосу́; *pl.* -осы, -о́с -оса́м); (*of chocolate*) пли́тка; (*of soap*) кусо́к (-ска́); (*barrier*) прегра́да, барье́р; (*leg.*) колле́гия юри́стов; (*counter*) сто́йка, (*room*) бар; (*mus.*) такт; *v.t.* (*obstruct*) прегражда́ть *imp.*, прегради́ть *perf.*; (*prohibit*) запреща́ть *imp.*, запрети́ть (-ещу́, -ети́шь) *perf.*

barb *n.* зубе́ц (-бца́); *barbed wire*, колю́чая про́волока.

barbarian *n.* ва́рвар; *adj.* ва́рварский. **barbaric, barbarous** *adj.* ва́рварский, гру́бый (груб, -а́, -о).

barber *n.* парикма́хер; *b.'s shop*, парикма́херская *sb.*

bard *n.* бард, певе́ц (-вца́).

bare *adj.* (*naked*) го́лый (гол, -а́, -о); (*barefoot*) бо́сой (бос, -а́, -о); (*exposed*) обнажённый (-ён, -ена́); (*unadorned*) неприкра́шенный (-ен); (*scanty*) минима́льный; *v.t.* обнажа́ть *imp.*, обнажи́ть *perf.*; *b. one's head*, снима́ть *imp.*, снять (сниму́, -мешь; снял, -а́, -о) *perf.* шля́пу, ша́пку. **barefaced** *adj.* на́глый (нагл, -а́, -о). **barely** *adv.* едва́, чуть не, е́ле-е́ле, лишь (с трудо́м).

bargain *n.* вы́годная сде́лка, дешёвая поку́пка; *v.i.* торгова́ться *imp.*, с~ *perf.*

barge *n.* ба́ржа, ба́рка; *v.i.*: *b. into*, ната́лкиваться *imp.*, натолкну́ться *perf.* на + *acc.* **bargee** *n.* ло́дочник.

baritone *n.* барито́н.

barium *n.* ба́рий.

bark[1] *n.* (*sound*) лай; *v.i.* ла́ять (ла́ю, ла́ешь) *imp.*

bark[2] *n.* (*of tree*) кора́; *v.t.* сдира́ть *imp.*, содра́ть (сдеру́, -рёшь; содра́л, -а́, -о) *perf.* ко́жу с + *gen.*

barley *n.* ячме́нь (-ня́) *m.*

barm *n.* заква́ска.

barmaid *n.* буфе́тчица. **barman** *n.* ба́рмен, буфе́тчик.

barn *n.* амба́р.

barometer *n.* баро́метр. **barometric(al)** *adj.* барометри́ческий.

baron *n.* баро́н. **baroness** *n.* баро́не́сса. **baronet** *n.* бароне́т. **baronial** *adj.* баро́нский.

baroque *n.* баро́кко *neut.indecl.*

barrack[1] *n.* каза́рма.

barrack[2] *v.t.* осви́стывать *imp.*, освиста́ть (-ищу́, -и́щешь) *perf.*

barrage *n.* загражде́ние, барра́ж.

barrel *n.* (*vessel*) бо́чка; (*of gun*) ду́ло; *b.-organ*, шарма́нка.

barren *adj.* беспло́дный.

barricade *n.* баррика́да, прегра́да; *v.t.* баррикади́ровать *imp.*, за~ *perf.*
barrier *n.* барье́р, прегра́да, шлагба́ум.
barring *prep.* за исключе́нием + *gen.*
barrister *n.* адвока́т.
barrow[1] *n.* (*tumulus*) курга́н.
barrow[2] *n.* (*cart*) та́чка.
barter *n.* менова́я торго́вля; *v.i.* обме́ниваться *imp.*, обменя́ться *perf.* това́рами.
base[1] *adj.* (*low*) ни́зкий (-зок, -зка́, -зко), по́длый (подл, -а́, -о); (*metal, also fig.*) низкопро́бный.
base[2] *n.* осно́ва, основа́ние, (*also mil.*) ба́за; *v.t.* осно́вывать *imp.*, основа́ть (-ную́, -нуёшь) *perf.* **baseless** *adj.* необосно́ванный. **baseline** *n.* (*sport*) за́дняя ли́ния площа́дки. **basement** *n.* цо́кольный эта́ж (-а́), подва́л.
bash *v.t.* колоти́ть (-очу́, -о́тишь) *imp.*, по~ *perf.*
bashful *adj.* засте́нчивый. **bashfulness** *n.* засте́нчивость.
basic *adj.* основно́й.
basil *n.* базили́к.
basin *n.* (*vessel*) ми́ска, таз (*loc.* -у́; *pl.* -ы́); (*geog., geol.*) бассе́йн; (*pool*) водоём.
basis *n.* ба́зис, осно́ва.
bask *v.i.* гре́ться *imp.*; (*fig.*) наслажда́ться *imp.*, наслади́ться *perf.* (in, + *instr.*).
basket *n.* корзи́на, корзи́нка. **basketball** *n.* баскетбо́л; *adj.* баскетбо́льный.
bas-relief *n.* барелье́ф.
bass[1] *n.* (*mus.*) бас (*pl.* -ы́); *adj.* басо́вый; *b. drum*, большо́й бараба́н.
bass[2] *n.* (*fish*) о́кунь (*pl.* -ни, -не́й) *m.*
bassoon *n.* фаго́т.
bastard *n.* внебра́чный, побо́чный, ребёнок (-нка; *pl.* де́ти, дете́й); *adj.* незаконнорождённый.
baste[1] *v.t.* (*tack*) мета́ть *imp.*, на~, с~ *perf.*
baste[2] *v.t.* (*cul.*) полива́ть *imp.*, поли́ть (-лью́, -льёшь) *perf.* жи́ром.
baste[3] *v.t.* (*thrash*) дуба́сить *imp.*, от~ *perf.*
bastion *n.* бастио́н.
bat[1] *n.* (*zool.*) лету́чая мышь (*pl.* -ши, -ше́й).
bat[2] *n.* (*sport*) бита́; *v.i.* бить (бью, бьёшь) *imp.*, по~ *perf.* по мячу́.
bat[3] *v.t.* (*wink*) морга́ть *imp.*, моргну́ть *perf.* + *instr.*, *abs.*
batch *n.* па́чка; (*of loaves*) вы́печка.
bated *adj.* уме́ренный (-ен); *with b. breath*, затаи́в дыха́ние.
bath *n.* (*vessel*) ва́нна; *pl.* пла́вательный бассе́йн; *b. house*, ба́ня; *b. robe*, купа́льный хала́т; *v.t.* купа́ть *imp.*, вы́~, ис~ *perf.* **bathe** *v.i.* купа́ться *imp.*, вы́~, ис~ *perf.*; *v.t.* омыва́ть *imp.*, омы́ть (омо́ю, омо́ешь) *perf.* **bather** *n.* купа́льщик, -ица. **bathing** *n.* купа́ние; *b. costume*, купа́льный костю́м. **bathroom** *n.* ва́нная *sb.*
batiste *n.* бати́ст.
batman *n.* (*mil.*) денщи́к (-а́).
baton *n.* (*mil.*) жезл (-а́); (*police*) дуби́нка; (*sport*) эстафе́та; (*mus.*) дирижёрская па́лочка.
battalion *n.* батальо́н.
batten *n.* ре́йка; *v.t.* закола́чивать *imp.*, заколоти́ть (-очу́, -о́тишь) *perf.* доска́ми.
batter *n.* жи́дкое те́сто; *v.t.* разбива́ть *imp.*, разби́ть (разобью́, -ьёшь) *perf.*; размозжи́ть *perf.*; *battering-ram*, тара́н.
battery *n.* (*mil., tech.*) батаре́я; (*leg.*) оскорбле́ние де́йствием.
battle *n.* би́тва, сраже́ние, бой (*loc.* бою́; *pl.* бои́); *adj.* боево́й. **battlefield** *n.* по́ле (*pl.* -ля́) бо́я. **battlement** *n.* зубча́тая стена́ (*acc.* -ну; *pl.* -ны, -н, -на́м). **battleship** *n.* лине́йный кора́бль (-ля́) *m.*, линко́р.
bauble *n.* безделу́шка.
bawdy *adj.* непристо́йный; *b.-house*, публи́чный дом (*pl.* -а́).
bawl *v.i.* ора́ть (ору́, орёшь) *imp.*
bay[1] *n.* (*bot.*) ла́вр(овое де́рево); *pl.* лавро́вый вено́к (-нка́), ла́вры *m.pl.*; *adj.* лавро́вый.
bay[2] *n.* (*geog.*) зали́в, бу́хта.
bay[3] *n.* (*recess*) пролёт; *b. window*, фона́рь (-ря́) *m.*; *sick b.*, лазаре́т.
bay[4] *v.i.* (*bark*) ла́ять (ла́ю, ла́ешь) *imp.*; (*howl*) выть (во́ю, во́ешь) *imp.*; *n.* лай; вой.
bay[5] *adj.* (*colour*) гнедо́й.

bayonet *n.* штык (-á); *v.t.* колóть (-лю́, -лешь) *imp.*, за~ *perf.* штыкóм.
bazaar *n.* базáр.
be[1] *v.* **1.** быть (*fut.* бýду, -дешь; был, -á, -о; нé был, -á, -о): *usually omitted in pres.*: *he is a teacher*, он учи́тель; + *instr. or nom. in past and fut.*: *he was, will be, a teacher*, он был, бýдет, учи́телем. **2.** (*exist*) существовáть *imp.* **3.** (*frequentative*) бывáть *imp.* **4.** (*be situated*) находи́ться (-ожýсь, -óдишься) *imp.*: *where is the information office?* где нахóдится спрáвочное бюрó?; (*upright*) стоя́ть (-ою́, -ои́шь) *imp.*: *the piano is against the wall*, роя́ль стои́т у стены́; (*laid flat*) лежáть (-жý, -жи́шь) *imp.*: *the letter is on the table*, письмó лежи́т на столé. **5.** (*in general definitions*) явля́ться *imp.* + *instr.*: *Moscow is the capital of the USSR*, столи́цей СССР явля́ется гóрод Москвá. **6.** *there is, are*, имéется, имéются; (*emph.*) есть.
be[2] *v.aux.* **1.** *be + inf.*, *expressing duty, plan*: дóлжен (-жнá) + *inf.*: *he is to leave on Monday*, он дóлжен отпрáвится в понедéльник. **2.** *be + past part. pass.*, *expressing passive*: быть + *past part. pass. in short form*: *this was made by my son*, э́то бы́ло сдéлано мои́м сы́ном; *impersonal construction of 3 pl. + acc.*: *I was beaten*, меня́ би́ли; *reflexive construction*: *music was heard*, слы́шалась мýзыка. **3.** *be + pres. part. act.*, *expressing continuous tenses*: *imperfective aspect*: *I am reading*, я читáю.
beach *n.* пляж, бéрег (*loc.* -ý; *pl.* -á); *b.-head*, плацдáрм; *v.t.* вытáскивать *imp.*, вы́тащить *perf.* на бéрег.
beacon *n.* маяк (-á), сигнáльный огóнь (огня́) *m.*
bead *n.* бýсина; (*of liquid*) кáпля (*gen. pl.* -пель); *pl.* бýсы *f.pl.*
beadle *n.* церкóвный стóрож (*pl.* -á).
beagle *n.* (коротконóгая) гóнчая *sb.*
beak *n.* клюв.
beaker *n.* стакáн.
beam *n.* (*timber etc.*) бáлка; (*ray*) луч (-á); (*naut.*) бимс; (*breadth*) ширинá; *v.t.* испускáть *imp.*, испусти́ть (-ущý, -ýстишь) *perf.*; *v.i.* (*shine*) сия́ть *imp.*
bean *n.* фасóль, боб (-á).
bear[1] *n.* медвéдь *m.*, -дица; *Great, Little, B.*, Большáя, Мáлая, Медвéдица; *b.-cub*, медвежóнок (-жóнка; *pl.* -жáта, -жáт).
bear[2] *v.t.* (*carry*) носи́ть (ношý, нóсишь) *indet.*, нести́ (несý, -сёшь; нёс, -лá) *det.*, по~ *perf.*; (*support*) поддéрживать *imp.*, поддержáть (-жý, -жишь) *perf.*; (*endure*) терпéть (-плю́, -пишь) *imp.*; выноси́ть (-ошý, -óсишь) *imp.*, вы́нести (-су, -сешь; -с) *perf.*; (*give birth to*) рождáть *imp.*, роди́ть *imp.*, (роди́л, -á, -о) *perf.* **bearable** *adj.* снóсный, терпи́мый.
beard *n.* бородá (*acc.* -оду; *pl.* -оды, -óд, -одáм). **bearded** *adj.* бородáтый.
bearer *n.* носи́тель *m.*; (*of cheque*) предъяви́тель *m.*; (*of letter*) подáтель *m.*
bearing *n.* ношéние; (*behaviour*) поведéние; (*relation*) отношéние; (*position*) пéленг; (*tech.*) подши́пник, опóра.
beast *n.* живóтное *sb.*, зверь (*pl.* -ри, -рéй) *m.*; (*fig.*) скоти́на *m.* & *f.* **beastly** *adj.* (*coll.*) проти́вный, отврати́тельный.
beat *n.* бой; (*round*) обхóд; (*mus.*) такт; *v.t.* бить (бью, бьёшь) *imp.*, по~ *perf.*; (*cul.*) взбивáть *imp.*, взбить (взобью́, -ьёшь) *perf.*; *b. a carpet*, выбивáть *imp.*, вы́бить (-бью, -бьешь) *perf.* ковёр; *b. off*, отбивáть *imp.*, отби́ть (отобью́, -ьёшь) *perf.*; *b. time*, отбивáть *imp.*, отби́ть (отобью́, -ьёшь) *perf.* такт; *b. up*, избивáть *imp.*, изби́ть (изобью́, -ьёшь) *perf.* **beating** *n.* битьё; (*defeat*) поражéние; биéние.
beatific *adj.* блажéнный (-éн -éнна). **beatify** *v.t.* канонизи́ровать *imp.*, *perf.* **beatitude** *n.* блажéнство.
beau *n.* (*fop*) франт; (*ladies' man*) ухажёр.
beautiful *adj.* краси́вый, прекрáсный. **beautify** *v.t.* украшáть *imp.* укрáсить *perf.* **beauty** *n.* (*quality*) красотá; (*person*) красáвица.
beaver *n.* (*animal*) бобр (-á); (*fur*) бобёр (-брá), бобрóвый мех (-а(у), *loc.* -е & -ý; *pl.* -á).

becalmed *adj.*: *be b.* штилева́ть (-лю́ю, -лю́ешь) *imp.*

because *conj.* потому́ что, так как; *adv.*: *b. of*, из-за + *gen.*

beckon *v.t.* мани́ть (-ню́, -нишь) *imp.*, по~ *perf.* к себе́.

become *v.i.* станови́ться (-влю́сь, -вишься) *imp.*, стать (-а́ну, -а́нешь) *perf.* + *instr.*; *b. of*, ста́ться (-а́нется) *perf.* с + *instr.* **becoming** *adj.* подоба́ющий, иду́щий к лицу́ + *dat.*

bed *n.* крова́ть, посте́ль; (*garden*) гря́дка; (*sea*) дно *pl.* до́нья, -ьев; (*river*) ру́сло; (*geol.*) пласт (-а́, *loc.* -у́). **bedclothes, bedding** *n.* посте́льное бельё. **bedridden** *adj.* прико́ванный (-на) к посте́ли боле́знью. **bedrock** *n.* материко́вая поро́да. **bedroom** *n.* спа́льня (*gen.pl.* -лен). **bedtime** *n.* вре́мя *neut.* ложи́ться спать.

bedeck *v.t.* украша́ть *imp.*, укра́сить *perf.*

bedevil *v.t.* терза́ть *imp.*; му́чить *imp.*, за~ *perf.*

bedlam *n.* бедла́м, сумасше́дший дом.

bedraggled *adj.* заво́женный (-ен).

bee *n.* пчела́ (*pl.* -ёлы). **beehive** *n.* у́лей (у́лья).

beech *n.* бук.

beef *n.* говя́дина.

beer *n.* пи́во. **beer(y)** *adj.* пивно́й.

beet *n.* свёкла.

beetle[1] *n.* (*tool*) трамбо́вка, кува́лда.

beetle[2] *n.* (*insect*) жук (-а́).

beetle[3] *adj.* нависа́ющий.

beetroot *n.* свёкла.

befall *v.t.* & *i.* случа́ться *imp.*, случи́ться *perf.* (+ *dat.*).

befit *v.t.* подходи́ть (-ит) *imp.*, подойти́ (-ойдёт; -ошёл, -ошла́) *perf.* + *dat.*

before *adv.* пре́жде, ра́ньше; *prep.* пе́ред + *instr.*, до + *gen.*; *conj.* до того́ как, пре́жде чем; (*rather than*) скоре́е чем; *the day b. yesterday*, позавчера́. **beforehand** *adv.* зара́нее, вперёд.

befriend *v.t.* ока́зывать *imp.*, оказа́ть (-ажу́, -а́жешь) *perf.* дру́жескую по́мощь + *dat.*

beg *v.i.* ни́щенствовать *imp.*; *v.t.* (*ask*) проси́ть (-ошу́, -о́сишь) *imp.*, по~ *perf.*; (*of dog*) служи́ть (-ит) *imp.*; *b. pardon*, проси́ть (-ошу́, -о́сишь) *imp.* проще́ние.

beget *v.t.* порожда́ть *imp.*, породи́ть *perf.*

beggar *n.* ни́щий *sb.*; *v.t.* разоря́ть *imp.*, разори́ть *perf.* **beggarliness** *n.* нищета́. **beggarly** *adj.* (*poor*) бе́дный (-ден, -дна́, -дно); (*mean*) жа́лкий (-лок, -лка́, -лко).

begin *v.t.* начина́ть *imp.*, нача́ть (-чну́, -чнёшь; на́чал, -а́, -о) *perf.*; *v.i.* начина́ться *imp.*, нача́ться (-чну́сь, -чнёшься; -алс́я, -ала́сь) *perf.* **beginner** *n.* начина́ющий *sb.*, новичо́к (-чка́). **beginning** *n.* нача́ло.

begonia *n.* бего́ния.

begrudge *v.t.* (*spare*) скупи́ться *imp.*, по~ *perf.* на + *acc.*, + *inf.*

beguile *v.t.* (*amuse*) развлека́ть *imp.*, развле́чь (-еку́, -ечёшь; -ёк, -екла́) *perf.*

behalf *n.*: *on b. of*, от и́мени + *gen.*; (*in interest of*) в по́льзу + *gen.*

behave *v.i.* вести́ (веду́, -дёшь; вёл, -а́) *imp.* себя́. **behaviour** *n.* поведе́ние.

behead *v.t.* обезгла́вливать *imp.*, обезгла́вить *perf.*

behest *n.* заве́т.

behind *adv.*, *prep.* сза́ди (+ *gen.*), позади́ (+ *gen.*), за (+ *acc.*, *instr.*); *n.* зад (*loc.* -у́; *pl.* -ы́).

behold *interj.* се! **beholden** *predic.*: *b. to*, обя́зан + *dat.*

beige *adj.* беж *indecl.*, бе́жевый.

being *n.* (*existence*) бытие́ (*instr.* -ие́м, *prep.* -ии́); (*creature*) существо́; *for the time being*, на не́которое вре́мя; вре́менно.

belabour *v.t.* бить (бью, бьёшь) *imp.*, по~ *perf.*

belated *adj.* запозда́лый.

belch *n.* отры́жка; *v.i.* рыга́ть *imp.*, рыгну́ть *perf.*; *v.t.* изверга́ть *imp.*, изве́ргнуть (-г(нул), -гла) *perf.*

beleaguer *v.t.* осажда́ть *imp.*, осади́ть *perf.*

belfry *n.* колоко́льня (*gen.pl.* -лен).

belie *v.t.* противоре́чить *imp.* + *dat.*

belief *n.* (*faith*) ве́ра; (*confidence*) убежде́ние. **believable** *adj.* вероя́тный, правдоподо́бный. **believe** *v.t.* ве́рить

imp., по~ *perf.* + *dat.*; *I b. so*, ка́жется так; *I b. not*, ду́маю, что нет; едва́ ли.
belittle *v.t.* умаля́ть *imp.*, умали́ть *perf.*
bell *n.* ко́локол (*pl.* -а́); (*small*) колоко́льчик, бубе́нчик; *b.-bottomed trousers*, брю́ки (-к) *pl.* с растру́бами; *b.-ringer*, звона́рь (-ря́) *m.*; *b. tower*, колоко́льня (*gen.pl.* -лен).
belle *n.* краса́вица.
belles-lettres *n.* худо́жественная литерату́ра.
bellicose *adj.* вои́нственный (-ен, -енна), агресси́вный. **belligerency** *n.* вои́нственность. **belligerent** *n.* вою́ющая сторона́ (*acc.* -ону; *pl.* -оны, -о́н, -она́м); *adj.* вою́ющий.
bellow *n.* мыча́ние, рёв; *v.t.* & *i.* мыча́ть (-чу́, -чи́шь) *imp.*; реве́ть (-ву́, -вёшь) *imp.*
bellows *n.* мехи́ *m.pl.*
belly *n.* живо́т (-а́), брю́хо (*pl.* -хи).
belong *v.i.* принадлежа́ть (-жу́, -жи́шь) *imp.* (to, (к) + *dat.*). **belongings** *n.* пожи́тки (-ков) *pl.*, ве́щи (-ще́й) *f.pl.*
beloved *adj.* люби́мый, возлю́бленный (-ен, -енна).
below *adv.* вниз, внизу́, ни́же; *prep.* ни́же + *gen.*
belt *n.* (*strap*) по́яс (*pl.* -а́), реме́нь (-мня́); (*zone*) зо́на, полоса́ (*acc.* -осу; *pl.* -осы, -о́с, -оса́м); *v.t.* подпоя́сывать *imp.*, подпоя́сать (-я́шу, -я́шешь) *perf.*; (*thrash*) поро́ть (-рю́, -решь) *imp.*, вы́~ *perf.* ремнём.
bench *n.* (*seat*) скамья́ (*pl.* ска́мьи́, -ме́й), скаме́йка; (*for work*) стано́к (-нка́); (*court*) полице́йские су́дьи (*gen.* -де́й) *pl.*; (*parl.*) ме́сто (*pl.* -та́); *back benches*, ска́мьи́ рядовы́х чле́нов парла́мента.
bend *n.* сгиб, изги́б, накло́н; *v.t.* сгиба́ть *imp.*, согну́ть *perf.*
beneath *prep.* под + *instr.*
benediction *n.* благослове́ние.
benefaction *n.* ми́лость, дар (*pl.* -ы́). **benefactor** *n.* благоде́тель *m.* **benefactress** *n.* благоде́тельница.
benefice *n.* бенефи́ция. **beneficence** *n.* благодея́ние, милосе́рдие. **beneficent** *adj.* благотво́рный, поле́зный.
beneficial *adj.* поле́зный, вы́годный. **beneficiary** *n.* лицо́ (*pl.* -ца), получа́ющее дохо́ды; (*in will*) насле́дник.
benefit *n.* по́льза, вы́года; (*allowance*) посо́бие; (*theat.*) бенефи́с; *v.t.* приноси́ть (-ошу́, -о́сишь) *imp.*, принести́ (-есу́, -есёшь; -ёс, -есла́) *perf.* по́льзу + *dat.*; *v.i.* извлека́ть *imp.*, извле́чь (-еку́, -ечёшь; -ёк, -екла́) *perf.* вы́году.
benevolence *n.* благожела́тельность, благодея́ние. **benevolent** *adj.* благоскло́нный (-нен, -нна), благотвори́тельный.
benign *adj.* до́брый (добр, -а́, -о, -ы́), мя́гкий (мя́гок, мягка́, мя́гко, мя́гки́); (*of tumour*) доброка́чественный (-нен, -нна).
bent *n.* скло́нность, накло́нность.
benumbed *adj.* окочене́вший, оцепене́лый.
benzene *n.* бензо́л.
bequeath *v.t.* завеща́ть *imp.*, *perf.* (+ *acc.* & *dat.*). **bequest** *n.* насле́дство, посме́ртный дар (*pl.* -ы́).
berate *v.t.* руга́ть *imp.*, вы́~ *perf.*
bereave *v.t.* лиша́ть *imp.*, лиши́ть *perf.* (of, + *gen.*). **bereavement** *n.* поте́ря (бли́зкого).
berry *n.* я́года.
berserk *adj.* неи́стовый; *go b.*, неи́стовствовать *imp.*
berth *n.* (*bunk*) ко́йка; (*naut.*) стоя́нка; *give a wide b. to*, обходи́ть (-ожу́, -о́дишь) *imp.*; избега́ть *imp.*, избе́гнуть (избе́г(нул), -гла) *perf.* + *gen.*; *v.t.* ста́вить *imp.*, по~ *perf.* на я́корь, на прича́л.
beryl *n.* бери́лл.
beseech *v.t.* умоля́ть *imp.*, умоли́ть *perf.* **beseeching** *adj.* умоля́ющий.
beset *v.t.* осажда́ть *imp.*, осади́ть *perf.*
beside *prep.* о́коло + *gen.*, во́зле + *gen.*, ря́дом с + *instr.*; *b. the point*, некста́ти; *b. oneself*, вне себя́. **besides** *adv.* кро́ме того́, поми́мо; *prep.* кро́ме + *gen.*
besiege *v.t.* осажда́ть *imp.*, осади́ть *perf.*
besom *n.* садо́вая метла́ (*pl.* мётлы, -тел, -тлам), ве́ник.
besotted *adj.* одуре́лый.
bespoke *adj.* зака́занный (-ан); *b. tailor*, портно́й *sb.*, рабо́тающий на зака́з.
best *adj.* лу́чший, са́мый лу́чший; *adv.* лу́чше всего́, бо́льше всего́; *do one's b.*, де́лать *imp.*, с~ *perf.* всё возмож-

ное; *b. man*, ша́фер (*pl.* -а́); *b. seller*, хо́дкая кни́га.
bestial *adj.* ско́тский, зве́рский. **bestiality** *n.* ско́тство, зве́рство.
bestow *v.t.* дарова́ть *imp., perf.*
bestride *v.t.* (*sit*) сиде́ть (сижу́, сиди́шь) *imp.* верхо́м на + *prep.*; (*stand*) стоя́ть (-ою́, -ои́шь) *imp.*, расста́вив но́ги над + *instr.*
bet *n.* пари́ *neut.indecl.*; (*stake*) ста́вка; *v.t.* держа́ть (-жу́, -жишь) *imp.* пари́ (on, на + *acc.*). **betting** *n.* заключе́ние пари́.
betide *v.t. & i.* случа́ться *imp.*, случи́ться *perf.* (+ *dat.*); *whate'er b.*, что бы ни случи́лось; *woe b. you*, го́ре тебе́.
betray *v.t.* изменя́ть *imp.*, измени́ть (-ню́, -нишь) *perf.* + *dat.*; предава́ть (-даю́, -даёшь) *imp.*, преда́ть (-а́м, -а́шь, -а́ст, -ади́м; пре́дал, -а́, -о) *perf.* **betrayal** *n.* изме́на, преда́тельство.
betroth *v.t.* обруча́ть *imp.*, обручи́ть *perf.* **betrothal** *n.* обруче́ние.
better *adj.* лу́чший; *adv.* лу́чше; (*more*) бо́льше; *v.t.* улучша́ть *imp.*, улу́чшить *perf.*; *get the b. of*, брать (беру́, -рёшь; брал, -а́, -о) *imp.*, взять (возьму́, -мёшь; взял, -а́, -о) *perf.* верх над + *instr.*; *had b.*: *you had b. go*, вам (*dat.*) лу́чше бы пойти́; *think b. of*, переду́мывать *imp.*, переду́мать *perf.* **betterment** *n.* улучше́ние.
between, betwixt *prep.* ме́жду + *instr.*
bevel *n.* (*tool*) ма́ска.
beverage *n.* напи́ток (-тка).
bevy *n.* собра́ние, компа́ния.
bewail *v.t.* сокруша́ться *imp.*, сокруши́ться *perf.* о + *prep.*
beware *v.i.* остерега́ться *imp.*, остере́чься (-егу́сь, -ежёшься; -ёгся, -егла́сь) *perf.* (of, + *gen.*).
bewilder *v.t.* сбива́ть *imp.*, сбить (собью́, -ьёшь) *perf.* с то́лку. **bewildered** *adj.* смущённый (-ён, -ена́), озада́ченный (-ен). **bewilderment** *n.* смуще́ние, замеша́тельство.
bewitch *v.t.* заколдо́вывать *imp.*, заколдова́ть *perf.*; очаро́вывать *imp.*, очарова́ть *perf.* **bewitching** *adj.* очарова́тельный.
beyond *prep.* за + *acc.*, *instr.*, по ту сто́рону + *gen*; (*above*) сверх + *gen.*; (*outside*) вне + *gen.*; *the back of b.*, глушь (-ши́), край (*loc.* -аю́) све́та.
bias *n.* (*inclination*) укло́н; (*prejudice*) предубежде́ние; *to cut on the b.*, крои́ть *imp.*, с~ *perf.* по косо́й. **biased** *adj.* предубеждённый (-ён, -ена́).
bib *n.* нагру́дник.
Bible *n.* Би́блия. **biblical** *adj.* библе́йский.
bibliography *n.* библиогра́фия.
bibliophile *n.* библиофи́л.
bibulous *adj.* пья́нствующий.
bicarbonate (of soda) *n.* со́да.
bicentenary *n.* двухсотле́тие; *adj.* двухсотле́тний.
biceps *n.* би́цепс, двугла́вая мы́шца.
bicker *v.i.* препрека́ться *imp.*; препира́ться *imp.* **bickering** *n.* препрека́ния *neut. pl.*, ссо́ры *f.pl.* из-за мелоче́й.
bicycle *n.* велосипе́д.
bid *n.* предложе́ние цены́, зая́вка; *v.t. & i.* предлага́ть *imp.*, предложи́ть (-жу́, -жишь) *perf.* (це́ну) (for, за + *acc.*); *v.t.* (*command*) прика́зывать *imp.*, приказа́ть (-ажу́, -а́жешь) *perf.* + *dat.* **bidding** *n.* предложе́ние цены́, торги́ *m.pl.*; (*command*) приказа́ние.
bide *v.t.*: *b. one's time*, ожида́ть *imp.* подходя́щего моме́нта.
biennial *adj.* двухле́тний; *n.* двухле́тник.
bier *n.* (похоро́нные) дро́ги (-г) *pl.*
bifocal *adj.* двухфо́кусный.
big *adj.* большо́й, кру́пный (-пен, -пна́, -пно, кру́пны́); (*important*) ва́жный (-жен, -жна́, -жно, ва́жны́); *b. business*, де́ло большо́го масшта́ба; *b. end*, больша́я, ни́жняя, кривоши́пная голо́вка; *b. name*, знамени́тость; *b. noise*, ши́шка; *b. top*, цирк; *talk b.*, хва́статься *imp.*
bigamist *n.* (*man*) двоеже́нец (-нца), (*woman*) двуму́жница. **bigamous** *adj.* двубра́чный. **bigamy** *n.* двубра́чие.
bike *n.* велосипе́д.
bikini *n.* бики́ни *neut.indecl.*
bilateral *adj.* двусторо́нний.
bilberry *n.* черни́ка.
bile *n.* жёлчь. **bilious** *adj.* жёлчный.
bilge *n.* (*sl.*) ерунда́.
bilingual *adj.* двуязы́чный. **bilingualism** *n.* двуязы́чие.

bill *n.* (*account*) счёт (*pl.* -á); (*draft of law*) законопроéкт; (*b. of exchange*) вéксель (*pl.* -ля́); (*theat.*) прогрáмма; (*poster*) афи́ша; *v.t.* (*announce*) объявля́ть *imp.*, объяви́ть (-влю́, -вишь) *perf.* в афи́шах; расклéивать *imp.*, расклéить *perf.* афи́ши + *gen.*; *b. of fare*, меню́ *neut.indecl.*; *b. of health*, санитáрное удостоверéние; *b. of lading*, накладнáя *sb.*; *B. of Rights*, билль *m.* о правáх.
billet *n.* помещéние для постóя, кварти́ры *f.pl.*; *v.t.* расквартирóвывать *imp.*, расквартировáть *perf.*; *billeting officer*, квартирьéр.
billhead *n.* бланк.
billiard-ball *n.* билья́рдный шар (-á *with 2, 3, 4*; *pl.* -ы́). **billiard-cue** *n.* кий (ки́я; *pl.* кии́). **billiard-room** *n.* билья́рдная *sb.* **billiard-table, billiards** *n.* билья́рд.
billion *n.* миллиóн.
billow *n.* большáя волнá (*pl.* -ны, -н, -нáм), вал (*loc.* -ý; *pl.* -ы́); *v.i.* вздымáться *imp.* **billowy** *adj.* вздымáющийся, волни́стый.
billposter *n.* расклéйщик афи́ш.
bimonthly *adj.* (*twice a month*) выходя́щий два рáза в мéсяц; (*every two months*) выходя́щий раз в два мéсяца.
bin *n.* (*refuse*) мýсорное ведрó (*pl.* вёдра, -дер, -драм); (*corn*) зáкром (*pl.* -á), ларь (-ря́) *m.*
bind *v.t.* (*tie*) свя́зывать *imp.*, связáть (-яжý, -я́жешь) *perf.*; (*oblige*) обя́зывать *imp.*, обязáть (-яжý, -я́жешь) *perf.*; (*book*) переплетáть *imp.*, переплести́ (-етý, -етёшь; -ёл, -елá) *perf.* **binder** *n.* (*person*) переплётчик, -ица; (*agr.*) вязáльщик; (*for papers*) пáпка. **binding** *n.* (*book*) переплёт; (*braid*) оторóчка. **bindweed** *n.* вьюнóк (-нкá).
binge *n.* кутёж (-á).
bingo *n.* би́нго *neut.indecl.*
binoculars *n.* бинóкль *m.*
binomial *adj.* двучлéнный.
biochemical *adj.* биохими́ческий. **biochemist** *n.* биохи́мик. **biochemistry** *n.* биохи́мия. **biographer** *n.* биóграф. **biographical** *adj.* биографи́ческий. **biography** *n.* биогрáфия, жизнеописáние. **biological** *adj.* биологи́ческий. **biologist** *n.* биóлог. **biology** *n.* биолóгия.
bipartisan *adj.* двухпарти́йный. **bipartite** *adj.* двусторóнний. **biped** *n.* двунóгое живóтное *sb.* **biplane** *n.* биплáн.
birch *n.* (*tree*) берёза; (*rod*) рóзга (*gen.pl.* -зог); *v.t.* сечь (секý, сечёшь; сек, -лá) *imp.*, вы́~ *perf.* рóзгой.
bird *n.* пти́ца; *b. of passage*, перелётная пти́ца; *b. of prey*, хи́щная пти́ца; *b.'s-eye view*, вид с пти́чьего полёта.
birth *n.* рождéние; (*origin*) происхождéние; *b. certificate*, мéтрика; *b. control*, противозачáточные мéры *f.pl.* **birthday** *n.* день (дня) *m.* рождéния. **birthplace** *n.* мéсто (*pl.* -тá) рождéния. **birthright** *n.* прáво по рождéнию.
biscuit *n.* сухóе печéнье.
bisect *v.t.* разрезáть *imp.*, разрéзать (-éжу, -éжешь) *perf.* пополáм.
bishop *n.* епи́скоп; (*chess*) слон (-á). **bishopric** *n.* епáрхия.
bismuth *n.* ви́смут.
bison *n.* бизóн.
bit[1] *n.* (*tech.*) сверлó (*pl.* -ёрла), бурáв (-á); (*bridle*) удилá (-л) *pl.*
bit[2] *n.* (*piece*) кусóчек (-чка), дóля (*pl.* -ли, -лéй); *a b.*, немнóго; *not a b.*, ничýть.
bitch *n.* сýка.
bite *n.* укýс; (*fishing*) клёв; *v.t.* кусáть *imp.*, укуси́ть (-ушý, -ýсишь) *perf.*; (*fish*) клевáть (клюёт) *imp.*, клю́нуть *perf.* **biting** *adj.* éдкий (éдок, едкá, éдко), рéзкий (-зок, -зкá, -зко).
bitter *adj.* гóрький (-рек, -рькá, -рько). **bitterness** *n.* гóречь.
bittern *n.* выпь.
bitumen *n.* битýм. **bituminous** *adj.* битýм(инóз)ный.
bivouac *n.* бивáк.
bi-weekly *adj.* (*twice a week*) выходя́щий два рáза в недéлю; (*fortnightly*) выходя́щий раз в две нелéли, двухнедéльный.
bizarre *adj.* стрáнный (-нен, -ннá, -нно), причýдливый.
blab *v.t.* выбáлтывать *imp.*, вы́болтать *perf.*
black *adj.* чёрный (-рен, -рнá); (*dark-skinned*) чернокóжий; *b. currant*,

чёрная сморо́дина; *b. eye*, подби́тый глаз (*pl.* -á, глаз, -áм), фона́рь (-ря́) *m. n.* (*Negro*) чёрный *sb.*; (*mourning*) тра́ур. **blackberry** *n.* ежеви́ка (*collect.*). **blackbird** *n.* чёрный дрозд (-á). **blackboard** *n.* кла́ссная доска́ (*acc.* -ску; *pl.* -ски, -со́к, -ска́м). **blacken** *v.t.* черни́ть *imp.*, за~, на~, (*fig.*) о~ *perf.* **blackguard** *n.* полле́ц (-á), мерза́вец (-вца). **blackleg** *n.* штрейкбре́хер. **blackmail** *n.* шанта́ж (-á); *v.t.* шантажи́ровать *imp.*

bladder *n.* пузы́рь (-ря́) *m.*

blade *n.* (*knife etc.*) ле́звие, клино́к (-нка́); (*oar etc.*) ло́пасть (*pl.* -ти, -те́й); (*grass*) были́нка.

blame *n.* вина́, порица́ние; *v.t.* вини́ть *imp.* (for, в + *prep.*); *be to b.*, быть винова́тым. **blameless** *adj.* безупре́чный, неви́нный (-нен, -нна).

blanch *v.t.* бели́ть *imp.*, вы́~ *perf.*; (*food*) обва́ривать *imp.*, обвари́ть (-рю́, -ришь) *perf.*; *v.i.* бледне́ть *imp.*, по~ *perf.*

bland *adj.* мя́гкий (-гок, -гка́, -гко, мя́гки́); (*in manner*) ве́жливый.

blandishment *n.*: *pl.* льсти́вые ре́чи (-че́й) *pl.*

blank *n.* (*space*) пробе́л; (*form*) бланк; (*ticket*) пусто́й биле́т; *adj.* пусто́й (пуст, -á, -о, -ы́); незапо́лненный (-ен); чи́стый (чист, -á, -о, чи́сты́); *b. cartridge*, холосто́й патро́н; *b. wall*, глуха́я стена́ (*acc.* -ну; *pl.* -ны, -н, -на́м); *b. verse*, бе́лый стих (-á).

blanket *n.* одея́ло.

blare *n.* звук трубы́; *v.i.* труби́ть *imp.*, про~ *perf.*; (*shout*) ора́ть (ору́, орёшь) *imp.*

blasphemous *adj.* богоху́льный. **blasphemy** *n.* богоху́льство.

blast *n.* (*wind*) поры́в ве́тра; (*air*) струя́ (*pl.* -у́и); (*sound*) гудо́к (-дка́); (*of explosion*) взрывна́я волна́ (*pl.* -ны, -н, -на́м); *v.t.* взрыва́ть *imp.*, взорва́ть (-ву́, -вёшь; взорва́л, -á, -о) *perf.*; *b. off*, стартова́ть *imp.*, *perf.*; взлета́ть *imp.*, взлете́ть (-ечу́, -ети́шь) *perf.*; *b.-furnace*, до́менная печь (*pl.* -чи, -че́й).

blatant *adj.* (*clear*) я́вный; (*flagrant*) вопию́щий.

blaze[1] *n.* (*flame*) я́ркое пла́мя *neut.*; (*light*) я́ркий свет; *v.i.* (*flame*) пыла́ть *imp.*; (*with light*) сверка́ть *imp.*

blaze[2] *v.t.* (*mark*) ме́тить *imp.*, на~ *perf.*; *b. the trail*, прокла́дывать *imp.* путь.

blazer *n.* спорти́вная ку́ртка.

bleach *n.* хло́рная и́звесть; *v.t.* бели́ть *imp.*, вы́~ *perf.* **bleaching** *n.* отбе́ливание, беле́ние.

bleak *adj.* (*bare*) оголённый (-ён, -ена́); (*dreary*) уны́лый.

bleary *adj.* му́тный (-тен, -тна́, -тно, му́тны́), затума́ненный (-ен); *b.-eyed*, с затума́ненными глаза́ми.

bleat *v.i.* бле́ять (-е́ю, -е́ешь) *imp.*; *n.* бле́яние.

bleed *v.i.* кровоточи́ть *imp.*; *v.t.* пуска́ть *imp.*, пусти́ть (пущу́, пу́стишь) *perf.* кровь + *dat.*; *n.* кровотече́ние; кровопуска́ние; *my heart bleeds*, се́рдце облива́ется кро́вью.

bleep *n.* бип.

blemish *n.* недоста́ток (-тка), пятно́ (*pl.* -тна, -тен, -тнам), поро́к; *without b.*, непоро́чный, незапя́танный (-ан).

blench *v.i.* вздро́гнуть *perf.*

blend *n.* смесь; *v.t.* сме́шивать *imp.*, смеша́ть *perf.*; *v.i.* гармони́ровать *imp.* **blender** *n.* смеси́тель *m.*

bless *v.t.* благословля́ть *imp.*, благослови́ть *perf.* **blessed** *adj.* благослове́нный (-е́н, -е́нна), счастли́вый (сча́стлив). **blessing** *n.* (*action*) благослове́ние; (*object*) бла́го.

blind *adj.* слепо́й (слеп, -á, -о); *b. alley*, тупи́к (-á); *b. flying*, слепо́й полёт; *n.* што́ра; *v.t.* ослепля́ть *imp.*, ослепи́ть *perf.*

blink *v.i.* мига́ть *imp.*, мигну́ть *perf.*; морга́ть *imp.*, моргну́ть *perf.*; *n.* мига́ние. **blinkers** *n.* шо́ры (-р) *pl.*

blip *n.* сигна́л на экра́не.

bliss *n.* блаже́нство. **blissful** *adj.* блаже́нный (-е́н, -е́нна).

blister *n.* пузы́рь (-ря́) *m.*, волды́рь (-ря́) *m.*; *v.i.* покрыва́ться *imp.*, покры́ться (-ро́юсь, -ро́ешься) *perf.* пузыря́ми, волдыря́ми; *v.t.* вызыва́ть *imp.*, вы́звать (-зовет) *perf.* пузы́рь, волды́рь на + *prep.*, на ко́же + *gen.*

blithe *adj.* весёлый (вéсел, -á, -от вéселы́); (*carefree*) беспéчный.
blitz *n.* стреми́тельное нападéние; (*aerial*) стреми́тельный налёт. **blitzkrieg** *n.* молниенóсная войнá.
blizzard *n.* метéль, вью́га.
bloated *adj.* наду́тый, разду́тый.
bloater *n.* копчёная селёдка.
blob *n.* (*liquid*) кáпля (*gen.pl.* -пель); (*spot*) пя́тнышко (*pl.* -шки, -шек, -шкам).
bloc *n.* блок.
block *n.* (*of wood*) чурбáн, колóда; (*of stone*) глы́ба; (*obstruction*) затóр; (*traffic*) прóбка; (*tech.*) блок; (*b. of flats*) жилóй дом (*pl.* -á); *b. and tackle*, тáли (-лей) *pl.*; *b. letters*, печáтные бу́квы *f.pl.*; *v.t.* преграждáть *imp.*, прегради́ть *perf.*; *b. out*, набрáсывать *imp.*, набросáть *perf.* вчернé.
blockade *n.* блокáда; *v.t.* блоки́ровать *imp.*, *perf.*
blockage *n.* затóр.
blond *n.* блонди́н, ~ка; *adj.* белоку́рый.
blood *n.* кровь (*loc.* -ви́; *pl.* -ви, -вéй); (*descent*) происхождéние; *b. bank*, храни́лище крóви и плáзмы; *b.-donor*, дóнор; *b. orange*, королёк (-лькá); *b.-poisoning*, заражéние крóви; *b. pressure*, кровянóе давлéние; *b.-relation*, бли́зкий рóдственник, -ица; *b. transfusion*, переливáние крóви; *b.-vessel*, кровенóсный сосу́д. **bloodhound** *n.* ищéйка. **bloodless** *adj.* бескрóвный. **bloody** *adj.* кровáвый, окровáвленный (-ен).
bloom *n.* расцвéт; *v.i.* расцветáть *imp.*, расцвести́ (-ету́, -етёшь; -ёл, -елá) *perf.*
blossom *n.* цветóк (-ткá; *pl.* цветы́); *collect.* цвет; *in b.*, в цвету́.
blot *n.* кля́кса; пятнó (*pl.* -тна, -тен, -тнам); *v.t.* промокáть *imp.*, промокну́ть *perf.*; пáчкать *imp.*, за~ *perf.*
blotch *n.* пятнó (*pl.* -тна, -тен, -тнам). **blotchy** *adj.* запя́танный (-ан).
blotter, blotting-paper *n.* промокáтельная бумáга.
blouse *n.* кóфточка, блу́зка.
blow[1] *n.* удáр.
blow[2] *v.i.* & *t.* дуть (ду́ю, ду́ешь) *imp.*; вéять (вéет) *imp.*; выдувáть *imp.*, вы́дуть (-ую, -уешь) *perf.*; *b. away*, сноси́ть (-ошу́, -óсишь) *imp.*, снести́ (-есу́, -есёшь; снёс, -лá) *perf.*; *b. down*, свáливать *imp.*, свали́ть (-лю́, -лишъ) *perf.*; *b. up*, взрывáтв *imp.*, взорвáтъ (-ву́, -вёшь; взорвáл, -á, -о) *perf.*; *b.-up*, фотопаннó *neut.indecl.* **blowlamp** *n.* пая́льная лáмпа.
blubber[1] *n.* вóрвань.
blubber[2] *v.i.* ревéть (-ву́, -вёшь) *imp.*
bludgeon *n.* дуби́нка.
blue *adj.* (*dark*) си́ний (-нь, -ня́, -не); (*light*) голубóй; *n.* си́ний, голубóй, цвет; (*sky*) нéбо. **bluebell** *n.* колокóльчик. **bluebottle** *n.* си́няя му́ха. **blueprint** си́нька, светокóпия.
bluff[1] *n.* (*cliff*) отвéсный бéрег (*loc.* -у́; *pl.* -á); *adj.* (*person*) грубовáто-добродýшный.
bluff[2] *n.* (*deceit*) обмáн, блеф; *v.i.* притворя́ться *imp.*, притвори́ться *perf.*
blunder *n.* грýбая оши́бка; *v.i.* ошибáться *imp.*, ошиби́ться (-бу́сь, -бёшься; -бся) *perf.*; (*stumble*) спотыкáться *imp.*, споткну́ться *perf.*
blunt *adj.* (*knife*) тупóй (туп, -á, -о, ту́пы́); (*person*) прямóй (прям, -á, -о, пря́мы́); (*words*) рéзкий (-зок, -зкá, -зко); *v.t.* тупи́ть (-плю́, -пишь) *imp.*, за~, ис~ *perf.*; притупля́ть *imp.*, притупи́ть (-плю́, -пишь) *perf.*
blur *n.* расплы́вчатая фóрма; *v.t.* тумáнить *imp.*, за~ *perf.*; изглáживать *imp.*, изглáдить *perf.*
blurb *n.* реклáмная нáдпись (на суперобло́жке).
blurred *adj.* расплы́вчатый, неясный (-сен, -снá, -сно, нея́сны́).
blurt *v.t.*: *b. out*, выбáлтывать *imp.*, вы́болтать *perf.*
blush *v.i.* краснéть *imp.*, по~ *perf.*; зардéться *perf.*; *n.* румя́нец (-нца).
bluster *v.i.* бушевáть (-шу́ю, -шу́ешь) *imp.*; *n.* пусты́е угрóзы *f.pl.*
boa *n.* боá *m.indecl.* (*snake*), *neut.indecl.* (*wrap*); *b. constrictor*, удáв.
boar *n.* бóров (*pl.* -ы, -óв); (*wild*) вепрь *m.*
board *n.* доскá (*acc.* -ску; *pl.* -ски, -сóк, -скáм); (*table*) стол (-á); (*food*) питáние; (*committee*) правлéние, со-

вёт; *pl.* сце́на, подмо́стки (-ков) *pl.*; (*naut.*) борт (*loc.* -у́; *pl.* -а́); *on b.*, на борт(у́); *v.i.* столова́ться *imp.*; *v.t.* сади́ться *imp.*, сесть (ся́ду, -дешь; сел) *perf.* (на кора́бль, в по́езд и т.д.); (*naut.*) брать (беру́, -рёшь; брал, -а́, -о) *imp.*, взять (возьму́, -мёшь; взял, -а́, -о) *perf.* на аборда́ж. **boarder** *n.* пансионе́р. **boarding-house** *n.* пансио́н. **boarding-school** *n.* интерна́т.

boast *v.i.* хва́статься *imp.*, по~ *perf.*; *v.t.* горди́ться *imp.*+*instr.*; *n.* хвастовство́. **boaster** *n.* хвасту́н (-а́). **boastful** *adj.* хвастли́вый.

boat *n.* ло́дка, су́дно (*pl.* -да́, -до́в), кора́бль (-ля́) *m.*; *b. building*, судострое́ние; *b.-hook*, баго́р (-гра́). **boatswain** *n.* бо́цман.

bob[1] *n.* (*weight*) баланси́р; (*hair*) стри́жка воло́с, покрыва́ющая у́ши.

bob[2] *v.i.* подпры́гивать *imp.*, подпры́гнуть *perf.*

bobbin *n.* кату́шка, шпу́лька.

bobby *n.* полисме́н, бо́бби *m.indecl.*

bobsleigh *n.* бо́бсле́й.

bobtail *n.* обре́занный хвост (-а́).

bode *v.t.* предвеща́ть *imp.*

bodice *n.* лиф, корса́ж.

bodily *adv.* целико́м; *adj.* теле́сный, физи́ческий.

bodkin *n.* тупа́я игла́ (*pl.* -лы).

body *n.* те́ло (*pl.* -ла́), ту́ловище; (*corpse*) труп; (*frame*) о́стов; (*troops etc.*) ко́рпус (*pl.* -а́); (*carriage*) ку́зов (*pl.* -а́); (*main part*) основна́я часть. **bodyguard** *n.* телохрани́тель *m.*; *collect.* ко́рпус телохрани́телей.

bog *n.* боло́то, тряси́на; *get bogged down*, увяза́ть *imp.*, увя́знуть (-з) *perf.* **boggy** *adj.* боло́тистый.

bogus *adj.* подде́льный, фальши́вый.

bogy *n.* пу́гало.

boil[1] *n.* (*med.*) фуру́нкул, нары́в.

boil[2] *v.i.* кипе́ть (-пи́т) *imp.*, вс~ *perf.*; *v.t.* кипяти́ть *imp.*, с~ *perf.*; (*cook*) вари́ть (-рю́, -ришь) *imp.*, с~ *perf.*; *n.* кипе́ние; *bring to the b.*, доводи́ть (-ожу́, -о́дишь) *imp.*, довести́ (-еду́, -едёшь; -ёл, -ела́) *perf.* до кипе́ния. **boiled** *adj.* варёный, кипячёный. **boiler** *n.* (*vessel*) котёл (-тла́); (*fowl*) ку́рица го́дная для ва́рки; *b. house*, коте́льная *sb.*; *b. suit*, комбинезо́н. **boiling** *n.* кипе́ние; *adj.* кипя́щий; *b. water*, кипято́к (-тка́).

boisterous *adj.* бу́рный (-рен, бу́рна́, -рно), шумли́вый.

bold *adj.* сме́лый (смел, -а́, -о), хра́брый (храбр, -а́, -о, хра́бры́), де́рзкий (-зок, -зка́, -зко); (*clear*) чёткий (-ток, -тка́, -тко); (*type*) жи́рный.

bole *n.* ствол (-а́).

bolster *n.* ва́лик; *v.t.*: *b. up*, подпира́ть *imp.*, подпере́ть (подопру́, -рёшь; подпёр) *perf.*

bolt *n.* засо́в, задви́жка; (*tech.*) болт (-а́); (*flight*) бе́гство; *v.t.* запира́ть *imp.*, запере́ть (-пру́, -прёшь; за́пер, -ла́, -ло) *perf.* на засо́в; скрепля́ть *imp.*, скрепи́ть *perf.* болта́ми; *v.i.* (*flee*) удира́ть *imp.*, удра́ть (удеру́, -рёшь; удра́л, -а́, -о) *perf.*; (*horse*) понести́ (-есёт; -ёс, -есла́) *perf.*

bomb *n.* бо́мба; *v.t.* бомби́ть *imp.*; бомбарди́ровать *imp.* **bombard** *v.t.* бомбарди́ровать *imp.* **bombardment** *n.* бомбардиро́вка. **bomber** *n.* бомбардиро́вщик.

bombastic *adj.* напы́щенный (-ен, -енна).

bonanza *n.* золото́е дно.

bond *n.* (*econ.*) облига́ция; связь; *pl.* око́вы (-в) *pl.*, (*fig.*) у́зы (уз) *pl.*

bone *n.* кость (*pl.* -ти, -те́й); *pl.* прах; *b. of contention*, я́блоко раздо́ра.

bonfire *n.* костёр (-тра́).

bonnet *n.* ка́пор, че́пчик; (*car*) капо́т.

bonny *adj.* здоро́вый, хоро́шенький.

bony *adj.* кости́стый.

booby *n.* болва́н, о́лух; *b. trap*, лову́шка.

book *n.* кни́га; *v.t.* (*order*) зака́зывать *imp.*, заказа́ть (-ажу́, -а́жешь) *perf.*; (*reserve*) брони́ровать *imp.*, за~ *perf.* **bookbinder** *n.* переплётчик, -ица. **bookkeeper** *n.* бухга́лтер. **bookmaker, bookie** *n.* букме́кер. **booking** *n.* (*order*) зака́з; (*sale*) прода́жа биле́тов; *b. clerk*, касси́р; *b. office*, ка́сса.

boom[1] *n.* (*barrier*) бон.

boom[2] *n.* (*sound*) гул; (*econ.*) бум, экономи́ческий подъём; *v.i.* гуде́ть (гужу́, гуди́шь) *imp.*; (*flourish*) процвета́ть *imp.*

boon[1] *n.* бла́го.
boon[2] *adj.*: *b. companion*, весёлый друг (*pl.* друзья́, -зе́й).
boor *n.* гру́бый, мужикова́тый челове́к. **boorish** *adj.* мужикова́тый.
boost *v.t.* (*raise*) поднима́ть *imp.*, подня́ть (-ниму́, -ни́мешь; по́днял, -а́, -о) *perf.*; (*increase*) увели́чивать *imp.*, увели́чить *perf.*
boot *n.* боти́нок (-нка; *gen.pl.* -нок), сапо́г (-а́; *gen.pl.* -г); (*football*) бу́тса; *v.t.*: *b. out*, выгоня́ть *imp.*, вы́гнать (вы́гоню, -нишь) *perf.* **bootee** *n.* де́тский вя́заный башмачо́к (-чка́). **boots** *n.* коридо́рный *sb.*
booth *n.* кио́ск, бу́дка; (*polling*) каби́на (для голосова́ния).
bootlegger *n.* торго́вец (-вца) контраба́ндными спиртны́ми напи́тками.
booty *n.* добы́ча; (*mil.*) трофе́и *m.pl.*
booze *n.* вы́пивка; *v.i.* выпива́ть *imp.*
boracic *adj.* бо́рный. **borax** *n.* бура́.
border *n.* (*boundary*) грани́ца; (*edge*) край (*loc.* -аю́; *pl.* -ая́); (*edging*) кайма́, бордю́р; *v.i.* грани́чить *imp.* (on, с + *instr.*); *v.t.* окаймля́ть *imp.*, окайми́ть *perf.* **borderline** *n.* грани́ца.
bore[1] *n.* (*calibre*) кана́л (ствола́), кали́бр (ору́жия); (*borehole*) бурова́я сква́жина; *v.t.* сверли́ть *imp.*, про ~ *perf.* **boring**[1] *adj.* сверля́щий, буро-во́й.
bore[2] *n.* (*tedium*) ску́ка; (*person*) ну́дный челове́к; *v.t.* надоеда́ть *imp.*, надое́сть (-е́м, -е́шь, -е́ст, -еди́м; -е́л) *perf.* **boredom** *n.* ску́ка. **boring**[2] *adj.* ску́чный (-чен, -чна́, -чно).
born *adj.* прирождённый; *be b.*, роди́ться *imp.*, (-и́лся́, -и́ла́сь) *perf.*
borough *n.* го́род (*pl.* -а́).
borrow *v.t.* занима́ть *imp.*, заня́ть (займу́, -мёшь; за́нял, -а́, -о) *perf.* (from (person), у + *gen.*); заимствова́ть *imp.*, *perf.*
bosh *n.* чепуха́.
bosom *n.* (*breast*) грудь (-ди́, *instr.* -дью; *pl.* -ди, -де́й); (*heart*) се́рдце; (*depths*) не́дра (-р) *pl.*; *b. friend*, закады́чный друг (*pl.* друзья́, -зе́й).
boss *n.* хозя́ин (*pl.* -я́ева, -я́ев), шеф; *v.t.* кома́ндовать *imp.*, с ~ *perf.* + *instr.*
bossy *adj.* вла́стный.
botanical *adj.* ботани́ческий. **botanist** *n.* бота́ник. **botany** *n.* бота́ника.
botch *v.t.* по́ртить *imp.*, ис ~ *perf.*
both *adj.*, *pron.* о́ба (обо́их, -им, -ими) *m.* & *neut.*, о́бе (обе́их, -им, -ими) *f.*; *adv.* то́же; *both . . . and*, и... и; не то́лько... но и; как... так и.
bother *n.* беспоко́йство, хло́поты (*gen.* -о́т) *pl.*; *v.t.* беспоко́ить *imp.*; надоеда́ть *imp.*, надое́сть (-е́м, -е́шь, -е́ст, -еди́м; -е́л) *perf.*
bottle *n.* буты́лка; *b.-neck*, у́зкое ме́сто (*pl.* -та́), зато́р; *v.t.* разлива́ть *imp.* разли́ть (разолью́, -ьёшь; разли́л, -а́, -о) *perf.* по буты́лкам; *b. up*, (*conceal*) зата́ивать *imp.*, затаи́ть *perf.*; (*restrain*) подавля́ть *imp.*, подави́ть (-влю́, -вишь) *perf.*
bottom *n.* ни́жняя часть (*pl.* -ти, -те́й); (*of river etc.*) дно (*pl.* до́нья, -ьев); (*buttocks*) зад (*loc.* -у́; *pl.* -ы́); *adj.* са́мый ни́жний. **bottomless** *adj.* бездо́нный (-нен, -нна); *b. pit*, ад (*loc.* -у́).
bough *n.* сук (-а́, *loc.* -у́; *pl.* -и́, -о́в & су́чья, -ьев), ветвь (*pl.* -ви, -ве́й).
boulder *n.* валу́н (-а́), глы́ба.
bounce *n.* прыжо́к (-жка́), скачо́к (-чка́); *v.i.* подпры́гивать *imp.*, подпры́гнуть *perf.* **bouncing** *adj.* ро́слый, здоро́вый.
bound[1] *n.* (*limit*) преде́л; *v.t.* ограни́чивать *imp.*, ограни́чить *perf.*
bound[2] *n.* (*spring*) прыжо́к (-жка́), скачо́к (-чка́); *v.i.* пры́гать *imp.*, пры́гнуть *perf.*; скака́ть (-ачу́, -а́чешь) *imp.*
bound[3] *adj.* (*tied*) свя́занный (-ан); *he is b. to be there*, он обяза́тельно там бу́дет.
bound[4] *adj.*: *to be b. for*, направля́ться *imp.*, напра́виться *perf.* на + *acc.*
boundary *n.* грани́ца, межа́ (*pl.* -жи, -ж, -жа́м).
bounder *n.* хам.
boundless *adj.* беспреде́льный, безграни́чный.
bounteous, bountiful *adj.* (*generous*) ще́дрый (щедр, -а́, -о); (*ample*) оби́льный. **bounty** *n.* ще́дрость; (*gratuity*) пре́мия.
bouquet *n.* буке́т.
bourgeois *n.* буржуа́ *m.indecl.*; *adj.* буржуа́зный. **bourgeoisie** *n.* буржуази́я.

bout *n.* (*of illness*) при́ступ; (*sport*) схва́тка, встре́ча.
bovine *adj.* быча́чий (-чья, -чье); (*fig.*) тупо́й (туп, -а́, -о, ту́пы́).
bow[1] *n.* (*weapon*) лук; (*knot*) бант; (*mus.*) смычо́к (-чка́).
bow[2] *n.* (*obeisance*) покло́н; *v.i.* кла́няться *imp.*, поклони́ться (-ню́сь, -нишься). *perf.*
bow[3] *n.* (*naut.*) нос (*loc.* -у́; *pl.* -ы́); (*rowing*) пе́рвый но́мер (*pl.* -а́).
bowdlerize *v.t.* очища́ть *imp.*, очи́стить *perf.*
bowels *n.* кише́чник; (*depths*) не́дра (-р) *pl.*
bower *n.* бесе́дка.
bowl[1] *n.* (*vessel*) ми́ска, таз (*loc.* -у́; *pl.* -ы́), ча́ша.
bowl[2] *n.* (*ball*) шар (-а́ *with 2, 3, 4*; *pl.* -ы́); *v.i.* мета́ть (мечу́, -чешь) *imp.*, метну́ть *perf.* мяч; подава́ть (-даю́, -даёшь) *imp.*, пода́ть (-а́м, -а́шь, -а́ст, -ади́м; по́дал, -а́, -о) *perf.* мяч. **bowler (hat)** *n.* котело́к (-лка́). **bowling-alley** *n.* кегельба́н. **bowls** *n.* игра́ в шары́; *play b.*, игра́ть *imp.*, сыгра́ть *perf.* в шары́.
box[1] *n.* (*container*) коро́бка, я́щик, сунду́к (-а́); (*theat.*) ло́жа; (*coach*) ко́злы (-зел) *pl.*; (*horse*) сто́йло; *b.-office*, ка́сса; *b.-pleat*, бантова́я скла́дка.
box[2], **boxwood** *n.* (*bot.*) самши́т.
box[3] *n.* (*blow*) уда́р; *v.i.* бокси́ровать *imp.* **boxer** *n.* боксёр. **boxing** *n.* бокс.
boy *n.* ма́льчик, ю́ноша *m.*; *b. friend*, друг (*pl.* друзья́, -зе́й); *b. scout*, бойска́ут. **boyhood** *n.* о́трочество. **boyish** *adj.* мальчи́шеский.
boycott *n.* бойко́т; *v.t.* бойкоти́ровать *imp.*, *perf.*
bra *n.* бюстга́лтер.
brace *n.* (*clamp*) скре́па; *pl.* подтя́жки *f.pl.*; (*pair*) па́ра; *v.t.* скрепля́ть *imp.*, скрепи́ть *perf.*; *b. oneself*, напряга́ть *imp.*, напря́чь (-ягу́, -яжёшь; -я́г, -ягла́) *perf.* си́лы.
bracelet *n.* брасле́т.
bracing *adj.* бодря́щий.
bracket *n.* (*support*) кронште́йн; *pl.* ско́бки *f.pl.*; (*category*) катего́рия, ру́брика.
brad *n.* штифтик. **bradawl** *n.* ши́ло (*pl.* ши́лья, -ьев).
brag *v.i.* хва́статься *imp.*, по~ *perf.*
braggart *n.* хвасту́н (-а́).
braid *n.* тесьма́.
Braille *n.* шрифт Бра́йля.
brain *n.* мозг (-а(у), *loc.* -е & -у́; *pl.* -и́); (*intellect*) ум (-а́); *b. drain*, уте́чка умо́в; *v.t.* размозжи́ть *perf.* го́лову + *dat.* **brainstorm** *n.* припа́док (-дка) безу́мия. **brainwashing** *n.* идеологи́ческая обрабо́тка. **brainwave** *n.* блестя́щая иде́я.
braise *v.t.* туши́ть (-шу́, -шишь) *imp.*, с~ *perf.*
brake *n.* то́рмоз (*pl.* -а́, *fig.* -ы); *v.t.* тормози́ть *imp.*, за~ *perf.*
bramble *n.* ежеви́ка.
brambling *n.* вьюро́к (-рка́).
bran *n.* о́труби (-бе́й) *pl.*
branch *n.* ве́тка; (*subject*) о́трасль; (*department*) отделе́ние, филиа́л; *v.i.* разветвля́ться *imp.*, разветви́ться *perf.*
brand *n.* (*mark*) клеймо́ (*pl.* -ма); (*make*) ма́рка; (*sort*) сорт (*pl.* -а́); *v.t.* клейми́ть *imp.*, за~ *perf.*
brandish *v.t.* разма́хивать *imp.* + *instr.*
brandy *n.* коnья́к (-а́(у́)).
brass *n.* лату́нь, жёлтая медь; (*mus.*) ме́дные инструме́нты *m.pl.*; *adj.* лату́нный, ме́дный; *b. band*, ме́дный духово́й орке́стр; *bold as b.*, на́глый (нагл, -а́, -о); *b. hats*, нача́льство, ста́ршие офице́ры *m.pl.*; *top b.*, вы́сшее нача́льство.
brassière *n.* бюстга́лтер.
brat *n.* ребёнок (-нка; *pl.* де́ти, -те́й); (*derog.*) постре́л.
bravado *n.* брава́да.
brave *adj.* хра́брый (храбр, -а́, -о, хра́бры́), сме́лый (смел, -а́, -о); *v.t.* хра́бро встреча́ть *imp.*, встре́тить *perf.* **bravery** *n.* хра́брость, сме́лость.
brawl *n.* у́личная дра́ка, сканда́л; *v.i.* дра́ться (деру́сь, -рёшься; дра́лся, -ала́сь, -а́ло́сь) *imp.*, по~ *perf.*; сканда́лить *imp.*, на~ *perf.*
brawn *n.* му́скульная си́ла; (*cul.*) свино́й сту́день (-дня) *m.* **brawny** дю́жий (дюж, -а́, -е), си́льный (си́лён, -льна́, -льно, си́льны́).
bray *n.* крик осла́; *v.i.* крича́ть (-чи́т) *imp.*; издава́ть (-даю́, -даёшь) *imp.*,

изда́ть (-а́м, -а́шь, -а́ст, -ади́м; изда́л, -а́, -о) *perf.* ре́зкий звук.

brazen *adj.* ме́дный, бро́нзовый; (*b.-faced*) бессты́дный.

brazier *n.* жаро́вня (*gen.pl.* -вен).

breach *n.* наруше́ние; (*break*) проло́м; (*mil.*) брешь; *v.t.* прола́мывать *imp.*, пролома́ть, пролом́ить (-млю́, -мишь) *perf.*

bread *n.* хлеб; (*white*) бу́лка; *b.-winner*, корми́лец (-льца).

breadth *n.* ширина́, широта́.

break *n.* проло́м, разры́в; (*pause*) переры́в, па́уза; *b. of day*, рассве́т; *v.t.* лома́ть *imp.*, с~ *perf.*; разбива́ть *imp.*, разби́ть (разобью́, -ьёшь) *perf.*; (*violate*) наруша́ть *imp.*, нару́шить *perf.*; *b. in*(*to*), вла́мываться *imp.*, вломи́ться (-млю́сь, -мишься) *perf.* в+*acc.*; *b. off*, отла́мывать *imp.*, отломи́ть (-млю́, -мишь) *perf.*; (*interrupt*) прерыва́ть *imp.*, прерва́ть (-ву́, -вёшь; -вал, -вала́, -ва́ло) *perf.*; *b. out*, вырыва́ться *imp.*, вы́рваться (-вусь, -вешься) *perf.*; *b. through*, пробива́ться *imp.*, проби́ться (-бью́сь, -бьёшься) *perf.*; *b. up*, разбива́ть(ся) *imp.*, разби́ть(ся) (разобью́, -бьёт(ся)) *perf.*; *b. with*, порыва́ть *imp.*, порва́ть (-ву́, -вёшь; порва́л, -а́, -о) *perf.* с+*instr.* **breakage** *n.* поло́мка. **breakdown** *n.* ава́рия; *nervous b.*, не́рвное расстро́йство. **breaker** *n.* буру́н (-а́). **breakfast** *n.* у́тренний за́втрак; *v.i.* за́втракать *imp.*, по~ *perf.* **breakneck** *adj.*: *at b. speed*, сломя́ го́лову. **breakwater** *n.* мол (*loc.* -у́).

breast *n.* грудь (-ди́, *instr.* -дью; *pl.* -ди, -де́й); *b.-feeding*, кормле́ние гру́дью; *b. stroke*, брасс.

breath *n.* дыха́ние, дунове́ние. **breathe** *v.i.* дыша́ть (-шу́, -шишь) *imp.*; *b. in*, вдыха́ть *imp.*, вдохну́ть *perf.*; *b. out*, выдыха́ть *imp.*, вы́дохнуть *perf.* **breather, breathing-space** *n.* переды́шка. **breathless** *adj.* запыха́вшийся.

breeches *n.* бри́джи (-жей) *pl.*, брю́ки (-к) *pl.*

breed *n.* поро́да; *v.i.* размножа́ться *imp.*, размно́житься *perf.*; *v.t.* разводи́ть (-ожу́, -о́дишь) *imp.*, развести́ (-еду́, -едёшь; -ёл, -ела́) *perf.* **breeder** *n.* -во́д: *cattle b.*, скотово́д; *poultry b.*, птицево́д. **breeding** *n.* разведе́ние, -во́дство; (*upbringing*) воспи́танность.

breeze *n.* ветеро́к (-рка́); (*naut.*) бриз. **breezy** *adj.* све́жий (свеж, -а́, -о́, све́жи́); (*lively*) живо́й (жив, -а́, -о).

breviary *n.* тре́бник.

brevity *n.* кра́ткость.

brew *v.t.* (*beer*) вари́ть (-рю́, -ришь) *imp.*, с~ *perf.*; (*tea*) зава́ривать *imp.*, завари́ть (-рю́, -ришь) *perf.* **brewer** *n.* пивова́р. **brewery** *n.* пивова́ренный заво́д.

bribe *n.* взя́тка; *v.t.* дава́ть (даю́, даёшь) *imp.*, дать (дам, дашь, даст, дади́м; дал, -а́, да́ло́, -и) *perf.* взя́тку +*dat.*; подкупа́ть *imp.*, подкупи́ть (-плю́, -пишь) *perf.* **bribery** *n.* по́дкуп.

brick *n.* кирпи́ч (-а́) (*also collect.*); (*toy*) (де́тский) ку́бик; *adj.* кирпи́чный. **brickbat** *n.* обло́мок (-мка) кирпича́. **brick-field, -yard** *n.* кирпи́чный заво́д. **bricklayer** *n.* ка́менщик.

bridal *adj.* сва́дебный. **bride** *n.* неве́ста; (*after wedding*) новобра́чная *sb.* **bridegroom** *n.* жени́х (-а́); новобра́чный *sb.* **bridesmaid** *n.* подру́жка неве́сты.

bridge[1] *n.* мост (мо́ста́, *loc.* -у́; *pl.* -ы́), мо́стик; (*of nose*) перено́сица; *v.t.* наводи́ть (-ожу́, -о́дишь) *imp.*, навести́ (-еду́, -едёшь; -ёл, -ела́) *perf.* мост че́рез+*acc.*; стро́ить *imp.*, по~ *perf.* мост че́рез+*acc.* **bridgehead** *n.* плацда́рм.

bridge[2] *n.* (*cards*) бридж.

bridle *n.* узда́ (*pl.* -ды), узде́чка; *v.t.* обу́здывать *imp.*, обузда́ть *perf.*; *v.i.* возмуща́ться *imp.*, возмути́ться (-ущу́сь, -ути́шься) *perf.*

brief *adj.* недо́лгий (-лог, -лга́, -лго), кра́ткий (-ток, -тка́, -тко); *n.* инстру́кция; *v.t.* инструкти́ровать *imp.*, *perf.* **brief-case** *n.* портфе́ль *m.* **briefing** *n.* инструкти́рование, **briefly** *adv.* кра́тко, сжа́то. **briefs** *n.* шо́рты (-т & -тов) *pl.*

brier *n.* шипо́вник.

brig *n.* бриг.

brigade *n.* брига́да. **brigadier** *n.* бригади́р.

bright *adj.* я́ркий (я́рок, ярка́, я́рко), блестя́щий; (*clever*) смышлёный (-ён). **brighten** *v.i.* проясня́ться *imp.*, про-

ясни́ться *perf.*; *v.t.* придава́ть (-даю́, -даёшь) *imp.*, прида́ть (-а́м, -а́шь, -а́ст, -ади́м; -при́дал, -а́, -о) *perf.* блеск, красоту́. **brightness** *n.* я́ркость.
brilliant *adj.* блестя́щий.
brim *n.* край (*pl.* -ая́); (*hat*) поля́ (-ле́й) *pl.* **brimful** *adj.* по́лный (-лон, -лна́, по́лно́) до краёв.
brimstone *n.* саморо́дная се́ра.
brine *n.* рассо́л.
bring *v.t.* (*carry*) приноси́ть (-ошу́, -о́сишь) *imp.*, принести́ (-есу́, -есёшь; -ёс, -есла́) *perf.*; (*lead*) приводи́ть (-ожу́, -о́дишь) *imp.*, привести́ (-еду́, -едёшь; -ёл, -ела́) *perf.*; (*transport*) привози́ть (-ожу́, -о́зишь) *imp.*, привезти́ (-езу́, -езёшь; -ёз, -езла́) *perf.*; *b. about*, быть причи́ной + *gen.*; *b. back*, возвраща́ть *imp.*, возврати́ть (-ащу́, -ати́шь) *perf.*; *b. down*, сва́ливать *imp.*, свали́ть (-лю́, -лишь) *perf.*; *b. forward*, переноси́ть (-ошу́, -о́сишь) *imp.*, перенести́ (-есу́, -есёшь; -ёс, -есла́) *perf.* на сле́дующую страни́цу; *b. up*, (*educate*) воспи́тывать *imp.*, воспита́ть *perf.*; (*question*) поднима́ть *imp.*, подня́ть (-ниму́, -ни́мешь; по́днял, -а́, -о) *perf.*
brink *n.* край (*pl.* -ая́), грань.
brisk *adj.* (*lively*) живо́й (жив, -а́, -о), оживлённый (-ён, -ённа); (*air etc.*) све́жий (свеж, -а́, -о́, све́жи́), бодря́щий.
brisket *n.* груди́нка.
brisling *n.* бри́слинг, шпро́та.
bristle *n.* щети́на; *v.i.* ощети́ниваться *imp.*, ощети́ниться *perf.*; *b. with*, изоби́ловать *imp.* + *instr.*
British *adj.* брита́нский, англи́йский. **Britisher, Briton** *n.* брита́нец (-нца), -нка; англича́нин (*pl.* -а́не, -а́н), -а́нка.
brittle *adj.* хру́пкий (-пок, -пка́, -пко). **brittleness** *n.* хру́пкость.
broach *v.t.* начина́ть *imp.*, нача́ть (-чну́, -чнёшь; на́чал, -а́, -о) *perf.* обсужда́ть; затра́гивать *imp.*, затро́нуть. *perf.*
broad *adj.* (*wide*) широ́кий (о́к, -ока́, -о́ко́); (*general*) о́бщий (общ, -а́); (*clear*) я́сный (я́сен, ясна́, я́сно, я́сны́); *in b. daylight*, средь бе́ла дня; *in b. outline*, в о́бщих черта́х; *b.-minded*, с широ́кими взгля́дами. **broadly** *adv.*: *b. speaking*, вообще́ говоря́.
broadcast *n.* радио-, теле-, переда́ча, радио-, теле-, програ́мма; *adj.* радио-, теле-; *v.t.* передава́ть (-даю́, -даёшь) *imp.*, переда́ть *perf.* (-а́м, -а́шь, -а́ст, -ади́м; пе́редал, -а́, -о) по ра́дио, по телеви́дению; (*seed*) се́ять (се́ю, се́ешь) *imp.*, по~ *perf.* вразбро́с. **broadcaster** *n.* ди́ктор. **broadcasting** *n.* радио-, теле-, веща́ние.
brocade *n.* парча́; *adj.* парчо́вый.
broccoli *n.* спа́ржевая капу́ста.
brochure *n.* брошю́ра.
brogue *n.* (*shoe*) спорти́вный боти́нок (-нка; *gen.pl.* -нок); (*accent*) ирла́ндский акце́нт.
broiler *n.* бро́йлер.
broke *predic.* разорён (-а́); *be b. to the world*, не име́ть *imp.* ни гроша́. **broken** *adj.* сло́манный (-ан), разби́тый, нару́шенный (-ен); *b.-hearted*, уби́тый го́рем.
broker *n.* бро́кер, ма́клер. **brokerage** *n.* комиссио́нное вознагражде́ние.
bromide *n.* броми́д. **bromine** *n.* бром (-а(у)).
bronchitis *n.* бронхи́т.
bronze *n.* бро́нза; *adj.* бро́нзовый; *v.t.* бронзирова́ть *imp.*, *perf.*
brooch *n.* брошь, бро́шка.
brood *n.* вы́водок (-дка); *v.i.* мра́чно размышля́ть *imp.* **broody** *adj.* сидя́щий на я́йцах; *b. hen*, насе́дка.
brook[1] *n.* руче́й (-чья́).
brook[2] *v.t.* терпе́ть (-плю́, -пишь) *imp.*
broom *n.* метла́ (*pl.* мётлы, -тел, -тлам); (*plant*) раки́тник, дрок. **broomstick** *n.* (*witches'*) помело́ (*pl.* -лья, -льев).
broth *n.* суп, похлёбка.
brothel *n.* публи́чный дом (*pl.* -а́).
brother *n.* брат (*pl.* -ья, -ьев); *b. in arms*, собра́т (*pl.* -ья, -ьев) по ору́жию. *b.-in-law*, (*sister's husband*) зять (*pl.* -я́, -ёв); (*husband's brother*) де́верь (*pl.* -рья́, -ре́й); (*wife's brother*) шу́рин *pl.* (шурья́, -ьёв); (*wife's sister's husband*) своя́к (-а́). **brotherhood** *n.* бра́тство. **brotherly** *adj.* бра́тский.
brow *n.* (*eyebrow*) бровь (*pl.* -ви, -ве́й);

(*forehead*) лоб (лба, *loc.* лбу); (*of cliff*) вы́ступ. **browbeaten** *adj.* запу́ганный (-ан).

brown *adj.* кори́чневый; (*eyes*) ка́рий; *b. paper*, обёрточная бума́га; *v.t.* (*cul.*) подрумя́нивать *imp.*, подрумя́нить *perf.*

browse *v.i.* (*feed*) пасти́сь (пасётся; па́сся, пасла́сь) *imp.*; (*read*) чита́ть *imp.* бессисте́мно.

bruise *n.* синя́к (-а́), уши́б; *v.t.* ушиба́ть *imp.*, ушиби́ть (-бу́, -бёшь; -б) *perf.* **bruised** *adj.* (*fruit*) повреждённый (-ён, -ена́).

brunette *n.* брюне́тка.

brush *n.* щётка; (*paint*) кисть (*pl.* -ти, -те́й); *v.t.* (*clean*) чи́стить *imp.*, вы́~, по~ *perf.* щёткой; (*touch*) легко́ каса́ться *imp.*, косну́ться *perf.* + *gen.*; *b. one's hair*, причёсываться *imp.*, причеса́ться (-ешу́сь, -е́шешься) *perf.* щёткой; *b. aside*, отстраня́ть *imp.*, отстрани́ть *perf.*; *b.-off n.*: *give the b.-off*, отма́хиваться *imp.*, отмахну́ться *perf.* + *gen.*; *b. up*, собира́ть *imp.*, собра́ть (соберу́, -рёшь; собра́л, -а́, -о) *perf.* щёткой; (*renew*) возобновля́ть *imp.*, возобнови́ть *perf.* знако́мство с + *instr.*

brushwood *n.* хво́рост (-а(у)).

Brussels sprouts *n.* брюссе́льская капу́ста.

brutal *adj.* жесто́кий (-о́к, -о́ка́, о́ко), зве́рский, гру́бый (груб, -а́, -о). **brutality** *n.* жесто́кость, зве́рство. **brutalize** *v.t.* (*treat brutally*) гру́бо обраща́ться *imp.*, с + *instr.*; (*make brutal*) доводи́ть (-ожу́, -о́дишь) *imp.*, довести́ (-еду́, -едёшь; -ёл, -ела́) *perf.* до озвере́ния. **brute** *n.* живо́тное *sb.*, скоти́на, жесто́кий челове́к. **brutish** *adj.* гру́бый (груб, -а́, -о), жесто́кий (-о́к, -о́ка́, -о́ко).

bubble *n.* пузы́рь (-ря́) *m.*, пузырёк (-рька́); *v.i.* пузы́риться *imp.*; кипе́ть (-пи́т) *imp.*, вс~ *perf.* **bubbly** *n.* шампа́нское *sb.*

buccaneer *n.* пира́т.

buck *n.* саме́ц (-мца́) оле́ня, кро́лика *etc.*; *v.i.* брыка́ться *imp.*

bucket *n.* ведро́ (*pl.* вёдра, -дер, -драм), ведёрко (*pl.* -рки, -рок, -ркам).

buckle *n.* пря́жка; *v.t.* застёгивать *imp.*, застегну́ть *perf.* пря́жкой; *v.i.* (*crumple*) коро́биться *imp.*, по~, с~ *perf.*

buckshot *n.* карте́чь.

buckskins *n.* лоси́ны (-н) *pl.*

buckthorn *n.* круши́на.

buckwheat *n.* гречи́ха.

bucolic *adj.* буколи́ческий, дереве́нский.

bud *n.* по́чка, буто́н; *v.i.* развива́ться *imp.* **budding** *n.* окулиро́вка, почкова́ние.

Buddha *n.* Бу́дда. **Buddhism** *n.* будди́зм. **Buddhist** *n.* будди́ст; *adj.* будди́йский.

budge *v.t.* & *i.* шевели́ть(ся) (-елю́(сь), -е́лишь(ся)) *imp.*, по~ *perf.*

budgerigar *n.* попуга́йчик.

budget *n.* бюдже́т; *v.i.*: *b. for*, предусма́тривать *imp.*, предусмотре́ть (-рю́, -ришь) *perf.* в бюдже́те.

buff *n.* (*leather*) ко́жа; *in, to, the b.*, нагишо́м; *adj.* желтова́то-бе́жевый.

buffalo *n.* бу́йвол.

buffoon *n.* шут (-а́); *act the b.*, паясни́чать *imp.*

bug *n.* (*bedbug*) клоп (-а́); (*virus*) ви́рус; (*microphone*) потайно́й микрофо́н; *v.t.* (*install b.*) устана́вливать *imp.*, установи́ть (-влю́, -вишь) *perf.* аппарату́ру для подслу́шивания в + *prep.*; (*listen*) подслу́шивать *imp.*

bugle *n.* рог (*pl.* -а́), горн. **bugler** *n.* горни́ст.

build *n.* (*person*) телосложе́ние; *v.t.* стро́ить *imp.*, вы́~, по~ *perf.* **builder** *n.* строи́тель *m.* **building** *n.* (*edifice*) зда́ние; (*action*) строи́тельство; *b. society*, о́бщество, предоставля́ющее сре́дства для поку́пки жилы́х помеще́ний.

bulb *n.* лу́ковица; (*electric*) ла́мпочка. **bulbous** *adj.* лу́ковичный.

bulge *n.* вы́пуклость, вы́ступ; *v.i.* выпя́чиваться *imp.*; выпира́ть *imp.* **bulging** *adj.* разбу́хший, оттопы́ривающийся; *b. eyes*, глаза́ (-з) *pl.* на вы́кате.

bulk *n.* (*size*) объём; (*greater part*) бо́льшая часть; (*mass*) основна́я ма́сса; (*large object*) грома́да; *b. buying*, заку́пки *f.pl.* гурто́м; *b. cargo*, груз нава́лом.

bull *n.* (*ox*) бык (-á); (*male animal*) самéц (-мцá); *adj.* бычáчий (-чья, -чье). **bulldog** *n.* бульдóг. **bulldoze** *v.t.* расчищáть *imp.*, расчи́стить *perf.* бульдóзером. **bulldozer** *n.* бульдóзер. **bullfinch** *n.* снеги́рь (-ря́) *m.* **bullock** *n.* вол (-á). **bull's-eye** *n.* (*target*) я́блоко.

bullet *n.* пу́ля; *b.-proof*, пулестóйкий.

bulletin *n.* бюллетéнь *m.*

bullion *n.* сли́ток (-тка).

bully *n.* зади́ра *m.* & *f.*, забия́ка *m.* & *f.*; *v.t.* запу́гивать *imp.*, запугáть *perf.*; задирáть *imp.*

bulrush *n.* камы́ш (-á).

bulwark *n.* бастиóн, оплóт.

bum *n.* зад (*loc.* -у́; *pl.* -ы́).

bumble-bee *n.* шмель (-ля́) *m.*

bump *n.* (*blow*) удáр, толчóк (-чкá); (*swelling*) ши́шка; *v.i.* ударя́ться *imp.*, удáриться *perf.*; *b. into, against*, налетáть *imp.*, налетéть (-ечу́, -ети́шь) *perf.* на + *acc.*; натáлкиваться *imp.*, натолкну́ться *perf.* на + *acc.* **bumper** *n.* бáмпер; *adj.* óчень кру́пный, оби́льный.

bumpkin *n.* неотёсанный пáрень (-рня; *pl.* -рни, -рнéй) *m.*; *country b.*, деревéнщина *m.* & *f.*

bumptious *adj.* нахáльный, самоувéренный (-ен, -енна).

bun *n.* сдóбная бу́лка.

bunch *n.* пучóк (-чкá), свя́зка, гроздь (*pl.* -ди, -дéй & -дья, -дьев); *v.t.* собирáть *imp.*, собрáть (соберу́, -рёшь; собрáл, -á, -о) *perf.* в пучки́.

bundle *n.* у́зел (узлá), узелóк (-лкá); *v.t.* свя́зывать *imp.*, связáть (-яжу́, -я́жешь) *perf.* в у́зел; *b. away, off*, спровáживать *imp.*, спровáдить *perf.*

bung *n.* вту́лка.

bungalow *n.* бу́нгало *neut.indecl.*

bungle *v.t.* пóртить *imp.*, ис~ *perf.*; *n.* пу́таница. **bungler** *n.* пу́таник.

bunk *n.* (*berth*) кóйка.

bunker *n.* бу́нкер (*pl.* -á & -ы).

bunkum *n.* чепухá.

buoy *n.* буй (*pl.* буи́), бáкен. **buoyancy** *n.* плаву́честь; (*fig.*) бóдрость, оживлéние. **buoyant** *adj.* плаву́чий; бóдрый (бодр, -á, -о), жизнерáдостный.

bur(r) *n.* колю́чка.

burden *n.* брéмя *neut.*; *v.t.* обременя́ть *imp.*, обремени́ть *perf.*

bureau *n.* бюрó *neut.indecl.* **bureaucracy** *n.* бюрократи́я (*also collect.*), бюрократи́зм. **bureaucrat** *n.* бюрокрáт. **bureaucratic** *adj.* бюрократи́ческий.

burglar *n.* взлóмщик. **burglary** *n.* крáжа со взлóмом. **burgle** *v.i.* совершáть *imp.*, соверши́ть *perf.* крáжу со взлóмом; *v.t.* грáбить *imp.*, о~ *perf.*

burial *n.* погребéние; *b.-service*, заупокóйная слу́жба.

burlesque *n.* парóдия; *v.t.* пароди́ровать *imp.*, *perf.*; *adj.* пароди́ческий, пароди́йный.

burly *adj.* здоровéнный.

burn *v.t.* жечь (жгу, жжёшь, жгут; жёг, жгла) *imp.*, с~ (сожгу́, сожжёшь, сожгу́т; сжёг, сожглá) *perf.*; *v.t.* & *i.* (*injure*) обжигáть(ся) *imp.*, обжéчь(ся) (обожгу́(сь), обожжёшь(ся), обожгу́т(ся); обжёг(ся), обожглá(сь)) *perf.*; *v.i.* горéть (-рю́, -ри́шь) *imp.*, с~ *perf.*; (*by sun*) загорáть *imp.*, загорéть (-рю́, -ри́шь) *perf.*; *n.* ожóг. **burner** *n.* горéлка. **burning** *adj.* горя́чий (-ч, -чá).

burnish *v.t.* полировáть *imp.*, на~, от~ *perf.* **burnishing** *n.* полирóвка; *adj.* полировáльный.

burr *n. see* **bur(r)**.

burrow *n.* норá (*pl.* -ры), нóрка; *v.i.* рыть (рóю, рóешь) *imp.*, вы́~ *perf.* нору́; (*fig.*) ры́ться (рóюсь, рóешься) *imp.*

bursar *n.* казначéй, завхóз. **bursary** *n.* стипéндия.

burst *n.* разры́в, вспы́шка; *v.i.* разрывáться *imp.*, разорвáться (-вётся; -вáлся, -валáсь, -валóсь) *perf.*; лóпаться *imp.*, лóпнуть *perf.*; *v.t.* разрывáть *imp.*, разорвáть (-ву́, -вёшь; разорвáл, -á, -о) *perf.*

bury *v.t.* (*dead*) хорони́ть (-ню́, -нишь) *imp.*, по~ *perf.*; (*hide*) зарывáть *imp.*, зары́ть (-рóю, -рóешь) *perf.*

bus *n.* автóбус; *b.-conductor*, конду́ктор (*pl.* -á).

bush *n.* куст (-á); (*collect.*) кустáрник. **bushy** *adj.* густóй (густ, -á, -о, гу́сты́).

business *n.* (*matter*) дéло; (*occupation*) заня́тие; (*firm*) коммéрческое предприя́тие; *big b.*, кру́пный капита́л; *mind your own b.*, не ва́ше де́ло; *no monkey b.*, без фо́кусов; *on b.*, по де́лу.

busker *n.* у́личный музыка́нт.

bust *n.* (*sculpture*) бюст; (*bosom*) грудь (-ди́, *instr.* -дью; *pl.* -ди, -де́й).

bustle[1] *n.* (*fuss*) сумато́ха, суета́; *v.i.* суети́ться *imp.*

bustle[2] *n.* (*garment*) турню́р.

busy *adj.* занято́й (за́нят, -а́, -о); *v.t.*: *b. oneself*, занима́ться *imp.*, заня́ться (займу́сь, -мёшься; заня́лся́, -ла́сь) *perf.* (with, + *instr.*). **busybody** *n.* челове́к, сую́щий нос в чужи́е дела́.

but *conj.* но, а, кро́ме; *b. then*, но зато́; *prep.* кро́ме + *gen.*

butcher *n.* мясни́к (-а́); *v.t.* ре́зать (ре́жу, -жешь) *imp.*, за~ *perf.*; *b.'s shop*, мясна́я *sb.* **butchery** *n.* резня́.

butler *n.* дворе́цкий *sb.*

butt[1] *n.* (*cask*) бо́чка.

butt[2] *n.* (*of gun*) прикла́д; (*end*) то́лстый коне́ц (-нца́).

butt[3] *n.* (*target*) мише́нь.

butt[4] *v.t.* бода́ть *imp.*, за~ *perf.*; *v.i.* бода́ться *imp.*

butter *n.* (сли́вочное) ма́сло; *v.t.* нама́зывать *imp.*, намаза́ть (-ажу́, -а́жешь) *perf.* ма́слом. **buttercup** *n.* лю́тик. **butterfly** *n.* ба́бочка.

buttock *n.* я́годица.

button *n.* пу́говица; (*knob*) кно́пка; *v.t.* застёгивать *imp.*, застегну́ть *perf.*

buttress *n.* контрфо́рс; *v.t.* подпира́ть *imp.*, подпере́ть (подопру́, -рёшь; подпёр) *perf.*

buy *n.* поку́пка; *v.t.* покупа́ть *imp.*, купи́ть (-плю́, -пишь) *perf.* **buyer** *n.* покупа́тель *m.*

buzz *n.* жужжа́ние; *v.i.* жужжа́ть (-жи́т) *imp.*; гуде́ть (гужу́, гуди́шь) *imp.*

buzzard *n.* каню́к (-а́).

buzzer *n.* зу́ммер.

by *adv.* ми́мо; *by and by*, вско́ре; *prep.* (*near*) о́коло + *gen.*, у + *gen.*; (*beside*) ря́дом с + *instr.*; (*via*) че́рез + *acc.*; (*past*) ми́мо + *gen.*; (*time*) к + *dat.*; (*means*) *instr. without prep.*; *by means of*, посре́дством + *gen.*

bye-bye *interj.* пока́! всего́!

by-election *n.* дополни́тельные вы́боры *m.pl.* **bygone** *adj.* пережи́тый, про́шлый; *n.*: *pl.* про́шлое *sb.*; (*objects*) предме́ты, *m.pl.* вы́шедшие из употребле́ния; *let b. be b.*, что пропа́ло, то быльём поросло́. **by-law** *n.* постановле́ние ме́стной вла́сти. **bypass** *n.* (*road*) обхо́д, обхо́дный путь (-ти́, -тём) *m.*; (*pipe*) обво́дный кана́л; *v.t.* обходи́ть (-ожу́, -о́дишь) *imp.*, обойти́ (обойду́, -дёшь; обошёл, -шла́) *perf.*; объезжа́ть *imp.*, объе́хать (-е́ду, -е́дешь) *perf.* **by-product** *n.* побо́чный проду́кт. **bystander** *n.* наблюда́тель *m.* **byway** *n.* просёлочная доро́га. **byword** *n.* (*proverb*) погово́рка; (*example*) приме́р.

Byzantine *adj.* византи́йский.

C

C *n.* (*mus.*) до *neut.indecl.*

cab *n.* (*taxi*) такси́ *neut.indecl.*; (*of lorry*) каби́на; *c.-rank*, стоя́нка такси́.

cabaret *n.* эстра́дное представле́ние.

cabbage *n.* капу́ста; *c. white*, капу́стница.

cabin *n.* (*hut*) хи́жина; (*bathing etc.*) каби́на; (*ship's*) каю́та; *c.-boy*, ю́нга *m.*

cabinet *n.* (*polit.*) кабине́т; (*cupboard*) (застеклённый) шкаф (*loc.* -у́; *pl.* -ы́); *c.-maker*, краснодере́вец (-вца); *C. Minister*, мини́стр-член кабине́та.

cable *n.* (*rope*) кана́т, трос; (*electric*)

ка́бель *m.*; (*cablegram*) каблогра́мма; *c. stitch*, жгут (-а́); *v.t.* & *i.* телеграфи́ровать *imp.*, *perf.* (по подво́дному ка́белю).

cabotage *n.* кабота́ж.

cacao *n.* кака́о *neut.indecl.*

cache *n.* укры́тый, та́йный, запа́с.

cackle *n.* (*geese*) го́гот, гогота́нье; (*hens*) куда́хтанье; *v.i.* гогота́ть (-очу́, -о́чешь) *imp.*; куда́хтать (-хчу, -хчешь) *imp.*

cactus *n.* ка́ктус; *adj.* ка́ктусовый.

cad *n.* хам.

cadaverous *adj.* мёртвенно-бле́дный (-ден, -дна́, -дно, -бле́дны́).

caddie *n.* челове́к, прислу́живающий при игре́ в гольф.

caddish *adj.* ха́мский.

caddy *n.* (*box*) ча́йница.

cadence *n.* (*rhythm*) ритм, такт; (*mus.*) каде́нция. **cadenced** *adj.* ме́рный, ритми́чный. **cadenza** *n.* каде́нция.

cadet *n.* каде́т (*gen.pl.* -т & -тов); *adj.* каде́тский.

cadge *v.t.* выпра́шивать *imp.*, вы́просить *perf.*

cadre *n.* ка́дры *m.pl.*

Caesarean (section) *n.* ке́сарево сече́ние.

caesura *n.* цезу́ра.

cafe *n.* кафе́ *neut.indecl.* **cafeteria** *n.* кафете́рий.

caffeine *n.* кофеи́н.

cage *n.* кле́тка; (*in mine*) клеть (*loc.* -ети́; *pl.* -ти, -те́й); *v.t.* сажа́ть *imp.*, посади́ть (-ажу́, -а́дишь) *perf.* в кле́тку; *caged*, в кле́тке.

cairn *n.* гру́да камне́й.

caisson *n.* кессо́н.

cajole *v.t.* ума́сливать *imp.*, ума́слить *perf.* **cajolery** *n.* лесть, ума́сливание.

cake *n.* торт, пиро́жное *sb.*; (*fruit-c.*) кекс; (*soap*) кусо́к (-ска́); *v.i.* тверде́ть *imp.*, за~ *perf.*; отвердева́ть *imp.*, отверде́ть *perf.*

calamitous *adj.* па́губный, бе́дственный (-ен, -енна). **calamity** *n.* бе́дствие.

calcareous *adj.* известко́вый. **calcium** *n.* ка́льций; *adj.* ка́льциевый.

calculate *v.t.* вычисля́ть *imp.*, вы́числить *perf.*; *v.i.* рассчи́тывать *imp.*, рассчита́ть *perf.* (on, на + *acc.*); *calculated*, преднаме́ренный (-ен, -енна); *calculating-machine*, вычисли́тельная маши́на. **calculation** *n.* вычисле́ние, расчёт. **calculus** *n.* (*math.*) исчисле́ние; (*stone*) ка́мень (-мня; *pl.* -мни, -мне́й) *m.*

calendar *n.* календа́рь (-ря́) *m.*; (*register*) спи́сок (-ска).

calf[1] *n.* (*cow*) телёнок (-нка; *pl.* теля́та, -т); (*other animal*) детёныш; (*leather*) теля́чья ко́жа; *c.-love*, ребя́ческая любо́вь (-бви́, -бо́вью).

calf[2] *n.* (*leg*) икра́ (*pl.* -ры).

calibrate *v.t.* калибри́ровать *imp. perf.*; калиброва́ть *imp.* **calibration** *n.* калибро́вка. **calibre** *n.* кали́бр.

calico *n.* коленко́р (-а(у)), митка́ль (-ля́) *m.*

call *v.* звать (зову́, -вёшь; звал, -а́, -о) *imp.*, по~ *perf.*; (*name*) называ́ть *imp.*, назва́ть (назову́, -вёшь; назва́л, -а́, -о) *perf.*; (*cry*) крича́ть (-чу́, -чи́шь) *imp.*, кри́кнуть *perf.*; (*wake*) буди́ть (бужу́, бу́дишь) *imp.*, раз~ *perf.*; (*visit*) заходи́ть (-ожу́, -о́дишь) *imp.*, зайти́ (зайду́, -дёшь; зашёл, -шла́) *perf.* (on, к + *dat.*; at, в + *acc.*); (*stop at*) остана́вливаться *imp.*, останови́ться (-вится) *perf.* (at, в, на, + *prep.*); (*summon*) вызыва́ть *imp.*, вы́звать (вы́зову, -вешь) *perf.*; (*ring up*) звони́ть *imp.*, по~ *perf.* + *dat.*; *c. for*, (*require*) тре́бовать *imp.*, по~ *perf.* + *gen.*; (*fetch*) заходи́ть (-ожу́, -о́дишь) *imp.* зайти́ (зайду, -дёшь; зашёл, -шла́) *perf.* за + *instr.*; *c. off*, отменя́ть *imp.*, отмени́ть (-ню́, -нишь) *perf.*; *c. out*, вскри́кивать *imp.*, вскри́кнуть *perf.*; *c. up*, призыва́ть *imp.*, призва́ть (призову́, -вёшь; призва́л, -а́, -о) *perf.*; *n.* (*cry*) крик; (*summons*) зов, призы́в; (*telephone*) (телефо́нный) вы́зов, разгово́р; (*visit*) визи́т; (*signal*) сигна́л; *c.-box*, телефо́н-автома́т; *c.-boy*, ма́льчик, вызыва́ющий актёров на сце́ну; *c.-over*, перекли́чка; *c.-sign*, позывно́й сигна́л, позывны́е *sb.*; *c.-up*, призы́в. **caller** *n.* посети́тель *m.*, ~ница; гость (*pl.* -ти, -те́й) *m.*, го́стья (*gen.pl.* -тий). **calling** *n.* (*summons*) призва́ние; (*profession*) профе́ссия; (*occupation*) заня́тие; (*trade*) ремесло́.

callous *adj.* (*person*) бессерде́чный, бесчу́вственный (-ен(ен), -енна).
callow *adj.* (*unfledged*) неопери́вшийся; (*raw*) нео́пытный.
callus *n.* мозо́ль.
calm *adj.* (*tranquil*) споко́йный, хладнокро́вный; (*quiet*) ти́хий (тих, -а́, -о); (*windless*) безве́тренный (-ен, -енна); *n.* споко́йствие; безве́трие; *v.t.* & *i.* (*c. down*) успока́ивать(ся) *imp.*, успоко́ить(ся) *perf.*
calorie *n.* кало́рия.
calumniate *v.t.* клевета́ть (-ещу́, -е́щешь) *imp.*, на ~ *perf.* на + *acc.*
calumniation, calumny *n.* клевета́.
calve *v.i.* тели́ться (-ится) *imp.*, о ~ *perf.*
calypso *n.* кали́псо *neut.indecl.*
calyx *n.* ча́шечка.
cam *n.* кулачо́к (-чка́), кула́к (-а́). **camshaft** *n.* распредели́тельный, кулачко́вый, вал (*loc.* -у́; *pl.* -ы́).
camber *n.* вы́пуклость. **cambered** *adj.* вы́пуклый.
camel *n.* верблю́д; *camel('s)-hair*, верблю́жья шерсть.
cameo *n.* каме́я.
camera *n.* фотоаппара́т; кино-, теле-, ка́мера. **cameraman** *n.* кинооперáтор.
camomile *n.* рома́шка.
camouflage *n.* маскиро́вка; камуфля́ж; *adj.* маскиро́вочный; *v.t.* маскирова́ть *imp.*, за ~ *perf.*
camp *n.* ла́герь (*pl.* -я́, -е́й) *m.*; *v.i.* располага́ться *imp.*, расположи́ться (-жу́сь, -жишься) *perf.* ла́герем; *c.-bed*, раскладна́я крова́ть, раскладу́шка; *c.-chair*, складно́й стул (*pl.* -ья, -ьев); *c.-fire*, бива́чный костёр (-тра́).
campaign *n.* кампа́ния; похо́д; *v.i.* (*conduct c.*) проводи́ть (-ожу́, -о́дишь) *imp.*, провести́ (-еду́, -едёшь; -ёл, -ела́) *perf.* кампа́нию; (*serve in c.*) уча́ствовать *imp.* в похо́де, в кампа́нии.
campanula *n.* колоко́льчик.
camphor *n.* камфара́. **camphorated oil** *n.* камфо́рное ма́сло.
campus *n.* академи́ческий городо́к (-дка́), академгородо́к (-дка́).
camshaft *see* **cam.**
can[1] *n.* жестя́нка, (консе́рвная) коро́бка, ба́нка; *v.t.* консерви́ровать *imp.*, за ~ *perf.*
can[2] *v. aux.* (*be able*) мочь (могу́, мо́жешь; мог, -ла́) *imp.*, с ~ *perf.* + *inf.*; (*know how*) уме́ть *imp.*, с ~ *perf.* + *inf.*
Canadian *n.* кана́дец (-дца), -дка; *adj.* кана́дский.
canal *n.* кана́л.
canary *n.* канаре́йка.
cancel *v.t.* аннули́ровать *imp.*, *perf.*; отменя́ть *imp.*, отмени́ть (-ню́, -нишь) *perf.*; (*math.*) сокраща́ть *imp.*, сократи́ть (-ащу́, -ати́шь) *perf.*; (*print.*) вычёркивать *imp.*, вы́черкнуть *perf.*; (*stamp*) гаси́ть (гашу́, га́сишь) *imp.*, по ~ *perf.*; *n.* (*print.*) перепеча́танный лист (-а́). **cancellation** *n.* аннули́рование, отме́на; (*math.*) сокраще́ние; (*print.*) перепеча́тка.
cancer *n.* рак; (*C.*) Рак; *adj.* ра́ковый; *c. patient*, больно́й ра́ком. **cancerous** *adj.* ра́ковый.
candelabrum *n.* канделя́бр.
candid *adj.* открове́нный (-нен, -нна), и́скренний (-нен, -нна, -нне & -нно); *c. camera*, скры́тый фотоаппара́т.
candidacy *n.* кандидату́ра. **candidate** *n.* кандида́т. **candidature** *n.* кандидату́ра.
candied *adj.* заса́харенный; *c. peel*, цука́т(ы).
candle *n.* свеча́ (*pl.* -чи, -че́й); *c.-end*, ога́рок (-рка). **candlestick** *n.* подсве́чник. **candlewick** *n.* фити́ль (-ля́) *m.*, вы́шивка фитилька́ми.
candour *n.* открове́нность, и́скренность.
candy *n.* сла́дости *f.pl.*; *v.t.* заса́харивать *imp.*, заса́харить *perf.*
cane *n.* (*plant*) тростни́к (-а́); (*stick*) трость (*pl.* -ти, -те́й), па́лка; *c. sugar*, тростнико́вый са́хар (-а(у)); *v.t.* бить (бью, бьёшь) *imp.*, по ~ *perf.* тро́стью, па́лкой.
canine *adj.* соба́чий (-чья, -чье); *n.* (*tooth*) клык (-а́).
canister *n.* жестяна́я коро́бка.
canker *n.* рак.
cannibal *n.* каннниба́л, людое́д; *adj.* каннниба́льский, людое́дский. **cannibalism** *n.* каннибали́зм, людое́дство.

cannibalistic *adj.* каннибáльский, людоéдский. **cannibalize** *v.t.* снимáть *imp.*, снять (сниму́, -мешь; снял, -á, -о) *perf.* чáсти с + *gen.*

cannon *n.* (*gun*) пу́шка; (*billiards*) карамбóль *m.*; *adj.* пу́шечный; *c.-ball*, пу́шечное ядрó (*pl.* я́дра, я́дер, я́драм); *c.-ball service*, пу́шечная подáча; *c.-fodder*, пу́шечное мя́со; *v.i.*: *c. into*, налетáть *imp.*, налетéть (-лечу́, -лети́шь) *perf.* на + *acc.*; *c. off*, отскáкивать *imp.*, отскочи́ть (-очу́, -óчишь) *perf.* от + *gen.* **cannonade** *n.* канонáда

canoe *n.* канóэ *neut.indecl.*; челнóк (-á); *v.i.* плáвать *indet.*, плыть (плыву́, -вёшь; плыл, -á, -о) *det.* в челнокé, на канóэ.

canon *n.* канóн; (*person*) канóник; *c. law*, канони́ческое прáво. **canonical** *adj.* канони́ческий; *c. hours*, устáвные часы́ *m.pl.* моли́тв. **canonicals** *n.* церкóвное облачéние. **canonization** *n.* канонизáция. **canonize** *v.t.* канонизовáть *imp.*, *perf.*

canopy *n.* балдахи́н.

cant[1] *n.* (*slant*) наклóн, наклóнное положéние; *v.t.* наклоня́ть *imp.*, наклони́ть (-ню́, -нишь) *perf.*; придавáть (-даю́, -даёшь) *imp.*, придáть (-áм, -áшь, -áст, -ади́м; при́дал, -á, -о) *perf.* + *dat.* наклóнное положéние.

cant[2] *n.* (*hypocrisy*) хáнжество; (*jargon*) жаргóн, аргó *neut.indecl.*

cantaloup *n.* канталу́па.

cantankerous *adj.* ворчли́вый.

cantata *n.* кантáта.

canteen *n.* столóвая *sb.*, буфéт; (*case*) я́щик; (*flask*) фля́га.

canter *n.* кéнтер, лёгкий галóп; *v.i.* (*rider*) éздить *indet.*, éхать (éду, éдешь) *det.* лёгким галóпом; (*horse*) ходи́ть (-дит) *indet.*, идти́ (идёт; шёл, шла) *det.* лёгким галóпом; *v.t.* пускáть *imp.*, пусти́ть (пущу́, пу́стишь) *perf.* лёгким галóпом.

cantilever *n.* консóль, укóсина; *c. bridge*, консóльный мост (мóстá, *loc.* -у́; *pl.* -ы́).

canto *n.* песнь.

canton *n.* кантóн.

canvas *n.* холст (-á), канвá, паруси́на; (*painting*) карти́на; (*sails*) парусá *m.pl.*; *under c.*, (*on ship*) под парусáми; (*in tent*) в палáтках.

canvass *v.i.* собирáть *imp.*, собрáть (соберу́, -рёшь; собрáл, -á, -о) *perf.* голосá; *c. for*, агити́ровать *imp.*, с~ *perf.* за + *acc.*; *n.* собирáние голосóв; агитáция. **canvasser** *n.* собирáтель *m.* голосóв.

canyon *n.* каньóн.

cap *n.* шáпка, фурáжка; (*cloth*) кéпка; (*woman's*) чепéц (-пцá); (*percussion*) кáпсюль *m.*, пистóн; (*lid*) кры́шка; *v.t.* (*surpass*) перещеголя́ть *perf.*; превосходи́ть (-ожу́, -óдишь) *imp.*, превзойти́ (-ойду́, -ойдёшь; -ошёл, -ошлá) *perf.*

capability *n.* спосóбность. **capable** *adj.* спосóбный; (*skilful*) умéлый; *c. of*, (*admitting*) поддаю́щийся + *dat.*; (*able*) спосóбный на + *acc.*

capacious *adj.* простóрный, вмести́тельный, ёмкий (ёмок, ёмка). **capacitance** *n.* ёмкость. **capacity** *n.* ёмкость, вмести́мость; (*ability*) спосóбность; (*power*) мóщность; *in the c. of*, в кáчестве + *gen.*

cape[1] *n.* (*geog.*) мыс (*loc.* -е & -у́; *pl.* мысы́).

cape[2] *n.* (*cloak*) пелери́на, плащ (-á). **caped** *adj.* с пелери́ной.

caper[1] *n.* (*plant*) кáперс; *pl.* кáперсы *m.pl.*

caper[2] *n.* (*leap*) прыжóк (-жкá); *cut capers*, вы́делывать *imp.* антрашá; *v.i.* дéлать *imp.* прыжки́.

capillary *n.* капилля́р; *adj.* капилля́рный.

capital *adj.* (*city*) столи́чный; (*letter*) прописнóй; (*main*) капитáльный; (*excellent*) отли́чный; *c. goods*, срéдства *neut.pl.* произвóдства; *c. punishment*, смéртная казнь; *c. ship*, кру́пный боевóй корáбль (-ля́) *m.*; *n.* (*town*) столи́ца; (*letter*) прописнáя бу́ква; (*econ.*) капитáл; (*arch.*) капитéль. **capitalism** *n.* капитали́зм. **capitalist** *n.* капитали́ст; *adj.* капиталисти́ческий. **capitalistic** *adj.* капиталисти́ческий. **capitalization** *n.* капитализáция. **capitalize** *v.t.* капитализи́ровать *imp.*, *perf.*

capitation *attrib.* поголóвный.

capitulate *v.i.* капитули́ровать *imp.*, *perf.* **capitulation** *n.* капитуля́ция.
capon *n.* каплу́н (-á).
caprice *n.* капри́з. **capricious** *adj.* капри́зный.
Capricorn *n.* Козеро́г.
capsize *v.t.* & *i.* опроки́дывать(ся) *imp.*, опроки́нуть(ся) *perf.*
capstan *n.* кабеста́н.
capsule *n.* ка́псула, обла́тка.
captain *n.* капита́н; *v.t.* быть капита́ном + *gen.* **captaincy** *n.* зва́ние, чин, до́лжность, капита́на.
caption *n.* на́дпись, по́дпись; (*cin.*) титр.
captious *adj.* приди́рчивый.
captivate *v.t.* пленя́ть *imp.*, плени́ть *perf.* **captivating** *adj.* плени́тельный. **captive** *adj.*, *n.* пле́нный. **captivity** *n.* нево́ля; (*esp. mil.*) плен (*loc.* -у́). **capture** *n.* взя́тие, захва́т, пои́мка; *v.t.* брать (беру́, -рёшь; брал, -á, -о) *imp.*, взять (возьму́, -мёшь; взял, -á, -о) *perf.* в плен; захва́тывать *imp.*, захвати́ть (-ачу́, -а́тишь) *perf.*
car *n.* маши́на, автомоби́ль *m.*; *attrib.* автомоби́льный.
caracul *n.* кара́куль *m.*
carafe *n.* графи́н.
caramel(s) *n.* караме́ль.
carat *n.* кара́т (*gen.pl.* -т & -тов).
caravan *n.* (*convoy*) карава́н; (*cart*) фурго́н; (*house*) дом-фурго́н.
caraway (seeds) *n.* тмин (-а(у)).
carbide *n.* карби́д.
carbine *n.* карби́на.
carbohydrate *n.* углево́д. **carbolic (acid)** *n.* карбо́ловая кислота́. **carbon** *n.* углеро́д; ко́пия; *c. copy*, ко́пия (че́рез копи́рку); *c. dioxide*, углекислота́; *c. paper*, копирова́льная бума́га. **carbonaceous** *adj.* (*carbon*) углеро́дистый; (*coal*) у́глистый. **carbonate** *n.* углеки́слая соль. **carboniferous** *adj.* углено́сный; *C.*, карбо́новый (пери́од). **carborundum** *n.* карбору́нд.
carboy *n.* буты́ль.
carbuncle *n.* карбу́нкул.
carburettor *n.* карбюра́тор.
carcase, carcass *n.* ту́ша, труп.
card *n.* ка́рта, ка́рточка; (*ticket*) биле́т; *a house of cards*, ка́рточный до́мик; *c. index*, картоте́ка; *c.-sharp(er)*, шу́лер (*pl.* -á); *c.-table*, ло́мберный, ка́рточный, стол (-á). **cardboard** *n.* карто́н; *adj.* карто́нный.
cardiac *adj.* серде́чный.
cardigan *n.* вя́заная ко́фта, кардига́н.
cardinal *adj.* (*important*) кардина́льный; (*scarlet*) а́лый; *c. number*, коли́чественное числи́тельное *sb.*; *n.* кардина́л.
care *n.* (*trouble*) забо́та, попече́ние; (*attention*) внима́тельность; (*tending*) ухо́д; *take c.*, осторо́жно! береги́(те)сь!; смотри́(те)!; *take c. of*, забо́титься *imp.*, по~ *perf.* о + *prep.*; *I don't c.*, мне всё равно́; *what do I c.? who cares?* а мне всё равно́! а мне-то что?
career *n.* (*movement*) карье́р; (*profession*) карье́ра.
carefree *adj.* беззабо́тный. **careful** *adj.* (*cautious*) осторо́жный; (*thorough*) тща́тельный; (*attentive*) внима́тельный. **careless** *adj.* (*negligent*) небре́жный; (*incautious*) неосторо́жный; (*carefree*) беззабо́тный.
caress *n.* ла́ска (*gen.pl.* -ск); *v.t.* ласка́ть *imp.*
caretaker *n.* смотри́тель *m.*, ~ница; сто́рож (*pl.* -á); *attrib.* вре́менный.
care-worn *adj.* измý́ченный (-ен) забо́тами.
cargo *n.* груз.
caricature *n.* карикату́ра; *v.t.* изобража́ть *imp.*, изобрази́ть *perf.* в карикату́рном ви́де.
caries *n.* карио́з.
carmine *n.* карми́н, карми́нный цвет; *adj.* карми́нный.
carnage *n.* резня́.
carnal *adj.* пло́тский.
carnation *n.* (садо́вая) гвозди́ка.
carnival *n.* карнава́л; (*Shrove-tide*) ма́сленица.
carnivore *n.* плотоя́дное живо́тное *sb.* **carnivorous** *adj.* плотоя́дный.
carol *n.* (рожде́ственский) гимн.
carotid artery *n.* со́нная арте́рия.
carousal *n.* попо́йка.
carp[1] *n.* (*wild*) саза́н; (*domesticated*) карп.

carp[2] *v.i.* придира́ться *imp.*, придра́ться (-деру́сь, -дерёшся; -дра́лся, -драла́сь, -дра́ло́сь) *perf.* (at, к + *dat.*).

carpenter *n.* пло́тник. **carpentry** *n.* пло́тничество.

carpet *n.* ковёр (-вра́); *v.t.* устила́ть *imp.*, устла́ть (-телю́, -те́лешь) *perf.* ковра́ми; *c.-bag*, саквоя́ж.

carping *adj.* приди́рчивый; *n.* приди́рки (-рок) *pl.*

carriage *n.* (*vehicle*) каре́та, экипа́ж; (*rly.*) ваго́н; (*of machine*) каре́тка; (*conveyance*) прово́з, перево́зка; (*bearing*) оса́нка; *c. forward*, с опла́той доста́вки получа́телем; *c. free*, беспла́тная пересы́лка; *c. paid*, за пересы́лку упла́чено. **carriageway** *n.* прое́зжая часть доро́ги, у́лицы. **carrier** *n.* (*person*) во́зчик; (*object*) бага́жник; *c. pigeon*, почто́вый го́лубь (*pl.* -би, -бе́й) *m.*; *c. wave*, несу́щая волна́ (*pl.* -ны, -н, -на́м).

carrion *n.* па́даль; *c. crow*, чёрная воро́на.

carrot *n.* морко́вка; *pl.* морко́вь (*collect.*).

carry *v.t.* (*by hand*) носи́ть (ношу́, но́сишь) *indet.*, нести́ (несу́, -сёшь; нёс, -ла́) *det.*; переноси́ть (-ошу́, -о́сишь) *imp.*, перенести́ (-есу́, -есёшь; -ёс, -есла́) *perf.*; (*in vehicle*) вози́ть (вожу́, во́зишь) *indet.*, везти́ (везу́, -зёшь; вёз, -ла́) *det.*; *v.i.* нести́сь (несётся; нёсся, несла́сь); (*sound*) быть слы́шен (-шна́, -шно); *c. forward*, переноси́ть (-ошу́, -о́сишь) *imp.*, перенести́ (-есу́, -есёшь; -ёс, -есла́) *perf.*; *c. on*, (*continue*) продолжа́ть *imp.*; (*behaviour*) вести́ (веду́, ведёшь; вёл, -а́) *imp.* себя́ несде́ржанно; *c. out*, выполня́ть *imp.*, вы́полнить *perf.*; доводи́ть (-ожу́, -о́дишь) *imp.*, довести́ (-еду́, -едёшь; -ёл, -ела́) *perf.* до конца́; *c. over*, переноси́ть (-ошу́, -о́сишь) *imp.*, перенести́ (-есу́, -есёшь; -ёс, -есла́) *perf.*

cart *n.* теле́га, пово́зка; *v.t.* вози́ть (вожу́, во́зишь) *indet.*, везти́ (везу́, -зёшь; вёз, -ла́) *det.* в теле́ге; *c.-horse*, ломова́я ло́шадь (*pl.* -ди, -де́й, *instr.* -дьми́); *c.-load*, воз; *c.-track*, гужева́я доро́га, просёлок (-лка); *c.-wheel*, колесо́ (*pl.* -ёса) теле́ги; (*somersault*) переворо́т бо́ком в сто́рону. **cartage** *n.* сто́имость перево́зки.

cartel *n.* карте́ль *m.*

cartilage *n.* хрящ (-а́). **cartilaginous** *adj.* хрящево́й.

cartographer *n.* карто́граф. **cartographic** *adj.* картографи́ческий. **cartography** *n.* картогра́фия.

carton *n.* коро́бка из карто́на, пластма́ссы и т.д.

cartoon *n.* карикату́ра; (*design*) карто́н; (*cin.*) мультфи́льм. **cartoonist** *n.* карикатури́ст, ~ка.

cartridge *n.* патро́н; *c. belt*, патронта́ш.

carve *v.t.* ре́зать (ре́жу, -жешь) *imp.* по + *dat.*; (*wood*) выреза́ть *imp.*, вы́резать (-ежу, -ежешь) *perf.*; (*stone*) высека́ть *imp.*, вы́сечь (-еку, -ечешь; -ек); (*meat etc.*) нареза́ть *imp.* наре́зать (-е́жу, -е́жешь) *perf.* **carver** *n.* (*person*) ре́зчик; *pl.* (*cutlery*) большо́й нож (-а́) и ви́лка. **carving** *n.* резьба́; резно́й орна́мент; *c.-knife*, нож (-а́) для нареза́ния мя́са.

cascade *n.* каска́д.

case[1] *n.* (*instance*) слу́чай; (*leg.*) де́ло (*pl.* -ла́); (*med.*) больно́й *sb.*; (*gram.*) паде́ж (-а́); *as the c. may be*, в зави́симости от обстоя́тельств; *in c.*, (в слу́чае) е́сли; *in any c.*, во вся́ком слу́чае; *in no c.*, ни в ко́ем слу́чае; *just in c.*, на вся́кий слу́чай, на аво́сь.

case[2] *n.* (*box*) я́щик, коро́бка; (*suitcase*) чемода́н; (*casing*) футля́р, чехо́л (-хла́); (*print.*) ка́сса; *v.t.* покрыва́ть *imp.*, покры́ть (-ро́ю, -ро́ешь) *perf.*; *c.-harden*, цементи́ровать *imp.*, *perf.*

casement window *n.* ство́рное окно́ (*pl.* о́кна, о́кон, о́кнам).

cash *n.* нали́чные *sb.*; де́ньги (-нег, -ньга́м) *pl.*; ка́сса; *c. and carry*, прода́жа за нали́чный расчёт без доста́вки на́ дом; *c. down*, де́ньги на бо́чку; *c. on delivery*, нало́жным платежо́м; *c. register*, ка́сса; *v.t.* превраща́ть *imp.*, преврати́ть (-ащу, -ати́шь) *perf.* в нали́чные *sb.*; *c. a cheque*, получа́ть *imp.*, получи́ть (-чу́, -чишь) *perf.* де́ньги по че́ку. **cashier**[1] *n.* касси́р. **cashier**[2] *v.t.* увольня́ть *imp.*, уво́лить *perf.* со слу́жбы.

cashmere *n.* кашеми́р.
casing *n.* (*tech.*) кожу́х (-а́).
casino *n.* казино́ *neut.indecl.*
cask *n.* бо́чка.
casket *n.* шкату́лка, ларе́ц (-рца́).
casserole *n.* тяжёлая кастрю́ля; блю́до, приготовля́емое в ней.
cassock *n.* ря́са.
cast *v.t.* (*throw*) броса́ть *imp.*, бро́сить *perf.*; (*shed*) сбра́сывать *imp.*, сбро́сить *perf.*; (*theat.*) распределя́ть *imp.*, распредели́ть *perf.* ро́ли + *dat.*; (*found*) лить (лью, льёшь; лил, -а́, -о) *imp.*, с~ (солью́, -ьёшь; слил, -а́, -о) *perf.*; (*horoscope*) составля́ть *imp.*, соста́вить *perf.*; *c. ashore*, выбра́сывать *imp.*, вы́бросить *perf.* на бе́рег; *c. off*, (*knitting*) спуска́ть *imp.*, спусти́ть (-ущу́, -у́стишь) *perf.* пе́тли; (*naut.*) отплыва́ть *imp.*, отплы́ть (-ыву́, -ывёшь; отплы́л, -а́, -о) *perf.*; *c. on*, (*knitting*) набира́ть *imp.*, набра́ть (наберу́, -рёшь; набра́л, -а́, -о) *perf.* пе́тли; *n.* (*throw*) бросо́к (-ска́), броса́ние; (*of mind etc.*) склад; (*mould*) фо́рма; (*med.*) ги́псовая повя́зка; (*theat.*) де́йствующие ли́ца (-ц) *pl.*; (*in eye*) лёгкое косогла́зие. **castaway** *n.* потерпе́вший *sb.* кораблекруше́ние. **cast iron** *n.* чугу́н (-а́). **cast-iron** *adj.* чугу́нный. **cast-offs** *n.* (*clothes*) но́шеное пла́тье.
castanet *n.* кастанье́та.
caste *n.* ка́ста; ка́стовая систе́ма.
castigate *v.t.* бичева́ть *imp.*
castle *n.* за́мок (-мка); (*chess*) ладья́.
castor *n.* (*wheel*) ро́лик, колёсико (*pl.* -ки, -ков); *c. sugar*, са́харная пу́дра.
castor oil *n.* касто́ровое ма́сло.
castrate *v.t.* кастри́ровать *imp.*, *perf.* **castration** *n.* кастра́ция.
casual *adj.* случа́йный; (*careless*) несерьёзный. **casualty** *n.* (*wounded*) ра́неный *sb.*; (*killed*) уби́тый *sb.*; *pl.* поте́ри (-рь) *pl.*; *c. ward*, пала́та ско́рой по́мощи.
casuist *n.* казуи́ст. **casuistic(al)** *adj.* казуисти́ческий. **casuistry** *n.* казуи́стика.
cat *n.* ко́шка; (*tom*) кот (-а́); *catcall*, свист, осви́стывание; *v.t.* & *i.* осви́стывать *imp.*, освиста́ть (-ищу́, -и́щешь) *perf.*; *c.-o'-nine-tails*, ко́шки *f.pl.*; *c.'s-eye*, (*min.*) коша́чий глаз (*loc.* -у́; *pl.* -за́, -з); (*on road*) (доро́жный) рефле́ктор; *c.'s-meat*, кони́на (для ко́шек); *catwalk*, у́зкий мо́стик; рабо́чий помо́ст.
cataclysm *n.* катакли́зм.
catalogue *n.* катало́г; (*price list*) прейскура́нт; *v.t.* каталогизи́ровать *imp.*, *perf.*
catalysis *n.* ката́лиз. **catalyst** *n.* катализа́тор. **catalytic** *adj.* каталити́ческий.
catamaran *n.* катамара́н.
catapult *n.* (*child's*) рога́тка; (*hist.*, *aeron.*) катапу́льта; *v.t.* катапульти́ровать *imp.*, *perf.*
cataract *n.* (*waterfall*) водопа́д; (*med.*) катара́кта.
catarrh *n.* ката́р.
catastrophe *n.* катастро́фа. **catastrophic** *adj.* катастрофи́ческий.
catch *v.t.* (*captive*) лови́ть (-влю́, -вишь) *imp.*, пойма́ть *perf.*; (*seize*) захва́тывать *imp.*, захвати́ть (-ачу́, -а́тишь) *perf.*; (*surprise*) застава́ть (-таю́, -таёшь) *imp.*, заста́ть (-а́ну, -а́нешь) *perf.*; (*disease*) заража́ться *imp.*, зарази́ться *perf.* + *instr.*; (*be in time for*) успева́ть *imp.*, успе́ть *perf.* на + *acc.*; *c. on*, зацепля́ть(ся) *imp.*, зацепи́ть(ся) (-плю́(сь), -пишь(ся)) *perf.* за + *acc.*; (*v.i.*) (*become popular*) привива́ться *imp.*, приви́ться (-вьётся; -ви́лся, -вила́сь) *perf.*; *c. up with*, догоня́ть *imp.*, догна́ть (догоню́, -нишь; догна́л, -а́, -о) *perf.*; *n.* (*action*) по́имка; (*of fish*) уло́в; (*trick*) уло́вка; (*on door etc.*) защёлка, задви́жка; *c. crops*, междупосевны́е культу́ры *f.pl.* **catching** *adj.* зара́зный; заразительный; привлека́тельный. **catchment area** *n.* водосбо́рная пло́щадь (*pl.* -ди, -де́й). **catchword** *n.* (*slogan*) ло́зунг; (*running title*) колонти́тул; (*headword*) загла́вное сло́во (*pl.* -ва́). **catchy** *adj.* привлека́тельный, легко́ запомина́ющийся.
catechism *n.* (*eccl.*) катехи́зис; допро́с.
catechize *v.t.* допра́шивать *imp.*, допроси́ть (-ошу́, -о́сишь) *perf.*
categorical *adj.* категори́ческий. **category** *n.* катего́рия.
catenary *n.* цепна́я ли́ния; *adj.* цепно́й.

cater *v.i.* поставля́ть *imp.* прови́зию; *c. for*, снабжа́ть *imp.*, снабди́ть *perf.*; обслу́живать *imp.*, обслужи́ть (-жу́, -жишь) *perf.* **caterer** *n.* поставщи́к (-а́) (прови́зии).

caterpillar *n.* гу́сеница; *adj.* гу́сеничный; *c. track*, гу́сеничная ле́нта.

caterwaul *v.i.* крича́ть (-чу́, -чи́шь) кото́м; задава́ть (-даёт) *imp.*, зада́ть (-а́ст; за́дал, -а́, -о) *perf.* коша́чий конце́рт. **caterwauling** *n.* коша́чий конце́рт.

catgut *n.* кетгу́т.

catharsis *n.* ка́тарсис.

cathedral *n.* (кафедра́льный) собо́р.

catheter *n.* кате́тер.

cathode *n.* като́д; *c. rays*, като́дные лучи́ *m.pl.*

Catholic *adj.* католи́ческий; *n.* като́лик, -ичка. **Catholicism** *n.* католи́чество, католици́зм.

catkin *n.* серёжка.

cattle *n.* скот (-а́).

cauldron *n.* котёл (-тла́).

cauliflower *n.* цветна́я капу́ста.

caulk *v.t.* конопа́тить *imp.*, за~ *perf.*

causal *adj.* причи́нный (-нен, -нна). **causality** *n.* причи́нность. **causation** *n.* причине́ние; причи́нность. **cause** *n.* причи́на, по́вод; (*leg. etc.*) де́ло (*pl.* -ла́); *v.t.* причиня́ть *imp.*, причини́ть *perf.*; вызыва́ть *imp.*, вы́звать (-зову, -зовешь) *perf.*; (*induce*) заставля́ть *imp.*, заста́вить *perf.* **causeless** *adj.* беспричи́нный (-нен, -нна).

caustic *adj.* каусти́ческий, е́дкий (е́док, едка́, е́дко); *c. soda*, е́дкий натр; *n.* е́дкое вещество́.

cauterization *n.* прижига́ние. **cauterize** *v.t.* прижига́ть *imp.*, прижéчь (-жгу́, -жжёшь; -жёг, -жгла́) *perf.* **cautery** *n.* термока́утер.

caution *n.* осторо́жность; (*warning*) предупрежде́ние; *v.t.* предостерега́ть *imp.*, предостере́чь (-егу́, -ежёшь; -ёг, -егла́) *perf.* **cautious** *adj.* осторо́жный. **cautionary** *adj.* предостерега́ющий.

cavalcade *n.* кавалька́да. **cavalier** *adj.* бесцеремо́нный (-нен, -нна); *C.*, (*hist.*) роя́листский; роя́лист. **cavalry** *n.* кавале́рия. **cavalryman** *n.* кавале́рист.

cave *n.* пеще́ра; *v.i.*: *c. in*, обва́ливаться *imp.*, обвали́ться (-ится) *perf.*; (*yield*) уступа́ть *imp.*, уступи́ть (-плю́, -пишь) *perf.* **caveman** *n.* пеще́рный челове́к. **cavern** *n.* пеще́ра. **cavernous** *adj.* пеще́ристый.

caviare *n.* икра́.

cavil *v.i.* придира́ться *imp.*, придра́ться (-деру́сь, -дерёшься; -а́лся, -ала́сь, -а́ло́сь) *perf.* (at, к + *dat.*).

cavity *n.* впа́дина, по́лость (*pl.* -ти, -те́й).

caw *v.i.* ка́ркать *imp.*, ка́ркнуть *perf.*; *n.* ка́рканье.

cayman *n.* kaйма́н.

cease *v.t.* & *i.* прекраща́ть(ся) *imp.*, прекрати́ть(ся) (-ащу́, -ати́т(ся)) *perf.*; *v.i.* перестава́ть (-таю́, -таёшь) *imp.*, переста́ть (-а́ну, -а́нешь) *perf.* (+ *inf.*); *c.-fire*, прекраще́ние огня́. **ceaseless** *adj.* непреста́нный (-а́нен, -а́нна).

cedar *n.* кедр.

ceiling *n.* потоло́к (-лка́); (*prices etc.*) максима́льная цена́ (*acc.* -ну), максима́льный у́ровень (-вня) *m.*

celandine *n.* чистоте́л.

celebrate *v.t.* пра́здновать *imp.*, от~ *perf.*; *be celebrated*, сла́виться *imp.* (for, + *instr.*). **celebrated** *adj.* знамени́тый. **celebration** *n.* пра́зднование. **celebrity** *n.* знамени́тость.

celery *n.* сельдере́й.

celestial *adj.* небе́сный.

celibacy *n.* безбра́чие. **celibate** *adj.* безбра́чный; (*person*) холосто́й (-ост), незаму́жняя.

cell *n.* (*room*) ке́лья; (*prison*) (тюре́мная) ка́мера; (*biol.*) кле́тка, кле́точка; (*polit.*) яче́йка.

cellar *n.* подва́л, по́греб (*pl.* -а́); *adj.* подва́льный.

cellist *n.* виолончели́ст. **cello** *n.* виолонче́ль.

cellophane *n.* целлофа́н; *adj.* целлофа́новый. **cellular** *adj.* кле́точный. **cellule** *n.* кле́точка. **celluloid** *n.* целлуло́ид; (кино)фи́льм. **cellulose** *n.* целлюло́за; клетча́тка.

Celsius: *C. scale*, шкала́ термоме́тра

Це́льсия; *C. thermometer*, термо́метр Це́льсия; *10° C.*, 10° по Це́льсию.

Celt *n.* кельт. **Celtic** *adj.* ке́льтский.

cement *n.* цеме́нт; *v.t.* цементи́ровать *imp.*, за~ *perf.*

cemetery *n.* кла́дбище.

cenotaph *n.* кенота́ф.

censer *n.* кади́ло.

censor *n.* це́нзор; *v.t.* подверга́ть *imp.*, подве́ргнуть (-г) *perf.* цензу́ре. **censorious** *adj.* стро́гий (строг, -а́, -о); скло́нный (-о́нен, -о́нна́, -о́нно) осужда́ть. **censorship** *n.* цензу́ра. **censure** *n.* осужде́ние; порица́ние; *v.t.* осужда́ть *imp.*, осуди́ть (-ужу́, -у́дишь) *perf.*; порица́ть *imp.*

census *n.* пе́репись (населе́ния).

cent *n.* цент; *per c.*, проце́нт.

centaur *n.* кента́вр.

centenarian *adj.* столе́тний; *n.* столе́тний челове́к, челове́к в во́зрасте ста лет. **centenary** *n.* столе́тие. **centennial** *adj.* столе́тний; *n.* столе́тняя годовщи́на. **centigrade** *adj.* стогра́дусный; *10° C.*, 10° по Це́льсию. **centigram** *n.* сантигра́мм. **centilitre** *n.* центили́тр. **centimetre** *n.* сантиме́тр. **centipede** *n.* сороконо́жка.

central *adj.* центра́льный; *c. heating*, центра́льное отопле́ние. **centralism** *n.* централи́зм. **centralization** *n.* централиза́ция. **centralize** *v.t.* централизова́ть *imp.*, *perf.* **centre** *n.* центр; середи́на; *c. back*, центр защи́ты; *c.-board*, опускно́й киль *m.*; *c. forward*, центр нападе́ния; *c. half*, центр полузащи́ты; *v.i.* сосредото́чиваться *imp.*, сосредото́читься *perf.* **centrifugal** *adj.* центробе́жный. **centrifuge** *n.* центрифу́га. **centripetal** *adj.* центростреми́тельный.

centurion *n.* центурио́н. **century** *n.* столе́тие, век (*loc.* в -е, на -у́; *pl.* -а́); (*sport*) сто очко́в.

ceramic *adj.* керами́ческий. **ceramics** *n.* кера́мика.

cereal *adj.* хле́бный; *n.*: *pl.* хлеба́ *m.pl.*, хле́бные, зерновы́е, зла́ки *m.pl.*; *breakfast cereals*, зерновы́е хло́пья (-ьев) *pl.*

cerebral *adj.* мозгово́й.

ceremonial *adj.* форма́льный; торже́ственный (-ен, -енна), пара́дный; *n.* церемониа́л. **ceremonious** *adj.* церемо́нный (-нен, -нна). **ceremony** *n.* церемо́ния.

cerise *adj.* (*n.*) све́тло-вишнёвый (цвет).

cert *n.* (*sl.*) ве́рное де́ло. **certain** *adj.* (*definite*) определённый (-ёнен, -ённа); (*reliable*) ве́рный (-рен, -рна́, -рно, ве́рны́); (*doubtless*) несомне́нный (-нен, -нна); *predic.* уве́рен (-нна); *for c.*, наверняка́. **certainly** *adv.* (*of course*) коне́чно, безусло́вно; (*without fail*) непреме́нно; (*beyond question*) несомне́нно. **certainty** *n.* (*conviction*) уве́ренность; (*undoubted fact*) несомне́нный факт; безусло́вность; *bet on a c.*, держа́ть (-жу́, -жишь) *imp.* пари́ наверняка́.

certificate *n.* удостовере́ние, свиде́тельство; сертифика́т; аттеста́т; *birth c.*, ме́трика. **certify** *v.t.* удостоверя́ть *imp.*, удостове́рить *perf.*; свиде́тельствовать *imp.*, за~ *perf.*; (*as insane*) признава́ть (-наю́, -наёшь) *imp.*, призна́ть *perf.* сумасше́дшим.

certitude *n.* уве́ренность.

cessation *n.* прекраще́ние.

cesspit *n.* помо́йная я́ма. **cesspool** *n.* выгребна́я я́ма; (*fig.*) клоа́ка.

chafe *v.t.* (*rub*) тере́ть (тру́, трёшь; тёр) *imp.*; (*rub sore*) натира́ть *imp.*, натере́ть (-тру́, -трёшь; -тёр); *v.i.* (*fret*) раздража́ться *imp.*, раздражи́ться *perf.*

chaff *n.* (*husks*) мяки́на; (*chopped straw*) се́чка; (*banter*) подшу́чивание; *v.t.* поддра́знивать *imp.*, поддразни́ть (-ню́, -нишь) *perf.*; подшу́чивать *imp.*, подшути́ть (-учу́, -у́тишь) *perf.* над + *instr.*

chaffinch *n.* зя́блик.

chagrin *n.* огорче́ние.

chain *n.* цепь (*loc.* -пи́; *pl.* -пи, -пе́й); (*crochet*) коси́чка; *c. reaction*, цепна́я реа́кция; *c. stitch*, тамбу́рный шов (шва), тамбу́рная стро́чка.

chair *n.* стул (*pl.* -ья, -ьев), кре́сло (*gen.pl.* -сел); (*chairmanship*) председа́тельство; (*chairman*) председа́тель *m.*, ~ница; (*univ.*) ка́федра; *v.t.* (*preside*) председа́тельствовать *imp.* на +

prep.; (*carry aloft*) поднимáть *imp.*, поднять (-нимý, -ни́мешь; пóднял, -á, -о) *perf.* и нести́ (несý, -сёшь; нёс, -лá) *imp.* **chairman, -woman** *n.* председáтель *m.*, ~ница.

chalice *n.* чáша.

chalk *n.* мел (-а(у), *loc.* -ý & -е); (*piece of c.*) мелóк (-лкá); *not by a long c.*, отню́дь нет, далекó не; *v.t.* писáть (пишý, пи́шешь) *imp.*, на~ *perf.* мéлом; черти́ть (-рчý, -ртишь) *imp.*, на~ *perf.* мéлом. **chalky** *adj.* меловóй, известкóвый.

challenge *n.* (*summons*) вы́зов; (*sentry's call*) óклик (часовóго); (*leg.*) отвóд; *v.t.* вызывáть *imp.*, вы́звать (вы́зову, -вешь) *perf.*; окликáть *imp.*, окли́кнуть *perf.*; отводи́ть (-ожý, -óдишь) *imp.*, отвести́ (-едý, -едёшь; -ёл, -елá) *perf.*

chalybeate *adj.* желéзистый.

chamber *n.* кóмната; (*polit.*) палáта; *pl.* меблирóванные кóмнаты *f.pl.*; *pl.* (*judge's*) кабинéт (судьи́); *c. music*, кáмерная мýзыка; *c.-pot*, ночнóй горшóк (-шкá). **chamberlain** *n.* камергéр; *C.*, гофмéйстер. **chambermaid** *n.* гóрничная *sb.*

chameleon *n.* хамелеóн.

chamois *n.* (*animal*) сéрна; (*c.-leather*) зáмша; *adj.* зáмшевый.

champ *v.i.* чáвкать *imp.*, чáвкнуть *perf.*; *c. the bit*, грызть (-зёт; -з) *imp.* удилá (*pl.*).

champagne *n.* шампáнское *sb.*

champion *n.* (*athletic etc.*) чемпиóн, ~ка; (*animal, plant etc.*) пéрвый призёр; (*upholder*) побóрник, -ица; *adj.* получи́вший пéрвый приз; *v.t.* защищáть *imp.*, защити́ть (-ищý, -ити́шь) *perf.* **championship** *n.* пéрвенство, чемпионáт; побóрничество.

chance *n.* случáйность; (*opportunity*) слýчай; (*possibility*) шанс; *adj.* случáйный; *v.i.* (*happen*) случáться *imp.*, случи́ться *perf.*; *c. it*, рискнýть *perf.*

chancel *n.* алтáрь (-ря́) *m.*

chancellery *n.* канцеля́рия. **chancellor** *n.* кáнцлер; (*univ.*) рéктор университéта; *Lord C.*, лорд-кáнцлер; *C. of the Exchequer*, кáнцлер казначéйства.

Chancery *n.* суд (-á) лóрда-кáнцлера; *c.*, канцеля́рия.

chancy *adj.* рискóванный (-ан, -анна).

chandelier *n.* лю́стра.

change *n.* перемéна, изменéние; (*of clothes etc.*) смéна; (*money*) сдáча; (*of trains etc.*) пересáдка; *c. for the better*, перемéна к лýчшему; *c. of air*, перемéна обстанóвки; *c. of life*, климактéрий; *c. of scene*, перемéна обстанóвки; *for a c.*, для разнообрáзия; *v.t. & i.* меня́ть(ся) *imp.*; изменя́ть(ся) *imp.*, измени́ть(ся) (-ню́(сь), -нишь(ся)) *perf.*; *v.i.* (*one's clothes*) переодевáться *imp.*, переодéться (-éнусь, -éнешься) *perf.*; (*trains etc.*) пересáживаться *imp.*, пересéсть (-ся́ду, -ся́дешь; -сéл) *perf.*; *v.t.* (*a baby*) перепелёнывать *imp.*, перепеленáть *perf.*; (*give c. for*) размéнивать *imp.*, разменя́ть *perf.*; *c. into* превращáться *imp.*, преврати́ться (-ащýсь, -ати́шься) *perf.* в + *acc.* **changeable** *adj.* непостоя́нный (-нен, -нна), неустóйчивый, измéнчивый. **changeless** *adj.* неизмéнный (-нен, -нна), постоя́нный (-нен, -нна).

channel *n.* канáл, проли́в, протóк; (*fig.*) рýсло (*gen.pl.* -сл & -сел), путь (-ти́, -тём) *m.*; *the* (*English*) *C.*, Ла-Мáнш; *v.t.* пускáть *imp.*, пусти́ть (пущý, пýстишь) *perf.* по канáлу; (*fig., direct*) направля́ть *imp.*

chaos *n.* хáос. **chaotic** *adj.* хаоти́чный.

chap[1] *n.* (*person*) мáлый *sb.*, пáрень (-рня; *pl.* -рни, -рнéй) *m.*

chap[2] *n.* (*crack*) трéщина; *v.i.* трéскаться *imp.*, по~ *perf.*

chapel *n.* часóвня (*gen.pl.* -вен), капéлла; молéльня (*gen.pl.* -лен).

chap-fallen *adj.* удручённый (-ён, -енá).

chaplain *n.* капеллáн.

chapter *n.* главá (*pl.* -вы); (*eccl.*) капи́тул; *c. house*, здáние капи́тула.

char[1] *n.* приходя́щая домрабóтница.

char[2] *v.t. & i.* обýгливать(ся) *imp.*, обýглить(ся) *perf.*

character *n.* харáктер; (*testimonial*) рекомендáция; (*personage*) персонáж; (*theat.*) дéйствующее лицó (*pl.* -ца); (*letter*) бýква; (*numeral*) ци́фра;

(*mark*) знак. **characteristic** *adj.* характе́рный; *n.* характе́рная черта́. **characterize** *v.t.* характеризова́ть *imp., perf.*

charade *n.* шара́да.

charcoal *n.* древе́сный у́голь (угля́) *m.*

charge *n.* (*load*) нагру́зка; (*for gun; electr.*) заря́д; (*fee*) пла́та; (*care*) попече́ние; (*person*) пито́мец (-мца), -мица; (*accusation*) обвине́ние; (*mil.*) ата́ка; *be in c. of*, заве́довать *imp.* + *instr.*; име́ть *imp.* на попече́нии; *in the c. of*, на попече́нии + *gen.*; *v.t.* (*gun; electr.*) заряжа́ть *imp.*, заряди́ть (-яжу́, -я́ди́шь) *perf.*; (*accuse*) обвиня́ть *imp.*, обвини́ть *perf.* (with, в + *prep.*); (*mil.*) атакова́ть *imp., perf.*; *v.i.* броса́ться *imp.*, бро́ситься *perf.* в ата́ку; *c.* (*for*), брать (беру́, -рёшь; брал, -а́, -о) *imp.*, взять (возьму́, -мёшь; взял, -а́, -о) *perf.* (за + *acc.*); назнача́ть *imp.*, назна́чить *perf.* пла́ту (за + *acc.*); *c. to* (*the account of*), запи́сывать *imp.*, записа́ть (-ишу́, -и́шешь) *perf.* на счёт + *gen.*

chargé d'affaires *n.* пове́ренный *sb.* в дела́х.

chariot *n.* колесни́ца.

charisma *n.* (*divine gift*) бо́жий дар; (*charm*) обая́ние. **charismatic** *adj.* боговдохнове́нный; вдохнове́нный; с бо́жьей и́скрой; обая́тельный.

charitable *adj.* благотвори́тельный; (*merciful*) милосе́рдный; (*lenient*) снисходи́тельный. **charity** *n.* (*kindness*) милосе́рдие; (*leniency*) снисходи́тельность; благотвори́тельность; (*organization*) благотвори́тельное о́бщество; *pl.* благотвори́тельная де́ятельность.

charlatan *n.* шарлата́н.

charlotte *n.*: *apple c.*, шарло́тка.

charm *n.* очарова́ние; пре́лесть; (*spell*) за́говор; *pl.* ча́ры (чар) *pl.*; (*amulet*) талисма́н; (*trinket*) брело́к; *act, work, like a c.*, твори́ть *imp.*, со ~ *perf.* чудеса́; *v.t.* очаро́вывать *imp.*, очарова́ть *perf.*; *c. away*, отгоня́ть *imp.*, отогна́ть (отгоню́, -нишь; отогна́л, -а́, -о) *perf.* (как бы) колдовство́м; *bear a charmed life*, быть неуязви́мым.

charming *adj.* очарова́тельный, преле́стный.

charring *n.* рабо́та по до́му; *do, go out, c.*, служи́ть (-жу́, -жишь) *imp.* приходя́щей домрабо́тницей.

chart *n.* (*naut.*) морска́я ка́рта; (*table*) гра́фик; *v.t.* наноси́ть (-ошу́, -о́сишь) *imp.*, нанести́ (-су́, -сёшь; нанёс, -ла́) *perf.* на ка́рту; составля́ть *imp.*, соста́вить *perf.* гра́фик + *gen.* **charter** *n.* (*document*) ха́ртия; (*statutes*) уста́в; (*c.-party*) ча́ртер; *v.t.* (*ship*) фрахтова́ть *imp.*, за ~ *perf.*; (*vehicle etc.*) нанима́ть *imp.*, наня́ть (найму́, -мёшь; на́нял, -а́, -о) *perf.*

charwoman *n.* приходя́щая домрабо́тница.

chase *v.t.* гоня́ться *indet.*, гна́ться (гоню́сь, го́нишься; гна́лся, -ла́сь, гна́ло́сь) *det.* за + *instr.*; *n.* (*pursuit*) пого́ня, пресле́дование; (*hunting*) охо́та.

chased *adj.* укра́шенный (-н) гравиро́ванием, релье́фом.

chasm *n.* (*abyss*) бе́здна; (*fissure*) глубо́кая рассе́лина.

chassis *n.* шасси́ *neut.indecl.*

chaste *adj.* целому́дренный (-ен, -енна).

chastise *v.t.* подверга́ть *imp.*, подве́ргнуть (-г) *perf.* наказа́нию.

chastity *n.* целому́дрие.

chat *n.* бесе́да, разгово́р; *v.i.* бесе́довать *imp.*; разгова́ривать *imp.*

chattels *n.* дви́жимость.

chatter *n.* болтовня́; трескотня́; *v.i.* болта́ть *imp.*; треща́ть (-щу́, -щи́шь) *imp.*; (*of teeth*) стуча́ть (-ча́т) *imp.* **chatterbox** *n.* болту́н (-а́), ~ья. **chatty** *adj.* разгово́рчивый.

chauffeur *n.* шофёр.

chauvinism *n.* шовини́зм. **chauvinist** *n.* шовини́ст, ~ка; *adj.* шовинисти́ческий.

cheap *adj.* дешёвый (дёшев, -а́, -о). **cheapen** *v.t.* & *i.* обесце́нивать(ся) *imp.*, обесце́нить(ся) *perf.*; удешевля́ть(ся) *imp.*, удешеви́ть(ся) *perf.* **cheaply** *adv.* дёшево. **cheapness** *n.* дешеви́зна.

cheat *v.t.* обма́нывать *imp.*, обману́ть (-ну́, -нешь) *perf.*; *v.i.* плутова́ть *imp.*, на ~, с ~ *perf.*; моше́нничать *imp.*, c~ *perf.*; *n.* (*person*) обма́нщик, -ица; (*act*) обма́н. **cheating** *n.* моше́нничество, плутовство́.

check[1] *n.* контро́ль *m.*, прове́рка; (*stoppage*) заде́ржка; (*chess*) шах; *adj.* контро́льный; *v.t.* (*examine*) проверя́ть *imp.*, прове́рить *perf.*; контроли́ровать *imp.*, про~ *perf.*; (*restrain*) сде́рживать *imp.*, сдержа́ть (-жу́, -жишь) *perf.*; *c.-list*, контро́льный спи́сок (-ска); *checkmate*, шах и мат; *v.t.* наноси́ть (-ошу́, -о́сишь) *imp.*, нанести́ (-су́, -сёшь; нанёс, -ла́) *perf.* + *dat.* пораже́ние; *c.-point*, контро́льно-пропускно́й пункт.

check[2] *n.* (*pattern*) кле́тка. **check(ed)** *adj.* кле́тчатый.

cheek *n.* щека́ (*acc.* щёку; *pl.* щёки, щёк, -а́м); (*impertinence*) наха́льство, де́рзость; *v.t.* дерзи́ть (-и́шь) *imp.*, на~ *perf.* + *dat.*; *c.-bone*, скула́ (*pl.* -лы). **cheeky** *adj.* де́рзкий (-зок, -зка́, -зко), наха́льный.

cheep *n.* писк; *v.i.* пища́ть (-щу́, -щи́шь) *imp.*, пи́скнуть *perf.*

cheer *n.* одобри́тельное восклица́ние; *pl.* (*applause*) аплодисме́нты (-тов) *pl.*; *cheers!* за (ва́ше) здоро́вье!; *three cheers for . . .*, да здра́вствует (-уют) + *nom.*; *v.t.* (*applaud*) аплоди́ровать *imp.* + *dat.*; *c. up*, ободря́ть(ся) *imp.*, ободри́ть(ся) *perf.* **cheerful** *adj.* весёлый (ве́сел, -а́, -о, ве́селы́), бо́дрый (бодр, -а́, -о). **cheerless** *adj.* уны́лый. **cheery** *adj.* бо́дрый (бодр, -а́, -о).

cheese *n.* сыр (-а(у); *pl.* -ы́); *c.-cake*, ватру́шка; *cheesecloth*, ма́рля; *c.-paring*, ску́пость, грошо́вая эконо́мия; скупо́й (скуп, -а́, -о); *c. straw*, сы́рная па́лочка.

cheetah *n.* гепа́рд.

chef *n.* (шеф-)по́вар (*pl.* -а́).

chef-d'oeuvre *n.* шеде́вр.

chemical *adj.* хими́ческий; *c. warfare*, хими́ческая война́; *n.* химика́т; *pl.* химика́лии (-ий) *pl.* **chemically** *adv.* хими́чески. **chemist** *n.* хи́мик; (*druggist*) апте́карь *m.*; *c.'s* (*shop*), апте́ка. **chemistry** *n.* хи́мия.

chenille *n.* сине́ль; *adj.* сине́льный.

cheque *n.* чек; *c.-book*, че́ковая кни́жка.

chequered *adj.* (*varied*) разнообра́зный; (*changing*) изме́нчивый.

cherish *v.t.* (*foster*) леле́ять (-е́ю, -е́ешь) *imp.*; (*hold dear*) дорожи́ть *imp.* + *instr.*; (*preserve in memory*) храни́ть *imp.* (в па́мяти); (*love*) не́жно люби́ть (-блю́, -бишь) *imp.* **cherished** *adj.* заве́тный.

cheroot *n.* мани́льская сига́ра.

cherry *n.* ви́шня (*gen.pl.* -шен); чере́шня (*gen.pl.* -шен); (*tree*) вишнёвое де́рево (*pl.* -е́вья, -е́вьев); (*colour*) вишнёвый цвет; *adj.* вишнёвый, вишнёвого цве́та; *c.-wood*, древеси́на вишнёвого де́рева.

cherub *n.* херуви́м, херуви́мчик. **cherubic** *adj.* пу́хлый и розовощёкий.

chervil *n.* ке́рвель *m.*

chess *n.* ша́хматы (-т) *pl.*; *adj.* ша́хматный; *c.-board*, ша́хматная доска́ (*acc.* -ску; *pl.* -ски, -со́к, -скам); *c.-champion*, чемпио́н по ша́хматам; *c.-player*, шахмати́ст, ~ка; *c.-men*, ша́хматы (-т) *pl.*

chest *n.* я́щик, сунду́к (-а́); (*anat.*) грудь (-ди́, *instr.* -дью; *pl.* -ди, -де́й); *c. of drawers*, комо́д.

chestnut *n.* (*tree, fruit*) кашта́н; (*colour*) кашта́новый цвет; (*horse*) гнеда́я *sb.*; *adj.* кашта́новый; (*horse*) гнедо́й.

chevron *n.* наши́вка.

chew *v.t.* жева́ть (жую́, жуёшь) *imp.*; *c. over*, пережёвывать *imp.*, пережева́ть (-жую́, -жуёшь) *perf.*; *c. the cud*, жева́ть (жую́, жуёшь) *imp.* жва́чку. **chewing** *n.* жева́ние; *c.-gum*, жева́тельная рези́нка, жва́чка.

chicane *n.* вре́менное или передвижно́е препя́тствие на доро́ге, го́ночном тре́ке. **chicanery** *n.* крючкотво́рство; махина́ция.

chick *n.* цыплёнок (-нка; *pl.* цепля́та, -т). **chicken** *n.* ку́рица (*pl.* ку́ры, кур); цыплёнок (-нка; *pl.* цепля́та, -т); (*meat*) куря́тина; *adj.* трусли́вый; *c.-hearted*, *-livered*, трусли́вый. **chicken-pox** *n.* ве́тряная о́спа, ветря́нка.

chicory *n.* цико́рий.

chief *n.* глава́ (*pl.* -вы) *m.*, *f.*; (*mil. etc.*) нача́льник; (*of tribe*) вождь (-дя́) *m.*; (*robber*) атама́н; *adj.* гла́вный; ста́рший. **chiefly** *adv.* гла́вным о́бразом.

chieftain *n.* вождь (-дя́) *m.*; (*robber*) атама́н.

chiffon *n.* шифо́н; *adj.* шифо́новый.

child *n.* ребёнок (-нка; *pl.* де́ти, -те́й); *c.-birth*, ро́ды (-дов) *pl.*; *c. prodigy*, вундерки́нд; *c.'s play*, де́тские игру́шки *f.pl.* **childrens'** *adj.* де́тский. **childhood** *n.* де́тство. **childish** *adj.* де́тский, ребя́ческий. **childless** *adj.* безде́тный. **childlike** *adj.* де́тский.

chili *n.* стручко́вый пе́рец (-рца(у)).

chill *n.* хо́лод (-а(у); *pl.* -а́), охлажде́ние; (*ailment*) просту́да, озно́б; (*fig.*) холодо́к (-дка́); *v.t.* охлажда́ть *imp.*, охлади́ть *perf.*; студи́ть (-ужу́, -у́дишь) *imp.*, о ~ *perf.* **chilled** *adj.* охлаждённый (-ён, ена́), моро́женый. **chilly** *adj.* холо́дный (хо́лоден, -дна́, -дно, хо́лодны́), прохла́дный.

chime *n.* (*set of bells*) набо́р колоколо́в; *pl.* (*sound*) колоко́льный перезво́н, (*of clock*) бой; *v.t.* звони́ть *imp.*, по ~ *perf.* в + *acc.*; *v.i.* звене́ть (-ни́т) *imp.*, про ~ *perf.*; (*correspond*) соотве́тствовать *imp.* (to, + *dat.*); *c. in*, вме́шиваться *imp.*, вмеша́ться *perf.*

chimera *n.* химе́ра. **chimerical** *adj.* химери́ческий.

chimney *n.* (*for smoke*) (дымова́я) труба́ (*pl.* -бы); (*lamp c.*) ла́мповое стекло́ (*pl.* стёкла, -кол, -клам); (*cleft*) расще́лина, ками́н; *c.-pot*, дефле́ктор; *c.-sweep*, трубочи́ст.

chimpanzee *n.* шимпанзе́ *m.indecl.*

chin *n.* подборо́док (-дка); *v.t.*: *c. the bar*, *oneself*, подтя́гиваться *imp.*, подтяну́ться (-ну́сь, -нешься) *perf.* до у́ровня подборо́дка.

China *adj.* кита́йский. **china** *n.* (*material*) фарфо́р; (*objects*) посу́да; *adj.* фарфо́ровый.

chinchilla *n.* (*animal*, *fur*) шинши́лла.

Chinese *n.* (*person*) кита́ец (-а́йца), -а́янка; *adj.* кита́йский; *C. lantern*, кита́йский фона́рик; *C. white*, кита́йские бели́ла (-л) *pl.*

chink[1] *n.* (*sound*) звон; *v.i.* звене́ть (-ни́т) *imp.*, про ~ *perf.*

chink[2] *n.* (*opening*, *crack*) щель (*pl.* -ли, -ле́й), сква́жина.

chintz *n.* глазиро́ванный си́тец (-тца(у)).

chip *v.t.* отбива́ть *imp.*, отби́ть (отобью́, -ьёшь) края́ + *gen.*; *n.* (*of wood*) щепа́ (*pl.* -пы, -п, -па́м), ще́пка, лучи́на; щерби́на, щерби́нка; (*in games*) фи́шка; *pl.* жа́реная карто́шка (*collect.*); *c.-basket*, корзи́на из стру́жек.

chiropody *n.* педикю́р.

chirp *v.i.* чири́кать *imp.*

chisel *n.* долото́ (*pl.* -та); стаме́ска; зуби́ло; резе́ц (-зца́); *v.t.* высека́ть *imp.*, вы́сечь (-еку, -ечешь; -ек) *perf.*; выреза́ть *imp.*, вы́резать (-ежу, -ежешь) *perf.* **chiseller** *n.* моше́нник.

chit *n.* (*note*) запи́ска.

chit-chat *n.* болтовня́.

chivalrous *adj.* ры́царский. **chivalry** *n.* ры́царство.

chive *n.* лук(-а)-ре́занец (-нца).

chloral *n.* хлоралгидра́т. **chloride** *n.* хлори́д. **chlorinate** *v.t.* хлори́ровать *imp.*, *perf.* **chlorine** *n.* хлор. **chloroform** *n.* хлорофо́рм; *v.t.* хлороформи́ровать *imp.*, *perf.* **chlorophyll** *n.* хлорофи́лл.

chock *n.* клин (*pl.* -ья, -ьев); (тормозна́я) коло́дка; *c.-a-block*, *c.-full*, битко́м наби́тый, перепо́лненный (-ен, -енна).

chocolate *n.* шокола́д (-а(у)); (*sweet*) шокола́дка; (*colour*) шокола́дный цвет; *adj.* шокола́дный; шокола́дного цве́та.

choice *n.* вы́бор; *adj.* отбо́рный.

choir *n.* хор (*pl.* хо́ры́); хорово́й анса́мбль *m.*; *c.-boy*, (ма́льчик) пе́вчий *sb.*

choke *n.* (*valve*) дро́ссель *m.*; (*artichoke*) сердцеви́на артишо́ка; *v.i.* дави́ться (-влю́сь, -вишься) *imp.*, по ~ *perf.*; задыха́ться *imp.*, задохну́ться (-о́х(ну́л)ся, -о́х(ну́)лась) *perf.*; *v.t.* (*suffocate*) души́ть (-шу́, -шишь) *imp.*, за ~ *perf.*; (*of plants*) заглуша́ть, глуши́ть *imp.*, за ~ *perf.* **choker** *n.* (*collar*) высо́кий крахма́льный воротничо́к (-чка́); (*necklace*) коро́ткое ожере́лье.

cholera *n.* холе́ра.

choleric *adj.* вспы́льчивый.

cholesterol *n.* холестери́н.

choose *v.t.* (*select*) выбира́ть *imp.*, вы́брать (-беру, -берешь) *perf.*;

(*decide*) реша́ть *imp.*, реши́ть *perf.* **choosy** *adj.* разбо́рчивый.

chop[1] *v.t.* руби́ть (-блю́, -бишь) *imp.*, рубну́ть, рубану́ть *perf.*; (*chop up*) кроши́ть (-шу́, -шишь) *imp.*, ис~, на~, рас~ *perf.*; коло́ть (-лю́, -лешь) *imp.*, рас~ *perf.*; *c. off*, отруба́ть *imp.*, отруби́ть (-блю́, -бишь) *perf.*; *n.* (*blow*) ру́бящий уда́р; (*cul.*) отбивна́я котле́та.

chop[2] *v.i.*: *c. and change*, постоя́нно меня́ться *imp.*; колеба́ться (-блюсь, -блешься) *imp.*

chopper *n.* (*knife*) се́чка, коса́рь (-ря́) *m.*; (*axe*) колу́н (-а́). **choppy** *adj.* неспоко́йный; *c. sea*, зыбь на́ море.

chops *n.* (*jaws*) че́люсти (-тей) *pl.*; *c. of the Channel*, вход в Ла-Ма́нш; *lick one's c.*, обли́зываться *imp.*, облиза́ться (-жу́сь, -жешься) *perf.*

chop-sticks *n.* па́лочки *f.pl.* для еды́. **chop-suey** *n.* кита́йское рагу́ *neut. indecl.*

choral *adj.* хорово́й. **chorale** *n.* хора́л.

chord[1] *n.* (*math.*) хо́рда; (*anat.*) свя́зка.

chord[2] *n.* (*mus.*) акко́рд.

choreographer *n.* хорео́граф. **choreographic** *adj.* хореографи́ческий. **choreography** *n.* хореогра́фия.

chorister *n.* пе́вчий *sb.*, хори́ст, ~ка.

chortle *v.i.* фы́ркать *imp.*, фы́ркнуть *perf.* от сме́ха.

chorus *n.* хор (*pl.* хо́ры); (*refrain*) припе́в; *c.-girl*, хори́стка; *v.i.* (*sing*) петь (поёт) *imp.*, про~ *perf.* хо́ром; (*speak*) говори́ть *imp.*, сказа́ть (-а́жет) *perf.* хо́ром.

christen *v.t.* (*baptise*) крести́ть (-ещу́, -е́стишь) *imp.*, *perf.*; (*give name*) дава́ть (даю́, даёшь) *imp.*, дать (дам, дашь, даст, дади́м; дал, -а́, да́ло́, -и) *perf.* + *dat.* и́мя при креще́нии. **Christian** *n.* христиани́н (*pl.* -а́не, -а́н), -а́нка; *adj.* христиа́нский; *C. name*, и́мя *neut.* **Christianity** *n.* христиа́нство. **Christmas** *n.* рождество́; *C. Eve*, соче́льник; *C.-tide*, свя́тки (-ток) *pl.*; *C. tree*, ёлка.

chromatic *adj.* хромати́ческий. **chrome** *n.* крон; *c. leather*, хроми́рованная ко́жа; *c. steel*, хро́мистая сталь; *c. yellow*, (жёлтый) крон. **chromium** *n.* хром; *c.-plated*, хромиро́ванный. **chromolithograph(y)** *n.* хромолитогра́фия. **chromosome** *n.* хромосо́ма.

chronic *adj.* хрони́ческий.

chronicle *n.* хро́ника, ле́топись; (*Book of*) *Chronicles*, Паралипомено́н; *v.t.* заноси́ть (-ошу́, -о́сишь) *imp.*, занести́ (-есу́, -есёшь; -ёс, -есла́) *perf.* (в дневни́к, в ле́топись); отмеча́ть *imp.*, отме́тить *perf.* **chronicler** *n.* летопи́сец (-сца).

chronological *adj.* хронологи́ческий. **chronology** *n.* хроноло́гия. **chronometer** *n.* хрономе́тр.

chrysalis *n.* ку́колка.

chrysanthemum *n.* хризанте́ма.

chub *n.* голя́вль (-ля́) *m.*

chubby *adj.* пу́хлый (пухл, -а́, -о).

chuck *v.t.* броса́ть *imp.*, бро́сить *perf.*; *c. it!* брось!; *c. out*, вышиба́ть *imp.*, вы́шибить (-бу, -бешь; -б) *perf.*; *c. under the chin*, трепа́ть (-плю́, -плешь) *imp.*, по~ *perf.* по подборо́дку; *c. up*, броса́ть *imp.*, бро́сить *perf.* **chucker-out** *n.* вышиба́ла *m.*

chuckle *v.i.* посме́иваться *imp.*

chug *v.i.* итти́ (идёт) *imp.* с пыхте́нием; *c. along*, пропыхте́ть (-ти́т) *perf.*

chum *n.* това́рищ.

chump *n.* чурба́н; то́лстый коне́ц (-нца́); *c. chop*, то́лстая бара́нья отбивна́я *sb.*; *off one's c.*, спя́тивший с ума́.

chunk *n.* ломо́ть (-мтя́) *m.*, кусо́к (-ска́). **chunky** *adj.* коро́ткий (ко́роток, -тка́, -тко, ко́ротки́) и то́лстый (толст, -а́, -о, то́лсты́); корена́стый.

church *n.* це́рковь (-кви, -ковью; *pl.* -кви, -кве́й, -ква́м); *C. of England*, англика́нская це́рковь. **churchyard** *n.* (церко́вное) кла́дбище.

churlish *adj.* гру́бый (груб, -а́, -о), нелюбе́зный.

churn *n.* маслобо́йка; *v.t.* сбива́ть *imp.*, сбить (собью́, -ьёшь) *perf.*; *v.i.* (*foam*) пе́ниться *imp.*, вс~ *perf.*; (*seethe*) кипе́ть (-пи́т) *imp.*, вс~ *perf.*

chute *n.* скат, жёлоб (*pl.* -а́); (*parachute*) парашю́т.

cicada *n.* цика́да.

cider *n.* сидр.

cigar *n.* сигáра. **cigarette** *n.* сигарéта, папирóса; *c. lighter*, зажигáлка.
cinder *n.* шлак; *pl.* золá; *c.-path*, *c.-track*, гаревáя дорóжка.
cine-camera *n.* киноаппарáт. **cinema** *n.* кинó *neut.indecl.*, кинематогрáфия. **cinematic** *adj.* кинематографи́ческий.
cinnamon *n.* кори́ца; (*colour*) свéтло-коричневый цвет.
cipher *n.* (*math.*) ноль (-ля́) *m.*, нуль (-ля́) *m.*; шифр.
circle *n.* круг (*loc.* -е & -ý; *pl.* -и́); (*theatre*) я́рус; *v.t.* & *i.* кружи́ть(ся) (-ужý(сь), -ýжишь(ся)) *imp.*; *v.i.* дви́гаться (-аюсь, -аешься & дви́жусь, -жешься) *imp.*, дви́нуться *perf.* по крýгу. **circlet** *n.* кружóк (-жкá); венóк (-нкá). **circuit** *n.* кругооборóт; объéзд, обхóд; (*tour*) турнé *neut.indecl.*; (*leg.*) выезднáя сéссия судá; (*electr.*) цепь, кóнтур; *short c.*, корóткое замыкáние. **circuitous** *adj.* крýжный, окóльный. **circular** *adj.* крýглый (кругл, -á, -о, крýглы́), кругóвóй; (*circulating*) циркуля́рный; *n.* циркуля́р. **circularize** *v.t.* рассылáть *imp.*, разослáть (-ошлю́, -ошлёшь) *perf.* + *dat.* циркуля́ры. **circulate** *v.i.* циркули́ровать *imp.*; *v.t.* рассылáть *imp.*, разослáть (-ошлю́, -ошлёшь) *perf.*; (*spread*) распространя́ть *imp.*, распространи́ть *perf.* **circulation** *n.* (*movement*) циркуля́ция; (*distribution*) распространéние; (*of newspaper*) тирáж (-á); (*econ.*) обращéние; (*med.*) кровообращéние.
circumcise *v.t.* обрезáть *imp.*, обрéзать (-éжу, -éжешь) *perf.* **circumcision** *n.* обрезáние.
circumference *n.* окрýжность.
circumscribe *v.t.* очéрчивать *imp.*, очерти́ть (-рчý, -ртишь) *perf.*; (*restrict*) ограни́чивать *imp.*, ограни́чить *perf.*
circumspect *adj.* осмотри́тельный. **circumspection** *n.* осмотри́тельность.
circumstance *n.* обстоя́тельство; *pl.* (*material situation*) материáльное положéние; *in*, *under*, *the circumstances*, при дáнных обстоя́тельствах, в такóм слýчае; *in*, *under*, *no circumstances*, ни при каки́х обстоя́тельствах, ни в кóем слýчае. **circumstantial** *adj.* (*detailed*) подрóбный; *c. evidence*, кóсвенные доказáтельства *neut.pl.*
circumvent *v.t.* (*outwit*) перехитри́ть *perf.*; (*evade*) обходи́ть (-ожý, -óдишь) *imp.*, обойти́ (обойдý, -дёшь; обошёл, -шлá) *perf.*
circus *n.* (*show*) цирк; (*arena*) крýглая плóщадь (*pl.* -ди, -дéй).
cirrhosis *n.* цирróз.
cistern *n.* бак; резервуáр.
citadel *n.* цитадéль.
citation *n.* (*quotation*) ссы́лка, цитáта. **cite** *v.t.* цити́ровать *imp.*, про~ *perf.*; ссылáться *imp.*, сослáться (сошлю́сь, -лёшься) *perf.* на + *acc.*
citizen *n.* граждани́н (*pl.* -ане, -ан), -áнка. **citizenship** *n.* граждáнство.
citric *adj.* лимóнный. **citron** *n.* цитрóн. **citronella** *n.* цитронéлла. **citrous** *adj.* ци́трусовый. **citrus** *n.* ци́трус; *adj.* ци́трусовый.
city *n.* гóрод (*pl.* -á).
civet *n.* (*perfume*) цибети́н; (*c. cat*) вивéрра.
civic *adj.* граждáнский. **civil** *adj.* граждáнский; (*polite*) вéжливый; *c. engineer*, граждáнский инженéр; *c. engineering*, граждáнское строи́тельство; *C. Servant*, госудáрственный граждáнский слýжащий *sb.*; чинóвник; *C. Service*, госудáрственная слýжба; *c. war*, граждáнская войнá. **civilian** *n.* штáтский *sb.*; *adj.* штáтский; граждáнский. **civility** *n.* вéжливость. **civilization** *n.* цивилизáция, культýра. **civilize** *v.t.* цивилизовáть *imp.*, *perf.*; дéлать *imp.*, с~ *perf.* культýрным. **civilized** *adj.* цивилизóванный; культýрный.
claim *n.* (*demand*) трéбование, притязáние, претéнзия; (*piece of land*) отведённый учáсток (-тка); *v.t.* заявля́ть *imp.*, заяви́ть (-влю́, -вишь) *perf.* правá *pl.* на + *acc.*; претендовáть *imp.* на + *acc.*
clairvoyance *n.* яснови́дение. **clairvoyant** *n.* яснови́дец (-дца), -дица; *adj.* яснови́дящий.
clam *n.* венéрка, рази́нька.
clamber *v.i.* карáбкаться *imp.*, вс~ *perf.*

clammy *adj.* холо́дный и вла́жный на о́щупь.

clamorous *adj.* крикли́вый. **clamour** *n.* кри́ки *m.pl.*, шум (-a(y)); *v.i.* крича́ть (-чу́, -чи́шь) *imp.*; *c. for*, шу́мно тре́бовать *imp.*, по~ *perf.* + *gen.*

clamp[1] *n.* (*clasp*) зажи́м, скоба́ (*pl.* -бы, -б, -ба́м), ско́бка; *v.t.* скрепля́ть *imp.*, скрепи́ть *perf.*

clamp[2] *n.* (*of potatoes*) бурт (бу́рта́; *pl.* -ы́).

clan *n.* клан.

clandestine *adj.* та́йный.

clang, clank *n.* лязг, бряца́ние; *v.t.* & *i.* ля́згать *imp.*, ля́згнуть *perf.* (+*instr.*); бряца́ть *imp.*, про~ *perf.* (+*instr.*, на+*prep.*).

clap *v.t.* хло́пать *imp.*, хло́пнуть *perf.* + *dat.*; аплоди́ровать *imp.* + *dat.*; *n.* хлопо́к (-пка́); рукоплеска́ния *neut. pl.*; (*thunder*) уда́р. **clapper** *n.* язы́к (-а́). **claptrap** *n.* треску́чая фра́за; (*nonsense*) вздор.

claret *n.* бордо́ *neut.indecl.*

clarification *n.* (*explanation*) разъясне́ние; (*of liquid, chem.*) осветле́ние; (*purification*) очище́ние. **clarify** *v.t.* разъясня́ть *imp.*, разъясни́ть *perf.*; осветля́ть *imp.*, осветли́ть *perf.*; очища́ть *imp.*, очи́стить *perf.*

clarinet *n.* кларне́т.

clarity *n.* я́сность.

clash *n.* (*conflict*) столкнове́ние; (*disharmony*) дисгармо́ния; (*sound*) гро́хот, лязг; *v.i.* ста́лкиваться *imp.*, столкну́ться *perf.*; (*coincide*) совпада́ть *imp.*, совпа́сть (-адёт; -а́л) *perf.*; не гармони́ровать *imp.*; (*sound*) ля́згать *imp.*, ля́згнуть *perf.*

clasp *n.* (*buckle etc.*) пря́жка, застёжка; (*handshake*) пожа́тие руки́; (*embrace*) объя́тие; *v.t.* обнима́ть *imp.*, обня́ть (обниму́, -мешь; о́бнял, -а́, -о) *perf.*; сжима́ть *imp.*, сжать (сожму́, -мёшь) *perf.* в объя́тиях; *c.-knife*, складно́й нож (-а́).

class *n.* класс; (*category*) разря́д; *c.-conscious*, (кла́ссово) созна́тельный; *c.-consciousness*, кла́ссовое созна́ние; *c.-room*, класс; *c. war*, кла́ссовая борьба́; *v.t.* причисля́ть *imp.*, причи́слить *perf.* (as, к+*dat.*); классифици́ровать *imp.*, *perf.*

classic *adj.* класси́ческий; (*renowned*) знамени́тый; *n.* кла́ссик; класси́ческое произведе́ние; *pl.* кла́ссика; класси́ческие языки́ *m.pl.* **classical** *adj.* класси́ческий.

classification *n.* классифика́ция. **classify** *v.t.* классифици́ровать *imp.*, *perf.*; (*c. as secret*) засекре́чивать *imp.*, засекре́тить *perf.*

classy *adj.* кла́ссный, первокла́ссный, пе́рвый сорт *predic.*

clatter *n.* стук, лязг; *v.i.* стуча́ть (-чу́, -чи́шь) *imp.*, по~ *perf.*; ля́згать *imp.*, ля́згнуть *perf.*

clause *n.* статья́; (*leg.*) кла́узула; (*gram.*) предложе́ние.

claw *n.* ко́готь (-гтя; *pl.* -гти, -гте́й); (*of crustacean*) клешня́; *v.t.* скрести́ (-ебу́, -ебёшь; -ёб, -ебла́) *imp.*

clay *n.* гли́на; (*pipe*) гли́няная тру́бка; *adj.* гли́няный. **clayey** *cdj.* гли́нистый.

clean *adj.* чи́стый (чист, -а́, -о, чи́сты́); *adv.* (*fully*) соверше́нно, по́лностью; *v.t.* чи́стить *imp.*, вы́~, по~ *perf.*; очища́ть *imp.*, очи́стить *perf.* **cleaner** *n.* чи́стильщик, -ица; убо́рщик, -ица. **cleaner's** *n.* химчи́стка. **cleaning** *n.* чи́стка, убо́рка; очи́стка. **clean(li)ness** *n.* чистота́. **cleanse** *v.t.* очища́ть *imp.*, очи́стить *perf.*

clear *adj.* я́сный (я́сен, ясна́, я́сно, я́сны́); (*transparent*) прозра́чный; (*distinct*) отчётливый; (*free*) свобо́дный (of, от+*gen.*); *v.t.* & *i.* очища́ть(ся) *imp.*, очи́стить(ся) *perf.*; *v.t.* (*jump over*) перепры́гивать *imp.*, перепры́гнуть *perf.*; (*acquit*) опра́вдывать *imp.*, оправда́ть *perf.*; *c. away*, убира́ть *imp.*, убра́ть (уберу́, -рёшь; убра́л, -а́, -о) *perf.* со стола́; *c. off*, (*go away*) убира́ться *imp.*, убра́ться (уберу́сь, -рёшься; убра́лся, -ала́сь, -а́ло́сь) *perf.*; *c. out*, (*v.t.*) вычища́ть *imp.*, вы́чистить *perf.*; (*v.i.*) (*make off*) удира́ть *imp.*, удра́ть (удеру́, -рёшь; удра́л, -а́, -о) *perf.*; *c. up*, (*make tidy*) приводи́ть (-ожу́, -о́дишь) *imp.*, привести́ (-еду́, -едёшь; -ёл, -ела́) *perf.* в поря́док; (*explain*) выясня́ть *imp.*, вы́яснить *perf.* **clearance** *n.* расчи́стка; (*permission*) разреше́ние. **clearing** *n.* расчи́стка; (*in forest*) поля́на. **clearly** *adv.* я́сно; отчётливо.

cleavage *n.* разделе́ние. **cleaver** *n.* нож (-а́) мясника́.

clef *n.* (*mus.*) ключ (-а́).

cleft *n.* тре́щина, расще́лина; *adj.*: *in a cleft stick*, в тупике́.

clematis *n.* ломоно́с.

clemency *n.* милосе́рдие.

clench *v.t.* (*fist*) сжима́ть *imp.*, сжать (сожму́, -мёшь) *perf.*; (*teeth*) сти́скивать *imp.*, сти́снуть *perf.*

clergy *n.* духове́нство. **clergyman** *n.* свяще́нник. **clerical** *adj.* (*of clergy*) духо́вный; (*of clerk*) канцеля́рский. **clerk** *n.* конто́рский слу́жащий *sb.*

clever *adj.* у́мный (умён, умна́, у́мно́), спосо́бный. **cleverness** *n.* уме́ние.

cliché *n.* клише́ *neut.indecl.*, изби́тая фра́за.

click *v.t.* щёлкать *imp.*, щёлкнуть *perf.* + *instr.*; *n.* щёлк.

client *n.* клие́нт. **clientele** *n.* клиенту́ра.

cliff *n.* утёс, отве́сная скала́ (*pl.* -лы).

climacteric *n.* климакте́рий; *adj.* климактери́ческий.

climate *n.* кли́мат. **climatic** *adj.* климати́ческий.

climax *n.* кульминацио́нный пункт.

climb *v.t.* & *i.* ла́зить *indet.*, лезть (ле́зу, -зешь; лез) *det.* на + *acc.*; влеза́ть *imp.*, влезть (вле́зу, -зешь, влез) *perf.* на + *acc.*; поднима́ться *imp.*, подня́ться (-ниму́сь, -ни́мешься; -ня́лся́, -няла́сь) *perf.* на + *acc.*; (*aeron.*) набира́ть *imp.*, набра́ть (наберу́, -рёшь; набра́л, -а́, -о) *perf.* высоту́; *c. down*, спуска́ться *imp.*, спусти́ться (-ущу́сь, -у́стишься) *perf.* с + *gen.*; (*give in*) уступа́ть *imp.*, уступи́ть (-плю́, -пишь) *perf.* **climber** *n.* (*mountain-c.*) альпини́ст, ~ка; (*social c.*) карьери́ст, ~ка; (*plant*) вью́щееся расте́ние. **climbing** *n.* (*sport*) альпини́зм; (*ascent*) восхожде́ние; *adj.* (*plant*) вью́щийся.

clinch *n.* (*boxing*) клинч, захва́т.

cling *v.i.* прилипа́ть *imp.*, прили́пнуть (-п) *perf.* (to, к + *dat.*); *c. to*, (*clothes*) облега́ть (-а́ет) *imp.*

clinic *n.* (*consultation*) консульта́ция; (*place*) кли́ника. **clinical** *adj.* клини́ческий.

clink *v.t.* & *i.* звене́ть (-ню́, -ни́шь) *imp.*, про~ *perf.* (+ *instr.*); *c. glasses*, чо́каться *imp.*, чо́кнуться *perf.*; *n.* звон.

clinker *n.* (*brick*) кли́нкер; (*slag*) шлак.

clip[1] *n.* зажи́м; (*mil.*) обо́йма; *v.t.* скрепля́ть *imp.*, скрепи́ть *perf.*

clip[2] *v.t.* стричь (-игу́, -ижёшь; -иг) *imp.*, об~, о~ *perf.*; подреза́ть *imp.*, подре́зать (-е́жу, -е́жешь) *perf.* **clipped** *adj.* подре́занный, подстри́женный; *c. tones*, отры́вочная речь. **clipper** *n.* (*naut.*) кли́пер; *pl.* но́жницы *f.pl.*

clipping *n.* стри́жка; (*newspaper c.*) газе́тная вы́резка; *pl.* настри́г, обре́зки *f.pl.*

clique *n.* кли́ка. **cliquish** *adj.* за́мкнутый.

cloak *n.* плащ (-а́); *v.t.* покрыва́ть *imp.*, покры́ть (-ро́ю, -ро́ешь) *perf.* **cloakroom** *n.* (*for clothing*) гардеро́б; (*for luggage*) ка́мера хране́ния; (*lavatory*) убо́рная *sb.*, туале́т.

clock *n.* часы́ *m.pl.*; *c. face*, цифербла́т; *clockmaker*, часовщи́к (-а́); *clockwise*, по часово́й стре́лке; *c.-work*, часово́й механи́зм; *v.i.*: *c. in*, регистри́ровать *imp.*, за~ *perf.* прихо́д на рабо́ту.

clod *n.* ком (*pl.* -ья, -ьев), глы́ба; *c.-hopper*, у́вален (-льня) *m.*, дереве́нщина *m.* & *f.*

clog *n.* башма́к (-а́) на деревя́нной подо́шве; *v.t.*: *c. up*, засоря́ть *imp.*, засори́ть *perf.*

cloister *n.* (*monastery*) монасты́рь (-ря́) *m.*; (*arcade*) кры́тая арка́да.

close *adj.* (*near*) бли́зкий (-зок, -зка́, -зко, бли́зки́); (*stuffy*) ду́шный (-шен, -шна́, -шно); (*secret*) скры́тый; *v.t.* (*shut*) закрыва́ть *imp.*, закры́ть (-ро́ю, -ро́ешь) *perf.*; (*conclude*) зака́нчивать *imp.*, зако́нчить *perf.*; *adv.* бли́зко (to, от + *gen.*). **closed** *adj.* закры́тый. **closeted** *adj.*: *be c. together*, совеща́ться *imp.* наедине́. **close-up** *n.* съёмка, сня́тая на кру́пном пла́не; *in c.*, кру́пным пла́ном. **closing** *n.* закры́тие; *adj.* заключи́тельный. **closure** *n.* закры́тие.

clot *n.* сгу́сток (-тка); *v.i.* сгуща́ться *imp.*, сгусти́ться *perf.* **clotted** *adj.* сгущённый; *c. cream*, густы́е топлёные сли́вки (-вок) *pl.*

cloth *n.* ткань, сукно́ (*pl.* -кна, -кон, -кнам); (*duster*) тря́пка; (*table-c.*) ска́терть (*pl.* -ти, -те́й).

clothe *v.t.* одева́ть *imp.*, оде́ть (-е́ну, -е́нешь) (in, +*instr.*, в+*acc.*) *perf.* **clothes** *n.* оде́жда, пла́тье.

cloud *n.* о́блако (*pl.* -ка́, -ко́в); (*rain, storm, c.*) ту́ча; *v.t.* затемня́ть *imp.*, затемни́ть *perf.*; омрача́ть *imp.*, омрачи́ть *perf.*; *c. over*, покрыва́ться *imp.*, покры́ться (-ро́ется) *perf.* облака́ми, ту́чами.

clout *v.t.* ударя́ть *imp.*, уда́рить *perf.*; *n.* затре́щина.

clove *n.* гвозди́ка; (*garlic*) зубо́к (-бка́).

cloven *adj.* раздво́енный (-ен, -енна).

clover *n.* кле́вер (*pl.* -а́).

clown *n.* кло́ун.

club *n.* (*stick*) дуби́нка; *pl.* (*cards*) тре́фы *f.pl.*; (*association*) клуб; *v.t.* (*beat*) бить (бью, бьёшь) *imp.*, по~ *perf.* дуби́нкой; *v.i.*: *c. together*, устра́ивать *imp.*, устро́ить *perf.* скла́дчину.

cluck *v.i.* куда́хтать (-а́хчет) *imp.*

clue *n.* (*evidence*) ули́ка; (*to puzzle*) ключ (-а́) (к разга́дке).

clump *n.* гру́ппа дере́вьев; *v.i.* тяжело́ ступа́ть *imp.*, ступи́ть (-плю́, -пишь) *perf.*

clumsiness *n.* неуклю́жесть; беста́ктность. **clumsy** *adj.* неуклю́жий.

cluster *n.* (*bunch*) пучо́к (-чка́); (*group*) гру́ппа; *v.i.* собира́ться *imp.*, собра́ться (-берётся; собра́лся, -ала́сь, -ало́сь) *perf.* гру́ппами.

clutch[1] *n.* (*grasp*) хва́тка; ко́гти (-те́й) *m.pl.*; (*tech.*) сцепле́ние, му́фта; *v.t.* зажима́ть *imp.*, зажа́ть (зажму́, -мёшь) *perf.*; *v.i.*: *c. at*, хвата́ться *imp.*, хвати́ться (-ачу́сь, -а́тишься) *perf.* за+*acc.*

clutch[2] *n.* (*of eggs*) яйца́ (*pl.* яи́ц, яйцам).

clutter *n.* беспоря́док (-дка); *v.t.* приводи́ть (-ожу́, -о́дишь) *imp.*, привести́ (-еду́, -едёшь; -ёл, -ела́) *perf.* в беспоря́док.

c/o *abbr.* по а́дресу+*gen.*; че́рез+*acc.*

coach *n.* (*carriage*) каре́та; (*rly.*) ваго́н; (*bus*) авто́бус; (*tutor*) репети́тор; (*sport*) тре́нер; *v.t.* репети́ровать *imp.*; тернирова́ть *imp.*, на~ *perf.*

coagulate *v.i.* сгуща́ться *imp.*, сгусти́ться *perf.*

coal *n.* у́голь (у́гля́; *pl.* у́гли, у́гле́й) *m.*; *c.-bearing*, углено́сный; *c.-face*, у́гольный забо́й; *coalfield*, каменноуго́льный бассе́йн; *c.-mine*, у́гольная ша́хта; *c.-miner*, шахтёр; *c.-owner*, шахтовладе́лец (-льца); *c.-scuttle*, ведёрко (*pl.* -рки, -рок, -ркам) для у́гля́; *c.-seam*, у́гольный пласт (-а́).

coalesce *v.i.* соединя́ться *imp.*, соедини́ться *perf.*

coalition *n.* коали́ция.

coarse *adj.* гру́бый (груб, -а́, -о); (*vulgar*) вульга́рный.

coast *n.* побере́жье, бе́рег (*loc.* -у́; *pl.* -а́); *c. guard*, берегова́я охра́на; *v.i.* (*trade*) кабота́жничать *imp.*; (*move without power*) дви́гаться (-и́гается & -и́жется) *imp.*, дви́нуться *perf.* по ине́рции. **coastal** *adj.* берегово́й, прибре́жный. **coaster** *n.* кабота́жное су́дно (*pl.* -да́, -до́в).

coat *n.* (*overcoat*) пальто́ *neut.indecl.*; (*jacket*) пиджа́к (-а́), ку́ртка; (*layer*) слой (*pl.* слои́); (*animal*) шерсть (*pl.* -ти, -те́й), мех (*loc.* -у́; *pl.* -а́); *c. of arms*, герб (-а́); *v.t.* покрыва́ть *imp.*, покры́ть (-ро́ю, -ро́ешь) *perf.* (with, сло́ем+*gen.*).

coax *v.t.* зада́бривать *imp.*, задо́брить *perf.*

cob *n.* (*corn-c.*) поча́ток (-тка) кукуру́зы; (*swan*) ле́бедь(-дя; *pl.* -ди, -де́й) -саме́ц (-мца́); (*horse*) ни́зкая верхова́я ло́шадь (*pl.* -ди, -де́й, *instr.* -дьми́).

cobalt *n.* ко́бальт.

cobble *n.* булы́жник (*also collect.*); *v.t.* мости́ть *imp.*, вы~, за~ *perf.* булы́жником.

cobbler *n.* сапо́жник.

cobra *n.* очко́вая змея́ (*pl.* зме́и).

cobweb *n.* паути́на.

cocaine *n.* кокаи́н.

cochineal *n.* кошени́ль.

cock *n.* (*bird*) петýх (-á); (*tap*) кран; (*of gun*) курóк (-ркá); *v.t.* (*gun*) взводи́ть (-ожý, -óдишь) *imp.*, взвести́ (-едý, -едёшь; -ёл, -елá) *perf.* курóк + *gen.*; *c. a snook*, покáзывать *imp.*, показáть (-ажý, -áжешь) *perf.* длинный нос. **cocked hat** *n.* треугóлка.

cockade *n.* кокáрда.

cockatoo *n.* какадý *m.indecl.*

cockchafer *n.* мáйский жук (-á).

cockerel *n.* петушóк (-шкá).

cockle *n.* съедóбная сердцеви́дка.

cockney *n.* урожéнец (-нца), -нка, Лóндона.

cockpit *n.* (*arena*) арéна; (*aeron.*) каби́на.

cockroach *n.* таракáн.

cocktail *n.* коктéйль *m.*

cocky *adj.* (*cheeky*) дéрзкий (-зок, -зкá, -зко); (*conceited*) чвáнный.

cocoa *n.* какáо *neut.indecl.*

coco(a)nut *n.* кокóс; *adj.* кокóсовый.

cocoon *n.* кóкон.

cod *n.* трескá; *c.-liver oil*, ры́бий жир (-а(у)).

coda *n.* (*mus.*) кóда.

coddle *v.t.* изнéживать *imp.*, изнéжить *perf.*

code *n.* (*collection of laws*) кóдекс, закóны *m.pl.*; (*cipher*) код, шифр; *civil c.*, граждáнский кóдекс; *c. of honour*, закóны *m.pl.* чéсти; *penal c.*, уголóвный кóдекс; *Morse c.*, áзбука Мóрзе; *v.t.* шифровáть *imp.*, за~ *perf.* **codicil** *n.* припи́ска. **codify** *v.t.* кодифици́ровать *imp.*, *perf.*

co-education *n.* совмéстное обучéние.

coefficient *n.* коэффициéнт.

coerce *v.t.* принуждáть *imp.*, принýдить *perf.* **coercion** *n.* принуждéние; *under c.*, по принуждéнию.

coexist *v.i.* сосуществовáть *imp.* **coexistence** *n.* сосуществовáние.

coffee *n.* кóфе *m.* (*neut.* (*coll.*)) *indecl.*; *c.-mill*, кофéйница; *c.-pot*, кофéйник.

coffer *n.* сундýк (-á); *pl.* казнá.

coffin *n.* гроб (*loc.* -ý; *pl.* -ы́).

cog *n.* зубéц (-бцá); *c. in the machine*, ви́нтик маши́ны. **cogwheel** *n.* зубчáтое колесó (*pl.* -ёса), шестерня́ (*gen.pl.* -рён).

cogent *adj.* убеди́тельный.

cogitate *v.i.* размышля́ть *imp.*, размы́слить *perf.* **cogitation** *n.*: *pl.* мы́сли (-лей) *f.pl.*, размышлéния *neut.pl.*

cognate *adj.* рóдственный (-ен, -енна); *n.* рóдственное слóво.

cohabit *v.i.* сожи́тельствовать *imp.* **cohabitation** *n.* сожи́тельство.

coherence *n.* свя́зность. **coherent** *adj.* свя́зный. **cohesion** *n.* сплочённость; сцеплéние. **cohesive** *adj.* спосóбной к сцеплéнию.

cohort *n.* когóрта.

coil *v.t.* свёртывать *imp.*, свернýть *perf.* кольцóм, спирáлью; уклáдывать *imp.*, уложи́ть (-жу, -жишь) *perf.* в бýхту; *n* кольцó (*pl.* -льца, -лец, -льцам), бýхта; (*electr.*) катýшка.

coin *n.* монéта; *v.t.* чекáнить *imp.*, от~ *perf.* **coinage** *n.* (*coining*) чекáнка; (*system*) монéта; монéтная систéма.

coincide *v.i.* совпадáть *imp.*, совпáсть (-адý, -адёшь; -áл) *perf.* **coincidence** *n.* совпадéние. **coincidental** *adj.* случáйный.

coke[1] *n.* кокс; *adj.* кóксовый; *v.t.* коксовáть *imp.*; *c. oven*, коксовáльная печь (*pl.* -чи, -чéй).

Coke[2] *n.* кóка-кóла.

colander *n.* дуршлáг.

cold *n.* хóлод (-а у); *pl.* -á); (*illness*) простýда, нáсморк; *adj.* холóдный (хóлоден, -днá, -дно, хóлодны́); *c.-blooded*, жестóкий (-óк, -óкá, -óко); (*zool.*) холоднокрóвный; *c. steel*, холóдное орýжие; *c. war*, холóдная войнá.

colic *n.* кóлики *f.pl.*

collaborate *v.i.* сотрýдничать *imp.* **collaboration** *n.* сотрýдничество. **collaborator** *n.* сотрýдник, -ица.

collapse *v.i.* рýшиться *imp.*, об~ *perf.*; вали́ться (-лю́сь, -лишься) *imp.*, по~, с~ *perf.*; *n.* падéние; крах; провáл. **collapsible** *adj.* разбóрный, складнóй, откиднóй.

collar *n.* воротни́к (-á), воротничóк (-чкá); (*dog-c.*) ошéйник; (*horse-c.*) хомýт (-á); *c.-bone*, ключи́ца; *v.t.* (*seize*) хватáть *imp.*, схвати́ть (-ачý, -áтишь) *perf.*

collate *v.t.* сличáть *imp.*, сличи́ть *perf.*

collateral *adj.* побо́чный, дополни́тельный; *n.* (*c. security*) дополни́тельное обеспе́чение.

collation *n.* лёгкая заку́ска.

colleague *n.* колле́га *m.* & *f.*

collect *v.t.* собира́ть *imp.*, собра́ть (соберу́, -рёшь; собра́л, -á, -o) *perf.*; (*as hobby*) коллекциони́ровать *imp.* **collected** *adj.* со́бранный; *c. works*, собра́ние сочине́ний. **collection** *n.* сбор, собира́ние; колле́кция. **collective** *n.* коллекти́в; *adj.* коллекти́вный; *c. farm*, колхо́з; *c. farmer*, колхо́зник, -ица; *c. noun*, собира́тельное существи́тельное *sb.* **collectivization** *n.* коллективиза́ция. **collector** *n.* сбо́рщик; коллекционе́р.

college *n.* колле́дж. **collegiate** *adj.* университе́тский.

collide *v.i.* ста́лкиваться *imp.*, столкну́ться *perf.* **collision** *n.* столкнове́ние.

collie *n.* шотла́ндская овча́рка.

collier *n.* (*miner*) шахтёр; (*ship*) у́гольщик. **colliery** *n.* каменноуго́льная ша́хта.

colloquial *adj.* разгово́рный. **colloquialism** *n.* разгово́рное выраже́ние.

collusion *n.* та́йный сго́вор.

colon[1] *n.* (*anat.*) то́лстая кишка́ (*gen.pl.* -шо́к).

colon[2] *n.* (*punctuation mark*) двоето́чие.

colonel *n.* полко́вник.

colonial *adj.* колониа́льный. **colonialism** *n.* колониали́зм. **colonist** *n.* колони́ст, ~ка. **colonization** *n.* колониза́ция. **colonize** *v.t.* колонизова́ть *imp.*, *perf.* **colony** *n.* коло́ния.

colonnade *n.* колонна́да.

coloration *n.* окра́ска, расцве́тка.

coloratura *n.* (*mus.*) колорату́ра.

colossal *adj.* колосса́льный, грома́дный.

colour *n.* цвет (*pl.* -á), кра́ска; (*pl.*) (*flag*) зна́мя (*pl.* -мёна) *neut.*; *c.-blind* страда́ющий дальтони́змом; *c. film*, цветна́я плёнка; *c. prejudice*, ра́совая дискримина́ция; *v.t.* кра́сить *imp.*, цы~, о~, по~ *perf.*; раскра́шивать *imp.*, раскра́сить *perf.*; *v.i.* красне́ть *imp.*, по~ *perf.* **colouration** *see* **coloration.** **coloured** *adj.* цветно́й, раскра́шенный, окра́шенный. **colouring.** *n.* кра́сящее вещество́; окра́ска.

colt *n.* жеребёнок (-бёнка; *pl.* -бя́та, -бя́т).

column *n.* (*archit.*, *mil.*) коло́нна; столб (-á); (*of print*) столбе́ц (-бцá). **columnist** *n.* журнали́ст.

coma *n.* ко́ма. **comatose** *adj.* комато́зный.

comb *n.* гребёнка; гре́бень (-бня) *m.*; *v.t.* чеса́ть (чешу́, -шешь) *imp.*; причёсывать *imp.*, причеса́ть (-ешу́, -е́шешь) *perf.*

combat *n.* бой (*loc.* бою́), сраже́ние; *v.t.* боро́ться (-рю́сь, -решься) *imp.* с + *instr.*, про́тив + *gen.* **combatant** *n.* комбата́нт; *adj.* строево́й.

combination *n.* сочета́ние; соедине́ние; комбина́ция. **combine** *n.* комбина́т; (*c.-harvester*) комба́йн; *v.t.* & *i.* совмеща́ть(ся) *imp.*, совмести́ть(ся) *perf.* **combined** *adj.* совме́стный.

combustible *adj.* горю́чий. **combustion** *n.* горе́ние; *internal c. engine*, дви́гатель *m.* вну́треннего сгора́ния.

come *v.i.* (*on foot*) приходи́ть (-ожу́, -о́дишь) *imp.*, прийти́ (приду́, -дёшь; пришёл, -шла́) *perf.*; (*by transport*) приезжа́ть *imp.*, прие́хать (-е́ду, -е́дешь) *perf.*; *c. about*, случа́ться *imp.*, случи́ться *perf.*; *c. across*, случа́йно ната́лкиваться *imp.*, натолкну́ться *perf.* на + *acc.*; *c. back*, возвраща́ться *imp.*, возврати́ться (-ащу́сь, -ати́шься) *perf.*; *c. from*, происходи́ть (-ожу́, -о́дишь) *imp.*, произойти́ (-ойду́, -ойдёшь; -ошёл, -ошла́) *perf.* из, от + *gen.*; *c. in*, входи́ть (-ожу́, -о́дишь) *imp.*, войти́ (войду́, -дёшь; вошёл, -шла́) *perf.*; *c. in handy*, пригоди́ться *perf.*; *c. through*, проника́ть *imp.*, прони́кнуть (-к) *perf.*; *c. up to*, доходи́ть (-ожу́, -о́дишь) *imp.*, дойти́ (дойду́, -дёшь; дошёл, -шла́) *perf.* до + *gen.* **come-back** *n.* возвра́т. **come-down** *n.* паде́ние, ухудше́ние.

comedian *n.* комеди́йный актёр, ко́мик. **comedienne** *n.* комеди́йная актри́са. **comedy** *n.* коме́дия.

comet *n.* коме́та.

comfort *n.* комфо́рт, удо́бство; (*consolation*) утеше́ние; *v.t.* утеша́ть *imp.*, уте́шить *perf.* **comfortable** *adj.* удо́бный. **comforter** *n.* (*person*) утеши́тель *m.*; (*dummy*) со́ска.

comic *adj.* коми́ческий, юмористи́ческий; *c. opera*, опере́тта; *n.* ко́мик; (*magazine*) ко́микс. **comical** *adj.* смешно́й, коми́чный.

coming *adj.* наступа́ющий.

comma *n.* запята́я *sb.*; *inverted c.*, кавы́чка.

command *n.* (*order*) прика́з; (*order, authority*) кома́нда; *v.t.* прика́зывать *imp.*, приказа́ть (-ажу́, -а́жешь) *perf.* + *dat.*; кома́ндовать *imp.*, с~ *perf.* + *instr.*, над (*terrain*) + *instr.*; (*have c. of, master*) владе́ть *imp.* + *instr.* **commandant** *n.* коменда́нт. **commandeer** *v.t.* (*men*) набира́ть *imp.*, набра́ть (наберу́, -рёшь; набра́л, -а́, -о) *perf.* в а́рмию; (*goods*) реквизи́ровать *imp.*, *perf.* **commander** *n.* команди́р; кома́ндующий *sb.* (of, + *instr.*); *c.-in-chief*, главнокома́ндующий *sb.* **commanding** *adj.* кома́ндующий. **commandment** *n.* за́поведь. **commandos** *n.* деса́нтно-диверсио́нные войска́ (*gen.* -к) *pl.*

commemorate *v.t.* ознамено́вывать *imp.*, ознаменова́ть *perf.* **commemoration** *n.* ознаменова́ние. **commemorative** *adj.* па́мятный, мемориа́льный.

commence *v.t.* начина́ть *imp.*, нача́ть (-чну́, -чнёшь; на́чал, -а́, -о) *perf.* **commencement** *n.* нача́ло.

commend *v.t.* (*praise*) хвали́ть (-лю́, -лишь) *imp.*, по~ *perf.* **commendable** *adj.* похва́льный. **commendation** *n.* похвала́.

commensurable *adj.* соизмери́мый. **commensurate** *adj.* соразме́рный.

comment *n.* замеча́ние; *v.i.* де́лать *imp.*, с~ *perf.* замеча́ния; *c. on*, комменти́ровать *imp.*, *perf.*, про~ *perf.* **commentary** *n.* коммента́рий. **commentator** *n.* коммента́тор.

commerce *n.* торго́вля, комме́рция. **commercial** *adj.* торго́вый, комме́рческий; *n.* рекла́мная переда́ча. **commercialize** *v.t.* превраща́ть *imp.*, преврати́ть (-ащу́, -ати́шь) *perf.* в исто́чник дохо́дов.

commiserate *v.i.*: *c. with*, соболе́зновать *imp.* + *dat.* **commiseration** *n.* соболе́знование.

commissar *n.* комисса́р. **commissariat** *n.* (*polit.*) комиссариа́т; (*mil. etc.*) интенда́нтство.

commission *n.* (*command*) поруче́ние; (*agent's fee*) комиссио́нные *sb.*; (*c. of inquiry etc.*) коми́ссия; (*mil.*) офице́рское зва́ние; *put into c.*, вводи́ть (-ожу́, -о́дишь) *imp.*, ввести́ (введу́, -дёшь; ввёл, -а́) *perf.* в строй; *v.t.* поруча́ть *imp.*, поручи́ть (-чу́, -чишь) *perf.* + *dat.* **commissionaire** *n.* швейца́р. **commissioner** *n.* уполномо́ченный представи́тель *m.*; комисса́р.

commit *v.t.* соверша́ть *imp.*, соверши́ть *perf.*; *c. oneself*, обя́зываться *imp.*, обяза́ться (-яжу́сь, -я́жешься) *perf.*; *c. to*, предава́ть (-даю́, -даёшь) *imp.*, преда́ть (-а́м, -а́шь, -а́ст, -ади́м; пре́дал, -а́, -о) *perf.* + *dat.*; *c. to prison*, помеща́ть *imp.*, помести́ть *perf.* в тюрьму́. **commitment** *n.* обяза́тельство.

committee *n.* комите́т, коми́ссия.

commodity *n.* това́р; *scarce c.*, дефици́тный това́р.

commodore *n.* (*officer*) коммодо́р.

common *adj.* о́бщий, просто́й; обыкнове́нный; *n.* общи́нная земля́ (*acc.* -млю; *pl.* -мли, -ме́ль, -млям); *c.-room*, о́бщая ко́мната, учи́тельская *sb.*; *c. sense*, здра́вый смысл. **commonly** *adv.* обы́чно, обыкнове́нно. **commonplace** *adj.* изби́тый, бана́льный. **commonwealth** *n.* содру́жество, федера́ция.

commotion *n.* сумато́ха, волне́ние.

communal *adj.* общи́нный, коммуна́льный. **commune** *n.* комму́на; *v.i.* обща́ться *imp.*

communicate *v.t.* передава́ть (-даю́, -даёшь) *imp.*, переда́ть (-а́м, -а́шь, -а́ст, -ади́м; пе́редал, -а́, -о) *perf.*; сообща́ть *imp.*, сообщи́ть *perf.* **communication** *n.* сообще́ние; связь; коммуника́ция. **communicative** *adj.* разгово́рчивый.

communion *n.* (*eccl.*) прича́стие.

communiqué *n.* коммюнике́ *neut.indecl.*

Communism *n.* коммуни́зм. **Communist** *n.* коммуни́ст, ~ка; *adj.* коммунисти́ческий.

community *n.* о́бщи́на; содру́жество; о́бщность.

commute *v.t.* заменя́ть *imp.*, замени́ть (-ню́, -нишь) *perf.* **commuter** *n.* пассажи́р, име́ющий сезо́нный биле́т.

compact[1] *n.* (*agreement*) соглаше́ние.

compact[2] *adj.* компа́ктный; пло́тный (-тен, -тна́, -тно, пло́тны́); *n.* пу́дреница.

companion *n.* това́рищ; компаньо́н, ~ка; (*fellow traveller*) спу́тник; (*lady's c.*) компаньо́нка; (*handbook*) спра́вочник. **companionable** *adj.* общи́тельный, компане́йский. **companionship** *n.* дру́жеское обще́ние.

company *n.* о́бщество, компа́ния; (*theat.*) тру́ппа; (*mil.*) ро́та; *ship's c.*, экипа́ж.

comparable *adj.* сравни́мый. **comparative** *adj.* сравни́тельный; *n.* сравни́тельная сте́пень (*pl.* -ни, -не́й). **compare** *v.t.* & *i.* сра́внивать(ся) *imp.*, сравни́ть(ся) *perf.* (to, with, с + *instr.*). **comparison** *n.* сравне́ние.

compartment *n.* отделе́ние; (*rly.*) купе́ *neut.indecl.*

compass *n.* ко́мпас; *pl.* ци́ркуль *m.*; (*extent*) преде́лы *m.pl.*

compassion *n.* сострада́ние, жа́лость. **compassionate** *adj.* сострада́тельный.

compatibility *n.* совмести́мость. **compatible** *adj.* совмести́мый.

compatriot *n.* соотe‌́чественник, -ица.

compel *v.t.* заставля́ть *imp.*, заста́вить *perf.*; принужда́ть *imp.*, прину́дить *perf.* **compelling** *adj.* неотрази́мый.

compendium *n.* кра́ткое руково́дство; конспе́кт.

compensate *v.t.*: *c. for*, вознагражда́ть *imp.*, вознагради́ть *perf.* за + *acc.*; возмеща́ть *imp.*, возмести́ть *perf.* + *dat.*; компенси́ровать *imp.*, *perf.* **compensation** *n.* возмеще́ние, вознагражде́ние, компенса́ция.

compete *v.i.* конкури́ровать *imp.*; соревнова́ться *imp.*; состяза́ться *imp.*

competence *n.* компете́нция; компете́нтность; правомо́чие. **competent** *adj.* компете́нтный; правомо́чный.

competition *n.* соревнова́ние, состяза́ние; конкуре́нция; ко́нкурс. **competitive** *adj.* соревну́ющийся, конкури́рующий; *c. examination*, ко́нкурсный экза́мен. **competitor** *n.* соревну́ющийся *sb.*; конкуре́нт, ~ка.

compilation *n.* компиля́ция; составле́ние. **compile** *v.t.* составля́ть *imp.*, соста́вить *perf.*; компили́ровать *imp.*, с~ *perf.* **compiler** *n.* состави́тель *m.*, ~ница; компиля́тор.

complacency *n.* самодово́льство. **complacent** *adj.* самодово́льный.

complain *v.i.* жа́ловаться *imp.*, по~ *perf.* **complaint** *n.* жа́лоба; (*ailment*) боле́знь, неду́г.

complement *n.* дополне́ние; (*full number*) (ли́чный) соста́в. **complementary** *adj.* дополни́тельный.

complete *v.t.* заверша́ть *imp.*, заверши́ть *perf.*; *adj.* по́лный (-лон, -лна́, по́лно́); зако́нченный (-ен). **completion** *n.* заверше́ние, оконча́ние.

complex *adj.* сло́жный (-жен, -жна́, -жно); *n.* ко́мплекс. **complexity** *n.* сло́жность.

complexion *n.* цвет лица́.

compliance *n.* усту́пчивость. **compliant** *adj.* усту́пчивый.

complicate *v.t.* осложня́ть *imp.*, осложни́ть *perf.* **complicated** *adj.* сло́жный (-жен, -жна́, -жно). **complication** *n.* осложне́ние.

complicity *n.* соуча́стие.

compliment *n.* комплиме́нт; *pl.* приве́т; *v.t.* говори́ть *imp.* комплиме́нт(ы) + *dat.*; хвали́ть (-лю́, -лишь) *imp.*, по~ *perf.* **complimentary** *adj.* ле́стный, хвале́бный; (*ticket*) беспла́тный.

comply *v.i.*: *c. with*, (*fulfil*) исполня́ть *imp.*, испо́лнить *perf.*; (*submit to*) подчиня́ться *imp.*, подчини́ться *perf.* + *dat.*

component *n.* компоне́нт, составна́я часть (*pl.* -ти, -те́й); *adj.* составно́й.

comport *v.t.*: *c. oneself*, вести́ (веду́, -дёшь; вёл, -а́) *imp.* себя́. **comportment** *n.* поведе́ние.

compose *v.t.* (*lit., mus.*) сочиня́ть *imp.*, сочини́ть *perf.*; (*institute*) составля́ть *imp.*, соста́вить *perf.*; (*print.*) набира́ть *imp.*, набра́ть (наберу́, -рёшь;

набра́л, -а́, -о) *perf.* **composed** *adj.* споко́йный; *be c. of*, состоя́ть (-ои́т) *imp.* из + *gen.* **composer** *n.* компози́тор. **composite** *adj.* составно́й. **composition** *n.* построе́ние; сочине́ние; соста́в. **compositor** *n.* набо́рщик.

compost *n.* компо́ст.

composure *n.* самооблада́ние.

compound[1] *n.* (*mixture*) соедине́ние, соста́в; *adj.* составно́й; сло́жный.

compound[2] *n.* (*enclosure*) огоро́женное ме́сто (*pl.* -та́).

comprehend *v.t.* понима́ть *imp.*, поня́ть (пойму́, -мёшь; по́нял, -а́, -о) *perf.* **comprehensible** *adj.* поня́тный. **comprehensive** *adj.* всесторо́нний (-нен, -ння); всеобъе́млющий; *c. school*, общеобразова́тельная шко́ла.

compress *v.t.* сжима́ть *imp.*, сжать (сожму́, -мёшь) *perf.*; сда́вливать *imp.*, сдави́ть (-влю́, -вишь) *perf.*; *n.* компре́сс. **compressed** *adj.* сжа́тый. **compression** *n.* сжа́тие. **compressor** *n.* компре́ссор.

comprise *v.t.* заключа́ть *imp.* в себе́; состоя́ть (-ою́, -ои́шь) *imp.* из + *gen.*

compromise *n.* компроми́сс; *v.t.* компромети́ровать *imp.*, с ~ *perf.*; *v.i.* идти́ (иду́, идёшь; шёл, шла) *imp.*, пойти́ (пойду́, -дёшь; пошёл, -шла́) *perf.* на компроми́сс.

compulsion *n.* принужде́ние. **compulsory** *adj.* обяза́тельный.

compunction *n.* угрызе́ние со́вести.

computation *n.* вычисле́ние. **compute** *v.t.* вычисля́ть *imp.*, вы́числить *perf.* **computer** *n.* вычисли́тельная маши́на; (*electronic*) ЭВМ; компью́тер.

comrade *n.* това́рищ; *c.-in-arms*, сора́тник **comradeship** *n.* това́рищество.

concave *adj.* во́гнутый. **concavity** *n.* во́гнутая пове́рхность.

conceal *v.t.* скрыва́ть *imp.*, скрыть (-ро́ю, -ро́ешь) *perf.* **concealment** *n.* сокры́тие, ута́ивание.

concede *v.t.* уступа́ть *imp.*, уступи́ть (-плю́, -пишь) *perf.*

conceit *n.* самомне́ние; чва́нство. **conceited** *adj.* чва́нный (-нен, -нна).

conceivable *adj.* постижи́мый; мысли́мый. **conceive** *v.t.* (*plan, contemplate*) замышля́ть *imp.*, замы́слить *perf.*; (*become pregnant*) зачина́ть *imp.* зача́ть (-чну́, -чнёшь; зача́л, -а́, -о) *perf.*

concentrate *n.* концентра́т; *v.t & i.* сосредото́чивать(ся) *imp.*, сосредото́чить(ся) *perf.* (on, на + *prep.*); *v.t.* концентри́ровать *imp.*, с ~ *perf.* **concentrated** *adj.* концентри́рованный, сосредото́ченный (-ен, -енна). **concentration** *n.* сосредото́ченность, концентра́ция.

concentric *adj.* концентри́ческий.

concept *n.* поня́тие; конце́пция. **conception** *n.* понима́ние; представле́ние; (*physiol.*) зача́тие.

concern *n.* (*worry*) забо́та; (*business*) предприя́тие; *v.t.* каса́ться *imp.* + *gen.*; *c. oneself with*, занима́ться *imp.*, заня́ться (займу́сь, -мёшься; заня́лся́, -яла́сь) *perf.* + *instr.* **concerned** *adj.* озабо́ченный (-ен, -енна); *c. with*, свя́занный (-ан) с + *instr.*; за́нятый (-т, -та́, -то) + *instr.* **concerning** *prep.* относи́тельно + *gen.*

concert *n.* конце́рт; *v.t.* согласо́вывать *imp.*, согласова́ть *perf.* **concerted** *adj.* согласо́ванный.

concertina *n.* гармо́ника.

concession *n.* усту́пка; (*econ.*) конце́ссия. **concessionaire** *n.* концессионе́р.

conch *n.* ра́ковина.

conciliate *v.t.* умиротворя́ть *imp.*, умиротвори́ть *perf.* **conciliation** *n.* умиротворе́ние. **conciliatory** *adj.* примири́тельный.

concise *adj.* сжа́тый, кра́ткий (-ток, -тка́, -тко). **conciseness** *n.* сжа́тость, кра́ткость.

conclave *n.* конкла́в.

conclude *v.t.* (*complete*) зака́нчивать *imp.*, зако́нчить *perf.*; (*infer, arrange, complete*) заключа́ть *imp.*, заключи́ть *perf.* **concluding** *adj.* заключи́тельный; заверша́ющий. **conclusion** *n.* заключе́ние, оконча́ние; (*deduction*) вы́вод. **conclusive** *adj.* заключи́тельный; (*decisive*) реша́ющий.

concoct *v.t.* стря́пать *imp.*, со ~ *perf.* **concoction** *n.* стряпня́.

concomitant *adj.* сопу́тствующий.

concord *n.* согла́сие; согласова́ние. **concordance** *n.* согла́сие; соответствие; (*to Bible etc.*) слова́рь (-ря́) *m.* **concordat** *n.* конкорда́т.

concourse *n.* скопле́ние; (*area*) откры́тое ме́сто.

concrete *n.* бето́н; *c.-mixer*, бетономеша́лка; *adj.* (*made of c.*) бето́нный; (*not abstract*) конкре́тный.

concubine *n.* любо́вница.

concur *v.i.* соглаша́ться *imp.*, согласи́ться *perf.*

concussion *n.* сотрясе́ние.

condemn *v.t.* осужда́ть *imp.*, осуди́ть (-ужу́, -у́дишь) *perf.*; (*as unfit for use*) бракова́ть *imp.*, за~ *perf.* **condemnation** *n.* осужде́ние.

condensation *n.* конденса́ция. **condense** *v.t* (*liquid etc.*) конденси́ровать *imp.*, *perf.*; (*text etc.*) сжа́то излага́ть *imp.*, изложи́ть (-жу́, -жишь) *perf.* **condensed** *adj.* сжа́тый, кра́ткий (-ток, -тка́, -тко); сгущённый (-ён, -ена́); конденси́рованный. **condenser** *n.* конденса́тор.

condescend *v.i.* снисходи́ть (-ожу́, -о́дишь) *imp.*, снизойти́ (-ойду́, -ойдёшь; -ошёл, -ошла́) *perf.* **condescending** *adj.* снисходи́тельный. **condescension** *n.* снисхожде́ние.

condiment *n.* припра́ва.

condition *n.* усло́вие; (*state of being*) состоя́ние; положе́ние; *v.t.* обусло́вливать *imp.*, обусло́вить *perf.* **conditional** *adj.* усло́вный. **conditioned** *adj.* обусло́вленный (-ен); *c. reflex*, усло́вный рефле́кс.

condole *v.i.*: *c. with*, соболе́зновать *imp.* + *dat.* **condolence** *n.*: *pl.* соболе́знование.

condone *v.t.* закрыва́ть *imp.*, закры́ть (-ро́ю, -ро́ешь) *perf.* глаза́ на + *acc.*

conduce *v.i.*: *c. to*, спосо́бствовать *imp.* + *dat.* **conducive** *adj.* спосо́бствующий (to, + *dat.*).

conduct *n.* веде́ние; (*behaviour*) поведе́ние; *v.t.* вести́ (веду́, -дёшь; вёл, -а́) *imp.*, по~, про~ *perf.*; (*mus.*) дирижи́ровать *imp.* + *instr.*; (*phys.*) проводи́ть (-ит) *imp.* **conduction** *n.* проводи́мость. **conductor** *n.* (*bus, tram*) конду́ктор (*pl.* -а́); (*phys.*) проводни́к (-а́); (*mus.*) дирижёр.

conduit *n.* трубопрово́д; (*for wires*) кабелепрово́д.

cone *n.* ко́нус; (*of pine, fir*) ши́шка.

confection *n.* изготовле́ние; конди́терское изде́лие. **confectioner** *n.* конди́тер; *c.'s*, конди́терская *sb.* **confectionery** *n.* конди́терские изде́лия *neut.pl.*

confederacy *n.* конфедера́ция. **confederate** *adj.* конфедерати́вный; *n.* сообщни́к. **confederation** *n.* конфедера́ция.

confer *v.t.* жа́ловать *imp.*, по~ *perf.* (+ *acc.* & *instr.*, + *dat.* & *acc.*); присужда́ть *imp.*, присуди́ть (-ужу́, -у́дишь) (on, + *dat.*) *perf.*; *v.i.* совеща́ться *imp.* **conference** *n.* совеща́ние, конфере́нция; *c. hall*, конфере́нц-за́л. **conferment** *n.* присвое́ние; присужде́ние.

confess *v.t.* (*acknowledge*) признава́ть (-наю́ ,-наёшь) *imp.*, призна́ть *perf.*; (*eccl., of sinner & priest*) испове́довать *imp.*, *perf.* **confession** *n.* призна́ние; и́споведь. **confessor** *n.* духовни́к (-а́).

confidant(e) *n.* дове́ренное лицо́ (*pl.* -ца). **confide** *v.t.* поверя́ть *imp.*, пове́рить *perf.* **confidence** *n.* (*trust*) дове́рие; (*certainty*) уве́ренность; *c. trick*, моше́нничество. **confident** *adj.* уве́ренный (-ен, -енна). **confidential** *adj.* секре́тный; конфиденциа́льный.

configuration *n.* конфигура́ция.

confine *v.t.* ограни́чивать *imp.*, ограни́чить *perf.*; (*in prison*) заключа́ть *imp.*, заключи́ть *perf.* **confinement** *n.* (*for birth*) ро́ды (-дов) *pl.*; заключе́ние. **confines** *n.* преде́лы *m.pl.*

confirm *v.t.* подтвержда́ть *imp.*, подтверди́ть *perf.* **confirmation** *n.* подтвержде́ние; (*eccl.*) конфирма́ция. **confirmed** *adj.* закорене́лый.

confiscate *v.t.* конфискова́ть *imp.*, *perf.* **confiscation** *n.* конфиска́ция.

conflagration *n.* пожа́рище.

conflict *n.* конфли́кт; противоре́чие; *v.i.*: *c. with*, (*contradict*) противоре́чить *imp.* + *dat.* **conflicting** *adj.* противоречи́вый.

confluence *n.* слия́ние.

conform *v.i.*: *c. to*, подчиня́ться *imp.*, подчини́ться *perf.* + *dat.* **conformity** *n.*

соотве́тствие; (*compliance*) подчине́ние.
confound *v.t.* сбива́ть *imp.*, сбить (собью́, -ьёшь) *perf.* с то́лку; *c. it!* к чёрту! **confounded** *adj.* прокля́тый.
confront *v.t.* стоя́ть (-ою́, -ои́шь) *imp.* лицо́м к лицу́ с+*instr.*; *be confronted with*, быть поста́вленным пе́ред+*instr.*
confuse *v.t.* приводи́ть (-ожу́, -о́дишь) *imp.*, привести́ (-еду́, -едёшь; -ёл, -ела́) *perf.* в замеша́тельство; пу́тать *imp.*, за~, с~ *perf.* **confusion** *n.* замеша́тельство, пу́таница.
congeal *v.t.* застыва́ть *imp.*, засты́(ну)ть (-ы́ну, -ы́нешь; -ы́(ну)л, -ы́ла) *perf.*
congenial *adj.* бли́зкий (-зок, -зка́, -зко, бли́зки́) по ду́ху.
congenital *adj.* врождённый (-ён, -ена́).
conger (eel) *n.* морско́й у́горь (угря́) *m.*
congested *adj.* перепо́лненный (-ен); (*med.*) засто́йный. **congestion** *n.* (*population*) перенаселённость; (*traffic*) зато́р; (*med.*) засто́й кро́ви.
congratulate *v.t.* поздравля́ть *imp.*, поздра́вить *perf.* (on, с+*instr.*). **congratulation** *n.* поздравле́ние. **congratulatory** *adj.* поздрави́тельный.
congregate *v.i.* собира́ться *imp.*, собра́ться (-берётся; -бра́лся, -брала́сь, -бра́ло́сь) *perf.* **congregation** *n.* собра́ние; (*eccl.*) прихожа́не (-н) *pl.*
congress *n.* конгре́сс, съе́зд. **congressional** *adj.* относя́щийся к конгре́ссу. **Congressman** *n.* конгрессме́н.
congruent *adj.* конгруэ́нтный.
conic(al) *adj.* кони́ческий.
conifer *n.* хво́йное *sb.* **coniferous** *adj.* хво́йный, шишконо́сный.
conjectural *adj.* предположи́тельный. **conjecture** *n.* предположе́ние; *v.t.* предполага́ть *imp.*, предположи́ть (-жу́, -жишь) *perf.*
conjugal *adj.* супру́жеский.
conjugate *v.t.* (*gram.*) спряга́ть *imp.*, про~ *perf.* **conjugation** *n.* (*gram.*) спряже́ние.
conjunction *n.* (*gram.*) сою́з.
conjure *v.i.*: *c. up*, (*in mind*) вызыва́ть *imp.*, вы́звать (-зову, -зовешь) *perf.* в воображе́нии. **conjurer** *n.* фо́кусник. **conjuring** *n.* пока́зывание фо́кусов; *c. trick*, фо́кус.
conker *n.* ко́нский кашта́н; *pl.* де́тская игра́ в кашта́ны.
connect *v.t.* свя́зывать *imp.*, связа́ть (-яжу́, -я́жешь) *perf.*; соединя́ть *imp.*, соедини́ть *perf.* **connected** *adj.* свя́занный (-ан). **connecting** *adj.* соедини́тельный, связу́ющий; *c.-rod*, шату́н (-а́). **connection, -exion** *n.* связь (*loc.* связи́).
conning-tower *n.* боева́я ру́бка.
connivance *n.* попусти́тельство. **connive** *v.i.*: *c. at*, попусти́тельствовать *imp.*+*dat.*
connoisseur *n.* знато́к (-а́).
conquer *v.t.* (*country*) завоёвывать *imp.*, завоева́ть (-ою́ю, -ою́ешь) *perf.*; (*enemy*) побежда́ть *imp.*, победи́ть (-еди́шь, -еди́т) *perf.*; (*habit*) преодолева́ть *imp.*, преодоле́ть *perf.* **conqueror** *n.* завоева́тель *m.*; победи́тель *m.* **conquest** *n.* завоева́ние; покоре́ние.
consanguinity *n.* кро́вное родство́.
conscience *n.* со́весть; *pangs of c.*, угрызе́ние со́вести. **conscientious** *adj.* добросо́вестный. **conscious** *adj.* созна́тельный; *predic.* в созна́нии; *be c. of*, сознава́ть (-аю́, -аёшь) *imp.*+*acc.* **consciousness** *n.* созна́ние.
conscript *v.t.* призыва́ть *imp.*, призва́ть (призову́, -вёшь; призва́л, -а́, -о) *perf.* на вое́нную слу́жбу; *n.* новобра́нец (-нца), призывни́к (-а́). **conscription** *n.* во́инская пови́нность.
consecrate *v.t.* (*church etc.*) освяща́ть *imp.*, освяти́ть (-ящу́, -яти́шь) *perf.*; (*bishop etc.*) посвяща́ть *imp.*, посвяти́ть (-ящу́, -яти́шь) *perf.* (в епи́скопы и т.д.). **consecration** *n.* освяще́ние; посвяще́ние.
consecutive *adj.* после́довательный.
consensus *n.* согла́сие.
consent *v.i.* дава́ть (даю́, даёшь) *imp.*, дать (дам, дашь, даст, дади́м; дал, -а́, да́ло́, -и) *perf.* согла́сие; соглаша́ться *imp.*, согласи́ться *perf.* (to, +*inf.*, на+*acc.*); *n.* согла́сие.
consequence *n.* после́дствие; *of great c.*, большо́го значе́ния; *of some c.*, дово́льно ва́жный. **consequent** *adj.*

последовательный; *c. on*, вытекающий из + *gen.* **consequently** *adv.* следовательно. **consequential** *adj.* важный (-жен, -жна, -жно, -жны).

conservancy *n.* охрана (рек и лесов). **conservation** *n.* сохранение; охрана природы. **conservative** *adj.* консервативный; *n.* консерватор. **conservatory** *n.* оранжерея. **conserve** *v.t.* сохранять *imp.*, сохранить *perf.*

consider *v.t.* обдумывать *imp.*, обдумать *perf.*; рассматривать *imp.*, рассмотреть (-рю, -ришь) *perf.*; (*regard as, be of opinion that*) считать *imp.*, счесть (сочту, -тёшь; счёл, сочла) *perf.* + *instr.*, за + *acc.*, что. **considerable** *adj.* значительный. **considerate** *adj.* внимательный. **consideration** *n.* рассмотрение; внимание; *take into c.*, принимать *imp.*, принять (приму, -мешь; принял, -а, -о) *perf.* во внимание. **considered** *adj.* продуманный (-ан). **considering** *prep.* принимая + *acc.* во внимание.

consign *v.t.* отправлять *imp.*, отправить *perf.* **consignee** *n.* грузополучатель *m.* **consignment** *n.* (*goods consigned*) партия; (*consigning*) отправка товаров; *c. note*, накладная *sb.* **consignor** *n.* грузоотправитель *m.*

consist *v.i.*: *c. of*, состоять *imp.* из + *gen.* **consistency, -ce** *n.* последовательность; консистенция. **consistent** *adj.* последовательный; *c. with*, совместимый с + *instr.* **consistently** *adv.* последовательно; согласно с + *instr.*

consolation *n.* утешение. **consolatory** *adj.* утешительный. **console**[1] *v.t.* утешать *imp.*, утешить *perf.* **consoling** *adj.* утешительный.

console[2] *n.* (*arch.*) консоль; (*control panel*) пульт управления.

consolidate *v.t.* укреплять *imp.*, укрепить *perf.* **consolidated** *adj.* (*econ.*) консолидированный (-ан, -анна). **consolidation** *n.* укрепление; (*econ.*) консолидация.

consonance *n.* созвучие. **consonant** *n.* согласный *sb.*; *adj.* созвучный; согласный; совместимый.

consort *v.i.* общаться *imp.*; *n.* супруг, ~а; *Prince C.*, супруг царствующей королевы.

consortium *n.* консорциум.

conspicuous *adj.* заметный; видный (-ден, -дна, -дно, видны). **conspicuously** *adv.* ясно, заметно.

conspiracy *n.* заговор. **conspirator** *n.* заговорщик, -ица. **conspiratorial** *adj.* заговорщицкий. **conspire** *v.i.* устраивать *imp.*, устроить *perf.* заговор.

constable *n.* полицейский *sb.* **constabulary** *n.* полиция.

constancy *n.* постоянство. **constant** *adj.* постоянный (-нен, -нна); (*faithful*) верный (-рен, -рна, -рно, верны). **constantly** *adv.* постоянно.

constellation *n.* созвездие.

consternation *n.* тревога.

constipation *n.* запор.

constituency *n.* (*area*) избирательный округ (*pl.* -а); (*voters*) избиратели *m.pl.* **constituent** *n.* (*component*) составная часть (*pl.* -ти, -тей); (*voter*) избиратель *m.*; *adj.* составной; *c. assembly*, учредительное собрание.

constitute *v.t.* составлять *imp.*, составить *perf.* **constitution** *n.* (*polit.*, *med.*) конституция; (*composition*) составление. **constitutional** *adj.* (*med.*) конституциональный; (*polit.*) конституционный (-нен, -нна). **constitutionally** *adv.* законно; в соответствии с конституцией.

constrain *v.t.* принуждать *imp.*, принудить *perf.* **constrained** *adj.* принуждённый (-ён, -ена). **constraint** *n.* принуждение; *without c.*, свободно, непринуждённо.

constrict *v.t.* (*compress*) сжимать *imp.*, сжать (сожму, -мёшь) *perf.*; (*narrow*) суживать *imp.*, сузить *perf.* **constriction** *n.* сжатие, сужение.

construct *v.t.* строить *imp.*, по~ *perf.* **construction** *n.* строительство; (*also gram.*) конструкция; (*interpretation*) истолкование; *c. site*, стройка. **constructional** *adj.* строительный; (*structural*) структурный. **constructive** *adj.* конструктивный. **constructor** *n.* строитель *m.*, конструктор.

construe *v.t.* истолковывать *imp.*, истолковать *perf.*

consul *n.* ко́нсул; *honorary c.*, почётный ко́нсул; *C.-general*, генера́льный ко́нсул. **consular** *adj.* ко́нсульский. **consulate** *n.* ко́нсульство.

consult *v.t.* консульти́ровать *imp.*, про~ *perf.* с + *instr.*; сове́товаться *imp.*, по~ *perf.* с + *instr.* **consultation** *n.* консульта́ция, совеща́ние. **consultative** *adj.* консультати́вный, совеща́тельный. **consulting** *adj.* консульти́рующий; *c. room*, враче́бный кабине́т.

consume *v.t.* потребля́ть *imp.*, потреби́ть *perf.*; расхо́довать *imp.*, из~ *perf.* **consumer** *n.* потреби́тель *m.*; *c. goods*, това́ры *m.pl.* широ́кого потребле́ния, ширпотре́б; *c. society*, о́бщество потребле́ния.

consummate *adj.* зако́нченный (-ен, -енна); соверше́нный (-нен, -нна); *v.t.* заверша́ть *imp.*, заверши́ть *perf.*; доводи́ть (-ожу́, -о́дишь) *imp.*, довести́ (-еду́, -едёшь; довёл, -а́) *perf.* до конца́. **consummation** *n.* заверше́ние.

consumption *n.* потребле́ние, расхо́д; (*disease*) чахо́тка. **consumptive** *adj.* чахо́точный, туберкулёзный; *n.* больно́й *sb.* чахо́ткой, туберкулёзом.

contact *n.* конта́кт, соприкоснове́ние; *v.t.* соприкаса́ться *imp.*, соприкосну́ться *perf.* с + *instr.*; входи́ть (-ожу́, -о́дишь) *imp.*, войти́ (войду́, -дёшь; вошёл, -шла́) *perf.* в конта́кт с + *instr.*

contagion *n.* зара́за, инфе́кция. **contagious** *adj.* зара́зный, инфекцио́нный; *c. laughter*, зарази́тельный смех.

contain *v.t.* содержа́ть (-жу́, -жишь) *imp.*; вмеща́ть *imp.*, вмести́ть *perf.*; (*restrain*) сде́рживать *imp.*, сдержа́ть (-жу́, -жишь) *perf.* **container** *n.* (*vessel*) сосу́д; (*transport*) конте́йнер. **containment** *n.* сде́рживание.

contaminate *v.t.* заража́ть *imp.*, зарази́ть *perf.*; загрязня́ть *imp.*, загрязни́ть *perf.* **contamination** *n.* зараже́ние, загрязне́ние.

contemplate *v.t.* созерца́ть *imp.*; размышля́ть *imp.*; (*intend*) предполага́ть *imp.*, предположи́ть (-жу́, -жишь) *perf.* **contemplation** *n.* созерца́ние; размышле́ние. **contemplative** *adj.* созерца́тельный.

contemporary *n.* совреме́нник; *adj.* совреме́нный (-нен, -нна).

contempt *n.* презре́ние; *c. of court*, неуваже́ние к суду́; *hold in c.*, презира́ть *imp.* **contemptible** *adj.* презре́нный (-ен, -енна). **contemptuous** *adj.* презри́тельный.

contend *v.i.* (*compete*) состяза́ться *imp.*; *c. for*, оспа́ривать *imp.*; *v.t.* утвержда́ть *imp.* **contender** *n.* соревну́ющийся *sb.*

content[1] *n.* содержа́ние; *pl.* содержи́мое *sb.*; (*table of*) *contents*, содержа́ние.

content[2] *n.* дово́льство; *predic.* дово́лен (-льна); *v.t.*: *c. oneself with*, дово́льствоваться *imp.*, у~ *perf.* + *instr.* **contented** *adj.* дово́льный; удовлетворённый (-ён, -ена́).

contention *n.* (*dispute*) спор, разногла́сие; (*claim*) утвержде́ние. **contentious** *adj.* (*disputed*) спо́рный; (*quarrelsome*) вздо́рный.

contest *n.* соревнова́ние, состяза́ние; *v.t.* оспа́ривать *imp.*, оспо́рить *perf.* **contestant** *n.* уча́стник, -ица, соревнова́ния; конкуре́нт, ~ка.

context *n.* конте́кст.

contiguity *n.* соприкоснове́ние; бли́зость. **contiguous** *adj.* (*adjoining*) прилега́ющий (to, к + *dat.*); (*touching*) соприкаса́ющийся (to, с + *instr.*); (*near*) бли́зкий (-зок, -зка́, -зко, бли́зки́) (to, от + *gen.*).

continence *n.* воздержа́ние. **continent**[1] *adj.* возде́ржанный (-ан, -анна).

continent[2] *n.* матери́к (-а́), контине́нт. **continental** *adj.* материко́вый, континента́льный.

contingency *n.* случа́йность. **contingent** *adj.* случа́йный, непредви́денный (-ен, -енна); *c. on*, в зави́симости от + *gen.*; *n.* континге́нт.

continual *adj.* непреста́нный (-нен, -нна). **continuance, continuation** *n.* продолже́ние. **continue** *v.t.* & *i.* продолжа́ть(ся) *imp.*, продо́лжить(ся) *perf.* **continuous** *adj.* непреры́вный.

contort *v.t.* искажа́ть *imp.*, искази́ть

perf. **contortion** *n*. искаже́ние; искривле́ние. **contortionist** *n*. акроба́т.
contour *n*. ко́нтур, очерта́ние; *c. line*, горизонта́ль.
contraband *n*. контраба́нда; *adj*. контраба́ндный.
contraception *n*. предупрежде́ние бере́менности. **contraceptive** *n*. противозача́точное сре́дство; *adj*. противозача́точный.
contract *n*. контра́кт, догово́р; *v.i.* (*make a c.*) заключа́ть *imp*., заключи́ть *perf*. контра́кт, догово́р; *v.t.* & *i*. сокраща́ть(ся) *imp*., сократи́ть(ся) (-ащу́(сь), -ати́шь(ся)) *perf*. **contracting** *adj*. догова́ривающийся; *c. parties*, догова́ривающиеся сто́роны (-о́н, -она́м) *f.pl*. **contraction** *n*. сокраще́ние, сжа́тие. **contractor** *n*. подря́дчик.
contradict *v.t.* противоре́чить *imp*. + *dat*. **contradiction** *n*. противоре́чие. **contradictory** *adj*. противоречи́вый.
contralto *n*. контра́льто (*voice*) *neut*. & (*person*) *f.indecl*.
contraption *n*. штуко́вина; устро́йство.
contrariness *n*. своенра́вие, упря́мство.
contrary *adj*. (*opposite*) противополо́жный; (*perverse*) упря́мый; *c. to*, вопреки́ + *dat*.; *n*.: *on the c*., наоборо́т.
contrast *n*. контра́ст, противополо́жность; *v.t.* противопоставля́ть *imp*., противопоста́вить *perf*. (with, + *dat*.).
contravene *v.t.* наруша́ть *imp*., нару́шить *perf*. **contravention** *n*. наруше́ние.
contribute *v.t.* (*to fund etc.*) же́ртвовать *imp*., по~ *perf*. (to, в + *acc*.); *c. to*, (*further*) соде́йствовать *imp*., *perf*. по~ *perf*. + *dat*.; (*to publication etc.*) сотру́дничать *imp*. в + *prep*. **contribution** *n*. поже́ртвование; вклад. **contributor** *n*. же́ртвователь *m*.; сотру́дник; соуча́стник.
contrite *adj*. сокруша́ющийся, ка́ющийся. **contrition** *n*. раска́яние.
contrivance *n*. приспособле́ние; вы́думка. **contrive** *v.t.* умудря́ться *imp*., умудри́ться *perf*. + *inf*.
control *n*. (*check*) контро́ль, прове́рка; (*direction*) управле́ние; (*restraint*) сде́ржанность; (*remote c.*) телеуправле́ние; *c.-gear*, механи́зм управле́ния; *c. point*, контро́льный пункт; *c. tower*, диспе́тчерская вы́шка; *v.t.* (*check*) контроли́ровать *imp*., про~ *perf*.; управля́ть *imp*. + *instr*.; *c. oneself*, сде́рживаться *imp*., сдержа́ться (-жу́сь, -жишься) *perf*. **controllable, controlled** *adj*. управля́емый, регули́руемый. **controller** *n*. контролёр; (*electr*.) контро́ллер.
controversial *adj*. спо́рный. **controversy** *n*. спор, диску́ссия.
contuse *v.t.* конту́зить *perf*. **contusion** *n*. конту́зия.
conundrum *n*. головоло́мка.
convalesce *v.i.* поправля́ться *imp*. **convalescence** *n*. попра́вка, выздора́вливание. **convalescent** *n*., *adj*. выздора́вливающий.
convection *n*. конве́кция.
convene *v.t.* созыва́ть *imp*., созва́ть (созову́, -вёшь; созва́л, -а́, -о) *perf*.
convenience *n*. удо́бство; (*public c.*), убо́рная *sb*.; *c. foods*, полуфабрика́ты *m.pl*. **convenient** *adj*. удо́бный.
convent *n*. же́нский монасты́рь (-ря́) *m*.
convention *n*. (*assembly*) съезд, собра́ние; (*agreement*) конве́нция; (*practice, use, custom*) обы́чай; (*conventionality*) усло́вность. **conventional** *adj*. общепри́нятый, обы́чный; усло́вный; *c. weapons*, обы́чные ви́ды *m.pl*. ору́жия.
converge *v.i.* сходи́ться (-дятся) *imp*., сойти́сь (-йду́тся; сошли́сь) *perf*. в одну́ то́чку. **convergence** *n*. сходи́мость, конверге́нция. **converging** *adj*. сходя́щийся в одно́й то́чке.
conversant *predic*.: *c. with*, осведомлён (-а́) в + *prep*.; знако́м с + *instr*.
conversation *n*. разгово́р, бесе́да. **conversational** *adj*. разгово́рный. **converse**[1] *v.i.* разгова́ривать *imp*.; бесе́довать *imp*.
converse[2] *adj*. обра́тный, противополо́жный. **conversely** *adv*. наоборо́т. **conversion** *n*. (*change*) превраще́ние; (*of faith*) обраще́ние; (*of building*) перестро́йка. **convert** *v.t.* (*change*) превраща́ть *imp*., преврати́ть (-ащу́, -ати́шь) *perf*. (into, в + *acc*.); (*to faith*) обраща́ть *imp*., обрати́ть (-ащу́, -ати́шь) *perf*. (to, в + *acc*.); (*a building*) перестра́ивать *imp*., перестро́ить

perf. **convertible** *adj.* обрати́мый; *n.* кабриоле́т, фаэто́н.

convex *adj.* вы́пуклый.

convey *v.t.* (*transport*) перевози́ть (-ожу́, -о́зишь) *imp.*, перевезти́ (-езу́, -езёшь; -ёз, -езла́) *perf.*; (*communicate*) сообща́ть *imp.*, сообщи́ть *perf.*; (*transmit*) передава́ть (-даю́, -даёшь) *imp.*, переда́ть (-а́м, -а́шь, -а́ст, -ади́м; пе́редал, -а́, -о) *perf.* **conveyance** *n.* перево́зка, переда́ча. **conveyancing** *n.* оформле́ние перехо́да пра́ва на недви́жимость. **conveyer** *n.* конве́йер, транспортёр.

convict *n.* осуждённый *sb.*, ка́торжник; *v.t.* осужда́ть *imp.*, осуди́ть (-ужу́, -у́дишь) *perf.* **conviction** *n.* (*leg.*) осужде́ние; (*belief*) убежде́ние. **convince** *v.t.* убежда́ть *imp.*, убеди́ть (-и́шь, -и́т) *perf.* **convincing** *adj.* убеди́тельный.

convivial *adj.* пра́здничный.

convocation *n.* созы́в; собра́ние; (*eccl.*) собо́р, сино́д. **convoke** *v.t.* созыва́ть *imp.*, созва́ть (созову́, -вёшь; созва́л, -а́, -о) *perf.*

convoluted *adj.* свёрнутый спира́лью, изви́листый.

convolvulus *n.* вьюно́к (-нка́).

convoy *n.* конво́й; коло́нна под конво́ем; *v.t.* конвои́ровать *imp.*

convulse *v.t.*: *be convulsed with*, содрога́ться *imp.*, содрогну́ться *perf.* от + *gen.* **convulsion** *n.* (*med.*) конву́льсия; су́дороги *f.pl.*

coo *n.* воркова́ние; *v.i.* воркова́ть *imp.*

cooee *interj.* ау́!

cook *n.* куха́рка, по́вар (*pl.* -а́), ~и́ха; *v.t.* стря́пать *imp.*, со~ *perf.*; (*roast*) жа́рить *imp.*, за~, из~ *perf.*; (*boil*) вари́ть (-рю́, -ришь) *imp.*, с~ *perf.* **cooker** *n.* плита́ (*pl.* -ты), печь (*loc.* -чи́; *pl.* -чи, -че́й). **cookery** *n.* кулина́рия, стряпня́. **cooking** *adj.* ку́хонный; *c. salt*, пова́ренная соль.

cool *adj.* прохла́дный; (*of persons*) хладнокро́вный; *v.t.* студи́ть (-ужу́, -у́дишь) *imp.*, о~ *perf.*; охлажда́ть *imp.*, охлади́ть *perf.*; *c. down, off*, остыва́ть *imp.*, осты́(ну)ть (-ы́ну, -ы́нешь; -ы́(ну)л, -ы́ла) *perf.* **coolant** *n.* сма́зочно-охлажда́ющая жи́дкость. **cooler** *n.* охлади́тель *m.* **cooling** *adj.* охлажда́ющий.

coop *n.* куря́тник; *v.t.*: *c. up*, держа́ть (-жу́, -жишь) *imp.* взаперти́.

cooper *n.* бо́нда́рь (бо́ндаря́) *m.*, боча́р (-а́).

co-operate *v.i.* сотру́дничать *imp.*; коопери́роваться *imp.*, *perf.* **co-operation** *n.* сотру́дничество; коопера́ция. **co-operative, co-op.** *n.* кооперати́в; *adj.* совме́стный, кооперати́вный. **co-operator** *n.* коопера́тор.

co-opt *v.t.* коопти́ровать *imp.*, *perf.*

co-ordinate *v.t.* координи́ровать *imp.*, *perf.*; согласо́вывать *imp.*, согласова́ть *perf.*; *n.* координа́та; *adj.* согласо́ванный (-ан), координи́рованный (-ан, -анна). **co-ordination** *n.* координа́ция.

coot *n.* лысу́ха.

co-owner *n.* совладе́лец (-льца).

cop *n.* полице́йский *sb.*; *v.t.* пойма́ть *perf.*

cope[1] *n.* ри́за.

cope[2] *v.i.*: *c. with*, справля́ться *imp.*, спра́виться *perf.* с + *instr.*

copious *adj.* оби́льный. **copiousness** *n.* изоби́лие.

copper *n.* (*metal*) медь; (*vessel*) ме́дный котёл (-тла́); (*coin*) медя́к (-а́); (*policeman*) полице́йский *sb.* **copperplate** *n.* (*handwriting*) каллиграфи́ческий по́черк.

coppice, copse *n.* ро́щица.

Copt *n.* копт. **Coptic** *adj.* ко́птский.

copulate *v.i.* спа́риваться *imp.*, спа́риться *perf.* **copulation** *n.* копуля́ция.

copy *n.* ко́пия; (*specimen of book etc.*) экземпля́р; *c.-book*, тетра́дь; *copyright*, а́вторское пра́во; *fair c.*, чистови́к (-а́); *rough c.*, чернови́к (-а́); *v.t.* копи́ровать *imp.*, с~ *perf.*; (*transcribe*) переписывать *imp.*, переписа́ть (-ишу́, -и́шешь) *perf.*

coquetry *n.* коке́тство. **coquette** *n.* коке́тка. **coquettish** *adj.* коке́тливый, игри́вый.

coracle *n.* ло́дка из ивняка́, обтя́нутая ко́жей или паруси́ной.

coral *n.* кора́лл; *adj.* кора́лловый.

corbel *n.* вы́ступ; консо́ль; кроншта́йн.

cord *n.* шнур (-á), верёвка; *umbilical c.*, пуповина; *vocal cords*, голосовые связки *f.pl.*; *v.t.* связывать *imp.*, связать (-яжу́, -я́жешь) *perf.* верёвкой. **cordage** *n.* снасти (-тей) *pl.*, такелаж.
cordial *adj.* сердечный, радушный; *n.* (*drink*) фруктовый напиток (-тка). **cordiality** *n.* сердечность, радушие.
corduroy *n.* вельвет (-а(у)) в рубчик; плис; *pl.* вельветовые штаны (-нов) *pl.*
core *n.* сердцевина; (*fig.*) суть; *v.t.* удалять *imp.*, удалить *perf.* сердцевину из + *gen.*
cork *n.* (*stopper*) пробка; (*float*) поплавок (-вка́); *attrib.* пробковый; *v.t.* закупоривать *imp.*, закупорить *perf.* **corkscrew** *n.* штопор; *v.i.* двигаться (-игается & -ижется) *imp.*, двинуться *perf.* по спирали.
corm *n.* клубнелуковица.
cormorant *n.* баклан.
corn[1] *n.* зерно, зерновые хлеба *m.pl.*; (*wheat*) пшеница, (*oats*) овёс (овса́), (*maize*) кукуруза; *c.-cob*, початок (-тка). **cornflakes** *n.* кукурузные хлопья (-ьев) *pl.* **cornflour** *n.* кукурузная мука. **cornflower** *n.* василёк (-лька́). **corny** *adj.* зерновой; (*coll.*) банальный.
corn[2] *v.t.* засаливать *imp.*, засолить (-олю́, -о́ли́шь) *perf.*; *corned beef*, солонина.
corn[3] *n.* (*on foot*) мозоль.
cornea *n.* роговая оболочка.
cornelian *n.* сердолик.
corner *n.* угол (угла́, *loc.* углу́); *c.-stone*, краеугольный камень (-мня; *pl.* -мни, -мне́й) *m.*; *v.t.* загонять *imp.*, загнать (-гоню́, -го́нишь; загна́л, -а́, -о) *perf.* в угол.
cornet *n.* (*mus., mil.*) корнет; (*paper*) фунтик; (*ice-cream*) рожок (-жка́).
cornice *n.* карниз.
cornucopia *n.* рог изобилия.
corolla *n.* венчик.
corollary *n.* следствие; вывод.
corona *n.* корона, венец (-нца́). **coronary (thrombosis)** *n.* венечный тромбоз. **coronation** *n.* коронация. **coroner** *n.* следователь *m.* **coronet** *n.* небольшая корона; (*garland*) венок (-нка́).

corporal[1] *n.* капрал.
corporal[2] *adj.* телесный; *c. punishment*, телесное наказание.
corporate *adj.* корпоративный. **corporation** *n.* корпорация.
corps *n.* корпус (*pl.* -а́).
corpse *n.* труп.
corpulence *n.* тучность. **corpulent** *adj.* тучный (-чен, -чна́, -чно).
corpuscle *n.* частица, тельце (*pl.* -льца́, -ле́ц, -льца́м); *red, white, c.*, красные, белые, шарики *m.pl.* **corpuscular** *adj.* корпускулярный.
corral *n.* загон; *v.t.* загонять *imp.*, загнать (-гоню́, -го́нишь; загна́л, -а́, -о) *perf.* в загон.
correct *adj.* правильный, верный (-рен, -рна́, -рно, ве́рны́); (*conduct*) корректный; *v.t.* исправлять *imp.*, исправить *perf.* **correction** *n.* исправление; поправка. **corrective** *adj.* исправительный. **corrector** *n.* корректор (*pl.* -ы & -а́).
correlate *v.t.* соотносить (-ошу́, -о́сишь) *imp.*, соотнести (-есу́, -есёшь; -ёс, -есла́) *perf.* **correlation** *n.* соотношение, корреляция.
correspond *v.i.* соответствовать *imp.* (to, with, + *dat.*); (*by letter*) переписываться *imp.* **correspondence** *n.* соответствие; корреспонденция. **correspondent** *n.* корреспондент. **corresponding** *adj.* соответствующий (to, + *dat.*).
corridor *n.* коридор.
corroborate *v.t.* подтверждать *imp.*, подтвердить *perf.* **corroboration** *n.* подтверждение.
corrode *v.t.* разъедать *imp.*, разъесть (-е́ст, -едя́т; -е́л) *perf.* **corrosion** *n.* разъедание, коррозия. **corrosive** *adj.* едкий (е́док, едка́, е́дко); *n.* едкое, разъедающее, вещество.
corrugate *v.t.* гофрировать *imp., perf.*; *corrugated iron*, рифлёное железо.
corrupt *adj.* испорченный (-ен, -енна); развратный; *v.t.* развращать *imp.*, развратить (-ащу́, -ати́шь) *perf.*; портить *imp.*, ис~ *perf.* **corruption** *n.* порча; развращённость; коррупция.
corsage *n.* корсаж.
corsair *n.* корсар; пират.

corset *n.* корсе́т.
cortège *n.* торже́ственное ше́ствие, корте́ж.
cortex *n.* кора́.
corundum *n.* кору́нд.
corvette *n.* корве́т.
cos *n.* ромэ́н-сала́т.
cosh *n.* дуби́нка; *v.t.* ударя́ть *imp.*, уда́рить *perf.* дуби́нкой.
cosine *n.* ко́синус.
cosmetic *adj.* космети́ческий; *n.* космети́ческое сре́дство; *pl.* косме́тика.
cosmic *adj.* косми́ческий. **cosmonaut** *n.* космона́вт.
cosmopolitan *adj.* космополити́ческий; *n.* космополи́т.
Cossack *n.* каза́к (-а́; *pl.* -аки́), -а́чка; *adj.* каза́чий (-чья, -чье), каза́цкий.
cosset *v.t.* не́жить *imp.*
cost *n.* сто́имость, цена́ (*acc.* -ну; *pl.* -ны); *pl.* (*leg.*) суде́бные изде́ржки *f.pl.*; *c. price*, себесто́имость; *v.t.* сто́ить *imp.*
costermonger *n.* у́личный торго́вец (-вца).
costly *adj.* дорого́й (до́рог, -а́, -о), це́нный (-нен, -нна).
costume *n.* костю́м, оде́жда; *c. jewellery*, ювели́рное украше́ние без драгоце́нных камне́й; *c. play*, истори́ческая пье́са.
cosy *adj.* ую́тный; *n.* тёплая покры́шка.
cot *n.* (*child's*) де́тская крова́тка; (*hospital bed*) ко́йка.
cottage *n.* котте́дж.
cotton *n.* хло́пок (-пка); (*cloth*) хлопчатобума́жная ткань; (*thread*) (бума́жная) ни́тка; *c.-plant*, хлопча́тник; *c. wool*, ва́та; *adj.* хло́пковый, хлопчатобума́жный.
couch *n.* куше́тка, ло́же.
couch-grass *n.* пыре́й.
cough *n.* ка́шель (-шля) *m.*; *v.i.* ка́шлять *imp.*
council *n.* сове́т; (*eccl.*) собо́р. **councillor** *n.* сове́тник; член сове́та.
counsel *n.* (*consultation*) обсужде́ние; (*advice*) сове́т; (*lawyer*) адвока́т; *c. for the defence*, защи́тник; *c. for the prosecution*, обвини́тель *m.*; *v.t.* сове́товать *imp.*, по~ *perf.* + *dat.*
count[1] *v.t.* счита́ть *imp.*, со~, сче́сть (сочту́, -тёшь; счёл, сочла́) *perf.*; *n.* счёт (-а(у)), подсчёт. **countdown** *n.* отсчёт вре́мени.
count[2] *n.* (*title*) граф.
countenance *n.* лицо́ (*pl.* -ца); *v.t.* одобря́ть *imp.*, одо́брить *perf.*
counter *n.* прила́вок (-вка), сто́йка; (*token*) фи́шка, жето́н; *adj.* обра́тный; *adv.*: *run c. to*, де́йствовать *imp.* про́тив + *gen.*; *v.t.* пари́ровать *imp.*, от~ *perf.* **counteract** *v.t.* противоде́йствовать *imp.* **counteraction** *n.* противоде́йствие. **counterbalance** *n.* противове́с; *v.t.* уравнове́шивать *imp.*, уравнове́сить *perf.* **counterfeit** *adj.* подло́жный, фальши́вый. **counterintelligence** *n.* контрразве́дка. **countermand** *v.t.* отменя́ть *imp.*, отмени́ть (-ню́, -нишь) *perf.* **counterpane** *n.* покрыва́ло, **counterpart** *n.* соотве́тственная часть (*pl.* -ти, -те́й). **counterpoint** *n.* контрапу́нкт. **counter-revolutionary** *n.* контрреволюционе́р; *adj.* контрреволюцио́нный. **countersign** *n.* паро́ль *m.*
countess *n.* графи́ня.
counting-house *n.* бухгалте́рия.
countless *adj.* несчётный, бесчи́сленный (-ен, -енна).
countrified *adj.* деревенский. **country** *n.* (*nation*) страна́; (*land of birth*) ро́дина; (*rural areas*) дере́вня; *adj.* дереве́нский, се́льский. **countryman, -woman** *n.* земля́к, -я́чка; се́льский жи́тель *m.*, ~ница.
county *n.* гра́фство.
couple *n.* па́ра; два *m.* & *neut.*, две *f*, (двух, двум, двумя́); *married c.*, супру́ги *m.pl.*; *v.t.* сцепля́ть *imp.*, сцепи́ть (-плю́, -пишь) *perf.* **couplet** *n.* двусти́шье. **coupling** *n.* соедине́ние, сцепле́ние.
coupon *n.* купо́н; тало́н.
courage *n.* му́жество, хра́брость; **courageous** *adj.* хра́брый (храбр, -а́, -о, хра́бры́).
courier *n.* (*messenger*) курье́р; (*guide*) гид.
course *n.* курс, ход, путь (-ти́, -тём) *m.*; (*of meal*) блю́до; *of c.*, коне́чно; *v.t.* гна́ться (гоню́сь, го́нишься; гна́лся,

гнала́сь, гна́ло́сь) *imp.* за + *instr.* **coursing** *n.* охо́та с го́нчими.

court *n.* двор (-а́); (*sport*) корт, площа́дка; (*law*) суд (-а́); *c. martial*, вое́нный трибуна́л; *v.t.* уха́живать *imp.* за + *instr.* **courteous** *adj.* ве́жливый, любе́зный. **courtesy** *n.* ве́жливость. **courtier** *n.* придво́рный *sb.*

cousin *n.* двою́родный брат (*pl.* -ья, -ьев), -ная сестра́ (*pl.* сёстры, -тёр, -трам); *second c.*, троюро́дный брат (*pl.* -ья, -ьев), -ная сестра́ (*pl.* сёстры, -тёр, -трам).

cove *n.* небольша́я бу́хта.

covenant *n.* догово́р; *v.i.* заключа́ть *imp.*, заключи́ть *perf.* догово́р.

cover *n.* покры́шка; покро́в; укры́тие; чехо́л (-хла́); (*bed*) покрыва́ло; (*book*) переплёт, обло́жка; *under separate c.*, в отде́льном конве́рте; *v.t.* покрыва́ть *imp.*, покры́ть (-ро́ю, -ро́ешь) *perf.*; скрыва́ть *imp.*, скрыть (-ро́ю, -ро́ешь) *perf.* **coverage** *n.* репорта́ж, информа́ция. **covering** *n.* покры́шка, оболо́чка; *adj.* покрыва́ющий; *c. letter*, сопроводи́тельное письмо́ (*pl.* -сьма, -сем, -сьмам). **covert** *adj.* скры́тый, та́йный.

covet *v.t.* домога́ться *imp.*+*gen.*; пожела́ть *perf.* + *gen.* **covetous** *adj.* зави́стливый, а́лчный.

covey *n.* вы́водок (-дка).

cow[1] *n.* коро́ва. **cowboy** *n.* ковбо́й. **cowshed** *n.* хлев (*loc.* -е & -у́; *pl.* -а́).

cow[2] *v.t.* запу́гивать *imp.*, запуга́ть *perf.*

coward *n.* трус. **cowardice** *n.* тру́сость. **cowardly** *adj.* трусли́вый.

cower *v.i.* съёживаться *imp.*, съёжиться *perf.*

cowl *n.* (*hood*) капюшо́н; (*of chimney*) колпа́к (-а́) дымово́й трубы́.

cowslip *n.* первоцве́т.

cox(swain) *n.* рулево́й *m.*

coxcomb *n.* фат.

coy *adj.* скро́мный (-мен, -мна́, -мно).

crab *n.* краб; *catch a c.*, пойма́ть *perf.* леща́.

crab-apple *n.* (*fruit*) ди́кое я́блоко (*pl.* -ки, -к); (*tree*) ди́кая я́блоня.

crack *n.* тре́щина; треск; уда́р; *adj.* первокла́ссный, великоле́пный; *v.t.* (*break*) коло́ть (-лю́, -лешь) *imp.*, рас~ *perf.*; *v.i.* (*sound*) тре́снуть *perf.* **cracker** *n.* (*Christmas c.*) хлопу́шка; (*firework*) фе́йерверк. **crackle** *v.i.* потре́скивать *imp.*; хрусте́ть (-щу́, -сти́шь) *imp.*; *n.* потре́скивание, хруст (-а(у)). **crackpot** *n.* поме́шанный *sb.*

cradle *n.* колыбе́ль, лю́лька; *v.t.* убаю́кивать *imp.*

craft *n.* (*trade*) ремесло́ (*pl.* -ёсла, -ёсел, -ёслам); (*boat*) су́дно (*pl.* суда́, -до́в). **craftiness** *n.* хи́трость, лука́вство. **craftsman** *n.* реме́сленник. **crafty** *adj.* хи́трый (-тёр, -тра́, хи́тро́), кова́рный.

crag *n.* утёс. **craggy** *adj.* скали́стый.

cram *v.t.* набива́ть *imp.*, наби́ть (набью́, -ьёшь) *perf.*; впи́хивать *imp.*, впихну́ть *perf.*; пи́чкать *imp.*, на~ *perf.*; (*coach*)ната́скивать *imp.*, натаска́ть *perf.* **crammed** *adj.* битко́м наби́тый.

cramp[1] *n.* (*med.*) су́дорога.

cramp[2] *n.* зажи́м, скоба́ (*pl.* -бы, -б, -ба́м); *v.t.* стесня́ть *imp.*, стесни́ть *perf.*; ограни́чивать *imp.*, ограни́чить *perf.* **cramped** *adj.* сти́снутый; ограни́ченный (-ен, -енна).

cranberry *n.* клю́ква.

crane *n.* (*bird*) жура́вль (-ля́) *m.*; (*machine*) кран; *v.t.* (& *i.*) вытя́гивать *imp.*, вы́тянуть *perf.* (ше́ю).

cranium *n.* че́реп (*pl.* -а́).

crank[1] *n.* кривоши́п, заводна́я ру́чка; *c.-shaft*, коле́нчатый вал (*loc.* -у́; *pl.* -ы́); *v.t.* заводи́ть (-ожу́, -о́дишь) *imp.*, завести́ (-еду́, -едёшь; -ёл, -ела́) *perf.*

crank[2] *n.* (*eccentric*) чуда́к (-а́). **cranky** *adj.* чуда́ческий; эксцентри́чный.

cranny *n.* щель (*loc.* щели́; *pl.* ще́ли, щеле́й).

crape *n.* креп; (*mourning*) тра́ур.

crash[1] *n.* (*noise*) гро́хот, треск; (*accident*) круше́ние, ава́рия; (*financial*) крах, банкро́тство; *c. helmet*, защи́тный шлем; *c. landing*, вы́нужденная поса́дка; *v.i.* ру́шиться *imp.* с тре́ском; разбива́ться *imp.*, разби́ться (разобью́сь, -ьёшься) *perf.*

crash[2] *n.* (*linen*) холст (-а́), гру́бое полотно́.

crass *adj.* по́лный (-лон, -лна́, по́лно́), соверше́нный (-нен, -нна).
crate *n.* упако́вочный я́щик.
crater *n.* кра́тер, жерло́ (*pl.* -ла).
crave *v.t.* стра́стно жела́ть *imp.* + *gen.*; *c. for*, жа́ждать (-ду, -дешь) *imp.* + *gen.* **craving** *n.* стра́стное жела́ние.
craven *adj.* трусли́вый, малоду́шный.
crawl *v.i.* по́лзать *indet.*, ползти́ (-зу́, -зёшь; -з, -зла́) *det.*; тащи́ться (-щу́сь, -щишься) *imp.*; *n.* полза́ние; ме́дленный ход (-а(у)); (*sport*) кроль.
crayfish *n.* речно́й рак.
crayon *n.* цветно́й мело́к (-лка́), цветно́й каранда́ш (-а́); (*drawing*) пасте́ль; *v.t.* рисова́ть *imp.*, на~ *perf.* цветны́м мелко́м, карандашо́м.
craze *n.* ма́ния. **crazy** *adj.* поме́шанный (-ан).
creak *n.* скрип; *v.i.* скрипе́ть (-плю́, -пи́шь) *imp.* **creaking, creaky** *adj.* скрипу́чий.
cream *n.* сли́вки (-вок) *pl.*, крем; *c. cheese*, сли́вочный сыр (-а(у)); *soured c.*, смета́на; *v.t.* сбива́ть *imp.*, сбить (собью́, -ьёшь) *perf.* **creamed** *adj.* взби́тый, стёртый. **creamy** *adj.* сли́вочный, кре́мовый, густо́й.
crease *n.* мя́тая скла́дка; *v.t.* мять (мну, мнёшь) *imp.*, из~ (изомну́, -нёшь), с~ (сомну́, -нёшь) *perf.* **creased** *adj.* мя́тый.
create *v.t.* создава́ть (-даю́, -даёшь) *imp.*, созда́ть (-а́м, -а́шь, -а́ст, -ади́м; со́зда́л, -а́, -о) *perf.*; твори́ть *imp.*, со~ *perf.* **creation** *n.* творе́ние; созда́ние. **creative** *adj.* тво́рческий, созда́тельный. **creator** *n.* творе́ц (-рца́), созда́тель *m.* **creature** *n.* существо́; созда́ние; тварь.
crêche *n.* (де́тские) я́сли (-лей) *pl.*
credence *n.* дове́рие; *letter of c.*, рекоменда́тельное письмо́ (*pl.* -сьма, -сем, -сьмам); *give c.*, ве́рить *imp.* (to, + *dat.*). **credentials** *n.* манда́т; удостовере́ние ли́чности; вери́тельные гра́моты *f.pl.* **credibility** *n.* правдоподо́бие. **credible** *adj.* заслу́живающий дове́рия. **credibly** *adv.* достове́рно.
credit *n.* дове́рие; креди́т; прихо́д; *v.t.*: *credit with*, припи́сывать *imp.*, приписа́ть (-ишу́, -и́шешь) *perf.* + *dat.*; *give c.*, кредитова́ть *imp.*, *perf.* + *acc.*; отдава́ть (-даю́, -даёшь) *imp.*, отда́ть (-а́м, -а́шь, -а́ст, -ади́м; о́тдал, -а́, -о) *perf.* до́лжное + *dat.*; *it is to your c.*, э́то вам де́лает честь. **creditable** *adj.* де́лающий честь. **creditor** *n.* кредито́р. **credit-worthy** *adj.* кредитоспосо́бный.
credulity *n.* легкове́рие. **credulous** *adj.* легкове́рный.
creed *n.* убежде́ние; (*eccl.*) вероиспове́дание.
creep *v.i.* по́лзать *indet.*, ползти́ (-зу́, -зёшь; -з, -зла́) *det.*; кра́сться (-аду́сь, -адёшься, -а́лся) *imp.* **creeper** *n.* (*plant*) ползу́чее расте́ние. **creeping** *adj.* ползу́чий; *c. paralysis*, прогресси́вный парали́ч (-а́).
cremate *v.t.* креми́ровать *imp.*, *perf.* **cremation** *n.* крема́ция. **crematorium** *n.* кремато́рий.
Creole *n.* крео́л, ~ка.
crêpe *n.* креп; *c. de Chine*, крепдеши́н.
crescendo *adv.*, *adj.*, *n.* креще́ндо *indecl.*
crescent *n.* полуме́сяц; *adj.* серпови́дный.
cress *n.* кресс-сала́т.
crest *n.* гре́бень (-бня) *m.*; верши́на. *c.-fallen*, удручённый (-ён, -ённа).
cretin *n.* крети́н.
cretonne *n.* крето́н.
crevasse, crevice *n.* расще́лина, рассе́лина.
crew *n.* бригада; (*of ship*) экипа́ж, кома́нда.
crib *n.* (*bed*) де́тская крова́тка; (*in school*) шпарга́лка; *v.i.* спи́сывать *imp.*, списа́ть (-ишу́, -и́шешь) *perf.* (from, с + *gen.*).
crick *n.* растяже́ние мышц.
cricket[1] *n.* (*insect*) сверчо́к (-чка́).
cricket[2] *n.* (*sport*) кри́кет; *c.-bat*, бита́.
crier *n.* глаша́тай.
crime *n.* преступле́ние. **criminal** *n.* престу́пник; *adj.* престу́пный, уголо́вный.
crimp *v.t.* ме́лко завива́ть *imp.*, зави́ть (-вью́, -вьёшь; зави́л, -а́, -о) *perf.*
crimson *adj.* мали́новый, кармази́нный.
cringe *v.i.* (*cower*) съёживаться *imp.*, съёжиться *perf.*; (*of behaviour*) рабо-

ле́пствовать *imp.* **cringing** *adj.* подобостра́стный.
crinkle *n.* морщи́на.
crinoline *n.* криноли́н.
cripple *n.* кале́ка *m.* & *f.*; *v.t.* кале́чить *imp.*, ис~ *perf.*; (*fig.*) наноси́ть (-ошу́, -о́сишь) *imp.*, нанести́ (нанесу́, -сёшь; нанёс, -ла́) вред, поврежде́ние, + *dat.*
crisis *n.* кри́зис.
crisp *adj.* (*brittle*) хрустя́щий; (*fresh*) све́жий (свеж, -а́, -о́, све́жи́); (*abrupt*) ре́зкий (-зок, -зка́, -зко); *n.*: *pl.* чи́псы (-сов) *pl.*
criss-cross *adv.* крест-на́крест.
criterion *n.* крите́рий.
critic *n.* кри́тик. **critical** *adj.* крити́ческий; (*dangerous*) опа́сный. **criticism** *n.* кри́тика. **criticize** *v.t.* критикова́ть *imp.* **critique** *n.* кри́тика.
croak *n.* ква́канье; *v.i.* ква́кать *imp.*, ква́кнуть *perf.*; хрипе́ть (-плю́, -пи́шь) *imp.*
Croat, Croatian *n.* хорва́т, ~ка; *adj.* хорва́тский.
crochet *n.* вяза́ние крючко́м; *v.t.* вяза́ть (вяжу́, вя́жешь) *imp.*, с~ *perf.* (крючко́м).
crock *n.* (*broken pottery*) гли́няный черепо́к (-пка́). **crockery** *n.* гли́няная, фая́нсовая, посу́да.
crocodile *n.* (*animal*) крокоди́л; (*of children*) хожде́ние па́рами.
crocus *n.* кро́кус.
croft *n.* ме́лкое хозя́йство. **crofter** *n.* ме́лкий аренда́тор.
crone *n.* ста́рая карга́.
crony *n.* закады́чный друг (*pl.* друзья́, -зе́й, -зья́м).
crook *n.* (*staff*) по́сох; (*bend*) изги́б; (*swindler*) жу́лик, моше́нник; *v.t.* сгиба́ть *imp.*, согну́ть *perf.* **crooked** *adj.* криво́й (крив, -а́, -о); (*dishonest*) нече́стный. **crookedness** *n.* кривизна́; (*dishonesty*) жу́льничество.
croon *v.t.* & *i.* напева́ть *imp.*; мурлы́кать (-ы́чу, -ы́чешь) *imp.* **crooner** *n.* эстра́дный певе́ц (-вца́).
crop *n.* (*yield*) урожа́й; *pl.* культу́ры *f.pl.*; (*bird's*) зоб (*pl.* -ы́); (*haircut*) коро́ткая стри́жка; *v.t.* (*cut*) подстрига́ть *imp.*, подстри́чь (-игу́, -ижёшь; -и́г) *perf.*; *c. up*, неожи́данно возника́ть *imp.*, возни́кнуть (-к) *perf.*
croquet *n.* кроке́т.
cross *n.* крест (-а́); (*biol.*) (*action*) скре́щивание, (*result*) по́месь; *adj.* (*transverse*) попере́чный; (*angry*) серди́тый; *v.t.* пересека́ть *imp.*, пересе́чь (-еку́, -ечёшь; -е́к, -екла́) *perf.*; (*biol.*) скре́щивать *imp.*, скрести́ть *perf.*; *c. off, out*, вычёркивать *imp.*, вы́черкнуть *perf.*; *c. oneself*, крести́ться (-ещу́сь, -е́стишься) *imp.*, пере~ *perf.*; *c. over*, переходи́ть (-ожу́, -о́дишь) *imp.*, перейти́ (-ейду́, -ейдёшь; -ешёл, -ешла́) *perf.* (че́рез) + *acc.*; *crossbar*, попере́чина; *crossbow*, самостре́л; *c.-breed*, *n.* по́месь; *v.t.* скре́щивать *imp.*, скрести́ть *perf.*; *c.-country race*, кросс; *c.-examination*, перекрёстный допро́с; *c.-examine*, *c.-question*, подверга́ть *imp.*, подве́ргнуть (-г) *perf.* перекрёстному допро́су; *c.-eyed*, косогла́зый; *c.-legged*: *sit c.*, сиде́ть (сижу́, сиди́шь) *imp.* по-туре́цки; *c.-reference*, перекрёстная ссы́лка; *crossroad(s)*, перекрёсток (-тка); (*fig.*) распу́тье; *c.-section*, перекрёстное сече́ние; *crossways*, *-wise*, крест-на́крест; *crossword* (*puzzle*), кроссво́рд. **crossing** *n.* (*intersection*) перекрёсток (-тка); (*foot*) перехо́д; (*transport*; *rly.*) перее́зд.
crotch *n.* (*anat.*) промéжность.
crotchet *n.* (*mus.*) четвертна́я но́та.
crotchety *adj.* сварли́вый, приди́рчивый.
crouch *v.i.* пригиба́ться *imp.*, пригну́ться *perf.*; *n.* (*sport*) полуприсе́д, ни́зкая сто́йка.
croup *n.* круп.
crow *n.* воро́на; *as the c. flies*, по прямо́й ли́нии; *v.i.* кукаре́кать *imp.*; (*exult*) ликова́ть *imp.* **crowbar** *n.* лом (*pl.* ло́мы, ломо́в).
crowd *n.* толпа́ (*pl.* -пы); *v.i.* тесни́ться *imp.*, с~ *perf.*; *c. into*, вти́скиваться *imp.*, вти́снуться *perf.*; *c. out*, вытесня́ть *imp.*, вы́теснить *perf.* **crowded** *adj.* перепо́лненный (-ен).
crown *n.* коро́на, вене́ц (-нца́); (*tooth*) коро́нка; (*head*) маку́шка; (*hat*) тулья́; (*coin*) кро́на; *v.t.* короновать

imp., *perf.*; (*fig.*) венча́ть *imp.*, у~ *perf.*; *C. prince*, кронпри́нц.
crucial *adj.* (*decisive*) реша́ющий; (*critical*) крити́ческий.
crucible *n.* плави́льный ти́гель (-гля) *m.*
crucifix, crucifixion *n.* распя́тие. **crucify** *v.t.* распина́ть *imp.*, распя́ть (-пну́, -пнёшь) *perf.*
crude *adj.* (*rude*) гру́бый (груб, -а́, -о); (*raw*) сыро́й (сыр, -а́, -о). **crudeness, crudity** *n.* гру́бость.
cruel *adj.* жесто́кий (-о́к, -о́ка́, -о́ко). **cruelty** *n.* жесто́кость.
cruet *n.* судо́к (-дка́).
cruise *n.* круи́з; морско́е путеше́ствие; *v.i.* крейси́ровать *imp.*; *cruising speed*, сре́дняя, экономи́ческая, ско́рость; *cruising taxi*, свобо́дное такси́ *neut. indecl.* **cruiser** *n.* кре́йсер (*pl.* -а́ & -ы).
crumb *n.* кро́шка; *v.t.* обсыпа́ть *imp.*, обсы́пать (-плю, -плешь) *perf.* кро́шками.
crumble *v.t.* кроши́ть (-ошу́, -о́шишь) *imp.*, ис~, на~, рас~ *perf.*; *v.i.* обва́ливаться *imp.*, обвали́ться (-ится) *perf.* **crumbling** *adj.* осыпа́ющийся, обва́ливающийся. **crumbly** *adj.* рассы́пчатый, кроша́щийся.
crumpet *n.* сдо́бная лепёшка.
crumple *v.t.* мять (мну, мнёшь) *imp.*, с~ (сомну́, -нёшь) *perf.*; ко́мкать *imp.*, с~ *perf.*
crunch *n.* хруст; треск; *v.t.* грызть (-зу́, -зёшь; -з) *imp.*, раз~ *perf.*; *v.i.* хрусте́ть (-ущу́, -усти́шь) *imp.*, хру́стнуть *perf.*
crusade *n.* кресто́вый похо́д; (*fig.*) кампа́ния (в защи́ту + *gen.*); *v.i.* боро́ться (-рю́сь, -решься) *imp.* (for, за + *acc.*). **crusader** *n.* крестоно́сец (-сца); (*fig.*) боре́ц (-рца́) (за + *acc.*).
crush *n.* да́вка, толкотня́; (*infatuation*) си́льное увлече́ние; *v.t.* дави́ть (-влю́, -вишь) *imp.*, за~, раз~ *perf.*; мять (мну, мнёшь) *imp.*, с~ (сомну́, -нёшь) *perf.*; (*fig.*) подавля́ть *imp.*, подави́ть (-влю́, -вишь) *perf.* **crusher** *n.* дроби́лка. **crushing** *adj.* сокруши́тельный, уничтожа́ющий.
crust *n.* (*of earth*) кора́; (*bread etc.*) ко́рка.
crustacean *n.* ракообра́зное *sb.*
crusty *adj.* с твёрдой ко́ркой; (*irritable*) сварли́вый, раздражи́тельный.
crutch *n.* косты́ль (-ля́) *m.*
crux *n.* затрудни́тельный вопро́с; *c. of the matter*, суть де́ла.
cry *n.* плач; крик; *a far cry to*, далеко́ от + *gen.*; *v.i.* (*weep*) пла́кать (-а́чу, -а́чешь) *imp.*; (*shout*) крича́ть (-чу́, -чи́шь) *imp.*; *c. off*, отка́зываться *imp.*, отказа́ться (-ажу́сь, -а́жешься) *perf.* (от + *gen.*). **crying** *adj.* пла́чущий, вопию́щий; *it's a c. shame*, позо́рно! жа́лко.
crypt *n.* склеп. **cryptic** *adj.* зага́дочный. **cryptogram** *n.* та́йнопись.
crystal *n.* криста́лл; (*mineral*) хруста́ль (-ля́) *m.* **crystallize** *v.t.* & *i.* кристаллизова́ть(ся) *imp.*, *perf.*; *v.t.* (*fruit*) заса́харивать *imp.*, заса́харить *perf.*
cub *n.* детёныш ди́кого зве́ря; *bear c.*, медвежо́нок (-жо́нка; *pl.* -жа́та, -жа́т); *fox c.*, лисёнок (-нка; *pl.* лися́та, -т); *lion c.*, львёнок (-нка; *pl.* львя́та, -т); *wolf c.*, волчёнок (-нка; *pl.* волча́та, -т).
cubby-hole *n.* чула́н.
cube *n.* куб. **cubic** *adj.* куби́ческий.
cubicle *n.* отгоро́женная спа́льня (*gen. pl.* -лен).
cuckoo *n.* (*bird*) куку́шка; (*fool*) глупе́ц (-пца́); *v.i.* кукова́ть *imp.*, про~ *perf.*
cucumber *n.* огуре́ц (-рца́).
cud *n.* жва́чка.
cuddle *v.t.* обнима́ть *imp.*, обня́ть (обниму́, -мешь; о́бнял, -а́, -о) *perf.*; *v.i.* обнима́ться *imp.*, обня́ться (обниму́сь, -мешься; обня́лся́, -ла́сь) *perf.*
cudgel *n.* дуби́на, дуби́нка.
cue[1] *n.* (*theat.*) ре́плика.
cue[2] *n.* (*billiards*) кий (кия́; *pl.* кии́).
cuff[1] *n.* манже́та, обшла́г (-а́; *pl.* -а́); *off the c.*, экспро́мтом; *c.-link*, за́понка.
cuff[2] *v.t.* (*hit*) дава́ть (даю́, даёшь) *imp.*, дать (дам, дашь, даст, дади́м; дал, -а́, да́ло́, -и) *perf.* пощёчину + *dat.*
cul-de-sac *n.* тупи́к (-а́).
culinary *adj.* кулина́рный.

cull *v.t.* отбира́ть *imp.*, отобра́ть (отберу́, -рёшь; отобра́л, -а́, -о) *perf.*
culminate *v.i.* достига́ть *imp.*, дости́чь & дости́гнуть (-и́гну, -и́гнешь; -и́г) *perf.* вы́сшей то́чки. **culmination** *n.* кульминацио́нный пункт.
culpability *n.* вино́вность. **culpable** *adj.* вино́вный. **culprit** *n.* вино́вный *sb.*
cult *n.* культ; *c. of personality*, культ ли́чности.
cultivate *v.t.* (*land*) обраба́тывать *imp.*, обрабо́тать *perf.*; (*crops*; *fig.*) культиви́ровать *imp.*; (*develop*) развива́ть *imp.*, разви́ть (разовью́, -ьёшь; разви́л, -а́, -о) *perf.* **cultivated** *adj.* (*land*) обрабо́танный (-ан); (*plants*) вы́ращенный (-ен); (*person*) культу́рный; *c. crop*, пропашна́я культу́ра. **cultivation** *n.* обрабо́тка, возде́лывание; культива́ция; выра́щивание; *area under c.*, посевна́я пло́щадь. **cultivator** *n.* культива́тор.
cultural *adj.* культу́рный. **culture** *n.* культу́ра; (*of land*) возде́лывание; (*of animals*) разведе́ние; (*of bacteria*) выра́щивание. **cultured** *adj.* культу́рный; развито́й (ра́звит, -а́, -о); *c. pearls*, культиви́рованный же́мчуг (-а(у); *pl.* -а́).
culvert *n.* водопропускна́я труба́ (*pl.* -бы).
cumbersome *adj.* обремени́тельный; громо́здкий.
cumulative *adj.* постепе́нно увели́чивающийся. **cumulus** *n.* кучевы́е облака́ (-ко́в) *pl.*
cuneiform *adj.* клинообра́зный; *n.* кли́нопись.
cunning *n.* хи́трость, лука́вство; *adj.* хи́трый (-тёр, -тра́, хи́тро́), лука́вый.
cup *n.* ча́шка, ча́ша; (*prize*) ку́бок (-бка).
cupboard *n.* шкаф (*loc.* -у́; *pl.* -ы́).
cupid *n.* купидо́н.
cupidity *n.* а́лчность.
cupola *n.* ку́пол (*pl.* -а́).
cur *n.* (*dog*) дворня́жка; (*person*) гру́бый, ни́зкий, челове́к.
curable *adj.* излечи́мый.
curate *n.* свяще́нник (мла́дшего са́на).
curative *adj.* целе́бный.
curator *n.* храни́тель *m.* музе́я.
curb *v.t.* обу́здывать *imp.*, обузда́ть *perf.*; *n.* (*check*) обузда́ние, узда́ (*pl.* -ды); (*kerb*) край (*loc.* краю́; *pl.* края́) тротуа́ра.
curd (*cheese*) *n.* тво́ро́г (тво́рога́(у́)). **curdle** *v.t.* & *i.* свёртывать(ся) *imp.*, сверну́ть(ся) *perf.*; *v.t.* (*blood*) леденить *imp.*, о~ *perf.*
cure *n.* (*treatment*) лече́ние; (*means*) сре́дство (for, про́тив + *gen.*); *v.t.* (*person*) выле́чивать *imp.*, вы́лечить *perf.*; (*smoke*) копти́ть *imp.*, за~ *perf.*; (*salt*) соли́ть (солю́, со́ли́шь) *imp.*, по~ *perf.*
curfew *n.* коменда́нтский час.
curing *n.* лече́ние; (*cul.*) копче́ние, соле́ние.
curio *n.* ре́дкая антиква́рная вещь (*pl.* -щи, -ще́й).
curiosity *n.* любопы́тство. **curious** *adj.* любопы́тный.
curl *n.* (*hair*) ло́кон; (*spiral*; *hair*) завито́к (-тка́); *v.t.* завива́ть *imp.*, зави́ть (-вью́, -вьёшь; зави́л, -а́, -о) *perf.*; крути́ть (-учу́, -у́тишь) *imp.*, за~ *perf.*
curlew *n.* кро́ншнеп.
curling *n.* кэ́рлинг.
curly *adj.* вью́щийся; кудря́вый; *c.-haired*, *c.-headed*, курча́вый.
curmudgeon *n.* скря́га *m.* & *f.*
currants *n.* (*collect.*) кори́нка; *black c.*, чёрная сморо́дина; *red c.*, кра́сная сморо́дина.
currency *n.* валю́та; (*prevalence*) распространённость. **current** *adj.* теку́щий; *n.* тече́ние; (*air*) струя́ (*pl.* -у́и); (*water*; *electr.*) ток (-а(у)).
curriculum *n.* курс обуче́ния; *c. vitae*, жизнеописа́ние.
curry[1] *n.* кэ́рри *neut.indecl.*
curry[2] *v.t.*: *c. favour with*, заи́скивать *imp.* пе́ред + *instr.*, у + *gen.*
curse *n.* прокля́тие, руга́тельство; *v.t.* проклина́ть *imp.*, прокля́сть (-яну́, -янёшь; про́клял, -а́, -о) *perf.*; *v.i.* руга́ться *imp.*, по~ *perf.* **cursed** *adj.* прокля́тый, окая́нный.
cursive *n.* ско́ропись; *adj.* скорописный.
cursory *adj.* бе́глый; пове́рхностный.

curt *adj.* краткий (-ток, -тка́, -тко); ре́зкий (-зок, -зка́, -зко).
curtail *v.t.* сокраща́ть *imp.*, сократи́ть (-ащу́, -ати́шь) *perf.* **curtailment** *n.* сокраще́ние.
curtain *n.* за́навес; занаве́ска; *c. call*, вы́зов актёра; *v.t.* занаве́шивать *imp.*, занаве́сить *perf.*
curts(e)y *n.* ревера́нс.
curvature *n.* кривизна́; искривле́ние.
curve *n.* изги́б; (*math. etc.*) крива́я *sb.*; *v.t.* гнуть *imp.*, со~ *perf.*; *v.i.* изгиба́ться *imp.*, изогну́ться *perf.*
curvilinear *adj.* криволине́йный.
cushion *n.* поду́шка; *v.t.* смягча́ть *imp.*, смягчи́ть *perf.*
cusp *n.* о́стрый вы́ступ; (*geom.*) то́чка пересе́чения двух кривы́х.
custard *n.* сла́дкий заварно́й крем, со́ус; *c. powder*, концентра́т.
custodian *n.* храни́тель *m.*; сто́рож (*pl.* -а́). **custody** *n.* опе́ка; хране́ние; (*of police*) аре́ст; *to be in c.*, находи́ться (-ожу́сь, -о́дишься) *imp.* под стра́жей, аре́стом; *to take into c.*, арестова́ть *perf.*
custom *n.* обы́чай; привы́чка; (*customers*) клиенту́ра; *pl.* (*duty*) тамо́женные по́шлины *f.pl.*; *to go through the c.*, проходи́ть (-ожу́, -о́дишь) *imp.*, пройти́ (пройду́, -дёшь; прошёл, -шла́) *perf.* тамо́женный осмо́тр; *c.-house*, тамо́жня. **customary** *adj.* обы́чный, привы́чный. **customer** *n.* клие́нт; покупа́тель *m.*; зака́зчик.
cut *v.t.* ре́зать (ре́жу, -жешь) *imp.*, по~ *perf.*; (*hair*) стричь (-игу́, -ижёшь; -иг) *imp.*, о~ *perf.*; (*hay*) коси́ть (кошу́, ко́сишь) *imp.*, с~ *perf.*; (*price*) снижа́ть *imp.*, сни́зить *perf.*; (*cards*) снима́ть *imp.*, снять (сниму́, -мешь; снял, -а́, -о) *perf.* коло́ду; *c. down*, сруба́ть *imp.*, сруби́ть (-блю́, -бишь) *perf.*; *c. off*, отреза́ть *imp.*, отре́зать (-е́жу, -е́жешь) *perf.*; (*interrupt*) прерыва́ть *imp.*, прерва́ть (-ву́, -вёшь; -ва́л, -вала́, -ва́ло) *perf.*; *c. out*, выре́зывать *imp.*, вы́резать (-ежу, -ежешь) *perf.*; кро́ить *imp.*, вы́~, с~ *perf.*; *c.-out*, (*switch*) предохрани́тель *m.*, выключа́тель *m.*; (*figure*) вы́резанная фигу́ра; *c. up*, разреза́ть *imp.*, разре́зать (-е́жу, -е́жешь) *perf.*; *n.* поре́з, разре́з; покро́й; сниже́ние; *adj.* разре́занный (-ан); сре́занный (-ан); поре́занный (-ан); (*glass etc.*) гранёный; *c. out*, скро́енный (-ен); *c. rate*, сни́женная цена́ (*acc.* -ну); *c. up*, огорчённый (-ён, -ена́).
cute *adj.* привлека́тельный, преле́стный, заба́вный.
cuticle *n.* ко́жица.
cutlass *n.* аборда́жная са́бля (*gen.pl.* -бель).
cutler *n.* ножо́вщик. **cutlery** *n.* ножевы́е изде́лия *neut.pl.*; ножи́, ви́лки и ло́жки *pl.*
cutlet *n.* отбивна́я котле́та.
cutter *n.* (*tailor*) закро́йщик, -ица; (*naut.*) ка́тер (*pl.* -а́).
cutthroat *n.* головоре́з; *adj.* ожесточённый (-ён, -ённа).
cutting *n.* ре́зание; разреза́ние; (*press*) вы́резка; (*from plant*) черено́к (-нка́); (*rly.*) вы́емка; *adj.* ре́жущий; прони́зывающий; ре́зкий (-зок, -зка́, -зко).
cuttlefish *n.* карака́тица.
cyanide *n.* циани́д.
cybernetics *n.* киберне́тика.
cyclamen *n.* цикламе́н.
cycle *n.* цикл; (*electr.*) герц (*gen.pl.* -ц); (*bicycle*) велосипе́д; *v.i.* е́здить *imp.* на велосипе́де. **cyclic(al)** *adj.* цикли́ческий. **cycling** *n.* езда́ на велосипе́де; велоспо́рт. **cyclist** *n.* велосипеди́ст.
cyclone *n.* цикло́н.
cyclotron *n.* циклотро́н.
cygnet *n.* лебедёнок (-нка; *pl.* лебедя́та, -т).
cylinder *n.* цили́ндр. **cylindrical** *adj.* цилиндри́ческий.
cymbals *n.* таре́лки *f.pl.*
cynic *n.* ци́ник. **cynical** *adj.* цини́чный. **cynicism** *n.* цини́зм.
cynosure *n.* центр внима́ния.
cypress *n.* кипари́с.
Cypriot *n.* киприо́т, ~ка; *Greek* (*Turkish*) *C.*, киприо́т, ~ка, гре́ческого (туре́цкого) происхожде́ния.
Cyrillic *n.* кири́ллица.
cyst *n.* киста́.
czar, czarina *see* **tsar, tsarina**
Czech *n.* чех, че́шка; *adj.* че́шский.

D

D *n.* (*mus.*) ре *neut.indecl.*
dab[1] *n.* лёгкое каса́ние; мазо́к (-зка́); *v.t.* легко́ прикаса́ться *imp.*, прикосну́ться *perf.* к + *dat.*; *d. on*, накла́дывать *imp.*, наложи́ть (-жу́, -жишь) *perf.* мазка́ми.
dab[2] *n.* (*fish*) ка́мбала-лима́нда.
dab[3] *adj.*: *be a d. hand at*, соба́ку съесть (-ем, -ешь, -ест, -еди́м; -ел) *perf.* на + *prep.*
dabble *v.i.* плеска́ться (-ещу́сь, -е́щешься) *imp.*; *d. in*, пове́рхностно, по-люби́тельски, занима́ться *imp.*, заня́ться (займу́сь, -мёшься; -я́лся, -яла́сь) *perf.* + *instr.* **dabbler** *n.* диле-та́нт.
dace *n.* елёц (ельца́).
dachshund *n.* та́кса.
dad, daddy *n.* па́па; *d.-long-legs*, долго-но́жка.
dado *n.* вну́тренняя пане́ль.
daffodil *n.* жёлтый нарци́сс.
daft *adj.* глу́пый (глуп, -á, -o); бессмы́сленный (-ен, -енна).
dagger *n.* кинжа́л; (*print.*) кре́стик.
dahlia *n.* георги́н.
daily *adv.* ежедне́вно; *adj.* ежедне́вный, повседне́вный; *d. bread*, хлеб насу́щный; *d. dozen*, заря́дка; *n.* (*charwoman*) приходя́щая домрабо́тница; (*newspaper*) ежедне́вная газе́та.
daintiness *n.* изя́щество. **dainty** *adj.* изя́щный; изы́сканный (-ан, -анна).
dairy *n.* маслобо́йня; (*shop*) моло́чная *sb.*; *d. farm*, моло́чное хозя́йство. **dairymaid** *n.* доя́рка.
dais *n.* помо́ст.
daisy *n.* маргари́тка.
dale *n.* доли́на.
dalliance *n.* пра́здное времяпрепровожде́ние. **dally** *v.i.* развлека́ться *imp.*, развле́чься (-еку́сь, -ечёшся; -ёкся, -екла́сь) *perf.*
Dalmatian *n.* далма́тский дог.
dam[1] *n.* (*barrier*) плоти́на; перемы́чка; *v.t.* прегражда́ть *imp.*, прегради́ть *perf.* плоти́ной; пруди́ть (-ужу́, -у́дишь) *imp.*, за ~ *perf.*
dam[2] *n.* (*animal*) ма́тка.
damage *n.* поврежде́ние; уще́рб; *pl.* убы́тки *m.pl.*; *v.t.* поврежда́ть *imp.*, повреди́ть *perf.*; по́ртить *imp.*, ис ~ *perf.*
damascene *v.t.* насека́ть *imp.*, насе́чь (-еку́, -ечёшь; -ёк, -екла́) *perf.* зо́лотом, серебро́м.
damask *n.* камча́тная ткань; *adj.* дама́сский; камча́тный.
damn *v.t.* проклина́ть *imp.*, прокля́сть (-яну́, -янёшь; про́клял, -á, -o) *perf.*; (*censure*) осужда́ть *imp.*, осуди́ть (-ужу́, -у́дишь) *perf.* **damnable** *adj.* отврати́тельный, прокля́тый. **damnation** *n.* прокля́тие. **damned** *adj.* прокля́тый.
damp *n.* сы́рость, вла́жность; *adj.* сыро́й (сыр, -á, -o); вла́жный (-а́жен, -ажна́, -а́жно, -а́жны́); *v.t.* сма́чивать *imp.*, смочи́ть (-чу́, -чишь) *perf.*; увлажня́ть *imp.*, увлажни́ть *perf.*; *d.-course*, гидроизоля́ция; *d.-proof*, влагонепроница́емый.
damson *n.* тернosли́ва.
dance *v.i.* танцева́ть *imp.*; пляса́ть (-яшу́, -я́шешь) *imp.*, с ~ *perf.*; *n.* та́нец (-нца), пля́ска; (*party*) танцева́льный ве́чер (*pl.* -á). **dancer** *n.* танцо́р, ~ ка; (*ballet*) танцо́вщик, -ица, балери́на.
dandelion *n.* одува́нчик.
dandruff *n.* пе́рхоть.
dandy *n.* де́нди *m.indecl.*, франт.
Dane *n.* датча́нин (*pl.* -а́не, -а́н), -а́нка; *Great D.*, дог. **Danish** *adj.* да́тский.
danger *n.* опа́сность. **dangerous** *adj.* опа́сный.
dangle *v.t.* болта́ть *imp.* + *instr.*; *v.i.* болта́ться *imp.*; свиса́ть *imp.*
dank *adj.* промо́зглый.
dapper *adj.* аккура́тный; франтова́тый.
dappled *adj.* пятни́стый. **dapple-grey** *adj.* се́рый (сер, -á, -o) в я́блоках.
dare *v.i.* сметь *imp.*, по ~ *perf.*; отва́живаться *imp.*, отва́житься *perf.*; *I d. say*, полага́ю; *n.* вы́зов. **daredevil** *n.* сорвиголова́ *m.* & *f.* (*pl.* -о́вы, -о́в, -ова́м). **daring** *n.* сме́лость; *adj.* сме́лый (смел, -á, -o); де́рзкий (-зок, -зка́, -зко).

dark *adj.* тёмный (-мен, -мна́); *D. Ages*, ра́ннее средневеко́вье; *d.-room*, тёмная ко́мната; *d. secret*, вели́кая та́йна; *n.* темнота́, тьма, мрак. **darken** *v.t.* затемня́ть *imp.*, затемни́ть *perf.* **darkly** *adv.* мра́чно. **darkness** *n.* темнота́, тьма, мрак.
darling *n.* дорого́й *sb.*, ми́лый *sb.*; люби́мец (-мца); *adj.* дорого́й (до́рог, -а́, -о), люби́мый.
darn *v.t.* што́пать *imp.*, за~ *perf.*; *n.* зашто́панное ме́сто (*pl.* -та́). **darning** *n.* што́пка; *adj.* што́пальный; *d. thread, wool*, што́пка.
darnel *n.* пле́вел.
dart *n.* стрела́ (*pl.* -лы); стре́лка; (*tuck*) вы́тачка; *v.t.* мета́ть (мечу́, ме́чешь) *imp.*; броса́ть *imp.*, бро́сить *perf.*; *v.i.* носи́ться (ношу́сь, но́сишься) *indet.*, нести́сь (несу́сь, -сёшься; нёсся, несла́сь) *det.*, по~ *perf.*
dash *n.* (*hyphen*) тире́ *neut.indecl.*; (*admixture*) при́месь; (*rush*) рыво́к (-вка́); *v.t.* швыря́ть *imp.*, швырну́ть *perf.*; *v.i.* броса́ться *imp.*, бро́ситься *perf.*; носи́ться (ношу́сь, но́сишься) *indet.*, нести́сь (несу́сь, -сёшься; нёсся, несла́сь) *det.*, по~ *perf.*; мча́ться (мчусь, мчи́шься) *imp.* **dashboard** *n.* прибо́рная доска́ (*acc.* -ску; *pl.* -ски, -со́к, -ска́м). **dashing** *adj.* лихо́й (лих, -а́, -о, ли́хи́), удало́й (удал, -а́, -о).
data *n.* да́нные *sb.*; фа́кты *m.pl.*
date[1] *n.* (*fruit*) фи́ник(овая па́льма).
date[2] *n.* число́ (*pl.* -сла, -сел, -слам), да́та; (*engagement*) свида́ние; *out of d.*, устаре́лый; (*overdue*) просро́ченный (-ен); *up-to-d.*, совреме́нный (-нен, -нна); в ку́рсе де́ла; *v.t.* & *i.* дати́ровать(ся) *imp.*, *perf.*; (*make engagement*) назнача́ть *imp.*, назна́чить *perf.* свида́ние с + *instr.*
dative *adj.* (*n.*) да́тельный (паде́ж (-а́)).
daub *v.t.* ма́зать (ма́жу, -жешь) *imp.*, на~ *perf.*; малева́ть (-лю́ю, -лю́ешь) *imp.*, на~ *perf.*; *n.* плоха́я карти́на.
daughter *n.* дочь (до́чери, *instr.* -рью; *pl.* -ри, -ре́й, *instr.* -рьми́); *d.-in-law*, неве́стка (*in rel. to mother*), сноха́ (*pl.* -хи) (*in rel. to father*).
dauntless *adj.* неустраши́мый.
davit *n.* шлюпба́лка.
dawdle *v.i.* безде́льничать *imp.*
dawn *n.* рассве́т; заря́ (*pl.* зо́ри, зорь, зо́рям); *v.i.* (*day*) рассвета́ть *imp.*, рассвести́ (-етёт; -ело́) *perf.impers.*; *d.* (*up*)*on*, осеня́ть *imp.*, осени́ть *perf.*; *it dawned on me*, меня́ осени́ло.
day *n.* день (дня) *m.*; (*working d.*) рабо́чий день (дня) *m.*; (*24 hours*) су́тки (-ток) *pl.*; *pl.* (*period*) пери́од, вре́мя *neut.*; *d. after d.*, изо дня́ в де́нь; *the d. after tomorrow*, послеза́втра; *all d. long*, день-деньско́й; *the d. before*, накану́не; *the d. before yesterday*, позавчера́; *by d.*, днём; *every other day*, че́рез день; *d. off*, выходно́й день (дня) *m.*; *one d.*, одна́жды; *this d. week*, че́рез неде́лю; *carry, win, the d.*, оде́рживать *imp.*, одержа́ть (-жу́, -жишь) *perf.* побе́ду; *lose the d.*, потерпе́ть (-плю́, -пишь) *perf.* пораже́ние. **daybreak** *n.* рассве́т. **day-dreams** *n.* мечты́ (*gen.* мечта́ний) *f.pl.*, грёзы *f.pl.* **day-labourer** *n.* подёнщик, -ица. **daylight** *n.* дневно́й свет; *in broad d.*, средь бе́ла дня́.
daze *v.t.* ошеломля́ть *imp.*, ошеломи́ть *perf.*; *n.* изумле́ние **dazed** *adj.* изумлённый (-ён, -ена́), потрясённый (-ён, -ена́).
dazzle *v.t.* ослепля́ть *imp.*, ослепи́ть *perf.* **dazzling** *adj.* блестя́щий, ослепи́тельный.
deacon *n.* дья́кон (*pl.* -а́).
dead *adj.* мёртвый (мёртв, -а, -о & (*fig.*) -о́), уме́рший; (*animals*) до́хлый; (*plants*) увя́дший; (*numb*) онеме́вший; (*lifeless*) безжи́зненный (-ен, -енна); (*sound*) глухо́й (глух, -а́, -о); (*complete*) соверше́нный (-нен, -нна); *d. to*, глухо́й (глух, -а́, -о) к + *dat.*; *n.*: *the d.*, мёртвые *sb.*, уме́ршие *sb.*; *d. of night*, глубо́кая ночь (*loc.* -чи́); *adv.* соверше́нно; *d.-beat*, смерте́льно уста́лый; *d. calm*, (*naut.*) мёртвый штиль *m.*; *d. drunk*, мертве́цки пья́ный (пьян, -а́, -о); *d. end*, тупи́к (-а́); *d.-end*, безвы́ходный; *d. heat*, одновре́ме́нный фи́ниш; *deadline*, (*time*) преде́льный срок (-а(у)); *deadlock*, тупи́к (-а́); *reach d.*, зайти́ (зайду́, -дёшь; зашёл, -шла́) *perf.* в тупи́к; *d. march*, похоро́нный марш;

d. nettle, глуха́я крапи́ва; *d. reckoning*, счисле́ние пути́; *d. set*, мёртвая сто́йка; *d. weight*, мёртвый груз.
deaden *v.t.* & *i.* притупля́ть(ся) *imp.*, притупи́ть(ся) (-плю́(сь), -пишь(ся)) *perf.*
deadly *adj.* смерте́льный, смертоно́сный; *d. nightshade*, белладо́нна; *d. sin*, сме́ртный грех (-а́).
deaf *adj.* глухо́й (глух, -а́, -о); *d. and dumb*, *d. mute*, глухонемо́й (*sb.*). **deafen** *v.t.* оглуша́ть *imp.*, оглуши́ть *perf.* **deafness** *n.* глухота́.
deal[1] *n.*: *a great, good, d.*, мно́го (+ *gen.*); (*with compar.*) гора́здо.
deal[2] *n.* (*bargain*) сде́лка; (*cards*) сда́ча; *v.t.* (*cards*) сдава́ть (сдаю́, -аёшь) *imp.*, сдать (-ам, -ашь, -аст, -ади́м; сдал, -а́, -о) *perf.*; (*blow*) наноси́ть (-ошу́, -о́сишь) *imp.*, нанести́ (-есу́, -есёшь; -ёс, -есла́) *perf.*; *d. in*, торгова́ть *imp.* + *instr.*; *d. out*, распределя́ть *imp.*, распредели́ть *perf.*; *d. with*, (*engage in*) занима́ться *imp.*, заня́ться (займу́сь, -мёшься; заня́лся́, -ла́сь) *perf.* + *instr.*; (*behave towards*) обходи́ться (-ожу́сь, -о́дишься) *imp.*, обойти́сь (обойду́сь, -дёшься; обошёлся, -шла́сь) *perf.* с + *instr.* **dealer** *n.* (*trader*) торго́вец (-вца) (in, + *instr.*).
deal[3] *n.* (*wood*) ело́вая, сосно́вая, древеси́на; *adj.* ело́вый, (*pine*) сосно́вый.
dean *n.* (*univ.*) дека́н; (*church*) настоя́тель *m.* собо́ра. **deanery** *n.* декана́т.
dear *adj.* дорого́й (до́рог, -а́, -о); (*also n.*) ми́лый (мил, -а́, -о, ми́лы́) (*sb.*).
dearth *n.* недоста́ток (-тка); нехва́тка.
death *n.* смерть (*pl.* -ти, -те́й); *adj.* сме́ртный, смерте́льный; *at d.'s door*, при́ смерти; *put to d.*, казни́ть *imp.*, *perf.*; *deathbed*, сме́ртное ло́же; *d.-blow*, смерте́льный уда́р; *d. certificate*, свиде́тельство о сме́рти; *d. duty*, нало́г на насле́дство; *d. penalty*, сме́ртная ка́знь; *d. rate*, сме́ртность; *d.-roll*, спи́сок (-ска) уби́тых; *d.-warrant*, сме́ртный пригово́р (*also fig.*). **deathless** *adj.* бессме́ртный. **deathly** *adj.* смерте́льный.
debar *v.t.*: *d. from*, не допуска́ть *imp.* до + *gen.*
debase *v.t.* понижа́ть *imp.*, пони́зить *perf.* ка́чество + *gen.*
debatable *adj.* спо́рный. **debate** *n.* пре́ния (-ий) *pl.*, деба́ты (-тов) *pl.*; *v.t.* обсужда́ть *imp.*, обсуди́ть (-ужу́, -у́дишь) *perf.*; дебати́ровать *imp.*
debauch *v.t.* развраща́ть *imp.*, разврати́ть (-ащу́, -ати́шь) *perf.*; *n.* о́ргия. **debauched** *adj.* развращённый (-ён, -ённа), развра́тный. **debauchery** *n.* развра́т.
debenture *n.* долгово́е обяза́тельство.
debilitate *v.t.* рас-, о-, слабля́ть *imp.*, рас-, о-, сла́бить *perf.* **debility** *n.* бесси́лие, тщеду́шие.
debit *n.* де́бет; *debits and credits*, прихо́д и расхо́д; *v.t.* дебетова́ть *imp.*, *perf.*; запи́сывать *imp.*, записа́ть (-ишу́, -и́шешь) *perf.* в де́бет + *dat.*
debouch *v.i.* (*mil.*) дебуши́ровать *imp.*, *perf.*; (*river*) впада́ть *imp.*, впасть (впадёт; впал) *perf.*
debris *n.* оско́лки *m.pl.*, обло́мки *m.pl.*
debt *n.* долг (-а(у), *loc.* -у́; *pl.* -и́). **debtor** *n.* должни́к (-а́).
debunk *v.t.* разве́нчивать *imp.*, развенча́ть *perf.*
début *n.* дебю́т; *make one's d.*, дебюти́ровать *imp.*, *perf.* **debutante** *n.* дебюта́нтка.
deca- *in comb.* дека-, десяти-.
decade *n.* десятиле́тие.
decadence *n.* декаде́нтство; упа́дочничество. **decadent** *adj.* декаде́нтский; упа́дочный.
decamp *v.i.* удира́ть *imp.*, удра́ть (удеру́, -рёшь; удра́л, -а́, -о) *perf.*
decant *v.t.* сце́живать *imp.*, сцеди́ть (-ежу́, -е́дишь) *perf.*; (*wine*) перелива́ть *imp.*, перели́ть (-лью́, льёшь; перели́л, -а́, -о) *perf.* (в графи́н). **decanter** *n.* графи́н.
decapitate *v.t.* обезгла́вливать *imp.*, обезгла́вить *perf.*
decarbonize *v.t.* очища́ть *imp.*, очи́стить *perf.* от нага́ра.
decathlon *n.* десятибо́рье.
decay *v.i.* гнить (-ию́, -иёшь; гнил, -а́, -о) *imp.*, с ~ *perf.*; *n.* гние́ние; распа́д (*also phys.*). **decayed** *adj.* прогни́вший, гнило́й (гнил, -а́, -о). **decaying** *adj.* гнию́щий.

decease *n.* кончи́на. **deceased** *adj.* поко́йный; *n.* поко́йный *sb.*, поко́йник, -ица.

deceit *n.* обма́н. **deceitful** *adj.* лжи́вый. **deceive** *v.t.* обма́нывать *imp.*, обману́ть (-ну́, -нешь) *perf.*

deceleration *n.* замедле́ние.

December *n.* дека́брь (-ря́) *m.*; *attrib.* дека́брьский.

decency *n.* прили́чие, поря́дочность. **decent** *adj.* прили́чный, поря́дочный.

decentralization *n.* децентрализа́ция. **decentralize** *v.t.* децентрализова́ть *imp.*, *perf.*

deception *n.* обма́н. **deceptive** *adj.* обма́нчивый.

deci- *in comb.* деци-.

decibel *n.* децибе́л.

decide *v.t.* реша́ть *imp.*, реши́ть *perf.* **decided** *adj.* (*resolute*) реши́тельный; (*definite*) несомне́нный (-нен, -нна). **decidedly** *adv.* реши́тельно, бесспо́рно, я́вно.

deciduous *adj.* листопа́дный.

decimal *n.* десяти́чная дробь (*pl.* -би, -бе́й); *adj.* десяти́чный; *d. point*, запята́я *sb.*

decimate *v.t.* (*fig.*) коси́ть (-ит) *imp.*, с~ *perf.*

decipher *v.t.* расшифро́вывать *imp.*, расшифрова́ть *perf.*

decision *n.* реше́ние. **decisive** *adj.* реша́ющий, реши́тельный.

deck *n.* па́луба; (*bus etc.*) эта́ж (-а́); *d.-chair*, шезло́нг; *d.-hand*, па́лубный матро́с; *d.-house*, ру́бка; *v.t.*: *d. out*, украша́ть *imp.*, укра́сить *perf.*

declaim *v.t.* деклами́ровать *imp.*, про~ *perf.*

declaration *n.* объявле́ние; (*document*) деклара́ция. **declare** *v.t.* за-, объ-, являть *imp.*, за-, объ-, яви́ть (-влю́, -вишь) *perf.*

declassify *v.t.* рассекре́чивать *imp.*, рассекре́чить *perf.*

declension *n.* склоне́ние. **decline** *n.* упа́док (-дка); (*price*) пониже́ние; *v.i.* приходи́ть (-ит) *imp.*, прийти́ (придёт; пришёл, -шла́) *perf.* в упа́док; *v.t.* (*refuse*) отклоня́ть *imp.*, отклони́ть (-ню́, -нишь) *perf.*; (*gram.*) склоня́ть *imp.*, про~ *perf.* **declining** *adj.*: *d. years*, преклóнный во́зраст.

declivity *n.* укло́н.

decoction *n.* отва́р (-а(у)).

decode *v.t.* расшифро́вывать *imp.*, расшифрова́ть *perf.*

decompose *v.t.* разлага́ть *imp.*, разложи́ть (-жу́, -жишь) *perf.*; *v.i.* распада́ться *imp.*, распа́сться (-адётся; -а́лся) *perf.*; (*rot*) гнить (-ию́, -иёшь; гнил, -а́, -о) *imp.*, с~ *perf.*

decompress *v.t.* снижа́ть *imp.*, сни́зить *perf.* давле́ние на + *acc.* **decompression** *n.* декомпре́ссия.

decontaminate *v.t.* (*gas*) дегази́ровать *imp.*, *perf.*; (*radioactivity*) дезактиви́ровать *imp.*, *perf.*

decontrol *v.t.* снима́ть *imp.*, снять (сниму́, -мешь; снял, -а́, -о) *perf.* контро́ль *m.* с + *gen.*

decorate *v.t.* украша́ть *imp.*, укра́сить *perf.*; (*with medal etc.*) награжда́ть *imp.*, награди́ть *perf.* о́рденом (-на́ми). **decoration** *n.* украше́ние, отде́лка; о́рден (*pl.* -а́). **decorative** *adj.* декорати́вный. **decorator** *n.* маля́р (-а́).

decorous *adj.* прили́чный; чи́нный (-нен, -нна́, -нно). **decorum** *n.* прили́чие, деко́рум; (*etiquette*) этике́т.

decoy *n.* (*trap*) западня́; (*bait*) прима́нка; *v.t.* за-, при-, ма́нивать *imp.*, за-, при-, мани́ть (-ню́, -нишь) *perf.*

decrease *v.t.* & *i.* уменьша́ть(ся) *imp.*, уме́ньши́ть(ся) *perf.*; *n.* уменьше́ние, пониже́ние.

decree *n.* ука́з, декре́т, постановле́ние; *v.t.* постановля́ть *imp.*, постанови́ть (-влю́, -вишь) *perf.*

decrepit *adj.* дря́хлый (дряхл, -а́, -о); (*dilapidated*) ве́тхий (ветх, -а́, -о). **decrepitude** *n.* дря́хлость; ве́тхость.

dedicate *v.t.* посвяща́ть *imp.*, посвяти́ть (-ящу́, -яти́шь) *perf.* **dedication** *n.* посвяще́ние.

deduce *v.t.* заключа́ть *imp.*, заключи́ть *perf.*; де́лать *imp.*, с~ *perf.* вы́вод.

deduct *v.t.* вычита́ть *imp.*, вы́честь (-чту, -чтешь; -чел, -чла) *perf.* **deduction** *n.* (*amount*) вы́чет; (*deducting*) вычита́ние; (*inference*) вы́вод.

deed *n.* посту́пок (-пка); (*heroic*) по́двиг; (*leg.*) акт.
deem *v.t.* счита́ть *imp.*, счесть (сочту́, -тёшь; счёл, сочла́) *perf.* + *acc.* & *instr.*
deep *adj.* глубо́кий (-о́к, -ока́, -о́ко́); (*colour*) тёмный (-мен, -мна́); (*sound*) ни́зкий (-зок, -зка́, -зко, ни́зки́); *n.* мо́ре; *d.-rooted*, закорене́лый; *d.-seated*, укорени́вшийся. **deepen** *v.t.* углубля́ть *imp.*, углуби́ть *perf.*; сгуща́ть *imp.*, сгусти́ть *perf.*
deer *n.* оле́нь *m.* **deerskin** *n.* лоси́на. **deer-stalker** *n.* охо́тничья ша́пка.
deface *v.t.* по́ртить *imp.*, ис~ *perf.*; (*erase*) стира́ть *imp.*, стере́ть (сотру́, -рёшь; стёр) *perf.* **defacement** *n.* по́рча; стира́ние.
defamation *n.* диффама́ция, клевета́. **defamatory** *adj.* дискредити́рующий, позо́рящий. **defame** *v.t.* поро́чить *imp.*, о~ *perf.*; позо́рить *imp.*, о~ *perf.*
default *n.* невыполне́ние обяза́тельств; (*leg.*) нея́вка в суд; *v.i.* не выполня́ть *imp.* обяза́тельств.
defeat *n.* пораже́ние; *v.t.* побежда́ть *imp.*, победи́ть (-и́шь) *perf.* **defeatism** *n.* пораже́нчество. **defeatist** *n.* пораже́нец (-нца).
defecate *v.i.* испражня́ться *imp.*, испражни́ться *perf.* **defecation** *n.* испражне́ние.
defect *n.* дефе́кт, недоста́ток (-тка), изъя́н; *v.i.* дезерти́ровать *imp.*, *perf.* **defection** *n.* дезерти́рство. **defective** *adj.* неиспра́вный, повреждённый (-ён, -ена́); дефе́ктный, с изъя́ном. **defector** *n.* дезерти́р, невозвращéнец (-нца).
defence *n.* защи́та (*also leg.*, *sport*), оборо́на (*also mil.*); *pl.* (*mil.*) закрепле́ния *neut.pl.* **defenceless** *adj.* беззащи́тный. **defend** *v.t.* защища́ть *imp.*, защити́ть (-ищу́, -ити́шь) *perf.*; обороня́ть *imp.*, оборони́ть *perf.*; (*uphold*) подде́рживать *imp.*, поддержа́ть (-жу́, -жишь) *perf.* **defendant** *n.* подсуди́мый *sb.* **defender** *n.* защи́тник. **defensive** *adj.* оборони́тельный.
defer[1] *v.t.* (*postpone*) отсро́чивать *imp.*, отсро́чить *perf.*
defer[2] *v.i.*: *d. to*, подчиня́ться *imp.* + *dat.* **deference** *n.* уваже́ние, почте́ние. **deferential** *adj.* почти́тельный.
defiance *n.* откры́тое неповинове́ние; *in d. of*, вопреки́ + *dat.*, наперекóр + *dat.* **defiant** *adj.* вызыва́ющий, непоко́рный.
deficiency *n.* нехва́тка, дефици́т. **deficient** *adj.* недоста́точный; (*mentally d.*) слабоу́мный. **deficit** *n.* дефици́т, недочёт.
defile *v.t.* оскверня́ть *imp.*, оскверни́ть *perf.* **defilement** *n.* оскверне́ние, профана́ция.
define *v.t.* определя́ть *imp.*, определи́ть *perf.* **definite** *adj.* определённый (-нен, -нна). **definitely** *adv.* несомне́нно. **definition** *n.* определе́ние. **definitive** *adj.* оконча́тельный.
deflate *v.t.* & *i.* спуска́ть *imp.*, спусти́ть (-ущу́, -у́стишь) *perf.*; *v.t.* (*person*) сбива́ть *imp.*, сбить (собью́, -ьёшь) *perf.* спесь с + *gen.*; *v.i.* (*econ.*) проводи́ть (-ожу́, -о́дишь) *imp.*, провести́ (-еду́, -едёшь; -ёл, -ела́) *perf.* поли́тику дефля́ции. **deflation** *n.* дефля́ция.
deflect *v.t.* отклоня́ть *imp.*, отклони́ть (-ню́, -нишь) *perf.* **deflection** *n.* отклоне́ние.
defoliate *v.t.* уничтожа́ть *imp.*, уничто́жить *perf.* расти́тельность + *gen.* **defoliation** *n.* дефолиа́ция.
deforest *v.t.* обезле́сивать *imp.*, обезле́сить *perf.*
deform *v.t.* уро́довать *imp.*, из~ *perf.*; деформи́ровать *imp.*, *perf.* **deformity** *n.* уро́дство.
defraud *v.t.* обма́нывать *imp.*, обману́ть (-ну́, -нешь) *perf.*; *d. of*, выма́нивать *imp.*, вы́манить *perf.* + *acc.* & у + *gen.* (*of person*).
defray *v.t.* опла́чивать *imp.*, оплати́ть (-ачу́, -а́тишь) *perf.*
defrost *v.t.* размора́живать *imp.*, разморо́зить *perf.*
deft *adj.* ло́вкий (-вок, -вка́, -вко, ло́вки́).
defunct *adj.* усо́пший.
defy *v.t.* (*challenge*) вызыва́ть *imp.* вы́звать (вы́зову, -вешь) *perf.*; (*resist*) откры́то не повинова́ться *imp.* + *dat.*

degeneracy *n.* вырожде́ние, дегенера́тивность. **degenerate** *n.* дегенера́т, вы́родок (-дка); *adj.* дегенерати́вный; *v.i.* вырожда́ться *imp.*, вы́родиться *perf.* **degenerative** *adj.* дегенерати́вный.

degradation *n.* деграда́ция; униже́ние. **degrade** *v.t.* унижа́ть *imp.*, уни́зить *perf.* **degrading** *adj.* унизи́тельный.

degree *n.* сте́пень (*pl.* -ни, -не́й); (*math. etc.*) гра́дус; (*univ.*) учёная сте́пень (*pl.* -ни, -не́й).

dehydrate *v.t.* обезво́живать *imp.*, обезво́дить *perf.* **dehydration** *n.* дегидрата́ция.

deify *v.t.* обожествля́ть *imp.*, обожестви́ть *perf.*

deign *v.i.* соизволя́ть *imp.*, соизво́лить *perf.*

deity *n.* божество́.

dejected *adj.* удручённый (-ён, -ённа & -ена́), уны́лый. **dejection** *n.* уны́ние.

delay *n.* заде́ржка; замедле́ние; *without d.*, неме́дленно; *v.t.* заде́рживать *imp.*, задержа́ть (-жу́, -жишь) *perf.*; замедля́ть *imp.*, заме́длить *perf.*

delegate *n.* делега́т; *v.t.* делеги́ровать *imp., perf.* **delegation** *n.* делега́ция.

delete *v.t.* вычёркивать *imp.*, вы́черкнуть *perf.*

deliberate *adj.* (*intentional*) предна́ме́ренный (-ен, -енна); (*unhurried*) нетороплúвый; *v.t.* & *i.* размышля́ть *imp.*, размы́слить *perf.* (о + *prep.*). **deliberation** *n.* размышле́ние; (*discussion*) обсужде́ние, совеща́ние.

delicacy *n.* (*tact*) делика́тность; (*dainty*) ла́комство. **delicate** *adj.* то́нкий (-нок, -нка́, -нко, то́нки́); лёгкий (лёгок, -гка́, -гко́, лёгки́); (*health*) боле́зненный (-ен, -енна).

delicious *adj.* восхити́тельный; (*tasty*) о́чень вку́сный (-сен, -сна́, -сно).

delight *n.* наслажде́ние, пре́лесть. **delightful** *adj.* преле́стный.

delimit *v.t.* размежёвывать *imp.*, размежева́ть (-жу́ю, -жу́ешь) *perf.* **delimitation** *n.* размежева́ние.

delinquency *n.* правонаруше́ние, престу́пность. **delinquent** *n.* правонаруши́тель *m.*, ~ница.

delirious *adj.* бредово́й; *be d.*, бре́дить *imp.* **delirium** *n.* бред (-а(у), *loc.*, -у́); *d. tremens*, бе́лая горя́чка.

deliver *v.t.* доставля́ть *imp.*, доста́вить *perf.*; (*rescue*) избавля́ть *imp.*, изба́вить *perf.* (from, от + *gen.*); (*lecture*) прочита́ть *imp.*, проче́сть (-чту́, -чтёшь; -чёл, -чла́) *perf.*; (*letters*) разноси́ть (-ошу́, -о́сишь) *imp.*, разнести́ (-есу́, -есёшь; -ёс, -есла́) *perf.*; (*speech*) произноси́ть (-ошу́, -о́сишь) *imp.*, произнести́ (-есу́, -есёшь; -ёс, -есла́) *perf.* **deliverance** *n.* избавле́ние, освобожде́ние. **delivery** *n.* доста́вка.

dell *n.* лощи́на.

delphinium *n.* дельфи́ниум.

delta *n.* де́льта.

delude *v.t.* вводи́ть (-ожу́, -о́дишь) *imp.*, ввести́ (-еду́, -едёшь; ввёл, -а́) *perf.* в заблужде́ние.

deluge *n.* (*flood*) пото́п; (*rain*) ли́вень (-вня) *m.*

delusion *n.* заблужде́ние; *delusions of grandeur*, ма́ния вели́чия.

demagogue *n.* демаго́г. **demagogic** *adj.* демагоги́ческий. **demagogy** *n.* демаго́гия.

demand *n.* тре́бование; (*econ.*) спрос (for, на + *acc.*); *v.t.* тре́бовать *imp.*, по~ *perf.* + *gen.*

demarcate *v.t.* разграни́чивать *imp.*, разграни́чить *perf.* **demarcation** *n.* демарка́ция; *line of d.*, демаркацио́нная ли́ния.

demented *adj.* умалишённый (-ён, -ённа). **dementia** *n.* слабоу́мие.

demi- *in comb.* полу-.

demigod *n.* полубо́г (*pl.* -и, -о́в).

demilitarization *n.* демилитариза́ция. **demilitarize** *v.t.* демилитаризова́ть *imp., perf.*

demise *n.* кончи́на.

demobbed *adj.* демобилизо́ванный (-ан). **demobilization** *n.* демобилиза́ция. **demobilize** *v.t.* демобилизова́ть *imp., perf.*

democracy *n.* демокра́тия. **democrat** *n.* демокра́т. **democratic** *adj.* демократи́ческий, демократи́чный.

demolish *v.t.* разруша́ть *imp.*, разру́шить *perf.*; (*building*) сноси́ть

(-ошу́, -о́сишь) *imp.*, снести́ (-су́, -сёшь; снёс, -ла́) *perf.*; (*refute*) опроверга́ть *imp.*, опрове́ргнуть (-ве́рг(нул), -ве́ргла) *perf.* **demolition** *n.* разруше́ние, снос.

demon *n.* де́мон. **demonic** *adj.* дья́вольский, демони́ческий.

demonstrable *adj.* доказу́емый. **demonstrably** *adv.* очеви́дно, нагля́дно. **demonstrate** *v.t.* демонстри́ровать *imp.*, *perf.*; *v.i.* уча́ствовать *imp.* в демонстра́ции. **demonstration** *n.* демонстра́ция, пока́з. **demonstrative** *adj.* (*behaviour etc.*) экспанси́вный, несде́ржанный (-ан, -анна); (*gram.*) указа́тельный. **demonstrator** *n.* (*laboratory*) демонстра́тор; (*polit.*) демонстра́нт.

demoralization *n.* деморализа́ция. **demoralize** *v.t.* деморализова́ть *imp.*, *perf.*

demote *v.t.* понижа́ть *imp.*, пони́зить *perf.* в до́лжности; (*mil.*) разжа́ловать *perf.* **demotion** *n.* пониже́ние.

demur *v.i.* возража́ть *imp.*, возрази́ть *perf.* (at, to, про́тив + *gen.*); *n.*: *without d.*, без возраже́ний.

demure *adj.* (притво́рно) скро́мный (-мен, -мна́, -мно).

den *n.* (*animal's*) ло́гово, берло́га; (*thieves' etc.*) прито́н.

denial *n.* отрица́ние, опроверже́ние; (*refusal*) отка́з.

denigrate *v.t.* черни́ть *imp.*, о~ *perf.*

denomination *n.* (*name*) назва́ние; (*category*) катего́рия; (*relig.*) вероисповеда́ние. **denominator** *n.* знамена́тель *m.*

denote *v.t.* означа́ть *imp.*, означа́ть *perf.*

dénouement *n.* развя́зка.

denounce *v.t.* (*accuse*) облича́ть *imp.*, обличи́ть *perf.*; (*inform on*) доноси́ть (-ошу́, -о́сишь) *imp.*, донести́ (-есу́, -есёшь; -ёс, -есла́) *perf.* на + *acc.*; (*treaty*) денонси́ровать *imp.*, *perf.*

dense *adj.* (*thick*) густо́й (густ, -а́, -о, гу́сты́); (*stupid*) тупо́й (туп, -а́, -о, ту́пы́). **density** *n.* (*phys. etc.*) пло́тность.

dent *n.* вы́боина, вмя́тина; *v.t.* вмина́ть *imp.*, вмять (вомну́, -нёшь) *perf.*

dental *adj.* зубно́й. **dentifrice** *n.* (*paste*) зубна́я па́ста; (*powder*) зубно́й порошо́к (-шка́). **dentist** *n.* зубно́й врач (-а́). **dentistry** *n.* зубоврачева́ние.

denture *n.* зубно́й проте́з.

denunciation *n.* (*accusation*) обличе́ние; (*informing*) доно́с; (*treaty*) денонса́ция.

deny *v.t.* отрица́ть *imp.*; *d. oneself*, отка́зывать *imp.*, отказа́ть (-ажу́, -а́жешь) *perf.* себе́ в + *prep.*

deodorant *n.* дезодора́тор; *adj.* уничтожа́ющий за́пах.

depart *v.i.* отбыва́ть *imp.*, отбы́ть (отбу́ду, -дешь; о́тбы́л, -а́, -о) *perf.*; *d. from*, отклоня́ться *imp.*, отклони́ться (-ню́сь, -нишься) *perf.* от + *gen.*

department *n.* отде́л; (*government*) департа́мент, ве́домство; (*univ.*) факульте́т, ка́федра; *d. store*, универма́г. **departmental** *adj.* ве́домственный.

departure *n.* отбы́тие; отклоне́ние.

depend *v.i.* зави́сеть (-и́шу, -и́сишь) *imp.* (on, от + *gen.*); (*rely*) полага́ться *imp.*, положи́ться (-жу́сь, -жишься) *perf.* (on, на + *acc.*). **dependable** *adj.* надёжный. **dependant** *n.* иждиве́нец (-нца); *pl.* семья́ и дома́шние *sb.* **dependence** *n.* зави́симость. **dependent** *adj.* зави́симый, зави́сящий.

depict *v.t.* изобража́ть *imp.*, изобрази́ть *perf.*; (*in words*) опи́сывать *imp.*, описа́ть (-ишу́, -и́шешь) *perf.*

deplete *v.t.* истоща́ть *imp.*, истощи́ть *perf.* **depleted** *adj.* истощённый, (-ён, -ённа). **depletion** *n.* истоще́ние.

deplorable *adj.* приско́рбный, плаче́вный. **deplore** *v.t.* сожале́ть *imp.* о + *prep.*

deploy *v.t.* & *i.* развёртывать(ся) *imp.*, разверну́ть(ся) *perf.* **deployment** *n.* развёртывание.

depopulate *v.t.* истребля́ть *imp.*, истреби́ть *perf.* населе́ние + *gen.*

deport *v.t.* высыла́ть *imp.*, вы́слать (вы́шлю, -лешь) *perf.*; (*internal exile*) ссыла́ть *imp.*, сосла́ть (сошлю́, -лёшь) *perf.* **deportation** *n.* вы́сылка; сы́лка.

deportee *n.* высыла́емый *sb.*; ссы́льный *sb.*

deportment *n.* поведе́ние, оса́нка.

depose *v.t.* свергáть *imp.*, свéргнуть (-г(нул), -гла) *perf.* (с престóла); *v.i.* (*leg.*) покáзывать *imp.*, показáть (-ажý, -áжешь) *perf.* **deposit** *n.* (*econ.*) вклад; (*pledge*) взнос; (*sediment*) осáдок (-дка); (*coal etc.*) месторождéние; *v.t.* (*econ.*) вноси́ть (-ошý, -óсишь) *imp.*, внести́ (-есý, -есёшь; -ёс, -еслá) *perf.*; (*geol.*) отлагáть *imp.*, отложи́ть (-жý, -жишь) *perf.* **deposition** *n.* свержéние (с престóла); (*leg.*) показáние; (*geol.*) отложéние. **depositor** *n.* вклáдчик. **depository** *n.* храни́лище.

depot *n.* склад; депó *neut.indecl.*; *d. ship*, сýдно-бáза (*pl.* судá-бáзы, судóв-бáз).

deprave *v.t.* развращáть *imp.*, разврати́ть (-ащý, -ати́шь) *perf.* **depraved** *adj.* развращённый (-ён, -ённа). **depravity** *n.* разврáт.

deprecate *v.t.* возражáть *imp.*, возрази́ть *perf.* прóтив + *gen.* **deprecation** *n.* неодобрéние.

depreciate *v.t.* & *i.* обесцéнивать(ся) *imp.*, обесцéнить(ся) *perf.* **depreciation** *n.* обесцéнение. **depreciatory** *adj.* обесцéнивающий.

depress *v.t.* (*lower*) понижáть *imp.*, пони́зить *perf.*; (*dispirit*) удручáть *imp.*, удручи́ть *perf.* **depressed** *adj.* удручённый (-ён, -ённа & -енá). **depressing** *adj.* нагоня́ющий тоскý. **depression** *n.* (*hollow*) впáдина; (*econ.*, *med.*, *meteor.*, *etc.*) депрéссия.

deprivation *n.* лишéние. **deprive** *v.t.* лишáть *imp.*, лиши́ть *perf.* (of, + *gen.*).

depth *n.* глубинá (*pl.* -ны); *d. of feeling*, си́ла переживáния; *depths of the country*, глушь (-ши́); *in the d. of winter*, в разгáре зимы́; *d.-bomb*, *-charge*, глуби́нная бóмба.

deputation *n.* делегáция, депутáция. **depute** *v.t.* делеги́ровать *imp.*, *perf.* **deputize** *v.i.* замещáть *imp.*, замести́ть *perf.* (for, + *acc.*). **deputy** *n.* замести́тель *m.*; помóщник, -ица; (*parl.*) депутáт.

derail *v.t.* спускáть *imp.*, спусти́ть (-ущý, -ýстишь) *perf.* под откóс; *be derailed*, сходи́ть (-ожý, -óдишь) *imp.*, сойти́ (сойдý, -дёшь; сошёл, -шлá) *perf.* с рéльсов. **derailment** *n.* кружéние, сход с рéльсов.

derange *v.t.* расстрáивать *imp.*, расстрóить *perf.* **deranged** *adj.* (*mentally*) душевнобольнóй, ненормáльный. **derangement** *n.* (психи́ческое) расстрóйство.

derelict *adj.* брóшенный (-шен). **dereliction** *n.* упущéние; (*of duty*) нарушéние дóлга.

deride *v.t.* высмéивать *imp.*, вы́смеять (-ею, -еешь) *perf.* **derision** *n.* высмéивание; *object of d.*, посмéшище. **derisive** *adj.* (*mocking*) насмéшливый. **derisory** *adj.* (*ridiculous*) смехотвóрный.

derivation *n.* происхождéние. **derivative** *n.* производнóе *sb.*; *adj.* произвóдный. **derive** *v.t.* извлекáть *imp.*, извлéчь (-екý, -ечёшь; -ёк, -еклá) *perf.*; *v.i.*: *d. from*, происходи́ть (-ожý, -óдишь) *imp.*, произойти́ (-ойдý, -ойдёшь; -ошёл, -ошлá) *perf.* от + *gen.*

dermatitis *n.* дермати́т.

derogatory *adj.* умаля́ющий, унижáющий.

derrick *n.* дéррик; (*oil-well etc.*) буровáя вы́шка.

dervish *n.* дéрви́ш.

descend *v.t.* спускáться *imp.*, спусти́ться (-ущýсь, -ýстишься) *perf.* с + *gen.*; сходи́ть (-ожý, -óдишь) *imp.*, сойти́ (сойдý, -дёшь; сошёл, -шлá) *perf.* с + *gen.*; *v.i.* (*go down*) спускáться *imp.*, спусти́ться (-ущýсь, -ýстишься) *perf.*; (*sink*) понижáться *imp.*, пони́зиться *perf.*; *d. on*, (*attack*) обрýшиваться *imp.*, обрýшиться *perf.* на + *acc.*; *d. to*, (*property*; *to details etc.*) переходи́ть (-ожý, -óдишь) *imp.*, перейти́ (-йдý, -йдёшь; перешёл, -шлá) *perf.* к + *dat.* *be descended from*, происходи́ть (-ожý, -óдишь) *imp.*, произойти́ (-ойдý, -ойдёшь; -ошёл, -шлá) *perf.* из, от, + *gen.* **descendant** *n.* потóмок (-мка). **descent** *n.* спуск; (*sinking*) понижéние; (*lineage*) происхождéние; (*property*) наслéдование.

describe *v.t.* опи́сывать *imp.*, описáть (-ишý, -и́шешь) *perf.* **description** *n.* описáние. **descriptive** *adj.* описáтельный.

descry *v.t.* различа́ть *imp.*, различи́ть *perf.*
desecrate *v.t.* оскверня́ть *imp.*, оскверни́ть *perf.* **desecration** *n.* оскверне́ние, профана́ция.
desert[1] *n.* (*wilderness*) пусты́ня; *adj.* пусты́нный (-нен, -нна).
desert[2] *v.t.* покида́ть *imp.*, поки́нуть *perf.*; (*mil.*) дезерти́ровать *imp.*, *perf.* **deserter** *n.* дезерти́р. **desertion** *n.* дезерти́рство.
desert[3] *n.*: *pl.* заслу́ги *f.pl.* **deserve** *v.t.* заслу́живать *imp.*, заслужи́ть (-жу́, -жишь) *perf.* **deserving** *adj.* заслу́живающий (of, +*gen.*), досто́йный (-о́ин, -о́йна) (of, +*gen.*).
desiccated *adj.* сушёный.
design *n.* (*scheme*) за́мысел (-сла); (*sketch*) рису́нок (-нка); (*model*) констру́кция, прое́кт; *school of d.*, шко́ла изобрази́тельных иску́сств; *v.t.* конструи́ровать *imp.*, с~ *perf.*; создава́ть (-даю́, -даёшь) *imp.*, созда́ть (-а́м, -а́шь, -а́ст, -ади́м; со́зда́л, -а́, -о) *perf.*
designate *adj.* назна́ченный (-чен); *v.t.* обознача́ть *imp.*, обозна́чить *perf.*; (*appoint*) назнача́ть *imp.*, назна́чить *perf.* **designation** *n.* обозначе́ние, назва́ние.
designer *n.* констру́ктор, проектиро́вщик, диза́йнер; (*of clothes*) моделье́р.
desirable *adj.* жела́тельный. **desire** *n.* жела́ние; *v.t.* жела́ть *imp.*, по~ *perf.* +*gen.* **desirous** *adj.* жела́ющий.
desist *v.i.* перестава́ть (-таю́, -таёшь) *imp.*, переста́ть (-а́ну, -а́нешь) *perf.*
desk *n.* пи́сьменный стол (-а́); конто́рка; (*school*) па́рта.
desolate *adj.* (*deserted*) поки́нутый; (*dreary*) уны́лый. **desolation** *n.* запусте́ние.
despair *n.* отча́яние; *v.i.* отча́иваться *imp.*, отча́яться (-а́юсь, -а́ешься) *perf.* **despairing** *adj.* отча́янный (-ян, -янна). **desperado** *n.* сорвиголова́ (*pl.* -овы, -о́в, -ова́м). **desperate** *adj.* отча́янный (-ян, -янна). **desperation** *n.* отча́яние.
despatch *see* **dispatch.**
despicable *adj.* презре́нный (-е́н, -е́нна), жа́лкий (-лок, -лка́, -лко). **despise** *v.t.* презира́ть *imp.*, презре́ть (-рю́, -ри́шь) *perf.*
despite *prep.* вопреки́+*dat.*, несмотря́ на+*acc.*
despondency *n.* уны́ние, пода́вленность. **despondent** *adj.* уны́лый.
despot *n.* де́спот. **despotic** *adj.* деспоти́ческий, деспоти́чный. **despotism** *n.* деспоти́зм, деспоти́чность.
dessert *n.* десе́рт; сла́дкое *sb.*
destination *n.* ме́сто (*pl.* -та́) назначе́ния, цель. **destiny** *n.* судьба́, у́часть.
destitute *adj.* си́льно нужда́ющийся; без вся́ких средств. **destitution** *n.* нищета́, нужда́.
destroy *v.t.* уничтожа́ть *imp.*, уничто́жить *perf.*; губи́ть (-блю́, -бишь) *imp.*, по~ *perf.* **destroyer** *n.* (*naut.*) эсми́нец (-нца). **destruction** *n.* разруше́ние, уничтоже́ние. **destructive** *adj.* разруши́тельный, уничтожа́ющий.
desultory *adj.* беспоря́дочный.
detach *v.t.* отделя́ть *imp.*, отдели́ть *perf.* **detachable** *adj.* съёмный, отделя́емый. **detached** *adj.* отде́льный; *d. house*, особня́к (-а́). **detachment** *n.* отделе́ние, разъедине́ние; (*mil.*) отря́д.
detail *n.* дета́ль, подро́бность; (*mil.*) наря́д; *in d.*, подро́бно; *v.t.* подро́бно расска́зывать *imp.*, рассказа́ть (-ажу́, -а́жешь) *perf.*; выделя́ть *imp.*, вы́делить *perf.*; назнача́ть *imp.*, назна́чить *perf.* в наря́д; *d. for guard duty*, назна́чить *perf.* в карау́л. **detailed** *adj.* дета́льный, подро́бный.
detain *v.t.* заде́рживать *imp.*, задержа́ть (-жу́, -жишь) *perf.*; аресто́вывать *imp.*, арестова́ть *perf.* **detainee** *n.* аресто́ванный *sb.*, (челове́к) под стра́жей.
detect *v.t.* обнару́живать *imp.*, обнару́жить *perf.* **detection** *n.* обнару́же́ние; рассле́дование. **detective** *n.* сы́щик, детекти́в; *adj.* сыскно́й, детекти́вный; *d. film, story, etc.*, детекти́в. **detector** *n.* дете́ктор, обнаружи́тель *m.*
détente *n.* разря́дка.
detention *n.* задержа́ние, аре́ст.
deter *v.t.* уде́рживать *imp.*, удержа́ть (-жу́, -жишь) *perf.* (from, от+*gen.*).

detergent *n.* мо́ющее сре́дство; *adj.* мо́ющий, очища́ющий.
deteriorate *v.i.* ухудша́ться *imp.*, уху́дшиться *perf.* **deterioration** *n.* ухудше́ние.
determination *n.* (*resoluteness*) реши́тельность, реши́мость. **determine** *v.t.* устана́вливать *imp.*, установи́ть (-влю́, -вишь) *perf.*; определя́ть *imp.*, определи́ть *perf.* **determined** *adj.* (*resolute*) реши́тельный.
deterrent *n.* уде́рживающее сре́дство, сре́дство устраше́ния; *adj.* сде́рживающий, уде́рживающий.
detest *v.t.* ненави́деть (-и́жу, -и́дишь) *imp.* **detestable** *adj.* отврати́тельный. **detestation** *n.* отвраще́ние, не́нависть.
dethrone *v.t.* сверга́ть *imp.*, све́ргнуть (-г(нул), -гла) *perf.* с престо́ла; разве́нчивать *imp.*, развенча́ть *perf.* **dethronement** *n.* сверже́ние с престо́ла; развенча́ние.
detonate *v.t.* & *i.* взрыва́ть(ся) *imp.*, взорва́ть(ся) (-ву́, -вёт(ся); взорва́л(ся), -а́(сь) -о/-а́ло́сь) *perf.* **detonation** *n.* детона́ция, взрыв. **detonator** *n.* детона́тор.
detour *n.* обхо́д, объе́зд.
detract *v.i.*: *d. from*, умаля́ть *imp.*, умали́ть *perf.* + *acc.*
detriment *n.* уще́рб, вред (-а́). **detrimental** *adj.* вре́дный (-ден, -дна́, -дно), па́губный.
detritus *n.* детри́т.
deuce *n.* (*tennis*) ра́вный счёт; (*what*) *the d.*, чёрт возьми́!
devaluation *n.* девальва́ция. **devalue** *v.t.* проводи́ть (-ожу́, -о́дишь) *imp.*, провести́ (-еду́, -едёшь; -ёл, -ела́) *perf.* девальва́цию + *gen.*
devastate *v.t.* опустоша́ть *imp.*, опустоши́ть *perf.* **devastation** опустоше́ние.
develop *v.t.* & *i.* развива́ть(ся) *imp.*, разви́ть(ся) (разовью́(сь), -вёшь(ся); разви́л(ся), -а́(сь), -о/-и́ло́сь) *perf.*; *v.t.* (*phot.*) проявля́ть *imp.*, прояви́ть (-влю́, -вишь) *perf.*; (*nat. resources*) разраба́тывать *imp.*, разрабо́тать *perf.* **developer** *n.* (*of land etc.*) застро́йщик но́вого райо́на; (*phot.*) прояви́тель *m.* **development** *n.* разви́тие; (*phot.*) проявле́ние.
deviate *v.i.* отклоня́ться *imp.*, отклони́ться (-ню́сь, -нишься) *perf.* (from, от + *gen.*). **deviation** *n.* отклоне́ние; (*polit.*) укло́н.
device *n.* устро́йство, прибо́р.
devil *n.* дья́вол, чёрт (*pl.* че́рти, -те́й), бес; *d.-may-care*, бесшаба́шный. **devilish** *adj.* дья́вольский, черто́вский.
devious *adj.* (*indirect*) непрямо́й (-м, -ма́, -мо); (*person*) хи́трый (-тёр, -тра́, хитро́).
devise *v.t.* приду́мывать *imp.*, приду́мать *perf.*
devoid *adj.* лишённый (-ён, -ена́) (of, + *gen.*).
devolution *n.* переда́ча; перехо́д. **devolve** *v.t.* передава́ть (-даю́, -даёшь) *imp.*, переда́ть (-а́м, -а́шь, -а́ст, -ади́м; пе́редал, -а́, -о) *perf.*; *v.i.* переходи́ть (-ожу́, -о́дишь) *imp.*, перейти́ (-йду́, -йдёшь; перешёл, -шла́) *perf.*
devote *v.t.* посвяща́ть *imp.*, посвяти́ть (-ящу́, -яти́шь) *perf.* **devoted** *adj.* пре́данный (-ан). **devotion** *n.* пре́данность, приве́рженность; *pl.* религио́зные обя́занности *f.pl.* **devotional** *adj.* религио́зный.
devour *v.t.* пожира́ть *imp.*, пожра́ть (-ру́, -рёшь; пожра́л, -а́, -о) *perf.*
devout *adj.* на́божный, благочести́вый. **devoutness** *n.* на́божность, благоче́стие.
dew *n.* роса́. **dewdrop** *n.* роси́нка. **dewy** *adj.* вла́жный (-жен, -жна́, -жно), роси́стый.
dexterity *n.* прово́рство, ло́вкость; сноро́вка. **dext(e)rous** *adj.* прово́рный; ло́вкий (-вок, -вка́, -вко, ло́вки́).
diabetes *n.* са́харная боле́знь, диабе́т. **diabetic** *n.* диабе́тик; *adj.* диабети́ческий.
diabolic(al) *adj.* дья́вольский; зве́рский.
diagnose *v.t.* ста́вить *imp.*, по~ *perf.* диа́гноз + *gen.* **diagnosis** *n.* диа́гноз.
diagonal *n.* диагона́ль; *adj.* диагона́льный. **diagonally** *adv.* по диагона́ли.
diagram *n.* диагра́мма; чертёж (-а́); схе́ма.
dial *n.* цифербла́т; шкала́ (*pl.* -лы); (*tel.*) диск набо́ра; *v.t.* набира́ть *imp.*, набра́ть (наберу́, -рёшь; набра́л, -а́, -о) *perf.*

dialect *n.* диале́кт, наре́чие; *adj.* диале́ктный. **dialectical** *adj.* диалекти́ческий.
dialogue *n.* диало́г.
diameter *n.* диа́метр. **diametrical** *adj.* диаметра́льный; *diametrically opposed*, диаметра́льно противополо́жный.
diamond *n.* алма́з, бриллиа́нт; (*rhomb*) ромб; (*cards*) бу́бна (*pl.* бу́бны, бу́бён, бу́бна́м); *play a d.*, ходи́ть (хожу́, хо́дишь) *imp.*, пойти́ (пойду́, -дёшь; пошёл, -шла́) *perf.* с бубён; *adj.* алма́зный, бриллиа́нтовый; бубно́вый.
diaper *n.* пелёнка.
diaphanous *adj.* прозра́чный.
diaphragm *n.* диафра́гма; мембра́на.
diarrhoeia *n.* поно́с.
diary *n.* дневни́к (-а́).
diatribe *n.* обличи́тельная речь (*pl.* -чи, -че́й).
dice *n. see* **die**[1].
dicey *adj.* риско́ванный (-ан, -анна).
dictaphone *n.* диктафо́н. **dictate** *n.* веле́ние; *v.t.* диктова́ть *imp.*, про~ *perf.* **dictation** *n.* дикто́вка, дикта́нт. **dictator** *n.* дикта́тор. **dictatorial** *adj.* дикта́торский, повели́тельный. **dictatorship** *n.* диктату́ра.
diction *n.* ди́кция.
dictionary *n.* слова́рь (-ря́) *m.*
dictum *n.* авторите́тное заявле́ние; (*maxim*) изрече́ние.
didactic *adj.* дидакти́ческий.
diddle *v.t.* надува́ть *imp.*, наду́ть (-у́ю, -у́ешь) *perf.*
die[1] *n.* (*pl.* **dice**) игра́льная кость (*pl.* -ти, -те́й); (*pl.* **dies**) (*stamp*) штамп, ште́мпель (*pl.* -ля́) *m.*; (*mould*) ма́трица.
die[2] *v.i.* (*person*) умира́ть *imp.*, умере́ть (умру́, умрёшь; у́мер, -ла́, -ло) *perf.*; (*animal*) до́хнуть (до́х(нул), до́хла) *imp.*, из~, по~ *perf.*; (*plant*) вя́нуть (вя́(ну)л, вя́ла) *imp.*, за~ *perf.*; сконча́ться *perf.*; *d.-hard*, твердоло́бый *sb.*
diesel *n.* (*engine*) ди́зель *m.*; *attrib.* ди́зельный.
diet *n.* дие́та; (*habitual food*) пита́ние, стол (-а́); *v.i.* соблюда́ть *imp.*, соблюсти́ (-юду́, -юдёшь; -ю́л, -юла́) *perf.* дие́ту. **dietary** *adj.* диети́ческий.
differ *v.i.* отлича́ться *imp.*; различа́ться *imp.*; (*disagree*) не соглаша́ться *imp.* **difference** *n.* ра́зница; (*disagreement*) разногла́сие. **different** *adj.* разли́чный, ра́зный. **differential** *n.* (*math.*) дифференциа́л; ра́зница; *adj.* дифференциа́льный. **differentiate** *v.t.* различа́ть *imp.*, различи́ть *perf.* **differentiation** *n.* различе́ние, дифференциа́ция.
difficult *adj.* тру́дный (-ден, -дна́, -дно, тру́дны́), затрудни́тельный. **difficulty** *n.* тру́дность; затрудне́ние; *without d.*, без труда́.
diffidence *n.* неуве́ренность в себе́. **diffident** *adj.* ро́бкий (-бок, -бка́, -бко), неуве́ренный (-ен) в себе́.
diffused *adj.* рассе́янный (-ян, -янна).
dig *n.* (*archaeol.*) раско́пки *f.pl.*; (*poke*) тычо́к (-чка́); *pl.* (*lodgings*) кварти́ра; *give a d. in the ribs*, ткнуть *perf.* ло́ктем под ребро́; *v.t.* копа́ть *imp.*, вы́~ *perf.*; рыть (ро́ю, ро́ешь) *imp.*, вы́~ *perf.*; (*prod*) ты́кать (ты́чу, -чешь) *imp.*, ткнуть *perf.*
digest *n.* (*synopsis*) кра́ткое изложе́ние, резюме́ *neut.indecl.*; (*collection*) сбо́рник резюме́; *v.t.* перева́ривать *imp.*, перевари́ть (-рю́, -ришь) *perf.* **digestible** *adj.* удобовари́мый. **digestion** *n.* пищеваре́ние. **digestive** *adj.* пищевари́тельный.
digger *n.* копа́тель *m.*, землеко́п. **digging** *n.* копа́ние, рытьё; *pl.* земляны́е рабо́ты *f.pl.*
digit *n.* (*math.*) ци́фра, однозна́чное число́ (*pl.* -сла, -сел, -слам); (*anat.*) па́лец (-льца).
dignified *adj.* с чу́вством со́бственного досто́нства. **dignify** *v.t.* облагора́живать *imp.*, облагоро́дить *perf.* **dignitary** *n.* сано́вник. **dignity** *n.* досто́инство.
digress *v.i.* отклоня́ться *imp.*, отклони́ться (-ню́сь, -нишься) *perf.* (from, от + *gen.*). **digression** *n.* отступле́ние, отклоне́ние.
dike *n.* на́сыпь; (*ditch*) ров (рва, *loc.* во рву́).
dilapidated *adj.* обветша́лый. **dilapidation** *n.* (*eccl.*) поврежде́ние.
dilate *v.t.* & *i.* расширя́ть(ся) *imp.*, расши́рить(ся) *perf.*

dilatory *adj.* оття́гивающий.
dilemma *n.* диле́мма.
dilettante *n.* дилета́нт; *adj.* дилета́нтский, люби́тельский.
diligence *n.* прилежа́ние, усе́рдие. **diligent** *adj.* приле́жный, усе́рдный.
dill *n.* укро́п (-а(у)).
dilly-dally *v.i.* ме́шкать *imp.*
dilute *v.t.* разбавля́ть *imp.*, разба́вить *perf.*; *adj.* разба́вленный (-ен). **dilution** *n.* разбавле́ние.
dim *adj.* ту́склый (тускл, -а́, -о), сму́тный (-тен, -тна́, -тно); *d.-sighted*, недальнови́дный; *d.-witted*, тупо́й (туп, -а́, -о, ту́пы́).
dimension *n.* величина́; *pl.* разме́ры *m.pl.*; (*math.*) измере́ние. **-dimensional** *in comb.* -ме́рный; *three-d.*, трёхме́рный; *two-d.*, двухме́рный.
diminish *v.t.* & *i.* уменьша́ть(ся) *imp.*, уме́ньши́ть(ся) *perf.* **diminished** *adj.* уме́ньшенный (-ен). **diminution** *n.* уменьше́ние. **diminutive** *adj.* ма́ленький; (*gram.*) уменьши́тельный; *n.* уменьши́тельное *sb.*
dimity *n.* канифа́с.
dimness *n.* ту́склость; полусве́т.
dimple *n.* я́мочка.
din *n.* шум и гам; *v.t.*: *d. into one's ears*, прожужжа́ть (-жу́, -жи́шь) у́ши + *dat.*
dine *v.i.* обе́дать *imp.*, по ~ *perf.*; *v.t.* угоща́ть *imp.*, угости́ть *perf.* обе́дом. **diner** *n.* обе́дающий *sb.*; (*rly.*) ваго́н(-а)-рестора́н (-а).
ding-dong *adj.* череду́ющийся.
dinghy *n.* шлю́пка, я́лик.
dingy *adj.* (*drab*) ту́склый (тускл, -а́, -о); (*dirty*) гря́зный (-зен, -зна́, -зно).
dining-car *n.* ваго́н(-а)-рестора́н (-а). **dining-room** *n.* столо́вая *sb.* **dinner** *n.* обе́д; *d.-hour*, обе́денный переры́в; *d.-jacket*, смо́кинг; *d.-time*, обе́денное вре́мя *neut.*
dinosaur *n.* диноза́вр.
dint *n.*: *by d. of*, посре́дством + *gen.*; с по́мощью + *gen.*
diocesan *adj.* епархиа́льный. **diocese** *n.* епа́рхия.
diode *n.* дио́д.
dioxide *n.* двуо́кись.
dip *v.t.* & *i.* окуна́ть(ся) *imp.*, окуну́ть(ся) *perf.*; *v.t.* (*flag*) приспуска́ть *imp.*, приспусти́ть (-ущу́, -у́стишь) *perf.*; *d. into*, (*book*) перели́стывать *imp.*, перелиста́ть *perf.*; *n.* окуна́ние; (*depression*) впа́дина; (*slope*) укло́н; (*phys.*; *astr.*) наклоне́ние; *have a d.*, (*bathe*) купа́ться *imp.*, вы́ ~ *perf.*
diphtheria *n.* дифтери́я.
diphthong *n.* дифто́нг.
diploma *n.* дипло́м. **diplomacy** *n.* диплома́тия. **diplomat(ist)** *n.* диплома́т. **diplomatic** *adj.* дипломати́ческий, дипломати́чный; *d. bag*, дипломати́ческая по́чта.
dipper *n.* (*ladle*) ковш (-а́); (*bird*) оля́пка.
dipsomania *n.* алкоголи́зм.
dire *adj.* стра́шный (-шен, -шна́, -шно, стра́шны́); (*ominous*) злове́щий.
direct *adj.* прямо́й (прям, -а́, -о, пря́мы́); непосре́дственный (-ен, -енна); *d. current*, постоя́нный ток (-а(у)); *v.t.* направля́ть *imp.*, напра́вить *perf.*; (*guide, manage*) руководи́ть *imp.* + *instr.*; (*film*) режисси́ровать *imp.* **direction** *n.* направле́ние; (*guidance*) руково́дство; (*instruction*) указа́ние; (*film*) режиссу́ра; *stage d.*, рема́рка. **directive** *n.* директи́ва, указа́ние. **directly** *adv.* пря́мо; (*at once*) сра́зу. **director** *n.* дире́ктор (*pl.* -а́), член правле́ния; (*film*) режиссёр; *board of directors*, правле́ние. **directory** *n.* спра́вочник, указа́тель *m.*; *telephone d.*, телефо́нная кни́га.
dirge *n.* погреба́льная песнь.
dirt *n.* грязь (*loc.* -зи́); *d. cheap*, дешевле па́реной ре́пы; *d. floor*, земляно́й пол (*loc.* -у́; *pl.* -ы́). **dirty** *adj.* гря́зный (-зен, -зна́, -зно); (*mean*) по́длый (подл, -а́, -о); (*obscene*) непристо́йный; *v.t.* & *i.* па́чкать(ся) *imp.*, за ~ *perf.*
disability *n.* (*physical*) нетрудоспосо́бность. **disable** *v.t.* де́лать *imp.*, с ~ *perf.* неспосо́бным; (*cripple*) кале́чить *imp.*, ис ~ *perf.* **disabled** *adj.* искале́ченный (-ен); *d. serviceman*, инвали́д войны́. **disablement** *n.* инвали́дность.
disabuse *v.t.* выводи́ть (-ожу́, -о́дишь) *imp.*, вы́вести (-еду, -едешь; -ел) *perf.* из заблужде́ния; *d. of*, освобожда́ть *imp.*, освободи́ть *perf.* от + *gen.*

disadvantage *n.* невы́годное положе́ние; (*defect*) недоста́ток (-тка). **disadvantageous** *adj.* невы́годный.

disaffected *adj.* недово́льный, нелоя́льный. **disaffection** *n.* недово́льство, нелоя́льность.

disagree *v.i.* не соглаша́ться *imp.*, согласи́ться *perf.*; расходи́ться (-ожу́сь, -о́дишься) *imp.*, разойти́сь (-ойду́сь, -ойдёшься; -ошёлся, -ошла́сь) *perf.* **disagreeable** *adj.* неприя́тный. **disagreement** *n.* расхожде́ние, несогла́сие; (*quarrel*) ссо́ра.

disallow *v.t.* отка́зывать *imp.*, отказа́ть (-ажу́, -а́жешь) *perf.* в + *prep.*

disappear *v.i.* исчеза́ть *imp.*, исче́знуть (-е́з) *perf.*; пропада́ть *imp.*, пропа́сть (-аду́, -адёшь; -а́л) *perf.*; скрыва́ться *imp.*, скры́ться (-ро́юсь, -ро́ешься) *perf.* **disappearance** *n.* исчезнове́ние, пропа́жа.

disappoint *v.t.* разочаро́вывать *imp.*, разочарова́ть *perf.* **disappointed** *adj.* разочаро́ванный (-ан, -ан(н)а). **disappointing** *adj.* вызыва́ющий разочарова́ние. **disappointment** *n.* разочарова́ние; доса́да.

disapproval *n.* неодобре́ние. **disapprove** *v.t.* не одобря́ть *imp.*

disarm *v.t.* разоружа́ть *imp.*, разоружи́ть *perf.*; обезору́живать *imp.*, обезору́жить *perf.* **disarmament** *n.* разоруже́ние.

disarray *n.* беспоря́док (-дка), смяте́ние.

disaster *n.* бе́дствие, несча́стье. **disastrous** *adj.* бе́дственный (-ен, -енна); ги́бельный, губи́тельный.

disavow *v.t.* отрека́ться *imp.*, отре́чься (-еку́сь, -ечёшься; -ёкся, -екла́сь) *perf.* от + *gen.*; отрица́ть *imp.*

disband *v.t.* распуска́ть *imp.*, распусти́ть (-ущу́, -у́стишь) *perf.*; (*mil.*) расформиро́вывать *imp.*, расформирова́ть *perf.*; *v.i.* расходи́ться (-ожу́сь, -о́дишься) *imp.*, разойти́сь (-ойду́сь, -ойдёшься; -ошёлся, -ошла́сь) *perf.*

disbelief *n.* неве́рие. **disbelieve** *v.t.* не ве́рить *imp.* + *dat.*

disburse *v.t.* выпла́чивать *imp.*, вы́платить *perf.* **disbursement** *n.* вы́плата.

disc, disk *n.* диск, круг (*pl.* -и́); (*gramophone record*) грампласти́нка; *d. brake*, ди́сковый то́рмоз (*pl.* -а́); *d. jockey*, веду́щий *sb.* переда́чу.

discard *v.t.* отбра́сывать *imp.*, отбро́сить *perf.*; (*cards*) сбра́сывать *imp.*, сбро́сить *perf.*; *n.* (*card*) сбро́шенная ка́рта.

discern *v.t.* различа́ть *imp.*, различи́ть *perf.*; разгляде́ть (-яжу́, -ядишь) *perf.* **discernible** *adj.* различи́мый. **discerning** *adj.* проница́тельный. **discernment** *n.* распозна́ние; уме́ние различа́ть.

discharge *v.t.* (*ship etc.*) разгружа́ть *imp.*, разгрузи́ть (-ужу́, -у́зишь) *perf.* (*gun*; *electr.*) разряжа́ть *imp.*, разряди́ть *perf.*; (*dismiss*) увольня́ть *imp.*, уво́лить *perf.*; (*prisoner*) освобожда́ть *imp.*, освободи́ть *perf.*; (*debt*; *duty*) выполня́ть *imp.*, вы́полнить *perf.*; (*med.*) выделя́ть *imp.*, вы́делить *perf.*; *n.* разгру́зка; (*gun*) вы́стрел; (*electr.*) разря́д; увольне́ние; освобожде́ние; выполне́ние; (*med.*) (*action*) выделе́ние, (*matter*) выделе́ния *neut.pl.*

disciple *n.* учени́к (-а́).

disciplinarian *n.* сторо́нник стро́гой дисципли́ны. **disciplinary** *adj.* дисциплина́рный. **discipline** *n.* дисципли́на; *v.t.* дисциплини́ровать *imp.*, *perf.*

disclaim *v.t.* отрека́ться *imp.*, отре́чься (-еку́сь, -ечёшься; -ёкся, -екла́сь) *perf.* от + *gen.* **disclaimer** *n.* отрече́ние.

disclose *v.t.* обнару́живать *imp.*, обнару́жить *perf.* **disclosure** *n.* обнаруже́ние.

discoloured *adj.* измени́вший цвет, обесцве́ченный (-ен, -енна), вы́цветший.

discomfit *v.t.* приводи́ть (-ожу́, -о́дишь) *imp.*, привести́ (-еду́, -едёшь; -ёл, -ела́) *perf.* в замеша́тельство. **discomfiture** *n.* замеша́тельство.

discomfort *n.* неудо́бство, нело́вкость.

disconcert *v.t.* (*plans*) расстра́ивать *imp.*, расстро́ить *perf.*; (*person*) смуща́ть *imp.*, смути́ть (-ущу́, -ути́шь) *perf.*

disconnect *v.t.* разъединя́ть *imp.*, разъедини́ть *perf.*; (*electr.*) выключа́ть *imp.*, вы́ключить *perf.* **disconnected** *adj.* (*incoherent*) бессвя́зный.

disconsolate *adj.* неуте́шный.

discontent *n.* недово́льство. **discontented** *adj.* недово́льный.

discontinue *v.t.* & *i.* прекраща́ть(ся) *imp.*, прекрати́ть(ся) (-ащу́, -ати́т(ся)) *perf.*

discord *n.* (*disagreement*) разногла́сие, разла́д; (*mus.*) диссона́нс. **discordant** *adj.* несогласу́ющийся; диссони́рующий.

discount *n.* ски́дка; *v.t.* (*econ.*) учи́тывать *imp.*, уче́сть (учту́, -тёшь; учёл, учла́) *perf.*; (*disregard*) не принима́ть *imp.*, приня́ть (-иму́, -и́мешь; при́нял, -á, -о) *perf.* в расчёт, во внима́ние.

discountenance *v.t.* не одобря́ть *imp.*, одо́брить *perf.*

discourage *v.t.* обескура́живать *imp.*, обескура́жить *perf.* **discouragement** *n.* обескура́живание.

discourteous *adj.* нелюбе́зный, невоспи́танный (-ан, -анна). **discourtesy** *n.* нелюбе́зность, невоспи́танность.

discover *v.t.* открыва́ть *imp.*, откры́ть (-ро́ю, -ро́ешь) *perf.*; обнару́живать *imp.*, обнару́жить *perf.* **discoverer** *n.* иссле́дователь *m.* **discovery** *n.* откры́тие.

discredit *n.* позо́р; *v.t.* дискредити́ровать *imp.*, *perf.*

discreet *adj.* осмотри́тельный, благоразу́мный. **discretion** *n.* усмотре́ние; (*prudence*) благоразу́мие; *at one's d.*, по своему́ усмотре́нию.

discrepancy *n.* ра́зница, несоотве́тствие.

discriminate *v.t.* различа́ть *imp.*, различи́ть *perf.*; *d. against*, дискримини́ровать *imp.*, *perf.* **discrimination** *n.* установле́ние разли́чия; дискримина́ция.

discursive *adj.* непосле́довательный, сби́вчивый.

discus *n.* диск; *d. throwing*, мета́ние ди́ска.

discuss *v.t.* обсужда́ть *imp.*, обсуди́ть (-ужу́, -у́дишь) *perf.* **discussion** *n.* обсужде́ние, диску́ссия.

disdain *n.* презре́ние. **disdainful** *adj.* презри́тельный, надме́нный (-е́нен, -е́нна).

disease *n.* боле́знь. **diseased** *adj.* больно́й (-лен, -льна́).

disembark *v.t.* & *i.* выса́живать(ся) *imp.*, вы́садить(ся) *perf.* **disembarkation** *n.* вы́садка.

disembodied *adj.* беспло́тный.

disembowel *v.t.* потроши́ть *imp.*, вы́~ *perf.*

disenchantment *n.* разочарова́ние.

disengage *v.t.* высвобожда́ть *imp.*, вы́свободить *perf.*; (*tech.*) разобща́ть *imp.*, разобщи́ть *perf.*; выключа́ть *imp.*, вы́ключить *perf.* **disengaged** *adj.* свобо́дный. **disengagement** *n.* освобожде́ние; разобще́ние, выключе́ние.

disentangle *v.t.* распу́тывать *imp.*, распу́тать *perf.*

disestablishment *n.* отделе́ние це́ркви от госуда́рства.

disfavour *n.* неми́лость, неприя́знь.

disfigure *v.t.* уро́довать *imp.*, из~ *perf.*

disfranchise *v.t.* лиша́ть *imp.*, лиши́ть *perf.* (гражда́нских, избира́тельных) прав, привиле́гий. **disfranchisement** *n.* лише́ние гражда́нских, избира́тельных, прав.

disgorge *v.t.* изверга́ть *imp.*, изве́ргнуть (-г(нул), -гла) *perf.*

disgrace *n.* позо́р; (*disfavour*) неми́лость, опа́ла; *v.t.* позо́рить *imp.*, о~ *perf.* **disgraceful** *adj.* позо́рный.

disgruntled *adj.* недово́льный.

disguise *n.* маскиро́вка; измене́ние вне́шности; *v.t.* маскирова́ть *imp.*, за~ *perf.*; изменя́ть *imp.*, измени́ть (-ню́, -нишь) *perf.* вне́шность + *gen.*; (*conceal*) скрыва́ть *imp.*, скрыть (-ро́ю, -ро́ешь) *perf.* **disguised** *adj.* замаскиро́ванный (-ан, -анна); *d. as*, переоде́тый в + *acc.*

disgust *n.* отвраще́ние; *v.t.* внуша́ть *imp.*, внуши́ть *perf.* отвраще́ние + *dat.* **disgusting** *adj.* отврати́тельный, проти́вный.

dish *n.* блю́до; *pl.* посу́да *collect.*; *d.-towel*, ку́хонное полоте́нце (*gen.pl.* -нец); *d.-washer*, (посу́до)мо́ечная маши́на; *d.-water*, помо́и (-о́ев) *pl.*; *v.t.*: *d. up*, класть (-аду́, -адёшь; -ал) *imp.*, положи́ть (-ожу́, -о́жишь) *perf.* на блю́до.

disharmony *n.* дисгармо́ния; (*disagreement*) разногла́сие.

dishearten *v.t.* обескура́живать *imp.*, обескура́жить *perf.*
dishevelled *adj.* растрёпанный (-ан, -анна).
dishonest *adj.* нече́стный, недобросо́вестный. **dishonesty** *n.* нече́стность.
dishonour *n.* бесче́стье; *v.t.* бесче́стить *imp.*, о ~ *perf.* **dishonourable** *adj.* бесче́стный, по́длый (подл, -а́, -о).
disillusion *v.t.* разочаро́вывать *imp.*, разочарова́ть *perf.* **disillusionment** *n.* разочаро́ванность.
disinclination *n.* несклонность, неохо́та. **disinclined** *adj.*: *be d.*, не хоте́ться (хо́чется) *impers.* + *dat.*
disinfect *v.t.* дезинфици́ровать *imp.*, *perf.* **disinfectant** *n.* дезинфици́рующее сре́дство; *adj.* дезинфици́рующий. **disinfection** *n.* дезинфе́кция, обеззара́живание.
disingenuous *adj.* нейскренный (-нен, -нна, -нне & -нно).
disinherit *v.t.* лиша́ть *imp.*, лиши́ть *perf.* насле́дства.
disintegrate *v.t.* дезинтегри́ровать *imp.*, *perf.*; *v.i.* разлага́ться *imp.*, разложи́ться (-жу́сь, -жишься) *perf.* **disintegration** *n.* разложе́ние, дезинтегра́ция, распа́д.
disinterested *adj.* бескоры́стный.
disjointed *adj.* бессвя́зный.
disk *see* **disc.**
dislike *n.* нелюбо́вь (-бви́, *instr.* -бо́вью) (for, к + *dat.*); нерасположе́ние (for, к + *dat.*); *v.t.* не люби́ть (-блю́, -бишь) *imp.*
dislocate *v.t.* (*med.*) выви́хивать *imp.*, вы́вихнуть *perf.*; расстра́ивать *imp.*, расстро́ить *perf.* **dislocation** *n.* вы́вих; беспоря́док (-дка).
dislodge *v.t.* смеща́ть *imp.*, смести́ть *perf.*
disloyal *adj.* нелоя́льный, неве́рный (-рен, -рна́, -рно, неве́рны́). **disloyalty** *n.* нелоя́льность, неве́рность.
dismal *adj.* мра́чный (-чен, -чна́, -чно), уны́лый.
dismantle *v.t.* разбира́ть *imp.*, разобра́ть (разберу́, -рёшь; разобра́л, -а́, -о) *perf.*; демонти́ровать *imp.*, *perf.*
dismay *v.t.* приводи́ть (-ожу́, -о́дишь) *imp.*, привести́ (-еду́, -едёшь; -ёл, -ела́) *perf.* в у́жас, уны́ние; *n.* (*alarm*) испу́г (-а(у)); (*despair*) уны́ние.
dismember *v.t.* расчленя́ть *imp.*, расчлени́ть *perf.* **dismemberment** *n.* расчлене́ние.
dismiss *v.t.* (*discharge*) увольня́ть *imp.*, уво́лить *perf.*; (*disband*) распуска́ть *imp.*, распусти́ть (-ущу́, -у́стишь) *perf.*; *d.! interj.* (*mil.*) разойди́сь! **dismissal** *n.* увольне́ние; ро́спуск.
dismount *v.i.* (*from horse*) спе́шиваться *imp.*, спе́шиться *perf.*
disobedience *n.* непослуша́ние. **disobedient** *adj.* непослу́шный. **disobey** *v.t.* не слу́шаться *imp.* + *gen.*
disobliging *adj.* нелюбе́зный, не услу́жливый.
disorder *n.* беспоря́док (-дка). **disordered** *adj.* расстро́енный (-ен). **disorderly** *adj.* (*untidy*) беспоря́дочный; (*unruly*) бу́йный (бу́ен, буйна́, -но).
disorganization *n.* дезорганиза́ция. **disorganize** *v.t.* дезорганизова́ть *imp.*, *perf.*
disorientation *n.* дезориента́ция.
disown *v.t.* не признава́ть (-наю́, -наёшь) *imp.*, призна́ть *perf.*; отрица́ть *imp.*
disparage *v.t.* умаля́ть *imp.*, умали́ть *perf.* **disparagement** *n.* умале́ние.
disparity *n.* нера́венство.
dispassionate *adj.* беспристра́стный.
dispatch, des- *v.t.* (*send*) отправля́ть *imp.*, отпра́вить *perf.*; (*deal with*) расправля́ться *imp.*, распра́виться *perf.* с + *instr.*; *n.* отпра́вка; (*message*) донесе́ние; (*rapidity*) быстрота́; *d.-box*, вали́за; *d.-rider*, мотоцикли́ст свя́зи.
dispel *v.t.* рассе́ивать *imp.*, рассе́ять (-е́ю, -е́ешь) *perf.*
dispensary *n.* апте́ка.
dispensation *n.* (*exemption*) освобожде́ние (от обяза́тельства, обе́та). **dispense** *v.t.* (*distribute*) раздава́ть (-даю́, -даёшь) *imp.*, разда́ть (-а́м, -а́шь, -а́ст, -ади́м; ро́здал & разда́л, раздала́, ро́здало & разда́ло) *perf.*; (*justice, medicine*) отпуска́ть *imp.*, отпусти́ть (-ущу́, -у́стишь) *perf.*; *d. with*, (*do without*) обходи́ться (-ожу́сь, -о́дишься) *imp.*, обойти́сь (обойду́сь, -дёшься; обошёлся, -шла́сь) *perf.*

без + *gen.* **dispenser** *n.* (*person*) фармацéвт; (*device*) торгóвый автомáт.
dispersal *n.* распространéние. **disperse** *v.t.* разгонять *imp.*, разогнáть (разгоню, -нишь; разогнáл, -á, -о) *perf.*; рассéивать *imp.*, рассéять (-éю, -éешь) *perf.*; *v.i.* расходи́ться (-дится) *imp.*, разойти́сь (-ойдётся; -ошёлся, -ошлáсь) *perf.*
dispirited *adj.* удручённый (-ён, -енá).
displaced *adj.*: *d. persons*, перемещённые ли́ца *neut. pl.* **displacement** *n.* (*of fluid*) водоизмещéние.
display *n.* покáз; проявлéние; демонстрáция; *v.t.* покáзывать *imp.*, показáть (-ажу́, -áжешь) *perf.*; проявля́ть *imp.*, прояви́ть (-влю́, -вишь) *perf.*; демонстри́ровать *imp.*, *perf.*
displease *v.t.* раздражáть *imp.*, раздражи́ть *perf.* **displeased** *predic.* недовóлен (-льна).
disposable *adj.* могу́щий быть вы́брошенным. **disposal** *n.* удалéние, избавлéние (of, от + *gen.*); *at your d.*, (*service*) к вáшим услу́гам; (*use*) в вáшем распоряжéнии. **dispose** *v.i.*: *d. of*, избавля́ться *imp.*, избáвиться *perf.* от + *gen.* **disposed** *predic.*: *d. to*, склóнен, (-óннá, -óнно) к + *dat.*, располóжен + *inf.* or к + *dat.* **disposition** *n.* расположéние, склóнность; (*temperament*) нрав.
disproof *n.* опровержéние.
disproportionate *adj.* непропорционáльный.
disprove *v.t.* опровергáть *imp.*, опровéргнуть (-г(нул), -гла) *perf.*
disputation *n.* ди́спут. **dispute** *n.* (*debate*) спор; (*quarrel*) ссóра; *v.t.* оспáривать *imp.*, оспóрить *perf.*
disqualification *n.* дисквалификáция. **disqualify** *v.t.* лишáть *imp.*, лиши́ть *perf.* прáва + *inf.*; дисквалифици́ровать *imp.*, *perf.*
disquiet *n.* беспокóйство, тревóга. **disquieting** *adj.* тревóжный.
disregard *n.* невнимáние к + *dat.*; пренебрежéние + *instr.*; *v.t.* игнори́ровать *imp.*, *perf.*; пренебрегáть *imp.*, пренебрéчь (-егу́, -ежёшь; -ёг, -еглá) *perf.* + *instr.*
disrepair *n.* неисправность.
disreputable *adj.* пóльзующийся дурнóй слáвой, дурнóй репутáцией. **disrepute** *n.* дурнáя слáва.
disrespect *n.* неуважéние, непочтéние. **disrespectful** *adj.* непочти́тельный.
disrupt *v.t.* срывáть *imp.*, сорвáть (-ву́, -вёшь; сорвáл, -á, -о) *perf.* **disruptive** *adj.* подрывнóй, разруши́тельный.
dissatisfaction *n.* неудовлетворённость; недовóльство. **dissatisfied** *adj.* неудовлетворённый (-ён, -енá & -ённа), недовóльный.
dissect *v.t.* разрезáть *imp.*, разрéзать (-éжу, -éжешь) *perf.*; (*med. etc.*) вскрывáть *imp.*, вскрыть (-рóю, -рóешь) *perf.*
dissemble *v.t.* скрывáть *imp.*, скрыть (-рóю, -рóешь) *perf.*; *v.i.* притворя́ться *imp.*, притвори́ться *perf.*
dissemination *n.* рассéивание; распространéние.
dissension *n.* разноглáсие, раздóр. **dissent** *n.* расхождéние, несоглáсие; (*eccl.*) раскóл. **dissenter** *n.* (*eccl.*) раскóльник, сектáнт.
dissertation *n.* диссертáция.
disservice *n.* плохáя услу́га.
dissident *n.* диссидéнт, инакомы́слящий *sb.*
dissimilar *adj.* несхóдный, непохóжий, разли́чный. **dissimilation** *n.* диссимиля́ция.
dissipate *v.t.* (*dispel*) рассéивать *imp.*, рассéять (-éю, -éешь) *perf.*; (*squander*) промáтывать *imp.*, промотáть *perf.* **dissipated** *adj.* распу́тный, беспу́тный.
dissociate *v.t.*: *d. oneself*, отмежёвываться *imp.*, отмежевáться (-жу́юсь, -жу́ешься) *perf.* (from, от + *gen.*). **dissociation** *n.* разобщéние, отмежевáние.
dissolute *adj.* распу́щенный (-ен, -енна), разврáтный. **dissolution** *n.* (*treaty etc.*) расторжéние; (*parl.*) рóспуск; (*solution*) растворéние. **dissolve** *v.t.* & *i.* (*in liquid*) растворя́ть(ся) *imp.*, раствори́ть(ся) *perf.*; *v.t.* (*annul*) расторгáть *imp.*, растóргнуть (-г(нул), -гла) *perf.*; (*parl.*) распускáть *imp.*, распусти́ть (-ущу́, -у́стишь) *perf.*
dissonance *n.* диссонáнс. **dissonant** *adj.* диссони́рующий.

dissuade *v.t.* отгова́ривать *imp.*, отговори́ть *perf.* **dissuasion** *n.* отгова́ривание.

distaff *n.* пря́лка; *on the d. side*, по же́нской ли́нии.

distance *n.* расстоя́ние; (*distant point*) даль (*loc.* -ли́); (*sport*) диста́нция; *at a great d.*, вдали́. **distant** *adj.* да́льний, далёкий (-ёк, -ека́, -ёко́); (*reserved*) сде́ржанный (-ан, -анна).

distaste *n.* неприя́знь. **distasteful** *adj.* проти́вный, неприя́тный.

distemper[1] *n.* (*vet.*) чума́.

distemper[2] *n.* (*paint*) те́мпера; *v.t.* кра́сить *imp.*, по~ *perf.* те́мперой.

distend *v.t.* расширя́ть *imp.*, расши́рить *perf.*; надува́ть *imp.*, наду́ть (-у́ю, -у́ешь) *perf.* **distension** *n.* расшире́ние, надува́ние.

distil *v.t.* перегоня́ть *imp.*, перегна́ть (-гоню́, -го́нишь; перегна́л, -а́, -о) *perf.*; дистилли́ровать *imp.*, *perf.* **distillation** *n.* перего́нка, дистилля́ция. **distillary** *n.* виноку́ренный, перего́нный, заво́д.

distinct *adj.* (*separate*) отде́льный; (*clear*) отчётливый; (*definite*) определённый (-ёнен, -ённа); *d. from*, отлича́ющийся от + *gen.* **distinction** *n.* отли́чие, разли́чие. **distinctive** *adj.* осо́бенный, отличи́тельный. **distinctly** *adj.* я́сно, определённо.

distinguish *v.t.* различа́ть *imp.*, различи́ть *perf.*; *d. oneself*, отлича́ться *imp.*, отличи́ться *perf.* **distinguished** *adj.* выдаю́щийся.

distort *v.t.* искажа́ть *imp.*, искази́ть *perf.*; (*misrepresent*) извраща́ть *imp.*, изврати́ть (-ащу́, -ати́шь) *perf.* **distortion** *n.* искаже́ние, искривле́ние.

distract *v.t.* отвлека́ть *imp.*, отвле́чь (-еку́, -ечёшь; -ёк, -екла́) *perf.* **distracted** *adj.* (*maddened*) обезу́мевший. **distraction** *n.* (*amusement*) развлече́ние; (*madness*) безу́мие.

distrain *v.i.*: *d. upon*, накла́дывать *imp.*, наложи́ть (-жу́, -жишь) *perf.* аре́ст на + *acc.* **distraint** *n.* наложе́ние аре́ста.

distraught *adj.* обезу́мевший.

distress *n.* (*calamity*) беда́; (*ship etc.*) бе́дствие; (*poverty*) нужда́; (*physical*) недомога́ние; *v.t.* огорча́ть *imp.*, огорчи́ть *perf.*; му́чить *imp.*, из~ *perf.*

distribute *v.t.* распределя́ть *imp.*, распредели́ть *perf.* **distribution** *n.* распределе́ние, разда́ча. **distributive** *adj.* распредели́тельный. **distributor** *n.* распредели́тель *m.*; (*cin.*) кинопрока́тчик.

district *n.* о́круг (*pl.* -а́), райо́н.

distrust *n.* недове́рие; *v.t.* не доверя́ть *imp.* **distrustful** *adj.* недове́рчивый.

disturb *v.t.* беспоко́ить *imp.*, о~ *perf.* **disturbance** *n.* наруше́ние поко́я; *pl.* (*polit. etc.*) беспоря́дки *m.pl.*

disuse *n.* неупотребле́ние; *fall into d.*, выходи́ть (-ит) *imp.*, вы́йти (-йдет; вы́шел, -шла) *perf.* из употребле́ния. **disused** *adj.* вы́шедший из употребле́ния.

ditch *n.* кана́ва, ров (рва, *loc.* во рву́).

dither *v.i.* колеба́ться (-блюсь, -блешься) *imp.*; *n.*: *all of a d.*, в си́льном возбужде́нии.

ditto *n.* то же са́мое; *adv.* так же.

ditty *n.* пе́сенка.

diuretic *n.* мочего́нное сре́дство; *adj.* мочего́нный.

diurnal *adj.* дневно́й.

divan *n.* тахта́.

dive *v.i.* ныря́ть *imp.*, нырну́ть *perf.*; пры́гать *imp.*, пры́гнуть *perf.* в во́ду; (*aeron.*) пики́ровать *imp.*, *perf.*; (*submarine*) погружа́ться *imp.*, погрузи́ться *perf.*; *n.* ныро́к (-рка́), прыжо́к (-жка́) в во́ду; *d.-bomber*, пики́рующий бомбардиро́вщик. **diver** *n.* водола́з; (*bird*) гага́ра.

diverge *v.i.* расходи́ться (-ится) *imp.*, разойти́сь (-ойдётся; -ошёлся, -ошла́сь) *perf.*; (*deviate*) отклоня́ться *imp.*, отклони́ться (-ню́сь, -нишься) *perf.* (from, от + *gen.*). **divergence** *n.* расхожде́ние; отклоне́ние. **divergent** *adj.* расходя́щийся.

diverse *adj.* различный, разнообра́зный. **diversification** *n.* расшире́ние ассортиме́нта. **diversified** *adj.* многообра́зный. **diversify** *v.t.* разнообра́зить *imp.* **diversion** *n.* (*deviation*) отклоне́ние: (*detour*) объе́зд; (*amusement*) развлече́ние; (*mil.*) дивéрсия. **diversionist** *n.* диверса́нт.

diversity *n.* разнообра́зие; разли́чие. **divert** *v.t.* отклоня́ть *imp.*, отклони́ть (-ню́, -нишь) *perf.*; отводи́ть (-ожу́, -о́дишь) *imp.*, отвести́ (-еду́, -едёшь; -ёл, -ела́) *perf.*; (*amuse*) развлека́ть *imp.*, развле́чь (-еку́, -ечёшь; -ёк, -екла́) *perf.* **diverting** *adj.* заба́вный.

divest *v.t.* (*unclothe*) разоблача́ть *imp.*, разоблачи́ть *perf.*, (*deprive*) лиша́ть *imp.*, лиши́ть *perf.* (of, +*gen.*).

divide *v.t.* дели́ть (-лю́, -лишь) *imp.*, по~ *perf.*; разделя́ть *imp.*, раздели́ть (-лю́, -лишь) *perf.* **dividend** *n.* диви-де́нд. **dividers** *n.* ци́ркуль *m.*

divination *n.* гада́ние; предсказа́ние. **divine** *adj.* боже́ственный (-ен, -енна); *n.* богосло́в; *v.t.* предска́зывать *imp.*, предсказа́ть (-ажу́, -а́жешь) *perf.* **diviner** *n.* предсказа́тель *m.*

diving *n.* ныря́ние; (*profession*) водола́зное де́ло; (*aeron.*) пики́рование; (*naut.*) погруже́ние; *d.-board*, трампли́н.

divining-rod *n.* волше́бная лоза́ (*pl.* -зы).

divinity *n.* божество́; (*theology*) богосло́вие, теоло́гия.

divisible *adj.* дели́мый. **division** *n.* (*dividing*) деле́ние, разделе́ние; (*section*) отде́л, подразделе́ние; (*mil.*) диви́зия. **divisional** *adj.* дивизио́нный. **divisive** *adj.* разделя́ющий, вызыва́ющий разногла́сия. **divisor** *n.* дели́тель *m.*

divorce *n.* разво́д; *v.i.* разводи́ться (-ожу́сь, -о́дишься) *imp.*, развести́сь (-еду́сь, -едёшься; -ёлся, -ела́сь) *perf.* **divorced** *adj.* разведённый (-ён, -ена́). **divorcee** *n.* разведённая жена́ (*pl.* жёны).

divulge *v.t.* разглаша́ть *imp.*, разгласи́ть *perf.*

dizziness *n.* головокруже́ние. **dizzy** *adj.* головокружи́тельный; *I am d.*, у меня́ кру́жится голова́.

do *v.t.* де́лать *imp.*, с~ *perf.*; выполня́ть *imp.*, вы́полнить *perf.*; (*coll.*) (*cheat*) надува́ть *imp.*, наду́ть (-у́ю, -у́ешь) *perf.*; *v.i.* (*be suitable*) годи́ться *imp.*; (*suffice*) быть доста́точным; *that will do*, хва́тит! *how do you do*, здра́вствуйте! как вы пожива́ете? *do away with*, (*abolish*) уничтожа́ть *imp.*, уничто́жить *perf.*; *do in*, (*kill*) убива́ть *imp.*, уби́ть (убью́, -ьёшь) *perf.*; *do up*, (*restore*) ремонти́ровать *imp.*, от~ *perf.*; (*wrap up*) завёртывать *imp.*, заверну́ть *perf.*; (*fasten*) застёгивать *imp.*, застегну́ть *perf.*; *do without*, обходи́ться (-ожу́сь, -о́дишься) *imp.*, обойти́сь (обойду́сь, -дёшься; обошёлся, -шла́сь) *perf.* без+*gen.*

docile *adj.* поко́рный. **docility** *n.* поко́рность.

dock[1] *n.* (*bot.*) щаве́ль (-ля́) *m.*

dock[2] *v.t.* (*tail*) отруба́ть *imp.*, отруби́ть (-блю́, -бишь) *perf.*; (*money*) уре́зывать, уреза́ть *imp.*, уре́зать (-е́жу, -е́жешь) *perf.*

dock[3] *n.* (*naut.*) док; *v.t.* ста́вить *imp.*, по~ *perf.* в док; *v.i.* входи́ть (-ожу́, -о́дишь) *imp.*, войти́ (войду́, -дёшь; вошёл, -шла́) *perf.* в док; *v.t.* & *i.* (*spacecraft*) стыкова́ть(ся) *imp.*, со~ *perf.* **docker** *n.* до́кер, порто́вый рабо́чий *sb.* **docking** *n.* (*ship*) постано́вка в док; (*spacecraft*) стыко́вка. **dockyard** *n.* верфь.

dock[4] *n.* (*leg.*) скамья́ (*pl.* ска́мьи́, -ме́й) подсуди́мых.

docket *n.* квита́нция; (*label*) ярлы́к (-а́), этике́тка.

doctor *n.* врач (-а́); (*also univ. etc.*) до́ктор (*pl.* -а́); *v.t.* (*med.*) лечи́ть (-чу́, -чишь) *imp.*; (*falsify*) фальсифици́ровать *imp.*, *perf.* **doctor(i)al** *adj.* до́кторский. **doctorate** *n.* сте́пень (*pl.* -ни, -не́й) до́ктора.

doctrinaire *n.* доктринёр; *adj.* доктринёрский. **doctrine** *n.* доктри́на.

document *n.* докуме́нт; *v.t.* документи́ровать *imp.*, *perf.* **documentary** *adj.* документа́льный; *n.* документа́льный фильм. **documentation** *n.* документа́ция.

dodder *v.i.* дрожа́ть (-жу́, -жи́шь) *imp.* **dodderer** *n.* старый копу́н (-а́), ~ья.

dodge *n.* (*trick*) ло́вкий приём, увёртка; *v.t.* уклоня́ться *imp.*, уклони́ться (-ню́сь, -нишься) *perf.* от+*gen.*; увиливать *imp.*, увильну́ть *perf.* от+*gen.*

doe *n.* са́мка. **doeskin** *n.* за́мша.

dog *n.* соба́ка, пёс (пса); (*male dog*) кобе́ль (-ля́) *m.*; (*male animal*) саме́ц (-мца́); *d.-collar*, оше́йник; *d.-fight*, возду́шный бой (*loc.* бою́; *pl.* бои́); *v.t.* сле́довать *imp.*, по~ *perf.* по пята́м за + *instr.*; (*fig.*) пресле́довать *imp.*

doggerel *n.* ви́рши (-шей) *pl.*

dogma *n.* до́гма. **dogmatic** *adj.* догмати́ческий.

doing *n.*: *pl.* дела́ *neut.pl.*; (*events*) собы́тия *neut.pl.*

doldrums *n.*: *be in the d.*, хандри́ть *imp.*

dole *n.* посо́бие по безрабо́тице.

doleful *adj.* ско́рбный.

doll *n.* ку́кла (*gen.pl.* -кол).

dollar *n.* до́ллар.

dollop *n.* здоро́вый кусо́к (-ска́).

dolly *n.* ку́колка; (*stick*) валёк (-лька́); (*cin.*) опера́торская теле́жка.

dolphin *n.* дельфи́н, белобо́чка.

dolt *n.* болва́н. **doltish** *adj.* тупо́й (туп, -а́, -о, ту́пы́).

domain *n.* (*estate*) владе́ние; (*field*) о́бласть, сфе́ра.

dome *n.* ку́пол (*pl.* -а́). **domed** *adj.* с ку́полом.

domestic *adj.* (*of household; animals*) дома́шний; (*of family*) семе́йный; (*polit.*) вну́тренний; *n.* прислу́га. **domesticate** *v.t.* приуча́ть *imp.*, приучи́ть *perf.* **domesticity** *n.* дома́шняя, семе́йная, жизнь.

domicile *n.* постоя́нное местожи́тельство; *v.t.* сели́ть *imp.*, по~ *perf.* на постоя́нное жи́тельство. **domiciliary** *adj.* дома́шний.

dominance *n.* госпо́дство. **dominant** *adj.* преоблада́ющий; госпо́дствующий; *n.* домина́нта. **dominate** *v.t.* госпо́дствовать *imp.* над + *instr.* **domineering** *adj.* высокоме́рный.

dominion *n.* доминио́н; влады́чество.

domino *n.* кость (*pl.* -ти, -те́й) домино́; *pl.* (*game*) домино́ *neut.indecl.*

don[1] *n.* (*D., title*) дон; (*univ.*) преподава́тель *m.*

don[2] *v.t.* надева́ть *imp.*, наде́ть (-е́ну, -е́нешь) *perf.*

donate *v.t.* же́ртвовать *imp.*, по~ *perf.* **donation** *n.* дар (*pl.* -ы́), поже́ртвование.

donkey *n.* осёл (-сла́); *d. engine*, вспомога́тельный дви́гатель *m.*

donnish *adj.* педанти́чный.

donor *n.* же́ртвователь *m.*; (*med.*) до́нор.

doom *n.* рок, судьба́; (*ruin*) ги́бель; *v.t.* обрека́ть *imp.*, обре́чь (-еку́, -ечёшь; -ёк, -екла́) *perf.* **doomsday** *n.* стра́шный суд (-а́); коне́ц (-нца́) све́та.

door *n.* (*house*) дверь (*loc.* -ри́; *pl.* -ри, -ре́й, *instr.* -рьми́ & -ря́ми); (*smaller*) две́рца (*gen.pl.* -рец). **doorbell** *n.* (дверно́й) звоно́к (-нка́). **doorknob** *n.* (дверна́я) ру́чка. **doorman** *n.* швейца́р. **doormat** *n.* полови́к (-а́). **doorpost** *n.* (дверно́й) կося́к (-а́). **doorstep** *n.* поро́г. **doorway** *n.* дверно́й проём.

dope *n.* (*drug*) нарко́тик; информа́ция; *d.-fiend*, наркома́н, ~ка; *v.t.* дава́ть (даю́, даёшь) *imp.*, дать (дам, дашь, даст, дади́м; дал, -а́, да́ло́, -и) *perf.* нарко́тик + *dat.*

dormant *adj.* (*sleeping*) спя́щий; (*inactive*) безде́йствующий.

dormer window *n.* манса́рдное окно́ (*pl.* о́кна, о́кон, о́кнам).

dormitory *n.* дортуа́р.

dormouse *n.* со́ня.

dorsal *adj.* спинно́й.

dose *n.* до́за; *v.t.* дава́ть (даю́, даёшь) *imp.*, дать (дам, дашь, даст, дади́м; дал, -а́, да́ло́, -и) *perf.* лека́рство + *dat.*

doss-house *n.* ночле́жный дом (*pl.* -а́).

dossier *n.* досье́ *neut.indecl.*

dot *n.* то́чка; *v.t.* ста́вить *imp.*, по~ *perf.* то́чки на + *acc.*; (*scatter*) усе́ивать *imp.*, усе́ять (-е́ю, -е́ешь) *perf.* (with, + *instr.*); *dotted line*, пункти́р.

dotage *n.* (ста́рческое) слабоу́мие. **dotard** *n.* вы́живший из ума́ стари́к (-а́). **dote** *v.i.*: *d. on*, обожа́ть *imp.*

dotty *adj.* рехну́вшийся.

double *adj.* двойно́й, па́рный; (*doubled*) удво́енный (-ен); *d.-barrelled*, двуство́льный; *d.-bass*, контраба́с; *d. bed*, двуспа́льная крова́ть; *d.-breasted*, двубо́ртный; *d.-cross*, обма́нывать *imp.*, обману́ть (-ну́, -нешь) *perf.*; *d.-dealer*, двуру́шник; *d.-dealing*, двуру́шничество; двуру́шнический; *d.-decker*, двухэта́жный авто́бус; *d.-edged*, обоюдоо́стрый; *d.-faced*, двули́чный; *adv.* вдво́е; (*two together*) вдвоём; *n.* двойно́е коли́чество; (*person's*) двойни́к (-а́); (*understudy*) дублёр; *pl.* (*sport*) па́рная игра́; *at the d.*, бе́глым ша́гом; *v.t.* удва́ивать *imp.*, удво́ить *perf.*; (*fold*) скла́дывать *imp.*, сложи́ть (-жу́, -жишь) *perf.* вдво́е; *d. the parts of*, (*theat.*) игра́ть *imp.*, сыгра́ть *perf.* ро́ли + *gen.*

doubt *n.* сомне́ние; *v.t.* сомнева́ться *imp.* в + *prep.* **doubtful** *adj.* сомни́тельный. **doubting** *adj.* сомнева́ющийся. **doubtless** *adv.* несомне́нно.

douche *n.* душ; *v.t.* облива́ть *imp.*, обли́ть (оболью́, -ьёшь; о́бли́л, -а́, -о) *perf.* водо́й.

dough *n.* те́сто. **doughnut** *n.* по́нчик, пы́шка.

dour *adj.* угрю́мый, мра́чный (-чен, -чна́, -чно).

douse *v.t.* (*light*) туши́ть (-шу́, -шишь) *imp.*, за ~, по ~ *perf.*

dove *n.* го́лубь (*pl.* -би, -бе́й) *m.*, го́рлица; *d.-coloured*, си́зый (сиз, -а́, -о). **dovecot(e)** *n.* голубя́тня (*gen.pl.* -тен). **dovetail** *n.* ла́сточкин хвост (-а́); *v.i.*: *d.* (*into one another*), соотве́тствовать *imp.* друг дру́гу.

dowager *n.* вдова́ (*pl.* -вы); *in comb.* вдо́вствующая.

dowdy *adj.* безвку́сный, неэлега́нтный.

down[1] *n.* (*geog.*) безле́сная возвы́шенность; *pl.* Да́унс.

down[2] *n.* (*fluff*) пух (-а(у), *loc.* -у́), пушо́к (-шка́).

down[3] *adv.* (*motion*) вниз; (*position*) внизу́; *be d. with*, (*ill*) боле́ть *imp.* + *instr.*; *d. with*, (*interj.*) доло́й + *acc.*; *prep.* вниз с + *gen.*, по + *dat.*; (*along*) (вдоль) по + *dat.*; *v.t.*: *d. tools*, (*strike*) бастова́ть *imp.*, за ~ *perf.*; *d.-and-out*, бедня́к (-а́), оборва́нец (-нца); *downcast*, *d.-hearted*, уны́лый. **downfall** *n.* (*ruin*) ги́бель. **downpour** *n.* ли́вень (-вня) *m.* **downright** *adj.* прямо́й (прям, -а́, -о, пря́мы́); (*out-and-out*) я́вный; *adv.* соверше́нно. **downstream** *adv.* вниз по тече́нию.

dowry *n.* прида́ное *sb.*

doyen *n.* старшина́ (*pl.* -ны) *m.*

doze *v.i.* дрема́ть (-млю́, -млешь) *imp.*

dozen *n.* дю́жина; *baker's d.*, чёртова дю́жина.

drab *adj.* бесцве́тный; (*boring*) ску́чный (-чен, -чна́, -чно).

draft *n.* (*sketch*) чернови́к (-а́); (*of document*) прое́кт; (*econ.*) тра́тта; *see also* **draught**; *v.t.* составля́ть *imp.*, соста́вить *perf.* план, прое́кт, + *gen.*

drag *v.t.* & *i.* тащи́ть(ся) (-щу́(сь), -щишь(ся)) *imp.*; волочи́ть(ся) (-чу́(сь), -чишь(ся)) *imp.*; *v.t.* (*river etc.*) драги́ровать *imp.*, *perf.*; *n.* (*grapnel*) ко́шка; (*lure*) прима́нка; (*burden*) обу́за; (*brake*) тормозно́й башма́к (-а́); (*aeron.*) лобово́е сопротивле́ние; *d.-net*, бре́день (-дня) *m.*

dragon *n.* драко́н; *d.-fly*, стрекоза́ (*pl.* -зы).

dragoon *n.* драгу́н (*gen.pl.* -н (*collect.*) & -нов).

drain *n.* водосто́к; (*leakage*, *also fig.*) уте́чка; *d.-pipe*, водосто́чная труба́ (*pl.* -бы); *v.t.* осуша́ть *imp.*, осуши́ть (-шу́, -шишь) *perf.* **drainage** *n.* сток; канализа́ция; дрена́ж.

drake *n.* се́лезень (-зня) *m.*

dram *n.* глото́к (-тка́).

drama *n.* дра́ма. **dramatic** *adj.* драмати́ческий. **dramatis personae** *n.* де́йствующие ли́ца *neut.pl.* **dramatist** *n.* драмату́рг. **dramatize** *v.t.* инсцени́ровать *imp.*, *perf.*; (*fig.*) преувели́чивать *imp.*, преувели́чить *perf.*

drape *v.t.* драпирова́ть *imp.*, за ~ *perf.*; *n.* драпиро́вка. **draper** *n.* торго́вец (-вца) тка́нями. **drapery** *n.* драпиро́вка; (*cloth*; *collect.*) тка́ни *f.pl.*

drastic *adj.* круто́й (крут, -а́, -о), радика́льный.

drat *interj.* чёрт возьми́! **dratted** *adj.* прокля́тый.

draught *n.* (*drink*) глото́к (-тка́); (*air*) тя́га, сквозня́к (-а́); (*naut.*) оса́дка; *pl.* (*game*) ша́шки *f.pl.*; *see also* **draft**; *be in a d.*, быть на сквозняке́; *d. animals*, тя́гло *collect.*; *d. beer*, пи́во из бо́чки; *d. horse*, ломова́я ло́шадь (*pl.* -ди, -де́й, *instr.* -дьми́). **draughtsman** *n.* (*person*) чертёжник; (*counter*) ша́шка. **draughty** *adj.*: *it is d. here*, здесь ду́ет.

draw *n.* (*action*) вытя́гивание; (*lottery*) лотере́я; (*attraction*) прима́нка; (*drawn game*) ничья́; *v.t.* (*pull*) тяну́ть (-ну́, -нешь) *imp.*, по ~ *perf.*; таска́ть *indet.*, тащи́ть (-щу́, -щишь) *det.*; (*curtains*) задёргивать *imp.*, задёрнуть *perf.* (занаве́ски); (*attract*) привлека́ть *imp.*, привле́чь (-еку́, -ечёшь; -ёк, -екла́) *perf.*; (*pull out*) вытаскивать *imp.*, вы́тащить *perf.*; (*sword*) обнажа́ть *imp.*, обнажи́ть *perf.*; (*lots*) броса́ть *imp.*, бро́сить *perf.* (жре́бий); (*water*; *inspiration*) че́рпать *imp.*, черпну́ть *perf.*; (*game*) конча́ть *imp.*, ко́нчить *perf.* (игру́) вничью́; (*evoke*) вызыва́ть *imp.*, вы́звать (вы́зову, -вешь) *perf.*; (*conclusion*) выводи́ть (-ожу́, -о́дишь) *imp.*, вы́вести (-еду, -едешь; -ел) *perf.* (заключе́ние); (*fowl*) потроши́ть *imp.*, вы́ ~ *perf.*; (*diagram*) черти́ть (-рчу́, -ртишь) *imp.*, на ~ *perf.*; (*picture*) рисова́ть *imp.*, на ~ *perf.*; *d. aside*, отводи́ть (-ожу́, -о́дишь) *imp.*, отвести́ (-еду́, -едёшь; -ёл, -ела́) *perf.* в сто́рону; *d. back*, (*withdraw*) отступа́ть *imp.*, отступи́ть (-плю́, -пишь) *perf.*; *d. in*, (*involve*) вовлека́ть *imp.*, вовле́чь (-еку́, -ечёшь; -ёк, -екла́) *perf.*; *d. up*, (*document*) составля́ть *imp.*, соста́вить *perf.* **drawback** *n.* недоста́ток (-тка), поме́ха. **drawbridge** *n.* подъёмный мост (моста́, *loc.* -у́; *pl.* -ы́). **drawer** *n.* (*person*) чертёжник, рисова́льщик; (*of table etc.*) выдвижно́й я́щик; *pl.* кальсо́ны (-н) *pl.* **drawing** *n.* (*action*) рисова́ние, черче́ние; (*object*) рису́нок (-нка), чертёж (-а́); *d.-board*, чертёжная доска́ (*acc.* -ску; *pl.* -ски, -со́к, -ска́м); *d.-pen*, рейсфе́дер; *d.-pin*, кно́пка; *d.-room*, гости́ная *sb.*

drawl *n.* протя́жное, медли́тельное, произноше́ние; *v.i.* растя́гивать *imp.*, растяну́ть (-ну́, -нешь) *perf.* слова́.

dray *n.* подво́да; *d.-horse*, ломова́я ло́шадь (*pl.* -ди, -де́й, *instr.* -дьми́). **drayman** *n.* ломово́й изво́зчик.

dread *n.* страх; *v.t.* боя́ться (бою́сь, бои́шься) *imp.* + *gen.* **dreadful** *adj.* стра́шный (-шен, -шна́, -шно, стра́шны́).

dreadnought *n.* дредно́ут.

dream *n.* сон (сна); мечта́ (*gen.pl.* -а́ний); *v.i.* ви́деть (ви́жу, -дишь) *imp.*, у ~ *perf.* сон; *d. of*, ви́деть (ви́жу, ви́дишь) *imp.*, у ~ *perf.* во сне́; (*fig.*) мечта́ть *imp.* о + *prep.* **dreamer** *n.* мечта́тель *m.*, фантазёр.

dreariness *n.* тоскли́вость. **dreary** *adj.* тоскли́вый, ску́чный (-чен, -чна́, -чно).

dredge[1] *v.t.* (*river etc.*) драги́ровать *imp.*, *perf.* **dredger**[1] *n.* землечерпа́лка; дра́га.

dredge[2] *v.t.* (*sprinkle*) посыпа́ть *imp.*,, посы́пать (-плю, -плешь) *perf.* **dredger**[2] *n.* си́течко (*pl.* -чки, -чек, -чкам).

dreg *n.*: *pl.* оса́дки (-ков) *pl.*, отбро́сы (-сов) *pl.*; *d. of society*, подо́нки (-ков) *pl.* о́бщества.

drench *v.t.* (*wet*) прома́чивать *imp.*, промочи́ть (-чу́, -чишь) *perf.*; *get drenched*, промока́ть *imp.*, промо́кнуть (-к) *perf.*

dress *n.* пла́тье (*gen.pl.* -в), оде́жда; *d. circle*, бельэта́ж; *d. coat*, фрак; *dressmaker*, портни́ха; *d. rehearsal*, генера́льная репети́ция; *v.t.* & *i.* одева́ть(ся) *imp.*, оде́ть(ся) (-е́ну(сь), -е́нешь(ся)) *perf.*; *v.t.* (*cul.*) приправля́ть *imp.*, припра́вить *perf.*; (*med.*) перевя́зывать *imp.*, перевяза́ть (-яжу́, -я́жешь) *perf.*; *v.i.* (*mil.*) равня́ться *imp.* **dresser**[1] *n.* (*theat.*) костюме́р, ~ ша.

dresser[2] *n.* ку́хонный шкаф (*loc.* -у́; *pl.* -ы́).

dressing *n.* (*cul.*) припра́ва; (*med.*) перевя́зка; *d.-case*, несессе́р; *d. down*, вы́говор; *d.-gown*, хала́т; *d.-room*, убо́рная *sb.*; *d.-station*, перевя́зочный пункт; *d.-table*, туале́тный стол (-а́).

dribble *v.i.* (*water*) ка́пать *imp.*; (*child*) пуска́ть *imp.*, пусти́ть (пущу́, пу́стишь) *perf.* слю́ни; (*sport*) вести́ (веду́, -дёшь; -вёл, -а́) *imp.* мяч. **driblet** *n.* ка́пелька.

dried *adj.* сушёный. **drier** *n.* суши́лка.

drift *n.* тече́ние; (*naut.*) дрейф; (*aeron.*) снос; (*inaction*) безде́йствие; (*purpose*) тенде́нция; (*meaning*) смысл; (*snow*) сугро́б; (*sand*) нано́с; *v.i.* плыть (плыву́, -вёшь; плыл, -а́, -о) *imp.* по течéнию; (*naut.*) дрейфовáть *imp.*; (*snow etc.*) скопля́ться *imp.*, скопи́ться (-ится) *perf.*; *v.t.* (*snow*) наноси́ть (-ит) *imp.*, нанести́ (-есёт; -ёс, -еслá) *perf.*; заноси́ть (-ит) *imp.*, занести́ (-сёт; -слó) *perf.* (снéгом, пескóм) *impers.*+*acc.*

drill[1] *n.* сверлó (*pl.* -ёрла), дрель, бур; *v.t.* сверли́ть *imp.*, про~ *perf.*

drill[2] *n.* (*agr. machine*) сéялка.

drill[3] *v.t.* (*mil.*) обучáть *imp.*, обучи́ть (-чý, -чишь) *perf.* стрóю; муштровáть *imp.*, вы́~ *perf.*; *v.i.* проходи́ть (-ожý, -óдишь) *imp.*, пройти́ (-ойдý, -ойдёшь; -ошёл, -ошлá) *perf.* строевýю подготóвку; *n.* строевáя подготóвка.

drink *n.* питьё, напи́ток (-тка); (*mouthful*) глотóк (-ткá); (*strong*) *d.*, спиртнóй напи́ток (-тка); *soft d.*, безалкогóльный напи́ток (-тка); *v.t.* пить (пью, пьёшь; пил, -á, -о) *imp.*, вы́~ *perf.* (*to excess*, си́льно); (*plants*; *fig.*) впи́тывать *imp.*, впитáть *perf.* **drinking** *in comb.*: *d.-bout*, запóй; *d.-song*, застóльная пéсня (*gen.pl.* -сен); *d.-water*, питьевáя водá (*acc.* -ду).

drip *n.* (*action*) кáпанье; (*object*) кáпля (*gen.pl.* -пель); *v.i.* кáпать *imp.*, кáпнуть *perf.*; *d.-dry*, быстросóхнущий. **dripping** *n.* (*fat*) жир (-а(у), *loc.* -е & -ý); *d. wet*, промóкший насквóзь.

drive *n.* (*journey*) ездá; (*excursion*) катáнье, прогýлка; (*campaign*) похóд, кампáния; (*energy*) энéргия; (*tech.*) привóд; (*driveway*) подъезднáя дорóга; *v.t.* (*urge*; *chase*) гоня́ть *indet.*, гнать (гоню́, -нишь; гнал, -á, -о) *det.*; (*vehicle*) води́ть (вожý, вóдишь) *indet.*, вести́ (ведý, -дёшь; вёл, -á) *det.*; управля́ть *imp.*+*instr.*; (*convey*) вози́ть (вожý, вóзишь) *indet.*, везти́ (везý, -зёшь; вёз, -лá) *det.*, по~ *perf.*; *v.i.* (*travel*) éздить *indet.*, éхать (éду, éдешь) *det.*, по~ *perf.*; *v.t.* (*compel*) заставля́ть *imp.*, застáвить *perf.*; (*nail etc.*) вбивáть *imp.*, вбить (вобью́, -ьёшь) *perf.* (into, в+*acc.*); (*machine*) приводи́ть (-ожý, -óдишь) *imp.*, привести́ (-едý, -едёшь; -ёл, -елá) *perf.* в движéние (*by steam etc.*, +*instr.*); *d. away*, *v.t.* прогоня́ть *imp.*, прогнáть (прогоню́, -нишь; прогнáл, -á, -о) *perf.*; *v.i.* уезжáть *imp.*, уéхать (-éду, -éдешь) *perf.*; *d. out*, *v.t.* (*knock out*) выбивáть *imp.*, вы́бить (вы́бью, -ьешь) *perf.*; (*expel*) выгоня́ть *imp.*, вы́гнать (вы́гоню, -нишь) *perf.*; *d. up*, подъезжáть *imp.*, подъéхать (-éду, -éдешь) *perf.* (to, к+*dat.*).

drivel *n.* чепухá; *v.i.* порóть (-рю́, -решь) *imp.* чепухý.

driver *n.* (*of vehicle*) води́тель *m.*, шофёр. **driving** *n.* вождéние; катáние; *adj.* дви́жущий; *d.-belt*, приводнóй ремéнь (-мня́) *m.*; *d. force*, дви́жущая си́ла; *d. licence*, води́тельские правá *neut.pl.*; *d.-wheel*, ведýщее колесó (*pl.* -ёса).

drizzle *n.* мéлкий дождь (-дя́) *m.*; *v.i.* мороси́ть *imp.*

droll *adj.* смешнóй (-шóн, -шнá), забáвный. **drollery** *n.* шýтка.

dromedary *n.* дромадéр.

drone *n.* (*bee*; *idler*) трýтень (-тня) *m.*; (*buzz*) жужжáние; *v.i.* (*buzz*) жужжáть (-жжý, -жжи́шь) *imp.*; (*mutter*) бубни́ть *imp.*

drool *v.i.* пускáть *imp.*, пусти́ть (пущý, пýстишь) *perf.* слю́ни.

droop *v.i.* ни́кнуть (ник) *imp.*, по~, с~ *perf.*

drop *n.* (*of liquid*) кáпля (*gen.pl.* -пель); (*pendant*) висю́лька; (*sweet*) леденéц (-нцá); (*fall*) падéние, понижéние; *v.t.* & *i.* кáпать *imp.*, кáпнуть *perf.*; (*price*) снижáть(ся) *imp.*, сни́зить(ся) *perf.*; *v.i.* (*fall*) пáдать *imp.*, упáсть (-адý, -адёшь; -áл) *perf.*; *v.t.* роня́ть *imp.*, урони́ть (-ню́, -нишь) *perf.*; (*abandon*) бросáть *imp.*, брóсить *perf.*; (*eyes*) опускáть *imp.*, опусти́ть (-ущý, -ýстишь) *perf.*; *d. behind*, отставáть (-таю́, -таёшь) *imp.*, отстáть (-áну, -áнешь) *perf.*; *d. in*, заходи́ть (-ожý, -óдишь) *imp.*, зайти́ (зайдý, -дёшь; зашёл, -шлá) *perf.* (on, к+*dat.*); *d. off*, (*fall asleep*) засыпáть *imp.*, заснýть *perf.*; *d. out*, выбывáть *imp.*, вы́быть (-буду, -будешь) *perf.* (of, из+*gen.*); *d.-out*, вы́бывший *sb.* **droplet** *n.* кáпелька. **dropper** *n.* пипéтка. **droppings** *n.* помёт, навóз (-а(у)).

dropsy *n.* водя́нка.

dross *n.* шлак; (*refuse*) отбро́сы (-сов) *pl.*
drought *n.* за́суха; *d.-resistant*, засухоусто́йчивый.
drove *n.* ста́до (*pl.* -да́), гурт (-а́). **drover** *n.* гуртовщи́к (-а́).
drown *v.t.* топи́ть (-плю́, -пишь) *imp.*, у~ *perf.*; (*sound*) заглуша́ть *imp.*, заглуши́ть *perf.*; *v.i.* тону́ть (-ну́, -нешь) *imp.*, у~ *perf.*
drowse *v.i.* дрема́ть (-млю́, -млешь) *imp.* **drowsiness** *n.* сонли́вость, дремо́та. **drowsy** *adj.* сонли́вый, дре́млющий.
drub *v.t.* поро́ть (-рю́, -решь) *imp.* вы́~ *perf.*
drudge *n.* работя́га. **drudgery** *n.* тяжёлая, ну́дная рабо́та.
drug *n.* медикаме́нт; нарко́тик; *d. addict*, наркома́н, ~ка; *v.t.* дава́ть (даю́, даёшь) *imp.*, дать (дам, дашь, даст, дади́м; дал, -а́, да́ло́, -и) *perf.* нарко́тик + *dat.*
druid *n.* друи́д.
drum *n.* бараба́н; *v.i.* бить (бью́, бьёшь) *imp.* в бараба́н; бараба́нить *imp.* **drummer** *n.* бараба́нщик.
drunk *adj.* пья́ный (пья́н, -а́, -о). **drunkard** *n.* пья́ница *m.* & *f.* **drunken** *adj.* пья́ный. **drunkenness** *n.* пья́нство.
dry *adj.* сухо́й (сух, -а́, -о); *d.-cleaning*, химчи́стка; *d. land*, су́ша; *v.t.* суши́ть (-шу́, -шишь) *imp.*, вы́~ *perf.*; (*wipe dry*) вытира́ть *imp.*, вы́тереть (-тру, -трешь; -тер) *perf.*; *v.i.* со́хнуть (сох) *imp.*, вы́~, про~ *perf.* **drying** *n.* су́шка; *adj.* суши́льный. **dryness** *n.* су́хость.
dual *adj.* двойно́й, дво́йственный (-ен, -енна); *d.-purpose*, двойно́го назначе́ния. **duality** *n.* дво́йственность, раздво́енность.
dub[1] *v.t.* (*nickname*) дава́ть (даю́, даёшь) *imp.*, дать (дам, дашь, даст, дади́м; дал, -а́, да́ло́, -и) про́звище + *dat.*
dub[2] *v.t.* (*cin.*) дубли́ровать *imp.*, *perf.* **dubbing** *n.* дубля́ж.
dubious *adj.* сомни́тельный.
ducal *adj.* ге́рцогский. **duchess** *n.* герцоги́ня. **duchy** *n.* ге́рцогство.
duck[1] *n.* (*bird*) у́тка.
duck[2] *v.t.* окуна́ть *imp.*, окуну́ть *perf.*; *v.i.* увёртываться *imp.*, уверну́ться *perf.* от уда́ра.
duck[3] *n.* (*cloth*) паруси́на.
duckling *n.* утёнок (-нка; *pl.* утя́та, -т).
duct *n.* прохо́д, трубопрово́д; (*anat.*) прото́к.
ductile *adj.* (*metal*) ко́вкий (-вок, -вка́, -вко); (*clay*) пласти́чный. **ductility** *n.* ко́вкость, пласти́чность.
dud *n.* (*forgery*) подде́лка; (*shell*) неразорва́вшийся снаря́д; *adj.* подде́льный; (*worthless*) него́дный (-ден, -дна́, -дно).
dudgeon *n.* оби́да, возмуще́ние; *in high d.*, в глубо́ком возмуще́нии.
due *n.* до́лжное *sb.*; *pl.* сбо́ры *m.pl.*, взно́сы *m.pl.*; *adj.* до́лжный, надлежа́щий; *predic.* до́лжен (-жна́); *in d. course*, со вре́менем; *adv.* то́чно, пря́мо; *d. to*, благодаря́ + *dat.*, всле́дствие + *gen.*
duel *n.* дуэ́ль, поеди́нок (-нка).
duet *n.* дуэ́т.
duffer *n.* дура́к (-а́), недотёпа *m.* & *f.*
dug-out *n.* (*boat*) челно́к (-а́); (*mil.*) блинда́ж (-а́).
duke *n.* ге́рцог; *Grand D.*, вели́кий князь (*pl.* -зья́, -зе́й) *m.* **dukedom** *n.* ге́рцогство.
dulcet *adj.* сла́дкий (-док, -дка́, -дко), не́жный (-жен, -жна́, -жно, не́жны́).
dulcimer *n.* цимба́лы (-л) *pl.*
dull *adj.* тупо́й (туп, -а́, -о, ту́пы́); (*tedious*) ску́чный (-чен, -чна́, -чно); (*colour*) ту́склый (-л, -ла́, -ло), ма́товый; (*weather*) па́смурный; *v.t.* притупля́ть *imp.*, притупи́ть (-плю́, -пишь) *perf.* **dullard** *n.* тупи́ца *m.* & *f.* **dullness** *n.* ту́пость; ску́чность.
duly *adv.* надлежа́щим о́бразом; (*punctually*) в до́лжное вре́мя, своевре́менно.
dumb *adj.* немо́й (нем, -а́, -о); (*taciturn*) молчали́вый; *deaf and d.*, глухонемо́й; *d.-bell*, ганте́ль. **dumbfound** *v.t.* ошеломля́ть *imp.*, ошеломи́ть *perf.*
dummy *n.* маке́т; (*tailor's*) манеке́н; (*cards*) болва́н; (*baby's*) со́ска(-пус-

ты́шка); *adj.* ненастоя́щий, фальши́вый.

dump *n.* сва́лка; *v.t.* сва́ливать *imp.*, свали́ть (-лю́, -лишь) *perf.* **dumping** *n.* (*econ.*) де́мпинг, бро́совый э́кспорт.

dumpling *n.* клёцка.

dumpy *adj.* то́лстый (толст, -á, -о, то́лсты́), корена́стый.

dun *adj.* серова́то-кори́чневый.

dunce *n.* болва́н, тупи́ца *m.* & *f.*

dune *n.* дю́на.

dung *n.* помёт, наво́з (-а(у)).

dungarees *n.* рабо́чие брю́ки (-к) *pl.* на по́моча́х.

dungeon *n.* темни́ца.

dunk *v.t.* мака́ть *imp.*, макну́ть *perf.*

dupe *v.t.* обма́нывать *imp.*, обману́ть (-ну́, -нешь) *perf.*; *n.* же́ртва обма́на, простофи́ля *m.* & *f.*

duplicate *n.* дублика́т, ко́пия; *in. d.*, в двух экземпля́рах; *adj.* (*double*) двойно́й; (*identical*) иденти́чный; *v.t.* дубли́ровать *imp.*; снима́ть *imp.*, снять (сниму́, -мешь; снял, -á, -о) *perf.* ко́пию с + *gen.* **duplicator** *n.* копирова́льный аппара́т. **duplicity** *n.* двули́чность.

durability *n.* про́чность. **durable** *adj.* про́чный (-чен, -чна́, -чно, про́чны́). **duration** *n.* продолжи́тельность; срок (-а(у)).

duress *n.* принужде́ние; *under d.*, под давле́нием.

during *prep.* в тече́ние + *gen.*, во вре́мя + *gen.*

dusk *n.* су́мерки (-рек) *pl.*, су́мрак. **dusky** *adj.* су́меречный; тёмный (-мен, -мна́); (*complexion*) сму́глый (смугл, -á, -о).

dust *n.* пыль (*loc.* -ли́); *dustbin*, му́сорный я́щик; *d.-jacket*, суперобло́жка; *dustman*, му́сорщик; *d.-pan*, сово́к (-вка́); *v.t.* (*clean*) стира́ть *imp.*, стере́ть (сотру́, -рёшь; стёр) *perf.* пыль с + *gen.*; (*sprinkle*) посыпа́ть *imp.*, посы́пать (-плю, -плешь) *perf.* + *instr.* **duster** *n.* пы́льная тря́пка. **dusting** *n.* вытира́ние, сма́хивание, пы́ли. **dusty** *adj.* пы́льный (-лен -льна́, -льно), запылённый (-ён, -ена́)

Dutch *adj.* голла́ндский; *D. courage*, хра́брость во хмелю́; *D. treat*, скла́дчина; *n.*: *the D.*, голла́ндцы *m.pl.* **Dutchman** *n.* голла́ндец (-дца).

dutiable *adj.* подлежа́щий обложе́нию по́шлиной. **dutiful** *adj.* послу́шный. **duty** *n.* (*obligation*) долг (-а(у), *loc.* -у́; *pl.* -и́), обя́занность; (*office*) дежу́рство; (*tax*) по́шлина; *on d.*, дежу́рный; *be on d.*, дежу́рить *imp.*; *do one's d.*, исполня́ть *imp.*, испо́лнить *perf.* свой долг; *d.-free*, беспо́шлинный; *d.-paid*, опла́ченный по́шлиной.

dwarf *n.* ка́рлик, -ица; *adj.* ка́рликовый; *v.t.* (*stunt*) остана́вливать *imp.*, останови́ть (-влю́, -вишь) *perf.* рост, разви́тие, + *gen.*; (*tower above*) возвыша́ться *imp.*, возвы́ситься *perf.* над + *instr.*

dwell *v.i.* обита́ть *imp.*; *d. upon*, остана́вливаться *imp.* на + *prep.* **dweller** *n.* жи́тель *m.*, ~ница. **dwelling** *n.* (*d.-place*) местожи́тельство; *d.-house*, жило́й дом (-а(у); *pl.* -а́).

dwindle *v.i.* убыва́ть *imp.*, убы́ть (убу́ду, -дешь; у́был, -á, -о) *perf.*

dye *n.* краси́тель *m.*, кра́ска; *d.-works*, краси́льня (*gen.pl.* -лен); *v.t.* окра́шивать *imp.*, окра́сить *perf.*; *dyed-in-the-wool*, (*fig.*) закорене́лый. **dyeing** *n.* кра́шение. **dyer** *n.* краси́льщик.

dying *adj.* умира́ющий; (*at time of death*) предсме́ртный; *n.* умира́ние, угаса́ние; *d.-out*, вымира́ние.

dynamic *adj.* динами́ческий. **dynamics** *n.* дина́мика.

dynamite *n.* динами́т; *v.t.* взрыва́ть, *imp.*, взорва́ть (-ву́, -вёшь; взорва́л, -á, -о) *perf.* динами́том.

dynamo *n.* дина́мо-маши́на.

dynastic *adj.* династи́ческий; *n.* дина́стия.

dysentery *n.* дизентери́я.

dyspepsia диспепси́я. **dyspeptic** *n.*, *adj.* страда́ющий (*sb.*) диспе́псией.

E

E *n.* (*mus.*) ми *neut.indecl.*

each *adj., pron.* ка́ждый; *e. other*, друг дру́га (*dat.* -гу, *etc.*).

eager *adj.* стремя́щийся (for, к + *dat.*); (*impatient*) нетерпели́вый. **eagerness** *n.* пыл (-а(у), *loc.* -у́), рве́ние.

eagle *n.* орёл (орла́), орли́ца; *e.-eyed*, зо́ркий (-рок, -рка́, -рко); *e.-owl*, фи́лин. **eaglet** *n.* орлёнок (-нка; *pl.* орля́та, -т).

ear[1] *n.* (*corn*) ко́лос (*pl.* -о́сья, -о́сьев); *v.i.* колоси́ться *imp.*, вы~ *perf.*

ear[2] *n.* (*organ*) у́хо (*pl.* у́ши, уше́й); (*sense*) слух; *by e.*, по слу́ху; *to be all ears*, слу́шать *imp.* во все у́ши; *earache*, боль в у́хе; *e.-drum*, бараба́нная перепо́нка; *earless*, безу́хий; *e.-lobe*, мо́чка; *earmark*, клеймо́ (*pl.* -ма); клейми́ть *imp.*, за~ *perf.*; (*assign*) предназнача́ть *imp.*, предназна́чить *perf.*; *earphone*, нау́шник; *e.-ring*, серьга́ (*pl.* -рьги, -рёг, -рьга́м); *earshot*: *within e.*, в преде́лах слы́шимости; *out of e.*, вне преде́лов слы́шимости; *e.-splitting*, оглуши́тельный.

earl *n.* граф. **earldom** *n.* гра́фство, ти́тул гра́фа.

early *adj.* ра́нний; (*initial*) нача́льный; *adv.* ра́но.

earn *v.t.* зараба́тывать *imp.*, зарабо́тать *perf.*; (*deserve*) заслу́живать *imp.*, заслужи́ть (-жу́, -жишь) *perf.* **earnings** *n.* за́работок (-тка).

earnest *adj.* серьёзный; *n.*: *in e.*, всерьёз.

earth *n.* земля́ (*acc.* -лю); (*soil*) по́чва; (*fox's*) нора́ (*pl.* -ры); (*electr.*) заземле́ние; *v.t.* заземля́ть *imp.*, заземли́ть *perf.*; *e. up*, оку́чивать *imp.*, оку́чить *perf.* **earthen** *adj.* земляно́й. **earthenware** *n.* гли́няная посу́да (*collect.*); *adj.* гли́няный. **earthly** *adj.* земно́й, жите́йский. **earth-moving** *adj.* землеро́йный. **earthquake** *n.* землетрясе́ние. **earthwork** *n.* земляно́е укрепле́ние. **earthworm** *n.* земляно́й червь (-вя́; *pl.* -ви, -ве́й) *m.* **earthy** *adj.* земляно́й, земли́стый; (*coarse*) гру́бый (груб, -а́, -о).

earwig *n.* уховёртка.

ease *n.* (*facility*) лёгкость; (*unconstraint*) непринуждённость; *at e.*, *interj.* во́льно! *with e.*, легко́, без труда́; *v.t.* облегча́ть *imp.*, облегчи́ть *perf.*

easel *n.* мольбе́рт.

east *n.* восто́к; (*naut.*) ост; *adj.* восто́чный; о́стовый. **eastern** *adj.* восто́чный. **eastwards** *adv.* на восто́к, к восто́ку.

Easter *n.* па́сха.

easy *adj.* лёгкий (-гок, -гка́, -гко́, лёгки́); (*unconstrained*) непринуждённый (-ён, -ённа); *e.-going*, доброду́шный.

eat *v.t.* есть (ем, ешь, ест, еди́м; ел) *imp.*, съ~ *perf.*; ку́шать *imp.*, по~, с~ *perf.*; *e. away*, разъеда́ть *imp.*, разъе́сть (-е́ст; -е́л) *perf.*; *e. into*, въеда́ться *imp.*, въе́сться (-е́стся; -е́лся) *perf.* в + *acc.*; *e. up*, доеда́ть *imp.*, дое́сть (-е́м, -е́шь, -е́ст, -еди́м; -е́л) *perf.* **eatable** *adj.* съедо́бный.

eau-de-Cologne *n.* одеколо́н.

eaves *n.* стреха́ (*pl.* -и). **eavesdrop** *v.t.* подслу́шивать *imp.*, подслу́шать *perf.*

ebb *n.* (*tide*) отли́в; (*fig.*) упа́док (-дка).

ebony *n.* чёрное де́рево.

ebullience *n.* кипу́честь. **ebullient** *adj.* кипу́чий.

eccentric *n.* чуда́к (-а́), -а́чка; (*tech.*) эксце́нтрик; *adj.* эксцентри́чный. **eccentricity** *n.* эксцентри́чность, чуда́чество.

ecclesiastic *n.* духо́вное лицо́ (*pl.* -ца). **ecclesiastical** *adj.* духо́вный, церко́вный.

echelon *n.* эшело́н; *v.t.* эшелони́ровать *imp., perf.*

echo *n.* э́хо; (*imitation*) о́тклик; *e.-sounder*, эхоло́т; *v.i.* (*resound*) оглаша́ться *imp.*, огласи́ться *perf.* э́хом; *v.t. & i.* (*repeat*) повторя́ть(ся) *imp.*, повтори́ть(ся) *perf.*

eclipse *n.* затме́ние; (*fig.*) упа́док (-дка); *v.t.* затмева́ть *imp.*, затми́ть *perf.*

economic *adj.* экономи́ческий, хозя́йственный; (*profitable*) рента́бельный. **economical** *adj.* эконо́мный, бережли́вый. **economist** *n.* экономи́ст. **economize** *v.t.* & *i.* эконо́мить *imp.*, с~ *perf.* **economy** *n.* хозя́йство, эконо́мика; (*saving*) эконо́мия, сбереже́ние.

ecstasy *n.* экста́з, восхище́ние. **ecstatic** *adj.* исступлённый (-ён, -ённа).

eddy *n.* (*water*) водоворо́т; (*wind*) вихрь *m.*; *v.i.* (*water*) крути́ться (-ится) *imp.*; (*wind*) клуби́ться *imp.*

edelweiss *n.* эдельве́йс.

edge *n.* край (*loc.* -áе & -аю́; *pl.* -ая́), кро́мка; (*blade*) ле́звие; *on e.*, (*excited*) взволно́ванный (-ан); (*irritable*) раздражённый (-ён, -ена́); *v.t.* (*sharpen*) точи́ть (-чу́, -чишь) *imp.*, на~ *perf.*; (*border*) окаймля́ть *imp.*, окайми́ть *perf.*; *v.i.* пробира́ться *imp.*, пробра́ться (-беру́сь, -берёшься; -а́лся, -ала́сь, -а́ло́сь) *perf.* **edging** *n.* каймá. **edgy** *adj.* раздражи́тельный.

edible *adj.* съедо́бный.

edict *n.* ука́з.

edification *n.* назида́ние. **edifice** *n.* зда́ние, сооруже́ние. **edify** *v.t.* наставля́ть *imp.*, наста́вить *perf.* **edifying** *adj.* назида́тельный.

edit *v.t.* редакти́ровать *imp.*, от~ *perf.*; (*cin.*) монти́ровать *imp.*, с~ *perf.* **edition** *n.* изда́ние; (*number of copies*) тира́ж (-а́). **editor** *n.* реда́ктор. **editorial** *n.* передова́я статья́; *adj.* реда́кторский, редакцио́нный.

educate *v.t.* воспи́тывать *imp.*, воспита́ть *perf.* **educated** *adj.* образо́ванный (-ан, -анна). **education** *n.* образова́ние, воспита́ние; (*instruction*) обуче́ние. **educational** *adj.* образова́тельный, воспита́тельный; уче́бный.

eel *n.* у́горь (угря́) *m.*

eerie *adj.* (*gloomy*) мра́чный (-чен, -чна́, -чно); (*strange*) стра́нный (-нен, -нна́, -нно).

efface *v.t.* изгла́живать *imp.*, изгла́дить *perf.*; *e. oneself*, стушёвываться *imp.*, стушева́ться (-шу́юсь, -шу́ешься) *perf.*

effect *n.* (*result*) сле́дствие; (*efficacy*) де́йствие; (*impression*; *theat.*, *cin.*) эффе́кт; *pl.* иму́щество, (*personal*) ли́чные ве́щи (-ще́й) *f.pl.*; *in e.*, факти́чески; *bring into e.*, осуществля́ть *imp.*, осуществи́ть *perf.*; *take e.*, вступа́ть *imp.*. вступи́ть (-ит) *perf.* в си́лу; *v.t.* производи́ть (-ожу́, -о́дишь) *imp.*, произвести́ (-еду́, -едёшь; -ёл, -ела́) *perf.* **effective** *adj.* де́йственный (-ен, -енна), эффекти́вный; (*striking*) эффе́ктный; (*actual*) факти́ческий. **effectiveness** *n.* де́йственность, эффекти́вность. **effectual** *adj.* де́йственный (-ен, -енна).

effeminate *adj.* изне́женный (-ен, -енна).

effervesce *v.i.* пе́ниться *imp.* **effervescent** *adj.* шипу́чий.

efficacious *adj.* де́йственный (-ен, -енна), эффекти́вный. **efficacy** *n.* де́йственность, эффекти́вность. **efficiency** *n.* де́йственность, эффекти́вность; (*of person*) уме́ние; (*mech.*) коэффицие́нт поле́зного де́йствия. **efficient** *adj.* де́йственный (-ен, -енна), эффекти́вный; (*person*) уме́лый.

effigy *n.* изображе́ние.

effort *n.* (*exertion*) уси́лие; (*attempt*) попы́тка.

effrontery *n.* на́глость.

egg[1] *n.* яйцо́ (*pl.* я́йца, яи́ц, я́йцам); *attrib.* яи́чный; *e.-beater*, взбива́лка; *e.-cup*, рю́мка для яйца́; *e.-plant*, баклажа́н; *eggshell*, яи́чная скорлупа́ (*pl.* -пы).

egg[2] *v.t.*: *e. on*, подстрека́ть *imp.*, подстрекну́ть *perf.*

egret *n.* бе́лая ца́пля (*gen.pl.* -пель).

Egyptian *n.* египтя́нин (*pl.* -я́не, -я́н), -я́нка; *adj.* еги́петский.

eider *n.* (*duck*) га́га; (*e.-down*), гага́чий пух (*loc.* -у́). **eiderdown** *n.* (*quilt*) пухо́вое одея́ло.

eight *adj.*, *n.* во́семь (-сьми́, -семью́ & -сьмю́); (*collect.*; *8 pairs*) во́сьмеро (-ры́х); (*cards*; *boat*; *number 8*) восьмёрка; (*time*) во́семь (часо́в); (*age*) во́семь лет. **eighteen** *adj.*, *n.* восемна́дцать (-ти, -тью); (*age*) восемна́дцать лет. **eighteenth** *adj.*, *n.* восемна́дцатый; (*date*) восемна́дцатое (число́). **eighth** *adj.*, *n.* восьмо́й; (*fraction*) восьма́я (часть (*pl.* -ти, -те́й)); (*date*) восьмо́е (число́). **eightieth** *adj.*, *n.* восьмидеся́тый. **eighty** *adj.*, *n.* во́семьдесят

(-сьми́десяти, -сьмью́десятью); (*age*) во́семьдесят лет; *pl.* (*decade*) восьмидеся́тые го́ды (-до́в) *m.pl.*

either *adj.*, *pron.* (*one of two*) оди́н из двух, тот или друго́й; (*each of two*) и тот, и друго́й; о́ба; любо́й; *adv.*, *conj.*: *e. . . . or*, и́ли...и́ли, ли́бо...ли́бо.

eject *v.t.* изверга́ть *imp.*, изве́ргнуть (-г(ну)л, -гла) *perf.* **ejection** *n.* изверже́ние; *e. seat*, катапульти́руемое кре́сло (*gen.pl.* -сел).

eke *v.t.*: *e. out a living*, перебива́ться *imp.*, переби́ться (-бью́сь, -бьёшься) *perf.* ко́е-как.

elaborate *adj.* (*complicated*) сло́жный (-жен, -жна́, -жно); (*detailed*) подро́бный; *v.t.* разраба́тывать *imp.*, разрабо́тать *perf.*; уточня́ть *imp.*, уточни́ть *perf.* **elaboration** *n.* разрабо́тка, уточне́ние.

elapse *v.i.* проходи́ть (-о́дит) *imp.*, пройти́ (пройдёт; прошёл, -шла́) *perf.*; истека́ть *imp.*, исте́чь (-ечёт; -ёк, -екла́) *perf.*

elastic *n.* рези́нка; *adj.* эласти́чный, упру́гий. **elasticity** *n.* эласти́чность, упру́гость.

elate *v.t.* возбужда́ть *imp.*, возбуди́ть *perf.* **elation** *n.* восто́рг.

elbow *n.* ло́коть (-ктя; *pl.* -кти, -ктей) *m.*; *v.t.* толка́ть *imp.*, толкну́ть *perf.* ло́ктем, -тя́ми; *e.* (*one's way*) *through*, прота́лкиваться *imp.*, протолкну́ться *perf.* че́рез + *acc.*

elder[1] *n.* (*tree*) бузина́; *e.-berry*, я́года бузины́.

elder[2] *n.* (*person*) ста́рец (-рца); *pl.* ста́ршие *sb.*; *adj.* ста́рший. **elderly** *adj.* пожило́й. **eldest** *adj.* ста́рший.

elect *adj.* и́збранный; *v.t.* выбира́ть *imp.*, вы́брать (вы́беру, -решь) *perf.*; избира́ть *imp.*, избра́ть (изберу́, -рёшь; избра́л, -а́, -о) *perf.* **election** *n.* вы́боры *m.pl.*, избра́ние; *adj.* избира́тельный. **elective** *adj.* вы́борный. **elector** *n.* избира́тель *m.* **electoral** *adj.* избира́тельный, вы́борный. **electorate** *n.* избира́тели *m.pl.*

electric(al) *adj.* электри́ческий; *e. light*, электри́чество; *e. shock*, уда́р электри́ческим то́ком. **electrician** *n.* эле́ктрик, электромонтёр. **electricity** *n.* электри́чество. **electrify** *v.t.* (*convert to electricity*) электрифици́ровать *imp.*, *perf.*; (*charge with electricity*; *fig.*) электризова́ть *imp.*, на ~ *perf.* **electrode** *n.* электро́д. **electron** *n.* электро́н. **electronic** *adj.* электро́нный. **electronics** *n.* электро́ника.

electro- *in comb.* электро-. **electrocute** *v.t.* убива́ть *imp.*, уби́ть (убью́, -ьёшь) *perf.* электри́ческим то́ком; (*execute*) казни́ть *imp.*, *perf.* на электри́ческом сту́ле. **electrolysis** *n.* электро́лиз. **electrolyte** *n.* электроли́т. **electromagnetic** *adj.* электромагни́тный. **electrotype** *n.* (*print.*) гальва́но *neut.indecl.*

elegance *n.* элега́нтность, изя́щество. **elegant** *adj.* элега́нтный, изя́щный.

elegiac *adj.* элеги́ческий. **elegy** *n.* эле́гия.

element *n.* элеме́нт; (*4 e.s*) стихи́я; *pl.* (*rudiments*) нача́тки (-ков) *pl.*; *be in one's e.*, быть в свое́й стихи́и. **elemental** *adj.* стихи́йный. **elementary** *adj.* (*rudimentary*) элемента́рный; (*school etc.*) нача́льный.

elephant *n.* слон (-а́), ~ и́ха. **elephantine** *adj.* слоно́вый; (*clumsy*) тяжелове́сный, неуклю́жий.

elevate *v.t.* поднима́ть *imp.*, подня́ть (подниму́, -мешь; по́днял, -а́, -о) *perf.*; (*in rank*) возводи́ть (-ожу́, -о́дишь) *imp.*, возвести́ (-еду́, -едёшь; -ёл, -ела́) *perf.* **elevation** *n.* подня́тие; возведе́ние; (*height*) высота́; (*angle*) у́гол (угла́) возвыше́ния; (*drawing*) вертика́льная прое́кция. **elevator** *n.* подъёмник; (*for grain*) элева́тор.

eleven *adj.*, *n.* оди́ннадцать (-ти, -тью); (*time*) оди́ннадцать (часо́в); (*age*) оди́ннадцать лет; (*team*) кома́нда (из оди́ннадцати челове́к). **eleventh** *adj.*, *n.* оди́ннадцатый; (*date*) оди́ннадцатое (число́); *at the e. hour*, в после́днюю мину́ту.

elf *n.* эльф.

elicit *v.t.* извлека́ть *imp.*, извле́чь (-еку́, -ечёшь; -ёк, -екла́) *perf.* (from, из + *gen.*); (*evoke*) вызыва́ть *imp.*, вы́звать (вы́зову, -вешь) *perf.*

eligibility *n.* пра́во на избра́ние. **eligible** *adj.* могу́щий, име́ющий пра́во, быть и́збранным.
eliminate *v.t.* (*exclude*) устраня́ть *imp.*, устрани́ть *perf.*; (*remove*) уничтожа́ть *imp.*, уничто́жить *perf.* **elimination** *n.* устране́ние; уничтоже́ние.
élite *n.* эли́та; *adj.* эли́тный.
elk *n.* лось (*pl.* -си, -се́й) *m.*
ellipse *n.* э́ллипс. **ellipsis** *n.* э́ллипсис. **elliptic(al)** *adj.* эллипти́ческий.
elm *n.* вяз.
elocution *n.* ора́торское иску́сство.
elongate *v.t.* удлиня́ть *imp.*, удлини́ть *perf.*
elope *v.i.* сбега́ть *imp.*, сбежа́ть (-егу́, -ежи́шь) *perf.* **elopement** *n.* (та́йный) побе́г.
eloquence *n.* красноре́чие. **eloquent** *adj.* красноречи́вый, вырази́тельный.
else *adv.* (*besides*) ещё; (*instead*) друго́й; (*with neg.*) бо́льше; *nobody e.*, никто́ бо́льше; *or e.*, ина́че; а (не) то; и́ли же; *somebody e.*, кто́-нибудь друго́й; *something e.?* ещё что́-нибудь? **elsewhere** *adv.* (*place*) в друго́м ме́сте; (*direction*) в друго́е ме́сто.
elucidate *v.t.* по-, разъ-, ясня́ть *imp.*, по-, разъ-, ясни́ть *perf.* **elucidation** *n.* по-, разъ-, ясне́ние.
elude *v.t.* избега́ть *imp.* + *gen.*; уклоня́ться *imp.*, уклони́ться (-ню́сь, -ни́шься) *perf.* от + *gen.* **elusive** *adj.* неулови́мый.
emaciate *v.t.* истоща́ть *imp.*, истощи́ть *perf.* **emaciation** *n.* истоще́ние.
emanate *v.i.* исходи́ть (-ит) *imp.* (from, из, от, + *gen.*); (*light*) излуча́ться *imp.*, излучи́ться *perf.* **emanation** *n.* излуче́ние, эмана́ция.
emancipate *v.t.* освобожда́ть *imp.*, освободи́ть *perf.*; эмансипи́ровать *imp.*, *perf.* **emancipation** *n.* освобожде́ние, эмансипа́ция.
emasculate *v.t.* кастри́ровать *imp.*, *perf.*; (*fig.*) выхола́щивать *imp.*, вы́холостить *perf.* **emasculation** *n.* выхола́щивание.
embalm *v.t.* бальзами́ровать *imp.*, на~ *perf.* **embalmer** *n.* бальзамиро́вщик. **embalmment** *n.* бальзамиро́вка.
embankment *n.* (*river*) да́мба, на́бережная *sb.*; (*rly.*) на́сыпь.
embargo *n.* эмба́рго *neut.indecl.*; *v.t.* накла́дывать *imp.*, наложи́ть (-жу́, -жишь) *perf.* эмба́рго на + *acc.*
embark *v.t.* грузи́ть (-ужу́, -у́зишь) *imp.*, по~ *perf.* на кора́бль; *v.i.* сади́ться *imp.*, сесть (ся́ду, -дешь; сел) *perf.* на кора́бль; *e. upon*, пре́дпринимать *imp.*, предприня́ть (-иму́, -и́мешь; предпри́нял, -а́, -о) *perf.* **embarkation** *n.* поса́дка (на кора́бль).
embarrass *v.t.* смуща́ть *imp.*, смути́ть (-ущу́, -ути́шь) *perf.*; (*impede*) затрудня́ть *imp.*, затрудни́ть *perf.*; стесня́ть *imp.*, стесни́ть *perf.* **embarrassing** *adj.* неудо́бный. **embarrassment** *n.* смуще́ние, замеша́тельство.
embassy *n.* посо́льство.
embed *v.t.* вставля́ть *imp.*, вста́вить *perf.*; вде́лывать *imp.*, вде́лать *perf.*
embellish *v.t.* (*adorn*) украша́ть *imp.*, укра́сить *perf.*; (*story*) прикра́шивать *imp.*, прикра́сить *perf.* **embellishment** *n.* украше́ние; преувеличе́ние.
embers *n.* горя́чая зола́, тле́ющие угольки́ *m.pl.*
embezzle *v.t.* растра́чивать *imp.*, растра́тить *perf.* **embezzlement** *n.* растра́та. **embezzler** *n.* растра́тчик.
embitter *v.t.* ожесточа́ть *imp.*, ожесточи́ть *perf.*
emblem *n.* эмбле́ма, си́мвол.
embodiment *n.* воплоще́ние, олицетворе́ние. **embody** *v.t.* воплоща́ть *imp.*, воплоти́ть (-ощу́, -оти́шь) *perf.*; олицетворя́ть *imp.*, олицетвори́ть *perf.*
emboss *v.t.* чека́нить *imp.*, вы́~, от~ *perf.* **embossed** *adj.* чека́нный (-нен, -нна).
embrace *n.* объя́тие; *v.i.* обнима́ться *imp.*, обня́ться (обни́мемся, -етесь; -ня́лся́, -няла́сь) *perf.*; *v.t.* обнима́ть *imp.*, обня́ть (обниму́, -мешь; о́бнял, -а́, -о) *perf.*; (*accept*) принима́ть *imp.*, приня́ть (приму́, -мешь; при́нял, -а́, -о) *perf.*; (*comprise*) охва́тывать *imp.*, охвати́ть (-ачу́, -а́тишь) *perf.*
embrasure *n.* амбразу́ра.
embrocation *n.* жи́дкая мазь.

embroider *v.t.* (*cloth*) вышива́ть *imp.*, вы́шить (вы́шью, -ьешь) *perf.*; (*story*) прикра́шивать *imp.*, прикра́сить *perf.* **embroidery** *n.* вышива́ние, вы́шивка; преувеличе́ние; *e. frame*, пя́льцы (-лец) *pl.*

embryo *n.* заро́дыш, эмбрио́н. **embryonic** *adj.* заро́дышевый, эмбриона́льный; (*fig.*) элемента́рный.

emend *v.t.* исправля́ть *imp.*, испра́вить *perf.* **emendation** *n.* исправле́ние.

emerald *n.* изумру́д; *adj.* изумру́дный.

emerge *v.i.* появля́ться *imp.*, появи́ться (-влю́сь, -вишься) *perf.* **emergence** *n.* появле́ние. **emergency** *n.* непредви́денный слу́чай; *in case of e.*, в слу́чае кра́йней необходи́мости; *state of e.*, чрезвыча́йное положе́ние; *e. brake*, э́кстренный то́рмоз (*pl.* -а́); *e. exit*, запа́сный вы́ход; *e. landing*, вы́нужденная поса́дка; *e. powers*, чрезвыча́йные полномо́чия *neut.pl.* **emergent** *adj.* появля́ющийся; (*nation*) неда́вно получи́вший незави́симость.

emeritus *adj.*: *e. professor*, заслу́женный профе́ссор (*pl.* -а́) в отста́вке.

emery *n.* нажда́к (-а́); *e. paper*, нажда́чная бума́га.

emetic *adj.* рво́тный; *n.* рво́тное *sb.*

emigrant *n.* эмигра́нт, ~ка. **emigrate** *v.i.* эмигри́ровать *imp.*, *perf.* **emigration** *n.* эмигра́ция. **émigré** *n.* эмигра́нт; *adj.* эмигра́нтский.

eminence *n.* высота́, возвы́шенность; (*title*) высокопреосвяще́нство. **eminent** *adj.* выдаю́щийся. **eminently** *adv.* чрезвыча́йно.

emission *n.* испуска́ние, излуче́ние. **emit** *v.t.* испуска́ть *imp.*, испусти́ть (-ущу́, -у́стишь) *perf.*; (*light*) излуча́ть *imp.*, излучи́ть *perf.*; (*sound*) издава́ть (-даю́, -даёшь) *imp.*, изда́ть (-а́м, -а́шь, -а́ст, -ади́м; изда́л, -а́, -о) *perf.*

emotion *n.* (*state*) волне́ние; (*feeling*) эмо́ция, чу́вство. **emotional** *adj.* эмоциона́льный, волну́ющий.

emperor *n.* импера́тор.

emphasis *n.* ударе́ние; (*expressiveness*) вырази́тельность. **emphasize** *v.t.* подчёркивать *imp.*, подчеркну́ть *perf.*; выделя́ть *imp.*, вы́делить *perf.* **emphatic** *adj.* вырази́тельный, подчёркнутый; (*person*) насто́йчивый.

empire *n.* импе́рия.

empirical *adj.* эмпири́ческий, -чный. **empiricism** *n.* эмпири́зм. **empiricist** *n.* эмпи́рик.

employ *v.t.* (*thing*) по́льзоваться *imp.* + *instr.*; (*person*) нанима́ть *imp.*, наня́ть (найму́, -мёшь; на́нял, -а́, -о) *perf.*; (*busy*) занима́ть *imp.*, заня́ть (займу́, -мёшь; за́нял, -а́, -о) *perf.*; *e. oneself*, занима́ться *imp.*, заня́ться (займу́сь, -мёшься; заня́лся́, -ла́сь) *perf.* **employee** *n.* рабо́чий *sb.*, слу́жащий *sb.* **employer** *n.* работода́тель *m.* **employment** *n.* рабо́та, слу́жба; испо́льзование; *e. exchange*, би́ржа труда́; *full e.*, по́лная за́нятость.

empower *v.t.* уполномо́чивать *imp.*, уполномо́чить *perf.* (to, на + *acc.*).

empress *n.* императри́ца.

emptiness *n.* пустота́. **empty** *adj.* пусто́й (пуст, -а́, -о, пу́сты́); *e.-headed*, пустоголо́вый; *v.t.* опорожня́ть *imp.*, опоро́жни́ть *perf.*; (*solid*) высыпа́ть *imp.*, вы́сыпать (-плю, -плешь) *perf.*; (*liquid*) вылива́ть *imp.*, вы́лить (-лью, -льешь) *perf.*; *v.i.* пусте́ть *imp.*, о~ *perf.*; (*river*) впада́ть *imp.*, впасть (-адёт; -ал) *perf.*

emu *n.* э́му *m.indecl.*

emulate *v.t.* соревнова́ться *imp.* с + *instr.*; подража́ть *imp.* + *dat.* **emulation** *n.* соревнова́ние, подража́ние.

emulsion *n.* эму́льсия.

enable *v.t.* дава́ть (даю́, даёшь) *imp.*, дать (дам, дашь, даст, дади́м; дал, -а́, да́ло́, -и) *perf.* возмо́жность + *dat.* & *inf.*

enact *v.t.* (*ordain*) постановля́ть *imp.*, постанови́ть (-влю́, -вишь) *perf.*; (*law etc.*) вводи́ть (-ожу́, -о́дишь) *imp.*, ввести́ (введу́, -дёшь; ввёл, -а́) *perf.* в де́йствие; (*part, scene*) игра́ть *imp.*, сыгра́ть *perf.*

enamel *n.* эма́ль; *adj.* эма́левый; *v.t.* эмалирова́ть *imp.*, *perf.*

enamoured *predic.*: *be e. of*, быть влюблённым (-ён, -ена́) в + *acc.*; увлека́ться *imp.*, увле́чься (-еку́сь, -ечёшься; -ёкся, -екла́сь) *perf.* + *instr.*

encamp *v.i.* располага́ться *imp.*, расположи́ться (-жу́сь, -жи́шься) *perf.* ла́герем. **encampment** *n.* ла́герь (*pl.* -ря́) *m.*

enchant *v.t.* (*bewitch*) заколдо́вывать *imp.*, заколдова́ть *perf.*; (*charm*) очаро́вывать *imp.*, очарова́ть *perf.* **enchanting** *adj.* очарова́тельный, волше́бный. **enchantment** *n.* очарова́ние, волшебство́. **enchantress** *n.* волше́бница.

encircle *v.t.* окружа́ть *imp.*, окружи́ть *perf.* **encirclement** *n.* окруже́ние.

enclave *n.* анкла́в.

enclose *v.t.* огора́живать *imp.*, огороди́ть (-ожу́, -о́ди́шь) *perf.*; обноси́ть (-ошу́, -о́сишь) *imp.*, обнести́ (-есу́, -есёшь; -ёс, -есла́) *perf.*; (*in letter*) вкла́дывать *imp.*, вложи́ть (-жу́, -жишь) *perf.*; *please find enclosed*, прилага́ется (-а́ются) + *nom.* **enclosure** *n.* огоро́женное ме́сто (*pl.* -та́); в-, при-, ложе́ние.

encode *v.t.* шифрова́ть *imp.*, за~ *perf.*

encompass *v.t.* (*encircle*) окружа́ть *imp.*, окружи́ть *perf.*; (*contain*) заключа́ть *imp.*, заключи́ть *perf.*

encore *interj.* бис! *n.* вы́зов на бис; *give an e.*, биси́ровать *imp.*, *perf.*; *v.t.* вызыва́ть *imp.*, вы́звать (вы́зову, -вешь) *perf.* на бис.

encounter *n.* встре́ча; (*in combat*) столкнове́ние; *v.t.* встреча́ть *imp.*, встре́тить *perf.*; ста́лкиваться *imp.*, столкну́ться *perf.* с + *instr.*

encourage *v.t.* ободря́ть *imp.*, ободри́ть *perf.*; поощря́ть *imp.*, поощри́ть *perf.* **encouragement** *n.* ободре́ние, поощре́ние, подде́ржка. **encouraging** *adj.* ободри́тельный.

encroach *v.t.* вторга́ться *imp.*, вто́ргнуться (-г(нул)ся, -глась) *perf.* (on, в + *acc.*); (*fig.*) посяга́ть *imp.*, посягну́ть *perf.* (on, на + *acc.*). **encroachment** *n.* вторже́ние; посяга́тельство.

encumber *v.t.* загроможда́ть *imp.*, загромозди́ть *perf.*; обременя́ть *imp.*, обремени́ть *perf.* **encumbrance** *n.* обу́за, препя́тствие.

encyclopaedia *n.* энциклопе́дия. **encyclopaedic** *adj.* энциклопеди́ческий.

end *n.* коне́ц (-нца́), край (*loc.* -аю́; *pl.* -ая́); (*conclusion*) оконча́ние; (*death*) смерть; (*purpose*) цель; *e.-game*, (*chess*) э́ндшпиль *m.*; *e.-product*, гото́вое изде́лие; *an e. in itself*, самоце́ль; *in the e.*, в конце́ концо́в; *no e.*, без конца́; *no e. of*, ма́сса + *gen.*; *on e.*, (*upright*) стоймя́, ды́бом; (*continuously*) подря́д; *at a loose e.*, не у дел; *to the bitter e.*, до после́дней ка́пли кро́ви; *come to the e. of one's tether* дойти́ (дойду́, -дёшь; дошёл, -шла́) *perf.* до то́чки, *make ends meet*, своди́ть (-ожу́, -о́дишь) *imp.*, свести́ (сведу́, -дёшь; свёл, -а́) *perf.* концы́ с конца́ми; *v.t.* конча́тъ *imp.*, ко́нчить *perf.*; зака́нчивать *imp.*, зако́нчить *perf.*; прекраща́ть *imp.*, прекрати́ть (-ащу́, -ати́шь) *perf.*; *v.i.* конча́ться *imp.*, ко́нчиться *perf.*

endanger *v.t.* подверга́ть *imp.*, подве́ргнуть (-г) *perf.* опа́сности.

endear *v.t.* внуша́ть *imp.*, внуши́ть *perf.* любо́вь к + *dat.* (to, + *dat.*). **endearing** *adj.* привлека́тельный. **endearment** *n.* ла́ска (*gen.pl.* -ск).

endeavour *n.* попы́тка, стара́ние; *v.i.* стара́ться *imp.*, по~ *perf.*

endemic *adj.* эндеми́ческий.

ending *n.* оконча́ние (*also gram.*), заключе́ние. **endless** *adj.* бесконе́чный, беспреде́льный.

endorse *v.t.* (*document*) подпи́сывать *imp.*, подписа́ть (-ишу́, -и́шешь) *perf.*; (*bill*) индосси́ровать *imp.*, *perf.* (to, в по́льзу + *gen.*); (*approve*) одобря́ть *imp.*, одо́брить *perf.* **endorsement** *n.* по́дпись (на оборо́те + *gen.*); индоссаме́нт; одобре́ние.

endow *v.t.* обеспе́чивать *imp.*, обеспе́чить *perf.* постоя́нным дохо́дом; (*fig.*) одаря́ть *imp.*, одари́ть *perf.*; **endowment** *n.* вклад, поже́ртвование; (*talent*) дарова́ние.

endurance *n.* (*of person*) выно́сливость, терпе́ние; (*of object*) про́чность. **endure** *v.t.* выноси́ть (-ошу́, -о́сишь) *imp.*, вы́нести (-есу, -есешь; -ес) *perf.*; терпе́ть (-плю́, -пишь) *imp.*, по~ *perf.*; *v.i.* продолжа́ться *imp.*, продо́лжиться *perf.*

enema *n.* кли́зма.

enemy *n.* враг (-á), проти́вник, неприя́тель *m.*; *adj.* вра́жеский.

energetic *adj.* энерги́чный, си́льный (си́лён, -льна́, -льно, си́льны́). **energy** *n.* эне́ргия, си́ла; *pl.* уси́лия *neut.pl.*

enervate *v.t.* расслабля́ть *imp.*, рассла́бить *perf.*

enfeeble *v.t.* ослабля́ть *imp.*, осла́бить *perf.*

enfilade *n.* продо́льный ого́нь (огня́) *m.*; *v.t.* обстре́ливать *imp.*, обстреля́ть *perf.* продо́льным огнём.

enforce *v.t.* принужда́ть *imp.*, принуди́ть *perf.* к + *dat.* (upon, + *acc.*); (*law*) проводи́ть (-ожу́, -о́дишь) *imp.*, провести́ (-еду́, -едёшь; -ёл, -ела́) *perf.* в жизнь. **enforcement** *n.* принужде́ние; (*law etc.*) осуществле́ние, наблюде́ние за + *instr.*, за соблюде́нием + *gen.*

enfranchise *v.t.* предоставля́ть *imp.*, предоста́вить *perf.* избира́тельные права́ (*neut.pl.*) + *dat.*; (*set free*) освобожда́ть *imp.*, освободи́ть *perf.*

engage *v.t.* (*hire*) нанима́ть *imp.*, наня́ть (найму́, -мёшь; на́нял, -а́, -о) *perf.*; (*tech.*) зацепля́ть *imp.*, зацепи́ть (-ит) *perf.*; *e. the enemy in battle*, завя́зывать *imp.*, завяза́ть (-яжу́, -я́жешь) *perf.* бой с проти́вником. **engaged** *adj.* (*occupied*) за́нятый (-т, -та́, -то); *be e. in*, занима́ться *imp.*, заня́ться (займу́сь, -мёшься; заня́лся́, -ла́сь) *perf.* + *instr.*; *become e.*, обруча́ться *imp.*, обручи́ться *perf.* (to, с + *instr.*). **engagement** *n.* (*appointment*) свида́ние; (*obligation*) обяза́тельство; (*betrothal*) обруче́ние; (*battle*) бой (*loc.* бою́; *pl.* бои́); *e. ring*, обруча́льное кольцо́ (*pl.* -льца, -ле́ц, -льцам). **engaging** *adj.* привлека́тельный.

engender *v.t.* порожда́ть *imp.*, породи́ть *perf.*

engine *n.* мото́р, маши́на, дви́гатель *m.*; (*rly.*) парово́з; *e.-driver*, (*rly.*) машини́ст; *e.-room*, маши́нное отделе́ние. **engineer** *n.* инжене́р; *pl.* (*mil.*) инжене́рные войска́ (-к) *pl.*; *v.t.* (*construct*) сооружа́ть *imp.*, сооруди́ть *perf.*; (*arrange*) устра́ивать *imp.*, устро́ить *perf.* **engineering** *n.* инжене́рное де́ло, те́хника, машинострое́ние; *adj.* инжене́рный, техни́ческий.

English *adj.* англи́йский; *n.*: *the E.*, *pl.* англича́не (-н) *pl.* **Englishman, -woman** *n.* англича́нин (*pl.* -а́не, -а́н), -а́нка.

engrave *v.t.* гравирова́ть *imp.*, вы~ *perf.*; (*fig.*) запечатлева́ть *imp.*, запечатле́ть *perf.* **engraver** *n.* гравёр. **engraving** *n.* (*picture*) гравю́ра; (*action*) гравиро́вка; *adj.* гравирова́льный, гравёрный.

engross *v.t.* завладева́ть *imp.*, завладе́ть *perf.* + *instr.*; поглоща́ть *imp.*, поглоти́ть (-ощу́, -о́тишь) *perf.*; *be engrossed in*, быть поглощённым + *instr.* **engrossing** *adj.* увлека́тельный.

engulf *v.t.* заса́сывать *imp.*, засоса́ть (-су́, -сёшь) *perf.*

enhance *v.t.* увели́чивать *imp.*, увели́чить *perf.*

enigma *n.* зага́дка. **enigmatic** *adj.* зага́дочный.

enjoin *v.t.* предпи́сывать *imp.*, предписа́ть (-ишу́, -и́шешь) *perf.* + *dat.*; прика́зывать *imp.*, приказа́ть (-ажу́, -а́жешь) *perf.* + *dat.*; (*leg.*) запреща́ть *imp.*, запрети́ть (-ещу́, -ети́шь) *perf.* + *dat.* (from, + *inf.*).

enjoy *v.t.* получа́ть *imp.*, получи́ть (-чу́, -чишь) *perf.* удово́льствие от + *gen.*; наслажда́ться *imp.*, наслади́ться *perf.* + *instr.*; (*have use of*) по́льзоваться *imp.* + *instr.*; облада́ть *imp.* + *instr.* **enjoyable** *adj.* прия́тный. **enjoyment** *n.* удово́льствие, наслажде́ние; облада́ние (of, + *instr.*).

enlarge *v.t.* & *i.* увели́чивать(ся) *imp.*, увели́чить(ся) *perf.*; (*widen*) расширя́ть(ся) *imp.*, расши́рить(ся) *perf.*; *e. upon*, распространя́ться *imp.*, распространи́ться *perf.* о + *prep.* **enlargement** *n.* увеличе́ние; расшире́ние. **enlarger** *n.* (*phot.*) увеличи́тель *m.*

enlighten *v.t.* просвеща́ть *imp.*, просвети́ть (-ещу́, -ети́шь) *perf.*; (*inform*) осведомля́ть *imp.*, осве́домить *perf.* **enlightenment** *n.* просвеще́ние.

enlist *v.i.* поступа́ть *imp.*, поступи́ть (-плю́, -пишь) *perf.* на вое́нную слу́жбу; *v.t.* (*mil.*) вербова́ть *imp.*, за~ *perf.*; (*support etc.*) заруча́ться *imp.*, заручи́ться *perf.* + *instr.*

enliven *v.t.* оживля́ть *imp.*, оживи́ть *perf.*
enmesh *v.t.* опу́тывать *imp.*, опу́тать *perf.*
enmity *n.* вражда́, неприя́знь.
ennoble *v.t.* облагора́живать *imp.*, облагоро́дить *perf.*
ennui *n.* тоска́.
enormity *n.* чудо́вищность. **enormous** *adj.* грома́дный, огро́мный. **enormously** *adv.* кра́йне, чрезвыча́йно.
enough *adj.* доста́точный; *adv.* доста́точно, дово́льно; *e. money*, доста́точно де́нег (*gen.*); *be e.*, хвата́ть *imp.*, хвати́ть (-ит) *perf.impers.* + *gen.*; *I've had e. of him*, он мне надое́л.
enquire, enquiry *see* **inquire, inquiry.**
enrage *v.t.* беси́ть (бешу́, бе́сишь) *imp.*, вз~ *perf.*
enrapture *v.t.* восхища́ть *imp.*, восхити́ть (-ищу́, -ити́шь) *perf.*
enrich *v.t.* обогаща́ть *imp.*, обогати́ть (-ащу́, -ати́шь) *perf.*
enrol *v.t.* & *i.* запи́сывать(ся) *imp.*, записа́ть(ся) (-ишу́(сь), -и́шешь(ся)) *perf.*; *v.t.* (*mil.*) вербова́ть *imp.*, за~ *perf.*; *v.i.* (*mil.*) поступа́ть *imp.*, поступи́ть (-плю́, -пишь) *perf.* на вое́нную слу́жбу. **enrolment** *n.* регистра́ция, за́пись.
en route *adv.* по пути́ (to, for, в + *acc.*).
ensconce *v.t.*: *e. oneself*, заса́живаться *imp.*, засе́сть (募ся́ду, -дешь; засе́л) *perf.* (with, за + *acc.*).
ensemble *n.* (*mus.*) анса́мбль *m.*
enshrine *v.t.* (*relic*) класть (кладу́, -дёшь; клал) *imp.*, положи́ть (-жу́, -жишь) *perf.* в ра́ку; (*fig.*) храни́ть *imp.*
ensign *n.* (*flag*) флаг; (*rank*) пра́порщик.
enslave *v.t.* порабоща́ть *imp.*, поработи́ть (-ощу́, -оти́шь) *perf.* **enslavement** *n.* порабоще́ние.
ensnare *v.t.* опу́тывать *imp.*, опу́тать *perf.*
ensue *v.i.* сле́довать *imp.*; вытека́ть *imp.* **ensuing** *adj.* после́дующий.
ensure *v.t.* обеспе́чивать *imp.*, обеспе́чить *perf.*
entail *n.* майора́т(ное насле́дование); *v.t.* (*leg.*) определя́ть *imp.*, определи́ть *perf.* насле́дование + *gen.*; (*necessitate*) влечь (влечёт; влёк, -ла́) *imp.* за собо́й.
entangle *v.t.* запу́тывать *imp.*, запу́тать *perf.*
enter *v.t.* & *i.* входи́ть (-ожу́, -о́дишь) *imp.*, войти́ (войду́, -дёшь; вошёл, -шла́) *perf.* в + *acc.*; (*by transport*) въезжа́ть *imp.*, въе́хать (въе́ду, -дешь) *perf.* в + *acc.*; *v.t.* (*join*) поступа́ть *imp.*, поступи́ть (-плю́, -пишь) *perf.* в, на, + *acc.*; (*competition*) вступа́ть *imp.*, вступи́ть (-плю́, -пишь) *perf.* в + *acc.*; (*in list*) вноси́ть (-ошу́, -о́сишь) *imp.*, внести́ (внесу́, -сёшь; внёс, -ла́) *perf.* в + *acc.*
enteric *adj.* кише́чный. **enteritis** *n.* энтери́т.
enterprise *n.* (*undertaking*) предприя́тие; (*initiative*) предприи́мчивость; *free, private, e.*, ча́стное предпринима́тельство. **enterprising** *adj.* предприи́мчивый.
entertain *v.t.* (*amuse*) развлека́ть *imp.*, развле́чь (-еку́, -ечёшь; -ёк, -екла́) *perf.*; (*guests*) принима́ть *imp.*, приня́ть (приму́, -мешь; при́нял, -а́, -о) *perf.*; угоща́ть *imp.*, угости́ть *perf.* (to, + *instr.*); (*hopes*) пита́ть *imp.* **entertaining** *adj.* занима́тельный, развлека́тельный. **entertainment** *n.* развлече́ние; приём; угоще́ние; (*show*) дивертисме́нт.
enthral *v.t.* порабоща́ть *imp.*, поработи́ть (-ощу́, -оти́шь) *perf.*
enthrone *v.t.* возводи́ть (-ожу́, -о́дишь) *imp.*, возвести́ (-еду́, -едёшь; -ёл, -ела́) *perf.* на престо́л. **enthronement** *n.* возведе́ние на престо́л.
enthusiasm *n.* энтузиа́зм, воодушевле́ние. **enthusiast** *n.* энтузиа́ст, ~ка. **enthusiastic** *adj.* восто́рженный (-ен, -енна), воодушевлённый (-ён, -ённа).
entice *v.t.* зама́нивать *imp.*, замани́ть (-ню́, -нишь) *perf.*; соблазня́ть *imp.*, соблазни́ть *perf.* **enticement** *n.* собла́зн, прима́нка, зама́нивание. **enticing** *adj.* соблазни́тельный, зама́нчивый.
entire *adj.* по́лный, це́лый, весь (вся, всё; все). **entirely** *adv.* вполне́, соверше́нно; (*solely*) исключи́тельно. **en-**

tirety *n.* це́льность, полнота́; *in its e.*, по́лностью, в це́лом.

entitle *v.t.* (*book*) озагла́вливать *imp.*, озагла́вить *perf.*; (*give right to*) дава́ть (даю́, даёшь) *imp.*, дать (дам, дашь, даст, дади́м; дал, -а́, да́ло́, -и) *perf.* пра́во + *dat.* (to, на + *acc.*); *be entitled to*, име́ть *imp.* пра́во на + *acc.*

entity *n.* существо́; (*existence*) бытие́ (*prep.* -ии́, *instr.* -ие́м).

entomb *v.t.* погреба́ть *imp.*, погрести́ (-ебу́, -ебёшь; -ёб, -ебла́) *perf.* **entombment** *n.* погребе́ние.

entomological *adj.* энтомологи́ческий. **entomologist** *n.* энтомо́лог. **entomology** *n.* энтомоло́гия.

entrails *n.* вну́тренности (-тей) *pl.*, кишки́ (-шо́к) *pl.*; (*fig.*) не́дра (-р) *pl.*

entrance[1] *v.t.* приводи́ть (-ожу́, -о́дишь) *imp.*, привести́ (-еду́, -едёшь; -ёл, -ела́) *perf.* в состоя́ние тра́нса; (*charm*) очаро́вывать *imp.*, очарова́ть *perf.* **entrancing** *adj.* очарова́тельный.

entrance[2] *n.* вход, въезд; (*theat.*) вы́ход; (*into office etc.*) вступле́ние, поступле́ние; *e. examinations*, вступи́тельные экза́мены *m.pl.*; *e. hall*, вестибю́ль *m.*; *back e.*, чёрный вход; *front e.*, пара́дный вход. **entrant** *n.* (*sport*) уча́стник (for, + *gen.*).

entrap *v.t.* пойма́ть *perf.* в лову́шку; (*fig.*) запу́тывать *imp.*, запу́тать *perf.*

entreat *v.t.* умоля́ть *imp.*, умоли́ть *perf.* **entreaty** *n.* мольба́, про́сьба.

entrench *v.t.* ока́пывать *imp.*, окопа́ть *perf.*; *be, become, entrenched*, (*fig.*) укореня́ться *imp.*, укорени́ться *perf.*

entropy *n.* энтропи́я.

entrust *v.t.* (*secret*) вверя́ть *imp.*, вве́рить *perf.* (to, + *dat.*); (*object; person*) поруча́ть *imp.*, поручи́ть (-чу́, -чишь) *perf.* (to, + *dat.*).

entry *n.* вход, въезд; вступле́ние; (*theat.*) вы́ход; (*in book etc.*) за́пись, статья́; (*sport*) записа́вшийся.

entwine *v.t.* (*interweave*) сплета́ть *imp.*, сплести́ (-ету́, -етёшь; -ёл, -ела́) *perf.*; (*wreathe*) обвива́ть *imp.*, обви́ть (обовью́, -ьёшь; обви́л, -а́, -о) *perf.*

enumerate *v.t.* перечисля́ть *imp.*, перечи́слить *perf.* **enumeration** *n.* перечисле́ние, пе́речень (-чня) *m.*

enunciate *v.t.* (*proclaim*) объявля́ть *imp.*, объяви́ть (-влю́, -вишь) *perf.*; (*express*) излага́ть *imp.*, изложи́ть (-жу́, -жишь) *perf.*; (*pronounce*) произноси́ть (-ошу́, -о́сишь) *imp.*, произнести́ (-есу́, -есёшь; -ёс, -есла́) *perf.* **enunciation** *n.* объявле́ние; изложе́ние; произноше́ние.

envelop *v.t.* оку́тывать *imp.*, оку́тать *perf.*; завёртывать *imp.*, заверну́ть *perf.* **envelope** *n.* (*letter*) конве́рт; (*other senses*) обёртка, оболо́чка.

envenom *v.t.* отравля́ть *imp.*, отрави́ть (-влю́, -вишь) *perf.*; (*embitter*) озлобля́ть *imp.*, озло́бить *perf.*

enviable *adj.* зави́дный. **envious** *adj.* зави́стливый.

environment *n.* окружа́ющая обстано́вка, среда́ (*pl.* -ды). **environs** *n.* окре́стности *f.pl.*

envisage *v.t.* предусма́тривать *imp.*, предусмотре́ть (-рю́, -ришь) *perf.*

envoy *n.* посла́нник, аге́нт.

envy *n.* за́висть; *v.t.* зави́довать *imp.*, по~ *perf.* + *dat.*

enzyme *n.* энзи́м.

epaulette *n.* эполе́т(а).

ephemeral *adj.* эфеме́рный, недолгове́чный.

epic *n.* эпи́ческая поэ́ма, эпопе́я; *adj.* эпи́ческий.

epicentre *n.* эпице́нтр.

epicure *n.* эпикуре́ец (-е́йца). **epicurean** *adj.* эпикуре́йский.

epidemic *n.* эпиде́мия; *adj.* эпидеми́ческий.

epigram *n.* эпигра́мма. **epigrammatic(al)** *adj.* эпиграммати́ческий.

epigraph *n.* эпигра́ф.

epilepsy *n.* эпиле́псия. **epileptic** *n.* эпиле́птик; *adj.* эпилепти́ческий.

epilogue *n.* эпило́г.

Epiphany *n.* (*eccl.*) Богоявле́ние.

episcopal *adj.* епи́скопский. **episcopate** *n.* епи́скопство.

episode *n.* эпизо́д. **episodic** *adj.* эпизоди́ческий.

epistle *n.* посла́ние. **epistolary** *adj.* эпистоля́рный.

epitaph *n.* эпита́фия, надгро́бная на́дпись.

epithet *n.* эпи́тет.

epitome *n.* (*summary*) конспéкт; (*embodiment*) воплощéние. **epitomize** *v.t.* конспектúровать *imp.*, за ~, про ~ *perf.*; воплощáть *imp.*, воплотúть (-ощý, -отúшь) *perf.*

epoch *n.* эпóха, век (*pl.* -á), перúод.

equable *adj.* равномéрный, рóвный (-вен, -внá, -вно).

equal *adj.* рáвный (-вен, -внá), одинáковый; (*capable of*) спосóбный (to, на + *acc.*, + *inf.*); *n.* рáвный *sb.*, ровня́ *m.* & *f.*; *v.t.* равня́ться *imp.* + *dat.* **equality** *n.* рáвенство, равнопрáвие. **equalization** *n.* уравнéние. **equalize** *v.t.* урáвнивать *imp.*, уравня́ть *perf.*; *v.i.* (*sport*) равня́ть *imp.*, с ~ *perf.* счёт. **equally** *adv.* равнó, рáвным óбразом.

equanimity *n.* хладнокрóвие, невозмутúмость.

equate *v.t.* приравнивать *imp.*, приравня́ть *perf.* (with, к + *dat.*).

equation *n.* (*math.*) уравнéние.

equator *n.* эквáтор. **equatorial** *adj.* экваториáльный.

equestrian *n.* всáдник; *adj.* кóнный. **equestrienne** *n.* всáдница.

equidistant *adj.* равностоя́щий. **equilateral** *adj.* равносторóнний (-нен, -ння). **equilibrium** *n.* равновéсие.

equine *adj.* лошадúный.

equinox *n.* равнодéнствие.

equip *v.t.* оборýдовать *imp.*, *perf.*; снаряжáть *imp.*, снарядúть *perf.* **equipment** *n.* оборýдование, снаряжéние.

equitable *adj.* справедлúвый, беспристрáстный. **equity** *n.* справедлúвость, беспристрáстность; (*econ.*) мáржа; *pl.* (*econ.*) обыкновéнные áкции *f.pl.*

equivalence *n.* эквивалéнтность, равноцéнность. **equivalent** *adj.* эквивалéнтный, равноцéнный (-нен, -нна), равносúльный; *n.* эквивалéнт.

equivocal *adj.* (*ambiguous*) двусмы́сленный (-ен, -енна); (*suspicious*) сомнúтельный. **equivocate** *v.i.* говорúть *imp.* двусмы́сленно.

era *n.* э́ра, эпóха.

eradicate *v.t.* искореня́ть *imp.*, искоренúть *perf.* **eradication** *n.* искоренéние.

erase *v.t.* стирáть *imp.*, стерéть (сотрý, -рёшь; стёр) *perf.*; подчищáть *imp.*, подчúстить *perf.* **eraser** *n.* лáстик. **erasure** *n.* стирáние, подчúстка.

erect *adj.* прямóй (прям, -á, -о, пря́мы́); *v.t.* (*building*) сооружáть *imp.*, соорудúть *perf.*; воздвигáть *imp.*, воздвúгнуть (-г) *perf.*; (*straighten*) выпрямля́ть *imp.*, вы́прямить *perf.* **erection** *n.*острóйка, сооружéние; выпрямлéние.

erg *n.* эрг (*gen.pl.* эрг & -ов).

ergot *n.* спорынья́.

ermine *n.* горностáй.

erode *v.t.* разъедáть *imp.*, разъéсть (-éст, -едя́т; -éл) *perf.*; (*geol.*) эродúровать *imp.*, *perf.* **erosion** *n.* разъедáние; эрóзия.

erotic *adj.* эротúческий, любóвный.

err *v.i.* ошибáться *imp.*, ошибúться (-бýсь, -бёшься; -бся) *perf.*; заблуждáться *imp.*; (*sin*) грешúть *imp.*, со ~ *perf.*

errand *n.* поручéние; *run errands*, быть на посы́лках (for, у + *gen.*).

errant *adj.* (*knight*) стрáнствующий; (*thoughts*) блуждáющий.

erratic *adj.* непостоя́нный (-нен, -нна), измéнчивый.

erratum *n.* (*print.*) опечáтка; (*in writing*) опúска. **erroneous** *adj.* ошúбочный, лóжный. **error** *n.* ошúбка, заблуждéние.

erudite *adj.* учёный. **erudition** *n.* эрудúция, учёность.

erupt *v.i.* прорывáться *imp.*, прорвáться (-вýсь, -вёшься; -вáлся, -валáсь, -вáлóсь) *perf.*; (*volcano*) извергáться *imp.*, извéргнуться (-гся) *perf.* **eruption** *n.* (*volcano*) извержéние; (*mirth*) взрыв; (*med.*) сыпь.

erysipelas *n.* рóжа.

escalator *n.* эскалáтор.

escapade *n.* вы́ходка, продéлка. **escape** *n.* (*from prison*) бéгство, побéг; (*from danger*) спасéние; (*from reality*) ухóд; (*of gas*) утéчка; *have a narrow e.*, быть на волосóк (from, от + *gen.*); *v.i.* (*flee*) бежáть (бегý, бежúшь) *imp.*, *perf.*; убегáть *imp.*, убежáть (-егý, -ежúшь) *perf.*; (*save oneself*) спасáться *imp.*, спастúсь (-сýсь, -сёшься; -сся, -слáсь) *perf.*; (*leak*) утекáть *imp.*, утéчь (-ечёт; -ёк, -еклá) *perf.*; *v.t.*

избега́ть *imp.*, избежа́ть (-егу́, -ежи́шь) *perf.* + *gen.*; (*groan*) вырыва́ться *imp.*, вы́рваться (-вется) *perf.* из, у, + *gen.* **escapee** *n.* бегле́ц (-а́).

escort *n.* конво́й, эско́рт; *v.t.* сопровожда́ть *imp.*, сопроводи́ть *perf.*; (*mil.*) конвои́ровать *imp.*, от~ *perf.*; эскорти́ровать *imp.*, *perf.*

escutcheon *n.* щит (-а́) герба́.

Eskimo *n.* эскимо́с, ~ка; *adj.* эскимо́сский.

especial *adj.* осо́бенный, осо́бый; (*particular*) ча́стный. **especially** *adv.* осо́бенно; в ча́стности.

espionage *n.* шпиона́ж.

espousal *n.* (*fig.*) подде́ржка. **espouse** *v.t.* (*fig.*) подде́рживать *imp.*, поддержа́ть (-жу́, -жишь) *perf.*

espy *v.t.* уви́деть (-и́жу, -и́дишь) *perf.*; (*detect*) замеча́ть *imp.*, заме́тить *perf.*

essay *n.* о́черк, эссе́ *neut.indecl.*; (*attempt*) попы́тка, про́ба; *v.t.* пыта́ться *imp.*, по~ *perf.* + *inf.* **essayist** *n.* очерки́ст, ~ка; эссеи́ст.

essence *n.* су́щность, существо́; (*extract*) эссе́нция. **essential** *adj.* суще́ственный, необходи́мый, неотъе́млемый; *n.* основно́е *sb.*; *pl.* предме́ты *m.pl.* пе́рвой необходи́мости. **essentially** *adv.* по существу́, в основно́м.

establish *v.t.* (*set up*) учрежда́ть *imp.*, учреди́ть *perf.*; (*fact etc.*) устана́вливать *imp.*, установи́ть (-влю́, -вишь) *perf.*; (*appoint*) устра́ивать *imp.*, устро́ить *perf.*; (*secure*) упро́чивать *imp.*, упро́чить *perf.* **establishment** *n.* (*action*) учрежде́ние, установле́ние; (*institution*) учрежде́ние, заведе́ние; (*staff*) штат.

estate *n.* (*property*) поме́стье (*gen.pl.* -тий), име́ние; (*class*) сосло́вие; *real e.*, недви́жимость; *e. agent*, аге́нт по прода́же недви́жимости; *e. duty*, нало́г на насле́дство.

esteem *n.* уваже́ние, почте́ние; *v.t.* уважа́ть *imp.*; почита́ть *imp.* **estimable** *adj.* досто́йный (-о́ин, -о́йна) уваже́ния. **estimate** *n.* (*of quality*) оце́нка; (*of cost*) сме́та; *v.t.* оце́нивать *imp.*, оцени́ть (-ню́, -нишь) *perf.* **estimated** *adj.* предполага́емый, приме́рный. **estimation** *n.* оце́нка, мне́ние.

estrange *v.t.* отдаля́ть *imp.*, отдали́ть *perf.* **estrangement** *n.* отчужде́ние, отчуждённость.

estuary *n.* у́стье (*gen.pl.* -в).

etc. *abbr.* и т.д., и т.п. **etcetera** и так да́лее, и тому́ подо́бное.

etch *v.t.* трави́ть (-влю́, -вишь) *imp.*, вы́~ *perf.* **etching** *n.* (*action*) травле́ние; (*object*) офо́рт.

eternal *adj.* ве́чный. **eternity** *n.* ве́чность.

ether *n.* эфи́р. **ethereal** *adj.* эфи́рный.

ethical *adj.* эти́ческий, эти́чный. **ethics** *n.* э́тика.

ethnic *adj.* этни́ческий. **ethnography** *n.* этногра́фия.

etiquette *n.* этике́т.

étude *n.* этю́д.

etymological *adj.* этимологи́ческий. **etymologist** *n.* этимо́лог. **etymology** *n.* этимоло́гия.

eucalyptus *n.* эвкали́пт.

Eucharist *n.* евхари́стия, прича́стие.

eulogise *v.t.* превозноси́ть (-ошу́, -о́сишь) *imp.*, превознести́ (-есу́, -есёшь; -ёс, -есла́) *perf.* **eulogy** *n.* похвала́.

eunuch *n.* е́внух.

euphemism *n.* эвфеми́зм. **euphemistic** *adj.* эвфемисти́ческий.

euphonious *adj.* благозву́чный. **euphony** *n.* благозву́чие.

Eurasian *adj.* еврази́йский.

European *n.* европе́ец (-е́йца); *adj.* европе́йский.

evacuate *v.t.* (*person*) эвакуи́ровать *imp.*, *perf.*; (*med.*) опорожня́ть *imp.*, опоро́жни́ть *perf.* **evacuation** *n.* эваку́ация; опорожне́ние. **evacuee** *n.* эвакуи́рованный *sb.*

evade *v.t.* уклоня́ться *imp.*, уклони́ться (-ню́сь, -нишься) *perf.* от + *gen.*; (*law*) обходи́ть (-ожу́, -о́дишь) *imp.*, обойти́ (обойду́, -дёшь; обошёл, -шла́) *perf.*

evaluate *v.t.* оце́нивать *imp.*, оцени́ть (-ню́, -нишь) *perf.* **evaluation** *n.* оце́нка.

evangelical *adj.* ева́нгельский. **evangelist** *n.* евангели́ст.

evaporate *v.t.* & *i.* испаря́ть(ся) *imp.*, испари́ть(ся) *perf.*; *v.i.* (*lose moisture*) улету́чиваться *imp.*, улету́читься *perf.* **evaporation** *n.* испаре́ние.

evasion *n.* уклоне́ние (of, от + *gen.*); (*of law*) обхо́д; (*subterfuge*) увёртка. **evasive** *adj.* укло́нчивый.

eve *n.* кану́н; *on the e.*, накану́не.

even *adj.* ро́вный (-вен, -вна́, -вно); (*uniform*) равноме́рный; (*balanced*) уравнове́шенный; (*number*) чётный; *get e.*, расквита́ться *perf.* (with, с + *instr.*); *adv.* да́же; (*just*) как раз; (*with comp.*) ещё; *e. if*, да́же е́сли, хотя́ бы и; *e. though*, хотя́ бы; *e. so*, всё-таки; *not e.*, да́же не; *v.t.* выра́внивать *imp.*, вы́ровнять *perf.*

evening *n.* ве́чер (*pl.* -а́); *adj.* вече́рний.

evenly *adv.* по́ровну, ро́вно, одина́ково. **evenness** *n.* ро́вность; равноме́рность.

evensong *n.* вече́рня.

event *n.* собы́тие, происше́ствие, слу́чай; *in the e. of*, в слу́чае + *gen.*; *at all events*, во вся́ком слу́чае. **eventual** *adj.* (*possible*) возмо́жный; (*final*) коне́чный. **eventuality** *n.* возмо́жность. **eventually** *adv.* в конце́ концо́в.

ever *adv.* (*at any time*) когда́-либо, когда́-нибудь; (*always*) всегда́; (*emph.*) же; *e. since*, с тех пор (как); *e. so*, о́чень; *for e.*, навсегда́; *hardly e.*, почти́ никогда́. **evergreen** *adj.* вечнозелёный; *n.* вечнозелёное расте́ние. **everlasting** *adj.* ве́чный, постоя́нный. **evermore** *adv.*: *for e.*, навсегда́, наве́ки.

every *adj.* ка́ждый, вся́кий, все (*pl.*); *e. now and then*, вре́мя от вре́мени; *e. other*, ка́ждый второ́й; *e. other day*, че́рез день. **everybody, everyone** *pron.* ка́ждый, все (*pl.*). **everyday** *adj.* (*daily*) ежедне́вный; (*commonplace*) повседне́вный. **everything** *pron.* всё. **everywhere** *adv.* всю́ду, везде́.

evict *v.t.* выселя́ть *imp.*, вы́селить *perf.* **eviction** *n.* выселе́ние.

evidence *n.* свиде́тельство, доказа́тельство, ули́ка; *in e.*, (*predic.*) заме́тен (-тна, -тно); *give e.*, свиде́тельствовать *imp.* (о + *prep.*; + *acc.*; + что). **evident** *adj.* очеви́дный, я́сный (я́сен, ясна́, я́сно, ясны́).

evil *n.* зло (*gen.pl.* зол), поро́к; *adj.* злой (зол, зла), дурно́й (ду́рён, -рна́, -рно, ду́рны́); *e.-doer*, злоде́й.

evince *v.t.* проявля́ть *imp.*, прояви́ть (-влю́, -вишь) *perf.*

evoke *v.t.* вызыва́ть *imp.*, вы́звать (вы́зову, -вешь) *perf.*

evolution *n.* разви́тие, эволю́ция. **evolutionary** *adj.* эволюцио́нный. **evolve** *v.t.* & *i.* развива́ть(ся) *imp.*, разви́ть(ся) (разовью́(сь), -ьёшь(ся); разви́л(ся), -ила́(сь), -и́ло/-и́ло́сь) *perf.*; *v.i.* эволюциони́ровать *imp.*, *perf.*

ewe *n.* овца́ (*pl.* о́вцы, ове́ц, о́вцам).

ewer *n.* кувши́н.

ex- *in comb.* бы́вший.

exacerbate *v.t.* обостря́ть *imp.*, обостри́ть *perf.* **exacerbation** *n.* обостре́ние.

exact *adj.* то́чный (-чен, -чна́, -чно), аккура́тный; *v.t.* взы́скивать *imp.*, взыска́ть (взыщу́, -щешь) *perf.* (from, of, с + *gen.*). **exacting** *adj.* (*person*) взыска́тельный, требова́тельный; (*circumstance*) суро́вый. **exactitude, exactness** *n.* то́чность. **exactly** *adv.* то́чно, как раз, и́менно.

exaggerate *v.t.* преувели́чивать *imp.*, преувели́чить *perf.* **exaggeration** *n.* преувеличе́ние.

exalt *v.t.* возвыша́ть *imp.*, возвы́сить *perf.*; (*extol*) превозноси́ть (-ошу́, -о́сишь) *imp.*, превознести́ (-есу́, -есёшь; -ёс, -есла́) *perf.* **exaltation** *n.* возвыше́ние; (*elation*) восто́рг.

examination *n.* осмо́тр, иссле́дование; (*of knowledge*) экза́мен; (*leg.*) допро́с. **examine** *v.t.* осма́тривать *imp.*, осмотре́ть (-рю́, -ришь) *perf.*; иссле́довать *imp.*, *perf.*; экзаменова́ть *imp.*, про~ *perf.*; допра́шивать *imp.*, допроси́ть (-ошу́, -о́сишь) *perf.* **examiner** *n.* экзамена́тор.

example *n.* приме́р, образе́ц (-зца́); *for e.*, наприме́р.

exasperate *v.t.* раздража́ть *imp.*, раздражи́ть *perf.* **exasperation** *n.* раздраже́ние.

excavate *v.t.* выка́пывать *imp.*, вы́копать *perf.*; (*archaeol.*) раска́пывать *imp.*, раскопа́ть *perf.* **excavation** *n.* выка́пывание; раско́пки *f.pl.* **excavator** *n.* экскава́тор.

exceed *v.t.* превыша́ть *imp.*, превы́сить *perf.* **exceedingly** *adv.* чрезвыча́йно.

excel *v.t.* превосходи́ть (-ожу́, -о́дишь) *imp.*, превзойти́ (-о йду́, -ойдёшь; -ошёл, -ошла́) *perf.* (in, в+*prep.*, + *instr.*); *v.i.* отлича́ться *imp.* отличи́ться *perf.* (at, in, в+*prep.*). **excellence** *n.* превосхо́дство. **excellency** *n.* превосходи́тельство. **excellent** *adj.* превосхо́дный, отли́чный.

except *v.t.* исключа́ть *imp.*, исключи́ть *perf.*; *prep.* исключа́я + *acc.*, за исключе́нием + *gen.*, кро́ме + *gen.* **exception** *n.* исключе́ние; *take e. to*, возража́ть *imp.*, возрази́ть *perf.* про́тив + *gen.* **exceptional** *adj.* исключи́тельный.

excerpt *n.* отры́вок (-вка), вы́держка.

excess *n.* избы́ток (-тка), изли́шек (-шка), изли́шество; *e. fare* допла́та. **excessive** *adj.* чрезме́рный, изли́шний (-шен, -шня).

exchange *n.* обме́н (of, +*instr.*); (*of currency*) разме́н; (*rate of e.*) курс; (*building*) би́ржа; (*telephone*) центра́льная телефо́нная ста́нция; *v.t.* обме́нивать *imp.*, обменя́ть *perf.* (for, на + *acc.*); обме́ниваться *imp.*, обменя́ться *perf.* + *instr.*

Exchequer *n.* казначе́йство, казна́.

excise[1] *n.* (*duty*) акци́з(ный сбор); *v.t.* облага́ть *imp.*, обложи́ть (-жу́, -жишь) *perf.* акци́зным сбо́ром.

excise[2] *v.t.* (*cut out*) выреза́ть *imp.*, вы́резать (-ежу, -ежешь) *perf.* **excision** *n.* вы́резка.

excitable *adj.* возбуди́мый. **excite** *v.t.* возбужда́ть *imp.*, возбуди́ть *perf.*; волнова́ть *imp.*, вз~ *perf.* **excitement** *n.* возбужде́ние, волне́ние.

exclaim *v.i.* восклица́ть *imp.*, воскли́кнуть *perf.* **exclamation** *n.* восклица́ние; *e. mark*, восклица́тельный знак.

exclude *v.t.* исключа́ть *imp.*, исключи́ть *perf.* **exclusion** *n.* исключе́ние. **exclusive** *adj.* исключи́тельный; *e. of*, за исключе́нием + *gen.*, не счита́я + *gen.*

excommunicate *v.t.* отлуча́ть *imp.*, отлучи́ть *perf.* (от це́ркви). **excommunication** *n.* отлуче́ние.

excrement *n.* экскреме́нты (-тов) *pl.*

excrescence *n.* наро́ст.

excrete *v.t.* выделя́ть *imp.*, вы́делить *perf.* **excretion** *n.* выделе́ние.

excruciating *adj.* мучи́тельный.

exculpate *v.t.* опра́вдывать *imp.*, оправда́ть *perf.* **exculpation** *n.* оправда́ние.

excursion *n.* экску́рсия. **excursus** *n.* э́кскурс.

excusable *adj.* извини́тельный, прости́тельный. **excuse** *n.* извине́ние, оправда́ние, отгово́рка; *v.t.* извиня́ть *imp.*, извини́ть *perf.*; проща́ть *imp.*, прости́ть *perf.*; (*release*) освобожда́ть *imp.*, освободи́ть *perf.* (from, от + *gen.*); *e. me!* извини́те (меня́)! прости́те (меня́)! прошу́ проще́ния!

execrable *adj.* отврати́тельный, ме́рзкий (-зок, -зка́, -зко).

execute *v.t.* исполня́ть *imp.*, испо́лнить *perf.*; выполня́ть *imp.*, вы́полнить *perf.*; (*criminal*) казни́ть *imp.*, *perf.* **execution** *n.* выполне́ние, исполне́ние; казнь. **executioner** *n.* пала́ч (-а́). **executive** *n.* исполни́тельный орга́н; (*person*) руководи́тель *m.*; *adj.* исполни́тельный; *e. committee*, исполни́тельный комите́т, исполко́м.

exegesis *n.* толкова́ние.

exemplary *adj.* приме́рный, образцо́вый. **exemplify** *v.t.* (*illustrate by example*) поясня́ть *imp.*, поясни́ть *perf.* приме́ром, на приме́ре; (*serve as example*) служи́ть (-жу́, -жишь) *imp.*, по~ *perf.* приме́ром + *gen.*

exempt *adj.* освобождённый (-ён, -ена́) (from, от + *gen.*), свобо́дный (from, от + *gen.*); *v.t.* освобожда́ть *imp.*, освободи́ть *perf.* (from, от + *gen.*). **exemption** *n.* освобожде́ние (from, от + *gen.*).

exercise *n.* (*application*) примене́ние, осуществле́ние; (*physical e.*; *task*) упражне́ние; *take e.*, упражня́ться *imp.*; *e.-book*, тетра́дь; *v.t.* (*apply*) применя́ть *imp.*, примени́ть (-ню́, -нишь) *perf.*; (*employ*) испо́льзовать *imp.*, *perf.*; (*train*) упражня́ть *imp.*

exert *v.t.* ока́зывать *imp.*, оказа́ть (-ажу́, -а́жешь) *perf.*; *e. oneself*, стара́ться *imp.*, по~ *perf.* **exertion** *n.* напряже́ние, уси́лие.

exhalation *n.* выдыха́ние, вы́дох; (*vapour*) испаре́ние. **exhale** *v.t.* (*breathe out*) выдыха́ть *imp.*, вы́дохнуть *perf.*; (*as vapour*) испаря́ть *imp.*, испари́ть *perf.*

exhaust *n.* вы́хлоп; *e. pipe*, выхлопна́я труба́ (*pl.* -бы); *v.t.* (*use up*) истоща́ть *imp.*, истощи́ть *perf.*; (*person*) изнуря́ть *imp.*, изнури́ть *perf.*; (*subject*) исче́рпывать *imp.*, исче́рпать *perf.* **exhausted** *adj.*: *be e.*, (*person*) изнемога́ть *imp.*, изнемо́чь (-огу́, -о́жешь; -о́г, -огла́) *perf.* **exhausting** *adj.* изнури́тельный. **exhaustion** *n.* изнуре́ние, истоще́ние, изнеможе́ние. **exhaustive** *adj.* исче́рпывающий.

exhibit *n.* экспона́т; (*leg.*) веще́ственное доказа́тельство; *v.t.* (*show*) пока́зывать *imp.*, показа́ть (-ажу́, -а́жешь) *perf.*; (*manifest quality*) проявля́ть *imp.*, прояви́ть (-влю́, -вишь) *perf.*; (*publicly*) выставля́ть *imp.*, вы́ставить *perf.* **exhibition** *n.* пока́з, проявле́ние; (*public e.*) вы́ставка. **exhibitor** *n.* экспоне́нт.

exhilarate *v.t.* (*gladden*) весели́ть *imp.*, раз~ *perf.*; (*enliven*) оживля́ть *imp.*, оживи́ть *perf.* **exhilaration** *n.* весе́лье, оживле́ние.

exhort *v.t.* увещева́ть *imp.* **exhortation** *n.* увещева́ние.

exhume *v.t.* выка́пывать *imp.*, вы́копать *perf.*

exile *n.* изгна́ние, ссы́лка; (*person*) изгна́нник, ссы́льный *sb.*; *v.t.* изгоня́ть *imp.*, изгна́ть (изгоню́, -нишь; изгна́л, -а́, -о) *perf.*; ссыла́ть *imp.*, сосла́ть (сошлю́, -лёшь) *perf.*

exist *v.i.* существова́ть *imp.*; (*live*) жить (живу́, -вёшь; жил, -а́, -о) *imp.* **existence** *n.* существова́ние, нали́чие. **existent, existing** *adj.* существу́ющий, нали́чный.

exit *n.* вы́ход; (*theat.*) ухо́д (со сце́ны); (*death*) смерть; *e. visa*, выездна́я ви́за; *v.i.* уходи́ть (-ожу́, -о́дишь) *imp.*, уйти́ (уйду́, -дёшь; ушёл, ушла́) *perf.*

exonerate *v.t.* освобожда́ть *imp.*, освободи́ть *perf.* (from, от + *gen.*); (*from blame*) снима́ть *imp.*, снять (сниму́, -мешь; снял, -а́, -о) *perf.* обвине́ние с + *gen.*

exorbitant *adj.* непоме́рный, чрезме́рный.

exorcism *n.* изгна́ние ду́хов. **exorcize** *v.t.* (*spirits*) изгоня́ть *imp.*, изгна́ть (изгоню́, -нишь; изгнал, -а́, -о) *perf.*

exotic *adj.* экзоти́ческий.

expand *v.t.* & *i.* (*broaden*) расширя́ть(ся) *imp.*, расши́рить(ся) *perf.*; (*develop*) развива́ть(ся) *imp.*, разви́ть(ся) (разовью́(сь), -ьёшь(ся); разви́л(ся), -ила́(сь), -и́ло/-и́ло́сь) *perf.*; (*increase*) увели́чивать(ся) *imp.*, увели́чить(ся) *perf.* **expanse** *n.* простра́нство. **expansion** *n.* расшире́ние; разви́тие; увеличе́ние; (*of territory*) экспа́нсия. **expansive** *adj.* (*extensive*) обши́рный; (*effusive*) экспанси́вный.

expatiate *v.i.* распространя́ться *imp.*, распространи́ться *perf.* (on, о + *prep.*).

expatriate *n.* экспатриа́нт.

expect *v.t.* (*await*) ожида́ть *imp.* + *gen.*; ждать (жду, ждёшь; ждал, -а́, -о) *imp.* + *gen.*, что; (*anticipate*) наде́яться (-е́юсь, -е́ешься) *imp.*, по~ *perf.*; (*require*) тре́бовать *imp.* + *gen.*, что́бы. **expectant** *adj.* ожида́ющий (of, + *gen.*); *e. mother*, бере́менная же́нщина. **expectation** *n.* ожида́ние, наде́жда.

expectorant *n.* отха́ркивающее (сре́дство) *sb.* **expectorate** *v.t.* отха́ркивать *imp.*, отха́ркать *perf.*

expediency *n.* целесообра́зность. **expedient** *n.* сре́дство, приём; *adj.* целесообра́зный. **expedite** *v.t.* ускоря́ть *imp.*, ускорить *perf.*; бы́стро выполня́ть *imp.*, вы́полнить *perf.* **expedition** *n.* экспеди́ция; (*promptness*) сро́чность. **expeditionary** *adj.* экспедицио́нный. **expeditious** *adj.* бы́стрый (быстр, -а́, -о, бы́стры́).

expel *v.t.* выгоня́ть *imp.*, вы́гнать (вы́гоню, -нишь) *perf.* (*from school etc.*) исключа́ть *imp.*, исключи́ть *perf.*

expend *v.t.* тра́тить *imp.*, ис~, по~ *perf.*; расхо́довать *imp.*, из~ *perf.* **expenditure** *n.* расхо́дование, расхо́д, тра́та. **expense** *n.* расхо́д; *pl.* расхо́ды *m.pl.*, изде́ржки *f.pl.*; *at the e. of*, ценою + *gen.*, за счёт + *gen.* **expensive** *adj.* дорого́й (до́рог, -а́, -о).

experience *n.* о́пыт, о́пытность; (*incident*) пережива́ние; *v.t.* испы́тывать *imp.*, испыта́ть *perf.*; (*undergo*) пережива́ть *imp.*, пережи́ть (-иву́, -ивёшь;

пе́режи́л, -а́, -о) *perf.* **experienced** *adj.* о́пытный.

experiment *n.* о́пыт, экспериме́нт; *v.i.* производи́ть (-ожу́, -о́дишь) *imp.*, произвести́ (-еду́, -едёшь; -ёл, -ела́) *perf.* о́пыты (on, на + *acc.*); эксперименти́ровать *imp.* (on, with, над, с, + *instr.*). **experimental** эксперимента́льный, о́пытный. **experimentation** *n.* эксперименти́рование.

expert *n.* специали́ст (at, in, в + *prep.*, по + *dat.*), знато́к (-а́) (+ *gen.*); *adj.* о́пытный. **expertise** *n.* (*opinion*) эксперти́за; (*knowledge*) специа́льные зна́ния *neut.pl.*

expiate *v.t.* искупа́ть *imp.*, искупи́ть (-плю́, -пишь) *perf.* **expiation** *n.* искупле́ние.

expiration *n.* (*breathing out*) выдыха́ние; (*termination*) истече́ние. **expire** *v.t.* (*exhale*) выдыха́ть *imp.*, вы́дохнуть *perf.*; *v.i.* (*period*) истека́ть *imp.*, исте́чь (-ечёт; -ёк, -екла́) *perf.*; (*die*) умира́ть *imp.*, умере́ть (умру́, -рёшь; у́мер, -ла́, -ло) *perf.* **expiry** *n.* истече́ние.

explain *v.t.* объясня́ть *imp.*, объясни́ть *perf.*; (*justify*) опра́вдывать *imp.*, оправда́ть *perf.* **explanation** *n.* объясне́ние. **explanatory** *adj.* объясни́тельный.

expletive *adj.* вставно́й; *n.* вставно́е сло́во (*pl.* -ва́); (*oath*) бра́нное сло́во (*pl.* -ва́).

explicit *adj.* я́вный, определённый (-ёнен, -ённа).

explode *v.t.* & *i.* взрыва́ть(ся) *imp.*, взорва́ть(ся) (-ву́, -вётся; взорва́л(ся), -ала́(сь), -а́ло/-а́ло́сь) *perf.*; *v.t.* (*discredit*) разоблача́ть *imp.*, разоблачи́ть *perf.*; *v.i.* (*with anger etc.*) разража́ться *imp.*, разрази́ться *perf.*

exploit *n.* по́двиг; *v.t.* эксплуати́ровать *imp.*; (*mine etc.*) разраба́тывать *imp.*, разрабо́тать *perf.* **exploitation** *n.* эксплуата́ция; разрабо́тка. **exploiter** *n.* эксплуата́тор.

exploration *n.* иссле́дование. **exploratory** *adj.* иссле́довательский. **explore** *v.t.* иссле́довать *imp.*, *perf.* **explorer** *n.* иссле́дователь *m.*

explosion *n.* взрыв; (*anger etc.*) вспы́шка. **explosive** *n.* взры́вчатое вещество́; *adj.* взры́вчатый, взрывно́й.

exponent *n.* (*interpreter*) истолкова́тель *m.*; (*representative*) представи́тель *m.*; (*math.*) показа́тель *m.* сте́пени. **exponential** *adj.* (*math.*) показа́тельный.

export *n.* вы́воз, э́кспорт; *v.t.* вывози́ть (-ожу́, -о́зишь) *imp.*, вы́везти (-езу, -езешь; -ез) *perf.*; экспорти́ровать *imp.*, *perf.* **exporter** *n.* экспортёр.

expose *v.t.* (*to risk etc.*) подверга́ть *imp.*, подве́ргнуть (-г) *perf.* (to, + *dat.*); (*phot.*) экспони́ровать *imp.*, *perf.*; (*display*) выставля́ть *imp.*, вы́ставить *perf.*; (*discredit*) разоблача́ть *imp.*, разоблачи́ть *perf.*

exposition *n.* изложе́ние, толкова́ние.

exposure *n.* подверга́ние (to, + *dat.*); (*phot.*) вы́держка; выставле́ние; разоблаче́ние.

expound *v.t.* толкова́ть *imp.*; излага́ть *imp.*, изложи́ть (-жу́, -жишь) *perf.*

express *n.* (*train*) экспре́сс; (*messenger*) на́рочный *sb.*, курье́р; *adj.* (*definite*) определённый (-ёнен, -ённа), то́чный (-чен, -чна́, -чно); *v.t.* выража́ть *imp.*, вы́разить *perf.* **expression** *n.* выраже́ние; (*expressiveness*) вырази́тельность. **expressive** *adj.* вырази́тельный. **expressly** *adv.* наро́чно, наме́ренно.

expropriate *v.t.* экспроприи́ровать *imp.*, *perf.* **expropriation** *n.* экспроприа́ция.

expulsion *n.* изгна́ние; (*from school etc.*) исключе́ние.

expunge *v.t.* вычёркивать *imp.*, вы́черкнуть *perf.*

exquisite *adj.* утончённый (-ён, -ённа).

extant *adj.* сохрани́вшийся, существу́ющий.

extemporaneous *adj.* неподгото́вленный (-ен), импровизи́рованный (-ан). **extempore** *adv.* без подгото́вки, экспро́мтом. **extemporize** *v.t.* & *i.* импровизи́ровать *imp.*, сымпровизи́ровать *perf.*

extend *v.t.* простира́ть *imp.*, простере́ть (-тру́, -трёшь; -тёр) *perf.*; протя́гивать *imp.*, протяну́ть (-ну́, -нешь) *perf.*; (*enlarge*) расширя́ть *imp.*, расши́рить *perf.*; (*prolong*) продлева́ть *imp.*, продли́ть *perf.*; *v.i.* простира́ться *imp.*, простере́ться (-трётся; -тёрся) *perf.*; тяну́ться (-нется) *imp.*, по~ *perf.* **extension** *n.* расшире́ние; продле́ние. **extensive** *adj.* обши́рный, простра́нный (-нен, -нна), протяжённый (-ён, -ённа). **extent** *n.* протяже́ние; (*degree*) сте́пень (*pl.* -ни, -не́й); (*large space*) простра́нство.

extenuate *v.t.* уменьша́ть *imp.*, уме́ньшить *perf.*; *extenuating circumstances*, смягча́ющие вину́ обстоя́тельства *neut.pl.*

exterior *n.* вне́шность, нару́жность; *adj.* вне́шний, нару́жный.

exterminate *v.t.* уничтожа́ть *imp.*, уничто́жить *perf.*; истребля́ть *imp.*, истреби́ть *perf.* **extermination** *n.* уничтоже́ние, истребле́ние.

external *adj.* вне́шний, нару́жный.

extinct *adj.* (*volcano*) поту́хший; (*species*) вы́мерший; *become e.*, ту́хнуть (-х) *imp.*, по~ *perf.*; вымира́ть *imp.*, вы́мереть (-мрет; -мер) *perf.* **extinction** *n.* потуха́ние, вымира́ние.

extinguish *v.t.* гаси́ть (гашу́, га́сишь) *imp.*, по~ *perf.*; туши́ть (-шу́, -шишь) *imp.*, по~ *perf.*; (*debt*) погаша́ть *imp.*, погаси́ть (-ашу́, -а́сишь) *perf.* **extinguisher** *n.* гаси́тель *m.*; (*fire e.*) огнетуши́тель *m.*

extirpate *v.t.* истребля́ть *imp.*, истреби́ть *perf.*; искореня́ть *imp.*, искорени́ть *perf.* **extirpation** *n.* истребле́ние, искорене́ние.

extol *v.t.* превозноси́ть *imp.*, превознести́ (-есу́, -есёшь; -ёс, -есла́) *perf.*

extort *v.t.* вымога́ть *imp.* (from, у+*gen.*); (*information etc.*) выпы́тывать *imp.*, вы́пытать *perf.* (from, у+*gen.*). **extortion** *n.* вымога́тельство. **extortionate** *adj.* вымога́тельский, граби́тельский.

extra *n.* (*theat.*) стати́ст, ~ка; (*payment*) припла́та, добавле́ние; *adj.* доба́вочный, дополни́тельный, э́кстренный; осо́бый; *adv.* осо́бо, осо́бенно, дополни́тельно.

extra- *in comb.* вне-.

extract *n.* экстра́кт; (*from book etc.*) вы́держка; *v.t.* извлека́ть *imp.*, извле́чь (-еку́, -ечёшь; -ёк, -екла́) *perf.*; (*pull out*) выта́скивать *imp.*, вы́тащить *perf.*; (*tooth*) удаля́ть *imp.*, удали́ть *perf.* **extraction** *n.* извлече́ние; выта́скивание; удале́ние; (*descent*) происхожде́ние.

extradite *v.t.* выдава́ть (-даю́, -даёшь) *imp.*, вы́дать (-ам, -ашь, -аст, -адим) *perf.* **extradition** *n.* вы́дача.

extraneous *adj.* чу́ждый (чужд, -а́, -о) (to, +*dat.*), посторо́нний.

extraordinary *adj.* необыча́йный, чрезвыча́йный; (*surprising*) удиви́тельный.

extravagance *adj.* (*wild spending*) расточи́тельность; (*wildness*) сумасбро́дство. **extravagant** *adj.* расточи́тельный; сумасбро́дный.

extreme *n.* кра́йность; *adj.* кра́йний, чрезвыча́йный. **extremity** *n.* (*end*) край (*loc.* -а́е & -аю́; *pl.* -ая́), коне́ц (-нца́); (*adversity*) кра́йность; *pl.* (*hands & feet*) коне́чности *f.pl.*

extricate *v.t.* (*disentangle*) распу́тывать *imp.*, распу́тать *perf.*; *e. oneself*, выпу́тываться *imp.*, вы́путаться *perf.*

exuberance *n.* изоби́лие, ро́скошь; (*of person*) жизнера́достность. **exuberant** *adj.* оби́льный, роско́шный; жизнера́достный.

exude *v.t.* & *i.* выделя́ть(ся) *imp.*, вы́делить(ся) *perf.*

exult *v.i.* ликова́ть *imp.* **exultant** *adj.* лику́ющий. **exultation** *n.* ликова́ние.

eye *n.* глаз (*loc.* -зу́; *pl.* -за́, -з, -за́м); (*poet.*) о́ко (*pl.* о́чи, оче́й); (*needle etc.*) ушко́ (*pl.* -ки́, -ко́в); *an eye for an eye*, о́ко за о́ко; *up to the eyes in*, по́ уши, по го́рло, в+*prep.*; *v.t.* всма́триваться *imp.*, всмотре́ться (-рю́сь, -ришься) *perf.* в+*acc.* **eyeball** *n.* глазно́е я́блоко (*pl.* -ки, -к). **eyebrow** *n.* бровь (*pl.* -ви, -ве́й). **eyelash** *n.* ресни́ца. **eyelid** *n.* ве́ко (*pl.* -ки, -к). **eyepiece** *n.* окуля́р. **eyesight** *n.* зре́ние. **eyewitness** *n.* очеви́дец (-дца).

eyrie *n.* (орли́ное) гнездо́ (*pl.* -ёзда).

F

F *n.* (*mus.*) фа *neut.indecl.*
fable *n.* ба́сня (*gen.pl.* -сен), небыли́ца.
fabric *n.* (*structure*) структу́ра, устро́йство; (*cloth*) ткань. **fabricate** *v.t.* (*invent*) выду́мывать *imp.*, вы́думать *perf.*; (*forge*) подде́лывать *imp.*, подде́лать *perf.* **fabrication** *n.* вы́думка; подде́лка.
fabulous *adj.* ска́зочный.
façade *n.* фаса́д.
face *n.* лицо́ (*pl.* -ца); (*expression*) выраже́ние; (*grimace*) грима́са; (*outward aspect*) вне́шний вид; (*surface*) пове́рхность; (*clock etc.*) цифербла́т; *have the f.*, име́ть *imp.* наха́льство; *make faces*, ко́рчить *imp.* ро́жи; *f. down*, (*cards*) руба́шкой вверх; *f. to f.*, лицо́м к лицу́; *in the f. of*, пе́ред лицо́м + *gen.*, вопреки́ + *dat.*; *on the f. of it*, на пе́рвый взгля́д; *f. card*, фигу́ра; *f. value*, номина́льная сто́имость; *take at f. value*, принима́ть *imp.*, приня́ть (приму́, -мешь; при́нял, -а́, -о) *perf.* за чи́стую моне́ту; *v.t.* (*be turned towards*) быть обращённым к + *dat.*; (*meet firmly*) смотре́ть (-рю́, -ришь) *imp.* в лицо́ + *dat.*; (*cover*) облицо́вывать *imp.*, облицева́ть (-цу́ю, -цу́ешь) *perf.*; *f. the music*, расхлёбывать *imp.*, расхлеба́ть *perf.* ка́шу. **faceless** *adj.* безли́чный.
facet *n.* грань; (*aspect*) аспе́кт.
facetious *adj.* шутли́вый.
facial *adj.* лицево́й.
facile *adj.* лёгкий (-гок, -гка́, -гко́, лёгки́), свобо́дный; (*derog.*) пове́рхностный. **facilitate** *v.t.* облегча́ть *imp.*, облегчи́ть *perf.* **facility** *n.* (*ease*) лёгкость; (*ability*) спосо́бность; (*opportunity*) возмо́жность.
facing *n.* облицо́вка; (*of garment*) отде́лка, обши́вка.
facsimile *n.* факси́миле *neut.indecl.*
fact *n.* факт; (*reality*) действи́тельность; *pl.* (*information*) да́нные *sb.*; *the f. is that . . .*, де́ло в том, что...; *as a matter of f.*, со́бственно говоря́; *in f.*, действи́тельно, на са́мом де́ле.
faction *n.* фра́кция. **factional** *adj.* фракцио́нный.
factitious *adj.* иску́сственный (-вен(ен), -венна).
factor *n.* (*circumstance*) фа́ктор; (*merchant*) комиссионе́р; (*math.*) мно́житель *m.*; (*of safety etc.*) коэффицие́нт.
factory *n.* фа́брика, заво́д; *f.-ship*, плаву́чий рыбозаво́д.
factual *adj.* факти́ческий, действи́тельный.
faculty *n.* спосо́бность, дар (*pl.* -ы́); (*univ.*) факульте́т.
fade *v.i.* вя́нуть (вял) *imp.*, за ~ *perf.*; увяда́ть *imp.*, увя́нуть (-я́л) *perf.*; (*colour*) выцвета́ть *imp.*, вы́цвести (-етет; -ел) *perf.*; (*sound*) замира́ть *imp.*, замере́ть (-мрёт; за́мер, -ла́, -ло) *perf.*
faeces *n.* кал.
fag *v.i.* корпе́ть (-плю́, -пишь) (over, над + *instr.*); *v.t.* утомля́ть *imp.*, утоми́ть *perf.*; *n.* (*drudgery*) тяжёлая рабо́та; (*cigarette*) сигаре́тка; *f.-end*, оку́рок (-рка).
faggot *n.* (*wood*) вяза́нка хво́роста, -ту.
faience *n.* фая́нс.
fail *n.*: *without f.*, обяза́тельно, непреме́нно; *v.t.* & *i.* (*be insufficient*) не хвата́ть *imp.*, не хвати́ть (-ит) *perf. impers.* + *gen.* (*subject*) & у + *gen.* (*object*); *v.i.* (*weaken*) ослабева́ть *imp.*, ослабе́ть *perf.*; *v.i.* (*not succeed*) терпе́ть (-плю́, -пишь) *imp.*, по ~ *perf.* неуда́чу; не удава́ться (удаётся) *imp.*, уда́ться (-а́стся; -ало́сь) *perf.impers.* + *dat.* (in, + *inf.*); *v.t.* & *i.* (*examination*) прова́ливать(ся) *imp.*, провали́ть(ся) (-лю́(сь), -лишь(ся)) *perf.* **failing** *n.* недоста́ток (-тка), сла́бость; *prep.* за неиме́нием + *gen.*, в слу́чае отсу́тствия + *gen.* **failure** *n.* неуда́ча, прова́л; (*person*) неуда́чник, -ица.
faint *n.* о́бморок; *adj.* (*weak*) сла́бый (слаб, -а́, -о); (*pale*) бле́дный (-ден, -дна́, -дно, бле́дны́); *f.-hearted*, малоду́шный; *v.i.* па́дать *imp.*, упа́сть (упаду́, -дёшь; упа́л) *perf.* в о́бморок.
fair[1] *n.* я́рмарка.

fair[2] *adj.* (*beautiful*) краси́вый; (*just*) че́стный (-тен, -тна́, -тно), справедли́вый; (*considerable*) поря́дочный; (*blond*) белоку́рый; *f. copy*, чистови́к (-а́). **fairly** *adv.* (*tolerably*) дово́льно; (*completely*) соверше́нно. **fairway** *n.* фарва́тер.

fairy *n.* фе́я; *f.-tale*, ска́зка.

faith *n.* (*belief*) ве́ра; (*trust*) дове́рие; (*loyalty*) ве́рность. **faithful** *adj.* ве́рный (-рен, -рна́, -рно, ве́рны́). **faithless** *adj.* вероло́мный, неве́рный (-е́рен, -ерна́, -е́рно, -е́рны́).

fake *n.* подде́лка; *v.t.* подде́лывать *imp.*, подде́лать *perf.*

falcon *n.* со́кол. **falconry** *n.* соколи́ная охо́та.

fall *n.* паде́ние; *pl.* водопа́д; *v.i.* па́дать *imp.*, (у)па́сть ((у)паду́, -дёшь; (у)па́л) *perf.*; понижа́ться *imp.*, пони́зиться *perf.*; *f. apart*, распада́ться *imp.*, распа́сться (-адётся; -а́лся) *perf.*; *f. asleep*, засыпа́ть *imp.*, засну́ть *perf.*; *f. back on*, прибега́ть *imp.*, прибе́гнуть (-г(нул), -гла) *perf.* к + *dat.*; *f. off*, отпада́ть *imp.*, отпа́сть (-аду́, -адёшь; -а́л) *perf.*; *f. over*, опроки́дываться *imp.*, опроки́нуться *perf.*; *f. through*, прова́ливаться *imp.*, провали́ться (-ится) *perf.*; *f.-out*, радиоакти́вные оса́дки (-ков) *pl.*

fallacious *adj.* оши́бочный, ло́жный. **fallacy** *n.* оши́бка, заблужде́ние.

fallibility *n.* оши́бочность. **fallible** *adj.* подве́рженный (-ен) оши́бкам.

fallow *n.* пар (*pl.* -ы́), земля́ (*acc.* -лю) под па́ром; *adj.* под па́ром; *lie f.*, лежа́ть (-жи́т) *imp.* под па́ром.

fallow deer *n.* лань.

false *adj.* ло́жный, фальши́вый. **falsehood** *n.* ложь (лжи, *instr.* ло́жью). **falsetto** *n.* фальце́т. **falsification** *n.* фальсифика́ция, подде́лка. **falsify** *v.t.* фальсифици́ровать *imp.*, *perf.*; подде́лывать *imp.*, подде́лать *perf.* **falsity** *n.* ло́жность.

falter *v.i.* (*stumble*) спотыка́ться *imp.*, споткну́ться *perf.*; (*stammer*) запина́ться *imp.*, запну́ться *perf.*; (*waver*) колеба́ться (-блюсь, -блешься) *imp.*

fame *n.* сла́ва, репута́ция. **famed** *adj.* изве́стный.

familiar *adj.* (*close*) бли́зкий (-зок, -зка́, -зко, бли́зки́); (*well known*) знако́мый; (*usual*) обы́чный; (*informal*) фамилья́рный. **familiarity** *n.* бли́зость; знако́мство; фамилья́рность. **familiarize** *v.t.* ознакомля́ть *imp.*, ознако́мить *perf.* (with, с + *instr.*).

family *n.* семья́ (*pl.* -мьи, -ме́й, -мьям); (*lineage etc.*) род (-а(у), *loc.* -у́; *pl.* -ы́); (*generic group*) семе́йство; *attrib.* семе́йный, фами́льный; *f. tree*, родосло́вная *sb.*

famine *n.* (*scarcity of food*) го́лод (-а(у)); (*dearth*) недоста́ток (-тка). **famish** *v.t.* мори́ть *imp.*, у~ *perf.* го́лодом; *v.i.*, *be famished*, голода́ть *imp.*

famous *adj.* знамени́тый, изве́стный, просла́вленный.

fan[1] *n.* (*device etc.*) ве́ер (*pl.* -а́); (*ventilator*) вентиля́тор; *v.t.* обма́хивать *imp.*, обмахну́ть *perf.*; (*flame*) раздува́ть *imp.*, разду́ть (-у́ю, -у́ешь) *perf.*

fan[2] *n.* (*devotee*) боле́льщик, -ица. **fanatic** *n.* фана́тик, -и́чка. **fanatical** *adj.* фанати́ческий.

fanciful *adj.* (*capricious*) прихотли́вый; (*imaginary*) вообража́емый. **fancy** *n.* фанта́зия, воображе́ние; (*whim*) причу́да; *adj.* орнамента́льный; *v.t.* (*imagine*) представля́ть *imp.*, предста́вить *perf.* себе́; (*suppose*) каза́ться (ка́жется; каза́лось) *imp.*, по~ *perf.* *impers.* + *dat.*; (*like*) нра́виться *imp.*, по~ *perf.impers.* + *dat.*; *f. dress*, маскара́дный костю́м; *f.-dress*, костюмиро́ванный.

fanfare *n.* фанфа́ра.

fang *n.* клык (-а́); (*serpent's*) ядови́тый зуб (*pl.* -ы, -о́в).

fantastic *adj.* фантасти́ческий, причу́дливый. **fantasy** *n.* фанта́зия, воображе́ние.

far *adj.* да́льний, далёкий (-ёк, -ека́, -ёко́); (*remote*) отдалённый; *adv.* далёко́; (*fig.*) намно́го; *as f. as*, (*prep.*) до + *gen.*; (*conj.*) поско́льку; *by f.*, намно́го; (*in*) *so f. as*, поско́льку; *so f.*, до сих пор; *f.-fetched*, натя́нутый; притя́нутый за́ волосы, за́ уши; *f.-reaching*, далеко́ иду́щий;

f.-seeing, дальнови́дный; *f.-sighted*, дальнови́дный; (*physically*) дальнозо́ркий.

farce *n.* фарс. **farcical** *adj.* фа́рсовый, смехотво́рный.

fare *n.* (*price*) проездна́я пла́та; (*passenger*) пассажи́р; (*food*) пи́ща; *v.i.* пожива́ть *imp.* **farewell** *interj.* проща́й(те)! *n.* проща́ние; *attrib.* проща́льный; *bid f.*, проща́ться *imp.*, прости́ться *perf.* (to, с + *instr.*).

farinaceous *adj.* мучни́стый, мучно́й.

farm *n.* фе́рма, хозя́йство. **farmer** *n.* фе́рмер. **farming** *n.* се́льское хозя́йство.

farrier *n.* (*smith*) кузне́ц (-а́); (*horse-doctor*) конова́л.

farther *comp.adj.* бо́лее отдалённый (-ён, -ённа); дальне́йший; (*additional*) дополни́тельный; *adv.* да́льше. **farthermost** *adj.* са́мый да́льний. **farthest** *superl.adj.* са́мый да́льний, са́мый отдалённый; *adv.* да́льше всего́.

fascicle *n.* (*bot.*) пучо́к (-чка́); (*book*) вы́пуск.

fascinate *v.t.* очаро́вывать *imp.*, очарова́ть *perf.* **fascinating** *adj.* очарова́тельный. **fascination** *n.* очарова́ние.

Fascism *n.* фаши́зм. **Fascist** *n.* фаши́ст, ~ка; *adj.* фаши́стский.

fashion *n.* (*manner*) мане́ра; (*pattern*) фасо́н; (*style*) стиль *m.*; (*style of dress etc.*) мо́да; *after a f.*, не́которым о́бразом; *after the f. of*, по образцу́ + *gen.*; *v.t.* придава́ть (-даю́, -даёшь) *imp.*, прида́ть (-а́м, -а́шь, -а́ст, -ади́м; при́дал, -а́, -о) *perf.* фо́рму + *dat.*; формирова́ть *imp.*, с~ *perf.* **fashionable** *adj.* мо́дный (-ден, -дна́, -дно), фешене́бельный.

fast[1] *n.* пост (-а́, *loc.* -у́); *v.i.* пости́ться *imp.*; *break* (*one's*) *f.*, разговля́ться *imp.*, разгове́ться *perf.*

fast[2] *adj.* (*firm*) про́чный (-чен, -чна́, -чно, про́чны́), кре́пкий (-пок, -пка́, -пко), твёрдый (-д, -да́, -до), сто́йкий (-о́ек, -ойка́, -о́йко); (*rapid*) ско́рый (скор, -а́, -о), бы́стрый (быстр, -а́, -о, бы́стры́); (*immoral*) беспу́тный; *be f.*, (*timepiece*) спеши́ть *imp.* **fasten** *v.t.* (*attach*) прикрепля́ть *imp.*, прикрепи́ть *perf.* (to, к + *dat.*); (*tie*) привя́зывать *imp.*, привяза́ть (-яжу́, -я́жешь) *perf.* (to, к + *dat.*); (*garment*) застёгивать *imp.*, застегну́ть *perf.* **fastener, fastening** *n.* запо́р, задви́жка; (*on garment*) застёжка.

fastidious *adj.* брезгли́вый.

fat *n.* жир (-а(у), *loc.* -у́; *pl.* -ы́), са́ло; *adj.* (*greasy*) жи́рный (-рен, -рна́, -рно); (*plump*) то́лстый (-т, -та́, -то, то́лсты́), ту́чный (-чен, -чна́, -чно); *get, grow, f.*, толсте́ть *imp.*, по~ *perf.*

fatal *adj.* фата́льный, рокова́й; (*deadly*) па́губный, смерте́льный. **fatality** *n.* па́губность, фата́льность; (*calamity*) несча́стье; (*death*) смерть. **fate** *n.* судьба́ (*pl.* -дьбы, -деб, -дьбам), рок, жре́бий. **fated** *predic.* обречён (-а́). **fateful** *adj.* рокова́й.

father *n.* оте́ц (-тца́); *f.-in-law*, (*husband's f.*) свёкор (-кра); (*wife's f.*) тесть *m.* **fatherland** *n.* оте́чество. **fatherly** *adj.* оте́ческий.

fathom *n.* шесть (-ти́, -тью) фу́тов (глубины́ воды́); *v.t.* измеря́ть *imp.*, изме́рить *perf.* глубину́ (воды́); (*understand*) понима́ть *imp.*, поня́ть (пойму́, -мёшь; по́нял, -а́, -о) *perf.*

fatigue *n.* уста́лость, утомле́ние; *v.t.* утомля́ть *imp.*, утоми́ть *perf.*

fatness *n.* ту́чность. **fatten** *v.t.* отка́рмливать *imp.*, откорми́ть (-млю́, -мишь) *perf.*; *v.i.* толсте́ть *imp.*, по~ *perf.* **fatty** *adj.* жи́рный (-рен, -рна́, -рно), жирово́й.

fatuous *adj.* тупо́й (туп, -а́, -о, ту́пы́).

fault *n.* недоста́ток (-тка), дефе́кт; (*blame*) вина́; (*geol.*) сброс. **faultless** *adj.* безупре́чный, безоши́бочный. **faulty** *adj.* дефе́ктный.

fauna *n.* фа́уна.

favour *n.* (*goodwill*) благоскло́нность; (*aid*) одолже́ние; *in* (*somebody's*) *favour*, в по́льзу + *gen.*; *be in f. of*, стоя́ть (-ою́, -ои́шь) *imp.* за + *acc.*; *v.t.* благоволи́ть *imp.* к + *dat.*; благоприя́тствовать *imp.* + *dat.* **favourable** *adj.* (*propitious*) благоприя́тный; (*approving*) благоскло́нный (-нен, -нна). **favourite** *n.* люби́мец (-мца), -мица, фавори́т, ~ка; *adj.* люби́мый.

fawn[1] *n.* оленёнок (-нка; *pl.* оленя́та, -т); *adj.* (*f.-coloured*) желтова́то-коричневый.

fawn[2] *v.i.* (*animal*) ласка́ться *imp.* (upon, к + *dat.*); (*person*) подли́зываться *imp.*, подлиза́ться (-ижу́сь, -и́жешься) *perf.* (upon, к + *dat.*).

fealty *n.* (прися́га на) ве́рность.

fear *n.* страх, боя́знь, опасе́ние; *v.t.* & *i.* боя́ться (бою́сь, бои́шься) *imp.* + *gen.*; опаса́ться *imp.* + *gen.* **fearful** *adj.* (*terrible*) стра́шный (-шен, -шна́, -шно, стра́шны́); (*timid*) пугли́вый. **fearless** *adj.* бесстра́шный. **fearsome** *adj.* гро́зный (-зен, -зна́, -зно).

feasibility *n.* осуществи́мость, возмо́жность. **feasible** *adj.* осуществи́мый, возмо́жный.

feast *n.* (*meal*) пир (*loc.* -е & -у́; *pl.* -ы́); (*festival*) пра́здник; *v.i.* пирова́ть *imp.*; *v.t.* угоща́ть *imp.*, угости́ть *perf.*; *f. one's eyes on*, любова́ться *imp.*, по~ *perf.* + *instr.*, на + *acc.*

feat *n.* по́двиг.

feather *n.* перо́ (*pl.* пе́рья, -ьев); *pl.* (*plumage*) опере́ние; *v.t.* оперя́ть *imp.*, опери́ть *perf.*; *f. bed*, пери́на; *f.-brained*, ве́треный. **feathery** *adj.* перна́тый.

feature *n.* осо́бенность, черта́; (*newspaper*) статья́; *pl.* (*of face*) черты́ *f.pl.* лица́; *f. film*, худо́жественный фильм; *v.t.* (*in film*) пока́зывать *imp.*, показа́ть (-ажу́, -а́жешь) *perf.* (на экра́не); *v.i.* (*take part*) уча́ствовать *imp.* (in, в + *prep.*).

febrile *adj.* лихора́дочный.

February *n.* февра́ль (-ля́) *m.*; *attrib.* февра́льский.

fecund *adj.* плодоро́дный. **fecundity** *n.* плодоро́дие.

federal *adj.* федерати́вный. **federation** *n.* федера́ция.

fee *n.* гонора́р; (*entrance f. etc.*) взнос; *pl.* (*regular payment, school, etc.*) пла́та.

feeble *adj.* сла́бый (слаб, -а́, -о), не́мощный; *f.-minded*, слабоу́мный. **feebleness** *n.* сла́бость.

feed *n.* корм (-а(у), *loc.* -е & -у́; *pl.* -а́); *v.t.* корми́ть (-млю́, -мишь) *imp.*, на~, по~ *perf.*; пита́ть *imp.*, на~ *perf.*; *v.i.* корми́ться (-млю́сь, -мишься) *imp.*, по~ *perf.*; пита́ться *imp.* (on, + *instr.*); *f. up*, (*fatten*) отка́рмливать *imp.*, откорми́ть (-млю́, -мишь) *perf.*; *I am fed up with*, мне надое́л (-а, -о, -и) + *nom.* **feedback** *n.* обра́тная связь.

feel *v.t.* осяза́ть *imp.*; ощуща́ть *imp.*, ощути́ть (-ущу́, -ути́шь) *perf.*; чу́вствовать *imp.*, по~ *perf.*; (*undergo*) испы́тывать *imp.*, испыта́ть *perf.*; *v.i.* (*feel bad etc.*) чу́вствовать *imp.*, по~ *perf.* себя́ + *adv.*, + *instr.*; *f. like*, хоте́ться (хо́чется) *imp.impers.* + *dat.* **feeling** *n.* (*sense*) ощуще́ние; (*emotion*) чу́вство, эмо́ция; (*impression*) впечатле́ние; (*mood*) настрое́ние.

feign *v.t.* притворя́ться *imp.*, притвори́ться *perf.* + *instr.* **feigned** *adj.* притво́рный.

feint *n.* ло́жный уда́р; (*pretence*) притво́рство.

felicitate *v.t.* поздравля́ть *imp.*, поздра́вить *perf.* (on, с + *instr.*). **felicitation** *n.* поздравле́ние.

felicitous *adj.* уда́чный, счастли́вый (сча́стли́в). **felicity** *n.* сча́стье, блаже́нство.

feline *adj.* коша́чий (-чья, -чье).

fell[1] *n.* (*animal's skin*) шку́ра.

fell[2] *v.t.* (*tree*) сруба́ть *imp.*, сруби́ть (-блю́, -бишь) *perf.*; (*person*) сбива́ть *imp.*, сбить (собью́, -ьёшь) *perf.* с ног.

fellow *n.* челове́к, па́рень (-рня; *pl.* -рни, -рне́й) *m.*, това́рищ; член (колле́джа, нау́чного о́бщества и т.п.). **fellowship** *n.* това́рищество, сооо́бщество, содру́жество.

felon *n.* уголо́вный престу́пник, -ица. **felonious** *adj.* престу́пный. **felony** *n.* уголо́вное преступле́ние.

fel(d)spar *n.* полево́й шпат.

felt *n.* фетр, во́йлок; *adj.* фе́тровый, во́йлочный; *f. boots*, ва́ленки (-нок) *pl.*

female *n.* (*animal*) са́мка; (*person*) же́нщина; *adj.* же́нский. **feminine** *adj.* же́нский, же́нственный (-ен, -енна); (*gram.*) же́нского ро́да.

femoral *adj.* бе́дренный. **femur** *n.* бедро́ (*pl.* бёдра, -дер, -драм).

fen *n.* боло́то, болоти́стая ме́стность.

fence *n.* огра́да, забо́р, и́згородь; (*receiver of stolen goods*) бары́га, ску́пщик кра́деного; *v.t.*: *f. in*, огора́живать *imp.*, огороди́ть (-ожу́, -о́ди́шь) *perf.*; *f. off*, отгора́живать *imp.*, отгороди́ть (-ожу́, -о́ди́шь) *perf.*; *v.i.* (*sport*) фехтова́ть *imp.* **fencer** *n.* фехтова́льщик, -ица. **fencing** *n.* огора́живание; (*enclosure*) забо́р, и́згородь; (*sport*) фехтова́ние; *adj.* фехтова́льный.

fend *v.t.*: *f. off*, отража́ть *imp.*, отрази́ть *perf.*; (*blow*) пари́ровать *imp.*, от~ *perf.*; *f. for oneself*, забо́титься *imp.*, по~ *perf.* о себе́. **fender** *n.* (*guard*) решётка; (*naut.*) кра́нец (-нца).

fennel *n.* фе́нхель *m.*

ferment *n.* (*substance*) заква́ска; (*action, also fig.*) броже́ние; *v.i.* броди́ть (-дит) *imp.*; *v.t.* ква́сить (-а́шу, -а́сишь) *imp.*, за~ *perf.*; (*excite*) возбужда́ть *imp.*, возбуди́ть *perf.* **fermentation** *n.* броже́ние; (*excitement*) возбужде́ние.

fern *n.* па́поротник.

ferocious *adj.* свире́пый, лю́тый (лют, -а́, -о). **ferocity** *n.* свире́пость, лю́тость.

ferret *n.* хорёк (-рька́); *v.t.*: *f. out*, выгоня́ть *imp.*, вы́гнать (вы́гоню, -нишь) *perf.*; (*search out*) разню́хивать *imp.*, разню́хать *perf.*; *v.i.*: *f. about*, (*rummage*) ры́ться (ро́юсь, ро́ешься) *imp.*

ferro- *in comb.* ферро-, железо-; *f.-concrete*, железобето́н. **ferrous** *adj.* желе́зный; *f. metals*, чёрные мета́ллы *m.pl.*

ferry *n.* паро́м, перево́з; *v.t.* перевози́ть (-ожу́, -о́зишь) *imp.*, перевезти́ (-езу́, -езёшь; -ёз, -езла́) *perf.* **ferryman** *n.* паро́мщик, перево́зчик.

fertile *adj.* плодоро́дный, плодови́тый. **fertility** *n.* плодоро́дие, плодови́тость. **fertilize** *v.t.* (*soil*) удобря́ть *imp.*, удо́брить *perf.*; (*egg*) оплодотворя́ть *imp.*, оплодотвори́ть *perf.* **fertilizer** *n.* удобре́ние.

fervent, fervid *adj.* горя́чий, пы́лкий (-лок, -лка́, -лко). **fervour** *n.* пыл (-а(у), *loc.* -у́), горя́чность, рве́ние.

festal *adj.* (*of feast*) пра́здничный; (*gay*) весёлый (ве́сел, -а́, -о, ве́селы́).

fester *v.i.* гнои́ться *imp.*

festival *n.* пра́здник, фестива́ль *m.* **festive** *adj.* пра́здничный; (*jovial*) весёлый (ве́сел, -а́, -о, ве́селы́). **festivity** *n.* весе́лье; *pl.* торжества́ *neut.pl.*

festoon *n.* гирля́нда; (*archit.*) фесто́н; *v.t.* украша́ть *imp.*, укра́сить *perf.* гирля́ндами, фесто́нами.

fetch *v.t.* (*carrying*) приноси́ть (-ошу́, -о́сишь) *imp.*, принести́ (-есу́, -есёшь; -ёс, -есла́) *perf.*; (*leading*) приводи́ть (-ожу́, -о́дишь) *imp.*, привести́ (-еду́, -едёшь; -ёл, -ела́) *perf.*; (*go and come back with*) (*on foot*) сходи́ть (-ожу́, -о́дишь) *perf.* за + *instr.*; заходи́ть (-ожу́, -о́дишь) *imp.*, зайти́ (зайду́, -дёшь; зашёл, -шла́) *perf.* за + *instr.*; (*by vehicle*) заезжа́ть *imp.*, зае́хать (-е́ду, -е́дешь) *perf.* за + *instr.*; (*cause*) вызыва́ть *imp.*, вы́звать (вы́зову, -вешь) *perf.*; (*price*) выруча́ть *imp.*, вы́ручить *perf.* **fetching** *adj.* привлека́тельный.

fetid *adj.* злово́нный (-нен, -нна).

fetish *n.* фети́ш.

fetlock *n.* щётка.

fetter *v.t.* ско́вывать *imp.*, скова́ть (скую́, скуёшь) *perf.*; *n.*: *pl.* кандалы́ (-ло́в) *pl.*, око́вы (-в) *pl.*

fettle *n.* состоя́ние.

feud *n.* кро́вная месть.

feudal *adj.* феода́льный. **feudalism** *n.* феодали́зм.

fever *n.* (*med.*) жар (-а(у), *loc.* -у́), лихора́дка; (*agitation*) возбужде́ние. **feverish** *adj.* лихора́дочный; возбуждённый (-ён, -ена́).

few, a f. *adj.*, *pron.* немно́гие (-их) *pl.*; немно́го + *gen.*, ма́ло + *gen.*, не́сколько + *gen.*; *quite a f.*, нема́ло + *gen.*

fez *n.* фе́ска.

fiancé *n.* жени́х (-а́). **fiancée** *n.* неве́ста.

fiasco *n.* прова́л.

fiat *n.* (*sanction*) са́нкция; (*decree*) декре́т.

fib *n.* вранье́; *v.i.* привира́ть *imp.*, привра́ть (-ру́, -рёшь; привра́л, -а́, -о) *perf.* **fibber** *n.* врал́ь (-ля́) *m.*

fibre *n.* фи́бра, волокно́ (*pl.* -о́кна, -о́кон, -о́кнам); (*character*) хара́ктер. **fibreglass** *n.* стекловолокно́. **fibrous** *adj.* фибро́зный, волокни́стый.

fickle *adj.* непостоя́нный (-нен, -нна), изме́нчивый. **fickleness** *n.* непостоя́нство, изме́нчивость.

fiction *n.* (*literature*) беллетри́стика, худо́жественная литерату́ра; (*invention*) вы́думка. **fictional** *adj.* беллетристи́ческий; вы́мышленный. **fictitious** *adj.* вы́мышленный, фикти́вный.

fiddle *n.* (*violin*) скри́пка; (*swindle*) обма́н; *v.i.* игра́ть *imp.* (with, с + *instr.*); *f. about*, безде́льничать *imp.*; *v.t.* (*cheat*) надува́ть *imp.*, наду́ть (-у́ю, -у́ешь) *perf.*

fidelity *n.* ве́рность.

fidget *n.* непосе́да *m.* & *f.*; *v.i.* ёрзать *imp.*; не́рвничать *imp.* **fidgety** *adj.* непосе́дливый.

field *n.* по́ле (*pl.* -ля́, -ле́й); (*sport*) площа́дка; (*sphere*) о́бласть, сфе́ра; *attrib.* полево́й; *f.-glasses*, полево́й бино́кль *m.*; *F. Marshal*, фельдма́ршал; *f.-mouse*, полева́я мышь (*pl.* -ши, -ше́й).

fiend *n.* (*demon*) дья́вол, де́мон; (*cruel person*) и́зверг. **fiendish** *adj.* дья́вольский.

fierce *adj.* свире́пый, лю́тый (лют, -а́, -о); (*strong*) си́льный (силён, -льна́, -льно, си́льны́).

fiery *adj.* о́гненный.

fife *n.* ду́дка.

fifteen *adj.*, *n.* пятна́дцать (-ти, -тью); (*age*) пятна́дцать лет. **fifteenth** *adj.*, *n.* пятна́дцатый; (*date*) пятна́дцатое (число́). **fifth** *adj.*, *n.* пя́тый; (*fraction*) пя́тая (часть (*pl.*-ти, -те́й)); (*date*) пя́тое (число́); (*mus.*) кви́нта. **fiftieth** *adj.*, *n.* пятидеся́тый. **fifty** *adj.*, *n.* пятьдеся́т (-ти́десяти, -тью́десятью); (*age*) пятьдеся́т лет; *pl.* (*decade*) пятидеся́тые го́ды (-до́в) *m.pl.*; *f.-f.*, *adj.* ра́вный (-вен, -вна́); *adv.* по́ровну.

fig *n.* фи́га, ви́нная я́года, инжи́р.

fight *n.* дра́ка; (*battle*) бой (*loc.* бою́; *pl.* бои́); (*fig.*) борьба́; *v.t.* боро́ться (-рю́сь, -решься) *imp.* с + *instr.*; сража́ться *imp.*, срази́ться *perf.* с + *instr.*; *v.i.* дра́ться (деру́сь, -рёшься; дра́лся, -ла́сь, дра́ло́сь) *imp.* **fighter** *n.* бое́ц (бойца́); (*aeron.*) истреби́тель *m.* **fighting** *n.* бои́ *m.pl.*, сраже́ние, дра́ка; *adj.* боево́й.

figment *n.* вы́мысел (-сла), плод (-а́) воображе́ния.

figuration *n.* оформле́ние; (*ornamentation*) орнамента́ция. **figurative** *adj.* о́бразный, перено́сный. **figure** *n.* (*form, body, person*) фигу́ра; (*number*) ци́фра; (*diagram*) рису́нок (-нка); (*image*) изображе́ние; (*person*) ли́чность; (*of speech*) оборо́т ре́чи; *f.-head*, (*naut.*) носово́е украше́ние; (*person*) подставно́е лицо́ (*pl.* -ца); *v.t.* (*represent*) изобража́ть *imp.*, изобрази́ть *perf.*; (*imagine*) представля́ть *imp.*, предста́вить *perf.* себе́; *f. out*, вычисля́ть *imp.*, вы́числить *perf.* **figurine** *n.* статуэ́тка.

filament *n.* волокно́ (*pl.* -о́кна, -о́кон, -о́кнам), нить.

filch *v.t.* стяну́ть (-ну́, -нешь) *perf.*

file[1] *n.* (*tool*) напи́льник; *v.t.* подпи́ливать *imp.*, подпили́ть (-лю́, -лишь) *perf.*

file[2] *n.* (*folder*) подши́вка, па́пка; (*set of papers*) де́ло (*pl.* -ла); *v.t.* подшива́ть *imp.*, подши́ть (подошью́, -ьёшь) *perf.*; влага́ть *imp.*, вложи́ть (-жу́, -жишь) *perf.* в па́пки.

file[3] *n.* (*row*) ряд (-а́ *with* 2, 3, 4, *loc.* -у́; *pl.* -ы́), шере́нга; *in* (*single*) *f.*, гусько́м.

filial *adj.* (*of son*) сыно́вный; (*of daughter*) доче́рний.

filigree *n.* филигра́нь; *adj.* филигра́нный.

fill *v.t.* & *i.* наполня́ть(ся) *imp.*, напо́лнить(ся) *perf.*; *v.t.* заполня́ть *imp.*, запо́лнить *perf.*; (*tooth*) пломбирова́ть *imp.*, за~ *perf.*; (*occupy*) занима́ть *imp.*, заня́ть (займу́, -мёшь; за́нял, -а́, -о) *perf.*; (*satiate*) насыща́ть *imp.*, насы́тить (-ы́щу, -ы́тишь) *perf.*; *f. in*, (*v.t.*) заполня́ть *imp.*, запо́лнить *perf.*; (*words*) впи́сывать *imp.*, вписа́ть (-ишу́, -и́шешь) *perf.*; (*v.i.*) замеща́ть *imp.*, замести́ть *perf.*

fillet *n.* (*ribbon*) повя́зка; (*cul.*) филе́ *neut.indecl.*

filling *n.* наполне́ние; (*tooth*) пло́мба; (*cul.*) начи́нка.

fillip *n.* щелчо́к (-чка́); толчо́к (-чка́).

filly *n.* кобы́лка.

film *n.* (*haze*) ды́мка; (*layer*; *phot.*) плёнка; (*cin.*) фильм; *f. star*, кинозвезда́ (*pl.* -ёзды); *v.t.* экранизи́ровать *imp.*, *perf.*; *v.i.* производи́ть (-ожу́, -о́дишь) *imp.*, произвести́ (-еду́, -едёшь; -ёл, -ела́) *perf.* киносъёмку; снима́ть *imp.*, снять (сниму́, -мешь; снял, -а́, -о) *perf.* фильм. **filmy** *adj.* тума́нный (-нен, -нна).

filter *n.* фильтр; *v.t.* фильтрова́ть *imp.*, про~ *perf.*; проце́живать *imp.*, процеди́ть *perf.*; *f. through*, *out*, проса́чиваться *imp.*, просочи́ться *perf.*

filth *n.* грязь (*loc.* -зи́); (*obscenity*) непристо́йность. **filthy** *adj.* гря́зный (-зен, -зна́, -зно); непристо́йный.

fin *n.* плавни́к (-а́); (*aeron.*) киль *m.*

final *n.* фина́л; *pl.* выпускны́е экза́мены *m.pl.*; *adj.* после́дний, оконча́тельный. **finale** *n.* фина́л, развя́зка. **finality** *n.* зако́нченность. **finally** *adv.* в конце́ концо́в, оконча́тельно.

finance *n.* фина́нсы (-сов) *pl.*; *pl.* дохо́ды *m.pl.*; *v.t.* финанси́ровать *imp.*, *perf.* **financial** *adj.* фина́нсовый. **financier** *n.* финанси́ст.

finch *n. see comb.*, *e.g.* **bullfinch.**

find *n.* нахо́дка; *v.t.* находи́ть (-ожу́, -о́дишь) *imp.*, найти́ (найду́, -дёшь; нашёл, -шла́) *perf.*; (*person*) застава́ть (-таю́, -таёшь) *imp.*, заста́ть (-а́ну, -а́нешь) *perf.*; *f. out*, узнава́ть (-наю́, -наёшь) *imp.*, узна́ть *perf.*; *f. fault with*, придира́ться *imp.*, придра́ться (придеру́сь, -рёшься; придра́лся, -ала́сь, -а́ло́сь) *perf.* к + *dat.* **finding** *n.* (*leg.*) пригово́р; *pl.* (*of inquiry*) вы́воды *m.pl.*

fine[1] *n.* (*penalty*) штраф; *v.t.* штрафова́ть *imp.*, о~ *perf.*

fine[2] *adj.* (*excellent*) прекра́сный, превосхо́дный; (*delicate*) то́нкии (-нок, -нка́, -нко, то́нки́); (*of sand etc.*) ме́лкий (-лок, -лка́, -лко); *f. arts*, изобрази́тельные иску́сства *neut.pl.* **fineness** *n.* то́нкость, изя́щество, острота́. **finery** *n.* наря́д, украше́ние. **finesse** *n.* хи́трость.

finger *n.* па́лец (-льца) (*index*, указа́тельный; *middle*, сре́дний; *ring*, безымя́нный; *little*, мизи́нец (-нца)); *f.-print*, отпеча́ток (-тка) па́льца; *f.-tip*, ко́нчик па́льца; *have at* (*one's*) *f.-tips*, знать *imp.* как свои пять па́льцев; *v.t.* тро́гать *imp.*, тро́нуть *perf.*

finish *n.* коне́ц (-нца́), оконча́ние; (*of furniture etc.*) отде́лка; (*sport*) фи́ниш; *v.t.* & *i.* конча́ть(ся) *imp.* ко́нчить(ся) *perf.*; *v.t.* ока́нчивать *imp.*, око́нчить *perf.*; *finishing touches*, после́дние штрихи́ *m.pl.*

finite *adj.* определённый (-нен, -нна); (*gram.*) ли́чный.

Finn *n.* финн, фи́нка. **Finnish** *adj.* фи́нский.

fir *n.* ель, пи́хта; *f.-cone*, ело́вая ши́шка.

fire *n.* ого́нь (огня́) *m.*; (*grate*) ками́н; (*conflagration*) пожа́р; (*bonfire*) костёр (-тра́); (*fervour*) пыл (-а(у), *loc.* -у́); *be on f.*, горе́ть (-рю́, -ри́шь) *imp.*; *catch f.*, загора́ться *imp.*, загоре́ться (-рю́сь, -ри́шься) *perf.*; *set f. to*, *set on f.*, поджига́ть *imp.*, подже́чь (подожгу́, -жжёшь; поджёг, подожгла́) *perf.*; *v.t.* зажига́ть *imp.*, заже́чь (-жгу́, -жжёшь; -жёг, -жгла́) *perf.*; воспламеня́ть *imp.*, воспламени́ть *perf.*; (*gun*) стреля́ть *imp.* из + *gen.* (at, в + *acc.*, по + *dat.*); (*dismiss*) увольня́ть *imp.*, уво́лить *perf.*; *f.-alarm*, пожа́рная трево́га; *firearm*(*s*), огнестре́льное ору́жие; *f. brigade*, пожа́рная кома́нда; *f.-engine*, пожа́рная маши́на; *f.-escape* пожа́рная ле́стница; *f. extinguisher*, огнетуши́тель *m.*; *firefly*, светля́к (-а́); *f.-guard*, ками́нная решётка; *fireman*, пожа́рный *sb.*; (*tending furnace*) кочега́р; *f. place*, ками́н; *fireproof*, *f.-resistant*, огнеупо́рный; *fireside*, ме́сто у ками́на; *f. station*, пожа́рное депо́ *neut.indecl.*; *firewood*, дрова́ (-в) *pl.*; *firework*, фейерве́рк. **firing** *n.* (*of gun*) стрельба́.

firm[1] *n.* (*business*) фи́рма.

firm[2] *adj.* твёрдый (твёрд, -а́, -о), кре́пкий (-пок, -пка́, -пко), сто́йкий (-о́ек, -ойка́, -о́йко). **firmament** *n.* небе́сный свод. **firmness** *n.* твёрдость.

first *adj.* пе́рвый; (*foremost*) выдаю́щийся; *n.* (*date*) пе́рвое (число́); пе́рвый *sb.*; *adv.* сперва́, снача́ла, в пе́рвый раз; *in the f. place*, во-пе́рвых; *f. of all*, пре́жде всего́; *at f. sight*, на пе́рвый взгляд, с пе́рвого взгля́да; *f. aid*, пе́рвая по́мощь; *give f. aid*, ока́зывать *imp.*, оказа́ть (-ажу́, -а́жешь) *perf.* пе́рвую по́мощь (to, + *dat.*); *f.-born*, пе́рвенец (-нца); *f.-class*, первокла́ссный, превосхо́дный; *f. cousin*, двою́родный брат (*pl.* -ья, -ьев), двою́родная сестра́ (*pl.* сёстры, сестёр, сёстрам); *f.-hand*, из пе́рвых рук; *f.-rate*, первокла́ссный, превосхо́дный.

fiscal *adj.* фина́нсовый, фиска́льный.

fish *n.* ры́ба; *adj.* ры́бный, ры́бий (-бья, -бье); *v.i.* лови́ть (-влю́, -вишь) *imp.* ры́бу; уди́ть (ужу́, у́дишь) *imp.* ры́бу; *f. for*, (*compliments etc.*) напра́шиваться *imp.*, напроси́ться (-ошу́сь, -о́сишься) *perf.* на + *acc.*; *f. out*, выта́скивать *imp.*, вы́таскать *perf.* **fisherman** *n.* рыба́к (-а́), рыболо́в. **fishery** *n.* ры́бный про́мысел (-сла). **fishing** *n.* ры́бная ло́вля; *f. boat*, рыболо́вное су́дно (*pl.* суда́, -до́в); *f. line*, ле́са́ (*pl.* лёсы); *f. rod*, уди́лище, у́дочка. **fishmonger** *n.* торго́вец (-вца) ры́бой. **fishy** *adj.* ры́бный, ры́бий (-бья, -бье); (*dubious*) подозри́тельный.

fission *n.* расщепле́ние; *nuclear f.* деле́ние ядра́; *cell f.*, деле́ние кле́ток. **fissure** *n.* трещи́на.

fist *n.* кула́к (-а́). **fisticuffs** *n.* кула́чный бой (*loc.* бою́; *pl.* бои́).

fit[1] *n.*: *be a good f.*, (*clothes*) хорошо́ сиде́ть (-ди́т, -дя́т) *imp.*; *adj.* подходя́щий, го́дный (-ден, -дна́, -дно); (*healthy*) здоро́вый; *v.t.* (*be suitable*) годи́ться *imp.* + *dat.*, на + *acc.*, для + *gen.*; подходи́ть (-ожу́, -о́дишь) *imp.*, подойти́ (подойду́, -дёшь; подошёл, -шла́) *perf.* + *dat.*; (*adjust*) прила́живать *imp.*, прила́дить *perf.* (to, к + *dat.*); *v.t.* & *i.* приспоса́бливать(ся) *imp.*; приспосо́бить(ся) *perf.*; *f. out*, снабжа́ть *imp.*, снабди́ть *perf.*

fit[2] *n.* (*attack*) припа́док (-дка), при́ступ; (*fig.*) поры́в. **fitful** *adj.* поры́вистый.

fitter *n.* монтёр, устано́вщик. **fitting** *n.* (*of clothes*) приме́рка; прила́живание, монта́ж; *pl.* армату́ра; *adj.* подходя́щий, го́дный (-ден, -дна́, -дно); *f.-room*, приме́рочная *sb.*

five *adj.*, *n.* пять (-ти́, -тью́); (*collect.*; *5 pairs*) пя́теро (-ры́х); (*cards*; *number 5*) пятёрка; (*time*) пять (часо́в); (*age*) пять лет; *f.-year plan*, пятиле́тка.

fix *n.* (*dilemma*) диле́мма; (*radio etc.*) засе́чка; *v.t.* устана́вливать *imp.*, установи́ть (-влю́, -вишь) *perf.*; (*arrange*) устра́ивать *imp.*, устро́ить *perf.*; (*repair*) поправля́ть *imp.*, попра́вить *perf.*; *v.t.* & *i.* остана́вливать(ся) *imp.*, останови́ть(ся) (-влю́(сь), -вишь(ся)) *perf.* (on, на + *acc.*). **fixation** *n.* викса́ция. **fixed** *adj.* неподви́жный, постоя́нный (-нен, -нна).

fizz *v.i.* шипе́ть (-плю́, -пи́шь) *imp.*, *n.* (*coll.*) шипу́чка. **fizzy** *adj.* шипу́чий.

flabbergast *v.t.* ошеломля́ть *imp.*, ошеломи́ть *perf.*

flabby, flaccid *adj.* дря́блый (-л, -ла́, -ло), вя́лый.

flag[1] *n.* (*standard*) флаг, зна́мя (*pl.* -мёна) *neut.*; *v.t.* (*signal*) сигнализи́ровать *imp.*, *perf.*, про~ *perf.* фла́гами.

flag[2] *n.* (*stone*) плита́ (*pl.* -ты); *v.t.* мости́ть *imp.*, вы́~, за~ *perf.* пли́тами.

flag[3] *v.i.* (*droop*) поника́ть *imp.*, пони́кнуть (-к) *perf.*

flagellate *v.t.* бичева́ть (-чу́ю, -чу́ешь) *imp.*

flagon *n.* кувши́н.

flagrant *adj.* вопию́щий, очеви́дный, сканда́льный.

flagship *n.* флагма́н. **flagstaff** *n.* флагшто́к.

flail *n.* цеп (-а́).

flair *n.* чутьё.

flake *n.* слой (*pl.* -ои́); *pl.* хло́пья (-ьев) *pl.*; *v.i.* слои́ться *imp.*; лупи́ться (-пится) *imp.*, об~ *perf.* **flaky** *adj.* слои́стый.

flamboyant *adj.* цвети́стый.

flame *n.* пла́мя *neut.*, ого́нь (огня́) *m.*; (*passion*) пыл (-а(у), *loc.* -у́); *f.-thrower* огнемёт; *v.i.* пыла́ть *imp.*; *f. up*, разгора́ться *imp.*, разгоре́ться (-ри́тся) *perf.*

flamingo *n.* флами́нго *m. indecl.*

flange *n.* фла́нец (-нца).

flank *n.* бок (*loc.* -у́; *pl.* -а́), фланг; *v.t.* быть располо́женным сбо́ку, на фла́нге, +*gen.*; (*mil.*) фланки́ровать *imp.*, *perf.*

flannel *n.* флане́ль; *attrib.* флане́левый.

flap *n.* мах; (*wings*) взмах; (*board*) отки́дная доска́ (*acc.* -ску; *pl.* -ски, -со́к, -ска́м); *v.t.* маха́ть (машу́, -шешь) *imp.*, махну́ть *perf.*+*instr.*; взма́хивать *imp.*, взмахну́ть *perf.*+*instr.*; *v.i.* развева́ться *imp.*

flare *n.* вспы́шка; (*signal*) светово́й сигна́л; *v.i.* вспы́хивать *imp.*, вспы́хнуть *perf.*; *f. up*, вспыли́ть *perf.*

flash *n.* вспы́шка, пробле́ск; *in a f.*, ми́гом; *v.i.* сверка́ть *imp.*, сверкну́ть *perf.* **flashy** *adj.* показно́й.

flask *n.* фля́жка.

flat[1] *n.* (*dwelling*) кварти́ра.

flat[2] *n.* (*f. region*) равни́на; (*mus.*) бемо́ль *m.*; (*tyre*) спу́щенная ши́на; *adj.* пло́ский (-сок, -ска́, -ско), ро́вный (-вен, -вна́, -вно); (*dull*) ску́чный (-чен, -чна́, -чно); *f.-fish*, ка́мбала; *f. foot*, плоскосто́пие; *f.-iron*, утю́г (-а́). **flatten** *v.t.* де́лать *imp.*, с~ *perf.* пло́ским; *v.i.* станови́ться (-ится) *imp.*, стать (ста́нет) *perf.* пло́ским; *v.t.* & *i.* выра́внивать(ся) *imp.*, вы́ровнять(ся) *perf.*

flatter *v.t.* льсти́ть *imp.*, по~ *perf.*+*dat.* **flatterer** *n.* льстец (-а́). **flattering** *adj.* льсти́вый, ле́стный. **flattery** *n.* лесть.

flaunt *v.t.* щеголя́ть *imp.*, щегольну́ть *perf.*+*instr.*; *f. oneself*, выставля́ться *imp.*, вы́ставиться *perf.*

flautist *n.* флейти́ст.

flavour *n.* арома́т, вкус; (*fig.*) при́вкус, отте́нок (-нка); *v.t.* приправля́ть *imp.*, припра́вить *perf.* **flavourless** *adj.* безвку́сный.

flaw *n.* (*crack*) трещи́на; (*defect*) изъя́н.

flax *n.* лён (льна). **flaxen** *adj.* льняно́й; (*colour*) соло́менный.

flay *v.t.* сдира́ть *imp.*, содра́ть (сдеру́, -рёшь; содра́л, -а́, -о) *perf.* ко́жу с+*gen.*

flea *n.* блоха́ (*pl.* -хи, -х, -ха́м); *f.-bite*, блоши́ный уку́с.

fleck *n.* пятно́ (*pl.* -тна, -тен, -тнам), кра́пина.

fledge *v.t.* оперя́ть *imp.*, опери́ть *perf.*; *be*(*come*) *fledged*, оперя́ться *imp.*, опери́ться *perf.* **fledg(e)ling** *n.* птене́ц (-нца́).

flee *v.i.* бежа́ть (бегу́, бежи́шь) *imp.*, *perf.* (from, от+*gen.*); (*vanish*) исчеза́ть *imp.*, исче́знуть (-з) *perf.*

fleece *n.* ове́чья шерсть, руно́ (*pl.* -на); *v.t.* обдира́ть *imp.*, ободра́ть (обдеру́, -рёшь; ободра́л, -а́, -о) *perf.* **fleecy** *adj.* шерсти́стый.

fleet[1] *n.* флот (*pl.* -о́ты, -о́то́в); (*vehicles*) парк.

fleet[2] *adj.* бы́стрый (быстр, -а́, -о, бы́стры́); *f. of foot*, быстроно́гий. **fleeting** *adj.* мимолётный.

flesh *n.* (*as opp. to mind*) плоть; (*meat*) мя́со; (*of fruit*) мя́коть; *in the f.*, во плоти́. **fleshly** *adj.* пло́тский. **fleshy** *adj.* мяси́стый.

flex *n.* электрошну́р (-а́); *v.t.* сгиба́ть *imp.*, согну́ть *perf.* **flexibility** *adj.* ги́бкость, пода́тливость. **flexible** *adj.* ги́бкий (-бок, -бка́, -бко), пода́тливый. **flexion** *n.* сгиб(а́ние); (*gram.*) фле́ксия.

flick *n.* щелчо́к (-чка́); *f.-knife*, фи́нка; *v.t.* & *i.* щёлкать *imp.*, щёлкнуть *perf.* (+*instr.*); *f. off*, сма́хивать *imp.*, смахну́ть *perf.*

flicker *n.* мерца́ние; *v.i.* мерца́ть *imp.*

flier *see* **flyer.**

flight[1] *n.* (*fleeing*) бе́гство; *put to f.*, обраща́ть *imp.*, обрати́ть (-ащу́, -ати́шь) *perf.* в бе́гство.

flight[2] *n.* (*flying*) полёт, перелёт; (*trip*) рейс; (*flock*) стая́; (*aeron. unit*) звено́ (*pl.* -нья, -ньев); *f. of stairs*, ле́стничный марш. **flighty** *adj.* ве́треный.

flimsy *adj.* непро́чный (-чен, -чна́, -чно).

flinch *v.i.* уклоня́ться *imp.*, уклони́ться (-ню́сь, -ни́шься) *perf.* (from, от+

gen.); (*wince*) вздрáгивать *imp.*, вздрóгнуть *perf.*
fling *v.t.* швырять *imp.*, швырнýть *perf.*; *v.i.* (*also f. oneself*) бросáться *imp.*, брóситься *perf.*
flint *n.* кремéнь (-мня́) *m.*; *attrib.* кремнёвый.
flip *n.* щелчóк (-чкá); *v.t.* щёлкать *imp.*, щёлкнуть *perf.* + *instr.*
flippancy *n.* легкомы́слие. **flippant** *adj.* легкомы́сленный (-ен, -енна).
flipper *n.* плавни́к (-á), ласт.
flirt *n.* кокéтка; *v.i.* флиртовáть *imp.* (with, с + *instr.*); (*fig.*) заигрывать *imp.* (with, с + *instr.*). **flirtation** *n.* флирт.
flit *v.i.* (*migrate*) переезжáть *imp.*, переéхать (-éду, -éдешь) *perf.*; (*fly*) порхáть *imp.*, порхнýть *perf.*
float *n.* поплавóк (-вкá), плот (-á); *v.i.* плáвать *indet.*, плыть (плывý, -вёшь; плыл, -á, -о) *det.*; *v.t.* (*loan*) выпускáть *imp.*, вы́пустить *perf.*; (*company*) пускáть *imp.*, пусти́ть (пущý, пýстишь) *perf.* в ход.
flock *n.* (*animals*) стáдо (*pl.* -дá); (*birds*) стáя; (*people*) толпá (*pl.* -пы); *v.i.* стекáться *imp.*, стéчься (стечётся; стёкся, -клáсь) *perf.*; толпи́ться *imp.*
floe *n.* плавýчая льди́на.
flog *v.t.* сечь (секý, сечёшь; сек, -лá) *imp.*, вы́~ *perf.*
flood *n.* наводнéние, разли́в, потóп; *f.-tide*, прили́в; *v.i.* (*river etc.*) выступáть *imp.*, вы́ступить *perf.* из берегóв; *v.t.* наводня́ть *imp.*, наводни́ть *perf.*; затопля́ть *imp.*, затопи́ть (-плю́, -пишь) *perf.* **floodgate** *n.* шлюз. **floodlight** *n.* прожéктор (*pl.* -ы & -á).
floor *n.* пол (*loc.* -ý; *pl.* -ы́); (*of sea*) дно (*no pl.*); (*storey*) этаж (-á); *ground, first*, (*etc.*) *f.*, пéрвый, вторóй, (и т.д.) этаж (-á); *take the f.*, брать (берý, -рёшь; брал, -á, -о) *imp.*, взять (возьмý, -мёшь; взял, -á, -о) *perf.* слóво; *f.-board*, полови́ца; *f.-cloth*, половáя тря́пка; *v.t.* настилáть *imp.*, настлáть (-телю́, -тéлешь) *perf.* пол + *gen.*; (*knock down*) вали́ть (-лю́, -лишь) *imp.*, по~ *perf.* нá пол; (*confound*) стáвить *imp.*, по~ *perf.* в тупи́к. **flooring** *n.* насти́л(ка).
flop *v.i.* шлёпаться *imp.*, шлёпнуться *perf.*; (*fail*) провáливаться *imp.*, провали́ться (-ится) *perf.*
flora *n.* флóра. **floral** *adj.* цветóчный. **florescence** *n.* цветéние. **florid** *adj.* цвети́стый; (*ruddy*) румя́ный. **florist** *n.* торгóвец (-вца) цветáми.
flotilla *n.* флоти́лия.
flotsam *n.* плáвающие oблóмки *m.pl.*
flounce[1] *v.i.* бросáться *imp.*, брóситься *perf.*
flounce[2] *n.* (*of skirt*) обóрка.
flounder[1] *n.* (*fish*) кáмбала.
flounder[2] *v.i.* барáхтаться *imp.*; пýтаться *imp.*, с~ *perf.*
flour *n.* мукá; *f.-mill*, мéльница.
flourish *n.* (*movement*) размáхивание (+ *instr.*); (*of pen*) рóсчерк; (*mus.*) туш; *v.i.* (*thrive*) процветáть *imp.*; *v.t.* (*wave*) размáхивать *imp.*, размахнýть *perf.* + *instr.*
floury *adj.* мучни́стый.
flout *v.t.* пренебрегáть *imp.*, пренебрéчь (-егý, -ежёшь; -ёг, -еглá) *perf.* + *instr.*
flow *v.i.* течь (течёт; тёк, -лá) *imp.*; ли́ться (льётся; ли́лся, лилáсь, ли́лось) *imp.*; *n.* течéние, потóк; (*tide*) прили́в.
flower *n.* цветóк (-ткá; *pl.* -ты́); (*pick; prime*) цвет; *f.-bed*, клýмба; *flowerpot*, цветóчный горшóк (-шкá); *v.i.* цвести́ (цветёт; цвёл, -á) *imp.* **flowery** *adj.* покры́тый цветáми; (*florid*) цвети́стый.
fluctuate *v.i.* колебáться (-блюсь, -блешься) *imp.*, по~ *perf.* **fluctuation** *n.* колебáние.
flue *n.* дымохóд.
fluency *n.* плáвность, бéглость. **fluent** *adj.* плáвный, бéглый. **fluently** *adv.* бéгло, свобóдно.
fluff *n.* пух (-а(у), *loc.* -ý), пушóк (-шкá). **fluffy** *adj.* пуши́стый.
fluid *n.* жи́дкость; *adj.* жи́дкий (-док, -дкá, -дко), текýчий.
flunkey *n.* лакéй.
fluorescence *n.* флюоресцéнция. **fluorescent** *adj.* флюоресци́рующий.
fluoride *n.* фтори́д. **fluorine** *n.* фтор.

flurry *n.* (*squall*) поры́в ве́тра; (*commotion*) сумато́ха; *v.t.* (*agitate*) волнова́ть *imp.*, вз~ *perf.*
flush *n.* прили́в; (*redness*) румя́нец (-нца); *v.i.* (*redden*) красне́ть *imp.*, по~ *perf.*; *v.t.* спуска́ть *imp.*, спусти́ть (-ущу́, -у́стишь) *perf.* во́ду в+*acc.*
fluster *n.* волне́ние; *v.t.* волнова́ть *imp.*, вз~ *perf.*
flute *n.* (*mus.*) фле́йта; (*groove*) желобо́к (-бка́); (*archit.*) каннелю́ра.
flutter *v.i.* порха́ть *imp.*, порхну́ть *perf.*; развева́ться *imp.*; (*with excitement*) трепета́ть (-ещу́, -е́щешь) *imp.*; *n.* порха́ние; тре́пет.
fluvial *adj.* речно́й.
flux *n.* тече́ние; *in a state of f.*, в состоя́нии измене́ния.
fly[1] *n.* (*insect*) му́ха.
fly[2] *v.i.* лета́ть *indet.*, лете́ть (лечу́, лети́шь) *det.*, по~ *perf.*; (*flag*) развева́ться *imp.*; (*hasten*) нести́сь (несу́сь, -сёшься; нёсся, несла́сь) *imp.*, по~ *perf.*; (*flee*) бежа́ть (бегу́, бежи́шь) *imp.*, *perf.*; *v.t.* (*aircraft*) управля́ть *imp.*+*instr.*; (*transport*) перевози́ть (-ожу́, -о́зишь) *imp.*, перевезти́ (-езу́, -езёшь; -ёз, -езла́) *perf.* (самолётом); (*flag*) поднима́ть *imp.*, подня́ть (-ниму́, -ни́мешь; по́днял, -а́, -о) *perf.*
flyer, flier *n.* лётчик. **flying** *n.* полёт(ы).
flywheel *n.* махови́к (-а́).
foal *n.* (*horse*) жеребёнок (-нка; *pl.* жеребя́та, -т); (*ass*) ослёнок (-нка; *pl.* ословя́та, -т); *in f.*, жерёбая; *v.i.* жереби́ться *imp.*, о~ *perf.*
foam *n.* пе́на; *f. plastic*, пенопла́ст; *f. rubber*, пенорези́на; *v.i.* пе́ниться *imp.*, вс~ *perf.* **foamy** *adj.* пени́стый.
focal *adj.* фо́кусный.
fo'c's'le *see* **forecastle.**
focus *n.* фо́кус, центр; *v.t.* фокуси́ровать *imp.*, с~ *perf.*; (*concentrate*) сосредото́чивать *imp.*, сосредото́чить *perf.*
fodder *n.* корм (*loc.* -е & -у́; *pl.* -а́), фура́ж (-а́).
foe *n.* враг (-а́).
fog *n.* тума́н, мгла. **foggy** *adj.* тума́нный (-нен, -нна), нея́сный (-сен, -сна́, -сно).
foible *n.* сла́бость.
foil[1] *n.* (*metal*) фо́льга; (*contrast*) контра́ст.
foil[2] *v.t.* (*frustrate*) расстра́ивать *imp.*, расстро́ить *perf.* (пла́ны+*gen.*); *n.* (*track*) след (*pl.* -ы́) зве́ря.
foil[3] *n.* (*sword*) рапи́ра.
foist *v.t.* навя́зывать *imp.*, навяза́ть (-яжу́, -я́жешь) *perf.* (on, +*dat.*).
fold[1] *n.* (*sheep-f.*) овча́рня (*gen.pl.* -рен).
fold[2] *n.* скла́дка, сгиб; *v.t.* скла́дывать *imp.*, сложи́ть (-жу́, -жишь) *perf.*; сгиба́ть *imp.*, согну́ть *perf.* **folder** *n.* па́пка. **folding** *adj.* складно́й, откидно́й, створ́чатый.
foliage *n.* листва́.
folk *n.* наро́д (-а(у)), лю́ди (-де́й, -дям, -дьми́) *pl.*; *pl.* (*relatives*) родня́ *collect.*; *attrib.* наро́дный. **folklore** *n.* фолькло́р.
follow *v.t.* сле́довать *imp.*, по~ *perf.*+*dat.*, за+*instr.*; идти́ (иду́, идёшь; шёл, шла) *det.* за+*instr.*; следи́ть *imp.* за+*instr.* **follower** *n.* после́дователь *m.*, ~ница. **following** *adj.* сле́дующий.
folly *n.* глу́пость, безу́мие.
fond *adj.* лю́бящий, не́жный; *be f. of*, люби́ть (-блю́, -бишь) *imp.*+*acc.*
fondle *v.t.* ласка́ть *imp.*
fondness *n.* не́жность, любо́вь (-бви́, *instr.* -бо́вью).
font *n.* (*eccl.*) купе́ль.
food *n.* пи́ща, еда́; *f. value*, пита́тельность. **foodstuff** *n.* пищево́й проду́кт.
fool *n.* дура́к (-а́), глупе́ц (-пца́); *v.t.* дура́чить *imp.*, о~ *perf.*; *v.i.*: *f. about*, *play the f.*, дура́читься *imp.* **foolery** *n.* дура́чество. **foolhardy** *adj.* безрассу́дно хра́брый (храбр, -а́, -о). **foolish** *adj.* глу́пый (глуп, -а́, -о). **foolishness** *n.* глу́пость.
foot *n.* нога́ (*acc.* -гу; *pl.* -ги, -г, -га́м), ступня́; (*measure*) фут; (*of hill etc.*) подно́жие; (*mil.*) пехо́та; *on f.*, пешко́м; *put one's foot in it*, сесть (ся́ду, -дешь; сел) *perf.* в лу́жу. **football** *n.* футбо́л; *attrib.* футбо́льный. **footballer** *n.* футболи́ст. **footfall** *n.* по́ступь. **footlights** *n.* ра́мпа. **footman** *n.* лаке́й. **footnote** *n.* сно́ска, примеча́ние. **footpath** *n.* тропи́нка; (*pavement*)

тротуа́р. **footprint** *n.* след (*pl.* -ы́) (ноги́). **footstep** *n.* (*tread*) шаг (-а(у) & (*with 2, 3, 4*) -а́, *loc.* -у́; *pl.* -и́); (*footprint*) след (*pl.* -ы́) (ноги́). **footwear** *n.* о́бувь.

fop *n.* щёголь *m.*, фат. **foppish** *adj.* щегольско́й, фатова́тый.

for *prep.* (*of time*) в тече́ние + *gen.*, на + *acc.*; (*of purpose*) для + *gen.*, за + *acc.*, + *instr.*; (*of destination*) в + *acc.*; (*on account of*) из-за + *gen.*; (*in place of*) вме́сто + *gen.*; *for the sake of*, ра́ди + *gen.*; *as for*, что каса́ется + *gen.*; *conj.* так как, и́бо.

forage *n.* фура́ж (-а́), корм (*loc.* -е & -у́; *pl.* -а́); *v.i.* фуражи́ровать *imp.*

foray *n.* набе́г.

forbear[1] *n.* (*ancestor*) пре́док (-дка).

forbear[2] *v.i.* (*refrain*) возде́рживаться *imp.*, воздержа́ться (-жу́сь, -жишься) *perf.* (from, от + *gen.*). **forbearance** *n.* возде́ржанность.

forbid *v.t.* запреща́ть *imp.*, запрети́ть (-ещу́, -ети́шь) *perf.* (+ *dat.* (*person*) & *acc.* (*thing*)); воспреща́ть *imp.*, воспрети́ть (-ещу́, -ети́шь) *perf.* + *acc.*, + *inf.*

force *n.* (*strength*) си́ла; (*violence*) наси́лие; (*meaning*) смысл; *pl.* (*armed f.*) вооружённые си́лы *f.pl.*; *by f.*, си́лой; *by f. of*, в си́лу + *gen.*; *in f.*, в си́ле; (*in large numbers*) толпа́ми; *v.t.* (*compel*) заставля́ть *imp.*, заста́вить *perf.*; принужда́ть *imp.*, принуди́ть *perf.*; (*lock etc.*) взла́мывать *imp.*, взлома́ть *perf.*; (*hasten*) форси́ровать *imp.*, *perf.* **forceful** *adj.* си́льный (си́лён, -льна́, -льно, си́льны́); (*speech*) убеди́тельный. **forcible** *adj.* наси́льственный.

forceps *n.* щипцы́ (-цо́в) *pl.*

ford *n.* брод; *v.t.* переходи́ть (-ожу́, -о́дишь) *imp.*, перейти́ (-ейду́, -ейдёшь; -ешёл, -ешла́) *perf.* вброд + *acc.*, че́рез + *acc.*

fore *n.*: *to the f.*, на пере́днем пла́не.

forearm *n.* предпле́чье (*gen.pl.* -чий). **forebode** *v.t.* (*betoken*) предвеща́ть *imp.*; (*have presentiment*) предчу́вствовать *imp.* **foreboding** *n.* предчу́вствие. **forecast** *n.* предсказа́ние; (*of weather*) прогно́з; *v.t.* предска́зывать *imp.*, предсказа́ть (-ажу́, -а́жешь) *perf.* **forecastle, fo'c's'le** *n.* (*naut.*) бак. **forefather** *n.* пре́док (-дка). **forefinger** *n.* указа́тельный па́лец (-льца). **foreground** *n.* пере́дний план. **forehead** *n.* лоб (лба, *loc.* лбу).

foreign *adj.* (*from abroad*) иностра́нный (-нен, -нна); (*alien*) чужо́й; (*external*) вне́шний; *f. body*, иноро́дное те́ло (*pl.* -ла́). **foreigner** *n.* иностра́нец (-нца).

forelock *n.* чёлка. **foreman** *n.* (*jury*) старшина́ (*pl.* -ны) *m.* прися́жных; (*factory*) ма́стер (*pl.* -а́).

foremost *adj.* передово́й, пере́дний; (*notable*) выдаю́щийся.

forensic *adj.* суде́бный.

forerunner *n.* предве́стник. **foresee** *v.t.* предви́деть (-и́жу, -и́дишь) *imp.* **foreshadow** *v.t.* предвеща́ть *imp.* **foresight** *n.* предви́дение; (*caution*) предусмотри́тельность.

forest *n.* лес (-а(у), *loc.* -у́; *pl.* -а́).

forestall *v.t.* предупрежда́ть *imp.*, предупреди́ть *perf.*

forester *n.* лесни́к (-а́), лесни́чий *sb.* **forestry** *n.* лесово́дство.

foretaste *n.* предвкуше́ние; *v.t.* предвкуша́ть *imp.*, предвкуси́ть (-ушу́, -у́сишь) *perf.* **foretell** *v.t.* предска́зывать *imp.*, предсказа́ть (-ажу́, -а́жешь) *perf.* **forethought** *n.* (*intention*) предна́меренность; (*caution*) предусмотри́тельность. **forewarn** *v.t.* предостерега́ть *imp.*, предостере́чь (-егу́, -ежёшь; -ёг, -егла́) *perf.* **foreword** *n.* предисло́вие.

forfeit *n.* (*fine*) штраф; (*deprivation*) лише́ние, конфиска́ция; (*in game*) фант; *pl.* (*game*) игра́ в фа́нты; *v.t.* лиша́ться *imp.*, лиши́ться *perf.* + *gen.*; (*pay with*) плати́ться (-ачу́сь, -а́тишься) *imp.*, по~ *perf.* + *instr.* **forfeiture** *n.* лише́ние, конфиска́ция, поте́ря.

forge[1] *n.* (*smithy*) кузни́ца; (*furnace*) горн; *v.t.* кова́ть (кую́, куёшь) *imp.*, вы́~ *perf.*; (*fabricate*) подде́лывать *imp.*, подде́лать *perf.*

forge[2] *v.i.*: *f. ahead* продвига́ться *imp.*, продви́нуться *perf.* вперёд.

forger *n.* подде́лыватель *m.*; (*of money*) фальшивомоне́тчик. **forgery** *n.* подде́лка, подло́г.

forget *v.t.* забывáть *imp.*, забы́ть (забу́ду, -дешь) *perf.*; *f.-me-not.* незабу́дка. **forgetful** *adj.* забы́вчивый,
forgive *v.t.* прощáть *imp.*, прости́ть *perf.* **forgiveness** *n.* прощéние.
forgo *v.t.* воздéрживаться *imp.*, воздержáться (-жу́сь, -жи́шься) *perf.* от + *gen.*
fork *n.* (*eating*) ви́лка; (*digging*) ви́лы (-л) *pl.*; разветвлéние; *v.i.* рабóтать *imp.* ви́лами; (*form fork*) разветвля́ться *imp.*, разветви́ться *perf.*
forlorn *adj.* уны́лый.
form *n.* фóрма, вид, фигу́ра; (*formality*) формáльность; (*class*) класс; (*document*) бланк, анкéта; (*bench*) скамéйка; *v.t.* (*shape*) придавáть (-даю́, -даёшь) *imp.*, придáть (-áм, -áшь, -áст, -ади́м; при́дал, -á, -о) *perf.* фóрму + *dat.*; (*make up*) составля́ть *imp.*, состáвить *perf.*; образóвывать *imp.*, образовáть *perf.*; формировáть *imp.*, с ~ *perf.*; *v.i.* принимáть *imp.*, приня́ть (-и́мет; при́нял, -á, -о) *perf.* фóрму; образóвываться *imp.*, образовáться *perf.* **formal** *adj.* официáльный, формáльный. **formality** *n.* формáльность. **formation** *n.* образовáние, формировáние, формáция.
former *adj.* бы́вший, прéжний; *the f.*, (*of two*) пéрвый. **formerly** *adv.* прéжде.
formidable *adj.* (*dread*) грóзный (-зен, -знá, -зно); (*arduous*) тру́дный (-ден, -днá, -дно, тру́дны́).
formless *adj.* бесфóрменный (-ен, -енна).
formula *n.* фóрмула. **formulate** *v.t.* формули́ровать *imp.*, с ~ *perf.* **formulation** *n.* формулирóвка.
forsake *v.t.* (*desert*) покидáть *imp.*, поки́нуть *perf.*; (*renounce*) откáзываться *imp.*, отказáться (-ажу́сь, -áжешься) *perf.* от + *gen.*
forswear *v.t.* отрекáться *imp.*, отрéчься (-еку́сь, -ечёшься; -ёкся, -еклáсь) *perf.* от + *gen.*
fort *n.* форт (*loc.* -у́; *pl.* -ы́).
forth *adv.* вперёд, дáльше; *back and f.*, взад и вперёд; *and so f.*, и так дáлее. **forthcoming** *adj.* предстоя́щий. **forthwith** *adv.* немéдленно.
fortieth *adj.*, *n.* сороковóй.
fortification *n.* фортификáция, укреплéние. **fortify** *v.t.* укрепля́ть *imp.*, укрепи́ть *perf.*; подкрепля́ть *imp.*, подкрепи́ть *perf.* **fortitude** *n.* му́жество.
fortnight *n.* две недéли. **fortnightly** *adj.* двухнедéльный; *adv.* раз в две недéли.
fortress *n.* крéпость.
fortuitous *adj.* случáйный.
fortunate *adj.* счастли́вый (счáстли́в). **fortunately** *adv.* к счáстью. **fortune** *n.* (*destiny*) судьбá (*pl.* -дьбы, -деб, -дьбам); (*good f.*) счáстье; (*wealth*) состоя́ние; *f.-teller*, гадáльщик, -ица, гадáлка; *f.-telling*, гадáние.
forty *adj.*, *n.* сóрок (*oblique cases* -á); (*age*) сóрок лет; *pl.* (*decade*) сороковы́е гóды (-дóв) *m.pl.*
forward *adj.* перéдний, передовóй; (*early*) рáнний; *n.* (*sport*) нападáющий *sb.*; *adv.* вперёд, дáльше; *v.t.* (*promote*) спосóбствовать *imp.*, по ~ *perf.* + *dat.*; (*letter etc.*) пересылáть *imp.*, переслáть (перешлю́, -лёшь) *perf.*
fossil *n.* окаменéлость, ископáемое *sb.*; *adj.* окаменéлый, ископáемый. **fossilize** *v.t.* & *i.* превращáть(ся) *imp.*, преврати́ть(ся) (-ащу́(сь), -ати́шь(ся)) *perf.* в окаменéлость.
foster *v.t.* воспи́тывать *imp.*, воспитáть *perf.*; (*feeling*) лелéять (-éю, -éешь) *imp.*; *adj.* приёмный; *f.-child*, приёмыш.
foul *adj.* (*dirty*) гря́зный (-зен, -знá, -зно); (*repulsive*) отврати́тельный; (*obscene*) непристóйный; *n.* (*collision*) столкновéние; (*sport*) нарушéние прáвил; *v.t.* & *i.* (*dirty*) пáчкать(ся) *imp.*, за ~, ис ~ *perf.*; (*entangle*) запу́тывать(ся) *imp.*, запу́тать(ся) *perf.*
found[1] *v.t.* (*establish*) оснóвывать *imp.*, основáть (-ную́, -нуёшь) *perf.*; (*building*) заклáдывать *imp.*, заложи́ть (-жу́, -жишь) *perf.*
found[2] *v.t.* (*metal*) отливáть *imp.*, отли́ть (отолью́, -ьёшь; óтли́л, -á, -о) *perf.*
foundation *n.* (*of building*) фундáмент; (*basis*) оснóва, основáние; (*institution*)

учреждéние; (*funds*) фонд. **founder**[1] *n.* основáтель *m.*, ~ница.

founder[2] *n.* (*of metal*) литéйщик, плавúльщик.

founder[3] *v.i.* (*naut.*) идтú (идёт; шёл, шла) *imp.*, пойтú (пойдёт; пошёл, -шлá) *perf.* ко днý.

foundling *n.* подкúдыш.

foundry *n.* литéйная *sb.*

fount[1] *n.* (*print.*) комплéкт шрúфта.

fount[2] *n.* истóчник. **fountain** *n.* фонтáн, истóчник; *f.-pen*, авторýчка.

four *adj.*, *n.* четы́ре (-рёх, -рём, -рьмя́); (*collect.*; *4 pairs*) чéтверо (-ры́х); (*cards*; *boat*; *number 4*) четвёрка; (*time*) четы́ре (часá); (*age*) четы́ре гóда; *on all fours*, на четверéньках. **fourteen** *adj.*, *n.* четы́рнадцать (-ти, -тью); (*age*) четы́рнадцать лет. **fourteenth** *adj.*, *n.* четы́рнадцатый; (*date*) четы́рнадцатое (числó). **fourth** *adj.*, *n.* четвёртый; (*quarter*) чéтверть (*pl.* -ти, -тéй); (*date*) четвёртое (числó); (*mus.*) квáрта.

fowl *n.* (*bird*) птúца; (*domestic*) домáшняя птúца; (*wild*) дичь *collect.*

foyer *n.* фойé *neut.indecl.*

fox *n.* лисá (*pl.* -сы), лисúца; *attrib.* лúсий (-сья, -сье); *v.t.* обмáнывать *imp.*, обманýть (-нý, -нешь) *perf.* **foxglove** *n.* наперстя́нка. **foxhole** *n.* (*mil.*) ячéйка. **foxy** *adj.* лúсий (-сья, -сье); (*crafty*) хúтрый (-тёр, -трá, хúтрó).

fraction *n.* (*math.*) дробь (*pl.* -би, -бéй); (*portion*) частúца. **fractional** *adj.* дрóбный.

fractious *adj.* раздражúтельный.

fracture *n.* перелóм; *v.t.* & *i.* ломáть(ся) *imp.*, с~ *perf.*

fragile *adj.* лóмкий (-мок, -мкá, -мко), хрýпкий (-пок, -пкá, -пко). **fragility** *n.* лóмкость, хрýпкость.

fragment *n.* облóмок (-мка), оскóлок (-лка); (*of writing etc.*) отры́вок (-вка), фрагмéнт. **fragmentary** *adj.* отры́вочный.

fragrance *n.* аромáт. **fragrant** *adj.* аромáтный, душúстый.

frail *adj.* хрýпкий (-пок, -пкá, -пко).

frame *n.* óстов; (*body*) тéло (*pl.* -лá); (*build*) телосложéние; (*picture*) рáма, рáмка; (*cin.*) кадр; *f. of mind*, настроéние; *v.t.* (*devise*) создавáть (-даю́, -даёшь) *imp.*, создáть (-áм, -áшь, -áст, -адúм; сóздал, -á, -о) *perf.*; (*adapt*) приспосáбливать *imp.*, приспособля́ть *perf.*; (*picture*) вставля́ть *imp.*, встáвить *perf.* в рáму; (*surround*) обрамля́ть *imp.*, обрамúть *perf.* **framework** *n.* óстов, структýра; (*fig.*) рáмки *f.pl.*

franc *n.* франк.

franchise *n.* (*privilege*) привилéгия; (*right to vote*) прáво гóлоса.

frank[1] *adj.* (*open*) откровéнный (-нен, -нна).

frank[2] *v.t.* (*letter*) франкúровать *imp.*, *perf.*

frantic *adj.* нéистовый, бéшеный.

fraternal *adj.* брáтский. **fraternity** *n.* брáтство, общúна. **fraternize** *v.t.* брáтаться *imp.*, по~ *perf.* (with, с + *instr.*).

fraud *n.* (*deception*) обмáн; (*person*) обмáнщик. **fraudulent** *adj.* обмáнный (-нен, -нна).

fraught *adj.*: *f. with*, чревáтый + *instr.*, пóлный (-лон, -лнá, пóлнó) + *gen.*, *instr.*

fray[1] *v.t.* & *i.* обтрёпывать(ся) *imp.*, обтрепáть(ся) (-плю́(сь), -плешь(ся)) *perf.*

fray[2] *n.* (*brawl*) дрáка.

freak *n.* (*caprice*) причýда; (*monstrosity*) урóд.

freckle *n.* веснýшка. **freckled** *adj.* веснýшчатый.

free *adj.* свобóдный, вóльный; (*gratis*) бесплáтный; *of one's own f. will*, по дóброй вóле; *f.-lance*, внештáтный; *f. speech*, свобóда слóва; *f. thinker*, вольнодýмец (-мца); *v.t.* освобождáть *imp.*, освободúть *perf.* **freedom** *n.* свобóда. **Freemason** *n.* франкмасóн.

freeze *v.i.* замерзáть *imp.*, мёрзнуть (-з) *imp.*, за~ *perf.*; *v.t.* заморáживать *imp.*, заморóзить *perf.*

freight *n.* фрахт, груз. **freighter** *n.* (*ship*) грузовóе сýдно (*pl.* -дá, -дóв).

French *adj.* францýзский; *F. bean*, фасóль; *F. leave*, ухóд без прощáния, без разрешéния. **Frenchman** *n.* францýз. **Frenchwoman** *n.* францýженка.

frenetic *adj.* неистовый.

frenzied *adj.* неистовый. **frenzy** *n.* неистовство.

frequency *n.* частота́ (*pl.* -ты). **frequent** *adj.* ча́стый (част, -а́, -о); *v.t.* ча́сто посеща́ть *imp.*

fresco *n.* фре́ска.

fresh *adj.* све́жий (свеж, -а́, -о́, све́жи́); (*new*) но́вый (нов, -а́, -о); (*vigorous*) бо́дрый (бодр, -а́, -о, бо́дры́); *f. water*, пре́сная вода́ (*acc.* -ду). **freshen** *v.t.* освежа́ть *imp.*, освежи́ть *perf.*; *v.i.* свеже́ть *imp.*, по~ *perf.* **freshly** *adv.* свежо́; (*recently*) неда́вно. **freshness** *n.* све́жесть; бо́дрость. **freshwater** *adj.* пресново́дный.

fret[1] *n.* (*irritation*) раздраже́ние; *v.t.* (*eat away*) разъеда́ть *imp.*, разъе́сть (-е́м, -е́шь, -е́ст, -еди́м; -е́л) *perf.*; *v.t.* & *i.* (*distress*) беспоко́ить(ся) *imp.*, о~ *perf.* **fretful** *adj.* беспоко́йный.

fret[2] *n.* (*mus.*) лад (*loc.* -у́; *pl.* -ы́).

fretsaw *n.* ло́бзик.

friar *n.* мона́х. **friary** *n.* мужско́й монасты́рь (-ря́) *m.*

friction *n.* тре́ние; (*fig.*) тре́ния *neut.pl.*

Friday *n.* пя́тница; *Good F.*, страстна́я пя́тница.

friend *n.* друг (*pl.* друзья́, -зе́й), подру́га; прия́тель *m.*, ~ница; (*acquaintance*) знако́мый *sb.* **friendly** *adj.* дру́жеский, дру́жественный. **friendship** *n.* дру́жба.

frigate *n.* фрега́т.

fright *n.* испу́г (-а(у)). **frighten** *v.t.* пуга́ть *imp.*, ис~, на~ *perf.* **frightful** *adj.* стра́шный (-шен, -шна́, -шно, стра́шны́), ужа́сный.

frigid *adj.* холо́дный (хо́лоден, -дна́, -дно, хо́лодны́). **frigidity** *n.* хо́лодность.

frill *n.* обо́рка.

fringe *n.* бахрома́.

frisk *n.* (*leap*) прыжо́к (-жка́); *v.i.* (*frolic*) резви́ться *imp.*; *v.t.* (*search*) шмона́ть *imp.* **frisky** *adj.* игри́вый, ре́звый (резв, -а́, -о).

fritter[1] *n.* ола́дья (*gen.pl.* -дий).

fritter[2] *v.t.*: *f. away*, растра́чивать *imp.*, растра́тить *perf.* (по мелоча́м и т.п.).

frivolity *n.* легкомы́сленность. **frivolous** *adj.* легкомы́сленный (-ен, -енна).

fro *adv.*: *to and f.*, взад и вперёд.

frock *n.* пла́тье (*gen.pl.* -в); *f.-coat*, сюрту́к (-а́).

frog *n.* лягу́шка.

frolic *v.i.* резви́ться *imp.*; (*play pranks*) прока́зничать *imp.*, на~ *perf.*; *n.* весе́лье; (*prank*) прока́за.

from *prep. expressing*: **1.** *starting-point*: (*away f.*; *f. person*) от + *gen.*; (*f. off*, *down f.*; *in time*) с + *gen.*; (*out of*) из + *gen.*; **2.** *change of state*; *distinction*: от + *gen.*, из + *gen.*; **3.** *escape*, *avoidance*: от + *gen.*; **4.** *source*: из + *gen.*; **5.** *giving*, *sending*: от + *gen.*; (*stressing sense of possession*) у + *gen.*; **6.** *model*: по + *dat.*; **7.** *reason*, *cause*: от + *gen.*; **8.** *motive*: из-за + *gen.*; **9.**: *in phrasal verbs*: *see verbs*; **10.**: *from . . . to*, (*time*) с + *gen.* . . . до + *gen.*; (*with strictly defined starting-point*) от + *gen.* . . . до + *gen.*; (*up to and including*) с + *gen.* . . . по + *acc.*; (*space*) (*emphasizing distance*) от + *gen.* . . . до + *gen.*; (*emphasizing journey*) из + *gen.* . . . в + *acc.*; **11.** *f. above*, свépху; *f. abroad*, из-за грани́цы; *f. afar*, и́здали; *f. among*, из числа́ + *gen.*; *f. behind*, из-за + *gen*; *f. day to day*, изо дня́ в де́нь; *f. everywhere*, отовсю́ду; *f. here*, отсю́да; *f. long ago*, и́здавна; *f. memory*, по па́мяти; *f. nature*, с нату́ры; *f. now on*, отны́не; *f. off*, с + *gen.*; *f. there*, отту́да; *f. time to time*, вре́мя от вре́мени; *f. under*, из-под + *gen.*

front *n.* фаса́д, пере́дняя сторона́ (*acc.* -ону; *pl.* -оны, -о́н, -она́м); (*mil.*) фронт (*pl.* -ы, -о́в); *in f. of*, впереди́ + *gen.*, пе́ред + *instr.*; *adj.* пере́дний, пара́дный. **frontal** *adj.* (*anat.*) ло́бный; (*mil.*) лобово́й, фронта́льный.

frontier *n.* грани́ца. *adj.* пограни́чный.

frost *n.* моро́з; *f.-bite*, отмороже́ние; *f.-bitten*, отморо́женный (-ен). **frosted** *adj.*: *f. glass*, ма́товое стекло́. **frosty** *adj.* моро́зный; (*fig.*) ледяно́й.

froth *n.* пе́на; *v.t.* & *i.* пе́нить(ся) *imp.*, вс~ *perf.* **frothy** *adj.* пе́нистый.

frown *n.* хму́рый взгляд; *v.i.* хму́риться *imp.*, на~ *perf.*

frugal *adj.* (*careful*) бережли́вый; (*scanty*) ску́дный (-ден, -дна́, -дно).

fruit *n.* плод (-á); *collect.* фру́кты *m.pl.* **fruitful** *adj.* плодови́тый, плодотво́рный. **fruition** *n.* осуществле́ние; *come to f.*, осуществи́ться *perf.* **fruitless** *adj.* беспло́дный, бесполе́зный.

frustrate *v.t.* расстра́ивать *imp.*, расстро́ить *perf.* **frustration** *n.* расстро́йство.

fry[1] *n.* (*collect.*, *fishes*) мальки́ *m.pl.*

fry[2] *v.t.* & *i.* жа́рить(ся) *imp.*, за ~, из ~ *perf.* **frying-pan** *n.* сковорода́ (*pl.* ско́вороды, -о́д, -ода́м).

fuel *n.* то́пливо, горю́чее *sb.*

fugitive *n.* бегле́ц (-á); *adj.* (*transient*) мимолётный.

fugue *n.* фу́га.

fulcrum *n.* то́чка опо́ры, враще́ния.

fulfil *v.t.* (*perform*) вы-, ис-, полня́ть *imp.*, вы́-, ис-, по́лнить *perf.*; (*bring about*) осуществля́ть *imp.*, осуществи́ть *perf.* **fulfilment** *n.* вы-, ис-, полне́ние; осуществле́ние.

full *adj.* по́лный (-лон, -лна́, по́лно́) (of, + *gen.*, *instr.*); (*complete*) це́лый; (*abundant*) изоби́лующий, бога́тый; (*replete*) сы́тый (сыт, -á, -о); *f. back*, защи́тник; *f.-blooded*, полнокро́вный; *f. stop*, то́чка; *n.*: *in f.*, по́лностью; *to the f.*, в по́лной ме́ре; *adv.* (*very*) о́чень; (*exactly*) пря́мо, как раз. **fullness** *n.* полнота́. **fully** *adv.* по́лностью, вполне́.

fulsome *adj.* чрезме́рный.

fumble *v.i.*: *f. for*, нащу́пывать *imp.* + *acc.*; *f. with*, нело́вко обраща́ться *imp.* с + *instr.*

fume *n.* испаре́ние; *v.i.* испаря́ться *imp.*, испари́ться *perf.*; (*with anger*) кипе́ть (-плю́, -пи́шь) *imp.*, вс ~ *perf.* от зло́сти. **fumigate** *v.t.* оку́ривать *imp.*, окури́ть (-рю́, -ришь) *perf.* **fumigation** *n.* оку́ривание.

fun *n.* заба́ва, весе́лье; *make f. of*, смея́ться (-ею́сь, -еёшься) *imp.*, по ~ *perf.* над + *instr.*

function *n.* фу́нкция, назначе́ние; *pl.* (*duties*) обя́занности *f.pl.*; *v.i.* функциони́ровать *imp.*; де́йствовать *imp.* **functional** *adj.* функциона́льный. **functionary** *n.* должностно́е лицо́ (*pl.* -ца).

fund *n.* запа́с; (*of money*) фонд, капита́л.

fundamental *n.* осно́ва; *adj.* основно́й.

funeral *n.* по́хороны (-о́н, -она́м) *pl.*; *adj.* похоро́нный, тра́урный. **funereal** *adj.* (*gloomy*) мра́чный (-чен, -чна́, -чно).

fungoid *adj.* грибно́й. **fungus** *n.* гриб (-á).

funnel *n.* воро́нка; (*chimney*) дымова́я труба́ (*pl.* -бы).

funny *adj.* смешно́й (-шо́н, -шна́), заба́вный; (*odd*) стра́нный (-нен, -нна́, -нно).

fur *n.* мех (*loc.* -у́; *pl.* -á); *pl.* (*collect.*) пушни́на, меха́ *m.pl.*; *attrib.* мехово́й; *f. coat*, шу́ба.

furbish *v.t.* полирова́ть *imp.*, от ~ *perf.*; (*renovate*) подновля́ть *imp.*, поднови́ть *perf.*

furious *adj.* бе́шеный, я́ростный.

furl *v.t.* свёртывать *imp.*, сверну́ть *perf.*

furnace *n.* то́пка, горн; *blast-f.*, до́менная печь (*pl.* -чи, -че́й).

furnish *v.t.* (*provide*) снабжа́ть *imp.*, снабди́ть *perf.* (with, с + *instr.*); доставля́ть *imp.*, доста́вить *perf.*; (*house*) меблирова́ть *imp.*, *perf.*; обставля́ть *imp.*, обста́вить *perf.* **furniture** *n.* ме́бель, обстано́вка.

furrier *n.* меховщи́к (-á), скорня́к (-á).

furrow *n.* борозда́ (*acc.* бо́розду́; *pl.* бо́розды, -о́зд, -озда́м); (*wrinkle*) морщи́на; *v.t.* борозди́ть *imp.*, вз ~, из ~ *perf.*

furry *adj.* мехово́й, пуши́стый.

further *compar.adj.* дальне́йший; (*additional*) доба́вочный; *adv.* да́льше, да́лее; *v.t.* продвига́ть *imp.*, продви́нуть *perf.*; соде́йствовать *imp.*, *perf.* + *dat.*; спосо́бствовать *imp.*, по ~ *perf.* + *dat.* **furthermore** *adv.* к тому́ же. **furthest** *superl.adj.* са́мый да́льний.

furtive *adj.* скры́тый, та́йный. **furtively** *adv.* укра́дкой, кра́дучись.

fury *n.* я́рость, неи́стовство, бе́шенство.

furze *n.* утёсник.

fuse[1] *v.t.* & *i.* (*of metal*) сплавля́ть(ся) *imp.*, спла́вить(ся) *perf.*

fuse[2] *n.* (*in bomb*) запáл, фити́ль (-ля́) *m.*, взрывáтель *m.*; *v.t.* вставля́ть *imp.*, встáвить *perf.* взрывáтель в + *acc.*
fuse[3] *n.* (*electr.*) плáвкая прóбка, плáвкий предохрани́тель *m.*; *f. wire*, плáвкая прóволока.
fuselage *n.* фюзеля́ж.
fusible *adj.* плáвкий (-вок, -вка).
fusillade *n.* расстрéл.
fusion *n.* плáвка, слия́ние; (*nuclear f.*) си́нтез (я́дер).
fuss *n.* суетá; *v.i.* суети́ться *imp.* **fussy** *adj.* суетли́вый.
fusty *adj.* зáтхлый.
futile *adj.* бесполéзный, тщéтный. **futility** *n.* бесполéзность, тщéтность.
future *n.* бýдущее *sb.*, бýдущность; (*gram.*) бýдущее врéмя *neut.*; *adj.* бýдущий.

G

G *n.* (*mus.*) соль *neut.indecl.*
gab *n.* болтовня́.
gabble *v.i.* таратóрить *imp.*
gable *n.* щипéц (-пцá).
gad *v.i.*: *g. about*, шатáться *imp.*
gadfly *n.* óвод (*pl.* -ы & -á), слепéнь (-пня́) *m.*
gadget *n.* приспособлéние.
gag *n.* кляп; *v.t.* засóвывать *imp.*, засýнуть *perf.* кляп в рот + *dat.*
gaggle *n.* (*flock*) стáя; (*cackle*) гоготáнье; *v.i.* гоготáть (-очý, -óчешь) *imp.*
gaiety *n.* весéлье, весёлость. **gaily** *adv.* вéсело.
gain *n.* при́быль; *pl.* дохóды *m.pl.*; (*increase*) прирóст; *v.t.* получáть *imp.*, получи́ть (-чý, -чишь) *perf.*; приобретáть *imp.*, приобрести́ (-етý, -етёшь; -ёл, -елá) *perf.*; *g. on*, нагоня́ть *imp.*, нагнáть (нагоню́, -нишь; нагнáл, -á, -о) *perf.*
gainsay *v.t.* (*deny*) отрицáть *imp.*; (*contradict*) противорéчить *imp.* + *dat.*
gait *n.* похóдка.
gala *n.* прáзднество.
galaxy *n.* галáктика; (*G., Milky Way*) Млéчный путь (-ти́, -тём) *m.*; (*fig.*) плея́да.
gale *n.* си́льный вéтер (-тра; *loc.* на -трý); (*naut.*) шторм.
gall[1] *n.* (*bile*) жёлчь; (*bitterness*) жёлчность; *g.-bladder*, жёлчный пузы́рь (-ря́) *m.*
gall[2] *n.* (*sore*) ссáдина; (*irritation*) раздражéние; *v.t.* (*vex*) раздражáть *imp.*, раздражи́ть *perf.*
gallant *adj.* (*brave*) хрáбрый (храбр, -á, -о); (*courtly*) галáнтный. **gallantry** *n.* хрáбрость; галáнтность.
gallery *n.* галерéя; (*theat.*) галёрка.
galley *n.* (*ship*) галéра; (*kitchen*) кáмбуз; *g. proof*, грáнка.
gallon *n.* галлóн.
gallop *n.* галóп; *v.i.* скакáть (-ачý, -áчешь) *imp.* (галóпом).
gallows *n.* ви́селица.
gallstone *n.* жёлчный кáмень (-мня; *pl.* -мни, -мнéй) *m.*
galore *adv.* в изоби́лии.
galosh *n.* галóша.
galvanic *adv.* гальвани́ческий. **galvanize** *v.t.* гальванизи́ровать *imp.*, *perf.*; (*coat with zinc*) оцинкóвывать *imp.*, оцинковáть *perf.*
gambit *n.* гамби́т.
gamble *n.* азáртная игрá (*pl.* -ры); (*undertaking*) рискóванное предприя́тие; *v.i.* игрáть *imp.* в азáртные и́гры; рисковáть *imp.* (with, + *instr.*); *g. away*, проигрывать *imp.*, проигрáть *perf.* **gambler** *n.* игрóк (-á). **gambling** *n.* азáртные и́гры *f.pl.*
gambol *v.i.* резви́ться *imp.*

game *n.* игра́ (*pl.* -ры); (*single g.*) па́ртия; (*collect., animals*) дичь; *adj.* (*ready*) гото́вый. **gamekeeper** *n.* лесни́к (-а́). **gaming-house** *n.* иго́рный дом (*pl.* -а́). **gaming-table** *n.* иго́рный стол (-а́).

gammon *n.* о́корок.

gamut *n.* га́мма, диапазо́н.

gander *n.* гуса́к (-а́).

gang *n.* брига́да, ба́нда, ша́йка.

gangrene *n.* гангре́на.

gangster *n.* га́нгстер, банди́т.

gangway *n.* (*passage*) прохо́д; (*naut.*) схо́дни (-ней) *pl.*

gaol *n.* тюрьма́ (*pl.* -рьмы, -рем, -рьмам); *v.t.* заключа́ть *imp.*, заключи́ть *perf.* в тюрьму́. **gaoler** *n.* тюре́мщик.

gap *n.* (*breach*) брешь, проло́м; (*crack*) щель (*pl.* -ли, -ле́й); (*blank space*) пробе́л.

gape *v.i.* (*person*) разева́ть *imp.*, рази́нуть *perf.* рот; (*chasm*) зия́ть *imp.*; *g. at*, глазе́ть *imp.*, по~ *perf.* на + *acc.*

garage *n.* гара́ж (-а́).

garb *n.* одея́ние.

garbage *n.* му́сор.

garble *v.t.* подтасо́вывать *imp.*, подтасова́ть *perf.*

garden *n.* сад (*loc.* -у́; *pl.* -ы́); (*kitchen g.*) огоро́д; *pl.* парк; *attrib.* садо́вый. **gardener** *n.* садо́вник, садово́д. **gardening** *n.* садово́дство.

gargle *n.* полоска́ние; *v.i.* полоска́ть (-ощу́, -о́щешь) *imp.*, про~ *perf.* го́рло.

gargoyle *n.* горгу́лья.

garish *adj.* я́ркий (я́рок, ярка́, я́рко), крича́щий.

garland *n.* гирля́нда, вено́к (-нка́); *v.t.* украша́ть *imp.*, укра́сить *perf.* гирля́ндой, венко́м.

garlic *n.* чесно́к (-а́(у́)).

garment *n.* предме́т оде́жды; *pl.* оде́жда *collect.*

garnish *n.* (*dish*) гарни́р; (*embellishment*) украше́ние; *v.t.* гарни́ровать *imp.*, *perf.*; украша́ть *imp.*, укра́сить *perf.*

garret *n.* манса́рда.

garrison *n.* гарнизо́н.

garrulous *adj.* болтли́вый.

garter *n.* подвя́зка.

gas *n.* газ (-а(у)); (*talk*) болтовня́; *attrib.* га́зовый; *g. cooker*, га́зовая плита́ (*pl.* -ты); *g. main*, газопрово́д; *g. mask*, противога́з; *gasworks*, га́зовый заво́д; *v.t.* отравля́ть *imp.*, отрави́ть (-влю́, -вишь) *perf.* га́зом. **gaseous** *adj.* газообра́зный.

gash *n.* глубо́кая ра́на, разре́з.

gasket *n.* прокла́дка.

gasp *v.i.* задыха́ться *imp.*, задохну́ться (-х(ну́л)ся, -х(ну́)лась) *perf.*; (*exclaim*) а́хнуть *perf.*

gastric *adj.* желу́дочный.

gate *n.* (*large*) воро́та (-т) *pl.*; (*small*) кали́тка. **gatekeeper** *n.* приври́тник. **gateway** *n.* (*gate*) воро́та (-т) *pl.*; (*entrance*) вход.

gather *v.t.* на-, со-, бира́ть *imp.*, на-, со-, бра́ть (-беру́, -берёшь; -бра́л, -брала́, -бра́ло) *perf.*; (*infer*) заключа́ть *imp.*, заключи́ть *perf.*; *v.i.* собира́ться *imp.*, собра́ться (-берётся; -бра́лся, -брала́сь, -бра́ло́сь) *perf.* **gathering** *n.* (*action*) собира́ние; (*assembly*) собра́ние.

gaudy *adj.* я́ркий (я́рок, ярка́, я́рко), крича́щий.

gauge *n.* (*measure*) ме́ра; (*instrument*) кали́бр, измери́тельный прибо́р; (*rly.*) колея́; (*criterion*) крите́рий; *v.t.* измеря́ть *imp.*, изме́рить *perf.*; (*estimate*) оце́нивать *imp.*, оцени́ть (-ню́, -нишь) *perf.*

gaunt *adj.* то́щий (тощ, -а́, -е).

gauntlet *n.* рукави́ца.

gauze *n.* ма́рля, газ.

gay *adj.* весёлый (ве́сел, -а́, -о, ве́селы́); (*bright*) пёстрый (пёстр, -а́, пёстро́).

gaze *n.* при́стальный взгляд; *v.t.* при́стально гляде́ть (-яжу́, -яди́шь) *imp.* (at, на + *acc.*).

gazelle *n.* газе́ль.

gazette *n.* официа́льная газе́та; *v.t.* опублико́вывать *imp.*, опубликова́ть *perf.* в официа́льной газе́те. **gazetteer** *n.* географи́ческий спра́вочник.

gear *n.* (*appliance*) приспособле́ние, механи́зм, устро́йство; (*in motor*) переда́ча; (*high, low, g. etc.*) ско́рость (*pl.* -ти, -те́й); *in g.*, включённый (-ён, -ена́). **gearbox** *n.* коро́бка скоро-

стéй. **gearwheel** *n.* зубчáтое колесó (*pl.* -ёса), шестерня́ (*gen.pl.* -рён).
geld *v.t.* кастри́ровать *imp.*, *perf.* **gelding** *n.* мéрин.
gelignite *n.* гелигни́т.
gem *n.* драгоцéнный кáмень (-мня; *pl.* -мни, -мнéй) *m.*; (*fig.*) драгоцéнность.
Gemini *n.* Близнецы́ *m.pl.*
gender *n.* род (*pl.* -ы́).
gene *n.* ген.
genealogical *adj.* генеалоги́ческий. **genealogy** *n.* генеалóгия, родослóвная *sb.*
general *n.* генерáл; *adj.* óбщий (общ, -á, -е), всеóбщий; (*chief*) генерáльный, глáвный; *in g.*, вообщé. **generality** *n.* всеóбщность; (*majority*) большинствó. **generalization** *n.* обобщéние. **generalize** *v.t.* обобщáть *imp.*, обобщи́ть *perf.*; *v.i.* говори́ть *imp.* неопределённо. **generally** *adv.* обы́чно, вообщé.
generate *v.t.* порождáть *imp.*, породи́ть *perf.*; производи́ть (-ожу́, -óдишь) *imp.*, произвести́ (-еду́, -едёшь; -ёл, -елá) *perf.* **generation** *n.* порождéние, произвóдство; (*in descent*) поколéние. **generator** *n.* генерáтор.
generic *adj.* родовóй; (*general*) óбщий (общ, -á, -е).
generosity *n.* (*magnanimity*) великоду́шие; (*munificence*) щéдрость. **generous** *adj.* великоду́шный; щéдрый (щедр, -á, -о); (*abundant*) оби́льный.
genesis *n.* происхождéние; (*G.*) Кни́га Бытия́.
genetic *adj.* генети́ческий. **genetics** *n.* генéтика.
genial *adj.* (*of person*) доброду́шный. **geniality** *n.* доброду́шие.
genital *adj.* половóй. **genitals** *n.* половы́е óрганы *m.pl.*
genitive *adj.* (*n.*) роди́тельный (падéж (-á)).
genius *n.* (*person*) гéний; (*ability*) гениáльность; (*spirit*) дух.
genocide *n.* геноци́д.
genre *n.* жанр.
genteel *adj.* благовоспи́танный (-ан, -анна).
gentian *n.* горечáвка.
gentile *adj.* нееврéйский; *n.* нееврéй.
gentility *n.* благовоспи́танность.
gentle *adj.* (*mild*) мя́гкий (-гок, -гкá, -гко); (*meek*) крóткий (-ток, -ткá, -тко); (*quiet*) ти́хий (тих, -á, -о); (*light*) лёгкий (-гок, -гкá, -гкó, лёгки́). **gentleman** *n.* джентльмéн; господи́н (*pl.* -одá, -óд, -одáм). **gentleness** *n.* мя́гкость.
genuine *adj.* (*authentic*) пóдлиный (-нен, -нна), настоя́щий; (*sincere*) и́скренний (-нен, -нна, -нно & -нне). **genuineness** *n.* пóдлинность; и́скренность.
genus *n.* род (*pl.* -ы́).
geo- *in comb.* гео-. **geographer** *n.* геóграф. **geographical** *adj.* географи́ческий. **geography** *n.* геогрáфия. **geological** *adj.* геологи́ческий. **geologist** *n.* геóлог. **geology** *n.* геолóгия. **geometric(al)** *adj.* геометри́ческий. **geometrician** *n.* геóметр. **geometry** *n.* геомéтрия.
Georgian *n.* (*USSR*) грузи́н (*gen.pl.* -н), ~ка; *adj.* грузи́нский.
geranium *n.* герáнь.
germ *n.* микрóб; (*fig.*) зарóдыш.
German *n.* нéмец (-мца), нéмка; *adj.* немéцкий; *G. measles*, красну́ха. **Germanic** *adj.* германский.
germane *adj.* умéстный.
germinate *v.i.* прорастáть *imp.*, прорасти́ (-тёт; прорóс, -лá) *perf.*
gesticulate *v.i.* жестикули́ровать *imp.* **gesticulation** *n.* жестикуля́ция. **gesture** *n.* жест.
get *v.t.* (*obtain*) доставáть (-таю́, -таёшь) *imp.*, достáть (-áну, -áнешь) *perf.*; добивáться *imp.*, доби́ться (добью́сь, -ьёшься) *perf.* + *gen.*; (*receive*) получáть *imp.*, получи́ть (-чу́, -чишь) *perf.*; (*understand*) понимáть *imp.*, поня́ть (пойму́, -мёшь; пóнял, -á, -о) *perf.*; (*disease*) схвáтывать *imp.*, схватáть (-ачу́, -áтишь) *perf.*; (*induce*) уговáривать *imp.*, уговори́ть *perf.* (to do, + *inf.*); *v.i.* (*become*) станови́ться (-влю́сь, -вишься) *imp.*, стать (стáну, -нешь) *perf.* + *instr.*; *have got*, (*have*) имéть *imp.*; *have got to*, быть дóлжен (-жнá) + *inf.*; *g. about*, (*spread*) распространя́ться *imp.*, распространи́ться *perf.*; *g. away*, ускользáть *imp.*,

ускользну́ть *perf.*; *g. back*, (*recover*) получа́ть *imp.*, получи́ть (-чу́, -чишь) *perf.* обра́тно; (*return*) возвраща́ться *imp.*, верну́ться *perf.*; *g. down to*, принима́ться *imp.*, приня́ться (приму́сь, -мешься; приня́лся́, -ла́сь) *perf.* за + *acc.*; *g. off*, слеза́ть *imp.*, слезть (-зу, -зешь; -з) *perf.* с + *gen.*; *g. on*, сади́ться *imp.*, сесть (ся́ду, -дешь; сел) *perf.* в, на, + *acc.*; (*prosper*) преуспева́ть *imp.*, преуспе́ть *perf.*; *g. on with*, (*person*) ужива́ться *imp.*, ужи́ться (уживу́сь, -вёшься; ужи́лся, -ла́сь) *perf.* с + *instr.*; *g. out of*, (*avoid*) избавля́ться *imp.*, изба́виться *perf.* от + *gen.*; *g. to*, (*reach*) достига́ть *imp.*, дости́гнуть & дости́чь (-и́гну, -и́гнешь; -и́г) *perf.* + *gen.*; *g. up*, (*from bed*) встава́ть (-таю́, -таёшь) *imp.*, встать (-а́ну, -а́нешь) *perf.*

geyser *n.* (*spring*) ге́йзер; (*water-heater*) (га́зовая) коло́нка.

ghastly *adj.* стра́шный (-шен, -шна́, -шно, стра́шны́), ужа́сный.

gherkin *n.* огуре́ц (-рца́).

ghetto *n.* ге́тто *neut.indecl.*

ghost *n.* привиде́ние, при́зрак, дух, тень (*pl.* -ни, -не́й). **ghostly** *adj.* при́зрачный.

giant *n.* велика́н, гига́нт; *adj.* грома́дный.

gibber *v.i.* тарато́рить *imp.* **gibberish** *n.* тараба́рщина.

gibbet *n.* ви́селица.

gibe *n.* насме́шка; *v.i.* насмеха́ться *imp.* (at, над + *instr.*).

giblets *n.* потроха́ (-хо́в) *pl.*

giddiness *n.* головокруже́ние; (*frivolity*) легкомы́слие. **giddy** *adj.* (*frivolous*) легкомы́сленный (-ен, -енна); *predic.*: *I am, feel, giddy*, у меня́ кру́жится голова́.

gift *n.* (*present*) пода́рок (-рка); (*donation*; *ability*) дар (*pl.* -ы́); (*talent*) тала́нт (к + *dat.*); (*ability*) спосо́бность (к + *dat.*). **gifted** *adj.* одарённый (-ён, -ённа), тала́нтливый.

gig *n.* (*carriage*) кабриоле́т; (*boat*) ги́чка.

gigantic *adj.* гига́нтский, грома́дный.

giggle *n.* хихи́канье; *v.i.* хихи́кать *imp.*, хихи́кнуть *perf.*

gild *v.t.* золоти́ть *imp.*, вы́~, по~ *perf.*

gill *n.* (*of fish*) жа́бра.

gilt *n.* позоло́та; *adj.* золочённый, позоло́ченный.

gimlet *n.* бура́вчик.

gin[1] *n.* (*snare*) западня́; (*winch*) лебёдка; (*cotton-g.*) джин.

gin[2] *n.* (*spirit*) джин.

ginger *n.* имби́рь (-ря) *m.*; *attrib.* имби́рный; (*in colour*) ры́жий (рыж, -а́, -е). **gingerbread** *n.* имби́рный пря́ник.

gingerly *adv.* осторо́жно.

gipsy *n.* цыга́н (*pl.* -не, -н), ~ка; *attrib.* цыга́нский.

giraffe *n.* жира́ф.

gird *v.t.* опоя́сывать *imp.*, опоя́сать (-я́шу, -я́шешь) *perf.*; (*encircle*) окружа́ть *imp.*, окружи́ть *perf.* **girder** *n.* ба́лка, фе́рма. **girdle** *n.* по́яс (*pl.* -а́); *v.t.* подпоя́сывать *imp.*, подпоя́сать (-я́шу, -я́шешь) *perf.*

girl *n.* де́вочка, де́вушка; *g.-friend*, подру́га. **girlish** *adj.* де́вичий (-чья, -чье).

girth *n.* (*band*) подпру́га; (*measurement*) обхва́т.

gist *n.* суть, су́щность.

give *v.t.* дава́ть (даю́, даёшь) *imp.*, дать (дам, дашь, даст, дади́м; дал, -а́, да́ло́, -и) *perf.*; дари́ть (-рю́, -ришь) *imp.*, по~ *perf.*; *g. away*, выдава́ть (-даю́, -даёшь) *imp.*, вы́дать (-ам, -ашь, -аст, -адим) *perf.*; *g. back*, возвраща́ть *imp.*, возврати́ть (-ащу́, -ати́шь) *perf.*; *g. in*, (*yield, v.i.*) уступа́ть *imp.*, уступи́ть (-плю́, -пишь) *perf.* (to, + *dat.*); (*hand in, v.t.*) вруча́ть *imp.*, вручи́ть *perf.*; *g. out*, (*emit*) издава́ть (-даю́, -даёшь) *imp.*, изда́ть (-а́м, -а́шь, -а́ст, -ади́м; изда́л, -а́, -о) *perf.*; (*distribute*) раздава́ть (-даю́, -даёшь) *imp.*, разда́ть (-а́м, -а́шь, -а́ст, -ади́м; ро́здал & разда́л, раздала́, ро́здало & разда́ло) *perf.*; (*cease*) конча́ться *imp.*, ко́нчиться *perf.*; *g. up*, отка́зываться *imp.*, отказа́ться (-ажу́сь, -а́жешься) *perf.* от + *gen.*; (*habit etc.*) броса́ть *imp.*, бро́сить *perf.*; *g. oneself up*, сдава́ться (сдаю́сь, сдаёшься) *imp.*, сда́ться (-а́мся, -а́шься, -а́стся, -ади́мся;

сда́лся, -ла́сь, сдало́сь) *perf.* **given** *predic.* (*inclined*) скло́нен (-о́нна́, -о́нно) (to, к+*dat.*); (*devoted*) пре́дан (-а) (to, +*dat.*).

gizzard *n.* (*of bird*) му́скульный желу́док (-дка).

glacial *adj.* леднико́вый; (*fig.*) ледяно́й. **glacier** *n.* ледни́к (-а́), гле́тчер.

glad *adj.* ра́достный, весёлый; *predic.* рад. **gladden** *v.t.* ра́довать *imp.*, об~ *perf.* **gladness** *n.* ра́дость.

glade *n.* прога́лина, поля́на.

gladiolus *n.* шпа́жник.

glamorous *adj.* (*charming*) обая́тельный; (*attractive*) привлека́тельный. **glamour** *n.* обая́ние; привлека́тельность.

glance *n.* (*look*) бе́глый взгляд; *v.i.*: *g. at*, взгля́дывать *imp.*, взгляну́ть (-ну́, -нешь) *perf.* на+*acc.*; *g. off*, скользи́ть *imp.*, скользну́ть *perf.* по пове́рхности+*gen.*

gland *n.* железа́ (*pl.* же́лезы, -ёз, -еза́м). **glandular** *adj.* желе́зистый.

glare *n.* (*light*) ослепи́тельный блеск; (*look*) при́стальный, свире́пый, взгляд; *v.i.* ослепи́тельно сверка́ть *imp.*; при́стально, свире́по, смотре́ть (-рю́, -ришь) *imp.* (at, на+*acc.*). **glaring** *adj.* (*bright*) я́ркий; (*dazzling*) ослепи́тельный; (*mistake*) гру́бый.

glass *n.* (*substance*) стекло́; (*drinking vessel*) стака́н, рю́мка; (*glassware*) стекля́нная посу́да; (*mirror*) зе́ркало (*pl.* -ла́); *pl.* (*spectacles*) очки́ (-ко́в) *pl.*; *attrib.* стекля́нный; *g.-blower*, стеклоду́в; *g. fibre*, стекловолокно́; *glasshouse*, тепли́ца. **glassy** *adj.* (*of glass*) стекля́нный; (*water*) зерка́льный, гла́дкий (-док, -дка́, -дко); (*look*) ту́склый (тускл, -а́, -о).

glaze *n.* глазу́рь; *v.t.* (*picture*) застекля́ть *imp.*, застекли́ть *perf.*; (*cover with g.*) покрыва́ть *imp.*, покры́ть (-ро́ю, -ро́ешь) *perf.* глазу́рью. **glazier** *n.* стеко́льщик.

gleam *n.* сла́бый свет; (*also of hope etc.*) про́блеск; *v.i.* свети́ться (-ится) *imp.*

glean *v.t.* тща́тельно собира́ть *imp.*, собра́ть (соберу́, -рёшь; собра́л, -а́, -о) *perf.*; *v.i.* подбира́ть *imp.*, подобра́ть (подберу́, -рёшь; подобра́л, -а́, -о) *perf.* коло́сья.

glee *n.* весе́лье. **gleeful** *adj.* весёлый (ве́сел, -а́, -о, ве́селы́).

glib *adj.* бо́йкий (бо́ек, бойка́, бо́йко).

glide *v.i.* скользи́ть *imp.*; (*aeron.*) плани́ровать *imp.*, с~ *perf.* **glider** *n.* (*aircraft*) планёр; (*person*) планери́ст.

glimmer *n.* мерца́ние; *v.i.* мерца́ть *imp.*

glimpse *n.* (*appearance*) про́блеск; (*view*) мимолётный взгляд; *v.t.* ме́льком ви́деть (ви́жу, ви́дишь) *imp.*, у~ *perf.*

glint, glitter *n.* блеск; *v.i.* блесте́ть (-ещу́, -ести́шь & -е́щешь) *imp.*; сверка́ть *imp.*

gloat *v.i.* пожира́ть *imp.*, пожра́ть (-ру́, -рёшь; пожра́л, -а́, -о) *perf.* глаза́ми (over, +*acc.*); (*maliciously*) злора́дствовать *imp.*

global *adj.* (*world-wide*) мирово́й; (*total*) всео́бщий. **globe** *n.* (*sphere*) шар (-а́ *with 2, 3, 4*; *pl.* -ы́); (*the earth*) земно́й шар; (*chart*) гло́бус. **globular** *adj.* шарови́дный, сфери́ческий. **globule** *n.* ша́рик.

gloom *n.* мрак. **gloomy** *adj.* мра́чный (-чен, -чна́, -чно).

glorification *n.* прославле́ние. **glorify** *v.t.* прославля́ть *imp.*, просла́вить *perf.* **glorious** *adj.* сла́вный (-вен, -вна́, -вно); (*splendid*) великоле́пный. **glory** *n.* сла́ва; *v.i.* торжествова́ть *imp.*

gloss[1] *n.* (*word*) гло́сса; (*explanation*) толкова́ние.

gloss[2] *n.* (*lustre*) лоск, гля́нец (-нца); (*appearance*) ви́димость; *v.t.* наводи́ть (-ожу́, -о́дишь) *imp.*, навести́ (-еду́, -едёшь; навёл, -а́) *perf.* лоск, гля́нец, на+*acc.*; *g. over*, зама́зывать *imp.*, зама́зать (-а́жу, -а́жешь) *perf.*

glossary *n.* глосса́рий, слова́рь (-ря́) *m.*

glove *n.* перча́тка. **glover** *n.* перча́точник, -ица.

glow *n.* нака́л, за́рево; (*of cheeks*) румя́нец (-нца); (*ardour*) пыл (-а(у), *loc.* -у́); *v.i.* (*incandescence*) накаля́ться *imp.*, накали́ться *perf.*; (*shine*) сия́ть *imp.*; *g.-worm*, светля́к (-а́).

glucose *n.* глюко́за.

glue *n.* клей (-е́я (-е́ю), *loc.* -ее́ & -ею́; *pl.* -е́й); *v.t.* кле́ить *imp.*, с~ *perf.*;

(*attach*) приклéивать *imp.*, приклéить *perf.* (to, к + *dat.*).
glum *adj.* угрюмый.
glut *n.* (*surfeit*) пресыщéние; (*excess*) избы́ток (-тка); (*in market*) затовáривание (ры́нка); *v.t.* пресыщáть *imp.*, пресы́тить (-ы́щу, -ы́тишь) *perf.*; (*overstock*) затовáривать *imp.*, затовáрить *perf.*
glutton *n.* обжóра *m.* & *f.* **gluttonous** *adj.* обжóрливый. **gluttony** *n.* обжóрство.
gnarled *adj.* (*hands*) шишковáтый; (*tree*) сучковáтый.
gnash *v.t.* скрежетáть (-ещу́, -éщешь) *imp.* + *instr.* **gnashing** *n.* скрéжет.
gnat *n.* комáр (-á).
gnaw *v.t.* глодáть (-ожу́, -óжешь) *imp.*; грызть (-зу́, -зёшь; -з) *imp.*
gnome *n.* гном.
go *n.* (*movement*) движéние; (*energy*) энéргия; (*attempt*) попы́тка; *be on the go*, быть в движéнии; *have a go*, пытáться *imp.*, по ~ *perf.*; *v.i.* (*on foot*) ходи́ть (хожу́, хóдишь) *indet.*, идти́ (иду́, идёшь; шёл, шла) *det.*, пойти́ (пойду́, -дёшь; пошёл, -шлá) *perf.*; (*by transport*) éздить *indet.*, éхать (éду, éдешь) *det.*, по ~ *perf.*; (*work*) рабóтать *imp.*; (*become*) станови́ться (-влю́сь, -вишься) *imp.*, стать (стáну, -нешь) *perf.* + *instr.*; *be going* (*to do*), собирáться *imp.*, собрáться (соберу́сь, -рёшься; собрáлся, -алáсь, -áлóсь) *perf.* (+ *inf.*); *go about*, (*set to work at*) брáться (беру́сь, -рёшься; брáлся, -лáсь) *imp.*, взя́ться (возьму́сь, -мёшься; взя́лся, -лáсь) *perf.* за + *acc.*; (*wander*) броди́ть (-ожу́, -óдишь) *indet.*; *go at*, (*attack*) набрáсываться *imp.*, набрóситься *perf.* на + *acc.*; *go away*, (*on foot*) уходи́ть (-ожу́, -óдишь) *imp.*, уйти́ (уйду́, -дёшь; ушёл, ушлá) *perf.*; (*by transport*) уезжáть *imp.*, уéхать (уéду, -дешь) *perf.*; *go down*, спускáться *imp.*, спусти́ться (-ущу́сь, -у́стишься) *perf.*; *go into*, (*enter*) входи́ть (-ожу́, -óдишь) *imp.*, войти́ (войду́, -дёшь; вошёл, -шлá) *perf.* в + *acc.*; (*investigate*) расслéдовать *imp.*, *perf.*; *go off*, (*go away*) уходи́ть (-ожу́, -óдишь) *imp.*, уйти́ (уйду́, -дёшь; ушёл, ушлá) *perf.*; (*deteriorate*) пóртиться *imp.*, ис ~ *perf.*; *go on*, (*continue*) продолжáть(ся) *imp.*, продóлжить(ся) *perf.*; *go out*, выходи́ть (-ожу́, -óдишь) *imp.*, вы́йти (вы́йду, -дешь; вы́шел, -шла) *perf.*; (*flame etc.*) гáснуть (-с) *imp.*, по ~ *perf.*; *go over*, (*inspect*) пересмáтривать *imp.*, пересмотрéть (-рю́, -ришь) *perf.*; (*rehearse*) повторя́ть *imp.*, повтори́ть *perf.*; (*change allegiance etc.*) переходи́ть (-ожу́, -óдишь) *imp.*, перейти́ (перейду́, -дёшь; перешёл, -шлá) *perf.* (to, в, на, + *acc.*, к + *dat.*); *go through*, (*scrutinize*) разбирáть *imp.*, разобрáть (разберу́, -рёшь; разобрáл, -á, -о) *perf.*; *go through with*, доводи́ть (-ожу́, -óдишь) *imp.*, довести́ (-еду́, -едёшь; -ёл, -елá) *perf.* до концá; *go without*, обходи́ться (-ожу́сь, -óдишься) *imp.*, обойти́сь (обойду́сь, -дёшься; обошёлся, -шлáсь) *perf.* без + *gen.*; *go-ahead*, предприи́мчивый; *go-between*, посрéдник.
goad *v.t.* подгоня́ть *imp.*, подогнáть (подгоню́, -нишь; подогнáл, -á, -о) *perf.*; *g. on*, (*instigate*) подстрекáть *imp.*, подстрекну́ть *perf.* (to, к + *dat.*).
goal *n.* (*aim*) цель; (*sport*) ворóта (-т) *pl.*, (*also point(s) won*) гол (*pl.* -ы́); *score a g.*, забивáть *imp.*, заби́ть (-бью́, -бьёшь) *perf.* гол. **goalkeeper** *n.* вратáрь (-ря́) *m.*
goat *n.* козá (*pl.* -зы), козёл (-злá); *attrib.* кóзий (-зья, -зье). **goatherd** *n.* кóзий пасту́х (-á).
gobble[1] *v.t.* (*eat*) жрать (жру, жрёшь; жрал, -á, -о) *imp.*; *g. up*, пожирáть *imp.*, пожрáть (-ру́, -рёшь; пожрáл, -á, -о) *perf.*
gobble[2] *v.i.* (*of turkeys*) кулды́кать *imp.*
goblet *n.* бокáл, ку́бок (-бка).
god *n.* бог (*pl.* -и, -óв); (*idol*) куми́р; (*G.*) Бог (*voc.* Бóже); *pl.* (*theat.*) галёрка. **godchild** *n.* крéстник, -ица. **god-daughter** *n.* крéстница. **goddess** *n.* боги́ня. **godfather** *n.* крёстный *sb.* **God-fearing** *adj.* богобоя́зненный (-ен, -енна). **godless** *adj.* безбóжный. **godlike** *adj.* богоподóбный. **godly** *adj.* нáбожный. **godmother** *n.* крёстная

sb. **godparent** *n.* крёстный *sb.* **godson** крéстник.

goggle *v.i.* тарáщить *imp.* глазá (at, на + *acc.*); *g.-eyed*, пучеглáзый; *n.*: *pl.* защи́тные очки́ (-кóв) *pl.*

going *adj.* дéйствующий. **goings-on** *n.* поведéние; делá *neut.pl.*

goitre *n.* зоб (*loc.* -е & -ý; *pl.* -ы́).

gold *n.* зóлото; *adj.* золотóй; *g.-bearing*, золотонóсный; *g.-beater*, золотобóй; *g.-digger*, золотоискáтель *m.*; (*sl.*) авантюри́стка; *g.-dust*, золотонóсный песóк (-скá (-скý)); *g.-field*, золотóй при́иск; *g. leaf*, золотáя фóльга; *g.-mine*, золотóй рудни́к (-á); (*fig.*) золотóе дно; *g. plate*, золотáя посýда *collect.*; *g.-plate*, золоти́ть *imp.*, по ~ *perf.*; *g.-smith*, золоты́х дел мáстер (*pl.* -á). **golden** *adj.* золотóй, золоти́стый; *g. eagle*, бéркут. **goldfinch** *n.* щегóл (-глá). **goldfish** *n.* золотáя ры́бка.

golf *n.* гольф. **golfer** *n.* игрóк (-á) в гольф.

gondola *n.* гондóла. **gondolier** *n.* гондольéр.

gong *n.* гонг.

good *n.* добрó, блáго; *pl.* (*wares*) товáр(ы); *do g.*, (*benefit*) идти́ (идёт; шёл, шла) *imp.*, пойти́ (пойдёт; пошёл, -шлá) *perf.* на пóльзу + *dat.*; *adj.* хорóший (-ш, -шá), дóбрый (добр, -á, -о, дóбры́); *g.-humoured*, добродýшный; *g.-looking*, краси́вый; *g. morning*, дóброе ýтро! *g. night*, спокóйной нóчи! **goodbye** *interj.* прощáй(те)! до свидáния! **goodness** *n.* добротá.

goose *n.* гусь (*pl.* -си, -сéй) *m.*, гусы́ня; (*cul.*) гуся́тина; (*fool*) простофи́ля *m.* & *f.*; (*iron*) портнóвский утю́г (-á); *g.-flesh*, гуси́ная кóжа.

gooseberry *n.* крыжóвник (*plant or* (*collect.*) *berries*).

gore[1] *n.* (*blood*) запёкшаяся кровь (*loc.* -ви́).

gore[2] *n.* (*cloth*) клин (*pl.* -ья, -ьев).

gore[3] *v.t.* (*pierce*) бодáть *imp.*, за ~ *perf.*

gorge *n.* глóтка; (*narrow opening*) ущéлье (*gen.pl.* -лий); *v.t.* жрать (жру, жрёшь; жрал, -á, -о) *imp.*, со ~ *perf.*; *v.i.* объедáться *imp.*, объéсться (-éмся, -éшься, -éстся, -еди́мся; -éлся) *perf.* (on, + *instr.*).

gorgeous *adj.* пы́шный (-шен, -шнá, -шно), великолéпный.

gorilla *n.* гори́лла.

gormandize *v.i.* объедáться *imp.*, объéстся (-éмся, -éшься, -éстся, -еди́мся; -éлся) *perf.*

gorse *n.* утёсник.

gory *adj.* окровáвленный.

gosh *interj.* бóже мой!

goshawk *n.* большóй я́стреб (*pl.* -ы & -á).

gosling *n.* гусёнок (-нка; *pl.* гуся́та, -т).

Gospel *n.* Евáнгелие.

gossamer *n.* (*web*) паути́на; (*gauze*) тóнкая ткань.

gossip *n.* (*talk*) болтовня́, сплéтня (*gen. pl.* -тен); (*person*) болтýн (-á), ~ ья (*gen.pl.* -ний), сплéтник, -ица; *v.i.* болтáть *imp.*; сплéтничать *imp.*, на ~ *perf.*

Goth *n.* гот. **Gothic** гóтский; (*archit.*; *print.*) готи́ческий.

gouache *n.* гуáшь.

gouge *n.* полукрýглое долотó (*pl.* -та); *v.t.*: *g. out*, выдáлбливать *imp.*, вы́долбить *perf.*; (*eyes*) выкáлывать *imp.*, вы́колоть (-лю, -лешь) *perf.*

goulash *n.* гуля́ш (-яшá).

gourd *n.* ты́ква.

gourmand *n.* лакóмка *m.* & *f.*

gourmet *n.* гурмáн.

gout *n.* подáгра. **gouty** *adj.* подагри́ческий.

govern *v.t.* прáвить *imp.* + *instr.*; управля́ть *imp.* + *instr.* **governess** *n.* гувернáнтка. **government** *n.* (*of state*) прави́тельство; управлéние (of, + *instr.*). **governmental** *adj.* прави́тельственный. **governor** *n.* прави́тель *m.*, губернáтор; (*head of institution*) завéдующий *sb.* (of, + *instr.*).

gown *n.* (*woman's*) плáтье (*gen.pl.* -в); (*official's*) мáнтия.

grab *n.* (*grasp*) захвáт; (*device*) черпáк (-á); *v.t.* хватáть *imp.*, (с)хвати́ть (-ачý, -áтишь) *perf.*; захвáтывать *imp.*, захвати́ть (-ачý, -áтишь) *perf.*

grace *n.* (*gracefulness*) грáция; (*refinement*) изя́щество; (*kindness*) любéзность; (*favour*) ми́лость; (*theol.*) благода́ть; *v.t.* (*adorn*) украша́ть *imp.*, укра́сить *perf.*; (*confer*) удоста́ивать *imp.*, удосто́ить *perf.* (with, +*gen.*). **graceful** *adj.* грацио́зный, изя́щный. **graceless** *adj.* (*improper*) неприли́чный; (*inelegant*) неуклю́жий.

gracious *adj.* ми́лостивый, снисходи́тельный.

gradation *n.* града́ция.

grade *n.* (*level*) сте́пень (*pl.* -ни, -не́й); (*quality*) ка́чество; (*sort*) сорт (*pl.* -а́); (*slope*) укло́н; *v.t.* распределя́ть *imp.*, распредели́ть *perf.* по степеня́м, гру́ппам и т.п.; сортирова́ть *imp.* рас~ *perf.*; (*road etc.*) нивели́ровать *imp.*, *perf.*

gradient *n.* укло́н.

gradual *adj.* постепе́нный (-нен, -нна).

graduate *n.* око́нчивший *sb.* университет, вуз; *v.i.* конча́ть *imp.*, око́нчить *perf.* (университе́т, вуз); *v.t.* градуи́ровать *imp.*, *perf.*

graffito *n.* стенна́я на́дпись, стенно́й рису́нок (-нка).

graft[1] *n.* (*agric.*) приво́й, риви́вка; (*med.*) переса́дка (живо́й тка́ни); *v.t.* (*agric.*) привива́ть *imp.*, приви́ть (-вью́, -вьёшь; прив́ил, -а́, -о) *perf.* (to, +*dat.*); (*med.*) переса́живать *imp.*, пересади́ть (-ажу́, -а́дишь) *perf.*

graft[2] *n.* (*bribe*) взя́тка, по́дкуп; *v.i.* (*give*) дава́ть (даю́, даёшь) *imp.*, дать (дам, дашь, даст, дади́м; дал, -а́, да́ло́, -и) *perf.* взя́тки; (*take*) брать (беру́, -рёшь; брал, -а́, -о) *imp.*, взять (возьму́, -мёшь; взял, -а́, -о) *perf.* взя́тки.

grain *n.* (*seed*; *collect.*) зерно́ (*pl.* зёрна, -рен, -рнам); (*particle*) крупи́нка; (*of sand*) песчи́нка; (*measure*) гран (*gen. pl.* -н); (*smallest amount*) крупи́ца; (*of wood*) (древе́сное) волокно́; *against the g.*, не по нутру́; *not a g. of*, ни гра́на + *gen.*

gram(me) *n.* грамм (*gen.pl.* -м & -мов).

grammar *n.* грамма́тика; *g. school*, гимна́зия. **grammarian** *n.* грамма́тик. **grammatical** *adj.* граммати́ческий.

gramophone *n.* граммофо́н, проигрыватель *m.*; *g. record*, грампласти́нка.

grampus *n.* се́рый дельфи́н.

granary *n.* амба́р.

grand *adj.* (*in titles*) вели́кий; (*main*) гла́вный; (*majestic*) вели́чественный (-ен, -енна); (*splendid*) великоле́пный; *g. duke*, вели́кий ге́рцог; (*in Russia*) вели́кий князь (*pl.* -зья́, -зе́й); *g. master*, гроссме́йстер; *g. piano*, роя́ль *m.* **grandchild** *n.* внук, вну́чка; *pl.* внуча́та (-т) *pl.* **granddaughter** *n.* вну́чка. **grandfather** *n.* де́душка *m.* **grandmother** *n.* ба́бушка. **grandparents** *n.* ба́бушка и де́душка. **grandson** *n.* внук. **grandstand** *n.* трибу́на.

grandee *n.* (*Span.*, *Portug.*) гранд; вельмо́жа *m.*

grandeur *n.* вели́чие.

grandiloquence *n.* напы́щенность. **grandiloquent** *adj.* напы́щенный (-ен, -енна).

grandiose *adj.* грандио́зный.

grange *n.* фе́рма.

granite *n.* грани́т; *attrib.* грани́тный.

grannie, granny *n.* ба́бушка.

grant *n.* дар (*pl.* -ы́); (*financial*) дота́ция, субси́дия; *v.t.* дарова́ть *imp.*, *perf.*; предоставля́ть *imp.*, предоста́вить *perf.*; (*concede*) допуска́ть *imp.*, допусти́ть (-ущу́, -у́стишь) *perf.*; *take for granted*, счита́ть *imp.*, счесть (сочту́, -тёшь; счёл, сочла́) *perf.* само́ собо́й разуме́ющимся.

granular *adj.* зерни́стый.

granulate *v.t.* гранули́ровать *imp.*, *perf.*; *granulated sugar*, са́харный песо́к (-ска́(у́)).

granule *n.* зёрнышко (*pl.* -шки, -шек, -шкам).

grape *n.* виноград (-а(у)) (*collect.*); *g.-shot*, карте́чь; *g.-vine*, виногра́дная лоза́ (*pl.* -зы). **grapefruit** *n.* гре́йпфрут.

graph *n.* гра́фик.

graphic *adj.* графи́ческий; (*vivid*) я́ркий (я́рок, ярка́, я́рко).

graphite *n.* графи́т.

grapnel *n.* дрек, ко́шка.

grapple *n.* (*grapnel*) дрек, ко́шка; (*grip*) захва́т; *v.i.* сцепля́ться *imp.*, сцепи́ться (-плю́сь, -пишься) *perf.* (with, с + *instr.*); боро́ться (-рю́сь, -решься) *imp.* (with, с + *instr.*); *grappling-hook*, *-iron*, дрек, ко́шка.

grasp *n.* (*grip*) хва́тка; (*control*) власть; (*mental hold*) схва́тывание; *v.t.* (*clutch*) хвата́ть *imp.*, схвати́ть (-ачу́, -а́тишь) *perf.*; (*comprehend*) понима́ть *imp.*, поня́ть (пойму́, -мёшь; по́нял, -а́, -о) *perf.* **grasping** *adj.* жа́дный (-ден, -дна́, -дно).

grass *n.* трава́ (*pl.* -вы), злак; (*pasture*) па́стбище; *g. snake*, уж (-а́); *g. widow*, соло́менная вдова́ (*pl.* -вы). **grasshopper** *n.* кузне́чик. **grassy** *adj.* травяни́стый, травяно́й.

grate[1] *n.* (*in fireplace*) (ками́нная) решётка.

grate[2] *v.t.* (*rub*) тере́ть (тру, трёшь; тёр) *imp.*, на~ *perf.*; *v.i.* (*sound*) скрипе́ть (-пи́т) *imp.*; *g.* (*up*)*on*, (*irritate*) раздража́ть *imp.*, раздражи́ть *perf.*

grateful *n.* благода́рный.

grater *n.* тёрка.

gratify *v.t.* удовлетворя́ть *imp.*, удовлетвори́ть *perf.*

grating *n.* решётка.

gratis *adv.* беспла́тно, да́ром.

gratitude *n.* благода́рность.

gratuitous *adj.* (*free*) дарово́й; (*motiveless*) беспричи́нный (-нен, -нна).

gratuity *n.* де́нежный пода́рок (-рка); (*tip*) чаевы́е *sb.*; (*mil.*) наградны́е *sb.*

grave[1] *n.* моги́ла; *g.-digger*, моги́льщик. **gravestone** *n.* надгро́бный ка́мень (-мня; *pl.* -мни, -мне́й) *m.* **graveyard** *n.* кла́дбище.

grave[2] *adj.* (*serious*) серьёзный, ва́жный (-жен, -жна́, -жно, -жны́).

gravel *n.* гра́вий; *g. pit*, грави́йный карье́р.

gravitate *v.i.* тяготе́ть *imp.* (towards, к + *dat.*). **gravitation** *n.* тяготе́ние.

gravity *n.* (*seriousness*) серьёзность; (*force*) тя́жесть; *specific g.*, уде́льный вес.

gravy *n.* (мясна́я) подли́вка; *g.-boat*, со́усник.

grayling *n.* ха́риус.

graze[1] *v.t.* & *i.* (*feed*) пасти́ (пасу́(сь), пасёшь(ся); па́с(ся), пасла́(сь)) *imp.*

graze[2] *n.* (*abrasion*) цара́пина; *v.t.* (*touch lightly*) задева́ть *imp.*, заде́ть (-е́ну, -е́нешь) *perf.*; (*abrade*) цара́пать *imp.*, о~ *perf.*

grease *n.* жир (-а(у), *loc.* -е & -у́), топлёное са́ло; (*lubricant*) сма́зка; *g.-gun*, таво́тный шприц; *g.-paint*, грим; *v.t.* сма́зывать *imp.*, сма́зать (-а́жу, -а́жешь) *perf.* **greasy** *adj.* жи́рный (-рен, -рна́, -рно), са́льный.

great *adj.* (*large*) большо́й; (*eminent*) вели́кий; (*long*) до́лгий (-лог, -лга́, -лго); (*strong*) си́льный (си́лён, -льна́, -льно, си́льны́); *to a g. extent*, в большо́й сте́пени; *a g. deal*, мно́го (+ *gen.*); *a g. many*, мно́гие; мно́жество (+ *gen.*); *g.-aunt*, двою́родная ба́бушка; *g.-granddaughter*, пра́внучка; *g.-grandfather*, пра́дед; *g.-grandmother*, праба́бка; *g.-grandson*, пра́внук; *g.-uncle*, двою́родный де́душка *m.* **greatly** *adv.* о́чень.

grebe *n.* пога́нка.

Grecian *adj.* гре́ческий.

greed *n.* жа́дность (for, к + *dat.*), а́лчность. **greedy** *adj.* жа́дный (-ден, -дна́, -дно) (for, к + *dat.*), а́лчный; (*for food*) прожо́рливый.

Greek *n.* грек, греча́нка; *adj.* гре́ческий.

green *n.* (*colour*) зелёный цвет; (*piece of land*) лужо́к (-жка́); *pl.* зе́лень *collect.*; *adj.* зелёный (зе́лен, -а́, -о); (*inexperienced*) нео́пытный. **greenery** *n.* зе́лень. **greenfinch** *n.* зелену́шка. **greenfly** *n.* тля (*gen.pl.* тлей). **greengage** *n.* ренкло́д. **greengrocer** *n.* зеленщи́к (-а́). **greenhorn** *n.* новичо́к (-чка́). **greenhouse** *n.* тепли́ца, оранжере́я.

greet *v.t.* кла́няться *imp.*, поклони́ться (-ню́сь, -нишься) *perf.* + *dat.*; приве́тствовать *imp.* (& *perf.* *in past tense*). **greeting** *n.* приве́т(ствие).

gregarious *adj.* ста́дный; (*person*) общи́тельный.

grenade *n.* грана́та.

grey *adj.* се́рый (сер, -а́, -о); (*hair*) седо́й (сед, -а́, -о); *g. hair*, седниа́ (*pl.* -ы).

greyhound *n.* борза́я *sb.*

grid *n.* (*grating*) решётка; (*network*) сеть (*pl.* -ти, -те́й); (*map*) координа́тная се́тка.

grief *n.* го́ре, печа́ль; *come to g.*, попада́ть *imp.*, попа́сть (попаду́, -дёшь; попа́л) *perf.* в беду́.

grievance *n.* жалоба, обида.

grieve *v.t.* огорчать *imp.*, огорчить *perf.*; *v.i.* горевать (-рюю, -рюешь) *imp.* (for, о + *prep.*).

grievous *adj.* тяжкий (-жек, -жка, -жко); (*flagrant*) вопиющий.

grill[1] *n.* рашпер; *v.t.* (*cook*) жарить *imp.*, за ~, из ~ *perf.* (на рашпере, решётке); (*question*) допрашивать, *imp.*, допросить (-ошу, -осишь) *perf.*

grille, grill[2] *n.* (*grating*) решётка.

grim *adj.* (*stern*) суровый; (*sinister*) мрачный (-чен, -чна, -чно); (*unpleasant*) неприятный.

grimace *n.* гримаса; *v.i.* гримасничать *imp.*

grime *n.* (*soot*) сажа; (*dirt*) грязь (*loc.* -зи). **grimy** *adj.* грязный (-зен, -зна, -зно).

grin *n.* усмешка; *v.i.* усмехаться *imp.*, усмехнуться *perf.*

grind *v.t.* (*flour etc.*) молоть (мелю, -лешь) *imp.*, с ~ *perf.*; (*axe*) точить (-чу, -чишь) *imp.*, на ~ *perf.*; (*oppress*) мучить *imp.*, за ~, из ~ *perf.*; *g. one's teeth*, скрежетать (-ещу, -ещешь) *imp.* зубами.

grip *n.* схватывание; (*control*) власть; *v.t.* схватывать *imp.*, схватить (-ачу, -атишь) *perf.*

grisly *adj.* ужасный.

gristle *n.* хрящ (-а). **gristly** *adj.* хрящеватый.

grit *n.* крупный песок (-ска(у)); (*firmness*) стойкость. **gritty** *adj.* песчаный.

grizzly *adj.* серый (сер, -а, -о); *g. bear*, гризли *m. indecl.*

groan *n.* стон; *v.i.* стонать (-ну, -нешь) *imp.*

grocer *n.* бакалейщик; *g.'s shop*, бакалейная лавка, гастроном(ический магазин). **groceries** *n.* бакалея *collect.*

groin *n.* (*anat.*) пах (*loc.* -у); (*arch.*) ребро (*pl.* рёбра, -бер, -брам) крестового свода.

groom *n.* грум, конюх; (*bridegroom*) жених (-а); *v.t.* (*horse*) чистить *imp.*, по ~ *perf.*; (*person*) холить *imp.*, вы ~ *perf.*; (*prepare*) готовить *imp.*, под ~ *perf.* (for, к + *dat.*); *well-groomed*, выхоленный (-ен).

groove *n.* желобок (-бка), паз (*loc.* -у; *pl.* -ы); (*routine*) колея.

grope *v.i.* нащупывать *imp.* (for, after, + *acc.*); *g. one's way*, идти (иду, идёшь; шёл, шла) *imp.*, пойти (пойду, -дёшь; пошёл, -шла) *perf.* ощупью.

gross[1] *n.* (*12 dozen*) гросс; *by the g.*, оптом.

gross[2] *adj.* (*luxuriant*) пышный (-шен, -шна, -шно); (*fat*) тучный (-чен, -чна, -чно); (*coarse*) грубый (груб, -а, -о); (*total*) валовой; *g. weight*, вес брутто.

grotesque *adj.* гротескный; (*absurd*) нелепый.

grotto *n.* грот, пещера.

ground *n.* земля (*acc.* -лю), почва, грунт; *pl.* (*dregs*) гуща; (*sport*) площадка; *pl.* (*of house*) парк; (*background*) фон; (*reason*) основание, причина; *break fresh g.*, прокладывать *imp.*, проложить (-жу, -жишь) *perf.* новые пути; *gain g.*, делать *imp.*, с ~ *perf.* успехи; *give, lose, g.*, уступать *imp.*, уступить (-плю, -пишь) *perf.* (to, + *dat.*); *stand one's g.*, стоять (-ою, -оишь) *imp.* на своём; *g. floor*, цокольный, первый, этаж (-а); *g.-nut*, земляной орех; *v.t.* (*base*) обосновывать *imp.*, обосновать (-ную, -нуёшь) *perf.*; (*instruct*) обучать *imp.*, обучить (-чу, -чишь) *perf.* основам (in, + *gen.*); *v.i.* (*naut.*) садиться *imp.*, сесть (сядет; сел) *perf.* на мель. **groundless** *adj.* беспричинный (-нен, -нна), необоснованный (-ан, -анна). **groundsheet** *n.* полотнище палатки. **groundwork** *n.* фундамент, основа, основание.

groundsel *n.* крестовник.

group *n.* группа; *g. captain*, полковник авиации; *v.t.* & *i.* группировать(ся) *imp.*, с ~ *perf.*

grouse[1] *n.* (*bird*) тетерев (*pl.* -а); (*red*) *g.*, шотландская куропатка.

grouse[2] *v.i.* (*grumble*) ворчать (-чу, -чишь) *imp.*

grove *n.* роща.

grovel *v.i.* пресмыкаться *imp.* (before, перед + *instr.*).

grow *v.i.* расти́ (-ту́, -тёшь; рос, -ла́) *imp.*; (*become*) станови́ться (-влю́сь, -вишься) *imp.*, стать (ста́ну, -нешь) *perf.* + *instr.*; *v.t.* (*cultivate*) выра́щивать *imp.*, вы́растить *perf.*; *g. up*, (*person*) выраста́ть *imp.*, вы́расти (-ту, -тешь; вы́рос, -ла) *perf.*; (*custom*) возника́ть *imp.*, возни́кнуть (-к) *perf.*
growl *n.* ворча́ние; *v.i.* ворча́ть (-чу́, -чи́шь) *imp.* (at, на + *acc.*).
grown-up *adj.*, *n.* взро́слый *sb.*
growth *n.* рост (-а(у)); (*tumour*) о́пухоль.
groyne *n.* волноре́з.
grub *n.* (*larva*) личи́нка; (*sl.*) (*food*) жратва́; *v.i.*: *g. about*, ры́ться (ро́юсь, ро́ешься) *imp.* **grubby** *adj.* чума́зый.
grudge *n.* недово́льство, за́висть; *have a g. against*, име́ть *imp.* зуб про́тив + *gen.*; *v.t.* жале́ть *imp.*, по~ *perf.* + *acc.*, + *gen.*; неохо́тно дава́ть (даю́, даёшь) *imp.*, дать (дам, дашь, даст, дади́м; дал, -а́, да́ло́, -и) *perf.*; неохо́тно де́лать *imp.*, с~ *perf.* **grudgingly** *adv.* неохо́тно.
gruel *n.* жи́дкая ка́ша; *v.t.* утомля́ть *imp.*, утоми́ть *perf.* **gruelling** *adj.* изнури́тельный, суро́вый.
gruesome *adj.* отврати́тельный.
gruff *adj.* (*surly*) грубова́тый; (*voice*) хри́плый (-л, -ла́, -ло).
grumble *n.* ворча́ние, ро́пот; *v.i.* ворча́ть (-чу́, -чи́шь) *imp.* (at, на + *acc.*).
grumpy *adj.* брюзгли́вый.
grunt *n.* хрю́канье; *v.i.* хрю́кать *imp.*, хрю́кнуть *perf.*
guarantee *n.* (*person*) поручи́тель *m.*, ~ница; (*security*) гара́нтия, зало́г; *v.t.* гаранти́ровать *imp.*, *perf.* (against, от + *gen.*); руча́ться *imp.*, поручи́ться (-чу́сь, -чишься) *perf.* за + *acc.* **guarantor** *n.* поручи́тель *m.*, ~ница. **guaranty** *n.* гара́нтия.
guard *n.* (*protection*) охра́на; (*watch*; *body of soldiers*) карау́л; (*sentry*) часово́й *sb.*; (*watchman*) сто́рож (*pl.* -а́); (*rly.*) конду́ктор (*pl.* -а́); *pl.* (*G.*) гва́рдия; *g. of honour*, почётный карау́л; *v.t.* охраня́ть *imp.*, охрани́ть *perf.*; *v.i.*: *g. against*, остерега́ться *imp.*, остере́чься (-егу́сь, -ежёшься; -ёгся, -егла́сь) *perf.* + *gen.*, *inf.* **guard-house, -room** *n.* гауптва́хта. **guardsman** *n.* гварде́ец (-е́йца).
guardian *n.* храни́тель *m.*, ~ница; (*leg.*) опеку́н (-а́).
guer(r)illa *n.* партиза́н; *g. warfare*, партиза́нская война́.
guess *n.* дога́дка; *v.t.* & *i.* дога́дываться *imp.*, догада́ться *perf.* (о + *prep.*); *v.t.* (*g. correctly*) уга́дывать *imp.*, угада́ть *perf.*
guest *n.* гость (*pl.* -ти, -те́й) *m.*, ~я (*gen.pl.* -тий).
guffaw *n.* хо́хот; *v.i.* хохота́ть (-очу́, -о́чешь) *imp.*
guidance *n.* руково́дство. **guide** *n.* проводни́к (-а́), -и́ца; гид; (*adviser*) сове́тчик; (*manual*) руково́дство; (*guidebook*) путеводи́тель *m.*; *g.-post*, указа́тельный столб (-а́); *v.t.* води́ть (вожу́, во́дишь) *indet.*, вести́ (веду́, -дёшь; вёл, -а́) *det.*; (*direct*) руководи́ть *imp.* + *instr.*; (*control*) управля́ть *imp.* + *instr.*; *guided missile*, управля́емая раке́та.
guild *n.* ги́льдия, цех.
guile *n.* кова́рство, хи́трость. **guileful** *adj.* кова́рный. **guileless** *adj.* простоду́шный.
guillemot *n.* ка́йра, чи́стик.
guillotine *n.* гильоти́на; *v.t.* гильотини́ровать *imp.*, *perf.*
guilt *n.* вина́, вино́вность. **guiltless** *adj.* неви́нный (-нен, -нна), невино́вный. **guilty** *adj.* вино́вный (of, в + *prep.*), винова́тый.
guinea *n.* гине́я; *g.-fowl*, *-hen*, цеса́рка; *g.-pig*, морска́я сви́нка; (*fig.*) подо́пытный кро́лик.
guise *n.* вид, о́блик; *under the g. of*, под ви́дом + *gen.*
guitar *n.* гита́ра.
gulf *n.* зали́в; (*chasm*) про́пасть; *G. Stream*, гольфстри́м.
gull *n.* ча́йка.
gullet *n.* пищево́д; (*throat*) го́рло.
gullible *adj.* легкове́рный.
gully *n.* (*ravine*) овра́г; (*channel*) кана́ва.
gulp *n.* глото́к (-тка́); *v.t.* жа́дно глота́ть *imp.*
gum[1] *n.* (*anat.*) десна́ (*pl.* дёсны, -сен, -снам).

gum[2] *n.* (*glue*) каме́дь, клей (-е́я(ю), *loc.* -е́е & -е́ю; *pl.* -е́й); *v.t.* скле́ивать *imp.*, скле́ить *perf.* **gumboot** *n.* рези́новый сапо́г (-а́; *gen.pl.* -г). **gum-tree** *n.* эвкали́пт.

gumption *n.* нахо́дчивость.

gun *n.* (*piece of ordnance*) ору́дие, пу́шка; (*rifle etc.*) ружьё (*pl.* -жья, -жей); (*pistol*) пистоле́т; *starting g.*, ста́ртовый пистоле́т; *v.t.*: *g. down*, расстре́ливать *imp.*, расстреля́ть *perf.* **gunboat** *n.* каноне́рская ло́дка. **gun-carriage** *n.* лафе́т. **gunner** *n.* артиллери́ст; (*aeron.*) стрело́к (-лка́). **gunpowder** *n.* по́рох (-а(у)). **gunsmith** *n.* оруже́йный ма́стер (*pl.* -а́).

gunwale *n.* планши́рь *m.*

gurgle *v.i.* бу́лькать *imp.*, бу́лькнуть *perf.*

gush *n.* си́льный пото́к; излия́ние; *v.i.* хлы́нуть *perf.*; излива́ться *imp.*, изли́ться (изолью́сь, -ьёшься; изли́лся, -ила́сь, -и́ло́сь) *perf.*

gusset *n.* клин (*pl.* -ья, -ьев), ла́стовица.

gust *n.* поры́в. **gusty** *adj.* поры́вистый.

gusto *n.* удово́льствие, смак.

gut *n.* кишка́ (*gen.pl.* -шо́к); *pl.* (*entrails*) вну́тренности *f.pl.*; *pl.* (*coll.*, *bravery*) мужество́; *v.t.* потроши́ть *imp.*, вы́~ *perf.*; (*devastate*) опустоша́ть *imp.*, опустоши́ть *perf.*

gutta-percha *n.* гуттапе́рча.

gutter *n.* (водосто́чный) жёлоб (*pl.* -а́), сто́чная кана́ва; *g. press*, бульва́рная пре́сса.

guttural *adj.* горта́нный, горлово́й.

guy[1] *n.* (*rope*) оття́жка.

guy[2] *n.* (*fellow*) па́рень (-рня; *pl.* -рни, -рне́й) *m.*

guzzle *v.t.* (*food*) пожира́ть *imp.*, пожра́ть (-ру́, -рёшь; пожра́л, -а́, -о) *perf.*; (*liquid*) хлеба́ть *imp.*, хлебну́ть *perf.*

gym *n.* (*gymnasium*) гимнасти́ческий зал; (*gymnastics*) гимна́стика. **gymnasium** *n.* гимнасти́ческий зал; (*school*) гимна́зия. **gymnast** *n.* гимна́ст, ~ка. **gymnastic** *adj.* гимнасти́ческий. **gymnastics** *n.* гимна́стика.

gynaecology *n.* гинеколо́гия.

gypsum *n.* гипс.

gyrate *v.i.* враща́ться *imp.* по кру́гу; дви́гаться (дви́гается & дви́жется) *imp.* по спира́ли.

gyro(scope) *n.* гироско́п. **gyro-compass** *n.* гироко́мпас.

H

haberdasher *n.* торго́вец (-вца) галантере́ей. **haberdashery** *n.* (*articles*) галантере́я; (*shop*) галантере́йный магази́н.

habit *n.* привы́чка; (*constitution*) сложе́ние; (*dress*) одея́ние.

habitable *adj.* го́дный (-ден, -дна́, -дно) для жилья́. **habitation** *n.* жили́ще.

habitual *adj.* обы́чный, привы́чный. **habitué** *n.* завсегда́тай.

hack[1] *n.* (*mattock*) моты́га; (*miner's pick*) кайла́ (*pl.* -лы), кайло́ (*pl.* -ла); *v.t.* руби́ть (-блю́, -бишь) *imp.*; дроби́ть *imp.*, раз~ *perf.*; *h.-saw*, ножо́вка.

hack[2] *n.* (*hired horse*) наёмная ло́шадь (*pl.* -ди, -де́й, *instr.* -дьми́); (*jade*) кля́ча; (*person*) подёнщик, писа́ка *m.* & *f.* **hackneyed** *adj.* изби́тый, бана́льный.

haddock *n.* пи́кша.

haematology *n.* гематоло́гия. **haemophilia** *n.* гемофили́я. **haemorrhage** *n.* кровоизлия́ние, кровотече́ние. **haemorrhoids** *n.* геморро́й *collect.*

haft *n.* рукоя́тка.

hag *n.* ве́дьма, карга́.

haggard *adj.* измождённый (-ён, -ена́)

haggle *v.i.* торгова́ться *imp.*, с~ *perf.*

hail[1] *n.* град; *v.i.*: *it is hailing*, идёт (*past* пошёл) град; *v.t.* осыпа́ть *imp.*, осы́пать (-плю, -плешь) *perf.* + *acc.* & *instr.*; *v.i.* сы́паться (-плется) *imp.* гра́дом. **hailstone** *n.* гра́дина.

hail[2] *v.t.* (*greet*) приве́тствовать *imp.* (& *perf. in past*); (*call*) оклика́ть *imp.*, окли́кнуть *perf.*; *v.i.*: *h. from*, (*of persons only*) быть ро́дом из + *gen.*; происходи́ть (-ожу́, -о́дишь) *imp.*, произойти́ (произойду́, -дёшь; произошёл, -шла́) *perf.* из + *gen.*

hair *n.* (*single h.*) во́лос (*pl.* -осы, -о́с, -оса́м); *collect.* (*human*) во́лосы (-о́с, -оса́м) *pl.*; (*animal*) шерсть; *do one's hair*, причёсываться *imp.*, причеса́ться (-ешу́сь, -е́шешься) *perf.* **haircut** *n.* стри́жка. **hair-do** *n.* причёска. **hairdresser** *n.* парикма́хер. **hairy** *adj.* волоса́тый.

hake *n.* хек.

halberd *n.* алеба́рда.

hale *adj.* здоро́вый.

half *n.* полови́на; (*sport*) тайм; *in comb.* пол(у)-; *adj.* полови́нный; *in h.*, попола́м; *one and a h.*, полтора́ *m.* & *neut.*, -ры́ *f.* + *gen. sing.* (*obl. cases*: полу́тора + *pl.*); *h. past* (*one etc.*), полови́на (второ́го и т.д.); *h.-back*, полузащи́тник; *h.-hearted*, равноду́шный; *h.-hour*, полчаса́ (*obl. cases*: полу́часа); *h.-mast*: *flag at h.-mast*, приспущённый флаг; *h. moon*, полуме́сяц; *h.-time*, переры́в ме́жду та́ймами; *h.-way*, на полпути́; *h.-witted*, слабоу́мный.

halibut *n.* па́лтус.

hall *n.* (*large room*) зал; (*entrance h.*) холл, вестибю́ль *m.*; (*dining h.*) столо́вая (колле́джа); (*h. of residence*) общежи́тие. **hallmark** *n.* пробі́рное клеймо́ (*pl.* -ма); (*fig.*) при́знак.

halliard *see* **halyard.**

hallow *v.t.* освяща́ть *imp.*, освяти́ть (-ящу́, -яти́шь) *perf.*

hallucination *n.* галлюцина́ция.

halo *n.* гало́ *neut. indecl.*; (*around Saint*) ве́нчик, нимб; (*fig.*) орео́л.

halogen *n.* гало́ге́н.

halt[1] *n.* (*stoppage*) остано́вка; (*rly.*) полуста́нок (-нка); *v.t.* & *i.* остана́вливать(ся) *imp.*, останови́ть(ся) (-влю́(сь), -вишь(ся)) *perf.*; *interj.* (*mil.*) стой(те)!

halt[2] *v.i.* (*hesitate*) колеба́ться (-блюсь, блешься) *imp.*

halter *n.* недоу́здок (-дка).

halve *v.t.* дели́ть (-лю́, -лишь) *imp.*, раз~ *perf.* попола́м.

halyard, halliard *n.* фал.

ham *n.* (*cul.*) ветчина́, о́корок; (*theat.*) плохо́й актёр; (*radio h.*) радиолюби́тель *m.*; *v.i.* (*theat.*) переигрыва́ть *imp.*, переигра́ть *perf.*

hamlet *n.* дереву́шка.

hammer *n.* мо́лот, молото́к (-тка́); *come under the h.*, продава́ться (-даётся) *imp.*, прода́ться (-да́стся; -да́лся, -дала́сь) *perf.* с молотка́.; *vt.* бить (бью, бьёшь) *imp.* мо́лотом, молотко́м.

hammock *n.* гама́к (-а́); (*naut.*) ко́йка.

hamper[1] *n.* (*basket*) корзи́на с кры́шкой.

hamper[2] *v.t.* (*hinder*) меша́ть *imp.*, по~ *perf.* + *dat.*

hamster *n.* хомя́к (-а́).

hand *n.* рука́ (*acc.* -ку; *pl.* -ки, -к, -ка́м); (*worker*) рабо́чий *sb.*; (*handwriting*) по́черк; (*clock h.*) стре́лка; *at h.*, под руко́й; *on hands and knees*, на четвере́ньках; *v.t.* передава́ть (-даю́, -даёшь) *imp.*, переда́ть (-а́м, -а́шь, -а́ст, -ади́м; пе́редал, -а́, -о) *perf.*; вруча́ть *imp.*, вручи́ть *perf.* **handbag** *n.* су́мка, су́мочка. **handbook** *n.* спра́вочник, руково́дство. **handcuffs** *n.* нару́чники *m.pl.* **handful** *n.* горсть (*pl.* -ти, -те́й).

handicap *n.* (*sport*) гандика́п; (*hindrance*) поме́ха. **handicapped** *adj.*: *h. person*, инвали́д.

handicraft *n.* ремесло́ (*pl.* -ёсла, -ёсел, -ёслам).

handiwork *n.* ручна́я рабо́та.

handkerchief *n.* носово́й плато́к (-тка́).

handle *n.* ру́чка, рукоя́тка; *v.t.* (*treat*) обраща́ться *imp.* с + *instr.*; (*manage*) управля́ть *imp.* + *instr.*; (*touch*) тро́гать *imp.*, тро́нуть *perf.* руко́й, рука́ми. **handlebar(s)** *n.* руль (-ля́) *m.*

handsome *adj.* краси́вый; (*generous*) ще́дрый (щедр, -а́, -о).

handwriting *n.* по́черк.

handy *adj.* (*convenient*) удо́бный; (*skilful*) ло́вкий (-вок, -вка́, -вко, ло́вки́); *come in h.*, пригоди́ться *perf.*
hang *v.t.* ве́шать *imp.*, пове́сить *perf.*; подве́шивать *imp.*, подве́сить *perf.*; *v.i.* висе́ть (вишу́, виси́шь) *imp.*; *h. about*, слоня́ться *imp.*; *h. back*, колеба́ться (-блюсь, -блешься) *imp.*; *h. on*, (*remain*) держа́ться (-жу́сь, -жишься) *imp.* **hanger-on** *n.* прижива́льщик. **hangman** *n.* пала́ч (-а́).
hangar *n.* анга́р.
hangover *n.* похме́лье.
hanker *v.i.*: *h. after*, стра́стно жела́ть *imp.*, по~ *perf.*+*gen.*
hansom *n.* двухколёсный экипа́ж.
haphazard *adj.* случа́йный; *adv.* случа́йно, науда́чу.
hapless *adj.* злополу́чный.
happen *v.i.* (*occur*) случа́ться *imp.*, случи́ться *perf.*; происходи́ть (-ит) *imp.*, произойти́ (-ойдёт; -ошёл, -ошла́) *perf.*; (*h. to be somewhere*) ока́зываться *imp.*, оказа́ться (-ажу́сь, -а́жешься) *perf.*; *h. upon*, ната́лкиваться *imp.*, натолкну́ться *perf.* на+*acc.*
happiness *n.* сча́стье. **happy** *adj.* счастли́вый (сча́стли́в); (*apt*) уда́чный.
harass *v.t.* беспоко́ить *imp.*, о~ *perf.*
harbinger *n.* предве́стник.
harbour *n.* га́вань, порт (*loc.* -у́; *pl.* -ы, -о́в); (*shelter*) убе́жище; *v.t.* (*person*) укрыва́ть *imp.*, укры́ть (-ро́ю, -ро́ешь) *perf.*; (*thoughts*) зата́ивать *imp.*, затаи́ть *perf.*
hard *adj.* твёрдый (твёрд, -а́, -о), жёсткий (-ток, -тка́, -тко); (*difficult*) тру́дный (-ден, -дна́, -дно, тру́дны́); (*difficult to bear*) тяжёлый (-л, -ла́); (*severe*) суро́вый; *h.-boiled egg*, яйцо́ (*pl.* я́йца, яи́ц, я́йцам) вкруту́ю; *h.-headed*, практи́чный; *h.-hearted*, жестокосе́рдный; *h.-working*, приле́жный.
harden *v.t.* де́лать *imp.*, с~ *perf.* твёрдым; закаля́ть *imp.*, закали́ть *perf.*; *v.i.* затвердева́ть *imp.*, затверде́ть *perf.*; (*become callous*) ожесточа́ться *imp.*, ожесточи́ться *perf.*
hardly *adv.* (*scarcely*) едва́ (ли); (*with difficulty*) с трудо́м.
hardship *n.* (*privation*) нужда́.
hardware *n.* скобяны́е изде́лия *neut.pl.*
hardy *adj.* (*bold*) сме́лый (смел, -а́, -о); (*robust*) выно́сливый.
hare *n.* за́яц (за́йца); *h.-brained*, опроме́тчивый. **harelip** *n.* за́ячья губа́.
harem *n.* гаре́м.
haricot (bean) *n.* фасо́ль.
hark *v.i.*: *h. to, at*, слу́шать *imp.*, по~ *perf.*+*acc.*; *h. back to*, возвраща́ться *imp.*, верну́ться *perf.* к+*dat.*; *interj.* чу!
harlot *n.* проститу́тка.
harm *n.* вред (-а́), зло; *v.t.* вреди́ть *imp.*, по~ *perf.*+*dat.* **harmful** *adj.* вре́дный (-ден, -дна́, -дно). **harmless** *adj.* безвре́дный.
harmonic *adj.* гармони́ческий. **harmonica** *n.* губна́я гармо́ника. **harmonious** *adj.* гармони́чный; (*amicable*) дру́жный (-жен, -жна́, -жно). **harmonium** *n.* фисгармо́ния. **harmonize** *v.t.* гармонизи́ровать *imp.*, *perf.*; *v.i.* гармони́ровать *imp.* (with, с+*instr.*).
harmony *n.* гармо́ния, созву́чие, согла́сие.
harness *n.* у́пряжь, сбру́я; *v.t.* за-, в-, пряга́ть *imp.*, за-, в-, пря́чь (-ягу́, -яжёшь; -я́г, -ягла́) *perf.*; (*fig.*) испо́льзовать *imp.*, *perf.* как исто́чник эне́ргии.
harp *n.* а́рфа; *v.i.* игра́ть *imp.* на а́рфе; *harp on*, распространя́ться *imp.*, распространи́ться *perf.* о+*prep.* **harpist** *n.* арфи́ст, ~ка.
harpoon *n.* гарпу́н (-а́), острога́.
harpsichord *n.* клавеси́н.
harpy *n.* га́рпия; (*fig.*) хи́щник.
harridan *n.* ве́дьма, карга́.
harrier[1] *n.* (*hound*) го́нчая *sb.*
harrier[2] *n.* (*falcon*) лунь (-ня́) *m.*
harrow *n.* борона́ (*acc.* -ону; *pl.* -оны, -о́н, -она́м); *v.t.* борони́ть *imp.*, вз~ *perf.*; (*torment*) терза́ть *imp.*
harry *v.t.* (*ravage*) опустоша́ть *imp.*, опустоши́ть *perf.*; (*worry*) трево́жить *imp.*, вс~ *perf.*
harsh *adj.* гру́бый (груб, -а́, -о); (*sound*) ре́зкий (-зок, -зка́, -зко); (*cruel*) суро́вый.
hart *n.* оле́нь *m.*

harvest *n.* жáтва, сбор (плодóв); (*yield*) урожáй; (*fig.*) плоды́ *m.pl.*; *v.t.* & *abs.* собирáть *imp.*, собрáть (соберý, -рёшь; собрáл, -á, -о) *perf.* (урожáй).
hash *n.* рýбленое мя́со; (*medley*) мешанúна; *make a h. of*, напýтать *perf.* + *acc.*, в + *prep.*; *v.t.* рубúть (-блю́, -бишь) *imp.*
hasp *n.* застёжка.
hassock *n.* (*cushion*) подýшечка; (*tuft of grass*) кóчка.
haste *n.* поспéшность, торопли́вость, спéшка. **hasten** *v.i.* спешúть *imp.*, по~ *perf.*; *v.t.* & *i.* торопúть(ся) (-плю́(сь), -пишь(ся)) *imp.*, по~ *perf.*; *v.t.* ускоря́ть *imp.*, ускóрить *perf.* **hasty** *adj.* (*hurried*) поспéшный; (*rash*) опромéтчивый; (*quick-tempered*) вспы́льчивый.
hat *n.* шля́па; *top h.*, цили́ндр.
hatch[1], **-way** *n.* (*naut.*) люк.
hatch[2] *n.* (*brood*) вы́водок (-дка); *v.t.* выси́живать *imp.*, вы́сидеть (-ижу, -идишь) *perf.*; *v.i.* вылýпливаться, вылупля́ться *imp.*, вы́лупиться *perf.*
hatch[3] *v.t.* (*line*) штриховáть *imp.*, за~ *perf.*
hatchet *n.* топóрик.
hate *n.* нéнависть; *v.t.* ненави́деть (-и́жу, -и́дишь) *imp.* **hateful** *adj.* ненави́стный. **hatred** *n.* нéнависть.
haughty *adj.* надмéнный (-нен, -нна), высокомéрный.
haul *n.* добы́ча; (*distance*) ездá; *v.t.* тянýть (-нý, -нешь) *imp.*; таскáть *indet.*, тащи́ть (-щý, -щишь) *det.*; (*transport*) перевози́ть (-ожý, -óзишь) *imp.*, перевезти́ (-езý, -езёшь; -ёз, -езлá) *perf.*
haunch *n.* бедрó (*pl.* бёдра, -дер, -драм), ля́жка.
haunt *n.* чáсто посещáемое мéсто; (*of criminals*) притóн; *v.t.* (*frequent*) чáсто посещáть *imp.*
have *v.t.* имéть *imp.*; (*cheat*) надувáть *imp.*, надýть (-ýю, -ýешь) *perf.*; *I have*, (*possess*) у меня́ (есть; был, -á, -о) + *nom.*; *I have not*, у меня́ нет (*past* нé было) + *gen.*; *I have* (*got*) *to*, я дóлжен (-жнá) + *inf.*; *you had better*, вам лýчше бы + *inf.*; *h. on* (*wear*) быть одéтым в + *prep.*; (*be engaged in*) быть зáнятым (-т, -тá, -то) + *instr.*
haven *n.* гáвань; (*refuge*) убéжище.
haversack *n.* рáнец (-нца).
havoc *n.* (*devastation*) опустошéние; (*disorder*) беспоря́док (-дка).
hawk[1] *n.* (*bird*) я́стреб (*pl.* -ы & -á).
hawk[2] *v.t.* (*trade*) торговáть *imp.* вразнóс + *instr.* **hawker** *n.* разнóсчик.
hawk[3] (*cough*) *v.t.* откáшливать *imp.*, откáшлянуть *perf.*; *v.i.* откáшливаться *imp.*, откáшляться *perf.*
hawse(-hole) *n.* (*naut.*) клюз.
hawser *n.* трос.
hawthorn *n.* боя́рышник.
hay *n.* сéно; *make h.*, коси́ть (кошý, кóсишь) *imp.*, с~ *perf.* сéно; *h. fever*, сéнная лихорáдка. **haycock** *n.* копнá (*pl.* -пны, -пён, -пнáм). **hayloft** *n.* сеновáл. **haystack** *n.* стог (*loc.* -е & -ý; *pl.* -á).
hazard *n.* риск; *v.t.* рисковáть *imp.* + *instr.* **hazardous** *adj.* рискóванный (-ан, -анна).
haze *n.* тумáн, ды́мка.
hazel *n.* лещи́на. **hazelnut** *n.* леснóй орéх.
hazy *adj.* (*misty*) тумáнный (-нен, -нна); (*vague*) смýтный (-тен, -тнá, -тно).
H-bomb *n.* водорóдная бóмба.
he *pron.* он (егó, емý, им, о нём).
head *n.* головá (*acc.* -ову; *pl.* -овы, -óв, -овáм); (*mind*) ум (-á); (*h. of cattle*) головá скотá; (*h. of coin*) лицевáя сторонá (*acc.* -ону) монéты; *heads or tails?* орёл или рéшка? (*chief*) главá (*pl.* -вы) *m.*, начáльник; *attrib.* глáвный; *v.t.* (*lead*) возглавля́ть *imp.*, возглáвить *perf.*; (*h. chapter*) озаглáвливать *imp.*, озаглáвить *perf.*; *v.i.*: *h. for*, направля́ться *imp.*, напрáвиться *perf.* в, на, + *acc.*, к + *dat.* **headache** *n.* головнáя боль. **head-dress** *n.* головнóй убóр. **heading** *n.* (*title*) заголóвок (-вка). **headland** *n.* мыс (*loc.* -е & -ý; *pl.* мы́сы́). **headlight** *n.* фáра. **headline** *n.* заголóвок (-вка). **headlong** *adj.* (*precipitate*) опромéтчивый; *adv.* стремглáв. **headmaster, -mistress** *n.* дирéктор (*pl.* -á) шкóлы. **headphone** *n.* наýшник. **headquarters** *n.* штаб-квартúра. **headstone** *n.* надгрóбный

ка́мень (-мня; *pl.* -мни, -мне́й) *m.* **headstrong** *adj.* своево́льный. **headway** *n.* движе́ние вперёд. **heady** *adj.* стреми́тельный; (*liquor*) хмельно́й (-лён, -льна́).

heal *v.t.* излечивать *imp.*, излечи́ть (-чу́, -чишь) *perf.*; исцеля́ть *imp.*, исцели́ть *perf.*; *v.i.* зажива́ть *imp.*, зажи́ть (-ивёт; за́жил, -а́, -о) *perf.* **healing** *adj.* целе́бный.

health *n.* здоро́вье. **healthy** *adj.* здоро́вый; (*beneficial*) поле́зный.

heap *n.* ку́ча, гру́да; *v.t.* нагроможда́ть *imp.*, нагромозди́ть *perf.*; (*load*) нагружа́ть *imp.*, нагрузи́ть (-ужу́, -у́зи́шь) *perf.* (with, + *instr.*).

hear *v.t.* слы́шать (-шу, -шишь) *imp.*, у~ *perf.*; (*listen to*) слу́шать *imp.*, по~ *perf.*; (*learn*) узнава́ть (-наю́, -наёшь) *imp.*, узна́ть *perf.*; *h. out*, выслу́шивать *imp.*, вы́слушать *perf.* **hearing** *n.* слух; (*limit*) преде́л слы́шимости; (*leg.*) слуша́ние, разбо́р де́ла. **hearsay** *n.* слух.

hearken *v.i.* внима́ть *imp.*, внять (*past only*: внял, -а́, -о) *perf.* (to, + *dat.*).

hearse *n.* катафа́лк.

heart *n.* (*organ*; *fig.*) се́рдце (*pl.* -дца́, -де́ц, -дца́м) (*fig.*) душа́ (*acc.* -шу; *pl.* -ши); (*courage*) му́жество; (*of tree etc.*) сердцеви́на; (*essence*) суть; *pl.* (*cards*) че́рви (-ве́й) *pl.*; *at h.*, в глубине́ души́; *by h.*, наизу́сть; *h. attack*, серде́чный при́ступ. **heartburn** *n.* изжо́га. **hearten** *v.t.* ободря́ть *imp.*, ободри́ть *perf.* **heartfelt** *adj.* и́скренний (-нен, -нна, -нно & -нне), серде́чный. **heartless** *adj.* бессерде́чный. **heart-rending** *adj.* душераздира́ющий. **hearty** *adj.* (*cordial*) серде́чный; (*vigorous*) здоро́вый.

hearth *n.* оча́г (-а́).

heat *n.* жар (*loc.* -е & -у́), жа́ра; (*phys.*) теплота́; (*of feeling*) пыл (*loc.* -у́); (*sport*) забе́г, зае́зд; *v.t.* & *i.* нагрева́ть(ся) *imp.*, нагре́ть(ся) *perf.*; *v.t.* топи́ть (-плю́, -пишь) *imp.* **heater** *n.* нагрева́тель *m.* **heating** *n.* отопле́ние.

heath *n.* пу́стошь; (*shrub*) ве́реск.

heathen *n.* язы́чник; *adj.* язы́ческий.

heather *n.* ве́реск.

heave *v.t.* (*lift*) поднима́ть *imp.*, подня́ть (подниму́, -мешь; по́днял, -а́, -о) *perf.*; (*pull*) тяну́ть (-ну́, -нешь) *imp.*, по~ *perf.*

heaven *n.* не́бо, рай (*loc.* раю́); *pl.* небеса́ *neut.pl.* **heavenly** *adj.* небе́сный, боже́ственный.

heaviness *n.* тя́жесть. **heavy** *adj.* тяжёлый (-л, -ла́); (*strong*) си́льный (си́лён, -льна́, -льно, си́льны́); (*abundant*) оби́льный; (*gloomy*) мра́чный (-чен, -чна́, -чно); (*sea*) бу́рный (-рен, бу́рна́, -рно). **heavyweight** *n.* тяжелове́с.

Hebrew *n.* евре́й; *adj.* (древне)евре́йский.

heckle *v.t.* пререка́ться *imp.* с + *instr.*

hectare *n.* гекта́р.

hectic *adj.* лихора́дочный.

hedge *n.* (*fence*) жива́я и́згородь; (*barrier*) прегра́да; *v.t.* огора́живать *imp.*, огороди́ть (-ожу́, -о́ди́шь) *perf.*; *v.i.* верте́ться (-рчу́сь, -ртишься) *imp.* **hedgerow** *n.* шпале́ра. **hedge-sparrow** *n.* лесна́я завиру́шка.

hedgehog *n.* ёж (-а́).

heed *n.* внима́ние; *v.t.* обраща́ть *imp.*, обрати́ть (-ащу́, -ати́шь) *perf.* внима́ние на + *acc.* **heedful** *adj.* внима́тельный. **heedless** *adj.* небре́жный.

heel[1] *n.* (*of foot*) пята́ (*pl.* -ты, -т, -та́м); (*of foot, sock*) пя́тка; (*of shoe*) каблу́к (-а́).

heel[2] *n.* (*of ship*) крен; *v.t.* & *i.* крени́ть(ся) *imp.*, на~ *perf.*

hefty *adj.* дю́жий (дюж, -а́, -е).

hegemony *n.* гегемо́ния.

heifer *n.* тёлка.

height *n.* высота́ (*pl.* -ты), вышина́ (*no pl.*); (*elevation*) возвы́шенность. **heighten** *v.t.* повыша́ть *imp.*, повы́сить *perf.*; (*strengthen*) уси́ливать *imp.*, уси́лить *perf.*

heinous *adj.* гну́сный (-сен, -сна́, -сно).

heir *n.* насле́дник. **heiress** *n.* насле́дница. **heirloom** *n.* фами́льная вещь (*pl.* -щи, -ще́й).

helicopter *n.* вертолёт.

heliograph *n.* гелио́граф. **heliotrope** *n.* гелиотро́п.

helium *n.* ге́лий.

helix *n.* спира́ль.

hell *n.* ад (*loc.* -ý). **hellish** *adj.* áдский.
Hellene *n.* э́ллин. **Hellenic** *adj.* э́ллинский. **Hellenistic** *adj.* эллинисти́ческий.
helm *n.* руль (-ля́) *m.*, корми́ло (правле́ния). **helmsman** *n.* рулевóй *sb.*; (*fig.*) кóрмчий *sb.*
helmet *n.* шлем.
help *n.* пóмощь; (*person*) помóщник, -ица; *v.t.* помогáть *imp.*, помóчь (-огý, -óжешь; -óг, -оглá) *perf.* + *dat.*; (*with negative*) не мочь (могý, мóжешь; мог, -лá) *imp.* не + *inf.*; *h. oneself*, брать (берý, -рёшь; брал, -á, -о) *imp.*, взять (возьмý, -мёшь; взял, -á, -о) *perf.* себé. **helpful** *adj.* полéзный. **helping** *n.* (*of food*) пóрция. **helpless** *adj.* беспомóщный.
helter-skelter *adv.* как попáло.
helve *n.* рукоя́тка, черенóк (-нкá).
hem *n.* рубéц (-бцá), каймá (*gen.pl.* каём); *v.t.* подрубáть *imp.*, подруби́ть (-блю́, -бишь) *perf.*; *h. about, in*, окружáть *imp.*, окружи́ть *perf.*
hemisphere *n.* полушáрие.
hemlock *n.* болиголóв.
hemp *n.* (*plant*) конопля́; (*fibre*) пенькá. **hempen** *adj.* конопля́ный; пенькóвый.
hen *n.* (*female bird*) сáмка; (*domestic fowl*) кýрица (*pl.* кýры, кур). **henbane** *n.* беленá. **hen-coop** *n.* куря́тник. **henpecked** *adj.*: *be h.*, быть у жены́ под башмакóм, под каблукóм.
hence *adv.* (*from here*) отсю́да; (*from this time*) с э́тих пóр; (*as a result*) слéдовательно. **henceforth, henceforward** *adv.* отны́не.
henchman *n.* привéрженец (-нца).
henna *n.* хна.
hepatic *adj.* печёночный.
her *poss.pron.* её; свой (-оя́, -оё; -ои́).
herald *n.* герóльд, предвéстник; *v.t.* возвещáть *imp.*, возвести́ть *perf.*
herb *n.* травá (*pl.* -вы). **herbaceous** *adj.* травяни́стый. **herbal** *adj.* травянóй. **herbivorous** *adj.* травоя́дный.
herd *n.* стáдо (*pl.* -дá); (*of people*) толпá (*pl.* -пы); *v.i.* ходи́ть (-ит) *imp.* стáдом; (*people*) толпи́ться *imp.*, с~ *perf.*; *v.t.* собирáть *imp.*, собрáть (соберý, -рёшь; собрáл, -á, -о) *perf.* в стáдо. **herdsman** *n.* пастýх (-á).
here *adv.* (*position*) здесь, тут; (*direction*) сюдá; *h. is* . . ., вот (+ *nom.*); *h. and there*, там и сям. **hereabout(s)** *adv.* поблизости. **hereafter** *adv.* в бýдущем. **hereby** *adv.* э́тим; таки́м óбразом. **hereupon** *adv.* (*in consequence*) вслéдствие э́того; (*after*) пóсле э́того. **herewith** *adv.* при сём, при э́том, чéрез э́то.
hereditary *adj.* наслéдственный.
heredity *n.* наслéдственность.
heresy *n.* éресь. **heretic** *n.* ерети́к (-á). **heretical** *adj.* ерети́ческий.
heritable *adj.* наслéдуемый.
heritage *n.* наслéдство, наслéдие.
hermaphrodite *n.* гермафроди́т.
hermetic *adj.* гермети́ческий.
hermit *n.* отшéльник, пусты́нник. **hermitage** *n.* пýстынь; хили́ще (отшéльника, пусты́нника).
hernia *n.* гры́жа.
hero *n.* герóй. **heroic** *adj.* герои́ческий. **heroine** *n.* герои́ня. **heroism** *n.* герои́зм.
heron *n.* цáпля (*gen.pl.* -пель).
herpes *n.* лишáй (-ая́).
herring *n.* сельдь (*pl.* -ди, -дéй), селёдка; *h.-bone*, ёлочка; (*attrib.*) ёлочкой, в ёлочку.
hers *poss.pron.* её; свой (-оя́, -оё; -ои́).
herself *pron.* (*emph.*) (онá) самá (-мóй, *acc.* -мý); (*refl.*) себя́ (себé, собóй); -ся (*suffixed to v.t.*).
hertz *n.* герц (*gen.pl.* -ц).
hesitant *adj.* нереши́тельный. **hesitate** *v.i.* колебáться (-блюсь, -блешься) *imp.*, по~ *perf.*; (*in speech*) запинáться *imp.*, запнýться *perf.* **hesitation** *n.* колебáние, нереши́тельность.
hessian *n.* мешкови́на.
heterogeneous *adj.* разнорóдный.
hew *v.t.* руби́ть (-блю́, -бишь) *imp.*
hexa- *in comb.* шести-, гекза-. **hexagon** *n.* шестиугóльник. **hexameter** *n.* гекзáметр.
hey *interj.* эй!
heyday *n.* расцвéт.
hi *interj.* эй! привéт!
hiatus *n.* пробéл; (*ling.*) зия́ние.
hibernate *v.i.* находи́ться (-ожýсь, -óдишься) *imp.* в зи́мней спя́чке; зимовáть *imp.*, пере~, про~ *perf.*

hibernation *n.* зи́мняя спя́чка, зимо́вка.
hiccough, hiccup *v.i.* ика́ть *imp.*, икну́ть *perf.*; *n.*: *pl.* ико́та.
hide[1] *n.* (*animal's skin*) шку́ра, ко́жа.
hide[2] *v.t.* & *i.* (*conceal*) пря́тать(ся) (-я́чу(сь), -я́чешь(ся)) *imp.*, с~ *perf.*; скрыва́ть(ся) *imp.*, скры́ть(ся) (скро́ю(сь), -о́ешь(ся)) *perf.*
hideous *adj.* отврати́тельный, безобра́зный.
hiding *n.* (*flogging*) по́рка.
hierarchy *n.* иера́рхия.
hieroglyph *n.* иеро́глиф. **hieroglyphic** *adj.* иероглифи́ческий.
higgledy-piggledy *adv.* как придётся.
high *adj.* высо́кий (-о́к, -ока́, -о́ко́); (*elevated*) возвы́шенный; (*higher*) вы́сший; (*intense*) си́льный (си́лён, -льна́, -льно, си́льны́); *h.-class*, высокока́чественный; *higher education*, вы́сшее образова́ние; *h. fidelity*, высо́кая то́чность воспроизведе́ния; *h.-handed*, повели́тельный; *h. jump*, прыжо́к (-жка́) в высоту́; *h.-minded*, благоро́дный; *h.-pitched*, высо́кий (-о́к, -ока́, -о́ко́); *h.-strung*, чувстви́тельный, не́рвный (-вен, не́рвна́, -вно). **highland(s)** *n.* го́рная страна́. **highly** *adv.* в вы́сшей сте́пени. **highness** *n.* возвы́шенность; (*title*) высо́чество. **highway** *n.* больша́я доро́га, шоссе́ *neut.indecl.* **highwayman** *n.* разбо́йник (с большо́й доро́ги).
hijack *v.t.* похища́ть *imp.*, похи́тить (-и́щу, -и́тишь) *perf.* **hijacker** *n.* похити́тель *m.*
hike *n.* похо́д.
hilarious *adj.* весёлый (ве́сел, -а́, -о, ве́селы́). **hilarity** *n.* весе́лье.
hill *n.* холм (-а́). **hillock** *n.* хо́лмик. **hilly** *adj.* холми́стый.
hilt *n.* рукоя́тка.
himself *pron.* (*emph.*) (он) сам (-ого́, -ому́, -и́м, -о́м); (*refl.*) себя́ (себе́, собо́й); -ся (*suffixed to v.t.*).
hind[1] *n.* (*deer*) са́мка (благоро́дного) оле́ня.
hind[2] *adj.* (*rear*) за́дний. **hindmost** *adj.* са́мый за́дний.
hinder *v.t.* меша́ть *imp.*, по~ *perf.* + *dat.* **hindrance** *n.* поме́ха, препя́тствие.
Hindu *n.* инду́с; *adj.* инду́сский.
hinge *n.* шарни́р, пе́тля (*gen.pl.* -тель); *v.t.* прикрепля́ть *imp.*, прикрепи́ть *perf.* на пе́тлях; *v.i.* враща́ться *imp.* на пе́тлях; *h. on*, (*fig.*) зави́сеть (-сит) *imp.* от + *gen.*
hint *n.* намёк; *v.i.* намека́ть *imp.*, намекну́ть *perf.* (at, на + *acc.*).
hinterland *n.* глубина́ страны́.
hip[1] *n.* (*anat.*) бедро́ (*pl.* бёдра, -дер, -драм).
hip[2] *n.* (*fruit*) я́года шипо́вника.
hippopotamus *n.* гиппопота́м.
hire *n.* наём (на́йма), прока́т; *h.-purchase*, поку́пка в рассро́чку; *v.t.* нанима́ть *imp.*, наня́ть (найму́, -мёшь; на́нял, -а́, -о) *perf.*; брать (беру́, -рёшь; брал, -а́, -о) *imp.*, взять, (возьму́, -мёшь; взял, -а́, -о) *perf.* напрока́т; *h. out*, отдава́ть (-даю́, -даёшь) *imp.*, отда́ть (-а́м, -а́шь, -а́ст, -ади́м; о́тдал, -а́, -о) *perf.* внаймы́, напрока́т.
hireling *n.* наёмник.
hirsute *adj.* волоса́тый.
his *poss.pron.* его́; свой (-оя́, -оё; -ои́).
hiss *n.* шипе́ние, свист; *v.i.* шипе́ть (-плю́, -пи́шь) *imp.*; свисте́ть (-ищу́, -исти́шь) *imp.*; *v.t.* осви́стывать *imp.*, освиста́ть (-ищу́, -и́щешь) *perf.*
historian *n.* исто́рик. **historic(al)** *adj.* истори́ческий. **history** *n.* исто́рия.
histrionic *adj.* театра́льный.
hit *n.* (*blow*) уда́р; (*on target*) попада́ние (в цель); (*success*) успе́х; *v.t.* (*strike*) ударя́ть *imp.*, уда́рить *perf.*; (*target*) попада́ть *imp.*, попа́сть (-аду́, -адёшь; -а́л) *perf.* (в цель); *h. (up)on*, находи́ть (-ожу́, -о́дишь) *imp.*, найти́ (найду́, -дёшь; нашёл, -шла́) *perf.*
hitch *n.* (*jerk*) толчо́к (-чка́); (*knot*) у́зел (узла́); (*stoppage*) заде́ржка; *v.t.* (*move*) подта́лкивать *imp.*, подтолкну́ть *perf.*; (*fasten*) зацепля́ть *imp.*, зацепи́ть (-плю́, -пишь) *perf.*; привя́зывать *imp.*, привяза́ть (-яжу́, -я́жешь) *perf.*; *h. up*, подтя́гивать *imp.*, подтяну́ть (-ну́, -нешь) *perf.*; *h.-hike*, голосова́ть *imp.*
hither *adv.* сюда́. **hitherto** *adv.* до сих по́р.
hive *n.* у́лей (у́лья).

hoard *n.* запа́с; *v.t.* накопля́ть *imp.*, накопи́ть (-плю́, -пишь) *perf.*

hoarding *n.* рекла́мный щит (-а́).

hoar-frost *n.* и́ней.

hoarse *adj.* хри́плый (-л, -ла́, -ло).

hoary *adj.* седо́й (сед, -а́, -о).

hoax *n.* мистифика́ция; *v.t.* мистифици́ровать *imp.*, *perf.*

hobble *n.* (*for horse*) (ко́нские) пу́ты (-т) *pl.*; *v.i.* прихра́мывать *imp.*; *v.t.* (*horse*) трено́жить *imp.*, с~ *perf.*

hobby *n.* конёк (-нька́), хо́бби *neut. indecl.*

hobnail *n.* сапо́жный гвоздь (-дя́; *pl.* -ди, -де́й) *m.*

hob-nob *v.i.* пить (пью, пьёшь) *imp.* вме́сте; *h. with*, якша́ться *imp.* с+*instr.*

hock *n.* (*wine*) рейнве́йн (-а(у)).

hockey *n.* хокке́й; *ice h.*, хокке́й с ша́йбой; *h. stick*, клю́шка.

hod *n.* (*for bricks*) лото́к (-тка́); (*for coal*) ведёрко (*pl.* -рки, -рок, -ркам).

hoe *n.* моты́га; *v.t.* моты́жить *imp.*

hog *n.* бо́ров (*pl.* -ы, -о́в), свинья́ (*pl.* -ньи, -не́й, -ньям).

hoist *n.* подъёмник; *v.t.* поднима́ть *imp.*, подня́ть (-ниму́, -ни́мешь; по́днял, -а́, -о) *perf.*

hold[1] (*naut.*) трюм.

hold[2] *n.* (*grasp*) хва́тка; (*influence*) влия́ние (on, на+*acc.*); *v.t.* (*grasp*) держа́ть (-жу́, -жишь) *imp.*; (*contain*) вмеща́ть *imp.*, вмести́ть *perf.*; (*possess*) владе́ть *imp.*+*instr.*; (*conduct*) проводи́ть (-ожу́, -о́дишь) *imp.*, провести́ (-еду́, -едёшь; -ёл, -ела́) *perf.*; (*consider*) счита́ть *imp.*, счесть (сочту́, -тёшь; счёл, сочла́) *perf.* (+*acc.* & *instr.*, за+*acc.*); *v.i.* держа́ться (-жу́сь, -жишься) *imp.*; (*continue*) продолжа́ться *imp.*, продо́лжиться *perf.*; *h. back*, сде́рживать(ся) *imp.*, сдержа́ть(ся) (-жу́(сь), -жишь(ся)) *perf.*; *h. forth*, разглаго́льствовать *imp.*; *h. out*, (*stretch out*) протя́гивать *imp.*, протяну́ть (-ну́, -нешь) *perf.*; (*resist*) не сдава́ться (сдаю́сь, сдаёшься) *imp.*; *h. over*, (*postpone*) откла́дывать *imp.*, отложи́ть (-жу́, -жишь) *perf.*; *h. up*, (*support*) подде́рживать *imp.*, поддержа́ть (-жу́, -жишь) *perf.*; (*display*) выставля́ть *imp.*, вы́ставить *perf.*; (*impede*) заде́рживать *imp.*, задержа́ть (-жу́, -жишь) *perf.* **holdall** *n.* портпле́д. **hold-up** *n.* (*robbery*) налёт; (*delay*) заде́ржка.

hole *n.* дыра́ (*pl.* -ры), я́ма, отве́рстие; (*animal's*) нора́ (*pl.* -ры); *full of holes*, дыря́вый; *pick holes in*, придира́ться *imp.*, придра́ться (придеру́сь, -рёшься; придра́лся, -ала́сь, -а́ло́сь) *perf.* к+*dat.*; *v.t.* (*make h. in*) продыря́вливать *imp.*, продыря́вить *perf.*

holiday *n.* (*festival*) пра́здник; (*from work*) о́тпуск; *pl.* кани́кулы (-л) *pl.*; *on h.*, ьо́тупске, -ку́.

holiness *n.* свя́тость; (*H.*, *title*) святе́йшество.

hollow *n.* впа́дина; (*valley*) лощи́на; (*in tree*) дупло́ (*pl.* -пла, -пел, -плам); *adj.* пусто́й (пуст, -а́, -о, пу́сты́), по́лый; (*sunken*) впа́лый; (*sound*) глухо́й (глух, -а́, -о); *v.t.* (*h. out*) выда́лбливать *imp.*, вы́долбить *perf.*

holly *n.* остроли́ст.

hollyhock *n.* штокро́за.

holm[1] *n.* (*islet*) острово́к (-вка́).

holm[2], **-oak** *n.* ка́менный дуб (*loc.* -е & -у́; *pl.* -ы́).

holocaust *n.* (*sacrifice*) всесожже́ние; (*destruction*) уничтоже́ние (в огне́).

holograph *adj.* собственнору́чный.

holster *n.* кобура́.

holy *adj.* свято́й (свят, -а́, -о), свяще́нный (-е́н, -е́нна); *H. Week*, страстна́я неде́ля.

homage *n.* почте́ние, уваже́ние; *do, pay, h. to*, отдава́ть (-даю́, -даёшь) *imp.*, отда́ть (-а́м, -а́шь, -а́ст, -ади́м; о́тдал, -а́, -о) *perf.* до́лжное+*dat.*

home *n.* дом (-а(у); *pl.* -а́); (*native land*) ро́дина; *at h.*, до́ма; *feel at h.*, чу́вствовать *imp.* себя́ как до́ма; *adj.* дома́шний, родно́й; *H. Affairs*, вну́тренние дела́ *neut.pl.*; *adv.* (*direction*) домо́й; (*position*) до́ма; (*as aimed*) в цель. **homeland** *n.* ро́дина. **homeless** *adj.* бчдо́мный **home-made** *adj.* дома́шний, самоде́льный. **homesick** *adj.*: *to be h.*, тоскова́ть *imp.* по ро́дине. **homewards** *adv.* домо́й, восвоя́си.

homely *adj.* просто́й (прост, -а́, -о, про́сты́).

homicide *n.* (*person*) убийца *m.* & *f.*; (*action*) убийство.
homily *n.* проповедь, поучение.
homogeneous *adj.* однородный.
homonym *n.* омоним.
hone *n.* точильный камень (-мня; *pl.* -мни, -мней) *m.*; *v.t.* точить (-чу, -чишь) *imp.*, на~ *perf.*
honest *n.* (*fair*) честный (-тен, -тна, -тно); (*righteous*) правдивый; (*sincere*) искренний (-нен, -нна, -нне & -нно). **honesty** *n.* честность; правдивость; искренность.
honey *n.* мёд (-а(у), *loc.* -у & -е; *pl.* -ы). **honeycomb** *n.* медовые соты (-тов) *pl.*; *attrib.* сотовый, сотовидный. **honeymoon** *n.* медовый месяц; *v.i.* проводить (-ожу, -одишь) *imp.*, провести (-еду, -едёшь; -ёл, -ела) *perf.* медовый месяц. **honeysuckle** *n.* жимолость.
honk *v.i.* гоготать (-очу, -очешь) *imp.*; (*siren etc.*) гудеть (-дит) *imp.*
honorarium *n.* гонорар.
honorary *adj.* почётный.
honour *n.* честь, почёт; *pl.* почести *f.pl.*; (*up*)*on my h.*, честное слово; *v.t.* (*respect*) почитать *imp.*; (*confer*) удостаивать *imp.*, удостоить *perf.* (with, +*gen.*). **honourable** *adj.* честный (-тен, -тна, -тно); (*respected*) почтенный (-нен, -нна).
hood[1] *n.* капюшон; (*tech.*) капот.
hood[2], **hoodlum** *n.* громила *m.*
hoodwink *v.t.* втирать *imp.*, втереть (вотру, -рёшь; втёр) *perf.* очки+*dat.*
hoof *n.* копыто.
hook *n.* крюк (-а, *loc.* -е & -у), крючок (-чка); (*trap*) ловушка; (*cutting instrument*) серп (-а); *v.t.* зацеплять *imp.*, зацепить (-плю, -пишь) *perf.*; (*catch*) ловить (-влю, -вишь) *imp.*, поймать *perf.*
hookah *n.* кальян.
hooligan *n.* хулиган.
hoop *n.* обруч (*pl.* -и, -ей).
hoot *v.i.* кричать (-чу, -чишь) *imp.*, крикнуть *perf.*; (*owl*) ухать *imp.*, ухнуть *perf.*; (*horn*) гудеть (-дит) *imp.*
hop[1] *n.* (*plant*; *collect. hops*) хмель (-ля (-лю)) *m.*
hop[2] *n.* (*jump*) прыжок (-жка); *v.i.* прыгать *imp.*, прыгнуть *perf.* (на одной ноге).
hope *n.* надежда; *v.i.* надеяться (-еюсь, -еешься) *imp.*, по~ *perf.* (for, на+*acc.*). **hopeful** *adj.* (*hoping*) надеющийся; (*promising*) многообещающий. **hopeless** *adj.* безнадёжный.
hopper *n.* бункер (*pl.* -а & -ы); (*rly.*) хоппер.
horde *n.* (*hist.*, *fig.*) орда (*pl.* -ды).
horizon *n.* горизонт; (*fig.*) кругозор. **horizontal** *n.* горизонталь; *adj.* горизонтальный.
hormone *n.* гормон.
horn *n.* рог (*pl.* -а); (*mus.*) рожок (-жка); (*motor h.*) гудок (-дка); *attrib.* роговой. **hornbeam** *n.* граб. **horned** *adj.* рогатый.
hornet *n.* шершень (-шня) *m.*
horny *adj.* роговой; (*calloused*) мозолистый.
horoscope *n.* гороскоп; *cast a h.*, составлять *imp.*, составить *perf.* гороскоп.
horrible *adj.* ужасный, страшный (-шен, -шна, -шно, страшны). **horrid** *adj.* ужасный, противный. **horrify** *v.t.* ужасать *imp.*, ужаснуть *perf.* **horror** *n.* ужас, отвращение.
hors-d'oeuvre *n.* закуска (*usu. in pl.*).
horse *n.* лошадь (*pl.* -ди, -дей, *instr.* -дьми), конь (-ня; *pl.* -ни, -ней) *m.*; (*collect.*, *cavalry*) конница; *attrib.* лошадиный, конский. **horse-chestnut** *n.* конский каштан. **horseflesh** *n.* конина. **horse-fly** *n.* слепень (-пня) *m.* **horsehair** *n.* конский волос. **horseman, -woman** *n.* всадник, -ица. **horseplay** *n.* возня. **horsepower** *n.* лошадиная сила. **horse-radish** *n.* хрен (-а(у)). **horseshoe** *n.* подкова. **horsewhip** *n.* хлыст (-а); *v.t.* хлестать (-ещу, -ещешь) *imp.*, хлестнуть *perf.*
horticulture *n.* садоводство.
hose *n.* (*stockings*) чулки (*gen.* -лок) *pl.*; (*h.-pipe*) шланг, рукав (-а; *pl.* -а).
hosier *n.* торговец (-вца) трикотажными изделиями. **hosiery** *n.* чулочные изделия *neut.pl.*, трикотаж.
hospitable *adj.* гостеприимный.
hospital *n.* больница; (*military h.*) госпиталь (*pl.* -ли, -лей) *m.*

hospitality *n.* гостеприимство.
host[1] *n.* (*multitude*) множество; (*army*) войско (*pl.* -ка́).
host[2] *n.* (*landlord etc.*) хозя́ин (*pl.* -я́ева, -я́ев).
host[3] *n.* (*eccl.*) обла́тка.
hostage *n.* зало́жник, -ица.
hostel *n.* (*students'*) общежи́тие; (*tourists'*) турба́за.
hostelry *n.* постоя́лый двор (-а́).
hostess *n.* хозя́йка; (*air h.*) бортпроводни́ца.
hostile *adj.* вражде́бный. **hostility** *n.* вражде́бность; *pl.* вое́нные де́йствия *neut.pl.*
hot *adj.* горя́чий (-ч, -ча́), жа́ркий (-рок, -рка́, -рко); (*pungent*) о́стрый (остр & остёр, остра́, о́стро́); (*fresh*) све́жий (свеж, -а́, -о́, све́жи́), *h. air*, бахва́льство; *h.-blooded*, пы́лкий (-лок, -лка́, -лко); *h.-headed*, вспы́льчивый; *h.-water bottle*, гре́лка. **hotbed** *n.* парни́к (-а́); (*fig.*) расса́дник. **hotfoot** *adv.* поспе́шно. **hothouse** *n.* тепли́ца. **hotplate** *n.* пли́тка.
hotel *n.* гости́ница, оте́ль *m.*
hound *n.* (*dog*) го́нчая *sb.*; (*person*) подле́ц (-а́); *v.t.* трави́ть (-влю́, -вишь) *imp.*, за~ *perf.*; *h. on*, подстрека́ть *imp.*, подстрекну́ть *perf.*
hour *n.* (*period, specific time*) час (-а́ *with 2, 3, 4, loc.* -у́; *pl.* -ы́); (*time in general*) вре́мя *neut.* **hourly** *adj.* ежеча́сный.
house *n.* дом (-а(у); *pl.* -а́); (*parl.*) пала́та; (*theatre*) теа́тр; (*audience*) пу́блика; (*performance*) сеа́нс; (*dynasty*) дом (*pl.* -а́), дина́стия; *attrib.* дома́шний; *v.t.* помеща́ть *imp.*, помести́ть *perf.*; (*provide houses for*) обеспе́чивать *imp.*, обеспе́чить *perf.* жильём. **housebreaker** *n.* взло́мщик. **household** *n.* (*people*) дома́шние *sb.*; (*establishment*) дома́шнее хозя́йство. **house-keeper** *n.* эконо́мка. **housemaid** *n.* го́рничная *sb.* **house-warming** *n.* новосе́лье. **housewife** *n.* хозя́йка. **housework** *n.* дома́шняя рабо́та. **housing** *n.* (*accommodation*) жильё; (*provision of h.*) жили́щное строи́тельство; (*casing*) кожу́х (-а́); *h. estate*, жило́й масси́в.
hovel *n.* лачу́га.
hover *v.i.* (*bird*) пари́ть *imp.*; (*helicopter*) висе́ть (-си́т) *imp.*; (*hesitate*) колеба́ться (-блюсь, -блешься) *imp.* **hovercraft** *n.* су́дно (*pl.* -да́, -до́в) на возду́шной поду́шке, СВП.
how *adv.* как, каки́м о́бразом; *h. do you do?* здра́вствуйте! *h. many, h. much*, ско́лько (+*gen.*). **however** *adv.* как бы ни (+*past*); *conj.* одна́ко, тем не ме́нее; *however much*, ско́лько бы ни (+*gen.* & *past*).
howitzer *n.* га́убица.
howl *n.* вой, рёв; *v.i.* выть (во́ю, во́ешь) *imp.*; реве́ть (-ву́, -вёшь) *imp.* **howler** *n.* (*mistake*) грубе́йшая оши́бка.
hub *n.* (*of wheel*) ступи́ца; (*fig.*) центр (внима́ния); *h. of the universe*, пуп (-а́) земли́.
hubbub *n.* шум (-а(у)), гам (-а(у)).
huddle *n.* (*heap*) ку́ча; (*confusion*) сумато́ха; *v.t.* (*heap together*) сва́ливать *imp.*, свали́ть (-лю́, -лишь) *perf.* в ку́чу; *v.i.*: *h. together*, съёживаться *imp.*, съёжиться *perf.*
hue *n.* (*tint*) отте́нок (-нка).
huff *n.* припа́док (-дка) раздраже́ния; *v.t.* & *i.* обижа́ть(ся) *imp.*, оби́деть(ся) (-и́жу(сь), -и́дишь(ся)) *perf.*
hug *n.* объя́тие; (*wrestling*) хва́тка; *v.t.* (*embrace*) обнима́ть *imp.*, обня́ть (обниму́, -мешь; о́бнял, -а́, -о) *perf.*; (*keep close to*) держа́ться (-жу́сь, -жишься) *imp.* + *gen.*
huge *adj.* огро́мный.
hulk *n.* ко́рпус (*pl.* -а́) (корабля́). **hulking** *adj.* (*bulky*) грома́дный; (*clumsy*) неуклю́жий.
hull[1] *n.* (*of pea etc.*) стручо́к (-чка́); (*of grain*) шелуха́; *v.t.* лущи́ть *imp.*, об~ *perf.*
hull[2] *n.* (*of ship*) ко́рпус (*pl.* -а́); (*of aeroplane*) фюзеля́ж.
hum *n.* жужжа́ние, гуде́ние; *v.i.* жужжа́ть (-жу́, -жи́шь) *imp.*; гуде́ть (гужу́, гуди́шь) *imp.*; *v.t.* напева́ть *imp.*; *interj.* гм!
human *adj.* челове́ческий, людско́й; *n.* челове́к. **humane** *adj.* челове́чный, гума́нный (-нен, -нна). **humanism** *n.* гумани́зм. **humanist** *n.* гумани́ст. **humanity** *n.* (*human race*) челове́-

чество; (*humaneness*) гума́нность; *the Humanities*, гуманита́рные нау́ки *f.pl.*
humble *adj.* смире́нный (-е́н, -е́нна), скро́мный (-мен, -мна́, -мно); *v.t.* унижа́ть *imp.*, уни́зить *perf.*
humdrum *adj.* (*banal*) бана́льный; (*dull*) ску́чный (-чен, -чна́, -чно).
humid *adj.* вла́жный (-жен, -жна́, -жно). **humidity** *n.* вла́жность.
humiliate *v.t.* унижа́ть *imp.*, уни́зить *perf.* **humiliation** *n.* униже́ние.
humility *n.* смире́ние.
humming-bird *n.* коли́бри *m.* & *f. indecl.*
hummock *n.* (*hillock*) буго́р (-гра́); (*in ice*) (ледяно́й) торо́с.
humorist *n.* юмори́ст. **humorous** *adj.* юмористи́ческий. **humour** *n.* ю́мор; (*mood*) настрое́ние; *out of h.*, не в ду́хе; *v.t.* потака́ть *imp.* + *dat.*
hump *n.* горб (-а́, *loc.* -у́); (*of earth*) буго́р (-гра́); *v.t.* го́рбить *imp.*, с~ *perf.* **humpback** *n.* горб (-а́, *loc.* -у́); (*person*) горбу́н (-а́), ~ья. **humpbacked** *adj.* горба́тый.
humus *n.* перегно́й.
hunch *n.* (*hump*) горб (-а́, *loc.* -у́); (*thick piece*) ломо́ть (-мтя́) *m.*; (*suspicion*) подозре́ние; *v.t.* го́рбить *imp.*, с~ *perf.* **hunchback** *n.* горб (-а́, *loc.* -у́); (*person*) горбу́н (-а́), ~ья. **hunchbacked** *adj.* горба́тый.
hundred *adj.*, *n.* сто (*in oblique cases* ста); (*collect.*) со́тня (*gen.pl.* -тен); (*age*) сто лет; *two h.*, две́сти (двухсо́т, двумста́м, двумяста́ми, двухста́х); *three h.*, три́ста (трёхсо́т трёмста́м, тремяста́ми, трёхста́х); *four h.*, четы́реста (-рёхсо́т, -рёмста́м, -рьмяста́ми, -рёхста́х); *five h.*, пятьсо́т (пятисо́т, пятиста́м, пятьюста́ми, пятиста́х). **hundredfold** *adj.* стокра́тный; *adv.* в сто раз. **hundredth** *adj.*, *n.* со́тый.
Hungarian *n.* венгр, венге́рка; *adj.* венге́рский.
hunger *n.* го́лод; (*fig.*) жа́жда (for, + *gen.*); *h.-strike*, голодо́вка; *v.i.* голода́ть *imp.*; *h. for*, жа́ждать (-ду, -дешь) *imp.* + *gen.* **hungry** *adj.* голо́дный (го́лоден, -дна́, -дно, го́лодны́).
hunk *n.* ломо́ть (-мтя́) *m.*
hunt *n.* охо́та; (*fig.*) по́иски *m.pl.* (for, + *gen.*); *v.t.* охо́титься *imp.* на + *acc.*, за + *instr.*; трави́ть (-влю́, -вишь) *imp.*, за~ *perf.*; *h. down*, вы́следить *perf.*; *h. out*, отыска́ть (-ыщу́, -ы́щешь) *perf.* **hunter** *n.* охо́тник. **hunting** *n.* охо́та; *attrib.* охо́тничий (-чья, -чье). **huntsman** *n.* охо́тник, е́герь (*pl.* -ря́) *m.*
hurdle *n.* (*fence*) плете́нь (-тня́) *m.*; (*sport*) барье́р; (*fig.*) препя́тствие. **hurdler** *n.* барьери́ст. **hurdles, hurdling** *n.* (*sport*) барье́рный бег.
hurl *v.t.* швыря́ть *imp.*, швырну́ть *perf.*
hurly-burly *n.* сумато́ха.
hurrah, hurray *interj.* ура́!
hurricane *n.* урага́н.
hurried *adj.* торопли́вый. **hurry** *n.* спе́шка, торопли́вость; *in a h.*, второпя́х; *v.t.* & *i.* торопи́ть(ся) (-плю́(сь), -пишь(ся)) *imp.*, по~ *perf.*; *v.i.* спеши́ть *imp.*, по~ *perf.*
hurt *n.* вред (-а́), уще́рб, поврежде́ние; *v.i.* боле́ть (-ли́т) *imp.*; *v.t.* поврежда́ть *imp.*, повреди́ть *perf.*; *h. the feelings of*, задева́ть *imp.*, заде́ть (-е́ну, -е́нешь) *perf.* + *acc.*
hurtle *v.i.* (*move swiftly*) нести́сь (несу́сь, -сёшься; нёсся, -сла́сь) *imp.*, по~ *perf.*
husband *n.* муж (*pl.* -ья́, -е́й, -ья́м); *v.t.* эконо́мить *imp.*, с~ *perf.*
hush *n.* тишина́, молча́ние; *v.t.* успока́ивать *imp.*, успоко́ить *perf.*; *interj.* ти́ше! тсс!
husk *n.* шелуха́; *v.t.* шелуши́ть *imp.*
husky[1] *adj.* (*voice*) хри́плый (хрипл, -а́, -о).
husky[2] *n.* (*dog*) эскимо́сская ла́йка.
hussar *n.* гуса́р (*gen.pl.* -р (*as collect.*) & -ров).
hustle *n.* толкотня́; *v.t.* & *i.* (*push*) толка́ть(ся) *imp.*, толкну́ть(ся) *perf.*; (*hurry*) торопи́ть(ся) (-плю́(сь), -пишь(ся)) *imp.*, по~ *perf.*
hut *n.* хи́жина, бара́к.
hutch *n.* кле́тка.
hyacinth *n.* гиаци́нт.
hybrid *n.* гибри́д; *adj.* гибри́дный.
hydra *n.* ги́дра.
hydrangea *n.* горте́нзия.

hydrant *n.* гидрáнт.
hydrate *n.* гидрáт.
hydraulic *adj.* гидравли́ческий; *h. engineering*, гидротéхника. **hydraulics** *n.* гидрáвлика.
hydro- *in comb.* гидро-. **hydrocarbon** *n.* углеводорóд. **hydrochloric acid** *n.* солянáя кислотá. **hydrodynamics** *n.* гидродинáмика. **hydroelectric** *adj.* гидроэлектри́ческий; *h. plant*, гидроэлектростáнция, ГЭС *f.indecl.* **hydrofoil** *n.* подвóдное крылó (*pl.* -лья, -льев); (*vessel*) сýдно (*pl.* -дá, -дóв), корáбль (-ля́) *m.*, на подвóдных кры́льях, СПК, КПК. **hydrogen** *n.* водорóд; *h. bomb*, водорóдная бóмба. **hydrolysis** *n.* гидрóлиз. **hydrophobia** *n.* водобоя́знь. **hydroplane** *n.* (*fin*) горизонтáльный руль (-ля́) *m.*; (*motor boat*) гли́ссер; (*seaplane*) гидросамолёт. **hydroxide** *n.* гидроóкись.
hyena *n.* гиéна.
hygiene *n.* гигиéна. **hygienic** *adj.* гигиени́ческий.
hymn *n.* гимн; *v.t.* славослóвить *imp.*
hyperbola *n.* гипербóла. **hyperbolic** *adj.* гиперболи́ческий.
hyperbole *n.* гипербóла. **hyperbolical** *adj.* гиперболи́ческий.
hypercritical *adj.* придирчивый.
hypersensitive *adj.* сверхчувстви́тельный.
hyphen *n.* дефи́с. **hyphen(ate)** *v.t.* писáть (пишý, -шешь) *imp.*, на~ *perf.* чéрез дефи́с.
hypnosis *n.* гипнóз. **hypnotic** *adj.* гипноти́ческий; (*soporific*) снотвóрный. **hypnotism** *n.* гипноти́зм. **hypnotist** *n.* гипнотизёр. **hypnotize** *v.t.* гипнотизи́ровать *imp.*, за~ *perf.*
hypocrisy *n.* лицемéрие. **hypocrite** *n.* лицемéр. **hypocritical** *adj.* лицемéрный.
hypodermic *adj.* подкóжный.
hypotenuse *n.* гипотенýза.
hypothesis *n.* гипотéза, предположéние. **hypothesize** *v.i.* стрóить *imp.*, по~ *perf.* гипотéзу; дéлать *imp.*, с~ *perf.* предположéние. **hypothetical** *adj.* гипотети́ческий, предположи́тельный.
hysteria *n.* истери́я. **hysterical** *adj.* истери́чный, истери́ческий. **hysterics** *n.* истéрика, истери́ческий припáдок (-дка).

I

I *pron.* я (меня́, мне, мной & мнóю, обо мне).
iambic *adj.* ямби́ческий. **iambus** *n.* ямб.
ib. *abbr.*, **ibidem** *adv.* там же.
ice *n.* лёд (льда(у), *loc.* льду); (*i. cream*) морóженое *sb.*; *i.-age*, леднико́вый пери́од; *i.-axe*, ледорýб; *i.-boat*, бýер (*pl.* -á); *i.-breaker*, ледокóл; *i. cream*, морóженое *sb.*; *i.-floe*, плавýчая льди́на; *i. hockey*, хоккéй с шáйбой; *v.t.* заморáживать *imp.*, заморóзить *perf.*; (*cul.*) глазировáть *imp.*, *perf.*; *v.i.*: *i. over, up*, обледеневáть *imp.*, обледенéть *perf.* **iceberg** *n.* áйсберг. **icicle** *n.* сосýлька. **icing** *n.* (*cul.*) глазýрь. **icy** *adj.* ледянóй; (*also fig.*) холóдный (хóлоден, -днá, -дно, хóлодны́) (как лёд).
icon *n.* икóна.
idea *n.* идéя, мысль; (*conception*) поня́тие; (*intention*) намерéние.
ideal *n.* идеáл; *adj.* идеáльный. **idealism** *n.* идеали́зм. **idealist** *n.* идеали́ст. **idealize** *v.t.* идеализи́ровать *imp.*, *perf.*
identical *adj.* (*of one thing*) тот же сáмый; (*of different things*) тождéственный (-ен, -енна), одинáковый. **identification** *n.* отождествлéние; (*recognition*) опознáние; (*of person*) установлéние ли́чности. **identify** *v.t.* отождествля́ть *imp.*, отождестви́ть *perf.*; (*recognize*) опознавáть (-наю́,

-наёшь) *imp.*, опознáть *perf.* **identity** *n.* (*sameness*) тождéственность; (*of person*) ли́чность; (*math.*) тóждество; *i. card*, удостоверéние ли́чности.
ideogram, ideograph *n.* идеогрáмма.
ideological *adj.* идеологи́ческий. **ideologist, ideologue** *n.* идеóлог. **ideology** *n.* идеолóгия.
idiocy *n.* идиоти́зм.
idiom *n.* (*expression*) идиóма; (*language*) язы́к (-á), гóвор. **idiomatic** *adj.* идиомати́ческий.
idiosyncrasy *n.* склад умá, идиосинкрази́я.
idiot *n.* идиóт. **idiotic** *adj.* идиóтский.
idle *adj.* (*vain*) тщéтный; (*useless*) бесполéзный; (*unoccupied*) незáнятый; (*lazy*) лени́вый; (*machine*) холостóй (хóлост, -á, -о); *v.i.* бездéльничать *imp.*; (*engine*) рабóтать *imp.* вхолостýю; *v.t.*: *i. away*, прáздно проводи́ть (-ожý, -óдишь) *imp.*, провести́ (-едý, -едёшь; -ёл, -елá) *perf.* **idleness** *n.* тщéтность; бесполéзность; прáздность, бездéлье. **idler** *n.* бездéльник, -ица.
idol *n.* и́дол, куми́р. **idolater, -tress** *n.* идолопоклóнник, -ица. **idolatrous** *adj.* идолопоклóннический. **idolatry** *n.* идолопоклóнство; (*fig.*) обожáние. **idolize** *v.t.* боготвори́ть *imp.*
idyll *n.* иди́ллия. **idyllic** *adj.* идилли́ческий.
i.e. *abbr.* т.е., то есть.
if *conj.* (*conditions*) éсли, éсли бы; (*whether*) ли; *as if*, как бýдто; *even if*, дáже éсли; *if only*, éсли бы тóлько.
igloo *n.* и́глу *neut.indecl.*
igneous *adj.* óгненный, огневóй; (*rock*) вулкани́ческий. **ignite** *v.t.* зажигáть *imp.*, зажéчь (-жгý, жжёшь; -жёг, -жглá) *perf.*; *v.i.* загорáться *imp.*, загорéться (-рю́сь, -ри́шься) *perf.* **ignition** *n.* зажигáние.
ignoble *adj.* ни́зкий (-зок, -зкá, -зко).
ignominious *adj.* позóрный. **ignominy** *n.* позóр.
ignoramus *n.* невéжда *m.* **ignorance** *n.* невéжество, невéдение. **ignorant** *adj.* невéжественный (-ен, -енна); (*uninformed*) несвéдущий (of, в + *prep.*).
ignore *v.t.* не обращáть *imp.* внимáния на + *acc.*; игнори́ровать *imp., perf.*
ilex *n.* пáдуб.
ill *n.* (*evil*) зло; (*harm*) вред (-á); *pl.* (*misfortunes*) несчáстья (-тий) *pl.*; *adj.* (*sick*) больнóй (-лен, -льнá); (*evil*) дурнóй (дýрён, -рнá, -рно, дýрны́), злой (зол, злá); *adv.* плóхо, дýрно; (*scarcely*) едвá ли; *fall i.*, заболевáть *imp.*, заболéть *perf.*; *i.-advised*, неблагоразýмный; *i.-bred*, невоспи́танный (-ан, -анна); *i.-disposed*, недоброжелáтельный (towards, к + *dat.*); *i.-mannered*, невéжливый; *i.-natured*, злóбный; *i.-tempered*, раздражи́тельный; *i.-treat*, плóхо обращáться *imp.* с + *instr.*
illegal *adj.* незакóнный (-нен, -нна), нелегáльный. **illegality** *n.* незакóнность, нелегáльность.
illegible *adj.* неразбóрчивый.
illegitimacy *n.* незакóнность; (*of child*) незаконнорождённость. **illegitimate** *adj.* незакóнный (-нен, -нна); незаконнорождённый (-ён, -ённа).
illiberal *adj.* непросвещённый; (*bigoted*) нетерпи́мый; (*stingy*) скупóй (скуп, -á, -о).
illicit *adj.* незакóнный (-нен, -нна), недозвóленный (-ен, -енна).
illimitable *adj.* безграни́чный.
illiteracy *n.* негрáмотность. **illiterate** *adj.* негрáмотный.
illness *n.* болéзнь.
illogical *adj.* нелоги́чный.
illuminate *v.t.* освещáть *imp.*, освети́ть (-ещý, -ети́шь) *perf.*; (*building*) иллюмини́ровать *imp., perf.*; (*manuscript*) украшáть *imp.*, укрáсить *perf.* **illumination** *n.* освещéние; (*also pl.*) иллюминáция; украшéние (рýкописи).
illusion *n.* иллю́зия. **illusory** *adj.* обмáнчивый, иллюзóрный.
illustrate *v.t.* иллюстри́ровать *imp., perf.*, про ~ *perf.* **illustration** *n.* иллюстрáция. **illustrative** *adj.* иллюстрати́вный.
illustrious *adj.* знамени́тый.
image *n.* (*statue etc.*) изображéние; (*optical i.*) отражéние; (*semblance*) подóбие; (*literary i. etc.*) óбраз. **imagery** *n.* óбразность.

imaginable *adj.* вообрази́мый. **imaginary** *adj.* воображáемый, мни́мый. **imagination** *n.* воображéние, фантáзия. **imagine** *v.t.* воображáть *imp.*, вообрази́ть *perf.*; (*conceive*) представля́ть *imp.*, представить *perf.* себé.
imbecile *n.* слабоу́мный *sb.*; (*fool*) глупéц (-пцá); *adj.* слабоу́мный.
imbed *see* **embed.**
imbibe *v.t.* (*absorb*) впи́тывать *imp.*, впитáть *perf.*
imbroglio *n.* пу́таница.
imbue *v.t.* пропи́тывать *imp.*, пропитáть *perf.* (with, +*instr.*); внушáть *imp.*, внуши́ть *perf.*+*dat.* (with, +*acc.*).
imitate *v.t.* подражáть *imp.*+*dat.* **imitation** *n.* подражáние (of, +*dat.*), имитáция; *attrib.* (*counterfeit*) поддéльный; (*artificial*) иску́сственный (-ен(ен), -енна). **imitative** *adj.* подражáтельный.
immaculate *adj.* незапя́тнанный (-ан, -анна); (*irreproachable*) безупрéчный.
immanent *adj.* прису́щий (in, +*dat.*), имманéнтный.
immaterial *adj.* невещéственный (-ен(ен), -енна); (*unimportant*) несущéственный (-ен(ен), -енна).
immature *adj.* незрéлый.
immeasurable *adj.* неизмери́мый.
immediate *adj.* (*direct*) непосрéдственный (-ен, -енна); (*swift*) немéдленный (-ен, -енна). **immediately** *adv.* тóтчас, немéдленно; непосрéдственно.
immemorial *adj.* незапáмятный.
immense *adj.* необъя́тный, огрóмный.
immerse *v.t.* погружáть *imp.*, погрузи́ть *perf.* **immersion** *n.* погружéние.
immigrant *n.* иммигрáнт, ~ка. **immigrate** *v.i.* иммигри́ровать *imp.*, *perf.* **immigration** *n.* иммигрáция.
imminent *adj.* бли́зкий (-зок, -зкá, -зко, бли́зки́); (*danger*) грозя́щий.
immobile *adj.* неподви́жный. **immobility** *n.* неподви́жность.
immoderate *adj.* неумéренный (-ен, -енна).
immodest *adj.* нескрóмный (-мен, -мнá, -мно).
immolate *v.t.* приноси́ть (-ошу́, -óсишь) *imp.*, принести́ (-есу́, -есёшь; -ёс, -еслá) *perf.* в жéртву; жéртвовать *imp.*, по~ *perf.*+*instr.*
immoral *adj.* безнрáвственный (-ен(ен), -енна). **immorality** *n.* безнрáвственность.
immortal *adj.* бессмéртный. **immortality** *n.* бессмéртие. **immortalize** *v.t.* обессмéртить *perf.*
immovable *adj.* неподви́жный, недви́жимый; (*steadfast*) непоколеби́мый.
immune *adj.* (*to illness*) невосприи́мчивый (to, к+*dat.*); (*free from*) свобóдный (from, от+*gen.*). **immunity** *n.* невосприи́мчивость (to, к+*dat.*), иммунитéт; освобождéние (from, от+*gen.*); (*diplomatic etc.*) неприкосновéнность.
immure *v.t.* заточáть *imp.*, заточи́ть *perf.*
immutable *adj.* неизмéнный (-нен, -нна).
imp *n.* бесёнок (-нка; *pl.* -ня́та, -ня́т).
impact *n.* (*striking*) удáр; (*collision*) столкновéние; (*influence*) влия́ние.
impair *v.t.* (*damage*) повреждáть *imp.*, повреди́ть *perf.*; (*weaken*) ослабля́ть *imp.*, ослáбить *perf.*
impale *v.t.* прокáлывать *imp.*, проколóть (-лю́, -лешь) *perf.*; (*as torture etc.*) сажáть *imp.*, посади́ть (-ажу́, -áдишь) *perf.* нá кол.
impalpable *adj.* неосязáемый.
impart *v.t.* дели́ться (-лю́сь, -лишься) *imp.*, по~ *perf.*+*instr.* (to, с+*instr.*).
impartial *adj.* беспристрáстный.
impassable *adj.* непроходи́мый, непроéзжий.
impasse *n.* тупи́к (-á).
impassioned *adj.* стрáстный (-тен, -тнá, -тно).
impassive *adj.* бесстрáстный.
impatience *n.* нетерпéние. **impatient** *adj.* нетерпели́вый.
impeach *v.t.* обвиня́ть *imp.*, обвини́ть *perf.* (of, with, в+*prep.*).
impeccable *adj.* безупрéчный.
impecunious *adj.* бездéнежный.
impedance *n.* пóлное сопротивлéние. **impede** *v.t.* препя́тствовать *imp.*, вос~ *perf.*+*dat.*; задéрживать *imp.*, задержáть (-жу́, -жишь) *perf.* **impediment** *n.* препя́тствие, задéржка; (*in speech*) заикáние.

impel *v.t.* побуждáть *imp.*, побудúть *perf.* (to + *inf.*, к + *dat.*).
impend *v.i.* нависáть *imp.*, навúснуть (-с) *perf.*
impenetrable *adj.* непроницáемый.
imperative *adj.* (*imperious*) повелúтельный; (*obligatory*) необходúмый; *n.* (*gram.*) повелúтельное наклонéние.
imperceptible *adj.* незамéтный.
imperfect *n.* имперфéкт; *adj.* (*incomplete*) несовершéнный (-нен, -нна), непóлный (-лон, -лнá, -лно); (*faulty*) дефéктный. **imperfection** *n.* несовершéнство; (*fault*) недостáток (-тка). **imperfective** *adj.* (*n.*) несовершéнный (вид).
imperial *adj.* (*of empire*) импéрский; (*of emperor*) императóрский. **imperialism** *n.* империалúзм. **imperialist** *n.* империалúст; *attrib.* империалистúческий.
imperil *v.t.* подвергáть *imp.*, подвéргнуть (-г) *perf.* опáсности.
imperious *adj.* влáстный; (*urgent*) настоя́тельный.
imperishable *adj.* вéчный; (*food*) непóртящийся.
impersonal *adj.* безлúчный.
impersonate *v.t.* (*personify*) олицетворя́ть *imp.*, олицетворúть *perf.*; (*play part*) исполня́ть *imp.*, испóлнить *perf.* роль + *gen.*; (*pretend to be*) выдавáть (-даю́, -даёшь) *imp.*, вы́дать (-ам, -ашь, -аст, -адим) *perf.* себя́ за + *acc.*
impertinence *n.* дéрзость. **impertinent** *adj.* (*insolent*) дéрзкий (-зок, -зкá, -зко); (*out of place*) неумéстный.
imperturbable *adj.* невозмутúмый.
impervious *adj.* непроницáемый (to, для + *gen.*); (*not responsive*) глухóй (глух, -á, -о) (to, к + *dat.*).
impetuous *adj.* стремúтельный.
impetus *n.* двúжущая сúла; (*fig.*) úмпульс.
impiety *n.* нечестúвость.
impinge *v.i.*: *i.* (*up*)*on*, (*strike*) ударя́ться *imp.*, удáриться *perf.* о + *acc.*; (*encroach*) покушáться *imp.*, покусúться *perf.* на + *acc.*
impious *adj.* нечестúвый.
impish *adj.* прокáзливый.
implacable *adj.* неумолúмый.
implant *v.t.* насаждáть *imp.*, насадúть *perf.*
implement[1] *n.* (*tool*) орýдие, инструмéнт; *pl.* принадлéжности *f.pl.*
implement[2] *v.t.* (*fulfil*) выполня́ть *imp.*, вы́полнить *perf.*
implicate *v.t.* впýтывать *imp.*, впýтать *perf.* **implication** *n.* вовлечéние; (*meaning*) смысл.
implicit *adj.* подразумевáемый; (*absolute*) безоговóрочный.
implore *v.t.* умоля́ть *imp.*
imply *v.t.* подразумевáть *imp.*
impolite *adj.* невéжливый.
imponderable *adj.* невесóмый.
import *n.* (*meaning*) значéние; (*of goods*) úмпорт, ввоз; *v.t.* импортúровать *imp.*, *perf.*; ввозúть (-ожý, -óзишь) *imp.*, ввезтú (ввезý, -зёшь; ввёз, -лá) *perf.*
importance *n.* вáжность. **important** *adj.* вáжный (-жен, -жнá, -жно, -жны́), значúтельный.
importunate *adj.* назóйливый.
impose *v.t.* (*tax*) облагáть *imp.*, обложúть (-жý, -жишь) *perf.* + *instr.* (on, + *acc.*); (*obligation*) налагáть *imp.*, наложúть (-жý, -жишь) *perf.* (on, на + *acc.*); (*force* (*oneself*) *on*) навя́зывать(ся) *imp.*, навязáть(ся) (-яжý(сь), -я́жешь(ся)) *perf.* (on, + *dat.*). **imposing** *adj.* внушúтельный. **imposition** *n.* обложéние, наложéние.
impossibility *n.* невозмóжность. **impossible** *adj.* невозмóжный.
imposter *n.* самозвáнец (-нца). **imposture** *n.* самозвáнство, обмáн.
impotence *n.* бессúлие; (*med.*) импотéнция. **impotent** *adj.* бессúльный; (*med.*) импотéнтный.
impound *v.t.* (*cattle*) загоня́ть *imp.*, загнáть (загоню́, -нишь; загнáл, -á, -о) *perf.*; (*confiscate*) конфисковáть *imp.*, *perf.*
impoverish *v.t.* обедня́ть *imp.*, обеднúть *perf.*
impracticable *adj.* невыполнúмый; (*impassable*) непроходúмый.
imprecation *n.* прокля́тие.
impregnable *adj.* неприступный.
impregnate *v.t.* (*fertilize*) оплодотворя́ть *imp.*, оплодотворúть *perf.*;

(*saturate*) пропи́тывать *imp.*, пропита́ть *perf.*
impresario *n.* импреса́рио *m.indecl.*, антрепренёр.
impress[1] *n.* отпеча́ток (-тка), печа́ть; *v.t.* (*imprint*) отпеча́тывать *imp.*, отпеча́тать *perf.*; (*affect person*) производи́ть (-ожу́, -о́дишь) *imp.*, произвести́ (-еду́, -едёшь; -ёл, -ела́) *perf.* (како́е-либо) впечатле́ние на + *acc.*
impression *n.* (*notion etc.*) впечатле́ние; (*printing*) о́ттиск; (*reprint*) (стерео-ти́пное) изда́ние, перепеча́тка.
impressionism *n.* импрессиони́зм.
impressive *adj.* вырази́тельный; (*producing great effect*) порази́тельный.
imprint *n.* отпеча́ток (-тка); *v.t.* отпеча́тывать *imp.*, отпеча́тать *perf.*; (*on memory etc.*) запечатлева́ть *imp.*, запечатле́ть *perf.*
imprison *v.t.* заключа́ть *imp.*, заключи́ть *perf.* (в тюрьму́). **imprisonment** *n.* тюре́мное заключе́ние.
improbable *adj.* невероя́тный, неправдоподо́бный.
impromptu *n.* экспро́мт; *adj.* импровизи́рованный (-ан, -ан(н)а); *adv.* без подгото́вки, экспро́мтом.
improper *adj.* (*inaccurate*) непра́вильный; (*indecent*) неприли́чный.
improve *v.t.* & *i.* улучша́ть(ся) *imp.*, улу́чшить(ся) *perf.* **improvement** *n.* улучше́ние, усовершенствова́ние.
improvidence *n.* непредусмотри́тельность. **improvident** *adj.* непредусмотри́тельный.
improvisation *n.* импровиза́ция. **improvise** *v.t.* импровизи́ровать *imp.*, сымпровизи́ровать *perf.*
imprudence *n.* неосторо́жность. **imprudent** *adj.* неосторо́жный.
impudence *n.* на́глость. **impudent** *adj.* на́глый (нагл, -а́, -о).
impugn *v.t.* оспа́ривать *imp.*, оспо́рить *perf.*
impulse *n.* (*push*) толчо́к (-чка́); (*impetus*) и́мпульс; (*sudden tendency*) поры́в. **impulsive** *adj.* импульси́вный.
impunity *n.* безнака́занность; *with i.*, безнака́занно.
impure *adj.* нечи́стый (-т, -та́, -то).
impute *v.t.* припи́сывать *imp.*, приписа́ть (-ишу́, -и́шешь) *perf.* (to, + *dat.*); (*fault*) вменя́ть *imp.*, вмени́ть *perf.* в + *acc.* (to, + *dat.*).
in *prep.* (*place*) в + *prep.*, на + *prep.*; (*into*) в + *acc.*, на + *acc.*; (*point in time*) в + *prep.*, на + *prep.*; *in the morning* (*etc.*) у́тром (*instr.*); *in spring* (*etc.*), весно́й (*instr.*); (*at some stage in*; *throughout*) во вре́мя + *gen.*; (*duration*) за + *acc.*; (*after interval of*) че́рез + *acc.*; (*during course of*) в тече́ние + *gen.*; (*circumstance*) в + *prep.*, при + *prep.*; *adv.* (*place*) внутри́; (*motion*) внутрь; (*at home*) у себя́, до́ма; (*in fashion*) в мо́де; *in here, there*, (*place*) здесь, там; (*motion*) сюда́, туда́; *adj.* вну́тренний; (*fashionable*) мо́дный (-ден, -дна́, -дно); *in*(-)*patient*, стациона́рный больно́й *sb.*; *n.*: *the ins and outs*, все закоу́лки *m.pl.*; дета́ли *f.pl.*
inability *n.* неспосо́бность, невозмо́жность.
inaccessible *adj.* недосту́пный.
inaccurate *adj.* нето́чный (-чен, -чна́, -чно).
inaction *n.* безде́йствие. **inactive** *adj.* безде́ятельный. **inactivity** *n.* безде́ятельность.
inadequate *adj.* недоста́точный, неадеква́тный.
inadmissible *adj.* недопусти́мый.
inadvertent *adj.* (*inattentive*) невнима́тельный; (*unintentional*) ненаме́ренный (-ен, -енна).
inalienable *adj.* неотъе́млемый, неотчужда́емый.
inane *adj.* (*empty*) пусто́й (пуст, -а́, -о, пу́сты́); (*silly*) глу́пый (глуп, -а́, -о).
inanimate *adj.* (*lifeless*) неодушевлённый (-ён, -ённа); (*dull*) безжи́зненный (-ен, -енна).
inapplicable *adj.* неприме́нимый.
inapposite *adj.* неуме́стный.
inappreciable *adj.* незаме́тный.
inappropriate *adj.* неуме́стный.
inapt *adj.* (*unsuitable*) неподходя́щий; (*unskilful*) неиску́сный. **inaptitude** *n.* неуме́стность; неспосо́бность.
inarticulate *adj.* (*not jointed*) нечленоразде́льный; (*indistinct*) невня́тный.

inasmuch *adv.*: *i. as*, так как; ввиду́ того́, что.
inattention *n.* невнима́ние. **inattentive** *adj.* невнима́тельный.
inaudible *adj.* неслы́шный.
inaugural *adj.* (*lecture etc.*) вступи́тельный. **inaugurate** *v.t.* (*admit to office*) торже́ственно вводи́ть (-ожу́, -о́дишь) *imp.*, ввести́ (введу́, -дёшь; ввёл, -а́) *perf.* в до́лжность; (*open*) открыва́ть *imp.*, откры́ть (-ро́ю, -ро́ешь) *perf.*; (*begin*) начина́ть *imp.*, нача́ть (начну́, -нёшь; на́чал, -а́, -о) *perf.* **inauguration** *n.* торже́ственное введе́ние, вступле́ние, в до́лжность; откры́тие.
inauspicious *adj.* неблагоприя́тный.
inborn, inbred *adj.* врождённый (-ён, -ена́), приро́дный.
incalculable *adj.* неисчисли́мый.
incandesce *v.t.* & *i.* накаля́ть(ся) *imp.*, накали́ть(ся) *perf.* добела́. **incandescence** *n.* бе́лое кале́ние. **incandescent** *adj.* накалённый (-ён, -ена́) добела́.
incantation *n.* заклина́ние.
incapability *n.* неспосо́бность. **incapable** *adj.* неспосо́бный (of, к + *dat.*, на + *acc.*).
incapacitate *v.t.* де́лать *imp.*, с ~ *perf.* неспосо́бным.
incapacity *n.* неспосо́бность.
incarcerate *v.t.* заключа́ть *imp.*, заключи́ть *perf.* (в тюрьму́). **incarceration** *n.* заключе́ние (в тюрьму́).
incarnate *adj.* воплощённый (-ён, -ена́); *v.t.* воплоща́ть *imp.*, воплоти́ть (-ошу́, -оти́шь) *perf.* **incarnation** *n.* воплоще́ние.
incautious *adj.* неосторо́жный.
incendiary *adj.* зажига́тельный; *n.* поджига́тель *m.*; (*fig.*) подстрека́тель *m.*; (*bomb*) зажига́тельная бо́мба.
incense[1] *n.* фимиа́м, ла́дан.
incense[2] *v.t.* (*enrage*) разъяря́ть *imp.*, разъяри́ть *perf.*
incentive *n.* побужде́ние.
inception *n.* нача́ло.
incessant *adj.* непреста́нный (-нен, -нна).
incest *n.* кровосмеше́ние.
inch *n.* дюйм; *i. by i.*, ма́ло-пома́лу.
incidence *n.* (*falling*) паде́ние; (*range of action*) сфе́ра де́йствия. **incident** *n.* слу́чай, инциде́нт. **incidental** *adj.* (*casual*) случа́йный; *i. to*, прису́щий + *dat.* **incidentally** *adv.* случа́йно; (*by the way*) ме́жду про́чим.
incinerate *v.t.* испепеля́ть *imp.*, испепели́ть *perf.* **incineration** *n.* испепеле́ние. **incinerator** *n.* мусоросжига́тельная печь (*pl.* -чи, -че́й).
incipient *adj.* начина́ющийся.
incise *v.t.* надре́зывать, надреза́ть *imp.*, надре́зать (-е́жу, -е́жешь) *perf.* **incision** *n.* надре́з (in, на + *acc.*). **incisive** *adj.* ре́жущий; (*fig.*) о́стрый (остр & остёр, остра́, о́стро́). **incisor** *n.* резе́ц (-зца́).
incite *v.t.* побужда́ть *imp.*, побуди́ть *perf.* (to, к + *dat.*, + *inf.*); подстрека́ть *imp.*, подстрекну́ть *perf.* (to, к + *dat.*). **incitement** *n.* подстрека́тельство.
incivility *n.* неве́жливость.
inclement *adj.* суро́вый.
inclination *n.* (*slope*) накло́н; (*propensity*) скло́нность (for, to, к + *dat.*). **incline** *n.* накло́н; *v.t.* & *i.* склоня́ть(ся) *imp.*, склони́ть(ся) (-ню́(сь), -нишь(ся)) *perf.* **inclined** *adj.* (*disposed*) скло́нный (-о́нен, -о́нна́, -о́нно) (to, к + *dat.*).
include *v.t.* включа́ть *imp.*, включи́ть *perf.* (in, в + *acc.*); заключа́ть *imp.*, заключи́ть *perf.* в себе́. **including** *prep.* включа́я + *acc.* **inclusion** *n.* включе́ние. **inclusive** *adj.* включа́ющий (в себе́); *adv.* включи́тельно.
incognito *adv.*, *n.* инко́гнито *adv.*, *m.* & *neut.indecl.*
incoherence *n.* бессвя́зность. **incoherent** *adj.* бессвя́зный.
incombustible *adj.* несгора́емый.
income *n.* дохо́д; *i. tax*, подохо́дный нало́г.
incommensurable *adj.* несоизмери́мый. **incommensurate** *adj.* несоразме́рный.
incommode *v.t.* беспоко́ить *imp.*, о ~ *perf.*
incommodious *adj.* неудо́бный.
incomparable *adj.* несравни́мый (to, with, с + *instr.*); (*matchless*) несравне́нный (-нен, -нна).
incompatible *adj.* несовмести́мый.
incompetence *n.* неспосо́бность; (*leg.*)

неправомо́чность. **incompetent** *adj.* неспосо́бный; (*leg.*) неправомо́чный.
incomplete *adj.* непо́лный (-лон, -лна́, -лно), незако́нченный (-ен, -енна).
incomprehensible *adj.* непоня́тный.
inconceivable *adj.* невообрази́мый.
inconclusive *adj.* неубеди́тельный.
incongruity *n.* несоотве́тствие. **incongruous** *adj.* несоотве́тственный (-ен, -енна) (with, +*dat.*); (*out of place*) неуме́стный.
inconsequent *adj.* непосле́довательный. **inconsequential** *adj.* незначи́тельный.
inconsiderable *adj.* незначи́тельный.
inconsiderate *adj.* (*person*) невнима́тельный; (*action*) необду́манный (-ан, -анна).
inconsistency *n.* непосле́довательность; (*incompatibility*) несовмести́мость. **inconsistent** *adj.* непосле́довательный; (*incompatible*) несовмести́мый.
inconsolable *adj.* безуте́шный.
inconsonant *adj.* несозву́чный (with, +*dat.*).
inconspicuous *adj.* незаме́тный.
inconstant *adj.* непостоя́нный (-нен, -нна).
incontestable *adj.* неоспори́мый.
incontinence *n.* невозде́ржанность; (*med.*) недержа́ние. **incontinent** *adj.* невозде́ржанный (-ан, -анна).
incontrovertible *adj.* неопровержи́мый.
inconvenience *n.* неудо́бство; *v.t.* причиня́ть *imp.*, причини́ть *perf.* неудо́бство + *dat.* **inconvenient** *adj.* неудо́бный.
incorporate *v.t.* (*include*) включа́ть *imp.*, включи́ть *perf.*; *v.t.* & *i.* (*unite*) объединя́ть(ся) *imp.*, объедини́ть(ся) *perf.*; соединя́ть(ся) *imp.*, соедини́ть(ся) *perf.*
incorporeal *adj.* бестеле́сный.
incorrect *adj.* непра́вильный.
incorrigible *adj.* неисправи́мый.
incorruptible *adj.* неподку́пный; (*not decaying*) непо́ртящийся.
increase *n.* рост, увеличе́ние; (*in pay etc.*) приба́вка; *v.t.* & *i.* увели́чивать(ся) *imp.*, увели́чить(ся) *perf.*; (*intensify*) уси́ливать(ся) *imp.*, уси́лить(ся) *perf.*
incredible *adj.* невероя́тный.
incredulous *adj.* недове́рчивый.
increment *n.* приба́вка; (*profit*) при́быль.
incriminate *v.t.* обвиня́ть *imp.*, обвини́ть *perf.* (в преступле́нии).
incubate *v.t.* (*eggs*) выводи́ть (-ожу́, -о́дишь) *imp.*, вы́вести (-еду, -едешь; -ел) *perf.* (в инкуба́торе); (*bacteria*) выра́щивать *imp.*, вы́растить *perf.* **incubator** *n.* инкуба́тор.
inculcate *v.t.* внедря́ть *imp.*, внедри́ть *perf.*
incumbent *adj.*: *it is i.* (*up*)*on you*, на вас лежи́т обя́занность.
incur *v.t.* навлека́ть *imp.*, навле́чь (-еку́, -ечёшь; -ёк, -екла́) *perf.* на себя́.
incurable *adj.* неизлечи́мый.
incurious *adj.* нелюбопы́тный.
incursion *n.* (*invasion*) вторже́ние; (*attack, raid*) набе́г.
indebted *predic.* (*owing money*) в долгу́ (to, у + *gen.*); (*owing gratitude*) обя́зан (-а, -о) (to, +*dat.*).
indecency *n.* неприли́чие, непристо́йность. **indecent** *adj.* неприли́чный, непристо́йный.
indecision *n.* нереши́тельность. **indecisive** *adj.* нереши́тельный.
indeclinable *adj.* несклоня́емый.
indecorous *adj.* неприли́чный.
indecorum *n.* неприли́чие.
indeed *adv.* в са́мом де́ле, действи́тельно; (*interrog.*) неуже́ли?
indefatigable *adj.* неутоми́мый.
indefeasible *adj.* неотъе́млемый.
indefensible *adj.* (*by arms*) неприго́дный для оборо́ны; (*by argument*) не могу́щий быть опра́вданным.
indefinable *adj.* неопредели́мый. **indefinite** *adj.* неопределённый (-нен, -нна).
indelible *adj.* неизглади́мый, несмыва́емый; *i. pencil*, хими́ческий каранда́ш (-а́).
indelicacy *n.* неделика́тность, беста́ктность. **indelicate** *adj.* неделика́тный, беста́ктный.
indemnify *v.t.*: *i. against*, страхова́ть *imp.*, за~ *perf.* от + *gen.*; обезопа́сить *perf.* от + *gen.*; *i. for*, (*compensate*) компенси́ровать *imp.*, *perf.* **indemnity**

n. (*against loss*) гара́нтия от убы́тков; (*compensation*) компенса́ция; (*war i.*) контрибу́ция.
indent *v.t.* (*notch*) зазу́бривать *imp.*, зазубри́ть *perf.*; (*print.*) де́лать *imp.*, с~ *perf.* о́тступ; (*order goods*) зака́зывать *imp.*, заказа́ть (-ажу́, -а́жешь) *perf.* (for, +*acc.*). **indentation** *n.* (*notch*) зубе́ц (-бца́); (*print.*) о́тступ. **indenture** *n.* контра́кт.
independence *n.* незави́симость, самостоя́тельность. **independent** *adj.* незави́симый, самостоя́тельный.
indescribable *adj.* неопису́емый.
indestructible *adj.* неразруши́мый.
indeterminate *adj.* неопределённый (-нен, -нна).
index *n.* и́ндекс, указа́тель *m.*, показа́тель *m.*; (*pointer*) стре́лка; (*finger*) указа́тельный па́лец (-льца); *v.t.* (*provide i.*) снабжа́ть *imp.*, снабди́ть *perf.* указа́телем; (*enter in i.*) заноси́ть (-ошу́, -о́сишь) *imp.*, занести́ (-есу́, -есёшь; -ёс, -есла́) *perf.* в указа́тель.
Indian *n.* (*from India*) инди́ец (-и́йца), индиа́нка; (*from America*) инде́ец (-е́йца), индиа́нка; *adj.* инди́йский; инде́йский; *I. club*, булава́; *I. corn*, кукуру́за; *I. ink*, тушь; *I. summer*, ба́бье ле́то.
indiarubber *n.* каучу́к; (*eraser*) рези́нка.
indicate *v.t.* ука́зывать *imp.*, указа́ть (-ажу́, -а́жешь) *perf.*; пока́зывать *imp.*, показа́ть (-ажу́, -а́жешь) *perf.*
indication *n.* указа́ние; (*sign*) при́знак.
indicative *adj.* ука́зывающий; (*gram.*) изъяви́тельный; *n.* изъяви́тельное наклоне́ние. **indicator** *n.* указа́тель *m.*
indict *v.t.* обвиня́ть *imp.*, обвини́ть *perf.* (for, в+*prep.*).
indifference *n.* равноду́шие, безразли́чие; (*unimportance*) незначи́тельность. **indifferent** *adj.* равноду́шный, безразли́чный; (*mediocre*) посре́дственный (-ен, -енна).
indigenous *adj.* тузе́мный, ме́стный.
indigent *adj.* нужда́ющийся, бе́дный (-ден, -дна́, -дно, бедны́).
indigestible *adj.* неудобовари́мый. **indigestion** *n.* несваре́ние желу́дка.
indignant *adj.* негоду́ющий; *be i.*, негодова́ть *imp.* (with, на+*acc.*, про́тив+*gen.*). **indignation** *n.* негодова́ние.
indignity *n.* оскорбле́ние.
indirect *adj.* непрямо́й (-м, -ма́, -мо); (*lighting*) отражённый; (*econ.*; *gram.*) ко́свенный.
indiscernible *adj.* неразличи́мый.
indiscreet *adj.* нескро́мный (-мен, -мна́, -мно), неосторо́жный. **indiscretion** *n.* нескро́мность, неосторо́жность, неосмотри́тельность.
indiscriminate *adj.* неразбо́рчивый, огу́льный; (*confused*) беспоря́дочный. **indiscriminately** *adv.* беспоря́дочно; без разбо́ру.
indispensible *adj.* необходи́мый, незамени́мый.
indisposed *predic.* (*unwell*) нездоро́в (-а, -о); (*averse*) не скло́нен (склонна́, -но). **indisposition** *n.* (*ill health*) нездоро́вье; (*ailment*) неду́г; (*disinclination*) нерасположе́ние.
indisputable *adj.* бесспо́рный.
indissoluble *adj.* неразры́вный; (*in liquid*) нераствори́мый.
indistinct *adj.* нея́сный (-сен, -сна́, -сно); (*sound only*) невня́тный.
indistinguishable *adj.* неразличи́мый.
indite *v.t.* сочиня́ть *imp.*, сочини́ть *perf.*
individual *n.* индиви́дуум, ли́чность; *adj.* индивидуа́льный, ли́чный. **individualism** *n.* индивидуали́зм. **individualist** *n.* индивидуали́ст. **individualistic** *adj.* индивидуалисти́ческий. **individuality** *n.* индивидуа́льность.
indivisible *adj.* недели́мый.
indoctrinate *v.t.* внуша́ть *imp.*, внуши́ть *perf.* + *dat.* (with, +*acc.*).
indolence *n.* ле́ность. **indolent** *adj.* лени́вый.
indomitable *adj.* неукроти́мый.
indoor *adj.* ко́мнатный, (находя́щийся) внутри́ до́ма. **indoors** *adv.* внутри́ до́ма.
indubitable *adj.* несомне́нный (-е́нен, -е́нна).
induce *v.t.* (*prevail on*) заставля́ть *imp.*, заста́вить *perf.*; (*bring about*) вызыва́ть *imp.*, вы́звать (вы́зову, -вешь) *perf.* **inducement** *n.* побужде́ние.

induct *v.t.* вводи́ть (-ожу́, -о́дишь) *imp.*, ввести́ (введу́, -дёшь; ввёл, -а́) *perf.* (в до́лжность).
induction *n.* инду́кция; (*inducting*) введе́ние в до́лжность.
indulge *v.t.* потво́рствовать *imp.* + *dat.*; *v.i.* предава́ться (-даю́сь, -даёшься) *imp.*, преда́ться (-а́мся, -а́шься, -а́стся, -ади́мся; -а́лся, -ала́сь) *perf.* (in, + *dat.*). **indulgence** *n.* снисхожде́ние, потво́рство. **indulgent** *adj.* снисходи́тельный.
industrial *adj.* промы́шленный. **industrialist** *n.* промы́шленник. **industrious** *adj.* трудолюби́вый, приле́жный. **industry** *n.* промы́шленность, инду́стри́я; (*diligence*) прилежа́ние.
inebriate *n.* пья́ница *m.* & *f.*; *adj.* пья́ный (пьян, -а́, -о); *v.t.* опьяня́ть *imp.*, опьяни́ть *perf.*
inedible *adj.* несъедо́бный.
ineffable *adj.* несказа́нный.
ineffective *adj.* безрезульта́тный; (*person*) неспосо́бный.
ineffectual *adj.* безрезульта́тный.
inefficiency *n.* неэффекти́вность; (*of person*) неспосо́бность. **inefficient** *adj.* неэффекти́вный; неспосо́бный.
inelegant *adj.* неэлега́нтный.
ineligible *adj.* не могу́щий быть и́збранным.
inept *adj.* (*out of place*) неуме́стный; (*silly*) глу́пый (глуп, -а́, -о); (*unskilful*) неуме́лый.
inequality *n.* нера́венство, неро́вность.
inequitable *adj.* несправедли́вый.
ineradicable *adj.* неискорени́мый.
inert *adj.* ине́ртный; (*sluggish*) ко́сный. **inertia** *n.* (*phys.*) ине́рция; (*sluggishness*) ине́ртность.
inescapable *adj.* неизбе́жный.
inessential *adj.* несуще́ственный (-ен(ен), -енна).
inestimable *adj.* неоцени́мый.
inevitable *adj.* неизбе́жный.
inexact *adj.* нето́чный (-чен, -чна́, -чно).
inexcusable *adj.* непрости́тельный.
inexhaustible *adj.* неистощи́мый.
inexorable *adj.* неумоли́мый.
inexpedient *adj.* нецелесообра́зный.
inexpensive *adj.* недорого́й (недо́рог, -а́, -о).
inexperience *n.* нео́пытность. **inexperienced** *adj.* нео́пытный.
inexpert *adj.* неиску́сный.
inexplicable *adj.* необъясни́мый.
inexpressible *adj.* невырази́мый. **inexpressive** *adj.* невырази́тельный.
inextinguishable *adj.* неугаси́мый.
inextricable *adj.* (*of state*) безвы́ходный; (*of problem*) запу́танный (-ан, -анна).
infallible *adj.* непогреши́мый.
infamous *adj.* (*person*) бесла́вный, гну́сный (-сен, -сна́, -сно); (*action*) позо́рный. **infamy** *n.* позо́р, дурна́я сла́ва.
infancy *n.* младе́нчество. **infant** *n.* младе́нец (-нца). **infanticide** *n.* (*action*) детоуби́йство; (*person*) детоуби́йца *m.* & *f.* **infantile** *adj.* младе́нческий, инфанти́льный.
infantry *n.* пехо́та; *adj.* пехо́тный. **infantryman** *n.* пехоти́нец (-нца).
infatuate *v.t.* вскружи́ть (-ужу́, -у́жи́шь) *perf.* го́лову + *dat.* **infatuation** *n.* си́льное увлече́ние.
infect *v.t.* заража́ть *imp.*, зарази́ть *perf.* (with, + *instr.*). **infection** *n.* зара́за, инфе́кция. **infectious** *adj.* зара́зный; (*fig.*) зарази́тельный.
infelicitous *adj.* несча́стный, неуда́чный. **infelicity** *n.* несча́стье.
infer *v.t.* заключа́ть *imp.*, заключи́ть *perf.*; подразумева́ть *imp.* **inference** *n.* заключе́ние.
inferior *adj.* ни́зший; (*in quality*) ху́дший, плохо́й (плох, -а́, -о, пло́хи́); *n.* подчинённый *sb.* **inferiority** *n.* бо́лее ни́зкое положе́ние, бо́лее ни́зкое ка́чество; *i. complex*, ко́мплекс неполноце́нности.
infernal *adj.* а́дский. **inferno** *n.* (*hell*) ад (*loc.* -у́); (*conflagration*) пожа́рище.
infertile *adj.* неплодоро́дный.
infested *adj.*: *be i. with*, кише́ть (-шу́, -ши́шь) *imp.* + *instr.*
infidel *n.* неве́рный *sb.*, неве́рующий *sb.*; *adj.* неве́рующий. **infidelity** *n.* (*disloyalty*) неве́рность; (*disbelief*) неве́рие.
infiltrate *v.t.* (*fluid*) фильтрова́ть *imp.*, про~ *perf.*; (*of persons*) постепе́нно проника́ть *imp.*, прони́кнуть (-к) *perf.* в + *acc.*

infinite *adj.* бесконе́чный, безграни́чный. **infinitesimal** *adj.* бесконе́чно ма́лый. **infinitive** *n.* инфинити́в. **infinity** *n.* бесконе́чность, безграни́чность.

infirm *adj.* не́мощный, сла́бый (слаб, -á, -о). **infirmary** *n.* больни́ца. **infirmity** *n.* не́мощь, сла́бость.

inflame *v.t.* & *i.* воспламеня́ть(ся) *imp.*, воспламени́ть(ся) *perf.*; (*excite*) возбужда́ть(ся) *imp.*, возбуди́ть(ся) *perf.*; (*med.*) воспаля́ть(ся) *imp.*, воспали́ть(ся) *perf.* **inflammable** *adj.* огнеопа́сный. **inflammation** *n.* воспламене́ние; (*med.*) воспале́ние. **inflammatory** *adj.* подстрека́тельский; (*med.*) воспали́тельный.

inflate *v.t.* надува́ть *imp.*, наду́ть (-у́ю, -у́ешь) *perf.*; (*econ.*) проводи́ть (-ожу́, -о́дишь) *imp.*, провести́ (-еду́, -едёшь; -ёл, -ела́) *perf.* инфля́цию + *gen.* **inflated** *adj.* (*bombastic*) напы́щенный (-ен, -енна). **inflation** *n.* надува́ние; (*econ.*) инфля́ция.

inflect *v.t.* вгиба́ть *imp.*, вогну́ть *perf.*; (*gram.*) изменя́ть *imp.*, измени́ть (-ню́, -нишь) *perf.* (оконча́ние + *gen.*). **inflection, -xion** *n.* вгиба́ние; (*gram.*) фле́ксия.

inflexible *adj.* неги́бкий (-бок, -бка́, -бко); (*fig.*) непреклóнный (-нен, -нна).

inflict *v.t.* (*blow*) наноси́ть (-ошу́, -о́сишь) *imp.*, нанести́ (-есу́, -есёшь; -ёс, -есла́) *perf.* ((up)on, + *dat.*); (*suffering*) причиня́ть *imp.*, причи́инть *perf.* ((up)on, + *dat.*); (*penalty*) налага́ть *imp.*, наложи́ть (-жу́, -жишь) *perf.* ((up)on, на + *acc.*); *i. oneself* (*up*)*on*, навя́зываться *imp.*, навяза́ться (-яжу́сь, -я́жешься) *perf.* + *dat.*

inflow *n.* втека́ние, прито́к.

influence *n.* влия́ние; *v.t.* влия́ть *imp.*, по~ *perf.* на + *acc.* **influential** *adj.* влия́тельный.

influenza *n.* грипп.

influx *n.* (*of stream*) впаде́ние; (*of persons*) напл́ыв.

inform *v.t.* сообща́ть *imp.*, сообщи́ть *perf.* + *dat.* (of, about, + *acc.*, о + *prep.*); *v.i.* доноси́ть (-ошу́, -о́сишь) *imp.*, донести́ (-есу́, -есёшь; -ёс, -есла́) *perf.* (against, на + *acc.*).

informal *adj.* неофициа́льный, неформа́льный.

informant *n.* осведоми́тель *m.* **information** *n.* информа́ция, све́дения *neut. pl.* **informer** *n.* доно́счик.

infraction *n.* наруше́ние.

infra-red *adj.* инфракра́сный.

infrequent *adj.* ре́дкий (-док, -дка́, -дко).

infringe *v.t.* (*violate*) наруша́ть *imp.*, нару́шить *perf.*; *v.i.*: *i.* (*up*)*on*, посяга́ть *imp.*, посягну́ть *perf.* на + *acc.* **infringement** *n.* наруше́ние; посяга́тельство.

infuriate *v.t.* разъяря́ть *imp.*, разъяри́ть *perf.*

infuse *v.t.* влива́ть *imp.*, влить (волью́, -ьёшь; влил, -á, -о) *perf.*; (*fig.*) внуша́ть *imp.*, внуши́ть *perf.* (into, + *dat.*); (*steep*) наста́ивать *imp.*, настоя́ть (-ою́, -ои́шь) *perf.* **infusion** *n.* влива́ние; внуше́ние; насто́й.

ingenious *adj.* изобрета́тельный. **ingenuity** *n.* изобрета́тельность.

ingenuous *adj.* открове́нный (-нен, -нна), бесхи́тростный.

inglorious *adj.* бессла́вный.

ingot *n.* сли́ток (-тка).

ingrained *adj.* закорене́лый.

ingratiate *v.t.*: *i. oneself*, вкра́дываться *imp.*, вкра́сться (-аду́сь, -адёшься; -а́лся) *perf.* в ми́лость (with, + *dat.*).

ingratitude *n.* неблагода́рность.

ingredient *n.* составна́я часть (*pl.* -ти, -те́й).

ingress *n.* вход; (*right*) пра́во вхо́да.

inhabit *v.t.* жить (живу́, -вёшь; жил, -á, -о) *imp.* в, на, + *prep.*; обита́ть *imp.* в, на, + *prep.* **inhabitant** *n.* жи́тель *m.*, ~ница, обита́тель *m.*, ~ница.

inhalation *n.* вдыха́ние. **inhale** *v.t.* вдыха́ть *imp.*, вдохну́ть *perf.*

inherent *adj.* прису́щий (in, + *dat.*).

inherit *v.t.* насле́довать *imp.*, *perf.*, у~ *perf.* **inheritance** *n.* насле́дство. **inheritor** *n.* насле́дник. **inheritress, -trix** *n.* насле́дница.

inhibit *v.t.* (*forbid*) запреща́ть *imp.*, запрети́ть (-ещу́, -ети́шь) *perf.* (+ *dat.* & *inf.*); (*hinder*) препя́тствовать *imp.*, вос~ *perf.* + *dat.* **inhibition** *n.* запреще́ние; сде́рживание; (*psych.*) торможе́ние.

inhospitable *adj.* негостеприи́мный.

inhuman *adj.* (*brutal*) бесчелове́чный; (*not human*) нечелове́ческий.

inimical *adj.* вражде́бный; (*harmful*) вре́дный (-ден, -дна́, -дно).

inimitable *adj.* неподража́емый.

iniquitous *adj.* несправедли́вый. **iniquity** *n.* несправедли́вость.

initial *adj.* (перво)нача́льный; *n.* нача́льная бу́ква; *pl.* инициа́лы *m.pl.*; *v.t.* ста́вить *imp.*, по~ *perf.* инициа́лы на + *acc.* **initially** *adv.* в нача́ле.

initiate *v.t.* (*begin*) начина́ть *imp.*, нача́ть (начну́, -нёшь; на́чал, -а́, -о) *perf.*; (*admit*) посвяща́ть *imp.*, посвяти́ть (-ящу́, -яти́шь) *perf.* (into, в + *acc.*).

initiative *n.* почи́н, инициати́ва.

inject *v.t.* впры́скивать *imp.*, впры́снуть *perf.* **injection** *n.* впры́скивание, инъе́кция.

injudicious *adj.* неблагоразу́мный.

injunction *n.* предписа́ние; (*leg.*) суде́бное постановле́ние, суде́бный запре́т.

injure *v.t.* вреди́ть *imp.*, по~ *perf.* + *dat.*; поврежда́ть *imp.*, повреди́ть *perf.*; (*physically*) ра́нить *imp.*, *perf.* **injurious** *adj.* вре́дный (-ден, -дна́, -дно); (*insulting*) оскорби́тельный. **injury** *n.* вред (-а́), поврежде́ние; (*physical*) ра́на.

injustice *n.* несправедли́вость.

ink *n.* черни́ла (-л) *pl.*; (*printer's i.*) типогра́фская кра́ска; *i.-well*, черни́льница.

inkling *n.* (*hint*) намёк (of, на + *acc.*); (*suspicion*) подозре́ние.

inland *adj.* вну́тренний; *adv.* (*motion*) внутрь страны́; (*place*) внутри́ страны́.

inlay *n.* инкруста́ция; *v.t.* инкрусти́ровать *imp.*, *perf.*

inlet *n.* (*of sea*) у́зкий зали́в; впуск.

inmate *n.* жиле́ц (-льца́), жили́ца; (*of prison*) заключённый *sb.*; (*of hospital*) больно́й *sb.*

inmost *adj.* са́мый вну́тренний; (*fig.*) глубоча́йший, сокрове́нный (-е́н, -е́нна).

inn *n.* гости́ница.

innate *adj.* врождённый (-ён, -ена́).

inner *adj.* вну́тренний.

innkeeper *n.* хозя́ин (*pl.* -я́ева, -я́ев) гости́ницы.

innocence *n.* неви́нность, невино́вность. **innocent** *adj.* неви́нный (-нен, -нна), невино́вный (of, в + *prep.*).

innocuous *adj.* безвре́дный.

innovate *v.i.* вводи́ть (-ожу́, -о́дишь) *imp.*, ввести́ (введу́, -дёшь; ввёл, -а́) *perf.* но́вшества. **innovation** *n.* нововведе́ние, но́вшество. **innovator** *n.* нова́тор.

innuendo *n.* намёк, инсинуа́ция.

innumerable *adj.* бесчи́сленный (-ен, -енна).

inoculate *v.t.* привива́ть *imp.*, приви́ть (-вью́, -вьёшь; приви́л, -а́, -о) *perf.* + *dat.* (against, + *acc.*). **inoculation** *n.* приви́вка (against, от, про́тив, + *gen.*).

inoffensive *adj.* безоби́дный.

inoperative *adj.* неде́йствующий.

inopportune *adj.* несвоевре́менный (-нен, -нна).

inordinate *adj.* чрезме́рный.

inorganic *adj.* неоргани́ческий.

input *n.* (*action*) ввод, вход; (*power supplied*) вводи́мая мо́щность; (*electr. signal*) входно́й сигна́л; (*econ.*) затра́ты *f.pl.*; (*data*) входны́е да́нные *sb.*; (*device*) устро́йство вво́да.

inquest *n.* суде́бное сле́дствие, дозна́ние.

inquietude *n.* беспоко́йство.

inquire *v.t.* спра́шивать *imp.*, спроси́ть (-ошу́, -о́сишь) *perf.*; *v.i.* справля́ться *imp.*, спра́виться *perf.* (about, о + *prep.*); рассле́довать *imp.*, *perf.* (into, + *acc.*). **inquiry** *n.* вопро́с, спра́вка; (*investigation*) рассле́дование; *i. office*, спра́вочное бюро́ *neut.indecl.*

inquisition *n.* рассле́дование; *the I.*, инквизи́ция. **inquisitive** *adj.* пытли́вый, любозна́тельный. **inquisitor** *n.* следо́ватель *m.*; (*hist.*) инквизи́тор.

inroad *n.* набе́г; (*fig.*) посяга́тельство (on, into, на + *acc.*).

insane *adj.* душевнобольно́й, безу́мный. **insanity** *n.* безу́мие.

insatiable *adj.* ненасы́тный.

inscribe *v.t.* надпи́сывать *imp.*, надписа́ть (-ишу́, -и́шешь) *perf.*; впи́сывать *imp.*, вписа́ть (-ишу́, -и́шешь) *perf.*; (*dedicate*) посвяща́ть *imp.*, посвяти́ть (-ящу́, -яти́шь) *perf.* **inscription** *n.* на́дпись; посвяще́ние.

inscrutable *adj.* непостижи́мый, непроница́емый.

insect *n.* насеко́мое *sb.* **insecticide** *n.* инсектици́д. **insectivorous** *adj.* насекомоя́дный.

insecure *adj.* (*unsafe*) небезопа́сный; (*not firm*) непро́чный (-чен, -чна́, -чно).

insensate *adj.* бесчу́вственный (-ен, -енна); (*stupid*) глу́пый (глуп, -а́, -о).

insensibility *n.* бесчу́вствие. **insensible** *adj.* (*inappreciable*) незаме́тный; (*unconscious*) потеря́вший созна́ние; (*insensitive*) нечувстви́тельный.

insensitive *adj.* нечувстви́тельный.

inseparable *adj.* неотдели́мый, неразлу́чный.

insert *v.t.* вставля́ть *imp.*, вста́вить *perf.*; вкла́дывать *imp.*, вложи́ть (-жу́, -жишь) *perf.*; (*into newspaper etc.*) помеща́ть *imp.*, помести́ть *perf.* (in, в + *prep.*). **insertion** *n.* (*inserting*) вставле́ние, вкла́дывание; (*thing inserted*) вста́вка; (*in newspaper*) объявле́ние.

inset *n.* (*in book*) вкла́дка, вкле́йка; (*in dress*) вста́вка.

inshore *adj.* прибре́жный; *adv.* бли́зко к бе́регу.

inside *n.* вну́тренняя сторона́ (*acc.* -ону; *pl.* -оны, -о́н, -она́м), вну́тренность; *turn i. out*, вывёртывать *imp.*, вы́вернуть *perf.* наизна́нку; *adj.* вну́тренний; *i. left*, *right*, (*sport*) ле́вый, пра́вый, полусре́дний *sb.*; *adv.* (*place*) внутри́; (*motion*) внутрь; *prep.* (*place*) внутри́ + *gen.*, в + *prep.*; (*motion*) внутрь + *gen.*, в + *acc.*

insidious *adj.* кова́рный.

insight *n.* проница́тельность.

insignia *n.* зна́ки *m.pl.* отли́чия, разли́чия.

insignificant *adj.* незначи́тельный.

insincere *adj.* неи́скренний (-нен, -нна).

insinuate *v.t.* постепе́нно вводи́ть (-ожу́, -о́дишь) *imp.*, ввести́ (введу́, -дёшь; ввёл, -а́) *perf.* (into, в + *acc.*); (*hint*) намека́ть *imp.*, намекну́ть *perf.* на + *acc.*; *i. oneself*, вкра́дываться *imp.*, вкра́сться (-аду́сь, -адёшься; -а́лся) *perf.* (into, в + *acc.*). **insinuation** *n.* инсинуа́ция.

insipid *adj.* (*tasteless*) безвку́сный; (*dull*) ску́чный (-чен, -чна́, -чно).

insist *v.t.* & *i.* утвержда́ть *imp.*; наста́ивать *imp.*, настоя́ть (-ою́, -ои́шь) *perf.* (on, на + *prep.*). **insistent** *adj.* насто́йчивый.

insolence *n.* на́глость. **insolent** *adj.* на́глый (нагл, -а́, -о).

insoluble *adj.* (*problem*) неразреши́мый; (*in liquid*) нераствори́мый.

insolvent *adj.* несостоя́тельный.

insomnia *n.* бессо́нница.

insomuch *adv.*: *i. that*, насто́лько..., что; *i. as*, ввиду́ того́, что; так как.

inspect *v.t.* осма́тривать *imp.*, осмотре́ть (-рю́, -ришь) *perf.*; инспекти́ровать *imp.*, про~ *perf.* **inspection** *n.* осмо́тр, инспе́кция. **inspector** *n.* инспе́ктор (*pl.* -а́), контролёр, ревизо́р.

inspiration *n.* вдохнове́ние; (*breathing in*) вдыха́ние. **inspire** *v.t.* вдохновля́ть *imp.*, вдохнови́ть *perf.*; внуша́ть *imp.*, внуши́ть *perf.* + *dat.* (with, + *acc.*); (*breathe in*) вдыха́ть *imp.*, вдохну́ть *perf.*

instability *n.* неусто́йчивость.

install *v.t.* (*person in office*) вводи́ть (-ожу́, -о́дишь) *imp.*, ввести́ (введу́, -дёшь; ввёл, -а́) *perf.* в до́лжность; (*apparatus*) устана́вливать *imp.*, установи́ть (-влю́, -вишь) *perf.* **installation** *n.* введе́ние в до́лжность; устано́вка; *pl.* сооруже́ния *neut.pl.*

instalment *n.* (*payment*) очередно́й взнос; (*serial publication*) отде́льный вы́пуск; часть (*pl.* -ти, -те́й); *by instalments*, в рассро́чку, по частя́м.

instance *n.* приме́р, слу́чай; (*leg.*) инста́нция; *at the i. of*, по тре́бованию + *gen.*; *for i.*, наприме́р.

instant *n.* мгнове́ние, моме́нт; *adj.* (*immediate*) неме́дленный (-ен, -енна); (*urgent*) настоя́тельный; (*of current month*) теку́щего ме́сяца; (*of coffee etc.*) раствори́мый. **instantaneous** *adj.*

мгнове́нный (-нен, -нна). **instantly** *adv.* неме́дленно, то́тчас.

instead *adv.* вме́сто (of, +*gen.*), взаме́н (of, +*gen.*); *i. of going*, вме́сто того́, что́бы пойти́.

instep *n.* подъём.

instigate *v.t.* подстрека́ть *imp.*, подстрекну́ть *perf.* (to, к+*dat.*). **instigation** *n.* подстрека́тельство. **instigator** *n.* подстрека́тель *m.*, ~ница.

instil *v.t.* (*liquid*) влива́ть *imp.*, влить (волью́, -ьёшь; влил, -а́, -о) *perf.* по ка́пле; (*ideas etc.*) внуша́ть *imp.*, внуши́ть *perf.* (into, +*dat.*).

instinct *n.* инсти́нкт. **instinctive** *adj.* инстинкти́вный.

institute *n.* институ́т, (нау́чное) учрежде́ние; *v.t.* устана́вливать *imp.*, установи́ть (-влю́, -вишь) *perf.*; учрежда́ть *imp.*, учреди́ть *perf.*; (*initiate*) начина́ть *imp.*, нача́ть (начну́, -нёшь; на́чал, -а́, -о) *perf.* **institution** *n.* установле́ние, учрежде́ние.

instruct *v.t.* (*teach*) обуча́ть *imp.*, обучи́ть (-чу́, -чишь) *perf.* (in, +*dat.*); (*inform*) сообща́ть *imp.*, сообщи́ть *perf.*+*dat.*; (*command*) прика́зывать *imp.*, приказа́ть (-ажу́, -а́жешь) *perf.*+*dat.* **instruction** *n.* инстру́кция; (*teaching*) обуче́ние. **instructive** *adj.* поучи́тельный. **instructor** *n.* инстру́ктор.

instrument *n.* ору́дие, инструме́нт; (*leg.*) докуме́нт, акт. **instrumental** *adj.* служа́щий ору́дием; (*mus.*) инструмента́льный; (*gram.*) твори́тельный; *be i. in*, спосо́бствовать *imp.*, по~ *perf.*+*dat.*; *n.* (*gram.*) твори́тельный паде́ж (-а́). **instrumentation** *n.* (*mus.*) инструменто́вка.

insubordinate *adj.* неподчиня́ющийся.

insufferable *adj.* невыноси́мый.

insular *adj.* (*of island*) островно́й; (*narrow-minded*) ограни́ченный (-ен, -енна).

insulate *v.t.* изоли́ровать *imp.*, *perf.*; *insulating tape*, изоляцио́нная ле́нта. **insulation** *n.* изоля́ция. **insulator** *n.* изоля́тор.

insulin *n.* инсули́н.

insult *n.* оскорбле́ние; *v.t.* оскорбля́ть *imp.*, оскорби́ть *perf.* **insulting** *adj.* оскорби́тельный.

insurance *n.* страхова́ние; *attrib.* страхово́й. **insure** *v.t.* страхова́ть *imp.*, за~ *perf.* (against, от+*gen.*).

insurgent *n.* повста́нец (-нца); *adj.* восста́вший.

insurmountable *adj.* непреодоли́мый.

insurrection *n.* восста́ние, мяте́ж (-а́).

intact *adj.* (*untouched*) нетро́нутый; (*entire*) це́лый (цел, -а́, -о).

intake *n.* (*action*) впуск, вход; (*mechanism*) впускно́е, приёмное, устро́йство; (*of water*) водозабо́р; (*airway in mine*) вентиляцио́нная вы́работка; (*of persons*) набо́р, о́бщее число́; (*quantity*) потребле́ние.

intangible *adj.* неосяза́емый.

integral *adj.* неотъе́млемый; (*whole*) це́льный (-лен, -льна́, -льно); (*math.*) интегра́льный; *n.* интегра́л. **integrate** *v.t.* (*combine*) объединя́ть *imp.*, объедини́ть *perf.*; (*math.*) интегри́ровать *imp.*, *perf.* **integration** *n.* объедине́ние, интегра́ция.

integrity *n.* (*wholeness*) це́лостность; (*honesty*) че́стность.

intellect *n.* интелле́кт, ум (-а́). **intellectual** *n.* интеллиге́нт; *adj.* у́мственный; интеллектуа́льный.

intelligence *n.* (*intellect*) ум (-а́); (*cleverness*) смышлёность; (*information*) све́дения *neut.pl.*; (*i. service*) разве́дка, разве́дывательная слу́жба. **intelligent** *adj.* у́мный (умён, умна́, у́мно́).

intelligentsia *n.* интеллиге́нция.

intelligible *adj.* поня́тный.

intemperate *adj.* невозде́ржанный.

intend *v.t.* намерева́ться *imp.*+*inf.*; быть наме́ренным (-ен)+*inf.*; собира́ться *imp.*, собра́ться (соберу́сь, -рёшься; собра́лся, -ала́сь, -а́ло́сь) *perf.*; (*design*) предназнача́ть *imp.*, предназна́чить *perf.* (for, для+*gen.*, на+*acc.*); (*mean*) име́ть *imp.* в виду́.

intense *adj.* си́льный (си́лён, -льна́, -льно, си́льны́); напряжённый (-ён, -ённа). **intensify** *v.t.* & *i.* уси́ливать(ся) *imp.*, уси́лить(ся) *perf.* **intensity** *n.* интенси́вность, напряжённость, си́ла. **intensive** *adj.* интенси́вный.

intent *n.* наме́рение, цель; *adj.* (*resolved*) стремя́щийся (on, к+*dat.*); (*occupied*) погружённый (-ён, -ена́) (on, в+*acc.*);

(*earnest*) внима́тельный. **intention** *n.* наме́рение, цель. **intentional** *adj.* наме́ренный (-ен, -енна), умы́шленный (-ен, -енна).

inter[1] *v.t.* (*bury*) хорони́ть (-ню́, -нишь) *imp.*, по~ *perf.*

inter-[2] *pref.* (*mutually*) взаимо-; (*between*) меж-, между-; (*in verbs*) пере-.

interact *v.i.* взаимоде́йствовать *imp.* **interaction** *n.* взаимоде́йствие.

inter alia *adv.* ме́жду про́чим.

interbreed *v.t.* & *i.* скре́щивать(ся) *imp.*, скрести́ть(ся) *perf.*

intercede *v.i.* хода́тайствовать *imp.*, по~ *perf.* (for, за + *acc.*; with, пе́ред + *instr.*).

intercept *v.t.* перехва́тывать *imp.*, перехвати́ть (-ачу́, -а́тишь) *perf.*; (*cut off*) прерыва́ть *imp.*, прерва́ть (-ву́, -вёшь; прерва́л, -а́, -о) *perf.* **interception** *n.* перехва́т.

intercession *n.* хода́тайство. **intercessor** *n.* хода́тай.

interchange *n.* (*exchange*) обме́н (of, + *instr.*); (*alternation*) чередова́ние; (*road junction*) тра́нспортная развя́зка; *v.t.* обме́ниваться *imp.*, обменя́ться *perf.* + *instr.*; чередова́ть *imp.* **interchangeable** *adj.* взаимозаменя́емый.

inter-city *adj.* междугоро́дный.

intercom *n.* вну́тренняя телефо́нная связь.

interconnection *n.* взаимосвя́зь.

inter-continental *adj.* межконтинента́льный.

intercourse *n.* (*social*) обще́ние; (*trade etc.*) сноше́ния *neut.pl.*; (*sexual*) половы́е сноше́ния *neut.pl.*

inter-departmental *adj.* меж(ду)ве́домственный.

interdependent *adj.* взаимозави́симый.

interdict *n.* запреще́ние; *v.t.* запреща́ть *imp.*, запрети́ть (-ещу́, -ети́шь) *perf.* (person, + *dat.*).

interdisciplinary *adj.* межотраслево́й.

interest *n.* интере́с (in, к + *dat.*); (*profit*) вы́года; (*econ.*) проце́нты *m.pl.*; *v.t.* интересова́ть *imp.*; (*i. person in*) заинтересо́вывать *imp.*, заинтересова́ть *perf.* (in, + *instr.*); *be interested in*, интересова́ться *imp.* + *instr.* **interesting** *adj.* интере́сный.

interfere *v.i.* меша́ть *imp.*, по~ *perf.* (with, + *dat.*); вме́шиваться *imp.*, вмеша́ться *perf.* (in, в + *acc.*). **interference** *n.* вмеша́тельство; (*radio*) поме́хи *f.pl.*

inter-governmental *adj.* межправи́тельственный.

interim *n.* промежу́ток (-тка) (вре́мени); *in the i.*, тем вре́менем; *adj.* промежу́точный; (*temporary*) вре́менный.

interior *n.* вну́тренность; (*polit.*) вну́тренние дела́ *neut.pl.*; *adj.* вну́тренний.

interjection *n.* восклица́ние; (*gram.*) междоме́тие.

interlace *v.t.* & *i.* переплета́ть(ся) *imp.*, переплести́(сь) (-ету́(сь), -етёшь(ся); -ёл(ся), -ела́(сь)) *perf.*

interlinear *adj.* междустро́чный.

interlock *v.t.* & *i.* сцепля́ть(ся) *imp.*, сцепи́ть(ся) (-плю́(сь), -пишь(ся)) *perf.*

interlocutor *n.* собесе́дник, -ица.

interlope *v.i.* вме́шиваться *imp.*, вмеша́ться *perf.* в чужи́е дела́.

interlude *n.* промежу́точный эпизо́д; (*theat.*) антра́кт.

intermediary *n.* посре́дник; *adj.* посре́днический; (*intermediate*) промежу́точный.

intermediate *adj.* промежу́точный.

interment *n.* погребе́ние.

interminable *adj.* бесконе́чный.

intermission *n.* переры́в, па́уза.

intermittent *adj.* преры́вистый.

intermix *v.t.* & *i.* переме́шивать(ся) *imp.*, перемеша́ть(ся) *perf.*

intern *v.t.* интерни́ровать *imp.*, *perf.*

internal *adj.* вну́тренний; *i. combustion engine*, дви́гатель *m.* вну́треннего сгора́ния.

international *n.* (*contest*) междунаро́дное состяза́ние; *adj.* междунаро́дный, интернациона́льный. **internationalism** *n.* интернационали́зм.

internecine *adj.* междоусо́бный.

internee *n.* интерни́рованный *sb.* **internment** *n.* интерни́рование.

interplanetary *adj.* межплане́тный.

interplay *n.* взаимоде́йствие.

interpolate *v.t.* (*insert*) вставля́ть *imp.*, вста́вить *perf.*; (*math.*) интерполи́ровать *imp.*, *perf.* **interpolation** *n.* вста́вка; (*math.*) интерполя́ция.
interpose *v.t.* (*insert*) вставля́ть *imp.*, вста́вить *perf.*; *v.i.* (*intervene*) вме́шиваться *imp.*, вмеша́ться *perf.*
interpret *v.t.* толкова́ть *imp.*; (*speech etc.*) у́стно переводи́ть (-ожу́, -о́дишь) *imp.*, перевести́ (-еду́, -едёшь; -ёл, -ела́) *perf.* **interpretation** *n.* толкова́ние. **interpreter** *n.* толкова́тель *m.*; перево́дчик, -ица.
interregnum *n.* междуца́рствие; (*interval*) переры́в.
interrogate *v.t.* допра́шивать *imp.*, допроси́ть (-ошу́, -о́сишь) *perf.* **interrogation** *n.* допро́с; (*question*) вопро́с. **interrogative** *adj.* вопроси́тельный.
interrupt *v.t.* прерыва́ть *imp.*, прерва́ть (-ву́, -вёшь; -ва́л, -вала́, -ва́ло) *perf.* **interruption** *n.* переры́в.
intersect *v.t.* & *i.* пересека́ть(ся) *imp.*, пересе́чь(ся) (-еку́(сь), -ечёшь(ся); -е́к(ся), -екла́(сь)) *perf.* **intersection** *n.* пересече́ние.
intersperse *v.t.* (*scatter*) рассыпа́ть *imp.*, рассы́пать (-плю, -плешь) *perf.* (between, among, ме́жду + *instr.*, среди́ + *gen.*); (*diversify*) разнообра́зить *imp.*
intertwine *v.t.* & *i.* переплета́ть(ся) *imp.*, переплести́(сь) (-ету́(сь), -етёшь(ся); -ёл(ся), -ела́(сь)) *perf.*
interval *n.* промежу́ток (-тка); (*also mus.*) интерва́л; (*school*) переме́на.
intervene *v.i.* (*occur*) происходи́ть (-ит) *imp.*, произойти́ (-ойдёт; -ошёл, -ошла́) *perf.*; *i. in*, вме́шиваться *imp.*, вмеша́ться *perf.* в + *acc.* **intervention** *n.* вмеша́тельство; (*polit.*) интерве́нция.
interview *n.* делово́е свида́ние, встре́ча; (*press i.*) интервью́ *neut.indecl.*; *v.t.* интервьюи́ровать *imp.*, *perf.*, про ~ *perf.* **interviewer** *n.* интервьюе́р.
interweave *v.t.* votка́ть (-ку́, -кёшь; -ка́л, -ка́ла́, -ка́ло) *perf.*
intestate *adj.* уме́рший без завеща́ния.
intestinal *adj.* кише́чный. **intestine**[1] *n.* кишка́ (*gen. pl.* -шо́к); *pl.* кише́чник.
intestine[2] *adj* вну́тренний, междоусо́бный.
intimacy *n.* инти́мность, бли́зость. **intimate**[1] *adj.* инти́мный, бли́зкий (-зок, -зка́, -зко, бли́зки́).
intimate[2] *v.t.* (*state*) сообща́ть *imp.*, сообщи́ть *perf.*; (*hint*) намека́ть *imp.*, намекну́ть *perf.* на + *acc.* **intimation** *n.* сообще́ние; намёк.
intimidate *v.t.* запу́гивать *imp.*, запуга́ть *perf.*
into *prep.* в, во + *acc.*, на + *acc.*
intolerable *adj.* невыноси́мый. **intolerance** *n.* нетерпи́мость. **intolerant** *adj.* нетерпи́мый.
intonation *n.* интона́ция. **intone** *v.t.* интони́ровать *imp.*
intoxicant *adj.* (*n.*) опьяня́ющий (напи́ток (-тка)). **intoxicate** *v.t.* опьяня́ть *imp.*, опьяни́ть *perf.* **intoxication** *n.* опьяне́ние; *in a state of i.*, в нетре́звом состоя́нии.
intra- *pref.* внутри-.
intractable *adj.* непода́тливый.
intransigent *adj.* непримири́мый.
intransitive *adj.* неперехо́дный.
intrepid *adj.* неустраши́мый.
intricacy *n.* запу́танность, сло́жность. **intricate** *adj.* запу́танный (-ан, -анна), сло́жный (-жен, -жна́, -жно).
intrigue *n.* интри́га; *v.i.* интригова́ть *imp.*; *v.t.* интригова́ть *imp.*, за ~ *perf.* **intriguer** *n.* интрига́н, ~ ка.
intrinsic *adj.* прису́щий, суще́ственный (-ен, -енна).
introduce *v.t.* вводи́ть (-ожу́, -о́дишь) *imp.*, ввести́ (введу́, -дёшь; ввёл, -а́) *perf.*; вноси́ть (-ошу́, -о́сишь) *imp.*, внести́ (внесу́, -сёшь; внёс, -ла́) *perf.*; (*person*) представля́ть *imp.*, предста́вить *perf.* **introduction** *n.* введе́ние, внесе́ние; представле́ние; (*to book*) предисло́вие. **introductory** *adj.* вво́дный, вступи́тельный.
introspection *n.* самонаблюде́ние.
intrude *v.i.* вторга́ться *imp.*, вто́ргнуться (-г(нул)ся, -глась) *perf.* (into, в + *acc.*); *v.t.* & *i.* навя́зывать(ся) *imp.*, навяза́ть(ся) (-яжу́(сь), -я́жешь(ся)) *perf.* (upon, + *dat.*). **intrusion** *n.* вторже́ние.
intuition *n.* интуи́ция. **intuitive** *adj.* интуити́вный.

inundate *v.t.* наводня́ть *imp.*, наводни́ть *perf.* **inundation** *n.* наводне́ние.

inure *v.t.* приуча́ть *imp.*, приучи́ть (-чу́, -чишь) *perf.* (to, к + *dat.*, + *inf.*).

invade *v.t.* вторга́ться *imp.*, вто́ргнуться (-г(нул)ся, -глась) *perf.* в + *acc.* **invader** *n.* захва́тчик.

invalid[1] *n.* (*disabled person*) инвали́д, больно́й *sb.*; *adj.* (*disabled*) нетрудоспосо́бный.

invalid[2] *adj.* (*not valid*) недействи́тельный. **invalidate** *v.t.* де́лать *imp.*, с ~ *perf.* недействи́тельным.

invaluable *adj.* неоцени́мый.

invariable *adj.* неизме́нный (-нен, -нна); (*math.*) постоя́нный (-нен, -нна).

invasion *n.* вторже́ние (в + *acc.*); (*encroachment*) посяга́тельство (на + *acc.*).

invective *n.* (*verbal attack*) обличи́тельная речь; (*abuse*) руга́тельства *neut.pl.*

inveigh *v.i.* поноси́ть (-ошу́, -о́сишь) *imp.* (against, + *acc.*).

inveigle *v.t.* завлека́ть *imp.*, завле́чь (-еку́, -ечёшь; -ёк, -екла́) *perf.*

invent *v.t.* изобрета́ть *imp.*, изобрести́ (-ету́, -етёшь; -ёл, -ела́) *perf.*; выду́мывать *imp.*, вы́думать *perf.* **invention** *n.* изобрете́ние; вы́думка. **inventive** *adj.* изобрета́тельный. **inventor** *n.* изобрета́тель *m.*

inventory *n.* инвента́рь (-ря́) *m.*, о́пись (иму́щества); *v.t.* инвентаризова́ть *imp.*, *perf.*

inverse *adj.* обра́тный. **inversion** *n.* перестано́вка.

invertebrate *adj.* беспозвоно́чный; *n.* беспозвоно́чное *sb.*

invest *v.t.* (*clothe*, *endue*) облека́ть *imp.*, обле́чь (-еку́, -ечёшь; -ёк, -екла́) *perf.* (in, в + *acc.*; with, + *instr.*); (*lay siege to*) осажда́ть *imp.*, осади́ть *perf.*; *v.t.* & *i.* (*econ.*) вкла́дывать *imp.*, вложи́ть (-жу́, -жишь) *perf.* (де́ньги) (in, в + *acc.*); инвести́ровать *imp.*, *perf.*

investigate *v.t.* иссле́довать *imp.*, *perf.*; (*leg.*) рассле́довать *imp.*, *perf.* **investigation** *n.* иссле́дование; рассле́дование. **investigator** *n.* иссле́дователь *m.*; (*leg.*) сле́дователь *m.*

investiture *n.* введе́ние в до́лжность.

investment *n.* (*econ.*) вложе́ние, вклад, инвести́ция; (*mil.*) оса́да. **investor** *n.* вкла́дчик.

inveterate *adj.* закорене́лый, застаре́лый.

invigorate *v.t.* укрепля́ть *imp.*, укрепи́ть *perf.*; (*animate*) оживля́ть *imp.*, оживи́ть *perf.*

invincible *adj.* непобеди́мый.

inviolable *adj.* неприкоснове́нный (-нен, -нна), неруши́мый. **inviolate** *adj.* нена-ру́шенный.

invisible *adj.* неви́димый; *i. ink*, симпати́ческие черни́ла (-л) *pl.*

invitation *n.* приглаше́ние. **invite** *v.t.* приглаша́ть *imp.*, пригласи́ть *perf.*; (*request*) проси́ть (-ошу́, -о́сишь) *imp.*, по ~ *perf.*; (*attract*) привлека́ть *imp.*, привле́чь (-еку́, -ечёшь; -ёк, -екла́) *perf.* **inviting** *adj.* привлека́тельный.

invocation *n.* призы́в.

invoice *n.* факту́ра, накладна́я *sb.*

invoke *v.t.* призыва́ть *imp.*, призва́ть (-зову́, -зовёшь; призва́л, -а́, -о); взыва́ть *imp.*, воззва́ть (-зову́, -зовёшь) *perf.*

involuntary *adj.* нево́льный; непроизво́льный.

involve *v.t.* (*entail*) вовлека́ть *imp.*, вовле́чь (-еку́, -ечёшь; -ёк, -екла́) *perf.*; (*include*) включа́ть *imp.*, включи́ть *perf.* в себе́. **involved** *adj.* (*complex*) сло́жный (-жен, -жна́, -жно).

invulnerable *adj.* неуязви́мый.

inward *adj.* вну́тренний. **inwardly** *adv.* внутри́, вну́тренне. **inwards** *adv.* вну́трь.

iodine *n.* йод; *attrib.* йо́дный.

ion *n.* ио́н. **ionic** *adj.* ио́нный.

iota *n.* йо́та; *not an i.*, ни на йо́ту.

IOU *n.* долгова́я распи́ска.

irascible *adj.* раздражи́тельный.

irate *adj.* гне́вный (-вен, -вна́, -вно).

ire *n.* гнев.

iridescent *adj.* ра́дужный.

iris *n.* (*anat.*) ра́дужная оболо́чка; (*bot.*) каса́тик.

Irish *adj.* ирла́ндский. **Irishman** *n.* ирла́ндец (-дца). **Irishwoman** *n.* ирла́ндка.

irk *v.t.* надоеда́ть *imp.*, надое́сть (-е́м, -е́шь, -е́ст, -еди́м; -е́л) *perf.* + *dat.* **irksome** *adj.* ску́чный (-чен, -чна́, -чно).

iron *n.* желе́зо; (*for clothes*) утю́г (-а́); *pl.* (*fetters*) кандалы́ (-ло́в) *pl.*; *adj.* желе́зный; *v.t.* (*clothes*) утю́жить *imp.*, вы́~, от~ *perf.*; гла́дить *imp.*, вы́~ *perf.*

ironic(al) *adj.* ирони́ческий. **irony** *n.* иро́ния.

irradiate *v.t.* (*light up*) освеща́ть *imp.*, освети́ть (-ещу́, -ети́шь) *perf.*; (*subject to radiation*) облуча́ть *imp.*, облучи́ть *perf.* **irradiation** *n.* освеще́ние; облуче́ние.

irrational *adj.* неразу́мный; (*math.*) иррациона́льный.

irreconcilable *adj.* (*persons*) непримири́мый; (*ideas*) несовмести́мый.

irrecoverable *adj.* невозвра́тный.

irredeemable *adj.* (*econ.*) не подлежа́щий вы́купу; (*hopeless*) безнадёжный.

irrefutable *adj.* неопровержи́мый.

irregular *adj.* нерегуля́рный; (*gram.*) непра́вильный; (*not even*) неро́вный (-вен, -вна́, -вно); (*disorderly*) беспоря́дочный.

irrelevant *adj.* неуме́стный.

irreligious *adj.* неве́рующий.

irremediable *adj.* непоправи́мый, неизлечи́мый.

irremovable *adj.* неустрани́мый; (*from office*) несменя́емый.

irreparable *adj.* непоправи́мый.

irreplaceable *adj.* незамени́мый.

irrepressible *adj.* неудержи́мый.

irreproachable *adj.* безупре́чный.

irresistible *adj.* неотрази́мый.

irresolute *adj.* нереши́тельный.

irrespective *adj.*: *i. of*, безотноси́тельно к + *dat.*, незави́симо от + *gen.*

irresponsible *adj.* (*of conduct etc.*) безотве́тственный (-ен, -енна); (*not responsible*) неотве́тственный (-ен, -енна); (*leg.*) невменя́емый.

irretrievable *adj.* непоправи́мый, невозвра́тный.

irreverent *adj.* непочти́тельный.

irreversible *adj.* необрати́мый.

irrevocable *adj.* неотменя́емый.

irrigate *v.t.* ороша́ть *imp.*, ороси́ть *perf.* **irrigation** *n.* ороше́ние, ирригáция.

irritable *adj.* раздражи́тельный. **irritate** *v.t.* раздража́ть *imp.*, раздражи́ть *perf.* **irritation** *n.* раздраже́ние.

irrupt *v.i.* вторга́ться *imp.*, вто́ргнуться (-г(нул)ся, -глась) *perf.* (into, в + *acc.*). **irruption** *n.* вторже́ние.

Islam *n.* исла́м. **Islamic** *adj.* мусульма́нский, исламúстский.

island, isle *n.* о́стров (*pl.* -а́); *adj.* островно́й. **islander** *n.* островитя́нин (*pl.* -я́не, -я́н), -я́нка. **islet** *n.* острово́к (-вка́).

iso- *in comb.* изо-, равно-. **isobar** *n.* изоба́ра. **isomer** *n.* изоме́р. **isosceles** *adj.* равнобе́дренный. **isotherm** *n.* изоте́рма. **isotope** *n.* изото́п.

isolate *v.t.* изоли́ровать *imp.*, *perf.*; обособля́ть *imp.*, обосо́бить *perf.*; (*chem.*) выделя́ть *imp.*, вы́делить *perf.* **isolation** *n.* изоля́ция; *i. hospital*, инфекцио́нная больни́ца; *i. ward*, изоля́тор.

Israeli *n.* израильтя́нин (*pl.* -я́не, -я́н), -я́нка; *adj.* изра́ильский.

issue *n.* (*outlet*) вы́ход, (*outflow*) вытека́ние; (*progeny*) пото́мство; (*outcome*) исхо́д, результа́т; (*question*) (спо́рный) вопро́с; (*of book etc.*) вы́пуск, изда́ние; *v.i.* выходи́ть (-ожу́, -о́дишь) *imp.*, вы́йти (вы́йду, -дешь; вы́шел, -шла) *perf.*; (*flow*) вытека́ть *imp.*, вы́течь (-еку, -ечешь; -ек) *perf.*; *v.t.* выпуска́ть *imp.*, вы́пустить *perf.*; выдава́ть (-даю́, -даёшь) *imp.*, вы́дать (-ам, -ашь, -аст, -адим) *perf.*

isthmus *n.* перешéек (-е́йка).

it *pron.* он, оно́ (его́, ему́, им, о нём), она́ (её, ей, ей & е́ю, о ней); *demonstr.* э́то.

Italian *n.* италья́нец (-нца), -нка; *adj.* италья́нский.

italic *adj.* (*I.*) итали́йский; (*print.*) курси́вный; *n.* курси́в. **italicize** *v.t.* выделя́ть *imp.*, вы́делить *perf.* курси́вом.

itch *n.* зуд, чесо́тка; *v.i.* зуде́ть (-ди́т) *imp.*; чеса́ться чéшется *imp.*

item *n.* (*on list*) предмéт; (*in account*) пункт; (*on agenda*) вопрóс; (*in programme*) нóмер (*pl.* -á); *adv.* тáкже, тóже.
iterate *v.t.* повторя́ть *imp.*, повтори́ть *perf.*
itinerant *adj.* стрáнствующий. **itinerary** *n.* (*route*) маршрýт; (*guidebook*) путеводи́тель *m.*
its *poss.pron.* егó, её; свой (-оя́, -оё; -ой).
itself *pron.* (*emph.*) (он(ó)) сам(ó) (-огó, -омý, -и́м, -óм), (онá) самá (-мóй, -мý); (*refl.*) себя́ (себé, собóй); -ся (*suffixed to v.t.*).
ivory *n.* слонóвая кость.
ivy *n.* плющ (-á).

J

jab *n.* укóл, толчóк (-чкá); *v.t.* ты́кать (ты́чу, -чешь) *imp.*, ткнуть *perf.* (+ *instr.* в + *acc.*; + *acc.* в + *acc.*).
jabber *n.* болтовня́; *v.t.* & *i.* болтáть *imp.*
jack[1] *n.* (*fellow*) пáрень (-рня; *pl.* -рни, -рнéй) *m.*; (*cards*) валéт; (*lifting machine*) домкрáт; *v.t.* (*j. up*) поднимáть *imp.*, подня́ть (-нимý, -ни́мешь; пóднял, -á, -о) *perf.* домкрáтом.
jack[2] *n.* (*naut.*) гюйс.
jackal *n.* шакáл.
jackass *n.* осёл (ослá).
jackdaw *n.* гáлка.
jacket *n.* кýртка; (*woman's*) жакéтка; (*animal's*) шкýра; (*tech.*) кожýх (-á); (*on boiler*) рубáшка; (*on book*) (супер)облóжка.
jack-knife *n.* большóй складнóй нож (-á).
jade[1] *n.* (*horse*) кля́ча. **jaded** *adj.* изнурённый (-ён, -ённа).
jade[2] *n.* (*mineral*) нефри́т.
jagged *adj.* зубчáтый, зазýбренный (-ен, -енна).
jaguar *n.* ягуáр.
jail *see* **gaol**.
jam[1] *n.* (*crush*) дáвка; (*of machine*) заедáние, перебóй; (*in traffic*) прóбка; *v.t.* (*squeeze*) сжимáть *imp.*, сжать (сожмý, -мёшь) *perf.*; (*thrust*) впи́хивать *imp.*, впихнýть *perf.* (into, в + *acc.*); (*block*) загромождáть *imp.*, загромозди́ть *perf.*; (*radio*) заглушáть *imp.*, заглуши́ть *perf.*; *v.i.* (*machine*) заедáть *imp.*, заéсть (-éст; -éло) *perf. impers.* + *acc.*
jam[2] *n.* (*conserve*) варéнье, джем.
jamb *n.* кося́к (-á).
jangle *n.* рéзкий звук; *v.i.* издавáть (-даю́, -даёшь) *imp.*, издáть (-áм, -áшь, -áст, -ади́м; издáл, -á, -о) *perf.* рéзкие звýки.
janissary, -izary *n.* янычáр (*gen.pl.* -ров & (*collect.*) -р).
janitor *n.* (*door-keeper*) привра́тник, -ица; (*caretaker*) двóрник.
January *n.* янвáрь (-ря́) *m.*; *attrib.* янвáрский.
Japanese *n.* япóнец (-нца), -нка; *adj.* япóнский.
jape *n.* шýтка; *v.i.* шути́ть (шучý, шýтишь) *imp.*, по~ *perf.*
jar[1] *n.* (*container*) бáнка.
jar[2] *v.i.* (*sound*) скрипéть (-пи́т) *imp.*; (*irritate*) раздражáть *imp.*, раздражи́ть *perf.* (upon, + *acc.*).
jargon *n.* жаргóн.
jasmin(e), jessamin(e) *n.* жасми́н.
jasper *n.* я́шма; *attrib.* я́шмовый.
jaundice *n.* желтýха; (*fig.*) зáвисть. **jaundiced** *adj.* желтýшный, больнóй (-лен, -льнá) желтýхой; (*fig.*) зави́стливый.
jaunt *n.* прогýлка, поéздка.
jaunty *adj.* бóдрый (бодр, -á, -о, бóдры́).
javelin *n.* копьё (*pl.* -пья, -пий, -пьям).

jaw *n.* чéлюсть; *pl.* пасть, рот (рта, *loc.* во ртý); *pl.* (*of valley etc.*) ýзкий вход; *pl.* (*of vice*) гýбка.
jay *n.* (*bird*) сóйка; (*fig.*) болтýн (-á), ~ья.
jazz *n.* джаз; *adj.* джáзовый.
jealous *adj.* ревни́вый, зави́стливый; *be j. of*, (*person*) ревновáть *imp.*; (*thing*) зави́довать *imp.*, по~ *perf.* + *dat.*; (*rights*) ревни́во оберегáть *imp.*, оберéчь (-егý, -ежёшь; -ёг, -еглá) *perf.* **jealousy** *n.* рéвность, зáвисть.
jeans *n.* джи́нсы (-сов) *pl.*
jeer *n.* насмéшка; *v.t.* & *i.* насмехáться *imp.* (над + *instr.*).
jejune *adj.* (*scanty*) скýдный (-ден, -днá, -дно); (*to mind*) неинтерéсный.
jelly *n.* (*sweet*) желé *neut.indecl.*; (*meat, fish*) стýдень (-дня) *m.* **jellyfish** *n.* медýза.
jemmy *n.* фóмка, лом (*pl.* -ы, -ов).
jeopardize *v.t.* подвергáть *imp.*, подвéргнуть (-г) *perf.* опáсности. **jeopardy** *n.* опáсность.
jerk *n.* толчóк (-чкá); (*of muscle*) вздрáгивание; *v.t.* дёргать *imp.* + *instr.*; *v.i.* (*twitch*) дёргаться *imp.*, дёрнуться *perf.* **jerky** *adj.* тря́ский (-сок, -ска), отры́вистый.
jersey *n.* (*garment*) фуфáйка; (*fabric*) джéрси́ *neut.indecl.*
jest *n.* шýтка, насмéшка; *v.i.* шути́ть (шучý, шýтишь) *imp.*, по~ *perf.* **jester** *n.* шутни́к (-á), -и́ца; (*hist.*) шут (-á).
Jesuit *n.* иезуи́т. **Jesuitical** *adj.* иезуи́тский.
jet[1] *n.* (*stream*) струя́ (*pl.* -ýи); (*nozzle*) форсýнка, соплó (*pl.* сóпла, сóп(е)л); *j. engine*, реакти́вный дви́гатель *m.*; *j. plane*, реакти́вный самолёт.
jet[2] *n.* (*min.*) гагáт; *adj.* гагáтовый; *j.-black*, чёрный (-рен, -рнá) как смоль.
jetsam *n.* товáры *m.pl.*, сбрóшенные с корабля́.
jettison *v.t.* выбрáсывать *imp.*, вы́бросить *perf.* зá борт.
jetty *n.* (*mole*) мол (*loc.* -ý); (*landing-pier*) при́стань (*pl.* -ни, -нéй).
Jew *n.* еврéй. **Jewess** *n.* еврéйка. **Jewish** *adj.* еврéйский. **Jewry** *n.* еврéйство.
jewel *n.* драгоцéнность, драгоцéнный кáмень (-мня; *pl.* -мни, -мнéй) *m.* **jeweller** *n.* ювели́р. **jewellery, jewelry** *n.* драгоцéнности *f.pl.*, ювели́рные издéлия *neut.pl.*
jib *n.* (*naut.*) кли́вер (*pl.* -á & -ы); (*of crane*) стрелá (*pl.* -лы) (крáна).
jingle *n.* звя́канье; *v.t.* & *i.* звя́кать *imp.*, звя́кнуть *perf.* (+ *instr.*).
jingo *n.* урá-патриóт. **jingoism** *n.* урá-патриоти́зм. **jingoistic** *adj.* урá-патриоти́ческий.
job *n.* (*work*) рабóта; (*task*) задáние; (*position*) мéсто (*pl.* -á). **jobless** *adj.* безрабóтный.
jockey *n.* жокéй; *v.t.* (*cheat*) надувáть *imp.*, надýть (-ýю, -ýешь) *perf.*
jocose *adj.* игри́вый.
jocular *adj.* шутли́вый.
jocund *adj.* весёлый (вéсел, -á, -о, вéселы́).
jog *n.* (*push*) толчóк (-чкá); (*movement*) мéдленная ходьбá, launch ездá; *v.t.* толкáть *imp.*, толкнýть *perf.*; (*nudge*) подтáлкивать *imp.*, подтолкнýть *perf.* **jog-trot** *n.* рысцá.
join *v.t.* & *i.* соединя́ть(ся) *imp.*, соедини́ть(ся) *perf.*; *v.t.* присоединя́ться *imp.*, присоедини́ться *perf.* к + *dat.*; (*become member of*) вступáть *imp.*, вступи́ть (-плю́, -пишь) *perf.* в + *acc.*; *v.i.*: *j. up*, вступáть *imp.*, вступи́ть (-плю́, -пишь) *perf.* в áрмию.
joiner *n.* столя́р (-á). **joinery** *n.* (*goods*) столя́рные издéлия *neut.pl.*; (*work*) столя́рная рабóта.
joint *n.* соединéние, мéсто (*pl.* -тá) соединéния; (*anat.*) сустáв; (*tech.*) стык, шов (шва), шарни́р; *adj.* соединённый, óбщий; *j. stock*, акционéрный капитáл; (*attrib.*) акционéрный; *v.t.* (*join*) сочленя́ть *imp.*, сочлени́ть *perf.*; (*divide*) расчленя́ть *imp.*, расчлени́ть *perf.*
joist *n.* переклáдина.
joke *n.* шýтка, острóта, анекдóт; *v.i.* шути́ть (шучý, шýтишь) *imp.*, по~ *perf.* **joker** *n.* шутни́к (-á), -и́ца.
jollity *n.* весéлье. **jolly** *adj.* весёлый (вéсел, -á, -о, вéселы́); *adv.* óчень.
jolt *n.* тря́ска; *v.t.* трясти́ (-сý, -сёшь; -с, -слá) *imp.*

jostle *n.* толкотня́; *v.t.* & *i.* толка́ть(ся) *imp.*, толкну́ть(ся) *perf.*

jot *n.* йо́та; *not a j.*, ни на йо́ту; *v.t.* (*j. down*) бы́стро, кра́тко, запи́сывать *imp.*, записа́ть (-ишу́, -и́шешь) *perf.*

joule *n.* джо́уль *m.*

journal *n.* журна́л, дневни́к (-а́); (*tech.*) ца́пфа, ше́йка. **journalese** *n.* газе́тный язы́к (-а́). **journalism** *n.* журнали́стика. **journalist** *n.* журнали́ст.

journey *n.* путеше́ствие, пое́здка; (*specific j. of vehicle*) рейс; *v.i.* путеше́ствовать *imp.*

jovial *adj.* (*merry*) весёлый (ве́сел, -а́, -о, ве́селы́); (*sociable*) общи́тельный.

jowl *n.* (*jaw*) че́люсть; (*cheek*) щека́ (*acc.* щёку; *pl.* щёки, щёк, -а́м).

joy *n.* ра́дость. **joyful, joyous** *adj.* ра́достный. **joyless** *adj.* безра́достный.

jubilant *adj.* лику́ющий. **jubilate** *v.i.* ликова́ть *imp.*

jubilee *n.* юбиле́й.

Judaic *adj.* иуде́йский.

judge *n.* судья́ (*pl.* -дьи, -де́й, -дьям) *m.*; (*connoisseur*) цени́тель *m.*; *v.t.* & *i.* суди́ть (сужу́, су́дишь) *imp.*; *v.t.* (*appraise*) оце́нивать *imp.*, оцени́ть (-ню́, -нишь) *perf.* **judgement** *n.* (*sentence*) пригово́р; (*decision*) реше́ние; (*opinion*) мне́ние; (*estimate*) оце́нка.

judicature *n.* отправле́ние правосу́дия; (*judiciary*) суде́йская корпора́ция. **judicial** *adj.* (*of law*) суде́бный; (*of judge*) суде́йский; (*impartial*) беспристра́стный. **judicious** *adj.* здравомы́слящий.

judo *n.* дзюдо́ *neut.indecl.*

jug *n.* кувши́н; *v.t.* туши́ть (-шу́, -шишь) *imp.*, с~ *perf.*

juggle *v.i.* жонгли́ровать *imp.* **juggler** *n.* жонглёр.

jugular *adj.* ше́йный; *j. vein*, яре́мная ве́на.

juice *n.* сок (-а(у), *loc.* -е & -у́); (*fig.*) су́щность. **juicy** *adj.* со́чный (-чен, -чна́, -чно).

July *n.* ию́ль *m.*; *attrib.* ию́льский.

jumble *n.* (*disorder*) беспоря́док (-дка); (*articles*) барахло́; *v.t.* перепу́тывать *imp.*, перепу́тать *perf.*

jump *n.* прыжо́к (-жка́), скачо́к (-чка́); (*in price etc.*) ре́зкое повыше́ние; *v.i.* пры́гать *imp.*, пры́гнуть *perf.*; ска-ка́ть (-ачу́, -а́чешь) *imp.*; (*from shock*) вздра́гивать *imp.*, вздро́гнуть *perf.*; (*of price etc.*) подска́кивать *imp.*, подскочи́ть (-ит) *perf.*; *v.t.* (*j. over*) перепры́гивать *imp.*, перепры́гнуть *perf.*; *j. at*, (*accept eagerly*) ухва́тываться *imp.*, ухвати́ться (-ачу́сь, -а́тишься) *perf.* за + *acc.*; *j. the rails*, сходи́ть (-ит) *imp.*, сойти́ (сойдёт; сошёл, -шла́) *perf.* с ре́льсов.

jumper *n.* (*garment*) дже́мпер.

jumpy *adj.* не́рвный (-вен, не́рвна́, -вно).

junction *n.* (*joining*) соедине́ние; (*rly.*) железнодоро́жный у́зел (узла́); (*roads*) перекрёсток (-тка).

juncture *n.* (*joining*) соедине́ние; (*state of affairs*) положе́ние дел; *at this j.*, в э́тот моме́нт.

June *n.* ию́нь *m.*; *attrib.* ию́ньский.

jungle *n.* джу́нгли (-лей) *pl.*

junior *adj.* мла́дший.

juniper *n.* можжеве́льник.

junk[1] *n.* (*rubbish*) барахло́.

junk[2] *n.* (*ship*) джо́нка.

junta *n.* ху́нта.

Jupiter *n.* Юпи́тер.

jurisdiction *n.* (*administration of law*) отправле́ние правосу́дия; (*legal authority*) юрисди́кция.

jurisprudence *n.* юриспруде́нция.

jurist *n.* юри́ст.

juror *n.* прися́жный *sb.*; (*in competition*) член жюри́. **jury** *n.* прися́жные *sb.*; жюри́ *neut.indecl.*

just *adj.* (*fair*) справедли́вый; (*deserved*) заслу́женный, до́лжный; *adv.* (*exactly*) то́чно, и́менно; (*barely*) едва́; (*at this, that, moment*) то́лько что; *j. in case*, на вся́кий слу́чай.

justice *n.* правосу́дие; (*fairness*) справедли́вость; (*judge*) судья́ (*pl.* -дьи, -де́й, -дьям); (*proceedings*) суд (-а́); *bring to j.*, отдава́ть (-даю́, -даёшь) *imp.*, отда́ть (-а́м, -а́шь, -а́ст, -адим; о́тдал, -а́, -о) *perf.* под суд; *do j. to*, отдава́ть (-аю́, -аёшь) *imp.*, отда́ть (-а́м, -а́шь, -а́ст, -адим; о́тдал, -а́, -о) *perf.* до́лжное + *dat.*

justify *v.t.* опра́вдывать *imp.*, оправда́ть *perf.* **justification** *n.* оправда́ние.
jut *v.i.* (*j. out, forth*) выдава́ться (-даётся) *imp.*, вы́даться (-астся, -адутся) *perf.*; выступа́ть *imp.*
jute *n.* джу́т.
juvenile *n.* ю́ноша *m.*, подро́сток (-тка); *adj.* ю́ный (юн, -а́, -о), ю́ношеский.
juxtapose *v.t.* помеща́ть *imp.*, помести́ть *perf.* ря́дом; сопоставля́ть *imp.*, сопоста́вить *perf.* (with, с + *instr.*).

K

kale, kail *n.* кормова́я капу́ста.
kaleidoscope *n.* калейдоско́п.
kangaroo *n.* кенгуру́ *m.indecl.*
keel *n.* киль *m.*; *v.t.* & *i.*: *k. over*, опроки́дывать(ся) *imp.*, опроки́нуть(ся) *perf.*
keen *adj.* (*sharp*) о́стрый (о́стр & остёр, остра́, о́стро́); (*strong*) си́льный (си́лён, -льна́, -льно, си́льны́); (*penetrating*) проница́тельный; (*ardent*) стра́стный (-тен, -тна́, -тно).
keep[1] *n.* (*of castle*) гла́вная ба́шня (*gen.pl.* -шен); (*maintenance*) содержа́ние; (*food*) пи́ща.
keep[2] *v.t.* (*observe*) соблюда́ть *imp.*, соблюсти́ (-юду́, -юдёшь; -ю́л, -юла́) *perf.* (*the law*); сде́рживать *imp.*, сдержа́ть (-жу́, -жишь) *perf.* (*one's word*); (*celebrate*) пра́здновать *imp.*, от~ *perf.*; (*possess, maintain*) держа́ть (-жу́, -жишь) *imp.*; храни́ть *imp.*; (*family*) содержа́ть (-жу́, -жишь) *imp.*; (*diary*) вести́ (веду́, -дёшь; вёл, -а́) *imp.*; (*detain*) заде́рживать *imp.*, задержа́ть (-жу́, -жишь) *perf.*; (*retain, reserve*) сохраня́ть *imp.*, сохрани́ть *perf.*; *v.i.* (*remain*) остава́ться (-таю́сь, -таёшься) *imp.*, оста́ться (-а́нусь, -а́нешься) *perf.*; (*of food*) не по́ртиться *imp.*; *k. away*, держа́ть(ся) (-жу́(сь), -жишь(ся)) *imp.* в отдале́нии; *k. back*, (*hold back*) уде́рживать *imp.*, удержа́ть (-жу́, -жишь) *perf.*; (*conceal*) скрыва́ть *imp.*, скры́ть (-ро́ю, -ро́ешь) *perf.*; *k. down*, подавля́ть *imp.*, подави́ть (-влю́, -вишь) *perf.*; *k. from*, уде́рживаться *imp.*, удержа́ться (-жу́сь, -жишься) *perf.* от + *gen.*; *k. on*, продолжа́ть *imp.*, продо́лжить *perf.* (+ *inf.*).
keepsake *n.* пода́рок (-рка) на па́мять.
keg *n.* бочо́нок (-нка).
ken *n.* (*knowledge*) преде́л позна́ний; (*sight*) кругозо́р.
kennel *n.* конура́.
kerb *n.* кра́й (*loc.* -аю́; *pl.* -ая́, -аёв) тротуа́ра. **kerbstone** *n.* бордю́рный ка́мень (-мня; *pl.* -мни, -мне́й) *m.*
kerchief *n.* (головно́й) плато́к (-тка́).
kernel *n.* (*nut*) ядро́ (*pl.* я́дра, я́дер, я́драм); (*grain*) зерно́ (*pl.* зёрна, -рен, -рнам); (*fig.*) суть.
kerosene *n.* кероси́н (-а(у)).
kestrel *n.* пустельга́.
kettle *n.* ча́йник. **kettledrum** *n.* лита́вра.
key *n.* ключ (-а́); (*piano, typewriter*) кла́виш(а); (*mus.*) тона́льность; *attrib.* веду́щий, ключево́й. **keyboard** *n.* клавиату́ра. **keyhole** *n.* замо́чная сква́жина. **keynote** *n.* (*mus.*) то́ника; (*fig.*) то́н. **keystone** *n.* (*archit.*) замко́вый ка́мень (-мня; *pl.* -мни, -мне́й) *m.*; (*fig.*) основно́й при́нцип.
khaki *n., adj.* ха́ки *neut., adj.indecl.*
khan *n.* ха́н. **khanate** *n.* ха́нство.
kick *n.* уда́р ного́й, пино́к (-нка́); (*recoil of gun*) отда́ча; *v.t.* ударя́ть *imp.*, уда́рить *perf.* ного́й; пина́ть *imp.*, пнуть *perf.*; (*score goal*) забива́ть *imp.*, заби́ть (-бью́, -бьёшь) *perf.* (гол, мяч); *v.i.* (*of horse etc.*) ляга́ться *imp.*; *k. out*, вышвы́ривать *imp.*, вы́швырнуть *perf.*

kid[1] *n.* (*goat*) козлёнок (-лёнка; *pl.* -ля́та, -ля́т); (*leather*) ла́йка; (*child*) малы́ш (-а́).

kid[2] *v.t.* (*deceive*) обма́нывать *imp.*, обману́ть (-ну́, -нешь) *perf.*; (*tease*) поддра́знивать *imp.*, поддразни́ть (-ню́, -нишь) *perf.*

kidnap *v.t.* похища́ть *imp.*, похи́тить (-и́щу, -и́тишь) *perf.*

kidney *n.* по́чка; *attrib.* по́чечный; *k. bean*, фасо́ль.

kill *v.t.* убива́ть *imp.*, уби́ть (убью́, -ьёшь) *perf.*; (*cattle*) ре́зать (ре́жу, -жешь) *imp.*, за~ *perf.*; *k. off*, ликвиди́ровать *imp.*, *perf.* **killer** *n.* убийца *m.* & *f.* **killing** *n.* уби́йство; *adj.* (*murderous*, *fig.*) уби́йственный (-ен, -енна); (*amusing*, *coll.*) умори́тельный.

kiln *n.* о́бжиговая печь (*pl.* -чи, -че́й).

kilo- *in comb.* ки́ло-. **kilocycle, kiloherz** *n.* килоге́рц (*gen.pl.* -ц). **kilogram(me)** *n.* килогра́мм. **kilometre** *n.* киломе́тр. **kiloton(ne)** *n.* килото́нна. **kilowatt** *n.* килова́тт (*gen.pl.* -т).

kimono *n.* кимоно́ *neut.indecl.*

kin *n.* (*family* семья́ (*pl.* -мьи, -ме́й, -мьям); (*collect.*, *relatives*) родня́.

kind[1] *n.* сорт (*pl.* -а́), род (*pl.* -ы, -о́в); *a k. of*, что́-то вро́де + *gen.*; *this k. of*, тако́й; *what k. of*, что (это, он, *etc.*) за + *nom.*; *k. of*, (*adv.*) как бу́дто, ка́к-то; *pay in k.*, плати́ть (-ачу́, -а́тишь) *imp.*, за~ *perf.* нату́рой; *return in k.*, отпла́чивать *imp.*, отплати́ть (-ачу́, -а́тишь) *perf.* той же моне́той + *dat.*

kind[2] *adj.* до́брый (добр, -а́, -о, до́бры́), любе́зный.

kindergarten *n.* де́тский сад (*loc.* -у́; *pl.* -ы́).

kindle *v.t.* зажига́ть *imp.*, заже́чь (-жгу́, -жжёшь; -жёг, -жгла́) *perf.*; *v.i.* загора́ться *imp.*, загоре́ться (-рю́сь, -ри́шься) *perf.* **kindling** *n.* расто́пка.

kindly *adj.* до́брый (добр, -а́, -о, до́бры́); *adv.* любе́зно; (*with imper.*), (*request*) бу́дьте добры́, + *imper.* **kindness** *n.* доброта́, любе́зность.

kindred *n.* (*relationship*) кро́вное родство́; (*relatives*) ро́дственники *m.pl.*; *adj.* ро́дственный (-ен, -енна); (*similar*) схо́дный (-ден, -дна́, -дно).

kinetic *adj.* кинети́ческий.

king *n.* коро́ль (-ля́) *m.* (*also chess*, *cards*, *fig.*); (*fig.*) царь (-ря́) *m.*; (*draughts*) да́мка. **kingdom** *n.* короле́вство; (*fig.*) ца́рство. **kingfisher** *n.* зимоpо́док (-дка). **kingpin** *n.* шкво́рень (-рня) *m.*

kink *n.* пе́тля (*gen.pl.* -тель), изги́б.

kinsfolk *n.* кро́вные ро́дственники *m.pl.* **kinship** *n.* родство́; (*similarity*) схо́дство. **kinsman, -woman** *n.* ро́дственник, -ица.

kiosk *n.* кио́ск; (*telephone*) бу́дка.

kip *v.i.* дры́хнуть (дры́х(ну)л, -хла) *imp.*

kipper *n.* копчёная селёдка.

kiss *n.* поцелу́й; *v.t.* целова́ть(ся) *imp.*, по~ *perf.*

kit *n.* (*soldier's*) ли́чное обмундирова́ние; (*clothing*) снаряже́ние; (*tools*) компле́кт. **kitbag** *n.* вещево́й мешо́к (-шка́).

kitchen *n.* ку́хня (*gen.pl.* -хонь); *attrib.* кухо́нный; *k. garden*, огоро́д; *k.-maid*, судомо́йка.

kite *n.* (*bird*) ко́ршун; (*person*) хи́щник; (*toy*) бума́жный змей.

kith *n.*: *k. and kin*, знако́мые *sb.* и родня́.

kitten *n.* котёнок (-тёнка; *pl.* -тя́та, -тя́т); *v.i.* коти́ться *imp.*, о~ *perf.*

kleptomania *n.* клептома́ния. **kleptomaniac** *n.* клептома́н.

knack *n.* сноро́вка, трюк.

knacker *n.* живодёр.

knapsack *n.* рюкза́к (-а́), ра́нец (-нца).

knave *n.* (*rogue*) плут (-а́); (*cards*) вале́т. **knavery** *n.* плутовство́. **knavish** *adj.* плутовско́й.

knead *v.t.* меси́ть (мешу́, ме́сишь) *imp.*, с~ *perf.*

knee *n.* коле́но (*pl.* (*anat.*) -ни, -ней; (*tech.*) -нья, -ньев); *k.-joint*, коле́нный суста́в. **kneecap** *n.* (*bone*) коле́нная ча́шка; (*protective covering*) наколе́нник.

kneel *v.i.* стоя́ть (-ою́, -ои́шь) *imp.* на коле́нях; (*k. down*) станови́ться (-влю́сь, -ви́шься) *imp.*, стать (-а́ну, -а́нешь) *perf.* на коле́ни.

knell *n.* похоро́нный звон.

knickers *n.* пантало́ны (-н) *pl.*

knick-knack *n.* безделу́шка.

knife *n.* нож (-á); *v.t.* колóть (-лю́, -лешь) *imp.*, за~ *perf.* ножóм.
knight *n.* ры́царь *m.*; (*holder of order*) кавалéр (óрдена); (*chess*) конь (-ня́; *pl.* -ни, -нéй) *m.* **knighthood** *n.* ры́царство. **knightly** *adj.* ры́царский.
knit *v.t.* (*garment*) вязáть (вяжу́, -жешь) *imp.*, с~ *perf.*; (*unite*) свя́зывать *imp.*, связáть (-яжу́, -я́жешь) *perf.*; *v.t.* & *i.* (*unite*) соединя́ть(ся) *imp.*, соедини́ть(ся) *perf.*; *v.i.* (*bones*) срастáться *imp.*, срасти́сь (-тётся; срóсся, сросла́сь) *perf.*; *k. one's brows*, хму́рить *imp.*, на~ *perf.* брóви. **knitting** *n.* (*action*) вязáние; (*object*) вязáнье; *k.-needle*, спи́ца. **knitwear** *n.* трикотáж.
knob *n.* ши́шка, кнóпка; (*door handle*) (кру́глая) ру́чка (двéри). **knobb(l)y** *adj.* шишковáтый.
knock *n.* (*noise*) стук; (*blow*) удáр; *v.t.* & *i.* (*strike*) ударя́ть *imp.*, удáрить *perf.*; (*strike door etc.*) стучáть (-чу́, -чи́шь) *imp.*, по~ *perf.* (at, в + *acc.*); *k. about*, (*treat roughly*) колоти́ть (-очу́, -óтишь) *imp.*, по~ *perf.*; (*wander*) шатáться *imp.*; *k. down*, (*person*) сбивáть *imp.*, сбить (собью́, -ьёшь) *perf.* с ног; (*building*) сноси́ть (-ошу́, -óсишь) *imp.*, снести́ (снесу́, -сёшь; снёс, -ла́) *perf.*; (*at auction*) продавáть (-даю́, -даёшь) *imp.*, продáть (-áм, -áшь, -áст, -ади́м; прóдал, -á, -о) *perf.* с молоткá; *k. in*, вбивáть *imp.*, вбить (вобью́, -ьёшь) *perf.* (в + *acc.*); *k. off*, сбивáть *imp.*, сбить (собью́, -ьёшь) *perf.*; (*leave work*) прекращáть *imp.*, прекрати́ть (-ащу́, -ати́шь) *perf.* (рабóту); *k. out*, выбивáть *imp.*, вы́бить (-бью, -бьешь) *perf.*; (*sport*) нокаути́ровать *imp.*, *perf.*; *k.-out*, нокáут. **knocker** *n.* (*door-k.*) двернóй молотóк (-ткá).
knoll *n.* бугóр (-гра́).
knot *n.* у́зел (узла́) (*also fig.*, *naut.*); (*hard lump*) нарóст; (*in wood*) сучóк (-чкá); (*group*) ку́чка; *v.t.* завя́зывать *imp.*, завязáть (-яжу́, -я́жешь) *perf.* узлóм. **knotty** *adj.* узловáтый; (*fig.*) запу́танный (-ан, -анна).
knout *n.* кнут (-á).
know *v.t.* знать *imp.*; (*k. how to*) умéть *imp.*, с~ *perf.* + *inf.*; (*be acquainted*) быть знакóмым с + *instr.*; (*recognize*) узнавáть (-наю́, -наёшь) *imp.*, узнáть *perf.*; *k.-all*, всезнáйка *m.* & *f.*; *k.-how*, умéние. **knowing** *adj.* (*cunning*) хи́трый (-тёр, -трá, хи́тро́). **knowingly** *adv.* сознáтельно. **knowledge** *n.* знáние, познáния (-ний) *pl.*; (*familiarity*) знакóмство (of, с + *instr.*); (*sum of what is known*) нау́ка; *to my k.*, наскóлько мне извéстно.
knuckle *n.* сустáв пáльца; (*cul.*) нóжка; *v.i.*: *k. down to*, реши́тельно брáться (беру́сь, -рёшься; брáлся, -ла́сь) *imp.*, взя́ться (возьму́сь, -мёшься; взя́лся, -ла́сь) *perf.* за + *acc.*; *k. under*, подчиня́ться *imp.*, подчини́ться *perf.* (to, + *dat.*).
ko(w)tow *n.* ни́зкий поклóн; *v.i.* ни́зко кла́няться *imp.*, поклони́ться (-ню́сь, -нишься) *perf.*; (*fig.*) раболéпствовать *imp.* (to, пéред + *instr.*).
Kremlin *n.* Кремль (-ля́) *m.*
kudos *n.* слáва.

L

label *n.* этикéтка; (*also fig.*) ярлы́к (-á); *v.t.* приклéивать *imp.*, приклéить *perf.* ярлы́к к + *dat.*
labial *adj.* (*n.*) губнóй (звук).
laboratory *n.* лаборатóрия; *l. assistant, technician*, лаборáнт, ~ка.
laborious *adj.* (*arduous*) тру́дный (-ден, -днá, -дно, тру́дны́); (*industrious*) трудолюби́вый; (*of style*) вы́мученный (-ен).
labour *n.* труд (-á), рабóта; (*workers*) рабóчие *sb.*; (*task*) задáча; (*childbirth*)

ро́ды (-дов) *pl.*; *attrib.* трудово́й, рабо́чий; *l. exchange*, би́ржа труда́; *l. force*, рабо́чая си́ла; *l.-intensive*, трудоёмкий; *l. pains*, родовы́е схва́тки *f.pl.*; *L. Party*, лейбори́стская па́ртия; *v.i.* труди́ться *imp.*; рабо́тать *imp.*; *v.t.* (*elaborate*) подро́бно разраба́тывать *imp.*, разрабо́тать *perf.* **laboured** *adj.* затруднённый (-ён, -ённа); (*style*) вы́мученный (-ен). **labourer** *n.* чернорабо́чий *sb.* **labourite** *n.* лейбори́ст.

laburnum *n.* раки́тник-золото́й до́ждь (-дя́) *m.*

labyrinth *n.* лабири́нт.

lace *n.* (*fabric*) кру́жево; (*cord*) шнур (-а́), шнуро́к (-рка́); *v.t.* (*l. up*) шнурова́ть *imp.*, за~ *perf.*

lacerate *v.t.* рвать (рву, рвёшь; рвал, -а́, -о) *imp.*; (*fig.*) раздира́ть *imp.* **laceration** *n.* (*wound*) рва́ная ра́на.

lachrymose *adj.* слезли́вый.

lack *n.* недоста́ток (-тка) (of, +*gen.*, в+*prep.*), отсу́тствие; *v.t.* испы́тывать *imp.*, испыта́ть *perf.* недоста́ток в+*prep.*; недостава́ть (-таёт) *imp.*, недоста́ть (-а́нет) *perf.impers.*+*dat.* (*person*), +*gen.* (*object*).

lackadaisical *adj.* (*languid*) то́мный (-мен, -мна́, -мно); (*affected*) жема́нный (-нен, -нна).

lackey *n.* лаке́й.

lack-lustre *adj.* ту́склый (-л, -ла́, -ло).

laconic *adj.* лакони́чный, -ческий.

lacquer *n.* лак; *v.t.* лакирова́ть *imp.*, от~ *perf.*

lactic *adj.* моло́чный.

lacuna *n.* пробе́л.

lad *n.* па́рень (-рня; *pl.* -рни, -рне́й) *m.*

ladder *n.* ле́стница; (*naut.*) трап.

laden *adj.* нагружённый (-ён, -ена́); (*fig.*) обременённый (-ён, -ена́).

ladle *n.* (*spoon*) поло́вник; (*for metal*) ковш (-а́); *v.t.* че́рпать *imp.*, черпну́ть *perf.*

lady *n.* да́ма, ле́ди *f.indecl.* **ladybird** *n.* бо́жья коро́вка.

lag[1] *v.i.*: *l. behind*, отстава́ть (-таю́, -таёшь) *imp.*, отста́ть (-а́ну, -а́нешь) *perf.* (от+*gen.*).

lag[2] *n.* (*convict*) ка́торжник.

lag[3] *v.t.* (*insulate*) покрыва́ть *imp.*, покры́ть (-ро́ю, -ро́ешь) *perf.* изоля́цией. **lagging** *n.* теплова́я изоля́ция.

lagoon *n.* лагу́на.

lair *n.* ло́говище, берло́га.

laity *n.* (*in religion*) миря́не (-н) *pl.*; (*in profession*) профа́ны (-нов) *pl.*

lake *n.* о́зеро (*pl.* озёра); *attrib.* озёрный.

lamb *n.* ягнёнок (-нка; *pl.* ягня́та, -я́т); (*eccl.*) а́гнец (-нца); *v.i.* ягни́ться *imp.*, о~ *perf.*

lame *adj.* хромо́й (хром, -а́, -о); (*fig.*) неубеди́тельный; *be l.*, хрома́ть *imp.*; *go l.*, хроме́ть *imp.*, о~ *perf.*; *v.t.* кале́чить *imp.*, о~ *perf.* **lameness** *n.* хромота́.

lament *n.* плач; *v.t.* опла́кивать *imp.*, опла́кать (-а́чу, -а́чешь) *perf.* **lamentable** *adj.* приско́рбный.

lamina *n.* то́нкая пласти́нка, то́нкий слой (*pl.* -о́и). **laminated** *adj.* листово́й, пласти́нчатый.

lamp *n.* ла́мпа, фона́рь (-ря́) *m.* **lamppost** *n.* фона́рный сто́лб (-а́). **lampshade** *n.* абажу́р.

lampoon *n.* пасквиль *m.*

lamprey *n.* мино́га.

lance *n.* пи́ка, копьё (*pl.* -пья, -пий, -пьям); (*fish-spear*) острога́; *l.-corporal*, ефре́йтор; *v.t.* пронза́ть *imp.*, пронзи́ть *perf.* пи́кой, копьём; (*med.*) вскрыва́ть *imp.*, вскры́ть (-ро́ю, -ро́ешь) *perf.* (ланце́том). **lancer** *n.* ула́н (*pl.* -нов & -н (*collect.*)). **lancet** *n.* ланце́т.

land *n.* земля́ (*acc.* -млю; *pl.* -мли, -ме́ль, -млям); (*dry l.*) су́ша; (*country*) страна́ (*pl.* -ны); (*soil*) по́чва; *pl.* (*estates*) поме́стья (-тий) *pl.*; *v.t.* (*unload*) выгружа́ть *imp.*, вы́грузить *perf.*; *v.t.* & *i.* (*persons*) выса́живать(ся) *imp.*, вы́садить(ся) *perf.*; (*aeron.*) приземля́ть(ся) *imp.*, приземли́ть(ся) *perf.* **landfall** *n.* подхо́д к бе́регу. **landing** *n.* вы́садка; (*aeron.*) поса́дка; (*mil.*) деса́нт; (*on stairs*) ле́стничная площа́дка; *l.-stage*, при́стань (*pl.* -ни, -не́й). **landlady** *n.* домовладе́лица; хозя́йка. **landlord** *n.* землевладе́лец (-льца); (*of house*) домовладе́лец (-льца); (*of inn*) хозя́ин (*pl.* -я́ева,

-я́ев). **landmark** *n.* (*boundary stone*; *fig.*) ве́ха; (*conspicuous object*) ориенти́р. **landowner** *n.* землевладе́лец (-льца). **landscape** *n.* ландша́фт; (*also picture*) пейза́ж; *l.-painter*, пейзажи́ст. **landslide, landslip** *n.* о́ползень (-зня) *m.*
landau *n.* ландо́ *neut.indecl.*
lane *n.* у́зкая доро́га; (*street*) переу́лок (-лка); (*passage*) прохо́д; (*on road*) ряд (-á *with 2, 3, 4, loc.* -ý; *pl.* -ы́); (*in race*) доро́жка; (*for ships*) морско́й путь (-ти́, -тём) *m.*; (*for aircraft*) тра́сса полёта.
language *n.* язы́к (-á); (*style, form of speech*) речь.
languid *adj.* то́мный (-мен, -мна́, -мно).
languish *v.i.* (*pine*) томи́ться *imp.*
languor *n.* томле́ние, то́мность; (*fatigue*) уста́лость. **languorous** *adj.* то́мный (-мен, -мна́, -мно); уста́лый.
lank *adj.* (*person*) худоща́вый; (*hair*) гла́дкий (-док, -дка́, -дко). **lanky** *adj.* долговя́зый.
lantern *n.* фона́рь (-ря́) *m.*
lanyard *n.* (*naut.*) тро́совый та́лреп; (*cord*) шнур (-á).
lap[1] *n.* (*flap*; *of skirt*) пола́ (*pl.* -лы); (*ear-lobe*) мо́чка; (*of person*) коле́ни (-ней) *pl.*; (*racing*) круг (*pl.* -и́).
lap[2] *v.t.* (*drink*) лака́ть *imp.*, вы́~ *perf.*; *v.i.* (*water*) плеска́ться (-е́щется) *imp.*
lapel *n.* отворо́т, ла́цкан.
lapidary *n.* грани́льщик; *adj.* грани́льный; (*fig.*) сжа́тый.
lapis lazuli *n.* ля́пис-лазу́рь.
lapse *n.* (*mistake*) оши́бка; (*of pen*) опи́ска; (*of memory*) прова́л па́мяти; (*decline*) паде́ние; (*expiry*) истече́ние; (*of time*) тече́ние, ход вре́мени; *v.i.* впада́ть *imp.*, впасть (-аду́, -адёшь; -ал) *perf.* (into, в+*acc.*); (*expire*) истека́ть *imp.*, исте́чь (-ечёт; -ёк, -екла́) *perf.*
lapwing *n.* чи́бис.
larceny *n.* воровство́.
larch *n.* ли́ственница.
lard *n.* свино́е са́ло; *v.t.* (*cul.*) шпигова́ть *imp.*, на~ *perf.*; (*fig.*) уснаща́ть *imp.*, уснасти́ть *perf.* (with, +*instr.*).
larder *n.* кладова́я *sb.*
large *adj.* большо́й, кру́пный (-пен, -пна́, -пно, кру́пны́); (*wide, broad*) широ́кий (-о́к, -ока́, -о́ко́); *n.*: *at l.* (*free*) на свобо́де; (*in detail*) подро́бно; (*as a whole*) цели́ко́м. **largely** *adj.* (*to a great extent*) в значи́тельной сте́пени.
largess(e) *n.* ще́дрость.
lark[1] *n.* (*bird*) жа́воронок (-нка).
lark[2] *n.* шу́тка, прока́за; *v.i.* (*l. about*) резви́ться *imp.*
larva *n.* личи́нка. **larval** *adj.* личи́ночный.
laryngeal *adj.* горта́нный. **laryngitis** *n.* ларинги́т. **larynx** *n.* горта́нь.
lascivious *adj.* похотли́вый.
laser *n.* ла́зер.
lash *n.* плеть (*pl.* -ти, -те́й), бич (-á); (*blow*) уда́р плётью, бичо́м; (*eyelash*) ресни́ца; *v.t.* (*beat*) хлеста́ть (хлещу́, -щешь) *imp.*, хлестну́ть *perf.*; (*with words*) бичева́ть (-чу́ю, -чу́ешь) *imp.*; (*fasten*) привя́зывать *imp.*, привяза́ть (-яжу́, -я́жешь) *perf.* (to, к+*dat.*); *l. together*, свя́зывать *imp.*, связа́ть (-яжу́, -я́жешь) *perf.*
lass *n.* де́вушка, де́вочка.
lassitude *n.* уста́лость.
lasso *n.* лассо́ *neut.indecl.*; *v.t.* лови́ть (-влю́, -вишь) *imp.*, пойма́ть *perf.* лассо́.
last[1] *n.* (*cobbler's*) коло́дка.
last[2] *adj.* (*final*) после́дний; (*most recent*) про́шлый; (*extreme*) кра́йний; *the year* (*etc.*) *before l.*, позапро́шлый год (и т.д.); *l. but one*, предпосле́дний; *l. but two*, тре́тий (-тья, -тье) с конца́; *l. night*, вчера́ ве́чером, но́чью; *n.* (*l.-mentioned*) после́дний *sb.*; (*end*) коне́ц (-нца́); *at l.*, наконе́ц, в конце́ концо́в; *adv.* (*after all others*) по́сле всех; (*on last occasion*) в после́дний раз; (*in last place*) в конце́.
last[3] *v.i.* (*go on*) продолжа́ться *imp.*, продо́лжиться *perf.*; дли́ться *imp.*, про~ *perf.*; (*food, health*) сохраня́ться *imp.*, сохрани́ться *perf.*; (*suffice*) хвата́ть *imp.*, хвати́ть (-ит) *perf.* **lasting** *adj.* (*enduring*) дли́тельный; (*permanent*) постоя́нный (-нен, -нна); (*durable*) про́чный (-чен, -чна́, -чно, про́чны́).
lastly *adj.* в конце́, в заключе́ние, наконе́ц.

latch *n.* щеко́лда.
late *adj.* по́здний; (*recent*) неда́вний; (*dead*) поко́йный; (*former*) бы́вший; *be l. for*, опа́здывать *imp.*, опозда́ть *perf.* на + *acc.*; *adv.* по́здно; *n.*: *of l.*, неда́вно, за после́днее вре́мя.
latent *adj.* скры́тый.
lateral *adj.* боково́й. **laterally** *adv.* (*from side*) сбо́ку; (*towards side*) вбок.
latex *n.* мле́чный со́к (-а(у), *loc.* -е & -у́); (*synthetic*) ла́текс.
lath *n.* ре́йка, дра́нка (*also collect.*).
lathe *n.* тока́рный стано́к (-нка́).
lather *n.* (мы́льная) пе́на; (*of horse*) мы́ло; *v.t.* & *i.* мы́лить(ся) *imp.*, на~ *perf.*; (*of horse*) взмы́ливаться *imp.*, взмы́литься *perf.*
Latin *adj.* лати́нский; (*Romance*) рома́нский; *n.* лати́нский язы́к (-а́); (*when qualified*) латы́нь; *L.-American*, латиноамерика́нский.
latitude *n.* свобо́да; (*geog.*) широта́.
latrine *n.* убо́рная *sb.*; (*esp. in camp*) отхо́жее ме́сто (*pl.* -та́).
latter *adj.* после́дний; *l.-day*, совреме́нный. **latterly** *adv.* (*towards end*) к концу́; (*of late*) неда́вно.
lattice *n.* решётка. **latticed** *adj.* решётчатый.
laud *n.* хвала́; *v.t.* хвали́ть (-лю́, -лишь) *imp.*, по~ *perf.* **laudable** *adj.* похва́льный. **laudatory** *adj.* хвале́бный.
laugh *n.* смех (-а(у)), хо́хот; *v.i.* смея́ться (-ею́сь, -ёшься) *imp.* (at, над + *instr.*); *l. it off*, отшу́чиваться *imp.*, отшути́ться (-учу́сь, -у́тишься) *perf.*; *laughing-stock*, посме́шище. **laughable** *adj.* смешно́й (-шо́н, -шна́). **laughter** *n.* сме́х (-а(у)), хо́хот.
launch[1] *v.t.* броса́ть *imp.*, бро́сить *perf.*; (*ship*) спуска́ть *imp.*, спусти́ть (-ущу́, -у́стишь) *perf.* на́ воду; (*rocket*) запуска́ть *imp.*, запусти́ть (-ущу́, -у́стишь) *perf.*; (*undertake*) предпринима́ть *imp.*, предприня́ть (-ниму́, -ни́мешь; предпри́нял, -а́, -о) *perf.*; *n.* спуск на́ воду; за́пуск. **launcher** *n.* (*for rocket*) пускова́я устано́вка. **launching pad** *n.* пускова́я площа́дка.
launch[2] *n.* (*naut.*) барка́с; (*motor-l.*) мото́рный ка́тер (*pl.* -а́).
launder *v.t.* стира́ть *imp.*, вы́~ *perf.* **laund(e)rette** *n.* пра́чечная *sb.* самообслу́живания. **laundress** *n.* пра́чка. **laundry** *n.* (*place*) пра́чечная *sb.*; (*articles*) бельё.
laurel *n.* ла́вр(овое де́рево); (*ornamental plant*, *Japanese l.*) золото́е де́рево (*pl.* -е́вья, -е́вьев); *pl.* ла́вры *m.pl.*, по́чести *f.pl.*
lava *n.* ла́ва.
lavatory *n.* убо́рная *sb.*
lavender *n.* лава́нда.
lavish *adj.* ще́дрый (щедр, -а́, -о); (*abundant*) оби́льный; *v.t.* расточа́ть *imp.* (upon, + *dat.*).
law *n.* зако́н, пра́во; (*jurisprudence*) юриспруде́нция; (*rule*) пра́вило; *l. and order*, правопоря́док (-дка). **lawcourt** *n.* суд (-а́). **lawful** *adj.* зако́нный (-нен, -нна). **lawgiver** *n.* законода́тель *m.* **lawless** *adj.* беззако́нный (-нен, -нна).
lawn[1] *n.* (*fabric*) бати́ст.
lawn[2] *n.* (*grass*) газо́н; *l.-mower*, газонокоси́лка.
lawsuit *n.* проце́сс.
lawyer *n.* адвока́т, юри́ст.
lax *adj.* (*loose*) сла́бый (слаб, -а́, -о); (*careless*) небре́жный; (*not strict*) нестро́гий. **laxity** *n.* сла́бость; небре́жность; (*moral l.*) распу́щенность.
laxative *adj.* слаби́тельный; *m.* слаби́тельное *sb.*
lay[1] *n.* пе́сенка, балла́да.
lay[2] *adj.* (*non-clerical*) све́тский; (*non-professional*) непрофессиона́льный.
lay[3] *n.* (*position*) положе́ние; *v.t.* (*place*) класть (кладу́, -дёшь; клал) *imp.*, положи́ть (-жу́, -жишь) *perf.*; (*impose*) налага́ть *imp.*, наложи́ть (-жу́, -жишь) *perf.*; (*present*) излага́ть *imp.*, изложи́ть (-жу́, -жишь) *perf.*; (*trap etc.*) устра́ивать *imp.*, устро́ить *perf.*; (*crops, dust*) прибива́ть *imp.*, приби́ть (-бью́, -бьёшь) *perf.*; (*calm*) успока́ивать *imp.*, успоко́ить *perf.*; (*ghost*) изгоня́ть *imp.*, изгна́ть (изгоню́, -нишь; изгна́л, -а́, -о) *perf.*; (*meal*) накрыва́ть *imp.*, накры́ть (-ро́ю, -ро́ешь) *perf.* стол к + *dat.*; (*eggs*) класть (-адёт; -ал) *imp.*, положи́ть (-ит) *perf.*; *v.abs.* (*lay eggs*)

нести́сь (несётся; нёсся, несла́сь) *imp.*, с~ *perf.*; *l. bare, open*, раскрыва́ть *imp.*, раскры́ть (-ро́ю, -ро́ешь) *perf.*; *l. a bet, wager*, держа́ть (-жу́, -жишь) *imp.* пари́ (on, на+*acc.*); *l. claim to*, име́ть *imp.* претéнзию на+*acc.*; *l. hands on*, (*seize*) завладева́ть *imp.*, завладе́ть *perf.*+*instr.*; *l. siege to*, осажда́ть *imp.*, осади́ть *perf.*; *l. table*, накрыва́ть *imp.*, накры́ть (-ро́ю, -ро́ешь) *perf.* стол (for (*meal*), к+*dat.*); *l. waste*, опустоша́ть *imp.*, опустоши́ть *perf.*; *l. aside*, (*put a.*) откла́дывать *imp.*, отложи́ть (-жу́, -жишь) *perf*; (*save*) приберега́ть *imp.*, прибере́чь (-егу́, -ежёшь; -ёг, -егла́) *perf.*; *l. down*, (*relinquish*) отка́зываться *imp.*, отказа́ться (-ажу́сь, -а́жешься) *perf.* от+*gen.*; (*formulate*) составля́ть *imp.*, соста́вить *perf.*; (*rule etc.*) устана́вливать *imp.*, установи́ть (-влю́, -вишь) *perf.*; (*ship etc.*) закла́дывать *imp.*, заложи́ть (-жу́, -жишь) *perf.*; *l. down one's arms*, скла́дывать, слага́ть *imp.*, сложи́ть (-жу́, -жишь) *perf.* ору́жие; *l. down one's life*, положи́ть (-жу́, -жишь) *perf.* жизнь (for, за+*acc.*); *l. in* (*stock of*), запаса́ть *imp.*, запасти́ (-су́, -сёшь; -с, -сла́) *perf.*+*acc.*, +*gen.*; *l. off*, (*workmen*) вре́менно увольня́ть *imp.*, уво́лить *perf.*; *l. out*, (*spread*) выкла́дывать *imp.*, вы́ложить *perf.*; (*arrange*) разбива́ть *imp.*, разби́ть (разобью́, -ьёшь) *perf.*; (*expend*) тра́тить *imp.*, ис~, по~ *perf.*; *l. up*, запаса́ть *imp.*, запасти́ (-су́, -сёшь; -с, -сла́) *perf.*+*acc.*, +*gen.*; *be laid up*, быть прико́ванным к посте́ли, к до́му. **layabout** *n.* безде́льник.

layer *n.* слой (*pl.* -о́й), пласт (-а́, *loc.* -у́); (*hort.*) отво́док (-дка); (*hen*) несу́шка.

layman *n.* миря́нин (*pl.* -я́не, -я́н); (*non-expert*) неспециали́ст.

laze *v.i.* безде́льничать *imp.* **laziness** *n.* лень. **lazy** *adj.* лени́вый; *l.-bones*, лентя́й, ~ка.

lea *n.* луг (*loc.* -у́; *pl.* -а́).

lead[1] *n.* (*example*) приме́р; (*leadership*) руково́дство; (*position*) пе́рвое ме́сто; (*theat.*) гла́вная роль (*pl.* -ли, -ле́й); (*cards*) пе́рвый ход; (*electr.*) про́вод (*pl.* -а́); (*dog's*) поводо́к (-дка́); *v.t.* води́ть (вожу́, во́дишь) *indet.*, вести́ (веду́, -дёшь; вёл, -а́) *det.*; (*guide*) руководи́ть *imp.*+*instr.*; (*army*) кома́ндовать *imp.*, с~ *perf.*+*instr.*; (*induce*) заставля́ть *imp.*, заста́вить *perf.*; *v.t.* & *i.* (*cards*) ходи́ть (хожу́, хо́дишь) *imp.* (с+*gen.*); *v.i.* (*sport*) занима́ть *imp.*, заня́ть (займу́, -мёшь; за́нял, -а́, -о) *perf.* пе́рвое ме́сто; *l. astray*, сбива́ть *imp.*, сбить (собью́, -ьёшь) *perf.* с пути́; *l. away*, уводи́ть (-ожу́, -о́дишь) *imp.*, увести́ (-еду́, -едёшь; увёл, -а́) *perf.*; *l. on*, увлека́ть *imp.*, увле́чь (-еку́, -ечёшь; -ёк, -екла́) *perf.*; *l. to*, (*result in*) приводи́ть (-ит) *imp.*, привести́ (-едёт; -ёл, -ела́) *perf.* к+*dat*.

lead[2] *n.* (*metal*) свине́ц (-нца́); (*naut.*) лот; (*print.*) шпон(а). **leaden** *adj.* свинцо́вый.

leader *n.* руководи́тель *m.*, ~ница, ли́дер, вождь (-дя́) *m.*; (*mus.*) концертме́йстер; (*editorial*) передова́я статья́. **leadership** *n.* руково́дство; *under the l. of*, во главе́ с+*instr.*

leading *adj.* веду́щий, выдаю́щийся; *l. article*, передова́я статья́.

leaf *n.* лист (-а́; *pl.* (*plant*) -ья, -ьев & (*paper*) -ы́, -о́в); (*of door*) створка; (*of table*) опускна́я доска́ (*acc.* -ску; *pl.* -ски, -со́к, -ска́м); *l.-mould*, листово́й перегно́й; *v.i.*: *l. through*, перели́стывать *imp.*, перелиста́ть *perf.* **leaflet** *n.* листо́вка. **leafy** *adj.* покры́тый ли́стьями.

league *n.* ли́га, сою́з; (*sport*) класс.

leak *n.* течь, уте́чка; *spring a l.*, дава́ть (даёт) *imp.*, дать (даст; дал, -а́, да́ло́, -и) *perf.* течь; *v.i.* (*escape*) течь (-чёт; тёк, -ла́) *imp.*; (*allow water to l.*) пропуска́ть *imp.* во́ду; *l. out*, проса́чиваться *imp.*, просочи́ться *perf.*

lean[1] *adj.* (*thin*) худо́й (худ, -а́, -о); (*meat*) по́стный (-тен, -тна́, -тно); (*meagre*) ску́дный (-ден, -дна́, -дно).

lean[2] *v.t.* & *i.* прислоня́ть(ся) *imp.*, прислони́ть(ся) (-оню́(сь), -о́нишь(ся)) *perf.* (against, к+*dat.*); *v.i.* (*l. on, rely on*) опира́ться *imp.*, опере́ться (обопру́сь, -рёшься; опёрся, опёрла́сь) *perf.* (on, на + *acc.*); (*be inclined*) быть склóнным (-óнен, -óнна́, -óнно) (to(wards), к + *dat.*); *l. back*, откѝдываться *imp.*, откѝнуться *perf.*; *l. out of*, высóвываться *imp.*, вы́сунуться *perf.* в + *acc.* **leaning** *n.* склóнность.

leap *n.* прыжóк (-жка́), скачóк (-чка́); *v.i.* пры́гать *imp.*, пры́гнуть *perf.*; скака́ть (-ачу́, -а́чешь) *imp.*; *v.t.* (*l. over*) перепры́гивать *imp.*, перепры́гнуть *perf.*; *l.-frog*, чехарда́; *l. year*, високóсный год (*loc.* -у́; *pl.* -ы & -а́, -óв).

learn *v.t.* учи́ться (учу́сь, у́чишься) *imp.*, об ~ *perf.* + *dat.*; (*find out*) узнава́ть (-на́ю, -наёшь) *imp.*, узна́ть *perf.* **learned** *adj.* учёный. **learner** *n.* уча́щийся *sb.*, учени́к (-а́), -и́ца. **learning** *n.* (*studies*) уче́ние; (*erudition*) учёность.

lease *n.* аре́нда; *v.t.* (*of owner*) сдава́ть (сдаю́, сдаёшь) *imp.*, сдать (-ам, -ашь, -аст, -ади́м; сдал, -а́, -о) *perf.* в аре́нду; (*of tenant*) брать (беру́, -рёшь; брал, -а́, -о) *imp.*, взять (возьму́, -мёшь; взял, -а́, -о) *perf.* в аре́нду. **leaseholder** *n.* арендáтор.

leash *n.* свóра, при́вязь.

least *adj.* наиме́ньший, мале́йший; *adv.* ме́нее всегó; *at l.*, по кра́йней ме́ре; *not in the l.*, ничу́ть.

leather *n.* кóжа; *attrib.* кóжаный.

leave[1] *n.* (*permission*) разреше́ние; (*l. of absence*) óтпуск (*loc.* -е & -у́); *on l.*, в óтпуске, -ку́; *take* (*one's*) *l.*, проща́ться *imp.*, прости́ться *perf.* (of, с + *instr.*).

leave[2] *v.t.& i.* оставля́ть *imp.*, оста́вить *perf.*; (*abandon*) покида́ть *imp.*, поки́нуть *perf.*; (*go away*) уходи́ть (-ожу́, -óдишь) *imp.*, уйти́ (уйду́, -дёшь; ушёл, ушла́) *perf.* (from, от + *gen.*); уезжа́ть *imp.*, уе́хат ь (уе́ду, -дешь) *perf.* from, от + *gen.*); (*entrust*) предоставля́ть *imp.*, предоста́вить *perf.* (to, + *dat.*); *l. out*, пропуска́ть *imp.*, пропусти́ть (-ущу́, -у́стишь) *perf.*

leaven *n.* (*yeast*) дрóжжи (-же́й) *pl.*; заква́ска; *v.t.* ста́вить *imp.*, по ~ *perf.* на дрожжа́х; заква́шивать *imp.*, заква́сить *perf.*

leavings *n.* оста́тки *m.pl.*; (*food*) объе́дки (-ков) *pl.*

lecherous *adj.* распу́тный.

lectern *n.* аналóй.

lecture *n.* (*discourse*) ле́кция; (*reproof*) нота́ция; *v.i.* (*deliver l.*(*s*)) чита́ть *imp.*, про ~ *perf.* ле́кцию (-ии) (on, по + *dat.*); *v.t.* (*admonish*) чита́ть *imp.*, про ~ *perf.* нота́цию + *dat.*; *l. room*, аудитóрия. **lecturer** *n.* ле́ктор; (*univ.*) преподава́тель *m.*, ~ ница.

ledge *n.* вы́ступ; (*under water*) риф.

ledger *n.* гла́вная кни́га, гроссбу́х.

lee *n.* защи́та; *l. side*, подве́тренная сторона́ (*acc.* -ону); *l. shore*, подве́тренный бе́рег (*loc.* -у́).

leech[1] *n.* (*doctor*) ле́карь (*pl.* -ри, -ре́й) *m.*

leech[2] *n.* (*worm*) пия́вка; (*person*) вымога́тель *m.*

leek *n.* лук-поре́й.

leer *v.i.* смотре́ть (-рю́, -ришь) *imp.*, по ~ *perf.* и́скоса (at, на + *acc.*).

lees *n.* оса́док (-дка), подóнки (-ков) *pl.*

leeward *n.* подве́тренная сторона́ (*acc.* -ону); *adj.* подве́тренный.

leeway *n.* (*naut.*) дрейф.

left *n.* ле́вая сторона́ (*acc.* -ону); (*L.*; *polit.*) ле́вые *sb.*; *adj.* ле́вый; *adv.* нале́во, сле́ва (of, от + *gen.*); *l.-hander*, левша́ *m.* & *f.*

left-luggage office *n.* ка́мера хране́ния.

left-overs *n.* оста́тки *m.pl.*; (*food*) объе́дки (-ков) *pl.*

leg *n.* нога́ (*acc.* -гу; *pl.* -ги, -г, -га́м); (*furniture etc.*) нóжка; (*support*) подста́вка; (*stage of journey etc.*) эта́п; *pull someone's l.*, морóчить *imp.* гóлову + *dat.*

legacy *n.* насле́дство.

legal *adj.* (*of the law*) правовóй; (*lawful*) закóнный; *l. adviser* юрискóнсульт. **legality** *n.* закóнность. **legalize** *v.t.* узакóнивать *imp.*, узакóнить *perf.*

legate *n.* лега́т.

legatee *n.* насле́дник.

legation *n.* (дипломати́ческая) ми́ссия.

legend *n.* леге́нда. **legendary** *adj.* легенда́рный.

leggings *n.* гама́ши *f.pl.*

legible *adj.* разбóрчивый.

legion *n.* легиóн; (*great number*) мнóжество. **legionary** *n.* легионе́р.

legislate *v.i.* издавáть (-даю́, -даёшь) *imp.*, издáть (-áм, -áшь, -áст, -ади́м; издáл, -á, -о) *perf.* закóны. **legislation** *n.* законодáтельство. **legislative** *adj.* законодáтельный. **legislator** *n.* законодáтель *m.*

legitimacy *n.* закóнность; (*of child*) законнорождённость. **legitimate** *adj.* закóнный (-нен, -нна); (*child*) законнорождённый (-ён, -ённа). **legitimize** *v.t.* узакóнивать *imp.*, узакóнить *perf.*

leguminous *adj.* бобóвый, стручкóвый.

leisure *n.* досýг; *at l.*, на досýге. **leisurely** *adj.* нетороплúвый; *adv.* не спешá.

leitmotiv *n.* лейтмоти́в.

lemon *n.* лимóн; *attrib.* лимóнный. **lemonade** *n.* лимонáд.

lend *v.t.* давáть (даю́, даёшь) *imp.*, дать (дам, дашь, даст, дади́м; дал, -á, дáлó, -и) *perf.* взаймы́ (to, +*dat.*); одáлживать *imp.*, одолжи́ть *perf.* (to, +*dat.*).

length *n.* длинá, расстоя́ние; (*duration*) продолжи́тельность; (*of cloth*) отрéз; *at l.*, (*at last*) наконéц; (*in detail*) подрóбно. **lengthen** *v.t.* & *i.* удлиня́ть(ся) *imp.*, удлини́ть(ся) *perf.* **lengthways, -wise** *adv.* в длинý, вдоль. **lengthy** *adj.* дли́нный (-нен, -ннá, длúннó).

lenience, -cy *n.* снисходи́тельность. **lenient** *adj.* снисходи́тельный.

lens *n.* ли́нза; (*anat.*) хрустáлик глáза.

Lent *n.* вели́кий пост (-á, *loc.* -ý). **Lenten** *adj.* великопóстный; (*food*) пóстный (-тен, -тнá, -тно).

lentil *n.* чечеви́ца.

Leo *n.* Лев (Льва).

leonine *adj.* льви́ный.

leopard *n.* леопáрд.

leper *n.* прокажённый *sb.* **leprosy** *n.* прокáза.

lesion *n.* повреждéние; (*med.*) поражéние.

less *adj.* мéньший; *adv.* мéньше, мéнее; *prep.* без+*gen.*, за вы́четом+*gen.*

lessee *n.* арендáтор.

lessen *v.t.* & *i.* уменьшáть(ся) *imp.*, умéньши́ть(ся) *perf.*

lesser *adj.* мéньший.

lesson *n.* урóк.

lest *conj.* (*in order that not*) чтóбы не; (*that*) как бы не.

let[1] *n.* (*hindrance*) помéха.

let[2] *n.* (*lease*) сдáча в наём; *v.t.* (*allow*) позволя́ть *imp.*, позвóлить *perf.*+*dat.*; разрешáть *imp.*, разреши́ть *perf*+*dat.*; (*allow to escape*) пускáть *imp.*, пусти́ть (пущý, пýстишь) *perf.*; (*rent out*) сдавáть (сдаю́, -аёшь) *imp.*, сдать (-ам, -ашь, -аст, -ади́м; сдал, -á, -о) *perf.* внаём (to, +*dat.*); *v.aux.* (*imperative*) (*1st person*) давáй(те); (*3rd person*) пусть; (*assumption*) допýстим; *l. alone*, оставля́ть *imp.*, остáвить *perf.* в покóе; (*in imperative*) не говоря́ ужé о+*prep.*; *l. down*, (*lower*) опускáть *imp.*, опусти́ть (-ущý, -ýстишь) *perf.*; (*fail*) подводи́ть (-ожý, -óдишь) *imp.*, подвести́ (-едý, -едёшь; -ёл, -елá) *perf.*; (*disappoint*) разочарóвывать *imp.*, разочаровáть *perf.*; *l. go*, выпускáть *imp.*, вы́пустить *perf.*; *let's go*, пойдёмте! пошли́! поéхали! *l. in*(*to*), (*admit*) впускáть *imp.*, впусти́ть (-ущý, -ýстишь) *perf.* в+*acc.*; (*into secret*) посвящáть *imp.*, посвяти́ть (-ящý, -яти́шь) *perf.* в+*acc.*; *l. know*, давáть (даю́, даёшь) *imp.*, дать (дам, дашь, даст, дади́м; дал, -á, дáлó, -и) *perf.* знать+*dat.*; *l. off*, (*gun*) вы́стрелить *perf.* из+*gen.*; (*not punish*) отпускáть *imp.*, отпусти́ть (-ущý, -ýстишь) *perf.* без наказáния; *l. out*, (*release, loosen*) выпускáть *imp.*, вы́пустить *perf.*

lethal *adj.* смертонóсный.

lethargic *adj.* летарги́ческий; (*inert*) вя́лый. **lethargy** *n.* летаргия; вя́лость.

letter *n.* (*symbol*) бýква; (*print*) ли́тера; (*missive*) письмó (*pl.* -сьма, -сем, -сьмам); *pl.* (*literature*) литератýра; *pl.* (*erudition*) учёность; *to the l.*, буквáльно; *l.-box*, почтóвый я́щик.

lettuce *n.* салáт.

leukaemia *n.* лейкеми́я.

level *n.* ýровень (-вня) *m.*; (*spirit-l.*) ватерпáс; (*surveyor's*) нивели́р; (*flat country*) равни́на; *adj.* горизонтáльный, рóвный (-вен, -внá, -вно); *l. crossing*, (железнодорóжный) переéзд; *l.-headed*, уравновéшенный (-ен, -енна); *v.t.* (*make l.*) вырáвнивать *imp.*, вы́ровнять *perf.*; (*make equal*) ура́внивать *imp.*, уравня́ть *perf.*; (*raze*) ровня́ть *imp.*, с~ *perf.* с землёй; (*gun*) наводи́ть (-ожу́, -о́дишь) *imp.*, навести́ (-еду́, -едёшь; -ёл, -ела́) *perf.* (at, в, на, +*acc.*); (*criticism*) направля́ть *imp.*, напра́вить *perf.* (at, про́тив+*gen.*); (*surveying*) нивели́ровать *imp.*, *perf.*

lever *n.* рыча́г (-а́). **leverage** *n.* де́йствие рычага́; (*influence*) влия́ние.

leveret *n.* зайчо́нок (-чо́нка; *pl.* -ча́та, -ча́т).

levity *n.* легкомы́слие.

levy *n.* (*tax*) сбор; (*mil.*) набо́р; *v.t.* (*tax*) взима́ть *imp.* (from, с+*gen.*); (*mil.*) набира́ть *imp.*, набра́ть (наберу́, -рёшь; набра́л, -а́, -о) *perf.*

lewd *adj.* (*lascivious*) похотли́вый; (*indecent*) непристо́йный.

lexicographer *n.* лексико́граф. **lexicography** *n.* лексикогра́фия.

lexicon *n.* слова́рь (-ря́) *m.*

liability *n.* (*responsibility*) отве́тственность (for, за+*acc.*); (*obligation*) обяза́тельство; *pl.* (*debts*) долги́ *m.pl.*; (*susceptibility*) подве́рженность (to, +*dat.*). **liable** *adj.* отве́тственный (-ен, -енна) (for, за+*acc.*); обя́занный (-ан); подве́рженный (-ен) (to, +*dat.*).

liaison *n.* любо́вная связь; (*mil.*) связь (взаимоде́йствия); *l. officer*, офице́р свя́зи.

liar *n.* лгун (-а́), ~ья.

libation *n.* возлия́ние.

libel *n.* клевета́; *v.t.* клевета́ть (-ещу́, -е́щешь) *imp.*, на~ *perf.* на+*acc.* **libellous** *adj.* клеветни́ческий.

liberal *n.* либера́л; *adj.* либера́льный; (*generous*) ще́дрый (щедр, -а́, -о); (*abundant*) оби́льный.

liberate *v.t.* освобожда́ть *imp.*, освободи́ть *perf.* **liberation** *n.* освобожде́ние; *attrib.* освободи́тельный. **liberator** *n.* освободи́тель *m.*

libertine *n.* (*profligate*) распу́тник; (*free-thinker*) вольноду́мец (-мца).

liberty *n.* свобо́да, во́льность; *at l.*, на свобо́де.

libidinous *adj.* похотли́вый.

Libra *n.* Весы́ (-со́в) *pl.*

librarian *n.* библиоте́карь *m.* **library** *n.* библиоте́ка.

libretto *n.* либре́тто *neut.indecl.*

licence[1] *n.* (*permission, permit*) разреше́ние, пра́во (*pl.* -ва́), лице́нзия; (*liberty*) (изли́шняя) во́льность. **license, -ce**[2] *v.t.* (*allow*) разреша́ть *imp.*, разреши́ть *perf.*+*dat.*; дава́ть (даю́, даёшь) *imp.*, дать (дам, дашь, даст, дади́м; дал, -а́, да́ло́, -и) *perf.* пра́во +*dat.*

licentious *adj.* похотли́вый, распу́щенный.

lichen *n.* (*bot.*) лиша́йник; (*med.*) лиша́й (-ая́).

lick *n.* лиза́ние; *go at full l.*, нести́сь (несу́сь, -сёшься; нёсся, несла́сь) *det.*, по~ *perf.*; *v.t.* лиза́ть (лижу́, -жешь) *imp.*, лизну́ть *perf.*; (*l. all over*) обли́зывать *imp.*, облиза́ть (-ижу́, -и́жешь) *perf.*; (*thrash*) колоти́ть (-очу́, -о́тишь) *imp.*, по~ *perf.*; (*defeat*) побежда́ть *imp.*, победи́ть (-и́шь) *perf.* **lickspittle** *n.* подхали́м.

lid *n.* (*cover*) кры́шка; (*eyelid*) ве́ко (*pl.* -ки, -к).

lie[1] *n.* (*untruth*) ложь (лжи, *instr.* ло́жью); (*deceit*) обма́н; *v.i.* лгать (лгу, лжёшь; лгал, -а́, -о) *imp.*, со~ *perf.*

lie[2] *n.* (*position*) положе́ние; *l. of the land*, (*fig.*) положе́ние веще́й; *v.i.* лежа́ть (-жу́, -жи́шь) *imp.*; (*be situated*) находи́ться (-ожу́сь, -о́дишься) *imp.*; *l. down*, ложи́ться *imp.*, лечь (ля́гу, ля́жешь; лёг, -ла́) *perf.*; *l. in wait for*, подстерега́ть *imp.*, подстере́чь (-егу́, -ежёшь; -ёг, -егла́) *perf.* +*acc.*

lieu *n.*: *in l. of*, вме́сто+*gen.*

lieutenant *n.* лейтена́нт; *l.-colonel*, подполко́вник; *l.-general*, генера́л-лейтена́нт.

life *n.* жизнь; (*way of l.*) о́браз жи́зни; (*energy*) жи́вость; (*biography*) жизнеописа́ние; (*of inanimate object*) срок рабо́ты, слу́жбы; *for l.*, на всю жизнь; *from l.*, с нату́ры. **lifebelt** *n.* спаса́тельный по́яс (*pl.* -а́). **lifeboat** *n.* спаса́тельная шлю́пка. **lifebuoy** *n.* спаса́тельный буй (*pl.* буи́). **life-guard** *n.* (*bodyguard*) ли́чная охра́на. **Life-Guards** *n.* лейб-гва́рдия. **life-jacket** *n.*

спаса́тельный жиле́т. **lifeless** *adj.* безжи́зненный (-ен, -енна). **lifelike** *adj.* сло́вно живо́й (жив, -а́, -о). **lifelong** *adj.* пожи́зненный (-ен, -енна). **life-size(d)** *adj.* в натура́льную величину́. **lifetime** *n.* продолжи́тельность жи́зни.

lift *n.* подня́тие; (*machine*) лифт, подъёмная маши́на, подъёмник; (*force*) подъёмная си́ла; *give a l.*, подвози́ть (-ожу́, -о́зишь) *imp.*, подвезти́ (-езу́, -езёшь; -ёз, -езла́) *perf.*; *v.t.* & *i.* поднима́ть(ся) *imp.*, подня́ть(ся) (-ниму́(сь), -ни́мешь(ся); по́днял/ подня́лся́, -ла́(сь), -ло/-ло́сь) *perf.*; *v.t.* (*steal*) красть (краду́, -дёшь; крал) *imp.*, у~ *perf.*

ligament *n.* свя́зка.

ligature *n.* лигату́ра; (*mus.*) ли́га.

light[1] *n.* свет, освеще́ние; (*source of l.*) ого́нь (огня́) *m.*, ла́мпа, фона́рь (-ря́) *m.*; *pl.* (*traffic l.*) светофо́р; *bring to l.*, выводи́ть (-ожу́, -о́дишь) *imp.*, вы́вести (-еду, -едешь; -ел) *perf.* на чи́стую во́ду; *come to l.*, обнару́живаться *imp.*, обнару́житься *perf.*; *shed l. on*, пролива́ть *imp.*, проли́ть (-лью́, -льёшь; про́ли́л, -а́, -о) *perf.* свет на + *acc.*; *l. meter*, (*phot.*) экспоно́метр; *l.-year*, светово́й год (*pl.* го́ды, лет, года́м); *adj.* (*bright*) све́тлый (-тел, -тла́, -тло); (*pale*) бле́дный (-ден, -дна́, -дно, бле́дны́); *it is l. in the room*, в ко́мнате светло́; *v.t.* & *i.* (*ignite*) зажига́ть(ся) *imp.*, заже́чь(ся) (-жгу́(сь), -жжёшь(ся); -жёг(ся), -жгла́(сь)) *perf.*; *v.t.* (*give l. to*) освеща́ть *imp.*, освети́ть (-ещу́, -ети́шь) *perf.*; *l. up*, (*begin to smoke*) закури́ть (-рю́, -ришь) *perf.*

light[2] *adj.* (*not heavy*) лёгкий (-гок, -гка́, -гко́, лёгки́); (*unimportant*) незначи́тельный; (*nimble*) бы́стрый (быстр, -а́, -о, бы́стры́); (*cheerful*) весёлый (ве́сел, -а́, -о, ве́селы́); *l.-fingered*, на́ руку нечи́стый (-т, -та́, -то); *l.-headed*, (*frivolous*) легкомы́сленный (-ен, -енна); (*delirious*) *predic.* в бреду́; *l.-hearted*, беззабо́тный; *l. industry*, лёгкая промы́шленность; *l. infantry*, лёгкая пехо́та; *l.-minded*, легкомы́сленный (-ен, -енна).

light[3] *v.i.*: *l. upon*, неожи́данно ната́лкиваться *imp.*, натолкну́ться *perf.* на + *acc.*

lighten[1] *v.t.* & *i.* (*make lighter*) облегча́ть(ся) *imp.*, облегчи́ть(ся) *perf.*; *v.t.* (*mitigate*) смягча́ть *imp.*, смягчи́ть *perf.*

lighten[2] *v.t.* (*illuminate*) освеща́ть *imp.*, освети́ть (-ещу́, -ети́шь) *perf.*; *v.i.* (*grow bright*) светле́ть *imp.*, по~ *perf.*; (*flash*) сверка́ть *imp.*, сверкну́ть *perf.*; *it lightens*, сверка́ет мо́лния.

lighter[1] *n.* (*cigarette l. etc.*) зажига́лка.

lighter[2] *n.* (*boat*) ли́хтер.

lighthouse *n.* мая́к (-а́).

lighting *n.* освеще́ние; (*lights*) освети́тельные устано́вки *f.pl.*

lightning *n.* мо́лния; *ball l.*, шарова́я мо́лния; *summer l.*, зарни́ца; *l.-conductor*, молниеотво́д.

lights *n.* (*cul.*) лёгкое *sb.*

lightship *n.* плаву́чий мая́к (-а́).

lightweight *n.* (*sport*) легкове́с; *adj.* легкове́сный.

ligneous *adj.* деревяни́стый.

lignite *n.* лигни́т.

like[1] *adj.* (*similar*) похо́жий (на + *acc.*), подо́бный; *what is he l.?* что он за челове́к? *n.*: *and the l.*, и тому́ подо́бное, и т.п.

like[2] *v.t.* нра́виться *imp.*, по~ *perf.* *impers.* + *dat.*; люби́ть (-блю́, -бишь) *imp.*; (*wish for*) хоте́ть (хочу́, -чешь, хоти́м) *imp.*; *I should l.*, я хоте́л бы; *I would l.*, мне хо́чется; *as you l.*, как вам удо́бно. **likeable** *adj.* симпати́чный.

likelihood *n.* вероя́тность. **likely** *adj.* (*probable*) вероя́тный; (*suitable*) подходя́щий.

liken *v.t.* уподобля́ть *imp.*, уподо́бить *perf.* (to, + *dat.*).

likeness *n.* (*resemblance*) схо́дство; (*semblance*) вид; (*portrait*) портре́т.

likewise *adv.* (*similarly*) подо́бно; (*also*) то́же, та́кже.

liking *n.* вкус (for, к + *dat.*).

lilac *n.* сире́нь; *adj.* сире́невый.

lily *n.* ли́лия; *l. of the valley*, ла́ндыш.

limb *n.* член те́ла; (*of tree*) сук (-а́, *loc.* -у́; *pl.* -и́, -о́в & су́чья, -ьев).

limber[1] *n.* (*mil.*) передóк (-дкá); *v.t.* & *abs.* (*l. up*) прицеплять *imp.*, прицепи́ть (-плю́, -пишь) *perf.* (ору́дие, -ия) к передкáм.
limber[2] *adj.* (*flexible*) ги́бкий (-бок, -бкá, -бко); (*nimble*) провóрный; *v.i.*: *l. up*, разминáться *imp.*, размя́ться (разомну́сь, -нёшься) *perf.*
limbo *n.* преддвéрие áда; (*fig.*) заброшенность, забвéние.
lime[1] *n.* (*min.*) и́звесть. **limekiln** *n.* печь (*loc.* печи́; *pl.* -чи, -чéй) для óбжига известнякá. **limelight** *n.* друммóндов свет; *in the l.*, (*fig.*) в цéнтре внимáния. **limestone** *n.* известня́к (-á).
lime[2] *n.* (*fruit*) лайм.
lime[3] *n.* (*l.-tree*) ли́па.
limit *n.* грани́ца, предéл; *v.t.* ограни́чивать *imp.*, ограни́чить *perf.* **limitation** *n.* ограничéние; (*leg.*) исковáя дáвность. **limitless** *adj.* безграни́чный.
limousine *n.* лимузи́н.
limp[1] *n.* (*lameness*) хромотá; *v.i.* хромáть *imp.*
limp[2] *adj.* (*not stiff*) мя́гкий (-гок, -гкá, -гко); (*fig.*) вя́лый.
limpet *n.* морскóе блю́дечко (*pl.* -чки, -чек, -чкам).
limpid *adj.* прозрáчный.
linchpin *n.* чекá.
linden *n.* ли́па.
line[1] *n.* ли́ния, чертá; (*cord*) верёвка; (*fishing l.*) лéсá (*pl.* лёсы); (*wrinkle*) морщи́на; (*limit*) грани́ца; (*row*) ряд (-á *with 2, 3, 4, loc.* -у́; *pl.* -ы́); (*of words*) строкá (*pl.* -ки, -к, -кáм); (*of verse*) стих (-á); *v.t.* (*paper*) линовáть *imp.*, раз~ *perf.*; *v.t.* & *i.* (*l. up*) выстрáивать(ся) *imp.*, вы́строить(ся) *perf.* в ряд.
line[2] *v.t.* (*clothes*) клáсть (кладу́, -дёшь; клал) *imp.*, положи́ть (-жу́, -жишь) *perf.* на подклáдку.
lineage *n.* происхождéние (по прямóй ли́нии).
lineal *adj.* (происходя́щий) по прямóй ли́нии.
linear *adj.* линéйный.
lined[1] *adj.* линóванный; (*face*) морщи́нистый.
lined[2] *adj.* (*garment*) на подклáдке, с подклáдкой.
linen *n.* полотнó (*pl.* -тна, -тен, -тнам); *collect.* бельё; *adj.* льнянóй, полотня́ный.
liner *n.* лáйнер.
linesman *n.* (*sport*) судья́ (*pl.* -дьи, -дéй, -дьям) *m.* на ли́нии.
ling[1] *n.* (*fish*) морскáя щу́ка.
ling[2] *n.* (*heather*) вéреск.
linger *v.i.* мéдлить *imp.*; задéрживаться *imp.*, задержáться (-жу́сь, -жишься) *perf.*
lingerie *n.* дáмское бельё.
lingering *adj.* (*illness*) затяжнóй.
lingo *n.* (*special language*) жаргóн.
linguist *n.* лингви́ст, языковéд. **linguistic** *adj.* лингвисти́ческий. **linguistics** *n.* лингви́стика, языкознáние.
liniment *n.* жи́дкая мазь.
lining *n.* (*clothing etc.*) подклáдка; (*tech.*) облицóвка.
link *n.* звенó (*pl.* -нья, -ньев), связь; *v.t.* соединя́ть *imp.*, соедини́ть *perf.*; свя́зывать *imp.*, связáть (свяжу́, -жешь) *perf.*
linnet *n.* коноплянка.
linoleum *n.* линóлеум.
linotype *n.* линоти́п.
linseed *n.* льнянóе сéмя (*gen.pl.* -мя́н) *neut.*; *l. cake*, льняны́е жмыхи́ (-хóв) *pl.*; *l. oil*, льнянóе мáсло.
lint *n.* кóрпия.
lintel *n.* перемы́чка.
lion *n.* лев (льва); *l.-cub*, львёнок (-нка; *pl.* львя́та, -т). **lioness** *n.* льви́ца.
lip *n.* губá (*pl.* -бы, -б, -бáм); (*of vessel*) край (*loc.* -аю́; *pl.* -ая́); (*fig.*) дéрзость. **lipstick** *n.* губнáя помáда.
liquefaction *n.* сжижéние. **liquefy** *v.t.* & *i.* превращáть(ся) *imp.*, преврати́ть(ся) (-ащу́, -ати́т(ся)) *perf.* в жи́дкое состоя́ние.
liqueur *n.* ликёр (-а(у)).
liquid *n.* жи́дкость; *adj.* жи́дкий (-док, -дкá, -дко); (*transparent*) прозрáчный; (*ling.*) плáвный; (*econ.*) ликви́дный.
liquidate *v.t.* ликвиди́ровать *imp.*, *perf.* **liquidation** *n.* ликвидáция; *go into l.*, ликвиди́роваться *imp.*, *perf.*
liquidity *n.* жи́дкое состоя́ние.
liquor *n.* (спиртнóй) напи́ток (-тка).

liquorice *n.* (*plant*) лакри́чник, соло́дка; (*root*) лакри́ца, солодко́вый ко́рень (-рня) *m.*
lissom *adj.* (*lithe*) ги́бкий (-бок, -бка́, -бко); (*agile*) прово́рный.
list[1] *n.* (*roll*) спи́сок (-ска), пе́речень (-чня) *m.*; *v.t.* вноси́ть (-ошу́, -о́сишь) *imp.*, внести́ (внесу́, -сёшь; внёс, -ла́) *perf.* в спи́сок.
list[2] *n.* (*naut.*) крен; *v.i.* накреня́ться *imp.*, крени́ться *imp.*, на~ *perf.*
listen *v.i.* слу́шать *imp.*, по~ *perf.* (to, +*acc.*); (*heed*) прислу́шиваться *imp.*, прислу́шаться *perf.* (to, к+*dat.*); *l. in*, (*telephone*) подслу́шивать *imp.*, подслу́шать *perf.* (to, +*acc.*); (*radio*) слу́шать *imp.* ра́дио.
listless *adj.* (*languid*) то́мный (-мен, -мна́, -мно); (*indifferent*) безразли́чный.
litany *n.* лита́ния.
literacy *n.* гра́мотность.
literal *adj.* (*in letters*) бу́квенный; (*sense etc.*) буква́льный.
literary *adj.* литерату́рный.
literate *adj.* гра́мотный.
literature *n.* литерату́ра.
lithe *adj.* ги́бкий (-бок, -бка́, -бко).
lithograph *n.* литогра́фия; *v.t.* литографи́ровать *imp.*, *perf.* **lithographer** *n.* лито́граф. **lithographic** *adj.* литогра́фский. **lithography** *n.* литогра́фия.
litigant *n.* сторона́ (*acc.* -ону; *pl.* -оны, -о́н, -она́м); *adj.* тя́жущийся. **litigate** *v.i.* суди́ться (сужу́сь, су́дишься) *imp.* **litigation** *n.* тя́жба. **litigious** *adj.* сутя́жнический.
litmus *n.* ла́кмус; *l. paper*, ла́кмусовая бума́га.
litre *n.* литр.
litter *n.* (*vehicle, stretcher*) носи́лки (-лок) *pl.*; (*bedding*) подсти́лка; (*disorder*) беспоря́док (-дка); (*rubbish*) сор (-а(у)); (*brood*) помёт; *v.t.* (*make untidy*) сори́ть *imp.*, на~ *perf.* (with, +*instr.*); (*scatter*) разбра́сывать *imp.*, разброса́ть *perf.*
little *n.* немно́гое; *l. by l.*, ма́ло-пома́лу; *a l.*, немно́го+*gen.*; *not a l.*, нема́ло+*gen.*; *adj.* ма́ленький, небольшо́й; (*in height*) небольшо́го ро́ста; (*in distance, time*) коро́ткий (ко́ро́ток, коротка́, ко́ро́тко́); (*unimportant*) незначи́тельный; *adv.* ма́ло, немно́го; (*not at all*) совсе́м не.
littoral *n.* побере́жье; *adj.* прибре́жный.
liturgical *adj.* литурги́ческий. **liturgy** *n.* литурги́я.
live[1] *adj.* живо́й (жив, -а́, -о); (*coals*) горя́щий; (*mil.*) боево́й; (*electr.*) под напряже́нием; (*active*) де́ятельный; (*real*) жи́зненный (-ен, -енна).
live[2] *v.i.* жить (живу́, -вёшь; жил, -а́, -о) *imp.*; существова́ть *imp.*; *l. down*, загла́живать *imp.*, загла́дить *perf.*; *l. on*, (*feed on*) пита́ться *imp.*+*instr.*; *l. through*, пережива́ть *imp.*, пережи́ть (-иву́, -ивёшь; пе́режи́л, -а́, -о) *perf.*; *l. until, to see*, дожива́ть *imp.*, дожи́ть (-иву́, -ивёшь; до́жил, -а́, -о) *perf.* до+*gen.*; *l. up to*, жить (живу́, -вёшь; жил, -а́, -о) *imp.* согла́сно+*dat.*
livelihood *n.* сре́дства *neut.pl.* к существова́нию.
lively *adj.* живо́й (жив, -а́, -о), весёлый (ве́сел, -а́, -о, ве́селы́).
liven (up) *v.t.* & *i.* оживля́ть(ся) *imp.*, оживи́ть(ся) *perf.*
liver *n.* пе́чень; (*cul.*) печёнка.
livery *n.* ливре́я.
livestock *n.* скот (-а́), живо́й инвента́рь (-ря́) *m.*
livid *adj.* (*colour*) синева́то-се́рый; *predic.* (*angry*) зол (зла).
living *n.* сре́дства *neut.pl.* к существова́нию; (*eccl.*) бенефи́ция; *earn a l.*, зараба́тывать *imp.*, зарабо́тать *perf.* на жизнь; *adj.* живо́й (жив, -а́, -о), живу́щий; (*of likeness*) то́чный; *l. image*, ко́пия; *l.-room*, гости́ная *sb.*
lizard *n.* я́щерица.
lo *interj.* вот! се!
loach *n.* голе́ц (-льца́).
load *n.* груз; (*also fig.*) бре́мя *neut.*; (*tech.*) нагру́зка; *pl.* (*lots*) ку́ча; *v.t.* нагружа́ть *imp.*, грузи́ть (-ужу́, -у́зи́шь) *imp.*, на~ *perf.*; (*fig.*) обременя́ть *imp.*, обремени́ть *perf.*; (*gun, camera*) заряжа́ть *imp.*, заряди́ть (-яжу́, -я́ди́шь) *perf.*
loadstar *see* **lodestar.**
loadstone, lode- *n.* магни́тный железня́к (-а́); (*magnet*) магни́т.
loaf[1] *n.* хлеб, бу́лка.

loaf[2] *v.i.* бездéльничать *imp.*; шатáться *imp.* **loafer** *n.* бездéльник.

loam *n.* суглúнок (-нка).

loan *n.* заём (зáйма); *v.t.* давáть (даю́, даёшь) *imp.*, дать (дам, дашь, даст, дадúм; дал, -á, дáлó, -и) *perf.* взаймы́.

loath, loth *predic.*: *be l. to*, не хотéть (хочу́, -чешь; хотúм) *imp.*+*inf.*

loathe *v.t.* питáть *imp.* отвращéние к+*dat.* **loathing** *n.* отвращéние. **loathsome** *adj.* отвратúтельный.

lob *n.* (*sport*) свечá (*pl.* -чи, -чéй).

lobar *adj.* долевóй.

lobby *n.* прихóжая *sb.*, вестибю́ль *m.*; (*parl.*) кулуáры (-ров) *pl.*

lobe *n.* дóля (*pl.* -ли, -лéй); (*of ear*) мóчка.

lobster *n.* омáр; *l.-pot*, вéрша для омáров.

local *adj.* мéстный; (*train*) прúгородный.

locality *n.* (*site*) местоположéние; (*district*) мéстность.

localize *v.t.* (*restrict*) локализовáть *imp., perf.*

locate *v.t.* (*place*) помещáть *imp.*, поместúть *perf.*; (*discover*) обнару́живать *imp.*, обнару́жить *perf.*; *be located*, находúться (-ится) *imp.*

location *n.* (*position*) местонахождéние; определéние мéста; *on l.*, (*cin.*) на нату́ре.

locative *adj.* (*n.*) мéстный (падéж (-á)).

loch, lough *n.* (*lake*) óзеро (*pl.* -ёра); (*sea l.*) (у́зкий) залúв.

lock[1] *n.* (*of hair*) лóкон; *pl.* вóлосы (волóс, -áм) *pl.*

lock[2] *n.* замóк (-мкá), запóр; (*tech.*) стóпор; (*canal*) шлюз; *l.-keeper*, начáльник шлю́за; *v.t.* запирáть *imp.*, заперéть (-пру́, -прёшь; зáпер, -лá, -ло) *perf.*; *v.i.* запирáться *imp.*, заперéться (-прётся; зáперся́, -рлáсь, зáперлóсь) *perf.*; *l.-out*, локáут; *l.-up*, (*cell*) арестáнтская *sb.*

locker *n.* шкáфчик.

locket *n.* медальóн.

lockjaw *n.* столбня́к (-á).

locksmith *n.* слéсарь (*pl.* -ри & -ря́) *m.*

locomotion *n.* передвижéние. **locomotive** *adj.* двúжущий(ся); *n.* (*rly.*) локомотúв.

locum (tenens) *n.* врéменный заместúтель *m.*

locust *n.* саранчá (*also collect.*; *fig.*).

locution *n.* оборóт рéчи.

lode *n.* ру́дная жúла. **lodestar, load-** *n.* Поля́рная звездá; (*fig.*) путевóдная звездá (*pl.* звёзды). **lodestone** *see* **loadstone.**

lodge *n.* (*hunting*) (охóтничий) дóмик; (*porter's*) швейцáрская *sb.*, сторóжка; (*Masonic*) лóжа; *v.t.* (*accommodate*) помещáть *imp.*, поместúть *perf.*; (*deposit*) давáть (даю́, даёшь) *imp.*, дать (дам, дашь, даст, дадúм; дал, -á, дáлó, -и) *perf.* на хранéние (with, +*dat.*); (*complaint*) подавáть (-даю́, -даёшь) *imp.*, подáть (-áм, -áшь, -áст, -адúм; пóдал, -á, -о) *perf.*; *v.i.* (*reside*) жить (живу́, -вёшь; жил, -á, -о) *imp.* (with, у+*gen.*); (*stick*) засáживать *imp.*, засéсть (-ся́дет; -сéл) *perf.* **lodger** *n.* жилéц (-льцá), жилúца. **lodging** *n.* (*also pl.*) квартúра, (снимáемая) кóмната.

loft *n.* (*attic*) чердáк (-á); (*for hay*) сеновáл; (*for pigeons*) голубя́тня (*gen.pl.* -тен); (*gallery*) галерéя.

lofty *adj.* óчень высóкий (-óк, -окá, -óкó); (*elevated*) возвы́шенный.

log *n.* бревнó (*pl.* брёвна, -вен, -внам); (*for fire*) полéно (*pl.* -нья, -ньев); (*naut.*) лаг; *l.-book*, (*naut.*) вáхтенный журнáл; (*aeron.*) бортовóй журнáл; (*registration book*) формуля́р.

logarithm *n.* логарúфм. **logarithmic** *adj.* логарифмúческий.

loggerhead *n.*: *be at l.s*, ссóриться *imp.*, по~ *perf.* (with, с+*instr.*).

logic *n.* лóгика. **logical** *adj.* (*of logic*) логúческий; (*consistent*) логúчный. **logician** *n.* лóгик.

logistics *n.* материáльно-техни́ческое обеспéчение.

loin *n.* (*pl.*) пояснúца; (*cul.*) филéйная часть.

loiter *v.i.* слоня́ться *imp.*

lone, lonely *adj.* одинóкий, уединённый (-ён, -ённа). **loneliness** *n.* одинóчество, уединённость.

long[1] *v.i.* стра́стно жела́ть *imp.*, по~ *perf.* (for, + *gen.*); тоскова́ть *imp.* (for, по + *dat.*).

long[2] *adj.* (*space*) дли́нный (-нен, -нна́, дли́нно́); (*time*) до́лгий (-лог, -лга́, -лго); (*protracted*) дли́тельный; (*in measurements*) длино́й в + *acc.*; *in the l. run*, в коне́чном счёте; *l.-boat*, барка́с; *l.-lived*, долгове́чный; *l.-sighted*, дальнозо́ркий (-рок, -рка); (*fig.*) дальнови́дный; *l.-suffering*, долготерпе́ние; долготерпели́вый; *l.-term*, долгосро́чный; *l.-winded*, многоречи́вый; *adv.* до́лго; *l. after*, спустя́ мно́го вре́мени; *l. ago*, (уже́) давно́; *as l. as*, пока́; *l. before*, задо́лго до + *gen.*

longevity *n.* долгове́чность.

longing *n.* стра́стное жела́ние (for, + *gen.*); тоска́ (for, по + *dat.*).

longitude *n.* долгота́ (*pl.* -ты).

longways *adv.* в длину́.

look *n.* (*glance*) взгляд; (*appearance*) вид; (*expression*) выраже́ние; *v.i.* смотре́ть (-рю́, -ришь) *imp.*, по~ *perf.* (at, на, в, + *acc.*); гляде́ть (-яжу́, -яди́шь) *imp.*, по~ *perf.* (at, на + *acc.*); (*appear*) вы́глядеть (-яжу, -ядишь) *imp.* + *instr.*; (*face*) выходи́ть (-ит) *imp.* (towards, onto, на + *acc.*); *l. about*, осма́триваться *imp.*, осмотре́ться (-рю́сь, -ришься) *perf.*; *l. after*, (*attend to*) присма́тривать *imp.*, присмотре́ть (-рю́, -ришь) *perf.* за + *instr.*; *l. down on*, презира́ть *imp.*; *l. for*, иска́ть (ищу́, и́щешь) *imp.* + *acc.*, + *gen.*; *l. forward to*, предвкуша́ть *imp.*, предвкуси́ть (-ушу́, -у́сишь) *perf.*; *l. in on*, загля́дывать *imp.*, загляну́ть (-ну́, -нешь) *perf.* к + *dat.*; *l. into*, (*investigate*) разбира́ться *imp.*, разобра́ться (разберу́сь, -рёшься; -а́лся, -ала́сь, -а́ло́сь) *perf.* в + *prep.*; *l. like*, быть похо́жим на + *acc.*; *it looks like rain*, похо́же на (то, что бу́дет) дождь; *l. on*, (*regard*) счита́ть *imp.*, счесть (сочту́, -тёшь; счёл, сочла́) *perf.* (as, + *instr.*, за + *instr.*); *l. out*, выгля́дывать *imp.*, вы́глянуть *perf.* (в окно́); быть настороже́; *imper.* осторо́жно! береги́(те)сь!; *l. over*, *through*, просма́тривать *imp.*, просмотре́ть (-рю́, -ришь) *perf.*; *l. up*, (*raise eyes*) поднима́ть *imp.*, подня́ть (подниму́, -мешь; по́дня́л, -а́, -о) *perf.* глаза́; (*in dictionary etc.*) иска́ть (ищу́, и́щешь) *imp.*; (*improve*) улучша́ться *imp.*, улу́чшиться *perf.*; *l. up to*, уважа́ть *imp.* **looker-on** *n.* зри́тель *m.*, ~ница. **looking-glass** *n.* зе́ркало (*pl.* -ла́).

loom[1] *n.* тка́цкий стано́к (-нка́).

loom[2] *v.i.* нея́сно вырисо́вываться *imp.*, вы́рисоваться *perf.*; (*fig.*) гото́виться *imp.*

loop *n.* пе́тля (*gen.pl.* -тель); *v.i.* образо́вывать *imp.*, образова́ть *perf.* пе́тлю; *l. the l.*, (*aeron.*) де́лать *imp.*, с~ *perf.* мёртвую пе́тлю.

loophole *n.* бойни́ца; (*fig.*) лазе́йка.

loose *adj.* (*free*) свобо́дный; (*not fixed*) неприкреплённый; (*inexact*) нето́чный (-чен, -чна́, -чно); (*not compact*) ры́хлый (рыхл, -а́, -о); (*lax*) распу́щенный (-ен, -енна); *be at a l. end*, безде́льничать *imp.*; *v.t.* (*free*) освобожда́ть *imp.*, освободи́ть *perf.*; (*untie*) отвя́зывать *imp.*, отвяза́ть (-яжу́, -я́жешь) *perf.* **loosen** *v.t.* & *i.* ослабля́ть(ся) *imp.*, осла́бить(ся) *perf.*

loot *n.* добы́ча; *v.t.* гра́бить *imp.*, о~ *perf.*

lop[1] *v.t.* (*tree*) подреза́ть *imp.*, подре́зать (-е́жу, -е́жешь) *perf.*; (*l. off*) отруба́ть *imp.*, отруби́ть (-блю́, -бишь) *perf.*

lop[2] *v.i.* (*hang*) свиса́ть *imp.*, сви́снуть (-с) *perf.*

lope *v.i.* бе́гать *indet.*, бежа́ть (бегу́, бежи́шь) *det.* вприпры́жку.

lopsided *adj.* кривобо́кий.

loquacious *adj.* болтли́вый. **loquacity** *n.* болтли́вость.

lord *n.* (*master*) господи́н (*pl.* -да́, -д, -да́м), влады́ка *m.*; (*the L.*; *eccl.*) Госпо́дь (-ода, *voc.* -оди); (*peer*; *title*) лорд; *v.t.*: *l. it over*, помыка́ть *imp.* + *instr.* **lordly** *adj.* (*haughty*) высокоме́рный. **lordship** *n.* власть (over, над + *instr.*); (*title*) све́тлость.

lore *n.* зна́ния *neut.pl.*

lorgnette *n.* лорне́т.

lorry *n.* грузови́к (-а́).

lose *v.t.* терять *imp.*, по~ *perf.*; (*forfeit*) лишаться *imp.*, лишиться *perf.* + *gen.*; (*game etc.*) проигрывать *imp.*, проиграть *perf.*; *v.i.* (*suffer loss*) терпеть (-плю, -пишь) *imp.*, по~ *perf.* ущерб (by, от + *gen.*); (*clock*) отставать (-таёт) *imp.*, отстать (-анет) *perf.* **loss** *n.* потеря, ущерб; (*in game*) проигрыш; *at a l.*, (*puzzled*) в затруднении.

lot *n.* жребий; (*destiny*) участь; (*of goods*) партия; *a l., lots*, много, масса; *the l.*, всё (всего), все (всех) *pl.*

loth *see* **loath.**

lotion *n.* примочка.

lottery *n.* лотерея.

lotto *n.* лото *neut.indecl.*

lotus *n.* лотос.

loud *adj.* (*sound*) громкий (-мок, -мка, -мко); (*noisy*) шумный (-мен, -мна, -мно); (*colour*) кричащий; *out l.*, вслух. **loudspeaker** *n.* громкоговоритель *m.*

lough *see* **loch.**

lounge *n.* фойе *neut.indecl.*; (*sitting-room*) гостиная *sb.*; *v.i.* сидеть (сижу, сидишь) *imp.* развалясь; (*idle*) бездельничать *imp.*

lour, lower[2] *v.i.* (*person, sky*) хмуриться *imp.*, на~ *perf.*

louse *n.* вошь (вши, *instr.* вошью). **lousy** *adj.* вшивый; (*coll.*) паршивый.

lout *n.* увалень (-льня) *m.*, грубиян. **loutish** *adj.* неотёсанный (-ан, -анна).

lovable *adj.* милый (мил, -а, -о, милы). **love** *n.* любовь (-бви, *instr.* -бовью) (of, for, к + *dat.*); (*sweetheart*) возлюбленный *sb.*; *in l. with*, влюблённый (-ён, -ена) в + *acc.*; *v.t.* любить (-блю, -бишь) *imp.* **lovely** *adj.* красивый; (*delightful*) прелестный. **lover** *n.* любовник, -ица.

low[1] *n.* (*of cow*) мычание; *v.i.* мычать (-чу, -чишь) *imp.*

low[2] *adj.* низкий (-зок, -зка, -зко), невысокий (-ок, -ока, -око); (*quiet*) тихий (тих, -а, -о); (*coarse*) грубый (груб, -а, -о); (*weak*) слабый (слаб, -а, -о).

lower[1] *v.t.* опускать *imp.*, опустить (-ущу, -устишь) *perf.*; снижать *imp.*, снизить *perf.*

lower[2] *see* **lour.**

lower[3] *adj.* низший, нижний.

lowland *n.* низменность.

lowly *adj.* скромный (-мен, -мна, -мно).

loyal *adj.* верный (-рен, -рна, -рно, верны), лояльный. **loyalty** *n.* верность, лояльность.

lozenge *n.* (*shape*) ромб; (*tablet*) лепёшка.

lubber *n.* увалень (-льня) *m.*

lubricant *n.* смазка, смазочный материал. **lubricate** *v.t.* смазывать *imp.*, смазать (-ажу, -ажешь) *perf.* **lubrication** *n.* смазка.

lubricity *n.* скользкость; (*lewdness*) похотливость.

lucerne *n.* люцерна.

lucid *adj.* ясный (ясен, ясна, ясно, ясны).

luck *n.* (*chance*) случай; (*good l.*) счастье, удача; (*bad l.*) неудача. **luckily** *adv.* к счастью. **luckless** *adj.* несчастный. **lucky** *adj.* счастливый (счастлив); (*successful*) удачный.

lucrative *adj.* прибыльный.

lucre *n.* прибыль.

ludicrous *adj.* смехотворный.

lug[1] *v.t.* (*drag*) таскать *indet.*, тащить (-щу, -щишь) *det.*

lug[2] *n.* (*ear*) ухо (*pl.* уши, ушей); (*tech.*) ушко (*pl.* -ки, -ков), выступ, прилив.

luggage *n.* багаж (-а).

lugubrious *adj.* печальный.

lukewarm *adj.* тепловатый; (*fig.*) равнодушный.

lull *n.* (*in storm*) затишье; (*interval*) перерыв; *v.t.* (*to sleep*) убаюкивать *imp.*, убаюкать *perf.*; (*suspicions*) усыплять *imp.*, усыпить *perf.*; *v.i.* затихать *imp.*, затихнуть (-х) *perf.*

lullaby *n.* колыбельная песня (*gen.pl.* -сен).

lumbago *n.* люмбаго *neut.indecl.*

lumbar *adj.* поясничный.

lumber[1] *v.i.* (*move*) двигаться (-аюсь, -аешься & движусь, -жешься) *imp.*, двинуться *perf.* тяжело, шумно, неуклюже.

lumber[2] *n.* (*domestic*) рухлядь; (*timber*) лесоматериалы *m.pl.*; *l.-room*, чулан;

v.t. загромождáть *imp.*, загромоздить *perf.* **lumberjack** *n.* лесорýб.
luminary *n.* светило.
luminous *adj.* светящийся.
lump *n.* ком (*pl.* -ья, -ьев), кусóк (-скá); (*swelling*) óпухоль; (*lot*) кýча; *v.t.*: *l. together*, смéшивать *imp.*, смешáть *perf.* (в кýчу).
lunacy *n.* безýмие.
lunar *adj.* лýнный.
lunatic *adj.* (*n.*) сумасшéдший (*sb.*); безýмный (*sb.*).
lunch *n.* обéд, вторóй зáвтрак; *l.-hour*, *-time*, обéденный перерыв; *v.i.* обéдать *imp.*, по~ *perf.*
lung *n.* лёгкое *sb.*
lunge *n.* (*sport*) вы́пад; толчóк (-чкá); *v.i.* (*fencing*) дéлать *imp.*, с~ *perf.* вы́пад; наносить (-ошý, -óсишь) *imp.*, нанести (-есý, -есёшь; -ёс, -еслá) *perf.* удáр (с плечá) (at + *dat.*).
lupin(e) *n.* люпин.
lupine *adj.* вóлчий (-чья, -чье).
lupus *n.* волчáнка.
lurch[1] *n.*: *leave in the l.*, покидáть *imp.*, покинуть *perf.* в бедé.
lurch[2] *v.i.* (*stagger*) ходить (хожý, хóдишь) *indet.*, идти (идý, идёшь; шёл, шла) *det.* шатáясь.
lure *n.* примáнка; *v.t.* примáнивать *imp.*, приманить (-ню́, -нишь) *perf.*
lurid *adj.* мрáчный (-чен, -чнá, -чно); (*sensational*) сенсациóнный.
lurk *v.i.* прятаться (-ячусь, -ячешься) *imp.*, с~ *perf.*; (*fig.*) таиться *imp.*
luscious *adj.* прíторный.
lush *adj.* сóчный (-чен, -чнá, -чно).
lust *n.* пóхоть, вожделéние (of, for, к + *dat.*); *v.i.* стрáстно желáть *imp.*, по~ *perf.* (for, + *gen.*). **lustful** *adj.* похотливый.
lustre *n.* (*gloss*) глянец (-нца); (*splendour*) блеск; (*chandelier*) лю́стра. **lustrous** *adj.* глянцевитый, блестящий.
lusty *adj.* (*healthy*) здорóвый; (*lively*) живóй (жив, -á, -о).
lute[1] *n.* (*mus.*) лю́тня (*gen.pl.* -тен).
lute[2] *n.* (*clay etc.*) замáзка.
luxuriant *adj.* пы́шный (-шен, -шнá, -шно).
luxuriate *v.i.* наслаждáться *imp.*, насладиться *perf.* (in, + *instr.*).
luxurious *adj.* роскóшный. **luxury** *n.* рóскошь.
lye *n.* щёлок (-а(у)).
lymph *n.* лимфа. **lymphatic** *adj.* лимфатический.
lynch *v.t.* линчевáть (-чýю, -чýешь) *imp.*, *perf.*; *l. law*, суд (-á) Линча.
lynx *n.* рысь.
lyre *n.* лира.
lyric *n.* лирика; *pl.* словá *neut.pl.* пéсни. **lyrical** *adj.* лирический. **lyricism** *n.* лиризм.

M

macabre *adj.* жýткий (-ток, -ткá, -тко).
macadam *n.* щéбень (-бня) *m.* **macadamize** *v.t.* мостить *imp.*, вы~, за~ *perf.* щéбнем.
macaroni *n.* макарóны (-н) *pl.*
macaroon *n.* миндáльное печéнье.
macaw *n.* макáо *m.indecl.*
mace *n.* (*weapon*) булавá; (*staff of office*) жезл; *m.-bearer*, жезлонóсец (-сца).
Mach (number) *n.* числó М(áха).
machete *n.* мачéте *neut.indecl.*
machination *n.* махинáция, интрига, кóзни (-ней) *pl.*
machine *n.* машина, станóк (-нкá); (*state m.*) аппарáт; *attrib.* машинный; *m.-gun*, пулемёт; *m.-made*, машинного произвóдства, машинной вырaбoтки; *m. tool*, станóк (-нкá); *v.t.* обрабáтывать *imp.*, обрабóтать *perf.*

на станке́; (*sew*) шить (шью, шьёшь) *imp.*, с ~ *perf.* (на маши́не). **machinery** *n.* (*machines*) маши́ны *f.pl.*; (*mechanism*) механи́зм; (*of state*) аппара́т. **machinist** *n.* машини́ст; (*sewing*) шве́йник, -ица, швея́.

mackerel *n.* ску́мбрия, макре́ль; *m. sky*, не́бо бара́шками.

mackintosh *n.* (*material*) прорези́ненная мате́рия; (*coat*) непромока́емое пальто́ *neut.indecl.*

macrocephalic *adj.* макроцефали́ческий. **macrocosm** *n.* макроко́см, вселе́нная *sb.*

mad *adj.*, сумасше́дший, поме́шанный (-ан, -анна); (*animal*) бе́шеный; (*fig.*) безу́мный. **madcap** *n.* сорване́ц (-нца́). **madden** *v.t.* своди́ть (-ожу́, -о́дишь) *imp.*, свести́ (сведу́, -дёшь; свёл, -а́) *perf.* с ума́; (*irritate*) выводи́ть (-ожу́, -о́дишь) *imp.*, вы́вести (-еду, -едешь; -ел) *perf.* из себя́. **madhouse** *n.* сумасше́дший дом (-а(у); *pl.* -а́). **madly** *adv.* безу́мно. **madman** *n.* сумасше́дший *sb.*, безу́мец (-мца). **madness** *n.* сумасше́ствие, безу́мие. **madwoman** *n.* сумасше́дшая *sb.*, безу́мная *sb.*

made *see* **make.**

madder *n.* (*plant*) маре́на; (*dye*) крапп.

madrigal *n.* мадрига́л.

maestro *n.* маэ́стро *m.indecl.*

mafia *n.* ма́фия.

magazine *n.* журна́л; (*mil.*) скла́д боеприпа́сов, вещево́й склад; (*of gun*) магази́н.

maggot *n.* личи́нка. **maggoty** *adj.* черви́вый.

magic *n.* ма́гия, волшебство́, колдовство́; *adj.* волше́бный, маги́ческий. **magician** *n.* волше́бник, колду́н (-а́); (*conjurer*) фо́кусник.

magisterial *adj.* авторите́тный.

magistracy *n.* магистрату́ра. **magistrate** *n.* полице́йский судья́ (*pl.* -дьи, -де́й, -дьям) *m.*

magma *n.* ма́гма.

magnanimous *adj.* великоду́шный.

magnate *n.* магна́т.

magnesia *n.* о́кись ма́гния. **magnesium** *n.* ма́гний.

magnet *n.* магни́т. **magnetic** *adj.* магни́тный; (*attractive*) притяга́тельный. **magnetism** *n.* магнети́зм; притяга́тельность. **magnetize** *v.t.* намагни́чивать *imp.*, намагни́тить *perf.* **magneto** *n.* магне́то *neut.indecl.*

magnification *n.* увеличе́ние.

magnificence *n.* великоле́пие, пы́шность. **magnificent** *adj.* великоле́пный, пы́шный (-шен, -шна́, -шно).

magnify *v.t.* увели́чивать *imp.*, увели́чить *perf.*; (*exaggerate*) преувели́чивать *imp.*, преувели́чить *perf.*

magnitude *n.* величина́.

magnolia *n.* магно́лия.

magpie *n.* соро́ка.

maharajah *n.* магара́джа *m.* **maharanee** *n.* магара́ни *f.indecl.*

mahogany *n.* кра́сное де́рево.

maid *n.* служа́нка, го́рничная *sb.*; *m. of honour*, фре́йлина. **maiden** *adj.* незаму́жняя, де́вичий; (*first*) пе́рвый; *m. name*, деви́чья фами́лия.

mail[1] *n.* (*letters etc.*) по́чта; (*train*) почто́вый по́езд (*pl.* -а́); *m. order*, почто́вый зака́з, зака́з по по́чте; *v.t.* посыла́ть *imp.*, посла́ть (пошлю́, -лёшь) *perf.* по по́чте.

mail[2] *n.* (*armour*) кольчу́га; броня́; *mailed fist*, вое́нная, физи́ческая, си́ла.

maim *v.t.* кале́чить *imp.*, ис ~ *perf.*; уве́чить *imp.*

main *n.* (*sea*) откры́тое мо́ре; (*gas m.*; *pl.*) магистра́ль; *in the m.*, в основно́м; гла́вным о́бразом; *with might and m.*, не щадя́ сил; *adj.* основно́й, гла́вный; (*road*) магистра́льный; *by m. force*, изо всех сил; *the m. chance*, путь (-ти́, -тём) *m.* к нажи́ве; *m. line*, (*rly.*) магистра́ль. **mainland** *n.* матери́к (-а́); *attrib.* материко́вый. **mainly** *adv.* в основно́м; гла́вным о́бразом; (*for most part*) бо́льшей ча́стью. **mainmast** *n.* грот-ма́чта. **mainsail** *n.* грот. **mainspring** *n.* ходова́я пружи́на. **mainstay** *n.* гро́та-штаг; (*fig.*) гла́вная опо́ра.

maintain *v.t.* (*continue*) продолжа́ть *imp.*, продо́лжить *perf.*; (*support*) подде́рживать *imp.*, поддержа́ть (-жу́, -жишь) *perf.*; (*family*) содержа́ть (-жу́, -жишь) *imp.*; (*machine*) обслу́живать *imp.*, обслужи́ть (-жу́,

-жишь) *perf.*; (*assert*) утверждать *imp.* **maintenance** *n.* поддержка; содержание; обслуживание, уход.

maize *n.* кукуруза.

majestic *adj.* величественный (-ен, -енна). **majesty** *n.* величественность; (*title*) величество.

majolica *n.* майолика.

major[1] *n.* (*mil.*) майор; *m.-general*, генерал-майор.

major[2] *adj.* (*greater*) бóльший; (*more important*) более важный; (*main*) главный; (*mus.*) мажорный; (*senior*) старший; *n.* совершеннолетний *sb.*; (*mus.*) мажор. **majority** *n.* (*greater number*) большинство; (*rank*) чин майора; (*full age*) совершеннолетие.

make *v.t.* делать *imp.*, с~ *perf.*; (*create*) создавать (-даю, -даёшь) *imp.*, создать (-ам, -ашь, -аст, -адим; создал, -а, -о) *perf.*; (*produce*) производить (-ожу, -одишь) *imp.*, произвести (-еду, -едёшь; -ёл, -ела) *perf.*; (*compose*) составлять *imp.*, составить *perf.*; (*prepare*) готовить *imp.*, при~ *perf.*; (*amount to*) равняться *imp.* + *dat.*; (*become*) становиться (-влюсь, -вишься) *imp.*, стать (стану, -нешь) *perf.* + *instr.*; (*earn*) зарабатывать *imp.*, заработать *perf.*; (*compel*) заставлять *imp.*, заставить *perf.*; *made in the USSR*, изготовлено в СССР; *be made of*, состоять (-ою, -оишь) *imp.* из + *gen.*; *m. as if, though*, делать *imp.*, с~ *perf.* вид, что; *m. a bed*, стелить (стелю, -лешь) *imp.*, по~ *perf.* постель; *m. believe*, притворяться *imp.*, притвориться *perf.*; *m.-believe*, притворство; притворный; *m. do with*, довольствоваться *imp.*, у~ *perf.* + *instr.*; *m. fun of*, высмеивать *imp.*, высмеять (-ею, -еешь) *perf.*; *m. oneself at home*, быть как дома; *m. oneself scarce*, исчезать *imp.*, исчезнуть (-з) *perf.*; *m. sure of*, удостоверяться *imp.*, удостовериться *perf.* в + *prep.*; *m. way for*, уступать *imp.*, уступить (-плю, -пишь) *perf.* дорогу + *dat.*; *m. away with*, покончить *perf.* с + *instr.*; *m. off*, удирать *imp.*, удрать (удеру, -рёшь; удрал, -а, -о) *perf.*; *m. out*, (*document*) составлять *imp.*, составить *perf.*; (*cheque*) выписывать *imp.*, выписать (-ишу, -ишешь) *perf.*; (*understand*) разбирать *imp.*, разобрать (разберу, -рёшь; разобрал, -а, -о) *perf.*; *m. over*, передавать (-даю, -даёшь) *imp.*, передать (-ам, -ашь, -аст, -адим; передал, -а, -о) *perf.*; *m. up*, (*compound*) составлять *imp.*, составить *perf.*; (*theat.*) гримировать(ся) *imp.*, на(за)~ *perf.*; *m.-up*, (*theat.*) грим; (*cosmetics*) косметика; (*composition*) состав; *m. it up*, мириться *imp.*, по~ *perf.* (with, с + *instr.*); *m. up for*, возмещать *imp.*, возместить *perf.*; *m. up one's mind*, решаться *imp.*, решиться *perf.*; *m. up to*, заискивать *imp.* перед + *instr.* **make** *n.* марка, тип, сорт (*pl.* -а). **makeshift** *adj.* временный. **makeweight** *n.* довесок (-ска).

malachite *n.* малахит.

maladjusted *adj.* плохо приспособленный (-ен).

maladministration *n.* плохое управление.

maladroit *adj.* неловкий (-овок, -овка, -овко); (*tactless*) бестактный.

malady *n.* болезнь.

malaria *n.* малярия.

malcontent *n.* недовольный *sb.*

male *n.* (*animal*) самец (-мца); (*person*) мужчина *m.*; *adj.* мужской.

malevolence *n.* недоброжелательность. **malevolent** *adj.* недоброжелательный.

malformation *n.* неправильное образование.

malice *n.* злоба; (*leg.*) злой умысел (-сла); *with m. aforethought*, со злым умыслом. **malicious** *adj.* злобный.

malign *adj.* пагубный; *v.t.* клеветать (-ещу, -ещешь) *imp.*, на~ *perf.* на + *acc.* **malignant** *adj.* (*harmful*) зловредный; (*malicious*) злобный; (*med.*) злокачественный.

malinger *v.i.* притворяться *imp.*, притвориться *perf.* больным. **malingerer** *n.* симулянт.

mallard *n.* кряква.

malleable *adj.* ковкий (-вок, -вка, -вко); (*fig.*) податливый.

mallet *n.* (деревянный) молоток (-тка).

mallow *n.* мальва, просвирник.

malnutrition *n.* недоеда́ние.

malpractice *n.* (*wrongdoing*) противозако́нное де́йствие; (*negligence*) престу́пная небре́жность.

malt *n.* со́лод; *v.t.* солоди́ть *imp.*, на~ *perf.*

maltreat *v.t.* пло́хо обраща́ться *imp.* с + *instr.*

mamba *n.* ма́мба.

mambo *n.* ма́мбо *neut.indecl.*

mamma *n.* ма́ма.

mammal *n.* млекопита́ющее *sb.* **mammalian** *adj.* млекопита́ющий.

mammary *adj.* грудно́й.

mammon *n.* мамо́на, бога́тство.

mammoth *n.* ма́монт; *adj.* грома́дный.

man *n.* (*human*; *person*) челове́к (*pl.* лю́ди, -де́й, -дям, -дьми́); (*human race*) челове́чество; (*male*) мужчи́на *m.*; (*husband*) муж (*pl.* -ья́, -е́й, -ья́м); (*servant*) слуга́ *m.*; (*labourer*) рабо́чий *sb.*; *pl.* (*soldiers*) солда́ты *m.pl.*, рядовы́е *sb.*; *pl.* (*sailors*) матро́сы *m.pl.*; (*draughts*) ша́шка; *m. in the street*, зауря́дный челове́к; *m.-hour*, челове́ко-час (*pl.* -ы́); *m.-of-war*, вое́нный кора́бль (-ля́) *m.*; *v.t.* (*furnish with men*) укомплекто́вывать *imp.*, укомплектова́ть *perf.* ли́чным соста́вом; ста́вить *imp.*, по~ *perf.* люде́й к + *dat.*; (*act thus*) станови́ться (-влю́сь, -ви́шься) *imp.*, стать (ста́ну, -нешь) *perf.* к + *dat.*

manacle *n.* нару́чник; *v.t.* надева́ть *imp.*, наде́ть (-е́ну, -е́нешь) *perf.* нару́чники на + *acc.*

manage *v.t.* (*control*) управля́ть *imp.* + *instr.*; заве́довать *imp.* + *instr.*; (*cope*) справля́ться *imp.*, спра́виться *perf.* с + *instr.* **management** *n.* управле́ние (of, + *instr.*), заве́дование (of, + *instr.*); (*the m.*) администра́ция, дире́кция. **manager** *n.* управля́ющий *sb.* (of, + *instr.*), заве́дующий *sb.* (of, + *instr.*), администра́тор, дире́ктор (*pl.* -а́); (*good*, *bad*, *m.*) хозя́ин; (*in entertainment*) импреса́рио *m.indecl.*; (*sport*) ме́неджер. **managerial** *adj.* администрати́вный, дире́кторский.

mandarin *n.* мандари́н.

mandatary *n.* мандата́рий. **mandate** *n.* манда́т. **mandated** *adj.* подманда́тный. **mandatory** *adj.* обяза́тельный.

mandible *n.* ни́жняя че́люсть; (*of insect*) жва́ло.

mandolin(e) *n.* мандоли́на.

mane *n.* гри́ва.

manful *adj.* му́жественный (-ен, -енна).

manganese *n.* ма́рганец (-нца).

manger *n.* я́сли (-лей) *pl.*; *dog in the m.*, соба́ка на се́не.

mangle[1] *n.* (*for clothes*) като́к (-тка́); *v.t.* ката́ть *imp.*, вы́~ *perf.*

mangle[2] *v.t.* (*mutilate*) кале́чить *imp.*, ис~ *perf.*; (*words*) кове́ркать *imp.*, ис~ *perf.*

mango *n.* ма́нго *neut.indecl.*

mangrove *n.* ма́нгровое де́рево (*pl.* -е́вья, -е́вьев).

manhandle *v.t.* передвига́ть *imp.*, передви́нуть *perf.* вручну́ю; (*treat roughly*) гру́бо обраща́ться *imp.* с + *instr.*

manhole *n.* смотрово́й коло́дец (-дца).

manhood *n.* возмужа́лость; (*courage*) му́жественность.

mania *n.* ма́ния. **maniac** *n.* манья́к, -я́чка. **maniacal** *adj.* маниака́льный.

manicure *n.* маникю́р; *v.t.* де́лать *imp.*, с~ *perf.* маникю́р + *dat.* **manicurist** *n.* маникю́рша.

manifest *adj.* очеви́дный; *v.t.* де́лать *imp.*, с~ *perf.* очеви́дным; (*display*) проявля́ть *imp.*, прояви́ть (-влю́, -вишь) *perf.*; *n.* манифе́ст. **manifestation** *n.* проявле́ние. **manifesto** *n.* манифе́ст.

manifold *adj.* разнообра́зный; *n.* (*tech.*) колле́ктор, трубопрово́д.

manikin *n.* (*little man*) челове́чек (-чка); (*lay figure*) манеке́н.

Manil(l)a *n.* (*hemp*), мани́льская пенька́; (*paper*), мани́льская бума́га.

manipulate *v.t.* манипули́ровать *imp.* + *instr.* **manipulation** *n.* манипуля́ция.

manly *adj.* му́жественный (-ен, -енна).

mankind *n.* челове́чество.

manna *n.* ма́нна (небе́сная).

mannequin *n.* манеке́нщица.

manner *n.* спо́соб, о́браз, мане́ра; *pl.* нра́вы *m.pl.*; *pl.* (*good m.*) (хоро́шие) мане́ры *f.pl.* **mannered** *adj.* вычурный, мане́рный. **mannerism** *n.* мане́ра; мане́рность.

mannish *adj.* (*masculine*) мужеподо́бный; (*characteristic of man*) сво́йственный (-ен, -енна) мужчи́не.
manoeuvrable *adj.* легко́ управля́емый.
manoeuvre *n.* манёвр; *v.i.* маневри́ровать *imp.*, с ~ *perf.*; проводи́ть (-ожу́, -о́дишь) *imp.*, провести́ (-еду́, -едёшь; -ёл, -ела́) *perf.* манёвры.
manor *n.* (*estate*) поме́стье (*gen.pl.* -тий); (*house*) поме́щичий дом (-а(у); *pl.* -а́). **manorial** *adj.* манориа́льный
manpower *n.* людски́е ресу́рсы *m.pl.*
mansard (roof) *n.* манса́рдная кры́ша.
manservant *n.* слуга́ *m.*
mansion *n.* большо́й дом (*pl.* -а́); *pl.* многокварти́рный дом.
manslaughter *n.* человекоуби́йство; (*leg.*) непредумы́шленное уби́йство.
mantelpiece *n.* ками́нная доска́ (*acc.* -ску; *pl.* -ски, -со́к, -ска́м). **mantelshelf** *n.* ками́нная по́лка.
mantis *n.* богомо́л.
mantle *n.* (*cloak*) наки́дка; (*gas m.*) газокали́льная се́тка; (*earth's*) ма́нтия.
manual *adj.* ручно́й; *m. labour*, физи́ческий, ручно́й, труд (-а́); *n.* спра́вочник, руково́дство, уче́бник; (*of organ*) мануа́л. **manually** *adv.* вручну́ю.
manufacture *n.* произво́дство, изготовле́ние; *v.t.* производи́ть (-ожу́, -о́дишь) *imp.*, произвести́ (-еду́, -едёшь; -ёл, -ела́) *perf.*; изготовля́ть *imp.*, изгото́вить *perf.*; (*fabricate*) фабрикова́ть *imp.*, с ~ *perf.* **manufacturer** *n.* фабрика́нт, промы́шленник, производи́тель *m.*
manure *n.* наво́з; *v.t.* унаво́живать *imp.*, унаво́зить *perf.*
manuscript *n.* ру́копись; *adj.* рукопи́сный.
many *adj.*, *n.* мно́го + *gen.*, мно́гие *pl.*; *how m.*, ско́лько + *gen.*
Maoism *n.* мао́изм. **Maoist** *n.* мао́ист; *adj.* мао́истский.
map *n.* ка́рта; *v.t.* черти́ть (-рчу́, -ртишь) *imp.*, на ~ *perf.* план + *gen.*; *m. out*, составля́ть *imp.*, соста́вить *perf.* план + *gen.*
maple *n.* клён; *attrib.* клено́вый.
mar *v.t.* по́ртить *imp.*, ис ~ *perf.*
marathon *n.* марафо́н.
marauder *n.* мародёр. **marauding** *adj.* мародёрский.
marble *n.* мра́мор; (*toy*) ша́рик; *pl.* (*game*) игра́ в ша́рики; *attrib.* мра́морный. **marbled** *adj.* мра́морный.
March[1] *n.* март; *attrib.* ма́ртовский.
march[2] *v.i.* маршировáть *imp.*, про ~ *perf.*; *n.* марш; ход; *m. past*, прохожде́ние торже́ственным ма́ршем.
mare *n.* кобы́ла; *m.'s nest*, иллю́зия; *find a m.'s nest*, попа́сть (-аду́, -адёшь; -а́л) *perf.* па́льцем в не́бо.
margarine *n.* маргари́н (-а(у)).
margin *n.* край (*loc.* -аю́; *pl.* -ая́), кайма́ (*gen.pl.* каём); (*on page*) по́ле (*pl.* -ля́); *m. of error*, преде́лы *m.pl.* погре́шности; *profit m.*, при́быль; *safety m.*, запа́с про́чности.
marigold *n.* (*Tagetes*) ба́рхатцы (-цев) *pl.*; (*Calendula*) ноготки́ (-ко́в) *pl.*
marijuana *n.* марихуа́на.
marinade *n.* марина́д; *v.t.* марино**ва́**ть *imp.*, за ~ *perf.*
marine *adj.* (*maritime*) морско́й; (*naval*) вое́нно-морско́й; *n.* (*fleet*) морско́й флот; (*soldier*) солда́т морско́й пехо́ты; *pl.* морска́я пехо́та. **mariner** *n.* моря́к (-а́), матро́с.
marionette *n.* марионе́тка.
marital *adj.* супру́жеский, бра́чный.
maritime *adj.* морско́й; (*near sea*) примо́рский.
marjoram *n.* (*Majorana*) майора́н; (*Origanum*) души́ца.
mark[1] *n.* (*coin*) ма́рка.
mark[2] *n.* (*target, aim*) цель; (*sign*) знак; (*school*) отме́тка, (*numerical*) балл; (*trace*) след (*pl.* -ы́); (*level*) у́ровень (-вня) *m.*; *high-, low-, water m.*, отме́тка у́ровня по́лной, ма́лой, воды́; *hit the m.*, попада́ть *imp.*, попа́сть (-аду́, -адёшь; -а́л) *perf.* в то́чку; *make one's m.*, отлича́ться *imp.*, отличи́ться *perf.*; *on your marks*, на старт! *v.t.* отмеча́ть *imp.*, отме́тить *perf.*; ста́вить *imp.*, по ~ *perf.* знак, (*goods*) расце́нку, на + *acc.*, (*school*) отме́тку, балл, за + *acc.*; (*leave trace(s)*) оставля́ть *imp.*, оста́вить *perf.* след(ы́) на + *prep.*; (*football*) закрыва́ть *imp.*, закры́ть (-ро́ю, -ро́ешь) *perf.*; *m. my words*, попо́мни(те) мои́ слова́! *m.*

time, топта́ться (-пчу́сь, -пчешься) *imp.* на ме́сте; *m. off*, отделя́ть *imp.*, отдели́ть (-лю́, -лишь) *perf.*; *m. out*, размеча́ть *imp.*, разме́тить *perf.* **marker** *n.* знак, указа́тель *m.*; (*in book*) закла́дка.

market *n.* ры́нок (-нка), база́р; (*demand*) спрос; (*trade*) торго́вля; (*conditions*) конъюнкту́ра; *black m.*, чёрный ры́нок (-нка); *buyer's, seller's, m.*, конъюнкту́ра ры́нка, вы́годная для покупа́теля, для продавца́; (*European*) *Common M.*, (европе́йский) о́бщий ры́нок (-нка); *find a m.*, находи́ть (-ожу́, -о́дишь) *imp.*, найти́ (найду́, -дёшь; нашёл, -шла́) *perf.* сбыт; *m.-day*, база́рный день (дня) *m.*; *m. garden*, огоро́д; *m.-place*, база́рная пло́щадь (*pl.* -ди, -де́й); *m. price*, ры́ночная цена́ (*acc.* -ну; *pl.* -ны); *v.t.* продава́ть (-даю́, -даёшь) *imp.*, прода́ть (-а́м, -а́шь, -а́ст, -ади́м; про́дал, -а́, -о) *perf.* **marketable** *adj.* хо́дкий (-док, -дка́, -дко); (*econ.*) това́рный.

marksman *n.* ме́ткий стрело́к (-лка́). **marksmanship** *n.* ме́ткая стрельба́.

marl *n.* ме́ргель *m.*

marmalade *n.* апельси́новый джем.

marmoset *n.* игру́нка.

marmot *n.* суро́к (-рка́).

maroon[1] *adj.* (*n.*) (*colour*) тёмно-бордо́вый (цвет).

maroon[2] *v.t.* (*put ashore*) выса́живать *imp.*, вы́садить *perf.* (на необита́емом о́строве); (*cut off*) отреза́ть *imp.*, отре́зать (-е́жет) *perf.*

marquee *n.* шатёр (-тра́).

marquis *n.* марки́з.

marriage *n.* брак; (*wedding*) сва́дьба; *attrib.* бра́чный. **marriageable** *adj.* взро́слый; *m. age*, бра́чный во́зраст. **married** *adj.* (*man*) жена́тый; (*woman*) заму́жняя, за́мужем; (*of m. persons*) супру́жеский.

marrow *n.* ко́стный мозг (*loc.* -у́); (*essence*) су́щность; (*vegetable*) кабачо́к (-чка́). **marrowbone** *n.* мозгова́я кость (*pl.* -ти, -те́й).

marry *v.t.* (*of man*) жени́ться (-ню́сь, -нишься) *imp.*, *perf.* на + *prep.*; (*of woman*) выходи́ть (-ожу́, -о́дишь) *imp.*, вы́йти (вы́йду, -дешь; вы́шла) *perf.* за́муж за + *acc.*; (*give in marriage*) (*man*) жени́ть (-ню́, -нишь) *imp.*, *perf.*, по ~ *perf.* (to, на + *prep.*); (*woman*) выдава́ть (-даю́, -даёшь) *imp.*, вы́дать (-ам, -ашь, -аст, -адим) *perf.* за́муж (to, за + *acc.*).

Mars *n.* Марс.

marsh *n.* боло́то; *m.-gas*, боло́тный газ; *m. mallow*, алте́й лека́рственный; *m. marigold*, калу́жница боло́тная. **marshy** *adj.* боло́тистый.

marshal *n.* ма́ршал; *v.t.* выстра́ивать *imp.*, вы́строить *perf.*; приводи́ть (-ожу́, -о́дишь) *imp.*, привести́ (-еду́, -едёшь; -ёл, -ела́) *perf.* в поря́док; *marshalling yard*, сортиро́вочная ста́нция.

marsupial *adj.* су́мчатый; *n.* су́мчатое живо́тное *sb.*

marten *n.* куни́ца.

martial *adj.* вое́нный; (*warlike*) во́инский; *m. law*, вое́нное положе́ние.

Martian *n.* марсиа́нин (*pl.* -а́не, -а́н); *adj.* марсиа́нский.

martin *n.* стриж (-а́); (*house-m.*) городска́я ла́сточка.

martinet *n.* сторо́нник стро́гой дисципли́ны.

martyr *n.* му́ченик, -ица; *v.t.* му́чить *imp.*, за ~ *perf.* **martyrdom** *n.* му́ченичество.

marvel *n.* чу́до (*pl.* -деса́), ди́во; *v.i.* изумля́ться *imp.*, изуми́ться *perf.*; удивля́ться *imp.*, удиви́ться *perf.* **marvellous** *adj.* чуде́сный, изуми́тельный, удиви́тельный.

Marxian, Marxist *n.* маркси́ст; *adj.* маркси́стский. **Marxism** *n.* маркси́зм.

marzipan *n.* марципа́н; *adj.* марципа́нный.

mascot *n.* талисма́н.

masculine *adj.* мужско́й; (*gram.*) мужско́го ро́да; (*of woman*) мужеподо́бный; *n.* (*gram.*) мужско́й род.

maser *n.* ма́зер.

mash *n.* (*of malt*) су́сло; (*of bran*) по́йло; (*mashed potatoes*) карто́фельное пюре́ *neut.indecl.*; *v.t.* размина́ть *imp.*, размя́ть (разомну́, -нёшь) *perf.*

mask *n.* ма́ска; (*gas-m.*) противога́з;

v.t. маскирова́ть *imp.*, за~ *perf.*; *masked ball*, бал-маскара́д.
masochism *m.* мазохи́зм. **masochist** *n.* мазохи́ст. **masochistic** *adj.* мазохи́стский.
mason *n.* ка́менщик; (*M.*) масо́н. **Masonic** *adj.* масо́нский. **masonry** *n.* ка́менная кла́дка; (*M.*) масо́нство.
masque *n.* ма́ска. **masquer** *n.* уча́стник, -ица, ба́ла-маскара́да. **masquerade** *n.* маскара́д; *v.i.*: *m. as*, притворя́ться *imp.*, притвори́ться *perf.* + *instr.*; выдава́ть (-даю́, -даёшь) *imp.*, вы́дать (-ам, -ашь, -аст, -адим) *perf.* себя́ за + *acc.*
mass[1] *n.* (*eccl.*) обе́дня (*gen.pl.* -ден), ме́сса.
mass[2] *n.* ма́сса; (*majority*) большинство́; *pl.* (*the m.*) наро́дные ма́ссы *f.pl.*; *attrib.* ма́ссовый; *m. media*, сре́дства *neut.pl.* ма́ссовой информа́ции; *m. meeting*, ми́тинг; *m.-produced*, ма́ссового произво́дства; *m. production*, ма́ссовое произво́дство; *v.t.* масси́ровать *imp.*, *perf.*
massacre *n.* резня́; *v.t.* ре́зать (ре́жу, -жешь) *imp.*, за~ *perf.*
massage *n.* масса́ж; *v.t.* масси́ровать *imp.*, *perf.* **masseur, -euse** *n.* массажи́ст, ~ка.
massif *n.* го́рный масси́в.
massive *adj.* масси́вный.
mast *n.* ма́чта; *m.-head*, топ ма́чты.
master *n.* (*owner*) хозя́ин (*pl.* -я́ева, -я́ев), владе́лец (-льца); (*of household, college*) глава́ (*pl.* -вы) *m.* (семьи́, ко́лледжа); (*of ship*) капита́н; (*teacher*) учи́тель (*pl.* -ля́) *m.*; (*M., univ.*) маги́стр; (*workman*; *artist*) ма́стер (*pl.* -а́); (*of film*) контро́льная ко́пия; (*of record*) пе́рвый оригина́л; *be m. of*, владе́ть *imp.* + *instr.*; *M. of Arts*, маги́стр гуманита́рных нау́к; *m.-key*. отмы́чка; *m.-switch*, гла́вный выключа́тель *m.*; *v.t.* (*overcome*) преодолева́ть *imp.*, преодоле́ть *perf.*; справля́ться *imp.*, спра́виться *perf.* с + *instr.*; (*subjugate*) подчиня́ть *imp.*, подчини́ть *perf.* себе́; (*acquire knowledge of*) овладева́ть *imp.*, овладе́ть *perf.* + *instr.* **masterful** *adj.* вла́стный. **masterly** *adj.* мастерско́й. **masterpiece** *n.* шеде́вр. **mastery** *n.* (*dominion*) госпо́дство; (*skill*) мастерство́; (*knowledge*) соверше́нное владе́ние (of, + *instr.*).
masticate *v.t.* жева́ть (жую́, жуёшь) *imp.*
mastiff *n.* ма́стифф.
mastodon *n.* мастодо́нт.
mat[1] *n.* ко́врик, полови́к (-а́); (*of rushes, straw*) цино́вка; (*under dish etc.*) подста́вка.
mat[2] *adj. see* **matt.**
match[1] *n.* спи́чка. **matchbox** *n.* спи́чечная коро́бка.
match[2] *n.* (*equal*) ро́вня *m.* & *f.*; (*contest*) матч, состяза́ние; (*marriage*) брак; *a m. for*, па́ра + *dat.*; *meet one's m.*, встреча́ть *imp.*, встре́тить *perf.* ра́вного себе́, досто́йного, проти́вника; *v.t.* (*correspond*) соотве́тствовать *imp.* + *dat.*; (*of colour*) гармони́ровать *imp.* с + *instr.*; (*select*) подбира́ть *imp.*, подобра́ть (подберу́, -рёшь; подобра́л, -а́, -о) *perf.* **matchboard** *n.* шпунтова́я доска́ (*acc.* -ску; *pl.* -ски, -со́к, -ска́м). **matchless** *adj.* несравне́нный (-нен, -нна). **matchmaker** *n.* сват, сва́ха.
mate[1] *n.* (*chess*) мат; *v.t.* объявля́ть *imp.*, объяви́ть (-влю́, -вишь) *perf.* мат + *dat.*
mate[2] *n.* (*one of a pair*) саме́ц (-мца́), са́мка; (*fellow worker*) напа́рник, това́рищ; (*assistant*) помо́щник; (*naut.*) помо́щник капита́на; *v.i.* (*of animals*) спа́риваться *imp.*, спа́риться *perf.*
material *adj.* материа́льный; (*essential*) суще́ственный (-ен, -енна); *n.* материа́л; (*cloth*) мате́рия; *pl.* (*necessary articles*) принадле́жности *f.pl.* **materialism** *n.* материали́зм; материалисти́чность. **materialist** *n.* материали́ст. **materialistic** *adj.* материалисти́чный, -ческий. **materialization** *n.* материализа́ция. **materialize** *v.t.* & *i.* материализова́ть(ся) *imp.*, *perf.*; осуществля́ть(ся) *imp.*, осуществи́ть(ся) *perf.*
maternal *adj.* матери́нский; (*kinship*) по ма́тери; *m. grandfather*, де́душка с матери́нской стороны́. **maternity** *n.* матери́нство; *m. benefit*, посо́бие роже́нице; *m. dress*, пла́тье (*gen.pl.* -в)

для беременных; *m. home, hospital*, родильный дом (-а(у); *pl.* -á); *m. ward*, родильная палата.

mathematical *adj.* математический. **mathematician** *n.* математик. **mathematics** *n.* математика.

matinée *n.* дневной спектакль *m.*; *m. coat*, распашонка.

matins *n.* утреня.

matriarchal *adj.* матриархальный. **matriarchy** *n.* матриархат. **matricidal** *adj.* матереубийственный. **matricide** *n.* (*action*) матереубийство; (*person*) матереубийца *m.* & *f.*

matriculate *v.t.* принимать *imp.*, принять (приму, -мешь; принял, -á, -о) *perf.* в вуз; *v.i.* быть принятым в вуз. **matriculation** *n.* зачисление в вуз; (*examination*) вступительный экзамен в вуз.

matrimonial *adj.* супружеский. **matrimony** *n.* брак, супружество.

matrix *n.* (*womb*) матка; (*rock*) маточная порода; (*mould*) матрица.

matron *n.* замужняя женщина; (*hospital*) сестра-хозяйка; (*school*) заведующая *sb.* хозяйством.

matt *adj.* матовый.

matted *adj.* спутанный (-ан).

matter *n.* (*substance*) вещество; (*philos., med.*) материя; (*content*) содержание; (*affair*) дело (*pl.* -лá); (*question*) вопрос; *a m. of form*, формальность; *a m. of life and death*, вопрос жизни и смерти; *a m. of opinion*, спорное дело; *a m. of taste*, дело вкуса; *an easy m.*, простое дело; *as a m. of fact*, фактически; собственно говоря; *for that m.*, что касается этого; в этом отношении; *money matters*, денежные делá *neut.pl.*; *no laughing m.*, не шуточное дело; *what's the m.?* в чём дело? что случилось? *what's the m. with him?* что с ним? *m.-of-fact*, прозаичный; *v.i.* иметь *imp.* значение; (*med.*) гноиться *imp.*; *it doesn't m.*, это не имеет значения; *it matters a lot to me*, для меня это очень важно; *what does it m.?* какое это имеет значение?

matting *n.* (*rushes*) циновка; (*bast*) рогожа.

mattock *n.* мотыга.

mattress *n.* матрас, тюфяк (-á).

mature *adj.* зрелый (зрел, -á, -о); (*well-considered*) хорошо обдуманный (-ан, -анна); *v.i.* зреть *imp.*, со~ *perf.*; *v.t.* доводить (-ожу, -одишь) *imp.*, довести (-еду, -едёшь; -ёл, -елá) *perf.* до зрелости; (*plan*) обдумывать *imp.*, обдумать *perf.* **maturity** *n.* зрелость.

maul *v.t.* терзать *imp.*; калечить *imp.*, ис~ *perf.*; (*criticize*) раскритиковать *perf.*

mausoleum *n.* мавзолей.

mauve *adj.* (*n.*) розовато-лиловый (цвет).

maxim *n.* сентенция.

maximum *n.* максимум; *adj.* максимальный.

may[1] *v.aux.* (*possibility; permission*) мочь (могу, можешь; мог, -лá) *imp.*, с~ *perf.*; (*possibility*) возможно, что + *indicative*; (*wish*) пусть + *indicative.*

May[2] *n.* (*month*) май; (*m., hawthorn*) боярышник; *m.-bug*, майский жук (-á); *M. Day*, Первое *sb.* мая; *attrib.* майский. **mayfly** *n.* подёнка.

maybe *adv.* может быть.

mayonnaise *n.* майонез.

mayor *n.* мэр. **mayoress** *n.* женá (*pl.* жёны) мэра; женщина-мэр.

maze *n.* лабиринт; (*fig.*) путаница.

mazurka *n.* мазурка.

mead *n.* мёд (-а(у), *loc.* -ý; *pl.* -ы́).

meadow *n.* луг (*loc.* -ý; *pl.* -á). **meadowsweet** *n.* таволга.

meagre *adj.* (*thin*) худой (худ, -á, -о); (*scanty*) скудный (-ден, -днá, -дно).

meal[1] *n.* едá; *at mealtimes*, во время еды́.

meal[2] *n.* (*ground grain*) мукá крупного помола. **mealy** *adj.* рассыпчатый; *m.-mouthed*, сладкоречивый.

mean[1] *adj.* (*average*) средний; *n.* (*middle point*) середина, среднее *sb.*; *pl.* (*method*) средство, способ; *pl.* (*resources*) средства *neut.pl.*, состояние; *by all means*, конечно, пожалуйста; *by means of*, при помощи + *gen.*, посредством + *gen.*; *by no means*, совсем не; *means test*, проверка нуждаемости.

mean[2] *adj.* (*ignoble*) подлый (подл, -á,

-о), ни́зкий (-зок, -зка́, -зко); (*miserly*) скупо́й (скуп, -а́, -о); (*poor*) убо́гий.
mean[3] *v.t.* (*have in mind*) име́ть *imp.* в виду́; (*intend*) намерева́ться *imp.* + *inf.*; (*signify*) зна́чить *imp.*
meander *v.i.* (*stream*) извива́ться *imp.*; (*person*) броди́ть (-ожу́, -о́дишь) *imp.* без це́ли. **meandering** *adj.* изви́листый.
meaning *n.* значе́ние, смысл; *adj.* значи́тельный. **meaningful** *adj.* (много)значи́тельный. **meaningless** *adj.* бессмы́сленный (-ен, -енна).
meantime, meanwhile *adv.* тем вре́менем, ме́жду тем.
measles *n.* корь. **measly** *adj.* ничто́жный.
measurable *adj.* измери́мый. **measure** *n.* ме́ра; (*size*) ме́рка; (*degree*) сте́пень (*pl.* -ни, -не́й); (*limit*) преде́л; *made to m.*, сши́тый по ме́рке; сде́ланный (-ан) на зака́з; *v.t.* измеря́ть *imp.*, изме́рить *perf.*; ме́рить *imp.*, с~ *perf.*; (*for clothes*) снима́ть *imp.*, снять (сниму́, -мешь; снял, -а́, -о) *perf.* ме́рку с + *gen.*; (*estimate*) оце́нивать *imp.*, оцени́ть (-ню́, -нишь) *perf.*; *v.i.* (*be of specified size*) име́ть *imp.* + *acc.*; *the room measures 30 feet in length*, ко́мната име́ет три́дцать фу́тов в длину́; *m. off*, отмеря́ть *imp.*, отме́рить *perf.*; *m. out*, (*deal out*) распределя́ть *imp.*, распредели́ть *perf.*; *m. up to*, соотве́тствовать *imp.* + *dat.* **measured** *adj.* (*rhythmical*) ме́рный. **measurement** *n.* (*action*) измере́ние; *pl.* (*dimensions*) разме́ры *m.pl.*
meat *n.* мя́со. **meaty** *adj.* мясно́й, мяси́стый.
mechanic *n.* меха́ник. **mechanical** *adj.* механи́ческий; (*automatic*) машина́льный; *m. engineer*, инжене́р-меха́ник; *m. engineering*, машинострое́ние. **mechanics** *n.* меха́ника. **mechanism** *n.* механи́зм. **mechanistic** *adj.* механисти́ческий. **mechanization** *n.* механиза́ция. **mechanize** *v.t.* механизи́ровать *imp.*, *perf.*
medal *n.* меда́ль. **medallion** *n.* медальо́н. **medallist** *n.* (*recipient*) медали́ст.
meddle *v.i.* вме́шиваться *imp.*, вмеша́ться *perf.* (in, with, в + *acc.*).
media *pl. of* **medium.**
mediaeval *adj.* средневеко́вый.
mediate *v.i.* посре́дничать *imp.* **mediation** *n.* посре́дничество. **mediator** *n.* посре́дник.
medical *adj.* медици́нский; *m. jurisprudence*, суде́бная медици́на; *m. man*, врач (-а́); *m. student*, ме́дик, -и́чка. **medicated** *adj.* (*impregnated*) пропи́танный (-ан) лека́рством. **medicinal** *adj.* (*of medicine*) лека́рственный; (*healing*) целе́бный. **medicine** *n.* медици́на; (*substance*) лека́рство; *m.-man*, зна́харь *m.*, шама́н.
mediocre *adj.* посре́дственный (-ен, -енна), зауря́дный. **mediocrity** *n.* посре́дственность.
meditate *v.i.* размышля́ть *imp.* **meditation** *n.* размышле́ние. **meditative** *adj.* заду́мчивый.
Mediterranean *adj.* средиземномо́рский; *n.* Средизе́мное мо́ре.
medium *n.* (*middle*) середи́на; (*means*) сре́дство; (*environment*; *phys.*) среда́ (*pl.* -ды); (*person*) ме́диум; *pl.* (*mass media*) сре́дства *neut.pl.* ма́ссовой информа́ции; *adj.* сре́дний.
medley *n.* смесь, вся́кая вся́чина.
meek *adj.* кро́ткий (-ток, -тка́, -тко), смире́нный (-е́н, -е́нна). **meekness** *n.* кро́тость, смире́нность.
meet *v.t.* & *i.* встреча́ть(ся) *imp.*, встре́тить(ся) *perf.*; *v.t.* (*make acquaintance*) знако́миться *imp.*, по~ *perf.* с + *instr.*; *v.i.* (*assemble*) собира́ться *imp.*, собра́ться (соберётся; собра́лся, -ала́сь, -а́ло́сь) *perf.* **meeting** *n.* встре́ча; собра́ние, заседа́ние, ми́тинг.
mega- *in comb.* ме́га-. **megacycle, megahertz** *n.* мегаге́рц (*gen.pl.* -ц). **megalith** *n.* мегали́т. **megalithic** *adj.* мегалити́ческий. **megaphone** *n.* мегафо́н. **megaton(ne)** *n.* мегато́нна. **megavolt** *n.* мегаво́льт (*gen.pl.* -т). **megawatt** *n.* мегава́тт (*gen.pl.* -т). **megohm** *n.* мего́м (*gen.pl.* -м).
megalomania *n.* мегалома́ния.
melancholia *n.* меланхо́лия. **melancholic** *adj.* меланхоли́ческий. **melancholy** *n.* грусть, тоска́; *adj.* уны́лый, гру́стный (-тен, -тна́, -тно).
mêlée *n.* сва́лка.
mellow *adj.* (*ripe*) спе́лый (спел, -а́, -о); (*juicy*) со́чный (-чен, -чна́, -чно);

(*soft*) мя́гкий (-гок, -гка́, -гко); (*intoxicated*) подвы́пивший; *v.i.* спеть *imp.*; смягча́ться *imp.*, смягчи́ться *perf.*

melodic *adj.* мелоди́ческий. **melodious** *adj.* мелоди́чный. **melody** *n.* мело́дия, напе́в.

melodrama *n.* мелодра́ма. **melodramatic** *adj.* мелодрамати́ческий.

melon *n.* ды́ня; (*water-m.*) арбу́з.

melt *v.t.* & *i.* раста́пливать(ся) *imp.*, растопи́ть(ся) (-плю́, -пит(ся)) *perf.*; (*smelt*) пла́вить(ся) *imp.*, рас~ *perf.*; (*dissolve*) растворя́ть(ся) *imp.*, раствори́ть(ся) *perf.*; *v.i.* (*thaw*) та́ять (та́ет) *imp.*, рас~ *perf.*; *melting-point*, то́чка плавле́ния.

member *n.* член. **membership** *n.* чле́нство; (*number of members*) коли́чество чле́нов; *attrib.* чле́нский.

membrane *n.* перепо́нка. **membran(e)ous** *adj.* перепо́нчатый.

memento *n.* напомина́ние. **memoir** *n.* кра́ткая биогра́фия; *pl.* мемуа́ры (-ров) *pl.*; воспомина́ния *neut.pl.* **memorable** *adj.* достопа́мятный. **memorandum** *n.* па́мятная запи́ска; (*diplomatic m.*) мемора́ндум. **memorial** *adj.* па́мятный, мемориа́льный; *n.* па́мятник. **memorize** *v.t.* зау́чивать *imp.*, заучи́ть (-чу́, -чишь) *perf.* наизу́сть. **memory** *n.* па́мять; (*recollection*) воспомина́ние; (*computer*) запомина́ющее устро́йство.

menace *n.* угро́за; *v.t.* угрожа́ть *imp.* + *dat.* **menacing** *adj.* угрожа́ющий.

menagerie *n.* звери́нец (-нца).

mend *v.t.* чини́ть (-ню́, -нишь) *imp.*, по~ *perf.*; (*clothes*) што́пать *imp.*, за~ *perf.*; (*road*) ремонти́ровать *imp.*, от~ *perf.*; *m. one's ways*, исправля́ться *imp.*, испра́виться *perf.*

mendacious *adj.* лжи́вый. **mendacity** *n.* лжи́вость.

mendicancy *n.* ни́щенство. **mendicant** *adj.* ни́щий, ни́щенствующий; *n.* ни́щий *sb.*

menial *adj.* лаке́йский, ни́зкий (-зок, -зка́, -зко).

meningitis *n.* менинги́т.

menopause *n.* кли́макс.

menstrual *adj.* менструа́льный. **menstruation** *n.* менструа́ция.

mental *adj.* у́мственный, психи́ческий, душе́вный; *m. arithmetic*, счёт в уме́; *m. deficiency*, у́мственная отста́лость; *m. home, hospital, institution*, психиатри́ческая больни́ца. **mentality** *n.* ум (-а́); (*character*) склад ума́. **mentally** *adv.* у́мственно, мы́сленно.

menthol *n.* менто́л.

mention *v.t.* упомина́ть *imp.*, упомяну́ть (-ну́, -нешь) *perf.*; *not to m.*, не говоря́ уже́ о + *prep.*; *n.* упомина́ние.

mentor *n.* ме́нтор.

menu *n.* меню́ *neut.indecl.*

mercantile *adj.* торго́вый; *m. marine*, торго́вый флот.

mercenary *adj.* коры́стный; (*hired*) наёмный; *n.* наёмник.

mercerize *v.t.* мерсеризова́ть *imp.*, *perf.*

merchandise *n.* това́ры *m.pl.* **merchant** *n.* купе́ц (-пца́); торго́вец (-вца); *attrib.* торго́вый; *m. navy*, торго́вый флот; *m. ship*, торго́вое су́дно (*pl.* -да́, -до́в).

merciful *adj.* милосе́рдный. **mercifully** *adv.* к сча́стью. **merciless** *adj.* беспоща́дный.

mercurial *adj.* (*person*) живо́й (жив, -а́, -о); (*of mercury*) рту́тный. **mercury** *n.* (*metal*) ртуть; (*M., planet*) Мерку́рий.

mercy *n.* милосе́рдие; поща́да; *at the m. of*, во вла́сти + *gen.*

mere *adj.* просто́й, чи́стый, су́щий; *a m. child*, су́щий ребёнок, всего́ лишь ребёнок. **merely** *adv.* то́лько, про́сто.

meretricious *adj.* показно́й, мишу́рный.

merge *v.t.* & *i.* слива́ть(ся) *imp.*, сли́ть(ся) (солью́(сь), -ьёшь(ся); сли́л(ся), -ила́(сь), -и́ло/и́ло́сь) *perf.* **merger** *n.* объедине́ние.

meridian *n.* меридиа́н.

meringue *n.* мере́нга.

merit *n.* заслу́га, досто́инство; *v.t.* заслу́живать *imp.*, заслужи́ть (-жу́, -жишь) *perf.* + *gen.* **meritorious** *adj.* похва́льный.

mermaid *n.* руса́лка. **merman** *n.* водяно́й *sb.*

merrily *adv.* ве́село. **merriment** *n.* весе́лье. **merry** *adj.* весёлый (ве́сел, -а́, -о, ве́селы́); *m.-go-round*, карусе́ль; *m.-making*, весе́лье.

mesh *n.* пéтля (*gen.pl.* -тель); *pl.* (*network*) сéти (-тéй) *pl.*; *pl.* (*fig.*) западня́; *v.i.* сцепля́ться *imp.*, сцепи́ться (-ится) *perf.*
mesmeric *adj.* гипноти́ческий. **mesmerize** *v.t.* гипнотизи́ровать *imp.*, за~ *perf.*
meson *n.* мезóн.
mess *n.* (*disorder*) беспоря́док (-дка); (*trouble*) бедá; (*eating-place*) столóвая *sb.*; *v.i.* столовáться *imp.* (with, вмéсте с + *instr.*); *m. about*, лóдырничать *imp.*; *m. up*, пóртить *imp.*, ис~ *perf.*
message *n.* сообщéние; (*errand*) поручéние. **messenger** *n.* посы́льный *sb.*, курьéр.
Messiah *n.* месси́я *m.* **Messianic** *adj.* мессиáнский.
Messrs. *abbr.* господá (*gen.* -д) *m.pl.*
messy *adj.* (*untidy*) беспоря́дочный; (*dirty*) гря́зный (-зен, -знá, -зно).
metabolism *n.* метаболи́зм, обмéн веществ.
metal *n.* метáлл; (*road-m.*) щéбень (-бня) *m.*; (*rly.*) баллáст; *pl.* (*rails*) рéльсы *m.pl.*; *adj.* металли́ческий; *v.t.* (*road*) шосси́ровать *imp.*, *perf.*; *metalled road*, шоссé *neut.indecl.* **metallic** *adj.* металли́ческий. **metallurgical** *adj.* металлурги́ческий. **metallurgy** *n.* металлу́ргия.
metamorphose *v.t.* подвергáть *imp.*, подвéргнуть (-г) *perf.* метаморфóзе. **metamorphosis** *n.* метаморфóза; (*biol.*) метаморфóз.
metaphor *n.* метáфора. **metaphorical** *adj.* метафори́ческий.
metaphysical *adj.* метафизи́ческий. **metaphysician** *n.* метафи́зик. **metaphysics** *n.* метафи́зика.
meteor *n.* метеóр. **meteoric** *adj.* метеори́ческий, метеóрный. **meteorite** *n.* метеори́т. **meteorological** *adj.* метеорологи́ческий. **meteorologist** *n.* метеорóлог. **meteorology** *n.* метеорóлогия.
meter *n.* счётчик; *v.t.* измеря́ть *imp.*, измéрить *perf.* при пóмощи счётчика.
methane *n.* метáн.
method *n.* мéтод, спóсоб; (*system*) систéма. **methodical** *adj.* системати́ческий, методи́чный.
Methodism *n.* методи́зм. **Methodist** *n.* методи́ст; *adj.* методи́стский.
methyl *n.* мети́л; *m. alcohol*, мети́ловый спирт. **methylated** *adj.*: *m. spirit(s)* денатурáт.
meticulous *adj.* тщáтельный.
metre *n.* метр. **metric(al)** *adj.* метри́ческий.
metronome *n.* метронóм.
metropolis *n.* (*capital*) столи́ца. **metropolitan** *adj.* столи́чный; *n.* (*eccl.*) митрополи́т.
mettle *n.* темперáмент; (*ardour*) пыл (-а(у)). **mettlesome** *adj.* горя́чий (-ч, -чá).
mew *see* **miaow.**
mezzanine *n.* антресóли *f.pl.*
mezzo-soprano *n.* мéццо-сопрáно (*voice*) *neut.* & (*person*) *f.indecl.*
miaow *interj.* мя́у; *n.* мяу́канье; *v.i.* мяу́кать *imp.*, мяу́кнуть *perf.*
mica *n.* слюдá.
Michaelmas *n.* Михáйлов день (дня) *m.*
micro- *in comb.* ми́кро-. **microbe** *n.* микрóб. **microcosm** *n.* микрокóсм. **microfilm** *n.* микрофи́льм. **micron** *n.* микрóн (*gen.pl.* -н). **micro-organism** *n.* микрооргани́зм. **microphone** *n.* микрофóн. **microscope** *n.* микроскóп. **microscopic** *adj.* микроскопи́ческий. **microsecond** *n.* микросеку́нда. **microwave** *adj.* микроволнóвый; *n.* микроволнá (*pl.* -óлны, *dat.* -óлнáм).
mid *adj.* срéдний, середи́нный. **midday** *n.* пóлдень (полу́дня & пóлдня) *m.*; *attrib.* полу́денный. **middle** *n.* середи́на; *adj.* срéдний; *m.-aged*, срéдних лет; *M. Ages*, срéдние векá *m.pl.*; *m. man*, посрéдник; *m.-sized*, срéднего размéра. **middleweight** *n.* срéдний вес.
midge *n.* мóшка.
midget *n.* кáрлик, -ица; *adj.* óчень мáленький, миниатю́рный.
Midlands *n.* центрáльные грáфства *neut.pl.* Áнглии. **midnight** *n.* пóлночь (полу́ночи & пóлночи); *attrib.* полу́ночный. **midriff** *n.* диафрáгма. **midshipman** *n.* корабéльный гардемари́н. **midst** *n.* середи́на. **midsummer** *n.* середи́на лéта. **midway** *adv.* на полпути́, на полдорóге. **mid-week** *n.*

середи́на неде́ли. **midwinter** *n.* середи́на зимы́.
midwife *n.* акуше́рка. **midwifery** *n.* акуше́рство.
might *n.* мощь, могу́щество; си́ла; *with all one's m., with m. and main*, не щадя́ сил. **mighty** *adj.* могу́щественный (-ен, -енна), мо́щный (-щен, -щна́, -щно).
mignonette *n.* резеда́.
migraine *n.* мигре́нь.
migrant *adj.* кочу́ющий; (*bird*) перелётный; *n.* (*person*) переселе́нец (-нца); (*bird*) перелётная пти́ца. **migrate** *v.i.* мигри́ровать *imp., perf.*; переселя́ться *imp.*, пересели́ться *perf.* **migration** *n.* мигра́ция. **migratory** *adj.* кочу́ющий; (*bird*) перелётный.
mike *n.* микрофо́н.
milch *adj.* моло́чный; *m.-cow*, до́йная коро́ва.
mild *adj.* (*soft*) мя́гкий (-гок, -гка́, -гко); (*light*) лёгкий (-гок, -гка́, -гко́, лёгки́); (*not sharp*) нео́стрый (не остр & остёр, остра́, о́стро́); (*not strong*) некре́пкий (-пок, -пка́, -пко); *m. steel*, мя́гкая сталь.
mildew *n.* (*fungi*) мильдю́ *neut.indecl.*; (*on paper etc.*) пле́сень.
mile *n.* ми́ля. **mileage** *n.* расстоя́ние в ми́лях; (*distance travelled*) коли́чество про́йденных миль; (*expenses*) де́ньги (-нег, -ньга́м) *pl.* на прое́зд. **milestone** *n.* ми́льный ка́мень (-мня; *pl.* -мни, -мне́й) *m.*; (*fig.*) ве́ха.
militancy *n.* вои́нственность. **militant** *adj.* во́инствующий; (*combative*) боево́й; *n.* боец (бойца́); активи́ст. **military** *adj.* вое́нный; *m. band*, духово́й орке́стр; *n.* вое́нные *sb.* **militate** *v.i.*: *m. against*, говори́ть *imp.* про́тив + *gen.* **militia** *n.* ополче́ние; (*USSR*) мили́ция. **militiaman** *n.* ополче́нец (-нца); (*USSR*) милиционе́р.
milk *n.* молоко́; (*of plants*) мле́чный сок; *attrib.* моло́чный; *v.t.* дои́ть *imp.*, по~ *perf.* **milkmaid** *n.* доя́рка. **milkman** *n.* продаве́ц (-вца́) молока́. **milksop** *n.* тря́пка. **milk-tooth** *n.* моло́чный зуб (*pl.* -ы, -о́в). **milky** *adj.* моло́чный; *M. Way*, Мле́чный Путь (-ти́, -тём) *m.*
mill *n.* ме́льница; (*factory*) фа́брика, заво́д; (*rolling-m.*) прока́тный стан; *m.-hand*, фабри́чный рабо́чий *sb.*; *m.-pond*, ме́льничный пруд (-а́, *loc.* -у́); *m.-race*, ме́льничный лото́к (-тка́); *m.-wheel*, ме́льничное колесо́ (*pl.* -ёса); *v.t.* (*grain etc.*) моло́ть (мелю́, -лешь) *imp.*, с~ *perf.*; (*cloth*) валя́ть *imp.*, с~ *perf.*; (*metal*) фрезерова́ть *imp.*, от~ *perf.*; (*coin*) гурти́ть *imp.*; *milled edge*, (*of coin*) гурт; *v.i.* кружи́ть (-ужу́, -у́жи́шь) *imp.* **miller** *n.* ме́льник.
millenium *n.* тысячеле́тие.
millepede, milli- *n.* многоно́жка.
millet *n.* (*plant*) про́со; (*grain*) пшено́.
milli- *in comb.* милли-. **milliard** *n.* миллиа́рд. **millibar** *n.* миллиба́р. **milligram(me)** *n.* миллигра́мм. **millimetre** *n.* миллиме́тр.
milliner *n.* моди́стка; шля́пница. **millinery** *n.* да́мские шля́пы *f.pl.*
million *n.* миллио́н. **millionaire** *n.* миллионе́р. **millionth** *adj.* миллио́нный.
millipede *see* **mille-**.
millstone *n.* жёрнов (*pl.* -а́); (*fig.*) бре́мя *neut.*
milt *n.* моло́ки (-к) *pl.*
mime *n.* мим; *v.t.* изобража́ть *imp.*, изобрази́ть *perf.* мими́чески; *v.i.* исполня́ть *imp.*, испо́лнить *perf.* роль в пантоми́ме. **mimic** *adj.* мими́ческий, подража́тельный; *n.* мими́ст; *v.t.* имити́ровать *imp.*, сымити́ровать *perf.*; (*ape*) обезья́нничать *imp.*, с~ *perf.* с + *gen.* **mimicry** *n.* имита́ция; (*biol.*) мимикри́я.
mimosa *n.* мимо́за; (*acacia*) ака́ция.
minaret *n.* минаре́т.
mince *n.* (*meat*) ру́бленое мя́со; *v.t.* руби́ть (-блю́, -бишь) *imp.*; (*in machine*) пропуска́ть *imp.*, пропусти́ть (-ущу́, -у́стишь) *perf.* че́рез мясору́бку; *v.i.* (*speak*) говори́ть *imp.* жема́нно; (*walk*) семени́ть *imp.*; *not to m. matters*, говори́ть *imp.* пря́мо, без обиняко́в. **mincemeat** *n.* начи́нка из изю́ма, миндаля́ и т.п. **mincer** *n.* мясору́бка.
mind *n.* ум (-а́), ра́зум; (*memory*) па́мять; (*opinion*) мне́ние; *absence of m.*, забы́вчивость, рассе́янность;

bear in m., иметь *imp.* в виду́; по́мнить *imp.*; *be in one's right m.*, быть в здра́вом уме́; *be out of one's m.*, быть не в своём уме́; *change one's m.*, переду́мывать *imp.*, переду́мать *perf.*; *make up one's m.*, реша́ться *imp.*, реши́ться *perf.*; *presence of m.*, прису́тствие ду́ха; *v.t.* (*give heed to*) обраща́ть *imp.*, обрати́ть (-ащу́, -ати́шь) *perf.* внима́ние на + *acc.*; (*look after*) присма́тривать *imp.*, присмотре́ть (-рю́, -ришь) *perf.* за + *instr.*; *I don't m.*, я не возража́ю; я ничего́ не име́ю про́тив; *don't m. me*, не обраща́й(те) внима́ния на меня́! *m. you don't forget*, смотри́ не забу́дь! *m. your own business*, не вме́шивайтесь в чужи́е дела́! *never m.*, не беспоко́йтесь! ничего́! **minded** *adj.* (*disposed*) располо́женный (-ен). **mindful** *adj.* по́мнящий, внима́тельный (of, к + *dat.*).

mine[1] *poss.pron.* мой (моя́, моё; мои́); свой (-оя́, -оё; -ои́).

mine[2] *n.* ша́хта, рудни́к (-а́); (*fig.*) исто́чник; (*mil.*) ми́на; *v.t.* (*obtain from m.*) добыва́ть *imp.*, добы́ть (добу́ду, -дешь; до́был, -а́, -о) *perf.*; (*mil.*) мини́ровать *imp.*, *perf.* **minefield** *n.* ми́нное по́ле (*pl.* -ля́). **minelayer** *n.* ми́нный загради́тель *m.* **miner** *n.* шахтёр, горня́к (-а́). **minesweeper** *n.* ми́нный тра́льщик.

mineral *n.* минера́л; *adj.* минера́льный; *m.-water*, минера́льная вода́ (*acc.* -ду). **mineralogist** *n.* минерало́г. **mineralogy** *n.* минерало́гия.

mingle *v.t.* & *i.* сме́шивать(ся) *imp.*, смеша́ть(ся) *perf.*

miniature *n.* миниатю́ра; *adj.* миниатю́рный. **miniaturist** *n.* миниатюри́ст.

minibus *n.* микроавто́бус.

minim *n.* (*mus.*) полови́нная но́та. **minimal** *adj.* минима́льный. **minimize** *v.t.* (*reduce*) доводи́ть (-ожу́, -о́дишь) *imp.*, довести́ (-еду́, -едёшь; -ёл, -ела́) *perf.* до ми́нимума; (*underestimate*) преуменьша́ть *imp.*, преуме́ньши́ть *perf.* **minimum** *n.* ми́нимум; *adj.* минима́льный.

mining *n.* го́рное де́ло.

miniskirt *n.* ми́ни-ю́бка.

minister *n.* (*polit.*) мини́стр; (*diplomat*) посла́нник; (*eccl.*) свяще́нник. **ministerial** *adj.* министе́рский; (*eccl.*) па́стырский. **ministration** *n.* по́мощь. **ministry** *n.* (*polit.*) министе́рство; (*eccl.*) духове́нство.

mink *n.* но́рка; *attrib.* но́рковый.

minnow *n.* голья́н.

minor *adj.* (*lesser*) ме́ньший; (*less important*) второстепе́нный (-нен, -нна); (*mus.*) мино́рный; *n.* (*person under age*) несовершенноле́тний *n.*; (*mus.*) мино́р. **minority** *n.* (*small number*) меньшинство́ (*pl.* -ва); (*age*) несовершенноле́тие; *national m.*, нацменьшинство́ (*pl.* -ва).

minstrel *n.* менестре́ль *m.*

mint[1] *n.* (*plant*) мя́та; (*peppermint*) пе́речная мя́та; *attrib.* мя́тный.

mint[2] *n.* (*econ.*) моне́тный двор (-а́); *in m. condition*, блестя́щий, но́вый (нов, -а́, -о); (*book etc.*) непотрёпанный (-ан); *v.t.* чека́нить *imp.*, от~, вы́~ *perf.*

minuet *n.* менуэ́т.

minus *prep.* ми́нус + *acc.*; без + *gen.*; *n.* ми́нус; *adj.* (*math.*, *electr.*) отрица́тельный.

minuscule *adj.* минуску́льный; (о́чень) ма́ленький; *n.* минуску́л.

minute[1] *n.* мину́та; *pl.* протоко́л; *v.t.* заноси́ть (-ошу́, -о́сишь) *imp.*, занести́ (-есу́, -есёшь; -ёс, -есла́) *perf.* в протоко́л.

minute[2] *adj.* ме́лкий (-лок, -лка́, -лко), мельча́йший. **minutiae** *n.* ме́лочи (-че́й) *f.pl.*

minx *n.* коке́тка.

miracle *n.* чу́до (*pl.* -деса́). **miraculous** *adj.* чуде́сный.

mirage *n.* мира́ж.

mire *n.* (*mud*) грязь (*loc.* -зи́); (*swamp*) боло́то. **miry** *adj.* гря́зный (-зен, -зна́, -зно).

mirror *n.* зе́ркало (*pl.* -ла́); (*fig.*) отображе́ние; *m. image*, зерка́льное изображе́ние; *v.t.* отража́ть *imp.*, отрази́ть *perf.*

mirth *n.* весе́лье.

misadventure *n.* несча́стный слу́чай.

misanthrope *n.* мизантро́п. **misanthropic** *adj.* мизантропи́ческий. **misanthropy** *n.* мизантро́пия.

misapplication *n.* непра́вильное испо́льзование. **misapply** *v.t.* непра́вильно испо́льзовать *imp., perf.* **misapprehend** *v.t.* непра́вильно понима́ть *imp.*, поня́ть (пойму́, -мёшь; по́нял, -а́, -о) *perf.* **misapprehension** *n.* непра́вильное понима́ние. **misappropriate** *v.t.* незако́нно присва́ивать *imp.*, присво́ить *perf.* **misappropriation** *n.* незако́нное присвое́ние. **misbehave** *v.i.* ду́рно вести́ (веду́, -дёшь; вёл, -а́) *imp.* себя́.

miscalculate *v.t.* непра́вильно рассчи́тывать *imp.*, рассчита́ть *perf.*; (*fig., abs.*) просчи́тываться *imp.*, просчита́ться *perf.* **miscarriage** *n.* (*mistake*) оши́бка; (*med.*) вы́кидыш, або́рт; *m. of justice*, суде́бная оши́бка. **miscarry** *v.i.* терпе́ть (-плю́, -пишь) *imp.*, по~ *perf.* неуда́чу; (*med.*) име́ть *imp.* вы́кидыш. **miscast** *v.t.* непра́вильно распределя́ть *imp.*, распредели́ть *perf.* роль + *dat.*

miscellaneous *adj.* ра́зный, разнообра́зный. **miscellany** *n.* (*mixture*) смесь; (*book*) сбо́рник.

mischance *n.* несча́стный слу́чай. **mischief** *n.* (*harm*) вред (-а́); (*naughtiness*) озорство́; (*pranks*) прока́зы *f.pl.* **mischievous** *adj.* озорно́й. **misconception** *n.* непра́вильное представле́ние. **misconduct** *n.* дурно́е поведе́ние; (*adultery*) супру́жеская неве́рность; *v.t.*: *m. oneself*, ду́рно вести́ (веду́, -дёшь; вёл, -а́) *imp.* себя́. **misconstruction** *n.* непра́вильное истолкова́ние. **misconstrue** *v.t.* непра́вильно истолко́вывать *imp.*, истолкова́ть *perf.* **miscount** *n.* оши́бка при подсчёте; непра́вильный подсчёт; *v.t.* ошиба́ться *imp.*, ошиби́ться (-бу́сь, -бёшься; -бся) *perf.* при подсчёте + *gen.*

misdeal *v.i.* ошиба́ться *imp.*, ошиби́ться (-бу́сь, -бёшься; -бся) *perf.* при сда́че карт. **misdeed** *n.* злодея́ние. **misdirect** *v.t.* непра́вильно направля́ть *imp.*, напра́вить *perf.*; (*letter*) непра́вильно адресова́ть *imp., perf.* **misdirection** *n.* непра́вильное указа́ние, руково́дство.

miser *n.* скупе́ц (-пца́), скря́га *m.* & *f.* **miserable** *adj.* (*unhappy*) несча́стный; (*wretched*) жа́лкий (-лок, -лка́, -лко), убо́гий. **miserly** *adj.* скупо́й (скуп, -а́, -о). **misery** *n.* страда́ние, несча́стье.

misfire *v.i.* дава́ть (даёт) *imp.*, дать (даст; дал, -а́, да́ло́, -и) *perf.* осе́чку; *n.* осе́чка. **misfit** *n.* (*garment*) пло́хо сидя́щее пла́тье (*gen.pl.* -в); (*person*) неуда́чник. **misfortune** *n.* несча́стье, беда́. **misgiving** *n.* опасе́ние. **misgovern** *v.t.* пло́хо управля́ть *imp.* + *instr.* **misgovernment** *n.* плохо́е управле́ние. **misguided** *adj.* введённый (-ён, -ена́) в заблужде́ние.

mishap *n.* неуда́ча, несча́стье. **misinform** *v.t.* дезинформи́ровать *imp., perf.* **misinformation** *n.* дезинформа́ция. **misinterpret** *v.t.* неве́рно понима́ть *imp.*, поня́ть (пойму́, -мёшь; по́нял, -а́, -о) *perf.* **misjudge** *v.t.* неве́рно оце́нивать *imp.*, оцени́ть (-ню́, -нишь) *perf.* **misjudgement** *n.* неве́рная оце́нка. **mislay** *v.t.* класть (-аду́, -адёшь; -ал) *imp.*, положи́ть (-жу́, -жишь) *perf.* не на ме́сто; затеря́ть *perf.* **mislead** *v.t.* вводи́ть (-ожу́, -о́дишь) *imp.*, ввести́ (введу́, -дёшь; ввёл, -а́) *perf.* в заблужде́ние. **mismanage** *v.t.* пло́хо управля́ть *imp.* + *instr.* **mismanagement** *n.* плохо́е управле́ние. **misnomer** *n.* непра́вильное назва́ние.

misogynist *n.* женоненави́стник. **misogyny** *n.* женоненави́стничество.

misplace *v.t.* класть (-аду́, -адёшь; -ал) *imp.*, положи́ть (-жу́, -жишь) *perf.* не на ме́сто; *misplaced confidence*, незаслу́женное дове́рие. **misprint** *n.* опеча́тка; *v.t.* непра́вильно печа́тать *imp.*, на~ *perf.* **mispronounce** *v.t.* непра́вильно произноси́ть (-ошу́, -о́сишь) *imp.*, произнести́ (-есу́, -есёшь; -ёс, -есла́) *perf.* **mispronunciation** *n.* непра́вильное произноше́ние. **misquotation** *n.* непра́вильная цита́та; непра́вильное цити́рование. **misquote** *v.t.* непра́вильно цити́ровать *imp.*, про~ *perf.* **misread** *v.t.* непра́вильно чита́ть *imp.*, про~ *perf.* **misrepresent**

v.t. искажа́ть *imp.*, искази́ть *perf.* **misrepresentation** *n.* искаже́ние.

Miss[1] *n.* (*title*) мисс.

miss[2] *n.* про́мах, неуда́ча; *v.i.* прома́хиваться *imp.*, промахну́ться *perf.*; *v.t.* (*let slip*) упуска́ть *imp.*, упусти́ть (-ущу́, -у́стишь) *perf.*; (*train*) опа́здывать *imp.*, опозда́ть *perf.* на + *acc.*; *m. out*, пропуска́ть *imp.*, пропусти́ть (-ущу́, -у́стишь) *perf.*; *m. the point*, не понима́ть *imp.*, поня́ть (пойму́, -мёшь; по́нял, -а́, -о) *perf.* су́ти.

missel-thrush *n.* дрозд-деря́ба.

misshapen *adj.* уро́дливый.

missile *n.* снаря́д, раке́та.

missing *adj.* отсу́тствующий, недостаю́щий; (*person*) пропа́вший бе́з вести.

mission *n.* ми́ссия; командиро́вка. **missionary** *n.* миссионе́р; *adj.* миссионе́рский. **missive** *n.* письмо́ (*pl.* -сьма, -сем, -сьмам); посла́ние.

misspell *v.t.* непра́вильно писа́ть (пишу́ -шешь) *imp.*, на~ *perf.* **misspelling** *n.* непра́вильное написа́ние. **misspent** *adj.* растра́ченный (-ен) (впусту́ю). **misstatement** *n.* непра́вильное заявле́ние.

mist *n.* тума́н, мгла.

mistake *v.t.* непра́вильно понима́ть *imp.*, поня́ть (пойму́, -мёшь; по́нял, -а́, -о) *perf.*; *m. for*, принима́ть *imp.*, приня́ть (приму́, -мешь; при́нял, -а́, -о) *perf.* за + *acc.*; *n.* оши́бка; *make a m.*, ошиба́ться *imp.*, ошиби́ться (-бу́сь, -бёшься; -бся) *perf.* **mistaken** *adj.* оши́бочный; *be m.*, ошиба́ться *imp.*, ошиби́ться (-бу́сь, -бёшься; -бся) *perf.*

mister *n.* ми́стер, господи́н.

mistletoe *n.* оме́ла.

mistranslate *v.t.* непра́вильно переводи́ть (-ожу́, -о́дишь) *imp.*, перевести́ (-еду́, -едёшь; -ёл, -ела́) *perf.* **mistranslation** *n.* непра́вильный перево́д.

mistress *n.* хозя́йка; (*teacher*) учи́тельница; (*lover*) любо́вница.

mistrust *v.t.* не доверя́ть *imp.* + *dat.*; *n.* недове́рие. **mistrustful** *adj.* недове́рчивый.

misty *adj.* тума́нный.

misunderstand *v.t.* непра́вильно понима́ть *imp.*, поня́ть (пойму́, -мёшь; по́нял, -а́, -о) *perf.* **misunderstanding** *n.* непра́вильное понима́ние, недоразуме́ние; (*disagreement*) размо́лвка.

misuse *v.t.* непра́вильно употребля́ть *imp.*, употреби́ть *perf.*; (*ill-treat*) ду́рно обраща́ться *imp.* с + *instr.*; *n.* непра́вильное употребле́ние.

mite *n.* (*cheese-m.*) (сы́рный) клещ (-а́); (*child*) ма́ленький ребёнок (-нка; *pl.* де́ти, -те́й, -тям, -тьми́), кро́шка; *widow's m.*, ле́пта вдови́цы; *not a m.*, ничу́ть.

mitigate *v.t.* смягча́ть *imp.*, смягчи́ть *perf.* **mitigation** *n.* смягче́ние.

mitre *n.* ми́тра.

mitten *n.* рукави́ца, мите́нка; *pl.* (*boxing-gloves*) боксёрские перча́тки *f.pl.*

mix *v.t.* меша́ть *imp.*, с~ *perf.*; *v.i.* сме́шиваться *imp.*, смеша́ться *perf.*; (*person*) обща́ться *imp.*; *m. up*, (*confuse*) пу́тать *imp.*, с~ *perf.*; *get mixed up in*, впу́тываться *imp.*, впу́таться *perf.* в + *acc.*; *n.* смесь; (*food m.*) (пищево́й) полуфабрика́т. **mixer** *n.* смеси́тель *m.* **mixture** *n.* смесь; (*medicine*) миксту́ра.

mnemonic *adj.* мнемони́ческий; *n.* мнемони́ческий приём; *pl.* мнемо́ника.

mo *n.* мину́тка; *half a mo*, (одну́) мину́тку!

moan *n.* стон; *v.i.* стона́ть (-ну́, -нешь) *imp.*, про~ *perf.*

moat *n.* (крепостно́й) ров (рва, *loc.* во рву́). **moated** *adj.* обнесённый (-ён, -ена́) рвом.

mob *n.* (*populace*) чернь; (*crowd*) толпа́ (*pl.* -пы); (*gang*) ша́йка; *v.t.* (*attack*) напада́ть *imp.*, напа́сть (-адёт; -а́л) *perf.* толпо́й на + *acc.*; (*crowd around*) толпи́ться *imp.* вокру́г + *gen.* **mobster** *n.* га́нгстер.

mobile *adj.* подвижно́й, передвижно́й. **mobility** *n.* подви́жность. **mobilization** *n.* мобилиза́ция. **mobilize** *v.t.* & *i.* мобилизова́ть(ся) *imp.*, *perf.*

moccasin *n.* мокаси́н (*gen.pl.* -н).

mocha *n.* мо́кко *m.* & *neut.indecl.*

mock *v.t.* & *i.* издева́ться *imp.* над + *instr.*; осме́ивать *imp.*, осмея́ть (-ею́

-еёшь) *perf.*; *adj.* (*sham*) подде́льный; (*pretended*) мни́мый; *mocking-bird*, пересме́шник; *m. turtle soup*, суп из теля́чьей головы́; *m.-up*, маке́т, моде́ль. **mockery** *n.* (*derision*) издева́тельство, насме́шка; (*travesty*) паро́дия (of, на+*acc.*; +*gen.*).

mode *n.* (*manner*) о́браз; (*method*) спо́соб.

model *n.* (*representation*) моде́ль, маке́т; (*pattern*) образе́ц (-зца́); (*artist's*) нату́рщик, -ица; (*mannequin*) манеке́нщик, -ица; *adj.* образцо́вый, приме́рный; *v.t.* лепи́ть (-плю́, -пишь) *imp.*, вы́~, с~ *perf.*; (*document*) оформля́ть *imp.*, офо́рмить *perf.*; *v.i.* (*act as m.*) быть нату́рщиком, -ицей; быть манеке́нщиком, -ицей; *m. after, on*, создава́ть (-даю́, -даёшь) *imp.*, созда́ть (-а́м, -а́шь, -а́ст, -ади́м; со́зда́л, -а́, -о) *perf.* по образцу́+*gen.*; *m. oneself on*, брать (беру́, -рёшь; брал, -а́, -о) *imp.*, взять (возьму́, -мёшь; взял, -а́, -о) *perf.*+*acc.* за образе́ц, приме́р.

moderate *adj.* (*var. senses*; *polit.*) уме́ренный (-ен, -енна); (*person, conduct*) сде́ржанный (-ан, -анна); (*quantity*) небольшо́й; *v.t.* умеря́ть *imp.*, уме́рить *perf.*; *v.i.* стиха́ть *imp.*, сти́хнуть (-х) *perf.* **moderation** *n.* уме́ренность; *in m.*, уме́ренно.

modern *adj.* совреме́нный (-нен, -нна), но́вый (нов, -а́, -о). **modernism** *n.* модерни́зм. **modernistic** *adj.* модерни́стский. **modernity** *n.* совреме́нность. **modernization** *n.* модерниза́ция. **modernize** *v.t.* модернизи́ровать *imp.*, *perf.*

modest *adj.* скро́мный (-мен, -мна́, -мно). **modesty** *n.* скро́мность.

modification *n.* видоизмене́ние, модифика́ция. **modify** *v.t.* (*soften*) смягча́ть *imp.*, смягчи́ть *perf.*; (*partially change*) модифици́ровать *imp.*, *perf.*

modish *adj.* мо́дный (-ден, -дна́, -дно).

modular *adj.* мо́дульный. **modulate** *v.t.* модули́ровать *imp.* **modulation** *n.* модуля́ция. **module** *n.* (*measure*) едини́ца измере́ния; (*unit*) мо́дульный, автоно́мный, отсе́к; *lunar excursion m.*, лу́нная ка́псула. **modulus** *n.* мо́дуль *m.*

mohair *n.* мохе́р.

Mohammedan *adj.* мусульма́нский; *n.* мусульма́нин (*pl.* -а́не, -а́н), -а́нка. **Mohammedanism** *n.* исла́м.

moiré *adj.* муа́ровый.

moist *adj.* сыро́й (сыр, -а́, -о), вла́жный (-жен, -жна́, -жно). **moisten** *v.t.* & *i.* увлажня́ть(ся) *imp.*, увлажни́ть(ся) *perf.* **moisture** *n.* вла́га.

mol *see* **mole**[4].

molar[1] *n.* (*tooth*) коренно́й зуб (*pl.* -ы, -о́в); *adj.* коренно́й.

molar[2] *adj.* (*chem.*) мо́льный, моля́рный.

molasses *n.* чёрная па́тока.

mole[1] *n.* (*on skin*) ро́динка.

mole[2] *n.* (*animal*) крот (-а́). **molehill** *n.* кротови́на. **moleskin** *n.* кро́то́вый мех; (*fabric*) молески́н; *pl.* молески́новые брю́ки (-к) *pl.*

mole[3] *n.* (*pier*) мол (*loc.* -у́).

mole[4] *n.* (*chem.*) моль *m.*

molecular *adj.* молекуля́рный. **molecule** *n.* моле́кула.

molest *v.t.* пристава́ть (-таю́, -таёшь) *imp.*, приста́ть (-а́ну, -а́нешь) *perf.* к+*dat.* **molestation** *n.* пристава́ние.

mollify *v.t.* смягча́ть *imp.*, смягчи́ть *perf.*

mollusc *n.* моллю́ск.

mollycoddle *n.* не́женка *m.* & *f.*; *v.t.* не́жить *imp.*

molten *adj.* распла́вленный (-ен).

moment *n.* моме́нт, миг, мгнове́ние; (*phys.*) моме́нт; (*importance*) значе́ние; *a m. ago*, то́лько что; *at a m.'s notice*, по пе́рвому тре́бованию; *at the last m.*, в после́днюю мину́ту; *just a m.*, сейча́с! погоди́! **momentarily** *adv.* на мгнове́ние. **momentary** *adj.* преходя́щий, кратковре́менный (-нен, -нна). **momentous** *adj.* ва́жный (-жен, -жна́, -жно, ва́жны́). **momentum** *n.* коли́чество движе́ния; (*impetus*) дви́жущая си́ла; *gather m.*, набира́ть *imp.*, набра́ть (наберу́, -рёшь; набра́л, -а́, -о) *perf.* ско́рость.

monarch *n.* мона́рх, ~иня. **monarchical** *adj.* монархи́ческий. **monarchism** *n.*

монархи́зм. **monarchist** *n.* монархи́ст. **monarchy** *n.* мона́рхия.

monastery *n.* (мужско́й) монасты́рь (-ря́) *m.* **monastic** *adj.* (*of monastery*) монасты́рский; (*of monks*) мона́шеский. **monasticism** *n.* мона́шество.

Monday *n.* понеде́льник.

monetary *adj.* де́нежный. **money** *n.* де́ньги (-нег, -ньга́м) *pl.*; *m.-box*, копи́лка; *m.-changer*, меня́ла *m.*; *m.-grubbing*, стяжа́тельский; *m.-lender*, ростовщи́к (-а́), -и́ца; *m.-market*, де́нежный ры́нок (-нка); *m. order*, (де́нежный) почто́вый перево́д. **moneyed** *adj.* бога́тый.

Mongol *n.* монго́л, ~ка; *adj.* монго́льский.

mongoose *n.* мангу́ста.

mongrel *adj.* нечистокро́вный, сме́шанный; *n.* дворня́жка; (*also fig.*) ублю́док (-дка).

monitor *n.* (*school*) ста́роста *m.* (кла́сса); (*lizard*) вара́н; (*naut.*; *TV*) монито́р; (*of broadcasts etc.*) слуха́ч (-а́); (*of radioactivity*) дозиме́тр; *v.t.* проверя́ть *imp.*, прове́рить *perf.*; контроли́ровать *imp.*, про~ *perf.*; *v.i.* вести́ (веду́, -дёшь; вёл, -а́) *imp.* радиоперехва́т.

monk *n.* мона́х.

monkey *n.* обезья́на; *v.i.*: *m.* (*about*) *with*, неуме́ло обраща́ться *imp.* с+*instr.*; *m. business*, прока́за; *m.-jacket*, коро́ткая (матро́сская) ку́ртка; *m.-nut*, земляно́й оре́х; *m.-puzzle*, арауќария; *m. tricks*, ша́лости *f.pl.*; *m.-wrench*, разводно́й га́ечный ключ (-а́).

mono- *in comb.* одно- моно-, едино-. **monochrome** *adj.* одноцве́тный; *n.* однокра́сочное изображе́ние. **monocle** *n.* моно́кль *m.* **monogamous** *adj.* единобра́чный. **monogamy** *n.* единобра́чие. **monogram** *n.* моногра́мма. **monograph** *n.* моногра́фия. **monolith** *n.* моноли́т. **monolithic** *adj.* моноли́тный. **monologue** *n.* моноло́г. **monomania** *n.* монома́ния. **monomaniac** *n.* манья́к. **monoplane** *n.* монопла́н. **monopolist** *n.* монополи́ст. **monopolize** *v.t.* монополизи́ровать *imp.*, *perf.* **monopoly** *n.* монопо́лия. **monorail** *n.* моноре́льсовая доро́га. **monosyllabic** *adj.* односло́жный. **monosyllable** *n.* односло́жное сло́во (*pl.* -ва́). **monotheism** *n.* единобо́жие, монотеи́зм. **monotheistic** *adj.* монотеисти́ческий. **monotone** *n.* моното́нность; *in a m.*, моното́нно. **monotonous** *adj.* моното́нный, однообра́зный. **monotony** *n.* моното́нность, однообра́зие. **monoxide** *n.* однооќись.

monsoon *n.* (*wind*) муссо́н; (*rainy season*) дождли́вый сезо́н.

monster *n.* чудо́вище, уро́д; *adj.* грома́дный. **monstrosity** *n.* уро́дство, чудо́вищность; чудо́вище. **monstrous** *adj.* чудо́вищный; (*huge*) грома́дный; (*atrocious*) безобра́зный.

montage *n.* (*cin.*) монта́ж; (*of photographs*) фотомонта́ж.

month *n.* ме́сяц. **monthly** *adj.* ежеме́сячный, ме́сячный; *n.* ежеме́сячник; *adv.* ежеме́сячно.

monument *n.* па́мятник. **monumental** *adj.* монумента́льный; (*stupendous*) изуми́тельный, колосса́льный.

moo *v.i.* мыча́ть (-чу́, -чи́шь); *n.* мыча́ние.

mood[1] *n.* (*gram.*) наклоне́ние.

mood[2] *n.* настрое́ние. **moody** *adj.* уны́лый, в дурно́м настрое́нии.

moon *n.* (*of earth*) луна́; (*of other planets*) спу́тник; *v.i.* бесце́льно слоня́ться *imp.* **moonlight** *n.* лу́нный свет; *v.i.* халту́рить *imp.* **moonshine** *n.* фанта́зия; (*liquor*) самого́н. **moonstone** *n.* лу́нный ка́мень (-мня) *m.* **moonstruck** *adj.* поме́шанный (-ан).

moor[1] *n.* ме́стность, поро́сшая ве́реском. **moorcock** *n.* саме́ц (-мца́) шотла́ндской курола́тки. **moorhen** *n.* (*water-hen*) водяна́я ку́рочка. **moorland** *n.* ве́ресковая пу́стошь.

Moor[2] *n.* мавр. **Moorish** *adj.* маврита́нский.

moor[3] *v.t.* & *i.* швартова́ть(ся) *imp.*, при~ *perf.* **mooring** *n.*: *pl.* швартовы *m.pl.*; (*place*) прича́л; *m.-mast*, прича́льная ма́чта.

moose *n.* америка́нский лось (*pl.* -си, -се́й) *m.*

moot *adj.* спо́рный.

mop *n.* шва́бра; (*of hair*) копна́ воло́с; *v.t.* протира́ть *imp.*, протере́ть (-тру́, -трёшь; -тёр) *perf.* (шва́брой); *m. one's brow*, вытира́ть *imp.*, вы́тереть (-тру, -трешь; -тер) *perf.* лоб; *m. up*, вытира́ть *imp.*, вы́тереть (-тру, -трешь; -тер) *perf.*; (*mil.*) очища́ть *imp.*, очи́стить *perf.* (от проти́вника).

mope *v.i.* хандри́ть *imp.*

moped *n.* мопе́д.

moraine *n.* море́на.

moral *adj.* мора́льный, нра́вственный (-ен, -енна); *n.* мора́ль; *pl.* нра́вы *m.pl.*, нра́вственность. **morale** *n.* мора́льное состоя́ние; (*of troops*) боево́й дух. **moralist** *n.* морали́ст, ~ка. **moralistic** *adj.* моралисти́ческий. **morality** *n.* нра́вственность, мора́ль. **moralize** *v.i.* морализи́ровать *imp.*

morass *n.* боло́то, тряси́на.

moratorium *n.* морато́рий.

morbid *adj.* боле́зненный (-ен, -енна), нездоро́вый; (*med.*) патологи́ческий.

mordant *adj.* е́дкий (е́док, едка́, е́дко).

more *adj.* (*larger*) бо́льший; (*greater quantity*) бо́льше + *gen.*; (*additional*) ещё; *adv.* бо́льше; (*in addition*) ещё; (*forming comparative*) бо́лее; *and what is m.*, и вдоба́вок; и бо́льше того́; *m. fool you*, тем ху́же для тебя́; *m. or less*, бо́лее и́ли ме́нее; *once m.*, ещё раз; *what m. do you want?* что ещё ты хо́чешь? *without m. ado*, без дальне́йших церемо́ний. **moreover** *adv.* сверх того́; кро́ме того́.

mores *n.* нра́вы *m.pl.*

morganatic *adj.* морганати́ческий.

morgue *n.* морг; (*journ.*) спра́вочный отде́л.

moribund *adj.* умира́ющий.

morning *n.* у́тро; *in the mornings*, по утра́м; *since m.*, с утра́; *towards m.*, к утру́; *until m.*, до утра́; *at seven o'clock in the m.*, в семь часо́в утра́; *attrib.* у́тренний; *m. coat*, визи́тка.

morocco *n.* сафья́н; *attrib.* сафья́новый.

moron *n.* у́мственно отста́лый *sb.* **moronic** *adj.* отста́лый.

morose *adj.* угрю́мый.

morpheme *n.* морфе́ма.

morphine *n.* мо́рфий.

morphology *n.* морфоло́гия.

Morse (code) *n.* а́збука Мо́рзе.

morsel *n.* кусо́чек (-чка).

mortal *adj.* сме́ртный, смерте́льный; *n.* сме́ртный *sb.* **mortality** *n.* смерте́льность; (*death-rate*) сме́ртность.

mortar *n.* (*vessel*) сту́па, сту́пка; (*cannon*) миномёт, морти́ра; (*cement*) (известко́вый) раство́р; *m.-board*, (*cap*) академи́ческая ша́почка с пло́ским квадра́тным ве́рхом.

mortgage *n.* ипоте́ка; (*deed*) закладна́я *sb.*; *v.t.* закла́дывать *imp.*, заложи́ть (-жу́, -жишь) *perf.*

mortification *n.* (*humiliation*) униже́ние; (*of the flesh*) умерщвле́ние. **mortify** *v.t.* унижа́ть *imp.*, уни́зить *perf.*; умерщвля́ть *imp.*, умертви́ть (-рщвлю́, -ртви́шь) *perf.*

mortise *n.* гнездо́ (*pl.* -ёзда), паз (*loc.* -у́; *pl.* -ы́); *m. lock*, врезно́й замо́к (-мка́).

mortuary *adj.* похоро́нный; *n.* морг, поко́йницкая *sb.*

mosaic[1] *n.* моза́ика; *adj.* моза́ичный.

Mosaic[2] *adj.* Моисе́ев.

Moslem *n.* мусульма́нин (*pl.* -а́не, -а́н), -а́нка; *adj.* мусульма́нский.

mosque *n.* мече́ть.

mosquito *n.* моски́т; *m.-net*, моски́тная се́тка.

moss *n.* мох (м(о́)ха, *loc.* м(о́)хе & мху́; *pl.* мхи); *m.-grown*, поро́сший мхом. **mossy** *adj.* мши́стый.

most *adj.* наибо́льший; *n.* наибо́льшее коли́чество; *adj.* & *n.* (*majority*) большинство́ + *gen.*; бо́льшая часть + *gen.*; *adv.* бо́льше всего́, наибо́лее; (*forming superlative*) са́мый. **mostly** *adv.* гла́вным о́бразом.

mote *n.* пыли́нка.

motel *n.* моте́ль *m.*

moth *n.* моль, ночна́я ба́бочка; *m.-ball*, нафтали́новый ша́рик; *m.-eaten*, изъе́денный мо́лью.

mother *n.* мать (-тери, *instr.* -терью; *pl.* -тери, -тере́й); *v.t.* относи́ться (-ошу́сь, -о́сишься) *imp.* по-матери́нски к + *dat.*; *m. country*, метропо́лия; *m.-in-law*, (*wife's m.*) тёща; (*husband's m.*) свекро́вь; *m. of pearl*, перламу́тр; перламу́тровый; *m. tongue*, родно́й язы́к (-а́). **motherhood** *n.* матери́нство.

motherland *n.* ро́дина. **motherless** *adj.* лишённый (-ён, -ена́) ма́тери. **motherly** *adj.* матери́нский.
motif *n.* основна́я те́ма.
motion *n.* движе́ние, ход; (*gesture*) жест; (*proposal*) предложе́ние; (*of bowels*) испражне́ние; *in m.*, в движе́нии, на ходу́; *v.t.* пока́зывать *imp.*, показа́ть (-ажу́, -а́жешь) *perf.* + *dat.* же́стом, что́бы... **motionless** *adj.* неподви́жный. **motivate** *v.t.* побужда́ть *imp.*, побуди́ть *perf.* **motivation** *n.* побужде́ние. **motive** *n.* по́вод, моти́в; *adj.* дви́жущий, дви́гательный.
motley *adj.* (*in colour*) разноцве́тный; (*varied*) пёстрый (-р, -ра́, пёстро́); *n.* вся́кая вся́чина; (*costume*) шутовско́й костю́м.
motor *n.* дви́гатель *m.*, мото́р; *adj.* дви́гательный, мото́рный; (*of m. vehicles*) автомоби́льный; *m. boat*, мото́рная ло́дка; *m. bus*, авто́бус; *m. car*, (легково́й) автомоби́ль *m.*; *m. cycle* мотоци́кл; *m. racing*, автомоби́льные го́нки *f.pl.*; *m. scooter*, моторо́ллер; *m. vehicle*, автомоби́ль *m.* **motoring** *n.* автомобили́зм. **motorist** *n.* автомобили́ст, ~ка. **motorize** *v.t.* моторизова́ть *imp.*, *perf.* **motorway** *n.* автостра́да.
mottled *adj.* испещрённый (-ён, -ена́), кра́пчатый.
motto *n.* деви́з.
mould[1] *n.* (*earth*) взрыхлённая земля́ (*acc.* -лю).
mould[2] *n.* (*shape*) фо́рма, фо́рмочка; *v.t.* формова́ть *imp.*, с~ *perf.*; лепи́ть (-плю́, -пишь) *imp.*, вы́~, с~ *perf.* **moulding** *n.* (*action*) формо́вка; (*decoration*) лепно́е украше́ние; (*in wood*) баге́т.
mould[3] *n.* (*fungi*) пле́сень. **mouldy** *adj.* заплесневе́лый; (*coll.*) дрянно́й (-нен, -нна́, -нно).
moulder *v.i.* разлага́ться *imp.*, разложи́ться (-ится) *perf.*
moult *v.i.* линя́ть *imp.*, вы́~ *perf.*; *n.* ли́нька.
mound *n.* холм (-а́); (*heap*) на́сыпь.
Mount[1] *n.* (*in names*) гора́ (*acc.* -ру).
mount[2] *v.t.* (*ascend*) поднима́ться *imp.*, подня́ться (-ниму́сь, -ни́мешься; -ня́лся́, -няла́сь) *perf.* на + *acc.*; (*m. a horse etc.*) сади́ться *imp.*, сесть (ся́ду, -дешь; сел) *perf.* на + *acc.*; (*picture*) накле́ивать *imp.*, накле́ить *perf.* на карто́н; (*gem*) вставля́ть *imp.*, вста́вить *perf.* в опра́ву; (*gun*) устана́вливать *imp.*, установи́ть (-влю́, -вишь) *perf.* на лафе́т; *m. up*, (*accumulate*) нака́пливаться *imp.*, накопи́ться (-ится) *perf.*; *m. guard*, стоя́ть (-ою́, -ои́шь) *imp.* на часа́х; *n.* (*for picture*) карто́н, подло́жка; (*for gem*) опра́ва; (*horse*) верхова́я ло́шадь (*pl.* -ди, -де́й, *instr.* дьми́).
mountain *n.* гора́ (*acc.* -ру; *pl.* -ры, -р, -ра́м); *attrib.* го́рный; *m. ash*, ряби́на. **mountaineer** *n.* альпини́ст, ~ка. **mountaineering** *n.* альпини́зм. **mountainous** *adj.* гори́стый; (*huge*) грома́дный.
mountebank *n.* (*clown*) шут (-а́); (*charlatan*) шарлата́н.
mourn *v.t.* опла́кивать *imp.*, опла́кать (-а́чу, -а́чешь) *perf.*; *v.i.* скорбе́ть (-блю́, -би́шь) *imp.* (over, о + *prep.*). **mournful** *adj.* печа́льный, ско́рбный. **mourning** *n.* (*sorrow*) печа́ль; (*dress*) тра́ур.
mouse *n.* мышь (*pl.* -ши, -ше́й); *v.i.* лови́ть (-влю́, -вишь) *imp.*, пойма́ть *perf.* мыше́й. **mouser** *n.* мышело́в. **mousetrap** *n.* мышело́вка.
mousse *n.* мусс.
moustache *n.* усы́ (усо́в) *pl.*
mousy *adj.* мыши́ный; (*timid*) ро́бкий (-бок, -бка́, -бко).
mouth *n.* рот (рта, *loc.* во рту́); (*poet.*) уста́ (-т) *pl.*; (*entrance*) вход; (*of river*) у́стье (*gen.pl.* -в); (*of gun, volcano*) жерло́ (*pl.* -ла); *m. to feed*, едо́к (-а́); *by word of m.*, у́стно; *v.t.* говори́ть *imp.*, сказа́ть (-ажу́, -а́жешь) *perf.* напы́щенно. **mouthful** *n.* по́лный рот (рта); (*small amount*) кусо́к (-ска́), глото́к (-тка́). **mouth-organ** *n.* губна́я гармо́ника. **mouthpiece** *n.* мундшту́к (-а́); (*person*) ру́пор.
movable *adj.* подвижно́й; (*property*) дви́жимый.
move *n.* (*in game*) ход (-а(у); *pl.* хо́ды́); (*change of location*) переме́на ме́ста; (*step*) шаг (*loc.* -у́; *pl.* -и́); *v.t.* & *i.* дви́-

гать(ся) (-аю(сь), -аешь(ся) & дви́жу(сь), -жешь(ся)) *imp.*, дви́нуть(ся) *perf.*; *v.t.* (*affect*) тро́гать *imp.*, тро́нуть *perf.*; (*propose*) вноси́ть (-ошу́, -о́сишь) *imp.*, внести́ (внесу́, -сёшь; внёс, -ла́) *perf.*; *v.i.* (*events*) развива́ться *imp.*, разви́ться (разовьётся; разви́лся, -ила́сь, -и́ло́сь) *perf.*; (*m. house*) переезжа́ть *imp.*, перее́хать (-е́ду, -е́дешь) *perf.*; *m. away*, (*v.i.*) уезжа́ть *imp.*, уе́хать (уе́ду, -дешь) *perf.*; *m. in*, въезжа́ть *imp.*, въе́хать (-е́ду, -е́дешь) *perf.*; *m. on*, идти́ (иду́, идёшь; шёл, шла) *imp.*, пойти́ (пойду́, -дёшь; пошёл, -шла́) *perf.* да́льше; *m. on!* проходи́те (да́льше)! *m. out*, съезжа́ть *imp.*, съе́хать (-е́ду, -е́дешь) *perf.* (of, с + *gen.*). **movement** *n.* движе́ние; (*mus.*) часть (*pl.* -ти, -те́й). **moving** *n.* дви́жущийся; (*touching*) тро́гательный; *m. staircase*, эскала́тор.

mow *v.t.* (*also m. down*) коси́ть (кошу́, ко́сишь) *imp.*, с~ *perf.* **mower** *n.* (*person*) косе́ц (-сца́); (*machine*) коси́лка.

Mr. *abbr.* ми́стер, господи́н. **Mrs.** *abbr.* ми́ссис *f.indecl.*, госпожа́.

MS. *abbr.* ру́копись.

Mt. *abbr.* гора́.

much *adj.*, *n.* мно́го + *gen.*; мно́гое *sb.*; *adv.* о́чень; (*with comp. adj.*) гора́здо.

muck *n.* (*dung*) наво́з; (*dirt*) грязь (*loc.* -зи́); *v.t.* (*dirty*) па́чкать *imp.*, за~, ис~ *perf.*; *m. out*, чи́стить *imp.*, вы́~ *perf.*; *m. up*, изга́живать *imp.*, изга́дить *perf.*

mucous *adj.* слизи́стый. **mucus** *n.* слизь.

mud *n.* грязь (*loc.* -зи́). **mudguard** *n.* крыло́ (*pl.* -лья, -льев). **mudslinger** *n.* клеветни́к (-а́).

muddle *v.t.* пу́тать *imp.*, с~ *perf.*; *v.i.*: *m. along*, де́йствовать *imp.* наобу́м; *m. through*, ко́е-ка́к доводи́ть (-ожу́, -о́дишь) *imp.*, довести́ (-еду́, -едёшь; -ёл, -ела́) *perf.* де́ло до конца́; *n.* неразбери́ха, пу́таница; *m.-headed*, бестолко́вый.

muddy *adj.* гря́зный (-зен, -зна́, -зно); (*of liquid*) му́тный (-тен, -тна́, -тно); (*of light*) ту́склый (-л, -ла́, -ло); *v.t.* обры́згивать *imp.*, обры́згать *perf.* грязью; (*water*) мути́ть (мучу́, му́тишь) *imp.*, вз~, за~ *perf.*

muezzin *n.* муэдзи́н.

muff *n.* му́фта.

muffle *v.t.* заку́тывать *imp.*, заку́тать *perf.*; (*sound*) глуши́ть *imp.*, за~ *perf.*; *muffled oars*, обмо́танные вёсла (*gen.* -сел) *neut.pl.* **muffler** *n.* кашне́ *neut. indecl.*, шарф.

mufti *n.*: *in m.*, в шта́тском.

mug *n.* (*vessel*) кру́жка; (*face*) мо́рда.

muggy *adj.* сыро́й (сыр, -а́, -о) и тёплый (-пел, -пла́).

mulatto *n.* мула́т, ~ка.

mulberry *n.* (*tree*) шелкови́ца, ту́товое де́рево (*pl.* -е́вья, -е́вьев); (*fruit*) ту́товая я́года.

mulch *n.* му́льча; *v.t.* мульчи́ровать *imp.*, *perf.* **mulching** *n.* мульчи́рование.

mule *n.* мул; (*machine*) мюль-маши́на. **muleteer** *n.* пого́нщик му́лов. **mulish** *adj.* упря́мый как осёл.

mull *v.t.* подогрева́ть *imp.*, подогре́ть *perf.* с пря́ностями; *mulled wine*, глинтве́йн.

mullah *n.* мулла́ *m.*

mullet *n.* (*grey m.*) кефа́ль; (*red m.*) бараб́улька.

mullion *n.* сре́дник.

multi- *in comb.* много-. **multicoloured** *adj.* многокра́сочный. **multifarious** *adj.* разнообра́зный. **multilateral** *adj*, многосторо́нний. **multimillionaire** *n.* мультимиллионе́р.

multiple *adj.* составно́й, сло́жный (-жен, -жна́, -жно); (*varied*) разнообра́зный; (*numerous*) многочи́сленный; (*math.*) кра́тный; *m. sclerosis*, рассе́янный склеро́з; *m. shop*, магази́н с филиа́лами; *n.* кра́тное число́ (*pl.* -сла, -сел, -слам); *least common m.*, о́бщее наиме́ньшее кра́тное *sb.* **multiplication** *n.* размноже́ние; (*math.*) умноже́ние. **multiplicity** *n.* многочи́сленность, многообра́зие. **multiply** *v.t.* & *i.* размножа́ть(ся) *imp.*, размно́жить(ся) *perf.*; *v.t.* (*math.*) умножа́ть *imp.*, умно́жить *perf.*

multitude *n.* мно́жество; (*crowd*) толпа́ (*pl.* -пы).

mum[1] *interj.* ти́ше! *mum's the word!*

(об э́том) ни гугу́! *keep m.*, молча́ть (-чу́, -чи́шь) *imp.*
mum[2] *n.* (*mother*) ма́ма.
mumble *v.t.* & *i.* мя́млить *imp.*, про~ *perf.*
mummify *v.t.* мумифици́ровать *imp.*, *perf.* **mummy**[1] *n.* му́мия.
mummy[2] *n.* (*mother*) ма́ма, ма́мочка.
mumps *n.* сви́нка.
munch *v.t.* жева́ть (жую́, жуёшь) *imp.*
mundane *adj.* земно́й.
municipal *adj.* муниципа́льный, городско́й. **municipality** *n.* муниципалите́т.
munificence *n.* ще́дрость. **munificent** *adj.* ще́дрый (щедр, -а́, -о).
munitions *n.* вое́нное иму́щество.
mural *adj.* стенно́й; *n.* стенна́я ро́спись.
murder *n.* уби́йство; *v.t.* убива́ть *imp.*, уби́ть (убью́, -ьёшь) *perf.*; (*language*) кове́ркать *imp.*, ис~ *perf.* **murderer, murderess** *n.* уби́йца *m.* & *f.* **murderous** *adj.* уби́йственный (-ен, -енна), смертоно́сный.
murky *adj.* тёмный (-мен, -мна́), мра́чный (-чен, -чна́, -чно).
murmur *n.* (*of water*) журча́ние; (*of voices*) шёпот; (*of discontent*) ро́пот; *without a m.*, безро́потно; *v.i.* журча́ть (-чи́т) *imp.*; ропта́ть (ропщу́, -щешь) *imp.* (at, на + *acc.*); *v.t.* шепта́ть (шепчу́, -чешь) *imp.*, шепну́ть *perf.*
muscle *n.* мы́шца, му́скул. **muscular** *adj.* мы́шечный, му́скульный; (*person*) му́скулистый.
Muscovite *n.* москви́ч (-а́), ~ка.
muse[1] *v.i.* размышля́ть *imp.*
muse[2] *n.* му́за.
museum *n.* музе́й.
mushroom *n.* гриб (-а́); *m. cloud*, грибови́дное о́блако (*pl.* -ка́, -ко́в).
music *n.* му́зыка; (*sheet m.*) но́ты *f.pl.*; *play without m.*, игра́ть *imp.*, сыгра́ть *perf.* без нот; *m.-hall*, мю́зик-хо́лл; *m.-paper*, но́тная бума́га; *m.-stand*, пюпи́тр. **musical** *adj.* музыка́льный; *m. comedy*, музыка́льная коме́дия; *n.* музыка́льная (кино)коме́дия. **musician** *n.* музыка́нт; (*composer*) компози́тор. **musicologist** *n.* музыкове́д. **musicology** *n.* музыкове́дение.
musk *n.* му́скус; *m.-deer*, кабарга́ (*gen. pl.* -ро́г); *m.-melon*, ды́ня; *m.-rat*, онда́тра. **musky** *adj.* му́скусный.
musket *n.* мушке́т. **musketeer** *n.* мушкетёр.
muslin *n.* musли́н, кисея́; *adj.* мусли́новый, кисе́йный.
mussel *n.* съедо́бная ми́дия.
must[1] *n.* муст; (*new wine*) молодо́е вино́.
must[2] *v.aux.* (*obligation*) до́лжен (-жна́) *predic.* + *inf.*; на́до *impers.* + *dat.* & *inf.*; (*necessity*) ну́жно *impers.* + *dat.* & *inf.*; *m. not*, (*prohibition*) нельзя́ *impers.* + *dat.* & *inf.*; *n.* необходи́мость.
mustard *n.* горчи́ца; *m. gas*, горчи́чный газ; *m. plaster*, горчи́чник; *m.-pot*, горчи́чница.
musty *adj.* за́тхлый.
mutant *adj.* мута́нтный; *n.* мута́нт. **mutation** *n.* мута́ция.
mute *adj.* (*dumb*) немо́й (нем, -а́, -о); (*silent*) безмо́лвный; *n.* немо́й *sb.*; (*mus.*) surди́нка. **muted** *adj.* приглушённый (-ён, -ена́); *with m. strings*, под сурди́нку.
mutilate *v.t.* уве́чить *imp.*, из~ *perf.* кале́чить *imp.*, ис~ *perf.* **mutilation** *n.* уве́чье.
mutineer *n.* мятéжник. **mutinous** *adj.* мяте́жный. **mutiny** *n.* мяте́ж (-а́); *v.i.* бунтова́ть *imp.*, взбунтова́ться *perf.*
mutism *n.* немота́.
mutter *v.i.* бормота́ть (-очу́, -о́чешь) *imp.*; ворча́ть (-чу́, -чи́шь) *imp.*; *n.* бормота́ние, ворча́ние.
mutton *n.* бара́нина.
mutual *adj.* взаи́мный, взаимо-; (*common*) о́бщий; *m. benefit*, ка́сса взаимопо́мощи; *m. friend*, о́бщий друг (*pl.* друзья́, -зе́й).
muzzle *n.* (*animal's*) мо́рда; (*on animal*) намо́рдник; (*of gun*) ду́ло; *v.t.* надева́ть *imp.*, наде́ть (-е́ну, -е́нешь) *perf.* намо́рдник на + *acc.*; (*impose silence*) заставля́ть *imp.*, заста́вить *perf.* молча́ть.
muzzy *adj.* тума́нный (-нен, -нна).
my *poss.pron.* мой (моя́, моё; мои́); свой (-оя́, -оё; -ои́).
myopia *n.* близору́кость. **myopic** *adj.* близору́кий.

myriad *n.* мириáды (-д) *pl.*; *adj.* бесчи́сленный (-ен, -енна).

myrrh *n.* ми́рра.

myrtle *n.* мирт; *attrib.* ми́ртовый.

myself *pron.* (*emph.*) (я) сам (-огó, -омý, -и́м, -óм), самá (-мóй, *acc.* -мý); (*refl.*) себя́ (себé, собóй); -ся (*suffixed to v.t.*).

mysterious *adj.* таи́нственный (-ен, -енна). **mystery** *n.* тáйна; (*relig. rite; play*) мисте́рия.

mystic(al) *adj.* мисти́ческий; *n.* ми́стик. **mysticism** *n.* мистици́зм. **mystification** *n.* мистификáция. **mystify** *v.t.* озадáчивать *imp.*, озадáчить *perf.*

myth *n.* миф. **mythical** *adj.* мифи́ческий. **mythological** *adj.* мифологи́ческий. **mythologist** *n.* мифóлог. **mythology** *n.* мифолóгия.

N

nacre *n.* перламýтр. **nacr(e)ous** *adj.* перламýтровый.

nadir *n.* нади́р; (*lowest point*) сáмый ни́зкий ýровень (-вня) *m.*

nag[1] *n.* (*horse*) лóшадь (*pl.* -ди, -дéй, *instr.* -дьми́).

nag[2] *v.i.*: *n. at*, пили́ть (-лю́, -лишь) *imp.* + *acc.*; (*of pain*) ныть (нóет) *imp.*

naiad *n.* ная́да.

nail *n.* (*finger-, toe-n.*) нóготь (-гтя; *pl.* -гти, -гтéй) *m.*; (*claw*) кóготь (-гтя; *pl.* -гти, -гтéй) *m.*; (*metal spike*) гвоздь (-дя́; *pl.* -ди, -дéй) *m.*; *n.-brush*, щёточка для ногтéй; *n.-file*, пи́лка для ногтéй; *n.-scissors*, нóжницы (-ц) *pl.* для ногтéй; *n.-varnish*, лак для ногтéй; *v.t.* прибивáть *imp.*, приби́ть (-бью́, -бьёшь) *perf.* (гвоздя́ми).

naive *adj.* наи́вный. **naivety** *n.* наи́вность.

naked *adj.* гóлый (гол, -á, -о), нагóй (наг, -á, -о); обнажённый (-ён, -енá); *n. eye*, невооружённый глаз; *n. light*, незащищённый свет; *n. sword*, обнажённый меч (-á); *n. truth*, чи́стая прáвда. **nakedness** *n.* наготá.

name *n.* назвáние; (*forename*) и́мя *neut.*; (*surname*) фами́лия; (*reputation*) репутáция; *what is his n.?* как егó зовýт? *in the n. of*, во и́мя + *gen.*; *n.-day*, имени́ны (-н) *pl.*; *n.-part*, заглáвная роль; *n.-plate*, дощéчка с фами́лией; *namesake*, тёзка *m.* & *f.*; *v.t.* называ́ть *imp.*, назвáть (назовý, -вёшь; назвáл, -á, -о) *perf.*; (*appoint*) назначáть *imp.*, назнáчить *perf.* **nameless** *adj.* безымя́нный. **namely** *adv.* (а) и́менно; то есть.

nanny *n.* ня́ня; *n.-goat*, козá (*pl.* -зы).

nano-second *n.* нáно-секýнда.

nap[1] *n.* (*sleep*) корóткий сон (сна); *v.i.* вздремнýть *perf.*

nap[2] *n.* (*on cloth*) ворс.

napalm *n.* напáлм.

nape *n.* загри́вок (-вка).

napkin *n.* (*table-n.*) салфéтка; (*nappy*) пелёнка.

narcissus *n.* нарци́сс.

narcosis *n.* наркóз. **narcotic** *adj.* наркоти́ческий; *n.* наркóтик.

nark *n.* (*spy*) легáвый *sb.*, стукáч (-á); *v.t.* (*irritate*) раздражáть *imp.*, раздражи́ть *perf.*

narrate *v.t.* расскáзывать *imp.*, рассказáть (-ажý, -áжешь) *perf.*; повествовáть *imp.* о + *prep.* **narration** *n.* повествовáние. **narrative** *n.* расскáз, пóвесть (*pl.* -ти, -тéй); *adj.* повествовáтельный. **narrator** *n.* расскáзчик, повествовáтель *m.*

narrow *adj.* ýзкий (ýзок, узкá, ýзко; ýзки́), тéсный (-сен, -снá, -сно); (*restricted*) ограни́ченный (-ен, -енна), *n.-gauge*, узкоколéйный; *n.-minded*, ограни́ченный (-ен, -енна); *n.*: *pl.* ýзкая часть; (*strait*) ýзкий проли́в; *v.t.* & *i.* сýживать(ся) *imp.*, сýзить(ся) *perf.* **narrowly** *adv.* (*hardly*) чуть, éле-

-éле; *he n. escaped drowning*, он чуть не утону́л. **narrowness** *n.* у́зость, ограни́ченность.

narwhal *n.* нарва́л.

nasal *adj.* носово́й; (*voice*) гнуса́вый.

nascent *adj.* рожда́ющийся.

nasturtium *n.* насту́рция.

nasty *adj.* га́дкий (-док, -дка́, -дко), проти́вный; (*dirty*) гря́зный (-зен, -зна́, -зно); (*person*) зло́бный.

nation *n.* на́ция; (*people*) наро́д; (*country*) страна́ (*pl.* -ны). **national** *adj.* национа́льный, наро́дный; (*of the state*) госуда́рственный; *n.* по́дданный *sb.* **nationalism** *n.* национали́зм. **nationalist** *n.* национали́ст, ~ка. **nationalistic** *adj.* националисти́ческий. **nationality** *n.* национа́льность; (*citizenship*) гражда́нство, по́дданство. **nationalization** *n.* национализа́ция. **nationalize** *v.t.* национализи́ровать *imp., perf.*

native *n.* (*n. of*) уроже́нец (-нца), -нка (+*gen.*); тузе́мец (-мца), -мка; *adj.* (*natural*) приро́дный; (*of one's birth*) родно́й; (*indigenous*) тузе́мный; (*local*) ме́стный; *n. land*, ро́дина; *n. language*, родно́й язы́к (-а́); *n. speaker*, носи́тель *m.* языка́.

nativity *n.* рождество́ (Христо́во).

natter *v.i.* болта́ть *imp.*; *n.* болтовня́.

natural *adj.* есте́ственный (-ен, -енна), приро́дный; *n. death*, есте́ственная смерть; *n. resources*, приро́дные бога́тства *neut.pl.*; *n. selection*, есте́ственный отбо́р; *n.* (*person*) самоdoро́док (-дка); (*mus.*) бека́р. **naturalism** *n.* натурали́зм. **naturalist** *n.* натурали́ст. **naturalistic** *adj.* натуралисти́ческий. **naturalization** *n.* (*of alien*) натурализа́ция; (*of plant, animal*) акклиматиза́ция. **naturalize** *v.t.* натурализи́ровать *imp., perf.*; акклиматизи́ровать *imp., perf.* **naturally** *adv.* есте́ственно, по приро́де; (*of course*) коне́чно, как и сле́довало ожида́ть. **nature** *n.* приро́да; (*character*) хара́ктер; *by n.*, по приро́де; *in the n. of*, вро́де+*gen.*; *second n.*, втора́я нату́ра; *state of n.*, первобы́тное состоя́ние.

naughtiness *n.* (*disobedience*) непослуша́ние; (*mischief*) ша́лости *f.pl.*

naughty *adj.* непослу́шный; шаловли́вый.

nausea *n.* тошнота́; (*loathing*) отвраще́ние. **nauseate** *v.t.* тошни́ть *imp. impers.* от+*gen.*; быть проти́вным+*dat.*; *the idea nauseates me*, меня́ тошни́т от э́той мы́сли; э́та мысль мне проти́вна. **nauseous** *adj.* тошнотво́рный; (*loathsome*) отврати́тельный.

nautical *n.* морско́й.

naval *adj.* (вое́нно-)морско́й, фло́тский.

nave *n.* неф.

navel *n.* пупо́к (-пка́); *n.-string*, пупови́на.

navigable *adj.* судохо́дный. **navigate** *v.t.* (*ship*) вести́ (веду́, -дёшь; вёл, -а́) *imp.*; (*sea*) пла́вать *imp.* **navigation** *n.* навига́ция. **navigator** *n.* шту́рман.

navvy *n.* землеко́п.

navy *n.* вое́нно-морско́й флот (*pl.* -о́ты, -о́то́в); *n. blue*, тёмно-си́ний.

Nazi *n.* наци́ст, ~ка; *adj.* наци́стский. **Nazism** *n.* наци́зм.

near *adv.* бли́зко, недалёко́; *far and n.*, повсю́ду; *n. at hand*, под руко́й; *n. by*, ря́дом; *prep.* во́зле+*gen.*, о́коло+*gen.*, у+*gen.*; *adj.* бли́зкий (-зок, -зка́, -зко, близки́), недалёкий (-ёк, -ека́, -ёко́); *n. miss*, бли́зкий про́мах; *n.-sighted*, близору́кий; *v.t. & i.*, приближа́ться *imp.*, прибли́зиться *perf.* к+*dat.*; подходи́ть (-ожу́, -о́дишь) *imp.*, подойти́ (-ойду́, -ойдёшь; -ошёл, -ошла́) *perf.* к+*dat.*

nearly *adv.* почти́, приблизи́тельно.

neat *adj.* (*tidy*) опря́тный, аккура́тный; (*clear*) чёткий (-ток, -тка́, -тко); (*undiluted*) неразба́вленный (-ен).

nebula *n.* тума́нность. **nebular** *adj.* небуля́рный. **nebulous** *adj.* нея́сный (-сен, -сна́, -сно), тума́нный (-нен, -нна).

necessarily *adv.* неизбе́жно. **necessary** *adj.* ну́жный (-жен, -жна́, -жно, -жны́), необходи́мый; (*inevitable*) неизбе́жный; *n.* необходи́мое *sb.* **necessitate** *v.t.* де́лать *imp.*, с~ *perf.* необходи́мым; (*involve*) влечь (-ечёт, -еку́т; влёк, -ла́) *imp.* за собо́й. **necessity** *n.* необходи́мость; неизбе́жность; (*object*) предме́т пе́рвой необходи́мости; (*poverty*) нужда́.

neck *n.* ше́я; (*of garment*) вы́рез; (*of bottle*) го́рлышко (*pl.* -шки, -шек, -шкам); (*isthmus*) перешеек (-е́йка); *get it in the n.*, получи́ть *perf.* по ше́е; *risk one's n.*, рискова́ть *imp.* голово́й; *up to one's n.*, по го́рло, по́ уши; *n. and n.*, голова́ в го́лову; *n. or nothing*, ли́бо пан, ли́бо пропа́л. **neckband** *n.* во́рот. **neckerchief** *n.* ше́йный плато́к (-тка́). **necklace** *n.* ожере́лье (*gen.pl.* -лий). **necklet** *n.* ожере́лье (*gen.pl.* -лий); (*fur*) горже́тка. **neckline** *n.* вы́рез. **necktie** *n.* га́лстук.

necromancer *n.* колду́н (-а́). **necromancy** *n.* чёрная ма́гия, колдовство́.

nectar *n.* некта́р.

née *adj.* урождённая.

need *n.* нужда́, на́добность, потре́бность; *v.t.* нужда́ться *imp.* в + *prep.*; *I* (*etc.*) *n.*, мне (*dat.*) ну́жен (-жна́, -жно, -жны́) + *nom.*; *I n. five roubles*, мне ну́жно пять рубле́й.

needle *n.* игла́ (*pl.* -лы), иго́лка; (*knitting*) спи́ца; (*pointer*) стре́лка; *pl.* (*pine-n.*) хво́я; *v.t.* раздража́ть *imp.*, раздражи́ть *perf.*

needless *adj.* нену́жный, изли́шний; *n. to say*, не прихо́дится и говори́ть. **needy** *adj.* нужда́ющийся, бе́дствующий.

negation *n.* отрица́ние. **negative** *adj.* отрица́тельный; негати́вный; *n. quantity*, отрица́тельная величина́; *n. result*, негати́вный результа́т; *n.* отрица́ние; (*gram.*) отрица́тельное сло́во (*pl.* -ва́); (*phot.*) негати́в; *in the n.*, отрица́тельно; отрица́тельный.

neglect *v.t.* пренебрега́ть *imp.*, пренебре́чь (-егу́, -ежёшь; -ёг, -егла́) *perf.* + *instr.*; не забо́титься *imp.* о + *prep.*; (*abandon*) забра́сывать *imp.*, забро́сить *perf.*; (*not fulfil*) не выполня́ть *imp.* + *gen.*; *n.* пренебреже́ние; (*condition*) забро́шенность. **neglectful** *adj.* небре́жный, невнима́тельный (of, к + *dat.*). **negligence** *n.* небре́жность, неради́вость. **negligent** *adj.* небре́жный, неради́вый. **negligible** *adj.* незначи́тельнный.

negotiate *v.i.* вести́ (веду́, -дёшь; вёл, -а́) *imp.* перегово́ры; *v.t.* (*arrange*) заключа́ть *imp.*, заключи́ть *perf.*; (*overcome*) преодолева́ть *imp.*, преодоле́ть *perf.* **negotiation** *n.* (*discussion*) перегово́ры *m.pl.*

Negress *n.* негритя́нка. **Negro** *n.* негр; *adj.* негритя́нский.

neigh *n.* ржа́ние; *v.i.* ржать (ржу, ржёшь) *imp.*

neighbour *n.* сосе́д (*pl.* -и, -ей), ~ка. **neighbourhood** *n.* (*vicinity*) сосе́дство; (*area*) ме́стность; *in the n. of*, о́коло + *gen.* **neighbouring** *adj.* сосе́дний. **neighbourly** *adj.* добрососе́дский.

neither *adv.* та́кже не, то́же не; *pron.* ни тот, ни друго́й; *n. . . . nor*, ни…ни.

nemesis *n.* возме́здие.

neocolonialism *n.* неоколониали́зм.

neolithic *adj.* неолити́ческий.

neologism *n.* неологи́зм.

neon *n.* нео́н; *attrib.* нео́новый.

nephew *n.* племя́нник.

nepotism *n.* кумовство́.

Neptune *n.* Непту́н. **neptunium** *n.* непту́ний.

nerve *n.* нерв; (*assurance*) самооблада́ние; (*impudence*) на́глость; *pl.* (*nervousness*) нерво́зность; *get on the nerves of*, де́йствовать *imp.*, по~ *perf.* + *dat.* на не́рвы. **nerveless** *adj.* бесси́льный. **nervous** *adj.* не́рвный (не́рвен, нервна́, не́рвно); *n. breakdown*, не́рвное расстро́йство. **nervy** *adj.* нерво́зный.

nest *n.* гнездо́ (*pl.* -ёзда); *n.-egg*, сбереже́ния *neut.pl.*; *v.i.* гнезди́ться *imp.*; вить (вью, вьёшь; вил, -а́, -о) *imp.*, свить (совью́, -ьёшь; свил, -а́, -о) *perf.* (себе́) гнездо́. **nestle** *v.i.* льнуть *imp.*, при~ *perf.* **nestling** *n.* птене́ц (-нца́).

net[1] *n.* сеть (*loc.* сети́; *pl.* -ти, -те́й), се́тка; *v.t.* (*catch*) лови́ть (-влю́, -вишь) *imp.*, пойма́ть *perf.* сетя́ми; (*cover*) закрыва́ть *imp.*, закры́ть (-ро́ю, -ро́ешь) *perf.* се́ткой.

net[2], **nett** *adj.* не́тто *indecl.*, чи́стый (чист, -а́, -о, чи́сты́); *n. price*, цена́ не́тто; *n. profit*, чи́стая при́быль; *n. weight*, чи́стый вес, вес не́тто; *v.t.* получа́ть *imp.*, получи́ть (-чу́, -чишь) *perf.* …чи́стого дохо́да.

nettle *n.* крапи́ва; *n.-rash*, крапи́вница; *v.t.* (*fig.*) раздража́ть *imp.*, раздражи́ть *perf.*
network *n.* сеть (*loc.* се́ти́; *pl.* -ти, -те́й).
neuralgia *n.* невралги́я. **neurasthenia** *n.* неврастени́я. **neuritis** *n.* неври́т. **neurologist** *n.* невро́лог. **neurology** *n.* невроло́гия. **neurosis** *n.* невро́з. **neurotic** *adj.* невроти́ческий; *n.* невро́тик, нервнобольно́й *sb.*
neuter *adj.* сре́дний, сре́днего ро́да; *n.* (*gender*) сре́дний род; (*word*) сло́во (*pl.* -ва́) сре́днего ро́да; (*animal*) кастри́рованное живо́тное *sb.*; *v.t.* кастри́ровать *imp.*, *perf.* **neutral** *adj.* нейтра́льный; (*indifferent*) безуча́стный; *n.* (*state*) нейтра́льное госуда́рство; (*person*) граждани́н (*pl.* -ане, -ан), -а́нка, нейтра́льного госуда́рства; (*gear*) нейтра́льное положе́ние рычага́ коро́бки переда́ч; *in n.*, не включённый (-ён, -ена́). **neutrality** *n.* нейтралите́т; безуча́стность. **neutralization** *n.* нейтрализа́ция. **neutralize** *v.t.* нейтрализова́ть *imp.*, *perf.* **neutrino** *n.* нейтри́но *neut.indecl.* **neutron** *n.* нейтро́н.
never *adv.* никогда́; *n.!* не мо́жет быть! *n. again*, никогда́ бо́льше, бо́льше не; *n. fear!* бу́дь(те) уве́рен(ы)! *n. mind*, ничего́! всё равно́! *n. once*, ни ра́зу; *on the n.-n.*, в рассро́чку. **nevertheless** *conj.*, *adv.* тем не ме́нее.
new *adj.* но́вый (нов, -а́, -о); (*fresh*) све́жий (свеж, -а́, -о́, све́жи́); (*young*) молодо́й (мо́лод, -а́, -о). **new-born** *adj.* новорождённый. **newcomer** *n.* прише́лец (-льца). **newfangled** *adj.* новомо́дный. **newly** *adv.* (*recently*) неда́вно; (*in new manner*) за́ново, вновь.
newel *n.* коло́нка винтово́й ле́стницы.
Newfoundland *n.* ньюфаундле́нд, водола́з.
news *n.* но́вость, -ти *pl.*, изве́стие, -ия *pl.* **newsagent** *n.* газе́тчик. **news-letter** *n.* информацио́нный бюллете́нь *m.* **newspaper** *n.* газе́та. **newsprint** *n.* газе́тная бума́га. **newsreel** *n.* кинохро́ника. **news-vendor** *n.* газе́тчик, продаве́ц (-вца́) газе́т.
newt *n.* трито́н.
next *adj.* сле́дующий, бу́дущий; *adv.* в сле́дующий раз; пото́м, зате́м; *n. door*, по сосе́дству; (*house*) в сосе́днем до́ме; (*flat*) в сосе́дней кварти́ре; *n.-door*, сосе́дний; *n. door to*, (*fig.*) почти́; *n. of kin*, ближа́йший ро́дственник; *n. to*, ря́дом с + *instr.*, о́коло + *gen.*; (*fig.*) почти́.
nexus *n.* связь.
nib *n.* перо́ (*pl.* пе́рья, -ьев).
nibble *v.t.* & *i.* грызть (-зу́, -зёшь; -з) *imp.*; обгрыза́ть *imp.*, обгры́зть (-зу́, -зёшь; -з) *perf.*; (*grass*) щипа́ть (-плет) *imp.*; (*fish*) клева́ть (клюёт) *imp.*
nice *adj.* (*precise*) то́чный (-чен, -чна́, -чно); (*subtle*) то́нкий (-нок, -нка́, -нко, то́нки́); (*pleasant*) прия́тный (*also iron.*); хоро́ший (-ш, -ша́); (*person*) ми́лый (мил, -а́, -о, ми́лы́), любе́зный. **nicety** *n.* то́чность; то́нкость; *to a n.*, то́чно, вполне́.
niche *n.* ни́ша; (*fig.*) своё, надлежа́щее, ме́сто.
nick *n.* зару́бка, засе́чка; *in the n. of time*, в са́мый после́дний моме́нт; как раз во́время; *v.t.* де́лать *imp.*, с~ *perf.* зару́бку, засе́чку, на + *acc.*
nickel *n.* ни́кель *m.*; *attrib.* ни́келевый; *n.-plate*, никелирова́ть *imp.*, *perf.*
nickname *n.* про́звище, прозва́ние; *v.t.* прозыва́ть *imp.*, прозва́ть (прозову́, -вёшь; прозва́л, -а́, -о) *perf.*
nicotine *n.* никоти́н. **nicotinic acid** *n.* никоти́новая кислота́.
niece *n.* племя́нница.
niggardly *adj.* (*miserly*) скупо́й (скуп, -а́, -о); (*scanty*) ску́дный (-ден, -дна́, -дно).
niggling *adj.* ме́лочный.
night *n.* ночь (*loc.* -чи́; *pl.* -чи, -че́й); (*evening*) ве́чер (*pl.* -а́); *at n.*, но́чью; *first n.*, премье́ра; *last n.*, вчера́ ве́чером; *n. and day*, непреста́нно; *attrib.* ночно́й; *n.-club*, ночно́й клуб; *n.-dress*, *-gown*, ночна́я руба́шка; *n.-light*, ночни́к (-а́). **nightcap** *n.* ночно́й колпа́к (-а́); (*drink*) стака́нчик спиртно́го на́ ночь. **nightfall** *n.* наступле́ние но́чи. **nightingale** *n.* солове́й (-вья́). **nightjar** *n.* козодо́й. **nightly** *adj.* ночно́й; (*every night*) ежено́шный; *adv.*

еженóщно. **nightmare** *n.* кошмáр. **nightmarish** *adj.* кошмáрный.
nihilism *n.* нигилúзм. **nihilist** *n.* нигилúст. **nihilistic** *adj.* нигилистúческий.
nil *n.* ноль (-ля́) *m.*
nimble *adj.* провóрный; (*mind*) гúбкий (-бок, -бкá, -бко).
nimbus *n.* нимб; (*cloud*) дождевóе óблако (*pl.* -кá, -кóв).
nine *adj., n.* дéвять (-тú, -тью); (*collect.*; *9 pairs*) дéвятеро (-рых); (*cards*; *number 9*) девя́тка; (*time*) дéвять (часóв); (*age*) дéвять лет. **ninepins** *n.* кéгли (-лей) *pl.* **nineteen** *adj., n.* девятнáдцать (-ти, -тью); (*age*) девятнáдцать лет. **nineteenth** *adj., n.* девятнáдцатый; (*date*) девятнáдцатое (числó). **ninetieth** *adj., n.* девянóстый. **ninety** *adj., n.* девянóсто (-та); (*age*) девянóсто лет; *pl.* (*decade*) девянóстые гóды (-дóв) *m.pl.* **ninth** *adj., n.* девя́тый; (*fraction*) девя́тая (часть (*pl.* -ти, -тéй)); (*date*) девя́тое (числó); (*mus.*) нóна.
nip[1] *v.t.* (*pinch*) щипáть (-плю, -плешь) *imp.*, щипнýть *perf.*; (*bite*) кусáть *imp.*, укусúть (-ушý, -ýсишь) *perf.*; *n. along*, слетáть *perf.*; *n. in the bud*, пресекáть *imp.*, пресéчь (-екý, -ечёшь; -ёк, -еклá) *perf.* в кóрне; *n.* щипóк (-пкá); укýс; *there's a n. in the air*, вóздух пáхнет морóзцем. **nipper** *n.* (*boy*) мальчугáн.
nip[2] *n.* (*drink*) глотóк (-ткá), рю́мочка.
nipple *n.* сосóк (-скá); (*tech.*) нúппель (*pl.* -ли & -ля́) *m.*
nirvana *n.* нирвáна.
nit *n.* гнúда.
nitrate *n.* нитрáт. **nitre** *n.* селúтра. **nitric** *adj.* азóтный. **nitrogen** *n.* азóт. **nitrogenous** *adj.* азóтный. **nitroglycerine** *n.* нитроглицерúн. **nitrous** *adj.* азóтистый; *n. oxide*, зáкись азóта.
nitwit *n.* простофúля *m.* & *f.*
no *adj.* (*not any*) никакóй, не одúн; (*not a*) (совсéм) не; *adv.* нет; (нискóлько) не + *compar.*; *n.* отрицáние, откáз; (*in vote*) гóлос (*pl.* -á) „прóтив"; *no doubt*, конéчно, несомнéнно; *no fear*, конéчно, нет! *no longer*, ужé не, бóльше не; *no one*, никтó, *no wonder*, не удивúтельно.
Noah's ark *n.* Нóев ковчéг.
nobelium *n.* нóбелий.
nobility *n.* (*class*) дворя́нство; (*quality*) благорóдство. **noble** *adj.* дворя́нский, знáтный; благорóдный. **nobleman** *n.* дворянúн (*pl.* -я́не, -я́н).
nobody *pron.* никтó; *n.* ничтóжество.
nocturnal *adj.* ночнóй. **nocturne** *n.* ноктю́рн.
nod *v.i.* кивáть *imp.*, кивнýть *perf.* головóй; (*drowsily*) клевáть (клюю́, клюёшь) *imp.* нóсом; *nodding acquaintance*,повéрхностное знакóмство; *n.* кивóк (-вкá).
nodule *n.* узелóк (-лкá).
noggin *n.* крýжечка.
noise *n.* шум (-а(у)); (*radio*) помéхи *f.pl.* **noiseless** *adj.* бесшýмный. **noisy** *adj.* шýмный (-мен, -мнá, -мно).
nomad *n.* кочéвник. **nomadic** *adj.* кочевóй, кочýющий.
nomenclature *n.* номенклатýра. **nominal** *adj.* номинáльный; (*gram.*) именнóй. **nominate** *v.t.* (*propose*) выдвигáть *imp.*, вы́двинуть *perf.*; (*appoint*) назначáть *imp.*, назнáчить *perf.* **nomination** *n.* выдвижéние; назначéние. **nominative** *adj.* (*n.*) именúтельный (падéж (-á)). **nominee** *n.* кандидáт.
non- *pref.* не-, без-. **non-acceptance** *n.* непринятие.
nonage *n.* несовершеннолéтие.
nonagenarian *n.* девяностолéтний старúк (-á), -няя старýха.
non-aggression *n.* ненападéние; *n. pact*, пакт о ненападéнии. **non-alcoholic** *adj.* безалкогóльный. **non-alignment** *n.* неприсоединéние. **non-appearance** *n.* (*leg.*) неявка (в суд). **non-arrival** *n.* неприбы́тие.
nonchalance *n.* (*indifference*) безразлúчие; (*carelessness*) беспéчность. **nonchalant** *n.* безразлúчный; беспéчный.
non-combatant *adj.* нестроевóй. **non-commissioned** *adj.*; *n. officer*, ýнтерофицéр. **non-committal** *adj.* уклóнчивый. **non-conductor** *n.* непроводнúк (-á).
nonconformist *n.* диссидéнт; *adj.* диссидéнтский.
nondescript *adj.* неопределённый (-нен, -нна), неопределённого вúда.
none *pron.* (*no one*) никтó; (*nothing*) ничтó; (*not one*) не одúн; *adv.* совсéм

не; ничу́ть не; *n. the less*, тем не ме́нее.
nonentity *n.* ничто́жество.
non-essential *adj.* несуще́ственный (-ен(ен), -енна). **non-existence** *n.* небытие́ (*instr.* -ие́м, *prep.* -ии́). **non-existent** *adj.* несуществу́ющий. **non-ferrous** *adj.* цветно́й. **non-interference, -intervention** *n.* невмеша́тельство. **non-party** *adj.* беспарти́йный. **non-payment** *n.* неплатёж (-а́).
nonplus *v.t.* ста́вить *imp.*, по~ *perf.* в тупи́к.
non-proliferation *n.* нераспростране́ние (я́дерного ору́жия). **non-productive** *adj.* непроизводи́тельный. **non-resident** *adj.* не прожива́ющий по ме́сту слу́жбы. **non-resistance** *n.* непротивле́ние.
nonsense *n.* вздор, ерунда́, чепуха́. **nonsensical** *adj.* бессмы́сленный (-ен, -енна).
non sequitur *n.* нелоги́чное заключе́ние.
non-skid, -slip *adj.* нескользя́щий. **non-smoker** *n.* (*person*) некуря́щий *sb.*; (*compartment*) ваго́н, купе́ *neut. indecl.*, для некуря́щих. **non-stop** *adj.* безостано́вочный; (*flight*) беспоса́дочный; *adv.* без остано́вок; без поса́док.
noodles *n.* лапша́.
nook *n.* укро́мный уголо́к (-лка́); *every n. and cranny*, все углы́ и закоу́лки *m.pl.*
noon *n.* по́лдень (-лу́дня & -лдня́) *m.*; *attrib.* полу́денный.
no one *see* **no.**
noose *n.* пе́тля (*gen.pl.* -тель); *v.t.* пойма́ть *perf.* арка́ном.
nor *conj.* и не; та́кже не, то́же не; *neither . . . n.*, ни...ни.
norm *n.* но́рма. **normal** *adj.* норма́льный. **normality** *n.* норма́льность. **normalize** *v.t.* нормализова́ть *imp.*, *perf.*
north *n.* се́вер; (*naut.*) норд; *adj.* се́верный; (*naut.*) но́рдовый; *adv.* к се́веру, на се́вер; *n.-east*, се́веро-восто́к; (*naut.*) норд-о́ст; *n.-easterly, -eastern*, се́веро-восто́чный; (*naut.*) норд-о́стовый; *N. Star*, Поля́рная звезда́; *n.-west*, се́веро-за́пад; (*naut.*) норд-ве́ст; *n.-westerly, -western*, се́веро-за́падный; (*naut.*) норд-ве́стовый; *n. wind*, норд. **northeaster** *n.* норд-о́ст. **northerly** *adj.* се́верный; (*naut.*) но́рдовый. **northern** *adj.* се́верный; *n. lights*, се́верное сия́ние. **northerner** *n.* северя́нин (*pl.* -я́не, -я́н); жи́тель *m.*, ~ница, се́вера. **northernmost** *adj.* са́мый се́верный. **northward(s)** *adv.* к се́веру, на се́вер. **northwester** *n.* норд-ве́ст.
Norwegian *adj.* норве́жский; *n.* норве́жец (-жца), -жка.
nose *n.* нос (*loc.* -у́; *pl.* -ы́); (*sense*) чутьё; (*of ship etc.*) носова́я часть (*pl.* -ти, -те́й); (*of rocket*) голо́вка; *v.t.* ню́хать *imp.*, по~ *perf.*; *n. out*, разню́хать *perf.*; *v.i.* (*of ship etc.*) осторо́жно продвига́ться *imp.*, продви́нуться *perf.* вперёд. **nosebag** *n.* то́рба. **nosebleed** *n.* кровотече́ние и́з носу. **nosedive** *n.* пике́ *neut.indecl.*; *v.i.* пики́ровать *imp.*, *perf.*
nostalgia *n.* тоска́ (по ро́дине, по пре́жнему). **nostalgic** *adj.* вызыва́ющий тоску́.
nostril *n.* ноздря́ (*pl.* -ри, -ре́й).
not *adv.* не; нет; ни; *n. at all*, ниско́лько, ничу́ть; (*reply to thanks*) не сто́ит (благода́рности); *n. half*, (*not at all*) совсе́м не; (*very much*) ужа́сно; *n. once*, ни ра́зу; *n. that*, не то, что́бы; *n. too*, дово́льно +*neg.*; *n. to say*, что́бы не сказа́ть; *n. to speak of*, не говоря́ уже́ о+*prep.*
notable *adj.* заме́тный, замеча́тельный. **notably** *adv.* осо́бенно, заме́тно.
notary (public) *n.* нота́риус.
notation *n.* нота́ция; (*mus.*) но́тное письмо́.
notch *n.* зару́бка; *v.t.* заруба́ть *imp.*, заруби́ть (-блю́, -бишь) *perf.*
note *n.* (*record*) заме́тка, запи́ска; (*annotation*) примеча́ние; (*letter*) запи́ска; (*banknote*) банкно́т; (*mus.*; *dipl.*) но́та; (*tone*) тон; (*attention*) внима́ние; *n. of hand*, ве́ксель (*pl.* -ля́) *m.*; *man of n.*, выдаю́щийся челове́к; *strike the right* (*a false*) *n.*, брать (беру́, -рёшь; брал, -а́, -о) *imp.*, взять (возьму́, -мёшь; взял, -а́, -о)

perf. (не)вéрный тон; *take n. of*, обращáть *imp.*, обратúть (-ащý, -атúшь) *perf.* внимáние на + *acc.*; *v.t.* отмечáть *imp.*, отмéтить *perf.*; *n. down*, запúсывать *imp.*, записáть (-ишý, -úшешь) *perf.* **notebook** *n.* записнáя кнúжка, блокнóт. **notecase** *n.* бумáжник. **noted** *adj.* знаменúтый; извéстный (for, + *instr.*). **notepaper** *n.* почтóвая бумáга. **noteworthy** *adj.* достóйный (-óин, -óйна) внимáния.

nothing *n.* ничтó, ничегó; *n. but*, ничегó крóме + *gen.*, тóлько; *n. of the kind*, ничегó подóбного; *come to n.*, кончáться *imp.*, кóнчиться *perf.* ничéм; *for n.*, (*free*) дáром; (*in vain*) зря, напрáсно; *have n. to do with*, не имéть *imp.* никакóго отношéния к + *dat.*; *there is* (*was*) *n. for it* (*but to*), ничегó другóго не остаётся (оставáлось) (как); придётся (пришлóсь) + *inf.*; *to say n. of*, не говорú уже о + *prep.*

notice *n.* (*sign*) объявлéние; (*intimation*) извещéние; (*warning*) предупреждéние; (*attention*) внимáние; (*review*) (печáтный) óтзыв; *at a moment's n.*, немéдленно; *give* (*in*) *one's n.*, подавáть (-даю, -даёшь) *imp.*, подáть (-áм, -áшь, -áст, -адúм; пóдал, -á, -о) *perf.* заявлéние об ухóде с рабóты; *give someone n.*, предупреждáть *imp.*, предупредúть *perf.* об увольнéнии; *take no n. of*, не обращáть *imp.* внимáния на + *acc.*; *n.-board*, доскá (*acc.* -ску; *pl.* -ски, -сóк, -скáм) для объявлéний; *v.t.* замечáть *imp.*, замéтить *perf.*; (*take n. of*) обращáть *imp.*, обратúть (-ащý, -атúшь) *perf.* внимáние на + *acc.* **noticeable** *adj.* замéтный. **notifiable** *adj.* подлежáщий регистрáции. **notification** *n.* извещéние, уведомлéние; (*of death etc.*) регистрáция. **notify** *v.t.* извещáть *imp.*, известúть *perf.* (of, о + *prep.*); уведомлять *imp.*, увéдомить *perf.* (of, о + *prep.*).

notion *n.* понятие, представлéние.

notoriety *n.* дурнáя слáва. **notorious** *adj.* пресловýтый.

notwithstanding *prep.* несмотрú на + *acc.*; *adv.* тем не мéнее.

nougat *n.* нугá.

nought *n.* (*nothing*) ничтó; (*figure 0*) нуль (-лú) *m.*, ноль (-лú) *m.*; *noughts and crosses*, крéстики и нóлики *m.pl.*

noun *n.* (úмя *neut.*) существúтельное *sb.*

nourish *v.t.* питáть *imp.*, на~ *perf.* **nourishing** *adj.* питáтельный. **nourishment** *n.* питáние.

nova *n.* нóвая звездá (*pl.* -ёзды).

novel *adj.* нóвый (нов, -á, -о); (*unusual*) необыкновéнный (-нен, -нна); *n.* ромáн. **novelist** *n.* романúст, áвтор ромáнов. **novelty** *n.* (*newness*) новизнá; (*new thing*) новúнка.

November *n.* ноябрь (-рú) *m.*; *attrib.* нóябрьский.

novice *n.* (*eccl.*) пóслушник, -ица; (*beginner*) новичóк (-чкá).

now *adv.* тепéрь, сейчáс; (*immediately*) тóтчас же; (*next*) тогдá; *conj.*: *n.* (*that*), раз, когдá; (*every*) *n. and again*, *then*, врéмя от врéмени; *n. . . . n. . . .*, то...то...; *by n.*, ужé; *from n. on*, в дальнéйшем, впредь. **nowadays** *adv.* в нáше врéмя.

nowhere *adv.* (*place*) нигдé; (*direction*) никудá; *pron.*: *I have n. to go*, мне нéкуда пойтú.

noxious *adj.* врéдный (-ден, -днá, -дно).

nozzle *n.* соплó (*pl.* -пла, -п(е)л), форсýнка, пáтрубок (-бка).

nuance *n.* нюáнс.

nuclear *adj.* ядерный. **nucleic** *adj.*: *n. acid*, нуклеúновая кислотá. **nucleus** *n.* ядрó (*pl.* ядра, ядер, ядрам).

nude *adj.* обнажённый (-ён, -енá), нагóй (наг, -á, -о); *n.* обнажённая фигýра.

nudge *v.t.* подтáлкивать *imp.*, подтолкнýть *perf.* лóктем; *n.* лёгкий толчóк (-чкá).

nudity *n.* наготá.

nugget *n.* (*gold*) саморóдок (-дка).

nuisance *n.* досáда, неприятность; (*person*) раздражáющий, надоéдливый, человéк.

null *adj.*: *n. and void*, недéйствительный. **nullify** *v.t.* аннулúровать *imp.*, *perf.* **nullity** *n.* недéйствительность.

numb *adj.* онемéлый, оцепенéлый; *v.t.* вызывáть *imp.*, вы́звать (-зовет) *perf.* онемéние в + *prep.*, у + *gen.*

number *n.* (*total*) колúчество; (*total*; *symbol*; *math.*; *gram.*) числó (*pl.* -сла,

-сел, -слам); (*item*) нóмер (*pl.* -á); *n.-plate*, номернáя дощéчка; *v.t.* (*count*) считáть *imp.*, со~, счесть (сочтý, -тёшь; счёл, сочлá) *perf.*; (*assign n. to*) нумеровáть *imp.*, за~, про~ *perf.*; (*contain*) начúтывать *imp.*; *n. among*, причислЯть *imp.*, причúслить *perf.* к+*dat.*; *his days are numbered*, егó дни сочтенЫ. **numberless** *adj.* бесчúсленный (-ен, -енна).

numeral *adj.* числовóй, цифровóй; *n.* цúфра; (*gram.*) (úмя *neut.*) числúтельное *sb.* **numerator** *n.* числúтель *m.* **numerical** *adj.* числовóй, цифровóй. **numerous** *adj.* многочúсленный (-ен, -енна); (*many*) мнóго+*gen.pl.*

numismatic *adj.* нумизматúческий. **numismatics** *n.* нумизмáтика. **numismatist** *n.* нумизмáт.

numskull *n.* тупúца *m.* & *f.*, óлух.

nun *n.* монáхиня. **nunnery** *n.* (жéнский) монастЫрь (-рЯ) *m.*

nuptial *adj.* брáчный, свáдебный; *n.*: *pl.* свáдьба (*gen.pl.* -деб).

nurse *n.* (*child's*) нЯня; (*medical*) медсестрá (*pl.* -ёстры, -естёр, -ёстрам), сидéлка; (*country*) колыбéль; *v.t.* (*suckle*) кормúть (-млЮ, -мишь) *imp.*, на~, по~ *perf.*; (*tend sick*) ухáживать *imp.* за+*instr.*; (*treat illness*) лечúть (-чý, -чишь) *imp.*; *nursing home*, чáстная лечéбница, чáстный санатóрий. **nursery** *n.* (*room*) дéтская *sb.*; (*day n.*) Ясли (-лей) *pl.*; (*for plants*) питóмник; *n. rhyme*, дéтские стишкú *m.pl.*; *n. school*, дéтский сад (*loc.* -ý; *pl.* -Ы). **nurs(e)ling** *n.* питóмец (-мца), -мица.

nut *n.* орéх; (*for bolt etc.*) гáйка; (*sl.*, *head*) башкá; (*sl.*, *person*) псих. **nutcrackers** *n.* щипцЫ (-цóв) *pl.* для орéхов. **nuthatch** *n.* пóползень (-зня) *m.* **nutshell** *n.* орéховая скорлупá (*pl.* -пы); *in a n.*, в двух словáх. **nut-tree** *n.* орéшник.

nutmeg *n.* мускáтный орéх.

nutria *n.* нýтрия.

nutriment *n.* питáтельная едá. **nutrition** *n.* питáние. **nutritious** *adj.* питáтельный.

nylon *n.* нейлóн; *pl.* нейлóновые чулкú (-лóк) *pl.*; *attrib.* нейлóновый.

nymph *n.* нúмфа. **nymphomaniac** *n.* нимфомáнка.

nystagmus *n.* нистáгм.

O

O *interj.* о! ах! ох!

oaf *n.* неуклЮжий, неотёсанный, человéк. **oafish** *adj.* неуклЮжий.

oak *n.* (*tree*) дуб (*loc.* -е & -ý; *pl.* -Ы); (*wood*) древесúна дýба; *attrib.* дубóвый.

oakum *n.* пáкля.

oar *n.* веслó (*pl.* вёсла, -сел, -слам). **oarsman** *n.* гребéц (-бцá).

oasis *n.* оáзис.

oast-house *n.* хмелесушúлка.

oat *n.*: *pl.* овёс (овсá) *collect.* **oatcake** *n.* овсЯная лепёшка. **oatmeal** *n.* овсЯнка.

oath *n.* клЯтва, присЯга; (*expletive*) ругáтельство; *on, under, o.*, под присЯгой.

obduracy *n.* упрЯмство. **obdurate** *adj.* упрЯмый.

obedience *n.* послушáние. **obedient** *adj.* послýшный.

obelisk *n.* обелúск; (*print.*; *obelus*) крéстик.

obese *n.* тýчный (-чен, -чнá, -чно). **obesity** *n.* тýчность.

obey *v.t.* слýшаться *imp.*, по~ *perf.*+*gen.*; повиновáться *imp.* (*also perf. in past*)+*dat.*

obituary *n.* некролóг; *adj.* некрологúческий.

object *n.* (*thing*) предмéт; (*aim*) цель; (*gram.*) дополнéние; *o.-glass*, объектив; *o.-lesson*, (*fig.*) наглядный примéр; *v.i.* возражáть *imp.*, возразить *perf.* (to, прóтив + *gen.*); протестовáть *imp.* (to, прóтив + *gen.*); *I don't o.*, я не прóтив. **objection** *n.* возражéние, протéст; *I have no o.*, я не возражáю. **objectionable** *adj.* неприятный. **objective** *adj.* объективный; (*gram.*) объéктный; *n.* (*mil.*) объéкт; (*aim*) цель; (*lens*) объектив; (*gram.*) объéктный падéж (-á). **objectivity** *n.* объективность. **objector** *n.* возражáющий *sb.*

obligation *n.* обязáтельство; *I am under an o.*, я обязан (-а). **obligatory** *adj.* обязáтельный. **oblige** *v.t.* обязывать *imp.*, обязáть (-яжý, -яжешь) *perf.*; заставлять *imp.*, застáвить *perf.*; *be obliged to*, (*grateful*) быть благодáрным + *dat.* **obliging** *adj.* услýжливый, любéзный.

oblique *adj.* косóй (кос, -á, -о); (*indirect*) непрямóй (-м, -мá, -мо); (*gram.*) кóсвенный.

obliterate *v.t.* (*efface*) стирáть *imp.*, стерéть (сотрý, -рёшь; стёр) *perf.*; (*destroy*) уничтожáть *imp.*, уничтóжить *perf.* **obliteration** *n.* стирáние; уничтожéние.

oblivion *n.* забвéние. **oblivious** *adj.* (*forgetful*) забывчивый; *to be o. of*, не замечáть *imp.* + *gen.*

oblong *adj.* продолговáтый.

obnoxious *adj.* противный.

oboe *n.* гобóй.

obscene *adj.* непристóйный. **obscenity** *n.* непристóйность.

obscure *adj.* (*dark*) тёмный (-мен, -мнá); (*unclear*) неясный (-сен, -снá, -сно); (*little known*) мáло извéстный; *v.t.* затемнять *imp.*, затемнить *perf.*; дéлать *imp.*, с~ *perf.* неясным. **obscurity** *n.* неясность, неизвéстность.

obsequious *adj.* подобострáстный.

observance *n.* соблюдéние; (*rite*) обряд. **observant** *adj.* наблюдáтельный. **observation** *n.* наблюдéние; (*remark*) замечáние. **observatory** *n.* обсерватóрия. **observe** *v.t.* (*law etc.*) соблюдáть *imp.*, соблюсти (-юдý, -юдёшь; -юл, -юлá) *perf.*; (*watch*) наблюдáть *imp.*; (*remark*) замечáть *imp.*, замéтить *perf.* **observer** *n.* наблюдáтель *m.*

obsess *v.t.* преслéдовать *imp.*; мýчить *imp.* **obsession** *n.* одержимость; (*idea*) навязчивая идéя. **obsessive** *adj.* навязчивый.

obsidian *n.* обсидиáн.

obsolescence *n.* устаревáние. **obsolescent** *adj.* устаревáющий. **obsolete** *adj.* устарéлый, вышедший из употреблéния.

obstacle *n.* препятствие, помéха; *o.-race*, бег с препятствиями.

obstetric(al) *adj.* акушéрский. **obstetrician** *n.* акушéр. **obstetrics** *n.* акушéрство.

obstinacy *n.* упрямство. **obstinate** *adj.* упрямый.

obstreperous *adj.* бýйный (бýен, буйнá, -но).

obstruct *v.t.* пре-, за-, граждáть *imp.*, пре-, за-, градить *perf.*; (*prevent, impede*) препятствовать *imp.*, вос~ *perf.* + *dat.*; мешáть *imp.*, по~ *perf.* + *dat.* **obstruction** *n.* пре-, за-, граждéние; (*obstacle*) препятствие. **obstructive** *adj.* пре-, за-, граждáющий; препятствующий, мешáющий.

obtain *v.t.* получáть *imp.*, получить (-чý, -чишь) *perf.*; доставáть (-таю, -таёшь) *imp.*, достáть (-áну, -áнешь) *perf.*

obtrude *v.t.* навязывать *imp.*, навязáть (-яжý, -яжешь) *perf.* ((up)on, + *dat.*). **obtrusive** *adj.* навязчивый.

obtuse *adj.* тупóй (туп, -á, -о, тýпы).

obverse *n.* (*of coin etc.*) лицевáя сторонá (*acc.* -ону; *pl.* -оны, -óн, -онáм).

obviate *v.t.* (*remove*) устранять *imp.*, устранить *perf.*; (*get round*) обходить (-ожý, -óдишь) *imp.*, обойти (обойдý, -дёшь; обошёл, -шлá) *perf.*

obvious *adj.* очевидный, явный.

ocarina *n.* окарина.

occasion *n.* (*juncture*) слýчай; (*cause*) пóвод; (*occurrence*) событие; *v.t.* причинять *imp.*, причинить *perf.* **occasional** *adj.* случáйный, рéдкий (-док, -дкá, -дко). **occasionally** *adv.* иногдá, врéмя от врéмени.

Occident *n.* Зáпад. **Occidental** *adj.* зáпадный.

occlude *v.t.* преграждáть *imp.*, преградúть *perf.* **occlusion** *n.* преграждéние.

occult *adj.* тáйный, оккýльтный.

occupancy *n.* занятие; (*possession*) владéние (of, +*instr.*). **occupant** *n.* (*of land*) владéлец (-льца), -лица; (*of house etc.*) жúтель *m.*, ~ница. **occupation** *n.* занятие; (*military o.*) оккупáция; (*profession*) профéссия. **occupational** *adj.* профессионáльный; *o. disease*, профессионáльное заболевáние; *o. therapy*, трудотерапúя. **occupy** *v.t.* занимáть *imp.*, занять (займý, -мёшь; зáнял, -á, -о) *perf.*; (*mil.*) оккупúровать *imp.*, *perf.*

occur *v.i.* (*happen*) случáться *imp.*, случúться *perf.*; (*be met with*) встречáться *imp.*; *o. to*, приходúть (-ит) *imp.*, прийтú (придёт; пришёл, -шлá) *perf.* в гóлову + *dat.* **occurrence** *n.* слýчай, происшéствие.

ocean *n.* океáн; (*fig.*) мáсса, мóре; *attrib.* океáнский; *o.-going*, океáнский. **oceanic** *adj.* океáнский, океанúческий.

ocelot *n.* оцелóт.

ochre *n.* óхра.

o'clock *adv.*: *at six o.*, в шесть часóв.

octagon *n.* восьмиугóльник. **octagonal** *adj.* восьмиугóльный.

octane *n.* октáн; *o. number*, октáновое числó.

octave *n.* (*mus.*) октáва.

octet *n.* октéт.

October *n.* октябрь (-ря́) *m.*; *attrib.* октябрьский.

octogenarian *n.* восьмидесятилéтний старúк (-á), -няя старýха.

octopus *n.* осьминóг, спрут.

ocular *adj.* глазнóй, окулярный. **oculist** *n.* окулúст.

odd *adj.* (*number*) нечётный; (*not paired*) непáрный; (*casual*) случáйный; (*strange*) стрáнный (-нен, -ннá, -нно); *five hundred o.*, пятьсóт с лúшним; *o. job*, случáйная рабóта; *o. man out*, (трéтий) лúшний *sb.* **oddity** *n.* стрáнность; (*person*) чудáк (-á), -áчка. **oddly** *adv.* стрáнно; *o. enough*, как это ни стрáнно. **oddment** *n.* остáток (-тка); *pl.* разрóзненные предмéты *m.pl.* **odds** *n.* (*advantage*) перевéс; (*variance*) разноглáсие; (*chance*) шáнсы *m.pl.*; *be at o. with*, (*person*) не лáдить с + *instr.*; (*things*) не соотвéтствовать *imp.* + *dat.*; *long* (*short*) *o.*, нерáвные (почтú рáвные) шáнсы *m.pl.*; *the o. are that*, верoятнее всегó, что; *o. and ends*, обрывки *m.pl.*

ode *n.* óда.

odious *adj.* ненавúстный, отвратúтельный. **odium** *n.* нéнависть, отвращéние.

odour *n.* зáпах; *be in good* (*bad*) *o. with*, быть в (не)мúлости у + *gen.* **odourless** *adj.* без зáпаха.

odyssey *n.* одиссéя.

oedema *n.* отёк.

oesophagus *n.* пищевóд.

of *prep.* expressing **1**. origin: из + *gen.*: *he comes of a working-class family*, он из рабóчей семьú; **2**. cause: от + *gen.*: *he died of hunger*, он ýмер от гóлода; **3**. authorship: *genitive: the works of Pushkin*, сочинéния Пýшкина; **4**. material: из + *gen.*: *made of wood*, сдéланный из дéрева; *adjective: a heart of stone*, кáменное сéрдце; **5**. identity: *apposition: the city of Moscow*, гóрод Москвá; *adjective: the University of Moscow*, Москóвский университéт; **6**. concern, reference: о + *prep.*: *he talked of Lenin*, он говорúл о Лéнине; **7**. quality: *genitive: a man of strong character*, человéк сúльного харáктера; *adjective: a man of importance*, вáжный человéк; **8**. partition: *genitive* (often in -у(-ю): see Introduction): *a glass of milk, tea*, стакáн молокá, чáю; из + *gen.*: *one of them*, одúн из них; **9**. belonging: *genitive: the capital of England*, столúца Áнглии; *poss. adj.*: *the house of his father*, отцóвский дом; **10**. following other parts of speech: see individual entries, e.g. *be afraid*, боя́ться (of, + *gen.*); *dispose of*, избавля́ться от + *gen.*

off *adv.*: in phrasal verbs, see verb, e.g. *clear o.*, убирáться; *prep.* (*from surface of*) с + *gen.*; (*away from*) от + *gen.*; *adj.* (*far*) дáльний; (*right hand*) прáвый; (*free*) свобóдный; *o. and on*, врéмя от врéмени; *on the o. chance*, на всякий слýчай; *o. colour*, нездорóвый;

o. the cuff, без подгото́вки; *o. the point*, не относя́щийся к де́лу; *o. white*, не совсе́м бе́лый (бел, -а́, бе́ло́).

offal *n.* (*food*) требуха́, потроха́ (-хо́в) *pl.*; (*carrion*) па́даль.

offence *n.* (*attack*) нападе́ние; (*insult*) оби́да; (*against law*) просту́пок (-пка), преступле́ние; *take o.*, обижа́ться *imp.*, оби́деться (-и́жусь, -и́дишься) *perf.* (at, на + *acc.*). **offend** *v.t.* оскорбля́ть *imp.*, оскорби́ть *perf.*; обижа́ть *imp.*, оби́деть (-и́жу, -и́дишь) *perf.*; *o. against*, наруша́ть *imp.*, нару́шить *perf.* **offender** *n.* правонаруши́тель *m.*, ~ница; престу́пник, -ица. **offensive** *adj.* (*attacking*) наступа́тельный; (*insulting*) оскорби́тельный, оби́дный; (*repulsive*) проти́вный; *n.* нападе́ние.

offer *v.t.* предлага́ть *imp.*, предложи́ть (-жу́, -жишь) *perf.*; *n.* предложе́ние; *on o.*, в прода́же.

offhand *adj.* бесцеремо́нный (-нен, -нна), небре́жный; *adv.* (*without preparation*) без подгото́вки, экспро́мтом.

office *n.* (*position*) до́лжность; (*place, room, etc.*) бюро́ *neut.indecl.*, конто́ра, канцеля́рия; (*eccl.*) (церко́вная) слу́жба. **officer** *n.* должностно́е лицо́ (*pl.* -ца); (*mil.*) офице́р. **official** *adj.* служе́бный, должностно́й; (*authorized*) официа́льный; *n.* должностно́е лицо́ (*pl.* -ца). **officiate** *v.i.* (*eccl.*) соверша́ть *imp.*, соверши́ть *perf.* богослуже́ние. **officious** *adj.* (*intrusive*) навя́зчивый.

offing *n.*: *in the o.*, в недалёком бу́дущем.

offprint *n.* отде́льный о́ттиск. **offscourings** *n.* отбро́сы (-сов) *pl.*, подо́нки (-ков) *pl.* **offset** *n.* (*compensation*) возмеще́ние; (*offshoot*) о́тпрыск; (*in pipe*) отво́д; *o. process*, (*print.*) офсе́тный спо́соб; *v.t.* возмеща́ть *imp.*, возмести́ть *perf.* **offshoot** *n.* о́тпрыск. **offside** *adv.* вне игры́. **offspring** *n.* пото́мок (-мка); (*collect.*) пото́мки *m.pl.*

often *adv.* ча́сто.

ogle *v.t.* & *i.* стро́ить *imp.* гла́зки + *dat.*

ogre *n.* велика́н-людое́д. **ogress** *n.* велика́нша-людое́дка.

oh *interj.* о! ах! ох!

ohm *n.* ом (*gen.pl.* ом).

oho *interj.* ого́!

oil *n.* ма́сло (*pl.* -сла́, -сел, -сла́м); (*petroleum*) нефть; (*lubricant*) жи́дкая сма́зка; *pl.* (*paint*) ма́сло, ма́сляные кра́ски *f.pl.*; *v.t.* сма́зывать *imp.*, сма́зать (сма́жу, -жешь) *perf.*; *o.-colour*, *-paint*, ма́сляная кра́ска; *o.-painting*, карти́на, напи́санная ма́сляными кра́сками; *o.-rig*, бурова́я устано́вка; *o.-tanker*, та́нкер; *o.-well*, нефтяна́я сква́жина. **oilcake** *n.* жмых (-а́). **oilcan** *n.* маслёнка. **oilcloth** *n.* клеёнка. **oilfield** *n.* месторожде́ние не́фти. **oilskin** *n.* то́нкая клеёнка; *pl.* дождево́е пла́тье. **oily** *adj.* масляни́стый; (*unctuous*) еле́йный.

ointment *n.* мазь.

O.K. *adv.* хорошо́; *interj.* ла́дно!; *v.t.* одобря́ть *imp.*, одо́брить *perf.*

okapi *n.* ока́пи *m.* & *f.indecl.*

old *adj.* ста́рый (стар, -а́, ста́ро́); (*ancient*; *of long standing*) стари́нный; (*former*) бы́вший; *how o. are you?* ско́лько тебе́, вам, (*dat.*) лет? *she is three years o.*, ей (*dat.*) три го́да; *the o.*, старики́ *m.pl.*; *o. age*, ста́рость; *o.-age pension*, пе́нсия по ста́рости; *O. Believer*, старообря́дец (-дца); *o. chap, fellow, etc.*, старина́; *the o. country*, ро́дина, оте́чество; *o.-fashioned*, старомо́дный; *o. maid*, ста́рая де́ва; *o. man*, (*also father, husband*) стари́к (-а́); (*boss*) шеф; *o. man's beard*, ломоно́с; *o.-time*, стари́нный, пре́жних времён; *o. woman*, стару́ха; (*coll.*) стару́шка; *o.-world*, стари́нный.

oleaginous *adj.* масляни́стый, жи́рный (-рен, -рна́, -рно).

oleander *n.* олеа́ндр.

olfactory *adj.* обоня́тельный.

oligarch *n.* олига́рх. **oligarchic(al)** *adj.* олигархи́ческий. **oligarchy** *n.* олига́рхия.

olive *n.* (*fruit*) масли́на, оли́вка; (*colour*) оли́вковый цвет; *adj.* оли́вковый; *o.-branch*, оли́вковая ветвь (*pl.* -ви, -ве́й); *o. oil*, оли́вковое ма́сло; *o.-tree*, масли́на, оли́вковое де́рево (*pl.* дере́вья, -ьев).

Olympic *adj.* олимпи́йский; *O. games*, Олимпи́йские и́гры *f.pl.*

omelet(te) *n.* омле́т.

omen *n.* предзнаменова́ние. **ominous** *adj.* злове́щий.
omission *n.* про́пуск; (*neglect*) упуще́ние. **omit** *v.t.* (*leave out*) пропуска́ть *imp.*, пропусти́ть (-ущу́, -у́стишь) *perf.*; (*neglect*) упуска́ть *imp.*, упусти́ть (-ущу́, -у́стишь) *perf.*
omnibus *n.* (*bus*) авто́бус; (*book*) однoто́мник.
omnipotence *n.* всемогу́щество. **omnipotent** *adj.* всемогу́щий. **omnipresent** *adj.* вездесу́щий. **omniscient** *adj.* всеве́дущий. **omnivorous** *adj.* всея́дный; (*fig.*) всепоглоща́ющий.
on *prep.* (*position*) на + *prep.*; *on the right of*, (*relative position*) с пра́вой стороны́ от + *gen.*; (*direction*) на + *acc.*; (*time*) в + *acc.*; *on the next day*, на сле́дующий день; *on Mondays*, (*repeated action*) по понеде́льникам (*dat.pl.*); *on* (*the morning of*) *the first of June*, (у́тром) пе́рвого ию́ня (*gen.*); *on arrival*, по прибы́тии (*prep.*); (*concerning*) по + *prep.*, о + *prep.*, на + *acc.*; *adv.* да́льше, вперёд; in phrasal verbs, see verbs, e.g. *move on*, идти́ да́льше; *and so on*, и так далее, и т.д.; *further on*, да́льше; *later on*, по́зже.
once *adv.* (оди́н) раз; (*on past occasion*) одна́жды; *all at o.*, неожи́данно; *at o.*, сра́зу, неме́дленно; (*if, when*) *o.*, как то́лько; *o. again, more*, ещё раз; *o. and for all*, раз и навсегда́; *o. or twice*, не́сколько раз; *o. upon a time there lived*, жил-был...
oncoming *n.* приближе́ние; *adj.* приближа́ющийся; *o. traffic*, встре́чное движе́ние.
one *adj.* оди́н (одна́, -но́); (*only, single*) еди́нственный; (*unified*) еди́ный; *n.* оди́н; (*unit*) едини́ца; *pron.*: not usu. translated; verb translated in 2nd pers. sing. or by impers. construction: *one never knows*, никогда́ не зна́ешь; *where can one buy this book?* где мо́жно купи́ть э́ту кни́гу? *chapter o.*, пе́рвая глава́; *I for o.*, что каса́ется меня́; я со свое́й стороны́; *o. after another*, оди́н за други́м; *o. and all*, все до одного́; все как оди́н; *o. and only*, еди́нственный; *o. and the same*, оди́н и тот же; *o. another*, друг дру́га (*dat.* -гу, *etc.*); *o. fine day*, в оди́н прекра́сный день; *o. o'clock*, час; *o.-armed, -handed*, однору́кий; *o.-eyed*, одногла́зый; *o.-legged*, одноно́гий; *o.-sided, -track, -way*, односторо́нний; *o.-time*, бы́вший; *o.-way street*, у́лица односторо́ннего движе́ния.
onerous *adj.* тя́гостный.
oneself *pron.* себя́ (себе́, собо́й); -ся (*suffixed to v.t.*).
onion *n.* (*plant*; *pl. collect.*) лук; (*single o.*) лу́ковица.
onlooker *n.* наблюда́тель *m.*, ~ница.
only *adj.* еди́нственный; *adv.* то́лько; *if o.*, е́сли бы то́лько; *o. just*, то́лько что; *conj.* но.
onomatopoeia *n.* звукоподража́ние. **onomatopoeic** *adj.* звукоподража́тельный.
onset, onslaught *n.* на́тиск, ата́ка.
onus *n.* (*burden*) бре́мя *neut.*; (*responsibility*) отве́тственность.
onward *adj.* дви́жущийся вперёд. **onwards** *adv.* вперёд.
onyx *n.* о́никс; *attrib.* о́никсовый.
ooze *n.* ил, ти́на; *v.t.* & *i.* сочи́ться *imp.* **oozy** *adj.* и́листый, ти́нистый.
opacity *n.* непрозра́чность.
opal *n.* опа́л; *o. glass*, моло́чное стекло́. **opalescence** *n.* опалесце́нция. **opalescent** *adj.* опалесци́рующий. **opaline** *adj.* опа́ловый.
opaque *adj.* непрозра́чный.
open *adj.* откры́тый; (*frank*) открове́нный (-нен, -нна); (*accessible*) досту́пный; (*boat*) беспа́лубный; *in the o. air*, на откры́том во́здухе; *opencast mining*, откры́тые го́рные рабо́ты *f.pl.*; *o.-handed*, ще́дрый (щедр, -á, -o); *o.-minded*, непредубеждённый (-ён, -ённа); *o.-mouthed*, с рази́нутым ртом; *o.-work*, ажу́рный; ажу́рная рабо́та; *v.t.* & *i.* открыва́ть(ся) *imp.*, откры́ть(ся) (-ро́ю(сь), -ро́ешь(ся)) *perf.*; (*o. wide*) раскрыва́ть(ся) *imp.*, раскры́ть(ся) (-ро́ю(сь), -ро́ешь(ся)) *perf.*; *v.i.* (*begin*) начина́ться *imp.*, нача́ться (-чнётся; начался́, -ла́сь) *perf.* **opening** *n.* откры́тие; (*aperture*) отве́рстие; (*beginning*) нача́ло; *adj.* вступи́тельный, нача́льный, пе́рвый.

opera *n.* óпера; *attrib.* óперный; *o.-glasses*, бинóкль *m.*; *o.-hat*, складнóй цили́ндр; *o.-house*, óпера, óперный теáтр.
operate *v.i.* дéйствовать *imp.* (upon, на + *acc.*); дéлать *imp.*, с~ *perf.* оперáцию; (*med.*) опери́ровать *imp.*, *perf.* (on, + *acc.*); *v.t.* управля́ть *imp.* + *instr.*
operatic *adj.* óперный.
operating-theatre *n.* операциóнная *sb.* **operation** *n.* дéйствие; (*med.*; *mil.*) оперáция. **operational** *adj.* операти́вный. **operative** *adj.* дéйствующий, операти́вный; *n.* рабóчий *sb.* **operator** *n.* оперáтор; (*telephone o.*) телефони́ст, ~ка.
operetta *n.* оперéтта.
ophthalmia *n.* офтальми́я. **ophthalmic** *adj.* глазнóй.
opiate *n.* опиáт.
opine *v.t.* полагáть *imp.* **opinion** *n.* мнéние; (*expert's o.*) заключéние (специали́ста); *o. poll*, опрóс общéственного мнéния. **opinionated** *adj.* упóрствующий в свои́х взгля́дах.
opium *n.* óпий, óпиум; *o. poppy*, снотвóрный мак.
opossum *n.* опóссум.
opponent *n.* проти́вник.
opportune *adj.* своеврéменный (-нен, -нна). **opportunism** *n.* оппортуни́зм. **opportunist** *n.* оппортуни́ст. **opportunity** *n.* слýчай, возмóжность.
oppose *v.t.* (*contrast*) противопоставля́ть *imp.*, противопостáвить *perf.* (to, + *dat.*); (*resist*) проти́виться *imp.*, вос~ *perf.* + *dat.*; (*speak etc. against*) выступáть *imp.*, вы́ступить *perf.* прóтив + *gen.* **opposed** *adj.* (*contrasted*) противопостáвленный (-ен); (*of person*) прóтив (to, + *gen.*); *as o. to*, в противополóжность + *dat.* **opposite** *adj.* противополóжный, обрáтный; *n.* противополóжность; *just the o.*, как раз наоборóт; *adv.* напрóтив; *prep.* (на)прóтив + *gen.* **opposition** *n.* (*contrast*) противопоставлéние; (*resistance*) сопротивлéние; (*polit.*) оппози́ция.
oppress *v.t.* притесня́ть *imp.*, притесни́ть *perf.*; угнетáть *imp.* **oppression** *n.* притеснéние, угнетéние. **oppressive** *adj.* гнетýщий, угнетáтельский; (*weather*) дýшный (-шен, -шнá, -шно). **oppressor** *n.* угнетáтель *m.*, ~ница.
opprobrious *adj.* оскорби́тельный. **opprobrium** *n.* позóр.
opt *v.i.* выбирáть *imp.*, вы́брать (вы́беру, -решь) *perf.* (for, + *acc.*); *o. out*, не принимáть *imp.* учáстия (of, в + *prep.*). **optative (mood)** *n.* оптати́в.
optic *adj.* глазнóй, зри́тельный. **optical** *adj.* опти́ческий. **optician** *n.* óптик. **optics** *n.* óптика.
optimism *n.* оптими́зм. **optimist** *n.* оптими́ст. **optimistic** *adj.* оптимисти́чный, -ческий. **optimum** *adj.* оптимáльный.
option *n.* вы́бор; *without the o.* (*of a fine*), без прáва замéны штрáфом. **optional** *adj.* необязáтельный, факультати́вный.
opulence *n.* богáтство. **opulent** *adj.* богáтый.
opus *n.* óпус.
or *conj.* и́ли; *or else*, инáче; *or so*, приблизи́тельно.
oracle *n.* орáкул. **oracular** *adj.* орáкульский; (*mysterious*) загáдочный.
oral *adj.* ýстный; *n.* ýстный экзáмен.
orange *n.* (*fruit*) апельси́н; (*colour*) орáнжевый цвет; *attrib.* апельси́нный, апельси́новый; *adj.* орáнжевый; *o.-blossom*, померáнцевый цвет; (*decoration*) флёрдорáнж; *o.-peel*, апельси́новая кóрка. **orangery** *n.* оранжерéя.
orang-(o)utan(g) *n.* орангутáнг.
oration *n.* речь. **orator** *n.* орáтор. **oratorical** *adj.* орáторский.
oratorio *n.* оратóрия.
oratory[1] *n.* (*chapel*) часóвня (*gen.pl.* -вен).
oratory[2] *n.* (*speech*) орáторское искýсство, красноречие.
orb *n.* шар (-á *with 2, 3, 4*; *pl.* -ы́); (*part of regalia*) держáва.
orbit *n.* орби́та; (*eye-socket*) глазнáя впáдина; *in o.*, на орби́те; *v.t.* вращáться *imp.* по орби́те вокрýг + *gen.* **orbital** *adj.* орбитáльный.
orchard *n.* фруктóвый сад (*loc.* -ý; *pl.* -ы́).

orchestra *n.* оркéстр. **orchestral** *adj.* оркестрóвый. **orchestrate** *v.t.* оркестровáть *imp.*, *perf.* **orchestration** *n.* оркестрóвка.

orchid *n.* орхидéя. **orchis** *n.* ятры́шник.

ordain *v.t.* предпи́сывать *imp.*, предписáть (-ишý, -и́шешь) *perf.*; (*eccl.*) посвящáть *imp.*, посвяти́ть (-ящý, -яти́шь) *perf.* (в духóвный сан (*v. abs.*); в + *nom.-acc.pl.* (*of rank*)).

ordeal *n.* испытáние.

order *n.* поря́док (-дка); (*system*) строй; (*command*) прикáз; (*for goods*) закáз; (*document*) óрдер (*pl.* -á); (*archit.*) óрдер; (*biol.*) отря́д; (*of monks, knights*) óрден; (*insignia*) óрден (*pl.* -á); *pl.* (*holy o.*) духóвный сан; *by o.*, по прикáзу; *in o. to*, для тогó чтóбы; *made to o.*, сдéланный (-ан) на закáз; *v.t.* (*command*) прикáзывать *imp.*, приказáть (-ажý, -áжешь) *perf.* + *dat.*; велéть (-лю́, -ли́шь) *imp.*, *perf.* + *dat.*; (*goods etc.*) закáзывать *imp.*, заказáть (-ажý, -áжешь) *perf.* **orderly** *adj.* аккурáтный, опря́тный; *o. officer*, дежýрный офицéр; *n.* (*med.*) санитáр; (*mil.*) ординáрец (-рца).

ordinal *adj.* поря́дковый; *n.* поря́дковое числи́тельное *sb.*

ordinance *n.* декрéт.

ordinary *adj.* обыкновéнный (-нен, -нна), обы́чный; (*mediocre*) зауря́дный.

ordination *n.* посвящéние.

ordnance *n.* артиллéрия; *attrib.* артиллери́йский.

ore *n.* рудá (*pl.* -ды).

organ *n.* óрган; (*mus.*) оргáн; *o.-grinder*, шармáнщик; *o.-stop*, реги́стр оргáна. **organic** *adj.* органи́ческий; *o. whole*, еди́ное цéлое *sb.* **organism** *n.* органи́зм. **organist** *n.* органи́ст. **organization** *n.* организáция. **organize** *v.t.* организóвывать *imp.* (*pres. not used*), организовáть *imp.* (*in pres.*), *perf.*; устрáивать *imp.*, устрóить *perf.*

orgy *n.* óргия.

oriel *n.* э́ркер; (*o. window*) окнó (*pl.* óкна, óкон, óкнам) э́ркера.

Orient[1] *n.* Востóк. **oriental** *adj.* востóчный.

orient[2], **orientate** *v.t.* ориенти́ровать *imp.*, *perf.* (oneself, -ся). **orientation** *n.* ориентáция, ориентирóвка.

orifice *n.* отвéрстие.

origin *n.* происхождéние, начáло. **original** *adj.* оригинáльный; (*initial*) первоначáльный; (*genuine*) пóдлинный (-нен, -нна); *n.* оригинáл, пóдлинник. **originality** *n.* оригинáльность; пóдлинность. **originate** *v.t.* порождáть *imp.*, породи́ть *perf.*; *v.i.* происходи́ть (-ожý, -óдишь) *imp.*, произойти́ (-ойдý, -ойдёшь; -ошёл, -ошлá) *perf.* (from, in, от + *gen.*); брать (берý, -рёшь; брал, -á, -о) *imp.*, взять (возьмý, -мёшь; взял, -á, -о) *perf.* начáло (from, in, в + *prep.*, от + *gen.*). **originator** *n.* áвтор, инициáтор.

oriole *n.* и́волга.

ormolu *n.* золочёная брóнза.

ornament *n.* украшéние, орнáмент; *v.t.* украшáть *imp.*, украсить *perf.* **ornamental** *adj.* орнаментáльный, декорати́вный.

ornate *adj.* разукрáшенный (-ен); (*lit. style*) витиевáтый.

ornithological *adj.* орнитологи́ческий. **ornithologist** *n.* орнитóлог. **ornithology** *n.* орнитолóгия.

orphan *n.* сиротá (*pl.* -ты) *m.* & *f.*; *v.t.* дéлать *imp.*, с~ *perf.* сиротóй; *be orphaned*, сиротéть *imp.*, о~ *perf.* **orphanage** *n.* прию́т, сирóтский дом (*pl.* -á). **orphaned** *adj.* осиротéлый.

orris-root *n.* фиáлковый кóрень (-рня) *m.*

orthodox *adj.* ортодоксáльный; (*eccl.*, *O.*) правослáвный. **orthodoxy** *n.* ортодóксия; (*O.*) правослáвие.

orthographic(al) *adj.* орфографи́ческий. **orthography** *n.* орфогрáфия, правописáние.

orthopaedic *adj.* ортопеди́ческий. **orthopaedics** *n.* ортопéдия.

oscillate *v.i.* вибри́ровать *imp.*; (*also of person*) колебáться (-блюсь, -блешься) *imp.*, по~ *perf.* **oscillation** *n.* вибрáция, осцилля́ция; колебáние. **oscilloscope** *n.* осциллоскóп.

osier *n.* (*tree*) и́ва; (*shoot*) лозá (*pl.* -зы); *pl.* ивня́к (-á) (*collect.*).

osmosis *n.* óсмос.

osprey *n.* (*bird*) скопá; (*plume*) эгрéт.
osseous *adj.* кóстный; (*bony*) кости́стый. **ossified** *adj.* окостенéлый.
ostensible *adj.* мни́мый. **ostensibly** *adv.* я́кобы.
ostentation *n.* показнóе проявлéние, выставлéние напокáз. **ostentatious** *adj.* показнóй.
osteopath *n.* остеопáт. **osteopathy** *n.* остеопáтия.
ostler *n.* кóнюх.
ostracism *n.* остраки́зм. **ostracize** *v.t.* подвергáть *imp.*, подвéргнуть (-г) *perf.* остраки́зму.
ostrich *n.* стрáус.
other *adj.* другóй, инóй; тот; *pl.* други́е *sb.*; *any o. business*, текýщие делá *neut.pl.*, рáзное *sb.*; *every o.*, кáждый вторóй; *every o. day*, чéрез дéнь; *in o. words*, ины́ми словáми; *on the o. hand*, с другóй стороны́; *on the o. side*, на той сторонé, по ту стóрону; *one after the o.*, оди́н за други́м; *one or the o.*, тот или инóй; *the o. day*, на днях, недáвно; *the o. way round*, наоборóт; *the others*, остальны́е. **otherwise** *adv.*, *conj.* инáче, а то.
otiose *adj.* ненýжный.
otter *n.* вы́дра.
ouch *interj.* ай!
ought *v.aux.* дóлжен (-жнá) (бы) + *inf.*; слéдовало (бы) *impers.* + *dat.* & *inf.*; (*probability*) верóятно, по всей верóятности + *finite verb*; *o. not*, не слéдовало (бы) *impers.* + *dat.* & *inf.*; нельзя́ + *dat.* & *inf.*
ounce *n.* ýнция.
our, ours *poss.pron.* наш (-а, -е; -и); свой (-оя́, -оё; -ои́). **ourselves** *pron.* (*emph.*) (мы) сáми (-и́х, -и́м, -и́ми); (*refl.*) себя́ (себé, собóй); -ся (*suffixed to v.t.*).
oust *v.t.* вытесня́ть *imp.*, вы́теснить *perf.*
out *adv.* **1**. нарýжу, вон; (*to the end*) до концá; in phrasal verbs often rendered by prefix вы- (вы́- in *perf.*), e.g. *pull o.*, вытáскивать *imp.*, вы́тащить *perf.*; **2**. *to be o.*, in various senses: *he is o.*, (*not at home*) егó нет дóма; (*not in office etc.*) он вы́шел; *they are o.*, (*on strike*) они бастýют; *the secret is o.*, тáйна раскры́та; *the truth will o.*, прáвды не скрыть; *to be o.* rendered by *perf.* verb in *past* (English *pres.*, *past*) or *fut.* (English *fut.*): (*be at an end*) кóнчиться *perf.*; (*be o. of fashion*) вы́йти (вы́йду, -дешь; вы́шел, -шла) *perf.* из мóды; (*of book, be published*) вы́йти (вы́йдет; вы́шел, -шла) *perf.* из печáти; (*of candle etc.*) потýхнуть (-х) *perf.*; (*of chicken etc.*) вы́лупиться *perf.*; (*of flower*) распусти́ться (-ится) *perf.*; (*of person, be unconscious*) потеря́ть *perf.* сознáние; (*of rash*) вы́ступить *perf.*; **3**.: *o. and o.*, отъя́вленный, совершéнный; *o. with you!* вон отсю́да! **4**.: *o. of*, из + *gen.*, вне + *gen.*; *o. of date*, устарéлый, старомóдный; *o. of doors*, на откры́том вóздухе; *o. of gear*, вы́ключенный (-ен); *o. of order*, неисправный; *o. of the way*, отдалённый (-ён, -ённа), трýдно находи́мый; *o. of work*, безрабóтный.
outbalance *v.t.* перевéшивать *imp.*, перевéсить *perf.* **outbid** *v.t.* предлагáть *imp.*, предложи́ть (-жý, -жишь) *perf.* бóлее высóкую цéну, чем + *nom.* **outboard** *adj.*: *o. motor*, подвеснóй дви́гатель *m.* **outbreak** *n.* (*of anger, disease*) вспы́шка; (*of war*) начáло. **outbuilding** *n.* надвóрная пострóйка. **outburst** *n.* взрыв, вспы́шка. **outcast** *n.* отвéрженец (-нца); *adj.* отвéрженный. **outclass** *v.t.* оставля́ть *imp.*, остáвить *perf.* далекó позади́. **outcome** *n.* результáт, исхóд. **outcrop** *n.* обнажённая порóда. **outcry** *n.* (шýмные) протéсты *m.pl.* **outdistance** *v.t.* обгоня́ть *imp.*, обогнáть (обгоню́, -нишь; обогнáл, -á, -о) *perf.* **outdo** *v.t.* превосходи́ть (-ожý, -óдишь) *imp.*, превзойти́ (-ойдý, -ойдёшь; -ошёл, -ошлá) *perf.*
outdoor *adj.*, **outdoors** *adv.* на откры́том вóздухе, на ýлице.
outer *adj.* (*external*) внéшний, нарýжный; (*far from centre*) отдалённый (от цéнтра). **outermost** *adj.* сáмый дáльний, крáйний.
outfit *n.* снаряжéние; (*set of things*) набóр; (*clothes*) одéжда. **outfitter** *n.* торгóвец (-вца) одéждой. **outgoings** *n.* из-

де́ржки *f.pl.* **outgrow** *v.t.* перераста́ть *imp.*, перерасти́ (-расту́, -растёшь; -ро́с, -росла́) *perf.*; (*clothes*) выраста́ть *imp.*, вы́расти (-ту, -тешь; вы́рос) *perf.* из + *gen.*; (*habit*) избавля́ться *imp.*, изба́виться *perf.* с во́зрастом от + *gen.* **outhouse** *n.* надво́рная постро́йка.

outing *n.* прогу́лка, экску́рсия.

outlandish *adj.* стра́нный (-нен, -нна́, -нно). **outlast** *v.t.* продолжа́ться *imp.*, продо́лжиться *perf.* до́льше, чем + *nom.* **outlaw** *n.* лицо́ (*pl.* -ца) вне зако́на; банди́т; *v.t.* объявля́ть *imp.*, объяви́ть (-влю́, -вишь) *perf.* вне зако́на. **outlay** *n.* изде́ржки *f.pl.*, расхо́ды *m.pl.* **outlet** *n.* вы́пуск; (*fig.*) вы́ход; (*for goods*) торго́вая то́чка. **outline** *n.* очерта́ние, ко́нтур; (*sketch, draft*) о́черк; *v.t.* оче́рчивать *imp.*, очерти́ть (-рчу́, -ртишь) *perf.* **outlive** *v.t.* пережи́ть (-иву́, -ивёшь; пе́режил, -а́, -о) *perf.* **outlook** *n.* вид, перспекти́вы *f.pl.* **outlying** *adj.* отдалённый (-ён, -ённа). **outmoded** *adj.* старомо́дный. **outnumber** *v.t.* чи́сленно превосходи́ть (-ожу́, -о́дишь) *imp.*, превзойти́ (-ойду́, -ойдёшь; -ошёл, -ошла́) *perf.* **out-patient** *n.* амбулато́рный больно́й *sb.* **outpost** *n.* аванпо́ст. **output** *n.* вы́пуск, проду́кция.

outrage *n.* (*violation of rights*) наси́льственное наруше́ние чужи́х прав; (*gross offence*) надруга́тельство (upon, над + *instr.*); *v.t.* оскорбля́ть *imp.*, оскорби́ть *perf.*; надруга́ться *perf.* над + *instr.*; (*infringe*) наруша́ть *imp.*, нару́шить *perf.* **outrageous** *adj.* (*immoderate*) возмути́тельный; (*offensive*) оскорби́тельный.

outrigger *n.* (*boat*) аутри́гер. **outright** *adv.* (*entirely*) вполне́; (*once for all*) раз на всегда́; (*openly*) откры́то; *adj.* прямо́й (прям, -а́, -о, пря́мы́). **outset** *n.* нача́ло; *at the o.*, внача́ле; *from the o.*, с са́мого нача́ла. **outshine** *v.t.* затмева́ть *imp.*, затми́ть *perf.*

outside *n.* (*external side*) нару́жная сторона́ (*acc.* -ону; *pl.* -оны, -о́н, -она́м); (*exterior, appearance*) нару́жность, вне́шность; *at the o.*, са́мое бо́льшее, в кра́йнем слу́чае; *from the o.*, извне́; *on the o.*, снару́жи; *adj.* нару́жный, вне́шний; (*sport*) кра́йний; *adv.* (*on the o.*) снару́жи; (*to the o.*) нару́жу; (*out of doors*) на откры́том во́здухе, на у́лице; *prep.* вне + *gen.*; за + *instr.*, за преде́лами + *gen.*; (*other than*) кро́ме + *gen.* **outsider** *n.* посторо́нний *sb.*; (*sport*) аутса́йдер.

outsize *adj.* бо́льше станда́ртного разме́ра. **outskirts** *n.* окра́ина. **outspoken** *adj.* открове́нный (-нен, -нна), прямо́й (прям, -а́, -о, пря́мы́). **outspread** *adj.* распростёртый. **outstanding** *adj.* (*person*) выдаю́щийся; (*debt*) неупла́ченный. **outstay** *v.t.* переси́живать *imp.*, пересиде́ть (-ижу́, -иди́шь) *perf.*; *o. one's welcome*, заси́живаться *imp.*, засиде́ться (-ижу́сь, -иди́шься) *perf.* **outstretched** *adj.*: *with o. arms*, с распростёртыми объя́тиями. **outstrip** *v.t.* обгоня́ть *imp.*, обогна́ть (обгоню́, -нишь; обогна́л, -а́, -о) *perf.* **outvote** *v.t.* побежда́ть *imp.*, победи́ть (-ди́шь) *perf.* большинство́м голосо́в.

outward *adj.* (*external*) вне́шний, нару́жный; *o. bound*, уходя́щий в пла́вание. **outwardly** *adv.* вне́шне, на вид. **outwards** *adv.* нару́жу.

outweigh *v.t.* переве́шивать *imp.*, переве́сить *perf.* **outwit** *v.t.* перехитри́ть *perf.*

oval *adj.* ова́льный; *n.* ова́л.

ovary *n.* (*anat.*) яи́чник; (*bot.*) за́вязь.

ovation *n.* ова́ция.

oven *n.* печь (*loc.* -чи́; *pl.* -чи, -че́й); духо́вка.

over *adv.*, *prep.* with verbs: see verbs, e.g. *jump o.*, перепры́гивать *imp.*; *think o.*, обду́мывать *imp.*; *adv.* (*in excess*) сли́шком; (*in addition*) вдоба́вок; (*again*) сно́ва; *prep.* (*above*) над + *instr.*; (*through*; *covering*) по + *dat.*; (*concerning*) о + *prep.*; (*across*) че́рез + *acc.*; (*on the other side of*) по ту сто́рону + *gen.*; (*more than*) свы́ше + *gen.*; бо́лее + *gen.*; (*with age*) за + *acc.*; *all o.*, (*finished*) всё ко́нчено; (*everywhere*) повсю́ду; *all o. the country*, по всей стране́; *o. again*, ещё раз; *o. against*, напро́тив + *gen.*; (*in contrast to*) по сравне́нию с + *instr.*; *o. and above*, сверх + *gen.*; не говоря́ уже́ о + *prep.*;

o. the radio, по ра́дио; *o. there*, вон там; *o. the way*, че́рез доро́гу.
overact *v.t.* & *i.* переи́грывать *imp.*, переигра́ть *perf.* **overall** *n.* хала́т; *pl.* комбинезо́н, спецоде́жда; *adj.* о́бщий. **overawe** *v.t.* внуша́ть *imp.*, внуши́ть *perf.* благогове́йный страх + *dat.* **overbalance** *v.i.* теря́ть *imp.*, по ~ *perf.* равнове́сие. **overbearing** *adj.* вла́стный, повели́тельный. **overboard** *adv.* (*motion*) за́ борт; (*position*) за бо́ртом. **overcast** *adj.* (*sky*) покры́тый облака́ми. **overcoat** *n.* пальто́ *neut. indecl.* **overcome** *v.t.* преодолева́ть *imp.*, преодоле́ть *perf.*; *adj.* охва́ченный (-ен). **overcrowded** *adj.* перепо́лненный (-ен), перенаселённый (-ён, -ена́). **overcrowding** *n.* перенаселённость. **overdo** *v.t.* (*cook*) пережа́ривать *imp.*, пережа́рить *perf.*; *o. it, things*, (*work too hard*) переутомля́ться *imp.*, переутоми́ться *perf.*; (*go too far*) перeба́рщивать *imp.*, переборщи́ть *perf.*
overdose *n.* чрезме́рная до́за. **overdraft** *n.* превыше́ние креди́та; (*amount*) долг ба́нку. **overdraw** *v.i.* превыша́ть *imp.*, превы́сить *perf.* креди́т (в ба́нке). **overdrive** *n.* ускоря́ющая переда́ча. **overdue** *adj.* просро́ченный (-ен); *be o.*, (*late*) запа́здывать *imp.*, запозда́ть *perf.* **overestimate** *v.t.* переоце́нивать *imp.*, переоцени́ть (-ню́, -нишь) *perf.*; *n.* переоце́нка. **overflow** *v.i.* перелива́ться *imp.*, перели́ться (-льётся; -ли́лся, -лила́сь, -ли́ло́сь) *perf.*; (*river etc.*) разлива́ться *imp.*, разли́ться (разольётся; разли́лся, -ила́сь, -и́ло́сь) *perf.*; *n.* разли́в; (*outlet*) переливна́я труба́ (*pl.* -бы). **overgrown** *adj.* заро́сший. **overhang** *v.t.* & *i.* выступа́ть *imp.* над + *instr.*; (*also fig.*) нависа́ть *imp.*, нави́снуть (-с) *perf.* над + *instr.*; *n.* свес, вы́ступ.
overhaul *v.t.* разбира́ть *imp.*, разобра́ть (разберу́, -рёшь; разобра́л, -а́, -о) *perf.*; (*repair*) капита́льно ремонти́ровать *imp., perf.*; (*overtake*) догоня́ть *imp.*, догна́ть (догоню́, -нишь; догна́л, -а́, -о) *perf.* **overhead** *adv.* наверху́, над голово́й; *adj.* возду́шный, подвесно́й; (*expenses*) накладно́й; *n.*: *pl.* накладны́е расхо́ды *m.pl.* **overhear** *v.t.* неча́янно слы́шать (-шу, -шишь) *imp.*, у ~ *perf.*; (*eavesdrop*) подслу́шивать *imp.*, подслу́шать *perf.* **overjoyed** *adj.* в восто́рге (at, от + *gen.*), о́чень дово́льный (at, + *instr.*). **overland** *adj.* сухопу́тный; *adv.* по су́ше. **overlap** *v.t.* & *i.* (*completely*) перекрыва́ть *imp.*, перекры́ть (-ро́ю, -ро́ешь) *perf.* (друг дру́га); *v.t.* (*in part*) части́чно покрыва́ть *imp.*, покры́ть (-ро́ю, -ро́ешь) *perf.*; *v.i.* части́чно совпада́ть *imp.*, совпа́сть (-аду́, -адёшь; -а́л) *perf.*
overleaf *adv.* на обра́тной стороне́ (листа́, страни́цы). **overlook** *v.t.* (*look down on*) смотре́ть (-рю́, -ришь) *imp.* све́рху на + *acc.*; (*of window*) выходи́ть (-ит) *imp.* на, в, + *acc.*; (*not notice*) не замеча́ть *imp.*, заме́тить *perf.* + *gen.*; (*o. offence etc.*) проща́ть *imp.*, прости́ть *perf.* **overlord** *n.* сюзере́н, влады́ка *m.* **overmaster** *v.t.* подчиня́ть *imp.*, подчини́ть *perf.* себе́; (*fig.*) всеце́ло овладева́ть *imp.*, овладе́ть *perf.* + *instr.* **overnight** *adv.* накану́не ве́чером; (*all night*) с ве́чера, всю ночь; (*suddenly*) неожи́данно, ско́ро; *stay o.*, ночева́ть (-чу́ю, -чу́ешь) *imp.*, пере ~ *perf.*; *adj.* ночно́й. **overpass** *n.* путепрово́д. **overpay** *v.t.* перепла́чивать *imp.*, переплати́ть (-ачу́, -а́тишь) *perf.*
over-populated *adj.* перенаселённый (-ён, -ена́). **over-population** *n.* перенаселённость. **overpower** *v.t.* переси́ливать *imp.*, переси́лить *perf.*; (*heat etc.*) одолева́ть *imp.*, одоле́ть *perf.* **over-production** *n.* перепроизво́дство. **overrate** *v.t.* переоце́нивать *imp.*, переоцени́ть (-ню́, -нишь) *perf.* **overreach** *v.t.* перехитри́ть *perf.*; *o. oneself*, зарыва́ться *imp.*, зарва́ться (-ву́сь, -вёшься; -ва́лся, -вала́сь, -ва́ло́сь) *perf.* **override** *v.t.* (*fig.*) отверга́ть *imp.*, отве́ргнуть (-г(нул), -гла) *perf.* **overrule** *v.t.* аннули́ровать *imp.*, *perf.* **overrun** *v.t.* (*flood*) наводня́ть *imp.*, наводни́ть *perf.*; (*ravage*) опустоша́ть *imp.*, опустоши́ть *perf.*
oversea(s) *adv.* за мо́рем, че́рез мо́ре; *adj.* замо́рский. **oversee** *v.t.* надзира́ть

imp. за + *instr.* **overseer** *n.* надзира́тель *m.*, ~ница. **overshadow** *v.t.* затмева́ть *imp.*, затми́ть *perf.* **oversight** *n.* (*supervision*) надзо́р; (*mistake*) недосмо́тр, оплóшность. **oversleep** *v.i.* просыпа́ть *imp.*, проспа́ть (-плю́, -пи́шь; -па́л, -пала́, -па́ло) *perf.* **overstate** *v.t.* преувели́чивать *imp.*, преувели́чить *perf.* **overstatement** *n.* преувеличе́ние. **overstep** *v.t.* переступа́ть *imp.*, переступи́ть (-плю́, -пишь) *perf.* + *acc.*, через + *acc.*

overt *adj.* я́вный, откры́тый.

overtake *v.t.* догоня́ть *imp.*, догна́ть (догоню́, -нишь; догна́л, -á, -о) *perf.*; (*of misfortune etc.*) постига́ть *imp.*, пости́чь & пости́гнуть (-и́гну, -и́гнешь; -и́г) *perf.* **overthrow** *v.t.* (*upset*) опроки́дывать *imp.*, опроки́нуть *perf.*; (*from power*) сверга́ть *imp.*, све́ргнуть (-г(нул), -гла) *perf.*; *n.* сверже́ние. **overtime** *n.* (*time*) сверхуро́чные часы́ *m.pl.*; (*payment*) сверхуро́чное *sb.*; *adv.* сверхуро́чно.

overtone *n.* (*mus.*) оберто́н; (*fig.*) скры́тый намёк.

overture *n.* предложе́ние, инициати́ва; (*mus.*) увертю́ра.

overturn *v.t.* & *i.* опроки́дывать(ся) *imp.*, опроки́нуть(ся) *perf.*; *v.t.* сверга́ть *imp.*, све́ргнуть (-г) *perf.* **overweening** *adj.* высокоме́рный, самонаде́янный (-ян, -янна). **overwhelm** *v.t.* подавля́ть *imp.*, подави́ть (-влю́, -вишь) *perf.*; (*of emotions*) овладева́ть *imp.*, овладе́ть *perf.* + *instr.* **overwhelming** *adj.* подавля́ющий. **overwork** *v.t.* & *i.* переутомля́ть(ся) *imp.*, переутоми́ть(ся) *perf.*

owe *v.t.* (*o. money*) быть до́лжным (-жен, -жна́) + *acc.* & *dat.*; (*be indebted*) быть обя́занным (-ан) + *instr.* & *dat.*; *he, she, owes me three roubles*, он до́лжен, она́ должна́, мне три рубля́; *she owes him her life*, она́ обя́зана ему́ жи́знью. **owing** *adj.*: *be o.*, причита́ться *imp.* (to, + *dat.*); *o. to*, из-за + *gen.*, по причи́не + *gen.*, вследствие + *gen.*

owl *n.* сова́ (*pl.* -вы). **owlet** *n.* совёнок (-нка; *pl.* совя́та, -т).

own *adj.* свой (-оя́, -оё; -ои́); (свой) со́бственный; (*relative*) родно́й; *on one's o.*, самостоя́тельно; *v.t.* (*possess*) владе́ть *imp.* + *instr.*; (*admit*) признава́ть (-наю́, -наёшь) *imp.*, призна́ть *perf.*; *o. up*, признава́ться (-наю́сь, -наёшься) *imp.*, призна́ться *perf.* **owner** *n.* владе́лец (-льца), со́бственник. **ownership** *n.* владе́ние (of, + *instr.*), со́бственность.

ox *n.* вол (-á).

oxalic *adj.*: *o. acid*, щаве́льная кислота́.

oxidation *n.* окисле́ние. **oxide** *n.* о́кись, о́кисел (-сла). **oxidize** *v.t.* & *i.* окисля́ть(ся) *imp.*, окисли́ть(ся) *perf.* **oxyacetylene** *adj.* кислоро́дно-ацетиле́новый. **oxygen** *n.* кислоро́д; *attrib.* кислоро́дный.

oyster *n.* у́стрица; *o.-catcher*, кули́к-соро́ка.

ozone *n.* озо́н.

P

pace *n.* шаг (-á *with 2, 3, 4, loc.* -у́; *pl.* -и́); (*fig.*) те́мп; *keep p. with*, идти́ (иду́, идёшь; шёл, шла́) *imp.* в но́гу с + *instr.*; *set the p.*, задава́ть (-даю́, -даёшь) *imp.*, зада́ть (-а́м, -а́шь, -а́ст, -ади́м; за́дал, -á, -о) *perf.* темп; *v.i.* шага́ть *imp.*, шагну́ть *perf.*; *v.t.*: *p. out*, измеря́ть *imp.*, изме́рить *perf.* шага́ми.

pachyderm *n.* толстоко́жее (живо́тное) *sb.*

pacific *adj.* ми́рный; *P.*, тихоокеа́нский; *n.* Ти́хий океа́н. **pacification** *n.* усмире́ние, умиротворе́ние. **pacifism**

n. пацифи́зм. **pacifist** *n.* пацифи́ст. **pacify** *v.t.* усмиря́ть *imp.*, усмири́ть *perf.*; умиротворя́ть *imp.*, умиротвори́ть *perf.*

pack *n.* у́зел (узла́), вьюк (*pl.* -ю́ки́); (*soldier's*) ра́нец (-нца); (*hounds*) сво́ра; (*wolves, birds*) ста́я; (*cards*) коло́да; *p.-horse*, вью́чная ло́шадь (*pl.* -ди, -де́й, *instr.* -дьми́); *p.-ice*, пак, па́ковый лёд (льда, *loc.* льду); *p. of lies*, сплошна́я ложь (лжи, *instr.* ло́жью); *v.t.* пакова́ть *imp.*, у~ *perf.*; укла́дывать *imp.*, уложи́ть (-жу́, -жишь) *perf.*; (*cram*) набива́ть *imp.*, наби́ть (-бью́, -бьёшь) *perf.* **package** *n.* паке́т, свёрток (-тка); (*packaging*) упако́вка. **packaging** *n.* упако́вка. **packet** *n.* паке́т; па́чка; (*money*) куш. **packing-case** *n.* я́щик. **packing-needle** *n.* упако́вочная игла́ (*pl.* -лы).

pact *n.* догово́р, пакт.

pad[1] *v.i.* (*walk*) идти́ (иду́, идёшь; шёл, шла) *imp.*, пойти́ (пойду́, -дёшь; пошёл, -шла́) *perf.* неслы́шным ша́гом.

pad[2] *n.* (*cushion*) поду́шка, поду́шечка; (*guard*) щито́к (-тка́); (*of paper*) блокно́т; (*paw*) ла́па; *v.t.* набива́ть *imp.*, наби́ть (-бью́, -бьёшь) *perf.*; подбива́ть *imp.*, подби́ть (подобью́, -ьёшь) *perf.* **padding** *n.* наби́вка.

paddle[1] *n.* (*oar*) (байда́рочное) весло́ (*pl.* вёсла, -сел, -слам); (*of p.-wheel*) ло́пасть (*pl.* -ти, -те́й); *p.-boat*, колёсный парохо́д; *p.-wheel*, гребно́е колесо́ (*pl.* -ёса); *v.i.* (*row*) грести́ (гребу́, -бёшь; грёб, -ла́) *imp.* байда́рочным весло́м.

paddle[2] *v.i.* (*wade*) ходи́ть (хожу́, хо́дишь) *indet.*, идти́ (иду́, идёшь; шёл, шла) *det.*, пойти́ (пойду́, -дёшь; пошёл, -шла́) *perf.* босико́м по воде́.

paddock *n.* небольшо́й луг (*loc.* -у́; *pl.* -а́).

padlock *n.* вися́чий замо́к (-мка́); *v.t.* запира́ть *imp.*, запере́ть (запру́, -рёшь; за́пер, -ла́, -ло) *perf.* на вися́чий замо́к.

padre *n.* полково́й свяще́нник.

paediatric *adj.* педиатри́ческий. **paediatrician** *n.* педиа́тор. **paediatrics** *n.* педиатри́я.

pagan *n.* язы́чник, -ица; *adj.* язы́ческий. **paganism** *n.* язы́чество.

page[1] *n.* (*p.-boy*) паж (-а́), ма́льчик-слуга́ *m.*; *v.t.* (*summon*) вызыва́ть *imp.*, вы́звать (вы́зову, -вешь) *perf.*

page[2] *n.* (*of book*) страни́ца.

pageant *n.* пы́шная проце́ссия; великоле́пное зре́лище. **pageantry** *n.* великоле́пие.

paginate *v.t.* нумерова́ть *imp.*, про~ *perf.* страни́цы + *gen.*

pagoda *n.* па́года.

paid, paid-up *adj.* опла́ченный (-ен); *see* **pay**.

pail *n.* ведро́ (*pl.* вёдра, -дер, -драм).

pain *n.* боль; *pl.* (*of childbirth*) родовы́е схва́тки *f.pl.*; *pl.* (*efforts*) уси́лия *neut. pl.*; *on p. of death*, под стра́хом сме́рти; *take pains over*, прилага́ть *imp.*, приложи́ть (-жу́, -жишь) *perf.* уси́лия к + *dat.*; *p.-killer*, болеутоля́ющее сре́дство; *v.t.* причиня́ть *imp.*, причини́ть *perf.* боль + *dat.*; (*fig.*) огорча́ть *imp.*, огорчи́ть *perf.* **painful** *adj.* боле́зненный (-ен, -енна); *be p.*, (*part of body*) боле́ть (-ли́т) *imp.* **painless** *adj.* безболе́зненный (-ен, -енна). **painstaking** *adj.* стара́тельный, усе́рдный.

paint *n.* кра́ска; *v.t.* кра́сить *imp.*, по~ *perf.*; (*portray*) писа́ть (пишу́, -шешь) *imp.*, на~ *perf.* кра́сками. **paintbrush** *n.* кисть (*pl.* -ти, -те́й). **painter**[1] *n.* (*artist*) худо́жник, -ица; (*decorator*) маля́р (-а́).

painter[2] *n.* (*rope*) фа́линь *m.*

painting *n.* (*art*) жи́вопись; (*picture*) карти́на.

pair *n.* па́ра; not translated with nouns denoting a single object, e.g. *a p. of scissors*, но́жницы (-ц) *pl.*; *one p. of scissors*, одни́ но́жницы; *v.t. & i.* располага́ть(ся) *imp.*, расположи́ть(ся) (-жу́, -жит(ся)) *perf.* па́рами; *p. off*, уходи́ть (-ожу́, -о́дишь) *imp.*, уйти́ (уйду́, -дёшь; ушёл, ушла́) *perf.* па́рами.

pal *n.* това́рищ, прия́тель *m.*; *p. up with*, дружи́ть (-жу́, -у́жи́шь) *imp.*, подружи́ться (-ужу́сь, -у́жи́шься) *perf.* с + *instr.*

palace *n.* дворе́ц (-рца́); *attrib.* дворцо́вый.

palaeographer *n.* палео́граф. **palaeography** *n.* палеогра́фия. **palaeolithic** *adj.* палеолити́ческий. **palaeontologist** *n.* палеонто́лог. **palaeontology** *n.* палеонтоло́гия. **palaeozoic** *adj.* палеозо́йский.

palatable *adj.* вку́сный (-сен, -сна́, -сно); (*fig.*) прия́тный. **palatal** *adj.* нёбный; (*ling. also*) палата́льный; *n.* палата́льный (звук) *sb.* **palatalize** *v.t.* палатализова́ть *imp., perf.* **palate** *n.* нёбо; (*taste*) вкус.

palatial *adj.* дворцо́вый; (*splendid*) великоле́пный.

palaver *n.* (*idle talk*) пуста́я болтовня́; (*affair*) де́ло.

pale¹ *n.* (*stake*) кол (-а́, *loc.* -у́; *pl.* -ья); (*boundary*) грани́ца; (*fig.*) преде́лы *m.pl.*

pale² *adj.* бле́дный (-ден, -дна́, -дно, бле́дны́); *p.-face*, бледноли́цый *sb.*; *v.i.* бледне́ть *imp.*, по~ *perf.*

palette *n.* пали́тра; *p.-knife*, мастихи́н, шта́пель *m.*

paling(s) *n.* частоко́л.

palisade *n.* частоко́л, палиса́д.

palish *adj.* бледнова́тый.

pall¹ *n.* покро́в. **pallbearer** *n.* несу́щий *sb.* гроб.

pall² *v.i.*: *p. on.*, надоеда́ть *imp.*, надое́сть (-е́м, -е́шь, -е́ст, -еди́м; -е́л) *perf.* + *dat.*

palliasse *n.* соло́менный тюфя́к (-а́).

palliative *adj.* смягча́ющий, паллиати́вный; *n.* смягча́ющее сре́дство, паллиати́в.

pallid *adj.* бле́дный (-ден, -дна́, -дно, бле́дны́). **pallor** *n.* бле́дность.

palm¹ *n.* (*tree*) па́льма; (*branch*) па́льмовая ветвь (*pl.* -ви, -ве́й); (*willow-branch as substitute*) ве́точка ве́рбы; *p.-oil*, па́льмовое ма́сло; *P. Sunday*, ве́рбное воскресе́нье.

palm² *n.* (*of hand*) ладо́нь; *v.t.* (*conceal*) пря́тать (-я́чу, -я́чешь) *imp.*, с~ *perf.* в руке́; *p. off*, всу́чивать *imp.*, всучи́ть (-учу́, -у́чи́шь) *perf.* (on, + *dat.*). **palmist** *n.* хирома́нт, ~ка. **palmistry** *n.* хирома́нтия.

palmy *adj.* (*flourishing*) цвету́щий.

palpable *adj.* осяза́емый.

palpitate *v.i.* (*throb*) (си́льно) би́ться (бьётся) *imp.*; (*tremble*) трепета́ть (-ещу́, -е́щешь) *imp.* **palpitations** *n.* (си́льное) сердцебие́ние, пульса́ция.

palsy *n.* парали́ч (-а́).

paltry *adj.* ничто́жный.

pampas *n.* пампа́сы (-сов) *pl.*; *p.-grass*, пампа́сная трава́.

pamper *v.t.* балова́ть *imp.*, из~ *perf.*

pamphlet *n.* брошю́ра.

pan¹ *n.* (*saucepan*) кастрю́ля; (*frying-p.*) сковорода́ (*pl.* ско́вороды, -о́д, -ода́м); (*bowl*; *of scales*) ча́шка; *v.t.*: *p. off, out*, промыва́ть *imp.*, промы́ть (-мо́ю, -мо́ешь) *perf.*

pan² *v.i.* (*cin.*) панорами́ровать *imp., perf.*

panama (hat) *n.* пана́ма.

panacea *n.* панаце́я.

pan-American *adj.* панамерика́нский.

pancake *n.* блин (-а́); *v.i.* (*aeron.*) парашюти́ровать *imp.*, с~ *perf.*

panchromatic *adj.* панхромати́ческий.

pancreas *n.* поджелу́дочная железа́ (*pl.* -езы, -ёз, -еза́м).

panda *n.* па́нда; *giant p.*, бамбу́ковый медве́дь *m.*

pandemonium *n.* гвалт.

pander *n.* сво́дник; *v.i.*: *p. to*, потво́рствовать *imp.* + *dat.*

pane *n.* око́нное стекло́ (*pl.* стёкла, -кол, -клам).

panel *n.* пане́ль, филёнка; (*control-p.*) щит (-а́) управле́ния; (*list of jurors*) спи́сок (-ска) прися́жных; (*jury*) прися́жные *sb.*; (*team in discussion, quiz*) уча́стники *m.pl.* (диску́ссии, виктори́ны); (*team of experts*) гру́ппа специали́стов; *v.t.* обшива́ть *imp.*, обши́ть (обошью́, -ьёшь) *perf.* пане́лями, филёнками. **panelling** *n.* пане́льная обши́вка.

pang *n.* о́страя боль; *pl.* му́ки (-к) *pl.*

panic *n.* па́ника; *p.-monger*, паникёр; *p.-stricken*, охва́ченный (-ен) па́никой; *adj.* пани́ческий; *v.i.* впада́ть *imp.*, впасть (-аду́, -адёшь; -ал) *perf.* в па́нику. **panicky** *adj.* пани́ческий.

panicle *n.* метёлка.

pannier *n.* корзи́нка.

panorama *n.* панора́ма. **panoramic** *adj.* панора́мный.

pansy *n.* аню́тины гла́зки (-зок) *pl.*
pant *v.i.* задыха́ться *imp.*, задохну́ться (-о́х(ну́л)ся, -о́х(ну́)лась) *perf.*; пыхте́ть (-хчу́, -хти́шь) *imp.*
pantheism *n.* пантеи́зм. **pantheist** *n.* пантеи́ст. **pantheistic** *adj.* пантеисти́ческий.
panther *n.* панте́ра, барс.
panties *n.* тру́сики (-ков) *pl.*
pantomime *n.* рожде́ственское представле́ние для дете́й; (*dumb show*) пантоми́ма.
pantry *n.* кладова́я *sb.*; (*butler's*) буфе́тная *sb.*
pants *n.* (*trousers*) брю́ки (-к) *pl.*; (*underpants*) кальсо́ны (-н) *pl.*, трусы́ (-со́в) *pl.*
papacy *n.* па́пство. **papal** *adj.* па́пский.
paper *n.* бума́га; *pl.* докуме́нты *m.pl.*; (*newspaper*) газе́та; (*wallpaper*) обо́и (-о́ев) *pl.*; (*dissertation*) докла́д; *adj.* бума́жный; *v.t.* окле́ивать *imp.*, окле́ить *perf.* обо́ями. **paperback** *n.* кни́га в бума́жной обло́жке. **paper-clip** *n.* скре́пка. **paper-hanger** *n.* обо́йщик. **paper-knife** *n.* разрезно́й нож (-а́). **paper-mill** *n.* бума́жная фа́брика. **paperweight** *n.* пресс-папье́ *neut.indecl.* **papery** *adj.* бума́жный.
papier mâché *n.* папье́-маше́ *neut.indecl.*
paprika *n.* кра́сный пе́рец (-рца(у)).
papyrus *n.* папи́рус.
par *n.* (*equality*) ра́венство; (*normal condition*) норма́льное состоя́ние; *p. of exchange*, парите́т; *above*, *below*, *p.*, вы́ше, ни́же, номина́льной цены́; *on a p. with*, наравне́ с + *instr.*
parable *n.* при́тча.
parabola *n.* пара́бола. **parabolic** *adj.* параболи́ческий.
parachute *n.* парашю́т; *v.t.* сбра́сывать *imp.*, сбро́сить *perf.* с парашю́том; *v.i.* спуска́ться *imp.*, спусти́ться (-ущу́сь, -у́стишься) *perf.* с парашю́том. **parachutist** *n.* парашюти́ст; *pl.* (*troops*) парашю́тно-деса́нтные войска́ *neut.indecl.*
parade *n.* пара́д; (*display*) выставле́ние напока́з; *p.-ground*, плац; *v.t.* & *i.* стро́ить(ся) *imp.*, по~ *perf.*; *v.t.* (*show off*) выставля́ть *imp.*, вы́ставить *perf.* напока́з.
paradigm *n.* паради́гма.
paradise *n.* рай (*loc.* раю́).
paradox *n.* парадо́кс. **paradoxical** *adj.* парадокса́льный.
paraffin *n.* парафи́н; (*p. oil*) кероси́н; *liquid p.*, парафи́новое ма́сло; *attrib.* парафи́новый; *p. wax*, твёрдый парафи́н.
paragon *n.* образе́ц (-зца́).
paragraph *n.* абза́ц; (*news item*) (газе́тная) заме́тка.
parakeet *n.* длиннохво́стый попуга́й.
parallax *n.* паралла́кс.
parallel *adj.* паралле́льный; *p. bars*, паралле́льные бру́сья *m. pl.*; *n.* паралле́ль. **parallelogram** *n.* параллелогра́мм.
paralyse *v.t.* парализова́ть *imp.*, *perf.* **paralysis** *n.* парали́ч (-а́). **paralytic** *n.* парали́тик; *adj.* парали́чный.
parameter *n.* пара́метр.
paramilitary *adj.* полувое́нный.
paramount *adj.* (*supreme*) верхо́вный; (*pre-eminent*) первостепе́нный (-нен, -нна).
paramour *n.* любо́вник, -ица.
paranoia *n.* парано́йя.
parapet *n.* парапе́т; (*mil.*) бру́ствер.
paraphernalia *n.* (*personal belongings*) ли́чное иму́щество; (*accessories*) принадле́жности *f.pl.*
paraphrase *n.* переска́з, парафра́за; *v.t.* переска́зывать *imp.*, пересказа́ть (-ажу́, -а́жешь) *perf.*; парафрази́ровать *imp.*, *perf.*
paraplegia *n.* параплеги́я.
parapsychology *n.* парапсихоло́гия.
parasite *n.* парази́т; (*person*) тунея́дец (-дца). **parasitic(al)** *adj.* паразити́ческий, парази́тный.
parasol *n.* зо́нтик.
paratrooper *n.* парашюти́ст. **paratroops** *n.* парашю́тно-деса́нтные войска́ *neut. pl.*
paratyphoid *n.* парати́ф.
parboil *v.t.* слегка́ отва́ривать *imp.*, отвари́ть (-рю́, -ришь) *perf.*
parcel *n.* паке́т, посы́лка; (*of land*) уча́сток (-тка); *p. post*, почто́во-посы́лочная слу́жба; *v.t.*: *p. out*, дели́ть (-лю́, -лишь) *imp.*, раз~ *perf.*;

p. up, завёртывать *imp.*, заверну́ть *perf.* в паке́т.

parch *v.t.* иссуша́ть *imp.*, иссуши́ть (-ит) *perf.*; *become parched*, пересыха́ть *imp.*, пересо́хнуть (-х) *perf.*

parchment *n.* перга́мент; *attrib.* перга́мен(т)ный.

pardon *n.* проще́ние; извине́ние; (*leg.*) поми́лование; *v.t.* проща́ть *imp.*, прости́ть *perf.*; (*leg.*) поми́ловать *perf.* **pardonable** *adj.* прости́тельный.

pare *v.t.* обреза́ть *imp.*, обре́зать (-е́жу, -е́жешь) *perf.*; (*fruit*) чи́стить *imp.*, о~ *perf.*; *p. away, down*, (*fig.*) сокраща́ть *imp.*, сократи́ть (-ащу́, -ати́шь) *perf.*

parent *n.* роди́тель *m.*, ~ница; (*forefather*) пре́док (-дка); (*origin*) причи́на. **parentage** *n.* происхожде́ние. **parental** *adj.* роди́тельский.

parenthesis *n.* (*word, clause*) вво́дное сло́во (*pl.* -ва́), предложе́ние; *pl.* (*brackets*) ско́бки *f.pl.*; *in p.*, в ско́бках.

pariah *n.* па́рия *m.* & *f.*

parings *n.* обре́зки *f.pl.*

parish *n.* (*area*) прихо́д; (*inhabitants*) прихожа́не (-н) *pl.*; *attrib.* прихо́дский. **parishioner** *n.* прихожа́нин (*pl.* -а́не, -а́н), -а́нка.

parity *n.* ра́венство; (*econ.*) парите́т.

park *n.* парк; (*national p.*) запове́дник; (*for cars etc.*) стоя́нка; *v.t.* & *abs.* ста́вить *imp.*, по~ *perf.* (маши́ну). **parking** *n.* стоя́нка.

parley *n.* перегово́ры (-ров) *pl.*; *v.i.* вести́ (веду́, -дёшь; вёл, -а́) *imp.* перегово́ры.

parliament *n.* парла́мент. **parliamentarian** *n.* знато́к (-а́) парла́ментской пра́ктики. **parliamentary** *adj.* парла́ментский.

parlour *n.* гости́ная *sb.*; приёмная *sb.* **parlourmaid** *n.* го́рничная *sb.*

parochial *adj.* прихо́дский; (*fig.*) ограни́ченный (-ен, -енна). **parochialism** *n.* ограни́ченность интере́сов.

parody *n.* паро́дия; *v.t.* пароди́ровать *imp.*, *perf.*

parole *n.* че́стное сло́во; освобожде́ние под че́стное сло́во; (*password*) паро́ль *m.*; *on p.*, освобождённый (-ён, -ена́) под че́стное сло́во.

paroxysm *n.* пароксі́зм, припа́док (-дка).

parquet *n.* парке́т; *attrib.* парке́тный; *v.t.* устила́ть *imp.*, устла́ть (устелю́, -лешь) *perf.* парке́том.

parricidal *adj.* отцеуби́йственный (-ен, -енна). **parricide** *n.* (*action*) отцеуби́йство; (*person*) отцеуби́йца *m.* & *f.*

parrot *n.* попуга́й; *v.t.* повторя́ть *imp.*, повтори́ть *perf.* как попуга́й.

parry *v.t.* пари́ровать *imp.*, *perf.*, от~ *perf.*

parse *v.t.* де́лать *imp.*, с~ *perf.* разбо́р +*gen.*

parsec *n.* парсе́к.

parsimonious *adj.* бережли́вый; (*mean*) скупо́й (скуп, -а́, -о). **parsimony** *n.* бережли́вость; ску́пость.

parsley *n.* петру́шка.

parsnip *n.* пастерна́к.

parson *n.* прихо́дский свяще́нник. **parsonage** *n.* дом (*pl.* -а́) прихо́дского свяще́нника.

part *n.* часть (*pl.* -ти, -те́й), до́ля (*pl.* -ли, -ле́й); (*taking p.*) уча́стие; (*in play*) роль (*pl.* -ли, -ле́й); (*mus.*) па́ртия; (*in dispute*) сторона́ (*acc.* -ону; *pl.* -оны, -о́н, -она́м); *for the most p.*, бо́льшей ча́стью; *in p.*, ча́стью; *for my p.*, что каса́ется меня́; *take p. in*, уча́ствовать *imp.* в+*prep.*; *p. and parcel*, неотъе́млемая часть; *p.-owner*, совладе́лец (-льца); *p.-time*, (за́нятый (-т, -та́, -то)) непо́лный рабо́чий день; *v.t.* & *i.* (*divide*) разделя́ть(ся) *imp.*, раздели́ть(ся) (-лю́(сь), -лишь(ся)) *perf.*; *v.i.* (*leave*) расстава́ться (-таю́сь, -таёшься) *imp.*, расста́ться (-а́нусь, -а́нешься) *perf.* (from, with, с+*instr.*); *p. one's hair*, де́лать *imp.*, с~ *perf.* себе́ пробо́р.

partake *v.i.* принима́ть *imp.*, приня́ть (приму́, -мешь; при́нял, -а́, -о) *perf.* уча́стие (in, of, в+*prep.*); (*eat*) есть (ем, ешь, ест, еди́м; ел) *imp.*, съ~ *perf.* (of, +*acc.*).

partial *adj.* (*incomplete*) части́чный, непо́лный (-лон, -лна́, -лно); (*biased*) пристра́стный; *p. to*, неравноду́шный

к + *dat*. **partiality** *n*. пристра́стие (for, к + *dat*.). **partially** *adv*. части́чно.
participant *n*. уча́стник, -ица (in, + *gen*.). **participate** *v.i*. уча́ствовать *imp*. (in, в + *prep*.). **participation** *n*. уча́стие (in, в + *prep*.).
participial *adj*. прича́стный. **participle** *n*. прича́стие.
particle *n*. части́ца.
particoloured *adj*. разноцве́тный.
particular *adj*. осо́бый, осо́бенный; (*careful*) тща́тельный; *n*. подро́бность; *pl*. подро́бный отчёт; *in p*., в ча́стности.
parting *n*. (*leave-taking*) проща́ние; (*of hair*) пробо́р.
partisan *n*. (*adherent*) сторо́нник; (*mil*.) партиза́н (*gen.pl*. -н); *attrib*. узкопарти́йный; партиза́нский.
partition *n*. разделе́ние, расчлене́ние; (*wall*) перегоро́дка, перебо́рка; *v.t*. разделя́ть *imp*., раздели́ть (-лю́, -лишь) *perf*.; *p. off*, отделя́ть *imp*., отдели́ть (-лю́, -лишь) *perf*. перегоро́дкой.
partitive *adj*. раздели́тельный; *p. genitive*, роди́тельный раздели́тельный *sb*.
partly *adv*. ча́стью, отча́сти.
partner *n*. (со)уча́стник; (*in business*) компаньо́н; (*in dance, game*) партнёр, ~ша. **partnership** *n*. (со)уча́стие, сотру́дничество; (*business*) това́рищество.
partridge *n*. куропа́тка.
party *n*. (*polit*.) па́ртия; (*group*) гру́ппа; (*social gathering*) вечери́нка; (*leg*.) сторона́ (*acc*. -ону; *pl*. -оны, -о́н, -она́м); (*accomplice*) (со)уча́стник; *be a p. to*, принима́ть *imp*., приня́ть (приму́, -мешь; при́нял, -а́, -о) *perf*. уча́стие в + *prep*.; *attrib*. парти́йный; *p. line*, (*polit*.) ли́ния па́ртии; (*telephone*) о́бщий телефо́нный про́вод (*pl*. -а́); *p. wall*, о́бщая стена́ (*acc*. -ну; *pl*. -ны, -н, -на́м).
paschal *adj*. пасха́льный.
pasha *n*. паша́ *m*.
pass *v.t*. & *i*. (*go past*; *p. test*; *of time*) проходи́ть (-ожу́, -о́дишь) *imp*., пройти́ (пройду́, -дёшь; прошёл, -шла́) *perf*. (by, ми́мо + *gen*.); (*travel past*) проезжа́ть *imp*., прое́хать (-е́ду, -е́дешь) *perf*. (by, мимо + *gen*.); (*go across*; *change*) переходи́ть (-ожу́, -о́дишь) *imp*., перейти́ (-ейду́, -ейдёшь; -ешёл, -ешла́) *perf*. (+ *acc*., че́рез + *acc*.; to, в + *acc*., к + *dat*.); (*p. examination*) сдава́ть (сдаю́, -аёшь) *imp*., сдать (-ам, -ашь, -аст, -ади́м; сдал, -а́, -о) *perf*. (экза́мен); *v.i*. (*happen*) происходи́ть (-ит) *imp*., произойти́ (-ойдёт; -ошёл, -ошла́) *perf*.; (*cards*) пасова́ть *imp*., с~ *perf*.; *v.t*. (*sport*) пасова́ть *imp*., пасну́ть *perf*.; (*overtake*) обгоня́ть *imp*., обогна́ть (обгоню́, -нишь; обогна́л, -а́, -о) *perf*.; (*time*) проводи́ть (-ожу́, -о́дишь) *imp*., провести́ (-еду́, -едёшь; -ёл, -ела́) *perf*.; (*hand on*) передава́ть (-даю́, -даёшь) *imp*., переда́ть (-а́м, -а́шь, -а́ст, -ади́м; пе́редал, -а́, -о) *perf*.; (*law, resolution*) принима́ть *imp*., приня́ть (приму́, -мешь; при́нял, -а́, -о) *perf*.; (*sentence*) выноси́ть (-ошу́, -о́сишь) *imp*., вы́нести (-су, -сешь; -с) *perf*. (upon, + *dat*.); *p. as, for*, слыть (слыву́, -вёшь; слыл, -а́, -о) *imp*., про~ *perf*. + *instr*., за + *acc*.; *p. away*, (*die*) сконча́ться *perf*.; *p. by*, (*omit*) пропуска́ть *imp*., пропусти́ть (-ущу́, -у́стишь) *perf*.; *p. off*, (постепе́нно; хорошо́) проходи́ть (-ит) *imp*., пройти́ (-йдёт; прошёл, -шла́) *perf*.; *p. out*, (*coll*.) отключа́ться *imp*., отключи́ться *perf*.; *p. over*, (*in silence*) обходи́ть (-ожу́, -о́дишь) *imp*., обойти́ (обойду́, -дёшь; обошёл, -шла́) *perf*. молча́нием; *p. through*, (*experience*) пережива́ть *imp*., пережи́ть (-иву́, -ивёшь; пе́режил, -а́, -о) *perf*.; *n*. (*permit*) про́пуск (*pl*. -а́); (*free p*.) беспла́тный биле́т; (*cards*; *sport*) пас; (*fencing*) вы́пад; (*juggling*) фо́кус; (*hypnotism*) пасс; (*mountain p*.) перева́л; *bring to p*., соверша́ть *imp*., соверши́ть *perf*.; *come to p*., случа́ться *imp*., случи́ться *perf*.; *make a p. at*, пристава́ть (-таю́, -таёшь) *imp*., приста́ть (-а́ну, -а́нешь) *perf*. к + *dat*.; *p. degree*, дипло́м без отли́чия; *p.-mark*, посре́дственная оце́нка.
passable *adj*. проходи́мый, прое́зжий; (*fairly good*) неплохо́й (-х, -ха́, -хо).

passage *n.* прохóд, проéзд; (*of time*) ход; (*sea trip*) рейс; (*in house*) коридóр; (*in book*) отры́вок (-вка); (*musical*) пассáж.

passenger *n.* пассажи́р.

passer-by *n.* прохóжий *sb.*

passing *adj.* (*transient*) мимолётный, преходя́щий; (*cursory*) бéглый; *n.*: *in p.*, мимохóдом.

passion *n.* страсть (*pl.* -ти, -тéй) (for, к + *dat.*); (*attraction*) увлечéние; (*anger*) вспы́шка гнéва; *P.* (*of Christ*; *mus.*) стрáсти (-тéй) *f.pl.* (Христóвы); *p.-flower*, страстноцвéт. **passionate** *adj.* стрáстный (-тен, -тнá, -тно), пы́лкий (-лок, -лкá, -лко).

passive *adj.* пасси́вный; (*gram.*) страдáтельный; *n.* страдáтельный залóг. **passivity** *n.* пасси́вность.

passkey *n.* отмы́чка.

Passover *n.* еврéйская пáсха.

passport *n.* пáспорт (*pl.* -á).

password *n.* парóль *m.*

past *adj.* прóшлый; (*gram.*) прошéдший; *n.* прóшлое *sb.*; (*gram.*) прошéдшее врéмя *neut.*; *prep.* ми́мо + *gen.*; (*beyond*) за + *instr.*; *adv.* ми́мо.

paste *n.* (*of flour*) тéсто; (*similar mixture*) пáста; (*adhesive*) клéйстер; (*of imitation gem*) страз; *v.t.* наклéивать *imp.*, наклéить *perf.*; *p. up*, расклéивать *imp.*, расклéить *perf.* **pasteboard** *n.* картóн.

pastel *n.* (*crayon*) пастéль; (*drawing*) рисýнок (-нка) пастéлью; *attrib.* пастéльный.

pastern *n.* бáбка.

pasteurization *n.* пастеризáция. **pasteurize** *v.t.* пастеризовáть *imp.*, *perf.*

pastiche *n.* смесь.

pastille *n.* лепёшка.

pastime *n.* развлечéние; (*game*) игрá (*pl.* -ры).

pastor *n.* пáстор. **pastoral** *adj.* (*bucolic*) пасторáльный; (*of pastor*) пáсторский; *n.* пасторáль.

pastry *n.* печéнье, пирóжное *sb.*

pasturage *n.* пастьбá. **pasture** *n.* (*land*) пáстбище; (*herbage*) поднóжный корм (*loc.* -е & -ý); *v.t.* пасти́ (-сý, -сёшь; -с, -слá) *imp.*

pasty [1] *n.* пирóг (-á).

pasty [2] *adj.* тестообрáзный; (*p.-faced*) блéдный (-ден, -днá, -дно, блéдны́).

pat *n.* шлепóк (-пкá); (*of butter etc.*) кусóк (-скá); *v.t.* хлопáть *imp.*, по~ *perf.*; *adj.* умéстный; *adv.* кстáти, своеврéменно.

patch *n.* заплáта; (*over eye*) повя́зка (на глазý); (*on face*) мýшка; (*spot*) пятнó (*pl.* -тна, -тен, -тнам); (*piece of land*) учáсток (-тка) земли́; *p.-pocket*, накладнóй кармáн; *v.t.* стáвить *imp.*, по~ *perf.* заплáту, -ты, на + *acc.*; *p. up*, (*fig.*) улáживать *imp.*, улáдить *perf.* **patchwork** *n.* лоскýтная рабóта; *attrib.* лоскýтный. **patchy** *adj.* пёстрый (пёстр, -á, пёстрó); (*uneven*) нерóвный (-вен, -внá, -вно).

pâté *n.* паштéт.

patella *n.* колéнная чáшка.

patent *adj.* патентóванный (-ан); (*obvious*) я́вный; *p. leather*, лакирóванная кóжа; *n.* патéнт; *v.t.* патентовáть *imp.*, за~ *perf.* **patentee** *n.* владéлец (-льца) патéнта.

paternal *adj.* отцóвский; (*fatherly*) отéческий; *p. uncle*, дя́дя *m.* со стороны́ отцá. **paternity** *n.* отцóвство.

path *n.* тропи́нка, тропá (*pl.* -пы, -п, трóпáм); (*way*) путь (-ти́, -тём) *m.*

pathetic *adj.* жáлостный, трóгательный.

pathless *adj.* бездорóжный.

pathological *adj.* патологи́ческий. **pathologist** *n.* патóлог. **pathology** *n.* патолóгия.

pathos *n.* пáфос.

pathway *n.* тропи́нка, тропá (*pl.* -пы, -п, трóпáм).

patience *n.* терпéние; (*persistence*) упóрство; (*cards*) пасья́нс. **patient** *adj.* терпели́вый; (*persistent*) упóрный; *n.* больнóй *sb.*, пациéнт, ~ка.

patina *n.* пати́на.

patio *n.* (*court*) внýтренний двóрик; (*terrace*) террáса.

patriarch *n.* патриáрх. **patriarchal** *adj.* патриархáльный; (*relig.*) патриáрший.

patrician *n.* аристокрáт, ~ка; (*hist.*) патри́ций; *adj.* аристократи́ческий; (*hist.*) патрициáнский.

patricidal *etc. see* **parricide**.

patrimonial *adj.* насле́дственный. **patrimony** *n.* насле́дство.

patriot *n.* патрио́т, ~ка. **patriotic** *adj.* патриоти́ческий. **patriotism** *n.* патриоти́зм.

patrol *n.* патру́ль (-ля́) *m.*; (*action*) патрули́рование; *v.t.* & *i.* патрули́ровать *imp.*

patron *n.* покрови́тель *m.*; (*of shop*) клие́нт, ~ка; *p. saint*, засту́пник, -ица. **patronage** *n.* покрови́тельство. **patroness** *n.* покрови́тельница. **patronize** *v.t.* покрови́тельствовать *imp.* + *dat.*; (*shop*) быть клие́нтом, клие́нткой, + *gen.*; (*treat condescendingly*) снисходи́тельно относи́ться (-ошу́сь, -о́сишься) *imp.* к + *dat.*

patronymic *n.* родово́е и́мя *neut.*; (*Russian name*) о́тчество.

patter[1] *v.i.* (*sound*) посту́кивать *imp.*; *n.* посту́кивание, лёгкий то́пот.

patter[2] *n.* (*speech*) скорогово́рка.

pattern *n.* (*paragon*) образе́ц (-зца́); (*model*) моде́ль; (*sewing*) вы́кройка; (*design*) узо́р.

patty *n.* пирожо́к (-жка́).

paunch *n.* брюшко́ (*pl.* -ки́, -ко́в), пу́зо.

pauper *n.* бедня́к (-а́), ни́щий *sb.*

pause *n.* па́уза, переры́в; *v.i.* де́лать *imp.*, с~ *perf.* па́узу; остана́вливаться *imp.*, останови́ться (-влю́сь, -ви́шься) *perf.*

pave *v.t.* мости́ть *imp.*, вы́~, за~ *perf.*; *p. the way*, подготовля́ть *imp.*, подгото́вить *perf.* по́чву (for, для + *gen.*). **pavement** *n.* тротуа́р, пане́ль.

pavilion *n.* (*building*) павильо́н; (*tent*) пала́тка, шатёр (-тра́).

paw *n.* ла́па; *v.t.* тро́гать *imp.* ла́пой; (*horse*) бить (бьёт) *imp.* копы́том.

pawl *n.* защёлка; (*naut.*) пал.

pawn[1] *n.* (*chess*) пе́шка.

pawn[2] *n.*: *in p.*, в закла́де; *v.t.* закла́дывать *imp.*, заложи́ть (-жу́, -жишь) *perf.*; отдава́ть (-даю́, -даёшь) *imp.*, отда́ть (-а́м, -а́шь, -а́ст, -ади́м; о́тдал, -а́, -о) *perf.* в зало́г. **pawnbroker** *n.* ростовщи́к (-а́), -и́ца. **pawnshop** *n.* ломба́рд.

pay *v.t.* плати́ть (-ачу́, -а́тишь) *imp.*, за~, у~ *perf.* (for, за + *acc.*); (*bill etc.*) опла́чивать *imp.*, оплати́ть (-ачу́, -а́тишь) *perf.*; *v.i.* (*be profitable*) окупа́ться *imp.*, окупи́ться (-ится) *perf.*; *n.* (*payment*) упла́та; (*wages*) жа́лованье, зарпла́та; *p. packet*, полу́чка; *p.-roll*, платёжная ве́домость. **payable** *adj.* подлежа́щий упла́те. **payee** *n.* получа́тель *m.*, ~ница; (*of cheque etc.*) предъяви́тель *m.*, ~ница. **payload** *n.* поле́зная нагру́зка. **payment** *n.* упла́та, платёж (-а́); *p. by instalments*, платёж (-а́) в рассро́чку; *p. in kind*, пла́та нату́рой.

pea *n.* (*also pl., collect.*) горо́х (-а(у)).

peace *n.* мир; (*treaty*) ми́рный догово́р; (*public order*; *tranquillity*) споко́йствие; (*quiet*) поко́й; *attrib.* ми́рный; *at p. with*, в ми́ре с + *instr.*; *in p.*, в поко́е; *make p.*, заключа́ть *imp.*, заключи́ть *perf.* мир; *make one's p.*, мири́ться *imp.*, по~ *perf.* (with, с + *instr.*); *p. and quiet*, мир и тишина́; *p.-loving*, миролюби́вый; *p.-offering*, искупи́тельная же́ртва; *p.-time*, ми́рное вре́мя *neut.* **peaceable, peaceful** *adj.* ми́рный.

peach *n.* пе́рсик; (*p.-tree*) пе́рсиковое де́рево (*pl.* дере́вья, -ьев); *p.-coloured*, пе́рсикового цве́та.

peacock *n.* павли́н; *p. butterfly*, дневно́й павли́ний глаз. **peafowl** *n.* павли́н. **peahen** *n.* па́ва.

pea-jacket *n.* бушла́т.

peak *n.* (*of cap*) козырёк (-рька́); (*summit*; *highest point*) верши́на; *p. hour*, часы́ *m.pl.* пик; *p.-load*, максима́льная, пи́ковая, нагру́зка.

peaky *adj.* (*worn out*) измождённый (-ён, -ена́).

peal *n.* (*sound*) звон колоколо́в, трезво́н; (*set of bells*) набо́р колоколо́в; (*of thunder*) раска́т; (*of laughter*) взрыв; *v.i.* (*bells*) трезво́нить *imp.*; (*thunder*) греме́ть (-ми́т) *imp.*, по~ *perf.*; *p. the bells*, звони́ть *imp.*, по~ *perf.* в колокола́.

peanut *n.* земляно́й оре́х, ара́хис.

pear *n.* гру́ша; (*p.-tree*) гру́шевое де́рево (*pl.* дере́вья, -ьев); *p.-shaped*, грушеви́дный.

pearl *n.* же́мчуг (-а(у); *pl.* -а́); (*single p., also fig.*) жемчу́жина; *p. barley*, перло́вая крупа́; *p. button*, перламу́тровая пу́говица; *p.-oyster*, жемчу́жница. **pearly** *adj.* жемчу́жный.

peasant *n.* крестья́нин (*pl.* -я́не, -я́н), -я́нка; *attrib.* крестья́нский; *p. woman*, крестья́нка. **peasantry** *n.* крестья́нство.

peat *n.* торф (-а(у)). **peatbog** *n.* торфяни́к (-а́). **peaty** *adj.* торфяно́й.

pebble *n.* га́лька. **pebbly** *adj.* покры́тый га́лькой.

peccadillo *n.* грешо́к (-шка́).

peck *v.t.* & *i.* клева́ть (клюю́, клюёшь) *imp.*, клю́нуть *perf.*; *n.* клево́к (-вка́).

pectoral *adj.* грудно́й; (*worn on chest*) нагру́дный.

peculiar *adj.* (*distinctive*) своеобра́зный; (*special*) осо́бенный; (*strange*) стра́нный (-нен, -нна́, -нно); *p. to*, сво́йственный (-ен(ен), -енна)+*dat.* **peculiarity** *n.* осо́бенность; стра́нность.

pecuniary *adj.* де́нежный.

pedagogical *adj.* педагоги́ческий. **pedagogics** *n.* педаго́гика. **pedagogue** *n.* учи́тель (*pl.* -ля́) *m.*, педаго́г.

pedal *n.* педа́ль; *v.i.* нажима́ть *imp.*, нажа́ть (-жму́, -жмёшь) *perf.* педа́ль; (*ride bicycle*) е́хать (е́ду, е́дешь) *imp.*, по~ *perf.* на велосипе́де.

pedant *n.* педа́нт, ~ка. **pedantic** *adj.* педанти́чный. **pedantry** *n.* педанти́чность.

peddle *v.t.* торгова́ть *imp.* вразно́с+*instr.*

pedestal *n.* пьедеста́л, подно́жие; (*of table*) ту́мба.

pedestrian *adj.* пе́ший, пешехо́дный; (*prosaic*) прозаи́ческий; *n.* пешехо́д; *p. crossing*, перехо́д.

pedicure *n.* педикю́р.

pedigree *n.* (*genealogy*) родосло́вная *sb.*; (*descent*) происхожде́ние; *adj.* поро́дистый, племенно́й.

pediment *n.* фронто́н.

pedlar *n.* разно́счик.

pedometer *n.* шагоме́р.

peek *v.i.* (*p. in*) загля́дывать *imp.*, загляну́ть (-ну́, -нешь) *perf.*; (*p. out*) выгля́дывать *imp.*, вы́глянуть *perf.*

peel *n.* ко́рка, ко́жица; *v.t.* очища́ть *imp.*, очи́стить *perf.*; *v.i.*: *p. off*, (*detach oneself*) сходи́ть (-ит) *imp.*, сойти́ (сойдёт; сошёл, -шла́) *perf.* **peelings** *n.* очи́стки (-ков) *pl.*, шелуха́.

peep *v.i.* (*p. in*) загля́дывать *imp.*, загляну́ть (-ну́, -нешь) *perf.*; (*p. out*) выгля́дывать *imp.*, вы́глянуть *perf.*; *n.* (*glance*) бы́стрый взгляд; *p. of day*, рассве́т; *p.-hole*, глазо́к (-зка́).

peer[1] *v.i.* всма́триваться *imp.*, всмотре́ться (-рю́сь, -ришься) *perf.* (at, в+*acc.*).

peer[2] *n.* (*noble*) пэр, лорд; (*equal*) ра́вный *sb.*, ро́вня́ *m.* & *f.* **peerage** *n.* (*class*) сосло́вие пэ́ров; (*rank*) зва́ние пэ́ра. **peeress** *n.* (*peer's wife*) супру́га пэ́ра; ле́ди, *f.indecl.* **peerless** *adj.* несравне́нный (-е́нен, -е́нна), бесподо́бный.

peeved *adj.* раздражённый (-ён, -ена́).

peevish *adj.* раздражи́тельный, брюзгли́вый.

peewit *see* **pewit**.

peg *n.* ко́лышек (-шка), деревя́нный гвоздь (-дя́; *pl.* -ди, -де́й) *m.*; (*for hat etc.*) ве́шалка; (*on violin etc.*) коло́к (-лка́); *off the p.*, гото́вый; *take down a p.*, оса́живать *imp.*, осади́ть (-ажу́, -а́дишь) *perf.*; *v.t.* прикрепля́ть *imp.*, прикрепи́ть *perf.* ко́лышком, -ками; (*price etc.*) иску́сственно поддéрживать *imp.*, поддержа́ть (-жу́, -жишь) *perf.*; *v.i.*: *p. away*, приле́жно рабо́тать *imp.* (at, над+*instr.*); *p. out*, (*die*) помира́ть *imp.*, помере́ть (-мру́, -мрёшь; по́мер, -ла́, -ло) *perf.*

pejorative *adj.* уничижи́тельный.

peke, Pekin(g)ese *n.* кита́йский мопс.

pelican *n.* пелика́н.

pellagra *n.* пелла́гра.

pellet *n.* ка́тышек (-шка); (*shot*) дроби́на.

pellicle *n.* ко́жица, плёнка.

pell-mell *adv.* (*in disorder*) беспоря́дочно; (*headlong*) очертя́, сломя́, го́лову.

pellucid *adj.* (*transparent*) прозра́чный; (*clear*) я́сный (я́сен, ясна́, я́сно, я́сны́).

pelmet *n.* ламбреке́н.

pelt[1] *n.* (*animal skin*) шку́ра, ко́жа.

pelt[2] *v.t.* забра́сывать *imp.*, заброса́ть *perf.*; *v.i.* (*rain*) бараба́нить (-ит) *imp.*; *n.*: (*at*) *full p.*, со всех ног.

pelvic *adj.* тáзовый. **pelvis** *n.* таз (*loc.* -е & -ý; *pl.* -ы́).

pen[1] *n.* (*for writing*) перó (*pl.* -рья, -рьев); *p. and ink*, пи́сьменные принадлéжности *f.pl.*; *slip of the p.*, опи́ска; *p.-friend*, знакóмый *sb.* по пи́сьмам; *p.-name*, псевдони́м.

pen[2] *n.* (*enclosure*) загóн; *v.t.* загоня́ть *imp.*, загнáть (загоню́, -нишь; загнáл, -á, -о) *perf.*

pen[3] *n.* (*female swan*) сáмка лéбедя.

penal *adj.* уголóвный; (*punishable*) наказу́емый; *p. battalion*, штрафнóй батальóн; *p. code*, уголóвный кóдекс; *p. servitude*, кáторжные рабóты *f.pl.* **penalize** *v.t.* накáзывать *imp.*, наказáть (-ажу́, -áжешь) *perf.*; (*sport*) штрафовáть *imp.*, о~ *perf.* **penalty** *n.* наказáние, взыскáние; (*sport*) штраф; *p. area*, штрафнáя площáдка; *p. kick*, штрафнóй удáр. **penance** *n.* епитимья́ (*gen.pl.* -ми́й).

penchant *n.* склóнность (for, к + *dat.*).

pencil *n.* карандáш (-á); *p.-case*, пенáл; *p.-sharpener*, точи́лка; *v.t.* (*write*) писáть (пишу́, -шешь) *imp.*, на~ *perf.* карандашóм; (*draw*) рисовáть *imp.*, на~ *perf.* карандашóм.

pendant *n.* подвéска, кулóн; *adj.* вися́чий.

pending *adj.* (*awaiting decision*) ожидáющий решéния; *patent p.*, патéнт зая́влен; *prep.* (*during*) во врéмя + *gen.*; (*until*) в ожидáнии + *gen.*, до + *gen.*

pendulous *adj.* вися́чий, отви́слый.

pendulum *n.* мáятник.

penetrate *v.t.* прони́зывать *imp.*, пронизáть (-ижу́, -и́жешь) *perf.*; *v.i.* проникáть *imp.*, прони́кнуть (-к) *perf.* (into, в + *acc.*; through, чéрез + *acc.*). **penetrating** *adj.* проницáтельный; (*sound*) прони́зительный. **penetration** *n.* проникновéние; (*insight*) проницáтельность.

penguin *n.* пингви́н.

penicillin *n.* пеницилли́н.

peninsula *n.* полуóстров (*pl.* -á). **peninsular** *adj.* полуостровнóй.

penis *n.* мужскóй половóй член.

penitence *n.* раскáяние, покая́ние. **penitent** *adj.* раскáивающийся; *n.* кáющийся грéшник. **penitential** *adj.* покая́нный.

penknife *n.* перочи́нный нож (-á).

pennant *n.* вы́мпел.

penniless *adj.* бездéнежный; (*predic.*) без грошá; (*poor*) бéдный (-ден, -днá, -дно, бéдны́).

pennon *n.* вы́мпел.

penny *n.* пéнни *neut.indecl.*, пенс.

pension *n.* пéнсия; *v.t.*: *p. off*, увольня́ть *imp.*, увóлить *perf.* на пéнсию. **pensionable** *adj.* даю́щий, имéющий, прáво на пéнсию; (*age*) пенсиóнный. **pensioner** *n.* пенсионéр, ~ка.

pensive *adj.* заду́мчивый.

penta- *in comb.* пяти-, пента-. **pentacle** *n.* маги́ческая фигу́ра. **pentagon** *n.* пятиугóльник; *the P.*, Пентагóн. **pentagonal** *adj.* пятиугóльный. **pentagram** *n.* пентагрáмма. **pentahedron** *n.* пятигрáнник. **pentameter** *n.* пентáметр. **pentathlon** *n.* пятибóрье. **pentatonic** *adj.* пентатóнный.

Pentecost *n.* пятидеся́тница.

penthouse *n.* особня́к (-á) на кры́ше многоэтáжного дóма.

pent-up *adj.* (*anger etc.*) сдéрживаемый.

penultimate *adj.* (*n.*) предпослéдний (слог).

penumbra *n.* полутéнь (*loc.* -éни́; *pl.* -éни, -енéй).

penurious *adj.* бéдный (-ден, -днá, -дно, бéдны́); (*stingy*) скупóй (скуп, -á, -о). **penury** *n.* нуждá.

peony *n.* пиóн.

people *n.* нарóд; (*as pl.*, *persons*) лю́ди (-дéй, -дям, -дьми́) *pl.*; (*relatives*) родны́е *sb.*; (*occupy*) населя́ть *imp.*, насели́ть *perf.*; (*populate*) заселя́ть *imp.*, засели́ть *perf.*

pepper *n.* пéрец (-рца(у)); *v.t.* пéрчить *imp.*, на~, по~ *perf.*; (*pelt*) забрáсывать *imp.*, забросáть *perf.* **peppercorn** *n.* перчи́нка. **pepper-pot** *n.* пéречница.

peppermint *n.* пéречная мя́та; (*sweet*) мя́тная конфéта.

peppery *adj.* напéрченный; (*fig.*) вспы́льчивый.

per *prep.* (*by means of*) *expressed by instrumental case*, по + *dat.*; (*person*) чéрез + *acc.*; (*for each*) (*person*) на + *acc.*; (*time*) в + *acc.*; (*quantity*) за +

acc.; *as p.*, согла́сно + *dat.*; *p. annum*, ежего́дно, в год; *p. capita*, *p. head*, на челове́ка; *p. diem*, в день; *p. hour*, в час; *p. se*, сам (-á, -ó) по себе́, по существу́.

perambulator *n.* де́тская коля́ска.

perceive *v.t.* воспринима́ть *imp.*, восприня́ть (-иму́, -и́мешь; воспри́нял, -á, -о) *perf.*

per cent *adv.*, *n.* проце́нт, на со́тню. **percentage** *n.* проце́нтное содержа́ние, проце́нт.

perceptible *adj.* воспринима́емый, заме́тный. **perception** *n.* восприя́тие, понима́ние. **perceptive** *adj.* воспринима́ющий, восприи́мчивый.

perch[1] *n.* (*fish*) о́кунь (*pl.* -ни, -не́й) *m.*

perch[2] *n.* (*roost*) насе́ст, жёрдочка; (*fig.*) высо́кое, про́чное, положе́ние; *v.i.* сади́ться *imp.*, сесть (ся́ду, -дешь; сел) *perf.*; *v.t.* сажа́ть *imp.*, посади́ть (-ажу́, -а́дишь) *perf.* (на насе́ст); высоко́ помеща́ть *imp.*, помести́ть *perf.* **perched** *adj.* высоко́ сидя́щий, располо́женный (-ен).

perchance *adv.* быть мо́жет.

percussion *n.* уда́р, столкнове́ние; (*mus. instruments*) уда́рные инструме́нты *m.pl.*; *p. cap*, уда́рный ка́псюль *m.* **percussive** *adj.* уда́рный.

perdition *n.* ги́бель.

peregrine (falcon) *n.* со́кол, сапса́н.

peremptory *adj.* повели́тельный.

perennial *adj.* ве́чный; (*plant*) многоле́тний; *n.* многоле́тнее расте́ние.

perfect *adj.* соверше́нный (-нен, -нна); (*exact*) то́чный (-чен, -чна́, -чно); (*gram.*) перфе́ктный; (*mus.*) чи́стый; *n.* перфе́кт; *v.t.* соверше́нствовать *imp.*, у ~ *perf.* **perfection** *n.* соверше́нство. **perfective** *adj.* (*n.*) соверше́нный (вид).

perfidious *adj.* вероло́мный, преда́тельский. **perfidy** *n.* вероло́мство, преда́тельство.

perforate *v.t.* перфори́ровать *imp.*, *perf.* **perforation** *n.* перфора́ция; (*hole*) отве́рстие.

perforce *adv.* по необходи́мости, во́лей-нево́лей.

perform *v.t.* (*carry out*) исполня́ть *imp.*, испо́лнить *perf.*; соверша́ть *imp.*, соверши́ть *perf.*; (*play*; *music*) игра́ть *imp.*, сыгра́ть *perf.*; *v.i.* выступа́ть *imp.*, вы́ступить *perf.* **performance** *n.* исполне́ние; (*of play etc.*) представле́ние, спекта́кль *m.*; (*of engine etc.*) эксплуатацио́нные ка́чества *neut.pl.* **performer** *n.* исполни́тель *m.* **performing** *adj.* (*animal*) дрессиро́ванный.

perfume *n.* (*sweet smell*) арома́т; (*smell*) за́пах; (*scent*) духи́ (-хо́в) *pl.*; *v.t.* души́ть (-шу́, -шишь) *imp.*, на ~ *perf.* **perfumery** *n.* парфюме́рия.

perfunctory *adj.* пове́рхностный.

pergola *n.* пе́ргола.

perhaps *adv.* мо́жет быть.

peri *n.* пе́ри *f.indecl.*

pericarp *n.* перика́рпий. **perigee** *n.* периге́й. **perihelion** *n.* периге́лий.

peril *n.* опа́сность, риск. **perilous** *adj.* опа́сный, риско́ванный (-ан, -анна).

perimeter *n.* (*geom.*) пери́метр; (*boundary*) вне́шняя грани́ца.

period *n.* пери́од; (*term*) срок (-а(у)); (*epoch*) эпо́ха; (*full stop*) то́чка; *adj.* относя́щийся к определённому пери́оду. **periodic** *adj.* периоди́ческий; *p. table*, периоди́ческая систе́ма элеме́нтов Менделе́ева. **periodical** *adj.* периоди́ческий; *n.* периоди́ческое изда́ние, журна́л. **periodicity** *n.* периоди́чность.

peripheral *adj.* перифери́йный. **periphery** *n.* (*outline*) ко́нтур; перифери́я.

periscope *n.* periско́п.

perish *v.i.* погиба́ть *imp.*, поги́бнуть (-б) *perf.*; (*die*) умира́ть *imp.*, умере́ть (умру́, -рёшь; у́мер, -ла́, -ло) *perf.*; (*spoil*) по́ртиться *imp.*, ис ~ *perf.* **perishable** *adj.* скоропо́ртящийся; *n.*: *pl.* скоропо́ртящиеся това́ры *m.pl.*

peristyle *n.* перисти́ль *m.*

peritoneum *adj.* брюши́на. **peritonitis** *n.* воспале́ние брюши́ны.

periwig *n.* пари́к (-а́).

periwinkle[1] *n.* (*plant*) барви́нок (-нка).

periwinkle[2] *n.* (*winkle*) литори́на.

perjure *v.*: *p. oneself*, наруша́ть *imp.*, нару́шить *perf.* кля́тву. **perjurer** *n.* лжесвиде́тель *m.*, ~ница. **perjury** *n.* ло́жное показа́ние под прися́гой, лжесвиде́тельство.

perk[1] *see* **perquisite.**

perk[2] *v.i.*: *p. up*, оживля́ться *imp.*, оживи́ться *perf.*; приободря́ться *imp.*, приободри́ться *perf.* **perky** *adj.* бо́йкий (бо́ек, бойка́, -ко); (*pert*) де́рзкий (-зок, -зка́, -зко).

permafrost *n.* ве́чная мерзлота́.

permanence *n.* постоя́нство. **permanency** *n.* постоя́нство; (*permanent employment*) постоя́нная рабо́та. **permanent** *adj.* постоя́нный; *p. wave*, пермане́нт.

permeable *adj.* проница́емый. **permeate** *v.t.* (*penetrate*) проника́ть *imp.*, прони́кнуть (-к) *perf.* в + *acc.*; (*saturate*) пропи́тывать *imp.*, пропита́ть *perf.*; *v.i.* распространя́ться *imp.*, распространи́ться *perf.* **permeation** *n.* проника́ние.

permissible *adj.* допусти́мый, позволи́тельный. **permission** *n.* разреше́ние, позволе́ние. **permissive** *adj.* разреша́ющий, позволя́ющий; (*liberal*) либера́льный. **permissiveness** *n.* (сексуа́льная) вседозво́ленность. **permit** *v.t.* разреша́ть *imp.*, разреши́ть *perf.* + *dat.*; позволя́ть *imp.*, позво́лить *perf.* + *dat.*; *v.i.*: *p. of*, допуска́ть *imp.*, допусти́ть (-ущу́, -у́стишь) *perf.* + *acc.*; *n.* про́пуск (*pl.* -а́); (*permission*) разреше́ние.

permutation *n.* перестано́вка.

pernicious *adj.* па́губный.

peroration *n.* заключи́тельная часть (*pl.* -ти, -те́й) (ре́чи).

peroxide *n.* пе́рекись; (*hydrogen p.*) пе́рекись водоро́да; *p. blonde*, хими́ческая блонди́нка.

perpendicular *adj.* перпендикуля́рный; (*cliff etc.*) отве́сный; *n.* перпендикуля́р.

perpetrate *v.t.* соверша́ть *imp.*, соверши́ть *perf.* **perpetration** *n.* соверше́ние.

perpetual *adj.* ве́чный, бесконе́чный; (*for life*) пожи́зненный; (*without limit*) бессро́чный. **perpetuate** *v.t.* увекове́чивать *imp.*, увекове́чить *perf.* **perpetuation** *n.* увекове́чение. **perpetuity** *n.* ве́чность, бесконе́чность; *in p.*, навсегда́, наве́чно.

perplex *v.t.* приводи́ть (-ожу́, -о́дишь) *imp.*, привести́ (-еду́, -едёшь; -ёл, -ела́) в недоуме́ние; озада́чивать *imp.*, озада́чить *perf.* **perplexity** *n.* недоуме́ние, озада́ченность.

perquisite, perk[1] *n.* случа́йный, дополни́тельный, дохо́д.

perry *n.* гру́шевый сидр.

persecute *v.t.* пресле́довать *imp.*; (*pester*) надоеда́ть *imp.*, надое́сть (-е́м, -е́шь, -е́ст, -еди́м; -е́л) *perf.* + *dat.* (with, + *instr.*). **persecution** *n.* пресле́дование.

perseverance *n.* насто́йчивость, сто́йкость. **persevere** *v.i.* сто́йко, насто́йчиво, продолжа́ть *imp.* (in, at, etc., + *acc.*, *inf.*).

Persian *n.* перс, ~ия́нка; (*cat*) перси́дская ко́шка; *adj.* перси́дский; *P. lamb*, кара́куль *m.*

persist *v.i.* упо́рствовать *imp.* (in, в + *prep.*); насто́йчиво продолжа́ть *imp.* (in, + *acc.*, *inf.*); (*continue to exist*) продолжа́ть *imp.* существова́ть. **persistence** *n.* упо́рство, насто́йчивость. **persistent** *adj.* упо́рный, насто́йчивый.

person *n.* челове́к (*pl.* лю́ди, -де́й, -дям, -дьми́), осо́ба; (*appearance*) вне́шность; (*in play*; *gram.*) лицо́ (*pl.* -ца); *in p.*, ли́чно. **personable** *adj*, привлека́тельный. **personage** *n.* осо́ба. (ва́жная) персо́на, выдаю́щаяся ли́чность. **personal** *adj.* ли́чный, персона́льный; *p. property*, дви́жимое иму́щество; *p. remarks*, ли́чности *f.pl.* **personality** *n.* ли́чность. **personally** *adv.* ли́чно; *I p.*, что каса́ется меня́. **personalty** *n.* дви́жимое иму́щество. **personate** *v.t.* игра́ть *imp.*, сыгра́ть *perf.* роль + *gen.*; (*pretend to be*) выдава́ть (-даю́, -даёшь) *imp.*, вы́дать (-ам, -ашь, -аст, -адим) *perf.* себя́ за + *acc.* **personification** *n.* олицетворе́ние. **personify** *v.t.* олицетворя́ть *imp.*, олицетвори́ть *perf.*

personnel *n.* ка́дры (-ров) *pl.*, персона́л; (*mil.*) ли́чный соста́в; *p. carrier*, транспортёр; *p. department*, отде́л ка́дров; *p. manager*, нача́льник отде́ла ка́дров.

perspective *n.* перспекти́ва; *adj.* перспекти́вный.

perspicacious *adj.* проница́тельный. **perspicacity** *n.* проница́тельность.

perspiration *n.* пот (*loc.* -ý; *pl.* -ы́), испа́рина; (*action*) поте́ние. **perspire** *v.i.* поте́ть *imp.*, вс~ *perf.*

persuade *v.t.* убежда́ть *imp.*, убеди́ть (-и́шь) *perf.* (of, в + *prep.*); угова́ривать *imp.*, уговори́ть *perf.* **persuasion** *n.* убежде́ние; (*religious belief*) религио́зные убежде́ния *neut.pl.*; (*joc.*) род, сорт. **persuasive** *adj.* убеди́тельный.

pert *adj.* де́рзкий (-зок, -зка́, -зко).

pertain *v.i.*: *p. to*, (*belong*) принадлежа́ть *imp.* + *dat.*; (*relate*) име́ть *imp.* отноше́ние к + *dat.*

pertinacious *adj.* упря́мый, неусту́пчивый. **pertinacity** *n.* упря́мство, неусту́пчивость.

pertinence *n.* уме́стность. **pertinent** *adj.* уме́стный.

perturb *v.t.* (*disturb*) трево́жить *imp.*, вс~ *perf.*; (*agitate*) волнова́ть *imp.*, вз~ *perf.* **perturbation** *n.* трево́га, волне́ние.

perusal *n.* внима́тельное чте́ние. **peruse** *v.t.* (*read*) внима́тельно чита́ть *imp.*, про~ *perf.*; (*fig.*) рассма́тривать *imp.*, рассмотре́ть (-рю́, -ришь) *perf.*

pervade *v.t.* (*permeate*) проника́ть *imp.*, прони́кнуть (-к) *perf.* в + *acc.*; (*spread*) распространя́ться *imp.*, распространи́ться *perf.* по + *dat.*

perverse *adj.* (*persistent*) упря́мый; (*wayward*) капри́зный; (*perverted*) извращённый (-ён, -ённа). **perversion** *n.* извраще́ние. **perversity** *n.* упря́мство извращённость. **pervert** *v.t.* извраща́ть *imp.*, изврати́ть (-ащу́, -ати́шь) *perf.*; *n.* извращённый челове́к.

pessimism *n.* пессими́зм. **pessimist** *n.* пессими́ст. **pessimistic** *adj.* пессимисти́ческий.

pest *n.* вреди́тель *m.*; (*fig.*) я́зва. **pester** *v.t.* надоеда́ть *imp.*, надое́сть (-е́м, -е́шь, -е́ст, -еди́м; -е́л) *perf.* + *dat.*; (*importune*) пристава́ть (-таю́, -таёшь) *imp.*, приста́ть (-а́ну, -а́нешь) *perf.* к + *dat.* **pesticide** *n.* пестици́д. **pestilence** *n.* чума́. **pestilent(ial)** *adj.* (*deadly*) смертоно́сный; (*injurious*) вре́дный (-ден, -дна́, -дно); (*of pestilence*) чумно́й; (*coll.*) несно́сный, надое́дливый.

pestle *n.* пест (-а́), пе́стик.

pet *n.* (*animal*) люби́мое, дома́шнее, живо́тное *sb.*; (*favourite*) люби́мец (-мца), -мица, ба́ловень (-вня) *m.*; *adj.* (*animal*) ко́мнатный, дома́шний; (*favourite*) люби́мый; *p. name*, ласка́тельное и́мя *neut.*; *p. shop*, зоомагази́н; *v.t.* ласка́ть *imp.*; балова́ть *imp.*, из~ *perf.*

petal *n.* лепесто́к (-тка́).

peter *v.i.*: *p. out*, истоща́ться *imp.*, истощи́ться *perf.*; (*stream*) иссяка́ть *imp.*, исся́кнуть (-к) *perf.*

petition *n.* хода́тайство, проше́ние; (*formal written p.*) пети́ция; (*leg.*) заявле́ние; *v.t.* подава́ть (-даю́, -даёшь) *imp.*, пода́ть (-а́м, -а́шь, -а́ст, -ади́м; по́дал, -а́, -о) *perf.* проше́ние, хода́тайство, + *dat.*; обраща́ться *imp.*, обрати́ться (-ащу́сь, -ати́шься) *perf.* с пети́цией в + *acc.* **petitioner** *n.* проси́тель *m.*

petrel *n.* буреве́стник, качу́рка.

petrifaction *n.* окамене́ние. **petrified** *adj.* окамене́лый; *be p.*, (*fig.*) оцепене́ть *perf.* (with, от + *gen.*). **petrify** *v.t.* превраща́ть *imp.*, преврати́ть (-ащу́, -ати́шь) *perf.* в ка́мень; *v.i.* камене́ть *imp.*, о~ *perf.*

petrochemical *adj.* нефтехими́ческий. **petrochemistry** *n.* нефтехи́мия. **petrodollar** *n.* нефтедо́ллар. **petrol** *n.* бензи́н; *attrib.* бензи́новый; *p. gauge*, бензоме́р; *p. pipe*, бензопрово́д; *p. pump*, (*in engine*) бензонасо́с; (*at p. station*) бензоколо́нка; *p. station*, бензозапра́вочная ста́нция; *p. tank*, бензоба́к. **petroleum** *n.* нефть.

petticoat *n.* ни́жняя ю́бка.

pettifogger *n.* крючкотво́р. **pettifoggery** *n.* крючкотво́рство. **pettifogging** *adj.* кляу́зный.

petty *adj.* ме́лкий (-лок, -лка́, -лко); *p. bourgeois*, мелкобуржуа́зный; *p. cash*, ме́лкие су́ммы *m.pl.*; *p. officer*, старшина́ (*pl.* -ны) *m.*

petulance *n.* нетерпели́вость, раздражи́тельность. **petulant** *adj.* нетерпели́вый, приди́рчивый.

pew *n.* церко́вная скамья́ (*pl.* ска́мьи́, -ме́й).

pewit *n.* чи́бис.

pewter *n.* сплав о́лова со свинцо́м; (*dishes*) оловя́нная посу́да.
phalanx *n.* фала́нга.
phallic *adj.* фалли́ческий. **phallus** *n.* фа́ллос.
phantom *n.* фанто́м, при́зрак.
Pharaoh *n.* фарао́н.
Pharisaic(al) *adj.* фарисе́йский. **Pharisee** *n.* фарисе́й.
pharmaceutical *adj.* фармацевти́ческий. **pharmacist** *n.* фармаце́вт. **pharmacology** *n.* фармаколо́гия. **pharmacopeia** *n.* фармакопе́я. **pharmacy** *n.* фармаци́я; (*dispensary*) апте́ка.
pharynx *n.* гло́тка.
phase *n.* фа́за, ста́дия.
pheasant *n.* фаза́н.
phenomenal *adj.* феномена́льный. **phenomenon** *n.* явле́ние; (*also person, event*) фено́мен.
phial *n.* скля́нка, пузырёк (-рька́).
philander *v.i.* волочи́ться (-чу́сь, -чишься) *imp.* (with, за + *instr.*). **philanderer** *n.* волоки́та *m.*
philanthrope, -pist *n.* филантро́п. **philanthropic** *adj.* филантропи́ческий. **philanthropy** *n.* филантро́пия.
philatelic *adj.* филателисти́ческий. **philatelist** *n.* филатели́ст. **philately** *n.* филатели́я.
philharmonic *adj.* (*in titles*) филармони́ческий.
philippic *n.* фили́ппика.
Philistine *n.* (*fig.*) фили́стер, меща́нин (*pl.* -а́не, -а́н), -а́нка; *adj.* фили́стерский, меща́нский. **philistinism** *n.* фили́стерство, меща́нство.
philological *adj.* филологи́ческий. **philologist** *n.* фило́лог. **philology** *n.* филоло́гия.
philosopher *n.* фило́соф. **philosophic(al)** *adj.* филосо́фский. **philosophize** *v.i.* филосо́фствовать *imp.* **philosophy** *n.* филосо́фия.
philtre *n.* привoро́тное зе́лье (*gen.pl.* -лий).
phlegm *n.* мокрота́; (*quality*) флéгма. **phlegmatic** *adj.* флегмати́ческий.
phlox *n.* флокс.
phobia *n.* фо́бия, страх.
phoenix *n.* фе́никс.
phone *n.* телефо́н; *v.t.* & *i.* звони́ть *imp.*, по~ *perf.* + *dat.* (по телефо́ну).
phoneme *n.* фоне́ма. **phonemic** *adj.* фонемати́ческий. **phonetic** *adj.* фонети́ческий. **phonetician** *n.* фoнети́ст. **phonetics** *n.* фоне́тика. **phonograph** *n.* фоно́граф. **phonological** *adj.* фонологи́ческий. **phonology** *n.* фонoло́гия.
phosphate *n.* фосфа́т. **phosphorescence** *n.* фосфоресце́нсия. **phosphorescent** *adj.* светя́щийся, фосфоресци́рующий. **phosphorous** *adj.* фо́сфористый. **phosphorus** *n.* фо́сфор.
photo *n.* сни́мок (-мка); *v.t.* снима́ть *imp.*, снять (сниму́, -мешь; снял, -а́, -о) *perf.*; *p. finish*, фотофи́ниш. **photocopy** *n.* фотоко́пия. **photoelectric** *adj.* фотоэлектри́ческий; *p. cell*, фотоэлеме́нт. **photogenic** *adj.* фотогени́чный. **photograph** *n.* фотогра́фия, сни́мок (-мка); *v.t.* фотографи́ровать *imp.*, с~ *perf.*; снима́ть *imp.*, снять (сниму́, -мешь; снял, -а́, -о) *perf.* **photographer** *n.* фото́граф. **photographic** *adj.* фотографи́ческий. **photography** *n.* фотогра́фия. **photogravure** *n.* фотогравю́ра. **photolithography** *n.* фотолитогра́фия. **photometer** *n.* фото́метр. **photosynthesis** *n.* фотоси́нтез.
phrase *n.* фра́за; (*diction*) стиль *m.*; (*expression*) оборо́т (ре́чи); *v.t.* выража́ть *imp.*, вы́разить *perf.* слова́ми. **phraseological** *adj.* фразеологи́ческий. **phraseology** *n.* фразеоло́гия.
phrenology *n.* френоло́гия.
physical *adj.* физи́ческий; *p. culture*, физкульту́ра; *p. examination*, медици́нский осмо́тр; *p. exercises*, заря́дка. **physician** *n.* врач (-а́). **physicist** *n.* фи́зик. **physics** *n.* фи́зика.
physiognomy *n.* физионо́мия.
physiological *n.* физиологи́ческий. **physiologist** *n.* физио́лог. **physiology** *n.* физиоло́гия. **physiotherapist** *n.* физиотерапе́вт. **physiotherapy** *n.* физиотерапи́я.
physique *n.* телосложе́ние.
pianist *n.* пиани́ст, ~ка. **piano** *n.* фортепья́но *neut.indecl.*; (*grand*) роя́ль *m.*; (*upright*) пиани́но *neut.indecl.* **pianoforte** *n.* фортепья́но *neut.indecl.*
piccolo *n.* пи́кколо *neut.indecl.*

pick[1] *v.t.* (*ground*) разрыхлять *imp.*, разрыхлить *perf.*; (*bone*) обгладывать *imp.*, обглодать (-ожу, -ожешь) *perf.*; (*flower*) срывать *imp.*, сорвать (-ву, -вёшь; сорвал, -а, -о) *perf.*; (*gather*) собирать *imp.*, собрать (соберу, -рёшь; собрал, -а, -о) *perf.*; (*select*) выбирать *imp.*, выбрать (выберу, -решь) *perf.*; *p. someone's brains*, присваивать *imp.*, присвоить *perf.* (чужие) мысли; *p. a lock*, открывать *imp.*, открыть (-рою, -роешь) *perf.* замок отмычкой; *p. one's nose, teeth*, ковырять *imp.*, ковырнуть *perf.* в носу, в зубах; *p. a quarrel*, искать (ищу, ищешь) *imp.* ссоры (with, с + *instr.*); *p. to pieces*, (*fig.*) раскритиковать *perf.*; *p. someone's pocket*, залезать *imp.*, залезть (-зу, -зешь; -з) *perf.* в карман + *dat.*; *p. one's way*, выбирать *imp.*, выбрать (выберу, -решь) *perf.* дорогу; *p. off*, (*pluck off*) обрывать *imp.*, оборвать (-ву, -вёшь; оборвал, -а, -о) *perf.*; (*shoot*) перестреливать *imp.*, перестрелять *perf.* (одного за другим); *p. on*, (*nag*) пилить (-лю, -лишь) *imp.*; *p. out*, отбирать *imp.*, отобрать (отберу, -рёшь; отобрал, -а, -о) *perf.*; *p. up*, (*lift*) поднимать *imp.*, поднять (подниму, -мешь; поднял, -а, -о) *perf.*; (*gain*) добывать *imp.*, добыть (добуду, -дешь; добыл, -а, -о) *perf.*; (*fetch*) заезжать *imp.*, заехать (заеду, -дешь) *perf.* за + *instr.*; (*recover*) поправляться *imp.*, поправиться *perf.*; *p. oneself up*, подниматься *imp.*, подняться (поднимусь, -мешься; поднялся, -лась) *perf.*; *p.-up*, (*truck*) пикап; (*electron.*) звукосниматель *m.*

pick[2] *n.* выбор; (*best part*) лучшая часть, самое лучшее; *take your p.*, выбирай(те)!

pick[3], **pickaxe** *n.* кирка (*pl.* кирки, -рок, киркам).

picket *n.* (*stake*) кол (-а, *loc.* -у; *pl.* -ья, -ьев); (*person*) пикетчик, -ица; (*collect.*) пикет; *v.t.* пикетировать *imp.*

pickle *n.* (*brine*) рассол; (*vinegar*) маринад; *pl.* соленье, маринады *m.pl.*, пикули (-лей) *pl.*; (*plight*) напасть; *v.t.* солить (солю, солишь) *imp.*, по ~ *perf.*; мариновать *imp.*, за ~ *perf.* **pickled** *adj.* солёный (солон, -а, -о); маринованный; (*drunk*) пьяный (пьян, -а, -о).

pickpocket *n.* карманник.

picnic *n.* пикник (-а); *v.i.* участвовать *imp.* в пикнике.

pictorial *adj.* изобразительный; (*illustrated*) иллюстрированный. **picture** *n.* картина; (*p. of health etc.*) воплощение; (*film*) фильм; *the pictures*, кино *neut.indecl.*; *p.-book*, книга с картинками; *p.-gallery*, картинная галерея; *p. postcard*, художественная открытка; *p. window*, целостенное окно (*pl.* окна, окон, окнам); *v.t.* изображать *imp.*, изобразить *perf.*; (*to oneself*) представлять *imp.*, представить *perf.* себе. **picturesque** *adj.* живописный; (*language etc.*) образный.

pie *n.* пирог (-а), пирожок (-жка).

piebald *adj.* пегий; *n.* (*horse*) пегая лошадь (*pl.* -ди, -дей, *instr.* -дьми).

piece *n.* кусок (-ска), часть (*pl.* -ти, -тей); (*one of set*) штука; (*of land*) участок (-тка); (*of paper*) листок (-тка); (*mus., lit.*) произведение; (*picture*) картина; (*drama*) пьеса; (*chess*) фигура; (*coin*) монета; *take to pieces*, разбирать *imp.*, разобрать (разберу, -рёшь; разобрал, -а, -о) *perf.* (на части); *p. of advice*, совет; *p. of information*, сведение; *p. of news*, новость; *p.-work*, сдельщина; *p.-worker*, сдельщик; *v.t.*: *p. together*, собирать *imp.*, собрать (соберу, -рёшь; собрал, -а, -о) *perf.* из кусочков; сводить (-ожу, -одишь) *imp.*, свести (сведу, -дёшь; свёл, -а) *perf.* воедино. **piecemeal** *adv.* по частям.

pied *adj.* разноцветный.

pier *n.* (*mole*) мол (*loc.* -у); (*in harbour*) пирс; (*of bridge*) бык (-а); (*between windows etc.*) простенок (-нка); *p.-glass*, трюмо *neut.indecl.*

pierce *v.t.* пронзать *imp.*, пронзить *perf.*; прокалывать *imp.*, проколоть (-лю, -лешь) *perf.*; (*of cold, look, etc.*) пронизывать *imp.*, пронизать (-ижу, -ижешь) *perf.* **piercing** *adj.* острый (остр & остёр, остра, остро), пронзительный.

piety *n.* на́божность.
piffle *n.* чепуха́, вздор. **piffling** *adj.* ничто́жный.
pig *n.* свинья́ (*pl.* -ньи, -не́й, -ньям) (*also of person*); (*of metal*) болва́нка, чу́шка; *v.t.*: *p. it*, жить (живу́, -вёшь; жил, -а́, -о) *imp.*, по-сви́нски; *v. abs.* порос́иться *imp.*, о~ *perf.* **pigheaded** *adj.* упря́мый. **pig-iron** *n.* чугу́н (-а́) в чу́шках. **piglet** *n.* поросёнок (-сёнка; *pl.* -ся́та, -ся́т). **pigskin** *n.* свина́я ко́жа.
pigsty *n.* свина́рник. **pigswill** *n.* помо́и (-о́ев) *pl.* **pigtail** *n.* коси́чка.
pigeon *n.* го́лубь (*pl.* -би, -бе́й) *m.*; *p.-hole*, (*n.*) отделе́ние для бума́г; (*v.t.*) раскла́дывать *imp.*, разложи́ть (-ожу́, -о́жишь) *perf.* по отделе́ниям, по я́щикам; (*put aside*) откла́дывать *imp.*, отложи́ть (-ожу́, -о́жишь) *perf.* в до́лгий я́щик.
pigment *n.* пигме́нт. **pigmentation** *n.* пигмента́ция.
pigmy *see* **pygmy**.
pike[1] *n.* (*weapon*) пи́ка.
pike[2] *n.* (*fish*) щу́ка;. *p-perch*, суда́к (-а́).
pilaster *n.* пиля́стр.
pilchard *n.* сарди́н(к)а.
pile[1] *n.* (*heap*) ку́ча, ки́па; (*funeral p.*) погреба́льный костёр (-тра́); (*building*) огро́мное зда́ние; (*electr.*) батаре́я; (*atomic p.*) я́дерный реа́ктор; *v.t.*: *p. up*, скла́дывать *imp.*, сложи́ть (-жу́, -жишь) *perf.* в ку́чу; сва́ливать *imp.*, свали́ть (-лю́, -лишь) *perf.* в ку́чу; (*load*) нагружа́ть *imp.*, нагрузи́ть (-ужу́, -у́зишь) *perf.* (with, + *instr.*); *v.i.*: *p. in(to)*, *on*, забира́ться *imp.*, забра́ться (заберу́сь, -рёшься; забра́лся, -ала́сь, -а́ло́сь) *perf.* в + *acc.*; *p. up*, накопля́ться, нака́пливаться *imp.*, накопи́ться (-ится) *perf.*
pile[2] *n.* (*support*) сва́я; *p.-driver*, копёр (-пра́).
pile[3] *n.* (*on cloth etc.*) ворс.
piles *n.* геморро́й.
pilfer *v.t.* ворова́ть *imp.* **pilfering** *n.* ме́лкая кра́жа.
pilgrim *n.* пилигри́м, пало́мник, -ица. **pilgrimage** *n.* пало́мничество.
pill *n.* пилю́ля; *the p.*, противозача́точная пилю́ля.
pillage *n.* мародёрство; *v.t.* гра́бить *imp.*, о~ *perf.*; *v. abs.* мародёрствовать *imp.*
pillar *n.* столб (-а́); (*fig.*) столп (-а́); *p.-box*, стоя́чий почто́вый я́щик.
pillion *n.* за́днее сиде́нье (мотоци́кла).
pillory *n.* позо́рный столб (-а́); *v.t.* (*fig.*) пригвожда́ть *imp.*, пригвозди́ть *perf.* к позо́рному столбу́.
pillow *n.* поду́шка; *v.t.* подпира́ть *imp.*, подпере́ть (подопру́, -рёшь; подпёр) *perf.* **pillowcase** *n.* на́волочка.
pilot *n.* (*naut.*) ло́цман; (*aeron.*) пило́т, лётчик; *adj.* о́пытный, про́бный; *v.t.* управля́ть *imp.* + *instr.*; (*aeron.*) пилоти́ровать *imp.*
pimento *n.* пе́рец (-рца(у)).
pimp *n.* сво́дник, -ица; *v.i.* сво́дничать *imp.*
pimpernel *n.* о́чный цвет.
pimple *n.* прыщ (-а́). **pimpled, pimply** *adj.* прыща́вый, прыщева́тый.
pin *n.* була́вка; (*peg*) па́лец (-льца); *p.-head*, (*fig.*) ме́лочь (*pl.* -чи, -че́й); (*person*) тупи́ца *m.* & *f.*; *p.-hole*, була́вочное отве́рстие; *p.-point*, то́чно определя́ть *imp.*, определи́ть *perf.*; *p.-prick*, (*fig.*) ме́лкая неприя́тность; *p.-stripe*, то́нкая поло́ска; *p.-tuck*, ме́лкая скла́дочка; *v.t.* прика́лывать *imp.*, приколо́ть (-лю́, -лешь) *perf.*; (*press*) прижима́ть *imp.*, прижа́ть (-жму́, -жмёшь) *perf.* (against, к + *dat.*); *p.-up*, карти́нка красо́тки, прикреплённая на сте́ну.
pinafore *n.* пере́дник.
pince-nez *n.* пенсне́ *neut.indecl.*
pincers *n.* клещи́ (-ще́й) *pl.*, пинце́т; (*crab's*) клешни́ *f.pl.*; *pincer movement*, захва́т в клещи́.
pinch *v.t.* щипа́ть (-плю́, -плешь) *imp.*, (у)щипну́ть *perf.*; прищемля́ть *imp.*, прищеми́ть *perf.*; (*of shoe*) жать (жмёт) *imp.*; (*steal*) стяну́ть (-ну́, -нешь) *perf.*; (*arrest*) сца́пать *perf.*; *v.i.* скупи́ться *imp.*; *where the shoe pinches*, в чём загво́здка; *n.* щипо́к (-пка́); (*of salt*) щепо́тка; (*of snuff*) поню́шка (табаку́); *at a p.*, в кра́йнем слу́чае.
pinchbeck *n.* томпа́к (-а́); *adj.* томпа́ковый.

pincushion *n.* поду́шечка для була́вок.

pine[1] *v.i.* томи́ться *imp.*; *p. for*, тоскова́ть *imp.* по + *dat.*, *prep.*

pine[2] *n.* (*tree*) сосна́ (*pl.* -сны, -сен, -снам); *attrib.* сосно́вый; *p.-cone*, сосно́вая ши́шка; *p.-needles*, сосно́вая хво́я *collect.*

pineal *adj.* шишкови́дный.

pineapple *n.* анана́с.

ping-pong *n.* насто́льный те́ннис, пинг-по́нг.

pinion[1] *n.* (*of wing*) оконе́чность пти́чьего крыла́; (*flight-feather*) махово́е перо́ (*pl.* -рья, -рьев); *v.t.* подреза́ть *imp.*, подре́зать (-е́жу, -е́жешь) *perf.* кры́лья + *dat.*; (*person*) свя́зывать *imp.*, связа́ть (-яжу́, -я́жешь) *perf.* ру́ки + *dat.*

pinion[2] *n.* (*cog-wheel*) шестерня́ (*gen.pl.* -рён).

pink[1] *n.* (*flower*) гвозди́ка; (*colour*) ро́зовый цвет; *the p.*, вы́сшая сте́пень, верх; *in the p.*, в прекра́сном состоя́нии; *adj.* ро́зовый.

pink[2] *v.t.* (*pierce*) протыка́ть *imp.*, проткну́ть *perf.*; *p. out*, украша́ть *imp.*, укра́сить *perf.* зубца́ми.

pink[3] *v.i.* (*of engine*) рабо́тать *imp.* с детона́цией.

pinnace *n.* пина́с.

pinnacle *n.* (*peak; fig.*) верши́на; (*turret*) остроконе́чная ба́шенка.

pint *n.* пи́нта.

pintail *n.* (*duck*) шилохво́сть.

piny *adj.* сосно́вый.

pioneer *n.* пионе́р, ~ка; (*mil.*) сапёр; *adj.* пионе́рский; сапёрный.

pious *adj.* на́божный.

pip[1] *n.* (*on dice etc.*) очко́ (*pl.* -ки́, -ко́в); (*star*) звёздочка.

pip[2] *n.* (*seed*) зёрнышко (*pl.* -шки, -шек, -шкам).

pip[3] *n.* (*sound*) бип.

pipe *n.* труба́ (*pl.* -бы); (*mus.*) ду́дка, свире́ль; *pl.* волы́нка; (*for smoking*) тру́бка; *p.-dream*, пуста́я мечта́ (*gen. pl.* -ний); *v.t.* (*play on p.*) игра́ть *imp.*, сыгра́ть *perf.* на ду́дке, на свире́ли; (*convey by p.*) пуска́ть *imp.*, пусти́ть (пущу́, пу́стишь) *perf.* по тру́бам, по трубопрово́ду; *v.i.*: *p. down*, замолка́ть *imp.*, замо́лкнуть (-к) *perf.*

pipeclay *n.* бе́лая тру́бочная гли́на.

pipeline *n.* трубопрово́д; (*oil p.*) нефтепрово́д. **piper** *n.* волы́нщик.

pipette *n.* пипе́тка. **piping** *n.* (*on dress etc.*) кант; *adj.* (*voice*) пискли́вый; *p. hot*, с пы́лу, с жа́ру.

pipit *n.* щеври́ца, конёк (-нька́).

piquancy *n.* пика́нтность. **piquant** *adj.* пика́нтный.

piqué *n.* пике́ *neut.indecl.*

piracy *n.* пира́тство. **pirate** *n.* пира́т; *v.t.* (*book*) самово́льно переиздава́ть (-даю́, -даёшь) *imp.*, переизда́ть (-а́м, -а́шь, -а́ст, -ади́м; -а́л, -ала́, -а́ло) *perf.* **piratical** *adj.* пира́тский.

pirouette *n.* пируэ́т; *v.i.* де́лать *imp.*, с~ *perf.* пируэ́т(ы).

piscatorial *adj.* рыболо́вный.

Pisces *n.* Ры́бы *f.pl.*

pistachio *n.* фиста́шка; *attrib.* фиста́шковый.

pistil *n.* пе́стик.

pistol *n.* пистоле́т.

piston *n.* по́ршень (-шня) *m.*; (*in cornet etc.*) писто́н; *adj.* поршнево́й; *p.-ring*, поршнево́е кольцо́ (*pl.* -льца, -ле́ц, -льцам); *p.-rod*, шток по́ршня.

pit *n.* я́ма; (*mine*) ша́хта; (*quarry*) карье́р; (*theat.*) парте́р; (*in workshop*) ремо́нтная я́ма; (*car-racing*) запра́вочно-ремо́нтный пу́нкт; *the bottomless p.*, преиспо́дняя *sb.*; *in the p. of the stomach*, под ло́жечкой; *p.-head*, надша́хтный копёр (-пра́); *v.t.*: *p. against*, выставля́ть *imp.*, вы́ставить *perf.* про́тив + *gen.*

pit-a-pat *adv.* с ча́стым бие́нием; *go p.*, (*heart*) затрепета́ть (-е́щет) *perf.*

pitch[1] *n.* (*resin*) смола́; *p.-black*, чёрный (-рен, -рна́) как смоль; *p.-dark*, о́чень тёмный (-мен, -мна́); *p.-darkness*, тьма кроме́шная; *v.t.* смоли́ть *imp.*, вы́~, о~ *perf.*

pitch[2] *v.t.* (*camp, tent*) разбива́ть *imp.*, разби́ть (разобью́, -ьёшь) *perf.*; (*ball*) подава́ть (-даю́, -даёшь) *imp.*, пода́ть (-а́м, -а́шь, -а́ст, -ади́м; по́дал, -а́, -о) *perf.*; (*fling*) кида́ть *imp.*, ки́нуть *perf.*; *v.i.* (*fall*) па́дать *imp.*, (у)па́сть (-аду́, -адёшь; -а́л) *perf.*; (*ship*) испы́тывать *imp.*, испыта́ть *perf.* килеву́ю ка́чку; *p. into*, набра́сываться *imp.*, набро́ситься *perf.* на + *acc.*; *pitched battle*, генера́льное сраже́ние; *n.* (*of ship*) килева́я ка́чка; (*of ball*) пода́ча; (*football p. etc.*) площа́дка; (*degree*) у́ровень (-вня) *m.*; (*mus.*) высота́ (*pl.* -ты); (*slope*) укло́н; *p.-pipe*, камерто́н-ду́дка.

pitchblende *n.* уранини́т.

pitcher[1] *n.* (*sport*) подаю́щий *sb.* (мяч).

pitcher[2] *n.* (*vessel*) кувши́н.

pitchfork *n.* ви́лы (-л) *pl.*

pitchy *adj.* смоли́стый.

piteous *adj.* жа́лостный, жа́лкий (-лок, -лка́, -лко).

pitfall *n.* западня́.

pith *n.* сердцеви́на; (*essence*) суть; (*vigour*) си́ла, эне́ргия. **pithy** *adj.* (*fig.*) сжа́тый, содержа́тельный.

pitiable *adj.* жа́лкий (-лок, -лка́, -лко), несча́стный. **pitiful** *adj.* жа́лостный, жа́лкий (-лок, -лка́, -лко). **pitiless** *adj.* безжа́лостный.

pittance *n.* ску́дное жа́лованье, жа́лкие гроши́ (-ше́й) *pl.*

pitted *adj.* (*of face*) изры́тый, рябо́й (ряб, -а́, -о).

pituitary *adj.* сли́зистый; *n.* (*gland*) гипо́физ.

pity *n.* сожале́ние; *it's a p.*, жа́лко, жаль; *take p. on*, сжа́литься *perf.* над + *instr.*; *what a p.*, как жа́лко! *v.t.* жале́ть *imp.*, по ~ *perf.*; *I p. you* мне жаль тебя́.

pivot *n.* сте́ржень (-жня) *m.*; (*fig.*) центр; *v.i.* враща́ться *imp.* **pivotal** *adj.* (*fig.*) центра́льный.

placard *n.* афи́ша, плака́т; *v.t.* (*wall*) раскле́ивать *imp.*, раскле́ить *perf.* афи́ши, плака́ты, на + *prep.*, по + *dat.*

placate *v.t.* умиротворя́ть *imp.*, умиротвори́ть *perf.*

place *n.* ме́сто (*pl.* -та́); *change places with*, обме́ниваться *imp.*, обменя́ться *perf.* места́ми с + *instr.*; *give p. to*, уступа́ть *imp.*, уступи́ть (-плю́, -пишь) *perf.* ме́сто + *dat.*; *in p.*, на ме́сте; (*suitable*) уме́стный; *in p. of*, вме́сто + *gen.*; *in the first, second, p.*, во-пе́рвых, во-вторы́х; *out of p.*, не на ме́сте; (*unsuitable*) неуме́стный; *take p.*, случа́ться *imp.*, случи́ться *perf.*; (*pre-arranged event*) состоя́ться (-ойтся) *perf.*; *take the p. of*, заменя́ть *imp.*, замени́ть (-ню́, -нишь) *perf.*; *p.-name*, географи́ческое назва́ние; *p.-setting*, столо́вый прибо́р; *v.t.* помеща́ть *imp.*, помести́ть *perf.*; (*stand*) ста́вить *imp.*, по ~ *perf.*; (*lay*) класть (кладу́, -дёшь; -ал) *imp.*, положи́ть (-жу́, -жишь) *perf.*; (*determine*) определя́ть *imp.*, определи́ть *perf.*

placenta *n.* плаце́нта.

placid *adj.* споко́йный. **placidity** *n.* споко́йствие.

plagiarism *n.* плагиа́т. **plagiarist** *n.* плагиа́тор. **plagiarize** *v.t.* заимствовать *imp., perf.*

plague *n.* чума́, морова́я я́зва; *v.t.* му́чить *imp.*, за ~, из ~ *perf.*

plaice *n.* ка́мбала.

plaid *n.* плед; (*cloth*) шотла́ндка; *adj.* в шотла́ндскую кле́тку.

plain *n.* равни́на; *adj.* (*clear*) я́сный (я́сен, ясна́, я́сно, я́сны́); (*simple*) просто́й (прост, -а́, -о, про́сты́); (*direct*) прямо́й (прям, -а́, -о, пря́мы́); (*ugly*) некраси́вый; *p.-clothes policeman*, шпик (-а́); *p.-spoken*, открове́нный (-нен, -нна); *p. stitch*, пряма́я пе́тля.

plaintiff *n.* исте́ц (-тца́), исти́ца.

plaintive *adj.* жа́лобный.

plait *n.* коса́ (*acc.* ко́су́; *pl.* -сы); *v.t.* плести́ (плету́, -тёшь; плёл, -а́) *imp.*, с ~ *perf.*

plan *n.* план; *v.t.* плани́ровать *imp.*, за ~, с ~ *perf.*; (*intend*) намерева́ться *imp.* + *inf.*

plane[1] *n.* (*tree*) плата́н.

plane[2] *n.* (*tool*) руба́нок (-нка); *v.t.* строга́ть *imp.*, вы́ ~ *perf.*

plane[3] *n.* (*surface*) пло́скость; (*level*) у́ровень (-вня) *m.*; (*aeroplane*) самолёт; *v.i.* плани́ровать *imp.*, с ~ *perf.*

plane[4] *adj.* (*level*) пло́ский (-сок, -ска́, -ско), плоскостно́й.

planet *n.* плане́та. **planetarium** *n.* планета́рий. **planetary** *adj.* плане́тный, планета́рный.

plank *n.* доска́ (*acc.* -ску; *pl.* -ски, -со́к, -ска́м); (*polit.*) пункт парти́йной програ́ммы; *p. bed*, на́ры (-р) *pl.*; *v.t.* выстила́ть *imp.*, вы́стлать (-телю,

-телешь) *perf.* досками. **planking** *n.* настил; (*collect.*) доски (-сок, -скам) *f.pl.*
plankton *n.* планктон.
plant *n.* растение; (*fixtures*) установка; (*factory*) завод; *v.t.* сажать *imp.*, посадить (-ажу, -адишь) *perf.*; насаждать *imp.*, насадить (-ажу, -адишь) *perf.*; (*fix firmly*) прочно ставить *imp.*, по~ *perf.*; (*garden etc.*) засаживать *imp.*, засадить (-ажу, -адишь) *perf.* (with, +*instr.*); (*palm off*) всучивать *imp.*, всучить (-учу, -учишь) *perf.* (on, +*dat.*); *p. out*, высаживать *imp.*, высадить *perf.* в грунт.
plantain *n.* подорожник.
plantation *n.* (*of trees*) (лесо)насаждение; (*of cotton etc.*) плантация. **planter** *n.* плантатор.
plaque *n.* дощечка, мемориальная доска (*acc.* -ску; *pl.* -ски, -сок, -скам); (*plate*) декоративная тарелка.
plasma *n.* плазма; протоплазма.
plaster *n.* пластырь *m.*; (*for walls etc.*) штукатурка; *p. of Paris*, (*n.*) гипс; (*attrib.*) гипсовый; *p. cast*, (*mould*) гипсовый слепок (-пка); (*for leg etc.*) гипсовая повязка; *v.t.* (*wall*) штукатурить *imp.*, от~, о~ *perf.*; (*daub*) замазывать *imp.*, замазать (-ажу, -ажешь) *perf.*; (*apply a p. to*) накладывать *imp.*, наложить (-жу, -жишь) *perf.* пластырь на+*acc.* **plasterboard** *n.* сухая штукатурка. **plastered** *adj.* (*drunk*) пьяный (пьян, -á. -о). **plasterer** *n.* штукатур.
plastic *n.* пластмасса; *adj.* пластичный, пластический; (*made of p.*) пластмассовый; *p. arts*, пластика; *p. surgery*, пластическая хирургия.
plate *n.* пластинка; (*for food*) тарелка, (*collect.*; *silver, gold p.*) столовое серебро, золото; (*metal sheet*) лист (-á); (*print.*) печатная форма; (*illustration*) (вкладная) иллюстрация; (*name-p. etc.*) дощечка; (*phot.*) фотопластинка; *p.-armour*, броневые плиты *f.pl.*; *p. glass*, зеркальное стекло; *p.-rack*, сушилка для посуды; *v.t.* плакировать *imp.*, *perf.* **plateful** *n.* полная тарелка. **platelayer** *n.* путевой рабочий *sb.*
plateau *n.* плато *neut.indecl.*, плоскогорье.
platform *n.* платформа; (*rly.*) перрон; *p. ticket* перронный билет.
platinum *n.* платина; *attrib.* платиновый.
platitude *n.* банальность, плоскость. **platitudinous** *adj.* банальный, плоский (-сок, -ска, -ско).
platoon *n.* взвод.
platypus *n.* утконос.
plaudits *n.* аплодисменты (-тов) *pl.*
plausibility *n.* (*probability*) правдоподобие; (*speciosity*) благовидность. **plausible** *adj.* правдоподобный; благовидный.
play *v.t.* & *i.* играть *imp.*, сыграть *perf.* (*game*) в+*acc.*, (*instrument*) на+*prep.*, (*in p.*) в+*prep.*, (*for prize*) на+*acc.*, (*opponent*) с+*instr.*; *v.t.* (*p. part of*; *also fig.*) играть *imp.*, сыграть *perf.* роль+*gen.*; (*mus. composition*) исполнять *imp.*, исполнить *perf.*; (*chessman, card*) ходить (хожу, ходишь) *imp.*+*instr.*; (*record*) ставить *imp.*, по~ *perf.*; (*searchlight*) направлять *imp.*, направить *perf.* (on, на+*acc.*); *v.i.* (*frolic*) резвиться *imp.*; (*fountain*) бить (бьёт) *imp.*; (*light*) переливаться *imp.*; *p. down*, преуменьшать *imp.*, преуменьшить *perf.*; *p. fair*, честно поступать *imp.*, поступить (-плю, -пишь) *perf.*; *p. false*, изменять *imp.*, изменить (-ню, -нишь) *perf.* (+*dat.*); *p. the fool*, валять *imp.* дурака; *p. into the hands of*, играть *imp.*, сыграть *perf.* на руку+*dat.*; *p. a joke, trick, on* подшучивать *imp.*, подшутить (-учу, -утишь) *perf.* над+*instr.*; *p. off*, играть *imp.*, сыграть *perf.* решающую партию; *p.-off*, решающая встреча; *p. off against*, стравливать *imp.*, стравить (-влю, -вишь) *perf.* с+*instr.*; *p. safe*, действовать *imp.* наверняка; *played out*, измотанный (-ан); *n.* игра; (*theat.*) пьеса. **playbill** *n.* театральная афиша. **playboy** *n.* прожигатель *m.* жизни. **player** *n.* игрок (-á); (*actor*) актёр, актриса; (*musician*) музыкант. **playfellow, playmate** *n.* друг (*pl.* друзья, -зей) детства. **playful** *adj.* игривый. **playgoer** *n.* театрал. **play-**

ground *n.* площадка для игр. **playhouse** *n.* театр. **playing** *n.*: *p.-card*, игральная карта; *p.-field*, спортплощадка. **plaything** *n.* игрушка. **playwright** *n.* драматург.

plea *n.* (*appeal*) обращение; (*entreaty*) мольба; (*statement*) заявление; *on a p. of*, под предлогом + *gen.* **plead** *v.i.* умолять *imp.* (with, + *acc.*); *v.t.* ссылаться *imp.*, сослаться (сошлюсь, -лёшься) *perf.* на + *acc.*; *p. (not) guilty*, (не) признавать (-наю, -наёшь) *imp.*, признать *perf.* себя виновным.

pleasant *adj.* приятный. **pleasantry** *n.* шутка. **please** *v.t.* нравиться *imp.*, по~ *perf.* + *dat.*; угождать *imp.*, угодить *perf.* + *dat.*, на + *acc.*; *v.i.*: *as you p.*, как вам угодно; *if you p.*, пожалуйста, будьте добры; (*iron.*) представьте себе! *imper.* пожалуйста; будьте добры. **pleased** *adj.* довольный; *predic.* рад. **pleasing, pleasurable** *adj.* приятный. **pleasure** *n.* (*enjoyment*) удовольствие; (*will, desire*) воля, желание.

pleat *n.* складка; *pl.* плиссе *neut.indecl.*; *v.t.* делать *imp.*, с~ *perf.* складки на + *prep.*; плиссировать *imp.* **pleated** *adj.* плиссе *indecl.* (*follows noun*).

plebeian *adj.* плебейский; *n.* плебей.

plebiscite *n.* плебисцит.

plectrum *n.* плектр.

pledge *n.* (*security*) залог; (*promise*) зарок, обещание; *sign, take, the p.*, дать (дам, дашь, даст, дадим; дал, -а, дало, -и) *perf.* зарок не пить; *v.t.* отдавать (-даю, -даёшь) *imp.*, отдать (-ам, -ашь, -аст, -адим; отдал, -а, -о) *perf.* в залог; *p. oneself*, брать (беру, -рёшь; брал, -а, -о) *imp.*, взять (возьму, -мёшь; взял, -а, -о) *perf.* на себя обязательство; *p. one's word*, давать (даю, даёшь) *imp.*, дать (дам, дашь, даст, дадим; дал, -а, дало, -и) *perf.* слово.

plenary *adj.* полный (-лон, -лна, полно); (*assembly*) пленарный. **plenipotentiary** *adj.* (*n.*) полномочный (представитель *m.*). **plenteous, plentiful** *adj.* обильный. **plenty** *n.* изобилие, избыток (-тка).

plethora *n.* (*med.*) полнокровие; (*fig.*) изобилие.

pleurisy *n.* плеврит.

plexus *n.* сплетение.

pliability, pliancy *n.* гибкость; (*fig.*) податливость. **pliable, pliant** *adj.* гибкий (-бок, -бка, -бко); (*fig.*) податливый.

pliers *n.* плоскогубцы (-цев) *pl.*; клещи (-щей) *pl.*

plight *n.* (бедственное, трудное) положение.

Plimsoll line *n.* грузовая марка. **plimsolls** *n.* спортивные тапочки *f.pl.*, кеды (-д(ов)) *m.pl.*

plinth *n.* плинтус; (*of wall*) цоколь *m.*

plod *v.i.* плестись (плетусь, -тёшься; плёлся, -лась) *imp.*; тащиться (-щусь, -щишься) *imp.*; (*work*) упорно работать *imp.* (at, над + *instr.*). **plodder** *n.* работяга *m.* & *f.*

plot *n.* (*of land*) участок (-тка) (земли); (*of book etc.*) фабула; (*conspiracy*) заговор; *v.t.* (*on graph, map, etc.*) наносить (-ошу, -осишь) *imp.*, нанести (-су, -сёшь; нанёс, -ла) на график, на карту; (*a course*) прокладывать *imp.*, проложить (-ожу, -ожишь) *perf.*; *v. abs.* (*conspire*) составлять *imp.*, составить *perf.* заговор. **plotter** *n.* заговорщик, -ица.

plough *n.* плуг (*pl.* -и); *the P.*, (*astron.*) Большая Медведица; (*land*) пашня; *v.t.* пахать (пашу, -шешь) *imp.*, вс~ *perf.*; *v.t.* & *i.* (*fail in examination*) проваливать(ся) *imp.*, провалить(ся) (-лю(сь), -лишь(ся)) *perf.*; *v.i.*: *p. through*, пробиваться *imp.*, пробиться (-бьюсь, -бьёшься) *perf.* сквозь + *acc.*

plover *n.* ржанка.

ploy *n.* уловка.

pluck *n.* (*cul.*) потроха (-хов) *pl.*, ливер; (*courage*) мужество; *v.t.* (*chicken*) щипать (-плю, -плешь) *imp.*, об~ *perf.*; *p. up (one's) courage*, собираться *imp.*, собраться (соберусь, -рёшься; собрался, -алась, -алось) *perf.* с духом; *v.i.*: *p. at*, дёргать *imp.*, дёрнуть *perf.* **plucky** *adj.* смелый (смел, -а, -о).

plug *n.* пробка; (*electr.*) штепсельная вилка; (*electr. socket*) штепсель (*pl.*

-лй) *m.*; (*sparking-p.*) (запáльная) свечá (*pl.* -чи, -чéй); (*tobacco*) прессóванный табáк (-á(ý)); (*advertisement*) реклáма; *v.t.* (*p. up*) затыкáть *imp.*, заткнýть *perf.*; (*sl.*, *shoot*) бáхать *imp.*, бáхнуть *perf.*; (*advertise*) реклами́ровать *imp.*, *perf.*; *p. in*, включáть *imp.*, включи́ть *perf.*; *v.i.*: *p. away at*, корпéть (-плю́, -пи́шь) *imp.* над + *instr*.

plum *n.* (*fruit*) сли́ва; (*colour*) тёмно-фиолéтовый цвет; *p.-cake*, кекс.

plumage *n.* оперéние, пéрья (-ьев) *neut. pl.*

plumb *n.* отвéс; (*naut.*) лот; *adj.* вертикáльный; (*fig.*) я́вный; *adv.* вертикáльно; (*fig.*) тóчно; *v.t.* измеря́ть *imp.*, измéрить *perf.* глубинý + *gen.*; (*fig.*) проникáть *imp.*, прони́кнуть (-к) *perf.* в + *acc.*

plumbago *n.* графи́т.

plumber *n.* водопровóдчик. **plumbing** *n.* (*work*) водопровóдное дéло; (*system of pipes*) водопровóдная систéма.

plume *n.* (*feather*) перó (*pl.* -рья, -рьев); (*on hat etc.*) султáн, плюмáж; *p. of smoke*, дымóк (-мкá); *v.t.*: *p. oneself on*, кичи́ться *imp.* + *instr*.

plummet *n.* (*plumb*) отвéс; (*sounding-lead*) лот; (*on fishing-line*) грузи́ло; *v.i.* слетáть *imp.*, слетéть (-ечý, -ети́шь) *perf.*

plump[1] *adj.* пóлный (-лон, -лнá, пóлнó), пýхлый (пухл, -á, -о).

plump[2] *v.t.* & *i.* бýхать(ся) *imp.*, бýхнуть(ся) *perf.*; *v.i.*: *p. for*, (*vote for*) голосовáть *imp.*, про ~ *perf.* тóлько за + *acc.*; (*fig.*) выбирáть *imp.*, вы́брать (вы́беру, -решь) *perf.*

plunder *v.t.* грáбить *imp.*, о ~ *perf.*; *n.* добы́ча.

plunge *v.t.* & *i.* (*immerse*) погружáть(ся) *imp.*, погрузи́ть(ся) *perf.* (into, в + *acc.*); *v.i.* (*dive*) ныря́ть *imp.*, нырнýть *perf.*; (*rush*) бросáться *imp.*, брóситься *perf.* **plunger** *n.* плýнжер.

pluperfect *adj.* предпрошéдший; *n.* предпрошéдшее врéмя *neut.*

plural *n.* мнóжественное числó; *adj.* мнóжественный. **pluralism** *n.* плюрали́зм. **pluralistic** *adj.* плюралисти́ческий.

plus *prep.* плюс + *acc.*; *adj.* (*additional*) добáвочный; (*positive*) положи́тельный; *n.* (знак) плюс.

plush *n.* плюш; *adj.* плю́шевый. **plushy** *adj.* шикáрный.

Pluto *n.* Плутóн.

plutocracy *n.* плутокрáтия. **plutocrat** *n.* плутокрáт. **plutocratic** *adj.* плутократи́ческий.

plutonium *n.* плутóний.

ply[1] *v.i.* курси́ровать *imp.*; *v.t.* (*tool*) рабóтать *imp.* + *instr.*; (*task*) занимáться *imp.* + *instr.*; *p. with questions*, засыпáть *imp.*, засы́пать (-плю, -плешь) *perf.* вопрóсами.

ply[2] *n.* (*layer*) слой (*pl.* слои́); (*strand*) прядь. **plywood** *n.* фанéра.

p.m. *adv.* пóсле полýдня.

pneumatic *adj.* пневмати́ческий.

pneumonia *n.* пневмони́я, воспалéние лёгких.

poach[1] *v.t.* (*cook*) вари́ть (-рю́, -ришь) *imp.*, опускáя в кипятóк; кипяти́ть *imp.* на мéдленном огнé; *poached egg*, яйцó-пашóт.

poach[2] *v.i.* (*hunt*) незакóнно охóтиться *imp.*; (*trespass*) вторгáться *imp.*, втóргнуться (-г(нул)ся, -глась) *perf.* в чужи́е владéния; *v.t.* охóтиться *imp.* на + *acc.* на чужóй землé. **poacher** *n.* браконьéр.

pochard *n.* нырóк (-ркá).

pocket *n.* кармáн; (*billiards*) лýза; (*air-p.*) воздýшная я́ма; *in p.*, в вы́игрыше; *in person's p.* в рукáх у + *gen.*; *out of p.*, в убы́тке; *adj.* кармáнный; *v.t.* класть (-адý, -адёшь; -ал) *imp.*, положи́ть (-жý, -жишь) *perf.* в кармáн; (*appropriate*) прикармáнивать *imp.*, прикармáнить *perf.*; (*billiards*) загоня́ть *imp.*, загнáть (загоню́, -нишь; загнáл, -á, -о) *perf.* в лýзу. **pocketful** *n.* пóлный кармáн.

pock-marked *adj.* рябóй (ряб, -á, -о).

pod *n.* стручóк (-чкá), шелухá; *v.t.* лущи́ть *imp.*, об ~ *perf.*

podgy *adj.* тóлстенький, пýхлый (пухл, -á, -о).

podium *n.* (*conductor's*) пульт.

poem *n.* стихотворéние; (*longer p.*) поэ́ма. **poet** *n.* поэ́т; *P. Laureate*, поэ́т-лауреáт. **poetaster** *n.* стихоплёт.

poetess *n.* поэте́сса. **poetic(al)** *adj.* поэти́ческий, поэти́чный; (*in verse*) стихотво́рный. **poetry** *n.* поэ́зия, стихи́ *m.pl.*; (*quality*) поэти́чность.

pogrom *n.* погро́м.

poignancy *n.* острота́. **poignant** *adj.* о́стрый (остр & остёр, остра́, о́стро́).

point[1] *n.* то́чка; (*place*; *in list*; *print.*) пункт; (*in score*) очко́ (*pl.* -ки́, -ко́в); (*in time*) моме́нт; (*in space*) ме́сто (*pl.* -та́); (*essence*) суть; (*sense*) смысл; (*sharp p.*) остриё; (*tip*) ко́нчик; (*promontory*) мыс (*loc.* -е & -у́; *pl.* мысы́); (*decimal p.*) запята́я *sb.*; (*power p.*) ште́псель (*pl.* -ля́) *m.*; *pl.* (*rly.*) стре́лка; *be on the p. of* (*doing*), собира́ться *imp.*, собра́ться (соберу́сь, -рёшься; собра́лся, -ала́сь, -ало́сь) *perf.* + *inf.*; *beside*, *off*, *the p.*, некста́ти; *in p. of fact*, факти́чески; *that is the p.*, в э́том и де́ло; *the p. is that*, де́ло в том, что; *there is no point* (*in doing*), не име́ет смы́сла (+ *inf.*); *to the p.*, кста́ти; *p.-blank*, прямо́й (прям, -а́, -о, пря́мы́); *p.-duty*, регули́рование движе́ния; *p. of view*, то́чка зре́ния.

point[2] *v.t.* (*wall*) расшива́ть *imp.*, расши́ть (разошью́, -ьёшь) *perf.* швы + *gen.*; (*gun etc.*) наводи́ть (-ожу́, -о́дишь) *imp.*, навести́ (-еду́, -едёшь; -ёл, -ела́) *perf.* (at, на + *acc.*); *v. abs.* (*dog*) де́лать *imp.*, с~ *perf.* сто́йку; *v.i.* (*with finger*) по-, у-, ка́зывать *imp.*, по-, у-, каза́ть (-ажу́, -а́жешь) *perf.* па́льцем (at, to, на + *acc.*); (*draw attention*; *p. out*) обраща́ть *imp.*, обрати́ть (-ащу́, -ати́шь) *perf.* внима́ние (to, на + *acc.*). **pointed** *adj.* (*sharp*) о́стрый (остр & остёр, остра́, о́стро́); (*of arch etc.*) стре́льчатый; (*of remark*) ко́лкий (-лок, -лка́, -лко). **pointer** *n.* указа́тель *m.*; (*of clock etc.*) стре́лка; (*dog*) по́йнтер (*pl.* -ы & -а́). **pointless** *adj.* (*meaningless*) бессмы́сленный (-ен, -енна); (*without score*) с неоткры́тым счётом.

poise *v.t.* уравнове́шивать *imp.*, уравнове́сить *perf.*; *be poised*, (*hover*) висе́ть (-си́т) *imp.* в во́здухе; *n.* уравнове́шенность.

poison *n.* яд (-а(у)), отра́ва; *p. gas*, ядови́тый газ; *p. ivy*, ядоно́сный сума́х; *p. pen*, а́втор анони́мных пи́сем; *v.t.* отравля́ть *imp.*, отрави́ть (-влю́, -вишь) *perf.* **poisoner** *n.* отрави́тель *m.* **poisonous** *adj.* ядови́тый.

poke *v.t.* ты́кать (ты́чу, -чешь) *imp.*, ткнуть *perf.*; *p. fun at*, подшу́чивать *imp.*, подшути́ть (-учу́, -у́тишь) *perf.* над + *instr.*; *p. one's nose into*, сова́ть (сую́, суёшь) *imp.*, су́нуть *perf.* нос в + *acc.*; *p. the fire*, меша́ть *imp.*, по~ *perf.* (кочерго́й) у́гли в ками́не; *n.* тычо́к (-чка́). **poker**[1] *n.* (*metal rod*) кочерга́ (*gen.pl.* -рёг).

poker[2] *n.* (*cards*) по́кер; *p.-face*, бесстра́стное лицо́.

poky *adj.* те́сный (-сен, -сна́, -сно).

polar *adj.* поля́рный; (*phys.*) по́люсный; *p. bear*, бе́лый медве́дь *m.* **polarity** *n.* поля́рность. **polarize** *v.t.* поляризова́ть *imp.*, *perf.* **pole**[1] *n.* (*geog.*; *phys.*) по́люс; *p.-star*, Поля́рная звезда́.

pole[2] *n.* (*rod*) столб (-а́), шест (-а́); *p.-vaulting*, прыжо́к (-жка́) с шесто́м.

Pole[3] *n.* поля́к, по́лька.

pole-axe *n.* секи́ра, берды́ш (-а́).

polecat *n.* хорёк (-рька́).

polemic *adj.* полеми́ческий; *n.* поле́мика.

police *n.* поли́ция; (*as pl.*) полице́йские *sb.*; *p. constable*, полице́йский *sb.*; *p. court*, полице́йский суд (-а́); *p. station*, полице́йский уча́сток (-тка). **policeman** *n.* полице́йский *sb.*, полисме́н.

policy[1] *n.* (*course of action*) поли́тика.

policy[2] *n.* (*document*) по́лис.

polio(myelitis) *n.* полиомиели́т.

Polish[1] *adj.* по́льский.

polish[2] *n.* (*gloss*) гля́нец (-нца); (*process*) полиро́вка; (*substance*) политу́ра; (*fig.*) изы́сканность; *v.t.* полирова́ть *imp.*, на~, от~ *perf.*; *p. off*, расправля́ться *imp.*, распра́виться *perf.* с + *instr.* **polished** *adj.* (*refined*) изы́сканный (-ан, -анна).

polite *adj.* ве́жливый. **politeness** *n.* ве́жливость.

politic *adj.* полити́чный. **political** *adj.* полити́ческий; (*of the state*) госуда́рственный; *p. economy*, политэконо́мика; *p. prisoner*, политзаключённый *sb.* **politician** *n.* поли́тик. **politics** *n.* поли́тика.

polka *n.* по́лька.

poll *n.* (*voting*) голосова́ние; (*number of votes*) число́ голосо́в; (*opinion p.*) опро́с; *v.t.* (*receive votes*) получа́ть *imp.*, получи́ть (-чу́, -чишь) *perf.*; *v.i.* голосова́ть *imp.*, про~ *perf.*

pollard *v.t.* подстрига́ть *imp.*, подстри́чь (-игу́, -ижёшь; -и́г) *perf.*

pollen *n.* пыльца́. **pollinate** *v.t.* опыля́ть *imp.*, опыли́ть *perf.*

polling *attrib.*: *p. booth*, каби́на для голосова́ния; *p. station*, избира́тельный уча́сток (-тка).

pollute *v.t.* загрязня́ть *imp.*, загрязни́ть *perf.* **pollution** *n.* загрязне́ние.

polo *n.* по́ло *neut.indecl.*; *p.-necked*, с высо́ким воротнико́м.

polonaise *n.* полоне́з.

polyandry *n.* полиа́ндрия, многому́жие. **polychromatic** *adj.* многокра́сочный. **polychrome** *n.* (*statue*) раскра́шенная ста́туя. **polyester** *n.* полиэфи́р. **polyethylene** *n.* полиэтиле́н. **polygamous** *adj.* многобра́чный. **polygamy** *n.* многобра́чие. **polyglot** *n.* полигло́т; *adj.* многоязы́чный; (*person*) говоря́щий на мно́гих языка́х. **polygon** *n.* многоуго́льник. **polygonal** *adj.* многоуго́льный. **polyhedral** *adj.* многогра́нный. **polyhedron** *n.* многогра́нник. **polymer** *n.* полиме́р. **polymeric** *adj.* полиме́рный. **polymerize** *v.t.* & *i.* полимеризи́ровать(ся) *imp.*

polyp *n.* поли́п.

polyphonic *adj.* полифони́ческий. **polyphony** *n.* полифони́я. **polystyrene** *n.* полистиро́л. **polysyllabic** *adj.* многосло́жный. **polysyllable** *n.* многосло́жное сло́во (*pl.* -ва́). **polytechnic** *adj.* политехни́ческий; *n.* полите́хникум. **polytheism** *n.* многобо́жие. **polythene** *n.* полиэтиле́н. **polyurethane** *n.* полиурета́н. **polyvalent** *adj.* многовале́нтный.

pom *n.* шпиц.

pomade *n.* пома́да; *v.t.* пома́дить *imp.*, на~ *perf.*

pomegranate *n.* грана́т.

Pomeranian *n.* шпиц.

pommel *n.* (*hilt*) голо́вка; (*of saddle*) лука́ (*pl.* -ки).

pomp *n.* пы́шность, великоле́пие. **pomposity** *n.* напы́щенность. **pompous** *adj.* напы́щенный (-ен, -енна).

pom-pom, pompon *n.* помпо́н.

poncho *n.* по́нчо *neut.indecl.*

pond *n.* пруд (-а́, *loc.* -у́). **pondweed** *n.* рдест.

ponder *v.t.* обду́мывать *imp.*, обду́мать *perf.*; *v.i.* размышля́ть *imp.*, размы́слить *perf.* (over, о + *prep.*).

ponderous *adj.* тяжелове́сный.

poniard *n.* кинжа́л.

pontiff *n.* (*pope*) ри́мский па́па *m.*; (*bishop*) епи́скоп; (*chief priest*) первосвяще́нник.

pontoon[1] *n.* понто́н; *p. bridge*, понто́нный мост (мо́ста́, *loc.* -у́; *pl.* -ы́).

pontoon[2] *n.* (*cards*) два́дцать одно́.

pony *n.* по́ни *m.indecl.*

poodle *n.* пу́дель (*pl.* -ли & -ля́) *m.*

pooh *interj.* фу! **pooh-pooh** *v.t.* пренебрега́ть *imp.*, пренебре́чь (-егу́, -ежёшь; -ёг, -егла́) *perf.* + *instr.*

pool[1] *n.* (*of water*) прудо́к (-дка́), лу́жа; (*swimming p.*) бассе́йн.

pool[2] *n.* (*collective stakes*) совоку́пность ста́вок; (*common fund*) о́бщий фонд; (*common resources*) объединённые запа́сы *m.pl.*; *car p.*, автоба́за; *typing p.*, машинопи́сное бюро́ *neut. indecl.*; *v.t.* объединя́ть *imp.*, объедини́ть *perf.*

poop *n.* полую́т; (*stern*) корма́.

poor *adj.* бе́дный (-ден, -дна́, -дно, бе́дны́); (*bad*) плохо́й (плох, -а́, -о, пло́хи́); (*scanty*) ску́дный (-ден, -дна́, -дно); (*weak*) сла́бый (слаб, -а́, -о); *n.*: *the p.*, беднота́, бедняки́ *m.pl.*; *p.-house*, рабо́тный дом (*pl.* -а́); *p.-spirited*, малоду́шный. **poorly** *predic.* нездоро́в (-а, -о).

pop[1] *v.i.* хло́пать *imp.*, хло́пнуть *perf.*; щёлкать *imp.*, щёлкнуть *perf.*; *v.t.* бы́стро всу́нуть *perf.* (into, в + *acc.*); *p. in on*, забега́ть *imp.*, забежа́ть (-егу́, -ежи́шь) *perf.* к + *dat.*; *n.* хлопо́к (-пка́), щёлк; (*drink*) шипу́чий напи́ток (-тка). **popgun** *n.* (*toy*) пуга́ч (-а́).

pop[2] *adj.* популя́рный, поп-; *p. art*,

поп-а́рт; *p. concert*, конце́рт поп-му́зыки; *p. music*, поп-му́зыка.
pope *n.* па́па ри́мский *m.* **popery** *n.* папи́зм. **popish** *adj.* папи́стский.
poplar *n.* то́поль (*pl.* -ля́) *m.*
poppet *n.* кро́шка.
poppy *n.* мак; *p.-seed*, (*collect.*) мак (-а(у)).
poppycock *n.* чепуха́.
populace *n.* просто́й наро́д. **popular** *adj.* наро́дный; (*liked*) популя́рный. **popularity** *n.* популя́рность. **popularize** *v.t.* популяризи́ровать *imp.*, *perf.* **populate** *v.t.* населя́ть *imp.*, насели́ть *perf.* **population** *n.* населе́ние. **populous** *adj.* (много)лю́дный.
porcelain *n.* фарфо́р; *attrib.* фарфо́ровый.
porch *n.* подъе́зд, крыльцо́ (*pl.* -льца, -ле́ц, -льца́м).
porcupine *n.* дикобра́з.
pore[1] *n.* по́ра.
pore[2] *v.i.*: *p. over*, погружа́ться *imp.*, погрузи́ться (-ужу́сь, -у́зи́шься) *perf.* в + *acc.*
pork *n.* свини́на; *p.-butcher*, колба́сник; *p. pie*, пиро́г (-а́) со свини́ной.
pornographic *adj.* порнографи́ческий. **pornography** *n.* порногра́фия.
porous *adj.* по́ристый.
porphyry *n.* порфи́р.
porpoise *n.* морска́я свинья́ (*pl.* -ньи, -не́й, -ньям).
porridge *n.* ка́ша.
port[1] *n.* (*harbour*) порт (*loc.* -у́; *pl.* -ы, -о́в); (*town*) порто́вый го́род (*pl.* -а́).
port[2] *n.* (*naut.*, *aeron.*) ле́вый борт (*loc.* -у́).
port[3] *n.* (*wine*) портве́йн (-а(у)).
portable *adj.* портати́вный.
portal *n.* порта́л.
portcullis *n.* опускна́я решётка.
portend *v.t.* предвеща́ть *imp.* **portent** *n.* предзнаменова́ние. **portentous** *adj.* злове́щий.
porter[1] *n.* (*gate-*, *door-*, *keeper*) швейца́р, приврáтник; *p.'s lodge*, швейца́рская *sb.*, до́мик приврáтника.
porter[2] *n.* (*carrier*) носи́льщик.
porter[3] *n.* (*beer*) по́ртер.
portfolio *n.* портфе́ль *m.*
porthole *n.* иллюмина́тор.
portico *n.* по́ртик.
portion *n.* часть (*pl.* -ти, -те́й), до́ля (*pl.* -ли, -ле́й); (*of food*) по́рция; *v.t.*: *p. out*, разделя́ть *imp.*, раздели́ть (-лю́, -лишь) *perf.*
portly *adj.* доро́дный.
portmanteau *n.* чемода́н; *p. word*, сло́во-гибри́д.
portrait *n.* портре́т. **portraiture** *n.* портре́тная жи́вопись. **portray** *v.t.* рисова́ть *imp.*, на~ *perf.*; изобража́ть *imp.*, изобрази́ть *perf.* **portrayal** *n.* рисова́ние, изображе́ние.
Portuguese *n.* португа́лец (-льца), -лка; *adj.* португа́льский.
pose *n.* по́за; *v.t.* (*question*) ста́вить *imp.*, по~ *perf.*; *v.i.* пози́ровать *imp.*; *p. as*, принима́ть *imp.*, приня́ть (приму́, -мешь; при́нял, -а́, -о) *perf.* по́зу + *gen.*
poser *n.* тру́дный вопро́с, тру́дная зада́ча.
poseur *n.* позёр. **poseuse** *n.* позёрка.
posh *adj.* шика́рный.
posit *v.t.* (*assume*) постули́ровать *imp.*, *perf.*
position *n.* положе́ние, пози́ция; *in a p. to*, в состоя́нии + *inf.*; *v.t.* ста́вить *imp.*, по~ *perf.* **positional** *adj.* позицио́нный.
positive *adj.* положи́тельный; (*person*) уве́ренный (-ен, -енна); (*proof*) несомне́нный (-нен, -нна); (*phot.*) позити́вный; *n.* (*phot.*) позити́в. **positivism** *n.* позитиви́зм. **positron** *n.* позитро́н.
posse *n.* отря́д (шери́фа).
possess *v.t.* облада́ть *imp.* + *instr.*; владе́ть *imp.* + *instr.*; (*of feeling etc.*) овладева́ть *imp.*, овладе́ть *perf.* + *instr.* **possessed** *adj.* одержи́мый. **possession** *n.* владе́ние (of, + *instr.*); *pl.* со́бственность. **possessive** *adj.* со́бственнический; (*gram.*) притяжа́тельный. **possessor** *n.* облада́тель *m.*, ~ница.
possibility *n.* возмо́жность. **possible** *adj.* возмо́жный; *as much as p.*, ско́лько возмо́жно; *as soon as p.*, как мо́жно скоре́е; *n.* возмо́жное *sb.* **possibly** *adv.* возмо́жно, мо́жет (быть).
post[1] *n.* (*pole*) столб (-а́); *v.t.* (*p. up*) выве́шивать *imp.*, вы́весить *perf.*

post[2] *n.* (*station*) пост (-á, *loc.* на -ý); (*trading-p.*) фактóрия; *v.t.* (*station*) расставлять *imp.*, расстáвить *perf.*; (*appoint*) назначáть *imp.*, назнáчить *perf.*

post[3] *n.* (*letters, p. office, etc.*) пóчта; *by return of p.*, с обрáтной пóчтой; *attrib.* почтóвый; *p.-box*, почтóвый ящик; *p.-code*, почтóвый индекс; *p.-free*, без почтóвой оплáты; *P. Office*, (*ministry*) Министéрство связи; *p. office*, пóчта, почтóвое отделéние; *General P. Office*, (глáвный) почтáмт; *p.-paid*, с оплáченными почтóвыми расхóдами; *v.t.* (*send by p.*) отправлять *imp.*, отпрáвить *perf.* по пóчте; (*put in p.-box*) опускáть *imp.*, опустить (-ущý, -ýстишь) в почтóвый ящик. **postage** *n.* почтóвая оплáта, почтóвые расхóды *m.pl.*; *p. stamp*, почтóвая мáрка. **postal** *adj.* почтóвый; *p.-order*, почтóвый перевóд. **postcard** *n.* открытка.

post-date *v.t.* датировать *imp., perf.* бóлее пóздним числóм.

poster *n.* афиша, плакáт.

poste restante *n.* (*in address*) до востребования.

posterior *adj.* (*later*) послéдующий; (*hinder*) зáдний; *n.* зад (*loc.* -ý; *pl.* -ы́).

posterity *n.* (*descendants*) потóмство; (*later generations*) послéдующие поколéния *neut.pl.*

postern *n.* зáдняя дверь (*loc.* -ри́; *pl.* -ри, -рéй, *instr.* -рями & -рьми́).

postface *n.* послеслóвие.

post-graduate *n.* аспирáнт; *adj.* аспирáнтский; *p. course*, аспирантýра.

posthumous *adj.* посмéртный.

postlude *n.* постлю́дия.

postman *n.* почтальóн. **postmark** *n.* почтóвый штéмпель (*pl.* -ля́) *m.*; *v.t.* штемпелевáть (-лю́ю, -лю́ешь) *imp.*, за~ *perf.* **postmaster, -mistress** *n.* начáльник почтóвого отделéния.

post-mortem *adj.* посмéртный; *n.* вскрытие трýпа.

postpone *v.t.* отсрóчивать *imp.*, отсрóчить *perf.* **postponement** *n.* отсрóчка.

postprandial *adj.* послеобéденный.

postscript *n.* постскри́птум.

postulate *n.* постулáт; *v.t.* постули́ровать *imp., perf.*

posture *n.* пóза, положéние; *v.i.* рисовáться *imp.*

post-war *adj.* послевоéнный.

posy *n.* букéтик.

pot *n.* горшóк (-шкá), котелóк (-лкá); (*as prize*) кýбок (-бка); *pots of money*, кýча дéнег; *p.-bellied*, пузáтый; *p.-belly*, пýзо; *p.-boiler*, халтýра; (*person*) халтýрщик; *p.-roast*, тушёное мясо; тушить (-шý, -шишь) *imp.*; *p.-shot*, выстрел наугáд; *v.t.* (*food*) консерви́ровать *imp.*, за~ *perf.*; (*plant*) сажáть *imp.*, посади́ть (-ажý, -áдишь) *perf.* в горшóк; (*billiards*) загонять *imp.*, загнáть (загоню́, -нишь; загнáл, -á, -о) *perf.* в лýзу.

potash *n.* потáш (-á). **potassium** *n.* кáлий.

potato *n.* (*plant*; *pl. collect.*) картóфель *m.* (*no pl.*); картóфелина; картóшка (also *collect.*; *coll.*); *two potatoes*, две картóфелины, картóшки.

potence, -cy *n.* си́ла, могýщество; (*of drug etc.*) дéйственность. **potent** *adj.* (*reason etc.*) убеди́тельный; (*drug etc.*) сильнодéйствующий; (*mighty*) могýщественный (-ен, -енна). **potentate** *n.* властели́н.

potential *adj.* потенциáльный, возмóжный; *n.* потенциáл, возмóжность. **potentially** *n.* потенциáльность.

pot-hole *n.* пещéра; (*in road*) выбоина. **pot-holer** *n.* пещéрник.

potion *n.* дóза лекáрства, зéлье.

pot-pourri *n.* попурри́ *neut.indecl.*

potsherd *n.* черепóк (-пкá).

potter[1] *v.i.*: *p. at, in*, рабóтать *imp.* кóе-как над+*instr.*; *p. about*, лóдырничать *imp.*

potter[2] *n.* гончáр (-á). **pottery** *n.* (*goods*) гончáрные издéлия *neut.pl.*; (*place*) гончáрная *sb.*

potty[1] *adj.* (*trivial*) пустякóвый; (*crazy*) помéшанный (-ан) (about, на+*prep.*).

potty[2] *n.* ночнóй горшóк (-шкá).

pouch *n.* сýмка, мешóк (-шкá).

pouffe *n.* пуф.

poulterer *n.* торгóвец (-вца) домáшней пти́цей.

poultice *n.* припа́рка; *v.t.* ста́вить *imp.*, по~ *perf.* припа́рку + *dat.*
poultry *n.* дома́шняя пти́ца; *p.-farm*, птицефе́рма.
pounce *v.i.*: *p.* (*up*)*on*, налета́ть *imp.*, налете́ть (-ечу́, -ети́шь) *perf.* на + *acc.*; набра́сываться *imp.*, набро́ситься *perf.* на + *acc.*; (*fig.*) ухвати́ться (-ачу́сь, -а́тишься) *perf.* за + *acc.*
pound[1] *n.* (*measure*) фунт; *p. sterling*, фунт сте́рлингов.
pound[2] *n.* (*enclosure*) заго́н.
pound[3] *v.t.* (*crush*) толо́чь (-лку́, -лчёшь; -ло́к, -лкла́) *imp.*, ис~, рас~ *perf.*; (*strike*) колоти́ть (-очу́, -о́тишь) *imp.*, по~ *perf.* по + *dat.*, в + *acc.*; *v.i.* (*heart*) колоти́ться (-ится) *imp.*; *p. along*, тяжело́ ходи́ть (хожу́, хо́дишь) *imp.*; (*run*) тяжело́ бе́гать *imp.*; *p. away at*, (*with guns*) обстре́ливать *imp.*, обстреля́ть *perf.*
pour *v.t.* лить (лью, льёшь; лил, -а́, -о); *p. out*, налива́ть *imp.*, нали́ть (налью, -ьёшь; на́ли́л, -а́, -о) *perf.*; *v.i.* ли́ться (льётся; ли́лся, лила́сь, ли́ло́сь) *imp.*; *it is pouring*, (*with rain*) дождь льёт как из ведра́. **pouring** *adj.* (*rain*) проливно́й.
pout *v.t.* & *i.* надува́ть(ся) *imp.*, наду́ть(ся) (-у́ю(сь), -у́ешь(ся)) *perf.*
poverty *n.* бе́дность, убо́гость; *p.-stricken*, убо́гий.
P.O.W. *abbr.* военнопле́нный *sb.*
powder *n.* порошо́к (-шка́); (*cosmetic*) пу́дра; (*gun-p.*) по́рох (-а(у)); *p.-blue*, се́ро-голубо́й; *p. compact*, пу́дреница; *p.-flask*, пороховни́ца; *p.-magazine*, пороховой по́греб (*pl.* -а́); *p.-puff*, пухо́вка; *v.t.* (*sprinkle with p.*) посыпа́ть *imp.*, посы́пать (-плю, -плешь) *perf.* порошко́м; (*nose etc.*) пу́дрить *imp.*, на~ *perf.*; *powdered milk*, моло́чный порошо́к (-шка́). **powdery** *adj.* порошкообра́зный.
power *n.* (*vigour*) си́ла; (*might*) могу́щество; (*ability*) спосо́бность; (*control*) власть; (*authorization*) полномо́чие; (*State*) держа́ва; (*math.*) сте́пень (*pl.* -ни, -не́й); *attrib.* силово́й, механи́ческий; *party in p.*, па́ртия у вла́сти; *p. of attorney*, дове́ренность; *p. cut*, прекраще́ние пода́чи эне́ргии; *p. point*, ште́псель (*pl.* -ля́) *m.*; *p.-station*, электроста́нция. **powerful** *adj.* си́льный (си́лён, -льна́, -льно, си́льны́); могу́щественный (-ен, -енна). **powerless** *adj.* бесси́льный.
practicable *adj.* осуществи́мый; (*theat.*) настоя́щий. **practical** *adj.* (*of practice*) практи́ческий; (*useful in practice*; *person*) практи́чный; *p. joke*, гру́бая шу́тка. **practically** *adv.* (*in effect*) факти́чески; (*almost*) почти́. **practice** *n.* пра́ктика; (*custom*) обы́чай; (*exercise*) упражне́ние; *in p.*, на де́ле; *put into p.*, осуществля́ть *imp.*, осуществи́ть *perf.*; *attrib.* уче́бный. **practise** *v.t.* (*carry out*) применя́ть *imp.*, примени́ть (-ню́, -нишь) *perf.* на пра́ктике; (*also abs. of doctor etc.*) практикова́ть *imp.*; (*engage in*) занима́ться *imp.*, заня́ться (займу́сь, -мёшься; заня́лся́, -яла́сь) *perf.* + *instr.*; упражня́ться *imp.* в + *prep.*, (*mus. instrument*, в игре́ на + *prep.*). **practised** *adj.* о́пытный. **practitioner** *n.* (*doctor*) практику́ющий врач (-а́); (*lawyer*) практику́ющий юри́ст; *general p.*, врач (-а́) о́бщей пра́ктики.
pragmatic *adj.* прагмати́ческий. **pragmatism** *n.* прагмати́зм. **pragmatist** *n.* прагма́тик.
prairie *n.* степь (*loc.* -пи́; *pl.* -пи, -пе́й); (*in N. America*) пре́рия.
praise *v.t.* хвали́ть (-лю́, -лишь) *imp.*, по~ *perf.*; *n.* похвала́. **praiseworthy** *adj.* похва́льный.
pram *n.* де́тская коля́ска.
prance *v.i.* (*horse*) станови́ться (-ится) *imp.*, стать (ста́нет) *perf.* на дыбы́; (*fig.*) задава́ться (-даю́сь, -даёшься) *imp.*
prank *n.* вы́ходка, ша́лость.
prate *v.i.* болта́ть *imp.*
prattle *v.i.* лепета́ть (-ечу́, -е́чешь); *n.* ле́пет.
prawn *n.* креве́тка.
pray *v.t.* моли́ть (-лю́, -лишь) *imp.* (for, о + *prep.*); *v.i.* моли́ться (-лю́сь, -лишься) *imp.*, по~ *perf.* (to, + *dat.*; for, о + *prep.*). **prayer** *n.* моли́тва; *p.-book*, моли́твенник.

preach *v.t.* пропове́довать *imp.*; *v.i.* произноси́ть (-ошу́, -о́сишь) *imp.*, произнести́ (-есу́, -есёшь; -ёс, -есла́) *perf.* про́поведь. **preacher** *n.* пропове́дник.
preamble *n.* преа́мбула.
pre-arrange *v.t.* зара́нее плани́ровать *imp.*, за~ *perf.* **pre-arrangement** *n.* предвари́тельная договорённость.
precarious *adj.* ненадёжный; (*insecure*) непро́чный (-чен, -чна́, -чно).
pre-cast *adj.* сбо́рный.
precaution *n.* предосторо́жность; (*action*) ме́ра предосторо́жности.
precede *v.t.* предше́ствовать *imp.* + *dat.* **precedence** *n.* предше́ствование; (*seniority*) старшинство́. **precedent** *n.* преце́дент.
precept *n.* наставле́ние.
precinct *n.* огоро́женное ме́сто; *pl.* окре́стности *f.pl.*; (*boundary*) преде́л.
precious *adj.* драгоце́нный (-нен, -нна); (*beloved*) дорого́й (до́рог, -а́, -о); (*refined*) изы́сканный (-ан, -анна); *adv.* о́чень, весьма́.
precipice *n.* обры́в; (*also fig.*) про́пасть. **precipitate** *n.* оса́док (-дка); *adj.* стреми́тельный; (*person*) опроме́тчивый; *v.t.* (*throw down*) низверга́ть *imp.*, низве́ргнуть (-г) *perf.*; (*hurry*) ускоря́ть *imp.*, уско́рить *perf.*; (*chem.*) осажда́ть *imp.*, осади́ть (-ажу́, -а́дишь) *perf.* **precipitation** *n.* низверже́ние; ускоре́ние; осажде́ние; (*hastiness*) стреми́тельность; (*meteorol.*) оса́дки *m.pl.* **precipitous** *adj.* обры́вистый.
précis *n.* конспе́кт.
precise *adj.* то́чный (-чен, -чна́, -чно). **precisely** *adv.* то́чно; (*in answer*) и́менно, то́чно так. **precision** *n.* то́чность; *adj.* то́чный.
pre-classical *adj.* доклассѝческий.
preclude *v.t.* предотвраща́ть *imp.*, предотврати́ть (-ащу́, -ати́шь) *perf.*
precocious *adj.* не по года́м развито́й (ра́звит, -а́, -о); ра́но разви́вшийся. **precocity** *n.* ра́ннее разви́тие.
preconceived *adj.* предвзя́тый. **preconception** *n.* предвзя́тое мне́ние.
pre-condition *n.* предпосы́лка.
precursor *n.* предте́ча *m.* & *f.*, предше́ственник.
predator *n.* хи́щник. **predatory** *adj.* хи́щнический; (*animal*) хи́щный.
predecease *v.t.* умира́ть *imp.*, умере́ть (умру́, -рёшь; у́мер, -ла́, -ло) *perf.* ра́ньше + *gen.*
predecessor *n.* предше́ственник, -ица.
predestination *n.* предопределе́ние. **predestine** *v.t.* предопределя́ть *imp.*, предопредели́ть *perf.*
predetermine *v.t.* предреша́ть *imp.*, предреши́ть *perf.*; предопределя́ть *imp.*, предопредели́ть *perf.*
predicament *n.* затрудни́тельное положе́ние.
predicate *n.* (*gram.*) сказу́емое *sb.*, предика́т. **predicate** *v.t.* утвержда́ть *imp.* **predicative** *adj.* предикати́вный.
predict *v.t.* предска́зывать *imp.*, предсказа́ть (-ажу́, -а́жешь) *perf.* **prediction** *n.* предсказа́ние.
predilection *n.* пристра́стие (for, к + *dat.*).
predispose *v.t.* предрасполага́ть *imp.*, предрасположи́ть (-ожу́, -о́жишь) *perf.* (to, к + *dat.*). **predisposition** *n.* предрасположе́ние (to, к + *dat.*).
predominance *n.* преоблада́ние. **predominant** *adj.* преоблада́ющий. **predominate** *v.i.* преоблада́ть *imp.*
pre-eminence *n.* превосхо́дство. **pre-eminent** *adj.* выдаю́щийся.
pre-empt *v.t.* покупа́ть *imp.*, купи́ть (-плю́, -пишь) *perf.* пре́жде други́х; (*fig.*) завладева́ть *imp.*, завладе́ть *perf.* + *instr.* пре́жде други́х. **pre-emption** *n.* поку́пка пре́жде други́х; (*right*) преиму́щественное пра́во на поку́пку. **pre-emptive** *adj.* преиму́щественный; (*mil.*) упрежда́ющий.
preen *v.t.* (*of bird*) чи́стить *imp.*, по~ *perf.* клю́вом; *p. oneself*, (*smarten*) прихора́шиваться *imp.*; (*be proud*) горди́ться *imp.* собо́й.
pre-fab *n.* сбо́рный дом (*pl.* -а́). **prefabricated** *adj.* заводско́го изготовле́ния; сбо́рный.
preface *n.* предисло́вие; *v.t.* де́лать *imp.*, с~ *perf.* предвари́тельные замеча́ния к + *dat.* **prefatory** *adj.* вступи́тельный.
prefect *n.* префе́кт; (*school*) ста́роста *m.* **prefecture** *n.* префекту́ра.

prefer *v.t.* (*promote*) продвигáть *imp.*, продвúнуть *perf.* (по слýжбе); (*like better*) предпочитáть *imp.*, предпочéсть (-чтý, -чтёшь; -чёл, -члá) *perf.*; *p. a charge against*, выдвигáть *imp.*, вы́двинуть *perf.* обвинéние прóтив + *gen.* **preferable** *adj.* предпочтúтельный. **preference** *n.* предпочтéние; *p. share*, привилегирóванная áкция. **preferential** *adj.* предпочтúтельный; (*econ.*) преференциáльный. **preferment** *n.* продвижéние по слýжбе.

prefiguration *n.* прообраз. **prefigure** *v.t.* служúть (-жý, -жишь) *imp.* прообразом + *gen.*

prefix *n.* пристáвка, прéфикс.

pregnancy *n.* берéменность. **pregnant** *adj.* (*woman*) берéменная; чревáтый (with, + *instr.*), пóлный (-лон, -лнá, пóлнó) (with, + *gen.*).

prehensile *adj.* хватáтельный.

prehistoric *adj.* доисторúческий. **prehistory** *n.* (*of situation etc.*) предыстóрия.

pre-ignition *n.* преждеврéменное зажигáние.

prejudge *v.t.* предрешáть *imp.*, предрешúть *perf.*

prejudice *n.* предрассýдок (-дка); (*bias*) предубеждéние; (*injury*) ущéрб; *without p. to*, без ущéрба для + *gen.*; *v.t.* наносúть (-ошý, -óсишь) *imp.*, нанестú (-есý, -есёшь; -ёс, -еслá) *perf.* ущéрб + *dat.*; *p. against*, восстанáвливать *imp.*, восстановúть (-влю́, -вишь) *perf.* прóтив + *gen.*; *p. in favour of*, располагáть *imp.*, расположúть (-жý, -жишь) *perf.* в пóльзу + *gen.*

prelate *n.* прелáт.

prelim *n.*: *pl.* (*print.*) сбóрный лист (-á). **preliminary** *adj.* предварúтельный; *n.*: *pl.* (*discussion*) предварúтельные переговóры *m.pl.*

prelude *n.* вступлéние; (*mus.*; *fig.*) прелю́дия.

pre-marital *adj.* добрáчный.

premature *adj.* преждеврéменный (-нен, -нна).

premeditated *adj.* преднамéренный (-ен, -енна). **premeditation** *n.* преднамéренность.

premier *adj.* пéрвый; *n.* премьéр-минúстр. **première** *n.* премьéра.

premise, premiss *n.* (*logic*) (пред)посы́лка. **premises** *n.* помещéние.

premium *n.* прéмия.

premonition *n.* предчýвствие. **premonitory** *adj.* предупреждáющий.

pre-natal *adj.* предродовóй.

preoccupation *n.* озабóченность. **preoccupied** *adj.* озабóченный (-ен, -енна). **preoccupy** *v.t.* поглощáть *imp.*, поглотúть (-ощý, -óтишь) *perf.* внимáние + *gen.*

pre-ordain *v.t.* предопределя́ть *imp.*, предопределúть *perf.*

prep *n.* приготовлéние урóков; *adj.*: *p. school*, приготовúтельная шкóла.

pre-pack(age) *v.t.* расфасóвывать *imp.*, расфасовáть *perf.*

prepaid *adj.* оплáченный (-ен) вперёд.

preparation *n.* приготовлéние; *pl.* подготóвка (for, к + *dat.*); (*medicine etc.*) препарáт. **preparatory** *adj.* под-, при-, готовúтельный; *p. to*, прéжде чем. **prepare** *v.t.* & *i.* при-, под-, готáвливать(ся) *imp.*, при-, под-, готóвить(ся) *perf.* (for, к + *dat.*). **prepared** *adj.* готóвый.

preponderance *n.* перевéс. **preponderant** *adj.* преобладáющий. **preponderate** *v.i.* имéть *imp.* перевéс.

preposition *n.* предлóг. **prepositional** *adj.* предлóжный.

prepossess *v.t.* предрасполагáть *imp.*, предрасположúть (-жý, -жишь) *perf.* (in favour of, к + *dat.*). **prepossessing** *adj.* привлекáтельный.

preposterous *adj.* (*absurd*) нелéпый, абсýрдный.

prepuce *n.* крáйняя плоть.

pre-record *v.t.* предварúтельно записывать *imp.*, записáть (-ишý, -úшешь) *perf.*

prerequisite *n.* предпосы́лка.

prerogative *n.* прерогатúва.

presage *n.* предвéстник, предзнаменовáние; (*foreboding*) предчýвствие; *v.t.* предвещáть *imp.*

presbyter *n.* пресвúтер. **Presbyterian** *n.* пресвитериáнин (*pl.* -áне, -áн), -áнка; *adj.* пресвитериáнский. **presbytery** *n.* пресвитéрия.

prescience *n.* предви́дение. **prescient** *adj.* предви́дящий.

prescribe *v.t.* устана́вливать *imp.*, установи́ть (-влю́, -вишь) *perf.*; (*med.*) пропи́сывать *imp.*, прописа́ть (-ишу́, -и́шешь) *perf.* (to, for, (*person*) + *dat.*; for, (*complaint*) про́тив + *gen.*). **prescription** *n.* устано́вка; (*med.*) реце́пт.

presence *n.* прису́тствие; (*appearance*) (вне́шний) вид; *p. of mind*, прису́тствие ду́ха. **present** *adj.* прису́тствующий; (*being dealt with*) да́нный; (*existing now*) ны́нешний; (*also gram.*) настоя́щий; *predic.* налицо́; *be p.*, прису́тствовать *imp.* (at, на + *prep.*); *p.-day*, ны́нешний, совреме́нный (-нен, -нна); *n.*: *the p.*, настоя́щее *sb.*; (*gram.*) настоя́шее вре́мя *neut.*; (*gift*) пода́рок (-рка); *at p.*, в настоя́щее, да́нное, вре́мя *neut.*; *for the p.*, пока́; *v.t.* (*introduce*) представля́ть *imp.*, предста́вить *perf.* (to, + *dat.*); (*hand in*) подава́ть (-даю́, -даёшь) *imp.*, пода́ть (-а́м, -а́шь, -а́ст, -ади́м; по́дал, -а́, -о) *perf.*; (*a play*) ста́вить *imp.*, по~ *perf.*; (*a gift*) подноси́ть (-ошу́, -о́сишь) *imp.*, поднести́ (-есу́, -есёшь; -ёс, -есла́) *perf.* + *dat.* (with, + *acc.*); *p. arms*, брать (беру́, -рёшь; брал, -а́, -о) *imp.*, взять (возьму́, -мёшь; взял, -а́, -о) *perf.* ору́жие на карау́л; (*command*) на карау́л!; *p. oneself*, явля́ться *imp.*, яви́ться (явлю́сь, я́вишься) *perf.* **presentable** *adj.* прили́чный. **presentation** *n.* представле́ние, подноше́ние.

presentiment *n.* предчу́вствие.

presently *adv.* вско́ре, сейча́с.

preservation *n.* сохране́ние, предохране́ние; (*state of p.*) сохра́нность; (*of game etc.*) охра́на. **preservative** *adj.* предохрани́тельный; *n.* предохраня́ющее сре́дство. **preserve** *v.t.* (*keep safe*) сохраня́ть *imp.*, сохрани́ть *perf.*; (*maintain*; *p. fruit etc.*) храни́ть *imp.*; (*food*) консерви́ровать *imp.*, за~ *perf.*; (*game*) охраня́ть *imp.*, охрани́ть *perf.*; *n.* (*for game, fish*) охо́тничий, рыболо́вный, запове́дник; *pl.* консе́рвы (-вов) *pl.*; (*jam*) джем, варе́нье.

preside *v.i.* председа́тельствовать *imp.* (at, на + *prep.*). **presidency** *n.* председа́тельство, президе́нтство. **president** *n.* председа́тель *m.*, президе́нт. **presidential** *adj.* президе́нтский. **presidium** *n.* прези́диум.

press[1] *n.* (*of people*) толпа́; (*of affairs*) спе́шка; (*machine*) пресс; (*printing-p.*) печа́тный стано́к (-нка́); (*printing firm*) типогра́фия; (*publishing house*) изда́тельство; (*the p.*) пре́сса, печа́ть; (*cupboard*) шкаф (*loc.* -у́; *pl.* -ы́); *p. attaché*, пресс-атташе́ *m.indecl.*; *p. conference*, пресс-конфере́нция; *p.-cutting*, газе́тная вы́резка; *p.-mark*, шифр; *p. photographer* фотокорреспонде́нт; *v.t.* жать (жму, жмёшь) *imp.*; (*p. down on*) нажима́ть *imp.*, нажа́ть (-жму́, -жмёшь) *perf.* + *acc.*, на + *acc.*; (*clasp*) прижима́ть *imp.*, прижа́ть (-жму́, -жмёшь) *perf.* (to, к + *dat.*); (*with iron*) гла́дить *imp.*, вы́~ *perf.*; (*oppress, p. on*) тяготи́ть (-ощу́, -оти́шь) *imp.*; (*insist on*) наста́ивать *imp.*, настоя́ть (-ою́, -ои́шь) *perf.* на + *prep.*; *p. forward*, продвига́ться *imp.*, продви́нуться *perf.* вперёд; *p.-stud*, кно́пка.

press[2] *v.t.* (*hist.*) наси́льственно вербова́ть *imp.*, за~, на~ *perf.* во флот; *p. into service*, по́льзоваться *imp.* + *instr.*; *p.-gang*, отря́д вербо́вщиков.

pressing *adj.* (*urgent*) неотло́жный; (*persistent*) настоя́тельный. **pressure** *n.* давле́ние, нажи́м; *p.-cooker*, скорова́рка; *p.-gauge*, мано́метр. **pressurized** *adj.* (*aircraft cabin etc.*) гермети́ческий.

prestige *n.* прести́ж.

pre-stressed *adj.* предвари́тельно напряжённый (-ён, -ённа).

presumably *adv.* вероя́тно, предположи́тельно. **presume** *v.t.* счита́ть *imp.* дока́занным; полага́ть *imp.*; (*venture*) позволя́ть *imp.* себе́. **presumption** *n.* предположе́ние; (*arrogance*) самонаде́янность. **presumptive** *adj.* предполага́емый. **presumptuous** *adj.* самонаде́янный (-ян, -янна), наха́льный.

presuppose *v.t.* предполага́ть *imp.*

pretence *n.* притво́рство. **pretend** *v.t.* притворя́ться *imp.*, притвори́ться *perf.* (to be, +*instr.*); де́лать *imp.*, с~ *perf.* вид (что); *v.i.*: *p. to*, претендова́ть *imp.* на+*acc.* **pretender** *n.* претенде́нт. **pretension** *n.* прете́нзия. **pretentious** *adj.* претенцио́зный.

preternatural *adj.* сверхъесте́ственный (-ен, -енна).

pretext *n.* предло́г.

pretonic *adj.* предуда́рный.

prettiness *n.* милови́дность. **pretty** *adj.* милови́дный; (*also iron.*) хоро́шенький; *a p. penny*, кру́гленькая су́мма; *adv.* дово́льно.

prevail *v.i.* (*predominate*) преоблада́ть *imp.*; *p.* (*up*)*on*, угова́ривать *imp.*, уговори́ть *perf.* **prevailing** *adj.* преоблада́ющий. **prevalent** *adj.* распространённый (-ён, -ена́).

prevaricate *v.i.* говори́ть *imp.* уклончиво.

prevent *v.t.* предупрежда́ть *imp.*, предупреди́ть *perf.*; меша́ть *imp.*, по~ *perf.* +*dat.* **prevention** *n.* предупрежде́ние. **preventive** *adj.* предупреди́тельный; (*med.*) профилакти́ческий.

preview *n.* предвари́тельный просмо́тр.

previous *adj.* предыду́щий; *adv.*: *p. to*, пре́жде чем. **previously** *adv.* зара́нее, пре́жде.

pre-war *adj.* довое́нный.

prey *n.* (*animal*) добы́ча; (*victim*) же́ртва (to, +*gen.*); *bird of p.*, хи́щная пти́ца; *v.i.*: *p.* (*up*)*on*, (*emotion etc.*) му́чить *imp.*

price *n.* цена́ (*acc.* -ну; *pl.* -ны); *at any p.*, любо́й ценой, во что́ бы то ни ста́ло; *at a p.*, по дорого́й цене́; *not at any p.*, ни за что́; *what p. . . .*, каки́е ша́нсы на+*acc.*; *p.-list*, прейскура́нт; *v.t.* назнача́ть *imp.*, назна́чить *perf.* це́ну+*gen.*; (*fig.*) оце́нивать *imp.*, оцени́ть (-ню́, -нишь) *perf.* **priceless** *adj.* бесце́нный.

prick *v.t.* коло́ть (-лю́, -лешь) *imp.*, ука́лывать *imp.*, уколо́ть (-лю́, -лешь) *perf.*; (*conscience*) му́чить *imp.*; *p. out*, (*plants*) пики́ровать *imp.*, *perf.*; *p. up one's ears*, навостри́ть *perf.* у́ши; *n.* уко́л. **pricker** *n.* ши́ло (*pl.* -лья, -льев). **prickle** *n.* (*thorn*) колю́чка; (*spine*) игла́ (*pl.* -лы). **prickly** *adj.* колю́чий; *p. heat*, потни́ца; *p. pear*, опу́нция.

pride *n.* го́рдость; (*of lions*) прайд; *take a p. in*, *p. oneself on*, горди́ться *imp.*+*instr.*

priest *n.* свяще́нник; (*non-Christian*) жрец (-а́). **priestess** *n.* жри́ца. **priesthood** *n.* свяще́нство. **priestly** *adj.* свяще́ннический.

prig *n.* самодово́льный педа́нт. **priggish** *adj.* педанти́чный.

prim *adj.* чо́порный.

primacy *n.* пе́рвенство. **primarily** *adv.* первонача́льно; (*above all*) пре́жде всего́. **primary** *adj.* перви́чный; (*chief*) основно́й; *p. colour*, основно́й цвет (*pl.* -а́); *p. feather*, махово́е перо́ (*pl.* -рья, -рьев); *p. school*, нача́льная шко́ла. **primate** *n.* при́ма́с; (*zool.*) прима́т. **prime** *n.* расцве́т; *in one's p.*, *in the p. of life*, в расцве́те сил; *adj.* (*chief*) гла́вный; (*excellent*) превосхо́дный; (*primary*) перви́чный; *p. cost*, себесто́имость; *p. minister*, премье́р-мини́стр; *p. number*, просто́е число́ (*pl.* -сла, -сел, -слам); *v.t.* (*engine*) заправля́ть *imp.*, запра́вить *perf.*; (*with information etc.*) зара́нее снабжа́ть *imp.*, снабди́ть *perf.* (with, +*instr.*); (*with paint etc.*) грунтова́ть *imp.*, за~ *perf.* **primer** *n.* буква́рь (-ря́) *m.*; (*textbook*) уче́бник; (*paint etc.*) грунт. **prim(a)eval** *adj.* первобы́тный. **priming** *n.* (*with paint etc.*) грунто́вка. **primitive** *adj.* первобы́тный, примити́вный. **primogeniture** *n.* первоstartро́дство. **primordial** *adj.* первобы́тный; (*original*) иско́нный.

primrose *n.* первоцве́т; (*colour*) бле́дно-жёлтый цвет.

primula *n.* первоцве́т.

primus (stove) *n.* при́мус (*pl.* -ы & -а́).

prince *n.* (*in W. Europe*) принц; (*in Russia*) князь (*pl.* -зья́, -зе́й). **princely** *adj.* кня́жеский; (*splendid*) великоле́пный. **princess** *n.* принце́сса; (*wife*) княги́ня; (*daughter*) княжна́ (*gen.pl.* -жо́н). **principality** *n.* кня́жество.

principal *adj.* гла́вный, основно́й; *n.* нача́льник, -ица; (*of school*) дире́ктор (*pl.* -а́); (*econ.*) капита́л. **principally**

adv. гла́вным о́бразом, преиму́щественно.

principle *n.* при́нцип; *in p.*, в при́нципе; *on p.*, принципиа́льно. **principled** *adj.* принципиа́льный.

print *n.* (*mark*) след (*pl.* -ы́); (*also phot.*) отпеча́ток (-тка); (*fabric*) си́тец (-тца(у)); (*print.*) печа́ть; (*picture*) гравю́ра, эста́мп; *in p.*, в прода́же; *out of p.*, распро́данный (-ан); *v.t.* (*impress*) запечатлева́ть *imp.*, запечатле́ть *perf.*; (*book etc.*) печа́тать *imp.*, на~ *perf.*; (*write*) писа́ть (пишу́, -шешь) *imp.*, на~ *perf.* печа́тными бу́квами; (*fabric*) набива́ть *imp.*, наби́ть (-бью́, -бьёшь) *perf.*; (*phot.*; *p. out*, *off*) отпеча́тывать *imp.*, отпеча́тать *perf.*; *p. out*, (*of computer etc.*) распеча́тывать *imp.*, распеча́тать *perf.*; *p.-out*, распеча́тка, табуляграмма. **printed** *adj.* печа́тный; (*fabric*) набивно́й; *p. circuit*, печа́тная схе́ма; *p. matter*, бандеро́ль. **printer** *n.* печа́тник, типо́граф; (*of fabric*) набо́йщик; *p.'s ink*, типогра́фская кра́ска. **printing** *n.* печа́тание, печа́ть; *p.-press*, печа́тный стано́к (-нка́).

prior *n.* настоя́тель *m.*; *adj.* (*earlier*) пре́жний, предше́ствующий; (*more important*) бо́лее ва́жный; *adv.*: *p. to*, до+*gen.* **prioress** *n.* настоя́тельница. **priority** *n.* приорите́т; *in order of p.*, в поря́дке очерёдности. **priory** *n.* монасты́рь (-ря́) *m.*

prise *see* **prize**[3].

prism *n.* при́зма. **prismatic** *adj.* призмати́ческий.

prison *n.* тюрьма́ (*pl.* -рьмы, -рем, -рьмам); *attrib.*; тюре́мный; *p.-breaking*, побе́г из тюрьмы́; *p. camp*, ла́герь (*pl.* -ря́) *m.* **prisoner** *n.* заключённый *sb.*; (*p. of war*) (военно)пле́нный *sb.*; *p. of State*, политзаключённый *sb.*

pristine *adj.* (*ancient*) первонача́льный; (*untouched*) нетро́нутый.

privacy *n.* (*seclusion*) уедине́ние; (*private life*) ча́стная жизнь. **private** *adj.* (*personal*) ча́стный, ли́чный; (*unofficial*) неофициа́льный; (*confidential*) конфиденциа́льный; *in p.*, наедине́; в ча́стной жи́зни; *p. view*, закры́тый просмо́тр; *n.* рядово́й *sb.* **privateer** *n.* ка́пер.

privation *n.* лише́ние. **privative** *adj.* (*gram.*) привати́вный.

privet *n.* бирючи́на.

privilege *n.* привиле́гия. **privileged** *adj.* привилегиро́ванный.

privy *adj.* та́йный; *p. to*, прича́стный к+*dat.*, посвящённый (-ён, -ена́) в+*acc.*; *P. Council*, та́йный сове́т.

prize[1] *n.* (*reward*) пре́мия, приз, награ́да; *adj.* удосто́енный пре́мии, награ́ды; *p.-fight*, состяза́ние на приз; *p.-fighter*, боксёр-профессиона́л; *p.-winner*, призёр, лауреа́т; *v.t.* высоко́ цени́ть (-ню́, -нишь) *imp.*

prize[2] *n.* (*ship*) приз.

prize[3] *v.t.*: *p. open*, взла́мывать *imp.*, взлома́ть *perf.* с по́мощью рычага́.

pro[1] *n.*: *pros and cons*, до́воды *m.pl.* за и про́тив.

pro[2] *n.* (*professional*) профессиона́л; (спортсме́н-)профессиона́л.

probability *n.* вероя́тность, правдоподо́бие; *in all p.*, по всей вероя́тности. **probable** *adj.* вероя́тный, правдоподо́бный. **probably** *adv.* вероя́тно.

probate *n.* утвержде́ние завеща́ния.

probation *n.* испыта́ние, стажиро́вка; (*leg.*) усло́вный пригово́р. **probationary** *adj.* испыта́тельный. **probationer** *n.* стажёр.

probe *n.* (*med.*) зонд; (*spacecraft*) иссле́довательская раке́та; (*fig.*) рассле́дование; *v.t.* зонди́ровать *imp.*; (*fig.*) рассле́довать *imp.*, *perf.*

probity *n.* че́стность.

problem *n.* пробле́ма, вопро́с; (*math.*, *chess*, *etc.*) зада́ча; *p. child*, тру́дный ребёнок (-нка; *pl.* де́ти, -те́й, -тям, -тьми́). **problematic(al)** *adj.* проблемати́чный, проблемати́ческий.

proboscis *n.* хо́бот; (*of insects*) хобото́к (-тка́).

procedural *adj.* процеду́рный. **procedure** *n.* процеду́ра. **proceed** *v.i.* (*go further*) идти́ (иду́, идёшь; шёл, шла) *imp.*, пойти́ (пойду́, -дёшь; пошёл, -шла́) *perf.* да́льше; (*act*) поступа́ть *imp.*, поступи́ть (-плю́, -пишь) *perf.*; (*abs.*, *p. to say*) продолжа́ть *imp.*

продо́лжить *perf.*; (*of action*) продолжа́ться *imp.*, продо́лжиться *perf.*; *p. against*, возбужда́ть *imp.*, возбуди́ть *perf.* де́ло, проце́сс, про́тив + *gen.*; *p. from*, исходи́ть (-ожу́, -о́дишь) *imp.* из, от, + *gen.*; *p. in*, *with*, возобновля́ть *imp.*, возобнови́ть *perf.*; продолжа́ть *imp.*, продо́лжить *perf.*; *p. to*, приступа́ть *imp.*, притупи́ть (-плю́, -пишь) *perf.* к + *dat.* **proceeding** *n.* (*action*) посту́пок (-пка); *pl.* (*legal p.*) судопроизво́дство; *pl.* (*published report*) труды́ *m.pl.*, запи́ски *f.pl.* **proceeds** *n.* вы́ручка. **process** *n.* (*course*), ход; проце́сс; *v.t.* обраба́тывать *imp.*, обрабо́тать *perf.*; *processed cheese*, пла́вленный сыр (-а(у); *pl.* -ы́). **processing** *n.* обрабо́тка. **procession** *n.* проце́ссия, ше́ствие.

proclaim *v.t.* провозглаша́ть *imp.*, провозгласи́ть *perf.*; объявля́ть *imp.*, объяви́ть (-влю́, -вишь) *perf.* **proclamation** *n.* провозглаше́ние; объявле́ние.

proclivity *n.* накло́нность (to(wards), к + *dat.*).

procrastinate *v.i.* ме́длить *imp.* **procrastination** *n.* оття́жка.

procreation *n.* деторожде́ние.

proctor *n.* про́ктор. **proctorial** *adj.* про́кторский.

procuration *n.* (*obtaining*) получе́ние; (*pimping*) сво́дничество. **procure** *v.t.* добыва́ть *imp.*, добы́ть (добу́ду, -дешь; до́был, -а́, до́было) *perf.*; достава́ть (-таю́, -таёшь) *imp.*, доста́ть (-а́ну, -а́нешь) *perf.*; *v.i.* (*pimp*) сво́дничать *imp.* **procurer** *n.* сво́дник. **procuress** *n.* сво́дница.

prod *v.t.* ты́кать (ты́чу, -чешь) *imp.*, ткнуть *perf.*; *n.* тычо́к (-чка́).

prodigal *adj.* (*wasteful*) расточи́тельный; (*lavish*) ще́дрый (щедр, -а́, -о) (of, на + *acc.*); *p. son*, блу́дный сын; *n.* мот. **prodigality** *n.* мотовство́; изоби́лие.

prodigious *adj.* (*amazing*) удиви́тельный; (*enormous*) огро́мный. **prodigy** *n.* чу́до (*pl.* -деса́); *infant p.*, вундерки́нд.

produce *v.t.* (*evidence etc.*) представля́ть *imp.*, предста́вить *perf.*; (*ticket etc.*) предъявля́ть *imp.*, предъяви́ть (-влю́, -вишь) *perf.*; (*play etc.*) ста́вить *imp.*, по ~ *perf.*; (*manufacture*; *cause*) производи́ть (-ожу́, -о́дишь) *imp.*, произвести́ (-еду́, -едёшь; -ёл, -ела́) *perf.*; *n.* проду́кция; (*collect.*) проду́кты *m.pl.* **producer** *n.* (*econ.*) производи́тель *m.*; (*of play etc.*) постано́вщик, режиссёр; *p. gas*, генера́торный газ.

product *n.* проду́кт, фабрика́т; (*result*) результа́т; (*math.*) произведе́ние.

production *n.* произво́дство; (*yield*) проду́кция; (*artistic p.*) произведе́ние; (*of play etc.*) постано́вка. **productive** *adj.* производи́тельный, продукти́вный; (*fruitful*) плодоро́дный. **productivity** *n.* производи́тельность.

profanation *n.* профана́ция, оскверне́ние. **profane** *adj.* све́тский; (*blasphemous*) богоху́льный; *v.t.* оскверня́ть *imp.*, оскверни́ть *perf.* **profanity** *n.* богоху́льство.

profess *v.t.* (*pretend*) притворя́ться *imp.*, притвори́ться *perf.* (*to be*, + *instr.*); (*declare*) заявля́ть *imp.*, заяви́ть (-влю́, -вишь) *perf.*; (*affirm faith*) испове́довать *imp.*; (*engage in*) занима́ться *imp.*, заня́ться (займу́сь, -мёшься; заня́лся́, -ла́сь) *perf.* + *instr.* **professed** *adj.* откры́тый; (*alleged*) мни́мый. **profession** *n.* (*declaration*) заявле́ние; (*of faith*) испове́дание; (*vocation*) профе́ссия. **professional** *n.* профессиона́льный; *n.* (спортсме́н-) профессиона́л. **professor** *n.* профе́ссор (*pl.* -а́). **professorial** *adj.* профе́ссорский.

proffer *v.t.* предлага́ть *imp.*, предложи́ть (-ожу́, -о́жишь) *perf.*; *n.* предложе́ние.

proficiency *n.* уме́ние. **proficient** *adj.* уме́лый.

profile *n.* про́филь *m.*; (*biographical sketch*) кра́ткий биографи́ческий о́черк.

profit *n.* (*advantage*) по́льза, вы́года; (*gain*) при́быль; *at a p.*, с при́былью; *v.t.* приноси́ть (-ит) *imp.*, принести́ (-есёт; -ёс, -есла́) *perf.* по́льзу + *dat.*; *v.i.* получа́ть *imp.*, получи́ть (-чу́, -чишь) *perf.* при́быль; *p. by*, по́льзоваться *imp.*, вос ~ *perf.* + *instr.* **profitable** *adj.* вы́годный, при́быльный.

profiteer *v.i.* спекули́ровать *imp.*; *n.* спекуля́нт, ~ка. **profiteering** *n.* спекуля́ция. **profitless** *adj.* бесполе́зный.
profligacy *n.* распу́тство. **profligate** *n.* распу́тник; *adj.* распу́тный.
pro forma *adv.* для профо́рмы.
profound *adj.* глубо́кий (-о́к, -ока́, -о́ко́). **profundity** *n.* глубина́.
profuse *adj.* (*lavish*) ще́дрый (щедр, -а́, -о) (in, на + *acc.*); (*abundant*) изоби́льный. **profusion** *n.* изоби́лие.
progenitor *n.* прароди́тель *m.* **progeny** *n.* пото́мок (-мка); (*collect.*) пото́мство.
prognathous *adj.* (*jaw*) выдаю́щийся.
prognosis *n.* прогно́з. **prognosticate** *v.t.* предска́зывать *imp.*, предсказа́ть (-ажу́, -а́жешь) *perf.* **prognostication** *n.* предсказа́ние.
programme *n.* програ́мма; *adj.* програ́ммный; *v.t.* программи́ровать *imp.*, за ~ *perf.* **programmer** *n.* программи́ст.
progress *n.* прогре́сс; (*success*) успе́хи *m.pl.*; *make p.*, де́лать *imp.*, с ~ *perf.* успе́хи; *v.i.* продвига́ться *imp.*, продви́нуться *perf.* вперёд. **progression** *n.* продвиже́ние; (*math.*) прогре́ссия. **progressive** *adj.* прогресси́вный.
prohibit *v.t.* запреща́ть *imp.*, запрети́ть (-ещу́, -ети́шь) *perf.* **prohibition** *n.* запреще́ние; (*on alcohol*) сухо́й зако́н. **prohibitive** *adj.* запрети́тельный; (*price*) недосту́пный.
project *v.t.* (*plan*) проекти́ровать *imp.* с ~ *perf.*; (*cast*) броса́ть *imp.*, бро́сить *perf.*; (*a film*) демонстри́ровать *imp.*, про ~ *perf.*; *v.i.* (*jut out*) выступа́ть *imp.*; *n.* прое́кт. **projectile** *n.* снаря́д. **projection** *n.* прое́кция; (*protrusion*) вы́ступ. **projectionist** *n.* киномеха́ник. **projector** *n.* (*apparatus*) проекцио́нный аппара́т.
proletarian *adj.* пролета́рский; *n.* пролета́рий, -рка. **proletariat** *n.* пролетариа́т.
proliferate *v.i.* размножа́ться *imp.*, размно́житься; (*spread*) распространя́ться *imp.*, распространи́ться *perf.*
prolific *adj.* плодови́тый; (*abounding*) изоби́лующий (in, + *instr.*).
prolix *adj.* многосло́вный. **prolixity** *n.* многосло́вие.
prologue *n.* проло́г.
prolong *v.t.* продлева́ть *imp.*, продли́ть *perf.* **prolongation** *n.* продле́ние.
promenade *n.* ме́сто (*pl.* -та́) для гуля́нья; (*at seaside*) на́бережная *sb.*; *p. deck*, ве́рхняя па́луба; *v.i.* прогу́ливаться *imp.*, прогуля́ться *perf.*
prominence *n.* возвыше́ние, вы́пуклость; (*distinction*) изве́стность; *solar p.*, протубера́нец (-нца). **prominent** *adj.* вы́пуклый; (*conspicuous*) ви́дный; (*distinguished*) выдаю́щийся.
promiscuity *n.* разноро́дность; (*sexual p.*) промискуите́т. **promiscuous** *adj.* (*varied*) разноро́дный; (*indiscriminate*) беспоря́дочный; (*casual*) случа́йный.
promise *n.* обеща́ние; *v.t.* обеща́ть *imp.*, *perf.*; *promised land*, земля́ (*acc.* -лю) обетова́нная. **promising** *adj.* многообеща́ющий, перспекти́вный. **promissory** *adj.*: *p. note*, долгово́е обяза́тельство.
promontory *n.* мыс (*loc.* -е & -у́; *pl.* мы́сы́).
promote *v.t.* (*advance*) продвига́ть *imp.* продви́нуть *perf.*; (*assist*) спосо́бствовать *imp.*, *perf.* + *dat.*; (*product*) соде́йствовать *imp.*, *perf.* прода́же + *gen.*; *p. to*, (*mil.*) производи́ть (-ожу́, -о́дишь) *imp.*, произвести́ (-еду́, -едёшь; -ёл, -ела́) *perf.* в + *nom.-acc.pl.* **promoter** *n.* (*company p.*) учреди́тель *m.*; (*of sporting event etc.*) антрепренёр. **promotion** *n.* продвиже́ние, повыше́ние; соде́йствие.
prompt *adj.* бы́стрый (быстр, -а́, -о, бы́стры́), неме́дленный (-ен, -енна); *adv.* ро́вно; *v.t.* (*incite*) побужда́ть *imp.*, побуди́ть *perf.* (to, к + *dat.*; + *inf.*); (*speaker*; *also fig.*) подска́зывать *imp.*, подсказа́ть (-ажу́, -а́жешь) *perf.* + *dat.*; (*theat.*) суфли́ровать *imp.* + *dat.*; *n.* подска́зка; *p.-box*, суфлёрская бу́дка. **prompter** *n.* суфлёр.
promulgate *v.t.* обнаро́довать *perf.*; публикова́ть *imp.*, о ~ *perf.*; (*disseminate*) распространя́ть *imp.*, распространи́ть *perf.* **promulgation** *n.* обнаро́дование, опубликова́ние; распростране́ние.

prone *adj.* (лежа́щий) ничко́м; *predic.*: *p. to*, скло́нен (-о́нна́, -о́нно) к + *dat.*
prong *n.* зубе́ц (-бца́).
pronominal *adj.* местоиме́нный. **pronoun** *n.* местоиме́ние.
pronounce *v.t.* (*declare*) объявля́ть *imp.*, объяви́ть (-влю́, -вишь) *perf.*; (*articulate*) произноси́ть (-ошу́, -о́сишь) *imp.*, произнести́ (-есу́, -есёшь; -ёс, -есла́) *perf.*; *v.i.* (*give opinion*) выска́зываться *imp.*, вы́сказаться (-ажусь, -ажешься) *perf.* **pronounced** *adj.* ре́зко вы́раженный (-ен). **pronouncement** *n.* выска́зывание. **pronunciation** *n.* произноше́ние.
proof *n.* доказа́тельство; (*test*) испыта́ние; (*strength of alcohol*) устано́вленный гра́дус; (*print.*) корректу́ра; (*phot.*) про́бный отпеча́ток (-тка); (*of engraving*) про́бный о́ттиск; *p.-reader*, корре́ктор (*pl.* -ы & -а́); *adj.* (*impenetrable*) непроница́емый (against, для + *gen.*); (*not yielding*) неподдаю́щийся (against, + *dat.*).
prop[1] *n.* (*support*) подпо́рка, сто́йка; (*fig.*) опо́ра; *v.t.* (*p. up*) подпира́ть *imp.*, подпере́ть (-допру́, -допрёшь; -дпёр) *perf.*; (*fig.*) подде́рживать *imp.*, поддержа́ть (-жу́, -жишь) *perf.*
prop[2] *n.* (*theat.*): *pl.* (*collect.*) реквизи́т, бутафо́рия.
prop[3] *n.* (*aeron.*) пропе́ллер.
propaganda *n.* пропага́нда. **propagandist** *n.* пропаганди́ст.
propagate *v.t.* & *i.* размножа́ть(ся) *imp.*, размно́жить(ся) *perf.*; (*disseminate*) распространя́ть(ся) *imp.*, распространи́ть(ся) *perf.* **propagation** *n.* размноже́ние; распростране́ние.
propane *n.* пропа́н.
propel *v.t.* приводи́ть (-ожу́, -о́дишь) *imp.*, привести́ (-еду́, -едёшь; -ёл, -ела́) *perf.* в движе́ние; (*fig.*) дви́гать (-аю, -аешь & дви́жу, -жешь) *imp.*, дви́нуть *perf.*; *propelling pencil*, винтово́й каранда́ш (-а́). **propellant** *n.* (*in firearm*) по́рох; (*in rocket engine*) то́пливо. **propeller** *n.* (*aeron.*) пропе́ллер; (*aeron.*; *naut.*) винт (-а́).
propensity *n.* накло́нность (to, к + *dat.*; + *inf.*).
proper *adj.* (*characteristic*) сво́йственный (-ен(ен), -енна) (to, + *dat.*); (*gram.*) со́бственный; (*correct*) пра́вильный; (*strictly so called*; *after n.*) в у́зком смы́сле сло́ва; (*suitable*) надлежа́щий, до́лжный; (*decent*) присто́йный; *p. fraction*, пра́вильная дробь (*pl.* -би, -бе́й). **properly** *adv.* (*fittingly*, *duly*) до́лжным о́бразом, как сле́дует; (*correctly*) со́бственно; (*decently*) прили́чно.
property *n.* (*possessions*) со́бственность, иму́щество; (*attribute*) сво́йство; *pl.* (*theat.*) реквизи́т, бутафо́рия; *p.-man*, реквизи́тор, бутафо́р.
prophecy *n.* проро́чество. **prophesy** *v.t.* проро́чить *imp.*, на~ *perf.* **prophet** *n.* проро́к. **prophetess** *n.* проро́чица. **prophetic** *adj.* проро́ческий.
prophylactic *adj.* профилакти́ческий; *n.* профилакти́ческое сре́дство. **prophylaxis** *n.* профила́ктика.
propinquity *n.* (*nearness*) бли́зость; (*kinship*) родство́.
propitiate *v.t.* умиротворя́ть *imp.*, умиротвори́ть *perf.* **propitiation** *n.* умиротворе́ние.
propitious *adj.* благоприя́тный.
proponent *n.* сторо́нник, -ица.
proportion *n.* пропо́рция; (*correct relation*) пропорциона́льность; *pl.* разме́ры *m.pl.* **proportional** *adj.* пропорциона́льный; *p. representation*, пропорциона́льное представи́тельство. **proportionate** *adj.* соразме́рный (to, + *dat.*; с + *instr.*).
proposal *n.* предложе́ние. **propose** *v.t.* предлага́ть *imp.*, предложи́ть (-жу́, -жишь) *perf.*; (*intend*) предполага́ть *imp.*; *v.i.* (*p. marriage*) де́лать *imp.*, с~ *perf.* предложе́ние (to, + *dat.*). **proposition** *n.* (*assertion*) утвержде́ние; (*math.*) теоре́ма; (*proposal*) предложе́ние; (*undertaking*) (*coll.*) де́ло.
propound *v.t.* предлага́ть *imp.*, предложи́ть (-жу́, -жишь) *perf.* на обсужде́ние.
proprietary *adj.* (*of owner*) со́бственнический; (*medicine*) патенто́ванный. **proprietor** *n.* со́бственник, хозя́ин (*pl.* -я́ева, -я́ев). **proprietress** *n.* со́бственница, хозя́йка.
propriety *n.* присто́йность, прили́чие.

propulsion *n.* движéние вперёд; (*fig*). движущая сила.
prorogue *v.t.* назначáть *imp.*, назнáчить *perf.* перерыв в рабóте + *gen.*
prosaic *adj.* прозаи́ческий, прозаи́чный.
proscenium *n.* авансцéна.
proscribe *v.t.* (*put outside the law*) объявля́ть *imp.*, объяви́ть (-влю́, -вишь) *perf.* вне закóна; (*banish*) изгоня́ть *imp.*, изгнáть (изгоню́, -нишь; изгнáл, -á, -о) *perf.*; (*forbid*) запрещáть *imp.*, запрети́ть (-ещу́, -ети́шь) *perf.*
prose *n.* прóза.
prosecute *v.t.* (*pursue*) вести́ (веду́, -дёшь; вёл, -á) *imp.*; (*leg.*) преслéдовать *imp.* **prosecution** *n.* ведéние; (*leg.*) судéбное преслéдование; (*prosecuting party*) обвинéние. **prosecutor** *n.* обвини́тель *m.*
proselyte *n.* прозели́т. **proselytize** *v.t.* обращáть *imp.*, обрати́ть (-ащу́, -ати́шь) *perf.* в другу́ю вéру.
prosody *n.* просóдия.
prospect *n.* вид, перспекти́ва; *v.t.* & *i.* развéдывать *imp.*, развéдать *perf.* (for, на + *acc.*). **prospective** *adj.* бу́дущий, предполагáемый. **prospector** *n.* развéдчик. **prospectus** *n.* проспéкт.
prosper *v.i.* процветáть *imp.*; преуспевáть *imp.* **prosperity** *n.* процветáние, преуспевáние. **prosperous** *adj.* процветáющий, преуспевáющий; (*wealthy*) зажи́точный.
prostate (gland) *n.* предстáтельная железá (*pl.* жéлезы, -лёз, -лезáм).
prostitute *n.* проститу́тка; *v.t.* проституи́ровать *imp.*, *perf.* **prostitution** *n.* проститу́ция.
prostrate *adj.* распростёртый, (лежáщий) ничкóм; (*exhausted*) обесси́ленный (-ен); (*with grief*) уби́тый (with, + *instr.*); *v.t.* (*exhaust*) истощáть *imp.*, истощи́ть *perf.*; *p. oneself*, пáдать *imp.*, пасть (паду́, -дёшь; пал) *perf.* ниц. **prostration** *n.* прострáция.
prosy *adj.* прозаи́чный, прозаи́ческий.
protagonist *n.* глáвный герóй; (*advocate*) сторóнник.
protean *adj.* (*having many forms*) многообрáзный; (*versatile*) многосторóнний (-нен, -нння).
protect *v.t.* защищáть *imp.*, защити́ть (-ищу́, -ити́шь) *perf.* (from, от + *gen.*; against, прóтив + *gen.*). **protection** *n.* защи́та, охрáна; (*patronage*) покрови́тельство. **protectionism** *n.* протекциони́зм. **protective** *adj.* защи́тный, покрови́тельственный. **protector** *n.* защи́тник, покрови́тель *m.*; (*regent*) протéктор. **protectorate** *n.* протекторáт.
protégé(e) *n.* протежé *m.* & *f. indecl.*
protein *n.* протеи́н, белóк (-лкá).
protest *n.* протéст; *v.i.* протестовáть *imp.*, *perf.*; *v.t.* (*affirm*) заявля́ть *imp.*, заяви́ть (-влю́, -вишь) *perf.* + *acc.*, о + *prep.*, что.
Protestant *n.* протестáнт, ~ка; *adj.* протестáнтский. **Protestantism** *n.* протестáнтство.
protestation *n.* (торжéственное) заявлéние (о + *prep.*; что); (*protest*) протéст.
protocol *n.* протокóл.
proton *n.* протóн.
protoplasm *n.* протоплáзма.
prototype *n.* прототи́п.
protozoon *n.* простéйшее (живóтное) *sb.*
protract *v.t.* тяну́ть (-ну́, -нешь) *imp.*; (*plan*) черти́ть (-рчу́, -ртишь) *imp.*, на~ *perf.* **protracted** *adj.* дли́тельный. **protraction** *n.* промедлéние; начертáние. **protractor** *n.* (*instrument*) транспорти́р; (*muscle*) разгибáтельная мы́шца.
protrude *v.t.* высóвывать *imp.*, вы́сунуть *perf.*; *v.i.* выдавáться (-даёшься) *imp.*, вы́даться (-астся) *perf.* **protrusion** *n.* вы́ступ.
protuberance *n.* вы́пуклость, вы́ступ, бугорóк (-ркá). **protuberant** *adj.* вы́пуклый; *p. eyes*, глазá (-з, -зáм) *m.pl.* навы́кате.
proud *adj.* гóрдый (горд, -á, -о, гóрды́); *be p. of*, горди́ться *imp.* + *instr.*
provable *adj.* доказу́емый. **prove** *v.t.* докáзывать *imp.*, доказáть (-ажу́, -áжешь) *perf.*; удостоверя́ть *imp.*, удостовéрить *perf.*; (*a will*) утверждáть *imp.*, утверди́ть *perf.*; *v.i.* окáзываться *imp.*, оказáться (-ажу́сь, -áжешься) *perf.* (to be, + *instr.*).

proven *adj.* дока́занный (-ан).
provenance *n.* происхожде́ние.
provender *n.* корм (*loc.* -е & -у́; *pl.* -а́).
proverb *n.* посло́вица. **proverbial** *adj.* воше́дший в погово́рку; (*well-known*) общеизве́стный; *p. saying*, погово́рка.
provide *v.t.* (*stipulate*) ста́вить *imp.*, по~ *perf.* усло́вием (that, что); (*supply person*) снабжа́ть *imp.*, снабди́ть *perf.* (with, +*instr.*); обеспе́чивать *imp.*, обеспе́чить *perf.* (with, +*instr.*); (*supply thing*) предоставля́ть *imp.*, предоста́вить *perf.* (to, for, +*dat.*); дава́ть (даю́, даёшь) *imp.*, дать (дам, дашь, даст, дади́м; дал, -а́, да́ло́, -и) *perf.* (to, for, +*dat.*); *v.i.*: *p. against*, принима́ть *imp.*, приня́ть (приму́, -мешь; при́нял, -а́, -о) *perf.* ме́ры про́тив+*gen.*; *p. for*, предусма́тривать *imp.*, предусмотре́ть (-рю́, -ришь) *perf.*+*acc.*; (*p. for family etc.*) содержа́ть (-жу́, -жишь) *imp.*+*acc.* **provided (that)** *conj.* при усло́вии, что; е́сли то́лько. **providence** *n.* провиде́ние; (*foresight*) предусмотри́тельность. **provident** *adj.* предусмотри́тельный; (*thrifty*) бережли́вый. **providential** *adj.* (*lucky*) счастли́вый (сча́стли́в). **providing** *see* **provided (that)**.
province *n.* о́бласть (*pl.* -ти, -те́й) (*also fig.*); прови́нция; *pl.* (*the p.*) прови́нция. **provincial** *adj.* провинциа́льный; *n.* провинциа́л, ~ка. **provincialism** *n.* провинциа́льность; (*expression*) областно́е выраже́ние.
provision *n.* снабже́ние, обеспече́ние; *pl.* прови́зия; (*in agreement etc.*) положе́ние; *make p. against*, принима́ть *imp.*, приня́ть (приму́, -мешь; при́нял, -а́, -о) *perf.* ме́ры про́тив+*gen.*; *make p. for*, предусма́тривать *imp.*, предусмотре́ть (-рю́, -ришь) *perf.*+*acc.*; *v.t.* снабжа́ть *imp.*, снабди́ть *perf.* прови́зией. **provisional** *adj.* вре́менный. **proviso** *n.* усло́вие, огово́рка. **provisory** *adj.* усло́вный.
provocation *n.* провока́ция. **provocative** *adj.* провокацио́нный; *p. of*, вызыва́ющий+*acc.* **provoke** *v.t.* провоци́ровать *imp.*, с~ *perf.*; (*call forth, cause*) вызыва́ть *imp.* вы́звать (вы́зову, -вешь) *perf.*; (*irritate*) раздража́ть *imp.*, раздражи́ть *perf.*
provost *n.* (*univ.*) ре́ктор; (*mayor*) мэр; *p. marshal*, нача́льник вое́нной поли́ции.
prow *n.* нос (*loc.* -у́; *pl.* -ы́).
prowess *n.* (*valour*) до́блесть; (*skill*) уме́ние.
prowl *v.i.* ры́скать (ры́щу, -щешь) *imp.*; *v.t.* броди́ть (-ожу́, -о́дишь) *imp.* по+*dat.*
proximity *n.* бли́зость.
proxy *n.* полномо́чие, дове́ренность; (*person*) уполномо́ченный *sb.*, замести́тель *m.*; *by p.*, по дове́ренности; *stand p. for*, быть *imp.* замести́телем+*gen.*
prude *n.* скро́мник, -ица.
prudence *n.* благоразу́мие. **prudent** *adj.* благоразу́мный.
prudery *n.* притво́рная стыдли́вость. **prudish** *adj.* не в ме́ру стыдли́вый.
prune[1] *n.* (*plum*) черносли́вина; *pl.* черносли́в (-а(у)) (*collect.*).
prune[2] *v.t.* (*trim*) об-, под-, реза́ть *imp.*, об-, под-, ре́зать (-е́жу, -е́жешь) *perf.*; (*fig.*) сокраща́ть *imp.*, сократи́ть (-ащу́, -ати́шь) *perf.* **pruning-hook** *n.* приви́вочный нож (-а́).
prurience *n.* похотли́вость. **prurient** *adj.* похотли́вый.
Prussian *n.* прусса́к (-а́), -а́чка; *adj.* пру́сский; *P. blue*, берли́нская лазу́рь. **prussic** *adj.*: *p. acid*, сини́льная кислота́.
pry *v.i.* сова́ть (сую́, суёшь) *imp.* нос (into, в+*acc.*). **prying** *adj.* пытли́вый, любопы́тный.
psalm *n.* псало́м (-лма́). **psalter** *n.* псалты́рь (-ри & -ря́) *f.* & *m.*
pseudo- *in comb.* псевдо-. **pseudonym** *n.* псевдони́м.
psyche *n.* пси́хика. **psychiatric** *adj.* психиатри́ческий. **psychiatrist** *n.* психиа́тр. **psychiatry** *n.* психиатри́я. **psychic(al)** *adj.* психи́ческий, душе́вный. **psycho** *n.* псих. **psycho-** *in comb.* психо-. **psycho-analyse** *v.t.* подверга́ть *imp.*, подве́ргнуть (-г) *perf.* психоана́лизу. **psycho-analysis** *n.* психоана́лиз. **psycho-analyst** *n.* специали́ст по психоана́лизу. **psycho-analytic(al)** *adj.*

психоаналити́ческий. **psychological** *adj.* психологи́ческий. **psychologist** *n.* психо́лог. **psychology** *n.* психоло́гия; (*coll.*) пси́хика. **psychomotor** *adj.* психомото́рный. **psychoneurosis** *n.* психоневро́з. **psychopath** *n.* психопа́т. **psychopathic** *adj.* психопати́ческий. **psychopathology** *n.* психопатоло́гия. **psychosis** *n.* психо́з. **psychotherapy** *n.* психотерапи́я.

ptarmigan *n.* тундря́нка.

pterodactyl *n.* птерода́ктиль *m.*

pub *n.* пивна́я *sb.*, каба́к (-а́).

puberty *n.* полова́я зре́лость.

public *adj.* обще́ственный; (*open*) публи́чный, откры́тый; *p. health*, здравоохране́ние; *p. house*, пивна́я *sb.*; *p. relations officer*, слу́жащий *sb.* отде́ла информа́ции; *p. school*, ча́стная сре́дняя шко́ла; *p. servant*, госуда́рственный слу́жащий *sb.*; *p. spirit*, обще́ственный дух; *p. utility*, предприя́тие обще́ственного по́льзования; *n.* пу́блика, обще́ственность; *in p.*, откры́то, публи́чно. **publication** *n.* (*action*) опубликова́ние; (*also book etc.*) изда́ние. **publicist** *n.* публици́ст. **publicity** *n.* рекла́ма; *p. agent*, аге́нт по рекла́ме. **publicize** *v.t.* реклами́ровать *imp., perf.* **publicly** *adv.* публи́чно, откры́то. **publish** *v.t.* публикова́ть *imp.*, о~ *perf.*; (*book*) издава́ть (-даю́, -даёшь) *imp.*, изда́ть (-а́м, -а́шь, -а́ст, -ади́м; изда́л, -а́, -о) *perf.* **publisher** *n.* изда́тель *m.* **publishing** *n.* (*business*) изда́тельское де́ло; *p. house*, изда́тельство.

puce *adj.* (*n.*) краснова́то-кори́чневый (цвет).

puck *n.* (*in ice hockey*) ша́йба.

pucker *v.t.* & *i.* мо́рщить(ся) *imp.*, с~ *perf.*; *n.* морщи́на.

pudding *n.* пу́динг, запека́нка; *p.-head*, болва́н; *p.-stone*, конгломера́т.

puddle *n.* лу́жа.

pudgy *adj.* пу́хлый (пухл, -а́, -о).

puerile *adj.* ребя́ческий. **puerility** *n.* ребя́чество.

puff *n.* (*of wind*) поры́в; (*of smoke*) дымо́к (-мка́); (*on dress*) бу́фы (-ф) *pl. only*; *p.-ball*, (*fungus*) дождеви́к (-а́); *p. pastry*, слоёное те́сто; *p. sleeves*, рукава́ *m.pl.* с бу́фами; *v.i.* пыхте́ть (-хчу́, -хти́шь) *imp.*; *p. at*, (*pipe etc.*) попы́хивать *imp.* + *instr.*; *v.t.*: *p. up, out*, (*inflate*) надува́ть *imp.*, наду́ть (-у́ю, -у́ешь) *perf.*

puffin *n.* ту́пик.

pug[1] *n.* (*dog*) мопс; *p.-nosed*, курно́сый.

pug[2] *n.* (*clay*) мя́тая гли́на.

pugilism *n.* бокс. **pugilist** *n.* боксёр.

pugnacious *adj.* драчли́вый. **pugnacity** *n.* драчли́вость.

puissant *adj.* могу́щественный (-ен, -енна).

puke *v.i.* рвать (рвёт; рва́ло) *imp.*, вы́~ *perf. impers.* + *acc.*; *n.* рво́та.

pull *v.t.* тяну́ть (-ну́, -нешь) *imp.*, по~ *perf.*; таска́ть *indet.*, тащи́ть (-щу́, -щишь) *det.*, по~ *perf.*; (*a muscle*) растя́гивать *imp.*, растяну́ть (-ну́, -нешь) *perf.*; (*a cork*) выта́скивать *imp.*, вы́тащить *perf.*; (*a tooth*) удаля́ть *imp.*, удали́ть *perf.*; *v.t.* & *i.* дёргать *imp.*, дёрнуть *perf.* (at, (за) + *acc.*); *p. faces*, грима́сничать *imp.*; *p. someone's leg*, моро́чить *imp.* го́лову + *dat.*; *p.* (*the*) *strings, wires*, нажима́ть *imp.*, нажа́ть (нажму́, -мёшь) *perf.* на та́йные пружи́ны; *p. the trigger*, спуска́ть *imp.*, спусти́ть (-ущу́, -у́стишь) *perf.* куро́к; *p. apart, to pieces*, разрыва́ть *imp.*, разорва́ть (-ву́, -вёшь; -ва́л, -вала́, -ва́ло) *perf.*; (*fig.*) раскритикова́ть *perf.*; *p. at*, (*pipe etc.*) затя́гиваться *imp.*, затяну́ться (-ну́сь, -нешься) *perf.* + *instr.*; *p. down*, (*demolish*) сноси́ть (-ошу́, -о́сишь) *imp.*, снести́ (снесу́, -сёшь; снёс, -ла́) *perf.*; *p. in*, (*earn*) зараба́тывать *imp.*, зарабо́тать *perf.*; (*of train*) прибыва́ть *imp.*, прибы́ть (-бу́дет; при́был, -а́, -о) *perf.*; (*of vehicle*) подъезжа́ть *imp.*, подъе́хать (-е́дет) *perf.* к обо́чине доро́ги; *p. off*, (*garment*) стя́гивать *imp.*, стяну́ть (-ну́, -нешь) *perf.*; (*achieve*) успе́шно заверша́ть *imp.*, заверши́ть *perf.*; (*win*) выи́грывать *imp.*, вы́играть *perf.*; *p. on*, (*garment*) натя́гивать *imp.*, натяну́ть (-ну́, -нешь) *perf.*; *p. out*, (*v.t.*) (*remove*) выта́скивать *imp.*, вы́тащить *perf.*; (*v.i.*) (*withdraw*) отка́зываться *imp.*, отказа́ться (-ажу́сь, -а́жешься) *perf.* от уча́стия (of, в+*prep.*); (*of vehicle*) отъезжа́ть *imp.*, отъе́хать (-е́дет) *perf.* от обо́чины (доро́ги); (*of train*) отходи́ть (-ит) *imp.*, отойти́ (-йдёт; отошёл, -шла́) *perf.* (от ста́нции); *p. through*, выжива́ть *imp.*, вы́жить (вы́живу, -вешь) *perf.*; *p. oneself together*, брать (беру́, -рёшь; брал, -а́, -о) *imp.*, взять (возьму́, -мёшь; взял, -а́, -о) *perf.* себя́ в ру́ки; *p. up*, (*v.t.*) подтя́гивать *imp.*, подтяну́ть (-ну́, -нешь) *perf.*; (*v.t.* & *i.*) (*stop*) остана́вливать(ся) *imp.*, останови́ть(ся) (-влю́(сь), -вишь(ся)) *perf.*; *p.-in*, *p.-up*, заку́сочная *sb.* на доро́ге; *p.-through*, проти́рка; *n.* тя́га; (*fig.*) зару́чка.

pullet *n.* моло́дка.

pulley *n.* блок, шкив (*pl.* -ы́).

Pullman *n.* пу́льман(овский ваго́н).

pullover *n.* пуло́вер.

pulmonary *adj.* лёгочный.

pulp *n.* (*of fruit*) мя́коть; (*anat.*) пу́льпа; (*of paper*) бума́жная ма́сса; *v.t.* превраща́ть *imp.*, преврати́ть (-ащу́, -ати́шь) *perf.* в мя́гкую ма́ссу.

pulpit *n.* ка́федра.

pulsar *n.* пульса́р. **pulsate** *v.i.* пульси́ровать *imp.* **pulsation** *n.* пульса́ция.
pulse[1] *n.* (*throbbing*) пульс; *v.i.* пульси́ровать *imp.*

pulse[2] *n.* (*food*) бобо́вые *sb.*

pulverize *v.t.* размельча́ть *imp.*, размельчи́ть *perf.*; (*fig.*) сокруша́ть *imp.*, сокруши́ть *perf.*

puma *n.* пу́ма.

pumice(-stone) *n.* пе́мза.

pummel *v.t.* колоти́ть (-очу́, -о́тишь) *imp.*, по~ *perf.*; тузи́ть *imp.*, от~ *perf.*

pump[1] *n.* (*machine*) насо́с; *v.t.* (*use p.*) кача́ть *imp.*; (*person*) выпра́шивать *imp.*, вы́просить *perf.* у+*gen.*; *p. in(to)*, вка́чивать *imp.*, вкача́ть *perf.*; *p. out*, выка́чивать *imp.*, вы́качать *perf.*; *p. up*, нака́чивать *imp.*, накача́ть *perf.*

pump[2] *n.* (*shoe*) ту́фля (*gen.pl.* -фель).

pumpkin *n.* ты́ква.

pun *n.* каламбу́р; *v.i.* каламбу́рить *imp.*, с~ *perf.*

punch[1] *v.t.* (*with fist*) ударя́ть *imp.*, уда́рить *perf.* кулако́м; (*pierce*) пробива́ть *imp.*, проби́ть (-бью́, -бьёшь) *perf.*; (*a ticket*) компости́ровать *imp.*, про~ *perf.*; *p.-ball*, пенчингбо́л, гру́ша; *p.-up*, дра́ка; *n.* (*blow*) уда́р кулако́м; (*for tickets*) компо́стер; (*for piercing*) пробо́йник; (*for stamping*) пуансо́н.

punch[2] *n.* (*drink*) пунш.

punctilio *n.* форма́льность. **punctilious** *adj.* соблюда́ющий форма́льности, щепети́льный.

punctual *adj.* пунктуа́льный. **punctuality** *n.* пунктуа́льность.

punctuate *v.t.* ста́вить *imp.*, по~ *perf.* зна́ки препина́ния в+*acc.*; прерыва́ть *imp.*, прерва́ть (-ву́, -вёшь; прерва́л, -а́, -о) *perf.* **punctuation** *n.* пунктуа́ция; *p. marks*, зна́ки *m.pl.* препина́ния.

puncture *n.* проко́л; *v.t.* прока́лывать *imp.*, проколо́ть (-лю́, -лешь) *perf.*; *v.i.* получа́ть *imp.*, получи́ть (-чу́, -чишь) *perf.* проко́л.

pundit *n.* (*fig.*) знато́к (-а́).

pungency *n.* е́дкость. **pungent** *adj.* е́дкий (е́док, едка́, е́дко).

punish *v.t.* нака́зывать *imp.*, наказа́ть (-ажу́, -а́жешь) *perf.* **punishable** *adj.* наказу́емый. **punishment** *n.* наказа́ние.
punitive *adj.* кара́тельный.

punnet *n.* корзи́нка.

punster *n.* каламбури́ст.

punt *n.* (*boat*) плоскодо́нка.

punter *n.* (*gambler*) игро́к (-а́).

puny *adj.* хи́лый (хил, -а́, -о), тщеду́шный.

pup *n.* щено́к (-нка́; *pl.* щенки́, -ко́в & щеня́та, -т); *v.i.* щени́ться *imp.*, о~ *perf.*

pupa *n.* ку́колка.

pupil *n.* учени́к (-а́), -и́ца; (*of eye*) зрачо́к (-чка́).

puppet *n.* марионе́тка, ку́кла (*gen.pl.* -кол); *p. regime*, марионе́точный режи́м; *p.-theatre*, ку́кольный теа́тр.

puppy *n.* щено́к (-нка́; *pl.* щенки́, -ко́в & щеня́та, -т).

purblind *adj.* близору́кий.

purchase *n.* поку́пка; (*leverage*) то́чка опо́ры; *v.t.* покупа́ть *imp.*, купи́ть

(-плю́, -пишь) *perf.* **purchaser** *n.* покупа́тель *m.*, ~ница.

pure *adj.* чи́стый (чист, -а́, -о, чи́сты́); (*of science*) теорети́ческий; *p.-blooded*, чистокро́вный; *p.-bred*, поро́дистый; *p.-minded*, чи́стый (чист, -а́, -о, чи́сты́) душо́й.

purée *n.* пюре́ *neut.indecl.*

purely *adv.* чи́сто; (*entirely*) соверше́нно.

purgative *adj.* слаби́тельный; (*purifying*) очисти́тельный; *n.* слаби́тельное *sb.* **purgatory** *n.* чисти́лище. **purge** *v.t.* (*cleanse*) очища́ть *imp.*, очи́стить *perf.*; (*of medicine*; *abs.*) сла́бить *imp.*; (*atone for*) искупа́ть *imp.*, искупи́ть (-плю́, -пишь) *perf.*; (*p. party*, *army*, *etc.*) проводи́ть (-ожу́, -о́дишь) *imp.*, провести́ (-еду́, -едёшь; -ёл, -ела́) *perf.* чи́стку в+*acc.*; *n.* очище́ние; (*of party*, *army*, *etc.*) чи́стка.

purification *n.* очище́ние, очи́стка. **purify** *v.t.* очища́ть *imp.*, очи́стить *perf.*

purism *n.* пури́зм. **purist** *n.* пури́ст.

puritan, P., *n.* пурита́нин (*pl.* -а́не, -а́н), -а́нка. **puritanical** *adj.* пурита́нский.

purity *n.* чистота́.

purlieu *n.*: *pl.* окре́стности *f.pl.*

purloin *v.t.* похища́ть *imp.*, похи́тить (-и́щу, -и́тишь) *perf.*

purple *adj.* (*n.*) пу́рпу́рный, фиоле́товый (цвет).

purport *n.* смысл.

purpose *n.* цель, наме́рение; *on p.*, наро́чно; *to no p.*, напра́сно; *to the p.*, кста́ти. **purposeful** *adj.* целеустремлённый (-ён, -ённа). **purposeless** *adj.* бесце́льный. **purposely** *adv.* наро́чно.

purr *n.* мурлы́канье; *v.i.* мурлы́кать (-ы́чу, -ы́чешь) *imp.*

purse *n.* кошелёк (-лька́); *v.t.* поджима́ть *imp.*, поджа́ть (подожму́, -мёшь) *perf.* **purser** *n.* казначе́й.

pursuance *n.* выполне́ние. **pursuant** *adv.*: *p. to*, в соотве́тствии с+*instr.*; согла́сно+*dat.* **pursue** *v.t.* пресле́довать *imp.* **pursuit** *n.* пресле́дование; (*occupation*) заня́тие.

purulent *adj.* гно́йный.

purvey *v.t.* поставля́ть *imp.*, поста́вить *perf.* **purveyor** *n.* поставщи́к (-а́).

purview *n.* кругозо́р.

pus *n.* гной (-о́я(ю), *loc.* -о́е & -ою́).

push *v.t.* толка́ть *imp.*, толкну́ть *perf.*; (*goods*) реклами́ровать *imp.*, *perf.*; *v.i.* толка́ться *imp.*; *be pushed for*, име́ть *imp.* ма́ло+*gen.*; *he is pushing fifty*, ему́ ско́ро сту́кнет пятьдеся́т; *p. one's way*, проти́скиваться *imp.*, проти́снуться *perf.*; *p. ahead*, *on*, продвига́ться *imp.*, продви́нуться *perf.*; *p. around*, (*person*) помыка́ть *imp.*, +*instr.*; *p. aside*, (*also fig.*) отстраня́ть *imp.*, отстрани́ть *perf.*; *p. away*, отта́лкивать *imp.*, оттолкну́ть *perf.*; *p. into*, (*v.t.*) вта́лкивать *imp.*, втолкну́ть *perf.* в+*acc.*; (*urge*) толка́ть *imp.*, толкну́ть *perf.* на+*acc.*; *p. off*, (*v.i.*) (*in boat*) отта́лкиваться *imp.*, оттолкну́ться *perf.* (от бе́рега); (*go away*) убира́ться *imp.*, убра́ться (уберу́сь, -рёшься; убра́лся,- ала́сь, -а́лось) *perf.*; *p. through*, (*v.t.*) прота́лкивать *imp.*, протолкну́ть *perf.*; (*conclude*) доводи́ть (-ожу́, -о́дишь) *imp.*, довести́ (-еду́, -едёшь; -ёл, -ела́) *perf.* до конца́; *n.* толчо́к (-чка́); (*energy*) эне́ргия; *p.-ball*, пушбо́л; *p.-bike*, велосипе́д. **pushing** *adj.* (*of person*) напо́ристый.

puss, pussy(-cat) *n.* ко́шечка, ки́ска; *p. willow*, ве́рба.

pustular *adj.* пустулёзный, прыща́вый. **pustule** *n.* пу́стула, прыщ (-а́).

put *v.t.* класть (кладу́, -дёшь; клал) *imp.*, положи́ть (-жу́, -жишь) *perf.*; (*upright*) ста́вить *imp.*, по~ *perf.*; помеща́ть *imp.*, помести́ть *perf.*; (*into specified state*) приводи́ть (-ожу́, -о́дишь) *imp.*, привести́ (-еду́, -едёшь; -ёл, -ела́) *perf.*; (*estimate*) определя́ть *imp.*, определи́ть *perf.* (at, в+*acc.*); (*express*) выража́ть *imp.*, вы́разить *perf.*; (*translate*) переводи́ть (-ожу́, -о́дишь) *imp.*, перевести́ (-еду́, -едёшь; -ёл, -ела́) *perf.* (into, на+*acc.*); (*a question*) задава́ть (-даю́, -даёшь) *imp.*, зада́ть (-а́м, -а́шь, -а́ст, -ади́м; за́дал, -а́, -о) *perf.*; *p. an end*, *a stop*, *to*, класть (кладу́, -дёшь; клал) *imp.*, положи́ть (-жу́, -жишь) *perf.* коне́ц+*dat.*; *p. oneself in another's place*, ста́вить *imp.*, по~ *perf.* себя́ на ме́сто

+*gen.*; *p. the shot*, толка́ть *imp.*, толкну́ть *perf.* ядро́; *p. to death*, казни́ть *imp.*, *perf.*; *p. to flight*, обраща́ть *imp.*, обрати́ть (-ащу́, -ати́шь) *perf.* в бе́гство; *p. to shame*, стыди́ть *imp.*, при~ *perf.*; *p. about*, (*of ship*) лечь (ля́жет, ля́гут; лёг, -ла́) *perf.* на друго́й галс; (*rumour etc.*) распространя́ть *imp.*, распространи́ть *perf.*; *p. away*, (*for future*) откла́дывать *imp.*, отложи́ть (-жу́, -жишь) *perf.*; (*in prison*) сажа́ть *imp.*, посади́ть (-ажу́, -а́дишь) *perf.*; *p. back*, (*in place*) ста́вить *imp.*, по~ *perf.* на ме́сто; *p. the clock back*, передвига́ть *imp.*, передви́нуть *perf.* стре́лки часо́в наза́д; *p. by*, (*money*) откла́дывать *imp.*, отложи́ть (-жу́, -жишь) *perf.*; *p. down*, (*suppress*) подавля́ть *imp.*, подави́ть (-влю́, -вишь) *perf.*; (*write down*) запи́сывать *imp.*, записа́ть (-ишу́, -и́шешь) *perf.*; (*passengers*) выса́живать *imp.*, вы́садить *perf.*; (*attribute*) припи́сывать *imp.*, приписа́ть (-ишу́, -и́шешь) *perf.* (to, +*dat.*); *p. forth*, (*of plant*) пуска́ть *imp.*, пусти́ть (-ит) *perf.* (побе́ги); *p. forward*, (*proposal*) предлага́ть *imp.*, предложи́ть (-жу́, -жишь) *perf.*; *p. the clock forward*, передвига́ть *imp.*, передви́нуть *perf.* стре́лки часо́в вперёд; *p. in*, (*install*) устана́вливать *imp.*, установи́ть (-влю́, -вишь) *perf.*; (*a claim*) предъявля́ть *imp.*, предъяви́ть (-влю́, -вишь) *perf.*; (*interpose*) вставля́ть *imp.*, вста́вить *perf.*; (*spend time*) проводи́ть (-ожу́, -о́дишь) *imp.*, провести́ (-еду́, -едёшь; -ёл, -ела́) *perf.*; *p. in an appearance*, появля́ться *imp.*, появи́ться (-влю́сь, -вишься) *perf.*; *p. off*, (*postpone*) откла́дывать *imp.*, отложи́ть (-жу́, -жишь) *perf.*; (*evade*) отде́лываться *imp.*, отде́латься *perf.* от+*gen.*; (*dissuade*) отгова́ривать *imp.*, отговори́ть *perf.* от+*gen.*, +*inf.*; *p. on*, (*clothes*) надева́ть *imp.*, наде́ть (-е́ну, -е́нешь) *perf.*; (*appearance*) принима́ть *imp.*, приня́ть (приму́, -мешь; при́нял, -а́, -о) *perf.*; (*a play*) ста́вить *imp.*, по~ *perf.*; (*turn on*) включа́ть *imp.*, включи́ть *perf.*; (*add to*) прибавля́ть *imp.*, приба́вить *perf.*; *p. on airs*, ва́жничать *imp.*; *p. on weight*, толсте́ть *imp.*, по~ *perf.*; *p. out*, (*dislocate*) вы́вихнуть *perf.*; (*a fire etc.*) туши́ть (-шу́, -шишь) *imp.*, по~ *perf.*; (*annoy*) раздража́ть *imp.*, раздражи́ть *perf.*; *p. out to sea*, (*of ship*) выходи́ть (-ит) *imp.*, вы́йти (вы́йдет; вы́шел, -шла) *perf.* в мо́ре; *p. through*, (*carry out*) выполня́ть *imp.*, вы́полнить *perf.*; (*on telephone*) соединя́ть *imp.*, соедини́ть *perf.* по телефо́ну; *p. up*, (*building*) стро́ить *imp.*, по~ *perf.*; (*price*) повыша́ть *imp.*, повы́сить *perf.*; (*a guest*) дава́ть (даю́, даёшь) *imp.*, дать (дам, дашь, даст, дади́м; дал, -а́, да́ло́, -и) *perf.* прию́т +*gen.*; (*as guest*) остана́вливаться *imp.*, останови́ться (-влю́сь, -вишься) *perf.*; *p. up to*, (*instigate*) подстрека́ть *imp.*, подстрекну́ть *perf.* к+*dat.*; *p. up with*, терпе́ть (-плю́, -пишь) *imp.*

putative *adj.* предполага́емый.

putrefaction *n.* гние́ние. **putrefy** *v.i.* гнить (-ию́, -иёшь; гнил, -а́, -о) *imp.*, с~ *perf.* **putrid** *adj.* гнило́й (гнил, -а́, -о), гни́лостный.

putsch *n.* путч.

puttee *n.* обмо́тка.

putty *n.* зама́зка, шпаклёвка; *v.t.* шпаклева́ть (-лю́ю, -лю́ешь) *imp.*, за~ *perf.*

puzzle *n.* (*perplexity*) недоуме́ние; (*enigma*) зага́дка; (*toy etc.*) головоло́мка; *v.t.* озада́чивать *imp.*, озада́чить *perf.*; *p. out*, разгада́ть *perf.*; *v.i.*: *p. over*, лома́ть *imp.* себе́ го́лову над +*instr.*

pygmy *n.* пигме́й; *adj.* ка́рликовый.

pyjamas *n.* пижа́ма.

pylon *n.* пило́н, опо́ра.

pyorrhoea *n.* пиоре́я.

pyramid *n.* пирами́да. **pyramidal** *adj.* пирамида́льный.

pyre *n.* погреба́льный костёр (-тра́).

pyrites *n.*: (*iron*) *p.*, пири́т; *copper p.*, халькопири́т.

pyromania *n.* пирома́ния.

pyrotechnic(al) *adj.* пиротехни́ческий. **pyrotechnics** *n.* пироте́хника.

Pyrrhic *adj.*: *P. victory*, пи́ррова побе́да.

python *n.* пито́н.

Q

qua *conj.* в ка́честве + *gen.*
quack[1] *n.* (*sound*) кря́канье; *v.i.* кря́кать *imp.*, кря́кнуть *perf.*
quack[2] *n.* зна́харь *m.*, шарлата́н. **quackery** *n.* зна́харство, шарлата́нство.
quad *n.* (*quadrangle*) четырёхуго́льный двор (-а́); (*quadrat*) шпа́ция; *pl.* (*quadruplets*) че́тверо (-ры́х) близнецо́в. **quadrangle** *n.* (*figure*) четырёхуго́льник; (*court*) четырёхуго́льный двор (-а́). **quadrangular** *adj.* четырёхуго́льный. **quadrant** *n.* квадра́нт. **quadrat** *n.* шпа́ция. **quadratic** *adj.* квадра́тный; *q. equation*, квадра́тное уравне́ние. **quadrilateral** *adj.* четырёхсторо́нний.
quadrille *n.* кадри́ль.
quadroon *n.* квартеро́н.
quadruped *n.* четвероно́гое живо́тное *sb.* **quadruple** *adj.* четверно́й, учетверённый (-ён, -ена́); *v.t.* & *i.* учетверя́ть(ся) *imp.*, учетвери́ть(ся) *perf.* **quadruplets** *n.* че́тверо (-ры́х) близнецо́в.
quaff *v.t.* пить (пью́, пьёшь; пил, -а́, -о) *imp.*, вы́~ *perf.* больши́ми глотка́ми.
quag, quagmire *n.* тряси́на; (*also fig.*) боло́то.
quail[1] *n.* (*bird*) пе́репел (*pl.* -а́), -ёлка.
quail[2] *v.i.* (*flinch*) дро́гнуть *perf.*; тру́сить *imp.*, с~ *perf.* (before, + *acc.*, пе́ред + *instr.*).
quaint *adj.* причу́дливый, оригина́льный.
quake *v.i.* трясти́сь (трясу́сь, -сёшься; тря́сся, -сла́сь) *imp.*; дрожа́ть (-жу́, -жи́шь) *imp.* (for, with, от + *gen.*); *n.* землетрясе́ние.
Quaker *n.* ква́кер, ~ка.
qualification *n.* (*restriction*) ограниче́ние, огово́рка; (*for post etc.*) квалифика́ция; (*for citizenship etc.*) ценз; (*description*) характери́стика. **qualify** *v.t.* (*describe*) квалифици́ровать *imp.*, *perf.*; (*restrict*) ограни́чивать *imp.*, ограни́чить *perf.*; *v.t.* & *i.* (*prepare for*) гото́вить(ся) *imp.* (for, к + *dat.*; + *inf.*).
qualitative *adj.* ка́чественный. **quality** *n.* ка́чество; сорт; (*excellence*) высо́кое ка́чество; (*ability*) спосо́бность.
qualm *n.* (*queasiness*) при́ступ тошноты́; (*doubt, scruple*) колеба́ние, угрызе́ние со́вести.
quandary *n.* затрудни́тельное положе́ние, диле́мма.
quantify *v.t.* определя́ть *imp.*, определи́ть *perf.* коли́чество + *gen.* **quantitative** *adj.* коли́чественный. **quantity** *n.* коли́чество; (*math.*) величина́ (*pl.* -ны).
quantum *n.* (*amount*) коли́чество; (*share*) до́ля (*pl.* -ли, -ле́й); (*phys.*) квант; *attrib.* ква́нтовый.
quarantine *n.* каранти́н; *v.t.* подверга́ть *imp.*, подве́ргнуть (-г) *perf.* каранти́ну.
quark *n.* кварк.
quarrel *n.* ссо́ра; *v.i.* ссо́риться *imp.*, по~ *perf.* (with, с + *instr.*; about, for, из-за + *gen.*). **quarrelsome** *adj.* вздо́рный.
quarry[1] *n.* (*for stone etc.*) каменоло́мня (*gen.pl.* -мен), карье́р; *v.t.* добыва́ть *imp.*, добы́ть (добу́ду, -дешь; до́был, -а́, -о) *perf.*
quarry[2] *n.* (*object of pursuit*) пресле́дуемый зве́рь (*pl.* -ри, -ре́й) *m.*
quart *n.* ква́рта. **quarter** *n.* че́тверть (*pl.* -ти, -те́й); (*of year; of town*) кварта́л; (*direction*) сторона́ (*acc.* -ону; *pl.* -оны, -о́н, -она́м); (*mercy*) поща́да; *pl.* кварти́ры *f.pl.*; *a q. to one*, без че́тверти час; *q.-day*, пе́рвый день (дня) *m.* кварта́ла; *q.-final*, четверть-

фина́л(ьная игра́); *v.t.* (*divide*) дели́ть (-лю́, -лишь) *imp.*, раз~ *perf.* на четы́ре (ра́вные) ча́сти; (*traitor's body*) четвертова́ть *imp.*, *perf.*; (*lodge*) расквартиро́вывать *imp.*, расквартирова́ть *perf.* **quarterdeck** *n.* шка́нцы (-цев) *pl.* **quarterly** *adj.* трёхме́сячный, кварта́льный; *n.* журна́л, выходя́щий раз в три ме́сяца; *adv.* раз в кварта́л, раз в три ме́сяца. **quartermaster** *n.* квартирме́йстер. **quartet(te)** *n.* кварте́т. **quarto** *n.* (ин-)ква́рто *neut.indecl.*

quartz *n.* кварц.

quasar *n.* кваза́р.

quash *v.t.* (*annul*) аннули́ровать *imp.*, *perf.*; (*crush*) подавля́ть *imp.*, подави́ть (-влю́, -вишь) *perf.*

quasi *adv.* как бу́дто.

quasi- *in comb.* квази-.

quater-centenary *n.* четырёхсотле́тие.

quatrain *n.* четверости́шие.

quaver *v.i.* дрожа́ть (-жу́, -жи́шь) *imp.*; *n.* дрожа́ние; (*mus.*) восьма́я *sb.* но́ты.

quay *n.* на́бережная *sb.*

queasy *adj.* (*stomach*) сла́бый (слаб, -а́, -о); (*person*) испы́тывающий тошноту́.

queen *n.* короле́ва; (*cards*) да́ма; (*chess*) ферзь (-зя́) *m.*; *q. bee*, ма́тка; *q. mother*, вдо́вствующая короле́ва; *v.t.* (*chess*) проводи́ть (-ожу́, -о́дишь) *imp.*, провести́ (-еду́, -едёшь; -ёл, -ела́) *perf.* в ферзи́. **queenly** *adj.* ца́рственный (-ен(ен), -енна).

queer *adj.* стра́нный (-нен, -нна́, -нно); *feel q.*, чу́вствовать *imp.* недомога́ние.

quell *v.t.* подавля́ть *imp.*, подави́ть (-влю́, -вишь) *perf.*

quench *v.t.* (*thirst*) утоля́ть *imp.*, утоли́ть *perf.*; (*fire, desire*) туши́ть (-шу́, -шишь) *imp.*, по~ *perf.*

querulous *adj.* ворчли́вый.

query *n.* вопро́с, сомне́ние; *v.t.* (*express doubt*) выража́ть *imp.*, вы́разить *perf.* сомне́ние в+*prep.* **quest** *n.* по́иски *m.pl.*; *in q. of*, в по́исках+*gen.* **question** *n.* вопро́с; (*doubt*) сомне́ние; *beyond all q.*, вне сомне́ния; *it is (merely) a q. of*, э́то вопро́с+*gen.*; де́ло то́лько в том, что́бы+*inf.*; *it is out of the q.*, об э́том не мо́жет быть и ре́чи; *the person in q.*, челове́к, о кото́ром идёт речь; *the q. is this*, де́ло в э́том; *q. mark*, вопроси́тельный знак; *v.t.* (*ask*) спра́шивать *imp.*, спроси́ть (-ошу́, -о́сишь) *perf.*; (*doubt*) сомнева́ться *imp.* в+*prep.* **questionable** *adj.* сомни́тельный. **questionnaire** *n.* анке́та, вопро́сник.

queue *n.* о́чередь (*pl.* -ди, -де́й); *v.i.* стоя́ть (-ою́, -ои́шь) *imp.* в о́череди.

quibble *n.* софи́зм, увёртка; *v.i.* уклоня́ться *imp.*, уклони́ться (-ню́сь, -ни́шься) *perf.* от су́ти вопро́са, от прямо́го отве́та.

quick *adj.* ско́рый (скор, -а́, -о), бы́стрый (быстр, -а́, -о, бы́стры́); (*nimble*) прово́рный; (*clever*) смышлёный; *q.-tempered*, вспы́льчивый; *q.-witted*, остроу́мный; *n.*: *to the q.*, за живо́е, до мя́са; *the q. and the dead*, живы́е и мёртвые *sb.*; *adv.* ско́ро, бы́стро; *as imper.* скоре́е! **quicken** *v.t.* & *i.* (*accelerate*) ускоря́ть(ся) *imp.*, уско́рить(ся) *perf.*; *v.t.* (*animate*) оживля́ть *imp.*, оживи́ть *perf.* **quicklime** *n.* негашёная и́звесть. **quickness** *n.* быстрота́; прово́рство. **quicksand** *n.* плыву́н (-а́), зыбу́чий песо́к (-ска́). **quickset** *n.* (*hedge*) жива́я и́згородь. **quicksilver** *n.* ртуть.

quid *n.* фунт.

quiescence *n.* неподви́жность, поко́й. **quiescent** *adj.* неподви́жный, в состоя́нии поко́я. **quiet** *n.* (*silence*) тишина́; (*calm*) споко́йствие; *adj.* ти́хий (тих, -а́, -о); споко́йный; *interj.* ти́ше!; *v.t.* & *i.* успока́ивать(ся) *imp.*, успоко́ить(ся) *perf.*

quill *n.* (*feather*) перо́ (*pl.* -рья, -рьев); (*spine*) игла́ (*pl.* -лы).

quilt *n.* (стёганое) одея́ло; *v.t.* стега́ть *imp.*, вы́~ *perf.* **quilting** *n.* стёжка.

quince *n.* айва́.

quincentenary *n.* пятисотле́тие.

quinine *n.* хини́н.

quinquennial *adj.* пятиле́тний.

quintessence *n.* квинтэссе́нция.

quintet(te) *n.* квинте́т. **quintuple** *adj.* пятикра́тный. **quins, quintuplets** *n.* пять (-ти́, -тью́) близнецо́в.

quip *n.* острóта.
quire *n.* (*in manuscript*) тетрáдь; (*24 sheets*) рýсская дéсть (*pl.* -ти, -тéй).
quirk *n.* причýда.
quisling *n.* квúслинг.
quit *v.t.* покидáть *imp.*, покúнуть *perf.*; (*dwelling*) выезжáть *imp.*, вы́ехать (-еду, -едешь) *perf.* из + *gen.*
quite *adv.* (*wholly*) совсéм, вполнé; (*somewhat*) довóльно; *q. a few*, довóльно мнóго.
quits *predic.*: *we are q.*, мы с тобóй квúты; *I am q. with him*, я расквитáлся (*past*) с ним.
quiver[1] (*for arrows*) колчáн.
quiver[2] *v.i.* (*tremble*) трепетáть (-ещý, -éщешь) *imp.*; дрожáть (-жý, -жúшь) *imp.* (мéлкой дрóжью); *n.* трéпет, мéлкая дрожь.
quixotic *adj.* донкихóтский.
quiz *n.* викторúна. **quizzical** *adj.* насмéшливый.
quod *n.* тюрьмá.
quoit *n.* метáтельное кольцó (*pl.* -льца, -лéц, -льцам); *pl.* (*game*) метáние колéц в цель.
quondam *adj.* бы́вший.
quorum *n.* квóрум.
quota *n.* квóта.
quotation *n.* (*quoting*) цитúрование; (*passage quoted*) цитáта; (*estimate*) смéта; (*of stocks etc.*) котирóвка; *q.-marks*, кавы́чки (-чек) *pl.* **quote** *v.t.* цитúровать *imp.*, про ~ *perf.*; ссылáться *imp.*, сослáться (сошлю́сь, -лёшься) *perf.* на + *acc.*; (*price*) назначáть *imp.*, назнáчить *perf.*
quotidian *adj.* (*daily*) ежеднéвный; (*commonplace*) обы́денный.
quotient *n.* чáстное *sb.*

R

rabbet *n.* шпунт (-á).
rabbi *n.* раввúн. **rabbinical** *adj.* раввúнский.
rabbit *n.* крóлик; *r. punch*, удáр в заты́лок.
rabble *n.* сброд, чернь.
rabid *adj.* бéшеный. **rabies** *n.* водобоя́знь, бéшенство.
raccoon *see* **racoon.**
race[1] *n.* (*ethnic r.*) рáса; род.
race[2] *n.* (*contest*) (*on foot*) бег; (*of cars etc.*; *fig.*) гóнка, гóнки *f.pl.*; (*of horses*) скáчки *f.pl.*; *r.-meeting*, скáчки *f.pl.*; *r.-track*, трек; (*for horse r.*) скаковáя дорóжка; *v.i.* (*compete*) состязáться *imp.* в скóрости; (*rush*) мчáться (мчусь, мчúшься) *imp.*; *v.t.* гнать (гоню́, -нишь; гнал, -á, -о). **racecard** *n.* прогрáмма скáчек. **racecourse** *n.* ипподрóм. **racehorse** *n.* скаковáя лóшадь (*pl.* -ди, -дéй, *instr.* -дьмú). **racer** *n.* (*person*) гóнщик; (*car*) гóночный автомобúль *m.*
racial *adj.* рáсовый. **rac(ial)ism** *n.* расúзм. **rac(ial)ist** *n.* расúст, ~ка; *adj.* расúстский.
rack[1] *n.* (*for fodder*) кормýшка; (*for hats etc.*) вéшалка; (*for plates etc.*) стеллáж (-á); (*in train etc.*) сéтка для вещéй; (*for torture*) ды́ба; (*cogged bar*) зубчáтая рéйка; *v.t.* мýчить *imp.*; пытáть *imp.*; *r. one's brains*, ломáть *imp.* себé гóлову.
rack[2] *n.*: *go to r. and ruin*, разоря́ться *imp.*, разорúться *perf.*
racket[1] *n.* (*bat*) ракéтка.
racket[2] *n.* (*uproar*) шум (-а(у)); (*illegal activity*) рэ́кет. **racketeer** *n.* рэкетúр.
rac(c)oon *n.* енóт.
racy *adj.* колорúтный.
rad *n.* рад.
radar *n.* (*system*) радиолокáция;

(*apparatus*) радиолока́тор, рада́р; *attrib.* радиолокацио́нный, рада́рный.

radial *adj.* радиа́льный, лучево́й.

radiance *n.* сия́ние. **radiant** *adj.* сия́ющий; лучи́стый; *n.* исто́чник (лучи́стого) тепла́, све́та. **radiate** *v.t.* излуча́ть *imp.*; лучи́ться *imp.* + *instr.*; *v.i.* исходи́ть (-ит) *imp.* из одно́й то́чки; (*diverge*) расходи́ться (-ятся) *imp.* луча́ми. **radiation** *n.* излуче́ние, радиа́ция; *r. sickness*, лучева́я боле́знь. **radiator** *n.* радиа́тор; (*in central heating*) батаре́я.

radical *adj.* коренно́й; (*polit.*) радика́льный; (*ling.*) корнево́й; *n.* (*polit.*, *chem.*) радика́л; (*math.*, *ling.*) ко́рень (-рня; *pl.* -рни, -рне́й) *m.* **radically** *adv.* коренны́м о́бразом, соверше́нно.

radicle *n.* корешо́к (-шка́).

radio *n.* ра́дио *neut.indecl.*; *adj.* радио-; *v.t.* ради́ровать *imp.*, *perf.*

radio- *in comb.* радио-; *r. astronomy*, радиоастроно́мия; *r.-carbon*, радиоакти́вный изото́п углеро́да; *r.-carbon dating*, дати́рование радиоуглеро́дным ме́тодом; *r.-chemistry*, радиохи́мия; *r.-element*, радиоакти́вный элеме́нт; *r.-frequency*, (*n.*) радиочастота́ (*pl.* -ты); (*adj.*) радиочасто́тный; *r. star*, радиозвезда́ (*pl.* -ёзды); *r.-telegraphy*, радиотелеграфи́я; *r.-telephone*, радиотелефо́н; *r. telescope*, радиотелеско́п; *r. wave*, радиоволна́ (*pl.* -о́лны, *dat.* -о́лна́м). **radioactive** *adj.* радиоакти́вный. **radioactivity** *n.* радиоакти́вность. **radiogram** *n.* (*X-ray picture*) рентгеногра́мма; (*radio-telegram*) радиогра́мма; (*radio and gramophone*) радио́ла. **radiographer** *n.* рентгено́лог. **radiography** *n.* радиогра́фия; (*spec. X-ray*) рентгеногра́фия. **radioisotope** *n.* радиоизото́п. **radiolocation** *n.* радиолока́ция. **radiologist** *n.* радио́лог; (*spec. X-ray*) рентгено́лог. **radiology** *n.* радиоло́гия; рентгеноло́гия. **radiometer** *n.* радиоме́тр. **radioscopy** *n.* рентгеноскопи́я. **radiosonde** *n.* радиозо́нд. **radiotherapy** *n.* радиотерапи́я; (*spec. X-ray*) рентгенотерапи́я.

radish *n.* реди́ска; реди́с (*no pl.*: *plant*; *collect.*).

radium *n.* ра́дий.

radius *n.* (*math.*) ра́диус; (*bone*) лучева́я кость.

radon *n.* радо́н.

raffia *n.* ра́фия.

raffish *adj.* беспу́тный.

raffle *n.* лотере́я; *v.t.* разы́грывать *imp.*, разыгра́ть *perf.* в лотере́е.

raft *n.* плот (-а́, *loc.* -у́).

rafter *n.* (*beam*) стропи́ло.

raftsman *n.* плотовщи́к (-а́).

rag[1] *n.* тря́пка, лоску́т (-а́; *pl.* -а́, -о́в & -ья, -ьев); *pl.* (*clothes*) лохмо́тья (-ьев) *pl.*; *r.-and-bone man*, тряпи́чник; *r. doll*, тряпи́чная ку́кла (*gen. pl.* -кол).

rag[2] *v.t.* (*tease*) дразни́ть (-ню́, -нишь) *imp.*

ragamuffin *n.* оборва́нец (-нца).

rage *n.* (*anger*) я́рость, гнев; (*desire*) страсть (for, к + *dat.*); *all the r.*, после́дний крик мо́ды; *v.i.* беси́ться (бешу́сь, бе́сишься) *imp.*; (*storm etc.*) свире́пствовать *imp.*

ragged *adj.* (*jagged*) зазу́бренный (-ен); (*of clothes*) изо́дранный (-ан, -анна); (*of person*) в лохмо́тьях.

raglan *n.* регла́н; *r. sleeve*, рука́в (-а́; *pl.* -а́) регла́н (*indecl.*).

ragout *n.* рагу́ *neut.indecl.*

ragtime *n.* ре́гтайм.

ragwort *n.* кресто́вник.

raid *n.* набе́г, налёт; (*by police*) обла́ва; *v.t.* де́лать *imp.*, с~ *perf.* налёт на + *acc.*

rail *n.* пери́ла (-л) *pl.*; (*rly.*) рельс; (*railway*) желе́зная доро́га; *by r.*, по́ездом, по желе́зной доро́ге; *v.t.*: *r. in*, *off*, обноси́ть (-ошу́, -о́сишь) *imp.*, обнести́ (-есу́, -есёшь; -ёс, -есла́) *perf.* пери́лами. **railhead** *n.* коне́чный пункт (желе́зной доро́ги). **railing** *n.* пери́ла (-л) *pl.*, огра́да.

raillery *n.* доброду́шное подшу́чивание.

railway *n.* желе́зная доро́га; *attrib.* железнодоро́жный. **railwayman** *n.* железнодоро́жник.

raiment *n.* одея́ние.

rain *n.* дождь (-дя́) *m.*; *pl.* (*the r.*) пери́од (тропи́ческих) дожде́й; *r.-gauge*, дождеме́р; *r.-water*, дождева́я вода́ (*acc.* -ду); *v.impers.* *it is* (*was*) *raining*, идёт (шёл) дождь; *v.t.* осыпа́ть *imp.*, осы́пать (-плю, -плешь) *perf.* + *instr.* (upon, + *acc.*); *v.i.* осыпа́ться *imp.*, осы́паться (-плется) *perf.* **rainbow** *n.* ра́дуга; *r. trout*, ра́дужная форе́ль. **raincoat** *n.* непромока́емое пальто́ *neut.indecl.*, плащ (-а́). **raindrop** *n.* дождева́я ка́пля (*gen.pl.* -пель). **rainfall** *n.* (*shower*) ли́вень (-вня) *m.*; (*amount of rain*) коли́чество оса́дков. **rainproof** *adj.* непромока́емый. **rainy** *adj.* дождли́вый; *r. day*, чёрный день (дня) *m.*

raise *v.t.* (*lift*) поднима́ть *imp.*, подня́ть (подниму́, -мешь; по́днял, -а́, -о) *perf.*; (*heighten*) повыша́ть *imp.*, повы́сить *perf.*; (*erect*) воздвига́ть *imp.*, воздви́гнуть (-г) *perf.*; (*provoke*) вызыва́ть *imp.*, вы́звать (вы́зову, -вешь) *perf.*; (*procure*) добыва́ть *imp.*, добы́ть (добу́ду, -дешь; до́бы́л, -а́, -о) *perf.*; (*children*) расти́ть *imp.*

raisin *n.* изю́минка; *pl.* (*collect.*) изю́м (-а(у)).

raja(h) *n.* ра́джа (*gen.pl.* -жей) *m.*

rake[1] (*tool*) гра́бли (-блей & -бель) *pl.*; *v.t.* (*r. together*, *up*) сгреба́ть *imp.*, сгрести́ (сгребу́, -бёшь; сгрёб, -бла́) *perf.*; (*with shot*) обстре́ливать *imp.*, обстреля́ть *perf.* продо́льным огнём.

rake[2] *n.* (*person*) пове́са *m.* **rakish** *adj.* распу́тный.

rally[1] *v.t.* & *i.* спла́чивать(ся) *imp.*, сплоти́ть(ся) *perf.*; *v.i.* (*after illness etc.*) оправля́ться *imp.*, опра́виться *perf.*; *n.* (*meeting*) слёт; ма́ссовый ми́тинг; (*motoring r.*) (авто)ра́лли *neut.indecl.*; (*tennis*) обме́н уда́рами.

rally[2] *v.t.* (*ridicule*) подшу́чивать *imp.*, подшути́ть (-учу́, -у́тишь) *perf.* над + *instr.*

ram *n.* (*sheep*) бара́н; (*the R.*, *Aries*) Ове́н (Овна́); (*machine*) тара́н; *v.t.* (*beat down*) трамбова́ть *imp.*, у~ *perf.*; (*drive in*) вбива́ть *imp.*, вбить (вобью́, -ьёшь) *perf.*; (*strike with r.*) тара́нить *imp.*, про~ *perf.*

ramble *v.i.* (*walk*) броди́ть (-ожу́, -о́дишь) *imp.*; (*speak*) говори́ть *imp.* несвя́зно; *n.* прогу́лка. **rambler (rose)** *n.* вью́щаяся ро́за. **rambling** *adj.* (*scattered*) разбро́санный; (*incoherent*) бессвя́зный.

ramification *n.* разветвле́ние. **ramify** *v.i.* разветвля́ться *imp.*, разветви́ться *perf.*

ramp *n.* скат, укло́н.

rampage *v.i.* неи́стовствовать *imp.*; *n.* неи́стовство.

rampant *adj.* (*of lion etc.*) стоя́щий на за́дних ла́пах; (*raging*) свире́пствующий.

rampart *n.* вал (*loc.* -у́; *pl.* -ы́).

ramrod *n.* шо́мпол (*pl.* -а́).

ramshackle *adj.* ве́тхий (ветх, -а́, -о).

ranch *n.* ра́нчо *neut.indecl.*

rancid *adj.* прого́рклый.

rancour *n.* зло́ба. **rancorous** *adj.* зло́бный.

random *n.*: *at r.*, науда́чу, науга́д, набу́м; *adj.* сде́ланный (-ан), вы́бранный (-ан), науга́д; случа́йный.

range *n.* (*of mountains*) цепь (*pl.* -пи, -пе́й); (*grazing ground*) неогоро́женное па́стбище; (*artillery r.*) полиго́н; (*of voice*) диапазо́н; (*scope*) круг (*loc.* -у́; *pl.* -и́), преде́лы *m.pl.*; (*distance*) да́льность; *r.-finder*, дальноме́р; *v.t.* (*arrange in row*) выстра́ивать *imp.*, вы́строить *perf.* в ряд; *v.i.* (*extend*) тяну́ться (-нется) *imp.*; (*occur*) встреча́ться *imp.*, встре́титься *perf.*; (*vary*) колеба́ться (-блется) *imp.*, по~ *perf.*; (*wander*) броди́ть (-ожу́, -о́дишь) *imp.*

rank[1] *n.* (*row*) ряд (-а́ *with* 2, 3, 4; *loc.* -у́; *pl.* -ы́); (*taxi r.*) стоя́нка такси́; (*grade*) зва́ние, чин, ранг; *v.t.* (*classify*) классифици́ровать *imp.*, *perf.*; (*consider*) счита́ть *imp.* (as, + *instr.*); *v.i.*: *r. with*, быть (*fut.* бу́ду, -дешь; был, -а́, -о; не́ был, -а́, -о) в числе́ + *gen.*, на у́ровне + *gen.*

rank[2] *adj.* (*luxuriant*) бу́йный (бу́ен, буйна́, -но); (*in smell*) зловонный (-нен, -нна); (*repulsive*) отврати́тельный; (*clear*) я́вный.

rankle *v.i.* причиня́ть *imp.*, причини́ть *perf.* боль.

ransack *v.t.* (*search*) обша́ривать *imp.*, обша́рить *perf.*; (*plunder*) гра́бить *imp.*, о~ *perf.*

ransom *n.* вы́куп; *v.t.* выкупа́ть *imp.*, вы́купить *perf.*

rant *v.t.* & *i.* напыщенно деклами́ровать *imp.*
rap[1] *n.* (*blow*) стук, ре́зкий уда́р; *v.t.* (ре́зко) ударя́ть *imp.*, уда́рить *perf.*; *v.i.* стуча́ть (-чу́, -чи́шь) *imp.*, сту́кнуть *perf.*; *r. out*, (*words*) отчека́нивать *imp.*, отчека́нить *perf.*
rap[2] *n.*: *not a r.*, ниско́лько; *I don't care a r.*, мне наплева́ть.
rapacious *adj.* неуме́ренно жа́дный (-ден, -дна́, -дно), хи́щнический.
rape[1] *v.t.* наси́ловать *imp.*, из~ *perf.*; *n.* изнаси́лование; (*abduction*) похище́ние.
rape[2] *n.* (*plant*) рапс; *r.-oil*, ра́псовое ма́сло.
rapid *adj.* бы́стрый (быстр, -á, -о, бы́стры́); *n.*: *pl.* поро́г, быстрина́ (*pl.* -ны). **rapidity** *n.* быстрота́.
rapier *n.* рапи́ра.
rapt *adj.* восхищённый (-ён, -ённа); (*absorbed*) поглощённый (-ён, -ена́). **rapture** *n.* восто́рг. **rapturous** *adj.* восто́рженный (-ен, -енна).
rare[1] *adj.* (*of meat*) недожа́ренный (-ен).
rare[2] *adj.* ре́дкий (-док, -дка́, -дко), ре́дкостный. **rarefy** *v.t.* разрежа́ть *imp.*, разреди́ть *perf.* **rarity** *n.* ре́дкость.
rascal *n.* плут (-á).
rase *see* **raze.**
rash[1] *n.* сыпь.
rash[2] *adj.* опроме́тчивый.
rasher *n.* ло́мтик (беко́на, ветчины́).
rasp *n.* (*file*) ра́шпиль *m.*; (*sound*) ре́жущий звук; *a r. in the voice*, скрипу́чий го́лос; *v.t.*: *r. the nerves*, де́йствовать *imp.*, по~ *perf.* на не́рвы.
raspberry *n.* (*plant*) мали́на (*also collect.*, *fruit*); *attrib.* мали́новый.
rasping *adj.* (*sound*) ре́жущий, скрипу́чий.
rat *n.* кры́са; (*turncoat*) перебе́жчик; *r.-catcher* крысоло́в; *r.-race*, бе́шеная пого́ня за успе́хом; *r.-trap*, крысоло́вка; *v.i.*: *r. on*, предава́ть (-даю́, -даёшь) *imp.*, преда́ть (-а́м, -а́шь, -а́ст, -ади́м; пре́дал, -á, -о) *perf.* + *acc.*
ratchet *n.* храпови́к (-á); *attrib.* храпово́й.
rate *n.* но́рма, ста́вка; (*speed*) ско́рость; *pl.* ме́стные нало́ги *m.pl.*; *at any r.*, во вся́ком слу́чае, по ме́ньшей ме́ре; *at the r. of*, по + *dat.*, со ско́ростью + *gen.*; *v.t.* оце́нивать *imp.*, оцени́ть (-ню́, -нишь) *perf.*; (*consider*) счита́ть *imp.* **rateable** *adj.* подлежа́щий обложе́нию ме́стным нало́гом; *r. value*, облага́емая сто́имость. **ratepayer** *n.* налогоплате́льщик, -ица.
rather *adv.* лу́чше, скоре́е; (*somewhat*) не́сколько, дово́льно; (*as answer*) ещё бы!; *he* (*she*) *had* (*would*) *r.*, он (она́) предпочёл (-чла́) бы + *inf.*; *or r.*, (и́ли) верне́е (сказа́ть), точне́е (сказа́ть); *r. . . . than*, скоре́е ... чем.
ratification *n.* ратифика́ция. **ratify** *v.t.* ратифици́ровать *imp.*, *perf.*
rating *n.* оце́нка; (*naut.*) рядово́й *sb.*
ratio *n.* пропо́рция.
ration *n.* паёк (пайка́), рацио́н; *v.t.* нормирова́ть *imp.*, *perf.*; *be rationed*, выдава́ться (-даётся) *imp.*, вы́даться (-астся, -адутся) *perf.* по ка́рточкам.
rational *adj.* разу́мный; (*also math.*) рациона́льный. **rationalism** *n.* рационали́зм. **rationalist** *n.* рационали́ст. **rationalize** *v.t.* дава́ть (даю́, даёшь) *imp.*, дать (дам, дашь, даст, дади́м; дал, -á, да́ло́, -и) *perf.* рационалисти́ческое объясне́ние + *gen.*; (*industry etc.*) рационализи́ровать *imp.*, *perf.*
rattan *n.* рота́нг.
rattle *v.i.* & *t.* (*sound*) греме́ть (-млю́, -ми́шь) *imp.* (+ *instr.*); бря́цать *imp.* (+ *instr.*); *v.i.* (*speak*) болта́ть *imp.*; *v.t.* (*fluster*) смуща́ть *imp.*, смути́ть (-ущу́, -ути́шь) *perf.*; *r. along*, (*move*) мча́ться (мчусь, мчи́шься) *imp.* с гро́хотом; *r. off*, (*utter*) отбараба́нить *perf.*; *n.* (*sound*) треск, гро́хот; (*instrument*) трещо́тка; (*toy*) погрему́шка. **rattlesnake** *n.* грему́чая змея́ (*pl.* -е́и, -е́й). **rattling** *adj.* (*brisk*) бы́стрый; *r. good*, великоле́пный.
raucous *adj.* ре́зкий (-зок, -зка́, -зко).
ravage *v.t.* опустоша́ть *imp.*, опустоши́ть *perf.*; *n.*: *pl.* разруши́тельное де́йствие.
rave *v.i.* бре́дить *imp.*; (*wind*, *sea*) реве́ть (-вёт) *imp.*; *r. about*, бре́дить *imp.* + *instr.*; восторга́ться *imp.* + *instr.*

raven *n.* во́рон.
ravenous *adj.* прожо́рливый; (*famished*) голо́дный (го́лоден, -дна́, -дно, го́лодны́) как волк; *r. appetite*, во́лчий аппети́т.
ravine *n.* уще́лье (*gen.pl.* -лий).
ravish *v.t.* (*rape*) наси́ловать *imp.*, из~ *perf.*; (*charm*) восхища́ть *imp.*, восхити́ть (-ищу́, -ити́шь) *perf.* **ravishing** *adj.* восхити́тельный.
raw *adj.* сыро́й (сыр, -а́, -о); (*brick*) необожжённый; (*alcohol*) неразба́вленный; (*style*) неотде́ланный; (*inexperienced*) нео́пытный; (*stripped of skin*) обо́дранный; (*sensitive*) чувстви́тельный; (*edge of cloth*) неподру́бленный; *r.-boned*, костля́вый; *r. material(s)*, сырьё (*no pl.*); *r. place*, (*abrasion*) цара́пина; *r. silk*, шёлк-сыре́ц (-рца́); *r. wound*, жива́я ра́на; *n.* больно́е ме́сто; *touch on the r.*, задева́ть *imp.*, заде́ть (-е́ну, -е́нешь) *perf.* за живо́е. **rawhide** *n.* недублёная ко́жа.
ray[1] *n.* (*beam*) луч (-а́); (*fig.*) про́блеск.
ray[2] *n.* (*fish*) скат.
rayon *n.* виско́за.
raze *v.t.*: *r. to the ground*, ровня́ть *imp.*, с~ *perf.* с землёй.
razor *n.* бри́тва; *r.-back*, (*ridge*) о́стрый хребе́т (-бта́); (*whale*) полоса́тик; *r.-bill*, гага́рка.
reach *v.t.* (*extend*) протя́гивать *imp.*, протяну́ть (-ну́, -нешь) *perf.*; (*attain, arrive at*) достига́ть *imp.*, дости́чь & дости́гнуть (-и́гну, -и́гнешь; -и́г) *perf.* + *gen.*, до + *gen.*; доходи́ть (-ожу́, -о́дишь) *imp.*, дойти́ (дойду́, -дёшь; дошёл, -шла́) *perf.* до + *gen.*; *v.i.* (*extend*) простира́ться *imp.*; *n.* досяга́емость; (*of river*) плёс.
react *v.i.* реаги́ровать *imp.*, от~, про~ *perf.* (to, на + *acc.*). **reaction** *n.* реа́кция. **reactionary** *adj.* реакцио́нный; *n.* реакционе́р, ~ка. **reactive** *adj.* реаги́рующий; (*tech.*) реакти́вный. **reactor** *n.* реа́ктор.
read *v.t.* чита́ть *imp.*, про~, проче́сть (-чту́, -чтёшь; -чёл, -чла́) *perf.*; (*piece of music*) разбира́ть *imp.*, разобра́ть (разберу́, -рёшь; разобра́л, -а́, -о) *perf.*; (*of meter etc.*) пока́зывать *imp.*, показа́ть (-а́жет) *perf.*; (*r. a meter etc.*) снима́ть *imp.*, снять (сниму́, -мешь; снял, -а́, -о) *perf.* показа́ния + *gen.*; (*univ.*) изуча́ть *imp.*; (*interpret*) толкова́ть *imp.*; *v.i.* чита́ться *imp.* **readable** *adj.* интере́сный, хорошо́ напи́санный (-ан); (*legible*) разбо́рчивый. **reader** *n.* чита́тель *m.*, ~ница; (*publisher's r.*) рецензе́нт; (*printer's r.*) корре́ктор (*pl.* -ы & -а́); (*univ.*) ста́рший преподава́тель *m.*; (*book*) хрестома́тия.
readily *adv.* (*willingly*) охо́тно; (*easily*) легко́. **readiness** *n.* гото́вность.
reading *n.* чте́ние; (*erudition*) начи́танность; (*variant*) вариа́нт; (*interpretation*) толкова́ние; *r.-desk*, пюпи́тр; *r.-lamp*, насто́льная ла́мпа; *r. matter*, литерату́ра; *r.-room*, чита́льня (*gen. pl.* -лен), чита́льный зал.
ready *adj.* гото́вый (for, к + *dat.*, на + *acc.*); *r.-made*, гото́вый; *r. money*, нали́чные де́ньги (-нег, -ньга́м) *pl.*; *r. reckoner*, арифмети́ческие табли́цы *f.pl.*
reagent *n.* реакти́в.
real *adj.* настоя́щий, действи́тельный, реа́льный; *r. estate*, недви́жимость. **realism** *n.* реали́зм. **realist** *n.* реали́ст. **realistic** *adj.* реалисти́чный, -и́ческий. **reality** *n.* действи́тельность; *in r.*, действи́тельно. **realization** *n.* (*of plan etc.*) осуществле́ние; (*of assets*) реализа́ция; (*understanding*) осозна́ние. **realize** *v.t.* (*plan etc.*) осуществля́ть *imp.*, осуществи́ть *perf.*; (*assets*) реализова́ть *imp.*, *perf.*; (*apprehend*) осознава́ть (-на́ю, -наёшь) *imp.*, осозна́ть *perf.* **really** *adv.* действи́тельно, в са́мом де́ле.
realm *n.* (*kingdom*) короле́вство; (*sphere*) о́бласть (*pl.* -ти, -те́й).
ream[1] *n.* стопа́ (*pl.* -пы).
ream[2] *v.t.* развёртывать *imp.*, разверну́ть *perf.*
reap *v.t.* жать (жну, жнёшь) *imp.*, сжать (сожну́, -нёшь) *perf.*; (*fig.*) пожина́ть *imp.*, пожа́ть (-жну́, -жнёшь) *perf.* **reaper** *n.* (*person*) жнец (-а́), жни́ца; (*machine*) жа́тка; *r. and binder*, жа́тка-сноповяза́лка. **reaping-hook** *n.* серп (-а́).
rear[1] *v.t.* (*lift*) поднима́ть *imp.*, подня́ть (-ниму́, -ни́мешь; по́днял, -а́, -о)

perf.; (*children*) воспи́тывать *imp.*, воспита́ть *perf.*; *v.i.* (*of horse*) станови́ться (-ится) *imp.*, стать (-а́нет) *perf.* на дыбы́.

rear[2] *n.* тыл (*loc.* -у́; *pl.* -ы́); *bring up the r.*, замыка́ть *imp.*, замкну́ть *perf.* ше́ствие; *adj.* за́дний; (*also mil.*) ты́льный; (*mil.*) тылово́й; *r.-admiral*, контр-адмира́л; *r.-light*, (*of car*) за́дний фона́рь (-ря́) *m.*; *r.-view mirror*, зе́ркало (*pl.* -ла́) за́дней обзо́рности. **rearguard** *n.* арьерга́рд; *r. action*, арьерга́рдный бой (*pl.* бои́). **rearwards** *adv.* наза́д, в тыл.

rearm *v.t.* & *i.* перевооружа́ть(ся) *imp.*, перевооружи́ть(ся) *perf.* **rearmament** *n.* перевооруже́ние.

reason *n.* (*cause*) причи́на, основа́ние; (*intellect*) ра́зум, рассу́док (-дка); *it stands to r.*, разуме́ется; *not without r.*, не без основа́ния; *v.t.* (*discuss*) обсужда́ть *imp.*, обсуди́ть (-ужу́, -у́дишь) *perf.*; *v.i.* рассужда́ть *imp.*; *r. with*, (*person*) угова́ривать *imp.* + *acc.* **reasonable** *adj.* (*sensible*) разу́мный; (*well-founded*) основа́тельный; (*inexpensive*) недорого́й (недо́рог, -а́, -о).

reassurance *n.* успока́ивание. **reassure** *v.t.* успока́ивать *imp.*, успоко́ить *perf.*

rebate *n.* ски́дка.

rebel *n.* повста́нец (-нца), бунтовщи́к (-а́); *adj.* повста́нческий; *v.i.* бунтова́ть *imp.*, взбунтова́ться *perf.* **rebellion** *n.* восста́ние, бунт. **rebellious** *adj.* мяте́жный, повста́нческий.

rebirth *n.* возрожде́ние.

rebound *v.i.* отска́кивать *imp.*, отскочи́ть (-чу́, -чишь) *perf.*; *n.* рикоше́т, отско́к.

rebuff *n.* отпо́р; *v.t.* дава́ть (даю́, даёшь) *imp.*, дать (дам, дашь, даст, дади́м; дал, -а́, да́ло́, -и) *perf.* + *dat.* отпо́р.

rebuke *v.t.* упрека́ть *imp.*, упрекну́ть *perf.*; *n.* упрёк.

rebut *v.t.* (*refute*) опроверга́ть *imp.*, опрове́ргнуть (-г(нул), -гла) *perf.* **rebuttal** *n.* опроверже́ние.

recalcitrant *adj.* непоко́рный.

recall *v.t.* (*summon*) призыва́ть *imp.*, призва́ть (призову́, -вёшь; призва́л, -а́, -о) *perf.* обра́тно; (*an official*) отзыва́ть *imp.*, отозва́ть (отзову́, -вёшь, отозва́л, -а́, -о) *perf.*; (*remember*) вспомина́ть *imp.*, вспо́мнить *perf.*; (*remind*) напомина́ть *imp.*, напо́мнить *perf.*; (*r. to life*) возвраща́ть *imp.*, верну́ть *perf.* к жи́зни; *n.* призы́в верну́ться; о́тзыв.

recant *v.t.* & *i.* отрека́ться *imp.*, отре́чься (-еку́сь, -ечёшься; -ёкся, -екла́сь) *perf.* (от + *gen.*). **recantation** *n.* отрече́ние.

recapitulate *v.t.* резюми́ровать *imp.*, *perf.* **recapitulation** *n.* резюме́ *neut. indecl.*

recast *v.t.* перераба́тывать *imp.*, перерабо́тать *perf.*; переде́лывать *imp.*, переде́лать *perf.*

recede *v.i.* отходи́ть (-ожу́, -о́дишь) *imp.*, отойти́ (отойду́, -дёшь; отошёл, -шла́) *perf.*; отступа́ть *imp.*, отступи́ть (-плю́, -пишь) *perf.*

receipt *n.* (*receiving*) получе́ние; *pl.* (*amount*) прихо́д; (*written r.*) распи́ска, квита́нция; *v.t.* распи́сываться *imp.*, расписа́ться (-ишу́сь, -и́шешься) *perf.* на + *prep.* **receive** *v.t.* (*accept, admit, entertain*) принима́ть *imp.*, приня́ть (приму́, -мешь; при́нял, -а́, -о) *perf.*; (*acquire, be given, be sent*) получа́ть *imp.*, получи́ть (-чу́, -чишь) *perf.*; (*stolen goods*) укрыва́ть *imp.*, укры́ть (-ро́ю, -ро́ешь) *perf.* **receiver** *n.* (*official r.*) управля́ющий *sb.* иму́ществом (банкро́та); (*of stolen goods*) укрыва́тель *m.* кра́деного; (*radio, television*) приёмник; (*telephone*) тру́бка.

recension *n.* изво́д.

recent *adj.* неда́вний; (*new*) но́вый (нов, -а́, -о). **recently** *adv.* неда́вно.

receptacle *n.* вмести́лище. **reception** *n.* приём; *r.-room*, приёмная *sb.* **receptionist** *n.* секрета́рь (-ря́) *m.*, -рша, в приёмной. **receptive** *adj.* восприи́мчивый.

recess *n.* переры́в в рабо́те; (*parl.*) кани́кулы (-л) *pl.*; (*niche*) ни́ша; *pl.* (*of the heart*) тайники́ *m.pl.* **recession** *n.* спад.

recidivist *n.* рецидиви́ст.

recipe *n.* реце́пт.

recipient *n.* получа́тель *m.*, ~ница. **reciprocal** *adj.* взаи́мный; (*corresponding*) соотве́тственный; *n.* (*math.*) обра́тная величина́ (*pl.* -ны). **reciprocate** *v.t.* отвеча́ть *imp.* (взаи́мностью) на + *acc.* **reciprocating** *adj.* (*motion*) возвра́тно-поступа́тельный; (*engine*) поршнево́й. **reciprocity** *n.* взаи́мность.

recital *n.* (*account*) изложе́ние, подро́бное перечисле́ние; (*concert*) (со́льный) конце́рт. **recitation** *n.* публи́чное чте́ние. **recitative** *n.* речитати́в. **recite** *v.t.* деклами́ровать *imp.*, про~ *perf.*; чита́ть *imp.*, про~ *perf.* вслух; (*enumerate*) перечисля́ть *imp.*, перечи́слить *perf.*

reckless *adj.* (*rash*) опроме́тчивый; (*careless*) неосторо́жный.

reckon *v.t.* подсчи́тывать *imp.*, подсчита́ть *perf.*; (*also regard as*) счита́ть *imp.*, счесть (сочту́, -тёшь; счёл, сочла́) *perf.* (+ *instr.*, за + *acc.*); *v.i.*: *r. with*, счита́ться *imp.* с + *instr.* **reckoning** *n.* счёт, расчёт; *day of r.*, час распла́ты.

reclaim *v.t.* (*reform*) исправля́ть *imp.*, испра́вить *perf.*; (*land*) осва́ивать *imp.*, осво́ить *perf.*

recline *v.i.* отки́дываться *imp.*, отки́нуться *perf.*; полулежа́ть (-жу́, -жи́шь) *imp.*

recluse *n.* затво́рник, -ица.

recognition *n.* узнава́ние; (*acknowledgement*) призна́ние. **recognize** *v.t.* (*know again*) узнава́ть (-наю́, -наёшь) *imp.*, узна́ть *perf.*; (*acknowledge*) признава́ть (-наю́, -наёшь) *imp.*, призна́ть *perf.*

recoil *v.i.* отпря́дывать *imp.*, отпря́нуть *perf.*; отша́тываться *imp.*, отшатну́ться *perf.* (from, от + *gen.*); (*of gun*) отдава́ть (-даёт) *imp.*, отда́ть (-а́ст, -аду́т; о́тдал, -а́, -о) *perf.*; *n.* отско́к; отда́ча.

recollect *v.t.* вспомина́ть *imp.*, вспо́мнить *perf.* **recollection** *n.* воспомина́ние.

recommend *v.t.* рекомендова́ть *imp.*, *perf.*; (*for prize etc.*) представля́ть *imp.*, предста́вить *perf.* (for, к + *dat.*). **recommendation** *n.* рекоменда́ция; представле́ние.

recompense *n.* вознагражде́ние; *v.t.* вознагражда́ть *imp.*, вознагради́ть *perf.*

reconcile *v.t.* примиря́ть *imp.*, примири́ть *perf.*; *r. oneself*, примиря́ться *imp.*, примири́ться *perf.* (to, с + *instr.*). **reconciliation** *n.* примире́ние.

recondition *v.t.* приводи́ть (-ожу́, -о́дишь) *imp.*, привести́ (-еду́, -едёшь; -ёл, -ела́) *perf.* в испра́вное состоя́ние.

reconnaissance *n.* разве́дка. **reconnoitre** *v.t.* разве́дывать *imp.*, разве́дать *perf.*

reconstruct *v.t.* перестра́ивать *imp.*, перестро́ить *perf.*; реконструи́ровать *imp.*, *perf.*; воссоздава́ть (-даю́, -даёшь) *imp.*, воссозда́ть (-а́м, -а́шь, -а́ст, -ади́м; -а́л, -ала́, -а́ло) *perf.* **reconstruction** *n.* перестро́йка; реконстру́кция; воссозда́ние.

record *v.t.* запи́сывать *imp.*, записа́ть (-ишу́, -и́шешь) *perf.*; *n.* за́пись; (*minutes*) протоко́л; (*gramophone r.*) грампласти́нка; (*sport etc.*) реко́рд; *pl.* архи́в; *off the r.*, неофициа́льно; *adj.* реко́рдный; *r.-breaker*, *-holder*, рекордсме́н, ~ка; *r.-player*, проигрыватель *m.* **recorder** *n.* (*person who records*) регистра́тор; (*judge*) рико́рдер; (*tech.*) регистри́рующий, самопи́шущий, прибо́р; (*flute*) блок-флейта. **recording** *n.* за́пись; (*sound r.*) звукоза́пись.

recount[1] *v.t.* (*narrate*) переска́зывать *imp.*, пересказа́ть (-ажу́, -а́жешь) *perf.*

re-count[2] *v.t.* (*count again*) пересчи́тывать *imp.*, пересчита́ть *perf.*; *n.* пересчёт.

recoup *v.t.* возмеща́ть *imp.*, возмести́ть *perf.* (*person*, + *dat.*; *loss etc.*, + *acc.*). **recoupment** *n.* возмеще́ние.

recourse *n.*: *have r. to*, прибега́ть *imp.*, прибе́гнуть (-г(нул), -гла) *perf.* к по́мощи + *gen.*

recover *v.t.* (*regain possession*) получа́ть *imp.*, получи́ть (-чу́, -чишь) *perf.* обра́тно; (*debt etc.*) взы́скивать *imp.*, взыска́ть *perf.* (-ыщу́, -ы́щешь) *perf.* (from, с + *gen.*); *v.i.* (*r. health*) поправля́ться *imp.*, попра́виться *perf.* (from, по́сле + *gen.*). **recovery** *n.* получе́ние обра́тно; выздоровле́ние.

re-create *v.t.* вновь создава́ть (-даю́, -даёшь) *imp.*, созда́ть (-а́м, -а́шь, -аст, -ади́м; со́зда́л, -а́, -о) *perf.*
recreation *n.* развлече́ние, о́тдых.
recrimination *n.* взаи́мное обвине́ние.
recruit *n.* новобра́нец (-нца); *v.t.* вербова́ть *imp.*, за~ *perf.* **recruitment** *n.* вербо́вка.
rectangle *n.* прямоуго́льник. **rectangular** *adj.* прямоуго́льный.
rectification *n.* исправле́ние; (*chem.*) ректифика́ция; (*electr.*) выпрямле́ние.
rectify *v.t.* исправля́ть *imp.*, испра́вить *perf.*; ректифици́ровать *imp.*, *perf.*; выпрямля́ть *imp.*, вы́прямить *perf.*
rectilinear *adj.* прямолине́йный.
rectitude *n.* че́стность.
recto *n.* нечётная пра́вая страни́ца; (*of folio*) лицева́я сторона́ (*acc.* -ону; *pl.* -оны, -о́н, -она́м).
rector *n.* (*priest*) прихо́дский свяще́нник; (*univ. etc.*) ре́ктор. **rectorship** *n.* ре́кторство. **rectory** *n.* дом (*pl.* -а́) прихо́дского свяще́нника.
rectum *n.* пряма́я кишка́ (*gen.pl.* -шо́к).
recumbent *adj.* лежа́чий.
recuperate *v.i.* восстана́вливать *imp.*, восстанови́ть (-влю́, -вишь) *perf.* своё здоро́вье. **recuperation** *n.* восстановле́ние здоро́вья.
recur *v.i.* повторя́ться *imp.*, повтори́ться *perf.*; *recurring decimal*, периоди́ческая дробь (*pl.* -би, -бе́й). **recurrence** *n.* повторе́ние. **recurrent** *adj.* повторя́ющийся.
red *adj.* (*in colour*; *fig.*, *polit.*) кра́сный (-сен, -сна́, -сно); (*of hair*) ры́жий (рыж, -а́, -е); *n.* (*colour*) кра́сный цвет; (*fig.*, *polit.*) кра́сный *sb.*; *in the r.*, в долгу́; *r. admiral*, адмира́л; *r.-blooded*, энерги́чный; *r. cabbage*, краснокоча́нная капу́ста; *r. currant*, кра́сная сморо́дина (*also collect.*); *r. deer*, благоро́дный оле́нь *m.*; *r.-handed*, с поли́чным; *r. herring*, ло́жный след (*pl.* -ы́); *draw a r. herring across the track*, сбива́ть *imp.*, сбить (собью́, -ьёшь) *perf.* с то́лку; *r.-hot*, раскалённый (-ён, -ена́) до́красна́; *R. Indian*, инде́ец (-е́йца), индиа́нка; *r. lead*, свинцо́вый су́рик; *r. light*, кра́сный фона́рь (-ря́) *m.*; *see the r. light*, предчу́вствовать *imp.* приближе́ние опа́сности; *r. pepper*, стручко́вый пе́рец (-рца); *r. tape*, волоки́та. **redbreast** *n.* мали́новка. **redden** *v.t.* окра́шивать *imp.*, окра́сить *perf.* в кра́сный цвет; *v.i.* красне́ть *imp.*, по~ *perf.* **reddish** *adj.* красноватый; (*hair*) рыжева́тый.
redeem *v.t.* (*buy back*) выкупа́ть *imp.*, вы́купить *perf.*; (*from sin*) искупа́ть *imp.*, искупи́ть (-плю́, -пишь) *perf.* **redeemer** *n.* искупи́тель *m.* **redemption** *n.* вы́куп; искупле́ние.
redolent *adj.*: *r. of*, па́хнущий + *instr.*; *be r. of*, па́хнуть (-х(нул), -хла) *imp.* + *instr.*
redouble *v.t.* удва́ивать *imp.*, удво́ить *perf.*
redoubt *n.* реду́т.
redoubtable *adj.* гро́зный (-зен, -зна́, -зно).
redound *v.i.* спосо́бствовать *imp.*, по~ *perf.* (to, + *dat.*); *r. to someone's credit*, де́лать *imp.*, с~ *perf.* честь + *dat.*
redox *n.* окисле́ние-восстановле́ние.
redpoll *n.* чечётка.
redress *v.t.* исправля́ть *imp.*, испра́вить *perf.*; *r. the balance*, восстана́вливать *imp.*, восстанови́ть (-влю́, -вишь) *perf.* равнове́сие; *n.* возмеще́ние.
redshank *n.* тра́вник. **redskin** *n.* красноко́жий *sb.* **redstart** *n.* горихво́стка (-лысу́шка).
reduce *v.t.* (*decrease*) уменьша́ть *imp.*, уме́ньши́ть *perf.*; (*lower*) снижа́ть *imp.*, сни́зить *perf.*; (*shorten*) сокраща́ть *imp.*, сократи́ть (-ащу́, -ати́шь) *perf.*; (*bring to*) приводи́ть (-ожу́, -о́дишь) *imp.*, привести́ (-еду́, -едёшь; -ёл, -ела́) *perf.* (to, в + *acc.*); *v.i.* худе́ть *imp.*, по~ *perf.* **reduction** *n.* уменьше́ние, сниже́ние, сокраще́ние; (*amount of r.*) ски́дка.
redundancy *n.* (*excess of workers*) изли́шек (-шка) рабо́чей си́лы; (*dismissal*) увольне́ние (рабо́чих, слу́жащих). **redundant** *adj.* (*excessive*) изли́шний; (*dismissed*) уво́ленный (-ен) (по сокраще́нию шта́тов).
reduplicate *v.t.* удва́ивать *imp.*, удво́ить *perf.* **reduplication** *n.* удвое́ние.

redwing *n.* белобро́вик. **redwood** *n.* секво́йя.

reed *n.* (*plant*) тростни́к (-а́), камы́ш (-а́); (*in mus. instrument*) язычо́к (-чка́); (*mus.*) язычко́вый инструме́нт; *a broken r.*, ненадёжная опо́ра; *attrib.* тростнико́вый, камышо́вый; (*mus.*) язычко́вый; *r.-pipe*, свире́ль. **reedy** *adj.* (*slender*) то́нкий (-нок, -нка́, -нко, то́нки́); (*voice*) пронзи́тельный.

reef *n.* (*of sail; ridge*) риф; *r.-knot*, ри́фовый у́зел (узла́); *v.abs.* брать (беру́, -рёшь; брал, -а́, -о) *imp.*, взять (возьму́, -мёшь; взял, -а́, -о) *perf.* ри́фы. **reefer** *n.* (*jacket*) бушла́т; (*cigarette*) сигаре́та с марихуа́ной.

reek *n.* вонь, дурно́й за́пах; *v.i.*: *r.* (*of*), воня́ть *imp.* (+ *instr.*).

reel[1] *n.* кату́шка; (*of film*) руло́н; (*straight*) *off the r.*, (*fig.*) сра́зу, без переры́ва; *v.t.* (*on to r.*) нама́тывать *imp.*, намота́ть *perf.* на кату́шку; *r. off*, разма́тывать *imp.*, размота́ть *perf.*; (*story etc.*) отбараба́нить *perf.*

reel[2] *v.i.* (*be dizzy*) кружи́ться (-ится) *imp.*, за~ *perf.*; (*stagger*) поша́тываться *imp.*, пошатну́ться *perf.*

reel[3] *n.* (*dance*) рил.

refectory *n.* (*in monastery*) тра́пезная *sb.*; (*in college*) столо́вая *sb.*; *r. table*, дли́нный у́зкий обе́денный стол (-а́).

refer *v.t.* (*direct*) отсыла́ть *imp.*, отосла́ть (отошлю́, -лёшь) *perf.* (to, к + *dat.*); *v.i.*: *r. to*, (*cite*) ссыла́ться *imp.*, сосла́ться (сошлю́сь, -лёшься) *perf.* на + *acc.*; (*mention*) упомина́ть *imp.*, упомяну́ть (-ну́, -нешь) *perf.* + *acc.*; *r. to drawer*, обрати́тесь к чекода́телю. **referee** *n.* судья́ (*pl.* -дьи, -де́й, -дьям) *m.*; *v.t.* суди́ть (сужу́, су́дишь) *imp.* **reference** *n.* (*to book etc.*) ссы́лка; (*mention*) упомина́ние; (*testimonial*) рекоменда́ция; *r. book*, спра́вочник; *r. library*, спра́вочная библиоте́ка (без вы́дачи книг на́ дом). **referendum** *n.* рефере́ндум.

refine *v.t.* очища́ть *imp.*, очи́стить *perf.*; рафини́ровать *imp.*, *perf.* **refined** *adj.* (*in style etc.*) утончённый (-ён, -ённа); (*in manners*) культу́рный; *r. sugar*, рафина́д. **refinery** *n.* (*oil-r.*) нефтеочисти́тельный заво́д; (*sugar-r.*) рафина́дный заво́д.

refit *n.* переоборудование; *v.t.* переобору́довать *imp.*, *perf.*

reflect *v.t.* отража́ть *imp.*, отрази́ть *perf.*; *v.i.* (*meditate*) размышля́ть *imp.*, размы́слить *perf.* (on, о + *prep.*). **reflection** *n.* отраже́ние; размышле́ние; *on r.*, поду́мав. **reflector** *n.* рефле́ктор. **reflex** *n.* рефле́кс; *adj.* рефле́кторный; *r. camera*, зерка́льный фотоаппара́т. **reflexive** *adj.* (*gram.*) возвра́тный.

reform *v.t.* реформи́ровать *imp.*, *perf.*; *v.t.* & *i.* (*of people*) исправля́ть(ся) *imp.*, испра́вить(ся) *perf.*; *n.* рефо́рма, исправле́ние. **reformation** *n.* рефо́рма; *the R.*, Реформа́ция. **reformatory** *adj.* исправи́тельный; *n.* исправи́тельное заведе́ние.

refract *v.t.* преломля́ть *imp.*, преломи́ть (-ит) *perf.* **refraction** *n.* рефра́кция, преломле́ние. **refractive** *adj.* преломля́ющий. **refractory** *adj.* (*person*) упря́мый, непоко́рный; (*substance*) тугопла́вкий.

refrain[1] *n.* припе́в.

refrain[2] *v.i.* уде́рживаться *imp.*, удержа́ться (-жу́сь, -жишься) *perf.* (from, от + *gen.*).

refresh *v.t.* освежа́ть *imp.*, освежи́ть *perf.*; *r. oneself*, подкрепля́ться *imp.*, подкрепи́ться *perf.* **refreshment** *n.* (*drink*) освежа́ющий напи́ток (-тка); *pl.* заку́ска; *r. room*, буфе́т.

refrigerate *v.t.* охлажда́ть *imp.*, охлади́ть *perf.* **refrigeration** *n.* охлажде́ние. **refrigerator** *n.* холоди́льник.

refuge *n.* убе́жище, прибе́жище; *take r.*, находи́ть (-ожу́, -о́дишь) *imp.*, найти́ (найду́, -дёшь; нашёл, -шла́) *perf.* убе́жище. **refugee** *n.* бе́женец (-нца), -нка.

refund *v.t.* возвраща́ть *imp.*, возврати́ть (-ащу́, -ати́шь) *perf.*; (*expenses*) возмеща́ть *imp.*, возмести́ть *perf.*; *n.* возвраще́ние (де́нег); возмеще́ние.

refusal *n.* отка́з; *first r.*, пра́во пе́рвого вы́бора. **refuse**[1] *v.t.* отка́зывать *imp.*, отказа́ть (-ажу́, -а́жешь) *perf.*

refuse[2] *n.* отбро́сы (-сов) *pl.*, му́сор.

refutation *n.* опровержéние. **refute** *v.t.* опровергáть *imp.*, опровéргнуть (-г(нул), -гла) *perf.*

regain *v.t.* (*recover*) снóва приобретáть *imp.*, приобрести́ (-етý, -етёшь, -ёл, -ела́) *perf.*; (*reach*) снóва достигáть *imp.*, дости́гнуть & дости́чь (-и́гну, -и́гнешь; -и́г) *perf.*

regal *adj.* королéвский.

regale *v.t.* угощáть *imp.*, угости́ть *perf.* (with, + *instr.*).

regalia *n.* регáлии *f.pl.*

regard *v.t.* смотрéть (-рю́, -ришь) *imp.*, по~ *perf.* на + *acc.*; (*take into account*) считáться *imp.* с + *instr.*; *r. as*, считáть *imp.* + *instr.*, за + *instr.*; *as regards*, что касáется + *gen.*; *n.* (*esteem*) уважéние; (*attention*) внимáние; *pl.* поклóн, привéт; *with r. to*, относи́тельно + *gen.*; что касáется + *gen.* **regarding** *prep.* относи́тельно + *gen.*; что касáется + *gen.* **regardless** *adv.* не обращáя внимáния; *r. of*, не считáясь с + *instr.*

regatta *n.* регáта.

regency *n.* регéнтство.

regenerate *v.t.* перерождáть *imp.*, перероди́ть *perf.*; *adj.* перерождённый (-ён, -енá). **regeneration** *n.* перерождéние.

regent *n.* рéгент.

regicide *n.* (*action*) цареуби́йство; (*person*) цареуби́йца *m.* & *f.*

régime *n.* режи́м. **regimen** *n.* (*med.*) режи́м; (*gram.*) управлéние.

regiment *n.* полк (-á, *loc.* -ý). **regimental** *adj.* полковóй. **regimentation** *n.* регламентáция.

region *n.* óбласть (*pl.* -ти, -тéй). **regional** *adj.* областнóй, регионáльный, мéстный.

register *n.* реéстр, кни́га зáписей; (*also mus.*) реги́стр; *v.t.* регистри́ровать *imp.*, за~ *perf.*; (*express*) выражáть *imp.*, вы́разить *perf.*; (*a letter*) отправля́ть *imp.*, отпрáвить *perf.* заказны́м. **registered** *adj.* (*letter*) заказнóй. **registrar** *n.* регистрáтор. **registration** *n.* регистрáция, зáпись; *r. mark*, номернóй знак. **registry** *n.* регистратýра; (*r. office*) отдéл зáписей áктов граждáнского состоя́ния, загс.

regression *n.* регрéсс. **regressive** *adj.* регресси́вный.

regret *v.t.* сожалéть *imp.* о + *prep.*; *I r. to say*, к сожалéнию, дóлжен сказáть; *n.* сожалéние. **regretful** *adj.* пóлный (-лон, -лнá, пóлнó) сожалéния. **regrettable** *adj.* прискóрбный.

regular *adj.* реглу́ярный; (*also gram.*) прáвильный; (*recurring*) очереднóй; (*of officer*) кáдровый; *n.* (*coll.*) завсегдáтай. **regularity** *n.* регуля́рность. **regularize** *v.t.* упоря́дочивать *imp.*, упоря́дочить *perf.* **regulate** *v.t.* регули́ровать *imp.*, у~ *perf.* **regulation** *n.* регули́рование; *pl.* прáвила *neut.pl.*, устáв; *adj.* установлéнный.

rehabilitate *v.t.* реабилити́ровать *imp.*, *perf.* **rehabilitation** *n.* реабилитáция.

rehash *v.t.* передéлывать *imp.*, передéлать *perf.*; *n.* передéлка.

rehearsal *n.* репети́ция. **rehearse** *v.t.* репети́ровать *imp.*, от~ *perf.*

reign *n.* цáрствование; *v.i.* цáрствовать *imp.*; (*prevail*) цари́ть *imp.*

reimburse *v.t.* возмещáть *imp.*, возмести́ть *perf.* (+ *dat. of person*). **reimbursement** *n.* возмещéние.

rein *n.* пóвод (*loc.* -ý; *pl.* повóдья, -ьев); *pl.* вóжжи (-жéй) *pl.*

reincarnation *n.* перевоплощéние.

reindeer *n.* сéверный олéнь *m.*; *r. moss*, олéний мох (м(ó)ха, *loc.* мху & м(ó)хе).

reinforce *v.t.* подкрепля́ть *imp.*, подкрепи́ть (-плю́, -пишь) *perf.*; уси́ливать *imp.*, уси́лить *perf.*; *reinforced concrete*, железобетóн. **reinforcement** *n.* (*also pl.*) подкреплéние, усилéние.

reinstate *v.t.* восстанáвливать *imp.*, восстанови́ть (-влю́, -вишь) *perf.* **reinstatement** *n.* восстановлéние.

reinsurance *n.* перестрахóвка. **reinsure** *v.t.* перестрахóвывать *imp.*, перестраховáть *perf.*

reiterate *v.t.* повторя́ть *imp.*, повтори́ть *perf.* **reiteration** *n.* повторéние.

reject *v.t.* отвергáть *imp.*, отвéргнуть (-г(нул), -гла) *perf.*; (*as defective*) браковáть *imp.*, за~ *perf.*; *n.* бракóванное издéлие. **rejection** *n.* откáз (of, от + *gen.*); бракóвка.

rejoice *v.t.* ра́довать *imp.*, об~ *perf.*; *v.i.* ра́доваться *imp.*, об~ *perf.* (in, at, +*dat.*). **rejoicing** *n.* ликова́ние.

rejoin *v.t.* (вновь) присоединя́ться *imp.*, присоедини́ться *perf.* к+*dat.*

rejoinder *n.* отве́т.

rejuvenate *v.t.* & *i.* омола́живать(ся) *imp.*, омолоди́ть(ся) *perf.* **rejuvenation** *n.* омоложе́ние.

relapse *n.* рециди́в; *v.i.* сно́ва впада́ть *imp.*, впасть (-аду́, -адёшь, -ал) *perf.* (into, в+*acc.*); (*into illness*) сно́ва заболева́ть *imp.*, заболе́ть *perf.*

relate *v.t.* (*narrate*) расска́зывать *imp.*, рассказа́ть (-ажу́, -а́жешь) *perf.*; (*establish relation*) устана́вливать *imp.*, установи́ть (-влю́, -вишь) *perf.* связь ме́жду+*instr.*; *v.i.* относи́ться (-ится) *imp.* (to, к+*dat.*). **related** *adj.* ро́дственный (-ен, -енна). **relation** *n.* (*narration*) повествова́ние; (*connection etc.*) связь, отноше́ние; (*person*) ро́дственник, -ица; *in r. to*, относи́тельно+*gen.* **relationship** *n.* родство́. **relative** *adj.* относи́тельный; *n.* ро́дственник, -ица. **relativity** *n.* относи́тельность; (*phys.*) тео́рия относи́тельности.

relax *v.t.* & *i.* ослабля́ть(ся) *imp.*, осла́бить(ся) *perf.*; смягча́ть(ся) *imp.*, смягчи́ть(ся) *perf.* **relaxation** *n.* ослабле́ние, смягче́ние; (*rest*) о́тдых.

relay *n.* сме́на; (*sport*) эстафе́та; (*electr.*) реле́ *neut.indecl.*; (*broadcast etc.*) трансля́ция; *v.t.* сменя́ть *imp.*, смени́ть (-ню́, -нишь) *perf.*; (*radio*) трансли́ровать *imp.*, *perf.*

release *v.t.* (*set free*) освобожда́ть *imp.*, освободи́ть *perf.*; отпуска́ть *imp.*, отпусти́ть (-ущу́, -у́стишь) *perf.*; (*film etc.*) выпуска́ть *imp.*, вы́пустить *perf.*; *n.* освобожде́ние; вы́пуск.

relegate *v.t.* переводи́ть (-ожу́, -о́дишь) *imp.*, перевести́ (-еду́, -едёшь; -ёл, -ела́) *perf.* (в бо́лее ни́зкий класс, (*sport*) в ни́зшую ли́гу). **relegation** *n.* перево́д (в бо́лее ни́зкий класс, в ни́зшую ли́гу).

relent *v.i.* смягча́ться *imp.*, смягчи́ться *perf.* **relentless** *adj.* неумоли́мый, непрекло́нный (-нен, -нна).

relevance *n.* уме́стность. **relevant** *adj.* относя́щийся к де́лу; уме́стный.

reliable *adj.* надёжный. **reliance** *n.* дове́рие. **reliant** *adj.* уве́ренный (-ен, -енна).

relic *n.* оста́ток (-тка), рели́квия; *pl.* (*of saint*) мо́щи (-ще́й) *pl.*

relief[1] *n.* (*art, geol.*) релье́ф.

relief[2] *n.* (*alleviation*) облегче́ние; (*assistance*) по́мощь; (*in duty*) сме́на; (*raising of siege*) сня́тие оса́ды. **relieve** *v.t.* (*alleviate*) облегча́ть *imp.*, облегчи́ть *perf.*; (*help*) ока́зывать *imp.*, оказа́ть (-ажу́, -а́жешь) *perf.* по́мощь +*dat.*; (*replace*) сменя́ть *imp.*, смени́ть (-ню́, -нишь) *perf.*; (*raise siege*) снима́ть *imp.*, снять (сниму́, -мешь; снял, -а́, -о) *perf.* оса́ду с+*gen.*

religion *n.* рели́гия. **religious** *adj.* религио́зный.

relinquish *v.t.* оставля́ть *imp.*, оста́вить *perf.*; (*right etc.*) отка́зываться *imp.*, отказа́ться (-ажу́сь, -а́жешься) *perf.* от+*gen.*

reliquary *n.* ра́ка.

relish *n.* (*enjoyment*) смак, наслажде́ние; (*condiment*) припра́ва; *v.t.* смакова́ть *imp.*

reluctance *n.* неохо́та. **reluctant** *adj.* неохо́тный; *be r. to*, не жела́ть *imp.*+*inf.*

rely *v.i.* полага́ться *imp.*, положи́ться (-жу́сь, -жишься) *perf.* (on, на+*acc.*).

remain *v.i.* остава́ться (-аю́сь, -аёшься) *imp.*, оста́ться (-а́нусь, -а́нешься) *perf.* **remainder** *n.* оста́ток (-тка); (*books*) кни́жные оста́тки *m.pl.*; *v.t.* распродава́ть (-даю́, -даёшь) *imp.*, распрода́ть (-а́м, -а́шь, -а́ст, -ади́м; распро́дал, -а́, -о) *perf.* по дешёвой цене́. **remains** *n.* оста́тки *m.pl.*; (*human r.*) оста́нки (-ков) *pl.*

remand *v.t.* отсыла́ть *imp.*, отосла́ть (отошлю́, -лёшь) *perf.* под стра́жу; *n.* отсы́лка под стра́жу; *prisoner on r.*, подсле́дственный *sb.*

remark *v.t.* замеча́ть *imp.*, заме́тить *perf.*; *n.* замеча́ние. **remarkable** *adj.* замеча́тельный.

remedial *adj.* лече́бный. **remedy** *n.* сре́дство (for, от, про́тив, +*gen.*); *v.t.* исправля́ть *imp.*, испра́вить *perf.*

remember *v.t.* вспомина́ть *imp.*, вспо́мнить *perf.* о + *prep.*; по́мниться *imp. impers.* + *dat.*; (*greet*) передава́ть (-даю́, -даёшь) *imp.*, переда́ть (-а́м, -а́шь, -а́ст, -ади́м; пе́редал, -а́, -о) *perf.* приве́т от + *gen.* (to, + *dat.*). **remembrance** *n.* па́мять; *pl.* приве́т.

remind *v.t.* напомина́ть *imp.*, напо́мнить *perf.* + *dat.* (of, + *acc.*, о + *prep.*). **reminder** *n.* напомина́ние.

reminiscence *n.* воспомина́ние. **reminiscent** *adj.* напомина́ющий.

remiss *predic.* небре́жен (-жна). **remission** *n.* отпуще́ние. **remit** *v.t.* пересыла́ть *imp.*, пересла́ть (-ешлю́, -ешлёшь) *perf.* **remittance** *n.* пересы́лка; (*money*) де́нежный перево́д.

remnant *n.* оста́ток (-тка).

remonstrance *n.* проте́ст. **remonstrate** *v.i.*: *r. with*, увещева́ть *imp.* + *acc.*

remorse *n.* угрызе́ния *neut.pl.* со́вести. **remorseful** *adj.* по́лный (-лон, -лна́, по́лно́) раска́яния. **remorseless** *adj.* беспоща́дный.

remote *adj.* да́льний, отдалённый (-ён, -ённа); *r. control*, дистанцио́нное управле́ние, телеуправле́ние.

removal *n.* смеще́ние, устране́ние; (*change of house*) перее́зд. **remove** *v.t.* смеща́ть *imp.*, смести́ть *perf.*; устраня́ть *imp.*, устрани́ть *perf.*; *v.i.* переезжа́ть *imp.*, перее́хать (-е́ду, -е́дешь) *perf.*; *n.* шаг, сте́пень (*pl.* -ни, -не́й) (отдале́ния). **removed** *adj.* далёкий (-ёк, -ека́, -ёко́); *once r.*, двою́родный; *twice r.*, троюро́дный.

remuneration *n.* вознагражде́ние. **remunerative** *adj.* вы́годный.

renaissance *n.* возрожде́ние; *the R.*, Ренесса́нс.

renal *adj.* по́чечный.

renascence *n.* возрожде́ние.

render *v.t.* воздава́ть (-даю́, -даёшь) *imp.*, возда́ть (-а́м, -а́шь, -а́ст, -ади́м; возда́л, -а́, -о) *perf.*; (*help etc.*) ока́зывать *imp.*, оказа́ть (-ажу́, -а́жешь) *perf.*; (*role etc.*) исполня́ть *imp.*, испо́лнить *perf.*; (*transmit*) передава́ть (-даю́, -даёшь) *imp.*, переда́ть (-а́м, -а́шь, -а́ст, -ади́м; пе́редал, -а́, -о) *perf.*; (*fat*) топи́ть (-плю́, -пишь) *imp.*; (*stone*) штукату́рить *imp.*, о~, от~ *perf.* **rendering** *n.* исполне́ние; переда́ча; вытаплива́ние.

rendezvous *n.* (*meeting*) свида́ние, встре́ча; (*meeting-place*) ме́сто (*pl.* -та́) свида́ния, встре́чи; *v.i.* встреча́ться *imp.*, встре́титься *perf.*; собира́ться *imp.*, собра́ться (-берётся; собра́лся, -ала́сь, -а́ло́сь) *perf.*

renegade *n.* ренега́т, ~ка.

renew *v.t.* (воз)обновля́ть *imp.*, (воз)обнови́ть *perf.*; (*of agreement etc.*) продлева́ть *imp.*, продли́ть *perf.* срок де́йствия + *gen.* **renewal** *n.* (воз)обновле́ние; продле́ние (сро́ка де́йствия).

rennet *n.* сычу́жина.

renounce *v.t.* отка́зываться *imp.*, отказа́ться (-ажу́сь, -а́жешься) *perf.* от + *gen.*; отрека́ться *imp.*, отре́чься (-еку́сь, -ечёшься; -ёкся, -екла́сь) *perf.* от + *gen.*

renovate *v.t.* ремонти́ровать *imp.*, от~ *perf.* **renovation** *n.* ремо́нт.

renown *n.* изве́стность, сла́ва. **renowned** *adj.* изве́стный; *be r. for*, сла́виться *imp.* + *instr.*

rent[1] *n.* (*tear*) проре́ха, дыра́ (*pl.* -ры).

rent[2] *n.* (*for premises*) аре́нда; аре́ндная, кварти́рная, пла́та; (*for land*) ре́нта; *v.t.* (*of tenant*) арендова́ть *imp.*, *perf.*; брать (беру́, -рёшь; брал, -а́, -о) *imp.*, взять (возьму́, -мёшь; взял, -а́, -о) *perf.* в аре́нду; (*of owner*) сдава́ть (сдаю́, сдаёшь) *imp.*, сдать (-а́м, -а́шь, -а́ст, -ади́м; сдал, -а́, -о) *perf.* в аре́нду.

renunciation *n.* отка́з, отрече́ние (of, от + *gen.*).

rep(p)[1] *n.* (*fabric*) репс.

rep[2] *n.* (*commercial traveller*) коммивояжёр.

repair[1] *v.i.* (*resort*) направля́ться *imp.*, напра́виться *perf.*

repair[2] *v.t.* (*restore*) ремонти́ровать *imp.*, от~ *perf.*; (*clothing etc.*) чини́ть (-ню́, -нишь) *imp.*, по~ *perf.*; (*error etc.*) исправля́ть *imp.*, испра́вить *perf.*; *n.* (*also pl.*) ремо́нт (*only sing.*); почи́нка; (*good condition*) испра́вность; *out of r.*, в неиспра́вном состоя́нии; *attrib.* ремо́нтный; почи́ночный.

reparation *n.* возмеще́ние; *pl.* репара́ции *f.pl.*
repartee *n.* остроу́мный, нахо́дчивый, отве́т.
repatriate *v.t.* репатрии́ровать *imp., perf.* **repatriation** *n.* репатриа́ция.
repay *v.t.* отпла́чивать *imp.*, отплати́ть (-ачу́, -а́тишь) *perf.* (person, + *dat.*); вознагражда́ть *imp.*, вознагради́ть *perf.* (action, за + *instr.*). **repayment** *n.* отпла́та; вознагражде́ние.
repeal *v.t.* отменя́ть *imp.*, отмени́ть (-ню́, -нишь) *perf.*; *n.* отме́на.
repeat *v.t.* & *i.* повторя́ть(ся) *imp.*, повтори́ть(ся) *perf.*; *n.* повторе́ние. **repeatedly** *adv.* неоднокра́тно.
repel *v.t.* отта́лкивать *imp.*, оттолкну́ть *perf.*; отража́ть *imp.*, отрази́ть *perf.*
repent *v.i.* раска́иваться *imp.*, раска́яться (-а́юсь, -а́ешься) *perf.* (of, в + *prep.*). **repentance** *n.* раска́яние. **repentant** *adj.* раска́ивающийся.
repercussion *n.* (*of event*) после́дствие.
repertoire *n.* репертуа́р. **repertory** *n.* (*store*) запа́с; (*repertoire*) репертуа́р; *r. company*, постоя́нная тру́ппа.
repetition *n.* повторе́ние. **repetitious, repetitive** *adj.* (беспреста́нно) повторя́ющийся.
replace *v.t.* (*put back*) класть (-аду́, -адёшь; -ал) *imp.*, положи́ть (-жу́, -жишь) *perf.* обра́тно (на ме́сто); (*substitute*) заменя́ть *imp.*, замени́ть (-ню́, -нишь) *perf.* (by, + *instr.*); замеща́ть *imp.*, замести́ть *perf.* **replacement** *n.* заме́на, замеще́ние.
replenish *v.t.* пополня́ть *imp.*, попо́лнить *perf.* **replenishment** *n.* пополне́ние.
replete *adj.* пресы́щенный (-ен), напо́лненный (-ен); (*sated*) сы́тый (сыт, -а́, -о).
replica *n.* то́чная ко́пия.
reply *v.t.* & *i.* отвеча́ть *imp.*, отве́тить *perf.* (to, на + *acc.*); *n.* отве́т; *r. paid*, с опла́ченным отве́том.
report *v.t.* (*relate*) сообща́ть *imp.*, сообщи́ть *perf.*; (*formally*) докла́дывать *imp.*, доложи́ть (-жу́, -жишь) *perf.*; *v.i.* (*present oneself*) явля́ться *imp.*, яви́ться (явлю́сь, я́вишься) *perf.*; *n.* сообще́ние; докла́д; (*school*) та́бель *m.* успева́емости; (*sound*) звук взры́ва, вы́стрела. **reporter** *n.* репортёр, корреспонде́нт.
repose *v.i.* (*lie*) лежа́ть (-жу́, -жи́шь) *imp.*; (*rest*) отдыха́ть *imp.*, отдохну́ть *perf.*; *n.* (*rest*) о́тдых; (*peace*) поко́й.
repository *n.* храни́лище.
repp *see* **rep**[1].
reprehensible *adj.* предосуди́тельный.
represent *v.t.* представля́ть *imp.*; (*portray*) изобража́ть *imp.*, изобрази́ть *perf.* **representation** *n.* представи́тельство, представле́ние; изображе́ние. **representative** *adj.* изобража́ющий (of, + *acc.*); (*typical*) типи́чный; (*polit.*) представи́тельный; *n.* представи́тель *m.*
repress *v.t.* подавля́ть *imp.*, подави́ть (-влю́, -вишь) *perf.* репресси́ровать *imp., perf.* **repression** *n.* подавле́ние, репре́ссия. **repressive** *adj.* репресси́вный.
reprieve *v.t.* отсро́чивать *imp.*, отсро́чить *perf.* + *dat.* приведе́ние в исполне́ние (сме́ртного) пригово́ра; *n.* отсро́чка приведе́ния в исполне́ние (сме́ртного) пригово́ра.
reprimand *n.* вы́говор; *v.t.* де́лать *imp.*, с~ *perf.* вы́говор + *dat.*
reprint *v.t.* переиздава́ть (-даю́, -даёшь) *imp.*, переизда́ть (-а́м, -а́шь, -а́ст, -адим; -а́л, -ала́, -а́ло) *perf.*; перепеча́тывать *imp.*, перепеча́тать *perf.*; *n.* переизда́ние; перепеча́тка.
reprisal *n.* репресса́лия.
reproach *v.t.* упрека́ть *imp.*, упрекну́ть *perf.* (with, в + *prep.*); укоря́ть *imp.*, укори́ть *perf.* (with, в + *prep.*); *n.* упрёк, уко́р. **reproachful** *adj.* укори́зненный.
reproduce *v.t.* воспроизводи́ть (-ожу́, -о́дишь) *imp.*, воспроизвести́ (-еду́, -едёшь; -ёл, -ела́) *perf.* **reproduction** *n.* (*action*) воспроизведе́ние; (*object*) ко́пия, репроду́кция. **reproductive** *adj.* воспроизводи́тельный.
reproof *n.* порица́ние. **reprove** *v.t.* порица́ть *imp.*
reptile *n.* пресмыка́ющееся *sb.*
republic *n.* респу́блика. **republican** *adj.* республика́нский; *n.* республика́нец (-нца), -нка.

repudiate *v.t.* отка́зываться *imp.*, отказа́ться (-ажу́сь, -а́жешься) *perf.* от + *gen.*; (*reject*) отверга́ть *imp.*, отве́ргнуть (-г(нул), -гла) *perf.* **repudiation** *n.* отка́з (of, от + *gen.*).

repugnance *n.* отвраще́ние. **repugnant** *adj.* проти́вный.

repulse *v.t.* отража́ть *imp.*, отрази́ть *perf.* **repulsion** *n.* отвраще́ние. **repulsive** *adj.* отврати́тельный, проти́вный.

reputable *adj.* по́льзующийся хоро́шей репута́цией. **reputation, repute** *n.* репута́ция, сла́ва. **reputed** *adj.* предполага́емый.

request *n.* про́сьба; *by, on, r.*, по про́сьбе; *in (great) r.*, в (большо́м) спро́се; *r. stop*, остано́вка по тре́бованию; *v.t.* проси́ть (-ошу́, -о́сишь) *imp.*, по~ *perf.* + *acc.*, + *gen.*, о + *prep.* (*person*, + *acc.*).

requiem *n.* ре́квием.

require *v.t.* (*demand*; *need*) тре́бовать *imp.*, по~ *perf.* + *gen.*; (*need*) нужда́ться *imp.* в + *prep.* **requirement** *n.* тре́бование; (*necessity*) потре́бность.

requisite *adj.* необходи́мый; *n.* необходи́мое *sb.*, необходи́мая вещь (*pl.* -щи, -ще́й). **requisition** *n.* реквизи́ция; *v.t.* реквизи́ровать *imp.*, *perf.*

requite *v.t.* отпла́чивать *imp.*, отплати́ть (-ачу́, -а́тишь) *perf.* (for, за + *acc.*; with, + *instr.*).

rescind *v.t.* отменя́ть *imp.*, отмени́ть (-ню́, -нишь) *perf.*

rescue *v.t.* спаса́ть *imp.*, спасти́ (-су́, -сёшь; -с, -сла́) *perf.*; *n.* спасе́ние; *attrib.* спаса́тельный. **rescuer** *n.* спаси́тель *m.*

research *n.* иссле́дование (+ *gen.*); (*occupation*) нау́чно-иссле́довательская рабо́та; *v.i.* занима́ться *imp.*, заня́ться (займу́сь, -мёшься; заня́лся́, -ла́сь) *perf.* иссле́дованиями, нау́чно-иссле́довательской рабо́той; *r. into*, иссле́довать *imp.*, *perf.* + *acc.* **researcher** *n.* иссле́дователь *m.*

resemblance *n.* схо́дство. **resemble** *v.t.* походи́ть (-ожу́, -о́дишь) *imp.* на + *acc.*

resent *v.t.* (*be indignant*) негодова́ть *imp.* на + *acc.*, про́тив + *gen.*; (*take offence*) обижа́ться *imp.*, оби́деться (-и́жусь, -и́дишься) *perf.* на + *acc.* **resentful** *adj.* оби́дчивый. **resentment** *n.* негодова́ние; оби́да.

reservation *n.* (*proviso etc.*) огово́рка; (*booking*) предвари́тельный зака́з; (*tract of land*) резерва́ция. **reserve** *v.t.* (*postpone*) откла́дывать *imp.*, отложи́ть (-жу́, -жишь); (*keep in stock*) резерви́ровать *imp.*, *perf.*; (*book*) зара́нее зака́зывать *imp.*, заказа́ть (-ажу́, -а́жешь) *perf.*; брони́ровать *imp.*, за~ *perf.*; *n.* (*stock*; *mil.*) запа́с, резе́рв; (*sport*) запасно́й игро́к (-а́); (*nature r. etc.*) запове́дник; (*proviso*) огово́рка; (*r. price*) ни́зшая отплатна́я цена́ (*acc.* -ну); (*self-restraint*) сде́ржанность; *attrib.* запасно́й, запа́сный, резе́рвный. **reserved** *adj.* (*person*) сде́ржанный (-ан, -анна). **reservist** *n.* резерви́ст. **reservoir** *n.* резервуа́р, водохрани́лище; (*of knowledge etc.*) запа́с.

reside *v.i.* прожива́ть *imp.*; (*of right etc.*) принадлежа́ть (-жи́т) *imp.* (in, + *dat.*).

residence *n.* (*residing*) прожива́ние; (*abode*) местожи́тельство; (*official r. etc.*) резиде́нция. **resident** *n.* (постоя́нный) жи́тель *m.*, ~ница; *adj.* прожива́ющий; (*population*) постоя́нный; *r. physician*, врач, живу́щий при больни́це. **residential** *adj.* жило́й; *r. qualification*, ценз осе́длости.

residual *adj.* оста́точный. **residuary** *adj.* (*of estate*) оста́вшийся. **residue** *n.* оста́ток (-тка); (*of estate*) оста́вшееся насле́дство.

resign *v.t.* отка́зываться *imp.*, отказа́ться (-ажу́сь, -а́жешься) *perf.* от + *gen.*; *v.i.* уходи́ть (-ожу́, -о́дишь) *imp.*, уйти́ (уйду́, -дёшь; ушёл, ушла́) *perf.* в отста́вку; (*chess*) сдава́ть (сдаю́, сдаёшь) *imp.*, сдать (-а́м, -а́шь, -а́ст, -ади́м; сдал, -а́, -о) *perf.* па́ртию; *r. oneself to*, покоря́ться *imp.*, покори́ться *perf.* + *dat.* **resignation** *n.* отста́вка, заявле́ние об отста́вке; (*being resigned*) поко́рность; (*chess*) сда́ча. **resigned** *adj.* поко́рный.

resilient *adj.* упру́гий; (*person*) неунываю́щий.

resin *n.* смола́ (*pl.* -лы). **resinous** *adj.* смоли́стый.

resist *v.t.* сопротивля́ться *imp.*+*dat.*; не поддава́ться (-даю́сь, -даёшься) *imp.*+*dat.* **resistance** *n.* сопротивле́ние; (*r. movement*) движе́ние сопротивле́ния. **resistant** *adj.* про́чный (-чен, -чна́, -чно, про́чны́). **resistor** *n.* рези́стор.

resolute *adj.* реши́тельный. **resolution** *n.* (*character*) реши́тельность, реши́мость; (*at meeting etc.*) резолю́ция; (*of problem*; *mus.*) разреше́ние. **resolve** *v.t.* реша́ть *imp.*, реши́ть *perf.*; разреша́ть *imp.*, разреши́ть *perf.*; *v.t.* & *i.* (*decide*) реша́ться *imp.*, реши́ться *perf.*+*inf.*, на+*acc.*; (*of meeting etc.*) выноси́ть (-ит) *imp.*, вы́нести (-сет; -с) *perf.* резолю́цию; *n.* реше́ние.

resonance *n.* резона́нс. **resonant** *adj.* раздаю́щийся; зву́чный (-чен, -чна́, -чно). **resonate** *v.i.* резони́ровать *imp.*

resort *v.i.*: *r. to*, прибега́ть *imp.*, прибе́гнуть (-г(нул), -гла) *perf.* к+*dat.*; (*visit*) (ча́сто) посеща́ть *imp.*+*acc.*; *n.* (*expedient*) сре́дство; (*health r. etc.*) куро́рт; *in the last r.*, в кра́йнем слу́чае; *without r. to*, не прибега́я к+*dat.*

resound *v.i.* (*of sound etc.*) раздава́ться (-даётся) *imp.*, разда́ться (-а́стся, -аду́тся; -а́лся, -ала́сь) *perf.*; (*of place etc.*) оглаша́ться *imp.*, огласи́ться *perf.* (with, +*instr.*).

resource *n.* (*usu. pl.*) ресу́рс, сре́дство; (*expedient*) сре́дство, возмо́жность; (*ingenuity*) нахо́дчивость. **resourceful** *adj.* нахо́дчивый.

respect *n.* (*relation*) отноше́ние; (*esteem*) уваже́ние; *in r. of*, *with r. to*, что каса́ется+*gen.*, в отноше́нии+*gen.*; *v.t.* уважа́ть *imp.*; почита́ть *imp.* **respectability** *n.* почте́нность, респекта́бельность. **respectable** *adj.* почте́нный (-нен, -нна), респекта́бельный. **respectful** *adj.* почти́тельный. **respective** *adj.* соотве́тственный (-ен, -енна). **respectively** *adv.* соотве́тственно.

respiration *n.* дыха́ние; *artificial r.*, иску́сственное дыха́ние. **respirator** *n.* респира́тор.

respite *n.* переды́шка.

resplendent *adj.* блестя́щий; сверка́ющий.

respond *v.i.*: *r. to*, отзыва́ться *imp.*, отозва́ться (отзову́сь, -вёшься; отозва́лся, -ала́сь, -а́ло́сь) *perf.* на+*acc.*; реаги́ровать *imp.*, про~, от~ *perf.* на+*acc.* **respondent** *n.* отве́тчик, -ица.

response *n.* отве́т; о́тклик. **responsibility** *n.* отве́тственность, обя́занность. **responsible** *adj.* отве́тственный (-ен, -енна) (to, пе́ред+*instr.*; for, за+*acc.*). **responsive** *adj.* отзы́вчивый.

rest[1] *v.i.* отдыха́ть *imp.*, отдохну́ть *perf.*; поко́иться *imp.* (upon, на+*prep.*); *v.t.* (*place*) класть (-аду́, -адёшь; -ал) *imp.*, положи́ть (-жу́, -жишь) *perf.*; (*allow to r.*) дава́ть (даю́, даёшь) *imp.*, дать (дам, дашь, даст, дади́м; дал, -а́, да́ло́, -и) *perf.* о́тдых+*dat.*; *n.* (*repose*) о́тдых; (*peace*) поко́й; (*mus.*) па́уза; (*support*) опо́ра, подста́вка.

rest[2] *n.* (*the remainder*) оста́ток (-тка), остально́е *sb.*; (*the others*) остальны́е *sb.*, други́е *sb.*; *for the r.*, что каса́ется остально́го, что до остально́го.

restaurant *n.* рестора́н.

restful *adj.* споко́йный, ти́хий (тих, -а́, -о); (*soothing*) успока́ивающий.

restitution *n.* (*restoring*) возвраще́ние; (*reparation*) возмеще́ние убы́тков.

restive *adj.* (*horse*) норови́стый; (*person*; *restless*) беспоко́йный; (*wilful*) своенра́вный.

restless *adj.* беспоко́йный; (*uneasy*) неспоко́йный, трево́жный.

restoration *n.* реставра́ция, восстановле́ние. **restore** *v.t.* реставри́ровать *imp.*, *perf.*; восстана́вливать *imp.*, восстанови́ть (-влю́, -вишь) *perf.*

restrain *v.t.* сде́рживать *imp.*, сдержа́ть (-жу́, -жишь) *perf.*; уде́рживать *imp.*, удержа́ть (-жу́, -жишь) *perf.* (from, от+*gen.*). **restraint** *n.* (*reserve*) сде́ржанность; (*restriction*) ограниче́ние; (*confinement*) заключе́ние; *without r.*, свобо́дно, без у́держу.

restrict *v.t.* ограни́чивать *imp.*, ограни́чить *perf.* **restriction** *n.* ограниче́ние. **restrictive** *adj.* ограничи́тельный.

result *v.i.* сле́довать *imp.*; происходи́ть (-ит) *imp.*, произойти́ (-ойдёт; -ошёл, -ошла́) *perf.* в результа́те; *r. in*, конча́ться *imp.*, ко́нчиться *perf.*+*instr.*;

n. результа́т.
resume *v.t.* возобновля́ть *imp.*, возобнови́ть *perf.* **résumé** *n.* резюме́ *neut.indecl.* **resumption** *n.* возобновле́ние.
resurrect *v.t.* воскреша́ть *imp.*, воскреси́ть *perf.* **resurrection** *n.* (*of the dead*) воскресе́ние; (*to memory etc.*) воскреше́ние.
resuscitate *v.t.* приводи́ть (-ожу́, -о́дишь) *imp.*, привести́ (-еду́, -едёшь; -ёл, -ела́) *perf.* в созна́ние.
retail *n.* ро́зничная прода́жа; *attrib.* ро́зничный; *adv.* в ро́зницу; *v.t.* продава́ть (-даю́, -даёшь) *imp.*, прода́ть (-а́м, -а́шь, -а́ст, -ади́м; про́дал, -а́, -о) *perf.* в ро́зницу; *v.i.* продава́ться (-даётся) *imp.* в ро́зницу. **retailer** *n.* ро́зничный торго́вец (-вца).
retain *v.t.* уде́рживать *imp.*, удержа́ть (-жу́, -жишь) *perf.*; (*preserve*) сохраня́ть *imp.*, сохрани́ть *perf.*
retaliate *v.i.* отпла́чивать *imp.*, отплати́ть (-ачу́, -а́тишь) *perf.* тем же (са́мым); (*make reprisals*) применя́ть *imp.*, примени́ть (-ню́, -нишь) *perf.* репресса́лии. **retaliation** *n.* отпла́та, возме́здие.
retard *v.t.* замедля́ть *imp.*, заме́длить *perf.* **retarded** *adj.* отста́лый.
retch *v.i.* рвать (рвёт; рва́ло) *imp. impers.* + *acc.*
retention *n.* удержа́ние; (*preservation*) сохране́ние. **retentive** *adj.* уде́рживающий; (*memory*) хоро́ший.
reticence *n.* (*restraint*) сде́ржанность; (*secretiveness*) скры́тность. **reticent** *adj.* сде́ржанный. (-ан, -анна); скры́тный.
reticulated *adj.* се́тчатый. **reticulation** *n.* се́тчатый узо́р, се́тчатое строе́ние.
retina *n.* сетча́тка.
retinue *n.* сви́та.
retire *v.i.* (*withdraw*) уединя́ться *imp.*, уедини́ться *perf.*; (*from office etc.*) уходи́ть (-ожу́, -о́дишь) *imp.*, уйти́ (уйду́, -дёшь; ушёл, ушла́) *perf.* в отста́вку. **retired** *adj.* отставно́й, в отста́вке. **retirement** *n.* отста́вка. **retiring** *adj.* скро́мный (-мен, -мна́, -мно).
retort[1] *v.t.* отвеча́ть *imp.*, отве́тить *perf.* тем же (on, на + *acc.*); *v.i.* возража́ть *imp.*, возрази́ть *perf.*; *n.* возраже́ние; (*reply*) нахо́дчивый отве́т, остроу́мная ре́плика.
retort[2] *n.* (*vessel*) рето́рта.
retouch *v.t.* ретуши́ровать *imp.*, *perf.*, от~ *perf.*
retrace *v.t.*: **r.** *one's steps*, возвраща́ться *imp.*, возврати́ться (-ащу́сь, -ати́шься) *perf.*
retract *v.t.* (*draw in*) втя́гивать *imp.*, втяну́ть (-яну́, -я́нешь) *perf.*; (*take back*) брать (беру́, -рёшь; брал, -а́, -о) *imp.*, взять (возьму́, -мёшь; взял, -а́, -о) *perf.* наза́д.
retread *v.t.* (*tyre*) возобновля́ть *imp.*, возобнови́ть *perf.* проте́ктор + *gen.*; *n.* ши́на с возобновлённым проте́ктором.
retreat *v.i.* отступа́ть *imp.*, отступи́ть (-плю́, -пишь) *perf.*; *n.* отступле́ние; (*signal*) отбо́й; (*withdrawal*) уедине́ние; (*refuge*) убе́жище.
retrench *v.t.* & *i.* сокраща́ть *imp.*, сократи́ть (-ащу́, -ати́шь) *perf.* (расхо́ды). **retrenchment** *n.* сокраще́ние расхо́дов.
retribution *n.* возме́здие, ка́ра.
retrieval *n.* (*recovery*) восстановле́ние; (*computing*) по́иск (информа́ции); (*repair*) исправле́ние; *v.t.* восстана́вливать *imp.*, восстанови́ть (-влю́, -вишь) *perf.*; (*repair*) исправля́ть *imp.*, испра́вить *perf.*
retroactive *adj.* (*leg.*) име́ющий обра́тную си́лу. **retrograde** *adj.* ретрогра́дный. **retrogress** *v.i.* дви́гаться (-аюсь, -аешься & дви́жусь, -жешься) *imp.* наза́д; регресси́ровать *imp.* **retrorocket** *n.* ретрораке́та. **retrospect** *n.* ретроспекти́вный взгляд; *in r.*, ретроспекти́вно. **retrospective** *adj.* обращённый (-ён, -ена́) в про́шлое, ретроспекти́вный; (*leg.*) име́ющий обра́тную си́лу.
return *v.t.* & *i.* (*give back; come back*) возвра́щать(ся) *imp.*, возврати́ть(ся) (-ащу́(сь), -ати́шь(ся)) *imp.*, верну́ть(ся) *perf.*; *v.t.* (*reply to*) отвеча́ть *imp.*, отве́тить *perf.* на + *acc.*; (*elect*)

избира́ть *imp.*, избра́ть (изберу́, -рёшь; избра́л, -а́, -о) *perf.*; *n.* возвраще́ние; возвра́т; (*proceeds*) при́быль; *by r.*, обра́тной по́чтой; *in r.*, взаме́н (for, +*gen.*); *r. match*, отве́тный матч; *r. ticket*, обра́тный биле́т.

reunion *n.* встре́ча (друзе́й и т.п.); *family r.*, сбор всей семьи́. **reunite** *v.t.* воссоединя́ть *imp.*, воссоедини́ть *perf.*

rev *n.* оборо́т; *v.t.* & *i.*: *r. up*, ускоря́ть *imp.*, ускори́ть *perf.* (дви́гатель *m.*).

revanchism *n.* реванши́зм. **revanchist** *n.* реванши́ст.

reveal *v.t.* обнару́живать *imp.*, обнару́жить *perf.*; раскрыва́ть *imp.*, раскры́ть (-ро́ю, -ро́ешь) *perf.*

reveille *n.* подъём.

revel *v.i.* пирова́ть *imp.*; *r. in*, наслажда́ться *imp.* + *instr.*

revelation *n.* открове́ние; откры́тие; *R.* (*eccl.*) апокали́псис.

revenge *v.t.*: *r. oneself*, мстить *imp.*, ото~ *perf.* (for, за + *acc.*; on, + *dat.*); *n.* месть, отомще́ние. **revengeful** *adj.* мсти́тельный.

revenue *n.* дохо́д; *adj.* тамо́женный.

reverberate *v.t.* & *i.* отража́ть(ся) *imp.* **reverberation** *n.* отраже́ние; (*fig.*) о́тзвук.

revere *v.t.* почита́ть *imp.*, глубоко́ уважа́ть *imp.* **reverence** *n.* благогове́ние; почте́ние. **reverend** *adj.* (*in title*) (его́) преподо́бие. **reverential** *adj.* благогове́йный.

reverie *n.* мечты́ (*gen.* -та́ний) *f.pl.*

reversal *n.* по́лное измене́ние; (*of decision*) отме́на. **reverse** *adj.* обра́тный; *r. gear*, за́дний ход; *v.t.* изменя́ть *imp.*, измени́ть (-ню́, -нишь) *perf.* на обра́тный; (*revoke*) отменя́ть *imp.*, отмени́ть (-ню́, -нишь) *perf.*; *v.i.* дава́ть (даю́, даёшь) *imp.*, дать (дам, дашь, даст, дади́м; дал, -а́, да́ло́, -и) *perf.* за́дний ход; *n.* (*the r.*) обра́тное *sb.*, противополо́жное *sb.*; (*r. gear*) за́дний ход; (*r. side*) обра́тная сторона́ (*acc.* -ону, *pl.* -оны, -о́н, -она́м); (*misfortune*) неуда́ча; (*defeat*) пораже́ние. **reversible** *adj.* обрати́мый; (*cloth*) двусторо́нний. **reversion** *n.* возвраще́ние, реве́рсия. **revert** *v.i.* возвраща́ться (-ащу́сь, -ати́шься) *imp.* (to, в + *acc.*, к + *dat.*); (*leg.*) переходи́ть (-ит) *imp.*, перейти́ (-йдёт; -ешёл, -ешла́) *perf.* к пре́жнему владе́льцу.

review *n.* (*leg.*) пересмо́тр; (*mil.*) смотр, пара́д; (*survey*) обзо́р, обозре́ние; (*criticism*) реце́нзия; (*periodical*) журна́л; *v.t.* (*leg.*) пересма́тривать *imp.*, пересмотре́ть (-рю́, -ришь) *perf.*; (*survey*) обозрева́ть *imp.*, обозре́ть (-рю́, -ри́шь) *perf.*; (*of troops etc.*) принима́ть *imp.*, приня́ть (приму́, -мешь; при́нял, -а́, -о) *perf.* пара́д + *gen.*; (*book etc.*) рецензи́ровать *imp.*, про~ *perf.* **reviewer** *n.* рецензе́нт.

revise *v.t.* пересма́тривать *imp.*, пересмотре́ть (-рю́, -ришь) *perf.*; исправля́ть *imp.*, испра́вить *perf.*; *n.* втора́я корректу́ра. **revision** *n.* пересмо́тр, исправле́ние.

revival *n.* возрожде́ние; (*to life etc.*) оживле́ние. **revive** *v.t.* возрожда́ть *imp.*, возроди́ть *perf.*; оживля́ть *imp.*, оживи́ть *perf.*; *v.i.* ожива́ть *imp.*, ожи́ть (оживу́, -вёшь; о́жил, -а́, -о) *perf.*

revocation *n.* отме́на. **revoke** *v.t.* отменя́ть *imp.*, отмени́ть (-ню́, -нишь) *perf.*; *v.i.* (*cards*) объявля́ть *imp.*, объяви́ть (-влю́, -вишь) *perf.* рено́нс.

revolt *n.* бунт, мяте́ж (-а́); *v.t.* вызыва́ть *imp.*, вы́звать (вы́зову, -вешь) *perf.* отвраще́ние у + *gen.*; *v.i.* бунтова́ть *imp.*, взбунтова́ться *perf.* **revolting** *adj.* отврати́тельный.

revolution *n.* (*motion*) враще́ние; (*single turn*) оборо́т; (*polit. etc.*) револю́ция. **revolutionary** *adj.* революцио́нный; *n.* революционе́р. **revolutionize** *v.t.* революционизи́ровать *imp.*, *perf.* **revolve** *v.t.* & *i.* враща́ть(ся) *imp.* **revolver** *n.* револьве́р.

revue *n.* ревю́ *neut.indecl.*

revulsion *n.* (*change*) внеза́пное ре́зкое измене́ние; (*dislike*) отвраще́ние.

reward *n.* награ́да, вознагражде́ние; *v.t.* (воз)награжда́ть *imp.*, (воз)награди́ть *perf.*

rewrite *v.t.* (*recast*) переде́лывать *imp.*, переде́лать *perf.*

rhapsodize *v.i.*: *r. over*, восторга́ться *imp.* + *instr.* **rhapsody** *n.* (*mus.*) рапсо́дия; *pl.* восхище́ние.
rhesus *n.* ре́зус; *in comb.* ре́зус-.
rhetoric *n.* рито́рика. **rhetorical** *adj.* ритори́ческий.
rheumatic *adj.* ревмати́ческий. **rheumatism** *n.* ревмати́зм. **rheumatoid** *adj.* ревмато́идный.
rhinestone *n.* иску́сственный бриллиа́нт.
rhino, rhinoceros *n.* носоро́г.
rhizome *n.* ризо́ма, корневи́ще.
rhododendron *n.* рододе́ндрон.
rhomb *n.* ромб. **rhombic** *adj.* ромби́ческий. **rhomboid** *n.* ромбо́ид. **rhombus** *n.* ромб.
rhubarb *n.* реве́нь (-ня́) *m.*
rhyme *n.* ри́фма; *pl.* (*verse*) рифмо́ванные стихи́ *m.pl.*; *v.t.* рифмова́ть *imp.*, с~ *perf.*; *v.i.* рифмова́ться *imp.*
rhythm *n.* ритм, ритми́чность. **rhythmic(al)** *adj.* ритми́ческий, -чный.
rib *n.* ребро́ (*pl.* рёбра, -бер, -брам); (*of umbrella*) спи́ца; (*knitting etc.*) ру́бчик; (*of leaf*) жи́лка; (*of ship*) шпанго́ут (*also collect.*).
ribald *adj.* непристо́йный.
ribbon *n.* ле́нта; *pl.* (*reins*) во́жжи (-же́й) *pl.*; *pl.* (*shreds*) кло́чья (-ьев) *m.pl.*; *r. development*, ле́нточная застро́йка.
riboflavin *n.* рибофлави́н.
ribonucleic *adj.* рибонуклеи́новый.
rice *n.* рис; *attrib.* ри́совый.
rich *adj.* бога́тый; (*soil*) ту́чный (-чен, -чна́, -чно); (*food*) жи́рный (-рен, -рна́, -рно); (*amusing*) заба́вный. **riches** *n.* бога́тство. **richly** *adv.* (*fully*) вполне́.
rick[1] *n.* стог (*loc.* -е & -у́; *pl.* -а́), скирд(а́) (-а́ & -ы́; *pl.* ски́рды, -д(о́в), -да́м).
rick[2] *v.t.* растя́гивать *imp.*, растяну́ть (-ну́, -нешь) *perf.*
rickets *n.* рахи́т. **rickety** *adj.* рахити́чный; (*shaky*) расша́танный.
rickshaw *n.* ри́кша.
ricochet *n.* рикоше́т; *v.i.* рикошети́ровать *imp.*, *perf.*
rid *v.t.* освобожда́ть *imp.*, освободи́ть *perf.* (of, от + *gen.*); *get r. of*, избавля́ться *imp.*, изба́виться *perf.* от + *gen.*
riddance *n.*: *good r.!* ска́тертью доро́га!
riddle[1] *n.* (*enigma*) зага́дка.
riddle[2] *n.* (*sieve*) гро́хот; *v.t.* (*sift*) грохоти́ть *imp.*, про~ *perf.*; (*with bullets etc.*) изреше́чивать *imp.*, изрешети́ть *perf.*
ride *v.i.* е́здить *indet.*, е́хать (е́ду, е́дешь) *det.*, по~ *perf.* (*on horseback*, верхо́м); (*lie at anchor*) стоя́ть (-ои́т) *imp.* на я́коре; *v.t.* е́здить *indet.*, е́хать (е́ду, е́дешь) *det.*, по~ *perf.* в, на, + *prep.*; *n.* пое́здка, езда́. **rider** *n.* вса́дник, -ица; (*clause*) дополне́ние.
ridge *n.* хребе́т (-бта́), гре́бень (-бня) *m.*; (*of roof*) конёк (-нька́); *r.-pole*, (*of tent*) растя́жка; *r.-tile*, конько́вая черепи́ца.
ridicule *n.* насме́шка; *v.t.* осме́ивать *imp.*, осмея́ть (-ею́, -еёшь) *perf.* **ridiculous** *adj.* неле́пый, смешно́й (-шо́н, -шна́).
riding[1] *n.* (*division of county*) ра́йдинг.
riding[2] *n.* (*horse-r.*) (верхова́я) езда́; *r.-habit*, амазо́нка; *r.-light*, я́корный ого́нь (огня́) *m.*
Riesling *n.* ри́слинг (-а(у)).
rife *predic.* широко́ распространён (-а́), обы́чен (-чна); *be r. with*, изоби́ловать *imp.* + *instr.*
riff-raff *n.* подо́нки (-ков) *pl.*
rifle *v.t.* (*search*) обы́скивать *imp.*, обыска́ть (-ыщу́, -ы́щешь) *perf.*; (*a gun*) нареза́ть *imp.*, наре́зать (-е́жу, -е́жешь) *perf.*; *n.* винто́вка; *pl.* стрелки́ *m.pl.*; *r.-range*, стре́льбище.
rift *n.* тре́щина; (*dispute*) разры́в.
rig *v.t.* оснаща́ть *imp.*, оснасти́ть *perf.*; *r. out*, наряжа́ть *imp.*, наряди́ть (-яжу́, -я́дишь) *perf.*; *r. up*, стро́ить *imp.*, по~ *perf.* из чего́ попа́ло; *n.* бурова́я устано́вка. **rigging** *n.* такела́ж.
right *adj.* (*position*; *justified*; *polit.*) пра́вый (прав, -а́, -о); (*correct*) пра́вильный; (*appropriate*) ну́жный (-жен, -жна́, -жно, -жны́); (*suitable*) подходя́щий; *in one's r. mind*, в здра́вом уме́; *r. angle*, прямо́й у́гол (угла́); *r. side*, (*of cloth*) лицева́я сторона́ (*acc.* -ону); *v.t.* исправля́ть *imp.*, испра́вить *perf.*; *n.* пра́во (*pl.* -ва́); (*r.*

side) пра́вая сторона́ (*acc.* -ону); (*R.*; *polit.*) пра́вые *sb.*; *be in the r.*, быть (*fut.* бу́ду, -дешь; был, -а́, -о; не́ был, -а́, -о) пра́вым; *by r. of*, по пра́ву + *gen.*; *by rights*, по пра́ву, по справедли́вости; *reserve the r.*, оставля́ть *imp.*, оста́вить *perf.* за собо́й пра́во; *set to rights*, приводи́ть (-ожу́, -о́дишь) *imp.*, привести́ (-еду́, -едёшь; -ёл, -ела́) *perf.* в поря́док; *r. of way*, пра́во прохо́да, прое́зда; *adv.* (*straight*) пря́мо; (*exactly*) то́чно, как раз; (*to the full*) соверше́нно; (*correctly*) пра́вильно; как сле́дует; (*on the r.*) спра́во (of, от + *gen.*); (*to the r.*) напра́во.

righteous *adj.* (*person*) пра́ведный; (*action*) справедли́вый.

rightful *adj.* зако́нный.

rigid *adj.* жёсткий (-ток, -тка́, -тко), негну́щийся; (*strict*) стро́гий (-г, -га́, -го). **rigidity** *n.* жёсткость; стро́гость.

rigmarole *n.* бессмы́сленная, несвя́зная, болтовня́.

rigor mortis *n.* тру́пное окочене́ние.

rigorous *adj.* стро́гий (-г, -га́, -го), суро́вый. **rigour** *n.* стро́гость, суро́вость.

rill *n.* ручеёк (-ейка́).

rim *n.* (*of wheel*) о́бод (*pl.* обо́дья, -ьев); (*spectacles*) опра́ва. **rimless** *adj.* без опра́вы.

rind *n.* кожура́, ко́рка.

ring[1] *n.* кольцо́ (*pl.* -льца, -ле́ц, -льцам); (*circle*) круг (*loc.* -у́; *pl.* -и́); (*boxing*) ринг; (*circus*) (цирко́вая) аре́на; *r.-dove*, вя́хирь *m.*; *r.-finger*, безымя́нный па́лец (-льца); *r.-master*, инспе́ктор (*pl.* -а́ & -ы) мане́жа; *r. road*, кольцева́я доро́га; *v.t.* (*encircle*) окружа́ть *imp.*, окружи́ть *perf.* (кольцо́м).

ring[2] *v.i.* (*sound*) звене́ть (-ни́т) *imp.*, про ~ *perf.*; звони́ть *imp.*, по ~ *perf.*; (*of shot etc.*) раздава́ться (-даётся) *imp.*, разда́ться (-а́стся, -аду́тся; -а́лся, -ала́сь) *perf.*; (*of place*) оглаша́ться *imp.*, огласи́ться *perf.* (with, + *instr.*); *v.t.* звони́ть *imp.*, по ~ *perf.* в + *acc.*; *r. off*, дава́ть (даю́, даёшь) *imp.*, дать (дам, дашь, даст, дади́м; дал, -а́, да́ло́, -и) *perf.* отбо́й; *r. up*, звони́ть *imp.*, по ~ *perf.* + *dat.*; *n.* звон, звоно́к (-нка́).

ringleader *n.* глава́рь (-ря́) *m.*, зачи́нщик.

ringlet *n.* (*of hair*) ло́кон.

ringworm *n.* стригу́щий лиша́й (-ая́).

rink *n.* като́к (-тка́).

rinse *v.t.* полоска́ть (-ощу́, -о́щешь) *imp.*, вы́ ~, про ~ *perf.*; *n.* полоска́ние; (*for hair*) кра́ска для воло́с.

riot *n.* бунт; *run r.*, бу́йствовать *imp.*; переступа́ть *imp.*, переступи́ть (-плю́, -пишь) *perf.* все грани́цы; (*of plants*) бу́йно разраста́ться *imp.*, разрасти́сь (-тётся; разро́сся, -сла́сь) *perf.*; *v.i.* бунтова́ть *imp.*, взбунтова́ться *perf.* **riotous** *adj.* бу́йный (бу́ен, буйна́, -но).

rip *v.t.* & *i.* рвать(ся) (рву, рвёт(ся); -а́л(ся), -ала́(сь), -а́ло/-а́ло́сь) *imp.*; поро́ть(ся) (-рю́, -рет(ся)) *imp.*; *v.t.* (*tear up*) разрыва́ть *imp.*, разорва́ть (-ву́, -вёшь; разорва́л, -а́, -о) *perf.*; *v.i.* (*rush*) мча́ться (мчи́тся) *imp.*; *n.* проре́ха, разре́з; *r.-cord*, вытяжно́й трос.

ripe *adj.* зре́лый (зрел, -а́, -о), спе́лый (спел, -а́, -о). **ripen** *v.t.* де́лать *imp.*, с ~ *perf.* зре́лым; *v.i.* созрева́ть *imp.*, созре́ть *perf.* **ripeness** *n.* зре́лость.

ripple *n.* рябь; *v.t.* & *i.* покрыва́ть(ся) *imp.*, покры́ть(ся) (-ро́ет(ся)) *perf.* ря́бью.

rise *v.i.* поднима́ться *imp.*, подня́ться (-ниму́сь, -ни́мешься; -ня́лся́, -няла́сь) *perf.*; повыша́ться *imp.*, повы́ситься *perf.*; (*get up*) встава́ть (-таю́, -таёшь) *imp.*, встать (-а́ну, -а́нешь) *perf.*; (*rebel*) восстава́ть (-таю́, -таёшь) *imp.*, восста́ть (-а́ну, -а́нешь) *perf.*; (*sun etc.*) в(о)сходи́ть (-ит) *imp.*, взойти́ (-йдёт; взошёл, -шла́); (*wind*) уси́ливаться *imp.*, уси́литься *perf.*; *n.* подъём, возвыше́ние; (*in pay*) приба́вка; (*of sun etc.*) восхо́д. **riser** *n.* (*of stairs*) по́дступень; *he is an early r.*, он ра́но встаёт. **rising** *n.* (*revolt*) восста́ние.

risk *n.* риск; *v.t.* рискова́ть *imp.*, рискну́ть *perf.* + *instr.* **risky** *adj.* риско́ванный (-ан, -анна).

risqué *adj.* непристо́йный.

rissole *n.* котлéта.
rite *n.* обря́д. **ritual** *n.* ритуáл; *adj.* ритуáльный, обря́довый.
rival *n.* сопéрник, -ица; конкурéнт, ~ка; *adj.* сопéрничающий; *v.t.* сопéрничать *imp.* с + *instr.*; конкури́ровать *imp.* с + *instr.* **rivalry** *n.* сопéрничество.
river *n.* рекá (*acc.* рéку́; *pl.* рéки, рек, рéкáм); *adj.* речнóй. **riverside** *n.* прибрéжная полосá (*acc.* пóлосу́; *pl.* -осы, -óс, -осáм); *attrib.* прибрéжный.
rivet *n.* заклёпка; *v.t.* клепáть *imp.*; за-, с-, клёпывать *imp.*, за-, с-, клепáть *perf.*; (*attention etc.*) прикóвывать *imp.*, приковáть (-кую́, -куёшь) *perf.* (on, к + *dat.*).
rivulet *n.* рéчка, ручеёк (-ейкá).
RNA *abbr.* рибонуклеи́новая кислотá.
roach *n.* (*fish*) плотвá.
road *n.* дорóга, путь (-ти́, -тём) *m.*; (*highway*) шоссé *neut.indecl.*; (*central part*; *carriageway*) мостовáя *sb.*; (*street*) у́лица; (*naut.*; *usu. pl.*) рейд; *r.-block*, заграждéние на дорóге; *r.-hog*, лихáч (-á); *r.-house*, придорóжный буфéт, придорóжная гости́ница; *r.-map*, áтлас автомоби́льных дорóг; *r. sense*, чу́вство дорóги; *r. sign*, дорóжный знак. **roadman** *n.* дорóжный рабóчий *sb.* **roadside** *n.* обóчина; *attrib.* придорóжный. **roadstead** *n.* рейд. **roadway** *n.* мостовáя *sb.*
roam *v.t.* & *i.* броди́ть (-ожу́, -óдишь) *imp.* (по + *dat.*); скитáться *imp.* (по + *dat.*).
roan *adj.* чáлый.
roar *n.* (*animal's*) рёв; (*other noise*) грóхот, шум; *v.i.* ревéть (-ву́, -вёшь) *imp.*; грохотáть (-очу́, -óчешь) *imp.*, про~ *perf.*
roast *v.t.* & *i.* жáрить(ся) *imp.*, за~ из~ *perf.*; *adj.* жáреный; *r. beef*, рóстбиф; *n.* жаркóе *sb.*, жáреное *sb.*
rob *v.t.* грáбить *imp.*, о~ *perf.*; красть (-аду́, -адёшь; -ал) *imp.*, у~ *perf.* у + *gen.* (of, + *acc.*); (*deprive*) лишáть *imp.*, лиши́ть *perf.* (of, + *gen.*). **robber** *n.* грабитель *m.* **robbery** *n.* грабёж (-á).
robe *n.* (*also pl.*) мáнтия.
robin *n.* мали́новка.
robot *n.* рóбот.
robust *adj.* здорóвый (-в, -вá), крéпкий (-пок, -пкá, -пко).
rock[1] *n.* (*geol.*) (гóрная) порóда; (*cliff etc.*) скалá (*pl.* -лы); (*large stone*) большóй кáмень (-мня; -мни, -мнéй) *m.*; *on the rocks*, на мели́; (*drink*) со льдом; *r.-bottom*, сáмый ни́зкий; *r.-crystal*, гóрный хрустáль (-ля́) *m.*; *r.-salt*, кáменная соль.
rock[2] *v.t.* & *i.* качáть(ся) *imp.*, качну́ть(ся) *perf.*; (*sway*) колебáть(ся) (-блю(сь), -блешь(ся)) *imp.*, по~ *perf.*; *r. to sleep*, укáчивать *imp.*, укачáть *perf.*; *rocking-chair* (крéсло-)качáлка; *rocking-horse*, конь-качáлка; *r. and roll*, рок-н-рóлл.
rockery *n.* сад (*loc.* -у́; *pl.* -ы́) камнéй.
rocket *n.* ракéта. **rocketry** *n.* ракéтная тéхника.
rocky *adj.* скали́стый; (*unsteady*) неустóйчивый.
rococo *n.* рококó *neut.indecl.*; *adj.* в сти́ле рококó.
rod *n.* прут (-á; *pl.* -ья, -ьев); (*for caning*) рóзга; (*tech.*) стéржень (-жня) *m.*; (*fishing-r.*) у́дочка.
rodent *n.* грызу́н (-á).
rodeo *n.* родéо *neut.indecl.*
roe[1] *n.* (*hard*) икрá; (*soft*) молóки (-óк) *pl.*
roe[2] **(-deer)** *n.* косу́ля. **roebuck** *n.* самéц (-мцá) косу́ли.
roentgen *n.* рентгéн (*gen.pl.* -н & -нов). **roentgenography** *n.* рентгеногрáфия. **roentgenology** *n.* рентгенолóгия.
rogue *n.* плут (-á). **roguish** *adj.* плутовскóй; (*mischievous*) прокáзливый.
role *n.* роль (*pl.* -ли, -лéй).
roll[1] *n.* (*cylinder*) рулóн; (*document*) сви́ток (-ткa); (*register*) спи́сок (-скa), реéстр; (*bread r.*) бу́лочка; *r.-call*, перекли́чка.
roll[2] *v.t.* & *i.* катáть(ся) *indet.*, кати́ть(ся) (качу́(сь), кáтишь(ся)) *det.*, по~ *perf.*; (*r. up*) свёртывать(ся) *imp.*, сверну́ть(ся) *perf.*; *v.t.* (*road*) укáтывать *imp.*, укатáть *perf.*; (*metal*) прокáтывать *imp.*, прокатáть *perf.*; (*dough*) раскáтывать *imp.*, раскатáть *perf.*; *v.i.* (*sound*) гремéть (-ми́т) *imp.*; *n.* катáние; (*of thunder*) раскáт.

roller *n.* ва́лик; (*wave*) вал (*loc.* -у́; *pl.* -ы́); *pl.* (*for hair*) бигуди́ *neut.indecl.*; *r. bearing*, ро́ликовый подши́пник; *r.-skates*, ро́лики *m.pl.*, коньки́ *m.pl.* на ро́ликах; *r. towel*, полоте́нце на ро́лике.
rollicking *adj.* разуха́бистый.
rolling *adj.* (*of land*) холми́стый; *r.-mill*, прока́тный стан; *r.-pin*, ска́лка; *r.-stock*, подвижно́й соста́в.
Roman *n.* ри́млянин (*pl.* -яне, -ян), -янка; *adj.* ри́мский; *R. alphabet*, лати́нский алфави́т; *R. Catholic*, (*n.*) като́лик, -и́чка; (*adj.*) ри́мско-католи́ческий; *r. type*, прямо́й, све́тлый шрифт.
romance *n.* (*tale*; *love affair*) рома́н; (*quality*) рома́нтика; (*mus.*) рома́нс; *R. languages*, рома́нские языки́ *m.pl.*
Romanesque *adj.* рома́нский.
Romanian *n.* румы́н (*gen.pl.* -н), ~ка; *adj.* румы́нский.
romantic *adj.* романти́чный, -ческий. **romanticism** *n.* романти́зм.
romp *v.i.* вози́ться (вожу́сь, во́зишься) *imp.*; *r. home*, с лёгкостью вы́играть *perf.*
rondo *n.* (*mus.*) ро́ндо *neut.indecl.*
Röntgen *n.*: *R. rays*, рентге́новские лучи́ *m.pl.*; (*r.*) *see* **roentgen**.
rood *n.* распя́тие; *r.-loft*, хо́ры (-р & -ров) *pl.* в це́ркви; *r.-screen*, перего-ро́дка в це́ркви.
roof *n.* кры́ша, кро́вля (*gen.pl.* -вель); *r. of the mouth*, нёбо; *v.t.* крыть (кро́ю, -о́ешь) *imp.*, покрыва́ть *imp.*, покры́ть (-ро́ю, -ро́ешь) *perf.*
rook[1] *n.* (*chess*) ладья́.
rook[2] *n.* (*orn.*) грач (-а́). **rookery** *n.* грачо́вник.
room *n.* (*in house*) ко́мната; *pl.* помеще́ние; (*space*) ме́сто; (*opportunity*) возмо́жность. **roomy** *adj.* просто́рный.
roost *n.* насе́ст.
root[1] *n.* (*var. senses*) ко́рень (-рня; *pl.* -рни, -рне́й) *m.*; (*mus.*) основно́й тон (акко́рда); (*plant*) корнепло́д; *r. and branch*, коренны́м о́бразом; *r.-stock*, корневи́ще; *v.i.* пуска́ть *imp.*, пусти́ть (-ит) *perf.* ко́рни; *r. to the spot*, пригвожда́ть *imp.*, пригвозди́ть *perf.* к ме́сту.
root[2] *v.i.* (*rummage*) ры́ться (ро́юсь, ро́ешься) *imp.*
rope *n.* верёвка, кана́т, трос; *r.-dancer*, канатохо́дец (-дца); *r.-ladder*, верёвочная ле́стница; *v.t.* привя́зывать *imp.*, привяза́ть (-яжу́, -я́жешь) *perf.*; *r. in, off*, о(т)гора́живать *imp.*, о(т)городи́ть (-ожу́, -о́ди́шь) *perf.* кана́том.
rosary *n.* (*eccl.*) чётки (-ток) *pl.*
rose *n.* ро́за; (*nozzle*) се́тка; *pl.* (*complexion*) румя́нец (-нца); *r.-bud*, буто́н ро́зы; *r.-coloured*, ро́зовый; *r.-water*, ро́зовая вода́ (*acc.* -ду); *r.-window*, розе́тка.
rosemary *n.* розмари́н.
rosette *n.* розе́тка.
rosewood *n.* ро́зовое де́рево.
rosin *n.* канифо́ль; *v.t.* натира́ть *imp.*, натере́ть (-тру́, -трёшь; -тёр) *perf.* канифо́лью.
roster *n.* расписа́ние (наря́дов, дежу́рств).
rostrum *n.* трибу́на, ка́федра.
rosy *adj.* ро́зовый; (*complexion*) румя́ный.
rot *n.* гниль; (*nonsense*) вздор; *v.i.* гнить (-ию́, -иёшь; гнил, -а́, -о) *imp.*, с~ *perf.*; *v.t.* гнои́ть *imp.*, с~ *perf.*
rota *n.* расписа́ние дежу́рств. **rotary** *adj.* враща́тельный, ротацио́нный. **rotate** *v.t.* & *i.* враща́ть(ся) *imp.* **rotation** *n.* враще́ние; *in r.*, по о́череди.
rote *n.*: *by r.*, наизу́сть.
rotten *adj.* гнило́й (гнил, -а́, -о). **rotter** *n.* дрянь.
rotund *adj.* (*round*) кру́глый (-л, -ла́, -ло, кру́глы́); (*plump*) по́лный (-лон, -лна́, по́лно́). **rotunda** *n.* рото́нда. **rotundity** *n.* округлённость, полнота́.
rouble *n.* рубль (-ля́) *m.*
rouge *n.* румя́на (-н) *pl.*; *v.t.* & *i.* румя́нить(ся) *imp.*, на~ *perf.*
rough *adj.* (*uneven*) неро́вный (-вен, -вна́, -вно); (*coarse*) гру́бый (груб, -а́, -о); (*sea*) бу́рный (-рен, бу́рна́, -но); (*approximate*) приблизи́тельный; *r.-and-ready*, гру́бый но эффекти́вный; *r. copy*, чернови́к (-а́); *n.* (*r. ground*) неро́вное по́ле; (*person*) хулига́н.

roughage *n.* грýбая пи́ща. **roughcast** *n.* гáлечная штукатýрка. **roughly** *adv.* грýбо; *r. speaking*, примéрно.
roulette *n.* рулéтка.
round *adj.* крýглый (-л, -лá, -ло, крýглы́); (*plump*) пóлный (-лон, -лнá, пóлнó); *r. dance*, кругово́й тáнец (-нца); *in r. figures*, приблизи́тельно; *r.-shouldered*, сутýлый; *n.* (*r. object*) круг (*loc.* -ý; *pl.* -и́); (*circuit*; *also pl.*) обхóд; (*sport*) тур, рáунд; (*series*) ряд (*pl.* -ы́); (*ammunition*) патрóн, снаря́д; (*of applause*) взрыв; *adv.* вокрýг; (*in a circle*) по крýгу; *all r.*, кругóм; *all the year r.*, крýглый год; *prep.* вокрýг + *gen.*; кругóм + *gen.*; по + *dat.*; *r. the corner*, (*motion*) зá угол, (*position*) за углóм; *v.t.* & *i.* округля́ть(ся) *imp.*, округли́ть(ся) *perf.*; *v.t.* (*pass r.*) огибáть *imp.*, обогнýть *perf.*; *r. off*, (*complete*) завершáть *imp.*, заверши́ть *perf.*; *r. up*, сгоня́ть *imp.*, согнáть (сгоню́, -нишь; согнáл, -á, -о) *perf.*; *r.-up*, загóн; (*police*) облáва. **roundabout** *n.* (*merry-go-round*) карусéль; (*road junction*) трáнспортная развя́зка с односторóнним кругоы́м движéнием маши́н; *adj.* окóльный; *in a r. way*, окóльным путём.
rouse *v.t.* буди́ть (бужý, бýдишь) *imp.*, раз ~ *perf.*; (*to action etc.*) побуждáть *imp.*, побуди́ть (-ужý, -ýдишь) *perf.* (to, к + *dat.*). **rousing** *adj.* возбуждáющий.
rout *n.* (*defeat*) разгрóм; (*flight*) беспоря́дочное бéгство; *v.t.* обращáть *imp.*, обрати́ть (-ащý, -ати́шь) *perf.* в бéгство.
route *n.* маршрýт, путь (-ти́, -тём) *m.*; *r. march*, похóдное движéние; *v.t.* отправля́ть *imp.*, отпрáвить *perf.* (по определённому маршрýту).
routine *n.* заведённый поря́док (-дка), режи́м; (*pejor.*) рути́на; *adj.* установлéнный; очереднóй.
rove *v.i.* скитáться *imp.*; (*of thoughts etc.*) блуждáть *imp.* **rover** *n.* скитáлец (-льца).
row[1] *n.* (*line*) ряд (-á *with 2, 3, 4*, *loc.* -ý; *pl.* -ы́).
row[2] *v.i.* (*in boat*) грести́ (гребý, -бёшь; грёб, -лá) *imp.*; *v.t.* (*convey*) перевози́ть (-ожý, -óзишь) *imp.*, перевезти́ (-езý, -езёшь; -ёз, -езлá) *perf.* на лóдке.
row[3] *n.* (*dispute*) ссóра; (*brawl*) скандáл; *v.i.* ссóриться *imp.*, по ~ *perf.*; скандáлить *imp.*, на ~ *perf.*
rowan *n.* ряби́на.
rowdy *adj.* бýйный (бýен, буйнá, -но); *n.* буя́н.
rowlock *n.* уклю́чина.
royal *adj.* королéвский, цáрский; (*majestic*) великолéпный. **royalist** *n.* роя́ли́ст; *adj.* роялúстский. **royalty** *n.* член, члéны *pl.*, королéвской семьи́; (*author's fee*) áвторский гонорáр; (*patentee's fee*) отчислéние владéльцу патéнта.
rub *v.t.* & *i.* терéть(ся) (трý(сь), трёшь(ся); тёр(ся)) *imp.*; *v.t.* (*polish*; *chafe*) натирáть *imp.*, натерéть (-трý, -трёшь; -тёр) *perf.*; (*r. dry*) вытирáть *imp.*, вы́тереть (-тру, -трешь; -тер) *perf.*; *r. in, on*, втирáть *imp.*, втерéть (вотрý, -рёшь; втёр) *perf.*; *r. out*, стирáть *imp.*, стерéть (сотрý, -рёшь; стёр) *perf.*; *r. it in*, растравля́ть *imp.*, растрави́ть (-влю́, -вишь) *perf.* рáну; *r. one's hands*, потирáть *imp.* рýки (with (*joy etc.*), от + *gen.*); *r. up the wrong way*, глáдить *imp.* прóтив шéрсти.
rubber[1] *n.* (*cured*) рези́на; (*not cured*) каучýк; (*eraser*, *also r. band*) рези́нка, лáстик; *attrib.* рези́новый; *r.-stamp*, (*fig.*) штамповáть *imp.*
rubber[2] *n.* (*cards*) рóббер.
rubberize *v.t.* прорези́нивать *imp.*, прорези́нить *perf.*
rubbish *n.* мýсор, хлам; (*nonsense*) чепухá, вздор. **rubbishy** *adj.* дрянно́й (-нен, -ннá, -нно).
rubble *n.* бут.
rubella *n.* краснýха.
rubicund *n.* румя́ный.
rubric *n.* рýбрика.
ruby *n.* руби́н; *adj.* руби́новый.
ruche *n.* рюш.
ruck *v.t.* (*r. up*) мять (мну, мнёшь) *imp.*, из ~ (изомнý, -нёшь), с ~ (сомнý, -нёшь) *perf.*
rucksack *n.* рюкзáк (-á).
rudd *n.* краснопёрка.

rudder *n.* руль (-ля́) *m.*
ruddy *adj.* кра́сный (-сен, -сна́, -сно); (*face*) румя́ный; (*sl.*, *damnable*) проклятый.
rude *adj.* гру́бый (груб, -а́, -о); (*impolite also*) неве́жливый; *r. awakening*, глубо́кое разочарова́ние; *r. health*, кре́пкое здоро́вье; *r. shock*, внеза́пный уда́р.
rudimentary *adj.* зача́точный, рудимента́рный. **rudiments** *n.* (*elements*) нача́тки (-ков) *pl.*; (*beginning*) зача́тки *m.pl.*
rue[1] *n.* (*plant*) ру́та.
rue[2] *v.t.* сожале́ть *imp.* о + *prep.* **rueful** *adj.* печа́льный, уны́лый.
ruff[1] *n.* (*frill*) бры́жи (-жей) *pl.*; (*of feathers, hair*) кольцо́ (*pl.* -льца, -ле́ц, -льцам) (пе́рьев, ше́рсти) вокру́г ше́и.
ruff[2] *v.t.* (*cards*) покрыва́ть *imp.*, покры́ть (-ро́ю, -ро́ешь) *perf.* ко́зырем; *n.* покры́тие ко́зырем; ко́зырь (*pl.* -ри, -ре́й) *m.*
ruffian *n.* головоре́з, хулига́н. **ruffianly** *adj.* хулига́нский.
ruffle *v.t.* (*hair*) еро́шить *imp.*, взъ~ *perf.*; (*water*) ряби́ть *imp.*; (*person*) раздража́ть *imp.*, раздражи́ть *perf.*
rug *n.* (*mat*) ко́врик, ковёр (-вра́); (*wrap*) плед.
Rugby (football) *n.* ре́гби *neut.indecl.*
rugged *adj.* (*uneven*) неро́вный (-вен, -вна́, -вно); (*rocky*) скали́стый; (*rough*) гру́бый (груб, -а́, -о).
ruin *n.* (*downfall*) ги́бель; (*destruction*) разоре́ние; *pl.* разва́лины *f.pl.*, руи́ны *f.pl.*; *v.t.* губи́ть (-блю́, -бишь) *imp.*, по~ *perf.*; разоря́ть *imp.*, разори́ть *perf.* **ruinous** *adj.* губи́тельный, разори́тельный; (*state*) разру́шенный (-ен).
rule *n.* пра́вило; (*carpenter's, print.*) лине́йка; *as a r.*, как пра́вило, обы́чно; *v.t.* & *i.* пра́вить *imp.* (+ *instr.*); (*make lines*) линова́ть *imp.*, раз~ *perf.*; (*give decision*) постановля́ть *imp.*, постанови́ть (-влю́, -вишь) *perf.*; *r. out*, исключа́ть *imp.*, исключи́ть *perf.* **ruler** *n.* (*person*) прави́тель *m.*, ~ница; (*object*) лине́йка. **ruling** *n.* (*of court etc.*) постановле́ние.
rum[1] *n.* ром.
rum[2] *adj.* стра́нный (-нен, -нна́, -нно), чудно́й (-дён, -дна́).
Rumanian *see* **Romanian.**
rumba *n.* ру́мба.
rumble *v.i.* громыха́ть *imp.*; грохота́ть (-о́чет) *imp.*; *n.* громыха́ние, грохота́ние, гро́хот.
ruminant *n.* жва́чное (живо́тное) *sb.*; *adj.* жва́чный; (*contemplative*) заду́мчивый. **ruminate** *v.i.* жева́ть (жуёт) *imp.* жва́чку; (*fig.*) размышля́ть *imp.* (over, on, о + *prep.*). **rumination** *n.* размышле́ние.
rummage *v.i.* ры́ться (ро́юсь, ро́ешься) *imp.*
rumour *n.* слух; *v.t.*: *it is rumoured that*, хо́дят слу́хи (*pl.*), что.
rump *n.* огу́зок (-зка); *r. steak*, ромште́кс.
rumple *v.t.* мять (мну, мнёшь) *imp.*, из~ (изомну́, -нёшь), с~ (сомну́, -нёшь) *perf.*; (*hair*) еро́шить *imp.*, взъ~ *perf.*
run *v.i.* бе́гать *indet.*, бежа́ть (бегу́, бежи́шь) *det.*, по~ *perf.*; (*roll along*) ката́ться *indet.*, кати́ться (качу́сь, ка́тишься) *det.*, по~ *perf.*; (*work, of machines*) рабо́тать *imp.*; (*ply, of bus etc.*) ходи́ть (-ит) *indet.*, идти́ (идёт; шёл, шла) *det.*; (*compete in race*) уча́ствовать *imp.* (в бе́ге); (*seek election*) выставля́ть *imp.*, вы́ставить *perf.* свою́ кандидату́ру; (*be valid*) быть действи́тельным; (*of play etc.*) идти́ (идёт; шёл, шла) *imp.*; (*spread rapidly*) бы́стро распространя́ться *imp.*, распространи́ться *perf.*; (*of ink, dye*) расплыва́ться *imp.*, расплы́ться (-ывётся; -ы́лся, -ыла́сь) *perf.*; (*flow*) течь (течёт; тёк, -ла́) *imp.*; (*of document*) гласи́ть *imp.*; *v.t.* (*manage; operate a machine*) управля́ть *imp.* + *instr.*; (*a business etc.*) вести́ (веду́, -дёшь; вёл, -а́) *imp.*; *r. dry, low*, иссяка́ть *imp.*, исся́кнуть (-к) *perf.*; *r. errands*, быть на посы́лках (for, у + *gen.*); *r. risks*, рискова́ть *imp.*; *r. to earth*, (*fig.*) отыска́ть (отыщу́, -щешь) *perf.*; *r. across, into*, (*meet*) встреча́ться *imp.*, встре́титься *perf.* с + *instr.*; *r. after*, (*fig.*) уха́живать *imp.* за + *instr.*; *r. away*, (*flee*) убега́ть *imp.*, убежа́ть

(-егу́, -ежи́шь) *perf.*; *r. down*, (*knock down*) задави́ть (-влю́, -вишь) *perf.*; (*disparage*) умаля́ть *imp.*, умали́ть *perf.*; *be r. down*, (*of person*) переутоми́ться *perf.* (*in past tense*); *r.-down*, (*decayed*) захуда́лый; *r. in*, (*engine*) обка́тывать *imp.*, обката́ть *perf.*; *r. into* see *r. across*; *r. out*, конча́ться *imp.*, ко́нчиться *perf.*; *r. out of*, истоща́ть *imp.*, истощи́ть *perf.* свой запа́с + *gen.*; *r. over*, (*glance over*) бе́гло просма́тривать *imp.*, просмотре́ть (-рю́, -ришь) *perf.*; (*injure*) задави́ть (-влю́, -вишь) *perf.*; *r. through*, (*pierce*) прока́лывать *imp.*, проколо́ть (-лю́, -лешь) *perf.*; (*money*) прома́тывать *imp.*, промота́ть *perf.*; (*glance over*) see *r. over*; *r. to*, (*reach*) достига́ть *imp.*, дости́гнуть & дости́чь (-и́гну, -и́гнешь; -и́г) *perf.* + *gen.*; (*of money*) хвата́ть *imp.*, хвати́ть (-ит) *perf.impers.* + *gen.* на + *acc.*; *the money won't r. to a car*, э́тих де́нег не хва́тит на маши́ну; *r. up against*, ната́лкиваться *imp.*, натолкну́ться *perf.* на + *acc.*; *n.* бег; (*also distance covered*) пробе́г; (*direction*) направле́ние; (*course, motion*) ход, тече́ние; (*regular route*) маршру́т; (*mus.*) рула́да; (*bombing r.*) захо́д на цель; *at a r.*, бего́м; *r. on*, большо́й спрос на + *acc.*; *common r. of men*, обыкнове́нные лю́ди (-де́й, -дям, -дьми́) *pl.*; *in the long r.*, в конце́ концо́в.

rune *n.* ру́на.

rung *n.* ступе́нь, ступе́нька.

runner *n.* (*also tech.*) бегу́н (-а́); (*messenger*) посы́льный *sb.*; (*of sledge*) по́лоз (*pl.* поло́зья, -ьев); (*cloth*) доро́жка; (*stem*) сте́лющийся побе́г; *r. bean*, фасо́ль; *r.-up*, уча́стник состяза́ния, заня́вший второ́е ме́сто. **running** *n.* бег; (*of machine*) ход, рабо́та; *be in the r.*, име́ть *imp.* ша́нсы на вы́игрыш; *make the r.*, задава́ть (-даю́, -даёшь) *imp.*, зада́ть (-а́м, -а́шь, -а́ст, -ади́м; за́дал, -а́, -о) *perf.* темп; *adj.* бегу́щий; (*of r.*) бегово́й, (*after pl. n.*, *in succession*) подря́д; *r. account*, теку́щий счёт; *r.-board*, подно́жка; *r. commentary*, (ра́дио)репорта́ж; *r. title*, колонти́тул; *r. water*, прото́чная вода́ (*acc.* -ду). **runway** *n.* (*aeron.*) взлётно-поса́дочная полоса́ (*acc.* по́лосу́; *pl.* -осы, -о́с, -оса́м).

rupee *n.* ру́пия.

rupture *n.* разры́в; (*hernia*) гры́жа.

rural *adj.* се́льский, дереве́нский.

ruse *n.* хи́трость, уло́вка.

rush[1] *n.* (*plant*) (*also collect.*) камы́ш (-а́), тростни́к (-а́); (*bot.*) си́тник.

rush[2] *v.t.* бы́стро проводи́ть (-ожу́, -о́дишь) *imp.*, провести́ (-еду́, -едёшь; -ёл, -ела́) *perf.*; торопи́ть (-плю́, -пишь) *imp.*, по~ *perf.*; *v.i.* броса́ться *imp.*, бро́ситься *perf.*; мча́ться (мчусь, мчи́шься) *imp.*; *n.* стреми́тельное движе́ние, поры́в; (*influx*) наплы́в; (*of blood etc.*) прили́в; (*hurry*) спе́шка; *r.-hour(s)*, часы́ *m.pl.* пик; *r. job*, авра́л.

rusk *n.* суха́рь (-ря́) *m.*

russet *adj.* краснова́то-кори́чневый.

Russia (leather) *n.* ю́фть. **Russian** *n.* ру́сский *sb.*; *adj.* ру́сский; *R. salad*, винегре́т.

rust *n.* ржа́вчина; *r.-proof*, нержаве́ющий; *v.i.* ржаве́ть *imp.*, за~ *perf.*

rustic *adj.* дереве́нский; (*unpolished, uncouth*) неотёсанный (-ан, -анна); *n.* дереве́нский, се́льский, жи́тель *m.*, ~ница. **rusticate** *v.t.* (*univ.*) вре́менно исключа́ть *imp.*, исключи́ть *perf.* из университе́та; (*arch.*) рустова́ть *imp.*; жить (живу́, -вёшь; жил, -а́, -о) *imp.* в дере́вне. **rustication** *n.* (*arch.*) русто́вка.

rustle *n.* ше́лест, шо́рох, шурша́ние; *v.i.* шелесте́ть (-ти́шь) *imp.*; *v.t. & i.* шурша́ть (-шу́, -ши́шь) *imp.* (+ *instr.*); *v.t.* (*r. cattle*) красть (-аду́, -адёшь; -а́л) *imp.*, у~ *perf.*

rusty *adj.* ржа́вый.

rut *n.* (*groove*) колея́.

ruthless *adj.* безжа́лостный.

rye *n.* рожь (ржи); *attrib.* ржано́й.

S

Sabbath *n.* (*Jewish*) суббо́та; (*Christian*) воскресе́нье; (*witches'*) ша́баш. **sabbatical** *adj.*: *s.* (*year*) годи́чный о́тпуск.

sable *n.* (*animal*; *fur*) со́боль (*pl.* (*animal*) -ли, -ле́й & (*fur*) -ля́) *m.*; (*fur*) собо́лий мех (*loc.* -е & -у́; *pl.* -а́); *attrib.* соболи́ный, собо́лий.

sabotage *n.* сабота́ж, дивéрсия; *v.t.* саботи́ровать *imp.*, *perf.* **saboteur** *n.* сабота́жник, диверса́нт.

sabre *n.* са́бля (*gen.pl.* -бель), ша́шка; *s.-rattling*, бряца́ние ору́жием.

sac *n.* мешо́чек (-чка).

saccharin *n.* сахари́н.

saccharine *adj.* са́харистый.

sacerdotal *adj.* свяще́ннический.

sachet *n.* поду́шечка.

sack[1] *v.t.* (*plunder*) разгра́бить *perf.*

sack[2] *n.* куль (-ля́) *m.*, мешо́к (-шка́); *the s.*, (*dismissal*) увольне́ние; *v.t.* увольня́ть *imp.*, уво́лить *perf.* **sacking** *n.* (*hessian*) мешкови́на.

sacrament *n.* та́инство; (*Eucharist*) прича́стие. **sacred** *adj.* свяще́нный (-е́н, -е́нна), свято́й (свят, -а́, -о). **sacrifice** *n.* же́ртва; *v.t.* же́ртвовать *imp.*, по~ *perf.* + *instr.* **sacrificial** *adj.* же́ртвенный. **sacrilege** *n.* святота́тство. **sacrilegious** *adj.* святота́тственный. **sacristy** *n.* ри́зница. **sacrosanct** *adj.* свяще́нный (-е́н, -е́нна).

sad *adj.* печа́льный, гру́стный (-тен, -тна́, -тно). **sadden** *v.t.* печа́лить *imp.*, о~ *perf.*

saddle *n.* седло́ (*pl.* сёдла, -дел, -длам;) *v.t.* седла́ть *imp.*, о~ *perf.*; (*burden*) обременя́ть *imp.*, обремени́ть *perf.* (with, + *instr.*). **saddler** *n.* седе́льник, шо́рник.

sadism *n.* сади́зм. **sadist** *n.* сади́ст. **sadistic** *adj.* сади́стский.

sadness *n.* печа́ль, грусть.

safe *n.* сейф, несгора́емый шкаф (*loc.* -у́; *pl.* -ы́); *adj.* (*uninjured*) невреди́мый; (*out of danger*) в безопа́сности; (*secure*) безопа́сный; (*reliable*) надёжный; *s. and sound*, цел (-а́, -о) и невреди́м. **safeguard** *n.* предохрани́тельная ме́ра; *v.t.* предохраня́ть *imp.*, предохрани́ть *perf.* **safety** *n.* безопа́сность; *s.-belt*, предохрани́тельный реме́нь (-мня́) *m.*; *s.-catch*, предохрани́тель *m.*; *s. lamp*, рудни́чная ла́мпа; *s.-pin*, англи́йская була́вка; *s. razor*, безопа́сная бри́тва; *s.-valve*, предохрани́тельный кла́пан; (*fig.*) отду́шина.

saffron *n.* шафра́н; *adj.* шафра́нный, шафра́новый.

sag *v.i.* провиса́ть *imp.*, прови́снуть (-с) *perf.*; прогиба́ться *imp.*, прогну́ться *perf.*; *n.* прове́с, проги́б.

saga *n.* са́га.

sagacious *adj.* проница́тельный. **sagacity** *n.* проница́тельность.

sage[1] *n.* (*herb*) шалфе́й; *s.-green*, серова́то-зелёный.

sage[2] *n.* (*person*) мудре́ц (-а́); *adj.* му́дрый (мудр, -а́, -о).

Sagittarius *n.* Стреле́ц (-льца́).

sago *n.* са́го *neut.indecl.*; (*palm*) са́говая па́льма.

sail *n.* па́рус (*pl.* -а́); (*collect.*) паруса́ *m.pl.*; (*of windmill*) крыло́ (*pl.* -лья, -льев); *v.t.* (*a ship*) управля́ть *imp.* + *instr.*; *v.t.* пла́вать *indet.*, плыть (плыву́, -вёшь; плыл, -а́, -о) *det.*; (*depart*) отплыва́ть *imp.*, отплы́ть (-ыву́, -ывёшь; -ы́л, -ыла́, -ы́ло) *perf.* **sailcloth** *n.* паруси́на. **sailing** *n.* (*sport*) па́русный спорт; *s.-ship*, па́русное су́дно (*pl.* -да́, -до́в). **sailor** *n.* матро́с, моря́к (-а́).

saint *n.* свято́й *sb.* **saintly** *adj.* свято́й (свят, -а́, -о), безгре́шный.

sake *n.*: *for the s. of*, ра́ди + *gen.*, для + *gen.*
salacious *adj.* непристо́йный; (*lustful*) похотли́вый.
salad *n.* сала́т, винегре́т; *s. days*, зелёная ю́ность; *s.-dressing*, припра́па к сала́ту; *s.-oil*, расти́тельное, оли́вковое, ма́сло.
salamander *n.* саламáндра.
salami *n.* саля́ми *f.indecl.*
salaried *adj.* получа́ющий жа́лованье. **salary** *n.* жа́лованье.
sale *n.* прода́жа; (*also amount sold*) сбыт (*no pl.*); (*at reduced price*) распрода́жа по сни́женным це́нам; *be for s.*, продава́ться (-даётся) *imp.*; *s.-room*, аукцио́нный зал. **saleable** *adj.* хо́дкий (-док, -дка́, -дко). **salesman** *n.* продаве́ц (-вца́). **saleswoman** *n.* продавщи́ца.
salient *adj.* (*projecting*) выдаю́щийся, выступа́ющий; (*conspicuous*) заме́тный, я́ркий; *n.* вы́ступ.
saline *n.* соляно́й.
saliva *n.* слюна́. **salivary** *adj.* слю́нный. **salivate** *v.i.* выделя́ть *imp.*, вы́делить *perf.* слюну́. **salivation** *n.* слюнотече́ние.
sallow *adj.* желтова́тый.
sally *n.* вы́лазка; (*witticism*) остро́та; *v.i.*: *s. forth, out*, отправля́ться *imp.*, отпра́виться *perf.*; *s. out*, (*mil.*) де́лать *imp.*, с ~ *perf.* вы́лазку.
salmon *n.* ло́сось *m.*, сёмга; (*cul.*) лососи́на, сёмга.
salon *n.* сало́н. **saloon** *n.* (*hall*) зал; (*on ship*) сало́н; (*rly.*) сало́н-ваго́н; (*bar*) бар; *s. deck*, па́луба пе́рвого кла́сса.
salt *n.* соль; *s.-cellar*, соло́нка; *s. lake*, солено́е о́зеро (*pl.* -ёра); *s.-marsh*, солонча́к (-а́); *s.-mine*, соляны́е ко́пи (-пей) *pl.*; *s. water*, морска́я вода́ (*acc.* -ду); *s.-water*, морско́й; *adj.* солёный (со́лон, -а́, -о); (*preserved in salt also*) засо́ленный (-ен); *v.t.* соли́ть (солю́, со́ли́шь) *imp.*, по ~ *perf.*; заса́ливать *imp.*, засоли́ть (-олю́, -о́ли́шь) *perf.*; *s. away*, припря́тывать *imp.*, припря́тать (-я́чу, -я́чешь) *perf.*
saltpetre *n.* сели́тра.
salty *adj.* (*also fig.*) солёный (со́лон, -а́, -о).
salubrious *adj.* здоро́вый.
salutary *adj.* благотво́рный. **salutation** *n.* приве́тствие. **salute** *n.* приве́тствие; (*mil.*) салю́т; *v.t.* приве́тствовать *imp.* (*in past also perf.*); салютова́ть *imp.*, *perf.*, от ~ *perf.* + *dat.*
salvage *n.* спасе́ние; (*property*) спасённое иму́щество; (*ship*) спасённое су́дно (*pl.* -да́, -до́в); (*cargo*) спасённый груз; (*waste material*) ути́ль; *v.t.* спаса́ть *imp.*, спасти́ (-су́, -сёшь; -с, -сла́, -сло) *perf.*
salvation *n.* спасе́ние; *S. Army*, А́рмия спасе́ния.
salve *n.* мазь, бальза́м; *v.t.*: *s. one's conscience*, успока́ивать *imp.*, успоко́ить *perf.* со́весть.
salver *n.* подно́с.
salvo *n.* залп.
sal volatile *n.* ню́хательная соль.
same *adj.* (*monotonous*) однообра́зный; *the s.*, тот же са́мый; тако́й же, одина́ковый; *just the s.*, то́чно тако́й же; *much the s.*, почти́ тако́й же; *pron.*: *the s.*, одно́ и то́ же, то же са́мое; *adv.*: *the s.*, таки́м же о́бразом, так же; *all the s.*, всё-таки, тем не ме́нее. **sameness** *n.* однообра́зие.
samovar *n.* самова́р.
sample *n.* образе́ц (-зца́), про́ба; *v.t.* про́бовать *imp.*, по ~ *perf.* **sampler** *n.* обра́зчик вы́шивки.
sanatorium *n.* санато́рий.
sanctify *v.t.* освяща́ть *imp.*, освяти́ть (-ящу́, -яти́шь) *perf.* **sanctimonious** *adj.* ха́нжеский. **sanction** *n.* са́нкция; *v.t.* санкциони́ровать *imp.*, *perf.* **sanctity** *n.* (*holiness*) свя́тость; (*sacredness*) свяще́нность. **sanctuary** *n.* святи́лище, алта́рь (-ря́) *m.*; (*refuge*) убе́жище; (*for animals etc.*) запове́дник. **sanctum** *n.* свята́я *sb.* святы́х; (*joc.*) рабо́чий кабине́т.
sand *n.* песо́к (-ска́(у́)); (*grain of s., usu. pl.*) песчи́нка; (*shoal, sing. or pl.*) о́тмель; *pl.* (*beach*) пляж; *pl.* (*expanse of s.*) пески́ *m.pl.*; *attrib.* песо́чный, песча́ный; *s.-bar*, песча́ный бар; *s.-blast*, обдува́ть *imp.*, обду́ть (-у́ю, -у́ешь) *perf.* песо́чной струёй; *s.-dune*, дю́на; *s.-glass*, песо́чные часы́ (-со́в)

pl.; *s.-martin*, береговáя лáсточка; *s.-pit*, (*children's*) песóчница.
sandal[1] *n.* сандáлия.
sandal[2], **-wood** *n.* сандáловое дéрево.
sandbag *n.* мешóк (-шкá) с пескóм; (*as ballast*) баллáстный мешóк (-шкá); *v.t.* защищáть *imp.*, защити́ть (-ищý, -ити́шь) *perf.* мешкáми с пескóм.
sandbank *n.* óтмель.
sandpaper *n.* шкýрка; *v.t.* шлифовáть *imp.*, от ~ *perf.* шкýркой.
sandpiper *n.* перевóзчик.
sandstone *n.* песчáник.
sandstorm *n.* песчáная бýря.
sandwich *n.* сáндвич, бутербрóд; (*cake*) торт с прослóйкой; *s.-board*, реклáмные щиты́ *m.pl.*; *s.-man*, человéк-реклáма; *v.t.*: *s. between*, вставля́ть *imp.*, встáвить *perf.* мéжду + *instr.*
sandy *adj.* песчáный, песóчный; (*hair*) рыжевáтый.
sane *adj.* нормáльный; (*of views*) разýмный.
sang-froid *n.* самообладáние.
sanguinary *adj.* кровáвый. **sanguine** *adj.* сангвини́ческий, оптимисти́ческий.
sanitary *adj.* санитáрный; гигиени́ческий; *s. towel*, гигиени́ческая подýшка. **sanitation** *n.* санитари́я; (*disposal of sewage*) водопровóд и канализáция. **sanity** *n.* нормáльная пси́хика; (*good sense*) здрáвый ум (-á).
Santa Claus *n.* Сáнта Клáус; (*Russian equivalent*) дед-морóз.
sap[1] *n.* (*juice*) сок (*loc.* -е & -ý); *v.t.* (*exhaust*) истощáть *imp.*, истощи́ть *perf.* (*cf.* **sap**[2]).
sap[2] *n.* (*mil.*) сáпа; *v.t.* (*undermine*) подрывáть *imp.*, подорвáть (-вý, -вёшь; -вáл, -валá, -вáло) *perf.* (*cf.* **sap**[1]).
sapling *n.* молодóе дéревце (*pl.* -вцá, -вéц, -вцáм).
sapper *n.* сапёр.
sapphire *n.* сапфи́р; *adj.* (*colour*) си́ний (синь, -ня́, -не).
Saracen *n.* сараци́н (*gen.pl.* -н).
sarcasm *n.* саркáзм. **sarcastic** *adj.* саркасти́ческий.
sarcoma *n.* саркóма.
sarcophagus *n.* саркофáг.
sardine *n.* сарди́на.
sardonic *adj.* сардони́ческий.
sari *n.* сáри *neut.indecl.*
sartorial *adj.* портня́жный.
sash[1] *n.* (*scarf*) пóяс (*pl.* -á), кушáк (-á).
sash[2] *n.* (*frame*) окóнный переплёт, скользя́щая рáма; *s.-window*, подъёмное окнó (*pl.* óкна, óкон, óкнам).
Satan *n.* сатанá *m.* **satanic** *adj.* сатани́нский; (*devilish*) дья́вольский.
satchel *n.* рáнец (-нца), сýмка.
sate *v.t.* насыщáть *imp.*, насы́тить (-ы́щу, -ы́тишь) *perf.*
sateen *n.* сати́н.
satellite *n.* спýтник, сателли́т (*also fig.*).
satiate *v.t.* насыщáть *imp.*, насы́тить (-ы́щу, -ы́тишь) *perf.*; *be satiated*, пресыщáться *imp.*, пресы́титься (-ы́щусь, -ы́тишься) *perf.* **satiation** *n.* насыщéние. **satiety** *n.* пресыщéние, сы́тость.
satin *n.* атлáс; *adj.* атлáсный; *s.-stitch*, гладь. **satinet(te)** *n.* сатинéт. **satiny** *adj.* атлáсный, шелкови́стый.
satire *n.* сати́ра. **satirical** *adj.* сатири́ческий. **satirist** *n.* сати́рик. **satirize** *v.t.* высмéивать *imp.*, вы́смеять (-ею, -еешь) *perf.*
satisfaction *n.* удовлетворéние. **satisfactory** *adj.* удовлетвори́тельный. **satisfy** *v.t.* удовлетворя́ть *imp.*, удовлетвори́ть *perf.*; (*hunger*, *curiosity*) утоля́ть *imp.*, утоли́ть *perf.*
saturate *v.t.* пропи́тывать *imp.*, пропитáть *perf.*; насыщáть *imp.*, насы́тить (-ы́щу, -ы́щешь) *perf.* **saturation** *n.* насыщéние, насы́щенность.
Saturday *n.* суббóта.
Saturn *n.* Сатýрн. **saturnine** *adj.* мрáчный (-чен, -чнá, -чно), угрю́мый.
satyr *n.* сати́р.
sauce *n.* сóус; (*insolence*) нáглость; *apple s.*, я́блочное пюрé *neut.indecl.*; *s.-boat*, сóусник. **saucer** *n.* блю́дце (*gen.pl.* -дец). **saucepan** *n.* кастрю́ля. **saucy** *adj.* нáглый (нагл, -á, -о).
sauna *n.* фи́нская бáня.
saunter *v.i.* прогýливаться *imp.*; *n.* прогýлка.
sausage *n.* колбасá (*pl.* -сы), соси́ска; *s.-meat*, колбáсный фарш; *s. roll*, пирожóк (-жкá) с колбáсным фáршем.

savage *adj.* ди́кий (дик, -á, -о); (*cruel*) жесто́кий (-óк, -óкá, -óко); *n.* дика́рь (-ря́) *m.*; *v.t.* свире́по напада́ть *imp.*, напа́сть (-аду́, -адёшь; -а́л) *perf.* на + *acc.* **savagery** *n.* ди́кость; жесто́кость.

savanna(h) *n.* сава́нна.

savant *n.* учёный *sb.*

save *v.t.* (*rescue*) спаса́ть *imp.*, спасти́ (-су́, -сёшь; -с, -сла́, -сло) *perf.*; (*put aside*) откла́дывать *imp.*, отложи́ть (-жу́, -жишь) *perf.*; (*spare*) бере́чь (-егу́, -ежёшь; -ёг, -егла́) *imp.*; *v.i.*: *s. up*, копи́ть (-плю́, -пишь) *imp.*, на ~ *perf.* де́ньги. **savings** *n.* сбереже́ния *neut.pl.*; *s.-bank*, сберега́тельная ка́сса. **saviour** *n.* спаси́тель *m.*

savour *n.* вкус; *v.t.* смакова́ть *imp.*; наслажда́ться *imp.*, наслади́ться *perf.* + *instr.*

savoury *adj.* (*sharp*) о́стрый (остр & остёр, остра́, о́стро́); (*salty*) солёный (со́лон, -á, -о); (*spicy*) пря́ный.

savoy *n.* саво́йская капу́ста.

saw *n.* пила́ (*pl.* -лы); *v.t.* пили́ть (-лю́, -лишь) *imp.*; *s. up*, распи́ливать *imp.*, распили́ть (-лю́, -лишь) *perf.* **sawdust** *n.* опи́лки (-лок) *pl.* **saw-edged** *adj.* пилообра́зный. **sawfish** *n.* пила́-ры́ба. **sawmill** *n.* лесопи́льный заво́д, лесопи́лка. **sawyer** *n.* пи́льщик.

saxhorn *n.* саксго́рн.

saxifrage *n.* камнело́мка.

saxophone *n.* саксофо́н.

say *v.t.* говори́ть *imp.*, сказа́ть (-ажу́, -а́жешь) *perf.*; *to s. nothing of*, не говоря́ уже́ о + *prep.*; *that is to s.*, то есть; (*let us*) *s.*, ска́жем; *it is said* (*that*), говоря́т (что); *n.* сло́во; (*opinion*) мне́ние; (*influence*) влия́ние; *have one's s.*, вы́сказаться (-ажусь, -ажешься) *perf.* **saying** *n.* погово́рка.

scab *n.* (*on wound*) струп (*pl.* -ья, -ьев), ко́рка; (*mange*) парша́; (*strike-breaker*) штрейкбре́хер.

scabbard *n.* но́жны (*gen.* -жен) *pl.*

scabies *n.* чесо́тка.

scabious *n.* скабио́за.

scabrous *adj.* скабрёзный.

scaffold *n.* эшафо́т. **scaffolding** *n.* леса́ (-со́в) *pl.*, по́дмости (-тей) *pl.*

scald *v.t.* обва́ривать *imp.*, обвари́ть (-рю́, -ришь) *perf.*; *n.* ожо́г.

scale[1] *n.* (*of fish*) чешу́йка; *pl.* чешуя́ (*collect.*); (*on boiler etc.*) на́кипь; *v.t.* чи́стить *imp.*, о ~ *perf.*; соска́бливать *imp.*, соскобли́ть (-облю́, -о́бли́шь) *perf.* чешую́ с + *gen.*; *v.i.* шелуши́ться *imp.*

scale[2] *n.* (*s.-pan*) ча́ша весо́в; *pl.* весы́ (-со́в) *pl.*

scale[3] *n.* (*relative dimensions*) масшта́б; (*set of marks*) шкала́ (*pl.* -лы); (*mus.*) га́мма; (*math.*; *s. of notation*) систе́ма счисле́ния; *v.t.* (*climb*) взбира́ться *imp.*, взобра́ться (взберу́сь, -рёшься; взобра́лся, -ала́сь, -а́ло́сь) *perf.* (по ле́стнице) на + *acc.*; *s. down*, понижа́ть *imp.*, пони́зить *perf.*; *s. up*, повыша́ть *imp.*, повы́сить *perf.*

scalene *adj.* неравносторо́нний.

scallop *n.* (*mollusc*) гребешо́к (-шка́); *pl.* (*decoration*) фесто́ны *m.pl.*; *s.-shell*, ра́ковина гребешка́; *v.t.* (*cook*) запека́ть *imp.*, запе́чь (-еку́, -ечёшь; -ёк, -екла́) *perf.* в ра́ковине; (*decorate*) украша́ть *imp.*, укра́сить *perf.* фесто́нами.

scalp *n.* ко́жа че́репа; (*as trophy*) скальп; *v.t.* скальпи́ровать *imp.*, *perf.*

scalpel *n.* ска́льпель *m.*

scaly *adj.* чешу́йчатый; (*of boiler etc.*) покры́тый на́кипью.

scamp *n.* плути́шка *m.*

scamper *v.i.* бы́стро бе́гать *imp.*; (*playfully*) резви́ться *imp.*

scampi *n.* креве́тки *f.pl.*

scan *v.t.* & *i.* (*verse*) сканди́ровать(ся) *imp.*; *v.t.* (*intently*) внима́тельно рассма́тривать *imp.*; (*quickly*) бе́гло просма́тривать *imp.*, просмотре́ть (-рю́, -ришь) *perf.*

scandal *n.* сканда́л; (*gossip*) спле́тни (-тен) *pl.* **scandalize** *v.t.* шоки́ровать *imp.*, *perf.* **scandalmonger** *n.* спле́тник, -ица. **scandalous** *adj.* сканда́льный.

Scandinavian *adj.* скандина́вский.

scansion *n.* сканди́рование.

scanty *adj.* ску́дный (-ден, -дна́, -дно); (*insufficient*) недоста́точный.

scapegoat *n.* козёл (-зла́) отпуще́ния.

scapula *n.* лопа́тка.

scar *n.* рубе́ц (-бца́), шрам. **scarred** *adj.* обезобра́женный (-ен) рубца́ми, шра́мами.

scarab *n.* скарабе́й.
scarce *adj.* дефици́тный, недоста́точный; (*rare*) ре́дкий (-док, -дка́, -дко); *make oneself s.*, улизну́ть *perf.* **scarcely** *adv.* (*only just*) едва́; (*surely not*) едва́ ли. **scarcity** *n.* недоста́ток (-тка), дефици́т.
scare *v.t.* пуга́ть *imp.*, ис~, на~ *perf.*; *s. away, off*, отпу́гивать *imp.*, отпугну́ть *perf.*; *n.* па́ника. **scarecrow** *n.* пу́гало, чу́чело. **scaremonger** *n.* паникёр.
scarf *n.* шарф.
scarlet *adj.* (*n.*) а́лый (цвет); *s. fever*, скарлати́на; *s. runner*, фасо́ль многоцве́тковая.
scathing *adj.* е́дкий (е́док, едка́, е́дко), уничтожа́ющий.
scatter *v.t.* & *i.* рассыпа́ть(ся) *imp.*, рассы́пать(ся) (-плю, -плет(ся)) *perf.*; (*disperse*) рассе́ивать(ся) *imp.*, рассе́ять(ся) (-е́ю, -е́ет(ся)) *perf.*; *v.t.* (*disperse, drive away*) разгоня́ть *imp.*, разогна́ть (разгоню́, -нишь; разогна́л, -а́, -о) *perf.*; *v.i.* (*run*) разбега́ться *imp.*, разбежа́ться (-ежи́тся, -егу́тся) *perf.*; *s.-brained*, легкомы́сленный (-ен, -енна). **scattered** *adj.* разбро́санный (-ан); (*sporadic*) отде́льный.
scavenger *n.* (*person*) му́сорщик; (*animal*) живо́тное *sb.*, пита́ющееся па́далью.
scenario *n.* сцена́рий. **scenarist** *n.* сценари́ст. **scene** *n.* сце́на; (*part of play also*) явле́ние; (*place of action*) ме́сто де́йствия; (*scenery*) декора́ция; *behind the scenes*, за кули́сами; *make a s.*, устра́ивать *imp.*, устро́ить *perf.* сце́ну; *s.-painter*, худо́жник-декора́тор; *s.-shifter*, рабо́чий *sb.* сце́ны. **scenery** *n.* (*theat.*) декора́ция; (*landscape*) пейза́ж. **scenic** *adj.* сцени́ческий.
scent *n.* (*smell*) арома́т; (*perfume*) духи́ (-хо́в) *pl.*; (*trail*) след (-а(у); *pl.* -ы́); *v.t.* (*discern*) чу́ять (чу́ю, чу́ешь) *imp.*; (*apply perfume*) души́ть (-шу́, -шишь) *imp.*, на~ *perf.*; (*make fragrant*) наполня́ть *imp.*, напо́лнить *perf.* арома́том.
sceptic *n.* ске́птик. **sceptical** *adj.* скепти́ческий. **scepticism** *n.* скептици́зм.
sceptre *n.* ски́петр.
schedule *n.* (*timetable*) расписа́ние; (*inventory*) о́пись; *v.t.* составля́ть *imp.*, соста́вить *perf.* расписа́ние, о́пись, + *gen.*
schematic *adj.* схемати́ческий. **scheme** *n.* (*plan*) прое́кт; (*intention*) за́мысел (-сла); (*intrigue*) махина́ция; *v.i.* стро́ить *imp.* та́йные пла́ны. **schemer** *n.* интрига́н. **scheming** *adj.* интригу́ющий.
scherzo *n.* ске́рцо *neut.indecl.*
schism *n.* раско́л. **schismatic** *adj.* раско́льнический; *n.* раско́льник.
schizophrenia *n.* шизофрени́я. **schizophrenic** *adj.* шизофрени́ческий; *n.* шизофре́ник.
scholar *n.* учёный *sb.*; (*scholarship-holder*) стипендиа́т, ~ка. **scholarly** *adj.* учёный, нау́чный. **scholarship** *n.* учёность, нау́ка; (*payment*) стипе́ндия.
school *n.* шко́ла; (*specialist s.*) учи́лище; (*univ.*) факульте́т; *attrib.* шко́льный; *v.t.* (*curb*) обу́здывать *imp.*, обузда́ть *perf.*; (*accustom*) приуча́ть *imp.*, приучи́ть (-чу́, -чишь) *perf.* (to, к + *dat.*, + *inf.*). **school-book** *n.* уче́бник. **schoolboy** *n.* шко́льник, учени́к (-а́). **schoolgirl** *n.* шко́льница, учени́ца. **schooling** *n.* обуче́ние. **school-leaver** *n.* выпускни́к (-а́), -и́ца. **schoolmaster** *n.* шко́льный учи́тель (*pl.* -ля́) *m.* **schoolmistress** *n.* шко́льная учи́тельница.
schooner *n.* шху́на.
sciatic *adj.* седа́лищный. **sciatica** *n.* и́шиас.
science *n.* нау́ка; (*natural s.*) есте́ственные нау́ки *f.pl.*; *s. fiction*, нау́чная фанта́стика. **scientific** *adj.* нау́чный. **scientist** *n.* учёный *sb.*; (*natural s.*) есте́ственник, -ица.
scintillate *v.i.* и́скри́ться *imp.* **scintillating** *adj.* блиста́тельный.
scion *n.* о́тпрыск.
scissors *n.* но́жницы (-ц) *pl.*
sclerosis *n.* склеро́з.
scoff[1] *v.i.* (*mock*) издева́ться *imp.* (at, над + *instr.*).
scoff[2] *v.t.* (*eat*) жрать (жру, жрёшь; жрал, -а́, -о) *imp.*, со~ *perf.*

scold *v.t.* бранить *imp.*, вы~ *perf.* **scolding** *n.* нагоняй.

scollop *see* **scallop.**

sconce *n.* (*bracket*) бра *neut.indecl.*; (*candlestick*) подсвечник.

scone *n.* сдобная лепёшка.

scoop *n.* черпак (-á), ковш (-á); *v.t.* (*s. out, up*) вычерпывать *imp.*, вычерпать *perf.*

scooter *n.* (*child's*) самокат, роллер; (*motor s.*) мотороллер.

scope *n.* пределы *m.pl.*, простор, размах.

scorbutic *adj.* цинготный.

scorch *v.t.* палить *imp.*, с~ *perf.*; подпаливать *imp.*, подпалить *perf.*; *scorched earth policy*, тактика выжженной земли; *n.* ожог. **scorching** *adj.* палящий, знойный.

score *n.* (*notch*) зарубка; (*account; number of points etc.*) счёт; (*mus.*) партитура; (*twenty*) два десятка; *pl.* (*great numbers*) десятки *m.pl.*, множество; *v.t.* (*notch*) делать *imp.*, с~ *perf.* зарубки на+*prep.*; (*points etc.*) получать *imp.*, получить (-чу, -чишь) *perf.*; (*mus.*) оркестровать *imp.*, *perf.*; *v.i.* (*keep s.*) вести (веду, -дёшь; вёл, -á) *imp.*, с~ *perf.* счёт.

scorn *n.* презрение; *v.t.* презирать *imp.* презреть (-рю, -ришь) *perf.* **scornful** *adj.* презрительный.

Scorpio *n.* Скорпион.

scorpion *n.* скорпион.

Scot *n.* шотландец (-дца), -дка. **Scotch** *adj.* шотландский; *n.* (*whisky*) шотландское виски *neut.indecl.*; *the S.*, шотландцы *m.pl.*

scot-free *adv.* безнаказанно.

Scots, Scottish *adj.* шотландский; *see* **Scotch.**

scoundrel *n.* негодяй, подлец (-á).

scour[1] *v.t.* (*cleanse*) отчищать *imp.*, отчистить *perf.* **scourer** *n.* металлическая мочалка.

scour[2] *v.t.* & *i.* (*rove*) рыскать (рыщу, -щешь) *imp.* (по+*dat.*).

scourge *n.* бич (-á); *v.t.* бичевать (-чую, -чуешь) *imp.*

scout *n.* разведчик; (*S.*) бойскаут; *v.i.*: *s. about*, рыскать (рыщу, -щешь) *imp.* (for, в поисках+*gen.*).

scowl *v.i.* хмуриться *imp.*, на~ *perf.*; *n.* хмурый вид, взгляд.

scrabble *v.i.*: *s. about*, рыться (роюсь, роешься) *imp.*

scramble *v.i.* карабкаться *imp.*, вс~ *perf.*; (*struggle*) драться (дерусь, -рёшься; дрался, -алась, -алось) *imp.* (for, за+*acc.*); *v.t.* (*mix together*) перемешивать *imp.*, перемешать *perf.*; *scrambled eggs*, яичница-болтунья.

scrap[1] *n.* (*fragment etc.*) клочок (-чка), обрезок (-зка), кусочек (-чка); *pl.* остатки *m.pl.*; *pl.* (*of food*) объедки (-ков) *pl.*; *s.-metal*, металлический лом, скрап; *v.t.* превращать *imp.*, превратить (-ащу, -атишь) *perf.* в лом; пускать *imp.*, пустить (пущу, пустишь) *perf.* на слом.

scrap[2] *n.* (*fight*) драка; *v.i.* драться (дерусь, -рёшься; дрался, -алась, -алось) *imp.*

scrape *v.t.* скрести (скребу, -бёшь; скрёб, -ла) *imp.*; скоблить (-облю, -облишь) *imp.*; *s. off*, отскребать *imp.*, отскрести (-ребу, -ребёшь; -рёб, -ребла) *perf.*; *s. through*, (*examination*) с трудом выдерживать *imp.*, выдержать (-жу, -жишь) *perf.*; *s. together*, наскребать *imp.*, наскрести (-ребу, -ребёшь; -рёб, -ребла) *perf.*

scratch *v.t.* царапать *imp.*, о~ *perf.*; *v.t.* & *abs.* чесать(ся) (чешу(сь), -шешь(ся)) *imp.*, по~ *perf.*; *v. abs.* царапаться *imp.*; *v.t.* (*erase, s. off, through, etc.*) вычёркивать *imp.*, вычеркнуть *perf.*; *n.* царапина; *adj.* случайный.

scrawl *n.* каракули *f.pl.*; *v.t.* писать (пишу, -шешь) *imp.*, на~ *perf.* каракулями.

scrawny *adj.* тощий (тощ, -á, -е), сухопарый.

scream *n.* крик, визг; *v.i.* кричать (-чу, -чишь) *imp.*, крикнуть *perf.*; *v.t.* выкрикивать *imp.*, выкрикнуть *perf.*

screech *n.* визг; *v.i.* визжать (-жу, -жишь) *imp.*

screen *n.* ширма; (*cin., television, radio, etc.*) экран; (*sieve*) грохот; *s.-play*, сценарий; *v.t.* (*shelter*) защищать *imp.*, защитить (-ищу, -итишь) *perf.*;

заслоня́ть *imp.*, заслони́ть *perf.*; (*show film etc.*) демонстри́ровать *imp.*, *perf.*; (*sieve*) просе́ивать *imp.*, просе́ять (-е́ю, -е́ешь) *perf.*; *s. off*, отгора́живать *imp.*, отгороди́ть (-ожу́, -о́ди́шь) *perf.* ши́рмой.

screw *n.* (*male s.*; *propeller*) винт (-а́); (*female s.*) га́йка; (*s.-bolt*) болт (-а́); *v.t.* (*s. on*) приви́нчивать *imp.*, привинти́ть *perf.*; (*s. up*) зави́нчивать *imp.*, завинти́ть *perf.*; *s. up one's eyes*, щу́риться *imp.*, со~ *perf.* **screwdriver** *n.* отвёртка.

scribble *v.t.* небре́жно, бы́стро, писа́ть (пишу́, -шешь) *imp.*, на~ *perf.*; *n.* кара́кули *f.pl.* **scribbler** *n.* писа́ка *m.* & *f.*

scribe *n.* пи́сец (-сца́); (*Bibl.*) кни́жник.

scrimmage *n.* сва́лка.

script *n.* по́черк, шрифт; (*of film etc.*) сцена́рий; *s.-writer*, сценари́ст.

Scripture *n.* свяще́нное писа́ние.

scrofula *n.* золоту́ха.

scroll *n.* сви́ток (-тка); (*design*) завито́к (-тка́); *s.-work*, орна́мент в ви́де завитко́в.

scrounge *v.t.* (*steal*) ти́брить *imp.*, с~ *perf.*; (*cadge*) выкля́нчивать *imp.*, вы́клянчить *perf.*; *v.i.* попроша́йничать *imp.*

scrub[1] *n.* (*brushwood*) куста́рник; (*area*) поро́сшая куста́рником ме́стность.

scrub[2] *v.t.* мыть (мо́ю, мо́ешь) *imp.*, вы́~ *perf.* щёткой; *scrubbing-brush*, жёсткая щётка; *n.* чи́стка.

scruff *n.* загри́вок (-вка); *take by the s. of the neck*, брать (беру́, -рёшь; брал, -а́, -о) *imp.*, взять (возьму́, -мёшь; взял, -а́, -о) *perf.* за ши́ворот.

scruffy *adj.* (*of clothes*) потрёпанный (-ан, -анна); (*of person*) неря́шливый.

scrum(mage) *n.* схва́тка вокру́г мяча́.

scruple *n.* (*also pl.*) колеба́ние, угрызе́ния *neut.pl.* со́вести; *v.i.* колеба́ться (-блюсь, -блешься) *imp.* **scrupulous** *adj.* скрупулёзный, щепети́льный.

scrutineer *n.* прове́рщик, -ица. **scrutinize** *v.t.* рассма́тривать *imp.* **scrutiny** *n.* рассмотре́ние, прове́рка.

scud *v.i.* нести́сь (несётся; нёсся, несла́сь) *imp.*, по~ *perf.*; скользи́ть *imp.*

scuffed *adj.* потёртый, поцара́панный.

scuffle *n.* сва́лка; *v.i.* дра́ться (деру́сь, -рёшься; дра́лся, -ала́сь, -а́ло́сь) *imp.*

scull *n.* весло́ (*pl.* вёсла, -сел, -слам); (*stern oar*) кормово́е весло́; *v.i.* грести́ (гребу́, -бёшь; грёб, -ла́) *imp.* (па́рными вёслами); гала́нить *imp.*

scullery *n.* судомо́йня (*gen.pl.* -о́ен).

sculptor *n.* ску́льптор. **sculptural** *adj.* скульпту́рный. **sculpture** *n.* скульпту́ра.

scum *n.* пе́на, на́кипь; (*fig.*, *people*) подо́нки (-ков) *pl.*

scupper[1] *n.* шпига́т.

scupper[2] *v.t.* (*ship*) потопля́ть *imp.*, потопи́ть (-плю́, -пишь) *perf.*

scurf *n.* пе́рхоть.

scurrility *n.* непристо́йность, гру́бость. **scurrilous** *adj.* непристо́йный, гру́бый (груб, -а́, -о).

scurry *v.i.* поспе́шно, суетли́во, бе́гать *indet.*, бежа́ть (бегу́, бежи́шь) *det.*

scurvy *n.* цинга́; *adj.* по́длый (подл, -а́, -о).

scuttle[1] *n.* (*coal-box*) ведёрко (*pl.* -рки, -рок, -ркам) для у́гля́.

scuttle[2] *v.t.* (*ship*) затопля́ть *imp.*, затопи́ть (-плю́, -пишь) *perf.*

scuttle[3] *v.i.* (*run away*) удира́ть *imp.*, удра́ть (удеру́, -рёшь; удра́л, -а́, -о) *perf.*

scythe *n.* коса́ (*acc.* ко́су́; *pl.* -сы).

sea *n.* мо́ре (*pl.* -ря́); *at s.*, в (откры́том) мо́ре; *by s.*, мо́рем; *attrib.* морско́й; *s. anchor*, плаву́чий я́корь (*pl.* -ря́) *m.*; *s. anemone*, акти́ния; *s.-breeze*, ве́тер (-тра) с мо́ря; *s.-coast*, побере́жье; *s.-dog*, (*person*) морско́й волк (*pl.* -и, -о́в); *s. front*, на́бережная *sb.*; *s.-gull*, ча́йка; *s.-horse*, морско́й конёк (-нька́); *s. lane*, морско́й путь (-ти́, -тём) *m.*; *s.-level*, у́ровень (-вня) *m.* мо́ря; *s.-lion*, морско́й лев (льва); *s.-shore*, побере́жье; *s.-urchin*, морско́й ёж (-а́); *s.-wall*, да́мба. **seaboard** *n.* побере́жье. **seafaring** *n.* морепла́вание. **seagoing** *adj.* да́льнего пла́вания.

seal[1] *n.* (*on document etc.*) печа́ть; *v.t.* скрепля́ть *imp.*, скрепи́ть *perf.* печа́тью; запеча́тывать *imp.*, запеча́тать *perf.*; *sealing-wax*, сургу́ч (-а́).

seal[2] *n.* (*animal*) тюле́нь *m.*; (*fur-s.*) ко́тик. **sealskin** *n.* ко́тиковый мех (*loc.* -е & -у́); *attrib.* ко́тиковый.

seam *n.* шов (шва), рубе́ц (-бца́); (*stratum*) пласт (-а́, *loc.* -у́); *v.t.* сшива́ть *imp.*, сшить (сошью́, -ьёшь) *perf.* шва́ми.

seaman *n.* моря́к (-а́); (*also rank*) матро́с.

seamstress *n.* швея́.

seamy *adj.* со шва́ми нару́жу; *the s. side*, (*also fig.*) изна́нка.

seance *n.* спирити́ческий сеа́нс.

seaplane *n.* гидросамолёт. **seaport** *n.* порто́вый го́род (*pl.* -а́).

sear *v.t.* прижига́ть *imp.*, приже́чь (-жгу́, -жжёшь, -жгу́т; -жёг, -жгла́) *perf.*

search *v.t.* обы́скивать *imp.*, обыска́ть (-ыщу́, -ы́щешь) *perf.*; *v.i.* иска́ть (ищу́, и́щешь) *imp.* (for, + *acc.*); производи́ть (-ожу́, -о́дишь) *imp.*, произвести́ (-еду́, -едёшь; -ёл, -ела́) *perf.* о́быск; *n.* по́иски *m.pl.*; о́быск; *s.-party*, по́исковая гру́ппа; *s.-warrant*, о́рдер (*pl.* -а́) на о́быск. **searching** *adj.* (*thorough*) тща́тельный; (*look*) испыту́ющий. **searchlight** *n.* проже́ктор (*pl.* -ы & -а́).

seascape *n.* мари́на. **seasickness** *n.* морска́я боле́знь. **seaside** *n.* бе́рег (*loc.* -у́) мо́ря; (*resort*) морско́й куро́рт.

season *n.* сезо́н; (*period in general*) пери́од; (*one of four*) вре́мя *neut.* го́да; *in s.*, по сезо́ну; *s.-ticket*, сезо́нный биле́т; *v.t.* (*mature*) выде́рживать *imp.*, вы́держать (-жу, -жишь) *perf.*; (*flavour*) приправля́ть *imp.*, припра́вить *perf.* **seasonable** *adj.* по сезо́ну; (*timely*) своевре́менный (-нен, -нна). **seasonal** *adj.* сезо́нный. **seasoning** *n.* припра́ва.

seat *n.* ме́сто (*pl.* -та́), сиде́нье; (*chair*) стул (*pl.* -ья, -ьев); (*bench*) скаме́йка; (*buttocks*) седа́лище; (*of trousers*) зад (*loc.* -у́; *pl.* -ы́); (*country s.*) уса́дьба; (*ticket*) биле́т; *s. belt*, привязно́й реме́нь (-мня́) *m.*; *v.t.* сажа́ть *imp.*, посади́ть (-ажу́, -а́дишь) *perf.*; (*of room etc.*) вмеща́ть *imp.*, вмести́ть *perf.*; *be seated*, сади́ться *imp.*, сесть (ся́ду, -дешь; сел) *perf.*

seaweed *n.* морска́я во́доросль.

sebaceous *adj.* са́льный.

sec *n.*: *half a s.!* мину́тку! оди́н моме́нт!

secateurs *n.* сека́тор.

secede *v.i.* отка́лываться *imp.*, отколо́ться (-лю́сь, -лешься) *perf.* **secession** *n.* отко́л.

secluded *adj.* укро́мный. **seclusion** *n.* укро́мность; (*place*) укро́мное ме́сто.

second *adj.* второ́й; *be s. to*, (*inferior*) уступа́ть *imp.*, уступи́ть (-плю́, -пишь) *perf.* + *dat.*; *s. ballot*, перебаллотиро́вка; *s.-best*, второсо́ртный; *s.-class*, второкла́ссный, второсо́ртный; *s.-hand*, подде́ржанный (-ан, -анна); (*of information*) из вторы́х рук; *s.-rate*, второразря́дный; *s. sight*, ясновиде́ние; *on s. thoughts*, взве́сив всё ещё раз; *have s. thoughts*, переду́мывать *imp.*, переду́мать *perf.* (about, + *acc.*); *s. wind*, второ́е дыха́ние; *n.* второ́й *sb.*; (*date*) второ́е (число́) *sb.*; (*mus.*; *time*; *angle*) секу́нда; (*coll.*, *moment*) моме́нт; (*in duel*) секунда́нт; *pl.* това́р второ́го со́рта; *pl.* (*flour*) мука́ гру́бого помо́ла; (*s. helping*) втора́я по́рция; *s. in command*, замести́тель *m.* команди́ра; *s. hand*, (*of clock etc.*) секу́ндная стре́лка; *v.t.* (*support*) подде́рживать *imp.*, поддержа́ть (-жу́, -жишь) *perf.*; (*transfer*) откомандиро́вывать *imp.*, откомандирова́ть *perf.* **secondary** *adj.* втори́чный, второстепе́нный (-нен, -нна); (*education*) сре́дний. **secondly** *adv.* во-вторы́х.

secrecy *n.* секре́тность. **secret** *n.* та́йна, секре́т; *adj.* та́йный, секре́тный; (*hidden*) потайно́й.

secretarial *adj.* секрета́рский. **secretariat** *n.* секретариа́т. **secretary** *n.* секрета́рь (-ря́) *m.*, -рша; (*minister*) мини́стр.

secrete *v.t.* (*conceal*) пря́тать (-я́чу, -я́чешь) *imp.*, с~ *perf.*; (*med.*) выделя́ть *imp.*, вы́делить *perf.* **secretion** *n.* укрыва́ние; (*med.*) секре́ция, выделе́ние.

secretive *adj.* скры́тный.

sect *n.* се́кта. **sectarian** *adj.* секта́нтский; *n.* секта́нт.
section *n.* се́кция, отре́зок (-зка); (*of book*) разде́л; (*of solid*) сече́ние, про́филь, разре́з. **sectional** *adj.* секцио́нный. **sector** *n.* се́ктор (*pl.* -ы & -а́), уча́сток (-тка).
secular *adj.* све́тский, мирско́й; *s. clergy*, бе́лое духове́нство. **secularization** *n.* секуляриза́ция. **secularize** *v.t.* секуляризова́ть *imp., perf.*
secure *adj.* безопа́сный, надёжный; *v.t.* (*fasten*) закрепля́ть *imp.*, закрепи́ть *perf.*; (*guarantee*) обеспе́чивать *imp.*, обеспе́чить *perf.*; (*obtain*) достава́ть (-таю́, -таёшь) *imp.*, доста́ть (-а́ну, -а́нешь) *perf.* **security** *n.* безопа́сность; (*guarantee*) зало́г; *pl.* це́нные бума́ги *f.pl.*; *S. Council*, Сове́т Безопа́сности; *s. risk*, неблагонадёжный челове́к (*pl.* лю́ди, -де́й, -дям, -дьми́); *social s.*, социа́льное обеспе́чение.
sedan(-chair) *n.* портше́з.
sedate *adj.* степе́нный (-нен, -нна).
sedation *n.* успокое́ние. **sedative** *adj.* успока́ивающий; *n.* успока́ивающее сре́дство.
sedentary *adj.* сидя́чий.
sedge *n.* осо́ка.
sediment *n.* оса́док (-дка), отсто́й. **sedimentary** *adj.* оса́дочный.
sedition *n.* подстрека́тельство к мятежу́. **seditious** *adj.* подстрека́тельский, мяте́жный.
seduce *v.t.* соблазня́ть *imp.*, соблазни́ть *perf.*; совраща́ть *imp.*, соврати́ть (-ащу́, -ати́шь) *perf.* **seducer** *n.* соблазни́тель *m.* **seduction** *n.* обольще́ние. **seductive** *adj.* соблазни́тельный, обольсти́тельный. **seductress** *n.* соблазни́тельница.
sedulous *adj.* приле́жный.
see[1] *n.* епа́рхия; *Holy S.*, па́пский престо́л.
see[2] *v.t.* & *i.* ви́деть (ви́жу, ви́дишь) *imp.*, у ~ *perf.*; *v.t.* (*watch, look*) смотре́ть (-рю́, -ришь) *imp.* по ~ *perf.*; (*find out*) узнава́ть (-наю́, -наёшь) *imp.*, узна́ть *perf.*; (*understand*) понима́ть *imp.*, поня́ть (пойму́, -мёшь; по́нял, -а́, -о) *perf.*; (*meet*) ви́деться (ви́жусь, ви́дишься) *imp.*, у ~ *perf.* с + *instr.*; (*imagine*) представля́ть *imp.*, предста́вить *perf.* себе́; (*escort*) провожа́ть *imp.*, проводи́ть *perf.*; *s. about*, (*attend to*) забо́титься *imp.*, по ~ *perf.* о + *prep.*; *s. over*, осма́тривать *imp.*, осмотре́ть (-рю́, -ришь) *perf.*; *s. through*, (*fig.*) ви́деть (ви́жу, ви́дишь) *imp.* насквозь + *acc.*
seed *n.* се́мя (*gen.pl.* -мя́н) *neut.*; (*grain*) зерно́; *s.-bed*, парни́к (-а́); *s.-cake*, бу́лочка с тми́ном; *s.-corn*, посевно́е зерно́; *s.-pearl(s)*, ме́лкий же́мчуг. **seedling** *n.* сея́нец (-нца); *pl.* расса́да. **seedy** *adj.* (*shabby*) потрёпанный (-ан, -анна); (*ill*) нездоро́вый.
seeing (that) *conj.* ввиду́ того́, что.
seek *v.t.* иска́ть (ищу́, -щешь) *imp.* + *acc., gen.*
seem *v.i.* каза́ться (кажу́сь, -жешься) *imp.*, по ~ *perf.* (+ *instr.*) (*often used parenthetically in impers. forms*). **seeming** *adj.* мни́мый. **seemingly** *adv.* по-ви́димому, на вид.
seemly *adj.* прили́чный.
seep *v.i.* проса́чиваться *imp.*, просочи́ться *perf.* **seepage** *n.* проса́чивание, течь.
seer *n.* прови́дец (-дца).
see-saw *n.* (*game*) кача́ние на доске́; (*board*) де́тские каче́ли (-лей) *pl.*; *v.i.* кача́ться *imp.* (на доске́).
seethe *v.i.* кипе́ть (-плю́, -пи́шь) *imp.*, вс ~ *perf.*
segment *n.* отре́зок (-зка); (*of orange etc.*) до́лька; (*geom.*) сегме́нт.
segregate *v.t.* отделя́ть *imp.*, отдели́ть (-лю́, -лишь) *perf.* **segregation** *n.* отделе́ние, сегрега́ция.
seine *n.* не́вод (*pl.* -а́).
seismic *adj.* сейсми́ческий. **seismograph** *n.* сейсмо́граф. **seismology** *n.* сейсмоло́гия.
seize *v.t.* хвата́ть *imp.*, схвати́ть (-ачу́, -а́тишь) *perf.*; *v.i.*: *s. up*, заеда́ть *imp.*, зае́сть (-е́ст; -е́ло) *perf. impers.* + *acc.*; *s. upon*, ухва́тываться *imp.*, ухвати́ться (-ачу́сь, -а́тишься) *perf.* за + *acc.* **seizure** *n.* захва́т; заеда́ние; (*stroke*) уда́р.
seldom *adv.* ре́дко.
select *adj.* и́збранный; *v.t.* отбира́ть *imp.*, отобра́ть (отберу́, -рёшь; ото-

бра́л, -а́, -о) *perf.*; выбира́ть *imp.*, вы́брать (вы́беру, -решь) *perf.* **selection** *n.* вы́бор; (*biol.*) отбо́р. **selective** *adj.* селекти́вный.

self *n.* со́бственная ли́чность; (*one's interests*) свои́ ли́чные интере́сы *m.pl.*

self- *in comb.* само-; *s.-absorbed*, эгоцентри́чный; *s.-assured*, самоуве́ренный (-ен, -енна); *s.-centred*, эгоцентри́чный; *s.-confidence*, самоуве́ренность; *s.-confident*, самоуве́ренный (-ен, -енна); *s.-conscious*, засте́нчивый; *s.-contained*, (*person*) за́мкнутый; (*flat etc.*) отде́льный; *s.-control*, самооблада́ние; *s.-defence*, самооборо́на, самозащи́та; *s.-denial*, самоотрече́ние; *s.-determination*, самоопределе́ние; *s.-effacing*, скро́мный (-мен, -мна́, -мно); *s.-esteem*, самоуваже́ние; *s.-evident*, очеви́дный; *s.-government*, самоуправле́ние; *s.-help*, самопо́мощь; *s.-importance*, самомне́ние; *s.-interest*, своекоры́стие; *s.-made*, (*man*) вы́бившийся из низо́в; *s.-portrait*, автопортре́т; *s.-possessed*, хладнокро́вный; *s.-preservation*, самосохране́ние; *s.-propelled*, самохо́дный; *s.-respect*, чу́вство со́бственного досто́инства; *s.-reliant*, наде́ющийся то́лько на себя́; *s.-righteous*, уве́ренный (-ен, -енна) в свое́й righteous правоте́, фарисе́йский; *s.-sacrifice*, самопоже́ртвование; *s.-satisfied*, самодово́льный; *s.-service*, самообслу́живание (*attrib.*, *in gen. after n.*); *s.-starter*, самопу́ск; *s.-styled*, самозва́нный; *s.-sufficient*, самостоя́тельный; *s.-willed*, самово́льный.

selfish *adj.* эгоисти́чный, себялюби́вый. **selfless** *adj.* самоотве́рженный (-ен, -енна).

sell *v.t.* & *i.* продава́ть(ся) (-даю́, -даёт(ся)) *imp.*, прода́ть(ся) (-а́м, -а́шь, -а́ст(ся), -ади́м; -ал/-а́лся, -ала́(сь), -ало/-ало́сь) *perf.*; *v.t.* (*deal in*) торгова́ть *imp.* + *instr.*; *s. off*, *out*, распродава́ть (-даю́, -даёшь) *imp.*, распрода́ть (-а́м, -а́шь, -а́ст, -ади́м; -ал, -ала́, -ало) *perf.* **seller** *n.* торго́вец (-вца) (of, + *instr.*), продаве́ц (-вца́). **selling** *n.* прода́жа.

selvage *n.* кро́мка.

semantic *adj.* семанти́ческий. **semantics** *n.* сема́нтика.

semaphore *n.* семафо́р.

semblance *n.* вне́шний вид.

semen *n.* се́мя *neut.*

semi- *in comb.* полу-; *s.-conscious*, полубессозна́тельный; *s.-detached house*, дом, разделённый о́бщей стено́й; *s.-official*, полуофициа́льный; официо́зный; *s.-precious stone*, самоцве́т. **semibreve** *n.* це́лая но́та. **semicircle** *n.* полукру́г. **semicircular** *adj.* полукру́глый. **semicolon** *n.* то́чка с запято́й. **semiconductor** *n.* полупроводни́к (-а́). **semifinal** *n.* полуфина́л. **semifinalist** *n.* полуфинали́ст.

seminar *n.* семина́р. **seminary** *n.* (духо́вная) семина́рия.

semiquaver *n.* шестна́дцатая но́та.

Semite *n.* семи́т, ~ка. **Semitic** *adj.* семити́ческий.

semitone *n.* полуто́н. **semivowel** *n.* полугла́сный *sb.*

semolina *n.* ма́нная крупа́.

sempstress *see* **seamstress.**

senate *n.* сена́т; (*univ.*) (учёный) сове́т. **senator** *n.* сена́тор. **senatorial** *adj.* сена́торский.

send *v.t.* посыла́ть *imp.*, посла́ть (пошлю́, -лёшь) *perf.*; *s. down*, (*univ.*) исключа́ть *imp.*, исключи́ть *perf.* из университе́та; *s. off*, отправля́ть *imp.*, отпра́вить *perf.*; *s. up*, (*ridicule*) высме́ивать *imp.*, вы́смеять (-ею, -еешь) *perf.*; *s.-off*, про́воды (-дов) *pl.* **sender** *n.* отправи́тель *m.*

senile *adj.* ста́рческий, дря́хлый (-л, -ла́, -ло). **senility** *n.* ста́рость, дря́хлость.

senior *adj.* (*n.*) ста́рший (*sb.*); *s. citizen*, стари́к (-а́), стару́ха; *s. partner*, глава́ (*pl.* -вы) фи́рмы. **seniority** *n.* старшинство́.

senna *n.* александри́йский лист (-а́).

sensation *n.* сенса́ция; (*feeling*) ощуще́ние, чу́вство. **sensational** *adj.* сенсацио́нный (-нен, -нна).

sense *n.* чу́вство, ощуще́ние; (*good s.*) здра́вый смысл; (*meaning*) смысл; *in one's senses*, в своём уме́; *v.t.* ощуща́ть *imp.*, ощути́ть (-ущу́, -ути́шь) *perf.*; чу́вствовать *imp.* **senseless** *adj.* бессмы́сленный (-ен, -енна).

sensibility *n.* чувстви́тельность.
sensible *adj.* благоразу́мный.
sensitive *adj.* чувстви́тельный; (*touchy*) оби́дчивый. **sensitivity** *n.* чувстви́тельность.
sensory *adj.* чувстви́тельный.
sensual, sensuous *adj.* чу́вственный (-ен, -енна).
sentence *n.* фра́за; (*gram.*) предложе́ние; (*leg.*) пригово́р; *v.t.* осужда́ть *imp.*, осуди́ть (-ужу́, -у́дишь) *perf.* (to, к + *dat.*); пригова́ривать *imp.*, приговори́ть *perf.* (to, к + *dat.*).
sententious *adj.* сентенцио́зный.
sentiment *n.* (*feeling*) чу́вство; (*opinion*) мне́ние. **sentimental** *adj.* сентимента́льный. **sentimentality** *n.* сентимента́льность.
sentinel, sentry *n.* часово́й *sb.*
sepal *n.* чашели́стник.
separable *adj.* отдели́мый. **separate** *adj.* отде́льный; (*independent*) самостоя́тельный; *n.* отде́льный о́ттиск; *v.t.* & *i.* отделя́ть(ся) *imp.*, отдели́ть(ся) (-лю́(сь), -лишь(ся)) *perf.* **separation** *n.* отделе́ние. **separatism** *n.* сепарати́зм. **separatist** *n.* сепарати́ст. **separator** *n.* сепара́тор.
sepia *n.* се́пия.
sepoy *n.* сипа́й.
sepsis *n.* се́псис.
September *n.* сентя́брь (-ря́) *m.*; *attrib.* сентя́брьский.
septet *n.* септе́т.
septic *adj.* септи́ческий; *s. tank*, се́птик. **septicaemia** *n.* се́псис, септицеми́я.
septuple *adj.* семикра́тный.
sepulchral *adj.* моги́льный, гробово́й. **sepulchre** *n.* моги́ла.
sequel *n.* (*result*) после́дствие; (*continuation*) продолже́ние. **sequence** *n.* после́довательность; (*cin.*) эпизо́д; *s. of events*, ход собы́тий.
sequester *v.t.* (*isolate*) уединя́ть *imp.*, уедини́ть *perf.*; (*confiscate*) секвестрова́ть *imp.*, *perf.* **sequestered** *adj.* уединённый. **sequestration** *n.* секве́стр.
sequin *n.* блёстка.
sequoia *n.* секво́йя.
seraph *n.* серафи́м.
Serb(ian) *adj.* се́рбский; *n.* серб, ~ка; **Serbo-Croat(ian)** *adj.* сербскохорва́тский.
serenade *n.* серена́да; *v.t.* исполня́ть *imp.*, испо́лнить *perf.* серена́ду + *dat.*
serene *adj.* (*calm*) споко́йный; (*clear*) я́сный (я́сен, ясна́, я́сно, я́сны́). **serenity** *n.* споко́йствие; я́сность.
serf *n.* крепостно́й *sb.* **serfdom** *n.* крепостно́е пра́во, крепостни́чество.
serge *n.* са́ржа.
sergeant *n.* сержа́нт; *s.-major*, старшина́ (*pl.* -ны) *m.*
serial *adj.* сери́йный; (*of story etc.*) выходя́щий отде́льными вы́пусками; *n.* (*story*) рома́н в не́скольких частя́х; (*film*) сери́йный фильм; (*periodical*) периоди́ческое изда́ние. **serialize** *v.t.* издава́ть (-даю́, -даёшь) *imp.*, изда́ть (-а́м, -а́шь, -а́ст, -ади́м; изда́л, -а́, -о) *perf.* вы́пусками, се́риями. **series** *n.* ряд (-á *with* 2, 3, 4, *loc.* -у́; *pl.* -ы́), се́рия.
serious *adj.* серьёзный. **seriousness** *n.* серьёзность.
sermon *n.* про́поведь.
serpent *n.* змея́ (*pl.* -е́и). **serpentine** *adj.* (*coiling*) изви́листый.
serrated *adj.* зазу́бренный, зубча́тый.
serried *adj.* со́мкнутый.
serum *n.* сы́воротка.
servant *n.* слуга́ (*pl.* -ги) *m.*, служа́нка. **serve** *v.t.* служи́ть (-жу́, -жишь) *imp.*, по~ *perf.* + *dat.* (as, for, + *instr.*); (*attend to*) обслу́живать *imp.*, обслужи́ть (-жу́, -жишь) *perf.*; (*food, ball*) подава́ть (-даю́, -даёшь) *imp.*, пода́ть (-а́м, -а́шь, -а́ст, -ади́м; по́дал, -а́, -о) *perf.*; (*period*) отбыва́ть *imp.*, отбы́ть (-бу́ду, -бу́дешь; о́тбы́л, -а́, -о) *perf.*; (*writ etc.*) вруча́ть *imp.*, вручи́ть *perf.* (on, + *dat.*); *v.i.* (*be suitable*) годи́ться (for, на + *acc.*, для + *gen.*); (*sport*) подава́ть (-даю́, -даёшь) *imp.*, пода́ть (-а́м, -а́шь, -а́ст, -ади́м; по́дал, -а́, -о) *perf.* мяч; *it serves him right*, подело́м ему́ (*dat.*). **service** *n.* слу́жба; (*attendance*) обслу́живание; (*set of dishes etc.*) серви́з; (*sport*) пода́ча; (*transport*) сообще́ние; *at your s.*, к ва́шим услу́гам; *v.t.* обслу́живать *imp.*, обслужи́ть (-жу́, -жишь) *perf.* **serviceable** *n.* (*useful*) поле́зный; (*durable*)

про́чный (-чен, -чна́, -чно, про́чны́). **serviceman** *n.* военнослу́жащий *sb.* **serviette** *n.* салфе́тка. **servile** *adj.* ра́бский; (*cringing*) раболе́пный. **servility** *n.* раболе́пие. **servo-** *in comb.* серво-; *s.-mechanism*, сервомехани́зм; *s.-motor*, сервомото́р.

sesame *n.* кунжу́т; (*open*) *s.*, сеза́м, откро́йся.

session *n.* заседа́ние, се́ссия.

set[1] *v.t.* (*put*; *s. trap*) ста́вить *imp.*, по~ *perf.*; (*establish*; *s. clock*) устана́вливать *imp.*, установи́ть (-влю́, -вишь) *perf.*; (*table*) накрыва́ть *imp.*, накры́ть (-ро́ю, -ро́ешь) *perf.*; (*plant*) сажа́ть *imp.*, посади́ть (-ажу́, -а́дишь) *perf.*; (*bone*) вправля́ть *imp.*, впра́вить *perf.*; (*hair*) укла́дывать *imp.*, уложи́ть (-жу́, -жишь) *perf.*; (*jewel*) оправля́ть *imp.*, опра́вить *perf.*; (*print.*, *s. up*) набира́ть *imp.*, набра́ть (наберу́, -рёшь; набра́л, -а́, -о) *perf.*; (*bring into state*) приводи́ть (-ожу́, -о́дишь) *imp.*, привести́ (-еду́, -едёшь; -ёл, -ела́) *perf.* (in, to, в + *acc.*); (*example*) подава́ть (-даю́, -даёшь) *imp.*, пода́ть (-а́м, -а́шь, -а́ст, -ади́м; по́дал, -а́, -о) *perf.*; (*task*) задава́ть (-даю́, -даёшь; за́дал, -а́, -о) *perf.*; *v.i.* (*solidify*) тверде́ть *imp.*, за~ *perf.*; застыва́ть *imp.*, засты́(ну)ть (-ы́нет; -ы́л) *perf.*; (*fruit*) завя́зываться *imp.*, завяза́ться (-я́жется) *perf.*; (*sun etc.*) заходи́ть (-ит) *imp.*, зайти́ (зайдёт; зашёл, -шла) *perf.*; сади́ться *imp.*, сесть (ся́дет; сел) *perf.*; *s. eyes on*, уви́деть (-и́жу, -и́дишь) *perf.*; *s. free*, освобожда́ть *imp.*, освободи́ть *perf.*; *s. one's heart on*, стра́стно жела́ть *imp.* + *gen.*; *s. to music*, положи́ть (-жу́, -жишь) *perf.* на му́зыку; *s. sail*, пуска́ться *imp.*, пусти́ться (пущу́сь, пу́стишься) *perf.* в пла́вание; *s. about*, (*begin*) начина́ть *imp.*, нача́ть (начну́, -нёшь; на́чал, -а́, -о) *perf.*; (*attack*) напада́ть *imp.*, напа́сть (-аду́, -адёшь; -а́л) *perf.* на + *acc.*; *s. back*, (*impede*) препя́тствовать *imp.*, вос~ *perf.* + *dat.*; *s.-back*, неуда́ча; *s. down*, (*passenger*) выса́живать *imp.*, вы́садить *perf.*; (*in writing*) запи́сывать *imp.*, записа́ть (-ишу́, -и́шешь) *perf.*; (*attribute*) припи́сывать *imp.*, приписа́ть (-ишу́, -и́шешь) *perf.* (to, + *dat.*); *s. forth*, (*expound*) излага́ть *imp.*, изложи́ть (-жу́, -жишь) *perf.*; (*on journey*) *see s. off*; *s. in*, наступа́ть *imp.*, наступи́ть (-ит) *perf.*; *s. off*, (*on journey*) отправля́ться *imp.*, отпра́виться *perf.*; (*enhance*) оттеня́ть *imp.*, оттени́ть *perf.*; *s. out*, (*state*) излага́ть *imp.*, изложи́ть (-жу́, -жишь) *perf.*; (*on journey*) *see s. off*; *s. up*, (*business*) осно́вывать *imp.*, основа́ть (-ную́, -нуёшь) *perf.*; (*person*) обеспе́чивать *imp.*, обеспе́чить *perf.* (with, + *instr.*).

set[2] *n.* набо́р, компле́кт, прибо́р; (*of dishes etc.*) серви́з; (*of people*) круг (*loc.* -у́; *pl.* -и́); (*radio*) приёмник; (*television*) телеви́зор; (*tennis*) сет; (*theat.*) декора́ция; (*cin.*) съёмочная площа́дка.

set[3] *adj.* (*established*) устано́вленный (-ен); (*fixed*, *of smile etc.*) засты́вший; (*of intention*) обду́манный (-ан); *s. phrase*, усто́йчивое словосочета́ние; *s. square*, уго́льник.

settee *n.* дива́н.

setter *n.* (*dog*) се́ттер; (*person*) устано́вщик.

setting *n.* (*frame*) опра́ва; (*theat.*) декора́ция, постано́вка; (*mus.*) му́зыка на слова́; (*of sun etc.*) захо́д, зака́т.

settle *v.t.* (*decide*) реша́ть *imp.*, реши́ть *perf.*; (*arrange*) ула́живать *imp.*, ула́дить *perf.*; (*a bill etc.*) опла́чивать *imp.*, оплати́ть (-ачу́, -а́тишь) *perf.*; (*colonize*) заселя́ть *imp.*, засели́ть *perf.*; *v.i.* сели́ться *imp.*, по~ *perf.*; (*subside*) оседа́ть *imp.*, осе́сть (ося́дет; осе́л) *perf.*; *s. down*, уса́живаться *imp.*, усе́сться (уся́дусь, -дешься; усе́лся) *perf.* **settlement** *n.* поселе́ние; (*of dispute*) разреше́ние; (*payment*) упла́та; (*subsidence*) оса́дка, оседа́ние; *marriage s.*, бра́чный контра́кт. **settler** *n.* поселе́нец (-нца).

seven *adj.*, *n.* семь (-ми́, -мью́); (*collect.*; *7 pairs*) се́меро (-ры́х); (*cards*; *number 7*) семёрка; (*time*) семь (часо́в); (*age*) семь лет. **seventeen** *adj.*, *n.* семна́дцать; (*age*) семна́дцать лет. **seventeenth** *adj.*, *n.* семна́дцатый; (*date*) семна́дцатое (число́). **seventh**

adj., *n.* седьмóй; (*fraction*) седьмáя (часть (*pl.* -ти, -тéй)); (*date*) седьмóе (числó). **seventieth** *adj.*, *n.* семидесятый. **seventy** *adj.*, *n.* сéмьдесят (-мидесяти, -мьюдесятью); (*age*) сéмьдесят лет; *pl.* (*decade*) семидесятые гóды (-дóв) *m.pl.*

sever *v.t.* (*cut off*) отрезáть *imp.*, отрéзать (-éжу, -éжешь) *perf.*; (*relations*) разрывáть *imp.*, разорвáть (-вý, -вёшь; -вáл, -валá, -вáло) *perf.*; (*friendship*) порывáть *imp.*, порвáть (-вý, -вёшь; порвáл, -á, -о) *perf.*

several *pron.* (*adj.*) нéсколько (+*gen.*).

severance *n.* разрыв; *s. pay*, выходнóе посóбие.

severe *adj.* стрóгий (строг, -á, -о), сурóвый; (*illness etc.*) тяжёлый (-л, -лá). **severity** *n.* стрóгость, сурóвость.

sew *v.t.* шить (шью, шьёшь) *imp.*, с~ (сошью, -ьёшь) *perf.*; *s. on*, пришивáть *imp.*, пришить (-шью, -шьёшь) *perf.*; *s. up*, зашивáть *imp.*, зашить (-шью, -шьёшь) *perf.*

sewage *n.* стóчные вóды *f.pl.*, нечистóты (-т) *pl.*; *s.-farm*, поля *neut.pl.* орошéния. **sewer** *n.* стóчная, канализациóнная, трубá (*pl.* -бы). **sewerage** *n.* канализáция.

sewing *n.* шитьё; *s.-machine*, швéйная машина.

sex *n.* (*gender*) пол; секс; *adj.* сексуáльный.

sexcentenary *n.* шестисотлéтие.

sextant *n.* секстáнт.

sextet *n.* секстéт.

sexton *n.* пономáрь (-ря) *m.*, могильщик.

sextuple *adj.* шестикрáтный.

sexual *adj.* половóй, сексуáльный. **sexuality** *n.* сексуáльность. **sexy** *adj.* (*alluring*) соблазительный; (*erotic*) эротический.

sh *interj.* тише! тсс!

shabby *adj.* понóшенный (-ен), потрёпанный (-ан, -анна); (*mean*) пóдлый (подл, -á, -о).

shack *n.* лачýга, хижина.

shackle *n.*: *pl.* кандалы (-лóв) *pl.*; (*also fig.*) окóвы (-в) *pl.*; *v.t.* закóвывать *imp.*, заковáть (-кую, -куёшь) *perf.*

shade *n.* тень (*loc.* -ни; *pl.* -ни, -нéй), полумрáк; (*of colour*, *meaning*) оттéнок (-нка); (*lamp-s.*) абажýр; *a s.*, чуть-чуть; *v.t.* затенять *imp.*, затенить *perf.*; заслонять *imp.* заслонить (-оню, -óнишь) *perf.*; (*drawing*) тушевáть (-шýю, -шýешь) *imp.*, за~ *perf.*; *v.i.* незамéтно переходить (-ит) *imp.* (into, в+*acc.*). **shadow** *n.* тень (*loc.* -ни; *pl.* -ни, -нéй); *v.t.* (*follow*) тáйно следить *imp.* за+*instr.* **shadowy** *adj.* тёмный (-мен, -мнá), неясный (-сен, -снá, -сно). **shady** *adj.* тенистый; (*suspicious*) подозрительный.

shaft *n.* (*of spear*) дрéвко (*pl.* -ки, -ков); (*arrow*; *fig.*) стрелá (*pl.* -лы); (*of light*) луч (-á); (*of cart*) оглóбля (*gen.pl.* -бель); (*axle*) вал (*loc.* -ý; *pl.* -ы); (*mine s.*) ствол (-á) (шáхты).

shag *n.* (*tobacco*) махóрка; (*bird*) баклáн. **shaggy** *adj.* лохмáтый, космáтый.

shah *n.* шах.

shake *v.t.* & *i.* трясти(сь) (-сý(сь), -сёшь(ся); -с(ся), -слá(сь)) *imp.*; *v.i.* (*tremble*) дрожáть (-жý, -жишь) *imp.*; *v.t.* (*impair*) колебáть (-блю, -блешь) *imp.*, по~ *perf.*; *s. hands*, пожимáть *imp.*, пожáть (-жмý, -жмёшь) *perf.* рýку+*dat.*; *s. one's head*, покачáть *perf.* головóй; *s. off*, стряхивать *imp.*, стряхнýть *perf.*; (*fig.*) избавляться *imp.*, избáвиться *perf.* от+*gen.*; *s. up*, (*fig.*) встряхивать *imp.*, встряхнýть *perf.*

shako *n.* кивер (*pl.* -á).

shaky *adj.* шáткий (-ток, -тка), непрóчный (-чен, -чнá, -чно).

shale *n.* слáнец (-нца).

shallot *n.* лук-шалóт.

shallow *adj.* мéлкий (-лок, -лкá, -лко); (*superficial*) повéрхностный; *n.* мелковóдье, мель (*loc.* -ли).

sham *v.t.* & *i.* притворяться *imp.*, притвориться *perf.*+*instr.*; *n.* притвóрство; (*person*) притвóрщик, -ица; *adj.* притвóрный; (*fake*) поддéльный.

shaman *n.* шамáн.

shamble *v.i.* волочить (-чý, -чишь) *imp.* нóги.

shambles *n.* бóйня; (*muddle*) хаóс.

shame *n.* стыд, позóр; *v.t.* стыдить

imp., при ~ *perf.* **shamefaced** *adj.*) стыдли́вый. **shameful** *adj.* позо́рный. **shameless** *adj.* бессты́дный.

shampoo *v.t.* мыть (мо́ю, мо́ешь) *imp.*, по ~ *perf.*; *n.* шампу́нь *m.*

shamrock *n.* трили́стник.

shandy *n.* смесь (просто́го) пи́ва с лимона́дом, с имби́рным.

shank *n.* (*leg*) нога́ (*acc.* -гу; *pl.* -ги, -г, -га́м), го́лень; (*shaft*) сте́ржень (-жня) *m.*

shanty[1] *n.* (*hut*) хиба́рка, лачу́га; *s. town*, бидонви́ль, трущо́ба.

shanty[2] *n.* (*song*) матро́сская пе́сня (*gen. pl.* -сен).

shape *n.* фо́рма, вид, о́браз; *v.t.* придава́ть (-даю́, -даёшь) *imp.*, прида́ть (-а́м, -а́шь, -а́ст, -ади́м; при́дал, -а́, -о) *perf.* фо́рму + *dat.*; *v.i.* принима́ть *imp.*, приня́ть (-и́мет; при́нял, -а́, -о) *perf.* фо́рму. **shapeless** *adj.* бесфо́рменный (-ен, -енна). **shapely** *adj.* стро́йный (-о́ен, -ойна́, -о́йно).

share *n.* до́ля (*pl.* -ли, -ле́й), часть (*pl.* -ти, -те́й); (*participation*) уча́стие; (*econ.*) а́кция, пай (*pl.* паи́, паёв); *v.t.* дели́ть (-лю́, -лишь) *imp.*, по ~ *perf.*; разделя́ть *imp.*, раздели́ть (-лю́, -лишь) *perf.* **shareholder** *n.* акционе́р, ~ ка; па́йщик, -ица.

shark *n.* аку́ла.

sharp *adj.* о́стрый (остр & остёр, остра́, о́стро́); (*steep*) круто́й (крут, -а́, -о); (*sudden*; *harsh*) ре́зкий (-зок, -зка́, -зко); (*fine*) то́нкий (-нок, -нка́, -нко, то́нки́); *n.* (*mus.*) дие́з; *adv.* (*with time*) ро́вно; (*of angle*) кру́то. **sharpen** *v.t.* точи́ть (-чу́, -чишь) *imp.*, на ~ *perf.*; обостря́ть *imp.*, обостри́ть *perf.*

shatter *v.t.* & *i.* разбива́ть(ся) *imp.*, разби́ть(ся) (разобью́, -ьёт(ся)) *perf.* вдре́безги; *v.t.* (*hopes etc.*) разруша́ть *imp.*, разру́шить *perf.*

shave *v.t.* & *i.* бри́ть(ся) (бре́ю(сь), -е́ешь(ся)) *imp.*, по ~ *perf.*; *v.t.* (*plane*) строга́ть *imp.*, вы́ ~ *perf.*; *n.* бритьё; *close s.*, едва́ избе́гнутая опа́сность. **shaver** *n.* электри́ческая бри́тва.

shawl *n.* шаль.

she *pron.* она́ (её, ей, ей & е́ю, о ней).

sheaf *n.* сноп (-а́); (*of papers etc.*) свя́зка.

shear *v.t.* стричь (-игу́, -ижёшь; -иг) *imp.*, о ~ *perf.* **shearer** *n.* стрига́льщик. **shears** *n.* но́жницы (-ц) *pl.*

sheath *n.* (*for sword etc.*) но́жны (*gen.* -жен) *pl.*; (*anat.*) оболо́чка; (*for cable etc.*) обши́вка. **sheathe** *v.t.* вкла́дывать *imp.*, вложи́ть (-жу́, -жишь) *perf.* в но́жны; обшива́ть *imp.*, обши́ть (обошью́, -ьёшь) *perf.* **sheathing** *n.* обши́вка.

sheave *n.* шкив (*pl.* -ы́).

shed[1] *n.* сара́й.

shed[2] *v.t.* (*tears, blood, light*) пролива́ть *imp.*, проли́ть (-лью́, -льёшь; про́ли́л, -а́, -о) *perf.*; (*skin, clothes*) сбра́сывать *imp.*, сбро́сить *perf.*

sheen *n.* блеск.

sheep *n.* овца́ (*pl.* о́вцы, ове́ц, о́вцам); *s.-dog*, овча́рка; *s.-fold*, овча́рня (*gen.pl.* -рен). **sheepish** *adj.* (*bashful*) засте́нчивый; (*abashed*) сконфу́женный (-ен). **sheepskin** *n.* овчи́на.

sheer *adj.* абсолю́тный, су́щий; (*textile*) прозра́чный; (*rock etc.*) отве́сный.

sheet[1] *n.* (*on bed*) простыня́ (*pl.* про́стыни, -ы́нь, -ыня́м); (*of glass, paper, etc.*) лист (-а́); (*wide expanse*) пелена́ (*gen.pl.* -ён); *attrib.* (*metal, glass, etc.*) листово́й; *s. lightning*, зарни́ца.

sheet[2] *n.* (*naut.*) шкот; *s.-anchor*, запасно́й станово́й я́корь (*pl.* -ря́) *m.*; (*fig.*) я́корь (*pl.* -ря́) *m.* спасе́ния.

sheikh *n.* шейх.

sheldrake, shelduck *n.* пега́нка.

shelf *n.* по́лка; (*of cliff etc.*) усту́п; *s.-mark*, шифр.

shell *n.* (*of mollusc etc.*) ракови́на; (*of tortoise*) щит (-а́); (*of egg, nut*) скорлупа́ (*pl.* -пы); (*of building etc.*) о́стов; (*explosive s.*) снаря́д; *v.t.* очища́ть *imp.*, очи́стить *perf.*; лущи́ть *imp.*, об ~ *perf.*; (*bombard*) обстре́ливать *imp.*, обстреля́ть *perf.*; *s. out*, (*abs.*) раскоше́ливаться *imp.*, раскоше́литься *perf.*

shellac *n.* шелла́к.

shellfish *n.* (*mollusc*) моллю́ск; (*crustacean*) ракообра́зное *sb.*

shelter *n.* прию́т, убе́жище, укры́тие; *v.t.* дава́ть (даю́, даёшь) *imp.*, дать (дам, дашь, даст, дади́м; дал, -а́, да́ло́, -и) *perf.* прию́т + *dat.*; служи́ть

(-жу́, -жишь) *imp.*, по~ *perf.* убе́жищем, укры́тием, +*dat.*; *v.t.* & *i.* укрыва́ть(ся) *imp.*, укры́ть(ся) (-ро́ю-(сь), -ро́ешь(ся)) *perf.*

shelve[1] *v.t.* (*defer*) откла́дывать *imp.*, отложи́ть (-жу́, -жишь) *perf.* (в до́лгий я́щик).

shelve[2] *v.i.* (*of land*) отло́го спуска́ться *imp.* **shelving**[1] *adj.* отло́гий.

shelving[2] *n.* (*shelves*) стелла́ж (-а́).

shepherd *n.* пасту́х (-а́); (*fig.*) па́стырь *m.*; *v.t.* проводи́ть (-ожу́, -о́дишь) *imp.*, провести́ (-еду́, -едёшь; -ёл, -ела́) *perf.* **shepherdess** *n.* пасту́шка.

sherbet *n.* шербе́т.

sheriff *n.* шери́ф.

sherry *n.* хе́рес.

shield *n.* щит (-а́); *v.t.* прикрыва́ть *imp.*, прикры́ть (-ро́ю, -ро́ешь) *perf.*; заслоня́ть *imp.*, заслони́ть *perf.*

shift *v.t.* & *i.* (*change position*) перемеща́ть(ся) *imp.*, перемести́ть(ся) *perf.*; (*change form*) меня́ть(ся) *imp.*; *v.t.* (*move*; *s. responsibility etc.*) перекла́дывать *imp.*, переложи́ть (-жу́, -жишь) *perf.*; *n.* перемеще́ние; переме́на; (*of workers*) сме́на. **shiftless** *adj.* неуме́лый. **shifty** *adj.* ненадёжный, нече́стный.

shilly-shally *n.* нереши́тельность; *v.i.* колеба́ться (-блюсь, -блешься) *imp.*, по~ *perf.*

shimmer *v.i.* мерца́ть *imp.*; *n.* мерца́ние.

shin *n.* го́лень; *s.-bone*, большеберцо́вая кость (*pl.* -ти, -те́й); *s.-guard*, *-pad*, щито́к (-тка́); *v.i.*: *s. up*, ла́зить *imp.* по+*dat.*

shindy *n.* шум, сва́лка.

shine *v.i.* свети́ть(ся) (-ит(ся)) *imp.*; блесте́ть (-ещу́, -е́щешь & -ести́шь) *imp.*; (*of sun etc.*) сия́ть *imp.*; *v.t.* полирова́ть *imp.*, от~ *perf.*; *n.* свет, сия́ние, блеск; (*polish*) гля́нец (-нца).

shingle[1] *n.* (*for roof*) (кро́вельная) дра́нка.

shingle[2] *n.* (*pebbles*) га́лька.

shingles *n.* опоя́сывающий лиша́й (-ая́).

shining, shiny *adj.* блестя́щий.

ship *n.* кора́бль (-ля́) *m.*; су́дно (*pl.* -да́, -до́в); *v.t.* (*transport*) перевози́ть (-ожу́, -о́зишь) *imp.*, перевезти́ (-езу́, -езёшь; -ёз, -езла́) *perf.* (по воде́); (*dispatch*) отправля́ть *imp.*, отпра́вить *perf.* (по воде́). **shipbuilding** *n.* судострои́тельство. **shipment** *n.* (*loading*) погру́зка; (*consignment*) груз. **shipping** *n.* суда́ (-до́в) *pl.* **shipshape** *adv.* в по́лном поря́дке. **shipwreck** *n.* кора́блекруше́ние. **shipwright** *n.* (*shipbuilder*) судострои́тель *m.*; (*carpenter*) корабе́льный пло́тник. **shipyard** *n.* верфь.

shire *n.* гра́фство.

shirk *v.t.* уви́ливать *imp.*, увильну́ть *perf.* от+*gen.*

shirt *n.* руба́шка; *in s.-sleeves*, без пиджака́.

shiver[1] *v.i.* (*tremble*) дрожа́ть (-жу́, -жи́шь) *imp.*; *n.* дрожь.

shiver[2] *n.* (*splinter etc.*) оско́лок (-лка).

shoal[1] *adj.* (*shallow*) ме́лкий; *n.* (*bank*) мель (*loc.* -ли́).

shoal[2] *n.* (*of fish*) ста́я, кося́к (-а́).

shock[1] *n.* (*impact etc.*) уда́р, толчо́к (-чка́); (*med.*) шок; *attrib.* (*troops*, *brigade*, *wave*) уда́рный; *s. absorber*, амортиза́тор; *s. tactics*, та́ктика сокруши́тельных уда́ров; *s. therapy*, шокотерапи́я; *s.-worker*, уда́рник; *v.t.* шоки́ровать *imp.* **shocking** *adj.* возмути́тельный, ужа́сный.

shock[2] *n.* (*of sheaves*) копна́ (*pl.* -пны, -пён, -пна́м).

shock[3] *n.* (*of hair*) копна́ воло́с.

shod *adj.* обу́тый.

shoddy *adj.* дрянно́й (-нен, -нна́, -нно).

shoe *n.* ту́фля (*gen.pl.* -фель); (*horseshoe*) подко́ва; (*tech.*) башма́к (-а́); *v.t.* подко́вывать *imp.*, подкова́ть (-кую́, -куёшь) *perf.* **shoeblack** *n.* чисти́льщик сапо́г. **shoehorn** *n.* рожо́к (-жка́). **shoe-lace** *n.* шнуро́к (-рка́) для боти́нок. **shoemaker** *n.* сапо́жник. **shoe-string** *n.*: *on a s.*, с небольши́ми сре́дствами.

shoo *interj.* кш! *v.t.* прогоня́ть *imp.*, прогна́ть (прогоню́, -нишь; прогна́л, -а́, -о) *perf.*

shoot *v.t.* & *i.* (*discharge*) стреля́ть *imp.* (a gun, из+*gen.*; at, в+*acc.*, по+*dat.*); (*arrow*) пуска́ть *imp.*, пусти́ть (пущу́, пу́стишь) *perf.*; (*kill*) застре́ливать *imp.*, застрели́ть (-лю́, -лишь) *perf.*; (*execute*) расстре́ливать *imp.*, расстреля́ть *perf.*; (*hunt*) охо́титься *imp.* на + *acc.*; (*football*) бить (бью, бьёшь) *imp.* (по воро́там); (*cin.*) снима́ть *imp.*, снять (сниму́, -мешь; снял, -á, -о) *perf.* (фильм); *v.i.* (*go swiftly*) проноси́ться (-ошу́сь, -о́сишься) *imp.*, пронести́сь (-есу́сь, -есёшься; -ёсся, -есла́сь) *perf.*; (*of plant*) пуска́ть *imp.*, пусти́ть (-ит) *perf.* ростки́; *s. down*, (*aircraft*) сбива́ть *imp.*, сбить (собью́, -бёшь) *perf.*; *n.* (*branch*) росто́к (-тка́), побе́г; (*hunt*) охо́та. **shooting** *n.* стрельба́; (*hunting*) охо́та; *s.-box*, охо́тничий до́мик; *s.-gallery*, тир; *s.-range*, стре́льбище.

shop *n.* (*for sales*) магази́н, ла́вка; (*for repairs, manufacture*) мастерска́я *sb.*, цех (*loc.* -е & -у́; *pl.* -и & -á); *talk s.*, говори́ть *imp.* на узкопрофессиона́льные те́мы, о дела́х; *s. assistant*, продаве́ц (-вца́), -вщи́ца; *s.-floor*, (*fig.*) рабо́чие *sb.pl.*; *s.-lifter*, магази́нщик; *s.-steward*, цехово́й ста́роста *m.*; *s.-window*, витри́на; *v.i.* де́лать *imp.*, с~ *perf.* поку́пки (*f.pl.*); *v.t.* (*imprison*) сажа́ть *imp.*, посади́ть (-ажу́, -а́дишь) *perf.* в тюрьму́; (*inform against*) доноси́ть (-ошу́, -о́сишь) *imp.*, донести́ (-су́, -сёшь; донёс, -ла́) *perf.* на + *acc.* **shopkeeper** *n.* ла́вочник. **shopper** *n.* покупа́тель *m.*, ~ница. **shopping** *n.* поку́пки *f.pl.*; *go, do one's, s.*, де́лать *imp.*, с~ *perf.* поку́пки. **shopwalker** *n.* дежу́рный администра́тор магази́на.

shore[1] *n.* бе́рег (*loc.* -у́; *pl.* -á); *s. leave*, о́тпуск на бе́рег.

shore[2] *v.t.*: *s. up*, подпира́ть *imp.*, подпере́ть (подопру́, -рёшь; подпёр) *perf.*

shorn *adj.* остри́женный (-ен).

short *adj.* коро́ткий (ко́ро́ток, -тка́, ко́ро́тко́); (*concise*) кра́ткий (-ток, -тка́, -тко); (*not tall*) ни́зкий (-зок, -зка́, -зко, ни́зки́); (*of person*) ни́зкого ро́ста; (*deficient*) недоста́точный; *be s. of*, (*have too little*) испы́тывать *imp.*, испыта́ть *perf.* недоста́ток в + *prep.*; (*not amount to*) быть (*fut.* бу́ду, -дешь; был, -á, -о; не́ был, -á, -о) ме́ньше + *gen.*; (*uncivil*) гру́бый (груб, -á, -о); (*crumbling*) рассы́пчатый; *in s.*, одни́м сло́вом; *s.-change*, недодава́ть (-даю́, -даёшь) *imp.*, недода́ть (-а́м, -а́шь, -а́ст, -ади́м; недо́дал, -á, -о) *perf.* сда́чу + *dat.*; *s. circuit*, коро́ткое замыка́ние; *s.-circuit*, замыка́ть *imp.*, замкну́ть *perf.* на́коротко; *s. cut*, коро́ткий путь (-ти́, -тём) *m.*; *s. list*, оконча́тельный спи́сок (-ска); *s.-list*, включа́ть *imp.*, включи́ть *perf.* в оконча́телный спи́сок; *s.-lived*, недолгове́чный, мимолётный; *s. measure*, недоме́р; *at s. notice*, неме́дленно; *s.-range*, краткосро́чный; *s. sight*, близору́кость; *s.-sighted*, близору́кий; (*fig.*) недальнови́дный; *s. story*, расска́з, нове́лла; *in s. supply*, дефици́тный; *s.-tempered*, вспы́льчивый; *s.-term*, краткосро́чный; *s.-wave*, коротковолно́вый; *s. weight*, недове́с; *s.-winded*, страда́ющий оды́шкой; *n.* (*film*) короткометра́жный фильм; (*drink*) спиртно́е *sb.*; (*s. circuit*) коро́ткое замыка́ние; *pl.* шо́рты (-т) *pl.*; *v.t.* замыка́ть *imp.*, замкну́ть *perf.* на́коротко. **shortage** *n.* недоста́ток (-тка); дефици́т. **shortbread** *n.* песо́чное пече́нье. **shortcoming** *n.* недоста́ток (-тка). **shorten** *v.t.* & *i.* укора́чивать(ся) *imp.*, укороти́ть(ся) *perf.*; сокраща́ть(ся) *imp.*, сократи́ть(ся) (-ащу́, -ати́т(ся)) *perf.*; *s. sail*, убавля́ть *imp.*, уба́вить *perf.* парусо́в. **shortfall** *n.* дефици́т. **shorthand** *n.* стеногра́фия. **shorthorn** *n.* шортго́рнская поро́да скота́. **shortly** *adv.*: *s. after*, вско́ре (по́сле + *gen.*); *s. before*, незадо́лго (до + *gen.*).

shot[1] *n.* (*discharge of gun*) вы́стрел; (*for cannon; sport*) ядро́ (*pl.* я́дра, я́дер, я́драм); (*pellet*) дроби́нка; (*as pl., collect.*) дробь; (*person*) стрело́к (-лка́); (*attempt*) попы́тка; (*injection*) уко́л; (*phot.*) сни́мок (-мка); (*cin.*) съёмка; *like a s.*, очень охо́тно, неме́дленно; *a s. in the arm*, (*fig.*) сти́мул; *s.-gun*, дробови́к (-á).

shot[2] *adj.* (*of material*) перели́вчатый.

shoulder *n.* плечо́ (*pl.* -чи, -ч, -ча́м); (*cul.*) лопа́тка; (*of road*) обо́чина; *straight from the s.*, сплеча́; *s. to s.*, плечо́м к плечу́; *s.-blade*, лопа́тка; *s.-strap*, брете́лька; (*on uniform*) пого́н (*gen.pl.* -н); *v.t.* взва́ливать *imp.*, взвали́ть (-лю́, -лишь) *perf.* на пле́чи.

shout *n.* крик; *v.i.* кричáть (-чý, -чи́шь) *imp.*, кри́кнуть *perf.*; *s. down*, перекри́кивать *imp.*, перекричáть (-чý, -чи́шь) *perf.*

shove *n.* толчóк (-чкá); *v.t.* & *i.* толкáть(ся) *imp.*, толкнýть *perf.*; *s. off*, (*coll.*) убирáться *imp.*, убрáться (уберýсь, -рёшься; убрáлся, -алáсь, -áлóсь) *perf.*

shovel *n.* совóк (-вкá), лопáта; *v.t.* копáть *imp.*, вы́~ *perf.*; (*s. up*) сгребáть *imp.*, сгрести́ (сгребý, -бёшь; сгрёб, -лá) *perf.*

show *v.t.* покáзывать *imp.*, показáть (-ажý, -áжешь) *perf.*; (*exhibit*) выставля́ть *imp.*, вы́ставить *perf.*; (*film etc.*) демонстри́ровать *imp.*, про~ *perf.*; *v.i.* быть ви́дным (-ден, -днá, -дно, ви́дны́), замéтным; *s. off*, (*v.i.*) рисовáться *imp.*; *n.* (*exhibition*) вы́ставка; (*theat.*) спектáкль *m.*; (*spectacle*; *pageant*) зрéлище; (*business*) дéло (*pl.* -лá); (*appearance*) ви́димость; *s. of hands*, голосовáние поднятием руки́; *s.-case*, витри́на; *s.-jumping*, соревновáние по скáчкам; *s.-room*, салóн. **showboat** *n.* плавýчий теáтр. **showgirl** *n.* стати́стка. **showman** *n.* балагáнщик.

shower *n.* (*rain*) дóждик; (*hail*; *fig.*) град; (*s.-bath*) душ; *v.t.* осыпáть *imp.*, осы́пать (-плю, -плешь) *perf.* + *instr.* (on, + *acc.*); *v.i.* принимáть *imp.*, приня́ть (примý, -мешь; при́нял, -á, -о) *perf.* душ. **showery** *adj.* дождли́вый.

showy *adj.* я́ркий (я́рок, яркá, я́рко); (*gaudy*) брóский (-сок, -скá, -ско).

shrapnel *n.* шрапнéль.

shred *n.* клочóк (-чкá), лоскутóк (-ткá); *not a s.*, ни кáпли; *tear to shreds*, (*fig.*) пóлностью опровергáть *imp.*, опровéргнуть (-г(нул), -гла) *perf.*; *v.t.* рéзать (рéжу, -жешь) *imp.* на клочки́; рвать (рву, рвёшь; рвал, -á, -о) *imp.* в клочки́.

shrew *n.* (*woman*) сварли́вая, стропти́вая, жéнщина; (*animal*) землерóйка.

shrewd *adj.* проницáтельный.

shrewish *adj.* сварли́вый.

shriek *n.* пронзи́тельный крик, визг; *v.i.* визжáть (-жý, -жи́шь) *imp.*; кричáть (-чý, -чи́шь) *imp.*, кри́кнуть *perf.*

shrill *adj.* пронзи́тельный, рéзкий (-зок, -зкá, -зко).

shrimp *n.* кревéтка.

shrine *n.* (*casket*) рáка; (*tomb*) гробни́ца; (*sacred place*) святы́ня.

shrink *v.i.* сади́ться *imp.*, сесть (ся́дет; сел) *perf.*; *v.t.* вызывáть *imp.*, вы́звать (-зовет) *perf.* усáдку у + *gen.*; *s. from*, уклоня́ться *imp.* от + *gen.*; избегáть *imp.* + *gen.*; *s.-proof*, безусáдочный. **shrinkage** *n.* усáдка.

shrivel *v.t.* & *i.* съёживать(ся) *imp.*, съёжить(ся) *perf.*

shroud *n.* сáван; *pl.* (*naut.*) вáнты *f.pl.*; *v.t.* (*fig.*) окýтывать *imp.*, окýтать *perf.* (in, + *instr.*).

Shrove-tide *n.* мáсленица.

shrub *n.* куст (-á), кустáрник. **shrubbery** *n.* кустáрник.

shrug *v.t.* & *i.* пожимáть *imp.*, пожáть (-жмý, -жмёшь) *perf.* (плечáми).

shudder *n.* содрогáние; *v.i.* содрогáться *imp.*, содрогнýться *perf.*

shuffle *v.t.* & *i.* (*one's feet*) шáркать *imp.* (ногáми); *v.t.* (*cards*) тасовáть *imp.*, с~ *perf.*; (*intermingle*, *confuse*) перемéшивать *imp.*, перемешáть *perf.*; *s. off*, (*blame etc.*) свáливать *imp.*, свали́ть (-лю́, -лишь) *perf.* (on to, на + *acc.*); *n.* шáрканье; тасóвка.

shun *v.t.* избегáть *imp.* + *gen.*

shunt *v.i.* (*rly.*) маневри́ровать *imp.*, с~ *perf.*; *v.t.* (*rly.*) переводи́ть (-ожý, -óдишь) *imp.*, перевести́ (-едý, -едёшь; -ёл, -елá) *perf.* на запáсный путь.

shut *v.t.* & *i.* закрывáть(ся) *imp.*, закры́ть(ся) (-рóю, -рóет(ся)) *perf.*; *s. in*, запирáть *imp.*, заперéть (запрý, -рёшь; зáпер, -лá, -ло) *perf.*; *s. up*, (*v.i.*) замолчáть (-чý, -чи́шь) *perf.*; (*imper.*) заткни́сь!

shutter *n.* стáвень (-вня) *m.*, стáвня (*gen.pl.* -вен); (*phot.*) затвóр; *v.t.* закрывáть *imp.*, закры́ть (-рóю, -рóешь) *perf.* стáвнями.

shuttle *n.* челнóк (-á). **shuttlecock** *n.* волáн.

shy[1] *adj.* застéнчивый, рóбкий (-бок, -бкá, -бко).

shy[2] *v.i.* (*in alarm*) пугáться *imp.*, ис~ *perf.* (at, + *gen.*).

shy[3] *v.t.* (*throw*) бросáть *imp.*, брóсить *perf.*; *n.* бросóк (-скá).

Siamese *adj.* сиáмский; *S. twins*, сиáмские близнецы́ *m.pl.*

Siberian *adj.* сиби́рский; *n.* сибиря́к (-á), -я́чка.

sibilant *adj.* (*n.*) свистя́щий (звук) (*sb.*).

sic *adv.* так!

sick *adj.* больнóй (-лен, -льнá); *be, feel, s.*, тошни́ть *imp. impers.* + *acc.*; тóшно *impers.* + *dat.*; *be s. for*, (*pine*) тосковáть *imp.* по + *dat.*; *be s. of*, надоедáть *imp.*, надоéсть (-éм, -éшь, -éст, -еди́м; -éл) *perf.* + *nom.* (*object*) & *dat.* (*subject*); *I'm s. of her*, онá мне надоéла; *s.-bed*, постéль больнóго; *s.-benefit*, посóбие по болéзни; *s.-leave*, óтпуск по болéзни. **sicken** *v.t.* вызывáть *imp.*, вы́звать (-зовет) *perf.* тошнотý, (*disgust*) отвращéние, у + *gen.*; *v.i.* заболевáть *imp.*, заболéть *perf.* **sickening** *adj.* отврати́тельный.

sickle *n.* серп (-á).

sickly *adj.* (*ailing*) болéзненный (-ен, -енна), хи́лый (хил, -á, -о); (*nauseating*) тошнотвóрный. **sickness** *n.* болéзнь; (*vomiting*) тошнотá; *s. benefit*, посóбие по болéзни.

side *n.* сторонá (*acc.* -ону; *pl.* -оны, -óн, -онáм), бок (*loc.* на -ý; *pl.* -á); *s. by s.*, бок ó бок; ря́дом (with, с + *instr.*); *on the s.*, на сторонé, дополни́тельно; *v.i.*: *s. with*, вставáть (-таю́, -таёшь) *imp.*, встать (-áну, -áнешь) *perf.* на стóрону + *gen.*; *s.-car*, коля́ска (мотоци́кла); *s.-effect*, (*of medicine etc.*) побóчное дéйствие; *s.-saddle*, дáмское седлó (*pl.* сёдла, -дел, -длам); *s.-slip*, боковóе скольжéние; (*aeron.*) скольжéние на крылó; *s.-step*, (*fig.*) уклоня́ться *imp.*, уклони́ться (-ню́сь, -нишься) *perf.* от + *gen.*; *s.-stroke*, плáвание на бокý; *s.-track*, (*distract*) отвлекáть *imp.*, отвлéчь (-екý, -ечёшь; -ёк, -еклá) *perf.*; (*postpone*) откладывать *imp.*, отложи́ть (-жý, -жишь) *perf.* рассмотрéние + *gen.*; *s.-view*, прóфиль *m.*, вид сбóку. **sideboard** *n.* сервáнт, буфéт; *pl.* бáки (-к) *pl.* **sidelight** *n.* боковóй фонáрь (-ря́) *m.* **sideline** *n.* (*work*) побóчная рабóта.

sidelong *adj.* (*glance*) косóй.

sidereal *adj.* звёздный.

sideways *adv.* бóком; (*from side*) сбóку.

siding *n.* запáсный путь (-ти́, -тём) *m.*

sidle *v.i.* ходи́ть (хожý, хóдишь) *imp.* бóком.

siege *n.* осáда; *lay s. to*, осаждáть *imp.*, осади́ть *perf.*; *raise the s. of*, снимáть *imp.*, снять (снимý, -мешь; снял, -á, -о) *perf.* осáду с + *gen.*

sienna *n.* сиéна; *burnt s.*, жжёная сиéна.

siesta *n.* сиéста.

sieve *n.* решетó (*pl.* -ёта), си́то; *v.t.* просéивать *imp.*, просéять (-éю, -éешь) *perf.*

sift *v.t.* просéивать *imp.*, просéять (-éю, -éешь) *perf.*; (*evidence etc.*) тщáтельно рассмáтривать *imp.*, рассмотрéть (-рю́, -ришь) *perf.* **sifter** *n.* си́то.

sigh *v.i.* вздыхáть *imp.*, вздохнýть *perf.*; *n.* вдох.

sight *n.* (*faculty*) зрéние; (*view*; *range*) вид; (*spectacle*) зрéлище; *pl.* достопримечáтельности *f.pl.*; (*on gun*) прицéл; *at, on, s.*, при ви́де (of, + *gen.*); *at first s.*, с пéрвого взгля́да; *in s. of*, в видý + *gen.*; *long s.*, дáльнозоркость; *short s.*, близорýкость; *catch s. of*, уви́деть (-и́жу, -и́дишь) *perf.*; *know by s.*, знать *imp.* в лицó; *lose s. of*, теря́ть *imp.*, по~ *perf.* и́з виду; (*fig.*) упускáть *imp.*, упусти́ть (-ущý, -ýстишь) *perf.* и́з виду; *s.-reading*, чтéние нот с листá. **sightless** *adj.* слепóй (слеп, -á, -о).

sign *n.* знак; (*indication*) при́знак; (*signboard*) вы́веска; *v.t.* & *abs.* подпи́сывать(ся) *imp.*, подписáть(ся) (-ишý(сь), -и́шешь(ся)) *perf.*; *v.i.* (*give s.*) подавáть (-даю́, -даёшь) *imp.*, подáть (-áм, -áшь, -áст, -ади́м; пóдал, -á, -о) *perf.* знак.

signal[1] *adj.* выдаю́щийся, замечáтельный.

signal[2] *n.* сигнáл; *pl.* (*mil.*) связь; *v.t.* & *i.* сигнализи́ровать *imp.*, *perf.*, про~ *perf.* **signal-box** *n.* сигнáльная бýдка. **signalman** *n.* сигнáльщик.

signatory *n.* подписáвший *sb.*; (*of treaty*) сторонá (*acc.* -ону; *pl.* -оны, -óн, -онáм), подписáвшая договóр.

signature *n.* по́дпись; (*print.*) сигнату́ра; (*mus.*) ключ (-а́); *s. tune*, музыка́льная ша́пка.
signboard *n.* вы́веска.
signet *n.* печа́тка; *s.-ring*, кольцо́ (*pl.* -льца, -ле́ц, -льцам) с печа́ткой.
significance *n.* значе́ние. **significant** *adj.* значи́тельный. **signify** *v.t.* означа́ть *imp.*; (*express*) выража́ть *imp.*, вы́разить *perf.*; *v.i.* быть (*fut.* бу́ду, -дешь; был, -а́, -о; не́ был, -а́, -о) *imp.* ва́жным.
signpost *n.* указа́тельный столб (-а́).
silage *n.* си́лос.
silence *n.* молча́ние, тишина́; *v.t.* заста́вить *perf.* замолча́ть. **silencer** *n.* глуши́тель *m.* **silent** *adj.* (*not speaking*) безмо́лвный; (*taciturn*) молчали́вый; (*of film*) немо́й; (*without noise*) ти́хий (тих, -а́, -о), бесшу́мный; *be s.*, молча́ть (-чу́, -чи́шь) *imp.*
silhouette *n.* силуэ́т; *v.t.*: *be silhouetted*, вырисо́вываться *imp.*, вы́рисоваться *perf.* (against, на фо́не + *gen.*).
silica *n.* кремнезём. **silicate** *n.* силика́т. **silicon** *n.* кре́мний. **silicone** *n.* силико́н. **silicosis** *n.* силико́з.
silk *n.* шёлк (-а(у), *loc.* -е & -у́; *pl.* -а́); *take s.*, станови́ться (-влю́сь, -ви́шься) *imp.*, стать (-а́ну, -а́нешь) *perf.* короле́вским адвока́том; *attrib.* шёлковый; *s. hat*, цили́ндр. **silkworm** *n.* шелкови́чный червь (-вя́; *pl.* -ви, -ве́й) *m.* **silky** *adj.* шелкови́стый.
sill *n.* подоко́нник.
silly *adj.* глу́пый (глуп, -а́, -о).
silo *n.* си́лос; *v.t.* силосова́ть *imp.*, *perf.*, за ~ *perf.*
silt *n.* ил (-а(у)); *v.i.*: *s. up*, засоря́ться *imp.*, засори́ться *perf.* и́лом.
silver *n.* серебро́; (*cutlery*) столо́вое серебро́; *adj.* (*of s.*) сере́бряный; (*silvery*) серебри́стый; (*hair*) седо́й (сед, -а́, -о); *s. foil*, сере́бряная фо́льга; *s. fox*, черно-бу́рая лиса́; *s. paper*, (*tin foil*) станио́ль *m.*; *s. plate*, столо́вое серебро́; *v.t.* серебри́ть *imp.*, вы́ ~ , по ~ *perf.*; (*mirror*) покрыва́ть *imp.*, покры́ть (-ро́ю, -ро́ешь) *perf.* амальга́мой рту́ти. **silversmith** *n.* сере́бряных дел ма́стер (*pl.* -а́). **silverware** *n.* столо́вое серебро́. **silvery** *adj.* серебри́стый; (*hair*) седо́й (сед, -а́, -о).
silviculture *n.* лесово́дство.
simian *adj.* обезья́ний.
similar *adj.* подо́бный (to, + *dat.*), схо́дный (-ден, -дна́, -дно) (to, с + *instr.*; in, по + *dat.*). **similarity** *n.* схо́дство; (*math.*) подо́бие. **similarly** *adv.* подо́бным о́бразом.
simile *n.* сравне́ние.
simmer *v.t.* кипяти́ть *imp.* на ме́дленном огне́; *v.i.* кипе́ть (-пи́т) *imp.* на ме́дленном огне́; *s. down*, успока́иваться *imp.*, успоко́иться *perf.*
simper *v.i.* жема́нно улыба́ться *imp.*, улыбну́ться *perf.*; *n.* жема́нная улы́бка.
simple *adj.* просто́й (прост, -а́, -о, про́сты́); *s.-hearted*, простоду́шный; *s.-minded*, тупова́тый. **simpleton** *n.* проста́к (-а́). **simplicity** *n.* простота́. **simplify** *v.t.* упроща́ть *imp.*, упрости́ть *perf.* **simply** *adv.* про́сто.
simulate *v.t.* притворя́ться *imp.*, притвори́ться *perf.* + *instr.*; (*conditions etc.*) модели́ровать *imp.*, *perf.* **simulated** *adj.* (*pearls etc.*) иску́сственный.
simultaneous *adj.* одновре́ме́нный (-нен, -нна).
sin *n.* грех (-а́); *v.i.* греши́ть *imp.*, со ~ *perf.*; *s. against*, наруша́ть *imp.*, нару́шить *perf.*
since *adv.* с тех пор; (*ago*) (тому́) наза́д; *prep.* с + *gen.*; *conj.* с тех пор как; (*reason*) так как.
sincere *adj.* и́скренний (-нен, -нна, -нно & -нне). **sincerely** *adv.* и́скренне; *yours s.*, и́скренне Ваш. **sincerity** *n.* и́скренность.
sine *n.* си́нус.
sinecure *n.* синеку́ра.
sine die *adv.* на неопределённый срок.
sine qua non *n.* обяза́тельное усло́вие.
sinew *n.* сухожи́лие. **sinewy** *adj.* жи́листый.
sinful *adj.* гре́шный (-шен, -шна́, -шно, гре́шны́). **sinfully** *adv.* грешно́.
sing *v.t.* & *i.* петь (пою́, поёшь) *imp.*, про ~ , с ~ *perf.*
singe *v.t.* пали́ть *imp.*, о ~ *perf.*; *n.* ожо́г.
singer *n.* певе́ц (-вца́), -ви́ца.

single *adj.* оди́н (одна́); (*unmarried*) холосто́й, незаму́жняя; (*solitary*) одино́кий; (*bed*) односпа́льный; *s. combat*, единобо́рство; *in s. file*, гусько́м; *s.-handed*, без посторо́нней по́мощи; *s.-minded*, целеустремлён-ный (-ён, -ённа); *s. room*, ко́мната на одного́; *s.-seater*, одноме́стный автомоби́ль *m.*; *n.* (*ticket*) биле́т в оди́н коне́ц; *pl.* (*tennis etc.*) одино́чная игра́; *v.t.*: *s. out*, выделя́ть *imp.*, вы́делить *perf.* **singlet** *n.* ма́йка.

singsong *adj.* моното́нный.

singular *n.* еди́нственное число́; *adj.* еди́нственный; (*unusual*) необыча́й-ный; (*strange*) стра́нный (-нен, -нна́, -нно). **singularity** *n.* (*peculiarity*) своео-бра́зие.

sinister *adj.* (*ominous*) злове́щий; (*evil*) злой (зол, зла).

sink *v.i.* опуска́ться *imp.*, опусти́ться (-ущу́сь, -у́стишься) *perf.*; (*subside*) оседа́ть *imp.*, осе́сть (ося́дет; осе́л) *perf.*; (*of ship*) тону́ть (-нет) *imp.*, по~ *perf.*; (*of sick person*) умира́ть *imp.*; *v.t.* (*ship*) топи́ть (-плю́, -пишь) *imp.*, по~ *perf.*; (*well*) рыть (ро́ю, ро́ешь) *imp.*, вы́~ *perf.*; (*shaft*) проходи́ть (-ожу́, -о́дишь) *imp.*, пройти́ (пройду́, -дёшь; прошёл, -шла́) *perf.*; *n.* (*also fig.*) клоа́ка; (*basin*) ра́ковина. **sinker** *n.* грузи́ло.

sinner *n.* гре́шник, -ица.

Sino- *in comb.* кита́йско-. **sinologist** *n.* китаеве́д, сино́лог. **sinology** *n.* китаеве́дение, синоло́гия.

sinuous *adj.* изви́листый.

sinus *n.* (ло́бная) па́зуха. **sinusitis** *n.* синуси́т.

sip *v.t.* пить (пью, пьёшь; пил, -а́, -о) *imp.*, ма́ленькими глотка́ми; *n.* ма́ленький глото́к (-тка́).

siphon *n.* сифо́н.

sir *n.* сэр.

sire *n.* (*as vocative*) сир; (*stallion etc.*) производи́тель *m.*; *v.t.* быть (*fut.* бу́ду, -дешь; был, -а́, -о; не́ был, -а́, -о) *imp.* производи́телем + *gen.*

siren *n.* сире́на.

sirloin *n.* филе́ *neut.indecl.*

sister *n.* сестра́ (*pl.* сёстры, -тёр, -трам); *s.-in-law*, (*husband's sister*) золо́вка; (*wife's sister*) своя́ченица; (*brother's wife*) неве́стка. **sisterhood** *n.* (*relig.*) сестри́нская о́бщи́на.

sit *v.i.* (*be sitting*) сиде́ть (сижу́, сиди́шь) *imp.*; (*s. down*) сади́ться *imp.*, сесть (ся́ду, -дешь; сел) *perf.*; (*parl., leg.*) заседа́ть *imp.*; (*pose*) пози́ровать *imp.* (for, для + *gen.*); *v.t.* уса́живать *imp.*, усади́ть (-ажу́, -а́дишь) *perf.*; (*examination*) сдава́ть (сдаю́, -аёшь) *imp.*; *s. back*, отки́дываться *imp.*, отки́нуться *perf.*; *s. down*, сади́ться *imp.*, сесть (ся́ду, -дешь; сел) *perf.*; *s.-down strike*, италья́нская забасто́вка; *s. on*, (*committee etc.*) быть (*fut.* бу́ду, -дешь; был, -а́, -о; не́ был, -а́, -о) *imp.* чле́ном + *gen.*; *s. up*, приподнима́ться *imp.*, приподня́ться (-ниму́сь, -ни́мешься; -ня́лся, -няла́сь) *perf.*; (*stay out of bed*) не ложи́ться *imp.* спать.

site *n.* ме́сто (*pl.* -та́), местоположе́ние; *building s.*, строи́тельная площа́дка.

sitter *n.* пози́рующий *sb.*; (*model*) нату́рщик, -ица; *s.-in*, приходя́щая ня́ня. **sitting** *n.* (*parl. etc.*) заседа́ние; (*for portrait*) сеа́нс; (*for meal*) сме́на; *adj.* сидя́чий, сидя́щий; *s.-room*, гости́ная *sb.*

situated *adj.*: *be s.*, находи́ться (-ожу́сь, -о́дишься) *imp.* **situation** *n.* местоположе́ние; (*circumstances*) положе́ние; (*work etc.*) ме́сто (*pl.* -та́).

six *adj., n.* шесть (-ти́, -тью́); (*collect.*; *6 pairs*) ше́стеро (-ры́х); (*cards*; *number 6*) шестёрка; (*time*) шесть (часо́в); (*age*) шесть лет. **sixteen** *adj., n.* шестна́дцать (-ти, -тью); (*age*) шестна́дцать лет. **sixteenth** *adj., n.* шестна́дцатый; (*date*) шестна́дцатое (число́). **sixth** *adj., n.* шесто́й; (*fraction*) шеста́я (часть (*pl.* -ти, -те́й)); (*date*) шесто́е (число́); (*mus.*) се́кста. **sixtieth** *adj., n.* шестидеся́тый. **sixty** *adj., n.* шестьдеся́т (-ти́десяти, -тью́десятью); (*age*) шестьдеся́т лет; *pl.* (*decade*) шестидеся́тые го́ды (-до́в) *m.pl.*

size[1] *n.* (*dimensions*; *of garment etc.*) разме́р; (*magnitude*) величина́; (*capacity*) объём; (*format*) форма́т; *v.t.*: *s. up*, оце́нивать *imp.*, оцени́ть (-ню́,

-нишь) *perf.* **sizeable** *adj.* поря́дочных разме́ров.
size[2] *n.* (*solution*) шли́хта; *v.t.* шлихтова́ть *imp.*
sizzle *v.i.* шипе́ть (-пи́т) *imp.*
skate[1] *n.* (*fish*) скат.
skate[2] *n.* (*ice-s.*) конёк (-нька́); (*roller-s.*) конёк (-нька́) на ро́ликах; *v.i.* ката́ться *imp.* на конька́х; *skating-rink*, като́к (-тка́).
skein *n.* мото́к (-тка́).
skeleton *n.* скеле́т, о́стов; *s. key*, отмы́чка.
sketch *n.* набро́сок (-ска), зарисо́вка; (*theat.*) скетч; *s.-book*, альбо́м для зарисо́вок; *s.-map*, кроки́ *neut.indecl.*; *v.t.* & *i.* де́лать *imp.*, с~ *perf.* набро́сок, -ски (+*gen.*). **sketchy** *adj.* отры́вочный; (*superficial*) пове́рхностный.
skew *adj.* косо́й; *n.* укло́м; *on the s.*, ко́со; *v.t.* перека́шивать *imp.*, перекоси́ть *perf.*; *v.i.* уклоня́ться *imp.*, уклони́ться (-ню́сь, -нишься) *perf.*
skewbald *adj.* пе́гий.
skewer *n.* ве́ртел (*pl.* -а́); *v.t.* наса́живать *imp.*, насади́ть (-ажу́, -а́дишь) *perf.* на ве́ртел.
ski *n.* лы́жа; *s.-jump*, трампли́н; *s.-run*, лыжня́; *v.i.* ходи́ть (хожу́, хо́дишь) *imp.* на лы́жах.
skid *n.* зано́с; *v.i.* заноси́ть (-ошу́, -о́сишь) *imp.*, занести́ (-сёт; -сло́) *perf.impers.*+*acc.*
skier *n.* лы́жник.
skiff *n.* я́лик, скиф.
skiing *n.* лы́жный спорт.
skilful *adj.* иску́сный, уме́лый. **skill** *n.* мастерство́, иску́сство, уме́ние. **skilled** *adj.* иску́сный; (*worker*) квалифици́рованный.
skim *v.t.* снима́ть *imp.*, снять (сниму́, -мешь; снял, -а́, -о) *perf.* (*cream*) сли́вки *pl.*; (*skin on milk*) пе́нки *pl.*; (*scum*) на́кипь, с+*gen.*; *v.i.* скользи́ть *imp.* (over, along, по+*dat.*); *s. through*, бе́гло просма́тривать *imp.*, просмотре́ть (-рю́, -ришь) *perf.*; *adj.*: *s. milk*, снято́е молоко́.
skimp *v.t.* & *i.* скупи́ться *imp.* (на+*acc.*). **skimpy** *adj.* ску́дный (-ден, -дна́, -дно).
skin *n.* ко́жа; (*hide*) шку́ра; (*of fruit etc.*) кожура́; (*on milk*) пе́нка; *s.-deep*, пове́рхностный; *s.-diver*, аквалангист; *s.-tight*, в обтя́жку; *v.t.* сдира́ть *imp.*, содра́ть (сдеру́, -рёшь; содра́л, -а́, -о) *perf.* ко́жу, шку́ру, с+*gen.*; снима́ть *imp.*, снять (сниму́, -мешь; снял, -а́, -о) *perf.* кожуру́ с+*gen.* **skinflint** *n.* скря́га *m.* & *f.* **skinny** *adj.* то́щий (тощ, -а́, -е).
skint *adj.* без гроша́ в карма́не.
skip[1] *v.i.* скака́ть (-ачу́, -а́чешь) *imp.*; (*with rope*) пры́гать *imp.* че́рез скака́лку; *v.t.* (*omit*) пропуска́ть *imp.*, пропусти́ть (-ущу́, -у́стишь) *perf.*; *skipping-rope*, скака́лка.
skip[2] *n.* (*container*) скип.
skipper *n.* (*naut.*) шки́пер (*pl.* -ы & -а́); (*naut., other senses*) капита́н.
skirmish *n.* схва́тка, сты́чка; *v.i.* сража́ться *imp.*
skirt *n.* ю́бка; *v.t.* обходи́ть (-ожу́, -о́дишь) *imp.*, обойти́ (обойду́, -дёшь; обошёл, -шла́) *perf.* стороно́й; *skirting-board*, пли́нтус.
skit *n.* скетч.
skittish *adj.* (*horse*) норови́стый; (*person*) игри́вый.
skittle *n.* ке́гля; *pl.* ке́гли *f.pl.*
skulk *v.i.* (*hide*) скрыва́ться *imp.*; (*creep*) кра́сться (краду́сь, -дёшься; кра́лся) *imp.*
skull *n.* че́реп (*pl.* -а́); *s.-cap*, ермо́лка.
skunk *n.* скунс, воню́чка.
sky *n.* не́бо (*pl.* -беса́). **sky-blue** *adj.* лазу́рный. **skyjack** *v.t.* похища́ть *imp.*, похи́тить (-и́щу, -и́тишь) *perf.* **skylark** *n.* жа́воронок (-нка). **skylight** *n.* окно́ (*pl.* о́кна, о́кон, о́кнам) в кры́ше. **skyline** *n.* горизо́нт. **skyscraper** *n.* небоскрёб. **skyway** *n.* авиатра́сса.
slab *n.* плита́ (*pl.* -ты); (*of cake etc.*) кусо́к (-ска́).
slack[1] *n.* (*coal-dust*) у́гольная пыль.
slack[2] *adj.* (*loose*) сла́бый (слаб, -а́, -о); (*sluggish*) вя́лый; (*inactive*) неакти́вный; (*negligent*) небре́жный; (*of rope*) ненатя́нутый; *n.* (*of rope*) слабина́; *pl.* повседне́вные брю́ки (-к) *pl.* **slacken** *v.t.* ослабля́ть *imp.*, осла́бить *perf.*; *v.t.* & *i.* (*slow down*) замедля́ть(ся) *imp.*, заме́длить(ся) *perf.*; *v.i.* ослабева́ть *imp.*, ослабе́ть *perf.* **slacker** *n.* безде́льник, ло́дырь *m.*

slag *n.* шлак.
slake *v.t.* (*thirst*) утоля́ть *imp.*, утоли́ть *perf.*; (*lime*) гаси́ть (гашу́, га́сишь) *imp.*, по~ *perf.*
slalom *n.* сла́лом.
slam *v.t.* & *i.* (*door*) захло́пывать(ся) *imp.*, захло́пнуть(ся) *perf.*; *n.* (*cards*) шлем.
slander *n.* клевета́; *v.t.* клевета́ть (-ещу́, -е́щешь) *imp.*, на~ *perf.* на+ *acc.* **slanderous** *adj.* клеветни́ческий.
slang *n.* сленг, жарго́н; *v.t.* брани́ть *imp.*, вы́~ *perf.* **slangy** *adj.* жарго́нный, вульга́рный.
slant *v.t.* & *i.* наклоня́ть(ся) *imp.*, наклони́ть(ся) (-ню́, -нит(ся)) *perf.*; *n.* укло́н. **slanting** *adj.* пока́тый, косо́й (кос, -а́, -о).
slap *v.t.* хло́пать *imp.*, хло́пнуть *perf.* + *acc.*, *instr.*, по+*dat.*; шлёпать *imp.*, шлёпнуть *perf.*; *n.* шлепо́к (-пка́); *adv.* пря́мо. **slapdash** *adj.* поспе́шный, небре́жный. **slapstick** *n.* балага́н.
slash *v.t.* руби́ть (-блю́, -бишь) *imp.*; (*prices etc.*) ре́зко снижа́ть *imp.*, сни́зить *perf.*; *n.* разре́з, про́рез.
slat *n.* пла́нка, филёнка.
slate[1] *n.* сла́нец (-нца); (*for roofing*) ши́фер (*no pl.*), ши́ферная пли́тка; (*for writing*) гри́фельная доска́ (*acc.* -ску; *pl.* -ски, -со́к, -ска́м); *s.-pencil*, гри́фель *m.*; *v.t.* (*roof*) крыть (кро́ю, -о́ешь) *imp.*, по~ *perf.* ши́ферными пли́тками.
slate[2] *v.t.* (*criticize*) раскритикова́ть *perf.*
slattern *n.* неря́ха. **slatternly** *adj.* неря́шливый.
slaughter *n.* (*of animals*) убо́й; (*massacre*) резня́; *v.t.* ре́зать (ре́жу, -жешь) *imp.*, за~ *perf.*; (*people*) убива́ть *imp.*, уби́ть (убью́, -ьёшь) *perf.* **slaughter-house** *n.* бо́йня (*gen.pl.* бо́ен).
Slav *n.* славяни́н (*pl.* -я́не, -я́н), -я́нка; *adj.* славя́нский.
slave *n.* раб (-а́), рабы́ня (*gen.pl.* -нь); *s.-trade*, работорго́вля; *v.i.* рабо́тать *imp.* как раб.
slaver *v.i.* пуска́ть *imp.*, пусти́ть (пущу́, пу́стишь) *perf.* слю́ни; *n.* слю́ни (-ней) *pl.*
slavery *n.* ра́бство.
Slavic *adj.* славя́нский.
slavish *adj.* ра́бский.
Slavonic *adj.* славя́нский.
slay *v.t.* убива́ть *imp.*, уби́ть (убью́, -ьёшь) *perf.*
sleazy *adj.* (*person*) неря́шливый.
sledge *n.* са́ни (-не́й) *pl.*
sledge-hammer *n.* кува́лда.
sleek *adj.* гла́дкий (-док, -дка́, -дко).
sleep *n.* сон (сна); *go to s.*, засыпа́ть *imp.*, засну́ть *perf.*; *v.i.* спать (сплю, спишь; спал, -а́, -о) *imp.*; (*spend the night*) ночева́ть (-чу́ю, -чу́ешь) *imp.*, пере~ *perf.*; *s.-walker*, луна́тик. **sleeper** *n.* спя́щий *sb.*; (*rly.*, *beam*) шпа́ла; (*sleeping-car*) спа́льный ваго́н. **sleeping** *adj.* спя́щий, спа́льный; *s.-bag*, спа́льный мешо́к (-шка́); *s.-car*(*riage*), спа́льный ваго́н; *s. partner*, пасси́вный партнёр; *s.-pill*, снотво́рная табле́тка; *s. sickness*, со́нная боле́знь. **sleepless** *adj.* бессо́нный (-нен, -нна). **sleepy** *adj.* со́нный (-нен, -нна).
sleet *n.* мо́крый снег (-а(у), *loc.* -у́).
sleeve *n.* рука́в (-а́; *pl.* -а́); (*tech.*) му́фта; (*of record*) конве́рт.
sleigh *n.* са́ни (-не́й) *pl.*; *s.-bell*, бубе́нчик.
sleight-of-hand *n.* ло́вкость рук.
slender *adj.* (*slim*) то́нкий (-нок, -нка́, -нко, то́нки́); (*meagre*) ску́дный (-ден, -дна́, -дно); (*of hope etc.*) сла́бый (слаб, -а́, -о).
sleuth *n.* сы́щик.
slew *v.t.* & *i.* бы́стро повора́чивать(ся) *imp.*, поверну́ть(ся) *perf.*
slice *n.* ло́мтик, ломо́ть (-мтя́) *m.*; (*share*) часть (*pl.* -ти, -те́й); *v.t.* (*s. up*) нареза́ть *imp.*, наре́зать (-е́жу, -е́жешь) *perf.*
slick *adj.* (*dextrous*) ло́вкий (-вок, -вка́, -вко, ло́вки́); (*crafty*) хи́трый (-тёр, -тра́, хи́тро́); (*sleek*) гла́дкий (-док, -дка́, -дко); *n.* нефтяна́я плёнка.
slide *v.i.* скользи́ть *imp.*; (*on ice*) кати́ться (качу́сь, ка́тишься) *imp.*, по~ *perf.* по льду; *v.t.* (*drawer etc.*) задвига́ть *imp.*, задви́нуть *perf.* (into, в + *acc.*); *n.* (*on ice*) ледяна́я гора́ (*acc.* -ру; *pl.* -ры, -р, -ра́м), ледяна́я

доро́жка; (*children's s.*) де́тская го́рка; (*chute*) жёлоб (*pl.* -а́); (*microscope s.*) предме́тное стекло́ (*pl.* стёкла, -кол, -клам); (*phot.*) диапозити́в, слайд; *s.-rule*, логарифми́ческая лине́йка; *s.-valve*, золотни́к (-а́). **sliding** *adj.* скользя́щий; (*door*) задвижно́й; *s. seat*, слайд.

slight[1] *adj.* (*slender*) то́нкий (-нок, -нка́, -нко, то́нки́); (*inconsiderable*) незначи́тельный; (*light*) лёгкий (-гок, -гка́, -гко́, лёгки́); *not the slightest*, ни мале́йшего, -шей (*gen.*); *not in the slightest*, ничу́ть.

slight[2] *v.t.* пренебрега́ть *imp.*, пренебре́чь (-егу́, -ежёшь; -ёг, -егла́) *perf.* + *instr.*; *n.* пренебреже́ние, неуваже́ние.

slightly *adv.* слегка́, немно́го.

slim *adj.* то́нкий (-нок, -нка́, -нко, то́нки́); (*chance etc.*) сла́бый (слаб, -а́, -о); *v.i.* худе́ть *imp.*, по~ *perf.*

slime *n.* слизь. **slimy** *adj.* сли́зистый; (*person*) еле́йный.

sling *v.t.* (*throw*) броса́ть *imp.*, бро́сить *perf.*; швыря́ть *imp.*, швырну́ть *perf.*; (*suspend*) подве́шивать *imp.*, подве́сить *perf.*; *n.* (*for throwing*) праща́; (*bandage*) пе́ревязь; (*rope*) строп.

slink *v.i.* кра́сться (-аду́сь, -адёшься; -а́лся) *imp.* **slinky** *adj.* (*garment*) облега́ющий.

slip *n.* (*slipping*) скольже́ние; (*mistake*) оши́бка; (*garment*) комбина́ция; (*pillowcase*) на́волочка; (*building s.*) ста́пель (*pl.* -ля́ & -ли); (*landing*) э́ллинг; (*of paper etc.*) поло́ска; (*print.*) гра́нка; (*cutting*) черено́к (-нка́); (*glaze*) поливна́я глазу́рь; *s. of the pen*, опи́ска; *s. of the tongue*, обмо́лвка; *give the s.*, ускользну́ть *perf.* от + *gen.*; *v.i.* скользи́ть *imp.*, скользну́ть *perf.*; поскользну́ться *perf.*; (*from hands etc.*) выска́льзывать *imp.*, вы́скользнуть *perf.*; *v.t.* (*let go*) спуска́ть *imp.*, спусти́ть (-ущу́, -у́стишь) *perf.*; (*insert*) сова́ть (сую́, суёшь) *imp.*, су́нуть *perf.*; *s. off*, (*depart, v.i.*) ускольза́ть *imp.*, ускользну́ть *perf.*; (*clothes, v.t.*) сброса́ть *imp.*, сбро́сить *perf.*; *s. on*, (*clothes*) наки́дывать *imp.*, наки́нуть *perf.*; *s. up*, (*make mistake*) ошиба́ться *imp.*, ошиби́ться (-бу́сь, -бёшься; -бся) *perf.* **slipper** *n.* (house, дома́шняя) ту́фля (*gen. pl.* -фель); та́почка (*coll.*). **slippery** *adj.* ско́льзкий (-зок, -зка́, -зко); (*fig., shifty*) увёртливый. **slipshod** *adj.* неря́шливый, небре́жный. **slipway** *n.* (*for building*) ста́пель (*pl.* -ля́ & -ли); (*for landing*) э́ллинг.

slit *v.t.* разреза́ть *imp.*, разре́зать (-е́жу, -е́жешь) *perf.*; *n.* щель (*pl.* -ли, -ле́й), разре́з.

slither *v.i.* скользи́ть *imp.*

sliver *n.* ще́пка.

slob *n.* неря́ха *m.* & *f.*

slobber *v.i.* пуска́ть *imp.*, пусти́ть (пущу́, пу́стишь) *perf.* слю́ни; *n.* слю́ни (-ней) *pl.*

sloe *n.* тёрн.

slog *v.t.* (*hit*) си́льно ударя́ть *imp.*, уда́рить *perf.*; (*work*) упо́рно рабо́тать *imp.*

slogan *n.* ло́зунг.

sloop *n.* шлюп.

slop *n.*: *pl.* (*water*) помо́и (-о́ев) *pl.*; (*food*) жи́дкая пи́ща; *s.-basin*, полоска́тельница; *s.-pail*, помо́йное ведро́ (*pl.* вёдра, -дер, -драм); *v.t.* & *i.* выплёскивать(ся) *imp.*, вы́плескать(ся) (-ещу, -ещет(ся)) *perf.*

slope *n.* накло́н, склон; *v.i.* име́ть *imp.* накло́н. **sloping** *adj.* накло́нный (-нен, -нна), пока́тый.

sloppy *adj.* (*ground*) мо́крый (мокр, -а́, -о); (*food*) жи́дкий (-док, -дка́, -дко); (*work*) неря́шливый; (*sentimental*) сентимента́льный.

slot *n.* щель (*pl.* -ли, -ле́й), паз (*loc.* -у́; *pl.* -ы́); *s.-machine*, автома́т.

sloth *n.* лень; (*zool.*) лени́вец (-вца). **slothful** *adj.* лени́вый.

slouch *v.i.* (*stoop*) суту́литься *imp.*

slough *v.t.* сбра́сывать *imp.*, сбро́сить *perf.*

sloven *n.* неря́ха *m.* & *f.* **slovenly** *adj.* неря́шливый.

slow *adj.* ме́дленный (-ен(ен), -енна); (*tardy*) медли́тельный; (*stupid*) тупо́й (туп, -а́, -о, ту́пы́); (*business*) вя́лый; *be slow*, (*clock*) отстава́ть (-таёт) *imp.*, отста́ть (-а́нет) *perf.*; *adv.* ме́дленно; *v.t.* & *i.* (*s. down, up*) замедля́ть(ся)

imp., замéдлить(ся) *perf.* **slowcoach** *n.* *n.* копýн (-á), ~ья.
slow-worm *n.* беретéница, медяни́ца.
sludge *n.* (*mud*) грязь (*loc.* -зи́); (*sediment*) отстóй.
slug *n.* (*zool.*) слизня́к (-á); (*bullet*) пýля; (*piece of metal*) кусóк (-ска́) метáлла.
sluggard *n.* лентя́й. **sluggish** *adj.* (*inert*) инéртный; (*torpid*) вя́лый.
sluice *n.* шлюз; *v.t.* заливáть *imp.*, зали́ть (-лью́, -льёшь; зáли́л, -á, -о) *perf.*; *v.i.* ли́ться (льётся; ли́лся, лилáсь, ли́лóсь) *imp.*
slum *n.* трущóба.
slumber *n.* сон (сна); *v.i.* спать (сплю, спишь; спал, -á, -о) *imp.*
slump *n.* рéзкое падéние (цен, спрóса, интерéса); *v.i.* рéзко пáдать *imp.*, (у)пáсть (-адёт; -áл) *perf.*; (*of person*) тяжелó опускáться *imp.*, опусти́ться (-ущýсь, -ýстишься) *perf.*
slur *v.t.* (*speak indistinctly*) невня́тно произноси́ть (-ошý, -óсишь) *imp.*, произнести́ (-есý, -есёшь; -ёс, -еслá) *perf.*; *s. over*, обходи́ть (-ожý, -óдишь) *imp.*, обойти́ (обойдý, -дёшь; обошёл, -шлá) *perf.* молчáнием; *n.* (*stigma*) пятнó (*pl.* -тна, -тен, -тнам); (*mus.*) ли́га.
slush *n.* сля́коть. **slushy** *adj.* сля́котный; (*fig.*) сентиментáльный.
slut *n.* неря́ха. **sluttish** *adj.* неря́шливый.
sly *adj.* хи́трый (-тёр, -трá, хи́трó), лукáвый; *on the s.*, тайкóм.
smack[1] *n.* (*flavour*) при́вкус; *v.i.*: *s. of*, пáхнуть *imp.* + *instr.*
smack[2] *n.* (*slap*) шлепóк (-пкá); *v.t.* шлёпать *imp.*, шлёпнуть *perf.*
smack[3] *n.* (*boat*) смэк.
small *adj.* мáленький, небольшóй, мáлый (мал, -á); (*of agent*, *particles*; *petty*) мéлкий (-лок, -лкá, -лко); (*unimportant*) незначи́тельный; *s. capitals*, капитéль; *s. change*, мéлочь; *s. fry*, мéлкая сóшка; *s.-minded*, мéлкий (-лок, -лкá, -лко); *s.-scale*, мелкомасштáбный; *s. talk*, свéтская беcéда; *n.*: *s. of the back*, поясни́ца; *pl.* мéлочь.
smart[1] *v.i.* сáднить *imp. impers.*
smart[2] *adj.* (*brisk*) бы́стрый (быстр, -á, -о, бы́стры́); (*cunning*) лóвкий (-вок, -вкá, -вко, лóвки́); (*sharp*) смекáлистый (*coll.*); (*in appearance*) элегáнтный.
smash *v.t.* & *i.* разбивáть(ся) *imp.*, разби́ть(ся) (разобью́, -ьёт(ся)) *perf.*; *v.i.* (*collide*) стáлкиваться *imp.*, столкнýться *perf.* (into, с + *instr.*); *n.* (*disaster*) катастрóфа; (*collision*) столкновéние; (*blow*) тяжёлый удáр.
smattering *n.* повéрхностное знáние.
smear *v.t.* смáзывать *imp.*, смáзать (-áжу, -áжешь) *perf.*; (*dirty*) пáчкать *imp.*, за~, ис~ *perf.*; (*discredit*) порóчить *imp.*, о~ *perf.*; *n.* (*slander*) клеветá; (*med.*) мазóк (-зкá).
smell *n.* (*sense*) обоня́ние; (*odour*) зáпах; *v.t.* чýвствовать *imp.* зáпах + *gen.*; ню́хать *imp.*, по~ *perf.*; *v.i.*: *s. of*, пáхнуть (пáх(нул), пáхла) *imp.* + *instr.*; *s. out*, (*also fig.*) разню́хивать *imp.*, разню́хать *perf.*; *smelling-salts*, ню́хательная соль. **smelly** *adj.* воню́чий.
smelt[1] *v.t.* (*ore*) плáвить *imp.*; (*metal*) выплавля́ть *imp.*, вы́плавить *perf.*
smelt[2] *n.* (*fish*) кóрюшка.
smile *v.i.* улыбáться *imp.*, улыбнýться *perf.*; *n.* улы́бка.
smirk *v.i.* ухмыля́ться *imp.*, ухмыльнýться *perf.*; *n.* ухмы́лка.
smith *n.* кузнéц (-á).
smithereens *n.*: (*in*)*to s.*, вдрéбезги.
smithy *n.* кýзница.
smock *n.* блýза.
smog *n.* тумáн с ды́мом.
smoke *n.* дым (-а(у), *loc.* -ý); (*cigarette etc.*) кýрево; *s.-bomb*, дымовáя бóмба; *s.-screen*, дымовáя завéса; *v.i.* дыми́ть *imp.*, на~ *perf.*; (*of lamp*) копти́ть *imp.*, на~ *perf.*; *v.t.* & *i.* (*cigarette etc.*) кури́ть (-рю́, -ришь) *imp.*, по~ *perf.*; *v.t.* (*cure*; *colour*) копти́ть *imp.*, за~ *perf.*; *s. out*, выкýривать *imp.*, вы́курить *perf.* **smokeless** *adj.* безды́мный. **smoker** *n.* кури́льщик, -ица, куря́щий *sb.* **smoking** *n.*: *s.-compartment*, купé *neut. indecl.* для куря́щих; *s.-room*, кури́тельная *sb.* **smoky** *adj.* ды́мный; (*room*) прокýренный; (*colour*) ды́мчатый.
smooth *adj.* (*surface etc.*) глáдкий (-док, -дкá, -дко); (*movement etc.*) плáвный; (*flattering*) льсти́вый; *v.t.*

приглáживать *imp.*, приглáдить *perf.*; *s. over*, сглáживать *imp.*, сглáдить *perf.*

smother *v.t.* (*stifle, also fig.*) души́ть (-шу́, -шишь) *imp.*, за~ *perf.*; (*cover*) покрывáть *imp.*, покры́ть (-рóю, -рóешь) *perf.*

smoulder *v.i.* тлеть *imp.*

smudge *v.t.* пáчкать *imp.*, за~, ис~ *perf.*

smug *adj.* самодовóльный.

smuggle *v.t.* провози́ть (-ожу́, -óзишь) *imp.*, провезти́ (-езу́, -езёшь; -ёз, -езлá) *perf.* контрабáндой; (*convey secretly*) тáйно проноси́ть (-ошу́, -óсишь) *imp.*, пронести́ (-есу́, -есёшь; -ёс, -еслá) *perf.* **smuggler** *n.* контрабанди́ст.

smut *n.* части́ца сáжи, кóпоти; (*indecency*) непристóйность. **smutty** *adj.* гря́зный (-зен, -знá, -зно); непристóйный.

snack *n.* закýска; *s.-bar*, закýсочная *sb.*, буфéт.

snaffle *n.* трéнзель (*pl.* -ли & -ля́) *m.*; *v.t.* (*steal*) стащи́ть (-щу́, -щишь) *perf.*

snag *n.* (*branch*) сучóк (-чкá); (*in river*) коря́га; (*fig.*) загвóздка; *v.t.* зацепля́ть *imp.*, зацепи́ть (-плю́, -пишь) *perf.*

snail *n.* ули́тка; *at s.'s pace*, черепáхой.

snake *n.* змея́ (*pl.* -éи); *s.-charmer*, заклинáтель *m.*, ~ница, змей; *s.-skin*, змеи́ная кóжа. **snaky** *adj.* змеи́ный; (*winding*) изви́листый.

snap *v.i.* (*of dog etc.*) огрызáться *imp.*, огрызну́ться *perf.* (at, на+*acc.*); *v.t.* & *i.* говори́ть *imp.* серди́то, раздражённо; (*break*) обрывáть(ся) *imp.*, оборвáть(ся) (-ву́, -вёт(ся); -вáл(ся), -валá(сь), -вáло/-валóсь) *perf.*; *v.t.* (*make sound*) щёлкать *imp.*, щёлкнуть *perf.*+*instr.*; *s. up*, (*buy*) расхвáтывать *imp.*, расхватáть *perf.*; *n.* (*sound*) щёлк; (*fastener*) кнóпка, застёжка; (*cards*) дéтская кáрточная игрá; *cold s.*, рéзкое внезáпное похолодáние; *adj.* скоропали́тельный; (*parl.*) внеочереднóй. **snapdragon** *n.* льви́ный зев. **snap-fastener** *n.* кнóпка. **snapshot** *n.* моментáльный сни́мок (-мка).

snare *n.* ловýшка; *v.t.* лови́ть (-влю́, -вишь) *imp.*, поймáть *perf.* в ловýшку.

snarl *v.i.* рычáть (-чи́т) *imp.*; (*person*) ворчáть (-чу́, -чи́шь) *imp.*; *n.* рычáние; ворчáние.

snatch *v.t.* хватáть *imp.*, (с)хвати́ть (-ачу́, -áтишь) *perf.*; (*opportunity etc.*) ухвати́ться (-ачу́сь, -áтишься) *perf.* за+*acc.*; *v.i.*: *s. at*, хватáться *imp.*, (с)хвати́ться (-ачу́сь, -áтишься) *perf.* за+*acc.*; *n.* попы́тка схвати́ть; (*fragment*) обры́вок (-вка); *in, by, snatches*, уры́вками.

sneak *v.i.* (*slink*) крáсться (-аду́сь, -адёшься; -áлся) *imp.*; (*tell tales*) я́бедничать *imp.*, на~ *perf.* (*coll.*); *v.t.* (*steal*) стащи́ть (-щу́, -щишь) *perf.*; *n.* я́бедник, -ица (*coll.*); *s.-thief*, вори́шка *m.* **sneaking** *adj.* (*hidden*) тáйный; (*of feeling etc.*) неосóзнанный.

sneer *v.i.* (*smile*) насмéшливо улыбáться *imp.*; (*speak*) насмéшливо говори́ть *imp.*; *n.* насмéшливая улы́бка.

sneeze *v.i.* чихáть *imp.*, чихну́ть *perf.*; *n.* чихáнье.

snick *n.* зару́бка.

snide *adj.* (*sneering*) насмéшливый.

sniff *v.i.* шмы́гать *imp.*, шмыгну́ть *perf.* нóсом; *v.t.* ню́хать *imp.*, по~ *perf.*

snigger *v.i.* хихи́кать *imp.*, хихи́кнуть *perf.*; *n.* хихи́канье.

snip *v.t.* рéзать (рéжу, -жешь) *imp.* (нóжницами); *s. off*, срезáть *imp.*, срéзать (-éжу, -éжешь) *perf.*; *n.* (*purchase*) вы́годная покýпка.

snipe *n.* (*bird*) бекáс; *v.i.* стреля́ть *imp.* из укры́тия (at, в+*acc.*). **sniper** *n.* снáйпер.

snippet *n.* отрéзок (-зка); *pl.* (*of knowledge etc.*) обры́вки *m.pl.*

snivel *v.i.* (*run at nose*) распускáть *imp.*, распусти́ть (-ущу́, -ýстишь) *perf.* сóпли; (*whimper*) хны́кать (хны́чу, -чешь & хны́каю, -аешь) *imp.*

snob *n.* сноб. **snobbery** *n.* сноби́зм. **snobbish** *adj.* сноби́стский.

snook *n.*: *cock a s. at*, показáть (-ажу́, -áжешь) *perf.* дли́нный нос+*dat.*

snoop *v.i.* совáть (сую́, суёшь) *imp.* нос в чужи́е делá; *s. about*, шпиóнить *imp.*

snooty *adj.* чвáнный (-нен, -нна).

snooze *v.i.* вздремну́ть *perf.*; *n.* коро́ткий сон (сна).
snore *v.i.* храпе́ть (-плю́, -пи́шь) *imp.*; *n.* храп.
snorkel *n.* шно́ркель *m.*; (*diver's*) тру́бка (аквала́нга).
snort *v.i.* фы́ркать *imp.*, фы́ркнуть *perf.*; *n.* фы́рканье.
snot *n.* со́пли (-ле́й) *pl.*
snout *n.* ры́ло, мо́рда.
snow *n.* снег (-а(у), *loc.* -у́; *pl.* -а́); *s.-blindness*, сне́жная слепота́; *s.-boot*, бот (*gen.pl.* -т & -тов); *s.-bound*, заснежённый (-ён, -ена́); *s.-drift*, сугро́б; *s.-plough*, снегоочисти́тель *m.*; *s.-shoes*, снегосту́пы (-пов) *pl.*; *s.-white*, белосне́жный; *v.i.*: *it is snowing*, *it snows*, идёт (*past* шёл) снег; *snowed up*, *in*, занесённый (-ён, -ена́) сне́гом. **snowball** *n.* снежо́к (-жка́). **snowdrop** *n.* подсне́жник. **snowflake** *n.* снежи́нка. **snowman** *n.* сне́жная ба́ба. **snowstorm** *n.* мете́ль, вью́га. **snowy** *adj.* сне́жный; (*snow-white*) белосне́жный.
snub[1] *v.t.* относи́ться (-ошу́сь, -о́сишься) *imp.*, отнести́сь (-есу́сь, -есёшься; -ёсся, -есла́сь) *perf.* пренебрежи́тельно к + *dat.*; (*humiliate*) унижа́ть *imp.*, уни́зить *perf.*
snub[2] *adj.* вздёрнутый; *s.-nosed*, курно́сый.
snuff[1] *n.* (*tobacco*) ню́хательный таба́к (-а́(у́)); *take s.*, ню́хать *imp.*, по~ *perf.* таба́к; *s.-box*, табаке́рка.
snuff[2] *n.* (*on candle*) нага́р на свече́; *v.t.* снима́ть *imp.*, снять (сниму́, -мешь; снял, -а́, -о) *perf.* нага́р с + *gen.*; *s. out* (*candle*) туши́ть (-шу́, -шишь) *imp.*, по~ *perf.*; (*hopes etc.*) разруша́ть *imp.*, разру́шить *perf.*
snuffle *v.i.* (*noisily*) сопе́ть (-плю́, -пи́шь) *imp.*
snug *adj.* ую́тный, удо́бный.
snuggle *v.i.*: *s. up to*, прижима́ться *imp.*, прижа́ться (-жму́сь, -жмёшься) *perf.* к + *dat.*
so *adv.* так; (*in this way*) так, таки́м о́бразом; (*thus, at beginning of sentence*) ита́к; (*also*) та́кже, то́же; *conj.* (*therefore*) поэ́тому; *and so on*, и так да́лее; *if so*, в тако́м слу́чае; *or so*, или о́коло э́того; *so-and-so*, тако́й-то; *so . . . as*, так(о́й)...как; *so as to*, с тем что́бы; *so be it*, быть по сему́; *so-called*, так называ́емый; *so far*, до сих пор; (*in*) *so far as*, насто́лько, поско́льку; *so long!* пока́! *so long as*, поско́льку; *so much*, насто́лько; *so much so*, до тако́й сте́пени; *so much the better*, тем лу́чше; *so-so*, так себе́; *so that*, что́бы; *so . . . that*, так...что; *so to say, speak*, так сказа́ть; *so what?* ну и что?
soak *v.t.* & *i.* пропи́тывать(ся) *imp.*, пропита́ть(ся) *perf.* (in, + *instr.*); *v.t.* мочи́ть (-чу́, -чишь) *imp.*, на~ *perf.*; (*drench*) прома́чивать *imp.*, промочи́ть (-чу́, -чишь) *perf.*; *s. up*, впи́тывать *imp.*, впита́ть *perf.*; *v.i.*: *s. through*, проса́чиваться *imp.*, просочи́ться *perf.*; *get soaked*, промока́ть *imp.*, промо́кнуть (-к) *perf.*; *n.* (*drinker*) пья́ница *m.* & *f.*
soap *n.* мы́ло (*pl.* -ла́); *attrib.* мы́льный; *v.t.* мы́лить *imp.*, на~ *perf.*; *s.-boiler*, мылова́р; *s.-box*, (*stand*) импровизи́рованная трибу́на; *s.-bubble*, мы́льный пузы́рь (-ря́) *m.*; *s.-dish*, мы́льница; *s.-flakes*, мы́льные хло́пья (-ьев) *pl.*; *s. powder*, стира́льный порошо́к (-шка́); *s.-works*, мылова́ренный заво́д. **soapy** *adj.* мы́льный.
soar *v.i.* пари́ть *imp.*; (*aeron.*) плани́ровать *imp.*, с~ *perf.*; (*building etc.*) вы́ситься *imp.*; (*prices*) подска́кивать *imp.*, подскочи́ть (-ит) *perf.*
sob *v.i.* рыда́ть *imp.*; *n.* рыда́ние.
sober *adj.* тре́звый (трезв, -а́, -о); *v.t.* & *i.*: *s. up*, (*also fig.*) отрезвля́ть(ся) *imp.*, отрезви́ть(ся) *perf.*; *v.i.*: *s. up*, трезве́ть *imp.*, о~ *perf.* **sobriety** *n.* тре́звость.
sobriquet *n.* про́звище.
soccer *n.* футбо́л.
sociable *adj.* общи́тельный; (*meeting etc.*) дру́жеский. **social** *adj.* обще́ственный, социа́льный; *S. Democrat*, социа́л-демокра́т; *s. sciences*, обще́ственные нау́ки *f.pl.*; *s. security*, социа́льное обеспе́чение; *n.* вечери́нка. **socialism** *n.* социали́зм. **socialist** *n.* социали́ст; *adj.* социалисти́ческий.

socialize *v.t.* социализи́ровать *imp.*, *perf.* **society** *n.* о́бщество; (*beau monde*) свет; *attrib.* све́тский. **sociolinguistics** *n.* социолингви́стика. **sociological** *adj.* социологи́ческий. **sociologist** *n.* социо́лог. **sociology** *n.* социоло́гия.

sock[1] *n.* носо́к (-ска́).

sock[2] *v.t.* тузи́ть *imp.*, от ~ *perf.*

socket *n.* впа́дина; (*electr.*) ште́псель (*pl.* -ля́) *m.*; (*for bulb*) патро́н; (*tech.*) гнездо́ (*pl.* -ёзда), растру́б.

sod *n.* (*turf*) дёрн; (*piece of turf*) дерни́на.

soda *n.* со́да; *s.-water*, со́довая вода́ (*acc.* -ду).

sodden *adj.* промо́кший, пропи́танный (-ан) вла́гой.

sodium *n.* на́трий.

sodomite *n.* педера́ст. **sodomy** *n.* педера́стия.

sofa *n.* дива́н, софа́ (*pl.* -фы).

soft *adj.* мя́гкий (-гок, -гка́, -гко); (*sound*) ти́хий (тих, -а́, -о); (*colour*) нея́ркий (-рок, -рка́, -рко); (*malleable*) ко́вкий (-вок, -вка́, -вко); (*tender*) не́жный (-жен, -жна́, -жно, не́жны́); *s.-boiled*, всмя́тку; *s. drink*, безалкого́льный напи́ток (-тка); *s. fruit*, я́года; *s. goods*, тексти́ль *m.*; *s.-headed*, придурькова́тый; *s.-hearted*, мягкосерде́чный; *s.-pedal*, преуменьша́ть *imp.*, преуме́ньшить *perf.* (значе́ние + *gen.*). **soften** *v.t.* & *i.* смягча́ть(ся) *imp.*, смягчи́ть(ся) *perf.* **softness** *n.* мя́гкость. **software** *n.* програ́ммное обеспе́чение. **softwood** *n.* хво́йная древеси́на.

soggy *adj.* пропи́танный (-ан) водо́й; (*ground*) боло́тистый.

soil[1] *n.* по́чва; *s. science*, почвове́дение.

soil[2] *v.t.* па́чкать *imp.*, за ~, ис ~ *perf.*

sojourn *n.* вре́менное пребыва́ние; *v.i.* вре́менно жить (живу́, -вёшь; жил, -а́, -о *imp.*

solace *n.* утеше́ние; *v.t.* утеша́ть *imp.*, уте́шить *perf.*

solar *adj.* со́лнечный.

solarium *n.* соля́рий.

solder *n.* припо́й; *v.t.* пая́ть *imp.*; спа́ивать *imp.*, спая́ть *perf.* **soldering-iron** *n.* пая́льник.

soldier *n.* солда́т (*gen.pl.* -т), вое́нный *sb.*; (*toy s.*) солда́тик; *s. of fortune*, кондотье́р. **soldierly** *adj.* во́инский.

sole[1] *n.* (*of foot, shoe*) подо́шва; (*of foot*) ступня́; (*of shoe*) подмётка; *v.t.* ста́вить *imp.*, по ~ *perf.* подмётку к + *dat.*, на + *acc.*

sole[2] *n.* (*fish*) морско́й язы́к (-а́).

sole[3] *adj.* еди́нственный; (*exclusive*) исключи́тельный.

solecism *n.* солеци́зм.

solemn *adj.* торже́ственный (-ен, -енна). **solemnity** *n.* торже́ственность; (*celebration*) торжество́.

solenoid *n.* солено́ид.

solicit *v.t.* проси́ть (-ошу́, -о́сишь) *imp.*, по ~ *perf.* + *acc.*, *gen.*, о + *prep.*; выпра́шивать *imp.*; (*of prostitute*) пристава́ть (-таю́, -таёшь) *imp.*, приста́ть (-а́ну, -а́нешь) *perf.* к + *dat.* (*v. abs.*, к мужчи́нам). **solicitor** *n.* соли́ситор. **solicitous** *adj.* забо́тливый. **solicitude** *n.* забо́тливость.

solid *adj.* (*not liquid*) твёрдый (твёрд, -а́, -о); (*not hollow*; *continuous*) сплошно́й; (*of time*) без переры́ва; (*firm*) про́чный (-чен, -чна́, -чно, про́чны́), пло́тный (-тен, -тна́, -тно, пло́тны́); (*pure*) чи́стый (чист, -а́, -о, чи́сты́); (*of reason etc.*) убеди́тельный; *s.-state physics*, фи́зика твёрдого те́ла; *n.* твёрдое те́ло (*pl.* -ла́); *pl.* твёрдая пи́ща. **solidarity** *n.* солида́рность. **solidify** *v.t.* & *i.* де́лать(ся) *imp.*, с ~ *perf.* твёрдым; *v.i.* затвердева́ть *imp.*, затверде́ть *perf.* **solidity** *n.* твёрдость; про́чность.

solidus *n.* дели́тельная черта́.

soliloquy *n.* моноло́г.

solipsism *n.* солипси́зм.

solitaire *n.* (*gem*) солите́р.

solitary *adj.* одино́кий, уединённый (-ён, -ённа); *s. confinement*, одино́чное заключе́ние. **solitude** *n.* одино́чество, уедине́ние.

solo *n.* со́ло *neut.indecl.*; (*aeron.*) самостоя́тельный полёт; *adj.* со́льный; *adv.* со́ло. **soloist** *n.* соли́ст, ~ка.

solstice *n.* солнцестоя́ние.

soluble *adj.* раствори́мый. **solution** *n.* раство́р; (*action*) растворе́ние; (*of puzzle etc.*) реше́ние, разреше́ние.

solve *v.t.* решáть *imp.*, решúть *perf.*
solvency *n.* платёжеспосóбность. **solvent** *adj.* растворя́ющий; (*financially*) платёжеспосóбный; *n.* раствори́тель *m.*
sombre *adj.* мрáчный (-чен, -чнá, -чно).
sombrero *n.* сомбрéро *neut.indecl.*
some *adj.*, *pron.* (*any*) какóй-нибудь; (*a certain*) какóй-то; (*a certain amount or number of*) нéкоторый, *or often expressed by noun in* (*partitive*) *gen.*; (*several*) нéсколько + *gen.*; (*approximately*) óколо + *gen.*; *often expressed by inversion of noun and numeral*; (*s. people, things*) нéкоторые *pl.*; *s. day*, когдá-нибудь; *s. more*, ещё; *s. other day*, другóй раз; *s.... others*, одни́... други́е; *to s. extent*, до извéстной стéпени. **somebody, someone** *n.*, *pron.* (*definite*) ктó-то; (*indefinite*) ктó-нибудь; (*important person*) вáжная персóна. **somehow** *adv.* кáк-то; кáк-нибудь; (*for some reason*) почемý-то; *s. or other*, так и́ли инáче.
somersault *n.* прыжóк (-жкá) кувыркóм; *v.i.* кувыркáться *imp.*, кувыр(к)нýться *perf.*
something *n.*, *pron.* (*definite*) чтó-то; (*indefinite*) чтó-нибудь; *s. like*, (*approximately*) приблизи́тельно; (*a thing like*) чтó-то врóде + *gen.* **sometime** *adv.* нéкогда; *adj.* бы́вший. **sometimes** *adv.* иногдá. **somewhat** *adv.* нéсколько, довóльно. **somewhere** *adv.* (*position*) (*definite*) гдé-то; (*indefinite*) гдé-нибудь; (*motion*) кудá-то; кудá-нибудь.
somnolent *adj.* сóнный.
son *n.* сын (*pl.* -овья́, -овéй); *s.-in-law*, зять (*pl.* -я́, -ёв) *m.*
sonar *n.* гидролокáтор.
sonata *n.* сонáта.
sonde *n.* зонд.
song *n.* пéсня (*gen.pl.* -сен); (*singing*) пéние; *s.-bird*, пéвчая пти́ца; *s.-thrush*, пéвчий дрозд (-á).
sonic *adj.* звуковóй, акусти́ческий.
sonnet *n.* сонéт.
sonny *n.* сынóк.
sonorous *adj.* звýчный (-чен, -чнá, -чно).
soon *adv.* скóро, вскóре; (*early*) рáно; *as s. as*, как тóлько; *as s. as possible*, как мóжно скорée; *no sooner said than done*, скáзано — сдéлано; *sooner or later*, рáно и́ли пóздно; *the sooner the better*, чем рáньше, тем лýчше.
soot *n.* сáжа, кóпоть.
soothe *v.t.* успокáивать *imp.*, успокóить *perf.*; (*pain*) облегчáть *imp.*, облегчи́ть *perf.*
soothsayer *n.* предсказáтель *m.*, ~ница.
sooty *adj.* запáчканный (-ан) сáжей, закоптéлый.
sophism *n.* софи́зм.
sophisticated *adj.* (*person*) искушённый; (*tastes*) изощрённый (-ён, -ённа); (*equipment*) усовершéнствованный.
soporific *adj.* снотвóрный; *n.* снотвóрное *sb.*
soprano *n.* сопрáно (*voice*) *neut.* & (*person*) *f.indecl.*, ди́скант.
sorbet *n.* шербéт.
sorcerer *n.* колдýн (-á). **sorceress** *n.* колдýнья (*gen.pl.* -ний). **sorcery** *n.* колдовствó.
sordid *adj.* (*dirty*) гря́зный (-зен, -знá, -зно); (*wretched*) убóгий; (*base*) пóдлый (подл, -á, -о).
sore *n.* боля́чка, я́зва; *adj.* больнóй (-лен, -льнá); *my throat is s.*, у меня́ боли́т гóрло.
sorrel[1] *n.* (*herb*) щавéль (-ля́) *m.*
sorrel[2] *adj.* (*of horse*) гнедóй; *n.* гнедáя лóшадь (*pl.* -ди, -дéй, *instr.* -дьми́).
sorrow *n.* печáль, гóре, скорбь. **sorrowful** *adj.* печáльный, скóрбный. **sorry** *adj.* жáлкий (-лок, -лкá, -лко); *predic.*: *be s.*, жалéть *imp.* (about, о + *prep.*); жаль *impers.* + *dat.* (for, + *gen.*); *s.!* извини́(те)!
sort *n.* род (*pl.* -ы́), вид, сорт (*pl.* -á); *v.t.* сорти́ровать *imp.*; разбирáть *imp.*, разобрáть (разберý, -рёшь; разобрáл, -á, -о) *perf.* **sorter** *n.* сорти́рóвщик, -ица.
sortie *n.* вы́лазка.
SOS *n.* (рáдио)сигнáл бéдствия.
sot *n.* пья́ница *m.* & *f.*
sotto voce *adv.* вполгóлоса.
soubriquet *see* **sobriquet**.
soufflé *n.* суфлé *neut.indecl.*
soul *n.* душá (*acc.* -шу; *pl.* -ши).
sound[1] *adj.* (*healthy*) здорóвый; (*strong*; *of sleep*) крéпкий (-пок, -пкá, -пко);

(*firm*) прóчный (-чен, -чнá, -чно, прóчны́); *adv.* крéпко.
sound[2] *n.* (*noise*) звук, шум; *attrib.* звуковóй; *s. barrier*, звуковóй барьéр; *s. effects*, звуковóе сопровождéние; *s.-proof*, звуконепроницáемый; *s.-track*, звуковáя дорóжка; *s.-wave*, звуковáя волнá (*pl.* -ны, -н, вóлнáм); *v.i.* звучáть (-чи́т) *imp.*, про~ *perf.*
sound[3] *v.t.* (*test depth*) измеря́ть *imp.*, измéрить *perf.* глубинý + *gen.*; (*med.*, *fig.*) зонди́ровать *imp.*, по~ *perf.*; *n.* зонд.
sound[4] *n.* (*strait*) проли́в.
soup *n.* суп (-а(у), *loc.* -е & -ý; *pl.* -ы́); *s.-kitchen*, бесплáтная столóвая *sb.*; *v.t.*: *s. up*, повышáть *imp.*, повы́сить *perf.* мóщность + *gen.*
sour *adj.* ки́слый (-сел, -слá, -сло); (*of milk etc.*) проки́сший; *s. cream*, сметáна; *v.i.* прокисáть *imp.*, проки́снуть (-с) *perf.*; *v.t.* & *i.* озлобля́ть(ся) *imp.*, озлóбить(ся) *perf.*
source *n.* истóчник; (*of river*) истóки *m.pl.*
south *n.* юг; (*naut.*) зюйд; *adj.* ю́жный; (*naut.*) зю́йдовый; *adv.* к ю́гу, на юг; *s.-east*, ю́го-востóк; (*naut.*) зюйд-óст; *s.-easterly*, *-eastern*, ю́го-востóчный; (*naut.*) зюйд-óстовый; *s.-west*, ю́го-зáпад; (*naut.*) зюйд-вéст; *s.-westerly*, *-western*, ю́го-зáпадный; (*naut.*) зюйд-вéстовый; *s. wind*, зюйд. **southeaster** *n.* зюйд-óст. **southerly** *adj.* ю́жный; (*naut.*) зю́йдовый. **southern** *adj.* ю́жный. **southerner** *n.* южáнин (*pl.* -áне, -áн), -áнка; жи́тель *m.*, ~ница, ю́га. **southernmost** *adj.* сáмый ю́жный. **southpaw** *n.* левшá *m.* & *f.* **southward(s)** *adv.* к ю́гу, на юг. **southwester** *n.* зюйд-вéст.
souvenir *n.* сувени́р.
sou'wester *n.* (*hat*) зюйдвéстка.
sovereign *adj.* суверéнный; *n.* суверéн, монáрх; (*coin*) соверéн. **sovereignty** *n.* суверенитéт.
soviet *n.* совéт; *Supreme S.*, Верхóвный Совéт; *S. Union*, Совéтский Сою́з; *adj.* (*S.*) совéтский.
sow[1] *n.* свинья́ (*pl.* -ньи, -нéй, -ньям), свиномáтка.
sow[2] *v.t.* (*seed*) сéять (сéю, сéешь) *imp.*, по~ *perf.*; (*field*) засéивать *imp.*, засéять (-éю, -éешь) *perf.*; *sowing-machine*, сéялка. **sower** *n.* сéятель *m.*
soy *n.* сóевый сóус. **soya** *n.* сóя; *s. bean*, сóевый боб (-á).
sozzled *predic.* в дóску пьян (-á, -о).
spa *n.* вóды *f.pl.*, курóрт.
space *n.* прострáнство; (*distance*) протяжéние; (*interval*) промежýток (-тка); (*place*) мéсто; (*outer s.*) кóсмос; *attrib.* косми́ческий; *s.-bar*, клáвиша для интервáлов; *s. station*, косми́ческая стáнция; *s.-time*, прострáнство-врéмя *neut.*; прострáнственно-временнóй; *v.t.* расставля́ть *imp.*, расстáвить *perf.* с промежýтками. **spacecraft** *n.* косми́ческий корáбль (-ля́) *m.* **spaceman** *n.* космонáвт, астронáвт. **spaceship** *n.* косми́ческий корáбль (-ля́) *m.* **spacesuit** *n.* скафáндр (космонáвта). **spacious** *adj.* простóрный, помести́тельный.
spade[1] *n.* (*tool*) лопáта, зáступ.
spade[2] *n.* (*cards*) пи́ка.
spaghetti *n.* спагéтти *neut.indecl.*
span *n.* (*of bridge*) пролёт; (*aeron.*) размáх; (*as measure*) пядь (*pl.* пя́ди, пя́дéй); *v.t.* (*of bridge*) соединя́ть *imp.*, соедини́ть *perf.* стóроны + *gen.*, (*river*) берегá + *gen.*
spangle *n.* блёстка.
Spaniard *n.* испáнец (-нца), -нка.
spaniel *n.* спаниéль *m.*
Spanish *adj.* испáнский.
spank *v.t.* шлёпать *imp.*, шлёпнуть *perf.*; *n.* шлепóк (-пкá).
spanner *n.* гáечный ключ (-á).
spar[1] *n.* (*naut.*) рангóутное дéрево (*pl.* -éвья, -éвьев); (*aeron.*) лонжерóн.
spar[2] *v.i.* бокси́ровать *imp.*; (*fig.*) препирáться *imp.*
spare *adj.* (*in reserve*) запаснóй, запáсный; (*extra, to s.*) ли́шний; (*of seat, time*) свобóдный; (*thin*) худощáвый; *s. parts*, запасны́е чáсти (-тéй) *f.pl.*; *s. room*, кóмната для гостéй; *n.*: *pl.* запчáсти (-тéй) *pl.*; *v.t.* (*grudge*) жалéть *imp.*, по~ *perf.* + *acc.*, *gen.*; *he spared no pains*, он не жалéл трудóв; (*do without*) обходи́ться (-ожýсь, -óдишься) *imp.*, обойти́сь (обойдýсь, -дёшься; обошёлся, -шлáсь) *perf.* без

+*gen.*; (*time*) уделя́ть *imp.*, удели́ть *perf.*; (*person*, *feelings*, *etc.*) щади́ть *imp.*, по~ *perf.*
spare-rib *n.* (свино́е) рёбрышко (*pl.* -шки, -шек, -шкам).
spark *n.* и́скра; *v.i.* искри́ть *imp.*; *sparking-plug* запа́льная свеча́ (*pl.* -чи, -че́й).
sparkle *v.i.* и́скри́ться *imp.*; сверка́ть *imp.*
sparrow *n.* воробе́й (-бья́); *s.-hawk*, перепеля́тник.
sparse *adj.* ре́дкий (-док, -дка́, -дко); (*population*) разбро́санный (-ан).
spasm *n.* спазм, су́дорога. **spasmodic** *adj.* спазмоди́ческий, су́дорожный.
spastic *adj.* спасти́ческий.
spate *n.* разли́в; (*fig.*) пото́к.
spatial *adj.* простра́нственный.
spatio-temporal *adj.* простра́нственно-временно́й.
spatter *v.t.* (*liquid*) бры́згать (-зжу, -зжешь) *imp.*+*instr.*; (*person etc.*) забры́згивать *imp.*, забры́згать *perf.* (with, +*instr.*); *n.* бры́зги (-г) *pl.*
spatula *n.* шпа́тель *m.*
spavin *n.* ко́стный шпат.
spawn *v.t.* & *abs.* мета́ть (ме́чет) *imp.* (икру́); *v.t.* (*fig.*) порожда́ть *imp.*, породи́ть *perf.*; *n.* икра́; (*mushroom s.*) грибни́ца; (*offspring*) отро́дье.
speak *v.t.* & *i.* говори́ть *imp.*, сказа́ть (-ажу́, -а́жешь) *perf.*; *v.i.* (*make speech*) выступа́ть *imp.*, вы́ступить *perf.* (с ре́чью); выска́зываться *imp.*, вы́сказаться (-ажусь, -ажешься) *perf.* (for, за+*acc.*; against, про́тив+*gen.*). **speaker** *n.* ора́тор; (*at conference etc.*) докла́дчик; (*S.*, *parl.*) спи́кер; (*loud-speaker*) громкоговори́тель *m.* **speaking** *n.*: *not be on s. terms*, не разгова́ривать *imp.* (with, с+*instr.*); *s.-trumpet*, ру́пор; *s.-tube*, перегово́рная тру́бка.
spear *n.* копьё (*pl.* -пья, -пий, -пьям); *v.t.* пронза́ть *imp.*, пронзи́ть *perf.* копьём. **spearhead** *n.* передово́й отря́д.
special *adj.* осо́бый, специа́льный; (*extra*) э́кстренный. **specialist** *n.* специали́ст, ~ка. **speciality** *n.* специа́льность. **specialization** *n.* специализа́ция. **specialize** *v.t.* & *i.* специализи́ровать(ся) *imp.*, *perf.* **specially** *adv.* осо́бенно.
specie *n.* зво́нкая моне́та.
species *n.* вид.
specific *adj.* специфи́ческий; (*biol.*) видово́й; (*phys.*) уде́льный. **specification(s)** *n.* спецификация. **specify** *v.t.* (*mention*) специа́льно упомина́ть *imp.*, упомяну́ть (-ну́, -нешь)+*acc.*, о+*prep.*; (*include in specifications*) специфици́ровать *imp.*, *perf.*
specimen *n.* образе́ц (-зца́), экземпля́р; *s. page*, про́бная страни́ца.
specious *adj.* благови́дный, правдоподо́бный.
speck *n.* кра́пинка, пя́тнышко (*pl.* -шки, -шек, -шкам). **speckled** *adj.* кра́пчатый.
spectacle *n.* зре́лище; *pl.* очки́ (-ко́в) *pl.*
spectacular *adj.* эффе́ктный.
spectator *n.* зри́тель *m.*, ~ница.
spectral *adj.* (*ghostlike*) при́зрачный; (*phys.*) спектра́льный. **spectre** *n.* при́зрак.
spectroscope *n.* спектроско́п. **spectroscopic** *adj.* спектроскопи́ческий.
spectrum *n.* спектр.
speculate *v.i.* (*meditate*) размышля́ть *imp.*, размы́слить *perf.* (on, о+*prep.*); (*in shares etc.*) спекули́ровать *imp.* **speculation** *n.* теория, предположе́ние; спекуля́ция. **speculative** *adj.* гипотети́ческий; спекуляти́вный. **speculator** *n.* спекуля́нт, ~ка.
speech *n.* (*faculty*) речь; (*address*) речь (*pl.* -чи, -че́й), выступле́ние; (*language*) язы́к (-а́); *s. day*, акт; *s. therapy*, логопе́дия. **speechify** *v.i.* ора́торствовать *imp.* **speechless** *adj.* немо́й (нем, -а́, -о); (*with emotion*) онеме́вший.
speed *n.* ско́рость, быстрота́; (*phot.*) светочувстви́тельность; *at full s.*, по́лным хо́дом; *s. limit*, дозво́ленная ско́рость; *v.i.* спеши́ть *imp.*, по~ *perf.*; *v.t.*: *s. up*, ускоря́ть *imp.*, уско́рить *perf.* **speedboat** *n.* быстрохо́дный ка́тер (*pl.* -а́). **speedometer** *n.* спидо́метр. **speedway** *n.* доро́жка для мотоцикле́тных го́нок. **speedwell** *n.* веро́ника. **speedy** *adj.* бы́стрый (быстр, -а́, -о, бы́стры́), ско́рый (скор, -а́, -о).
speleologist *n.* спелео́лог. **speleology** *n.* спелеоло́гия.
spell[1] *n.* (*incantation*) заклина́ние.

spell[2] *v.t.* (*write*) писа́ть (пишу́, -шешь) *imp.*, на ~ *perf.* по бу́квам; (*say*) произноси́ть (-ошу́, -о́сишь) *imp.*, произнести́ (-есу́, -есёшь; -ёс, -есла́) *perf.* по бу́квам; *how do you s. that word?* как пи́шется э́то сло́во?

spell[3] *n.* (*period*) промежу́ток (-тка) вре́мени.

spellbound *adj.* зачаро́ванный (-ан, -ан(н)а).

spelling *n.* правописа́ние.

spend *v.t.* (*money*; *effort*) тра́тить *imp.*, ис ~, по ~ *perf.*; (*time*) проводи́ть (-ожу́, -о́дишь) *imp.*, провести́ (-еду́, -едёшь; -ёл, -ела́) *perf.* **spendthrift** *n.* расточи́тель *m.*, ~ница; мот, ~о́вка.

sperm[1] *n.* спе́рма.

sperm[2] **(whale)** *n.* кашало́т.

spermaceti *n.* спермаце́т.

spermatic *adj.* семенно́й.

spermatozoon *n.* сперматозо́ид.

sphere *n.* (*var. senses*) сфе́ра; (*ball*) шар (-а́ *with 2, 3, 4*; *pl.* -ы́). **spherical** *adj.* сфери́ческий, шарообра́зный. **spheroid** *n.* сферо́ид.

sphincter *n.* сфи́нктер.

sphinx *n.* сфинкс.

spice *n.* спе́ция, пря́ность; *v.t.* приправля́ть *imp.*, припра́вить *perf.* спе́циями.

spick *adj.*: *s. and span*, чи́стый (чист, -а́, -о, чи́сты́), опря́тный; (*of person*) оде́тый с иго́лочки.

spicy *adj.* пря́ный; (*fig.*) пика́нтный.

spider *n.* пау́к (-а́). **spidery** *adj.* то́нкий (-нок, -нка́, -нко, то́нки́).

spike[1] *n.* (*bot.*) ко́лос (*pl.* коло́сья, -ьев).

spike[2] *n.* (*point*) остриё; (*nail*) гвоздь (-дя́; *pl.* -ди, -де́й) *m.*; (*on shoes*) шип (-а́); (*for papers*) на́колка; *v.t.* снабжа́ть *imp.*, снабди́ть *perf.* шипа́ми; (*gun*) заклёпывать *imp.*, заклепа́ть *perf.*; (*drink*) добавля́ть *imp.*, доба́вить *perf.* спиртно́е в + *acc.*

spill *v.t.* & *i.* пролива́ть(ся) *imp.*, проли́ть(ся) (-лью́, -льёт(ся); про́ли́л/проли́лся, -а́(сь), -о/проли́ло́сь) *perf.*; рассыпа́ть(ся) *imp.*, рассы́пать(ся) (-плю, -плет(ся)) *perf.*; *n.* проли́тие, рассы́пка; (*fall*) паде́ние.

spin *v.t.* (*thread etc.*) прясть (пряду́, -дёшь; -ял, -я́ла́, -я́ло) *imp.*, с ~ *perf.*; (*top*) запуска́ть *imp.*, запусти́ть (-ущу́, -у́стишь) *perf.*; (*coin*) подбра́сывать *imp.*, подбро́сить *perf.*; *v.t.* & *i.* (*turn*) крути́ть(ся) (-учу́(сь), -у́тишь(ся)) *imp.*; кружи́ть(ся) (-ужу́(сь), -у́жи́шь(ся)) *imp.*; *s. out*, (*prolong*) затя́гивать *imp.*, затяну́ть (-ну́, -нешь) *perf.*; *n.* круже́ние; (*aeron.*) што́пор; (*excursion*) пое́здка; *go for a s.*, прока́тываться *imp.*, прокати́ться (-ачу́сь, -а́тишься) *perf.*

spinach *n.* шпина́т.

spinal *adj.* спинно́й; *s. column*, спинно́й хребе́т (-бта́); *s. cord*, спинно́й мозг.

spindle *n.* веретено́ (*pl.* -ёна); (*axis, pin*) ось (*pl.* о́си, осе́й) *m.*, шпи́ндель *m.* **spindly** *adj.* дли́нный (-нен, -нна́, дли́нно́) и то́нкий (-нок, -нка́, -нко, то́нки́).

spine *n.* (*backbone*) позвоно́чник, хребе́т (-бта́); (*bot.*) шип (-а́); (*zool.*) игла́ (*pl.* -лы); (*of book*) корешо́к (-шка́). **spineless** *adj.* (*fig.*) мягкоте́лый, бесхара́ктерный.

spinet *n.* спине́т.

spinnaker *n.* спи́накер.

spinner *n.* пряди́льщик, -ица; (*fishing*) блесна́.

spinney *n.* ро́щица.

spinning *n.* пряде́ние; *s.-machine*, пряди́льная маши́на; *s.-top*, волчо́к (-чка́); *s.-wheel*, пря́лка.

spinster *n.* незаму́жняя же́нщина.

spiny *adj.* колю́чий; (*fig.*) затрудни́тельный.

spiral *adj.* спира́льный, винтово́й; *n.* спира́ль.

spire *n.* шпиль *m.*

spirit *n.* дух, душа́; *pl.* (*mood*) настрое́ние; (*liquid*) спирт (*loc.* -е & -у́; *pl.* -ы́); *pl.* (*drinks*) спиртно́е *sb.*; *s.-lamp*, спирто́вка; *s.-level*, ватерпа́с; *v.t.*: *s. away*, та́йно уноси́ть (-ошу́, -о́сишь) *imp.*, унести́ (унесу́, -сёшь; унёс, -ла́) *perf.* **spirited** *adj.* энерги́чный, пы́лкий (-лок, -лка́, -лко). **spiritless** *adj.* безжи́зненный (-ен, -енна). **spiritual** *adj.* духо́вный. **spiritualism** *n.* спирити́зм. **spiritualist** *n.* спири́т. **spirituous** *adj.* спиртно́й.

spit[1] *n.* (*skewer*) ве́ртел (*pl.* -а́); (*of land*) стре́лка, коса́ (*acc.* ко́су́; *pl.*

-сы); *v.t.* насáживать *imp.*, насадúть (-ажý, -áдишь) *perf.* на вéртел; (*fig.*) пронзáть *imp.*, пронзúть *perf.*

spit[2] *v.i.* плевáть (плюю, -юёшь) *imp.*, плю́нуть *perf.*; (*of rain*) моросúть *imp.*; (*of fire etc.*) шипéть (-пúт) *imp.*; *v.t.*: *s. out*, выплёвывать *imp.*, вы́плюнуть *perf.*; *spitting image*, тóчная кóпия; *n.* слюнá, плевóк (-вкá).

spite *n.* злóба, злость; *in s. of*, несмотря́ на + *acc.* **spiteful** *adj.* злóбный.

spittle *n.* слюнá, плевóк (-вкá).

spittoon *n.* плевáтельница.

spitz *n.* шпиц.

splash *v.t.* (*person*) забры́згивать *imp.*, забры́згать *perf.* (with, + *instr.*); (*s. liquid*) бры́згать (-зжу, -зжешь) *imp.* + *instr.*; *v.i.* плескáть(ся) (-ещý(сь), -éщешь(ся)) *imp.*, плеснýть *perf.*; (*move*) шлёпать *imp.*, шлёпнуть *perf.* (through, по + *dat.*); *s. money about*, сорúть *imp.* деньгáми; *n.* бры́зги (-г) *pl.*, плеск; *s.-down*, приводнéние.

splatter *v.i.* плескáться (-éщется) *imp.*

spleen *n.* селезёнка; (*spite*) злóба.

splendid *adj.* великолéпный. **splendour** *n.* блеск, великолéпие.

splenetic *adj.* жёлчный.

splice *v.t.* (*ropes*) срáщивать *imp.*, срастúть *perf.* концы́ + *gen.*; (*film, tape*) склéивать *imp.*, склéить *perf.* концы́ + *gen.*; *n.* (*naut.*) сплéсень (-сня) *m.*; (*film, tape*) склéйка, мéсто склéйки.

splint *n.* лубóк (-бкá), шúна; *v.t.* наклáдывать *imp.*, наложúть (-жý, -жишь) *perf.* шúну на + *acc.*; класть (-адý, -адёшь; -ал) *imp.*, положúть (-жý, -жишь) *perf.* в лубóк.

splinter *n.* оскóлок (-лка), щéпка; (*in skin*) занóза; *s. group*, отколóвшаяся грýппа; *v.t.* & *i.* расщепля́ть(ся) *imp.*, расщепúть(ся) *perf.*

split *n.* расщéлина, расщéп; (*schism*) раскóл; *pl.* шпагáт; *v.t.* & *i.* расщепля́ть(ся) *imp.*, расщепúть(ся) *perf.*; раскáлывать(ся) *imp.*, расколóть(ся) (-лю́, -лет(ся)) *perf.*; (*divide*) делúть(ся) (-лю́, -лит(ся)) *imp.*, раз~ *perf.* (на чáсти); *v.i.*: *s. on*, доносúть (-ошý, -óсишь) *imp.*, донестú (-есý, -есёшь; -ёс, -еслá) *perf.* на + *acc.*; *s. hairs*, спóрить *imp.* о мелочáх; *s. one's sides*, надрывáться *imp.* от хóхота; *s.-level*, на рáзных ýровнях; *s. pea(s)*, лущёный горóх (-а(у)); *s. personality*, раздвоéние лúчности; *s. pin*, шплинт (шплúнтá); *s. second*, мгновéние óка.

splotch *n.* нерóвное пятнó (*pl.* -тна, -тен, -тнам), мазóк (-зкá).

splutter *v.i.* бры́згать (-зжу, -зжешь) *imp.* слюнóй; *v.t.* (*utter*) говорúть *imp.* невня́тно.

spoil *n.* (*pl. or collect.*) добы́ча; (*of war*) трофéи *m.pl.*; *v.t.* & *i.* (*damage*; *decay*) пóртить(ся) *imp.*, ис~ *perf.*; *v.t.* (*indulge*) баловáть *imp.*, из~ *perf.*; *be spoiling for a fight*, рвáться (рвусь, рвёшься; рвáлся, -алáсь, -áлóсь) *imp.* в дрáку.

spoke *n.* спúца.

spoken *adj.* (*language*) ýстный. **spokesman, -woman** *n.* представúтель *m.*, ~ ница.

sponge *n.* гýбка; *s.-cake*, бисквúт; *s. rubber*, гýбчатая резúна; *v.t.* (*wash*) мыть (мóю, мóешь) *imp.*, вы́ ~, по ~ *perf.* гýбкой; (*obtain*) выпрáшивать *imp.*, вы́просить *perf.*; *v.i.*: *s. on*, жить (живý, -вёшь; жил, -á, -о) *imp.* на счёт + *gen.* **sponger** *n.* приживáльщик, паразúт. **spongy** *adj.* гýбчатый.

sponsor *n.* поручúтель *m.*, ~ ница; *v.t.* ручáться *imp.*, поручúться (-чýсь, -чишься) *perf.* за + *acc.*; (*finance*) финансúровать *imp.*, *perf.*

spontaneity *n.* непосрéдственность, самопроизвóльность. **spontaneous** *adj.* непосрéдственный (-ен, -енна), самопроизвóльный.

spoof *n.* (*hoax*) мистификáция; (*parody*) парóдия.

spook *n.* привидéние.

spool *n.* шпýлька, катýшка.

spoon *n.* лóжка; *s.-bait*, блеснá; *v.t.* чéрпать *imp.*, черпнýть *perf.* лóжкой. **spoonbill** *n.* колпúца. **spoonful** *n.* пóлная лóжка.

spoor *n.* след (-а(у); *pl.* -ы́).

sporadic *adj.* спорадúческий.

spore *n.* спóра.

sport *n.* спорт; *pl.* спортúвные соревновáния *neut.pl.*; (*fun*) забáва, потéха;

(*person*) сла́вный ма́лый *sb.*; *sports car*, спорти́вный автомоби́ль *m.*; *sports coat*, спорти́вная ку́ртка; *v.t.* щеголя́ть *imp.*, щегольну́ть *perf.*+*instr.* **sportsman** *n.* спортсме́н. **sportsmanlike** *adj.* спортсме́нский.

spot *n.* (*place*) ме́сто (*pl.* -та́); (*mark*) пятно́ (*pl.* -тна, -тен, -тнам) (*also fig.*), кра́пинка; (*pimple*) пры́щик; (*on dice etc.*) очко́ (*pl.* -ки́, -ко́в); *on the s.*, на ме́сте; (*without delay*) неме́дленно; *s. check*, вы́борочная прове́рка; *v.t.* (*mark*; *fig.*) пятна́ть *imp.*, за~ *perf.*; (*recognize*) узнава́ть (-наю́, -наёшь) *imp.*, узна́ть *perf.*; (*notice*) замеча́ть *imp.*, заме́тить *perf.*; *v.i.*: *it's spotting with rain*, накра́пывает дождь. **spotless** *adj.* чи́стый (чист, -а́, -о, чи́сты́); (*fig.*) безупре́чный. **spotlight** *n.* проже́ктор (*pl.* -ы & -а́); *v.t.* освеща́ть *imp.*, освети́ть (-ещу́, -ети́шь) *perf.* проже́ктором. **spotty** *adj.* прыщева́тый.

spouse *n.* супру́г, ~а.

spout *v.i.* бить (бьёт) *imp.* струёй; хлы́нуть *perf.*; *v.t.* выпуска́ть *imp.*, вы́пустить *perf.* струю́+*gen.*; (*verses etc.*) деклами́ровать *imp.*, про~ *perf.*; *n.* (*tube*) но́сик; (*jet*) струя́ (*pl.* -у́и).

sprain *v.t.* растя́гивать *imp.*, растяну́ть (-ну́, -нешь) *perf.*; *n.* растяже́ние.

sprat *n.* ки́лька, шпро́та.

sprawl *v.i.* (*of person*) разва́ливаться *imp.*, развали́ться (-лю́сь, -лишься) *perf.*; (*of town*) раски́дываться *imp.*, раски́нуться *perf.*

spray[1] *n.* (*of flowers etc.*) ве́т(оч)ка.

spray[2] *n.* (*liquid*) бры́зги (-г) *pl.*; (*water*) водяна́я пыль; (*atomizer*) распыли́тель *m.*; *v.t.* опры́скивать *imp.*, опры́скать *perf.* (with, +*instr.*); (*cause to scatter*) распыля́ть *imp.*, распыли́ть *perf.*; *s.-gun*, краскопу́льт.

spread *v.t.* & *i.* (*s. out*) расстила́ть(ся) *imp.*, разостла́ть(ся) (расстелю́, -лет(ся)) *perf.*; (*unfurl*, *unroll*) развёртывать(ся) *imp.*, разверну́ть(ся) *perf.*; (*rumour*, *disease*, *etc.*) распространя́ть(ся) *imp.*, распространи́ть(ся) *perf.*; *v.i.* (*extend*) простира́ться *imp.*, простере́ться (-трётся; -тёрся) *perf.*; *v.t.* (*bread etc.*, *acc.*; *butter etc.*, *instr.*) нама́зывать, ма́зать (ма́жу, -жешь) *imp.*, на~ *perf.*; *n.* распростране́ние; (*span*) разма́х; (*feast*) пир; (*paste*) па́ста; (*double page*) разворо́т.

spree *n.* (*drinking*) кутёж (-а́); *go on the s.*, кути́ть (кучу́, ку́тишь) *imp.*, кутну́ть *perf.*

sprig *n.* ве́точка.

sprightly *adj.* бо́дрый (бодр, -а́, -о), бо́дры́).

spring *v.i.* (*jump*) пры́гать *imp.*, пры́гнуть *perf.*; *v.t.* (*disclose unexpectedly*) неожи́данно сообща́ть *imp.*, сообщи́ть *perf.* (on, +*dat.*); *s. a leak*, дава́ть (даёт) *imp.*, дать (даст, даду́т; дал, -а́, да́ло́, -и) *perf.* течь; *s. a surprise on*, де́лать *imp.*, с~ *perf.* сюрпри́з+*dat.*; *s. from*, (*originate*) происходи́ть (-ожу́, -о́дишь) *imp.*, произойти́ (-ойду́, -ойдёшь; -ошёл, -ошла́) *perf.* из+*gen.*; *s. up*, (*jump up*) вска́кивать *imp.*, вскочи́ть (-чу́, -чишь) *perf.*; (*arise*) возника́ть *imp.*, возни́кнуть (-к) *perf.*; *n.* (*jump*) прыжо́к (-жка́); (*season*) весна́ (*pl.* вёсны, -сен, -снам), *attrib.* весе́нний; (*source*) исто́чник, ключ (-а́), родни́к (-а́); (*elasticity*) упру́гость; (*coil*) пружи́на; (*on vehicle*) рессо́ра; (*fig.*, *motive*) моти́в; *s. balance*, пружи́нные весы́ (-со́в) *pl.*; *s.-clean*, генера́льная убо́рка; (*v.t.*) производи́ть (-ожу́, -о́дишь) *imp.*, произвести́ (-еду́, -едёшь; -ёл, -ела́) *perf.* генера́льную убо́рку+*gen.*; *s. mattress*, пружи́нный матра́с; *s. tide*, сизиги́йный прили́в; *s. water*, ключева́я вода́ (*acc.* -ду). **springboard** *n.* трампли́н. **springbok** *n.* прыгу́н (-а́). **springy** *adj.* упру́гий.

sprinkle *v.t.* (*with liquid*) опры́скивать *imp.*, опры́скать *perf.* (with, +*instr.*); (*with solid*) посыпа́ть *imp.*, посы́пать (-плю, -плешь) *perf.* (with, +*instr.*). **sprinkler** *n.* (*for watering*) опры́скиватель *m.*; (*fire-extinguisher*) спри́нклер.

sprint *v.i.* бежа́ть (бегу́, бежи́шь) *imp.* на коро́ткую диста́нцию; *n.* спринт. **sprinter** *n.* спри́нтер.

sprit *n.* шприто́в.

sprocket *n.* зубе́ц (-бца́); *s.-wheel*, звёздочка, цепно́е колесо́ (*pl.* -ёса).
sprout *v.i.* пуска́ть *imp.*, пусти́ть (-ит) *perf.* ростки́; *n.* росто́к (-тка́), побе́г; *pl.* брюссе́льская капу́ста.
spruce[1] *adj.* наря́дный, элега́нтный; *v.t.*: *s. oneself up*, принаряжа́ться *imp.*, принаряди́ться (-яжу́сь, -я́дишься) *perf.*
spruce[2] *n.* ель.
spry *adj.* живо́й (жив, -а́, -о), бо́дрый (бодр, -а́, -о, бо́дры́).
spud *n.* (*tool*) моты́га; (*potato*) карто́шка (*also collect.*).
spume *n.* пе́на.
spur *n.* (*rider's*) шпо́ра; (*fig.*) сти́мул; (*of mountain*) отро́г; *on the s. of the moment*, экспро́мтом; *v.t.*: *s. on*, толка́ть *imp.*, толкну́ть *perf.* (to, на + *acc.*).
spurge *n.* молоча́й.
spurious *adj.* подде́льный, подло́жный.
spurn *v.t.* отверга́ть *imp.*, отве́ргнуть (-г(нул), -гла) *perf.*
spurt *n.* (*jet*) струя́ (*pl.* -у́и); (*effort*) рыво́к (-вка́); *v.i.* бить (бьёт) *imp.* струёй; де́лать *imp.*, с~ *perf.* рыво́к.
sputter *v.t.* (*utter*) невня́тно говори́ть *imp.*; *v.i.* шипе́ть (-пит) *imp.*
sputum *n.* слюна́.
spy *n.* шпио́н; *v.i.* шпио́нить *imp.* (on, за + *instr.*). **spyglass** *n.* подзо́рная труба́ (*pl.* -бы). **spyhole** *n.* глазо́к (-зка́).
squabble *n.* перебра́нка; *v.i.* вздо́рить *imp.*, по~ *perf.*
squad *n.* кома́нда, гру́ппа.
squadron *n.* (*mil.*) эскадро́н; (*naut.*) эска́дра; (*aeron.*) эскадри́лья; *s.-leader*, майо́р авиа́ции.
squalid *adj.* гря́зный (-зен, -зна́, -зно), убо́гий.
squall *n.* шквал; *v.i.* визжа́ть (-жу́, -жи́шь) *imp.* **squally** *adj.* шква́листый.
squalor *n.* грязь (*loc.* -зи́), убо́гость.
squander *v.t.* растра́чивать *imp.*, растра́тить *perf.*; (*fortune*) прома́тывать *imp.*, промота́ть *perf.*
square *n.* (*math.*) квадра́т; (*in town*) пло́щадь (*pl.* -ди, -де́й), сквер; (*on paper, material*) кле́тка; (*chess*) по́ле; (*mil.*) каре́ *neut.indecl.*; (*instrument*) науго́льник; *set s.*, уго́льник; *T-s.*, рейсши́на; *adj.* квадра́тный; (*meal*) пло́тный (-тен, -тна́, -тно, пло́тны́); *s. root*, квадра́тный ко́рень (-рня) *m.*; *s. sail*, прямо́й па́рус (*pl.* -а́); *v.t.* де́лать *imp.*, с~ *perf.* квадра́тным; (*math.*) возводи́ть (-ожу́, -о́дишь) *imp.*, возвести́ (-еду́, -едёшь; -ёл, -ела́) *perf.* в квадра́т; (*bribe*) подкупа́ть *imp.*, подкупи́ть (-плю́, -пишь) *perf.*; *s. accounts with*, распла́чиваться *imp.*, расплати́ться (-ачу́сь, -а́тишься) *perf.* с + *instr.*
squash *n.* (*crowd*) толку́ча; (*drink*) (фрукто́вый) сок (-а(у), *loc.* -е & -у́); *v.t.* разда́вливать *imp.*, раздави́ть (-влю́, -вишь) *perf.*; (*silence*) заставля́ть *imp.*, заста́вить *perf.* замолча́ть; (*suppress*) подавля́ть *imp.*, пода́вить (-влю́, -вишь) *perf.*; *v.i.* вти́скиваться *imp.*, вти́снуться *perf.*
squat *adj.* корена́стый, призе́мистый; *v.i.* сиде́ть (сижу́, сиди́шь) *imp.* на ко́рточках; *s. down*, сади́ться *imp.*, сесть (ся́ду, -дешь; сел) *perf.* на ко́рточки.
squatter *n.* лицо́, самово́льно поселя́ющееся в чужо́м до́ме.
squaw *n.* индиа́нка (в Се́верной Аме́рике).
squawk *n.* пронзи́тельный крик; (*of bird*) клёкот; *v.i.* пронзи́тельно крича́ть (-чу́, -чи́шь) *imp.*, кри́кнуть *perf.*; (*of bird*) клекота́ть (-о́чет) *imp.*
squeak *n.* писк, скрип; *v.i.* пища́ть (-щу́, -щи́шь) *imp.*, пи́скнуть *perf.*; скрипе́ть (-плю́, -пи́шь) *imp.*, скри́пнуть *perf.* **squeaky** *adj.* пискли́вый, скрипу́чий.
squeal *n.* визг; *v.i.* визжа́ть (-жу́, -жи́шь) *imp.*, ви́згнуть *perf.*
squeamish *adj.* брезгли́вый, приверéдливый.
squeeze *n.* (*crush*) да́вка; (*pressure*) сжа́тие; (*hand*) пожа́тие; *v.t.* дави́ть (давлю́, да́вишь) *imp.*; сжима́ть *imp.*, сжать (сожму́, -мёшь) *perf.*; пожима́ть *imp.*, пожа́ть (пожму́, -мёшь) *perf.*; *s. in*, впи́хивать(ся) *imp.*, впихну́ть(ся) *perf.*; вти́скивать(ся) *imp.*, вти́снуть(ся) *perf.*; *s. out*, выжима́ть *imp.*, вы́жать (вы́жму, -мешь) *perf.*; *s.*

through, проти́скивать(ся) *imp.*, проти́снуть(ся) *perf.*
squelch *n.* хлю́панье; *v.i.* хлю́пать *imp.*, хлю́пнуть *perf.*
squib *n.* (*firework*) пета́рда.
squid *n.* кальма́р.
squiggle *n.* (*flourish*) загогу́лина; (*scribble*) кара́кули *f.pl.*
squint *n.* косогла́зие; *adj.* косо́й (кос, -а́, -о), косогла́зый; *v.i.* коси́ть *imp.*; смотре́ть (-рю́, -ришь) *imp.*, по~ *perf.* и́скоса.
squire *n.* сквайр, поме́щик.
squirm *v.i.* (*wriggle*) извива́ться *imp.*, изви́ться (изовью́сь, -вьёшься; изви́лся, извила́сь) *perf.*; (*fidget*) ёрзать *imp.*
squirrel *n.* бе́лка.
squirt *n.* струя́ (*pl.* -у́и); *v.i.* бить (бьёт) *imp.* струёй; *v.t.* пуска́ть *imp.*, пусти́ть (пущу́, пу́стишь) *perf.* струю́ (*substance*, + *gen.*; at, на + *acc.*).
stab *n.* уда́р (ножо́м *etc.*); (*pain*) внеза́пная о́страя боль; *v.i.* наноси́ть (-ошу́, -о́сишь) *imp.*, нанести́ (-есу́, -есёшь; -ёс, -есла́) *perf.* уда́р (ножо́м *etc.*) (at, *dat.*); *v.t.* коло́ть (-лю́, -лешь) *imp.*, кольну́ть *perf.*
stability *n.* усто́йчивость, про́чность, стаби́льность, постоя́нство. **stabilization** *n.* стабилиза́ция. **stabilize** *v.t.* стабилизи́ровать *imp.*, *perf.* **stabilizer** *n.* стабилиза́тор.
stable *adj.* (*steady*; *of prices*, *family life etc.*) усто́йчивый; (*lasting*, *durable*) про́чный (-чен, -чна́, -чно, про́чны́); (*unwavering*) стаби́льный; (*psych.*) уравнове́шенный (-ен, -енна); *n.* коню́шня; *v.t.* ста́вить *imp.*, по~ *perf.* в коню́шню.
staccato *n.* (*mus.*) стакка́то *neut.indecl.*; *adv.* (*mus.*) стакка́то.
stack *n.* (*hay*) скирд(а́) (-а́ & -ы́; *pl.* ски́рды́, -д(о́в), -да́м), стог (*loc.* -е & -у́; *pl.* -а́); (*heap*) ку́ча, ки́па; (*building materials etc.*) шта́бель (*pl.* -ля́) *m.*; (*chimney*) (дымова́я) труба́ (*pl.* -бы); (*s.-room*) (книго)храни́лище; *pl.* ма́сса, мно́жество; *v.t.* скла́дывать *imp.*, сложи́ть (-жу́, -жишь) *perf.* в ку́чу; укла́дывать *imp.*, уложи́ть (-жу́, -жишь) *perf.* штабеля́ми.
stadium *n.* стадио́н.
staff *n.* (*personnel*) штат, шта́ты (-тов) *pl.*, персона́л, ка́дры (-ров) *pl.*; (*mil.*) штаб (*pl.* -ы́); (*stick*) посо́х, жезл (-а́); (*mus.*) но́тные лине́йки *f.pl.*; *adj.* шта́тный; (*mil.*) штабно́й.
stag *n.* саме́ц-оле́нь (самца́-оле́ня) *m.*; *s.-beetle*, рога́ч (-а́); *s.-party*, вечери́нка без же́нщин.
stage *n.* (*theat.*) сце́на, подмо́стки (-ков) *pl.*, эстра́да; (*platform*) платфо́рма; (*period*) ста́дия, фа́за, эта́п; *v.t.* (*theat.*) ста́вить *imp.*, по~ *perf.*; (*dramatize*, *feign*) инсцени́ровать *imp.*, *perf.*; (*organize*) организова́ть *imp.*, *perf.*; *s.-manager*, режиссёр; *s. whisper*, театра́льный шёпот.
stagger *n.* поша́тывание, шата́ние; *v.i.* шата́ться *imp.*, шатну́ться *perf.*; кача́ться *imp.*, качну́ться *perf.*; *v.t.* (*surprise*) поража́ть *imp.*, порази́ть *perf.*; потряса́ть *imp.*, потрясти́ (-су́, -сёшь; потря́с, -ла́) *perf.*; (*hours of work etc.*) распределя́ть *imp.*, распредели́ть *perf.* **be staggered** *v.i.* поража́ться *imp.*, порази́ться *perf.* **staggering** *adj.* потряса́ющий, порази́тельный.
stagnancy, stagnation *n.* засто́й, ко́сность, ине́ртность. **stagnant** *adj.* (*water*) стоя́чий; (*fig.*) засто́йный, ко́сный, ине́ртный. **stagnate** *v.i.* заста́иваться *imp.*, застоя́ться (-ою́сь, -ои́шься) *perf.*; косне́ть *imp.*, за~ *perf.*
staid *adj.* степе́нный (-нен, -нна), тре́звый (трезв, -а́, -о), соли́дный.
stain *n.* пятно́ (*pl.* -тна, -тен, -тнам); (*dye*) кра́ска; *v.t.* па́чкать *imp.*, за~, ис~ *perf.*; пятна́ть *imp.*, за~ *perf.*; (*dye*) окра́шивать *imp.*, окра́сить *perf.*; *stained glass*, цветно́е стекло́. **stainless** *adj.* незапя́танный, безупре́чный; *s. steel*, нержаве́ющая сталь.
stair *n.* ступе́нь, ступе́нька. **staircase, stairs** *n.* ле́стница. **stair well** *n.* ле́стничная кле́тка. **flight of stairs** *n.* ле́стничный марш.
stake *n.* (*stick*) кол (-а́, *loc.* -у́; *pl.* -ья, -ьев), столб (-а́); (*landmark*) ве́ха; (*bet*) ста́вка, закла́д; *be at s.*, быть поста́вленным на ка́рту; *v.t.* (*mark*

out) огора́живать *imp.*, огороди́ть (-ожу́, -о́ди́шь) *perf.* ко́льями; отмеча́ть *imp.*, отме́тить *perf.* ве́хами; (*risk*) ста́вить *imp.*, по~ *perf.* на ка́рту; рискова́ть *imp.* + *instr.*

stalactite *n.* сталакти́т.

stalagmite *n.* сталагми́т.

stale *adj.* несве́жий (несве́ж, -á, -е); (*hard, dry*) чёрствый (чёрств, -á, -о), сухо́й (сух, -á, -о); (*musty, damp*) за́тхлый; (*hackneyed*) изби́тый; *become, grow s.*, черстве́ть *imp.*, за~, по~ *perf.*

stalemate *n.* пат; (*fig.*) тупи́к (-á).

stalk *n.* сте́бель (-ля; *gen.pl.* -бле́й) *m.*; *v.t.* высле́живать *imp.*; (*stride*) ше́ствовать *imp.*

stall *n.* сто́йло; (*booth*) ларёк (-рька́) кио́ск, пала́тка; (*theat.*) кре́сло (*gen. pl.* -сел) в парте́ре; *pl.* (*theat.*) парте́р; *v.t.* & *i.* остана́вливать(ся) *imp.*, останови́ть(ся) (-влю́(сь), -вишь(ся)) *perf.*; *v.i.* теря́ть *imp.*, по~ *perf.* ско́рость; (*play for time*) оття́гивать *imp.*, оття́нуть (-ну́, -нешь) *perf.* вре́мя.

stallion *n.* жеребе́ц (-бца́).

stalwart *adj.* сто́йкий (-о́ек, -ойка́, -о́йко); *n.* сто́йкий приве́рженец (-нца), -кая -нка.

stamen *n.* тычи́нка.

stamina *n.* выно́сливость.

stammer *v.i.* заика́ться *imp.*; *n.* заика́ние. **stammerer** *n.* за́ика *m.* & *f.*

stamp *n.* печа́ть, штамп, ште́мпель (*pl.* -ля́) *m.*; (*hallmark*) клеймо́ (*pl.* -ма); (*postage*) (почто́вая) ма́рка; (*feet*) то́панье; *s.-duty*, ге́рбовый сбор; *v.t.* ста́вить *imp.*, по~ *perf.* печа́ть на + *acc.*; штампова́ть *imp.*, штемпелева́ть (-лю́ю, -лю́ешь) *imp.*, за~ *perf.*; клейми́ть *imp.*, за~ *perf.*; (*trample*) топта́ть (-пчу́, -пчешь) *imp.*, по~ *perf.*; *v.i.* то́пать *imp.*, то́пнуть *perf.* (нога́ми); *s. out*, подавля́ть *imp.*, подави́ть (-влю́, -вишь) *perf.*; ликвиди́ровать *imp.*, *perf.*

stampede *n.* пани́ческое бе́гство; *v.t.* & *i.* обраща́ть(ся) *imp.* в пани́ческое бе́гство.

stanch *v.t.* остана́вливать *imp.*, останови́ть (-влю́, -вишь) *perf.*

stanchion *n.* подпо́рка, сто́йка.

stand *n.* (*hat, coat*) ве́шалка; (*music*) пюпи́тр; (*umbrella, support*) подста́вка; (*counter*) сто́йка; (*booth*) ларёк (-рька́), кио́ск; (*taxi, bicycle*) стоя́нка; (*tribune*) ка́федра, трибу́на; (*at stadium*) трибу́на; (*position*) пози́ция, ме́сто (*pl.* -тá), положе́ние; (*resistance*) сопротивле́ние; *v.i.* стоя́ть (-ою́, -ои́шь) *imp.*; (*remain in force*) остава́ться (-аю́сь, -аёшься) *imp.*, оста́ться (-а́нусь, -а́нешься) в си́ле; *the matter stands thus*, де́ло обстои́т так; *it stands to reason*, разуме́ется; *v.t.* (*put*) ста́вить *imp.*, по~ *perf.*; (*endure*) выде́рживать *imp.*, вы́держать (-жу, -жишь) *perf.*; выноси́ть (-ошу́, -о́сишь) *imp.*, вы́нести (-су, -сешь; -с) *perf.*; терпе́ть (-плю́ -пишь) *imp.*, по~ *perf.*; (*treat to*) угоща́ть *imp.*, угости́ть *perf.* (*s.b.*, + *acc.*; *s.th.*, + *instr.*); *s. back*, отходи́ть (-ожу́, -о́дишь) *imp.*, отойти́ (-йду́, -йдёшь; отошёл, отошла́) *perf.* (from, от + *gen.*); (*not go forward*) держа́ться (-жу́сь, -жишься) *imp.* позади́; *s.-by*, (*store*) запа́с; (*reliable person*) надёжный челове́к (*pl.* лю́ди, -де́й, -дям, -дьми́); (*support*) опо́ра; *s. by*, (*v.i.*) (*not interfere*) не вме́шиваться *imp.*, вмеша́ться *perf.*; (*prepare*) пригота́вливаться *imp.*, пригото́виться *perf.*; (*v.t.*) (*support*) подде́рживать *imp.*, поддержа́ть (-жу́, -жишь) *perf.*; (*fulfil*) выполня́ть *imp.*, вы́полнить *perf.*; *s. for*, (*signify*) означа́ть *imp.*; (*tolerate*): *I shall not s. for it*, я не потерплю́; *s.-in*, замести́тель *m.*, ~ница; *s. in* (*for*), замеща́ть *imp.*, замести́ть *perf.*; *s.-offish*, высокоме́рный; *s. out*, выдава́ться (выдаётся), *imp.*, вы́даться (-астся, -адутся) *perf.*; выделя́ться *imp.*, вы́делиться *perf.*; *s. up*, встава́ть (встаю́, встаёшь) *imp.*, встать (-а́ну, -а́нешь) *perf.*; *s. up for*, (*defend*) отста́ивать *imp.*, отстоя́ть (-ою́, -ои́шь) *perf.*; защища́ть *imp.*, защити́ть (-ищу́, -ити́шь) *perf.*; *s. up to*, (*endure*) выде́рживать *imp.*, вы́держать (-жу, -жишь) *perf.*; (*not give in to*) не пасова́ть *imp.*, с~ *perf.* пе́ред+*instr*.

standard *n.* (*flag*) зна́мя (*pl.* -мёна) *neut.*, штанда́рт; (*norm*) станда́рт, норм; *s. of living*, жи́зненный у́ровень (-вня) *m.*; *of high s.* высо́кого ка́чества; *s.-bearer*, знамено́сец (-сца); *s. lamp*, торше́р; *adj.* норма́льный, станда́ртный, нормати́вный; (*generally accepted*) общепри́нятый; (*exemplary*) образцо́вый. **standardization** *n.* нормализа́ция, стандартиза́ция. **standardize** *v.t.* стандартизи́ровать *imp.*, *perf.*; нормализова́ть *imp.*, *perf.*

standing *n.* положе́ние, ранг, репута́ция; *to be in good s.* (*with s.b.*), быть на хоро́шем счету́ (у кого́-л.); *adj.* (*upright*) стоя́чий; (*permanent*) посто́янный; *s. army*, постоя́нная а́рмия; *s. committee*, постоя́нный комите́т.

stand-pipe *n.* стоя́к (-а́).

standpoint *n.* то́чка зре́ния.

standstill *n.* остано́вка, засто́й, па́уза; *be at a s.*, стоя́ть (-ою́, -ои́шь) *imp.* на мёртвой то́чке; *bring* (*come*) *to a s.* остана́вливать(ся) *imp.*, останови́ть(ся) (-влю́(сь), -вишь(ся)) *perf.*

stanza *n.* строфа́ (*pl.* -фы, -ф, -фа́м), станс.

staple[1] *n.* (*fastening*) скоба́ (*pl.* -бы, -б, -ба́м).

staple[2] *n.* (*principal product*) гла́вный проду́кт, основно́й това́р; (*principal element*) гла́вный элеме́нт; *adj.* основно́й, гла́вный.

star *n.* звезда́ (*pl.* звёзды); (*asterisk*) звёздочка; *adj.* звёздный; (*chief*) гла́вный; (*celebrated*) знамени́тый; *v.i.* игра́ть *imp.*, сыгра́ть *perf.* гла́вную роль. **starfish** *n.* морска́я звезда́ (*pl.* звёзды). **star-gazer** *n.* астро́лог, звездочёт.

starboard *n.* пра́вый борт (*loc.* -у́).

starch *n.* крахма́л; *v.t.*, крахма́лить *imp.*, на~ *perf.* **starched** *adj.* крахма́льный, накрахма́ленный. **starchy** *adj.* крахмали́стый; (*prim*) чо́порный.

stare *n.* при́стальный взгляд; *v.i.* при́стально смотре́ть (-трю́, -тришь) (at, на+*acc.*); *s.* (*one*) *in the face*, (*be obvious*) броса́ться *imp.*, бро́ситься *perf.* (+*dat.*) в глаза́.

stark *adj.* (*bare*) го́лый (гол, -а́, -о); (*desolate*) пусты́нный (-нен, -нна); (*sharp*) ре́зкий (-зок, -зка́, -зко); *adv.* соверше́нно.

starling *n.* скворе́ц (-рца́).

starry *adj.* звёздный; *s.-eyed*, (*coll.*) мечта́тельный.

start *n.* нача́ло; (*setting out*) отправле́ние; (*sport*) старт; (*advantage*) преиму́щество; (*shudder*) рыво́к (-вка́); *v.i.* начина́ться *imp.*, нача́ться (начнётся; начался́, -ла́сь) *perf.*; (*engine*) заводи́ться (-о́дится) *imp.*, завести́сь (-едётся; -ёлся, -ела́сь) *perf.*; (*set out*) отправля́ться *imp.*, отпра́виться *perf.*; (*shudder*) вздра́гивать *imp.*, вздро́гнуть *perf.*; (*sport*) ста́ртовать *imp.*, *perf.*; *v.t.* начина́ть *imp.*, нача́ть (-чну́, -чнёшь; на́чал, -а́, -о) *perf.* (gerund, inf., +*inf.*; by+gerund, с того́, что ...; with, +*instr.*, с+*gen.*; from the beginning, с нача́ла); (*set in motion*) пуска́ть *imp.*, пусти́ть (пущу́, пу́стишь) *perf.*; запуска́ть *imp.*, запусти́ть (-ущу́, -у́стишь) *perf.* **starter** *n.* (*tech.*) пуска́тель *m.*, ста́ртёр; (*sport*) ста́ртёр. **starter, starting** *adj.* пусково́й. **starting-point** *n.* отправно́й пункт.

startle *v.t.* испуга́ть *perf.*; поража́ть *imp.*, порази́ть *perf.* **startled** *adj.* испу́ганный (-ан), потрясённый (-ён, -ена́). **startling** *adj.* порази́тельный, потряса́ющий.

starvation *n.* го́лод, голода́ние. **starve** *v.i.* страда́ть *imp.*, по~ *perf.* от го́лода; (*to death*) умира́ть *imp.*, умере́ть (умру́, -рёшь; у́мер, -ла́, -ло) с го́лоду; *v.t.* мори́ть *imp.*, по~, у~ *perf.* го́лодом. **starving** *adj.* голода́ющий; (*hungry*) голо́дный (го́лоден, -дна́, -дно, голодны́).

state *n.* (*condition*) состоя́ние, положе́ние; (*pomp*) великоле́пие, по́мпа; (*nation, government*) госуда́рство, штат; *lie in s.*, поко́иться *imp.* в откры́том гробу́; *adj.* (*ceremonial*) торже́ственный (-ен, -енна); (*apart-*

ments) пара́дный; (*of State*) госуда́рственный; *v.t.* (*announce*) заявля́ть *imp.*, заяви́ть (-влю́, -вишь) *perf.*; (*expound*) излага́ть *imp.*, изложи́ть (-жу́, -жишь) *perf.*; (*maintain*) утверждать *imp.* **stated** *adj.* (*appointed*) назна́ченный. **stateless** *adj.* не име́ющий гражда́нства. **stately** *adj.* вели́чественный (-ен, -енна), велича́вый. **statement** *n.* (*announcement*) заявле́ние; (*exposition*) изложе́ние; (*assertion*) утвержде́ние. **statesman** *n.* госуда́рственный де́ятель *m.*

static *adj.* стати́чный, неподви́жный. **statics** *n.* ста́тика.

station *n.* (*rly.*) вокза́л, ста́нция; (*position*) ме́сто (*pl.* -та́); (*social*) obще́ственное положе́ние; (*naval etc.*) ба́за; (*meteorological*, *hydro-electric power*, *radio etc.*) ста́нция; (*post*) пост (-а́, *loc.* -у́); *v.t.* ста́вить *imp.*, по~ *perf.*; помеща́ть *imp.*, помести́ть *perf.*; (*mil.*) размеща́ть *imp.*, размести́ть *perf.* **station-master** *n.* нача́льник вокза́ла, ста́нции.

stationary *adj.* неподви́жный; (*tech.*) стациона́рный; (*constant*) постоя́нный (-нен, -нна), усто́йчивый.

stationer *n.* продаве́ц (-вца́), -вщи́ца канцеля́рского магази́на. **stationery** *n.* канцеля́рские това́ры *m.pl.*; (*writing-paper*) почто́вая бума́га; *s. shop*, канцеля́рский магази́н.

statistic *n.* статисти́ческое да́нное, ци́фра. **statistical** *adj.* статисти́ческий. **statistician** *n.* стати́стик. **statistics** *n.* стати́стика.

statue *n.* ста́туя. **statuesque** *adj.* велича́вый. **statuette** *n.* статуэ́тка.

stature *n.* рост, стан; (*merit*) досто́инство, ка́чество.

status *n.* ста́тус; (*social*) обще́ственное положе́ние; (*state*) состоя́ние. **status quo** *n.* ста́тус-кво́.

statute *n.* стату́т; законода́тельный акт; *pl.* уста́в; *s.-book*, свод зако́нов. **statutory** *adj.* устано́вленный (-ен) зако́ном.

staunch *v.t. see* **stanch**; *adj.* (*loyal*) ве́рный (-рен, -рна́, -рно); (*steadfast*) сто́йкий (-о́ек, -ойка́, -о́йко), твёрдый (твёрд, -а́, -о); про́чный (-чен, -чна́, -чно, про́чны́).

stave *n.* (*of cask*) клёпка; *v.t.* пробива́ть *imp.*, проби́ть (-бью́, -бьёшь) *perf.*; разбива́ть *imp.*, разби́ть (разобью́, -бьёшь) *perf.*; *s. off*, предотвраща́ть *imp.*, предотврати́ть (-ащу́, -ати́шь) *perf.*

stay[1] *n.* (*time spent*) пребыва́ние; (*suspension*) приостановле́ние; (*postponement*) отсро́чка; *v.i.* (*remain*) остава́ться (-аю́сь, -аёшься) *imp.*, оста́ться (-а́нусь, -а́нешься) *perf.* (*to dinner*, обе́дать); (*put up*) остана́вливаться *imp.*, останови́ться (-влю́сь, -вишься) *perf.* (at (*place*), в + *prep.*; at (*friends' etc.*), у + *gen.*); гости́ть *imp.* (with, у + *gen.*); (*live*) жить (живу́, живёшь; жил, -а́, -о); *s. a moment!* подожди́те мину́тку!; *s. away*, отсу́тствовать *imp.*; *s. behind*, остава́ться (-аю́сь, -аёшься) *imp.*, оста́ться (-а́нусь, -а́нешься) *perf.*; *v.t.* (*check*) заде́рживать *imp.*, задержа́ть (-жу́, -жишь) *perf.*; (*hunger*, *thirst*) утоля́ть *imp.*, утоли́ть *perf.*; (*suspend*) приостана́вливать *imp.*, приостанови́ть (-влю́, -вишь) *perf.*; (*postpone*) отсро́чивать *imp.*, отсро́чить *perf.*; *s. the course*, подде́рживаться *imp.*, поддержа́ться (-жу́сь, -жишься) до конца́. **stay-at-home** *n.* домосе́д, ~ка. **staying-power** *n.* выно́сливость.

stay[2] *n.* (*naut.*) штаг; (*support*) подде́ржка; *v.t.* (*support*) подде́рживать *imp.*, поддержа́ть (-жу́, -жишь) *perf.* **stays** *n.* корсе́т.

stead *n.*: *to stand s.b. in good s.*, оказываться *imp.*, оказа́ться (-ажу́сь, -а́жешься) *perf.* поле́зным кому́-л.

steadfast *adj.* (*firm*, *steady*) про́чный (-чен, -чна́, -чно, про́чны́), усто́йчивый; (*unshakeable*) сто́йкий (-о́ек, -ойка́, -о́йко), непоколеби́мый.

steady *adj.* (*firm*) про́чный (-чен, -чна́, -чно, про́чны́), усто́йчивый, твёрдый (твёрд, -а́, -о); (*continuous*) непреры́вный; (*prices*) усто́йчивый; (*wind*, *temperature*) ро́вный (-вен, -вна́, -вно); (*speed*) постоя́нный (-нен, -нна); (*unshakeable*) непоколеби́мый; (*staid*) степе́нный (-нен, -нна); *s. hand*, твёрдая рука́ (*acc.* -ку; *pl.* -ки, -к, -ка́м); *v.t.* (*boat*) приводи́ть (-ожу́, -о́дишь) *imp.*, привести́ (-еду́, -едёшь; -ёл, -ела́) *perf.* в равнове́сие.

steak *n.* (*before cooking*) то́лстый кусо́к (-ска́) мя́са (*meat*), говя́дины (*beef*), ры́бы (*fish*), для жа́ренья; (*dish*) то́лстый кусо́к (-ска́) жа́реного мя́са (*meat*), жа́реной ры́бы (*fish*); (*beefsteak*) бифште́кс.

steal *v.t.* ворова́ть *imp.*, с~ *perf.*; красть (краду́, -дёшь; крал) *imp.*, у~ *perf.* (*also a kiss*); *s. a glance*, укра́дкой взгля́дывать *imp.*, взгляну́ть (-ну́, -нешь) *perf.* (at, на + *acc.*); *v.i.* кра́сться (краду́сь, -дёшься; кра́лся) *imp.*; подкра́дываться *imp.*, подкра́сться (-аду́сь, -адёшься; -а́лся) *perf.* **stealing** *n.* воровство́. **stealth** *n.* хи́трость, уло́вка; *by s.*, укра́дкой, тайко́м. **stealthy** *adj.* ворова́тый, та́йный, скры́тый.

steam *n.* пар (*loc.* -у́; *pl.* -ы́); *at full s.*, на всех пара́х; *get up s.*, разводи́ть (-ожу́, -о́дишь) *imp.*, развести́ (-еду́, -едёшь; -ёл, -ела́) пары́; (*fig.*) собира́ться *imp.*, собра́ться (-берётся; -бра́лся, -брала́сь, -бра́ло́сь) с си́лами; *let off s.*, (*fig.*) дава́ть (даю́, даёшь) *imp.*, дать (дам, дашь, даст, дади́м; дал, -а́, да́ло́, -и) *perf.* вы́ход свои́м чу́вствам; *under one's own s.*, сам (-а́, -о́, -и); свои́м хо́дом; *adj.* парово́й, паро- *in comb.*; *v.t.* па́рить *imp.*; *v.i.* па́риться *imp.*, по~ *perf.*; (*vessel*) ходи́ть (хо́дит) *indet.*, идти́ (идёт; шёл, шла) *det.* на пара́х; *s. up*, (*mist over*) запотева́ть *imp.*, запоте́ть *perf.*; поте́ть *imp.*, за~, от~ *perf.*; *s. engine*, парова́я маши́на. **steamer** *n.* парохо́д. **steaming** *adj.* дымя́щийся. **steam-roller** *n.* парово́й като́к (-тка́). **steamship** *n.* парохо́д.

steed *n.* конь (-ня́, *pl.* -ни, -не́й) *m.*

steel *n.* сталь; *adj.* стально́й; *v.t.* (*make resolute*) ожесточа́ть *imp.*, ожесточи́ть *perf.*; *to s. one's (own) heart*, ожесточа́ться *imp.*, ожесточи́ться *perf.*; *s. foundry*, сталелите́йный заво́д; *s.-making*, сталеплави́льный; *s.-rolling*, сталепрока́тный; *s. works*, сталеплави́льный заво́д. **steely** *adj.* стально́й; (*cold*) холо́дный (хо́лоден, -дна́, -дно, хо́лодны́); (*stern*) суро́вый. **steelyard** *n.* безме́н.

steep[1] *v.t.* (*immerse*) погружа́ть *imp.*, погрузи́ть *perf.* (in, в + *acc.*); (*saturate*) пропи́тывать *imp.*, пропита́ть *perf.* (in, + *instr.*); *be steeped in*, (*also fig.*) погружа́ться *imp.*, погрузи́ться *perf.* (in, в + *acc.*).

steep[2] *adj.* круто́й (крут, -а́, -о); (*excessive*) чрезме́рный; (*improbable*) невероя́тный. **steepness** *n.* крутизна́.

steeple *n.* шпиль *m.* **steeplechase** *n.* ска́чки *f.pl.* с препя́тствиями. **steeplejack** *n.* верхола́з.

steer[1] *n.* молодо́й вол (-а́), бычо́к (-чка́).

steer[2] *v.t.* (*control, navigate*) управля́ть *imp.*, пра́вить *imp.* + *instr.*; (*guide*) руководи́ть *imp.* + *instr.*; *v.abs.* пра́вить *imp.* рулём; рули́ть *imp.* (*coll.*); *s. clear of*, избега́ть *imp.*, избежа́ть (-егу́, -ежи́шь) *perf.* + *gen.* **steering-column** *n.* рулева́я коло́нка. **steering-wheel** *n.* руль (-ля́) *m.*, бара́нка (*coll.*); (*naut.*) штурва́л.

stellar *adj.* звёздный. **stellate** *adj.* звездообра́зный.

stem[1] *n.* сте́бель (-бля; *pl.* -бли, -бле́й) *m.*; (*trunk*) ствол (-а́); (*wine-glass*) но́жка; (*ling.*) осно́ва; (*naut.*) нос (*loc.* -у́; *pl.* -ы́); *from s. to stern*, от но́са до кормы́; *v.i.*: *s. from*, происходи́ть (-ожу́, -о́дишь) *imp.*, произойти́ (-ойдёт; -ошёл, -ошла́) *perf.* от + *gen.*

stem[2] *v.t.* (*dam*) запру́живать *imp.*, запруди́ть (-ужу́, -у́дишь) *perf.*; (*stop*) остана́вливать *imp.*, останови́ть (-влю́, -вишь) *perf.*

stench *n.* злово́ние, смрад.

stencil *n.* трафаре́т; (*tech.*) шабло́н; *v.t.* наноси́ть (-ошу́, -о́сишь) *imp.*, нанести́ (-есу́, -есёшь; -ёс, -есла́) *perf.* узо́р по трафаре́ту. **stencilled** *adj.* трафаре́тный.

stentorian *adj.* громогла́сный.

step *n.* (*pace, action*) шаг (-а́ *with* 2, 3, 4, *loc.* -у́; *pl.* -и́); (*gait*) похо́дка; (*dance*) па *neut.indecl.*; (*of stairs, ladder*) ступе́нь (*gen.pl.* -е́ней); (*measure*) ме́ра; *s. by s.*, шаг за шаго́м; *in s.*, в но́гу; *out of s.*, не в но́гу; *watch one's s.*, де́йствовать *imp.* осторо́жно; *take steps*, принима́ть *imp.*, приня́ть (приму́, -мешь; при́нял, -á, -о) *perf.* ме́ры; *v.i.* шага́ть *imp.*, шагну́ть *perf.*; ступа́ть *imp.*, ступи́ть (-плю́, -пишь) *perf.*; *s. aside*, сторони́ться (-ню́сь, -нишься) *imp.*, по~ *perf.*; *s. back*, отступа́ть *imp.*, отступи́ть (-плю́, -пишь) *perf.*; *s. down*, (*resign*) уходи́ть (-ожу́, -о́дишь) *imp.*, уйти́ (уйду́, -дёшь; ушёл, ушла́) *perf.* в отста́вку; *s. forward*, выступа́ть *imp.*, вы́ступить *perf.*; *s. in*, (*intervene*) вме́шиваться *imp.*, вмеша́ться *perf.*; *s. on*, наступа́ть *imp.*, наступи́ть (-плю́, -пишь) *perf.* на + *acc.* (s.b.'s foot, кому́-л. на́ ногу); *s. over*, переша́гивать *imp.*, перешагну́ть *perf.* + *acc.*, че́рез + *acc.*; *s. up*, (*increase*, *promote*) повыша́ть *imp.*, повы́сить *perf.*; (*strengthen*) уси́ливать *imp.*, уси́лить *perf.* **step-ladder** *n.* стремя́нка. **stepped** *adj.* ступе́нчатый. **stepping-stone** *n.* ка́мень (-мня; *pl.* -мни, -мне́й) *m.* для перехо́да че́рез ре́чку *etc.*; (*fig.*) сре́дство к достиже́нию це́ли. **steps** *n.* ле́стница.

stepbrother *n.* сво́дный брат (*pl.* -ья, -ьев). **stepdaughter** *n.* па́дчерица. **stepfather** *n.* о́тчим. **stepmother** *n.* ма́чеха. **stepsister** *n.* сво́дная сестра́ (*pl.* сёстры, сестёр, сёстрам). **stepson** *n.* па́сынок (-нка).

steppe *n.* степь (*loc.* -пи́; *pl.* -пи, -пе́й); *adj.* степно́й.

stereo *n.* (*record-player*) стереофони́ческий прои́грыватель *m.*; (*stereophony*) стереофо́ния; *adj.* (*recorded in stereo*) сте́рео. **stereophonic** *adj.* стереофони́ческий. **stereophony** *n.* стереофо́ния. **stereoscope** *n.* стереоско́п. **stereoscopic** *adj.* стереоскопи́ческий. **stereotype** *n.* стереоти́п; (*tech.*) шабло́н. **stereotyped** *adj.* (*also banal*) стереоти́пный, шабло́нный.

sterile *adj.* (*barren*, *germ-free*) стери́льный. **sterility** *n.* стери́льность. **sterilization** *n.* стерилиза́ция. **sterilize** *v.t.* стерилизова́ть *imp.*, *perf.* **sterilizer** *n.* стерилиза́тор.

sterling *n.* сте́рлинг; *pound s.*, фунт сте́рлингов; *adj.* сте́рлинговый; (*irreproachable*) безупре́чный; (*reliable*) надёжный.

stern[1] *n.* корма́.

stern[2] *adj.* суро́вый, стро́гий (-г, -га́, -го).

sternum *n.* груди́на.

stethoscope *n.* стетоско́п.

stevedore *n.* стивидо́р, гру́зчик.

stew *n.* (*cul.*) мя́со тушёное вме́сте с овоща́ми; *be in a s.*, (*coll.*) волнова́ться *imp.*; *v.t.* & *i.* туши́ть(ся) (-шу́(сь), -шишь(ся)) *imp.*, с~ *perf.*; томи́ть(ся) *imp.*; *to s. in one's own juice*, расхлёбывать *imp.* ка́шу, кото́рую сам завари́л. **stewed** *adj.* тушёный; *s. fruit*, компо́т. **stewpan, stewpot** *n.* кастрю́ля, соте́йник.

steward *n.* стю́ард, бортпроводни́к (-á); (*master of ceremonies*) распоряди́тель *m.* **stewardess** *n.* стюарде́сса, бортпроводни́ца.

stick[1] *n.* па́лка; (*of chalk etc.*) па́лочка; (*hockey*, *walking*) клю́шка; *sticks*, (*collect.*) хво́рост (-а(у)).

stick[2] *v.t.* (*spear*) зака́лывать *imp.*, заколо́ть (-лю́, -лешь) *perf.*; (*make adhere*) прикле́ивать *imp.*, прикле́ить *perf.* (to, к + *dat.*); прилепля́ть *imp.*, прилепи́ть (-плю́, -пишь) *perf.* (to, к + *dat.*); (*coll.*) (*put*) ста́вить *imp.*, по~ *perf.*; (*lay*) класть (кладу́, -дёшь; клал) *imp.*, положи́ть (-жу́, -жишь) *perf.*; *v.i.* (*adhere*) ли́пнуть (лип) *imp.* (to, к + *dat.*); прилипа́ть *imp.*, прили́пнуть (-нет; прили́п) *perf.* (to, к + *dat.*); прикле́иваться *imp.*, прикле́иться *perf.* (to, к + *dat.*); *s. in*, (*thrust in*) втыка́ть *imp.*, воткну́ть *perf.*; вка́лывать *imp.*, вколо́ть (-лю́, -лешь) *perf.*; *the arrow stuck into the ground*, стрела́ воткну́лась в зе́млю; (*into opening*) всо́вывать *imp.*, всу́нуть *perf.*; *s. on*, (*glue on*) накле́ивать *imp.*, накле́ить *perf.*; *s. out*, (*thrust out*) высо́вывать *imp.*, вы́сунуть *perf.* (from, из + *gen.*); (*project*) торча́ть (-чу́, -чи́шь) *imp.*; *s. to*, (*keep to*) приде́рживаться *imp.*, придержа́ться (-жу́сь, -жишься) *perf.* + *gen.*; (*remain at*) не отвлека́ться *imp.* от + *gen.*; *s. together*, держа́ться (-жимся) *imp.* вме́сте; *s. up for*, защищáть *imp.*, защити́ть (-ищу́, -ити́шь) *perf.*; *be, get, stuck*, застревáть *imp.*, застря́ть (-я́ну, -я́нешь) *perf.* **sticker** *n.* (*label*) этикéтка, ярлы́к (-á). **sticking-plaster** *n.* ли́пкий плáстырь *m.*

stickleback *n.* кóлюшка.

stickler *n.* (я́рый) сторóнник, -ица; привéрженец (-нца), -нка (for, + *gen.*).

sticky *adj.* ли́пкий (-пок, -пкá, -пко), клéйкий; *he will come to a s. end*, он плóхо кóнчит.

stiff *adj.* жёсткий (-ток, -ткá, -тко), неги́бкий (-бок, -бкá, -бко); (*with cold*) окоченéлый; (*prim*) чóпорный; (*difficult*) трýдный (-ден, -днá, -дно, трýдны́); (*breeze*) си́льный (си́лён, -льнá, -льно, си́льны́); *be s.*, (*ache*) болéть (-ли́т) *imp.* **stiffen** *v.t.* дéлать *imp.*, с~ *perf.* жёстким; *v.i.* станови́ться (-влю́сь, -вишься) *imp.*, стать (-áну, -áнешь) *perf.* жёстким. **stiffness** *n.* жёсткость; (*primness*) чóпорность.

stifle *v.t.* души́ть (-шу́, -шишь) *imp.*, за~ *perf.*; (*suppress*) подавля́ть *imp.*, подави́ть (-влю́, -вишь) *perf.*; (*sound*) заглушáть *imp.*, заглуши́ть *perf.*; *v.i.* задыхáться *imp.*, задохнýться (-óх(нýл)ся, -óх(нý)лась) *perf.* **stifling** *adj.* удýшливый, дýшный (-шен, -шнá, -шно).

stigma *n.* клеймó (*pl.* -ма) позóра. **stigmatize** *v.t.* клейми́ть *imp.*, за~ *perf.*

stile *n.* ступéньки *f.pl.* для перехóда чéрез забóр, перелáз (*coll.*).

stiletto *n.* стилéт; *s. heels*, гвóздики *m.pl.*, шпи́льки *f.pl.*

still[1] *adv.* (всё) ещё, до сих пóр, по-прéжнему; *s. better*, ещё лýчше; (*nevertheless*) всё же, тем не мéнее, однáко; (*motionless*) неподви́жно; (*quietly*) спокóйно; *stand s.*, не дви́гаться (-аюсь, -аешься & дви́жусь, -жешься) *imp.*, дви́нуться *perf.*; *time stood s.* врéмя останови́лось; *sit s.*, сидéть (сижý, сиди́шь) *imp.* сми́рно.

still[2] *n.* (*quiet*) тишинá; (*film*) кадр; *adj.* ти́хий (тих, -á, -о), спокóйный; (*immobile*) неподви́жный; (*not fizzy*) не шипýчий; *v.t.* успокáивать *imp.*, успокóить *perf.*

still[3] *n.* перегóнный куб (*pl.* -ы́).

still-born *adj.* мертворождённый.

still life *n.* натюрмóрт.

stillness *n.* тишинá, спокóйствие; (*immobility*) неподви́жность.

stilt *n.* ходýля; (*tech.*) стóйка, свáя. **stilted** *adj.* ходýльный.

stimulant *n.* возбуждáющее срéдство. **stimulate** *v.t.* возбуждáть *imp.*, возбуди́ть *perf.*; стимули́ровать *imp.*, *perf.* **stimulating** *adj.* возбуди́тельный. **stimulation** *n.* возбуждéние. **stimulus** *n.* сти́мул, возбуди́тель *m.*, побуди́тельная причи́на.

sting *n.* жáло (*also fig.*); укýс (*also wound*); *v.t.* жáлить *imp.*, у~ *perf.*; укуси́ть (-ушý, -ýсишь); *v.i.* (*burn*) жечь (жжёт, жгут; жёг, жгла) *imp.* **stinging** *adj.* (*caustic*) язви́тельный; *s. nettle*, жгýчая крапи́ва. **sting-ray** *n.* скат дазиáтис.

stinginess *n.* скýпость, скáредность. **stingy** *adj.* скупóй (скуп, -á, -о), скáредный.

stink *n.* зловóние, вонь, смрад; *v.i.* воня́ть *imp.* (of, + *instr.*); смердéть (-ржý, -рди́шь) *imp.* (of, + *instr.*). **stinking** *adj.* вонючий, зловóнный (-нен, -нна), смрáдный.

stint *n.* нóрма; *v.t.* скупи́ться *imp.*, по~ *perf.* на + *acc.*

stipend *n.* (*salary*) жáлование; (*grant*) стипéндия. **stipendiary** *adj.* получáющий жáлование.

stipple *n.* рабóта, гравировáние пункти́ром; *v.t.* & *i.* рисовáть *imp.*, на~ *perf.*, гравировáть *imp.*, вы́~ *perf.*, пункти́ром.

stipulate *v.i.* стáвить *imp.*, по~ *perf.* услóвием (that, что); *v.t.* обуслóвливать *imp.*, обуслóвить *perf.* + *instr.*; (*demand*) трéбовать *imp.* + *gen.* **stipulation** *n.* услóвие.

stir *n.* шевелéние, движéние; (*uproar*) суматóха; *cause a s.*, вызывáть *imp.*, вы́звать (вы́зову, -вешь) *perf.* волнéние; *v.t.* (*move*) шевели́ть (шевелю́, -éли́шь) *imp.*, шевельнýть *perf.* + *instr.*; дви́гать *imp.*, дви́нуть *perf.* + *instr.*; (*mix*) мешáть *imp.*, по~ *perf.*;

размéшивать *imp.*, размешáть *perf.*; (*excite*) волновáть *imp.*, вз~ *perf.*; *v.i.* (*move*) шевели́ться (шевелю́сь, -е́ли́шься) *imp.*, шевельну́ться *perf.*; дви́гаться *imp.*, дви́нуться *perf.*; (*be excited*) волновáться; *s. up*, возбуждáть *imp.*, возбуди́ть *perf.* **stirring** *adj.* волну́ющий.

stirrup *n.* стрéмя (-мени; *pl.* -менá, -мя́н, -менáм) *neut.*

stitch *n.* стежóк (-жкá); (*knitting*) пéтля (*gen.pl.* -тель); (*med.*) шов (шва); (*pain*) кóлотье (*coll.*); *v.t.* (*embroider, make line of stitches*) строчи́ть (-очу́, -óчи́шь) *imp.*, про~ *perf.*; (*join by sewing, make, suture*) сшивáть *imp.*, сшить (сошью́, сошьёшь) *perf.*; (*med.*) наклáдывать *imp.*, наложи́ть (-жу́, -жишь) *perf.* швы на + *acc.*; *s. up*, зашивáть *imp.*, заши́ть (-шью́, -шьёшь) *perf.* **stitching** *n.* (*sewing*) шитьё; (*stitches*) стрóчка.

stoat *n.* горностáй.

stock *n.* (*store*) запáс; (*equipment*) инвентáрь (-ря́) *m.*; (*livestock*) скот (-á); (*cul.*) бульóн; (*family*) семья́ (*pl.* -мьи, -мéй, -мьям); (*origin, clan*) род (*loc.* -у́; *pl.* -ы́); (*fin.*) áкции *f.pl.*; *pl.* (*fin.*) фóнды *m.pl.*; (*punishment*) колóдки *f.pl.*; *in s.*, в нали́чии; *out of s.*, распрóдан; *take s. of*, обду́мывать *imp.*, обду́мать *perf.*; *adj.* стандáртный; (*banal*) изби́тый; *v.t.* имéть в нали́чии; *s. up*, запасáть *imp.*, запасти́ (-су́, -сёшь; запáс, -слá) *perf.* **stock-breeder** *n.* скотовóд. **stock-breeding** *n.* скотовóдство. **stockbroker** *n.* биржевóй мáклер. **stock-exchange** *n.* фóндовая би́ржа. **stock-in-trade** *n.* (торгóвый) инвентáрь (-ря́) *m.* **stockpile** *n.* запáс; *v.t.* накáпливать *imp.*, накопи́ть (-плю́, -пишь) *perf.* **stock-still** *adj.* неподви́жный. **stock-taking** *n.* переучёт товáра, провéрка инвентаря́. **stockyard** *n.* скотопригóнный двор (-á).

stockade *n.* частокóл.

stocking *n.* чулóк (-лкá; *gen.pl.* чулóк).

stocky *adj.* приземи́стый, коренáстый.

stodgy *adj.* (*food*) тяжёлый (-л, -лá); (*boring*) ску́чный (-чен, -чнá, -чно).

stoic *n.* стóик. **stoic(al)** *adj.* стои́ческий. **stoicism** *n.* стоици́зм.

stoke *v.t.* топи́ть (-плю́, -пишь) *imp.* **stokehold, stokehole** *n.* кочегáрка.

stoker *n.* кочегáр, истопни́к (-á).

stole *n.* паланти́н.

stolid *adj.* флегмати́чный.

stomach *n.* желу́док (-дка), (*also surface of body*) живóт (-á); *adj.* желу́дочный; *v.t.* терпéть (-плю́, -пишь) *imp.*, по~ *perf.* **stomach-ache** *n.* боль в животé.

stone *n.* (*material, piece of it*) кáмень (-мня; *pl.* -мни, -мнéй) *m.*; (*fruit*) кóсточка; *adj.* кáменный; *v.t.* побивáть *imp.*, поби́ть (-бью́, -бьёшь) *perf.* камня́ми; (*fruit*) вынимáть *imp.*, вы́нуть *perf.* кóсточки из + *gen.*; *s. to death*, заби́ть (-бью́, -бьёшь) *perf.* камня́ми нáсмерть. **Stone Age** *n.* кáменный век (*loc.* -у́). **stone-cold** *adj.* совершéнно холóдный (хóлоден, -днá, -дно, хóлодны́). **stone-deaf** *adj.* совершéнно глухóй (глух, -á, -о). **stonemason** *n.* кáменщик. **stonewall** *v.i.* устрáивать *imp.*, устрóить *perf.* обстру́кцию; мешáть *imp.*, по~ *perf.* диску́ссии. **stonily** *adv.* с кáменным выражéнием, хóлодно. **stony** *adj.* камени́стый; (*fig.*) кáменный, холóдный (хóлоден, -днá, -дно, хóлодны́). **stony-broke** *predic.*: *I am s.*, у меня́ нет ни грошá.

stool *n.* табурéт, табурéтка.

stoop *n.* суту́лость; *v.t.* & *i.* суту́лить(ся) *imp.*, с~ *perf.*; (*bend* (*down*)) наклоня́ть(ся) *imp.*, наклони́ть(ся) (-ню́(сь), -нишь(ся)) *perf.*; *s. to*, (*abase oneself*) унижáться *imp.*, уни́зиться *perf.* до + *gen.*; (*condescend*) снисходи́ть (-ожу́, -óдишь) *imp.*, снизойти́ (-ойду́, -ойдёшь; -ошёл, -ошлá) *perf.* до + *gen.* **stooped, stooping** *adj.* суту́лый.

stop *n.* остановка; (*discontinuance*) прекращéние; (*organ*) реги́стр; (*full s.*) тóчка; *request s.*, останóвка по трéбованию; *v.t.* остáнавливать *imp.*, останови́ть (-влю́, -вишь) *perf.*; (*discontinue*) прекращáть *imp.*, прекрати́ть (-ащу́, -ати́шь) *perf.*; (*restrain*) удéрживать *imp.*, удержáть (-жу́, -жишь) *perf.* (from, от + *gen.*);

v.i. остана́вливаться *imp.*, останови́ться (-влю́сь, -ви́шься) *perf.*; (*discontinue*) прекраща́ться *imp.*, прекрати́ться (-и́тся) *perf.*; (*cease*) перестава́ть (-таю́, -таёшь) *imp.*, переста́ть (-а́ну, -а́нешь) *perf.* (+*inf.*); *s. up*, *v.t.* затыка́ть *imp.*, заткну́ть *perf.*; *s. at nothing*, ни перед че́м не остана́вливаться *imp.*, останови́ться (-влю́сь, -ви́шься) *perf.* **stopcock** *n.* запо́рный кран. **stopgap** *n.* заты́чка. **stop-light** *n.* стоп-сигна́л. **stoppage** *n.* остано́вка; (*strike*) забасто́вка. **stopper** *n.* про́бка; (*tech.*) сто́пор. **stop-press** *n.* э́кстренное сообще́ние в газе́те. **stop-watch** *n.* секундоме́р.

storage *n.* хране́ние. **store** *n.* запа́с; (*storehouse*) склад; (*shop*) магази́н; *set s. by*, цени́ть (-ню́, -нишь) *imp.*; *what is in s. for me?* что ждёт меня́ впереди́? *v.t.* запаса́ть *imp.*, запасти́ (-су́, -сёшь; запа́с, -сла́) *perf.*; (*put into storage*) сдава́ть (сдаю́, сдаёшь) *imp.*, сдать (сдам, сдашь, сдаст, сдади́м; сдал, -а́, -о) *perf.* на хране́ние. **storehouse** *n.* склад, амба́р, храни́лище. **store-room** кладова́я *sb.*

storey, story[1] *n.* эта́ж (-а́).

stork *n.* а́ист.

storm *n.* бу́ря, гроза́ (*pl.* -зы); (*naut.*) шторм; (*mil.*) штурм, при́ступ; (*outburst*) взрыв; *v.t.* (*mil.*) штурмова́ть *imp.*; брать (беру́, берёшь) *imp.*, взять (возьму́, -мёшь; взял, -а́, -о) *perf.* при́ступом; *v.i.* бушева́ть (-шу́ю, -шу́ешь) *imp.* **storm-cloud** *n.* ту́ча. **stormy** *adj.* бу́рный (-рен, бу́рна́, -рно), бу́йный (бу́ен, буйна́, -но). **stormy petrel** *n.* качу́рка ма́лая.

story[1] *see* **storey**.

story[2] *n.* расска́з, по́весть; (*anecdote*) анекдо́т; (*plot*) фа́була, сюже́т; (*history, event*) исто́рия; *s.-teller*, расска́зчик.

stout *adj.* (*solid*) пло́тный (-тен, -тна́, -тно, пло́тны́); (*portly*) доро́дный; *n.* кре́пкий по́ртер; *s.-hearted*, отва́жный. **stoutly** *adv.* (*stubbornly*) упо́рно; (*energetically*) энерги́чно; (*strongly*) кре́пко. **stoutness** *n.* (*strength*) про́чность; (*portliness*) доро́дство; (*courage*) отва́га; (*firmness*) сто́йкость.

stove *n.* (*with fire inside*) печь (*loc.* -чи́; *pl.* -чи, -че́й); (*cooker*) плита́ (*pl.* -ты).

stow *v.t.* укла́дывать *imp.*, уложи́ть (-жу́, -жишь) *perf.*; *s. away*, (*travel free*) е́хать (е́ду, е́дешь) *imp.*, по~ *perf.* за́йцем, без биле́та. **stowaway** *n.* за́яц (за́йца), безбиле́тный пассажи́р.

straddle *v.i.* широко́ расставля́ть *imp.*, расста́вить *perf.* но́ги; *v.t.* (*sit astride*) сиде́ть (сижу́, сиди́шь) *imp.* верхо́м на+*prep.*; (*stand astride*) стоя́ть (-ою́, -ои́шь) *imp.*, расста́вив но́ги над+*instr.*

straggle *v.i.* (*drop behind*) отстава́ть (-стаю́, -стаёшь) *imp.*, отста́ть (-а́ну, -а́нешь) *perf.* **straggler** *n.* отста́вший *sb.* **straggling** *adj.* (*scattered*) разбро́санный; (*untidy*) беспоря́дочный.

straight *adj.* (*unbent*) прямо́й (-м, -ма́, -мо, пря́мы́); (*honest*) че́стный (-тен, -тна́, -тно); (*undiluted*) неразба́вленный; *predic.* (*properly arranged*) в поря́дке; *adv.* пря́мо; *s. away*, сра́зу. **straighten** *v.t.* & *i.* выпрямля́ть(ся) *imp.*, вы́прямить(ся) *perf.*; *v.t.* (*smooth out*) расправля́ть *imp.*, распра́вить *perf.* **straightforward** *adj.* прямо́й (-м, -ма́, -мо, пря́мы́); (*simple*) просто́й (-т, -та́, -то); (*honest*) че́стный (-тен, -тна́, -тно). **straightness** *n.* прямизна́.

strain[1] *n.* (*pull, tension*) натяже́ние; (*also sprain*) растяже́ние; (*phys., tech.*) напряже́ние; (*tendency*) скло́нность; (*sound*) напе́в, звук; *in the same s.*, в том же ду́хе; *v.t.* (*stretch*) натя́гивать *imp.*, натяну́ть (-ну́, -нешь) *perf.*; (*also sprain*) растя́гивать *imp.*, растяну́ть (-ну́, -нешь) *perf.*; (*phys., tech.*) напряга́ть *imp.*, напря́чь (-ягу́, -яжёшь; -яг, -ягла́) *perf.*; (*filter*) проце́живать *imp.*, процеди́ть (-ежу́, -е́дишь) *perf.*; *v.i.* (*also exert oneself*) напряга́ться *imp.*, напря́чься (-ягу́сь, -яжёшься; -я́гся, -ягла́сь) *perf.* **strained** *adj.* натя́нутый (*also fig.*); растя́нутый (*also sprained*). **strainer** *n.* (*tea s.*) си́течко; (*filter*) фильтр; (*sieve*) си́то.

strain[2] *n.* (*breed*) поро́да; (*hereditary trait*) насле́дственная черта́.

strait(s) *n.* (*geog.*) проли́в. **straiten** *v.t.* ограни́чивать *imp.*, ограни́чить *perf.*

straitened *adj.*: *in s. circumstances*, в стеснённых обстоя́тельствах. **strait-jacket** *n.* смири́тельная руба́шка. **strait-laced** *adj.* пурита́нский. **straits** *n.* (*difficulties*) затрудни́тельное положе́ние.

strand[1] *n.* (*hair*, *rope*) прядь; (*rope*, *cable*) стре́нга; (*thread*, *also fig.*) нить.

strand[2] *n.* (*of sea etc.*) бе́рег (*loc.* -у́; *pl.* -а́); *v.t.* сажа́ть *imp.*, посади́ть (-ажу́, -а́дишь) *perf.* на мель. **stranded** *adj.* (*fig.*) без средств.

strange *adj.* стра́нный (-нен, -нна́, -нно); (*unfamiliar*) незнако́мый; (*alien*) чужо́й. **strangely** *adv.* стра́нно. **strangeness** *n.* стра́нность. **stranger** *n.* незнако́мец (-мца), -о́мка; неизве́стный *sb.*; чужо́й *sb.*

strangle *v.t.* души́ть (-шу́, -шишь) *imp.*, за~ *perf.* **stranglehold** *n.* мёртвая хва́тка. **strangulate** *v.t.* сжима́ть *imp.*, сжать (сожму́, -мёшь) *perf.* **strangulation** *n.* (*strangling*) удуше́ние; (*strangulating*) зажима́ние.

strap *n.* реме́нь (-мня́) *m.*; *v.t.* (*tie up*) стя́гивать *imp.*, стяну́ть (-ну́, -нешь) *perf.* ремнём. **strapping** *adj.* ро́слый.

stratagem *n.* стратаге́ма, хи́трость. **strategic** *adj.* стратеги́ческий. **strategist** *n.* страте́г. **strategy** *n.* страте́гия.

stratification *n.* расслое́ние. **stratified** *adj.* слои́стый. **stratosphere** *n.* стратосфе́ра. **stratum** *n.* слой (*pl.* -о́й), пласт (-а́, *loc.* -у́).

straw *n.* соло́ма; (*drinking*) соло́минка; *the last s.*, после́дняя ка́пля; *adj.* соло́менный.

strawberry *n.* клубни́ка; (*wild s.*) земляни́ка *collect.*; *adj.* клубни́чный; земляни́чный.

stray *v.i.* сбива́ться *imp.*, сби́ться (собью́сь, -ьёшься) *perf.*; (*roam*) блужда́ть *imp.*; (*digress*) отклоня́ться *imp.*, отклони́ться (-ню́сь, -нишься) *perf.*; *adj.* (*lost*) заблуди́вшийся; (*homeless*) бездо́мный; *n.* (*waif*) беспризо́рный *sb.*; (*from flock*) отби́вшееся от ста́да живо́тное *sb.*; *s. bullet*, шальна́я пу́ля.

streak *n.* полоса́ (*acc.* по́лосу́; *pl.* -осы, -о́с, -оса́м) (of luck, везе́ния); (*tendency*) жи́лка; (*lightning*) вспы́шка; *v.t.* испещря́ть *imp.*, испещри́ть *perf.*; *v.i.* (*rush*) проноси́ться (-ошу́сь, -о́сишься) *imp.*, пронести́сь (-есу́сь, -есёшься; -ёсся, -есла́сь) *perf.* **streaked** *adj.* с полоса́ми, с прожи́лками (with, + *gen.*). **streaky** *adj.* полоса́тый; (*meat*) с просло́йками жи́ра.

stream *n.* (*brook*, *tears*) руче́й (-чья́); (*brook*, *flood*, *tears*, *people etc.*) пото́к; (*jet*) струя́ (*pl.* -у́и); (*current*) тече́ние; *up/down s.*, вверх/вниз по тече́нию; *with/against the s.*, по тече́нию, про́тив тече́ния; *v.i.* течь (течёт, теку́т; тёк, текла́) *imp.*; струи́ться (-и́тся) *imp.*; (*rush*) проноси́ться (-ошу́сь, -о́сишься) *imp.*, пронести́сь (-есу́сь, -есёшься; -ёсся, -есла́сь) *perf.*; (*blow*) развева́ться (-а́ется). **streamer** *n.* вы́мпел. **stream-lined** *adj.* обтека́емый; (*fig.*) хорошо́ нала́женный.

street *n.* у́лица; *adj.* у́личный; *s. lamp*, у́личный фона́рь (-ря́) *m.*

strength *n.* си́ла, кре́пость; (*numbers*) чи́сленность; *in full s.*, в по́лном соста́ве; *on the s. of*, в си́лу + *gen.* **strengthen** *v.t.* уси́ливать *imp.*, уси́лить *perf.*; укрепля́ть *imp.*, укрепи́ть *perf.* **strengthening** *n.* усиле́ние, укрепле́ние.

strenuous *adj.* тре́бующий уси́лий, энерги́чный.

stress *n.* (*pressure*, *fig.*) давле́ние; (*tech.*) напряже́ние; (*emphasis*) ударе́ние; *v.t.* де́лать *imp.*, с~ *perf.* ударе́ние на + *acc.*; подчёркивать *imp.*, подчеркну́ть *perf.*

stretch *n.* (*expanse*) протяже́ние, простра́нство; *at a s.*, (*in succession*) подря́д; *v.t.* & *i.* (*widen*, *spread out*) растя́гивать(ся) *imp.*, растяну́ть(ся) (-ну́(сь), -нешь(ся)) *perf.*; (*in length*, *s. out limbs*) вытя́гивать(ся) *imp.*, вы́тянуть(ся) *perf.*; (*tauten e.g. bow*) натя́гивать(ся) *imp.*, натяну́ть(ся) (-ну́(сь), -нешь(ся)) *perf.*; (*extend e.g. rope*, *s. forth limbs*) протя́гивать(ся) *imp.*, протяну́ть(ся) (-ну́(сь), -нешь(ся)) *perf.*; *v.i.* (*material*, *land*) тяну́ться (-нется) *imp.*; *v.t.* (*exaggerate*) преувели́чивать *imp.*, преувели́чить *perf.*; *s. a point*, допуска́ть *imp.*, допусти́ть (-ущу́, -у́стишь) *perf.* натя́жку; *s.*

oneself, потя́гиваться *imp.*, потяну́ться (-ну́сь, -нешься) *perf.*; *s. one's legs*, (*coll.*) размина́ть *imp.*, размя́ть (разомну́, -нёшь) *perf.* но́ги. **stretcher** *n.* носи́лки (-лок) *pl.*

strew *v.t.* разбра́сывать *imp.*, разброса́ть *perf.*; *s. with*, посыпа́ть *imp.*, посы́пать (-плю, -плешь) *perf.* + *instr.*; усыпа́ть *imp.*, усы́пать (-плю, -плешь) *perf.* + *instr.*

stricken *adj.* поражённый (-ён, -ена́), охва́ченный (-ен).

strict *adj.* стро́гий (-г, -га́, -го); (*precise*) то́чный (-чен, -чна́, -чно). **strictly** *adv.* стро́го, то́чно. **strictness** *n.* стро́гость, то́чность. **stricture(s)** *n.* (стро́гая) кри́тика, осужде́ние.

stride *n.* (большо́й) шаг (-а́ *with* 2, 3, 4, *loc.* -у́; *pl.* -и́); *pl.* (*fig.*) успе́хи *m.pl.*; *to get into one's s.*, принима́ться *imp.*, приня́ться (приму́сь, -мешься; -ня́лся́, -няла́сь) *perf.* за де́ло; *to take s.th. in one's s.*, преодолева́ть *imp.*, преодоле́ть *perf.* что-л. без уси́лий; *v.i.* шага́ть *imp.* (больши́ми шага́ми).

stridency *n.* ре́зкость. **strident** *adj.* ре́зкий (-зок, -зка́, -зко).

strife *n.* (*conflict*) борьба́; (*discord*) раздо́р.

strike *n.* (*refusal to work*) забасто́вка, ста́чка; (*discovery*) откры́тие; (*blow*) уда́р; *adj.* забасто́вочный; *v.i.* (*be on s.*) бастова́ть *imp.*; (*go on s.*) забастова́ть *perf.*; объявля́ть *imp.*, объяви́ть (-влю́, -вишь) *perf.* забасто́вку; (*clock*) бить (бьёт) *imp.*, про ~ *perf.*; *v.t.* (*hit*) ударя́ть *imp.*, уда́рить *perf.*; (*mil.*, *surprise*) поража́ть *imp.*, порази́ть *perf.*; (*discover*) открыва́ть *imp.*, откры́ть (-ро́ю, -ро́ешь) *perf.*; (*match*) зажига́ть *imp.*, заже́чь (-жгу́, -жжёшь, -жгу́т; -жёг, -жгла́) *perf.*; (*clock*) бить (бьёт) *imp.*, про ~ *perf.*; (*occur to*) приходи́ть (-ит) *imp.*, прийти́ (придёт; пришёл, -шла́) *perf.* в го́лову + *dat.*; *s. off*, вычёркивать *imp.*, вы́черкнуть *perf.*; *s. up*, начина́ть *imp.*, нача́ть (-чну́, -чнёшь; на́чал, -а́, -о); *s. upon*, напада́ть *imp.*, напа́сть (-аду́, -адёшь; -а́л) на + *acc.* **strike-breaker** *n.* штрейкбре́хер. **striker** *n.* забасто́вщик, -ица. **striking** *adj.* порази́тельный; *s. distance*, досяга́емость.

string *n.* бечёвка, верёвка, завя́зка; (*mus.*) струна́ (*pl.* -ны); (*series*) верени́ца, ряд (-а́ *with* 2, 3, 4, *loc.* -у́; *pl.* -ы́); (*beads*) ни́тка; *pl.* (*instruments*) стру́нные инструме́нты *m.pl.*; *second s.*, запасно́й ресу́рс; *pull strings*, нажима́ть *imp.*, нажа́ть (нажму́, -мёшь) *perf.* на та́йные пружи́ны; *without strings attached*, без каки́х-либо усло́вий; *adj.* стру́нный; *v.t.* (*tie up*) завя́зывать *imp.*, завяза́ть (-яжу́, -я́жешь) *perf.*; (*thread*) низа́ть (нижу́, -жешь) *imp.*, на ~ *perf.*; (*beans*) чи́стить *imp.*, о ~ *perf.*; *s. along*, (*coll.*) (*deceive*) обма́нывать *imp.*, обману́ть (-ну́, -нешь) *perf.*; *s. out*, (*prolong*) растя́гивать *imp.*, растяну́ть (-ну́, -нешь) *perf.*; *strung up*, (*tense*) напряжённый; *s.-bag*, *s. vest*, се́тка. **stringed** *adj.* стру́нный. **stringy** *adj.* (*fibrous*) волокни́стый; (*meat*) жи́листый.

stringency *n.* стро́гость. **stringent** *adj.* стро́гий (-г, -га́, -го).

strip[1] *n.* полоса́ (*acc.* по́лосу́; *pl.* -осы, -о́с, -оса́м), поло́ска, ле́нта; *s. cartoon*, расска́з в рису́нках; *s. light*, ла́мпа дневно́го све́та.

strip[2] *v.t.* (*undress*) раздева́ть *imp.*, разде́ть (-е́ну, -е́нешь) *perf.*; (*deprive*) лиша́ть *imp.*, лиши́ть *perf.* (of, + *gen.*); (*lay bare*) обнажа́ть *imp.*, обнажи́ть *perf.*; *s. off*, (*tear off*) сдира́ть *imp.*, содра́ть (сдеру́, -рёшь; -а́л, -ала́, -а́ло); *v.i.* раздева́ться *imp.*, разде́ться (-е́нусь, -е́нешься) *perf.* **strip-tease** *n.* стрипти́з.

stripe *n.* полоса́ (*acc.* по́лосу́; *pl.* -осы, -о́с, -оса́м). **striped** *adj.* полоса́тый.

stripling *n.* подро́сток (-тка), ю́ноша *m.*

strive *v.i.* (*endeavour*) стара́ться *imp.*, по ~ *perf.*; стреми́ться *imp.* (for, к + *dat.*); (*struggle*) боро́ться (-рю́сь, -решься) *imp.* (for, за + *acc.*; against, про́тив + *gen.*).

stroke *n.* (*blow*, *med.*) уда́р; (*of oar*) взмах; (*oarsman*) загребно́й *sb.*; (*drawing*) штрих (-а́); (*clock*) бой (*pl.* бои́); (*piston*) ход (*pl.* -ы, -о́в);

(*swimming*) стиль *m.*; *v.t.* гла́дить *imp.*, по~ *perf.*
stroll *n.* прогу́лка; *v.i.* прогу́ливаться *imp.*, прогуля́ться *perf.*
strong *adj.* (*also able*; *gram.*) си́льный (си́лён, -льна́, -льно, си́льны́); (*also drinks*) кре́пкий (-пок, -пка́, -пко); (*healthy*) здоро́вый; (*opinion etc.*) твёрдый (-д, -да́, -до). **stronghold** *n.* кре́пость; (*fig.*) опло́т. **strong-minded, strong-willed** *adj.* реши́тельный. **strong-room** ко́мната-сейф.
strontium *n.* стро́нций.
strop *n.* реме́нь (-мня́) *m.* (для пра́вки бритв); *v.t.* пра́вить *imp.* (бри́тву).
structural *adj.* структу́рный; (*building*) конструкти́вный, строи́тельный. **structure** *n.* (*composition, arrangement*) структу́ра; (*system*) строй, устро́йство; (*building*) сооруже́ние.
struggle *n.* борьба́; *v.i.* боро́ться (-рю́сь, -решься) *imp.* (for, за + *acc.*; against, про́тив + *gen.*); (*writhe*, *s. with* (*fig.*)) би́ться (бью́сь, бьёшься) (with, над + *instr.*).
strum *v.i.* бренча́ть (-чу́, -чи́шь) *imp.* (on, на + *prep.*).
strut[1] *n.* (*vertical*) подпо́ра, сто́йка; (*horizontal*) распо́рка; (*angle brace*) подко́с.
strut[2] *v.i.* ходи́ть (хожу́, хо́дишь) *indet.*, идти́ (иду́, идёшь; шёл, шла) *det.* го́голем.
stub *n.* (*stump*) пень (пня) *m.*; (*pencil*) огры́зок (-зка); (*cigarette*) оку́рок (-рка); (*counterfoil*) корешо́к (-шка́); *v.t.*: *s. one's toe*, ударя́ться *imp.*, уда́риться *perf.* ного́й (on, на + *acc.*); *s. out*, гаси́ть (гашу́, га́сишь) *imp.*, по~ *perf.* (cigarette *etc.*, оку́рок).
stubble *n.* стерня́, жнивьё; (*hair*) щети́на.
stubborn *adj.* упря́мый, упо́рный. **stubbornness** *n.* упря́мство, упо́рство.
stucco *n.* штукату́рка; *adj.* штукату́рный.
stuck-up *adj.* (*coll.*) надму́тый.
stud[1] *n.* (*press-button*) кно́пка; (*collar, cuff*) за́понка; (*large-headed nail*) гвоздь (-дя́; *pl.* -ди, -де́й) *m.* с большо́й шля́пкой; *v.t.* (*set with studs*) обива́ть *imp.*, оби́ть (обью́, -ьёшь) *perf.* гвоздя́ми; (*bestrew*) усе́ивать *imp.*, усе́ять (-е́ю, -е́ешь) *perf.* (with, + *instr.*).
stud[2] *n.* (*horses*) ко́нный заво́д. **stud-horse** *n.* племенно́й жеребе́ц (-бца́).
student *n.* студе́нт, ~ка.
studied *adj.* обду́манный (-ан, -анна).
studio *n.* (*artist's, broadcasting, cinema*) сту́дия; (*artist's*) ателье́ *neut. indecl.*, мастерска́я *sb.*
studious *adj.* (*diligent*) приле́жный; (*liking study*) лю́бящий нау́ку.
study *n.* изуче́ние, иссле́дование; *pl.* заня́тия *neut.pl.*; (*essay*) о́черк; (*art*) эски́з, этю́д; (*mus.*) этю́д; (*room*) кабине́т; *v.t.* изуча́ть *imp.*, изучи́ть (-чу́, -чишь) *perf.*; учи́ться (учу́сь, у́чишься) *imp.*, об~ *perf.* + *dat.*; занима́ться *imp.*, заня́ться (займу́сь, -мёшься; заня́лся́, -яла́сь) *perf.* + *instr.*; (*research*) иссле́довать *imp.*, *perf.*; (*scrutinize*) рассма́тривать *imp.*, рассмотре́ть (-рю́, -ришь) *perf.*; *v.i.* учи́ться (учу́сь, у́чишься) *imp.*, об~ *perf.*
stuff *n.* (*material*) материа́л; (*substance*) вещество́; ((*woollen*) *fabric*) (шерстяна́я) мате́рия; *s. and nonsense*, вздор; *v.t.* набива́ть *imp.*, наби́ть (набью́, -ьёшь) *perf.*; (*cul.*) начиня́ть *imp.*, начини́ть *perf.*; (*cram into*) запи́хивать *imp.*, запиха́ть *perf.* (into, в + *acc.*); (*thrust, shove into*) сова́ть (сую́, суёшь) *imp.*, су́нуть *perf.* (into, в + *acc.*); *v.i.* (*overeat*) объеда́ться *imp.*, объе́сться (-е́мся, -е́шься, -е́стся, -еди́мся; -е́лся) *perf.* **stuffiness** *n.* духота́, спёртость. **stuffing** *n.* наби́вка; (*cul.*) начи́нка. **stuffy** *adj.* спёртый, ду́шный (-шен, -шна́, -шно).
stumble *v.i.* (*also fig.*) спотыка́ться *imp.*, споткну́ться *perf.* (over, о + *acc.*); *s. upon*, натыка́ться *imp.*, наткну́ться *perf.* на + *acc.* **stumbling-block** *n.* ка́мень (-мня; *pl.* -мни, -мне́й) *m.* преткнове́ния.
stump *n.* (*tree*) пень (пня) *m.*; (*pencil*) огры́зок (-зка); (*limb*) обру́бок (-бка), культя́; *v.t.* (*perplex*) ста́вить *imp.*, по~ *perf.* в тупи́к; *v.i.* (*coll.*) ковыля́ть *imp.*

stun *v.t.* (*also fig.*) оглуша́ть *imp.*, оглуши́ть *perf.*; (*also fig.*) ошеломля́ть *imp.*, ошеломи́ть *perf.* **stunning** *adj.* (*also fig.*) ошеломи́тельный; (*fig.*) сногсшиба́тельный (*coll.*).

stunt[1] *n.* трюк.

stunt[2] *v.t.* заде́рживать *imp.*, задержа́ть (-жу́, -жишь) *perf.* рост + *gen.* **stunted** *adj.* ча́хлый, низкоро́слый.

stupefaction *n.* ошеломле́ние. **stupefy** *v.t.* ошеломля́ть *imp.*, ошеломи́ть *perf.* **stupendous** *adj.* изуми́тельный; (*huge*) грома́дный. **stupid** *adj.* (*foolish*) глу́пый (-п, -па́, -по), дура́цкий (*coll.*); (*dull-witted*) тупо́й (туп, -а́, -о, ту́пы́). **stupidity** *n.* глу́пость, ту́пость. **stupor** *n.* оцепене́ние; (*med.*) сту́пор.

sturdy *adj.* (*robust*) кре́пкий (-пок, -пка́, -пко), здоро́вый (-в, -ва́); (*solid, firm*) твёрдый (-д, -да́, -до).

sturgeon *n.* осётр (-а́); (*dish*) осетри́на.

stutter *n.* заика́ние; *v.i.* заика́ться *imp.* **stutterer** *n.* зáйка *m.* & *f.*

sty[1] *n.* (*pigsty*) свина́рник.

sty[2] *n.* (*on eye*) ячме́нь (-ня́) *m.*

style *n.* стиль *m.*; (*manner*) мане́ра; (*taste*) вкус; (*fashion*) мо́да; (*sort*) род (*pl.* -ы́); *in* (*grand*) *s.*, с ши́ком; *v.t.* конструи́ровать *imp., perf.* по мо́де. **stylish** *adj.* мо́дный (-ден, -дна́, -дно), шика́рный. **stylist** *n.* стили́ст. **stylistic** *adj.* стилисти́ческий. **stylistics** *n.* стили́стика. **stylize** *v.t.* стилизова́ть *imp., perf.*

stylus *n.* грамофо́нная иго́лка.

suave *adj.* обходи́тельный. **suavity** *n.* обходи́тельность.

subaltern *n.* (*mil.*) мла́дший офице́р. **subcommittee** *n.* подкоми́ссия, подкомите́т. **subconscious** *adj.* подсозна́тельный; *n.* подсозна́ние. **subcutaneous** *adj.* подко́жный. **subdivide** *v.t.* подразделя́ть *imp.*, подраздели́ть *perf.* **subdivision** *n.* подразделе́ние. **subdue** *v.t.* покоря́ть *imp.*, покори́ть *perf.* **subdued** *adj.* (*suppressed, dispirited*) пода́вленный; (*soft*) мя́гкий (-гок, -гка́, -гко); (*indistinct*) приглушённый. **sub-editor** *n.* помо́щник, -ица реда́ктора. **sub-heading** *n.* подзаголо́вок (-вка). **subhuman** *adj.* не дости́гший челове́ческого у́ровня.

subject *n.* (*theme*) те́ма, сюже́т; (*discipline, theme*) предме́т; (*question*) вопро́с; (*logic, philos., bearer of certain characteristic*) субъе́кт; (*thing on to which action is directed*) объе́кт; (*gram.*) подлежа́щее *sb.*; (*national*) по́дданный *sb.*; *adj.* (*subordinate*) подчинённый (-ён, -ена́) (to, + *dat.*); (*dependent*) подвла́стный (to, + *dat.*); *s. to*, (*susceptible to*) подве́рженный + *dat.*; (*on condition that*) при усло́вии, что..., е́сли; *s. to his agreeing*, при усло́вии, что он согласи́тся, е́сли он согласи́тся; *be s. to* (*change etc.*), подлежа́ть (-жи́т) *imp.* + *dat.*; *v.t.*: *s. to*, подчиня́ть *imp.*, подчини́ть *perf.* + *dat.*; подверга́ть *imp.*, подве́ргнуть (подве́рг, -ла) *perf.* + *dat.* **subjection** *n.* подчине́ние. **subjective** *adj.* субъекти́вный. **subjectivity** *n.* субъекти́вность. **subject-matter** *n.* (*book, lecture*) содержа́ние, те́ма; (*discussion*) предме́т.

sub judic *adj.* на рассмотре́нии суда́.

subjugate *v.t.* покоря́ть *imp.*, покори́ть *perf.* **subjugation** *n.* покоре́ние.

subjunctive (mood) *n.* сослага́тельное наклоне́ние.

sublet *v.t.* передава́ть (-даю́, -даёшь) *imp.*, переда́ть (-а́м, -а́шь, -а́ст, -ади́м; пе́редал, -а́, -о) *perf.* в суба-ре́нду.

sublimate *v.t.* (*chem., psych.*) сублими́ровать; (*fig.*) возвыша́ть *imp.*, возвы́сить *perf.* **sublimation** *n.* (*chem., psych.*) сублима́ция; (*fig.*) возвыше́ние. **sublime** *adj.* возвы́шенный.

subliminal *adj.* подсозна́тельный. **sub-machine-gun** *n.* пистоле́т-пулемёт, автома́т. **submarine** *adj.* подво́дный; *n.* подво́дная ло́дка. **submerge** *v.t.* погружа́ть *imp.*, погрузи́ть *perf.*; затопля́ть *imp.*, затопи́ть (-плю́, -пишь) *perf.* **submission** *n.* подчине́ние; (*for inspection*) представле́ние. **submissive** *adj.* поко́рный. **submit** *v.i.* подчиня́ться *imp.*, подчини́ться *perf.* (to, + *dat.*); покоря́ться *imp.*, покори́ться *perf.* (to, + *dat.*); *v.t.* представля́ть *imp.*, предста́вить *perf.* (на рассмотре́ние). **subordinate** *n.* подчинённый *sb.*; *adj.* подчинённый

(-ён, -ена́); (*secondary*) второстепе́нный; (*gram.*) прида́точный; *v.t.* подчиня́ть *imp.*, подчини́ть *perf.* **subordination** *n.* подчине́ние. **suborn** *v.t.* подкупа́ть *imp.*, подкупи́ть (-плю́, -пишь) *perf.* **subpoena** *n.* вы́зов, пове́стка в суд; *v.t.* вызыва́ть *imp.*, вы́звать (-зову, -зовешь) *perf.* в суд. **subscribe** *v.i.* подпи́сываться *imp.*, подписа́ться (-ишу́сь, -и́шешься) *perf.* (to, на + *acc.*); *s. to*, (*opinion*) присоединя́ться *imp.*, присоедини́ться *perf.* к + *dat.* **subscriber** *n.* (*to newspaper etc.*) подпи́счик, -ица; абоне́нт, ~ка. **subscription** *n.* (*to newspaper etc.*) подпи́ска, абонеме́нт; (*fee*) взнос. **subsection** *n.* подразде́л. **subsequent** *adj.* после́дующий. **subsequently** *adv.* впосле́дствии. **subservience** *n.* раболе́пие, раболе́пство. **subservient** *adj.* раболе́пный. **subside** *v.i.* (*water*) убыва́ть *imp.*, убы́ть (убу́ду, -дешь; у́был, -а́, -о) *perf.*; (*calm down, abate*) укла́дываться *imp.*, уле́чься (уля́жется, уля́гутся; улёгся, улегла́сь); (*soil*) оседа́ть *imp.*, осе́сть (ося́дет; осе́л) *perf.*; (*collapse*) обва́ливаться *imp.*, обвали́ться (-ится) *perf.* **subsidence** *n.* (*abatement*) спад; (*soil*) оседа́ние. **subsidiary** *adj.* вспомога́тельный; (*secondary*) второстепе́нный. **subsidize** *v.t.* субсиди́ровать *imp.*, *perf.* **subsidy** *n.* субси́дия, дота́ция. **subsist** *v.i.* (*exist*) существова́ть *imp.*; (*live*) жить (живу́, -вёшь; жил, -а́, -о) *imp.* (on, + *instr.*). **subsistence** *n.* существова́ние; (*livelihood*) пропита́ние. **subsoil** *n.* подпо́чва. **subsonic** *adj.* дозвуково́й. **substance** *n.* вещество́; (*essence*) су́щность, суть; (*content*) содержа́ние. **substantial** *adj.* (*durable*) про́чный (-чен, -чна́, -чно, про́чны́); (*considerable*) значи́тельный; (*food*) пло́тный (-тен, -тна́, -тно, пло́тны́); (*real*) реа́льный; (*material*) веще́ственный. **substantially** *adv.* (*basically*) в основно́м; (*considerably*) в значи́тельной сте́пени. **substantiate** *v.t.* приводи́ть (-ожу́, -о́дишь) *imp.*, привести́ (-еду́, -едёшь; -ёл, -ела́) *perf.* доста́точные основа́ния + *gen.* **substantive** *n.* (и́мя *neut.*) существи́тельное. **substitute** *n.* (*person*) замести́тель *m.*, ~ница; (*thing*) заме́на; (*tech.*) замени́тель *m.*; *v.t.* заменя́ть *imp.*, замени́ть (-ню́, -нишь) *perf.* + *instr.* (for, + *acc.*); *I s. water for milk*, заменя́ю молоко́ водо́й. **substitution** *n.* заме́на, замеще́ние. **substructure** *n.* фунда́мент. **subsume** *v.t.* относи́ть (-ошу́, -о́сишь) *imp.*, отнести́ (-су́, -сёшь; -ёс, -есла́) к како́й-л. катего́рии. **subtenant** *n.* субаренда́тор. **subterfuge** *n.* увёртка, отгово́рка, уло́вка. **subterranean** *adj.* подзе́мный. **subtitle** *n.* подзаголо́вок (-вка); (*cinema*) субти́тр.

subtle *adj.* (*fine, delicate*) то́нкий (-нок, -нка́, -нко); (*mysterious*) таи́нственный (-ен, -енна); (*ingenious*) иску́сный; (*cunning*) хи́трый (-тёр, -тра́, хи́тро́). **subtlety** *n.* (*fineness, delicacy*) то́нкость; (*mystery*) таи́нственность; (*ingenuity*) иску́сность; (*cunning*) хи́трость.

subtract *v.t.* вычита́ть *imp.*, вы́честь (-чту, -чтешь; -чел, -чла) *perf.* **subtraction** *n.* вычита́ние. **suburb** *n.* при́город. **suburban** *adj.* при́городный. **subversion** *n.* (*overthrow*) сверже́ние; (*subversive activities*) подрывна́я де́ятельность. **subversive** *adj.* подрывно́й. **subvert** *v.t.* сверга́ть *imp.*, све́ргнуть (-г(нул), -гла) *perf.* **subway** *n.* тонне́ль *m.*; (*pedestrian s.*) подзе́мный перехо́д.

succeed *v.i.* удава́ться (удаётся) *imp.*, уда́ться (уда́стся, удаду́тся; уда́лся, -ла́сь) *perf.*; *the plan will s.*, план уда́стся; *he succeeded in buying the book*, ему́ удало́сь купи́ть кни́гу; (*be successful*) преуспева́ть *imp.*, преуспе́ть *perf.* (in, в + *prep.*); (*follow*) сменя́ть *imp.*, смени́ть (-ню́, -нишь) *perf.*; (*be heir*) насле́довать *imp.*, *perf.* (to, + *dat.*). **succeeding** *adj.* после́дующий. **success** *n.* успе́х, уда́ча. **successful** *adj.* успе́шный, уда́чный. **succession** *n.* преéмственность; (*sequence*) после́довательность; (*series*) (непреры́вная) цепь (*loc.* -пи́; *pl.* -пи, -пе́й); (*to throne*) престолонасле́дие; *right of s.*, пра́во насле́дования; *in s.*, подря́д, оди́н за други́м. **successive** *adj.* (*consecutive*) после́довательный.

successor *n.* наслéдник -ица; преéмник, -ица.

succinct *adj.* сжáтый.

succour *n.* пóмощь; *v.t.* приходи́ть (-ожу́, -óдишь) *imp.*, прийти́ (приду́, -дёшь; пришёл, -шлá) *perf.* на пóмощь + *gen.*

succulent *adj.* сóчный (-чен, -чнá, -чно).

succumb *v.i.* уступáть *imp.*, уступи́ть (-плю́, -пишь) *perf.* (to, + *dat.*); поддавáться (-даю́сь, -даёшься) *imp.*, поддáться (-áмся, -áшься, -áстся, -ади́мся; -áлся, -алáсь) *perf.* (to, + *dat.*).

such *adj.* такóй, подóбный; *s. people*, таки́е лю́ди; *in s. cases*, в таки́х, в подóбных, слу́чаях; *in such a way*, таки́м óбразом, так; *such as*, (*for example*) так напримéр; (*of such a kind as*) такóй как; *s. beauty as yours*, такáя красотá как вáша; (*that which*) тот (та, то, те), котóрый; *I shall read such books as I like*, я бу́ду читáть те кни́ги, котóрые мне нрáвятся; *such as to*, такóй, чтóбы; *his illness was not such as to cause anxiety*, егó болéзнь былá не такóй (серьёзной), чтóбы вы́звать беспокóйство; *s. and s.*, такóй-то; *pron.* такóв (-á, -ó, -ы́); тот (та, то, те), такóй; *s. was his character*, такóв был егó харáктер; *s. as are of my opinion*, те, кто соглáсен со мной; *as s.*, сам по сéбе, как таковóй, по существу́; *s. is not the case*, э́то не так. **suchlike** *adj.* подóбный, такóй; *pron.* (*inanim.*) тому́ подóбное; (*people*) таки́е лю́ди (-дéй, -дям, -дьми́) *pl.*

suck *v.t.* сосáть (сосу́, сосёшь) *imp.*; *s. in*, всáсывать *imp.*, всосáть (-су́, -сёшь) *perf.*; (*engulf*) засáсывать *imp.*, засосáть (-су́, -сёшь) *perf.*; *s. out*, высáсывать *imp.*, вы́сосать (-су, -сешь) *perf.*; *s. up to*, (*coll.*) подли́зываться *imp.*, подлизáться (-ижу́сь, -и́жешься) *perf.* к + *dat.* **sucker** *n.* (*biol.*, *rubber device*) присóска; (*bot.*) корневóй óтпрыск. **suckle** *v.t.* корми́ть (-млю́, -мишь) *imp.*, на ~ *perf.* гру́дью. **suckling** *n.* груднóй ребёнок (-нка) (*pl.* дéти, -тéй), сосу́н (-á). **suction** *n.* сосáние, всáсывание.

sudden *adj.* внезáпный, неожи́данный (-ан, -анна); *s. death*, скоропости́жная смерть. **suddenly** *adv.* внезáпно, вдруг, неожи́данно. **suddenness** *n.* внезáпность, неожи́данность.

suds *n.* мы́льная пéна.

sue *v.t.* преслéдовать *imp.* судéбным поря́дком; возбуждáть *imp.*, возбуди́ть *perf.* дéло прóтив + *gen.* (for, о + *prep.*); *s. s.b. for damages*, предъявля́ть *imp.*, предъяви́ть (-влю́, -вишь) *perf.* (к) кому́-л. иск о возмещéнии ущéрба.

suede *n.* зáмша; *adj.* зáмшевый.

suet *n.* пóчечное сáло.

suffer *v.t.* страдáть *imp.*, по ~ *perf.* + *instr.*, от + *gen.*; (*experience*) испы́тывать *imp.*, испытáть *perf.*; (*loss, defeat*) терпéть (-плю́, -пишь) *imp.*, по ~ *perf.*; (*allow*) позволя́ть *imp.*, позвóлить *perf.* + *dat.*; дозволя́ть *imp.*, дозвóлить *perf.* + *dat.*; (*tolerate*) терпéть (-плю́, -пишь) *imp.*; *v.i.* страдáть *imp.*, по ~ *perf.* (from, + *instr.*, от + *gen.*). **sufferance** *n.* (*tacit consent*) молчали́вое соглáсие; *he is here on s.*, егó здесь тéрпят. **suffering** *n.* страдáние.

suffice *v.i.* (*t.*) быть достáточным (для + *gen.*); хватáть (-áет) *imp.*, хвати́ть (-ит) *perf.* *impers.* + *gen.* (+ *dat.*); *five pounds will s. me*, мне хвáтит пяти́ фу́нтов. **sufficiency** *n.* (*adequacy*) достáточность; (*prosperity*) достáток (-тка). **sufficient** *adj* .достáточный.

suffix *n.* су́ффикс.

suffocate *v.t.* удушáть *imp.*, удуши́ть (-шу́, -шишь) *perf.*; *v.i.* задыхáться *imp.*, задохну́ться (-óх(ну́л)ся, -óх(ну́)лась) *perf.* **suffocating** *adj.* ду́шный (-шен, -шнá, -шно), уду́шливый. **suffocation** *n.* удушéние; (*difficulty in breathing*) уду́шье.

suffrage *n.* (*right*) избирáтельное прáво.

suffuse *v.t.* (*light, tears*) заливáть *imp.*, зали́ть (-лью́, -льёшь; зáли́л, -á, зáли́ло) *perf.* (with, + *instr.*); (*colour*) покрывáть *imp.*, покры́ть (-рóю, -рóешь) *perf.* (with, + *instr.*). **suffusion**

n. покры́тие; (*colour*) кра́ска; (*flush*) румя́нец (-нца).

sugar *n.* са́хар (-а(у)); *adj.* са́харный; *v.t.* подсла́щивать *imp.*, подсласти́ть *perf.*; *s.-basin*, са́харница; *s.-beet*, са́харная свёкла; *s.-cane*, са́харный тростни́к; *s.-refinery*, (сахаро)рафина́дный заво́д. **sugary** *adj.* са́харный; (*sweet*) сла́дкий (-док, -дка́, -дко); (*saccharine*) сахари́стый; (*sickly sweet*) при́торный, слаща́вый.

suggest *v.t.* (*propose*) предлага́ть *imp.*, предложи́ть (-жу́, -жишь) *perf.*; (*advise*) сове́товать *imp.*, по~ *perf.*; (*call up*) внуша́ть *imp.*, внуши́ть *perf.*; *s. itself to*, приходи́ть (-ит) *imp.*, прийти́ (придёт; пришёл, -шла́) *perf.* кому́-л. в го́лову; *a solution suggested itself to me*, мне пришло́ в го́лову реше́ние. **suggestible** *adj.* поддаю́щийся внуше́нию. **suggestibility** *n.* внуша́емость. **suggestion** *n.* (*proposal*) предложе́ние; (*psych.*) внуше́ние. **suggestive** *adj.* вызыва́ющий мы́сли (of, о+*prep.*); (*slightly indecent*) соблазни́тельный.

suicidal *adj.* самоуби́йственный; (*fig.*) губи́тельный. **suicide** *n.* самоуби́йство; (*person*) самоуби́йца *m.* & *f.*; (*fig.*) крах по со́бственной вине́; *commit s.*, соверша́ть *imp.*, соверши́ть *perf.* самоуби́йство; поко́нчить *perf.* с собо́й (*coll.*).

suit *n.* (*clothing*) костю́м; (*leg.*) иск; (*request*) про́сьба; (*cards*) масть; *follow s.*, (*cards*) ходи́ть (хожу́, хо́дишь) *imp.* в масть; (*fig.*) сле́довать *imp.*, по~ *perf.* приме́ру; *in one's birthday s.*, в чём мать роди́ла; *v.t.* (*be convenient for*) устра́ивать *imp.*, устро́ить *perf.*; (*accommodate*) приспоса́бливать *imp.*, приспосо́бить *perf.*; (*be suitable for, match*) подходи́ть (-ожу́, -о́дишь) *imp.*, подойти́ (-йду́, -йдёшь; подошёл, -шла́) *perf.* (+*dat.*); (*look attractive on*) идти́ (идёт; шёл, шла) *imp.*+*dat.*; *s. oneself*, выбира́ть *imp.*, вы́брать (-беру, -берешь) *perf.* по вку́су. **suitability** *n.* приго́дность. **suitable** *adj.* (*fitting*) подходя́щий; (*convenient*) удо́бный. **suitably** *adv.* соотве́тственно. **suitcase** *n.* чемода́н.

suite *n.* (*retinue*) сви́та; (*furniture*) гарниту́р; (*rooms*) апарта́менты *m.pl.*; (*mus.*) сюи́та.

suitor *n.* (*admirer*) покло́нник; (*plaintiff*) исте́ц (истца́); (*petitioner*) проси́тель *m.*, -ница.

sulk *v.i.* ду́ться *imp.* **sulkiness** *n.* скве́рное настрое́ние. **sulky** *adj.* наду́тый, хму́рый (-р, -ра́, -ро).

sullen *adj.* угрю́мый, хму́рый (-р, -ра́, -ро). **sullenness** *n.* угрю́мость.

sully *v.t.* пятна́ть *imp.*, за~ *perf.*

sulphate *n.* сульфа́т. **sulphide** *n.* сульфи́д. **sulphite** *n.* сульфи́т. **sulphur** *n.* се́ра. **sulphureous** *adj.* серни́стый. **sulphuric** *adj.* се́рный; *s. acid*, се́рная кислота́.

sultan *n.* (*sovereign*) султа́н.

sultana *n.* (*raisin*) изю́мина без семя́н; *pl.* кишми́ш (-и́ша́) (*collect.*).

sultriness *n.* зной, духота́. **sultry** *adj.* зно́йный; ду́шный (-шен, -шна́, -шно); (*passionate*) стра́стный.

sum *n.* су́мма; (*arithmetical problem*) арифмети́ческая зада́ча; *pl.* арифме́тика; *v.t.* (*add up*) скла́дывать *imp.*, сложи́ть (-жу́, -жишь) *perf.*; *s. up*, (*summarize*) сумми́ровать *imp.*, *perf.*; резюми́ровать *imp.*, *perf.*; (*appraise*) оце́нивать *imp.*, оцени́ть (-ню́, -нишь) *perf.* **summing-up** *n.* (*leg.*) заключи́тельная речь (*pl.* -чи, -че́й) судьи́.

summarize *v.t.* сумми́ровать *imp.*, *perf.*; резюми́ровать *imp.*, *perf.* **summary** *n.* резюме́ *neut.indecl.*, конспе́кт, сво́дка; *adj.* сумма́рный, ско́рый (-р, -ра́, -ро).

summer *n.* ле́то (*pl.* -та́); *Indian s.*, ба́бье ле́то (*pl.* -та́); *attrib.* ле́тний; *v.i.* проводи́ть (-ожу́, -о́дишь) *imp.*, провести́ (-еду́, -едёшь; провёл, -а́) *perf.* ле́то (*pl.* -та́). **summer-house** *n.* бесе́дка. **summery** *adj.* ле́тний.

summit *n.* верши́на, верх (-а(у), *loc.* -у́; *pl.* -и́ & -а́); (*fig.*) зени́т, преде́л; *s. meeting*, встре́ча глав прави́тельств.

summon *v.t.* вызыва́ть *imp.*, вы́звать (-зову, -зовешь) *perf.*; (*call*) призыва́ть *imp.*, призва́ть (-зову́, -зовёшь; призва́л, -а́, -о) *perf.*; *s. up one's courage*, собира́ться *imp.*, собра́ться

(-берусь, -берёшься; -брался, -бралась, -брало́сь) *perf.* с ду́хом.

summons *n.* вы́зов; (*leg.*) пове́стка в суд; *v.t.* вызыва́ть *imp.*, вы́звать (-зову, -зовешь) *perf.* в суд.

sumptuous *adj.* роско́шный.

sun *n.* со́лнце; *in the s.*, на со́лнце. **sunbathe** *v.i.* гре́ться *imp.* на со́лнце, загора́ть *imp.* **sunbeam** *n.* со́лнечный луч (-а́). **sunburn** *n.* зага́р; (*inflammation*) со́лнечный ожо́г. **sunburnt** *adj.* загоре́лый; *become s.*, загора́ть *imp.*, загоре́ть (-рю́, -ри́шь) *perf.*

Sunday *n.* воскресе́нье; *adj.* воскре́сный.

sun-dial *n.* со́лнечные часы́ *m.pl.*

sundry *adj.* ра́зный; *all and s.*, все вме́сте и ка́ждый в отде́льности.

sunflower *n.* подсо́лнечник; *s. seeds*, се́мечки *neut.pl.* **sun-glasses** *n.* защи́тные очки́ (-ко́в) *pl.* от со́лнца.

sunken *adj.* (*hollow*) впа́лый; (*submerged*) погружённый; (*ship*) зато́пленный; (*below certain level*) ни́же (како́го-л. у́ровня).

sunlight *n.* со́лнечный свет. **sunny** *adj.* со́лнечный. **sunrise** *n.* восхо́д со́лнца. **sunset** *n.* захо́д со́лнца, зака́т. **sunshade** *n.* (*parasol*) зо́нтик; (*awning*) наве́с. **sunshine** *n.* со́лнечный свет. **sunstroke** *n.* со́лнечный уда́р. **sun-tan** *n.* зага́р. **sun-tanned** *adj.* загоре́лый.

superannuated *adj.* (*pensioner*) вы́шедший на пе́нсию; (*obsolete*) устаре́лый. **superb** *adj.* великоле́пный, превосхо́дный. **supercilious** *adj.* надме́нный (-нен, -нна), презри́тельный. **superficial** *adj.* пове́рхностный; (*outward*) вне́шний. **superficiality** *n.* пове́рхностность. **superfluity** *n.* (*surplus*) изли́шек (-шка); (*abundance*) оби́лие. **superfluous** *adj.* ли́шний, ненужный; (*abundant*) оби́льный. **superhuman** *adj.* сверхчелове́ческий. **superimpose** *v.t.* накла́дывать *imp.*, наложи́ть (-жу́, -жишь) *perf.* **superintend** *v.t.* заве́довать *imp.*+*instr.*; (*supervise*) надзира́ть *imp.* за+*instr.* **superintendent** *n.* заве́дующий *sb.* (of, +*instr.*), надзира́тель *m.*, ~ница (of, за+*instr.*); (*police*) ста́рший полице́йский офице́р. **superior** *n.* нача́льник, -ица; ста́рший *sb.*; (*relig.*) настоя́тель *m.*, ~ница; *adj.* (*better*) лу́чший, превосходя́щий; (*higher*) вы́сший, ста́рший; (*of better quality*) вы́сшего ка́чества; (*haughty*) высокоме́рный. **superiority** *n.* превосхо́дство. **superlative** *adj.* превосхо́дный; *n.* (*gram.*) превосхо́дная сте́пень. **superman** *n.* сверхчелове́к. **supermarket** *n.* универса́м. **supernatural** *adj.* сверхъесте́ственный (-ен, -енна). **supernumerary** *adj.* сверхшта́тный. **superpose** *v.t.* накла́дывать *imp.*, наложи́ть (-жу́ -жишь) *perf.* **superpower** *n.* одна́ из наибо́лее мо́щных вели́ких держа́в. **superscription** *n.* на́дпись. **supersede** *v.t.* заменя́ть *imp.*, замени́ть (-ню́, -нишь) *perf.* **supersonic** *adj.* сверхзвуково́й. **superstition** *n.* суеве́рие. **superstitious** *adj.* суеве́рный. **superstructure** *n.* надстро́йка. **supervene** *v.i.* сле́довать *imp.*, по~ *perf.* **supervise** *v.t.* наблюда́ть *imp.* за+*instr.*, надзира́ть *imp.* за+*instr.* **supervision** *n.* надзо́р, наблюде́ние. **supervisor** *n.* надзира́тель *m.*, ~ница; надсмо́трщик, -ица; (*of studies*) нау́чный руководи́тель *m.*

supine *adj.* (*lying on back*) лежа́щий на́взничь; (*indolent*) лени́вый.

supper *n.* у́жин; *have s.*, у́жинать *imp.*, по~ *perf.*; *the Last S.*, та́йная ве́черя.

supplant *v.t.* вытесня́ть *imp.*, вы́теснить *perf.*

supple *adj.* ги́бкий (-бок, -бка́, -бко). **suppleness** *n.* ги́бкость.

supplement *n.* (*to book*) дополне́ние; (*to periodical*) приложе́ние; *v.t.* дополня́ть *imp.*, допо́лнить *perf.* **supplementary** *adj.* дополни́тельный.

suppliant *n.* проси́тель *m.*, ~ница.

supplier *n.* поставщи́к (-а́) (*anim.* & *inanim.*). **supply** *n.* снабже́ние, поста́вка; (*stock*) запа́с; (*econ.*) предложе́ние; *pl.* припа́сы (-ов) *pl.*, (*provisions*) продово́льствие; *s. and demand*, спрос и предложе́ние; *s. line*, путь (-ти́, -тём) *m.* подво́за; *v.t.* снабжа́ть *imp.*, снабди́ть *perf.* (with, +*instr.*); поставля́ть *imp.*, поста́вить *perf.*

support *n.* подде́ржка, опо́ра; *v.t.*

поддéрживать *imp.*, поддержáть (-жý, -жишь) *perf.*; (*family*) содержáть (-жý, -жишь) *imp.* **supporter** *n.* сторóнник, -ица. **supporting** *adj.* (*tech.*) опóрный; *s. actor*, исполнитель *m.*, ~ница второстепéнной рóли.

suppose *v.t.* (*think*) полагáть *imp.*; (*presuppose*) предполагáть *imp.*, предположить (-жý, -жишь) *perf.*; (*assume*) допускáть *imp.*, допустить (-ущý, -ýстишь) *perf.* **supposed** *adj.* (*pretended*) мнимый. **supposition** *n.* предположéние. **suppositious** *adj.* предположительный.

suppress *v.t.* (*uprising*, *feelings*) подавлять *imp.*, подавить (-влю, -вишь) *perf.*; (*laughter*, *tears*) сдéрживать *imp.*, сдержáть (-жý, -жишь) *perf.*; (*forbid*) запрещáть *imp.*, запретить (-ещý, -етишь) *perf.* **suppression** *n.* подавлéние; (*prohibition*) запрещéние.

supremacy *n.* госпóдство, главéнство. **supreme** *adj.* верхóвный, вы́сший; (*greatest*) величáйший; *S. Soviet* (*of the U.S.S.R.*), Верхóвный Совéт (СССР); *S. Court*, Верхóвный суд (-á).

surcharge *n.* приплáта, доплáта.

sure *adj.* (*convinced*) увéренный (-ен, -ена) (of, в + *prep.*; that, что); (*unerring*) увéренный (-ен, -енна); (*certain*, *reliable*) вéрный (-рен, -рнá, -рно, вéрны́); (*steady*) твёрдый (твёрд, -á, -о); *s. enough*, действительно, на сáмом дéле; *he is s. to come*, он обязáтельно придёт; *make s. of*, (*convince oneself*) убеждáться *imp.*, убедиться (-дишься) *perf.* в + *prep.*; (*secure*) обеспéчивать *imp.*, обеспéчить *perf.*; *make s. that*, (*check up*) проверять *imp.*, провéрить *perf.* что; *for s.*, **surely** *adv.* навернякá, навéрное.

surety *n.* порýка; поручитель *m.*, ~ница; *stand s. for*, ручáться *imp.*, поручиться (-чýсь, -чишься) *perf.* за + *acc.*

surf *n.* прибóй; *v.i.* занимáться *imp.*, заняться (займýсь, -мёшься; занялся́, -лáсь) *perf.* сéрфингом.

surface *n.* повéрхность; (*exterior*) внéшность; *on the s.*, (*fig.*) внéшне; *under the s.*, (*fig.*) по существý; *adj.* повéрхностный; (*exterior*) внéшний; (*ground*) назéмный; *v.i.* всплывáть *imp.*, всплыть (-ывý, -ывёшь; всплыл, -á, -о) *perf.*

surfeit *n.* (*excess*) излишество; (*surplus*) излишек (-шка); *be surfeited*, пресыщáться *imp.*, пресы́титься (-ы́щусь, -ы́тишся) *perf.* (with, + *instr.*).

surge *n.* прилив, (большáя) волнá (*pl.* -ы, вóлнáм); *v.i.* (*be agitated*, *choppy*) волновáться *imp.*, вз~ *perf.*; (*rise*, *heave*) вздымáться *imp.*; (*rush*, *gush*) хлы́нуть *perf.*; *s. forward*, ринуться *perf.* вперёд.

surgeon *n.* хирýрг; (*mil.*) воéнный врач (-á). **surgery** *n.* (*treatment*) хирургия; (*place*) кабинéт, приёмная *sb.*, (врачá); (*s. hours*) приёмные часы́ *m.pl.* (врачá). **surgical** *adj.* хирургический.

surly *adj.* (*morose*) угрю́мый; (*rude*) грýбый (груб, -á, -о).

surmise *n.* предположéние, догáдка; *v.t.* & *i.* предполагáть *imp.*, предположить (-жý, -жишь) *perf.*; *v.i.* догáдываться *imp.*, догадáться *perf.*

surmount *v.t.* преодолевáть *imp.*, преодолéть *perf.*

surname *n.* фамилия.

surpass *v.t.* превосходить (-ожý, -óдишь) *imp.*, превзойти (-ойдý, -ойдёшь; -ошёл, -ошлá) *perf.* **surpassing** *adj.* превосхóдный.

surplus *n.* излишек (-шка), избы́ток (-тка); *adj.* излишний (-шен, -шня), избы́точный.

surprise *n.* удивлéние, неожиданность, сюрприз; *by s.*, врасплóх; *to my s.*, к моемý удивлéнию; *s. attack*, внезáпное нападéние; *v.t.* удивлять *imp.*, удивить *perf.*; (*come upon suddenly*) заставáть (-таю́, -таёшь) *imp.*, застáть (-áну, -áнешь) *perf.* врасплóх; *be surprised* (*at*), удивляться *imp.*, удивиться *perf.* (+ *dat.*). **surprising** *adj.* удивительный, неожиданный (-ан, -анна).

surreal *adj.* сюрреалистический. **surrealism** *n.* сюрреализм. **surrealist** *n.* сюрреалист; *adj.* сюрреалистический.

surrender *n.* сдáча; (*renunciation*) откáз;

v.t. сдава́ть (сдаю́, сдаёшь) *imp.*, сдать (сдам, сдашь, сдаст, сдади́м; сдал, -а́, -о) *perf.*; (*renounce*) отка́зываться *imp.*, отказа́ться (-ажу́сь, -а́жешься) *perf.* от + *gen.*; *v.i.* сдава́ться (сдаю́сь, сдаёшься) *imp.*, сда́ться (сда́мся, сда́шься, сда́стся, сдади́мся; сда́лся, -ла́сь) *perf.*; *s. oneself to*, предава́ться (-даю́сь, -даёшься) *imp.*, преда́ться (-да́мся, -да́шься, -да́стся, -дади́мся; -да́лся, -ла́сь) *perf.* + *dat.*

surreptitious *adj.* та́йный, сде́ланный тайко́м. **surreptitiously** *adv.* та́йно, тайко́м, исподтишка́ (*coll.*).

surrogate *n.* (*person*) замести́тель *m.*, ~ ница; (*thing*) замени́тель *m.*, суррога́т.

surround *n.* (*frame*) обрамле́ние; (*edge, selvage*) кро́мка; *v.t.* окружа́ть *imp.*, окружи́ть *perf.* (with, + *instr.*); обступа́ть *imp.*, обступи́ть (-пит) *perf.*; *s. with*, (*enclose*) обноси́ть (-ошу́, -о́сишь) *imp.*, обнести́ (-есу́, -есёшь; -ёс, -есла́) *perf.* + *instr.* **surrounding** *adj.* окружа́ющий, окре́стный. **surroundings** *n.* (*environs*) окре́стности *f.pl.*; (*milieu*) среда́, окруже́ние; (*locality*) ме́стность.

surveillance *n.* надзо́р, наблюде́ние.

survey *n.* обозре́ние, осмо́тр, обзо́р; (*investigation*) обсле́дование; (*geol.*) изыска́ние; (*topog.*) межева́ние; *v.t.* обозрева́ть *imp.*, обозре́ть (-рю́, -ри́шь) *perf.*; осма́тривать *imp.*, осмотре́ть (-рю́, -ришь) *perf.*; (*investigate*) обсле́довать *imp.*, *perf.*; (*topog.*) межева́ть (-жу́ю, -жу́ешь) *imp.* **surveyor** *n.* землеме́р.

survival *n.* (*surviving*) выжива́ние; (*relic*) пережи́ток (-тка). **survive** *v.t.* пережива́ть *imp.*, пережи́ть (-иву́, -ивёшь; пе́режи́л, -а́, -о) *perf.*; *v.i.* выжива́ть *imp.*, вы́жить (-иву, -ивешь) *perf.*; остава́ться (-аю́сь, -аёшься) *imp.*, оста́ться (-а́нусь, -а́нешься) *perf.* в живы́х. **survivor** *n.* оста́вшийся *sb.* в живы́х.

susceptibility *n.* восприи́мчивость; (*sensitivity*) чувстви́тельность. **susceptible** *adj.* восприи́мчивый (to, к + *dat.*); (*sensitive*) чувстви́тельный (to, к + *dat.*); (*impressionable*) впечатли́тельный.

suspect *n.* подозрева́емый *sb.*; *adj.* подозри́тельный; *v.t.* подозрева́ть *imp.* (of, в + *prep.*); (*mistrust*) не доверя́ть *imp.* + *dat.*; (*foresee*) предчу́вствовать *imp.*; (*have reason to believe*) полага́ть *imp.* (that, что).

suspend *v.t.* (*hang up*) подве́шивать *imp.*, подве́сить *perf.*; (*call a halt to*) приостана́вливать *imp.*, приостанови́ть (-влю́, -вишь) *perf.*; (*repeal temporarily*) вре́менно отменя́ть *imp.*, отмени́ть (-ню́, -нишь) *perf.*; (*dismiss temporarily*) вре́менно отстраня́ть *imp.*, отстрани́ть *perf.*; *suspended sentence*, усло́вный пригово́р. **suspender** *n.* (*stocking*) подвя́зка. **suspense** *n.* (*uncertainty*) неизве́стность, неопределённость; (*anxiety*) беспоко́йство; *keep in s.*, держа́ть (-жу́, -жишь) *imp.* в напряжённом ожида́нии. **suspension** *n.* (*halt*) приостано́вка; (*temporary repeal*) вре́менная отме́на; (*temporary dismissal*) вре́менное отстране́ние; (*hanging up*) подве́шивание; (*tech.*) подве́с; *s. bridge*, вися́чий мост (мо́ста́, *loc.* -у́; *pl.* -ы́).

suspicion *n.* подозре́ние; *on s.*, по подозре́нию (of, в + *loc.*); (*trace*) отте́нок (-нка). **suspicious** *adj.* подозри́тельный.

sustain *v.t.* (*support*) подде́рживать *imp.*, поддержа́ть (-жу́, -жишь) *perf.*; (*stand up to*) выде́рживать *imp.*, вы́держать (-жу, -жишь) *perf.*; (*suffer*) потерпе́ть (-плю́, -пишь) *perf.* **sustained** *adj.* (*uninterrupted*) непреры́вный. **sustenance** *n.* пи́ща, пита́ние.

swab *n.* шва́бра; (*med.*) тампо́н; (*smear, specimen*) мазо́к (-зка́); *v.t.* мыть (мо́ю, мо́ешь) *imp.*, вы́ ~, по ~ *perf.* шва́брой; *s. the decks*, (*naut.*) дра́ить (-а́ю, -а́ишь) *imp.*, на ~ *perf.* па́лубы.

swaddle *v.t.* пелена́ть *imp.*, за ~, с ~ *perf.* **swaddling-clothes** *n.* пелёнки (*gen.* -нок) *pl.*

swagger *v.i.* (*walk with s.*) расха́живать *imp.* с ва́жным ви́дом; (*put on airs*) ва́жничать *imp.*

swallow[1] *n.* глото́к (-тка́); *v.t.* глота́ть *imp.*, глотну́ть *perf.*; прогла́тывать

imp., проглотить (-очу́, -о́тишь) *perf.*; *s. up*, поглоща́ть *imp.*, поглоти́ть (-ощу́, -о́тишь) *perf.*
swallow[2] *n.* (*bird*) ла́сточка.
swamp *n.* боло́то, топь; *v.t.* залива́ть *imp.*, зали́ть (-лью́, -льёшь; за́ли́л, -а́, -о) *perf.*; *s. with* (*letters etc.*), засыпа́ть *imp.*, засы́пать (-плю, -плешь) *perf.* + *instr.* **swampy** *adj.* боло́тистый, то́пкий (-пок, -пка́, -пко).
swan *n.* ле́бедь (*pl.* -ди, -де́й) *m.*; *s.-song*, лебеди́ная песнь.
swank *v.i.* хва́статься *imp.*, по~ *perf.* (about, + *instr.*); (*coll.*) бахва́литься *imp.* (about, + *instr.*).
swap *n.* обме́н; *v.t.* меня́ть *imp.*, об~, по~ *perf.*; обме́нивать *imp.*, обменя́ть *perf.*; обме́ниваться *imp.*, обменя́ться *perf.* + *instr.*
sward *n.* лужа́йка, дёрн.
swarm *n.* рой (ро́я, *loc.* рою́; *pl.* рои́, роёв), (*crowd*) толпа́ (*pl.* -пы); *v.i.* рои́ться (-и́тся) *imp.*; толпи́ться (-и́тся) *imp.*; кише́ть (-ши́т) *imp.* (with, + *instr.*).
swarthy *adj.* сму́глый (-л, -ла́, -ло).
swastika *n.* сва́стика.
swat *v.t.* прихло́пнуть *perf.*; убива́ть *imp.*, уби́ть (убью́, -ьёшь) *perf.*
swathe *n.* (*bandage*) бинт (-а́); (*puttee*) обмо́тка; *v.t.* (*bandage*) бинтова́ть *imp.*, за~ *perf.*; (*wrap up*) заку́тывать *imp.*, заку́тать *perf.*
sway *n.* колеба́ние, кача́ние; (*influence*) влия́ние; (*power*) власть; *v.t.* & *i.* колеба́ть(ся) (-блю(сь), -блешь(ся)) *imp.*, по~ *perf.*; кача́ть(ся) *imp.*, качну́ть(ся) *perf.*; *v.t.* (*influence*) име́ть *imp.* влия́ние на + *acc.*
swear *v.i.* (*vow*) кля́сться (кляну́сь, -нёшься; кля́лся, -ла́сь) *imp.*, по~ *perf.*; (*curse*) руга́ться *imp.*, ругну́ться *perf.*; *v.t.*: *s. in*, приводи́ть (-ожу́, -о́дишь) *imp.*, привести́ (-еду́, -едёшь; -ёл, -ела́) *perf.* к прися́ге; *s.-word*, руга́тельство, бра́нное сло́во (*pl.* -ва́).
sweat *n.* пот (*loc.* -у́; *pl.* -ы́); (*perspiration*) испа́рина; *v.i.* поте́ть *imp.*, вс~ *perf.* **sweater** *n.* сви́тер. **sweaty** *adj.* по́тный (-тен, -тна́, -тно).
swede[1] *n.* брю́ква.
Swede[2] *n.* швед, шве́дка. **Swedish** *adj.* шве́дский.
sweep *n.* вымета́ние; (*span*) разма́х; (*scope*) охва́т; (*chimney-sweep*) трубочи́ст; *v.t.* мести́ (мету́, -тёшь; мёл, -а́) *imp.*; подмета́ть *imp.*, подмести́ (-ету́, -етёшь; подмёл, -ела́) *perf.*; (*mil.*) обстре́ливать *imp.*, обстреля́ть *perf.*; (*naut.*) (*drag*) тра́лить *imp.*, про~ *perf.*; *v.i.* (*go majestically*) ходи́ть (хожу́, хо́дишь) *indet.*, идти́ (иду́, идёшь; шёл, шла) *det.*, пойти́ (пойду́, -дёшь; пошёл, -шла́) *perf.* велича́во; (*move swiftly*) мча́ться (мчусь, мчи́шься) *imp.*; *s. away*, смета́ть *imp.*, смести́ (смету́, -тёшь; смёл, -а́) *perf.* **sweeping** *n.* подмета́ние; (*naut.*) трале́ние; *adj.* широ́кий (-к, -ка́, -о́ко́); (*wholesale*) огу́льный. **sweepstake** *n.* тотализа́тор.
sweet *n.* (*sweetmeat*) конфе́та; (*dessert*) сла́дкое *sb.*; *adj.* сла́дкий (-док, -дка́, -дко); (*fragrant*) души́стый; (*dear*) ми́лый (мил, -а́, -о, ми́лы́). **sweetbread** *n.* (*cul.*) сла́дкое мя́со. **sweeten** *v.t.* подсла́щивать *imp.*, подсласти́ть *perf.* **sweetheart** *n.* возлю́бленный, -нная *sb.* **sweetness** *n.* сла́дость. **sweet pea** *n.* души́стый горо́шек (-шка(у)) (*collect.*).
swell *v.i.* (*up*) опуха́ть *imp.*, опу́хнуть (-х) *perf.*; пу́хнуть (-х) *imp.*, вс~, о~ *perf.*; распуха́ть *imp.*, распу́хнуть (-х) *perf.*; (*a sail*) надува́ться *imp.*, наду́ться (-у́ется) *perf.*; (*a bud*) набуха́ть *imp.*, набу́хнуть (-нет; -х) *perf.*; (*increase*) увели́чиваться *imp.*, увели́читься *perf.*; (*sound*) нараста́ть *imp.*, нарасти́ (-тёт; наро́с, -ла́) *perf.*; *v.t.* (*a sail*) надува́ть *imp.*, наду́ть (-у́ю, -у́ешь) *perf.*; (*increase*) увели́чивать *imp.*, увели́чить *perf.*; *n.* вы́пуклость; (*naut.*) мёртвая зыбь (*pl.* -би, -бе́й). **swelling** *n.* о́пухоль; (*bud*) набуха́ние; (*increase*) увеличе́ние.
swelter *v.i.* томи́ться *imp.*, ис~ *perf.* от жары́. **sweltering** *adj.* зно́йный.
swerve *v.i.* отклоня́ться *imp.*, отклони́ться (-ню́сь, -ни́шься) *perf.*; (*sudden*) ре́зко свора́чивать *imp.*, свороти́ть (-очу́, -о́тишь) *perf.*, сверну́ть *perf.*, в сто́рону.

swift *n.* стриж (-á); *adj.* бы́стрый (быстр, -á, -о, бы́стры́). **swiftness** *n.* быстрота́.
swig *n.* глото́к (-тка́); *v.t.* потя́гивать *imp.* (*coll.*).
swill *n.* по́йло; *v.t.* (*rinse*) полоска́ть (-ощу́, -о́щешь) *imp.*, вы́~ *perf.*; (*sluice*) облива́ть *imp.*, обли́ть (оболью́, -льёшь; о́бли́л, облила́, о́бли́ло) *perf.*
swim *v.i.* пла́вать *indet.*, плыть (плыву́, -вёшь; плыл, -á, -о) *det.*; (*head*) кружи́ться (кру́жи́тся) *imp.*; *v.t.* (*across*) переплыва́ть *imp.*, переплы́ть (-ыву́, -ывёшь; переплы́л, -á, -о) *perf.* + *acc.*, че́рез + *acc.*; *n.*: *in the s.*, в ку́рсе де́ла. **swimmer** *n.* плове́ц (-вца́), пловчи́ха. **swimming** *n.* пла́вание. **swimming-pool** *n.* бассе́йн для пла́вания. **swim-suit** *n.* купа́льный костю́м.
swindle *v.t.* обма́нывать *imp.*, обману́ть (-ну́, -нешь) *perf.*; (*coll.*) надува́ть *imp.*, наду́ть (-у́ю, -у́ешь) *perf.*; *n.* обма́н; надува́тельство (*coll.*). **swindler** *n.* плут (-á), ~о́вка; моше́нник, -ица.
swine *n.* свинья́ (*pl.* -ньи, -не́й). **swineherd** *n.* свинопа́с.
swing *v.i.* кача́ться *imp.*, качну́ться *perf.*; колеба́ться (-блюсь, -блешься) *imp.*, по~ *perf.*; раска́чиваться *imp.*, раскача́ться *perf.*; *v.t.* кача́ть *imp.*, качну́ть *perf.* + *acc.*, *instr.*; (*arms*) разма́хивать *imp.* + *instr.*; раска́чивать *imp.*, раскача́ть *perf.*; *n.* кача́ние; (*stroke*) мах (-а(у)); (*seat*) каче́ли (-лей) *pl.*; *in full s.*, в по́лном разга́ре; *s. bridge*, разводно́й мост (мо́ста́, *loc.* -у́; *pl.* -ы́). **swing-door** *n.* дверь (*loc.* -ри́; *pl.* -ри, -ре́й, *instr.* -рьми́ & -ря́ми) открыва́ющаяся в любу́ю сто́рону.
swingeing *adj.* (*huge*) грома́дный; (*forcible*) си́льный (си́лён, -льна́, -льно, си́льны́).
swinish *adj.* сви́нский (*coll.*). **swinishness** *n.* сви́нство (*coll.*).
swipe *n.* уда́р сплеча́; *v.t.* ударя́ть *imp.*, уда́рить *perf.* сплеча́.
swirl *v.i.* кружи́ться (-ужу́сь, -у́жи́шься) *imp.*, верте́ться (-рчу́сь, -ртишься) *imp.*; *v.t.* кружи́ть (-ужу́, -у́жи́шь) *imp.*; *n.* круже́ние; (*whirlpool*) водоворо́т; (*whirlwind*) вихрь *m.*
swish *v.i.* (*cut the air*) рассека́ть *imp.*, рассе́чь (-секу́, -сечёшь; -се́к, -ла́) *perf.* во́здух со сви́стом; *v.t.* (*brandish*) разма́хивать *imp.* + *instr.*; *v.t.* & *i.* (*rustle*) шелесте́ть (-ти́шь) *imp.* (+ *instr.*); шурша́ть (-шу́, -ши́шь) *imp.* (+ *instr.*); *n.* (*of whip*) свист; (*of scythe*) взмах со сви́стом; (*rustle*) ше́лест, шурша́ние.
Swiss *n.* швейца́рец (-рца), -ца́рка; *adj.* швейца́рский; *s. roll*, руле́т (с варе́ньем).
switch *n.* (*electr.*) выключа́тель *m.*, переключа́тель *m.*; (*rly.*) стре́лка; (*change*) измене́ние; (*twig*) прут (пру́та́; *pl.* -тья, -тьев); (*whip*) хлыст (-á); *v.t.* (*whip*) ударя́ть *imp.*, уда́рить *perf.* пруто́м, хлысто́м; (*electr.*; *fig.*; *also s. over*) переключа́ть *imp.*, переключи́ть *perf.*; (*wave*) маха́ть (машу́, ма́шешь) *imp.*, махну́ть *perf.* + *instr.*; (*change direction*) (*of conversation etc.*) направля́ть *imp.*, напра́вить *perf.* (разгово́р) в другу́ю сто́рону; (*rly.*) переводи́ть (-ожу́, -о́дишь) *imp.*, перевести́ (-еду́, -едёшь; перевёл, -á) *perf.* (train, по́езд (*pl.* -á)) на друго́й путь; *s. off*, выключа́ть *imp.*, вы́ключить *perf.*; *s. on*, включа́ть *imp.*, включи́ть *perf.* **switchback** *n.* америка́нские го́ры *f. pl.* **switchboard** *n.* коммута́тор, распредели́тельный щит (-á).
swivel *v.t.* & *i.* враща́ть(ся) *imp.*; *n.* вертлю́г; *s. chair*, враща́ющийся стул (*pl.* -ья, -ьев).
swollen *adj.* взду́тый. **swollen-headed** *adj.* чванли́вый.
swoon *n.* о́бморок; *v.i.* па́дать *imp.*, упа́сть (упаду́, -дёшь; упа́л) *perf.* в о́бморок.
swoop *v.i.*: *s. down*, налета́ть *imp.*, налете́ть (-ечу́, -ети́шь) *perf.* (on, на + *acc.*); *n.* налёт; *at one fell s.*, одни́м уда́ром, одни́м ма́хом.
sword *n.* меч (-á), шпа́га; *s.-fish*, меч-ры́ба. **swordsman** *n.* (иску́сно) владе́ющий *sb.* холо́дным ору́жием; (*fencer*) фехтова́льщик.

sworn *adj.* (*on oath*) под прися́гой; (*enemy*) закля́тый; (*friend*) закады́чный; (*brother*) на́званый.
sybaritic *adj.* сибари́тский.
sycamore *n.* я́вор.
sycophancy *n.* лесть. **sycophant** *n.* льстéц (-á). **sycophantic** *adj.* льсти́вый.
syllabic *adj.* слогово́й; (*lit.*) силлаби́ческий. **syllable** *n.* слог (*pl.* -и, -о́в).
syllabus *n.* програ́мма.
symbiosis *n.* симбио́з.
symbol *n.* си́мвол, знак. **symbolic(al)** *adj.* символи́ческий. **symbolism** *n.* символи́зм. **symbolist** *n.* символи́ст. **symbolize** *v.t.* символизи́ровать *imp.*
symmetrical *adj.* симметри́ческий. **symmetry** *n.* симметри́я.
sympathetic *adj.* сочу́вственный (-ен, -енна); (*well-disposed*) благожела́тельный; (*physiol.*) симпати́ческий; (*likeable*) симпати́чный. **sympathize** *v.i.* сочу́вствовать *imp.* (with, + *dat.*). **sympathizer** *n.* (*supporter*) сторо́нник, -ица. **sympathy** *n.* сочу́вствие; (*condolence*) соболéзнование; (*favour, liking*) симпа́тия.
symphonic *adj.* симфони́ческий. **symphony** *n.* симфо́ния.
symposium *n.* симпо́зиум, совеща́ние.
symptom *n.* симпто́м, при́знак. **symptomatic** *adj.* симптомати́ческий.
synagogue *n.* синаго́га.
synchronism *n.* синхрони́зм. **synchronization** *n.* синхрониза́ция. **synchronize** *v.t.* синхронизи́ровать *imp., perf.*; (*cinema*) совмеща́ть *imp.*, совмести́ть *perf.* (with, с + *instr.*).
syncopate *v.t.* (*mus.*) синкопи́ровать.
syncopation *n.* синко́па.
syndicate *n.* синдика́т; *v.t.* синдици́ровать *imp., perf.*
syndrome *n.* синдро́м.
synod *n.* сино́д, собо́р. **synodal** *adj.* синода́льный.
synonym *n.* синони́м. **synonymous** *adj.* синоними́ческий.
synopsis *n.* конспéкт. **synoptic(al)** *adj.* синопти́ческий.
syntactic(al) *adj.* синтакси́ческий. **syntax** *n.* си́нтаксис.
synthesis *n.* си́нтез. **synthesize** *v.t.* синтези́ровать *imp., perf.* **synthetic(al)** *adj.* синтети́ческий. **synthetics** *n.* синтéтика.
syphilis *n.* си́филис.
Syrian *n.* сири́ец (-и́йца), сири́йка; *adj.* сири́йский.
syringe *n.* шприц, спринцо́вка; *v.t.* спринцева́ть *imp.*
syrup *n.* сиро́п, па́тока. **syrupy** *adj.* подо́бный сиро́пу.
system *n.* систéма; (*order*) стро́й; (*network*) сеть (*loc.* сéти́; *pl.* -ти, -тéй); (*organism*) органи́зм. **systematic** *adj.* системати́ческий. **systematize** *v.t.* систематизи́ровать *imp., perf.* **systemic** *adj.* относя́щийся к всему́ органи́зму.

T

T *n.*: *to a T*, точь-в-то́чь (*coll.*), как раз; *T-shirt*, тéнниска (*coll.*); *T-square*, рейсши́на.
tab *n.* (*loop*) пéтелька; (*on uniform*) петли́ца; (*of boot*) ушко́ (*pl.* -ки́, -ко́в); *keep tabs on*, следи́ть *imp.* за + *instr.*
tabby *n.* (*cat*) полоса́тая ко́шка; (*gossip*) зла́я сплетни́ца; (*cloth*) муа́р.
tabernacle *n.* (*Jewish hist.*) ски́ния; (*receptacle*) дарохрани́тельница.
table *n.* (*furniture*; *food*) стол (-á); (*company*) о́бщество за столо́м; (*list*) табли́ца; (*slab*) доска́ (*acc.* -ску; *pl.* -ски, -со́к, -ска́м), плита́ (*pl.* -ты); *bedside-t.*, ту́мбочка; *t.-cloth*, ска́терть; *t. of contents*, оглавлéние; *t.-spoon*, столо́вая ло́жка; *t. tennis*,

насто́льный те́ннис; *v.t.* (*for discussion*) предлага́ть *imp.*, предложи́ть (-жу́, -жишь) *perf.* на обсужде́ние.
tableau *n.* жива́я карти́на; (*dramatic situation*) драмати́ческая ситуа́ция.
tableland *n.* плоского́рье.
tablet *n.* (*medicine*) табле́тка; (*memorial t.*) мемориа́льная доска́ (*acc.* -ску; *pl.* -ски, -со́к, -ска́м); (*name-plate*) доще́чка; (*notebook*) блокно́т; (*of soap*) кусо́к (-ска́).
tabloid *n.* (*newspaper*) малоформа́тная газе́та; (*popular newspaper*) бульва́рная газе́та; *in t. form*, сжа́то.
taboo *n.* табу́ *neut.indecl.*, запреще́ние; *adj.* (*prohibited*) запрещённый (-ён, -ена́); (*consecrated*) свяще́нный (-е́н, -е́нна); *v.t.* налага́ть *imp.*, наложи́ть (-жу́, -жишь) *perf.* табу́ на + *acc.*
tabular *adj.* табли́чный; (*flat*) пло́ский (-сок, -ска́, -ско); (*geol.*) слои́стый, пласти́нчатый. **tabulate** *v.t.* располага́ть *imp.*, расположи́ть (-жу́, -жишь) *perf.* в ви́де табли́ц. **tabulator** *n.* (*on typewriter*) табуля́тор; (*person*) состави́тель *m.* табли́ц.
tacit *adj.* (*silent*; *implied*) молчали́вый; (*implied*) подразумева́емый. **taciturn** *adj.* молчали́вый, неразгово́рчивый. **taciturnity** *n.* молчали́вость, неразгово́рчивость.
tack[1] *n.* (*nail*) гво́здик; (*stitch*) намётка; (*naut.*) галс; (*fig.*) курс; *v.t.* (*fasten*) прикрепля́ть *imp.*, прикрепи́ть *perf.* гво́здиками; (*stitch*) смётывать *imp.*, смета́ть *perf.* на живу́ю ни́тку; (*fig.*) добавля́ть *imp.*, доба́вить *perf.* ((on)to, + *dat.*); *v.i.* (*naut.*; *fig.*) лави́ровать *imp.*
tack[2] *n.* (*for riding*) сбру́я (*collect.*).
tackle *n.* (*requisites*) снасть (*collect.*), принадле́жности *f.pl.*; (*equipment*) обору́дование; (*naut.*) такела́ж; (*block and t.*) та́ли (-лей) *pl.*; (*tech.*, *t.-block*) полиспа́ст; (*sport*) блокиро́вка; *v.t.* (*try to overcome*) пыта́ться *imp.*, по~ *perf.* преодоле́ть; (*get down to*) бра́ться (беру́сь, -рёшься) *imp.*, взя́ться (возьму́сь, -мёшься; взя́лся, -ла́сь) *perf.* за + *acc.*; (*work on*) занима́ться *imp.*, заня́ться (займу́сь, -мёшься; заня́лся́, -ла́сь) *perf.* + *instr.*; (*sport*) (*intercept*) перехва́тывать *imp.* перехвати́ть (-ачу́, -а́тишь) *perf.*; блоки́ровать *imp.*, *perf.*; (*secure ball from*) отнима́ть *imp.*, отня́ть (отниму́, -мешь; о́тнял, -а́, -о) *perf.* мяч у + *gen.*
tacky *adj.* ли́пкий (-пок, -пка́, -пко), кле́йкий.
tact *n.* такт(и́чность). **tactful** *adj.* такти́чный.
tactical *adj.* такти́ческий; (*artful*) ло́вкий (-вок, -вка́, -вко, ло́вки́). **tactician** *n.* та́ктик. **tactics** *n.* та́ктика.
tactile *adj.* осяза́тельный; (*tangible*) осяза́емый.
tactless *adj.* беста́ктный.
tadpole *n.* голова́стик.
taffeta *n.* тафта́; *attrib.* тафтяно́й.
taffrail *n.* гакабо́рт.
tag *n.* (*label*) ярлы́к (-а́), этике́тка, би́рка; (*of lace*) наконе́чник; (*of boot*) ушко́ (*pl.* -ки́, -ко́в); (*quotation*) изби́тая цита́та; *v.t.* (*label*) прикрепля́ть *imp.*, прикрепи́ть *perf.* ярлы́к на + *acc.*; *v.i.*: *t. along*, (*follow*) сле́довать *imp.*, по~ *perf.* по пята́м (after, за + instr.); *may I t. along?* мо́жно с ва́ми?
tail *n.* (*of animal*, *aircraft*, *kite*, *procession*, *etc.*) хвост; (*of shirt*) ни́жний коне́ц (-нца́); (*of hair*; *of letter*; (*mus.*) *of note*) хво́стик; (*of coat*) фа́лда; (*of coin*) обра́тная сторона́ (*acc.* -ону) моне́ты; *heads or tails?* орёл и́ли ре́шка? *pl.* (*coat*) фрак; *t.-board*, (*of cart*) откидна́я доска́ (*acc.* -ску; *pl.* -ски, -со́к, -ска́м); (*of lorry*) откидно́й борт (*loc.* -у́; *pl.* -а́); *t.-lamp*, *-light*, за́дний фона́рь (-ря́) *m.*; *t.-spin*, што́пор; *t. wind*, попу́тный ве́тер (-тра); *v.t.* (*fruit etc.*) острига́ть *imp.*, остри́чь (-игу́, -ижёшь; -и́г) *perf.* хво́стики + *gen.*; (*shadow*) высле́живать *imp.*; *v.i.*: *t. away*, *off*, постепе́нно уменьша́ться *imp.*; (*disappear*) исчеза́ть *imp.*; (*grow silent*, *abate*) затиха́ть *imp.* **tailcoat** *n.* фрак.
tailor *n.* портно́й *sb.*; *v.t.* шить (шью, шьёшь) *imp.*, сшить (сошью́, -ьёшь) *perf.*; *v.i.* портня́жничать *imp.* (*coll.*); *t.-made*, сши́тый, изгото́вленный на

зака́з; (*fig.*) приспосо́бленный. **tailoring** *n.* портня́жное де́ло.

tailpiece *n.* (*typ.*) концо́вка; (*appendage*) за́дний коне́ц (-нца́).

taint *n.* пятно́ (*pl.* -тна, -тен, -тнам), поро́к; (*trace*) налёт; (*infection*) зара́за; *v.t.* & *i.* (*spoil*) по́ртить(ся) *imp.*, ис~ *perf.*; (*infect*) заража́ть(ся) *imp.*, зарази́ть(ся) *perf.* **tainted** *adj.* испо́рченный (-ен).

take *v.t.* (*var. senses*) брать (беру́, -рёшь; брал, -а́, -о) *imp.*, взять (возьму́, -мёшь; взял, -а́, -о) *perf.*; (*also seize, capture*) захва́тывать *imp.*, захвати́ть (-ачу́, -а́тишь) *perf.*; (*receive, accept*; *t. breakfast*; *t. medicine*; *t. steps*) принима́ть *imp.*, приня́ть (приму́, -мешь; при́нял, -а́, -о) *perf.*; (*convey, escort*) провожа́ть *imp.*, проводи́ть (-ожу́, -о́дишь) *perf.*; (*public transport*) е́здить *indet.*, е́хать (е́ду, е́дешь) *det.*, по~ *perf.* + *instr.*, на + *prep.*; (*photograph*) снима́ть *imp.*, снять (сниму́, -мешь; снял, -а́, -о) *perf.*; (*occupy*; *t. time*) занима́ть *imp.*, заня́ть (займу́, -мёшь; за́нял, -а́, -о) *perf.*; (*impers.*) *how long does it take?* ско́лько вре́мени ну́жно? (*size in clothing*) носи́ть (ношу́, но́сишь) *imp.*; (*exam*) сдава́ть (-аю́, -аёшь) *imp.*; *t. courage, heart*, мужа́ться *imp.*; *t. cover*, пря́таться (-я́чусь, -я́чешься) *imp.*, с~ *perf.*; *t. to heart*, принима́ть *imp.*, приня́ть (приму́, -мешь; при́нял, -а́, -о) *perf.* бли́зко к се́рдцу; *t. a liking to*, полюби́ться (-блю́сь, -бишься) *perf. impers.* + *dat.* (*coll.*); *t. a turning*, свора́чивать *imp.*, сверну́ть *perf.* на у́лицу (*street*), доро́гу (*road*); *v.i.* (*be successful*) име́ть *imp.* успе́х; (*of injection*) привива́ться *imp.*, приви́ться (-вьётся; -ви́лся, -вила́сь) *perf.*; *t. after*, походи́ть (-ожу́, -о́дишь) *imp.* на + *acc.*; *t. away*, (*remove*) убира́ть *imp.*, убра́ть (уберу́, -рёшь; убра́л, -а́, -о) *perf.*; (*subtract*) вычита́ть *imp.*, вы́честь (-чту, -чтешь; -чел, -чла) *perf.*; *t.-away*, магази́н, где продаю́т на вы́нос; *t. back*, брать (беру́, берёшь; брал, -а́, -о) *imp.*, взять (возьму́, -мёшь; взял, -а́, -о) *perf.* обра́тно, наза́д; *t. down* (*in writing*) запи́сывать *imp.*, записа́ть (-ишу́, -и́шешь) *perf.*; *t. s.b., s.th. for, to be*, принима́ть *imp.*, приня́ть (приму́, -мешь; при́нял, -а́, -о) *perf.* за + *acc.*; счита́ть *imp.*, счесть (сочту́, -тёшь; счёл, сочла́) *perf.* + *instr.*, за + *instr.*; *t. from*, отнима́ть *imp.*, отня́ть (отниму́, -мешь; о́тнял, -а́, -о) *perf.* у, от + *gen.*; *t. in*, (*clothing*) ушива́ть *imp.*, уши́ть (ушью́, -ьёшь) *perf.*; (*understand*) понима́ть *imp.*, поня́ть (пойму́, -мёшь; по́нял, -а́, -о) *perf.*; (*deceive*) обма́нывать *imp.*, обману́ть (-ну́, -нешь) *perf.*; *t. off*, (*clothing*) снима́ть *imp.*, снять (сниму́, -мешь; снял, -а́, -о) *perf.*; (*mimic*) передра́знивать *imp.*, передразни́ть (-ню́, -нишь) *perf.*; (*aeroplane*) взлета́ть *imp.*, взлете́ть (-ечу́, -ети́шь) *perf.*; *t.-off*, (*imitation*) подража́ние, карикату́ра; (*aeron.*) взлёт; *t. on*, (*undertake*) брать (беру́, -рёшь; брал, -а́, -о) *imp.*, взлять (возьму́, -мёшь; взял, -а́, -о) *perf.* на себя́; (*at game*) сража́ться *imp.*, срази́ться *perf.* с + *instr.* (at, в + *acc.*); *t. out*, вынима́ть *imp.*, вы́нуть *perf.*; (*dog*) выводи́ть (-ожу́, -о́дишь) *imp.*, вы́вести (-еду, -едешь; -ел) *perf.* (for a walk, на прогу́лку); (*person*) води́ть (вожу́, во́дишь) *indet.*, вести́ (веду́, -дёшь; вёл, -а́) *det.*, по~ *perf.*; (*to theatre, restaurant etc.*) приглаша́ть *imp.*, пригласи́ть *perf.* (to, в + *acc.*); *we took them out every night*, мы приглаша́ли их куда́-нибудь ка́ждый ве́чер; *t. over*, принима́ть *imp.*, приня́ть (приму́, -мешь; при́нял, -а́, -о) *perf.*; (*seize*) завладева́ть *imp.*, завладе́ть *perf.* + *instr.*; *t. to*, (*thing*) пристрасти́ться *perf.* к + *dat.*; (*person*) привя́зываться *imp.*, привяза́ться (-яжу́сь, -я́жешься) *perf.* к + *dat.*; *t. up*, (*enter upon*) бра́ться (беру́сь, -рёшься) *imp.*, взя́ться (возьму́сь, -мёшься; взя́лся, -ла́сь) *perf.* за + *acc.*; (*challenge*) принима́ть *imp.*, приня́ть (приму́, -мешь; при́нял, -а́, -о) *perf.*; (*time*) занима́ть *imp.*, заня́ть (займу́, -мёшь; за́нял, -а́, -о) *perf.*; *n.* (*fishing*) уло́в; (*hunting*) добы́ча; (*cin.*) дубль *m.*, кинока́др.

taking *adj.* привлека́тельный.

takings *n.* сбор, барыши́ *m.pl.*
talc(um), t. powder *n.* тальк.
tale *n.* расска́з, ска́зка; (*gossip*) спле́тня (*gen.pl.* -тен); (*coll., lie*) вы́думка.
talent *n.* тала́нт. **talented** *adj.* тала́нтливый.
talisman *n.* талисма́н.
talk *v.i.* разгова́ривать *imp.* (to, with, с+*instr.*); (*gossip*) спле́тничать *imp.*, на~ *perf.*; *v.i.* & *t.* говори́ть *imp.*, по~ *perf.*; *t. down to*, говори́ть *imp.* свысока́ с+*instr.*; *t. into*, угова́ривать *imp.*, уговори́ть *perf.*+*inf.*; *t. over*, (*discuss*) обсужда́ть *imp.*, обсуди́ть (-ужу́, -у́дишь) *perf.*; *t. round*, (*persuade*) переубежда́ть *imp.*, переубеди́ть *perf.*; (*discuss, reaching no conclusion*) говори́ть *imp.*, по~ *perf.* о+*prep.* простра́нно, не каса́ясь существа́ де́ла; *t. to*, (*reprimand*) венгова́ривать *imp.*+*dat.*; *n.* (*conversation*) разгово́р, бесе́да; (*chatter, gossip*) болтовня́ (*coll.*); (*lecture*) бесе́да; *pl.* перегово́ры (-ров) *pl.* **talkative** *adj.* болтли́вый, разгово́рчивый. **talker** *n.* говоря́щий *sb.*; (*chatterer*) болту́н (-а́) (*coll.*); (*orator*) ора́тор. **talking-to** *n.* (*coll.*) вы́говор.
tall *adj.* высо́кий (-о́к, -ока́, -о́ко́); (*in measurements*) высото́й, ро́стом в+*acc.* **tallboy** *n.* высо́кий комо́д.
tallow *n.* са́ло. **tallowy** *adj.* са́льный.
tally *n.* (*score*) счёт (-а(у)); (*label*) би́рка, ярлы́к (-а́); (*duplicate*) ко́пия, дублика́т; *v.i.* соотве́тствовать (with, +*dat.*); *v.t.* подсчи́тывать *imp.*, подсчита́ть *perf.*
tally-ho *interj.* ату́!
talon *n.* ко́готь (-гтя; *pl.* -гти, -гте́й) *m.*
tamarisk *n.* тамари́ск.
tambourine *n.* бу́бен (-бна), тамбури́н.
tame *adj.* ручно́й, приручённый (-ён, -ена́); (*submissive*) поко́рный; (*insipid*) ску́чный (-чен, -чна́, -чно); *v.t.* прируча́ть *imp.*, приручи́ть *perf.*; (*also curb*) укроща́ть *imp.*, укроти́ть (-ощу́, -оти́шь) *perf.* **tameable** *adj.* укроти́мый. **tamer** *n.* укроти́тель *m.*; (*trainer*) дрессиро́вщик; (*fig.*) усмири́тель *m.*
tamp *v.t.* (*road etc.*) трамбова́ть *imp.*, у~ *perf.*; (*pack full*) набива́ть *imp.*, наби́ть (-бью́, -бьёшь) *perf.*
tamper *v.i.*: *t. with*, (*meddle*) вме́шиваться *imp.*, вмеша́ться *perf.* в+*acc.*; (*touch*) тро́гать *imp.*, тро́нуть *perf.*; (*forge*) подде́лывать *imp.*, подде́лать *perf.*
tampon *n.* тампо́н.
tan *n.* (*sun-t.*) зага́р; (*bark*) толчёная дубова́я кора́; *adj.* желтова́то-коpи́чневый; *v.t.* (*of sun*) обжига́ть *imp.*, обже́чь (обожжёт; обжёг, обожгла́) *perf.*; (*hide*) дуби́ть *imp.*, вы́~ *perf.*; (*beat*) (*coll.*) дуба́сить *imp.*, от~ *perf.*; *v.i.* загора́ть *imp.*, загоре́ть (-рю́, -ри́шь) *perf.*
tandem *n.* (*bicycle*) та́ндем; (*horses*) упря́жка цу́гом; *in t.*, (*horses*) цу́гом; (*single file*) гусько́м.
tang *n.* (*taste*) ре́зкий при́вкус; (*smell*) о́стрый за́пах; (*tech.*) хвостови́к; (*characteristic feature*) характе́рная черта́.
tangent *n.* (*math.*) каса́тельная *sb.*; (*trigon.*) та́нгенс; *go off at a t.*, (*in conversation etc.*) отклоня́ться *imp.*, отклони́ться (-ню́сь, -ни́шься) *perf.* от те́мы. **tangential** *adj.* (*diverging*) отклоня́ющийся.
tangerine *n.* мандари́н.
tangible *adj.* осяза́емый.
tangle *v.t.* & *i.* запу́тывать(ся) *imp.*, запу́тать(ся) *perf.*; *n.* пу́таница.
tango *n.* та́нго *neut.indecl.*
tangy *adj.* о́стрый (остр & остёр, остра́, о́стро́); ре́зкий (-зок, -зка́, -зко).
tank *n.* цисте́рна, бак; (*reservoir*) водоём; (*mil.*) танк; *attrib.* та́нковый; *t.-engine*, танк-паровоз.
tankard *n.* кру́жка.
tanker *n.* (*sea*) та́нкер; (*road*) автоцисте́рна.
tanner *n.* дуби́льщик. **tannery** *n.* коже́венный заво́д. **tannin** *n.* тани́н. **tanning** *n.* дубле́ние.
tantalize *v.t.* дразни́ть (-ню́, -нишь) *imp.* ло́жными наде́ждами; му́чить *imp.*, за~, из~ *perf.*
tantamount *predic.* равноси́лен (-льна, -льно, -льны) (to, +*dat.*).
tantrum *n.* вспы́шка гне́ва, при́ступ раздраже́ния.

tap[1] *n.* (*water etc.*) кран; *on t.*, распи́вочно; *v.t.* (*open*) открыва́ть *imp.*, откры́ть (-ро́ю, -ро́ешь) *perf.*; (*pour out*) налива́ть *imp.*, нали́ть (-лью́, -льёшь; на́ли́л, -á, -о) *perf.*; (*med.*) выка́чивать *imp.*, вы́качать *perf.*; (*draw sap from*) подса́чивать *imp.*, подсочи́ть *perf.*; (*telephone conversation*) подслу́шивать *imp.*; *t. telegraph wires*, перехва́тывать *imp.*, перехвати́ть (-ачу́, -а́тишь) *perf.* телегра́фное сообще́ние; (*make use of*) испо́льзовать *imp.*, *perf.*

tap[2] *n.* (*knock*) лёгкий стук; *v.t.* стуча́ть (-чу́, -чи́шь) *imp.*, по ~ *perf.* в + *acc.*, по + *dat.*; *t.-dance*, (*v.i.*) отбива́ть *imp.*, отби́ть (отобью́, -ьёшь) *perf.* чечётку; (*n.*) чечётка; *t.-dancer*, чечёточник, -ица.

tape *n.* (*cotton strip*) тесьма́; (*adhesive, magnetic, measuring, etc.*) ле́нта; (*sport*) ле́нточка; *t.-measure*, рулётка; *t.-recorder*, магнитофо́н; *t.-recording*, за́пись; *v.t.* (*seal*) закле́ивать *imp.*, закле́ить *perf.*; (*record*) запи́сывать *imp.*, записа́ть (-ишу́, -и́шешь) *perf.* на ле́нту.

taper *n.* (*slender candle*) то́нкая све́чка; (*wick*) вощённый фити́ль (-ля́) *m.*; *v.t.* & *i.* су́живать(ся) *imp.*, су́зить(ся) *perf.* к концу́. **tapering** *adj.* су́живающийся к одному́ концу́.

tapestry *n.* гобеле́н.

tapeworm *n.* ле́нточный глист (-а́).

tapioca *n.* тапио́ка.

tapir *n.* тапи́р.

tappet *n.* толка́тель *m.*

tar *n.* дёготь (-гтя(-гтю)) *m.*; (*pitch*) смола́; (*tarmac*) гудро́н; *v.t.* ма́зать (ма́жу, -жешь) *imp.*, вы́ ~ , на ~ , по ~ *perf.* дёгтем; смоли́ть *imp.*, вы́ ~ , о ~ *perf.*; гудрони́ровать *imp.*, *perf.*

tarantella *n.* таранте́лла.

tarantula *n.* тара́нтул.

tardiness *n.* (*slowness*) медли́тельность; (*lateness*) опозда́ние. **tardy** *adj.* (*slow*) медли́тельный; (*late*) по́здний, запозда́лый.

tare[1] *n.* (*vetch*) ви́ка; *pl.* (*Bibl.*) пле́велы *m.pl.*

tare[2] *n.* (*comm.*) та́ра; (*allowance*) ски́дка на та́ру.

target *n.* мише́нь, цель.

tariff *n.* тари́ф; (*price-list*) прейскура́нт; *v.t.* тарифици́ровать *imp.*, *perf.*

tarmac *n.* (*material*) гудро́н; (*road*) гудрони́рованное шоссе́ *neut.indecl.*; (*runway*) бетони́рованная площа́дка; *v.t.* гудрони́ровать *imp.*, *perf.*

tarn *n.* го́рное озерко́ (*pl.* -ки́, -ко́в).

tarnish *v.t.* де́лать *imp.*, с ~ *perf.* ту́склым; (*discredit*) поро́чить *imp.*, о ~ *perf.*; *v.i.* тускне́ть *imp.*, по ~ *perf.*; *n.* (*dullness*) ту́склость; (*blemish*) пятно́ (*pl.* -тна, -тен, -тнам). **tarnished** *adj.* ту́склый (-л, -ла́, -ло).

tarpaulin *n.* брезе́нт.

tarragon *n.* эстраго́н.

tarry[1] *adj.* покры́тый дёгтем.

tarry[2] *v.i.* ме́длить *imp.*

tarsus *n.* предплюсна́ (*pl.* -сны, -сен).

tart[1] *adj.* (*taste*) ки́слый (-сел, -сла́, -сло), те́рпкий (-пок, -пка́, -пко); (*biting*) ко́лкий (-лок, -лка́, -лко). **tartness** *n.* кислота́; ко́лкость.

tart[2] *n.* (*pie*) сла́дкий пиро́г (-а́).

tart[3] *n.* (*girl*) шлю́ха.

tartan *n.* шотла́ндка.

tartar *n.* ви́нный ка́мень (-мня) *m.*

Tartar *n.* тата́рин (*pl.* -ры, -р), -рка; *to catch a T.*, встреча́ть *imp.*, встре́тить *perf.* проти́вника не по си́лам.

task *n.* зада́ча, зада́ние; *take to t.*, де́лать *imp.*, с ~ *perf.* вы́говор + *dat.*; отчи́тывать *imp.*, отчита́ть *perf.* (*coll.*); *t.-force*, операти́вная гру́ппа.

taskmaster *n.* эксплуата́тор.

tassel *n.* ки́сточка, кисть (*pl.* -ти, -те́й).

taste *n.* (*also fig.*) вкус; (*liking*) скло́нность (for, к + *dat.*); (*sample*) про́ба; (*small piece*) ма́ленький кусо́к (-ска́); (*sip*) ма́ленький глото́к (-тка́); *t.-bud*, вкусова́я лу́ковица; *v.t.* чу́вствовать *imp.*, по ~ *perf.* вкус + *gen.*; (*sample*) про́бовать *imp.*, по ~ *perf.*; (*fig.*) вкуша́ть *imp.*, вкуси́ть (-ушу́, -у́сишь) *perf.*; (*wine etc.*) дегусти́ровать *imp.*, *perf.*; *v.i.* име́ть *imp.* вкус, при́вкус (of, + *gen.*). **tasteful** *adj.* (сде́ланный) со вку́сом. **tasteless** *adj.* безвку́сный. **tasting** *n.* дегуста́ция. **tasty** *adj.* вку́сный (-сен, -сна́, -сно).

tatter *n.* (*shred*) лоску́т (-а́); *pl.* лохмо́тья (-ьев) *pl.* **tattered** *adj.* обо́рванный; в лохмо́тьях.

tattle *n.* (*chatter*) болтовня́; (*gossip*) спле́тни (-тен) *pl.*; *v.i.* (*chatter*) болта́ть *imp.*; (*gossip*) спле́тничать *imp.*, на~ *perf.*

tattoo[1] *n.* (*mil.*) (*in evening*) сигна́л вече́рней зари́; (*ceremonial*) торже́ственная заря́; *to beat the t.*, бить (бью, бьёшь) *imp.*, по~ *perf.* зо́рю; *v.i.* бараба́нить *imp.* па́льцами.

tattoo[2] *n.* (*design*) татуиро́вка; *v.t.* татуи́ровать *imp.*, *perf.*

taunt *n.* насме́шка, ко́лкость; *v.t.* насмеха́ться *imp.* над+*instr.* **taunting** *adj.* насме́шливый.

Taurus *n.* Теле́ц (-льца́).

taut *adj.* ту́го натя́нутый, туго́й (туг, -а́, -о); (*nerves*) взви́нченный. **tauten** *v.t.* & *i.* ту́го натя́гивать(ся) *imp.*, натяну́ть(ся) (-ну́(сь), -нешь(ся)) *perf.* **tautness** *n.* натяже́ние.

tautological *adj.* тавтологи́ческий. **tautology** *n.* тавтоло́гия.

tavern *n.* таве́рна.

tawdriness *n.* мишура́. **tawdry** *adj.* мишу́рный; (*showy*) показно́й.

tawny *adj.* рыжева́то-кори́чневый; *t. owl*, нея́сыть.

tax *n.* нало́г; (*strain*) напряже́ние; *direct* (*indirect*) *taxes*, прямы́е (ко́свенные) нало́ги; *t.-collector*, сбо́рщик нало́гов; *t.-dodger*, неплате́льщик; *t.-free*, освобождённый (-ён, -ена́) от нало́га; *v.t.* облага́ть *imp.*, обложи́ть (-жу́, -жишь) *perf.* нало́гом; (*strain*) напряга́ть *imp.*, напря́чь (-ягу́, -яжёшь; напря́г, -ла́) *perf.*; (*tire*) утомля́ть *imp.*, утоми́ть *perf.*; (*patience*) испы́тывать *imp.*, испыта́ть *perf.*; (*charge*) обвиня́ть *imp.*, обвини́ть *perf.* (with, в+*prep.*). **taxable** *adj.* подлежа́щий обложе́нию нало́гом. **taxation** *n.* обложе́ние нало́гом. **taxpayer** *n.* налогоплате́льщик.

taxi *n.* такси́ *neut.indecl.*; *t.-driver*, води́тель *m.* такси́; *t. rank*, стоя́нка такси́; *v.i.* (*aeron.*) рули́ть *imp.*

taxidermist *n.* наби́вщик чу́чел. **taxidermy** *n.* наби́вка чу́чел.

taximeter *n.* таксо́метр.

tea *n.* чай (ча́я(ю); *pl.* чаи́); *attrib.* ча́йный; *t.-bag*, паке́тик с сухи́м ча́ем; *t.-caddy*, ча́йница; *t.-cloth*, *t.-towel*, полоте́нце для посу́ды; *t.-cosy*, стёганый чехо́льчик (для ча́йника); *t.-cup*, ча́йная ча́шка; *t.-leaf*, ча́йный лист (-а́; *pl.* -ья, -ьев); *t.-pot*, ча́йник; *t.-spoon*, ча́йная ло́жка; *t.-strainer*, ча́йное си́течко.

teach *v.t.* учи́ть (учу́, у́чишь) *imp.*, на~ *perf.* (*person*, +*acc.*; *subject*, +*dat.*, *inf.*); обуча́ть *imp.*, обучи́ть (-чу́, -чишь) *perf.* (*person*, +*acc.*; *subject*, +*dat.*, *inf.*); преподава́ть (-даю́, -даёшь) *imp.* (*subject*, +*acc.*); (*coll.*) проу́чивать *imp.*, проучи́ть (-чу́, -чишь) *perf.* **teacher** *n.* учи́тель (*pl.* -ля́ & (*fig.*) -ли) *m.*, ~ница; преподава́тель *m.*, ~ница; *t.-training college*, педагоги́ческий институ́т. **teaching** *n.* (*instruction*) обуче́ние; (*doctrine*) уче́ние.

teak *n.* тик; *attrib.* ти́ковый.

teal *n.* чиро́к (-рка́).

team *n.* (*sport*) кома́нда; (*of people*) брига́да, гру́ппа; (*of horses etc.*) упря́жка; *t.-mate*, (*sport*) игро́к (-а́) той же кома́нды; (*at work*) това́рищ по рабо́те, член той же брига́ды; *t.-work*, брига́дная, совме́стная рабо́та; (*co-operation*) взаимоде́йствие, сотру́дничество; *v.i.* (*t. up*) объединя́ться *imp.*, объедини́ться *perf.* в кома́нду *etc.*; *v.t.* запряга́ть *imp.*, запря́чь (-ягу́, -я́жешь; -я́г, -ягла́) *perf.* в упря́жку.

tear[1] *n.* (*rent*) проре́ха; (*hole*) дыра́ (*pl.* -ры); (*cut*) разре́з; *v.t.* рвать (рву, рвёшь; рвал, -а́, -о) *imp.*; (*also t. to pieces*) разрыва́ть *imp.*, разорва́ть (-ву́, -вёшь; -ва́л, -вала́, -ва́ло) *perf.*; *v.i.* рва́ться (рвётся; рва́лся, -ала́сь, -а́ло́сь) *imp.*; разрыва́ться *imp.*, разорва́ться (-вётся; -ва́лся, -вала́сь, -ва́ло́сь) *perf.*; (*rush*) мча́ться (мчу́сь, мчи́шься) *imp.*; *t. down*, *off*, срыва́ть *imp.*, сорва́ть (-ву́, -вёшь; сорва́л, -а́, -о) *perf.*; *t. away*, *off*, отрыва́ть *imp.*, оторва́ть (-ву́, -вёшь; оторва́л, -а́, -о) *perf.*; *t. out*, вырыва́ть *imp.*, вы́рвать (-ву, -вешь) *perf.*; *t. up*, изрыва́ть *imp.*,

изорвáть (-вý, -вёшь; -вáл, -валá, -вáло) *perf.*
tear[2] *n.* (*t.-drop*) слезá (*pl.* -ёзы, -ёз, -езáм); *t.-gas*, слезоточи́вый газ (-а(у)). **tearful** *adj.* слезли́вый; (*sad*) печáльный.
tease *v.t.* дразни́ть (-ню́, -нишь) *imp.*; (*wool*) чесáть (чешý, -шешь) *imp.*; (*cloth*) ворсовáть *imp.*, на~ *perf.* **teaser** *n.* (*puzzle*) головолóмка.
teasel, teazle *n.* (*plant*) ворся́нка; (*device*) ворши́льная ши́шка.
teat *n.* сосóк (-скá).
technical *adj.* техни́ческий; (*specialist*) специáльный; (*formal*) формáльный; *t. college*, техни́ческое учи́лище. **technicality** *n.* техни́ческая сторонá (*acc.* -ону; *pl.* -оны, -óн, -онáм); формáльность. **technician** *n.* тéхник. **technique** *n.* тéхника; (*method*) мéтод. **technology** *n.* технолóгия, тéхника. **technological** *adj.* технологи́ческий. **technologist** *n.* технóлог.
teddy-bear *n.* медвежóнок (-жóнка; *pl.* -жáта, -жáт).
tedious *adj.* скýчный (-чен, -чнá, -чно), утоми́тельный. **tedium** *n.* скýка, утоми́тельность.
teem[1] *v.i.* (*abound in, be abundant*) кишéть (-ши́т) *imp.* (with, + *instr.*); (*abound in*) изоби́ловать *imp.* (with, + *instr.*).
teem[2] *v.i.*: *it is teeming*, дождь льёт как из ведрá.
teenage *adj.* ю́ношеский. **teenager** *n.* подрóсток (-тка). **teens** *n.* вóзраст от тринадцати́ до девятнадцати́ лет.
teeter *v.i.* качáться *imp.*, качнýться *perf.*; пошáтываться *imp.*
teethe *v.i.*: *the child is teething*, у ребёнка прорéзываются зýбы. **teething** *n.* подрéзывание зубóв; *t. ring*, дéтское зубнóе кольцó; *t. troubles*, (*fig.*) начáльные проблéмы.
teetotal *adj.* трéзвый (-в, -вá, -во). **teetotalism** *n.* трéзвенность. **teetotaller** *n.* трéзвенник.
tele- *in comb.* теле-. **telecommunication(s)** *n.* дáльняя связь. **telegram** *n.* телегрáмма. **telegraph** *n.* телегрáф; *attrib.* телегрáфный; *v.t.* телеграфи́ровать *imp.*, *perf.*; *t.-pole*, телегрáфный столб (-á). **telegraphese** *n.* телегрáфный стиль *m.* **telegraphic** *adj.* телегрáфный. **telegraphist** *n.* телеграфи́ст. **telegraphy** *n.* телеграфи́я. **telemeter** *n.* телемéтр. **telemetry** *n.* телеметри́я. **telepathic** *adj.* телепати́ческий. **telepathy** *n.* телепáтия. **telephone** *n.* телефóн; *attrib.* телефóнный; *v.t.* (*message*) телефони́ровать *imp.*, *perf.* + *acc.*, о + *prep.*; (*person*) звони́ть *imp.*, по~ *perf.* (по телефóну) + *dat.*; *t. box*, телефóнная бýдка; *t. directory*, телефóнная кни́га; *t. exchange*, телефóнная стáнция; *t. number*, нóмер (*pl.* -á) телефóна. **telephonic** *adj.* телефóнный. **telephonist** *n.* телефони́ст, ~ка. **telephony** *n.* телефони́я. **telephoto lens** *n.* телеобъекти́в. **telephotography** *n.* телефотогрáфия. **teleprinter, teletype** *n.* телетáйп. **telescope** *n.* телескóп; *v.t.* & *i.* телескопи́чески склáдывать(ся) *imp.*, сложи́ть(ся) (сложý, слóжишь) *perf.* **telescopic** *adj.* телескопи́ческий. **televise** *v.t.* покáзывать *imp.*, показáть (-ажý, -áжешь) *perf.* по телеви́дению; передавáть (-даю́, -даёшь) *imp.*, передáть (-áм, -áшь, -áст, -ади́м; пéредал, -á, -о) *perf.* по телеви́дению. **television** *n.* телеви́дение; (*set*) телеви́зор; *attrib.* телевизиóнный. **telex** *n.* тéлекс.
tell *v.t.* (*relate*) расскáзывать *imp.*, рассказáть (-ажý, -áжешь) *perf.* (*thing told*, + *acc.*; *person told*, + *dat.*); (*utter, inform*) говори́ть *imp.*, сказáть (скажý, -жешь) *perf.* (*thing uttered*, + *acc.*; *thing informed about*, о + *prep.*; *person informed*, + *dat.*); (*order*) велéть (-лю́, -ли́шь) *imp.*, *perf.* + *dat.*; *t. one thing from another*, отличáть *imp.*, отличи́ть *perf.* + *acc.* от + *gen.*; *v.i.* (*have an effect*) скáзываться *imp.*, сказáться (скажýсь, -жешься) *perf.* (on, на + *prep.*); *all told*, итогó; *t. fortunes*, гадáть *imp.*, по~ *perf.*; *t. off*, (*select*) отбирáть *imp.*, отобрáть (отберý, -рёшь; отобрáл, -á, -о) *perf.*; (*rebuke*) отдéлывать *imp.*, отдéлать *perf.*; *t. on, t. tales about*, ябéдничать *imp.*, на~*perf.* на + *acc.* **teller** *n.* (*of story*) расскáзчик, -ица; (*of votes*) счётчик голосóв; (*in bank*) касси́р, ~ша. **telling**

adj. (*effective*) эффе́ктный; (*significant*) многозначи́тельный; *t.-off*, вы́говор. **telltale** *n.* доно́счик, сплéтник; *adj.* преда́тельский.
temerity *n.* (*rashness*) безрассу́дство; (*audacity*) дёрзость.
temper *n.* (*metal*) зака́л; (*character*) нрав, хара́ктер; (*mood*) настрое́ние; (*anger*) гнев; *lose one's t.*, выходи́ть (-ожу́, -о́дишь) *imp.*, вы́йти (вы́йду, -дешь; вы́шел, -шла) *perf.* из себя́; *v.t.* (*metal*) отпуска́ть *imp.*, отпусти́ть (-ущу́, -у́стишь) *perf.*; (*moderate*) смягча́ть *imp.*, смягчи́ть *perf.*
temperance *n.* (*moderation*) уме́ренность; (*sobriety*) тре́звенность.
temperament *n.* темпера́мент; (*mus.*) темпера́ция. **temperamental** *adj.* темпера́ментный.
temperate *adj.* уме́ренный (-ен, -енна).
temperature *n.* температу́ра; (*high t.*) повы́шенная температу́ра; *take s.b.'s t.*, измеря́ть *imp.*, изме́рить *perf.* температу́ру + *dat.*
tempest *n.* бу́ря. **tempestuous** *adj.* бу́рный (-рен, бу́рна́, -рно), бу́йный (бу́ен, буйна́, -но).
template *n.* шабло́н.
temple[1] *n.* (*relig.*) храм.
temple[2] *n.* (*anat.*) висо́к (-ска́).
tempo *n.* темп.
temporal *adj.* (*secular*) мирско́й, све́тский; (*of time*) временно́й.
temporary *adj.* вре́менный.
temporize *v.i.* приспоса́бливаться *imp.*, приспосо́биться *perf.* ко вре́мени и обстоя́тельствам; (*hesitate*) ме́длить *imp.*
tempt *v.t.* искуша́ть *imp.*, искуси́ть *perf.*; соблазня́ть *imp.*, соблазни́ть *perf.*; *t. fate*, испы́тывать *imp.*, испыта́ть *perf.* судьбу́. **temptation** *n.* искуше́ние, собла́зн. **tempter, -tress** *n.* искуси́тель *m.*, ~ница. **tempting** *adj.* зама́нчивый, соблазни́тельный.
ten *adj., n.* де́сять (-ти́, -тью́); (*collect.*; *10 pairs*) де́сятеро (-ры́х); (*cards*; *number 10*) деся́тка; (*time*) де́сять (часо́в); (*age*) де́сять лет; (*set of 10*; *10 years, decade*) деся́ток (-тка); *in tens*, деся́тками. **tenth** *adj., n.* деся́тый; (*fraction*) деся́тая (часть (*pl.* -ти, -те́й)); (*date*) деся́тое (число́); (*mus.*) де́цима.
tenable *adj.* (*strong*) про́чный (-чен, -чна́, -чно, про́чны́); (*logical*) логи́чный; (*of office*) могу́щий быть за́нятым.
tenacious *adj.* це́пкий (-пок, -пка́, -пко); (*stubborn*) упо́рный. **tenacity** *n.* це́пкость; упо́рство.
tenancy *n.* (*renting of property*) наём помеще́ния; (*period*) срок (-а(у)) аре́нды. **tenant** *n.* нанима́тель *m.*, ~ница; аренда́тор.
tench *n.* линь (-ня́) *m.*
tend[1] *v.i.* (*be apt*) име́ть скло́нность (to, к + *dat.*, + *inf.*); (*move*) направля́ться *imp.*, напра́виться *perf.*
tend[2] *v.t.* (*look after*) (*person*) уха́живать *imp.* за + *instr.*; (*machine*) обслу́живать *imp.*, обслужи́ть (-жу́, -жишь) *perf.*
tendency *n.* тенде́нция, скло́нность. **tendentious** *adj.* тенденцио́зный.
tender[1] *v.t.* (*offer*) предлага́ть *imp.*, предложи́ть (-жу́, -жишь) *perf.*; (*money*) предоставля́ть *imp.*, предоста́вить *perf.*; *v.i.* (*make t. for*) подава́ть (-даю́, -даёшь) *imp.*, пода́ть (-а́м, -а́шь, -а́ст, -ади́м; по́дал, -а́, -о) *perf.* зая́вку (на торга́х); *n.* предложе́ние; *legal t.*, зако́нное платёжное сре́дство.
tender[2] *n.* (*rly.*) те́ндер; (*naut.*) посы́льное су́дно (*pl.* -да́, -до́в).
tender[3] *adj.* (*delicate, affectionate*) не́жный (-жен, -жна́, -жно, не́жны́); (*soft*) мя́гкий (-гок, -гка́, -гко); (*sensitive*) чувстви́тельный. **tenderness** *n.* не́жность; (*softness*) мя́гкость.
tendon *n.* сухожи́лие.
tendril *n.* у́сик.
tenement *n.* (*dwelling-house*) жило́й дом (-а(у); *pl.* -а́); (*flat*) кварти́ра; *t.-house*, многокварти́рный дом (-а(у); *pl.* -а́).
tenet *n.* до́гмат, при́нцип.
tennis *n.* те́ннис; *attrib.* те́ннисный; *t.-player*, теннис́ист, ~ка.
tenon *n.* шип (-а́).
tenor *n.* (*structure*) укла́д; (*direction*) направле́ние; (*purport*) о́бщее содержа́ние; (*mus.*) те́нор.

tense[1] *n.* врéмя *neut.*
tense[2] *v.t.* напрягáть *imp.*, напрячь (-ягý, -яжёшь; напрýг, -лá) *perf.*; *adj.* (*tight*) натянутый; (*strained*) напряжённый (-ён, -ённа); (*excited*) возбуждённый (-ён, -енá); (*nervous*) нéрвный (нéрвен, нéрвнá, нéрвно). **tenseness** *n.* натянутость, напряжённость. **tensile** *adj.* растяжимый. **tension** *n.* напряжéние (*also fig.*; *electr.*); натяжéние.
tent *n.* палáтка; *t.-peg*, кóлышек (-шка) для палáтки; *t. pole*, палáточная стóйка.
tentacle *n.* щýпальце (*gen.pl.* -лец & -льцев).
tentative *adj.* (*experimental*) прóбный; (*preliminary*) предварительный.
tenterhooks *n.*: *be on t.*, сидéть (сижý, сидишь) *imp.* как на игóлках.
tenth *see* **ten.**
tenuous *adj.* (*slender, subtle*) тóнкий (-нок, -нкá, -нко, тóнки́); (*flimsy*) непрóчный (-чен, -чнá, -чно); (*insignificant*) незначительный; (*rarefied*) разрежённый.
tenure *n.* (*possession*) владéние; (*office*) пребывáние в дóлжности; (*period*) срок (-а(у)) (*of possession*) владéния, (*of office*) пребывáния в дóлжности.
tepid *adj.* тепловáтый.
tercentenary, -ennial *n.* трёхсотлéтие; *adj.* трёхсотлéтний.
term *n.* (*period*) срок (-а(у)); (*univ.*) семéстр; (*school*) чéтверть (*pl.* -ти, -тéй); (*math.*) член; (*leg.*) сéссия; (*technical word, expression*) тéрмин; (*expression*) выражéние; (*med.*) нормáльный периóд берéменности; *pl.* (*conditions*) услóвия *neut.pl.* (of payment, оплáты); (*relations*) отношéния *neut.pl.*; *on good terms*, в хорóших отношéниях; (*language*) язык (-á), выражéния *neut.pl.*; *come to terms with*, (*resign oneself to*) покорýться *imp.*, покорíться *perf.* к + *dat.*; (*come to an agreement with*) приходить (-ожý, -óдишь) *imp.*, прийти (придý, -дёшь; пришёл, -шлá) *perf.* к соглашéниию с + *instr.*; *v.t.* называть *imp.*, назвáть (назовý, -вёшь; назвáл, -á, -о) *perf.*; *I do not t. impatience a shortcoming*, я не назывáю нетерпéние недостáтком.
termagant *n.* сварливая жéнщина; мегéра (*coll.*).
terminable *adj.* ограни́ченный срóком, срóчный (-чен, -чнá, -чно).
terminal *adj.* конéчный, заключительный; (*univ.*) семестрóвый; (*school*) четвертнóй; (*leg.*) сессиóнный; *n.* (*electr.*) зажим; (*computer*) терминáл; (*terminus*) (*rly.*) конéчная стáнция; (*bus etc.*) конéчная останóвка; (*aeron.*) (*airport buildings*) здáния *neut.pl.* аэропóрта; *air-t.*, аэровокзáл.
terminate *v.t.* & *i.* кончáть(ся) *imp.*, кóнчить(ся) *perf.* (in, + *instr.*). **termination** *n.* конéц (-нцá), окончáние.
terminology *n.* терминолóгия. **terminological** *adj.* терминологи́ческий.
terminus *n.* (*rly.*) конéчная стáнция; (*bus etc.*) конéчная останóвка.
termite *n.* термит.
tern *n.* крáчка.
terra *n.*: *t. firma*, сýша; *t. incognita*, неизвéстная странá.
terrace *n.* террáса; (*row of houses*) ряд (-á *with 2, 3, 4, loc.* -у; *pl.* -ы́) домóв; *v.t.* террасировать *imp., perf.*
terracotta *n.* терракóта; *adj.* терракóтовый.
terrain *n.* мéстность.
terrapin *n.* (*turtle*) вóдная черепáха.
terrestrial *adj.* земнóй; (*ground*) назéмный.
terrible *adj.* (*frightening, dreadful, very bad*) ужáсный; (*excessive*) стрáшный (-шен, -шнá, -шно, стрáшны́) (*coll.*). **terribly** *adv.* ужáсно, стрáшно.
terrier *n.* терьéр.
terrific *adj.* ужасáющий; (*coll.*) (*huge*) огрóмный; (*splendid*) великолéпный. **terrify** *v.t.* ужасáть *imp.*, ужаснýть *perf.*
territorial *adj.* территориáльный. **territory** *n.* территóрия, (*fig.*) óбласть, сфéра.
terror *n.* ýжас, страх; (*person, thing causing t.*) террóр. **terrorism** *n.* терроризм. **terrorist** *n.* террорист, ~ка. **terrorize** *v.t.* терроризировать *imp. perf.*

terse *adj.* сжа́тый, кра́ткий (-ток, -тка́, -тко). **terseness** *n.* сжа́тость, кра́ткость.
tertiary *adj.* трети́чный; (*education*) вы́сший.
tessellated *adj.* моза́ичный.
test *n.* испыта́ние, про́ба; (*exam*) экза́мен; контро́льная *sb.* (*coll.*); (*standard*) крите́рий; (*analysis*) ана́лиз; (*chem., reagent*) реакти́в; *t. ban*, запреще́ние испыта́ний я́дерного ору́жия; *t. case*, де́ло (*pl.* -ла́) име́ющее принципиа́льное значе́ние для разреше́ния аналоги́чных дел; *t. flight*, испыта́тельный полёт; *t. paper*, (*exam*) экзаменацио́нный биле́т; *t. pilot*, лётчик-испыта́тель *m.*; *t.-tube*, проби́рка; *v.t.* (*try out*) испы́тывать *imp.*, испыта́ть *perf.*; (*check up on*) проверя́ть *imp.*, прове́рить *perf.*; (*give exam to*) экзаменова́ть *imp.*, про~ *perf.*; (*chem.*) подверга́ть *imp.*, подве́ргнуть (-г) *perf.* де́йствию реакти́ва.
testament *n.* завеща́ние; *Old, New T.*, Ве́тхий, Но́вый заве́т. **testamentary** *adj.* завеща́тельный. **testator** *n.* завеща́тель *m.*, ~ница.
testicle *n.* яи́чко (*pl.* -чки, -чек).
testify *v.i.* свиде́тельствовать *imp.* (to, в по́льзу + *gen.*; against, про́тив + *gen.*); *v.t.* (*declare*) заявля́ть *imp.*, заяви́ть (-влю́, -вишь) *perf.*; (*be evidence of*) свиде́тельствовать о + *prep.*
testimonial *n.* рекоменда́ция, характери́стика. **testimony** *n.* показа́ние, -ния *pl.*, свиде́тельство; (*declaration*) заявле́ние.
testy *adj.* раздражи́тельный.
tetanus *n.* столбня́к (-а́).
tetchy *adj.* раздражи́тельный.
tête-à-tête *n., adv.* тет-а-те́т.
tether *n.* при́вязь; *be at, come to the end of one's t.*, дойти́ (дойду́, -дёшь; дошёл, -шла́) *perf.* до то́чки; *v.t.* привя́зывать *imp.*, привяза́ть (-яжу́, -я́жешь) *perf.*
tetra- *in comb.* четырёх-, тетра-. **tetrahedron** *n.* четырёхгра́нник. **tetralogy** *n.* тетрало́гия.
Teutonic *adj.* тевто́нский.
text *n.* текст; (*theme*) те́ма. **textbook** *n.* уче́бник.
textile *adj.* тексти́льный; *n.* ткань; *pl.* тексти́ль *m.* (*collect.*).
textual *adj.* текстово́й.
texture *n.* факту́ра; (*consistency*) консисте́нция; (*quality*) ка́чество; (*structure*) строе́ние.
thalidomide *n.* талидоми́д.
than *conj.* (*comparison*) чем; *other t.*, (*except*) кро́ме + *gen.*; *none other t.*, не кто ино́й, как; *nothing else t.*, не что ино́е, как.
thank *v.t.* благодари́ть *imp.*, по~ *perf.* (for, за + *acc.*); *t. God*, сла́ва Бо́гу; *t. you*, спаси́бо, благодарю́ вас; *n.pl.* благода́рность; *thanks to* (*good result*) благодаря́ + *dat.*; (*bad result*) из-за + *gen.* **thankful** *adj.* благода́рный. **thankless** *adj.* неблагода́рный. **thank-offering** *n.* благода́рственная же́ртва. **thanksgiving** *n.* (*service of*) благода́рственный моле́бен (-бна); благодаре́ние.
that *dem.adj., dem.pron.* тот (та, то; *pl.* те); э́тот (э́та, э́то; *pl.* э́ти); *t. which*, тот (та, то; те) кото́рый; *rel.pron.* кото́рый; *conj.* что; (*purpose*) что́бы; *adv.* так, до тако́й сте́пени.
thatch *n.* (*straw*) соло́менная, (*reed*) тростнико́вая кры́ша; *v.t.* крыть (кро́ю, кро́ешь) *imp.*, по~ *perf.* соло́мой (*straw*), тростнико́м (*reed*).
thaw *v.t.* раста́пливать *imp.*, растопи́ть (-плю́, -пишь) *perf.*; *v.i.* та́ять (та́ет) *imp.*, рас~ *perf.*; (*fig.*) смягча́ться *imp.*, смягчи́ться *perf.*; *n.* о́ттепель; (*fig.*) смягче́ние.
the *adj. definite article not translated*; *adv.* тем; *the . . . the*, чем...тем; *t. more t. better*, чем бо́льше тем лу́чше.
theatre *n.* теа́тр; (*lecture etc.*) аудито́рия; (*operating*) операцио́нная *sb.*; *t.-goer*, театра́л. **theatrical** *adj.* театра́льный.
theft *n.* воровство́, кра́жа.
their, theirs *poss.pron.* их; свой (-оя́, -оё; -ои́).
theism *n.* теи́зм. **theist** *n.* теи́ст. **theistic(al)** *adj.* теисти́ческий.

theme *n.* тéма, предмéт. **thematic** *adj.* тематúческий.
themselves *pron.* (*emph.*) (онú) сáми (-úх, -úм, -úми); (*refl.*) себя́ (себé, собóй); -ся (*suffixed to v.t.*).
then *adv.* (*at that time*) тогдá, в то врéмя; (*after that*) потóм, затéм; *now and t.*, врéмя от врéмени; *conj.* в такóм слу́чае, тогдá; *n.* то врéмя *neut.*; *adj.* тогдáшний.
thence *adv.* оттýда; (*from that*) из э́того. **thenceforth, -forward** *adv.* с тогó/э́того врéмени.
theodolite *n.* теодолúт.
theologian *n.* теóлог. **theological** *adj.* теологúческий. **theology** *n.* теолóгия.
theorem *n.* теорéма. **theoretical** *adj.* теоретúческий. **theorist** *n.* теорéтик. **theorize** *v.i.* теоретизúровать *imp.* **theory** *n.* теóрия.
theosophy *n.* теосóфия.
therapeutic(al) *adj.* терапевтúческий. **therapeutics** *n.* терапéвтика. **therapy** *n.* терапúя.
there *adv.* (*place*) там; (*direction*) тудá; *interj.* вот! ну! *t. is, are*, есть, имéется (-éются); *t. you are*, (*on giving s.th.*) пожáлуйста. **thereabouts** *adv.* (*near*) поблúзости; (*approximately*) приблизúтельно. **thereafter** *adv.* пóсле э́того. **thereby** *adv.* такúм óбразом. **therefore** *adv.* поэ́тому, слéдовательно. **therein** *adv.* в э́том; (*in that respect*) в э́том отношéнии. **thereupon** *adv.* затéм.
thermal *adj.* теплов́ой, термúческий; *t. capacity*, теплоёмкость; *t. springs*, горя́чие истóчники *m.pl.*; *t. unit*, единúца теплотьí.
thermo- *in comb.* термо-, тепло-. **thermocouple** *n.* термопáра. **thermodynamics** *n.* термодинáмика. **thermoelectric(al)** *adj.* термоэлектрúческий. **thermometer** *n.* термóметр, грáдусник. **thermonuclear** *adj.* термоя́дерный. **thermos** *n.* тéрмос. **thermostat** *n.* термостáт.
thesis *n.* (*proposition*) тéзис; (*dissertation*) диссертáция.
they *pron.* онú (их, им, úми, о них).
thick *adj.* тóлстый (-т, -тá, -то, тóлстьí), (*in measurements*) толщинóй в + *acc.*; (*line*) жúрный (-рен, -рнá, -рно); (*dense*) плóтный (-тен, -тнá, -тно, плóтньí); густóй (-т, -тá, -то, гу́стьí); (*turbid*) му́тный (-тен, -тнá, -тно, му́тньí); (*stupid*) тупóй (туп, -á, -о, ту́пьí); *t.-headed*, тупоголóвый (*coll.*); *t.-skinned*, толстокóжий; *n.* гу́ща; (*of fight*) разгáр; *through t. and thin*, не колéблясь; несмотря́ ни на какúе препя́тствия. **thicken** *v.t.* & *i.* утолщáть(ся) *imp.*, утолстúть(ся) *perf.*; (*make, become denser*) сгущáть(ся) *imp.*, сгустúть(ся) *perf.*; *v.i.* (*become more intricate*) усложня́ться *imp.*, усложнúться *perf.* **thicket** *n.* чáща. **thickness** *n.* (*also dimension*) толщинá; (*density*) плóтность, густотá; (*layer*) слой (*pl.* слоú). **thickset** *adj.* коренáстый.
thief *n.* вор (*pl.* -ы, -óв), ~óвка. **thieve** *v.i.* воровáть *imp.*; *v.t.* красть (-аду́, -адёшь; -ал) *imp.*, у ~ *perf.* **thievery** *n.* воровствó. **thievish** *adj.* воровáтый.
thigh *n.* бедрó (*pl.* бёдра, -дер, -драм). *t.-bone*, бéдренная кость (*pl.* -ти, -тéй).
thimble *n.* напёрсток (-тка).
thin *adj.* (*slender*; *not thick*) тóнкий (-нок, -нкá, -нко, тóнкú); (*lean*) худóй (худ, -á, -о, ху́дьí); (*too liquid*) жúдкий (-док, -дкá, -дко); (*sparse*) рéдкий (-док, -дкá, -дко); (*weak*) слáбый (-б, -бá, -бо); *v.t.* & *i.* дéлать(ся) *imp.*, с ~ *perf.* тóнким, жúдким; *v.i.*: *t. down*, худéть *imp.*, по ~ *perf.*; *t. out*, редéть *imp.*, по ~ *perf.*; *v.t.*: *t. out*, прорéживать *imp.*, проредúть *perf.*
thing *n.* вещь (*pl.* -щи, -щéй); (*object*) предмéт; (*matter*) дéло (*pl.* -лá); *poor t.*, (*person*) бедня́жка *m.* & *f.* (*coll.*); *pl.* (*belongings*) пожúтки (-ков) *pl.* (*coll.*); (*clothes*) одéжда; (*implements*) у́тварь (*collect.*); (*affairs*) делá *neut.pl.* **thingamy** *n.* (*person*) как бишь егó? (*thing*) штýка.
think *v.t.* & *i.* ду́мать *imp.*, по ~ *perf.* (about, of, о + *prep.*, над + *instr.*); (*consider*) считáть *imp.*, счесть (сочтý, -тёшь; счёл, сочлá) *perf.* (to be, + *instr.*, за + *acc.*; that, что); *v.i.* (*think, reason*) мы́слить *imp.*; (*intend*) намеревáться *imp.* (of doing, + *inf.*); *t. out*, проду́мывать *imp.*, проду́мать

perf.; *t. over*, обду́мывать *imp.*, обду́мать *perf.*; *t. up, of*, приду́мывать *imp.*, приду́мать *perf.* **thinker** *n.* мысли́тель *m.* **thinking** *adj.* мы́слящий; *n.* (*reflection*) размышле́ние; *to my way of t.*, по моему́ мне́нию.

thinly *adv.* то́нко. **thinness** *n.* то́нкость; (*leanness*) худоба́. **thin-skinned** *adj.* (*fig.*) оби́дчивый.

third *adj.*, *n.* тре́тий (-тья, -тье); (*fraction*) треть (*pl.* -ти, -те́й); (*date*) тре́тье (число́); (*mus.*) те́рция; *t. party*, тре́тья сторона́ (*acc.* -ону; *pl.* -оны, -о́н, -она́м); *t.-rate*, третьестепе́нный; *T. World*, стра́ны *f.pl.* тре́тьего ми́ра.

thirst *n.* жа́жда (for, + *gen.* (*fig.*)); *v.i.* (*fig.*) жа́ждать (-ду, -дешь) *imp.* (for, + *gen.*). **thirsty** *adj.*: *be t.*, хоте́ть (хочу́, -чешь; хоти́м) *imp.* пить.

thirteen *adj.*, *n.* трина́дцать (-ти, -тью); (*age*) трина́дцать лет. **thirteenth** *adj.*, *n.* трина́дцатый; (*date*) трина́дцатое (число́).

thirtieth *adj.*, *n.* тридца́тый; (*date*) тридца́тое (число́). **thirty** *adj.*, *n.* три́дцать (-ти́, -тью́); (*age*) три́дцать лет; *pl.* (*decade*) тридца́тые го́ды (-до́в) *m.pl.*

this *dem.adj.*, *dem.pron.* э́тот (э́та, э́то; *pl.* э́ти); *t. way*, сюда́; *like t.*, вот так.

thistle *n.* чертополо́х.

thither *adv.* туда́.

thong *n.* реме́нь (-мня́) *m.*

thorax *n.* грудна́я кле́тка.

thorn *n.* шип (-а́), колю́чка (*coll.*). **thorny** *adj.* колю́чий; (*fig.*) терни́стый; (*ticklish*) щекотли́вый.

thorough *adj.* основа́тельный, тща́тельный; (*complete*) по́лный (-лон, -лна́, по́лно́), соверше́нный (-нен, -нна). **thoroughbred** *adj.* чистокро́вный, поро́дистый. **thoroughfare** *n.* прое́зд, (*walking*) прохо́д. **thorough-going** *adj.* радика́льный. **thoroughly** *adv.* (*completely*) вполне́, соверше́нно. **thoroughness** *n.* основа́тельность, тща́тельность.

though *conj.* хотя́; несмотря́ на то, что; *as t.*, как бу́дто; *adv.* одна́ко, всё-таки.

thought *n.* мысль; (*heed*) внима́ние; (*meditation*) размышле́ние; (*intention*) наме́рение; *pl.* (*opinion*) мне́ние. **thoughtful** *adj.* заду́мчивый; (*considerate*) внима́тельный, забо́тливый. **thoughtless** *adj.* необду́манный (-ан, -анна); (*inconsiderate*) невнима́тельный. **thought-reader** *n.* тот, кто уме́ет чита́ть чужи́е мы́сли.

thousand *adj.*, *n.* ты́сяча (*instr.* -чей & -чью). **thousandth** *adj.*, *n.* ты́сячный; (*fraction*) ты́сячная (часть (*pl.* -ти, -те́й)).

thraldom, thrall *n.* (*state*) ра́бство; *in t.*, обращённый (-ён, -ена́) в ра́бство.

thrash *v.t.* бить (бью, бьёшь) *imp.*, по~ *perf.*; *t. out*, (*discuss*) тща́тельно обсужда́ть *imp.*, обсуди́ть (-ужу́ -у́дишь) *perf.*; *v.i.*: *t. about*, мета́ться (мечу́сь, -чешься) *imp.* **thrashing** *n.* (*beating*) взбу́чка (*coll.*).

thread *n.* ни́тка, нить (*also fig.*); (*of screw etc.*) наре́зка, резьба́; *v.t.* (*needle*) продева́ть *imp.*, проде́ть (-е́ну, -е́нешь) *perf.* ни́тку в + *acc.*; (*beads etc.*) нани́зывать *imp.*, наниза́ть (-ижу́, -и́зешь) *perf.*; *t. one's way*, пробира́ться *imp.*, пробра́ться (-беру́сь, -берёшься; -бра́лся, -брала́сь, -бра́ло́сь) *perf.* (through, че́рез + *acc.*). **threadbare** *adj.* (*clothes etc.*) потёртый, изно́шенный; (*hackneyed*) изби́тый.

threat *n.* угро́за. **threaten** *v.t.* угрожа́ть *imp.*, грози́ть *imp.*, при~ *perf.* (*person*, + *dat.*; with, + *instr.*; to do, + *inf.*).

three *adj.*, *n.* три (трёх, -ём, -емя́, -ёх); (*collect.*; *3 pairs*) тро́е (-ои́х); (*cards, number 3*) тро́йка; (*time*) три (часа́); (*age*) три го́да; *t. times*, три́жды; *t. times four*, три́жды четы́ре; *t.-cornered*, треуго́льный; *t.-dimensional*, трёхме́рный; *t.-ply*, (*wood*) трёхсло́йный; (*rope*) тройно́й; *t.-quarters*, три че́тверти. **threefold** *adj.* тройно́й; *adv.* втройне́. **threesome** *n.* тро́йка.

thresh *v.t.* молоти́ть (-очу́, -о́тишь) *imp.* **threshing** *n.* молотьба́; *t.-floor*, ток (*loc.* -у́; *pl.* -а́); *t.-machine*, молоти́лка.

threshold *n.* поро́г.

thrice *adv.* три́жды.

thrift *n.* бережли́вость; (*plant*) арме́-

рия. **thriftless** *adj.* расточи́тельный. **thrifty** *adj.* бережли́вый.

thrill *n.* (*trepidation, excitement*) тре́пет, волне́ние; (*s.th. thrilling*) что-л. захва́тывающее; *v.t.* & *i.* си́льно волнова́ть(ся) *imp.*, вз~ *perf.* **thriller** *n.* приключе́нческий, детекти́вный, (*novel*) рома́н, (*film*) фильм. **thrilling** *adj.* волну́ющий, захва́тывающий.

thrive *v.i.* процвета́ть *imp.*; (*grow*) разраста́ться *imp.*, разрасти́сь (-тётся; разро́сся, -сла́сь) *perf.*

throat *n.* го́рло. **throaty** *adj.* горта́нный; (*hoarse*) хри́плый (-л, -ла́, -ло).

throb *v.i.* (*heart*) си́льно би́ться (бьётся) *imp.*; пульси́ровать *imp.*; *his head throbbed*, кровь стуча́ла у него́ в виска́х; *n.* бие́ние; пульса́ция.

throe *n.* о́страя боль; *pl.* му́ки *f.pl.*; (*of birth*) родовы́е му́ки *f.pl.*; (*of death*) аго́ния.

thrombosis *n.* тромбо́з.

throne *n.* трон, престо́л; *come to the t.*, вступа́ть *imp.*, вступи́ть (-плю́, -пишь) *perf.* на престо́л.

throng *n.* толпа́ (*pl.* -пы); *v.i.* толпи́ться *imp.*; *v.t.* заполня́ть *imp.*, запо́лнить *perf.* (толпо́й).

throttle *n.* (*gullet*) гло́тка; (*tech.*) дро́ссель *m.*; *v.t.* (*strangle*) души́ть (-шу́, -шишь) *imp.*, за~ *perf.*; (*tech.*) дроссели́ровать *imp.*, *perf.*; *t. down*, сбавля́ть *imp.*, сба́вить *perf.* ско́рость + *gen.*

through *prep.* (*across, via, t. opening*) че́рез + *acc.*; (*esp. t. thick of*) сквозь + *acc.*; (*air, streets etc.*) по + *dat.*; (*agency*) посре́дством + *gen.*; (*reason*) из-за + *gen.*; *adv.* насквозь; (*from beginning to end*) с нача́ла до конца́; *be t. with*, (*s.th.*) ока́нчивать *imp.*, око́нчить *perf.*; (*s.b.*) порыва́ть *imp.*, порва́ть (-ву́, -вёшь; порва́л, -а́, -о) *perf.* с + *instr.*; *put t.*, (*on telephone*) соединя́ть *imp.*, соедини́ть *perf.*; *t. and t.*, до конца́, соверше́нно; *adj.* сквозно́й. **throughout** *adv.* повсю́ду, во всех отноше́ниях; *prep.* по всему́ (всей, всему́; *pl.* всем) + *dat.*; (*from beginning to end*) с нача́ла до конца́ + *gen.*

throw *n.* бросо́к (-ска́), броса́ние; *v.t.* броса́ть *imp.*, бро́сить *perf.*; кида́ть *imp.*, ки́нуть *perf.*; (*rider*) сбра́сывать *imp.*, сбро́сить *perf.*; (*pottery*) формова́ть *imp.*, с~ *perf.*; (*party*) устра́ивать *imp.*, устро́ить *perf.*; *t. oneself at*, набра́сываться *imp.*, набро́ситься *perf.* на + *acc.*; *t. oneself into*, броса́ться *imp.*, бро́ситься *perf.* в + *acc.*; *t. about*, разбра́сывать *imp.*, разброса́ть *perf.*; *t. money about*, сори́ть *imp.* деньга́ми; *t. aside, away*, отбра́сывать *imp.*, отбро́сить *perf.*; *t. away, out*, выбра́сывать *imp.*, вы́бросить *perf.*; *t. back*, отбра́сывать *imp.*, отбро́сить *perf.* наза́д; *t.-back*, регре́сс, возвра́т к про́шлому, атави́зм; *t. down*, сбра́сывать *imp.*, сбро́сить *perf.*; *t. in*, (*add*) добавля́ть *imp.*, доба́вить *perf.*; (*sport*) вбра́сывать *imp.*, вбро́сить *perf.*; *t.-in*, вбра́сывание мяча́; *t. off*, сбра́сывать *imp.*, сбро́сить *perf.*; *t. open*, распа́хивать *imp.*, распахну́ть *perf.*; *t. out*, (*see also t. away*) (*expel*) выгоня́ть *imp.*, вы́гнать (вы́гоню, -нишь) *perf.*; (*reject*) отверга́ть *imp.*, отве́ргнуть (-г(нул), -гла) *perf.*; *t. over, t. up*, (*abandon, renounce*) броса́ть *imp.*, бро́сить *perf.*

thrush[1] *n.* (*orn.*) дрозд (-а́).

thrush[2] *n.* (*disease*) моло́чница.

thrust *n.* (*shove*) толчо́к (-чка́); (*lunge*) вы́пад; (*blow, stroke, mil.*) уда́р; (*tech., of rocket*) тя́га; *v.t.* (*shove*) толка́ть *imp.*, толкну́ть *perf.*; (*t. into, out of; give quickly, carelessly*) сова́ть (сую́, суёшь) *imp.*, су́нуть *perf.*; *t. one's way*, пробива́ть *imp.*, проби́ть (-бью́, -бьёшь) *perf.* себе́ доро́гу; *t. aside*, отта́лкивать *imp.*, оттолкну́ть *perf.*; *t. out*, высо́вывать *imp.*, вы́сунуть *perf.*

thud *n.* глухо́й звук, стук; *v.i.* (*fall with t.*) па́дать *imp.*, (у)па́сть ((у)паду́, -дёшь; (у)па́л) *perf.* с глухи́м сту́ком; шлёпаться *imp.*, шлёпнуться *perf.* (*coll.*).

thug *n.* головоре́з (*coll.*).

thumb *n.* большо́й па́лец (-льца); *thumbs down*, знак отрица́ния; *thumbs up!* неду́рно! *under the t. of*, под башмако́м у + *gen.*; *v.t.*: *t. through*, перели́стывать *imp.*, перелиста́ть *perf.*; *t. a lift*, голосовáть *imp.*, про ~ *perf.* (*coll.*). **thumbscrew** *n.* тиски́ (-кóв) *pl.* для больши́х пáльцев.

thump *n.* (*heavy blow*) тяжёлый удáр; (*thud*) глухóй звук, стук; *v.t.* наноси́ть (-ошу́, -óсишь) *imp.*, нанести́ (-есу́, -есёшь; -ёс, -еслá) *perf.* удáр + *dat.*; колоти́ть (-очу́, -óтишь) *imp.*, по ~ *perf.* в + *acc.*, по + *dat.*; *v.i.* (*strike with t.*) би́ться (бьюсь, бьёшься) *imp.* с глухи́м шу́мом.

thunder *n.* гром (*pl.* -ы, -óв); (*fig.*) грóхот; *t.-cloud*, грозовáя ту́ча; *v.i.* греме́ть (-млю́, -ми́шь) *imp.*; грохотáть (-очу́, -óчешь) *imp.*; (*fulminate* (*fig.*)) метáть (мечу́, -чешь) *imp.* грóмы и мóлнии; *it thunders*, гром греми́т. **thunderbolt** *n.* удáр мóлнии; (*fig.*) гром среди́ я́сного нéба. **thunderclap** *n.* удáр грóма. **thunderous** *adj.* громовóй. **thunderstorm** *n.* грозá (*pl.* -зы). **thunderstruck** *adj.* (*fig.*) как грóмом поражённый (-ён, -енá). **thundery** *adj.* грозовóй.

Thursday *n.* четвéрг (-á).

thus *adv.* (*in this way*) так, таки́м óбразом; (*accordingly*) итáк; *t. far*, до сих пор.

thwack *n.* си́льный удáр; *v.t.* бить (бью, бьёшь) *imp.*, по ~ *perf.*

thwart *v.t.* мешáть *imp.*, по ~ *perf.* + *dat.*; (*plans*) расстрáивать *imp.*, расстрóить *perf.*; *n.* (*bench*) бáнка.

thyme *n.* тимья́н.

thyroid *n.* (*t. gland*) щитови́дная железá.

tiara *n.* тиáра.

tibia *n.* большáя берцóвая кость (*pl.* -ти, -тéй).

tic *n.* тик.

tick[1] *n.* (*noise*) ти́канье; (*moment*) момéнт, мину́точка; (*mark*) пти́чка; *v.i.* ти́кать *imp.*, ти́кнуть *perf.*; *v.t.* отмечáть *imp.*, отмéтить *perf.* пти́чкой; *t. off*, (*scold*) отдéлывать *imp.*, отдéлать *perf.* (*coll.*).

tick[2] *n.* (*mite*) клещ (-á).

tick[3] *n.* (*of mattress*) чехóл (-хлá); (*of pillow*) нáволо(ч)ка; (*ticking*) тик.

tick[4] *n.* (*coll.*) креди́т; *on t.*, в креди́т.

ticket *n.* билéт; (*label*) ярлы́к (-á); (*season t.*) кáрточка; (*cloakroom t.*) номерóк (-ркá); (*receipt*) квитáнция; *t.-collector*, контролёр; *t.-office*, (билéтная) кáсса; *t.-punch*, компóстер; *v.t.* прикрепля́ть *imp.*, прикрепи́ть *perf.* ярлы́к к + *dat.*

tickle *n.* щекóтка; *v.t.* щекотáть (-очу́, -óчешь) *imp.*, по ~ *perf.*; (*amuse*) весели́ть *imp.*, по ~, раз ~ *perf.*; *v.i.* щекотáть (-óчет) *imp.*, по ~ *perf. impers.*; *my throat tickles*, у меня́ щекóчет в гóрле. **ticklish** *adj.* щекотли́вый (*also fig.*); *to be t.*, боя́ться (бою́сь, бои́шься) *imp.* щекóтки.

tidal *adj.* прили́во-отли́вный; *t. wave*, прили́вная волнá (*pl.* -ны, -н, вóлнáм).

tiddlywinks *n.* (игрá в) блóшки (-шек) *pl.*

tide *n.* прили́в и отли́в; *high t.*, прили́в; *low t.*, отли́в; (*current, tendency*) течéние; *the t. turns*, (*fig.*) собы́тия принимáют другóй оборóт; *t.-mark*, отмéтка у́ровня пóлной воды́; *v.t.*: *t. over*, помогáть *imp.*, помóчь (-огу́, -óжешь; -óг, -оглá) *perf.* + *dat. of person* спрáвиться (*difficulty*, с + *instr.*); *will this money t. you over?* вы протя́нете с э́тими деньгáми?

tidiness *n.* опря́тность, аккурáтность. **tidy** *adj.* опря́тный, аккурáтный; (*considerable*) поря́дочный; *v.t.* убирáть *imp.*, убрáть (уберу́, -рёшь; убрáл, -á, -о) *perf.*; приводи́ть (-ожу́, -óдишь) *imp.*, привести́ (-еду́, -едёшь; -ёл, -елá) *perf.* в поря́док.

tie *n.* (*garment*) гáлстук; (*string, lace*) завя́зка; (*link, bond; tech.*) связь; (*equal points etc.*) рáвный счёт; *end in a t.*, закáнчиваться *imp.*, закóнчиться *perf.* вничью́; (*match*) матч; (*mus.*) ли́га; (*burden*) обу́за; *pl.* (*bonds*) у́зы (уз) *pl.*; *t.-pin*, булáвка для гáлстука; *v.t.* свя́зывать *imp.*, связáть (свяжу́, -жешь) *perf.* (*also fig.*); (*t. up*) завя́зывать *imp.*, завязáть (-яжу́, -я́жешь) *perf.*; (*restrict*) ограни́чивать *imp.*, ограни́чить *perf.*; *t. down*, (*fasten*) привя́зывать *imp.*, привязáть (-яжу́, -я́жешь) *perf.*; *t. up*, (*tether*) привя́зывать *imp.*, привязáть (-яжу́, -я́жешь) *perf.*; (*parcel*) перевя́зывать *imp.*, перевязáть (-яжу́, -я́жешь); *v.i.* (*be tied*) завя́зываться *imp.*, завязáться (-я́жется) *perf.*; (*sport*) равня́ть *imp.*, с ~

perf. счёт; сыгра́ть *perf.* вничью́; *t. in, up, with,* совпада́ть *imp.*, совпа́сть (-адёт; -а́л) *perf.* с + *instr.*

tier *n.* ряд (-а́ *with 2, 3, 4, loc.* -у́; *pl.* -ы́), я́рус.

tiff *n.* размо́лвка; *v.i.* ссо́риться *imp.*, по ~ *perf.* (with, с + *instr.*).

tiger *n.* тигр. **tigress** *n.* тигри́ца.

tight *adj.* (*compact*) пло́тный (-тен, -тна́, -тно, пло́тны́); (*cramped*) те́сный (-сен, -сна́, -сно), у́зкий (-зок, -зка́, -зко); (*impenetrable*) непрони-ца́емый; (*strict*) стро́гий (-г, -га́, -го); (*tense, taut*) туго́й (туг, -а́, -о), натя́нутый; *t.-fisted*, скупо́й (-п, -па́, -по); *t. corner*, (*fig.*) тру́дное поло-же́ние. **tighten** *v.t.* & *i.* натя́гивать(ся) *imp.*, натяну́ть(ся) *perf.*; (*clench, contract*) сжима́ть(ся) *imp.*, сжа́ть(ся) (сожму́(сь), -мёшь(ся)) *perf.*; *t. one's belt*, поту́же затя́гивать *imp.*, затя-ну́ть *perf.* по́яс (*also fig.*); *t. up,* (*discipline etc.*) подтя́гивать *imp.*, подтя́нуть *perf.* (*coll.*). **tightly** *adv.* (*strongly*) про́чно; (*closely, cramped*) те́сно. **tightness** *n.* теснота́; напря-жённость. **tightrope** *n.* ту́го натя́ну-тый кана́т. **tights** *n.* колго́тки (-ток) *pl.*

tilde *n.* ти́льда.

tile *n.* (*roof*) черепи́ца (*also collect.*); (*decorative*) ка́фель *m.* (*also collect.*); *v.t.* крыть (кро́ю, кро́ешь) *imp.*, по ~ *perf.* черепи́цей, ка́фелем. **tiled** *adj.* (*roof*) черепи́чный; (*floor*) ка́фель-ный.

till[1] *prep.* до + *gen.*; *not t.*, то́лько (Friday, в пя́тницу; the next day, на сле́дующий день); *conj.* пока́ не; *not t.*, то́лько когда́.

till[2] *n.* ка́сса.

till[3] *v.t.* возде́лывать *imp.*, возде́лать *perf.* **tillage** *n.* обрабо́тка земли́.

tiller[1] *n.* земледе́лец (-льца).

tiller[2] *n.* (*naut.*) ру́мпель *m.*

tilt *n.* накло́н; (*naut., aeron.*) крен; *on the t.*, в накло́нном положе́нии; *at full t.*, и́зо всех сил; по́лным хо́дом; *v.t.* & *i.* наклоня́ть(ся) *imp.*, накло-ни́ть(ся) (-ню́(сь), -нишь(ся)) *perf.*; (*heel (over)*) крени́ть(ся) *imp.*, на ~ *perf.*

timber *n.* лесоматериа́л, лес (-а(у)) (*collect.*); (*beam*) ба́лка; (*naut.*) ти́м-берс. **timbered** *adj.* обши́тый де́ревом; деревя́нный. **timbering** *n.* (*work*) пло́т-ничная рабо́та.

timbre *n.* тембр.

time *n.* вре́мя *neut.*; (*occasion*) раз (*pl.* -зы, -з); (*term*) срок (-а(у)); (*period*) перио́д, эпо́ха; (*mus.*) темп, такт; (*sport*) тайм; *pl.* (*period*) времена́ *pl.*; (*in comparison*) раз; *five times as big*, в пять раз бо́льше; (*multiplica-tion*) *four times four*, четы́режды четы́ре; *five times four*, пя́тью четы́ре; *t. and t. again, t. after t.*, не раз, ты́сячу раз; *at a t.*, ра́зом, одно-вре́ме́нно; *at the t.*, в э́то вре́мя; *at times*, по времена́м; *at the same t.*, в то же вре́мя; *before my t.*, до меня́; *for a long t.*, до́лго; (*up to now*) давно́; *for the t. being*, пока́; *from t. to t.*, вре́мя от вре́мени; *in t.*, (*early enough*) во́-время; (*with t.*) со вре́менем; *in good t.*, своевре́менно; *in t. with*, в такт + *dat.*; *in no t.*, момента́льно; *on t.*, во́-время; *one at a t.*, по одному́; *be in t.*, успева́ть *imp.*, успе́ть *perf.* (for, к + *dat.*, на + *acc.*); *I do not have t. for him*, (*fig.*) я не хочу́ тра́тить вре́мя на него́; *have t. to*, (*manage*) успева́ть *imp.*, успе́ть *perf.* + *inf.*; *have a good t.*, хорошо́ проводи́ть (-ожу́, -о́дишь) *imp.*, провести́ (-еду́, -едёшь; -ёл, -ела́) *perf.* вре́мя; *it is t.*, пора́ (to, + *inf.*); *what is the t.?* кото́рый час? *kill t.*, убива́ть *imp.*, уби́ть (убью́, -ьёшь) *perf.* вре́мя; *work full* (*part*) *t.*, рабо́тать *imp.* по́лный (непо́лный) рабо́чий день; *t.-bomb*, бо́мба заме́дленного де́йст-вия; *t.-consuming*, отнима́ющий мно́-го вре́мени; *t.-honoured*, освящённый века́ми; *t.-lag*, отстава́ние во вре́-мени; (*tech.*) запа́здывание; *t.-limit*, преде́льный срок (-а(у)); *t. off*, о́тпуск; *t.-signal*, сигна́л вре́мени; *t.-signature*, та́ктовый разме́р; *v.t.* (*choose t.*) выбира́ть *imp.*, вы́брать (-беру, -берешь) *perf.* вре́мя + *gen.*; (*arrange t.*) назнача́ть *imp.*, назна́чить *perf.* вре́мя + *gen.*; (*ascertain t.*) засека́ть *imp.*, засе́чь (-еку́, -ечёшь;

засе́к, -ла́, -ло) *perf.* вре́мя; хронометри́ровать *imp.*, *perf.* **timekeeper** *n.* (*person*) та́бельщик; (*sport*) хронометри́ст. **timeless** *adj.* ве́чный. **timely** *adj.* своевре́менный. **timepiece** *n.* часы́ (-со́в) *pl.*; хроно́метр. **timetable** *n.* расписа́ние; (*of work*) гра́фик.

timid *adj.* ро́бкий (-бок, -бка́, -бко), засте́нчивый. **timidity** *n.* ро́бкость, засте́нчивость. **timorous** *adj.* боязли́вый.

tin *n.* (*metal*) о́лово; *t. plate*, бе́лая жесть; *attrib.* оловя́нный, жестяно́й; (*container*) (консе́рвная) ба́нка, жестя́нка; (*cake-t.*) фо́рма; (*baking t.*) про́тивень (-вня) *m.*; *t. foil*, оловя́нная фо́льга; *t.-opener*, консе́рвный нож (-а́); *v.t.* (*coat with t.*) луди́ть (лужу́, лу́дишь) *imp.*, вы ~, по ~ *perf.*; (*pack in t.*) консерви́ровать *imp.*, *perf.*; *tinned food*, консе́рвы (-вов) *pl.* **tinny** *adj.* (*thin*) то́нкий (-нок, -нка́, -нко, то́нки́); (*piano etc.*) издаю́щий металли́ческий звук; (*sound*) металли́ческий. **tinsmith** *n.* жестя́нщик.

tincture *n.* (*colour*, *fig.*) отте́нок (-нка); (*taste*; *fig.*) при́вкус; (*fig.*) налёт; *v.t.* (*colour*; *fig.*) слегка́ окра́шивать *imp.*, окра́сить *perf.*; (*flavour*) придава́ть (-даю́, -даёшь) *imp.*, прида́ть (-а́м, -а́шь, -а́ст, -ади́м; при́дал, -а́, -о) *perf.* вкус + *dat.*

tinder *n.* трут; *t.-box*, тру́тница.

tinge *n.* (*colour*; *fig.*) отте́нок (-нка); (*taste*; *fig.*) при́вкус; (*fig.*) налёт; *v.t.* (*also fig.*) слегка́ окра́шивать *imp.*, окра́сить *perf.*

tingle *n.* пока́лывание, (*from cold*) пощи́пывание; *v.i.* (*sting*) коло́ть (ко́лет) *imp. impers.*; *my fingers t.*, у меня́ ко́лет па́льцы; *his nose tingled with the cold*, моро́з пощи́пывал ему́ нос; (*burn*) горе́ть (гори́т) *imp.*; (*jingle*) звене́ть (-ни́т) *imp.* в уша́х (*person*, у + *gen.*).

tinker *n.* ме́дник, луди́льщик; *v.i.* (*work as a t.*) рабо́тать *imp.* луди́льщиком; *t. with*, вози́ться (вожу́сь, во́зишься) *imp.* с + *instr.*

tinkle *n.* звон, звя́канье; *v.i.*(*t.*) звене́ть (-ню́, -ни́шь) *imp.* (+ *instr.*); звя́кать *imp.*, звя́кнуть *perf.* + *instr.*; (*on instrument*) бренча́ть (-чу́, -чи́шь) *imp.* (on, на + *prep.*).

tinsel *n.* мишура́ (*also fig.*); *attrib.* мишу́рный.

tint *n.* отте́нок (-нка); (*faint t.*) бле́дный тон (*pl.* -а́); *v.t.* слегка́ окра́шивать *imp.*, окра́сить *perf.* **tinted** *adj.* окра́шенный; *t. glasses*, тёмные очки́ (-ко́в) *pl.*

tiny *adj.* о́чень ма́ленький; кро́шечный (*coll.*).

tip[1] *n.* (*end*) ко́нчик; (*of stick*, *spear etc.*) наконе́чник; *v.t.* приставля́ть *imp.*, приста́вить *perf.* наконе́чник к + *dat.*; *be on the t. of s.b.'s tongue*, верте́ться (ве́ртиться) *imp.* на языке́ у + *gen.*

tip[2] *n.* (*money*) чаевы́е (-ы́х) *pl.*; (*advice*) сове́т, намёк; (*private information*) све́дения *neut.pl.*, полу́ченные ча́стным о́бразом; (*dump*) сва́лка; (*slight push*) лёгкий толчо́к (-чка́); *v.t.* & *i.* наклоня́ть(ся) *imp.*, наклони́ть(ся) (-ню́(сь), -нишь(ся)) *perf.*; *v.t.* (*hit lightly*) слегка́ ударя́ть *imp.*, уда́рить *perf.*; (*give t.*) дава́ть (даю́, даёшь) *imp.*, дать (дам, дашь, даст, дади́м; дал, -а́, да́ло́, -и) *perf.* (*person*, + *dat.*; *money*, де́ньги на чай, *information*, ча́стную информа́цию); *t. out*, выва́ливать *imp.*, вы́валить *perf.*; *t. over*, *up*, (*v.t.* & *i.*) опроки́дывать(ся) *imp.*, опроки́нуть(ся) *perf.*; *t. up*, *back*, (*seat*) отки́дывать *imp.*, отки́нуть *perf.*; *t. the scales*, (*fig.*) реша́ть *imp.*, реши́ть *perf.* исхо́д де́ла; *t.-up lorry*, самосва́л.

tipple *n.* (алкого́льный) напи́ток (-тка); *v.i.* выпива́ть *imp.*; *v.t.* & *i.* попива́ть *imp.* (*coll.*). **tippler** *n.* пья́ница *m.* & *f.*

tipster *n.* жучо́к (-чка́).

tipsy *adj.* подвы́пивший.

tiptoe *n.*: *on t.*, на цы́почках.

tip-top *adj.* первокла́ссный, превосхо́дный.

tirade *n.* тира́да.

tire[1] (*metal*) колёсный банда́ж (-а́).

tire[2] *see* **tyre.**

tire[3] *v.t.* (*weary*) утомля́ть *imp.*, утоми́ть *perf.*; (*bore*) надоеда́ть *imp.*, надое́сть (-е́м, -е́шь, -е́ст, -еди́м; -е́л) *perf.* + *dat.*; *v.i.* утомля́ться *imp.*, утоми́ться *perf.*; устава́ть (устаю́,

-аёшь) *imp.*, устáть (-áну, -áнешь) *perf.* **tired** *adj.* устáлый, утомлённый; *be t. of*: *I am t. of him*, он мне надоéл; *I am t. of playing*, мне надоéло игрáть; *t. out*, измýченный. **tiredness** *n.* устáлость. **tireless** *adj.* неутоми́мый. **tiresome** *adj.* утоми́тельный, надоéдливый. **tiring** *adj.* утоми́тельный.

tiro *n.* новичóк (-чкá).

tissue *n.* ткань; (*handkerchief*) бумáжная салфéтка; *t.-paper*, папирóсная бумáга.

tit[1] *n.* (*bird*) сини́ца.

tit[2] *n.*: *t. for tat*, зуб зá зуб.

titanic *adj.* (*huge*) титани́ческий.

titbit *n.* лáкомый кусóк (-скá); (*news*) пикáнтная нóвость.

tithe *n.* деся́тая часть (*pl.* -ти, -тéй); (*hist.*) десяти́на.

titillate *v.t.* щекотáть (-очý, -óчешь) *imp.*, по~ *perf.*; прия́тно возбуждáть *imp.*, возбуди́ть *perf.*

titivate *v.t.* & *i.* (*coll.*) прихорáшивать(ся) *imp.* (*coll.*).

title *n.* (*of book etc.*) назвáние; (*heading*) заглáвие; (*rank*) ти́тул, звáние; (*cin.*) титр; (*sport*) звáние чемпиóна; *t.-deed*, докумéнт, дáющий прáво сóбственности; *t.-holder*, чемпиóн; *t.-page*, ти́тульный лист (*pl.* -ы́); *t.-role*, заглáвная роль (*pl.* -ли, -лéй). **titled** *adj.* титулóванный.

titter *n.* хихи́канье; *v.i.* хихи́кать *imp.*, хихи́кнуть *perf.*

tittle *n.* чýточка, кáпелька; *t.-tattle*, болтовня́ (*coll.*).

titular *adj.* номинáльный; титулóванный.

to *prep.* (*town, a country, theatre, school, etc.*) в+*acc.*; (*the sea, the moon, the ground, post-office, meeting, concert, north, etc.*) на+*acc.*; (*the doctor; towards, up t.*; *t. one's surprise etc.*) к+*dat.*; (*with accompaniment of*) под+*acc.*; (*in toast*) за+*acc.*; (*time*): *ten minutes t. three*, без десяти́ три; (*compared with*) в сравнéнии с+*instr.*; *it is ten t. one that*, дéвять из десяти́ за то, что; *t. the left* (*right*), налéво (напрáво); (*in order t.*) чтóбы+*inf.*; *adv.*: *shut the door t.*, закрóйте дверь; *come t.*, приходи́ть (-ожý, -óдишь) *imp.*, прийти́ (-йдý, -йдёшь; пришёл, -шлá) *perf.* в сознáние; *bring t.*, приводи́ть (-ожý, -óдишь) *imp.*, привести́ (-едý, -едёшь; -ёл, -елá) *perf.* в сознáние; *t. and fro*, взад и вперёд.

toad *n.* жáба. **toadstool** *n.* погáнка.

toady *n.* подхали́м; *v.t.* льстить *imp.*, по~ *perf.* +*dat.*; *v.t.* & *i.* низкопоклóнничать *imp.* (to, пéред+*instr.*).

toast *n.* (*bread*) поджáренный хлеб; (*drink*) тост; *t.-master*, тамадá *m.*; *t.-rack*, подстáвка для поджáренного хлéба; *v.t.* (*bread*) поджáривать *imp.*, поджáрить *perf.*; (*drink*) пить (пью, пьёшь; пил, -á, -о) *imp.*, вы~ *perf.* за здорóвье+*gen.* **toaster** *n.* тóстер.

tobacco *n.* табáк; *attrib.* табáчный; *t.-pouch*, кисéт. **tobacconist** *n.* торгóвец (-вца) табáчными издéлиями; *t.'s shop*, табáчный магази́н.

toboggan *n.* табóгган, сáни (-нéй) *pl.*; *v.i.* катáться *imp.* на саня́х.

today *adv.* сегóдня; (*nowadays*) в нáши дни; *n.* сегóдняшний день (дня) *m.*; *today's newspaper*, сегóдняшняя газéта; *the writers of t.*, совремéнные писáтели *m.pl.*

toddle *v.i.* ковыля́ть *imp.* (*coll.*); (*learn to walk*) учи́ться (учýсь, ýчишься) *imp.* ходи́ть; (*stroll*) прогýливаться *imp.* **toddler** *n.* ребёнок (-нка; *pl.* дéти, -тéй), начинáющий ходи́ть; малы́ш (-á) (*coll.*).

toddy *n.* горя́чий пунш.

to-do *n.* суматóха, сутá.

toe *n.* пáлец (-льца) ноги́; (*of sock etc.*) носóк (-скá); *t.-cap*, носóк (-скá); *from top to t.*, с головы́ до пят; *v.t.* (*touch with t.*) касáться *imp.*, коснýться *perf.* noскóм+*gen.*; *t. the line*, (*fig.*) подчиня́ться *imp.*, подчини́ться *perf.* трéбованиям.

toffee *n.* (*substance*) ири́с; (*a t.*) ири́ска (*coll.*).

toga *n.* тóга.

together *adv.* вмéсте, сообщá; (*simultaneously*) одноврéмéнно; *t. with*, вмéсте с+*instr.*; *all t.*, все вмéсте; *get t.*, собирáть(ся) *imp.*, собрáть(ся) (-берý, -берёшь; -брáл(ся), -бралá(сь),

-бра́ло, -бра́ло́сь) *perf.*; *join t.* объединя́ть(ся) *imp.*, объедини́ть(ся) *perf.* (with, с+*instr.*).

toggle *n.* (*button*) продолгова́тая (деревя́нная) пу́говица.

toil *n.* тяжёлый труд; *v.i.* труди́ться (-ужу́сь, -у́дишься) *imp.*; (*drag oneself along*) тащи́ться (тащу́сь, -щишься) *imp.* **toiler** *n.* тру́женик, -ица.

toilet *n.* туале́т; *t.-paper*, туале́тная бума́га; *t. water*, туале́тная вода́ (*acc.* во́ду).

toilsome *adj.* утоми́тельный.

token *n.* (*sign*) знак; (*keepsake*) пода́рок (-рка) на па́мять; (*coupon, counter*) тало́н, жето́н; *as a t. of*, в знак+*gen.*; *attrib.* символи́ческий; *t. resistance*, ви́димость сопротивле́ния; *by the same t.*, (*similarly*) к тому́ же; (*moreover*) кро́ме того́.

tolerable *adj.* (*bearable*) терпи́мый; (*satisfactory*) удовлетвори́тельный, сно́сный (*coll.*). **tolerance** *n.* терпи́мость; (*tech.*) до́пуск; (*med.*) толера́нтность. **tolerant** *adj.* терпи́мый; (*med.*) толера́нтный. **tolerate** *v.t.* терпе́ть (-плю́, -пишь) *imp.*, по~ *perf.*; (*allow*) допуска́ть *imp.*, допусти́ть (-ущу́, -у́стишь) *perf.*; (*med.*) быть толера́нтным. **toleration** *n.* терпи́мость.

toll[1] *n.* (*duty*) по́шлина; *take its t.*, наноси́ть (-о́сит) *imp.*, нанести́ (-сёт; нанёс, -есла́) *perf.* тяжёлый уро́н; *t.-bridge*, пла́тный мост (мо́ста́, *loc.* -у́; *pl.* -ы́); *t.-gate*, заста́ва, где взима́ется сбор.

toll[2] *v.t.* (ме́дленно и ме́рно) ударя́ть *imp.*, уда́рить *perf.* в ко́локол; *v.i.* звони́ть *imp.*, по~ *perf.* (ме́дленно и ме́рно).

tom(-cat) *n.* кот (-а́).

tomahawk *n.* томага́вк; *v.t.* бить (бью, бьёшь) *imp.*, по~ *perf.* томага́вком.

tomato *n.* помидо́р; *attrib.* тома́тный.

tomb *n.* моги́ла. **tombstone** *n.* моги́льная плита́ (*pl.* -ты).

tomboy *n.* сорване́ц (-нца́).

tome *n.* больша́я (тяжёлая) кни́га.

tomfoolery *n.* дура́чества *neut.pl.*

tommy-gun *n.* автома́т.

tomorrow *adv.* за́втра; *n.* за́втрашний день (дня) *m.*; *t. morning*, за́втра у́тром; *the day after t.*, послеза́втра; *see you t.*, (*coll.*) до за́втра.

tom-tit *n.* сини́ца.

tom-tom *n.* тамта́м.

ton *n.* то́нна; (*a lot*) ма́сса.

tonal *adj.* тона́льный. **tonality** *n.* тона́льность. **tone** *n.* тон (*pl.* -ы (*mus. & fig.*), -а́ (*colour*)); (*atmosphere, mood*) атмосфе́ра, настрое́ние; (*med.*) то́нус; *t.-arm*, звукоснима́тель *m.*; *t. control*, регуля́ция те́мбра; *t.-deaf*, с сла́бым музыка́льным слу́хом; *v.t.* придава́ть (-даю́, -даёшь) *imp.*, прида́ть (-а́м, -а́шь, -а́ст, -ади́м; при́дал, -а́, -о) *perf.* жела́тельный тон+*dat.*; *v.i.* (*harmonize*) гармони́ровать *imp.* (with, с+*instr.*); *t. down*, смягча́ть(ся) *imp.*, смягчи́ть(ся) *perf.*; *t. up*, усиливать *imp.*, уси́лить *perf.*; (*med.*) тонизи́ровать *imp.*, *perf.*

tongue *n.* (*var. senses*) язы́к (-а́); (*of shoe*) язычо́к (-чка́); *t.-in-cheek*, с насме́шкой, ирони́чески; *t.-tied*, косноязы́чный; *t.-twister*, скорогово́рка; *give t.*, (*of dog*) поддава́ть (-аю́, -аёшь) *imp.*, подда́ть (-а́м, -а́шь, -а́ст, -ади́м; по́ддал, -а́, -о) *perf.* го́лос; (*of person*) гро́мко говори́ть *imp.*; *hold one's t.*, держа́ть (-жу́, -жишь) *imp.* язы́к за зуба́ми; *lose one's t.*, прогла́тывать *imp.*, проглоти́ть (-очу́, -о́тишь) *perf.* язы́к; *put out one's t.*, пока́зывать *imp.*, показа́ть (-ажу́, -а́жешь) *perf.* язы́к.

tongs *n.* щипцы́ (-цо́в) *pl.*

tonic *n.* (*med.*) тонизи́рующее сре́дство; (*mus.*) то́ника; *adj.* (*med.*) тонизи́рующий; (*mus.*) тони́ческий.

tonight *adv.* сего́дня ве́чером; *n.* сего́дняшний ве́чер.

tonnage *n.* тонна́ж, грузовмести́мость; (*charge*) корабе́льный сбор.

tonsil *n.* минда́лина. **tonsillitis** *n.* анги́на.

tonsure *n.* тонзу́ра; *v.t.* выбрива́ть *imp.*, вы́брить (-рею, -реешь) *perf.* тонзу́ру +*dat.*

too *adv.* сли́шком; (*also*) та́кже, то́же; (*very*) о́чень; (*indeed*) действи́тельно; (*moreover*) к тому́ же; *none t.*, не сли́шком.

tool *n.* инструме́нт; (*machine-t.*) стано́к (-нка́); (*implement*; *fig.*) ору́дие; *t.-box*, я́щик с инструме́нтами.

toot *n.* гудо́к (-дка́); *v.i.* гуде́ть (-ди́т) *imp.*; (*give a hoot*) дава́ть (даю́, даёшь) *imp.*, дать (дам, дашь, даст, дади́м; дал, -а́, да́ло́, -и) *perf.* гудо́к; *v.t.* (*blow*) труби́ть *imp.* в+*acc.*

tooth *n.* зуб (*pl.* -ы, -о́в); (*tech.*) зубе́ц (-бца́); *attrib.* зубно́й; *t.-brush*, зубна́я щётка; *t.-comb*, ча́стый гре́бень (-бня) *m.*; *false teeth*, вставны́е зу́бы (-бо́в) *pl.*; *first t.*, моло́чный зуб (*pl.* -ы, -о́в); *loose t.* шата́ющийся зуб (*pl.* -ы, -о́в); *second t.*, постоя́нный зуб (*pl.* -ы, -о́в); *t. and nail*, (*fiercely*) не на жи́знь, а на сме́рть; (*energetically*) энерги́чно; *in the teeth of*, (*in defiance of*) наперекóр+*dat.*; (*directly against*) пря́мо про́тив+*gen.*; *have one's teeth attended to*, лечи́ть (-чу́, -чишь) зу́бы (-бо́в) *pl.*; *he has cut a t.*, у него́ проре́зался зуб. **toothache** *n.* зубна́я боль. **toothed** *adj.* зубча́тый. **toothless** *adj.* беззу́бый. **toothpaste** *n.* зубна́я па́ста. **toothpick** *n.* зубочи́стка. **toothsome** *adj.* вку́сный (-сен, -сна́, -сно). **toothy** *adj.* зуба́стый (*coll.*).

top[1] *n.* (*toy*) волчо́к (-чка́).

top[2] *n.* (*of object*; *fig.*) верх (-а(у), *loc.* -у́; *pl.* -и́); (*of hill etc.*) верши́на; (*of tree*) верху́шка; (*of head*) маку́шка; (*of milk*) сли́вки (-вок) *pl.*; (*lid*) кры́шка; (*upper part*) ве́рхняя часть (*pl.* -ти, -те́й); *t. copy*, оригина́л; *t. drawer*, (*fig.*) вы́сшее о́бщество; *t. hat*, цили́ндр; *t.-heavy*, переве́шивающий в свое́й ве́рхней ча́сти; (*at*) *t. level*, на вы́сшем у́ровне; (*of high rank*) высокопоста́вленный; *t. secret*, соверше́нно секре́тный; *on t. of*, (*position*) на+*prep.*, сверх+*gen.*; (*on to*) на+*acc.*; *on t. of everything*, сверх всего́; *from t. to bottom*, све́рху до́низу; *at the t. of one's voice*, во всё го́рло; *at t. speed*, во весь опо́р; *adj.* ве́рхний, вы́сший, са́мый высо́кий; (*foremost*) пе́рвый; *v.t.* (*cover*) покрыва́ть *imp.*, покры́ть (-ро́ю, -ро́ешь) *perf.*; (*reach t. of*) поднима́ться *imp.*, подня́ться (-ниму́сь, -ни́мешься; -ня́лся́, -няла́сь) *perf.* на верши́ну+*gen.*; (*excel*) превосходи́ть (-ожу́, -о́дишь) *imp.*, превзойти́ (-ойду́, -ойдёшь; -ошёл, -ошла́) *perf.*; (*cut t. off*) обреза́ть *imp.*, обре́зать (-е́жу, -е́жешь) *perf.* верху́шку+*gen.*; *t. off*, заверша́ть *imp.*, заверши́ть *perf.*; *t. up*, (*with liquid*) долива́ть *imp.*, доли́ть (-лью́, -льёшь; до́ли́л, -а́, -о) *perf.*; (*with grain etc.*) досыпа́ть *imp.*, досы́пать (-плю, -плешь) *perf.*

topaz *n.* топа́з.

topcoat *n.* пальто́ *neut. indecl.*

topiary *n.* иску́сство фигу́рной стри́жки кусто́в.

topic *n.* те́ма, предме́т. **topical** *adj.* актуа́льный; *t. question*, злободне́вный вопро́с. **topicality** *n.* актуа́льность.

topknot *n.* (*tuft, crest*) хохо́л (-хла́); (*knot*) пучо́к (-чка́) лент (*of ribbons*), воло́с (*of hair*).

topmost *adj.* са́мый ве́рхний; са́мый ва́жный.

topographer *n.* топо́граф. **topographic(al)** *adj.* топографи́ческий. **topography** *n.* топогра́фия.

topology *n.* тополо́гия. **toponymy** *n.* топони́мия.

topple *v.t.* & *i.* опроки́дывать(ся) *imp.*, опроки́нуть(ся) *perf.*; *v.i.* вали́ться (-лю́сь, -лишься) *imp.*, по~, с~ *perf.*

topsail *n.* ма́рсель *m.*

topsoil *n.* ве́рхний слой по́чвы.

topsy-turvy *adj.* повёрнутый вверх дном; (*disorderly*) беспоря́дочный; *adv.* вверх дном, ши́ворот-навы́ворот.

torch *n.* фа́кел; (*electric t.*) электри́ческий фона́рик; (*fig.*) све́точ; *t.-bearer*, фа́кельщик, -ица. **torchlight** *n.* свет фа́кела, фона́рика.

toreador *n.* тореадо́р.

torment *n.* муче́ние, му́ка; *v.t.* му́чить *imp.*, за~, из~ *perf.* **tormentor** *n.* мучи́тель *m.*

tornado *n.* торна́до; (*fig.*) урага́н.

torpedo *n.* торпе́да; *t.-boat*, торпе́дный ка́тер (*pl.* -а́); *v.t.* торпеди́ровать *imp.*, *perf.*; (*fig.*) прова́ливать *imp.*, провали́ть (-лю́, -лишь) *perf.*

torpid *adj.* (*numb*) онеме́лый; (*sluggish*)

вя́лый; (*zool.*) находя́щийся в спя́чке. **torpor** *n.* онеме́лость; апа́тия.

torque *n.* (*phys.*, *mech.*) враща́ющий моме́нт.

torrent *n.* стреми́тельный пото́к; (*fig.*) пото́к; *pl.* ли́вень (-вня) *m.* **torrential** *adj.* теку́щий бы́стрым пото́ком; (*of rain*) проливно́й; (*fig.*) оби́льный.

torrid *adj.* зно́йный.

torsion *n.* скру́ченность; (*tech.*) круче́ние.

torso *n.* ту́ловище; (*of statue*) торс.

tort *n.* гражда́нское правонаруше́ние.

tortoise *n.* черепа́ха. **tortoise-shell** *n.* па́нцирь *m.* черепа́хи; (*material*) черепа́ха; *attrib.* черепа́ховый; (*cat*) пёстрый.

tortuous *adj.* изви́листый; (*evasive*) укло́нчивый.

torture *n.* пы́тка; *v.t.* пыта́ть *imp.*; (*torment*) му́чить *imp.*, за~, из~ *perf.*; (*distort*) искажа́ть *imp.*, искази́ть *perf.* **torturer** *n.* мучи́тель *m.*, пала́ч (-а́).

toss *n.* бросо́к (-ска́), броса́ние; *t. of coin*, подбра́сывание моне́ты, жеребьёвка (*fig.*); *win* (*lose*) *the t.*, (не) выпада́ть *imp.*, вы́пасть (-адет; -ал) *perf.* жре́бий *impers.* (*I won the t.*, мне вы́пал жре́бий); *v.t.* броса́ть *imp.*, бро́сить *perf.*; (*coin*) подбра́сывать *imp.*, подбро́сить *perf.*; (*rider*) сбра́сывать *imp.*, сбро́сить *perf.*; (*of bull etc.*) поднима́ть *imp.*, подня́ть (-ниму́, -ни́мешь; по́днял, -а́, -о) *perf.* на рога́; (*head*) вски́дывать *imp.*, вски́нуть *perf.*; (*salad*) переме́шивать *imp.*, перемеша́ть *perf.*; *t. a pancake*, перевора́чивать *imp.*, переверну́ть *perf.* блин, подбро́сив его́; *v.i.* (*of ship*) кача́ться *imp.*, качну́ться *perf.*; (*in bed*) мета́ться (мечу́сь, -чешься) *imp.*; *t. aside*, *away*, отбра́сывать *imp.*, отбро́сить *perf.*; *t. off*, (*work*) де́лать *imp.*, с~ *perf.* на́спех; (*drink*) пить (пью, пьёшь) *imp.*, вы~ *perf.* за́лпом; *t. up*, броса́ть *imp.*, бро́сить *perf.* жре́бий. **toss-up** *n.* жеребьёвка; (*doubtful matter*): *it is a t.*, э́то ещё вопро́с.

tot[1] *n.* (*coll.*) (*child*) малы́ш (-а́) (*coll.*); (*glass*) ма́ленькая рю́мка; (*dram*) ма́ленький глото́к (-тка́).

tot[2]: *t. up*, (*coll.*) (*v.t.*) скла́дывать *imp.*, сложи́ть (-жу́, -жишь) *perf.*; (*v.i.*) равня́ться *imp.* (to, + *dat.*).

total *n.* ито́г, су́мма; *adj.* о́бщий; (*complete*) по́лный (-лон, -лна́, по́лно́); *in t.*, в це́лом, вме́сте; *t. recall*, фотографи́ческая па́мять; *t. war*, тота́льная война́; *sum t.*, о́бщая су́мма; *v.t.* подсчи́тывать *imp.*, подсчита́ть *perf.*; *v.i.* равня́ться *imp.* + *dat.* **totalitarian** *adj.* тоталита́рный. **totality** *n.* вся су́мма целико́м; *the t. of*, весь (вся, всё; все); *in t.*, в це́лом вме́сте. **totalizator** *n.* тотализа́тор. **totalize** *v.t.* соединя́ть *imp.*, соедини́ть *perf.* воеди́но. **totally** *adv.* соверше́нно.

totem *n.* тоте́м; *t.-pole*, тоте́мный столб (-а́).

totter *v.i.* (*walk unsteadily*) ходи́ть (хожу́, хо́дишь) *indet.*, идти́ (иду́, идёшь; шёл, шла) *det.*, пойти́ (пойду́, -дёшь; пошёл, -шла́) *perf.* неве́рными шага́ми; (*reel*) шата́ться *imp.*; (*toddle*) ковыля́ть *imp.*; (*perish*) ги́бнуть (-б) *imp.*, по~ *perf.*

toucan *n.* тука́н.

touch *n.* прикоснове́ние; (*sense*) осяза́ние; (*stroke of brush etc.*) штрих (-а́); (*mus. or art style*) туше́; (*of piano etc.*) уда́р; (*shade*) отте́нок (-нка); (*taste*) при́вкус; (*small amount*) чу́точка; (*of illness*) лёгкий при́ступ; (*sport*) пло́щадь (*pl.* -ди, -де́й) за боковы́ми ли́ниями; (*personal t.*) ли́чный подхо́д; *get in t. with*, свя́зываться *imp.*, связа́ться (-яжу́сь, -я́жешься) *perf.* с + *instr.*; *keep in* (*lose*) *t. with*, подде́рживать *imp.*, поддержа́ть (-жу́, -жишь) *perf.* (теря́ть *imp.*, по~ *perf.*) связь, конта́кт с + *instr.*; *put the finishing touches to*, отде́лывать *imp.*, отде́лать *perf.*; *t.-line*, бокова́я ли́ния; *t. typing*, слепо́й ме́тод маши́нописи; *common t.*, чу́вство ло́ктя; *to the t.*, на о́щупь; *v.t.* (*lightly*) прикаса́ться *imp.*, прикосну́ться *perf.* к + *dat.*; каса́ться *imp.*, косну́ться *perf.* + *gen.*; (*also disturb*; *affect*) тро́гать *imp.*, тро́нуть *perf.*; (*momentarily reach*) подска́кивать *imp.*, подскочи́ть (-чит) *perf.* до + *gen.* (*coll.*); (*be comparable with*) идти́ (иду́, идёшь; шёл, шла) *imp.* в сравне́нии с + *instr.*; *v.i.* (*be contiguous*; *come into contact*) соприкаса́ться *imp.*, соприкосну́ться *perf.*; *t. down*, приземля́ться *imp.*, приземли́ться *perf.*; *t.-down*, поса́дка; *t. off*, (*provoke*) вызыва́ть *imp.*, вы́звать (вы́зову, -вешь) *perf.*; *t.* (*up*)*on*, (*fig.*) каса́ться *imp.*, косну́ться *perf.* + *gen.*; *t. up*, поправля́ть *imp.*, попра́вить *perf.*; *t.-and-go*, риско́ванное де́ло; *t. wood!* не сгла́зить бы! **touched** *adj.* тро́нутый. **touchiness** *n.* оби́дчивость. **touching** *adj.* тро́гательный. **touchstone** *n.* проби́рный ка́мень (-мня; *pl.* -мни, -мне́й) *m.* **touchy** *adj.* оби́дчивый.

tough *adj.* жёсткий (-ток, -тка́, -тко); (*durable*) про́чный (-чен, -чна́, -чно, про́чны́); (*strong*) кре́пкий (-пок, -пка́, -пко); (*difficult*) тру́дный (-ден, -дна́, -дно, тру́дны́); (*hardy*) выно́сливый; *n.* хулига́н, банди́т. **toughen** *v.t.* & *i.* де́лать(ся) *imp.*, с ~ *perf.* жёстким. **toughness** *n.* жёсткость; (*durability*) про́чность.

toupee *n.* небольшо́й пари́к (-а́).

tour *n.* (*journey*) путеше́ствие, пое́здка; (*excursion*) экску́рсия; (*of artistes*) турне́ *neut.indecl.*; (*of duty*) объе́зд; *t. de force*, проявле́ние си́лы (*strength*), ло́вкости (*skill*); *v.i.* (*t.*) соверша́ть *imp.*, соверши́ть *perf.* путеше́ствие, турне́, объе́зд (по + *dat.*). **tourism** *n.* тури́зм. **tourist** *n.* тури́ст, ~ка; путеше́ственник, -ица; *t. class*, второ́й класс.

tournament *n.* турни́р. **tourney** *v.i.* уча́ствовать *imp.* в турни́ре.

tourniquet *n.* турнике́т.

tousle *v.t.* взъеро́шивать *imp.*, взъеро́шить *perf.* (*coll.*).

tout *n.* навя́зчивый торго́вец (-вца); (*of horses*) челове́к (*pl.* лю́ди, -де́й, -дям, -дьми́) добыва́ющий и прода́ющий све́дения о лошадя́х пе́ред ска́чками; *v.t.* навя́зывать *imp.*, навяза́ть (-яжу́, -я́жешь) *perf.* (*thing*, + *acc.*; *person*, + *dat.*).

tow[1] *v.t.* букси́ровать *imp.*; *n.* буксиро́вка; *on t.*, на букси́ре; *t.-boat*, букси́рное су́дно (*pl.* -да́, -до́в); *t.-path*, бечевни́к (-а́); *t.-rope*, букси́р, бечева́ *no pl.*

tow[2] *n.* (*text.*) па́кля.

towards *prep.* (*in direction of*) (по направле́нию) к + *dat.*; (*fig.*) к + *dat.*; (*for*) для + *gen.*

towel *n.* полоте́нце; *t. rail*, ве́шалка для полоте́нец. **towelling** *n.* махро́вая ткань.

tower *n.* ба́шня; (*tech.*) вы́шка; (*fig.*): *t. of strength*, надёжная опо́ра; *v.i.* вы́ситься *imp.*, возвыша́ться *imp.* (above, над + *instr.*). **towering** *adj.* (*high*) высо́кий (-о́к, -ока́, -о́ко́); (*rising up*) возвыша́ющийся; (*furious*) неи́стовый.

town *n.* го́род (*pl.* -а́); *attrib.* городско́й; *t. clerk*, секрета́рь *m.* городско́й корпора́ции; *t. council*, городско́й сове́т; *t. councillor*, член городско́го сове́та; *t. crier*, глаша́тай; *t. hall*, ра́туша; *t. planning*, градострои́тельство. **townsman, -swoman** *n.* горожа́нин (*pl.* -а́не, -а́н), -а́нка.

toxic *adj.* ядови́тый, токси́ческий. **toxin** *n.* яд (-а(у)); (*med.*) токси́н.

toy *n.* игру́шка; *t. dog*, ма́ленькая ко́мнатная соба́чка; *t. soldier*, оловя́нный солда́тик; *v.i.*: *t. with*, (*s.th. in hands*) верте́ть (верчу́, -ртишь) *imp.* в рука́х; (*trifle with*) игра́ть *imp.* (с) + *instr.*

trace[1] *n.* (*track*, *mark*) след (*pl.* -ы́); (*small amount*) небольшо́е коли́чество; *t. element*, микроэлеме́нт; *v.t.* (*track* (*down*), *trace* (*through*)) просле́живать *imp.*, проследи́ть *perf.*; (*make copy*) калькирова́ть *imp.*, с ~ *perf.*; *t. back*, (*v.i.*) восходи́ть (-ожу́, -о́дишь) *imp.* (to, к + *dat.*); *t. out*, (*plan*) набра́сывать *imp.*, наброса́ть *perf.*; (*map*, *diagram*) черти́ть (черчу́, -ртишь) *imp.*, на ~ *perf.* **tracery** *n.* узо́р. **tracing** *n.* (*copy*) чертёж (-а́) на ка́льке; *t. paper*, ка́лька.

trace[2] *n.* (*of harness*) постро́мка.

trachea *n.* трахе́я.

track *n.* (*path*) доро́жка, тропи́нка; (*mark*) след (*pl.* -ы́); (*rly.*) путь (-ти́,

-тём) *m.*, колея́; (*sport*) трек, доро́жка; (*on tape*) (звукова́я) доро́жка; (*on record*) за́пись; *t. events*, соревнова́ния *neut.pl.* по бегу́; *t. suit*, трениро́вочный костю́м; *off the t.*, на ло́жном пути́; (*fig.*) отклони́вшийся от те́мы; *off the beaten t.*, в глуши́; *be on the t. of*, пресле́довать *imp.*; *go off the t.*, (*fig.*) отклоня́ться *imp.*, отклони́ться (-ню́сь, -ни́шься) *perf.* от те́мы; *keep t. of*, следи́ть *imp* за + *instr.*; *lose t. of*, теря́ть *imp.*, по~ *perf.* след + *gen.*; *v.t.* просле́живать *imp.*, проследи́ть *perf.*; *t. down*, высле́живать *imp.*, вы́следить *perf.*

tract[1] *n.* (*expanse*) простра́нство; (*anat.*) тракт.

tract[2] *n.* (*treatise*) тракта́т; (*pamphlet*) брошю́ра.

tractability *n.* (*of person*) сгово́рчивость; (*of material*) ко́вкость. **tractable** *adj.* (*person*) сгово́рчивый; (*material*) ко́вкий (-вок, -вка́, -вко). **traction** *n.* тя́га; (*therapy*) тра́кция; *t.-engine*, тра́ктор-тяга́ч (-а́). **tractor** *n.* тра́ктор; *t.-driver*, трактори́ст.

trade *n.* торго́вля; (*occupation*) профе́ссия, ремесло́ (*pl.* -ёсла, -ёсел, -ёслам); (*collect.*) торго́вцы *m.pl.*; *t. mark*, фабри́чная ма́рка; (*fig.*) отличи́тельный знак; *t. name*, (*of firm*) назва́ние фи́рмы; *t. secret*, секре́т фи́рмы; *t. union*, профсою́з; *t.-unionist*, член профсою́за; *t. wind*, пасса́т; *v.i.* торгова́ть *imp.* (in, + *instr.*); *v.t.* (*swap like things*) обме́ниваться *imp.*, обменя́ться *perf.* + *instr.*; (*t. for s.th. different*) обме́нивать *imp.*, обменя́ть *perf.* (for, на + *acc.*); *t. in*, сдава́ть (сдаю́, сдаёшь) *imp.*, сдать (сдам, сдашь, сдаст, сдади́м; сдал, -а́, -о) *perf.* в счёт поку́пки но́вого; *t. on*, (*exploit*) испо́льзовать *imp.*, *perf.* **trader, tradesman** *n.* торго́вец (-вца). **trading** *n.* торго́вля, комме́рция; *attrib.* торго́вый; *t. station*, факто́рия.

tradition *n.* тради́ция; (*legend*) преда́ние. **traditional** *adj.* традицио́нный (-нен, -нна). **traditionalism** *n.* приве́рженность к тради́циям. **traditionally** *adv.* по тради́ции.

traduce *v.t.* клевета́ть (-ещу́, -е́щешь) *imp.*, на~ *perf.* на + *acc.* **traducer** *n.* клеветни́к (-а́), -и́ца.

traffic *n.* движе́ние; (*trade*) торго́вля; (*transportation*) тра́нспорт; *t. island*, острово́к (-вка́) безопа́сности; *t. jam*, про́бка; *t. lights*, светофо́р; *v.i.* торгова́ть *imp.* (in, + *instr.*). **trafficator** *n.* указа́тель *m.* поворо́та. **trafficker** *n.* торго́вец (-вца) (in, + *instr.*).

tragedian *n.* тра́гик. **tragedy** *n.* траге́дия. **tragic** *adj.* траги́ческий. **tragicomedy** *n.* трагикоме́дия.

trail *n.* (*trace, track*) след (*pl.* -ы́); (*path*) тропи́нка; (*course; road*) путь (-ти́, -тём) *m.*; *v.t.* (*track*) высле́живать *imp.*, вы́следить *perf.*; *v.t.* & *i.* (*drag*) таска́ть(ся) *indet.*, тащи́ть(ся) (-щу́(сь), -щишь(ся)) *det.*; волочи́ть(ся) (-чу́(сь), -чишь(ся)) *imp.* **trailer** *n.* (*on vehicle*) прице́п; (*plant*) сте́лющееся расте́ние; (*cin.*) (кино)ро́лик.

train *n.* по́езд (*pl.* -а́); (*of dress*) шлейф; (*retinue*) сви́та; (*mil.*) обо́з; (*convoy*) карава́н; (*series*) цепь (*loc.* -пи́; *pl.* -пи, -пе́й); *v.t.* (*instruct*) обуча́ть *imp.*, обучи́ть (-чу́, -чишь) *perf.* (in, + *dat.*); (*prepare*) гото́вить *imp.* (for, к + *dat.*); (*sport*) тренирова́ть *imp.*, на~ *perf.*; (*animals*) дрессирова́ть *imp.*, вы~ *perf.*; (*break in*) объезжа́ть *imp.*, объе́здить *perf.*; (*aim, point*) направля́ть *imp.*, напра́вить *perf.*; (*plant*) направля́ть *imp.*, напра́вить *perf.* рост + *gen.*; *v.i.* (*prepare*) пригота́вливаться *imp.*, пригото́виться *perf.* (for, к + *dat.*); (*sport*) тренирова́ться *imp.*, на~ *perf.* **trainee** *n.* стажёр, практика́нт. **trainer** *n.* инстру́ктор; (*sport*) тре́нер; (*of animals*) дрессиро́вщик. **training** *n.* обуче́ние; (*sport*) трениро́вка; (*of animals*) дрессиро́вка; *t.-college*, (*teachers'*) педагоги́ческий институ́т; *t.-school*, специа́льное учи́лище.

traipse *v.i.* таска́ться *indet.*, тащи́ться (-щу́сь, -щишься) *det.*

trait *n.* (характе́рная) черта́; штрих (-а́).

traitor *n.* преда́тель *m.*, изме́нник. **traitorous** *adj.* преда́тельский. **traitress** *n.* преда́тельница, изме́нница.

trajectory *n.* траекто́рия.

tram *n.* трамва́й; *t.-driver*, вагоново́жа́тый *sb.*; *t.-line*, трамва́йная ли́ния. **trammel** *n.* (*net*) не́вод (*pl.* -а́), трал; (*fig.*) поме́ха, препя́тствие; *v.t.* (*fig.*) препя́тствовать *imp.*, вос~ *perf.* +*dat.*

tramp *n.* (*vagrant*) бродя́га *m.*; (*tread*) то́пот; (*journey on foot*) путеше́ствие пешко́м; *v.i.* (*of vagrant*) бродя́жничать *imp.*; (*go with heavy tread*) то́пать *imp.*; (*go on foot*) ходи́ть (хожу́, хо́дишь) *indet.*, идти́ (иду́, идёшь; шёл, шла) *det.*, пойти́ (пойду́, -дёшь; пошёл, -шла́) *perf.* пешко́м. **trample** *v.t.* топта́ть (топчу́, -чешь) *imp.*, по~, ис~ *perf.*; *t. down*, выта́птывать *imp.*, вы́топтать (-пчу, -пчешь) *perf.*; *t. on*, (*fig.*) попира́ть *imp.*, попра́ть (-ру́, -рёшь) *perf.*

trampoline *n.* бату́т, бату́д.

trance *n.* транс; (*rapture*) состоя́ние экста́за.

tranquil *adj.* споко́йный. **tranquillity** *n.* споко́йствие. **tranquillize** *v.t.* успока́ивать *imp.*, успоко́ить *perf.* **tranquillizer** *n.* транквилиза́тор.

transact *v.t.* (*business*) вести́ (веду́, -дёшь; вёл, -а́) *imp.*; (*a deal*) заключа́ть *imp.*, заключи́ть *perf.* **transaction** *n.* де́ло (*pl.* -ла́), сде́лка; *pl.* (*publications*) труды́ *m.pl.*; (*minutes*) прото́колы *m.pl.*

transatlantic *adj.* трансатланти́ческий.

transceiver *n.* приёмо-переда́тчик.

transcend *v.t.* преступа́ть *imp.*, преступи́ть (-плю́, -пишь) *perf.* преде́лы +*gen.*; (*excel*) превосходи́ть (-ожу́, -о́дишь) *imp.*, превзойти́ (-ойду́, -ойдёшь; -ошёл, -ошла́) *perf.* **transcendency** *n.* превосхо́дство. **transcendent** *adj.* превосхо́дный. **transcendental** *adj.* (*philos.*) трансцендента́льный.

transcontinental *adj.* трансконтинента́льный.

transcribe *v.t.* (*copy out*) перепи́сывать *imp.*, переписа́ть (-ишу́, -и́шешь) *perf.*; (*shorthand*) расшифро́вывать *imp.*, расшифрова́ть *perf.*; (*mus.*) аранжи́ровать *imp.*; (*phon.*) транскриби́ровать *imp.*, *perf.* **transcript** *n.* ко́пия; (*shorthand*) расшифро́вка. **transcription** *n.* (*copying out*) перепи́сывание; (*copy*) ко́пия; (*mus.*) аранжиро́вка; (*phon.*) транскри́пция.

transducer *n.* преобразова́тель *m.*, да́тчик.

transept *n.* трансе́пт.

transfer *n.* (*of objects*) перено́с, перемеще́ние; (*of money*; *of people*) перево́д; (*leg.*) переда́ча; (*design*) переводна́я карти́нка; *v.t.* (*objects*) переноси́ть (-ошу́, -о́сишь) *imp.*, перенести́ (-есу́, -есёшь; -ёс, -есла́) *perf.*; перемеща́ть *imp.*, перемести́ть *perf.*; (*money*; *people*; *design*) переводи́ть (-ожу́, -о́дишь) *imp.*, перевести́ (-еду́, -едёшь; -ёл, -ела́) *perf.*; (*leg.*) передава́ть (-даю́, -даёшь) *imp.*, переда́ть (-а́м, -а́шь, -а́ст, -ади́м; пе́редал, -а́, -о) *perf.*; *v.i.* (*to different job*) переходи́ть (-ожу́, -о́дишь) *imp.*, перейти́ (-ейду́, -ейдёшь; -ешёл, -ешла́) *perf.*; (*change trains etc.*) переса́живаться *imp.*, пересе́сть (-ся́ду, -ся́дешь; -се́л) *perf.* **transferable** *adj.* допуска́ющий переда́чу; (*replaceable*) заменя́емый, замени́мый. **transference** *n.* передача.

transfiguration *n.* преобразова́ние; (*spiritual*) преображе́ние. **transfigure** *v.t.* преобразо́вывать *imp.*, преобразова́ть *perf.*; (*in spirit*) преобража́ть *imp.*, преобрази́ть *perf.*

transfix *v.t.* (*pierce*) пронза́ть *imp.*, пронзи́ть *perf.*; (*fig.*) пригвожда́ть *imp.*, пригвозди́ть *perf.* к ме́сту.

transform *v.t.* & *i.* (*also electr.*) преобразо́вывать(ся) *imp.*, преобразова́ть(ся) *perf.*; *t. into*, *v.t.*(*i.*) превраща́ть(ся) *imp.*, преврати́ть(ся) (-ащу́(сь), -ати́шь(ся)) *perf.* в+*acc.* **transformation** *n.* преобразова́ние; превраще́ние. **transformer** *n.* (*electr.*) трансформа́тор.

transfuse *v.t.* (*med.*) перелива́ть *imp.*, перели́ть (-лью́, -льёшь; -ли́л, -лила́) *perf.*; (*steep*) пропи́тывать *imp.*, пропита́ть *perf.* (in, +*instr.*); (*convey*) передава́ть (-даю́, -даёшь) *imp.*, переда́ть (-а́м, -а́шь, -а́ст, -ади́м; пе́редал, -а́, -о) *perf.* **transfusion** *n.* перелива́ние (кро́ви).

transgress *v.t.* переступа́ть *imp.*, переступи́ть (-плю́, -пишь) *perf.*; нарушáть *imp.*, нарýшить *perf.* **transgression** *n.* простýпок (-пка), нарушéние; (*sin*) грех (-á). **transgressor** *n.* правонарушúтель *m.*; (*sinner*) грéшник, -ица.

transience *n.* быстротéчность, мимолётность. **transient** *adj.* преходя́щий; (*fleeting*) мимолётный.

transistor *n.* транзúстор; *t. radio*, транзúсторный приёмник. **transistorized** *adj.* на транзúсторах.

transit *n.* транзúт, прохождéние; (*astron.*) прохождéние планéты; *in t.*, в пути́; *t. camp*, лáгерь (*pl.* -ря́, -рéй) *m.* перемещённых лиц; *t. visa*, транзúтная вúза. **transition** *n.* перехóд. **transitional** *adj.* перехóдный; (*interim*) промежýточный. **transitive** *adj.* перехóдный. **transitory** *adj.* мимолётный; (*temporary*) врéменный.

translate *v.t.* переводúть (-ожý, -óдишь) *imp.*, перевестú (-едý, -едёшь; -ёл, -елá) *perf.*; (*explain*) объясня́ть *imp.*, объяснúть *perf.* **translation** *n.* перевóд. **translator** *n.* перевóдчик, -ица.

transliterate *v.t.* транслитерúровать *imp.*, *perf.* **transliteration** *n.* транслитерáция.

translucency *n.* полупрозрáчность. **translucent** *adj.* просвéчивающий, полупрозрáчный.

transmigration *n.* переселéние.

transmission *n.* передáча; (*tech.*) трансмúссия; *attrib.* передáточный. **transmit** *v.t.* передавáть (-даю́, -даёшь) *imp.*, передáть (-áм, -áшь, -áст, -адúм; пéредал, -á, -о) *perf.* **transmitter** *n.* (радио)передáтчик.

transmutation *n.* превращéние. **transmute** *v.t.* превращáть *imp.*, превратúть (-ащý, -атúшь) *perf.*

transom *n.* переплёт.

transparency *n.* прозрáчность; (*picture*) транспарáнт; (*phot.*) диапозитúв. **transparent** *adj.* прозрáчный; (*obvious*) очевúдный; (*frank*) откровéнный (-нен, -нна).

transpire *v.t.* & *i.* испаря́ть(ся) *imp.*, испарúть(ся) *perf.*; *v.i.* (*fig.*) обнарýживаться *imp.*, обнарýжиться *perf.*; (*occur*) случáться *imp.*, случúться *perf.*

transplant *v.t.* пересáживать *imp.*, пересадúть (-ажý, -áдишь) *perf.*; (*surg.*) дéлать *imp.*, с~ *perf.* пересáдку + *gen.*; *n.* (*surg.*) пересáдка.

transport *n.* (*var. senses*) трáнспорт; (*conveyance*) перевóзка; (*of rage etc.*) поры́в; *attrib.* трáнспортный; *v.t.* перевозúть (-ожý, -óзишь) *imp.*, перевезтú (-езý, -езёшь; -ёз, -езлá) *perf.*; (*exile*) ссылáть *imp.*, сослáть (сошлю́, -лёшь) *perf.* **transportation** *n.* трáнспорт, перевóзка; (*exile*) ссы́лка.

transpose *v.t.* перемещáть *imp.*, переместúть *perf.*; (*words*) переставля́ть *imp.*, перестáвить *perf.*; (*mus.*) транспонúровать *imp.*, *perf.* **transposition** *n.* перемещéние, перестанóвка; (*mus.*) транспонирóвка.

trans-ship *v.t.* перегружáть *imp.*, перегрузúть (-ужý, -ýзишь) *perf.*

transverse *adj.* поперéчный.

transvestism *n.* трансвестúзм. **transvestite** *n.* трансвестúт.

trap *n.* ловýшка (*also fig.*), западня́, капкáн; (*tech.*) сифóн; (*cart*) рессóрная двукóлка; *v.t.* (*catch*) ловúть (-влю́, -вишь) *imp.*, поймáть *perf.* (в ловýшку); (*fig.*) замáнивать *imp.*, заманúть (-ню́, -нишь) *perf.* в ловýшку. **trapdoor** *n.* люк.

trapeze *n.* трапéция. **trapezium** *n.* трапéция.

trapper *n.* охóтник, стáвящий капкáны.

trappings *n.* сбрýя (*collect.*); (*fig.*) (*exterior attributes*) внéшние атрибýты *m.pl.*; (*adornments*) украшéния *neut.pl.*

trash *n.* дрянь (*coll.*). **trashy** *adj.* дряннóй (-нен, -ннá, -нно).

trauma *n.* трáвма. **traumatic** *adj.* травматúческий.

travel *n.* путешéствие; (*tech.*) передвижéние; *t. bureau*, бюрó *neut.indecl.* путешéствий; *t.-sick*: *be t.-sick*, укáчивать *imp.*, укачáть *perf. impers.* + *acc.*; *I am t.-sick in cars*, меня́ в машúне укáчивает; *v.i.* путешéствовать *imp.*; (*tech.*) передвигáться *imp.*, передвúнуться *perf.*; *v.t.* объезжáть *imp.*, объéхать (-éду, -éдешь) *perf.* **traveller** *n.* путешéственник, -ица;

(*salesman*) коммивояжёр; *t.'s cheque*, доро́жный чек. **travelling** *n.* путеше́ствие; *attrib.* доро́жный; (*itinerant*) передвижно́й. **travelogue** *n.* (*film*) фильм о путеше́ствиях; (*lecture*) ле́кция о путеше́ствии с диапозити́вами.

traverse *v.t.* пересека́ть *imp.*, пересе́чь (-еку́, -ечёшь; -е́к, -екла́) *perf.*; (*discuss*) подро́бно обсужда́ть *imp.*, обсуди́ть (-ужу́, -у́дишь) *perf.*

travesty *n.* паро́дия; *v.t.* пароди́ровать *imp.*, *perf.*

trawl *n.* трал; *v.t.* тра́лить *imp.*; *v.i.* лови́ть (-влю́, -вишь) *imp.* ры́бу тра́ловой се́тью. **trawler** *n.* тра́улер. **trawling** *n.* трале́ние.

tray *n.* подно́с; *in-*(*out-*)*t.*, корзи́нка для входя́щих (исходя́щих) бума́г.

treacherous *adj.* преда́тельский; (*unreliable*) ненадёжный. **treachery** *n.* преда́тельство.

treacle *n.* па́тока. **treacly** *adj.* па́точный.

tread *n.* по́ступь, похо́дка; (*stair*) ступе́нька; (*of tyre*) проте́ктор; *v.i.* ступа́ть *imp.*, ступи́ть (-плю́, -пишь) *perf.*; шага́ть *imp.*, шагну́ть *perf.*; *v.t.* топта́ть (-пчу́, -пчешь) *imp.*; дави́ть (-влю́, -вишь) *imp.* **treadle** *n.* (*of bicycle*) педа́ль; (*of sewing-machine*) подно́жка.

treason *n.* изме́на; *high t.*, госуда́рственная изме́на. **treasonable** *adj.* изме́ннический.

treasure *n.* сокро́вище, клад; *t. trove*, на́йденный клад; *v.t.* (*preserve*) храни́ть *imp.*; (*value*) дорожи́ть *imp.* + *instr.*; высо́ко́ цени́ть (-ню́, -нишь) *imp.* **treasurer** *n.* казначе́й. **treasury** *n.* (*also fig.*) сокро́вищница; (*T.*) казна́ *no pl.*; *the T.*, госуда́рственное казначе́йство.

treat *n.* (*pleasure*) удово́льствие; (*entertainment*) угоще́ние; *v.t.* (*have as guest*) угоща́ть *imp.*, угости́ть *perf.* (to, + *instr.*); (*med.*) лечи́ть (-чу́, -чишь) *imp.* (for, от + *gen.*; with, + *instr.*); (*behave towards*) обраща́ться *imp.* с + *instr.*; (*process*) обраба́тывать *imp.*, обрабо́тать *perf.* (with, + *instr.*); (*discuss*) трактова́ть *imp.* о + *prep.*; (*regard*) относи́ться (-ошу́сь, -о́сишься) *imp.*, отнести́сь (-есу́сь, -есёшься; -ёсся, -есла́сь) *perf.* к + *dat.* (as, как к + *dat.*). **treatise** *n.* тракта́т. **treatment** *n.* (*behaviour*) обраще́ние; (*med.*) лече́ние; (*processing*) обрабо́тка; (*discussion*) тракто́вка. **treaty** *n.* догово́р.

treble *adj.* тройно́й; (*trebled*) утро́енный (-ен); (*mus.*) дисканто́вый; *adv.* втро́е, втройне́; *n.* тройно́е коли́чество; (*mus.*) ди́скант; *v.t.* & *i.* утра́ивать(ся) *imp.*, утро́ить(ся) *perf.*

tree *n.* де́рево (*pl.* дере́вья, -ьев). **treeless** *adj.* безле́сный.

trefoil *n.* трили́стник.

trek *n.* (*migration*) переселе́ние; (*journey*) путеше́ствие; *v.i.* (*migrate*) переселя́ться *imp.*, пересели́ться *perf.*; (*journey*) путеше́ствовать *imp.*

trellis *n.* шпале́ра; (*for creepers*) решётка.

tremble *v.i.* трепета́ть (-ещу́, -е́щешь) *imp.* (at, при + *prep.*); дрожа́ть (-жу́, -жи́шь) *imp.* (with, от + *gen.*); трясти́сь (-су́сь, -сёшься; -ся, -сла́сь) *imp.* (with, от + *gen.*). **trembling** *n.* тре́пет, дро́жь; *in fear and t.*, трепеща́.

tremendous *adj.* (*enormous*) огро́мный; (*excellent*, *remarkable*) потряса́ющий.

tremor *n.* дрожь, тре́пет; (*earthquake*) толчо́к (-чка́). **tremulous** *adj.* дрожа́щий; (*uneven*) неро́вный (-вен, -вна́, -вно); (*shy*) ро́бкий (-бок, -бка́, -бко).

trench *n.* кана́ва, ров (рва, *loc.* во рву́); (*mil.*) око́п; *t. coat*, тёплая полушине́ль; *v.t.* рыть (ро́ю, ро́ешь) *imp.*, вы~ *perf.* кана́вы, рвы, око́пы в + *prep.*; (*dig over*) перека́пывать *imp.*, перекопа́ть *perf.*

trenchant *adj.* о́стрый (остр & остёр, остра́, о́стро́), ре́зкий (-зок, -зка́, -зко). **trenchancy** *n.* острота́, ре́зкость.

trend *n.* направле́ние, тенде́нция. **trendy** *adj.* мо́дный (-ден, -дна́, -дно).

trepidation *n.* (*trembling*) тре́пет; (*alarm*) трево́га.

trespass *n.* (*on property*) наруше́ние грани́ц; (*misdemeanour*) просту́пок (-пка); *v.i.* наруша́ть *imp.*, нару́шить *perf.* пра́во владе́ния; *t. on*, (*property*) нарушáть *imp.*, нарýшить *perf.* грани́цу + *gen.*; (*selfishly exploit*) злоупотребля́ть *imp.*, злоупотреби́ть *perf.* + *instr.* **trespasser** *n.* наруши́тель *m.*, ~ница грани́ц.

tress *n.* лóкон, косá (*acc.* кóсу; *pl.* -сы).

trestle *n.* кóзлы (-зел, -злам) *pl.*

trial *n.* (*test*) испытáние (*also ordeal*), прóба; (*leg.*) процéсс, суд (-á); (*sport*) попы́тка; *on t.*, (*probation*) на испытáнии; (*of objects*) взя́тый на прóбу; (*leg.*) под судóм; *t. period*, испытáтельный срок (-а(у)); *t. run*, прóбный пробéг; (*of ship*) прóбное плáвание; (*of plane*) испытáтельный полёт; *t. and error*, мéтод подбóра.

triangle *n.* треугóльник. **triangular** *adj.* треугóльный; (*three-edged*) трёхгрáнный.

tribal *adj.* племеннóй, родовóй. **tribe** *n.* плéмя *neut.*, род (-а(у), *loc.* -ý; *pl.* -ы́). **tribesman** *n.* член плéмени, рóда.

tribulation *n.* гóре, несчáстье.

tribunal *n.* трибунáл; (*court*; *fig.*) суд (-á).

tribune[1] *n.* (*leader*) трибýн.

tribune[2] *n.* (*platform*) трибýна; (*throne*) кáфедра.

tributary *n.* (*geog.*) притóк; (*hist.*) дáнник. **tribute** *n.* дань (*also fig.*); *pay t.*, (*fig.*) отдавáть (-даю́, -даёшь) *imp.*, отдáть (-áм, -áшь, -áст, -ади́м; óтдал, -á, -о) *perf.* дань (уважéния) (to, + *dat.*).

trice *n.*: *in a t.*, мгновéнно.

trick *n.* (*ruse*) хи́трость; (*deception*) обмáн; (*conjuring t.*) фóкус; (*feat, stunt*) трюк; (*joke*) шýтка; (*of trade etc.*) приём; (*habit*) привы́чка; (*cards*) взя́тка; *play a t. on*, игрáть *imp.*, сыгрáть *perf.* шýтку с + *instr.*; *v.t.* обмáнывать *imp.*, обманýть (-нý, -нешь) *perf.* **trickery** *n.* обмáн, надувáтельство (*coll.*).

trickle *v.i.* кáпать *imp.*; сочи́ться *imp.*; *n.* стрýйка.

trickster *n.* обмáнщик, -ица. **tricky** *adj.* (*complicated*) слóжный (-жен, -жнá, -жно); (*crafty*) хи́трый (-тёр, -трá, хи́трó).

tricot *n.* трикó *neut.indecl.*

tricycle *n.* трёхколёсный велосипéд.

trident *n.* трезýбец (-бца).

triennial *adj.* трёхлéтний.

trifle *n.* пустя́к (-á), мéлочь (*pl.* -чи, -чéй); (*dish*) вид слáдкого блю́да; *a t.*, (*adv.*) немнóго + *gen.*; *v.i.* шути́ть (шучý, шýтишь) *imp.*, по~ *perf.* (with, с + *instr.*); относи́ться (-ошýсь, -óсишься) *imp.*, отнести́сь (-есýсь, -есёшься; -ёсся, -еслáсь) *perf.* несерьёзно (with, к + *dat.*). **trifling** *adj.* пустякóвый.

trigger *n.* (*of gun*) курóк (-ркá), спусковóй крючóк (-чкá); (*releasing catch*) защёлка; *v.t.*: *t. off*, вызывáть *imp.*, вы́звать (вы́зову, -вешь) *perf.*

trigonometry *n.* тригономéтрия.

trilby (hat) *n.* мя́гкая фéтровая шля́па.

trill *n.* трель; *v.i.* выводи́ть (-ожý, -óдишь) *imp.*, вы́вести (-еду, -едешь; -ел) *perf.* трель.

trilogy *n.* трилóгия.

trim *n.* поря́док (-дка), готóвность; *in fighting t.*, в боевóй готóвности; *in good t.*, (*sport*) в хорóшей фóрме; (*haircut*) подстри́жка; (*clipping, pruning*) подрéзка; *adj.* (*neat*) аккурáтный, опря́тный; (*smart*) наря́дный; *v.t.* (*cut, clip, cut off*) подрезáть *imp.*, подрéзать (-éжу, -éжешь) *perf.*; (*hair*) подстригáть *imp.*, подстри́чь (-игý, -ижёшь; -и́г) *perf.*; (*square*) обтёсывать *imp.*, обтесáть (-ешý, -éшешь) *perf.*; (*a dress etc.*) отдéлывать *imp.*, отдéлать *perf.*; (*a dish*) украшáть *imp.*, укрáсить *perf.* **trimming** *n.* (*on dress*) отдéлка; (*to food*) гарни́р, приправá.

trimaran *n.* тримарáн.

Trinity *n.* трóица; *T. Sunday*, трóицын день (дня) *m.*

trinket *n.* безделýшка, брелóк.

trio *n.* три́о *neut.indecl.*; (*of people*) трóйка.

trip *n.* поéздка, путешéствие, экскýрсия; (*business t.*) командирóвка; (*stumbling*) спотыкáние; (*sport*) поднóжка; (*light step*) лёгкая похóдка; (*mistake*) оши́бка; (*tech.*) расцепля́ющее устрóйство; *v.i.* (*run lightly*) бéгать *indet.*, бежáть (бегý, бежи́шь) *det.*, по~ *perf.* вприпры́жку; (*stumble*) спотыкáться *imp.*, споткнýться *perf.*

(over, о+*acc.*); (*make a mistake*) ошибáться *imp.*, ошибúться (-бýсь, -бёшься; -бся) *perf.*; *v.t.* подставля́ть *imp.*, подстáвить *perf.* нóжку+*dat.* (*also fig.*); (*confuse*) запýтывать *imp.*, запýтать *perf.*

tripartite *adj.* трёхсторóнний.

tripe *n.* (*dish*) рубéц (-бцá).

triple *adj.* тройнóй; (*tripled*) утрóенный (-ен); *v.t.* & *i.* утрáивать(ся) *imp.*, утрóить(ся) *perf.* **triplet** *n.* (*mus.*) триóль; (*one of triplets*) близнéц (-á) (из трóйни); *pl.* трóйня. **triplicate** *n.*: *in t.*, в трёх экземпля́рах.

tripod *n.* тренóжник.

triptych *n.* трúптих.

trite *adj.* банáльный, избúтый.

triumph *n.* триýмф (*also event*), торжествó, побéда; *v.i.* торжествовáть *imp.*, вос~ *perf.* (over, над+*instr.*). **triumphal** *adj.* триумфáльный. **triumphant** *adj.* (*exultant*) торжествýющий, ликýющий; (*victorious*) победонóсный.

trivia *n.* мéлочи (-чéй) *pl.* **trivial** *adj.* незначúтельный. **triviality** *n.* тривиáльность, банáльность. **trivialize** *v.t.* упрощáть *imp.*, упростúть *perf.*

troglodyte *n.* троглодúт.

troika *n.* трóйка.

Trojan *adj.* троя́нский; *n.*: *work like a T.*, рабóтать *imp.* энергúчно, усéрдно.

troll *n.* (*myth.*) тролль *m.*

trolley *n.* телéжка, вагонéтка; (*table on wheels*) стóлик на колёсиках. **trolleybus** *n.* троллéйбус.

trollop *n.* неря́ха; проститýтка.

trombone *n.* тромбóн.

troop *n.* грýппа, отря́д; *pl.* (*mil.*) войскá *neut.pl.*, солдáты *m.pl.*; *t.-ship*, войсковóй трáнспорт; *v.i.* (*move in a crowd*) двúгаться (-ается & двúжется) *imp.* толпóй. **trooper** *n.* кавалерúст. **trooping the colour**(s) *n.* торжéственный вы́нос знáмени (знамён).

trophy *n.* трофéй; (*prize*) приз (*pl.* -ы́).

tropic *n.* трóпик; *T. of Cancer*, трóпик Рáка; *T. of Capricorn*, трóпик Козерóга. **tropical** *adj.* тропúческий.

trot *n.* рысь (*loc.* -сú); *v.i.* рысúть *imp.*; (*rider*) éздить *indet.*, éхать (éду, éдешь) *det.*, по~ *perf.* ры́сью; (*horse*) ходúть (-дит) *indet.*, идтú (идёт; шёл, шла) *det.*, пойтú (пойдý, -дёшь; пошёл, -шлá) *perf.* ры́сью; *t. out*, (*present for inspection*) представля́ть *imp.*, представить *perf.* на рассмотрéние; (*show off*) щеголя́ть *imp.*, щегольнýть *perf.*+*instr.* **trotter** *n.* (*horse*) рысáк (-á); *pl.* (*dish*) нóжки *f.pl.*

troubadour *n.* трубадýр.

trouble *n.* (*worry*) беспокóйство, тревóга; (*misfortune*) бедá (*pl.* -ды), гóре; (*unpleasantness*) неприя́тности *f.pl.*; (*effort, pains*) хлóпоты (-óт) *pl.*, труд; (*care*) забóта; (*disrepair*) проблéма, неприя́тности *f.pl.* (with, с+*instr.*), неисправность (with, в+*prep.*); (*illness*) болéзнь; *heart t.*, больнóе сéрдце; *t.-maker*, нарушúтель *m.*, ~ница спокóйствия; *t.-shooter*, аварúйный монтёр; *ask for t.*, напрáшиваться *imp.*, напросúться (-ошýсь, -óсишься) *perf.* на неприя́тности; *be in t.*, имéть *imp.* неприя́тности; *cause t. to*, доставля́ть *imp.*, достáвить *perf.* хлóпоты+*dat.*; *get into t.*, попáсть (-адý, -адёшь; -áл) *perf.* в бедý; *make t. for*, причиня́ть *imp.*, причинúть *perf.* неприя́тности+*dat.*; *take t.*, старáться *imp.*, по~ *perf.*; *take the t.*, трудúться (-ужýсь, -ýдишься) *imp.*, по~ *perf.* (to, +*inf.*); *the t. is* (*that*), бедá в том, что; *v.t.* (*make anxious, disturb, give pain*) беспокóить *imp.*; *may I t. you for*, мóжно попросúть у вас+*acc.*; *may I t. you to*, мóжно попросúть вас+*inf.*; *v.i.* (*worry*) беспокóиться *imp.*; (*take the t.*) трудúться (тружýсь, трýдишься) *imp.* **troubled** *adj.* беспокóйный. **troublesome** *adj.* (*restless, fidgety*) беспокóйный; (*capricious*) капрúзный; (*difficult*) трýдный (-ден, -днá, -дно, трýдны́).

trough *n.* (*for food*) кормýшка, коры́то; (*gutter*) жёлоб (*pl.* -á); (*of wave*) подóшва; (*meteorol.*) ложбúна нúзкого давлéния.

trounce *v.t.* (*beat*) бить (бью, бьёшь) *imp.*, по~ *perf.*; (*punish*) сурóво накáзывать *imp.*, наказáть (-ажý,

-а́жешь) *perf.*; (*scold*) суро́во брани́ть *imp.*, вы~ *perf.* (*coll.*).
troupe *n.* тру́ппа.
trouser-leg *n.* штани́на (*coll.*). **trousers** *n.* брю́ки (-к) *pl.*, штаны́ (-но́в) *pl.* **trouser-suit** *n.* брю́чный костю́м.
trousseau *n.* прида́ное *sb.*
trout *n.* форе́ль.
trowel *n.* (*for plastering etc.*) лопа́тка; (*garden t.*) садо́вый сово́к (-вка́).
truancy *n.* прогу́л. **truant** *n.* прогу́льщик, -ица; *play t.*, прогу́ливать *imp.*, прогуля́ть *perf.*; *adj.* пра́здный.
truce *n.* переми́рие; (*respite*) передышка.
truck[1] *n.*: *have no t. with*, избега́ть *imp.*, избежа́ть (-егу́, -ежи́шь) *perf.* +*gen.*
truck[2] *n.* (*lorry*) грузови́к (-а́); (*rly.*) ваго́н-платфо́рма.
truckle *v.i.* раболе́пствовать *imp.* (to, пе́ред+*instr.*).
truculence *n.* свире́пость. **truculent** *adj.* свире́пый.
trudge *n.* утоми́тельная прогу́лка; *v.i.* уста́ло тащи́ться (-щу́сь, -щишься) *imp.*
true *adj.* (*faithful*, *correct*) ве́рный (-рен, -рна́, -рно, ве́рны́); (*correct*) пра́вильный; (*genuine*) по́длинный (-нен, -нна); (*exact*) то́чный (-чен, -чна́, -чно); *t. to life*, реалисти́ческий; *come t.*, сбыва́ться *imp.*, сбы́ться (сбу́дется; сбы́лся, -ла́сь) *perf.*
truffle *n.* трю́фель (*pl.* -ли, -ле́й) *m.*
truism *n.* трюи́зм. **truly** *adv.* (*sincerely*) и́скренне; (*faithfully*) ве́рно; (*really*, *indeed*) действи́тельно, пои́стине; (*accurately*) то́чно; *yours t.*, пре́данный Вам.
trump *n.* ко́зырь (*pl.* -ри, -ре́й) *m.* (*also fig.*); *v.i.* козыря́ть *imp.*, козырну́ть *perf.* (*coll.*); *v.t.* бить (бью, бьёшь) *imp.*, по~ *perf.* ко́зырем; *t. up*, выду́мывать *imp.*, вы́думать *perf.*; фабрикова́ть *imp.*, с~ *perf.*
trumpery *n.* мишура́; (*rubbish*) дрянь (*coll.*).
trumpet *n.* труба́ (*pl.* -бы); *v.i.* труби́ть *imp.* (on, в+*acc.*); (*elephant*) реве́ть (-ву́, -вёшь) *imp.*; *v.t.* (*proclaim*) возвеща́ть *imp.*, возвести́ть *perf.* **trumpeter** *n.* труба́ч (-а́).
truncate *v.t.* усека́ть *imp.*, усе́чь (-еку́, -ечёшь; усе́к, -ла́) *perf.*; (*cut top off*) среза́ть *imp.*, сре́зать (-е́жу, -е́жешь) *perf.* верху́шку+*gen.*; (*abbreviate*) сокраща́ть *imp.*, сократи́ть (-ащу́, -ати́шь) *perf.*
truncheon *n.* (*police*) дуби́нка; (*staff*, *baton*) жезл (-а́).
trundle *v.t.* & *i.* ката́ть(ся) *indet.*, кати́ть(ся) (качу́(сь), ка́тишь(ся)) *det.*, по~ *perf.*
trunk *n.* (*stem*) ствол (-а́); (*anat.*) ту́ловище; (*elephant's*) хо́бот; (*box*) сунду́к (-а́); *pl.* (*swimming*) пла́вки (-вок) *pl.*; (*boxing etc.*) трусы́ (-со́в) *pl.*; *t.-call*, вы́зов по междугоро́дному телефо́ну; *t.-line*, магистра́льная ли́ния; *t.-road*, магистра́льная доро́га.
truss *n.* (*girder*) ба́лка, фе́рма; (*med.*) грыжево́й банда́ж (-а́); (*sheaf*, *bunch*) свя́зка; *v.t.* (*tie* (*up*), *bird*) свя́зывать *imp.*, связа́ть (-яжу́, -я́жешь) *perf.*; (*reinforce*) укрепля́ть *imp.*, укрепи́ть *perf.*
trust *n.* дове́рие, ве́ра; (*body of trustees*) опе́ка; (*property held in t.*) довери́тельная со́бственность; (*econ.*) трест; (*credit*) креди́т; (*responsibility*) отве́тственность; *breach of t.*, злоупотребле́ние дове́рием; *on t.*, (*credit*) в креди́т; *take on t.*, принима́ть *imp.*, приня́ть (приму́, -мешь; при́нял, -а́, -о) *perf.* на ве́ру; *v.t.* доверя́ть *imp.*, дове́рить *perf.* +*dat.* (with, +*acc.*; to, +*inf.*); ве́рить *imp.*, по~ *perf.* +*dat.*, в+*acc.*; (*entrust*) (*object*) поруча́ть *imp.*, поручи́ть (-чу́, -чишь) *perf.* (to, +*dat.*); (*a secret etc.*) вверя́ть *imp.*, вве́рить *perf.* (to, +*dat.*); *v.i.* (*hope*) наде́яться *imp.*, по~ *perf.* **trustee** *n.* попечи́тель *m.*, ~ница, опеку́н, ~ша. **trustful, trusting** *adj.* дове́рчивый. **trustiness** *n.* ве́рность; (*reliability*) надёжность. **trustworthy, trusty** *adj.* надёжный, ве́рный (-рен, -рна́, -рно, ве́рны́).
truth *n.* и́стина, пра́вда; *tell the t.*, говори́ть *imp.*, сказа́ть (скажу́, -жешь) *perf.* пра́вду; *to tell you the t.*, по пра́вде говоря́. **truthful** *adj.* правди́вый.

try *n.* (*attempt*) попы́тка; (*test, trial*) испыта́ние, про́ба; *v.t.* (*taste*; *examine effectiveness of*) про́бовать *imp.*, по~ *perf.*; (*test*) испы́тывать *imp.*, испыта́ть *perf.*; (*leg.*) суди́ть (сужу́, су́дишь) *imp.* (for, за + *acc.*); *v.i.* (*endeavour*) стара́ться *imp.*, по~ *perf.*; (*make an attempt*) пыта́ться *imp.*, по~ *perf.*; *t. on*, (*clothes*) примеря́ть *imp.*, приме́рить *perf.* **trying** *adj.* тяжёлый (-л, -ла́); (*tiresome*) доку́чливый (*coll.*).

tsar *n.* царь (-ря́) *m.* **tsarina** *n.* цари́ца.

tub *n.* ка́дка, лоха́нь.

tuba *n.* ту́ба.

tubby *adj.* то́лстенький.

tube *n.* тру́бка, труба́ (*pl.* -бы); (*toothpaste etc.*) тю́бик; (*underground*) метро́ *neut.indecl.*; *cathode-ray t.*, электроннолучева́я тру́бка; *inner t.*, ка́мера.

tuber *n.* клу́бень (-бня) *m.* **tubercular** *adj.* туберкулёзный. **tuberculosis** *n.* туберкулёз. **tuberose** *n.* тубero´за.

tubing *n.* тру́бы *m.pl.*; (*pipe-line*) трубопрово́д. **tubular** *adj.* тру́бчатый.

tuck *n.* (*in garment*) скла́дка; *v.t.* (*make tucks in*) де́лать *imp.*, с~ *perf.* скла́дки на + *loc.*; (*thrust into, t. away*) засо́вывать *imp.*, засу́нуть *perf.*; (*hide away*) пря́тать (-я́чу, -я́чешь) *imp.*, с~ *perf.*; *t. in*, (*shirt etc.*) заправля́ть *imp.*, запра́вить *perf.*; *t. in, up*, (*blanket, skirt*) подтыка́ть *imp.*, подоткну́ть *perf.*; *t. up*, (*sleeves*) засу́чивать *imp.*, засучи́ть (-чу́, -чишь) *perf.*; (*in bed*) укрыва́ть *imp.*, укры́ть (-ро́ю, -ро́ешь) *perf.*; (*hair etc. out of the way*) подбира́ть *imp.*, подобра́ть (подберу́, -рёшь; подобра́л, -а́, -о) *perf.*

Tuesday *n.* вто́рник.

tuft *n.* пучо́к (-чка́). **tufted** *adj.* с хохолко́м.

tug *v.t.* (*sharply*) дёргать *imp.*, дёрнуть *perf.*; (*pull*) тяну́ть (-ну́, -нешь) *imp.*, по~ *perf.*; (*tow*) букси́ровать *imp.*; *n.* рыво́к (-вка́); (*tugboat*) букси́рное су́дно (*pl.* -да́, -до́в); *t. of war*, перетя́гивание на кана́те.

tuition *n.* обуче́ние (in, + *dat.*).

tulip *n.* тюльпа́н.

tulle *n.* тюль *m.*

tumble *v.i.* (*fall*) па́дать *imp.*, (у)па́сть ((у)паду́, -дёшь; (у)па́л) *perf.*; (*go head over heels*) кувырка́ться *imp.*, кувыркну́ться *perf.*; (*rush headlong*) броса́ться *imp.*, бро́ситься *perf.*; *v.t.* (*disarrange*) приводи́ть (-ожу́, -о́дишь) *imp.*, привести́ (-еду́, -едёшь; -ёл, -ела́) *perf.* в беспоря́док; *n.* паде́ние; кувырка́нье. **tumbledown** *adj.* полуразру́шенный (-ен), развали́вшийся. **tumbler** *n.* (*acrobat*) акроба́т; (*glass*) стака́н; (*pigeon*) ту́рман.

tumour *n.* о́пухоль.

tumult *n.* (*uproar*) сумато́ха, шум (-а(у)); (*agitation*) волне́ние. **tumultuous** *adj.* шу́мный (-мен, -мна́, -мно).

tumulus *n.* курга́н, моги́льный холм (-а́).

tun *n.* больша́я бо́чка.

tuna *n.* туне́ц (-нца́).

tundra *n.* ту́ндра.

tune *n.* мело́дия, моти́в; *in t.*, в тон, (*of instrument*) настро́енный (-ен); *out of t.*, не в тон, фальши́вый, (*of instrument*) расстро́енный (-ен); *be in t. with*, (*fig.*) гармони́ровать *imp.* с + *instr.*; *be out of t. with*, (*fig.*) (*thing*) идти́ (иду́, идёшь; шёл, шла) *imp.* вразре́з с + *instr.*; (*person*) быть не в ладу́ с + *instr.*; *call the t.*, распоряжа́ться *imp.*; *change one's t.*, (пере)меня́ть *imp.*, перемени́ть (-ню́, -нишь) *perf.* тон; *v.t.* (*instrument*; *radio*) настра́ивать *imp.*, настро́ить *perf.*; (*engine etc.*) регули́ровать *imp.*, от~ *perf.*; (*fig.*) приспособля́ть *imp.*, приспосо́бить *perf.*; *t. in*, настра́ивать *imp.*, настро́ить (*radio*) ра́дио (to, на + *acc.*); *v.i.*: *t. up*, настра́ивать *imp.*, настро́ить *perf.* инструме́нт(ы). **tuneful** *adj.* мелоди́чный, гармони́чный. **tuneless** *adj.* немелоди́чный. **tuner** *n.* настро́йщик.

tungsten *n.* вольфра́м.

tunic *n.* туни́ка; (*of uniform*) ки́тель (*pl.* -ля́ & -ли) *m.*

tuning *n.* настро́йка; (*of engine*) регулиро́вка; *t.-fork*, камерто́н.

tunnel *n.* тунне́ль *m.*; *v.i.* прокла́дывать *imp.*, проложи́ть (-жу́, -жишь) *perf.* тунне́ль *m.*

tunny *n.* туне́ц (-нца́).

turban *n.* тюрбáн, чалмá.
turbid *adj.* мýтный (-тен, -тнá, -тно); (*fig.*) тумáнный (-нен, -нна).
turbine *n.* турбúна. **turbo-jet** *adj.* (*n.*) турбореактúвный (самолёт). **turbo-prop** *adj.* (*n.*) турбовинтовóй (самолёт).
turbot *n.* тюрбó *neut.indecl.*
turbulence *n.* бýйность, бýрность; (*tech.*) турбулéнтность. **turbulent** *adj.* бýйный (бýен, буйнá, -но), бýрный (-рен, бýрнá, -но); (*tech.*) турбулéнтный.
tureen *n.* сýпник, сýпница.
turf *n.* дёрн; *the t.*, (*track*) беговáя дорóжка; (*races*) скáчки *f.pl.*; *v.t.* дерновáть *imp.*
turgid *adj.* (*swollen*) опýхший; (*pompous*) напы́щенный (-ен, -енна).
Turk *n.* тýрок (-рка), турчáнка.
turkey *n.* индюк (-á), -ю́шка; (*dish*) индéйка.
Turkic *adj.* тю́ркский. **Turkish** *adj.* турéцкий; *T. bath*, турéцкие бáни *f.pl.*; *T. delight*, рахáт-лукýм. **Turkoman, Turkmen** *n.* туркмéн, ~ка; *adj.* туркмéнский.
turmoil *n.* (*disorder*) беспорядок (-дка); (*uproar*) суматóха, шум (-а(у)).
turn *n.* (*change of direction*) поворóт; (*revolution*) оборóт; (*service*) услýга; (*change*) изменéние; (*one's t. to do s.th.*) óчередь; (*character*) склад харáктера; (*circus, variety*) нóмер (*pl.* -á); *t. of phrase*, оборóт рéчи; *at every t.*, на кáждом шагý; *by, in turn(s)*, по óчереди; *to a t.*, как раз в мéру; *take a bad t.*, принимáть *imp.*, принять (примý, -мешь; прúнял, -á, -о) *perf.* дурнóй оборóт; *take a t. for the worse*, изменяться *imp.*, измениться (-нюсь, -нишься) *perf.* к хýдшему; *v.t.* (*handle, key, car around etc.*) поворáчивать *imp.*, повернýть *perf.*; (*revolve, rotate*) вращáть *imp.*, (*spin, twirl*) вертéть (-рчý, -ртишь) *imp.* + *acc.*, *instr.*; (*page; on its face*) перевёртывать *imp.*, перевернýть *perf.*; (*direct*) направлять *imp.*, напрáвить *perf.*; (*cause to become*) дéлать *imp.*, с~ *perf.* + *instr.*; (*on lathe*) точúть (-чý, -чишь) *imp.*; *t. s.b.'s head*, кружúть (кружý, крýжишь) *imp.*, вс~ *perf.* гóлову + *dat.*; *t. one's stomach*: *that turns my stomach*, меня от этого тошнúт; *v.i.* (*change direction*) поворáчивать *imp.*, повернýть *perf.*; завёртывать *imp.*, завернýть *perf.*; (*rotate*) вращáться *imp.*; (*t. round*) поворáчиваться *imp.*, повернýться *perf.*; (*become*) становúться (-влю́сь, -вишься) *imp.*, стать (стáну, -нешь) *perf.*) + *instr.*; *t. against*, ополчáться *imp.*, ополчúться *perf.* на + *acc.*, прóтив + *gen.*; *t. around*, *see t. round*; *t. away*, (*v.t. & i.*) отворáчивать(ся) *imp.*, отвернýть(ся) *perf.*; *t. back*, (*v.i.*) поворáчивать *imp.*, повернýть *perf.* назáд; (*v.t.*) (*bend back*) отгибáть *imp.*, отогнýть *perf.*; *t. down*, (*refuse*) отклонять *imp.*, отклонúть (-ню́, -нишь) *perf.*; (*collar*) отгибáть *imp.*, отогнýть *perf.*; (*make quieter*) дéлать *imp.*, с~ *perf.* тúше; *t. grey*, (*v.i.*) седéть *imp.*, по~ *perf.*; *t. in*, (*v.t.*) (*hand back*) возвращáть *imp.*, вернýть *perf.*; (*so as to face inwards*) поворáчивать *imp.*, повернýть *perf.* вовнýтрь; *t. inside out*, выворáчивать *imp.*, вы́вернуть *perf.* наизнáнку; *t. into*, (*change into*) (*v.t. & i.*) превращáть(ся) *imp.*, превратúть(ся) (-ащý(сь), -атúшь(ся)) *perf.* в + *acc.*; (*street*) сворáчивать *imp.*, свернýть *perf.* на + *acc.*; *t. off*, (*light, radio, etc.*) выключáть *imp.*, вы́ключить *perf.*; (*tap*) закрывáть *imp.*, закры́ть (-рóю, -рóешь) *perf.*; (*branch off*) сворáчивать *imp.*, свернýть *perf.*; *t. on*, (*light, radio, etc.*) включáть *imp.*, включúть *perf.*; (*tap*) открывáть *imp.*, откры́ть (-рóю, -рóешь) *perf.*; (*attack*) нападáть *imp.*, напáсть (-адý, -адёшь; -ал) *perf.*; *t. out*, (*light etc.*) *see t. off*; (*prove to be*) окáзываться *imp.*, оказáться (-ажýсь, -áжешься) *perf.* (to be, + *instr.*); (*drive out*) выгонять *imp.*, вы́гнать (вы́гоню, -нишь) *perf.*; (*pockets*) вывёртывать *imp.*, вы́вернуть *perf.*; (*be present*) приходúть (-ожý, -óдишь) *imp.*, прийтú (придý, -дёшь; пришёл, -шлá) *perf.*; (*product*) выпускáть *imp.*, вы́пустить *perf.*; *t. over*, (*egg, page, on its face, roll over*)

(*v.t.* & *i.*) перевёртывать(ся) *imp.*, перевернýть(ся) *perf.*; (*hand over*) передавáть (-даю́, -даёшь) *imp.*, передáть (-áм, -áшь, -áст, -ади́м; пéредал, -á, -о) *perf.*; (*think about*) обдýмывать *imp.*, обдýмать *perf.*; (*overturn*) (*v.t.* & *i.*) опроки́дывать(ся) *imp.*, опроки́нуть(ся) *perf.*; (*switch over*) переключáть *imp.*, переключи́ть *perf.* (to, на + *acc.*); *t. pale*, бледнéть *imp.*, по ~ *perf.*; *t. red*, краснéть *imp.*, по ~ *perf.*; *t. round*, (*v.i.*) (*rotate*; *t. one's back*; *t. to face s.th.*) повёртываться *imp.*, повернýться *perf.*; (*t. to face*) оборáчиваться *imp.*, обернýться *perf.*; (*v.t.*) повёртывать *imp.*, повернýть *perf.*; *t. sour*, скисáть *imp.*, ски́снуть (скис) *perf.*; *t. to*, обращáться *imp.*, обрати́ться (-ащýсь, -ати́шься) *perf.* к + *dat.* (for, за + *instr.*); *t. up*, (*appear*) появля́ться *imp.*, появи́ться (-влю́сь, -вишься) *perf.*; (*be found*) находи́ться (-ожýсь, -óдишься) *imp.*, найти́сь (-йдýсь, -йдёшься; нашёлся, -шлáсь) *perf.*; (*shorten garment*) подшивáть *imp.*, подши́ть (-шью́, -шьёшь) *perf.*; (*crop up*) подвёртываться *imp.*, подвернýться *perf.*; (*bend up*; *stick up*) (*v.t.* & *i.*) загибáть(ся) *imp.*, загнýть(ся) *perf.*; (*make louder*) дéлать *imp.*, с ~ *perf.* грóмче; *t. up one's nose*, вороти́ть (-очý, -óтишь) *imp.* нос (at, от + *gen.*) (*coll.*); *t. upside down*, переворáчивать *imp.*, перевернýть *perf.* вверх дном. **turn-out** *n.* (*people*) коли́чество приходя́щих; (*goods*) вы́пуск. **turn-up** *n.* (*on trousers etc.*) отворóт, обшлáг (-á; *pl.* -á).

turncoat *n.* ренегáт, перебéжчик.

turner *n.* тóкарь (*pl.* -ри & -ря́) *m.*

turning *n.* (*road*) поворóт; *t.-point*, поворóтный пункт.

turnip *n.* рéпа.

turnover *n.* (*turning over*) опроки́дывание; (*econ.*) оборóт; (*fluctuation of manpower*) текýчесть рабóчей си́лы; (*pie*) полукрýглый пирóг (-á) с начи́нкой.

turnpike *n.* (*toll-gate*) застáва (где взимáется подорóжный сбор).

turnstile *n.* турникéт.

turntable *n.* (*rly.*) поворóтный круг (*loc.* -е & -ý; *pl.* -и́); (*gramophone*) диск.

turpentine *n.* скипидáр.

turpitude *n.* ни́зость, порóчность.

turquoise *n.* (*material*, *stone*) бирюзá; *adj.* бирюзóвый.

turret *n.* бáшенка; (*gun t.*) оруди́йная бáшня.

turtle *n.* черепáха.

turtle-dove *n.* гóрлица.

tusk *n.* би́вень (-вня) *m.*, клык (-á).

tussle *n.* дрáка; *v.i.* дрáться (дерýсь, -рёшься; дрáлся, -лáсь, дрáлóсь) *imp.* (for, за + *acc.*).

tut *interj.* ах ты!

tutelage *n.* (*guardianship*) опекýнство; (*instruction*) обучéние. **tutelar(y)** *adj.* опекýнский. **tutor** *n.* (*private teacher*) чáстный домáшний учи́тель (*pl.* -ля́) *m.*, ~ ница; (*coach*) репети́тор; (*univ.*) руководи́тель *m.*, ~ ница; (*primer*) учéбник; (*mus. primer*) шкóла игры́; *v.t.* (*instruct*) обучáть *imp.*, обучи́ть (-чý, -чишь) *perf.* (in, + *dat.*); (*give lessons to*) давáть (даю́, даёшь) *imp.*, дать (дам, дашь, даст, дади́м; дал, -á, дáлó, -и) *perf.* урóки + *dat.*; (*guide*) руководи́ть *imp.* + *instr.* **tutorial** *n.* консультáция, встрéча с руководи́телем.

tutu *n.* (*ballet*) пáчка.

twaddle *n.* пустáя болтовня́, чепухá.

twang *n.* (*string*) рéзкий звук (натя́нутой струны́); (*voice*) гнусáвость; *v.i.* (*string*) звучáть (-чý, -чи́шь) *imp.*, про ~ *perf.*; (*voice*) гнусáвить; *v.t.* (*pluck*) перебирáть *imp.*

tweak *n.* щипóк (-пкá); *v.t.* щипáть (-плю́, -плешь) *imp.*, (у)щипнýть *perf.*

tweed *n.* твид.

tweet *n.* щéбет; *v.i.* щебетáть (-ечý, -éчешь) *imp.*

tweezers *n.* пинцéт.

twelfth *adj.*, *n.* двенáдцатый; (*date*) двенáдцатое (числó); *T.-night*, канýн крещéния. **twelve** *adj.*, *n.* двенáдцать (-ти, -тью); (*time*) двенáдцать (часóв); (*age*) двенáдцать лет.

twentieth *adj.*, *n.* двадцáтый; (*date*) двадцáтое (числó). **twenty** *adj.*, *n.* двáдцать (-ти́, -тью́); (*age*) двáдцать лет; *pl.* (*decade*) двадцáтые гóды (-дóв) *m.pl.*

twice *adv.* (*2 times, on 2 occasions*) два́жды; *t. as*, вдвое, в два ра́за + *comp.*

twiddle *v.t.* (*turn, twirl*) верте́ть (-рчу́, -ртишь) *imp.*, + *acc.*, *instr.*; (*toy with*) игра́ть *imp.* + *instr.*; *t. one's thumbs*, (*fig.*) безде́льничать *imp.*

twig *n.* ве́точка, прут (пру́та́; *pl.* -тья, -тьев).

twilight *n.* су́мерки (-рек) *pl.*; (*decline*) упа́док (-дка). **twilit** *adj.* су́меречный.

twill *n.* твил, са́ржа.

twin *n.* близне́ц (-а́); *pl.* (*Gemini*) Близнецы́ *m.pl.*; *t. beds*, па́ра односпа́льных крова́тей; *t. brother*, брат (*pl.* -ья, -ьев) -близне́ц (-а́); *t.-engined*, двухмото́рный; *t. town*, го́род (*pl.* -а́) -побрати́м; *v.t.* (*unite*) соединя́ть *imp.*, соедини́ть *perf.*

twine *n.* бечёвка, шпага́т; *v.t.* (*twist, weave*) вить (вью, вьёшь; вил, -а́, -о) *imp.*, с~ *perf.*; *v.t.* & *i.* (*t. round*) обвива́ть(ся) *imp.*, обви́ть(ся) (обовью́(сь), -ьёшь(ся); обви́л(ся), -ла́(сь), -ло(сь)) *perf.*

twinge *n.* при́ступ (бо́ли), о́страя боль; (*of conscience*) угрызе́ние.

twinkle *n.* мерца́ние; (*of eyes*) огонёк (-нька́); *v.i.* мерца́ть *imp.*, сверка́ть *imp.* **twinkling** *n.* мерца́ние; *in the t. of an eye*, в мгнове́ние о́ка.

twirl *n.* враще́ние, круче́ние; (*flourish*) ро́счерк; *v.t.* & *i.* (*twist, turn*) верте́ть(ся) (-рчу́(сь), -ртишь(ся)) *imp.*; (*whirl, spin*) кружи́ть(ся) (-жу́(сь), кру́жи́шь(ся)) *imp.*

twist *n.* (*bend*) изги́б, поворо́т; (*twisting*) круче́ние; (*distortion*) искаже́ние; (*sprain*) вы́вих; (*dance*) твист; (*characteristic*) характе́рная осо́бенность; (*in story*) поворо́т фа́булы; *v.t.* скру́чивать *imp.*, крути́ть (-учу́, -у́тишь) *imp.*, с~ *perf.*; (*wind together*) вить (вью, вьёшь; вил, -а́, -о) *imp.*, с~ *perf.*; (*distort*) искажа́ть *imp.*, искази́ть *perf.*; (*sprain*) выви́хивать *imp.*, вы́вихнуть *perf.*; *v.i.* (*bend, curve*) изгиба́ться *imp.*, изогну́ться *perf.*; (*climb, meander, twine*) ви́ться (вьётся) *imp.* **twisted** *adj.* (*bent, distorted*) искривлённый (-ён, -ена́) (*also fig.*). **twister** *n.* обма́нщик, -ица.

twit *v.t.* упрека́ть *imp.*, упрекну́ть *perf.* (with, в + *prep.*).

twitch *n.* (*twitching, jerk*) подёргивание; (*spasm*) су́дорога; *v.t.* & *i.* дёргать(ся) *imp.*, дёрнуть(ся) *perf.* (at, за + *acc.*).

twitter *n.* ще́бет; *v.i.* щебета́ть (-ечу́, -е́чешь) *imp.*, чири́кать *imp.*

two *adj.*, *n.* два, две (*f.*) (двух, -ум, -умя́, -ух); (*collect.*; *2 pairs*) дво́е (-ои́х); (*cards, number 2*) дво́йка; (*time*) два (часа́); (*age*) два го́да; *t. times*, два́жды; *t. times four*, два́жды четы́ре; *in t.*, (*in half*) на́двое, попола́м; *t.-edged*, обоюдоо́стрый (*also fig.*); (*ambiguous*) двусмы́сленный (-ен, -енна); *t.-ply*, (*wood*) двухсло́йный; (*rope*) двойно́й; *t.-seater*, двухме́стный (автомоби́ль); *t.-stroke*, двухта́ктный; *t.-way*, двусторо́нний. **twofold** *adj.* двойно́й; *adv.* вдвойне́. **twosome** *n.* па́ра, дво́йка.

tycoon *n.* магна́т.

tympanum *n.* (*anat.*) бараба́нная перепо́нка.

type *n.* (*var. senses*) тип; (*model*) типи́чный образе́ц (-зца́); (*sort, kind*) род (*pl.* -ы́); (*letter*) ли́тера; (*collect.*) шрифт (*pl.* -ы́); *true to t.*, типи́чный; *v.t.* писа́ть (пишу́, -шешь) *imp.*, на~ *perf.* на маши́нке. **typescript** *n.* маши́нопись. **typewriter** *n.* пи́шущая маши́нка. **typewritten** *adj.* машинопи́сный.

typhoid fever *n.* брюшно́й тиф.

typhoon *n.* тайфу́н.

typhus *n.* сыпно́й тиф.

typical *adj.* типи́чный. **typify** *v.t.* служи́ть (-жу́, -жишь) *imp.*, по~ *perf.* типи́чным приме́ром + *gen.*; (*personify*) олицетворя́ть *imp.*, олицетвори́ть *perf.*

typist *n.* машини́стка.

typographical *adj.* типогра́фский, книгопеча́тный. **typography** *n.* книгопеча́тание; (*style*) оформле́ние.

tyrannical *adj.* тирани́ческий, деспоти́чный. **tyrannize** *v.i.* (*t.*) тира́нствовать *imp.* (над + *instr.*). **tyrant** *n.* тира́н, де́спот.

tyre *n.* ши́на; *t.-gauge*, мано́метр для шин.

U

U-boat *n.* неме́цкая подво́дная ло́дка; *U-tube*, U-обра́зная тру́бка; *U-turn*, разворо́т.
ubiquitous *adj.* вездесу́щий; (*universal*) повсеме́стный. **ubiquity** *n.* вездесу́щность; повсеме́стность.
udder *n.* вы́мя *neut*.
U.F.O. *abbr.* НЛО (неопо́знанный лета́ющий объе́кт); (*flying saucer*) лета́ющая таре́лка.
ugh *interj.* тьфу!
ugliness *n.* уро́дство. **ugly** *adj.* некраси́вый, уро́дливый, безобра́зный; (*unpleasant*) неприя́тный; (*repulsive*) проти́вный; *u. duckling*, (*fig.*) га́дкий утёнок (-нка; *pl.* утя́та, -т).
Ukrainian *n.* украи́нец (-нца), -нка; *adj.* украи́нский.
ukulele *n.* гава́йская гита́ра.
ulcer *n.* я́зва. **ulcerate** *v.t.* & *i.* изъязвля́ть(ся) *imp.*, изъязви́ть(ся) *perf.* **ulcered, ulcerous** *adj.* изъязвлённый.
ulna *n.* локтева́я кость (*pl.* -ти, -те́й).
ulterior *adj.* скры́тый.
ultimate *adj.* (*final*) после́дний, оконча́тельный; (*fundamental*) основно́й. **ultimately** *adv.* в коне́чном счёте, в конце́ концо́в. **ultimatum** *n.* ультима́тум.
ultra- *in comb.* ультра-, сверх-.
ultramarine *n.* ультрамари́н; *adj.* ультрамари́новый. **ultra-violet** *adj.* ультрафиоле́товый.
umber *n.* у́мбра; *adj.* тёмно-кори́чневый.
umbilical *adj.* пупо́чный; *u. cord* пупови́на.
umbra *n.* по́лная тень (*loc.* -ни́; *pl.* -ни, -не́й). **umbrage** *n.* оби́да; *take u.*, обижа́ться *imp.*, оби́деться (оби́жусь, -и́дишься) *perf.* (at, на + *acc.*).
umbrella *n.* зо́нтик, зонт (-а́); *u. stand*, подста́вка для зонто́в.
umpire *n.* судья́ (*pl.* -дьи, -де́й, -дьям) *m.*; *v.t.* & *i.* суди́ть (сужу́, су́дишь) *imp.*
unabashed *adj.* нерастеря́вшийся; без вся́кого смуще́ния. **unabated** *adj.* неосла́бленный, неосла́бный. **unable** *adj.*: *be u. to*, не мочь (могу́, мо́жешь; мог, -ла́) *imp.*, с~ *perf.*; быть не в состоя́нии; (*not know how to*) не уме́ть *imp.*, с~ *perf.* **unabridged** *adj.* несокращённый, без сокраще́ний.
unaccompanied *adj.* несопровожда́емый; (*mus.*) без аккомпанеме́нта.
unaccountable *adj.* (*inexplicable*) необъясни́мый. **unaccustomed** *adj.* (*not accustomed*) непривы́кший (to, к + *dat.*); (*unusual*) непривы́чный. **unadulterated** *adj.* настоя́щий, нефальсифици́рованный; чисте́йший. **unaffected** *adj.* и́скренний (-нен, -нна, -нне & -нно); (*not affected*) незатро́нутый. **unaided** *adj.* без по́мощи, самостоя́тельный. **unalloyed** *adj.* беспри́месный, чи́стый (чист, -а́, -о, чи́сты́). **unalterable** *adj.* неизменя́емый, неизме́нный (-нен, -нна).
unambiguous *adj.* недвусмы́сленный (-ен, -енна). **unanimity** *n.* единоду́шие.
unanimous *adj.* единоду́шный. **unanswerable** *adj.* (*irrefutable*) неопровержи́мый. **unapproachable** *adj.* непристу́пный; (*unmatched*) несравни́мый.
unarmed *adj.* безору́жный, невооружённый. **unashamed** *adj.* бессо́вестный, на́глый (нагл, -а́, -о). **unasked** *adj.* доброво́льный, непро́шеный (*coll.*). **unassailable** *adj.* непристу́пный; (*irrefutable*) неопровержи́мый. **unassuming** *adj.* скро́мный (-мен, -мна́, -мно), непритяза́тельный. **unattainable** *adj.* недосяга́емый. **unattended** *adj.* (*unaccompanied*) несопровожда́емый. **unattractive** *adj.* непривлека́тельный. **unauthorized** *adj.* неразрешённый; (*person*) неправомо́чный. **unavailable** *adj.* не име́ющийся в нали́чии, недосту́пный; *be u.*, в нали́чии нет + *gen.* **unavailing** *adj.* бесполе́зный, тще́тный. **unavoidable** *adj.* неизбе́жный, немину́емый. **unaware** *predic.*: *be u. of*, не сознава́ть (-аю́, -аёшь) *imp.* + *acc.*; не знать *imp.* о + *prep.* **unawares** *adv.* врасплóх, неожи́данно; (*unintentionally*) нечáянно.
unbalance *v.t.* (*psych.*) лиша́ть *imp.*,

лиши́ть *perf.* душе́вного равнове́сия. **unbalanced** *adj.* (*psych.*) неуравнове́шенный (-ен, -енна). **unbearable** *adj.* невыноси́мый. **unbeatable** *adj.* (*unsurpassable*) не могу́щий быть превзойдённым; (*invincible*) непобеди́мый. **unbeaten** *adj.* (*unsurpassed*) непревзойдённый (-ён, -ённа). **unbecoming** *adj.* (*inappropriate*) неподходя́щий; (*unseemly*) неприли́чный; *be u.*, быть не к лицу́ (to, +*dat.*). **unbelief** *n.* неве́рие. **unbelievable** *adj.* невероя́тный. **unbeliever** *n.* неве́рующий *sb.* **unbend** *v.t.* & *i.* (*straighten*) выпрямля́ть(ся) *imp.*, вы́прямиться *perf.*; разгиба́ть(ся) *imp.*, разогну́ть(ся) *perf.*; *v.i.* (*become affable*) станови́ться (-влю́сь, -вишься) *imp.*, стать (-а́ну, -а́нешь) *perf.* приве́тливым. **unbending** *adj.* непреклóнный (-нен, -нна). **unbias(s)ed** *adj.* беспристра́стный. **unblemished** *adj.* незапя́тнанный. **unblushing** *adj.* беззасте́нчивый. **unbolt** *v.t.* отпира́ть *imp.*, отпере́ть (отопру́, -рёшь; о́тпер, -ла́, -ло) *perf.* **unborn** *adj.* ещё не рождённый (-ён, -ена́). **unbosom** *v.t.*: *u. oneself*, открыва́ть *imp.*, откры́ть (-ро́ю, -ро́ешь) *perf.* ду́шу. **unbound** *adj.* (*free*) свобо́дный; (*book*) непереплетённый. **unbounded** *adj.* (*not limited*) неограни́ченный (-ен, -енна); (*joy*) безме́рный; (*infinite*) безграни́чный. **unbreakable** *adj.* небью́щийся. **unbridled** *adj.* разну́зданный (-ан, -анна). **unbroken** *adj.* (*intact*) неразби́тый, це́лый; (*continuous*) непреры́вный; (*unsurpassed*) непоби́тый; (*horse*) необъе́зженный. **unbuckle** *v.t.* расстёгивать *imp.*, расстегну́ть *perf.* **unburden** *v.t.*: *u. oneself*, отводи́ть (-ожу́, -о́дишь) *imp.*, отвести́ (-еду́, -едёшь; -ёл, -ела́) *perf.* ду́шу. **unbutton** *v.t.* расстёгивать *imp.*, расстегну́ть *perf.*

uncalled-for *adj.* неуме́стный. **uncanny** *adj.* жу́ткий (-ток, -тка́, -тко), сверхъесте́ственный (-ен, -енна). **uncared-for** *adj.* забро́шенный. **unceasing** *adj.* непреры́вный, безостано́вочный. **unceremonious** *adj.* бесцеремо́нный (-нен, -нна). **uncertain** *adj.* (*not certainly known*) то́чно неизве́стный, нея́сный (-сен, -сна́, -сно); (*indecisive, hesitating*) неуве́ренный (-ен, -енна); (*lacking belief, confidence*) неуве́ренный (-ен, -ена); (*indeterminate*) неопределённый (-нен, -нна); (*changeable*) изме́нчивый; *be u.*, (*not know for certain*) то́чно не знать *imp.*; *in no u. terms*, в недвусмы́сленных выраже́ниях. **uncertainty** *n.* неизве́стность; неуве́ренность; неопределённость; изме́нчивость. **unchain** *v.t.* спуска́ть *imp.* спусти́ть (-ущу́, -у́стишь) *perf.* с це́пи. **unchallenged** *adj.* не вызыва́ющий возраже́ний. **unchangeable** *adj.* неизмени́мый, неизменя́емый. **unchanged** *adj.* неизмени́вшийся. **unchanging** *adj.* неизменя́ющийся. **uncharacteristic** *adj.* нетипи́чный, нехаракте́рный. **uncharitable** *adj.* немилосе́рдный, жесто́кий (-о́к, -о́ка́, -о́ко). **uncharted** *adj.* (*fig.*) неиссле́дованный. **unchecked** *adj.* (*unrestrained*) необу́зданный (-ан, -анна). **uncivil** *adj.* неве́жливый. **uncivilized** *adj.* нецивилизо́ванный. **unclaimed** *adj.* невостре́бованный. **unclassified** *adj.* неклассифици́рованный; (*not secret*) несекре́тный.

uncle *n.* дя́дя (*pl.* -ди, -дей & -дья́, -дьёв) *m.*

unclean *adj.* (*not clean*; *Bibl. of food*) нечи́стый (-т, -та́, -то). **unclear** *adj.* нея́сный (-сен, -сна́, -сно), непоня́тный. **uncoil** *v.t.* & *i.* разма́тывать(ся) *imp.*, размота́ть(ся) *perf.* **uncomfortable** *adj.* неудо́бный; (*awkward*) нело́вкий (-вок, -вка́, -вко). **uncommon** *adj.* (*unusual, remarkable*) необыкнове́нный (-нен, -нна), замеча́тельный; (*rare*) ре́дкий (-док, -дка́, -дко). **uncommunicative** *adj.* необщи́тельный, молчали́вый. **uncomplaining** *adj.* безро́потный. **uncompleted** *adj.* неоко́нченный, незако́нченный. **uncomplimentary** *adj.* нелéстный. **uncompromising** *adj.* не иду́щий на компроми́ссы; (*inflexible*) непреклóнный (-нен, -нна). **unconcealed** *adj.* нескрыва́емый. **unconcern** *n.* (*freedom from anxiety*) беззабо́тность; (*indifference*) равноду́шие. **unconcerned** *adj.* беззабо́тный; равноду́шный. **unconditional**

adj. безоговóрочный, безуслóвный. **unconfirmed** *adj.* неподтверждённый. **unconnected** *adj.*: *u. with*, не свя́занный (-ан) с + *instr.* **unconquerable** *adj.* непобеди́мый. **unconscionable** *adj.* бессóвестный; (*excessive*) неумéренный (-ен, -енна). **unconscious** *adj.* (*also unintentional*) бессознáтельный; (*predic.*) без сознáния; (*unintentional*) невóльный; *be u. of*, не сознавáть (-аю́, -аёшь) *imp.* + *gen.*; *n.* подсознáтельное *sb.* **unconsciousness** *n.* бессознáтельное состоя́ние; бессознáтельность. **unconstitutional** *adj.* неконституциóнный (-нен, -нна). **unconstrained** *adj.* непринуждённый (-ён, -ённа). **uncontrollable** *adj.* неудержи́мый, неукроти́мый. **uncontrolled** *adj.* (*unbridled*) необу́зданный (-ан, -анна). **unconventional** *adj.* чу́ждый (-д, -дá, -до) услóвности; необы́чный. **unconvincing** *adj.* неубеди́тельный. **uncooked** *adj.* сырóй (-р, -рá, -ро). **unco-operative** *adj.* неотзы́вчивый, безучáстный. **uncork** *v.t.* откýпоривать *imp.*, откýпорить *perf.* **uncouple** *v.t.* расцепля́ть *imp.*, расцепи́ть (-плю́, -пишь) *perf.* **uncouth** *adj.* грýбый (-б, -бá, -бо). **uncover** *v.t.* (*remove cover from*) снимáть *imp.*, снять (сниму́, -мешь; снял, -á, -о) *perf.* кры́шку с + *gen.*; (*reveal*) открывáть *imp.*, откры́ть (-рóю, -рóешь) *perf.*; (*disclose*) обнарýживать *imp.*, обнарýжить *perf.* **uncovered** *adj.* незакры́тый, откры́тый. **uncritical** *adj.* некрити́чный.

unction *n.* (*ceremony*) помáзание; (*process*) втирáние мáзи; (*ointment*) мазь; (*balm*) елéй; (*piety*) нáбожность; (*affectedness*) елéйность; *extreme u.*, собóрование. **unctuous** *adj.* елéйный.

uncultivated *adj.* (*land*) невозделанный; (*talent*) неразвитóй (нерáзвит, -á, -о); (*uncultured*) некультýрный. **uncultured** *adj.* некультýрный. **uncurl** *v.t.* & *i.* развивáть(ся) *imp.*, разви́ть(ся) (разовью́, -ьёт(ся); разви́л(ся), -лá(сь), разви́лó(сь)) *perf.* **uncut** *adj.* (*unabridged*) несокращённый, без сокращéний.

undamaged *adj.* неповреждённый, неиспóрченный. **undaunted** *adj.* бесстрáшный. **undeceive** *v.t.* выводи́ть (-ожу́, -óдишь) *imp.*, вы́вести (-еду, -едешь; -ел) *perf.* из заблуждéния. **undecided** *adj.* (*not settled*) нерешённый; (*irresolute*) нереши́тельный. **undemanding** *adj.* нетрéбовательный. **undemocratic** *adj.* недемократи́ческий, антидемократи́ческий.. **undemonstrative** *adj.* сдéржанный (-ан, -анна). **undeniable** *adj.*, неоспори́мый, несомнéнный (-нен, -нна).

under *prep.* (*position*) под + *instr.*; (*direction*) под + *acc.*; (*fig.*) под + *instr.*; (*less than*) мéньше + *gen.*, ни́же + *gen.*; (*according to*) по + *dat.*; (*in view of, in the reign, time, of*) при + *prep.*; *u. age*, несовершеннолéтний; *u. repair*, в ремóнте; *u. way*, на ходу́; *from u.*, из-под + *gen.*; *adv.* (*position*) внизу́, ни́же; (*direction*) вниз; (*less*) мéньше; *adj.* ни́жний; (*subordinate*) ни́зший; *u.-secretary*, замести́тель *m.* мини́стра; *u.-side*, ни́жняя повéрхность.

undercarriage *n.* шасси́ *neut. indecl.* **underclothes, underclothing** *n.* ни́жнее бельё. **undercoat** *n.* (*of paint*) грунтóвка. **undercover** *adj.* тáйный, секрéтный. **undercurrent** *n.* подвóдное течéние; (*fig.*) скры́тая тендéнция. **undercut** *v.t.* (*cut away*) подрезáть *imp.*, подрéзать (-éжу, -éжешь) *perf.*; (*price*) назначáть *imp.*, назнáчить *perf.* бóлее ни́зкую цéну чем + *nom.* **underdeveloped** *adj.* недорáзвитый, слаборáзвитый; (*photog.*) недопроя́вленный. **underdog** *n.* неудáчник.

underdone *adj.* недожáренный (-ен). **underemployment** *n.* непóлная заня́тость. **underestimate** *v.t.* недооцéнивать *imp.*, недооцени́ть (-ню́, -нишь) *perf.*; *n.* недооцéнка. **underexpose** *v.t.* недодéрживать *imp.*, недодержáть (-жу́, -жишь) *perf.* **underfed** *adj.* недокóрмленный. **underfelt** *n.* грунт коврá. **underfloor** *adj.* находя́щийся под пóлом. **underfoot** *adv.* под ногáми. **undergarment** *n.* предмéт ни́жнего белья́.

undergo *v.t.* подвергáться *imp.*, подвéргнуться (-гся) *perf.* + *dat.*; (*endure*) переноси́ть (-ошу́, -óсишь) *imp.*, перенести́ (-есу́, -есёшь; -ёс, -есла́) *perf.* **undergraduate** *n.* студе́нт, ~ка. **underground** *n.* (*rly.*) метро́ *neut. indecl.*; (*fig.*) подпо́лье; *adj.* подзе́мный; (*fig.*) подпо́льный; *adv.* под землёй; (*fig.*) подпо́льно; *go u.*, уходи́ть (-ожу́, -о́дишь) *imp.*, уйти́ (уйду́, -дёшь; ушёл, ушла́) *perf.* в подпо́лье. **undergrowth** *n.* подле́сок (-ска). **underhand** *adj.* закули́сный, та́йный. **underlie** *v.t.* (*fig.*) лежа́ть (-жи́т) *imp.* в осно́ве + *gen.* **underline** *v.t.* подчёркивать *imp.*, подчеркну́ть *perf.* **underling** *n.* подчинённый *sb.*

undermanned *adj.* испы́тывающий недоста́ток в рабо́чей си́ле. **undermentioned** *adj.* нижеупомя́нутый. **undermine** *v.t.* де́лать *imp.*, с~ *perf.* подко́п под + *instr.*; (*wash away*) подмыва́ть *imp.*, подмы́ть (-мо́ю, -мо́ешь) *perf.*; (*authority*) подрыва́ть *imp.*, подорва́ть (-ву́, -вёшь; подорва́л, -а́, -о) *perf.*; (*health*) разруша́ть *imp.*, разру́шить *perf.* **underneath** *adv.* (*position*) внизу́; (*direction*) вниз; *prep.* (*position*) под + *instr.*; (*direction*) под + *acc.*; *n.* ни́жняя часть (*pl.* -ти, -те́й); *adj.* ни́жний. **undernourished** *adj.* недоко́рмленный; *be u.*, недоеда́ть *imp.* **undernourishment** *n.* недоеда́ние.

underpaid *adj.* низкоопла́чиваемый. **underpants** *n.* кальсо́ны (-н) *pl.*, трусы́ (-со́в) *pl.* **underpass** *n.* прое́зд под полотно́м доро́ги, тонне́ль *m.* **underpin** *v.t.* подводи́ть (-ожу́, -о́дишь) *imp.*, подвести́ (-еду́, -едёшь; -ёл, -ела́) *perf.* фунда́мент под + *acc.* **underpopulated** *adj.* малонаселённый (-ён, -ённа). **underprivileged** *adj.* по́льзующийся ме́ньшими права́ми; (*poor*) бе́дный (-ден, -дна́, -дно, бе́дны́). **underrate** *v.t.* недооце́нивать *imp.*, недооцени́ть *perf.*

undersell *v.t.* продава́ть (-даю́, -даёшь) *imp.*, прода́ть (-а́м, -а́шь, -а́ст, -ади́м; про́дал, -а́, -о) *perf.* дешёвле + *gen.* **undersigned** *adj.* (*n.*) нижеподписа́вшийся (*sb.*). **undersized** *adj.* маломе́рный, нестанда́ртный; (*dwarfish*) ка́рликовый. **underskirt** *n.* ни́жняя ю́бка.

understaffed *adj.* неукомплекто́ванный.

understand *v.t.* понима́ть *imp.*, поня́ть (пойму́, -мёшь; по́нял, -а́, -о) *perf.*; (*have heard say*) слы́шать *imp.* **understandable** *adj.* поня́тный. **understanding** *n.* понима́ние; (*intellect*) ра́зум; (*mutual u.*) взаимопонима́ние; (*agreement*) соглаше́ние; (*harmony*) согла́сие; *adj.* (*sympathetic*) чу́ткий (-ток, -тка́, -тко), отзы́вчивый.

understate *v.t.* преуменьша́ть *imp.*, преуме́ньши́ть *perf.* **understatement** *n.* преуменьше́ние.

understudy *n.* дублёр; *v.t.* дубли́ровать *imp.* роль + *gen.*

undertake *v.t.* (*engage in, enter upon*) предпринима́ть *imp.*, предприня́ть (-иму́, -и́мешь; предпри́нял, -а́, -о) *perf.*; (*responsibility*) брать (беру́, берёшь) *imp.*, взять (возьму́, -мёшь; взял, -а́, -о) *perf.* на себя́; (+ *inf.*) обя́зываться *imp.*, обяза́ться (-яжу́сь, -я́жешься) *perf.*; (*guarantee*) руча́ться *imp.*, поручи́ться (-чу́сь, -чишься) *perf.* (that, что). **undertaker** *n.* гробовщи́к (-а́). **undertaking** *n.* предприя́тие; (*obligation*) обяза́тельство.

undertone *n.* (*half-tint*) полуто́н (*pl.* -ы & -а́); (*nuance*) отте́нок (-нка); *speak in undertones*, говори́ть *imp.* вполго́лоса. **undertow**, *n.* глуби́нное тече́ние, противополо́жное пове́рхностному; подво́дное тече́ние. **underwater** *adj.* подво́дный. **underwear** *n.* ни́жнее бельё. **underworld** *n.* (*myth.*) преиспо́дняя *sb.*; (*criminals*) престу́пный мир (*pl.* -ы́). **underwrite** *v.t.* (*sign*) подпи́сывать *imp.*, подписа́ть (подпишу́, -шешь) *perf.*; (*accept liability for*) принима́ть *imp.*, приня́ть (приму́, -мешь; при́нял, -а́, -о) *perf.* на страх; (*guarantee*) гаранти́ровать *imp.*, *perf.* **underwriter** *n.* подпи́счик; страхо́вщик; (*company*) страхова́я компа́ния.

undeserved *adj.* незаслу́женный (-ен, -енна). **undeserving** *adj.* незаслу́живающий; *u. of*, не заслу́живающий + *gen.* **undesirable** *adj.* нежела́тельный; *n.* нежела́тельное лицо́ (*pl.* -ца). **undeveloped** *adj.* нера́звитый;

(*land*) незастро́енный. **undignified** *adj.* недосто́йный (-о́ин, -о́йна). **undiluted** *adj.* неразба́вленный. **undisciplined** *adj.* недисциплини́рованный (-ан, -анна). **undiscovered** *adj.* неоткры́тый; (*unknown*) неизве́стный. **undiscriminating** *adj.* непроница́тельный, неразбо́рчивый. **undisguised** *adj.* откры́тый, я́вный. **undismayed** *adj.* необескура́женный. **undisputed** *adj.* бесспо́рный. **undistinguished** *adj.* невыда́ющийся. **undisturbed** *adj.* (*untouched*) нетро́нутый; (*peaceful*) споко́йный; (*in order*) в поря́дке. **undivided** *adj.* (*unanimous*) единоду́шный; *give u. attention*, посвяща́ть *imp.*, посвяти́ть (-ящу́, -яти́шь) *perf.* все си́лы (to, +*dat.*). **undo** *v.t.* (*open*) открыва́ть *imp.*, откры́ть (-ро́ю, -ро́ешь) *perf.*; (*untie*) развя́зывать *imp.*, развяза́ть (-яжу́, -я́жешь) *perf.*; (*unbutton, unhook, unbuckle*) расстёгивать *imp.*, расстегну́ть *perf.*; (*destroy, cancel*) уничтожа́ть *imp.*, уничто́жить *perf.*; (*be the undoing of*) губи́ть (гублю́, -бишь) *imp.*, по~ *perf.* **undoing** *n.* (*ruin, downfall*) ги́бель; (*destruction*) уничтоже́ние. **undoubted** *adj.* несомне́нный (-нен, -нна). **undoubtedly** *adv.* несомне́нно. **undress** *v.t.* & *i.* раздева́ть(ся) *imp.*, разде́ть(ся) (-е́ну(сь), -е́нешь(ся)) *perf.* **undrinkable** *adj.* него́дный (-ден, -дна́, -дно) для питья́. **undue** *adj.* чрезме́рный. **unduly** *adv.* чрезме́рно.

undulate *v.i.* быть волни́стым, холми́стым. **undulating** *adj.* волни́стый. **undulation** *n.* волни́стость; (*motion*) волнообра́зное движе́ние; (*of surface*) неро́вность пове́рхности.

undying *adj.* (*eternal*) ве́чный.

unearned *adj.* незарабо́танный; (*undeserved*) незаслу́женный (-ен, -енна); *u. income*, нетрудово́й дохо́д. **unearth** *v.t.* (*dig up*) выка́пывать *imp.*, вы́копать *perf.* из земли́; (*fox etc.*) выгоня́ть *imp.*, вы́гнать (вы́гоню, -нишь) *perf.* из но́ры; (*fig.*) раска́пывать *imp.*, раскопа́ть *perf.* **unearthly** *adj.* неземно́й, сверхъесте́ственный (-ен, -енна); (*inconvenient*) кра́йне неудо́бный. **uneasiness** *n.* (*anxiety*) беспоко́йство, трево́га; (*awkwardness*) нело́вкость. **uneasy** *adj.* беспоко́йный, трево́жный; нело́вкий (-вок, нело́вка́, -вко). **uneatable** *adj.* несъедо́бный. **uneconomic** *adj.* нерента́бельный, неэкономи́чный. **uneconomical** *adj.* (*car etc.*) неэкономи́чный; (*person*) неэконо́мный. **uneducated** *adj.* необразо́ванный (-ан, -анна). **unemployed** *adj.* безрабо́тный; (*unoccupied*) неза́нятый (-т, -та́, -то); (*unused*) неиспо́льзованный. **unemployment** *n.* безрабо́тица; *u. benefit*, посо́бие по безрабо́тице. **unending** *adj.* бесконе́чный, нескончаемый. **unenlightened** *adj.* непросвещённый (-ён, -ённа); (*uninformed*) неосведомлённый. **unenterprising** *adj.* непредприи́мчивый, безынициати́вный. **unenviable** *adj.* незави́дный. **unequal** *adj.* нера́вный; (*of u. value*) неравноце́нный (-нен, -нна); (*unjust*) несправедли́вый; (*inadequate*) неадеква́тный; *u. to*, неподходя́щий для+*gen.* **unequalled** *adj.* бесподо́бный, непревзойдённый (-ён, -ённа). **unequivocal** *adj.* недвусмы́сленный (-ен, -енна). **unerring** *adj.* безоши́бочный.

UNESCO *abbr.* ЮНЕ́СКО.

uneven *adj.* неро́вный (-ве́н, -вна́, -вно). **uneventful** *adj.* не бога́тый собы́тиями, ти́хий (тих, -а́, -о). **unexceptionable** *adj.* безукори́зненный (-ен, -енна). **unexceptional** *adj.* обы́чный. **unexpected** *adj.* неожи́данный (-ан -анна); (*sudden*) внеза́пный. **unexplainable** *adj.* необъясни́мый. **unexplored** *adj.* неиссле́дованный. **unexpurgated** *adj.* без купю́р, неподве́ргшийся цензу́ре.

unfailing *adj.* неизме́нный (-нен, -нна); (*faithful*) ве́рный (-рен, -рна́, -рно, ве́рны́); (*reliable*) надёжный; (*inexhaustible*) неисчерпа́емый. **unfair** *adj.* несправедли́вый; (*dishonest*) нече́стный (-тен, -тна́, -тно). **unfaithful** *adj.* неве́рный (-рен, -рна́, -рно, неве́рны́); (*treacherous*) вероло́мный. **unfamiliar** *adj.* незнако́мый; (*unknown*) неве́домый. **unfashionable** *adj.* немо́дный (-ден, -дна́, -дно). **unfasten** *v.t.* (*detach untie*) открепля́ть *imp.*, открепи́ть *perf.*; (*detach, unbutton*) отстёгивать *imp.*, отстегну́ть *perf.*; (*undo, unbutton, unhook*) расстёгивать *imp.*, расстегну́ть *perf.* **unfathomable** *adj.* (*immeasurable*) неизмери́мый, бездо́нный; (*incomprehensible*) непостижи́мый. **unfavourable** *adj.* неблагоприя́тный; (*not approving*) неблагоскло́нный (-нен, -нна). **unfeeling** *adj.* бесчу́вственный (-ен, -енна). **unfeigned** *adj.* и́стинный (-нен, -нна), неподде́льный. **unfinished** *adj.* незако́нченный; (*crude*) необрабо́танный (-ан, -анна). **unfit** *adj.* него́дный (-ден, -дна́, -дно), неприго́дный, неподходя́щий; (*unhealthy*) нездоро́вый. **unfix** *v.t.* открепля́ть *imp.*, открепи́ть *perf.* **unflagging** *adj.* неослабева́ющий. **unfledged** *adj.* неопери́вшийся (*also fig.*). **unfold** *v.t.* & *i.* развёртывать(ся) *imp.*, разверну́ть(ся) *perf.*; (*open up*) раскрыва́ть(ся) *imp.*, раскры́ть(ся) (-ро́ю(сь), -ро́ешь(ся)) *perf.* **unforeseen** *adj.* непредви́денный. **unforgettable** *adj.* незабыва́емый. **unforgivable** *adj.* непрости́тельный. **unforgiving** *adj.* непроща́ющий. **unfortunate** *adj.* несчастли́вый, несча́стный; (*regrettable*) неуда́чный; *n.* несчастли́вец (-вца), неуда́чник, -ица. **unfortunately** *adv.* к несча́стью, к сожале́нию. **unfounded** *adj.* необосно́ванный (-ан, -анна). **unfreeze** *v.t.* & *i.* размора́живать(ся) *imp.*, разморо́зить(ся) *perf.* **unfriendly** *adj.* недружелю́бный, неприве́тливый. **unfrock** *v.t.* лиша́ть *imp.*, лиши́ть *perf.* духо́вного са́на. **unfruitful** *adj.* беспло́дный. **unfulfilled** *adj.* (*promise etc.*) невы́полненный; (*hopes etc.*) неосуществлённый. **unfurl** *v.t.* & *i.* развёртывать(ся) *imp.*, разверну́ть(ся) *perf.* **unfurnished** *adj.* немеблиро́ванный.

ungainly *adj.* нескла́дный, неуклю́жий. **ungentlemanly** *adj.* неблагоро́дный, неве́жливый. **ungodliness** *n.* безбо́жие. **ungodly** *adj.* (*also outrageous*) безбо́жный. **ungovernable** *adj.* необу́зданный (-ан, -анна), неукроти́мый. **ungracious** *adj.* нелюбе́зный. **ungrammatical** *adj.* граммати́чески непра́вильный. **ungrateful** *adj.* неблагода́рный. **unguarded** *adj.* (*incautious*) неосторо́жный.

unguent *n.* мазь.

unhappiness *n.* несча́стье. **unhappy** *adj.* несчастли́вый, несча́стный. **unharmed** *adj.* невреди́мый. **unhealthy** *adj.* (*in var. senses*) нездоро́вый, боле́зненный (-ен, -енна); (*harmful*) вре́дный (-ден, -дна́, -дно). **unheard-of** *adj.* несль́іханный (-ан, -анна). **unheeded** *adj.* незаме́ченный. **unheeding** *adj.* невнима́тельный. **unhelpful** *adj.* бесполе́зный. **unhesitating** *adj.* реши́тельный. **unhesitatingly** *adv.* без колеба́ния. **unhinge** *v.t.* снима́ть *imp.*, снять (сниму́, -мешь; снял, -а́, -о) *perf.* с пе́тли; (*fig.*) расстра́ивать *imp.*, расстро́ить *perf.* **unholy** *adj.* (*impious*) нечести́вый; (*awful*) ужа́сный. **unhook** *v.t.* снима́ть *imp.*, снять (сниму́, -мешь; снял, -а́, -о) *perf.* с крючка́; (*undo hooks*) расстёгивать *imp.*, расстегну́ть *perf.*; (*uncouple*) расцепля́ть *imp.*, расцепи́ть (-плю́, -пишь) *perf.* **unhoped-for** *adj.* неожи́данный (-ан, -анна). **unhorse** *v.t.* сбра́сывать *imp.*, сбро́сить *perf.* с ло́шади. **unhurt** *adj.* невреди́мый.

unicorn *n.* единоро́г.

unification *n.* объедине́ние, унифика́ция (*also standardization*).

uniform *n.* фо́рма, фо́рменная оде́жда; *adj.* единообра́зный; (*homogeneous*) одноро́дный; (*of u.*) фо́рменный. **uniformity** *n.* единообра́зие; одноро́дность.

unify *v.t.* объединя́ть *imp.*, объедини́ть *perf.*; унифици́ровать *imp.*, *perf.* (*also standardize*).

unilateral *adj.* односторо́нний.

unimaginable *adj.* невообрази́мый. **unimaginative** *adj.* лишённый (-ён, -ена́) воображе́ния, прозаи́чный. **unimpeachable** *adj.* безупре́чный. **unimportant** *adj.* нева́жный. **uninformed** *adj.* (*ignorant*) несве́дущий (about, в + *prep.*); (*ill-informed*) неосведомлённый. **uninhabitable** *adj.* неприго́дный для жилья́. **uninhabited** *adj.* необита́емый. **uninitiated** *adj.* непосвящённый. **uninspired** *adj.* бана́льный. **unintelligible** *adj.* неразбо́рчивый. **un-**

intentional *adj.* неумы́шленный (-ен, -енна). **unintentionally** *adv.* неумы́шленно. **uninterested** *adj.* незаинтересо́ванный. **uninteresting** *adj.* неинтере́сный. **uninterrupted** *adj.* непреры́вный. **uninviting** *adj.* непривлека́тельный.

union *n.* (*alliance*) сою́з; (*joining together*, *alliance*) объедине́ние; (*combination*) соедине́ние; (*marriage*) бра́чный сою́з; (*harmony*) согла́сие; (*trade u.*) профсою́з. **unionist** *n.* член профсою́за; (*polit.*) унио́ни́ст.

unique *adj.* еди́нственный (в своём ро́де), уника́льный.

unison *n.* (*mus.*) унисо́н; (*fig.*) согла́сие; *in u.*, (*mus.*) в унисо́н; (*fig.*) в согла́сии.

unit *n.* едини́ца; (*mil.*) часть (*pl.* -ти -те́й).

unite *v.t.* & *i.* соединя́ть(ся) *imp.*, соедини́ть(ся) *perf.*; объединя́ть(ся) *imp.*, объедини́ть(ся) *perf.* **united** *adj.* соединённый, объединённый; *U. Nations*, Организа́ция Объединённых На́ций; *U. States*, Соединённые Шта́ты *m.pl.* Аме́рики. **unity** *n.* еди́нство; (*cohesion*) сплочённость; (*math.*) еди ни́ца.

universal *adj.* (*general*) всео́бщий; (*world-wide*) всеми́рный; (*many-sided*) универса́льный. **universe** *n.* вселе́нная *sb.*; (*world*) мир; (*cosmos*) ко́смос.

university *n.* университе́т; *attrib.* университе́тский.

unjust *adj.* несправедли́вый. **unjustifiable** *adj.* не име́ющий оправда́ния. **unjustified** *adj.* неопра́вданный.

unkempt *adj.* нечёсаный (-ан); (*untidy*) неопря́тный. **unkind** *adj.* недо́брый, злой (зол, зла, зло). **unknown** *adj.* неизве́стный.

unlace *v.t.* расшнуро́вывать *imp.*, расшнурова́ть *perf.* **unlawful** *adj.* незако́нный (-нен, -нна). **unlearn** *v.t.* разу́чиваться *imp.*, разучи́ться (-чу́сь, -чишься) *perf.* (how to, +*inf.*); *v.t.* забыва́ть *imp.*, забы́ть (забу́ду, -дешь) *perf.* **unleash** *v.t.* (*dog*) спуска́ть *imp.*, спусти́ть (-ущу́, -у́стишь) *perf.* с при́вязи; (*also fig.*) развя́зывать *imp.*, развяза́ть (-яжу́, -я́жешь) *perf.* **unleavened** *adj.* бездрожжево́й, пре́сный (-сен, -сна́, -сно).

unless *conj.* е́сли...не.

unlike *adj.* непохо́жий (на + *acc.*); (*in contradistinction to*) в отли́чие от + *gen.* **unlikely** *adj.* маловероя́тный, неправдоподо́бный; *it is u. that*, вряд ли, едва́ ли. **unlimited** *adj.* (*unrestricted*) неограни́ченный (-ен, -енна); (*boundless*) безграни́чный. **unlined** *adj.* (*clothing*) без подкла́дки. **unload** *v.t.* (*remove load from*) разгружа́ть *imp.*, разгрузи́ть (-ужу́, -у́зишь) *perf.*; (*remove load from*, *remove from*) выгружа́ть *imp.*, вы́грузить *perf.*; (*gun*) разряжа́ть *imp.*, разряди́ть *perf.* **unlock** *v.t.* отпира́ть *imp.*, отпере́ть (отопру́, -рёшь; отпер, -ла́, -ло) *perf.*; открыва́ть *imp.*, откры́ть (-ро́ю, -ро́ешь) *perf.* **unlucky** *adj.* несчастли́вый; (*unsuccessful*, *unfortunate*) неуда́чный.

unmake *v.t.* (*destroy*) уничтожа́ть *imp.*, уничто́жить *perf.*; (*annul*) аннули́ровать *imp.*, *perf.*; (*depose*) понижа́ть *imp.*, пони́зить *perf.* **unman** *v.t.* (*discourage*) лиша́ть *imp.*, лиши́ть *perf.* му́жества. **unmanageable** *adj.* тру́дно подда́ющийся контро́лю; (*of child*) тру́дный (-ден, -дна́, -дно, тру́дны́). **unmanly** *adj.* недосто́йный (-о́ин, -о́йна) мужчи́ны. **unmannerly** *adj.* невоспи́танный (-ан, -анна). **unmarketable** *adj.* него́дный (-ден, -дна́, -дно) для прода́жи. **unmarried** *adj.* холосто́й (хо́лост, -а́, -о); (*of man*) нежена́тый; (*of woman*) незаму́жняя. **unmask** *v.t.* (*fig.*) разоблача́ть *imp.*, разоблачи́ть *perf.* **unmentionable** *adj.* незатра́гиваемый, необсужда́емый. **unmerciful** *adj.* безжа́лостный. **unmerited** *adj.* незаслу́женный (-ен, -енна). **unmethodical** *adj.* несистемати́ческий, неметоди́чный. **unmindful** *adj.* невнима́тельный (of, к + *dat.*). **unmistakable** *adj.* несомне́нный (-нен, -нна), я́сный (я́сен, ясна́, я́сно, ясны́). **unmitigated** *adj.* несмягчённый; (*absolute*) абсолю́тный; (*thorough*) отъя́вленный. **unmoved** *adj.* (*indifferent*) равноду́шный; (*adamant*) непреклонный (-нен, -нна).

unnatural *adj.* неесте́ственный (-ен.

-енна), противоесте́ственный (-ен, -енна). **unnecessary** *adj.* нену́жный, изли́шний (-шен, -шня). **unnerve** *v.t.* лиша́ть *imp.*, лиши́ть *perf.* реши́мости, му́жества. **unnoticed** *adj.* незаме́ченный.

unobjectionable *adj.* прие́млемый. **unobservant** *adj.* невнима́тельный, ненаблюда́тельный. **unobserved** *adj.* незаме́ченный. **unobtainable** *adj.* тако́й, кото́рого нельзя́ доста́ть; недосту́пный. **unobtrusive** *adj.* ненавя́зчивый. **unoccupied** *adj.* неза́нятый (-т, -та́, -то), свобо́дный; (*uninhabited*) необита́емый. **unofficial** *adj.* неофициа́льный. **unopposed** *adj.* не встре́тивший сопротивле́ния. **unorthodox** *adj.* неортодокса́льный.

unpack *v.t.* распако́вывать *imp.*, распакова́ть *perf.* **unpaid** *adj.* (*not receiving pay*) не получа́ющий пла́ты; (*work*) беспла́тный. **unpalatable** *adj.* невку́сный; (*unpleasant*) неприя́тный. **unpardonable** *adj.* непрости́тельный. **unpin** *v.t.* отка́лывать *imp.*, отколо́ть (-лю́, -лешь) *perf.* **unpleasant** *adj.* неприятный. **unpleasantness** *n.* непривлека́тельность; (*also occurrence*) неприя́тность; (*quarrel*) ссо́ра. **unpopular** *adj.* непопуля́рный. **unprecedented** *adj.* беспрецеде́нтный, бесприме́рный. **unpredictable** *adj.* не могу́щий быть предска́занный. **unprejudiced** *adj.* беспристра́стный. **unpremeditated** *adj.* непреднаме́ренный (-ен, -енна). **unprepared** *adj.* неподгото́вленный, негото́вый. **unprepossessing** *adj.* непривлека́тельный. **unpretentious** *adj.* просто́й (прост, -а́, -о, про́сты́), без прете́нзий. **unprincipled** *adj.* беспринци́пный; (*immoral*) безнра́вственный (-ен(ен), -енна). **unprintable** *adj.* нецензу́рный. **unproductive** *adj.* непродукти́вный. **unprofitable** *adj.* невы́годный. **unpromising** *adj.* не обеща́ющий ничего́ хоро́шего. **unpronounceable** *adj.* непроизноси́мый. **unpropitious** *adj.* неблагоприя́тный. **unprotected** *adj.* (*defenceless*) беззащи́тный; (*area*) откры́тый. **unproven** *adj.* недока́занный. **unprovoked** *adj.* ниче́м не вы́званный, непровоци́рованный. **unpublished** *adj.* неопублико́ванный, неи́зданный. **unpunctual** *adj.* непунктуа́льный. **unpunished** *adj.* безнака́занный (-ан, -анна).

unqualified *adj.* неквалифици́рованный (-ан, -анна); (*unconditional*) безогово́рочный. **unquenchable** *adj.* неутоли́мый; (*fig.*) неугаси́мый. **unquestionable** *adj.* несомне́нный (-нен, -нна), неоспори́мый. **unquestionably** *adv.* несомне́нно. **unquestioned** *adj.* не вызыва́ющий сомне́ния.

unravel *v.t.* & *i.* распу́тывать(ся) *imp.*, распу́тать(ся) *perf.*; *v.t.* (*solve*) разга́дывать *imp.*, разгада́ть *perf.* **unread** *adj.* (*book etc.*) непрочи́танный. **unreadable** *adj.* (*illegible*) неразбо́рчивый; (*boring*) ску́чный (-чен, -чна́, -чно). **unready** *adj.* негото́вый; (*slow-witted*) несообрази́тельный. **unreal** *adj.* ненастоя́щий. **unrealistic** *adj.* нереа́льный. **unreasonable** *adj.* (*unwise*) неблагоразу́мный; (*excessive*) непоме́рный; (*expensive*) непоме́рно дорого́й (до́рог, -а́, -о); (*of price*) непоме́рно высо́кий (-о́к, -ока́, -о́ко́); (*unfounded*; *of demand*) необосно́ванный (-ан, -анна). **unreasoned** *adj.* непроду́манный. **unreasoning** *adj.* немы́слящий. **unreceptive** *adj.* невосприи́мчивый. **unrecognizable** *adj.* неузнава́емый. **unrecognized** *adj.* непри́знанный. **unrefined** *adj.* неочи́щенный; (*manners etc.*) гру́бый (груб, -а́, -о). **unrelenting** *adj.* (*ruthless*) безжа́лостный; (*unremitting*) неосла́бный; (*not abating*) неуменьша́ющийся. **unreliable** *adj.* ненадёжный. **unremitting** *adj.* неосла́бный; (*incessant*) беспреста́нный (-нен, -нна). **unremunerative** *adj.* невы́годный. **unrepeatable** *adj.* (*unique*) неповтори́мый; (*indecent*) неприли́чный. **unrepentant** *adj.* нерася́вшийся. **unrepresentative** *adj.* нехаракте́рный. **unrequited** *adj.*: *u. love*, любо́вь без взаи́мности. **unreserved** *adj.* (*full*) по́лный (-лон, -лна́, по́лно́); (*open*) открове́нный (-нен, -нна); (*unconditional*) безогово́рочный; *u. seats*, незаброни́рованные места́ *neut.pl*

unresisting *adj.* несопротивля́ющийся. **unrest** *n.* беспоко́йство; (*polit.*) беспоря́дки *m.pl.*, волне́ния *neut.pl.* **unrestrained** *adj.* несде́ржанный (-ан, -анна). **unrestricted** *adj.* неограни́ченный (-ен, -енна). **unripe** *adj.* незре́лый, неспе́лый. **unrivalled** *adj.* бесподо́бный. **unroll** *v.t.* & *i.* развёртывать(ся) *imp.*, разверну́ть(ся) *perf.* **unruffled** *adj.* (*smooth*) гла́дкий (-док, -дка́, -дко); (*calm*) споко́йный. **unruly** *adj.* (*wild*) бу́йный (бу́ен, буйна́, -но), (*disobedient*) непослу́шный.

unsafe *adj.* опа́сный; (*insecure*) ненадёжный. **unsaid** *adj.*: *leave u.*, молча́ть (-чу́, -чи́шь) *imp.* о+*prep.* **unsaleable** *adj.* нехо́дкий. **unsalted** *adj.* несолёный (несо́лон, -а́, -о). **unsatisfactory** *adj.* неудовлетвори́тельный. **unsatisfied** *adj.* неудовлетворённый (-ён, -ена́ & -ённа). **unsatisfying** *adj.* неудовлетворя́ющий; (*food*) несы́тный (-тен, -тна́, -тно). **unsavoury** *adj.* невку́сный; (*distasteful*) проти́вный. **unscathed** *adj.* невреди́мый; (*fig.*) жив и невреди́м. **unscheduled** *adj.* внеочередно́й. **unscientific** *adj.* ненау́чный. **unscrew** *v.t.* & *i.* отви́нчивать(ся) *imp.*, отвинти́ть(ся) *perf.* **unscrupulous** *adj.* неразбо́рчивый в сре́дствах, беспринци́пный, бессо́вестный. **unseasonable** *adj.* не по сезо́ну; (*inopportune*) несвоевре́менный (-нен, -нна). **unseasoned** *adj.* (*food*) неприпра́вленный; (*wood*) невы́держанный; (*unaccustomed*) непривы́кший. **unseat** *v.t.* (*of horse*) сбра́сывать *imp.*, сбро́сить *perf.* с седла́; (*parl.*) лиша́ть *imp.*, лиши́ть *perf.* парла́ментского манда́та. **unseemly** *adj.* неподоба́ющий, непристо́йный. **unseen** *adj.* неви́данный; *u. translation*, перево́д с листа́. **unselfish** *adj.* бескоры́стный, неэгоисти́чный. **unserviceable** *adj.* неприго́дный. **unsettle** *v.t.* наруша́ть *imp.*, наруши́ть *perf.* распоря́док+*gen.*, выбива́ть *imp.*, вы́бить (-бью, -бьешь) *perf.* из колеи; (*upset*) расстра́ивать *imp.*, расстро́ить *perf.* **unsettled** *adj.*: *the weather is u.*, пого́да не установи́лась. **unshakeable** *adj.* непоколеби́мый. **unshaven** *adj.* небри́тый. **unsheathe** *v.t.* вынима́ть *imp.*, вы́нуть *perf.* из но́жен. **unship** *v.t.* (*cargo*) выгружа́ть *imp.*, вы́грузить *perf.*; (*passenger*) выса́живать *imp.*, вы́садить *perf.* на бе́рег. **unsightly** *adj.* непригля́дный, уро́дливый. **unskilful** *adj.* неуме́лый. **unskilled** *adj.* неквалифици́рованный (-ан, -анна). **unsociable** *adj.* необщи́тельный. **unsold** *adj.* непро́данный. **unsolicited** *adj.* непро́шеный. **unsolved** *adj.* нерешённый. **unsophisticated** *adj.* просто́й (прост, -а́, -о, про́сты́), безыску́сственный (-ен, -енна). **unsound** *adj.* (*unhealthy*, *unwholesome*) нездоро́вый; (*rotten*, *also fig.*) гнило́й (гнил, -а́, -о); (*unreliable*) ненадёжный; (*unfounded*) необосно́ванный (-ан, -анна); (*faulty*) дефе́ктный; *of u. mind*, душевнобольно́й. **unsparing** *adj.* (*lavish*) ще́дрый (щедр, -а́, -о); (*merciless*) беспоща́дный. **unspeakable** *adj.* (*inexpressible*) невырази́мый; (*very bad*) отврати́тельный. **unspecified** *adj.* то́чно не устано́вленный (-ен), неопределённый (-нен, -нна). **unspoilt** *adj.* неиспо́рченный. **unspoken** *adj.* невы́сказанный. **unsporting, unsportsmanlike** *adj.* неспорти́вный, недосто́йный (-о́ин, -о́йна) спортсме́на. **unstable** *adj.* неусто́йчивый; (*emotionally*) неуравнове́шенный (-ен, -енна). **unsteady** *adj.* неусто́йчивый. **unsuccessful** *adj.* неуда́чный, безуспе́шный. **unsuitable** *adj.* неподходя́щий, неподоба́ющий. **unsuited** *adj.* (*incompatible*) несовмести́мый. **unsullied** *adj.* незапя́тнанный. **unsupported** *adj.* неподде́ржанный. **unsure** *adj.* (*not convinced*) неуве́ренный (-ен, -ена) (of oneself, в себе́); (*hesitating*) неуве́ренный (-ен, -енна). **unsurpassed** *adj.* непревзойдённый (-ён, -ённа). **unsuspected** *adj.* не вызыва́ющий подозре́ний; (*unforeseen*) непредви́денный. **unsuspecting** *adj.* неподозрева́ющий. **unsweetened** *adj.* неподсла́щенный. **unswerving** *adj.* непоколеби́мый. **unsymmetrical** *adj.* несимметри́ческий. **unsympathetic** *adj.* несочу́вствующий; (*unattractive*) несимпати́чный. **unsystematic** *adj.* несистемати́чный.

untainted *adj.* неиспо́рченный. **untalented** *adj.* ненала́нтливый. **untameable** *adj.* не поддающийся прируче́нию; (*indomitable*) неукроти́мый. **untapped** *adj.*: *u. resources*, неиспо́льзованные ресу́рсы *m.pl.* **untarnished** *adj.* непотускне́вший; (*fig.*) незапя́тнанный. **untenable** *adj.* несостоя́тельный. **unthinkable** *adj.* (*inconceivable*) невообрази́мый; (*unlikely*) невероя́тный; (*out of the question*) исключённый (-ён, -ена́). **unthinking** *adj.* легкомы́сленный (-ен, -енна). **unthread** *v.t.* вынима́ть *imp.*, вы́нуть *perf.* ни́тку из + *gen.* **untidiness** *n.* неопря́тность; (*disorder*) беспоря́док (-дка). **untidy** *adj.* неопря́тный; (*in disorder*) в беспоря́дке. **untie** *v.t.* развя́зывать *imp.*, развяза́ть (-яжу́, -я́жешь) *perf.*; (*set free*) освобожда́ть *imp.*, освободи́ть *perf.*

until *prep.* до + *gen.*; *not u.*, не ра́ньше + *gen.*; *u. then*, до тех пор; *conj.* пока́, пока́...не; *not u.*, то́лько когда́.

untimely *adj.* (*premature*) безвре́менный; (*inopportune*) несвоевре́менный (-нен, -нна); (*inappropriate*) неуме́стный. **untiring** *adj.* неутоми́мый. **untold** *adj.* (*innumerable*) бессчётный, несме́тный; (*inexpressible*) невырази́мый. **untouched** *adj.* (*also pure*) нетро́нутый; (*indifferent*) равноду́шный. **untoward** *adj.* (*unfavourable*) неблагоприя́тный; (*refractory*) непоко́рный. **untrained** *adj.* необу́ченный. **untranslatable** *adj.* непереводи́мый. **untried** *adj.* неиспы́танный. **untroubled** *adj.* споко́йный. **untrue** *adj.* (*incorrect, disloyal*) неве́рный (-рен, -рна́, -рно, неве́рны́); (*incorrect*) непра́вильный; (*false*) ло́жный. **untrustworthy** *adj.* ненадёжный. **untruth** *n.* непра́вда, ложь. **untruthful** *adj.* лжи́вый.

unusable *adj.* неприго́дный. **unused** *adj.* (*not employed*) неиспо́льзованный; (*not accustomed*) непривы́кший (to, к + *dat.*); **unusual** *adj.* необыкнове́нный (-нен, -нна), необы́чный. **unusually** *adv.* необыкнове́нно. **unutterable** *adj.* невырази́мый.

unvarnished *adj.* (*fig.*) неприкра́шенный. **unvarying** *adj.* неизменя́ющийся. **unveil** *v.t.* снима́ть *imp.*, снять (сниму́, -мешь; снял, -а́, -о) *perf.* покрыва́ло с + *gen.*; (*statue*) торже́ственно открыва́ть *imp.*, откры́ть (-ро́ю, -ро́ешь) *perf.*; (*disclose*) открыва́ть *imp.*, откры́ть (-ро́ю, -ро́ешь) *perf.* **unversed** *adj.* несве́дущий (in, в + *prep.*); (*inexperienced*) нео́пытный (in, в + *prep.*).

unwanted *adj.* нежела́нный. **unwarranted** *adj.* (*unjustified*) неопра́вданный. **unwary** *adj.* неосторо́жный. **unwavering** *adj.* непоколеби́мый. **unwelcome** *adj.* нежела́нный, нежела́тельный; (*unpleasant*) неприя́тный. **unwell** *adj.* нездоро́вый. **unwholesome** *adj.* нездоро́вый, вре́дный (-ден, -дна́, -дно). **unwieldy** *adj.* громо́здкий, неуклю́жий. **unwilling** *adj.* нерасполо́женный. **unwillingly** *adv.* неохо́тно, про́тив жела́ния. **unwillingness** *n.* нерасположе́ние, неохо́та. **unwind** *v.t.* & *i.* разма́тывать(ся) *imp.*, размота́ться *perf.*; (*rest*) отдыха́ть *imp.*, отдохну́ть *perf.* **unwise** *adj.* не(благо)разу́мный. **unwitting** *adj.* нево́льный, нечаянный. **unwittingly** *adv.* нево́льно, неча́янно. **unwonted** *adj.* непривы́чный, необы́чный. **unworkable** *adj.* непримени́мый. **unworldly** *adj.* не от ми́ра сего́; (*spiritual*) духо́вный. **unworthy** *adj.* недосто́йный (-о́ин, -о́йна). **unwrap** *v.t.* развёртывать *imp.*, разверну́ть *perf.* **unwritten** *adj.*: *u. law*, непи́саный зако́н.

unyielding *adj.* упо́рный, непода́тливый.

unzip *v.t.* расстёгивать *imp.*, расстегну́ть *perf.* (мо́лнию + *gen.*).

up *adv.* (*motion*) наве́рх, вверх; (*position*) наверху́, вверху́; *up and down*, вверх и вниз; (*back and forth*) взад и вперёд; *up to*, (*towards*) к + *dat.*; (*time*) вплоть до + *gen.*; *up to now*, до сих пор; *be up against*, име́ть *imp.* де́ло с + *instr.*; *it is up to you* + *inf.*, э́то вам + *inf.*, вы должны́ + *inf.*; *not up to much*, нева́жный (-жен, -жна́, -жно); *what's up?* что случи́лось? в чём де́ло? *your time is up*, ва́ше вре́мя истекло́; *up and about*, на нога́х; *he isn't up yet*, он ещё не встал; *he isn't up to this job*, он не годи́тся для э́той рабо́ты; *prep.* вверх по + *dat.*; (*along*) (вдоль) по + *dat.*; *up wind*, про́тив ве́тра; *v.t.* & *i.* поднима́ть(ся) *imp.*, подня́ть(ся) (-ниму́(сь), -ни́мешь(ся); по́днял/подня́лся́, -ла́(сь), -ло/-ло́сь) *perf.*; (*leap up*) вска́кивать *imp.*, вскочи́ть (-чу́, -чишь) *perf.*; *adj.*: *up-to-date*, совреме́нный (-нен, -нна); (*fashionable*) мо́дный (-ден, -дна́, -дно); *up-and-coming*, напори́стый, многообеща́ющий; *n.*: *ups and downs*, (*fig.*) преврáтности *f.pl.* судьбы́.

upbraid *v.t.* брани́ть *imp.*, вы~ *perf.* (for, за + *acc.*).

upbringing *n.* воспита́ние.

update *v.t.* модернизи́ровать *imp.*, *perf.*; (*book*) дополня́ть *imp.*, допо́лнить *perf.*

upgrade *v.t.* повыша́ть *imp.*, повы́сить *perf.* (по слу́жбе).

upheaval *n.* сдвиг; (*revolution*) переворо́т; (*geol.*) смеще́ние пласто́в.

uphill *adj.* иду́щий в го́ру; (*fig.*) тяжёлый (-л, -ла́); *adv.* в го́ру.

uphold *v.t.* подде́рживать *imp.*, поддержа́ть (-жу́, -жишь) *perf.*; *u. a view*, приде́рживаться *imp.* взгля́да. **upholder** *n.* сторо́нник.

upholster *v.t.* обива́ть *imp.*, оби́ть (обобью́, -ьёшь) *perf.* (with, in, + *instr.*). **upholsterer** *n.* обо́йщик. **upholstery** *n.* оби́вка.

upkeep *n.* (*maintenance, support*) содержа́ние; (*repair(s)*) ремо́нт; (*cost of u.*) сто́имость содержа́ния.

upland *n.* гори́стая часть (*pl.* -ти, -те́й) страны́, наго́рная страна́ (*pl.* -ны); *adj.* наго́рный; (*inland*) лежа́щий внутри́ страны́.

uplift *v.t.* поднима́ть *imp.*, подня́ть (-ниму́, -ни́мешь; по́днял, -а́, -о) *perf.*; *n.* подъём.

upon *prep.* (*position*) на + *prep.*, (*motion*) на + *acc.*; *see* **on.**

upper *adj.* ве́рхний; (*socially, in rank*) вы́сший; *gain the u. hand*, оде́рживать *imp.*, одержа́ть (-жу́, -жишь) *perf.* верх (over, над + *instr.*); *u. crust*, верху́шка о́бщества; *the U. House*, ве́рхняя пала́та; *n.* передо́к (-дка́). **uppermost** *adj.* са́мый ве́рхний, вы́сший; *be u. in person's mind*, бо́льше всего́ занима́ть *imp.*, заня́ть (займу́, -мёшь; за́нял, -а́, -о) *perf.* мы́сли кого́-л.

uppish *adj.* спеси́вый, высокоме́рный.

upright *n.* подпо́рка, сто́йка; *adj.* вертика́льный; (*straight*) прямо́й (-м, -ма́, -мо, пря́мы́); (*honest*) че́стный (-тен, -тна́, -тно); *u. piano*, пиани́но *neut.indecl.*; *adv.* вертика́льно, пря́мо, стоймя́.

uprising *n.* восста́ние, бунт.

uproar *n.* шум (-а(у)), гам. **uproarious** *adj.* шу́мный (-мен, -мна́, -мно), бу́йный (бу́ен, буйна́, -но).

uproot *v.t.* вырыва́ть *imp.*, вы́рвать (-ву, -вешь) *perf.* с ко́рнем; (*eradicate*) искореня́ть *imp.*, искорени́ть *perf.*

upset *n.* (*disorder, confusion, discomposure*) расстро́йство; *v.t.* (*disorder, discompose, spoil* (*plans etc.*)) расстра́ивать *imp.*, расстро́ить *perf.*; *v.t.* & *i.* (*overturn*) опроки́дывать(ся) *imp.*, опроки́нуть(ся) *perf.*; *adj.* (*miserable*) расстро́енный (-ен); *u. stomach*, расстро́йство желу́дка.

upshot *n.* развя́зка, результа́т.

upside-down *adj.* перевёрнутый вверх дном; *adv.* вверх дном; (*in disorder*) в беспоря́дке.

upstairs *adv.* (*position*) наверху́; (*motion*) наве́рх; *n.* ве́рхний эта́ж (-а́); *adj.* находя́щийся в ве́рхнем этаже́.

upstart *n.* вы́скочка *m.* & *f.*

upstream *adv.* про́тив тече́ния; (*situation*) вверх по тече́нию.

upsurge *n.* подъём, волна́ (*pl.* -ны, -н, волна́м).

uptake *n.*: *be quick on the u.*, бы́стро соobража́ть *imp.*, сообрази́ть *perf.*

upturned *adj.* (*face etc.*) по́днятый (по́днят, -а́, -о) кве́рху; (*inverted*) перевёрнутый.

upward *adj.* напра́вленный (-ен) вверх, дви́жущийся вверх. **upwards** *adv.* вверх; *u. of*, свы́ше + *gen.*

uranium *n.* ура́н; *attrib.* ура́новый.

urban *adj.* городско́й.

urbane *adj.* ве́жливый, с изы́сканными мане́рами. **urbanity** *n.* ве́жливость.

urchin *n.* мальчи́шка *m.*

urge *n.* (*incitement*) побужде́ние, толчо́к (-чка́); (*desire*) жела́ние; *v.t.* (*impel, u. on*) подгоня́ть *imp.*, подогна́ть (подгоню́, -нишь; подогна́л, -а́, -о) *perf.*; (*induce, prompt*) побужда́ть *imp.*, побуди́ть *perf.*; (*advocate*) насто́йчиво убежда́ть *imp.*; (*give as reason*) обраща́ть *imp.*, обрати́ть (-ащу́, -ати́шь) *perf.* внима́ние на + *acc.* **urgency** *n.* (*also insistence*) настоя́тельность; (*immediate importance*) безотлага́тельность; *a matter of great u.*, сро́чное де́ло (*pl.* -ла́). **urgent** *adj.* сро́чный (-чен, -чна́, -чно); (*also insistent*) настоя́тельный; (*absolutely essential*) кра́йне необходи́мый. **urgently** *adv.* сро́чно.

uric *adj.* мочево́й. **urinal** *n.* писсуа́р. **urinate** *v.i.* мочи́ться (-чу́сь, -чишься) *imp.*, по ~ *perf.* **urination** *n.* мочеиспуска́ние. **urine** *n.* моча́.

urn *n.* у́рна.

usable *adj.* го́дный (-ден, -дна́, -дно) к употребле́нию. **usage** *n.* употребле́ние; (*custom*) обы́чай; (*treatment*) обраще́ние. **use** *n.* (*also benefit*) по́льза; (*application*) употребле́ние, примене́ние, испо́льзование; *it is of no u.*, бесполе́зно; *make u. of*, испо́льзовать *imp.*, *perf.*; по́льзоваться *imp.* + *instr.*; *v.t.* употребля́ть *imp.*, употреби́ть *perf.*; по́льзоваться *imp.* + *instr.*; применя́ть *imp.*, примени́ть (-ню́, -нишь) *perf.*; (*treat*) обраща́ться *imp.* с + *instr.*; *I used to see him often*, я ча́сто его́ встреча́л (*imp. p.t.*); *be, get, used to*, привыка́ть *imp.*, привы́кнуть (-к) *perf.* (to, к + *dat.*); *u. up*, расхо́довать *imp.*, из ~ *perf.* **used** *adj.* (*second-hand*) поде́ржанный, ста́рый (стар, -а́, ста́ро́). **useful** *adj.* поле́зный; *come in u., prove u.*, пригоди́ться *perf.* (to, + *dat.*). **useless** *adj.* бесполе́зный, никуда́ не го́дный (-ден, -дна́, -дно). **user** *n.* потреби́тель *m.*

usher *n.* (*door-keeper*) швейца́р; (*theat.*) билетёр; *v.t.* (*lead in*) вводи́ть (ввожу́, -о́дишь) *imp.*, ввести́ (-еду́, -едёшь; -ёл, -ела́) *perf.*; (*proclaim, u. in*) возвеща́ть *imp.*, возвести́ть *perf.* **usherette** *n.* билетёрша.

usual *adj.* обыкнове́нный (-нен, -нна), обы́чный; *as u.*, как обы́чно. **usually** *adv.* обыкнове́нно, обы́чно.

usurer *n.* ростовщи́к (-а́). **usurious** *adj.* ростовщи́ческий.

usurp *v.t.* узурпи́ровать *imp.*, *perf.*; незако́нно захва́тывать *imp.*, захвати́ть (-ачу́, -а́тишь) *perf.* **usurper** *n.* узурпа́тор, захва́тчик.

usury *n.* ростовщи́чество.

utensil *n.* инструме́нт, ору́дие; *pl.* у́тварь; принадле́жности *f.pl.*; (*kitchen utensils*) посу́да.

uterine *adj.* ма́точный; (*of one mother*) единоутро́бный. **uterus** *n.* ма́тка.

utilitarian *adj.* утилита́рный; *n.* утилитари́ст. **utilitarianism** *n.* утилитари́зм. **utility** *n.* поле́зность; (*profitableness*) вы́годность; *adj.* утилита́рный; (*practical*) практи́чный.

utilize *v.t.* испо́льзоваться *imp.*, *perf.*; утилизи́ровать *imp.*, *perf.*

utmost *adj.* (*extreme*) кра́йний, преде́льный; (*furthest*) са́мый отдалённый (-ён, -ённа); *this is of the u. importance to me*, э́то для меня́ кра́йне ва́жно; *n.*: *do one's u.*, де́лать *imp.*, с ~ *perf.* всё возмо́жное.

Utopia *n.* уто́пия. **utopian** *adj.* утопи́ческий; *n.* утопи́ст.

utter *attrib.* по́лный, соверше́нный, абсолю́тный; (*out-and-out*) отъя́вленный (*coll.*); *v.t.* произноси́ть (-ошу́, -о́сишь) *imp.*, произнести́ (-есу́, -есёшь; -ёс, -есла́) *perf.*; (*let out*) издава́ть (-даю́, -даёшь) *imp.*, изда́ть (-а́м, -а́шь, -а́ст, -ади́м; изда́л, -а́, -о) *perf.* **utterance** *n.* (*uttering*) произнесе́ние; (*pronouncement*) выска́зывание; (*diction*) ди́кция; (*pronunciation*) произноше́ние; *gift of u.*, дар сло́ва; *give u. to*, выража́ть *imp.*, вы́разить *perf.* слова́ми. **utterly** *adv.* кра́йне, соверше́нно.

uvula *n.* язычо́к (-чка́).

Uzbek *n.* узбе́к, -е́чка; *adj.* узбе́кский.

V

V-neck *n.* V-обра́зный вы́рез; *V sign*, (*victory*) знак побе́ды.
vacancy *n.* (*for job*) вака́нсия, свобо́дное ме́сто (*pl.* -та́); (*at hotel*) свобо́дный но́мер (*pl.* -а́); (*emptiness*) пустота́; (*apathy*) безуча́стность; (*absent-mindedness*) рассе́янность. **vacant** *adj.* (*post*) вака́нтный; (*post*; *not engaged, free*) свобо́дный; (*empty*) пусто́й (пуст, -а́, -о, пу́сты́); (*look*) рассе́янный (-ян, -янна); "*v. possession*", ,,помеще́ние гото́во для въе́зда". **vacantly** *adv.* рассе́янно. **vacate** *v.t.* освобожда́ть *imp.*, освободи́ть *perf.*; покида́ть *imp.*, поки́нуть *perf.* **vacation** *n.* (*school*, *univ.*) кани́кулы (-л) *pl.*; (*leave*) о́тпуск; (*vacating*) оставле́ние, освобожде́ние.
vaccinate *v.t.* привива́ть *imp.*, приви́ть (-вью́, -вьёшь; приви́л, -а́, -о) *perf.* + *dat.* (against, + *acc.*). **vaccination** *n.* приви́вка (against, от, про́тив + *gen.*). **vaccine** *n.* вакци́на.
vacillate *v.i.* колеба́ться (-блюсь, -блешься) *imp.* **vacillation** *n.* колеба́ние; (*inconstancy*) непостоя́нство.
vacuity *n.* пустота́. **vacuous** *adj.* пусто́й (пуст, -а́, -о, пу́сты́); (*foolish*) бессмы́сленный (-ен, -енна). **vacuum** *n.* ва́куум; (*fig.*) пустота́; *v. brake*, ва́куумный тормо́з; *v.-clean*, чи́стить *imp.*, вы ~, по ~ *perf.* пылесо́сом; *v. cleaner*, пылесо́с; *v. flask*, те́рмос; *vacuum-gauge*, вакуумме́тр; *v. pump*, ва́куум-насо́с.
vade-mecum *n.* путеводи́тель *m.*
vagabond *n.* бродя́га *m.*; *attrib.* бродя́чий. **vagabondage** *n.* бродя́жничество. **vagabondize** *v.i.* скита́ться *imp.*, бродя́жничать *imp.*
vagary *n.* капри́з, причу́да.
vagina *n.* влага́лище. **vaginal** *adj.* влага́лищный.
vagrancy *n.* бродя́жничество. **vagrant** *adj.* бродя́чий; *n.* бродя́га *m.*
vague *adj.* (*indeterminate*, *uncertain*) неопределённый (-нен, -нна); (*unclear*) нея́сный (-сен, -сна́, -сно); (*dim*) сму́тный (-тен, -тна́, -тно); (*absent-minded*) рассе́янный (-ян, -янна). **vagueness** *n.* неопределённость, нея́сность; (*absent-mindedness*) рассе́янность.
vain *adj.* (*futile*) тще́тный, напра́сный; (*empty*) пусто́й (пуст, -а́, -о, пу́сты́); (*conceited*) самовлюблённый, тщесла́вный; *in v.*, напра́сно, тще́тно, зря. **vainglorious** *adj.* тщесла́вный, хвастли́вый. **vainglory** *n.* тщесла́вие, хвастли́вость.
valance *n.* подзо́р, обо́рка, за́навеска.
vale *n.* дол, доли́на.
valediction *n.* проща́ние. **valedictory** *adj.* проща́льный.
valency *n.* вале́нтность.
valentine *n.* (*sweetheart*) возлю́бленный, -нная (выбира́ется 14-ого февраля́); (*card*) поздрави́тельная ка́рточка с днём свято́го Валенти́на.
valerian *n.* валериа́на; (*med.*) валериа́новые ка́пли (-пель) *pl.*
valet *n.* камерди́нер, слуга́ (*pl.* -ги) *m.*
valetudinarian *adj.* боле́зненный (-ен, -енна); (*hypochondriac*) мни́тельный.
valiant *adj.* хра́брый (храбр, -а́, -о), до́блестный.
valid *adj.* действи́тельный, име́ющий си́лу; (*weighty*) ве́ский. **validate** *v.t.* (*ratify*) утвержда́ть *imp.*, утверди́ть *perf.*; (*declare valid*) объявля́ть *imp.*, объяви́ть (-влю́, -вишь) *perf.* действи́тельным. **validity** *n.* действи́тельность; (*weightiness*) ве́скость.
valise *n.* саквоя́ж, чемода́н.
valley *n.* доли́на.
valorize *v.t.* устана́вливать *imp.*, установи́ть (-влю́, -вишь) *perf.* це́ны + *gen.* (by government action, путём госуда́рственных мероприя́тий).
valorous *adj.* до́блестный. **valour** *n.* до́блесть.
valuable *adj.* це́нный (-нен, -нна); (*costly*) дорого́й (до́рог, -а́, -о); *pl.* це́нные ве́щи (-що́й) *pl.*, драгоце́нности *f.pl.* **valuation** *n.* оце́нка. **value** *n.* це́нность; (*cost*, *worth*) цена́ (*pl.* -ны); (*worth*; *econ.*) сто́имость; (*significance*) значе́ние; (*math.*) вели-

чинá; (*mus.*) длúтельность; *pl.* цéнности *f.pl.*; *v.-added tax*, налóг на добáвленную стóимость; *v.-judgement*, субъектúвная оцéнка; *v.t.* (*estimate*) оцéнивать *imp.*, оценúть (-ню́, -нишь) *perf.*; (*hold dear*) ценúть (-ню́, -нишь) *imp.*, дорожúть *imp.*+*instr.* **valueless** *adj.* бесполéзный, ничегó не стóящий. **valuer** *n.* оцéнщик.

valve *n.* (*tech.*, *med.*, *mus.*) клáпан; (*tech.*) вентúль *m.*; (*bot.*) ствóрка; (*radio*) электрóнная лáмпа.

vamp[1] *n.* (*of shoe*) передóк (-дкá); (*patched-up article*) что-л. починённое на скóрую рýку; (*mus.*) импровизúрованный аккомпанемéнт; *v.t.* (*repair*) чинúть (-ню́, -нишь) *imp.*, по~ *perf.*; (*mus.*) импровизúровать *imp.*, сымпровизúровать *perf.* аккомпанемéнт к+*dat.*

vamp[2] *n.* (*flirt*) соблазнúтельница.

vampire *n.* (*also fig.*; *also v. bat*) вампúр.

van[1] *n.* (*road vehicle*, *caravan*) фургóн; (*rly.*) багáжный (*luggage*), товáрный (*goods*), служéбный (*guard's*), вагóн.

van[2] *n.* (*vanguard*) авангáрд.

vanadium *n.* ванáдий.

vandal *n.* вандáл, хулигáн. **vandalism** *n.* вандалúзм, варвáрство. **vandalize** *v.t.* разрушáть *imp.*, разрýшить *perf.*

vane *n.* (*weathercock*) флю́гер (*pl.* -á); (*of windmill*) крылó (*pl.* -лья, -льев); (*of propeller*) лóпасть (*pl.* -ти, -тéй); (*of turbine*) лопáтка.

vanguard *n.* авангáрд.

vanilla *n.* ванúль; *attrib.* ванúльный.

vanish *v.i.* исчезáть *imp.*, исчéзнуть (-éз) *perf.*; пропадáть *imp.*, пропáсть (-адý, -адёшь; -áл) *perf.*; *vanishing-point*, тóчка схóда.

vanity *n.* (*futility*) тщетá, суетá; (*vainglory*) тщеслáвие; *v. bag*, сýмочка, несессéр.

vanquish *v.t.* (*enemy*) побеждáть *imp.*, победúть (-едúшь, -едúт) *perf.*; (*fig.*) преодолевáть *imp.*, преодолéть *perf.*

vantage *n.* преимýщество; *v.-point*, вы́годная позúция; (*for observation*) пункт наблюдéния.

vapid *adj.* безвкýсный; (*also fig.*) прéсный (-сен, -снá, -сно); (*fig.*) скýчный (-чен, -чнá, -чно).

vaporize *v.t.* & *i.* испаря́ть(ся) *imp.*, испарúть(ся) *perf.* **vaporizer** *n.* испарúтель *m.* **vaporous** *adj.* парообрáзный; (*vague*) тумáнный (-нен, -нна).

vapour *n.* (*steam etc.*) пар (*loc.* -ý; *pl.* -ы́); (*mist*, *haze*) тумáн.

variable *adj.* измéнчивый, непостоя́нный (-нен, -нна); (*weather*) неустóйчивый, (*also math.*) перемéнный; *n.* (*math.*) перемéнная (величинá). **variance** *n.* (*disagreement*) разноглáсие; (*change*) изменéние; (*disparity*) несоответствие; *be at v. with*, расходúться (-ожýсь, -óдишься) *imp.*, разойтúсь (-ойдýсь, -ойдёшься; -ошёлся, -ошлáсь) *perf.* во мнéниях с+*instr.* **variant** *n.* вариáнт; *adj.* рáзный. **variation** *n.* (*varying*) изменéние, перемéна; (*variant*) вариáнт; (*variety*) разновúдность; (*mus.*, *math.*) вариáция.

varicose *adj.*: *v. veins*, расширéние вен.

variegate *v.t.* дéлать *imp.*, с~ *perf.* пёстрым; (*diversify*) разнообрáзить *imp.* **variegated** *adj.* разноцвéтный, пёстрый (-р, -рá, пёстрó); (*diverse*) разнообрáзный. **variety** *n.* разнообрáзие; (*sort*) разновúдность; (*multitude*) мнóжество; *v. show*, варьетé *neut.indecl.*, эстрáдный концéрт. **various** *adj.* (*of several kinds*) разлúчный; (*different*, *several*) рáзный; (*diverse*) разнообрáзный.

varnish *n.* лак; (*fig.*) лоск; *v.t.* лакировáть *imp.*, от~ *perf.* (*also fig.*). **varnishing** *n.* лакирóвка.

vary *v.t.* разнообрáзить *imp.*, меня́ть *imp.*; *v.i.* (*change*) меня́ться *imp.*, изменя́ться *imp.*, изменúться (-ню́сь, -нишься) *perf.*; (*differ*) рáзниться *imp.*; (*disagree*) не соглашáться *imp.*

vase *n.* вáза.

vaseline *n.* вазелúн.

vassal *n.* вассáл.

vast *adj.* громáдный, обшúрный. **vastly** *adv.* значúтельно. **vastness** *n.* громáдность, обшúрность.

vat *n.* чан (*pl.* -ы́), бак.

Vatican *n.* Ватикáн.

vaudeville *n.* водевúль *m.*; (*variety*) варьетé *neut.indecl.*

vault[1] *n.* (*leap*) прыжóк (-жкá); *v.t.*

перепрыгивать *imp.*, перепрыгнуть *perf.*; *v.i.* прыгать *imp.*, прыгнуть *perf.* **vaulting-horse** *n.* гимнастический конь (-ня́; *pl.* -ни, -не́й) *m.*

vault[2] *n.* (*arch, covering*) свод; (*cellar*) по́греб, подва́л; (*burial v.*) склеп; *v.t.* возводи́ть *imp.* (-ожу́, -о́дишь) *imp.*, возвести́ (-еду́, -едёшь; -ёл, -ела́) *perf.* свод над + *instr.* **vaulted** *adj.* сво́дчатый.

vaunt *n.* хвастовство́; *v.i.*(*t.*) хва́статься *imp.*, по~ *perf.* (+*instr.*).

veal *n.* теля́тина; *attrib.* теля́чий.

vector *n.* (*math.*) ве́ктор; (*carrier of disease*) перено́счик инфе́кции.

veer *v.i.* (*change direction*) изменя́ть *imp.*, измени́ть (-ню́, -нишь) *perf.* направле́ние; (*turn*) повора́чивать *imp.*, повороти́ть (-очу́, -о́тишь) *perf.*; *v. away from*, отша́тываться *imp.*, отшатну́ться *perf.* от + *gen.*

vegetable *n.* о́вощ; *adj.* расти́тельный; (*of vegetables*) овощно́й. **vegetarian** *n.* вегетариа́нец, -нка; *attrib.* вегетариа́нский. **vegetarianism** *n.* вегетариа́нство. **vegetate** *v.i.* расти́ (-ту́, -тёшь; рос, -ла́) *imp.*; (*fig.*) прозяба́ть *imp.* **vegetation** *n.* расти́тельность; (*fig.*) прозяба́ние. **vegetative** *adj.* расти́тельный; (*biol.*) вегетати́вный; (*fig.*) прозяба́ющий.

vehemence *n.* (*force*) си́ла; (*passion*) стра́стность. **vehement** *adj.* (*forceful*) си́льный (си́лён, -льна́, -льно, си́льны́); (*passionate*) стра́стный (-тен, -тна́, -тно).

vehicle *n.* сре́дство передвиже́ния/перево́зки; (*motor v.*) автомоби́ль *m.*; (*medium*) сре́дство; (*chem.*) носи́тель *m.* **vehicular** *adj.* (*conveying*) перево́зочный; (*of motor transport*) автомоби́льный; *v. transport*, автогружево́й тра́нспорт.

veil *n.* вуа́ль, покрыва́ло; (*fig.*) заве́са, покро́в; (*pretext*) предло́г; *v.t.* покрыва́ть *imp.*, покры́ть (-ро́ю, -ро́ешь) *perf.* вуа́лью, покрыва́лом; (*fig.*) скрыва́ть *imp.*, скрыть (-ро́ю, -ро́ешь) *perf.*

vein *n.* ве́на; (*of leaf; streak*) жи́лка; *in the same v.*, в том же ду́хе. **veined** *adj.* испещрённый (-ён, -ена́) жи́лками.

veld *n.* вельд.

vellum *n.* (*parchment*) то́нкий перга́мент; (*paper*) веле́невая бума́га.

velocity *n.* ско́рость.

velour(s) *n.* велю́р; (*attrib.*) велю́ровый.

velvet *n.* ба́рха́т; *adj.* бархáтный. **velveteen** *n.* вельве́т. **velvety** *adj.* бархати́стый.

venal *adj.* прода́жный, подку́пный. **venality** *n.* прода́жность.

vend *v.t.* продава́ть (-даю́, -даёшь) *imp.*, прода́ть (-а́м, -а́шь, -а́ст, -ади́м; про́дал, -а́, -о) *perf.* **vending-machine** *n.* торго́вый автома́т. **vendor** *n.* продаве́ц (-вца́), -вщи́ца.

vendetta *n.* венде́тта, кро́вная месть.

veneer *n.* фанеро́вка; (*fig.*) лоск; *v.t.* фанерова́ть *imp.*

venerable *adj.* почте́нный (-нен, -нна); (*V.*) преподо́бный. **venerate** *v.t.* благогове́ть *imp.* пе́ред + *instr.* **veneration** *n.* благогове́ние, почита́ние. **venerator** *n.* почита́тель *m.*

venereal *adj.* венери́ческий.

venetian blind *n.* жалюзи́ *neut.indecl.*

vengeance *n.* месть, мще́ние; *take v.*, мстить *imp.*, ото~ *perf.* (on, + *dat.*; for, за + *acc.*); *with a v.*, в по́лном смы́сле сло́ва; (*with might and main*) вовсю́. **vengeful** *adj.* мсти́тельный.

venial *adj.* прости́тельный.

venison *n.* оле́нина.

venom *n.* яд (-а(у)). **venomous** *adj.* ядови́тый.

vent[1] *n.* (*opening*) вы́ход (*also fig.*), отве́рстие; (*air-hole*) отду́шина; (*anus*) за́дний прохо́д; *v.t.* (*feelings*) дава́ть (даю́, даёшь) *imp.*, дать (дам, дашь, даст, дади́м; дал, -а́, да́ло́, -и) *perf.* вы́ход + *dat.*; излива́ть *imp.*, изли́ть (-лью́, -льёшь; изли́л, -а́, -о) *perf.* (on, на + *acc.*); (*smoke etc.*) выпуска́ть *imp.*, вы́пустить *perf.*; (*opinion*) выска́зывать *imp.*, вы́сказать (-ажу, -ажешь) *perf.*

vent[2] (*slit*) разре́з.

ventilate *v.t.* прове́тривать *imp.*, прове́трить *perf.*; (*fig.*) обсужда́ть *imp.*, обсуди́ть (-ужу́, -у́дишь) *perf.* **ventilation** *n.* вентиля́ция, прове́тривание. **ventilator** *n.* вентиля́тор.

ventral *adj.* брюшно́й.
ventricle *n.* желу́дочек (-чка).
ventriloquism, -quy *n.* чревовеща́ние. **ventriloquist** *n.* чревовеща́тель *m.* **ventriloquize** *v.i.* чревовеща́ть *imp.*
venture *n.* риско́ванное предприя́тие; (*speculation*) спекуля́ция; *at a v.*, наудáчу; *v.i.* (*hazard, dare*) отва́живаться *imp.*, отва́житься *perf.*; *v.t.* (*risk*) рискова́ть *imp.* + *instr.*, ста́вить *imp.*, по ~ *perf.* на ка́рту; *v. an opinion, guess*, осме́ливаться *imp.*, осме́литься *perf.* вы́сказать мне́ние, дога́дку. **venturesome** *adj.* (*person*) сме́лый (смел, -á, -о); (*enterprise*) риско́ванный (-ан, -анна).
venue *n.* ме́сто (*pl.* -тá) сбо́ра.
veracious *adj.* правди́вый. **veracity** *n.* правди́вость.
veranda(h) *n.* вера́нда.
verb *n.* глаго́л. **verbal** *adj.* (*oral*) у́стный; (*relating to words*) слове́сный; (*gram.*) отглаго́льный. **verbalize** *v.t.* выража́ть *imp.*, вы́разить *perf.* слова́ми; *v.i.* быть многосло́вным. **verbatim** *adj.* досло́вный; *adv.* досло́вно. **verbiage** *n.* многосло́вия. **verbose** *adj.* многосло́вный. **verbosity** *n.* многосло́вия.
verdant *adj.* зелёный (зе́лен, -á, -о).
verdict *n.* верди́кт, реше́ние; (*opinion*) мне́ние.
verdigris *n.* я́рь-медя́нка.
verdure *n.* зе́лень.
verge[1] *n.* (*also fig.*) край (*loc.* -áе & -аю́; *pl.* -ая́); (*of road*) обо́чина; (*fig.*) грань; (*eccl.*) жезл; *on the v. of*, на гра́ни + *gen.*; *he was on the v. of telling all*, он чуть не рассказа́л всё.
verge[2] *v.i.* клони́ться (-ню́сь, -нишься) *imp.* (towards, к + *dat.*); *v. on*, грани́чить *imp.* с + *instr.*
verger *n.* церко́вный служи́тель *m.*; (*bearer of staff*) жезлоно́сец (-сца).
verification *n.* прове́рка; (*confirmation*) подтвержде́ние. **verify** *v.t.* проверя́ть *imp.*, прове́рить *perf.*; (*confirm*) подтвержда́ть *imp.*, подтверди́ть *perf.* **verisimilitude** *n.* правдоподо́бие. **veritable** *adj.* настоя́щий. **verity** *n.* и́стина.
vermicelli *n.* вермише́ль.
vermilion *adj.* я́рко-кра́сный (-сен, -снá, -сно); *n.* ки́новарь.
vermin *n.* вреди́тели *m.pl.* паразиты *m.pl.*; (*fig.*) подо́нки (-ков) *pl.* **verminous** *adj.* кишáщий парази́тами; (*fig.*) отврати́тельный.
vermouth *n.* ве́рмут.
vernacular *adj.* (*native, of language*) родно́й; (*local, of dialect*) ме́стный; (*national, folk*) наро́дный; (*colloquial*) разгово́рный; *n.* родно́й язы́к (-á); ме́стный диале́кт; (*homely language*) разгово́рный язы́к (-á).
vernal *adj.* весе́нний.
vernier *n.* но́ниус, верньéр.
verruca *n.* борода́вка.
versatile *adj.* многосторо́нний; (*flexible, of mind*) ги́бкий (-бок, -бкá, -бко). **versatility** *n.* многосторо́нность; ги́бкость.
verse *n.* (*also Bibl.*) стих (-á); (*stanza*) строфá (*pl.* -фы); (*poetry*) стихи́ *m.pl.*, поэ́зия. **versed** *adj.* о́пытный, све́дущий (in, в + *prep.*). **versicle** *n.* во́зглас. **versify** *v.i.* писа́ть (пишу́, -шешь) *imp.*, на ~ *perf.* стихи́; *v.t.* перелага́ть *imp.*, переложи́ть (-жу́, -жишь) *perf.* в стихи́.
version *n.* (*variant*) вариа́нт; (*interpretation*) ве́рсия; (*text*) текст.
versus *prep.* про́тив + *gen.*
vertebra *n.* позвоно́к (-нкá); *pl.* позвоно́чник. **vertebral** *adj.* позвоно́чный. **vertebrate** *n.* позвоно́чное живо́тное *sb.*
vertex *n.* верши́на; (*anat.*) маку́шка. **vertical** *adj.* вертика́льный; *n.* вертика́ль.
vertiginous *adj.* (*dizzy*) головокружи́тельный; (*rotating*) крутя́щийся. **vertigo** *n.* головокруже́ние.
verve *n.* подъём, энтузиа́зм.
very *adj.* (*that v. same*) тот са́мый; (*this v. same*) э́тот са́мый; *at that v. moment*, в тот са́мый моме́нт; (*precisely*) как раз; *you are the v. person I was looking for*, как раз вас я иска́л; *the v.*, (*even the*) да́же, оди́н; *the v. thought frightens me*, однá, да́же, мысль об э́том меня́ пуга́ет; (*the extreme*) са́мый; *at the v. end*, в са́мом конце́; *adv.* о́чень; *v. much*, о́чень; *v. much* +

comp., гора́здо + *comp.*; *v.* + *superl.*, *superl.*; *v. first*, са́мый пе́рвый; *v. well*, (*agreement*) хорошо́, ла́дно; *not v.*, не о́чень, дово́льно + *neg.*
vesicle *n.* пузырёк (-рька́).
vespers *n.* вече́рня.
vessel *n.* сосу́д; (*ship*) кора́бль (-бля́) *m.*, су́дно (*pl.* суда́, -до́в).
vest[1] *n.* ма́йка; (*waistcoat*) жиле́т.
vest[2] *v.t.* (*with power*) облека́ть *imp.*, обле́чь (-еку́, -ечёшь; -ёк, -екла́) *perf.* (with, + *instr.*); (*rights*) наделя́ть *imp.*, надели́ть *perf.* + *instr.* (in, + *acc.*). **vested** *adj.*: *v. interest*, ли́чная заинтересо́ванность; *v. interests*, (*property rights*) иму́щественные права́ *neut. pl.*; (*entrepreneurs*) кру́пные предпринима́тели *m.pl.*; *v. rights*, безусло́вные права́ *neut.pl.*
vestal (virgin) *n.* веста́лка.
vestibule *n.* вестибю́ль *m.*, пере́дняя *sb.*
vestige *n.* (*trace*) след (*pl.* -ы́); (*sign*) при́знак.
vestments *n.* одея́ние, оде́жда; (*eccl.*) облаче́ние. **vestry** *n.* ри́зница. **vesture** *n.* одея́ние.
vet *n.* ветерина́р; *v.t.* (*fig.*) проверя́ть *imp.*, прове́рить *perf.*
vetch *n.* ви́ка *collect.*
veteran *n.* ветера́н; *adj.* ста́рый (стар, -а́, ста́ро́).
veterinary *adj.* ветерина́рный; *n.* ветерина́р.
veto *n.* ве́то *neut.indecl.*, запреще́ние; *v.t.* налага́ть *imp.*, наложи́ть (-жу́, -жишь) *perf.* ве́то на + *acc.*; запреща́ть *imp.*, запрети́ть (-ещу́, -ети́шь) *perf.*
vex *v.t.* досажда́ть *imp.*, досади́ть *perf.* + *dat.* **vexation** *n.* доса́да. **vexed** *adj.* (*annoyed*) раздоса́дованный (-ан); (*question*) спо́рный. **vexatious, vexing** *adj.* доса́дный.
via *prep.* че́рез + *acc.*
viable *adj.* жизнеспосо́бный; (*practicable*) осуществи́мый.
viaduct *n.* виаду́к.
vial *n.* пузырёк (-рька́).
vibrant *adj.* (*vibrating*) вибри́рующий; (*resonating*) резони́рующий; (*trembling*) дрожа́щий (with, от + *gen.*). **vibraphone** *n.* вибрафо́н. **vibrate** *v.i.* вибри́ровать *imp.*, дрожа́ть (-жу́, -жи́шь) *imp.*; (*to sound*) звуча́ть (-чу́, -чи́шь) *imp.*, про ~ *perf.*; *v.t.* (*make v.*) вызыва́ть *imp.*, вы́звать (вы́зову, -вешь) *perf.* вибра́цию в + *prep.* **vibration** *n.* вибра́ция, дрожа́ние. **vibrato** *n.* вибра́то *neut.indecl.*
vicar *n.* прихо́дский свяще́нник. **vicarage** *n.* дом (*pl.* -а́) свяще́нника.
vicarious *adj.* (*deputizing for another*) замеща́ющий друго́го; (*indirect*) ко́свенный.
vice[1] *n.* (*evil*) поро́к, зло; (*shortcoming*) недоста́ток (-тка).
vice[2] *n.* (*tech.*) тиски́ (-ко́в) *pl.*
vice- *in comb.* вице-, замести́тель *m.*; *v.-admiral*, вице-адмира́л; *v.-chairman*, замести́тель *m.* председа́теля; *v.-chancellor*, (*univ.*) проре́ктор; *v.-consul*, вице-ко́нсул; *v.-president*, вице-президе́нт. **viceroy** *n.* вице-коро́ль (-ля́) *m.*
vice versa *adv.* наоборо́т.
vicinity *n.* окре́стности *f.pl.*, сосе́дство, бли́зость; *in the v.*, побли́зости (of, от + *gen.*).
vicious *adj.* поро́чный; (*spiteful*) зло́бный; (*cruel, brutal*) жесто́кий (-о́к, -о́ка́, -о́ко); *v. circle*, поро́чный круг (*loc.* -е & -у́; *pl.* -и́). **viciousness** *n.* поро́чность; зло́бность.
vicissitude *n.* превра́тность.
victim *n.* же́ртва. **victimization** *n.* пресле́дование. **victimize** *v.t.* (*harass*) му́чить *imp.*, за ~, из ~ *perf.*; (*persecute*) пресле́довать *imp.*
victor *n.* победи́тель *m.*
Victorian *adj.* викториа́нский; (*fig.*) старомо́дный.
victorious *adj.* (*army*) победоно́сный; (*procession etc.*) побе́дный. **victory** *n.* побе́да.
victual *v.t.* снабжа́ть *imp.*, снабди́ть *perf.* прови́зией. **victualler** *n.* поставщи́к продово́льствия. **victuals** *n.* пи́ща, прови́зия *collect.*
vide imper. смотри́.
video *adj.* телевизио́нный. **videotape** *n.* магни́тная ле́нта для за́писи изображе́ния и зву́ка.
vie *v.i.* сопе́рничать *imp.* (with, с + *instr.*; for, в + *prep.*).

view *n.* (*prospect*, *picture*) вид; (*opinion*) взгляд, мнéние; (*viewing*) просмóтр; (*inspection*) осмóтр; *in v. of*, ввидý + *gen.*; *on v.*, вы́ставленный (-ен) для обозрéния; *with a v. to*, с цéлью + *gen.*, + *inf.*; *v.t.* (*pictures etc.*) рассмáтривать *imp.*; (*inspect*) осмáтривать *imp.*, осмотрéть (-рю́, -ришь) *perf.*; (*mentally*) смотрéть (-рю́, -ришь) *imp.* на + *acc.*; *v.i.* смотрéть (-рю́, -ришь) *imp.*, по~ *perf.* телевúзор. **viewer** *n.* зрúтель *m.*, ~ница; (*for slides*) проéктор. **viewfinder** *n.* видоискáтель *m.* **viewpoint** *n.* тóчка зрéния.

vigil *n.* бóдрствование; *keep v.*, бóдрствовать *imp.*, дежýрить *imp.* **vigilance** *n.* бдúтельность. **vigilant** *adj.* бдúтельный. **vigilante** *n.* дружúнник.

vignette *n.* виньéтка.

vigorous *adj.* сúльный (сúлён, -льнá, -льно, сúльны́), энергúчный. **vigour** *n.* сúла, энéргия.

vile *adj.* (*base*) пóдлый (подл, -á, -о), нúзкий (-зок, -зкá, -зко); (*disgusting*) отвратúтельный. **vileness** *n.* пóдлость; отвратúтельность. **vilify** *v.t.* чернúть *imp.*, о~ *perf.*

villa *n.* вúлла.

village *n.* дерéвня, селó; *attrib.* деревéнский, сéльский. **villager** *n.* деревéнский, сéльский, жúтель *m.*

villain *n.* злодéй. **villainous** *adj.* злодéйский; (*foul*) мéрзкий (-зок, -зкá, -зко). **villainy** *n.* злодéйство.

villein *n.* крепостнóй *sb.*

vim *n.* энéргия.

vinaigrette *n.* (*dressing*) припрáва из ýксуса и олúвкового мáсла.

vindicate *v.t.* (*justify*) оправдывать *imp.*, оправдáть *perf.*; (*stand up for*) отстáивать *imp.*, отстоя́ть (-ою́, -оúшь) *perf.* **vindication** *n.* (*justification*) оправдáние; (*defence*) защúта.

vindictive *adj.* мстúтельный.

vine *n.* виногрáдная лозá (*pl.* -зы).

vinegar *n.* ýксус; *attrib.* ýксусный. **vinegary** *adj.* кúслый (-сел, -слá, -сло).

vineyard *n.* виногрáдник.

vintage *n.* сбор, урожáй, виногрáда; (*wine*) винó из сбóра определённого гóда; *attrib.* (*wine*) мáрочный; (*car*) стáрый (стар, -á, стáрó).

viola[1] *n.* (*mus.*) альт.

viola[2] *n.* (*bot.*) фиáлка.

violate *v.t.* (*treaty*, *privacy*) нарушáть *imp.*, нарýшить *perf.*; (*grave*) осквернять *imp.*, осквернúть *perf.*; (*rape*) насúловать *imp.*, из~ *perf.* **violation** *n.* нарушéние; осквернéние; насúлие. **violator** *n.* нарушúтель *m.*

violence *n.* (*physical coercion*, *force*) насúлие; (*strength*, *force*) сúла. **violent** *adj.* (*person*) свирéпый, жестóкий (-óк, -óкá, -óко); (*storm etc.*) сúльный (сúлён, -льнá, -льно, сúльны́); (*quarrel*) бýрный (бýрен, бýрнá, -но), свирéпый; (*pain*) сúльный (сúлён, -льнá, -льно, сúльны́); (*epoch*) бýрный (бýрен, бýрнá, -но), жестóкий (-óк, -óкá, -óко); (*death*) насúльственный. **violently** *adv.* сúльно, óчень.

violet *n.* (*bot.*) фиáлка; (*colour*) фиолéтовый цвет; *adj.* фиолéтовый.

violin *n.* скрúпка. **violinist** *n.* скрипáч (-á), ~ка.

V.I.P. *abbr.* óчень вáжное лицó (*pl.* -ца).

viper *n.* гадю́ка; (*fig.*) змея́ (*pl.* -éи). **viperous** *adj.* ядовúтый.

virago *n.* мегéра.

viral *adj.* вúрусный.

virgin *n.* дéвственник, -ица; *V. Mary*, дéва Марúя; *adj.* (*also fig.*) дéвственный (-ен, -енна); *v. lands*, *soil*, целинá. **virginal** *adj.* дéвственный (-ен, -енна); (*innocent*) невúнный (-нен, -нна). **virginals** *n.* спинéт без нóжек. **virginity** *n.* дéвственность. **Virgo** *n.* Дéва.

virile *adj.* (*mature*) возмужáлый; (*manly*) мýжественный (-ен, -енна). **virility** *n.* возмужáлость; мýжество.

virtual *adj.* фактúческий. **virtually** *adv.* фактúчески. **virtue** *n.* (*excellence*) добродéтель; (*merit*) достóинство; *by v. of*, посрéдством + *gen.*, благодаря́ + *dat.* **virtuosity** *n.* виртуóзность. **virtuoso** *n.* виртуóз. **virtuous** *adj.* добродéтельный; (*chaste*) целомýдренный (-ен, -енна).

virulence *n.* (*toxicity*) ядовúтость; (*power*) сúла; (*med.*) вирулéнтность; (*fig.*) злóба. **virulent** *adj.* (*poisonous*)

ядови́тый; (*of disease*) опа́сный; (*fig.*) зло́бный.
virus *n.* ви́рус.
visa *n.* ви́за; *v.t.* визи́ровать *imp.*, *perf.*, за~ *perf.*
visage *n.* лицо́ (*pl.* -ца); (*aspect*) вид.
vis-à-vis *adv.* визави́, напро́тив; *n.* визави́ *neut.indecl.*; *prep.* (*with regard to*) в отноше́нии + *gen.*; (*opposite*) напро́тив + *gen.*
viscera *n.* вну́тренности *f.pl.*
viscose *n.* виско́за.
viscosity *n.* вя́зкость.
viscount *n.* вико́нт. **viscountess** *n.* виконте́сса.
viscous *adj.* вя́зкий (-зок, -зка́, -зко).
visibility *n.* ви́димость. **visible** *adj.* ви́димый. **visibly** *adv.* я́вно, заме́тно.
vision *n.* (*sense*) зре́ние; (*apparition*) виде́ние; (*insight*) проница́тельность; (*foresight*) предви́дение; (*on television screen*) изображе́ние. **visionary** *adj.* (*spectral*; *illusory*) при́зрачный; (*imaginary*, *fantastic*) вообража́емый, фантасти́ческий; (*impracticable*) неосуществи́мый; (*given to having visions*) скло́нный (-о́нен, -о́нна́, -о́нно) к галлюцина́циям; *n.* (*dreamer*) мечта́тель *m.*, ~ница, фантазёр; (*one who has visions*) визионе́р.
visit *n.* посеще́ние, визи́т; (*trip*) пое́здка; *v.t.* навеща́ть *imp.*, навести́ть *perf.*; посеща́ть *imp.*, посети́ть (-ещу́, -ети́шь) *perf.*; (*call on*) заходи́ть (-ожу́, -о́дишь) *imp.*, зайти́ (-йду́, -йдёшь; зашёл, -шла́) *perf.* к + *dat.*; ходи́ть (хожу́, хо́дишь) *indet.*, идти́ (иду́, идёшь; шёл, шла) *det.*, пойти́ (пойду́, -дёшь; пошёл, -шла́) *perf.* в го́сти к + *dat.*; *be visiting*, быть в гостя́х у + *gen.* **visitation** *n.* (*official visit*) официа́льное посеще́ние; (*eccl.*) бо́жье наказа́ние. **visiting-card** *n.* визи́тная ка́рточка. **visitor** *n.* гость (*pl.* -ти, -те́й) *m.*, посети́тель *m.*
visor *n.* (*of cap*) козырёк (-рька́); (*in car*) солнцезащи́тный щито́к (-тка́); (*of helmet*) забра́ло.
vista *n.* перспекти́ва, вид.
visual *adj.* (*of vision*) зри́тельный; (*graphic*) нагля́дный; *v. aids*, нагля́дные посо́бия *neut.pl.* **visualize** *v.t.* представля́ть *imp.*, предста́вить *perf.* себе́.
vital *adj.* (*also fig.*) жи́зненный (-ен, -енна); (*fig.*) суще́ственный (-ен, -енна); (*lively*) живо́й (жив, -а́, -о); *v. statistics*, стати́стика есте́ственного движе́ния населе́ния. **vitality** *n.* жизнеспосо́бность; (*liveliness*) жи́вость. **vitalize** *v.t.* оживля́ть *imp.*, оживи́ть *perf.* **vitals** *n.* жи́зненно ва́жные о́рганы *m.pl.*
vitamin *n.* витами́н.
vitiate *v.t.* по́ртить *imp.*, ис~ *perf.*; (*invalidate*) де́лать *imp.*, с~ *perf.* недействи́тельным; лиша́ть *imp.*, лиши́ть *perf.* си́лы. **vitiation** *n.* по́рча; (*leg.*) лише́ние си́лы; призна́ние недействи́тельным.
viticulture *n.* виногра́дарство.
vitreous *adj.* стеклови́дный; (*of glass*) стекля́нный. **vitrify** *v.t.* & *i.* превраща́ть(ся) *imp.*, преврати́ть(ся) (-ащу́(сь), -ати́шь(ся)) *perf.* в стекло́, в стеклови́дное вещество́.
vitriol *n.* купоро́с; (*fig.*) язви́тельность. **vitriolic** *adj.* купоро́сный; (*fig.*) язви́тельный.
vituperate *v.t.* брани́ть *imp.*, вы́~ *perf.* **vituperation** *n.* брань.
vivacious *adj.* живо́й (жив, -а́, -о) оживлённый (-ён, -ена́). **vivacity** *n.* жи́вость, оживлённость.
viva voce *adj.* у́стный; *n.* у́стный экза́мен.
vivid *adj.* (*bright*) я́ркий (я́рок, ярка́, я́рко); (*lively*) живо́й (жив, -а́, -о); (*imagination*) пы́лкий (пы́лок, -лка́, -лко). **vividness** *n.* я́ркость; жи́вость; пы́лкость.
vivify *v.t.* оживля́ть *imp.*, оживи́ть *perf.*
vivisection *n.* вивисе́кция.
vixen *n.* лиси́ца-са́мка; (*fig.*) меге́ра.
viz. *adv.* то есть, а и́менно.
vizier *n.* визи́рь *m.*
vocabulary *n.* слова́рь (-ря́) *m.*; (*range of language*) запа́с слов; (*of a language*) слова́рный соста́в.
vocal *adj.* голосово́й; (*mus.*) вока́льный; (*noisy*) шу́мный (шу́мен, -мна́, -мно); *v. cord*, голосова́я свя́зка. **vocalic** *adj.* гла́сный. **vocalist** *n.* певе́ц (-вца́), -ви́ца.

vocation *n.* призва́ние; (*profession*) профе́ссия. **vocational** *adj.* профессиона́льный. **vocative** *adj.* (*n.*) зва́тельный (паде́ж (-а́)).
vociferate *v.t.* крича́ть (-чу́, -чи́шь) *imp.*, кри́кнуть *perf.* **vociferous** *adj.* (*clamorous*) крикли́вый; (*noisy*) шу́мный (шу́мен, -мна́, -мно).
vodka *n.* во́дка.
vogue *n.* мо́да; (*popularity*) популя́рность; *in v.*, в мо́де.
voice *n.* го́лос; (*gram.*) зало́г; *v.t.* (*express*) выража́ть *imp.*, вы́разить *perf.* **voiced** *adj.* (*phon.*) зво́нкий (-нок, -нка́, -нко). **voiceless** *adj.* (*phon.*) глухо́й (глух, -а́, -о).
void *n.* пустота́; *adj.* пусто́й (пуст, -а́, -о, пу́сты́); (*invalid*) недействи́тельный; *v. of*, лишённый (-ён, -ена́) + *gen.*; *v.t.* (*render invalid*) де́лать *imp.*, с ~ *perf.* недействи́тельным; (*excrete*) опорожня́ть *imp.*, опоро́жнить *perf.*
volatile *adj.* (*chem.*) лету́чий; (*inconstant*) непостоя́нный (-нен, -нна); (*elusive*) неулови́мый. **volatility** *n.* лету́честь; непостоя́нство. **volatilize** *v.t.* & *i.* (*chem.*) улету́чивать(ся) *imp.*, улету́чить(ся) *perf.*; (*also fig.*) испаря́ть(ся) *imp.*, испари́ть(ся) *perf.*
vol-au-vent *n.* слоёный пирожо́к (-жка́).
volcanic *adj.* вулкани́ческий (*also fig.*). **volcano** *n.* вулка́н.
vole *n.* (*zool.*) полёвка.
volition *n.* во́ля; *by one's own v.*, по свое́й во́ле.
volley *n.* (*missiles*) залп; (*fig.*; *of arrows etc.*) град; (*sport*) уда́р с лёта; *v.t.* (*sport*) ударя́ть *imp.*, уда́рить *perf.* с лёта. **volley-ball** *n.* волейбо́л.
volt *n.* вольт. **voltage** *n.* вольта́ж, напряже́ние. **voltaic** *adj.* гальвани́ческий. **voltmeter** *n.* вольтме́тр.
volte-face *n.* (*fig.*) ре́зкая переме́на.
volubility *n.* говорли́вость. **voluble** *adj.* говорли́вый.
volume *n.* (*book*) том (*pl.* -а́); (*capacity, bulk*; *also fig.*) объём; (*loudness*) гро́мкость; (*mus., strength*) си́ла. **voluminous** *adj.* (*bulky*) объёмистый, обши́рный; (*of writer*) плодови́тый; (*of many volumes*) многото́мный.
voluntary *adj.* доброво́льный; (*deliberate*) умы́шленный (-ен, -енна); *n.* (*mus.*) со́ло *neut.indecl.* на орга́не. **volunteer** *n.* доброво́лец (-льца); *v.t.* предлага́ть *imp.*, предложи́ть (-жу́, -жишь) *perf.*; *v.i.* (*offer*) вызыва́ться *imp.*, вы́зваться (вы́зовусь, -вешься) *perf.* (*inf.*, + *inf.*; for, в + *acc.*); (*mil.*) идти́ (иду́, идёшь; шёл, шла) *imp.*, пойти́ (пойду́, -дёшь; пошёл, -шла́) *perf.* доброво́льцем.
voluptuary *n.* сластолю́бец (-бца). **voluptuous** *adj.* сластолюби́вый, чу́вственный (-ен, -енна). **voluptuousness** *n.* сластолю́бие.
volute *n.* (*archit.*) волю́та.
vomit *n.* рво́та; *v.t.* рвать (рвёт) *imp.*, вы́рвать (-вет) *perf. impers.* + *instr.*; *he was vomiting blood*, его рва́ло кро́вью; (*fig.*) изверга́ть *imp.*, изве́ргнуть *perf.*
voracious *adj.* прожо́рливый; (*fig.*) ненасы́тный. **voracity** *n.* прожо́рливость; ненасы́тность.
vortex *n.* (*whirlpool*; *also fig.*) водоворо́т; (*whirlwind*; *also fig.*) вихрь *m.*
votary *n.* почита́тель *m.*, ~ница; сторо́нник, -ица.
vote *n.* (*poll*) голосова́ние; (*individual v.*) го́лос (*pl.* -а́); *the v.*, (*suffrage*) пра́во го́лоса; (*resolution*) во́тум *no pl.*; *v. of no confidence*, во́тум недове́рия (in, + *dat.*); *v. of thanks*, выраже́ние благода́рности; *v.i.* голосова́ть *imp.*, про ~ *perf.* (for, за + *acc.*; against, про́тив + *gen.*); *v.t.* (*grant by v.*) ассигнова́ть *imp.*, *perf.*; (*deem*) признава́ть *imp.*, призна́ть *perf.*; *the film was voted a failure*, фильм был при́знан неуда́чным; *v. in*, избира́ть *imp.*, избра́ть (изберу́, -рёшь; избра́л, -а́, -о) *perf.* голосова́нием. **voter** *n.* избира́тель *m.* **voting-paper** *n.* избира́тельный бюллете́нь *m.*
votive *adj.* испо́лненный по обе́ту; *v. offering*, приноше́ние по обе́ту.
vouch *v.i.*; *v. for*, руча́ться *imp.*, поручи́ться *perf.* за + *acc.* **voucher** *n.* (*receipt*) распи́ска́; (*coupon*) тало́н. **vouchsafe** *v.t.* удоста́ивать *imp.*, удосто́ить + *instr.* (*person to whom granted*, + *acc.*).
vow *n.* кля́тва, обе́т; *v.t.* кля́сться

(клянýсь, -нёшься; клялся, -лáсь) *imp.*, по~ *perf.* в + *prep.*
vowel *n.* глáсный *sb.*
voyage *n.* путешéствие; *v.i.* путешéствовать *imp.*
vulcanization *n.* вулканизáция.
vulgar *adj.* вульгáрный, грýбый (груб, -á, -о), пóшлый (пошл, -á, -о); (*of the common people*) простонарóдный.
vulgarism *n.* вульгáрное выражéние.
vulgarity *n.* вульгáрность, пóшлость.
vulgarization *n.* вульгаризáция. **vulgarize** *v.t.* вульгаризи́ровать *imp.*, *perf.*
vulnerable *adj.* уязви́мый.
vulture *n.* гриф; (*fig.*) хи́щник.
vulva *n.* вýльва.

W

wad *n.* кусóк (-скá) вáты; (*in gun*) пыж (-á); *w. of money*, пáчка бумáжных дéнег; *v.t.* (*stuff with wadding*) набивáть *imp.*, наби́ть (набью́, -ьёшь) *perf.* вáтой. **wadding** вáта; (*padding, packing*) наби́вка.
waddle *v.i.* ходи́ть (хожý, хóдишь) *indet.*, идти́ (идý, идёшь; шёл, шла) *det.*, пойти́ (пойдý, -дёшь; пошёл, -шлá) *perf.* вперевáлку (*coll.*).
wade *v.t.* & *i.* (*river*) переходи́ть (-ожý, -óдишь) *imp.*, перейти́ (-йдý, -йдёшь; перешёл, -шлá) *perf.* вброд; *v.i.*: *w. through*, (*mud etc.*) пробирáться *imp.*, пробрáться (проберýсь, -рёшься; пробрáлся, -алáсь, -áлóсь) *perf.* по + *dat.*; (*s.th. boring etc.*) одолевáть *imp.*, одолéть *perf.* **wader** *n.* (*bird*) болóтная пти́ца; (*boot*) болóтный сапóг (-á; *gen.pl.* -г).
wafer *n.* вáфля (*gen.pl.* -фель); (*eccl.*; *paper seal*) облáтка.
waffle[1] *n.* (*dish*) вáфля (*gen.pl.* -фель).
waffle[2] *n.* (*blather*) трёп; *v.i.* трепáться (-плюсь, -плешься) *imp.*
waft *v.t.* & *i.* нести́(сь) (несý(сь), -сёшь(ся); нёс(ся), неслá(сь)) *imp.*, по~ *perf.*
wag[1] *n.* (*wave*) взмах; (*of tail*) виля́ние; *v.t.* (*tail*) виля́ть *imp.*, вильнýть *perf.* + *instr.*; (*finger*) грози́ть *imp.*, по~ *perf.* + *instr.*; *v.i.* качáться *imp.*, качнýться *perf.*
wag[2] *n.* (*joker*) шутни́к (-á).
wage[1] *n.* зáработная плáта; *w.-earner*, рабóчий *sb.*; (*bread-winner*) корми́лец (-льца); *w.-freeze*, заморáживание зáработной плáты; *living w.*, прожи́точный ми́нимум. **wages** *n.* *see* **wage**[1].
wage[2] *v.t.*: *w. war*, вести́ (ведý, -дёшь; вёл, -á) *imp.*, про~ *perf.* войнý.
wager *n.* пари́ *neut.indecl.*; (*stake*) стáвка; *v.i.*(*t.*) держáть (-жý, -жишь) *imp.* пари́ (на + *acc.*) (that, что).
waggish *n.* шаловли́вый.
wag(g)on *n.* (*carriage*) повóзка; (*cart*) телéга; (*rly.*) вагóн-платфóрма; (*van*) фургóн; (*trolley*) вагонéтка. **wag(g)oner** *n.* вóзчик.
wagtail *n.* трясогýзка.
waif *n.* беспризóрник.
wail *n.* вопль *m.*; *v.i.* вопи́ть *imp.* (*coll.*), выть (вóю, вóешь) *imp.* (*coll.*).
wainscot *n.* панéль; *v.t.* обшивáть *imp.*, обши́ть (обошью́, -ьёшь) *perf.* панéлью.
waist *n.* тáлия; (*level of w.*) пóяс (*pl.* -á); *w.-deep*, (*adv.*) по пóяс. **waistband** *n.* пóяс (*pl.* -á). **waistcoat** *n.* жилéт. **waistline** *n.* тáлия.
wait *n.* ожидáние; *lie in w.*, быть в засáде; *lie in w.* (*for*), поджидáть *imp.*; *v.i.*(*t.*) (*also w. for*) ждать (жду, ждёшь; ждал, -á, -о) *imp.* (+ *gen.*); *v.i.* (*be a waiter, waitress*) быть официáнтом, -ткой; *w. on*, обслýживать *imp.*, обслужи́ть (-жý, -жишь) *perf*

waiter *n.* официа́нт. **waiting** *n.* ожида́ние; *w.-list*, спи́сок (-ска) кандида́тов; *w.-room*, приёмная *sb.*; (*rly.*) зал ожида́ния. **waitress** *n.* официа́нтка.

waive *v.t.* отка́зываться *imp.*, отказа́ться (-ажу́сь, -а́жешься) *perf.* от + *gen.*

wake[1] *n.* (*at funeral*) поми́нки (-нок) *pl.*

wake[2] *n.* (*naut.*) кильва́тер; *in the w. of*, в кильва́тере + *dat.*, по пята́м за + *instr.*

wake[3] *v.t.* (*also w. up*) буди́ть (бужу́, бу́дишь) *imp.*, раз~ *perf.*; *v.i.* (*also w. up*) просыпа́ться *imp.*, просну́ться *perf.*; *v.t.* & *i.* (*also fig.*) пробужда́ть(ся) *imp.*, пробуди́ть(ся) (-ужу́(сь), -у́дишь(ся)) *perf.* **wakeful** *adj.* (*sleepless*) бессо́нный; (*vigilant*) бди́тельный. **wakefulness** *n.* бди́тельность.

waken *see* **wake**[3].

walk *n.* (*walking*) ходьба́; (*gait*) похо́дка; (*stroll*) прогу́лка пешко́м; (*path, avenue*) тропа́ (*pl.* -пы, -п, тро́па́м), алле́я; *w.-out*, (*strike*) забасто́вка; (*exit*) демонстрати́вный ухо́д; *w.-over*, лёгкая побе́да; *ten minutes' w. from here*, де́сять мину́т ходьбы́ отсю́да; *go for a w.*, идти́ (иду́, идёшь; шёл, шла) *imp.*, пойти́ (пойду́, -дёшь; пошёл, -шла́) *perf.* гуля́ть; *from all walks of life*, всех слоёв о́бщества; *v.i.* ходи́ть (хожу́, хо́дишь) *indet.*, идти́ (иду́, идёшь; шёл, шла) *det.*, пойти́ (пойду́, -дёшь; пошёл, -шла́) *perf.*; гуля́ть *imp.*, по~ *perf.*; *w. away, off*, уходи́ть (ухожу́, -о́дишь) *imp.*, уйти́ (уйду́, -дёшь; ушёл, ушла́) *perf.*; *w. in*, входи́ть (вхожу́, -о́дишь) *imp.*, войти́ (войду́, -дёшь; вошёл, -шла́) *perf.*; *w. out*, выходи́ть (-ожу́, -о́дишь) *imp.*, вы́йти (-йду, -йдешь; вы́шел, -шла) *perf.*; *v.t.* (*traverse*) обходи́ть (-ожу́, -о́дишь) *imp.*, обойти́ (-йду́, -йдёшь; обошёл, -шла́) *perf.*; (*take for w.*) выводи́ть (-ожу́, -о́дишь) *imp.*, вы́вести (-еду, -едешь; -ел) *perf.* гуля́ть. **walker** *n.* ходо́к (-а́). **walkie-talkie** *n.* (переносна́я) ра́ция. **walking** *n.* ходьба́; *w. stick*, трость (*pl.* -ти, -те́й); *adj.* гуля́ющий; (*med.*; *encyclopaedia*) ходя́чий; *w.-on part*, роль (*pl.* -ли, -ле́й) без слов.

wall *n.* стена́ (*acc.* -ну; *pl.* -ны, -н, -на́м); (*of object*) сте́нка; *attrib.* стенно́й; *v.t.* обноси́ть (-ошу́, -о́сишь) *imp.*, обнести́ (-есу́, -есёшь; -ёс, -есла́) *perf.* стено́й; *w. up*, (*door, window*) заде́лывать *imp.*, заде́лать; (*brick up*) замуро́вывать *imp.*, замурова́ть *perf.*

wallet *n.* бума́жник.

wallflower *n.* желтофио́ль.

wallop *n.* си́льный уда́р; *v.t.* си́льно ударя́ть *imp.*, уда́рить *perf.*; бить (бью, бьёшь) *imp.*, по~ *perf.*

wallow *v.i.* валя́ться *imp.*, бара́хтаться; *w. in*, (*give oneself up to*) предава́ться (-даю́сь, -даёшься) *imp.*, преда́ться (-а́мся, -а́шься, -а́стся, -ади́мся; преда́лся, -ла́сь) *perf.* + *dat.*

wallpaper *n.* обо́и (обо́ев) *pl.*

walnut *n.* гре́цкий оре́х; (*wood, tree*) оре́ховое де́рево (*pl.* (*tree*) -е́вья, -е́вьев), оре́х.

walrus *n.* морж (-а́).

waltz *n.* вальс; *v.i.* вальси́ровать *imp.*

wan *adj.* (*pale*) бле́дный (-ден, -дна́, -дно, бле́дны́); (*faint*) ту́склый (-л, -ла́, -ло).

wand *n.* (*of conductor, magician*) па́лочка; (*of official*) жезл (-а́).

wander *v.i.* броди́ть (брожу́, -о́дишь) *imp.*; (*also of thoughts etc.*) блужда́ть *imp.*; *w. from the point*, отклоня́ться *imp.*, отклони́ться (-ню́сь, -нишься) *perf.* от те́мы. **wanderer** *n.* стра́нник, скита́лец (-льца). **wandering** *adj.* бродя́чий; блужда́ющий; (*winding*) изви́листый.

wane *n.* убыва́ние; *v.i.* убыва́ть *imp.*, убы́ть (убу́дет; у́был, -а́, -о) *perf.*; (*diminish*) уменьша́ться *imp.*, уме́ньшиться *perf.*; (*weaken*) ослабева́ть *imp.*, ослабе́ть *perf.*

wangle *v.t.* ухитря́ться *imp.*, ухитри́ться *perf.* получи́ть.

want *n.* (*lack*) недоста́ток (-тка); (*need*) нужда́; (*requirement*) потре́бность; (*desire*) жела́ние; *v.t.* хоте́ть (хочу́, -чешь, хоти́м) *imp.*, за~ *perf.* + *gen.*, *acc.*; (*need*) нужда́ться *imp.* в + *prep.*; *I want you to come at six*, я хочу́, что́бы ты пришёл в шесть. **wanting**

adj. (*absent*) отсу́тствующий; *be w.*, недостава́ть (-таёт) *imp.* (*impers.* + *gen.*); *experience is w.*, недостаёт о́пыта.
wanton *adj.* (*licentious*) распу́тный; (*senseless*) бессмы́сленный (-ен, -енна); (*luxuriant*) бу́йный (бу́ен, буйна́, -но).
war *n.* война́ (*pl.* -ны); (*attrib.*) вое́нный (*in w. crime*, *w. correspondent*, *w. debts*, *w. loan etc.*); *at w.*, в состоя́нии войны́; *w.-cry*, боево́й клич; *w.-dance*, вои́нственный та́нец (-нца); *w.-game*, вое́нная игра́; *w.-horse*, боево́й конь (-ня́; *pl.* -ни, -не́й) *m.*; *w. memorial*, па́мятник па́вшим в войне́; *w.-paint*, раскра́ска те́ла пе́ред похо́дом; *w.-path*, (*fig.*): *be on the w.-path*, быть в вои́нственном настрое́нии; *v.i.* воева́ть (вою́ю, -ю́ешь) *imp.*
warble *n.* трель; *v.i.* издава́ть (-даю́, -даёшь) *imp.*, изда́ть (-а́м, -а́шь, -а́ст, -ади́м; изда́л, -а́, -о) *perf.* тре́ли.
ward[1] *n.* (*hospital*) пала́та; (*child etc.*) подопе́чный *sb.*; (*district*) администрати́вный райо́н го́рода.
ward[2] *v.t.*: *w. off*, отража́ть *imp.*, отрази́ть *perf.*
warden *n.* (*prison*) нача́льник; (*college*) ре́ктор.
warder *n.* тюре́мщик.
wardrobe *n.* гардеро́б.
warehouse *n.* склад, пакга́уз. **wares** *n.* изде́лия *neut.pl.*, това́ры *m.pl.*
warfare *n.* война́.
warhead *n.* боева́я голо́вка.
warily *adv.* осторо́жно. **wariness** *n.* осторо́жность.
warlike *adj.* вои́нственный (-ен, -енна).
warm *n.* тепло́; *adj.* (*also fig.*) тёплый (тёпел, -пла́, -пло́, -плы); *v.t.* & *i.* гре́ть(ся) *imp.*; согрева́ть(ся) *imp.*, согре́ть(ся) *perf.*; *w. up*, (*food etc.*) подогрева́ть(ся) *imp.*, подогре́ть(ся) *perf.*; (*liven up*) оживля́ть(ся) *imp.*, оживи́ть(ся) *perf.*; (*sport*) размина́ться *imp.*, размя́ться (разомну́сь, -нёшься) *perf.*; (*mus.*) разы́грываться *imp.*, разыгра́ться *perf.* **warmth** *n.* тепло́; (*cordiality*) серде́чность.
warmonger *n.* поджига́тель *m.* войны́.
warn *v.t.* предупрежда́ть *imp.*, предупреди́ть *perf.* (about, о + *prep.*). **warning** *n.* предупрежде́ние.
warp *n.* (*of cloth*) осно́ва; (*of wood*) коро́бление; *v.t.* & *i.* (*wood*) коро́бить(ся) *imp.*, по~, с~ *perf.*; *v.t.* (*pervert*, *distort*) извраща́ть *imp.*, изврати́ть (-ащу́, -ати́шь) *perf.*
warrant *n.* (*for arrest etc.*) о́рдер (*pl.* -а́); (*justification*) оправда́ние; (*proof*) доказа́тельство; *v.t.* (*justify*) опра́вдывать *imp.*, оправда́ть *perf.*; (*guarantee*) гаранти́ровать *imp.*, *perf.*; руча́ться *imp.*, поручи́ться (-чу́сь, -чишься) *perf.* за + *acc.* **warrantable** *adj.* допусти́мый. **warranty** *n.* (*basis*) основа́ние; (*guarantee*) гара́нтия.
warren *n.* уча́сток (-тка), где во́дятся кро́лики.
warring *adj.* противоречи́вый, непримири́мый.
warrior *n.* во́ин, бое́ц (бойца́).
warship *n.* вое́нный кора́бль (-ля́) *m.*
wart *n.* борода́вка; *w.-hog*, борода́вочник. **warty** *adj.* борода́вчатый.
wartime *n.*: *in w.*, во вре́мя войны́.
wary *adj.* осторо́жный.
wash *n.* мытьё; (*thin layer*) то́нкий слой (*pl.* -ои́); (*lotion*) примо́чка; (*surf*) прибо́й; (*backwash*) попу́тная струя́ (*pl.* -у́и); *at the w.*, в сти́рке; *have a w.*, мы́ться (мо́юсь, мо́ешься) *imp.*, по~ *perf.*; *w.-basin*, умыва́льник; *w.-house*, пра́чечная; *w.-out*, (*fiasco*) прова́л; *w.-room*, умыва́льная *sb.*; *w.-tub*, лоха́нь для сти́рки; *v.t.* & *i.* мы́ть(ся) (мо́ю(сь), мо́ешь(ся)) *imp.*, вы́~, по~ *perf.*; *v.t.* (*clothes*) стира́ть *imp.*, вы́~ *perf.*; (*of sea*) омыва́ть *imp.*; *v.i.* (*clothes*) стира́ться *imp.*; *w. ashore*: *the body was washed ashore*, труп приби́ло к бе́регу (*impers.*); *w. away*, *off*, *out*, смыва́ть(ся) *imp.*, смы́ть(ся) (смо́ю, -о́ешь, -о́ет(ся)) *perf.*; (*carry away*) сноси́ть (-ошу́, -о́сишь) *imp.*, снести́ (-есу́, -есёшь; -ёс, -есла́) *perf.*; *w. out*, (*rinse*) спола́скивать *imp.*, сполосну́ть *perf.*; *w. up*, (*dishes*) мыть (мо́ю, мо́ешь) *imp.*, вы́~, по~ *perf.* (посу́ду); *w. one's hands* (*of it*), умыва́ть *imp.*, умы́ть (умо́ю, -о́ешь) *perf.* ру́ки. **washed-out** *adj.* (*exhausted*) утомлённый. **washer** *n.* (*tech.*) ша́йба.

washerwoman *n.* пра́чка. **washing** *n.* (*of clothes*) сти́рка; (*clothes*) бельё; *w.-machine*, стира́льная маши́на; *w.-powder*, стира́льный порошо́к (-шка́); *w.-up*, (*action*) мытьё посу́ды; (*dishes*) гря́зная посу́да.

wasp *n.* оса́ (*pl.* о́сы); *w.'s nest*, оси́ное гнездо́ (*pl.* -ёзда). **waspish** *adj.* (*irritable*) раздражи́тельный; (*caustic*) язви́тельный.

wastage *n.* уте́чка. **waste** *n.* (*desert*) пусты́ня; (*wastage*) уте́чка; (*refuse*) отбро́сы *m.pl.*; (*of time, money etc.*) (бесполе́зная) тра́та; *go to w.*, пропада́ть *imp.*, пропа́сть (-аду́, -адёшь; -а́л) *perf.* да́ром; *w.-pipe*, сто́чная труба́ (*pl.* -бы); *adj.* (*desert*) пусты́нный (-нен, -нна); (*superfluous*) нену́жный; (*uncultivated*) невозде́ланный; *w. land*, пусты́рь (-ря́) *m.*; *lay w.*, опустоша́ть *imp.*, опустоши́ть *perf.*; *w. paper*, нену́жные бума́ги *f.pl.*; (*for recycling*) макулату́ра; *w. products*, отхо́ды (-дов) *pl.*; *w.-paper basket*, корзи́на для (нену́жных) бума́г; *v.t.* тра́тить *imp.*, по~, ис~ *perf.*; (*time*) теря́ть *imp.*, по~ *perf.*; *v.t.* & *i.* (*weaken*) истоща́ть(ся) *imp.*, истощи́ть(ся) *perf.*; *v.i.*; *w. away*, ча́хнуть (-х) *imp.*, за~ *perf.* **wasteful** *adj.* расточи́тельный. **wastrel** *n.* (*idler*) безде́льник.

watch *n.* (*timepiece*) часы́ (-со́в) *pl.*; (*duty*) дежу́рство; (*naut.*) ва́хта; *keep w. over*, наблюда́ть *imp.* за + *instr.*; *w.-chain*, цепо́чка для часо́в; *w.-dog*, сторожево́й пёс (пса); *w.-maker*, часовщи́к (-а́); *w.-spring*, часова́я пружи́на; *w.-tower*, сторожева́я ба́шня (*gen.pl.* -шен); *v.t.* наблюда́ть *imp.*; следи́ть *imp.* за + *instr.*; (*guard*, *w. over*) охраня́ть *imp.*, охрани́ть *perf.*; (*look after*) смотре́ть (-рю́, -ришь) *imp.*, по~ *perf.* за + *instr.*; *w. television, a film*, смотре́ть (-рю́, -ришь) *imp.*, по~ *perf.* телеви́зор, фильм; *w. out!* осторо́жно! **watchful** *adj.* бди́тельный. **watchman** *n.* (ночно́й) сто́рож (*pl.* -а́, -е́й). **watchword** *n.* ло́зунг.

water *n.* вода́ (*acc.* -ду; *pl.* -ды, -д, вода́м); *attrib.* водяно́й, во́дный; *w.-bath*, водяна́я ба́ня; *w.-bird*, водяна́я пти́ца; *w.-bottle*, графи́н для воды́; *w. bus*, речно́й трамва́й; *w.-butt*, бо́чка для дождево́й воды́; *W.-carrier*, Водоле́й; *w.-closet*, убо́рная *sb.*; *w.-colour*, акваре́ль; *w.-heater*, кипяти́льник; *w.-hole*, (*in desert*) ключ (-а́); *w.-jump*, во́дное препя́тствие; *w.-level*, у́ровень (-ня) *m.* воды́; *w.-lily*, водяна́я ли́лия; *w.-line*, ватерли́ния; *w.-main*, водопрово́дная магистра́ль; *w.-melon*, арбу́з; *w. mill*, водяна́я ме́льница; *w.-pipe*, водопрово́дная труба́ (*pl.* -бы); *w. polo*, во́дное по́ло *neut.indecl.*; *w.-power*, гидроэне́ргия; *w.-rat*, водяна́я кры́са; *w.-ski*, (*n.*) во́дная лы́жа; *w.-supply*, водоснабже́ние; *w.-tower*, водона́порная ба́шня (*gen.pl.* -шен); *w.-way*, во́дный путь (-ти́, -тём) *m.*; *w.-weed*, во́доросль; *w.-wheel*, водяно́е колесо́ (-ёса); *v.t.* (*flowers etc.*) полива́ть *imp.*, поли́ть (-лью́, -льёшь; по́лил, -а́, -о) *perf.*; (*animals*) пои́ть (пою́, по́ишь) *imp.*, на~ *perf.*; (*irrigate*) ороша́ть *imp.*, ороси́ть *perf.*; *v.i.* (*eyes*) слези́ться *imp.*; (*mouth*): *my mouth waters*, у меня́ слю́нки теку́т; *w. down*, разбавля́ть *imp.*, разба́вить *perf.* **watercourse** *n.* (*brook*) руче́й (-чья́); (*bed*) ру́сло (*gen.pl.* -л); (*channel*) кана́л. **watercress** *n.* кресс водяно́й. **waterfall** *n.* водопа́д. **waterfront** *n.* часть (*pl.* -ти, -те́й) го́рода примыка́ющая к бе́регу. **watering-can** *n.* ле́йка. **waterlogged** *adj.* заболо́ченный (-ен); пропи́танный (-ан) водо́й. **watermark** *n.* (*in paper*) водяно́й знак. **waterproof** *adj.* непромока́емый; *n.* непромока́емый плащ (-а́). **watershed** *n.* водора́здел. **waterside** *n.* бе́рег (*loc.* -у́; *pl.* -а́). **watertight** *adj.* водонепроница́емый; (*hermetic*) гермети́ческий. **waterworks** *n.* водопрово́дные сооруже́ния *neut.pl.* **watery** *adj.* водяни́стый; (*pale*) бле́дный (-ден, -дна́, -дно, бле́дны́).

watt *n.* ватт.

wattle *n.* (*fencing*) плете́нь (-тня́) *m.*; *attrib.* плетёный.

wave *v.t.* (*hand etc.*) маха́ть (машу́, -шешь) *imp.*, махну́ть *perf.* + *instr.*;

(*hair*) завива́ть *imp.*, зави́ть (-вью́, -вьёшь; зави́л, -а́, -о) *perf.*; *v.i.* (*flutter*) развева́ться *imp.*; (*rock, swing*) кача́ться *imp.*, качну́ться *perf.*; *w. aside*, (*spurn*) отверга́ть *imp.*, отве́ргнуть (-г) *perf.*; *w. down*, дава́ть (даю́, даёшь) *imp.*, дать (дам, дашь, даст, дади́м; дал, -а́, да́ло́, -ли) *perf.* знак остано́вки + *dat.*; *n.* (*in var. senses*) волна́ (*pl.* -ны, -н, во́лна́м); (*of hand*) взмах; (*in hair*) зави́вка. **wavelength** *n.* длина́ волны́. **waver** *v.i.* (*also fig.*) колеба́ться (-блюсь, -блешься) *imp.*; (*flicker, flutter*) колыха́ться (-ы́шется) *imp.*, колыхну́ться *perf.* **wavy** *adj.* волни́стый.

wax *n.* воск; (*in ear*) се́ра; *attrib.* восково́й; *v.t.* вощи́ть *imp.*, на ~ *perf.* **waxen, waxy** *adj.* восково́й; (*like wax*) похо́жий на воск. **waxwork** *n.* восковáя фигу́ра; *pl.* галере́я восковы́х фигу́р.

way *n.* (*road, path, route*; *fig.*) доро́га, путь (-ти́, -тём) *m.*; (*manner*) о́браз; (*method*) спо́соб; (*condition*) состоя́ние; (*respect*) отноше́ние; (*habit*) привы́чка; *by the w.*, (*fig.*) кста́ти, ме́жду про́чим; *on the w.*, по доро́ге, по пути́; *this w.* (*direction*) сюда́; (*in this w.*) таки́м о́бразом; *the other w. round*, наоборо́т; *under w.*, на ходу́; *be in the w.*, меша́ть *imp.*; *get out of the w.*, уходи́ть (-ожу́, -о́дишь) *imp.*, уйти́ (уйду́, -дёшь; ушёл, ушла́) *perf.* с доро́ги; *give w.*, (*yield*) поддава́ться (поддаю́сь, -аёшься) *imp.*, подда́ться (-а́мся, -а́шься, -а́стся, -ади́мся; подда́лся, -ла́сь) *perf.* (to, + *dat.*); (*collapse*) обру́шиваться *imp.*, обру́шиться *perf.*; *go out of one's w. to*, стара́ться *imp.*, по ~ *perf.* изо всех сил + *inf.*; *have it one's own w.*, де́йствовать *imp.* по-сво́ему; *make w.*, уступа́ть *imp.*, уступи́ть (-плю́, -пишь) *perf.* доро́гу (for, + *dat.*). **wayfarer** *n.* пу́тник. **waylay** *v.t.* (*lie in wait for*) подстерега́ть *imp.*, подстере́чь (-егу́, -ежёшь; подстерёг, -ла́) *perf.*; (*stop*) перехва́тывать *imp.*, перехвати́ть (-ачу́, -а́тишь) *perf.* по пути́. **wayside** *n.* обо́чина; *adj.* придоро́жный.

wayward *adj.* своенра́вный, капри́зный. **waywardness** *n.* своенра́вие, капри́зность.

we *pron.* мы (нас, нам, на́ми, нас).

weak *adj.* (*in var. senses*) сла́бый (слаб, -а́, -о); (*indecisive*) нереши́тельный; (*unconvincing*) неубеди́тельный. **weaken** *v.t.* ослабля́ть *imp.*, осла́бить *perf.*; *v.i.* слабе́ть *imp.*, о ~ *perf.* **weakling** *n.* сла́бый челове́к (*pl.* лю́ди, -де́й, -дям, -дьми́). **weakness** *n.* сла́бость; *have a w. for*, име́ть *imp.* сла́бость к + *dat.*

weal *n.* (*mark*) рубе́ц (-бца́).

wealth *n.* бога́тство; (*abundance*) изоби́лие. **wealthy** *adj.* бога́тый, состоя́тельный.

wean *v.t.* отнима́ть *imp.*, отня́ть (отниму́, -мешь) *perf.* от груди́; (*fig.*) отуча́ть *imp.*, отучи́ть (-чу́, -чишь) *perf.* (of, from, от + *gen.*).

weapon *n.* ору́жие. **weaponless** *adj.* безору́жный. **weaponry** *n.* вооруже́ние, ору́жие.

wear *n.* (*wearing*) но́ска; (*clothing*) оде́жда; (*w. and tear*) изна́шивание; *v.t.* носи́ть (ношу́, но́сишь) *imp.*; быть в + *prep.*; *v.i.* носи́ться (но́сится) *imp.*; *w. off*, (*cease to have effect*) перестава́ть (-таю́, -таёшь) *imp.*, переста́ть (-а́ну, -а́нешь) *perf.* де́йствовать; *w. out*, (*clothes*) изна́шивать(ся) *imp.*, износи́ть(ся) (-ошу́(сь), -о́сишь(ся)) *perf.*; (*exhaust, become exhausted*) истоща́ть(ся) *imp.*, истощи́ть(ся) *perf.*

weariness *n.* (*tiredness*) уста́лость, утомле́ние; (*tedium*) утоми́тельность. **wearing, wearisome** *adj.* утоми́тельный. **weary** *adj.* уста́лый, утомлённый (-ён, -ена́); *v.t.* & *i.* утомля́ть(ся) *imp.*, утоми́ть(ся) *perf.*

weasel *n.* ла́ска (*gen.pl.* -сок).

weather *n.* пого́да; *w.-beaten*, повреждённый (-ён, -ена́) бу́рями; (*of face*) обве́тренный (-ен); (*of person*) закалённый (-ён, -ена́); *w.-chart*, синопти́ческая ка́рта; *w. forecast*, прогно́з пого́ды; *w.-station*, метеорологи́ческая ста́нция; *v.t.* (*storm etc.*) выде́рживать *imp.*, вы́держать (-жу, -жишь) *perf.*; (*expose to atmosphere*) подвергáть *imp.*, подвéргнуть (-г) *perf.* атмосфéрным влия́ниям. **weathercock, weathervane** *n.* флю́гер (*pl.* -á). **weatherman** *n.* метеорóлог.

weave[1] *v.t.* & *i.* (*fabric*) ткать (тку, ткёшь; ткал, -á, -о) *imp.*, со~ *perf.*; *v.t.* (*fig.*; *also wreath etc.*) плести́ (плету́, -тёшь; плёл, -á) *imp.*, с~ *perf.*; *n.* узóр ткáни. **weaver** *n.* ткач, -и́ха. **weaving** *n.* (*the art of w.*) ткáчество; (*the w.*) тканьё.

weave[2] *v.i.* (*sway*) покáчиваться *imp.*

web *n.* (*cobweb, gossamer*; *fig.*) паути́на; (*membrane*) перепóнка; (*tissue*) ткань; (*fig.*) сплетéние. **webbed** *adj.* перепóнчатый. **webbing** *n.* ткáная лéнта, тесьмá.

wed *v.t.* (*of man*) жени́ться (-ню́сь, -ни́шься) *imp.*, *perf.* на + *prep.*; (*of woman*) выходи́ть (-ожу́, -óдишь) *imp.*, вы́йти (вы́йду, -дешь; вы́шла) *perf.* зáмуж за + *acc.*; (*unite*) сочетáть *imp.*, *perf.*; *v.i.* жени́ться (-ню́сь, -ни́шься) *perf.* (*coll.*); вступáть *imp.*, вступи́ть (-плю́, -пишь) *perf.* в брак. **wedded** *adj.* супру́жеский; *w. to*, (*fig.*) прéданный (-ан) + *dat.* **wedding** *n.* свáдьба, бракосочетáние; *w.-cake*, свáдебный торт; *w.-day*, день (дня) *m.* свáдьбы; *w.-dress*, подвенéчное плáтье (*gen.pl.* -в); *w.-ring*, обручáльное кольцó (*pl.* -льца, -лéц, -льцам).

wedge *n.* клин (*pl.* -ья, -ьев); *v.t.* (*w. open*) закли́нивать *imp.*, заклини́ть *perf.*; *v.t.* & *i.*: *w. in(to)*, вкли́нивать(ся) *imp.*, вкли́нить(ся) *perf.* (в + *acc.*).

wedlock *n.* брак, супру́жество; *born out of w.*, рождённый (-ён, -енá) вне брáка, внебрáчный.

Wednesday *n.* средá (*acc.* -ду; *pl.* -ды, -д, -дáм).

weed *n.* сорня́к (-á); *w.-killer*, гербици́д; *v.t.* полóть (полю́, -лешь) *imp.*, вы~ *perf.*; *w. out*, удаля́ть *imp.*, удали́ть *perf.* **weedy** *adj.* зарóсший сорнякáми; (*person*) тóщий (тощ, -á, -е).

week *n.* недéля; *w.-end*, суббóта и воскресéнье, уикэ́нд. **weekday** *n.* бу́дний день (дня) *m.* **weekly** *adj.* еженедéльный; (*wage*) недéльный; *adv.* раз в недéлю; еженедéльно; *n.* еженедéльник.

weep *v.i.* плáкать (плáчу, -чешь) *imp.*; *w. over*, оплáкивать *imp.*, оплáкать (оплáчу, -чешь) *perf.* **weeping** *n.* плач; *adj.*: *w. willow*, плаку́чая и́ва. **weepy** *adj.* слезли́вый.

weevil *n.* долгонóсик.

weft *n.* утóк (уткá).

weigh *v.t.* (*also fig.*) взвéшивать *imp.*, взвéсить *perf.*; (*consider*) обду́мывать *imp.*, обду́мать *perf.*; *v.t.* & *i.* (*so much*) вéсить *imp.*; *w. down*, отягощáть *imp.*, отяготи́ть (-ощу́, -оти́шь) *perf.*; *w. on*, тяготи́ть (-ощу́, -оти́шь) *imp.*; *w. out*, отвéшивать *imp.*, отвéсить *perf.*; *w. up*, (*appraise*) оцéнивать *imp.*, оцени́ть (-ню́, -нишь) *perf.*

weight *n.* (*also authority*) вес (*pl.* -á); (*load, also fig.*) тя́жесть; (*sport*) ги́ря, штáнга; (*influence*) влия́ние; *lose w.*, худéть *imp.*, по~ *perf.*; *put on w.*, толстéть *imp.*, по~ *perf.*; прибавля́ть *imp.*, прибáвить *perf.* в вéсе; *w.-lifter*, гиреви́к (-á), штанги́ст; *w.-lifting*, подня́тие тя́жестей; *v.t.* (*make heavier*) утяжеля́ть *imp.*, утяжели́ть *perf.* **weightless** *adj.* невесóмый. **weightlessness** *n.* невесóмость. **weighty** *adj.* (*also fig.*) вéский; (*heavy*) тяжёлый (-л, -лá); (*important*) вáжный (-жен, -жнá, -жно, -жны́).

weir *n.* плоти́на, запру́да.

weird *adj.* (*strange*) стрáнный (-нен, -ннá, -нно).

welcome *n.* (*greeting*) привéтствие; (*reception*) приём; *adj.* жéланный (-ан); (*pleasant*) прия́тный; *you are w.*, (*don't mention it*) не стóит благодáрности, пожáлуйста; *you are w. to use my bicycle*, мой велосипéд к вáшим услу́гам; *you are w. to stay the night*, вы мóжете переночевáть у меня́/нас; *v.t.* привéтствовать *imp.* (& *perf. in past tense*); *interj.* добрó пожáловать!

weld *n.* сварнóй шов (шва); *v.t.* & *i.* свáривать(ся) *imp.*, свари́ть(ся) *perf.*; (*fig.*) сплáчивать *imp.*, сплоти́ть *perf.* **welder** *n.* свáрщик. **welding** *n.* свáрка.

welfare *n.* благосостоя́ние, благополу́чие; *W. State*, госудáрство всеóбщего благосостоя́ния; *w. work*, рабо́та по социа́льному обеспе́чению.

well[1] *n.* коло́дец (-дца); (*for stairs*) ле́стничная кле́тка.

well[2] *v.i.*: *w. forth, up,* бить (бьёт) *imp.* ключо́м; хлы́нуть *perf.*

well[3] *adj.* (*healthy*) здоро́вый; *feel w.,* чу́вствовать *imp.*, по~ *perf.* себя́ хорошо́, здоро́вым; *get w.,* поправля́ться *imp.*, попра́виться *perf.*; *look w.,* хорошо́ вы́глядеть (-яжу, -ядишь) *imp.*; *all is w.,* всё в поря́дке; *interj.* ну(!); *adv.* хорошо́; (*very much*) о́чень; *as w.,* то́же; *as w. as,* (*in addition to*) кроме + *gen.*; *it may w. be true,* вполне́ возмо́жно, что э́то так; *very w.!* хорошо́! *w. done!* молоде́ц! *w.-advised,* благоразу́мный; *w.-balanced,* уравнове́шенный (-ен, -енна); *w.-behaved,* благонра́вный; *w.-being,* благополу́чие; *w.-bred,* благовоспи́танный (-ан, -анна); *w.-built,* кре́пкий (-пок, -пка́, -пко); *w.-defined,* чёткий (-ток, -тка́, -тко); *w.-disposed,* благоскло́нный (-нен, -нна), благожела́тельный; *w. done,* (*cooked*) (хорошо́) прожа́ренный (-ен); *w.-fed,* отко́рмленный (-ен); *w.-groomed,* (*person*) хо́леный; *w.-grounded,* обосно́ванный (-ан, -анна); (*versed*) све́дущий (in, в + *prep.*); *w.-informed,* (хорошо́) осведомлённый (-ён, -ена́) (about, в + *prep.*); *w.-known,* изве́стный; *w.-mannered,* воспи́танный (-ан); *w.-meaning,* име́ющий хоро́шие наме́рения; *w. paid,* хорошо́ опла́чиваемый; *w. preserved,* хорошо́ сохрани́вшийся; *w.-proportioned,* пропорциона́льный; *w.-read,* начи́танный (-ан, -анна); *w.-spoken,* уме́ющий изы́сканно говори́ть; *w. timed,* своевре́менный (-нен, -нна); *w.-wisher,* доброжела́тель *m.*; *w.-worn,* (*fig.*) изби́тый. **wellnigh** *adv.* почти́.

wellington (boot) *n.* рези́новый сапо́г (-а́; *gen.pl.* -г).

Welsh[1] *adj.* валли́йский, уэ́льский. **Welshman** *n.* валли́ец. **Welshwoman** *n.* валли́йка.

welsh[2] *v.t.*: *w. on,* (*swindle*) надува́ть *imp.*, наду́ть (-у́ю, -у́ешь) *perf.* (*coll.*); (*fail to keep*) не сде́рживать *imp.*, сдержа́ть (-жу́, -жишь) *perf.* + *gen.*

welt *n.* (*of shoe*) рант (*loc.* -у́); (*weal*) рубе́ц (-бца́).

welter *n.* (*confusion*) сумбу́р, пу́таница; *v.i.* валя́ться.

wench *n.* де́вка.

wend *v.t.*: *w. one's way,* держа́ть (-жу́, -жишь) *imp.* путь.

wer(e)wolf *n.* о́боротень (-тня) *m.*

west *n.* за́пад; (*naut.*) вест; *adj.* за́падный; *adv.* на за́пад, к за́паду. **westerly** *adj.* за́падный; *n.* за́падный ве́тер (-тра). **western** *adj.* за́падный; *n.* (*film*) ве́стерн. **westernize** *v.t.* европеизи́ровать *imp.*, *perf.* **westward(s)** *adv.* на за́пад, к за́даду.

wet *adj.* мо́крый (-р, -ра́, -ро); (*paint*) непросо́хший; (*rainy*) дождли́вый; *w.-nurse,* корми́лица; "*w. paint*", „осторо́жно окра́шено"; *w. through,* промо́кший до ни́тки; *w. suit,* водонепроница́емый костю́м; *n.* (*dampness*) вла́жность; (*rain*) дождь (-дя́) *m.*; *v.t.* мочи́ть (-чу́, -чишь) *imp.*, на~ *perf.* **wetness** *n.* вла́жность.

whack *n.* (*blow*) си́льный уда́р; *v.t.* колоти́ть (-очу́, -о́тишь) *imp.*, по~ *perf.*

whale *n.* кит (-а́).

wharf *n.* при́стань (*pl.* -ни, -не́й).

what *pron.* (*interrog., interj.*) что (чего́, чему́, чем, чём); (*how much*) ско́лько; (*rel.*) (то,) что (чего́, чему́, чем, чём); *what (...) for,* заче́м; *w. if,* а что е́сли; *w. is your name?* как вас зову́т? *adj.* (*interrog., interj.*) како́й; *w. kind of,* како́й. **whatever** *pron.* что бы ни + *past* (*w. you think,* что бы вы ни ду́мали); всё, что (*take w. you want,* возьми́те всё, что хоти́те); *adj.* како́й бы ни + *past* (*w. books he read(s),* каки́е бы кни́ги он ни прочита́л); (*at all*): *there is no chance w.,* нет никако́й возмо́жности; *is there any chance w.?* есть ли хоть кака́я-нибу́дь возмо́жность?

wheat *n.* пшени́ца. **wheaten** *adj.* пшени́чный.

wheedle *v.t.* (*coax into doing*) угова́ривать *imp.*, уговори́ть *perf.* с по́мощью ле́сти; *w. out of,* выма́нивать *imp.*, вы́манить *perf.* у + *gen.* **wheedling** *adj.* вкра́дчивый, льсти́вый.

wheel *n.* колесо́ (*pl.* -ёса); (*steering-w., helm*) руль (-ля́) *m.*, штурва́л; (*potter's*) гонча́рный круг; *v.t.* (*push*) ката́ть *indet.*, кати́ть (качу́, ка́тишь) *det.*, по~ *perf.*; *v.t. & i.* (*turn*) повёртывать(ся) *imp.*, поверну́ть(ся) *perf.*; *v.i.* (*circle*) кружи́ться (-ужу́сь, -у́жишься) *imp.* **wheelbarrow** *n.* та́чка. **wheelchair** *n.* инвали́дное кре́сло (*gen.pl.* -сел) (на колёсах). **wheelwright** *n.* коле́сник.

wheeze *n.* сопе́ние, хрип; *v.i.* сопе́ть (-плю́, -пи́шь) *imp.*, хрипе́ть (-плю́, -пи́шь) *imp.* **wheezy** *adj.* хри́плый (-л, -ла́, -ло).

whelk *n.* (*mollusc*) брюхоно́гий моллю́ск.

when *adv.* когда́; *conj.* когда́, в то вре́мя как; (*whereas*) тогда́ как; (*although*) хотя́. **whence** *adv.* отку́да. **whenever** *adv.* когда́ же; *conj.* (*every time*) вся́кий раз когда́; (*at any time*) в любо́е вре́мя, когда́; (*no matter when*) когда́ бы ни+*past*; *we shall have dinner w. you arrive*, во ско́лько бы вы ни прие́хали, мы пообе́даем.

where *adv., conj.* (*place*) где; (*whither*) куда́; *from w.*, отку́да. **whereabouts** *adv.* где; *n.* местонахожде́ние. **whereas** *conj.* тогда́ как; хотя́; (*official*) поско́льку. **whereby** *adv., conj.* посре́дством чего́. **wherein** *adv., conj.* в чём. **wherever** *adv., conj.* (*place*) где бы ни+*past*; (*whither*) куда́ бы ни+*past*; *w. he goes*, куда́ бы он ни пошёл; **wherewithal** *n.* сре́дства *neut. pl.*

whet *v.t.* точи́ть (-чу́, -чишь) *imp.*, на~ *perf.*; (*stimulate*) возбужда́ть *imp.*, возбуди́ть *perf.* **whetstone** *n.* точи́льный ка́мень (-мня; *pl.* -мни, -мне́й) *m.*

whether *conj.* ли; *I don't know w. he will come*, я не зна́ю, придёт ли он; *w. he comes or not*, придёт (ли) он и́ли нет.

whey *n.* сы́воротка.

which *adj.* (*interrog., rel.*) како́й; *pron.* (*interrog.*) како́й; (*person*) кто; (*rel.*) кото́рый; (*rel. to whole statement*) что; *w. is w.?* (*persons*) кто из них кто? (*things*) что-что? **whichever** *adj., pron.* како́й бы ни+*past* (*w. book you choose*, каку́ю бы кни́гу ты ни вы́брал); любо́й (*take w. book you want*, возьми́те любу́ю кни́гу).

whiff *n.* (*wind*) дунове́ние; (*smoke*) дымо́к (-мка́); (*odour*) за́пах.

while *n.* вре́мя *neut.*; промежу́ток (-тка) вре́мени; *a little w.*, недо́лго; *a long w.*, до́лго; *for a long w.*, (*up to now*) давно́; *for a w.*, на вре́мя; *in a little w.*, ско́ро; *once in a w.*, вре́мя от вре́мени; *it is worth w.*, сто́ит э́то сде́лать; *v.t.*: *w. away*, проводи́ть (-ожу́, -о́дишь) *imp.*, провести́ (-еду́, -едёшь; -ёл, -ела́) *perf.*; *conj.* пока́; в то вре́мя как; (*although*) хотя́; несмотря́ на то, что; (*contrast*) а; *we went to the cinema w. they went to the theatre*, мы ходи́ли в кино́, а они́ в теа́тр. **whilst** *see* **while**.

whim *n.* при́хоть, причу́да, капри́з.

whimper *n.* хны́канье; *v.i.* хны́кать (хны́чу, -чешь & хны́каю, -аешь) *imp.*

whimsical *adj.* капри́зный; (*odd*) причу́дливый. **whimsy** *n.* капри́з, при́хоть, причу́да.

whine *n.* (*wail*) вой; (*whimper*) хны́канье; *v.i.* скули́ть *imp.*; (*wail*) выть (во́ю, во́ешь); (*whimper*) хны́кать *imp.*

whinny *n.* ти́хое ржа́ние; *v.i.* ти́хо ржать (ржу, ржёшь) *imp.*

whip *n.* кнут (-а́), хлыст (-а́); *w. hand*, контро́ль (-ля) *m.*; *v.t.* (*lash*) хлеста́ть (-ещу́, -е́щешь) *imp.*, хлестну́ть *perf.*; (*urge on*) подгоня́ть *imp.*, подогна́ть (подгоню́, -нишь; подогна́л, -а́, -о) *perf.*; (*cream*) сбива́ть *imp.*, сбить (собью́, -ьёшь) *perf.*; *w. off*, ски́дывать *imp.*, ски́нуть *perf.*; *w. out*, выхва́тывать *imp.*, вы́хватить *perf.*; *w. round*, бы́стро повёртываться *imp.*, поверну́ться *perf.*; *w.-round*, сбор де́нег; *w. up*, (*stir up*) разжига́ть *imp.*, разже́чь (разожгу́, -ожжёшь; разжёг, разожгла́) *perf.* **whipper-snapper** *n.* ничто́жество. **whipping** *n.* побо́и (-о́ев) *pl.*

whirl *n.* круже́ние; (*of dust etc.*) вихрь (-ря) *m.*; (*turmoil*) сумато́ха, смяте́ние; *v.t. & i.* кружи́ть(ся) (кружу́(сь), кру́жишь(ся)) *imp.*, за~ *perf.* **whirlpool** *n.* водоворо́т. **whirlwind** *n.* вихрь (-ря) *m.*

whirr *n.* жужжа́ние; *v.i.* жужжа́ть (жужжу́, -жи́шь) *imp.*
whisk *n.* (*of twigs etc.*) ве́ничек (-чка); (*utensil*) муто́вка; (*movement*) пома́хивание; *v.t.* (*cream etc.*) сбива́ть *imp.*, сбить (собью́, -ьёшь) *perf.*; (*wag*, *wave*) маха́ть (машу́, -шешь) *imp.*, махну́ть *perf.* + *instr.*; *w. away*, *off*, (*brush off*) сма́хивать *imp.*, смахну́ть *perf.*; (*take away*) бы́стро уноси́ть (-ошу́, -о́сишь) *imp.*, унести́ (-есу́, -есёшь; -ёс, -есла́) *perf.*; *v.i.* (*scamper away*) юркну́ть *perf.*
whisker *n.* (*human*) во́лос (*pl.* -осы, -о́с, -оса́м) на лице́; (*animal*) ус (*pl.* -ы́); *pl.* (*human*) бакенба́рды *f.pl.*
whisky *n.* ви́ски *neut.indecl.*
whisper *n.* шёпот; (*rustle*) ше́лест; *v.t.* & *i.* шепта́ть (шепчу́, -чешь) *imp.*, шепну́ть *perf.*; (*rustle*) шелесте́ть (-ти́шь) *imp.*
whist *n.* вист.
whistle *n.* (*sound*) свист; (*instrument*) свисто́к (-тка́); *v.i.* свисте́ть (-ищу́, -исти́шь) *imp.*, сви́стнуть *perf.* (*also to dog etc.*); *v.t.* насви́стывать *imp.* **whistler** *n.* свисту́н (-а́) (*coll.*).
whit *n.*: *no w.*, *not a w.*, ничу́ть, ниско́лько.
white *adj.* бе́лый (бел, -а́, бе́ло́); (*hair*) седо́й (сед, -а́, -о); (*pale*) бле́дный (-ден, -дна́, -дно, бле́дны́); (*transparent*) прозра́чный; (*with milk*) с молоко́м; *paint w.*, кра́сить *imp.*, по~ *perf.* в бе́лый цвет; *w.-collar*, конто́рский; *w.-collar worker*, слу́жащий *sb.*; *w.-hot*, раскалённый добела́; *W. House*, Бе́лый дом; *w. lie*, неви́нная ложь (лжи, *instr.* ло́жью); *W. Russian*, (*n.*) белору́с, ~ка; (*adj.*) белору́сский; *n.* (*colour*) бе́лый цвет; (*egg*, *eye*) бело́к (-лка́); (*w. man*) бе́лый *sb.* **whitebait** *n.* малёк (-лька́); снето́к (-тка́). **whiten** *v.t.* бели́ть (белю́, бе́ли́шь) *imp.*, на~, по~, вы́~ *perf.*; (*blanch*, *bleach*) отбе́ливать *imp.*, отбели́ть *perf.*; *v.i.* беле́ть *imp.*, по~ *perf.* **whiteness** *n.* белизна́. **whitewash** *n.* раство́р для побе́лки; *v.t.* бели́ть (белю́, бе́ли́шь) *imp.*, по~ *perf.*; (*fig.*) обеля́ть *imp.*, обели́ть *perf.*
whither *adv.*, *conj.* куда́.
whiting *n.* (*fish*) мерла́нг.
Whitsun *n.* тро́ица.
whittle *v.t.* строга́ть *imp.*, вы́~ *perf.* ножо́м; *w. down*, (*decrease*) уменьша́ть *imp.*, уме́ньши́ть *perf.*
whiz(z) *n.* свист; *v.i.* свисте́ть (-ищу́, -исти́шь) *imp.*
who *pron.* (*interrog.*) кто (кого́, кому́, кем, ком); (*rel.*) кото́рый.
whoa *interj.* тпру!
whoever *pron.* кто бы ни + *past*; (*he who*) тот, кто.
whole *adj.* (*entire*) весь (вся, всё; все), це́лый; (*intact*, *of number*) це́лый; *w.-heartedly*, от всего́ се́рдца; *w. meal*, непросе́янная мука́; *n.* (*thing complete*) це́лое *sb.*; (*all there is*) весь (вся, всё; все) *sb.*; (*sum*) су́мма; *as a w.*, в це́лом; *on the w.*, в о́бщем. **wholesale** *adj.* опто́вый; (*fig.*) ма́ссовый; *n.* опто́вая торго́вля; *adv.* о́птом. **wholesaler** *n.* опто́вый торго́вец (-вца). **wholesome** *adj.* здоро́вый, благотво́рный. **wholly** *adv.* по́лностью, целико́м.
whom *pron.* (*interrog.*) кого́ *etc.* (*see* **who**); (*rel.*) кото́рого *etc.*
whoop *n.* крик, ги́канье (*coll.*); *v.i.* крича́ть (-чу́, -чи́шь) *imp.*, кри́кнуть *perf.*; ги́кать *imp.*, ги́кнуть *perf.* (*coll.*); *whooping cough*, коклю́ш.
whore *n.* проститу́тка.
whorl *n.* (*bot.*) муто́вка; (*on shell*) завито́к (-тка́); (*of spiral*) вито́к (-тка́).
whose *pron.* (*interrog.*, *rel.*) чей (чья, чьё; чьи); (*rel.*) кото́рого.
why *adv.* почему́; *n.* причи́на; *interj.* (*surprise*) да ведь!; (*impatience*) ну!
wick *n.* (*of lamp etc.*) фити́ль (-ля́) *m.*
wicked *adj.* злой (зол, зла); (*immoral*) безнра́вственный (-нен, -нна). **wickedness** *n.* зло́бность.
wicker *n.* пру́тья *m.pl.* для плете́ния; *attrib.* плетёный.
wicket *n.* кали́тка; (*cricket*) воро́тца.
wide *adj.* широ́кий (-к, -ка́, широ́ко́); (*extensive*) обши́рный; (*in measurements*) в + *acc.* ширино́й; *w. awake*, бо́дрствующий; (*wary*) бди́тельный; *w. open*, широко́ откры́тый; (*defenceless*) незащищённый; *adv.* (*off target*)

ми́мо це́ли. **widely** *adv.* широко́. **widen** *v.t.* & *i.* расширя́ть(ся) *imp.*, расши́рить(ся) *perf.* **widespread** *adj.* широко́ распространённый (-ён, -ена́).

wi(d)geon *n.* ди́кая у́тка.

widow *n.* вдова́ (*pl.* -вы). **widowed** *adj.* овдове́вший. **widower** *n.* вдове́ц (-вца́). **widowhood** *n.* вдовство́.

width *n.* ширина́; (*fig.*) широта́; (*of cloth*) поло́тнище.

wield *v.t.* держа́ть (-жу́, -жишь) *imp.* в рука́х; владе́ть + *instr.*

wife *n.* жена́ (*pl.* жёны).

wig *n.* пари́к (-а́).

wiggle *v.t.* & *i.* (*move*) шевели́ть(ся) *imp.*, по ~, шевельну́ть(ся) *perf.*

wigwam *n.* вигва́м.

wild *adj.* ди́кий (дик, -а́, -о); (*flower*) полево́й; (*uncultivated*) невозде́ланный; (*tempestuous*) бу́йный (бу́ен, буйна́, -но); (*furious*) неи́стовый; (*ill-considered*) необду́манный (-ан, -анна); *be w. about*, быть без ума́ от + *gen.*; *w.-goose chase*, сумасбро́дная зате́я; *n.*: *pl.* пусты́ня, де́бри (-рей) *pl.* **wildcat** *adj.* (*reckless*) риско́ванный; (*unofficial*) неофициа́льный. **wilderness** *n.* ди́кая ме́стность; (*desert*) пусты́ня. **wildfire** *n.*: *spread like w.*, распространя́ться *imp.*, распространи́ться *perf.* со сверхъесте́ственной быстрото́й. **wildlife** *n.* жива́я приро́да. **wildness** *n.* ди́кость.

wile *n.* хи́трость, уло́вка.

wilful *adj.* (*obstinate*) упря́мый; (*deliberate*) преднаме́ренный (-ен, -енна), умы́шленный (-ен, -енна). **wilfulness** *n.* упря́мство; преднаме́ренность.

will *n.* во́ля; (*w.-power*) си́ла во́ли; (*desire*) во́ля, жела́ние; (*at death*) завеща́ние; *against one's w.*, про́тив во́ли; *at w.*, по жела́нию; *of one's own free w.*, доброво́льно; *with a w.*, с энтузиа́змом; *good w.*, до́брая во́ля; *make one's w.*, писа́ть (пишу́, -шешь) *imp.*, на ~ *perf.* завеща́ние; *v.t.* (*want, desire*) хоте́ть (хочу́, -чешь, хоти́м) *imp.*, за ~ *perf.* + *gen.*, *acc.*; жела́ть *imp.*, по ~ *perf.* + *gen.*; (*order*) веле́ть (-лю́, -ли́шь) *imp.*, *perf.*; (*compel by one's w.*) заставля́ть *imp.*, заста́вить *perf.*; (*bequeath*) завеща́ть *imp.*, *perf.* **willing** *adj.* гото́вый, согла́сный; (*assiduous*) стара́тельный. **willingly** *adv.* охо́тно. **willingness** *n.* гото́вность.

will-o'-the-wisp *n.* блужда́ющий огонёк (-нька́).

willow *n.* и́ва.

willy-nilly *adv.* во́лей-нево́лей.

wilt *v.i.* вя́нуть (вял) *imp.*, за ~ *perf.*; поника́ть *imp.*, пони́кнуть (-к) *perf.*; (*weaken*) слабе́ть *imp.*, о ~ *perf.*

wily *adj.* хи́трый (-тёр, -тра́, хи́тро́), кова́рный.

win *n.* вы́игрыш, побе́да; *v.t.* & *i.* выи́грывать *imp.*, вы́играть *perf.*; *v.t.* (*obtain*) добива́ться *imp.*, доби́ться (-бью́сь, -бьёшься) *perf.* + *gen.*; *w. over*, (*convince*) убежда́ть *imp.*, убеди́ть (-ди́шь) *perf.*; (*gain favour of*) располага́ть *imp.*, расположи́ть (-жу́, -жишь) *perf.* к себе́; *w. through*, (*overcome*) преодолева́ть *imp.*, преодоле́ть *perf.*

wince *n.* содрога́ние, вздра́гивание; *v.i.* вздра́гивать *imp.*, вздро́гнуть *perf.*

winch *n.* (*windlass*) лебёдка.

wind[1] *n.* (*air*) ве́тер (-тра); (*breath*) дыха́ние; (*flatulence*) ве́тры *m.pl.*; *w. instrument*, духово́й инструме́нт; *w.-swept*, откры́тый ветра́м; *get w. of*, проню́хивать *imp.*, проню́хать *perf.*; *v.t.* (*make gasp*) заставля́ть *imp.*, заста́вить *perf.* задохну́ться.

wind[2] *v.i.* (*meander*) ви́ться (вьюсь, вьёшься; ви́лся, -ла́сь) *imp.*; извива́ться *imp.*; *v.t.* & *i.* (*coil*) нама́тывать(ся) *imp.*, намота́ть(ся) *perf.*; *v.t.* (*watch*) заводи́ть (-ожу́, -о́дишь) *imp.*, завести́ (-еду́, -едёшь; -ёл, -ела́) *perf.*; (*wrap*) уку́тывать *imp.*, уку́тать *perf.*; *w. down*, (*v.t.* & *i.*) разма́тывать(ся) *imp.*, размота́ть(ся) *perf.*; *w. up*, (*v.t.*) (*reel*) сма́тывать *imp.*, смота́ть *perf.*; (*watch*) *see* **wind**[2]; (*v.t.* & *i.*) (*end*) конча́ть(ся) *imp.*, ко́нчить(ся) *perf.* **winding** *adj.* (*twisted*) вито́й, спира́льный; (*meandering*) изви́листый.

windfall *n.* плод (-а́), сби́тый ве́тром; (*fig.*) неожи́данное сча́стье.

windlass *n.* лебёдка.

windmill *n.* ветряна́я ме́льница.

window *n.* окно́ (*pl.* о́кна, о́кон, о́кнам); (*of shop*) витри́на; *w.-box*, нару́жный я́щик для расте́ний; *w.-dressing*, украше́ние витри́н; *w.-frame*, око́нная ра́ма; *w.-ledge*, подоко́нник; *w.-pane*, око́нное стекло́ (*pl.* стёкла, -кол, -клам); *w.-shopping*, рассма́тривание витри́н; *w.-sill*, подоко́нник.
windpipe *n.* дыха́тельное го́рло, трахе́я.
windscreen *n.* пере́днее/ветрово́е стекло́ (*pl.* стёкла, -кол, -клам); *w. wiper*, стеклоочисти́тель *m.*, дво́рник (*coll.*).
windward *n.* наве́тренная сторона́ (*acc.* -ону); *adj.* наве́тренный. **windy** *adj.* ве́треный; (*verbose*) многосло́вный.
wine *n.* вино́ (*pl.* -на); *w.-cellar*, ви́нный по́греб (*pl.* -а́); *w.-coloured*, тёмно-кра́сный; *w.-grower*, виногра́дарь *m.*; *w.-growing*, виногра́дарство; *w.-list*, ка́рта вин; *w.-merchant*, торго́вец (-вца) вино́м; *w.-tasting*, дегуста́ция вин; *v.i.* пить (пью, пьёшь; пил, -а́, -о) *imp.*, вы~ *perf.* вино́; *v.t.* угоща́ть *imp.*, угости́ть *perf.* вино́м. **winebottle** *n.* ви́нная буты́лка. **wineglass** *n.* рю́мка. **winery** *n.* ви́нный заво́д. **winy** *adj.* ви́нный.
wing *n.* (*also polit.*) крыло́ (*pl.* -лья, -льев); (*archit.*) фли́гель (*pl.* -ля́, -ле́й) *m.*; (*sport*) фланг; *pl.* (*theat.*) кули́сы *f.pl.*; *w.-nut*, крыла́тая га́йка; *w.-span*, разма́х кры́льев; *v.i.* лета́ть *indet.*, лете́ть (лечу́, лети́шь) *det.*, по~ *perf.*; *v.t.* (*provide with wings*) снабжа́ть *imp.*, снабди́ть *perf.* кры́льями; (*quicken*) ускоря́ть *imp.*, уско́рить *perf.*; (*inspire*) окрыля́ть *imp.*, окрыли́ть *perf.* **winged** *adj.* крыла́тый.
wink *n.* (*blink*) морга́ние; (*as sign*) подми́гивание; *in a w.*, момента́льно; *v.i.* морга́ть *imp.*, моргну́ть *perf.*; мига́ть *imp.*, мигну́ть *perf.* (at, + *dat.*); подми́гивать *imp.*, подми́гнуть *perf.* (at, + *dat.*); (*fig.*) смотре́ть (-рю́, -ришь) *imp.*, по~ *perf.* сквозь па́льцы на + *acc.*
winkle *n.* берегова́я ули́тка; *v.t.*: *w. out*, выковы́ривать *imp.*, вы́ковырять *perf.*
winner *n.* победи́тель *m.*, ~ница. **winning** *adj.* вы́игрывающий, побежда́ющий; (*of shot etc.*) реша́ющий; (*charming*) обая́тельный; *n.*: *pl.* вы́игрыш; *w.-post*, фи́нишный столб (-а́).
winnow *v.t.* (*grain*) ве́ять (ве́ю, ве́ешь) *imp.*; (*sift*) просе́ивать *imp.*, просе́ять (-е́ю, -е́ешь) *perf.*
winsome *adj.* привлека́тельный, обая́тельный.
winter *n.* зима́; *attrib.* зи́мний; *v.i.* проводи́ть (-ожу́, -о́дишь) *imp.*, провести́ (-еду́, -едёшь: -ёл, -ела́) *perf.* зиму́; зимова́ть *imp.*, пере~ *perf.* **wintry** *adj.* зи́мний; (*cold*) холо́дный (хо́лоден, -дна́, -дно, хо́лодны́).
wipe *v.t.* (*also w. out inside of*) вытира́ть *imp.*, вы́тереть (вы́тру, -решь; вы́тер, -ла) *perf.*; *w. away*, *off*, стира́ть *imp.*, стере́ть (сотру́, -рёшь; стёр, -ла) *perf.*; *w. out*, (*exterminate*) уничтожа́ть *imp.*, уничто́жить *perf.*; (*disgrace etc.*) смыва́ть *imp.*, смыть (смо́ю, -о́ешь) *perf.*
wire *n.* про́волока; (*carrying current*) про́вод (*pl.* -а́); (*telegram*) телегра́мма; *attrib.* про́волочный; *w. netting*, про́волочная сеть; *v.t.* (*electr.*) де́лать *imp.*, с~ *perf.* электри́ческую прово́дку в + *acc.*; (*telegraph*) телеграфи́ровать *imp.*, *perf.* **wireless** *n.* ра́дио *neut.indecl.*; *w. set*, радиоприёмник. **wiring** *n.* электропрово́дка. **wiry** *adj.* жи́листый.
wisdom *n.* му́дрость; *w. tooth*, зуб (*pl.* -ы, -о́в) му́дрости. **wise** *adj.* му́дрый (-р, -ра́, -ро); (*prudent*) благоразу́мный.
wish *n.* жела́ние; *with best wishes*, всего́ хоро́шего, с наилу́чшими пожела́ниями; *v.t.* хоте́ть (хочу́, -чешь, хоти́м) *imp.*, за~ *perf.* (*I w. I could see him*, мне хоте́лось бы его́ ви́деть; *I w. to go*, я хочу́ пойти́; *I w. you to come early*, я хочу́, что́бы вы ра́но пришли́; *I w. the day were over*, хорошо́ бы день уже́ ко́нчился); жела́ть *imp.* + *gen.* (*I w. you luck*, жела́ю вам уда́чи); (*congratulate on*) поздравля́ть *imp.*, поздра́вить *perf.* (*I w. you a happy birthday*, поздравля́ю тебя́ с днём рожде́ния); *v.i.*: *w. for*, жела́ть *imp.* + *gen.*; хоте́ть (хочу́,

-чешь, хоти́м) *imp.*, за~ *perf.*+*gen.*, *acc.* **wishbone** *n.* ду́жка. **wishful** *adj.* жела́ющий; *w. thinking*, приня́тие жела́емого за действи́тельное.

wishy-washy *adj.* (*too liquid*) жи́дкий (-док, -дка́, -дко); (*fig.*) сла́бый (-б, -ба́, -бо), бесцве́тный.

wisp *n.* (*of straw*) пучо́к (-чка́); (*hair*) клочо́к (-чка́); (*smoke*) стру́йка.

wistaria *n.* глици́ния.

wistful *adj.* (*pensive*) заду́мчивый; (*melancholy*) тоскли́вый.

wit[1] *n.* (*mind*) ум (-а́); (*wittiness*) остроу́мие; (*person*) остря́к (-а́); *be at one's w.'s end*, не знать *imp.* что де́лать.

wit[2] *v.i.*: *to w.*, то́ есть, а и́менно.

witch *n.* ве́дьма, колду́нья (*gen.pl.* -ний); *w.-doctor*, зна́харь *m.*; *w.-hunt*, охо́та на ведьм. **witchcraft** *n.* колдовство́.

with *prep.* (*in company of, together w.*) (вме́сте) с+*instr.*; (*as a result of*) от+*gen.*; (*at house of, in keeping of*) у+*gen.*; (*by means of*) +*instr.*; (*in spite of*) несмотря́ на+*acc.*; (*including*) включа́я+*acc.*; *w. each/one another*, друг с дру́гом.

withdraw *v.t.* (*retract*) брать (беру́, -рёшь; брал, -а́, -о) *imp.*, взять (возьму́, -мёшь; взял, -а́, -о) *perf.* наза́д; (*curtain, hand*) отдёргивать *imp.*, отдёрнуть *perf.*; (*cancel*) снима́ть *imp.*, снять (сниму́, -мешь; снял, -а́, -о) *perf.*; (*mil.*) отводи́ть (-ожу́, -о́дишь) *imp.*, отвести́ (-еду́, -едёшь; -ёл, -ела́) *perf.*; (*money from circulation*) изыма́ть *imp.*, изъя́ть (изыму́, -ы́мешь) из обраще́ния; (*diplomatic representative*) отзыва́ть *imp.*, отозва́ть (отзову́, -вёшь; отозва́л, -а́, -о) *perf.*; (*from bank*) брать (беру́, -рёшь; брал, -а́, -о) *imp.*, взять (возьму́, -мёшь; взял, -а́, -о) *perf.*; *v.i.* удаля́ться *imp.*, удали́ться *perf.*; (*mil.*) отходи́ть (-ожу́, -о́дишь) *imp.*, отойти́ (-йду́, -йдёшь; отошёл, -шла́) *perf.* **withdrawal** *n.* (*retraction*) взя́тие наза́д; (*cancellation*) сня́тие; (*mil.*) отхо́д; (*money from circulation*) изъя́тие; (*departure*) ухо́д. **withdrawn** *adj.* за́мкнутый.

wither *v.i.* вя́нуть (вял) *imp.*, за~ *perf.*; высыха́ть *imp.*, вы́сохнуть (-х) *perf.*; *v.t.* иссуша́ть *imp.*, иссуши́ть (-шу́, -шишь) *perf.* **withering** *adj.* (*fig.*) испепеля́ющий.

withers *n.* хо́лка.

withhold *v.t.* (*refuse to grant*) не дава́ть (даю́, даёшь) *imp.*, дать (дам, дашь, даст, дади́м; дал, -а́, да́ло́, -и) *perf.*+*gen.*; (*hide*) скрыва́ть *imp.*, скрыть (скро́ю, -о́ешь) *perf.*; (*restrain*) уде́рживать *imp.*, удержа́ть (-жу́, -жишь) *perf.*

within *prep.* (*inside*) внутри́+*gen.*, в+*prep.*: (*w. the limits of*) в преде́лах+*gen.*; (*time*) в тече́ние+*gen.*; *adv.* внутри́; (*at home*) до́ма.

without *prep.* без+*gen.*; (*outside*) вне+*gen.*, за+*instr.*; *w. saying good-bye*, не проща́ясь; *do w.*, обходи́ться (-ожу́сь, -о́дишься) *imp.*, обойти́сь (-йду́сь, -йдёшься; обошёлся, -шла́сь) *perf.* без+*gen.*

withstand *v.t.* противостоя́ть (-ою́, -ои́шь) *imp.*+*dat.*; выде́рживать *imp.*, вы́держать (-жу, -жишь) *perf.*

witless *adj.* глу́пый (-п, -па́, -по).

witness *n.* (*person*) свиде́тель *m.*; (*eye-witness*) очеви́дец (-дца); (*to signature etc.*) завери́тель *m.*; (*evidence*) свиде́тельство; *bear w. to*, свиде́тельствовать *imp.*, за~ *perf.*; *w.-box*, ме́сто (*pl.* -та́) для свиде́телей; *v.t.* быть свиде́телем+*gen.*; (*document etc.*) заверя́ть *imp.*, заве́рить *perf.*

witticism *n.* остро́та. **wittiness** *n.* остроу́мие. **witty** *adj.* остроу́мный.

wizard *n.* волше́бник, колду́н (-а́). **wizardry** *n.* колдовство́.

wizened *adj.* (*wrinkled*) морщи́нистый.

wobble *v.t.* & *i.* шата́ть(ся) *imp.*, шатну́ть(ся) *perf.*; кача́ть(ся) *imp.*, качну́ть(ся) *perf.*; *v.i.* (*voice*) дрожа́ть (-жу́, -жи́шь) *imp.* **wobbly** *adj.* ша́ткий.

woe *n.* го́ре; *w. is me!* го́ре мне! **woebegone** *adj.* удручённый, мра́чный (-чен, -чна́, -чно). **woeful** *adj.* скорбный, го́рестный.

wolf *n.* волк (*pl.* -и, -о́в); *w.-cub*, волчо́нок (-нка; *pl.* волча́та, -т); *v.t.* пожира́ть *imp.*, пожра́ть (-ру́, -рёшь; пожра́л, -а́, -о) *perf.* (*coll.*). **wolfhound** *n.* волкода́в.

woman *n.* же́нщина. **womanhood** *n.* (*maturity*) же́нская зре́лость. **womanish** *adj.* женоподо́бный. **womanly** *adj.* же́нственный (-ен, -енна).

womb *n.* ма́тка; (*fig.*) чре́во.

womenfolk *n.* же́нщины *f.pl.*; (*of one's family*) же́нская полови́на семьи́.

wonder *n.* чу́до (*pl.* -деса́, -де́с); (*amazement*) изумле́ние; (*it's*) *no w.*, неудиви́тельно; *v.t.* интересова́ться *imp.* (*I w. who will come*, интере́сно, кто придёт); *v.i.*: *I shouldn't w. if*, неудиви́тельно бу́дет, е́сли; *I w. if you could help me*, не могли́ бы вы мне помо́чь? *w. at*, удивля́ться *imp.*, удиви́ться *perf.* + *dat.* **wonderful, wondrous** *adj.* замеча́тельный, удиви́тельный, чуде́сный.

wont *n.*; *as is his w.*, по своему́ обыкнове́нию; *predic.*: *be w. to*, име́ть привы́чку + *inf.* **wonted** *adj.* привы́чный.

woo *v.t.* уха́живать *imp.* за + *instr.*; (*fig.*) добива́ться + *gen.*

wood *n.* (*forest*) лес (-а(у), *loc.* -у́; *pl.* -а́); (*material*) де́рево; (*firewood*) дрова́ (-в, -ва́м) *pl.*; *w.-louse*, мокри́ца; *w.-pigeon*, лесно́й го́лубь (*pl.* -би, -бе́й) *m.*; *w.-pulp*, древе́сная ма́сса; *w.-shed*, сара́й для дров; *w.-wind*, деревя́нные духовы́е инструме́нты *m.pl.*; *w.-wool*, то́нкая, упако́вочная стру́жка. **woodbine** *n.* жимолость. **woodcock** *n.* вальдшне́п. **woodcut** *n.* гравю́ра на де́реве. **wooded** *adj.* леси́стый. **wooden** *adj.* (*also fig.*) деревя́нный. **woodland** *n.* леси́стая ме́стность; *attrib.* лесно́й. **woodman** *n.* лесни́к (-а́). **woodpecker** *n.* дя́тел (-тла). **woodwork** *n.* столя́рная рабо́та; (*wooden articles*) деревя́нные изде́лия *neut.pl.*; (*wooden parts of s.th.*) деревя́нные ча́сти (-те́й) *pl.* (строе́ния). **woodworm** *n.* (жук-)древото́чец (-чца). **woody** *adj.* (*plant etc.*) деревяни́стый; (*wooded*) леси́стый.

wool *n.* шерсть (*pl.* -ти, -те́й). **woollen** *adj.* шерстяно́й. **woolly** *adj.* (*covered with w.*) покры́тый ше́рстью; (*fleecy*) шерсти́стый; (*indistinct*) нея́сный (-сен, -сна́, -сно); *w. mind, thinking* пу́таница в голове́; *n.* (*coll.*) сви́тер.

word *n.* (*unit of language*; *utterance*; *promise*) сло́во (*pl.* -ва́); (*remark*) замеча́ние; (*news*) изве́стие; *have a w. with*, поговори́ть *perf.* с + *instr.*; *by w. of mouth*, на слова́х, у́стно; *in a w.*, одни́м сло́вом; *in other words*, други́ми слова́ми; *w. for w.*, сло́во в сло́во; *v.t.* выража́ть *imp.*, вы́разить *perf.* слова́ми; формули́ровать *imp.*, с~ *perf.* **wordiness** *n.* многосло́вие. **wording** *n.* формулиро́вка, реда́кция. **wordy** *adj.* многосло́вный.

work *n.* рабо́та; (*labour*; *toil*; *scholarly w.*) труд (-а́); (*occupation*) заня́тие; (*studies*) заня́тия *neut.pl.*; (*of art*) произведе́ние; (*book*) сочине́ние; *pl.* (*factory*) заво́д; (*mechanism*) механи́зм; *at w.*, (*doing w.*) за рабо́той; (*at place of w.*) на рабо́те; *out of w.*, безрабо́тный; *w.-bench*, верста́к (-а́); *w.-force*, рабо́чая си́ла; *w.-load*, нагру́зка; *w.-room*, рабо́чая ко́мната; *w.-shy*, лени́вый; *v.i.* (*also function*) рабо́тать *imp.* (at, on, над + *instr.*); (*study*) занима́ться *imp.*, заня́ться (займу́сь, -мёшься; за́нялся́, -ла́сь, -ло́сь) *perf.*; (*also toil, labour*) труди́ться (-ужу́сь, -у́дишься) *imp.*; (*function*) де́йствовать *imp.*; *w. to rule*, рабо́тать *imp.*, выполня́я сли́шком пунктуа́льно все пра́вила, с це́лью уме́ньши́ть производи́тельность; *v.t.* (*operate*) управля́ть *imp.* + *instr.*; обраща́ться *imp.* с + *instr.*; (*wonders*) твори́ть *imp.*, со~ *perf.*; (*soil*) обраба́тывать *imp.*, обрабо́тать *perf.*; (*mine*) разраба́тывать *imp.*, разрабо́тать *perf.*; (*compel to w.*) заставля́ть *imp.*, заста́вить *perf.* рабо́тать; *w. in*, вставля́ть *imp.*, вста́вить *perf.*; *w. out*, (*solve*) реша́ть *imp.*, реши́ть *perf.*; (*plans etc.*) разраба́тывать *imp.*, разрабо́тать *perf.*; (*exhaust*) истоща́ть *imp.*, истощи́ть *perf.*; *everything worked out well*, всё ко́нчилось хорошо́; *w. out at*, (*amount to*) составля́ть *imp.*, соста́вить *perf.*; *w. up*, (*perfect*) обраба́тывать *imp.*, обрабо́тать *perf.*; (*excite*) возбужда́ть *imp.*, возбуди́ть *perf.*; (*appetite*) нагу́ливать *imp.*, нагуля́ть *perf.* **workable** *adj.* осуществи́мый, реа́льный.

workaday *adj.* бу́дничный. **worker** *n.* рабо́чий *sb.*; рабо́тник, -ица. **working** *adj.*: *w. class*, рабо́чий класс; *w. conditions*, усло́вия *neut.pl.* труда́; *w. day*, рабо́чий день (дня) *m.*; *w. hours*, рабо́чее вре́мя *neut.*; *w. party*, коми́ссия. **workman** *n.* рабо́чий *sb.*, рабо́тник. **workmanlike** *adj.* иску́сный. **workmanship** *n.* иску́сство, мастерство́. **workshop** *n.* мастерска́я *sb.*

world *n.* мир (*pl.* -ы́), свет; *attrib.* мирово́й; *w.-famous*, всеми́рно изве́стный; *w.-view*, мировоззре́ние; *w. war*, мирова́я война́ (*pl.* -ны); *w.-weary*, уста́вший от жи́зни; *w.-wide*, распространённый (-ён, -ена́) по всему́ све́ту; всеми́рный. **worldly** *adj.* (*earthly*) земно́й; (*temporal*) мирско́й; (*experienced*) о́пытный.

worm *n.* червь (-вя́; *pl.* -ви, -ве́й) *m.*; (*also tech.*) червя́к (-а́); (*intestinal*) глист (-а́); *v.t.*: *w. oneself into*, вкра́дываться *imp.*, вкра́сться (-аду́сь, -адёшься; -а́лся) *perf.* в + *acc.*; *w. out*, выве́дывать *imp.*, вы́ведать *perf.* (of, у + *gen.*); *w. one's way*, пробира́ться *imp.*, пробра́ться (-беру́сь, -берёшься; -бра́лся, -брала́сь, -бра́ло́сь) *perf.* **worm-eaten** *adj.* исто́ченный (-ен) червя́ми. **wormwood** *n.* полы́нь.

worry *n.* (*anxiety*) беспоко́йство, трево́га; (*care*) забо́та; *v.t.* беспоко́ить *imp.*, о~ *perf.*; трево́жить *imp.*, вс~ *perf.*; (*of dog*) терза́ть *imp.*; *v.i.* беспоко́иться *imp.*, о~ *perf.* (about, о + *prep.*); му́читься *imp.*, за~, из~ *perf.* (about, из-за + *gen.*).

worse *adj.* ху́дший; *adv.* ху́же; *n.*: *from bad to w.*, всё ху́же и ху́же. **worsen** *v.t.* & *i.* ухудша́ться *imp.*, ухудши́ться *perf.*

worship *n.* поклоне́ние (of, + *dat.*); (*relig.*) богослуже́ние; *v.t.* поклоня́ться *imp.* + *dat.*; (*adore*) обожа́ть *imp.* **worshipper** *n.* покло́нник, -ица.

worst *adj.* наиху́дший, са́мый плохо́й; *adv.* ху́же всего́; *n.* са́мое плохо́е; *v.t.* побежда́ть *imp.*, победи́ть (-и́шь) *perf.*

worsted *n.* шерстяна́я/камво́льная пря́жа.

worth *n.* (*value*) цена́ (*acc.* -ну; *pl.* -ны); (*fig.*) це́нность; (*merit*) досто́инство; *give me a pound's w. of petrol*, да́йте мне бензи́на на фунт; *adj.*: *be w.*, (*of value equivalent to*) сто́ить *imp.* (*what is it w.?* ско́лько э́то сто́ит?); (*deserve*) сто́ить *imp.* + *gen.* (*is this film w. seeing?* сто́ит посмотре́ть э́тот фильм?); *for all one is w.*, изо все́х сил. **worthless** *adj.* ничего́ не сто́ящий; (*useless*) бесполе́зный. **worthwhile** *adj.* сто́ящий. **worthy** *adj.* досто́йный (-о́ин, -о́йна).

would-be *adj.*: *w. actor*, челове́к (*pl.* лю́ди, -де́й, -дям, -дьми́) мечта́ющий стать актёром.

wound *n.* ра́на, ране́ние; (*fig.*) оби́да; *v.t.* ра́нить *imp.*, *perf.*; (*fig.*) обижа́ть *imp.*, оби́деть (-и́жу, -и́дишь) *perf.* **wounded** *adj.* ра́неный.

wraith *n.* виде́ние.

wrangle *n.* пререка́ние, спор; *v.i.* пререка́ться *imp.*; спо́рить *imp.*, по~ *perf.*

wrap *n.* (*shawl*) шаль; (*stole*) паланти́н; *v.t.* (*also w. up*) завёртывать *imp.*, заверну́ть *perf.*; *w. up*, (*v.t.* & *i.*) (*in wraps*) заку́тывать(ся) *imp.*, заку́тать(ся) *perf.*; (*v.t.*) (*conclude*) заверша́ть *imp.*, заверши́ть *perf.*; *wrapped up in*, (*fig.*) поглощённый (-ён, -ена́) + *instr.* **wrapper** *n.* обёртка. **wrapping** *n.* обёртка; *w. paper*, обёрточная бума́га.

wrath *n.* гнев, я́рость. **wrathful** *adj.* гне́вный (-вен, -вна́, -вно).

wreak *v.t.*: *w. havoc*, производи́ть (-ожу́, -о́дишь) *imp.*, произвести́ (-еду́, -едёшь; -ёл, -ела́) *perf.* ужа́сные разруше́ния; *w. vengeance*, мстить *imp.*, ото~ *perf.* (on, + *dat.*).

wreath *n.* вено́к (-нка́); (*of smoke*) кольцо́ (*pl.* -льца, -ле́ц, -льцам). **wreathe** *v.t.* (*form into wreath*) сплета́ть *imp.*, сплести́ (-ету́, -етёшь; -ёл, -ела́) *perf.*; (*encircle*) обвива́ть *imp.*, обви́ть (обовью́, -ьёшь; обви́л, -ла́, -ло) *perf.* (with, + *instr.*); *v.i.* (*wind round*) обвива́ться *imp.*, обви́ться (обовью́сь, -ьёшься; обви́лся, -ла́сь) *perf.*; (*of smoke*) клуби́ться *imp.*

wreck *n.* (*destruction*) круше́ние, ава́-

рия; (*wrecked ship*) óстов разби́того сýдна; (*vehicle, person, building etc.*) развáлина; *v.t.* (*cause destruction of*) вызывáть *imp.*, вы́звать (вы́зову, -вешь) крушéние + *gen.*; (*ship*) топи́ть (топлю́, -пишь) *imp.*, по~ *perf.*; (*destroy, also hopes etc.*) разрушáть *imp.*, разрýшить *perf.*; *be wrecked*, терпéть (-плю́, -пишь) *imp.*, по~ *perf.* крушéние; (*of plans etc.*) рýхнуть *perf.* **wreckage** *n.* облóмки *m.pl.* крушéния.

wren *n.* крапи́вник.

wrench *n.* (*jerk*) дёрганье; (*sprain*) растяжéние; (*tech.*) гáечный ключ (-á); (*fig.*) боль; *v.t.* (*snatch, pull out*) вырывáть *imp.*, вы́рвать (-ву, -вешь) *perf.* (from, у + *gen.*); (*sprain*) растя́гивать *imp.*, растянýть (-нý, -нешь) *perf.*; *w. open*, взлáмывать *imp.*, взломáть *perf.*

wrest *v.t.* (*wrench*) вырывáть *imp.*, вы́рвать (-ву, -вешь) *perf.* (from, у + *gen.*); (*agreement etc.*) исторгáть *imp.*, истóргнуть (-г) *perf.* (from, у + *gen.*); (*distort*) искажáть *imp.*, искази́ть *perf.*

wrestle *v.i.* борóться (-рю́сь, -решься) *imp.* **wrestler** *n.* борéц (-рцá). **wrestling** *n.* борьбá.

wretch *n.* несчáстный *sb.*; (*scoundrel*) негодя́й. **wretched** *adj.* жáлкий (-лок, -лкá, -лко); (*unpleasant*) сквéрный (-рен, -рнá, -рно).

wriggle *v.i.* извивáться *imp.*, изви́ться (изовью́сь, -ьёшься; изви́лся, -лáсь) *perf.*; (*fidget*) ёрзать *imp.*; *v.t.* виля́ть *imp.*, вильнýть *perf.* + *instr.*; *w. out of*, увиливать *imp.*, увильнýть от + *gen.*

wring *v.t.* (*also w. out*) выжимáть *imp.*, вы́жать (вы́жму, -мешь) *perf.*; (*extort*) исторгáть *imp.*, истóргнуть (-г) *perf.* (from, у + *gen.*); (*hand*) крéпко пожимáть *imp.*, пожáть (пожмý, -мёшь) *perf.* (of, + *dat.*); (*neck*) свёртывать *imp.*, свернýть *perf.* (of, + *dat.*); *w. one's hands*, ломáть *imp.*, с~ *perf.* рýки. **wringer** *n.* маши́на для отжимáния белья́.

wrinkle *n.* морщи́на; (*tip*) полéзный совéт; *v.t.* & *i.* мóрщить(ся) *imp.*, с~ *perf.*

wrist *n.* запя́стье; *w.-watch*, нарýчные часы́ (-сóв) *pl.*

writ *n.* повéстка, предписáние.

write *v.t.* & *i.* (*also fig.*) писáть (пишý, -шешь) *imp.*, на~ *perf.*; *w. down*, запи́сывать *imp.*, записáть (запишý, -шешь) *perf.*; *w. off*, (*cancel*) аннули́ровать *imp.*, *perf.*; (*dispatch letter*) отсылáть *imp.*, отослáть (отошлю́, -шлёшь) *perf.*; *the car was a w.-off*, маши́на былá совершéнно испóрчена; *w. out*, выпи́сывать *imp.*, вы́писать (-ишу, -ишешь) *perf.* (in full, пóлностью); *w. up*, (*account of*) подрóбно опи́сывать *imp.*, описáть (-ишý, -и́шешь) *perf.*; (*notes*) перепи́сывать *imp.*, переписáть (-ишý, -и́шешь) *perf.*; *w.-up*, (*report*) отчёт. **writer** *n.* писáтель *m.*, ~ница.

writhe *v.i.* (*from pain*) кóрчиться *imp.*, с~ *perf.*; (*fig.*) мýчиться *imp.*, за~, из~ *perf.*

writing *n.* (*handwriting*) пóчерк; (*work*) произведéние; *in w.*, в пи́сьменной фóрме; *the w. on the wall*, зловéщее предзаменовáние; *w.-case*, несессéр для пи́сьменных принадлéжностей; *w.-desk*, контóрка, пи́сьменный стол (-á); *w.-paper*, почтóвая бумáга.

wrong *adj.* (*incorrect*) непрáвильный, невéрный (-рен, -рнá, -рно, невéрны́), оши́бочный; не тот (*I have bought the wrong book*, я купи́л не ту кни́гу; *you've got the wrong number*, (*telephone*) вы не тудá попáли); (*mistaken*) непрáвый (-в, -вá, -во) (*you are w.*, ты неправ); (*unjust*) несправедли́вый; (*sinful*) дурнóй (дýрён, -рнá, -рно, дýрны́); (*defective*) неисправный; (*side of cloth*) лéвый; *w. side out*, наизáнку; *w. way round*, наоборóт; *n.* зло; (*injustice*) несправедли́вость; *be in the w.*, быть непрáвым; *do w.*, греши́ть *imp.*, со~ *perf.*; *adv.* непрáвильно, невéрно; *go w.*, не получáться *imp.*, получи́ться (-ится) *perf.*; *v.t.* (*harm*) вреди́ть *imp.*, по~ *perf.* + *dat.*; обижáть *imp.*, оби́деть *perf.*; (*be unjust to*) быть несправедли́вым к + *dat.* **wrongdoer** *n.* престýпник, грéшник, -ица. **wrongful** *adj.* несправедли́вый, непра́вильный. **wrongly** *adv.* непра́вильно, неве́рно.

wrought *adj.*: *w. iron*, сва́рочное желе́зо.

wry *adj.* криво́й (-в, -ва́, -во), перeко́шенный; *w. face*, грима́са.

X

xenophobia *n.* ксенофо́бия.

Xerox *v.t.* размножа́ть *imp.*, размно́жить *perf.* на ксе́роксе. **Xerox copy** *n.* ксероко́пия.

X-ray *n.* (*picture*) рентге́н(овский сни́мок (-мка)); *pl.* (*radiation*) рентге́новы лучи́ *m.pl.*; *v.t.* (*photograph*) де́лать *imp.*, с~ *perf.* рентге́н + *gen.*; (*examine*) иссле́довать *imp.*, *perf.* рентге́новыми луча́ми.

xylophone *n.* ксилофо́н.

Y

yacht *n.* я́хта; *y.-club*, яхт-клу́б. **yachting** *n.* па́русный спорт. **yachtsman** *n.* яхтсме́н.

yak *n.* як.

Yale lock *n.* америка́нский замо́к (-мка́).

yam *n.* ям.

yank *n.* рыво́к (-вка́); *v.t.* рвану́ть *perf.*

yap *n.* тя́вканье; *v.i.* тя́вкать *imp.*, тя́вкнуть *perf.*

yard[1] *n.* (*piece of ground*) двор (-а́).

yard[2] *n.* (*measure*) ярд; (*naut.*) ре́й. **yardstick** *n.* (*fig.*) мери́ло.

yarn *n.* пря́жа; (*story*) расска́з.

yarrow *n.* тысячели́стник.

yashmak *n.* чадра́.

yawl *n.* ял.

yawn *n.* зево́к (-вка́); *v.i.* (*person*) зева́ть *imp.*, зевну́ть *perf.*; (*chasm etc.*) зия́ть *imp.*

year *n.* год (*loc.* -у́; *pl.* -ы & -а́, -о́в & лет, -а́м); *from y. to y.*, год о́т году; *y. in, y. out*, из го́да в го́д; *y.-book*, ежего́дник. **yearly** *adj.* ежего́дный, годово́й; *adv.* ежего́дно, раз в год.

yearn *v.i.* тоскова́ть *imp.*, (for, по + *dat.*, *prep.*). **yearning** *n.* тоска́ (for, по + *dat.*, *prep.*).

yeast *n.* дро́жжи (-же́й) *pl.*

yell *n.* крик; *v.i.* крича́ть (-чу́, -чи́шь) *imp.*, кри́кнуть *perf.*; *v.t.* выкри́кивать *imp.*, вы́крикнуть *perf.*

yellow *adj.* жёлтый (-т, -та́, жёлто́); (*cowardly*) трусли́вый; *n.* жёлтый цвет; *v.i.* желте́ть *imp.*, по~ *perf.* **yellowhammer** *n.* овся́нка. **yellowish** *adj.* желтова́тый.

yelp *n.* визг; *v.i.* визжа́ть (-жу́, -жи́шь) *imp.*, ви́згнуть *perf.*

yen *n.* (*money*) ие́на.

yes *adv.* да; *n.* утвержде́ние, согла́сие; (*in vote*) го́лос (*pl.* -а́) „за"; *y.-man*, подпева́ла *m.* & *f.* (*coll.*).

yesterday *adv.* вчера́; *n.* вчера́шний день (дня) *m.*; *y. morning*, вчера́ у́тром; *the day before y.*, позавчера́; *yesterday's newspaper*, вчера́шняя газе́та.

yet *adv.* (*still*) ещё; (*so far*) до сих пор; (*with compar.*) да́же, ещё; (*in questions*) уже́; (*nevertheless*) тем не ме́нее; *as y.*, пока́, до сих пор; *not y.*, ещё не; *conj.* одна́ко, но.

yew *n.* тис.

Yiddish *n.* и́диш.

yield *n.* (*harvest*) урожа́й; (*econ.*) дохо́д; *v.t.* (*fruit, revenue, etc.*) приноси́ть (-ошу́, -о́сишь) *imp.*, принести́ (-есу́, -есёшь; -ёс, -есла́) *perf.*; дава́ть (даю́, даёшь) *imp.*, дать (дам, дашь, даст, дади́м; дал, -а́, да́ло́, -и) *perf.*; (*give up*) сдава́ть (сдаю́, сдаёшь) *imp.*, сдать (-а́м, -а́шь, -а́ст, -ади́м; сдал, -а́, -о) *perf.*; *v.i.* (*give in*) (*to enemy etc.*) уступа́ть *imp.*, уступи́ть (-плю́, -пишь) *perf.* (to, +*dat.*); (*to temptation etc.*), поддава́ться (-даю́сь, -даёшься) *imp.*, подда́ться (-а́мся, -а́шься, -а́стся, -ади́мся; -а́лся, -ала́сь) *perf.* (to, +*dat.*).

yodel *n.* йо́дль *m.*; *v.i.* петь (пою́, поёшь) *imp.*, про~, с~ *perf.* йо́длем.

yoga *n.* йо́га. **yogi** *n.* йог.

yoghurt *n.* простоква́ша.

yoke *n.* (*also fig.*) ярмо́ (*pl.* -ма); (*fig.*) и́го; (*for buckets*) коромы́сло (*gen.pl.* -сел); (*of dress*) коке́тка; *y. of oxen*, па́ра запряжённых воло́в; *v.t.* впряга́ть *imp.*, впрячь (-ягу́, -яжёшь; -яг, -ягла́) *perf.* в ярмо́.

yokel *n.* дереве́нщина *m.* & *f.*

yolk *n.* желто́к (-тка́).

yonder *adv.* вон там; *adj.* вон тот (та, то; *pl.* те).

yore *n.*: (*in days*) *of y.*, во вре́мя о́но.

you *pron.* (*familiar sing.*) ты (тебя́, тебе́, тобо́й, тебе́); (*familiar pl., polite sing. & pl.*) вы (вас, вам, ва́ми, вас); (*one*) not usu. translated; verb translated in 2nd pers. sing. or by impers. construction: *y. never know*, никогда́ не зна́ешь.

young *adj.* молодо́й (мо́лод, -а́, -о), ю́ный (юн, -а́, -о); (*new*) но́вый (нов, -а́, -о); (*inexperienced*) нео́пытный; *the y.*, молодёжь; *n.* (*collect.*) молодня́к (-а́), детёныши *m.pl.* **youngish** *adj.* моложа́вый. **youngster** *n.* ма́льчик, ю́ноша *m.*

your(s) *poss. pron.* (*familiar sing.*; *also in letter*) твой (-оя́, -оё; -ои́); (*familiar pl., polite sing. & pl.*; *also in letter*) ваш; свой (-оя́, -оё; -ои́). **yourself** *pron.* (*emph.*) (*familiar sing.*) (ты) сам (-ого́, -ому́, -и́м, -о́м) (*m.*), сама́ (-мо́й, *acc.* -му́) (*f.*); (*familiar pl., polite sing. & pl.*) (вы) са́ми (-и́х, -и́м, -и́ми); (*refl.*) себя́ (себе́, собо́й); -ся (*suffixed to v.t.*); *by y.*, (*independently*) самостоя́тельно, сам (-а́; -и); (*alone*) оди́н (одна́; одни́).

youth *n.* (*age*) мо́лодость, ю́ность; (*young man*) ю́ноша *m.*; (*collect., as pl.*) молодёжь; *attrib.* молодёжный; *y. club*, молодёжный клуб; *y. hostel*, молодёжная турба́за. **youthful** *adj.* ю́ношеский.

yo-yo *n.* йо-йо́.

Yugoslav(ian) *adj.* югосла́вский; *n.* югосла́в, ~ка.

Z

zany *adj.* смешно́й (-шо́н, -шна́).

zeal *n.* рве́ние, усе́рдие. **zealot** *n.* фана́тик. **zealous** *adj.* ре́вностный, усе́рдный.

zebra *n.* зе́бра.

zenith *n.* зени́т.

zephyr *n.* зефи́р.

zero *n.* нуль (-ля́) *m.*, ноль (-ля́) *m.*; *attrib.* нулево́й; *z. hour*, час „Ч".

zest *n.* (*piquancy*) пика́нтность; (*ardour*) жар, энтузиа́зм; *z. for life*, жизнелю́бие.

zigzag *n.* зигза́г; *adj.* зигзагообра́зный; *v.i.* де́лать *imp.*, с~ *perf* зигза́ги.

zinc *n.* цинк; *attrib.* ци́нковый.

Zionism *n.* сиони́зм. **Zionist** *n.* сиони́ст.
zip *n.* (*z. fastener*) (застёжка-)мо́лния; *v.t.* & *i.*: *z. up*, застёгивать(ся) *imp.*, застегну́ть *perf.* на мо́лнию.
zither *n.* ци́тра.
zodiac *n.* зодиа́к; *sign of the z.*, знак зодиа́ка. **zodiacal** *adj.* зодиака́льный.
zonal *adj.* зона́льный. **zone** *n.* зо́на; (*geog.*) пояс (*pl.* -а́).
zoo *n.* зоопа́рк. **zoological** *adj.* зоологи́ческий; *z. garden(s)*, зоопа́рк, зоологи́ческий сад (*loc.* -у́; *pl.* -ы́).
zoologist *n.* зоо́лог. **zoology** *n.* зооло́гия.
zoom *v.i.* (*aeron.*) де́лать *imp.*, с~ *perf.* го́рку; *n.* го́рка; *z. lens*, объекти́в с переме́нным фо́кусным расстоя́нием.
Zulu *adj.* зулу́сский; *n.* зулу́с, ~ка.